The Norton Anthology
of World Masterpieces

THE WESTERN TRADITION

Seventh Edition

VOLUME 1

The Norton Anthology
of World Masterpieces

THE WESTERN TRADITION

Seventh Edition

Sarah Lawall, *General Editor*

PROFESSOR OF COMPARATIVE LITERATURE
AND ADJUNCT PROFESSOR OF FRENCH,
UNIVERSITY OF MASSACHUSETTS, AMHERST

Maynard Mack, *General Editor Emeritus*

STERLING PROFESSOR OF ENGLISH EMERITUS,
YALE UNIVERSITY

VOLUME 1
Literature of Western Culture Through the Renaissance

W • W • NORTON & COMPANY • *New York* • *London*

Editor: Peter Simon
Production Manager: Diane O'Connor
Project Editors: Kurt Wildermuth, Kathryn M. Talalay, Kate Lovelady
Manuscript Editors: Kurt Wildermuth, Candace Levy
Permissions: Kristin Sheerin
Editorial Assistant: Benjamin Reynolds
Cover and Text Design: Antonina Krass
Art Research: Neil Ryder Hoos

The text of this book is composed in Fairfield Medium
with the display set in Bernhard Modern.
Composition by Binghamton Valley Composition.
Manufacturing by R. R. Donnelley & Sons.

Cover illustration: Titian. *Bacchus and Ariadne* (detail). 1522/23. Oil on canvas, 175.2 x
190.5 cm. The National Gallery, London. Photograph © The National Gallery, London.

Library of Congress Cataloging-in-Publication Data

The Norton anthology of world masterpieces : the Western tradition /
    Sarah Lawall, general editor ; Maynard Mack, general editor
    emeritus. — 7th ed.
        p. cm.
    Includes bibliographical references and index.
    Contents: v. 1. Literature of Western culture through the
Renaissance — v. 2. Literature of Western culture since the
Renaissance.

ISBN 0-393-97289-5 (pbk.: v. 1). — ISBN 0-393-97300-X (pbk.: v. 2)

    1. Literature—Collections. I. Lawall, Sarah N.   II. Mack,
Maynard, 1909–   .
PN6014.N66   1998
808.8—dc21
                                                                98-35047
                                                                      CIP
W. W. Norton & Company, Inc., 500 Fifth Avenue, New York, N.Y. 10110
                    http://www.wwnorton.com

W. W. Norton & Company Ltd., 10 Coptic Street, London WC1A 1PU

2 3 4 5 6 7 8 9 0

Contents

Masterpieces of the Ancient World

MAP: GREECE AND WESTERN ASIA MINOR, CA. FIFTH CENTURY B.C.

Masterpieces of the Middle Ages

Masterpieces of the Renaissance

Preface to the Seventh Edition

The Seventh Edition of *The Norton Anthology of World Masterpieces* marks an exciting stage in the development of an anthology whose first appearance, in 1956, brought a fresh approach to the teaching of literature in North American colleges and universities. The readers of that First Edition were encouraged to focus on the literary work as a whole, not small samples; on the broad sweep of the Western tradition, not separate nations; on works treasured by generations of readers—in some cases, over thousands of years; and on the thought-provoking recurrence of themes, artistic forms, and diverse images of human identity. You will find the same indispensable features in this edition, as well as important changes that reflect the evolution both of the anthology and of educational expectations. This Seventh Edition is dedicated anew to exploring the Western tradition—a vital tapestry woven from Homer and Sappho, from Joyce and Akhmatova, from Ovid and Ariosto, from Beckett and Achebe. Throughout these volumes, you will encounter not only the canon of the First Edition (which remains part of the Seventh) but also new writers, women and men, from a variety of countries and cultural backgrounds, writing in a number of languages. You will also encounter more discussions of literature's cultural dimensions, improved translations, a detailed revision of all editorial apparatus, and new contextual aids such as maps, timelines, and pronouncing glossaries for unfamiliar words and names. Whether you are adding a few new selections to a tried and true list or striking out in new directions with different themes and combinations of works, you will find the Seventh Edition an eminently readable and teachable anthology.

Changes in this edition have taken several forms: introducing new authors and works for their intrinsic interest; adding small sections to existing larger pieces in order to fill out a theme or narrative line; choosing an alternate work by the same author when it speaks strongly to current concerns, or grouping several works to highlight features they share.

Most exciting, of course, are the many new selections and the opportunities they bring for different combinations among themselves and with the works you have already been teaching. Roman comedy is now represented by Plautus's *Pseudolus*, a perennial favorite whose farcical effects—the tricks and triumph of the wily servant, the bluster of the braggart soldier, the miserly father who stands in the way of his son's love affair—have been borrowed by generations of playwrights from Shakespeare and Molière to the authors of the twentieth-century Broadway hit *A Funny Thing Happened on the Way to the Forum*. With Lucian's *A True Story*, a marvelously comic narrative of its protagonist's impossible trials and tribulations, we introduce a vein of fantasy. This vein reappears, albeit more elegantly, with the epic parody of Ariosto's *Orlando Furioso*. Wild adventures involving numerous heroes and villains constitute this romantic poem, whose title character ("Orlando gone crazy"), driven mad by frustrated love for a Chinese princess, is a startling variant on the hero of *The Song of Roland*. Fantasy is also evident in *The Thousand and One Nights*, a chain-tale sequence as influential in Europe as in the Arab world for its magical creations and for the all-important character of Shahrazad, the eternal spinner of tales. On a harsher note, there are the medieval fabliaux and the famous adventures of Renard the Fox, whose trial at the court of King Lion and brutal revenge on his enemies is given here. Those of you who have enjoyed teaching the ever-popular *Sir Gawain and the Green Knight* will welcome two other tales from Arthurian legend, Sir Thomas Malory's *Morte Darthur*, which describes the tangled and ultimately fatal relationship of King Arthur, Queen Guinevere, and the noble knight Sir Lancelot, and Marie de France's *Lanval*, which gives an entirely different picture of Lancelot as he leaves Camelot for fairyland.

New to the Renaissance section is Lope de Vega's unusual play *Fuente Ovejuna*, a romantic comedy about consent, set during an actual peasant uprising of 1476 in a small village of Cordoba, Spain, that has disturbing political overtones. The play's happy ending arrives only after the entire village has withstood torture and refused to name the uprising's ringleader. Also new to that section, Shakespeare's *Othello* explores both the psychological and social drama of the Moor's jealousy and downfall and the way that cultural stereotypes play a role in establishing character from within and from without. New among the nineteenth-century selections, Dorothy Wordsworth's *Grasmere Journals* express the very personal world of the intimate journal, as the keen observation of details gradually reveals both the observer's own personality and those of her companions (including, in this case, her brother, the poet William Wordsworth). Selections of Zuni ritual poetry begin the twentieth-century sections, which also contain a variety of short fiction by Russian, American, Canadia, and Polish writers: Chekhov's famous tale of uncertain love, *The Lady with the Dog*; Faulkner's *The Bear*, printed complete to convey the full scope of its look at the legacy of slavery in the South; Richard Wright's story of adolescent coming-of-age (or just the reverse), *The Man Who Was Almost a Man*; Tadeusz Borowski's terrifying Holocaust story, *Ladies and Gentlemen, to the Gas Chamber*; Flannery O'Connor's chilling tale of multiple murders, *A Good Man Is Hard to Find*; Alice Munro's complex evocation of childhood memories, *Walker Brothers Cowboy*; and Leslie Marmon Silko's retelling of a Native American tale, *Yellow Woman*. Also included are the central chapters of a fascinating combination of fiction, autobiography, and essay: Virginia Woolf's passionate analysis of the woman writer's position in *A Room of One's Own*.

Complete pieces inserted into existing groups include the poignant tales of Abraham and Isaac and of Jacob and Esau in the Old Testament selections (Genesis 22, 25, 27), as well as the glorious love poetry of the Song of Songs; and Matthew 13 (*Why Jesus Teaches in Parables*) in the New Testament. Ovid (in a newly included translation by Allen Mandelbaum) is now represented by eight tales—the most recent additions being Europa and Jove, Ceres and Proserpina, Iphis and Ianthe, Pygmalion, Myrrha and Cinyras,

Venus and Adonis—that together explore different images of love and gender. Catullus and Petrarch appear in more-substantial selections, with three additional poems (and a new translation) by the Roman poet and five additional poems by the Italian. Marie de France is represented by two of her best-known and most poignant *lais*, *Lanval* and *Laüstic*. Newly appearing stories from Boccaccio include the paradoxical account of the making of a saint (*The First Story of the First Day*) and the influential tale of patient Griselda and her tyrannical husband (*The Tenth Story of the Tenth Day*); from Chaucer, the bawdy, popular *Wife of Bath's Prologue and Tale*. Many themes from these stories reappear, with special emphasis on the stereotyping of gender roles, in six stories of court and domestic intrigue (five of them new to this edition) from the *Heptameron* of Marguerite de Navarre. Adding to the fantastic twists of Rabelais's narrative *Gargantua and Pantagruel* are a rollicking debate conducted completely in body language and an impossible journey to another world flourishing inside Pantagruel's giant mouth. In the twentieth-century, Rilke's *Archaic Torso of Apollo* is complemented by three more poems of similar intensely physical description: *The Panther, The Swan,* and *Spanish Dancer.*

Among smaller narrative additions are the death of Patroclus in the *Iliad* (Book XVI); Augustine's departure from Carthage for Rome in the *Confessions* (Book V); Ganelon's trial at the end of *The Song of Roland* (especially interesting for its legal arguments and attempt to intimidate the jury); and, in *Paradise Lost,* the preliminary drama of Satan's malevolent entry into paradise, Adam and Eve's innocent conversation, and the angel's warning to Adam (Books 4 and 8).

Previous editions of this anthology have minimized the presence of lyric poetry in translation, recognizing—as so cogently argued in the Note on Translation printed at the end of each volume—that the precise language and music of an original poem will never be identical with its translation. Yet good translations often achieve a poetry of their own and occupy a pivotal position in their own language; read and appreciated for themselves, they simultaneously preserve and pass on important aspects of a major artistic imagination. Sappho, Catullus, Petrarch, Heine, and Baudelaire have had influence far beyond the range of those who could read the original poems. The images and emotions of European Romantic poetry and the abstract vision, liberated verse forms, and linguistic play of Symbolist poetry still echo in twentieth-century literature and will undoubtedly reverberate in that of the twenty-first.

New to this edition, therefore, is a series of poetry clusters representing the best and most influential work of a range of poets in four periods: medieval, Romantic, Symbolist, and Dada-Surrealist. The poems therein may be read for themselves (some have appeared separately in earlier editions) or as part of a significant spectrum of poetic expression. The medieval cluster includes familiar names from the Sixth Edition (Villon, Dante, and the Archpoet) and those less well known to the contemporary audience. Here, men and women from a variety of traditions—Arabic, Judaic, Welsh, Spanish, French, Provençal, Italian, English, German—demonstrate the multifarious vitality of medieval literature. To complement the considerable representation of English Romantic poetry we offer a cluster of continental poetry in translation: Victor Hugo, Giacomo Leopardi, and Heinrich Heine, included in earlier editions, are joined by the Spanish, Russian, French, and German writers Gustavo Adolfo Bécquer, Rosalía de Castro, Anna Petrovna Bunina, Alphonse de Lamartine, Friedrich Hölderlin, and Novalis (Friedrich von Hardenberg). Symbolist poets (or, more precisely, the great nineteenth-century poets Charles Baudelaire, Stéphane Mallarmé, Paul Verlaine, and Arthur Rimbaud, who inspired the Symbolist movement) are presented individually but may also be considered as a set of remarkable precursors of modern literature. Finally, a cluster of Dada-Surrealist poems that range from slashing, rebellious humor to ecstatic celebrations of love introduces the free association and dreamlike structures of this visionary movement with its strong links to modern art and film. Select as you will, whether within a group or by reaching out to writers in the larger anthology; we believe that you will find in each cluster a wealth of fascinating short texts and remarkable access into another period's emotional and intellectual horizons.

How to choose, as you turn from the virtual library before you to the inevitable constraint of available time? In the forty-one complete longer works printed here, and the scores of shorter works, substantial segments, and poems, you have an inexhaustible series of options to fit whatever course pattern you choose. Perhaps you have decided to proceed by theme or genre, in chronological order, or by comparative principle; you have only to select among a variety of works from different countries, languages, and cultural backgrounds. New entries in the Seventh Edition add to your options—and suggest further dimensions—in drama (Plautus's farce, Lope de Vega's romantic comedy), poetry (more individual poets as well as the new groupings), longer prose fiction (Lucian's comic novel, Ariosto's parody of chivalric romance), and shorter fiction from medieval to modern times (from *The Thousand and One Nights* to Flannery O'Connor's *A Good Man Is Hard to Find*). Many of the new inclusions—from any period—involve ethical, social, psychological, and political issues that are of contemporary concern, such as the impact of cultural stereotypes (*Othello* and *A Room of One's Own*) or of mass victimization (*Ladies and Gentlemen, to the Gas Chamber*). In each instance, the editors (who are all practicing teachers) have selected and prepared texts that are significant in their own areas of scholarly expertise, meaningful in the larger context of world literature, and able to delight, captivate, and challenge students.

From the beginning, the editors of *The Norton Anthology of World Masterpieces* have balanced the competing—and, we like to think, complementary—claims of teaching and scholarship, of the specialist's focused expertise and the generalist's broader perspectives. The founding editors set the example that guides their successors. In this edition, we welcome three new successor editors: William G. Thalmann (Ph.D., Yale), Professor of Classics at the University of Southern California; Lee Patterson (Ph.D., Yale), Professor of English at Yale University; and Heather James (Ph.D., University of California, Berkeley), Associate Professor of English at the University of Southern California. Three founding editors have recently assumed Emeritus status: Bernard M. W. Knox, eminent classical scholar and legendary teacher and lecturer; P. M. Pasinetti, who combines the intellectual breadth of the Renaissance scholar with a novelist's creative intuition; and, most notably, Maynard Mack, General Editor and presiding genius of all previous editions, a noted Enlightenment scholar whose wisdom, humanity, and gracefully worn knowledge have brought illumination to both editors and anthology. A fourth founding editor, Rene Wellek, died in 1995. A comparatist best known for his theoretical work and history of criticism, he was committed to the idea of teaching Western literary tradition in a truly international context, to the concept of literary masterpieces, and to the accessibility of these masterpieces for the enthusiastic and careful reader. It seems only appropriate, therefore, to dedicate this Seventh Edition to his memory.

Acknowledgments

Among our many critics, advisers, and friends, the following were of special help in providing suggestions and corrections: Joseph Barbarese (Rutgers University); Carol Clover (University of California, Berkeley); Patrick J. Cook (George Washington University); Janine Gerzanics (University of Southern California); Matthew Giancarlo (Yale University); Kevis Goodman (University of California at Berkeley); Roland Greene (University of Oregon); Dmitri Gutas (Yale University); John H. Hayes (Emory University); Suzanne Keen (Washington and Lee University); Charles S. Kraszewski (King's College); Gregory F. Kuntz; Michelle Latiolais (University of California at Irvine); Sharon L. James (Bryn Mawr College); Ivan Marcus (Yale University); Timothy Martin (Rutgers University, Camden); Fred C. Robinson (Yale University); John Rogers (Yale University); Robert Rothstein (University of Massachusetts); Lawrence Senelick (Boston University); Jack Shreve (Alleghany Community College); Frank Stringfellow (University of Miami); Nancy Vickers (Bryn Mawr College); and Jack Welch (Abilene Christian University).

We would also like to thank the following people who contributed to the planning of the Seventh Edition: Frank M. Acuna (Mount San Antonio Community College); Gene Antonio (DeKalb College); Julie Atkins (Marymount University); Robert Bagg (University of Massachusetts); Sandra C. Barnhill (South Plains College); Ronald Bogue (University of Georgia); Wendy Bashant (Coe College); Scott Boltwood (Emory and Henry College); John C. Bonnell (Macomb County Community College); Phyllis R. Brown (Santa Clara University); Ruth A. Cameron (Eastern Nazarene College); Mark Coleman (SUNY at Potsdam); Rosemary D. Cox (DeKalb College); Fara Darland (Scottsdale Community College); Catherine Callaway Dauterman (College of Notre Dame); William J. DeSaegher (Point Loma Nazarene University); John R. Dunlap (Santa Clara University); S. A. Eisenstein (Los Angeles City College); John H. Esperian (Community College of Southern Nevada); Anne M. Evans (Napa Valley College); Stephen D. Fox (Gallaudet University); Shearle Furnish (West Texas A & M University); C. Herbert Gilliland (United States Naval Academy); Tassie Gwilliam (University of Miami); Boyd Hagy (Marymount University); Mark Halperin (Central Washington University); Charles Heglan (University of South Florida); M. Susan Herdrich (Spokane Community College); Walter Hesford (University of Idaho); Alan Jacobs (Wheaton College); Alison Jasper (California Polytechnic State University); David L. Jeffrey (University of Ottawa); M. S. Johnston (Manhate State University); Martha Kallstrom (Georgia Southern University); Anne Kane-Lavin (Adirondack Community College); Jane M. Kinney (Valdosta State University); Alfred Kolb (Quinsigamond Community College); Alice S. Mandanis (Marymount University); Kay McClellan (South Plains College);

Victoria E. McClure (South Plains College); David McCracken (University of Washington); Patricia R. Menhart (Broward Community College); Robert I. Modica (Pima Community College); Michael W. Murphy (University of Wisconsin at Green Bay); Bradley Nystrom (California State University); Beryl Parker (John Abbot College); Sharon L. Romino (Fairmount State College); Merilyn L. Schiedat (Glendale Community College); Jonna G. Semeiks (Long Island University); Edward A. Shaw (University of Central Florida); Virginia L. Stein (Community College of Allegheny County); James Stokes (University of Wisconsin at Stevens Point); Gerard F. Strasser (Pennsylvania State University); Satya P. Tandon (Mohawk Valley Community College); Jon Thomson (United States Naval Academy); Burt Thorp (University of North Dakota); Robert Weathersby (Dalton College); David Whalen (Hillsdale College); Jack Williams (California State University); Katharine M. Wilson (University of Georgia); and L. Zancu (Millersville University).

Phonetic Equivalents

for use with the Pronouncing Glossaries preceding most
selections in this volume

a as in *cat*
ah as in *father*
ai as in *light*
ay as in *day*
aw as in *raw*
e as in *pet*
ee as in *street*
ehr as in *air*
er as in *bird*
eu as in *lurk*
g as in *good*
i as in *sit*
j as in *joke*
nh a nasal sound (as in French *vin, vĕ*)
o as in *pot*
oh as in *no*
oo as in *boot*
oy as in *toy*
or as in *bore*
ow as in *now*
s as in *mess*
ts as in *ants*
u as in *us*
zh as in *vision*

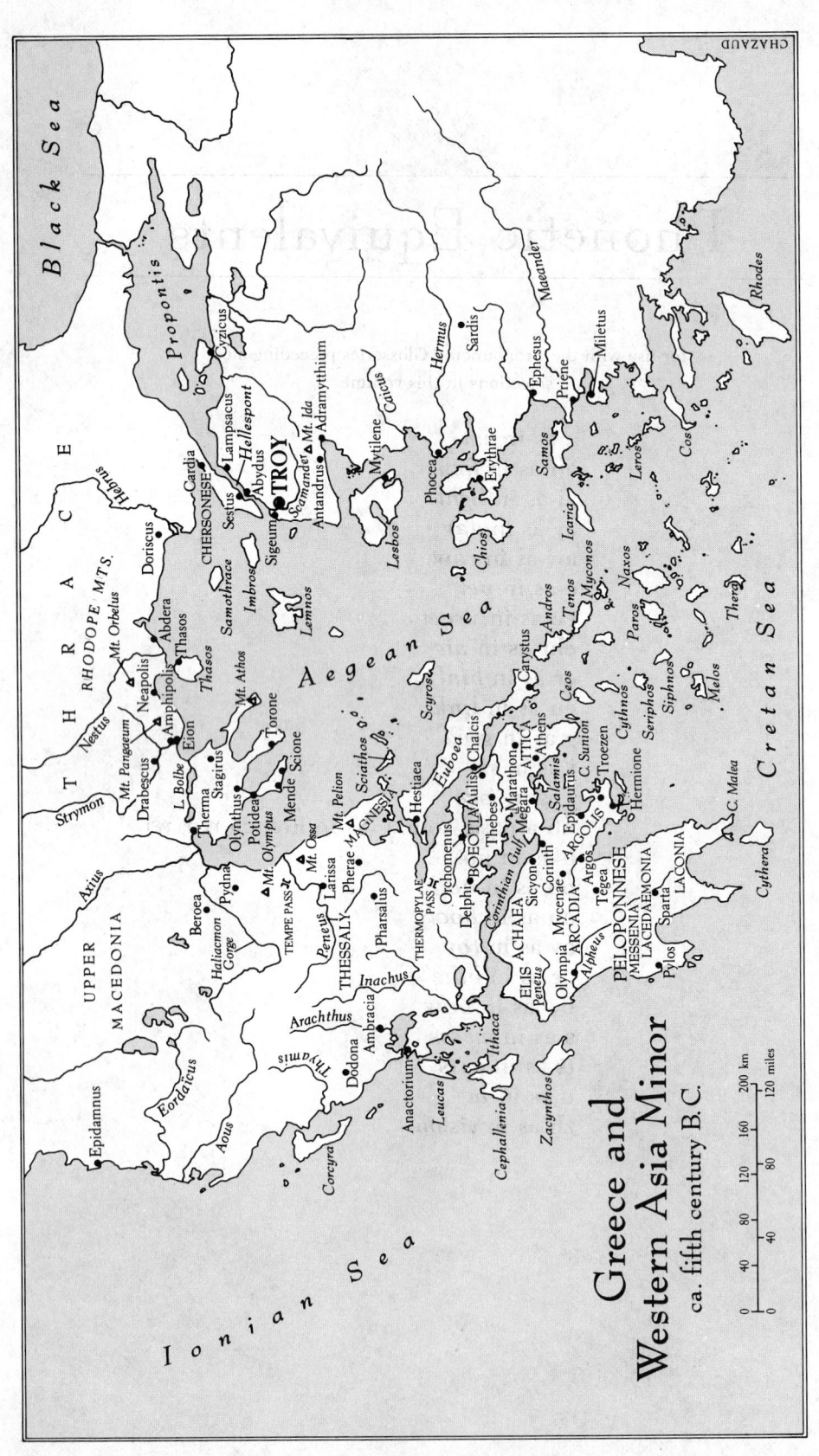

Greece and
Western Asia Minor
ca. fifth century B.C.

Masterpieces of the
Ancient World

This section represents, not the ancient world as a whole, but a particularly significant area and period. The area is the Mediterranean basin, and the period the twelve hundred years from, roughly, 800 B.C. to A.D. 400. In this place and time the intellectual and religious foundations of the modern Western outlook were laid.

The literature of that world, which, whether or not we are acquainted with it, still underlies many of our institutions, attitudes, and thought, was written in three languages—Hebrew, Greek, and Latin. The peoples who spoke these languages created their civilizations independently in place and time, but the development of the Mediterranean area into one economic and political unit brought them into contact with one another and produced a fusion of their typical attitudes that formed the basis of later European thought. This process of independent development, interaction, and final fusion is represented in the tripartite arrangement of this section. As the three separate lines converge, they finally meet in the figure of St. Augustine, who had the intellectual honesty and curiosity of the Greeks at their best, the social seriousness and sense of order of the Romans, and the Hebrews' feeling of human inadequacy and God's omnipotent justice.

THE ANCIENT WORLD

Though Rome at the height of her power was to extend her rule northward through France as far as Britain and eastward to the Euphrates, the ancient world was centered on the Mediterranean Sea. "We live around the sea," said the Greek philosopher Socrates, "like frogs around a pond." Climate and basic crops were (and still are) similar over most of the area: a dry hot summer and a comparatively mild winter, more favorable to sheep and goats than cattle, to vine and olive rather than cereal crops. Though metal was mined and worked, what we know as heavy industry did not exist. Coal and oil were not exploited for energy; the war galleys were propelled by sail and human oarsmen; and the armies moved on foot. All the advanced civilizations of the ancient world depended for their existence on slaves to do their heavy work on the land, in the mines, and in the house. The system of dependent labor, widely varied in its forms—peasants tied to the land as in Egypt, bought slaves as in Greece and Rome, or people enslaved for debt as in Greece and Israel—lasted until the end of the ancient world, to be gradually replaced in Europe by the feudal system with a peasantry technically free but in practice working the land for the benefit of an overlord.

Mediterranean civilization began, not on the coasts, but east and south of the sea: in Babylon and Egypt. Ancient civilization was based on agriculture and it flourished first in regions where the soil gave rich rewards: in the valley of the Nile, where annual floods left large tracts of land moist and fertile under the Egyptian sun, and in the valleys of the Euphrates and Tigris Rivers, which flowed through the "Fertile Crescent," the land now known as Iraq and Iran. Great cities—Thebes and Memphis in Egypt, Babylon and Nineveh in the Fertile Crescent—came into being as centers for the complicated administration of the irrigated fields. Supported by the surplus the land produced, they became centers also for government, religion, and the emerging cultures. As far back as 3000 B.C. the pharaohs of Egypt began to build their splendid temples and gigantic pyramids, as well as to record their political acts and religious beliefs in hieroglyphic script. The Sumerians, Babylonians, and Assyrians began to build the palaces and temples of Babylon, as well as to record their laws in cuneiform script on clay tablets.

These civilizations were already immemorially old when Israel, Greece, and, later, Rome became conscious of their national character and destiny. Whatever contributions they may have made to those younger cultures, however, Babylon, Nineveh, and Egypt, as the centuries went by, were all but lost to memory, as the modern rediscovery of *Gilgamesh* exemplifies. The pyramids and the Sphinx remained but it was not until the nineteenth century A.D. that the hieroglyphic writing of the Egyptians and the cuneiform records of Babylon and Nineveh were deciphered and their contents read again after a lapse of thousands of years. The cultural history of the ancient world came to medieval and Renaissance Europe in the languages not of Babylon and Egypt but in Hebrew, Greek, and Latin.

THE HEBREWS

There was, of course, contact between the old civilizations and the new. The Hebrews, in fact, early in their history, spent some years as government slaves in Egypt before their Exodus: their migration, under the leadership of Moses, through the Sinai desert to Palestine. In their period of independence, they progressed from their beginnings as a pastoral tribe to their high point as a kingdom with a splendid capital in Jerusalem. Their later history was a bitter and unsuccessful struggle for freedom against a series of foreign masters—Babylonian, Greek, and Roman.

After the period of expansion and prosperity under the great kings, David and Solomon (1005–925 B.C.), the kingdom fell apart again into warring factions, which called in outside powers. The melancholy end of a long period of internal and external struggle was the destruction of the cities and the deportation of the population to Babylon (586 B.C.). This period of exile (it ended in 539 B.C. when Cyrus, the Persian conqueror of Babylon, released the Hebrews from bondage) was a formative period for Hebrew religious thought, which was enriched and refined by the teachings of the prophet Ezekiel and the anonymous prophet known as the Second Isaiah. The return to Palestine was crowned by the rebuilding of the Temple and the creation of the canonical version of the Pentateuch or Torah, the first five books of the Hebrew Bible. The religious legacy of the Hebrew people was now codified for future generations.

Foreign domination, however, continued for the next several centuries. After encroachments by the Macedonian successors of Alexander the Great around 300 B.C., Palestine became part of a Hellenistic Greek-speaking kingdom. In 63 B.C., after a short period of independence, it was absorbed by the Roman Empire. A desperate revolt against Rome was crushed in A.D. 70 by the emperor Titus (on the arch of Titus in Rome a relief shows the legionaries carrying the menorah, the seven-branched candlestick, in Titus's triumph). A second revolt, against the emperor Hadrian (A.D. 131–34) resulted in the *diaspora*, the "scattering" of the Hebrew people. Religious communities in the great cities of the ancient world maintained local cohesion and universal religious solidarity but remained stateless, as they were to be all through the centuries until the creation, in 1948, of the state of Israel.

The ancient Hebrews left us a religious literature, written down probably between the eighth and second centuries B.C., which is informed by an attitude different from that of any other nation of the ancient world. It is founded on the idea of one God, the creator of all things, all-powerful and just—a conception revolutionary in its time.

THE GREEKS

The origin of the peoples who eventually called themselves Hellenes is still a mystery. The language they spoke belongs clearly to the great Indo-European family (which includes the Germanic, Celtic, Italic, and Sanskrit language groups), but many of the ancient Greek words and place names have terminations that are definitely not Indo-European—the word for sea (*thalassa*), for example. The Greeks of historic times were presumably a blend of the native tribes and the Indo-European invaders, en route from the European landmass.

In the last hundred years archeology has given us a clearer picture than our fore-bears had of the level of civilization in early Greece. The second millennium B.C. saw a brilliant culture, called Minoan after the mythical king Minos, flourishing on the large island of Crete, and the citadel of Mycenae and the palace at Pylos show that mainland Greece, in that same period, had centers of wealth and power unsuspected before the excavators discovered the gold masks of the buried kings and clay tablets covered with strange signs. The decipherment of these signs (published in 1953) revealed that the language of these Myceneans was an early form of Greek. It must have been the memory of these rich kingdoms that inspired Homer's vision of "Myce-nae rich in gold" and the splendid armed hosts that assembled for the attack on Troy.

It was a blurred memory (Homer does not remember the writing, for example, or the detailed bureaucratic accounting recorded on the tablets) and this is easy to understand: some time in the last century of the millennium the great palaces were destroyed by fire. With them disappeared not only the arts and skills that had created Mycenean wealth but even the system of writing. For the next few hundred years the Greeks were illiterate and so no written evidence survives for what, in view of our ignorance about so many aspects of it, we call the Dark Age of Greece.

One thing we do know about it: it produced a body of oral epic poetry that was the raw material Homer shaped into the two great poems, the *Iliad* and *Odyssey*. These Homeric poems seem from internal evidence to date from the eighth century B.C.— which is incidentally, or perhaps not incidentally, the century in which the Greeks learned how to write again. They played in the subsequent development of Greek civilization the same role that the Torah had played in Palestine: they became the basis of an education and therefore of a whole culture. Not only did the great characters of the epic serve as models of conduct for later generations of Greeks, but the figures of the Olympian gods retained, in the prayers, poems, and sculpture of the succeeding centuries, the shapes and attributes set down by Homer. The difference between the Greek and the Hebrew hero, between Achilles and Joseph, for example, is remarkable, but the difference between "the God of Abraham and of Isaac" and the Olympians who interfere capriciously in the lives of Hector or Achilles or Helen is an unbridgeable chasm. The two conceptions of the power that governs the universe are irreconcilable; and in fact the struggle between them ended, not in synthesis, but in the complete victory of the one and the disappearance of the other. The Greek conception of the nature of the gods and of their relation to humanity is so alien to us that it is difficult for the modern reader to take it seriously. The Hebrew basis of European religious thought has made it almost impossible for us to imagine a god who can be feared and laughed at, blamed and admired, and still sincerely worshiped. Yet all these are proper attitudes toward the gods on Olympus; they are all implicit in Homer's poems.

The Hebrew conception of God emphasizes those aspects of the universe that imply a harmonious order. The elements of disorder in the universe are, in the story of

Creation, blamed on humankind, and in all Hebrew literature the evidences of disorder are something the writer tries to reconcile with an *a priori* assumption of an all-powerful, just God; no one tampers with the fundamental datum. Just as clearly, the Greeks conceived their gods as an expression of the disorder of the world in which they lived. The Olympian gods, like the natural forces of sea and sky, follow their own will even to the extreme of conflict with each other, and always with a sublime disregard for the human beings who may be affected by the results of their actions. It is true that they are all subjects of a single more powerful god, Zeus. But his authority over them is based only on superior strength; though he cannot be openly resisted, he can be temporarily deceived by his fellow Olympians. And Zeus, although by virtue of his superior power his will is finally accomplished in the matter of Achilles' wrath, knows limits to his power too. He cannot save the life of his son the Lycian hero Sarpedon. Behind Zeus stands the mysterious power of Fate, to which even he must bow.

Such gods as these, representing as they do the blind forces of the universe that humans cannot control, are not always thought of as connected with morality. Morality is a human creation, and though the gods may approve of it, they are not bound by it. And violent as they are, they cannot feel the ultimate consequence of violence: death is a human fear, just as the courage to face it is a human quality. There is a double standard, one for gods, one for mortals, and the inevitable consequence is that our real admiration and sympathy are directed not toward the gods but toward the mortals. With Hector and Andromache, and even with Achilles at his worst, we can sympathize; but the gods, though they may excite terror or laughter, can never have our sympathy. We could as easily sympathize with a blizzard or the force of gravity. Homer imposed on Greek literature the anthropocentric emphasis that is its distinguishing mark and its great contribution to the Western mind. Though the gods are ever-present characters in the incidents of his poems, his true concern, first and last, is with men and women.

THE CITY-STATES OF GREECE

The stories told in the Homeric poems are set in the age of the Trojan War, which archeologists (those, that is, who believe that it happened at all) date to the twelfth century B.C. Though the poems do preserve some faded memories of the Mycenaean Age, as we have them they probably are the creation of later centuries, the tenth to the eighth B.C., the so-called Dark Age that succeeded the collapse (or destruction) of Mycenaean civilization. This was the time of the final settlement of the Greek peoples, an age of invasion perhaps and migration certainly, which saw the foundation and growth of many small independent cities. The geography of Greece—a land of mountain barriers and scattered islands—encouraged this fragmentation. The Greek cities never lost sight of their common Hellenic heritage, but it was not enough to unite them except in the face of unmistakable and overwhelming danger, and even then only partially and for a short time. They differed from each other in custom, political constitution, and even dialect: their relations with each other were those of rivals and fierce competitors.

These cities, constantly at war in the pursuit of more productive land for growing populations, were dominated from the late eighth century B.C. by aristocratic oligarchies, which maintained a stranglehold on the land and the economy of which it was the base. An important safety valve was colonization. In the eighth and seventh centuries B.C. landless Greeks founded new cities (always near the sea and generally owing little or no allegiance to the home base) all over the Mediterranean coast—in Spain, southern France (Marseilles, Nice, and Antibes were all Greek cities), in South Italy (Naples), Sicily (Syracuse), North Africa (Cyrene), all along the coast of Asia Minor (Smyrna, Miletus), and even on the Black Sea as far as Russian Crimea. Many of these new outposts of Greek civilization experienced a faster economic and cultural development than the older cities of the mainland. It was in the cities founded on the Asian coast that the Greeks adapted to their own language the Phoenician system of writing, adding signs for the vowels to create their alphabet, the forerunner of the Roman alphabet and of our own. Its first use was probably for commercial records and transactions, but as literacy became a general condition all over the Greek world in the course of the seventh century B.C., treaties and political decrees were inscribed on stone and literary works written on rolls of paper made from the Egyptian papyrus plant.

ATHENS AND SPARTA

By the beginning of the fifth century B.C. the two most prominent city-states were Athens and Sparta. These two cities led the combined Greek resistance to the Persian invasion of Europe in the years 490 to 479 B.C. The defeat of the solid Persian power by the divided and insignificant Greek cities surprised the world and inspired in Greece, and particularly in Athens, a confidence that knew no bounds.

Athens was at this time a democracy, the first in Western history. It was a direct, not a representative, democracy, for the number of free citizens was small enough to permit the exercise of power by a meeting of the citizens as a body in assembly. Athens's power lay in the fleet with which she had played her decisive part in the struggle against Persia, and with this fleet she rapidly became the leader of a naval alliance that included most of the islands of the Aegean Sea and many Greek cities on the coast of Asia Minor. Sparta, on the other hand, was rigidly conservative in government and policy. Because the individual citizen was reared and trained by the state for the state's business, war, the Spartan land army was superior to any other in Greece, and the Spartans controlled, by direct rule or by alliance, a majority of the city-states of the Peloponnese.

These two cities, allies for the war of liberation against Persia, became enemies when the external danger was eliminated. The middle years of the fifth century were disturbed by indecisive hostilities between them and haunted by the probability of full-scale war to come. As the years went by, this war came to be accepted as "inevitable" by both sides, and in 431 B.C. it began. It was to end in 404 B.C. with the total defeat of Athens.

Before the beginning of this disastrous war, known as the Peloponnesian War, Athenian democracy provided its citizens with a cultural and political environment that was without precedent in the ancient world. The institutions of Athens encouraged the maximum development of the individual's capacities and at the same time inspired the maximum devotion to the interests of the community. It was a moment in history of delicate and precarious balance between the freedom of the individual and the demands of the state. It was the proud boast of the Athenians that without sacrificing the cultural amenities of civilized life they could yet when called upon surpass in policy and war their adversary, Sparta, whose citizen body was an army in constant training. The Athenians were, in this respect as in others, a nation of amateurs. "The individual Athenian," said Pericles, Athens's great statesman at this time, "in his own person seems to have the power of adapting himself to the most varied forms of action with the utmost versatility and grace." But the freedom of the individual did not, in Athens's great days, produce anarchy. "While we are . . . unconstrained in our private intercourse," Pericles had observed earlier in his speech, "a spirit of reverence pervades our public acts."

There were limits on who could participate in the democracy. The "individual Athenian" of whom Pericles spoke was the adult male citizen. In his speech, he mentioned women only once, to tell them that the way for them to obtain glory was not to be worse than their nature made them, and to be least talked of among males for either praise or blame. Women could not own property, hold office, or vote. Peasant women may have had to work in the fields with their husbands, but affluent women were expected to remain inside the house except for funerals and religious festivals, rarely seen by men other than their husbands or male relatives. Their reputations for sexual chastity were fiercely protected; no suspicion of illegitimacy must fall on the sons they were expected to produce: future Athenian citizens, heirs to the family property and continuators of the family line (which was traced through the male side). There were, in addition, a number of men from other cities who settled in Athens, often for business reasons—*metics*, or "resident aliens." These could not own land or take part in civic affairs. A great deal of labor—in the houses and fields, in craftsmen's shops, in the silver mines that underlay Athens's wealth—was performed by slaves, who of course had no rights at all. And finally, even among citizens who participated in civic life on a footing of equality, there were marked divisions between the elite and the poorer classes and tensions between them. Still, although it was exclusionary in all these ways, and although it pursued a ruthless imperialist policy abroad, Athenian democracy represented a bold achievement of civic equality for those who belonged.

This democracy came under strain as the Peloponnesian War progressed. Under the mounting pressure of the long conflict, the Athenians lost the "spirit of reverence" that Pericles saw as the stabilizing factor in Athenian democracy. They subordinated all considerations to the immediate interest of the city and surpassed their enemy in the logical ferocity of their actions. They finally fell victim to leaders who carried the process one step further and subordinated all considerations to their own private interest. The war years saw the decay of that freedom in unity which is celebrated in Pericles' speech. By the end of the fifth century Athens was divided internally as well as defeated externally. The individual citizen no longer thought of himself and Athens as one and the same; the balance was gone forever.

One of the solvents of traditional values was an intellectual revolution that was taking place in the advanced Athenian democracy of the last half of the fifth century, a critical reevaluation of accepted ideas in every sphere of thought and action. It stemmed from innovations in education. Democratic institutions had created a demand for an education that would prepare men for public life, especially by training them in the art of public speaking. The demand was met by the appearance of the professional teacher, the Sophist, as he was called, who taught, for a handsome fee, not only the techniques of public speaking but also the subjects that gave a man something to talk about—government, ethics, literary criticism, even astronomy. The curriculum of the Sophists, in fact, marks the first appearance in European civilization of liberal education (for affluent males), just as they themselves were the first professors.

The Sophists were great teachers, but like most teachers they had little or no control over the results of their teaching. Their methods placed an inevitable emphasis on effective presentation of a point of view, to the detriment, and if necessary the exclusion, of anything that might make it less convincing. They produced a generation that had been trained to see both sides of any question and to argue the weaker side as effectively as the stronger, the false as effectively as the true. They taught how to argue inferentially from probability in the absence of concrete evidence; to appeal to the audience's sense of its own advantage rather than to accepted moral standards; and to justify individual defiance of general prejudice and even of law by making a distinction between "nature" and "convention." These methods dominated the thinking of the Athenians of the late fifth and fourth centuries B.C. Emphasis on the technique of effective presentation of both sides of any case encouraged a relativistic point of view. The canon of probability (which implies an appeal to human reason as the supreme authority) became a critical weapon for an attack on myth and on traditional conceptions of the gods; though it had its constructive side, too, for it was the base for historical reconstruction of the unrecorded past and of the stages of human progress from savagery to civilization. The rhetorical appeal to the self-interest of the audience, to expediency, became the method of the political leaders of the wartime democracy and the fundamental doctrine of new theories of power-politics. These theories served to justify the increasing severity of the measures Athens took to terrorize her rebellious subjects. The new spirit in Athens had magnificent achievements to its credit, but it undermined traditional moral convictions. At its roots was a supreme confidence in the human intelligence and a secular view of humanity's position in the universe that is best expressed in the statement of Protagoras, the most famous of the Sophists: "Man is the measure of all things." These shifts in worldview and moral beliefs led to new forms of creativity in art, literature, and thought, although they also caused bitter debates, and sometimes conflicts, between traditionalists and proponents of the new ideas.

THE DECLINE OF THE CITY-STATE

In the last quarter of the fifth century the whole traditional basis of individual conduct, which had been concern for the unity and cohesion of the city-state, was undermined—gradually at first by the critical approach of the Sophists and their pupils, and then rapidly, as the war accelerated the loosening of the old standards. "In peace and prosperity," says Thucydides, "both states and individuals are actuated by higher motives . . . but war, which takes away the comfortable provision of daily life, is a hard master, and tends to assimilate men's characters to their conditions." The war brought to Athens the rule of new politicians who were schooled in the doctrine of power-politics and initiated savage reprisals against Athens's rebellious subject-allies, launching the city on an expansionist course that ended in disaster in Sicily (413 B.C.) and a short-lived oligarchic revolution (411 B.C.). Seven years later Athens, her last fleet gone, surrendered to the Spartans. A pro-Spartan antidemocratic regime, the Thirty Tyrants, was installed, but soon overthrown. Athens became a democracy again but the confidence and unity of its great age were gone forever. Community and individual were no longer one. Yet despite a perceptible retreat into privacy, Athenian democracy continued to work through most of the fourth century, until the conquest of Philip (see below). That same century witnessed, in addition to continued creativity in poetry, painting, and sculpture, two new developments. It saw the flowering of Athenian rhetoric, a legacy of the Sophists and one of Greek culture's greatest contributions to Rome in turn. During the same time, Plato and Aristotle revolutionized philosophy and laid the foundations for later ancient and European philosophical thought. But they had a predecessor in Plato's great teacher, Socrates.

In the wake of their defeat by Sparta, Athenians began to feel more and more exasperation with a voice they had been listening to for many years. This was the voice of Socrates, a stonemason who for most of his adult life had made it his business to discuss with his fellow citizens such great issues as the nature of justice, of truth, of piety. Unlike the Sophists, he did not lecture nor did he charge a fee: his method was dialectic, a search for truth through questions and answers, and his dedication to his mission had kept him poor. But the initial results of his discussions were often infuriatingly like the results of sophistic teaching. By questions and answers he exposed the illogicality of his opponent's position, but did not often provide a substitute for the belief he had destroyed. Yet it is clear that he did believe in absolute standards, and what is more, believed they could be discovered by a process of logical inquiry and supported by logical proof. His ethics rested on an intellectual basis. The resentment against him, which came to a head in 399 B.C., is partly explained by his questioning of the old standards in order to establish new, and by his refusal to let the Athenians live in peace, for he preached that it was every person's duty to think through to the truth. In this last respect he was the prophet of the new age. For him, the city and the accepted code were no substitute for the task of self-examination that each individual must carry through to a conclusion. The characteristic statement of the old Athens was public, in the assembly or the theater; Socrates proclaimed the responsibility of each individual to work out a means to fulfillment and happiness and made clear his distrust of public life: "he who will fight for the right . . . must have a private station and not a public one."

The Athenians sentenced him to death on a charge of impiety. They hoped, no doubt, that he would go into exile to escape execution, but he remained, as he put it himself, at his post, and they were forced to have the sentence carried out. If they thought they were finished with him, they were sadly mistaken. In the next century Athens became the center for a large group of philosophical schools, all of them claiming to develop and interpret the ideas of Socrates.

The century that followed his death saw the exhaustion of the Greek city-states in constant internecine warfare. Politically and economically bankrupt, they fell under the power of Macedon in the north, whose king, Philip, combined a ferocious energy with a cynicism that enabled him to take full advantage of the disunity of the city-states. Greek liberty ended at the battle of Chaeronea in 338 B.C., and Philip's son Alexander inherited a powerful army and the political control of all Greece. He led his Macedonian and Greek armies against Persia, and in a few brilliant campaigns became master of an empire that extended into Egypt in the south and to the borders of India in the east. He died at Babylon in 323 B.C., and his empire broke up into a number of independent kingdoms ruled by his generals. One of these generals, Ptolemy, founded a Greek dynasty that ruled Egypt until after the Roman conquest and ended only with the death of the famous Cleopatra. The results of Alexander's fantastic achievements were more durable than might have been expected. Into the newly conquered territories came thousands of Greeks who wished to escape from the political futility and economic crisis of the homeland. Wherever they went they took with them their language, their culture, and their typical buildings, the gymnasium and the theater. At Alexandria in Egypt, for example, the Ptolemies formed a Greek library to preserve the texts of Greek literature for the scholars who edited them, a school of Greek poetry flourished, and Greek mathematicians and geographers made new advances in science. The Middle East became, as far as the cities were concerned, a Greek-speaking area; and when, some two or three centuries later, the first accounts of the life and teaching of Jesus of Nazareth were written down, they were written in Greek, the language on which the cultural homogeneity of the whole area was based.

ROME

When Alexander died in 323 B.C., the city of Rome, situated on the Tiber in the western coastal plain of Italy, was engaged in a struggle for the control of the surrounding areas. By the middle of the third century B.C., it dominated most of the Italian peninsula. Expansion southward brought Rome into collision with Carthage, a city in North Africa that was then the greatest power in the western Mediterranean. Two protracted wars resulted (264–41 and 218–01 B.C.), and it was only at the end of a third, shorter war (149–46 B.C.) that the Romans destroyed their great rival. The second Carthaginian (or Punic) War was particularly hard-fought, both in Spain and in Italy itself, where the Carthaginian general Hannibal, having made a spectacular crossing of the Alps, operated for years, and where Rome's southern Italian allies defected to Carthage and had to be slowly rewon. Rome, however, emerged from this war in 201 B.C. not merely victorious but a world power. The next two decades saw frequent wars—in Spain, in Greece, and in Asia Minor—that laid the foundations of the Roman Empire. These successes changed Roman social, cultural, and economic life profoundly.

From early on, the Romans had come into contact with Greek culture through the sophisticated Greek cities of southern Italy and Sicily; now, with their involvement

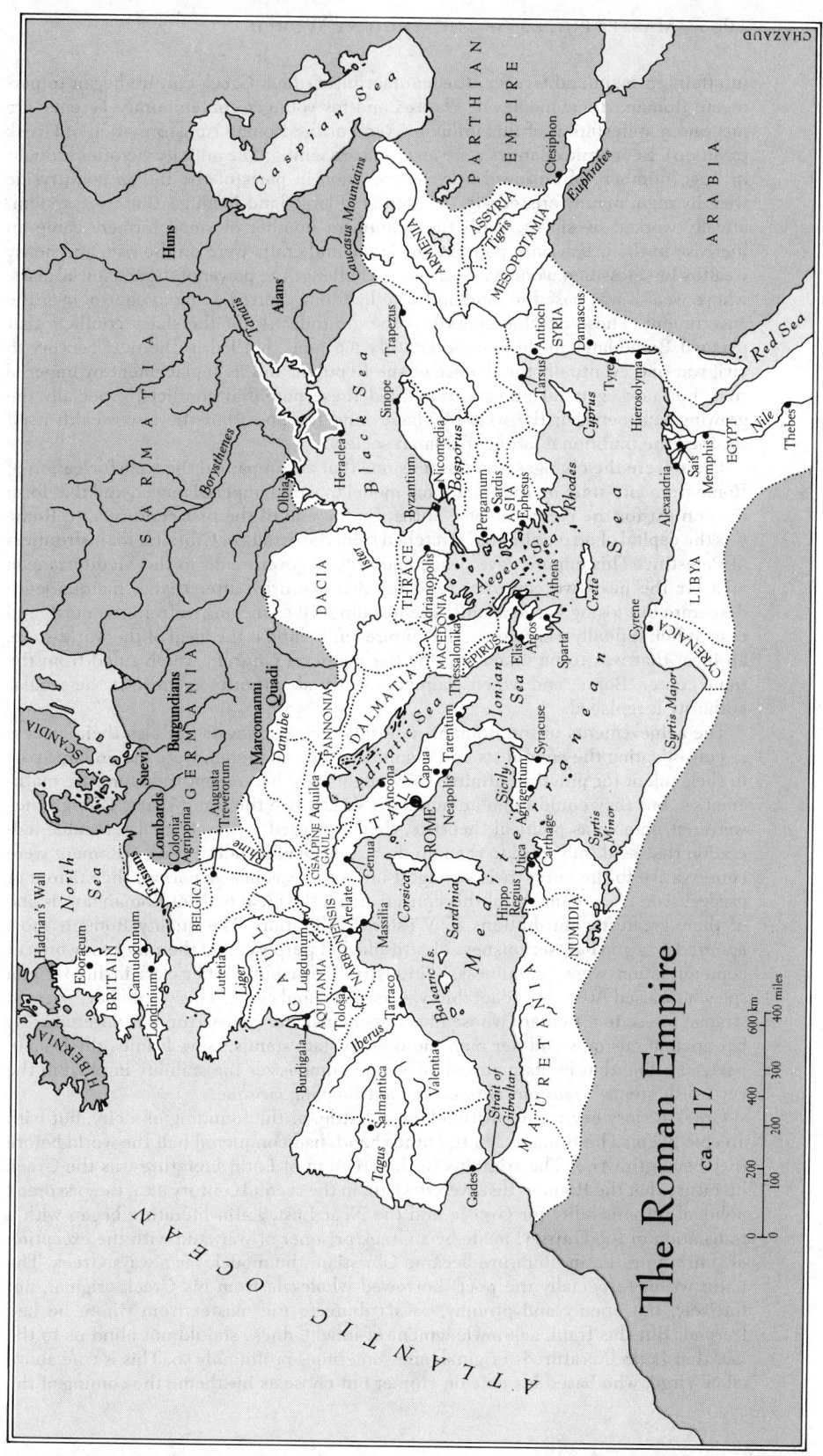

The Roman Empire

ca. 117

CHAZAUD

ATLANTIC OCEAN

HIBERNIA

BRITAIN
Hadrian's Wall
Eboracum
Camulodunum
Londinium

North Sea

SCANDIA
SCANDIA

Huns

Alans

SARMATIA

Caspian Sea

Tanais
Borysthenes
Olbia

Black Sea

Caucasus Mountains

PARTHIAN EMPIRE

ARMENIA

ASSYRIA
Tigris
MESOPOTAMIA
Euphrates
Ctesiphon

Heraclea
Sinope
Trapezus

ARABIA

Frisians
Lombards
Suevi
Burgundians
Marcomanni
Quadi

GERMANIA
Colonia
Agrippina
Augusta
Trevororum
Rhine

DACIA

Ister
Danube
PANNONIA

Byzantium
Nicomedia
Adrianopolis
THRACE
Bosporus
Pergamum
Sardis
ASIA
Ephesus

Antioch
SYRIA
Damascus
Tarsus
Tyre
Cyprus
Hierosolyma

Red Sea

BELGICA
Lutetia
Liger
Seine

GAUL
CISALPINE
GAUL
Aquileia
DALMATIA
Adriatic Sea
Ancona
Genua
ITALY
Capua
ROME
Neapolis
Tarentum
Thessalonika
MACEDONIA
EPIRUS
Ionian Sea
Elis
Argos
Sparta
Athens
Aegean Sea
Rhodes

Crete

Alexandria
Saïs
Memphis
EGYPT
Nile
Thebes

AQUITANIA
Tolosa
Burdigala
Lugdunum
Arelate
Massilia
NARBONENSIS

Corsica
Sardinia
Balearic Is.

Tarraco
Valentia
Iberus
Salmantica
Tagus
Gades
Strait of Gibraltar

Mediterranean Sea

Utica
Hippo
Regius
Carthage
NUMIDIA
Agrigentum
Syracuse
Sicily
Ionian Sea

Syrtis Minor
Syrtis Major

MAURETANIA

LIBYA
Cyrene
CYRENAICA

0   100   200   300   400   miles
0   200   400   600 km

in affairs in mainland Greece, this contact intensified. Greek culture began to permeate Roman; the comedies of Plautus and his younger contemporary Terence are just one manifestation of this influence (and of the Roman transformation of Greek tradition). Economic changes were just as far-reaching. The military victories brought in huge numbers of enslaved war-captives, and in parts of the Italian countryside wealthy men, mainly aristocrats, accumulated large land-holdings that were systematically worked by slaves. With the waning in number of small farmers came an increase in the urban poor population. Trade and crafts were on the rise, and newly wealthy businessmen were in a position to challenge the power of the senatorial class, whose wealth was based in land and who had long exerted de facto control over the government. These developments laid the groundwork for the sharp conflicts that plagued Rome later in the second century B.C. and that led in the next century to civil war and eventually the demise of the Republic and its replacement by imperial rule. For now, general prosperity masked these potential conflicts, especially the growing gulf between the wealthy classes and the poor, but the new wealth itself strained the traditional fabric of Roman society.

These were the changes and the tensions that accompanied the transformation of Rome from city-state on the traditional model to world imperial power, and that form the context for the comedies of Plautus. By the end of the first century B.C., Rome was the capital of an empire that stretched from the Straits of Gibraltar to the frontiers of Palestine. This empire gave peace and orderly government to the Mediterranean area for the next two centuries, and for two centuries after that it maintained a desperate but losing battle against the invading tribes moving in from the north and east. When it finally went down, the empire left behind it the ideal of the world-state, an ideal that was to be taken over by the medieval Church, which ruled from the same center, Rome, and which claimed a spiritual authority as great as the secular authority it replaced.

The achievements of the Romans, not only their conquests but also their success in consolidating the conquests and organizing the conquered, were due in large part to their talent for practical affairs. They might have had no aptitude for pure mathematics, but they could build an aqueduct to last two thousand years. Though they were not notable as political theorists, they organized a complicated yet stable federation that held Italy loyal to them in the presence of invading armies. Romans were conservative to the core; their strongest authority was *mos maiorum*, the custom of predecessors. A monument of this conservatism, the great body of Roman law, is one of their greatest contributions to Western civilization. The quality Romans most admired was *gravitas*, seriousness of attitude and purpose, and their highest words of commendation were "manliness," "industry," "discipline." Pericles, in his funeral speech, praised Athenian adaptability, versatility, and grace. This would have seemed strange praise to a Roman, whose idea of personal and civic virtue was different. "By her ancient customs and her men the Roman state stands," says Ennius the Roman poet, in a line that by its metrical heaviness emphasizes the stability implied in the key word "stands": *moribus antiquis res stat Romana virisque*.

Greek history begins, not with a king, a battle, or the founding of a city, but with an epic poem. The Romans, on the other hand, had conquered half the world before they began to write. The stimulus to the creation of Latin literature was the Greek literature that the Romans discovered when, in the second century B.C., they assumed political responsibility for Greece and the Near East. Latin literature began with a translation of the *Odyssey*, made by a Greek prisoner of war, and with the exception of satire, until Latin literature became Christian, the model was always Greek. The Latin writer (especially the poet) borrowed wholesale from his Greek original, not furtively, but openly and proudly, as a tribute to the master from whom he had learned. But this frank acknowledgment of indebtedness should not blind us to the fact that Latin literature is original, and sometimes profoundly so. This is true above all of Virgil, who based his epic on Homer but chose as his theme the coming of the

Trojan prince Aeneas to Italy, where he was to found a city from which, in the fullness of time, would come "the Latin race . . . and the walls of lofty Rome."

When Virgil was born in 70 B.C. the Roman republic, which had conquered and now governed the Mediterranean world, had barely recovered from one civil war and was drifting inexorably toward another. The institutions of the city-state proved inadequate for world government. The civil conflict that had disrupted the republic for more than a hundred years ended finally in the establishment of a powerful executive. Although the Senate, which had been the controlling body of the republic, retained an impressive share of the power, the new arrangement developed inevitably toward autocracy, the rule of the executive, the emperor, as he was called once the system was stabilized. The first of the long line of Roman emperors who gave stable government to the Roman world during the first two centuries A.D. was Octavius, known generally by his title, Augustus. He had made his way cautiously through the intrigues and bloodshed that followed the murder of his uncle Julius Caesar in 44 B.C. until by 31 B.C. he controlled the western half of the empire. In that year he fought a decisive battle with the ruler of the eastern half of the empire, Mark Antony, who was supported by Cleopatra, queen of Egypt. Octavius's victory at Actium united the empire under one authority and ushered in an age of peace and reconstruction.

For the next two hundred years the successors of Augustus, the Roman emperors, ruled the ancient world with only occasional disturbances, most of them confined to Rome, where emperors who flagrantly abused their immense power—Nero, for example—were overthrown by force. The second half of this period was described by Gibbon, the great historian of imperial Rome, as the period "in the history of the world during which the condition of the human race was most happy and prosperous." The years A.D. 96–180, those of the "five good emperors," were in fact remarkable: this was the longest period of peace that has ever been enjoyed by the inhabitants of an area that included Britain, France, all southern Europe, the Middle East, and the whole of North Africa. Trade and agriculture flourished, and the cities with their public baths, theaters, and libraries offered all the amenities of civilized life. Yet there was apparent, especially in the literature of the second century, a spiritual emptiness. Petronius's *Satyricon* paints a sardonic portrait of the vulgar display and intellectual poverty of the newly rich who can think only in terms of money and possessions. The old religion offered no comfort to those who looked beyond mere material ends; it had been too closely knit into the fabric of the independent city-state and was inadequate for a time in which men were citizens of the world. New religions arose or were imported from the East, universal religions that made their appeal to all nations and classes: the worship of the Egyptian goddess Isis, of the Persian god Mithras, who offered bliss in the life to come, and of the Hebrew prophet Jesus, crucified in Jerusalem and believed risen from the dead. This was the religion that, working underground and often suppressed (there was a persecution of the Christians under Nero in the first century, another under the last of the "good emperors" Marcus Aurelius in the second), finally triumphed and became the official and later the exclusive religion of the Roman world. As the empire in the third and fourth centuries disintegrated under the never-ending invasions by peoples from the north, the Church, with its center and spiritual head in Rome, converted the new inhabitants and so made possible the preservation of much of that Latin and Greek literature that was to serve the European Middle Ages and, later, the Renaissance, as a model and a basis for their own great achievements in the arts and letters.

FURTHER READING

H. M. Orlinsky, *Ancient Israel*, 2nd ed. (1960), is a short but clearly written outline of the history of Israel up to the return from Babylonian exile. John Boardman, Jasper Griffin, and Oswyn Murray, eds., *The Oxford History of the Classical World* (1986), is a handsomely illustrated survey, by many different specialists, of the whole sweep of classical culture—social, political, literary, artistic, and religious. For the history of Greece to the death of Alexander, see J. B. Bury, *A History of Greece*, 4th ed., revised by Russell Meiggs (1975), and Thomas R. Martin, *Ancient Greece* (1996)—the latter clearly written especially for the nonspecialist reader. Michael Grant, *History of Rome* (1978), presents a well-illustrated, eminently readable survey. For surveys of Greek and Roman civilization organized according to different types of people and their social experiences, see Jean-Pierre Vernant, ed., *The Greeks* (1995), and Andrea Giardina, ed., *The Romans* (1993). A rich and beautifully illustrated survey of women in Greece and Rome is Elaine Fantham, Helene Foley, Natalie Kampen, Sarah Pomeroy, and Alan Shapiro, eds., *Women in the Classical World* (1994). *Perseus* is a superb interactive CD-ROM program on Greek civilization, with a huge database of texts (in Greek and English), maps, images of sites and artifacts, and a short version of Martin's historical outline (above). Much of what is on the CD-ROM can be found at the excellent Perseus Website. For a wealth of links to other Websites on the ancient world, see the University of Michigan's Classics and Mediterranean Archaeology Home Page (this and the Perseus site can easily be located with standard Web search engines such as Lycos or WebCrawler).

ANCIENT GREECE AND THE FORMATION OF THE WESTERN MIND

TEXTS	CONTEXTS
	2200–1450 B.C. Minoan civilization flourishes on Crete
	ca. 1450 Mycenaeans from mainland Greece occupy Crete
	ca. 1150 Troy destroyed by the Achaeans
	776 Olympic Games founded in Greece
late 8th century B.C. Greek alphabetic scripts	
ca. 700 Homer, the *Iliad,* the *Odyssey*	
600 Sappho writing her **lyrics** on the island of Lesbos	
	594 Solon reforms laws at Athens, which becomes the world's first democracy (508), and defeats a Persian invasion at Marathon (490)
	480–479 Greece turns back a massive Persian invasion by sea at Salamis and by land at Plataea
458 Aeschylus's dramatic trilogy, *The Oresteia,* produced in Athens	
ca. 441 Sophocles, *Antigone*	
431 Euripides, *Medea*	**431–404** Peloponnesian War between Athens and Sparta; Athens surrenders (404)
429–347 Plato, author of *The Apology of Socrates* and *Phaedo*	
426? Sophocles, *Oedipus the King*	
411 Aristophanes, *Lysistrata*	
	399 Trial and execution of Socrates
	ca. 385 Plato founds the Academy
384–322 Aristotle, author of *Poetics*	
	ca. 350 Greek amphitheater built at Epidauros
	338 United Greeks defeated by Philip II of Macedon at Chaeronea

Boldface titles indicate works in the anthology.

ANCIENT GREECE AND THE FORMATION OF THE WESTERN MIND

TEXTS	CONTEXTS
	335 Aristotle founds Peripatetic school of philosophy and lectures in the Lyceum
	334 Alexander of Macedon, Philip's son, conquers Persian empire
	323 Euclid writes *Elements*, the first work of geometry
	307 Library and museum established at Alexandria, Egypt
ca. 254–184 Plautus, author of **Pseudolus**	148 Macedonia becomes a Roman province
ca. 84–54 Catullus	
70–19 Virgil, author of the **Aeneid**	
	47 Julius Caesar dictator; murdered in 44
43–ca. A.D. 17 Ovid, author of **Metamorphoses**	31 At Actium, Octavian Augustus Caesar defeats Antony and Cleopatra
	ca. 6 Birth of Jesus
	ca. A.D. 33 Crucifixion of Jesus
	ca. 35 Conversion of Paul
	47–58 Paul's missionary journeys
	64 Persecution of Christians under Nero
66 Petronius, author of the **Satyricon,** dies	66–70 Jewish revolt against Roman rule; Roman emperor Titus captures Jerusalem
ca. 75 Luke, Gospels and Acts of the Apostles	
ca. 80 Matthew, Gospels	
ca. 120–190 Lucian, author of **A True Story**	
354–430 Augustine, author of **Confessions**	

GILGAMESH

ca. 2500–1500 B.C.

Gilgamesh is a poem of unparalleled antiquity, the first great heroic narrative of world literature. Its origins stretch back to the margins of prehistory, and its evolution spans millennia. When it was known, it was widely known. Tablets containing portions of *Gilgamesh* have been found at sites throughout the Middle East and in all the languages written in cuneiform characters, wedge-shaped characters incised in clay or stone. But then, at a time when the civilizations of the Hebrews, Greeks, and Romans had only just developed beyond their infancy, *Gilgamesh* vanished from memory. For reasons that scholars have not yet fathomed, the literature of the cuneiform languages was not translated into the new alphabets that replaced them. Some portions of this once-famous work survived in subsequent traditions, but they did so as scattered and anonymous fragments. They became a kind of invisible substratum that was buried under what was previously believed to be the earliest level of our common tradition. Until Utnapishtim's "Story of the Flood," a portion of *Gilgamesh*, was accidentally rediscovered and published in 1872, no one suspected that the biblical story of Noah and the Great Flood was neither original nor unique.

A great lost work like *Gilgamesh* poses particular problems of understanding beyond those posed by the discovery of a lost masterpiece by a known author or of a known time. The meaning of a work of literature is partly contextual—it is established by the culture that produced that work. Yet the whole context of *Gilgamesh* was lost along with the text. The names of the gods and humans who people the epic, the cities and lands in which they lived, and the whole of their history vanished for thousands of years from common memory. The story of Gilgamesh and his companion, Enkidu, speaks to contemporary readers with astonishing immediacy. Its moving depiction of the bonds of friendship, of the quest for worldly renown, and of the tragic attempt to escape that death which is the common fate of humanity has a timeless resonance and appeal. Yet despite this immediate recognition of something profoundly familiar there is, because of this millennial gap in the history of its transmission, a strangeness and remoteness about the work that strikes us in virtually every line. That strangeness has diminished each year as more tablets have been discovered and translated and as our understanding of the languages and cultures of the ancient Middle East has increased, but what we know is still relatively slight compared with what we know of the cultures that succeeded them. Today the names of Ulysses and Achilles and the gods and goddesses of Mount Olympus are familiar even to many who have not read Homer. The names of Gilgamesh, Enkidu, Utnapishtim, Enlil, and Eanna are virtually unknown outside the poem itself.

Gilgamesh developed over a period of nearly a thousand years. The version discovered in the city of Nineveh amid the ruins of the great royal library of Assurbanipal, the last great king of the Assyrian empire—what modern scholars now call the Standard Version—circulated widely throughout the ancient Middle East for a millennium or more. While the history of the text is a long and complex one, and is still far from fully understood, it is possible to identify three principal stages in its development. The first begins in roughly 2700 B.C. when the historical Gilgamesh ruled in Uruk, a city in ancient Mesopotamia. Tales both mythical and legendary grew up around him and were repeated and copied for centuries. The stories that were later incorporated into the *Gilgamesh* epic existed in this literature, albeit in different form, as well as other material concerning the historical Gilgamesh that was not included in the epic. The earliest written versions of these stories date from roughly 2000 B.C., but oral versions of the stories both preceded them and continued on, parallel with the written tradition. The language of these materials was Sumerian, the earliest written language in Mesopotamia and one that has little if any connection to any other known language.

The history of the epic itself begins sometime before 1600 B.C., some eight cen-

turies before Homer, when a Babylonian author (Mesopotamian tradition identifies a priest-exorcist named Sîn-leqi-unninni) assembled free translations of the oral versions of some of these tales into a connected narrative. This new work was not simply a sequence of tales linked by the character of Gilgamesh but a conscious selection and recasting of the Sumerian materials into a new form. Some Gilgamesh tales were ignored, while elements from stories not associated with him in the Sumerian accounts were incorporated. This earliest version of the epic, which exists only in fragmentary form, continued to develop for the next few centuries. However, no comparable recasting of the poem was made. By the time of Assurbanipal (668–627 B.C.) the text was essentially stabilized.

Assurbanipal's synthetic version—the Standard Version—was also the first discovered. It was written on twelve hardened-clay tablets in Akkadian, a Semitic language like Hebrew and Arabic and one of the principal languages of Babylonia and Assyria. The first eleven of these tablets make up the story as printed here. The twelfth tells another story of Gilgamesh, "Gilgamesh and the Underworld," and since it is unclear how it is to be incorporated into the preceding tablets, it is usually presented as a kind of appendix to the story.

The tablets of the Standard Version are poorly preserved at a number of points, most notably in the adventure in the Cedar Forest, and the translation relies heavily on the earlier, Old Babylonian version and fragments from a number of other versions.

The epic narrates the legendary deeds of Gilgamesh, king of Uruk, but it begins with a prologue that emphasizes not his adventures but the wisdom he acquired and the monuments he constructed at the end of his epic journey. It also tells us that Gilgamesh was endowed by his divine creators with extraordinary strength, courage, and beauty. He is more god than man. His father, however, is mortal, and that fact is decisive in shaping the narrative that follows. The prologue also suggests that Gilgamesh himself has written this account and left the tablets in the foundation of the city wall of Uruk for all to read.

In our first view of him, Gilgamesh is the epitome of a bad ruler: arrogant, oppressive, and brutal. The people of Uruk complain of his oppression to the Sumerian gods, and the gods' response is to create Enkidu as a foil or counterweight to Gilgamesh. Where the latter is a mixture of human and divine, Enkidu, who also appears godlike, is a blend of human and wild animal, with the animal predominating at first. He is raised by wild beasts, lives as they do (eating only uncooked food), and embodies the conflict between animal and human natures that is a recurrent theme in Mesopotamian literature and myth. When he becomes a kind of protector of the animals, breaking the hunters' traps and filling in their pits, Enkidu poses a threat to the human community. This threat is neutralized by civilizing him. First a prostitute seduces him across the line separating animal from human and educates him in the elements of human society. Then shepherds teach him to eat prepared food, wear clothing, and anoint himself as humans do. He is weakened somewhat by this transformation and estranged from his animal companions, but he is also glorified and made greater than he was. The prostitute leads him to Uruk and the confrontation with Gilgamesh for which the gods have created him. His coming has been announced to Gilgamesh in one of the many dreams that play such an important role in the poem. Although the two are bent on destroying each other at first, their encounter results, as it was meant to, in a deep bond of friendship. Each finds in the other the true companion he has sought. The consequence of their union is that their prodigious energies are directed outward toward heroic achievements.

Gilgamesh proposes the first of their adventures both to gain them universal renown and to refresh the spirit of Enkidu, who has been weakened and confused by civilization. He suggests that they go to the great Cedar Forest in the Country of the Living and there slay the terrible giant Humbaba. Enkidu is reluctant at first because he knows the danger in this adventure better than Gilgamesh. But the latter prevails, and with the blessing of the sun god Shamash they succeed. Their victory is not a

simple, glorious triumph, however, and its meaning is unclear. Humbaba poses no apparent threat to Uruk and its people, and he curses them before he dies. Enlil, the god of wind and storm, is enraged by the slaying of his creature, curses the heroes, and gives to others the seven splendors that had been Humbaba's.

Their second adventure is not of their choosing and also leads to another ambiguous success. Gilgamesh's just but harsh rejection of Ishtar's advances provokes her to send the Bull of Heaven against the people of Uruk. The terrible destruction the Bull causes obliges Gilgamesh and Enkidu to destroy it, but that victory brings about the slow and painful death of Enkidu.

The death of his companion reveals to Gilgamesh the hollowness of mortal fame and leads him to undertake a solitary journey in search of immortality. This journey sets *Gilgamesh* apart from more straightforward heroic narratives and gives it a special appeal to modern readers. Gilgamesh's specific goal is to discover the secret of immortality from the one man, Utnapishtim, who has survived the Flood. His journey begins with a conventional challenge, the fierce lions who guard the mountain passes. But the challenges he faces subsequently—the dark tunnel that brings him to a prototypical garden of paradise, the puzzling and perilous voyage to Dilmun—have a different and more magical character. He is discouraged at every step, but Gilgamesh perseveres. Although he at last finds Utnapishtim and hears his story, his goal eludes him. He fails a simple test of his potential for immortality when he cannot remain awake for six days and seven nights. Moreover, he fails a second test as well when he first finds the plant that ensures eternal rejuvenation and then, in a moment of carelessness, loses it to the serpent. Discouraged and defeated, Gilgamesh returns at last to Uruk empty-handed. His consolation is the assurance that his worldly accomplishments will endure beyond his own lifetime.

In long, belated retrospect we can see that *Gilgamesh* explores many of the mysteries of the human condition for the first time in our literature—the complex and perilous relations between gods and mortals and between nature and civilization, the depths of friendship, and the immortality of art. It is both humbling and thrilling to hear so familiar a voice from so vast a distance.

The introduction to the present translation by N. K. Sandars in *The Epic of Gilgamesh* (1972) is readily available and contains a wealth of useful information. A. Leo Oppenheim gives a comprehensive interpretation of Mesopotamian civilization in *Ancient Mesopotamia* (1977), and Alexander Heidel addresses the importance of *Gilgamesh* for biblical studies in *The Gilgamesh Epic and Old Testament Parallels* (1963).

Gilgamesh[1]

PROLOGUE

Gilgamesh King in Uruk

I will proclaim to the world the deeds of Gilgamesh. This was the man to whom all things were known; this was the king who knew the countries of the world. He was wise, he saw mysteries and knew secret things, he brought us a tale of the days before the flood. He went on a long journey, was weary, worn-out with labour, returning he rested, he engraved on a stone the whole story.

When the gods created Gilgamesh they gave him a perfect body. Shamash[2] the glorious sun endowed him with beauty, Adad the god of the storm

---

1. Translated by N. K. Sandars.   2. Also judge and lawgiver, with some fertility attributes; he is the husband and brother of Ishtar, goddess of love, fertility, and war and queen of heaven.

endowed him with courage, the great gods made his beauty perfect, surpassing all others, terrifying like a great wild bull. Two thirds they made him god and one third man.

In Uruk[3] he built walls, a great rampart, and the temple of blessed Eanna for the god of the firmament Anu,[4] and for Ishtar the goddess of love. Look at it still today: the outer wall where the cornice runs, it shines with the brilliance of copper; and the inner wall, it has no equal. Touch the threshold, it is ancient. Approach Eanna the dwelling of Ishtar, our lady of love and war, the like of which no latter-day king, no man alive can equal. Climb upon the wall of Uruk; walk along it, I say; regard the foundation terrace and examine the masonry: is it not burnt brick and good? The seven sages[5] laid the foundations.

1

The Coming of Enkidu

Gilgamesh went abroad in the world, but he met with none who could withstand his arms till he came to Uruk. But the men of Uruk muttered in their houses, "Gilgamesh sounds the tocsin for his amusement, his arrogance has no bounds by day or night. No son is left with his father, for Gilgamesh takes them all, even the children; yet the king should be a shepherd to his people. His lust leaves no virgin to her lover, neither the warrior's daughter nor the wife of the noble; yet this is the shepherd of the city, wise, comely, and resolute."

The gods heard their lament, the gods of heaven cried to the Lord of Uruk, to Anu the god of Uruk: "A goddess made him, strong as a savage bull, none can withstand his arms. No son is left with his father, for Gilgamesh takes them all; and is this the king, the shepherd of his people? His lust leaves no virgin to her lover, neither the warrior's daughter nor the wife of the noble." When Anu had heard their lamentation the gods cried to Aruru, the goddess of creation, "You made him, O Aruru, now create his equal; let it be as like him as his own reflection, his second self, stormy heart for stormy heart. Let them contend together and leave Uruk in quiet."

So the goddess conceived an image in her mind, and it was of the stuff of Anu of the firmament. She dipped her hands in water and pinched off clay, she let it fall in the wilderness, and noble Enkidu was created. There was virtue in him of the god of war, of Ninurta himself. His body was rough, he had long hair like a woman's; it waved like the hair of Nisaba, the goddess of corn. His body was covered with matted hair like Samuqan's, the god of cattle. He was innocent of mankind; he knew nothing of the cultivated land.

Enkidu ate grass in the hills with the gazelle and lurked with wild beasts at the water-holes; he had joy of the water with the herds of wild game. But there was a trapper who met him one day face to face at the drinking-hole, for the wild game had entered his territory. On three days he met him face to face, and the trapper was frozen with fear. He went back to his house with

---

3. City in southern Babylonia between Fara and Ur. Shown by excavation to have been an important city from very early times, with great temples to the gods Anu and Ishtar. After the Flood it was the seat of a dynasty of kings, among whom Gilgamesh was the fifth and most famous.   4. Also father of the gods; he had an important temple in Uruk. Eanna was the temple precinct in Uruk, sacred to Anu and Ishtar.   5. Wise men who brought civilization to the seven oldest cities of Mesopotamia.

the game he had caught, and he was dumb, benumbed with terror. His face was altered like that of one who has made a long journey. With awe in his heart he spoke to his father: "Father, there is a man, unlike any other, who comes down from the hills. He is the strongest in the world, he is like an immortal from heaven. He ranges over the hills with wild beasts and eats grass; he ranges through your land and comes down to the wells. I am afraid and dare not go near him. He fills in the pits which I dig and tears up my traps set for the game; he helps the beasts to escape and now they slip through my fingers."

His father opened his mouth and said to the trapper, "My son, in Uruk lives Gilgamesh; no one has ever prevailed against him, he is strong as a star from heaven. Go to Uruk, find Gilgamesh, extol the strength of this wild man. Ask him to give you a harlot, a wanton from the temple of love; return with her, and let her woman's power overpower this man. When next he comes down to drink at the wells she will be there, stripped naked; and when he sees her beckoning he will embrace her, and then the wild beasts will reject him."

So the trapper set out on his journey to Uruk and addressed himself to Gilgamesh saying, "A man unlike any other is roaming now in the pastures; he is as strong as a star from heaven and I am afraid to approach him. He helps the wild game to escape; he fills in my pits and pulls up my traps." Gilgamesh said, "Trapper, go back, take with you a harlot, a child of pleasure. At the drinking-hole she will strip, and when he sees her beckoning he will embrace her and the game of the wilderness will surely reject him."

Now the trapper returned, taking the harlot with him. After a three days' journey they came to the drinking-hole, and there they sat down; the harlot and the trapper sat facing one another and waited for the game to come. For the first day and for the second day the two sat waiting, but on the third day the herds came; they came down to drink and Enkidu was with them. The small wild creatures of the plains were glad of the water, and Enkidu with them, who ate grass with the gazelle and was born in the hills; and she saw him, the savage man, come from far-off in the hills. The trapper spoke to her: "There he is. Now, woman, make your breasts bare, have no shame, do not delay but welcome his love. Let him see you naked, let him possess your body. When he comes near uncover yourself and lie with him; teach him, the savage man, your woman's art, for when he murmurs love to you the wild beasts that shared his life in the hills will reject him."

She was not ashamed to take him, she made herself naked and welcomed his eagerness; as he lay on her murmuring love she taught him the woman's art. For six days and seven nights they lay together, for Enkidu had forgotten his home in the hills; but when he was satisfied he went back to the wild beasts. Then, when the gazelle saw him, they bolted away; when the wild creatures saw him they fled. Enkidu would have followed, but his body was bound as though with a cord, his knees gave way when he started to run, his swiftness was gone. And now the wild creatures had all fled away; Enkidu was grown weak, for wisdom was in him, and the thoughts of a man were in his heart. So he returned and sat down at the woman's feet, and listened intently to what she said. "You are wise, Enkidu, and now you have become like a god. Why do you want to run wild with the beasts in the hills? Come with me. I will take you to strong-walled Uruk, to the blessed temple of Ishtar and of Anu, of love and of heaven: there Gilgamesh lives, who is very strong, and like a wild bull he lords it over men."

When she had spoken Enkidu was pleased; he longed for a comrade, for one who would understand his heart. "Come, woman, and take me to that holy temple, to the house of Anu and of Ishtar, and to the place where Gilgamesh lords it over the people. I will challenge him boldly, I will cry out aloud in Uruk, 'I am the strongest here, I have come to change the old order, I am he who was born in the hills, I am he who is strongest of all.'"

She said, "Let us go, and let him see your face. I know very well where Gilgamesh is in great Uruk. O Enkidu, there all the people are dressed in their gorgeous robes, every day is holiday, the young men and the girls are wonderful to see. How sweet they smell! All the great ones are roused from their beds. O Enkidu, you who love life, I will show you Gilgamesh, a man of many moods; you shall look at him well in his radiant manhood. His body is perfect in strength and maturity; he never rests by night or day. He is stronger than you, so leave your boasting. Shamash the glorious sun has given favours to Gilgamesh, and Anu of the heavens, and Enlil, and Ea the wise has given him deep understanding. I tell you, even before you have left the wilderness, Gilgamesh will know in his dreams that you are coming."

Now Gilgamesh got up to tell his dream to his mother, Ninsun, one of the wise gods. "Mother, last night I had a dream. I was full of joy, the young heroes were round me and I walked through the night under the stars of the firmament, and one, a meteor of the stuff of Anu, fell down from heaven. I tried to lift it but it proved too heavy. All the people of Uruk came round to see it, the common people jostled and the nobles thronged to kiss its feet; and to me its attraction was like the love of woman. They helped me, I braced my forehead and I raised it with thongs and brought it to you, and you yourself pronounced it my brother."

Then Ninsun, who is well-beloved and wise, said to Gilgamesh, "This star of heaven which descended like a meteor from the sky; which you tried to lift, but found too heavy, when you tried to move it it would not budge, and so you brought it to my feet; I made it for you, a goad and spur, and you were drawn as though to a woman. This is the strong comrade, the one who brings help to his friend in his need. He is the strongest of wild creatures, the stuff of Anu; born in the grass-lands and the wild hills reared him; when you see him you will be glad; you will love him as a woman and he will never forsake you. This is the meaning of the dream."

Gilgamesh said, "Mother, I dreamed a second dream. In the streets of strong-walled Uruk there lay an axe; the shape of it was strange and the people thronged round. I saw it and was glad. I bent down, deeply drawn towards it; I loved it like a woman and wore it at my side." Ninsun answered, "That axe, which you saw, which drew you so powerfully like love of a woman, that is the comrade whom I give you, and he will come in his strength like one of the host of heaven. He is the brave companion who rescues his friend in necessity." Gilgamesh said to his mother, "A friend, a counsellor has come to me from Enlil, and now I shall befriend and counsel him." So Gilgamesh told his dreams; and the harlot retold them to Enkidu.

And now she said to Enkidu, "When I look at you you have become like a god. Why do you yearn to run wild again with the beasts in the hills? Get up from the ground, the bed of a shepherd." He listened to her words with care.

It was good advice that she gave. She divided her clothing in two and with the one half she clothed him and with the other herself; and holding his hand she led him like a child to the sheepfolds, into the shepherds' tents. There all the shepherds crowded round to see him, they put down bread in front of him, but Enkidu could only suck the milk of wild animals. He fumbled and gaped, at a loss what to do or how he should eat the bread and drink the strong wine. Then the woman said, "Enkidu, eat bread, it is the staff of life; drink the wine, it is the custom of the land." So he ate till he was full and drank strong wine, seven goblets. He became merry, his heart exulted and his face shone. He rubbed down the matted hair of his body and anointed himself with oil. Enkidu had become a man; but when he had put on man's clothing he appeared like a bridegroom. He took arms to hunt the lion so that the shepherds could rest at night. He caught wolves and lions and the herdsmen lay down in peace; for Enkidu was their watchman, that strong man who had no rival.

He was merry living with the shepherds, till one day lifting his eyes he saw a man approaching. He said to the harlot, "Woman, fetch that man here. Why has he come? I wish to know his name." She went and called the man saying, "Sir, where are you going on this weary journey?" The man answered, saying to Enkidu, "Gilgamesh has gone into the marriage-house and shut out the people. He does strange things in Uruk, the city of great streets. At the roll of the drum work begins for the men, and work for the women. Gilgamesh the king is about to celebrate marriage with the Queen of Love, and he still demands to be first with the bride, the king to be first and the husband to follow, for that was ordained by the gods from his birth, from the time the umbilical cord was cut. But now the drums roll for the choice of the bride and the city groans." At these words Enkidu turned white in the face. "I will go to the place where Gilgamesh lords it over the people, I will challenge him boldly, and I will cry aloud in Uruk, 'I have come to change the old order, for I am the strongest here.'"

Now Enkidu strode in front and the woman followed behind. He entered Uruk, that great market, and all the folk thronged round him where he stood in the street in strong-walled Uruk. The people jostled; speaking of him they said, "He is the spit of Gilgamesh." "He is shorter." "He is bigger of bone." "This is the one who was reared on the milk of wild beasts. His is the greatest strength." The men rejoiced: "Now Gilgamesh has met his match. This great one, this hero whose beauty is like a god, he is a match even for Gilgamesh."

In Uruk the bridal bed was made, fit for the goddess of love. The bride waited for the bridegroom, but in the night Gilgamesh got up and came to the house. Then Enkidu stepped out, he stood in the street and blocked the way. Mighty Gilgamesh came on and Enkidu met him at the gate. He put out his foot and prevented Gilgamesh from entering the house, so they grappled, holding each other like bulls. They broke the doorposts and the walls shook, they snorted like bulls locked together. They shattered the doorposts and the walls shook. Gilgamesh bent his knee with his foot planted on the ground and with a turn Enkidu was thrown. Then immediately his fury died. When Enkidu was thrown he said to Gilgamesh, "There is not another like you in the world. Ninsun, who is as strong as a wild ox in the byre, she was the mother who bore you, and now you are raised above all men, and Enlil has given you the kingship, for your strength surpasses the strength of men." So Enkidu and Gilgamesh embraced and their friendship was sealed.

2

The Forest Journey

Enlil of the mountain, the father of the gods,[6] had decreed the destiny of Gilgamesh. So Gilgamesh dreamed and Enkidu said, "The meaning of the dream is this. The father of the gods has given you kingship, such is your destiny, everlasting life is not your destiny. Because of this do not be sad at heart, do not be grieved or oppressed. He has given you power to bind and to loose, to be the darkness and the light of mankind. He has given you unexampled supremacy over the people, victory in battle from which no fugitive returns, in forays and assaults from which there is no going back. But do not abuse this power, deal justly with your servants in the palace, deal justly before Shamash."

The eyes of Enkidu were full of tears and his heart was sick. He sighed bitterly and Gilgamesh met his eye and said, "My friend, why do you sigh so bitterly?" But Enkidu opened his mouth and said, "I am weak, my arms have lost their strength, the cry of sorrow sticks in my throat, I am oppressed by idleness." It was then that the lord Gilgamesh turned his thoughts to the Country of the Living; on the Land of Cedars the lord Gilgamesh reflected. He said to his servant Enkidu, "I have not established my name stamped on bricks as my destiny decreed; therefore I will go to the country where the cedar is felled. I will set up my name in the place where the names of famous men are written, and where no man's name is written yet I will raise a monument to the gods. Because of the evil that is in the land, we will go to the forest and destroy the evil; for in the forest lives Humbaba whose name is 'Hugeness,' a ferocious giant." But Enkidu sighed bitterly and said, "When I went with the wild beasts ranging through the wilderness I discovered the forest; its length is ten thousand leagues in every direction. Enlil has appointed Humbaba to guard it and armed him in sevenfold terrors, terrible to all flesh is Humbaba. When he roars it is like the torrent of the storm, his breath is like fire, and his jaws are death itself. He guards the cedars so well that when the wild heifer stirs in the forest, though she is sixty leagues distant, he hears her. What man would willingly walk into that country and explore its depths? I tell you, weakness overpowers whoever goes near it: it is not an equal struggle when one fights with Humbaba; he is a great warrior, a battering-ram. Gilgamesh, the watchman of the forest never sleeps."

Gilgamesh replied: "Where is the man who can clamber to heaven? Only the gods live for ever with glorious Shamash, but as for us men, our days are numbered, our occupations are a breath of wind. How is this, already you are afraid! I will go first although I am your lord, and you may safely call out, 'Forward, there is nothing to fear!' Then if I fall I leave behind me a name that endures; men will say of me, 'Gilgamesh has fallen in fight with ferocious Humbaba.' Long after the child has been born in my house, they will say it, and remember." Enkidu spoke again to Gilgamesh, "O my lord, if you will

6. The breath and "word" of Anu; he is also god of earth, wind, and spirit.

enter that country, go first to the hero Shamash, tell the Sun God, for the land is his. The country where the cedar is cut belongs to Shamash."

Gilgamesh took up a kid, white without spot, and a brown one with it; he held them against his breast, and he carried them into the presence of the sun. He took in his hand his silver sceptre and he said to glorious Shamash, "I am going to that country, O Shamash, I am going; my hands supplicate, so let it be well with my soul and bring me back to the quay of Uruk. Grant, I beseech, your protection, and let the omen be good." Glorious Shamash answered, "Gilgamesh, you are strong, but what is the Country of the Living to you?"

"O Shamash, hear me, hear me, Shamash, let my voice be heard. Here in the city man dies oppressed at heart, man perishes with despair in his heart. I have looked over the wall and I see the bodies floating on the river, and that will be my lot also. Indeed I know it is so, for whoever is tallest among men cannot reach the heavens, and the greatest cannot encompass the earth. Therefore I would enter that country: because I have not established my name stamped on brick as my destiny decreed, I will go to the country where the cedar is cut. I will set up my name where the names of famous men are written; and where no man's name is written I will raise a monument to the gods." The tears ran down his face and he said, "Alas, it is a long journey that I must take to the Land of Humbaba. If this enterprise is not to be accomplished, why did you move me, Shamash, with the restless desire to perform it? How can I succeed if you will not succour me? If I die in that country I will die without rancour, but if I return I will make a glorious offering of gifts and of praise to Shamash."

So Shamash accepted the sacrifice of his tears; like the compassionate man he showed him mercy. He appointed strong allies for Gilgamesh, sons of one mother, and stationed them in the mountain caves. The great winds he appointed: the north wind, the whirlwind, the storm and the icy wind, the tempest and the scorching wind. Like vipers, like dragons, like a scorching fire, like a serpent that freezes the heart, a destroying flood and the lightning's fork, such were they and Gilgamesh rejoiced.

He went to the forge and said, "I will give orders to the armourers; they shall cast us our weapons while we watch them." So they gave orders to the armourers and the craftsmen sat down in conference. They went into the groves of the plain and cut willow and box-wood; they cast for them axes of nine score pounds, and great swords they cast with blades of six score pounds each one, with pommels and hilts of thirty pounds. They cast for Gilgamesh the axe "Might of Heroes" and the bow of Anshan;[7] and Gilgamesh was armed and Enkidu; and the weight of the arms they carried was thirty score pounds.

The people collected and the counsellors in the streets and in the market-place of Uruk; they came through the gate of seven bolts and Gilgamesh spoke to them in the market-place: "I, Gilgamesh, go to see that creature of whom such things are spoken, the rumour of whose name fills the world. I will conquer him in his cedar wood and show the strength of the sons of Uruk, all the world shall know of it. I am committed to this enterprise: to climb the mountain, to cut down the cedar, and leave behind me an enduring

---

7. A district of Elam in southwest Persia; probably the source of wood for making bows.

name." The counsellors of Uruk, the great market, answered him, "Gilga-mesh, you are young, your courage carries you too far, you cannot know what this enterprise means which you plan. We have heard that Humbaba is not like men who die, his weapons are such that none can stand against them; the forest stretches for ten thousand leagues in every direction; who would willingly go down to explore its depths? As for Humbaba, when he roars it is like the torrent of the storm, his breath is like fire and his jaws are death itself. Why do you crave to do this thing, Gilgamesh? It is no equal struggle when one fights with Humbaba, that battering-ram."

When he heard these words of the counsellors Gilgamesh looked at his friend and laughed, "How shall I answer them; shall I say I am afraid of Humbaba, I will sit at home all the rest of my days?" Then Gilgamesh opened his mouth again and said to Enkidu, "My friend, let us go to the Great Palace, to Egalmah,[8] and stand before Ninsun the queen. Ninsun is wise with deep knowledge, she will give us counsel for the road we must go." They took each other by the hand as they went to Egalmah, and they went to Ninsun the great queen. Gilgamesh approached, he entered the palace and spoke to Ninsun. "Ninsun, will you listen to me; I have a long journey to go, to the Land of Humbaba, I must travel an unknown road and fight a strange battle. From the day I go until I return, till I reach the cedar forest and destroy the evil which Shamash abhors, pray for me to Shamash."

Ninsun went into her room, she put on a dress becoming to her body, she put on jewels to make her breast beautiful, she placed a tiara on her head and her skirts swept the ground. Then she went up to the altar of the Sun, standing upon the roof of the palace; she burnt incense and lifted her arms to Shamash as the smoke ascended: "O Shamash, why did you give this restless heart to Gilgamesh, my son; why did you give it? You have moved him and now he sets out on a long journey to the Land of Humbaba to travel an unknown road and fight a strange battle. Therefore from the day that he goes till the day he returns, until he reaches the cedar forest, until he kills Humbaba and destroys the evil thing which you, Shamash, abhor, do not forget him; but let the dawn, Aya, your dear bride, remind you always, and when day is done give him to the watchman of the night to keep him from harm." Then Ninsun the mother of Gilgamesh extinguished the incense, and she called to Enkidu with this exhortation: "Strong Enkidu, you are not the child of my body, but I will receive you as my adopted son; you are my other child like the foundlings they bring to the temple. Serve Gilgamesh as a foundling serves the temple and the priestess who reared him. In the pres-ence of my women, my votaries and hierophants,[9] I declare it." Then she placed the amulet for a pledge round his neck, and she said to him, "I entrust my son to you; bring him back to me safely."

And now they brought to them the weapons, they put in their hands the great swords in their golden scabbards, and the bow and the quiver. Gilga-mesh took the axe, he slung the quiver from his shoulder, and the bow of Anshan, and buckled the sword to his belt; and so they were armed and ready for the journey. Now all the people came and pressed on them and said, "When will you return to the city?" The counsellors blessed Gilgamesh and warned him, "Do not trust too much in your own strength, be watchful,

---

8. Home of the goddess Ninsun.   9. Priests.

restrain your blows at first. The one who goes in front protects his companion; the good guide who knows the way guards his friend. Let Enkidu lead the way, he knows the road to the forest, he has seen Humbaba and is experienced in battles; let him press first into the passes, let him be watchful and look to himself. Let Enkidu protect his friend, and guard his companion, and bring him safe through the pitfalls of the road. We, the counsellors of Uruk, entrust our king to you, O Enkidu; bring him back safely to us." Again to Gilgamesh they said, "May Shamash give you your heart's desire, may he let you see with your eyes the thing accomplished which your lips have spoken; may he open a path for you where it is blocked, and a road for your feet to tread. May he open the mountains for your crossing, and may the night-time bring you the blessings of night, and Lugulbanda, your guardian god, stand beside you for victory. May you have victory in the battle as though you fought with a child. Wash your feet in the river of Humbaba to which you are journeying; in the evening dig a well, and let there always be pure water in your water-skin. Offer cold water to Shamash and do not forget Lugulbanda."

Then Enkidu opened his mouth and said, "Forward, there is nothing to fear. Follow me, for I know the place where Humbaba lives and the paths where he walks. Let the counsellors go back. Here is no cause for fear." When the counsellors heard this they sped the hero on his way. "Go, Gilgamesh, may your guardian god protect you on the road and bring you safely back to the quay of Uruk."

After twenty leagues they broke their fast; after another thirty leagues they stopped for the night. Fifty leagues they walked in one day; in three days they had walked as much as a journey of a month and two weeks. They crossed seven mountains before they came to the gate of the forest. Then Enkidu called out to Gilgamesh, "Do not go down into the forest; when I opened the gate my hand lost its strength." Gilgamesh answered him, "Dear friend, do not speak like a coward. Have we got the better of so many dangers and travelled so far, to turn back at last? You, who are tried in wars and battles, hold close to me now and you will feel no fear of death; keep beside me and your weakness will pass, the trembling will leave your hand. Would my friend rather stay behind? No, we will go down together into the heart of the forest. Let your courage be roused by the battle to come; forget death and follow me, a man resolute in action, but one who is not foolhardy. When two go together each will protect himself and shield his companion, and if they fall they leave an enduring name."

Together they went down into the forest and they came to the green mountain. There they stood still, they were struck dumb; they stood still and gazed at the forest. They saw the height of the cedar, they saw the way into the forest and the track where Humbaba was used to walk. The way was broad and the going was good. They gazed at the mountain of cedars, the dwelling-place of the gods and the throne of Ishtar. The hugeness of the cedar rose in front of the mountain, its shade was beautiful, full of comfort; mountain and glade were green with brushwood.

There Gilgamesh dug a well before the setting sun. He went up the mountain and poured out fine meal on the ground and said, "O mountain, dwelling of the gods, bring me a favourable dream." Then they took each other by the hand and lay down to sleep; and sleep that flows from the night lapped over them. Gilgamesh dreamed, and at midnight sleep left him, and he told his dream to his friend. "Enkidu, what was it that woke me if you did not? My friend, I have dreamed a dream. Get up, look at the mountain precipice. The sleep that the gods sent me is broken. Ah, my friend, what a dream I have had! Terror and confusion; I seized hold of a wild bull in the wilderness. It bellowed and beat up the dust till the whole sky was dark, my arm was seized and my tongue bitten. I fell back on my knee; then someone refreshed me with water from his water-skin."

Enkidu said, "Dear friend, the god to whom we are travelling is no wild bull, though his form is mysterious. That wild bull which you saw is Shamash the Protector; in our moment of peril he will take our hands. The one who gave water from his water-skin, that is your own god who cares for your good name, your Lugulbanda.[1] United with him, together we will accomplish a work the fame of which will never die."

Gilgamesh said, "I dreamed again. We stood in a deep gorge of the mountain, and beside it we two were like the smallest of swamp flies; and suddenly the mountain fell, it struck me and caught my feet from under me. Then came an intolerable light blazing out, and in it was one whose grace and whose beauty were greater than the beauty of this world. He pulled me out from under the mountain, he gave me water to drink and my heart was comforted, and he set my feet on the ground."

Then Enkidu the child of the plains said, "Let us go down from the mountain and talk this thing over together." He said to Gilgamesh the young god, "Your dream is good, your dream is excellent, the mountain which you saw is Humbaba. Now, surely, we will seize and kill him, and throw his body down as the mountain fell on the plain."

The next day after twenty leagues they broke their fast, and after another thirty they stopped for the night. They dug a well before the sun had set and Gilgamesh ascended the mountain. He poured out fine meal on the ground and said, "O mountain, dwelling of the gods, send a dream for Enkidu, make him a favourable dream." The mountain fashioned a dream for Enkidu; it came, an ominous dream; a cold shower passed over him, it caused him to cower like the mountain barley under a storm of rain. But Gilgamesh sat with his chin on his knees till the sleep which flows over all mankind lapped over him. Then, at midnight, sleep left him; he got up and said to his friend, "Did you call me, or why did I wake? Did you touch me, or why am I terrified? Did not some god pass by, for my limbs are numb with fear? My friend, I saw a third dream and this dream was altogether frightful. The heavens roared and the earth roared again, daylight failed and darkness fell, lightning flashed, fire blazed out, the clouds lowered, they rained down death. Then the brightness departed, the fire went out, and all was turned to ashes fallen about us. Let us go down from the mountain and talk this over, and consider what we should do."

When they had come down from the mountain Gilgamesh seized the axe in his hand: he felled the cedar. When Humbaba heard the noise far off he was enraged; he cried out, "Who is this that has violated my woods and cut down my cedar?" But glorious Shamash called to them out of heaven, "Go forward, do not be afraid." But now Gilgamesh was overcome by weakness,

---

1. Hero of a cycle of Sumerian poems; protector of Gilgamesh.

for sleep had seized him suddenly, a profound sleep held him; he lay on the ground, stretched out speechless, as though in a dream. When Enkidu touched him he did not rise, when he spoke to him he did not reply. "O Gilgamesh, Lord of the plain of Kullab,[2] the world grows dark, the shadows have spread over it, now is the glimmer of dusk. Shamash has departed, his bright head is quenched in the bosom of his mother Ningal. O Gilgamesh, how long will you lie like this, asleep? Never let the mother who gave you birth be forced in mourning into the city square."

At length Gilgamesh heard him; he put on his breastplate, "The Voice of Heroes," of thirty shekels' weight; he put it on as though it had been a light garment that he carried, and it covered him altogether. He straddled the earth like a bull that snuffs the ground and his teeth were clenched. "By the life of my mother Ninsun who gave me birth, and by the life of my father, divine Lugulbanda, let me live to be the wonder of my mother, as when she nursed me on her lap." A second time he said to him, "By the life of Ninsun my mother who gave me birth, and by the life of my father, divine Lugul-banda, until we have fought this man, if man he is, this god, if god he is, the way that I took to the Country of the Living will not turn back to the city."

Then Enkidu, the faithful companion, pleaded, answering him, "O my lord, you do not know this monster and that is the reason you are not afraid. I who know him, I am terrified. His teeth are dragon's fangs, his countenance is like a lion, his charge is the rushing of the flood, with his look he crushes alike the trees of the forest and reeds in the swamp. O my Lord, you may go on if you choose into this land, but I will go back to the city. I will tell the lady your mother all your glorious deeds till she shouts for joy: and then I will tell the death that followed till she weeps for bitterness." But Gilgamesh said, "Immolation and sacrifice are not yet for me, the boat of the dead shall not go down, nor the three-ply cloth be cut for my shrouding. Not yet will my people be desolate, nor the pyre be lit in my house and my dwelling burnt on the fire. Today, give me your aid and you shall have mine: what then can go amiss with us two? All living creatures born of the flesh shall sit at last in the boat of the West, and when it sinks, when the boat of Magilum[3] sinks, they are gone; but we shall go forward and fix our eyes on this monster. If your heart is fearful throw away fear; if there is terror in it throw away terror. Take your axe in your hand and attack. He who leaves the fight unfinished is not at peace."

Humbaba came out from his strong house of cedar. Then Enkidu called out, "O Gilgamesh, remember now your boasts in Uruk. Forward, attack, son of Uruk, there is nothing to fear." When he heard these words his courage rallied; he answered, "Make haste, close in, if the watchman is there do not let him escape to the woods where he will vanish. He has put on the first of his seven splendours[4] but not yet the other six, let us trap him before he is armed." Like a raging wild bull he snuffed the ground; the watchman of the woods turned full of threatenings, he cried out. Humbaba came from his strong house of cedar. He nodded his head and shook it, menacing Gilgamesh; and on him he fastened his eye, the eye of death. Then Gilgamesh called to Shamash and his tears were flowing, "O glorious Shamash, I have followed the road you commanded but now if you send no succour how shall

2. In Uruk.   3. Unclear; perhaps the boat of the dead.   4. Unclear; perhaps warlike attributes.

I escape?" Glorious Shamash heard his prayer and he summoned the great wind, the north wind, the whirlwind, the storm and the icy wind, the tempest and the scorching wind; they came like dragons, like a scorching fire, like a serpent that freezes the heart, a destroying flood and the lightning's fork. The eight winds rose up against Humbaba, they beat against his eyes; he was gripped, unable to go forward or back. Gilgamesh shouted, "By the life of Ninsun my mother and divine Lugulbanda my father, in the Country of the Living, in this Land I have discovered your dwelling; my weak arms and my small weapons I have brought to this Land against you, and now I will enter your house."

So he felled the first cedar and they cut the branches and laid them at the foot of the mountain. At the first stroke Humbaba blazed out, but still they advanced. They felled seven cedars and cut and bound the branches and laid them at the foot of the mountain, and seven times Humbaba loosed his glory on them. As the seventh blaze died out they reached his lair. He slapped his thigh in scorn. He approached like a noble wild bull roped on the mountain, a warrior whose elbows are bound together. The tears started to his eyes and he was pale, "Gilgamesh, let me speak. I have never known a mother, no, nor a father who reared me. I was born of the mountain, he reared me, and Enlil made me the keeper of this forest. Let me go free, Gilgamesh, and I will be your servant, you shall be my lord; all the trees of the forest that I tended on the mountain shall be yours. I will cut them down and build you a palace." He took him by the hand and led him to his house, so that the heart of Gilgamesh was moved with compassion. He swore by the heavenly life, by the earthly life, by the underworld itself: "O Enkidu, should not the snared bird return to its nest and the captive man return to his mother's arms?" Enkidu answered, "The strongest of men will fall to fate if he has no judgement. Namtar, the evil fate that knows no distinction between men, will devour him. If the snared bird returns to its nest, if the captive man returns to his mother's arms, then you my friend will never return to the city where the mother is waiting who gave you birth. He will bar the mountain road against you, and make the pathways impassable."

Humbaba said, "Enkidu, what you have spoken is evil: you, a hireling, dependent for your bread! In envy and for fear of a rival you have spoken evil words." Enkidu said, "Do not listen, Gilgamesh: this Humbaba must die. Kill Humbaba first and his servants after." But Gilgamesh said, "If we touch him the blaze and the glory of light will be put out in confusion, the glory and glamour will vanish, its rays will be quenched." Enkidu said to Gilgamesh, "Not so, my friend. First entrap the bird, and where shall the chicks run then? Afterwards we can search out the glory and the glamour, when the chicks run distracted through the grass."

Gilgamesh listened to the word of his companion, he took the axe in his hand, he drew the sword from his belt, and he struck Humbaba with a thrust of the sword to the neck, and Enkidu his comrade struck the second blow. At the third blow Humbaba fell. Then there followed confusion for this was the guardian of the forest whom they had felled to the ground. For as far as two leagues the cedars shivered when Enkidu felled the watcher of the forest, he at whose voice Hermon and Lebanon[5] used to tremble. Now the moun-

5. Mountains in Lebanon.

tains were moved and all the hills, for the guardian of the forest was killed. They attacked the cedars, the seven splendours of Humbaba were extinguished. So they pressed on into the forest bearing the sword of eight talents. They uncovered the sacred dwellings of the Anunnaki[6] and while Gilgamesh felled the first of the trees of the forest Enkidu cleared their roots as far as the banks of Euphrates. They set Humbaba before the gods, before Enlil; they kissed the ground and dropped the shroud and set the head before him. When he saw the head of Humbaba, Enlil raged at them. "Why did you do this thing? From henceforth may the fire be on your faces, may it eat the bread that you eat, may it drink where you drink." Then Enlil took again the blaze and the seven splendours that had been Humbaba's: he gave the first to the river, and he gave to the lion, to the stone of execration, to the mountain and to the dreaded daughter of the Queen of Hell.

O Gilgamesh, king and conqueror of the dreadful blaze; wild bull who plunders the mountain, who crosses the sea, glory to him, and from the brave the greater glory is Enki's![7]

3

Ishtar and Gilgamesh, and the Death of Enkidu

Gilgamesh washed out his long locks and cleaned his weapons; he flung back his hair from his shoulders; he threw off his stained clothes and changed them for new. He put on his royal robes and made them fast. When Gilgamesh had put on the crown, glorious Ishtar lifted her eyes, seeing the beauty of Gilgamesh. She said, "Come to me Gilgamesh, and be my bridegroom; grant me seed of your body, let me be your bride and you shall be my husband. I will harness for you a chariot of lapis lazuli and of gold, with wheels of gold and horns of copper; and you shall have mighty demons of the storm for draft-mules. When you enter our house in the fragrance of cedar-wood, threshold and throne will kiss your feet. Kings, rulers, and princes will bow down before you; they shall bring you tribute from the mountains and the plain. Your ewes shall drop twins and your goats triplets; your pack-ass shall outrun mules; your oxen shall have no rivals, and your chariot horses shall be famous far-off for their swiftness."

Gilgamesh opened his mouth and answered glorious Ishtar, "If I take you in marriage, what gifts can I give in return? What ointments and clothing for your body? I would gladly give you bread and all sorts of food fit for a god. I would give you wine to drink fit for a queen. I would pour out barley to stuff your granary; but as for making you my wife—that I will not. How would it go with me? Your lovers have found you like a brazier which smoulders in the cold, a backdoor which keeps out neither squall of wind nor storm, a castle which crushes the garrison, pitch that blackens the bearer, a waterskin that chafes the carrier, a stone which falls from the parapet, a battering-ram turned back from the enemy, a sandal that trips the wearer. Which of your lovers did you ever love for ever? What shepherd of yours has pleased you for all time? Listen to me while I tell the tale of your lovers. There was Tammuz,[8] the lover of your youth, for him you decreed wailing, year after

---

6. Gods of the underworld, judges of the dead, and offspring of Anu.   7. Or Ea, god of the sweet waters and wisdom, a patron of arts, and one of the creators of humankind, toward whom he is usually well disposed.   8. The dying god of vegetation.

year. You loved the many-coloured roller, but still you struck and broke his wing; now in the grove he sits and cries, "Kappi, kappi, my wing, my wing." You have loved the lion tremendous in strength: seven pits you dug for him, and seven. You have loved the stallion magnificent in battle, and for him you decreed whip and spur and a thong, to gallop seven leagues by force and to muddy the water before he drinks; and for his mother Silili[9] lamentations. You have loved the shepherd of the flock; he made meal-cake for you day after day, he killed kids for your sake. You struck and turned him into a wolf; now his own herd-boys chase him away, his own hounds worry his flanks. And did you not love Ishullanu, the gardener of your father's palm-grove? He brought you baskets filled with dates without end; every day he loaded your table. Then you turned your eyes on him and said, 'Dearest Ishullanu, come here to me, let us enjoy your manhood, come forward and take me, I am yours.' Ishullanu answered, 'What are you asking from me? My mother has baked and I have eaten; why should I come to such as you for food that is tainted and rotten? For when was a screen of rushes sufficient protection from frosts?' But when you had heard his answer you struck him. He was changed to a blind mole deep in the earth, one whose desire is always beyond his reach. And if you and I should be lovers, should not I be served in the same fashion as all these others whom you loved once?"

When Ishtar heard this she fell into a bitter rage, she went up to high heaven. Her tears poured down in front of her father Anu, and Antum her mother. She said, "My father, Gilgamesh has heaped insults on me, he has told over all my abominable behaviour, my foul and hideous acts." Anu opened his mouth and said, "Are you a father of gods? Did not you quarrel with Gilgamesh the king, so now he has related your abominable behaviour, your foul and hideous acts?"

Ishtar opened her mouth and said again, "My father, give me the Bull of Heaven to destroy Gilgamesh. Fill Gilgamesh, I say, with arrogance to his destruction; but if you refuse to give me the Bull of Heaven I will break in the doors of hell and smash the bolts; there will be confusion of people, those above with those from the lower depths. I shall bring up the dead to eat food like the living; and the hosts of dead will outnumber the living." Anu said to great Ishtar, "If I do what you desire there will be seven years of drought throughout Uruk when corn will be seedless husks. Have you saved grain enough for the people and grass for the cattle?" Ishtar replied, "I have saved grain for the people, grass for the cattle; for seven years of seedless husks there is grain and there is grass enough."

When Anu heard what Ishtar had said he gave her the Bull of Heaven to lead by the halter down to Uruk. When they reached the gates of Uruk the Bull went to the river; with his first snort cracks opened in the earth and a hundred young men fell down to death. With his second snort cracks opened and two hundred fell down to death. With his third snort cracks opened, Enkidu doubled over but instantly recovered, he dodged aside and leapt on the Bull and seized it by the horns. The Bull of Heaven foamed in his face, it brushed him with the thick of its tail. Enkidu cried to Gilgamesh, "My friend, we boasted that we would leave enduring names behind us. Now thrust in your sword between the nape and the horns." So Gilgamesh fol-

9. Perhaps a divine horse.

lowed the Bull, he seized the thick of its tail, he thrust the sword between the nape and the horns and slew the Bull. When they had killed the Bull of Heaven they cut out its heart and gave it to Shamash, and the brothers rested.

But Ishtar rose up and mounted the great wall of Uruk; she sprang on to the tower and uttered a curse: "Woe to Gilgamesh, for he has scorned me in killing the Bull of Heaven." When Enkidu heard these words he tore out the Bull's right thigh and tossed it in her face saying, "If I could lay my hands on you, it is this I should do to you, and lash the entrails to your side." Then Ishtar called together her people, the dancing and singing girls, the prostitutes of the temple, the courtesans. Over the thigh of the Bull of Heaven she set up lamentation.

But Gilgamesh called the smiths and the armourers, all of them together. They admired the immensity of the horns. They were plated with lapis lazuli two fingers thick. They were thirty pounds each in weight, and their capacity in oil was six measures, which he gave to his guardian god, Lugulbanda. But he carried the horns into the palace and hung them on the wall. Then they washed their hands in Euphrates, they embraced each other and went away. They drove through the streets of Uruk where the heroes were gathered to see them, and Gilgamesh called to the singing girls, "Who is most glorious of the heroes, who is most eminent among men?" "Gilgamesh is the most glorious of heroes, Gilgamesh is most eminent among men." And now there was feasting, and celebrations and joy in the palace, till the heroes lay down saying, "Now we will rest for the night."

When the daylight came Enkidu got up and cried to Gilgamesh, "O my brother, such a dream I had last night. Anu, Enlil, Ea and heavenly Shamash took counsel together, and Anu said to Enlil, 'Because they have killed the Bull of Heaven, and because they have killed Humbaba who guarded the Cedar Mountain one of the two must die.' Then glorious Shamash answered the hero Enlil, 'It was by your command they killed the Bull of Heaven, and killed Humbaba, and must Enkidu die although innocent?' Enlil flung round in rage at glorious Shamash, 'You dare to say this, you who went about with them every day like one of themselves!' "

So Enkidu lay stretched out before Gilgamesh; his tears ran down in streams and he said to Gilgamesh, "O my brother, so dear as you are to me, brother, yet they will take me from you." Again he said, "I must sit down on the threshold of the dead and never again will I see my dear brother with my eyes."

While Enkidu lay alone in his sickness he cursed the gate as though it was living flesh, "You there, wood of the gate, dull and insensible, witless, I searched for you over twenty leagues until I saw the towering cedar. There is no wood like you in our land. Seventy-two cubits high and twenty-four wide, the pivot and the ferrule and the jambs are perfect. A master craftsman from Nippur has made you; but O, if I had known the conclusion! If I had known that this was all the good that would come of it, I would have raised the axe and split you into little pieces and set up here a gate of wattle instead. Ah, if only some future king had brought you here, or some god had fashioned you. Let him obliterate my name and write his own, and the curse fall on him instead of on Enkidu."

With the first brightening of dawn Enkidu raised his head and wept before the Sun God, in the brilliance of the sunlight his tears streamed down. "Sun God, I beseech you, about that vile Trapper, that Trapper of nothing because of whom I was to catch less than my comrade; let him catch least, make his game scarce, make him feeble, taking the smaller of every share, let his quarry escape from his nets."

When he had cursed the Trapper to his heart's content he turned on the harlot. He was roused to curse her also. "As for you, woman, with a great curse I curse you! I will promise you a destiny to all eternity. My curse shall come on you soon and sudden. You shall be without a roof for your commerce, for you shall not keep house with other girls in the tavern, but do your business in places fouled by the vomit of the drunkard. Your hire will be potter's earth, your thievings will be flung into the hovel, you will sit at the cross-roads in the dust of the potter's quarter, you will make your bed on the dunghill at night, and by day take your stand in the wall's shadow. Brambles and thorns will tear your feet, the drunk and the dry will strike your cheek and your mouth will ache. Let you be stripped of your purple dyes, for I too once in the wilderness with my wife had all the treasure I wished."

When Shamash heard the words of Enkidu he called to him from heaven: "Enkidu, why are you cursing the woman, the mistress who taught you to eat bread fit for gods and drink wine of kings? She who put upon you a magnificent garment, did she not give you glorious Gilgamesh for your companion, and has not Gilgamesh, your own brother, made you rest on a royal bed and recline on a couch at his left hand? He has made the princes of the earth kiss your feet, and now all the people of Uruk lament and wail over you. When you are dead he will let his hair grow long for your sake, he will wear a lion's pelt and wander through the desert."

When Enkidu heard glorious Shamash his angry heart grew quiet, he called back the curse and said, "Woman, I promise you another destiny. The mouth which cursed you shall bless you! Kings, princes and nobles shall adore you. On your account a man though twelve miles off will clap his hand to his thigh and his hair will twitch. For you he will undo his belt and open his treasure and you shall have your desire; lapis lazuli, gold and carnelian from the heap in the treasury. A ring for your hand and a robe shall be yours. The priest will lead you into the presence of the gods. On your account a wife, a mother of seven, was forsaken."

As Enkidu slept alone in his sickness, in bitterness of spirit he poured out his heart to his friend. "It was I who cut down the cedar, I who levelled the forest, I who slew Humbaba and now see what has become of me. Listen, my friend, this is the dream I dreamed last night. The heavens roared, and earth rumbled back an answer; between them stood I before an awful being, the sombre-faced man-bird; he had directed on me his purpose. His was a vampire face, his foot was a lion's foot, his hand was an eagle's talon. He fell on me and his claws were in my hair, he held me fast and I smothered; then he transformed me so that my arms became wings covered with feathers. He turned his stare towards me, and he led me away to the palace of Irkalla, the Queen of Darkness,[1] to the house from which none who enters ever returns, down the road from which there is no coming back.

---

1. Also Ereshkigal, queen of the underworld.

"There is the house whose people sit in darkness; dust is their food and clay their meat. They are clothed like birds with wings for covering, they see no light, they sit in darkness. I entered the house of dust and I saw the kings of the earth, their crowns put away for ever; rulers and princes, all those who once wore kingly crowns and ruled the world in the days of old. They who had stood in the place of the gods like Anu and Enlil, stood now like servants to fetch baked meats in the house of dust, to carry cooked meat and cold water from the water-skin. In the house of dust which I entered were high priests and acolytes, priests of the incantation and of ecstasy; there were servers of the temple, and there was Etana, that king of Kish whom the eagle carried to heaven in the days of old. I saw also Samuqan, god of cattle, and there was Ereshkigal the Queen of the Underworld; and Belit-Sheri squatted in front of her, she who is recorder of the gods and keeps the book of death. She held a tablet from which she read. She raised her head, she saw me and spoke: 'Who has brought this one here?' Then I awoke like a man drained of blood who wanders alone in a waste of rushes; like one whom the bailiff has seized and his heart pounds with terror."

Gilgamesh had peeled off his clothes, he listened to his words and wept quick tears, Gilgamesh listened and his tears flowed. He opened his mouth and spoke to Enkidu: "Who is there in strong-walled Uruk who has wisdom like this? Strange things have been spoken, why does your heart speak strangely? The dream was marvellous but the terror was great; we must treasure the dream whatever the terror; for the dream has shown that misery comes at last to the healthy man, the end of life is sorrow." And Gilgamesh lamented, "Now I will pray to the great gods, for my friend had an ominous dream."

This day on which Enkidu dreamed came to an end and he lay stricken with sickness. One whole day he lay on his bed and his suffering increased. He said to Gilgamesh, the friend on whose account he had left the wilderness, "Once I ran for you, for the water of life, and I now have nothing." A second day he lay on his bed and Gilgamesh watched over him but the sickness increased. A third day he lay on his bed, he called out to Gilgamesh, rousing him up. Now he was weak and his eyes were blind with weeping. Ten days he lay and his suffering increased, eleven and twelve days he lay on his bed of pain. Then he called to Gilgamesh, "My friend, the great goddess cursed me and I must die in shame. I shall not die like a man fallen in battle; I feared to fall, but happy is the man who falls in the battle, for I must die in shame." And Gilgamesh wept over Enkidu. With the first light of dawn he raised his voice and said to the counsellors of Uruk:

> Hear me, great ones of Uruk,
> I weep for Enkidu, my friend,
> Bitterly moaning like a woman mourning
> I weep for my brother.
> O Enkidu, my brother,   5
> You were the axe at my side,
> My hand's strength, the sword in my belt,
> The shield before me,
> A glorious robe, my fairest ornament;
> An evil Fate has robbed me.   10
> The wild ass and the gazelle

That were father and mother,
All long-tailed creatures that nourished you
Weep for you,
All the wild things of the plain and pastures;   15
The paths that you loved in the forest of cedars
Night and day murmur.
Let the great ones of strong-walled Uruk
Weep for you;
Let the finger of blessing   20
Be stretched out in mourning;
Enkidu, young brother. Hark,
There is an echo through all the country
Like a mother mourning.
Weep all the paths where we walked together;   25
And the beasts we hunted, the bear and hyena,
Tiger and panther, leopard and lion,
The stag and the ibex, the bull and the doe.
The river along whose banks we used to walk,
Weeps for you,   30
Ula of Elam and dear Euphrates
Where once we drew water for the water-skins.
The mountain we climbed where we slew the Watchman,
Weeps for you.
The warriors of strong-walled Uruk   35
Where the Bull of Heaven was killed,
Weep for you.
All the people of Eridu
Weep for you Enkidu.
Those who brought grain for your eating   40
Mourn for you now;
Who rubbed oil on your back
Mourn for you now;
Who poured beer for your drinking
Mourn for you now.   45
The harlot who anointed you with fragrant ointment
Laments for you now;
The women of the palace, who brought you a wife,
A chosen ring of good advice,
Lament for you now.   50
And the young men your brothers
As though they were women
Go long-haired in mourning.
What is this sleep which holds you now?
You are lost in the dark and cannot hear me.   55

He touched his heart but it did not beat, nor did he lift his eyes again. When Gilgamesh touched his heart it did not beat. So Gilgamesh laid a veil, as one veils the bride, over his friend. He began to rage like a lion, like a lioness robbed of her whelps. This way and that he paced round the bed, he tore out his hair and strewed it around. He dragged off his splendid robes and flung them down as though they were abominations.

In the first light of dawn Gilgamesh cried out, "I made you rest on a royal bed, you reclined on a couch at my left hand, the princes of the earth kissed your feet. I will cause all the people of Uruk to weep over you and raise the dirge of the dead. The joyful people will stoop with sorrow; and when you have gone to the earth I will let my hair grow long for your sake, I will wander through the wilderness in the skin of a lion." The next day also, in the first light, Gilgamesh lamented; seven days and seven nights he wept for Enkidu, until the worm fastened on him. Only then he gave him up to the earth, for the Anunnaki, the judges, had seized him.

Then Gilgamesh issued a proclamation through the land, he summoned them all, the coppersmiths, the goldsmiths, the stone-workers, and commanded them, "Make a statue of my friend." The statue was fashioned with a great weight of lapis lazuli for the breast and of gold for the body. A table of hard-wood was set out, and on it a bowl of carnelian filled with honey, and a bowl of lapis lazuli filled with butter. These he exposed and offered to the Sun; and weeping he went away.

4

The Search for Everlasting Life

Bitterly Gilgamesh wept for his friend Enkidu; he wandered over the wilderness as a hunter, he roamed over the plains; in his bitterness he cried, "How can I rest, how can I be at peace? Despair is in my heart. What my brother is now, that shall I be when I am dead. Because I am afraid of death I will go as best I can to find Utnapishtim[2] whom they call the Faraway, for he has entered the assembly of the gods." So Gilgamesh travelled over the wilderness, he wandered over the grasslands, a long journey, in search of Utnapishtim, whom the gods took after the deluge; and they set him to live in the land of Dilmun, in the garden of the sun; and to him alone of men they gave everlasting life.

At night when he came to the mountain passes Gilgamesh prayed: "In these mountain passes long ago I saw lions, I was afraid and I lifted my eyes to the moon; I prayed and my prayers went up to the gods, so now, O moon god Sin, protect me." When he had prayed he lay down to sleep, until he was woken from out of a dream. He saw the lions round him glorying in life; then he took his axe in his hand, he drew his sword from his belt, and he fell upon them like an arrow from the string, and struck and destroyed and scattered them.

So at length Gilgamesh came to Mashu, the great mountains about which he had heard many things, which guard the rising and the setting sun. Its twin peaks are as high as the wall of heaven and its paps reach down to the underworld. At its gate the Scorpions stand guard, half man and half dragon; their glory is terrifying, their stare strikes death into men, their shimmering halo sweeps the mountains that guard the rising sun. When Gilgamesh saw them he shielded his eyes for the length of a moment only; then he took courage and approached. When they saw him so undismayed the Man-Scorpion called to his mate, "This one who comes to us now is flesh of the

---

2. A wise king and priest who, like the biblical Noah, survived the Flood along with his family and with "the seed of all living creatures." Afterward he was taken by the gods to live forever in Dilmun, the Sumerian paradise.

gods." The mate of the Man-Scorpion answered, "Two thirds is god but one third is man."

Then he called to the man Gilgamesh, he called to the child of the gods: "Why have you come so great a journey; for what have you travelled so far, crossing the dangerous waters; tell me the reason for your coming?" Gilgamesh answered, "For Enkidu; I loved him dearly, together we endured all kinds of hardships; on his account I have come, for the common lot of man has taken him. I have wept for him day and night, I would not give up his body for burial, I thought my friend would come back because of my weeping. Since he went, my life is nothing; that is why I have travelled here in search of Utnapishtim my father; for men say he has entered the assembly of the gods, and has found everlasting life. I have a desire to question him concerning the living and the dead." The Man-Scorpion opened his mouth and said, speaking to Gilgamesh, "No man born of woman has done what you have asked, no mortal man has gone into the mountain; the length of it is twelve leagues of darkness; in it there is no light, but the heart is oppressed with darkness. From the rising of the sun to the setting of the sun there is no light." Gilgamesh said, "Although I should go in sorrow and in pain, with sighing and with weeping, still I must go. Open the gate of the mountain." And the Man-Scorpion said, "Go, Gilgamesh, I permit you to pass through the mountain of Mashu and through the high ranges; may your feet carry you safely home. The gate of the mountain is open."

When Gilgamesh heard this he did as the Man-Scorpion had said, he followed the sun's road to his rising, through the mountain. When he had gone one league the darkness became thick around him, for there was no light, he could see nothing ahead and nothing behind him. After two leagues the darkness was thick and there was no light, he could see nothing ahead and nothing behind him. After three leagues the darkness was thick, and there was no light, he could see nothing ahead and nothing behind him. After four leagues the darkness was thick and there was no light, he could see nothing ahead and nothing behind him. At the end of five leagues the darkness was thick and there was no light, he could see nothing ahead and nothing behind him. At the end of six leagues the darkness was thick and there was no light, he could see nothing ahead and nothing behind him. When he had gone seven leagues the darkness was thick and there was no light, he could see nothing ahead and nothing behind him. When he had gone eight leagues Gilgamesh gave a great cry, for the darkness was thick and he could see nothing ahead and nothing behind him. After nine leagues he felt the north wind on his face, but the darkness was thick and there was no light, he could see nothing ahead and nothing behind him. After ten leagues the end was near. After eleven leagues the dawn light appeared. At the end of twelve leagues the sun streamed out.

There was the garden of the gods; all round him stood bushes bearing gems. Seeing it he went down at once, for there was fruit of carnelian with the vine hanging from it, beautiful to look at; lapis lazuli leaves hung thick with fruit, sweet to see. For thorns and thistles there were haematite and rare stones, agate, and pearls from out of the sea. While Gilgamesh walked in the garden by the edge of the sea Shamash saw him, and he saw that he was dressed in the skins of animals and ate their flesh. He was distressed, and he spoke and said, "No mortal man has gone this way before, nor will, as long as the winds drive over the sea." And to Gilgamesh he said, "You will never find the life for which you are searching." Gilgamesh said to glorious Shamash, "Now that I have toiled and strayed so far over the wilderness, am I to sleep, and let the earth cover my head for ever? Let my eyes see the sun until they are dazzled with looking. Although I am no better than a dead man, still let me see the light of the sun."

Beside the sea she lives, the woman of the vine, the maker of wine; Siduri sits in the garden at the edge of the sea, with the golden bowl and the golden vats that the gods gave her. She is covered with a veil; and where she sits she sees Gilgamesh coming towards her, wearing skins, the flesh of the gods in his body, but despair in his heart, and his face like the face of one who has made a long journey. She looked, and as she scanned the distance she said in her own heart, "Surely this is some felon; where is he going now?" And she barred her gate against him with the cross-bar and shot home the bolt. But Gilgamesh, hearing the sound of the bolt, threw up his head and lodged his foot in the gate; he called to her, "Young woman, maker of wine, why do you bolt your door; what did you see that made you bar your gate? I will break in your door and burst in your gate, for I am Gilgamesh who seized and killed the Bull of Heaven, I killed the watchman of the cedar forest, I overthrew Humbaba who lived in the forest, and I killed the lions in the passes of the mountain."

Then Siduri said to him, "If you are that Gilgamesh who seized and killed the Bull of Heaven, who killed the watchman of the cedar forest, who overthrew Humbaba that lived in the forest, and killed the lions in the passes of the mountain, why are your cheeks so starved and why is your face so drawn? Why is despair in your heart and your face like the face of one who has made a long journey? Yes, why is your face burned from heat and cold, and why do you come here wandering over the pastures in search of the wind?"

Gilgamesh answered her, "And why should not my cheeks be starved and my face drawn? Despair is in my heart and my face is the face of one who has made a long journey, it was burned with heat and with cold. Why should I not wander over the pastures in search of the wind? My friend, my younger brother, he who hunted the wild ass of the wilderness and the panther of the plains, my friend, my younger brother who seized and killed the Bull of Heaven and overthrew Humbaba in the cedar forest, my friend who was very dear to me and who endured dangers beside me, Enkidu my brother, whom I loved, the end of mortality has overtaken him. I wept for him seven days and nights till the worm fastened on him. Because of my brother I am afraid of death, because of my brother I stray through the wilderness and cannot rest. But now, young woman, maker of wine, since I have seen your face do not let me see the face of death which I dread so much."

She answered, "Gilgamesh, where are you hurrying to? You will never find that life for which you are looking. When the gods created man they allotted to him death, but life they retained in their own keeping. As for you, Gilgamesh, fill your belly with good things; day and night, night and day, dance and be merry, feast and rejoice. Let your clothes be fresh, bathe yourself in water, cherish the little child that holds your hand, and make your wife happy in your embrace; for this too is the lot of man."

But Gilgamesh said to Siduri, the young woman, "How can I be silent, how can I rest, when Enkidu whom I love is dust, and I too shall die and be laid in the earth. You live by the sea-shore and look into the heart of it; young woman, tell me now, which is the way to Utnapishtim, the son of Ubara-Tutu? What directions are there for the passage; give me, oh, give me directions. I will cross the Ocean if it is possible; if it is not I will wander still farther in the wilderness." The wine-maker said to him, "Gilgamesh, there is no crossing the Ocean; whoever has come, since the days of old, has not been able to pass that sea. The Sun in his glory crosses the Ocean, but who beside Shamash has ever crossed it? The place and the passage are difficult, and the waters of death are deep which flow between. Gilgamesh, how will you cross the Ocean? When you come to the waters of death what will you do? But Gilgamesh, down in the woods you will find Urshanabi, the ferryman of Utnapishtim; with him are the holy things, the things of stone. He is fashioning the serpent prow of the boat. Look at him well, and if it is possible, perhaps you will cross the waters with him; but if it is not possible, then you must go back."

When Gilgamesh heard this he was seized with anger. He took his axe in his hand, and his dagger from his belt. He crept forward and he fell on them like a javelin. Then he went into the forest and sat down. Urshanabi saw the dagger flash and heard the axe, and he beat his head, for Gilgamesh had shattered the tackle of the boat in his rage. Urshanabi said to him, "Tell me, what is your name? I am Urshanabi, the ferryman of Utnapishtim the Far-away." He replied to him, "Gilgamesh is my name, I am from Uruk, from the house of Anu." Then Urshanabi said to him, "Why are your cheeks so starved and your face drawn? Why is despair in your heart and your face like the face of one who has made a long journey; yes, why is your face burned with heat and with cold, and why do you come here wandering over the pastures in search of the wind?"

Gilgamesh said to him, "Why should not my cheeks be starved and my face drawn? Despair is in my heart, and my face is the face of one who has made a long journey. I was burned with heat and with cold. Why should I not wander over the pastures? My friend, my younger brother who seized and killed the Bull of Heaven, and overthrew Humbaba in the cedar forest, my friend who was very dear to me, and who endured dangers beside me, Enkidu my brother whom I loved, the end of mortality has overtaken him. I wept for him seven days and nights till the worm fastened on him. Because of my brother I am afraid of death, because of my brother I stray through the wilderness. His fate lies heavy upon me. How can I be silent, how can I rest? He is dust and I too shall die and be laid in the earth for ever. I am afraid of death, therefore, Urshanabi, tell me which is the road to Utnapishtim? If it is possible I will cross the waters of death; if not I will wander still farther through the wilderness."

Urshanabi said to him, "Gilgamesh, your own hands have prevented you from crossing the Ocean; when you destroyed the tackle of the boat you destroyed its safety." Then the two of them talked it over and Gilgamesh said, "Why are you so angry with me, Urshanabi, for you yourself cross the sea by day and night, at all seasons you cross it." "Gilgamesh, those things you destroyed, their property is to carry me over the water, to prevent the waters of death from touching me. It was for this reason that I preserved them, but you have destroyed them, and the *urnu* snakes with them. But now, go into the forest, Gilgamesh; with your axe cut poles, one hundred and twenty, cut them sixty cubits long, paint them with bitumen, set on them ferrules and bring them back."

When Gilgamesh heard this he went into the forest, he cut poles one hundred and twenty; he cut them sixty cubits long, he painted them with bitumen, he set on them ferrules, and he brought them to Urshanabi. Then they boarded the boat, Gilgamesh and Urshanabi together, launching it out on the waves of Ocean. For three days they ran on as it were a journey of a month and fifteen days, and at last Urshanabi brought the boat to the waters of death. Then Urshanabi said to Gilgamesh, "Press on, take a pole and thrust it in, but do not let your hands touch the waters. Gilgamesh, take a second pole, take a third, take a fourth pole. Now, Gilgamesh, take a fifth, take a sixth and seventh pole. Gilgamesh, take an eighth, and ninth, a tenth pole. Gilgamesh, take an eleventh, take a twelfth pole." After one hundred and twenty thrusts Gilgamesh had used the last pole. Then he stripped himself, he held up his arms for a mast and his covering for a sail. So Urshanabi the ferryman brought Gilgamesh to Utnapishtim, whom they call the Faraway, who lives in Dilmun at the place of the sun's transit, eastward of the mountain. To him alone of men the gods had given everlasting life.

Now Utnapishtim, where he lay at ease, looked into the distance and he said in his heart, musing to himself, "Why does the boat sail here without tackle and mast; why are the sacred stones destroyed, and why does the master not sail the boat? That man who comes is none of mine; where I look I see a man whose body is covered with skins of beasts. Who is this who walks up the shore behind Urshanabi, for surely he is no man of mine?" So Utnapishtim looked at him and said, "What is your name, you who come here wearing the skins of beasts, with your cheeks starved and your face drawn? Where are you hurrying to now? For what reason have you made this great journey, crossing the seas whose passage is difficult? Tell me the reason for your coming."

He replied, "Gilgamesh is my name. I am from Uruk, from the house of Anu." Then Utnapishtim said to him, "If you are Gilgamesh, why are your cheeks so starved and your face drawn? Why is despair in your heart and your face like the face of one who has made a long journey? Yes, why is your face burned with heat and cold; and why do you come here, wandering over the wilderness in search of the wind?"

Gilgamesh said to him, "Why should not my cheeks be starved and my face drawn? Despair is in my heart and my face is the face of one who has made a long journey. It was burned with heat and with cold. Why should I not wander over the pastures? My friend, my younger brother who seized and killed the Bull of Heaven and overthrew Humbaba in the cedar forest, my friend who was very dear to me and endured dangers beside me, Enkidu, my brother whom I loved, the end of mortality has overtaken him. I wept for him seven days and nights till the worm fastened on him. Because of my brother I am afraid of death; because of my brother I stray through the wilderness. His fate lies heavy upon me. How can I be silent, how can I rest? He is dust and I shall die also and be laid in the earth for ever." Again Gilgamesh said, speaking to Utnapishtim, "It is to see Utnapishtim whom we call the Faraway that I have come this journey. For this I have wandered over the world, I have crossed many difficult ranges, I have crossed the seas, I have wearied myself with travelling; my joints are aching, and I have lost acquaintance with sleep which is sweet. My clothes were worn out before I came to the house of Siduri. I have killed the bear and hyena, the lion and panther, the tiger, the stag and the ibex, all sorts of wild game and the small creatures of the pastures. I ate their flesh and I wore their skins; and that was how I came to the gate of the young woman, the maker of wine, who barred her gate of pitch and bitumen against me. But from her I had news of the journey; so then I came to Urshanabi the ferryman, and with him I crossed over the waters of death. O, father Utnapishtim, you who have entered the assembly of the gods, I wish to question you concerning the living and the dead, how shall I find the life for which I am searching?"

Utnapishtim said, "There is no permanence. Do we build a house to stand for ever, do we seal a contract to hold for all time? Do brothers divide an inheritance to keep for ever, does the flood-time of rivers endure? It is only the nymph of the dragon-fly who sheds her larva and sees the sun in his glory. From the days of old there is no permanence. The sleeping and the dead, how alike they are, they are like a painted death. What is there between the master and the servant when both have fulfilled their doom? When the Anunnaki, the judges, come together, and Mammetun the mother of destinies, together they decree the fates of men. Life and death they allot but the day of death they do not disclose."

Then Gilgamesh said to Utnapishtim the Faraway, "I look at you now, Utnapishtim, and your appearance is no different from mine; there is nothing strange in your features. I thought I should find you like a hero prepared for battle, but you lie here taking your ease on your back. Tell me truly, how was it that you came to enter the company of the gods, and to possess everlasting life?" Utnapishtim said to Gilgamesh, "I will reveal to you a mystery, I will tell you a secret of the gods."

5

The Story of the Flood

"You know the city Shurrupak, it stands on the banks of Euphrates? That city grew old and the gods that were in it were old. There was Anu, lord of the firmament, their father, and warrior Enlil their counsellor, Ninurta the helper, and Ennugi watcher over canals; and with them also was Ea. In those days the world teemed, the people multiplied, the world bellowed like a wild bull, and the great god was aroused by the clamour. Enlil heard the clamour and he said to the gods in council, 'The uproar of mankind is intolerable and sleep is no longer possible by reason of the babel.' So the gods agreed to exterminate mankind. Enlil did this, but Ea because of his oath warned me in a dream. He whispered their words to my house of reeds, 'Reed-house, reed-house! Wall, O wall, hearken reed-house, wall reflect; O man of Shurrupak, son of Ubara-Tutu; tear down your house and build a boat, abandon possessions and look for life, despise worldly goods and save your soul alive. Tear down your house, I say, and build a boat. These are the measurements of the barque as you shall build her: let her beam equal her length, let her deck be roofed like the vault that covers the abyss; then take up into the boat the seed of all living creatures.'

"When I had understood I said to my lord, 'Behold what you have commanded I will honour and perform, but how shall I answer the people, the city, the elders?' Then Ea opened his mouth and said to me, his servant, 'Tell them this: I have learnt that Enlil is wrathful against me, I dare no longer walk in his land nor live in his city; I will go down to the Gulf to dwell with Ea my lord. But on you he will rain down abundance, rare fish and shy wild-fowl, a rich harvest-tide. In the evening the rider of the storm will bring you wheat in torrents.'

"In the first light of dawn all my household gathered round me, the children brought pitch and the men whatever was necessary. On the fifth day I laid the keel and the ribs, then I made fast the planking. The ground-space was one acre, each side of the deck measured one hundred and twenty cubits, making a square. I built six decks below, seven in all, I divided them into nine sections with bulkheads between. I drove in wedges where needed, I saw to the punt-poles, and laid in supplies. The carriers brought oil in baskets, I poured pitch into the furnace and asphalt and oil; more oil was consumed in caulking, and more again the master of the boat took into his stores. I slaughtered bullocks for the people and every day I killed sheep. I gave the shipwrights wine to drink as though it were river water, raw wine and red wine and oil and white wine. There was feasting then as there is at the time of the New Year's festival; I myself anointed my head. On the eleventh day the boat was complete.

"Then was the launching full of difficulty; there was shifting of ballast above and below till two thirds was submerged. I loaded into her all that I had of gold and of living things, my family, my kin, the beast of the field both wild and tame, and all the craftsmen. I sent them on board, for the time that Shamash had ordained was already fulfilled when he said, 'In the evening, when the rider of the storm sends down the destroying rain, enter the boat and batten her down.' The time was fulfilled, the evening came, the rider of the storm sent down the rain. I looked out at the weather and it was terrible, so I too boarded the boat and battened her down. All was now complete, the battening and the caulking; so I handed the tiller to Puzur-Amurri the steersman, with the navigation and the care of the whole boat.

"With the first light of dawn a black cloud came from the horizon; it thundered within where Adad, lord of the storm, was riding. In front over hill and plain Shullat and Hanish, heralds of the storm, led on. Then the gods of the abyss rose up; Nergal pulled out the dams of the nether waters, Ninurta the war-lord threw down the dykes, and the seven judges of hell, the Annunaki, raised their torches, lighting the land with their livid flame. A stupor of despair went up to heaven when the god of the storm turned daylight to darkness, when he smashed the land like a cup. One whole day the tempest raged, gathering fury as it went, it poured over the people like the tides of battle; a man could not see his brother nor the people be seen from heaven. Even the gods were terrified at the flood, they fled to the highest heaven, the firmament of Anu; they crouched against the walls, cowering like curs. Then Ishtar the sweet-voiced Queen of Heaven cried out like a woman in travail: 'Alas the days of old are turned to dust because I commanded evil; why did I command this evil in the council of all the gods? I commanded wars to destroy the people, but are they not my people, for I brought them forth? Now like the spawn of fish they float in the ocean.' The great gods of heaven and of hell wept, they covered their mouths.

"For six days and six nights the winds blew, torrent and tempest and flood overwhelmed the world, tempest and flood raged together like warring hosts. When the seventh day dawned the storm from the south subsided, the sea grew calm, the flood was stilled; I looked at the face of the world and there was silence, all mankind was turned to clay. The surface of the sea stretched as flat as a roof-top; I opened a hatch and the light fell on my face. Then I bowed low, I sat down and I wept, the tears streamed down my face, for on every side was the waste of water. I looked for land in vain, for fourteen leagues distant there appeared a mountain, and there the boat grounded; on the mountain of Nisir the boat held fast, she held fast and did not budge. One day she held, and a second day on the mountain of Nisir she held fast and did not budge. A third day, and a fourth day she held fast on the mountain and did not budge; a fifth day and a sixth day she held fast on the mountain. When the seventh day dawned I loosed a dove and let her go. She flew away, but finding no resting-place she returned. Then I loosed a swallow, and she flew away but finding no resting-place she returned. I loosed a raven, she saw that the waters had retreated, she ate, she flew around, she cawed, and she did not come back. Then I threw everything open to the four winds, I made a sacrifice and poured out a libation on the mountain top. Seven and again seven cauldrons I set up on their stands, I heaped up wood and cane and cedar and myrtle. When the gods smelled the sweet savour, they gathered like flies over the sacrifice. Then, at last, Ishtar also came, she lifted her necklace with the jewels of heaven that once Anu had made to please her. 'O you gods here present, by the lapis lazuli round my neck I shall remember these days as I remember the jewels of my throat; these last days I shall not forget. Let all the gods gather round the sacrifice, except Enlil. He shall not approach this offering, for without reflection he brought the flood; he consigned my people to destruction.'

"When Enlil had come, when he saw the boat, he was wrath and swelled with anger at the gods, the host of heaven, 'Has any of these mortals escaped? Not one was to have survived the destruction.' Then the god of the wells and canals Ninurta opened his mouth and said to the warrior Enlil, 'Who is there of the gods that can devise without Ea? It is Ea, alone who knows all things.' Then Ea opened his mouth and spoke to warrior Enlil, 'Wisest of gods, hero Enlil, how could you so senselessly bring down the flood?

> Lay upon the sinner his sin,
> Lay upon the transgressor his transgression,
> Punish him a little when he breaks loose,
> Do not drive him too hard or he perishes;
> Would that a lion had ravaged mankind   5
> Rather than the flood,
> Would that a wolf had ravaged mankind
> Rather than the flood,
> Would that famine had wasted the world
> Rather than the flood,   10
> Would that pestilence had wasted mankind
> Rather than the flood.

It was not I that revealed the secret of the gods; the wise man learned it in a dream. Now take your counsel what shall be done with him.'

"Then Enlil went up into the boat, he took me by the hand and my wife and made us enter the boat and kneel down on either side, he standing between us. He touched our foreheads to bless us saying, 'In time past Utnapishtim was a mortal man; henceforth he and his wife shall live in the distance at the mouth of the rivers.' Thus it was that the gods took me and placed me here to live in the distance, at the mouth of the rivers."

6

The Return

Utnapishtim said, "As for you, Gilgamesh, who will assemble the gods for your sake, so that you may find that life for which you are searching? But if you wish, come and put it to the test: only prevail against sleep for six days and seven nights." But while Gilgamesh sat there resting on his haunches, a mist of sleep like soft wool teased from the fleece drifted over him, and Utnapishtim said to his wife, "Look at him now, the strong man who would have everlasting life, even now the mists of sleep are drifting over him." His wife replied, "Touch the man to wake him, so that he may return to his own land in peace, going back through the gate by which he came." Utnapishtim said to his wife, "All men are deceivers, even you he will attempt to deceive; therefore bake loaves of bread, each day one loaf, and put it beside his head; and make a mark on the wall to number the days he has slept."

So she baked loaves of bread, each day one loaf, and put it beside his head, and she marked on the walls the days that he slept; and there came a day when the first loaf was hard, the second loaf was like leather, the third was soggy, the crust of the fourth had mould, the fifth was mildewed, the sixth was fresh, and the seventh was still on the embers. Then Utnapishtim touched him and he woke. Gilgamesh said to Utnapishtim the Faraway, "I hardly slept when you touched and roused me." But Utnapishtim said, "Count these loaves and learn how many days you slept, for your first is hard, your second like leather, your third is soggy, the crust of your fourth has mould, your fifth is mildewed, your sixth is fresh and your seventh was still over the glowing embers when I touched and woke you." Gilgamesh said, "What shall I do, O Utnapishtim, where shall I go? Already the thief in the night has hold of my limbs, death inhabits my room; wherever my foot rests, there I find death."

Then Utnapishtim spoke to Urshanabi the ferryman: "Woe to you Urshanabi, now and for ever more you have become hateful to this harbourage; it is not for you, nor for you are the crossings of this sea. Go now, banished from the shore. But this man before whom you walked, bringing him here, whose body is covered with foulness and the grace of whose limbs has been spoiled by wild skins, take him to the washing-place. There he shall wash his long hair clean as snow in the water, he shall throw off his skins and let the sea carry them away, and the beauty of his body shall be shown, the fillet on his forehead shall be renewed, and he shall be given clothes to cover his nakedness. Till he reaches his own city and his journey is accomplished, these clothes will show no sign of age, they will wear like a new garment."

So Urshanabi took Gilgamesh and led him to the washing-place, he washed his long hair as clean as snow in the water, he threw off his skins, which the sea carried away, and showed the beauty of his body. He renewed the fillet on his forehead, and to cover his nakedness gave him clothes which would show no sign of age, but would wear like a new garment til he reached his own city, and his journey was accomplished.

Then Gilgamesh and Urshanabi launched the boat on to the water and boarded it, and they made ready to sail away; but the wife of Utnapishtim the Faraway said to him, "Gilgamesh came here wearied out, he is worn out; what will you give him to carry him back to his own country?" So Utnapishtim spoke, and Gilgamesh took a pole and brought the boat in to the bank. "Gilgamesh, you came here a man wearied out, you have worn yourself out; what shall I give you to carry you back to your own country? Gilgamesh, I shall reveal a secret thing, it is a mystery of the gods that I am telling you. There is a plant that grows under the water, it has a prickle like a thorn, like a rose; it will wound your hands, but if you succeed in taking it, then your hands will hold that which restores his lost youth to a man."

When Gilgamesh heard this he opened the sluices so that a sweet-water current might carry him out to the deepest channel; he tied heavy stones to his feet and they dragged him down to the water-bed. There he saw the plant growing; although it pricked him he took it in his hands; then he cut the heavy stones from his feet, and the sea carried him and threw him on to the shore. Gilgamesh said to Urshanabi the ferryman, "Come here, and see this marvellous plant. By its virtue a man may win back all his former strength. I will take it to Uruk of the strong walls; there I will give it to the old men to eat. Its name shall be 'The Old Men Are Young Again'; and at last I shall eat it myself and have back all my lost youth." So Gilgamesh returned by the gate through which he had come, Gilgamesh and Urshanabi went together. They travelled their twenty leagues and then they broke their fast; after thirty leagues they stopped for the night.

Gilgamesh saw a well of cool water and he went down and bathed; but deep in the pool there was lying a serpent, and the serpent sensed the sweetness of the flower. It rose out of the water and snatched it away, and immediately it sloughed its skin and returned to the well. Then Gilgamesh sat down and wept, the tears ran down his face, and he took the hand of Urshanabi; "O Urshanabi, was it for this that I toiled with my hands, is it for this I have wrung out my heart's blood? For myself I have gained nothing; not I, but the beast of the earth has joy of it now. Already the stream has carried it twenty leagues back to the channels where I found it. I found a sign and now I have lost it. Let us leave the boat on the bank and go."

After twenty leagues they broke their fast, after thirty leagues they stopped for the night; in three days they had walked as much as a journey of a month and fifteen days. When the journey was accomplished they arrived at Uruk, the strong-walled city. Gilgamesh spoke to him, to Urshanabi the ferryman, "Urshanabi, climb up on to the wall of Uruk, inspect its foundation terrace, and examine well the brickwork; see if it is not of burnt bricks; and did not the seven wise men lay these foundations? One third of the whole is city, one third is garden, and one third is field, with the precinct of the goddess Ishtar. These parts and the precinct are all Uruk."

This too was the work of Gilgamesh, the king, who knew the countries of the world. He was wise, he saw mysteries and knew secret things, he brought us a tale of the days before the flood. He went a long journey, was weary, worn out with labour, and returning engraved on a stone the whole story.

7

The Death of Gilgamesh

The destiny was fulfilled which the father of the gods, Enlil of the mountain, had decreed for Gilgamesh: "In nether-earth the darkness will show him a light: of mankind, all that are known, none will leave a monument for generations to come to compare with his. The heroes, the wise men, like the new moon have their waxing and waning. Men will say, 'Who has ever ruled with might and with power like him?' As in the dark month, the month of shadows, so without him there is no light. O Gilgamesh, this was the meaning of your dream. You were given the kingship, such was your destiny, everlasting life was not your destiny. Because of this do not be sad at heart, do not be grieved or oppressed; he has given you power to bind and to loose, to be the darkness and the light of mankind. He has given unexampled supremacy over the people, victory in battle from which no fugitive returns, in forays and assaults from which there is no going back. But do not abuse this power, deal justly with your servants in the palace, deal justly before the face of the Sun."

> The king has laid himself down and will not rise again,
> The Lord of Kullab will not rise again;
> He overcame evil, he will not come again;
> Though he was strong of arm he will not rise again;
>
> He had wisdom and a comely face, he will not come again;   5
> He is gone into the mountain, he will not come again;
> On the bed of fate he lies, he will not rise again,
> From the couch of many colours he will not come again.

The people of the city, great and small, are not silent; they lift up the lament, all men of flesh and blood lift up the lament. Fate has spoken; like a hooked fish he lies stretched on the bed, like a gazelle that is caught in a noose. Inhuman Namtar is heavy upon him, Namtar that has neither hand nor foot, that drinks no water and eats no meat.

For Gilgamesh, son of Ninsun, they weighed out their offerings; his dear wife, his son, his concubine, his musicians, his jester, and all his household; his servants, his stewards, all who lived in the palace weighed out their offerings for Gilgamesh the son of Ninsun, the heart of Uruk. They weighed out their offerings to Ereshkigal, the Queen of Death, and to all the gods of the dead. To Namtar, who is fate, they weighed out the offering. Bread for Neti the Keeper of the Gate, bread for Ningizzida the god of the serpent, the lord of the Tree of Life; for Dumuzi also, the young shepherd, for Enki and Ninki, for Endukugga and Nindukugga, for Enmul and Ninmul, all the ancestral gods, forbears of Enlil. A feast for Shulpae the god of feasting. For Samuqan, god of the herds, for the mother Ninhursag, and the gods of creation in the place of creation, for the host of heaven, priest and priestess weighed out the offering of the dead.

Gilgamesh, the son of Ninsun, lies in the tomb. At the place of offerings he weighed the bread-offering, at the place of libation he poured out the wine. In those days the lord Gilgamesh departed, the son of Ninsun, the king, peerless, without an equal among men, who did not neglect Enlil his master. O Gilgamesh, lord of Kullab, great is thy praise.

THE BIBLE: THE OLD TESTAMENT
ca. 1000–300 B.C.

THE CREATION–THE FALL

The religious attitudes of the Hebrews appear in the story that they told of the creation of the world and of humankind. This creation is the work of one God, who is omnipotent and omniscient and who creates a perfect and harmonious order. The disorder that we see all around us, physical and moral, is not God's creation but Adam and Eve's; it is the consequence of humankind's disobedience. The story not only reconciles the undeniable existence of evil and disorder in the world with the conception of God's infinite justice but also attributes to humanity itself an independence of God, free will, which in this case had been used for evil. The Hebrew God is not limited in His power by other deities, who oppose His will (as in the Greek stories of Zeus and his undisciplined family); His power over inanimate nature is infinite. In all the range of His creation there is only one being able to resist Him—humankind.

Because God is all-powerful, even this resistance on Adam and Eve's part is in some mysterious way a manifestation of God's will. How this can be is not explained by the story, and we are left with the mystery that still eludes us, the coexistence of God's prescient power and humanity's unrestricted free will.

The story of the Fall ends with a situation in which Adam and Eve have earned for themselves and their descendants a short life of sorrow relieved only by death. It was the achievement of later Hebrew teachers to carry the story on and develop the concept of a God who is as merciful as He is just, who watches tenderly over the destinies of the creatures who have rebelled against Him, and who brings about the possibility of atonement and full reconciliation.

Adam and Eve's son Cain is the first person to shed human blood, but though God drives him out to be a wanderer on the face of the earth, He does not kill him. The brand on Cain's forehead, while it marks him as a murderer, also protects his life—no one is to touch him. Later when the descendants of Adam and Eve grow so wicked that God is sorry He has created the human race, He decides to destroy it by sending a universal flood. But He spares Noah and his family to beget a new human race, on which God pins His hopes. His rainbow in the sky reminds humankind of His promise that He will never again let loose the waters. But people do not learn their lesson: they start to build a tower high enough to reach to Heaven, and God is afraid that if they succeed they will then recognize no limit to their ambitions. Yet He does not destroy them; He merely frustrates their purpose by depriving them of their common language.

Intertwined with these lessons about humankind's proper relations to God is a generational process that eventually concentrates on the origins and development of the Hebrews as God's chosen people. This part of the story begins with Abraham's willingness to sacrifice his only son, Isaac. It continues through the rivalry in which Isaac's son Jacob supplants his brother Esau, and it culminates in the trials and ultimate prosperity of Jacob's son Joseph.

JOSEPH

Joseph, his father's favorite son, has a sense of his own great destiny, confirmed by his dreams, which represent him as the first of all his race. He is indeed to be the first, but to become so he must also be the last. He is sold into slavery by his brothers; the savior is rejected by those whom he is to save, as the Hebrews were rejected by their neighbors and as they rejected their own prophets.

With the loss of his liberty, Joseph's trials have only begun. In Egypt after making a new and successful life for himself, he is thrown into prison on a false accusation. He interprets the dream of Pharaoh's butler, who promises, if his interpretation is correct, to secure his release; the butler is restored to freedom and royal favor but, as is the way of the world, forgets his promise and leaves his comforter in jail. Joseph stays in prison two more years but finally obtains his freedom and becomes Pharaoh's most trusted adviser. When his brothers come from starving Palestine and bow down before him asking for help, he saves them; not only does he give them grain but he also provides a home for his people in Egypt. "I am Joseph your brother, whom ye sold into Egypt," he says to them when he reveals his identity. "God sent me before you to preserve you a posterity in the earth, and to save your lives by a great deliverance."

One of the essential points of this story is the distinction that it emphasizes between an external, secular standard of good and a spiritual, religious standard. In the eyes of the average person, prosperity and righteousness are connected, if not identified, and the sufferer is felt to be one whose misfortune must be explained as a punishment for his or her wickedness. This feeling is strong in ancient (and especially in Greek) literature, but we should not be unduly complacent about our superiority to the ancients in this respect, for the attitude is still with us. It is in fact a basic assumption of a competitive society—the view, seldom expressed but strongly rooted, that the plight of the unfortunate is the result of their own laziness, the wealth of the rich the reward of superior virtue.

The writer of the Joseph story sees in the unfortunate sufferer the savior who is the instrument of God's will. The story does not emphasize the sufferings of Joseph; he is pictured rather as the man of action who through native ability and divine protection turns the injuries done him into advantages. We are not made to feel the torment in his soul. When he weeps it is because of the memory of what he had suffered and his yearning for his youngest brother, and he is in full control of the situation. And his reward in the things of this world is great. Not only does he reveal himself as the savior of his nation but he becomes rich and powerful beyond his brothers' dreams, and in a great kingdom. The spiritual and secular standards are at the end of the story combined; Joseph's suffering is neatly balanced by his worldly reward.

JOB

Later Hebrew writers developed a sadder and profounder view. The greatest literary masterpiece of the Old Testament, the Book of Job, is also concerned with the inadequacy of worldly standards of happiness and righteousness; but the suffering of Job is so overwhelming and so magnificently expressed, that even with our knowledge of its purpose and its meaning it seems excessive. Joseph suffered slavery, exile, and imprisonment but turned them all to account. Job loses his family and wealth in a series of calamities, which strike one on the other like hammer blows, and is then plagued with a loathsome disease. Unlike Joseph, he is old; he cannot adapt himself and rise above adverse circumstances, and he no longer wishes to live. Except for one thing: he wishes to understand the reason for his suffering.

For his friends the explanation is simple. With the blindness of men who know no standards other than those of this world, they are sure that Job's misfortune must be the result of some wickedness on his part. But Job is confident in his righteousness; his torture is as much mental as physical. He cannot reconcile the fact of his innocence with the calamities that have come on him with all the decisive suddenness of the hand of God.

The full explanation is never given to him, but it is given to the reader in the two opening chapters of the book. This prologue to the dramatic section of the work gives us the knowledge that is hidden from the participants in the ensuing dialogue. The writer uses the method characteristic of Greek tragedy—irony, the deeper under- standing of the dramatic spoken word that is based on the superior knowledge of the audience. The prologue explains God's motive in allowing Job to suffer. It is an impor- tant one: God intends to use Job as a demonstration to His skeptical subordinate, Satan, of the fact that a human being can retain faith in God's justice in the face of the greatest imaginable suffering. This motive, which Job does not know and which is never revealed to him, gives to the dialogue between Job and his friends its suspense and its importance. God has rested His case—that humanity is capable of keeping faith in divine justice, against all appearances to the contrary—on this one man.

The arguments of Job's friends are based on the worldly equation that success equals virtue. They attempt to undermine Job's faith, not in God, but in himself. "Who ever perished, being innocent?" asks Eliphaz, "or where were the righteous cut off?" Job's misfortune is a proof that he must have sinned; all he has to do is to admit his guilt and ask God for pardon, which he will surely receive. He refuses to accept this easy way out, and we know that he is right. In fact, we know from the prologue that he has been selected for misfortune not because he has sinned, but precisely because of his outstanding virtue. "There is none like him in the earth," God says, "a perfect and an upright man, one that feareth God, and escheweth evil." What Job must do is to persevere not only in his faith in God's justice but also in the conviction of his own innocence. He must believe the illogical, accept a paradox. His friends are offering him an easy way out, one that seems to be the way of humility and submis- sion. But it is a false way. And God finally tells them so. "The Lord said to Eliphaz the Temanite, My wrath is kindled against thee, and against thy two friends: for ye have not spoken of me the thing that is right, as my servant Job hath."

Job's confidence in his own righteousness is not pride but intellectual honesty. He sees that the problem is much harder than his friends imagine. To let them persuade him of his own guilt would lighten his mental burden by answering the question that tortures him, but his intelligence will not let him yield. Like Oedipus, he refuses to stop short of the truth. He even uses the same words: "let me alone, that I may speak, and let come on me what will." He finally expresses his understanding and acceptance of the paradox involved in the combination of his suffering with his innocence, but he does so with a human independence and dignity: "Though he slay me, yet will I trust in him: but I will maintain mine own ways before him." He sums up his case with a detailed account of the righteousness of his ways, and it is clear that this account is addressed not only to his three friends but also to God. "My desire is, that the Almighty would answer me," he says. His friends are silenced by the majesty and firmness of his statement. They "ceased to answer Job, because he was righteous in his own eyes," but God is moved to reply.

The magnificent poetry of that reply, the voice out of the whirlwind, still does not give Job the full explanation, God's motive in putting him to the torture. It is a tri- umphant proclamation of God's power and also of His justice, and it silences Job, who accepts it as a sufficient answer. That God does not reveal the key to the riddle even to the man who has victoriously stood the test and vindicated His faith in human- ity is perhaps the most significant point in the story. It suggests that there is not and never will be an explanation of human suffering that humankind's intelligence can comprehend. Sufferers must, like Job, cling to their faith in themselves and in God; they must accept the inexplicable fact that their own undeserved suffering is the working of God's justice.

THE SONG OF SONGS

In this great dialogue between lovers, a man and a woman, frankly and in detail, express their appreciation of each other's bodies. The Song of Songs (or Song of Solomon) celebrates human sexuality and love in all their sensual splendor, and human life itself: "for love," it says, "is strong as death." Each of the lovers, again and again, takes inventory of the other's body, describing each part, comparing it to an animal, some feature of the natural landscape, or an aspect of the built human environment, so that we not only feel the power of physical desire but also appreciate the human body and love as harmonious parts of the world. Some of these comparisons are of great natural beauty ("thy belly is like a heap of wheat set about with lilies"); others are extravagant, fantastic ("thy hair is as a flock of goats," "thy teeth are like a flock of sheep," "thy neck is like the tower of David," "thy nose is as the tower of Lebanon"). The concreteness of the imagery and the piling of image upon image make the pair of bodies a figure of the world itself, to be contemplated in wonder.

But the incorporation of this poem in sacred scripture raises the possibility of further meanings, although what these might be is an open question. This challenging and beautiful text has had a long history of divergent interpretations; a medieval Jewish commentator described it as "locks to which the key has been lost." Is it an allegory, and if so, is it a religious or historical allegory? If the former, does it concern the love between God and his chosen people? On the other hand, Christians later understood it to describe the love between Christ and his church, or between God or Christ and the individual soul. The question of allegory is complicated by other uncertainties. Is the text as we have it a single composition or a collection of poems? How are passages to be divided between the pair of lovers? Are there other speakers as well? In addition, many words and phrases in the Hebrew text are ambiguous and obscure. For this reason, English translations differ markedly. The King James version is given here because of its beauty as an English poem and because of its influence on Anglophone literature and music, but readers should be aware that it is not as accurate as modern translations.

Many scholars today consider the Song of Songs one or several love poems, similar in important ways to Middle Eastern marriage songs that were were collected early in the twentieth century, and rooted, perhaps, in ancient fertility rituals of the great pagan religions of Asia Minor. But we may want to ask if there are not also aspects of this text that invite an allegorical reading, and whether we have to choose between sensual and more abstract meanings. Where do we draw the line between the literal and figurative meanings of words? Would we always want to? If the Song of Songs is an allegory, it is one that is wonderfully in touch with the world of the senses, as Dante's *Divine Comedy*, another great allegorical poem, is in a different way.

The student will find good background in R. R. Ackroyd and C. F. Evans, eds., *The Cambridge History of the Bible* (1970), vol. 1. R. H. Rowley, *The Growth of the Old Testament* (1950), concentrates on the Old Testament as a whole. The various volumes of *The Anchor Bible* contain modern translations and informative introductions and notes. The volume on the Song of Songs by Marvin Pope (1977) is especially helpful. For Job, see P. Sanders, ed., *Twentieth-Century Interpretations of the Book of Job* (1968). See also Robert Alter and Frank Kermode, eds., *The Literary Guide to the Bible* (1987), and Leland Ryken and Tremper Longman III, eds., *A Complete Literary Guide to the Bible* (1993).

PRONOUNCING GLOSSARY

The following list uses common English syllables and stress accents to provide rough equivalents of selected words whose pronunciation may be unfamiliar to the general reader.

Baalhamon: *bahl-ha'-mon*

Euphrates: *yoo-fray'-teez*

Canaan: *kay'-nuhn*

Job: *johb*

Esau: *ee'-saw*

Tirzah: *teer'-zah*

THE BIBLE: THE OLD TESTAMENT[1]

Genesis 1–3

[The Creation—The Fall]

1. In the beginning God created the heaven and the earth. And the earth was without form, and void; and darkness was upon the face of the deep. And the Spirit of God moved upon the face of the waters.

And God said, Let there be light: and there was light. And God saw the light, that it was good: and God divided the light from the darkness. And God called the light Day, and the darkness he called Night. And the evening and the morning were the first day.

And God said, Let there be a firmament in the midst of the waters, and let it divide the waters from the waters. And God made the firmament, and divided the waters which were under the firmament from the waters which were above the firmament:[2] and it was so. And God called the firmament Heaven. And the evening and the morning were the second day.

And God said, Let the waters under the heaven be gathered together unto one place, and let the dry land appear: and it was so. And God called the dry land Earth; and the gathering together of the waters called he Seas: and God saw that it was good. And God said, Let the earth bring forth grass, the herb yielding seed, and the fruit tree yielding fruit after his kind, whose seed is in itself, upon the earth: and it was so. And the earth brought forth grass, and herb yielding seed after his kind, and the tree yielding fruit, whose seed was in itself, after his kind: and God saw that it was good. And the evening and the morning were the third day.

And God said, Let there be lights in the firmament of the heaven to divide the day from the night; and let them be for signs, and for seasons, and for days, and years: and let them be for lights in the firmament of the heaven to give light upon the earth: and it was so. And God made two great lights; the greater light to rule the day, and the lesser light to rule the night: he made the stars also. And God set them in the firmament of the heaven to give light upon the earth, and to rule over the day and over the night, and to divide the light from the darkness: and God saw that it was good. And the evening and the morning were the fourth day. And God said, Let the waters bring forth abundantly the moving creature that hath life, and fowl that may fly above the earth in the open firmament of heaven. And God created great whales, and every living creature that moveth, which the waters brought forth

---

1. The text of these selections is that of the King James, or Authorized, Version of 1611, so called because it was the work of a team of fifty-four scholars named by King James I of England to produce a new translation "appointed to be read in churches." Since that time advances in biblical scholarship have corrected some of the translators' mistakes and substituted clearer versions where their prose is obscure. Yet the superiority of the Authorized Version as literature remains unquestioned; it is one of the greatest literary texts in the history of the English language. It was written at a time when English was at a creative peak—the age of William Shakespeare, Ben Jonson, and John Donne. It was written to be read aloud, as it was in churches and homes, and to be learned by heart, as it was in schools in the English-speaking world for centuries. The echoes of its magnificent rhythms and cadences can be heard in the verse of English poets from John Milton to T. S. Eliot, in the prose of John Bunyan and the speeches of Abraham Lincoln. 2. The sky, which seen from below has the appearance of a ceiling. The waters above are those that come down in the form of rain.

abundantly, after their kind, and every winged fowl after his kind: and God saw that it was good. And God blessed them, saying, Be fruitful, and multiply, and fill the waters in the seas, and let fowl multiply in the earth. And the evening and the morning were the fifth day.

And God said, Let the earth bring forth the living creature after his kind, cattle, and creeping thing, and beast of the earth after his kind: and it was so. And God made the beast of the earth after his kind, and cattle after their kind, and everything that creepeth upon the earth after his kind: and God saw that it was good.

And God said, Let us make man in our image, after our likeness: and let them have dominion over the fish of the sea, and over the fowl of the air, and over the cattle, and over all the earth, and over every creeping thing that creepeth upon the earth. So God created man in his own image, in the image of God created he him; male and female created he them. And God blessed them, and God said unto them, Be fruitful, and multiply, and replenish the earth, and subdue it: and have dominion over the fish of the sea, and over the fowl of the air, and over every living thing that moveth upon the earth.

And God said, Behold, I have given you every herb bearing seed, which is upon the face of all the earth, and every tree, in which is the fruit of a tree yielding seed; to you it shall be for meat. And to every beast of the earth, and to every fowl of the air, and to every thing that creepeth upon the earth, wherein there is life, I have given every green herb for meat: and it was so. And God saw every thing that he had made, and, behold, it was very good. And the evening and the morning were the sixth day.

2. Thus the heavens and the earth were finished, and all the host of them. And on the seventh day God ended his work which he had made; and he rested on the seventh day from all his work which he had made. And God blessed the seventh day, and sanctified it: because that in it he had rested from all his work which God created and made.

These are the generations of the heavens and of the earth when they were created,[3] in the day that the Lord God made the earth and the heavens, and every plant of the field before it was in the earth, and every herb of the field before it grew: for the Lord God had not caused it to rain upon the earth, and there was not a man to till the ground. But there went up a mist from the earth, and watered the whole face of the ground. And the Lord God formed man of the dust of the ground, and breathed into his nostrils the breath of life; and man became a living soul.

And the Lord God planted a garden eastward in Eden; and there he put the man whom he had formed. And out of the ground made the Lord God to grow every tree that is pleasant to the sight, and good for food; the tree of life also in the midst of the garden, and the tree of knowledge of good and evil. And a river went out of Eden to water the garden; and from thence it was parted, and became into four heads. The name of the first is Pison: that is it which compasseth the whole land of Havilah, where there is gold; and the gold of that land is good: there is bdellium and the onyx stone. And the

---

3. This is the beginning of a different account of the Creation, which does not agree in all respects with the first.

name of the second river is Gihon: the same is it that compasseth the whole land of Ethiopia. And the name of the third river is Hiddekel: that is it which goeth toward the east of Assyria. And the fourth river is Euphrates. And the Lord God took the man, and put him into the garden of Eden to dress it and to keep it. And the Lord God commanded the man, saying, Of every tree of the garden thou mayest freely eat: but of the tree of the knowledge of good and evil, thou shalt not eat of it: for in the day that thou eatest thereof thou shalt surely die.

And the Lord God said, It is not good that the man should be alone; I will make him an help meet for him. And out of the ground the Lord God formed every beast of the field, and every fowl of the air; and brought them unto Adam to see what he would call them: and whatsoever Adam called every living creature, that was the name thereof. And Adam gave names to all cattle, and to the fowl of the air, and to every beast of the field; but for Adam there was not found an help meet for him. And the Lord God caused a deep sleep to fall upon Adam, and he slept: and he took one of his ribs, and closed up the flesh instead thereof; and the rib, which the Lord God had taken from man, made he a woman, and brought her unto the man. And Adam said, This is now bone of my bones, and flesh of my flesh: she shall be called Woman, because she was taken out of Man. Therefore shall a man leave his father and his mother, and shall cleave unto his wife: and they shall be one flesh. And they were both naked, the man and his wife, and were not ashamed.

3. Now the serpent was more subtil than any beast of the field which the Lord God had made. And he said unto the woman, Yea, hath God said, Ye shall not eat of every tree of the garden? And the woman said unto the serpent, We may eat of the fruit of the trees of the garden: but of the fruit of the tree which is in the midst of the garden, God hath said, Ye shall not eat of it, neither shall ye touch it, lest ye die. And the serpent said unto the woman, Ye shall not surely die: for God doth know that in the day ye eat thereof, then your eyes shall be opened, and ye shall be as gods, knowing good and evil. And when the woman saw that the tree was good for food, and that it was pleasant to the eyes, and a tree to be desired to make one wise, she took of the fruit thereof, and did eat, and gave also unto her husband with her; and he did eat. And the eyes of them both were opened, and they knew that they were naked; and they sewed fig leaves together, and made themselves aprons. And they heard the voice of the Lord God walking in the garden in the cool of the day: and Adam and his wife hid themselves from the presence of the Lord God amongst the trees of the garden. And the Lord God called unto Adam, and said unto him, Where art thou? And he said, I heard thy voice in the garden, and I was afraid, because I was naked; and I hid myself. And he said, Who told thee that thou wast naked? Hast thou eaten of the tree, whereof I commanded thee that thou shouldest not eat? And the man said, The woman whom thou gavest to be with me, she gave me of the tree, and I did eat. And the Lord God said unto the woman, What is this that thou hast done? And the woman said, The serpent beguiled me, and I did eat. And the Lord God said unto the serpent, Because thou hast done this, thou art cursed above all cattle, and above every beast of

the field; upon thy belly shalt thou go, and dust shall thou eat all the days of thy life: and I will put enmity between thee and the woman, and between thy seed and her seed; it shall bruise thy head, and thou shalt bruise his heel. Unto the woman he said, I will greatly multiply thy sorrow and thy conception; in sorrow thou shalt bring forth children; and thy desire shall be to thy husband, and he shall rule over thee. And unto Adam he said, Because thou hast hearkened unto the voice of thy wife, and hast eaten of the tree, of which I commanded thee, saying, Thou shalt not eat of it: cursed is the ground for thy sake; in sorrow shalt thou eat of it all the days of thy life; thorns also and thistles shall it bring forth to thee; and thou shalt eat the herb of the field; in the sweat of thy face shalt thou eat bread, till thou return unto the ground; for out of it wast thou taken: for dust thou art, and unto dust shalt thou return. And Adam called his wife's name Eve; because she was the mother of all living. Unto Adam also and to his wife did the Lord God make coats of skins, and clothed them.

And the Lord God said, Behold, the man is become as one of us, to know good and evil: and now, lest he put forth his hand, and take also of the tree of life, and eat, and live forever: therefore the Lord God sent him forth from the garden of Eden, to till the ground from whence he was taken. So he drove out the man; and he placed at the east of the garden of Eden Cherubims, and a flaming sword which turned every way, to keep the way of the tree of life.

Genesis 4

[The First Murder]

4. And Adam knew Eve his wife; and she conceived, and bare Cain, and said, I have gotten a man from the Lord. And she again bare his brother Abel. And Abel was a keeper of sheep, but Cain was a tiller of the ground. And in process of time it came to pass, that Cain brought of the fruit of the ground an offering unto the Lord. And Abel, he also brought of the firstlings of his flock and of the fat thereof. And the Lord had respect unto Abel and to his offering: but unto Cain and to his offering he had not respect. And Cain was very wroth, and his countenance fell. And the Lord said unto Cain, Why art thou wroth? and why is thy countenance fallen? If thou doest well, shalt thou not be accepted? and if thou doest not well, sin lieth at the door. And unto thee shall be his desire, and thou shall rule over him.[1] And Cain talked with Abel his brother: and it came to pass, when they were in the field, that Cain rose up against Abel his brother, and slew him.

And the Lord said unto Cain, Where is Abel thy brother? And he said, I know not: am I my brother's keeper? And he said, What hast thou done? the voice of thy brother's blood crieth unto me from the ground. And now art thou cursed from the earth, which hath opened her mouth to receive thy brother's blood from thy hand; when thou tillest the ground, it shall not henceforth yield unto thee her strength, a fugitive and a vagabond shalt thou be in the earth. And Cain said unto the Lord, My punishment is greater than

1. Obscure; it seems to mean something like: Sin shall be eager for you, but you must master it.

I can bear. Behold, thou hast driven me out this day from the face of the earth; and from thy face shall I be hid; and I shall be a fugitive and a vagabond in the earth; and it shall come to pass, that every one that findeth me shall slay me. And the Lord said unto him, Therefore whosoever slayeth Cain, vengeance shall be taken on him sevenfold. And the Lord set a mark upon Cain, lest any finding him should kill him.

Genesis 6–9

[The Flood]

6. * * * And God saw that the wickedness of man was great in the earth, and that every imagination of the thoughts of his heart was only evil continually. And it repented the Lord that he had made man on the earth, and it grieved him at his heart. And the Lord said, I will destroy man whom I have created from the face of the earth; both man, and beast, and the creeping thing, and the fowls of the air; for it repenteth me that I have made them. But Noah found grace in the eyes of the Lord.

These are the generations of Noah: Noah was a just man and perfect in his generations, and Noah walked with God. And Noah begat three sons, Shem, Ham, and Japheth.

The earth also was corrupt before God, and the earth was filled with violence. And God looked upon the earth, and, behold, it was corrupt; for all flesh had corrupted his way upon the earth. And God said unto Noah, The end of all flesh is come before me; for the earth is filled with violence through them; and, behold, I will destroy them with the earth. Make thee an ark of gopher wood;[1] rooms shalt thou make in the ark, and shalt pitch it within and without with pitch. And this is the fashion which thou shalt make it of: The length of the ark shall be three hundred cubits,[2] the breadth of it fifty cubits, and the height of it thirty cubits. A window[3] shalt thou make to the ark, and in a cubit shalt thou finish it above; and the door of the ark shalt thou set in the side thereof; with lower, second, and third stories shalt thou make it. And, behold, I, even I, do bring a flood of waters upon the earth, to destroy all flesh, wherein is the breath of life, from under heaven; and every thing that is in the earth shall die. But with thee will I establish my covenant; and thou shalt come into the ark, thou, and thy sons, and thy wife, and thy sons' wives with thee. And of every living thing of all flesh, two of every sort shalt thou bring into the ark, to keep them alive with thee; they shall be male and female. Of fowls after their kind, and of cattle after their kind, of every creeping thing of the earth after his kind, two of every sort shall come unto thee, to keep them alive. And take thou unto thee of all food that is eaten, and thou shalt gather it to thee; and it shall be for food for thee, and for them. Thus did Noah; according to all that God commanded him, so did he.

7. * * * And Noah was six hundred years old when the flood of waters was upon the earth. And Noah went in, and his sons, and his wife, and his

---

1. Cypress. 2. A Hebrew measure of length, about one and a half feet. 3. Obscure; perhaps a skylight in the roof.

sons' wives with him, into the ark, because of the waters of the flood. Of clean beasts, and of beasts that are not clean, and of fowls, and of every thing that creepeth upon the earth, There went in two and two unto Noah into the ark, the male and the female, as God had commanded Noah. And it came to pass after seven days, that the waters of the flood were upon the earth. In the six hundredth year of Noah's life, in the second month, the seventeenth day of the month, the same day were all the fountains of the great deep broken up, and the windows of heaven were opened. And the rain was upon the earth forty days and forty nights. In the selfsame day entered Noah, and Shem, and Ham, and Japheth, the sons of Noah, and Noah's wife, and the three wives of his sons with them, into the ark; they, and every beast after his kind, and all the cattle after their kind, and every creeping thing that creepeth upon the earth after his kind, and every fowl after his kind, every bird of every sort. And they went in unto Noah into the ark, two and two of all flesh, wherein is the breath of life. And they that went in, went in male and female of all flesh, as God had commanded him: and the Lord shut him in. And the flood was forty days upon the earth; and the waters increased, and bare up the ark, and it was lift up above the earth. And the waters prevailed, and were increased greatly upon the earth; and the ark went upon the face of the waters. And the waters prevailed exceedingly upon the earth; and all the high hills, that were under the whole heaven, were covered. Fifteen cubits upward did the waters prevail; and the mountains were covered. And all flesh died that moved upon the earth, both of fowl, and of cattle, and of beast, and of every creeping thing that creepeth upon the earth, and every man: all in whose nostrils was the breath of life, of all that was in the dry land, died. And every living substance was destroyed which was upon the face of the ground, both man, and cattle, and the creeping things, and the fowl of the heaven; and they were destroyed from the earth: and Noah only remained alive, and they that were with him in the ark. And the waters prevailed upon the earth an hundred and fifty days.

8. And God remembered Noah, and every living thing, and all the cattle that was with him in the ark: and God made a wind to pass over the earth, and the waters assuaged; The fountains also of the deep and the windows of heaven were stopped, and the rain from heaven was restrained; And the waters returned from off the earth continually: and after the end of the hundred and fifty days the waters were abated. And the ark rested in the seventh month, on the seventeenth day of the month, upon the mountains of Ararat. And the waters decreased continually until the tenth month: in the tenth month, on the first day of the month, were the tops of the mountains seen.

And it came to pass at the end of forty days, that Noah opened the window of the ark which he had made: and he sent forth a raven, which went forth to and fro, until the waters were dried up from off the earth. Also he sent forth a dove from him, to see if the waters were abated from off the face of the ground; but the dove found no rest for the sole of her foot, and she returned unto him into the ark, for the waters were on the face of the whole earth: then he put forth his hand, and took her, and pulled her in unto him into the ark. And he stayed yet another seven days; and again he sent forth the dove out of the ark; and the dove came in to him in the evening; and, lo, in her mouth was an olive leaf plucked off: so Noah knew that the waters were abated from off the earth. And he stayed yet other seven days; and sent forth the dove; which returned not again unto him any more.

And it came to pass in the six hundredth and first year, in the first month, the first day of the month, the waters were dried up from off the earth: and Noah removed the covering of the ark, and looked, and, behold, the face of the ground was dry. And in the second month, on the seven and twentieth day of the month, was the earth dried.

And God spake unto Noah, saying, Go forth of the ark, thou, and thy wife, and thy sons, and thy sons' wives with thee. Bring forth with thee every living thing that is with thee, of all flesh, both of fowl, and of cattle, and of every creeping thing that creepeth upon the earth; that they may breed abundantly in the earth, and be fruitful, and multiply upon the earth. And Noah went forth, and his sons, and his wife, and his sons' wives with him: every beast, every creeping thing, and every fowl, and whatsoever creepeth upon the earth, after their kinds, went forth out of the ark. And Noah builded an altar unto the Lord; and took of every clean beast, and of every clean fowl, and offered burnt offerings on the altar. And the Lord smelled a sweet savour; and the Lord said in his heart, I will not again curse the ground any more for man's sake; for the imagination of man's heart is evil from his youth; neither will I again smite any more every thing living, as I have done. While the earth remaineth, seedtime and harvest, and cold and heat, and summer and winter, and day and night shall not cease.

9. And God blessed Noah and his sons, and said unto them, Be fruitful, and multiply, and replenish the earth. And the fear of you and the dread of you shall be upon every beast of the earth, and upon every fowl of the air, upon all that moveth upon the earth, and upon all the fishes of the sea; into your hand are they delivered. Every moving thing that liveth shall be meat for you; even as the green herb have I given you all things. But flesh with the life thereof, which is the blood thereof, shall ye not eat.[4] And surely your blood of your lives will I require; at the hand of every beast will I require it, and at the hand of man; at the hand of every man's brother will I require the life of man. Whoso sheddeth man's blood, by man shall his blood be shed, for in the image of God made he man. And you, be ye fruitful, and multiply; bring forth abundantly in the earth, and multiply therein.

And God spake unto Noah, and to his sons with him, saying, And I, behold, I establish my covenant with you, and with your seed after you; And with every living creature that is with you, of the fowl, of the cattle, and of every beast of the earth with you; from all that go out of the ark, to every beast of the earth. And I will establish my covenant with you; neither shall all flesh be cut off any more by the waters of a flood; neither shall there any more be a flood to destroy the earth. And God said, This is the token of the covenant which I make between me and you and every living creature that is with you, for perpetual generations: I do set my bow in the cloud, and it shall be for a token of a covenant between me and the earth. And it shall come to pass, when I bring a cloud over the earth, that the bow shall be seen in the cloud:

---

4. A reference to the biblical dietary laws: blood was supposed to be drained from a slaughtered animal.

and I will remember my covenant, which is between me and you and every living creature of all flesh; and the waters shall no more become a flood to destroy all flesh. And the bow shall be in the cloud; and I will look upon it, that I may remember the everlasting covenant between God and every living creature of all flesh that is upon the earth. And God said unto Noah, This is the token of the covenant, which I have established between me and all flesh that is upon the earth.

Genesis 11

[The Origin of Languages]

11. And the whole earth was of one language, and of one speech. And it came to pass, as they journeyed from the east, that they found a plain in the land of Shinar;[1] and they dwelt there. And they said one to another, Go to, let us make brick, and burn them thoroughly. And they had brick for stone, and slime[2] had they for mortar. And they said, Go to, let us build us a city and a tower,[3] whose top may reach unto heaven; and let us make us a name, lest we be scattered abroad upon the face of the whole earth. And the Lord came down to see the city and the tower, which the children of men builded. And the Lord said, Behold, the people is one, and they have all one language; and this they begin to do: and now nothing will be restrained from them, which they have imagined to do. Go to, let us go down, and there confound their language, that they may not understand one another's speech. So the Lord scattered them abroad from thence upon the face of all the earth: and they left off to build the city. Therefore is the name of it called Babel;[4] because the Lord did there confound the language of all the earth: and from thence did the Lord scatter them abroad upon the face of all the earth.

Genesis 22

[Abraham and Isaac]

22. And it came to pass after these things, that God did tempt Abraham, and said unto him, Abraham: and he said, Behold, here I am. And he said, Take now thy son, thine only son Isaac, whom thou lovest, and get thee into the land of Moriah; and offer him there for a burnt offering upon one of the mountains which I will tell thee of.

And Abraham rose up early in the morning, and saddled his ass, and took two of his young men with him, and Isaac his son, and clave the wood for the burnt offering, and rose up, and went unto the place of which God had told him. Then on the third day Abraham lifted up his eyes, and saw the place afar off. And Abraham said unto his young men, Abide ye here with the ass; and I and the lad will go yonder and worship, and come again to

1. In Mesopotamia. *They*: humankind.   2. Bitumen.   3. This story is based on the Babylonian practice of building temples in the form of terraced pyramids (ziggurats).   4. Babylon.

you. And Abraham took the wood of the burnt offering, and laid it upon Isaac his son; and he took the fire in his hand, and a knife; and they went both of them together. And Isaac spake unto Abraham his father, and said, My father: and he said, Here am I, my son. And he said, Behold the fire and the wood: but where is the lamb for a burnt offering? And Abraham said, My son, God will provide himself a lamb for a burnt offering: so they went both of them together.

And they came to the place which God had told him of; and Abraham built an altar there, and laid the wood in order, and bound Isaac his son, and laid him on the altar upon the wood. And Abraham stretched forth his hand, and took the knife to slay his son. And the Angel of the Lord called unto him out of heaven, and said, Abraham, Abraham: and he said, Here am I. And he said, Lay not thine hand upon the lad, neither do thou any thing unto him: for now I know that thou fearest God, seeing thou hast not withheld thy son, thine only son, from me. And Abraham lifted up his eyes, and looked, and behold behind him a ram caught in a thicket by his horns: and Abraham went and took the ram, and offered him up for a burnt offering in the stead of his son. And Abraham called the name of that place Jehovah-jireh: as it is said to this day, In the mount of the Lord it shall be seen.

And the Angel of the Lord called unto Abraham out of heaven the second time, and said, By myself have I sworn, saith the Lord, for because thou hast done this thing, and hast not withheld thy son, thine only son, that in blessing I will bless thee, and in multiplying I will multiply thy seed as the stars of the heaven, and as the sand which is upon the seashore; and thy seed shall possess the gate of his enemies; and in thy seed shall all the nations of the earth be blessed; because thou hast obeyed my voice.

Genesis 25, 27

[Jacob and Esau]

25. And Isaac entreated the Lord for his wife, because she was barren: and the Lord was entreated of him, and Rebekah his wife conceived. And the children struggled together within her; and she said, If it be so, why am I thus? And she went to inquire of the Lord. And the Lord said unto her, Two nations are in thy womb, and two manner of people shall be separated from thy bowels; and the one people shall be stronger than the other people; and the elder shall serve the younger.

And when her days to be delivered were fulfilled, behold, there were twins in her womb. And the first came out red, all over like a hairy garment; and they called his name Esau. And after that came his brother out, and his hand took hold on Esau's heel; and his name was called Jacob: and Isaac was threescore years old when he bare them. And the boys grew: and Esau was a cunning hunter, a man of the field; and Jacob was a plain man, dwelling in tents. And Isaac loved Esau, because he did eat of his venison: but Rebekah loved Jacob.

And Jacob sod pottage: and Esau came from the field, and he was faint: and Esau said to Jacob, Feed me, I pray thee, with that same red pottage; for I am faint: therefore was his name called Edom. And Jacob said, Sell me this day thy birthright. And Esau said, Behold, I am at the point to die: and what profit shall this birthright do to me? And Jacob said, Swear to me this day; and he sware unto him: and he sold his birthright unto Jacob. Then Jacob gave Esau bread and pottage of lentils; and he did eat and drink, and rose up, and went his way. Thus Esau despised his birthright.

27. And it came to pass, that when Isaac was old, and his eyes were dim, so that he could not see, he called Esau his eldest son, and said unto him, My son: and he said unto him, Behold, here am I. And he said, Behold now, I am old, I know not the day of my death: Now therefore take, I pray thee, thy weapons, thy quiver and thy bow, and go out to the field, and take me some venison; and make me savory meat, such as I love, and bring it to me, that I may eat; that my soul may bless thee before I die. And Rebekah heard when Isaac spake to Esau his son. And Esau went to the field to hunt for venison, and to bring it.

And Rebekah spake unto Jacob her son, saying, Behold, I heard thy father speak unto Esau thy brother, saying, Bring me venison, and make me savory meat, that I may eat, and bless thee before the Lord before my death. Now therefore, my son, obey my voice according to that which I command thee. Go now to the flock, and fetch me from thence two good kids of the goats; and I will make them savory meat for thy father, such as he loveth: and thou shalt bring it to thy father, that he may eat, and that he may bless thee before his death. And Jacob said to Rebekah his mother, Behold, Esau my brother is a hairy man, and I am a smooth man: My father peradventure will feel me, and I shall seem to him as a deceiver; and I shall bring a curse upon me, and not a blessing. And his mother said unto him, Upon me be thy curse, my son: only obey my voice, and go fetch me them. And he went, and fetched, and brought them to his mother: and his mother made savory meat, such as his father loved. And Rebekah took goodly raiment of her eldest son Esau, which were with her in the house, and put them upon Jacob her younger son: and she put the skins of the kids of the goats upon his hands, and upon the smooth of his neck: and she gave the savory meat and the bread, which she had prepared, into the hand of her son Jacob.

And he came unto his father, and said, My father: and he said, Here am I; who art thou, my son? And Jacob said unto his father, I am Esau thy firstborn; I have done according as thou badest me: arise, I pray thee, sit and eat of my venison, that thy soul may bless me. And Isaac said unto his son, How is it that thou hast found it so quickly, my son? And he said, Because the Lord thy God brought it to me. And Isaac said unto Jacob, Come near, I pray thee, that I may feel thee, my son, whether thou be my very son Esau or not. And Jacob went near unto Isaac his father; and he felt him, and said, The voice is Jacob's voice, but the hands are the hands of Esau. And he discerned him not, because his hands were hairy, as his brother Esau's hands: so he blessed him. And he said, Art thou my very son Esau? And he said, I am. And he said, Bring it near to me, and I will eat of my son's venison, that my soul may bless thee. And he brought it near to him, and he did eat: and he brought him wine, and he drank. And his father Isaac said unto him, Come near now, and kiss me, my son. And he came near, and kissed him: and he smelled the smell of his raiment, and blessed him, and said, See, the smell of my son is as the smell of a field which the Lord hath blessed: Therefore God give thee of the dew of heaven, and the fatness of the earth, and plenty of corn and wine: let people serve thee, and nations bow down to thee: be lord over thy brethren, and let thy mother's sons bow down to thee: cursed be every one that curseth thee, and blessed be he that blesseth thee.

And it came to pass, as soon as Isaac had made an end of blessing Jacob, and Jacob was yet scarce gone out from the presence of Isaac his father, that Esau his brother came in from his hunting. And he also had made savory meat, and brought it unto his father, and said unto his father, Let my father arise, and eat of his son's venison, that thy soul may bless me. And Isaac his father said unto him, Who art thou? And he said, I am thy son, thy firstborn, Esau. And Isaac trembled very exceedingly, and said, Who? where is he that hath taken venison, and brought it me, and I have eaten of all before thou camest, and have blessed him? yea, and he shall be blessed. And when Esau heard the words of his father, he cried with a great and exceeding bitter cry, and said unto his father, Bless me, even me also, O my father. And he said, Thy brother came with subtilty, and hath taken away thy blessing. And he said, Is not he rightly named Jacob?[1] for he hath supplanted me these two times: he took away my birthright; and, behold, now he hath taken away my blessing. And he said, Hast thou not reserved a blessing for me? And Isaac answered and said unto Esau, Behold, I have made him thy lord, and all his brethren have I given to him for servants; and with corn and wine have I sustained him: and what shall I do now unto thee, my son? And Esau said unto his father, Hast thou but one blessing, my father? bless me, even me also, O my father. And Esau lifted up his voice, and wept. And Isaac his father answered and said unto him, Behold, thy dwelling shall be the fatness of the earth, and of the dew of heaven from above; and by thy sword shalt thou live, and shalt serve thy brother: and it shall come to pass when thou shalt have the dominion, that thou shalt break his yoke from off thy neck.

Genesis 37, 39–46

[The Story of Joseph]

37.   * * * Joseph, being seventeen years old, was feeding the flock with his brethren; and the lad was with the sons of Bilhah, and with the sons of Zilpah, his father's wives: and Joseph brought unto his father their evil report.[1] Now Israel loved Joseph more than all his children, because he was the son of his old age: and he made him a coat of many colours. And when his brethren saw that their father loved him more than all his brethren, they hated him, and could not speak peaceably unto him.

And Joseph dreamed a dream, and he told it his brethren: and they hated him yet the more. And he said unto them, Hear, I pray you, this dream which I have dreamed: for, behold, we were binding sheaves in the field, and, lo, my sheaf arose, and also stood upright; and, behold, your sheaves stood round about, and made obeisance to my sheaf. And his brethren said to him, Shalt thou indeed reign over us? or shalt thou indeed have dominion over us? And they hated him yet the more for his dreams, and for his words.

And he dreamed yet another dream, and told it his brethren, and said,

1. Which means "he who supplants."   1. Joseph reported their misdeeds. *Father*: Israel.

Behold, I have dreamed a dream more; and, behold, the sun and the moon and the eleven stars made obeisance to me. And he told it to his father, and to his brethren: and his father rebuked him, and said unto him, What is this dream that thou hast dreamed? Shall I and thy mother and thy brethren indeed come to bow down ourselves to thee to the earth? And his brethren envied him; but his father observed the saying.

And his brethren went to feed their father's flock in Shechem. And Israel said unto Joseph, Do not thy brethren feed the flock in Shechem? come, and I will send thee unto them. And he said to him, Here am I. And he said to him, Go, I pray thee, see whether it be well with thy brethren, and well with the flocks; and bring me word again. So he sent him out of the vale of Hebron, and he came to Shechem.

And a certain man found him, and, behold, he was wandering in the field: and the man asked him, saying, What seekest thou? And he said, I seek my brethren: tell me, I pray thee, where they feed their flocks. And the man said, They are departed hence; for I heard them say, Let us go to Dothan. And Joseph went after his brethren, and found them in Dothan. And when they saw him afar off, even before he came near unto them, they conspired against him to slay him. And they said one to another, Behold, this dreamer cometh. Come now therefore, and let us slay him, and cast him into some pit, and we will say, Some evil beast hath devoured him: and we shall see what will become of his dreams. And Reuben heard it, and he delivered him out of their hands; and said, Let us not kill him. And Reuben said unto them, Shed no blood, but cast him into this pit that is in the wilderness, and lay no hand upon him; that he might rid him out of their hands, to deliver him to his father again.

And it came to pass, when Joseph was come unto his brethren, that they stripped Joseph out of his coat, his coat of many colours that was on him; and they took him, and cast him into a pit: and the pit was empty, there was no water in it. And they sat down to eat bread: and they lifted up their eyes and looked, and, behold, a company of Ishmeelites came from Gilead with their camels bearing spicery and balm and myrrh, going to carry it down to Egypt. And Judah said unto his brethren, What profit is it if we slay our brother, and conceal his blood? Come, and let us sell him to the Ishmeelites, and let not our hand be upon him; for he is our brother and our flesh. And his brethren were content. Then there passed by Midianites merchantmen; and they[2] drew and lifted up Joseph out of the pit, and sold Joseph to the Ishmeelites for twenty pieces of silver: and they[3] brought Joseph into Egypt.

And Reuben returned unto the pit; and, behold, Joseph was not in the pit; and he rent his clothes. And he returned unto his brethren, and said, The child is not; and I, whither shall I go? And they took Joseph's coat, and killed a kid of the goats, and dipped the coat in the blood; and they sent the coat of many colours, and they brought it to their father; and said, This have we found: know now whether it be thy son's coat or no. And he knew it, and said, It is my son's coat; an evil beast hath devoured him; Joseph is without doubt rent in pieces. And Jacob rent his clothes, and put sackcloth upon his loins, and mourned for his son many days. And all his sons and all his daughters rose up to comfort him; but he refused to be comforted; and he said,

2. The brothers. The confusion in this passage may be because the text we have is a composite of two different versions.   3. The Ishmeelites.

For I will go down into the grave unto my son mourning. Thus his father wept for him. * * *

39. And Joseph was brought down to Egypt; and Potiphar, an officer of Pharaoh, captain of the guard, an Egyptian, bought him of the hands of the Ishmeelites, which had brought him down thither. And the Lord was with Joseph, and he was a prosperous man; and he was in the house of his master the Egyptian. And his master saw that the Lord was with him, and that the Lord made all he did to prosper in his hand. And Joseph found grace in his sight, and he served him: and he made him overseer over his house, and all that he had he put into his hand. And it came to pass from the time that he had made him overseer in his house, and over all that he had, that the Lord blessed the Egyptian's house for Joseph's sake; and the blessing of the Lord was upon all that he had in the house, and in the field. And he left all that he had in Joseph's hand; and he knew not ought he had, save the bread which he did eat. And Joseph was a goodly person, and well favoured.

And it came to pass after these things, that his master's wife cast her eyes upon Joseph; and she said, Lie with me. But he refused, and said unto his master's wife, Behold, my master wotteth not what is with me in the house, and he hath committed all that he hath to my hand; there is none greater in this house than I; neither hath he kept back any thing from me but thee, because thou art his wife: how then can I do this great wickedness, and sin against God? And it came to pass, as she spake to Joseph day by day, that he hearkened not unto her, to lie by her, or to be with her. And it came to pass about this time, that Joseph went into the house to do his business; and there was none of the men of the house there within. And she caught him by his garment, saying, Lie with me: and he left his garment in her hand, and fled, and got him out. And it came to pass, when she saw that he had left his garment in her hand, and was fled forth, that she called unto the men of her house, and spoke unto them, saying, See, he hath brought in an Hebrew unto us to mock us; he came in unto me to lie with me, and I cried with a loud voice: and it came to pass, when he heard that I lifted up my voice and cried, that he left his garment with me, and fled, and got him out. And she laid up his garment by her, until his lord came home. And she spake unto him according to these words, saying, The Hebrew servant, which thou hast brought unto us, came in unto me to mock me: and it came to pass, as I lifted up my voice and cried, that he left his garment with me, and fled out. And it came to pass, when his master heard the words of his wife, which she spake unto him, saying, After this manner did thy servant to me; that his wrath was kindled. And Joseph's master took him, and put him into the prison, a place where the king's prisoners were bound: and he was there in the prison.

But the Lord was with Joseph, and showed him mercy, and gave him favour in the sight of the keeper of the prison. And the keeper of the prison committed to Joseph's hand all the prisoners that were in the prison; and whatsoever they did there, he was the doer of it. The keeper of the prison looked not to any thing that was under his hand; because the Lord was with him, and that which he did, the Lord made it to prosper.

40. And it came to pass after these things that the butler of the king of Egypt and his baker had offended their lord the king of Egypt. And Pharaoh

was wroth against two of his officers, against the chief of the butlers, and against the chief of the bakers. And he put them in ward in the house of the captain of the guard, into the prison, the place where Joseph was bound. And the captain of the guard charged Joseph with them, and he served them: and they continued a season in ward.

And they dreamed a dream both of them, each man his dream in one night, each man according to the interpretation of his dream, the butler and the baker of the king of Egypt, which were bound in the prison. And Joseph came in unto them in the morning, and looked upon them, and, behold, they were sad. And he asked Pharaoh's officers that were with him in the ward of his lord's house, saying, Wherefore look ye so sadly to day? And they said unto him, We have dreamed a dream, and there is no interpreter of it. And Joseph said unto them, Do not interpretations belong to God? tell me them, I pray you. And the chief butler told his dream to Joseph, and said to him, In my dream, behold, a vine was before me; and in the vine were three branches: and it was as though it budded, and her blossoms shot forth; and the clusters thereof brought forth ripe grapes: and Pharaoh's cup was in my hand: and I took the grapes, and pressed them into Pharaoh's cup, and I gave the cup into Pharaoh's hand. And Joseph said unto him, This is the interpretation of it: the three branches are three days: yet within three days shall Pharaoh lift up thine head, and restore thee unto thy place: and thou shalt deliver Pharaoh's cup into his hand, after the former manner when thou wast his butler. But think on me when it shall be well with thee, and shew kindness, I pray thee, unto me, and make mention of me unto Pharaoh, and bring me out of this house: for indeed I was stolen away out of the land of the Hebrews: and here also have I done nothing that they should put me into the dungeon. When the chief baker saw that the interpretation was good, he said unto Joseph, I also was in my dream, and, behold, I had three white baskets on my head: and in the uppermost basket there was of all manner of bakemeats for Pharaoh; and the birds did eat them out of the basket upon my head. And Joseph answered and said, This is the interpretation thereof: the three baskets are three days: yet within three days shall Pharaoh lift up thy head from off thee, and shall hang thee on a tree; and the birds shall eat thy flesh from off thee.

And it came to pass the third day, which was Pharaoh's birthday, that he made a feast unto all his servants: and he lifted up the head of the chief butler and of the chief baker among his servants. And he restored the chief butler unto his butlership again; and he gave the cup into Pharaoh's hand. But he hanged the chief baker: as Joseph had interpreted to them. Yet did not the chief butler remember Joseph, but forgat him.

41. And it came to pass at the end of two full years, that Pharaoh dreamed: and, behold, he stood by the river. And, behold, there came up out of the river seven well favoured kine[4] and fatfleshed; and they fed in a meadow. And, behold, seven other kine came up after them out of the river, ill favoured and leanfleshed; and stood by the other kine upon the brink of the river. And the ill favoured and leanfleshed kine did eat up the seven well favoured and fat kine. So Pharaoh awoke. And he slept and dreamed the second time: and, behold, seven ears of corn came up upon one stalk, rank[5]

4. Cattle.   5. Fat.

and good. And, behold, seven thin ears and blasted with the east wind sprung up after them. And the seven thin ears devoured the seven rank and full ears. And Pharaoh awoke, and, behold, it was a dream. And it came to pass in the morning that his spirit was troubled; and he sent and called for all the magicians of Egypt, and all the wise men thereof: and Pharaoh told them his dream; but there was none that could interpret them unto Pharaoh.

Then spake the chief butler unto Pharaoh, saying, I do remember my faults this day: Pharaoh was wroth with his servants, and put me in ward in the captain of the guard's house, both me and the chief baker: and we dreamed a dream in one night, I and he; we dreamed each man according to the interpretation of his dream. And there was there with us a young man, an Hebrew, servant to the captain of the guard; and we told him, and he interpreted to us our dreams; to each man according to his dream he did interpret. And it came to pass, as he interpreted to us, so it was; me he restored unto mine office, and him he hanged.

Then Pharaoh sent and called Joseph, and they brought him hastily out of the dungeon: and he shaved himself, and changed his raiment, and came in unto Pharaoh. And Pharaoh said unto Joseph, I have dreamed a dream, and there is none that can interpret it: and I have heard say of thee that thou canst understand a dream to interpret it. And Joseph answered Pharaoh, saying, It is not in me: God shall give Pharaoh an answer of peace. And Pharaoh said unto Joseph, In my dream, behold, I stood upon the bank of the river; and, behold, there came up out of the river seven kine, fatfleshed and well favoured; and they fed in a meadow: and, behold, seven other kine came up after them, poor and very ill favoured and lean-fleshed, such as I never saw in all the land of Egypt for badness: and the lean and the ill favoured kine did eat up the first seven fat kine: and when they had eaten them up, it could not be known that they had eaten them; but they were still ill favoured, as at the beginning. So I awoke. And I saw in my dream, and, behold, seven ears came up in one stalk, full and good: and, behold, seven ears, withered, thin, and blasted with the east wind, sprung up after them: and the thin ears devoured the seven good ears: and I told this unto the magicians; but there was none that could declare it to me.

And Joseph said unto Pharaoh, The dream of Pharaoh is one: God hath shewed Pharaoh what he is about to do. The seven good kine are seven years; and the seven good ears are seven years: the dream is one. And the seven thin and ill favoured kine that came up after them are seven years; and the seven empty ears blasted with the east wind shall be seven years of famine. This is the thing which I have spoken unto Pharaoh: what God is about to do he sheweth unto Pharaoh. Behold, there come seven years of great plenty throughout all the land of Egypt: and there shall arise after them seven years of famine; and all the plenty shall be forgotten in the land of Egypt; and the famine shall consume the land; and the plenty shall not be known in the land by reason of that famine following; for it shall be very grievous. And for that the dream was doubled unto Pharaoh twice; it is because the thing is established by God, and God will shortly bring it to pass. Now therefore let Pharaoh look out a man discreet and wise, and set him over the land of Egypt. Let Pharaoh do this, and let him appoint officers over the land, and take up the fifth part of the land[6] of Egypt in the seven plenteous years. And

6. Of the crop.

let them gather all the food of those good years that come, and lay up corn under the hand of Pharaoh, and let them keep food in the cities. And that food shall be for store to the land against the seven years of famine, which shall be in the land of Egypt; that the land perish not through the famine.

And the thing was good in the eyes of Pharaoh, and in the eyes of all his servants. And Pharaoh said unto his servants, Can we find such a one as this is, a man in whom the Spirit of God is? And Pharaoh said unto Joseph, Forasmuch as God hath shewed thee all this, there is none so discreet and wise as thou art: thou shalt be over my house, and according unto thy word shall all my people be ruled: only in the throne will I be greater than thou. And Pharaoh said unto Joseph, See, I have set thee over all the land of Egypt. And Pharaoh took off his ring from his hand, and put it upon Joseph's hand, and arrayed him in vestures of fine linen, and put a gold chain about his neck; and he made him to ride in the second chariot which he had; and they cried before him, Bow the knee: and he made him ruler over all the land of Egypt. And Pharaoh said unto Joseph, I am Pharaoh, and without thee shall no man lift up his hand or foot in all the land of Egypt. And Pharaoh called Joseph's name Zaphnath-paaneah; and he gave him to wife Asenath, the daughter of Poti-pherah priest of On. And Joseph went out over all the land of Egypt.

And Joseph was thirty years old when he stood before Pharaoh king of Egypt. And Joseph went out from the presence of Pharaoh, and went throughout all the land of Egypt. And in the seven plenteous years the earth brought forth by handfuls. And he gathered up all the food of the seven years, which were in the land of Egypt, and laid up the food in the cities: the food of the field, which was round about every city, laid he up in the same. And Joseph gathered corn as the sand of the sea, very much, until he left numbering; for it was without number. And unto Joseph were born two sons before the years of famine came, which Asenath, the daughter of Poti-pherah priest of On, bare unto him. And Joseph called the name of the first born Manasseh:[7] For God, said he, hath made me forget all my toil, and all my father's house. And the name of the second called he Ephraim:[8] For God hath caused me to be fruitful in the land of my affliction.

And the seven years of plenteousness, that was in the land of Egypt, were ended. And the seven years of dearth began to come, according as Joseph had said: and the dearth was in all lands; but in all the land of Egypt there was bread. And when all the land of Egypt was famished, the people cried to Pharaoh for bread: and Pharaoh said unto all the Egyptians, Go unto Joseph; what he saith to you, do. And the famine was over all the face of the earth. And Joseph opened all the storehouses, and sold unto the Egyptians; and the famine waxed sore in the land of Egypt. And all countries came into Egypt to Joseph for to buy corn; because that the famine was so sore in all lands.

42. Now when Jacob saw that there was corn in Egypt, Jacob said unto his sons, Why do ye look one upon another? And he said, Behold, I have heard that there is corn in Egypt: get you down thither, and buy for us from thence; that we may live, and not die.

---

7. Which means "causing to forget."   8. Which means "fruitfulness."

And Joseph's ten brethren went down to buy corn in Egypt. But Benjamin, Joseph's brother, Jacob sent not with his brethren; for he said, Lest peradventure mischief befall him. And the sons of Israel came to buy corn among those that came: for the famine was in the land of Canaan. And Joseph was the governor over the land, and he it was that sold to all the people of the land: and Joseph's brethren came, and bowed down themselves before him with their faces to the earth. And Joseph saw his brethren, and he knew them, but made himself strange unto them, and spake roughly unto them; and he said unto them, Whence come ye? And they said, From the land of Canaan to buy food. And Joseph knew his brethren, but they knew not him. And Joseph remembered the dreams which he dreamed of them, and said unto them, Ye are spies; to see the nakedness of the land ye are come. And they said unto him, Nay, my lord, but to buy food are thy servants come. We are all one man's sons; we are true men, thy servants are no spies. And he said unto them, Nay, but to see the nakedness of the land ye are come. And they said, Thy servants are twelve brethren, the sons of one man in the land of Canaan; and, behold, the youngest is this day with our father, and one is not. And Joseph said unto them, That is it that I spake unto you, saying, Ye are spies: Hereby ye shall be proved: By the life of Pharaoh ye shall not go forth hence, except your youngest brother come hither. Send one of you, and let him fetch your brother, and ye shall be kept in prison, that your words may be proved, whether there be any truth in you: or else by the life of Pharaoh surely ye are spies. And he put them all together into ward three days. And Joseph said unto them the third day, This do, and live; for I fear God: if ye be true men, let one of your brethren be bound in the house of your prison: go ye, carry corn for the famine of your houses: but bring your youngest brother unto me; so shall your words be verified, and ye shall not die. And they did so.

And they said one to another, We are verily guilty concerning our brother, in that we saw the anguish of his soul, when he besought us, and we would not hear; therefore is this distress come upon us. And Reuben answered them, saying, Spake I not unto you, saying, Do not sin against the child; and ye would not hear? therefore, behold, also his blood is required. And they knew not that Joseph understood them; for he spake unto them by an interpreter. And he turned himself about from them, and wept; and returned to them again, and communed with them, and took from them Simeon, and bound him before their eyes.

Then Joseph commanded to fill their sacks with corn, and to restore every man's money into his sack, and to give them provision for the way: and thus did he unto them. And they laded their asses with the corn, and departed thence. And as one of them opened his sack to give his ass provender in the inn, he espied his money; for, behold, it was in his sack's mouth. And he said unto his brethren, My money is restored; and, lo, it is even in my sack: and their heart failed them, and they were afraid, saying one to another, What is this that God hath done unto us?

And they came unto Jacob their father unto the land of Canaan, and told him all that befell unto them; saying, The man, who is lord of the land, spake roughly to us, and took us for spies of the country. And we said unto him, We are true men; we are no spies: we be twelve brethren, sons of our father; one is not, and the youngest is this day with our father in the land of Canaan.

And the man, the lord of the country, said unto us, Hereby shall I know that ye are true men; leave one of your brethren here with me, and take food for the famine of your households, and be gone: and bring your youngest brother unto me: then shall I know that ye are no spies, but that ye are true men: so will I deliver you your brother, and ye shall traffick in the land.

And it came to pass as they emptied their sacks, that, behold, every man's bundle of money was in his sack: and when both they and their father saw the bundles of money, they were afraid. And Jacob their father said unto them, Me have ye bereaved of my children: Joseph is not, and Simeon is not, and ye will take Benjamin away: all these things are against me.

And Reuben spake unto his father, saying, Slay my two sons, if I bring him not to thee: deliver him into my hand, and I will bring him to thee again. And he said, My son shall not go down with you; for his brother is dead, and he is left alone: if mischief befall him by the way in the which ye go, then shall ye bring down my gray hairs with sorrow to the grave.

43. And the famine was sore in the land. And it came to pass, when they had eaten up the corn which they had brought out of Egypt, their father said unto them, Go again, buy us a little food. And Judah spake unto him, saying, The man did solemnly protest unto us, saying, Ye shall not see my face, except your brother be with you. If thou wilt send our brother with us, we will go down and buy thee food: but if thou wilt not send him, we will not go down: for the man said unto us, Ye shall not see my face, except your brother be with you. And Israel said, Wherefore dealt ye so ill with me, as to tell the man whether ye had yet a brother? And they said, The man asked us straitly of our state, and of our kindred, saying, Is your father yet alive? have ye another brother? and we told him according to the tenor of these words: could we certainly know that he would say, Bring your brother down? And Judah said unto Israel his father, Send the lad with me, and we will arise and go; that we may live, and not die, both we, and thou, and also our little ones. I will be surety for him; of my hand shalt thou require him: if I bring him not unto thee, and set him before thee, then let me bear the blame for ever: for except we had lingered, surely now we had returned this second time. And their father Israel said unto them, If it must be so now, do this; take of the best fruits in the land in your vessels, and carry down the man a present, a little balm, and a little honey, spices, and myrrh, nuts, and almonds: and take double money in your hand: and the money that was brought again in the mouth of your sacks, carry it again in your hand; peradventure it was an oversight: take also your brother, and arise, go again unto the man: and God Almighty give you mercy before the man, that he may send away your other brother, and Benjamin. If I be bereaved of my children, I am bereaved.

And the men took that present, and they took double money in their hand, and Benjamin; and rose up, and went down to Egypt, and stood before Joseph. And when Joseph saw Benjamin with them, he said to the ruler of his house, Bring these men home, and slay,[9] and make ready; for these men shall dine with me at noon. And the man did as Joseph bade; and the man brought the men into Joseph's house. And the men were afraid, because they

9. Kill an animal for meat.

were brought into Joseph's house; and they said, Because of the money that was returned in our sacks at the first time are we brought in; that he may seek occasion against us, and fall upon us, and take us for bondmen, and our asses. And they came near to the steward of Joseph's house, and they communed with him at the door of the house, and said, O sir, we came indeed down at the first time to buy food; and it came to pass, when we came to the inn, that we opened our sacks, and behold, every man's money was in the mouth of his sack, our money in full weight: and we have brought it again in our hand. And other money have we brought down in our hands to buy food: we cannot tell who put our money in our sacks. And he said, Peace be to you, fear not: your God, and the God of your father, hath given you treasure in your sacks: I had your money. And he brought Simeon out unto them. And the man brought the men into Joseph's house, and gave them water, and they washed their feet; and he gave their asses provender. And they made ready the present against Joseph came at noon: for they heard that they should eat bread there.

And when Joseph came home, they brought him the present which was in their hand into the house, and bowed themselves to him to the earth. And he asked them of their welfare, and said, Is your father well, the old man of whom ye spake? Is he yet alive? And they answered, Thy servant our father is in good health, he is yet alive. And they bowed down their heads, and made obeisance. And he lifted up his eyes, and saw his brother Benjamin, his mother's son, and said, Is this your younger brother, of whom ye spake unto me? And he said, God be gracious unto thee, my son. And Joseph made haste; for his bowels did yearn upon his brother: and he sought where to weep; and he entered into his chamber, and wept there. And he washed his face, and went out, and refrained himself, and said, Set on bread. And they set on for him by himself, and for them by themselves, and for the Egyptians, which did eat with him, by themselves: because the Egyptians might not eat bread with the Hebrews; for that is an abomination unto the Egyptians. And they sat before him, the firstborn according to his birthright, and the youngest according to his youth: and the men marvelled one at another. And he took and sent messes[1] unto them from before him: but Benjamin's mess was five times so much as any of theirs. And they drank, and were merry with him.

44. And he commanded the steward of his house, saying, Fill the men's sacks with food, as much as they can carry, and put every man's money in his sack's mouth. And put my cup, the silver cup, in the sack's mouth of the youngest, and his corn money. And he did according to the word that Joseph had spoken. As soon as the morning was light, the men were sent away, they and their asses. And when they were gone out of the city, and not yet far off, Joseph said unto his steward, Up, follow after the men; and when thou dost overtake them, say unto them, Wherefore have ye rewarded evil for good? Is not this it in which my lord drinketh, and whereby indeed he divineth?[2] ye have done evil in so doing.

And he overtook them, and he spake unto them these same words. And

---

1. Portions.   2. Joseph's servant is to claim that this is the cup Joseph uses for clairvoyance; diviners stared into a cup of water and foretold the future.

they said unto him, Wherefore saith my lord these words? God forbid that thy servants should do according to this thing: behold, the money, which we found in our sacks' mouths, we brought again unto thee out of the land of Canaan: how then should we steal out of thy lord's house silver or gold? With whomsoever of thy servants it be found, both let him die, and we also will be my lord's bondmen. And he said, Now also let it be according unto your words: he with whom it is found shall be my servant; and ye shall be blameless. Then they speedily took down every man his sack to the ground, and opened every man his sack. And he searched, and began at the eldest, and left at the youngest: and the cup was found in Benjamin's sack. Then they rent their clothes, and laded every man his ass, and returned to the city.

And Judah and his brethren came to Joseph's house; for he was yet there: and they fell before him on the ground. And Joseph said unto them, What deed is this that ye have done? wot ye not that such a man as I can certainly divine? And Judah said, What shall we say unto my lord? what shall we speak? or how shall we clear ourselves? God hath found out the iniquity of thy servants: behold, we are my lord's servants, both we, and he also with whom the cup is found. And he said, God forbid that I should do so: but the man in whose hand the cup is found, he shall be my servant; and as for you, get you up in peace unto your father.

Then Judah came near unto him, and said, Oh my lord, let thy servant, I pray thee, speak a word in my lord's ears, and let not thine anger burn against thy servant: for thou art even as Pharaoh. My lord asked his servants, saying, Have ye a father, or a brother? And we said unto my lord, We have a father, an old man, and a child of his old age, a little one; and his brother is dead, and he alone is left of his mother, and his father loveth him. And thou saidst unto thy servants, Bring him down unto me, that I may set mine eyes upon him. And we said unto my lord, The lad cannot leave his father: for if he should leave his father, his father would die. And thou saidst unto thy servants, Except your youngest brother come down with you, ye shall see my face no more. And it came to pass when we came up unto thy servant my father, we told him the words of my lord. And our father said, Go again, and buy us a little food. And we said, We cannot go down: if our youngest brother be with us, then will we go down: for we may not see the man's face, except our youngest brother be with us. And thy servant my father said unto us, Ye know that my wife bare me two sons: and the one went out from me, and I said, Surely he is torn in pieces; and I saw him not since: and if ye take this also from me, and mischief befall him, ye shall bring down my gray hairs with sorrow to the grave. Now therefore when I come to thy servant my father, and the lad be not with us; seeing that his life is bound up in the lad's life; it shall come to pass, when he seeth that the lad is not with us, that he will die: and thy servants shall bring down the gray hairs of thy servant our father with sorrow to the grave. For thy servant became surety for the lad unto my father, saying, If I bring him not unto thee, then I shall bear the blame to my father for ever. Now therefore, I pray thee, let thy servant abide instead of the lad a bondman to my lord; and let the lad go up with his brethren. For how shall I go up to my father, and the lad be not with me? lest peradventure I see the evil that shall come on my father.

45. Then Joseph could not refrain himself before all them that stood by him; and he cried, Cause every man to go out from me. And there stood no man with him, while Joseph made himself known unto his brethren. And he wept aloud: and the Egyptians and the house of Pharaoh heard. And Joseph said unto his brethren, I am Joseph; doth my father yet live? And his brethren could not answer him; for they were troubled at his presence. And Joseph said unto his brethren, Come near to me, I pray you. And they came near. And he said, I am Joseph your brother, whom ye sold into Egypt. Now therefore be not grieved, nor angry with yourselves, that ye sold me hither: for God did send me before you to preserve life. For these two years hath the famine been in the land: and yet there are five years, in the which there shall neither be earing nor harvest. And God sent me before you to preserve you a posterity in the earth, and to save your lives by a great deliverance. So now it was not you that sent me hither, but God: and he hath made me a father to Pharaoh, and lord of all his house, and a ruler throughout all the land of Egypt. Haste ye, and go up to my father, and say unto him, Thus saith thy son Joseph, God hath made me lord of all Egypt: come down unto me, tarry not: and thou shalt dwell in the land of Goshen, and thou shalt be near unto me, thou, and thy children, and thy children's children, and thy flocks, and thy herds, and all that thou hast: and there will I nourish thee; for yet there are five years of famine; lest thou, and thy household, and all that thou hast, come to poverty. And, behold, your eyes see, and the eyes of my brother Benjamin, that it is my mouth that speaketh unto you. And ye shall tell my father of all my glory in Egypt, and of all that ye have seen; and ye shall haste and bring down my father hither. And he fell upon his brother Benjamin's neck, and wept; and Benjamin wept upon his neck. Moreover he kissed all his brethren, and wept upon them: and after that his brethren talked with him.

And the fame thereof was heard in Pharaoh's house, saying, Joseph's brethren are come: and it pleased Pharaoh well, and his servants. And Pharaoh said unto Joseph, Say unto thy brethren, This do ye; lade your beasts, and go, get you unto the land of Canaan; and take your father and your households, and come unto me: and I will give you the good of the land of Egypt, and ye shall eat the fat of the land. Now thou art commanded, this do ye; take you wagons out of the land of Egypt for your little ones, and for your wives, and bring your father, and come. Also regard not your stuff; for the good of all the land of Egypt is yours. And the children of Israel did so: and Joseph gave them wagons, according to the commandment of Pharaoh, and gave them provision for the way. To all of them he gave each man changes of raiment; but to Benjamin he gave three hundred pieces of silver, and five changes of raiment. And to his father he sent after this manner; ten asses laden with the good things of Egypt, and ten she-asses laden with corn and bread and meat for his father by the way. So he sent his brethren away, and they departed: and he said unto them, See that ye fall not out by the way.

And they went up out of Egypt, and came into the land of Canaan unto Jacob their father, and told him, saying, Joseph is yet alive, and he is governor over all the land of Egypt. And Jacob's heart fainted, for he believed them not. And they told him all the words of Joseph, which he had said unto them: and when he saw the wagons which Joseph had sent to carry him, the spirit of Jacob their father revived. And Israel said, It is enough; Joseph my son is yet alive: I will go and see him before I die.

46. And Israel took his journey with all that he had, and came to Beer-sheba, and offered sacrifices unto the God of his father Isaac. And God spake unto Israel in the visions of the night, and said, Jacob, Jacob. And he said, Here am I. And he said, I am God, the God of thy father: fear not to go down into Egypt; for I will there make of thee a great nation: I will go down with thee into Egypt; and I will also surely bring thee up again: and Joseph shall put his hand upon thine eyes. And Jacob rose up from Beer-sheba: and the sons of Israel carried Jacob their father, and their little ones, and their wives, in the wagons which Pharaoh had sent to carry him. And they took their cattle, and their goods, which they had gotten in the land of Canaan, and came into Egypt, Jacob, and all his seed with him: his sons, and his sons' sons with him, his daughters, and his sons' daughters, and all his seed brought he with him into Egypt.

From Job

1. There was a man in the land of Uz whose name was Job, and that man was perfect and upright, and one that feared God, and eschewed evil. And there were born unto him seven sons and three daughters. His substance also was seven thousand sheep, and three thousand camels, and five hundred yoke of oxen, and five hundred she asses, and a very great household; so that this man was the greatest of all the men of the east. And his sons went and feasted in their houses, every one his day;[1] and sent and called for their three sisters to eat and to drink with them. And it was so, when the days of their feasting were gone about, that Job sent and sanctified them, and rose up early in the morning, and offered burnt offerings according to the number of them all: for Job said, It may be that my sons have sinned, and cursed God in their hearts. Thus did Job continually.

Now there was a day when the sons of God came to present themselves before the Lord, and Satan came also among them. And the Lord said unto Satan, Whence comest thou? Then Satan answered the Lord, and said, From going to and fro in the earth, and from walking up and down in it. And the Lord said unto Satan, Hast thou considered my servant Job, that there is none like him in the earth, a perfect and an upright man, one that feareth God, and escheweth evil? Then Satan answered the Lord, and said, Doth Job fear God for nought? Hast not thou made an hedge about him, and about his house, and about all that he hath on every side? thou hast blessed the work of his hands, and his substance is increased in the land. But put forth thine hand now, and touch all that he hath, and he will curse thee to thy face. And the Lord said unto Satan, Behold, all that he hath is in thy power; only upon himself put not forth thine hand. So Satan went forth from the presence of the Lord.

---

1. In rotation at each son's house.

And there was a day when his sons and his daughters were eating and drinking wine in their eldest brother's house: and there came a messenger unto Job, and said, The oxen were plowing, and the asses feeding beside them: and the Sabeans fell upon them, and took them away; yea, they have slain the servants with the edge of the sword; and I only am escaped alone to tell thee. While he was yet speaking, there came also another, and said, The fire of God is fallen from heaven, and hath burned up the sheep, and the servants, and consumed them; and I only am escaped alone to tell thee. While he was yet speaking, there came also another, and said, The Chaldeans made out three bands,[2] and fell upon the camels, and have carried them away, yea, and slain the servants with the edge of the sword; and I only am escaped alone to tell thee. While he was yet speaking, there came also another, and said, Thy sons and thy daughters were eating and drinking wine in their eldest brother's house: and, behold, there came a great wind from the wilderness, and smote the four corners of the house, and it fell upon the young men, and they are dead; and I only am escaped alone to tell thee.

Then Job arose and rent his mantle,[3] and shaved his head, and fell down upon the ground, and worshipped, and said, Naked came I out of my mother's womb, and naked shall I return thither: the Lord gave, and the Lord hath taken away; blessed be the name of the Lord. In all this Job sinned not, nor charged God foolishly.

2. Again there was a day when the sons of God came to present themselves before the Lord, and Satan came also among them to present himself before the Lord. And the Lord said unto Satan, From whence comest thou? And Satan answered the Lord, and said, From going to and fro in the earth, and from walking up and down in it. And the Lord said unto Satan, Hast thou considered my servant Job, that there is none like him in the earth, a perfect and an upright man, one that feareth God, and escheweth evil? and still he holdeth fast his integrity, although thou movedst me against him, to destroy him without cause. And Satan answered the Lord, and said, Skin for skin, yea, all that a man hath will he give for his life. But put forth thine hand now, and touch his bone and his flesh, and he will curse thee to thy face. And the Lord said unto Satan, Behold, he is in thine hand; but save his life.

So went Satan forth from the presence of the Lord, and smote Job with sore boils from the sole of his foot unto his crown. And he took him a potsherd to scrape himself withal; and he sat down among the ashes.

Then said his wife unto him, Dost thou still retain thine integrity? curse God, and die. But he said unto her, Thou speakest as one of the foolish women speaketh. What? shall we receive good at the hand of God, and shall we not receive evil? In all this did not Job sin with his lips.

Now when Job's three friends heard of all this evil that was come upon him, they came every one from his own place; Eliphaz the Temanite, and Bildad the Shuhite, and Zophar the Naamathite: for they had made an appointment together to come to mourn with him and to comfort him. And when they lifted up their eyes afar off, and knew him not, they lifted up their voice, and wept; and they rent every one his mantle, and sprinkled dust upon

2. I.e., split up into three groups.   3. Tore his cloak.

their heads toward heaven. So they sat down with him upon the ground seven days and seven nights, and none spake a word unto him: for they saw that his grief was very great.

3. After this opened Job his mouth, and cursed his day. And Job spake, and said, Let the day perish wherein I was born, and the night in which it was said, There is a man child conceived. Let that day be darkness; let not God regard it from above, neither let the light shine upon it. Let darkness and the shadow of death stain it; let a cloud dwell upon it; let the blackness of the day terrify it. As for that night, let darkness seize upon it; let it not be joined unto the days of the year, let it not come into the number of the months. Lo, let that night be solitary, let no joyful voice come therein. Let them curse it that curse the day, who are ready to raise up their mourning.[4] Let the stars of the twilight thereof be dark; let it look for light, but have none; neither let it see the dawning of the day: because it shut not up the doors of my mother's womb, nor hid sorrow from mine eyes. Why died I not from the womb? Why did I not give up the ghost when I came out of the belly? Why did the knees prevent[5] me? or why the breasts that I should suck? For now should I have lain still and been quiet, I should have slept: then had I been at rest, with kings and counsellors of the earth, which built desolate places for themselves; or with princes that had gold, who filled their houses with silver: or as an hidden untimely birth I had not been; as infants which never saw light. There the wicked cease from troubling; and there the weary be at rest. There the prisoners rest together; they hear not the voice of the oppressor. The small and great are there; and the servant is free from his master. Wherefore is light given to him that is in misery, and life unto the bitter in soul; which long for death, but it cometh not; and dig for it more than for hid treasures; which rejoice exceedingly, and are glad, when they can find the grave? Why is light given to a man whose way is hid, and whom God hath hedged in? For my sighing cometh before I eat, and my roarings are poured out like the waters. For the thing which I greatly feared is come upon me, and that which I was afraid of is come unto me. I was not in safety, neither had I rest, neither was I quiet; yet trouble came.

4. Then Eliphaz the Temanite answered and said, If we assay to commune with thee, wilt thou be grieved? But who can withhold himself from speaking? Behold, thou hast instructed many, and thou hast strengthened the weak hands. Thy words have upholden him that was falling, and thou hast strengthened the feeble knees. But now it is come upon thee, and thou faintest; it toucheth thee, and thou art troubled. Is not this thy fear, thy confidence, thy hope, and the uprightness of thy ways?[6] Remember, I pray thee, who ever perished, being innocent? or where were the righteous cut off? Even as I have seen, they that plow iniquity, and sow wickedness, reap the same. By the blast of God they perish, and by the breath of his nostrils are they consumed. The roaring of the lion, and the voice of the fierce lion,

---

4. More literally: who are ready to rouse up leviathan, a dragon that was thought to produce darkness. *Them*: sorcerers, magicians.   **5.** Receive.   **6.** More literally: is not thy fear of God thy confidence, and thy hope the uprightness of thy ways?

and the teeth of the young lions, are broken. The old lion perisheth for lack
of prey, and the stout lion's whelps are scattered abroad. Now a thing was
secretly brought to me, and mine ear received a little thereof. In thoughts
from the visions of the night, when deep sleep falleth on men, fear came
upon me, and trembling, which made all my bones to shake. Then a spirit
passed before my face; the hair of my flesh stood up: It stood still, but I could
not discern the form thereof: an image was before mine eyes, there was
silence, and I heard a voice, saying, Shall mortal man be more just than God?
Shall a man be more pure than his maker? Behold, he put no trust in his
servants; and his angels he charged with folly: How much less in them that
dwell in houses of clay, whose foundation is in the dust, which are crushed
before the moth? They are destroyed from morning to evening: they perish
for ever without any regarding it. Doth not their excellency which is in them
go away? They die, even without wisdom.

    5. Call now, if there be any that will answer thee; and to which of the
saints wilt thou turn? For wrath killeth the foolish man, and envy slayeth the
silly one. I have seen the foolish taking root: but suddenly I cursed his habitation. His children are far from safety, and they are crushed in the gate,
neither is there any to deliver them. Whose harvest the hungry eateth up,
and taketh it even out of the thorns, and the robber swalloweth up their
substance. Although affliction cometh not forth of the dust, neither doth
trouble spring out of the ground; yet man is born unto trouble, as the sparks
fly upward. I would seek unto God, and unto God would I commit my cause:
which doeth great things and unsearchable; marvellous things without number: who giveth rain upon the earth, and sendeth waters upon the fields: to
set up on high those that be low; that those which mourn may be exalted to
safety. He disappointeth the devices of the crafty, so that their hands cannot
perform their enterprise. He taketh the wise in their own craftiness: and the
counsel of the froward is carried headlong. They meet with darkness in the
daytime, and grope in the noonday as in the night. But he saveth the poor
from the sword, from their mouth, and from the hand of the mighty. So the
poor hath hope, and iniquity stoppeth her mouth. Behold, happy is the man
whom God correcteth: therefore despise not thou the chastening of the
Almighty: for he maketh sore, and bindeth up: he woundeth, and his hands
make whole. He shall deliver thee in six troubles: yea, in seven there shall
no evil touch thee. In famine he shall redeem thee from death: and in war
from the power of the sword. Thou shalt be hid from the scourge of the
tongue: neither shalt thou be afraid of destruction when it cometh. At
destruction and famine thou shalt laugh: neither shalt thou be afraid of the
beasts of the earth. For thou shalt be in league with the stones of the field:
and the beasts of the field shall be at peace with thee. And thou shalt know
that thy tabernacle[7] shall be in peace; and thou shalt visit thy habitation, and
shalt not sin. Thou shalt know also that thy seed shall be great, and thine
offspring as the grass of the earth. Thou shalt come to thy grave in a full age,
like as a shock of corn cometh in in his season. Lo this, we have searched
it, so it is; hear it, and know thou it for thy good.

7. Tent.

6. But Job answered and said, Oh that my grief were thoroughly weighed, and my calamity laid in the balances together! For now it would be heavier than the sand of the sea: therefore my words are swallowed up.[8] For the arrows of the Almighty are within me, the poison whereof drinketh up my spirit: the terrors of God do set themselves in array against me. Doth the wild ass bray when he hath grass? or loweth the ox over his fodder?[9] Can that which is unsavoury be eaten without salt? or is there any taste in the white of an egg? The things that my soul refused to touch are as my sorrowful meat.[1] Oh that I might have my request; and that God would grant me the thing that I long for! Even that it would please God to destroy me; that he would let loose his hand, and cut me off! Then should I yet have comfort; yea, I would harden myself in sorrow: let him not spare; for I have not concealed[2] the words of the Holy One. What is my strength, that I should hope? and what is mine end, that I should prolong my life? Is my strength the strength of stones? or is my flesh of brass? Is not my help in me? and is wisdom driven quite from me?[3] To him that is afflicted pity should be shewed from his friend; but he forsaketh the fear of the Almighty. My brethren have dealt deceitfully as a brook, and as the stream of brooks they pass away; which are blackish by reason of the ice, and wherein the snow is hid: what time they wax warm, they vanish: when it is hot, they are consumed out of their place. The paths of their way are turned aside; they go to nothing, and perish. The troops of Tema looked, the companies of Sheba waited for them. They were confounded because they had hoped;[4] they came thither, and were ashamed. For now ye are nothing; ye see my casting down, and are afraid. Did I say, Bring unto me? or, Give a reward for me of your substance? or, Deliver me from the enemy's hand? or, Redeem me from the hand of the mighty? Teach me, and I will hold my tongue: and cause me to understand wherein I have erred. How forcible are right words! But what doth your arguing reprove? Do ye imagine to reprove words, and the speeches of one that is desperate, which are as wind? Yea, ye overwhelm the fatherless, and ye dig a pit for your friend. Now therefore be content, look upon me; for it is evident unto you if I lie. Return, I pray you, let it not be iniquity; yea, return again, my righteousness is in it. Is there iniquity in my tongue? Cannot my taste discern perverse things?

7. Is there not an appointed time to man upon earth? Are not his days also like the days of an hireling? As a servant earnestly desireth the shadow,[5] and as an hireling looketh for the reward of his work: so am I made to possess months of vanity, and wearisome nights are appointed to me. When I lie down, I say, When shall I arise, and the night be gone? and I am full of tossings to and fro unto the dawning of the day. My flesh is clothed with worms and clods of dust; my skin is broken, and become loathsome. My days are swifter than a weaver's shuttle, and are spent without hope. O remember that my life is wind: mine eye shall no more see good. The eye of him that

---

8. More literally: therefore have my words been rash; Job recognizes the exaggeration of his first outburst. 9. Animals do not complain without reason; therefore, when a rational person complains, he or she must have some justification for it. 1. More literally: my soul refuseth to touch them, they are as loathsome meat to me. He is referring to the statements of his friends. 2. Denied. 3. More literally: is not my help within me gone, and is not wisdom driven quite away from me. 4. The caravans reached the springs they had counted on and found them dry. 5. Evening, the end of the workday.

hath seen me shall see me no more: thine eyes are upon me, and I am not. As the cloud is consumed and vanisheth away: so he that goeth down to the grave shall come up no more. He shall return no more to his house, neither shall his place know him any more. Therefore I will not refrain my mouth; I will speak in the anguish of my spirit; I will complain in the bitterness of my soul. Am I a sea, or a whale, that thou settest a watch over me?[6] When I say, My bed shall comfort me, my couch shall ease my complaint; then thou scarest me with dreams, and terrifiest me through visions: so that my soul chooseth strangling, and death rather than my life. I loathe it; I would not live alway: let me alone; for my days are vanity. What is man, that thou shouldest magnify him? and that thou shouldest set thine heart upon him? and that thou shouldest visit him every morning, and try him every moment? How long wilt thou not depart from me, nor let me alone till I swallow down my spittle?[7] I have sinned; what shall I do unto thee, O thou preserver[8] of men? Why hast thou set me as a mark against thee, so that I am a burden to myself? And why dost thou not pardon my transgression, and take away mine iniquity? For now shall I sleep in the dust; and thou shalt seek me in the morning, but I shall not be.

8. Then answered Bildad the Shuhite, and said, How long wilt thou speak these things? and how long shall the words of thy mouth be like a strong wind? Doth God pervert judgment? or doth the Almighty pervert justice? If thy children have sinned against him, and he have cast them away for their transgression; if thou wouldest seek unto God betimes, and make thy supplication to the Almighty; if thou wert pure and upright; surely now he would awake for thee, and make the habitation of thy righteousness prosperous. Though thy beginning was small, yet thy latter end should greatly increase. For enquire, I pray thee, of the former age, and prepare thy self to the search of their fathers: (For we are but of yesterday, and know nothing, because our days upon earth are a shadow:) shall not they teach thee, and tell thee, and utter words out of their heart? Can the rush[9] grow up without mire? Can the flag grow without water? Whilst it is yet in his greenness, and not cut down, it withereth before any other herb. So are the paths of all that forget God; and the hypocrite's hope shall perish: whose hope shall be cut off, and whose trust shall be a spider's web. He shall lean upon his house, but it shall not stand: he shall hold it fast, but it shall not endure. He is green before the sun, and his branch shooteth forth in his garden. His roots are wrapped about the heap, and seeth the place of stones. If he destroy him from his place, then it shall deny him, saying, I have not seen thee. Behold, this is the joy of his way, and out of the earth shall others grow. Behold, God will not cast away a perfect man, neither will he help the evil doers: till he fill thy mouth with laughing, and thy lips with rejoicing. They that hate thee shall be clothed with shame; and the dwelling place of the wicked shall come to nought.

---

6. Job, now addressing God directly, compares his situation with that of the sea monster whom a god fought against in a Babylonian myth. He reproves God for exerting His power against anything as small as himself. 7. Even for a moment. 8. More literally: watcher. 9. Papyrus, which grows rapidly when the Nile is high but withers at once when the waters go down.

9. Then Job answered and said, I know it is so of a truth: but how should man be just with God? If he will contend with him, he cannot answer him one of a thousand.[1] He is wise in heart, and mighty in strength: who hath hardened himself against him, and hath prospered? Which removeth the mountains, and they know not: which overturneth them in his anger. Which shaketh the earth out of her place, and the pillars thereof tremble. Which commandeth the sun, and it riseth not; and sealeth up the stars. Which alone spreadeth out the heavens, and treadeth upon the waves of the sea. Which maketh Arcturus, Orion, and Pleiades, and the chambers of the south. Which doeth great things past finding out; yea, and wonders without number. Lo, he goeth by me, and I see him not: he passeth on also, but I perceive him not. Behold, he taketh away, who can hinder him? Who will say unto him, What doest thou? If God will not withdraw his anger, the proud helpers do stoop under him. How much less shall I answer him, and choose out my words to reason with him? Whom, though I were righteous, yet would I not answer, but I would make supplication to my judge. If I had called, and he had answered me; yet would I not believe that he had hearkened unto my voice. For he breaketh me with a tempest, and multiplieth my wounds without cause. He will not suffer me to take my breath, but filleth me with bitterness. If I speak of strength, lo, he is strong: and if of judgment, who shall set me a time to plead? If I justify myself, mine own mouth shall condemn me: if I say, I am perfect, it shall also prove me perverse. Though I were perfect, yet would I not know my soul: I would despise my life. This is one thing, therefore I said it, He destroyeth the perfect and the wicked. If the scourge slay suddenly, he will laugh at the trial of the innocent. The earth is given into the hand of the wicked: he covereth the faces of the judges thereof; if not, where, and who is he? Now my days are swifter than a post:[2] they flee away, they see no good. They are passed away as the swift ships: as the eagle that hasteth to the prey. If I say, I will forget my complaint, I will leave off my heaviness, and comfort myself: I am afraid of all my sorrows, I know that thou wilt not hold me innocent. If I be wicked, why then labour I in vain? If I wash myself with snow water, and make my hands never so clean; yet shalt thou plunge me in the ditch, and mine own clothes shall abhor me. For he is not a man, as I am, that I should answer him, and we should come together in judgment. Neither is there any daysman[3] betwixt us, that might lay his hand upon us both. Let him take his rod away from me, and let not his fear terrify me: then would I speak, and not fear him; but it is not so with me.

10. My soul is weary of my life; I will leave my complaint upon[4] myself; I will speak in the bitterness of my soul. I will say unto God, Do not condemn me; shew me wherefore thou contendest with me. Is it good unto thee that thou shouldest oppress, that thou shouldest despise the work of thine hands, and shine upon the counsel of the wicked? Hath thou eyes of flesh? or seest thou as man seeth? Are thy days as the days of man? Are thy years as man's days,[5] that thou enquirest after mine iniquity, and searchest after my sin? Thou knowest that I am not wicked; and there is none that can deliver out

1. One of a thousand questions.   2. Courier.   3. Arbitrator.   4. On behalf of. *Leave:* give free course to.   5. Is your time, like humankind's, short, so that you have to judge hastily?

of thine hand. Thine hands have made me and fashioned me together round about; yet thou dost destroy me. Remember, I beseech thee, that thou hast made me as the clay; and wilt thou bring me into dust again? Hast thou not poured me out as milk and curdled me like cheese? Thou hast clothed me with skin and flesh, and hast fenced me with bones and sinews. Thou hast granted me life and favour, and thy visitation hath preserved my spirit. And these things hast thou hid in thine heart: I know that this is with thee.[6] If I sin, then thou markest me, and thou wilt not acquit me from mine iniquity. If I be wicked, woe unto me; and if I be righteous, yet will I not lift up my head. I am full of confusion; therefore see thou mine affliction; for it increaseth. Thou huntest me as a fierce lion: and again thou shewest thyself marvellous upon me. Thou renewest thy witnesses[7] against me, and increasest thine indignation upon me; changes and war are against me. Wherefore then hast thou brought me forth out of the womb? Oh that I had given up the ghost, and no eye had seen me! I should have been as though I had not been; I should have been carried from the womb to the grave. Are not my days few? Cease then, and let me alone, that I may take comfort a little before I go whence I shall not return, even to the land of darkness and the shadow of death: a land of darkness, as darkness itself; and of the shadow of death, without any order, and where the light is as darkness.

11. Then answered Zophar the Naamathite, and said, Should not the multitude of words be answered? And should a man full of talk be justified? Should thy lies make men hold their peace? And when thou mockest, shall no man make thee ashamed? For thou hast said, My doctrine is pure, and I am clean in thine eyes. But oh that God would speak, and open his lips against thee; and that he would shew thee the secrets of wisdom, that they are double to that which is! Know therefore that God exacteth of thee less than thine iniquity deserveth. Canst thou by searching find out God? Canst thou find out the Almighty unto perfection? It is as high as heaven; what canst thou do? Deeper than hell; what canst thou know? The measure thereof is longer than the earth, and broader than the sea. If he cut off, and shut up, or gather together,[8] then who can hinder him? For he knoweth vain men: he seeth wickedness also; will he not then consider it? For vain man would be wise, though man be born like a wild ass's colt. If thou prepare thine heart, and stretch out thine hands toward him; if iniquity be in thine hand, put it far away, and let not wickedness dwell in thy tabernacles. For then shalt thou lift up thy face without spot; yea, thou shalt be stedfast, and shalt not fear: because thou shalt forget thy misery, and remember it as waters that pass away: and thine age shall be clearer than the noonday; thou shalt shine forth, thou shalt be as the morning. And thou shalt be secure, because there is hope; yea, thou shalt dig about thee,[9] and thou shalt take thy rest in safety. Also thou shalt lie down, and none shall make thee afraid; yea, many shall make suit unto thee. But the eyes of the wicked shall fail, and they shall not escape, and their hope shall be as the giving up of the ghost.

---

6. I.e., my destruction (*this*) is your purpose. Job accuses God of planning his destruction while showing favor to him. 7. Afflictions, which prove (to his friends) his guilt. 8. For judgment. 9. Search; the master inspects his property before retiring.

12. And Job answered and said, No doubt but ye are the people, and wisdom shall die with you. But I have understanding as well as you; I am not inferior to you: yea, who knoweth not such things as these? I am as one mocked of his neighbour, who calleth upon God, and he answered him: the just upright man is laughed to scorn. He that is ready to slip with his feet is as a lamp despised in the thought of him that is at ease. The tabernacles of robbers prosper, and they that provoke God are secure; into whose hand God bringeth abundantly. But ask now the beasts, and they shall teach thee; and the fowls of the air, and they shall tell thee: or speak to the earth, and it shall teach thee; and the fishes of the sea shall declare unto thee. Who knoweth not in all these that the hand of the Lord hath wrought this? In whose hand is the soul of every living thing, and the breath of all mankind. Doth not the ear try words? and the mouth taste his meat? With the ancient is wisdom; and in length of days understanding. With him is wisdom and strength, he hath counsel and understanding. Behold, he breaketh down, and it cannot be built again: he shutteth up a man, and there can be no opening. Behold, he withholdeth the waters, and they dry up: also he sendeth them out, and they overturn the earth. With him is strength and wisdom: the deceived and the deceiver are his. He leadeth counsellors away spoiled, and maketh the judges fools. He looseth the bond of kings, and girdeth their loins with a girdle. He leadeth princes away spoiled, and overthroweth the mighty. He removeth away the speech of the trusty, and taketh away the understanding of the aged. He poureth contempt upon princes, and weakeneth the strength of the mighty. He discovereth deep things out of darkness, and bringeth out to light the shadow of death. He increaseth the nations, and destroyeth them: he enlargeth the nations, and straiteneth them again.[1] He taketh away the heart of the chief of the people of the earth, and causeth them to wander in a wilderness where there is no way. They grope in the dark without light, and he maketh them to stagger like a drunken man.

13. Lo, mine eye hath seen all this, mine ear hath heard and understood it. What ye know, the same do I know also: I am not inferior unto you. Surely I would speak to the Almighty, and I desire to reason with God. But ye are forgers of lies, ye are all physicians of no value. O that ye would altogether hold your peace! and it should be your wisdom. Hear now my reasoning, and hearken to the pleadings of my lips. Will ye speak wickedly for God? and talk deceitfully for him? Will ye accept[2] his person? Will ye contend for God? Is it good that he should search you out? or as one man mocketh another, do ye so mock him? He will surely reprove you, if ye do secretly accept persons.[3] Shall not his excellency make you afraid? and his dread fall upon you? Your remembrances[4] are like unto ashes, your bodies to bodies of clay. Hold your peace, let me alone, that I may speak, and let come on me what will. Wherefore do I take my flesh in my teeth, and put my life in mine hand?[5] Though he slay me, yet will I trust in him: but I will maintain mine own ways before him. He also shall be my salvation: for an hypocrite shall not come before him. Hear diligently my speech, and my declaration with your ears.

---

1. Makes them small again.   2. Respect.   3. I.e., if you back the winning side for personal reasons.   4. Memorable sayings.   5. Like a wild beast at bay, defending its life with its teeth.

Behold now, I have ordered my cause; I know that I shall be justified. Who is he that will plead with me?[6] for now, if I hold my tongue, I shall give up the ghost. Only do not two things unto me: then will I not hide myself from thee.[7] Withdraw thine hand far from me: and let not thy dread make me afraid. Then call thou, and I will answer: or let me speak, and answer thou me. How many are mine iniquities and sins? Make me to know my transgression and my sin. Wherefore hidest thou thy face, and holdest me for thine enemy? Wilt thou break a leaf driven to and fro? and wilt thou pursue the dry stubble? For thou writest bitter things against me, and makest me to possess the iniquities of my youth. Thou puttest my feet also in the stocks, and lookest narrowly unto all my paths; thou settest a print upon the heels of my feet. And he, as a rotten thing, consumeth, as a garment that is moth eaten.

14. Man that is born of a woman is of few days, and full of trouble. He cometh forth like a flower, and is cut down: he fleeth also as a shadow, and continueth not. And dost thou open thine eyes upon such an one, and bringest me into judgment with thee? Who can bring a clean thing out of an unclean? not one. Seeing his days are determined, the number of his months are with thee, thou hast appointed his bounds that he cannot pass; turn from him, that he may rest, till he shall accomplish, as an hireling, his day. For there is hope of a tree, if it be cut down, that it will sprout again, and that the tender branch thereof will not cease. Though the root thereof wax old in the earth, and the stock thereof die in the ground; yet through the scent of water it will bud, and bring forth boughs like a plant. But man dieth, and wasteth away: yea, man giveth up the ghost, and where is he? As the waters fail from the sea, and the flood decayeth and drieth up: so man lieth down, and riseth not: till the heavens be no more, they shall not awake, nor be raised out of their sleep. O that thou wouldest hide me in the grave, that thou wouldest keep me secret, until thy wrath be past, that thou wouldest appoint me a set time, and remember me! If a man die, shall he live again? All the days of my appointed time will I wait, till my change[8] come. Thou shalt call, and I will answer thee: thou wilt have a desire to[9] the work of thine hands. For now thou numberest my steps: dost thou not watch over my sin? My transgression is sealed up in a bag, and thou sewest up mine iniquity. And surely the mountain falling cometh to nought, and the rock is removed out of his place. The waters wear the stones: thou washest away the things which grow out of the dust of the earth; and thou destroyest the hope of man. Thou prevailest for ever against him, and he passeth; thou changest his countenance, and sendest him away. His sons come to honour, and he knoweth it not; and they are brought low, but he perceiveth it not of them. But his flesh upon him shall have pain, and his soul within him shall mourn.

29. Moreover Job continued his parable, and said, Oh that I were as in months past, as in the days when God preserved me; when his candle shined upon my head, and when by his light I walked through darkness; as I was in the days of my youth, when the secret of God was upon my tabernacle; when the Almighty was yet with me, when my children were about me; when I

6. Accuse me.   7. He now addresses himself directly to God.   8. Release.   9. For.

washed my steps with butter and the rock poured me out rivers of oil; when I went out to the gate[1] through the city, when I prepared my seat in the street! The young men saw me, and hid themselves: and the aged arose, and stood up. The princes refrained talking, and laid their hand on their mouth. The nobles held their peace, and their tongue cleaved to the roof of their mouth. When the ear heard me, then it blessed me; and when the eye saw me, it gave witness to me: because I delivered the poor that cried, and the fatherless, and him that had none to help him. The blessing of him that was ready to perish came upon me: and I caused the widow's heart to sing for joy. I put on righteousness, and it clothed me: my judgment was as a robe and a diadem. I was eyes to the blind, and feet was I to the lame. I was a father to the poor: and the cause which I knew not I searched out. And I brake the jaws of the wicked, and plucked the spoil out of his teeth. Then I said, I shall die in my nest, and I shall multiply my days as the sand. My root was spread out by the waters, and the dew lay all night upon my branch. My glory was fresh in me, and my bow was renewed in my hand. Unto me men gave ear, and waited, and kept silence at my counsel. After my words they spake not again; and my speech dropped upon them. And they waited for me as for the rain; and they opened their mouth wide as for the latter rain. If I laughed on them, they believed it not; and the light of my countenance they cast not down. I chose out their way, and sat chief, and dwelt as a king in the army, as one that comforteth the mourners.

30. But now they that are younger than I have me in derision, whose fathers I would have disdained to have set with the dogs of my flock. Yea, whereto might the strength of their hands profit me, in whom old age was perished?[2] For want and famine they were solitary; fleeing into the wilderness in former time desolate and waste. Who cut up mallows by the bushes, and juniper roots for their meat. They were driven forth from among men, (they cried after them as after a thief;) to dwell in the cliffs of the valleys, in caves of the earth, and in the rocks. Among the bushes they brayed; under the nettles they were gathered together. They were children of fools, yea, children of base men: they were viler than the earth. And now am I their song, yea, I am their byword. They abhor me, they flee far from me, and spare not to spit in my face. Because he hath loosed my cord, and afflicted me, they have also let loose the bridle before me. Upon my right hand rise the youth; they push away my feet, and they raise up against me the ways of their destruction. They mar my path, they set forward my calamity, they have no helper. They came upon me as a wide breaking in of waters: in the desolation they rolled themselves upon me. Terrors are turned upon me: they pursue my soul as the wind: and my welfare passeth away as a cloud. And now my soul is poured out upon[3] me; the days of affliction have taken hold upon me. My bones are pierced in me in the night season: and my sinews take no rest. By the great force of my disease is my garment changed: it bindeth me about as the collar of my coat. He hath cast me into the mire, and I am become like dust and ashes. I cry unto thee, and thou dost not hear me: I stand up and thou regardest me not. Thou art become cruel to me: with thy strong

1. The town meeting place and law court was just inside the gate.　2. They were too old to work.
3. Within.

hand thou opposest thyself against me. Thou liftest me up to the wind; thou causest me to ride upon it, and dissolvest my substance. For I know that thou wilt bring me to death, and to the house appointed for all living. Howbeit he will not stretch out his hand to the grave, though they cry in his destruction. Did not I weep for him that was in trouble? Was not my soul grieved for the poor? When I looked for good, then evil came unto me: and when I waited for light, there came darkness. My bowels boiled, and rested not: the days of affliction prevented me. I went mourning without the sun: I stood up, and I cried in the congregation. I am a brother to dragons, and a companion to owls. My skin is black upon me, and my bones are burned with heat. My harp also is turned to mourning, and my organ[4] into the voice of them that weep.

31. I made a covenant with mine eyes; why then should I think upon a maid? For what portion of God is there from above? and what inheritance of the Almighty from on high? Is not destruction to the wicked? and a strange punishment to the workers of iniquity? Doth not he see my ways, and count all my steps? If I have walked with vanity, or if my foot hath hasted to deceit; let me be weighed in an even balance, that God may know mine integrity. If my step hath turned out of the way, and mine heart walked after mine eyes, and if any blot hath cleaved to mine hands; then let me sow, and let another eat; yea, let my offspring be rooted out. If mine heart have been deceived by a woman, or if I have laid wait at my neighbour's door; then let my wife grind unto another, and let others bow down upon her. For this is an heinous crime; yea, it is an iniquity to be punished by the judges. For it is a fire that consumeth to destruction, and would root out all mine increase.

If I did despise the cause of my manservant or of my maidservant, when they contended with me; what then shall I do when God riseth up? and when he visiteth, what shall I answer him? Did not he that made me in the womb make him? and did not one fashion us in the womb? If I have withheld the poor from their desire, or have caused the eyes of the widow to fail; or have eaten my morsel myself alone, and the fatherless hath not eaten thereof; (For from my youth he was brought up with me, as with a father, and I have guided her from my mother's womb;) if I have seen any perish for want of clothing, or any poor without covering; if his loins have not blessed me, and if he were not warmed with the fleece of my sheep; if I have lifted up my hand against the fatherless, when I saw my help in the gate:[5] then let mine arm fall from my shoulder blade, and mine arm be broken from the bone. For destruction from God was a terror to me, and by reason of his highness I could not endure. If I have made gold my hope, or have said to the fine gold, Thou art my confidence; if I rejoiced because my wealth was great, and because mine hand had gotten much; if I beheld the sun when it shined, or the moon walking in brightness; and my heart hath been secretly enticed, or my mouth hath kissed my hand:[6] this also were an iniquity to be punished by the judge: for I should have denied the God that is above.

If I rejoiced at the destruction of him that hated me, or lifted up myself when evil found him: neither have I suffered my mouth to sin by wishing a curse to his soul. If the men of my tabernacle said not, Oh that we had of

---

4. Pipe.   5. I.e., when I had influence in the court.   6. Idolatrous acts of worship of the sun and moon.

his flesh! We cannot be satisfied. The stranger did not lodge in the street: but I opened my doors to the traveller. If I covered my transgressions as Adam, by hiding mine iniquity in my bosom: did I fear a great multitude, or did the contempt of families terrify me, that I kept silence, and went not out of the door? Oh that one would hear me! Behold, my desire is, that the Almighty would answer me, and that mine adversary had written a book. Surely I would take it upon my shoulder, and bind it as a crown to me. I would declare unto him the number of my steps; as a prince would I go near unto him. If my land cry against me, or that the furrows likewise thereof complain; if I have eaten the fruits thereof without money, or have caused the owners thereof to lose their life: let thistles grow instead of wheat, and cockle instead of barley. The words of Job are ended.

38. Then the Lord answered Job out of the whirlwind, and said, Who is this that darkeneth counsel by words without knowledge? Gird up now thy loins like a man; for I will demand of thee, and answer thou me. Where wast thou when I laid the foundations of the earth? Declare, if thou hast understanding. Who hath laid the measures thereof, if thou knowest? or who hath stretched the line upon it? Whereupon are the foundations thereof fastened? or who laid the corner stone thereof; when the morning stars sang together, and all the sons of God shouted for joy? Or who shut up the sea with doors, when it brake forth, as if it had issued out of the womb? When I made the cloud the garment thereof, and thick darkness a swaddlingband for it, and brake up for it my decreed place,[7] and set bars and doors, and said, Hitherto shalt thou come, but no further: and here shall thy proud waves be stayed? Hast thou commanded the morning since thy days; and caused the dayspring[8] to know his place; that it might take hold of the ends of the earth, that the wicked might be shaken out of it? It is turned as clay to the seal; and they[9] stand as a garment. And from the wicked their light is withholden, and the high arm shall be broken. Hast thou entered into the springs of the sea? or hast thou walked in the search of the depth? Have the gates of death been opened unto thee? or hast thou seen the doors of the shadow of death? Hast thou perceived the breadth of the earth? Declare if thou knowest it all. Where is the way where light dwelleth? And as for darkness, where is the place thereof, that thou shouldest take it to the bound thereof, and that thou shouldest know the paths to the house thereof? Knowest thou it, because thou wast then born? or because the number of thy days is great? Hast thou entered into the treasures of the snow? or hast thou seen the treasures of the hail, which I have reserved against the time of trouble, against the day of battle and war? By what way is the light parted, which scattereth the east wind upon the earth? Who hath divided a watercourse for the overflowing of waters, or a way for the lightning of thunder; to cause it to rain on the earth, where no man is; on the wilderness, wherein there is no man; to satisfy the desolate and waste ground; and to cause the bud of the tender herb to spring forth? Hath the rain a father? or who hath begotten the drops of dew? Out of whose womb came the ice? And the hoary frost of heaven, who hath gendered it? The waters are hid as with a stone, and the face of the deep is

---

7. The broken coastline.   8. Dawn.   9. All things; God is describing the moment of the creation of the universe. *Turned as clay to the seal:* more literally, changed as clay under the seal.

frozen. Canst thou bind the sweet influences of Pleiades, or loose the bands of Orion? Canst thou bring forth Mazzaroth[1] in his season? or canst thou guide Arcturus with his sons? Knowest thou the ordinances of heaven? Canst thou set the dominion thereof in the earth? Canst thou lift up thy voice to the clouds, that abundance of waters may cover thee? Canst thou send lightnings, that they may go, and say unto thee, Here we are? Who hath put wisdom in the inward parts? or who hath given understanding to the heart? Who can number the clouds in wisdom? or who can stay the bottles of heaven, when the dust groweth into hardness, and the clods cleave fast together? Wilt thou hunt the prey for the lion? or fill the appetite of the young lions, when they couch in their dens, and abide in the covert to lie in wait? Who provideth for the raven his food? when his young ones cry unto God, they wander for lack of meat.

39. Knowest thou the time when the wild goats of the rock bring forth? or canst thou mark when the hinds do calve? Canst thou number the months that they fulfil? or knowest thou the time when they bring forth? They bow themselves, they bring forth their young ones, they cast out their sorrows. Their young ones are in good liking, they grow up with corn; they go forth, and return not unto them. Who hath sent out the wild ass free? or who hath loosed the bands of the wild ass? Whose house I have made the wilderness, and the barren land his dwellings. He scorneth the multitude of the city, neither regardeth he the crying of the driver. The range of the mountains is his pasture, and he searcheth after every green thing. Will the unicorn[2] be willing to serve thee, or abide by thy crib? Canst thou bind the unicorn with his band in the furrow? or will he harrow the valleys after thee? Wilt thou trust him, because his strength is great? or wilt thou leave thy labour to him? Wilt thou believe him, that he will bring home thy seed, and gather it into thy barn? Gavest thou the goodly wings unto the peacocks? or wings and feathers unto the ostrich? Which leaveth her eggs in the earth, and warmeth them in dust, and forgetteth that the foot may crush them, or that the wild beast may break them. She is hardened against her young ones, as though they were not hers: her labour is in vain without fear;[3] because God hath deprived her of wisdom, neither hath he imparted to her understanding. What time she lifteth up herself on high, she scorneth the horse and his rider. Hast thou given the horse strength? Hast thou clothed his neck with thunder? Canst thou make him afraid as a grasshopper? The glory of his nostrils is terrible. He paweth in the valley, and rejoiceth in his strength: he goeth on to meet the armed men. He mocketh at fear, and is not affrighted; neither turneth he back from the sword. The quiver rattleth against him, the glittering spear and the shield. He swalloweth the ground with fierceness and rage: neither believeth he that it is the sound of the trumpet. He saith among the trumpets, Ha, ha; and he smelleth the battle afar off, the thunder of the captains, and the shouting. Doth the hawk fly by thy wisdom, and stretch her wings toward the south? Doth the eagle mount up at thy command, and make her nest on high? She dwelleth and abideth on the rock, upon the crag of the rock, and the strong place. From thence she seeketh

---

1. Meaning disputed; it may be a name for the signs of the zodiac or for some particular constellation.   2. The Hebrew has "wild ox."   3. I.e., although her labor is in vain, she is without fear.

the prey, and her eyes behold afar off. Her young ones also suck up blood: and where the slain are, there is she.

40. Moreover the Lord answered Job, and said, Shall he that contendeth with the Almighty instruct him? He that reproveth God, let him answer it.

Then Job answered the Lord, and said, Behold, I am vile; what shall I answer thee? I will lay mine hand upon my mouth. Once have I spoken; but I will not answer: yea, twice; but I will proceed no further.

Then answered the Lord unto Job out of the whirlwind, and said, Gird up thy loins now like a man: I will demand of thee, and declare thou unto me. Wilt thou also disannul my judgment? Wilt thou condemn me, that thou mayest be righteous? Hast thou an arm like God: or canst thou thunder with a voice like him? Deck thyself now with majesty and excellency; and array thyself with glory and beauty. Cast abroad the rage of thy wrath: and behold every one that is proud, and abase him. Look on every one that is proud, and bring him low; and tread down the wicked in their place. Hide them in the dust together; and bind their faces in secret. Then will I also confess unto thee that thine own right hand can save thee.

Behold now behemoth,[4] which I made with thee; he eateth grass as an ox. Lo now, his strength is in his loins, and his force is in the navel of his belly. He moveth his tail like a cedar: the sinews of his stones[5] are wrapped together. His bones are as strong pieces of brass; his bones are like bars of iron. He is the chief of the ways of God: he that made him can make his sword to approach unto him. Surely the mountains bring him forth food, where all the beasts of the field play. He lieth under the shady trees, in the covert of the reed, and fens. The shady trees cover him with their shadow; the willows of the brook compass him about. Behold, he drinketh up a river, and hasteth not: he trusteth that he can draw up Jordan into his mouth. He taketh it with his eyes:[6] his nose pierceth through snares.

41. Canst thou draw out leviathan[7] with an hook? or his tongue with a cord which thou lettest down? Canst thou put an hook into his nose? or bore his jaw through with a thorn? Will he make many supplications unto thee? will he speak soft words unto thee? Will he make a covenant with thee? wilt thou take him for a servant for ever? Wilt thou play with him as with a bird? or wilt thou bind him for thy maidens? Shall the companions make a banquet of him? Shall they part him among the merchants? Canst thou fill his skin with barbed irons? or his head with fish spears? Lay thine hand upon him, remember the battle, do no more. Behold, the hope of him is in vain: shall not one be cast down even at the sight of him? None is so fierce that dare stir him up: who then is able to stand before me? Who hath prevented me,[8] that I should repay him? Whatsoever is under the whole heaven is mine. I will not conceal his parts, nor his power, nor his comely proportion. Who can discover the face of his garment?[9] or who can come to him with his double bridle? Who can open the doors of his face? His teeth are terrible round about. His scales are his pride, shut up together as with a close seal. One is so near to another, that no air can come between them. They are

---

4. Generally identified with the hippopotamus.   **5.** More literally: thighs.   **6.** Obscure; probably none can attack him in the eyes.   **7.** Here probably the crocodile.   **8.** Given anything to me first.   **9.** His scales. *Discover*: strip off.

joined one to another, they stick together, that they cannot be sundered. By his neesings[1] a light doth shine, and his eyes are like the eyelids of the morning. Out of his mouth go burning lamps, and sparks of fire leap out. Out of his nostrils goeth smoke, as out of a seething pot or caldron. His breath kindleth coals, and a flame goeth out of his mouth. In his neck remaineth strength, and sorrow is turned into joy before him. The flakes of his flesh are joined together: they are firm in themselves; they cannot be moved. His heart is as firm as a stone; yea, as hard as a piece of the nether millstone. When he raiseth up himself, the mighty are afraid: by reason of breakings they purify themselves.[2] The sword of him that layeth at him cannot hold: the spear, the dart, nor the habergeon. He esteemeth iron as straw, and brass as rotten wood. The arrow cannot make him flee: slingstones are turned with him into stubble. Darts are counted as stubble: he laugheth at the shaking of a spear. Sharp stones are under him: he spreadeth sharp pointed things upon the mire. He maketh the deep to boil like a pot: he maketh the sea like a pot of ointment. He maketh a path to shine after him; one would think the deep to be hoary.[3] Upon earth there is not his like, who is made without fear. He beholdeth all high things: he is a king over all the children of pride.

42. Then Job answered the Lord, and said, I know that thou canst do every thing, and that no thought can be withholden from thee. Who is he that hideth counsel without knowledge? Therefore have I uttered that I understood not; things too wonderful for me, which I knew not. Hear, I beseech thee, and I will speak: I will demand of thee, and declare thou unto me. I have heard of thee by the hearing of the ear: but now mine eye seeth thee. Wherefore I abhor myself, and repent in dust and ashes.

And it was so, that after the Lord had spoken these words unto Job, the Lord said to Eliphaz the Temanite, My wrath is kindled against thee, and against thy two friends: for ye have not spoken of me the thing that is right, as my servant Job hath. Therefore take unto you now seven bullocks and seven rams, and go to my servant Job, and offer up for yourselves a burnt offering; and my servant Job shall pray for you: for him will I accept: lest I deal with you after your folly, in that ye have not spoken of me the thing which is right, like my servant Job. So Eliphaz the Temanite and Bildad the Shuhite and Zophar the Naamathite went, and did according as the Lord commanded them: the Lord also accepted Job. And the Lord turned the captivity[4] of Job, when he prayed for his friends: also the Lord gave Job twice as much as he had before. Then came there unto him all his brethren, and all his sisters, and all they that had been of his acquaintance before, and did eat bread with him in his house: and they bemoaned him, and comforted him over all the evil that the Lord had brought upon him: every man also gave him a piece of money, and every one an earring of gold. So the Lord blessed the latter end of Job more than his beginning: for he had fourteen thousand sheep, and six thousand camels, and a thousand yoke of oxen, and a thousand she asses. He had also seven sons and three daughters. And he called the name of the first, Jemima; and the name of the second, Kezia; and

1. His breath (compare *sneeze*). The vapor exhaled by the crocodile appears luminous in the sunlight.   2. Corrupt text; probably in consternation they are beside themselves.   3. White (with foam).   4. Put an end to the suffering.

the name of the third, Kerenhappuch. And in all the land were no women found so fair as the daughters of Job: and their father gave them inheritance among their brethren. After this lived Job an hundred and forty years, and saw his sons, and his sons' sons, even four generations. So Job died, being old and full of days.

Psalm 8

1. O Lord our Lord, how excellent is thy name in all the earth! who hast set thy glory above the heavens.

2. Out of the mouth of babes and sucklings hast thou ordained strength because of thine enemies, that thou mightest still the enemy and the avenger.

3. When I consider thy heavens, the work of thy fingers, the moon and the stars, which thou hast ordained;

4. What is man, that thou art mindful of him? and the son of man, that thou visitest him?

5. For thou hast made him a little lower than the angels, and hast crowned him with glory and honour.

6. Thou madest him to have dominion over the works of thy hands; thou hast put all things under his feet:

7. All sheep and oxen, yea, and the beasts of the field;

8. The fowl of the air, and the fish of the sea, and whatsoever passeth through the paths of the seas.

9. O Lord our Lord, how excellent is thy name in all the earth!

Psalm 19

1. The heavens declare the glory of God; and the firmament sheweth his handywork.

2. Day unto day uttereth speech, and night unto night sheweth knowledge.

3. There is no speech nor language, where their voice is not heard.

4. Their line is gone out through all the earth, and their words to the end of the world. In them hath he set a tabernacle for the sun,

5. Which is as a bridegroom coming out of his chamber, and rejoiceth as a strong man to run a race.

6. His going forth is from the end of the heaven, and his circuit unto the ends of it: and there is nothing hid from the heat thereof.

7. The law of the Lord is perfect, converting the soul: the testimony of the Lord is sure, making wise the simple.

8. The statutes of the Lord are right, rejoicing the heart: the commandment of the Lord is pure, enlightening the eyes.

9. The fear of the Lord is clean, enduring for ever: the judgments of the Lord are true and righteous altogether.

10. More to be desired are they than gold, yea, than much fine gold: sweeter also than honey and the honeycomb.

11. Moreover by them is thy servant warned: and in keeping of them there is great reward.

12. Who can understand his errors? cleanse thou me from secret faults.

13. Keep back thy servant also from presumptuous sins; let them not have dominion over me: then shall I be upright, and I shall be innocent from the great transgression.

14. Let the words of my mouth, and the meditation of my heart, be acceptable in thy sight, O Lord, my strength, and my redeemer.

Psalm 23

1. The Lord is my shepherd; I shall not want.

2. He maketh me to lie down in green pastures: he leadeth me beside the still waters.

3. He restoreth my soul: he leadeth me in the paths of righteousness for his name's sake.

4. Yea, though I walk through the valley of the shadow of death, I will fear no evil: for thou art with me; thy rod and thy staff they comfort me.

5. Thou preparest a table before me in the presence of mine enemies: thou anointest my head with oil; my cup runneth over.

6. Surely goodness and mercy shall follow me all the days of my life: and I will dwell in the house of the Lord for ever.

Psalm 104

1. Bless the Lord, O my soul. O Lord my God, thou art very great; thou art clothed with honour and majesty.

2. Who coverest thyself with light as with a garment: who stretchest out the heavens like a curtain:

3. Who layeth the beams of his chambers in the waters: who maketh the clouds his chariot: who walketh upon the wings of the wind:

4. Who maketh his angels spirits; his ministers a flaming fire:

5. Who laid the foundations of the earth, that it should not be removed for ever.

6. Thou coveredst it with the deep as with a garment: the waters stood above the mountains.

7. At thy rebuke they fled; at the voice of thy thunder they hasted away.

8. They go up by the mountains; they go down by the valleys unto the place which thou hast founded for them.

9. Thou hast set a bound that they may not pass over; that they turn not again to cover the earth.

10. He sendeth the springs into the valleys, which run among the hills.

11. They give drink to every beast of the field: the wild asses quench their thirst.

12. By them shall the fowls of the heaven have their habitation, which sing among the branches.

13. He watereth the hills from his chambers: the earth is satisfied with the fruit of thy works.

14. He causeth the grass to grow for the cattle, and herb for the service of man: that he may bring forth food out of the earth;

15. And wine that maketh glad the heart of man, and oil to make his face to shine, and bread which strengtheneth man's heart.

16. The trees of the Lord are full of sap; the cedars of Lebanon, which he hath planted;

17. Where the birds make their nests: as for the stork, the fir trees are her house.

18. The high hills are a refuge for the wild goats; and the rocks for the conies.

19. He appointed the moon for seasons: the sun knoweth his going down.

20. Thou makest darkness, and it is night: wherein all the beasts of the forest do creep forth.

21. The young lions roar after their prey, and seek their meat from God.

22. The sun ariseth, they gather themselves together, and lay them down in their dens.

23. Man goeth forth unto his work and to his labour until the evening.

24. O Lord, how manifold are thy works! in wisdom hast thou made them all: the earth is full of thy riches.

25. So is this great and wide sea, wherein are things creeping innumerable, both small and great beasts.

26. There go the ships: there is that leviathan, whom thou hast made to play therein.

27. These wait all upon thee; that thou mayest give them their meat in due season.

28. That thou givest them they gather: thou openest thine hand, they are filled with good.

29. Thou hidest thy face, they are troubled: thou takest away their breath, they die, and return to their dust.

30. Thou sendest forth thy spirit, they are created: and thou renewest the face of the earth.

31. The glory of the Lord shall endure for ever: the Lord shall rejoice in his works.

32. He looketh on the earth, and it trembleth: he toucheth the hills, and they smoke.

33. I will sing unto the Lord as long as I live: I will sing praise to my God while I have my being.

34. My meditation of him shall be sweet: I will be glad in the Lord.

35. Let the sinners be consumed out of the earth, and let the wicked be no more. Bless thou the Lord, O my soul. Praise ye the Lord.

Psalm 137

1. By the rivers of Babylon,[1] there we sat down, yea, we wept, when we remembered Zion.

2. We hanged our harps upon the willows in the midst thereof.

3. For there they that carried us away captive required of us a song; and they that wasted us required of us mirth, saying, Sing us one of the songs of Zion.

4. How shall we sing the Lord's song in a strange land?

5. If I forget thee, O Jerusalem, let my right hand forget her cunning.

6. If I do not remember thee, let my tongue cleave to the roof of my mouth; if I prefer not Jerusalem above my chief joy.

7. Remember, O Lord, the children of Edom[2] in the day of Jerusalem; who said, Rase it, rase it, even to the foundation thereof.

8. O daughter of Babylon, who art to be destroyed; happy shall he be, that rewardeth thee as thou hast served us.

9. Happy shall he be, that taketh and dasheth thy little ones against the stones.

The Song of Songs

1. The song of songs, which is Solomon's.

Let him kiss me with the kisses of his mouth: for thy love is better than wine. Because of the savor of thy good ointments thy name is as ointment poured forth, therefore do the virgins love thee. Draw me, we will run after thee: the King hath brought me into his chambers: we will be glad and rejoice in thee, we will remember thy love more than wine: the upright love thee. I am black,[1] but comely, O ye daughters of Jerusalem, as the tents of Kedar,[2] as the curtains of Solomon. Look[3] not upon me, because I am black, because the sun hath looked upon me: my mother's children were angry with me; they made me the keeper of the vineyards; but mine own vineyard have I not kept. Tell me, O thou whom my soul loveth, where thou feedest, where thou makest thy flock to rest at noon: for why should I be as one that turneth aside by the flocks of thy companions?

If thou know not, O thou fairest among women, go thy way forth by the footsteps of the flock, and feed thy kids beside the shepherds' tents. I have compared thee, O my love, to a company of horses in Pharaoh's chariots. Thy cheeks are comely with rows of jewels, thy neck with chains of gold. We will make thee borders of gold with studs of silver.

While the King sitteth at his table, my spikenard[4] sendeth forth the smell thereof. A bundle of myrrh is my well-beloved unto me; he shall lie all night betwixt my breasts. My beloved is unto me as a cluster of camphire in the

---

1. On the Euphrates River. Jerusalem was captured and sacked by the Babylonians in 586 B.C. The Hebrews were taken away into captivity in Babylon. 2. The Edomites helped the Babylonians to capture Jerusalem. 1. Tanned from sun and weather; feminine beauty required a sheltered and fair skin. 2. A nomadic people of northern Arabia, living east of Palestine. 3. Better, *gaze* or *stare* (with fascination). 4. Fragrant oil made from an Indian plant.

vineyards of En-gedi.[5] Behold, thou art fair, my love; behold, thou art fair; thou hast doves' eyes. Behold, thou art fair, my beloved, yea, pleasant: also our bed is green. The beams of our house are cedar, and our rafters of fir.

2. I am the rose of Sharon,[6] and the lily of the valleys. As the lily among thorns, so is my love among the daughters. As the apple tree among the trees of the wood, so is my beloved among the sons. I sat down under his shadow with great delight, and his fruit was sweet to my taste. He brought me to the banqueting house, and his banner over me was love. Stay me with flagons, comfort me with apples: for I am sick of love. His left hand is under my head, and his right hand doth embrace me. I charge you, O ye daughters of Jerusalem, by the roes, and by the hinds of the field, that ye stir not up, nor awake my love, till he please. The voice of my beloved! behold he cometh leaping upon the mountains skipping upon the hills. My beloved is like a roe or a young hart: behold, he standeth behind our wall, he looketh forth at the windows, showing himself through the lattice. My beloved spake, and said unto me, Rise up, my love, my fair one, and come away. For, lo, the winter is past, the rain is over and gone; the flowers appear on the earth; the time of the singing of birds is come, and the voice of the turtle[7] is heard in our land; the fig tree putteth forth her green figs, and the vines with the tender grape give a good smell. Arise, my love, my fair one, and come away.

O my dove, that art in the clefts of the rock, in the secret places of the stairs, let me see thy countenance, let me hear thy voice; for sweet is thy voice, and thy countenance is comely. Take us the foxes, the little foxes, that spoil the vines: for our vines have tender grapes.

My beloved is mine, and I am his: he feedeth among the lilies. Until the day break, and the shadows flee away, turn, my beloved, and be thou like a roe or a young hart upon the mountains of Bether.[8]

3. By night on my bed I sought him whom my soul loveth: I sought him, but I found him not. I will rise now, and go about the city in the streets, and in the broad ways I will seek him whom my soul loveth: I sought him, but I found him not. The watchmen that go about the city found me: to whom I said, Saw ye him whom my soul loveth? It was but a little that I passed from them, but I found him whom my soul loveth: I held him, and would not let him go, until I had brought him into my mother's house, and into the chamber of her that conceived me. I charge you, O ye daughters of Jerusalem, by the roes, and by the hinds of the field, that ye stir not up, nor wake my love, till he please.

Who is this that cometh out of the wilderness like pillars of smoke, perfumed with myrrh and frankincense, with all powders of the merchant? Behold his bed, which is Solomon's; threescore valiant men are about it, of the valiant of Israel. They all hold swords, being expert in war: every man hath his sword upon his thigh because of fear in the night. King Solomon made himself a chariot of the wood of Lebanon. He made the pillars thereof of silver, the bottom thereof of gold, the covering of it of purple, the midst

---

5. An oasis on the western shore of the Dead Sea, a source of fragrant oil made from the camphire (henna) plant.   6. *Sharon:* a plain on the coast of Palestine, notable for its wildflowers.   7. The turtledove.   8. Name of a city of Judah, southwest of Jerusalem; the phrase may also mean "the cleft mountains" (a reference to female breasts or genitals).

thereof being paved with love, for the daughters of Jerusalem. Go forth, O ye daughters of Zion, and behold king Solomon with the crown wherewith his mother crowned him in the day of his espousals, and in the day of the gladness of his heart.

4. Behold, thou art fair, my love; behold, thou art fair; thou hast doves' eyes within thy locks: thy hair is as a flock of goats, that appear from mount Gilead.[9] Thy teeth are like a flock of sheep that are even shorn, which came up from the washing; whereof every one bear twins, and none is barren among them. Thy lips are like a thread of scarlet, and thy speech is comely: thy temples are like a piece of a pomegranate within thy locks. Thy neck is like the tower of David builded for an armory, whereon there hang a thousand bucklers, all shields of mighty men. Thy two breasts are like two young roes that are twins, which feed among the lilies. Until the day break, and the shadows flee away, I will get me to the mountain of myrrh, and to the hill of frankincense. Thou art all fair, my love; there is no spot in thee.

Come with me from Lebanon, my spouse, with me from Lebanon: look from the top of Amana, from the top of Shenir and Hermon,[1] from the lions' dens, from the mountains of the leopards. Thou hast ravished my heart, my sister, my spouse; thou hast ravished my heart with one of thine eyes, with one chain of thy neck. How fair is thy love, my sister, my spouse! how much better is thy love than wine! and the smell of thine ointments than all spices! Thy lips, O my spouse, drop as the honeycomb: honey and milk are under thy tongue; and the smell of thy garments is like the smell of Lebanon. A garden inclosed is my sister, my spouse; a spring shut up, a fountain sealed. Thy plants are an orchard of pomegranates, with pleasant fruits; camphire, with spikenard, spikenard and saffron; calamus[2] and cinnamon, with all trees of frankincense; myrrh and aloes, with all the chief spices: a fountain of gardens, a well of living waters, and streams from Lebanon.

Awake, O north wind; and come, thou south; blow upon my garden, that the spices thereof may flow out. Let my beloved come into his garden, and eat his pleasant fruits.

5. I am come into my garden, my sister, my spouse: I have gathered my myrrh with my spice; I have eaten my honeycomb with my honey; I have drunk my wine with my milk: eat, O friends; drink, yea, drink abundantly, O beloved.

I sleep, but my heart waketh: it is the voice of my beloved that knocketh, saying, Open to me, my sister, my love, my dove, my undefiled: for my head is filled with dew, and my locks with the drops of the night. I have put off my coat; how shall I put it on? I have washed my feet; how shall I defile them? My beloved put in his hand[3] by the hole of the door, and my bowels[4] were moved for him. I rose up to open to my beloved; and my hands dropped with myrrh, and my fingers with sweet smelling myrrh, upon the handles of the lock. I opened to my beloved; but my beloved had withdrawn himself, and was gone: my soul failed when he spake: I sought him, but I could not find him; I called him, but he gave me no answer. The watchmen that went

9. Location uncertain; perhaps a high inland plateau.   1. Mountains in the Antilebanon range of Syria.   2. Cane, an aromatic spice.   3. Possibly a euphemism for phallus.   4. Entrails, considered the seat of tender emotions.

about the city found me, they smote me, they wounded me; the keepers of the walls took away my veil from me. I charge you, O daughters of Jerusalem, if ye find my beloved, that ye tell him, that I am sick of love. What is thy beloved more than another beloved, O thou fairest among women? what is thy beloved more than another beloved, that thou dost so charge us? My beloved is white and ruddy, the chiefest among ten thousand. His head is as the most fine gold; his locks are bushy, and black as a raven: his eyes are as the eyes of doves by the rivers of waters, washed with milk, and fitly set: his cheeks are as a bed of spices, as sweet flowers: his lips like lilies, dropping sweet smelling myrrh: his hands are as gold rings set with the beryl: his belly is as bright ivory overlaid with sapphires: his legs are as pillars of marble, set upon sockets of fine gold: his countenance is as Lebanon, excellent as the cedars: his mouth is most sweet: yea, he is altogether lovely. This is my beloved, and this is my friend, O daughters of Jerusalem.

6. Whither is thy beloved gone, O thou fairest among women? whither is thy beloved turned aside? that we may seek him with thee. My beloved is gone down into his garden, to the beds of spices, to feed in the gardens, and to gather lilies. I am my beloved's, and my beloved is mine: he feedeth among the lilies.

Thou art beautiful, O my love, as Tirzah,[5] comely as Jerusalem, terrible as an army with banners. Turn away thine eyes from me, for they have overcome me: thy hair is as a flock of goats that appear from Gilead: thy teeth are as a flock of sheep which go up from the washing, whereof every one beareth twins, and there is not one barren among them. As a piece of a pomegranate are thy temples within thy locks. There are threescore queens, and fourscore concubines, and virgins without number. My dove, my undefiled, is but one; she is the only one of her mother, she is the choice one of her that bare her. The daughters saw her, and blessed her; yea, the queens and the concubines, and they praised her. Who is she that looketh forth as the morning, fair as the moon, clear as the sun, and terrible as an army with banners? I went down into the garden of nuts to see the fruits of the valley, and to see whether the vine flourished, and the pomegranates budded. Or ever I was aware, my soul made me like the chariots of Amminadib. Return, return, O Shulamite;[6] return, return, that we may look upon thee. What will ye see in the Shulamite? As it were the company of two armies.

7. How beautiful are thy feet with shoes, O prince's daughter! the joints of thy thighs are like jewels, the work of the hands of a cunning workman. Thy navel is like a round goblet, which wanteth not liquor: thy belly is like a heap of wheat set about with lilies. Thy two breasts are like two young roes that are twins. Thy neck is as a tower of ivory; thine eyes like the fishpools in Heshbon, by the gate of Bathrabbim:[7] thy nose is as the tower of Lebanon which looketh toward Damascus. Thine head upon thee is like Carmel,[8] and the hair of thine head like purple; the King is held in the galleries. How fair

---

5. A Canaanite city.　　6. The name, often taken as the feminine counterpart to Solomon, may also be the name or epithet of a Near Eastern goddess or a reference to the town Shunem.　　7. *Heshbon*: a city east of the northern end of the Dead Sea. *Bathrabbim*: another name for Heshbon, or one of its gates.　　8. A high promontory on the seacoast of Palestine.

and how pleasant art thou, O love, for delights! This thy stature is like to a palm tree, and thy breasts to clusters of grapes. I said, I will go up to the palm tree, I will take hold of the boughs thereof: now also thy breasts shall be as clusters of the vine, and the smell of thy nose like apples: and the roof of thy mouth like the best wine for my beloved, that goeth down sweetly, causing the lips of those that are asleep to speak.

I am my beloved's, and his desire is toward me. Come, my beloved, let us go forth into the field; let us lodge in the villages. Let us get up early to the vineyards; let us see if the vine flourish, whether the tender grape appear, and the pomegranates bud forth: there will I give thee my loves. The mandrakes[9] give a smell, and at our gates are all manner of pleasant fruits, new and old, which I have laid up for thee, O my beloved.

8. O that thou wert as my brother, that sucked the breasts of my mother! when I should find thee without, I would kiss thee; yea, I should not be despised. I would lead thee, and bring thee into my mother's house, who would instruct me: I would cause thee to drink of spiced wine of the juice of my pomegranate. His left hand should be under my head, and his right hand should embrace me. I charge you, O daughters of Jerusalem, that ye stir not up, nor awake my love, until he please. Who is this that cometh up from the wilderness, leaning upon her beloved? I raised thee up under the apple tree: there thy mother brought thee forth; there she brought thee forth that bare thee. Set me as a seal upon thine heart, as a seal upon thine arm: for love is strong as death; jealousy is cruel as the grave: the coals thereof are coals of fire, which hath a most vehement flame. Many waters cannot quench love, neither can the floods drown it: if a man would give all the substance of his house for love, it would utterly be contemned.

We have a little sister, and she hath no breasts: what shall we do for our sister in the day when she shall be spoken for? If she be a wall, we will build upon her a palace of silver: and if she be a door, we will inclose her with boards of cedar. I am a wall, and my breasts like towers: then was I in his eyes as one that found favor. Solomon had a vineyard at Baalhamon;[1] he let out the vineyard unto keepers; every one for the fruit thereof was to bring a thousand pieces of silver. My vineyard, which is mine, is before me: thou, O Solomon, must have a thousand, and those that keep the fruit thereof two hundred. Thou that dwellest in the gardens, the companions hearken to thy voice: cause me to hear it. Make haste, my beloved, and be thou like to a roe or to a young hart upon the mountains of spices.

Jonah

1. Now the word of the Lord came unto Jonah the son of Amittai, saying, Arise, go to Nineveh,[1] that great city, and cry against it; for their wickedness is come up before me. But Jonah rose up to flee unto Tarshish from the presence of the Lord, and went down to Joppa;[2] and he found a ship going

---

9. A common plant in Palestine, known for its narcotic or aphrodisiac effect, whose root was thought to look like the female genitalia.   1. Otherwise unknown. The name means "lord of a crowd."   1. On the Tigris River, the capital city of the Assyrians.   2. Seaport on the coast of Palestine. Tarshish is probably Tartessus in Spain. Jonah intends to go west (instead of east to Nineveh), as far away as he can.

to Tarshish: so he paid the fare thereof, and went down into it, to go with them unto Tarshish from the presence of the Lord. But the Lord sent out a great wind into the sea, and there was a mighty tempest in the sea, so that the ship was like to be broken. Then the mariners were afraid, and cried every man unto his god, and cast forth the wares that were in the ship into the sea, to lighten it of them. But Jonah was gone down into the sides of the ship; and he lay, and was fast asleep. So the shipmaster came to him, and said unto him, What meanest thou, O, sleeper? arise, call upon thy God, if so be that God will think upon us, that we perish not. And they said every one to his fellow, Come, and let us cast lots, that we may know for whose cause this evil is upon us. So they cast lots, and the lot fell upon Jonah. Then said they unto him, Tell us, we pray thee, for whose cause this evil is upon us; What is thine occupation? and whence comest thou? what is thy country? and of what people art thou? And he said unto them, I am an Hebrew; and I fear the Lord, the God of heaven, which hath made the sea and the dry land. Then were the men exceedingly afraid, and said unto him, Why hast thou done this? For the men knew that he fled from the presence of the Lord, because he had told them. Then said they unto him, What shall we do unto thee, that the sea may be calm unto us? for the sea wrought, and was tempestuous. And he said unto them, Take me up, and cast me forth into the sea; so shall the sea be calm unto you: for I know that for my sake this great tempest is upon you. Nevertheless the men rowed hard to bring it to the land; but they could not: for the sea wrought, and was tempestuous against them. Wherefore they cried unto the Lord, and said, We beseech thee, O Lord, we beseech thee, let us not perish for this man's life, and lay not upon us innocent blood: for thou, O Lord, hast done as it pleased thee. So they took up Jonah, and cast him forth into the sea: and the sea ceased from her raging. Then the men feared the Lord exceedingly, and offered a sacrifice unto the Lord, and made vows.

Now the Lord had prepared a great fish to swallow up Jonah. And Jonah was in the belly of the fish three days and three nights.

2. Then Jonah prayed unto the Lord his God out of the fish's belly, and said, I cried by reason of mine affliction unto the Lord, and he heard me; out of the belly of hell cried I, and thou heardest my voice. For thou hadst cast me into the deep, in the midst of the seas; and the floods compassed me about; all thy billows and thy waves passed over me. Then I said, I am cast out of thy sight; yet I will look again toward thy holy temple. The waters compassed me about, even to the soul: the depth closed me round about, the weeds were wrapped about my head. I went down to the bottoms of the mountains; the earth with her bars was about me for ever: yet hast thou brought up my life from corruption, O Lord my God. When my soul fainted within me I remembered the Lord: and my prayer came in unto thee, into thine holy temple. They that observe lying vanities forsake their own mercy.[3] But I will sacrifice unto thee with the voice of thanksgiving; I will pay that that I have vowed. Salvation is of the Lord. And the Lord spake unto the fish, and it vomited out Jonah upon the dry land.

3. Or those that worship false gods forfeit their claim to mercy.

3. And the word of the Lord came unto Jonah the second time, saying, Arise, go unto Nineveh, that great city, and preach unto it the preaching that I bid thee. So Jonah arose, and went unto Nineveh, according to the word of the Lord. Now Nineveh was an exceeding great city of three days' journey. And Jonah began to enter into the city a day's journey, and he cried, and said, Yet forty days, and Nineveh shall be overthrown.

So the people of Nineveh believed God, and proclaimed a fast, and put on sackcloth, from the greatest of them even to the least of them. For word came unto the king of Nineveh, and he arose from his throne, and he laid his robe from him, and covered him with sackcloth, and sat in ashes. And he caused it to be proclaimed and published through Nineveh by the decree of the king and his nobles, saying, Let neither man nor beast, herd nor flock, taste any thing: let them not feed, nor drink water: but let man and beast be covered with sackcloth, and cry mightily unto God: yea, let them turn every one from his evil way, and from the violence that is in their hands. Who can tell if God will turn and repent, and turn away from his fierce anger, that we perish not?

And God saw their works, that they turned from their evil way; and God repented of the evil, that he had said that he would do unto them; and he did it not.

4. But it displeased Jonah exceedingly, and he was very angry. And he prayed unto the Lord, and said, I pray thee, O Lord, was not this my saying, when I was yet in my country? Therefore I fled before unto Tarshish: for I knew that thou art a gracious God, and merciful, slow to anger, and of great kindness, and repentest thee of the evil.[4] Therefore now, O Lord, take, I beseech thee, my life from me; for it is better for me to die than to live. Then said the Lord, Doest thou well to be angry? So Jonah went out of the city, and sat on the east side of the city, and there made him a booth,[5] and sat under it in the shadow, till he might see what would become of the city. And the Lord God prepared a gourd,[6] and made it to come up over Jonah, that it might be a shadow over his head, to deliver him from his grief. So Jonah was exceeding glad of the gourd. But God prepared a worm when the morning rose the next day, and it smote the gourd that it withered. And it came to pass, when the sun did arise, that God prepared a vehement east wind; and the sun beat upon the head of Jonah, that he fainted, and wished in himself to die, and said, It is better for me to die than to live. And God said to Jonah, Doest thou well to be angry for the gourd? And he said, I do well to be angry, even unto death. Then said the Lord, Thou hast had pity on the gourd, for the which thou hast not laboured, neither madest it grow; which came up in a night, and perished in a night: and should not I spare Nineveh, that great city, wherein are more than sixscore thousand persons that cannot discern between their right hand and their left hand;[7] and also much cattle?

---

4. Jonah is quoting Scripture (Exodus 34.6).   5. A tent shelter.   6. Some kind of climbing plant.
7. I.e., children.

HOMER

eighth century B.C.

Greek literature begins with two masterpieces, the *Iliad* and *Odyssey*, which cannot be accurately dated (the conjectural dates range over three centuries) and which are attributed to the poet Homer, about whom nothing is known except his name. The Greeks believed that he was blind, perhaps because the bard Demodocus in the *Odyssey* was blind (see pp. 290–91), and seven different cities put forward claims to be his birthplace. They are all in what the Greeks called Ionia, the western coast of Asia Minor, which was heavily settled by Greek colonists. It does seem likely that he came from this area; the *Iliad* contains several accurate descriptions of natural features of the Ionian landscape, but his grasp of the geography of mainland, especially western, Greece is unsure. But even this is a guess, and all the other stories the Greeks told about him are obvious inventions.

The two great epics that have made his name supreme among poets may have been fixed in something like their present form before the art of writing was in general use in Greece; it is certain that they were intended not for reading but for oral recitation. The earliest stages of their composition date from around the beginnings of Greek literacy—the late eighth century B.C. The poems exhibit the unmistakable characteristics of oral composition.

The oral poet had at his disposal not reading and writing but a vast and intricate system of metrical formulas—phrases that would fit in at different places in the line—and a repertoire of standard scenes (the arming of the warrior, the battle of two champions) as well as the known outline of the story. Of course he could and did invent new phrases and scenes as he recited—but his base was the immense poetic reserve created by many generations of singers who lived before him. When he told again for his hearers the old story of Achilles and his wrath, he was recreating a traditional story that had been recited, with variations, additions, and improvements, by a long line of predecessors. The poem was not, in the modern sense, the poet's creation, still less an expression of his personality. Consequently, there is no trace of individual identity to be found in it; the poet remains as hidden behind the action and speech of his characters as if he were a dramatist.

The *Iliad* and *Odyssey* as we have them, however, are unlike most of the oral literature we know from other times and places. The poetic organization of each of these two epics, the subtle interrelationship of the parts, which creates their structural and emotional unity, suggests that they owe their present form to the shaping hand of a single poet, the architect who selected from the enormous wealth of the oral tradition and fused what he took with original material to create, perhaps with the aid of the new medium of writing, the two magnificently ordered poems known as the *Iliad* and *Odyssey*.

THE ILIAD

Of the two poems the *Iliad* is perhaps the earlier. Its subject is war; its characters are men in battle and women whose fate depends on the outcome. The war is fought by the Achaeans* against the Trojans for the recovery of Helen, the wife of the Achaean chieftain Menelaus; the combatants are heroes who in their chariots engage in individual duels before the supporting lines of infantry and archers. There is no senti-

---

*The transcription of Greek names is, unfortunately, a game with no rules. It used to be the convention that Greek names would be spelled according to the form they were given in Latin (and as they appear in our selections from Virgil and Ovid): Achaeans, Achilles. Recently, it has become fashionable to stay closer to the Greek—Akhaians, Akhilleus; this is the system followed by Robert Fitzgerald in his translation of the *Odyssey*. Robert Fagles, in our selections from the *Iliad*, has turned back to the old conventions, the Latin forms that have been standard in English verse and prose for many centuries. These are the forms used in this headnote.

mentality in Homer's descriptions of these battles. "Patroclus rising beside him stabbed his right jawbone, ramming the spearhead square between his teeth so hard he hooked him by that spearhead over the chariot-rail, hoisted, dragged the Trojan out as an angler perched on a jutting rock ledge drags some fish from the sea, some noble catch, with line and glittering bronze hook. So with the spear Patroclus gaffed him off his car, his mouth gaping round the glittering point and flipped him down facefirst, dead as he fell, his life breath blown away." This is meticulously accurate; there is no attempt to suppress the ugliness of Thestor's death. The bare, careful description creates the true nightmare quality of battle, in which men perform monstrous actions with the same matter-of-fact efficiency they display in their normal occupations, and the simile reproduces the grotesque appearance of violent death— the simple spear thrust takes away Thestor's dignity as a human being even before it takes his life. He is gaping, like a fish on the hook.

The simile does something else too. The comparison of Patroclus to an angler emphasizes another aspect of battle, its excitement. Homer's lines here combine two contrary emotions: the human revulsion from the horror of violent death and the human attraction to the excitement of violent action. This passage is typical of the poem as a whole. Everywhere in it we are conscious of these two poles, of war's ugly brutality and its "terrible beauty." The poet accepts violence as a basic aspect of human life and accepts it not without questioning it but without sentimentality; for it is equally sentimental to pretend that war is not ugly or to pretend that it does not have its beauty. After three thousand years, Homer is still one of war's greatest interpreters.

The *Iliad* describes the events of a few weeks in the ten-year siege of Troy. The particular subject of the poem, as its first line announces, is the anger of Achilles, the bravest of the Achaean chieftains encamped outside the city. Achilles is a man who comes to live by and for violence. His anger cuts him off from his commander and his fellow princes; to spite them he withdraws from the fighting. He is brought back into it at last by the death of his closest friend, Patroclus; the consequences of his wrath and withdrawal fall heavily on the Achaeans but most heavily on himself.

The great champion of the Trojans, Hector, fights bravely, but reluctantly. War, for him, is a necessary evil, and he thinks nostalgically of the peaceful past, though he has little hope of peace to come. His preeminence in peace is emphasized by the tenderness of his relations with his wife and child and also by his kindness to Helen, the cause of the war that he knows in his heart will bring his city to destruction. We see Hector, as we do not see Achilles, against the background of the patterns of civilized life—the rich city with its temples and palaces, the continuity of the family. The duel between these two men is the inevitable crisis of the poem, and just as inevitable is Hector's defeat and death.

At the climactic moment of Hector's death, as everywhere in the poem, Homer's firm control of his material preserves the balance in which our contrary emotions are held; pity for Hector does not entirely rob us of sympathy for Achilles. His brutal words to the dying Hector and the insults he inflicts on Hector's corpse are truly savage, but we are never allowed to forget that this inflexible hatred is the expression of his love for Patroclus. And the final book of the poem shows us an Achilles whose iron heart is moved at last; he is touched by the sight of Hector's father clasping in supplication the terrible hands that have killed so many of his sons. He remembers that he has a father and that he will never see him again; Achilles and Priam, the slayer and the father of the slain, weep together. Achilles gives Hector's body to Priam for honorable burial. His anger has run its full course and been appeased. It has brought death, first to the Achaeans and then to the Trojans, to Patroclus and to Hector, and so to Achilles himself, for his death is fated to come "soon after Hector's."

This tragic action is the center of the poem, but it is surrounded by scenes that remind us that the organized destruction of war, though an integral part of human life, is still only a part of it. The yearning for peace and its creative possibilities is never far below the surface. This is most poignantly expressed by the scenes that take place in Troy, especially the farewell between Hector and Andromache, but it is made clear that the Achaeans too are conscious of what they have sacrificed. Early in the poem, when Agamemnon, the Achaean commander, tests the morale of his troops by suggesting that the war be abandoned, they rush for the ships so eagerly and with such heartfelt relief that their commanders are hard put to stop them. These two poles of the human condition—war and peace, with their corresponding aspects of human nature, the destructive and the creative—are implicit in every situation and statement of the poem, and they are put before us, in symbolic form, in the shield that the god Hephaestus makes for Achilles, with its scenes of human life in both peace and war. Whether these two sides of life can ever be integrated, or even reconciled, is a question that the *Iliad* raises but cannot answer.

THE ODYSSEY

The other Homeric epic, the *Odyssey*, is concerned with the peace that followed the war and in particular with the return of the heroes who survived. Its subject is the long, drawn-out return of one of the heroes, Odysseus of Ithaca, who was destined to spend ten years wandering in unknown seas before he returned to his rocky kingdom. When Odysseus's wanderings began, Achilles had already received, at the hands of Apollo, the death that he had chosen. Odysseus struggles for life, and his outstanding quality is a probing and versatile intelligence that, combined with long experience, keeps him safe and alive through the trials and dangers of twenty years of war and seafaring. To stay alive he has to do things that Achilles would never have done and use an ingenuity and experience that Achilles did not possess, but his life is just as much a struggle.

Although Odysseus has become for us the archetypal adventurer, the *Odyssey* gives us a hero whose one goal is to get home. He struggles not simply for his own and his shipmates' personal survival but also to preserve and complete the heroic reputation that he won in war at Troy. It may seem ironic that Odysseus succeeds by concealing his name, as when he tricks the Cyclops by presenting himself as "Nobody," or when, at home on Ithaca, he tricks his wife's suitors by disguising himself as a beggar. But Odysseus's shiftiness, his talent for disguise, deception, and plain lying, is part of his versatility. It complements his strength and courage in battle—qualities he demonstrated at Troy as he will do again when he fights the suitors in his own hall. It makes this complex hero dangerous to his enemies, and sometimes to his friends, as the Phaeacians discover when Poseidon punishes them for helping him.

The adventures on the voyage home test these mental qualities, as well as Odysseus's physical endurance, by tempting him to lapse from the struggle homeward. The Lotos flower offers forgetfulness of home and family. Circe gives him a life of ease and self-indulgence on an enchanted island. In Phaeacia, Odysseus is offered the love of a young princess and her hand in marriage. The Sirens tempt him to live in the memory of the glorious past. Calypso, the goddess with whom he spends seven years, offers him the greatest temptation of all: immortality. In refusing, Odysseus chooses the human condition, with all its struggle, its disappointments, and its inevitable end. And the end, death, is ever-present. But he hangs on tenaciously and, in the midst of his ordeals, he is sent living to the world of the dead to see for himself what death means. Dark and comfortless, Homer's land of the dead is the most frightening picture of the afterlife in European literature. Odysseus talks to the dead, and when he consoles the shade of Achilles with talk of everlasting glory Achilles replies that it is better to be the most insignificant person on Earth than lord of the dead. Here the heroes of the two great epics confront one another over the chasm of death. Through them, the *Odyssey* defines its values by contrast with those of the *Iliad*. Against the dark background of Achilles' regret for life Odysseus's dedication to life—his acceptance of its limitations and his ability to seize its possibilities—shines out. His death, Teiresias assures him in this same episode, will come late and gently. Odysseus gets both long life and glory; Achilles could have only either one.

The *Odyssey* celebrates return to ordinary life and makes it seem a worthy prize after excitement, toil, and danger. The adventures occupy only four of twenty-four books (or eight if we include Calypso and the Phaeacians). For the entire second half of the poem, Odysseus is back on Ithaca, winning his way, by deceit that only paves the way for force, from the swineherd Eumaios's hut to the center of his own house. There, and in books 1–4, we see the social disorder on Ithaca that Odysseus's return is to set right. We also see Telemachus, his son, emerging from adolescence and impatient with all that keeps him from assuming a man's role (his mother as well as her suitors). In his aspirations a foil to Odysseus's mature wisdom, he is his father's potential rival, though in the end his willing subordinate. And we see Penelope's dealings with her son, with her suitors, and with the beggar who is really her husband in disguise. Penelope is a challenging figure, because the narrative does not give us full access to her thoughts and motives. But she seems, with a cunning that matches Odysseus's, to keep in balance two contradictory requirements of her situation. First, she has a duty to herself. If Odysseus, absent twenty years now, is lost for good, then she ought to remarry instead of devoting herself to a house without a head (and in Homeric and later Greek culture, a woman as head of a household was unthinkable). More immediately, she seems to take a natural pleasure in being wooed. On the other hand, she has a duty to her former marriage. If she remarries and Odysseus then returns, she will seem to have betrayed him and, in his and society's eyes, she will be classed with those other adulterers Helen and Clytemnestra. In its ambivalence, Penelope's trick of the web (she promised the suitors to choose one of them when she had finished a shroud for Odysseus's father, Laertes, and for three years she unwove each night what she had woven by day) perfectly encapsulates the way she is forced to play loyal wife and available bride at the same time; it is both a delaying tactic and a way of stringing the suitors along. Odysseus evidently interprets the trick simply as an expression of Penelope's faithfulness to him, and so have readers over the ages. But that only shows how Penelope's interests are folded into his at the end, how his restoration to home and authority retrospectively arranges potentially disorderly elements within a patriarchal order. That is not to say that Penelope lacks autonomy or initiative, at least in the shorter term. To a large extent she controls the timing and means of Odysseus's final homecoming (and therefore she controls key stages in the plot of the poem), not only by her famous trick of the marriage bed in book 23 but also by deciding in book 19 to set the contest of the bow, which will ultimately get a weapon into the beggar's hands (book 21). Why she does so, after the beggar has assured her that Odysseus is about to return, is one of the poem's mysteries. Has she recognized this beggar as her husband, consciously or not, so that she helps him against the suitors? Does she neither recognize nor believe the beggar, so that she acts in despair? Or is she again calculating probabilities to her best advantage?

The period in which the *Iliad* and the *Odyssey* probably took shape, 750–700 B.C. or a little after, saw enormous cultural, political, and social developments in Greece, especially the formation, in many areas, of the *polis*, or "city-state" (see pp. 4–5 above). As often happens, these changes occurred amid sharp conflicts and debates, in which the Homeric epics, publicly performed as they were, must have taken part. Along with the issue of peace and war, for instance, a central conflict of the *Iliad* concerns the nature of political authority. Which has the stronger claim, acknowledged position (Agamemnon) or merit (Achilles)? It is difficult to tell which side wins in the end, if either does, but the poem examines the ramifications of this debate, even while showing, paradoxically, the Greeks maintaining enough unity to destroy a tightly knit and orderly city. The problems of violence and order in this poem are as much political as individual. They involve profound questions about the nature of a political community.

The *Odyssey* offers a more positive meditation on the nature of civilization and of the structures of daily political life as the Greeks experienced it. It does so by showing what a community has to lose by the absence of those structures and to gain by their affirmation, as we see in the contrast between the disorder created by the suitors and Odysseus's restoration of hierarchical and patriarchal order in house and polity. In addition, Odysseus's adventures explore alternatives to "ordinary" (that is, Greek) civilization. Odysseus experiences nature itself as the threatening antithesis to human culture, and he encounters other cultural forms that seem defective or excessive when measured against Ithaca. The richest contrast is provided by the Cyclopes, who lack many of the features of the evolving Greek civilization: houses (they live in caves), agriculture (they are herders), ships for trade and colonization, political integration (their highest political unit is the family), and the key institution of hospitality. (This episode is complex, however, since the Cyclopes enjoy a golden-age existence on which Odysseus intrudes, and Polyphemus has the last word, his curse on Odysseus.) The Laestrygonians are organized as a community and not just by families—they have a ruler and an assembly place—but they share the Cyclopes' unfortunate habit of eating guests. Aeolus, like the Phaeacians, offers Odysseus flawless hospitality, but he lives isolated with his family and marries his daughters to his sons (in contrast to the Greek practice of knitting households together by exchanging women in marriage). Calypso lives in a cave, Circe in a house (she weaves like Penelope), but both live alone. Both are heads of households without husbands, and this, besides the fact that they are sexually threatening to males, makes them "strong" female figures intended to show the need for women's subordination. The Phaeacians, on the other hand, represent an idealized form of "normal" culture but are isolated from other communities and excessively civilized, with no opportunity for heroic achievement. When Odysseus finally is restored to Ithaca, he, and his Greek audience, can appreciate the familiar for having explored alternatives to it in these and many other ways. This self-fashioning by reference to the foreign, which was to have a long history among the Greeks, must have been especially important during this formative period of their culture.

But the *Odyssey* is a much more complex poem than this account suggests, its resolution of issues anything but tidy. One enormous contradiction underlies the final books: Odysseus restores order by killing men from his own community, within his house, and he is prepared to prolong internal warfare by killing the suitors' relatives in the final book. In fact, this struggle recapitulates the Trojan War and resembles the dispute between Achilles and Agamemnon in book 1 of the *Iliad*. In all three cases, men compete for honor over a woman. What is more, Odysseus kills the suitors within his own house, which should be exempt from competition and conflict, as the *Odyssey*'s many scenes of feasting in this same hall show. The *Odyssey* is no more successful than the *Iliad*, then, in resolving the problem of violence. Both poems leave us with questions. How can human aggression be controlled, if not eliminated? Can violence within the community be channeled into safe, perhaps even socially creative, forms? Can it be successfully controlled by being turned outward, against other communities? If so, does that justify the human suffering and waste that external wars cause? And what about the more refined forms of violence at the heart of social hierarchies that create asymmetries of gender and class? Such are the issues raised by the epics amid the formation of the polis, which was to lead, through a long process, to the modern state. Thousands of years later, we cannot claim to have solved them.

A sensitive exploration of Homer's vision of human life and the nature of the gods is Jasper Griffin, *Homer on Life and Death* (1980). Mark W. Edwards, *Homer: Poet of the Iliad* (1987), discusses the oral style and gives a detailed commentary on selected books of the poem, including all of those printed here. Martin Mueller, *The Iliad* (1984), is a highly readable discussion of almost every aspect of the poem, and Seth Schein, *The Mortal Hero: An Introduction to Homer's Iliad* (1987), is an eloquent reading. The psychiatrist Jonathan Shay, in *Achilles in Vietnam: Combat Trauma and the Undoing of Character* (1994), gives a highly interesting discussion of violence and its effects in Homer and in modern warfare based on his work with Vietnam veterans. Basic introductions to the *Odyssey* are J. Griffin, *Homer: The Odyssey* (1987), and W. G. Thalmann, *The Odyssey: An Epic of Return* (1992). An excellent companion to the poem is Ralph Hexter, *A Guide to the Odyssey: A Companion to the Translation by Robert Fitzgerald* (1993). Essays covering various aspects of the poem may be found in Charles Segal, *Singers, Heroes, and Gods in the Odyssey* (1994); Seth Schein, *Reading the Odyssey: Selected Interpretive Essays* (1996); and (on women) Beth Cohen, *The Distaff Side: Representing the Female in Homer's Odyssey* (1995). An excellent discussion of gender in the poem is Nancy Felson-Rubin, *Regarding Penelope: From Character to Poetics* (1994), with further bibliography.

PRONOUNCING GLOSSARY

The following list uses common English syllables and stress accents to provide rough equivalents of selected words whose pronunciation may be unfamiliar to the general reader.

Achaeans: *a-kee'-unz*

Achelous: *a-ke-loh'-us*

Achilles: *a-kil'-eez*

Aeantes: *ee-an'-teez*

Aepea: *ee-pee'-a*

Alkinoös: *al-kin-oh'-uhs*

Andromache: *an-dro'-ma-kee*

Atreus: *ay'-tree-uhs*

Atrides: *a-trai'-deez*

Caeneus: *seen'-yoos*

Chiron: *kai'-ron*

Chryseis: *krai-see'-is*

Chryses: *krai'-seez*

Circe: *ser'-see*

Danaans: *da'-nay-unz*

Deiphobus: *dee-i'-foh-bus*

Demodokos: *dee-mo'-do-kuhs*

Eetion: *ee-e'-tee-on*

Eurystheus: *yoo-ris'-thyoos*

Glaucus: *Glow'-kus*

Helios/Hêlios: *hee'-lee-os*

Hephaistos: *he-fess'-tus*

Hermes/Hermês: *her'-meez*

Idaeus: *ai-dee'-us*

Idomeneus: *ai-do'-men-yoos*

Laertes/Laërtês: *lay-er'-teez*

Laodice: *lay-o'-di-see*

Laothoë: *lay-o'-thoh-ee*

Menelaus/Meneláos: *me-ne-lay'-us*

Myrmidons: *mer'-mi-donz*

Mysians: *mee'-shunz*

Nausicaa: *naw-si'-kay-ah*

Odysseus: *oh-dis'-yoos*

Oeneus: *een'-yoos*

Orestes: *o-res'-teez*

Panthous: *pan'-tho-us*

Patroclus: *pa-troh'-klus*

Peleus: *peel'-yoos*

Phaeacians: *fee-ay'-shunz*

Pherae: *fee'-ree*

Phoebus: *fee'-bus*

Phthia: *fthai'-uh*

Polyphêmus: *po-li-fee'-mus*

Pirithous: *pai-ri'-tho-us*

Priam: *prai'-am*

Sarpedon: *sar-pee'-don*

Scaean: *see'-an*

Scylla/Skylla: *si'-lah/skil'-ah*

Scyros: *skai'-ros*

Smintheus: *smin'-thyoos*

Telêmakhos: *te-le'-ma-kos*

Theseus: *thee'-see-uhs*

Xanthus: *zan'-thus*

The Iliad[1]

BOOK I

[The Rage of Achilles]

Rage—Goddess,[2] sing the rage of Peleus' son Achilles,
murderous, doomed, that cost the Achaeans[3] countless losses,
hurling down to the House of Death so many sturdy souls,
great fighters' souls, but made their bodies carrion,
feasts for the dogs and birds,   5
and the will of Zeus was moving toward its end.
Begin, Muse, when the two first broke and clashed,
Agamemnon lord of men and brilliant Achilles.

    What god drove them to fight with such a fury?
Apollo the son of Zeus and Leto. Incensed at the king   10
he swept a fatal plague through the army—men were dying
and all because Agamemnon spurned Apollo's priest.
Yes, Chryses[4] approached the Achaeans' fast ships
to win his daughter back, bringing a priceless ransom
and bearing high in hand, wound on a golden staff,   15
the wreaths of the god, the distant deadly Archer.
He begged the whole Achaean army but most of all
the two supreme commanders, Atreus' two sons,
"Agamemnon, Menelaus—all Argives geared for war!
May the gods who hold the halls of Olympus give you   20
Priam's[5] city to plunder, then safe passage home.
Just set my daughter free, my dear one . . . here,
accept these gifts, this ransom. Honor the god
who strikes from worlds away—the son of Zeus, Apollo!"

    And all ranks of Achaeans cried out their assent: 25
"Respect the priest, accept the shining ransom!"
But it brought no joy to the heart of Agamemnon.
The king dismissed the priest with a brutal order
ringing in his ears: "Never again, old man,
let me catch sight of you by the hollow ships!   30
Not loitering now, not slinking back tomorrow.
The staff and the wreaths of god will never save you then.
The girl—I won't give up the girl. Long before that,
old age will overtake her in *my* house, in Argos,
far from her fatherland, slaving back and forth   35
at the loom, forced to share my bed!
               Now go,
don't tempt my wrath—and you may depart alive."

    The old man was terrified. He obeyed the order,
trailing away in silence down the shore

---

1. Translated by Robert Fagles.   2. The Muse, inspiration for epic poetry.   3. The Greeks. Homer also calls them Danaans and Argives.   4. His daughter is called Chryseis, and the place where he lives, Chryse.   5. King of Troy. Olympus is the mountain in northern Greece that was supposed to be the home of the gods.

where the battle lines of breakers crash and drag.   40
And moving off to a safe distance, over and over
the old priest prayed to the son of sleek-haired Leto,
lord Apollo, "Hear me, Apollo! God of the silver bow
who strides the walls of Chryse and Cilla sacrosanct—
lord in power of Tenedos—Smintheus,[6] god of the plague!   45
If I ever roofed a shrine to please your heart,
ever burned the long rich bones of bulls and goats
on your holy altar, now, now bring my prayer to pass.
Pay the Danaans back—your arrows for my tears!"

His prayer went up and Phoebus Apollo heard him.   50
Down he strode from Olympus' peaks, storming at heart
with his bow and hooded quiver slung across his shoulders.
The arrows clanged at his back as the god quaked with rage,
the god himself on the march and down he came like night.
Over against the ships he dropped to a knee, let fly a shaft   55
and a terrifying clash rang out from the great silver bow.
First he went for the mules and circling dogs but then,
launching a piercing shaft at the men themselves,
he cut them down in droves—
and the corpse-fires burned on, night and day, no end in sight.   60

Nine days the arrows of god swept through the army.
On the tenth Achilles called all ranks to muster—
the impulse seized him, sent by white-armed Hera[7]
grieving to see Achaean fighters drop and die.
Once they'd gathered, crowding the meeting grounds,   65
the swift runner Achilles rose and spoke among them:
"Son of Atreus, now we are beaten back, I fear,
the long campaign is lost. So home we sail . . .
if we can escape our death—if war and plague
are joining forces now to crush the Argives.   70
But wait: let us question a holy man,
a prophet, even a man skilled with dreams—
dreams as well can come our way from Zeus—
come, someone to tell us why Apollo rages so,
whether he blames us for a vow we failed, or sacrifice.   75
If only the god would share the smoky savor of lambs
and full-grown goats, Apollo might be willing, still,
somehow, to save us from this plague."
                                So he proposed
and down he sat again as Calchas rose among them,
Thestor's son, the clearest by far of all the seers   80
who scan the flight of birds. He knew all things that are,
all things that are past and all that are to come,
the seer who had led the Argive ships to Troy
with the second sight that god Apollo gave him.
For the armies' good the seer began to speak: 85
"Achilles, dear to Zeus . . .

6. A cult name of Apollo, probably a reference to his role as the destroyer of field mice. The Greek *smin-thos* means "mouse." Chryse and Chilla are cities near Troy. Tenedos is an island off the Tro-jan coast.   7. Sister and wife of Zeus (the father of the gods); she was hostile to the Trojans.

you order me to explain Apollo's anger,
the distant deadly Archer? I will tell it all.
But strike a pact with me, swear you will defend me
with all your heart, with words and strength of hand. 90
For there is a man I will enrage—I see it now—
a powerful man who lords it over all the Argives,
one the Achaeans must obey . . . A mighty king,
raging against an inferior, is too strong.
Even if he can swallow down his wrath today, 95
still he will nurse the burning in his chest
until, sooner or later, he sends it bursting forth.
Consider it closely, Achilles. Will you save me?"

    And the matchless runner reassured him: "Courage!
Out with it now, Calchas. Reveal the will of god, 100
whatever you may know. And I swear by Apollo
dear to Zeus, the power you pray to, Calchas,
when you reveal god's will to the Argives—no one,
not while I am alive and see the light on earth, no one
will lay his heavy hands on you by the hollow ships. 105
None among all the armies. Not even if you mean
Agamemnon here who now claims to be, by far,
the best of the Achaeans."
                          The seer took heart
and this time he spoke out, bravely: "Beware—
he casts no blame for a vow we failed, a sacrifice. 110
The god's enraged because Agamemnon spurned his priest,
he refused to free his daughter, he refused the ransom.
That's why the Archer sends us pains and he will send us more
and never drive this shameful destruction from the Argives,
not till we give back the girl with sparkling eyes 115
to her loving father—no price, no ransom paid—
and carry a sacred hundred bulls to Chryse town.
Then we can calm the god, and only then appease him."

    So he declared and sat down. But among them rose
the fighting son of Atreus, lord of the far-flung kingdoms, 120
Agamemnon—furious, his dark heart filled to the brim,
blazing with anger now, his eyes like searing fire.
With a sudden, killing look he wheeled on Calchas first:
"Seer of misery! Never a word that works to my advantage!
Always misery warms your heart, your prophecies— 125
never a word of profit said or brought to pass.
Now, again, you divine god's will for the armies,
bruit it out, as fact, why the deadly Archer
multiplies our pains: because I, I refused
that glittering price for the young girl Chryseis. 130
Indeed, I prefer *her* by far, the girl herself,
I want her mine in my own house! I rank her higher
than Clytemnestra, my wedded wife—she's nothing less
in build or breeding, in mind or works of hand.
But I am willing to give her back, even so, 135

if that is best for all. What I really want
is to keep my people safe, not see them dying.
But fetch me another prize, and straight off too,
else I alone of the Argives go without my honor.
That would be a disgrace. You are all witness,   140
look—*my* prize is snatched away!"

                       But the swift runner
Achilles answered him at once, "Just how, Agamemnon,
great field marshal . . . most grasping man alive,
how can the generous Argives give you prizes now?
I know of no troves of treasure, piled, lying idle,   145
anywhere. Whatever we dragged from towns we plundered,
all's been portioned out. But collect it, call it back
from the rank and file? *That* would be the disgrace.
So return the girl to the god, at least for now.
We Achaeans will pay you back, three, four times over,   150
if Zeus will grant us the gift, somehow, someday,
to raze Troy's massive ramparts to the ground."

    But King Agamemnon countered, "Not so quickly,
brave as you are, godlike Achilles—trying to cheat *me*.
Oh no, you won't get past me, take me in that way!   155
What do you want? To cling to your own prize
while I sit calmly by—empty-handed here?
Is that why you order me to give her back?
No—if our generous Argives *will* give me a prize,
a match for my desires, equal to what I've lost,   160
well and good. But if they give me nothing
I will take a prize myself—your own, or Ajax'
or Odysseus'[8] prize—I'll commandeer her myself
and let that man I go to visit choke with rage!
Enough. We'll deal with all this later, in due time.   165
Now come, we haul a black ship down to the bright sea,
gather a decent number of oarsmen along her locks
and put aboard a sacrifice, and Chryseis herself,
in all her beauty . . . we embark her too.
Let one of the leading captains take command.   170
Ajax, Idomeneus, trusty Odysseus or you, Achilles,
you—the most violent man alive—so you can perform
the rites for us and calm the god yourself."

                      A dark glance
and the headstrong runner answered him in kind: "Shameless—
armored in shamelessness—always shrewd with greed!   175
How could any Argive soldier obey your orders,
freely and gladly do your sailing for you
or fight your enemies, full force? Not I, no.
It wasn't Trojan spearmen who brought me here to fight.
The Trojans never did *me* damage, not in the least,   180
they never stole my cattle or my horses, never

8. The most subtle and crafty of the Greeks. Ajax was the bravest of the Greeks after Achilles.

in Phthia[9] where the rich soil breeds strong men
did they lay waste my crops. How could they?
Look at the endless miles that lie between us . . .
shadowy mountain ranges, seas that surge and thunder.   185
No, you colossal, shameless—we all followed you,
to please you, to fight for you, to win your honor
back from the Trojans—Menelaus[1] and you, you dog-face!
What do *you* care? Nothing. You don't look right or left.
And now you threaten to strip me of my prize in person—   190
the one I fought for long and hard, and sons of Achaea
handed her to me.

            My honors never equal yours,
whenever we sack some wealthy Trojan stronghold—
my arms bear the brunt of the raw, savage fighting,
true, but when it comes to dividing up the plunder   195
the lion's share is yours, and back I go to my ships,
clutching some scrap, some pittance that I love,
when I have fought to exhaustion.

                      No more now—
back I go to Phthia. Better that way by far,
to journey home in the beaked ships of war.   200
I have no mind to linger here disgraced,
brimming your cup and piling up your plunder."

   But the lord of men Agamemnon shot back,
"*Desert,* by all means—if the spirit drives you home!
I will never beg you to stay, not on *my* account.   205
Never—others will take my side and do me honor,
Zeus above all, whose wisdom rules the world.
You—I hate you most of all the warlords
loved by the gods. Always dear to your heart,
strife, yes, and battles, the bloody grind of war.   210
What if you are a great soldier? That's just a gift of god.
Go home with your ships and comrades, lord it over your Myrmidons![2]
You *are* nothing to me—you and your overweening anger!
But let this be my warning on your way:
since Apollo insists on taking my Chryseis,   215
I'll send her back in my own ships with *my* crew.
But I, I will be there in person at your tents
to take Briseis in all her beauty, your own prize—
so you can learn just how much greater I am than you
and the next man up may shrink from matching words with me,   220
from hoping to rival Agamemnon strength for strength!"

   He broke off and anguish gripped Achilles.
The heart in his rugged chest was pounding, torn . . .
Should he draw the long sharp sword slung at his hip,
thrust through the ranks and kill Agamemnon now?—   225

---

9. Achilles' home in northern Greece.   1. The aim of the expedition was to recapture Menelaus's wife,
Helen, who had run off to Troy with Priam's son Paris.   2. The name of Achilles' people.

or check his rage and beat his fury down?
As his racing spirit veered back and forth,
just as he drew his huge blade from its sheath,
down from the vaulting heavens swept Athena,[3]
the white-armed goddess Hera sped her down: 230
Hera loved both men and cared for both alike.
Rearing behind him Pallas seized his fiery hair—
only Achilles saw her, none of the other fighters—
struck with wonder he spun around, he knew her at once,
Pallas Athena! the terrible blazing of those eyes,   235
and his winged words went flying: "Why, why now?
Child of Zeus with the shield of thunder,[4] why come now?
To witness the outrage Agamemnon just committed?
I tell you this, and so help me it's the truth—
he'll soon pay for his arrogance with his life!"   240

   Her gray eyes clear, the goddess Athena answered,
"Down from the skies I come to check your rage
if only you will yield.
The white-armed goddess Hera sped me down:
she loves you both, she cares for you both alike.   245
Stop this fighting, now. Don't lay hand to sword.
Lash him with threats of the price that he will face.
And I tell you this—and I *know* it is the truth—
one day glittering gifts will lie before you,
three times over to pay for all his outrage.   250
Hold back now. Obey us both."
             So she urged
and the swift runner complied at once: "I must—
when the two of you hand down commands, Goddess,
a man submits though his heart breaks with fury.
Better for him by far. If a man obeys the gods   255
they're quick to hear his prayers."
                 And with that
Achilles stayed his burly hand on the silver hilt
and slid the huge blade back in its sheath.
He would not fight the orders of Athena.
Soaring home to Olympus, she rejoined the gods   260
aloft in the halls of Zeus whose shield is thunder.

   But Achilles rounded on Agamemnon once again,
lashing out at him, not relaxing his anger for a moment:
"Staggering drunk, with your dog's eyes, your fawn's heart!
Never once did you arm with the troops and go to battle   265
or risk an ambush packed with Achaea's picked men—
you lack the courage, you can see death coming.
Safer by far, you find, to foray all through camp,

---

3. A goddess, daughter of Zeus, and a patron of human ingenuity and resourcefulness, whether exemplified by handicrafts (such as spinning) or by skill in human relations (such as her favorite among the Greeks, Odysseus, possessed). She supported the Greek side in the war.   **4.** A terrible shield with which Zeus (or any other god to whom it was entrusted) stirred up storms or threw panic into human beings.

commandeering the prize of any man who speaks against you.
King who devours his people! Worthless husks, the men you rule— 270
if not, Atrides,[5] this outrage would have been your last.
I tell you this, and I swear a mighty oath upon it . . .
by this, this scepter, look,
that never again will put forth crown and branches,
now it's left its stump on the mountain ridge forever, 275
nor will it sprout new green again, now the brazen ax
has stripped its bark and leaves, and now the sons of Achaea
pass it back and forth as they hand their judgments down,
upholding the honored customs whenever Zeus commands—
This scepter will be the mighty force behind my oath: 280
someday, I swear, a yearning for Achilles will strike
Achaea's sons and all your armies! But then, Atrides,
harrowed as you will be, *nothing* you do can save you—
not when your hordes of fighters drop and die,
cut down by the hands of man-killing Hector![6] Then— 285
then you will tear your heart out, desperate, raging
that you disgraced the best of the Achaeans!"

                                           Down on the ground
he dashed the scepter studded bright with golden nails,
then took his seat again. The son of Atreus smoldered,
glaring across at him, but Nestor rose between them, 290
the man of winning words, the clear speaker of Pylos[7] . . .
Sweeter than honey from his tongue the voice flowed on and on.
Two generations of mortal men he had seen go down by now,
those who were born and bred with him in the old days,
in Pylos' holy realm, and now he ruled the third. 295
He pleaded with both kings, with clear good will,
"No more—or enormous sorrow comes to all Achaea!
How they would exult, Priam and Priam's sons
and all the Trojans. Oh they'd leap for joy
to hear the two of you battling on this way, 300
you who excel us all, first in Achaean councils,
first in the ways of war.

                        Stop. Please.
Listen to Nestor. You are both younger than I,
and in my time I struck up with better men than you,
even you, but never once did they make light of me. 305
I've never seen such men, I never will again . . .
men like Pirithous, Dryas, that fine captain,
Caeneus and Exadius, and Polyphemus, royal prince,
and Theseus,[8] Aegeus' boy, a match for the immortals.
They were the strongest mortals ever bred on earth, 310
the strongest, and they fought against the strongest too,
shaggy Centaurs, wild brutes of the mountains—
they hacked them down, terrible, deadly work.
And I was in their ranks, fresh out of Pylos,
far away from home—they enlisted me themselves 315

5. Son of Atreus, i.e., Agamemnon.   6. Son of Priam; the foremost warrior of the Trojans.   7. On the
western shore of the Peloponnese.   8. Names of heroes of an older generation.

and I fought on my own, a free lance, single-handed.
And none of the men who walk the earth these days
could battle with those fighters, none, but they,
they took to heart my counsels, marked my words.
So now you listen too. Yielding is far better . . .   320
Don't seize the girl, Agamemnon, powerful as you are—
leave her, just as the sons of Achaea gave her,
his prize from the very first.
And you, Achilles, never hope to fight it out
with your king, pitting force against his force: 325
no one can match the honors dealt a king, you know,
a sceptered king to whom great Zeus gives glory.
Strong as you are—a goddess was your mother[9]—
he has more power because he rules more men.
Atrides, end your anger—look, it's Nestor!   330
I beg you, cool your fury against Achilles.
Here the man stands over all Achaea's armies,
our rugged bulwark braced for shocks of war."

But King Agamemnon answered him in haste,
"True, old man—all you say is fit and proper—   335
but this soldier wants to tower over the armies,
he wants to rule over all, to lord it over all,
give out orders to every man in sight. Well,
there's one, I trust, who will never yield to him!
What if the everlasting gods have made a spearman of him?   340
Have they entitled him to hurl abuse at *me*?"

"Yes!"—blazing Achilles broke in quickly—
"What a worthless, burnt-out coward I'd be called
if I would submit to you and all your orders,
whatever you blurt out. Fling them at others,   345
don't give me commands!
Never again, *I* trust, will Achilles yield to *you*.
And I tell you this—take it to heart, I warn you—
my hands will never do battle for that girl,
neither with you, King, nor any man alive.   350
You Achaeans gave her, now you've snatched her back.
But all the rest I possess beside my fast black ship—
not one bit of it can you seize against my will, Atrides.
Come, try it! So the men can see, that instant,
your black blood gush and spurt around my spear!"   355

Once the two had fought it out with words,
battling face-to-face, both sprang to their feet
and broke up the muster beside the Argive squadrons.
Achilles strode off to his trim ships and shelters,
back to his friend Patroclus and their comrades.   360
Agamemnon had a vessel hauled down to the sea,

9. Thetis, a sea nymph, who was married to the mortal Peleus (Achilles' father); she later left humankind
and went to live with her father, Nereus, in the depths of the Aegean Sea.

he picked out twenty oarsmen to man her locks,
put aboard the cattle for sacrifice to the god
and led Chryseis in all her beauty amidships.
Versatile Odysseus took the helm as captain.
                                        All embarked,   365
the party launched out on the sea's foaming lanes
while the son of Atreus told his troops to wash,
to purify themselves from the filth of plague.
They scoured it off, threw scourings in the surf
and sacrificed to Apollo full-grown bulls and goats   370
along the beaten shore of the fallow barren sea
and savory smoke went swirling up the skies.

    So the men were engaged throughout the camp.
But King Agamemnon would not stop the quarrel,
the first threat he hurled against Achilles.   375
He called Talthybius and Eurybates briskly,
his two heralds, ready, willing aides:
"Go to Achilles' lodge. Take Briseis at once,
his beauty Briseis by the hand and bring her here.
But if he will not surrender her, I'll go myself,   380
I'll seize her myself, with an army at my back—
and all the worse for him!'
                                    He sent them off
with the strict order ringing in their ears.
Against their will the two men made their way
along the breaking surf of the barren salt sea   385
and reached the Myrmidon shelters and their ships.
They found him beside his lodge and black hull,
seated grimly—and Achilles took no joy
when he saw the two approaching.
They were afraid, they held the king in awe   390
and stood there, silent. Not a word to Achilles,
not a question. But he sensed it all in his heart,
their fear, their charge, and broke the silence for them:
"Welcome, couriers! Good heralds of Zeus and men,
here, come closer. You have done nothing to me.   395
You are not to blame. No one but Agamemnon—
he is the one who sent you for Briseis.
Go, Patroclus, Prince, bring out the girl
and hand her to them so they can take her back.
But let them both bear witness to my loss . . .   400
in the face of blissful gods and mortal men,
in the face of that unbending, ruthless king—
if the day should come when the armies need *me*
to save their ranks from ignominious, stark defeat.
The man is raving—with all the murderous fury in his heart. 405
He lacks the sense to see a day behind, a day ahead,
and safeguard the Achaeans battling by the ships."

    Patroclus obeyed his great friend's command.
He led Briseis in all her beauty from the lodge

and handed her over to the men to take away.   410
And the two walked back along the Argive ships
while she trailed on behind, reluctant, every step.
But Achilles wept, and slipping away from his companions,
far apart, sat down on the beach of the heaving gray sea
and scanned the endless ocean. Reaching out his arms,   415
again and again he prayed to his dear mother: "Mother!
You gave me life, short as that life will be,
so at least Olympian Zeus, thundering up on high,
should give me honor—but now he gives me nothing.
Atreus' son Agamemnon, for all his far-flung kingdoms—   420
the man disgraces me, seizes and keeps my prize,
he tears her away himself!"

                    So he wept and prayed
and his noble mother heard him, seated near her father,
the Old Man of the Sea in the salt green depths.
Suddenly up she rose from the churning surf   425
like mist and settling down beside him as he wept,
stroked Achilles gently, whispering his name, "My child—
why in tears? What sorrow has touched your heart?
Tell me, please. Don't harbor it deep inside you.
We must share it all."

                    And now from his depths   430
the proud runner groaned:"You know, you know,
why labor through it all? You know it all so well . . .
We raided Thebe once, Eetion's[1] sacred citadel,
we ravaged the place, hauled all the plunder here
and the armies passed it round, share and share alike,   435
and they chose the beauty Chryseis for Agamemnon.
But soon her father, the holy priest of Apollo
the distant deadly Archer, Chryses approached
the fast trim ships of the Argives armed in bronze
to win his daughter back, bringing a priceless ransom   440
and bearing high in hand, wound on a golden staff,
the wreaths of the god who strikes from worlds away.
He begged the whole Achaean army but most of all
the two supreme commanders, Atreus' two sons,
and all ranks of Achaeans cried out their assent,   445
'Respect the priest, accept the shining ransom!'
But it brought no joy to the heart of Agamemnon,
our high and mighty king dismissed the priest
with a brutal order ringing in his ears.
And shattered with anger, the old man withdrew   450
but Apollo heard his prayer—he loved him, deeply—
he loosed his shaft at the Argives, withering plague,
and now the troops began to drop and die in droves,
the arrows of god went showering left and right,
whipping through the Achaeans' vast encampment.   455
But the old seer who knew the cause full well
revealed the will of the archer god Apollo.

---

1. King of the Cilicians and father of Hector's wife, Andromache. Thebe was the Cilician capital city.

And I was the first, mother, I urged them all,
'Appease the god at once!' That's when the fury
gripped the son of Atreus. Agamemnon leapt to his feet   460
and hurled his threat—his threat's been driven home.
One girl, Chryseis, the fiery-eyed Achaeans
ferry out in a fast trim ship to Chryse Island,
laden with presents for the god.[2] The other girl,
just now the heralds came and led her away from camp,   465
Briseus' daughter, the prize the armies gave me.
But you, mother, if you have any power at all,
protect your son! Go to Olympus, plead with Zeus,
if you ever warmed his heart with a word or any action . . .

    Time and again I heard your claims in father's halls,   470
boasting how you and you alone of all the immortals
rescued Zeus,[3] the lord of the dark storm cloud,
from ignominious, stark defeat.
That day the Olympians tried to chain him down,
Hera, Poseidon[4] lord of the sea, and Pallas Athena—   475
you rushed to Zeus, dear Goddess, broke those chains,
quickly ordered the hundred-hander to steep Olympus,
that monster whom the immortals call Briareus[5]
but every mortal calls the Sea-god's son, Aegaeon,
though he's stronger than his father. Down he sat,   480
flanking Cronus' son, gargantuan in the glory of it all,
and the blessed gods were struck with terror then,
they stopped shackling Zeus.
                  Remind him of that,
now, go and sit beside him, grasp his knees . . .
persuade him, somehow, to help the Trojan cause,   485
to pin the Achaeans back against their ships,
trap them round the bay and mow them down.
So all can reap the benefits of their king—
so even mighty Atrides can see how mad he was
to disgrace Achilles, the best of the Achaeans!"   490

    And Thetis answered, bursting into tears,
"O my son, my sorrow, why did I ever bear you?
All I bore was doom . . .
Would to god you could linger by your ships
without a grief in the world, without a torment!   495
Doomed to a short life, you have so little time.
And not only short, now, but filled with heartbreak too,
more than all other men alive—doomed twice over.
Ah to a cruel fate I bore you in our halls!
Still, I shall go to Olympus crowned with snow   500
and repeat your prayer to Zeus who loves the lightning.
Perhaps he will be persuaded.
              But you, my child,

---

2. Apollo.   3. As god of the sky he controlled rain and sunshine.   4. Brother of Zeus.   5. A giant, son of Poseidon.

stay here by the fast ships, rage on at the Achaeans,
just keep clear of every foray in the fighting.
Only yesterday Zeus went off to the Ocean River   505
to feast with the Aethiopians,[6] loyal, lordly men,
and all the gods went with him. But in twelve days
the Father returns to Olympus. Then, for your sake,
up I go to the bronze floor, the royal house of Zeus—
I'll grasp his knees, I think I'll win him over."
                                          With that vow   510
his mother went away and left him there, alone,
his heart inflamed for the sashed and lovely girl
they'd wrenched away from him against his will.
Meanwhile Odysseus drew in close to Chryse Island,
bearing the splendid sacrifice in the vessel's hold.   515
And once they had entered the harbor deep in bays
they furled and stowed their sails in the black ship,
they lowered the mast by the forestays, smoothly,
quickly let it down on the forked mast-crutch
and rowed her into a mooring under oars.   520
Out went the bow-stones—cables fast astern—
and the crew themselves climbed out in the breaking surf,
leading out the sacrifice for the archer god Apollo,
and out of the deep-sea ship Chryseis stepped too.
Then tactful Odysseus led her up to the altar,   525
placing her in her loving father's arms, and said,
"Chryses, the lord of men Agamemnon sent me here
to bring your daughter back and perform a sacrifice,
a grand sacrifice to Apollo—for all Achaea's sake—
so we can appease the god   530
who's loosed such grief and torment on the Argives."

    With those words he left her in Chryses' arms
and the priest embraced the child he loved, exultant.
At once the men arranged the sacrifice for Apollo,
making the cattle ring his well-built altar,   535
then they rinsed their hands and took up barley.
Rising among them Chryses stretched his arms to the sky
and prayed in a high resounding voice, "Hear me, Apollo!
God of the silver bow who strides the walls of Chryse
and Cilla sacrosanct—lord in power of Tenedos!   540
If you honored me last time and heard my prayer
and rained destruction down on all Achaea's ranks,
now bring my prayer to pass once more. Now, at last,
drive this killing plague from the armies of Achaea!"

    His prayer went up and Phoebus Apollo heard him.   545
And soon as the men had prayed and flung the barley,
first they lifted back the heads of the victims,
slit their throats, skinned them and carved away

---

6. Or Ethiopians, who were thought to live at the extreme edges of the world. It was believed that a river (*Ocean River*) encircled the entire world.

the meat from the thighbones and wrapped them in fat,
a double fold sliced clean and topped with strips of flesh.   550
And the old man burned these on a dried cleft stick
and over the quarters poured out glistening wine
while young men at his side held five-pronged forks.
Once they had charred the thighs and tasted the organs
they cut the rest into pieces, pierced them with spits,   555
roasted them to a turn and pulled them off the fire.
The work done, the feast laid out, they ate well
and no man's hunger lacked a share of the banquet.
When they had put aside desire for food and drink,
the young men brimmed the mixing bowls with wine   560
and tipping first drops for the god in every cup
they poured full rounds for all. And all day long
they appeased the god with song, raising a ringing hymn
to the distant archer god who drives away the plague,
those young Achaean warriors singing out his power,   565
and Apollo listened, his great heart warm with joy.

   Then when the sun went down and night came on
they made their beds and slept by the stern-cables . . .
When young Dawn with her rose-red fingers shone once more,
they set sail for the main encampment of Achaea.   570
The Archer sent them a bracing following wind,
they stepped the mast, spread white sails wide,
the wind hit full and the canvas bellied out
and a dark blue wave, foaming up at the bow,
sang out loud and strong as the ship made way,   575
skimming the whitecaps, cutting toward her goal.
And once offshore of Achaea's vast encampment
they eased her in and hauled the black ship high,
far up on the sand, and shored her up with timbers.
Then they scattered, each to his own ship and shelter.   580

   But he raged on, grimly camped by his fast fleet,
the royal son of Peleus, the swift runner Achilles.
Now he no longer haunted the meeting grounds
where men win glory, now he no longer went to war
but day after day he ground his heart out, waiting there,   585
yearning, always yearning for battle cries and combat.

   But now as the twelfth dawn after this shone clear
the gods who live forever marched home to Olympus,
all in a long cortege, and Zeus led them on.
And Thetis did not forget her son's appeals.   590
She broke from a cresting wave at first light
and soaring up to the broad sky and Mount Olympus,
found the son of Cronus gazing down on the world,
peaks apart from the other gods and seated high
on the topmost crown of rugged ridged Olympus.   595
And crouching down at his feet,
quickly grasping his knees with her left hand,

her right hand holding him underneath the chin,[7]
she prayed to the lord god Zeus, the son of Cronus:
"Zeus, Father Zeus! If I ever served you well   600
among the deathless gods with a word or action,
bring this prayer to pass: honor my son Achilles!—
doomed to the shortest life of any man on earth.
And now the lord of men Agamemnon has disgraced him,
seizes and keeps his prize, tears her away himself. But you—   605
exalt him, Olympian Zeus: your urgings rule the world!
Come, grant the Trojans victory after victory
till the Achaean armies pay my dear son back,
building higher the honor he deserves!"
                                            She paused
but Zeus who commands the storm clouds answered nothing.   610
The Father sat there, silent. It seemed an eternity . . .
But Thetis, clasping his knees, held on, clinging,
pressing her question once again: "Grant my prayer,
once and for all, Father, bow your head in assent!
Or deny me outright. What have you to fear?   615
So I may know, too well, just how cruelly
I am the most dishonored goddess of them all."
                                            Filled with anger
Zeus who marshals the storm clouds answered her at last:
"Disaster. You will drive me into war with Hera.
She will provoke me, she with her shrill abuse.   620
Even now in the face of all the immortal gods
she harries me perpetually, Hera charges *me*
that I always go to battle for the Trojans.
Away with you now. Hera might catch us here.
I will see to this. I will bring it all to pass.   625
Look, I will bow my head if that will satisfy you.
That, I remind you, that among the immortal gods
is the strongest, truest sign that I can give.
No word or work of mine—nothing can be revoked,
there is no treachery, nothing left unfinished   630
once I bow my head to say it shall be done."

    So he decreed. And Zeus the son of Cronus bowed
his craggy dark brows and the deathless locks came pouring
down from the thunderhead of the great immortal king
and giant shock waves spread through all Olympus.   635

    So the two of them made their pact and parted.
Deep in the sea she dove from radiant Mount Olympus.
Zeus went back to his own halls, and all the gods
in full assembly rose from their seats at once
to meet the Father striding toward them now.   640
None dared remain at rest as Zeus advanced,
they all sprang up to greet him face-to-face

---

7. She takes on the posture of the suppliant, the physical pressure of which emphasizes the desperation
and urgency of the request. Zeus was, above all other gods, the protector of suppliants.

as he took his place before them on his throne.
But Hera knew it all. She had seen how Thetis,
the Old Man of the Sea's daughter, Thetis quick   645
on her glistening feet was hatching plans with Zeus.
And suddenly Hera taunted the Father, son of Cronus:
"So, who of the gods this time, my treacherous one,
was hatching plans with you?
Always your pleasure, whenever my back is turned,   650
to settle things in your grand clandestine way.
You never deign, do you, freely and frankly,
to share your plots with me—never, not a word!"

          The father of men and gods replied sharply,
"Hera—stop hoping to fathom all my thoughts.   655
You will find them a trial, though you are my wife.
Whatever is right for you to hear, no one, trust me,
will know of it before you, neither god nor man.
Whatever I choose to plan apart from all the gods—
no more of your everlasting questions, probe and pry no more."   660

          And Hera the Queen, her dark eyes wide, exclaimed,
"Dread majesty, son of Cronus, what are you saying?
Now surely I've never probed or pried in the past.
Why, you can scheme to your heart's content
without a qualm in the world for me. But now   665
I have a terrible fear that she has won you over,
Thetis, the Old Man of the Sea's daughter, Thetis
with her glistening feet. I know it. Just at dawn
she knelt down beside you and grasped your knees
and I suspect you bowed your head in assent to her—   670
you granted once and for all to exalt Achilles now
and slaughter hordes of Achaeans pinned against their ships."

          And Zeus who marshals the thunderheads returned,
"Maddening one . . . you and your eternal suspicions—
I can never escape you. Ah but tell me, Hera,   675
just what can you *do* about all this? Nothing.
Only estrange yourself from me a little more—
and all the worse for you.
If what you say is true, that must be my pleasure.
Now go sit down. Be quiet now. Obey my orders,   680
for fear the gods, however many Olympus holds,
are powerless to protect you when I come
to throttle you with my irresistible hands."
                                        He subsided
but Hera the Queen, her eyes wider, was terrified.
She sat in silence. She wrenched her will to his.   685
And throughout the halls of Zeus the gods of heaven
quaked with fear. Hephaestus[8] the Master Craftsman
rose up first to harangue them all, trying now

8. The lame god of fire and the patron of craftspeople, especially metalworkers.

to bring his loving mother a little comfort,
the white-armed goddess Hera: "Oh disaster . . .   690
that's what it is, and it will be unbearable
if the two of you must come to blows this way,
flinging the gods in chaos just for mortal men.
No more joy for us in the sumptuous feast
when riot rules the day.   695
I urge you, mother—you know that I am right—
work back into his good graces, so the Father,
our beloved Father will never wheel on us again,
send our banquets crashing! The Olympian lord of lightning—
what if he would like to blast us from our seats?   700
He is far too strong. Go back to him, mother,
stroke the Father with soft, winning words—
at once the Olympian will turn kind to us again."

   Pleading, springing up with a two-handled cup,
he reached it toward his loving mother's hands   705
with his own winning words: "Patience, mother!
Grieved as you are, bear up, or dear as you are,
I have to see you beaten right before my eyes.
I would be shattered—what could I do to save you?
It's hard to fight the Olympian strength for strength.   710
You remember the last time I rushed to your defense?
He grabbed my foot, he hurled me off the tremendous threshold
and all day long I dropped, I was dead weight and then,
when the sun went down, down I plunged on Lemnos,[9]
little breath left in me. But the mortals there   715
soon nursed a fallen immortal back to life."

   At that the white-armed goddess Hera smiled
and smiling, took the cup from her child's hands.
Then dipping sweet nectar[1] up from the mixing bowl
he poured it round to all the immortals, left to right.   720
And uncontrollable laughter broke from the happy gods
as they watched the god of fire breathing hard
and bustling through the halls.
                                   That hour then
and all day long till the sun went down they feasted
and no god's hunger lacked a share of the handsome banquet   725
or the gorgeous lyre Apollo struck or the Muses[2] singing
voice to voice in choirs, their vibrant music rising.

   At last, when the sun's fiery light had set,
each immortal went to rest in his own house,
the splendid high halls Hephaestus built for each   730
with all his craft and cunning, the famous crippled Smith.
And Olympian Zeus the lord of lightning went to his own bed
where he had always lain when welcome sleep came on him.

9. An island in the Aegean Sea.   1. The drink of the gods.   2. The Nine Muses were goddesses of
the arts and sources of artistic inspiration.

There he climbed and there he slept and by his side
lay Hera the Queen, the goddess of the golden throne.   735

Summary   The Greeks, in spite of Achilles' withdrawal, continued to fight. They
did not suffer immoderately from Achilles' absence; on the contrary, they pressed the
Trojans so hard that Hector, the Trojan leader, after rallying his men, returned to the
city to urge the Trojans to offer special prayers and sacrifices to the gods.

FROM BOOK VI

[Hector Returns to Troy]

As Hector turned for home his helmet flashed
and the long dark hide of his bossed shield, the rim
running the metal edge, drummed his neck and ankles.
                                                    And now
Glaucus son of Hippolochus and Tydeus' son Diomedes[3]
met in the no man's land between both armies: 5
burning for battle, closing, squaring off
and the lord of the war cry Diomedes opened up,
"Who are you, my fine friend?—another born to die?
I've never noticed you on the lines where we win glory,
not till now. But here you come, charging out   10
in front of all the rest with such bravado—
daring to face the flying shadow of my spear.
Pity the ones whose sons stand up to me in war!
But if you are an immortal come from the blue,
I'm not the man to fight the gods of heaven.   15
Not even Dryas' indestructible son Lycurgus,[4]
not even he lived long . . .
that fellow who tried to fight the deathless gods.
He rushed at the maenads once, nurses of wild Dionysus,[5]
scattered them breakneck down the holy mountain Nysa.   20
A rout of them strewed their sacred staves on the ground,
raked with a cattle prod by Lycurgus, murderous fool!
And Dionysus was terrified, he dove beneath the surf
where the sea-nymph Thetis pressed him to her breast—
Dionysus numb with fear: shivers racked his body,   25
thanks to the raucous onslaught of that man.
But the gods who live at ease lashed out against him—
worse, the son of Cronus[6] struck Lycurgus blind.
Nor did the man live long, not with the hate
of all the gods against him.
                              No, my friend,   30
I have no desire to fight the blithe immortals.
But if you're a man who eats the crops of the earth,
a mortal born for death—here, come closer,
the sooner you will meet your day to die!"

    The noble son of Hippolochus answered staunchly, 35
"High-hearted son of Tydeus, why ask about my birth?

---

3. One of the foremost Greek leaders. *Glaucus*: from Lycia in Asia Minor, and a Trojan ally.   4. King
of Thrace, a half-wild region along the north shore of the Aegean Sea.   5. God of the vine.   6. Zeus.

Like the generations of leaves, the lives of mortal men.
Now the wind scatters the old leaves across the earth,
now the living timber bursts with the new buds
and spring comes round again. And so with men: 40
as one generation comes to life, another dies away.
But about my birth, if you'd like to learn it well,
first to last—though many people know it—
here's my story . . .
                            There is a city, Corinth,
deep in a bend of Argos, good stallion-country   45
where Sisyphus used to live, the wiliest man alive.
Sisyphus, Aeolus' son, who had a son called Glaucus,
and in his day Glaucus sired brave Bellerophon,
a man without a fault. The gods gave him beauty
and the fine, gallant traits that go with men.   50
But Proetus[7] plotted against him. Far stronger,
the king in his anger drove him out of Argos,
the kingdom Zeus had brought beneath his scepter.
Proetus' wife, you see, was mad for Bellerophon,
the lovely Antea lusted to couple with him,   55
all in secret. Futile—she could never seduce
the man's strong will, his seasoned, firm resolve.
So straight to the king she went, blurting out her lies:
'I wish you'd die, Proetus, if you don't kill Bellerophon!
Bellerophon's bent on dragging me down with him in lust   60
though I fight him all the way!'
                            All of it false
but the king seethed when he heard a tale like that.
He balked at killing the man—he'd some respect at least—
but he quickly sent him off to Lycia, gave him tokens,
murderous signs, scratched in a folded tablet,   65
and many of them too, enough to kill a man.
He told him to show them to Antea's father:
that would mean his death.
                            So off he went to Lycia,
safe in the escort of the gods, and once he reached
the broad highlands cut by the rushing Xanthus,[8]   70
the king of Lycia gave him a royal welcome.
Nine days he feasted him, nine oxen slaughtered.
When the tenth Dawn shone with her rose-red fingers,
he began to question him, asked to see his credentials,
whatever he brought him from his in-law, Proetus.   75
But then, once he received that fatal message
sent from his own daughter's husband, first
he ordered Bellerophon to kill the Chimaera—
grim monster sprung of the gods, nothing human,
all lion in front, all snake behind, all goat between,   80
terrible, blasting lethal fire at every breath!
But he laid her low, obeying signs from the gods.
Next he fought the Solymi, tribesmen bent on glory,

7. King of Argos.   8. River in Lycia.

roughest battle of men he ever entered, so he claimed.
Then for a third test he brought the Amazons down,   85
a match for men in war. But as he turned back,
his host spun out the tightest trap of all:
picking the best men from Lycia far and wide
he set an ambush—that never came home again!
Fearless Bellerophon killed them all.
                    Then, yes,   90
when the king could see the man's power at last,
a true son of the gods, he pressed him hard to stay,
he offered his own daughter's hand in marriage,
he gave him half his royal honors as the king.
And the Lycians carved him out a grand estate,   95
the choicest land in the realm, rich in vineyards
and good tilled fields for him to lord it over.
And his wife bore good Bellerophon three children:
Isander, Hippolochus and Laodamia. Laodamia
lay in the arms of Zeus who rules the world   100
and she bore the god a son, our great commander,
Sarpedon helmed in bronze.
                    But the day soon came
when even Bellerophon was hated by all the gods.
Across the Alean plain he wandered, all alone,
eating his heart out, a fugitive on the run   105
from the beaten tracks of men. His son Isander?
Killed by the War-god, never sated—a boy fighting
the Solymi always out for glory. Laodamia? Artemis,
flashing her golden reins, cut her down in anger.
But Hippolochus fathered me, I'm proud to say.   110
He sent me off to Troy . . .
and I hear his urgings ringing in my ears:
'Always be the best, my boy, the bravest,
and hold your head up high above the others.
Never disgrace the generation of your fathers.   115
They were the bravest champions born in Corinth,
in Lycia far and wide.'
                    There you have my lineage.
That is the blood I claim, my royal birth."

When he heard that, Diomedes' spirits lifted.
Raising his spear, the lord of the war cry drove it home,   120
planting it deep down in the earth that feeds us all
and with winning words he called out to Glaucus,
the young captain, "Splendid—you are my friend,
my guest from the days of our grandfathers long ago!
Noble Oeneus hosted your brave Bellerophon once,   125
he held him there in his halls, twenty whole days,
and they gave each other handsome gifts of friendship.
My kinsman offered a gleaming sword-belt, rich red,
Bellerophon gave a cup, two-handled, solid gold—
I left it at home when I set out for Troy.   130
My father, Tydeus, I really don't remember.

I was just a baby when father left me then,
that time an Achaean army went to die at Thebes.[9]
So now I am your host and friend in the heart of Argos,
you are mine in Lycia when I visit in your country.   135
Come, let us keep clear of each other's spears,
even there in the thick of battle. Look,
plenty of Trojans there for me to kill,
your famous allies too, any soldier the god
will bring in range or I can run to ground.   140
And plenty of Argives too—kill them if you can.
But let's trade armor. The men must know our claim:
we are sworn friends from our fathers' days till now!"[1]

   Both agreed. Both fighters sprang from their chariots,
clasped each other's hands and traded pacts of friendship.   145
But the son of Cronus, Zeus, stole Glaucus' wits away.
He traded his gold armor for bronze with Diomedes,
the worth of a hundred oxen just for nine.
                   And now,
when Hector reached the Scaean Gates[2] and the great oak,
the wives and daughters of Troy came rushing up around him,   150
asking about their sons, brothers, friends and husbands.
But Hector told them only, "Pray to the gods"—
all the Trojan women, one after another . . .
Hard sorrows were hanging over many.
                    And soon
he came to Priam's palace, that magnificent structure   155
built wide with porches and colonnades of polished stone.
And deep within its walls were fifty sleeping chambers
masoned in smooth, lustrous ashlar, linked in a line
where the sons of Priam slept beside their wedded wives,
and facing these, opening out across the inner courtyard,   160
lay the twelve sleeping chambers of Priam's daughters,
masoned and roofed in lustrous ashlar, linked in a line
where the sons-in-law of Priam slept beside their wives.
And there at the palace Hector's mother[3] met her son,
that warm, goodhearted woman, going in with Laodice,   165
the loveliest daughter Hecuba ever bred. His mother
clutched his hand and urged him, called his name:
"My child—why have you left the bitter fighting,
why have you come home? Look how they wear you out,
the sons of Achaea—curse them—battling round our walls!   170
And that's why your spirit brought you back to Troy,
to climb the heights and stretch your arms to Zeus.
But wait, I'll bring you some honeyed, mellow wine.
First pour out cups to Father Zeus and the other gods,
then refresh yourself, if you'd like to quench your thirst.   175

9. Tydeus was one of the seven heroes who attacked Thebes, led by Oedipus's son Polyneices, who was
attempting to dislodge his brother Eteocles from the kingship. The brothers killed each other, and the rest
of the seven also perished. Diomedes, along with the sons of the other champions, later sacked
Thebes.   1. It was customary for guest-friends to exchange gifts.   2. One of the entrances to
Troy.   3. Hecuba, Priam's queen.

When a man's exhausted, wine will build his strength—
battle-weary as *you* are, fighting for your people."

But Hector shook his head, his helmet flashing:
"Don't offer me mellow wine, mother, not now—
you'd sap my limbs, I'd lose my nerve for war.   180
And I'd be ashamed to pour a glistening cup to Zeus
with unwashed hands. I'm splattered with blood and filth—
how could I pray to the lord of storm and lightning?
No, mother, you are the one to pray.
Go to Athena's shrine, the queen of plunder,   185
go with offerings, gather the older noble women
and take a robe, the largest, loveliest robe
that you can find throughout the royal halls,
a gift that far and away you prize most yourself,
and spread it out across the sleek-haired goddess' knees.   190
Then promise to sacrifice twelve heifers in her shrine,
yearlings never broken, if only she'll pity Troy,
the Trojan wives and all our helpless children,
if only she'll hold Diomedes[4] back from the holy city—
that wild spearman, that invincible headlong terror!   195
Now, mother, go to the queen of plunder's shrine
and I'll go hunt for Paris,[5] summon him to fight
if the man will hear what *I* have to say . . .
Let the earth gape and swallow him on the spot!
A great curse Olympian Zeus let live and grow in him,   200
for Troy and high-hearted Priam and all his sons.
That man—if I could see him bound for the House of Death,
I could say my heart had forgot its wrenching grief!"

But his mother simply turned away to the palace.
She gave her servants orders and out they strode   205
to gather the older noble women through the city.
Hecuba went down to a storeroom filled with scent
and there they were, brocaded, beautiful robes . . .
the work of Sidonian women. Magnificent Paris
brought those women back himself from Sidon,[6]   210
sailing the open seas on the same long voyage
he swept Helen off, her famous Father's child.
Lifting one from the lot, Hecuba brought it out
for great Athena's gift, the largest, loveliest,
richly worked, and like a star it glistened,   215
deep beneath the others. Then she made her way
with a file of noble women rushing in her train.

Once they reached Athena's shrine on the city crest
the beauty Theano opened the doors to let them in,
Cisseus' daughter, the horseman Antenor's wife   220
and Athena's priestess chosen by the Trojans. Then—

4. One of the Greek champions, who has just distinguished himself in the fighting.   5. Hector's brother, whose seduction and abduction of Helen, the wife of Menelaus, is the cause of the war.   6. A Phoenician city on the coast of what is now Lebanon.

with a shrill wail they all stretched their arms to Athena
as Theano, her face radiant, lifting the robe on high,
spread it out across the sleek-haired goddess' knees
and prayed to the daughter of mighty Father Zeus: 225
"Queen Athena—shield of our city—glory of goddesses!
Now shatter the spear of Diomedes! That wild man—
hurl him headlong down before the Scaean Gates!
At once we'll sacrifice twelve heifers in your shrine,
yearlings never broken, if only you'll pity Troy,   230
the Trojan wives and all our helpless children!'
     But Athena refused to hear Theano's prayers.
And while they prayed to the daughter of mighty Zeus
Hector approached the halls of Paris, sumptuous halls
he built himself with the finest masons of the day,   235
master builders famed in the fertile land of Troy.
They'd raised his sleeping chamber, house and court
adjoining Priam's and Hector's aloft the city heights.
Now Hector, dear to Zeus, strode through the gates,
clutching a thrusting-lance eleven forearms long;   240
the bronze tip of the weapon shone before him,
ringed with a golden hoop to grip the shaft.
And there in the bedroom Hector came on Paris
polishing, fondling his splendid battle-gear,
his shield and breastplate, turning over and over   245
his long curved bow. And there was Helen of Argos,
sitting with all the women of the house, directing
the rich embroidered work they had in hand.

                              Seeing Paris,
Hector raked his brother with insults, stinging taunts:[7]
"What on earth are you doing? Oh how wrong it is,   250
this anger you keep smoldering in your heart! Look,
your people dying around the city, the steep walls,
dying in arms—and all for you, the battle cries
and the fighting flaring up around the citadel.
You'd be the first to lash out at another—anywhere—   255
you saw hanging back from this, this hateful war.
                              Up with you—
before all Troy is torched to a cinder here and now!"

     And Paris, magnificent as a god, replied,
"Ah Hector, you criticize me fairly, yes,
nothing unfair, beyond what I deserve. And so   260
I will try to tell you something. Please bear with me,
hear me out. It's not so much from anger or outrage
at our people that I keep to my rooms so long.
I only wanted to plunge myself in grief.
But just now my wife was bringing me round,   265
her winning words urging me back to battle.

---

7. Paris, like Achilles, was sulking. He had been worsted in a duel with Menelaus, but the goddess Aphrodite saved him from the consequences of his defeat and brought him to his house in Troy. Paris was hated by his compatriots as the cause of the war.

And it strikes me, even me, as the better way.
Victory shifts, you know, now one man, now another.
So come, wait while I get this war-gear on,
or you go on ahead and I will follow—   270
I think I can overtake you."
       Hector, helmet flashing,
answered nothing. And Helen spoke to him now,
her soft voice welling up: "My dear brother,
dear to me, bitch that I am, vicious, scheming—
horror to freeze the heart! Oh how I wish   275
that first day my mother brought me into the light
some black whirlwind had rushed me out to the mountains
or into the surf where the roaring breakers crash and drag
and the waves had swept me off before all this had happened!
But since the gods ordained it all, these desperate years,   280
I wish I had been the wife of a better man, someone
alive to outrage, the withering scorn of men.
This one has no steadiness in his spirit,
not now, he never will . . .
and he's going to reap the fruits of it, I swear.   285
But come in, rest on this seat with me, dear brother.
You are the one hit hardest by the fighting, Hector,
you more than all—and all for me, slut that I am,
and this blind mad Paris. Oh the two of us!
Zeus planted a killing doom within us both,   290
so even for generations still unborn
we will live in song."
      Turning to go,
his helmet flashing, tall Hector answered,
"Don't ask me to sit beside you here, Helen.
Love me as you do, you can't persuade me now.   295
No time for rest. My heart races to help our Trojans—
they long for me, sorely, whenever I am gone.
But rouse this fellow, won't you?
And let him hurry himself along as well,
so he can overtake me before I leave the city.   300
For I must go home to see my people first,
to visit my own dear wife and my baby son.
Who knows if I will ever come back to them again?—
or the deathless gods will strike me down at last
at the hands of Argive fighters."
       A flash of his helmet   305
and off he strode and quickly reached his sturdy,
well-built house. But white-armed Andromache—
Hector could not find her in the halls.
She and the boy and a servant finely gowned
were standing watch on the tower, sobbing, grieving.   310
When Hector saw no sign of his loyal wife inside
he went to the doorway, stopped and asked the servants,
"Come, please, tell me the truth now, women.
Where's Andromache gone? To my sisters' house?
To my brothers' wives with their long flowing robes?   315

Or Athena's shrine where the noble Trojan women
gather to win the great grim goddess over?"

A busy, willing servant answered quickly,
"Hector, seeing you want to know the truth,
she hasn't gone to your sisters, brothers' wives   320
or Athena's shrine where the noble Trojan women
gather to win the great grim goddess over.
Up to the huge gate-tower of Troy she's gone
because she heard our men are so hard-pressed,
the Achaean fighters coming on in so much force.   325
She sped to the wall in panic, like a madwoman—
the nurse went with her, carrying your child."

At that, Hector spun and rushed from his house,
back by the same way down the wide, well-paved streets
throughout the city until he reached the Scaean Gates,   330
the last point he would pass to gain the field of battle.
There his warm, generous wife came running up to meet him,
Andromache the daughter of gallant-hearted Eetion
who had lived below Mount Placos rich with timber,
in Thebe below the peaks, and ruled Cilicia's people.   335
His daughter had married Hector helmed in bronze.
She joined him now, and following in her steps
a servant holding the boy against her breast,
in the first flush of life, only a baby,
Hector's son, the darling of his eyes   340
and radiant as a star . . .
Hector would always call the boy Scamandrius,
townsmen called him Astyanax,[8] Lord of the City,
since Hector was the lone defense of Troy.
The great man of war breaking into a broad smile,   345
his gaze fixed on his son, in silence. Andromache,
pressing close beside him and weeping freely now,
clung to his hand, urged him, called him: "Reckless one,
my Hector—your own fiery courage will destroy you!
Have you no pity for him, our helpless son? Or me,   350
and the destiny that weighs me down, your widow,
now so soon. Yes, soon they will kill you off,
all the Achaean forces massed for assault, and then,
bereft of you, better for me to sink beneath the earth.
What other warmth, what comfort's left for me,   355
once you have met your doom? Nothing but torment!
I have lost my father. Mother's gone as well.
Father . . . the brilliant Achilles laid him low
when he stormed Cilicia's city filled with people,
Thebe with her towering gates. He killed Eetion,   360
not that he stripped his gear—he'd some respect at least—
for he burned his corpse in all his blazoned bronze,

---

8. The name does literally mean "lord of the city." *Scamandrius*: after the Trojan river Scamander.

then heaped a grave-mound high above the ashes
and nymphs of the mountain planted elms around it,
daughters of Zeus whose shield is storm and thunder.   365
And the seven brothers I had within our halls . . .
all in the same day went down to the House of Death,
the great godlike runner Achilles butchered them all,
tending their shambling oxen, shining flocks.

                              And mother,
who ruled under the timberline of woody Placos once—   370
he no sooner haled her here with his other plunder
than he took a priceless ransom, set her free
and home she went to her father's royal halls
where Artemis,[9] showering arrows, shot her down.
You, Hector—you are my father now, my noble mother,   375
a brother too, and you are my husband, young and warm and strong!
Pity me, please! Take your stand on the rampart here,
before you orphan your son and make your wife a widow.
Draw your armies up where the wild fig tree stands,
there, where the city lies most open to assault,   380
the walls lower, easily overrun. Three times
they have tried that point, hoping to storm Troy,
their best fighters led by the Great and Little Ajax,
famous Idomeneus, Atreus' sons, valiant Diomedes.
Perhaps a skilled prophet revealed the spot—   385
or their own fury whips them on to attack."

    And tall Hector nodded, his helmet flashing:
"All this weighs on my mind too, dear woman.
But I would die of shame to face the men of Troy
and the Trojan women trailing their long robes   390
if I would shrink from battle now, a coward.
Nor does the spirit urge me on that way.
I've learned it all too well. To stand up bravely,
always to fight in the front ranks of Trojan soldiers,
winning my father great glory, glory for myself.   395
For in my heart and soul I also know this well:
the day will come when sacred Troy must die,
Priam must die and all his people with him,
Priam who hurls the strong ash spear . . .
                          Even so,
it is less the pain of the Trojans still to come   400
that weighs me down, not even of Hecuba herself
or King Priam, or the thought that my own brothers
in all their numbers, all their gallant courage,
may tumble in the dust, crushed by enemies—
That is nothing, nothing beside your agony   405
when some brazen Argive hales you off in tears,
wrenching away your day of light and freedom!
Then far off in the land of Argos you must live,

9. A virgin goddess, dispenser of natural and painless death to women.

laboring at a loom, at another woman's beck and call,
fetching water at some spring, Messeis or Hyperia,[1]   410
resisting it all the way—
the rough yoke of necessity at your neck.
And a man may say, who sees you streaming tears,
'There is the wife of Hector, the bravest fighter
they could field, those stallion-breaking Trojans,   415
long ago when the men fought for Troy.' So he will say
and the fresh grief will swell your heart once more,
widowed, robbed of the one man strong enough
to fight off your day of slavery.
                              No, no,
let the earth come piling over my dead body   420
before I hear your cries, I hear you dragged away!"

   In the same breath, shining Hector reached down
for his son—but the boy recoiled,
cringing against his nurse's full breast,
screaming out at the sight of his own father,   425
terrified by the flashing bronze, the horsehair crest,
the great ridge of the helmet nodding, bristling terror—
so it struck his eyes. And his loving father laughed,
his mother laughed as well, and glorious Hector,
quickly lifting the helmet from his head,   430
set it down on the ground, fiery in the sunlight,
and raising his son he kissed him, tossed him in his arms,
lifting a prayer to Zeus and the other deathless gods:
"Zeus, all you immortals! Grant this boy, my son,
may be like me, first in glory among the Trojans,   435
strong and brave like me, and rule all Troy in power
and one day let them say, 'He is a better man than his father!'—
when he comes home from battle bearing the bloody gear
of the mortal enemy he has killed in war—
a joy to his mother's heart."
                              So Hector prayed   440
and placed his son in the arms of his loving wife.
Andromache pressed the child to her scented breast,
smiling through her tears. Her husband noticed,
and filled with pity now, Hector stroked her gently,
trying to reassure her, repeating her name: "Andromache,   445
dear one, why so desperate? Why so much grief for me?
No man will hurl me down to Death, against my fate.
And fate? No one alive has ever escaped it,
neither brave man nor coward, I tell you—
it's born with us the day that we are born.   450
So please go home and tend to your own tasks,
the distaff and the loom, and keep the women
working hard as well. As for the fighting,
men will see to that, all who were born in Troy

1. In central and northern Greece.

but I most of all."

              Hector aflash in arms   455
took up his horsehair-crested helmet once again.
And his loving wife went home, turning, glancing
back again and again and weeping live warm tears.
She quickly reached the sturdy house of Hector,
man-killing Hector,   460
and found her women gathered there inside
and stirred them all to a high pitch of mourning.
So in his house they raised the dirges for the dead,
for Hector still alive, his people were so convinced
that never again would he come home from battle,   465
never escape the Argives' rage and bloody hands.

    Nor did Paris linger long in his vaulted halls.
Soon as he buckled on his elegant gleaming bronze
he rushed through Troy, sure in his racing stride.
As a stallion full-fed at the manger, stalled too long,   470
breaking free of his tether gallops down the plain,
out for his favorite plunge in a river's cool currents,
thundering in his pride—his head flung back, his mane
streaming over his shoulders, sure and sleek in his glory,
knees racing him on to the fields and stallion-haunts he loves—   475
so down from Pergamus'[2] heights came Paris, son of Priam,
glittering in his armor like the sun astride the skies,
exultant, laughing aloud, his fast feet sped him on.
Quickly he overtook his brother, noble Hector
still lingering, slow to turn from the spot   480
where he had just confided in his wife . . .
Magnificent Paris spoke first: "Dear brother,
look at me, holding you back in all your speed—
dragging my feet, coming to you so late,
and you told me to be quick!"   485

    A flash of his helmet as Hector shot back,
"Impossible man! How could anyone fair and just
underrate your work in battle? You're a good soldier.
But you hang back of your own accord, refuse to fight.
And that, that's why the heart inside me aches   490
when I hear our Trojans heap contempt on you,
the men who bear such struggles all for you.

                        Come,
now for attack! We'll set all this to rights,
someday, if Zeus will ever let us raise
the winebowl of freedom high in our halls,   495
high to the gods of cloud and sky who live forever—
once we drive these Argives geared for battle out of Troy!"

Summary   The Trojans rallied successfully and went over to the offensive. They
drove the Greeks back to the light fortifications they had built around their beached

2. The citadel of Troy.

ships. The Trojans lit their watchfires on the plain, ready to deliver the attack in the morning.

FROM BOOK VIII

[The Tide of Battle Turns]

And so their spirits soared
as they took positions down the passageways of battle
all night long, and the watchfires blazed among them.
Hundreds strong, as stars in the night sky glittering
round the moon's brilliance blaze in all their glory   5
when the air falls to a sudden, windless calm . . .
all the lookout peaks stand out and the jutting cliffs
and the steep ravines and down from the high heavens bursts
the boundless bright air and all the stars shine clear
and the shepherd's heart exults—so many fires burned   10
between the ships and the Xanthus'[3] whirling rapids
set by the men of Troy, bright against their walls.
A thousand fires were burning there on the plain
and beside each fire sat fifty fighting men
poised in the leaping blaze, and champing oats   15
and glistening barley, stationed by their chariots,
stallions waited for Dawn to mount her glowing throne.

BOOK IX

[The Embassy to Achilles]

So the Trojans held their watch that night but not the Achaeans—
godsent Panic seized them, comrade of bloodcurdling Rout:
all their best were struck by grief too much to bear.
As crosswinds chop the sea where the fish swarm,
the North Wind and the West Wind blasting out of Thrace[4]   5
in sudden, lightning attack, wave on blacker wave, cresting,
heaving a tangled mass of seaweed out along the surf—
so the Achaeans' hearts were torn inside their chests.

Distraught with the rising anguish, Atreus' son
went ranging back and forth, commanding heralds   10
to sound out loud and clear and call the men to muster,
each by name, but no loud outcry now. The king himself
pitched in with the lead heralds, summoning troops.
They grouped on the meeting grounds, morale broken.
Lord marshal Agamemnon rose up in their midst,   15
streaming tears like a dark spring running down
some desolate rock face, its shaded currents flowing.
So, with a deep groan, the king addressed his armies:
"Friends . . . lords of the Argives, all my captains!
Cronus' son has entangled me in madness, blinding ruin—   20
Zeus is a harsh, cruel god. He vowed to me long ago,
he bowed his head that I should never embark for home

3. One of the rivers of the Trojan plain.   4. The region northwest of Troy.

till I had brought the walls of Ilium crashing down.
But now, I see, he only plotted brutal treachery:
now he commands me back to Argos in disgrace,   25
whole regiments of my men destroyed in battle,
So it must please his overweening heart, who knows?
Father Zeus has lopped the crowns of a thousand cities,
true, and Zeus will lop still more—his power is too great.
So come, follow my orders. Obey me, all you Argives.   30
Cut and run! Sail home to the fatherland we love!
We'll never take the broad streets of Troy."

    Silence held them all, struck dumb by his orders.
A long while they said nothing, spirits dashed.
Finally Diomedes lord of the war cry broke forth: 35
"Atrides—I will be first to oppose you in your folly,
here in assembly, King, where it's the custom.
Spare me your anger. My courage—
mine was the first you mocked among the Argives,
branding me a coward, a poor soldier.[5] Yes, well,   40
they know all about that, the Argives young and old.
But you—the son of Cronus with Cronus' twisting ways
gave you gifts by halves: with that royal scepter
the Father gave you honor beyond all other men alive
but he never gave you courage, the greatest power of all.   45
Desperate man! So certain, are you, the sons of Achaea
are cowards, poor soldiers, just because you say so?
Desert—if your spirit drives you to sail home,
then sail away, my King! The sea-lanes are clear,
there are your ships of war, crowded down the surf,   50
those that followed you from Mycenae,[6] your own proud armada.
But the rest of the long-haired Achaeans will hold out,
right here, until we've plundered Troy. And they,
if they go running home to the land they love,
then the two of us, I and Sthenelus[7] here   55
will fight our way to the fixed doom of Troy.
Never forget—we all sailed here with god."

    And all the Achaeans shouted their assent,
stirred by the stallion-breaking Diomedes' challenge.
But Nestor the old driver rose and spoke at once: 60
"Few can match your power in battle, Diomedes,
and in council you excel all men your age.
So no one could make light of your proposals,
not the whole army—who could contradict you?
But you don't press on and reach a useful end.   65
How young you are . . . why, you could be my son,
my youngest-born at that, though you urge our kings
with cool clear sense: what you've said is right.
But it's my turn now, Diomedes.

---

5. This happened during Agamemnon's review of his forces before the battle.   6. A city near Argos.
7. Diomedes' companion.

I think I can claim to have some years on you.   70
So I *must* speak up and drive the matter home.
And no one will heap contempt on what I say,
not even mighty Agamemnon. Lost to the clan,
lost to the hearth, lost to the old ways, that one
who lusts for all the horrors of war with his own people.   75
But now, I say, let us give way to the dark night,
set out the evening meal. Sentries take up posts,
squads fronting the trench we dug outside the rampart.[8]
That's the command I give the younger fighters.
                                            Then,
Atrides, lead the way—you are the greatest king—   80
spread out a feast for all your senior chiefs.
That is your duty, a service that becomes you.
Your shelters overflow with the wine Achaean ships
bring in from Thrace, daily, down the sea's broad back.
Grand hospitality is yours, you rule so many men.   85
Come, gather us all and we will heed that man
who gives the best advice. That's what they need,
I tell you—all the Achaeans—good sound advice,
now our enemies, camping hard against the ships,
kindle their watchfires round us by the thousands.   90
What soldier could warm to that? Tonight's the night
that rips our ranks to shreds or pulls us through."

     The troops hung on his words and took his orders.
Out they rushed, the sentries in armor, forming
under the son of Nestor, captain Thrasymedes,   95
under Ascalaphus, Ialmenus, sons of Ares,[9]
under Meriones, Aphareus and Deipyrus,
under the son of Creon, trusty Lycomedes.
Seven chiefs of the guard, a hundred under each,
fighters marching, grasping long spears in their hands,   100
took up new positions between the trench and rampart.
There they lit their fires, each man made his meal.

     Meanwhile marshal Agamemnon led his commanders,
a file of senior chiefs, toward his own lodge
and set before them a feast to please their hearts.   105
They reached out for the good things that lay at hand
but when they had put aside desire for food and drink
the old man began to weave his counsel among them:
Nestor was first to speak—from the early days
his plans and tactics always seemed the best.   110
With good will to the chiefs he rose and spoke,
"Great marshal Atrides, lord of men Agamemnon . . .
with you I will end, my King, with you I will begin,
since you hold sway over many warriors, vast armies,
and Zeus has placed in your hands the royal scepter   115

8. The Greeks are now besieged beside their ships; Zeus's promise to Thetis is being fulfilled.   9. God of war.

and time-honored laws, so you will advise them well.
So you above all must speak your mind, and listen,
and carry out the next man's counsel too,
whenever his spirit leads him on to speak
for the public good. Credit will go to you   120
for whatever he proposes.
Now I will tell you what seems best to me.
No one will offer a better plan than this . . .
the plan I still retain, and I've been forming,
well, for a good long while now, from the very day   125
that you, my illustrious King, infuriated Achilles—
you went and took from his tents the girl Briseis,
and not with any applause from us, far from it:
I for one, I urged you against it, strenuously.
But you, you gave way to your overbearing anger,   130
disgraced a great man the gods themselves esteem—
you seized his gift of honor and keep her still.
But even so, late as it is, let us contrive
to set all this to rights, to bring him round
with gifts of friendship and warm, winning words."   135

   And Agamemnon the lord of men consented quickly:
"That's no lie, old man—a full account you give
of all my acts of madness. Mad, blind I was!
Not even I would deny it.
Why look, that man is worth an entire army,   140
the fighter Zeus holds dear with all his heart—
how he exalts him now and mauls Achaea's forces!
But since I was blinded, lost in my own inhuman rage,
now, at last, I am bent on setting things to rights:
I'll give a priceless ransom paid for friendship.
                                        Here,   145
before you all, I'll name in full the splendid gifts I offer.
Seven tripods[1] never touched by fire, ten bars of gold,
twenty burnished cauldrons, a dozen massive stallions,
racers who earned me trophies with their speed.
He is no poor man who owns what they have won,   150
not strapped for goods with all that lovely gold—
what trophies those high-strung horses carried off for me!
Seven women I'll give him, flawless, skilled in crafts,
women of Lesbos[2]—the ones I chose, my privilege,
that day he captured the Lesbos citadel himself: 155
they outclassed the tribes of women in their beauty.
These I will give, and along with them will go
the one I took away at first, Briseus' daughter,
and I will swear a solemn, binding oath in the bargain:
I never mounted her bed, never once made love with her—   160
the natural thing for mankind, men and women joined.
Now all these gifts will be handed him at once.

---

1. Three-footed kettles; such metal equipment was rare and highly valued.   2. A large island off the coast of what is now Turkey.

But if, later, the gods allow us to plunder
the great city of Priam, let him enter in
when we share the spoils, load the holds of his ship   165
with gold and bronze—as much as his heart desires—
and choose for his pleasure twenty Trojan women
second only to Argive Helen in their glory.
And then, if we can journey home to Achaean Argos,
pride of the breasting earth, he'll be my son-by-marriage!   170
I will even honor him on a par with my Orestes,
full-grown by now, reared in the lap of luxury.
Three daughters are mine in my well-built halls—
Chrysothemis and Laodice and Iphianassa—
and he may lead away whichever one he likes,   175
with no bride-price asked, home to Peleus' house.
And I will add a dowry, yes, a magnificent treasure
the likes of which no man has ever offered with his daughter!
Seven citadels I will give him, filled with people,
Cardamyle, Enope, and the grassy slopes of Hire,   180
Pherae the sacrosanct, Anthea deep in meadows,
rolling Aepea and Pedasus green with vineyards.
All face the sea at the far edge of sandy Pylos
and the men who live within them, rich in sheep-flocks,
rich in shambling cattle, will honor him like a god   185
with hoards of gifts and beneath his scepter's sway
live out his laws in sleek and shining peace.
                                        All this—
I would extend to him if he will end his anger.
Let him submit to me! Only the god of death[3]
is so relentless, Death submits to no one—   190
so mortals hate him most of all the gods.
Let him bow down to me! I am the greater king,
I am the elder-born, I claim—the greater man."

      Nestor the noble charioteer embraced his offer:
"Generous marshal Atrides, lord of men Agamemnon!   195
No one could underrate these gifts of yours, not now,
the treasure trove you offer Prince Achilles.
Come—we'll send a detail of picked men.
They'll go to Achilles' tent with all good speed.
Quick, whomever my eye will light on in review,   200
the mission's theirs. And old Phoenix[4] first—
Zeus loves the man, so let him lead the way.
Then giant Ajax and tactful royal Odysseus.
Heralds? Odius and Eurybates, you escort them.
Water for their hands! A reverent silence now . . .   205
a prayer to Zeus. Perhaps he'll show us mercy."

      The brisk commands he issued pleased them all.
Heralds brought the water at once and rinsed their hands,
and the young men brimmed the mixing bowls with wine

3. Hades.   4. He is especially suited for this embassy because he was tutor to the young Achilles.

and tipping first drops for the god in every cup   210
they poured full rounds for all. Libations finished,
each envoy having drunk to his heart's content,
the party moved out from Atrides' shelters.
Nestor the old driver gave them marching orders—
a sharp glance at each, Odysseus most of all: 215
"Try hard now, bring him round—invincible Achilles!"

      So Ajax and Odysseus made their way at once
where the battle lines of breakers crash and drag,
praying hard to the god who moves and shakes the earth[5]
that they might bring the proud heart of Achilles   220
round with speed and ease.
Reaching the Myrmidon shelters and their ships,
they found him there, delighting his heart now,
plucking strong and clear on the fine lyre—
beautifully carved, its silver bridge set firm—   225
he won from the spoils when he razed Eetion's city.
Achilles was lifting his spirits with it now,
singing the famous deeds of fighting heroes . . .
Across from him Patroclus sat alone, in silence,
waiting for Aeacus' son to finish with his song.   230
And on they came, with good Odysseus in the lead,
and the envoys stood before him. Achilles, startled,
sprang to his feet, the lyre still in his hands,
leaving the seat where he had sat in peace.
And seeing the men, Patroclus rose up too   235
as the famous runner called and waved them on:
"Welcome! Look, dear friends have come our way—
I must be sorely needed now—my dearest friends
in all the Achaean armies, even in my anger."

      So Prince Achilles hailed and led them in,   240
sat them down on settles with purple carpets
and quickly told Patroclus standing by, "Come,
a bigger winebowl, son of Menoetius, set it here.
Mix stronger wine. A cup for the hands of each guest—
here beneath my roof are the men I love the most."   245

      He paused. Patroclus obeyed his great friend,
who put down a heavy chopping block in the firelight
and across it laid a sheep's chine, a fat goat's
and the long back cut of a full-grown pig,
marbled with lard. Automedon[6] held the meats   250
while lordly Achilles carved them into quarters,
cut them well into pieces, pierced them with spits
and Patroclus raked the hearth, a man like a god
making the fire blaze. Once it had burned down
and the flames died away, he scattered the coals   255
and stretching the spitted meats across the embers,

---

5. Poseidon, who was believed to be responsible for earthquakes.   6. Achilles' charioteer.

raised them onto supports and sprinkled clean pure salt.
As soon as the roasts were done and spread on platters,
Patroclus brought the bread, set it out on the board
in ample wicker baskets. Achilles served the meat.   260
Then face-to-face with his noble guest Odysseus
he took his seat along the farther wall,
he told his friend to sacrifice to the gods
and Patroclus threw the first cuts[7] in the fire.
They reached out for the good things that lay at hand   265
and when they had put aside desire for food and drink,
Ajax nodded to Phoenix. Odysseus caught the signal,
filled his cup and lifted it toward Achilles,
opening with this toast: "Your health, Achilles!
We have no lack of a handsome feast, I see that,   270
either in Agamemnon's tents, the son of Atreus,
or here and now, in yours. We can all banquet here
to our heart's content.
                          But it's not the flowing feast
that is on our minds now—no, a stark disaster,
too much to bear, Achilles bred by the gods,   275
that is what we are staring in the face
and we are afraid. All hangs in the balance now:
whether we save our beached ships or they're destroyed,
unless, of course, you put your fighting power in harness.
They have pitched camp right at our ships and rampart,   280
those brazen Trojans, they and their far-famed allies,
thousands of fires blaze throughout their armies . . .
Nothing can stop them now—that's their boast—
they'll hurl themselves against our blackened hulls.
And the son of Cronus sends them signs on the right,   285
Zeus's firebolts flashing. And headlong Hector,
delirious with his strength, rages uncontrollably,
trusting to Zeus—no fear of man or god, nothing—
a powerful rabid frenzy has him in its grip!
Hector prays for the sacred Dawn to break at once,   290
he threatens to lop the high horns of our sterns
and gut our ships with fire, and all our comrades
pinned against the hulls, panicked by thick smoke,
he'll rout and kill in blood!
A nightmare—I fear it, with all my heart—   295
I fear the gods will carry out his threats
and then it will be our fate to die in Troy,
far from the stallion-land of Argos . . .
                                      Up with you—
now, late as it is, if you *want* to pull our Argives,
our hard-hit armies, clear of the Trojan onslaught.   300
Fail us now? What a grief it will be to you
through all the years to come. No remedy,
no way to cure the damage once it's done.
Come, while there's still time, think hard:

7. The portion of the meat reserved for the gods.

how can you fight off the Argives' fatal day? 305
Oh old friend, surely your father Peleus urged you,
that day he sent you out of Phthia to Agamemnon,
'My son, victory is what Athena and Hera will give,
if they so choose. But you, you hold in check
that proud, fiery spirit of yours inside your chest! 310
Friendship is much better. Vicious quarrels are deadly—
put an end to them, at once. Your Achaean comrades,
young and old, will exalt you all the more.'
That was your aged father's parting advice.
It must have slipped your mind.
                                        But now at last, 315
stop, Achilles—let your heart-devouring anger go!
The king will hand you gifts to match his insults
if only you'll relent and end your anger . . .
So come then, listen, as I count out the gifts,
the troves in his tents that Agamemnon vows to give you. 320
Seven tripods never touched by fire, ten bars of gold,
twenty burnished cauldrons, a dozen massive stallions,
racers who earned him trophies with their speed.
He is no poor man who owns what they have won,
not strapped for goods with all that lovely gold— 325
what trophies those high-strung horses carried off for him!
Seven women he'll give you, flawless, skilled in crafts,
women of Lesbos—the ones he chose, his privilege,
that day you captured the Lesbos citadel yourself:
they outclassed the tribes of women in their beauty. 330
These he will give, and along with them will go
the one he took away at first, Briseus' daughter,
and he will swear a solemn, binding oath in the bargain:
he never mounted her bed, never once made love with her . . .
the natural thing, my lord, men and women joined. 335
Now all these gifts will be handed you at once.
But if, later, the gods allow us to plunder
the great city of Priam, you shall enter in
when we share the spoils, load the holds of your ship
with gold and bronze—as much as your heart desires— 340
and choose for your pleasure twenty Trojan women
second only to Argive Helen in their glory.
And then, if we can journey home to Achaean Argos,
pride of the breasting earth, you'll be his son-by-marriage . . .
He will even honor you on a par with his Orestes, 345
full-grown by now, reared in the lap of luxury.
Three daughters are his in his well-built halls,
Chrysothemis and Laodice and Iphianassa—
and you may lead away whichever one you like,
with no bride-price asked, home to Peleus' house. 350
And he will add a dowry, yes, a magnificent treasure
the likes of which no man has ever offered with his daughter . . .
Seven citadels he will give you, filled with people,
Cardamyle, Enope, and the grassy slopes of Hire,
Pherae the sacrosanct, Anthea deep in meadows, 355

rolling Aepea and Pedasus green with vineyards.
All face the sea at the far edge of sandy Pylos
and the men who live within them, rich in sheep-flocks,
rich in shambling cattle, will honor you like a god
with hoards of gifts and beneath your scepter's sway   360
live out your laws in sleek and shining peace.
                          All this . . .
he would extend to you if you will end your anger.
But if you hate the son of Atreus all the more,
him and his troves of gifts, at least take pity
on all our united forces mauled in battle here—   365
they will honor you, honor you like a god.
Think of the glory you will gather in their eyes!
Now you can kill Hector—seized with murderous frenzy,
certain there's not a single fighter his equal,
no Achaean brought to Troy in the ships—   370
now, for once, you can meet the man head-on!"

    The famous runner Achilles rose to his challenge:
"Royal son of Laertes, Odysseus, great tactician . . .
I must say what I have to say straight out,
must tell you how I feel and how all this will end—   375
so you won't crowd around me, one after another,
coaxing like a murmuring clutch of doves.
I hate that man like the very Gates of Death
who says one thing but hides another in his heart.
I will say it outright. That seems best to me.   380
Will Agamemnon win me over? Not for all the world,
I swear it—nor will the rest of the Achaeans.
No, what lasting thanks in the long run
for warring with our enemies, on and on, no end?
One and the same lot for the man who hangs back   385
and the man who battles hard. The same honor waits
for the coward and the brave. They both go down to Death,
the fighter who shirks, the one who works to exhaustion.
And what's laid up for me, what pittance? Nothing—
and after suffering hardships, year in, year out,   390
staking my life on the mortal risks of war.

    Like a mother bird hurrying morsels back
to her wingless young ones—whatever she can catch—
but it's all starvation wages for herself.
                           So for me.
Many a sleepless night I've bivouacked in harness,   395
day after bloody day I've hacked my passage through,
fighting other soldiers to win their wives as prizes.
Twelve cities of men I've stormed and sacked from shipboard,
eleven I claim by land, on the fertile earth of Troy.
And from all I dragged off piles of splendid plunder,   400
hauled it away and always gave the lot to Agamemnon,
that son of Atreus—always skulking behind the lines,
safe in his fast ships—and he would take it all,

he'd parcel out some scraps but keep the lion's share.
Some he'd hand to the lords and kings—prizes of honor—   405
and they, they hold them still. From me alone, Achilles
of all Achaeans, he seizes, he keeps the wife I love . . .
Well *let* him bed her now—
enjoy her to the hilt!

        Why must we battle Trojans,
men of Argos? Why did he muster an army, lead us here,   410
that son of Atreus? Why, why in the world if not
for Helen with her loose and lustrous hair?
Are *they* the only men alive who love their wives,
those sons of Atreus? Never! Any decent man,
a man with sense, loves his own, cares for his own   415
as deeply as I, I loved that woman with all my heart,
though I won her like a trophy with my spear . . .
But now that he's torn my honor from my hands,
robbed me, lied to me—don't let him try me now.
I know *him* too well—he'll never win me over!

        No, Odysseus,   420
let him rack his brains with you and the other captains
how to fight the raging fire off the ships. Look—
what a mighty piece of work he's done without *me*!
Why, he's erected a rampart, driven a trench around it,
broad, enormous, and planted stakes to guard it. No use!   425
He still can't block the power of man-killing Hector!
No, though as long as *I* fought on Achaea's lines
Hector had little lust to charge beyond his walls,
never ventured beyond the Scaean Gates and oak tree.
There he stood up to me alone one day—   430
and barely escaped my onslaught.

        Ah but now,
since I have no desire to battle glorious Hector,
tomorrow at daybreak, once I have sacrificed
to Zeus and all the gods and loaded up my holds
and launched out on the breakers—watch, my friend,   435
if you'll take the time and care to see me off,
and you will see my squadrons sail at dawn,
fanning out on the Hellespont that swarms with fish,
my crews manning the oarlocks, rowing out with a will,
and if the famed god of the earthquake grants us safe passage,   440
the third day out we raise the dark rich soil of Phthia.
There lies my wealth, hoards of it, all I left behind
when I sailed to Troy on this, this insane voyage—
and still more hoards from here: gold, ruddy bronze,
women sashed and lovely, and gleaming gray iron,   445
and I will haul it home, all I won as plunder.
All but my prize of honor . . .
he who gave that prize has snatched it back again—
what outrage! That high and mighty King Agamemnon,
that son of Atreus!

        Go back and tell him all,   450
all I say—out in the open too—so other Achaeans

can wheel on him in anger if he still hopes—
who knows?—to deceive some other comrade.
                               Shameless,
inveterate—armored in shamelessness! Dog that he is,
he'd never dare to look me straight in the eyes again.   455
No, I'll never set heads together with that man—
no planning in common, no taking common action.
He cheated me, did me damage, wrong! But never again,
he'll never rob me blind with his twisting words again!
Once is enough for him. Die and be damned for all I care!   460
Zeus who rules the world has ripped his wits away.
His gifts, I loathe his gifts . . .
I wouldn't give you a splinter for that man!
Not if he gave me ten times as much, twenty times over, all
he possesses now, and all that could pour in from the world's end—   465
not all the wealth that's freighted into Orchomenos,[8] even into Thebes,
Egyptian Thebes where the houses overflow with the greatest troves of
      treasure,
Thebes with the hundred gates and through each gate battalions,
two hundred fighters surge to war with teams and chariots—
no, not if his gifts outnumbered all the grains of sand   470
and dust in the earth—no, not even then could Agamemnon
bring my fighting spirit round until he pays me back,
pays full measure for all his heartbreaking outrage!

    His daughter . . . I will marry no daughter of Agamemnon.
Not if she rivaled Aphrodite in all her golden glory,   475
not if she matched the crafts of clear-eyed Athena,
not even then would I make *her* my wife! No,
let her father pitch on some other Argive—
one who can please *him*, a greater king than I.
If the gods pull me through and I reach home alive,   480
Peleus needs no help to fetch a bride for me himself.
Plenty of Argive women wait in Hellas and in Phthia
daughters of lords who rule their citadels in power.
Whomever I want I'll make my cherished wife—at home.
Time and again my fiery spirit drove me to win a wife,   485
a fine partner to please my heart, to enjoy with her
the treasures my old father Peleus piled high.
I say no wealth is worth my life! Not all they claim
was stored in the depths of Troy, that city built on riches,
in the old days of peace before the sons of Achaea came—   490
not all the gold held fast in the Archer's rocky vaults,
in Phoebus Apollo's house on Pytho's[9] sheer cliffs!
Cattle and fat sheep can all be had for the raiding,
tripods all for the trading, and tawny-headed stallions.
But a man's life breath cannot come back again—   495
no raiders in force, no trading brings it back,
once it slips through a man's clenched teeth.

---

8. Great city north of Athens.   9. Apollo's shrine at Delphi. The treasures consisted of offerings made
to the god by grateful worshipers.

                                      Mother tells me,
the immortal goddess Thetis with her glistening feet,
that two fates bear me on to the day of death.
If I hold out here and I lay siege to Troy,   500
my journey home is gone, but my glory never dies.
If I voyage back to the fatherland I love,
my pride, my glory dies . . .
true, but the life that's left me will be long,
the stroke of death will not come on me quickly.   505

    One thing more. To the rest I'd pass on this advice:
sail home now! You will never set your eyes
on the day of doom that topples looming Troy.
Thundering Zeus has spread his hands above her—
her armies have taken heart!
                              So you go back   510
to the great men of Achaea. You report my message—
since this is the privilege of senior chiefs—
let *them* work out a better plan of action,
use their imaginations now to save the ships
and Achaea's armies pressed to their hollow hulls.   515
This maneuver will never work for them, this scheme
they hatched for the moment as I raged on and on.
But Phoenix can stay and rest the night with us,
so he can voyage home, home in the ships with me
to the fatherland we love. Tomorrow at dawn.   520
But only if Phoenix wishes.
I will never force the man to go."
                              He stopped.
A stunned silence seized them all, struck dumb—
Achilles' ringing denials overwhelmed them so.
At last Phoenix the old charioteer spoke out,   525
he burst into tears, terrified for Achaea's fleet:
"Sail home? Is *that* what you're turning over in your mind,
my glorious one, Achilles? Have you no heart at all
to fight the gutting fire from the fast trim ships?
The spirit inside you overpowered by anger!   530
How could I be severed from you, dear boy,
left behind on the beachhead here—alone?
The old horseman Peleus had me escort you,
that day he sent you out of Phthia to Agamemnon,
a youngster still untrained for the great leveler, war,   535
still green at debate where men can make their mark.
So he dispatched me, to teach you all these things,
to make you a man of words and a man of action too.
Cut off from you with a charge like that, dear boy?
I have no heart to be left behind, not even   540
if Zeus himself would swear to scrape away
the scurf of age and make me young again . . .
As fresh as I was that time I first set out
from Hellas where the women are a wonder,
fleeing a blood feud with my father, Amyntor,   545

Ormenus' son. How furious father was with me,
over his mistress with her dark, glistening hair.
How he would dote on her and spurn his wedded wife,
my own mother! And time and again she begged me,
hugging my knees, to bed my father's mistress down   550
and kill the young girl's taste for an old man.
Mother—I did your bidding, did my work . . .
But father, suspecting at once, cursed me roundly,
he screamed out to the cruel Furies[1]—'Never,
never let me bounce on my knees a son of his,   555
sprung of his loins!'—and the gods drove home that curse,
mighty Zeus of the Underworld and grim Persephone.[2]
So I, I took it into my head to lay him low
with sharp bronze! But a god checked my anger,
he warned me of what the whole realm would say,   560
the loose talk of the people, rough slurs of men—
they must not call me a father-killer, our Achaeans!
Then nothing could keep me there, my blood so fired up.
No more strolling about the halls with father raging.
But there was a crowd of kin and cousins round me,   565
holding me in the house, begging me to stay . . .
they butchered plenty of fat sheep, banquet fare,
and shambling crook-horned cattle, droves of pigs,
succulent, rich with fat—they singed the bristles,
splaying the porkers out across Hephaestus' fire,   570
then wine from the old man's jars, all we could drink.
Nine nights they passed the hours, hovering over me,
keeping the watch by rounds. The fires never died,
one ablaze in the colonnade of the walled court,
one in the porch outside my bedroom doors.

But then,   575
when the tenth night came on me, black as pitch,
I burst the doors of the chamber bolted tight
and out I rushed, I leapt the walls at a bound,
giving the slip to guards and women servants.
And away I fled through the whole expanse of Hellas   580
and gaining the good dark soil of Phthia, mother of flocks,
I reached the king, and Peleus gave me a royal welcome.
Peleus loved me as a father loves a son, I tell you,
his only child, the heir to his boundless wealth,
he made me a rich man, he gave me throngs of subjects,   585
I ruled the Dolopes, settling down on Phthia's west frontier.
And I made you what you are—strong as the gods, Achilles—
I loved you from the heart. You'd never go with another
to banquet on the town or feast in your own halls.
Never, until I'd sat you down on my knees   590
and cut you the first bits of meat, remember?
You'd eat your fill, I'd hold the cup to your lips
and all too often you soaked the shirt on my chest,

1. Avenging spirits, particularly concerned with crimes committed by kin against kin.   2. Wife of Hades
(the *Zeus of the Underworld*).

spitting up some wine, a baby's way . . . a misery.
Oh I had my share of troubles for you, Achilles,   595
did my share of labor. Brooding, never forgetting
the gods would bring no son of mine to birth,
not from my own loins.
                            So you, Achilles—
great godlike Achilles—I made you my son, I tried,
so someday *you* might fight disaster off my back.   600
But now, Achilles, beat down your mounting fury!
It's wrong to have such an iron, ruthless heart.
Even the gods themselves can bend and change,
and theirs is the greater power, honor, strength.
Even the gods, I say, with incense, soothing vows,   605
with full cups poured and the deep smoky savor
men can bring them round, begging for pardon
when one oversteps the mark, does something wrong.
We do have Prayers, you know, Prayers for forgiveness,
daughters of mighty Zeus . . . and they limp and halt,   610
they're all wrinkled, drawn, they squint to the side,
can't look you in the eyes, and always bent on duty,
trudging after Ruin, maddening, blinding Ruin.
But Ruin is strong and swift—
She outstrips them all by far, stealing a march,   615
leaping over the whole wide earth to bring mankind to grief.
And the Prayers trail after, trying to heal the wounds.
And then, if a man reveres these daughters of Zeus
as they draw near him, they will help him greatly
and listen to his appeals. But if one denies them,   620
turns them away, stiff-necked and harsh—off they go
to the son of Cronus, Zeus, and pray that Ruin
will strike the man down, crazed and blinded
until he's paid the price.
                            Relent, Achilles—you too!
See that honor attend these good daughters of Zeus,   625
honor that sways the minds of others, even heroes.
If Agamemnon were not holding out such gifts,
with talk of more to come, that son of Atreus,
if the warlord kept on blustering in his anger, why,
I'd be the last to tell you, 'Cast your rage to the winds!   630
Defend your friends!'—despite their desperate straits.
But now, look, he gives you a trove of treasures
right away, and vows there are more to follow.
He sends the bravest captains to implore you,
leaders picked from the whole Achaean army,   635
comrades-in-arms that you love most yourself.
Don't dismiss their appeal, their expedition here—
though no one could blame your anger, not before.
So it was in the old days too. So we've heard
in the famous deeds of fighting men, of heroes,   640
when seething anger would overcome the great ones.
Still you could bring them round with gifts and winning words.
There's an old tale I remember, an ancient exploit,

nothing recent, but this is how it went . . .
We are all friends here—let me tell it now.   645

    The Curetes were fighting the combat-hard Aetolians,
armies ringing Calydon,[3] slaughtering each other,
Aetolians defending their city's handsome walls
and Curetes primed to lay them waste in battle.
It all began when Artemis throned in gold   650
loosed a disaster on them, incensed that Oeneus[4]
offered her no first fruits, his orchard's crowning glory.
The rest of the gods had feasted full on oxen, true,
but the Huntress alone, almighty Zeus's daughter—
Oeneus gave her nothing. It slipped his mind   655
or he failed to care, but what a fatal error!
How she fumed, Zeus's child who showers arrows,
she loosed a bristling wild boar, his tusks gleaming,
crashing his savage, monstrous way through Oeneus' orchard,
ripping up whole trunks from the earth to pitch them headlong,   660
rows of them, roots and all, appleblossoms and all!
But the son of Oeneus, Meleager, cut him down—
mustering hunters out of a dozen cities,
packs of hounds as well. No slim band of men
could ever finish him off, that rippling killer,   665
he stacked so many men atop the tear-soaked pyre.
But over his body the goddess raised a terrific din,
a war for the prize, the huge beast's head and shaggy hide—
Curetes locked to the death with brave Aetolians.
                                              Now,
so long as the battle-hungry Meleager fought,   670
it was deadly going for the Curetes. No hope
of holding their ground outside their *own* city walls,
despite superior numbers. But then, when the wrath
came sweeping over the man, the same anger that swells
the chests of others, for all their care and self-control—   675
then, heart enraged at his own dear mother Althaea,
Meleager kept to his bed beside his wedded wife,
Cleopatra . . . that great beauty. Remember her?
The daughter of trim-heeled Marpessa,[5] Euenus' child,
and her husband Idas, strongest man of the men   680
who once walked the earth—he even braved Apollo,
he drew his bow at the Archer, all for Marpessa
the girl with lovely ankles. There in the halls
her father and mother always called Cleopatra Halcyon,
after the seabird's name . . . grieving once for her own fate   685
her mother had raised the halcyon's thin, painful cry,
wailing that lord Apollo the distant deadly Archer

---

3. A city in northwestern Greece. The Curetes and Aetolians were the local tribes, once allied, now at odds.   4. King of Calydon.   5. The story to which Homer alludes runs as follows: Idas, the famous archer, carried off and married Marpessa, daughter of Euenus. Apollo also had been her suitor, and he overtook Idas and carried off Marpessa. Idas defied Apollo to combat, but Zeus decided that the choice was up to Marpessa, who preferred Idas. They gave their daughter Cleopatra the nickname Halcyon, the name of a seabird that is supposed to mourn for its mate, to commemorate the time when Marpessa, carried off by Apollo, mourned for Idas.

had whisked her[6] far from Idas.
              Meleager's Cleopatra—
she was the one he lay beside those days,
brooding over his heartbreaking anger.   690
He was enraged by the curses of his mother,
volleys of curses she called down from the gods.
So racked with grief for her brother he had killed[7]
she kept pounding fists on the earth that feeds us all,
kept crying out to the god of death and grim Persephone,   695
flung herself on the ground, tears streaking her robes
and she screamed out, 'Kill Meleager, kill my son!'
And out of the world of darkness a Fury heard her cries,
stalking the night with a Fury's brutal heart, and suddenly—
thunder breaking around the gates, the roar of enemies,   700
towers battered under assault. And Aetolia's elders
begged Meleager, sent high priests of the gods,
pleading, 'Come out now! defend your people now!'—
and they vowed a princely gift.
Wherever the richest land of green Calydon lay,   705
there they urged him to choose a grand estate,
full fifty acres, half of it turned to vineyards,
half to open plowland, and carve it from the plain.
And over and over the old horseman Oeneus begged him,
he took a stand at the vaulted chamber's threshold,   710
shaking the bolted doors, begging his own son!
Over and over his brothers and noble mother
implored him—he refused them all the more—
and troops of comrades, devoted, dearest friends.
Not even they could bring his fighting spirit round   715
until, at last, rocks were raining down on the chamber,
Curetes about to mount the towers and torch the great city!
And then, finally, Meleager's bride, beautiful Cleopatra
begged him, streaming tears, recounting all the griefs
that fall to people whose city's seized and plundered—   720
the men slaughtered, citadel burned to rubble, enemies
dragging the children, raping the sashed and lovely women.
How his spirit leapt when he heard those horrors—
and buckling his gleaming armor round his body,
out he rushed to war. And so he saved them all   725
from the fatal day, he gave way to his own feelings,
but too late. No longer would they make good the gifts,
those troves of gifts to warm his heart, and even so
he beat off that disaster . . . empty-handed.

    But you, you wipe such thoughts from your mind.   730
Don't let your spirit turn you down that path, dear boy.
Harder to save the warships once they're up in flames.
Now—while the gifts still wait—go out and fight!
Go—the Achaeans all will honor you like a god!
But enter this man-killing war without the gifts—   735

6. Marpessa.   7. In the course of the battles Meleager had killed one of his mother's brothers.

your fame will flag, no longer the same honor,
even though you hurl the Trojans home!'

   But the swift runner Achilles answered firmly,
"Phoenix, old father, bred and loved by the gods,
what do I need with honor such as that?   740
I say my honor lies in the great decree of Zeus.
That gift will hold me here by the beaked ships
as long as the life breath remains inside my chest
and my springing knees will lift me. Another thing—
take it to heart, I urge you. Stop confusing   745
my fixed resolve with this, this weeping and wailing
just to serve his pleasure, Atreus' mighty son.
It degrades you to curry favor with that man,
and I will hate you for it, I who love you.
It does you proud to stand by me, my friend,   750
to attack the man who attacks me—
be king on a par with me, take half my honors!
These men will carry their message back, but you,
you stay here and spend the night in a soft bed.
Then, tomorrow at first light, we will decide   755
whether we sail home or hold out here.'
                         With that,
he gave Patroclus a sharp glance, a quiet nod
to pile the bedding deep for Phoenix now,
a sign to the rest to think of leaving quickly.
Giant Ajax rose to his feet, the son of Telamon,   760
tall as a god, turned and broke his silence:
"Ready, Odysseus? Royal son of Laertes,
great tactician—come, home we go now.
There's no achieving our mission here, I see,
not with this approach. Best to return at once,   765
give the Achaeans a full report, defeating as it is.
They must be sitting there, waiting for us now.
                       Achilles—
he's made his own proud spirit so wild in his chest,
so savage, not a thought for his comrades' love—
we honored him past all others by the ships.   770
Hard, ruthless man . . .
Why, any man will accept the blood-price paid
for a brother murdered, a child done to death.
And the murderer lives on in his own country—
the man has paid enough, and the injured kinsman   775
curbs his pride, his smoldering, vengeful spirit,
once he takes the price.
                   You—the gods have planted
a cruel, relentless fury in your chest! All for a girl,
just one, and here we offer you seven—outstanding beauties—
that, and a treasure trove besides. Achilles,   780
put some human kindness in your heart.
Show respect for your own house. Here we are,
under your roof, sent from the whole Achaean force!

Past all other men, all other Achaean comrades,
we long to be your closest, dearest friends."   785

    And the swift runner Achilles answered warmly,
"Ajax, royal son of Telamon, captain of armies,
all well said, after my own heart, or mostly so.
But my heart still heaves with rage
whenever I call to mind that arrogance of his—   790
how he mortified me, right in front of the Argives—
that son of Atreus treating me like some vagabond,
like some outcast stripped of all my rights!
You go back to him and declare my message:
I will not think of arming for bloody war again,   795
not till the son of wise King Priam, dazzling Hector
batters all the way to the Myrmidon ships and shelters,
slaughtering Argives, gutting the hulls with fire.
But round my own black ship and camp this Hector
will be stopped, I trust, blazing for battle   800
as he goes—stopped dead in his tracks!"
                                       So he finished.
Then each man, lifting his own two-handled cup,
poured it out to the gods, and back they went
along the ships, Odysseus in the lead.
Patroclus told his friends and serving-women   805
to pile a deep warm bed for Phoenix, quickly.
They obeyed and spread the bed as he ordered,
with fleeces, woolen throws and soft linen sheets.
There the old man lay, awaiting shining Dawn.
And deep in his well-built lodge Achilles slept   810
with the woman he brought from Lesbos, Phorbas' daughter,
Diomede in all her beauty sleeping by his side.
And over across from him Patroclus slept
with the sashed and lovely Iphis by his side,
whom Prince Achilles gave him the day he took   815
the heights of Scyros, Enyeus' rocky stronghold.

    But once the envoys reached Atrides' shelters,
comrades leapt to their feet, welcomed them back
and clustering round them, lifted golden cups.
One after another pressed them with questions,
King Agamemnon most urgent of all: "Come—   820
tell me, famous Odysseus, Achaea's pride and glory—
will he fight the fire off the ships? Or does he refuse,
does rage still grip his proud, mighty spirit?"

    And the steady, long-enduring Odysseus replied,   825
"Great marshal Atrides, lord of men Agamemnon,
that man has no intention of quenching his rage.
He's still bursting with anger, more than ever—
he spurns you, spurns all your gifts. Work out
your own defense, he says, you and your captains   830
save the Argive armies and the ships. Himself?

Achilles threatens, tomorrow at first light,
to haul his well-benched warships out to sea.
And what's more, he advises all the rest,
'Sail home now. You will never set your eyes   835
on the day of doom that topples looming Troy.
Thundering Zeus has spread his hands above her . . .
her armies have taken heart.'
                                                   That's his answer.
And here are men to confirm it, fellow envoys.
Ajax and two heralds, both clear-headed men.   840
But old Phoenix passes the night in camp
as Achilles bids him, so he can voyage home,
home in the ships with him to the fatherland they love.
Tomorrow at dawn. But only if Phoenix wishes.
He will never force the man to go.'
                                                   So he reported.   845
Silence held them all, struck dumb by his story,
Odysseus' words still ringing in their ears.
A long while they said nothing, spirits dashed.
Finally Diomedes lord of the war cry broke forth:
"Great marshal Atrides, lord of men Agamemnon—   850
if only you'd never begged the dauntless son of Peleus,
holding out to Achilles trove on trove of gifts!
He's a proud man at the best of times, and now
you've only plunged him deeper in his pride.
I say have done with the man—   855
whether he sails for home or stays on here.
He'll fight again—in his own good time—whenever
the courage in him flares and a god fires his blood.
So come, follow my orders. And all of us unite.
Go to sleep now, full to your heart's content   860
with food and wine, a soldier's strength and nerve.
Then when the Dawn's red fingers shine in all their glory,
quickly deploy your chariots and battalions, Agamemnon,
out in front of the ships—you spur them on
and you yourself, you fight in the front ranks!'   865

    And Achaea's kings all shouted their assent,
stirred by the stallion-breaking Diomedes' challenge.
Pouring cups to the gods, each warlord sought his shelter.
There they spent the night and took the gift of sleep.

Summary   After Achilles' refusal, the situation of the Greeks worsened rapidly.
Agamemnon, Diomedes, and Odysseus were all wounded. The Trojans breached the
stockade and fought beside the ships. Patroclus tried to bring Achilles to the aid of
the Greeks, but the most he could obtain was permission for himself to fight, clad in
Achilles' armor, at the head of the Myrmidons.

FROM BOOK XVI

[*Patroclus Fights and Dies*]

But now Sarpedon,[8] watching his comrades drop and die,
war-shirts billowing free as Patroclus killed them,
dressed his godlike Lycians down with a harsh shout:
"Lycians, where's your pride? Where are you running?
Now be fast to attack! I'll take him on myself,   5
see who he is who routs us, wreaking havoc against us—
cutting the legs from under squads of good brave men."

    With that he leapt from his chariot fully armed
and hit the ground and Patroclus straight across,
as soon as he saw him, leapt from his car too.   10
As a pair of crook-clawed, hook-beaked vultures
swoop to fight, screaming above some jagged rock—
so with their battle cries they rushed each other there.
And Zeus the son of Cronus[9] with Cronus' twisting ways,
filling with pity now to see the two great fighters,   15
said to Hera, his sister and his wife, "My cruel fate . . .
my Sarpedon, the man I love the most, my own son—
doomed to die at the hands of Menoetius' son Patroclus.
My heart is torn in two as I try to weigh all this.
Shall I pluck him up, now, while he's still alive   20
and set him down in the rich green land of Lycia,
far from the war at Troy and all its tears?
Or beat him down at Patroclus' hands at last?"

    But Queen Hera, her eyes wide, protested strongly:
"Dread majesty, son of Cronus—what are you saying?   25
A man, a mere mortal, his doom sealed long ago?
You'd set him free from all the pains of death?
Do as you please, Zeus . . .
but none of the deathless gods will ever praise you.
And I tell you this—take it to heart, I urge you—   30
if you send Sarpedon home, living still, beware!
Then surely some other god will want to sweep
his own son clear of the heavy fighting too.
Look down. Many who battle round King Priam's
mighty walls are sons of the deathless gods—   35
you will inspire lethal anger in them all.
                                                    No,
dear as he is to you, and your heart grieves for him,
leave Sarpedon there to die in the brutal onslaught,
beaten down at the hands of Menoetius' son Patroclus.
But once his soul and the life force have left him,   40
send Death to carry him home, send soothing Sleep,[1]
all the way till they reach the broad land of Lycia."

---

8. King of Lycia in Asia Minor and a Trojan ally; son of Zeus and a mortal woman (see 6.98–102, above).
9. King of the earlier generation of gods, the Titans, who were overthrown by the Olympian gods under
Zeus.   1. In Greek belief, the brother of Death.

There his brothers and countrymen will bury the prince
with full royal rites, with mounded tomb and pillar.
These are the solemn honors owed the dead."

                               So she pressed   45
and Zeus the father of men and gods complied at once.
But he showered tears of blood that drenched the earth,
showers in praise of him, his own dear son,
the man Patroclus was just about to kill
on Troy's fertile soil, far from his fatherland.   50
    Now as the two came closing on each other
Patroclus suddenly picked off Thrasymelus
the famous driver, the aide who flanked Sarpedon—
he speared him down the guts and loosed his limbs.
But Sarpedon hurled next with a flashing lance   55
and missed his man but he hit the horse Bold Dancer,
stabbing his right shoulder and down the stallion went,
screaming his life out, shrieking down in the dust
as his life breath winged away. And the paired horses[2]
reared apart—a raspy creak of the yoke, the reins flying,   60
fouled as the trace horse[3] thrashed the dust in death-throes.
But the fine spearman Automedon[4] found a cure for that—
wrenching his long sharp sword from his sturdy thigh
he leapt with a stroke to cut the trace horse free—
it worked. The team righted, pulled at the reins   65
and again both fighters closed with savage frenzy,
dueling now to the death.

                      Again Sarpedon missed—
over Patroclus' left shoulder his spearhead streaked,
it never touched his body. Patroclus hurled next,
the bronze launched from his hand—no miss, a mortal hit.   70
He struck him right where the midriff packs the pounding heart
and down Sarpedon fell as an oak or white poplar falls
or towering pine that shipwrights up on a mountain
hew down with whetted axes for sturdy ship timber—
so he stretched in front of his team and chariot,   75
sprawled and roaring, clawing the bloody dust.
As the bull a marauding lion cuts from the herd,
tawny and greathearted among the shambling cattle,
dies bellowing under the lion's killing jaws—
so now Sarpedon, captain of Lycia's shieldsmen,   80
died at Patroclus' hands and died raging still,
crying out his beloved comrade's name: "Glaucus[5]—
oh dear friend, dear fighter, soldier's soldier!
Now is the time to prove yourself a spearman,
a daring man of war—now, if you are brave,   85
make grueling battle your one consuming passion.
First find Lycia's captains, range the ranks,
spur them to fight and shield Sarpedon's body.
Then you, Glaucus, you fight for me with bronze!

---

2. Achilles' immortal horses, who shy away from contact with death.   3. A third horse that ran alongside
the pair pulling the chariot to help maneuver; here the mortal horse Bold Dancer.   4. Patroclus's charioteer.   5. Sarpedon's cousin and comrade, who has been temporarily disabled by a wound.

You'll hang your head in shame—every day of your life— 90
if the Argives strip my armor here at the anchored ships
where I have gone down fighting. Hold on, full force—
spur all our men to battle!"

Death cut him short.
The end closed in around him, swirling down his eyes,
choking off his breath. Patroclus planted a heel 95
against his chest, wrenched the spear from his wound
and the midriff came out with it—so he dragged out both
the man's life breath and the weapon's point together.
Close by, the Myrmidons[6] clung to the panting stallions
straining to bolt away, free of their masters' chariot. 100

But grief came over Glaucus, hearing his comrade's call.
His heart was racing—what could he do to help him?
Wounded himself, he gripped his right arm hard,
aching where Teucer's[7] arrow had hit him squarely,
assaulting the Argive wall, when Teucer saved his men. 105
Glaucus cried a prayer to the distant deadly Archer:[8]
"Hear me, Lord Apollo! Wherever you are now—
in Lycia's rich green country or here in Troy,
wherever on earth, you can hear a man in pain,
you have that power, and pain comes on me now. 110
Look at this ugly wound—
my whole arm rings with the stabbing pangs,
the blood won't clot, my shoulder's a dead weight.
I can't take up my spear, can't hold it steady—
no wading into enemy ranks to fight it out . . . 115
and our bravest man is dead, Sarpedon, Zeus's son—
did Zeus stand by him? Not even his own son!
I beg you, Apollo, heal this throbbing wound,
lull the pain now, lend me power in battle—
so I can rally our Lycians, drive them into war 120
and fight to save my comrade's corpse myself."
So Glaucus prayed and Apollo heard his prayer.
He stopped the pains at once, stanched the dark blood
in his throbbing wound and filled his heart with courage.
And Glaucus sensed it all and the man glowed with joy 125
that the mighty god had heard his prayer so quickly.
First he hurried to spur his Lycian captains on,
ranging his own ranks, to fight around Sarpedon,
then he ran for the Trojan lines with long strides.
He found Polydamas, Panthous' son, and Prince Agenor 130
and reaching Aeneas and Hector helmed in bronze,
shoulder-to-shoulder let his challenge fly:
"Hector, you've wiped your allies from your mind!
And all for you, Hector, far from their loved ones,
far from native land they bleed their lives away. 135
But you won't lift a hand to fight beside them.
There lies Sarpedon, lord of Lycia's shieldsmen,

6. Troops of Achilles and Patroclus.   7. Greek archer.   8. Apollo.

who defended his realm with just decrees and power—
Ares has cut him down with Patroclus' brazen spear.
Quick, my friends, stand by him! Cringe with shame   140
at the thought they'll strip his gear and maim his corpse—
these Myrmidons, seething for all the Argive troops we killed,
we speared to death against their fast trim ships!"

Hard grief came sweeping over the Trojans' heads—
unbearable, irrepressible. He was their city's bastion,   145
always, even though he came from foreign parts,
and a mass of allies marched at his command
but he excelled them all in battle, always.
So now they went at the Argives, out for blood,
and furious for Sarpedon Hector swung them round.   150
But the Argives surged to Patroclus' savage spirit—
he spurred the Aeantes[9] first, both ablaze for battle:
"Ajax, Ajax! Come—now thrill to fight as before,
brave among the brave, but now be braver still!
Their captain's down, the first to storm our wall,   155
the great Sarpedon. If only we could seize his body,
mutilate him, shame him, tear his gear from his back
and any comrade of his who tries to shield his corpse—
bring that enemy down with ruthless bronze!"
                                        Urging so
but his men already burned to drive the Trojans off.   160
And both armies now, pulling their lines tighter,
Trojans and Lycians, Myrmidons and Achaeans
closed around the corpse to lunge in battle—
terrible war cries, stark clashing of armored men.
And across the onslaught Zeus swept murderous night   165
to make the pitched battle over his own dear son
a brutal, blinding struggle.
                        Here at the first assault
the Trojans shouldered back the fiery-eyed Achaeans—
a Myrmidon had been hit, and not their least man,
dauntless Agacles' son, renowned Epigeus . . .   170
He ruled Budion's fortress town in the old days
but then, having killed some highborn cousin, fled
to Peleus and glistening Thetis, begged for his own life
and they sent him off with Achilles, breaker of men,
east to stallion-country to fight and die in Troy.   175
He had just grasped the corpse
when shining Hector smashed his head with a rock
and his whole skull split in his massive helmet—
down he slammed on Sarpedon's body, facefirst
and courage-shattering Death engulfed his corpse.   180
Grief for his dead companion seized Patroclus now,
he tore through frontline fighters swift as a hawk
diving to scatter crows and fear-struck starlings—
straight at the Lycians, Patroclus O my rider,

9. The two Greek warriors named Ajax.

straight at the pressing Trojan ranks you swooped,   185
enraged at your comrade's death! and struck Sthenelaus,
Ithaemenes' favorite son—a big rock to the neck
snapped the tendons strung to the skull's base.
So the front gave ground and flashing Hector too,
though only as far as a long slim spear can fly   190
when a man tests his hurling strength in the games
or in war when enemy fighters close to crush his life—
so far the Trojans gave as the Argives drove them back.
But Glaucus was first, lord of Lycia's shieldsmen now,
the first to turn and he killed the gallant Bathycles,   195
Chalcon's prize son who had made his home in Hellas,
excelling the Myrmidons all in wealth and fortune.
Now, just as the man was about to catch Glaucus
Glaucus suddenly spun and struck, he stabbed his chest,
ripped him down with a crash. A heavy blow to the Argives,   200
one of the brave ones down. A great joy to the Trojans,
massing packs of them swarming round the corpse
but Achaean forces never slacked their drive,
their juggernaut fury bore them breakneck on.
And there—Meriones[1] killed a Trojan captain,   205
Laogonus, daring son of Onetor, priest of Zeus,
Idaean Zeus, and his land revered him like a god—
Meriones gouged him under the jaw and ear, his spirit
flew from his limbs and the hateful darkness gripped him.
Just then Aeneas hurled his brazen spear at Meriones,   210
hoping to hit the man as he charged behind his shield.
But he eyed Aeneas straight on, he dodged the bronze,
ducking down with a quick lunge, and behind his back
the heavy spearshaft plunged and stuck in the earth,
the butt end quivering into the air till suddenly   215
rugged Ares snuffed its fury out, dead still.
The weapon shaking, planted fast in the ground,
his whole arm's power poured in a wasted shot,
Aeneas flared in anger, shouting out, "Meriones—
great dancer[2] as you are, my spear would have stopped   220
your dancing days for good if only I had hit you!"

     The hardy spearman Meriones shot back, "Aeneas—
great man of war as you are, you'll find it hard
to quench the fire of every man who fights you.
You too are made of mortal stuff, I'd say. And I,   225
if I'd lanced your guts with bronze—strong as you are
and cocksure of your hands—you'd give me glory now,
you'd give your life to the famous horseman Death!"

     But Patroclus nerved for battle dressed him down:
"Meriones, brave as you are, why bluster on this way?   230
Trust me, my friend, you'll never force the Trojans
back from this corpse with a few stinging taunts—

---

1. A warrior from Crete on the Greek side.   2. In Homer, the opposite of a warrior.

Earth will bury many a man before that. Come—
the proof of battle is action, proof of words, debate.
No time for speeches now, it's time to fight."   235

    Breaking off, he led the way as Meriones followed,
staunch as a god. And loud as the roar goes up
when men cut timber deep in the mountain glades
and the pounding din of axes echoes miles away—
so the pound and thud of blows came rising up   240
from the broad earth, from the trampled paths of war
and the bronze shields and tough plied hides struck hard
as the swords and two-edged spearheads stabbed against them.
Not even a hawk-eyed scout could still make out Sarpedon,
the man's magnificent body covered over head to toe,   245
buried under a mass of weapons, blood and dust.
But they still kept swarming round and round the corpse
like flies in a sheepfold buzzing over the brimming pails
in the first spring days when the buckets flood with milk.
So veteran troops kept swarming round that corpse,   250
never pausing—nor did mighty Zeus for a moment
turn his shining eyes from the clash of battle.
He kept them fixed on the struggling mass forever,
the Father's spirit churning, thrashing out the ways,
the numberless ways to cause Patroclus' slaughter . . .   255
To kill him too in this present bloody rampage
over Sarpedon's splendid body? Hector in glory
cutting Patroclus down with hacking bronze
then tearing the handsome war-gear off his back?
Or let him take still more, piling up his kills?   260
As Zeus turned things over, that way seemed the best:
the valiant friend-in-arms of Peleus' son Achilles
would drive the Trojans and Hector helmed in bronze
back to Troy once more, killing them by platoons—
and Zeus began with Hector, he made the man a coward.   265
Hector leaping back in his chariot, swerving to fly,
shouted out fresh orders—"Retreat, Trojans, now!"
He knew that Zeus had tipped the scales against him.
A rout—not even the die-hard Lycians stood their ground,
they all scattered in panic, down to the last man   270
when they saw their royal king speared in the heart,
Sarpedon sprawled there in the muster of the dead,
for men by the squad had dropped across his corpse
once Zeus stretched tight the lethal line of battle.
So then the Achaeans ripped the armor off his back,   275
Sarpedon's gleaming bronze that Menoetius' son
the brave Patroclus flung in the arms of cohorts
poised to speed those trophies back to the beaked ships.
And storming[3] Zeus was stirring up Apollo: "On with it now—
sweep Sarpedon clear of the weapons, Phoebus my friend,   280
and once you wipe the dark blood from his body,

---

3. I.e., the storm god.

bear him far from the fighting, off and away,
and bathe him well in a river's running tides
and anoint him with deathless oils . . .
dress his body in deathless, ambrosial robes.   285
Then send him on his way with the wind-swift escorts,
twin brothers Sleep and Death, who with all good speed
will set him down in the broad green land of Lycia.
There his brothers and countrymen will bury the prince
with full royal rites, with mounded tomb and pillar.   290
These are the solemn honors owed the dead."
                                                So he decreed
and Phoebus did not neglect the Father's strong desires.
Down from Ida's[4] slopes he dove to the bloody field
and lifting Prince Sarpedon clear of the weapons,
bore him far from the fighting, off and away,   295
and bathed him well in a river's running tides
and anointed him with deathless oils . . .
dressed his body in deathless, ambrosial robes
then sent him on his way with the wind-swift escorts,
twin brothers Sleep and Death, who with all good speed   300
set him down in Lycia's broad green land.
                                            But Patroclus,
giving a cry to Automedon whipping on his team,
Patroclus went for Troy's and Lycia's lines,
blind in his fatal frenzy—luckless soldier.
If only he had obeyed Achilles' strict command   305
he might have escaped his doom, the stark night of death.
But the will of Zeus will always overpower the will of men,
Zeus who strikes fear in even the bravest man of war
and tears away his triumph, all in a lightning flash,
and at other times he will spur a man to battle,   310
just as he urged Patroclus' fury now.
                                        Patroclus—
who was the first you slaughtered, who the last
when the great gods called you down to death?
First Adrestus, then Autonous, then Echeclus,
then Perimus, Megas' son, Epistor and Melanippus,   315
then in a flurry Elasus, Mulius and Pylartes—
he killed them all but the rest were bent on flight.

    And then and there the Achaeans might have taken Troy,
her towering gates toppling under Patroclus' power
heading the vanguard, storming on with his spear.   320
But Apollo took his stand on the massive rampart,
his mind blazing with death for him but help for Troy.
Three times Patroclus charged the jut of the high wall,
three times Apollo battered the man and hurled him back,
the god's immortal hands beating down on the gleaming shield.   325
Then at Patroclus' fourth assault like something superhuman,

---

4. High mountain near Troy, from which Zeus has been watching the fighting on the plain.

the god shrieked down his winging words of terror: "Back—
Patroclus, Prince, go back! It is not the will of fate
that the proud Trojans' citadel fall before your spear,
not even before Achilles—far greater man than you!"   330

And Patroclus gave ground, backing a good way off,
clear of the deadly Archer's wrath.
                          But now Hector,
reining his high-strung team at the Scaean Gates,
debated a moment, waiting . . .
should he drive back to the rout and soldier on?   335
Or call his armies now to rally within the ramparts?
As he turned things over, Apollo stood beside him,
taking the shape of that lusty rugged fighter
Asius, an uncle of stallion-breaking Hector,
a blood brother of Hecuba, son of Dymas   340
who lived in Phrygia near Sangarius'[5] rapids.
Like him, Apollo the son of Zeus incited Hector:
"Hector, why stop fighting? Neglecting your duty!
If only I outfought *you* as you can outfight *me*,
I'd soon teach you to shirk your work in war—   345
you'd pay the price, I swear. Up with you—fast!
Lash those pounding stallions straight at Patroclus—
you might kill him still—Apollo might give you glory!"

And back Apollo strode, a god in the wars of men
while glorious Hector ordered skilled Cebriones,[6]   350
"Flog the team to battle!" Apollo pressed on,
wading into the ruck, hurling Argives back in chaos
and handing glory to Hector and all the Trojan forces.
But Hector ignored the Argive masses, killing none,
he lashed his pounding stallions straight at Patroclus.   355
Patroclus, over against him, leapt down from his car
and hit the ground, his left hand shaking a spear
and seized with his right a jagged, glittering stone
his hand could just cover—Patroclus flung it hard,
leaning into the heave, not backing away from Hector,   360
no, and no wasted shot. But he hit his driver—
a bastard son of famed King Priam, Cebriones
yanking the reins back taut—right between the eyes.
The sharp stone crushed both brows, the skull caved in
and both eyes burst from their sockets, dropping down   365
in the dust before his feet as the reinsman vaulted,
plunging off his well-wrought car like a diver—
Cebriones' life breath left his bones behind
and you taunted his corpse, Patroclus O my rider:
"Look what a springy man, a nimble, flashy tumbler!   370
Just think what he'd do at sea where the fish swarm—
why, the man could glut a fleet, diving for oysters!

5. A river in Phrygia, a district of Asia Minor inland from Troy.   6. Hector's half brother and charioteer.

Plunging overboard, even in choppy, heaving seas,
just as he dives to ground from his war-car now.
Even these Trojans have their tumblers—what a leap!"   375

And he leapt himself at the fighting driver's corpse
with the rushing lunge of a lion struck in the chest
as he lays waste pens of cattle—
his own lordly courage about to be his death.
So you sprang at Cebriones, full fury, Patroclus,   380
as Hector sprang down from his chariot just across
and the two went tussling over the corpse as lions
up on the mountain ridges over a fresh-killed stag—
both ravenous, proud and savage—fight it out to the death.
So over the driver here and both claw-mad for battle,   385
Patroclus son of Menoetius, Hector ablaze for glory
strained to slash each other with ruthless bronze.
Hector seized the corpse's head, would not let go—
Patroclus clung to a foot and other fighters clashed,
Trojans, Argives, all in a grueling, maiming onset.   390

As the East and South Winds fight in killer-squalls
deep in a mountain valley thrashing stands of timber,
oak and ash and cornel with bark stretched taut and hard
and they whip their long sharp branches against each other,
a deafening roar goes up, the splintered timber crashing— 395
so Achaeans and Trojans crashed,
hacking into each other, and neither side now
had a thought of flight that would have meant disaster.
Showers of whetted spears stuck fast around Cebriones,
bristling winged arrows whipped from the bowstrings,   400
huge rocks by the salvo battering shields on shields
as they struggled round the corpse. And there he lay
in the whirling dust, overpowered in all his power
and wiped from memory all his horseman's skills.

So till the sun bestrode the sky at high noon   405
the weapons hurtled side-to-side and men kept falling.
But once the sun wheeled past the hour for unyoking oxen,
then the Argives mounted a fiercer new attack,
fighting beyond their fates . . .
They dragged the hero Cebriones out from under   410
the pelting shafts and Trojans' piercing cries
and they tore the handsome war-gear off his back
and Patroclus charged the enemy, fired for the kill.
Three times he charged with the headlong speed of Ares,
screaming his savage cry, three times he killed nine men. 415
Then at the fourth assault Patroclus like something superhuman—
then, Patroclus, the end of life came blazing up before you,
yes, the lord Apollo met you there in the heart of battle,
the god, the terror! Patroclus never saw him coming,
moving across the deadly rout, shrouded in thick mist   420
and on he came against him and looming up behind him now—

slammed his broad shoulders and back with the god's flat hand
and his eyes spun as Apollo knocked the helmet off his head
and under his horses' hoofs it tumbled, clattering on
with its four forged horns and its hollow blank eyes   425
and its plumes were all smeared in the bloody dust.
Forbidden before this to defile its crest in dust,[7]
it guarded the head and handsome brow of a god,
a man like a god, Achilles. But now the Father
gave it over to Hector to guard his head in war   430
since Hector's death was closing on him quickly.
Patroclus though—the spear in his grip was shattered,
the whole of its rugged bronze-shod shadow-casting length
and his shield with straps and tassels dropped from his shoulders,
flung down on the ground—and lord Apollo the son of Zeus   435
wrenched his breastplate off. Disaster seized him—
his fine legs buckling—
        he stood there, senseless—
                         And now,
right at his back, close-up, a Dardan[8] fighter speared him
squarely between the shoulder blades with a sharp lance.
Panthous' son Euphorbus, the best of his own age   440
at spears and a horseman's skill and speed of foot,
and even in this, his first attack in chariots—
just learning the arts of war—
he'd brought down twenty drivers off their cars.
He was the first to launch a spear against you,   445
Patroclus O my rider, but did not bring you down.
Yanking out his ashen shaft from your body,
back he dashed and lost himself in the crowds—
the man would not stand up to Patroclus here
in mortal combat, stripped, defenseless as he was.   450
Patroclus stunned by the spear and the god's crushing blow
was weaving back to his own thronging comrades,
trying to escape death . . .
                Hector waiting, watching
the greathearted Patroclus trying to stagger free,
seeing him wounded there with the sharp bronze   455
came rushing into him right across the lines
and rammed his spearshaft home,
stabbing deep in the guts, and the brazen point
went jutting straight out through Patroclus' back.
Down he crashed—horror gripped the Achaean armies.   460
As when some lion overpowers a tireless wild boar
up on a mountain summit, battling in all their fury
over a little spring of water, both beasts craving
to slake their thirst, but the lion beats him down
with sheer brute force as the boar fights for breath—   465
so now with a close thrust Hector the son of Priam
tore the life from the fighting son of Menoetius,

7. Because it was divinely made and part of the armor given by the gods to Peleus on his marriage to Thetis.   8. Trojan.

from Patroclus who had killed so many men in war,
and gloried over him, wild winging words: "Patroclus—
surely you must have thought you'd storm my city down,   470
you'd wrest from the wives of Troy their day of freedom,
drag them off in ships to your own dear fatherland—
you fool! Rearing in their defense my war-team,
Hector's horses were charging out to battle,
galloping, full stretch. And I with my spear,   475
Hector, shining among my combat-loving comrades,
I fight away from them the fatal day—but you,
the vultures will eat your body raw!

                    Poor, doomed . . .
not for all his power could Achilles save you now—
and how he must have filled your ears with orders   480
as you went marching out and the hero stayed behind:
'Now don't come back to the hollow ships, you hear?—
Patroclus, master horseman—
not till you've slashed the shirt around his chest
and soaked it red in the blood of man-killing Hector!'   485
So he must have commanded—you maniac, you obeyed."[9]

      Struggling for breath, you answered, Patroclus O my rider,
"Hector! Now is your time to glory to the skies . . .
now the victory is yours.
A gift of the son of Cronus, Zeus—Apollo too—   490
they brought me down with all their deathless ease,
they are the ones who tore the armor off my back.
Even if twenty Hectors had charged against me—
they'd all have died here, laid low by my spear.
No, deadly fate in league with Apollo killed me.   495
From the ranks of men, Euphorbus. You came third,
and all you could do was finish off my life . . .
One more thing—take it to heart, I urge you—
you too, you won't live long yourself, I swear.
Already I see them looming up beside you—death   500
and the strong force of fate, to bring you down
at the hands of Aeacus'[1] great royal son . . .

                              Achilles!"

      Death cut him short. The end closed in around him.
Flying free of his limbs
his soul went winging down to the House of Death,   505
wailing his fate, leaving his manhood far behind,
his young and supple strength. But glorious Hector
taunted Patroclus' body, dead as he was, "Why, Patroclus—
why prophesy my doom, my sudden death? Who knows?—
Achilles the son of sleek-haired Thetis may outrace me—   510
struck by *my* spear first—and gasp away his life!"

___

9. Hector is wrong. Achilles warned Patroclus only to drive the Trojans from the Greek ships and not to chase them back to the city.   1. Grandfather of Achilles (*son* is used loosely here).

With that he planted a heel against Patroclus' chest,
wrenched his brazen spear from the wound, kicked him over,
flat on his back, free and clear of the weapon.
At once he went for Automedon with that spear—   515
quick as a god, the aide of swift Achilles—
keen to cut him down but his veering horses
swept him well away—magnificent racing stallions,
gifts of the gods to Peleus, shining immortal gifts.

Summary   Hector stripped Achilles' divine armor from Patroclus's corpse. A fierce fight for the body itself ended in partial success for the Greeks; they took Patroclus's body but had to retreat to their camp, with the Trojans at their heels.

BOOK XVIII

[The Shield of Achilles]

So the men fought on like a mass of whirling fire
as swift Antilochus[2] raced the message toward Achilles.
Sheltered under his curving, beaked ships he found him,
foreboding, deep down, all that had come to pass.
Agonizing now he probed his own great heart: 5
"Why, why? Our long-haired Achaeans routed again,
driven in terror off the plain to crowd the ships, but why?
Dear gods, don't bring to pass the grief that haunts my heart—
the prophecy that mother revealed to me one time . . .
she said the best of the Myrmidons—while I lived—   10
would fall at Trojan hands and leave the light of day.
And now he's dead, I know it. Menoetius' gallant son,[3]
my headstrong friend! And I told Patroclus clearly,
'Once you have beaten off the lethal fire, quick,
come back to the ships—you must not battle Hector!' "   15
    As such fears went churning through his mind
the warlord Nestor's son drew near him now,
streaming warm tears, to give the dreaded message:
'Ah son of royal Peleus, what you must hear from me!
What painful news—would to god it had never happened!   20
Patroclus has fallen. They're fighting over his corpse.
He's stripped, naked—Hector with that flashing helmet,
Hector has your arms!'
                          So the captain reported.
A black cloud of grief came shrouding over Achilles.
Both hands clawing the ground for soot and filth,   25
he poured it over his head, fouled his handsome face
and black ashes settled onto his fresh clean war-shirt.
Overpowered in all his power, he sprawled in the dust.
Achilles lay there, fallen . . .
tearing his hair, defiling it with his own hands.   30
And the women he and Patroclus carried off as captives

2. A son of Nestor.   3. Patroclus.

caught the grief in their hearts and keened and wailed,
out of the tents they ran to ring the great Achilles,
all of them beat their breasts with clenched fists,
sank to the ground, each woman's knees gave way.   35
Antilochus kneeling near, weeping uncontrollably,
clutched Achilles' hands as he wept his proud heart out—
for fear he would slash his throat with an iron blade.
Achilles suddenly loosed a terrible, wrenching cry
and his noble mother heard him, seated near her father,   40
the Old Man of the Sea in the salt green depths,
and she cried out in turn. And immortal sea-nymphs
gathered round their sister, all the Nereids swelling
down the sounding depths, they all came rushing now—
Glitter, blossoming Spray and the swells' Embrace,   45
Fair-Isle and shadowy Cavern, Mist and Spindrift,
ocean nymphs of the glances pooling deep and dark,
Race-with-the-Waves and Headlands' Hope and Safe Haven,
Glimmer of Honey, Suave-and-Soothing, Whirlpool, Brilliance,
Bounty and First Light and Speeder of Ships and buoyant Power,   50
Welcome Home and Bather of Meadows and Master's Lovely Consort,
Gift of the Sea, Eyes of the World and the famous milk-white Calm
and Truth and Never-Wrong and the queen who rules the tides in beauty
and in rushed Glory and Healer of Men and the one who rescues kings
and Sparkler, Down-from-the-Cliffs, sleek-haired Strands of Sand   55
and all the rest of the Nereids swelling down the depths.
The silver cave was shimmering full of sea-nymphs,
all in one mounting chorus beating their breasts
as Thetis launched the dirge: "Hear me, sisters,
daughters of Nereus, so you all will know it well—   60
listen to all the sorrows welling in my heart!
I am agony—
                    mother of grief and greatness—O my child!
Yes, I gave birth to a flawless, mighty son . . .
the splendor of heroes, and he shot up like a young branch,
like a fine tree I reared him—the orchard's crowning glory—   65
but only to send him off in the beaked ships to Troy
to battle Trojans! Never again will I embrace him
striding home through the doors of Peleus' house.
And long as I have him with me, still alive,
looking into the sunlight, he is racked with anguish.   70
And I, I go to his side—nothing I do can help him.
Nothing. But go I shall, to see my darling boy,
to hear what grief has come to break his heart
while he holds back from battle."
                    So Thetis cried
as she left the cave and her sisters swam up with her,   75
all in a tide of tears, and billowing round them now
the ground swell heaved open. And once they reached
the fertile land of Troy they all streamed ashore,
row on row in a long cortege, the sea-nymphs
filing up where the Myrmidon ships lay hauled,   80
clustered closely round the great runner Achilles . . .

As he groaned from the depths his mother rose before him
and sobbing a sharp cry, cradled her son's head in her hands
and her words were all compassion, winging pity: "My child—
why in tears? What sorrow has touched your heart?
Tell me, please. Don't harbor it deep inside you.   85
Zeus has accomplished everything you wanted,
just as you raised your hands and prayed that day.
All the sons of Achaea are pinned against the ships
and all for want of you—they suffer shattering losses."   90

    And groaning deeply the matchless runner answered,
"O dear mother, true! All those burning desires
Olympian Zeus has brought to pass for me—
but what joy to me now? My dear comrade's dead—
Patroclus—the man I loved beyond all other comrades,   95
loved as my own life—I've lost him—Hector's killed him,
stripped the gigantic armor off his back, a marvel to behold—
my burnished gear! Radiant gifts the gods presented Peleus
that day they drove you into a mortal's marriage bed . . . .
I wish you'd lingered deep with the deathless sea-nymphs,   100
lived at ease, and Peleus carried home a mortal bride.
But now, as it is, sorrows, unending sorrows must surge
within your heart as well—for your own son's death.
Never again will you embrace him striding home.
My spirit rebels—I've lost the will to live,   105
to take my stand in the world of men—unless,
before all else, Hector's battered down by my spear
and gasps away his life, the blood-price for Patroclus,
Menoetius' gallant son he's killed and stripped!"

    But Thetis answered, warning through her tears,   110
"You're doomed to a short life, my son, from all you say!
For hard on the heels of Hector's death your death
must come at once—"

               "Then let me die at once"—
Achilles burst out, despairing—"since it was not my fate
to save my dearest comrade from his death! Look,   115
a world away from his fatherland he's perished,
lacking me, my fighting strength, to defend him.
But now, since I shall not return to my fatherland . . .
nor did I bring one ray of hope to my Patroclus,
nor to the rest of all my steadfast comrades,   120
countless ranks struck down by mighty Hector—
No, no, here I sit by the ships . . .
a useless, dead weight on the good green earth—
I, no man my equal among the bronze-armed Achaeans,
not in battle, only in wars of words that others win.   125
If only strife could die from the lives of gods and men
and anger that drives the sanest man to flare in outrage—
bitter gall, sweeter than dripping streams of honey,

that swarms in people's chests and blinds like smoke—
just like the anger Agamemnon king of men   130
has roused within me now . . .
                      Enough.
Let bygones be bygones. Done is done.
Despite my anguish I will beat it down,
the fury mounting inside me, down by force.
But now I'll go and meet that murderer head-on,   135
that Hector who destroyed the dearest life I know.
For my own death, I'll meet it freely—whenever Zeus
and the other deathless gods would like to bring it on!
Not even Heracles⁴ fled his death, for all his power,
favorite son as he was to Father Zeus the King.   140
Fate crushed him, and Hera's savage anger.
And I too, if the same fate waits for me . . .
I'll lie in peace, once I've gone down to death.
But now, for the moment, let me seize great glory!—
and drive some woman of Troy or deep-breasted Dardan⁵   145
to claw with both hands at her tender cheeks and wipe away
her burning tears as the sobs come choking from her throat—
they'll learn that I refrained from war a good long time!
Don't try to hold me back from the fighting, mother,
love me as you do. You can't persuade me now."   150

   The goddess of the glistening feet replied,
"Yes, my son, you're right. No coward's work,
to save your exhausted friends from headlong death.
But your own handsome war-gear lies in Trojan hands
bronze and burnished—and Hector in that flashing helmet,   155
Hector glories in your armor, strapped across his back.
Not that he will glory in it long, I tell you:
his own destruction hovers near him now. Wait—
don't fling yourself in the grind of battle yet,
not till you see me coming back with your own eyes.   160
Tomorrow I will return to you with the rising sun,
bearing splendid arms from Hephaestus, god of fire!"

   With that vow she turned away from her son
and faced and urged her sisters of the deep,
"Now down you go in the Ocean's folding gulfs   165
to visit father's halls—the Old Man of the Sea—
and tell him all. I am on my way to Olympus heights,
to the famous Smith Hephaestus—I pray he'll give my son
some fabulous armor full of the god's great fire!"

   And under a foaming wave her sisters dove   170
as glistening-footed Thetis soared toward Olympus

---

4. The son of Zeus by a mortal woman; pursued by the jealousy of Hera, he was forced to undertake twelve great labors and finally died in agony from the effects of a poisoned garment.   5. Trojan.

to win her dear son an immortal set of arms.

And now,
as her feet swept her toward Olympus, ranks of Achaeans,
fleeing man-killing Hector with grim, unearthly cries,
reached the ships and the Hellespont's long shore.   175
As for Patroclus, there seemed no hope that Achaens
could drag the corpse of Achilles' comrade out of range.
Again the Trojan troops and teams overtook the body
with Hector son of Priam storming fierce as fire.
Three times illustrious Hector shouted for support,   180
seized his feet from behind, wild to drag him off,
three times the Aeantes, armored in battle-fury
fought him off the corpse. But Hector held firm,
staking all on his massive fighting strength—
again and again he'd hurl himself at the melee,   185
again and again stand fast with piercing cries
but he never gave ground backward, not one inch.
The helmed Aeantes could no more frighten Hector,
the proud son of Priam, back from Patroclus' corpse
than shepherds out in the field can scare a tawny lion   190
off his kill when the hunger drives the beast claw-mad.
And now Hector would have hauled the body away
and won undying glory . . .
if wind-swift Iris[6] had not swept from Olympus
bearing her message—Peleus' son must arm—   195
but all unknown to Zeus and the other gods
since Hera spurred her on. Halting near
she gave Achilles a flight of marching orders:
"To arms—son of Peleus! Most terrifying man alive!
Defend Patroclus! It's all for him, this merciless battle   200
pitched before the ships. They're mauling each other now,
Achaeans struggling to save the corpse from harm,
Trojans charging to haul it back to windy Troy.
Flashing Hector far in the lead, wild to drag it off,
furious to lop the head from its soft, tender neck   205
and stake it high on the city's palisade.

Up with you—
no more lying low! Writhe with shame at the thought
Patroclus may be sport for the dogs of Troy!
Yours, the shame will be yours
if your comrade's corpse goes down to the dead defiled!"   210

    But the swift runner replied, "Immortal Iris—
what god has sped you here to tell me this?"

    Quick as the wind the rushing Iris answered,
"Hera winged me on, the illustrious wife of Zeus.
But the son of Cronus throned on high knows nothing,   215
nor does any other immortal housed on Olympus

---

6. Messenger of the gods, particularly of Hera.

shrouded deep in snow."
                             Achilles broke in quickly—
"How can I go to war? The Trojans have my gear.
And my dear mother told me I must not arm for battle,
not till I see her coming back with my own eyes—   220
she vowed to bring me burnished arms from the god of fire.
I know of no other armor. Whose gear could I wear?
None but Telamonian Ajax'[7] giant shield.
But he's at the front, I'm sure, engaging Trojans,
slashing his spear to save Patroclus' body."   225

    Quick as the wind the goddess had a plan:
"We know—we too—they hold your famous armor.
Still, just as you are, go out to the broad trench
and show yourself to the Trojans. Struck with fear
at the sight of you, they might hold off from attack   230
and Achaea's fighting sons get second wind,
exhausted as they are . . .
Breathing room in war is all too brief."

    And Iris racing the wind went veering off
as Achilles, Zeus's favorite fighter, rose up now   235
and over his powerful shoulder Pallas slung the shield,
the tremendous storm-shield with all its tassels flaring—
and crowning his head the goddess swept a golden cloud
and from it she lit a fire to blaze across the field.
As smoke goes towering up the sky from out a town   240
cut off on a distant island under siege . . .
enemies battling round it, defenders all day long
trading desperate blows from their own city walls
but soon as the sun goes down the signal fires flash,
rows of beacons blazing into the air to alert their neighbors—   245
if only they'll come in ships to save them from disaster—
so now from Achilles' head the blaze shot up the sky.
He strode from the rampart, took his stand at the trench
but he would not mix with the milling Argive ranks.
He stood in awe of his mother's strict command.   250
So there he rose and loosed an enormous cry
and off in the distance Pallas shrieked out too
and drove an unearthly panic through the Trojans.
Piercing loud as the trumpet's battle cry that blasts
from murderous raiding armies ringed around some city—   255
so piercing now the cry that broke from Aeacides.
And Trojans hearing the brazen voice of Aeacides,
all their spirits quaked—even sleek-maned horses,
sensing death in the wind, slewed their chariots round
and charioteers were struck dumb when they saw that fire,   260
relentless, terrible, burst from proud-hearted Achilles' head,
blazing as fiery-eyed Athena fueled the flames. Three times
the brilliant Achilles gave his great war cry over the trench,

---

7. The more famous of the two heroes called Ajax was the son of Telamon.

three times the Trojans and famous allies whirled in panic—
and twelve of their finest fighters died then and there,   265
crushed by chariots, impaled on their own spears.
And now the exultant Argives seized the chance
to drag Patroclus' body quickly out of range
and laid him on a litter . . .
Standing round him, loving comrades mourned,   270
and the swift runner Achilles joined them, grieving,
weeping warm tears when he saw his steadfast comrade
lying dead on the bier, mauled by tearing bronze,
the man he sent to war with team and chariot
but never welcomed home again alive.   275

     Now Hera the ox-eyed queen of heaven drove the sun,
untired and all unwilling, to sink in the Ocean's depths
and the sun went down at last and brave Achaeans ceased
the grueling clash of arms, the leveling rout of war.

     And the Trojans in turn, far across the field,   280
pulling forces back from the last rough assault,
freed their racing teams from under chariot yokes
but before they thought of supper, grouped for council.
They met on their feet. Not one of them dared to sit
for terror seized them all—the great Achilles   285
who held back from the brutal fighting so long
had just come blazing forth.
Panthous' son Polydamas led the debate,
a good clear head, and the only man who saw
what lay in the past and what the Trojans faced.[8]   290
He was Hector's close comrade, born on the same night,
but excelled at trading words as he at trading spear-thrusts.
And now, with all good will, Polydamas rose and spoke:
"Weigh both sides of the crisis well, my friends.
What I urge is this: draw back to the city now.   295
Don't wait for the holy Dawn to find us here afield,
ranged by the ships—we're too far from our walls.
As long as that man kept raging at royal Agamemnon
the Argive troops were easier game to battle down.
I too was glad to camp the night on the shipways,   300
hopes soaring to seize their heavy rolling hulls.
But now racing Achilles makes my blood run cold.
So wild the man's fury he will never rest content,
holding out on the plain where Trojans and Argives
met halfway, exchanging blows in the savage onset—   305
never: *he* will fight for our wives, for Troy itself!
So retreat to Troy. Trust me—we will face disaster.
Now, for the moment, the bracing godsent night
has stopped the swift Achilles in his tracks.
But let him catch us lingering here tomorrow,   310
just as he rises up in arms—there may be some

8. I.e., he was a prophet and knew the past and foresaw the future.

who will sense his fighting spirit all too well.
You'll thank your stars to get back to sacred Troy,
whoever escapes him. Dogs and birds will have their fill—
of Trojan flesh, by heaven. Battalions of Trojans!   315
Pray god such grief will never reach my ears.
So follow my advice, hard as it may seem . . .
Tonight conserve our strength in the meeting place,
and the great walls and gates and timbered doors we hung,
well-planed, massive and bolted tight, will shield the city.   320
But tomorrow at daybreak, armed to the hilt for battle,
we man the towering ramparts. All the worse for him—
if Achilles wants to venture forth from the fleet,
fight us round our walls. Back to the ships he'll go,
once he's lashed the power out of his rippling stallions,   325
whipping them back and forth beneath our city walls.
Not even *his* fury will let him crash our gates—
he'll never plunder Troy.
Sooner the racing dogs will eat him raw!"

   Helmet flashing, Hector wheeled with a dark glance: 330
"No more, Polydamas! Your pleading repels me now.
You say go back again—be crammed inside the city.
Aren't you sick of being caged inside those walls?
Time was when the world would talk of Priam's Troy
as the city rich in gold and rich in bronze—but now   335
our houses are stripped of all their sumptuous treasures,
troves sold off and shipped to Phrygia, lovely Maeonia,
once great Zeus grew angry . . .
but now, the moment the son of crooked Cronus
allows me to seize some glory here at the ships   340
and pin these Argives back against the sea—
you fool, enough! No more thoughts of retreat
paraded before our people. Not that one Trojan
will ever take your lead—I'll never permit it.
Come, follow my orders! All obey me now.   345
Take supper now. Take your posts through camp.
And no forgetting the watch, each man wide awake.
And any Trojan so weighed down, so oppressed
by his own possessions, let him collect the lot,
pass them round to the people—a grand public feast.   350
Far better for one of ours to reap the benefits
than all the marauding Argives. Then, as you say,
'tomorrow at daybreak, armed to the hilt for battle'—
we slash to attack against their deep curved hulls!
If it really *was* Achilles who reared beside the ships,   355
all the worse for him—if he wants his fill of war.
I for one, I'll never run from his grim assault,
I'll stand up to the man—see if he bears off glory
or I bear it off myself! The god of war is impartial:
he hands out death to the man who hands out death."   360

   So Hector finished. The Trojans roared assent,
lost in folly. Athena had swept away their senses.

They gave applause to Hector's ruinous tactics,
none to Polydamas, who gave them sound advice.
And now their entire army settled down to supper   365
but all night long the Argives raised Patroclus' dirge.
And Achilles led them now in a throbbing chant of sorrow,
laying his man-killing hands on his great friend's chest,
convulsed with bursts of grief. Like a bearded lion
whose pride of cubs a deer-hunter has snatched away,   370
out of some thick woods, and back he comes, too late,
and his heart breaks but he courses after the hunter,
hot on his tracks down glen on twisting glen—
where can he find him?—gripped by piercing rage . . .
so Achilles groaned, deeply, crying out to his Myrmidons,   375
"O my captains! How empty the promise I let fall
that day I reassured Menoetius in his house—
I promised the king I'd bring him back his son,
home to Opois,⁹ covered in glory, Troy sacked,
hauling his rightful share of plunder home at last.   380
But Zeus will never accomplish all our best-laid plans.
Look at us. Both doomed to stain red with our blood
the same plot of earth, a world away in Troy!
For not even I will voyage home again. Never.
No embrace in his halls from the old horseman Peleus   385
nor from mother, Thetis—this alien earth I stride
will hold me down at last.

          But now, Patroclus,
since I will follow you underneath the ground,
I shall not bury you, not till I drag back here
the gear and head of Hector, who slaughtered you,   390
my friend, greathearted friend . . .
Here in front of your flaming pyre I'll cut the throats
of a dozen sons of Troy in all their shining glory,
venting my rage on them for your destruction!
Till then you lie as you are beside my beaked ships   395
and round you the Trojan women and deep-breasted Dardans
will mourn you night and day, weeping burning tears,
women we fought to win—strong hands and heavy lance—
whenever we sacked rich cities held by mortal men."

    With that the brilliant Achilles ordered friends   400
to set a large three-legged cauldron over the fire
and wash the clotted blood from Patroclus' wounds
with all good speed. Hoisting over the blaze
a cauldron filled to the brim with bathing water,
they piled fresh logs beneath and lit them quickly.   405
The fire lapped at the vessel's belly, the water heated
and soon as it reached the boil in the glowing bronze
they bathed and anointed the body sleek with olive oil,
closed each wound with a soothing, seasoned unguent
and then they laid Patroclus on his bier . . .   410
covered him head to foot in a thin light sheet

9. Ancient city on the eastern coast of the Greek mainland and home of Menoetius, father of Patroclus.

and over his body spread the white linen shroud.
Then all night long, ringing the great runner Achilles,
Myrmidon fighters mourned and raised Patroclus' dirge.

But Zeus turned to Hera, his wife and sister, saying,   415
"So, my ox-eyed Queen, you've had your way at last,
setting the famous runner Achilles on his feet.
Mother Hera—look, these long-haired Achaeans
must be sprung of your own immortal loins."

But her eyes widening, noble Hera answered,   420
"Dread majesty, son of Cronus, what are you saying?
Even a mortal man will act to help a friend,
condemned as a mortal always is to death
and hardly endowed with wisdom deep as ours.
So how could I, claiming to be the highest goddess—   425
both by birth and since I am called your consort
and you in turn rule all the immortal gods—
how could I hold back from these, these Trojans,
men I loathe, and fail to weave their ruin?"

Now as the King and Queen provoked each other,   430
glistening-footed Thetis reached Hephaestus' house,
indestructible, bright as stars, shining among the gods,
built of bronze by the crippled Smith with his own hands.
There she found him, sweating, wheeling round his bellows,
pressing the work on twenty three-legged cauldrons,   435
an array to ring the walls inside his mansion.
He'd bolted golden wheels to the legs of each
so all on their own speed, at a nod from him,
they could roll to halls where the gods convene
then roll right home again—a marvel to behold.   440
But not quite finished yet . . .
the god had still to attach the inlaid handles.
These he was just fitting, beating in the rivets.
As he bent to the work with all his craft and cunning,
Thetis on her glistening feet drew near the Smith.   445
But Charis[1] saw her first, Charis coming forward,
lithe and lovely in all her glittering headdress,
the Grace the illustrious crippled Smith had married.
Approaching Thetis, she caught her hand and spoke her name:
"Thetis of flowing robes! What brings you to our house?   450
A beloved, honored friend—but it's been so long,
your visits much too rare. Follow me in, please,
let me offer you all a guest could want."
                                    Welcome words,
and the radiant goddess Charis led the way inside.
She seated her on a handsome, well-wrought chair,   455
studded with silver, under it slipped a stool

1. Her name means grace or beauty.

and called the famous Smith: "Hephaestus, come—
look who's here! Thetis would ask a favor of you!"

And the famous crippled Smith exclaimed warmly,
"Thetis—here? Ah then a wondrous, honored goddess   460
comes to grace our house! Thetis saved my life
when the mortal pain came on me after my great fall,
thanks to my mother's will, that brazen bitch,
she wanted to hide me—because I was a cripple.
What shattering anguish I'd have suffered then   465
if Thetis had not taken me to her breast, Eurynome too,
the daughter of ocean's stream that runs around the world.
Nine years I lived with both, forging bronze by the trove,
elegant brooches, whorled pins, necklaces, chokers, chains—
there in the vaulted cave—and round us Ocean's currents   470
swirled in a foaming, roaring rush that never died.
And no one knew. Not a single god or mortal,
only Thetis and Eurynome knew—they saved me.
And here is Thetis now, in our own house!
So I *must* do all I can to pay her back,   475
the price for the life she saved . . .
the nymph of the sea with sleek and lustrous locks.
Quickly, set before her stranger's generous fare
while I put away my bellows and all my tools."
                                           With that
he heaved up from the anvil block—his immense hulk   480
hobbling along but his shrunken legs moved nimbly.
He swung the bellows aside and off the fires,
gathered the tools he'd used to weld the cauldrons
and packed them all in a sturdy silver strongbox.
Then he sponged off his brow and both burly arms,   485
his massive neck and shaggy chest, pulled on a shirt
and grasping a heavy staff, Hephaestus left his forge
and hobbled on. Handmaids ran to attend their master,
all cast in gold but a match for living, breathing girls.
Intelligence fills their hearts, voice and strength their frames,   490
from the deathless gods they've learned their works of hand.
They rushed to support their lord as he went bustling on
and lurching nearer to Thetis, took his polished seat,
reached over to clutch her hand and spoke her name:
"Thetis of flowing robes! What brings you to our house?   495
A beloved, honored friend—but it's been so long,
your visits much too rare.
Tell me what's on your mind. I am eager to do it—
whatever I *can* do . . . whatever can be done."

But Thetis burst into tears, her voice welling: 500
"Oh Hephaestus—who of all the goddesses on Olympus,
who has borne such withering sorrows in her heart?
Such pain as Zeus has given me, above all others!
Me out of all the daughters of the sea he chose
to yoke to a mortal man, Peleus, son of Aeacus,   505

and I endured his bed, a mortal's bed, resisting
with all my will. And now he lies in the halls,
broken with grisly age, but now my griefs are worse.
Remember? Zeus also gave me a son to bear and breed,
the splendor of heroes, and he shot up like a young branch,   510
like a fine tree I reared him—the orchard's crowning glory—
but only to send him off in the beaked ships to Troy
to battle Trojans! Never again will I embrace him
striding home through the doors of Peleus' house.
And long as I have him with me, still alive,   515
looking into the sunlight, he is racked with anguish.
I go to his side—nothing I do can help him. Nothing.
That girl the sons of Achaea picked out for his prize—
right from his grasp the mighty Agamemnon tore her,
and grief for her has been gnawing at his heart.   520
But then the Trojans pinned the Achaeans tight
against their sterns, they gave them no way out,
and the Argive warlords begged my son to help,
they named in full the troves of glittering gifts
they'd send his way. But at that point he refused   525
to beat disaster off—refused himself, that is—
but he buckled his own armor round Patroclus,
sent him into battle with an army at his back.
And all day long they fought at the Scaean Gates,
that very day they would have stormed the city too,   530
if Apollo had not killed Menoetius' gallant son
as he laid the Trojans low—Apollo cut him down
among the champions there and handed Hector glory.
So now I come, I throw myself at your knees,
please help me! Give my son—he won't live long—   535
a shield and helmet and tooled greaves with ankle-straps
and armor for his chest. All that he had was lost,
lost when the Trojans killed his steadfast friend.
Now he lies on the ground—his heart is breaking."

    And the famous crippled Smith replied, "Courage!   540
Anguish for all that armor—sweep it from your mind.
If only I could hide him away from pain and death,
that day his grim destiny comes to take Achilles,
as surely as glorious armor shall be his, armor
that any man in the world of men will marvel at   545
through all the years to come—whoever sees its splendor."
    With that he left her there and made for his bellows,
turning them on the fire, commanding, "Work—to work!"
And the bellows, all twenty, blew on the crucibles,
breathing with all degrees of shooting, fiery heat   550
as the god hurried on—a blast for the heavy work,
a quick breath for the light, all precisely gauged
to the god of fire's wish and the pace of the work in hand.
Bronze he flung in the blaze, tough, durable bronze
and tin and priceless gold and silver, and then,   555

planting the huge anvil upon its block, he gripped
his mighty hammer in one hand, the other gripped his tongs.

And first Hephaestus makes a great and massive shield,
blazoning well-wrought emblems all across its surface,
raising a rim around it, glittering, triple-ply   560
with a silver shield-strap run from edge to edge
and five layers of metal to build the shield itself,
and across its vast expanse with all his craft and cunning
the god creates a world of gorgeous immortal work.

There he made the earth and there the sky and the sea   565
and the inexhaustible blazing sun and the moon rounding full
and there the constellations, all that crown the heavens,
the Pleiades and the Hyades, Orion in all his power too
and the Great Bear[2] that mankind also calls the Wagon:
she wheels on her axis always fixed, watching Orion,   570
and she alone is denied a plunge in the Ocean's baths.

And he forged on the shield two noble cities filled
with mortal men. With weddings and wedding feasts in one
and under glowing torches they brought forth the brides
from the women's chambers, marching through the streets   575
while choir on choir the wedding song rose high
and the young men came dancing, whirling round in rings
and among them the flutes and harps kept up their stirring call—
women rushed to the doors and each stood moved with wonder.
And the people massed, streaming into the marketplace   580
where a quarrel had broken out and two men struggled
over the blood-price for a kinsman just murdered.
One declaimed in public, vowing payment in full—
the other spurned him, he would not take a thing—
so both men pressed for a judge to cut the knot.   585
The crowd cheered on both, they took both sides,
but heralds held them back as the city elders sat
on polished stone benches, forming the sacred circle,
grasping in hand the staffs of clear-voiced heralds,
and each leapt to his feet to plead the case in turn.   590
Two bars of solid gold shone on the ground before them,
a prize for the judge who'd speak the straightest verdict.

But circling the other city camped a divided army
gleaming in battle-gear, and two plans split their ranks:
to plunder the city or share the riches with its people,   595
hoards the handsome citadel stored within its depths.
But the people were not surrendering, not at all.
They armed for a raid, hoping to break the siege—
loving wives and innocent children standing guard

2. The Big Dipper, which never descends below the horizon. It is a female bear (Ursa Major), hence *she*
in line 570. Pleiades, Hyades, and Orion are all constellations. Orion was a giant hunter of Greek mythology.

on the ramparts, flanked by elders bent with age   600
as men marched out to war. Ares and Pallas led them,
both burnished gold, gold the attire they donned, and great,
magnificent in their armor—gods for all the world,
looming up in their brilliance, towering over troops.
And once they reached the perfect spot for attack,   605
a watering place where all the herds collected,
there they crouched, wrapped in glowing bronze.
Detached from the ranks, two scouts took up their posts,
the eyes of the army waiting to spot a convoy,
the enemy's flocks and crook-horned cattle coming . . .   610
Come they did, quickly, two shepherds behind them,
playing their hearts out on their pipes—treachery
never crossed their minds. But the soldiers saw them,
rushed them, cut off at a stroke the herds of oxen
and sleek sheep-flocks glistening silver-gray   615
and killed the herdsmen too. Now the besiegers,
soon as they heard the uproar burst from the cattle
as they debated, huddled in council, mounted at once
behind their racing teams, rode hard to the rescue,
arrived at once, and lining up for assault   620
both armies battled it out along the river banks—
they raked each other with hurtling bronze-tipped spears.
And Strife and Havoc plunged in the fight, and violent Death—
now seizing a man alive with fresh wounds, now one unhurt,
now hauling a deadman through the slaughter by the heels,   625
the cloak on her back stained red with human blood.
So they clashed and fought like living, breathing men
grappling each other's corpses, dragging off the dead.

    And he forged a fallow field, broad rich plowland
tilled for the third time, and across it crews of plowmen   630
wheeled their teams, driving them up and back and soon
as they'd reach the end-strip, moving into the turn,
a man would run up quickly
and hand them a cup of honeyed, mellow wine
as the crews would turn back down along the furrows,   635
pressing again to reach the end of the deep fallow field
and the earth churned black behind them, like earth churning,
solid gold as it was—that was the wonder of Hephaestus' work.

    And he forged a king's estate where harvesters labored,
reaping the ripe grain, swinging their whetted scythes.   640
Some stalks fell in line with the reapers, row on row,
and others the sheaf-binders girded round with ropes,
three binders standing over the sheaves, behind them
boys gathering up the cut swaths, filling their arms,
supplying grain to the binders, endless bundles.   645
And there in the midst the king,
scepter in hand at the head of the reaping-rows,
stood tall in silence, rejoicing in his heart.
And off to the side, beneath a spreading oak,

the heralds were setting out the harvest feast,   650
they were dressing a great ox they had slaughtered,
while attendant women poured out barley, generous,
glistening handfuls strewn for the reapers' midday meal.

    And he forged a thriving vineyard loaded with clusters,
bunches of lustrous grapes in gold, ripening deep purple   655
and climbing vines shot up on silver vine-poles.
And round it he cut a ditch in dark blue enamel
and round the ditch he staked a fence in tin.
And one lone footpath led toward the vineyard
and down it the pickers ran   660
whenever they went to strip the grapes at vintage—
girls and boys, their hearts leaping in innocence,
bearing away the sweet ripe fruit in wicker baskets.
And there among them a young boy plucked his lyre,
so clear it could break the heart with longing,   665
and what he sang was a dirge for the dying year,
lovely . . . his fine voice rising and falling low
as the rest followed, all together, frisking, singing,
shouting, their dancing footsteps beating out the time.

    And he forged on the shield a herd of longhorn cattle,   670
working the bulls in beaten gold and tin, lowing loud
and rumbling out of the farmyard dung to pasture
along a rippling stream, along the swaying reeds.
And the golden drovers kept the herd in line,
four in all, with nine dogs at their heels,   675
their paws flickering quickly—a savage roar!—
a crashing attack—and a pair of ramping lions
had seized a bull from the cattle's front ranks—
he bellowed out as they dragged him off in agony.
Packs of dogs and the young herdsmen rushed to help   680
but the lions ripping open the hide of the huge bull
were gulping down the guts and the black pooling blood
while the herdsmen yelled the fast pack on—no use.
The hounds shrank from sinking teeth in the lions,
they balked, hunching close, barking, cringing away.   685

    And the famous crippled Smith forged a meadow
deep in a shaded glen for shimmering flocks to graze,
with shepherds' steadings, well-roofed huts and sheepfolds.

    And the crippled Smith brought all his art to bear
on a dancing circle, broad as the circle Daedalus   690
once laid out on Cnossos' spacious fields
for Ariadne[3] the girl with lustrous hair.
Here young boys and girls, beauties courted
with costly gifts of oxen, danced and danced,

3. Daughter of Minos, king of Crete. Daedalus was the "fabulous artificer" who built the labyrinth and,
with his son, Icarus, escaped from Crete on wings. Cnossos was the site of Minos's great palace.

linking their arms, gripping each other's wrists.   695
And the girls wore robes of linen light and flowing,
the boys wore finespun tunics rubbed with a gloss of oil,
the girls were crowned with a bloom of fresh garlands,
the boys swung golden daggers hung on silver belts.
And now they would run in rings on their skilled feet,   700
nimbly, quick as a crouching potter spins his wheel,
palming it smoothly, giving it practice twirls
to see it run, and now they would run in rows,
in rows crisscrossing rows—rapturous dancing.
A breathless crowd stood round them struck with joy   705
and through them a pair of tumblers dashed and sprang,
whirling in leaping handsprings, leading out the dance.

    And he forged the Ocean River's mighty power girdling
round the outmost rim of the welded indestructible shield.

    And once the god had made that great and massive shield   710
he made Achilles a breastplate brighter than gleaming fire,
he made him a sturdy helmet to fit the fighter's temples,
beautiful, burnished work, and raised its golden crest
and made him greaves of flexing, pliant tin.
                                   Now,
when the famous crippled Smith had finished off   715
that grand array of armor, lifting it in his arms
he laid it all at the feet of Achilles' mother Thetis—
and down she flashed like a hawk from snowy Mount Olympus
bearing the brilliant gear, the god of fire's gift.

Summary   Achilles finally accepted gifts of restitution from Agamemnon, as he
had refused to do earlier. His return to the fighting brought terror to the Trojans and
turned the battle into a rout in which Achilles killed every Trojan that crossed his
path. As he pursued Agenor, Apollo tricked him by rescuing his intended victim (he
spirited him away in a mist) and assumed Agenor's shape to lead Achilles away from
the walls of Troy. The Trojans took refuge in the city, all except Hector.

BOOK XXII

[The Death of Hector]

So all through Troy the men who had fled like panicked fawns
were wiping off their sweat, drinking away their thirst,
leaning along the city's massive ramparts now
while Achaean troops, sloping shields to shoulders,
closed against the walls. But there stood Hector,   5
shackled fast by his deadly fate, holding his ground,
exposed in front of Troy and the Scaean Gates.
And now Apollo turned to taunt Achilles:
"Why are you chasing *me*? Why waste your speed?—
son of Peleus, you a mortal and I a deathless god.   10
You still don't know that I am immortal, do you?—
straining to catch me in your fury! Have you forgotten?

There's a war to fight with the Trojans you stampeded,
look, they're packed inside their city walls, but you,
you've slipped away out here. You can't kill *me*—   15
I can never die—it's not my fate!"
                                        Enraged at that,
Achilles shouted in mid-stride, "You've blocked my way,
you distant, deadly Archer, deadliest god of all—
you made me swerve away from the rampart there.
Else what a mighty Trojan army had gnawed the dust   20
before they could ever straggle through their gates!
Now you've robbed me of great glory, saved their lives
with all your deathless ease. Nothing for you to fear,
no punishment to come. Oh I'd pay you back
if I only had the power at my command!"   25

    No more words—he dashed toward the city,
heart racing for some great exploit, rushing on
like a champion stallion drawing a chariot full tilt,
sweeping across the plain in easy, tearing strides—
as Achilles hurtled on, driving legs and knees.   30

    And old King Priam was first to see him coming,
surging over the plain, blazing like the star
that rears at harvest, flaming up in its brilliance—
far outshining the countless stars in the night sky,
that star they call Orion's Dog[4]—brightest of all   35
but a fatal sign emblazoned on the heavens,
it brings such killing fever down on wretched men.
So the bronze flared on his chest as on he raced—
and the old man moaned, flinging both hands high,
beating his head and groaning deep he called,   40
begging his dear son who stood before the gates,
unshakable, furious to fight Achilles to the death.
The old man cried, pitifully, hands reaching out to him,
"Oh Hector! Don't just stand there, don't, dear child,
waiting that man's attack—alone, cut off from friends!   45
You'll meet your doom at once, beaten down by Achilles,
so much stronger than you—that hard, headlong man.
Oh if only the gods loved him as much as I do . . .
dogs and vultures would eat his fallen corpse at once!—
with what a load of misery lifted from my spirit.   50
That man who robbed me of my sons, brave boys,
cutting them down or selling them off as slaves,
shipped to islands half the world away . . .
Even now there are two, Lycaon and Polydorus—
I cannot find them among the soldiers crowding Troy,   55
those sons Laothoë[5] bore me, Laothoë queen of women.
But if they are still alive in the enemy's camp,
then we'll ransom them back with bronze and gold.

---

4. Sirius, the "dog star," in the constellation Canis Major.   **5.** Priam had more than one wife. Achilles killed Lycaon and Polydorus in the fighting outside the city.

We have hoards inside the walls, the rich dowry
old and famous Altes[6] presented with his daughter.   60
But if they're dead already, gone to the House of Death,
what grief to their mother's heart and mine—we gave them life.
For the rest of Troy, though, just a moment's grief
unless you too are battered down by Achilles.
Back, come back! Inside the walls, my boy!   65
Rescue the men of Troy and the Trojan women—
don't hand the great glory to Peleus' son,
bereft of your own sweet life yourself.
                                        Pity me too!—
still in my senses, true, but a harrowed, broken man
marked out by doom—past the threshold of old age . . .   70
and Father Zeus will waste me with a hideous fate,
and after I've lived to look on so much horror!
My sons laid low, my daughters dragged away
and the treasure-chambers looted, helpless babies
hurled to the earth in the red barbarity of war . . .   75
my sons' wives hauled off by the Argives' bloody hands!
And I, I last of all—the dogs before my doors
will eat me raw, once some enemy brings me down
with his sharp bronze sword or spits me with a spear,
wrenching the life out of my body, yes, the very dogs   80
I bred in my own halls to share my table, guard my gates—
mad, rabid at heart they'll lap their master's blood
and loll before my doors.
                              Ah for a young man
all looks fine and noble if he goes down in war,
hacked to pieces under a slashing bronze blade—   85
he lies there dead . . . but whatever death lays bare,
all wounds are marks of glory. When an old man's killed
and the dogs go at the gray head and the gray beard
and mutilate the genitals—that is the cruelest sight
in all our wretched lives!"
                              So the old man groaned   90
and seizing his gray hair tore it out by the roots
but he could not shake the fixed resolve of Hector.
And his mother wailed now, standing beside Priam,
weeping freely, loosing her robes with one hand
and holding out her bare breast with the other,   95
her words pouring forth in a flight of grief and tears:
"Hector, my child! Look—have some respect for *this*!
Pity your mother too, if I ever gave you the breast
to soothe your troubles, remember it now, dear boy—
beat back that savage man from safe inside the walls!   100
Don't go forth, a champion pitted against him—
merciless, brutal man. If he kills you now,
how can I ever mourn you on your deathbed?—
dear branch in bloom, dear child I brought to birth!—

6. Laothoë's father.

Neither I nor your wife, that warm, generous woman . . .   105
Now far beyond our reach, now by the Argive ships
the rushing dogs will tear you, bolt your flesh!"

    So they wept, the two of them crying out
to their dear son, both pleading time and again
but they could not shake the fixed resolve of Hector.   110
No, he waited Achilles, coming on, gigantic in power.
As a snake in the hills, guarding his hole, awaits a man—
bloated with poison, deadly hatred seething inside him,
glances flashing fire as he coils round his lair . . .
so Hector, nursing his quenchless fury, gave no ground,   115
leaning his burnished shield against a jutting wall,
but harried still, he probed his own brave heart:
"No way out. If I slip inside the gates and walls,
Polydamas will be first to heap disgrace on me—
he was the one who urged me to lead our Trojans   120
back to Ilium just last night, the disastrous night
Achilles rose in arms like a god. But did I give way?
Not at all. And how much better it would have been!
Now my army's ruined, thanks to my own reckless pride,
I would die of shame to face the men of Troy   125
and the Trojan women trailing their long robes . . .
Someone less of a man than I will say, 'Our Hector—
staking all on his own strength, he destroyed his army!'
So they will mutter. So now, better by far for me
to stand up to Achilles, kill him, come home alive   130
or die at his hands in glory out before the walls.
But wait—what if I put down my studded shield
and heavy helmet, prop my spear on the rampart
and go forth, just as I am, to meet Achilles,
noble Prince Achilles . . .   135
why, I could promise to give back Helen, yes,
and all her treasures with her, all those riches
Paris once hauled home to Troy in the hollow ships—
and they were the cause of all our endless fighting—
Yes, yes, return it all to the sons of Atreus now   140
to haul away, and then, at the same time, divide
the rest with all the Argives, all the city holds,
and then I'd take an oath for the Trojan royal council
that we will hide nothing! Share and share alike the hoards
our handsome citadel stores within its depths and—   145
Why debate, my friend? Why thrash things out?
I must not go and implore him. He'll show no mercy,
no respect for me, my rights—he'll cut me down
straight off—stripped of defenses like a woman
once I have loosed the armor off my body.   150
No way to parley with that man—not now—
not from behind some oak or rock to whisper,
like a boy and a young girl, lovers' secrets
a boy and girl might whisper to each other . . .
Better to clash in battle, now, at once—   155

see which fighter Zeus awards the glory!"
                           So he wavered,
waiting there, but Achilles was closing on him now
like the god of war, the fighter's helmet flashing,
over his right shoulder shaking the Pelian ash spear,
that terror, and the bronze around his body flared   160
like a raging fire or the rising, blazing sun.
Hector looked up, saw him, started to tremble,
nerve gone, he could hold his ground no longer,
he left the gates behind and away he fled in fear—
and Achilles went for him, fast, sure of his speed   165
as the wild mountain hawk, the quickest thing on wings,
launching smoothly, swooping down on a cringing dove
and the dove flits out from under, the hawk screaming
over the quarry, plunging over and over, his fury
driving him down to beak and tear his kill—   170
so Achilles flew at him, breakneck on in fury
with Hector fleeing along the walls of Troy,
fast as his legs would go. On and on they raced,
passing the lookout point, passing the wild fig tree
tossed by the wind, always out from under the ramparts   175
down the wagon trail they careered until they reached
the clear running springs where whirling Scamander
rises up from its double wellsprings bubbling strong—
and one runs hot and the steam goes up around it,
drifting thick as if fire burned at its core   180
but the other even in summer gushes cold
as hail or freezing snow or water chilled to ice . . .
And here, close to the springs, lie washing-pools
scooped out in the hollow rocks and broad and smooth
where the wives of Troy and all their lovely daughters   185
would wash their glistening robes in the old days,
the days of peace before the sons of Achaea came . . .
Past these they raced, one escaping, one in pursuit
and the one who fled was great but the one pursuing
greater, even greater—their pace mounting in speed   190
since both men strove, not for a sacrificial beast
or oxhide trophy, prizes runners fight for, no,
they raced for the life of Hector breaker of horses.
Like powerful stallions sweeping round the post for trophies,
galloping full stretch with some fine prize at stake,   195
a tripod, say, or woman offered up at funeral games
for some brave hero fallen—so the two of them
whirled three times around the city of Priam,
sprinting at top speed while all the gods gazed down,
and the father of men and gods broke forth among them now: 200
"Unbearable—a man I love, hunted round his own city walls
and right before my eyes. My heart grieves for Hector.
Hector who burned so many oxen in my honor, rich cuts,
now on the rugged crests of Ida,[7] now on Ilium's heights.

---

7. The great mountain range near Troy.

But now, look, brilliant Achilles courses him round   205
the city of Priam in all his savage, lethal speed.
Come, you immortals, think this through. Decide.
Either we pluck the man from death and save his life
or strike him down at last, here at Achilles' hands—
for all his fighting heart."
                          But immortal Athena,   210
her gray eyes wide, protested strongly: "Father!
Lord of the lightning, king of the black cloud,
what are you saying? A man, a mere mortal,
his doom sealed long ago? You'd set him free
from all the pains of death?
                        Do as you please—   215
but none of the deathless gods will ever praise you."

And Zeus who marshals the thunderheads replied,
"Courage, Athena, third-born of the gods, dear child.
Nothing I said was meant in earnest, trust me,
I mean you all the good will in the world. Go.   220
Do as your own impulse bids you. Hold back no more."

So he launched Athena already poised for action—
down the goddess swept from Olympus' craggy peaks.

And swift Achilles kept on coursing Hector, nonstop
as a hound in the mountains starts a fawn from its lair,   225
hunting him down the gorges, down the narrow glens
and the fawn goes to ground, hiding deep in brush
but the hound comes racing fast, nosing him out
until he lands his kill. So Hector could never throw
Achilles off his trail, the swift racer Achilles—   230
time and again he'd make a dash for the Dardan Gates,
trying to rush beneath the rock-built ramparts, hoping
men on the heights might save him, somehow, raining spears
but time and again Achilles would intercept him quickly,
heading him off, forcing him out across the plain   235
and always sprinting along the city side himself—
endless as in a dream . . .
when a man can't catch another fleeing on ahead
and he can never escape nor his rival overtake him—
so the one could never run the other down in his speed   240
nor the other spring away. And how could Hector have fled
the fates of death so long? How unless one last time,
one final time Apollo had swept in close beside him,
driving strength in his legs and knees to race the wind?
And brilliant Achilles shook his head at the armies,   245
never letting them hurl their sharp spears at Hector—
someone might snatch the glory, Achilles come in second.
But once they reached the springs for the fourth time,
then Father Zeus held out his sacred golden scales:
in them he placed two fates of death that lays men low—   250

one for Achilles, one for Hector breaker of horses—
and gripping the beam mid-haft the Father raised it high
and down went Hector's day of doom, dragging him down
to the strong House of Death—and god Apollo left him.
Athena rushed to Achilles, her bright eyes gleaming,   255
standing shoulder-to-shoulder, winging orders now:
"At last our hopes run high, my brilliant Achilles—
Father Zeus must love you—
we'll sweep great glory back to Achaea's fleet,
we'll kill this Hector, mad as he is for battle!   260
No way for him to escape us now, no longer—
not even if Phoebus the distant deadly Archer
goes through torments, pleading for Hector's life,
groveling over and over before our storming Father Zeus.
But you, you hold your ground and catch your breath   265
while I run Hector down and persuade the man
to fight you face-to-face."

                So Athena commanded
and he obeyed, rejoicing at heart—Achilles stopped,
leaning against his ashen spearshaft barbed in bronze.
and Athena left him there, caught up with Hector at once,   270
and taking the build and vibrant voice of Deiphobus
stood shoulder-to-shoulder with him, winging orders:
"Dear brother, how brutally swift Achilles hunts you—
coursing you round the city of Priam in all his lethal speed!
Come, let us stand our ground together—beat him back."   275

    "Deiphobus!"—Hector, his helmet flashing, called out to her—
"dearest of all my brothers, all these warring years,
of all the sons that Priam and Hecuba produced!
Now I'm determined to praise you all the more,
you who dared—seeing me in these straits—   280
to venture out from the walls, all for *my* sake,
while the others stay inside and cling to safety."

    The goddess answered quickly, her eyes blazing,
"True, dear brother—how your father and mother both
implored me, time and again, clutching my knees,   285
and the comrades round me begging me to stay!
Such was the fear that broke them, man for man,
but the heart within me broke with grief for you.
Now headlong on the fight! No letup, no lance spared!
So now, now we'll *see* if Achilles kills us both   290
and hauls our bloody armor back to the beaked ships
or he goes down in pain beneath your spear."

    Athena luring him on with all her immortal cunning—
and now, at last, as the two came closing for the kill
it was tall Hector, helmet flashing, who led off: 295
"No more running from you in fear, Achilles!
Not as before. Three times I fled around

the great city of Priam—I lacked courage then
to stand your onslaught. Now my spirit stirs me
to meet you face-to-face. Now kill or be killed!   300
Come, we'll swear to the gods, the highest witnesses—
the gods will oversee our binding pacts. I swear
I will never mutilate you—merciless as you are—
if Zeus allows me to last it out and tear your life away.
But once I've stripped your glorious armor, Achilles,   305
I will give your body back to your loyal comrades.
Swear you'll do the same."
                          A swift dark glance
and the headstrong runner answered, "Hector, stop!
You unforgivable, you . . . don't talk to me of pacts.
There are no binding oaths between men and lions—   310
wolves and lambs can enjoy no meeting of the minds—
they are all bent on hating each other to the death.
So with you and me. No love between us. No truce
till one or the other falls and gluts with blood
Ares who hacks at men behind his rawhide shield.   315
Come, call up whatever courage you can muster.
Life or death—now prove yourself a spearman,
a daring man of war! No more escape for you—
Athena will kill you with my spear in just a moment.
Now you'll pay at a stroke for all my comrades' grief,   320
all you killed in the fury of your spear!"
                                      With that,
shaft poised, he hurled and his spear's long shadow flew
but seeing it coming glorious Hector ducked away,
crouching down, watching the bronze tip fly past
and stab the earth—but Athena snatched it up   325
and passed it back to Achilles
and Hector the gallant captain never saw her.
He sounded out a challenge to Peleus' princely son:
"You missed, look—the great godlike Achilles!
So you knew nothing at all from Zeus about my death—   330
and yet how sure you were! All bluff, cunning with words,
that's all you are—trying to make me fear you,
lose my nerve, forget my fighting strength.
Well, you'll never plant your lance in my back
as I flee *you* in fear—plunge it through my chest   335
as I come charging in, if a god gives you the chance!
but now it's for you to dodge *my* brazen spear—
I wish you'd bury it in your body to the hilt.
How much lighter the war would be for Trojans then
if you, their greatest scourge, were dead and gone!"   340

    Shaft poised, he hurled and his spear's long shadow flew
and it struck Achilles' shield—a dead-center hit—
but off and away it glanced and Hector seethed,
his hurtling spear, his whole arm's power poured
in a wasted shot. He stood there, cast down . . .   345

he had no spear in reserve. So Hector shouted out
to Deiphobus bearing his white shield—with a ringing shout
he called for a heavy lance—
                          but the man was nowhere near him,
vanished—
            yes and Hector knew the truth in his heart
and the fighter cried aloud, "My time has come!   350
At last the gods have called me down to death.
I thought he was at my side, the hero Deiphobus—
he's safe inside the walls, Athena's tricked me blind.
And now death, grim death is looming up beside me,
no longer far away. No way to escape it now. This,   355
this was their pleasure after all, sealed long ago—
Zeus and the son of Zeus, the distant deadly Archer—
though often before now they rushed to my defense.
So now I meet my doom. Well let me die—
but not without struggle, not without glory, no,   360
in some great clash of arms that even men to come
will hear of down the years!"
                          And on that resolve
he drew the whetted sword that hung at his side,
tempered, massive, and gathering all his force
he swooped like a soaring eagle   365
launching down from the dark clouds to earth
to snatch some helpless lamb or trembling hare.
So Hector swooped now, swinging his whetted sword
and Achilles charged too, bursting with rage, barbaric,
guarding his chest with the well-wrought blazoned shield,   370
head tossing his gleaming helmet, four horns strong
and the golden plumes shook that the god of fire
drove in bristling thick along its ridge.
Bright as that star amid the stars in the night sky,
star of the evening, brightest star that rides the heavens,   375
so fire flared from the sharp point of the spear Achilles
brandished high in his right hand, bent on Hector's death,
scanning his splendid body—where to pierce it best?
The rest of his flesh seemed all encased in armor,
burnished, brazen—*Achilles'* armor that Hector stripped   380
from strong Patroclus when he killed him—true,
but one spot lay exposed,
where collarbones lift the neckbone off the shoulders,
the open throat, where the end of life comes quickest—*there*
as Hector charged in fury brilliant Achilles drove his spear   385
and the point went stabbing clean through the tender neck
but the heavy bronze weapon failed to slash the windpipe—
Hector could still gasp out some words, some last reply . . .
he crashed in the dust—
                          godlike Achilles gloried over him:
"Hector—surely you thought when you stripped Patroclus' armor   390
that you, you would be safe! Never a fear of me—
far from the fighting as I was—you fool!
Left behind there, down by the beaked ships

his great avenger waited, a greater man by far—
that man was I, and I smashed your strength! And you—   395
the dogs and birds will maul you, shame your corpse
while Achaeans bury my dear friend in glory!"

Struggling for breath, Hector, his helmet flashing,
said, "I beg you, beg you for your life, your parents—
don't let the dogs devour me by the Argive ships!   400
Wait, take the princely ransom of bronze and gold,
the gifts my father and noble mother will give you—
but give my body to friends to carry home again,
so Trojan men and Trojan women can do me honor
with fitting rites of fire once I am dead."   405

Staring grimly, the proud runner Achilles answered,
"Beg no more, you fawning dog—begging me by my parents!
Would to god my rage, my fury would drive me now
to hack your flesh away and eat you raw—
such agonies you have caused me! Ransom?   410
No man alive could keep the dog-packs off you,
not if they haul in ten, twenty times that ransom
and pile it here before me and promise fortunes more—
no, not even if Dardan Priam should offer to weigh out
your bulk in gold! Not even then will your noble mother   415
lay you on your deathbed, mourn the son she bore . . .
The dogs and birds will rend you—blood and bone!"

At the point of death, Hector, his helmet flashing,
said, "I know you well—I see my fate before me.
Never a chance that I could win you over . . .   420
Iron inside your chest, that heart of yours.
But now beware, or my curse will draw god's wrath
upon your head, that day when Paris and lord Apollo—
for all your fighting heart—destroy you at the Scaean Gates!"

Death cut him short. The end closed in around him.   425
Flying free of his limbs
his soul went winging down to the House of Death,
wailing his fate, leaving his manhood far behind,
his young and supple strength. But brilliant Achilles
taunted Hector's body, dead as he was, "Die, die!   430
For my own death, I'll meet it freely—whenever Zeus
and the other deathless gods would like to bring it on!"

With that he wrenched his bronze spear from the corpse,
laid it aside and ripped the bloody armor off the back.
And the other sons of Achaea, running up around him,   435
crowded closer, all of them gazing wonder-struck
at the build and marvelous, lithe beauty of Hector.
And not a man came forward who did not stab his body,
glancing toward a comrade, laughing: "Ah, look here—

how much softer he is to handle now, this Hector,   440
than when he gutted our ships with roaring fire!"

    Standing over him, so they'd gloat and stab his body.
But once he had stripped the corpse the proud runner Achilles
took his stand in the midst of all the Argive troops
and urged them on with a flight of winging orders: 445
"Friends—lords of the Argives, O my captains!
Now that the gods have let me kill this man
who caused us agonies, loss on crushing loss—
more than the rest of all their men combined—
come, let us ring their walls in armor, test them,   450
see what recourse the Trojans still may have in mind.
Will they abandon the city heights with this man fallen?
Or brace for a last, dying stand though Hector's gone?
But wait—what am I saying? Why this deep debate?
Down by the ships a body lies unwept, unburied—   455
Patroclus . . . I will never forget him,
not as long as I'm still among the living
and my springing knees will lift and drive me on.
Though the dead forget their dead in the House of Death,
I will remember, even there, my dear companion.
                                        Now,   460
come, you sons of Achaea, raise a song of triumph!
Down to the ships we march and bear this corpse on high—
we have won ourselves great glory. We have brought
magnificent Hector down, that man the Trojans
glorified in their city like a god!"
                        So he triumphed   465
and now he was bent on outrage, on shaming noble Hector.
Piercing the tendons, ankle to heel behind both feet,
he knotted straps of rawhide through them both,
lashed them to his chariot, left the head to drag
and mounting the car, hoisting the famous arms aboard,   470
he whipped his team to a run and breakneck on they flew,
holding nothing back. And a thick cloud of dust rose up
from the man they dragged, his dark hair swirling round
that head so handsome once, all tumbled low in the dust—
since Zeus had given him over to his enemies now   475
to be defiled in the land of his own fathers.

    So his whole head was dragged down in the dust.
And now his mother began to tear her hair . . .
she flung her shining veil to the ground and raised
a high, shattering scream, looking down at her son.   480
Pitifully his loving father groaned and round the king
his people cried with grief and wailing seized the city—
for all the world as if all Troy were torched and smoldering
down from the looming brows of the citadel to her roots.
Priam's people could hardly hold the old man back,   485
frantic, mad to go rushing out the Dardan Gates.
He begged them all, groveling in the filth,

crying out to them, calling each man by name,
"Let go, my friends! Much as you care for me,
let me hurry out of the city, make my way,   490
all on my own, to Achaea's waiting ships!
I must implore that terrible, violent man . . .
Perhaps—who knows?—he may respect my age,
may pity an old man. He has a father too,
as old as I am—Peleus sired him once,   495
Peleus reared him to be the scourge of Troy
but most of all to me—he made my life a hell.
So many sons he slaughtered, just coming into bloom . . .
but grieving for all the rest, one breaks my heart the most
and stabbing grief for him will take me down to Death—   500
my Hector—would to god he had perished in my arms!
Then his mother who bore him—oh so doomed,
she and I could glut ourselves with grief."

    So the voice of the king rang out in tears,
the citizens wailed in answer, and noble Hecuba   505
led the wives of Troy in a throbbing chant of sorrow:
"O my child—my desolation! How can I go on living?
What agonies must I suffer now, now *you* are dead and gone?
You were my pride throughout the city night and day—
a blessing to us all, the men and women of Troy;   510
throughout the city they saluted you like a god.
You, you were their greatest glory while you lived—
now death and fate have seized you, dragged you down!"

    Her voice rang out in tears, but the wife of Hector
had not heard a thing. No messenger brought the truth   515
of how her husband made his stand outside the gates.
She was weaving at her loom, deep in the high halls,
working flowered braiding into a dark red folding robe.
And she called her well-kempt women through the house
to set a large three-legged cauldron over the fire   520
so Hector could have his steaming hot bath
when he came home from battle—poor woman,
she never dreamed how far he was from bathing,
struck down at Achilles' hands by blazing-eyed Athena.
But she heard the groans and wails of grief from the rampart now   525
and her body shook, her shuttle dropped to the ground,
she called out to her lovely waiting women, "Quickly—
two of you follow me—I must see what's happened.
that cry—that was Hector's honored mother I heard!
My heart's pounding, leaping up in my throat,   530
the knees beneath me paralyzed—Oh I know it . . .
something terrible's coming down on Priam's children.
Pray god the news will never reach my ears!
Yes but I dread it so—what if great Achilles
has cut my Hector off from the city, daring Hector,   535
and driven him out across the plain, and all alone?—
He may have put an end to that fatal headstrong pride

that always seized my Hector—never hanging back
with the main force of men, always charging ahead,
giving ground to no man in his fury!"
So she cried, 540
dashing out of the royal halls like a madwoman,
her heart racing hard, her women close behind her.
But once she reached the tower where soldiers massed
she stopped on the rampart, looked down and saw it all—
saw him dragged before the city, stallions galloping, 545
dragging Hector back to Achaea's beaked warships—
ruthless work. The world went black as night
before her eyes, she fainted, falling backward,
gasping away her life breath . . .
She flung to the winds her glittering headdress, 550
the cap and the coronet, braided band and veil,
all the regalia golden Aphrodite gave her once,
the day that Hector, helmet aflash in sunlight,
led her home to Troy from her father's house
with countless wedding gifts to win her heart. 555
But crowding round her now her husband's sisters
and brothers' wives supported her in their midst,
and she, terrified, stunned to the point of death,
struggling for breath now and coming back to life,
burst out in grief among the Trojan women: "O Hector— 560
I am destroyed! Both born to the same fate after all!
You, you at Troy in the halls of King Priam—
I at Thebes, under the timberline of Placos,
Eetion's house . . . He raised me as a child,
that man of doom, his daughter just as doomed— 565
would to god he'd never fathered *me!*
Now you go down
to the House of Death, the dark depths of the earth,
and leave me here to waste away in grief, a widow
lost in the royal halls—and the boy only a baby,
the son we bore together, you and I so doomed. 570
Hector, what help are you to him, now you are dead?—
what help is he to you? Think, even if he escapes
the wrenching horrors of war against the Argives,
pain and labor will plague him all his days to come.
Strangers will mark his lands off, stealing his estates. 575
The day that orphans a youngster cuts him off from friends.
And he hangs his head low, humiliated in every way . . .
his cheeks stained with tears, and pressed by hunger
the boy goes up to his father's old companions,
tugging at one man's cloak, another's tunic, 580
and some will pity him, true,
and one will give him a little cup to drink,
enough to wet his lips, not quench his thirst.
But then some bully with both his parents living
beats him from the banquet, fists and abuses flying: 585
'You, get out—you've got no father feasting with us here!'
And the boy, sobbing, trails home to his widowed mother . . .

Astyanax!
    And years ago, propped on his father's knee,
he would only eat the marrow, the richest cuts of lamb,
and when sleep came on him and he had quit his play,   590
cradled warm in his nurse's arms he'd drowse off,
snug in a soft bed, his heart brimmed with joy.
Now what suffering, now he's lost his father—
             Astyanax!
The Lord of the City, so the Trojans called him,
because it was you, Hector, you and you alone   595
who shielded the gates and the long walls of Troy.
But now by the beaked ships, far from your parents,
glistening worms will wriggle through your flesh,
once the dogs have had their fill of your naked corpse—
though we have such stores of clothing laid up in the halls, 600
fine things, a joy to the eye, the work of women's hands.
Now, by god, I'll burn them all, blazing to the skies!
No use to you now, they'll never shroud your body—
but they will be your glory
burned by the Trojan men and women in your honor!" 605

  Her voice rang out in tears and the women wailed in answer.

Summary Achilles buried Patroclus, and the Greeks celebrated the dead hero's
fame with athletic games, for which Achilles gave the prizes.

BOOK XXIV

[*Achilles and Priam*]

The games were over now. The gathered armies scattered,
each man to his fast ship, and fighters turned their minds
to thoughts of food and the sweet warm grip of sleep.
But Achilles kept on grieving for his friend,
the memory burning on . . .   5
and all-subduing sleep could not take him,
not now, he turned and twisted, side to side,
he longed for Patroclus' manhood, his gallant heart—
What rough campaigns they'd fought to an end together,
what hardships they had suffered, cleaving their way 10
through wars of men and pounding waves at sea.
The memories flooded over him, live tears flowing,
and now he'd lie on his side, now flat on his back,
now facedown again. At last he'd leap to his feet,
wander in anguish, aimless along the surf, and dawn on dawn 15
flaming over the sea and shore would find him pacing.
Then he'd yoke his racing team to the chariot-harness,
lash the corpse of Hector behind the car for dragging
and haul him three times round the dead Patroclus' tomb,
and then he'd rest again in his tents and leave the body 20
sprawled facedown in the dust. But Apollo pitied Hector—
dead man though he was—and warded all corruption off
from Hector's corpse and round him, head to foot,

the great god wrapped the golden shield of storm
so his skin would never rip as Achilles dragged him on.   25

And so he kept on raging, shaming noble Hector,
but the gods in bliss looked down and pitied Priam's son.
They kept on urging the sharp-eyed giant-killer Hermes
to go and steal the body, a plan that pleased them all,
but not Hera, Poseidon or the girl with blazing eyes.[8]   30
They clung to their deathless hate of sacred Troy,
Priam and Priam's people, just as they had at first
when Paris in all his madness launched the war.
He offended Athena and Hera—both goddesses.
When they came to his shepherd's fold he favored Love   35
who dangled before his eyes the lust that loosed disaster.[9]
But now, at the twelfth dawn since Hector's death,
lord Apollo rose and addressed the immortal powers:
"Hard-hearted you are, you gods, you live for cruelty!
Did Hector never burn in your honor thighs of oxen   40
and flawless, full-grown goats? Now you cannot
bring yourselves to save him—even his corpse—
so his wife can see him, his mother and his child,
his father Priam and Priam's people: how they'd rush
to burn the body on the pyre and give him royal rites!   45
But murderous Achilles—you gods, you *choose* to help Achilles.
That man without a shred of decency in his heart . . .
his temper can never bend and change—like some lion
going his own barbaric way, giving in to his power,
his brute force and wild pride, as down he swoops   50
on the flocks of men to seize his savage feast.
Achilles has lost all pity! No shame in the man,
shame that does great harm or drives men on to good.
No doubt some mortal has suffered a dearer loss than this,
a brother born in the same womb, or even a son . . .   55
he grieves, he weeps, but then his tears are through.
The Fates have given mortals hearts that can endure.
But this Achilles—first he slaughters Hector,
he rips away the noble prince's life
then lashes him to his chariot, drags him round   60
his beloved comrade's tomb. But why, I ask you?
What good will it do him? What honor will he gain?
Let that man beware, or great and glorious as he is,
we mighty gods will wheel on him in anger—look,
he outrages the senseless clay in all his fury!"   65

But white-armed Hera flared at him in anger:
"Yes, there'd be some merit even in what *you* say,
lord of the silver bow—if all you gods, in fact,
would set Achilles and Hector high in equal honor.
But Hector is mortal. He sucked a woman's breast.   70

8. Athena.   9. Paris had been appointed judge in a contest of beauty between Aphrodite, Hera, and Athena. All three goddesses offered bribes, but Aphrodite's promise to give him Helen proved the most attractive.

Achilles sprang from a goddess—one I reared myself:
I brought her up and gave her in marriage to a man,
to Peleus, dearest to all your hearts, you gods.
All you Gods, you shared in the wedding rites,
and so did you, Apollo—there you sat at the feast 75
and struck your lyre. What company you keep now,
these wretched Trojans. You—forever faithless!"

    But Zeus who marshals the storm clouds warned his queen,
"Now, Hera, don't fly into such a rage at fellow gods.
These two can never attain the same degree of honor. 80
Still, the immortals loved Prince Hector dearly,
best of all the mortals born in Troy . . .
so I loved him, at least:
he never stinted with gifts to please my heart.
Never once did my altar lack its share of victims, 85
winecups tipped and the deep smoky savor. These,
these are the gifts we claim—they are our rights.
But as for stealing courageous Hector's body,
we must abandon the idea—not a chance in the world
behind Achilles' back. For Thetis is always there, 90
his mother always hovering near him night and day.
Now would one of you gods call Thetis to my presence?—
so I can declare to her my solemn, sound decree:
Achilles must receive a ransom from King Priam,
Achilles must give Hector's body back."

                        So he decreed 95
and Iris, racing a gale-wind down with Zeus's message,
mid-sea between Samos and Imbros'[1] rugged cliffs
dove in a black swell as groaning breakers roared.
Down she plunged to the bottom fast as a lead weight
sheathed in a glinting lure of wild bull's horn,[2] 100
bearing hooked death to the ravenous fish.
And deep in a hollow cave she came on Thetis.
Gathered round her sat the other immortal sea-nymphs
while Thetis amidst them mourned her brave son's fate,
doomed to die, she knew, on the fertile soil of Troy, 105
far from his native land. Quick as the wind now
Iris rushed to the goddess, urging, "Rise, Thetis—
Zeus with his everlasting counsels calls you now!"
Shifting on her glistening feet, the goddess answered,
"Why . . . what does the great god want with me? 110
I cringe from mingling with the immortals now—
Oh the torment—never-ending heartbreak!
But go I shall. A high decree of the Father
must not come to nothing—whatever he commands."

    The radiant queen of sea-nymphs seized a veil, 115
blue-black, no robe darker in all the Ocean's depths,

---

1. Two islands in the North Aegean.   2. A lure for big fish.

and launched up and away with wind-swift Iris leading—
the ground swell round them cleaved and opened wide.
And striding out on shore they soared to the high sky
and found farseeing Zeus, and around him all the gods   120
who live in bliss forever sat in a grand assembly.
And Thetis took a seat beside the Father,
a throne Athena yielded. Hera placed in her hand
a burnished golden cup and said some words of comfort,
and taking a few quick sips, Thetis gave it back . . .   125
The father of men and gods began to address them:
"You have come to Olympus now, immortal Thetis,
for all your grief—what unforgettable sorrow
seizes on your heart. I know it well myself.
Even so, I must tell you why I called you here.   130
For nine whole days the immortals have been feuding
over Hector's corpse and Achilles, scourge of cities.
They keep urging the sharp-eyed giant-killer Hermes
to go and steal the body. But that is not my way.
I will grant Achilles glory and so safeguard   135
your awe and love of me for all the years to come.
Go at once to the camp, give your son this order:
tell him the gods are angry with him now
and I am rising over them all in deathless wrath
that he in heartsick fury still holds Hector's body,   140
there by his beaked ships, and will not give him back—
perhaps in fear of me he'll give him back at once.
Then, at the same time, I am winging Iris down
to greathearted Priam, commanding the king
to ransom his dear son, to go to Achaea's ships,   145
bearing gifts to Achilles, gifts to melt his rage."
                                              So he decreed
and Thetis with her glistening feet did not resist a moment.
Down the goddess flashed from the peaks of Mount Olympus,
made her way to her son's camp, and there he was,
she found him groaning hard, choked with sobs.   150
Around him trusted comrades swung to the work,
preparing breakfast, steadying in their midst
a large fleecy sheep just slaughtered in the shelter.
But his noble mother, settling down at his side,
stroked Achilles gently, whispering his name: "My child—   155
how long will you eat your heart out here in tears and torment?
All wiped from your mind, all thought of food and bed?
It's a welcome thing to make love with a woman . . .
You don't have long to live now, well I know:
already I see them looming up beside you—death   160
and the strong force of fate. Listen to me,
quickly! I bring you a message sent by Zeus:
he says the gods are angry with you now
and he is rising over them all in deathless wrath
that you in heartsick fury still hold Hector's body,   165
here by your beaked ships, and will not give him back.
O give him back at once—take ransom for the dead!"

The swift runner replied in haste, "So be it.
The man who brings the ransom can take away the body,
if Olympian Zeus himself insists in all earnest."   170

While mother and son agreed among the clustered ships,
trading between each other many winged words,
Father Zeus sped Iris down to sacred Troy:
"Quick on your way now, Iris, shear the wind!
Leave our Olympian stronghold—   175
take a message to greathearted Priam down in Troy:
he must go to Achaea's ships and ransom his dear son,
bearing gifts to Achilles, gifts to melt his rage.
But let him go alone, no other Trojan attend him,
only a herald with him, a seasoned, older one   180
who can drive the mules and smooth-running wagon
and bring the hero's body back to sacred Troy,
the man that brilliant Achilles killed in battle.
Let him have no fear of death, no dread in his heart,
such a powerful escort we will send him—the giant-killer   185
Hermes will guide him all the way to Achilles' presence.
And once the god has led him within the fighter's shelter,
Achilles will not kill him—he'll hold back all the rest:
Achilles is no madman, no reckless fool, not the one
to defy the gods' commands. Whoever begs his mercy   190
he will spare with all the kindness in his heart."
                                            So he decreed
and Iris ran his message, racing with gale force
to Priam's halls where cries and mourning met her.
Sons huddled round their father deep in the courtyard,
robes drenched with tears, and the old man amidst them,   195
buried, beaten down in the cloak that wrapped his body . . .
Smeared on the old man's head and neck the dung lay thick
that he scraped up in his own hands, groveling in the filth.
Throughout the house his daughters and sons' wives wailed,
remembering all the fine brave men who lay dead now,   200
their lives destroyed at the fighting Argives' hands.
And Iris, Zeus's crier, standing alongside Priam,
spoke in a soft voice, but his limbs shook at once—
"Courage, Dardan Priam, take heart! Nothing to fear.
No herald of doom, I come on a friendly mission—   205
I come with all good will.
I bring you a message sent by Zeus, a world away
but he has you in his heart, he pities you now . . .
Olympian Zeus commands you to ransom royal Hector,
to bear gifts to Achilles, gifts to melt his rage.   210
But you must go alone, no other Trojan attend you,
only a herald with you, a seasoned, older one
who can drive the mules and smooth-running wagon
and bring the hero's body back to sacred Troy,
the man that brilliant Achilles killed in battle.   215
But have no fear of death, no dread in your heart,
such a powerful escort will conduct you—the giant-killer

Hermes will guide you all the way to Achilles' presence.
And once the god has led you within the fighter's shelter,
Achilles will not kill you—he'll hold back all the rest: 220
Achilles is no madman, no reckless fool, not the one
to defy the gods' commands. Whoever begs his mercy
he will spare with all the kindness in his heart!"

      And Iris racing the wind went veering off
and Priam ordered his sons to get a wagon ready,   225
a good smooth-running one, to hitch the mules
and strap a big wicker cradle across its frame.
Then down he went himself to his treasure-chamber,
high-ceilinged, paneled, fragrant with cedarwood
and a wealth of precious objects filled its chests.   230
He called out to his wife, Hecuba, "Dear woman!
An Olympian messenger came to me from Zeus—
I must go to Achaea's ships and ransom our dear son,
bearing gifts to Achilles, gifts to melt his rage.
Tell me, what should I do? What do *you* think?   235
Myself—a terrible longing drives me, heart and soul,
down to the ships, into the vast Achaean camp."

      But his wife cried out in answer, "No, no—
where have your senses gone?—that made you famous once,
both among outland men and those you rule in Troy!   240
How can you think of going down to the ships, alone,
and face the glance of the man who killed your sons,
so many fine brave boys? You have a heart of iron!
If he gets you in his clutches, sets his eyes on you—
that savage, treacherous man—he'll show no mercy,   245
no respect for your rights!
                  Come, all we can do now
is sit in the halls, far from our son, and wail for Hector . . .
So this, this is the doom that strong Fate spun out,
our son's life line drawn with his first breath—
the moment I gave him birth—   250
to glut the wild dogs, cut off from his parents,
crushed by the stronger man. Oh would to god
that I could sink my teeth in his liver, eat him raw!
That would avenge what he has done to Hector—
no coward the man Achilles killed—my son stood   255
an fought for the men of Troy and their deep-breasted wives
with never a thought of flight or run for cover!"

      But the old and noble Priam answered firmly,
"I will go. My mind's made up. Don't hold me back.
And don't go flying off on your own across the halls,   260
a bird of evil omen—you can't dissuade me now.
If someone else had commanded me, some mortal man,
some prophet staring into the smoke, some priest,
I'd call it a lie and turn my back upon it.
Not now. I heard her voice with my own ears,   265

I looked straight at the goddess, face-to-face.
So I am going—her message must not come to nothing.
And if it is my fate to die by the beaked ships
of Achaeans armed in bronze, then die I shall.
Let Achilles cut me down straightway—   270
once I've caught my son in my arms and wept my fill!"

    He raised back the carved lids of the chests
and lifted out twelve robes, handsome, rich brocades,
twelve cloaks, unlined and light, as many blankets,
as many big white capes and shirts to go with them.   275
He weighed and carried out ten full bars of gold
and took two burnished tripods, four fine cauldrons
and last a magnificent cup the Thracians gave him once—
he'd gone on an embassy and won that priceless treasure—
but not even *that* did the old man spare in his halls,   280
not now, consumed with desire to ransom back his son.
Crowds of Trojans were mobbing his colonnades—
he gave them a tongue-lashing, sent them packing:
"Get out—you good-for-nothings, public disgraces!
Haven't you got enough to wail about at home   285
without coming here to add to all my griefs?
You think it nothing, the pain that Zeus has sent me?—
he's destroyed my best son! You'll learn too, in tears—
easier game you'll be for Argive troops to slaughter,
now my Hector's dead. But before I have to see   290
my city annihilated, laid waste before my eyes—
oh let me go down to the House of Death!"

    He herded them off with his staff—they fled outside
before the old man's fury. So he lashed out at his sons,
cursing the sight of Helenus, Paris, noble Agathon,   295
Pammon, Antiphonus, Polites loud with the war cry,
Deiphobus and Hippothous, even lordly Dius—
the old man shouted at all nine, rough commands:
"Get to your work! My vicious sons—my humiliations!
If only you'd all been killed at the fast ships   300
instead of my dear Hector . . .
But I—dear god, my life so cursed by fate!—
I fathered hero sons in the wide realm of Troy
and now, now not a single one is left, I tell you.
Mestor the indestructible, Troilus, passionate horseman   305
and Hector, a god among men—no son of a mortal man,
he seemed a deathless god's. But Ares killed them all
and all he left me are these, these disgraces—liars,
dancers, heroes only at beating the dancing-rings,
you plunder your own people for lambs and kids!   310
Why don't you get my wagon ready—now, at once?
Pack all these things aboard! We must be on our way!"

    Terrified by their father's rough commands
the sons trundled a mule-wagon out at once,

a good smooth-running one,   315
newly finished, balanced and bolted tight,
and strapped a big wicker cradle across its frame.
They lifted off its hook a boxwood yoke for the mules,
its bulging pommel fitted with rings for guide-reins,
brought out with the yoke its yoke-strap nine arms long   320
and wedged the yoke down firm on the sanded, tapered pole,
on the front peg, and slipped the yoke-ring onto its pin,
strapped the pommel with three good twists, both sides,
then lashed the assembly round and down the shaft
and under the clamp they made the lashing fast.   325
Then the priceless ransom for Hector's body:
hauling it up from the vaults they piled it high
on the wagon's well-made cradle, then they yoked the mules—
stamping their sharp hoofs, trained for heavy loads—
that the Mysians[3] once gave Priam, princely gifts.   330
And last they yoked his team to the king's chariot,
stallions he bred himself in his own polished stalls.

         No sooner were both men harnessed up beneath the roofs,
Priam and herald, minds set on the coming journey,
than Hecuba rushed up to them, gaunt with grief,   335
holding a gold cup of mellow wine in her right hand
so the men might pour libations before they left.
She stood in front of the horses, crying up at Priam,
"Here, quickly—pour a libation out to Father Zeus!
Pray for a safe return from all our mortal enemies,   340
seeing you're dead set on going down to the ships—
though you go against my will. But if go you must,
pray, at least, to the great god of the dark storm cloud,
up there on Ida, gazing down on the whole expanse of Troy!
Pray for a bird of omen, Zeus's wind-swift messenger,   345
the dearest bird in the world to his prophetic heart,
the strongest thing on wings—clear on the right
so you can see that sign with your own eyes
and trust your life to *it* as you venture down
to Achaea's ships and the fast chariot-teams.   350
But if farseeing Zeus does *not* send you that sign—
his own messenger—then I urge you, beg you,
don't go down to the ships—
not for all the passion in your heart!"

         The old majestic Priam gave his answer: 355
"Dear woman, surely I won't resist your urging now.
It's well to lift our hands and ask great Zeus for mercy."

         And the old king motioned a steward standing by
to pour some clear pure water over his hands,
and she came forward, bearing a jug and basin.   360
He rinsed his hands, took the cup from his wife

3. A people of central Asia Minor.

and taking a stand amidst the forecourt, prayed,
pouring the wine to earth and scanning the high skies,
Priam prayed in his rich resounding voice: "Father Zeus!
Ruling over us all from Ida, god of greatness, god of glory!   365
Grant that Achilles will receive me with kindness, mercy.
Send me a bird of omen, your own wind-swift messenger,
the dearest bird in the world to your prophetic heart,
the strongest thing on wings—clear on the right
so I can see that sign with my own eyes   370
and trust my life to *it* as I venture down
to Achaea's ships and the fast chariot-teams!"

    And Zeus in all his wisdom heard that prayer
and straightaway the Father launched an eagle—
truest of Zeus's signs that fly the skies—   375
the dark marauder that mankind calls the Black-wing.
Broad as the door of a rich man's vaulted treasure-chamber,
well-fitted with sturdy bars, so broad each wing of the bird
spread out on either side as it swept in through the city
flashing clear on the right before the king and queen.   380
All looked up, overjoyed—the people's spirits lifted.

    And the old man, rushing to climb aboard his chariot,
drove out through the gates and echoing colonnades.
The mules in the lead hauled out the four-wheeled wagon,
driven on by seasoned Idaeus. The horses came behind   385
as the old man cracked the lash and urged them fast
throughout the city with all his kinsmen trailing . . .
weeping their hearts out, as if he went to his death.
But once the two passed down through crowded streets
and out into open country, Priam's kin turned back,   390
his sons and in-laws straggling home to Troy.
But Zeus who beholds the world could hardly fail
to see the two men striking out across the plain.
As he watched the old man he filled with pity
and quickly summoned Hermes, his own dear son: 395
"Hermes—escorting men is your greatest joy,
you above all the gods,
and you listen to the wish of those you favor.
So down you go. Down and conduct King Priam there
through Achaea's beaked ships, so none will see him,   400
none of the Argive fighters recognize him now,
not till he reaches Peleus' royal son."
                              So he decreed
and Hermes the giant-killing guide obeyed at once.
Under his feet he strapped the supple sandals,
never-dying gold, that wing him over the waves   405
and boundless earth with the speed of gusting winds.
He seized the wand that enchants the eyes of men
whenever Hermes wants, or wakes them up from sleep.
That wand in his grip he flew, the mighty giant-killer
touching down on Troy and the Hellespont in no time   410

and from there he went on foot, for all the world
like a young prince, sporting his first beard,
just in the prime and fresh warm pride of youth.

And now,
as soon as the two drove past the great tomb of Ilus[4]
they drew rein at the ford to water mules and team.   415
A sudden darkness had swept across the earth
and Hermes was all but on them when the herald
looked up, saw him, shouted at once to Priam,
"Danger, my king—think fast! I see a man—
I'm afraid we'll both be butchered on the spot—   420
into the chariot, hurry! Run for our lives
or fling ourselves at his knees and beg for mercy!"

    The old man was stunned, in a swirl of terror,
the hairs stood bristling all over his gnarled body—
he stood there, staring dumbly. Not waiting for welcome   425
the running god of luck went straight up to Priam,
clasped the old king's hands and asked him warmly,
"Father—where do you drive these mules and team
through the godsent night while other mortals sleep?
Have you no fear of the Argives breathing hate and fury?   430
Here are your deadly enemies, camping close at hand.
Now what if one of them saw you, rolling blithely
on through the rushing night with so much tempting treasure—
how would you feel then? You're not so young yourself,
and the man who attends you here is far too old   435
to drive off an attacker spoiling for a fight.
But I would never hurt you—and what's more,
I'd beat off any man who'd do you harm:
you remind me of my dear father, to the life."

    And the old and noble Priam said at once,   440
"Our straits are hard, dear child, as you say.
But a god still holds his hands above me, even me.
Sending such a traveler here to meet me—
what a lucky omen! Look at your build . . .
your handsome face—a wonder. And such good sense—   445
your parents must be blissful as the gods!"

    The guide and giant-killer answered quickly,
"You're right, old man, all straight to the mark.
But come, tell me the truth now, point by point:
this treasure—a king's ransom—do you send it off   450
to distant, outland men, to keep it safe for you?
Or now do you all abandon sacred Troy,
all in panic—such was the man who died,
your finest, bravest man . . . your own son
who never failed in a fight against the Argives."   455

---

4. Priam's grandfather. The tomb was a landmark on the Trojan plain.

But the old majestic Priam countered quickly,
"Who are *you*, my fine friend?—who are your parents?
How can you speak so well of my doomed son's fate?"

And the guide and giant-killer answered staunchly,
"You're testing me, old man—asking of noble Hector.   460
Ah, how often I watched him battling on the lines
where men win glory, saw the man with my own eyes!
And saw him drive Achaeans against the ships that day
he kept on killing, cutting them down with slashing bronze
while we stood by and marveled—Achilles reined us in: 465
no fighting for us while he raged on at Agamemnon.
I am Achilles' aide, you see,
one and the same good warship brought us here.
I am a Myrmidon, and my father is Polyctor,
and a wealthy man he is, about as old as you . . .   470
He has six sons—I'm the seventh—we all shook lots
and it fell to me to join the armies here at Troy.
I've just come up from the ships to scout the plain—
at dawn the fiery-eyed Achaeans fight around the city.
They chafe, sitting in camp, so bent on battle now   475
the kings of Achaea cannot hold them back."

And the old and noble Priam asked at once,
"If you really are the royal Achilles' aide,
please, tell *me* the whole truth, point by point.
My son—does he still lie by the beached ships,   480
or by now has the great Achilles hacked him
limb from limb and served him to his dogs?"

The guide and giant-killer reassured him:
"So far, old man, no birds or dogs have eaten him.
No, there he lies—still there at Achilles' ship,   485
still intact in his shelters.
This is the twelfth day he's lain there, too,
but his body has not decayed, not in the least,
nor have the worms begun to gnaw his corpse,
the swarms that devour men who fall in battle.   490
True, dawn on fiery dawn he drags him round
his beloved comrade's tomb, drags him ruthlessly
but he cannot mutilate his body. It's marvelous—
go see for yourself how he lies there fresh as dew,
the blood washed away, and no sign of corruption.   495
All his wounds sealed shut, wherever they struck . . .
and many drove their bronze blades through his body.
Such pains the blissful gods are lavishing on your son,
dead man though he is—the gods love him dearly!"

And the old man rejoiced at that, bursting out,   500
"O my child, how good it is to give the immortals
fit and proper gifts! Now take my son—

or was he all a dream? Never once in his halls
did he forget the gods who hold Olympus, never,
so now they remember *him* . . . if only after death. 505
Come, this handsome cup: accept it from me, I beg you!
Protect me, escort me now—if the gods will it so—
all the way till I reach Achilles' shelter."

　　The guide and giant-killer refused him firmly,
"You test me again, old man, since I am young, 510
but you will not persuade me,
tempting me with a gift behind Achilles' back.
I fear the man, I'd die of shame to rob him—
just think of the trouble I might suffer later.
But I'd escort you with all the kindness in my heart, 515
all the way till I reached the shining hills of Argos
bound in a scudding ship or pacing you on foot—
and no marauder on earth, scorning your escort,
would dare attack you then."
　　　　　　　　　　　　And the god of luck,
leaping onto the chariot right behind the team, 520
quickly grasped the whip and reins in his hands
and breathed fresh spirit into the mules and horses.
As they reached the trench and rampart round the fleet,
the sentries had just begun to set out supper there
but the giant-killer plunged them all in sleep . . . 525
he spread the gates at once, slid back the bars
and ushered Priam in with his wagon-load of treasure.
Now, at last, they approached royal Achilles' shelter,
the tall, imposing lodge the Myrmidons built their king,
hewing planks of pine, and roofed it high with thatch, 530
gathering thick shaggy reeds from the meadow banks,
and round it built their king a spacious courtyard
fenced with close-set stakes. A single pine beam
held the gates, and it took three men to ram it home,
three to shoot the immense bolt back and spread the doors— 535
three average men. Achilles alone could ram it home himself.
But the god of luck now spread the gates for the old man,
drove in the glinting gifts for Peleus' swift son,
climbed down from behind the team and said to Priam,
"Old man, look, I am a god come down to you, 540
I am immortal Hermes—
my Father sent me here to be your escort.
But now I will hasten back. I will not venture
into Achilles' presence: it would offend us all
for a mortal man to host an immortal face-to-face. 545
But you go in yourself and clasp Achilles' knees,
implore him by his father, his mother with lovely hair,
by his own son—so you can stir his heart!"
　　　　　　　　　　　　　　　With that urging
Hermes went his way to the steep heights of Olympus.

But Priam swung down to earth from the battle-car   550
and leaving Idaeus there to rein in mules and team,
the old king went straight up to the lodge
where Achilles dear to Zeus would always sit.
Priam found the warrior there inside . . .
many captains sitting some way off, but two,   555
veteran Automedon and the fine fighter Alcimus
were busy serving him. He had just finished dinner,
eating, drinking, and the table still stood near.
The majestic king of Troy slipped past the rest
and kneeling down beside Achilles, clasped his knees   560
and kissed his hands, those terrible, man-killing hands
that had slaughtered Priam's many sons in battle.
Awesome—as when the grip of madness seizes one
who murders a man in his own fatherland and flees
abroad to foreign shores, to a wealthy, noble host,   565
and a sense of marvel runs through all who see him—
so Achilles marveled, beholding majestic Priam.
His men marveled too, trading startled glances.
But Priam prayed his heart out to Achilles:
"Remember your own father, great godlike Achilles—   570
as old as I am, past the threshold of deadly old age!
No doubt the countrymen round about him plague him now,
with no one there to defend him, beat away disaster.
No one—but at least he hears you're still alive
and his old heart rejoices, hopes rising, day by day,   575
to see his beloved son come sailing home from Troy.
But I—dear god, my life so cursed by fate . . .
I fathered hero sons in the wide realm of Troy
and now not a single one is left, I tell you.
Fifty sons I had when the sons of Achaea came,   580
nineteen born to me from a single mother's womb
and the rest by other women in the palace. Many,
most of them violent Ares cut the knees from under.
But one, one was left me, to guard my walls, my people—
the one you killed the other day, defending his fatherland,   585
my Hector! It's all for him I've come to the ships now,
to win him back from you—I bring a priceless ransom.
Revere the gods, Achilles! Pity me in my own right,
remember your own father! I deserve more pity . . .
I have endured what no one on earth has ever done before—   590
I put to my lips the hands of the man who killed my son."

     Those words stirred within Achilles a deep desire
to grieve for his own father. Taking the old man's hand
he gently moved him back. And overpowered by memory
both men gave way to grief. Priam wept freely   595
for man-killing Hector, throbbing, crouching
before Achilles' feet as Achilles wept himself,
now for his father, now for Patroclus once again,

and their sobbing rose and fell throughout the house.
Then, when brilliant Achilles had had his fill of tears   600
and the longing for it had left his mind and body,
he rose from his seat, raised the old man by the hand
and filled with pity now for his gray head and gray beard,
he spoke out winging words, flying straight to the heart:
"Poor man, how much you've borne—pain to break the spirit!   605
What daring brought you down to the ships, all alone,
to face the glance of the man who killed your sons,
so many fine brave boys? You have a heart of iron.
Come, please, sit down on this chair here . . .
Let us put our griefs to rest in our own hearts,   610
rake them up no more, raw as we are with mourning.
What good's to be won from tears that chill the spirit?
So the immortals spun our lives that we, we wretched men
live on to bear such torments—the gods live free of sorrows.
There are two great jars that stand on the floor of Zeus's halls   615
and hold his gifts, our miseries one, the other blessings.
When Zeus who loves the lightning mixes gifts for a man,
now he meets with misfortune, now good times in turn.
When Zeus dispenses gifts from the jar of sorrows only,
he makes a man an outcast—brutal, ravenous hunger   620
drives him down the face of the shining earth,
stalking far and wide, cursed by gods and men.
So with my father, Peleus. What glittering gifts
the gods rained down from the day that he was born!
He excelled all men in wealth and pride of place,   625
he lorded the Myrmidons, and mortal that he was,
they gave the man an immortal goddess for a wife.
Yes, but even on him the Father piled hardships,
no powerful race of princes born in his royal halls,
only a single son he fathered, doomed at birth,   630
cut off in the spring of life—
and I, I give the man no care as he grows old
since here I sit in Troy, far from my fatherland,
a grief to you, a grief to all your children . . .
And you too, old man, we hear you prospered once: 635
as far as Lesbos, Macar's[5] kingdom, bounds to seaward,
Phrygia east and upland, the Hellespont vast and north—
that entire realm, they say, you lorded over once,
you excelled all men, old king, in sons and wealth.
But then the gods of heaven brought this agony on you—   640
ceaseless battles round your walls, your armies slaughtered.
You must bear up now. Enough of endless tears,
the pain that breaks the spirit.
Grief for your son will do no good at all.
You will never bring him back to life—   645
sooner you must suffer something worse."

5. The legendary first king of Lesbos.

But the old and noble Priam protested strongly:
"Don't make me sit on a chair, Achilles, Prince,
not while Hector lies uncared-for in your camp!
Give him back to me, now, no more delay—   650
I must see my son with my own eyes.
Accept the ransom I bring you, a king's ransom!
Enjoy it, all of it—return to your own native land,
safe and sound . . . since now you've spared my life."

A dark glance—and the headstrong runner answered,   655
"No more, old man, don't tempt my wrath, not now!
My own mind's made up to give you back your son.
A messenger brought me word from Zeus—my mother,
Thetis who bore me, the Old Man of the Sea's daughter.
And what's more, I can see through you, Priam—   660
no hiding the fact from me: one of the gods
has led you down to Achaea's fast ships.
No man alive, not even a rugged young fighter,
would dare to venture into our camp. Never—
how could he slip past the sentries unchallenged?   665
Or shoot back the bolt of my gates with so much ease?
So don't anger me now. Don't stir my raging heart still more.
Or under my own roof I may not spare your life, old man—
suppliant that you are—may break the laws of Zeus!"

The old man was terrified. He obeyed the order.   670
But Achilles bounded out of doors like a lion—
not alone but flanked by his two aides-in-arms,
veteran Automedon and Alcimus, steady comrades,
Achilles' favorites next to the dead Patroclus.
They loosed from harness the horses and the mules,   675
they led the herald in, the old king's crier,
and sat him down on a bench. From the polished wagon
they lifted the priceless ransom brought for Hector's corpse
but they left behind two capes and a finely-woven shirt
to shroud the body well when Priam bore him home.   680
Then Achilles called the serving-women out:
"Bathe and anoint the body—
bear it aside first. Priam must not see his son."
He feared that, overwhelmed by the sight of Hector,
wild with grief, Priam might let his anger flare   685
and Achilles might fly into fresh rage himself,
cut the old man down and break the laws of Zeus.
So when the maids had bathed and anointed the body
sleek with olive oil and wrapped it round and round
in a braided battle-shirt and handsome battle-cape,   690
then Achilles lifted Hector up in his own arms
and laid him down on a bier, and comrades helped him
raise the bier and body onto the sturdy wagon . . .
Then with a groan he called his dear friend by name:
"Feel no anger at me, Patroclus, if you learn—   695

even there in the House of Death—I let his father
have Prince Hector back. He gave me worthy ransom
and you shall have your share from me, as always,
your fitting, lordly share."
                              So he vowed   700
and brilliant Achilles strode back to his shelter,
sat down on the well-carved chair that he had left,
at the far wall of the room, leaned toward Priam
and firmly spoke the words the king had come to hear:
"Your son is now set free, old man, as you requested.   705
Hector lies in state. With the first light of day
you will see for yourself as you convey him home.
Now, at last, let us turn our thoughts to supper.
Even Niobe[6] with her lustrous hair remembered food,
though she saw a dozen children killed in her own halls,   710
six daughters and six sons in the pride and prime of youth.
True lord Apollo killed the sons with his silver bow
and Artemis showering arrows killed the daughters.
Both gods were enraged at Niobe. Time and again
she placed herself on a par with their[7] own mother,   715
Leto in her immortal beauty—how she insulted Leto:
'All you have borne is two, but I have borne so many!'
So, two as they were, they slaughtered all her children.
Nine days they lay in their blood, no one to bury them—
Cronus' son had turned the people into stone . . .   720
then on the tenth the gods of heaven interred them.
And Niobe, gaunt, worn to the bone with weeping,
turned her thoughts to food. And now, somewhere,
lost on the crags, on the lonely mountain slopes,
on Sipylus where, they say, the nymphs who live forever,   725
dancing along the Achelous River run to beds of rest—
there, struck into stone, Niobe still broods
on the spate of griefs the gods poured out to her.[8]

     So come—we too, old king, must think of food.
Later you can mourn your beloved son once more,
when you bear him home to Troy, and you'll weep many tears."   730

     Never pausing, the swift runner sprang to his feet
and slaughtered a white sheep as comrades moved in
to skin the carcass quickly, dress the quarters well.
Expertly they cut the meat in pieces, pierced them with spits,
roasted them to a turn and pulled them off the fire.   735
Automedon brought the bread, set it out on the board
in ample wicker baskets. Achilles served the meat.
They reached out for the good things that lay at hand
and when they had put aside desire for food and drink,
Priam the son of Dardanus gazed at Achilles, marveling   740

---

6. Wife of Amphion, one of the two founders of the great Greek city of Thebes.   7. Apollo and Artemis's.   8. The legend of Niobe being turned into stone is thought to have had its origin in a rock face
on Sipylus (in Asia Minor) that resembled a woman who cried inconsolably for the loss of her children.
The Achelous River runs near Mount Sipylus.

now at the man's beauty, his magnificent build—
face-to-face he seemed a deathless god . . .
and Achilles gazed and marveled at Dardan Priam,
beholding his noble looks, listening to his words.
But once they'd had their fill of gazing at each other,   745
the old majestic Priam broke the silence first:
"Put me to bed quickly, Achilles, Prince.
Time to rest, to enjoy the sweet relief of sleep.
Not once have my eyes closed shut beneath my lids
from the day my son went down beneath your hands . . .   750
day and night I groan, brooding over the countless griefs,
groveling in the dung that fills my walled-in court.
But now, at long last, I have tasted food again
and let some glistening wine go down my throat.
Before this hour I had tasted nothing."
                                                    He shook his head   755
as Achilles briskly told his men and serving-women
to make beds in the porch's shelter, to lay down
some heavy purple throws for the beds themselves
and over them spread blankets and thick woolly robes,
a warm covering laid on top. Torches held in hand,   760
they went from the hall and fell to work at once
and in no time two good beds were spread and made.
Then Achilles nodded to Priam, leading the king on
with brusque advice: "Sleep outside, old friend,
in case some Achaean captain comes to visit.   765
They keep on coming now, huddling beside me,
making plans for battle—it's their duty.
But if one saw you here in the rushing dark night
he'd tell Agamemnon straightaway, our good commander.
Then you'd have real delay in ransoming the body.   770
One more point. Tell me, be precise about it—
how many days do you need to bury Prince Hector?
I will hold back myself
and keep the Argive armies back that long."

     And the old and noble Priam answered slowly,   775
"If you truly want me to give Prince Hector burial,
full, royal honors, you'd show me a great kindness,
Achilles, if you would do exactly as I say.
You know how crammed we are inside our city,
how far it is to the hills to haul in timber,   780
and our Trojans are afraid to make the journey.
Well, nine days we should mourn him in our halls,
on the tenth we'd bury Hector, hold the public feast,
on the eleventh build the barrow high above his body—
on the twelfth we'd fight again . . . if fight we must."   785

     The swift runner Achilles reassured him quickly:
"All will be done, old Priam, as you command.
I will hold our attack as long as you require."

With that he clasped the old king by the wrist,
by the right hand, to free his heart from fear.
Then Priam and herald, minds set on the journey home,   790
bedded down for the night within the porch's shelter.
And deep in his sturdy well-built lodge Achilles slept
with Briseis in all her beauty sleeping by his side.

Now the great array of gods and chariot-driving men   795
slept all night long, overcome by gentle sleep.
But sleep could never hold the running Escort—
Hermes kept on turning it over in his mind . . .
how could he convoy Priam clear of the ships,
unseen by devoted guards who held the gates?   800
Hovering at his head the Escort rose and spoke:
"Not a care in the world, old man? Look at you,
how you sleep in the midst of men who'd kill you—
and just because Achilles spared your life. Now, yes,
you've ransomed your dear son—for a king's ransom.   805
But wouldn't the sons you left behind be forced
to pay three times as much for *you* alive?
What if Atrides Agamemnon learns you're here—
what if the whole Achaean army learns you're here?"

The old king woke in terror, roused the herald.   810
Hermes harnessed the mules and team for both men,
drove them fast through the camp and no one saw them.

Once they reached the ford where the river runs clear,
the strong, whirling Xanthus sprung of immortal Zeus,
Hermes went his way to the steep heights of Olympus   815
as Dawn flung out her golden robe across the earth,
and the two men, weeping, groaning, drove the team
toward Troy and the mules brought on the body.
No one saw them at first, neither man nor woman,
none before Cassandra, golden as goddess Aphrodite.   820
She had climbed to Pergamus heights and from that point
she saw her beloved father swaying tall in the chariot,
flanked by the herald, whose cry could rouse the city.
And Cassandra saw *him* too . . .
drawn by the mules and stretched out on his bier.   825
She screamed and her scream rang out through all Troy:
"Come, look down, you men of Troy, you Trojan women!
Behold Hector now—if you ever once rejoiced
to see him striding home, home alive from battle!
He was the greatest joy of Troy and all our people!"   830

Her cries plunged Troy into uncontrollable grief
and not a man or woman was left inside the walls.
They streamed out at the gates to meet Priam
bringing in the body of the dead. Hector—
his loving wife and noble mother were first   835
to fling themselves on the wagon rolling on,

the first to tear their hair, embrace his head
and a wailing throng of people milled around them.
And now, all day long till the setting sun went down
they would have wept for Hector there before the gates   840
if the old man, steering the car, had not commanded,
"Let me through with the mules! Soon, in a moment,
you can have your fill of tears—once I've brought him home."

    So he called and the crowds fell back on either side,
making way for the wagon. Once they had borne him   845
into the famous halls, they laid his body down
on his large carved bed and set beside him singers
to lead off the laments, and their voices rose in grief—
they lifted the dirge high as the women wailed in answer.
And white-armed Andromache led their songs of sorrow,   850
cradling the head of Hector, man-killing Hector
gently in her arms: "O my husband . . .
cut off from life so young! You leave me a widow,
lost in the royal halls—and the boy only a baby,
the son we bore together, you and I so doomed.   855
I cannot think he will ever come to manhood.
Long before *that* the city will be sacked,
plundered top to bottom! Because you are dead,
her great guardian, you who always defended Troy,
who kept her loyal wives and helpless children safe,   860
all who will soon be carried off in the hollow ships
and I with them—
                  And you, my child, will follow me
to labor, somewhere, at harsh, degrading work,
slaving under some heartless master's eye—that,
or some Achaean marauder will seize you by the arm   865
and hurl you headlong down from the ramparts[9]—horrible death—
enraged at you because Hector once cut down his brother,
his father or his son, yes, hundreds of armed Achaeans
gnawed the dust of the world, crushed by Hector's hands!
Your father, remember, was no man of mercy . . .   870
not in the horror of battle, and that is why
the whole city of Troy mourns you now, my Hector—
you've brought your parents accursed tears and grief
but to me most of all you've left the horror, the heartbreak!
For you never died in bed and stretched your arms to me   875
or said some last word from the heart I can remember,
always, weeping for you through all my nights and days!"

    Her voice rang out in tears and the women wailed in answer
and Hecuba led them now in a throbbing chant of sorrow:
"Hector, dearest to me by far of all my sons . . .   880
and dear to the gods while we still shared this life—
and they cared about you still, I see, even after death.
Many the sons I had whom the swift runner Achilles

9. After the fall of Troy, Astyanax was, in fact, hurled from the walls.

caught and shipped on the barren salt sea as slaves
to Samos, to Imbros, to Lemnos shrouded deep in mist!   885
But you, once he slashed away your life with his brazen spear
he dragged you time and again around his comrade's tomb,
Patroclus whom you killed—not that he brought Patroclus
back to life by that. But I have you with me now . . .
fresh as the morning dew you lie in the royal halls   890
like one whom Apollo, lord of the silver bow,
has approached and shot to death with gentle shafts."

     Her voice rang out in tears and an endless wail rose up
and Helen, the third in turn, led their songs of sorrow:
"Hector! Dearest to me of all my husband's brothers—   895
my husband, Paris, magnificent as a god . . .
he was the one who brought me here to Troy—
Oh how I wish I'd died before that day!
But this, now, is the twentieth year for me
since I sailed here and forsook my own native land,   900
yet never once did I hear from *you* a taunt, an insult.
But if someone else in the royal halls would curse me,
one of your brothers or sisters or brothers' wives
trailing their long robes, even your own mother—
not your father, always kind as my own father—   905
why, you'd restrain them with words, Hector,
you'd win them to my side . . .
you with your gentle temper, all your gentle words.
And so in the same breath I mourn for you and me,
my doom-struck, harrowed heart! Now there is no one left   910
in the wide realm of Troy, no friend to treat me kindly—
all the countrymen cringe from me in loathing!"

     Her voice rang out in tears and vast throngs wailed
and old King Priam rose and gave his people orders:
"Now, you men of Troy, haul timber into the city!   915
Have no fear of an Argive ambush packed with danger—
Achilles vowed, when he sent me home from the black ships,
not to do us harm till the twelfth dawn arrives."

     At this command they harnessed oxen and mules to wagons,
they assembled before the city walls with all good speed   920
and for nine days hauled in a boundless store of timber.
But when the tenth Dawn brought light to the mortal world
they carried gallant Hector forth, streaming tears,
and they placed his corpse aloft the pyre's crest,
flung a torch and set it all aflame.
                              At last,   925
when young Dawn with her rose-red fingers shone once more,
the people massed around illustrious Hector's pyre . . .
And once they'd gathered, crowding the meeting grounds,
they first put out the fires with glistening wine,
wherever the flames still burned in all their fury.   930
Then they collected the white bones of Hector—

all his brothers, his friends-in-arms, mourning,
and warm tears came streaming down their cheeks.
They placed the bones they found in a golden chest,
shrouding them round and round in soft purple cloths.   935
They quickly lowered the chest in a deep, hollow grave
and over it piled a cope of huge stones closely set,
then hastily heaped a barrow, posted lookouts all around
for fear the Achaean combat troops would launch their attack
before the time agreed. And once they'd heaped the mound   940
they turned back home to Troy, and gathering once again
they shared a splendid funeral feast in Hector's honor,
held in the house of Priam, king by will of Zeus.

And so the Trojans buried Hector breaker of horses.

The Odyssey[1]

BOOK I

[A Goddess Intervenes]

Sing in me, Muse, and through me tell the story
of that man skilled in all ways of contending,
the wanderer, harried for years on end,
after he plundered the stronghold
on the proud height of Troy.
                              He saw the townlands   5
and learned the minds of many distant men,
and weathered many bitter nights and days
in his deep heart at sea, while he fought only
to save his life, to bring his shipmates home.
But not by will nor valor could he save them,   10
for their own recklessness destroyed them all—
children and fools, they killed and feasted on
the cattle of Lord Hêlios,[2] the Sun,
and he who moves all day through heaven
took from their eyes the dawn of their return.   15

Of these adventures, Muse, daughter of Zeus,
tell us in our time, lift the great song again.
Begin when all the rest who left behind them
headlong death in battle or at sea
had long ago returned,[3] while he alone still hungered   20
for home and wife. Her ladyship Kalypso[4]
clung to him in her sea-hollowed caves—
a nymph, immortal and most beautiful,
who craved him for her own.
                              And when long years and seasons

1. Translated by Robert Fitzgerald. Fitzgerald's translation provides its own pronunciation symbols. Thus
ê is pronounced like ee and accented syllables are indicated.   2. This is described in book 12.   3. From
the siege of Troy.   4. Her name is formed from a Greek verb that means "cover, hide."

wheeling brought around that point of time   25
ordained for him to make his passage homeward,
trials and dangers, even so, attended him
even in Ithaka,[5] near those he loved.
Yet all the gods had pitied Lord Odysseus,
all but Poseidon,[6] raging cold and rough   30
against the brave king till he came ashore
at last on his own land.
                                But now that god
had gone far off among the sunburnt races,
most remote of men, at earth's two verges,
in sunset lands and lands of the rising sun,   35
to be regaled by smoke of thighbones burning,
haunches of rams and bulls, a hundred fold.
He lingered delighted at the banquet side.

In the bright hall of Zeus upon Olympos
the other gods were all at home, and Zeus,   40
the father of gods and men, made conversation.
For he had meditated on Aigísthos, dead
by the hand of Agamémnon's[7] son, Orestês,
and spoke his thought aloud before them all:

"My word, how mortals take the gods to task!   45
All their afflictions come from us, we hear.
And what of their own failings? Greed and folly
double the suffering in the lot of man.
See how Aigísthos, for his double portion,
stole Agamémnon's wife and killed the soldier   50
on his homecoming day. And yet Aigísthos
knew that his own doom lay in this. We gods
had warned him, sent down Hermês Argeiphontês,[8]
our most observant courier, to say:
'Don't kill the man, don't touch his wife,   55
or face a reckoning with Orestês
the day he comes of age and wants his patrimony.'
Friendly advice—but would Aigísthos take it?
Now he has paid the reckoning in full."

The grey-eyed goddess Athena replied to Zeus: 60

"O Majesty, O Father of us all,
that man is in the dust indeed, and justly.
So perish all who do what he had done.
But my own heart is broken for Odysseus,
the master mind of war, so long a castaway   65
upon an island in the running sea;
a wooded island, in the sea's middle,

5. An island off the northwest coast of Greece, Odysseus's home.   6. The reason for his rage is given
by Zeus in lines 87–90.   7. The story of Agamémnon's return and death is told in detail in book 11.
8. Both the meaning and origin of this epithet are uncertain.

and there's a goddess in the place, the daughter
of one whose baleful mind knows all the deeps
of the blue sea—Atlas,[9] who holds the columns   70
that bear from land the great thrust of the sky.
His daughter[1] will not let Odysseus go,
poor mournful man; she keeps on coaxing him
with her beguiling talk, to turn his mind
from Ithaka. But such desire is in him   75
merely to see the hearthsmoke leaping upward
from his own island, that he longs to die.
Are you not moved by this, Lord of Olympos?
Had you no pleasure from Odysseus' offerings
beside the Argive[2] ships, on Troy's wide seaboard?   80
O Zeus, what do you hold against him now?"

To this the summoner of cloud replied:

"My child, what strange remarks you let escape you.
Could I forget that kingly man, Odysseus?
There is no mortal half so wise; no mortal   85
gave so much to the lords of open sky.
Only the god who laps the land in water,
Poseidon, bears the fighter an old grudge
since he poked out the eye of Polyphêmos,
brawniest of the Kyklopês.[3] Who bore   90
that giant lout? Thoösa, daughter of Phorkys,
an offshore sea lord: for this nymph had lain
with Lord Poseidon in her hollow caves.
Naturally, the god, after the blinding—
mind you, he does not kill the man;   95
he only buffets him away from home.
But come now, we are all at leisure here,
let us take up this matter of his return,
that he may sail. Poseidon must relent
for being quarrelsome will get him nowhere,   100
one god, flouting the will of all the gods."

The grey-eyed goddess Athena answered him:

"O Majesty, O Father of us all,
if it now please the blissful gods
that wise Odysseus reach his home again,   105
let the Wayfinder, Hermês, cross the sea
to the island of Ogýgia; let him tell
our fixed intent to the nymph with pretty braids,
and let the steadfast man depart for home.
For my part, I shall visit Ithaka   110

9. A Titan, whose punishment for his part in the war against Zeus was to hold up the sky on his shoulders.   1. Kalypso, who lives on the island of Ogýgia.   2. One of the collective names for the Greeks fighting at Troy.   3. Or Cyclopes; these giants had a single eye in the middle of their foreheads. This encounter is told in detail in book 9.

to put more courage in the son, and rouse him
to call an assembly of the islanders,
Akhaian[4] gentlemen with flowing hair.
He must warn off that wolf pack of the suitors
who prey upon his flocks and dusky cattle.   115
I'll send him to the mainland then, to Sparta
by the sand beach of Pylos; let him find
news of his dear father where he may
and win his own renown about the world."

She bent to tie her beautiful sandals on,   120
ambrosial, golden, that carry her over water
or over endless land on the wings of the wind,
and took the great haft of her spear in hand—
that bronzeshod spear this child of Power can use
to break in wrath long battle lines of fighters.   125

Flashing down from Olympos' height she went
to stand in Ithaka, before the Manor,
just at the doorsill of the court. She seemed
a family friend, the Taphian[5] captain, Mentês,
waiting, with a light hand on her spear.   130
Before her eyes she found the lusty suitors
casting dice inside the gate, at ease
on hides of oxen—oxen they had killed.

Their own retainers made a busy sight
with houseboys mixing bowls of water and wine,   135
or sopping water up in sponges, wiping
tables to be placed about in hall,
or butchering whole carcasses for roasting.

Long before anyone else, the prince Telémakhos
now caught sight of Athena—for he, too,   140
was sitting there unhappy among the suitors,
a boy, daydreaming. What if his great father
came from the unknown world and drove these men
like dead leaves through the place, recovering
honor and lordship in his own domains?   145
Then he who dreamed in the crowd gazed out at Athena.

Straight to the door he came, irked with himself
to think a visitor had been kept there waiting,
and took her right hand, grasping with his left
her tall bronze-bladed spear. Then he said warmly: 150

"Greetings, stranger! Welcome to our feast.
There will be time to tell your errand later."

He led the way, and Pallas Athena followed
into the lofty hall. The boy reached up

---

4. Another of the collective names for the Greeks.   5. The name of a nearby seafaring people.

and thrust her spear high in a polished rack 155
against a pillar where tough spear on spear
of the old soldier, his father, stood in order.
Then, shaking out a splendid coverlet,
he seated her on a throne with footrest—all
finely carved—and drew his painted armchair 160
near her, at a distance from the rest.
To be amid the din, the suitors' riot,
would ruin his guest's appetite, he thought,
and he wished privacy to ask for news
about his father, gone for years.
               A maid 165
brought them a silver finger bowl and filled it
out of a beautiful spouting golden jug,
then drew a polished table to their side.
The larder mistress with her tray came by
and served them generously. A carver lifted 170
cuts of each roast meat to put on trenchers
before the two. He gave them cups of gold,
and these the steward as he went his rounds
filled and filled again.
            Now came the suitors,
young bloods trooping in to their own seats 175
on thrones or easy chairs. Attendants poured
water over their fingers, while the maids
piled baskets full of brown loaves near at hand,
and houseboys brimmed the bowls with wine.
Now they laid hands upon the ready feast 180
and thought of nothing more. Not till desire
for food and drink had left them were they mindful
of dance and song, that are the grace of feasting.
A herald gave a shapely cithern harp
to Phêmios,[6] whom they compelled to sing— 185
and what a storm he plucked upon the strings
for prelude! High and clear the song arose.

Telémakhos now spoke to grey-eyed Athena,
his head bent close, so no one else might hear:

"Dear guest, will this offend you, if I speak? 190
It is easy for these men to like these things,
harping and song; they have an easy life,
scot free, eating the livestock of another—
a man whose bones are rotting somewhere now,
white in the rain on dark earth where they lie, 195
or tumbling in the groundswell of the sea.
If he returned, if these men ever saw him,
faster legs they'd pray for, to a man,
and not more wealth in handsome robes or gold.
But he is lost; he came to grief and perished, 200

6. He was a member of Odysseus's household.

and there's no help for us in someone's hoping
he still may come; that sun has long gone down.
But tell me now, and put it for me clearly—
who are you? Where do you come from? Where's your home
and family? What kind of ship is yours,   205
and what course brought you here? Who are your sailors?
I don't suppose you walked here on the sea.
Another thing—this too I ought to know—
is Ithaka new to you, or were you ever
a guest here in the old days? Far and near   210
friends knew this house; for he whose home it was
had much acquaintance in the world."

                                    To this
the grey-eyed goddess answered:

                                    "As you ask,
I can account most clearly for myself.
Mentês I'm called, son of the veteran   215
Ankhíalos; I rule seafaring Taphos.
I came by ship, with a ship's company,
sailing the winedark sea for ports of call
on alien shores—to Témesê, for copper,
bringing bright bars of iron in exchange.   220
My ship is moored on a wild strip of coast
in Reithron Bight, under the wooded mountain.
Years back, my family and yours were friends,
as Lord Laërtês[7] knows; ask when you see him.
I hear the old man comes to town no longer,   225
stays up country, ailing, with only one
old woman to prepare his meat and drink
when pain and stiffness take him in the legs
from working on his terraced plot, his vineyard.
As for my sailing here—   230
the tale was that your father had come home,
therefore I came. I see the gods delay him.
But never in this world is Odysseus dead—
only detained somewhere on the wide sea,
upon some island, with wild islanders;   235
savages, they must be, to hold him captive.
Well, I will forecast for you, as the gods
put the strong feeling in me—I see it all,
and I'm no prophet, no adept in bird-signs.
He will not, now, be long away from Ithaka,   240
his father's dear land; though he be in chains
he'll scheme a way to come; he can do anything.

But tell me this now, make it clear to me:
You must be, by your looks, Odysseus' boy?
The way your head is shaped, the fine eyes—yes,   245

7. Odysseus's father.

how like him! We took meals like this together
many a time, before he sailed for Troy
with all the lords of Argos in the ships.
I have not seen him since, nor has he seen me."

And thoughtfully Telémakhos replied: 250

"Friend, let me put it in the plainest way.
My mother says I am his son: I know not
surely. Who has known his own engendering?
I wish at least I had some happy man
as father, growing old in his own house—   255
but unknown death and silence are the fate
of him that, since you ask, they call my father."

Then grey-eyed Athena said:

                              "The gods decreed
no lack of honor in this generation:
such is the son Penélopê bore in you.   260
But tell me now, and make this clear to me:
what gathering, what feast is this? Why here?
A wedding? Revel? At the expense of all?
Not that, I think. How arrogant they seem,
these gluttons, making free here in your house!   265
A sensible man would blush to be among them."

To this Telémakhos answered:

"Friend, now that you ask about these matters,
our house was always princely, a great house,
as long as he of whom we speak remained here.   270
But evil days the gods have brought upon it,
making him vanish, as they have, so strangely.
Were his death known, I could not feel such pain—
if he had died of wounds in Trojan country
or in the arms of friends, after the war.   275
They would have made a tomb for him, the Akhaians,
and I should have all honor as his son.
Instead, the whirlwinds got him, and no glory.
He's gone, no sign, no word of him; and I inherit
trouble and tears—and not for him alone,   280
the gods have laid such other burdens on me.
For now the lords of the islands,
Doulíkhion and Samê, wooded Zakýnthos,[8]
and rocky Ithaka's young lords as well,
are here courting my mother; and they use   285
our house as if it were a house to plunder.
Spurn them she dare not, though she hates that marriage,
nor can she bring herself to choose among them.

8. Islands close to Ithaka.

Meanwhile they eat their way through all we have,
and when they will, they can demolish me."   290

Pallas Athena was disturbed, and said:

"Ah, bitterly you need Odysseus, then!
High time he came back to engage these upstarts.
I wish we saw him standing helmeted
there in the doorway, holding shield and spear,   295
looking the way he did when I first knew him.
That was at our house, where he drank and feasted
after he left Ephyra, homeward bound
from a visit to the son of Mêrmeris, Ilos.
He took his fast ship down the gulf that time   300
for a fatal drug to dip his arrows in
and poison the bronze points; but young Ilos
turned him away, fearing the gods' wrath.
My father gave it, for he loved him well.
I wish these men could meet the man of those days!   305
They'd know their fortune quickly: a cold bed.
Aye! but it lies upon the gods' great knees
whether he can return and force a reckoning
in his own house, or not.
                                If I were you,
I should take steps to make these men disperse.   310
Listen, now, and attend to what I say:
at daybreak call the islanders to assembly,
and speak your will, and call the gods to witness:
the suitors must go scattering to their homes.
Then here's a course for you, if you agree: 315
get a sound craft afloat with twenty oars
and go abroad for news of your lost father—
perhaps a traveller's tale, or rumored fame
issued from Zeus abroad in the world of men.
Talk to that noble sage at Pylos, Nestor,   320
then go to Meneláos, the red-haired king
at Sparta, last man home of all the Akhaians.
If you should learn your father is alive
and coming home, you could hold out a year.
Or if you learn that he is dead and gone,   325
then you can come back to your own dear country
and raise a mound for him, and burn his gear,
with all the funeral honors due the man,
and give your mother to another husband.
When you have done all this, or seen it done,   330
it will be time to ponder
concerning these contenders in your house—
how you should kill them, outright or by guile.
You need not bear this insolence of theirs,
you are a child no longer. Have you heard   335
what glory young Orestês won
when he cut down that two-faced man, Aigísthos,

for killing his illustrious father?
Dear friend, you are tall and well set-up, I see;
be brave—you, too—and men in times to come   340
will speak of you respectfully.
                Now I must join my ships;
my crew will grumble if I keep them waiting.
Look to yourself; remember what I told you."

Telémakhos replied:

                "Friend, you have done me
kindness, like a father to his son,   345
and I shall not forget your counsel ever.
You must get back to sea, I know, but come
take a hot bath, and rest; accept a gift
to make your heart lift up when you embark—
some precious thing, and beautiful, from me,   350
a keepsake, such as dear friends give their friends."

But the grey-eyed goddess Athena answered him:

"Do not delay me, for I love the sea ways.
As for the gift your heart is set on giving,
let me accept it on my passage home,   355
and you shall have a choice gift in exchange."

With this Athena left him
as a bird rustles upward, off and gone.
But as she went she put new spirit in him,
a new dream of his father, clearer now,   360
so that he marvelled to himself
divining that a god had been his guest.
Then godlike in his turn he joined the suitors.

The famous minstrel still sang on before them,
and they sat still and listened, while he sang   365
that bitter song, the Homecoming of Akhaians—
how by Athena's will they fared from Troy;
and in her high room careful Penélopê,
Ikários' daughter, heeded the holy song.
She came, then, down the long stairs of her house,   370
this beautiful lady, with two maids in train
attending her as she approached the suitors;
and near a pillar of the roof she paused,
her shining veil drawn over across her cheeks,
the two girls close to her and still,   375
and through her tears spoke to the noble minstrel:
"Phêmios, other spells you know, high deeds
of gods and heroes, as the poets tell them;
let these men hear some other; let them sit
silent and drink their wine. But sing no more   380
this bitter tale that wears my heart away.

It opens in me again the wound of longing
for one incomparable, ever in my mind—
his fame all Hellas[9] knows, and midland Argos."

But Telémakhos intervened and said to her: 385

"Mother, why do you grudge our own dear minstrel
joy of song, wherever his thought may lead?
Poets are not to blame, but Zeus who gives
what fate he pleases to adventurous men.
Here is no reason for reproof: to sing   390
the news of the Danaans![1] Men like best
a song that rings like morning on the ear.
But you must nerve yourself and try to listen.
Odysseus was not the only one at Troy
never to know the day of his homecoming.   395
Others, how many others, lost their lives!"

The lady gazed in wonder and withdrew,
her son's clear wisdom echoing in her mind.
But when she had mounted to her rooms again
with her two handmaids, then she fell to weeping   400
for Odysseus, her husband. Grey-eyed Athena
presently cast a sweet sleep on her eyes.

Meanwhile the din grew loud in the shadowy hall
as every suitor swore to lie beside her,
but Telémakhos turned now and spoke to them: 405

"You suitors of my mother! Insolent men,
now we have dined, let us have entertainment
and no more shouting. There can be no pleasure
so fair as giving heed to a great minstrel
like ours, whose voice itself is pure delight.   410
At daybreak we shall sit down in assembly
and I shall tell you—take it as you will—
you are to leave this hall. Go feasting elsewhere,
consume your own stores. Turn and turn about,
use one another's houses. If you choose   415
to slaughter one man's livestock and pay nothing,
this is rapine; and by the eternal gods
I beg Zeus you shall get what you deserve:
a slaughter here, and nothing paid for it!"

By now their teeth seemed fixed in their under-lips,   420
Telémakhos' bold speaking stunned them so.
Antínoös, Eupeithês' son, made answer:
"Telémakhos, no doubt the gods themselves
are teaching you this high and mighty manner.

9. The ancient name for Greece.   1. Another name for the Greeks as a whole.

Zeus forbid you should be king in Ithaka,   425
though you are eligible as your father's son."

Telémakhos kept his head and answered him:

"Antínoös, you may not like my answer,
but I would happily be king, if Zeus
conferred the prize. Or do you think it wretched?   430
I shouldn't call it bad at all. A king
will be respected, and his house will flourish.
But there are eligible men enough,
heaven knows, on the island, young and old,
and one of them perhaps may come to power   435
after the death of King Odysseus.
All I insist on is that I rule our house
and rule the slaves my father won for me."

Eurýmakhos, Pólybos' son, replied:

"Telémakhos, it is on the gods' great knees   440
who will be king in sea-girt Ithaka.
But keep your property, and rule your house,
and let no man, against your will, make havoc
of your possessions, while there's life on Ithaka.
But now, my brave young friend,   445
a question or two about the stranger.
Where did your guest come from? Of what country?
Where does he say his home is, and his family?
Has he some message of your father's coming,
or business of his own, asking a favor?   450
He left so quickly that one hadn't time
to meet him, but he seemed a gentleman."

Telémakhos made answer, cool enough:

"Eurýmakhos, there's no hope for my father.
I would not trust a message, if one came,   455
nor any forecaster my mother invites
to tell by divination of time to come.
My guest, however, was a family friend,
Mentês, son of Ankhíalos.
He rules the Taphian people of the sea."   460

So said Telémakhos, though in his heart
he knew his visitor had been immortal.
But now the suitors turned to play again
with dance and haunting song. They stayed till nightfall,
indeed, black night came on them at their pleasure,   465
and half asleep they left, each for his home.

Telémakhos' bedroom was above the court,
a kind of tower, with a view all round;

here he retired to ponder in the silence,
while carrying brands of pine alight beside him   470
Eurýkleia went padding, sage and old.
Her father had been Ops, Peisênor's son,
and she had been a purchase of Laërtês
when she was still a blossoming girl. He gave
the price of twenty oxen for her, kept her   475
as kindly in his house as his own wife,
though, for the sake of peace, he never touched her.
No servant loved Telémakhos as she did,
she who had nursed him in his infancy.
So now she held the light, as he swung open   480
the door of his neat freshly painted chamber.
There he sat down, pulling his tunic off,
and tossed it into the wise old woman's hands.
She folded it and smoothed it, and then hung it
beside the inlaid bed upon a bar;   485
then, drawing the door shut by its silver handle
she slid the catch in place and went away.
And all night long, wrapped in the finest fleece,
he took in thought the course Athena gave him.

BOOK II

[A Hero's Son Awakens]

When primal Dawn spread on the eastern sky
her fingers of pink light, Odysseus' true son
stood up, drew on his tunic and his mantle,
slung on a sword-belt and a new-edged sword,
tied his smooth feet into good rawhide sandals,   5
and left his room, a god's brilliance upon him.
He found the criers with clarion voices and told them
to muster the unshorn Akhaians in full assembly.
The call sang out, and the men came streaming in;
and when they filled the assembly ground, he entered,   10
spear in hand, with two quick hounds at heel;
Athena lavished on him a sunlit grace
that held the eye of the multitude. Old men
made way for him as he took his father's chair.

Now Lord Aigýptios, bent down and sage with years,   15
opened the assembly. This man's son
had served under the great Odysseus, gone
in the decked ships with him to the wild horse country
of Troy—a spearman, Ántiphos by name.
The ravenous Kyklops in the cave destroyed him   20
last in his feast of men. Three other sons
the old man had, and one, Eurýnomos,
went with the suitors; two farmed for their father;
but even so the old man pined, remembering
the absent one, and a tear welled up as he spoke: 25

"Hear me, Ithakans! Hear what I have to say.
No meeting has been held here since our king,
Odysseus, left port in the decked ships.
Who finds occasion for assembly, now?
one of the young men? one of the older lot?   30
Has he had word our fighters are returning—
news to report if he got wind of it—
or is it something else, touching the realm?
The man has vigor, I should say; more power to him.
Whatever he desires, may Zeus fulfill it."   35

The old man's words delighted the son of Odysseus,
who kept his chair no longer but stood up,
eager to speak, in the midst of all the men.
The crier, Peisênor, master of debate,
brought him the staff and placed it in his hand;[2]   40
then the boy touched the old man's shoulder, and said:

"No need to wonder any more, Sir,
who called this session. The distress is mine.
As to our troops returning, I have no news—
news to report if I got wind of it—   45
nor have I public business to propose;
only my need, and the trouble of my house—
the troubles.

              My distinguished father is lost,
who ruled among you once, mild as a father,
and there is now this greater evil still: 50
my home and all I have are being ruined.
Mother wanted no suitors, but like a pack
they came—sons of the best men here among them—
lads with no stomach for an introduction
to Ikários, her father across the sea;   55
he would require a wedding gift, and give her
to someone who found favor in her eyes.
No; these men spend their days around our house
killing our beeves and sheep and fatted goats,
carousing, soaking up our good dark wine,   60
not caring what they do. They squander everything.
We have no strong Odysseus to defend us,
and as to putting up a fight ourselves—
we'd only show our incompetence in arms.
Expel them, yes, if I only had the power;   65
the whole thing's out of hand, insufferable.
My house is being plundered: is this courtesy?
Where is your indignation? Where is your shame?
Think of the talk in the islands all around us,

2. As in the assembly in book 1 of the *Iliad*, the herald hands the person who is given the floor to speak a staff, the symbol of authority.

and fear the wrath of the gods, 70
or they may turn, and send you some devilry.
Friends, by Olympian Zeus and holy Justice
that holds men in assembly and sets them free,
make an end of this! Let me lament in peace
my private loss. Or did my father, Odysseus, 75
ever do injury to the armed Akhaians?
Is this your way of taking it out on me,
giving free rein to these young men?
I might as well—might better—see my treasure
and livestock taken over by you all; 80
then, if you fed on them, I'd have some remedy,
and when we met, in public, in the town,
I'd press my claim; you might make restitution.
This way you hurt me when my hands are tied."

And in hot anger now he threw the staff to the ground, 85
his eyes grown bright with tears. A wave of sympathy
ran through the crowd, all hushed; and no one there
had the audacity to answer harshly
except Antínoös, who said:

                    "What high and mighty
talk, Telémakhos! No holding you! 90
You want to shame us, and humiliate us,
but you should know the suitors are not to blame—
it is your own dear, incomparably cunning mother.
For three years now—and it will soon be four—
she has been breaking the hearts of the Akhaians, 95
holding out hope to all, and sending promises
to each man privately[3]—but thinking otherwise.

Here is an instance of her trickery:
she had her great loom standing in the hall
and the fine warp of some vast fabric on it; 100
we were attending her, and she said to us:
"Young men, my suitors, now my lord is dead,
let me finish my weaving before I marry,
or else my thread will have been spun in vain.
It is a shroud I weave for Lord Laërtês, 105
when cold death comes to lay him on his bier.
The country wives would hold me in dishonor
if he, with all his fortune, lay unshrouded.'
We have men's hearts; she touched them; we agreed.
So every day she wove on the great loom— 110
but every night by torchlight she unwove it;
and so for three years she deceived the Akhaians.
But when the seasons brought the fourth around,
one of her maids, who knew the secret, told us;

---

3. Her tactic is to divide the suitors and so put off the day that they will unanimously demand a decision.

we found her unraveling the splendid shroud.   115
She had to finish then, although she hated it.

Now here is the suitors' answer—
you and all the Akhaians, mark it well:
dismiss your mother from the house, or make her marry
the man her father names and she prefers.   120
Does she intend to keep us dangling forever?
She may rely too long on Athena's gifts—
talent in handicraft and a clever mind;
so cunning—history cannot show the like
among the ringleted ladies of Akhaia,   125
Mykênê with her coronet, Alkmênê, Tyro.[4]
Wits like Penélopê's never were before,
but this time—well, she made poor use of them.
For here are suitors eating up your property
as long as she holds out—a plan some god   130
put in her mind. She makes a name for herself,
but you can feel the loss it means for you.
Our own affairs can wait; we'll never go anywhere else,
until she takes an Akhaian to her liking."

But clear-headed Telémakhos replied: 135

"Antínoös, can I banish against her will
the mother who bore me and took care of me?
My father is either dead or far away,
but dearly I should pay for this
at Ikários' hands, if ever I sent her back.   140
The powers of darkness would requite it, too,
my mother's parting curse would call hell's furies[5]
to punish me, along with the scorn of men.
No: I can never give the word for this.
But if your hearts are capable of shame,   145
leave my great hall, and take your dinner elsewhere,
consume your own stores. Turn and turn about,
use one another's houses. If you choose
to slaughter one man's livestock and pay nothing,
this is rapine; and by the eternal gods   150
I beg Zeus you shall get what you deserve:
a slaughter here, and nothing paid for it!"

Now Zeus who views the wide world sent a sign to him,
launching a pair of eagles[6] from a mountain crest
in gliding flight down the soft blowing wind,   155
wing-tip to wing-tip quivering taut, companions,

---

4. Famous women of the past. Alkmênê was the mother of Herakles. Odysseus sees the ghosts of Tyro and Alkmênê in the underworld in book 9.   **5.** Spirits who avenge injured parents, especially (because they themselves are female) mothers. In Greek they are known as Erinyes.   **6.** The royal bird, the emblem of Zeus.

till high above the assembly of many voices
they wheeled, their dense wings beating, and in havoc
dropped on the heads of the crowd—a deathly omen—
wielding their talons, tearing cheeks and throats;   160
then veered away on the right hand through the city.
Astonished, gaping after the birds, the men
felt their hearts flood, foreboding things to come.
And now they heard the old lord Halithersês,
son of Mastor, keenest among the old   165
at reading birdflight into accurate speech;
in his anxiety for them, he rose and said:

"Hear me, Ithakans! Hear what I have to say,
and may I hope to open the suitors' eyes
to the black wave towering over them. Odysseus   170
will not be absent from his family long:
he is already near, carrying in him
a bloody doom for all these men, and sorrow
for many more on our high seamark, Ithaka.
Let us think how to stop it; let the suitors   175
drop their suit; they had better, without delay.
I am old enough to know a sign when I see one,
and I say all has come to pass for Odysseus
as I foretold when the Argives massed on Troy,
and he, the great tactician, joined the rest.   180
My forecast was that after nineteen years,
many blows weathered, all his shipmates lost,
himself unrecognized by anyone,
he would come home. I see this all fulfilled."

But Pólybos' son, Eurýmakhos, retorted: 185

"Old man, go tell the omens for your children
at home, and try to keep them out of trouble.
I am more fit to interpret this than you are.
Bird life aplenty is found in the sunny air,
not all of it significant. As for Odysseus,   190
he perished far from home. You should have perished with him—
then we'd be spared this nonsense in assembly,
as good as telling Telémakhos to rage on;
do you think you can gamble on a gift from him?
Here is what I foretell, and it's quite certain: 195
if you, with what you know of ancient lore,
encourage bitterness in this young man,
it means, for him, only the more frustration—
he can do nothing whatever with two eagles—
and as for you, old man, we'll fix a penalty   200
that you will groan to pay.
Before the whole assembly I advise Telémakhos
to send his mother to her father's house;
let them arrange her wedding there, and fix

a portion[7] suitable for a valued daughter.   205
Until he does this, courtship is our business,
vexing though it may be; we fear no one,
certainly not Telémakhos, with his talk;
and we care nothing for your divining, uncle,
useless talk; you win more hatred by it.   210
We'll share his meat, no thanks or fee to him,
as long as she delays and maddens us.
It is a long, long time we have been waiting
in rivalry for this beauty. We could have gone
elsewhere and found ourselves very decent wives."   215

Clear-headed Telémakhos replied to this:

"Eurýmakhos, and noble suitors all,
I am finished with appeals and argument.
The gods know, and the Akhaians know, these things.
But give me a fast ship and a crew of twenty   220
who will see me through a voyage, out and back.
I'll go to sandy Pylos, then to Sparta,
for news of Father since he sailed from Troy—
some traveller's tale, perhaps, or rumored fame
issued from Zeus himself into the world.   225
If he's alive, and beating his way home,
I might hold out for another weary year;
but if they tell me that he's dead and gone,
then I can come back to my own dear country
and raise a mound for him, and burn his gear,   230
with all the funeral honors that befit him,
and give my mother to another husband."

The boy sat down in silence. Next to stand
was Mentor, comrade in arms of the prince Odysseus,
an old man now. Odysseus left him authority   235
over his house and slaves, to guard them well.
In his concern, he spoke to the assembly:

"Hear me, Ithakans! Hear what I have to say.
Let no man holding scepter as a king
be thoughtful, mild, kindly, or virtuous;   240
let him be cruel, and practice evil ways;
it is so clear that no one here remembers
how like a gentle father Odysseus ruled you.
I find it less revolting that the suitors
carry their malice into violent acts;   245
at least they stake their lives
when they go pillaging the house of Odysseus—
their lives upon it, he will not come again.
What sickens me is to see the whole community

7. A dowry; in other passages (for example, 8.333–34) it is the suitors who offer gifts to the bride's father. Such a cultural amalgam, customs from different periods or places side by side, is characteristic of oral epic traditions.

sitting still, and never a voice or a hand raised   250
against them—a mere handful compared with you."

Leókritos, Euênor's son, replied to him:

"Mentor, what mischief are you raking up?
Will this crowd risk the sword's edge over a dinner?
Suppose Odysseus himself indeed   255
came in and found the suitors at his table:
he might be hot to drive them out. What then?
Never would he enjoy his wife again—
the wife who loves him well; he'd only bring down
abject death on himself against those odds.   260
Madness, to talk of fighting in either case.
Now let all present go about their business!
Halithersês and Mentor will speed the traveller;
they can help him: they were his father's friends.
I rather think he will be sitting here   265
a long time yet, waiting for news of Ithaka;
that seafaring he spoke of is beyond him."

On this note they were quick to end their parley.
The assembly broke up; everyone went home—
the suitors home to Odysseus' house again.   270
But Telémakhos walked down along the shore
and washed his hands in the foam of the grey sea,
then said this prayer:

                    "O god of yesterday,
guest in our house, who told me to take ship
on the hazy sea for news of my lost father,   275
listen to me, be near me:
the Akhaians only wait, or hope to hinder me,
the damned insolent suitors most of all."

Athena was nearby and came to him,
putting on Mentor's figure and his tone,   280
the warm voice in a lucid flight of words:

"You'll never be fainthearted or a fool,
Telémakhos, if you have your father's spirit;
he finished what he cared to say,
and what he took in hand he brought to pass.   285
The sea routes will yield their distances
to his true son, Penélopê's true son,—
I doubt another's luck would hold so far.
The son is rare who measures with his father,
and one in a thousand is a better man,   290
but you will have the sap and wit
and prudence—for you get that from Odysseus—
to give you a fair chance of winning through.
So never mind the suitors and their ways,

there is no judgment in them, neither do they 295
know anything of death and the black terror
close upon them—doom's day on them all.
You need not linger over going to sea.
I sailed beside your father in the old days,
I'll find a ship for you, and help you sail her. 300
So go on home, as if to join the suitors,
but get provisions ready in containers—
wine in two-handled jugs and barley meal,
the staying power of oarsmen,
in skin bags, watertight. I'll go the rounds 305
and call a crew of volunteers together.
Hundreds of ships are beached on sea-girt Ithaka;
let me but choose the soundest, old or new,
we'll rig her and take her out on the broad sea."

This was the divine speech Telémakhos heard 310
from Athena, Zeus's daughter. He stayed no longer,
but took his heartache home,
and found the robust suitors there at work,
skinning goats and roasting pigs in the courtyard.
Antínoös came straight over, laughing at him, 315
and took him by the hand with a bold greeting:

"High-handed Telémakhos, control your temper!
Come on, get over it, no more grim thoughts,
but feast and drink with me, the way you used to.
The Akhaians will attend to all you ask for— 320
ship, crew, and crossing to the holy land
of Pylos, for the news about your father."

Telémakhos replied with no confusion:

"Antínoös, I cannot see myself again
taking a quiet dinner in this company. 325
Isn't it enough that you could strip my house
under my very nose when I was young?
Now that I know, being grown, what others say,
I understand it all, and my heart is full.
I'll bring black doom upon you if I can— 330
either in Pylos, if I go, or in this country.
And I will go, go all the way, if only
as someone's passenger. I have no ship,
no oarsmen: and it suits you that I have none."

Calmly he drew his hand from Antínoös' hand. 335
At this the suitors, while they dressed their meat,
began to exchange loud mocking talk about him.
One young toplofty gallant set the tone:

                              "Well, think of that!
Telémakhos has a mind to murder us.

He's going to lead avengers out of Pylos,   340
or Sparta, maybe; oh, he's wild to do it.
Or else he'll try the fat land of Ephyra—
he can get poison there, and bring it home,
doctor the wine jar and dispatch us all."

Another took the cue:

                              "Well now, who knows?   345
He might be lost at sea, just like Odysseus,
knocking around in a ship, far from his friends.
And what a lot of trouble that would give us,
making the right division of his things!
We'd keep his house as dowry for his mother—   350
his mother and the man who marries her."

That was the drift of it. Telémakhos
went on through to the storeroom of his father,
a great vault where gold and bronze lay piled
along with chests of clothes, and fragrant oil.   355
And there were jars of earthenware in rows
holding an old wine,
mellow, unmixed, and rare; cool stood the jars
against the wall, kept for whatever day
Odysseus, worn by hardships, might come home.   360
The double folding doors were tightly locked
and guarded, night and day, by the serving woman,
Eurýkleia, grand-daughter of Peisênor,
in all her duty vigilant and shrewd.
Telémakhos called her to the storeroom, saying: 365

"Nurse, get a few two-handled travelling jugs
filled up with wine—the second best, not that
you keep for your unlucky lord and king,
hoping he may have slipped away from death
and may yet come again—royal Odysseus.   370
Twelve amphorai will do; seal them up tight.
And pour out barley into leather bags—
twenty bushels of barley meal ground fine.
Now keep this to yourself! Collect these things,
and after dark, when mother has retired   375
and gone upstairs to bed, I'll come for them.
I sail to sandy Pylos, then to Sparta,
to see what news there is of Father's voyage."

His loving nurse Eurýkleia gave a cry,
and tears sprang to her eyes as she wailed softly: 380

'Dear child, whatever put this in your head?
Why do you want to go so far in the world—
and you our only darling? Lord Odysseus
died in some strange place, far from his homeland.
Think how, when you have turned your back, these men   385

will plot to kill you and share all your things!
Stay with your own, dear, do. Why should you suffer
hardship and homelessness on the wild sea?"

But seeing all clear, Telémakhos replied:

"Take heart, Nurse, there's a god behind this plan.   390
And you must swear to keep it from my mother,
until the eleventh day, or twelfth, or till
she misses me, or hears that I am gone.
She must not tear her lovely skin lamenting."

So the old woman vowed by all the gods,   395
and vowed again, to carry out his wishes;
then she filled up the amphorai with wine
and sifted barley meal into leather bags.
Telémakhos rejoined the suitors.
                              Meanwhile
the goddess with grey eyes had other business: 400
disguised as Telémakhos, she roamed the town
taking each likely man aside and telling him:
"Meet us at nightfall at the ship!" Indeed,
she asked Noêmon, Phronios' wealthy son,
to lend her a fast ship, and he complied.   405
Now when at sundown shadows crossed the lanes
she dragged the cutter to the sea and launched it,
fitted out with tough seagoing gear,
and tied it up, away at the harbor's edge.
The crewmen gathered, sent there by the goddess.   410
Then it occurred to the grey-eyed goddess Athena
to pass inside the house of the hero Odysseus,
showing a sweet drowsiness on the suitors,
whom she had presently wandering in their wine;
and soon, as they could hold their cups no longer,   415
they straggled off to find their beds in town,
eyes heavy-lidded, laden down with sleep.
Then to Telémakhos the grey-eyed goddess
appeared again with Mentor's form and voice,
calling him out of the lofty emptied hall: 420

"Telémakhos, your crew of fighting men
is ready at the oars, and waiting for you;
come on, no point in holding up the sailing."

And Pallas Athena turned like the wind, running
ahead of him. He followed in her footsteps   425
down to the seaside, where they found the ship,
and oarsmen with flowing hair at the water's edge.
Telémakhos, now strong in the magic, cried:

"Come with me, friends, and get our rations down!
They are all packed at home, and my own mother   430
knows nothing!—only one maid was told."

He turned and led the way, and they came after,
carried and stowed all in the well-trimmed ship
as the dear son of Odysseus commanded.
Telémakhos then stepped aboard; Athena   435
took her position aft, and he sat by her.
The two stroke oars cast off the stern hawsers
and vaulted over the gunnels to their benches.
Grey-eyed Athena stirred them a following wind,
soughing from the north-west on the winedark sea,   440
and as he felt the wind, Telémakhos
called to all hands to break out mast and sail.
They pushed the fir mast high and stepped it firm
amidships in the box, made fast the forestays,
then hoisted up the white sail on its halyards   445
until the wind caught, booming in the sail;
and a flushing wave sang backward from the bow
on either side, as the ship got way upon her,
holding her steady course.
Now they made all secure in the fast black ship,   450
and, setting out the winebowls all a-brim,
they made libation to the gods,
                              the undying, the ever-new,
most of all to the grey-eyed daughter of Zeus.
And the prow sheared through the night into the dawn.

BOOK III

[*The Lord of the Western Approaches*]

The sun rose on the flawless brimming sea
into a sky all brazen—all one brightening
for gods immortal and for mortal men
on plowlands kind with grain.
                              And facing sunrise
the voyagers now lay off Pylos town,   5
compact stronghold of Neleus.[8] On the shore
black bulls were being offered by the people
to the blue-maned god[9] who makes the islands tremble:
nine congregations, each five hundred strong,
led out nine bulls apiece to sacrifice,   10
taking the tripes to eat, while on their altars
thighbones in fat lay burning for the god.
Here they put in, furled sail, and beached the ship;
but Telémakhos hung back in disembarking,
so that Athena turned and said: 15

"Not the least shyness, now, Telémakhos.
You came across the open sea for this—
to find out where the great earth hides your father
and what the doom was that he came upon.
Go to old Nestor,[1] master charioteer,   20

---

8. Mortal son of the god Poseidon and father of Nestor.   9. Poseidon.   1. The oldest of the warriors
at the siege of Troy.

so we may broach the storehouse of his mind.
Ask him with courtesy, and in his wisdom
he will tell you history and no lies."

But clear-headed Telémakhos replied:

"Mentor, how can I do it, how approach him?   25
I have no practice in elaborate speeches, and
for a young man to interrogate an old man
seems disrespectful—"

        But the grey-eyed goddess said:

"Reason and heart will give you words, Telémakhos;
and a spirit will counsel others. I should say   30
the gods were never indifferent to your life."

She went on quickly, and he followed her
to where the men of Pylos had their altars.
Nestor appeared enthroned among his sons,
while friends around them skewered the red beef   35
or held it scorching. When they saw the strangers
a hail went up, and all that crowd came forward
calling out invitations to the feast.
Peisístratos in the lead, the young prince,
caught up their hands in his and gave them places   40
on curly lambskins flat on the sea sand
near Thrasymêdês, his brother, and his father;
he passed them bits of the food of sacrifice,
and, pouring wine in a golden cup,
he said to Pallas Athena, daughter of Zeus: 45

"Friend, I must ask you to invoke Poseidon:
you find us at this feast, kept in his honor.
Make the appointed offering then, and pray,
and give the honeyed winecup to your friend
so he may do the same. He, too,   50
must pray to the gods on whom all men depend,
but he is just my age, you are the senior,
so here, I give the goblet first to you."

And he put the cup of sweet wine in her hand.
Athena liked his manners, and the equity   55
that gave her precedence with the cup of gold,
so she besought Poseidon at some length:

"Earthshaker, listen and be well disposed.
Grant your petitioners everything they ask:
above all, honor to Nestor and his sons;   60
second, to every man of Pylos town
a fair gift in exchange for this hekatomb;[2]

2. Strictly, a sacrifice of one hundred animals, but often used to refer to smaller offerings.

third, may Telémakhos and I perform
the errand on which last night we put to sea."

This was the prayer of Athena—   65
granted in every particular by herself.
She passed the beautiful wine cup to Telémakhos,
who tipped the wine and prayed as she had done.
Meanwhile the spits were taken off the fire,
portions of crisp meat for all. They feasted,   70
and when they had eaten and drunk their fill, at last
they heard from Nestor, prince of charioteers:

"Now is the time," he said, "for a few questions,
now that our young guests have enjoyed their dinner.
Who are you, strangers? Where are you sailing from,   75
and where to, down the highways of sea water?
Have you some business here? or are you, now,
reckless wanderers of the sea, like those corsairs
who risk their lives to prey on other men?"

Clear-headed Telémakhos responded cheerfully,   80
for Athena gave him heart. By her design
his quest for news about his father's wandering
would bring him fame in the world's eyes. So he said:

"Nestor, pride of Akhaians, Neleus' son,
you ask where we are from, and I can tell you: 85
our home port is under Mount Neion, Ithaka.
We are not here on Ithakan business, though,
but on my own. I want news of my father,
Odysseus, known for his great heart, and I
will comb the wide world for it. People say   90
he fought along with you when Troy was taken.
As to the other men who fought that war,
we know where each one died, and how he died;
but Zeus allotted my father death and mystery.
No one can say for sure where he was killed,   95
whether some hostile landsmen or the sea,
the stormwaves on the deep sea, got the best of him.
And this is why I come to you for help.
Tell me of his death, sir, if perhaps
you witnessed it, or have heard some wanderer   100
tell the tale. The man was born for trouble.
Spare me no part of it for kindness' sake,
but put the scene before me as you saw it.
If ever Odysseus my noble father
served you by promise kept or work accomplished   105
in the land of Troy, where you Akhaians suffered,
recall those things for me the way they were."

Then Nestor, prince of charioteers, made answer:

"Dear friend, you take me back to all the trouble
we went through in that country, we Akhaians: 110
rough days aboard ship on the cloudy sea
cruising away for pillage after Akhilleus;
rough days of battle around Priam's town.
Our losses, then—so many good men gone:
Arês' great Aias lies there, Akhilleus lies there,   115
Patróklos, too, the wondrous counselor,
and my own strong and princely son, Antílokhos[3]—
fastest man of them all, and a born fighter.
Other miseries, and many, we endured there.
Could any mortal man tell the whole story?   120
Not if you stayed five years or six to hear
how hard it was for the flower of the Akhaians;
you'd go home weary, and the tale untold.
Think: we were there nine years, and we tried everything,
all stratagems against them,   125
up to the bitter end that Zeus begrudged us.
And as to stratagems, no man would claim
Odysseus' gift for those. He had no rivals,
your father, at the tricks of war.
                                   Your father?
Well, I must say I marvel at the sight of you: 130
your manner of speech couldn't be more like his;
one would say No; no boy could speak so well.
And all that time at Ilion,[4] he and I
were never at odds in council or assembly—
saw things the same way, had one mind between us   135
in all the good advice we gave the Argives.
But when we plundered Priam's town and tower
and took to the ships, God scattered the Akhaians.
He had a mind to make homecoming hard for them,
seeing they would not think straight nor behave,   140
or some would not. So evil days came on them,
and she who had been angered,[5]
Zeus's dangerous grey-eyed daughter, did it,
starting a fight between the sons of Atreus.[6]
First they were fools enough to call assembly   145
at sundown, unheard of hour;
the Akhaian soldiers turned out, soaked with wine,
to hear talk, talk about it from their commanders:
Meneláos harangued them to get organized—
time to ride home on the sea's broad back, he said;   150
but Agamémnon wouldn't hear of it. He wanted
to hold the troops, make sacrifice, a hekatomb,

3. Nestor lists the great heroes who fell at Troy. Akhilleus (Achilles) was the bravest of the Greeks. Priam,
king of Troy, was killed when the city fell. Aias (Ajax) tried to kill Odysseus and the kings Meneláos and
Agamémnon, because the dead Akhilleus's armor (a prize awarded the bravest warrior after Akhilleus) was
given to Odysseus. He then committed suicide. Patróklos (Patroclus) was Akhilleus's closest friend. Odysseus will meet the ghosts of Akhilleus and Aias in the underworld (in book 11).   4. Troy.   5. Athena.
The Trojan princess Cassandra took refuge in Athena's temple when the Akhaians captured Troy, but she
was raped by Aias (not the great Aias but another chieftain of the same name). Athena was angry not just
with him, but with the whole Akhaian army because they did not punish him.   6. Meneláos and
Agamémnon.

something to pacify Athena's rage.
Folly again, to think that he could move her.
Will you change the will of the everlasting gods   155
in a night or a day's time?
The two men stood there hammering at each other
until the army got to its feet with a roar,
and no decision, wanting it both ways.
That night no one slept well, everyone cursing   160
someone else. Here was the bane from Zeus.
At dawn we dragged our ships to the lordly water,
stowed aboard all our plunder
and the slave women in their low hip girdles.
But half the army elected to stay behind   165
with Agamémnon as their corps commander;
the other half embarked and pulled away.
We made good time, the huge sea smoothed before us,
and held our rites when we reached Ténedos,[7]
being wild for home. But Zeus, not willing yet,   170
now cruelly set us at odds a second time,
and one lot turned, put back in the rolling ships,
under command of the subtle captain, Odysseus;
their notion was to please Lord Agamémnon.
Not I. I fled, with every ship I had;   175
I knew fate had some devilment brewing there.
Diomêdês[8] roused his company and fled, too,
and later Meneláos, the red-haired captain,
caught up with us at Lesbos,
while we mulled over the long sea route, unsure   180
whether to lay our course northward of Khios,
keeping the Isle of Psyria off to port,
or inside Khios, coasting by windy Mimas.
We asked for a sign from heaven, and the sign came
to cut across the open sea to Euboia,   185
and lose no time putting our ills behind us.
The wind freshened astern, and the ships ran
before the wind on paths of the deep sea fish,
making Geraistos before dawn.[9] We thanked Poseidon
with many a charred thighbone for that crossing.   190
On the fourth day, Diomêdês' company
under full sail put in at Argos port,
and I held on for Pylos. The fair wind,
once heaven set it blowing, never failed.

So this, dear child, was how I came from Troy,   195
and saw no more of the others, lost or saved.
But you are welcome to all I've heard since then
at home; I have no reason to keep it from you.

7. An island off the coast, southwest of Troy.   8. One of the Greek champions; his home was
Argos.   9. In their frail ships and without benefit of compass, Greek sailors preferred to hug the shore;
the normal route would have been inside (to the east) of the island of Khios, past the headland of Mimas
on the coast of Asia Minor, and across the Aegean Sea along the island chain of the Cyclades. But Nestor
was in a hurry; he went north of Khios and directly across the northern Aegean to Geraistos on the long
island of Euboia, which hugs the coast of the Greek mainland.

The Myrmidon[1] spearfighters returned, they say,
under the son of lionhearted Akhilleus;   200
and so did Poias' great son, Philoktête.[2]
Idómeneus[3] brought his company back to Krete;
the sea took not a man from him, of all
who lived through the long war.
And even as far away as Ithaka   205
you've heard of Agamémnon—how he came
home, how Aigísthos waited to destroy him
but paid a bitter price for it in the end.
That is a good thing, now, for a man to leave
a son behind him, like the son who punished   210
Aigísthos for the murder of his great father.
You, too, are tall and well set-up, I see;
be brave, you too, so men in times to come
will speak well of you."

                 Then Telémakhos said:

"Nestor, pride of Akhaians, Neleus' son,   215
that was revenge, and far and wide the Akhaians
will tell the tale in song for generations.
I wish the gods would buckle his arms on me!
I'd be revenged for outrage
on my insidious and brazen enemies.   220
But no such happy lot was given to me
or to my father. Still, I must hold fast."

To this Lord Nestor of Gerênia said:

"My dear young friend, now that you speak of it,
I hear a crowd of suitors for your mother   225
lives with you, uninvited, making trouble.
Now tell me how you take this. Do the people
side against you, hearkening to some oracle?
Who knows, your father might come home someday
alone or backed by troops, and have it out with them.   230
If grey-eyed Athena loved you
the way she did Odysseus in the old days,
in Troy country, where we all went through so much—
never have I seen the gods help any man
as openly as Athena did your father—   235
well, as I say, if she cared for you that way,
there would be those to quit this marriage game."

But prudently Telémakhos replied:

1. The tribal contingent led by Akhilleus, whose son, Neoptólemos, came to Troy to avenge his father; it
was he who killed Priam on the altar in his palace.   2. He had been abandoned on a desert island by
the Greeks because he fell sick of a loathsome disease; cured, he was brought to Troy for the final
assault.   3. Leader of the Greek troops from Krete (Crete).

"I can't think what you say will ever happen, sir.
It is a dazzling hope. But not for me.   240
It could not be—even if the gods willed it."

At this grey-eyed Athena broke in, saying:

"What strange talk you permit yourself, Telémakhos.
A god could save the man by simply wishing it—
from the farthest shore in the world.   245
If I were he, I should prefer to suffer
years at sea, and then be safe at home;
better that than a knife at my hearthside
where Agamémnon found it—killed by adulterers.
Though as for death, of course all men must suffer it: 250
the gods may love a man, but they can't help him
when cold death comes to lay him on his bier."

Telémakhos replied:

"Mentor, grievously though we miss my father, why
go on as if that homecoming could happen?   255
You know the gods had settled it already,
years ago, when dark death came for him.
But there is something else I imagine Nestor
can tell us, knowing as he does the ways of men.
They say his rule goes back over three generations,   260
so long, so old, it seems death cannot touch him.
Nestor, Neleus' son, true sage, say how
did the Lord of the Great Plains, Agamémnon, die?
What was the trick Aigísthos used
to kill the better man? And Meneláos,   265
where was he? Not at Argos in Akhaia,
but blown off course, held up in some far country,
is that what gave the killer nerve to strike?"

Lord Nestor of Gerênia made answer:

"Well, now, my son, I'll tell you the whole story.   270
You know, yourself, what would have come to pass
if red-haired Meneláos, back from Troy,
had caught Aigísthos in that house alive.
There would have been no burial mound for him,
but dogs and carrion birds to huddle on him   275
in the fields beyond the wall, and not a soul
bewailing him, for the great wrong he committed.
While we were hard-pressed in the war at Troy
he stayed safe inland in the grazing country,
making light talk to win Agamémnon's queen.   280
But the Lady Klytaimnéstra, in the first days,
rebuffed him, being faithful still;

then, too, she had at hand as her companion
a minstrel Agamémnon left attending her,
charged with her care, when he took ship for Troy.   285
Then came the fated hour when she gave in.
Her lover tricked the poet and marooned him
on a bare island for the seabirds' picking,
and took her home, as he and she desired.
Many thighbones he burned on the gods' altars   290
and many a woven and golden ornament
hung to bedeck them, in his satisfaction;
he had not thought life held such glory for him.

Now Meneláos and I sailed home together
on friendly terms, from Troy,   295
but when we came off Sunion Point[4] in Attika,
the ships still running free, Onêtor's son
Phrontis, the steersman of Meneláos' ship,
fell over with a death grip on the tiller:
some unseen arrow from Apollo hit him.[5]   300
No man handled a ship better than he did
in a high wind and sea, so Meneláos
put down his longing to get on, and landed
to give this man full honor in funeral.
His own luck turned then. Out on the winedark sea   305
in the murmuring hulls again, he made Cape Malea,[6]
but Zeus who views the wide world sent a gloom
over the ocean, and a howling gale
came on with seas increasing, mountainous,
parting the ships and driving half toward Krete   310
where the Kydonians live by Iardanos river.
Off Gortyn's coastline in the misty sea there
a reef, a razorback, cuts through the water,
and every westerly piles up a pounding
surf along the left side, going toward Phaistos—   315
big seas buffeted back by the narrow stone.
They were blown here, and fought in vain for sea room;
the ships kept going in to their destruction,
slammed on the reef. The crews were saved. But now
those five that weathered it got off to southward,   320
taken by wind and current on to Egypt;
and there Meneláos stayed.[7] He made a fortune
in sea traffic among those distant races,
but while he did so, the foul crime was planned
and carried out in Argos by Aigísthos,   325

---

4. The southern cape of Attica; they would round this to go toward the Peloponnese.   5. A formula for
a sudden death that has no obvious explanation; for women the arrow comes from Artemis.   6. The
easternmost of the three capes in which the Peloponnese ends. Meneláos would have to round it to get
into a harbor for Sparta. It is still a place of storms.   7. Meneláos is blown southeast, toward Egypt,
where he eventually arrives. Gortyn and Phaistos (site of a Minoan palace) are inland from the south coast
of Krete.

who ruled over golden Mykênai[8] seven years.
Seven long years, with Agamémnon dead,
he held the people down, before the vengeance.
But in the eighth year, back from exile in Attika,
Orestês killed the snake who killed his father. 330
He gave his hateful mother and her soft man
a tomb together, and proclaimed the funeral day
a festal day for all the Argive people.
That day Lord Meneláos of the great war cry
made port with all the gold his ships could carry. 335
And this should give you pause, my son:
don't stay too long away from home, leaving
your treasure there, and brazen suitors near;
they'll squander all you have or take it from you,
and then how will your journey serve? 340
I urge you, though, to call on Meneláos,
he being but lately home from distant parts
in the wide world. A man could well despair
of getting home at all, if the winds blew him
over the Great South Sea—that weary waste, 345
even the wintering birds delay
one winter more before the northward crossing.
Well, take your ship and crew and go by water,
or if you'd rather go by land, here are
horses, a car, and my own sons for company 350
as far as the ancient land of Lakedaimon[9]
and Meneláos, the red-haired captain there.
Ask him with courtesy, and in his wisdom
he will tell you history and no lies."

While Nestor talked, the sun went down the sky 355
and gloom came on the land,
and now the grey-eyed goddess Athena said:

"Sir, this is all most welcome and to the point,
but why not slice the bulls' tongues[1] now, and mix
libations for Poseidon and the gods? 360
Then we can all retire; high time we did;
the light is going under the dark world's rim,
better not linger at the sacred feast."

When Zeus's daughter spoke, they turned to listen,
and soon the squires brought water for their hands, 365
while stewards filled the winebowls and poured out
a fresh cup full for every man. The company
stood up to fling the tongues and a shower of wine
over the flames, then drank their thirst away.

8. Argos and Mykênai (Mycenae) are close to each other, and Homer sometimes does not discriminate between them. 9. Sparta. Car: a horsedrawn chariot. 1. The tongue was one of the parts of the meat reserved for the gods; it was thrown on the fire.

Now finally Telémakhos and Athena   370
bestirred themselves, turning away to the ship,
but Nestor put a hand on each, and said:

"Now Zeus forbid, and the other gods as well,
that you should spend the night on board, and leave me
as though I were some pauper without a stitch,   375
no blankets in his house, no piles of rugs,
no sleeping soft for host or guest! Far from it!
I have all these, blankets and deep-piled rugs,
and while I live the only son of Odysseus
will never make his bed on a ship's deck—   380
no, not while sons of mine are left at home
to welcome any guest who comes to us."

The grey-eyed goddess Athena answered him:

"You are very kind, sir, and Telémakhos
should do as you ask. That is the best thing.   385
He will go with you, and will spend the night
under your roof. But I must join our ship
and talk to the crew, to keep their spirits up,
since I'm the only senior in the company.
The rest are boys who shipped for friendship's sake,   390
no older than Telémakhos, any of them.
Let me sleep out, then, by the black hull's side,
this night at least. At daybreak I'll be off
to see the Kaukonians about a debt they owe me,
an old one and no trifle. As for your guest,   395
send him off in a car, with one of your sons,
and give him thoroughbreds, a racing team."

Even as she spoke, Athena left them—seeming
a seahawk, in a clap of wings—and all
the Akhaians of Pylos town looked up astounded.   400
Awed then by what his eyes had seen, the old man
took Telémakhos' hand and said warmly:

"My dear child, I can have no fears for you,
no doubt about your conduct or your heart,
if, at your age, the gods are your companions.   405
Here we had someone from Olympos—clearly
the glorious daughter of Zeus, his third child,
who held your father dear among the Argives.
O, Lady, hear me! Grant an illustrious name
to me and to my children and my dear wife!   410
A noble heifer shall be yours in sacrifice,
one that no man has ever yoked or driven;
my gift to you—her horns all sheathed in gold."

So he ended, praying; and Athena heard him.
Then Nestor of Gerênia led them all,   415
his sons and sons-in-law, to his great house;
and in they went to the famous hall of Nestor,
taking their seats on thrones and easy chairs,
while the old man mixed water in a wine bowl
with sweet red wine, mellowed eleven years   420
before his housekeeper uncapped the jar.
He mixed and poured his offering, repeating
prayers to Athena, daughter of royal Zeus.
The others made libation, and drank deep,
then all the company went to their quarters,   425
and Nestor of Gerênia showed Telémakhos
under the echoing eastern entrance hall
to a fine bed near the bed of Peisístratos,
captain of spearmen, his unmarried son.
Then he lay down in his own inner chamber   430
where his dear faithful wife had smoothed his bed.

When Dawn spread out her finger tips of rose,
Lord Nestor of Gerênia, charioteer,
left his room for a throne of polished stone,
white and gleaming as though with oil, that stood   435
before the main gate of the palace; Neleus here
had sat before him—masterful in kingship,
Neleus, long ago a prey to death, gone down
to the night of the underworld.
So Nestor held his throne and scepter now,   440
lord of the western approaches to Akhaia.
And presently his sons came out to join him,
leaving the palace: Ekhéphron and Stratíos,
Perseus and Arêtós and Thrasymêdês,
and after them the prince Peisístratos,   445
bringing Telémakhos along with him.
Seeing all present, the old lord Nestor said:

"Dear sons, here is my wish, and do it briskly
to please the gods, Athena first of all,
my guest in daylight at our holy feast.   450
One of you must go for a young heifer
and have the cowherd lead her from the pasture.
Another call on Lord Telémakhos' ship
to invite his crewmen, leaving two behind;
and someone else again send for the goldsmith,   455
Laerkês, to gild the horns.
The rest stay here together. Tell the servants
a ritual feast will be prepared in hall.
Tell them to bring seats, firewood and fresh water."

Before he finished, they were about these errands.   460
The heifer came from pasture,

the crewmen of Telémakhos from the ship,
the smith arrived, bearing the tools of his trade—
hammer and anvil, and the precision tongs
he handled fiery gold with,—and Athena   465
came as a god comes, numinous, to the rites.

The smith now gloved each horn in a pure foil
beaten out of the gold that Nestor gave him—
a glory and delight for the goddess' eyes—
while Ekhéphron and Stratíos held the horns.   470
Arêtós brought clear lustral water[2]
in a bowl quivering with frest-cut flowers,
a basket of barley in his other hand.
Thrasymêdês, who could stand his ground in war,
stood ready, with a sharp two-bladed axe,   475
for the stroke of sacrifice, and Perseus
held a bowl for the blood. And now Nestor,
strewing the barley grains, and water drops,
pronounced his invocation to Athena
and burned a pinch of bristles from the victim.   480
When prayers were said and all the grain was scattered
great-hearted Thrasymêdês in a flash
swung the axe, at one blow cutting through
the neck tendons. The heifer's spirit failed.
Then all the women gave a wail of joy[3]—   485
daughters, daughters-in-law, and the Lady Eurydíkê,
Klyménos' eldest daughter. But the men
still held the heifer, shored her up
from the wide earth where the living go their ways,
until Peisístratos cut her throat across,   490
the black blood ran, and life ebbed from her marrow.
The carcass now sank down, and they disjointed
shoulder and thigh bone, wrapping them in fat,
two layers, folded, with raw strips of flesh.
These offerings Nestor burned on the split-wood fire   495
and moistened with red wine. His sons took up
five-tined forks in their hands, while the altar flame
ate through the bones, and bits of tripe went round.
Then came the carving of the quarters, and they spitted
morsels of lean meat on the long sharp tines   500
and broiled them at arm's length upon the fire.

Polykástê, a fair girl, Nestor's youngest,
had meanwhile given a bath to Telémakhos—
bathing him first, then rubbing him with oil.
She held fine clothes and a cloak to put around him   505
when he came godlike from the bathing place;
then out he went to take his place with Nestor.
When the best cuts were broiled and off the spits,

2. Used for sprinkling.   3. The ritual cry at the moment of sacrifice.

they all sat down to banquet. Gentle squires
kept every golden wine cup brimming full.   510
And so they feasted to their heart's content,
until the prince of charioteers commanded:

"Sons, harness the blood mares for Telémakhos;
hitch up the car, and let him take the road."

They swung out smartly to do the work, and hooked   515
the handsome horses to a chariot shaft.
The mistress of the stores brought up provisions
of bread and wine, with victuals fit for kings,
and Telémakhos stepped up on the painted car.
Just at his elbow stood Peisístratos,   520
captain of spearmen, reins in hand. He gave
a flick to the horses, and with streaming manes
they ran for the open country. The tall town
of Pylos sank behind them in the distance,
as all day long they kept the harness shaking.   525

The sun was low and shadows crossed the lanes
when they arrived at Phêrai. There Dióklês,
son of Ortílokhos whom Alpheios fathered,
welcomed the young men, and they slept the night.
But up when the young Dawn's finger tips of rose   530
opened in the east, they hitched the team
once more to the painted car,
and steered out eastward through the echoing gate,
whipping their fresh horses into a run.
That day they made the grainlands of Lakedaimon,   535
where, as the horses held to a fast clip,
they kept on to their journey's end. Behind them
the sun went down and all the roads grew dark.

BOOK IV

[The Red-Haired King and His Lady]

By vales and sharp ravines in Lakedaimon
the travellers drove to Meneláos' mansion,
and found him at a double wedding feast
for son and daughter.
                        Long ago at Troy
he pledged her to the heir[4] of great Akhilleus,   5
breaker of men—a match the gods had ripened;
so he must send her with a chariot train
to the town and glory of the Myrmidons.
And that day, too, he brought Alektor's daughter
to marry his tall scion, Megapénthês,   10

---

4. Akhilleus's son, Neoptólemos. In the underworld (book 11), Akhilleus asks for news of him from
Odysseus.

born of a slave girl during the long war—
for the gods had never after granted Helen
a child to bring into the sunlit world
after the first, rose-lipped Hermionê,
a girl like the pale-gold goddess Aphroditê. 15
Down the great hall in happiness they feasted,
neighbors of Meneláos, and his kin,
for whom a holy minstrel harped and sang;
and two lithe tumblers moved out on the song
with spins and handsprings through the company. 20
Now when Telémakhos and Nestor's son
pulled up their horses at the main gate,
one of the king's companions in arms, Eteóneus,
going outside, caught sight of them. He turned
and passed through court and hall to tell the master, 25
stepping up close to get his ear. Said he:

"Two men are here—two strangers, Meneláos,
but nobly born Akhaians, they appear.
What do you say, shall we unhitch their team,
or send them on to someone free to receive them?" 30

The red-haired captain answered him in anger:

"You were no idiot before, Eteóneus,
but here you are talking like a child of ten.
Could we have made it home again—and Zeus
gave us no more hard roving!—if other men 35
had never fed us, given us lodging?
                              Bring
these men to be our guests: unhitch their team!"

Eteóneus left the long room like an arrow,
calling equerries after him, on the run.
Outside, they freed the sweating team from harness, 40
stabled the horses, tied them up, and showered
bushels of wheat and barley in the feed box;
then leaned the chariot pole
against the gleaming entry wall of stone
and took the guests in. What a brilliant place 45
that mansion of the great prince seemed to them!
A-glitter everywhere, as though with fiery
points of sunlight, lusters of the moon.
The young men gazed in joy before they entered
into a room of polished tubs to bathe. 50
Maidservants gave them baths, anointed them,
held out fresh tunics, cloaked them warm; and soon
they took tall thrones beside the son of Atreus.
Here a maid tipped out water for their hands
from a golden pitcher into a silver bowl, 55
and set a polished table near at hand;
the larder mistress with her tray of loaves

and savories came, dispensing all her best,
and then a carver heaped their platters high
with various meats, and put down cups of gold.   60
Now said the red-haired captain, Meneláos,
gesturing:

        "Welcome; and fall to; in time,
when you have supped, we hope to hear your names,
forebears and families—in your case, it seems,
no anonymities, but lordly men.   65
Lads like yourselves are not base born."

                          At this,
he lifted in his own hands the king's portion,
a chine of beef, and set it down before them.
Seeing all ready then, they took their dinner;
but when they had feasted well,   70
Telémakhos could not keep still, but whispered,
his head bent close, so the others might not hear:

"My dear friend, can you believe your eyes?—
the murmuring hall, how luminous it is
with bronze, gold, amber, silver, and ivory!   75
This is the way the court of Zeus must be,
inside, upon Olympos. What a wonder!"

But splendid Meneláos had overheard him
and spoke out on the instant to them both:

"Young friends, no mortal man can vie with Zeus.   80
His home and all his treasures are for ever.
But as for men, it may well be that few
have more than I. How painfully I wandered
before I brought it home! Seven years at sea,
Kypros, Phoinikia, Egypt, and still farther   85
among the sun-burnt races.
I saw the men of Sidon and Arabia
and Libya, too, where lambs are horned at birth.
In every year they have three lambing seasons,
so no man, chief or shepherd, ever goes   90
hungry for want of mutton, cheese, or milk—
all year at milking time there are fresh ewes.
But while I made my fortune on those travels
a stranger killed my brother, in cold blood,—
tricked blind, caught in the web of his deadly queen.   95
What pleasure can I take, then, being lord
over these costly things?
You must have heard your fathers tell my story,
whoever your fathers are; you must know of my life,
the anguish I once had, and the great house   100
full of my treasure, left in desolation.
How gladly I should live one third as rich

to have my friends back safe at home!—my friends
who died on Troy's wide seaboard, far
from the grazing lands of Argos.   105
But as things are, nothing but grief is left me
for those companions. While I sit at home
sometimes hot tears come, and I revel in them,
or stop before the surfeit makes me shiver.
And there is one I miss more than the other   110
dead I mourn for; sleep and food alike
grow hateful when I think of him. No soldier
took on so much, went through so much, as Odysseus.
That seems to have been his destiny, and this mine—
to feel each day the emptiness of his absence,   115
ignorant, even, whether he lived or died.
How his old father and his quiet wife,
Penélopê, must miss him still!
And Telémakhos, whom he left as a new-born child."

Now hearing these things said, the boy's heart rose   120
in a long pang for his father, and he wept,
holding his purple mantle with both hands
before his eyes. Meneláos knew him now,
and so fell silent with uncertainty
whether to let him speak and name his father   125
in his own time, or to inquire, and prompt him.
And while he pondered, Helen came
out of her scented chamber, a moving grace
like Artemis,[5] straight as a shaft of gold.
Beside her came Adrastê, to place her armchair,   130
Alkippê, with a rug of downy wool,
and Phylo, bringing a silver basket, once
given by Alkandrê, the wife of Pólybos,
in the treasure city, Thebes of distant Egypt.
He gave two silver bathtubs to Meneláos   135
and a pair of tripods, with ten pure gold bars,
and she, then, made these beautiful gifts to Helen:
a golden distaff, and the silver basket
rimmed in hammered gold, with wheels to run on.
So Phylo rolled it in to stand beside her,   140
heaped with fine spun stuff, and cradled on it
the distaff swathed in dusky violet wool.
Reclining in her light chair with its footrest,
Helen gazed at her husband and demanded:

"Meneláos, my lord, have we yet heard   145
our new guests introduce themselves? Shall I
dissemble what I feel? No, I must say it.
Never, anywhere, have I seen so great a likeness
in man or woman—but it is truly strange!

5. A virgin goddess, sister of Apollo, and associated with wild animals; women called on her for help in childbirth. Helen, Meneláos's wife, was the daughter of Leda, whom Zeus seduced when he was in the shape of a swan. Her kidnapping by Paris was the cause of the Trojan War.

This boy must be the son of Odysseus,
Telémakhos, the child he left at home
that year the Akhaian host made war on Troy—
daring all for the wanton that I was." 150

And the red-haired captain, Meneláos, answered:

"My dear, I see the likeness as well as you do. 155
Odysseus' hands and feet were like this boy's;
his head, and hair, and the glinting of his eyes.
Not only that, but when I spoke, just now,
of Odysseus' years of toil on my behalf
and all he had to endure—the boy broke down 160
and wept into his cloak."

             Now Nestor's son,
Peisístratos, spoke up in answer to him:

"My lord marshal, Meneláos, son of Atreus,
this is that hero's son as you surmise,
but he is gentle, and would be ashamed 165
to clamor for attention before your grace
whose words have been so moving to us both.
Nestor, Lord of Gerênia, sent me with him
as guide and escort; he had wished to see you,
to be advised by you or assisted somehow. 170
A father far from home means difficulty
for an only son, with no one else to help him;
so with Telémakhos:
his father left the house without defenders."

The king with flaming hair now spoke again: 175

"His son, in my house! How I loved the man,
and how he fought through hardship for my sake!
I swore I'd cherish him above all others
if Zeus, who views the wide world, gave us passage
homeward across the sea in the fast ships. 180
I would have settled him in Argos, brought him
over with herds and household out of Ithaka,
his child and all his people. I could have cleaned out
one of my towns to be his new domain.
And so we might have been together often 185
in feasts and entertainments, never parted
till the dark mist of death lapped over one of us.
But God himself must have been envious,
to batter the bruised man so that he alone
should fail in his return." 190

A twinging ache of grief rose up in everyone,
and Helen of Argos wept, the daughter of Zeus,
Telémakhos and Meneláos wept,
and tears came to the eyes of Nestor's son—

remembering, for his part, Antílokhos,   195
whom the son of shining Dawn had killed in battle.
But thinking of that brother, he broke out:

"O son of Atreus, when we spoke of you
at home, and asked about you, my old father
would say you have the clearest mind of all.   200
If it is not too much to ask, then, let us not
weep away these hours after supper;
I feel we should not: Dawn will soon be here!
You understand, I would not grudge a man
right mourning when he comes to death and doom: 205
what else can one bestow on the poor dead?—
a lock of hair sheared, and a tear let fall.
For that matter, I, too,
lost someone in the war at Troy—my brother,
and no mean soldier, whom you must have known,   210
although I never did,—Antílokhos.
He ranked high as a runner and fighting man."

The red-haired captain Meneláos answered:

"My lad, what you have said is only sensible,
and you did well to speak. Yes, that was worthy   215
a wise man and an older man than you are:
you speak for all the world like Nestor's son.
How easily one can tell the man whose father
had true felicity, marrying and begetting!
And that was true of Nestor, all his days,   220
down to his sleek old age in peace at home,
with clever sons, good spearmen into the bargain.
Come, we'll shake off this mourning mood of ours
and think of supper. Let the men at arms
rinse our hands again! There will be time   225
for a long talk with Telémakhos in the morning."

The hero Meneláos' companion in arms,
Asphalion, poured water for their hands,
and once again they touched the food before them.
But now it entered Helen's mind   230
to drop into the wine that they were drinking
an anodyne, mild magic of forgetfulness.
Whoever drank this mixture in the wine bowl
would be incapable of tears that day—
though he should lose mother and father both,   235
or see, with his own eyes, a son or brother
mauled by weapons of bronze at his own gate.
The opiate of Zeus's daughter bore
this canny power. It had been supplied her
by Polydamna, mistress of Lord Thôn,   240
in Egypt,⁶ where the rich plantations grow

---

6. The Greeks had great respect for Egyptian doctors, and Egyptian papyri document their skill as surgeons and their expertise with drugs.

herbs of all kinds, maleficent and healthful;
and no one else knows medicine as they do,
Egyptian heirs of Paian, the healing god.
She drugged the wine, then, had it served, and said—   245
taking again her part in the conversation—

"O Meneláos, Atreus' royal son,
and you that are great heroes' sons, you know
how Zeus gives all of us in turn
good luck and bad luck, being all powerful.   250
So take refreshment, take your ease in hall,
and cheer the time with stories. I'll begin.
Not that I think of naming, far less telling,
every feat of that rugged man, Odysseus,
but here is something that he dared to do   255
at Troy, where you Akhaians endured the war.
He had, first, given himself an outrageous beating
and thrown some rags on—like a household slave—
then slipped into that city of wide lanes
among his enemies. So changed, he looked   260
as never before upon the Akhaian beachhead,
but like a beggar, merged in the townspeople;
and no one there remarked him. But I knew him—
even as he was, I knew him,
and questioned him. How shrewdly he put me off!   265
But in the end I bathed him and anointed him,
put a fresh cloak around him, and swore an oath
not to give him away as Odysseus to the Trojans,
till he got back to camp where the long ships lay.
He spoke up then, and told me   270
all about the Akhaians, and their plans—
then sworded many Trojans through the body
on his way out with what he learned of theirs.
The Trojan women raised a cry—but my heart
sang—for I had come round, long before,   275
to dreams of sailing home, and I repented
the mad day Aphroditê
drew me away from my dear fatherland,
forsaking all—child, bridal bed, and husband—
a man without defect in form or mind."   280

Replied the red-haired captain, Meneláos:

"An excellent tale, my dear, and most becoming.
In my life I have met, in many countries,
foresight and wit in many first rate men,
but never have I seen one like Odysseus   285
for steadiness and a stout heart. Here, for instance,
is what he did—had the cold nerve to do—
inside the hollow horse, where we were waiting,
picked men all of us, for the Trojan slaughter,
when all of a sudden, you came by—I dare say   290

drawn by some superhuman
power that planned an exploit for the Trojans;
and Deïphobos,[7] that handsome man, came with you.
Three times you walked around it, patting it everywhere,
and called by name the flower of our fighters,   295
making your voice sound like their wives, calling.
Diomêdês and I crouched in the center
along with Odysseus; we could hear you plainly;
and listening, we two were swept
by waves of longing—to reply, or go.   300
Odysseus fought us down, despite our craving,
and all the Akhaians kept their lips shut tight,
all but Antiklos. Desire moved his throat
to hail you, but Odysseus' great hands clamped
over his jaws, and held. So he saved us all,   305
till Pallas Athena led you away at last."

Then clear-headed Telémakhos addressed him:

"My lord marshal, Meneláos, son of Atreus,
all the more pity, since these valors
could not defend him from annihilation—   310
not if his heart were iron in his breast.
But will you not dismiss us for the night now?
Sweet sleep will be a pleasure, drifting over us."

He said no more, but Helen called the maids
and sent them to make beds, with purple rugs   315
piled up, and sheets outspread, and fleecy
coverlets, in the porch inside the gate.
The girls went out with torches in their hands,
and presently a squire led the guests—
Telémakhos and Nestor's radiant son—   320
under the entrance colonnade, to bed.
Then deep in the great mansion, in his chamber,
Meneláos went to rest, and Helen,
queenly in her long gown, lay beside him.

When the young Dawn with finger tips of rose   325
made heaven bright, the deep-lunged man of battle
stood up, pulled on his tunic and his mantle,
slung on a swordbelt and a new edged sword,
tied his smooth feet into fine rawhide sandals
and left his room, a god's brilliance upon him.   330
He sat down by Telémakhos, asking gently:

"Telémakhos, why did you come, sir, riding
the sea's broad back to reach old Lakedaimon?
A public errand or private? Why, precisely?"

7. A Trojan prince whom Helen married after Paris was killed in battle.

Telémakhos replied: 335

"My lord marshal Meneláos, son of Atreus,
I came to hear what news you had of Father.
My house, my good estates are being ruined.
Each day my mother's bullying suitors come
to slaughter flocks of mine and my black cattle;   340
enemies crowd our home. And this is why
I come to you for news of him who owned it.
Tell me of his death, sir, if perhaps
you witnessed it, or have heard some wanderer
tell the tale. The man was born for trouble.   345
Spare me no part for kindness' sake; be harsh;
but put the scene before me as you saw it.
If ever Odysseus my noble father
served you by promise kept or work accomplished
in the land of Troy, where you Akhaians suffered,   350
recall those things for me the way they were."

Stirred now to anger, Meneláos said:

"Intolerable—that soft men, as those are,
should think to lie in that great captain's bed.
Fawns in a lion's lair! As if a doe   355
put down her litter of sucklings there, while she
quested a glen or cropped some grassy hollow.
Ha! Then the lord returns to his own bed
and deals out wretched doom on both alike.
So will Odysseus deal out doom on these.   360
O Father Zeus, Athena, and Apollo!
I pray he comes as once he was, in Lesbos,
when he stood up to wrestle Philomeleidês[8]—
champion and Island King—
and smashed him down. How the Akhaians cheered!   365
If only that Odysseus met the suitors,
they'd have their consummation, a cold bed!
Now for your questions, let me come to the point.
I would not misreport it for you; let me
tell you what the Ancient of the Sea,   370
who is infallible, said to me—every word.

During my first try at a passage homeward
the gods detained me, tied me down to Egypt—
for I had been too scant in hekatombs,
and gods will have the rules each time remembered.   375
There is an island washed by the open sea
lying off Nile mouth—seamen call it Pharos—
distant a day's sail in a clean hull
with a brisk land breeze behind. It has a harbor,
a sheltered bay, where shipmasters   380

8. A king of Lesbos who challenged all comers to wrestle with him.

take on dark water for the outward voyage.
Here the gods held me twenty days becalmed.
No winds came up, seaward escorting winds
for ships that ride the sea's broad back, and so
my stores and men were used up; we were failing   385
had not one goddess intervened in pity—
Eidothea, daughter of Proteus,
the Ancient of the Sea. How I distressed her!
I had been walking out alone that day—
my sailors, thin-bellied from the long fast,   390
were off with fish hooks, angling on the shore—
then she appeared to me, and her voice sang:

'What fool is here, what drooping dunce of dreams?
Or can it be, friend, that you love to suffer?
How can you linger on this island, aimless   395
and shiftless, while your people waste away?'

To this I quickly answered:

                    'Let me tell you,
goddess, whatever goddess you may be,
these doldrums are no will of mine. I take it
the gods who own broad heaven are offended.   400
Why don't you tell me—since the gods know everything—
who has me pinned down here?
How am I going to make my voyage home?'

Now she replied in her immortal beauty:

'I'll put it for you clearly as may be, friend.   405
The Ancient of the Salt Sea haunts this place,
immortal Proteus of Egypt; all the deeps
are known to him; he serves under Poseidon,
and is, they say, my father.
If you could take him by surprise and hold him,   410
he'd give you course and distance for your sailing
homeward across the cold fish-breeding sea.
And should you wish it, noble friend, he'd tell you
all that occurred at home, both good and evil,
while you were gone so long and hard a journey.'   415

To this I said:

                    'But you, now—you must tell me
how I can trap this venerable sea-god.
He will elude me if he takes alarm;
no man—god knows—can quell a god with ease.'

That fairest of unearthly nymphs replied: 420

'I'll tell you this, too, clearly as may be.
When the sun hangs at high noon in heaven,
the Ancient glides ashore under the Westwind,
hidden by shivering glooms on the clear water,
and rests in caverns hollowed by the sea.   425
There flippered seals, brine children, shining come
from silvery foam in crowds to lie around him,
exhaling rankness from the deep sea floor.
Tomorrow dawn I'll take you to those caves
and bed you down there. Choose three officers   430
for company—brave men they had better be—
the old one has strange powers, I must tell you.
He goes amid the seals to check their number,
and when he sees them all, and counts them all,
he lies down like a shepherd with his flock.   435
Here is your opportunity: at this point
gather yourselves, with all your heart and strength,
and tackle him before he bursts away.
He'll make you fight—for he can take the forms
of all the beasts, and water, and blinding fire;   440
but you must hold on, even so, and crush him
until he breaks the silence. When he does,
he will be in that shape you saw asleep.
Relax your grip, then, set the Ancient free,
and put your questions, hero: 445
Who is the god so hostile to you,
and how will you go home on the fish-cold sea.'

At this she dove under a swell and left me.
Back to the ships in the sandy cove I went,
my heart within me like a high surf running;   450
but there I joined my men once more
at supper, as the sacred Night came on,
and slept at last beside the lapping water.
When Dawn spread out her finger tips of rose
I started, by the sea's wide level ways,   455
praying the gods for help, and took along
three lads I counted on in any fight.
Meanwhile the nereid[9] swam from the lap of Ocean
laden with four sealskins, new flayed
for the hoax she thought of playing on her father.   460
In the sand she scooped out hollows for our bodies
and sat down, waiting. We came close to touch her,
and, bedding us, she threw the sealskins over us—
a strong disguise; oh, yes, terribly strong
as I recall the stench of those damned seals.   465
Would any man lie snug with a sea monster?
But here the nymph, again, came to our rescue,
dabbing ambrosia under each man's nose—
a perfume drowning out the bestial odor.

9. Sea nymph.

So there we lay with beating hearts all morning   470
while seals came shoreward out of ripples, jostling
to take their places, flopping on the sand.
At noon the Ancient issued from the sea
and held inspection, counting off the sea-beasts.
We were the first he numbered; he went by,   475
detecting nothing. When at last he slept
we gave a battlecry and plunged for him,
locking our hands behind him. But the old one's
tricks were not knocked out of him; far from it.
First he took on a whiskered lion's shape,   480
a serpent then; a leopard; a great boar;
then sousing water; then a tall green tree.
Still we hung on, by hook or crook, through everything,
until the Ancient saw defeat, and grimly
opened his lips to ask me:

                        'Son of Atreus,   485
who counselled you to this? A god: what god?
Set a trap for me, overpower me—why?'

He bit it off, then, and I answered:

                    'Old one,
you know the reason—why feign not to know?
High and dry so long upon this island   490
I'm at my wits' end, and my heart is sore.
You gods know everything; now you can tell me:
which of the immortals chained me here?
And how will I get home on the fish-cold sea?'

He made reply at once:

                    'You should have paid   495
honor to Zeus and the other gods, performing
a proper sacrifice before embarking:
that was your short way home on the winedark sea.
You may not see your friends, your own fine house,
or enter your own land again,   500
unless you first remount the Nile in flood
and pay your hekatomb to the gods of heaven.
Then, and then only,
the gods will grant the passage you desire.'

Ah, how my heart sank, hearing this—   505
hearing him send me back on the cloudy sea
in my own track, the long hard way of Egypt.
Nevertheless, I answered him and said:

'Ancient, I shall do all as you command.
But tell me, now, the others—   510
had they a safe return, all those Akhaians

who stayed behind when Nestor and I left Troy?
Or were there any lost at sea—what bitterness!—
any who died in camp, after the war?'

To this he said:

'For you to know these things   515
goes beyond all necessity, Meneláos.
Why must you ask?—you should not know my mind,
and you will grieve to learn it, I can tell you.
Many there were who died, many remain,
but two high officers alone were lost—   520
on the passage home, I mean; you saw the war.
One is alive, a castaway at sea;
the other, Aias,[1] perished with all hands—
though first Poseidon landed him on Gyrai
promontory, and saved him from the ocean.   525
Despite Athena's hate, he had lived on,
but the great sinner in his insolence
yelled that the gods' will and the sea were beaten,
and this loud brag came to Poseidon's ears.
He swung the trident in his massive hands   530
and in one shock from top to bottom split
that promontory, toppling into the sea
the fragment where the great fool sat.
So the vast ocean had its will with Aias,
drunk in the end on salt spume as he drowned.   535
Meanwhile your brother left that doom astern
in his decked ships—the Lady Hera[2] saved him;
but as he came round Malea
a fresh squall caught him, bearing him away
over the cold sea, groaning in disgust,   540
to the Land's End of Argos, where Thyestês
lived in the days of old, and then his son,
Aigísthos. Now, again, return seemed easy:
the high gods wound the wind into the east,
and back he sailed, this time to his own coast.   545
He went ashore and kissed the earth in joy,
hot tears blinding his eyes at sight of home.
But there were eyes that watched him from a height—
a lookout, paid two bars of gold to keep
vigil the year round for Aigísthos' sake,   550
that he should be forewarned, and Agamémnon's
furious valor sleep unroused.
Now this man with his news ran to the tyrant,
who made his crooked arrangements in a flash,
stationed picked men at arms, a score of men   555
in hiding; set a feast in the next room;
then he went out with chariots and horses
to hail the king and welcome him to evil.

1. The lesser Aias.   2. The wife and sister of Zeus. *Your brother*: Agamémnon.

He led him in to banquet, all serene,
and killed him, like an ox felled at the trough;   560
and not a man of either company
survived that ambush in Aigísthos' house.'

Before the end my heart was broken down.
I slumped on the trampled sand and cried aloud,
caring no more for life or the light of day,   565
and rolled there weeping, till my tears were spent.
Then the unerring Ancient said at last:

'No more, no more; how long must you persist?
Nothing is gained by grieving so. How soon
can you return to Argos? You may take him   570
alive there still—or else meanwhile Orestês
will have despatched him. You'll attend the feast.'

At this my heart revived, and I recovered
the self command to question him once more:

'Of two companions now I know. The third?   575
Tell me his name, the one marooned at sea;
living, you say, or dead? Even in pain
I wish to hear.'

                  And this is all he answered:

'Laërtês' son, whose home is Ithaka.
I saw him weeping, weeping on an island.   580
The nymph Kalypso has him, in her hall.
No means of faring home are left him now;
no ship with oars, and no ship's company
to pull him on the broad back of the sea.
As to your own destiny, prince Meneláos,   585
you shall not die in the bluegrass land of Argos;
rather the gods intend you for Elysion
with golden Rhadamanthos[3] at the world's end,
where all existence is a dream of ease.
Snowfall is never known there, neither long   590
frost of winter, nor torrential rain,
but only mild and lulling airs from Ocean
bearing refreshment for the souls of men—
the West Wind always blowing.
                            For the gods
hold you, as Helen's lord, a son of Zeus.'   595

At this he dove under a swell and left me,
and I went back to the ship with my companions,
feeling my heart's blood in me running high;

---

3. A son of Zeus by the mortal Europa, and brother to King Minos of Krete. Elysion is the paradise reserved
for a few of the heroes who were related to gods (Meneláos is Zeus's son-in-law).

but in the long hull's shadow, near the sea,
we supped again as sacred Night came on   600
and slept at last beside the lapping water.

When Dawn spread out her finger tips of rose,
in first light we launched on the courtly breakers,
setting up masts and yards in the well-found ships;
went all on board, and braced on planks athwart   605
oarsmen in line dipped oars in the grey sea.
Soon I drew in to the great stream[4] fed by heaven
and, laying by, slew bulls in the proper number,
until the immortal gods were thus appeased;
then heaped a death mound on that shore against   610
all-quenching time for Agamémnon's honor,
and put to sea once more. The gods sent down
a sternwind for a racing passage homeward.

So ends the story. Now you must stay with me
and be my guest eleven or twelve days more.   615
I'll send you on your way with gifts, and fine ones:
three chariot horses, and a polished car;
a hammered cup, too, so that all your days,
tipping the red wine for the deathless gods,
you will remember me."

                          Telémakhos answered: 620

"Lord, son of Atreus, no, you must not keep me.
Not that a year with you would be too long:
I never could be homesick here—I find
your tales and all you say so marvellous.
But time hangs heavy on my shipmates' hands   625
at holy Pylos, if you make me stay.
As for your gift, now, let it be some keepsake.
Horses I cannot take to Ithaka;
let me bestow them back on you, to serve
your glory here. My lord, you rule wide country,   630
rolling and rich with clover, galingale
and all the grains: red wheat and hoary barley.
At home we have no level runs or meadows,
but highland, goat land—prettier than plains, though.
Grasses, and pasture land, are hard to come by   635
upon the islands tilted in the sea,
and Ithaka is the island of them all."

At this the deep-lunged man of battle smiled.
Then he said kindly, patting the boy's hand:

"You come of good stock, lad. That was well spoken.   640
I'll change the gift, then—as indeed I can.

4. The Nile River.

Let me see what is costliest and most beautiful
of all the precious things my house contains:
a wine bowl, mixing bowl, all wrought of silver,
but rimmed with hammered gold. Let this be yours.   645
It is Hephaistos'[5] work, given me by Phaidimos,
captain and king of Sidon. He received me
during my travels. Let it be yours, I say."

This was their discourse on that morning. Meanwhile
guests were arriving at the great lord's house,   650
bringing their sheep, and wine, the ease of men,
with loaves their comely kerchiefed women sent,
to make a feast in hall.
                              At that same hour,
before the distant manor of Odysseus,
the suitors were competing at the discus throw   655
and javelin, on a measured field they used,
arrogant lords at play. The two best men,
Antínoös and Eurýmakhos, presided.
Now Phronios' son, Noêmon, came to see them
with a question for Antínoös. He said: 660

"Do any of us know, or not, Antínoös,
what day Telémakhos will be home from Pylos?
He took my ship, but now I need it back
to make a cruise to Elis, where the plains are.
I have a dozen mares at pasture there   665
with mule colts yet unweaned. My notion is
to bring one home and break him in for labor."

His first words made them stare—for they knew well
Telémakhos could not have gone to Pylos,
but inland with his flocks, or to the swineherd.   670
Eupeithês' son, Antínoös, quickly answered:

"Tell the story straight. He sailed? Who joined him—
a crew he picked up here in Ithaka,
or his own slaves? He might have done it that way.
And will you make it clear   675
whether he took the ship against your will?
Did he ask for it, did you lend it to him?"

Now said the son of Phronios in reply:

"Lent it to him, and freely. Who would not,
when a prince of that house asked for it, in trouble?   680
Hard to refuse the favor, it seems to me.
As for his crew, the best men on the island,
after ourselves, went with him. Mentor I noted

5. God of the forge and patron of metalworkers; he made Akhilleus's armor and was married to the goddess Aphrodite.

going aboard—or a god who looked like Mentor.
The strange thing is, I saw Lord Mentor here   685
in the first light yesterday—although he sailed
five days ago for Pylos."

                    Turning away,
Noêmon took the path to his father's house,
leaving the two men there, baffled and hostile.
They called the rest in from the playing field   690
and made them all sit down, so that Antínoös
could speak out from the stormcloud of his heart,
swollen with anger; and his eyes blazed:

"A bad business. Telémakhos had the gall
to make that crossing, though we said he could not.   695
So the young cub rounds up a first rate crew
in spite of all our crowd, and puts to sea.
What devilment will he be up to next time?—
Zeus blast the life out of him before he's grown!
Just give me a fast ship and twenty men;   700
I'll intercept him, board him in the strait
between the crags of Samê and this island.
He'll find his sea adventure after his father
swamping work in the end!"

                    They all cried "Aye!"   705
and "After him!" and trailed back to the manor.

Now not much time went by before Penélopê
learned what was afoot among the suitors.
Medôn the crier told her. He had been
outside the wall, and heard them in the court
conspiring. Into the house and up the stairs   710
he ran to her with his news upon his tongue—
but at the door Penélopê met him, crying:

"Why have they sent you up here now? To tell
the maids of King Odysseus—'Leave your spinning:
Time to go down and slave to feed those men'?   715
I wish this were the last time they came feasting,
courting me or consorting here! The last!
Each day you crowd this house like wolves
to eat away my brave son's patrimony.
When you were boys, did your own fathers tell you   720
nothing of what Odysseus was for them?
In word and act impeccable, disinterested
toward all the realm—though it is king's justice
to hold one man abhorred and love another;
no man alive could say Odysseus wronged him.   725
But your own hearts—how different!—and your deeds!
How soon are benefactions all forgotten!"

Now Medôn, the alert and cool man, answered:

"I wish that were the worst of it, my Lady,
but they intend something more terrible—   730
may Zeus forfend and spare us!
They plan to drive the keen bronze through Telémakhos
when he comes home. He sailed away, you know,
to hallowed Pylos and old Lakedaimon
for news about his father."

                         Her knees failed,   735
and her heart failed as she listened to the words,
and all her power of speech went out of her.
Tears came; but the rich voice could not come.
Only after a long while she made answer:

"Why has my child left me? He had no need   740
of those long ships on which men shake out sail
to tug like horses, breasting miles of sea.
Why did he go? Must he, too, be forgotten?"

Then Medôn, the perceptive man, replied:

"A god moved him—who knows?—or his own heart   745
sent him to learn, at Pylos, if his father
roams the wide world still, or what befell him."

He left her then, and went down through the house.
And now the pain around her heart benumbed her;
chairs were a step away, but far beyond her;   750
she sank down on the door sill of the chamber,
wailing, and all her women young and old
made a low murmur of lament around her,
until at last she broke out through her tears:

"Dearest companions, what has Zeus given me?   755
Pain—more pain than any living woman.
My lord, my lion heart, gone, long ago—
the bravest man, and best, of the Danaans,
famous through Hellas and the Argive midlands—
and now the squalls have blown my son, my dear one,   760
an unknown boy, southward. No one told me.
O brute creatures, not one soul would dare
to wake me from my sleep; you knew
the hour he took the black ship out to sea!
If I had seen that sailing in his eyes   765
he should have stayed with me, for all his longing,
stayed—or left me dead in the great hall.
Go, someone, now, and call old Dólios,
the slave my father gave me before I came,
my orchard keeper—tell him to make haste   770
and put these things before Laërtês; he

may plan some kind of action; let him come
to cry shame on these ruffians who would murder
Odysseus' son and heir, and end his line!"

The dear old nurse, Eurýkleia, answered her: 775

"Sweet mistress, have my throat cut without mercy
or what you will; it's true, I won't conceal it,
I knew the whole thing; gave him his provisions;
grain and sweet wine I gave, and a great oath
to tell you nothing till twelve days went by,   780
or till you heard of it yourself, or missed him;
he hoped you would not tear your skin lamenting.
Come, bathe and dress your loveliness afresh,
and go to the upper rooms with all your maids
to ask help from Athena, Zeus's daughter.   785
She it will be who saves this boy from death.
Spare the old man this further suffering;
the blissful gods cannot so hate his line,
heirs of Arkêsios;[6] one will yet again
be lord of the tall house and the far fields."   790

She hushed her weeping in this way, and soothed her.
The Lady Penélopê arose and bathed,
dressing her body in her freshest linen,
filled a basket with barley, and led her maids
to the upper rooms, where she besought Athena: 795

"Tireless child of Zeus, graciously hear me!
If ever Odysseus burned at our altar fire
thighbones of beef or mutton in sacrifice,
remember it for my sake! Save my son!
Shield him, and make the killers go astray!"   800

She ended with a cry, and the goddess heard her.
Now voices rose from the shadowy hall below
where the suitors were assuring one another:
"Our so-long-courted Queen is even now
of a mind to marry one of us, and knows   805
nothing of what is destined for her son."

Of what was destined they in fact knew nothing,
but Antínoös addressed them in a whisper:

"No boasting—are you mad?—and no loud talk:
someone might hear it and alarm the house.   810
Come along now, be quiet, this way; come,
we'll carry out the plan our hearts are set on."

Picking out twenty of the strongest seamen,
he led them to a ship at the sea's edge,

6. Laërtês' father and Odysseus's grandfather.

and down they dragged her into deeper water,   815
stepping a mast in her, with furled sails,
and oars a-trail from thongs looped over thole pins,
ready all; then tried the white sail, hoisting,
while men at arms carried their gear aboard.
They moored the ship some way off shore, and left her   820
to take their evening meal there, waiting for night to come.

Penélopê at that hour in her high chamber
lay silent, tasting neither food nor drink,
and thought of nothing but her princely son—
could he escape, or would they find and kill him?—   825
her mind turning at bay, like a cornered lion
in whom fear comes as hunters close the ring.
But in her sick thought sweet sleep overtook her,
and she dozed off, her body slack and still.

Now it occurred to the grey-eyed goddess Athena   830
to make a figure of dream in a woman's form—
Iphthimê, great Ikários' other daughter,
whom Eumêlos of Phêrai took as bride.
The goddess sent this dream to Odysseus' house
to quiet Penélopê and end her grieving.   835
So, passing by the strap-slit[7] through the door,
the image came a-gliding down the room
to stand at her bedside and murmur to her:

"Sleepest thou, sorrowing Penélopê?
The gods whose life is ease no longer suffer thee   840
to pine and weep, then; he returns unharmed,
thy little one; no way hath he offended."

Then pensive Penélopê made this reply,
slumbering sweetly in the gates of dream:

"Sister, hast thou come hither? Why? Aforetime   845
never wouldst come, so far away thy dwelling.
And am I bid be done with all my grieving?
But see what anguish hath my heart and soul!
My lord, my lion heart, gone, long ago—
the bravest man, and best, of the Danaans,   850
famous through Hellas and the Argive midlands—
and now my son, my dear one, gone seafaring,
a child, untrained in hardship or in council.
Aye,'tis for him I weep, more than his father!
Aye, how I tremble for him, lest some blow   855
befall him at men's hands or on the sea!
Cruel are they and many who plot against him,
to take his life before he can return.'

---

7. We would say, "through the keyhole." The inside bolt could be closed from outside by means of a strap
that came through a slit in the door.

Now the dim phantom spoke to her once more:

"Lift up thy heart, and fear not overmuch.   860
For by his side one goes whom all men else
invoke as their defender, one so powerful—
Pallas Athena; in thy tears she pitied thee
and now hath sent me that I so assure thee."

Then said Penélopê the wise:

                                                 "If thou art   865
numinous and hast ears for divine speech,
O tell me, what of Odysseus, man of woe?
Is he alive still somewhere, seeth he day light still?
Or gone in death to the sunless underworld?"

The dim phantom said only this in answer: 870

"Of him I may not tell thee in this discourse,
alive or dead. And empty words are evil."
The wavering form withdrew along the doorbolt
into a draft of wind, and out of sleep
Penélopê awoke, in better heart   875
for that clear dream in the twilight of the night.

Meanwhile the suitors had got under way,
planning the death plunge for Telémakhos.
Between the Isles of Ithaka and Samê
the sea is broken by an islet, Asteris,   880
with access to both channels from a cove.
In ambush here that night the Akhaians lay.

BOOK V

[Sweet Nymph and Open Sea]

Dawn came up from the couch of her reclining,
leaving her lord Tithonos'[8] brilliant side
with fresh light in her arms for gods and men.
And the master of heaven and high thunder, Zeus,
went to his place among the gods assembled   5
hearing Athena tell Odysseus' woe.
For she, being vexed that he was still sojourning
in the sea chambers of Kalypso, said:

"O Father Zeus and gods in bliss forever,
let no man holding scepter as a king
think to be mild, or kind, or virtuous;   10
let him be cruel, and practice evil ways,
for those Odysseus ruled cannot remember
the fatherhood and mercy of his reign.

8. A mortal man whom Eos, the dawn goddess, took for her husband.

Meanwhile he lives and grieves upon that island 15
in thralldom to the nymph; he cannot stir,
cannot fare homeward, for no ship is left him,
fitted with oars—no crewmen or companions
to pull him on the broad back of the sea.
And now murder is hatched on the high sea 20
against his son, who sought news of his father
in the holy lands of Pylos and Lakedaimon."

To this the summoner of cloud replied:

"My child, what odd complaints you let escape you.
Have you not, you yourself, arranged this matter— 25
as we all know—so that Odysseus
will bring these men to book, on his return?
And are you not the one to give Telémakhos
a safe route for sailing? Let his enemies
encounter no one and row home again." 30

He turned then to his favorite son and said:

"Hermês, you have much practice on our missions,
go make it known to the softly-braided nymph
that we, whose will is not subject to error,
order Odysseus home; let him depart. 35
But let him have no company, gods or men,
only a raft that he must lash together,
and after twenty days, worn out at sea,
he shall make land upon the garden isle,
Skhería,[9] of our kinsmen, the Phaiákians. 40
Let these men take him to their hearts in honor
and berth him in a ship, and send him home,
with gifts of garments, gold, and bronze—
so much he had not counted on from Troy
could he have carried home his share of plunder. 45
His destiny is to see his friends again
under his own roof, in his father's country."

No words were lost on Hermês the Wayfinder,
who bent to tie his beautiful sandals on,
ambrosial, golden, that carry him over water 50
or over endless land in a swish of the wind,
and took the wand with which he charms asleep—
or when he wills, awake—the eyes of men.
So wand in hand he paced into the air,
shot from Pieria[1] down, down to sea level, 55
and veered to skim the swell. A gull patrolling
between the wave crests of the desolate sea
will dip to catch a fish, and douse his wings;

9. Later Greeks identified it as the island of Corcyra (modern Corfu) off the northwest coast of mainland Greece.   1. The vicinity of Mount Olympus.

no higher above the whitecaps Hermês flew
until the distant island lay ahead,   60
then rising shoreward from the violet ocean
he stepped up to the cave. Divine Kalypso,
the mistress of the isle, was now at home.
Upon her hearthstone a great fire blazing
scented the farthest shores with cedar smoke   65
and smoke of thyme, and singing high and low
in her sweet voice, before her loom a-weaving,
she passed her golden shuttle to and fro.
A deep wood grew outside, with summer leaves
of alder and black poplar, pungent cypress.   70
Ornate birds here rested their stretched wings—
horned owls, falcons, cormorants—long-tongued
beachcombing birds, and followers of the sea.
Around the smoothwalled cave a crooking vine
held purple clusters under ply of green;   75
and four springs, bubbling up near one another
shallow and clear, took channels here and there
through beds of violets and tender parsley.
Even a god who found this place
would gaze, and feel his heart beat with delight: 80
so Hermês did; but when he had gazed his fill
he entered the wide cave. Now face to face
the magical Kalypso recognized him,
as all immortal gods know one another
on sight—though seeming strangers, far from home.   85
But he saw nothing of the great Odysseus,
who sat apart, as a thousand times before,
and racked his own heart groaning, with eyes wet
scanning the bare horizon of the sea.
Kalypso, lovely nymph, seated her guest   90
in a bright chair all shimmering, and asked:

"O Hermês, ever with your golden wand,
what brings you to my island?
Your awesome visits in the past were few.
Now tell me what request you have in mind;   95
for I desire to do it, if I can,
and if it is a proper thing to do.
But wait a while, and let me serve my friend."

She drew a table of ambrosia near him
and stirred a cup of ruby-colored nectar—   100
food and drink for the luminous Wayfinder,
who took both at his leisure, and replied:[2]

"Goddess to god, you greet me, questioning me?
Well, here is truth for you in courtesy.
Zeus made me come, and not my inclination;   105

2. The translator put Hermês' speech into rhymed couplets; there is no rhyme in the original Greek.

who cares to cross that tract of desolation,
the bitter sea, all mortal towns behind
where gods have beef and honors from mankind?
But it is not to be thought of—and no use—
for any god to elude the will of Zeus.   110
He notes your friend, most ill-starred by renown
of all the peers who fought for Priam's town—
nine years of war they had, before great Troy was down.
Homing, they wronged the goddess with grey eyes,
who made a black wind blow and the seas rise,   115
in which his troops were lost, and all his gear,
while easterlies and current washed him here.
Now the command is: send him back in haste.
His life may not in exile go to waste.
His destiny, his homecoming, is at hand,   120
when he shall see his dearest, and walk on his own land."

That goddess most divinely made
shuddered before him, and her warm voice rose:

"Oh you vile gods, in jealousy supernal!
You hate it when we choose to lie with men—   125
immortal flesh by some dear mortal side.
So radiant Dawn once took to bed Orion
until you easeful gods grew peevish at it,
and holy Artemis, Artemis throned in gold,
hunted him down in Delos with her arrows.   130
Then Dêmêtêr[3] of the tasseled tresses yielded
to Iasion, mingling and making love
in a furrow three times plowed; but Zeus found out
and killed him with a white-hot thunderbolt.
So now you grudge me, too, my mortal friend.   135
But it was I who saved him—saw him straddle
his own keel board, the one man left afloat
when Zeus rent wide his ship with chain lightning
and overturned him in the winedark sea.
Then all his troops were lost, his good companions,   140
but wind and current washed him here to me.
I fed him, loved him, sang that he should not die
nor grow old, ever, in all the days to come.
But now there's no eluding Zeus's will.
If this thing be ordained by him, I say   145
so be it, let the man strike out alone
on the vast water. Surely I cannot 'send' him.
I have no long-oared ships, no company
to pull him on the broad back of the sea.
My counsel he shall have, and nothing hidden,   150
to help him homeward without harm."

To this the Wayfinder made answer briefly:

3. Goddess associated with the growth of the crops, especially wheat.

"Thus you shall send him, then. And show more grace
in your obedience, or be chastised by Zeus."

The strong god glittering left her as he spoke,⁣⁣⁣⁣⁣   155
and now her ladyship, having given heed
to Zeus's mandate, went to find Odysseus
in his stone seat to seaward—tear on tear
brimming his eyes. The sweet days of his life time
were running out in anguish over his exile,   160
for long ago the nymph had ceased to please.
Though he fought shy of her and her desire,
he lay with her each night, for she compelled him.
But when day came he sat on the rocky shore
and broke his own heart groaning, with eyes wet   165
scanning the bare horizon of the sea.
Now she stood near him in her beauty, saying:

"O forlorn man, be still.
Here you need grieve no more; you need not feel

your life consumed here; I have pondered it,   170
and I shall help you go.
Come and cut down high timber for a raft
or flatboat; make her broad-beamed, and decked over,
so you can ride her on the misty sea.
Stores I shall put aboard for you—bread, water,   175
and ruby-colored wine, to stay your hunger—
give you a seacloak and a following wind
to help you homeward without harm—provided
the gods who rule wide heaven wish it so.
Stronger than I they are, in mind and power."   180

For all he had endured, Odysseus shuddered.
But when he spoke, his words went to the mark:

"After these years, a helping hand? O goddess,
what guile is hidden here?
A raft, you say, to cross the Western Ocean,   185
rough water, and unknown? Seaworthy ships
that glory in god's wind will never cross it.
I take no raft you grudge me out to sea.
Or yield me first a great oath, if I do,
to work no more enchantment to my harm."   190

At this the beautiful nymph Kalypso smiled
and answered sweetly, laying her hand upon him:

"What a dog you are! And not for nothing learned,
having the wit to ask this thing of me!
My witness then be earth and sky   195
and dripping Styx⁴ that I swear by—

---

4. One of the rivers of the underworld.

the gay gods cannot swear more seriously—
I have no further spells to work against you.
But what I shall devise, and what I tell you,
will be the same as if your need were mine. 200
Fairness is all I think of. There are hearts
made of cold iron—but my heart is kind."

Swiftly she turned and led him to her cave,
and they went in, the mortal and immortal.
He took the chair left empty now by Hermês, 205
where the divine Kalypso placed before him
victuals and drink of men; then she sat down
facing Odysseus, while her serving maids
brought nectar and ambrosia to her side.
Then each one's hands went out on each one's feast 210
until they had had their pleasure; and she said:

"Son of Laërtês, versatile Odysseus,
after these years with me, you still desire
your old home? Even so, I wish you well.
If you could see it all, before you go— 215
all the adversity you face at sea—
you would stay here, and guard this house, and be
immortal—though you wanted her forever,
that bride for whom you pine each day.
Can I be less desirable than she is? 220
Less interesting? Less beautiful? Can mortals
compare with goddesses in grace and form?"

To this the strategist Odysseus answered:

"My lady goddess, here is no cause for anger.
My quiet Penélopê—how well I know— 225
would seem a shade before your majesty,
death and old age being unknown to you,
while she must die. Yet, it is true, each day
I long for home, long for the sight of home.
If any god has marked me out again 230
for shipwreck, my tough heart can undergo it.
What hardship have I not long since endured
at sea, in battle! Let the trial come."

Now as he spoke the sun set, dusk drew on,
and they retired, this pair, to the inner cave 235
to revel and rest softly, side by side.

When Dawn spread out her finger tips of rose
Odysseus pulled his tunic and his cloak on,
while the sea nymph dressed in a silvery gown
of subtle tissue, drew about her waist 240
a golden belt, and veiled her head, and then
took thought for the great-hearted hero's voyage.

A brazen axehead first she had to give him,
two-bladed, and agreeable to the palm
with a smooth-fitting haft of olive wood;   245
next a well-polished adze; and then she led him
to the island's tip where bigger timber grew—
besides the alder and poplar, tall pine trees,
long dead and seasoned, that would float him high.
Showing him in that place her stand of timber   250
the loveliest of nymphs took her way home.
Now the man fell to chopping; when he paused
twenty tall trees were down. He lopped the branches,
split the trunks, and trimmed his puncheons true.
Meanwhile Kalypso brought him an auger tool   255
with which he drilled through all his planks, then drove
stout pins to bolt them, fitted side by side.
A master shipwright, building a cargo vessel,
lays down a broad and shallow hull; just so
Odysseus shaped the bottom of his craft.   260
He made his decking fast to close-set ribs
before he closed the side with longer planking,
then cut a mast pole, and a proper yard,
and shaped a steering oar to hold her steady.
He drove long strands of willow in all the seams   265
to keep out waves, and ballasted with logs.
As for a sail, the lovely nymph Kalypso
brought him a cloth so he could make that, too.
Then he ran up his rigging—halyards, braces—
and hauled the boat on rollers to the water.   270

This was the fourth day, when he had all ready;
on the fifth day, she sent him out to sea.
But first she bathed him, gave him a scented cloak,
and put on board a skin of dusky wine
with water in a bigger skin, and stores—   275
boiled meats and other victuals—in a bag.
Then she conjured a warm landbreeze to blowing—
joy for Odysseus when he shook out sail!
Now the great seaman, leaning on his oar,
steered all the night unsleeping, and his eyes   280
picked out the Pleiadês, the laggard Ploughman,[5]
and the Great Bear, that some have called the Wain,[6]
pivoting in the sky before Orion;
of all the night's pure figures, she alone
would never bathe or dip in the Ocean stream.[7]   285
These stars the beautiful Kalypso bade him
hold on his left hand as he crossed the main.
Seventeen nights and days in the open water
he sailed, before a dark shoreline appeared;
Skhería then came slowly into view   290
like a rough shield of bull's hide on the sea.

5. Another name for the constellation Boötes. Pleiadês is a cluster of stars in the constellation Taurus.
6. The Big Dipper.   7. I.e., it is visible all year long. Orion, the Hunter, also is a constellation.

But now the god of earthquake,[8] storming home
over the mountains of Asia from the Sunburned land,
sighted him far away. The god grew sullen
and tossed his great head, muttering to himself: 295

"Here is a pretty cruise! While I was gone,
the gods have changed their minds about Odysseus.
Look at him now, just offshore of that island
that frees him from the bondage of his exile!
Still I can give him a rough ride in, and will."   300

Brewing high thunderheads, he churned the deep
with both hands on his trident—called up wind
from every quarter, and sent a wall of rain
to blot out land and sea in torrential night.
Hurricane winds now struck from the South and East   305
shifting North West in a great spume of seas,
on which Odysseus' knees grew slack, his heart
sickened, and he said within himself:

"Rag of man that I am, is this the end of me?
I fear the goddess told it all too well—   310
predicting great adversity at sea
and far from home. Now all things bear her out:
the whole rondure of heaven hooded so
by Zeus in woeful cloud, and the sea raging
under such winds. I am going down, that's sure.   315
How lucky those Danaans were who perished
on Troy's wide seaboard, serving the Atreidai!
Would God I, too, had died there—met my end
that time the Trojans made so many casts at me
when I stood by Akhilleus after death.   320
I should have had a soldier's burial
and praise from the Akhaians—not this choking
waiting for me at sea, unmarked and lonely."

A great wave drove at him with toppling crest
spinning him round, in one tremendous blow,   325
and he went plunging overboard, the oar-haft
wrenched from his grip. A gust that came on howling
at the same instant broke his mast in two,
hurling his yard and sail far out to leeward.
Now the big wave a long time kept him under,   330
helpless to surface, held by tons of water,
tangled, too, by the seacloak of Kalypso.
Long, long, until he came up spouting brine,
with streamlets gushing from his head and beard;
but still bethought him, half-drowned as he was,   335
to flounder for the boat and get a handhold
into the bilge—to crouch there, foiling death.

8. Poseidon.

Across the foaming water, to and fro,
the boat careered like a ball of tumbleweed
blown on the autumn plains, but intact still.   340
So the winds drove this wreck over the deep,
East Wind and North Wind, then South Wind and West,
coursing each in turn to the brutal harry.

But Ino saw him—Ino, Kadmos' daughter,
slim-legged, lovely, once an earthling girl,   345
now in the seas a nereid, Leukothea.
Touched by Odysseus' painful buffeting
she broke the surface, like a diving bird,
to rest upon the tossing raft and say:

"O forlorn man, I wonder   350
why the Earthshaker, Lord Poseidon, holds
this fearful grudge—father of all your woes.
He will not drown you, though, despite his rage.
You seem clear-headed still; do what I tell you.
Shed that cloak, let the gale take your craft,   355
and swim for it—swim hard to get ashore
upon Skhería, yonder,
where it is fated that you find a shelter.
Here: make my veil your sash; it is not mortal;
you cannot, now, be drowned or suffer harm.   360
Only, the instant you lay hold of earth,
discard it, cast it far, far out from shore
in the winedark sea again, and turn away."

After she had bestowed her veil, the nereid
dove like a gull to windward   365
where a dark waveside closed over her whiteness.
But in perplexity Odysseus
said to himself, his great heart laboring:

"O damned confusion! Can this be a ruse
to trick me from the boat for some god's pleasure?   370
No I'll not swim; with my own eyes I saw
how far the land lies that she called my shelter.
Better to do the wise thing, as I see it.
While this poor planking holds, I stay aboard;
I may ride out the pounding of the storm,   375
or if she cracks up, take to the water then;
I cannot think it through a better way."

But even while he pondered and decided,
the god of earthquake heaved a wave against him
high as a rooftree and of awful gloom.   380
A gust of wind, hitting a pile of chaff,
will scatter all the parched stuff far and wide;
just so, when this gigantic billow struck
the boat's big timbers flew apart. Odysseus

clung to a single beam, like a jockey riding,   385
meanwhile stripping Kalypso's cloak away;
then he slung round his chest the veil of Ino
and plunged headfirst into the sea. His hands
went out to stroke, and he gave a swimmer's kick.

But the strong Earthshaker had him under his eye,   390
and nodded as he said:

        "Go on, go on;
wander the high seas this way, take your blows,
before you join that race[9] the gods have nurtured.
Nor will you grumble, even then, I think,
for want of trouble."

        Whipping his glossy team   395
he rode off to his glorious home at Aigai.[1]
But Zeus's daughter Athena countered him:
she checked the course of all the winds but one,
commanding them, "Be quiet and go to sleep."
Then sent a long swell running under a norther   400
to bear the prince Odysseus, back from danger,
to join the Phaiákians, people of the sea.
Two nights, two days, in the solid deep-sea swell
he drifted, many times awaiting death,
until with shining ringlets in the East   405
the dawn confirmed a third day, breaking clear
over a high and windless sea; and mounting
a rolling wave he caught a glimpse of land.
What a dear welcome thing life seems to children
whose father, in the extremity, recovers   410
after some weakening and malignant illness:
his pangs are gone, the gods have delivered him.
So dear and welcome to Odysseus
the sight of land, of woodland, on that morning.
It made him swim again, to get a foothold   415
on solid ground. But when he came in earshot
he heard the trampling roar of sea on rock,
where combers, rising shoreward, thudded down
on the sucking ebb—all sheeted with salt foam.
Here were no coves or harborage or shelter,   420
only steep headlands, rockfallen reefs and crags.
Odysseus' knees grew slack, his heart faint,
a heaviness came over him, and he said:

"A cruel turn, this. Never had I thought
to see this land, but Zeus has let me see it—   425
and let me, too, traverse the Western Ocean—
only to find no exit from these breakers.

9. The Phaiákians, favored by the gods.   1. Town on the coast of Euboia, where there was a temple of
Poseidon.

Here are sharp rocks off shore, and the sea a smother
rushing around them; rock face rising sheer
from deep water; nowhere could I stand up   430
on my two feet and fight free of the welter.
No matter how I try it, the surf may throw me
against the cliffside; no good fighting there.
If I swim down the coast, outside the breakers,
I may find shelving shore and quiet water—   435
but what if another gale comes on to blow?
Then I go cursing out to sea once more.
Or then again, some shark of Amphitritê's[2]
may hunt me, sent by the genius of the deep.
I know how he who makes earth tremble hates me."   440

During this meditation a heavy surge
was taking him, in fact, straight on the rocks.
He had been flayed there, and his bones broken,
had not grey-eyed Athena instructed him:
he gripped a rock-ledge with both hands in passing   445
and held on, groaning, as the surge went by,
to keep clear of its breaking. Then the backwash
hit him, ripping him under and far out.
An octopus, when you drag one from his chamber,
comes up with suckers full of tiny stones: 450
Odysseus left the skin of his great hands
torn on that rock-ledge as the wave submerged him.
And now at last Odysseus would have perished,
battered inhumanly, but he had the gift
of self-possession from grey-eyed Athena.   455
So, when the backwash spewed him up again,
he swam out and along, and scanned the coast
for some landspit that made a breakwater.
Lo and behold, the mouth of a calm river
at length came into view, with level shores   460
unbroken, free from rock, shielded from wind—
by far the best place he had found.
But as he felt the current flowing seaward
he prayed in his heart:

                    "O hear me, lord of the stream:
how sorely I depend upon your mercy!   465
derelict as I am by the sea's anger.
Is he not sacred, even to the gods,
the wandering man who comes, as I have come,
in weariness before your knees, your waters?
Here is your servant; lord, have mercy on me."   470

Now even as he prayed the tide at ebb
had turned, and the river god made quiet water,
drawing him in to safety in the shallows.

2. A sea goddess.

His knees buckled, his arms gave way beneath him,
all vital force now conquered by the sea.   475
Swollen from head to foot he was, and seawater
gushed from his mouth and nostrils. There he lay,
scarce drawing breath, unstirring, deathly spent.
In time, as air came back into his lungs
and warmth around his heart, he loosed the veil,   480
letting it drift away on the estuary
downstream to where a white wave took it under
and Ino's hands received it. Then the man
crawled to the river bank among the reeds
where, face down, he could kiss the soil of earth,   485
in his exhaustion murmuring to himself:

"What more can this hulk suffer? What comes now?
In vigil through the night here by the river
how can I not succumb, being weak and sick,
to the night's damp and hoarfrost of the morning?   490
The air comes cold from rivers before dawn.
But if I climb the slope and fall asleep
in the dark forest's undergrowth—supposing
cold and fatigue will go, and sweet sleep come—
I fear I make the wild beasts easy prey."   495

But this seemed best to him, as he thought it over.
He made his way to a grove above the water
on open ground, and crept under twin bushes
grown from the same spot—olive and wild olive—
a thicket proof against the stinging wind   500
or Sun's blaze, fine soever the needling sunlight;
nor could a downpour wet it through, so dense
those plants were interwoven. Here Odysseus
tunnelled, and raked together with his hands
a wide bed—for a fall of leaves was there,   505
enough to save two men or maybe three
on a winter night, a night of bitter cold.
Odysseus' heart laughed when he saw his leaf-bed,
and down he lay, heaping more leaves above him.

A man in a distant field, no hearthfires near,   510
will hide a fresh brand in his bed of embers
to keep a spark alive for the next day;
so in the leaves Odysseus hid himself,
while over him Athena showered sleep
that his distress should end, and soon, soon.   515
In quiet sleep she sealed his cherished eyes.

BOOK VI

[The Princess at the River]

Far gone in weariness, in oblivion,
the noble and enduring man slept on;

but Athena in the night went down the land
of the Phaiákians, entering their city.
In days gone by, these men held Hypereia,[3]   5
a country of wide dancing grounds, but near them
were overbearing Kyklopês, whose power
could not be turned from pillage. So the Phaiákians
migrated thence under Nausíthoös
to settle a New World across the sea,   10
Skhería Island. That first captain walled
their promontory, built their homes and shrines,
and parcelled out the black land for the plow.
But he had gone down long ago to Death.
Alkínoös ruled, and Heaven gave him wisdom,   15
so on this night the goddess, grey-eyed Athena,
entered the palace of Alkínoös
to make sure of Odysseus' voyage home.
She took her way to a painted bedchamber
where a young girl lay fast asleep—so fine   20
in mould and feature that she seemed a goddess—
the daughter of Alkínoös, Nausikaa.
On either side, as Graces[4] might have slept,
her maids were sleeping. The bright doors were shut,
but like a sudden stir of wind, Athena   25
moved to the bedside of the girl, and grew
visible as the shipman Dymas' daughter,
a girl the princess' age, and her dear friend.
In this form grey-eyed Athena said to her:

"How so remiss, and yet thy mother's daughter?   30
leaving thy clothes uncared for, Nausikaa,
when soon thou must have store of marriage linen,
and put thy minstrelsy in wedding dress!
Beauty, in these, will make the folk admire,
and bring thy father and gentle mother joy.   35
Let us go washing in the shine of morning!
Beside thee will I drub, so wedding chests
will brim by evening. Maidenhood must end!
Have not the noblest born Phaiákians
paid court to thee, whose birth none can excel?   40
Go beg thy sovereign father, even at dawn,
to have the mule cart and the mules brought round
to take thy body-linen, gowns and mantles.
Thou shouldst ride, for it becomes thee more,
the washing pools are found so far from home."   45

On this word she departed, grey-eyed Athena,
to where the gods have their eternal dwelling—
as men say—in the fastness of Olympos.
Never a tremor of wind, or a splash of rain,

---

3. Probably an imaginary place; however, the migration under pressure and the founding of the new city (described below) suggest the atmosphere of the great age of Greek colonization (eighth century B.C.).   4. Goddesses (usually three) personifying charm and beauty.

no errant snowflake comes to stain that heaven,   50
so calm, so vaporless, the world of light.
Here, where the gay gods live their days of pleasure,
the grey-eyed one withdrew, leaving the princess.

And now Dawn took her own fair throne, awaking
the girl in the sweet gown, still charmed by dream.   55
Down through the rooms she went to tell her parents,
whom she found still at home: her mother seated
near the great hearth among her maids—and twirling
out of her distaff yarn dyed like the sea—;
her father at the door, bound for a council   60
of princes on petition of the gentry.
She went up close to him and softly said:

"My dear Papà, could you not send the mule cart
around for me—the gig with pretty wheels?
I must take all our things and get them washed   65
at the river pools; our linen is all soiled.
And you should wear fresh clothing, going to council
with counselors and first men of the realm.
Remember your five sons at home: though two
are married, we have still three bachelor sprigs;   70
they will have none but laundered clothes each time
they go to the dancing. See what I must think of!"

She had no word to say of her own wedding,
though her keen father saw her blush. Said he:

"No mules would I deny you, child, nor anything.   75
Go along, now; the grooms will bring your gig
with pretty wheels and the cargo box upon it."

He spoke to the stableman, who soon brought round
the cart, low-wheeled and nimble;
harnessed the mules, and backed them in the traces.   80
Meanwhile the girl fetched all her soiled apparel
to bundle in the polished wagon box.
Her mother, for their luncheon, packed a hamper
with picnic fare, and filled a skin of wine,
and, when the princess had been handed up,   85
gave her a golden bottle of olive oil
for softening girls' bodies, after bathing.
Nausikaa took the reins and raised her whip,
lashing the mules. What jingling! What a clatter!
But off they went in a ground-covering trot,   90
with princess, maids, and laundry drawn behind.
By the lower river where the wagon came
were washing pools, with water all year flowing
in limpid spillways that no grime withstood.
The girls unhitched the mules, and sent them down   95
along the eddying stream to crop sweet grass.

Then sliding out the cart's tail board, they took
armloads of clothing to the dusky water,
and trod them in the pits, making a race of it.
All being drubbed, all blemish rinsed away,   100
they spread them, piece by piece, along the beach
whose pebbles had been laundered by the sea;
then took a dip themselves, and, all anointed
with golden oil, ate lunch beside the river
while the bright burning sun dried out their linen.   105
Princess and maids delighted in that feast;
then, putting off their veils,
they ran and passed a ball to a rhythmic beat,
Nausikaa flashing first with her white arms.

So Artemis goes flying after her arrows flown   110
down some tremendous valley-side—
                                Taÿgetos, Erymanthos[5]—
chasing the mountain goats or ghosting deer,
with nymphs of the wild places flanking her;
and Lêto's[6] heart delights to see them running,
for, taller by a head than nymphs can be,   115
the goddess shows more stately, all being beautiful.
So one could tell the princess from the maids.

Soon it was time, she knew, for riding homeward—
mules to be harnessed, linen folded smooth—
but the grey-eyed goddess Athena made her tarry,   120
so that Odysseus might behold her beauty
and win her guidance to the town.
                        It happened
when the king's daughter threw her ball off line
and missed, and put it in the whirling stream,—
at which they all gave such a shout, Odysseus   125
awoke and sat up, saying to himself:

"Now, by my life, mankind again! But who?
Savages, are they, strangers to courtesy?
Or gentle folk, who know and fear the gods?
That was a lusty cry of tall young girls—   130
most like the cry of nymphs, who haunt the peaks,
and springs of brooks, and inland grassy places.
Or am I amid people of human speech?
Up again, man; and let me see for myself."

He pushed aside the bushes, breaking off   135
with his great hand a single branch of olive,
whose leaves might shield him in his nakedness;
so came out rustling, like a mountain lion,
rain-drenched, wind-buffeted, but in his might at ease,

5. A mountain in Arcadia. Taÿgetos is the mountain range west of Sparta. Both places are rich in
game.   6. Mother of Artemis and Apollo.

with burning eyes—who prowls among the herds 140
or flocks, or after game, his hungry belly
taking him near stout homesteads for his prey.
Odysseus had this look, in his rough skin
advancing on the girls with pretty braids;
and he was driven on by hunger, too. 145
Streaked with brine, and swollen, he terrified them,
so that they fled, this way and that. Only
Alkínoös' daughter stood her ground, being given
a bold heart by Athena, and steady knees.

She faced him, waiting. And Odysseus came, 150
debating inwardly what he should do:
embrace this beauty's knees in supplication?
or stand apart, and, using honeyed speech,
inquire the way to town, and beg some clothing?
In his swift reckoning, he thought it best 155
to trust in words to please her—and keep away;
he might anger the girl, touching her knees.
So he began, and let the soft words fall:

"Mistress: please: are you divine, or mortal?
If one of those who dwell in the wide heaven, 160
you are most near to Artemis, I should say—
great Zeus's daughter—in your grace and presence.
If you are one of earth's inhabitants,
how blest your father, and your gentle mother,
blest all your kin. I know what happiness 165
must send the warm tears to their eyes, each time
they see their wondrous child go to the dancing!
But one man's destiny is more than blest—
he who prevails, and takes you as his bride.
Never have I laid eyes on equal beauty 170
in man or woman. I am hushed indeed.
So fair, one time, I thought a young palm tree
at Delos[7] near the altar of Apollo—
I had troops under me when I was there
on the sea route that later brought me grief— 175
but that slim palm tree filled my heart with wonder:
never came shoot from earth so beautiful.
So now, my lady, I stand in awe so great
I cannot take your knees. And yet my case is desperate:
twenty days, yesterday, in the winedark sea, 180
on the ever-lunging swell, under gale winds,
getting away from the Island of Ogýgia.
And now the terror of Storm has left me stranded
upon this shore—with more blows yet to suffer,
I must believe, before the gods relent. 185
Mistress, do me a kindness!
After much weary toil, I come to you,

7. A small island in the middle of the Aegean Sea, the birthplace of Apollo and a center for his worship.

and you are the first soul I have seen—I know
no others here. Direct me to the town,
give me a rag that I can throw around me,   190
some cloth or wrapping that you brought along.
And may the gods accomplish your desire:
a home, a husband, and harmonious
converse with him—the best thing in the world
being a strong house held in serenity   195
where man and wife agree. Woe to their enemies,
joy to their friends! But all this they know best."

Then she of the white arms, Nausikaa, replied:

"Stranger, there is no quirk or evil in you
that I can see. You know Zeus metes out fortune   200
to good and bad men as it pleases him.
Hardship he sent to you, and you must bear it.
But now that you have taken refuge here
you shall not lack for clothing, or any other
comfort due to a poor man in distress.   205
The town lies this way, and the men are called
Phaiákians, who own the land and city.
I am daughter to the Prince Alkínoös,
by whom the power of our people stands."

Turning, she called out to her maids-in-waiting: 210

"Stay with me! Does the sight of a man scare you?
Or do you take this one for an enemy?
Why, there's no fool so brash, and never will be,
as to bring war or pillage to this coast,
for we are dear to the immortal gods,   215
living here, in the sea that rolls forever,
distant from other lands and other men.
No: this man is a castaway, poor fellow;
we must take care of him. Strangers and beggars
come from Zeus: a small gift, then, is friendly.   220
Give our new guest some food and drink, and take him
into the river, out of the wind, to bathe."

They stood up now, and called to one another
to go on back. Quite soon they led Odysseus
under the river bank, as they were bidden;   225
and there laid out a tunic, and a cloak,
and gave him olive oil in the golden flask.
"Here," they said, "go bathe in the flowing water."
But heard now from that kingly man, Odysseus:

"Maids," he said, "keep away a little; let me   230
wash the brine from my own back, and rub on
plenty of oil. It is long since my anointing.

I take no bath, however, where you can see me—
naked before young girls with pretty braids."

They left him, then, and went to tell the princess.   235
And now Odysseus, dousing in the river,
scrubbed the coat of brine from back and shoulders
and rinsed the clot of sea-spume from his hair;
got himself all rubbed down, from head to foot,
then he put on the clothes the princess gave him.   240
Athena lent a hand, making him seem
taller, and massive too, with crisping hair
in curls like petals of wild hyacinth,
but all red-golden. Think of gold infused
on silver by a craftsman, whose fine art   245
Hephaistos taught him, or Athena: one
whose work moves to delight: just so she lavished
beauty over Odysseus' head and shoulders.
Then he went down to sit on the sea beach
in his new splendor. There the girl regarded him,   250
and after a time she said to the maids beside her:

"My gentlewomen, I have a thing to tell you.
The Olympian gods cannot be all averse
to this man's coming here among our islanders.
Uncouth he seemed, I thought so, too, before;   255
but now he looks like one of heaven's people.
I wish my husband could be fine as he
and glad to stay forever on Skhería!

But have you given refreshment to our guest?"

At this the maids, all gravely listening, hastened   260
to set out bread and wine before Odysseus,
and ah! how ravenously that patient man
took food and drink, his long fast at an end.

The princess Nausikaa now turned aside
to fold her linens; in the pretty cart   265
she stowed them, put the mule team under harness,
mounted the driver's seat, and then looked down
to say with cheerful prompting to Odysseus:

"Up with you now, friend; back to town we go;
and I shall send you in before my father   270
who is wondrous wise; there in our house with him
you'll meet the noblest of the Phaiákians.
You have good sense, I think; here's how to do it:
while we go through the countryside and farmland
stay with my maids, behind the wagon, walking   275
briskly enough to follow where I lead.
But near the town—well, there's a wall with towers
around the Isle, and beautiful ship basins

right and left of the causeway of approach;
seagoing craft are beached beside the road   280
each on its launching ways. The agora,[8]
with fieldstone benches bedded in the earth,
lies either side Poseidon's shrine—for there
men are at work on pitch-black hulls and rigging,
cables and sails, and tapering of oars.   285
The archer's craft is not for the Phaiákians,
but ship designing, modes of oaring cutters
in which they love to cross the foaming sea.
From these fellows I will have no salty talk,
no gossip later. Plenty are insolent.   290
And some seadog might say, after we passed:
'Who is this handsome stranger trailing Nausikaa?
Where did she find him? Will he be her husband?
Or is she being hospitable to some rover
come off his ship from lands across the sea—   295
there being no lands nearer. A god, maybe?
a god from heaven, the answer to her prayer,
descending now—to make her his forever?
Better, if she's roamed and found a husband
somewhere else: none of our own will suit her,   300
though many come to court her, and those the best.'
This is the way they might make light of me.
And I myself should hold it shame
for any girl to flout her own dear parents,
taking up with a man, before her marriage.   305

Note well, now, what I say, friend, and your chances
are excellent for safe conduct from my father.
You'll find black poplars in a roadside park
around a meadow and fountain—all Athena's—
but Father has a garden in the place—   310
this within earshot of the city wall.
Go in there and sit down, giving us time
to pass through town and reach my father's house.
And when you can imagine we're at home,
then take the road into the city, asking   315
directions to the palace of Alkínoös.
You'll find it easily: any small boy
can take you there; no family has a mansion
half so grand as he does, being king.
As soon as you are safe inside, cross over   320
and go straight through into the mégaron[9]
to find my mother. She'll be there in firelight
before a column, with her maids in shadow,
spinning a wool dyed richly as the sea.
My father's great chair faces the fire, too;   325
there like a god he sits and takes his wine.
Go past him, cast yourself before my mother,

8. Place of assembly.   9. The great hall of the palace.

embrace her knees—and you may wake up soon
at home rejoicing, though your home be far.
On Mother's feeling much depends; if she   330
looks on you kindly, you shall see your friends
under your own roof in your father's country."

At this she raised her glistening whip, lashing
the team into a run; they left the river
cantering beautifully, then trotted smartly.   335
But then she reined them in, and spared the whip,
so that her maids could follow with Odysseus.
The sun was going down when they went by
Athena's grove. Here, then, Odysseus rested,
and lifted up his prayer to Zeus's daughter: 340

"Hear me, unwearied child of royal Zeus!
O listen to me now—thou so aloof
while the Earthshaker wrecked and battered me.
May I find love and mercy among these people."

He prayed for that, and Pallas Athena heard him—   345
although in deference to her father's brother
she would not show her true form to Odysseus,
at whom Poseidon smoldered on
until the kingly man came home to his own shore.

BOOK VII

[Gardens and Firelight]

As Lord Odysseus prayed there in the grove
the girl rode on, behind her strapping team,
and came late to the mansion of her father,
where she reined in at the courtyard gate. Her brothers
awaited her like tall gods in the court,   5
circling to lead the mules away and carry
the laundered things inside. But she withdrew
to her own bedroom, where a fire soon shone,
kindled by her old nurse, Eurymedousa.
Years ago, from a raid on the continent,   10
the rolling ships had brought this woman over
to be Alkínoös' share—fit spoil for him
whose realm hung on his word as on a god's.
And she had schooled the princess, Nausikaa,
whose fire she tended now, making her supper.   15

Odysseus, when the time had passed, arose
and turned into the city. But Athena
poured a sea fog around him as he went—
her love's expedient, that no jeering sailor
should halt the man or challenge him for luck.   20
Instead, as he set foot in the pleasant city,

the grey-eyed goddess came to him, in figure
a small girl child, hugging a water jug.

Confronted by her, Lord Odysseus asked:

"Little one, could you take me to the house   25
of that Alkínoös, king among these people?
You see, I am a poor old stranger here;
my home is far away; here there is no one
known to me, in countryside or city."

The grey-eyed goddess Athena replied to him: 30

"Oh yes, good grandfer, sir, I know, I'll show you
the house you mean; it is quite near my father's.
But come now, hush, like this, and follow me.
You must not stare at people, or be inquisitive.
They do not care for strangers in this neighborhood; 35
a foreign man will get no welcome here.
The only things they trust are the racing ships
Poseidon gave, to sail the deep blue sea
like white wings in the sky, or a flashing thought."

Pallas Athena turned like the wind, running   40
ahead of him, and he followed in her footsteps.
And no seafaring men of Phaiákia
perceived Odysseus passing through their town:
the awesome one in pigtails barred their sight
with folds of sacred mist. And yet Odysseus   45
gazed out marvelling at the ships and harbors,
public squares, and ramparts towering up
with pointed palisades along the top.
When they were near the mansion of the king,
grey-eyed Athena in the child cried out: 50

"Here it is, grandfer, sir—that mansion house
you asked to see. You'll find our king and queen
at supper, but you must not be dismayed;
go in to them. A cheerful man does best
in every enterprise—even a stranger.   55
You'll see our lady just inside the hall—
her name is Arêtê; her grandfather
was our good king Alkínoös' father—
Nausíthoös by name, son of Poseidon
and Periboia. That was a great beauty,   60
the daughter of Eurymedon, commander
of the Gigantês[1] in the olden days,
who led those wild things to their doom and his.
Poseidon then made love to Periboia,
and she bore Nausíthoös, Phaiákia's lord,   65
whose sons in turn were Rhêxênor and Alkínoös.

---

1. The Giants; an older race of gods who battled, unsuccessfully, against the Olympians.

Rhêxênor had no sons; even as a bridegroom
he fell before the silver bow of Apollo,
his only child a daughter, Arêtê.
When she grew up, Alkínoös married her   70
and holds her dear. No lady in the world,
no other mistress of a man's household,
is honored as our mistress is, and loved,
by her own children, by Alkínoös,
and by the people. When she walks the town   75
they murmur and gaze, as though she were a goddess.
No grace or wisdom fails in her; indeed
just men in quarrels come to her for equity.
Supposing, then, she looks upon you kindly,
the chances are that you shall see your friends   80
under your own roof, in your father's country."

At this the grey-eyed goddess Athena left him
and left that comely land, going over sea
to Marathon, to the wide roadways of Athens
and her retreat in the stronghold of Erekhtheus.[2]   85
Odysseus, now alone before the palace,
meditated a long time before crossing
the brazen threshold of the great courtyard.
High rooms he saw ahead, airy and luminous
as though with lusters of the sun and moon,   90
bronze-paneled walls, at several distances,
making a vista, with an azure molding
of lapis lazuli. The doors were golden
guardians of the great room. Shining bronze
plated the wide door sill; the posts and lintel   95
were silver upon silver; golden handles
curved on the doors, and golden, too, and silver
were sculptured hounds, flanking the entrance way,
cast by the skill and ardor of Hephaistos
to guard the prince Alkínoös' house—   100
undying dogs that never could grow old.
Through all the rooms, as far as he could see,
tall chairs were placed around the walls, and strewn
with fine embroidered stuff made by the women.
Here were enthroned the leaders of Phaiákia   105
drinking and dining, with abundant fare.
Here, too, were boys of gold on pedestals
holding aloft bright torches of pitch pine
to light the great rooms, and the night-time feasting.
And fifty maids-in-waiting of the household   110
sat by the round mill, grinding yellow corn,
or wove upon their looms, or twirled their distaffs,
flickering like the leaves of a poplar tree;
while drops of oil glistened on linen weft.
Skillful as were the men of Phaiákia   115

2. King of Athens. Marathon was a village north of Athens near the coast; later it was the site of the famous
battle at which the Athenians repulsed a Persian invasion force (490 B.C.).

in ship handling at sea, so were these women
skilled at the loom, having this lovely craft
and artistry as talents from Athena.

To left and right, outside, he saw an orchard
closed by a pale—four spacious acres planted   120
with trees in bloom or weighted down for picking:
pear trees, pomegranates, brilliant apples,
luscious figs, and olives ripe and dark.
Fruit never failed upon these trees: winter
and summer time they bore, for through the year   125
the breathing Westwind ripened all in turn—
so one pear came to prime, and then another,
and so with apples, figs, and the vine's fruit
empurpled in the royal vineyard there.
Currants were dried at one end, on a platform   130
bare to the sun, beyond the vintage arbors
and vats the vintners trod; while near at hand
were new grapes barely formed as the green bloom fell,
or half-ripe clusters, faintly coloring.
After the vines came rows of vegetables   135
of all the kinds that flourish in every season,
and through the garden plots and orchard ran
channels from one clear fountain, while another
gushed through a pipe under the courtyard entrance
to serve the house and all who came for water.   140
These were the gifts of heaven to Alkínoös.

Odysseus, who had borne the barren sea,
stood in the gateway and surveyed this bounty.
He gazed his fill, then swiftly he went in.
The lords and nobles of Phaiákia   145
were tipping wine to the wakeful god, to Hermês—
a last libation before going to bed—
but down the hall Odysseus went unseen,
still in the cloud Athena cloaked him in,
until he reached Arêtê, and the king.   150
He threw his great hands round Arêtê's knees,
whereon the sacred mist curled back;
they saw him; and the diners hushed amazed
to see an unknown man inside the palace.
Under their eyes Odysseus made his plea: 155

"Arêtê, admirable Rhêxênor's daughter,
here is a man bruised by adversity, thrown
upon your mercy and the king your husband's,
begging indulgence of this company—
may the gods' blessing rest on them! May life   160
be kind to all! Let each one leave his children
every good thing this realm confers upon him!
But grant me passage to my father land.
My home and friends lie far. My life is pain."

He moved, then, toward the fire, and sat him down 165
amid the ashes.[3] No one stirred or spoke
until Ekhenêos broke the spell—an old man,
eldest of the Phaiákians, an oracle,
versed in the laws and manners of old time.
He rose among them now and spoke out kindly: 170

"Alkínoös, this will not pass for courtesy:
a guest abased in ashes at our hearth?
Everyone here awaits your word; so come, then,
lift the man up; give him a seat of honor,
a silver-studded chair. Then tell the stewards 175
we'll have another wine bowl for libation
to Zeus, lord of the lightning—advocate
of honorable petitioners. And supper
may be supplied our friend by the larder mistress."

Alkínoös, calm in power, heard him out, 180
then took the great adventurer by the hand
and led him from the fire. Nearest his throne
the son whom he loved best, Laódamas,
had long held place; now the king bade him rise
and gave his shining chair to Lord Odysseus. 185
A serving maid poured water for his hands
from a gold pitcher into a silver bowl,
and spread a polished table at his side;
the mistress of provisions came with bread
and other victuals, generous with her store. 190
So Lord Odysseus drank, and tasted supper.
Seeing this done, the king in majesty
said to his squire:

                "A fresh bowl, Pontónoös;
we make libation to the lord of lightning,
who seconds honorable petitioners." 195

Mixing the honey-hearted wine, Pontónoös
went on his rounds and poured fresh cups for all,
whereof when all had spilt they drank their fill.
Alkínoös then spoke to the company:

"My lords and leaders of Phaiákia: 200
hear now, all that my heart would have me say.
Our banquet's ended, so you may retire;
but let our seniors gather in the morning
to give this guest a festal day, and make
fair offerings to the gods. In due course we 205
shall put our minds upon the means at hand
to take him safely, comfortably, well

3. The fire, or hearth, was the sacred center of the home; the suppliant who sits there is, so to speak, on consecrated ground and cannot be forcibly removed.

and happily, with speed, to his own country,
distant though it may lie. And may no trouble
come to him here or on the way; his fate   210
he shall pay out at home, even as the Spinners⁴
spun for him on the day his mother bore him.
If, as may be, he is some god, come down
from heaven's height, the gods are working strangely:
until now, they have shown themselves in glory   215
only after great hekatombs—those figures
banqueting at our side, throned like ourselves.
Or if some traveller met them when alone
they bore no least disguise; we are their kin; Gigantês,
Kyklopês, rank no nearer gods than we."   220

Odysseus' wits were ready, and he replied:

"Alkínoös, you may set your mind at rest.
Body and birth, a most unlikely god
am I, being all of earth and mortal nature.
I should say, rather, I am like those men   225
who suffer the worst trials that you know,
and miseries greater yet, as I might tell you—
hundreds; indeed the gods could send no more.
You will indulge me if I finish dinner—?
grieved though I am to say it. There's no part   230
of man more like a dog than brazen Belly,
crying to be remembered—and it must be—
when we are mortal weary and sick at heart;
and that is my condition. Yet my hunger
drives me to take this food, and think no more   235
of my afflictions. Belly must be filled.
Be equally impelled, my lords, tomorrow
to berth me in a ship and send me home!
Rough years I've had; now may I see once more
my hall, my lands, my people before I die!"   240

Now all who heard cried out assent to this:
the guest had spoken well; he must have passage.
Then tipping wine they drank their thirst away,
and one by one went homeward for the night.
So Lord Odysseus kept his place alone   245
with Arêtê and the king Alkínoös
beside him, while the maids went to and fro
clearing away the wine cups and the tables.
Presently the ivory-skinned lady
turned to him—for she knew his cloak and tunic   250
to be her own fine work, done with her maids—
and arrowy came her words upon the air:

---

4. The Fates, who spin the pattern of each individual destiny.

"Friend, I, for one, have certain questions for you.
Who are you, and who has given you this clothing?
Did you not say you wandered here by sea?" 255

The great tactician carefully replied:

"Ah, majesty, what labor it would be
to go through the whole story! All my years
of misadventures, given by those on high!
But this you ask about is quickly told: 260
in mid-ocean lies Ogýgia, the island
haunt of Kalypso, Atlas' guileful daughter,
a lovely goddess and a dangerous one.
No one, no god or man, consorts with her;
but supernatural power brought me there 265
to be her solitary guest: for Zeus
let fly with his bright bolt and split my ship,
rolling me over in the winedark sea.
There all my shipmates, friends were drowned, while I
hung on the keelboard of the wreck and drifted 270
nine full days. Then in the dead of night
the gods brought me ashore upon Ogýgia
into her hands. The enchantress in her beauty
fed and caressed me, promised me I should be
immortal, youthful, all the days to come; 275
but in my heart I never gave consent
though seven years detained. Immortal clothing
I had from her, and kept it wet with tears.
Then came the eighth year on the wheel of heaven
and word to her from Zeus, or a change of heart, 280
so that she now commanded me to sail,
sending me out to sea on a craft I made
with timber and tools of hers. She gave me stores,
victuals and wine, a cloak divinely woven,
and made a warm land breeze come up astern. 285
Seventeen days I sailed in the open water
before I saw your country's shore, a shadow
upon the sea rim. Then my heart rejoiced—
pitiable as I am! For blows aplenty
awaited me from the god who shakes the earth. 290
Cross gales he blew, making me lose my bearings,
and heaved up seas beyond imagination—
huge and foundering seas. All I could do
was hold hard, groaning under every shock,
until my craft broke up in the hurricane. 295
I kept afloat and swam your sea, or drifted,
taken by wind and current to this coast
where I went in on big swells running landward.
But cliffs and rock shoals made that place forbidding,
so I turned back, swimming off shore, and came 300
in the end to a river, to auspicious water,
with smooth beach and a rise that broke the wind.

I lay there where I fell till strength returned.
Then sacred night came on, and I went inland
to high ground and a leaf bed in a thicket.   305
Heaven sent slumber in an endless tide
submerging my sad heart among the leaves.
That night and next day's dawn and noon I slept;
the sun went west; and then sweet sleep unbound me,
when I became aware of maids—your daughter's—   310
playing along the beach; the princess, too,
most beautiful. I prayed her to assist me,
and her good sense was perfect; one could hope
for no behavior like it from the young,
thoughtless as they most often are. But she   315
gave me good provender and good red wine,
a river bath, and finally this clothing.
There is the bitter tale. These are the facts."

But in reply Alkínoös observed:

"Friend, my child's good judgment failed in this—   320
not to have brought you in her company home.
Once you approached her, you became her charge."

To this Odysseus tactfully replied:

"Sir, as to that, you should not blame the princess.
She did tell me to follow with her maids,   325
but I would not. I felt abashed, and feared
the sight would somehow ruffle or offend you.
All of us on this earth are plagued by jealousy."

Alkínoös' answer was a declaration:

"Friend, I am not a man for trivial anger: 330
better a sense of measure in everything.
No anger here. I say that if it should please
our father Zeus, Athena, and Apollo—
seeing the man you are, seeing your thoughts
are my own thoughts—my daughter should be yours   335
and you my son-in-law, if you remained.
A home, lands, riches you should have from me
if you could be contented here. If not,
by Father Zeus, let none of our men hold you!
On the contrary, I can assure you now   340
of passage late tomorrow: while you sleep
my men will row you through the tranquil night
to your own land and home or where you please.
It may be, even, far beyond Euboia—
called most remote by seamen of our isle   345
who landed there, conveying Rhadamanthos
when he sought Títyos,[5] the son of Gaia.

5. A giant who tried to rape Lêto. In book 11 Odysseus sees him in the underworld, eternally punished for
his crime. Why Rhadamanthos went to see Títyos we have no idea.

They put about, with neither pause nor rest,
and entered their home port the selfsame day.
But this you, too, will see: what ships I have,   350
how my young oarsmen send the foam a-scudding!"

Now joy welled up in the patient Lord Odysseus
who said devoutly in the warmest tones:

"O Father Zeus, let all this be fulfilled
as spoken by Alkínoös! Earth of harvests   355
remember him! Return me to my homeland!"

In this manner they conversed with one another;
but the great lady called her maids, and sent them
to make a kingly bed, with purple rugs
piled up, and sheets outspread, and fleecy   360
coverlets, in an eastern colonnade.
The girls went out with torches in their hands,
swift at their work of bedmaking; returning
they whispered at the lord Odysseus' shoulder:

"Sir, you may come; your bed has been prepared."   365

How welcome the word "bed" came to his ears!
Now, then, Odysseus laid him down and slept
in luxury under the Porch of Morning,
while in his inner chamber Alkínoös
retired to rest where his dear consort lay.   370

BOOK VIII

[The Songs of the Harper]

Under the opening fingers of the dawn
Alkínoös, the sacred prince, arose,
and then arose Odysseus, raider of cities.
As the king willed, they went down by the shipways
to the assembly ground of the Phaiákians.   5
Side by side the two men took their ease there
on smooth stone benches. Meanwhile Pallas Athena
roamed through the byways of the town, contriving
Odysseus' voyage home—in voice and feature
the crier of the king Alkínoös   10
who stopped and passed the word to every man:

"Phaiákian lords and counselors, this way!
Come to assembly: learn about the stranger,
the new guest at the palace of Alkínoös—
a man the sea drove, but a comely man;   15
the gods' own light is on him."

                    She aroused them,
and soon the assembly ground and seats were filled

with curious men, a throng who peered and saw
the master mind of war, Laërtês' son.
Athena now poured out her grace upon him,   20
head and shoulders, height and mass—a splendor
awesome to the eyes of the Phaiákians;
she put him in a fettle to win the day,
mastering every trial they set to test him.
When all the crowd sat marshalled, quieted,   25
Alkínoös addressed the full assembly:

"Hear me, lords and captains of the Phaiákians!
Hear what my heart would have me say!
Our guest and new friend—nameless to me still—
comes to my house after long wandering   30
in Dawn lands, or among the Sunset races.
Now he appeals to me for conveyance home.
As in the past, therefore, let us provide
passage, and quickly, for no guest of mine
languishes here for lack of it. Look to it: 35
get a black ship afloat on the noble sea,
and pick our fastest sailer; draft a crew
of two and fifty from our younger townsmen—
men who have made their names at sea. Loop oars
well to your tholepins, lads, then leave the ship,   40
come to our house, fall to, and take your supper:
we'll furnish out a feast for every crewman.
These are your orders. As for my older peers
and princes of the realm, let them foregather
in festival for our friend in my great hall;   45
and let no man refuse. Call in our minstrel,
Demódokos, whom God made lord of song,
heart-easing, sing upon what theme he will."

He turned, led the procession, and those princes
followed, while his herald sought the minstrel.   50
Young oarsmen from the assembly chose a crew
of two and fifty, as the king commanded,
and these filed off along the waterside
to where the ship lay, poised above open water.
They hauled the black hull down to ride the sea,   55
rigging a mast and spar in the black ship,
with oars at trail from corded rawhide, all
seamanly; then tried the white sail, hoisting,
and moored her off the beach. Then going ashore
the crew went up to the great house of Alkínoös.   60
Here the enclosures, entrance ways, and rooms
were filled with men, young men and old, for whom
Alkínoös had put twelve sheep to sacrifice,
eight tuskers and a pair of shambling oxen.
These, now, they flayed and dressed to make their banquet.   65
The crier soon came, leading that man of song
whom the Muse cherished; by her gift he knew

the good of life, and evil—
for she who lent him sweetness made him blind.
Pontónoös fixed a studded chair for him   70
hard by a pillar amid the banqueters,
hanging the taut harp from a peg above him,
and guided up his hands upon the strings;
placed a bread basket at his side, and poured
wine in a cup, that he might drink his fill.   75
Now each man's hand went out upon the banquet.

In time, when hunger and thirst were turned away,
the Muse brought to the minstrel's mind a song
of heroes whose great fame rang under heaven:
the clash between Odysseus and Akhilleus,   80
how one time they contended at the godfeast
raging, and the marshal, Agamémnon,
felt inward joy over his captains' quarrel;
for such had been foretold him by Apollo
at Pytho⁶—hallowed height—when the Akhaian   85
crossed that portal of rock to ask a sign—
in the old days when grim war lay ahead
for Trojans and Danaans, by God's will.
So ran the tale the minstrel sang. Odysseus
with massive hand drew his rich mantle down   90
over his brow, cloaking his face with it,
to make the Phaiákians miss the secret tears
that started to his eyes. How skillfully
he dried them when the song came to a pause!
threw back his mantle, spilt his gout of wine!   95
But soon the minstrel plucked his note once more
to please the Phaiákian lords, who loved the song;
then in his cloak Odysseus wept again.
His tears flowed in the mantle unperceived;
only Alkínoös, at his elbow, saw them,   100
and caught the low groan in the man's breathing.
At once he spoke to all the seafolk round him:

"Hear me, lords and captains of the Phaiákians.
Our meat is shared, our hearts are full of pleasure
from the clear harp tone that accords with feasting;   105
now for the field and track; we shall have trials
in the pentathlon. Let our guest go home
and tell his friends what champions we are
at boxing, wrestling, broadjump and foot racing."

On this he led the way and all went after.   110
The crier unslung and pegged the shining harp
and, taking Demódokos's hand,
led him along with all the rest—Phaiákian
peers, gay amateurs of the great games.

6. The oracular shrine of Apollo at Delphi, high up on the mountainside.

They gained the common, where a crowd was forming,   115
and many a young athlete now came forward
with seaside names like Tipmast, Tiderace, Sparwood,
Hullman, Sternman, Beacher and Pullerman,
Bluewater, Shearwater, Runningwake, Boardalee,
Seabelt, son of Grandfleet Shipwrightson;   120
Seareach stepped up, son of the Launching Master,
rugged as Arês,[7] bane of men: his build
excelled all but the Prince Laódamas;
and Laódamas made entry with his brothers,
Halios and Klytóneus, sons of the king.   125
The runners, first, must have their quarter mile.
All lined up tense; then Go! and down the track
they raised the dust in a flying bunch, strung out
longer and longer behind Prince Klytóneus.
By just so far as a mule team, breaking ground,   130
will distance oxen, he left all behind
and came up to the crowd, an easy winner.
Then they made room for wrestling—grinding bouts
that Seareach won, pinning the strongest men;
then the broadjump; first place went to Seabelt;   135
Sparwood gave the discus the mightiest fling,
and Prince Laódamas outboxed them all.
Now it was he, the son of Alkínoös,
who said when they had run through these diversions:

"Look here, friends, we ought to ask the stranger   140
if he competes in something. He's no cripple;
look at his leg muscles and his forearms.
Neck like a bollard; strong as a bull, he seems;
and not old, though he may have gone stale under
the rough times he had. Nothing like the sea   145
for wearing out the toughest man alive."

Then Seareach took him up at once, and said:

"Laódamas, you're right, by all the powers.
Go up to him, yourself, and put the question."

At this, Alkínoös' tall son advanced   150
to the center ground, and there addressed Odysseus:

"Friend, Excellency, come join our competition,
if you are practiced, as you seem to be.
While a man lives he wins no greater honor
than footwork and the skill of hands can bring him.   155
Enter our games, then; ease your heart of trouble.
Your journey home is not far off, remember;
the ship is launched, the crew all primed for sea."

7. The Greek war god.

Odysseus, canniest of men, replied:

"Laódamas, why do you young chaps challenge me?   160
I have more on my mind than track and field—
hard days, and many, have I seen, and suffered.
I sit here at your field meet, yes; but only
as one who begs your king to send him home."

Now Seareach put his word in, and contentiously: 165

"The reason being, as I see it, friend,
you never learned a sport, and have no skill
in any of the contests of fighting men.
You must have been the skipper of some tramp
that crawled from one port to the next, jam full   170
of chaffering hands: a tallier of cargoes,
itching for gold—not, by your looks, an athlete."

Odysseus frowned, and eyed him coldly, saying:

"That was uncalled for, friend, you talk like a fool.
The gods deal out no gift, this one or any—   175
birth, brains, or speech—to every man alike.
In looks a man may be a shade, a specter,
and yet be master of speech so crowned with beauty
that people gaze at him with pleasure. Courteous,
sure of himself, he can command assemblies,   180
and when he comes to town, the crowds gather.
A handsome man, contrariwise, may lack
grace and good sense in everything he says.
You now, for instance, with your fine physique—
a god's, indeed—you have an empty noddle.   185
I find my heart inside my ribs aroused
by your impertinence. I am no stranger
to contests, as you fancy. I rated well
when I could count on youth and my two hands.
Now pain has cramped me, and my years of combat   190
hacking through ranks in war, and the bitter sea.
Aye. Even so I'll give your games a trial.
You spoke heart-wounding words. You shall be answered."

He leapt out, cloaked as he was, and picked a discus,
a rounded stone, more ponderous than those   195
already used by the Phaiákian throwers,
and, whirling, let it fly from his great hand
with a low hum. The crowd went flat on the ground—
all those oar-pulling, seafaring Phaiákians—
under the rushing noise. The spinning disk   200
soared out, light as a bird, beyond all others.
Disguised now as a Phaiákian, Athena
staked it and called out:

                   "Even a blind man,
friend, could judge this, finding with his fingers
one discus, quite alone, beyond the cluster.   205
Congratulations; this event is yours;
not a man here can beat you or come near you."

That was a cheering hail, Odysseus thought,
seeing one friend there on the emulous field,
so, in relief, he turned among the Phaiákians   210
and said:

                  "Now come alongside that one, lads.
The next I'll send as far, I think, or farther.
Anyone else on edge for competition
try me now. By heaven, you angered me.
Racing, wrestling, boxing—I bar nothing   215
with any man except Laódamas,
for he's my host. Who quarrels with his host?
Only a madman—or no man at all—
would challenge his protector among strangers,
cutting the ground away under his feet.   220
Here are no others I will not engage,
none but I hope to know what he is made of.
Inept at combat, am I? Not entirely.
Give me a smooth bow; I can handle it,
and I might well be first to hit my man   225
amid a swarm of enemies, though archers
in company around me drew together.
Philoktêtês[8] alone, at Troy, when we
Akhaians took the bow, used to outshoot me.
Of men who now eat bread upon the earth   230
I hold myself the best hand with a bow—
conceding mastery to the men of old,
Heraklês, or Eurýtos of Oikhalía,[9]
heroes who vied with gods in bowmanship.
Eurýtos came to grief, it's true; old age   235
never crept over him in his long hall;
Apollo took his challenge ill, and killed him.
What then, the spear? I'll plant it like an arrow.
Only in sprinting, I'm afraid, I may
be passed by someone. Roll of the sea waves   240
wearied me, and the victuals in my ship
ran low; my legs are flabby."

                          When he finished,
the rest were silent, but Alkínoös answered:

"Friend, we take your challenge in good part,
for this man angered and affronted you   245

---

8. He inherited the bow of Herakles, which never missed its mark.   9. Eurýtos of Oikhalía (in central Greece) challenged Apollo (also an archer) and was killed by the god. Eurýtos's bow was given to Odysseus by his son Iphitos, and it is with that bow that Odysseus will kill the suitors in book 22.

here at our peaceful games. You'd have us note
the prowess that is in you, and so clearly,
no man of sense would ever cry it down!
Come, turn your mind, now, on a thing to tell
among your peers when you are home again, 250
dining in hall, beside your wife and children:
I mean our prowess, as you may remember it,
for we, too, have our skills, given by Zeus,
and practiced from our father's time to this—
not in the boxing ring nor the palestra¹ 255
conspicuous, but in racing, land or sea;
and all our days we set great store by feasting,
harpers, and the grace of dancing choirs,
changes of dress, warm baths, and downy beds.
O master dancers of the Phaiákians! 260
Perform now: let our guest on his return
tell his companions we excel the world
in dance and song, as in our ships and running.
Someone go find the gittern² harp in hall
and bring it quickly to Demódokos!" 265

At the serene king's word, a squire ran
to bring the polished harp out of the palace,
and place was given to nine referees—
peers of the realm, masters of ceremony—
who cleared a space and smoothed a dancing floor. 270
The squire brought down, and gave Demódokos,
the clear-toned harp; and centering on the minstrel
magical young dancers formed a circle
with a light beat, and stamp of feet. Beholding,
Odysseus marvelled at the flashing ring. 275

Now to his harp the blinded minstrel sang
of Arês' dalliance with Aphroditê:
how hidden in Hephaistos' house they played
at love together, and the gifts of Arês,
dishonoring Hephaistos' bed—and how 280
the word that wounds the heart came to the master
from Hélios,³ who had seen the two embrace;
and when he learned it, Lord Hephaistos went
with baleful calculation to his forge.
There mightily he armed his anvil block 285
and hammered out a chain whose tempered links
could not be sprung or bent; he meant that they should hold.
Those shackles fashioned, hot in wrath Hephaistos
climbed to the bower and the bed of love,
pooled all his net of chain around the bed posts 290
and swung it from the rafters overhead—
light as a cobweb even gods in bliss
could not perceive, so wonderful his cunning.

1. Wrestling ground.   2. Shaped like a guitar.   3. The Sun, who sees everything.

Seeing his bed now made a snare, he feigned
a journey to the trim stronghold of Lemnos,   295
the dearest of earth's towns to him.[4] And Arês?
Ah, golden Arês' watch had its reward
when he beheld the great smith leaving home.
How promptly to the famous door he came,
intent on pleasure with sweet Kythereia![5]   300
She, who had left her father's side but now,
sat in her chamber when her lover entered;
and tenderly he pressed her hand and said:

"Come and lie down, my darling, and be happy!
Hephaistos is no longer here, but gone   305
to see his grunting[6] Sintian friends on Lemnos."

As she, too, thought repose would be most welcome,
the pair went in to bed—into a shower
of clever chains, the netting of Hephaistos.
So trussed, they could not move apart, nor rise,   310
at last they knew there could be no escape,
they were to see the glorious cripple now—
for Hêlios had spied for him, and told him;
so he turned back this side of Lemnos Isle,
sick at heart, making his way homeward.   315
Now in the doorway of the room he stood
while deadly rage took hold of him; his voice,
hoarse and terrible, reached all the gods:

"O Father Zeus, O gods in bliss forever,
here is indecorous entertainment for you,   320
Aphroditê, Zeus's daughter,
caught in the act, cheating me, her cripple,
with Arês—devastating Arês.
Cleanlimbed beauty is her joy, not these
bandylegs I came into the world with: 325
no one to blame but the two gods[7] who bred me!
Come see this pair entwining here
in my own bed! How hot it makes me burn!
I think they may not care to lie much longer,
pressing on one another, passionate lovers;   330
they'll have enough of bed together soon.
And yet the chain that bagged them holds them down
till Father sends me back my wedding gifts—
all that I poured out for his damned pigeon,
so lovely, and so wanton."

                    All the others   335
were crowding in, now, to the brazen house—
Poseidon who embraces earth, and Hermês

---

4. When Zeus threw him off Olympus (*Iliad* 1.711ff.), Hephaistos landed on the island of Lemnos (off the coast of Asia Minor), where the inhabitants took care of him.   **5.** A name for Aphrodite.   **6.** They do not speak Greek.   **7.** Zeus and Hera.

the runner, and Apollo, lord of Distance.
The goddesses stayed home for shame; but these
munificences ranged there in the doorway,   340
and irrepressible among them all
arose the laughter of the happy gods.
Gazing hard at Hephaistos' handiwork
the gods in turn remarked among themselves:

"No dash in adultery now."

                "The tortoise tags the hare—   345
Hephaistos catches Arês—and Arês outran the wind."

"The lame god's craft has pinned him. Now shall he
pay what is due from gods taken in cuckoldry."

They made these improving remarks to one another,
but Apollo leaned aside to say to Hermês: 350

"Son of Zeus, beneficent Wayfinder,
would you accept a coverlet of chain, if only
you lay by Aphroditê's golden side?"

To this the Wayfinder replied, shining:

"Would I not, though, Apollo of distances!   355
Wrap me in chains three times the weight of these,
come goddesses and gods to see the fun;
only let me lie beside the pale-golden one!"

The gods gave way again to peals of laughter,
all but Poseidon, and he never smiled,   360
but urged Hephaistos to unpinion Arês,
saying emphatically, in a loud voice:

                      "Free him;
you will be paid, I swear; ask what you will;
he pays up every jot the gods decree."

To this the Great Gamelegs replied:

                    "Poseidon,   365
lord of the earth-surrounding sea, I should not
swear to a scoundrel's honor. What have I
as surety from you, if Arês leaves me
empty-handed, with my empty chain?"

The Earth-shaker for answer urged again: 370

"Hephaistos, let us grant he goes, and leaves
the fine unpaid; I swear, then, I shall pay it."

Then said the Great Gamelegs at last:

                                    "No more;
you offer terms I cannot well refuse."

And down the strong god bent to set them free,   375
till disencumbered of their bond, the chain,
the lovers leapt away—he into Thrace,[8]
while Aphroditê, laughter's darling, fled
to Kypros[9] Isle and Paphos, to her meadow
and altar dim with incense. There the Graces   380
bathed and anointed her with golden oil—
a bloom that clings upon immortal flesh alone—
and let her folds of mantle fall in glory.

So ran the song the minstrel sang.

                                  Odysseus,
listening, found sweet pleasure in the tale,   385
among the Phaiákian mariners and oarsmen.
And next Alkínoös called upon his sons,
Halios and Laódamas, to show
the dance no one could do as well as they—
handling a purple ball carven by Pólybos.   390
One made it shoot up under the shadowing clouds
as he leaned backward; bounding high in air
the other cut its flight far off the ground—
and neither missed a step as the ball soared.
The next turn was to keep it low, and shuttling   395
hard between them, while the ring of boys
gave them a steady stamping beat.
Odysseus now addressed Alkínoös:

"O majesty, model of all your folk,
your promise was to show me peerless dancers;   400
here is the promise kept. I am all wonder."

At this Alkínoös in his might rejoicing
said to the seafarers of Phaiákia:

"Attend me now, Phaiákian lords and captains:
our guest appears a clear-eyed man and wise.   405
Come, let him feel our bounty as he should.
Here are twelve princes of the kingdom—lords
paramount, and I who make thirteen;
let each one bring a laundered cloak and tunic,
and add one bar of honorable gold.   410
Heap all our gifts together; load his arms;
let him go joyous to our evening feast!
As for Seareach—why, man to man

---

8. Non-Greek territory to the north, which was supposed to be Arês' home.   9. Or Cyprus, where Aphrodite had a famous shrine at Paphos.

he'll make amends, and handsomely; he blundered."

Now all as one acclaimed the king's good pleasure,   415
and each one sent a squire to bring his gifts.
Meanwhile Seareach found speech again, saying:

"My lord and model of us all, Alkínoös,
as you require of me, in satisfaction,
this broadsword of clear bronze goes to our guest.   420
Its hilt is silver, and the ringed sheath
of new-sawn ivory—a costly weapon."

He turned to give the broadsword to Odysseus,
facing him, saying blithely:

                                            "Sir, my best
wishes, my respects; if I offended,   425
I hope the seawinds blow it out of mind.
God send you see your lady and your homeland
soon again, after the pain of exile."

Odysseus, the great tactician, answered:

"My hand, friend; may the gods award you fortune.   430
I hope no pressing need comes on you ever
for this fine blade you give me in amends."

He slung it, glinting silver, from his shoulder,
as the light shone from sundown. Messengers
were bearing gifts and treasure to the palace,   435
where the king's sons received them all, and made
a glittering pile at their grave mother's side;
then, as Alkínoös took his throne of power,
each went to his own high-backed chair in turn,
and said Alkínoös to Arêtê: 440

"Lady, bring here a chest, the finest one;
a clean cloak and tunic; stow these things;
and warm a cauldron for him. Let him bathe,
when he has seen the gifts of the Phaiákians,
and so dine happily to a running song.   445
My own wine-cup of gold intaglio
I'll give him, too; through all the days to come,
tipping his wine to Zeus or other gods
in his great hall, he shall remember me."

Then said Arêtê to her maids:
                                        "The tripod: 450
stand the great tripod legs about the fire."

They swung the cauldron on the fire's heart,
poured water in, and fed the blaze beneath

until the basin simmered, cupped in flame.
The queen set out a rich chest from her chamber   455
and folded in the gifts—clothing and gold
given Odysseus by the Phaiákians;
then she put in the royal cloak and tunic,
briskly saying to her guest:

                    "Now here, sir,
look to the lid yourself, and tie it down   460
against light fingers, if there be any,
on the black ship tonight while you are sleeping."

Noble Odysseus, expert in adversity,
battened the lid down with a lightning knot
learned, once, long ago, from the Lady Kirkê.[1]   465
And soon a call came from the Bathing Mistress
who led him to a hip-bath, warm and clear—
a happy sight, and rare in his immersions
after he left Kalypso's home—where, surely,
the luxuries of a god were ever his.   470
When the bath maids had washed him, rubbed him down,
put a fresh tunic and a cloak around him,
he left the bathing place to join the men
at wine in hall.

               The princess Nausikaa,
exquisite figure, as of heaven's shaping,   475
waited beside a pillar as he passed
and said swiftly, with wonder in her look:

"Fare well, stranger; in your land remember me
who met and saved you. It is worth your thought."

The man of all occasions now met this: 480

"Daughter of great Alkínoös, Nausikaa,
may Zeus the lord of thunder, Hera's consort,
grant me daybreak again in my own country!
But there and all my days until I die
may I invoke you as I would a goddess,   485
princess, to whom I owe my life."

                  He left her
and went to take his place beside the king.

Now when the roasts were cut, the winebowls full,
a herald led the minstrel down the room
amid the deference of the crowd, and paused   490
to seat him near a pillar in the center—

---

1. Or Circe, a divine sorceress on whose island Odysseus had spent some time during his travels (book 12).

whereupon that resourceful man, Odysseus,
carved out a quarter from his chine of pork,
crisp with fat, and called the blind man's guide:

"Herald! here, take this to Demódokos: 495
let him feast and be merry, with my compliments.
All men owe honor to the poets—honor
and awe, for they are dearest to the Muse
who puts upon their lips the ways of life."

Gentle Demódokos took the proffered gift   500
and inwardly rejoiced. When all were served,
every man's hand went out upon the banquet,
repelling hunger and thirst, until at length
Odysseus spoke again to the blind minstrel:

"Demódokos, accept my utmost praise.   505
The Muse, daughter of Zeus in radiance,
or else Apollo gave you skill to shape
with such great style your songs of the Akhaians—
their hard lot, how they fought and suffered war.
You shared it, one would say, or heard it all.   510
Now shift your theme, and sing that wooden horse
Epeios built, inspired by Athena—
the ambuscade Odysseus filled with fighters
and sent to take the inner town of Troy.
Sing only this for me, sing me this well,   515
and I shall say at once before the world
the grace of heaven has given us a song."

The minstrel stirred, murmuring to the god, and soon
clear words and notes came one by one, a vision
of the Akhaians in their graceful ships   520
drawing away from shore: the torches flung
and shelters flaring: Argive soldiers crouched
in the close dark around Odysseus: and
the horse, tall on the assembly ground of Troy.
For when the Trojans pulled it in, themselves,   525
up to the citadel, they sat nearby
with long-drawn-out and hapless argument—
favoring, in the end, one course of three:
either to stave the vault with brazen axes,
or haul it to a cliff and pitch it down,   530
or else to save it for the gods, a votive glory—
the plan that could not but prevail.
For Troy must perish, as ordained, that day
she harbored the great horse of timber; hidden
the flower of Akhaia lay, and bore   535
slaughter and death upon the men of Troy.
He sang, then, of the town sacked by Akhaians
pouring down from the horse's hollow cave,
this way and that way raping the steep city,

and how Odysseus came like Arês to 540
the door of Deïphobos, with Meneláos,
and braved the desperate fight there—
conquering once more by Athena's power.

The splendid minstrel sang it.

           And Odysseus
let the bright molten tears run down his cheeks, 545
weeping the way a wife mourns for her lord
on the lost field where he has gone down fighting
the day of wrath that came upon his children.
At sight of the man panting and dying there,
she slips down to enfold him, crying out; 550
then feels the spears, prodding her back and shoulders,
and goes bound into slavery and grief.
Piteous weeping wears away her cheeks:
but no more piteous than Odysseus' tears,
cloaked as they were, now, from the company. 555
Only Alkínoös, at his elbow, knew—
hearing the low sob in the man's breathing—
and when he knew, he spoke:

"Hear me, lords and captains of Phaiákia!
And let Demódokos touch his harp no more. 560
His theme has not been pleasing to all here.
During the feast, since our fine poet sang,
our guest has never left off weeping. Grief
seems fixed upon his heart. Break off the song!
Let everyone be easy, host and guest; 565
there's more decorum in a smiling banquet!
We had prepared here, on our friend's behalf,
safe conduct in a ship, and gifts to cheer him,
holding that any man with a grain of wit
will treat a decent suppliant like a brother. 570
Now by the same rule, friend, you must not be
secretive any longer! Come, in fairness,
tell me the name you bore in that far country;
how were you known to family, and neighbors?
No man is nameless—no man, good or bad, 575
but gets a name in his first infancy,
none being born, unless a mother bears him!
Tell me your native land, your coast and city—
sailing directions for the ships, you know—
for those Phaiákian ships of ours 580
that have no steersman, and no steering oar,
divining the crew's wishes, as they do,
and knowing, as they do, the ports of call
about the world. Hidden in mist or cloud
they scud the open sea, with never a thought 585
of being in distress or going down.
There is, however, something I once heard

Nausíthoös, my father, say: Poseidon
holds it against us that our deep sea ships
are sure conveyance for all passengers.   590
My father said, some day one of our cutters
homeward bound over the cloudy sea
would be wrecked by the god, and a range of hills
thrown round our city. So, in his age, he said,
and let it be, or not, as the god please.   595
But come, now, put it for me clearly, tell me
the sea ways that you wandered, and the shores
you touched; the cities, and the men therein,
uncivilized, if such there were, and hostile,
and those godfearing who had kindly manners.   600
Tell me why you should grieve so terribly
over the Argives and the fall of Troy.
That was all gods' work, weaving ruin there
so it should make a song for men to come!
Some kin of yours, then, died at Ilion,   605
some first rate man, by marriage near to you,
next your own blood most dear?
Or some companion of congenial mind
and valor? True it is, a wise friend
can take a brother's place in our affection."   610

BOOK IX

[*New Coasts and Poseidon's Son*]

Now this was the reply Odysseus made:

"Alkínoös, king and admiration of men,
how beautiful this is, to hear a minstrel
gifted as yours: a god he might be, singing!
There is no boon in life more sweet, I say,   5
then when a summer joy holds all the realm,
and banqueters sit listening to a harper
in a great hall, by rows of tables heaped
with bread and roast meat, while a steward goes
to dip up wine and brim your cups again.   10
Here is the flower of life, it seems to me!
But now you wish to know my cause for sorrow—
and thereby give me cause for more.
                              What shall I
say first? What shall I keep until the end?
The gods have tried me in a thousand ways.   15
But first my name: let that be known to you,
and if I pull away from pitiless death,
friendship will bind us, though my land lies far.

I am Laërtês' son, Odysseus.
                              Men hold me
formidable for guile in peace and war: 20
this fame has gone abroad to the sky's rim.

My home is on the peaked sea-mark of Ithaka
under Mount Neion's wind-blown robe of leaves,
in sight of other islands—Doulíkhion,
Samê, wooded Zakynthos—Ithaka   25
being most lofty in that coastal sea,
and northwest, while the rest lie east and south.
A rocky isle, but good for a boy's training;
I shall not see on earth a place more dear,
though I have been detained long by Kalypso,   30
loveliest among goddesses, who held me
in her smooth caves, to be her heart's delight,
as Kirkê of Aiaia, the enchantress,
desired me, and detained me in her hall.
But in my heart I never gave consent.   35
Where shall a man find sweetness to surpass
his own home and his parents? In far lands
he shall not, though he find a house of gold.

What of my sailing, then, from Troy?
                              What of those years
of rough adventure, weathered under Zeus?   40
The wind that carried west from Ilion
brought me to Ísmaros, on the far shore,
a strongpoint on the coast of the Kikonês.[2]
I stormed that place and killed the men who fought.
Plunder we took, and we enslaved the women,   45
to make division, equal shares to all—
but on the spot I told them: 'Back, and quickly!
Out to sea again!' My men were mutinous,
fools, on stores of wine. Sheep after sheep
they butchered by the surf, and shambling cattle,   50
feasting,—while fugitives went inland, running
to call to arms the main force of Kikonês.
This was an army, trained to fight on horseback
or, where the ground required, on foot. They came
with dawn over that terrain like the leaves   55
and blades of spring. So doom appeared to us,
dark word of Zeus for us, our evil days.
My men stood up and made a fight of it—
backed on the ships, with lances kept in play,
from bright morning through the blaze of noon   60
holding our beach, although so far outnumbered;
but when the sun passed toward unyoking time,
then the Akhaians, one by one, gave way.
Six benches were left empty in every ship
that evening when we pulled away from death.   65
And this new grief we bore with us to sea:
our precious lives we had, but not our friends.
No ship made sail next day until some shipmate
had raised a cry, three times, for each poor ghost
unfleshed by the Kikonês on that field.   70

2. Allies of the Trojans, but Odysseus does not even mention this fact to excuse the piratical raid; he did
not think any excuse was needed.

Now Zeus the lord of cloud roused in the north
a storm against the ships, and driving veils
of squall moved down like night on land and sea.
The bows went plunging at the gust; sails
cracked and lashed out strips in the big wind.   75
We saw death in that fury, dropped the yards,
unshipped the oars, and pulled for the nearest lee:
then two long days and nights we lay offshore
worn out and sick at heart, tasting our grief,
until a third Dawn came with ringlets shining.   80
Then we put up our masts, hauled sail, and rested,
letting the steersmen and the breeze take over.

I might have made it safely home, that time,
but as I came round Malea the current
took me out to sea, and from the north   85
a fresh gale drove me on, past Kythera.[3]
Nine days I drifted on the teeming sea
before dangerous high winds. Upon the tenth
we came to the coastline of the Lotos Eaters,[4]
who live upon that flower. We landed there   90
to take on water. All ships' companies
mustered alongside for the mid-day meal.
Then I sent out two picked men and a runner
to learn what race of men that land sustained.
They fell in, soon enough, with Lotos Eaters,   95
who showed no will to do us harm, only
offering the sweet Lotos to our friends—
but those who ate this honeyed plant, the Lotos,
never cared to report, nor to return:
they longed to stay forever, browsing on   100
that native bloom, forgetful of their homeland.
I drove them, all three wailing, to the ships,
tied them down under their rowing benches,
and called the rest: 'All hands aboard;
come, clear the beach and no one taste   105
the Lotos, or you lose your hope of home.'
Filing in to their places by the rowlocks
my oarsmen dipped their long oars in the surf,
and we moved out again on our sea faring.

In the next land we found were Kyklopês,[5]   110
giants, louts, without a law to bless them.
In ignorance leaving the fruitage of the earth in mystery
to the immortal gods, they neither plow
nor sow by hand, nor till the ground, though grain—
wild wheat and barley—grows untended, and   115
wine-grapes, in clusters, ripen in heaven's rain.
Kyklopês have no muster and no meeting,

3. A large island off Malea, the southeastern tip of the Peloponnese.   4. It is generally thought that this
story contains some memory of early Greek contact with North Africa. The north wind Odysseus describes
would have taken him to the area of Cyrenaica, or modern Libya. Identifications of the Lotos range from
dates to hashish.   5. According to ancient tradition the Kyklopês lived in Sicily.

no consultation or old tribal ways,
but each one dwells in his own mountain cave
dealing out rough justice to wife and child,   120
indifferent to what the others do.
                               Well, then:
across the wide bay from the mainland
there lies a desert island, not far out,
but still not close inshore. Wild goats in hundreds
breed there; and no human being comes   125
upon the isle to startle them—no hunter
of all who ever tracked with hounds through forests
or had rough going over mountain trails.
The isle, unplanted and untilled, a wilderness,
pastures goats alone. And this is why: 130
good ships like ours with cheekpaint at the bows[6]
are far beyond the Kyklopês. No shipwright
toils among them, shaping and building up
symmetrical trim hulls to cross the sea
and visit all the seaboard towns, as men do   135
who go and come in commerce over water.
This isle—seagoing folk would have annexed it
and built their homesteads on it: all good land,
fertile for every crop in season: lush
well-watered meads along the shore, vines in profusion,   140
prairie, clear for the plow, where grain would grow
chin high by harvest time, and rich sub-soil.
The island cove is landlocked, so you need
no hawsers out astern, bow-stones[7] or mooring:
run in and ride there till the day your crews   145
chafe to be under sail, and a fair wind blows.
You'll find good water flowing from a cavern
through dusky poplars into the upper bay.
Here we made harbor. Some god guided us
that night, for we could barely see our bows   150
in the dense fog around us, and no moonlight
filtered through the overcast. No look-out,
nobody saw the island dead ahead,
nor even the great landward rolling billow
that took us in: we found ourselves in shallows,   155
keels grazing shore: so furled our sails
and disembarked where the low ripples broke.
There on the beach we lay, and slept till morning.

When Dawn spread out her finger tips of rose
we turned out marvelling, to tour the isle,   160
while Zeus's shy nymph daughters flushed wild goats
down from the heights—a breakfast for my men.
We ran to fetch our hunting bows and long-shanked
lances from the ships, and in three companies
we took our shots. Heaven gave us game a-plenty: 165
for every one of twelve ships in my squadron

6. On a Greek ship an emblem (often shown as a huge eye on vase paintings) was painted on the bows.
7. A primitive anchor made up of a stone attached to a rope.

nine goats fell to be shared; my lot was ten.
So there all day, until the sun went down,
we made our feast on meat galore, and wine—
wine from the ship, for our supply held out,　　　　　　　170
so many jars were filled at Ísmaros
from stores of the Kikonês that we plundered.
We gazed, too, at Kyklopês Land, so near,
we saw their smoke, heard bleating from their flocks.
But after sundown, in the gathering dusk,　　　　　　　175
we slept again above the wash of ripples.
When the young Dawn with finger tips of rose
came in the east, I called my men together
and made a speech to them:

　　　　　　　　　'Old shipmates, friends,
the rest of you stand by; I'll make the crossing　　　　　180
in my own ship, with my own company,
and find out what the mainland natives are—
for they may be wild savages, and lawless,
or hospitable and god-fearing men.'

At this I went aboard, and gave the word　　　　　　　185
to cast off by the stern. My oarsmen followed,
filing in to their benches by the rowlocks,
and all in line dipped oars in the grey sea.

As we rowed on, and nearer to the mainland,
at one end of the bay, we saw a cavern　　　　　　　190
yawning above the water, screened with laurel,
and many rams and goats about the place
inside a sheepfold—made from slabs of stone
earthfast between tall trunks of pine and rugged
towering oak trees.
　　　　　　　A prodigious man　　　　　　　195
slept in this cave alone, and took his flocks
to graze afield—remote from all companions,
knowing none but savage ways, a brute
so huge, he seemed no man at all of those
who eat good wheaten bread; but he seemed rather　　200
a shaggy mountain reared in solitude.
We beached there, and I told the crew
to stand by and keep watch over the ship;
as for myself I took my twelve best fighters
and went ahead. I had a goatskin full　　　　　　　205
of that sweet liquor that Euanthês' son,
Maron, had given me. He kept Apollo's
holy grove at Ísmaros; for kindness
we showed him there, and showed his wife and child,
he gave me seven shining golden talents[8]　　　　　　210
perfectly formed, a solid silver winebowl,
and then this liquor—twelve two-handled jars

8. Ingots of gold. The talent was a standard weight.

of brandy, pure and fiery. Not a slave
in Maron's household knew this drink; only
he, his wife and the storeroom mistress knew;   215
and they would put one cupful—ruby-colored,
honey-smooth—in twenty more of water,
but still the sweet scent hovered like a fume
over the winebowl. No man turned away
when cups of this came round.
                                        A wineskin full   220
I brought along, and victuals in a bag,
for in my bones I knew some towering brute
would be upon us soon—all outward power,
a wild man, ignorant of civility.

We climbed, then, briskly to the cave. But Kyklops   225
had gone afield, to pasture his fat sheep,
so we looked round at everything inside:
a drying rack that sagged with cheeses, pens
crowded with lambs and kids, each in its class:
firstlings apart from middlings, and the 'dewdrops,'   230
or newborn lambkins, penned apart from both.
And vessels full of whey were brimming there—
bowls of earthenware and pails of milking.
My men came pressing round me, pleading:

                              'Why not
take these cheeses, get them stowed, come back,   235
throw open all the pens, and make a run for it?
We'll drive the kids and lambs aboard. We say
put out again on good salt water!'

                        Ah,
how sound that was! Yet I refused, I wished
to see the caveman, what he had to offer—   240
no pretty sight, it turned out, for my friends.
We lit a fire, burnt an offering,
and took some cheese to eat; then sat in silence
around the embers, waiting. When he came
he had a load of dry boughs on his shoulder   245
to stoke his fire at suppertime. He dumped it
with a great crash into that hollow cave,
and we all scattered fast to the far wall.
Then over the broad cavern floor he ushered
the ewes he meant to milk. He left his rams   250
and he-goats in the yard outside, and swung
high overhead a slab of solid rock
to close the cave. Two dozen four-wheeled wagons,
with heaving wagon teams, could not have stirred
the tonnage of that rock from where he wedged it   255
over the doorsill. Next he took his seat
and milked his bleating ewes. A practiced job
he made of it, giving each ewe her suckling;

thickened his milk, then, into curds and whey,
sieved out the curds to drip in withy baskets, 260
and poured the whey to stand in bowls
cooling until he drank it for his supper.
When all these chores were done, he poked the fire,
heaping on brushwood. In the glare he saw us.

'Strangers,' he said, 'who are you? And where from? 265
What brings you here by sea ways—a fair traffic?
Or are you wandering rogues, who cast your lives
like dice, and ravage other folk by sea?'

We felt a pressure on our hearts, in dread
of that deep rumble and that mighty man. 270
But all the same I spoke up in reply:

'We are from Troy, Akhaians, blown off course
by shifting gales on the Great South Sea;
homeward bound, but taking routes and ways
uncommon; so the will of Zeus would have it. 275
We served under Agamémnon, son of Atreus—
the whole world knows what city
he laid waste, what armies he destroyed.
It was our luck to come here; here we stand,
beholden for your help, or any gifts 280
you give—as custom is to honor strangers.[9]
We would entreat you, great Sir, have a care
for the gods' courtesy; Zeus will avenge
the unoffending guest.'

　　　　　　He answered this
from his brute chest, unmoved:

　　　　　　　　　　　'You are a ninny, 285
or else you come from the other end of nowhere,
telling me, mind the gods! We Kyklopês
care not a whistle for your thundering Zeus
or all the gods in bliss; we have more force by far.
I would not let you go for fear of Zeus— 290
you or your friends—unless I had a whim to.
Tell me, where was it, now, you left your ship—
around the point, or down the shore, I wonder?'

He thought he'd find out, but I saw through this,
and answered with a ready lie:

　　　　　　　　　　　'My ship? 295
Poseidon Lord, who sets the earth a-tremble,
broke it up on the rocks at your land's end.

---

9. It is the mark of civilized people in the *Odyssey*, like Meneláos and Alkínoös, that they welcome strangers
and send them on their way with gifts.

A wind from seaward served him, drove us there.
We are survivors, these good men and I.'

Neither reply nor pity came from him,   300
but in one stride he clutched at my companions
and caught two in his hands like squirming puppies
to beat their brains out, spattering the floor.
Then he dismembered them and made his meal,
gaping and crunching like a mountain lion—   305
everything: innards, flesh, and marrow bones.
We cried aloud, lifting our hands to Zeus,
powerless, looking on at this, appalled;
but Kyklops went on filling up his belly
with manflesh and great gulps of whey,   310
then lay down like a mast among his sheep.
My heart beat high now at the chance of action,
and drawing the sharp sword from my hip I went
along his flank to stab him where the midriff
holds the liver. I had touched the spot   315
when sudden fear stayed me: if I killed him
we perished there as well, for we could never
move his ponderous doorway slab aside.
So we were left to groan and wait for morning.

When the young Dawn with finger tips of rose   320
lit up the world, the Kyklops built a fire
and milked his handsome ewes, all in due order,
putting the sucklings to the mothers. Then,
his chores being all dispatched, he caught
another brace of men to make his breakfast,   325
and whisked away his great door slab
to let his sheep go through—but he, behind,
reset the stone as one would cap a quiver.
There was a din of whistling as the Kyklops
rounded his flock to higher ground, then stillness.   330
And now I pondered how to hurt him worst,
if but Athena granted what I prayed for.
Here are the means I thought would serve my turn:

a club, or staff, lay there along the fold—
an olive tree, felled green and left to season   335
for Kyklops' hand. And it was like a mast
a lugger of twenty oars, broad in the beam—
a deep-sea going craft—might carry:
so long, so big around, it seemed. Now I
chopped out a six foot section of this pole   340
and set it down before my men, who scraped it;
and when they had it smooth, I hewed again
to make a stake with pointed end. I held this
in the fire's heart and turned it, toughening it,
then hid it, well back in the cavern, under   345
one of the dung piles in profusion there.

Now came the time to toss for it: who ventured
along with me? whose hand could bear to thrust
and grind that spike in Kyklops' eye, when mild
sleep had mastered him? As luck would have it,   350
the men I would have chosen won the toss—
four strong men, and I made five as captain.

At evening came the shepherd with his flock,
his woolly flock. The rams as well, this time,
entered the cave: by some sheep-herding whim—   355
or a god's bidding—none were left outside.
He hefted his great boulder into place
and sat him down to milk the bleating ewes
in proper order, put the lambs to suck,
and swiftly ran through all his evening chores.   360
Then he caught two more men and feasted on them.
My moment was at hand, and I went forward
holding an ivy bowl of my dark drink,
looking up, saying:

                    'Kyklops, try some wine.
Here's liquor to wash down your scraps of men.   365
Taste it, and see the kind of drink we carried
under our planks. I meant it for an offering
if you would help us home. But you are mad,
unbearable, a bloody monster! After this,
will any other traveller come to see you?'   370

He seized and drained the bowl, and it went down
so fiery and smooth he called for more:

'Give me another, thank you kindly. Tell me,
how are you called? I'll make a gift will please you.
Even Kyklopês know the wine-grapes grow   375
out of grassland and loam in heaven's rain,
but here's a bit of nectar and ambrosia!'

Three bowls I brought him, and he poured them down.
I saw the fuddle and flush come over him,
then I sang out in cordial tones:

                    'Kyklops,   380
you ask my honorable name? Remember
the gift you promised me, and I shall tell you.
My name is Nohbdy: mother, father, and friends,
everyone calls me Nohbdy.'

                And he said:

'Nohbdy's my meat, then, after I eat his friends.   385
Others come first. There's a noble gift, now.'

Even as he spoke, he reeled and tumbled backward,
his great head lolling to one side: and sleep
took him like any creature. Drunk, hiccuping,
he dribbled streams of liquor and bits of men.   390

Now, by the gods, I drove my big hand spike
deep in the embers, charring it again,
and cheered my men along with battle talk
to keep their courage up: no quitting now.
The pike of olive, green though it had been,   395
reddened and glowed as if about to catch.
I drew it from the coals and my four fellows
gave me a hand, lugging it near the Kyklops
as more than natural force nerved them; straight
forward they sprinted, lifted it, and rammed it   400
deep in his crater eye, and I leaned on it
turning it as a shipwright turns a drill
in planking, having men below to swing
the two-handled strap that spins it in the groove.
So with our brand we bored that great eye socket   405
while blood ran out around the red hot bar.
Eyelid and lash were seared; the pierced ball
hissed broiling, and the roots popped.

                       In a smithy
one sees a white-hot axehead or an adze
plunged and wrung in a cold tub, screeching steam—   410
the way they make soft iron hale and hard—:
just so that eyeball hissed around the spike.
The Kyklops bellowed and the rock roared round him,
and we fell back in fear. Clawing his face
he tugged the bloody spike out of his eye,   415
threw it away, and his wild hands went groping;
then he set up a howl for Kyklopês
who lived in caves on windy peaks nearby.
Some heard him; and they came by divers ways
to clump around outside and call:

                              'What ails you,   420
Polyphêmos? Why do you cry so sore
in the starry night? You will not let us sleep.
Sure no man's driving off your flock? No man
has tricked you, ruined you?'

                        Out of the cave
the mammoth Polyphêmos roared in answer: 425

'Nohbdy, Nohbdy's tricked me, Nohbdy's ruined me!'

To this rough shout they made a sage reply:

'Ah well, if nobody has played you foul
there in your lonely bed, we are no use in pain

given by great Zeus. Let it be your father,   430
Poseidon Lord, to whom you pray.'

                              So saying
they trailed away. And I was filled with laughter
to see how like a charm the name deceived them.
Now Kyklops, wheezing as the pain came on him,
fumbled to wrench away the great doorstone   435
and squatted in the breach with arms thrown wide
for any silly beast or man who bolted—
hoping somehow I might be such a fool.
But I kept thinking how to win the game:
death sat there huge; how could we slip away?   440
I drew on all my wits, and ran through tactics,
reasoning as a man will for dear life,
until a trick came—and it pleased me well.
The Kyklops' rams were handsome, fat, with heavy
fleeces, a dark violet.
                              Three abreast   445
I tied them silently together, twining
cords of willow from the ogre's bed;
then slung a man under each middle one
to ride there safely, shielded left and right.
So three sheep could convey each man. I took   450
the woolliest ram, the choicest of the flock,
and hung myself under his kinky belly,
pulled up tight, with fingers twisted deep
in sheepskin ringlets for an iron grip.
So, breathing hard, we waited until morning.   455

When Dawn spread out her finger tips of rose
the rams began to stir, moving for pasture,
and peals of bleating echoed round the pens
where dams with udders full called for a milking.
Blinded, and sick with pain from his head wound,   460
the master stroked each ram, then let it pass,
but my men riding on the pectoral fleece
the giant's blind hands blundering never found.
Last of them all my ram, the leader, came,
weighted by wool and me with my meditations.   465
The Kyklops patted him, and then he said:

'Sweet cousin ram, why lag behind the rest
in the night cave? You never linger so,
but graze before them all, and go afar
to crop sweet grass, and take your stately way   470
leading along the streams, until at evening
you run to be the first one in the fold.
Why, now, so far behind? Can you be grieving
over your Master's eye? That carrion rogue
and his accurst companions burnt it out   475
when he had conquered all my wits with wine.

Nohbdy will not get out alive, I swear.
Oh, had you brain and voice to tell
where he may be now, dodging all my fury!
Bashed by this hand and bashed on this rock wall   480
his brains would strew the floor, and I should have
rest from the outrage Nohbdy worked upon me.'

He sent us into the open, then. Close by,
I dropped and rolled clear of the ram's belly,
going this way and that to untie the men.   485
With many glances back, we rounded up
his fat, stiff-legged sheep to take aboard,
and drove them down to where the good ship lay.
We saw, as we came near, our fellows' faces
shining; then we saw them turn to grief   490
tallying those who had not fled from death.
I hushed them, jerking head and eyebrows up,
and in a low voice told them: 'Load this herd;
move fast, and put the ship's head toward the breakers.'
They all pitched in at loading, then embarked   495
and struck their oars into the sea. Far out,
as far off shore as shouted words would carry,
I sent a few back to the adversary:

'O Kyklops! Would you feast on my companions?
Puny, am I, in a Caveman's hands?   500
How do you like the beating that we gave you,
you damned cannibal? Eater of guests
under your roof! Zeus and the gods have paid you!'

The blind thing in his doubled fury broke
a hilltop in his hands and heaved it after us.   505
Ahead of our black prow it struck and sank
whelmed in a spuming geyser, a giant wave
that washed the ship stern foremost back to shore.
I got the longest boathook out and stood
fending us off, with furious nods to all   510
to put their backs into a racing stroke—
row, row, or perish. So the long oars bent
kicking the foam sternward, making head
until we drew away, and twice as far.
Now when I cupped my hands I heard the crew   515
in low voices protesting:

                'Godsake, Captain!
Why bait the beast again? Let him alone!'

'That tidal wave he made on the first throw
all but beached us.'

                'All but stove us in!'

'Give him our bearing with your trumpeting,   520
he'll get the range and lob a boulder.'

                                        'Aye
He'll smash our timbers and our heads together!'

I would not heed them in my glorying spirit,
but let my anger flare and yelled:

                                        'Kyklops,
if ever mortal man inquire   525
how you were put to shame and blinded, tell him
Odysseus, raider of cities, took your eye:
Laërtês' son, whose home's on Ithaka!'

At this he gave a mighty sob and rumbled:

'Now comes the weird[1] upon me, spoken of old.   530
A wizard, grand and wondrous, lived here—Télemos,
a son of Eurymos; great length of days
he had in wizardry among the Kyklopês,
and these things he foretold for time to come:
my great eye lost, and at Odysseus' hands.   535
Always I had in mind some giant, armed
in giant force, would come against me here.
But this, but you—small, pitiful and twiggy—
you put me down with wine, you blinded me.
Come back, Odysseus, and I'll treat you well,   540
praying the god of earthquake to befriend you—
his son I am, for he by his avowal
fathered me, and, if he will, he may
heal me of this black wound—he and no other
of all the happy gods or mortal men.'   545

Few words I shouted in reply to him:

'If I could take your life I would and take
your time away, and hurl you down to hell!
The god of earthquake could not heal you there!'

At this he stretched his hands out in his darkness   550
toward the sky of stars, and prayed Poseidon:

'O hear me, lord, blue girdler of the islands,
if I am thine indeed, and thou art father:
grant that Odysseus, raider of cities, never
see his home: Laërtês' son, I mean,   555
who kept his hall on Ithaka. Should destiny
intend that he shall see his roof again
among his family in his father land,

1. Fate, destiny.

far be that day, and dark the years between.
Let him lose all companions, and return   560
under strange sail to bitter days at home.'

In these words he prayed, and the god heard him.
Now he laid hands upon a bigger stone
and wheeled around, titanic for the cast,
to let it fly in the black-prowed vessel's track.   565
But it fell short, just aft the steering oar,
and whelming seas rose giant above the stone
to bear us onward toward the island.
                                    There
as we ran in we saw the squadron waiting,
the trim ships drawn up side by side, and all   570
our troubled friends who waited, looking seaward.
We beached her, grinding keel in the soft sand,
and waded in, ourselves, on the sandy beach.
Then we unloaded all the Kyklops' flock
to make division, share and share alike,   575
only my fighters voted that my ram,
the prize of all, should go to me. I slew him
by the sea side and burnt his long thighbones
to Zeus beyond the stormcloud, Kronos' son,
who rules the world. But Zeus disdained my offering;   580
destruction for my ships he had in store
and death for those who sailed them, my companions.
Now all day long until the sun went down
we made our feast on mutton and sweet wine,
till after sunset in the gathering dark   585
we went to sleep above the wash of ripples.

When the young Dawn with finger tips of rose
touched the world, I roused the men, gave orders
to man the ships, cast off the mooring lines;
and filing in to sit beside the rowlocks   590
oarsmen in line dipped oars in the grey sea.
So we moved out, sad in the vast offing,
having our precious lives, but not our friends.

BOOK X

[The Grace of the Witch]

We made our landfall on Aiolia Island,
domain of Aiolos[2] Hippotadês,
the wind king dear to the gods who never die—
an isle adrift upon the sea, ringed round
with brazen ramparts on a sheer cliffside.   5
Twelve children had old Aiolos at home—

2. King of the winds (whose name in Greek means "shifting, changeable"). Aiolia was a moving island that has been located by modern geographers in the Lipari Islands off the Sicilian coast. The great ancient geographer Eratosthenes was not so confident. He once said that we would know exactly where Odysseus wandered after we had traced the leatherworker who made the bag in which the winds were contained.

six daughters and six lusty sons—and he
gave girls to boys to be their gentle brides;
now those lords, in their parents' company,
sup every day in hall—a royal feast   10
with fumes of sacrifice and winds that pipe
'round hollow courts; and all the night they sleep
on beds of filigree beside their ladies.
Here we put in, lodged in the town and palace,
while Aiolos played host to me. He kept me   15
one full month to hear the tale of Troy,
the ships and the return of the Akhaians,
all which I told him point by point in order.
When in return I asked his leave to sail
and asked provisioning, he stinted nothing,   20
adding a bull's hide sewn from neck to tail
into a mighty bag, bottling storm winds;
for Zeus had long ago made Aiolos
warden of winds, to rouse or calm at will.
He wedged this bag under my afterdeck,   25
lashing the neck with shining silver wire
so not a breath got through; only the west wind
he lofted for me in a quartering breeze
to take my squadron spanking home.
                        No luck:
the fair wind failed us when our prudence failed.   30

Nine days and nights we sailed without event,
till on the tenth we raised our land. We neared it,
and saw men building fires along the shore;
but now, being weary to the bone, I fell
into deep slumber; I had worked the sheet   35
nine days alone, and given it to no one,
wishing to spill no wind on the homeward run.
But while I slept, the crew began to parley:
silver and gold, they guessed, were in that bag
bestowed on me by Aiolos' great heart;   40
and one would glance at his benchmate and say:
'It never fails. He's welcome everywhere:
hail to the captain when he goes ashore!
He brought along so many presents, plunder
out of Troy, that's it. How about ourselves—   45
his shipmates all the way. Nigh home we are
with empty hands. And who has gifts from Aiolos?
He has. I say we ought to crack that bag,
there's gold and silver, plenty, in that bag!'

Temptation had its way with my companions,   50
and they untied the bag.
                  Then every wind
roared into hurricane; the ships went pitching
west with many cries; our land was lost.
Roused up, despairing in that gloom, I thought:

'Should I go overside for a quick finish   55
or clench my teeth and stay among the living?'
Down in the bilge I lay, pulling my sea cloak
over my head, while the rough gale blew the ships
and rueful crews clear back to Aiolia.

We put ashore for water; then all hands   60
gathered alongside for a mid-day meal.
When we had taken bread and drink, I picked
one soldier, and one herald, to go with me
and called again on Aiolos. I found him
at meat with his young princes and his lady,   65
but there beside the pillars, in his portico,
we sat down silent at the open door.
The sight amazed them, and they all exclaimed:

'Why back again, Odysseus?'
                                    'What sea fiend
rose in your path?'
                                    'Did we not launch you well   70
for home, or for whatever land you chose?'

Out of my melancholy I replied:

'Mischief aboard and nodding at the tiller—
a damned drowse—did for me. Make good my loss,
dear friends! You have the power!'

                                    Gently I pleaded,   75
but they turned cold and still. Said Father Aiolos:

'Take yourself out of this island, creeping thing—
no law, no wisdom, lays it on me now
to help a man the blessed gods detest—
out! Your voyage here was cursed by heaven!'   80

He drove me from the place, groan as I would,
and comfortless we went again to sea,
days of it, till the men flagged at the oars—
no breeze, no help in sight, by our own folly—
six indistinguishable nights and days   85
before we raised the Laistrygonian height
and far stronghold of Lamos.[3] In that land
the daybreak follows dusk, and so the shepherd
homing calls to the cowherd setting out;
and he who never slept could earn two wages,   90
tending oxen, pasturing silvery flocks,

3. Presumably the founder of the city of the Laistrygonians, a race of human-eating giants.

where the low night path of the sun is near
the sun's path by day.[4] Here, then, we found
a curious bay with mountain walls of stone
to left and right, and reaching far inland,—   95
a narrow entrance opening from the sea
where cliffs converged as though to touch and close.
All of my squadron sheltered here, inside
the cavern of this bay.
                              Black prow by prow
those hulls were made fast in a limpid calm   100
without a ripple stillness all around them.
My own black ship I chose to moor alone
on the sea side, using a rock for bollard;
and climbed a rocky point to get my bearings.
No farms, no cultivated land appeared,   105
but puffs of smoke rose in the wilderness;
so I sent out two picked men and a herald
to learn what race of men this land sustained.

My party found a track—a wagon road
for bringing wood down from the heights to town;   110
and near the settlement they met a daughter
of Antiphatês the Laistrygon—a stalwart
young girl taking her pail to Artakía,
the fountain where these people go for water.
My fellows hailed her, put their questions to her: 115
who might the king be? ruling over whom?
She waved her hand, showing her father's lodge,
so they approached it. In its gloom they saw
a woman like a mountain crag, the queen—
and loathed the sight of her. But she, for greeting,   120
called from the meeting ground her lord and master,
Antiphatês, who came to drink their blood.
He seized one man and tore him on the spot,
making a meal of him; the other two
leaped out of doors and ran to join the ships.   125
Behind, he raised the whole tribe howling, countless
Laistrygonês—and more than men they seemed,
gigantic when they gathered on the sky line
to shoot great boulders down from slings; and hell's own
crashing rose, and crying from the ships,   130
as planks and men were smashed to bits—poor gobbets
the wildmen speared like fish and bore away.
But long before it ended in the anchorage—
havoc and slaughter—I had drawn my sword
and cut my own ship's cable. 'Men,' I shouted,   135
'man the oars and pull till your hearts break
if you would put this butchery behind!'
The oarsmen rent the sea in mortal fear

---

4. Generally thought to be a confused reference to the short summer nights of the far north.

and my ship spurted out of range, far out
from that deep canyon where the rest were lost.   140
So we fared onward and death fell behind,
and we took breath to grieve for our companions.

Our next landfall was on Aiaia, island
of Kirkê, dire beauty and divine,
sister of baleful Aiêtês, like him   145
fathered by Hêlios the light of mortals
on Persê, child of the Ocean stream.
                          We came
washed in our silent ship upon her shore,
and found a cove, a haven for the ship—
some god, invisible, conned us in. We landed,   150
to lie down in that place two days and nights,
worn out and sick at heart, tasting our grief.
But when Dawn set another day a-shining
I took my spear and broadsword and I climbed
a rocky point above the ship, for sight   155
or sound of human labor. Gazing out
from that high place over a land of thicket,
oaks and wide watercourses, I could see
a smoke wisp from the woodland hall of Kirkê.
So I took counsel with myself: should I   160
go inland scouting out that reddish smoke?
No: better not, I thought, but first return
to waterside and ship, and give the men
breakfast before I sent them to explore.
Now as I went down quite alone, and came   165
a bowshot from the ship, some god's compassion
set a big buck in motion to cross my path—
a stag with noble antlers, pacing down
from pasture in the woods to the riverside,
as long thirst and the power of sun constrained him.   170
He started from the bush and wheeled: I hit him
square in the spine midway along his back
and the bronze point broke through it. In the dust
he fell and whinnied as life bled away.
I set one foot against him, pulling hard   175
to wrench my weapon from the wound, then left it,
butt-end on the ground. I plucked some withies
and twined a double strand into a rope—
enough to tie the hocks of my huge trophy;
then pickaback I lugged him to the ship,   180
leaning on my long spearshaft; I could not
haul that mighty carcass on one shoulder.
Beside the ship I let him drop, and spoke
gently and low to each man standing near:

'Come, friends, though hard beset, we'll not go down   185
into the House of Death before our time.

As long as food and drink remain aboard
let us rely on it, not die of hunger.'

At this those faces, cloaked in desolation
upon the waste sea beach, were bared;   190
their eyes turned toward me and the mighty trophy,
lighting, foreseeing pleasure, one by one.
So hands were washed to take what heaven sent us.
And all that day until the sun went down
we had our fill of venison and wine,   195
till after sunset in the gathering dusk
we slept at last above the line of breakers.
When the young Dawn with finger tips of rose
made heaven bright, I called them round and said:

'Shipmates, companions in disastrous time,   200
O my dear friends, where Dawn lies, and the West,
and where the great Sun, light of men, may go
under the earth by night, and where he rises—
of these things we know nothing.[5] Do we know
any least thing to serve us now? I wonder.   205
All that I saw when I went up the rock
was one more island in the boundless main,
a low landscape, covered with woods and scrub,
and puffs of smoke ascending in mid-forest.'

They were all silent, but their hearts contracted,   210
remembering Antiphatês the Laistrygon
and that prodigious cannibal, the Kyklops.
They cried out, and the salt tears wet their eyes.
But seeing our time for action lost in weeping,
I mustered those Akhaians under arms,   215
counting them off in two platoons, myself
and my godlike Eurýlokhos commanding.
We shook lots in a soldier's dogskin cap
and his came bounding out—valiant Eurýlokhos!—
So off he went, with twenty-two companions   220
weeping, as mine wept, too, who stayed behind.

In the wild wood they found an open glade,
around a smooth stone house—the hall of Kirkê—
and wolves and mountain lions lay there, mild
in her soft spell, fed on her drug of evil.   225
None would attack—oh, it was strange, I tell you—
but switching their long tails they faced our men
like hounds, who look up when their master comes
with tidbits for them—as he will—from table.
Humbly those wolves and lions with mighty paws   230

5. In view of the immediately preceding lines, this can hardly be taken literally. It is possibly a sailor's
metaphorical way of saying "We don't know where we are."

fawned on our men—who met their yellow eyes
and feared them.
     In the entrance way they stayed
to listen there: inside her quiet house
they heard the goddess Kirkê.
       Low she sang
in her beguiling voice, while on her loom   235
she wove ambrosial fabric sheer and bright,
by that craft known to the goddesses of heaven.
No one would speak, until Politês—most
faithful and likable of my officers, said:

'Dear friends, no need for stealth: here's a young weaver 240
singing a pretty song to set the air
a-tingle on these lawns and paven courts.
Goddess she is, or lady. Shall we greet her?'

So reassured, they all cried out together,
and she came swiftly to the shining doors   245
to call them in. All but Eurýlokhos—
who feared a snare—the innocents went after her.
On thrones she seated them, and lounging chairs,
while she prepared a meal of cheese and barley
and amber honey mixed with Pramnian wine,[6] 250
adding her own vile pinch, to make them lose
desire or thought of our dear father land.
Scarce had they drunk when she flew after them
with her long stick and shut them in a pigsty—
bodies, voices, heads, and bristles, all   255
swinish now, though minds were still unchanged.
So, squealing, in they went. And Kirkê tossed them
acorns, mast, and cornel berries—fodder
for hogs who rut and slumber on the earth.

Down to the ship Eurýlokhos came running 260
to cry alarm, foul magic doomed his men!
But working with dry lips to speak a word
he could not, being so shaken; blinding tears
welled in his eyes; foreboding filled his heart.
When we were frantic questioning him, at last 265
we heard the tale: our friends were gone. Said he:

'We went up through the oak scrub where you sent us,
Odysseus, glory of commanders,
until we found a palace in a glade,
a marble house on open ground, and someone 270
singing before her loom a chill, sweet song—
goddess or girl, we could not tell. They hailed her,
and then she stepped through shining doors and said,
"Come, come in!" Like sheep they followed her,

6. A harsh, dark wine.

but I saw cruel deceit, and stayed behind.   275
Then all our fellows vanished. Not a sound,
and nothing stirred, although I watched for hours.'

When I heard this I slung my silver-hilted
broadsword on, and shouldered my long bow,
and said, 'Come, take me back the way you came.'   280
But he put both his hands around my knees
in desperate woe, and said in supplication:

'Not back there, O my lord! Oh, leave me here!
You, even you, cannot return, I know it,
I know you cannot bring away our shipmates;   285
better make sail with these men, quickly too,
and save ourselves from horror while we may.'

But I replied:

              'By heaven, Eurýlokhos,
rest here then; take food and wine;
stay in the black hull's shelter. Let me go,   290
as I see nothing for it but to go.'

I turned and left him, left the shore and ship,
and went up through the woodland hushed and shady
to find the subtle witch in her long hall.
But Hermês met me, with his golden wand,   295
barring the way—a boy whose lip was downy
in the first bloom of manhood, so he seemed.
He took my hand and spoke as though he knew me:[7]

'Why take the inland path alone,
poor seafarer, by hill and dale
upon this island all unknown?   300
Your friends are locked in Kirkê's pale;
all are become like swine to see;
and if you go to set them free
you go to stay, and never more make sail   305
for your old home upon Thaki.[8]

But I can tell you what to do
to come unchanged from Kirkê's power
and disenthrall your fighting crew:
take with you to her bower   310
as amulet, this plant I know—
it will defeat her horrid show,
so pure and potent is the flower;
no mortal herb was ever so.

7. The four rhymed stanzas that follow are a translator's license; in the original there is no change of meter and, of course, no rhyme.   8. Ithaka.

Your cup with numbing drops of night   315
and evil, stilled of all remorse,
she will infuse to charm your sight;
but this great herb with holy force
will keep your mind and senses clear:
when she turns cruel, coming near   320
with her long stick to whip you out of doors,
then let your cutting blade appear,

Let instant death upon it shine,
and she will cower and yield her bed—
a pleasure you must not decline,   325
so may her lust and fear bestead
you and your friends, and break her spell;
but make her swear by heaven and hell
no witches' tricks, or else, your harness shed,
you'll be unmanned by her as well.'   330

He bent down glittering for the magic plant
and pulled it up, black root and milky flower—
a *molü* in the language of the gods—
fatigue and pain for mortals to uproot;
but gods do this, and everything, with ease.   335

Then toward Olympos through the island trees
Hermês departed, and I sought out Kirkê,
my heart high with excitement, beating hard.
Before her mansion in the porch I stood
to call her, all being still. Quick as a cat   340
she opened her bright doors and sighed a welcome;
then I strode after her with heavy heart
down the long hall, and took the chair she gave me,
silver-studded, intricately carved,
made with a low footrest. The lady Kirkê   345
mixed me a golden cup of honeyed wine,
adding in mischief her unholy drug.
I drank, and the drink failed. But she came forward
aiming a stroke with her long stick, and whispered:

'Down in the sty and snore among the rest!'   350

Without a word, I drew my sharpened sword
and in one bound held it against her throat.
She cried out, then slid under to take my knees,
catching her breath to say, in her distress:

'What champion, of what country, can you be?   355
Where are your kinsmen and your city?
Are you not sluggish with my wine? Ah, wonder!
Never a mortal man that drank this cup
but when it passed his lips he had succumbed.

Hale must your heart be and your tempered will.   360
Odysseus then you are, O great contender,
of whom the glittering god with golden wand[9]
spoke to me ever, and foretold
the black swift ship would carry you from Troy.
Put up your weapon in the sheath. We two   365
shall mingle and make love upon our bed.
So mutual trust may come of play and love.'

To this I said:

              'Kirkê, am I a boy,
that you should make me soft and doting now?
Here in this house you turned my men to swine;   370
now it is I myself you hold, enticing
into your chamber, to your dangerous bed,
to take my manhood when you have me stripped.
I mount no bed of love with you upon it.
Or swear me first a great oath, if I do,   375
you'll work no more enchantment to my harm.'

She swore at once, outright, as I demanded,
and after she had sworn, and bound herself,
I entered Kirkê's flawless bed of love.

Presently in the hall her maids were busy,   380
the nymphs who waited upon Kirkê: four,
whose cradles were in fountains, under boughs,
or in the glassy seaward-gliding streams.
One came with richly colored rugs to throw
on seat and chairback, over linen covers;   385
a second pulled the tables out, all silver,
and loaded them with baskets all of gold;
a third mixed wine as tawny-mild as honey
in a bright bowl, and set out golden cups.
The fourth came bearing water, and lit a blaze   390
under a cauldron. By and by it bubbled,
and when the dazzling brazen vessel seethed
she filled a bathtub to my waist, and bathed me,
pouring a soothing blend on head and shoulders,
warming the soreness of my joints away.   395
When she had done, and smoothed me with sweet oil,
she put a tunic and a cloak around me
and took me to a silver-studded chair
with footrest, all elaborately carven.
Now came a maid to tip a golden jug   400
of water into a silver finger bowl,
and draw a polished table to my side.
The larder mistress brought her tray of loaves

9. Hermês.

with many savory slices, and she gave
the best, to tempt me. But no pleasure came;   405
I huddled with my mind elsewhere, oppressed.

Kirkê regarded me, as there I sat
disconsolate, and never touched a crust.
Then she stood over me and chided me:

'Why sit at table mute, Odysseus?   410
Are you mistrustful of my bread and drink?
Can it be treachery that you fear again,
after the gods' great oath I swore for you?'

I turned to her at once, and said:

                                        'Kirkê,
where is the captain who could bear to touch   415
this banquet, in my place? A decent man
would see his company before him first.
Put heart in me to eat and drink—you may,
by freeing my companions. I must see them.'

But Kirkê had already turned away.   420
Her long staff in her hand, she left the hall
and opened up the sty, I saw her enter,
driving those men turned swine to stand before me.
She stroked them, each in turn, with some new chrism;
and then, behold! their bristles fell away,   425
the coarse pelt grown upon them by her drug
melted away, and they were men again,
younger, more handsome, taller than before.
Their eyes upon me, each one took my hands,
and wild regret and longing pierced them through,   430
so the room rang with sobs, and even Kirkê
pitied that transformation. Exquisite
the goddess looked as she stood near me, saying:

'Son of Laërtês and the gods of old,
Odysseus, master mariner and soldier,   435
go to the sea beach and sea-breasting ship;
drag it ashore, full length upon the land;
stow gear and stores in rock-holes under cover;
return; be quick; bring all your dear companions.'

Now, being a man, I could not help consenting.   440
So I went down to the sea beach and the ship,
where I found all my other men on board,
weeping, in despair along the benches.
Sometimes in farmyards when the cows return
well fed from pasture to the barn, one sees   445
the pens give way before the calves in tumult,
breaking through to cluster about mothers,

bumping together, bawling. Just that way
my crew poured round me when they saw me come—
their faces wet with tears as if they saw   450
their homeland, and the crags of Ithaka,
even the very town where they were born.
And weeping still they all cried out in greeting:

'Prince, what joy this is, your safe return!
Now Ithaka seems here, and we in Ithaka!   455
But tell us now, what death befell our friends?'

And, speaking gently, I replied:

'First we must get the ship high on the shingle,
and stow our gear and stores in clefts of rock
for cover. Then come follow me, to see   460
your shipmates in the magic house of Kirkê
eating and drinking, endlessly regaled.'

They turned back, as commanded, to this work;
only one lagged, and tried to hold the others;
Eurýlokhos it was, who blurted out: 465

'Where now, poor remnants? is it devil's work
you long for? Will you go to Kirkê's hall?
Swine, wolves, and lions she will make us all,
beasts of her courtyard, bound by her enchantment.
Remember those the Kyklops held, remember   470
shipmates who made that visit with Odysseus!
The daring man! They died for his foolishness!'

When I heard this I had a mind to draw
the blade that swung against my side and chop him,
bowling his head upon the ground—kinsman[1]   475
or no kinsman, close to me though he was.
But others came between, saying, to stop me,
'Prince, we can leave him, if you say the word;
let him stay here on guard. As for ourselves,
show us the way to Kirkê's magic hall.'   480

So all turned inland, leaving shore and ship,
and Eurýlokhos—he, too, came on behind,
fearing the rough edge of my tongue. Meanwhile
at Kirkê's hands the rest were gently bathed,
anointed with sweet oil, and dressed afresh   485
in tunics and new cloaks with fleecy linings.
We found them all at supper when we came.
But greeting their old friends once more, the crew
could not hold back their tears; and now again

1. Eurýlokhos was related to Odysseus by marriage.

the rooms rang with sobs. Then Kirkê, loveliest 490
of all immortals, came to counsel me:

'Son of Laërtês and the gods of old.
Odysseus, master mariner and soldier,
enough of weeping fits. I know—I, too—
what you endured upon the inhuman sea, 495
what odds you met on land from hostile men.
Remain with me, and share my meat and wine;
restore behind your ribs those gallant hearts
that served you in the old days, when you sailed
from stony Ithaka. Now parched and spent, 500
your cruel wandering is all you think of,
never of joy, after so many blows.'

As we were men we could not help consenting.
So day by day we lingered, feasting long
on roasts and wine, until a year grew fat. 505
But when the passing months and wheeling seasons
brought the long summery days, the pause of summer,
my shipmates one day summoned me and said:

'Captain, shake off this trance, and think of home—
if home indeed awaits us,
                          if we shall ever see 510
your own well-timbered hall on Ithaka.'

They made me feel a pang, and I agreed.
That day, and all day long, from dawn to sundown,
we feasted on roast meat and ruddy wine,
and after sunset when the dusk came on 515
my men slept in the shadowy hall, but I
went through the dark to Kirkê's flawless bed
and took the goddess' knees in supplication,
urging, as she bent to hear:

                          'O Kirkê,
now you must keep your promise; it is time. 520
Help me make sail for home. Day after day
my longing quickens, and my company
give me no peace, but wear my heart away
pleading when you are not at hand to hear.'

The loveliest of goddesses replied: 525

'Son of Laërtês and the gods of old,
Odysseus, master mariner and soldier,
you shall not stay here longer against your will;
but home you may not go
unless you take a strange way round and come 530
to the cold homes of Death and pale Perséphonê.[2]

2. Queen of the underworld.

You shall hear prophecy from the rapt shade
of blind Teirêsias of Thebes,[3] forever
charged with reason even among the dead;
to him alone, of all the flitting ghosts,   535
Perséphonê has given a mind undarkened.'

At this I felt a weight like stone within me,
and, moaning, pressed my length against the bed,
with no desire to see the daylight more.
But when I had wept and tossed and had my fill   540
of this despair, at last I answered her:

'Kirkê, who pilots me upon this journey?
No man has ever sailed to the land of Death.'

That loveliest of goddesses replied:

'Son of Laërtês and the gods of old,   545
Odysseus, master of land ways and sea ways,
feel no dismay because you lack a pilot;
only set up your mast and haul your canvas
to the fresh blowing North; sit down and steer,
and hold that wind, even to the bourne of Ocean,   550
Perséphonê's deserted stand and grove,
dusky with poplars and the drooping willow.
Run through the tide-rip, bring your ship to shore,
land there, and find the crumbling homes of Death.
Here, toward the Sorrowing Water, run the streams   555
of Wailing, out of Styx, and quenchless Burning[4]—
torrents that join in thunder at the Rock.
Here then, great soldier, setting foot obey me:
dig a well shaft a forearm square; pour out
libations round it to the unnumbered dead: 560
sweet milk and honey, then sweet wine, and last
clear water, scattering handfuls of white barley.
Pray now, with all your heart, to the faint dead;
swear you will sacrifice your finest heifer,
at home in Ithaka, and burn for them   565
her tenderest parts in sacrifice; and vow
to the lord Teirêsias, apart from all,
a black lamb, handsomest of all your flock—
thus to appease the nations of the dead.
Then slash a black ewe's throat, and a black ram,   570
facing the gloom of Erebos;[5] but turn
your head away toward Ocean. You shall see, now
souls of the buried dead in shadowy hosts,
and now you must call out to your companions
to flay those sheep the bronze knife has cut down,   575

3. A blind prophet who figures prominently in the legends of Thebes (he is a character in Sophocles' *Oedipus the King*).   4. Pyriphlegethon, a river of the underworld, as are the Sorrowing Water (Acheron), the stream of Wailing (Cocytus), and the Styx.   5. The darkest region of the underworld, usually imagined as below the underworld itself but here to the west.

for offerings, burnt flesh to those below,
to sovereign Death and pale Perséphonê.
Meanwhile draw sword from hip, crouch down, ward off
the surging phantoms from the bloody pit
until you know the presence of Teirêsias.   580
He will come soon, great captain; be it he
who gives you course and distance for your sailing
homeward across the cold fish-breeding sea.'

As the goddess ended, Dawn came stitched in gold.
Now Kirkê dressed me in my shirt and cloak,   585
put on a gown of subtle tissue, silvery,
then wound a golden belt about her waist
and veiled her head in linen,
while I went through the hall to rouse my crew.

I bent above each one, and gently said: 590

'Wake from your sleep; no more sweet slumber. Come,
we sail: the Lady Kirkê so ordains it.'

They were soon up, and ready at that word;
but I was not to take my men unharmed
from this place, even from this. Among them all   595
the youngest was Elpênor—
no mainstay in a fight nor very clever—
and this one, having climbed on Kirkê's roof[6]
to taste the cool night, fell asleep with wine.
Waked by our morning voices, and the tramp   600
of men below, he started up, but missed
his footing on the long steep backward ladder
and fell that height headlong. The blow smashed
the nape cord, and his ghost fled to the dark.
But I was outside, walking with the rest,   605
saying:

          'Homeward you think we must be sailing
to our own land; no, elsewhere is the voyage
Kirkê has laid upon me. We must go
to the cold homes of Death and pale Perséphonê
to hear Teirêsias tell of time to come.'   610

They felt so stricken, upon hearing this,
they sat down wailing loud, and tore their hair.
But nothing came of giving way to grief.
Down to the shore and ship at last we went,
bowed with anguish, cheeks all wet with tears,   615
to find that Kirkê had been there before us
and tied nearby a black ewe and a ram:
she had gone by like air.

---

6. A flat roof and the coolest place to sleep.

For who could see the passage of a goddess
unless she wished his mortal eyes aware? 620

BOOK XI

[A Gathering of Shades]

We bore down on the ship at the sea's edge
and launched her on the salt immortal sea,
stepping our mast and spar in the black ship;
embarked the ram and ewe and went aboard
in tears, with bitter and sore dread upon us. 5
But now a breeze came up for us astern—
a canvas-bellying landbreeze, hale shipmate
sent by the singing nymph with sun-bright hair;
so we made fast the braces, took our thwarts,
and let the wind and steersman work the ship 10
with full sail spread all day above our coursing,
till the sun dipped, and all the ways grew dark
upon the fathomless unresting sea.
                                        By night
our ship ran onward toward the Ocean's bourne,
the realm and region of the Men of Winter,[7] 15
hidden in mist and cloud. Never the flaming
eye of Hêlios lights on those men
at morning, when he climbs the sky of stars,
nor in descending earthward out of heaven;
ruinous night being rove[8] over those wretches. 20
We made the land, put ram and ewe ashore,
and took our way along the Ocean stream
to find the place foretold for us by Kirkê.
There Perimêdês and Eurýlokhos
pinioned the sacred beasts. With my drawn blade 25
I spaded up the votive pit, and poured
libations round it to the unnumbered dead:
sweet milk and honey, then sweet wine, and last
clear water; and I scattered barley down.
Then I addressed the blurred and breathless dead, 30
vowing to slaughter my best heifer for them
before she calved, at home in Ithaka,
and burn the choice bits on the altar fire;
as for Teirêsias, I swore to sacrifice
a black lamb, handsomest of all our flock. 35
Thus to assuage the nations of the dead
I pledged these rites, then slashed the lamb and ewe,
letting their black blood stream into the wellpit.
Now the souls gathered, stirring out of Erebos,
brides and young men, and men grown old in pain, 40
and tender girls whose hearts were new to grief;
many were there, too, torn by brazen lanceheads,

7. Although Homer usually places Hades below the earth, here he puts it across a great expanse of sea, apparently in the far north.   8. Stretched or spread.

battle-slain, bearing still their bloody gear.
From every side they came and sought the pit
with rustling cries; and I grew sick with fear.   45
But presently I gave command to my officers
to flay those sheep the bronze cut down, and make
burnt offerings of flesh to the gods below—
to sovereign Death, to pale Perséphonê.
Meanwhile I crouched with my drawn sword to keep   50
the surging phantoms from the bloody pit
till I should know the presence of Teirêsias.

One shade came first—Elpênor, of our company,
who lay unburied still on the wide earth
as we had left him—dead in Kirkê's hall,   55
untouched, unmourned, when other cares compelled us.
Now when I saw him there I wept for pity
and called out to him:

     'How is this, Elpênor,
how could you journey to the western gloom
swifter afoot than I in the black lugger?'   60

He sighed, and answered:

     'Son of great Laërtês,
Odysseus, master mariner and soldier,
bad luck shadowed me, and no kindly power;
ignoble death I drank with so much wine.
I slept on Kirkê's roof, then could not see   65
the long steep backward ladder, coming down,
and fell that height. My neck bone, buckled under,
snapped, and my spirit found this well of dark.
Now hear the grace I pray for, in the name
of those back in the world, not here—your wife   70
and father, he who gave you bread in childhood,
and your own child, your only son, Telémakhos,
long ago left at home.
     When you make sail
and put these lodgings of dim Death behind,
you will moor ship, I know, upon Aiaia Island;   75
there, O my lord, remember me, I pray,
do not abandon me unwept, unburied,
to tempt the gods' wrath, while you sail for home;
but fire my corpse, and all the gear I had,
and build a cairn for me above the breakers—   80
an unknown sailor's mark for men to come.
Heap up the mound there, and implant upon it
the oar I pulled in life with my companions.'

He ceased, and I replied:

     'Unhappy spirit,
I promise you the barrow and the burial.'   85

So we conversed, and grimly, at a distance,
with my long sword between, guarding the blood,
while the faint image of the lad spoke on.
Now came the soul of Antikleía, dead,
my mother, daughter of Autólykos,   90
dead now, though living still when I took ship
for holy Troy. Seeing this ghost I grieved,
but held her off, through pang on pang of tears,
till I should know the presence of Teirêsias.
Soon from the dark that prince of Thebes came forward   95
bearing a golden staff; and he addressd me:

'Son of Laërtês and the gods of old,
Odysseus, master of land ways and sea ways,
why leave the blazing sun, O man of woe,
to see the cold dead and the joyless region?   100
Stand clear, put up your sword;
let me but taste of blood, I shall speak true.'

At this I stepped aside, and in the scabbard
let my long sword ring home to the pommel silver,
as he bent down to the sombre blood. Then spoke   105
the prince of those with gift of speech:[9]

                          'Great captain,
a fair wind and the honey lights of home
are all you seek. But anguish lies ahead;
the god who thunders on the land prepares it,
not to be shaken from your track, implacable,   110
in rancor for the son whose eye you blinded.
One narrow strait may take you through his blows:
denial of yourself, restraint of shipmates.
When you make landfall on Thrinakia first
and quit the violet sea, dark on the land   115
you'll find the grazing herds of Hêlios
by whom all things are seen, all speech is known.
Avoid those kine, hold fast to your intent,
and hard seafaring brings you all to Ithaka.
But if you raid the beeves, I see destruction   120
for ship and crew. Though you survive alone,
bereft of all companions, lost for years,
under strange sail shall you come home, to find
your own house filled with trouble: insolent men
eating your livestock as they court your lady.   125
Aye, you shall make those men atone in blood!
But after you have dealt out death—in open
combat or by stealth—to all the suitors,
go overland on foot, and take an oar,
until one day you come where men have lived   130
with meat unsalted, never known the sea,

9. Tiresias here predicts the future of Odysseus. Like many Greek prophecies, it contains alternatives. The
second (lines 120ff.) is what happens. The journey inland to find a people who have never seen the sea
(and so mistake an oar for a winnowing fan, line 136) does not take place within the *Odyssey* itself.

nor seen seagoing ships, with crimson bows
and oars that fledge light hulls for dipping flight.
The spot will soon be plain to you, and I
can tell you how: some passerby will say,   135
"What winnowing fan is that upon your shoulder?"
Halt, and implant your smooth oar in the turf
and make fair sacrifice to Lord Poseidon:
a ram, a bull, a great buck boar; turn back,
and carry out pure hekatombs at home   140
to all wide heaven's lords, the undying gods,
to each in order. Then a seaborne death
soft as this hand of mist will come upon you
when you are wearied out with rich old age,
your country folk in blessed peace around you.   145
And all this shall be just as I foretell.'

When he had done, I said at once,

                                        'Teirêsias,
my life runs on then as the gods have spun it.
But come, now, tell me this; make this thing clear:
I see my mother's ghost among the dead   150
sitting in silence near the blood. Not once
has she glanced this way toward her son, nor spoken.
Tell me, my lord,
may she in some way come to know my presence?'

To this he answered:

                                'I shall make it clear   155
in a few words and simply. Any dead man
whom you allow to enter where the blood is
will speak to you, and speak the truth; but those
deprived will grow remote again and fade.'

When he had prophesied, Teirêsias' shade   160
retired lordly to the halls of Death;
but I stood fast until my mother stirred,
moving to sip the black blood; then she knew me
and called out sorrowfully to me:

                                'Child,
how could you cross alive into this gloom   165
at the world's end?—No sight for living eyes;
great currents run between, desolate waters,
the Ocean first, where no man goes a journey
without ship's timber under him.

                                Say, now,
is it from Troy, still wandering, after years,   170
that you come here with ship and company?
Have you not gone at all to Ithaka?
Have you not seen your lady in your hall?'

She put these questions, and I answered her:

'Mother, I came here, driven to the land of death   175
in want of prophecy from Teirêsias' shade;
nor have I yet coasted Akhaia's hills
nor touched my own land, but have had hard roving
since first I joined Lord Agamémnon's host
by sea for Ilion, the wild horse country,   180
to fight the men of Troy.
But come now, tell me this, and tell me clearly,
what was the bane that pinned you down in Death?
Some ravaging long illness, or mild arrows
a-flying down one day from Artemis?   185
Tell me of Father, tell me of the son
I left behind me; have they still my place,
my honors, or have other men assumed them?
Do they not say that I shall come no more?
And tell me of my wife: how runs her thought,   190
still with her child, still keeping our domains,
or bride again to the best of the Akhaians?'

To this my noble mother quickly answered:

'Still with her child indeed she is, poor heart,
still in your palace hall. Forlorn her nights   195
and days go by, her life used up in weeping.
But no man takes your honored place. Telémakhos
has care of all your garden plots and fields,
and holds the public honor of a magistrate,
feasting and being feasted. But your father   200
is country bound and comes to town no more.
He owns no bedding, rugs, or fleecy mantles,
but lies down, winter nights, among the slaves,
rolled in old cloaks for cover, near the embers.
Or when the heat comes at the end of summer,   205
the fallen leaves, all round his vineyard plot,
heaped into windrows, make his lowly bed.
He lies now even so, with aching heart,
and longs for your return, while age comes on him.
So I, too, pined away, so doom befell me,   210
not that the keen-eyed huntress[1] with her shafts
had marked me down and shot to kill me; not
that illness overtook me—no true illness
wasting the body to undo the spirit;
only my loneliness for you, Odysseus,   215
for your kind heart and counsel, gentle Odysseus,
took my own life away.'

                    I bit my lip,
rising perplexed, with longing to embrace her,

---

1. Artemis.

and tried three times, putting my arms around her,
but she went sifting through my hands, impalpable   220
as shadows are, and wavering like a dream.
Now this embittered all the pain I bore,
and I cried in the darkness:

       'O my mother,
will you not stay, be still, here in my arms,
may we not, in this place of Death, as well,   225
hold one another, touch with love, and taste
salt tears' relief, the twinge of welling tears?
Or is this all hallucination, sent
against me by the iron queen, Perséphonê,
to make me groan again?'

      My noble mother   230
answered quickly:

     'O my child—alas,
most sorely tried of men—great Zeus's daughter,
Perséphonê, knits no illusion for you.
All mortals meet this judgment when they die.
No flesh and bone are here, none bound by sinew,   235
since the bright-hearted pyre consumed them down—
the white bones long exanimate—to ash;
dreamlike the soul flies, insubstantial.

You must crave sunlight soon.
      Note all things strange
seen here, to tell your lady in after days.'   240

So went our talk; then other shadows came,
ladies in company, sent by Perséphonê—
consorts or daughters of illustrious men—
crowding about the black blood.
      I took thought
how best to separate and question them,   245
and saw no help for it, but drew once more
the long bright edge of broadsword from my hip,
that none should sip the blood in company
but one by one, in order; so it fell
that each declared her lineage and name.   250

Here was great loveliness of ghosts![2] I saw
before them all, that princess of great ladies,
Tyro,[3] Salmoneus' daughter, as she told me,
and queen to Krêtheus, a son of Aiolos.
She had gone daft for the river Enipeus,[4]   255
most graceful of all running streams, and ranged

2. Here follows a list of famous and beautiful women of former times. 3. A queen of Thessaly.
4. Tyro had fallen in love with the river god of the Enipeus (a river in Thessaly).

all day by Enipeus' limpid side,
whose form the foaming girdler of the islands,
the god who makes earth tremble, took[5] and so
lay down with her where he went flooding seaward,   260
their bower a purple billow, arching round
to hide them in a sea-vale, god and lady.
Now when his pleasure was complete, the god
spoke to her softly, holding fast her hand:

'Dear mortal, go in joy! At the turn of seasons,   265
winter to summer, you shall bear me sons;
no lovemaking of gods can be in vain.
Nurse our sweet children tenderly, and rear them.
Home with you now, and hold your tongue, and tell
no one your lover's name—though I am yours,   270
Poseidon, lord of surf that makes earth tremble.'

He plunged away into the deep sea swell,
and she grew big with Pelias and Neleus,[6]
powerful vassals, in their time, of Zeus.
Pelias lived on broad Iolkos seaboard   275
rich in flocks, and Neleus at Pylos.
As for the sons borne by that queen of women
to Krêtheus, their names were Aison,[7] Pherês,
and Amytháon, expert charioteer.

Next after her I saw Antiopê,   280
daughter of Ásopos.[8] She too could boast
a god for lover, having lain with Zeus
and borne two sons to him: Amphion and
Zêthos, who founded Thebes, the upper city,
and built the ancient citadel. They sheltered   285
no life upon that plain, for all their power,
without a fortress wall.

            And next I saw
Amphitrion's true wife, Alkmênê, mother,
as all men know, of lionish Heraklês,
conceived when she lay close in Zeus's arms;   290
and Megarê, high-hearted Kreon's daughter,
wife of Amphitrion's unwearying son.

I saw the mother of Oidipous, Epikastê,[9]
whose great unwitting deed it was
to marry her own son. He took that prize   295
from a slain father; presently the gods
brought all to light that made the famous story.
But by their fearsome wills he kept his throne
in dearest Thebes, all through his evil days,

5. Poseidon assumed his shape.   6. Father of Nestor of Pylos.   7. Father of Jason, the Argonaut.
8. A river in Boeotia, the territory of Thebes.   9. Usually known as Jocasta. *Oidipous:* Oedipus.

while she descended to the place of Death,   300
god of the locked and iron door. Steep down
from a high rafter, throttled in her noose,
she swung, carried away by pain, and left him
endless agony from a mother's Furies.

And I saw Khloris, that most lovely lady,   305
whom for her beauty in the olden time
Neleus wooed with countless gifts, and married.
She was the youngest daughter of Amphion,
son of Iasos. In those days he[1] held
power at Orkhómenos, over the Minyai.   310
At Pylos then as queen she bore her children—
Nestor, Khromios, Periklýmenos,
and Pêro, too, who turned the heads of men
with her magnificence. A host of princes
from nearby lands came courting her; but Neleus   315
would hear of no one, not unless the suitor
could drive the steers of giant Iphiklos
from Phylakê—longhorns, broad in the brow,
so fierce that one man only, a diviner,[2]
offered to round them up. But bitter fate   320
saw him bound hand and foot by savage herdsmen.
Then days and months grew full and waned, the year
went wheeling round, the seasons came again,
before at last the power of Íphiklos,
relenting, freed the prisoner, who foretold   325
all things to him. So Zeus's will was done.

And I saw Lêda, wife of Tyndareus,
upon whom Tyndareus had sired twins
indomitable: Kastor, tamer of horses,
and Polydeukês, best in the boxing ring.[3]   330
Those two live still, though life-creating earth
embraces them: even in the underworld
honored as gods by Zeus, each day in turn[4]
one comes alive, the other dies again.

Then after Lêda to my vision came   335
the wife of Aloeus, Iphimedeia,
proud that she once had held the flowing sea[5]
and borne him sons, thunderers for a day,
the world-renowned Otos and Ephialtês.
Never were men on such a scale   340
bred on the plowlands and the grainlands, never
so magnificent any, after Orion.
At nine years old they towered nine fathoms tall,
nine cubits in the shoulders, and they promised
furor upon Olympos, heaven broken by battle cries,   345

1. Amphion (not the same Amphion who founded Thebes, line 283).   **2.** Named Melampus.   **3.** They also had a daughter, Clytemnestra, who was Agamémnon's wife.   **4.** They shared, as it were, one immortality between them.   **5.** Poseidon.

the day they met the gods in arms.
                              With Ossa's
mountain peak they meant to crown Olympos
and over Ossa Pelion's forest pile
for footholds up the sky. As giants grown
they might have done it, but the bright son of Zeus[6]   350
by Lêto of the smooth braid shot them down
while they were boys unbearded; no dark curls
clustered yet from temples to the chin.

Then I saw Phaidra, Prokris; and Ariadnê,
daughter of Minos,[7] the grim king. Theseus took her   355
aboard with him from Krete for the terraced land
of ancient Athens; but he had no joy of her.
Artemis killed her on the Isle of Dia
at a word from Dionysos.[8]
                              Maira, then,
and Klymênê, and that detested queen,   360
Eríphylê,[9] who betrayed her lord for gold . . .
but how name all the women I beheld there,
daughters and wives of kings? The starry night
wanes long before I close.
                              Here, or aboard ship,
amid the crew, the hour for sleep has come.   365
Our sailing is the gods' affair and yours."[1]

Then he fell silent. Down the shadowy hall
the enchanted banqueters were still. Only
the queen with ivory pale arms, Arêtê, spoke,
saying to all the silent men:

                    "Phaiákians,   370
how does he stand, now, in your eyes, this captain,
the look and bulk of him, the inward poise?
He is my guest, but each one shares that honor.
Be in no haste to send him on his way
or scant your bounty in his need. Remember   375
how rich, by heaven's will, your possessions are."

Then Ekhenêos, the old soldier, eldest
of all Phaiákians, added his word:

"Friends, here was nothing but our own thought spoken,
the mark hit square. Our duties to her majesty.   380

6. Apollo. Ossa and Pelion are mountains near Olympus in Thessaly.   7. King of Krete and father of
Phaidra and Ariadnê. Phaidra was the wife of Theseus of Athens; she fell in love with her stepson Hippolytus. Prokris was the unfaithful wife of Cephalus, king of Athens. Ariadnê helped Theseus slay the Minotaur
on Krete.   8. We have no other account of this version of the episode that explains why Dionysus wanted
Ariadnê killed; the prevalent version of the story in later times is that Dionysus carried Ariadnê off to be
his bride.   9. Bribed with a golden necklace by Polynices, son of Oedipus, she persuaded her husband,
Amphiaraus, to take part in the attack on Thebes, where he was killed. Maira was a nymph of Artemis who
broke her vow of chastity and was killed by the goddess. Some story must have been attached to the name
Klymênê, but we do not know what it is.   1. Odysseus breaks off the story of his wanderings, and we are
transported back to the scene of the banqueting hall of the Phaiákians.

For what is to be said and done,
we wait upon Alkínoös' command."

At this the king's voice rang:

                               "I so command—
as sure as it is I who, while I live,
rule the sea rovers of Phaiákia. Our friend   385
longs to put out for home, but let him be
content to rest here one more day, until
I see all gifts bestowed. And every man
will take thought for his launching and his voyage,
I most of all, for I am master here."   390

Odysseus, the great tactician, answered:

"Alkínoös, king and admiration of men,
even a year's delay, if you should urge it,
in loading gifts and furnishing for sea—
I too could wish it; better far that I   395
return with some largesse of wealth about me—
I shall be thought more worthy of love and courtesy
by every man who greets me home in Ithaka."

The king said:

                      "As to that, one word, Odysseus:
from all we see, we take you for no swindler—   400
though the dark earth be patient of so many,
scattered everywhere, baiting their traps with lies
of old times and of places no one knows.
You speak with art, but your intent is honest.
The Argive troubles, and your own troubles,   405
you told as a poet would, a man who knows the world.
But now come tell me this: among the dead
did you meet any of your peers, companions
who sailed with you and met their doom at Troy?
Here's a long night—an endless night—before us,   410
and no time yet for sleep, not in this hall.
Recall the past deeds and the strange adventures.
I could stay up until the sacred Dawn
as long as you might wish to tell your story."

Odysseus the great tactician answered: 415

"Alkínoös, king and admiration of men,
there is a time for story telling; there is
also a time for sleep. But even so,
if, indeed, listening be still your pleasure,
I must not grudge my part. Other and sadder   420
tales there are to tell, of my companions,
of some who came through all the Trojan spears,

clangor and groan of war,
only to find a brutal death at home—
and a bad wife behind it.

       After Perséphonê,   425
icy and pale, dispersed the shades of women,
the soul of Agamémnon, son of Atreus,
came before me, sombre in the gloom,
and others gathered round, all who were with him
when death and doom struck in Aegísthos' hall.   430
Sipping the black blood, the tall shade perceived me,
and cried out sharply, breaking into tears;
then tried to stretch his hands toward me, but could not,
being bereft of all the reach and power
he once felt in the great torque of his arms.   435
Gazing at him, and stirred, I wept for pity,
and spoke across to him:

     'O son of Atreus,
illustrious Lord Marshal, Agamémnon,
what was the doom that brought you low in death?
Were you at sea, aboard ship, and Poseidon   440
blew up a wicked squall to send you under,
or were you cattle-raiding on the mainland
or in a fight for some strongpoint, or women,
when the foe hit you to your mortal hurt?'

But he replied at once:

     'Son of Laërtês,   445
Odysseus, master of land ways and sea ways,
neither did I go down with some good ship
in any gale Poseidon blew, nor die
upon the mainland, hurt by foes in battle.
It was Aigísthos who designed my death,   450
he and my heartless wife, and killed me, after
feeding me, like an ox felled at the trough.
That was my miserable end—and with me
my fellows butchered, like so many swine
killed for some troop, or feast, or wedding banquet   455
in a great landholder's household. In your day
you have seen men, and hundreds, die in war,
in the bloody press, or downed in single combat,
but these were murders you would catch your breath at:
think of us fallen, all our throats cut, winebowl   460
brimming, tables laden on every side,
while blood ran smoking over the whole floor.
In my extremity I heard Kassandra,[2]
Priam's daughter, piteously crying
as the traitress Klytaimnéstra made to kill her   465
along with me. I heaved up from the ground

---

2. She was part of Agamémnon's share of the booty at Troy.

and got my hands around the blade, but she
eluded me, that whore. Nor would she close
my two eyes[3] as my soul swam to the underworld
or shut my lips. There is no being more fell,   470
more bestial than a wife in such an action,
and what an action that one planned!
The murder of her husband and her lord.
Great god, I thought my children and my slaves
at least would give me welcome. But that woman,   475
plotting a thing so low, defiled herself
and all her sex, all women yet to come,
even those few who may be virtuous.'

He paused then, and I answered:

                              'Foul and dreadful.
That was the way that Zeus who views the wide world   480
vented his hatred on the sons of Atreus—
intrigues of women, even from the start.
                              Myriads
died by Helen's fault, and Klytaimnéstra
plotted against you half the world away.'

And he at once said:

                              'Let it be a warning   485
even to you. Indulge a woman never,
and never tell her all you know. Some things
a man may tell, some he should cover up.
Not that I see a risk for you, Odysseus,
of death at your wife's hands. She is too wise,   490
too clear-eyed, sees alternatives too well,
Penélopê, Ikários' daughter—
that young bride whom we left behind—think of it!—
when we sailed off to war. The baby boy
still cradled at her breast—now he must be   495
a grown man, and a lucky one. By heaven,
you'll see him yet, and he'll embrace his father
with old fashioned respect, and rightly.
                              My own
lady never let me glut my eyes
on my own son, but bled me to death first.   500
One thing I will advise, on second thought;
stow it away and ponder it.
                              Land your ship
in secret on your island; give no warning.
The day of faithful wives is gone forever.

But tell me, have you any word at all   505
about my son's life? Gone to Orkhómenos

---

3. She would not give me a proper burial.

or sandy Pylos, can he be? Or waiting
with Meneláos in the plain of Sparta?
Death on earth has not yet taken Orestês.'

But I could only answer:

                'Son of Atreus,   510
why do you ask these questions of me? Neither
news of home have I, nor news of him,
alive or dead. And empty words are evil.'

So we exchanged our speech, in bitterness,
weighed down by grief, and tears welled in our eyes,   515
when there appeared the spirit of Akhilleus,
son of Peleus; then Patróklos' shade,
and then Antílokhos,[4] and then Aias,
first among all the Danaans in strength
and bodily beauty, next to prince Akhilleus.   520
Now that great runner, grandson of Aíakhos,[5]
recognized me and called across to me:

'Son of Laërtês and the gods of old,
Odysseus, master mariner and soldier,
old knife, what next? What greater feat remains   525
for you to put your mind on, after this?
How did you find your way down to the dark
where these dimwitted dead are camped forever,
the after images of used-up men?'

                  I answered:

'Akhilleus, Peleus' son, strongest of all   530
among the Akhaians, I had need of foresight
such as Teirêsias alone could give
to help me, homeward bound for the crags of Ithaka.
I have not yet coasted Akhaia, not yet
touched my land; my life is all adversity.   535
But was there ever a man more blest by fortune
than you, Akhilleus? Can there ever be?
We ranked you with immortals in your lifetime,
we Argives did, and here your power is royal
among the dead men's shades. Think, then, Akhilleus: 540
you need not be so pained by death.'
                To this
he answered swiftly:
                'Let me hear no smooth talk
of death from you, Odysseus, light of councils.
Better, I say, to break sod as a farm hand
for some poor country man, on iron rations,   545
than lord it over all the exhausted dead.

4. Son of Nestor.   5. Akhilleus.

Tell me, what news of the prince my son:[6] did he
come after me to make a name in battle
or could it be he did not? Do you know
if rank and honor still belong to Peleus   550
in the towns of the Myrmidons? Or now, may be,
Hellas and Phthia spurn him, seeing old age
fetters him, hand and foot. I cannot help him
under the sun's rays, cannot be that man
I was on Troy's wide seaboard, in those days   555
when I made bastion for the Argives
and put an army's best men in the dust.
Were I but whole again, could I go now
to my father's house, one hour would do to make
my passion and my hands no man could hold   560
hateful to any who shoulder him aside.'

Now when he paused I answered:

                        'Of all that—
of Peleus' life, that is—I know nothing;
but happily I can tell you the whole story
of Neoptólemos, as you require.   565
In my own ship I brought him out from Skyros[7]
to join the Akhaians under arms.
                        And I can tell you,
in every council before Troy thereafter
your son spoke first and always to the point;
no one but Nestor and I could out-debate him.   570
And when we formed against the Trojan line
he never hung back in the mass, but ranged
far forward of his troops—no man could touch him
for gallantry. Aye, scores went down before him
in hard fights man to man. I shall not tell   575
all about each, or name them all—the long
roster of enemies he put out of action,
taking the shock of charges on the Argives.
But what a champion his lance ran through
in Eurýpolos the son of Télephos! Keteians[8]   580
in throngs around that captain also died—
all because Priam's gifts had won his mother
to send the lad to battle; and I thought
Memnon[9] alone in splendor ever outshone him.

But one fact more: while our picked Argive crew   585
still rode that hollow horse Epeios built,
and when the whole thing lay with me, to open
the trapdoor of the ambuscade or not,
at that point our Danaan lords and soldiers

6. Neoptólemos (the name means "new war").   7. The Greeks were told by a prophet that Troy would
fall only to the son of Akhilleus, who was living on the rocky island of Skyros.   8. Eurýpolos's people
(from Asia Minor), who came to the aid of the Trojans.   9. Son of the dawn goddess, king of the Ethiopians, and a Trojan ally.

wiped their eyes, and their knees began to quake,   590
all but Neoptólemos. I never saw
his tanned cheek change color or his hand
brush one tear away. Rather he prayed me,
hand on hilt, to sortie, and he gripped
his tough spear, bent on havoc for the Trojans.   595
And when we had pierced and sacked Priam's tall city
he loaded his choice plunder and embarked
with no scar on him; not a spear had grazed him
nor the sword's edge in close work—common wounds
one gets in war. Arês in his mad fits   600
knows no favorites.'

                But I said no more,
for he had gone off striding the field of asphodel,
the ghost of our great runner, Akhilleus Aíákidês,[1]
glorying in what I told him of his son.

Now other souls of mournful dead stood by,   605
each with his troubled questioning, but one
remained alone, apart: the son of Télamon,
Aîas, it was—the great shade burning still
because I had won favor on the beachhead
in rivalry over Akhilleus' arms.[2]   610
The Lady Thetis, mother of Akhilleus,
laid out for us the dead man's battle gear,
and Trojan children, with Athena,
named the Danaan fittest to own them. Would
god I had not borne the palm that day!   615
For earth took Aîas then to hold forever,
the handsomest and, in all feats of war,
noblest of the Danaans after Akhilleus.
Gently therefore I called across to him:

'Aîas, dear son of royal Télamon,   620
you would not then forget, even in death,
your fury with me over those accurst
calamitous arms?—and so they were, a bane
sent by the gods upon the Argive host.
For when you died by your own hand we lost   625
a tower, formidable in war. All we Akhaians
mourn you forever, as we do Akhilleus;
and no one bears the blame but Zeus.
He fixed that doom for you because he frowned
on the whole expedition of our spearmen.   630
My lord, come nearer, listen to our story!
Conquer your indignation and your pride.'

But he gave no reply, and turned away,
following other ghosts toward Erebos.

---

1. Akhilleus was son of Peleus, whose father was Aiakos.   **2.** See n. 3, page 233.

Who knows if in that darkness he might still   635
have spoken, and I answered?
                              But my heart
longed, after this, to see the dead elsewhere.
And now there came before my eyes Minos,
the son of Zeus, enthroned, holding a golden staff,
dealing out justice among ghostly pleaders   640
arrayed about the broad doorways of Death.

And then I glimpsed Orion,[3] the huge hunter,
gripping his club, studded with bronze, unbreakable,
with wild beasts he had overpowered in life
on lonely mountainsides, now brought to bay   645
on fields of asphodel.
                       And I saw Títyos,
the son of Gaia, lying
abandoned over nine square rods of plain.
Vultures, hunched above him, left and right,
rifling his belly, stabbed into the liver,   650
and he could never push them off.
                                  This hulk
had once committed rape of Zeus's mistress,
Léto, in her glory, when she crossed
the open grass of Panopeus toward Pytho.

Then I saw Tántalos[4] put to the torture: 655
in a cool pond he stood, lapped round by water
clear to the chin, and being athirst he burned
to slake his dry weasand with drink, though drink
he would not ever again. For when the old man
put his lips down to the sheet of water   660
it vanished round his feet, gulped underground,
and black mud baked there in a wind from hell.
Boughs, too, drooped low above him, big with fruit,
pear trees, pomegranates, brilliant apples,
luscious figs, and olives ripe and dark;   665
but if he stretched his hand for one, the wind
under the dark sky tossed the bough beyond him.

Then Sísyphos[5] in torment I beheld
being roustabout to a tremendous boulder.
Leaning with both arms braced and legs driving,   670
he heaved it toward a height, and almost over,
but then a Power spun him round and sent
the cruel boulder bounding again to the plain.
Whereon the man bent down again to toil,
dripping sweat, and the dust rose overhead.   675
Next I saw manifest the power of Heraklês—
a phantom, this, for he himself has gone

---

3. According to later legend he was transformed into the constellation that bears his name; Homer, however, has him in the underworld after his death.   4. King of Lydia. He was the confidant of the gods and ate at their table, but he betrayed their secrets.   5. King of Corinth, the archetype of the liar and trickster; we do know what misdeed he is being punished for in this passage.

feasting amid the gods, reclining soft
with Hêbê of the ravishing pale ankles,
daughter of Zeus and Hêra, shod in gold.   680
But, in my vision, all the dead around him
cried like affrighted birds; like Night itself
he loomed with naked bow and nocked arrow
and glances terrible as continual archery.
My hackles rose at the gold swordbelt he wore   685
sweeping across him: gorgeous intaglio
of savage bears, boars, lions with wildfire eyes,
swordfights, battle, slaughter, and sudden death—
the smith who had that belt in him, I hope
he never made, and never will make, another.   690
The eyes of the vast figure rested on me,
and of a sudden he said in kindly tones:

'Son of Laërtês and the gods of old,
Odysseus, master mariner and soldier,
under a cloud, you too? Destined to grinding   695
labors like my own in the sunny world?[6]
Son of Kroníon Zeus or not, how many
days I sweated out, being bound in servitude
to a man far worse than I, a rough master!
He made me hunt this place one time   700
to get the watchdog of the dead: no more
perilous task, he thought, could be; but I
brought back that beast, up from the underworld;
Hermês and grey-eyed Athena showed the way.'

And Heraklês, down the vistas of the dead,   705
faded from sight; but I stood fast, awaiting
other great souls who perished in times past.
I should have met, then, god-begotten Theseus
and Peirithoös,[7] whom both I longed to see,
but first came shades in thousands, rustling   710
in a pandemonium of whispers, blown together,
and the horror took me that Perséphonê
had brought from darker hell some saurian death's head.
I whirled then, made for the ship, shouted to crewmen
to get aboard and cast off the stern hawsers,   715
an order soon obeyed. They took their thwarts,
and the ship went leaping toward the stream of Ocean
first under oars, then with a following wind.

BOOK XII

[Sea Perils and Defeat]

The ship sailed on, out of the Ocean Stream,
riding a long swell on the open sea

6. Heraklês, son of Zeus, was made subject to the orders of Eurýstheus of Argos, who ordered him to perform the twelve famous labors.   7. After his adventures in Krete, Theseus went with his friend Perithoös to Hades to kidnap Perséphonê; the venture failed, and the two heroes, imprisoned in Hades, were rescued by Heraklês.

for the Island of Aiaia.
                        Summering Dawn
has dancing grounds there, and the Sun his rising;[8]
but still by night we beached on a sand shelf   5
and waded in beyond the line of breakers
to fall asleep, awaiting the Day Star.

When the young Dawn with finger tips of rose
made heaven bright, I sent shipmates to bring
Elpênor's body from the house of Kirkê.   10
We others cut down timber on the foreland,
on a high point, and built his pyre of logs,
then stood by weeping while the flame burnt through
corse and equipment.
                        Then we heaped his barrow,
lifting a gravestone on the mound, and fixed   15
his light but unwarped oar against the sky.
These were our rites in memory of him. Soon, then,
knowing us back from the Dark Land, Kirkê came
freshly adorned for us, with handmaids bearing
loaves, roast meats, and ruby-colored wine.   20
She stood among us in immortal beauty
jesting:

        'Hearts of oak, did you go down
alive into the homes of Death? One visit
finishes all men but yourselves, twice mortal!
Come, here is meat and wine, enjoy your feasting   25
for one whole day; and in the dawn tomorrow
you shall put out to sea. Sailing directions,
landmarks, perils, I shall sketch for you, to keep you
from being caught by land or water
in some black sack of trouble.'

                        In high humor   30
and ready for carousal, we agreed;
so all that day until the sun went down
we feasted on roast meat and good red wine,
till after sunset, at the fall of night,
the men dropped off to sleep by the stern hawsers.   35
She took my hand then, silent in that hush,
drew me apart, made me sit down, and lay
beside me, softly questioning, as I told
all I had seen, from first to last.
                        Then said the Lady Kirkê:

'So: all those trials are over.
                        Listen with care   40
to this, now, and a god will arm your mind.
Square in your ship's path are Seirênês,[9] crying

---

8. This places Kirkê's island in the east, whereas Odysseus's ship, when it was blown past Cape Malea, was headed west. It is one more indication that Odyssean geography is highly imaginative.   9. Or Sirens.

beauty to bewitch men coasting by;
woe to the innocent who hears that sound!
He will not see his lady nor his children   45
in joy, crowding about him, home from sea;
the Seirênês will sing his mind away
on their sweet meadow lolling. There are bones
of dead men rotting in a pile beside them
and flayed skins shrivel around the spot.

                                    Steer wide;   50
keep well to seaward; plug your oarsmen's ears
with beeswax kneaded soft; none of the rest
should hear that song.
                       But if you wish to listen,
let the men tie you in the lugger, hand
and foot, back to the mast, lashed to the mast,   55
so you may hear those harpies' thrilling voices;
shout as you will, begging to be untied,
your crew must only twist more line around you
and keep their stroke up, till the singers fade.
What then? One of two courses you may take,   60
and you yourself must weigh them. I shall not
plan the whole action for you now, but only
tell you of both.
               Ahead are beetling rocks
and dark blue glancing Amphitritê, surging,
roars around them. Prowling Rocks,[1] or Drifters,   65
the gods in bliss have named them—named them well.
Not even birds can pass them by, not even
the timorous doves that bear ambrosia
to Father Zeus; caught by downdrafts, they die
on rockwall smooth as ice.
                    Each time, the Father   70
wafts a new courier to make up his crew.

Still less can ships get searoom of these Drifters,
whose boiling surf, under high fiery winds,
carries tossing wreckage of ships and men.
Only one ocean-going craft, the far-famed   75
Argo, made it, sailing from Aiêta;
but she, too, would have crashed on the big rocks
if Hêra had not pulled her through, for love
of Iêson, her captain.
                A second course
lies between headlands. One is a sharp mountain   80
piercing the sky, with stormcloud round the peak
dissolving never, not in the brightest summer,
to show heaven's azure there, nor in the fall.
No mortal man could scale it, nor so much

---

1. Homer does not precisely identify them with the Symplegades, the Clashing Rocks that came together
and crushed whatever tried to pass between them. They were thought to be located at the entrance to the
Black Sea. Homer's Prowling Rocks seem to be located, like Scylla and Charybdis, near the straits between
Sicily and Italy. *Amphitritê:* the sea.

as land there, not with twenty hands and feet, 85
so sheer the cliffs are—as of polished stone.
Midway that height, a cavern full of mist
opens toward Erebos and evening.[2] Skirting
this in the lugger, great Odysseus,
your master bowman, shooting from the deck, 90
would come short of the cavemouth with his shaft;
but that is the den of Skylla, where she yaps
abominably, a newborn whelp's cry,
though she is huge and monstrous. God or man,
no one could look on her in joy. Her legs— 95
and there are twelve—are like great tentacles,
unjointed, and upon her serpent necks
are borne six heads like nightmares of ferocity,
with triple serried rows of fangs and deep
gullets of black death. Half her length, she sways 100
her heads in air, outside her horrid cleft,
hunting the sea around that promontory
for dolphins, dogfish, or what bigger game
thundering Amphitritê feeds in thousands.
And no ship's company can claim 105
to have passed her without loss and grief; she takes,
from every ship, one man for every gullet.
The opposite point seems more a tongue of land
you'd touch with a good bowshot, at the narrows.
A great wild fig, a shaggy mass of leaves, 110
grows on it, and Kharybdis lurks below
to swallow down the dark sea tide. Three times
from dawn to dusk she spews it up
and sucks it down again three times, a whirling
maelstrom; if you come upon her then 115
the god who makes earth tremble could not save you.
No, hug the cliff of Skylla, take your ship
through on a racing stroke. Better to mourn
six men than lose them all, and the ship, too.'

So her advice ran; but I faced her, saying: 120

'Only instruct me, goddess, if you will,
how, if possible, can I pass Kharybdis,
or fight off Skylla when she raids my crew?'

Swiftly that loveliest goddess answered me:

'Must you have battle in your heart forever? 125
The bloody toil of combat? Old contender,
will you not yield to the immortal gods?
That nightmare cannot die, being eternal
evil itself—horror, and pain, and chaos;
there is no fighting her, no power can fight her, 130

2. I.e., to the northwest.

all that avails is flight.
     Lose headway there
along that rockface while you break out arms,
and she'll swoop over you, I fear, once more,
taking one man again for every gullet.
No, no, put all your backs into it, row on;   135
invoke Blind Force, that bore this scourge of men,
to keep her from a second strike against you.

Then you will coast Thrinákia,[3] the island
where Hêlios' cattle graze, fine herds, and flocks
of goodly sheep. The herds and flocks are seven,   140
with fifty beasts in each.
      No lambs are dropped,
or calves, and these fat cattle never die.
Immortal, too, their cowherds are—their shepherds—
Phaëthousa and Lampetía, sweetly braided
nymphs that divine Neaira bore   145
to the overlord of high noon, Hêlios.
These nymphs their gentle mother bred and placed
upon Thrinákia, the distant land,
in care of flocks and cattle for their father.

Now give those kine a wide berth, keep your thoughts   150
intent upon your course for home,
and hard seafaring brings you all to Ithaka.
But if you raid the beeves, I see destruction
for ship and crew.
     Rough years then lie between
you and your homecoming, alone and old,   155
the one survivor, all companions lost.'

As Kirkê spoke, Dawn mounted her golden throne,
and on the first rays Kirkê left me, taking
her way like a great goddess up the island.
I made straight for the ship, roused up the men   160
to get aboard and cast off at the stern.
They scrambled to their places by the rowlocks
and all in line dipped oars in the grey sea.
But soon an off-shore breeze blew to our liking—
a canvas-bellying breeze, a lusty shipmate   165
sent by the singing nymph with sunbright hair.
So we made fast the braces, and we rested,
letting the wind and steersman work the ship.
The crew being now silent before me, I
addressed them, sore at heart:

       'Dear friends,   170
more than one man, or two, should know those things
Kirkê foresaw for us and shared with me,

---

3. Later Greeks identified this island as Sicily.

so let me tell her forecast: then we die
with our eyes open, if we are going to die,
or know what death we baffle if we can. Seirênês   175
weaving a haunting song over the sea
we are to shun, she said, and their green shore
all sweet with clover; yet she urged that I
alone should listen to their song. Therefore
you are to tie me up, tight as a splint,   180
erect along the mast, lashed to the mast,
and if I shout and beg to be untied,
take more turns of the rope to muffle me.'

I rather dwelt on this part of the forecast,
while our good ship made time, bound outward down   185
the wind for the strange island of Seirênês.
Then all at once the wind fell, and a calm
came over all the sea, as though some power
lulled the swell.
                    The crew were on their feet
briskly, to furl the sail, and stow it; then,   190
each in place, they poised the smooth oar blades
and sent the white foam scudding by. I carved
a massive cake of beeswax into bits
and rolled them in my hands until they softened—
no long task, for a burning heat came down   195
from Hêlios, lord of high noon. Going forward
I carried wax along the line, and laid it
thick on their ears. They tied me up, then, plumb
amidships, back to the mast, lashed to the mast,
and took themselves again to rowing. Soon,   200
as we came smartly within hailing distance,
the two Seirênês, noting our fast ship
off their point, made ready, and they sang:[4]

> This way, oh turn your bows,
>   Akhaia's glory,   205
> As all the world allows—
>   Moor and be merry.
>
> Sweet coupled airs we sing.
>   No lonely seafarer
> Holds clear of entering   210
>   Our green mirror.
>
> Pleased by each purling note
>   Like honey twining

---

4. The translator has turned the eight unrhymed lines of the original into a lyric poem. Here is a prose
version of the Greek: "Draw near, illustrious Odysseus, flower of Akhaian chivalry, and bring your ship to
rest so that you may hear our voices. No seaman ever sailed his black ship past this spot without listening
to the sweet tones that flow from our lips, and none that has listened has not been delighted and gone on
a wiser man. For we know all that the Argives and Trojans suffered on the broad plain of Troy by the will
of the gods, and we have foreknowledge of all that is going to happen on this fruitful earth."

From her throat and my throat,
   Who lies a-pining?   215

Sea rovers here take joy
   Voyaging onward,
As from our song of Troy
Greybeard and rower-boy
   Goeth more learnèd.   220

All feats on that great field
   In the long warfare,
Dark days the bright gods willed,
   Wounds you bore there,

Argos' old soldiery   225
   On Troy beach teeming,
Charmed out of time we see.
No life on earth can be
   Hid from our dreaming.

The lovely voices in ardor appealing over the water   230
made me crave to listen, and I tried to say
'Untie me!' to the crew, jerking my brows;
but they bent steady to the oars. Then Perimêdês
got to his feet, he and Eurýlokhos,
and passed more line about, to hold me still.   235
So all rowed on, until the Seirênês
dropped under the sea rim, and their singing
dwindled away.
         My faithful company
rested on their oars now, peeling off
the wax that I had laid thick on their ears;   240
then set me free.
         But scarcely had that island
faded in blue air than I saw smoke
and white water, with sound of waves in tumult—
a sound the men heard, and it terrified them.
Oars flew from their hands; the blades went knocking   245
wild alongside till the ship lost way,
with no oarblades to drive her through the water.

Well, I walked up and down from bow to stern,
trying to put heart into them, standing over
every oarsman, saying gently,

                  'Friends,   250
have we never been in danger before this?
More fearsome, is it now, than when the Kyklops
penned us in his cave? What power he had!
Did I not keep my nerve, and use my wits
to find a way out for us?
            Now I say   255
by hook or crook this peril too shall be

something that we remember.
                          Heads up, lads!
We must obey the orders as I give them.
Get the oarshafts in your hands, and lay back
hard on your benches; hit these breaking seas.   260
Zeus help us pull away before we founder.
You at the tiller, listen, and take in
all that I say—the rudders are your duty;
keep her out of the combers and the smoke;
steer for that headland; watch the drift, or we   265
fetch up in the smother, and you drown us.'

That was all, and it brought them round to action.
But as I sent them on toward Skylla, I
told them nothing, as they could do nothing.
They would have dropped their oars again, in panic,   270
to roll for cover under the decking. Kirkê's
bidding against arms had slipped my mind,
so I tied on my cuirass and took up
two heavy spears, then made my way along
to the foredeck—thinking to see her first from there,   275
the monster of the grey rock, harboring
torment for my friends. I strained my eyes
upon that cliffside veiled in cloud, but nowhere
could I catch sight of her.
                    And all this time,
in travail, sobbing, gaining on the current,   280
we rowed into the strait—Skylla to port
and on our starboard beam Kharybdis, dire
gorge of the salt sea tide. By heaven! when she
vomited, all the sea was like a cauldron
seething over intense fire, when the mixture   285
suddenly heaves and rises.
                  The shot spume
soared to the landside heights, and fell like rain.

But when she swallowed the sea water down
we saw the funnel of the maelstrom, heard
the rock bellowing all around, and dark   290
sand raged on the bottom far below.
My men all blanched against the gloom, our eyes
were fixed upon that yawning mouth in fear
of being devoured.
                Then Skylla made her strike,
whisking six of my best men from the ship.   295
I happened to glance aft at ship and oarsmen
and caught sight of their arms and legs, dangling
high overhead. Voices came down to me
in anguish, calling my name for the last time.

A man surfcasting on a point of rock   300
for bass or mackerel, whipping his long rod

to drop the sinker and the bait far out,
will hook a fish and rip it from the surface
to dangle wriggling through the air:
                              so these
were borne aloft in spasms toward the cliff.   305

She ate them as they shrieked there, in her den,
in the dire grapple, reaching still for me—
and deathly pity ran me through
at that sight—far the worst I ever suffered,
questing the passes of the strange sea.   We rowed on.   310
The Rocks were now behind; Kharybdis, too,
and Skylla dropped astern.
                              Then we were coasting
the noble island of the god, where grazed
those cattle with wide brows, and bounteous flocks
of Hêlios, lord of noon, who rides high heaven.   315

From the black ship, far still at sea, I heard
the lowing of the cattle winding home
and sheep bleating; and heard, too, in my heart
the words of blind Teirêsias of Thebes
and Kirkê of Aiaia: both forbade me   320
the island of the world's delight, the Sun.
So I spoke out in gloom to my companions:

'Shipmates, grieving and weary though you are,
listen: I had forewarning from Teirêsias
and Kirkê, too; both told me I must shun   325
this island of the Sun, the world's delight.
Nothing but fatal trouble shall we find here.
Pull away, then, and put the land astern.'

That strained them to the breaking point, and, cursing,
Eurýlokhos cried out in bitterness: 330

'Are you flesh and blood, Odysseus, to endure
more than a man can? Do you never tire?
God, look at you, iron is what you're made of.
Here we all are, half dead with weariness,
falling asleep over the oars, and you   335
say "No landing"—no firm island earth
where we could make a quiet supper. No:
pull out to sea, you say, with night upon us—
just as before, but wandering now, and lost.
Sudden storms can rise at night and swamp   340
ships without a trace.
                      Where is your shelter
if some stiff gale blows up from south or west—
the winds that break up shipping every time
when seamen flout the lord gods' will? I say

do as the hour demands and go ashore   345
before black night comes down.
                              We'll make our supper
alongside, and at dawn put out to sea.'

Now when the rest said 'Aye' to this, I saw
the power of destiny devising ill.
Sharply I answered, without hesitation: 350

'Eurýlokhos, they are with you to a man.
I am alone, outmatched.
                        Let this whole company
swear me a great oath: Any herd of cattle
or flock of sheep here found shall go unharmed;
no one shall slaughter out of wantonness   355
ram or heifer; all shall be content
with what the goddess Kirkê put aboard.'

They fell at once to swearing as I ordered,
and when the round of oaths had ceased, we found
a halfmoon bay to beach and moor the ship in,   360
with a fresh spring nearby. All hands ashore
went about skillfully getting up a meal.
Then, after thirst and hunger, those besiegers,
were turned away, they mourned for their companions
plucked from the ship by Skylla and devoured,   365
and sleep came soft upon them as they mourned.

In the small hours of the third watch, when stars
that shone out in the first dusk of evening
had gone down to their setting, a giant wind
blew from heaven, and clouds driven by Zeus   370
shrouded land and sea in a night of storm;
so, just as Dawn with finger tips of rose
touched the windy world, we dragged our ship
to cover in a grotto, a sea cave
where nymphs had chairs of rock and sanded floors.   375
I mustered all the crew and said:

                      'Old shipmates,
our stores are in the ship's hold, food and drink;
the cattle here are not for our provision,
or we pay dearly for it.
                        Fierce the god is
who cherishes these heifers and these sheep: 380
Hêlios; and no man avoids his eye.'

To this my fighters nodded. Yes. But now
we had a month of onshore gales, blowing
day in, day out—south winds, or south by east.
As long as bread and good red wine remained   385
to keep the men up, and appease their craving,

they would not touch the cattle. But in the end,
when all the barley in the ship was gone,
hunger drove them to scour the wild shore
with angling hooks, for fishes and sea fowl, 390
whatever fell into their hands; and lean days
wore their bellies thin.

The storms continued.

So one day I withdrew to the interior
to pray the gods in solitude, for hope
that one might show me some way of salvation. 395
Slipping away, I struck across the island
to a sheltered spot, out of the driving gale.
I washed my hands there, and made supplication
to the gods who own Olympos, all the gods—
but they, for answer, only closed my eyes 400
under slow drops of sleep.

Now on the shore Eurýlokhos

made his insidious plea:

'Comrades,' he said,

'You've gone through everything; listen to what I say.
All deaths are hateful to us, mortal wretches,
but famine is the most pitiful, the worst 405
end that a man can come to.

Will you fight it?

Come, we'll cut out the noblest of these cattle
for sacrifice to the gods who own the sky;
and once at home, in the old country of Ithaka,
if ever that day comes— 410
we'll build a costly temple and adorn it
with every beauty for the Lord of Noon.
But if he flares up over his heifers lost,
wishing our ship destroyed, and if the gods
make cause with him, why, then I say: Better 415
open your lungs to a big sea once for all
than waste to skin and bones on a lonely island!'

Thus Eurýlokhos; and they murmured 'Aye!'
trooping away at once to round up heifers.
Now, that day tranquil cattle with broad brows 420
were grazing near, and soon the men drew up
around their chosen beasts in ceremony.
They plucked the leaves that shone on a tall oak—
having no barley meal—to strew the victims,
performed the prayers and ritual, knifed the kine 425
and flayed each carcass, cutting thighbones free
to wrap in double folds of fat. These offerings,
with strips of meat, were laid upon the fire.
Then, as they had no wine, they made libation
with clear spring water, broiling the entrails first; 430
and when the bones were burnt and tripes shared,

they spitted the carved meat.
                              Just then my slumber
left me in a rush, my eyes opened,
and I went down the seaward path. No sooner
had I caught sight of our black hull, than savory   435
odors of burnt fat eddied around me;
grief took hold of me, and I cried aloud:

'O Father Zeus and gods in bliss forever,
you made me sleep away this day of mischief!
O cruel drowsing, in the evil hour!   440
Here they sat, and a great work they contrived.'

Lampetía in her long gown meanwhile
had borne swift word to the Overlord of Noon:

'They have killed your kine.'

                              And the Lord Hêlios
burst into angry speech amid the immortals: 445

'O Father Zeus and gods in bliss forever,
punish Odysseus' men! So overweening,
now they have killed my peaceful kine, my joy
at morning when I climbed the sky of stars,
and evening, when I bore westward from heaven.   450
Restitution or penalty they shall pay—
and pay in full—or I go down forever
to light the dead men in the underworld.'

Then Zeus who drives the stormcloud made reply:

'Peace, Hêlios: shine on among the gods,   455
shine over mortals in the fields of grain.
Let me throw down one white-hot bolt, and make
splinters of their ship in the winedark sea.'

—Kalypso later told me of this exchange,
as she declared that Hermês had told her.   460
Well, when I reached the sea cave and the ship,
I faced each man, and had it out; but where
could any remedy be found? There was none.
The silken beeves of Hêlios were dead.
The gods, moreover, made queer signs appear: 465
cowhides began to crawl, and beef, both raw
and roasted, lowed like kine upon the spits.

Now six full days my gallant crew could feast
upon the prime beef they had marked for slaughter
from Hêlios' herd; and Zeus, the son of Kronos,   470
added one fine morning.
                        All the gales

had ceased, blown out, and with an offshore breeze
we launched again, stepping the mast and sail,
to make for the open sea. Astern of us
the island coastline faded, and no land   475
showed anywhere, but only sea and heaven,
when Zeus Kroníon piled a thunderhead
above the ship, while gloom spread on the ocean.
We held our course, but briefly. Then the squall
struck whining from the west, with gale force, breaking   480
both forestays, and the mast came toppling aft
along the ship's length, so the running rigging
showered into the bilge.
                              On the after deck
the mast had hit the steersman a slant blow
bashing the skull in, knocking him overside,   485
as the brave soul fled the body, like a diver.
With crack on crack of thunder, Zeus let fly
a bolt against the ship, a direct hit,
so that she bucked, in reeking fumes of sulphur,
and all the men were flung into the sea.   490
They came up 'round the wreck, bobbing a while
like petrels on the waves.
                              No more seafaring
homeward for these, no sweet day of return;
the god had turned his face from them.
                                        I clambered
fore and aft my hulk until a comber   495
split her, keel from ribs, and the big timber
floated free; the mast, too, broke away.
A backstay floated dangling from it, stout
rawhide rope, and I used this for lashing
mast and keel together. These I straddled,   500
riding the frightful storm.
                              Nor had I yet
seen the worst of it: for now the west wind
dropped, and a southeast gale came on—one more
twist of the knife—taking me north again,
straight for Kharybdis. All that night I drifted,   505
and in the sunrise, sure enough, I lay
off Skylla mountain and Kharybdis deep.
There, as the whirlpool drank the tide, a billow
tossed me, and I sprang for the great fig tree,
catching on like a bat under a bough.   510
Nowhere had I to stand, no way of climbing,
the root and bole being far below, and far
above my head the branches and their leaves,
massed, overshadowing Kharybdis' pool.
But I clung grimly, thinking my mast and keel   515
would come back to the surface when she spouted.
And ah! how long, with what desire, I waited!
till, at the twilight hour, when one who hears
and judges pleas in the marketplace all day

between contentious men, goes home to supper,   520
the long poles at last reared from the sea.

Now I let go with hands and feet, plunging
straight into the foam beside the timbers,
pulled astride, and rowed hard with my hands
to pass by Skylla. Never could I have passed her   525
had not the Father of gods and men, this time,
kept me from her eyes. Once through the strait,
nine days I drifted in the open sea
before I made shore, buoyed up by the gods,
upon Ogýgia Isle. The dangerous nymph   530
Kalypso lives and sings there, in her beauty,
and she received me, loved me.

                    But why tell
the same tale that I told last night in hall
to you and to your lady? Those adventures
made a long evening, and I do not hold   535
with tiresome repetition of a story."

BOOK XIII

[One More Strange Island]

He ended it, and no one stirred or sighed
in the shadowy hall, spellbound as they all were,
until Alkínoös answered:

              "When you came
here to my strong home, Odysseus, under
my tall roof, headwinds were left behind you.   5
Clear sailing shall you have now, homeward now,
however painful all the past.
                  My lords,
ever my company, sharing the wine of Council,
the songs of the blind harper, hear me further:
garments are folded for our guest and friend   10
in the smooth chest, and gold
in various shaping of adornment lies
with other gifts, and many, brought by our peers;
let each man add his tripod and deep-bellied
cauldron: we'll make levy upon the realm   15
to pay us for the loss each bears in this."

Alkínoös had voiced their own hearts' wish.
All gave assent, then home they went to rest;
but young Dawn's finger tips of rose, touching
the world, roused them to make haste to the ship,   20
each with his gift of noble bronze. Alkínoös,
their ardent king, stepping aboard himself,
directed the stowing under the cross planks,
not to cramp the long pull of the oarsmen.

Going then to the great hall, lords and crew   25
prepared for feasting.
                As the gods' anointed,
Alkínoös made offering on their behalf—an ox
to Zeus beyond the stormcloud, Kronos' son,
who rules the world. They burnt the great thighbones
and feasted at their ease on fresh roast meat,   30
as in their midst the godlike harper sang—
Demódokos, honored by all that realm.
                      Only Odysseus
time and again turned craning toward the sun,
impatient for day's end, for the open sea.
Just as a farmer's hunger grows, behind   35
the bolted plow and share, all day afield,
drawn by his team of winedark oxen: sundown
is benison for him, sending him homeward
stiff in the knees from weariness, to dine;
just so, the light on the sea rim gladdened Odysseus,   40
and as it dipped he stood among the Phaiákians,
turned to Alkínoös, and said:

"O king and admiration of your people,
give me fare well, and stain the ground with wine;
my blessings on you all! This hour brings   45
fulfillment to the longing of my heart:
a ship for home, and gifts the gods of heaven
make so precious and so bountiful.
                    After this voyage
god grant I find my own wife in my hall
with everyone I love best, safe and sound!   50
And may you, settled in your land, give joy
to wives and children; may the gods reward you
every way, and your realm be free of woe."

Then all the voices rang out, "Be it so!"
and "Well spoken!" and "Let our friend make sail!"   55

Whereon Alkínoös gave command to his crier:

"Fill the winebowl, Pontónoös: mix and serve:
go the whole round, so may this company
invoke our Father Zeus, and bless our friend,
seaborne tonight and bound for his own country."   60

Pontónoös mixed the honey-hearted wine
and went from chair to chair, filling the cups;
then each man where he sat poured out his offering
to the gods in bliss who own the sweep of heaven.
With gentle bearing Odysseus rose, and placed   65
his double goblet in Arêtê's hands,
saying:

"Great Queen, farewell;
be blest through all your days till age comes on you,
and death, last end for mortals, after age.
Now I must go my way. Live in felicity,   70
and make this palace lovely for your children,
your countrymen, and your king, Alkínoös."

Royal Odysseus turned and crossed the door sill,
a herald at his right hand, sent by Alkínoös
to lead him to the sea beach and the ship.   75
Arêtê, too, sent maids in waiting after him,
one with a laundered great cloak and a tunic,
a second balancing the crammed sea chest,
a third one bearing loaves and good red wine.
As soon as they arrived alongside, crewmen   80
took these things for stowage under the planks,
their victualling and drink; then spread a rug
and linen cover on the after deck,
where Lord Odysseus might sleep in peace.
Now he himself embarked, lay down, lay still,   85
while oarsmen took their places at the rowlocks
all in order. They untied their hawser,
passing it through a drilled stone ring; then bent
forward at the oars and caught the sea
as one man, stroking.
     Slumber, soft and deep   90
like the still sleep of death, weighed on his eyes
as the ship hove seaward.
     How a four horse team
whipped into a run on a straightaway
consumes the road, surging and surging over it!
So ran that craft and showed her heels to the swell,   95
her bow wave riding after, and her wake
on the purple night-sea foaming.
     Hour by hour
she held her pace; not even a falcon wheeling
downwind, swiftest bird, could stay abreast of her
in that most arrowy flight through open water,   100
with her great passenger—godlike in counsel,
he that in twenty years had borne such blows
in his deep heart, breaking through ranks in war
and waves on the bitter sea.
     This night at last
he slept serene, his long-tried mind at rest.   105

When on the East the sheer bright star arose
that tells of coming Dawn, the ship made landfall
and came up islandward in the dim of night.
Phorkys, the old sea baron, has a cove
here in the realm of Ithaka; two points   110
of high rock, breaking sharply, hunch around it,
making a haven from the plunging surf
that gales at sea roll shoreward. Deep inside,

at mooring range, good ships can ride unmoored.
There, on the inmost shore, an olive tree   115
throws wide its boughs over the bay; nearby
a cave of dusky light is hidden
for those immortal girls, the Naiadês.[5]
Within are winebowls hollowed in the rock
and amphorai; bees bring their honey here;   120
and there are looms of stone, great looms, whereon
the weaving nymphs make tissues, richly dyed
as the deep sea is; and clear springs in the cavern
flow forever. Of two entrances,
one on the north allows descent of mortals,   125
but beings out of light alone, the undying,
can pass by the south slit; no men come there.

This cove the sailors knew. Here they drew in,
and the ship ran half her keel's length up the shore,
she had such way on her from those great oarsmen.   130
Then from their benches forward on dry ground
they disembarked. They hoisted up Odysseus
unruffled on his bed, under his cover,
handing him overside still fast asleep,
to lay him on the sand; and they unloaded   135
all those gifts the princes of Phaiákia
gave him, when by Athena's heart and will
he won his passage home. They bore this treasure
off the beach, and piled it close around
the roots of the olive tree, that no one passing   140
should steal Odysseus' gear before he woke.
That done, they pulled away on the homeward track.

But now the god that shakes the islands, brooding
over old threats of his against Odysseus,
approached Lord Zeus to learn his will. Said he: 145

"Father of gods, will the bright immortals ever
pay me respect again, if mortals do not?—
Phaiákians, too, my own blood kin?
                              I thought
Odysseus should in time regain his homeland;
I had no mind to rob him of that day—   150
no, no; you promised it, being so inclined;
only I thought he should be made to suffer
all the way.
              But now these islanders
have shipped him homeward, sleeping soft, and put him
on Ithaka, with gifts untold   155
of bronze and gold, and fine cloth to his shoulder.
Never from Troy had he borne off such booty
if he had got home safe with all his share."

Then Zeus who drives the stormcloud answered, sighing:

5. Nymphs of lake, river, and stream.

"God of horizons, making earth's underbeam 160
tremble, why do you grumble so?
The immortal gods show you no less esteem,
and the rough consequence would make them slow
to let barbs fly at their eldest and most noble.
But if some mortal captain, overcome 165
by his own pride of strength, cuts or defies you,
are you not always free to take reprisal?
Act as your wrath requires and as you will."

Now said Poseidon, god of earthquake:

                                    "Aye,
god of the stormy sky, I should have taken 170
vengeance, as you say, and on my own;
but I respect, and would avoid, your anger.
The sleek Phaiákian cutter, even now,
has carried out her mission and glides home
over the misty sea. Let me impale her, 175
end her voyage, and end all ocean-crossing
with passengers, then heave a mass of mountain
in a ring around the city."

Now Zeus who drives the stormcloud said benignly:

"Here is how I should do it, little brother: 180
when all who watch upon the wall have caught
sight of the ship, let her be turned to stone—
an island like a ship, just off the bay.
Mortals may gape at that for generations!
But throw no mountain round[6] the sea port city." 185

When he heard this, Poseidon, god of earthquake,
departed for Skhería, where the Phaiákians
are born and dwell. Their ocean-going ship
he saw already near, heading for harbor;
so up behind her swam the island-shaker 190
and struck her into stone, rooted in stone, at one
blow of his palm,
                        then took to the open sea.
Those famous ship handlers, the Phaiákians,
gazed at each other, murmuring in wonder;
you could have heard one say:

                            "Now who in thunder 195
has anchored, moored that ship in the seaway,
when everyone could see her making harbor?"

---

6. This translates a correction of the text made in antiquity by the Alexandrian scholar Aristophanes of
Byzantium. But another great Alexandrian scholar, Aristarchus, defended the original text, which means
"and throw a big mountain round." Zeus, in other words, approved of Poseidon's intention to cut the
Phaiákians off from the sea altogether and adds the proposal to turn the ship into a rock. It is a difficult
question to decide, because Homer does not tell us what happened to the Phaiákians in the end.

The god had wrought a charm beyond their thought.
But soon Alkínoös made them hush, and told them:

"This present doom upon the ship—on me—   200
my father prophesied in the olden time.
If we gave safe conveyance to all passengers
we should incur Poseidon's wrath, he said,
whereby one day a fair ship, manned by Phaiákians,
would come to grief at the god's hands; and great   205
mountains would hide our city from the sea.
So my old father forecast.
                              Use your eyes:
these things are even now being brought to pass.
Let all here abide by my decree:
                              We make
an end henceforth of taking, in our ships,   210
castaways who may land upon Skhería;
and twelve choice bulls we dedicate at once
to Lord Poseidon, praying him of his mercy
not to heave up a mountain round our city."

In fearful awe they led the bulls to sacrifice   215
and stood about the altar stone, those captains,
peers of Phaiákia, led by their king in prayer
to Lord Poseidon.

                    Meanwhile, on his island,
his father's shore, that kingly man, Odysseus,
awoke, but could not tell what land it was   220
after so many years away; moreover,
Pallas Athena, Zeus's daughter, poured
a grey mist all around him, hiding him
from common sight—for she had things to tell him
and wished no one to know him, wife or townsmen,   225
before the suitors paid up for their crimes.

The landscape then looked strange, unearthly strange
to the Lord Odysseus: paths by hill and shore,
glimpses of harbors, cliffs, and summer trees.
He stood up, rubbed his eyes, gazed at his homeland,   230
and swore, slapping his thighs with both his palms,
then cried aloud:

                    "What am I in for now?
Whose country have I come to this time? Rough
savages and outlaws, are they, or
godfearing people, friendly to castaways?   235
Where shall I take these things? Where take myself,
with no guide, no directions? These should be
still in Phaiákian hands, and I uncumbered,
free to find some other openhearted
prince who might be kind and give me passage.   240

I have no notion where to store this treasure;
first-comer's trove it is, if I leave it here.

My lords and captains of Phaiákia
were not those decent men they seemed, not honorable,
landing me in this unknown country—no,   245
by god, they swore to take me home to Ithaka
and did not! Zeus attend to their reward,
Zeus, patron of petitioners, who holds
all other mortals under his eye; he takes
payment from betrayers!   250
                                    I'll be busy.
I can look through my gear. I shouldn't wonder
if they pulled out with part of it on board."

He made a tally of his shining pile—
tripods, cauldrons, cloaks, and gold—and found
he lacked nothing at all.
                                    And then he wept,   255
despairing, for his own land, trudging down
beside the endless wash of the wide, wide sea,
weary and desolate as the sea. But soon
Athena came to him from the nearby air,
putting a young man's figure on—a shepherd,   260
like a king's son, all delicately made.
She wore a cloak, in two folds off her shoulders,
and sandals bound upon her shining feet.
A hunting lance lay in her hands.
                                    At sight of her
Odysseus took heart, and he went forward   265
to greet the lad, speaking out fair and clear:

"Friend, you are the first man I've laid eyes on
here in this cove. Greetings. Do not feel
alarmed or hostile, coming across me; only
receive me into safety with my stores.   270
Touching your knees I ask it, as I might
ask grace of a god.
                                    O sir, advise me,
what is this land and realm, who are the people?
Is it an island all distinct, or part
of the fertile mainland, sloping to the sea?"   275

To this grey-eyed Athena answered:

                                    "Stranger,
you must come from the other end of nowhere,
else you are a great booby, having to ask
what place this is. It is no nameless country.
Why, everyone has heard of it, the nations   280
over on the dawn side, toward the sun,
and westerners in cloudy lands of evening.

No one would use this ground for training horses,
it is too broken, has no breadth of meadow;
but there is nothing meager about the soil,   285
the yield of grain is wondrous, and wine, too,
with drenching rains and dewfall.
                                        There's good pasture
for oxen and for goats, all kinds of timber,
and water all year long in the cattle ponds.
For these blessings, friend, the name of Ithaka   290
has made its way even as far as Troy—
and they say Troy lies far beyond Akhaia."

Now Lord Odysseus, the long-enduring,
laughed in his heart, hearing his land described
by Pallas Athena, daughter of Zeus who rules   295
the veering stormwind; and he answered her
with ready speech—not that he told the truth,
but, just as she did, held back what he knew,
weighing within himself at every step
what he made up to serve his turn.

                        Said he: 300

"Far away in Krete I learned of Ithaka—
in that broad island over the great ocean.
And here I am now, come myself to Ithaka!
Here is my fortune with me. I left my sons
an equal part, when I shipped out. I killed   305
Orsílokhos, the courier, son of Idómeneus.
This man could beat the best cross country runners
in Krete, but he desired to take away
my Trojan plunder, all I had fought and bled for,
cutting through ranks in war and the cruel sea.   310
Confiscation is what he planned; he knew
I had not cared to win his father's favor
as a staff officer in the field at Troy,
but led my own command.
                            I acted: I
hit him with a spearcast from a roadside   315
as he came down from the open country. Murky
night shrouded all heaven and the stars.
I made that ambush with one man at arms.
We were unseen. I took his life in secret,
finished him off with my sharp sword. That night   320
I found asylum on a ship off shore
skippered by gentlemen of Phoinikia;[7] I gave
all they could wish, out of my store of plunder,
for passage, and for landing me at Pylos
or Elis Town, where the Epeioi[8] are in power.   325
Contrary winds carried them willy-nilly

7. Phoenicia.   8. The people of Elis Town, in the western Peloponnese.

past that coast; they had no wish to cheat me,
but we were blown off course.
                            Here, then, by night
we came, and made this haven by hard rowing.
All famished, but too tired to think of food,   330
each man dropped in his tracks after the landing,
and I slept hard, being wearied out. Before
I woke today, they put my things ashore
on the sand here beside me where I lay,
then reimbarked for Sidon, that great city.   335
Now they are far at sea, while I am left
forsaken here."

                    At this the grey-eyed goddess
Athena smiled, and gave him a caress,
her looks being changed now, so she seemed a woman,
tall and beautiful and no doubt skilled   340
at weaving splendid things. She answered briskly:

"Whoever gets around you must be sharp
and guileful as a snake; even a god
might bow to you in ways of dissimulation.
You! You chameleon!   345
Bottomless bag of tricks! Here in your own country
would you not give your stratagems a rest
or stop spellbinding for an instant?

You play a part as if it were your own tough skin.

No more of this, though. Two of a kind, we are,   350
contrivers, both. Of all men now alive
you are the best in plots and story telling.
My own fame is for wisdom among the gods—
deceptions, too.
                    Would even you have guessed
that I am Pallas Athena, daughter of Zeus,   355
I that am always with you in times of trial,
a shield to you in battle, I who made
the Phaiákians befriend you, to a man?
Now I am here again to counsel with you—
but first to put away those gifts the Phaiákians   360
gave you at departure—I planned it so.
Then I can tell you of the gall and wormwood
it is your lot to drink in your own hall.
Patience, iron patience, you must show;
so give it out to neither man nor woman   365
that you are back from wandering. Be silent
under all injuries, even blows from men."

His mind ranging far, Odysseus answered:

"Can mortal man be sure of you on sight,
even a sage, O mistress of disguises?   370

Once you were fond of me—I am sure of that—
years ago, when we Akhaians made
war, in our generation, upon Troy.
But after we had sacked the shrines of Priam
and put to sea, God scattered the Akhaians;   375
I never saw you after that, never
knew you aboard with me, to act as shield
in grievous times—not till you gave me comfort
in the rich hinterland of the Phaiákians
and were yourself my guide into that city.   380

Hear me now in your father's name, for I
cannot believe that I have come to Ithaka.
It is some other land. You made that speech
only to mock me, and to take me in.
Have I come back in truth to my home island?"   385

To this the grey-eyed goddess Athena answered:

"Always the same detachment! That is why
I cannot fail you, in your evil fortune,
coolheaded, quick, well-spoken as you are!
Would not another wandering man, in joy,   390
make haste home to his wife and children? Not
you, not yet. Before you hear their story
you will have proof about your wife.
                        I tell you,
she still sits where you left her, and her days
and nights go by forlorn, in lonely weeping.   395
For my part, never had I despaired; I felt
sure of your coming home, though all your men
should perish; but I never cared to fight
Poseidon, Father's brother, in his baleful
rage with you for taking his son's eye.   400

Now I shall make you see the shape of Ithaka.
Here is the cove the sea lord Phorkys owns,
there is the olive spreading out her leaves
over the inner bay, and there the cavern
dusky and lovely, hallowed by the feet   405
of those immortal girls, the Naiadês—
the same wide cave under whose vault you came
to honor them with hekatombs—and there
Mount Neion, with his forest on his back!"

She had dispelled the mist, so all the island   410
stood out clearly. Then indeed Odysseus'
heart stirred with joy. He kissed the earth,
and lifting up his hands prayed to the nymphs:

"O slim shy Naiadês, young maids of Zeus,
I had not thought to see you ever again!
                        O listen smiling   415

to my gentle prayers, and we'll make offering
plentiful as in the old time, granted I
live, granted my son grows tall, by favor
of great Athena, Zeus's daughter,
who gives the winning fighter his reward!"   420

The grey-eyed goddess said directly:

           "Courage;
and let the future trouble you no more.
We go to make a cache now, in the cave,
to keep your treasure hid. Then we'll consider
how best the present action may unfold."   425

The goddess turned and entered the dim cave,
exploring it for crannies, while Odysseus
carried up all the gold, the fire-hard bronze,
and well-made clothing the Phaiákians gave him.
Pallas Athena, daughter of Zeus the storm king,   430
placed them, and shut the cave mouth with a stone,
and under the old grey olive tree those two
sat down to work the suitors death and woe.
Grey-eyed Athena was the first to speak, saying:

"Son of Laërtês and the gods of old,   435
Odysseus, master of land ways and sea ways,
put your mind on a way to reach and strike
a crowd of brazen upstarts.
                Three long years
they have played master in your house: three years
trying to win your lovely lady, making   440
gifts as though betrothed. And she? Forever
grieving for you, missing your return,
she has allowed them all to hope, and sent
messengers with promises to each—
though her true thoughts are fixed elsewhere."

                     At this   445
the man of ranging mind, Odysseus, cried:

"So hard beset! An end like Agamémnon's
might very likely have been mine, a bad end,
bleeding to death in my own hall. You forestalled it,
goddess, by telling me how the land lies.   450
Weave me a way to pay them back! And you, too,
take your place with me, breathe valor in me
the way you did that night when we Akhaians
unbound the bright veil from the brow of Troy!
O grey-eyed one, fire my heart and brace me!   455
I'll take on fighting men three hundred strong
if you fight at my back, immortal lady!"

The grey-eyed goddess Athena answered him:

"No fear but I shall be there; you'll go forward
under my arm when the crux comes at last.   460
And I foresee your vast floor stained with blood,
spattered with brains of this or that tall suitor
who fed upon your cattle.
                          Now, for a while,
I shall transform you; not a soul will know you,
the clear skin of your arms and legs shriveled,   465
your chestnut hair all gone, your body dressed
in sacking that a man would gag to see,
and the two eyes, that were so brilliant, dirtied—
contemptible, you shall seem to your enemies,
as to the wife and son you left behind.   470

But join the swineherd first—the overseer
of all your swine, a good soul now as ever,
devoted to Penélopê and your son.
He will be found near Raven's Rock and the well
of Arethousa, where the swine are pastured,   475
rooting for acorns to their hearts' content,
drinking the dark still water. Boarflesh grows
pink and fat on that fresh diet. There
stay with him and question him, while I
am off to the great beauty's land of Sparta,   480
to call your son Telémakhos home again—
for you should know, he went to the wide land
of Lakedaimon, Meneláos' country,
to learn if there were news of you abroad."

Odysseus answered:

                          "Why not tell him, knowing   485
my whole history, as you do? Must he
traverse the barren sea, he too, and live
in pain, while others feed on what is his?"

At this the grey-eyed goddess Athena said:

"No need for anguish on that lad's account.   490
I sent him off myself, to make his name
in foreign parts—no hardship in the bargain,
taking his ease in Meneláos' mansion,
lapped in gold.
                          The young bucks here, I know,
lie in wait for him in a cutter, bent   495
on murdering him before he reaches home.
I rather doubt they will. Cold earth instead
will take in her embrace a man or two
of those who fed so long on what is his."

Speaking no more, she touched him with her wand,   500
shriveled the clear skin of his arms and legs,
made all his hair fall out, cast over him
the wrinkled hide of an old man, and bleared
both his eyes, that were so bright. Then she
clapped an old tunic, a foul cloak, upon him,   505
tattered, filthy, stained by greasy smoke,
and over that a mangy big buck skin.
A staff she gave him, and a leaky knapsack
with no strap but a loop of string.
                    Now then,
their colloquy at an end, they went their ways—   510
Athena toward illustrious Lakedaimon
far over sea, to join Odysseus' son.

BOOK XIV

[Hospitality in the Forest]

He went up from the cove through wooded ground,
taking a stony trail into the high hills, where
the swineherd lived, according to Athena.
Of all Odysseus' field hands in the old days
this forester cared most for the estate;   5
and now Odysseus found him
in a remote clearing, sitting inside the gate
of a stockade he built to keep the swine
while his great lord was gone.
                 Working alone,
far from Penélopê and old Laërtês,   10
he had put up a fieldstone hut and timbered it
with wild pear wood. Dark hearts of oak he split
and trimmed for a high palisade around it,
and built twelve sties adjoining in this yard
to hold the livestock. Fifty sows with farrows   15
were penned in each, bedded upon the earth,
while the boars lay outside—fewer by far,
as those well-fatted were for the suitors' table,
fine pork, sent by the swineherd every day.
Three hundred sixty now lay there at night,   20
guarded by dogs—four dogs like wolves, one each
for the four lads the swineherd reared and kept
as under-herdsmen.
             When Odysseus came,
the good servant sat shaping to his feet
oxhide for sandals, cutting the well-cured leather.   25
Three of his young men were afield, pasturing
herds in other woods; one he had sent
with a fat boar for tribute into town,
the boy to serve while the suitors got their fill.

The watch dogs, when they caught sight of Odysseus,   30
faced him, a snarling troop, and pelted out
viciously after him. Like a tricky beggar

he sat down plump, and dropped his stick. No use.
They would have rolled him in the dust and torn him
there by his own steading if the swineherd   35
had not sprung up and flung his leather down,
making a beeline for the open. Shouting,
throwing stone after stone,
he made them scatter; then turned to his lord
and said:

       "You might have got a ripping, man!   40
Two shakes more and a pretty mess for me
you could have called it, if you had the breath.
As though I had not trouble enough already,
given me by the gods, my master gone,
true king that he was. I hang on here,   45
still mourning for him, raising pigs of his
to feed foreigners, and who knows where the man is,
in some far country among strangers! Aye—
if he is living still, if he still sees the light of day.

Come to the cabin. You're a wanderer too.   50
You must eat something, drink some wine, and tell me
where you are from and the hard times you've seen."

The forester now led him to his hut
and made a couch for him, with tips of fir
piled for a mattress under a wild goat skin,   55
shaggy and thick, his own bed covering.
                  Odysseus,
in pleasure at this courtesy, gently said:

"May Zeus and all the gods give you your heart's desire
for taking me in so kindly, friend."

                Eumaios—
O my swineherd!⁹—answered him:

            "Tush, friend,   60
rudeness to a stranger is not decency,
poor though he may be, poorer than you.
               All wanderers
and beggars come from Zeus. What we can give
is slight but well-meant—all we dare. You know
that is the way of slaves, who live in dread   65
of masters—new ones like our own.
             I told you
the gods, long ago, hindered our lord's return.
He had a fondness for me, would have pensioned me

---

9. This direct address by the poet to one of his characters is confined to Eumaios; it occurs frequently in
connection with his name in books 14–17. A medieval commentator suggested that it showed a special
affection for Eumaios on Homer's part, but because in the *Iliad* a similar form of address is used for five
different characters (among them the god Apollo and the obscure Melanippos) this seems unlikely. In the
case of Eumaios it may have been a formula devised to avoid hiatus (clashing vowels).

with acres of my own, a house, a wife
that other men admired and courted; all   70
gifts good-hearted kings bestow for service,
for a life work the bounty of god has prospered—
for it does prosper here, this work I do.
Had he grown old in his own house, my master
would have rewarded me. But the man's gone.   75
God curse the race of Helen and cut it down,
that wrung the strength out of the knees of many!
And he went, too—for the honor of Agamémnon
he took ship overseas for the wild horse country
of Troy, to fight the Trojans."

                                    This being told,   80
he tucked his long shirt up inside his belt
and strode into the pens for two young porkers.
He slaughtered them and singed them at the fire,
flayed and quartered them, and skewered the meat
to broil it all; then gave it to Odysseus   85
hot on the spits. He shook out barley meal,
took a winebowl of ivy wood and filled it,
and sat down facing him, with a gesture, saying:

"There is your dinner, friend, the pork of slaves.
Our fat shoats are all eaten by the suitors,   90
cold-hearted men, who never spare a thought
for how they stand in the sight of Zeus. The gods
living in bliss are fond of no wrongdoing,
but honor discipline and right behavior.
Even the outcasts of the earth, who bring   95
piracy from the sea, and bear off plunder
given by Zeus in shiploads—even those men
deep in their hearts tremble for heaven's eye.
But the suitors, now, have heard some word, some oracle
of my lord's death, being so unconcerned   100
to pay court properly or to go about their business.
All they want is to prey on his estate,
proud dogs: they stop at nothing. Not a day
goes by, and not a night comes under Zeus,
but they make butchery of our beeves and swine—   105
not one or two beasts at a time, either.
As for swilling down wine, they drink us dry.
Only a great domain like his could stand it—
greater than any on the dusky mainland
or here in Ithaka. Not twenty heroes   110
in the whole world were as rich as he. I know:
I could count it all up: twelve herds in Elis,
as many flocks, as many herds of swine,
and twelve wide ranging herds of goats, as well,
attended by his own men or by others—   115
out at the end of the island, eleven herds
are scattered now, with good men looking after them,

and every herdsman, every day, picks out
a prize ram to hand over to those fellows.
I too as overseer, keeper of swine,   120
must go through all my boars and send the best."

While he ran on, Odysseus with zeal
applied himself to the meat and wine, but inwardly
his thought shaped woe and ruin for the suitors.
When he had eaten all that he desired   125
and the cup he drank from had been filled again
with wine—a welcome sight—,
he spoke, and the words came light upon the air:

"Who is this lord who once acquired you,
so rich, so powerful, as you describe him?   130
You think he died for Agamémnon's honor.
Tell me his name: I may have met someone
of that description in my time. Who knows?
Perhaps only the immortal gods could say
if I should claim to have seen him: I have roamed   135
about the world so long."

                    The swineherd answered
as one who held a place of trust:

                         "Well, man,
his lady and his son will put no stock
in any news of him brought by a rover.
Wandering men tell lies for a night's lodging,   140
for fresh clothing; truth doesn't interest them.
Every time some traveller comes ashore
he has to tell my mistress his pretty tale,
and she receives him kindly, questions him,
remembering her prince, while the tears run   145
down her cheeks—and that is as it should be
when a woman's husband has been lost abroad.
I suppose you, too, can work your story up
at a moment's notice, given a shirt or cloak.
No: long ago wild dogs and carrion   150
birds, most like, laid bare his ribs on land
where life had left him. Or it may be, quick fishes
picked him clean in the deep sea, and his bones
lie mounded over in sand upon some shore.
One way or another, far from home he died,   155
a bitter loss, and pain, for everyone,
certainly for me. Never again shall I
have for my lot a master mild as he was
anywhere—not even with my parents
at home, where I was born and bred. I miss them   160
less than I do him—though a longing comes
to set my eyes on them in the old country.
No, it is the lost man I ache to think of—

Odysseus. And I speak the name respectfully,
even if he is not here. He loved me, cared for me.   165
I call him dear my lord, far though he be."

Now royal Odysseus, who had borne the long war,
spoke again:

    "Friend, as you are so dead sure
he will not come—and so mistrustful, too—
let me not merely talk, as others talk,   170
but swear to it: your lord is now at hand.
And I expect a gift for this good news
when he enters his own hall. Till then I would not
take a rag, no matter what my need.
I hate as I hate Hell's own gate that weakness   175
that makes a poor man into a flatterer.
Zeus be my witness, and the table garnished
for true friends, and Odysseus' own hearth—
by heaven, all I say will come to pass!
He will return, and he will be avenged   180
on any who dishonor his wife and son."

Eumaios—O my swineherd!—answered him:

"I take you at your word, then: you shall have
no good news gift from me. Nor will Odysseus
enter his hall. But peace! drink up your wine.   185
Let us talk now of other things. No more
imaginings. It makes me heavy-hearted
when someone brings my master back to mind—
my own true master.
    No, by heaven,
let us have no oaths! But if Odysseus   190
can come again god send he may! My wish
is that of Penélopê and old Laërtês
and Prince Telémakhos.
    Ah, he's another
to be distressed about—Odysseus' child,
Telémakhos! By the gods' grace he grew   195
like a tough sapling, and I thought he'd be
no less a man than his great father—strong
and admirably made; but then someone,
god or man, upset him, made him rash,
so that he sailed away to sandy Pylos   200
to hear news of his father. Now the suitors
lie in ambush on his homeward track,
ready to cut away the last shoot of Arkêsios'
line, the royal stock of Ithaka.
    No good
dwelling on it. Either he'll be caught   205
or else Kroníon's[1] hand will take him through.

---

1. Zeus, son of Kronos.

Tell me, now, of your own trials and troubles.
And tell me truly first, for I should know,
who are you, where do you hail from, where's your home
and family? What kind of ship was yours,   210
and what course brought you here? Who are your sailors?
I don't suppose you walked here on the sea."

To this the master of improvisation answered:

"I'll tell you all that, clearly as I may.
If we could sit here long enough, with meat   215
and good sweet wine, warm here, in peace and quiet
within doors, while the work of the world goes on—
I might take all this year to tell my story
and never end the tale of misadventures
that wore my heart out, by the gods' will.   220

My native land is the wide seaboard of Krete
where I grew up. I had a wealthy father,
and many other sons were born to him
of his true lady. My mother was a slave,
his concubine; but Kastor Hylákidês,   225
my father, treated me as a true born son.
High honor came to him in that part of Krete
for wealth and ease, and sons born for renown,
before the death-bearing Kêrês drew him down
to the underworld. His avid sons thereafter   230
dividing up the property by lot
gave me a wretched portion, a poor house.
But my ability won me a wife
of rich family. Fool I was never called,
nor turn-tail in a fight.
                  My strength's all gone,   235
but from the husk you may divine the ear
that stood tall in the old days. Misery owns me
now, but then great Arês and Athena
gave me valor and man-breaking power,
whenever I made choice of men-at-arms   240
to set a trap with me for my enemies.
Never, as I am a man, did I fear Death
ahead, but went in foremost in the charge,
putting a spear through any man whose legs
were not as fast as mine. That was my element,   245
war and battle. Farming I never cared for,
nor life at home, nor fathering fair children.
I reveled in long ships with oars; I loved
polished lances, arrows in the skirmish,
the shapes of doom that others shake to see.   250
Carnage suited me; heaven put those things
in me somehow. Each to his own pleasure!
Before we young Akhaians shipped for Troy
I led men on nine cruises in corsairs
to raid strange coasts, and had great luck, taking   255

rich spoils on the spot, and even more
in the division. So my house grew prosperous,
my standing therefore high among the Kretans.
Then came the day when Zeus who views the wide world
drew men's eyes upon that way accurst   260
that wrung the manhood from the knees of many!
Everyone pressed me, pressed King Idómeneus
to take command of ships for Ilion.
No way out; the country rang with talk of it.
So we Akhaians had nine years of war.   265
In the tenth year we sacked the inner city,
Priam's town, and sailed for home; but heaven
dispersed the Akhaians. Evil days for me
were stored up in the hidden mind of Zeus.
One month, no more, I stayed at home in joy   270
with children, wife, and treasure. Lust for action
drove me to go to sea then, in command
of ships and gallant seamen bound for Egypt.
Nine ships I fitted out; my men signed on
and came to feast with me, as good shipmates,   275
for six full days. Many a beast I slaughtered
in the gods' honor, for my friends to eat.
Embarking on the seventh, we hauled sail
and filled away from Krete on a fresh north wind
effortlessly, as boats will glide down stream.   280
All rigging whole and all hands well, we rested,
letting the wind and steersmen work the ships,
for five days; on the fifth we made the delta.[2]
I brought my squadron in to the river bank
with one turn of the sweeps. There, heaven knows,   285
I told the men to wait and guard the ships
while I sent out patrols to rising ground.
But reckless greed carried them all away
to plunder the rich bottomlands; they bore off
wives and children, killed what men they found.   290

When this news reached the city, all who heard it
came at dawn. On foot they came, and horsemen,
filling the river plain with dazzle of bronze;
and Zeus lord of lightning
threw my men into blind panic: no one dared   295
stand against that host closing around us.
Their scything weapons left our dead in piles,
but some they took alive, into forced labor.
And I—ah, how I wish that I had died
in Egypt, on that field! So many blows   300
awaited me!—Well, Zeus himself inspired me;
I wrenched my dogskin helmet off my head,
dropped my spear, dodged out of my long shield,
ran for the king's chariot and swung on

2. Of the Nile.

to embrace and kiss his knees. He pulled me up,   305
took pity on me, placed me on the footboards,
and drove home with me crouching there in tears.
Aye—for the troops, in battle fury still,
made one pass at me after another, pricking me
with spears, hoping to kill me. But he saved me,   310
for fear of the great wrath of Zeus that comes
when men who ask asylum are given death.

Seven years, then, my sojourn lasted there,
and I amassed a fortune, going about
among the openhanded Egyptians.   315
But when the eighth came round, a certain
Phoinikian adventurer came too,
a plausible rat, who had already done
plenty of devilry in the world.

                      This fellow
took me in completely with his schemes,   320
and led me with him to Phoinikia,
where he had land and houses. One full year
I stayed there with him, to the month and day,
and when fair weather came around again
he took me in a deepsea ship for Libya,   325
pretending I could help in the cargo trade;
he meant, in fact, to trade me off, and get
a high price for me. I could guess the game
but had to follow him aboard. One day
on course due west, off central Krete, the ship   330
caught a fresh norther, and we ran southward
before the wind while Zeus piled ruin ahead.
When Krete was out of sight astern, no land
anywhere to be seen, but sky and ocean,
Kroníon put a dark cloud in the zenith   335
over the ship, and gloom spread on the sea.
With crack on crack of thunder, he let fly
a bolt against the ship, a direct hit,
so that she bucked, in sacred fumes of sulphur,
and all the men were flung into the water.   340
They came up round the wreck, bobbing a while
like petrels on the waves. No homecoming
for these, from whom the god had turned his face!
Stunned in the smother as I was, yet Zeus
put into my hands the great mast of the ship—   345
a way to keep from drowning. So I twined
my arms and legs around it in the gale
and stayed afloat nine days. On the tenth night,
a big surf cast me up in Thesprotia.[3]
Pheidon the king there gave me refuge, nobly,   350
with no talk of reward. His son discovered me

3. On the west coast of the Greek mainland, north of Ithaka.

exhausted and half dead with cold, and gave me
a hand to bear me up till he reached home
where he could clothe me in a shirt and cloak.
In that king's house I heard news of Odysseus,   355
who lately was a guest there, passing by
on his way home, the king said; and he showed me
the treasure that Odysseus had brought:
bronze, gold, and iron wrought with heavy labor—
in that great room I saw enough to last   360
Odysseus' heirs for ten long generations.
The man himself had gone up to Dodona⁴
to ask the spelling leaves of the old oak
the will of God: how to return, that is,
to the rich realm of Ithaka, after so long   365
an absence—openly, or on the quiet.
And, tipping wine out, Pheidon swore to me
the ship was launched, the seamen standing by
to take Odysseus to his land at last.
But he had passage first for me: Thesprotians   370
were sailing, as luck had it, for Doulíkhion,⁵
the grain-growing island; there, he said,
they were to bring me to the king, Akastos.
Instead, that company saw fit to plot
foul play against me; in my wretched life   375
there was to be more suffering.
                          At sea, then,
when land lay far astern, they sprang their trap.
They'd make a slave of me that day, stripping
cloak and tunic off me, throwing around me
the dirty rags you see before you now.   380
At evening, off the fields of Ithaka,
they bound me, lashed me down under the decking
with stout ship's rope, while they all went ashore
in haste to make their supper on the beach.
The gods helped me to pry the lashing loose   385
until it fell away. I wound my rags
in a bundle round my head and eased myself
down the smooth lading plank into the water,
up to the chin, then swam an easy breast stroke
out and around, putting that crew behind,   390
and went ashore in underbrush, a thicket,
where I lay still, making myself small.
They raised a bitter yelling, and passed by
several times. When further groping seemed
useless to them, back to the ship they went   395
and out to sea again. The gods were with me,
keeping me hid; and with me when they brought me
here to the door of one who knows the world.
My destiny is yet to live awhile."

The swineherd bowed and said:

4. An oracle of Zeus. The message of the god was supposed to come from the sacred oak, perhaps from the rushing of the leaves in the wind.   5. An island off the west coast of Greece.

                "Ah well, poor drifter,   400
you've made me sad for you, going back over it,
all your hard life and wandering. That tale
about Odysseus, though, you might have spared me;
you will not make me believe that.
Why must you lie, being the man you are,   405
and all for nothing?
                  I can see so well
what happened to my master, sailing home!
Surely the gods turned on him, to refuse him
death in the field, or in his friends' arms
after he wound up the great war at Troy.   410
They would have made a tomb for him, the Akhaians,
and paid all honor to his son thereafter. No,
stormwinds made off with him. No glory came to him.

I moved here to the mountain with my swine.
Never, now, do I go down to town   415
unless I am sent for by Penélopê
when news of some sort comes. But those who sit
around her go on asking the old questions—
a few who miss their master still,
and those who eat his house up, and go free.   420
For my part, I have had no heart for inquiry
since one year an Aitolian[6] made a fool of me.
Exiled from land to land after some killing,
he turned up at my door; I took him in.
My master he had seen in Krete, he said,   425
lodged with Idómeneus, while the long ships,
leaky from gales, were laid up for repairs.
But they were all to sail, he said, that summer,
or the first days of fall—hulls laden deep
with treasure, manned by crews of heroes.
                      This time   430
you are the derelict the Powers bring.
Well, give up trying to win me with false news
or flattery. If I receive and shelter you,
it is not for your tales but for your trouble,
and with an eye to Zeus, who guards a guest."   435

Then said that sly and guileful man, Odysseus:

"A black suspicious heart beats in you surely;
the man you are, not even an oath could change you.
Come then, we'll make a compact; let the gods
witness it from Olympos, where they dwell.   440
Upon your lord's homecoming, if he comes
here to this very hut, and soon—
then give me a new outfit, shirt and cloak,
and ship me to Doulíkhion—I thought it
a pleasant island. But if Odysseus   445

6. Aitolia is on the mainland, east of Ithaka.

fails to appear as I predict, then Swish!
let the slaves pitch me down from some high rock,
so the next poor man who comes will watch his tongue."

The forester gave a snort and answered:

                              "Friend,
if I agreed to that, a great name   450
I should acquire in the world for goodness—
at one stroke and forever: your kind host
who gave you shelter and the hand of friendship,
only to take your life next day!
How confidently, after that, should I   455
address my prayers to Zeus, the son of Kronos!
It is time now for supper. My young herdsmen
should be arriving soon to set about it.
We'll make a quiet feast here at our hearth."

At this point in their talk the swine had come   460
up to the clearing, and the drovers followed
to pen them for the night—the porkers squealing
to high heaven, milling around the yard.
The swineherd then gave orders to his men:

"Bring in our best pig for a stranger's dinner.   465
A feast will do our hearts good, too; we know
grief and pain, hard scrabbling with our swine,
while the outsiders live on our labor."

                           Bronze
axe in hand, he turned to split up kindling,
while they drove in a tall boar, prime and fat,   470
planting him square before the fire. The gods,
as ever, had their due in the swineherd's thought,
for he it was who tossed the forehead bristles
as a first offering on the flames, calling
upon the immortal gods to let Odysseus   475
reach his home once more.
                     Then he stood up
and brained the boar with split oak from the woodpile.
Life ebbed from the beast; they slaughtered him,
singed the carcass, and cut out the joints.
Eumaios, taking flesh from every quarter,   480
put lean strips on the fat of sacrifice,
floured each one with barley meal, and cast it
into the blaze. The rest they sliced and skewered,
roasted with care, then took it off the fire
and heaped it up on platters. Now their chief,   485
who knew best the amenities, rose to serve,
dividing all that meat in seven portions—
one to be set aside, with proper prayers,
for the wood nymphs and Hermês, Maia's son;

the others for the company. Odysseus   490
he honored with long slices from the chine—
warming the master's heart. Odysseus looked at him
and said:

       "May you be dear to Zeus
as you are dear to me for this, Eumaios,
favoring with choice cuts a man like me."   495

And—O my swineherd!—you replied, Eumaios:

"Bless you, stranger, fall to and enjoy it
for what it is. Zeus grants us this or that,
or else refrains from granting, as he wills;
all things are in his power."

              He cut and burnt   500
a morsel for the gods who are young forever,
tipped out some wine, then put it in the hands
of Odysseus, the old soldier, raider of cities,
who sat at ease now with his meat before him.
As for the loaves, Mesaúlios dealt them out,   505
a yard boy, bought by the swineherd on his own,
unaided by his mistress or Laërtês,
from Taphians, while Odysseus was away.
Now all hands reached for that array of supper,
until, when hunger and thirst were turned away   510
Mesaúlios removed the bread and, heavy
with food and drink, they settled back to rest.

Now night had come on, rough, with no moon,
but a nightlong downpour setting in, the rainwind
blowing hard from the west. Odysseus   515
began to talk, to test the swineherd, trying
to put it in his head to take his cloak off
and lend it, or else urge the others to.
He knew the man's compassion.
                "Listen," he said,
"Eumaios, and you others, here's a wishful   520
tale that I shall tell. The wine's behind it,
vaporing wine, that makes a serious man
break down and sing, kick up his heels and clown,
or tell some story that were best untold.
But now I'm launched, I can't stop now.
                   Would god I felt   525
the hot blood in me that I had at Troy!
Laying an ambush near the walls one time,
Odysseus and Meneláos were commanders
and I ranked third. I went at their request.
We worked in toward the bluffs and battlements   530
and, circling the town, got into canebreaks,
thick and high, a marsh where we took cover,

hunched under arms.
                              The northwind dropped, and night
came black and wintry. A fine sleet descending
whitened the cane like hoarfrost, and clear ice   535
grew dense upon our shields. The other men,
all wrapt in blanket cloaks as well as tunics,
rested well, in shields up to their shoulder,
but I had left my cloak with friends in camp,
foolhardy as I was. No chance of freezing hard,   540
I thought, so I wore kilts and a shield only.
But in the small hours of the third watch, when stars
that rise at evening go down to their setting,
I nudged Odysseus, who lay close beside me;
he was alert then, listening, and I said: 545

'Son of Laërtês and the gods of old,
Odysseus, master mariner and soldier,
I cannot hold on long among the living.
The cold is making a corpse of me. Some god
inveigled me to come without a cloak.   550
No help for it now; too late.'

                              Next thing I knew
he had a scheme all ready in his mind—
and what a man he was for schemes and battles!
Speaking under his breath to me, he murmured:

'Quiet; none of the rest should hear you.'

                                            Then,   555
propping his head on his forearm, he said:

'Listen, lads, I had an ominous dream,
the point being how far forward from our ships
and lines we've come. Someone should volunteer
to tell the corps commander, Agamémnon;   560
he may reinforce us from the base.'

                              At this,
Thoas jumped up, the young son of Andraimon,
put down his crimson cloak and headed off,
running shoreward.
                          Wrapped in that man's cloak
how gratefully I lay in the bitter dark   565
until the dawn came stitched in gold! I wish
I had that sap and fiber in me now!"

Then—O my swineherd!—you replied, Eumaios:

"That was a fine story, and well told,
not a word out of place, not a pointless word.   570
No, you'll not sleep cold for lack of cover,

or any other comfort one should give
to a needy guest. However, in the morning,
you must go flapping in the same old clothes.
Shirts and cloaks are few here; every man   575
has one change only. When our prince arrives,
the son of Odysseus, he will make you gifts—
cloak, tunic, everything—and grant you passage
wherever you care to go."

On this he rose
and placed the bed of balsam near the fire,   580
strewing sheepskins on top, and skins of goats.
Odysseus lay down. His host threw over him
a heavy blanket cloak, his own reserve
against the winter wind when it came wild.
So there Odysseus dropped off to sleep,   585
while herdsmen slept nearby. But not the swineherd:
not in the hut could he lie down in peace,
but now equipped himself for the night outside;
and this rejoiced Odysseus' heart, to see him
care for the herd so, while his lord was gone.   590
He hung a sharp sword from his shoulder, gathered
a great cloak round him, close, to break the wind,
and pulled a shaggy goatskin on his head.
Then, to keep at a distance dogs or men,
he took a sharpened lance, and went to rest   595
under a hollow rock where swine were sleeping
out of the wind and rain.

BOOK XV

[How They Came to Ithaka]

South into Lakedaimon
into the land where greens are wide for dancing
Athena went, to put in mind of home
her great-hearted hero's honored son,
rousing him to return.

And there she found him   5
with Nestor's lad in the late night at rest
under the portico of Meneláos,
the famous king. Stilled by the power of slumber
the son of Nestor lay, but honeyed sleep
had not yet taken in her arms Telémakhos.   10
All through the starlit night, with open eyes,
he pondered what he had heard about his father,
until at his bedside grey-eyed Athena
towered and said:

"The brave thing now, Telémakhos,
would be to end this journey far from home.   15
All that you own you left behind
with men so lost to honor in your house

they may devour it all, shared out among them.
How will your journey save you then?
                                        Go quickly
to the lord of the great war cry, Meneláos;   20
press him to send you back. You may yet find
the queen your mother in her rooms alone.
It seems her father and her kinsmen say
Eurýmakhos is the man for her to marry.
He has outdone the suitors, all the rest,   25
in gifts to her, and made his pledges double.
Check him, or he will have your lands and chattels[7]
in spite of you.
                    You know a woman's pride
at bringing riches to the man she marries.
As to her girlhood husband, her first children,   30
he is forgotten, being dead—and they
no longer worry her.
                        So act alone.
Go back; entrust your riches to the servant
worthiest in your eyes, until the gods
make known what beauty you yourself shall marry.   35

This too I have to tell you: now take heed:
the suitors' ringleaders are hot for murder,
waiting in the channel between Ithaka
and Samê's rocky side; they mean to kill you
before you can set foot ashore. I doubt   40
they'll bring it off. Dark earth instead
may take to her cold bed a few brave suitors
who preyed upon your cattle.
                              Bear well out
in your good ship, to eastward of the islands,
and sail again by night. Someone immortal   45
who cares for you will make a fair wind blow.
Touch at the first beach, go ashore, and send
your ship and crew around to port by sea,
while you go inland to the forester,
your old friend, loyal keeper of the swine.   50
Remain that night with him; send him to town
to tell your watchful mother Penélopê
that you are back from Pylos safe and sound."

With this Athena left him for Olympos.
He swung his foot across and gave a kick   55
and said to the son of Nestor:

                        "Open your eyes,
Peisístratos. Get our team into harness.
We have a long day's journey."

---

7. The Greek could also mean "be careful she [Penélopê] doesn't carry off, against your will, some of your property," i.e., for her new husband. This would explain why Athena tells Telémakhos (lines 33–34) to turn the property over to the servant he has most confidence in. The suggestion that Penélopê is planning to marry Eurýmakhos and take Telémakhos's property with her is not to be taken seriously; Athena uses it to get Telémakhos moving.

                    Nestor's son
turned over and answered him:

                        "It is still night,
and no moon. Can we drive now? We can not,   60
itch as we may for the road home. Dawn is near.
Allow the captain of spearmen, Meneláos,
time to pack our car with gifts and time
to speak a gracious word, sending us off.
A guest remembers all his days   65
that host who makes provision for him kindly."

The Dawn soon took her throne of gold, and Lord
Meneláos, clarion in battle,
rose from where he lay beside the beauty
of Helen with her shining hair. He strode   70
into the hall nearby.
                    Hearing him come,
Odysseus' son pulled on his snowy tunic
over the skin, gathered his long cape
about his breadth of shoulder like a captain,
the heir of King Odysseus. At the door   75
he stood and said:

                    "Lord Marshal, Meneláos,
send me home now to my own dear country:
longing has come upon me to go home."

The lord of the great war cry said at once:

"If you are longing to go home, Telémakhos,   80
I would not keep you for the world, not I.
I'd think myself or any other host
as ill-mannered for over-friendliness
as for hostility.
                    Measure is best in everything.
To send a guest packing, or cling to him   85
when he's in haste—one sin equals the other.
'Good entertaining ends with no detaining.'
Only let me load your car with gifts
and fine ones, you shall see.
                    I'll bid the women
set out breakfast from the larder stores;   90
honor and appetite—we'll attend to both
before a long day's journey overland.
Or would you care to try the Argive midlands
and Hellas, in my company? I'll harness
my own team, and take you through the towns.   95
Guests like ourselves no lord will turn away;
each one will make one gift, at least,
to carry home with us: tripod or cauldron
wrought in bronze, mule team, or golden cup."

Clearheaded Telémakhos replied:

                    "Lord Marshal   100
Meneláos, royal son of Atreus,
I must return to my own hearth. I left
no one behind as guardian of my property.
This going abroad for news of a great father—
heaven forbid it be my own undoing,   105
or any precious thing be lost at home."

At this the tall king, clarion in battle,
called to his lady and her waiting women
to give them breakfast from the larder stores.
Eteóneus, the son of Boethoös, came   110
straight from bed, from where he lodged nearby,
and Meneláos ordered a fire lit
for broiling mutton. The king's man obeyed.
Then down to the cedar chamber Meneláos
walked with Helen and Prince Megapénthês.   115
Amid the gold he had in that place lying
the son of Atreus picked a wine cup, wrought
with handles left and right, and told his son
to take a silver winebowl.   Helen lingered
near the deep coffers filled with gowns, her own   120
handiwork.
           Tall goddess among women,
she lifted out one robe of state so royal,
adorned and brilliant with embroidery,
deep in the chest it shimmered like a star.
Now all three turned back to the door to greet   125
Telémakhos. And red-haired Meneláos
cried out to him:

               "O prince Telémakhos,
may Hêra's Lord of Thunder see you home
and bring you to the welcome you desire!
Here are your gifts—perfect and precious things   130
I wish to make your own, out of my treasure."

And gently the great captain, son of Atreus,
handed him the goblet. Megapénthês
carried the winebowl glinting silvery
to set before him, and the Lady Helen   135
drew near, so that he saw her cheek's pure line.
She held the gown and murmured:

                   "I, too,
bring you a gift, dear child, and here it is;
remember Helen's hands by this; keep it
for your own bride, your joyful wedding day;   140
let your dear mother guard it in her chamber.

My blessing: may you come soon to your island,
home to your timbered hall."

                    So she bestowed it,
and happily he took it. These fine things
Peisístratos packed well in the wicker carrier,   145
admiring every one. Then Meneláos
led the two guests in to take their seats
on thrones and easy chairs in the great hall.
Now came a maid to tip a golden jug
of water over a silver finger bowl,   150
and drew the polished tables up beside them;
the larder mistress brought her tray of loaves,
with many savories to lavish on them;
viands were served by Eteóneus, and wine
by Meneláos' son. Then every hand   155
reached out upon good meat and drink to take them,
driving away hunger and thirst. At last,
Telémakhos and Nestor's son led out
their team to harness, mounted their bright car,
and drove down under the echoing entrance way,   160
while red-haired Meneláos, Atreus' son,
walked alongside with a golden cup—
wine for the wayfarers to spill at parting.
Then by the tugging team he stood, and spoke
over the horses' heads:

                    "Farewell, my lads.   165
Homage to Nestor, the benevolent king;
in my time he was fatherly to me,
when the flower of Akhaia warred on Troy."

Telémakhos made this reply:

                    "No fear
but we shall bear at least as far as Nestor   170
your messages, great king. How I could wish
to bring them home to Ithaka! If only
Odysseus were there, if he could hear me tell
of all the courtesy I have had from you,
returning with your finery and your treasure."   175
Even as he spoke, a beat of wings went skyward
off to the right—a mountain eagle, grappling
a white goose in his talons, heavy prey
hooked from a farmyard. Women and men-at-arms
made hubbub, running up, as he flew over,   180
but then he wheeled hard right before the horses—
a sight that made the whole crowd cheer, with hearts
lifting in joy. Peisístratos called out:

"Read us the sign, O Meneláos, Lord
Marshal of armies! Was the god revealing   185
something thus to you, or to ourselves?"

At this the old friend of the god of battle
groped in his mind for the right thing to say,
but regal Helen put in quickly:

                  "Listen:
I can tell you—tell what the omen means,   190
as light is given me, and as I see it
point by point fulfilled. The beaked eagle
flew from the wild mountain of his fathers
to take for prey the tame house bird. Just so,
Odysseus, back from his hard trials and wandering,   195
will soon come down in fury on his house.
He may be there today, and a black hour
he brings upon the suitors."

                    Telémakhos
gazed and said:

            "May Zeus, the lord of Hêra,
make it so! In far-off Ithaka, all my life,   200
I shall invoke you as a goddess, lady."

He let the whip fall, and the restive mares
broke forward at a canter through the town
into the open country.
                  All that day
they kept their harness shaking, side by side,   205
until at sundown when the roads grew dim
they made a halt at Pherai. There Dióklês
son of Ortílokhos whom Alpheios fathered,
welcomed the young men, and they slept the night.
Up when the young Dawn's finger tips of rose   210
opened in the east, they hitched the team
once more to the painted car
and steered out westward through the echoing gate,
whipping their fresh horses into a run.
Approaching Pylos Height at that day's end,   215
Telémakhos appealed to the son of Nestor:

"Could you, I wonder, do a thing I'll tell you,
supposing you agree?
We take ourselves to be true friends—in age
alike, and bound by ties between our fathers,   220
and now by partnership in this adventure.
Prince, do not take me roundabout,
but leave me at the ship, else the old king
your father will detain me overnight
for love of guests, when I should be at sea."   225

The son of Nestor nodded, thinking swiftly
how best he could oblige his friend.
Here was his choice: to pull the team hard over

along the beach till he could rein them in
beside the ship. Unloading Meneláos'   230
royal keepsakes into the stern sheets,
he sang out:

        "Now for action! Get aboard,
and call your men, before I break the news
at home in hall to father. Who knows better
the old man's heart than I? If you delay,   235
he will not let you go, but he'll descend on you
in person and imperious; no turning
back with empty hands for him, believe me,
once his blood is up."

        He shook the reins
to the lovely mares with long manes in the wind,   240
guiding them full tilt toward his father's hall.
Telémakhos called in the crew, and told them:

"Get everything shipshape aboard this craft;
we pull out now, and put sea miles behind us."

The listening men obeyed him, climbing in   245
to settle on their benches by the rowlocks,
while he stood watchful by the stern. He poured out
offerings there, and prayers to Athena.

Now a strange man came up to him, an easterner
fresh from spilling blood in distant Argos,   250
a hunted man. Gifted in prophecy,
he had as forebear that Melampous, wizard
who lived of old in Pylos, mother city
of western flocks.[8]

        Melampous, a rich lord,
had owned a house unmatched among the Pylians,   255
until the day came when king Neleus, noblest
in that age, drove him from his native land.
And Neleus for a year's term sequestered
Melampous' fields and flocks, while he lay bound
hand and foot in the keep of Phylakos.   260
Beauty of Neleus' daughter put him there
and sombre folly the inbreaking Fury

8. The complicated story that follows (obscure in some of its details) gives us the genealogical background
of the young man who comes up to Telémakhos. His name, as we learn only at the end of the genealogy,
is Theoklýmenos, and he has an important role to play in the last part of the *Odyssey*. His gift for prophecy
is hereditary; his ancestor Melampous had it. Melampous's brother (who lived in Pylos under King Neleus,
Nestor's father) asked for the hand of Neleus's daughter. Neleus demanded as bride-price the herds of
cattle of a neighboring lord, Phylakos. Melampous tried to steal the cattle for his brother, was caught, and
was imprisoned. In prison he heard the worms in the roof beams announce that the wood was almost eaten
through, and he predicted the collapse of the roof. Phylakos, impressed, released him, with the cattle; his
brother was given the bride. Melampous then left for Argos, where he settled and prospered. One of his
great-grandsons was the prophet Amphiaraos, who foresaw that if he joined the champions who went to
besiege Thebes (The Seven against Thebes) he would lose his life (see n. 9, p. 339). Melampous's son
Mantios had a son named Polypheidês, and it is his son Theoklýmenos who now begs Telémakhos for a
place in his ship.

thrust upon him. But he gave the slip
to death, and drove the bellowing herd of Iphiklos
from Phylakê to Pylos, there to claim   265
the bride that ordeal won him from the king.
He led her to his brother's house, and went on
eastward into another land, the bluegrass
plain of Argos. Destiny held for him
rule over many Argives. Here he married,   270
built a great manor house, fathered Antíphatês
and Mantios, commanders both, of whom
Antíphatês begot Oikleiês
and Oikleiês the firebrand Amphiaraos.
This champion the lord of stormcloud, Zeus,   275
and strong Apollo loved; nor had he ever
to cross the doorsill into dim old age.
A woman, bought by trinkets, gave him over
to be cut down in the assault on Thebes.
His sons were Alkmáon and Amphílokhos.   280
In the meantime Lord Mantios begot
Polypheidês, the prophet, and
Kleitos—famous name! For Dawn in silks
of gold carried off Kleitos for his beauty
to live among the gods. But Polypheidês,   285
high-hearted and exalted by Apollo
above all men for prophecy, withdrew
to Hyperesia[9] when his father angered him.
He lived on there, foretelling to the world
the shape of things to come.

                   His son it was,   290
Theoklýmenos, who came upon Telémakhos
as he poured out the red wine in the sand
near his trim ship, with prayer to Athena;
and he called out, approaching:

                   "Friend, well met
here at libation before going to sea.   295
I pray you by the wine you spend, and by
your god, your own life, and your company;
enlighten me, and let the truth be known.
Who are you? Of what city and what parents?"

Telémakhos turned to him and replied: 300

"Stranger, as truly as may be, I'll tell you.
I am from Ithaka, where I was born;
my father is, or he once was, Odysseus.
But he's a long time gone, and dead, may be;
and that is what I took ship with my friends   305
to find out—for he left long years ago."

Said Theoklýmenos in reply:

9. Near Argos.

"I too
have had to leave my home. I killed a cousin.
In the wide grazing lands of Argos live
many kinsmen of his and friends in power,   310
great among the Akhaians. These I fled.
Death and vengeance at my back, as Fate
has turned now, I came wandering overland.
Give me a plank aboard your ship, I beg,
or they will kill me. They are on my track."   315

Telémakhos made answer:

"No two ways
about it. Will I pry you from our gunnel
when you are desperate to get to sea?
Come aboard; share what we have, and welcome."

He took the bronze-shod lance from the man's hand   320
and laid it down full-length on deck; then swung
his own weight after it aboard the cutter,
taking position aft, making a place
for Theoklýmenos near him. The stern lines
were slacked off, and Telémakhos commanded: 325

"Rig the mast; make sail!" Nimbly they ran
to push the fir pole high and step it firm
amidships in the box, make fast the forestays,
and hoist aloft the white sail on its halyards.
A following wind came down from grey-eyed Athena,   330
blowing brisk through heaven, and so steady
the cutter lapped up miles of salt blue sea,
passing Krounoi abeam and Khalkis estuary[1]
at sundown when the sea ways all grew dark.
Then, by Athena's wind borne on, the ship   335
rounded Pheai by night and coasted Elis,
the green domain of the Epeioi; thence
he put her head north toward the running pack
of islets, wondering if by sailing wide
he sheered off Death, or would be caught.
                              That night   340
Odysseus and the swineherd supped again
with herdsmen in their mountain hut. At ease
when appetite and thirst were turned away,
Odysseus, while he talked, observed the swineherd
to see if he were hospitable still—   345
if yet again the man would make him stay
under his roof, or send him off to town.

"Listen," he said, "Eumaios; listen, lads.
At daybreak I must go and try my luck

---

1. The precise location of these places is disputed, but the mention of Elis in line 336 shows that they are all on the west coast of the Peloponnese, south of the Gulf of Corinth. The Olympic Games were held in Elis.

around the port. I burden you too long.   350
Direct me, put me on the road with someone.
Nothing else for it but to play the beggar
in populous parts. I'll get a cup or loaf,
maybe, from some householder. If I go
as far as the great hall of King Odysseus   355
I might tell Queen Penélopê my news.
Or I can drift inside among the suitors
to see what alms they give, rich as they are.
If they have whims, I'm deft in ways of service—
that I can say, and you may know for sure.   360
By grace of Hermês the Wayfinder, patron
of mortal tasks, the god who honors toil,
no man can do a chore better than I can.
Set me to build a fire, or chop wood,
cook or carve, mix wine and serve—or anything   365
inferior men attend to for the gentry."

Now you were furious at this, Eumaios,
and answered—O my swineherd!—

                              "Friend, friend,
how could this fantasy take hold of you?
You dally with your life, and nothing less,   370
if you feel drawn to mingle in that company—
reckless, violent, and famous for it
out to the rim of heaven. Slaves
they have, but not like you. No—theirs are boys
in fresh cloaks and tunics, with pomade   375
ever on their sleek heads, and pretty faces.
These are their minions, while their tables gleam
and groan under big roasts, with loaves and wine.
Stay with us here. No one is burdened by you,
neither myself nor any of my hands.   380
Wait here until Odysseus' son returns.
You shall have clothing from him, cloak and tunic,
and passage where your heart desires to go."

The noble and enduring man replied:

"May you be dear to Zeus for this, Eumaios,   385
even as you are to me. Respite from pain
you give me—and from homelessness. In life
there's nothing worse than knocking about the world,
no bitterness we vagabonds are spared
when the curst belly rages! Well, you master it   390
and me, making me wait for the king's son.
But now, come, tell me:
what of Odysseus' mother, and his father
whom he took leave of on the sill of age?
Are they under the sun's rays, living still,   395
or gone down long ago to lodge with Death?"

To this the rugged herdsman answered:

"Aye,
that I can tell you; it is briefly told.
Laërtês lives, but daily in his hall
prays for the end of life and soul's delivery,   400
heartbroken as he is for a son long gone
and for his lady. Sorrow, when she died,
aged and enfeebled him like a green tree stricken;
but pining for her son, her brilliant son,
wore out her life.
                    Would god no death so sad   405
might come to benefactors dear as she!
I loved always to ask and hear about her
while she lived, although she lived in sorrow.
For she had brought me up with her own daughter,
Princess Ktimenê, her youngest child.   410
We were alike in age and nursed as equals
nearly, till in the flower of our years
they gave her, married her, to a Samian prince,[2]
taking his many gifts. For my own portion
her mother gave new clothing, cloak and sandals,   415
and sent me to the woodland. Well she loved me.
Ah, how I miss that family! It is true
the blissful gods prosper my work; I have
meat and drink to spare for those I prize;
but so removed I am, I have no speech   420
with my sweet mistress, now that evil days
and overbearing men darken her house.
Tenants all hanker for good talk and gossip
around their lady, and a snack in hall,
a cup or two before they take the road   425
to their home acres, each one bearing home
some gift to cheer his heart."

                    The great tactician
answered:

                    "You were still a child, I see,
when exiled somehow from your parents' land.
Tell me, had it been sacked in war, the city   430
of spacious ways in which they made their home,
your father and your gentle mother? Or
were you kidnapped alone, brought here by sea
huddled with sheep in some foul pirate squadron,
to this landowner's hall? He paid your ransom?"   435

The master of the woodland answered:

                    "Friend,
now that you show an interest in that matter,

2. From Samê, a nearby island or town.

attend me quietly, be at your ease,
and drink your wine. These autumn nights are long,
ample for story-telling and for sleep.   440
You need not go to bed before the hour;
sleeping from dusk to dawn's a dull affair.
Let any other here who wishes, though,
retire to rest. At daybreak let him breakfast
and take the king's own swine into the wilderness.   445
Here's a tight roof; we'll drink on, you and I,
and ease our hearts of hardships we remember,
sharing old times. In later days a man
can find a charm in old adversity,
exile and pain. As to your question, now: 450

A certain island, Syriê by name—
you may have heard the name—lies off Ortýgia³
due west, and holds the sunsets of the year.
Not very populous, but good for grazing
sheep and kine; rich too in wine and grain.   455
No dearth is ever known there, no disease
wars on the folk, of ills that plague mankind;
but when the townsmen reach old age, Apollo
with his longbow of silver comes, and Artemis,
showering arrows of mild death.
                                        Two towns   460
divide the farmlands of that whole domain,
and both were ruled by Ktêsios, my father,
Orménos' heir, and a great godlike man.

Now one day some of those renowned seafaring
men, sea-dogs, Phoinikians, came ashore   465
with bags of gauds for trading. Father had
in our household a woman of Phoinikia,
a handsome one, and highly skilled. Well, she
gave in to the seductions of those rovers.
One of them found her washing near the mooring   470
and lay with her, making such love to her
as women in their frailty are confused by,
even the best of them.
                                In due course, then,
he asked her who she was and where she hailed from:
and nodding toward my father's roof, she said: 475

'I am of Sidon town, smithy of bronze
for all the East. Arubas Pasha's daughter.
Taphian pirates caught me in a byway
and sold me into slavery overseas
in this man's home. He could afford my ransom.'   480

---

3. Another name for Delos, the central island of the Cyclades, but also the name of the central island of
the city of Syracuse in Sicily. However, the fact that on Syriê there is no disease and that everyone there
dies painlessly suggests that it is not located in this world at all—like Phaiákia, it is in fairyland.

The sailor who had lain with her replied:

'Why not ship out with us on the run homeward,
and see your father's high-roofed hall again,
your father and your mother? Still in Sidon
and still rich, they are said to be.'

She answered: 485

'It could be done, that, if you sailors take
oath I'll be given passage home unharmed.'

Well, soon she had them swearing it all pat
as she desired, repeating every syllable,
whereupon she warned them:

                    'Not a word   490
about our meeting here! Never call out to me
when any of you see me in the lane
or at the well. Some visitor might bear
tales to the old man. If he guessed the truth,
I'd be chained up, your lives would be in peril.   495
No: keep it secret. Hurry with your peddling,
and when your hold is filled with livestock, send
a message to me at the manor hall.
Gold I'll bring, whatever comes to hand,
and something else, too, as my passage fee—   500
the master's child, my charge: a boy so high,
bright for his age; he runs with me on errands.
I'd take him with me happily; his price
would be I know not what in sale abroad.'

Her bargain made, she went back to the manor.   505
But they were on the island all that year,
getting by trade a cargo of our cattle;
until, the ship at length being laden full,
ready for sea, they sent a messenger
to the Phoinikian woman. Shrewd he was,   510
this fellow who came round my father's hall,
showing a golden chain all strung with amber,
a necklace. Maids in waiting and my mother
passed it from hand to hand, admiring it,
engaging they would buy it. But that dodger,   515
as soon as he had caught the woman's eye
and nodded, slipped away to join the ship.
She took my hand and led me through the court
into the portico. There by luck she found
winecups and tables still in place—for Father's   520
attendant counselors had dined just now
before they went to the assembly. Quickly
she hid three goblets in her bellying dress
to carry with her while I tagged along

in my bewilderment. The sun went down   525
and all the lanes grew dark as we descended,
skirting the harbor in our haste to where
those traders of Phoinikia held their ship.
All went aboard at once and put to sea,
taking the two of us. A favoring wind   530
blew from the power of heaven. We sailed on
six nights and days without event. Then Zeus
the son of Kronos added one more noon—and sudden
arrows from Artemis pierced the woman's heart.
Stone-dead she dropped   535
into the sloshing bilge the way a tern
plummets; and the sailors heaved her over
as tender pickings for the seals and fish.
Now I was left in dread, alone, while wind
and current bore them on to Ithaka.   540
Laërtês purchased me. That was the way
I first laid eyes upon this land."

                        Odysseus,
the kingly man, replied:

                    "You rouse my pity,
telling what you endured when you were young.
But surely Zeus put good alongside ill: 545
torn from your own far home, you had the luck
to come into a kind man's service, generous
with food and drink. And a good life you lead,
unlike my own, all spent in barren roaming
from one country to the next, till now."   550

So the two men talked on, into the night,
leaving few hours for sleep before the Dawn
stepped up to her bright chair.
                    The ship now drifting
under the island lee, Telémakhos'
companions took in sail and mast, unshipped   555
the oars and rowed ashore. They moored her stern
by the stout hawser lines, tossed out the bow stones,
and waded in beyond the wash of ripples
to mix their wine and cook their morning meal.
When they had turned back hunger and thirst, Telémakhos   560
arose to give the order of the day.

"Pull for the town," he said, "and berth our ship,
while I go inland across country. Later,
this evening, after looking at my farms,
I'll join you in the city. When day comes   565
I hope to celebrate our crossing, feasting
everyone on good red meat and wine."

His noble passenger, Theoklýmenos,
now asked:

"What as to me, my dear young fellow,
where shall I go? Will I find lodging here   570
with some one of the lords of stony Ithaka?
Or go straight to your mother's hall and yours?"

Telémakhos turned round to him and said:

"I should myself invite you to our hall
if things were otherwise; there'd be no lack   575
of entertainment for you. As it stands,
no place could be more wretched for a guest
while I'm away. Mother will never see you;
she almost never shows herself at home
to the suitors there, but stays in her high chamber   580
weaving upon her loom. No, let me name
another man for you to go to visit:
Eurýmakhos, the honored son of Pólybos.
In Ithaka they are dazzled by him now—
the strongest of their princes, bent on making   585
mother and all Odysseus' wealth his own.
Zeus on Olympos only knows
if some dark hour for them will intervene."

The words were barely spoken, when a hawk,
Apollo's courier, flew up on the right,   590
clutching a dove and plucking her—so feathers
floated down to the ground between Telémakhos
and the moored cutter. Theoklýmenos
called him apart and gripped his hand, whispering:

"A god spoke in this bird-sign on the right.   595
I knew it when I saw the hawk fly over us.
There is no kinglier house than yours, Telémakhos,
here in the realm of Ithaka. Your family
will be in power forever."

                    The young prince,
clear in spirit, answered:

                        "Be it so,   600
friend, as you say. And may you know as well
the friendship of my house, and many gifts
from me, so everyone may call you fortunate."

He called a trusted crewman named Peiraios,
and said to him:

                "Peiraios, son of Klýtios,   605
can I rely on you again as ever, most
of all the friends who sailed with me to Pylos?
Take this man home with you, take care of him,
treat him with honor, till I come."

To this
Peiraios the good spearman answered:

"Aye,   610
stay in the wild country while you will,
I shall be looking after him, Telémakhos.
He will not lack good lodging."

Down to the ship
he turned, and boarded her, and called the others
to cast off the stern lines and come aboard.   615
So the men climbed in to sit beside the rowlocks.
Telémakhos now tied his sandals on
and lifted his tough spear from the ship's deck;
hawsers were taken in, and they shoved off
to reach the town by way of the open sea   620
as he commanded them—royal Odysseus'
own dear son, Telémakhos.

On foot
and swiftly he went up toward the stockade
where swine were penned in hundreds, and at night
the guardian of the swine, the forester,   625
slept under arms on duty for his masters.

BOOK XVI

[*Father and Son*]

But there were two men in the mountain hut—
Odysseus and the swineherd. At first light
blowing their fire up, they cooked their breakfast
and sent their lads out, driving herds to root
in the tall timber.

When Telémakhos came,   5
the wolvish troop of watchdogs only fawned on him
as he advanced. Odysseus heard them go
and heard the light crunch of a man's footfall—
at which he turned quickly to say:

"Eumaios,
here is one of your crew come back, or maybe   10
another friend: the dogs are out there snuffling
belly down; not one has even growled.
I can hear footsteps—"

But before he finished
his tall son stood at the door.

The swineherd
rose in surprise, letting a bowl and jug
tumble from his fingers. Going forward,   15
he kissed the young man's head, his shining eyes
and both hands, while his own tears brimmed and fell.
Think of a man whose dear and only son,
born to him in exile, reared with labor,   20

has lived ten years abroad and now returns:
how would that man embrace his son! Just so
the herdsman clapped his arms around Telémakhos
and covered him with kisses—for he knew
the lad had got away from death. He said: 25

"Light of my days, Telémakhos,
you made it back! When you took ship for Pylos
I never thought to see you here again.
Come in, dear child, and let me feast my eyes;
here you are, home from the distant places!   30
How rarely anyway, you visit us,
your own men, and your own woods and pastures!
Always in the town, a man would think
you loved the suitors' company, those dogs!"

Telémakhos with his clear candor said: 35

"I am with you, Uncle. See now, I have come
because I wanted to see you first, to hear from you
if Mother stayed at home—or is she married
off to someone and Odysseus' bed
left empty for some gloomy spider's weaving?"   40

Gently the forester replied to this:

"At home indeed your mother is, poor lady,
still in the women's hall. Her nights and days
are wearied out with grieving."

                        Stepping back
he took the bronze-shod lance, and the young prince   45
entered the cabin over the worn door stone.
Odysseus moved aside, yielding his couch,
but from across the room Telémakhos checked him:

"Friend, sit down; we'll find another chair
in our own hut. Here is the man to make one!"   50

The swineherd, when the quiet man sank down,
built a new pile of evergreens and fleeces—
a couch for the dear son of great Odysseus—
then gave them trenchers of good meat, left over
from the roast pork of yesterday, and heaped up   55
willow baskets full of bread, and mixed
an ivy bowl of honey-hearted wine.
Then he in turn sat down, facing Odysseus,
their hands went out upon the meat and drink
as they fell to, ridding themselves of hunger,   60
until Telémakhos paused and said:

       "Oh, Uncle,
what's your friend's home port? How did he come?
Who were the sailors brought him here to Ithaka?
I doubt if he came walking on the sea."

And you replied, Eumaios—O my swineherd—   65

"Son, the truth about him is soon told.
His home land, and a broad land, too, is Krete,
but he has knocked about the world, he says,
for years, as the Powers wove his life. Just now
he broke away from a shipload of Thesprotians   70
to reach my hut. I place him in your hands.
Act as you will. He wishes your protection."

The young man said:

      "Eumaios, my protection!
The notion cuts me to the heart. How can I
receive your friend at home? I am not old enough   75
or trained in arms. Could I defend myself
if someone picked a fight with me?
         Besides,
mother is in a quandary, whether to stay with me
as mistress of our household, honoring
her lord's bed, and opinion in the town,   80
or take the best Akhaian who comes her way—
the one who offers most.
      I'll undertake,
at all events, to clothe your friend for winter,
now he is with you. Tunic and cloak of wool,
a good broadsword, and sandals—these are his.   85
I can arrange to send him where he likes
or you may keep him in your cabin here.
I shall have bread and wine sent up; you need not
feel any pinch on his behalf.
       Impossible
to let him stay in hall, among the suitors.   90
They are drunk, drunk on impudence, they might
injure my guest—and how could I bear that?
How could a single man take on those odds?
Not even a hero could.
      The suitors are too strong."

At this the noble and enduring man, Odysseus,   95
addressed his son:

      "Kind prince, it may be fitting
for me to speak a word. All that you say
gives me an inward wound as I sit listening.
I mean this wanton game they play, these fellows,
riding roughshod over you in your own house,   100

admirable as you are. But tell me,
are you resigned to being bled? The townsmen,
stirred up against you, are they, by some oracle?
Your brothers—can you say your brothers fail you?
A man should feel his kin, at least, behind him   105
in any clash, when a real fight is coming.
If my heart were as young as yours, if I were
son of Odysseus, or the man himself,
I'd rather have my head cut from my shoulders
by some slashing adversary, if I   110
brought no hurt upon that crew! Suppose
I went down, being alone, before the lot,
better, I say, to die at home in battle
than see these insupportable things, day after
day the stranger cuffed, the women slaves   115
dragged here and there, shame in the lovely rooms,
the wine drunk up in rivers, sheer waste
of pointless feasting, never at an end!"

Telémakhos replied:

                    "Friend, I'll explain to you.
There is no rancor in the town against me,   120
no fault of brothers, whom a man should feel
behind him when a fight is in the making;
no, no—in our family the First Born
of Heaven, Zeus, made single sons the rule.
Arkeísios had but one, Laërtês; he   125
in his turn fathered only one, Odysseus,
who left me in his hall alone, too young
to be of any use to him.
And so you see why enemies fill our house
in these days: all the princes of the islands,   130
Doulíkhion, Samê, wooded Zakýnthos,
Ithaka, too—lords of our island rock—
eating our house up as they court my mother.
She cannot put an end to it; she dare not
bar the marriage that she hates; and they   135
devour all my substance and my cattle,
and who knows when they'll slaughter me as well?
It rests upon the gods' great knees.
                                        Uncle,
go down at once and tell the Lady Penélopê
that I am back from Pylos, safe and sound.   140
I stay here meanwhile. You will give your message
and then return. Let none of the Akhaians
hear it; they have a mind to do me harm."

To this, Eumaios, you replied:

                    "I know.
But make this clear, now—should I not likewise   145

call on Laërtês with your news? Hard hit
by sorrow though he was, mourning Odysseus,
he used to keep an eye upon his farm.
He had what meals he pleased, with his own folk.
But now no more, not since you sailed for Pylos;   150
he has not taken food or drink, I hear,
sitting all day, blind to the work of harvest,
groaning, while the skin shrinks on his bones."

Telémakhos answered:

                    "One more misery,
but we had better leave it so.   155
If men could choose, and have their choice, in everything,
we'd have my father home.
                    Turn back
when you have done your errand, as you must,
not to be caught alone in the countryside.[4]
But wait—you may tell Mother   160
to send our old housekeeper on the quiet
and quickly; she can tell the news to Grandfather."

The swineherd, roused, reached out to get his sandals,
tied them on, and took the road.

                    Who else
beheld this but Athena? From the air   165
she walked, taking the form of a tall woman,
handsome and clever at her craft, and stood
beyond the gate in plain sight of Odysseus,
unseen, though, by Telémakhos, unguessed,
for not to everyone will gods appear.   170
Odysseus noticed her; so did the dogs,
who cowered whimpering away from her. She only
nodded, signing to him with her brows,
a sign he recognized. Crossing the yard,
he passed out through the gate in the stockade   175
to face the goddess. There she said to him:

"Son of Laërtês and the gods of old,
Odysseus, master of land ways and sea ways,
dissemble to your son no longer now.
The time has come: tell him how you together   180
will bring doom on the suitors in the town.
I shall not be far distant then, for I
myself desire battle."

                    Saying no more,
she tipped her golden wand upon the man,
making his cloak pure white, and the knit tunic   185

---

4. The Greek says something more like "and don't go wandering round the countryside after him [Laërtês]."

fresh around him. Lithe and young she made him,
ruddy with sun, his jawline clean, the beard
no longer grey upon his chin. And she
withdrew when she had done.
                    Then Lord Odysseus
reappeared—and his son was thunderstruck.   190
Fear in his eyes, he looked down and away
as though it were a god, and whispered:

                    "Stranger,
you are no longer what you were just now!
Your cloak is new; even your skin! You are
one of the gods who rule the sweep of heaven!   195
Be kind to us, we'll make you fair oblation
and gifts of hammered gold. Have mercy on us!"

The noble and enduring man replied:

"No god. Why take me for a god? No, no.
I am that father whom your boyhood lacked   200
and suffered pain for lack of. I am he."

Held back too long, the tears ran down his cheeks
as he embraced his son.
                    Only Telémakhos,
uncomprehending, wild
with incredulity, cried out:

                              "You cannot   205
be my father Odysseus! Meddling spirits
conceived this trick to twist the knife in me!
No man of woman born could work these wonders
by his own craft, unless a god came into it
with ease to turn him young or old at will.   210
I swear you were in rags and old,
and here you stand like one of the immortals!"

Odysseus brought his ranging mind to bear
and said:

                    "This is not princely, to be swept
away by wonder at your father's presence.   215
No other Odysseus will ever come,
for he and I are one, the same; his bitter
fortune and his wanderings are mine.
Twenty years gone, and I am back again
on my own island.
                    As for my change of skin,   220
that is a charm Athena, Hope of Soldiers,[5]
uses as she will; she has the knack

5. Athena was a warrior goddess.

to make me seem a beggar man sometimes
and sometimes young, with finer clothes about me.
It is no hard thing for the gods of heaven   225
to glorify a man or bring him low."

When he had spoken, down he sat.
                                    Then, throwing
his arms around this marvel of a father
Telémakhos began to weep. Salt tears
rose from the wells of longing in both men,   230
and cries burst from both as keen and fluttering
as those of the great taloned hawk,
whose nestlings farmers take before they fly.
So helplessly they cried, pouring out tears,
and might have gone on weeping so till sundown,   235
had not Telémakhos said:

                    "Dear father! Tell me
what kind of vessel put you here ashore
on Ithaka? Your sailors, who were they?
I doubt you made it, walking on the sea!"

Then said Odysseus, who had borne the barren sea: 240

"Only plain truth shall I tell you, child.
Great seafarers, the Phaiákians, gave me passage
as they give other wanderers. By night
over the open ocean, while I slept,
they brought me in their cutter, set me down   245
on Ithaka, with gifts of bronze and gold
and stores of woven things. By the gods' will
these lie all hidden in a cave. I came
to this wild place, directed by Athena,
so that we might lay plans to kill our enemies.   250
Count up the suitors for me, let me know
what men at arms are there, how many men.
I must put all my mind to it, to see
if we two by ourselves can take them on
or if we should look round for help."

                                    Telémakhos   255
replied:

            "O Father, all my life your fame
as a fighting man has echoed in my ears—
your skill with weapons and the tricks of war—
but what you speak of is a staggering thing,
beyond imagining, for me. How can two men   260
do battle with a houseful in their prime?
For I must tell you this is no affair
of ten or even twice ten men, but scores,
throngs of them. You shall see, here and now.

The number from Doulíkhion alone   265
is fifty-two picked men, with armorers,
a half dozen; twenty-four came from Samê,
twenty from Zakýnthos; our own island
accounts for twelve, high-ranked, and their retainers,
Medôn the crier, and the Master Harper,   270
besides a pair of handymen at feasts.
If we go in against all these
I fear we pay in salt blood for your vengeance.
You must think hard if you would conjure up
the fighting strength to take us through."

                                    Odysseus   275
who had endured the long war and the sea
answered:

                    "I'll tell you now.
Suppose Athena's arm is over us, and Zeus
her father's, must I rack my brains for more?"

Clearheaded Telémakhos looked hard and said: 280

"Those two are great defenders, no one doubts it,
but throned in the serene clouds overhead;
other affairs of men and gods they have
to rule over."

                And the hero answered:

"Before long they will stand to right and left of us   285
in combat, in the shouting, when the test comes—
our nerve against the suitors' in my hall.
Here is your part: at break of day tomorrow
home with you, go mingle with our princes.
The swineherd later on will take me down   290
the port-side trail—a beggar, by my looks,
hangdog and old. If they make fun of me
in my own courtyard, let your ribs cage up
your springing heart, no matter what I suffer,
no matter if they pull me by the heels   295
or practice shots at me, to drive me out.
Look on, hold down your anger. You may even
plead with them, by heaven! in gentle terms
to quit their horseplay—not that they will heed you,
rash as they are, facing their day of wrath.   300
Now fix the next step in your mind.
                            Athena,
counseling me, will give me word, and I
shall signal to you, nodding: at that point
round up all armor, lances, gear of war
left in our hall, and stow the lot away   305
back in the vaulted store room. When the suitors

miss those arms and question you, be soft
in what you say: answer:

              'I thought I'd move them
out of the smoke. They seemed no longer those
bright arms Odysseus left us years ago   310
when he went off to Troy. Here where the fire's
hot breath came, they had grown black and drear.
One better reason, too, I had from Zeus:
Suppose a brawl starts up when you are drunk,
you might be crazed and bloody one another,   315
and that would stain your feast, your courtship. Tempered
iron can magnetize a man.'
                  Say that.
But put aside two broadswords and two spears
for our own use, two oxhide shields nearby
when we go into action. Pallas Athena   320
and Zeus All Provident will see you through,
bemusing our young friends.
                  Now one thing more.
If son of mine you are and blood of mine,
let no one hear Odysseus is about.
Neither Laërtês, nor the swineherd here,   325
nor any slave, nor even Penélopê.
But you and I alone must learn how far
the women are corrupted; we should know
how to locate good men among our hands,
the loyal and respectful, and the shirkers   330
who take you lightly, as alone and young."

His admirable son replied:

              "Ah, Father,
even when danger comes I think you'll find
courage in me. I am not scatterbrained.
But as to checking on the field hands now,   335
I see no gain for us in that. Reflect,
you make a long toil, that way, if you care
to look men in the eye at every farm,
while these gay devils in our hall at ease
eat up our flocks and herds, leaving us nothing.   340

As for the maids I say, Yes: make distinction
between good girls and those who shame your house;
all that I shy away from is a scrutiny
of cottagers just now. The time for that
comes later—if in truth you have a sign   345
from Zeus the Stormking."

              So their talk ran on,
while down the coast, and round toward Ithaka,
hove the good ship that had gone out to Pylos

bearing Telémakhos and his companions.
Into the wide bay waters, on to the dark land,
they drove her, hauled her up, took out the oars
and canvas for light-hearted squires to carry
homeward—as they carried, too, the gifts
of Meneláos round to Klýtios'[6] house.
But first they sped a runner to Penélopê.
They knew that quiet lady must be told
the prince her son had come ashore, and sent
his good ship round to port; not one soft tear
should their sweet queen let fall.

                       Both messengers,
crewman and swineherd—reached the outer gate
in the same instant, bearing the same news,
and went in side by side to the king's hall.
He of the ship burst out among the maids:

"Your son's ashore this morning, O my Queen!"

But the swineherd calmly stood near Penélopê
whispering what her son had bade him tell
and what he had enjoined on her. No more.
When he had done, he left the place and turned
back to his steading in the hills.

                     By now,
sullen confusion weighed upon the suitors.
Out of the house, out of the court they went,
beyond the wall and gate, to sit in council.
Eurýmakhos, the son of Pólybos,
opened discussion:

             "Friends, face up to it;
that young pup, Telémakhos, has done it;
he made the round trip, though we said he could not.
Well—now to get the best craft we can find
afloat, with oarsmen who can drench her bows,
and tell those on the island to come home."

He was yet speaking when Amphínomos,
craning seaward, spotted the picket ship
already in the roadstead under oars
with canvas brailed up; and this fresh arrival
made him chuckle. Then he told his friends:

"Too late for messages. Look, here they come
along the bay. Some god has brought them news,
or else they saw the cutter pass—and could not
overtake her."

6. The father of Peiraios (15.604), the man to whom Telémakhos entrusted Theoklýmenos.

On their feet at once,
the suitors took the road to the sea beach,
where, meeting the black ship, they hauled her in.   390
Oars and gear they left for their light-hearted
squires to carry, and all in company
made off for the assembly ground. All others,
young and old alike, they barred from sitting.
Eupeithês' son, Antínoös, made the speech: 395

"How the gods let our man escape a boarding,
that is the wonder.
                    We had lookouts posted
up on the heights all day in the sea wind,
and every hour a fresh pair of eyes;
at night we never slept ashore   400
but after sundown cruised the open water
to the southeast, patrolling until Dawn.
We were prepared to cut him off and catch him,
squelch him for good and all. The power of heaven
steered him the long way home.   405

Well, let this company plan his destruction,
and leave him no way out, this time. I see
our business here unfinished while he lives.
He knows, now, and he's no fool. Besides,
his people are all tired of playing up to us.   410
I say, act now, before he brings the whole
body of Akhaians to assembly—
and he would leave no word unsaid, in righteous
anger speaking out before them all
of how we plotted murder, and then missed him.   415
Will they commend us for that pretty work?
Take action now, or we are in for trouble;
we might be exiled, driven off our lands.
Let the first blow be ours.
If we move first, and get our hands on him   420
far from the city's eye, on path or field,
then stores and livestock will be ours to share;
the house we may confer upon his mother—
and on the man who marries her. Decide
otherwise you may—but if, my friends,   425
you want that boy to live and have his patrimony,
then we should eat no more of his good mutton,
come to this place no more.
                    Let each from his own hall
court her with dower gifts. And let her marry
the destined one, the one who offers most."   430

He ended, and no sound was heard among them,
sitting all hushed, until at last the son
of Nísos Aretíadês arose—

Amphínomos.

    He led the group of suitors
who came from grainlands on Doulíkhion,   435
and he had lightness in his talk that pleased
Penélopê, for he meant no ill.
Now, in concern for them, he spoke:

          "O Friends
I should not like to kill Telémakhos.
It is a shivery thing to kill a prince   440
of royal blood.
    We should consult the gods.
If Zeus hands down a ruling for that act,
then I shall say, 'Come one, come all,' and go
cut him down with my own hand—
but I say Halt, if gods are contrary."   445

Now this proposal won them, and it carried.
Breaking their session up, away they went
to take their smooth chairs in Odysseus' house.
Meanwhile Penélopê the Wise,
decided, for her part, to make appearance   450
before the valiant young men.
        She knew now
they plotted her child's death in her own hall,
for once more Medôn, who had heard them, told her.
Into the hall that lovely lady came,
with maids attending, and approached the suitors, 455
till near a pillar of the well-wrought roof
she paused, her shining veil across her cheeks,
and spoke directly to Antínoös:

         "Infatuate,
steeped in evil! Yet in Ithaka they say
you were the best one of your generation   460
in mind and speech. Not so, you never were.
Madman, why do you keep forever knitting
death for Telémakhos? Have you no pity
toward men dependent on another's mercy?
Before Lord Zeus, no sanction can be found   465
for one such man to plot against another!
Or are you not aware that your own father
fled to us when the realm was up in arms
against him? He had joined the Taphian pirates
in ravaging Thesprotian folk, our friends.   470
Our people would have raided *him*, then—breached
his heart, butchered his herds to feast upon—
only Odysseus took him in, and held
the furious townsmen off. It is Odysseus'
house you now consume, his wife you court,   475
his son you kill, or try to kill. And me

you ravage now, and grieve. I call upon you
to make an end of it!—and your friends too!"

The son of Pólybos it was, Eurýmakhos,
who answered her with ready speech:

                "My lady   480
Penélopê, wise daughter of Ikários,
you must shake off these ugly thoughts. I say
that man does not exist, nor will, who dares
lay hands upon your son Telémakhos,
while I live, walk the earth, and use my eyes.   485
The man's life blood, I swear,
will spurt and run out black around my lancehead!
For it is true of me, too, that Odysseus,
raider of cities, took me on his knees
and fed me often—tidbits and red wine.   490
Should not Telémakhos, therefore, be dear to me
above the rest of men? I tell the lad
he must not tremble for his life, at least
alone in the suitors' company. Heaven
deals death no man avoids."
                   Blasphemous lies   495
in earnest tones he told—the one who planned
the lad's destruction!
              Silently the lady
made her way to her glowing upper chamber,
there to weep for her dear lord, Odysseus,
until grey-eyed Athena   500
cast sweet sleep upon her eyes.

              At fall of dusk
Odysseus and his son heard the approach
of the good forester. They had been standing
over the fire with a spitted pig,
a yearling. And Athena coming near   505
with one rap of her wand made of Odysseus
an old old man again, with rags about him—
for if the swineherd knew his lord were there
he could not hold the news; Penélopê
would hear it from him.
             Now Telémakhos   510
greeted him first:

           "Eumaios, back again!
What was the talk in town? Are the tall suitors
home again, by this time, from their ambush,
or are they still on watch for my return?"

And you replied, Eumaios—O my swineherd: 515

"There was no time to ask or talk of that;
I hurried through the town. Even while I spoke
my message, I felt driven to return.
A runner from your friends turned up, a crier,
who gave the news first to your mother. Ah!   520
One thing I do know; with my own two eyes
I saw it. As I climbed above the town
to where the sky is cut by Hermês' ridge,
I saw a ship bound in for our own bay
with many oarsmen in it, laden down   525
with sea provisioning and two-edged spears,
and I surmised those were the men.
                        Who knows?"

Telémakhos, now strong with magic, smiled
across at his own father—but avoided
the swineherd's eye.
                    So when the pig was done,   530
the spit no longer to be turned, the table
garnished, everyone sat down to feast
on all the savory flesh he craved. And when
they had put off desire for meat and drink,
they turned to bed and took the gift of sleep.   535

BOOK XVII

[The Beggar at the Manor]

When the young Dawn came bright into the East
spreading her finger tips of rose, Telémakhos
the king's son, tied on his rawhide sandals
and took the lance that bore his handgrip. Burning
to be away, and on the path to town,   5
he told the swineherd:

                    "Uncle, the truth is
I must go down myself into the city.
Mother must see me there, with her own eyes,
or she will weep and feel forsaken still,
and will not set her mind at rest. Your job   10
will be to lead this poor man down to beg.
Some householder may want to dole him out
a loaf and pint. I have my own troubles.
Am I to care for every last man who comes?
And if he takes it badly—well, so much   15
the worse for him. Plain truth is what I favor."

At once Odysseus the great tactician
spoke up briskly:

                    "Neither would I myself
care to be kept here, lad. A beggar man

fares better in the town. Let it be said   20
I am not yet so old I must lay up
indoors and mumble, 'Aye, Aye' to a master.
Go on, then. As you say, my friend can lead me
as soon as I have had a bit of fire
and when the sun grows warmer. These old rags   25
could be my death, outside on a frosty morning,
and the town is distant, so they say."

                              Telémakhos
with no more words went out, and through the fence,
and down hill, going fast on the steep footing,
nursing woe for the suitors in his heart.   30
Before the manor hall, he leaned his lance
against a great porch pillar and stepped in
across the door stone.
                              Old Eurýkleia
saw him first, for that day she was covering
handsome chairs nearby with clean fleeces.   35
She ran to him at once, tears in her eyes;
and other maidservants of the old soldier
Odysseus gathered round to greet their prince,
kissing his head and shoulders.
                              Quickly, then,
Penélopê the Wise, tall in her beauty   40
as Artemis or pale-gold Aphroditê,
appeared from her high chamber and came down
to throw her arms around her son. In tears
she kissed his head, kissed both his shining eyes,
then cried out, and her words flew:

                              "Back with me!   45
Telémakhos, more sweet to me than sunlight!
I thought I should not see you again, ever,
after you took the ship that night to Pylos—
against my will, with not a word! you went
for news of your dear father. Tell me now   50
of everything you saw!"

                    But he made answer:

"Mother, not now. You make me weep. My heart
already aches—I came near death at sea.
You must bathe, first of all, and change your dress,
and take your maids to the highest room to pray.   55
Pray, and burn offerings to the gods of heaven,
that Zeus may put his hand to our revenge.

I am off now to bring home from the square
a guest, a passenger I had. I sent him
yesterday with all my crew to town.   60

Peiraios was to care for him, I said,
and keep him well, with honor, till I came."

She caught back the swift words upon her tongue.
Then softly she withdrew
to bathe and dress her body in fresh linen,   65
and make her offerings to the gods of heaven,
praying Almighty Zeus
to put his hand to their revenge.

      Telémakhos
had left the hall, taken his lance, and gone
with two quick hounds at heel into the town,   70
Athena's grace in his long stride
making the people gaze as he came near.
And suitors gathered, primed with friendly words,
despite the deadly plotting in their hearts—
but these, and all their crowd, he kept away from.   75
Next he saw sitting some way off, apart,
Mentor, with Antiphos and Halithersês,
friends of his father's house in years gone by.
Near these men he sat down, and told his tale
under their questioning.

      His crewman, young Peiraios,   80
guided through town, meanwhile, into the Square,
the Argive exile, Theoklýmenos.
Telémakhos lost no time in moving toward him;
but first Peiraios had his say:

      "Telémakhos,
you must send maids to me, at once, and let me   85
turn over to you those gifts from Meneláos!"

The prince had pondered it, and said:

      "Peiraios,
none of us knows how this affair will end.
Say one day our fine suitors, without warning,
draw upon me, kill me in our hall,   90
and parcel out my patrimony—I wish
you, and no one of them, to have those things.
But if my hour comes, if I can bring down
bloody death on all that crew,
you will rejoice to send my gifts to me—   95
and so will I rejoice!"

      Then he departed,
leading his guest, the lonely stranger, home.

Over chair-backs in hall they dropped their mantles
and passed in to the polished tubs, where maids
poured out warm baths for them, anointed them,   100

and pulled fresh tunics, fleecy cloaks around them.
Soon they were seated at their ease in hall.
A maid came by to tip a golden jug
over their fingers into a silver bowl
and draw a gleaming table up beside them.   105
The larder mistress brought her tray of loaves
and savories, dispensing each.
                          In silence
across the hall, beside a pillar, propped
in a long chair, Telémakhos' mother
spun a fine wool yarn.
                          The young men's hands   110
went out upon the good things placed before them,
and only when their hunger and thirst were gone
did she look up and say:

                   "Telémakhos,
what am I to do now? Return alone
and lie again on my forsaken bed—   115
sodden how often with my weeping
since that day when Odysseus put to sea
to join the Atreidai[7] before Troy?
                          Could you not
tell me, before the suitors fill our house,
what news you have of his return?"

                          He answered: 120

"Now that you ask a second time, dear Mother,
here is the truth.
                   We went ashore at Pylos
to Nestor, lord and guardian of the West,
who gave me welcome in his towering hall.
So kind he was, he might have been my father   125
and I his long-lost son—so truly kind,
taking me in with his own honored sons.
But as to Odysseus' bitter fate,
living or dead, he had no news at all
from anyone on earth, he said. He sent me   130
overland in a strong chariot
to Atreus' son, the captain, Meneláos.
And I saw Helen there, for whom the Argives
fought, and the Trojans fought, as the gods willed.
Then Meneláos of the great war cry   135
asked me my errand in that ancient land
of Lakedaimon. So I told our story,
and in reply he burst out:

                   'Intolerable!
That feeble men, unfit as those men are,
should think to lie in that great captain's bed,   140

---

7. The sons of Atreus: Agamémnon and Meneláos.

fawns in the lion's lair! As if a doe
put down her litter of sucklings there, while she
sniffed at the glen or grazed a grassy hollow.
Ha! Then the lord returns to his own bed
and deals out wretched doom on both alike.   145

So will Odysseus deal out doom on these.
O Father Zeus, Athena, and Apollo!
I pray he comes as once he was, in Lesbos,
when he stood up to wrestle Philomeleidês—
champion and Island King—   150
and smashed him down. How the Akhaians cheered!
If that Odysseus could meet the suitors,
they'd have a quick reply, a stunning dowry!
Now for your questions, let me come to the point.
I would not misreport it for you; let me   155
tell you what the Ancient of the Sea,
that infallible seer, told me.
                    On an island
your father lies and grieves. The Ancient saw him
held by a nymph, Kalypso, in her hall;
no means of sailing home remained to him,   160
no ship with oars, and no ship's company
to pull him on the broad back of the sea."

I had this from the lord marshal, Meneláos,
and when my errand in that place was done
I left for home. A fair breeze from the gods   165
brought me swiftly back to our dear island.'

The boy's tale made her heart stir in her breast,
but this was not all. Mother and son now heard
Theoklýmenos, the diviner, say:

"He does not see it clear—
                    O gentle lady,   170
wife of Odysseus Laërtiadês,
listen to me, I can reveal this thing.
Zeus be my witness, and the table set
for strangers and the hearth to which I've come—
the lord Odysseus, I tell you,   175
is present now, already, on this island!
Quartered somewhere, or going about, he knows
what evil is afoot. He has it in him
to bring a black hour on the suitors. Yesterday,
still at the ship, I saw this in a portent.   180
I read the sign aloud, I told Telémakhos!"

The prudent queen, for her part, said:

                        "Stranger,
if only this came true—

our love would go to you, with many gifts;
aye, every man who passed would call you happy!" 185

So ran the talk between these three.
                                        Meanwhile,
swaggering before Odysseus' hall,
the suitors were competing at the discus throw
and javelin, on the level measured field.
But when the dinner hour drew on, and beasts 190
were being driven from the fields to slaughter—
as beasts were, every day—Medôn spoke out:
Medôn, the crier, whom the suitors liked;
he took his meat beside them.

                        "Men," he said,
"each one has had his work-out and his pleasure, 195
come in to Hall now; time to make our feast.
Are discus throws more admirable than a roast
when the proper hour comes?"

                        At this reminder
they all broke up their games, and trailed away
into the gracious, timbered hall. There, first, 200
they dropped their cloaks on chairs; then came their ritual:
putting great rams and fat goats to the knife—
pigs and a cow, too.
                        So they made their feast.

During these hours, Odysseus and the swineherd
were on their way out of the hills to town. 205
The forester had got them started, saying:

"Friend, you have hopes, I know, of your adventure
into the heart of town today. My lord
wishes it so, not I. No, I should rather
you stood by here as guardian of our steading. 210
But I owe reverence to my prince, and fear
he'll make my ears burn later if I fail.
A master's tongue has a rough edge. Off we go.
Part of the day is past; nightfall will be
early, and colder, too."

                        Odysseus, 215
who had it all timed in his head, replied:

"I know, as well as you do. Let's move on.
You lead the way—the whole way. Have you got
a staff, a lopped stick, you could let me use
to put my weight on when I slip? This path 220
is hard going, they said."

                        Over his shoulders
he slung his patched-up knapsack, an old bundle

tied with twine. Eumaios found a stick for him,
the kind he wanted, and the two set out,
leaving the boys and dogs to guard the place.   225
In this way good Eumaios led his lord
down to the city.
            And it seemed to him
he led an old outcast, a beggar man,
leaning most painfully upon a stick,
his poor cloak, all in tatters, looped about him.   230

Down by the stony trail they made their way
as far as Clearwater, not far from town—
a spring house where the people filled their jars.
Ithakos, Nêritos, and Polýktor[8] built it,
and round it on the humid ground a grove,   235
a circular wood of poplars grew. Ice cold
in runnels from a high rock ran the spring,
and over it there stood an altar stone
to the cool nymphs, where all men going by
laid offerings.
            Well, here the son of Dólios   240
crossed their path—Melánthios.
                     He was driving
a string of choice goats for the evening meal,
with two goatherds beside him; and no sooner
had he laid eyes upon the wayfarers
than he began to growl and taunt them both   245
so grossly that Odysseus' heart grew hot:

"Here comes one scurvy type leading another!
God pairs them off together, every time.
Swineherd, where are you taking your new pig,
that stinking beggar there, licker of pots?   250
How many doorposts has he rubbed his back on
whining for garbage, where a noble guest
would rate a cauldron or a sword?
                  Hand him
over to me, I'll make a farmhand of him,
a stall scraper, a fodder carrier! Whey   255
for drink will put good muscle on his shank!
No chance: he learned his dodges long ago—
no honest sweat. He'd rather tramp the country
begging, to keep his hoggish belly full.
Well, I can tell you this for sure: 260
in King Odysseus' hall, if he goes there,
footstools will fly around his head—good shots
from strong hands. Back and side, his ribs will catch it
on the way out!"

            And like a drunken fool
he kicked at Odysseus' hip as he passed by.   265

8. Presumably the first rulers of Ithaka. Ithakos gave the island its name. Nêritos's name was given to the
most prominent mountain on Ithaka. Polýktor's name may possibly mean "having great possessions."

Not even jogged off stride, or off the trail,
the Lord Odysseus walked along, debating
inwardly whether to whirl and beat
the life out of this fellow with his stick,
or toss him, brain him on the stony ground.   270
Then he controlled himself, and bore it quietly.
Not so the swineherd.
               Seeing the man before him,
he raised his arms and cried:

                   "Nymphs of the spring,
daughters of Zeus, if ever Odysseus
burnt you a thighbone in rich fat—a ram's   275
or kid's thighbone, hear me, grant my prayer:
let our true lord come back, let heaven bring him
to rid the earth of these fine courtly ways
Melánthios picks up around the town—
all wine and wind! Bad shepherds ruin flocks!"   280

Melánthios the goatherd answered:

                "Bless me!
The dog can snap: how he goes on! Some day
I'll take him in a slave ship overseas
and trade him for a herd!
             Old Silverbow
Apollo, if he shot clean through Telémakhos   285
in hall today, what luck! Or let the suitors
cut him down!
          Odysseus died at sea;
no coming home for him."

              He flung this out
and left the two behind to come on slowly,
while he went hurrying to the king's hall.   290
There he slipped in, and sat among the suitors,
beside the one he doted on—Eurýmakhos.
Then working servants helped him to his meat
and the mistress of the larder gave him bread.

Reaching the gate, Odysseus and the forester   295
halted and stood outside, for harp notes came
around them ripping on the air
as Phêmios picked out a song. Odysseus
caught his companion's arm and said:

               "My friend,
here is the beautiful place—who could mistake it?   300
Here is Odysseus' hall: no hall like this!
See how one chamber grows out of another;
see how the court is tight with wall and coping;
no man at arms could break this gateway down!

Your banqueting young lords are here in force,   305
I gather, from the fumes of mutton roasting
and strum of harping—harping, which the gods
appoint sweet friend of feasts!"

                  And—O my swineherd!
you replied:

          "That was quick recognition;
but you are no numbskull—in this or anything.   310
Now we must plan this action. Will you take
leave of me here, and go ahead alone
to make your entrance now among the suitors?
Or do you choose to wait?—Let me go forward
and go in first.

              Do not delay too long;   315
someone might find you skulking here outside
and take a club to you, or heave a lance.
Bear this in mind, I say."

                The patient hero
Odysseus answered:

              "Just what I was thinking.
You go in first, and leave me here a little.   320
But as for blows and missiles,
I am no tyro at these things. I learned
to keep my head in hardship—years of war
and years at sea. Let this new trial come.
The cruel belly, can you hide its ache?   325
How many bitter days it brings! Long ships
with good stout planks athwart—would fighters rig them
to ride the barren sea, except for hunger?
Seawolves—woe to their enemies!"

                While he spoke
an old hound, lying near, pricked up his ears   330
and lifted up his muzzle. This was Argos,
trained as a puppy by Odysseus,
but never taken on a hunt before
his master sailed for Troy. The young men, afterward,
hunted wild goats with him, and hare, and deer,   335
but he had grown old in his master's absence.
Treated as rubbish now, he lay at last
upon a mass of dung before the gates—
manure of mules and cows, piled there until
fieldhands could spread it on the king's estate.   340
Abandoned there, and half destroyed with flies,
old Argos lay.

             But when he knew he heard
Odysseus' voice nearby, he did his best
to wag his tail, nose down, with flattened ears,

having no strength to move nearer his master. 345
And the man looked away,
wiping a salt tear from his cheek; but he
hid this from Eumaios. Then he said:

"I marvel that they leave this hound to lie
here on the dung pile; 350
he would have been a fine dog, from the look of him,
though I can't say as to his power and speed
when he was young. You find the same good build
in house dogs, table dogs landowners keep
all for style."

    And you replied, Eumaios: 355

"A hunter owned him—but the man is dead
in some far place. If this old hound could show
the form he had when Lord Odysseus left him,
going to Troy, you'd see him swift and strong.
He never shrank from any savage thing 360
he'd brought to bay in the deep woods; on the scent
no other dog kept up with him. Now misery
has him in leash. His owner died abroad,
and here the women slaves will take no care of him.
You know how servants are: without a master 365
they have no will to labor, or excel.
For Zeus who views the wide world takes away
half the manhood of a man, that day
he goes into captivity and slavery."

Eumaios crossed the court and went straight forward 370
into the mégaron among the suitors;
but death and darkness in that instant closed
the eyes of Argos, who had seen his master,
Odysseus, after twenty years.

      Long before anyone else
Telémakhos caught sight of the grey woodsman 375
coming from the door, and called him over
with a quick jerk of his head. Eumaios'
narrowed eyes made out an empty bench
beside the one the carver used—that servant
who had no respite, carving for the suitors. 380
This bench he took possession of, and placed it
across the table from Telémakhos
for his own use. Then the two men were served
cuts from a roast and bread from a bread basket.

At no long interval, Odysseus came 385
through his own doorway as a mendicant,
humped like a bundle of rags over his stick.
He settled on the inner ash wood sill,

leaning against the door jamb—cypress timber
the skilled carpenter planed years ago   390
and set up with a plumbline.

             Now Telémakhos
took an entire loaf and a double handful
of roast meat; then he said to the forester:

"Give these to the stranger there. But tell him
to go among the suitors, on his own;   395
he may beg all he wants. This hanging back
is no asset to a hungry man."

The swineherd rose at once, crossed to the door,
and halted by Odysseus.

            "Friend," he said,
"Telémakhos is pleased to give you these,   400
but he commands you to approach the suitors;
you may ask all you want from them. He adds,
your shyness is no asset to a beggar."

The great tactician, lifting up his eyes,
cried:

      "Zeus aloft! A blessing on Telémakhos!   405
Let all things come to pass as he desires!"

Palms held out, in the beggar's gesture, he
received the bread and meat and put it down
before him on his knapsack—lowly table!—
then he fell to, devouring it. Meanwhile   410
the harper in the great room sang a song.
Not till the man was fed did the sweet harper
end his singing—whereupon the company
made the walls ring again with talk.

            Unseen,
Athena took her place beside Odysseus   415
whispering in his ear:

         "Yes, try the suitors.
You may collect a few more loaves, and learn
who are the decent lads, and who are vicious—
although not one can be excused from death!"

So he appealed to them, one after another,   420
going from left to right, with open palm,
as though his life time had been spent in beggary.
And they gave bread, for pity—wondering, though,
at the strange man. Who could this beggar be,
where did he come from? each would ask his neighbor;   425

till in their midst the goatherd, Melánthios,
raised his voice:

"Hear just a word from me,
my lords who court our illustrious queen!
                                            This man,
this foreigner, I saw him on the road;
the swineherd, here was leading him this way;   430
who, what, or whence he claims to be, I could not
say for sure."

                    At this, Antínoös
turned on the swineherd brutally, saying:

                                            "You famous
breeder of pigs, why bring this fellow here?
Are we not plagued enough with beggars,   435
foragers and such rats?
                        You find the company
too slow at eating up your lord's estate—
is that it? So you call this scarecrow in?"

The forester replied:

                    "Antínoös,
well born you are, but that was not well said.   440
Who would call in a foreigner?—unless
an artisan with skill to serve the realm,
a healer, or a prophet, or a builder,
or one whose harp and song might give us joy.
All these are sought for on the endless earth,   445
but when have beggars come by invitation?
Who puts a field mouse in his granary? My lord,
you are a hard man, and you always were,
more so than others of this company—hard
on all Odysseus' people and on me.   450
But this I can forget
as long as Penélopê lives on, the wise and tender
mistress of this hall; as long
as Prince Telémakhos—"

                    But he broke off
at a look from Telémakhos, who said:

                                    "Be still.   455
Spare me a long-drawn answer to this gentleman.
With his unpleasantness, he will forever make
strife where he can—and goad the others on."

He turned and spoke out clearly to Antínoös:

"What fatherly concern you show me! Frighten   460
this unknown fellow, would you, from my hall
with words that promise blows—may God forbid it!
Give him a loaf. Am I a niggard? No,
I call on you to give. And spare your qualms
as to my mother's loss, or anyone's—   465
not that in truth you have such care at heart:
your heart is all in feeding, not in giving."

Antínoös replied:

                     "What high and mighty
talk, Telémakhos! No holding you!
If every suitor gave what I may give him,   470
he could be kept for months—kept out of sight!"

He reached under the table for the footstool
his shining feet had rested on—and this
he held up so that all could see his gift.

But all the rest gave alms,   475
enough to fill the beggar's pack with bread
and roast meat.

                     So it looked as though Odysseus
had had his taste of what these men were like
and could return scot free to his own doorway—
but halting now before Antínoös   480
he made a little speech to him. Said he:

"Give a mite, friend. I would not say, myself,
you are the worst man of the young Akhaians.
The noblest, rather; kingly, by your look;
therefore you'll give more bread than others do.   485
Let me speak well of you as I pass on
over the boundless earth!

                     I, too, you know,
had fortune once, lived well, stood well with men,
and gave alms, often, to poor wanderers
like this one that you see—aye, to all sorts,   490
no matter in what dire want. I owned
servants—many, god knows—and all the rest
that goes with being prosperous, as they say.
But Zeus the son of Kronos brought me down.

                                        No telling
why he would have it, but he made me go   495
to Egypt with a company of rovers—
a long sail to the south—for my undoing.
Up the broad Nile and in to the river bank
I brought my dipping squadron. There, indeed,
I told the men to stand guard at the ships;   500
I sent patrols out—out to rising ground;

but reckless greed carried my crews away
to plunder the Egyptian farms; they bore off
wives and children, killed what men they found.
The news ran on the wind to the city, a night cry,   505
and sunrise brought both infantry and horsemen,
filling the river plain with dazzle of bronze;
then Zeus lord of lightning
threw my men into a blind panic; no one dared
stand against that host closing around us.   510
Their scything weapons left our dead in piles,
but some they took alive, into forced labor,
myself among them. And they gave me, then,
to one Dmêtor, a traveller, son of Iasos,
who ruled at Kypros.⁹ He conveyed me there.   515
From that place, working northward, miserably—"

But here Antínoös broke in, shouting:

                              "God!
What evil wind blew in this pest?
                              Get over,
stand in the passage! Nudge my table, will you?
Egyptian whips are sweet   520
to what you'll come to here, you nosing rat,
making your pitch to everyone!
These men have bread to throw away on you
because it is not theirs. Who cares? Who spares
another's food, when he has more than plenty?"   525

With guile Odysseus drew away, then said:

"A pity that you have more looks than heart.
You'd grudge a pinch of salt from your own larder
to your own handy man. You sit here, fat
on others' meat, and cannot bring yourself   530
to rummage out a crust of bread for me!"

Then anger made Antínoös' heart beat hard,
and, glowering under his brows, he answered:

                              "Now!
You think you'll shuffle off and get away
after that impudence? Oh, no you don't!"   535

The stool he let fly hit the man's right shoulder
on the packed muscle under the shoulder blade—
like solid rock, for all the effect one saw.
Odysseus only shook his head, containing
thoughts of bloody work, as he walked on,   540
then sat, and dropped his loaded bag again

9. Or Cyprus.

upon the door sill. Facing the whole crowd
he said, and eyed them all:

           "One word only,
my lords, and suitors of the famous queen.
One thing I have to say.   545
There is no pain, no burden for the heart
when blows come to a man, and he defending
his own cattle—his own cows and lambs.
Here it was otherwise. Antínoös
hit me for being driven on by hunger—   550
how many bitter seas men cross for hunger!
If beggars interest the gods, if there are Furies
pent in the dark to avenge a poor man's wrong, then may
Antínoös meet his death before his wedding day!"

Then said Eupeithês' son, Antínoös:

                 "Enough.   555
Eat and be quiet where you are, or shamble elsewhere,
unless you want these lads to stop your mouth
pulling you by the heels, or hands and feet,
over the whole floor, till your back is peeled!"

But now the rest were mortified, and someone   560
spoke from the crowd of young bucks to rebuke him:

"A poor show, that—hitting this famished tramp—
bad business, if he happened to be a god.
You know they go in foreign guise, the gods do,
looking like strangers, turning up   565
in towns and settlements to keep an eye
on manners, good or bad."

                  But at this notion
Antínoös only shrugged.
                Telémakhos,
after the blow his father bore, sat still
without a tear, though his heart felt the blow.   570
Slowly he shook his head from side to side,
containing murderous thoughts.
                Penélopê
on the higher level of her room had heard
the blow, and knew who gave it. Now she murmured:

"Would god you could be hit yourself, Antínoös—   575
hit by Apollo's bowshot!"

                And Eurýnomê
her housekeeper, put in:

"He and no other?
If all we pray for came to pass, not one
would live till dawn!"

Her gentle mistress said:

"Oh, Nan, they are a bad lot; they intend   580
ruin for all of us; but Antínoös
appears a blacker-hearted hound than any.
Here is a poor man come, a wanderer,
driven by want to beg his bread, and everyone
in hall gave bits, to cram his bag—only   585
Antínoös threw a stool, and banged his shoulder!"

So she described it, sitting in her chamber
among her maids—while her true lord was eating.
Then she called in the forester and said:

"Go to that man on my behalf, Eumaios,   590
and send him here, so I can greet and question him.
Abroad in the great world, he may have heard
rumors about Odysseus—may have known him!"

Then you replied—O swineherd!

       "Ah, my queen,
if these Akhaian sprigs would hush their babble   595
the man could tell you tales to charm your heart.
Three days and nights I kept him in my hut;
he came straight off a ship, you know, to me.
There was no end to what he made me hear
of his hard roving and I listened, eyes   600
upon him, as a man drinks in a tale
a minstrel sings—a minstrel taught by heaven
to touch the hearts of men. At such a song
the listener becomes rapt and still. Just so
I found myself enchanted by this man.   605
He claims an old tie with Odysseus, too—
in his home country, the Minoan land
of Krete. From Krete he came, a rolling stone
washed by the gales of life this way and that
to our own beach.
       If he can be believed   610
he has news of Odysseus near at hand
alive, in the rich country of Thesprotia,
bringing a mass of treasure home."

Then wise Penélopê said again:

"Go call him, let him come here, let him tell   615
that tale again for my own ears.
       Our friends

can drink their cups outside or stay in hall,
being so carefree. And why not? Their stores
lie intact in their homes, both food and drink,
with only servants left to take a little.   620
But these men spend their days around our house
killing our beeves, our fat goats and our sheep,
carousing, drinking up our good dark wine;
sparing nothing, squandering everything.
No champion like Odysseus takes our part.   625
Ah, if he comes again, no falcon ever
struck more suddenly than he will, with his son,
to avenge this outrage!"

>   The great hall below
at this point rang with a tremendous sneeze—
"kchaou!" from Telémakhos—like an acclamation.   630
And laughter seized Penélopê.
>   Then quickly,
lucidly she went on:

>   "Go call the stranger
straight to me. Did you hear that, Eumaios?
My son's thundering sneeze at what I said!
May death come of a sudden so; may death   635
relieve us, clean as that, of all the suitors!
Let me add one thing—do not overlook it—
if I can see this man has told the truth,
I promise him a warm new cloak and tunic."

With all this in his head, the forester   640
went down the hall, and halted near the beggar,
saying aloud:

>   "Good father, you are called
by the wise mother of Telémakhos,
Penélopê. The queen, despite her troubles,
is moved by a desire to hear your tales   645
about her lord—and if she finds them true,
she'll see you clothed in what you need, a cloak
and a fresh tunic.
>   You may have your belly
full each day you go about this realm
begging. For all may give, and all they wish."   650

Now said Odysseus, the old soldier:

>   "Friend,
I wish this instant I could tell my facts
to the wise daughter of Ikários, Penélopê—
and I have much to tell about her husband;
we went through much together.
>   But just now   655

this hard crowd worries me. They are, you said
infamous to the very rim of heaven
for violent acts: and here, just now, this fellow
gave me a bruise. What had I done to him?
But who would lift a hand for me? Telémakhos?   660
Anyone else?

         No; bid the queen be patient.
Let her remain till sundown in her room,
and then—if she will seat me near the fire—
inquire tonight about her lord's return.
My rags are sorry cover; you know that;   665
I showed my sad condition first to you."

The woodsman heard him out, and then returned;
but the queen met him on her threshold, crying:

"Have you not brought him? Why? What is he thinking?
Has he some fear of overstepping? Shy   670
about these inner rooms? A hangdog beggar?"

To this you answered, friend Eumaios:

            "No:
he reasons as another might, and well,
not to tempt any swordplay from these drunkards.
Be patient, wait—he says—till darkness falls.   675
And, O my queen, for you too that is better:
better to be alone with him, and question him,
and hear him out."

         Penélopê replied:

"He is no fool; he sees how it could be.
Never were mortal men like these   680
for bullying and brainless arrogance!"

Thus she accepted what had been proposed,
so he went back into the crowd. He joined
Telémakhos, and said at once in whispers—
his head bent, so that no one else might hear: 685

"Dear prince, I must go home to keep good watch
on hut and swine, and look to my own affairs.
Everything here is in your hands. Consider
your own safety before the rest; take care
not to get hurt. Many are dangerous here.   690
May Zeus destroy them first, before we suffer!"

Telémakhos said:

         "Your wish is mine, Uncle.
Go when your meal is finished. Then come back

at dawn, and bring good victims for a slaughter.
Everything here is in my hands indeed—   695
and in the disposition of the gods."

Taking his seat on the smooth bench again,
Eumaios ate and drank his fill, then rose
to climb the mountain trail back to his swine,
leaving the mégaron and court behind him   700
crowded with banqueters.
                                        These had their joy
of dance and song, as day waned into evening.

BOOK XVIII

[Blows and a Queen's Beauty]

Now a true scavenger came in—a public tramp
who begged around the town of Ithaka,
a by-word for his insatiable swag-belly,
feeding and drinking, dawn to dark. No pith
was in him, and no nerve, huge as he looked.   5
Arnaios, as his gentle mother called him,
he had been nicknamed "Iros" by the young
for being ready to take messages.[1]
                                        This fellow
thought he would rout Odysseus from his doorway,
growling at him:

                        "Clear out, grandfather,   10
or else be hauled out by the ankle bone.
See them all giving me the wink? That means,
'Go on and drag him out!' I hate to do it.
Up with you! Or would you like a fist fight?"

Odysseus only frowned and looked him over,   15
taking account of everything, then said:

"Master, I am no trouble to you here.
I offer no remarks. I grudge you nothing.
Take all you get, and welcome. Here is room
for two on this doorslab—or do you own it?   20
You are a tramp, I think, like me. Patience:
a windfall from the gods will come. But drop
that talk of using fists; it could annoy me.
Old as I am, I might just crack a rib
or split a lip for you. My life would go   25
even more peacefully, after tomorrow,
looking for no more visits here from you."

Iros the tramp grew red and hooted:

1. The goddess Iris often served as messenger for the gods.

                                    "Ho,
listen to him! The swine can talk your arm off,
like an old oven woman! With two punches   30
I'd knock him snoring, if I had a mind to—
and not a tooth left in his head, the same
as an old sow caught in the corn! Belt up!
And let this company see the way I do it
when we square off. Can you fight a fresher man?"   35

Under the lofty doorway, on the door sill
of wide smooth ash, they held this rough exchange.
And the tall full-blooded suitor, Antínoös,
overhearing, broke into happy laughter.
Then he said to the others:

                        "Oh, my friends,   40
no luck like this ever turned up before!
What a farce heaven has brought this house!
                                    The stranger
and Iros have had words, they brag of boxing!
Into the ring they go, and no more talk!"

All the young men got on their feet now, laughing,   45
to crowd around the ragged pair. Antínoös
called out:

                "Gentlemen, quiet! One more thing:
here are goat stomachs ready on the fire
to stuff with blood and fat, good supper pudding.
The man who wins this gallant bout   50
may step up here and take the one he likes.
And let him feast with us from this day on:
no other beggar will be admitted here
when we are at our wine."

                        This pleased them all.
But now that wily man, Odysseus, muttered: 55

"An old man, an old hulk, has no business
fighting a young man, but my belly nags me;
nothing will do but I must take a beating.
Well, then, let every man here swear an oath
not to step in for Iros. No one throw   60
a punch for luck. I could be whipped that way."

So much the suitors were content to swear,
but after they reeled off their oaths, Telémakhos
put in a word to clinch it, saying:

                        "Friend,
if you will stand and fight, as pride requires,   65
don't worry about a foul blow from behind.

Whoever hits you will take on the crowd.
You have my word as host; you have the word
of these two kings, Antínoös and Eurýmakhos—
a pair of thinking men."

All shouted, "Aye!" 70
So now Odysseus made his shirt a belt
and roped his rags around his loins, baring
his hurdler's thighs and boxer's breadth of shoulder,
the dense rib-sheath and upper arms. Athena
stood nearby to give him bulk and power, 75
while the young suitors watched with narrowed eyes—
and comments went around:

"By god, old Iros now retires."

"Aye,
he asked for it, he'll get it—bloody, too."

"The build this fellow had, under his rags!" 80

Panic made Iros' heart jump, but the yard-boys
hustled and got him belted by main force,
though all his blubber quivered now with dread.
Antínoös' angry voice rang in his ears:

"You sack of guts, you might as well be dead, 85
might as well never have seen the light of day,
if this man makes you tremble! Chicken-heart,
afraid of an old wreck, far gone in misery!
Well, here is what I say—and what I'll do.
If this ragpicker can outfight you, whip you, 90
I'll ship you out to that king in Epeíros,
Ékhetos[2]—he skins everyone alive.
Let him just cut your nose off and your ears
and pull your privy parts out by the roots
to feed raw to his hunting dogs!"

Poor Iros 95
felt a new fit of shaking take his knees.
But the yard-boys pushed him out. Now both contenders
put their hands up. Royal Odysseus
pondered if he should hit him with all he had
and drop the man dead on the spot, or only 100
spar, with force enough to knock him down.
Better that way, he thought—a gentle blow,
else he might give himself away.
The two
were at close quarters now, and Iros lunged
hitting the shoulder. Then Odysseus hooked him 105

2. All we know of him is what Homer tells us here. Epeíros (Epirus) is north of Ithaka.

under the ear and shattered his jaw bone,
so bright red blood came bubbling from his mouth,
as down he pitched into the dust, bleating,
kicking against the ground, his teeth stove in.
The suitors whooped and swung their arms, half dead   110
with pangs of laughter.
                              Then, by the ankle bone,
Odysseus hauled the fallen one outside,
crossing the courtyard to the gate, and piled him
against the wall. In his right hand he stuck
his begging staff, and said:

                              "Here, take your post.   115
Sit here to keep the dogs and pigs away.
You can give up your habit of command
over poor waifs and beggarmen—you swab.
Another time you may not know what hit you."

When he had slung his rucksack by the string   120
over his shoulder, like a wad of rags,
he sat down on the broad door sill again,
as laughing suitors came to flock inside;
and each young buck in passing gave him greeting,
saying, maybe,

                    "Zeus fill your pouch for this!   125
May the gods grant your heart's desire!"

                                        "Well done
to put that walking famine out of business."

"We'll ship him out to that king in Epeíros,
Ékhetos—he skins everyone alive."

Odysseus found grim cheer in their good wishes—   130
his work had started well.
                              Now from the fire
his fat blood pudding came, deposited
before him by Antínoös—then, to boot,
two brown loaves from the basket, and some wine
in a fine cup of gold. These gifts Amphínomos   135
gave him. Then he said:

                    "Here's luck, grandfather;
a new day; may the worst be over now."

Odysseus answered, and his mind ranged far:

"Amphínomos, your head is clear, I'd say;
so was your father's—or at least I've heard   140
good things of Nísos the Doulíkhion,
whose son you are, they tell me—an easy man.

And you seem gently bred.
                    In view of that,
I have a word to say to you, so listen.

Of mortal creatures, all that breathe and move,   145
earth bears none frailer than mankind. What man
believes in woe to come, so long as valor
and tough knees are supplied him by the gods?
But when the gods in bliss bring miseries on,
then willy-nilly, blindly, he endures.   150
Our minds are as the days are, dark or bright,
blown over by the father of gods and men.

So I, too, in my time thought to be happy;
but far and rash I ventured, counting on
my own right arm, my father, and my kin;   155
behold me now.
                    No man should flout the law,
but keep in peace what gifts the gods may give.

I see you young blades living dangerously,
a household eaten up, a wife dishonored—
and yet the master will return, I tell you,   160
to his own place, and soon; for he is near.
So may some power take you out of this,
homeward, and softly, not to face that man
the hour he sets foot on his native ground.
Between him and the suitors I foretell   165
no quittance, no way out, unless by blood,
once he shall stand beneath his own roof-beam."

Gravely, when he had done, he made libation
and took a sip of honey-hearted wine,
giving the cup, then, back into the hands   170
of the young nobleman. Amphínomos, for his part,
shaking his head, with chill and burdened breast,
turned in the great hall.
                    Now his heart foreknew
the wrath to come, but he could not take flight,
being by Athena bound there.
                    Death would have him   175
broken by a spear thrown by Telémakhos.
So he sat down where he had sat before.

And now heart-prompting from the grey-eyed goddess
came to the quiet queen, Penélopê:
a wish to show herself before the suitors;   180
for thus by fanning their desire again
Athena meant to set her beauty high
before her husband's eyes, before her son.
Knowing no reason, laughing confusedly,
she said:

"Eurýnomê, I have a craving   185
I never had at all—I would be seen
among those ruffians, hateful as they are.
I might well say a word, then, to my son,
for his own good—tell him to shun that crowd;
for all their gay talk, they are bent on evil."   190

Mistress Eurýnomê replied:

"Well said, child,
now is the time. Go down, and make it clear,
hold nothing back from him.
                    But you must bathe
and put a shine upon your cheeks—not this way,
streaked under your eyes and stained with tears.   195
You make it worse, being forever sad,
and now your boy's a bearded man! Remember
you prayed the gods to let you see him so."

Penélopê replied:

"Eurýnomê,
it is a kind thought, but I will not hear it—   200
to bathe and sleek with perfumed oil. No, no,
the gods forever took my sheen away
when my lord sailed for Troy in the decked ships.
Only tell my Autonoë to come,
and Hippodameía; they should be attending me   205
in hall, if I appear there. I could not
enter alone into that crowd of men."

At this the good old woman left the chamber
to tell the maids her bidding. But now too
the grey-eyed goddess had her own designs.   210
Upon the quiet daughter of Ikários
she let clear drops of slumber fall, until
the queen lay back asleep, her limbs unstrung,
in her long chair. And while she slept the goddess
endowed her with immortal grace to hold   215
the eyes of the Akhaians. With ambrosia
she bathed her cheeks and throat and smoothed her brow—
ambrosia, used by flower-crowned Kythereia[3]
when she would join the rose-lipped Graces dancing.
Grandeur she gave her, too, in height and form,   220
and made her whiter than carved ivory.
Touching her so, the perfect one was gone.
Now came the maids, bare-armed and lovely, voices
breaking into the room. The queen awoke
and as she rubbed her cheek she sighed:

3. Aphrodite.

"Ah, soft   225
that drowse I lay embraced in, pain forgot!
If only Artemis the Pure would give me
death as mild, and soon! No heart-ache more,
no wearing out my lifetime with desire
and sorrow, mindful of my lord, good man   230
in all ways that he was, best of the Akhaians!"

She rose and left her glowing upper room,
and down the stairs, with her two maids in train,
this beautiful lady went before the suitors.
Then by a pillar of the solid roof   235
she paused, her shining veil across her cheek,
the two girls close to her and still;
and in that instant weakness took those men
in the knee joints, their hearts grew faint with lust;
not one but swore to god to lie beside her.   240
But speaking for her dear son's ears alone
she said:

          "Telémakhos, what has come over you?
Lightminded you were not, in all your boyhood.
Now you are full grown, come of age; a man
from foreign parts might take you for the son   245
of royalty, to go by your good looks;
and have you no more thoughtfulness or manners?
How could it happen in our hall that you
permit the stranger to be so abused?
Here, in our house, a guest, can any man   250
suffer indignity, come by such injury?
What can this be for you but public shame?"

Telémakhos looked in her eyes and answered,
with his clear head and his discretion:

                              "Mother,
I cannot take it ill that you are angry.   255
I know the meaning of these actions now,
both good and bad. I had been young and blind.
How can I always keep to what is fair
while these sit here to put fear in me?—princes
from near and far whose interest is my ruin;   260
are any on my side?
                     But you should know
the suitors did not have their way, matching
the stranger here and Iros—for the stranger
beat him to the ground.
                        O Father Zeus!
Athena and Apollo! could I see   265
the suitors whipped like that! Courtyard and hall
strewn with our friends, too weak-kneed to get up,
chapfallen to their collarbones, the way

old Iros rolls his head there by the gate
as though he were pig-drunk! No energy   270
to stagger on his homeward path; no fight
left in his numb legs!"

               Thus Penélopê
reproached her son, and he replied. Now, interrupting,
Eurýmakhos called out to her:

                   "Penélopê,
deep-minded queen, daughter of Ikários,   275
if all Akhaians in the land of Argos
only saw you now! What hundreds more
would join your suitors here to feast tomorrow!
Beauty like yours no woman had before,
or majesty, or mastery."

               She answered: 280

"Eurýmakhos, my qualities—I know—
my face, my figure, all were lost or blighted
when the Akhaians crossed the sea to Troy,
Odysseus my lord among the rest.
If he returned, if he were here to care for me,   285
I might be happily renowned!
But grief instead heaven sent me—years of pain.
Can I forget?—the day he left this island,
enfolding my right hand and wrist in his,
he said:

               'My lady, the Akhaian troops   290
will not easily make it home again
full strength, unhurt, from Troy. They say the Trojans
are fighters too; good lances and good bowmen,
horsemen, charioteers—and those can be
decisive when a battle hangs in doubt.   295
So whether God will send me back, or whether
I'll be a captive there, I cannot tell.
Here, then, you must attend to everything.
My parents in our house will be a care for you
as they are now, or more, while I am gone.   300
Wait for the beard to darken our boy's cheek;
then marry whom you will, and move away.'

The years he spoke of are now past; the night
comes when a bitter marriage overtakes me,
desolate as I am, deprived by Zeus   305
of all the sweets of life.

               How galling, too,
to see newfangled manners in my suitors!
Others who go to court a gentlewoman,
daughter of a rich house, if they are rivals,

bring their own beeves and sheep along; her friends 310
ought to be feasted, gifts are due to her;
would any dare to live at her expense?"

Odysseus' heart laughed when he heard all this—
her sweet tones charming gifts out of the suitors
with talk of marriage, though she intended none. 315
Eupeithês' son, Antínoös, now addressed her:

"Ikários' daughter, O deep-minded queen!
If someone cares to make you gifts, accept them!
It is no courtesy to turn gifts away.
But we go neither to our homes nor elsewhere 320
until of all Akhaians here you take
the best man for your lord."

                    Pleased at this answer,
every man sent a squire to fetch a gift—
Antínoös, a wide resplendent robe,
embroidered fine, and fastened with twelve brooches, 325
pins pressed into sheathing tubes of gold;
Eurýmakhos, a necklace, wrought in gold,
with sunray pieces of clear glinting amber.
Eurýdamas' men came back with pendants,
ear-drops in triple clusters of warm lights; 330
and from the hoard of Lord Polýktor's son,
Peisándros, came a band for her white throat,
jewelled adornment. Other wondrous things
were brought as gifts from the Akhaian princes.
Penélopê then mounted the stair again, 335
her maids behind, with treasure in their arms.

And now the suitors gave themselves to dancing,
to harp and haunting song, as night drew on;
black night indeed came on them at their pleasure.
But three torch fires were placed in the long hall 340
to give them light. On hand were stores of fuel,
dry seasoned chips of resinous wood, split up
by the bronze hatchet blade—these were mixed in
among the flames to keep them flaring bright;
each housemaid of Odysseus took her turn. 345

Now he himself, the shrewd and kingly man,
approached and told them:

                    "Housemaids of Odysseus,
your master so long absent in the world,
go to the women's chambers, to your queen.
Attend her, make the distaff whirl, divert her, 350
stay in her room, comb wool for her.
                              I stand here
ready to tend these flares and offer light

to everyone. They cannot tire me out,
even if they wish to drink till Dawn.
I am a patient man."

            But the women giggled,   355
glancing back and forth—laughed in his face;
and one smooth girl, Melántho, spoke to him
most impudently. She was Dólios' daughter,
taken as ward in childhood by Penélopê
who gave her playthings to her heart's content   360
and raised her as her own. Yet the girl felt
nothing for her mistress, no compunction,
but slept and made love with Eurýmakhos.
Her bold voice rang now in Odysseus' ears:

"You must be crazy, punch drunk, you old goat.   365
Instead of going out to find a smithy
to sleep warm in—or a tavern bench—you stay
putting your oar in, amid all our men.
Numbskull, not to be scared! The wine you drank
has clogged your brain, or are you always this way,   370
boasting like a fool? Or have you lost
your mind because you beat that tramp, that Iros?
Look out, or someone better may get up
and give you a good knocking about the ears
to send you out all bloody."

            But Odysseus   375
glared at her under his brows and said :

                "One minute:
let me tell Telémakhos how you talk
in hall, you slut; he'll cut your arms and legs off!"

This hard shot took the women's breath away
and drove them quaking to their rooms, as though   380
knives were behind: they felt he spoke the truth.
So there he stood and kept the firelight high
and looked the suitors over, while his mind
roamed far ahead to what must be accomplished.

They, for their part, could not now be still   385
or drop their mockery—for Athena wished
Odysseus mortified still more.
            Eurýmakhos,
the son of Pólybos, took up the baiting,
angling for a laugh among his friends.

"Suitors of our distinguished queen," he said,   390
"hear what my heart would have me say.
              This man
comes with a certain aura of divinity

into Odysseus' hall. He shines.

                                    He shines
around the noggin, like a flashing light,
having no hair at all to dim his lustre."   395

Then turning to Odysseus, raider of cities,
he went on:

                "Friend, you have a mind to work,
do you? Could I hire you to clear stones
from wasteland for me—you'll be paid enough—
collecting boundary walls and planting trees?   400
I'd give you a bread ration every day,
a cloak to wrap in, sandals for your feet.
Oh no: you learned your dodges long ago—
no honest sweat. You'd rather tramp the country
begging, to keep your hoggish belly full."   405

The master of many crafts replied:

                                    "Eurýmakhos,
we two might try our hands against each other
in early summer when the days are long,
in meadow grass, with one good scythe for me
and one as good for you: we'd cut our way   410
down a deep hayfield, fasting to late evening.
Or we could try our hands behind a plow,
driving the best of oxen—fat, well-fed,
well-matched for age and pulling power, and say
four strips apiece of loam the share could break: 415
you'd see then if I cleft you a straight furrow.
Competition in arms? If Zeus Kroníon
roused up a scuffle now, give me a shield,
two spears, a dogskin cap with plates of bronze
to fit my temples, and you'd see me go   420
where the first rank of fighters lock in battle.
There would be no more jeers about my belly.
You thick-skinned menace to all courtesy!
You think you are a great man and a champion,
but up against few men, poor stuff, at that.   425
Just let Odysseus return, those doors
wide open as they are, you'd find too narrow
to suit you on your sudden journey out."

Now fury mounted in Eurýmakhos,
who scowled and shot back:

                                    "Bundle of rags and lice!   430
By god, I'll make you suffer for your gall,
your insolent gabble before all our men."

He had his foot-stool out: but now Odysseus
took to his haunches by Amphínomos' knees,

fearing Eurýmakhos' missile, as it flew.   435
It clipped a wine steward on the serving hand,
so that his pitcher dropped with a loud clang
while he fell backward, cursing, in the dust.
In the shadowy hall a low sound rose—of suitors
murmuring to one another.

                "Ai!" they said,   440
"This vagabond would have done well to perish
somewhere else, and make us no such rumpus.
Here we are, quarreling over tramps; good meat
and wine forgotten; good sense gone by the board."

Telémakhos, his young heart high, put in: 445

"Bright souls, alight with wine, you can no longer
hide the cups you've taken.[4] Aye, some god
is goading you. Why not go home to bed?—
I mean when you are moved to. No one jumps
at my command."

            Struck by his blithe manner,   450
the young men's teeth grew fixed in their under lips,
but now the son of Nísos, Lord Amphínomos
of Aretíadês, addressed them all:

"O friends, no ruffling replies are called for;
that was fair counsel.
              Hands off the stranger, now,   455
and hands off any other servant here
in the great house of King Odysseus. Come,
let my own herald wet our cups once more,
we'll make an offering, and then to bed.
The stranger can be left behind in hall;   460
Telémakhos may care for him; he came
to Telémakhos' door, not ours."

               This won them over.
The soldier Moulios, Doulíkhion herald,
comrade in arms of Lord Amphínomos,
mixed the wine and served them all. They tipped out   465
drops for the blissful gods, and drank the rest,
and when they had drunk their thirst away
they trailed off homeward drowsily to bed.

BOOK XIX

[Recognitions and a Dream]

Now by Athena's side in the quiet hall
studying the ground for slaughter, Lord Odysseus
turned to Telémakhos.

---

4. I.e., you cannot hide the fact that you are drunk.

"The arms," he said.
"Harness and weapons must be out of sight
in the inner room. And if the suitors miss them,   5
be mild; just say 'I had a mind to move them
out of the smoke. They seemed no longer
the bright arms that Odysseus left at home
when he went off to Troy. Here where the fire's
hot breath came, they had grown black and drear.   10
One better reason struck me, too:
suppose a brawl starts up when you've been drinking—
you might in madness let each other's blood,
and that would stain your feast, your courtship.
                           Iron
itself can draw men's hands.' "

                 Then he fell silent,   15
and Telémakhos obeyed his father's word.
He called Eurýkleia, the nurse, and told her:

"Nurse, go shut the women in their quarters
while I shift Father's armor back
to the inner rooms—these beautiful arms unburnished,   20
caked with black soot in his years abroad.
I was a child then. Well, I am not now.
I want them shielded from the draught and smoke."

And the old woman answered:

                    "It is time, child,
you took an interest in such things. I wish   25
you'd put your mind on all your house and chattels.
But who will go along to hold a light?
You said no maids, no torch-bearers."

                    Telémakhos
looked at her and replied:

                "Our friend here.
A man who shares my meat can bear a hand,   30
no matter how far he is from home."

                He spoke so soldierly
her own speech halted on her tongue. Straight back
she went to lock the doors of the women's hall.
And now the two men sprang to work—father
and princely son, loaded with round helms   35
and studded bucklers, lifting the long spears,
while in their path Pallas Athena
held up a golden lamp of purest light.
Telémakhos at last burst out:

              "Oh, Father,
here is a marvel! All around I see   40

the walls and roof beams, pedestals and pillars,
lighted as though by white fire blazing near.
One of the gods of heaven is in this place!"

Then said Odysseus, the great tactician,

"Be still: keep still about it: just remember it.   45
The gods who rule Olympos make this light.
You may go off to bed now. Here I stay
to test your mother and her maids again.
Out of her long grief she will question me."

Telémakhos went across the hall and out   50
under the light of torches—crossed the court
to the tower chamber where he had always slept.
Here now again he lay, waiting for dawn,
while in the great hall by Athena's side
Odysseus waited with his mind on slaughter.   55

Presently Penélopê from her chamber
stepped in her thoughtful beauty.
                          So might Artemis
or golden Aphroditê have descended;
and maids drew to the hearth her own smooth chair
inlaid with silver whorls and ivory. The artisan   60
Ikmálios had made it, long before,
with a footrest in a single piece, and soft
upon the seat a heavy fleece was thrown.
Here by the fire the queen sat down. Her maids,
leaving their quarters, came with white arms bare   65
to clear the wine cups and the bread, and move
the trestle boards where men had lingered drinking.
Fiery ashes out of the pine-chip flares
they tossed, and piled on fuel for light and heat.
And now a second time Melántho's voice   70
rang brazen in Odysseus' ears:

                    "Ah, stranger,
are you still here, so creepy, late at night
hanging about, looking the women over?
You old goat, go outside, cuddle your supper;
get out, or a torch may kindle you behind!"   75

At this Odysseus glared under his brows
and said:

          "Little devil, why pitch into me again?
Because I go unwashed and wear these rags,
and make the rounds? But so I must, being needy;
that is the way a vagabond must live.   80
And do not overlook this: in my time
I too had luck, lived well, stood well with men,

and gave alms, often, to poor wanderers
like him you see before you—aye, to all sorts,
no matter in what dire want. I owned   85
servants—many, I say—and all the rest
that goes with what men call prosperity.
But Zeus the son of Kronos brought me down.
Mistress, mend your ways, or you may lose
all this vivacity of yours. What if her ladyship   90
were stirred to anger? What if Odysseus came?—
and I can tell you, there is hope of that—
or if the man is done for, still his son
lives to be reckoned with, by Apollo's will.
None of you can go wantoning on the sly   95
and fool him now. He is too old for that."

Penélopê, being near enough to hear him,
spoke out sharply to her maid:

                              "Oh, shameless,
through and through! And do you think me blind,
blind to your conquest? It will cost your life.   100
You knew I waited—for you heard me say it—
waited to see this man in hall and question him
about my lord; I am so hard beset."

She turned away and said to the housekeeper:

"Eurýnomê, a bench, a spread of sheepskin,   105
to put my guest at ease. Now he shall talk
and listen, and be questioned."

                    Willing hands
brought a smooth bench, and dropped a fleece upon it.
Here the adventurer and king sat down;
then carefully Penélopê began: 110

"Friend, let me ask you first of all:
who are you, where do you come from, of what nation
and parents were you born?"

                    And he replied:

"My lady, never a man in the wide world
should have a fault to find with you. Your name   115
has gone out under heaven like the sweet
honor of some god-fearing king, who rules
in equity over the strong: his black lands bear
both wheat and barley, fruit trees laden bright,
new lambs at lambing time—and the deep sea   120
gives great hauls of fish by his good strategy,
so that his folk fare well.
                    O my dear lady,

this being so, let it suffice to ask me
of other matters—not my blood, my homeland.
Do not enforce me to recall my pain.   125
My heart is sore; but I must not be found
sitting in tears here, in another's house:
it is not well forever to be grieving.
One of the maids might say—or you might think—
I had got maudlin over cups of wine."   130

And Penélopê replied:

                           "Stranger, my looks,
my face, my carriage, were soon lost or faded
when the Akhaians crossed the sea to Troy,
Odysseus my lord among the rest.
If he returned, if he were here to care for me,   135
I might be happily renowned!
But grief instead heaven sent me—years of pain.
Sons of the noblest families on the islands,
Doulíkhion, Samê, wooded Zakýnthos,
with native Ithakans, are here to court me,   140
against my wish; and they consume this house.
Can I give proper heed to guest or suppliant
or herald on the realm's affairs?
                                    How could I?
wasted with longing for Odysseus, while here
they press for marriage.
                          Ruses served my turn   145
to draw the time out—first a close-grained web
I had the happy thought to set up weaving
on my big loom in hall. I said, that day:
'Young men—my suitors, now my lord is dead,
let me finish my weaving before I marry,   150
or else my thread will have been spun in vain.
It is a shroud I weave for Lord Laërtês
when cold Death comes to lay him on his bier.
The country wives would hold me in dishonor
if he, with all his fortune, lay unshrouded.'   155
I reached their hearts that way, and they agreed.
So every day I wove on the great loom,
but every night by torchlight I unwove it;
and so for three years I deceived the Akhaians.
But when the seasons brought a fourth year on,   160
as long months waned, and the long days were spent,
through impudent folly in the slinking maids
they caught me—clamored up to me at night;
I had no choice then but to finish it.
And now, as matters stand at last,   165
I have no strength left to evade a marriage,
cannot find any further way; my parents
urge it upon me, and my son
will not stand by while they eat up his property.

He comprehends it, being a man full grown,   170
able to oversee the kind of house
Zeus would endow with honor.
                      But you too
confide in me, tell me your ancestry.
You were not born of mythic oak or stone."

And the great master of invention answered: 175

"O honorable wife of Lord Odysseus,
must you go on asking about my family?
Then I will tell you, though my pain
be doubled by it: and whose pain would not
if he had been away as long as I have   180
and had hard roving in the world of men?
But I will tell you even so, my lady.

One of the great islands of the world
in midsea, in the winedark sea, is Krete:
spacious and rich and populous, with ninety   185
cities and a mingling of tongues.
Akhaians there are found, along with Kretan
hillmen of the old stock, and Kydonians,
Dorians in three blood-lines, Pelasgians—
and one among their ninety towns is Knossos.[5]   190
Here lived King Minos whom great Zeus received
every ninth year in private council—Minos,
the father of my father, Deukálion.
Two sons Deukálion had: Idómeneus,
who went to join the Atreidai before Troy   195
in the beaked ships of war; and then myself,
Aithôn by name—a stripling next my brother.
But I saw with my own eyes at Knossos once
Odysseus.
            Gales had caught him off Cape Malea,
driven him southward on the coast of Krete,   200
when he was bound for Troy. At Ámnisos,
hard by the holy cave of Eileithuía,[6]
he lay to, and dropped anchor, in that open
and rough roadstead riding out the blow.
Meanwhile he came ashore, came inland, asking   205
after Idómeneus: dear friends he said they were;
but now ten mornings had already passed,
ten or eleven, since my brother sailed.
So I played host and took Odysseus home,
saw him well lodged and fed, for we had plenty;   210
then I made requisitions—barley, wine,

5. The site of the great palace discovered by Evans, who called the civilization that produced it Minoan.
It is impossible to extract historical fact from this confused account of the population of Krete. Kydonians
may be the inhabitants of the western end of the island. Dorians were the people who, according to Greek
belief, invaded Greece and destroyed the Mycenaean palace-civilizations (but Homer does not mention
them elsewhere). Pelasgians were the pre-Greek inhabitants of the area.   6. Goddess of childbirth. Ámnisos is on the coast near Knossos.

and beeves for sacrifice—to give his company
abundant fare along with him.
                              Twelve days
they stayed with us, the Akhaians, while that wind
out of the north shut everyone inside—   215
even on land you could not keep your feet,
such fury was abroad. On the thirteenth,
when the gale dropped, they put to sea."

Now all these lies he made appear so truthful
she wept as she sat listening. The skin   220
of her pale face grew moist the way pure snow
softens and glistens on the mountains, thawed
by Southwind after powdering from the West,
and, as the snow melts, mountain streams run full:
so her white cheeks were wetted by these tears   225
shed for her lord—and he close by her side.
Imagine how his heart ached for his lady,
his wife in tears; and yet he never blinked;
his eyes might have been made of horn or iron
for all that she could see. He had this trick—   230
wept, if he willed to, inwardly.
                              Well, then,
as soon as her relieving tears were shed
she spoke once more:

                    "I think that I shall say, friend,
give me some proof, if it is really true
that you were host in that place to my husband   235
with his brave men, as you declare. Come, tell me
the quality of his clothing, how he looked,
and some particular of his company."

Odysseus answered, and his mind ranged far:

"Lady, so long a time now lies between,   240
it is hard to speak of it. Here is the twentieth year
since that man left the island of my father.
But I shall tell what memory calls to mind.
A purple cloak, and fleecy, he had on—
a double thick one. Then, he wore a brooch   245
made of pure gold with twin tubes for the prongs,
and on the face a work of art: a hunting dog
pinning a spotted fawn in agony
between his forepaws—wonderful to see
how being gold, and nothing more, he bit   250
the golden deer convulsed, with wild hooves flying.
Odysseus' shirt I noticed, too—a fine
closefitting tunic like dry onion skin,
so soft it was, and shiny.
                              Women there,
many of them, would cast their eyes on it.   255

But I might add, for your consideration,
whether he brought these things from home, or whether
a shipmate gave them to him, coming aboard,
I have no notion: some regardful host
in another port perhaps it was. Affection   260
followed him—there were few Akhaians like him.
And I too made him gifts: a good bronze blade,
a cloak with lining and a broidered shirt,
and sent him off in his trim ship with honor.
A herald, somewhat older than himself,   265
he kept beside him; I'll describe this man:
round-shouldered, dusky, woolly-headed;
Eurýbatês, his name was—and Odysseus
gave him preferment over the officers.
He had a shrewd head, like the captain's own."   270

Now hearing these details—minutely true—
she felt more strangely moved, and tears flowed
until she had tasted her salt grief again.
Then she found words to answer:

                            "Before this
you won my sympathy, but now indeed   275
you shall be our respected guest and friend.
With my own hands I put that cloak and tunic
upon him—took them folded from their place—
and the bright brooch for ornament.
                                        Gone now,
I will not meet the man again   280
returning to his own home fields. Unkind
the fate that sent him young in the long ship
to see that misery at Ilion, unspeakable!"

And the master improviser answered:

                                        "Honorable
wife of Odysseus Laërtiadês,   285
you need not stain your beauty with these tears,
nor wear yourself out grieving for your husband.
Not that I can blame you. Any wife
grieves for the man she married in her girlhood,
lay with in love, bore children to—though he   290
may be no prince like this Odysseus,
whom they compare even to the gods. But listen:
weep no more, and listen:
I have a thing to tell you, something true.
I heard but lately of your lord's return,   295
heard that he is alive, not far away,
among Thesprótians in their green land
amassing fortune to bring home. His company
went down in shipwreck in the winedark sea
off the coast of Thrinákia. Zeus and Hêlios   300

held it against him that his men had killed
the kine of Hêlios. The crew drowned for this.
He rode the ship's keel. Big seas cast him up
on the island of Phaiákians, godlike men
who took him to their hearts. They honored him   305
with many gifts and a safe passage home,
or so they wished. Long since he should have been here,
but he thought better to restore his fortune
playing the vagabond about the world;
and no adventurer could beat Odysseus   310
at living by his wits—no man alive.
I had this from King Phaidôn of Thesprótia;
and, tipping wine out, Phaidôn swore to me
the ship was launched, the seamen standing by
to bring Odysseus to his land at last,   315
but I got out to sea ahead of him
by the king's order—as it chanced a freighter
left port for the grain bins of Doulíkhion.
Phaidôn, however, showed me Odysseus' treasure.
Ten generations of his heirs or more   320
could live on what lay piled in that great room.
The man himself had gone up to Dodona
to ask the spelling leaves of the old oak
what Zeus would have him do—how to return to Ithaka
after so many years—by stealth or openly.   325
You see, then, he is alive and well, and headed
homeward now, no more to be abroad
far from his island, his dear wife and son.
Here is my sworn word for it. Witness this,
god of the zenith, noblest of the gods,   330
and Lord Odysseus' hearthfire, now before me:
I swear these things shall turn out as I say.
Between this present dark and one day's ebb,
after the wane, before the crescent moon,
Odysseus will come."

              Penélopê,   335
the attentive queen, replied to him:

                     "Ah, stranger,
if what you say could ever happen!
You would soon know our love! Our bounty, too:
men would turn after you to call you blessed.
But my heart tells me what must be.   340
Odysseus will not come to me; no ship
will be prepared for you. We have no master
quick to receive and furnish out a guest
as Lord Odysseus was.
              Or did I dream him?

Maids, maids: come wash him, make a bed for him,   345
bedstead and colored rugs and coverlets
to let him lie warm into the gold of Dawn.

In morning light you'll bathe him and anoint him
so that he'll take his place beside Telémakhos
feasting in hall. If there be one man there   350
to bully or annoy him, that man wins
no further triumph here, burn though he may.
How will you understand me, friend, how find in me,
more than in common women, any courage
or gentleness, if you are kept in rags   355
and filthy at our feast? Men's lives are short.
The hard man and his cruelties will be
cursed behind his back, and mocked in death.
But one whose heart and ways are kind—of him
strangers will bear report to the wide world,   360
and distant men will praise him."

                         Warily
Odysseus answered:

                    "Honorable lady,
wife of Odysseus Laërtiadês,
a weight of rugs and cover? Not for me.
I've had none since the day I saw the mountains   365
of Krete, white with snow, low on the sea line
fading behind me as the long oars drove me north.
Let me lie down tonight as I've lain often,
many a night unsleeping, many a time
afield on hard ground waiting for pure Dawn.   370
No: and I have no longing for a footbath
either; none of these maids will touch my feet,
unless there is an old one, old and wise,
one who has lived through suffering as I have:
I would not mind letting my feet be touched   375
by that old servant."

                    And Penélopê said:

"Dear guest, no foreign man so sympathetic
ever came to my house, no guest more likeable,
so wry and humble are the things you say.
I have an old maidservant ripe with years,   380
one who in her time nursed my lord. She took him
into her arms the hour his mother bore him.
Let her, then, wash your feet, though she is frail.
Come here, stand by me, faithful Eurýkleia,
and bathe—bathe your master, I almost said,   385
for they are of an age, and now Odysseus'
feet and hands would be enseamed like his.
Men grow old soon in hardship."

                         Hearing this,
the old nurse hid her face between her hands
and wept hot tears, and murmured:

"Oh, my child!   390
I can do nothing for you! How Zeus hated you,
no other man so much! No use, great heart,
O faithful heart, the rich thighbones you burnt
to Zeus who plays in lightning—and no man
ever gave more to Zeus—with all your prayers   395
for a green age, a tall son reared to manhood.
There is no day of homecoming for you.
Stranger, some women in some far off place
perhaps have mocked my lord when he'd be home
as now these strumpets mock you here. No wonder   400
you would keep clear of all their whorishness
and have no bath. But here am I. The queen
Penélopê, Ikários' daughter, bids me;
so let me bathe your feet to serve my lady—
to serve you, too.
                    My heart within me stirs,   405
mindful of something. Listen to what I say:
strangers have come here, many through the years,
but no one ever came, I swear, who seemed
so like Odysseus—body, voice and limbs—
as you do."

             Ready for this, Odysseus answered: 410

"Old woman, that is what they say. All who have seen
the two of us remark how like we are,
as you yourself have said, and rightly, too."

Then he kept still, while the old nurse filled up
her basin glittering in firelight; she poured   415
cold water in, then hot.
                         But Lord Odysseus
whirled suddenly from the fire to face the dark.
The scar: he had forgotten that. She must not
handle his scarred thigh, or the game was up.
But when she bared her lord's leg, bending near,   420
she knew the groove at once.
                             An old wound
a boar's white tusk inflicted, on Parnassos[7]
years ago. He had gone hunting there
in company with his uncles and Autólykos,
his mother's father—a great thief and swindler   425
by Hermês'[8] favor, for Autólykos pleased him
with burnt offerings of sheep and kids. The god
acted as his accomplice. Well, Autólykos
on a trip to Ithaka
arrived just after his daughter's boy was born.   430
In fact, he had no sooner finished supper

7. The mountain range above Apollo's oracular shrine at Delphi.   8. Not only the messenger of the gods and the god who guided the dead down to the lower world but also the god of the marketplace and so of trickery and swindling.

than Nurse Eurýkleia put the baby down
in his own lap and said:

                "It is for you, now,
to choose a name for him, your child's dear baby;
the answer to her prayers."

                Autólykos replied: 435

"My son-in-law, my daughter, call the boy
by the name I tell you. Well you know, my hand
has been against the world of men and women;
odium[9] and distrust I've won. Odysseus
should be his given name. When he grows up,   440
when he comes visiting his mother's home
under Parnassos, where my treasures are,
I'll make him gifts and send him back rejoicing."

Odysseus in due course went for the gifts,
and old Autólykos and his sons embraced him   445
with welcoming sweet words; and Amphithéa,
his mother's mother, held him tight and kissed him,
kissed his head and his fine eyes.
                    The father
called on his noble sons to make a feast,
and going about it briskly they led in   450
an ox of five years, whom they killed and flayed
and cut in bits for roasting on the skewers
with skilled hands, with care; then shared it out.
So all the day until the sun went down
they feasted to their hearts' content. At evening,   455
after the sun was down and dusk had come,
they turned to bed and took the gift of sleep.

When the young Dawn spread in the eastern sky
her finger tips of rose, the men and dogs
went hunting, taking Odysseus. They climbed   460
Parnassos' rugged flank mantled in forest,
entering amid high windy folds at noon
when Hêlios beat upon the valley floor
and on the winding Ocean whence he came.
With hounds questing ahead, in open order,   465
the sons of Autólykos went down a glen,
Odysseus in the lead, behind the dogs,
pointing his long-shadowing spear.
                    Before them
a great boar lay hid in undergrowth,
in a green thicket proof against the wind   470
or sun's blaze, fine soever the needling sunlight,

9. The translator is reproducing a pun in the original Greek; Autólykos speaks of himself as *odyssamenos*, one who is angry and gives cause for anger.

impervious too to any rain, so dense
that cover was, heaped up with fallen leaves.
Patter of hounds' feet, men's feet, woke the boar
as they came up—and from his woody ambush   475
with razor back bristling and raging eyes
he trotted and stood at bay. Odysseus,
being on top of him, had the first shot,
lunging to stick him; but the boar
had already charged under the long spear.   480
He hooked aslant with one white tusk and ripped out
flesh above the knee, but missed the bone.
Odysseus' second thrust went home by luck,
his bright spear passing through the shoulder joint;
and the beast fell, moaning as life pulsed away.   485
Autólykos' tall sons took up the wounded,
working skillfully over the Prince Odysseus
to bind his gash, and with a rune[1] they stanched
the dark flow of blood. Then downhill swiftly
they all repaired to the father's house, and there   490
tended him well—so well they soon could send him,
with Grandfather Autólykos' magnificent gifts,
rejoicing, over sea to Ithaka.
His father and the Lady Antikleía
welcomed him, and wanted all the news   495
of how he got his wound; so he spun out
his tale, recalling how the boar's white tusk
caught him when he was hunting on Parnassos.

This was the scar the old nurse recognized;
she traced it under her spread hands, then let go,   500
and into the basin fell the lower leg
making the bronze clang, sloshing the water out.
Then joy and anguish seized her heart; her eyes
filled up with tears; her throat closed, and she whispered,
with hand held out to touch his chin:

                                            "Oh yes!   505
You are Odysseus! Ah, dear child! I could not
see you until now—not till I knew
my master's very body with my hands!"

Her eyes turned to Penélopê with desire
to make her lord, her husband, known—in vain,   510
because Athena had bemused the queen,
so that she took no notice, paid no heed.
At the same time Odysseus' right hand
gripped the old throat; his left hand pulled her near,
and in her ear he said:

                                   "Will you destroy me,   515
nurse, who gave me milk at your own breast?

1. An incantation; magic to stop the flow of blood.

Now with a hard lifetime behind I've come
in the twentieth year home to my father's island.
You found me out, as the chance was given you.
Be quiet; keep it from the others, else   520
I warn you, and I mean it, too,
if by my hand god brings the suitors down
I'll kill you, nurse or not, when the time comes—
when the time comes to kill the other women."

Eurýkleia kept her wits and answered him: 525

"Oh, what mad words are these you let escape you!
Child, you know my blood, my bones are yours;
no one could whip this out of me. I'll be
a woman turned to stone, iron I'll be.
And let me tell you too—mind now—if god   530
cuts down the arrogant suitors by your hand,
I can report to you on all the maids,
those who dishonor you, and the innocent."

But in response the great tactician said:

"Nurse, no need to tell me tales of these.   535
I will have seen them, each one, for myself.
Trust in the gods, be quiet, hold your peace."

Silent, the old nurse went to fetch more water,
her basin being all spilt.
                                When she had washed
and rubbed his feet with golden oil, he turned,   540
dragging his bench again to the fire side
for warmth, and hid the scar under his rags.
Penélopê broke the silence, saying:

                                "Friend,
allow me one brief question more. You know,
the time for bed, sweet rest, is coming soon,   545
if only that warm luxury of slumber
would come to enfold us, in our trouble. But for me
my fate at night is anguish and no rest.
By day being busy, seeing to my work,
I find relief sometimes from loss and sorrow;   550
but when night comes and all the world's abed
I lie in mine alone, my heart thudding,
while bitter thoughts and fears crowd on my grief.
Think how Pandáreos' daughter, pale forever,
sings as the nightingale[2] in the new leaves   555
through those long quiet hours of night,

2. The reference is to one of the many Greek legends that explain the song of the nightingale. In this one
the daughter of Pandáreos, a Cretan king, was married to Zêthos, king of Thebes. She had only one son;
her sister-in-law Niobe had many. In a fit of jealousy she tried to kill Niobe's eldest son but by mistake (in
the dark) killed her own son, Itylos, instead. Zeus changed her into a nightingale, and she sings in mourning
for Itylos.

on some thick-flowering orchard bough in spring;
how she rills out and tilts her note, high now, now low,
mourning for Itylos whom she killed in madness—
her child, and her lord Zêthos' only child.   560
My forlorn thought flows variable as her song,
wondering: shall I stay beside my son
and guard my own things here, my maids, my hall,
to honor my lord's bed and the common talk?
Or had I best join fortunes with a suitor,   565
the noblest one, most lavish in his gifts?
Is it now time for that?
My son being still a callow boy forbade
marriage, or absence from my lord's domain;
but now the child is grown, grown up, a man,   570
he, too, begins to pray for my departure,
aghast at all the suitors gorge on.

                Listen:
interpret me this dream: From a water's edge
twenty fat geese have come to feed on grain
beside my house. And I delight to see them.   575
But now a mountain eagle with great wings
and crooked beak storms in to break their necks
and strew their bodies here. Away he soars
into the bright sky; and I cry aloud—
all this in dream—I wail and round me gather   580
softly braided Akhaian women mourning
because the eagle killed my geese.

                Then down
out of the sky he drops to a cornice beam
with mortal voice telling me not to weep.
'Be glad,' says he, 'renowned Ikários' daughter: 585
here is no dream but something real as day,
something about to happen. All those geese
were suitors, and the bird was I. See now,
I am no eagle but your lord come back
to bring inglorious death upon them all!"   590
As he said this, my honeyed slumber left me.
Peering through half-shut eyes, I saw the geese
in hall, still feeding at the self-same trough."

The master of subtle ways and straight replied:

"My dear, how can you choose to read the dream   595
differently? Has not Odysseus himself
shown you what is to come? Death to the suitors,
sure death, too. Not one escapes his doom."

Penélopê shook her head and answered:

                "Friend,
many and many a dream is mere confusion,   600

a cobweb of no consequence at all.
Two gates for ghostly dreams there are: one gateway
of honest horn, and one of ivory.
Issuing by the ivory gate are dreams
of glimmering illusion, fantasies,   605
but those that come through solid polished horn
may be borne out, if mortals only know them.
I doubt it came by horn, my fearful dream—
too good to be true, that, for my son and me.
But one thing more I wish to tell you: listen   610
carefully. It is a black day, this that comes.
Odysseus' house and I are to be parted.
I shall decree a contest for the day.
We have twelve axe heads. In his time, my lord
could line them up, all twelve, at intervals   615
like a ship's ribbing; then he'd back away
a long way off and whip an arrow through.[3]
Now I'll impose this trial on the suitors.
The one who easily handles and strings the bow
and shoots through all twelve axes I shall marry,   620
whoever he may be—then look my last
on this my first love's beautiful brimming house.
But I'll remember, though I dream it only."

Odysseus said:

      "Dear honorable lady,
wife of Odysseus Laërtiadês,   625
let there be no postponement of the trial.
Odysseus, who knows the shifts of combat,
will be here: aye, he'll be here long before
one of these lads can stretch or string that bow
or shoot to thread the iron!"

               Grave and wise,   630
Penélopê replied:

      "If you were willing
to sit with me and comfort me, my friend,
no tide of sleep would ever close my eyes.
But mortals cannot go forever sleepless.
This the undying gods decree for all   635
who live and die on earth, kind furrowed earth.
Upstairs I go, then, to my single bed,
my sighing bed, wet with so many tears
after my Lord Odysseus took ship
to see that misery at Ilion, unspeakable.   640

3. The nature of this archery contest is a puzzle that has never been satisfactorily solved. The axes were probably double-headed; the aperture through which the arrow passed must have been the socket in which the wood handle fit. If the twelve ax heads were lined up, fixed in the ground (Telémakhos later digs a trench for them) so that the empty sockets were in a straight line, an archer might be able to shoot through them. When Odysseus finally does so, he is sitting down (21.441).

Let me rest there, you here. You can stretch out
on the bare floor, or else command a bed."

So she went up to her chamber softly lit,
accompanied by her maids. Once there, she wept
for Odysseus, her husband, till Athena   645
cast sweet sleep upon her eyes.

BOOK XX

[Signs and a Vision]

Outside in the entry way he made his bed—
raw oxhide spread on level ground, and heaped up
fleeces, left from sheep the Akhaians killed.
And when he had lain down, Eurýnomê
flung out a robe to cover him. Unsleeping   5
the Lord Odysseus lay, and roved in thought
to the undoing of his enemies.

                                        Now came a covey of women
laughing as they slipped out, arm in arm,
as many a night before, to the suitors' beds;
and anger took him like a wave to leap   10
into their midst and kill them, every one—
or should he let them all go hot to bed
one final night? His heart cried out within him
the way a brach[4] with whelps between her legs
would howl and bristle at a stranger—so   15
the hackles of his heart rose at that laughter.
Knocking his breast he muttered to himself:

"Down; be steady. You've seen worse, that time
the Kyklops like a rockslide ate your men
while you looked on. Nobody, only guile,   20
got you out of that cave alive."

                                        His rage,
held hard in leash, submitted to his mind,
while he himself rocked, rolling from side to side,
as a cook turns a sausage, big with blood
and fat, at a scorching blaze, without a pause,   25
to broil it quick: so he rolled left and right,
casting about to see how he, alone,
against the false outrageous crowd of suitors
could press the fight.

                                        And out of the night sky
Athena came to him; out of the nearby dark   30
in body like a woman; came and stood
over his head to chide him:

                                        "Why so wakeful,
most forlorn of men? Here is your home,

4. Bitch (obsolete).

there lies your lady; and your son is here,
as fine as one could wish a son to be." 35

Odysseus looked up and answered:

                              "Aye,
goddess, that much is true; but still
I have some cause to fret in this affair.
I am one man; how can I whip those dogs?
They are always here in force. Neither 40
is that the end of it, there's more to come.
If by the will of Zeus and by your will
I killed them all, where could I go for safety?
Tell me that!"

         And the grey-eyed goddess said:

"Your touching faith! Another man would trust 45
some villainous mortal, with no brains—and what
am I? Your goddess-guardian to the end
in all your trials. Let it be plain as day:
if fifty bands of men surrounded us
and every sword sang for your blood, 50
you could make off still with their cows and sheep.
Now you, too, go to sleep. This all night vigil
wearies the flesh. You'll come out soon enough
on the other side of trouble."

                    Raining soft
sleep on his eyes, the beautiful one was gone 55
back to Olympos. Now at peace, the man
slumbered and lay still, but not his lady.
Wakeful again with all her cares, reclining
in the soft bed, she wept and cried aloud
until she had had her fill of tears, then spoke 60
in prayer first to Artemis:

              "O gracious
divine lady Artemis, daughter of Zeus,
if you could only make an end now quickly,
let the arrow fly, stop my heart,
or if some wind could take me by the hair 65
up into running cloud, to plunge in tides of Ocean,
as hurricane winds took Pandareos' daughters[5]
when they were left at home alone. The gods
had sapped their parents' lives. But Aphroditê
fed those children honey, cheese, and wine, 70
and Hêra gave them looks and wit, and Artemis,
pure Artemis, gave lovely height, and wise

5. The fate of these daughters was different from that of the one who married Zêthos and became a
nightingale (see n. 2, p. 455). They paid for the sin of their father, who stole a golden image from the
temple of Hephaistos. Though the gods showered gifts on them, in the end they were swept away to their
deaths by the stormwinds.

Athena made them practised in her arts—
till Aphroditê in glory walked on Olympos,
begging for each a happy wedding day   75
from Zeus, the lightning's joyous king, who knows
all fate of mortals, fair and foul—
but even at that hour the cyclone winds
had ravished them away
to serve the loathsome Furies.
        Let me be   80
blown out by the Olympians! Shot by Artemis,
I still might go and see amid the shades
Odysseus in the rot of underworld.
No coward's eye should light by my consenting!
Evil may be endured when our days pass   85
in mourning, heavy-hearted, hard beset,
if only sleep reign over nighttime, blanketing
the world's good and evil from our eyes.
But not for me: dreams too my demon sends me.
Tonight the image of my lord came by   90
as I remember him with troops. O strange
exultation! I thought him real, and not a dream."

Now as the Dawn appeared all stitched in gold,
the queen's cry reached Odysseus at his waking,
so that he wondered, half asleep: it seemed   95
she knew him, and stood near him! Then he woke
and picked his bedding up to stow away
on a chair in the mégaron. The oxhide pad
he took outdoors. There, spreading wide his arms,
he prayed:

    "O Father Zeus, if over land and water,   100
after adversity, you willed to bring me home,
let someone in the waking house give me good augury,
and a sign be shown, too, in the outer world."

He prayed thus, and the mind of Zeus in heaven
heard him. He thundered out of bright Olympos   105
down from above the cloudlands in reply—
a rousing peal for Odysseus. Then a token
came to him from a woman grinding flour
in the court nearby. His own handmills were there,
and twelve maids had the job of grinding out   110
whole grain and barley meal, the pith of men.
Now all the rest, their bushels ground, were sleeping;
one only, frail and slow, kept at it still.
She stopped, stayed her hand, and her lord heard
the omen from her lips:

      "Ah, Father Zeus   115
almighty over gods and men!
A great bang of thunder that was, surely,

out of the starry sky, and not a cloud in sight.
It is your nod to someone. Hear me, then,
make what I say come true: 120
let this day be the last the suitors feed
so dainty in Odysseus' hall!
They've made me work my heart out till I drop,
grinding barley. May they feast no more!"

The servant's prayer, after the cloudless thunder   125
of Zeus, Odysseus heard with lifting heart,
sure in his bones that vengeance was at hand.
Then other servants, wakening, came down
to build and light a fresh fire at the hearth.
Telémakhos, clear-eyed as a god, awoke,   130
put on his shirt and belted on his sword,
bound rawhide sandals under his smooth feet,
and took his bronze-shod lance. He came and stood
on the broad sill of the doorway, calling Eurýkleia:

"Nurse, dear Nurse, how did you treat our guest?   135
Had he a supper and a good bed? Has he lain
uncared for still? My mother is like that,
perverse for all her cleverness:
she'd entertain some riff-raff, and turn out
a solid man."

        The old nurse answered him: 140

"I would not be so quick to accuse her, child.
He sat and drank here while he had a mind to;
food he no longer hungered for, he said—
for she did ask him. When he thought of sleeping,
she ordered them to make a bed. Poor soul!   145
Poor gentleman! So humble and so miserable,
he would accept no bed with rugs to lie on,
but slept on sheepskins and a raw oxhide
in the entry way. We covered him ourselves."

Telémakhos left the hall, hefting his lance,   150
with two swift flickering hounds for company,
to face the island Akhaians in the square;
and gently born Eurýkleia the daughter
of Ops Peisenóridês, called to the maids:

"Bestir yourselves! you have your brooms, go sprinkle   155
the rooms and sweep them, robe the chairs in red,
sponge off the tables till they shine.
Wash out the winebowls and two-handled cups.
You others go fetch water from the spring;
no loitering; come straight back. Our company   160
will be here soon; morning is sure to bring them;
everyone has a holiday today."

The women ran to obey her—twenty girls
off to the spring with jars for dusky water,
the rest at work inside. Then tall woodcutters 165
entered to split up logs for the hearth fire,
the water carriers returned; and on their heels
arrived the swineherd, driving three fat pigs,
chosen among his pens. In the wide court
he let them feed, and said to Odysseus kindly: 170

"Friend, are they more respectful of you now,
or still insulting you?"

               Replied Odysseus:

"The young men, yes. And may the gods requite
those insolent puppies for the game they play
in a home not their own. They have no decency." 175

During this talk, Melánthios the goatherd
came in, driving goats for the suitors' feast,
with his two herdsmen. Under the portico
they tied the animals, and Melánthios
looked at Odysseus with a sneer. Said he:

                           "Stranger, 180
I see you mean to stay and turn our stomachs
begging in this hall. Clear out, why don't you?
Or will you have to taste a bloody beating
before you see the point? Your begging ways
nauseate everyone. There are feasts elsewhere." 185

Odysseus answered not a word, but grimly
shook his head over his murderous heart.
A third man came up now: Philoítios
the cattle foreman, with an ox behind him
and fat goats for the suitors. Ferrymen 190
had brought these from the mainland, as they bring
travellers, too—whoever comes along.
Philoítios tied the beasts under the portico
and joined the swineherd.

                   "Who is this," he said,
"Who is the new arrival at the manor? 195
Akhaian? or what else does he claim to be?
Where are his family and fields of home?
Down on his luck, all right: carries himself like a captain.
How the immortal gods can change and drag us down
once they begin to spin dark days for us!— 200
Kings and commanders, too."

                     Then he stepped over
and took Odysseus by the right hand, saying:

"Welcome, Sir. May good luck lie ahead
at the next turn. Hard times you're having, surely.
O Zeus! no god is more berserk in heaven   205
if gentle folk, whom you yourself begot,
you plunge in grief and hardship without mercy!
Sir, I began to sweat when I first saw you,
and tears came to my eyes, remembering
Odysseus: rags like these he may be wearing   210
somewhere on his wanderings now—
I mean, if he's alive still under the sun.
But if he's dead and in the house of Death,
I mourn Odysseus. He entrusted cows to me
in Kephallênia, when I was knee high,   215
and now his herds are numberless, no man else
ever had cattle multiply like grain.
But new men tell me I must bring my beeves
to feed them, who care nothing for our prince,
fear nothing from the watchful gods. They crave   220
partition of our lost king's land and wealth.
My own feelings keep going round and round
upon this tether: can I desert the boy
by moving, herds and all, to another country,
a new life among strangers? Yet it's worse   225
to stay here, in my old post, herding cattle
for upstarts.
                    I'd have gone long since,
gone, taken service with another king; this shame
is no more to be borne; but I keep thinking
my own lord, poor devil, still might come   230
and make a rout of suitors in his hall."

Odysseus, with his mind on action, answered:

"Herdsman, I make you out to be no coward
and no fool: I can see that for myself.
So let me tell you this. I swear by Zeus   235
all highest, by the table set for friends,
and by your king's hearthstone to which I've come,
Odysseus will return. You'll be on hand
to see, if you care to see it,
how those who lord it here will be cut down."   240

The cowman said:

                    "Would god it all came true!
You'd see the fight that's in me!"

                              Then Eumaios
echoed him, and invoked the gods, and prayed
that his great-minded master should return.
While these three talked, the suitors in the field   245
had come together plotting—what but death

for Telémakhos?—when from the left an eagle
crossed high with a rockdove in his claws.

Amphínomos got up. Said he, cutting them short:

"Friends, no luck lies in that plan for us,   250
no luck, knifing the lad. Let's think of feasting."

A grateful thought, they felt, and walking on
entered the great hall of the hero Odysseus,
where they all dropped their cloaks on chairs or couches
and made a ritual slaughter, knifing sheep,   255
fat goats and pigs, knifing the grass-fed steer.
Then tripes were broiled and eaten. Mixing bowls
were filled with wine. The swineherd passed out cups,
Philoítios, chief cowherd, dealt the loaves
into the panniers, Melánthios poured wine,   260
and all their hands went out upon the feast.

Telémakhos placed his father to advantage
just at the door sill of the pillared hall,
setting a stool there and a sawed-off table,
gave him a share of tripes, poured out his wine   265
in a golden cup, and said:

                    "Stay here, sit down
to drink with our young friends. I stand between you
and any cutting word or cuffing hand
from any suitor. Here is no public house
but the old home of Odysseus, my inheritance.   270
Hold your tongues then, gentlemen, and your blows,
and let no wrangling start, no scuffle either."

The others, disconcerted, bit their lips
at the ring in the young man's voice. Antínoös,
Eupeithês' son, turned round to them and said: 275

"It goes against the grain, my lords, but still
I say we take this hectoring by Telémakhos.
You know Zeus balked at it, or else
we might have shut his mouth a long time past,
the silvery speaker."

                    But Telémakhos   280
paid no heed to what Antínoös said.

Now public heralds wound through Ithaka
leading a file of beasts for sacrifice, and islanders
gathered under the shade trees of Apollo,
in the precinct of the Archer[6]—while in hall   285

6. An epithet of Apollo (see *Iliad* 1). The trees are in his open-air precinct.

the suitors roasted mutton and fat beef
on skewers, pulling off the fragrant cuts;
and those who did the roasting served Odysseus
a portion equal to their own, for so
Telémakhos commanded.
                But Athena   290
had no desire now to let the suitors
restrain themselves from wounding words and acts.
Laërtês' son again must be offended.
There was a scapegrace fellow in the crowd
named Ktésippos, a Samian, rich beyond   295
all measure, arrogant with riches, early
and late a bidder for Odysseus' queen.
Now this one called attention to himself:

"Hear me, my lords, I have a thing to say.
Our friend has had his fair share from the start   300
and that's polite; it would be most improper
if we were cold to guests of Telémakhos—
no matter what tramp turns up. Well then, look here,
let me throw in my own small contribution.
He must have prizes to confer, himself,   305
on some brave bathman or another slave
here in Odysseus' house."

                His hand went backward
and, fishing out a cow's foot from the basket,
he let it fly.
            Odysseus rolled his head
to one side softly, ducking the blow, and smiled   310
a crooked smile with teeth clenched. On the wall
the cow's foot struck and fell. Telémakhos
blazed up:

           "Ktésippos, lucky for you, by heaven,
not to have hit him! He took care of himself,
else you'd have had my lance-head in your belly;   315
no marriage, but a grave instead on Ithaka
for your father's pains.
              You others, let me see
no more contemptible conduct in my house!
I've been awake to it for a long time—by now
I know what is honorable and what is not.   320
Before, I was a child. I can endure it
while sheep are slaughtered, wine drunk up, and bread—
can one man check the greed of a hundred men?—
but I will suffer no more viciousness.
Granted you mean at last to cut me down: 325
I welcome that—better to die than have
humiliation always before my eyes,
the stranger buffeted, and the serving women
dragged about, abused in a noble house."

They quieted, grew still, under his lashing,   330
and after a long silence, Ageláos,
Damástor's son, spoke to them all:

                "Friends, friends,
I hope no one will answer like a fishwife.
What has been said is true. Hands off this stranger,
he is no target, neither is any servant   335
here in the hall of King Odysseus.
Let me say a word, though, to Telémakhos
and to his mother, if it please them both:
as long as hope remained in you to see
Odysseus, that great gifted man, again,   340
you could not be reproached for obstinacy,
tying the suitors down here; better so,
if still your father fared the great sea homeward.
How plain it is, though, now, he'll come no more!
Go sit then by your mother, reason with her,   345
tell her to take the best man, highest bidder,
and you can have and hold your patrimony,
feed on it, drink it all, while she
adorns another's house."

             Keeping his head,
Telémakhos replied:

             "By Zeus Almighty,   350
Ageláos, and by my father's sufferings,
far from Ithaka, whether he's dead or lost,
I make no impediment to Mother's marriage.
'Take whom you wish,' I say, 'I'll add my dowry.'
But can I pack her off against her will   355
from her own home? Heaven forbid!"

               At this,
Pallas Athena touched off in the suitors
a fit of laughter, uncontrollable.
She drove them into nightmare, till they wheezed
and neighed as though with jaws no longer theirs,   360
while blood defiled their meat, and blurring tears
flooded their eyes, heart-sore with woe to come.
Then said the visionary, Theoklýmenos:

"O lost sad men, what terror is this you suffer?
Night shrouds you to the knees, your heads, your faces;   365
dry retch of death runs round like fire in sticks;
your cheeks are streaming; these fair walls and pedestals
are dripping crimson blood. And thick with shades
is the entry way, the courtyard thick with shades
passing athirst toward Érebos, into the dark,   370
the sun is quenched in heaven, foul mist hems us in . . ."

The young men greeted this with shouts of laughter,
and Eurýmakhos, the son of Pólybos, crowed:

"The mind of our new guest has gone astray.
Hustle him out of doors, lads, into the sunlight;   375
he finds it dark as night inside!"

The man of vision looked at him and said:

"When I need help, I'll ask for it, Eurýmakhos.
I have my eyes and ears, a pair of legs,
and a straight mind, still with me. These will do   380
to take me out. Damnation and black night
I see arriving for yourselves: no shelter,
no defence for any in this crowd—
fools and vipers in the king's own hall."

With this he left that handsome room and went   385
home to Peiraios, who received him kindly.
The suitors made wide eyes at one another
and set to work provoking Telémakhos
with jokes about his friends. One said, for instance:

"Telémakhos, no man is a luckier host   390
when it comes to what the cat dragged in. What burning
eyes your beggar had for bread and wine!
But not for labor, not for a single heave—
he'd be a deadweight on a field. Then comes
this other, with his mumbo-jumbo. Boy,   395
for your own good, I tell you, toss them both
into a slave ship for the Sikels.[7] That would pay you."

Telémakhos ignored the suitors' talk.
He kept his eyes in silence on his father,
awaiting the first blow. Meanwhile   400
the daughter of Ikários, Penélopê,
had placed her chair to look across and down
on father and son at bay; she heard the crowd,
and how they laughed as they resumed their dinner,
a fragrant feast, for many beasts were slain—   405
but as for supper, men supped never colder
than these, on what the goddess and the warrior
were even then preparing for the suitors,
whose treachery had filled that house with pain.

BOOK XXI

[*The Test of the Bow*]

Upon Penélopê, most worn in love and thought,
Athena cast a glance like a grey sea

---

7. The ancient (pre-Greek) inhabitants of Sicily.

lifting her. Now to bring the tough bow out and bring
the iron blades. Now try those dogs at archery
to usher bloody slaughter in.
                                                    So moving stairward   5
the queen took up a fine doorhook of bronze,
ivory-hafted, smooth in her clenched hand,
and led her maids down to a distant room,
a storeroom where the master's treasure lay:
bronze, bar gold, black iron forged and wrought.   10
In this place hung the double-torsion bow
and arrows in a quiver, a great sheaf—
quills of groaning.
                            In the old time in Lakedaimon
her lord had got these arms from Íphitos,[8]
Eurýtos' son. The two met in Messenia   15
at Ortílokhos'[9] table, on the day
Odysseus claimed a debt owed by that realm—
sheep stolen by Messenians out of Ithaka
in their long ships, three hundred head, and herdsmen.
Seniors of Ithaka and his father sent him   20
on that far embassy when he was young.
But Íphitos had come there tracking strays,
twelve shy mares, with mule colts yet unweaned.
And a fatal chase they led him over prairies
into the hands of Heraklês. That massive   25
son of toil and mortal son of Zeus
murdered his guest[1] at wine in his own house—
inhuman, shameless in the sight of heaven—
to keep the mares and colts in his own grange.
Now Íphitos, when he knew Odysseus, gave him   30
the master bowman's arm; for old Eurýtos
had left it on his deathbed to his son.
In fellowship Odysseus gave a lance
and a sharp sword. But Heraklês killed Íphitos
before one friend could play host to the other.   35
And Lord Odysseus would not take the bow
in the black ships to the great war at Troy.
As a keepsake he put it by:
it served him well at home in Ithaka.

Now the queen reached the storeroom door and halted.   40
Here was an oaken sill, cut long ago
and sanded clean and bedded true. Foursquare
the doorjambs and the shining doors were set
by the careful builder. Penélopê untied the strap
around the curving handle, pushed her hook   45
into the slit, aimed at the bolts inside
and shot them back. Then came a rasping sound
as those bright doors the key had sprung gave way—
a bellow like a bull's vaunt in a meadow—
followed by her light footfall entering   50

8. Son of Eurýtos, king of Oekhalia in Thessaly.   9. King of Pherai in Thessaly (see 3.528).
1. Íphitos.

over the plank floor. Herb-scented robes
lay there in chests, but the lady's milkwhite arms
went up to lift the bow down from a peg
in its own polished bowcase.
              Now Penélopê
sank down, holding the weapon on her knees,   55
and drew her husband's great bow out, and sobbed
and bit her lip and let the salt tears flow.
Then back she went to face the crowded hall,
tremendous bow in hand, and on her shoulder hung
the quiver spiked with coughing death. Behind her   60
maids bore a basket full of axeheads, bronze
and iron implements for the master's game.
Thus in her beauty she approached the suitors,
and near a pillar of the solid roof
she paused, her shining veil across her cheeks,   65
her maids on either hand and still,
then spoke to the banqueters:

                "My lords, hear me:
suitors indeed, you commandeered this house
to feast and drink in, day and night, my husband
being long gone, long out of mind. You found   70
no justification for yourselves—none
except your lust to marry me. Stand up, then:
we now declare a contest for that prize.
Here is my lord Odysseus' hunting bow.
Bend and string it if you can. Who sends an arrow   75
through iron axe-helve sockets, twelve in line?
I join my life with his, and leave this place, my home,
my rich and beautiful bridal house, forever
to be remembered, though I dream it only."

Then to Eumaios:

              "Carry the bow forward.   80
Carry the blades."

             Tears came to the swineherd's eyes
as he reached out for the big bow. He laid it
down at the suitors' feet. Across the room
the cowherd sobbed, knowing the master's weapon.
Antínoös growled, with a glance at both:

                   "Clods.   85
They go to pieces over nothing.
                You two, there,
why are you sniveling? To upset the woman
even more? Has she not pain enough
over her lost husband? *Sit down.*
Get on with dinner quietly, or cry about it   90
outside, if you must. Leave us the bow.
A clean-cut game, it looks to me.

Nobody bends that bowstave easily
in this company. Is there a man here
made like Odysseus? I remember him   95
from childhood: I can see him even now."

That was the way he played it, hoping inwardly
to span the great horn bow with corded gut
and drill the iron with his shot—he, Antínoös,
destined to be the first of all to savor   100
blood from a biting arrow at his throat,
a shaft drawn by the fingers of Odysseus
whom he had mocked and plundered, leading on
the rest, his boon companions. Now they heard
a gay snort of laughter from Telémakhos,   105
who said then brilliantly:

                              "A queer thing, that!
Has Zeus almighty made me a half-wit?
For all her spirit, Mother has given in,
promised to go off with someone—and
is that amusing? What am I cackling for?   110
Step up, my lords, contend now for your prize.
There is no woman like her in Akhaia,
not in old Argos, Pylos, or Mykênê,
neither in Ithaka nor on the mainland,
and you all know it without praise of mine.   115
Come on, no hanging back, no more delay
in getting the bow bent. Who's the winner?
I myself should like to try that bow.
Suppose I bend it and bring off the shot,
my heart will be less heavy, seeing the queen my mother   120
go for the last time from this house and hall,
if I who stay can do my father's feat."

He moved out quickly, dropping his crimson cloak,
and lifted sword and sword belt from his shoulders.
His preparation was to dig a trench,   125
heaping the earth in a long ridge beside it
to hold the blades half-bedded. A taut cord
aligned the socket rings. And no one there
but looked on wondering at his workmanship,
for the boy had never seen it done.

                              He took his stand then   130
on the broad door sill to attempt the bow.
Three times he put his back into it and sprang it,
three times he had to slack off. Still he meant
to string that bow and pull for the needle shot.
A fourth try and he had it all but strung—   135
when a stiffening in Odysseus made him check.
Abruptly then he stopped and turned and said:

"Blast and damn it, must I be a milksop
all my life? Half-grown, all thumbs,

no strength or knack at arms, to defend myself   140
if someone picks a fight with me.
                                    Take over,
O my elders and betters, try the bow,
run off the contest."

                        And he stood the weapon
upright against the massy-timbered door
with one arrow across the horn aslant,   145
then went back to his chair. Antínoös
gave the word:

                "Now one man at a time
rise and go forward. Round the room in order;
left to right from where they dip the wine."

As this seemed fair enough, up stood Leódês   150
the son of Oinops. This man used to find
visions for them in the smoke of sacrifice.
He kept his chair well back, retired by the winebowl,
for he alone could not abide their manners
but sat in shame for all the rest. Now it was he   155
who had first to confront the bow,
standing up on the broad door sill. He failed.
The bow unbending made his thin hands yield,
no muscle in them. He gave up and said:

"Friends, I cannot. Let the next man handle it.   160
Here is a bow to break the heart and spirit
of many strong men. Aye. And death is less
bitter than to live on and never have
the beauty that we came here laying siege to
so many days. Resolute, are you still,   165
to win Odysseus' lady Penélopê?
Pit yourselves against the bow, and look
among Akhaians for another's daughter.
Gifts will be enough to court and take her.
Let the best offer win."

                        With this Leódês   170
thrust the bow away from him, and left it
upright against the massy-timbered door,
with one arrow aslant across the horn.
As he went down to his chair he heard Antínoös'
voice rising:

                "What is that you say?   175
It makes me burn. You cannot string the weapon,
so 'Here is a bow to break the heart and spirit
of many strong men.' Crushing thought!
You were not born—you never had it in you—
to pull that bow or let an arrow fly.   180
But here are men who can and will."

He called out to the goatherd, Melánthios:

"Kindle a fire there, be quick about it,
draw up a big bench with a sheepskin on it,
and bring a cake of lard out of the stores.   185
Contenders from now on will heat and grease the bow.
We'll try it limber, and bring off the shot."

Melánthios darted out to light a blaze,
drew up a bench, threw a big sheepskin over it,
and brought a cake of lard. So one by one   190
the young men warmed and greased the bow for bending,
but not a man could string it. They were whipped.
Antínoös held off; so did Eurýmakhos,
suitors in chief, by far the ablest there.
Two men had meanwhile left the hall: 195
swineherd and cowherd, in companionship,
one downcast as the other. But Odysseus
followed them outdoors, outside the court,
and coming up said gently:

                    "You, herdsman,
and you, too, swineherd, I could say a thing to you,   200
or should I keep it dark?
                    No, no; speak,
my heart tells me. Would you be men enough
to stand by Odysseus if he came back?
Suppose he dropped out of a clear sky, as I did?
Suppose some god should bring him?   205
Would you bear arms for him, or for the suitors?"

The cowherd said:

                    "Ah, let the master come!
Father Zeus, grant our old wish! Some courier
guide him back! Then judge what stuff is in me
and how I manage arms!"

                    Likewise Eumaios   210
fell to praying all heaven for his return,
so that Odysseus, sure at least of these,
told them:

                    "I am at home, for I am he.
I bore adversities, but in the twentieth year
I am ashore in my own land. I find   215
the two of you, alone among my people,
longed for my coming. Prayers I never heard
except your own that I might come again.
So now what is in store for you I'll tell you:
If Zeus brings down the suitors by my hand   220
I promise marriages to both, and cattle,

and houses built near mine. And you shall be
brothers-in-arms of my Telémakhos.
Here, let me show you something else, a sign
that I am he, that you can trust me, look: 225
this old scar from the tusk wound that I got
boar hunting on Parnassos—
Autólykos' sons and I."

          Shifting his rags
he bared the long gash. Both men looked, and knew,
and threw their arms around the old soldier, weeping,   230
kissing his head and shoulders. He as well
took each man's head and hands to kiss, then said—
to cut it short, else they might weep till dark—

"Break off, no more of this.
Anyone at the door could see and tell them.   235
Drift back in, but separately at intervals
after me.
       Now listen to your orders:
when the time comes, those gentlemen, to a man,
will be dead against giving me bow or quiver.
Defy them. Eumaios, bring the bow   240
and put it in my hands there at the door.
Tell the women to lock their own door tight.
Tell them if someone hears the shock of arms
or groans of men, in hall or court, not one
must show her face, but keep still at her weaving.   245
Philoítios, run to the outer gate and lock it.
Throw the cross bar and lash it."

              He turned back
into the courtyard and the beautiful house
and took the stool he had before. They followed
one by one, the two hands loyal to him.   250

Eurýmakhos had now picked up the bow.
He turned it round, and turned it round
before the licking flame to warm it up,
but could not, even so, put stress upon it
to jam the loop over the tip
          though his heart groaned to bursting.   255
Then he said grimly:

       "Curse this day.
What gloom I feel, not for myself alone,
and not only because we lose that bride.
Women are not lacking in Akhaia,
in other towns, or on Ithaka. No, the worst   260
is humiliation—to be shown up for children
measured against Odysseus—we who cannot

even hitch the string over his bow.
What shame to be repeated of us, after us!"

Antínoös said:

"Come to yourself. You know   265
that is not the way this business ends.
Today the islanders held holiday, a holy day,
no day to sweat over a bowstring.
                                        Keep your head.
Postpone the bow. I say we leave the axes
planted where they are. No one will take them.   270
No one comes to Odysseus' hall tonight.
Break out good wine and brim our cups again,
we'll keep the crooked bow safe overnight,
order the fattest goats Melánthios has
brought down tomorrow noon, and offer thighbones burning   275
to Apollo, god of archers,
while we try out the bow and make the shot."

As this appealed to everyone, heralds came
pouring fresh water for their hands, and boys
filled up the winebowls. Joints of meat went round,   280
fresh cuts for all, while each man made his offering,
tilting the red wine to the gods, and drank his fill.
Then spoke Odysseus, all craft and gall:

"My lords, contenders for the queen, permit me:
a passion in me moves me to speak out.   285
I put it to Eurýmakhos above all
and to that brilliant prince, Antínoös. Just now
how wise his counsel was, to leave the trial
and turn your thoughts to the immortal gods! Apollo
will give power tomorrow to whom he wills.   290
But let me try my hand at the smooth bow!
Let me test my fingers and my pull
to see if any of the oldtime kick is there,
or if thin fare and roving took it out of me."

Now irritation beyond reason swept them all,   295
since they were nagged by fear that he could string it.
Antínoös answered, coldly and at length:

"You bleary vagabond, no rag of sense is left you.
Are you not coddled here enough, at table
taking meat with gentlemen, your betters,   300
denied nothing, and listening to our talk?
When have we let a tramp hear all our talk?
The sweet goad of wine has made you rave!
Here is the evil wine can do
to those who swig it down. Even the centaur[2]   305

---

2. Half horse, half man. At a wedding in the house of the Lapíthai, their human neighbors, the centaurs
got drunk and tried to rape the women; a fight ensued. The great pediment at Olympia presents this scene,
and individual contests of Lapith and centaur are portrayed on the Parthenon at Athens.

Eurýtion, in Peiríthoös' hall
among the Lapíthai, came to a bloody end
because of wine; wine ruined him: it crazed him,
drove him wild for rape in that great house.
The princes cornered him in fury, leaping on him   310
to drag him out and crop his ears and nose.
Drink had destroyed his mind, and so he ended
in that mutilation—fool that he was.
Centaurs and men made war for this,
but the drunkard first brought hurt upon himself.   315
The tale applies to you: I promise you
great trouble if you touch that bow. You'll come by
no indulgence in our house; kicked down
into a ship's bilge, out to sea you go,
and nothing saves you. Drink, but hold your tongue.   320
Make no contention here with younger men."

At this the watchful queen Penélopê
interposed:

          "Antínoös, discourtesy
to a guest of Telémakhos—whatever guest—
that is not handsome. What are you afraid of?   325
Suppose this exile put his back into it
and drew the great bow of Odysseus—
could he then take me home to be his bride?
You know he does not imagine that! No one
need let that prospect weigh upon his dinner!   330
How very, very improbable it seems."

It was Eurýmakhos who answered her:

"Penélopê, O daughter of Ikários,
most subtle queen, we are not given to fantasy.
No, but our ears burn at what men might say   335
and women, too. We hear some jackal whispering:
'How far inferior to the great husband
her suitors are! Can't even budge his bow!
Think of it; and a beggar, out of nowhere,
strung it quick and made the needle shot!'   340
That kind of disrepute we would not care for."

Penélopê replied, steadfast and wary:

"Eurýmakhos, you have no good repute
in this realm, nor the faintest hope of it—
men who abused a prince's house for years,   345
consumed his wine and cattle. Shame enough.
Why hang your heads over a trifle now?
The stranger is a big man, well-compacted,
and claims to be of noble blood.
          Ai!

Give him the bow, and let us have it out!   350
What I can promise him I will:
if by the kindness of Apollo he prevails
he shall be clothed well and equipped.
A fine shirt and a cloak I promise him;
a lance for keeping dogs at bay, or men;   355
a broadsword; sandals to protect his feet;
escort, and freedom to go where he will."

Telémakhos now faced her and said sharply:

"Mother, as to the bow and who may handle it
or not handle it, no man here   360
has more authority than I do—not one lord
of our own stony Ithaka nor the islands lying
east toward Elis: no one stops me if I choose
to give these weapons outright to my guest.
Return to your own hall. Tend your spindle.   365
Tend your loom. Direct your maids at work.
This question of the bow will be for men to settle,
most of all for me. I am master here."

She gazed in wonder, turned, and so withdrew,
her son's clearheaded bravery in her heart.   370
But when she had mounted to her rooms again
with all her women, then she fell to weeping
for Odysseus, her husband. Grey-eyed Athena
presently cast a sweet sleep on her eyes.

The swineherd had the horned bow in his hands   375
moving toward Odysseus, when the crowd
in the banquet hall broke into an ugly din,
shouts rising from the flushed young men:

                              "Ho! Where
do you think you are taking that, you smutty slave?"

"What is this dithering?"

                    "We'll toss you back alone   380
among the pigs, for your own dogs to eat,
if bright Apollo nods and the gods are kind!"
He faltered, all at once put down the bow, and stood
in panic, buffeted by waves of cries,
hearing Telémakhos from another quarter   385
shout:

"Go on, take him the bow!
                    Do you obey this pack?
You will be stoned back to your hills! Young as I am
my power is over you! I wish to God
I had as much the upper hand of these!   390

There would be suitors pitched like dead rats
through our gate, for the evil plotted here!"

Telémakhos' frenzy struck someone as funny,
and soon the whole room roared with laughter at him,
so that all tension passed. Eumaios picked up   395
bow and quiver, making for the door,
and there he placed them in Odysseus' hands.
Calling Eurýkleia to his side he said:

                              "Telémakhos
trusts you to take care of the women's doorway.
Lock it tight. If anyone inside   400
should hear the shock of arms or groans of men
in hall or court, not one must show her face,
but go on with her weaving."

                    The old woman
nodded and kept still. She disappeared
into the women's hall, bolting the door behind her.   405
Philoítios left the house now at one bound,
catlike, running to bolt the courtyard gate.
A coil of deck-rope of papyrus[3] fiber
lay in the gateway; this he used for lashing,
and ran back to the same stool as before,   410
fastening his eyes upon Odysseus.
                    And Odysseus took his time,
turning the bow, tapping it, every inch,
for borings that termites might have made
while the master of the weapon was abroad.
The suitors were now watching him, and some   415
jested among themselves:

                    "A bow lover!"

"Dealer in old bows!"

                    "Maybe he has one like it
at home!"

          "Or has an itch to make one for himself."

"See how he handles it, the sly old buzzard!"

And one disdainful suitor added this: 420

"May his fortune grow an inch for every inch he bends it!"

But the man skilled in all ways of contending,
satisfied by the great bow's look and heft,

---

3. A plant grown in Egypt. Its fibers were used here for rope; they were also made into paper.

like a musician, like a harper, when
with quiet hand upon his instrument   425
he draws between his thumb and forefinger
a sweet new string upon a peg: so effortlessly
Odysseus in one motion strung the bow.
Then slid his right hand down the cord and plucked it,
so the taut gut vibrating hummed and sang   430
a swallow's note.
                        In the hushed hall it smote the suitors
and all their faces changed. Then Zeus thundered
overhead, one loud crack for a sign.
And Odysseus laughed within him that the son
of crooked-minded Kronos had flung that omen down.   435
He picked one ready arrow from his table
where it lay bare: the rest were waiting still
in the quiver for the young men's turn to come.
He nocked it, let it rest across the handgrip,
and drew the string and grooved butt of the arrow,   440
aiming from where he sat upon the stool.
                                            Now flashed
arrow from twanging bow clean as a whistle
through every socket ring, and grazed not one,
to thud with heavy brazen head beyond.
                                        Then quietly
Odysseus said:

          "Telémakhos, the stranger   445
you welcomed in your hall has not disgraced you.
I did not miss, neither did I take all day
stringing the bow. My hand and eye are sound,
not so contemptible as the young men say.
The hour has come to cook their lordships' mutton—   450
supper by daylight. Other amusements later,
with song and harping that adorn a feast."

He dropped his eyes and nodded, and the prince
Telémakhos, true son of King Odysseus,
belted his sword on, clapped hand to his spear,   455
and with a clink and glitter of keen bronze
stood by his chair, in the forefront near his father.

BOOK XXII

[Death in the Great Hall]

Now shrugging off his rags the wiliest fighter of the islands[4]
leapt and stood on the broad door sill, his own bow in his hand.
He poured out at his feet a rain of arrows from the quiver
and spoke to the crowd:

4. In the account of the battle in the hall the translator occasionally, as here, uses a longer line than usual.
There is no such variation of length in the original.

"So much for that. Your clean-cut game is over.
Now watch me hit a target that no man has hit before,　　5
if I can make this shot. Help me, Apollo."

He drew to his fist the cruel head of an arrow for Antínoös
just as the young man leaned to lift his beautiful drinking cup,
embossed, two-handled, golden: the cup was in his fingers:
the wine was even at his lips: and did he dream of death?　　10
How could he? In that revelry amid his throng of friends
who would imagine a single foe—though a strong foe indeed—
could dare to bring death's pain on him and darkness on his eyes?
Odysseus' arrow hit him under the chin
and punched up to the feathers through his throat.　　15

Backward and down he went, letting the winecup fall
from his shocked hand. Like pipes his nostrils jetted
crimson runnels, a river of mortal red,
and one last kick upset his table
knocking the bread and meat to soak in dusty blood.　　20
Now as they craned to see their champion where he lay
the suitors jostled in uproar down the hall,
everyone on his feet. Wildly they turned and scanned
the walls in the long room for arms; but not a shield,
not a good ashen spear was there for a man to take and throw.　　25
All they could do was yell in outrage at Odysseus:

"Foul! to shoot at a man! That was your last shot!"

"Your own throat will be slit for this!"

　　　　　　　　　　"Our finest lad is down!

You killed the best on Ithaka."

　　　　　　　　　"Buzzards will tear your eyes out!"

For they imagined as they wished—that it was a wild shot,　　30
an unintended killing—fools, not to comprehend
they were already in the grip of death.
But glaring under his brows Odysseus answered:

"You yellow dogs, you thought I'd never make it
home from the land of Troy. You took my house to plunder,　　35
twisted my maids to serve your beds. You dared
bid for my wife while I was still alive.
Contempt was all you had for the gods who rule wide heaven,
contempt for what men say of you hereafter.
Your last hour has come. You die in blood."　　40

As they all took this in, sickly green fear
pulled at their entrails, and their eyes flickered

looking for some hatch or hideaway from death.
Eurýmakhos alone could speak. He said:

"If you are Odysseus of Ithaka come back, 45
all that you say these men have done is true.
Rash actions, many here, more in the countryside.
But here he lies, the man who caused them all.
Antínoös was the ringleader; he whipped us on
to do these things. He cared less for a marriage 50
than for the power Kroníon has denied him
as king of Ithaka. For that
he tried to trap your son and would have killed him.
He is dead now and has his portion. Spare
your own people. As for ourselves, we'll make 55
restitution of wine and meat consumed,
and add, each one, a tithe of twenty oxen
with gifts of bronze and gold to warm your heart.
Meanwhile we cannot blame you for your anger."

Odysseus glowered under his black brows 60
and said:

                    "Not for the whole treasure of your fathers,
all you enjoy, lands, flocks, or any gold
put up by others, would I hold my hand.
There will be killing till the score is paid.
You forced yourselves upon this house. Fight your way out, 65
or run for it, if you think you'll escape death.
I doubt one man of you skins by."

They felt their knees fail, and their hearts—but heard
Eurýmakhos for the last time rallying them.

"Friends," he said, "the man is implacable. 70
Now that he's got his hands on bow and quiver
he'll shoot from the big door stone there
until he kills us to the last man.
                            Fight, I say,
let's remember the joy of it. Swords out!
Hold up your tables to deflect his arrows. 75
After me, everyone: rush him where he stands.
If we can budge him from the door, if we can pass
into the town, we'll call out men to chase him.
This fellow with his bow will shoot no more."

He drew his own sword as he spoke, a broadsword of fine bronze, 80
honed like a razor on either edge. Then crying hoarse and loud
he hurled himself at Odysseus. But the kingly man let fly
an arrow at that instant, and the quivering feathered butt
sprang to the nipple of his breast as the barb stuck in his liver.
The bright broadsword clanged down. He lurched and fell aside, 85
pitching across his table. His cup, his bread and meat,

were spilt and scattered far and wide, and his head slammed on the ground.
Revulsion, anguish in his heart, with both feet kicking out,
he downed his chair, while the shrouding wave of mist closed on his eyes.

Amphínomos now came running at Odysseus,   90
broadsword naked in his hand. He thought to make
the great soldier give way at the door.
But with a spear throw from behind Telémakhos hit him
between the shoulders, and the lancehead drove
clear through his chest. He left his feet and fell   95
forward, thudding, forehead against the ground.
Telémakhos swerved around him, leaving the long dark spear
planted in Amphínomos. If he paused to yank it out
someone might jump him from behind or cut him down with a sword
at the moment he bent over. So he ran—ran from the tables   100
to his father's side and halted, panting, saying:

"Father let me bring you a shield and spear,
a pair of spears, a helmet.
I can arm on the run myself; I'll give
outfits to Eumaios and this cowherd.   105
Better to have equipment."

                    Said Odysseus:

"Run then, while I hold them off with arrows
as long as the arrows last. When all are gone
if I'm alone they can dislodge me."

                    Quick
upon his father's word Telémakhos   110
ran to the room where spears and armor lay.
He caught up four light shields, four pairs of spears,
four helms of war high-plumed with flowing manes,
and ran back, loaded down, to his father's side.
He was the first to pull a helmet on   115
and slide his bare arm in a buckler strap.
The servants armed themselves, and all three took their stand
beside the master of battle.
                    While he had arrows
he aimed and shot, and every shot brought down
one of his huddling enemies.   120
But when all barbs had flown from the bowman's fist,
he leaned his bow in the bright entry way
beside the door, and armed: a four-ply shield
hard on his shoulder, and a crested helm,
horsetailed, nodding stormy upon his head,   125
then took his tough and bronze-shod spears.
                    The suitors
who held their feet, no longer under bowshot,
could see a window high in a recess of the wall,
a vent, lighting the passage to the storeroom.

This passage had one entry, with a door,   130
at the edge of the great hall's threshold, just outside.

Odysseus told the swineherd to stand over
and guard this door and passage. As he did so,
a suitor named Ageláos asked the others:

"Who will get a leg up on that window   135
and run to alarm the town? One sharp attack
and this fellow will never shoot again."

                              His answer
came from the goatherd, Melánthios:

                              "No chance, my lord.
The exit into the courtyard is too near them,
too narrow. One good man could hold that portal   140
against a crowd. No: let me scale the wall
and bring you arms out of the storage chamber.
Odysseus and his son put them indoors,
I'm sure of it; not outside."

                    The goatish goatherd
clambered up the wall, toes in the chinks,   145
and slipped through to the storeroom. Twelve light shields,
twelve spears he took, and twelve thick-crested helms,
and handed all down quickly to the suitors.
Odysseus, when he saw his adversaries
girded and capped and long spears in their hands   150
shaken at him, felt his knees go slack,
his heart sink, for the fight was turning grim.
He spoke rapidly to his son:

"Telémakhos, one of the serving women
is tipping the scales against us in this fight,   155
or maybe Melánthios.'

                    But sharp and clear
Telémakhos said:

                    "It is my own fault, Father,
mine alone. The storeroom door—I left it
wide open. They were more alert than I.
Eumaios, go and lock that door,   160
and bring back word if a woman is doing this
or Melánthios, Dólios' son. More likely he."

Even as they conferred, Melánthios
entered the storeroom for a second load,
and the swineherd at the passage entry saw him.   165
He cried out to his lord:

"Son of Laërtês,
Odysseus, master mariner and soldier,
there he goes, the monkey, as we thought,
there he goes into the storeroom.
                    Let me hear your will:
put a spear through him—I hope I am the stronger—   170
or drag him here to pay for his foul tricks
against your house?"

                    Odysseus said:

                              "Telémakhos and I
will keep these gentlemen in hall, for all their urge to leave.
You two go throw him into the storeroom, wrench his arms
and legs behind him, lash his hands and feet   175
to a plank, and hoist him up to the roof beams.
Let him live on there suffering at his leisure."

The two men heard him with appreciation
and ducked into the passage. Melánthios,
rummaging in the chamber, could not hear them   180
as they came up; nor could he see them freeze
like posts on either side the door.
He turned back with a handsome crested helmet
in one hand, in the other an old shield
coated with dust—a shield Laërtês bore   185
soldiering in his youth. It had lain there for years,
and the seams on strap and grip had rotted away.
As Melánthios came out the two men sprang,
jerked him backward by the hair, and threw him.
Hands and feet they tied with a cutting cord   190
behind him, so his bones ground in their sockets,
just as Laërtês' royal son commanded.
Then with a whip of rope they hoisted him
in agony up a pillar to the beams,
and—O my swineherd—you were the one to say: 195

"Watch through the night up there, Melánthios.
An airy bed is what you need.
You'll be awake to see the primrose Dawn
when she goes glowing from the streams of Ocean
to mount her golden throne.
                    No oversleeping   200
the hour for driving goats to feed the suitors."

They stopped for helm and shield and left him there
contorted, in his brutal sling,
and shut the doors, and went to join Odysseus,
whose mind moved through the combat now to come.   205
Breathing deep, and snorting hard, they stood
four at the entry, facing two score men.
But now into the gracious doorway stepped

Zeus's daughter Athena. She wore the guise of Mentor,
and Odysseus appealed to her in joy: 210

"O Mentor, join me in this fight! Remember
how all my life I've been devoted to you,
friend of my youth!"

               For he guessed it was Athena,
Hope of Soldiers. Cries came from the suitors,
and Ageláos, Damástor's son, called out: 215

"Mentor, don't let Odysseus lead you astray
to fight against us on his side.
Think twice: we are resolved—and we will do it—
after we kill them, father and son,
you too will have your throat slit for your pains   220
if you make trouble for us here. It means your life.
Your life—and cutting throats will not be all.
Whatever wealth you have, at home, or elsewhere,
we'll mingle with Odysseus' wealth. Your sons
will be turned out, your wife and daughters   225
banished from the town of Ithaka."

Athena's anger grew like a storm wind as he spoke
until she flashed out at Odysseus:

                  "Ah, what a falling off!
Where is your valor, where is the iron hand
that fought at Troy for Helen, pearl of kings,   230
no respite and nine years of war? How many foes
your hand brought down in bloody play of spears?
What stratagem but yours took Priam's town?
How is it now that on your own door sill,
before the harriers of your wife, you curse your luck   235
not to be stronger?
              Come here, cousin, stand by me,
and you'll see action! In the enemies' teeth
learn how Mentor, son of Álkimos,
repays fair dealing!"

               For all her fighting words
she gave no overpowering aid—not yet;   240
father and son must prove their mettle still.
Into the smoky air under the roof
the goddess merely darted to perch on a blackened beam—
no figure to be seen now but a swallow.

Command of the suitors had fallen to Ageláos.   245
With him were Eurýnomos, Amphímedon,
Demoptólemos, Peisándros, Pólybos,
the best of the lot who stood to fight for their lives

after the streaking arrows downed the rest.
Ageláos rallied them with his plan of battle: 250

"Friends, our killer has come to the end of his rope,
and much good Mentor did him, that blowhard, dropping in.
Look, only four are left to fight, in the light there at the door.
No scattering of shots, men, no throwing away good spears;
we six will aim a volley at Odysseus alone,   255
and may Zeus grant us the glory of a hit.
If he goes down, the others are no problem."

At his command, then, "Ho!" they all let fly
as one man. But Athena spoiled their shots.
One hit the doorpost of the hall, another   260
stuck in the door's thick timbering, still others
rang on the stone wall, shivering hafts of ash.
Seeing his men unscathed, royal Odysseus
gave the word for action.

                    "Now I say, friends,
the time is overdue to let them have it.   265
Battlespoil they want from our dead bodies
to add to all they plundered here before."

Taking aim over the steadied lanceheads
they all let fly together. Odysseus killed
Demoptólemos; Telémakhos   270
killed Eurýadês; the swineherd, Élatos;
and Peisándros went down before the cowherd.
As these lay dying, biting the central floor,
their friends gave way and broke for the inner wall.
The four attackers followed up with a rush   275
to take spears from the fallen men.

                    Re-forming,
the suitors threw again with all their strength,
but Athena turned their shots, or all but two.
One hit a doorpost in the hall, another
stuck in the door's thick timbering, still others   280
rang on the stone wall, shivering hafts of ash.
Amphímedon's point bloodied Telémakhos'
wrist, a superficial wound, and Ktésippos'
long spear passing over Eumaios' shield
grazed his shoulder, hurtled on and fell.   285
No matter: with Odysseus the great soldier
the wounded threw again. And Odysseus raider of cities
struck Eurýdamas down. Telémakhos
hit Amphímedon, and the swineherd's shot
killed Pólybos. But Ktésippos, who had last evening thrown   290
a cow's hoof at Odysseus, got the cowherd's heavy cast
full in the chest—and dying heard him say:

"You arrogant joking bastard!
Clown, will you, like a fool, and parade your wit?
Leave jesting to the gods who do it better.   295
This will repay your cow's-foot courtesy
to a great wanderer come home."

            The master
of the black herds had answered Ktésippos.
Odysseus, lunging at close quarters, put a spear
through Ageláos, Damastor's son. Telémakhos   300
hit Leókritos from behind and pierced him,
kidney to diaphragm. Speared off his feet,
he fell face downward on the ground.

At this moment that unmanning thunder cloud,
the aegis,[5] Athena's shield,   305
took form aloft in the great hall.
           And the suitors mad with fear
at her great sign stampeded like stung cattle by a river
when the dread shimmering gadfly strikes in summer,
in the flowering season, in the long-drawn days.
After them the attackers wheeled, as terrible as falcons   310
from eyries in the mountains veering over and diving down
with talons wide unsheathed on flights of birds,
who cower down the sky in chutes and bursts along the valley—
but the pouncing falcons grip their prey, no frantic wing avails,
and farmers love to watch those beakèd hunters.   315
So these now fell upon the suitors in that hall,
turning, turning to strike and strike again,
while torn men moaned at death, and blood ran smoking
over the whole floor.
           Now there was one
who turned and threw himself at Odysseus' knees—   320
Leódês, begging for his life:

               "Mercy,
mercy on a suppliant, Odysseus!
Never by word or act of mine, I swear,
was any woman troubled here. I told the rest
to put an end to it. They would not listen,   325
would not keep their hands from brutishness,
and now they are all dying like dogs for it.
I had no part in what they did: my part
was visionary—reading the smoke of sacrifice.
Scruples go unrewarded if I die."   330

The shrewd fighter frowned over him and said:

"You were diviner to this crowd? How often
you must have prayed my sweet day of return

---

5. A magical shield (or breastplate) used by Athena and Zeus; it created a panic when displayed.

would never come, or not for years!—and prayed
to have my dear wife, and beget children on her.   335
No plea like yours could save you
from this hard bed of death. Death it shall be!"

He picked up Ageláos' broadsword
from where it lay, flung by the slain man,
and gave Leódês' neck a lopping blow   340
so that his head went down to mouth in dust.

One more who had avoided furious death
was the son of Terpis, Phêmios, the minstrel,
singer by compulsion to the suitors.
He stood now with his harp, holy and clear,   345
in the wall's recess, under the window, wondering
if he should flee that way to the courtyard altar,
sanctuary of Zeus, the Enclosure God.[6]
Thighbones in hundreds had been offered there
by Laërtês and Odysseus. No, he thought;   350
the more direct way would be best—to go
humbly to his lord. But first to save
his murmuring instrument he laid it down
carefully between the winebowl and a chair,
then he betook himself to Lord Odysseus,   355
clung hard to his knees, and said:

                    "Mercy,
mercy on a suppliant, Odysseus!
My gift is song for men and for the gods undying.
My death will be remorse for you hereafter.
No one taught me: deep in my mind a god   360
shaped all the various ways of life in song.
And I am fit to make verse in your company
as in the god's. Put aside lust for blood.
Your own dear son Telémakhos can tell you,
never by my own will or for love   365
did I feast here or sing amid the suitors.
They were too strong, too many; they compelled me."

Telémakhos in the elation of battle
heard him. He at once called to his father:

"Wait: that one is innocent: don't hurt him.   370
And we should let our herald live—Medôn;
he cared for me from boyhood. Where is *he*?
Has he been killed already by Philoítios
or by the swineherd? Else he got an arrow
in that first gale of bowshots down the room."   375

Now this came to the ears of prudent Medôn
under the chair where he had gone to earth,

6. Zeus Herkeios, guardian of the inner space of the home.

pulling a new-flayed bull's hide over him.
Quiet he lay while blinding death passed by.
Now heaving out from under   380
he scrambled for Telémakhos' knees and said:

"Here I am, dear prince; but rest your spear!
Tell your great father not to see in me
a suitor for the sword's edge—one of those
who laughed at you and ruined his property!"   385

The lord of all the tricks of war surveyed
this fugitive and smiled. He said:

"Courage: my son has dug you out and saved you.
Take it to heart, and pass the word along:
fair dealing brings more profit in the end.   390
Now leave this room. Go and sit down outdoors
where there's no carnage, in the court,
you and the poet with his many voices,
while I attend to certain chores inside."

At this the two men stirred and picked their way   395
to the door and out, and sat down at the altar,
looking around with wincing eyes
as though the sword's edge hovered still.
And Odysseus looked around him, narrow-eyed,
for any others who had lain hidden   400
while death's black fury passed.
                              In blood and dust
he saw that crowd all fallen, many and many slain.

Think of a catch that fishermen haul in to a halfmoon bay
in a fine-meshed net from the white-caps of the sea:
how all are poured out on the sand, in throes for the salt sea,   405
twitching their cold lives away in Hêlios' fiery air:
so lay the suitors heaped on one another.

Odysseus at length said to his son:

"Go tell old Nurse I'll have a word with her.
What's to be done now weighs on my mind."   410

Telémakhos knocked at the women's door and called:

"Eurýkleia, come out here! Move, old woman.
You kept your eye on all our servant girls.
Jump, my father is here and wants to see you."

His call brought no reply, only the doors   415
were opened, and she came. Telémakhos
led her forward. In the shadowy hall
full of dead men she found his father

spattered and caked with blood like a mountain lion
when he has gorged upon an ox, his kill—
with hot blood glistening over his whole chest,
smeared on his jaws, baleful and terrifying—
even so encrimsoned was Odysseus
up to his thighs and armpits. As she gazed
from all the corpses to the bloody man
she raised her head to cry over his triumph,
but felt his grip upon her, checking her.
Said the great soldier then:

                    "Rejoice
inwardly. No crowing aloud, old woman.
To glory over slain men is no piety.
Destiny and the gods' will vanquished these,
and their own hardness. They respected no one,
good or bad, who came their way.
For this, and folly, a bad end befell them.
Your part is now to tell me of the women,
those who dishonored me, and the innocent."

His own old nurse Eurýkleia said:

                    "I will, then.
Child, you know you'll have the truth from me.
Fifty all told they are, your female slaves,
trained by your lady and myself in service,
wool carding and the rest of it, and taught
to be submissive. Twelve went bad,
flouting me, flouting Penélopê, too.
Telémakhos being barely grown, his mother
would never let him rule the serving women—
but you must let me go to her lighted rooms
and tell her. Some god sent her a drift of sleep."

But in reply the great tactician said:

"Not yet. Do not awake her. Tell those women
who were the suitors' harlots to come here."

She went back on this mission through his hall.
Then he called Telémakhos to his side
and the two herdsmen. Sharply Odysseus said:

"These dead must be disposed of first of all.
Direct the women. Tables and chairs will be
scrubbed with sponges, rinsed and rinsed again.
When our great room is fresh and put in order,
take them outside, these women,
between the roundhouse and the palisade,
and hack them with your swordblades till you cut
the life out of them, and every thought of sweet

420

425

430

435

440

445

450

455

460

Aphroditê under the rutting suitors,
when they lay down in secret."

          As he spoke
here came the women in a bunch, all wailing,
soft tears on their cheeks. They fell to work   465
to lug the corpses out into the courtyard
under the gateway, propping one
against another as Odysseus ordered,
for he himself stood over them. In fear
these women bore the cold weight of the dead.   470
The next thing was to scrub off chairs and tables
and rinse them down. Telémakhos and the herdsman
scraped the packed earth floor with hoes, but made
the women carry out all blood and mire.
When the great room was cleaned up once again,   475
at swordpoint they forced them out, between
the roundhouse and the palisade, pell-mell
to huddle in that dead end without exit.
Telémakhos, who knew his mind, said curtly:

"I would not give the clean death of a beast[7]   480
to trulls who made a mockery of my mother
and of me too—you sluts, who lay with suitors."

He tied one end of a hawser to a pillar
and passed the other about the roundhouse top,
taking the slack up, so that no one's toes   485
could touch the ground. They would be hung like doves
or larks in springe's triggered in a thicket,
where the birds think to rest—a cruel nesting.
So now in turn each woman thrust her head
into a noose and swung, yanked high in air,   490
to perish there most piteously.
Their feet danced for a little, but not long.

From storeroom to the court they brought Melánthios,
chopped with swords to cut his nose and ears off,
pulled off his genitals to feed the dogs   495
and raging hacked his hands and feet away.
As their own hands and feet called for a washing,
they went indoors to Odysseus again.
Their work was done. He told Eurýkleia:

                     "Bring me
brimstone and a brazier—medicinal   500
fumes to purify my hall. Then tell
Penélopê to come, and bring her maids.
All servants round the house must be called in."

7. I.e., by sword or spear. Hanging was considered an ignominious way to die.

His own old nurse Eurýkleia replied:

"Aye, surely that is well said, child. But let me   505
find you a good clean shirt and cloak and dress you.
You must not wrap your shoulders' breadth again
in rags in your own hall. That would be shameful."

Odysseus answered:

                    "Let me have the fire.
The first thing is to purify this place."   510

With no more chat Eurýkleia obeyed
and fetched out fire and brimstone. Cleansing fumes
he sent through court and hall and storage chamber.
Then the old woman hurried off again
to the women's quarters to announce her news,   515
and all the servants came now, bearing torches
in twilight, crowding to embrace Odysseus,
taking his hands to kiss, his head and shoulders,
while he stood there, nodding to every one,
and overcome by longing and by tears.   520

BOOK XXIII

[The Trunk of the Olive Tree]

The old nurse went upstairs exulting,
with knees toiling, and patter of slapping feet,
to tell the mistress of her lord's return,
and cried out by the lady's pillow:

                              "Wake,
wake up, dear child! Penélopê, come down,   5
see with your own eyes what all these years you longed for!
Odysseus is here! Oh, in the end, he came!
And he has killed your suitors, killed them all
who made his house a bordel and ate his cattle
and raised their hands against his son!"

                         Penélopê said: 10

"Dear nurse . . . the gods have touched you.
They can put chaos into the clearest head
or bring a lunatic down to earth. Good sense
you always had. They've touched you. What is this
mockery you wake me up to tell me,   15
breaking in on my sweet spell of sleep?
I had not dozed away so tranquilly
since my lord went to war, on that ill wind
to Ilion.
        Oh, leave me! Back down stairs!
If any other of my women came in babbling   20

things like these to startle me, I'd see her
flogged out of the house! Your old age spares you that."

Eurýkleia said:

"Would I play such a trick on you, dear child?
It is true, true, as I tell you, he has come!   25
That stranger they were baiting was Odysseus.
Telémakhos knew it days ago—
cool head, never to give his father away,
till he paid off those swollen dogs!"

The lady in her heart's joy now sprang up   30
with sudden dazzling tears, and hugged the old one,
crying out:

            "But try to make it clear!
If he came home in secret, as you say,
could he engage them singlehanded? How?
They were all down there, still in the same crowd."   35

To this Eurýkleia said:

            "I did not see it,
I knew nothing; only I heard the groans
of men dying. We sat still in the inner rooms
holding our breath, and marvelling, shut in,
until Telémakhos came to the door and called me—   40
your own dear son, sent this time by his father!
So I went out, and found Odysseus
erect, with dead men littering the floor
this way and that. If you had only seen him!
It would have made your heart glow hot!—a lion   45
splashed with mire and blood.
                                But now the cold
corpses are all gathered at the gate,
and he has cleansed his hall with fire and brimstone,
a great blaze. Then he sent me here to you.
Come with me: you may both embark this time   50
for happiness together, after pain,
after long years. Here is your prayer, your passion,
granted: your own lord lives, he is at home,
he found you safe, he found his son. The suitors
abused his house, but he has brought them down."   55

The attentive lady said:

            "Do not lose yourself
in this rejoicing: wait: you know
how splendid that return would be for us,
how dear to me, dear to his son and mine;
but no, it is not possible, your notion   60

must be wrong.
    Some god has killed the suitors,
a god, sick of their arrogance and brutal
malice—for they honored no one living,
good or bad, who ever came their way.
Blind young fools, they've tasted death for it.   65
But the true person of Odysseus?
He lost his home, he died far from Akhaia."

The old nurse sighed:

     "How queer, the way you talk!
Here he is, large as life, by his own fire,
and you deny he ever will get home!   70
Child, you always were mistrustful!
But there is one sure mark that I can tell you:
that scar left by the boar's tusk long ago.
I recognized it when I bathed his feet
and would have told you, but he stopped my mouth,   75
forbade me, in his craftiness.
     Come down,
I stake my life on it, he's here!
Let me die in agony if I lie!"

    Penélopê said:

"Nurse dear, though you have your wits about you,
still it is hard not to be taken in   80
by the immortals. Let us join my son, though,
and see the dead and that strange one who killed them."

She turned then to descend the stair, her heart
in tumult. Had she better keep her distance
and question him, her husband? Should she run   85
up to him, take his hands, kiss him now?
Crossing the door sill she sat down at once
in firelight, against the nearest wall,
across the room from the lord Odysseus.
     There
leaning against a pillar, sat the man   90
and never lifted up his eyes, but only waited
for what his wife would say when she had seen him.
And she, for a long time, sat deathly still
in wonderment—for sometimes as she gazed
she found him—yes, clearly—like her husband,   95
but sometimes blood and rags were all she saw.
Telémakhos' voice came to her ears:

     "Mother,
cruel mother, do you feel nothing,
drawing yourself apart this way from Father?
Will you not sit with him and talk and question him?   100

What other woman could remain so cold?
Who shuns her lord, and he come back to her
from wars and wandering, after twenty years?
Your heart is hard as flint and never changes!"

Penélopê answered:

      "I am stunned, child.   105
I cannot speak to him. I cannot question him.
I cannot keep my eyes upon his face.
If really he is Odysseus, truly home,
beyond all doubt we two shall know each other
better than you or anyone. There are   110
secret signs we know, we two."

      A smile
came now to the lips of the patient hero, Odysseus,
who turned to Telémakhos and said:

"Peace: let your mother test me at her leisure.
Before long she will see and know me best.   115
These tatters, dirt—all that I'm caked with now—
make her look hard at me and doubt me still.
As to this massacre, we must see the end.
Whoever kills one citizen, you know,
and has no force of armed men at his back,   120
had better take himself abroad by night
and leave his kin. Well, we cut down the flower of Ithaka,
the mainstay of the town. Consider that."

Telémakhos replied respectfully:

        "Dear Father,
enough that you yourself study the danger,   125
foresighted in combat as you are,
they say you have no rival.
       We three stand
ready to follow you and fight. I say
for what our strength avails, we have the courage."

And the great tactician, Odysseus, answered:

         "Good.   130
Here is our best maneuver, as I see it:
bathe, you three, and put fresh clothing on,
order the women to adorn themselves,
and let our admirable harper choose a tune
for dancing, some lighthearted air, and strum it.   135
Anyone going by, or any neighbor,
will think it is a wedding feast he hears.
These deaths must not be cried about the town

till we can slip away to our own woods. We'll see
what weapon, then, Zeus puts into our hands." 140

They listened attentively, and did his bidding,
bathed and dressed afresh; and all the maids
adorned themselves. Then Phêmios the harper
took his polished shell and plucked the strings,
moving the company to desire 145
for singing, for the sway and beat of dancing,
until they made the manor hall resound
with gaiety of men and grace of women.
Anyone passing on the road would say:

"Married at last, I see—the queen so many courted. 150
Sly, cattish wife! She would not keep—not she!—
the lord's estate until he came."

                        So travellers'
thoughts might run—but no one guessed the truth.
Greathearted Odysseus, home at last,
was being bathed now by Eurýnomê 155
and rubbed with golden oil, and clothed again
in a fresh tunic and a cloak. Athena
lent him beauty, head to foot. She made him
taller, and massive, too, with crisping hair
in curls like petals of wild hyacinth 160
but all red-golden. Think of gold infused
on silver by a craftsman, whose fine art
Hephaistos taught him, or Athena: one
whose work moves to delight: just so she lavished
beauty over Odysseus' head and shoulders. 165
He sat then in the same chair by the pillar,
facing his silent wife, and said:

                       "Strange woman,
the immortals of Olympos made you hard,
harder than any. Who else in the world
would keep aloof as you do from her husband 170
if he returned to her from years of trouble,
cast on his own land in the twentieth year?

Nurse, make up a bed for me to sleep on.
Her heart is iron in her breast."

                    Penélopê

spoke to Odysseus now. She said:
                          "Strange man, 175
if man you are . . . This is no pride on my part
nor scorn for you—not even wonder, merely.
I know so well how you—how he—appeared
boarding the ship for Troy. But all the same . . .

Make up his bed for him, Eurýkleia.   180
Place it outside the bedchamber my lord
built with his own hands. Pile the big bed
with fleeces, rugs, and sheets of purest linen."

With this she tried him to the breaking point,
and he turned on her in a flash raging: 185

"Woman, by heaven you've stung me now!
Who dared to move my bed?
No builder had the skill for that—unless
a god came down to turn the trick. No mortal
in his best days could budge it with a crowbar.   190
There is our pact and pledge, our secret sign,
built into that bed—my handiwork
and no one else's!
                              An old trunk of olive
grew like a pillar on the building plot,
and I laid out our bedroom round that tree,   195
lined up the stone walls, built the walls and roof,
gave it a doorway and smooth-fitting doors.
Then I lopped off the silvery leaves and branches,
hewed and shaped that stump from the roots up
into a bedpost, drilled it, let it serve   200
as model for the rest. I planed them all,
inlaid them all with silver, gold and ivory,
and stretched a bed between—a pliant web
of oxhide thongs dyed crimson.
                                      There's our sign!
I know no more. Could someone's else's hand   205
have sawn that trunk and dragged the frame away?"

Their secret! as she heard it told, her knees
grew tremulous and weak, her heart failed her.
With eyes brimming tears she ran to him,
throwing her arms around his neck, and kissed him,   210
murmuring:

                    "Do not rage at me, Odysseus!
No one ever matched your caution! Think
what difficulty the gods gave: they denied us
life together in our prime and flowering years,
kept us from crossing into age together.   215
Forgive me, don't be angry. I could not
welcome you with love on sight! I armed myself
long ago against the frauds of men,
impostors who might come—and all those many
whose underhanded ways bring evil on!   220
Helen of Argos, daughter of Zeus and Leda,
would she have joined the stranger, lain with him,
if she had known her destiny? known the Akhaians
in arms would bring her back to her own country?

Surely a goddess moved her to adultery,   225
her blood unchilled by war and evil coming,
the years, the desolation; ours, too.
But here and now, what sign could be so clear
as this of our own bed?
No other man has ever laid eyes on it—   230
only my own slave, Aktoris, that my father
sent with me as a gift—she kept our door.
You make my stiff heart know that I am yours."

Now from his breast into his eyes the ache
of longing mounted, and he wept at last,   235
his dear wife, clear and faithful, in his arms,
longed for
            as the sunwarmed earth is longed for by a swimmer
spent in rough water where his ship went down
under Poseidon's blows, gale winds and tons of sea.
Few men can keep alive through a big surf   240
to crawl, clotted with brine, on kindly beaches
in joy, in joy, knowing the abyss behind:
and so she too rejoiced, her gaze upon her husband,
her white arms round him pressed as though forever.

The rose Dawn might have found them weeping still   245
had not grey-eyed Athena slowed the night
when night was most profound, and held the Dawn
under the Ocean of the East. That glossy team,
Firebright and Daybright, the Dawn's horses
that draw her heavenward for men—Athena   250
stayed their harnessing.

                Then said Odysseus:

"My dear, we have not won through to the end.
One trial—I do not know how long—is left for me
to see fulfilled. Teirêsias' ghost forewarned me
the night I stood upon the shore of Death, asking   255
about my friends' homecoming and my own.

But now the hour grows late, it is bed time,
rest will be sweet for us; let us lie down."

To this Penélopê replied:

                "That bed,
that rest is yours whenever desire moves you,   260
now the kind powers have brought you home at last.
But as your thought has dwelt upon it, tell me:
what is the trial you face? I must know soon;
what does it matter if I learn tonight?"

The teller of many stories said:

"My strange one,   265
must you again, and even now,
urge me to talk? Here is a plodding tale;
no charm in it, no relish in the telling.
Teirêsias told me I must take an oar
and trudge the mainland, going from town to town,   270
until I discover men who have never known
the salt blue sea, nor flavor of salt meat—
strangers to painted prows, to watercraft
and oars like wings, dipping across the water.
The moment of revelation he foretold   275
was this, for you may share the prophecy:
some traveller falling in with me will say:
'A winnowing fan, that on your shoulder, sir?'
There I must plant my oar, on the very spot,
with burnt offerings to Poseidon of the Waters: 280
a ram, a bull, a great buck boar. Thereafter
when I come home again, I am to slay
full hekatombs to the gods who own broad heaven,
one by one.
            Then death will drift upon me
from seaward, mild as air, mild as your hand,   285
in my well-tended weariness of age,
contented folk around me on our island.
He said all this must come.'

            Penélopê said:

"If by the gods' grace age at least is kind,
we have that promise—trials will end in peace."   290

So he confided in her, and she answered.
Meanwhile Eurýnomê and the nurse together
laid soft coverlets on the master's bed,
working in haste by torchlight. Eurýkleia
retired to her quarters for the night,   295
and then Eurýnomê, as maid-in-waiting,
lighted her lord and lady to their chamber
with bright brands.

            She vanished.
                      So they came
into that bed so steadfast, loved of old,
opening glad arms to one another.[8]   300
Telémakhos by now had hushed the dancing,
hushed the women. In the darkened hall
he and the cowherd and the swineherd slept.

---

8. Two great Alexandrian critics said that this line was the "end" of the *Odyssey* (though one of the words they are said to have used could mean simply "culmination"). Modern critics are divided; some find the rest of the poem banal, unartistic, full of linguistic anomalies, and so on. But if the poem stops here we are left in suspense about many important themes that have been developed and demand a sequel—the question of reprisals for the slaughter in the hall, to mention only one.

The royal pair mingled in love again
and afterward lay revelling in stories: 305
hers of the siege her beauty stood at home
from arrogant suitors, crowding on her sight,
and how they fed their courtship on his cattle,
oxen and fat sheep, and drank up rivers
of wine out of the vats.
              Odysseus told 310
of what hard blows he had dealt out to others
and of what blows he had taken—all that story.
She could not close her eyes till all was told.

His raid on the Kikonês, first of all,
then how he visited the Lotos Eaters, 315
and what the Kyklops did, and how those shipmates,
pitilessly devoured, were avenged.
Then of his touching Aiolos's isle
and how that king refitted him for sailing
to Ithaka; all vain: gales blew him back 320
groaning over the fishcold sea. Then how
he reached the Laistrygonians' distant bay
and how they smashed his ships and his companions.
Kirkê, then: of her deceits and magic,
then of his voyage to the wide underworld 325
of dark, the house of Death, and questioning
Teirêsias, Theban spirit.
              Dead companions,
many, he saw there, and his mother, too.
Of this he told his wife, and told how later
he heard the choir of maddening Seirênês, 330
coasted the Wandering Rocks, Kharybdis' pool
and the fiend Skylla who takes toll of men.
Then how his shipmates killed Lord Hêlios' cattle
and how Zeus thundering in towering heaven
split their fast ship with his fuming bolt, 335
so all hands perished.
          He alone survived,
cast away on Kalypso's isle, Ogýgia.
He told, then, how that nymph detained him there
in her smooth caves, craving him for her husband,
and how in her devoted lust she swore 340
he should not die nor grow old, all his days,
but he held out against her.
              Last of all
what sea-toil brought him to the Phaiákians;
their welcome; how they took him to their hearts
and gave him passage to his own dear island 345
with gifts of garments, gold and bronze . . .
                 Remembering,
he drowsed over the story's end. Sweet sleep
relaxed his limbs and his care-burdened breast.

Other affairs were in Athena's keeping.
Waiting until Odysseus had his pleasure   350
of love and sleep, the grey-eyed one bestirred
the fresh Dawn from her bed of paling Ocean
to bring up daylight to her golden chair,
and from his fleecy bed Odysseus
arose. He said to Penélopê:

                    "My lady,   355
what ordeals have we not endured! Here, waiting
you had your grief, while my return dragged out—
my hard adventures, pitting myself against
the gods' will, and Zeus, who pinned me down
far from home. But now our life resumes: 360
we've come together to our longed-for bed.
Take care of what is left me in our house;
as to the flocks that pack of wolves laid waste
they'll be replenished: scores I'll get on raids
and other scores our island friends will give me   365
till all the folds are full again.
                    This day
I'm off up country to the orchards. I must see
my noble father, for he missed me sorely.
And here is my command for you—a strict one,
though you may need none, clever as you are.   370
Word will get about as the sun goes higher
of how I killed those lads. Go to your rooms
on the upper floor, and take your women. Stay there
with never a glance outside or a word to anyone."

Fitting cuirass and swordbelt to his shoulders,   375
he woke his herdsmen, woke Telémakhos,
ordering all in arms. They dressed quickly,
and all in war gear sallied from the gate,
led by Odysseus.
                  Now it was broad day
but these three men Athena hid in darkness,   380
going before them swiftly from the town.

BOOK XXIV

[Warriors, Farewell]

Meanwhile the suitors' ghosts were called away
by Hermês of Kyllênê,[9] bearing the golden wand
with which he charms the eyes of men or wakens
whom he wills.
               He waved them on, all squeaking
as bats will in a cavern's underworld,   5
all flitting, flitting criss-cross in the dark
if one falls and the rock-hung chain is broken.

9. A mountain in Arcadia, Hermês' birthplace.

So with faint cries the shades trailed after Hermês,
pure Deliverer.
                    He led them down dank ways,
over grey Ocean tides, the Snowy Rock,   10
past shores of Dream and narrows of the sunset,
in swift flight to where the Dead inhabit
wastes of asphodel at the world's end.

Crossing the plain they met Akhilleus' ghost,
Patróklos and Antílokhos, then Aias,   15
noblest of Danaans after Akhilleus
in strength and beauty. Here the newly dead
drifted together, whispering. Then came
the soul of Agamémnon, son of Atreus,
in black pain forever, surrounded by men-at-arms   20
who perished with him in Aigísthos' hall.

Akhilleus greeted him:

                    "My lord Atreidês,
we held that Zeus who loves the play of lightning
would give you length of glory, you were king
over so great a host of soldiery   25
before Troy, where we suffered, we Akhaians.
But in the morning of your life
you met that doom that no man born avoids.
It should have found you in your day of victory,
marshal of the army, in Troy country;   30
then all Akhaia would have heaped your tomb
and saved your honor for your son. Instead
piteous death awaited you at home."

And Atreus' son replied:

                    "Fortunate hero,
son of Pêleus, godlike and glorious,   35
at Troy you died, across the sea from Argos,
and round you Trojan and Akhaian peers
fought for your corpse and died. A dustcloud wrought
by a whirlwind hid the greatness of you slain,
minding no more the mastery of horses.   40
All that day we might have toiled in battle
had not a storm from Zeus broken it off.
We carried you out of the field of war
down to the ships and bathed your comely body
with warm water and scented oil. We laid you   45
upon your long bed, and our officers
wept hot tears like rain and cropped their hair.
Then hearing of it in the sea, your mother, Thetis,
came with nereids of the grey wave crying
unearthly lamentation over the water,   50
and trembling gripped the Akhaians to the bone.

They would have boarded ship that night and fled
except for one man's wisdom—venerable
Nestor, proven counselor in the past.
He stood and spoke to allay their fear: 'Hold fast,   55
sons of the Akhaians, lads of Argos.
His mother it must be, with nymphs her sisters,
come from the sea to mourn her son in death."

Veteran hearts at this contained their dread
while at your side the daughters of the ancient   60
seagod wailed and wrapped ambrosial shrouding
around you.
            Then we heard the Muses sing
a threnody in nine immortal voices.
No Argive there but wept, such keening rose
from that one Muse who led the song.
                              Now seven   65
days and ten, seven nights and ten, we mourned you,
we mortal men, with nymphs who know no death,
before we gave you to the flame, slaughtering
longhorned steers and fat sheep on your pyre.

Dressed by the nereids and embalmed with honey,   70
honey and unguent in the seething blaze,
you turned to ash. And past the pyre Akhaia's
captains paraded in review, in arms,
clattering chariot teams and infantry.
Like a forest fire the flame roared on, and burned   75
your flesh away. Next day at dawn, Akhilleus,
we picked your pale bones from the char to keep
in wine and oil. A golden amphora
your mother gave for this—Hephaistos' work,
a gift from Dionysos.[1] In that vase,   80
Akhilleus, hero, lie your pale bones mixed
with mild Patróklos' bones, who died before you,
and nearby lie the bones of Antílokhos,
the one you cared for most of all companions
after Patróklos.
                  We of the Old Army,   85
we who were spearmen, heaped a tomb for these
upon a foreland over Hellê's waters,[2]
to be a mark against the sky for voyagers
in this generation and those to come.
Your mother sought from the gods magnificent trophies   90
and set them down midfield for our champions. Often
at funeral games after the death of kings
when you yourself contended, you've seen athletes
cinch their belts when trophies went on view.
But these things would have made you stare—the treasures   95

---

1. A god of the countryside especially associated with wine. Rarely mentioned in Homer, he later presides, at the Athenian festivals, over tragedy and comedy.   2. The Hellespont, the strait separating Asia Minor from Europe, visible from Troy.

Thetis on her silver-slippered feet
brought to your games—for the gods held you dear.
You perished, but your name will never die.
It lives to keep all men in mind of honor
forever, Akhilleus.
          As for myself, what joy   100
is this, to have brought off the war? Foul death
Zeus held in store for me at my coming home;
Aigísthos and my vixen cut me down.'

While they conversed, the Wayfinder came near,
leading the shades of suitors overthrown   105
by Lord Odysseus. The two souls of heroes
advanced together, scrutinizing these.
Then Agamémnon recognized Amphímedon,
son of Meláneus—friends of his on Ithaka—
and called out to him:

          "Amphímedon,   110
what ruin brought you into this undergloom?
All in a body, picked men, and so young?
One could not better choose the kingdom's pride.
Were you at sea, aboard ship, and Poseidon
blew up a dire wind and foundering waves,   115
or cattle-raiding, were you, on the mainland,
or in a fight for some stronghold, or women,
when the foe hit you to your mortal hurt?
Tell me, answer my question. Guest and friend
I say I am of yours—or do you not remember   120
I visited your family there? I came
with Prince Meneláos, urging Odysseus
to join us in the great sea raid on Troy.
One solid month we beat our way, breasting
south sea and west, resolved to bring him round,   125
the wily raider of cities."

         The new shade said:

"O glory of commanders, Agamémnon,
all that you bring to mind I remember well.
As for the sudden manner of our death
I'll tell you of it clearly, first to last.   130
After Odysseus had been gone for years
we were all suitors of his queen. She never
quite refused, nor went through with a marriage,
hating it, ever bent on our defeat.
Here is one of her tricks: she placed her loom,   135
her big loom, out for weaving in her hall,
and the fine warp of some vast fabric on it.
We were attending her, and she said to us:
'Young men, my suitors, now my lord is dead,
let me finish my weaving before I marry,   140

or else my thread will have been spun in vain.
This is a shroud I weave for Lord Laërtês
when cold Death comes to lay him on his bier.
The country wives would hold me in dishonor
if he, with all his fortune, lay unshrouded.'   145
We had men's hearts; she touched them; we agreed.
So every day she wove on the great loom—
but every night by torchlight she unwove it,
and so for three years she deceived the Akhaians.
But when the seasons brought the fourth around,   150
as long months waned, and the slow days were spent,
one of her maids, who knew the secret, told us.
We found her unraveling the splendid shroud,
and then she had to finish, willy nilly—
finish, and show the big loom woven tight   155
from beam to beam with cloth. She washed the shrouding
clean as sun or moonlight.
                                    Then, heaven knows
from what quarter of the world, fatality
brought in Odysseus to the swineherd's wood
far up the island. There his son went too   160
when the black ship put him ashore from Pylos.
The two together planned our death-trap. Down
they came to the famous town—Telémakhos
long in advance: we had to wait for Odysseus.
The swineherd led him to the manor later   165
in rags like a foul beggar, old and broken,
propped on a stick. These tatters that he wore
hid him so well that none of us could know him
when he turned up, not even the older men.
We jeered at him, took potshots at him, cursed him.   170
Daylight and evening in his own great hall
he bore it, patient as a stone. That night
the mind of Zeus beyond the stormcloud stirred him
with Telémakhos at hand to shift his arms
from mégaron to storage room and lock it.   175
Then he assigned his wife her part: next day
she brought his bow and iron axeheads out
to make a contest. Contest there was none;
that move doomed us to slaughter. Not a man
could bend the stiff bow to his will or string it,   180
until it reached Odysseus. We shouted,
'Keep the royal bow from the beggar's hands
no matter how he begs!' Only Telémakhos
would not be denied.
                                So the great soldier
took his bow and bent it for the bowstring   185
effortlessly. He drilled the axeheads clean,
sprang, and decanted arrows on the door sill,
glared, and drew again. This time he killed
Antínoös.
                    There facing us he crouched

and shot his bolts of groaning at us, brought us 190
down like sheep. Then some god, his familiar,
went into action with him round the hall,
after us in a massacre. Men lay groaning,
mortally wounded, and the floor smoked with blood.

That was the way our death came, Agamémnon. 195
Now in Odysseus' hall untended still
our bodies lie, unknown to friends or kinsmen
who should have laid us out and washed our wounds
free of the clotted blood, and mourned our passing.
So much is due the dead.''

        But Agamémnon's 200
tall shade when he heard this cried aloud:

''O fortunate Odysseus, master mariner
and soldier, blessed son of old Laërtês!
The girl you brought home made a valiant wife!
True to her husband's honor and her own, 205
Penélopê, Ikários' faithful daughter!
The very gods themselves will sing her story
for men on earth—mistress of her own heart,
                   Penélopê!
Tyndáreus' daughter waited, too—how differently!
Klytaimnéstra, the adulteress, 210
waited to stab her lord and king. That song
will be forever hateful. A bad name
she gave to womankind, even the best.''

These were the things they said to one another
under the rim of earth where Death is lord. 215

Leaving the town, Odysseus and his men
that morning reached Laërtês garden lands,
long since won by his toil from wilderness—
his homestead, and the row of huts around it
where fieldhands rested, ate and slept. Indoors 220
he had an old slave woman, a Sikel, keeping
house for him in his secluded age.

Odysseus here took leave of his companions.

''Go make yourselves at home inside,'' he said.
''Roast the best porker and prepare a meal. 225
I'll go to try my father. Will he know me?
Can he imagine it, after twenty years?''

He handed spear and shield to the two herdsmen,
and in they went, Telémakhos too. Alone
Odysseus walked the orchard rows and vines. 230
He found no trace of Dólios and his sons

nor the other slaves—all being gone that day
to clear a distant field, and drag the stones
for a boundary wall.
                          But on a well-banked plot
Odysseus found his father in solitude   235
spading the earth around a young fruit tree.

He wore a tunic, patched and soiled, and leggings—
oxhide patches, bound below his knees
against the brambles; gauntlets on his hands
and on his head a goatskin cowl of sorrow.   240
This was the figure Prince Odysseus found—
wasted by years, racked, bowed under grief.
The son paused by a tall pear tree and wept,
then inwardly debated: should he run
forward and kiss his father, and pour out   245
his tale of war, adventure, and return,
or should he first interrogate him, test him?
Better that way, he thought—
first draw him out with sharp words, trouble him.
His mind made up, he walked ahead. Laërtês   250
went on digging, head down, by the sapling,
stamping the spade in. At his elbow then
his son spoke out:

                          "Old man, the orchard keeper
you work for is no townsman. A good eye
for growing things he has; there's not a nurseling,   255
fig tree, vine stock, olive tree or pear tree
or garden bed uncared for on this farm.
But I might add—don't take offense—your own
appearance could be tidier. Old age
yes—but why the squalor, and rags to boot?   260
It would not be for sloth, now, that your master
leaves you in this condition; neither at all
because there's any baseness in your self.
No, by your features, by the frame you have,
a man might call you kingly,   265
one who should bathe warm, sup well, and rest easy
in age's privilege. But tell me:
who are your masters? whose fruit trees are these
you tend here? Tell me if it's true this island
is Ithaka, as that fellow I fell in with   270
told me on the road just now? He had
a peg loose, that one: couldn't say a word
or listen when I asked about my friend,
my Ithakan friend. I asked if he were alive
or gone long since into the underworld.   275
I can describe him if you care to hear it:
I entertained the man in my own land
when he turned up there on a journey; never
had I a guest more welcome in my house.

He claimed his stock was Ithakan: Laërtês   280
Arkeísiadês, he said his father was.
I took him home, treated him well, grew fond of him—
though we had many guests—and gave him
gifts in keeping with his quality: seven
bars of measured gold, a silver winebowl   285
filigreed with flowers, twelve light cloaks,
twelve rugs, robes and tunics—not to mention
his own choice of women trained in service,
the four well-favored ones he wished to take."

His father's eyes had filled with tears. He said: 290

"You've come to that man's island, right enough,
but dangerous men and fools hold power now.
You gave your gifts in vain. If you could find him
here in Ithaka alive, he'd make
return of gifts and hospitality,   295
as custom is, when someone has been generous.
But tell me accurately—how many years
have now gone by since that man was your guest?
your guest, my son—if he indeed existed—
born to ill fortune as he was. Ah, far   300
from those who loved him, far from his native land,
in some sea-dingle fish have picked his bones,
or else he made the vultures and wild beasts
a trove ashore! His mother at his bier
never bewailed him, nor did I, his father,   305
nor did his admirable wife, Penélopê,
who should have closed her husband's eyes in death
and cried aloud upon him as he lay.
So much is due the dead.
                        But speak out, tell me further:
who are you, of what city and family?   310
where have you moored the ship that brought you here,
where is your admirable crew? Are you a peddler
put ashore by the foreign ship you came on?"

Again Odysseus had a fable ready.

"Yes," he said, "I can tell you all those things.   315
I come from Rover's Passage where my home is,
and I'm King Allwoes' only son. My name
is Quarrelman.
                        Heaven's power in the westwind
drove me this way from Sikania,[3]
off my course. My ship lies in a barren   320
cove beyond the town there. As for Odysseus,
now is the fifth year since he put to sea
and left my homeland—bound for death, you say.

3. Another name for Sicily.

Yet landbirds flying from starboard crossed his bow—
a lucky augury. So we parted joyously,   325
in hope of friendly days and gifts to come."

A cloud of pain had fallen on Laërtês.
Scooping up handfuls of the sunburnt dust
he sifted it over his grey head, and groaned,
and the groan went to the son's heart. A twinge   330
prickling up through his nostrils warned Odysseus
he could not watch this any longer.
He leaped and threw his arms around his father,
kissed him, and said:

                    "Oh, Father, I am he!
Twenty years gone, and here I've come again   335
to my own land!
                    Hold back your tears! No grieving!
I bring good news—though still we cannot rest.
I killed the suitors to the last man!
Outrage and injury have been avenged!"

Laërtês turned and found his voice to murmur: 340

"If you are Odysseus, my son, come back,
give me some proof, a sign to make me sure."

His son replied:

                    "The scar then, first of all.
Look, here the wild boar's flashing tusk
wounded me on Parnassos; do you see it?   345
You and my mother made me go, that time,
to visit Lord Autólykos, her father,
for gifts he promised years before on Ithaka.
Again—more proof—let's say the trees you gave me
on this revetted plot of orchard once.   350
I was a small boy at your heels, wheedling
amid the young trees, while you named each one.
You gave me thirteen pear, ten apple trees,
and forty fig trees. Fifty rows of vines
were promised too, each one to bear in turn   355
Bunches of every hue would hang there ripening,
weighed down by the god of summer days."

The old man's knees failed him, his heart grew faint,
recalling all that Odysseus calmly told.
He clutched his son. Odysseus held him swooning   360
until he got his breath back and his spirit
and spoke again:

                    "Zeus, Father! Gods above!—
you still hold pure Olympos, if the suitors

paid for their crimes indeed, and paid in blood!
But now the fear is in me that all Ithaka   365
will be upon us. They'll send messengers
to stir up every city of the islands."

Odysseus the great tactician answered:

"Courage, and leave the worrying to me.
We'll turn back to your homestead by the orchard.   370
I sent the cowherd, swineherd, and Telémakhos
ahead to make our noonday meal."

               Conversing
in this vein they went home, the two together,
into the stone farmhouse. There Telémakhos
and the two herdsmen were already carving   375
roast young pork, and mixing amber wine.
During these preparations the Sikel woman
bathed Laërtês and anointed him,
and dressed him in a new cloak. Then Athena,
standing by, filled out his limbs again,   380
gave girth and stature to the old field captain
fresh from the bathing place. His son looked on
in wonder at the godlike bloom upon him,
and called out happily:

                  "Oh, Father,
surely one of the gods who are young forever   385
has made you magnificent before my eyes!"

Clearheaded Laërtês faced him, saying:

"By Father Zeus, Athena and Apollo,
I wish I could be now as once I was,
commander of Kephallenians, when I took   390
the walled town, Nérikos,[4] on the promontory!
Would god I had been young again last night
with armor on me, standing in our hall
to fight the suitors at your side! How many
knees I could have crumpled, to your joy!"   395

While son and father spoke, cowherd and swineherd
attended, waiting, for the meal was ready.
Soon they were all seated, and their hands
picked up the meat and bread.

                 But now old Dólios
appeared in the bright doorway with his sons,   400
work-stained from the field. Laërtês' housekeeper,
who reared the boys and tended Dólios

---

4. On the mainland; its exact location is unknown.

in his bent age, had gone to fetch them in.
When it came over them who the stranger was
they halted in astonishment. Odysseus   405
hit an easy tone with them. Said he:

"Sit down and help yourselves. Shake off your wonder.
Here we've been waiting for you all this time,
and our mouths watering for good roast pig!"

But Dólios came forward, arms outstretched,   410
and kissed Odysseus' hand at the wrist bone,
crying out:

            "Dear master, you returned!
You came to us again! How we had missed you!
We thought you lost. The gods themselves have brought you!
Welcome, welcome; health and blessings on you!   415
And tell me, now, just one thing more: Penélopê,
does she know yet that you are on the island?
or should we send a messenger?"

Odysseus gruffly said,
                    "Old man, she knows.
Is it for you to think of her?"

                    So Dólios   420
quietly took a smooth bench at the table
and in their turn his sons welcomed Odysseus,
kissing his hands; then each went to his chair
beside his father. Thus our friends
were occupied in Laërtês' house at noon.   425

Meanwhile to the four quarters of the town
the news ran: bloody death had caught the suitors;
and men and women in a murmuring crowd
gathered before Odysseus' hall. They gave
burial to the piteous dead, or bore   430
the bodies of young men from other islands
down to the port, thence to be ferried home.
Then all the men went grieving to assembly
and being seated, rank by rank, grew still,
as old Eupeithês rose to address them. Pain   435
lay in him like a brand for Antínoös,
the first man that Odysseus brought down,
and tears flowed for his son as he began:

"Heroic feats that fellow did for us
Akhaians, friends! Good spearmen by the shipload   440
he led to war and lost—lost ships and men,
and once ashore again killed these, who were
the islands' pride.
                    Up with you! After him!—

before he can take flight to Pylos town
or hide at Elis, under Epeian law!   445
We'd be disgraced forever! Mocked for generations
if we cannot avenge our sons' blood, and our brothers'!
Life would turn to ashes—at least for me;
rather be dead and join the dead!
                                        I say
we ought to follow now, or they'll gain time   450
and make the crossing."

                        His appeal, his tears,
moved all the gentry listening there;
but now they saw the crier and the minstrel
come from Odysseus' hall, where they had slept.
The two men stood before the curious crowd,   455
and Medôn said:

                "Now hear me, men of Ithaka.
When these hard deeds were done by Lord Odysseus
the immortal gods were not far off. I saw
with my own eyes someone divine who fought
beside him, in the shape and dress of Mentor;   460
it was a god who shone before Odysseus,
a god who swept the suitors down the hall
dying in droves."

                At this pale fear assailed them,
and next they heard again the old forecaster,
Halithérsês Mastóridês. Alone   465
he saw the field of time, past and to come.
In his anxiety for them he said:

"Ithakans, now listen to what I say.
Friends, by your own fault these deaths came to pass.
You would not heed me nor the captain, Mentor;   470
would not put down the riot of your sons.
Heroic feats they did!—all wantonly
raiding a great man's flocks, dishonoring
his queen, because they thought he'd come no more.
Let matters rest; do as I urge; no chase,   475
or he who wants a bloody end will find it."

The greater number stood up shouting "Aye!"
But many held fast, sitting all together
in no mind to agree with him. Eupeithês
had won them to his side. They ran for arms,   480
clapped on their bronze, and mustered
under Eupeithês at the town gate
for his mad foray.
                Vengeance would be his,
he thought, for his son's murder; but that day
held bloody death for him and no return.   485

At this point, querying Zeus, Athena said:

"O Father of us all and king of kings,
enlighten me. What is your secret will?
War and battle, worse and more of it,
or can you not impose a pact on both?"   490

The summoner of cloud replied:

                              "My child,
why this formality of inquiry?
Did you not plan that action by yourself—
see to it that Odysseus, on his homecoming,
should have their blood?
                              Conclude it as you will.   495
There is one proper way, if I may say so:
Odysseus' honor being satisfied,
let him be king by a sworn pact forever,
and we, for our part, will blot out the memory
of sons and brothers slain. As in the old time   500
let men of Ithaka henceforth be friends;
prosperity enough, and peace attend them."

Athena needed no command, but down
in one spring she descended from Olympos
just as the company of Odysseus finished   505
wheat crust and honeyed wine, and heard him say:

"Go out, someone, and see if they are coming."

One of the boys went to the door as ordered
and saw the townsmen in the lane. He turned
swiftly to Odysseus.

                              "Here they come,"   510
he said, "best arm ourselves, and quickly."

All up at once, the men took helm and shield—
four fighting men, counting Odysseus,
with Dólios' half dozen sons. Laërtês
armed as well, and so did Dólios—   515
greybeards, they could be fighters in a pinch.
Fitting their plated helmets on their heads
they sallied out, Odysseus in the lead.
Now from the air Athena, Zeus's daughter,
appeared in Mentor's guise, with Mentor's voice,   520
making Odysseus' heart grow light. He said
to put cheer in his son:

                              "Telémakhos,
you are going into battle against pikemen
where hearts of men are tried. I count on you
to bring no shame upon your forefathers."   525

In fighting power we have excelled this lot
in every generation."

Said his son:

"If you are curious, Father, watch and see
the stuff that's in me. No more talk of shame."

And old Laërtês cried aloud: 530

"Ah, what a day for me, dear gods!
to see my son and grandson vie in courage!"

Athena halted near him, and her eyes
shone like the sea. She said:

"Arkeísiadês,
dearest of all my old brothers-in-arms,   535
invoke the grey-eyed one and Zeus her father,
heft your spear and make your throw."

Power flowed into him from Pallas Athena,
whom he invoked as Zeus's virgin child,
and he let fly his heavy spear.

                               It struck   540
Eupeithês on the cheek plate of his helmet,
and undeflected the bronze head punched through.
He toppled, and his armor clanged upon him.
Odysseus and his son now furiously
closed, laying on with broadswords, hand to hand,   545
and pikes: they would have cut the enemy down
to the last man, leaving not one survivor,
had not Athena raised a shout
that stopped all fighters in their tracks.

                            "Now hold!"
she cried, "Break off this bitter skirmish;   550
end your bloodshed, Ithakans, and make peace."

Their faces paled with dread before Athena,
and swords dropped from their hands unnerved, to lie
strewing the ground, at the great voice of the goddess.
Those from the town turned fleeing for their lives.   555
But with a cry to freeze their hearts
and ruffling like an eagle on the pounce,
the lord Odysseus reared himself to follow—
at which the son of Kronos dropped a thunderbolt
smoking at his daughter's feet.
                                 Athena   560
cast a grey glance at her friend and said:

"Son of Laërtês and the gods of old,
Odysseus, master of land ways and sea ways,
command yourself. Call off this battle now,
or Zeus who views the wide world may be angry."   565

He yielded to her, and his heart was glad.
Both parties later swore to terms of peace
set by their arbiter, Athena, daughter
of Zeus who bears the stormcloud as a shield—
though still she kept the form and voice of Mentor.   570

SAPPHO OF LESBOS
born ca. 630 B.C.

About Sappho's life we know very little: she was born about 630 B.C. on the fertile island of Lesbos off the coast of Asia Minor and spent most of her life there; she was married and had a daughter. Her lyric poems (poems sung to the accompaniment of the lyre) were so admired in the ancient world that a later poet called her the tenth Muse. In the third century B.C. scholars at the great library in Alexandria arranged her poems in nine books, of which the first contained more than a thousand lines. But what we have now is a pitiful remnant: one (or possibly two) complete short poems, and a collection of quotations from her work by ancient writers, supplemented by bits and pieces written on ancient scraps of papyrus found in excavations in Egypt. Yet these remnants fully justify the enthusiasm of the ancient critics; Sappho's poems (insofar as we can guess at their nature from the fragments) give us the most vivid evocation of the joys and sorrows of love in all Greek literature.

Her themes are those of a Greek woman's world—girlhood, marriage, and love, especially the love of young women for each other and the poignancy of their parting as they leave to assume the responsibilities of a wife. About the social context of these songs we can only guess; all that can be said is that they reflect a world in which women, at least women of the aristocracy, lived an intense communal life of their own, one of female occasions, functions, and festivities, in which their young passionate natures were fully engaged with each other; to most of them, presumably, this was a stage preliminary to their later career in that world as wife and mother.

The first two poems printed here were quoted in their entirety by ancient critics (though it is possible that there was another stanza at the end of the second); their text is not a problem. But the important recent additions to our knowledge of Sappho's poetry, the pieces of ancient books found in Egypt, are difficult to read and usually full of gaps. Our third selection, in fact, comes from the municipal rubbish heap of the Egyptian village Oxyrhyncus. Most of the gaps in the text are due to holes or tears in the papyrus and can easily be filled in from our knowledge of Sappho's dialect and the strict meter in which she wrote, but the end of the third stanza and the whole of the fourth are imaginative reconstructions by the translator. The papyrus, for instance, tells us only that someone or something led Helen astray; Lattimore's "Queen of Cyprus" (the love goddess, Aphrodite) may well be right but is not certain. In the next stanza all that we have is part of a word that means something like "flexible" (Lattimore's "hearts that can be persuaded"); an adverb, *lightly;* and "remembering Anaktoria who is not here." As a matter of fact we don't have that all-important *not,* but the sense demands it. Fortunately, the final stanza, with its telling echo of the opening theme, is almost intact.

A fine recent translation of Sappho's poetry, with excellent introduction and notes, is given in Diane Rayor, *Sappho's Lyre: Archaic Lyric and Women Poets of Ancient Greece* (1991). Accessible surveys from varying points of view may be found in Jane M. Snyder, *The Woman and the Lyre: Women Writers in Classical Greece and Rome* (1989), Richard Jenkyns, *Three Classical Poets: Sappho, Catullus, and Juvenal* (1982), and Anne Burnett, *Three Archaic Poets: Archilochus, Alcaeus, Sappho* (1983). An outstanding assessment of Sappho's position as a woman in Greek society is John J. Winkler, "Double Consciousness in Sappho's Lyrics," in his *The Constraints of Desire: The Anthropology of Sex and Gender in Ancient Greece* (1990). Page duBois, *Sappho Is Burning* (1995), is a challenging discussion of Sappho's poetry as resisting the categories of Western thought.

[Throned in Splendor, Deathless, O Aphrodite][1]

Throned in splendor, deathless, O Aphrodite,[2]
child of Zeus, charm-fashioner, I entreat you
not with griefs and bitternesses to break my
    spirit, O goddess:

standing by me rather, if once before now   5
far away you heard, when I called upon you,
left your father's dwelling place and descended,
    yoking the golden

chariot to sparrows,[3] who fairly drew you
down in speed aslant the black world, the bright air   10
trembling at the heart to the pulse of countless
    fluttering wingbeats.

Swiftly then they came, and you, blessed lady,
smiling on me out of immortal beauty,
asked me what affliction was on me, why I   15
    called thus upon you,

what beyond all else I would have befall my
tortured heart: "Whom then would you have Persuasion
force to serve desire in your heart? Who is it,
    Sappho, that hurt you?   20

Though she now escape, she soon will follow;
though she take not gifts from you, she will give them:
though she love not, yet she will surely love you
    even unwilling."

In such guise come even again and set me   25
free from doubt and sorrow; accomplish all those

---

1. All selections translated by Richmond Lattimore.   2. A prayer to the goddess of love, Aphrodite. The translator has skillfully reproduced the metrical form of the Greek, the "Sapphic" stanza.   3. Aphrodite's sacred birds.

things my heart desires to be done; appear and
    stand at my shoulder.

[Like the Very Gods in My Sight Is He]

Like the very gods in my sight is he who
sits where he can look in your eyes, who listens
close to you, to hear the soft voice, its sweetness
    murmur in love and

laughter, all for him. But it breaks my spirit;   5
underneath my breast all the heart is shaken.
Let me only glance where you are, the voice dies,
    I can say nothing,

but my lips are stricken to silence, underneath my skin the tenuous flame suffuses;   10
nothing shows in front of my eyes, my ears are
    muted in thunder.

And the sweat breaks running upon me, fever
shakes my body, paler I turn than grass is;
I can feel that I have been changed, I feel that   15
    death has come near me.

[Some There Are Who Say That the Fairest Thing Seen]

Some there are who say that the fairest thing seen
on the black earth is an array of horsemen;
some, men marching; some would say ships; but I say
    she whom one loves best

is the loveliest. Light were the work to make this   5
plain to all, since she, who surpassed in beauty
all mortality, Helen, once forsaking
    her lordly husband,

fled away to Troy—land across the water.
Not the thought of child nor beloved parents   10
was remembered, after the Queen of Cyprus[1]
    won her at first sight.

Since young brides have hearts that can be persuaded
easily, light things, palpitant to passion
as am I, remembering Anaktória   15
    who has gone from me

---

1. Aphrodite.

and whose lovely walk and the shining pallor
of her face I would rather see before my
eyes than Lydia's chariots in all their glory
armored for battle.   20

AESCHYLUS
524?–456 B.C.

The earliest documents in the history of the Western theater are the seven plays of
Aeschylus that have come down to us through the more than two thousand years
since his death. When he produced his first play in the opening years of the fifth
century B.C., the performance that we know as drama was still less than half a century
old, still open to innovation—and Aeschylus, in fact, made such significant contributions to its development that he has been called "the creator of tragedy."

The origins of the theatrical contests in Athens are obscure; they were a puzzle
even for Aristotle, who in the fourth century B.C. wrote a famous treatise on tragedy.
All that we know for certain is that the drama began as a religious celebration that
took the form of song and dance.

Such ceremonies are of course to be found in the communal life of many early
cultures, but it was in Athens, and in Athens alone, that the ceremony gave rise to
what we know as tragedy and comedy and produced dramatic masterpieces that are
still admired, read, and performed.

At some time in the late sixth century B.C. the Athenians converted what seems to
have been a rural celebration of Dionysus, a vegetation deity especially associated
with the vine, into an annual city festival at which dancing choruses, competing for
prizes, sang hymns of praise to the god. It was from this choral performance that
tragedy and comedy developed. Some unknown innovator (his name was probably
Thespis) combined the choral song with the speech of a masked actor, who, playing
a god or hero, engaged the chorus in dialogue. It was Aeschylus who added a second
actor and so created the possibility of conflict and the prototype of the drama as we
know it.

After the defeat of the Persian invaders (480–479 B.C.), as Athens with its fleets
and empire moved toward supremacy in the Greek world, this spring festival became
a splendid occasion. The Dionysia, as it was now called, lasted for four or five days,
during which public business (except in emergencies) was suspended and prisoners
were released on bail for the duration of the festival. In an open-air theater that could
seat seventeen thousand spectators, tragic and comic poets competed for the prizes
offered by the city. Poets in each genre had been selected by the magistrates for the
year. On each of three days of the festival, a tragic poet presented three tragedies and
a satyr play (a burlesque on a mythic theme), and a comic poet produced one comedy.

The three tragedies could deal with quite separate stories or, as in the case of
Aeschylus's Oresteia, with the successive stages of one extended action. By the time
this trilogy was produced (458 B.C.) the number of actors had been raised to three;
the spoken part of the performance became steadily more important. In the Oresteia
an equilibrium between the two elements of the performance has been established.
The actors, with their speeches, create the dramatic situation and its movement, the
plot; the chorus, while contributing to dramatic suspense and illusion, ranges free of
the immediate situation in its odes, which extend and amplify the significance of the
action.

In 458 B.C. Aeschylus was at the end of a great career; he died two years later in the Greek city Gela, in Sicily. He had begun his career as a dramatist before the Persian Wars, in the first days of the new Athenian democracy. He fought against the Persians at Marathon (where his brother was killed) and almost certainly also in the great sea fight at Salamis in 480 B.C. (his play the *Persians,* produced in 472 B.C., contains what sounds like an eyewitness account of that battle). Only seven of his plays survive (we know that he produced ninety); besides the *Persians* and the three plays of the *Oresteia,* we have the text of *Suppliants* (sometime in the 460s), *The Seven Against Thebes* (467), and the famous and influential play *Prometheus Bound* (date unknown).

The *Oresteia* is a trilogy. The first play, *Agamemnon,* was followed at its performance by two more plays, *The Libation Bearers* and *The Eumenides,* which carried on its story and theme to a conclusion. The theme of the trilogy is justice, and its story, like that of almost all Greek tragedies, is a legend that was already well known to the audience that saw the first performance of the play. This particular legend, the story of the house of Atreus, is rich in dramatic potential, for it deals with a series of retributive murders that stained the hands of three generations of a royal family, and it has also a larger significance, social and historical, of which Aeschylus took full advantage. The legend preserves the memory of an important historical process through which the Greeks had passed: the transition from tribal institutions of justice to communal justice, from a tradition that demanded that a murdered person's next of kin avenge the death to a system requiring settlement of the private quarrel by a court of law (the typical institution of the city-state, which replaced the primitive tribe). When Agamemnon returns victorious from Troy, he is killed by his wife, Clytemnestra, and her lover, Aegisthus, who is Agamemnon's cousin. Clytemnestra kills her husband to avenge her daughter Iphigenia, whom Agamemnon sacrificed to the goddess Artemis when he had to choose between his daughter's life and his ambition to conquer Troy. Aegisthus avenges the crime of a previous generation, the hideous murder of his brothers by Agamemnon's father, Atreus. The killing of Agamemnon is, by the standards of the old system, justice; but it is the nature of this justice that the process can never be arrested, that one act of violence must give rise to another. Agamemnon's murder must be avenged too, as it is in the second play of the trilogy by Orestes, his son, who kills both Aegisthus and Clytemnestra, his own mother. Orestes has acted justly according to the code of tribal society based on blood relationship, but in doing so he has violated the most sacred blood relationship of all, the bond between mother and son. The old system of justice has produced an insoluble dilemma.

At the end of *The Libation Bearers,* Orestes sees a vision of the Furies. They are serpent-haired female hunters, the avengers of blood. Agamemnon had a son to avenge him, but for Clytemnestra there was no one to exact payment. This task is taken up by the Furies, who are the guardians of the ancient tribal sanctities; they enforce the old dispensation when no earthly agent is at hand to do so. Female themselves, they assert the claim of the mother against the son who killed her to avenge his father. At the end of the second play they are only a vision in Orestes' mind— "You can't see them," he says to the chorus. "*I* can; they drive me on. I must move on." But in the final play we see them too; they are the chorus, and they have pursued Orestes to the great shrine of Apollo at Delphi where he has come to seek refuge.

Apollo can save him from immediate destruction at the Furies' hands, but he cannot resolve the dilemma. Orestes must go to Athens, where Athena, the patron goddess of the city, will set up the first court of law to try his case. At Athens, before the ancient court of the Areopagus, the Furies argue eloquently, but Apollo himself arrives to testify that he ordered Orestes to act. Athena tilts the judges' vote in Orestes' favor by either creating or breaking a tie with her own vote, and Orestes, acquitted, goes home to Argos. The Furies threaten to turn their dreadful wrath against Athens itself, but the goddess persuades them to accept a home deep in Athenian earth, to act as protectors of the court and of the land.

The arguments employed in the trial may not strike us as compelling, and may appear disappointing as an answer to the problems of guilt and justice raised by the trilogy. A possible reply is the "progressivist" argument. According to this argument, the fact of the court's establishment is more important than the particular judgment in Orestes' case. This is the end of an old era and the beginning of a new. The court institutes a system of communal justice, which punishes impersonally and has at last replaced the inconclusive anarchy of individual revenge. Besides, the trilogy not only is concerned with the history of human institutions but also makes a religious state-ment. The sequence of murderous acts and counter-acts over three generations, lead-ing to an important advance in human understanding and civilization, can be seen as the working out of the will of Zeus. The chorus of *Agamemnon*, celebrating the power of Zeus, tells us that he

> has led us on to know,
> the Helmsman lays it down as law
> that we must suffer, suffer into truth.

From suffering come understanding and progress. That is Zeus's design in the trilogy, whereas in the *Iliad,* where events also are guided by a plan of Zeus, nothing at all comes out of the suffering except the certainty of more suffering. The ending of the *Eumenides,* then, when the Furies call blessings down on Athens, gives a vision of a city ruled by law and living in harmony with its land and its gods. In this story of progress painfully won, Aeschylus offers Athenian democracy its charter myth just as it is entering the era of its greatest achievements and its greatest risks.

This "progressivist" reading of the *Oresteia* has considerable force, but it does not account for everything. It leaves out, for example, one of the costs of this progress that the trilogy also shows clearly: gender asymmetry. In *Agamemnon*, Clytemnestra is a powerful and transgressive figure, a woman who "maneuvers like a man," as the Watchman says the first time she is mentioned in the play. Her murder of her husband is, in Greek terms, only an intensified form of this self-assertion, and, by raising the specter of a woman out of control, it justifies women's normal subjugation in Greek culture. But in avenging Iphigeneia, Clytemnestra also defends the integrity of the family, and particularly the parent-child bond, against her husband's public ambition, to which he has sacrificed their daughter. She asserts this bond again in her last moments, when she bares her breast to Orestes to dissuade him from killing her. In murdering her husband in the name of her child, she has struck at the basis of marriage, but she does have a measure of justice on her side, not to mention a claim of vengeance against her son. Orestes' acquittal in the third play leaves her claims unsatisfied. Athena, the virgin warrior-goddess who represents the female as an ally of patriarchal order, declares as she casts her vote for Orestes, "no mother gave me birth. / I honor the male, in all things but marriage." From this point of view, the Furies' incorporation into Athens represents the appropriation and taming of female power, and it validates the exclusion of women from the civic processes of the democ-racy—a fact of Athenian daily life. On the other hand, in celebrating the Furies' role of maintaining obedience to law through inspiring fear and of promoting natural fertility, the text acknowledges the power of the female, which it associates with the Earth's natural processes, "primitive" and prior to the male-centered rationality of the city but vital still. The female is given a role in the city, even though she is excluded from its official public life, and that role is celebrated. There is no doubt, however, about the dominance of the patriarchal principle under the authority of the Olympian gods.

The full scope of these events, however we interpret them, is apparent only to the audience, which follows the pattern of its execution through the three plays of the trilogy. As in the Book of Job, the characters who act and suffer are in the dark. They claim a knowledge of Zeus's will and boast that their actions are its fulfillment (it is in these terms that Agamemnon speaks of the sack of Troy, and Clytemnestra of

Agamemnon's murder), and they are, of course, in one sense, right. But their knowledge is limited; Agamemnon does not realize that Zeus's will includes his death at the hands of Clytemnestra, nor Clytemnestra that it demands her death at the hands of her son. The chorus has, at times, a deeper understanding, but its knowledge of Zeus's laws is an abstraction that it cannot relate to the terrible facts.

In this murky atmosphere (made all the more terrible by the beacon fire of the opening lines, which brings not light but deeper darkness), one human being sees clear; she possesses the concrete vision of the future, which complements the chorus's abstract knowledge of the law. This is the prophet Cassandra, Priam's daughter, brought from Troy as Agamemnon's share of the spoils. She has been given the power of true prophecy by the god Apollo, but the gift is nullified by the condition that her prophecies will never be believed. She sees reality—past, present, and future—so clearly that she is cut off from ordinary human beings (represented by the chorus) by the clarity of her vision and the terrible burden of her knowledge. The great scene in which she sings her prophecies delays the action for which everything has been prepared—the death of Agamemnon. Before we hear his famous cry offstage, Cassandra presents us with a mysterious vision that combines cause, effect, and result: the murders that have led to this terrible moment, the death of Agamemnon, and the murders that will follow. The past, present, and future of Clytemnestra's action and Agamemnon's suffering are fused into a timeless unity in Cassandra's great lines, an unearthly unity that is dissolved only when Agamemnon, in the real world of time and space, screams in mortal agony.

The tremendous statement of the trilogy is made in a style that for magnificence and richness of suggestion can be compared only with the style of Shakespeare at the height of his poetic power, the Shakespeare of *King Lear* and *Antony and Cleopatra*. The language of the *Oresteia* is an Oriental carpet of imagery in which combinations of metaphor, which at first seem bombastic in their violence, take their place in the ordered pattern of the poem as a whole. An image, once introduced, recurs and reappears again, to run its course verbally and visually through the whole length of the trilogy, richer in meaning with each fresh appearance. In the second choral ode, for example, the chorus, welcoming the news of Agamemnon's victory at Troy, sings of the net that Zeus and Night threw over the city, trapping the inhabitants like animals. The net is here an image of Zeus's justice, a retributive justice, since Troy is paying for the crime of taking Helen, and the image identifies Zeus's justice with Agamemnon's action in sacking the city. This image occurs again, with a different emphasis, in the hypocritical speech of welcome that Clytemnestra makes to her husband on his return. She tells how she feared for his safety at Troy, how she trembled at the rumors of his death:

> and the rumors spread and fester,
> a runner comes with something dreadful,
> close on his heels the next and his news worse,
> and they shout it out and the whole house can hear;
> and wounds—if he took one wound for each report
> to penetrate these walls, he's gashed like a dragnet.

This vision of Agamemnon dead she speaks of as her fear, but we know that it represents her deepest desire and, more, the purpose that she is now preparing to execute. When, later, she stands in triumph over her husband's corpse, she uses the same image to describe the robe that she threw over his limbs to blind and baffle him before she stabbed him—"Inextricable like a net for fishes / I cast about him a vicious wealth of raiment"—and this time the image materializes into an object visible on stage. We can see the net, the gashed robe still folded round Agamemnon's body. We shall see it again, for in the second play Orestes, standing over his mother's body as she now stands over his father's, will display the robe before us, with its holes and bloodstains, as a justification for what he has just done. Elsewhere in *Agamemnon* the chorus compares Cassandra to a wild animal caught in the net, and later Aegisthus exults to see Agamemnon's body lying "in the nets of Justice." For each speaker the image has a different meaning, but not one realizes the terrible sense in which it applies to them all. They are all caught in the net, the system of justice by vengeance that only binds tighter the more its captives struggle to free themselves. Clytemnestra attempts to escape, to arrest the process of the chain of murders and the working out of the will of Zeus. "But I will swear a pact with the spirit born within us," she says, but Agamemnon's body and the net she threw over him are there on the stage to remind us that her appeal will not be heard; one more generation must act and suffer before the net will vanish, never to be seen again.

D. J. Conacher, *Aeschylus' Oresteia: A Literary Commentary* (1987), is a scene-by-scene (and sometimes line-by-line) commentary addressed as much to Greekless readers as to classical scholars. James Hogan, *A Commentary on the Complete Greek Tragedies: Aeschylus* (1987), contains a line-by-line commentary on Richmond Lattimore's translation of the *Oresteia* (1953). John Herington, *Aeschylus* (1986), deals with the political and religious background of the tragedies and provides a perceptive discussion of the plays (*Oresteia*, pp. 111–56). Oliver Taplin, *Greek Tragedy in Action* (1978), gives a sensitive scene-by-scene discussion of the significance of stage action and spectacle in all three plays. Simon Goldhill, *Aeschylus: The Oresteia* (1992), includes a chapter on the trilogy's historical and cultural context and is an excellent guide through the complexities of each play. Froma Zeitlin's *Playing the Other: Gender and Society in Classical Greek Literature* (1996) includes (pp. 87–119) her outstanding essay on the *Oresteia*, "The Dynamics of Misogyny."

PRONOUNCING GLOSSARY

The following list uses common English syllables and stress accents to provide rough equivalents of selected words whose pronunciation may be unfamiliar to the general reader.

Aegisthus: *ee-jis'-thus*

Aeschylus: *ess'-kel-us*

Areopagus: *a-ree-op'-aguhs*

Calchas: *kal'-kahs*

Clytaemnestra: *klai-tem-nes'-truh*

Dionysus: *dai-oh-nai'-sus*

Eumenides: *yoo-me'-ni-deez*

Hermes: *her'-meez*

Iphigeneia: *i-fe-jen-ai'-uh*

Menelaus: *me-ne-lay'-us*

Oresteia: *o-res-tai'-uh*

Orestes: *o-res'-teez*

Thyestes: *thai-es'-teez*

THE ORESTEIA[1]

Agamemnon

CHARACTERS

WATCHMAN
CLYTAEMNESTRA
HERALD
AGAMEMNON
CASSANDRA

AEGISTHUS
CHORUS, *the Old Men of Argos and their* LEADER
Attendants of Clytaemnestra and of Agamemnon, bodyguard of Aegisthus

1. Translated by Robert Fagles.

[TIME AND SCENE: *A night in the tenth and final autumn of the Trojan war. The house of Atreus in Argos. Before it, an altar stands unlit; a* WATCHMAN *on the high roofs fights to stay awake.*]

WATCHMAN   Dear gods, set me free from all the pain,
   the long watch I keep, one whole year awake . . .
   propped on my arms, crouched on the roofs of Atreus
   like a dog.
           I know the stars by heart,
   the armies of the night, and there in the lead   5
   the ones that bring us snow or the crops of summer,
   bring us all we have—
   our great blazing kings of the sky,
   I know them, when they rise and when they fall . . .
   and now I watch for the light, the signal-fire[2]   10
   breaking out of Troy, shouting Troy is taken.
   So she commands, full of her high hopes.
   That woman[3]—she maneuvers like a man.

   And when I keep to my bed, soaked in dew,
   and the thoughts go groping through the night   15
   and the good dreams that used to guard my sleep . . .
   not here, it's the old comrade, terror, at my neck.
   I mustn't sleep, no—
       [*Shaking himself awake.*]
               Look alive, sentry.
   And I try to pick out tunes, I hum a little,
   a good cure for sleep, and the tears start,   20
   I cry for the hard times come to the house,
   no longer run like the great place of old.

   Oh for a blessed end to all our pain,
   some godsend burning through the dark—
       [*Light appears slowly in the east; he struggles to his feet and scans it.*]
                              I salute you!
   You dawn of the darkness, you turn night to day—   25
   I see the light at last.
   They'll be dancing in the streets of Argos[4]
   thanks to you, thanks to this new stroke of—
                        Aieeeeee!
   There's your signal clear and true, my queen!

---

2. I.e., the bonfire nearest to Argos, the last in a chain extending all the way to Troy, each one visible, when fired at night, from the next.   3. Clytaemnestra.   4. In Homer, Agamemnon, son of Atreus, is king of Mycenae. Later Greek poets, however, referred to his kingdom as Argos or Mycenae, perhaps because the Achaeans in Homer are sometimes called Argives. In 463 B.C., just five years before the production of the play, Argos had defeated Mycenae in battle and put an end to the city, displacing the inhabitants or selling them into slavery. Soon after, Argos and Athens entered into an alliance, aimed, of course, at Sparta. Since this alliance will be alluded to in the last play of the trilogy, it is important for Aeschylus to establish the un-Homeric location of the action right at the beginning.

Rise up from bed—hurry, lift a cry of triumph   30
through the house, praise the gods for the beacon,
if they've taken Troy . . .
                    But there it burns,
fire all the way. I'm for the morning dances.
Master's luck is mine. A throw of the torch
has brought us triple-sixes[5]—we have won!   35
My move now—
        [Beginning to dance, then breaking off, lost in thought.]
             Just bring him home. My king,
I'll take your loving hand in mine and then . . .
the rest is silence. The ox is on my tongue.[6]
Aye, but the house and these old stones,
give them a voice and what a tale they'd tell.   40
And so would I, gladly . . .
I speak to those who know; to those who don't
my mind's a blank. I never say a word.
        [He climbs down from the roof and disappears into the palace
        through a side entrance. A CHORUS, the old men of Argos who have
        not learned the news of victory, enters and marches round the altar.]
CHORUS   Ten years gone, ten to the day
our great avenger went for Priam—   45
   Menelaus[7] and lord Agamemnon,
two kings with the power of Zeus,
the twin throne, twin sceptre,
Atreus' sturdy yoke of sons
launched Greece in a thousand ships,   50
armadas cutting loose from the land,
armies massed for the cause, the rescue—
       [From within the palace CLYTAEMNESTRA raises a cry of triumph.]
the heart within them screamed for all-out war!
Like vultures robbed of their young,
   the agony sends them frenzied,   55
soaring high from the nest, round and
round they wheel, they row their wings,
stroke upon churning thrashing stroke,
but all the labor, the bed of pain,
   the young are lost forever.   60
Yet someone hears on high—Apollo,
Pan or Zeus[8]—the piercing wail
these guests of heaven raise,
and drives at the outlaws, late
but true to revenge, a stabbing Fury![9]   65

---

5. The highest throw in the ancient Greek dice game.   6. A proverbial phrase for enforced silence.   7. Another son of Atreus, also a king of Argos and commander of the Greek expedition against Troy. Priam was the king of Troy. His son Paris abducted (or seduced) Menelaus's wife, Helen.   8. The movements of birds are regarded as prophetic signs; Apollo perhaps as a prophetic god; Pan as a god of the wild places; Zeus because eagles and vultures were symbolic of his power.   9. This is the first mention of one of these avenging spirits, who will actually appear on stage as the chorus of the final play. Furies are called Erinyes in Greek.

[CLYTAEMNESTRA *appears at the doors and pauses with her entourage.*][1]

So towering Zeus the god of guests[2]
drives Atreus' sons at Paris,
all for a woman manned by many
the generations wrestle, knees
grinding the dust, the manhood drains,   70
the spear snaps in the first blood rites
   that marry Greece and Troy.
And now it goes as it goes
and where it ends is Fate.
And neither by singeing flesh   75
nor tipping cups of wine[3]
nor shedding burning tears can you
enchant away the rigid Fury.
   [CLYTAEMNESTRA *lights the altar-fires.*]
We are the old, dishonoured ones,[4]
the broken husks of men.   80
Even then they cast us off,
the rescue mission left us here
to prop a child's strength upon a stick.
What if the new sap rises in his chest?
He has no soldiery in him,   85
   no more than we,
and we are aged past aging,
gloss of the leaf shriveled,
three legs[5] at a time we falter on.
Old men are children once again,   90
   a dream that sways and wavers
into the hard light of day.
                          But you,
daughter of Leda, queen Clytaemnestra,
what now, what news, what message
drives you through the citadel   95
   burning victims?[6] Look,
the city gods, the gods of Olympus,
gods of the earth and public markets—
all the altars blazing with your gifts!
   Argos blazes! Torches   100
race the sunrise up her skies—
drugged by the lulling holy oils,
   unadulterated,

---

1. There are no stage directions on the manuscript copies of the plays that have come down to us. Here the translator had the queen enter so that she will be visible on stage when the chorus addresses her by name in line 93. Other scholars, pointing out that in Greek tragedy characters who are offstage are often addressed, disagree, and bring Clytaemnestra on stage only at line 256.   2. Zeus was thought to be particularly interested in punishing those who violated the code of hospitality. Paris had been a guest in Menelaus's house.   3. Neither by burnt sacrifice nor by pouring libations.   4. The general sense of the passage is that only two classes of the male population are left in Argos: those who are too young to fight and those who, like the chorus, are too old.   5. Because they use a stick, or cane, to support them when they walk.   6. Clytaemnestra is sacrificing in thanksgiving for the news of Troy's fall; the chorus does not know that the news has come via the signal fires.

run from the dark vaults of kings.
 Tell us the news!   105
What you can, what is right—
Heal us, soothe our fears!
Now the darkness comes to the fore,
now the hope glows through your victims,
beating back this raw, relentless anguish   110
 gnawing at the heart.
   [CLYTAEMNESTRA *ignores them and pursues her rituals; they assemble for the opening chorus.*]
O but I still have power to sound the god's command at the roads
that launched the kings. The gods breathe power through my song,
 my fighting strength, Persuasion grows with the years—
I sing how the flight of fury hurled the twin command,   115
   one will that hurled young Greece
and winged the spear of vengeance straight for Troy!
The kings of birds to kings of the beaking prows, one black,
 one with a blaze of silver
  skimmed the palace spearhand right   120
   and swooping lower, all could see,
    plunged their claws in a hare, a mother
  bursting with unborn young—the babies spilling,
quick spurts of blood—cut off the race just dashing into life!
Cry, cry for death, but good win out in glory in the end.   125

But the loyal seer of the armies studied Atreus' sons,
two sons with warring hearts—he saw two eagle-kings
 devour the hare and spoke the things to come,[7]
"Years pass, and the long hunt nets the city of Priam,
  the flocks beyond the walls,   130
a kingdom's life and soul—Fate stamps them out.
Just let no curse of the gods lour on us first,
 shatter our giant armor
  forged to strangle Troy. I see
   pure Artemis bristle in pity—   135
    yes, the flying hounds of the Father
  slaughter for armies . . . their own victim . . . a woman
trembling young, all born to die—She[8] loathes the eagles' feast!"
Cry, cry for death, but good win out in glory in the end.
  "Artemis, lovely Artemis, so kind   140
to the ravening lion's tender, helpless cubs,
the suckling young of beasts that stalk the wilds—
  bring this sign for all its fortune,
   all its brutal torment home to birth!

---

7. The seer Calchas identified the two eagles (*kings of birds*) as symbolic of the two kings and their action as a symbolic prophecy of the destruction of Troy. The two eagles seized and tore a pregnant hare, which meant that the two kings would destroy Troy, thus killing not only the living Trojans but the Trojan generations yet unborn. 8. Artemis, a virgin goddess, patron of hunting, and the protectress of wildlife, is angry that the eagles (*the flying hounds*) have destroyed a pregnant animal. The prophet fears that she may turn her wrath against the kings whom the eagles represent. *A woman trembling young:* just as the eagles kill the hare, the kings will kill Agamemnon's daughter Iphigenia. The Greek text refers only to the hare, but the translator has made the allusion clear.

I beg you, Healing Apollo, soothe her before   145
her crosswinds hold us down and moor the ships too long,[9]
pressing us on to another victim . . .
    nothing sacred, no
      no feast to be eaten[1]
        the architect of vengeance   150
      [*Turning to the palace.*]
      growing strong in the house
    with no fear of the husband
here she waits
the terror raging back and back in the future
    the stealth, the law of the hearth, the mother—   155
      Memory womb of Fury child-avenging Fury!"
So as the eagles wheeled at the crossroads,
Calchas clashed out the great good blessings mixed with doom
    for the halls of kings, and singing with our fate
we cry, cry for death, but good win out in glory in the end.   160

        Zeus, great nameless all in all,
        if that name will gain his favor,
          I will call him Zeus.[2]
        I have no words to do him justice,
          weighing all in the balance,   165
            all I have is Zeus, Zeus—
        lift this weight, this torment from my spirit,
          cast it once for all.

        He who was so mighty once,[3]
        storming for the wars of heaven,   170
          he has had his day.
    And then his son[4] who came to power
      met his match in the third fall
      and he is gone. Zeus, Zeus—
raise your cries and sing him Zeus the Victor!   175
        You will reach the truth:

        Zeus has led us on to know,
        the Helmsman lays it down as law
      that we must suffer, suffer into truth.

9. Calchas foresees the future. Artemis will send unfavorable winds to prevent the sailing of the Greek expedition from Aulis, the port of embarkation. She will demand the sacrifice of Agamemnon's daughter Iphigenia as the price of the fleet's release. He prays that in spite of its bad aspects, the omen will be truly prophetic—that is, that the Achaeans will capture Troy. He goes on to anticipate and try to avert some of the evils it portends.   1. At an ordinary sacrifice the celebrants gave the gods their due portion and then feasted on the animal's flesh. The word *sacrifice* comes to have the connotation of "feast." There will be no feast at this sacrifice, since the victim will be a human being. The ominous phrase reminds us of a feast of human flesh that has already taken place, Thyestes' feasting on his own children.   2. It was important, in prayer, to address the divinity by his or her right name: here the chorus uses an inclusive formula—they call on Zeus by whatever name pleases him.   3. Uranus, father of Kronos, grandfather of Zeus, the first lord of heaven. This whole passage refers to a primitive legend that told how Uranus was violently supplanted by his son, Kronos, who was in his turn overthrown by his son, Zeus. This legend is made to bear new meaning by Aeschylus, for he suggests that it is not a meaningless series of acts of violence but a progression to the rule of Zeus, who stands for order and justice. Thus the law of human life that Zeus proclaims and administers—that wisdom comes through suffering—has its counterpart in the history of the establishment of the divine rule.   4. Kronos.

We cannot sleep, and drop by drop at the heart   180
    the pain of pain remembered comes again,
    and we resist, but ripeness comes as well.
From the gods enthroned on the awesome rowing-bench[5]
    there comes a violent love.

      So it was that day the king,   185
    the steersman at the helm of Greece,
    would never blame a word the prophet said—
    swept away by the wrenching winds of fortune
he conspired! Weatherbound we could not sail,
our stores exhausted, fighting strength hard-pressed,   190
and the squadrons rode in the shallows off Chalkis[6]
    where the riptide crashes, drags,

and winds from the north pinned down our hulls at Aulis,
port of anguish . . . head winds starving,
sheets and the cables snapped   195
   and the men's minds strayed,
     the pride, the bloom of Greece
  was raked as time ground on,
ground down, and then the cure for the storm
and it was harsher—Calchas cried,   200
"My captains, Artemis must have blood!"—
   so harsh the sons of Atreus
    dashed their scepters on the rocks,
   could not hold back the tears,

and I still can hear the older warlord saying,   205
"Obey, obey, or a heavy doom will crush me!—
Oh but doom *will* crush me
   once I rend my child,
    the glory of my house—
   a father's hands are stained,   210
blood of a young girl streaks the altar.
Pain both ways and what is worse?
Desert the fleets, fail the alliance?
   No, but stop the winds with a virgin's blood,
    feed their lust, their fury?—feed their fury!—   215
   Law is law!—
       Let all go well."

And once he slipped his neck in the strap of Fate,
his spirit veering black, impure, unholy,
once he turned he stopped at nothing,
   seized with the frenzy   220
    blinding driving to outrage—
wretched frenzy, cause of all our grief!

---

5. The bench of the ship where the helmsman sat.   6. The unruly water of the narrows between Aulis on the mainland and Chalkis on the island of Euboea.

Yes, he had the heart
 to sacrifice his daughter!—
to bless the war that avenged a woman's loss,   225
 a bridal rite that sped the men-of-war.

"My father, father!"—she might pray to the winds;
no innocence moves her judges mad for war.
Her father called his henchmen on,
 on with a prayer,   230
  "Hoist her over the altar
like a yearling, give it all your strength!
She's fainting—lift her,
 sweep her robes around her,
but slip this strap in her gentle curving lips . . .   235
 here, gag her hard, a sound will curse the house"—

and the bridle chokes her voice . . . her saffron robes
pouring over the sand
     her glance like arrows showering
wounding every murderer through with pity
 clear as a picture, live,   240
she strains to call their names . . .
I remember often the days with father's guests
when over the feast her voice unbroken,
 pure as the hymn her loving father
bearing third libations,[7] sang to Saving Zeus—   245
transfixed with joy, Atreus' offspring
 throbbing out their love.

What comes next? I cannot see it, cannot say.
The strong techniques of Calchas do their work.[8]
But Justice turns the balance scales,   250
 sees that we suffer
and we suffer and we learn.
And we will know the future when it comes.
Greet it too early, weep too soon.
 It all comes clear in the light of day.   255
Let all go well today, well as she could want,
 [*Turning to* CLYTAEMNESTRA.]
our midnight watch, our lone defender,
 single-minded queen.

LEADER   We've come,
Clytaemnestra. We respect your power.
Right it is to honor the warlord's woman   260
once he leaves the throne.
      But why these fires?
Good news, or more good hopes? We're loyal,

---

7. Offerings of wine. At a banquet three libations were poured, the third and last to Zeus the saviour; the last libation was accompanied by a hymn of praise. 8. This seems to refer to the sacrifice of Iphigenia. Some scholars take the Greek words to refer to the fulfillment of Calchas's prophecies.

we want to hear, but never blame your silence.
CLYTAEMNESTRA   Let the new day shine, as the proverb says,
  glorious from the womb of Mother Night.   265
      [*Lost in prayer, then turning to the* CHORUS.]
  You will hear a joy beyond your hopes.
  Priam's citadel—the Greeks have taken Troy!
LEADER   No, what do you mean? I can't believe it.
CLYTAEMNESTRA   Troy is ours. Is that clear enough?
LEADER   The joy of it,
  stealing over me, calling up my tears—   270
CLYTAEMNESTRA   Yes, your eyes expose your loyal hearts.
LEADER   And you have proof?
CLYTAEMNESTRA   I do,
  I must. Unless the god is lying.
LEADER   That,
  or a phantom spirit sends you into raptures.
CLYTAEMNESTRA   No one takes me in with visions—senseless
    dreams.   275
LEADER   Or giddy rumor, you haven't indulged yourself—
CLYTAEMNESTRA   You treat me like a child, you mock me?
LEADER   Then when did they storm the city?
CLYTAEMNESTRA   Last night, I say, the mother of this morning.
LEADER   And who on earth could run the news so fast?   280
CLYTAEMNESTRA   The god of fire—rushing fire from Ida![9]
  And beacon to beacon rushed it on to me,
  my couriers riding home the torch.
                              From Troy
  to the bare rock of Lemnos, Hermes' Spur,[1]
  and the Escort winged the great light west   285
  to the Saving Father's face, Mount Athos[2] hurled it
  third in the chain and leaping Ocean's back
  the blaze went dancing on to ecstasy—pitch-pine
  streaming gold like a new-born sun—and brought
  the word in flame to Mount Makistos'[3] brow.   290
  No time to waste, straining, fighting sleep,
  that lookout heaved a torch glowing over
  the murderous straits of Euripos to reach
  Messapion's[4] watchmen craning for the signal.
  Fire for word of fire! tense with the heather   295
  withered gray, they stack it, set it ablaze—
  the hot force of the beacon never flags,
  it springs the Plain of Asôpos, rears
  like a harvest moon to hit Kithairon's[5] crest
  and drives new men to drive the fire on.   300
  That relay pants for the far-flung torch,

9. The mountain range near Troy. The names that follow in this speech designate the places where beacon fires flashed the message of Troy's fall to Argos. The chain began at Ida.   1. Hermes' cliff is on the island of Lemnos (off the coast of Asia Minor).   2. On a rocky peninsula in north Greece.   3. On the island of Euboea off the coast of central Greece.   4. A mountain on the mainland.   5. A mountain near Thebes.

they swell its strength outstripping my commands
and the light inflames the marsh, the Gorgon's Eye,[6]
it strikes the peak where the wild goats range[7]—
my laws, my fire whips that camp!   305
They spare nothing, eager to build its heat,
and a huge beard of flame overcomes the headland
beetling down the Saronic Gulf,[8] and flaring south
it brings the dawn to the Black Widow's[9] face—
the watch that looms above your heads—and now   310
the true son of the burning flanks of Ida
crashes on the roofs of Atreus' sons!

And I ordained it all.
Torch to torch, running for their lives,
one long succession racing home my fire.
                            One,   315
first in the laps and last,[1] wins out in triumph.
There you have my proof, *my* burning sign, I tell you—
the power my lord passed on from Troy to me![2]
LEADER   We'll thank the gods, my lady—first this story,
let me lose myself in the wonder of it all!   320
Tell it start to finish, tell us all.
CLYTAEMNESTRA   The city's ours—in our hands this very day!
I can hear the cries in crossfire rock the walls.
Pour oil and wine in the same bowl,
what have you, friendship? A struggle to the end.   325
So with the victors and the victims—outcries,
you can hear them clashing like their fates.

They are kneeling by the bodies of the dead,
embracing men and brothers, infants over
the aged loins that gave them life, and sobbing,   330
as the yoke constricts their last free breath,
for every dear one lost.
                      And the others,
there, plunging breakneck through the night—
the labor of battle sets them down, ravenous;
to breakfast on the last remains of Troy.   335

6. Lake Gorgopis.   7. Mount Aegiplanctus on the Isthmus of Corinth.   8. The sea.   9. Mount Arachnaeus ("spider") in Argive territory. This is the fire seen by the watchman at the beginning of the play.   1. The chain of beacons is compared to a relay race in which the runners carry torches; the last runner (who runs the final lap) comes in first to win.   2. This speech has often been criticized as discursive, but it has great poetic importance. The image of the light that will dispel the darkness, first introduced by the watchman, is one of the dominant images of the trilogy and is here developed with magnificent ambiguous effect. For the watchman the light means the safe return of Agamemnon and the restoration of order in the house; for Clytaemnestra it means the return of Agamemnon to his death at her hands. Each swift jump of the racing light is one step nearer home and death for Agamemnon. The light the watchman longs for brings only greater darkness, but eventually it brings darkness for Clytaemnestra too. The final emergence of the true light comes in the glare of the torchlight procession that ends the last play of the trilogy, a procession that symbolizes perfect reconciliation on both the human and the divine levels and the working out of the will of Zeus in the substitution of justice for vengeance. The conception of the beacons as a chain of descendants (compare line 311) is also important; the fire at Argos that announces Agamemnon's imminent death is a direct descendant of the fire on Ida that announces the sack of Troy and Agamemnon's sacrilegious conduct there. The metaphor thus reminds us of the sequence of crimes from generation to generation that is the history of the house of Pelops.

Not by rank but the lots of chance they draw,
they lodge in the houses captured by the spear,
settling in so soon, released from the open sky,
the frost and dew. Lucky men, off guard at last,
they sleep away their first good night in years.   340

If only they are revering the city's gods,
the shrines of the gods who love the conquered land,
no plunderer will be plundered in return.
Just let no lust, no mad desire seize the armies[3]
to ravish what they must not touch—   345
overwhelmed by all they've won!
                   The run for home
and safety waits, the swerve at the post,[4]
the final lap of the gruelling two-lap race.
And even if the men come back with no offense
to the gods, the avenging dead may never rest—   350
Oh let no new disaster strike! And here
you have it, what a woman has to say.
Let the best win out, clear to see.
A small desire but all that I could want.
LEADER   Spoken like a man, my lady, loyal,   355
full of self-command. I've heard your sign
and now your vision.
     [*Reaching towards her as she turns and re-enters the palace.*]
              Now to praise the gods.
The joy is worth the labor.
CHORUS   O Zeus my king and Night, dear Night,[5]
queen of the house who covers us with glories,[6]   360
you slung your net on the towers of Troy,
neither young nor strong could leap
the giant dredge net of slavery,
    all-embracing ruin.
I adore you, iron Zeus of the guests   365
and your revenge—you drew your longbow
year by year to a taut full draw
till one bolt, not falling short
or arching over the stars,
    could split the mark of Paris!   370

The sky stroke of god!—it is all Troy's to tell,
but even I can trace it to its cause:
god does as god decrees.
    And still some say
that heaven would never stoop to punish men   375
who trample the lovely grace of things

---

3. She, of course, hopes for the opposite of what she prays for here. The audience was familiar with the
traditional account, according to which Agamemnon and his army failed signally to respect the gods and
temples of Troy.   **4.** Greek runners turned at a post and came back on a parallel track.   **5.** Troy fell
to a night attack.   **6.** Probably the moon and stars; an obscure expression in the original.

untouchable. How wrong they are!
  A curse burns bright on crime—
    full-blown, the father's crimes will blossom,
      burst into the son's.[7]   380
Let there be less suffering . . .
give us the sense to live on what we need.

          Bastions of wealth
          are no defense for the man
          who treads the grand altar of Justice   385
            down and out of sight.

Persuasion, maddening child of Ruin
overpowers him—Ruin plans it all.
And the wound will smolder on,
    there is no cure,   390
a terrible brilliance kindles on the night.
He is bad bronze scraped on a touchstone:
put to the test, the man goes black.[8]
  Like the boy who chases
    a bird on the wing, brands his city,   395
      brings it down and prays,
but the gods are deaf
to the one who turns to crime, they tear him down.

          So Paris learned:
          he came to Atreus' house   400
          and shamed the tables spread for guests,
            he stole away the queen.

And she left her land *chaos,* clanging shields,
companions tramping, bronze prows, men in bronze,
    and she came to Troy with a dowry, death,   405
strode through the gates
    defiant in every stride,
as prophets of the house[9] looked on and wept,
"Oh the halls and the lords of war,
    the bed and the fresh prints of love.   410
I *see* him, unavenging, unavenged,
the stun of his desolation is so clear—
  he longs for the one who lies across the sea
until her phantom seems to sway the house.

          Her curving images,   415
          her beauty hurts her lord,

---

7. The language throughout this passage is significantly general. The chorus refers to Paris, but everything it says is equally applicable to Agamemnon, who sacrificed his daughter for his ambitions. The original Greek is corrupt (that is, has been garbled in the handwritten tradition) but seems to proclaim the doctrine that the sins of the fathers are visited on the children. So Paris (and Agamemnon) pay for the misdeeds of their ancestors (as well as their own).   8. Inferior bronze, adulterated with lead, turns black with use.   9. Menelaus's.

the eyes starve and the touch
　　of love is gone,

and radiant dreams are passing in the night,
the memories throb with sorrow, joy with pain . . .　　　　420
　　it is pain to dream and see desires
slip through the arms,
　　　a vision lost forever
winging down the moving drifts of sleep."
So he grieves at the royal hearth　　　　425
　　yet others' grief is worse, far worse.
All through Greece for those who flocked to war
they are holding back the anguish now,
　　you can feel it rising now in every house;
I tell you there is much to tear the heart.　　　　430

　　　　They knew the men they sent,
　　　　but now in place of men
　　　　ashes and urns come back
　　　　to every hearth.[1]

War, War, the great gold-broker of corpses　　　　435
holds the balance of the battle on his spear!
Home from the pyres he sends them,
　　home from Troy to the loved ones,
weighted with tears, the urns brimmed full,
　　the heroes return in gold-dust,[2]　　　　440
dear, light ash for men; and they weep,
they praise them, "He had skill in the swordplay,"
　　　"He went down so tall in the onslaught,"
"All for another's woman." So they mutter
in secret and the rancor steals　　　　445
toward our staunch defenders, Atreus' sons.

　　　　And there they ring the walls, the young,
　　　　the lithe, the handsome hold the graves
　　　　they won in Troy; the enemy earth
　　　　rides over those who conquered.　　　　450

The people's voice is heavy with hatred,
now the curses of the people must be paid,
and now I wait, I listen . . .
　　there—there is something breathing
under the night's shroud. God takes aim　　　　455
　　at the ones who murder many;
the swarthy Furies stalk the man
gone rich beyond all rights—with a twist

1. This strikes a contemporary note. In Homer the fallen Achaeans are buried at Troy, but in Aeschylus's Athens the dead were cremated on the battlefield, and their ashes were brought home for burial.　2. I.e., in ashes. The war god is a broker who gives, in exchange for bodies, gold dust (the word used for "bodies" could mean living bodies or corpses).

of fortune grind him down, dissolve him
into the blurring dead—there is no help.   460
The reach for power can recoil,
the bolt of god can strike you at a glance.

        Make me rich with no man's envy,
        neither a raider of cities, no,
        nor slave come face to face with life   465
        overpowered by another.

    [*Speaking singly.*]
—Fire comes and the news is good,
    it races through the streets
but is it true? Who knows?
Or just another lie from heaven?[3]   470

—Show us the man so childish, wonderstruck,
    he's fired up with the first torch,
then when the message shifts
he's sick at heart.

        —Just like a woman
to fill with thanks before the truth is clear.   475

—So gullible. Their stories spread like wildfire,
    they fly fast and die faster;
rumors voiced by women come to nothing.
LEADER   Soon we'll know her fires for what they are,
her relay race of torches hand-to-hand—   480
know if they're real or just a dream,
the hope of a morning here to take our senses.
I see a herald running from the beach
and a victor's spray of olive shades his eyes
and the dust he kicks, twin to the mud of Troy,   485
shows he has a voice—no kindling timber
on the cliffs, no signal-fires for him.
He can shout the news and give us joy,
or else . . . please, not that.
               Bring it on,
good fuel to build the first good fires.   490
And if anyone calls down the worst on Argos
let him reap the rotten harvest of his mind.
    [*The* HERALD *rushes in and kneels on the ground.*]
HERALD   Good Greek earth, the soil of my fathers!
Ten years out, and a morning brings me back.
All hopes snapped but one—I'm home at last.   495

---

3. Later we will see Agamemnon come on stage with Cassandra (his Trojan captive) and the spoils of Troy.
The chorus, which started out to sing a hymn of praise for the fall of Troy (line 359), ends in fear and
despondency. It now questions the truth of Clytaemnestra's announcement; perhaps Troy has not fallen
after all (line 469).

Never dreamed I'd die in Greece, assigned
the narrow plot I love the best.
                              And now
I salute the land, the light of the sun,
our high lord Zeus and the king of Pytho[4]—
no more arrows, master, raining on our heads!   500
At Scamander's banks we took our share,
your longbow brought us down like plague.[5]
Now come, deliver us, heal us—lord Apollo!
Gods of the market, here, take my salute.
And you, my Hermes,[6] Escort,   505
loving Herald, the herald's shield and prayer!—
And the shining dead[7] of the land who launched the armies,
warm us home . . . we're all the spear has left.

You halls of the kings, you roofs I cherish,
sacred seats—you gods that catch the sun,   510
if your glances ever shone on him in the old days,
greet him well—so many years are lost.
He comes, he brings us light in the darkness,
free for every comrade, Agamemnon lord of men.

Give him the royal welcome he deserves!   515
He hoisted the pickax of Zeus who brings revenge,
he dug Troy down, he worked her soil down,
the shrines of her gods and the high altars, gone!—
and the seed of her wide earth he ground to bits.
That's the yoke he claps on Troy. The king,   520
the son of Atreus comes. The man is blest,
the one man alive to merit such rewards.

Neither Paris nor Troy, partners to the end,
can say their work outweighs their wages now.
Convicted of rapine, stripped of all his spoils,   525
and his father's house and the land that gave it life—
he's scythed them to the roots. The sons of Priam
pay the price twice over.
LEADER   Welcome home
from the wars, herald, long live your joy.
HERALD   *Our* joy—
now I could die gladly. Say the word, dear gods.   530
LEADER   Longing for your country left you raw?
HERALD   The tears fill my eyes, for joy.
LEADER   You too,
down the sweet disease that kills a man
with kindness . . .
HERALD   Go on, I don't see what you—
LEADER   Love

4. Apollo.   5. Compare the opening scene of the *Iliad* 1 (p. 105), where Apollo punishes the Greeks
with his arrows (a metaphor for plague).   6. The gods' messenger and patron deity of heralds.   7. The
heroes of the past, who are buried in Argos and worshiped.

for the ones who love you—that's what took you.
HERALD   You mean   535
the land and the armies hungered for each other?
LEADER   There were times I thought I'd faint with longing.
HERALD   So anxious for the armies, why?
LEADER   For years now,
only my silence kept me free from harm.
HERALD   What,
with the kings gone did someone threaten you?
LEADER   So much . . . [8]   540
now as you say, it would be good to die.
HERALD   True, we *have* done well.
Think back in the years and what have you?
A few runs of luck, a lot that's bad.
Who but a god can go through life unmarked?   545

A long, hard pull we had, if I would tell it all.
The iron rations, penned in the gangways
hock by jowl like sheep. Whatever miseries
break a man, our quota, every sunstarved day.

Then on the beaches it was worse. Dug in   550
under the enemy ramparts—deadly going.
Out of the sky, out of the marshy flats
the dews soaked us, turned the ruts we fought from
into gullies, made our gear, our scalps
crawl with lice.
                        And talk of the cold,   555
the sleet to freeze the gulls, and the big snows
come avalanching down from Ida. Oh but the heat,
the sea and the windless noons, the swells asleep,
dropped to a dead calm . . .

But why weep now?   560
It's over for us, over for them.
The dead can rest and never rise again;
no need to call their muster. We're alive,
do we have to go on raking up old wounds?
Good-by to all that. Glad I am to say it.   565

For us, the remains of the Greek contingents,
the good wins out, no pain can tip the scales,
not now. So shout this boast to the bright sun—
fitting it is—wing it over the seas and rolling earth:

"Once when an Argive expedition captured Troy   570
they hauled these spoils back to the gods of Greece,

8. Throughout this dialogue the chorus has been gearing itself up to warn the herald that there may be
danger for Agamemnon at home; at this point its nerve fails, and it abandons the attempt.

they bolted them high across the temple doors,
the glory of the past!"
                 And hearing that,
men will applaud our city and our chiefs,
and Zeus will have the hero's share of fame—   575
he did the work.
             That's all I have to say.
LEADER   I'm convinced, glad that I was wrong.
   Never too old to learn; it keeps me young.
      [CLYTAEMNESTRA *enters with her women.*]
   First the house and the queen, it's their affair,
   but I can taste the riches.
CLYTAEMNESTRA   I cried out long ago![9]—   580
for joy, when the first herald came burning
through the night and told the city's fall.
And there were some who smiled and said,
"A few fires persuade you Troy's in ashes.
Women, women, elated over nothing."   585

You made me seem deranged.
For all that I sacrificed—a woman's way,
you'll say—station to station on the walls
we lifted cries of triumph that resounded
in the temples of the gods. We lulled and blessed   590
the fires with myrrh and they consumed our victims.
      [*Turning to the* HERALD.]
But enough. Why prolong the story?
From the king himself I'll gather all I need.
Now for the best way to welcome home
my lord, my good lord . . .
                No time to lose!   595
What dawn can feast a woman's eyes like this?
I can see the light, the husband plucked from war
by the Saving God and open wide the gates.

Tell him that, and have him come with speed,
the people's darling—how they long for him.   600
And for his wife,
may he return and find her true at hall,
just as the day he left her, faithful to the last.
A watchdog gentle to him alone,
      [*Glancing towards the palace.*]
                  savage
to those who cross his path. I have not changed.   605
The strains of time can never break our seal.
In love with a new lord, in ill repute I am
as practiced as I am in dyeing bronze.[1]

---

9. As the watchman had told her to (line 30).   1. She claims she is no more capable of adultery than
she is of dyeing bronze; but she will later kill Agamemnon with a bronze weapon.

That is my boast, teeming with the truth.
I am proud, a woman of my nobility—   610
I'd hurl it from the roofs!
    [*She turns sharply, enters the palace.*]
LEADER   She speaks well, but it takes no seer to know
she only says what's right.
    [*The* HERALD *attempts to leave; the* LEADER *takes him by the arm.*]
                   Wait, one thing.
Menelaus, is he home too, safe with the men?[2]
The power of the land—dear king.   615
HERALD   I doubt that lies will help my friends,
in the lean months to come.
LEADER   Help us somehow, tell the truth as well.
But when the two conflict it's hard to hide—
out with it.
HERALD   He's lost, gone from the fleets![3]   620
He and his ship, it's true.
LEADER   After you watched him
pull away from Troy? Or did some storm
attack you all and tear him off the line?
HERALD   There,
like a marksman, the whole disaster cut to a word.
LEADER   How do the escorts give him out—dead or alive?   625
HERALD   No clear report. No one knows . . .
only the wheeling sun that heats the earth to life.
LEADER   But then the storm—how did it reach the ships?
How did it end? Were the angry gods on hand?
HERALD   This blessed day, ruin it with *them*?   630
Better to keep their trophies far apart.

When a runner comes, his face in tears,
saddled with what his city dreaded most,[4]
the armies routed, two wounds in one,
one to the city, one to hearth and home . . .   635
our best men, droves of them, victims
herded from every house by the two-barb whip
that Ares[5] likes to crack,
                  that charioteer
who packs destruction shaft by shaft,
careening on with his brace of bloody mares—   640
When he comes in, I tell you, dragging that much pain,
wail your battle-hymn to the Furies, and high time!

But when he brings salvation home to a city
singing out her heart—

2. The relevance of this question and the following speeches lies in the fact that Menelaus's absence makes Agamemnon's murder easier (his presence might have made it impossible) and in the fact that Menelaus is bringing Helen home.   3. For what happened to Menelaus see the *Odyssey* 4 (pp. 250ff.).   4. The herald creates a vivid picture of a messenger bringing news of disaster to his city—a role he wishes to avoid.   5. The war god.

how can I mix the good with so much bad   645
and blurt out this?—
                    "Storms swept the Greeks,
and not without the anger of the gods!"

Those enemies for ages, fire[6] and water,
sealed a pact and showed it to the world—
they crushed our wretched squadrons.
                                    Night looming,   650
breakers lunging in for the kill
and the black gales come brawling out of the north—
ships ramming, prow into hooking prow, gored
by the rush-and-buck of hurricane pounding rain
by the cloudburst—
                    ships stampeding into the darkness,   655
lashed and spun by the savage shepherd's hand![7]

But when the sun comes up to light the skies
I see the Aegean heaving into a great bloom
of corpses . . . Greeks, the pick of a generation
scattered through the wrecks and broken spars.   660

But not us, not our ship, our hull untouched.
Someone stole us away or begged us off.
No mortal—a god, death grip on the tiller,
or lady luck herself, perched on the helm,
she pulled us through, she saved us. Aye,   665
we'll never battle the heavy surf at anchor,
never shipwreck up some rocky coast.

But once we cleared that sea-hell, not even
trusting luck in the cold light of day,
we battened on our troubles, they were fresh—   670
the armada punished, bludgeoned into nothing.

And now if one of them still has the breath
he's saying *we* are lost. Why not?
We say the same of him. Well,
here's to the best.
                    And Menelaus?   675
Look to it, he's come back, and yet . . .
if a shaft of the sun can track him down,
alive, and his eyes full of the old fire—
thanks to the strategies of Zeus, Zeus
would never tear the house out by the roots—   680
then there's hope our man will make it home.

You've heard it all. Now you have the truth.
        [*Rushing out.*]

---

6. Lightning.   7. The ships were scattered like sheep dispersed by a cruel shepherd.

CHORUS Who—what power named the name[8] that drove your fate?—
what hidden brain could divine your future,
steer that word to the mark,   685
to the bride of spears,
    the whirlpool churning armies,
        Oh for all the world a Helen!
Hell at the prows, hell at the gates
hell on the men-of-war,   690
from her lair's sheer veils she drifted
    launched by the giant western wind,
        and the long tall waves of men in armor,
huntsmen[9] trailing the oar-blades' dying spoor
slipped into her moorings,   695
    Simois'[1] mouth that chokes with foliage,
        bayed for bloody strife,

for Troy's Blood Wedding Day—she drives her word,
her burning will to the birth, the Fury
late but true to the cause,   700
to the tables shamed
    and Zeus who guards the hearth[2]—
        the Fury makes the Trojans pay!
Shouting their hymns, hymns for the bride
hymns for the kinsmen doomed   705
to the wedding march of Fate.
    Troy changed her tune in her late age,
        and I think I hear the dirges mourning
"Paris, born and groomed for the bed of Fate!"
They mourn with their life breath,   710
    they sing their last, the sons of Priam
        born for bloody slaughter.

    So a man once reared
a lion cub at hall, snatched
from the breast, still craving milk   715
    in the first flush of life.
A captivating pet for the young,
and the old men adored it, pampered it
    in their arms, day in, day out,
like an infant just born.   720
Its eyes on fire, little beggar,
fawning for its belly, slave to food.

    But it came of age
and the parent strain broke out
and it paid its breeders back.   725

8. Helen. The name contains the Greek root *hele*, which means "destroy." The chorus is so obsessed with Helen's guilt that it fails to recognize the true responsibility for the war and the imminence of disaster. 9. The Achaean army, which came after her. 1. A river in Troy. 2. I.e., protects the host and guest.

Grateful it was, it went
through the flock to prepare a feast,
an illicit orgy—the house swam with blood,
   none could resist that agony—
      massacre vast and raw!   730
From god there came a priest of ruin,
adopted by the house to lend it warmth.

And the first sensation Helen brought to Troy . . .
call it a spirit
   shimmer of winds dying   735
      glory light as gold
   shaft of the eyes dissolving, open bloom
that wounds the heart with love.
But veering wild in mid-flight
she whirled her wedding on to a stabbing end,   740
slashed at the sons of Priam—hearthmate, friend to the death,
   sped by Zeus who speeds the guest,
a bride of tears, a Fury.

There's an ancient saying, old as man himself:
men's prosperity   745
   never will die childless,
      once full-grown it breeds.
   Sprung from the great good fortune in the race
  comes bloom on bloom of pain—
insatiable wealth. But not I,   750
I alone say this. Only the reckless act
can breed impiety, multiplying crime on crime,
   while the house kept straight and just
is blessed with radiant children.[3]

       But ancient Violence longs to breed,   755
         new Violence comes
     when its fatal hour comes, the demon comes
    to take her toll—no war, no force, no prayer
     can hinder the midnight Fury stamped
    with parent Fury moving through the house.   760

       But Justice shines in sooty hovels,[4]
        loves the decent life.
   From proud halls crusted with gilt by filthy hands
    she turns her eyes to find the pure in spirit—
spurning the wealth stamped counterfeit with praise,   765
   she steers all things toward their destined end.[5]

3. These lines begin with the traditional Greek view that immoderate good fortune (or excellence of any kind beyond the average) is itself the cause of disaster. The chorus, however, rejects this view and states that only an act of evil produces evil consequences. 4. The homes of the poor. 5. Here the chorus admits, by implication, that the poor are less likely to commit evil acts.

[AGAMEMNON *enters in his chariot, his plunder borne before him by his entourage; behind him, half hidden, stands* CASSANDRA. *The old men press toward him.*]

Come, my king, the scourge of Troy,
   the true son of Atreus—
How to salute you, how to praise you
neither too high nor low, but hit   770
the note of praise that suits the hour?
So many prize some brave display,
they prefer some flaunt of honor
   once they break the bounds.
When a man fails they share his grief,   775
but the pain can never cut them to the quick.
When a man succeeds they share his glory,
torturing their faces into smiles.
But the good shepherd knows his flock.
When the eyes seem to brim with love   780
   and it is only unction,
he will know, better than we can know.
That day you marshaled the armies
all for Helen—no hiding it now—
I drew you in my mind in black;   785
you seemed a menace at the helm,
   sending men to the grave
to bring her home, that hell on earth.
But now from the depths of trust and love
I say Well fought, well won—   790
   the end is worth the labor!
Search, my king, and learn at last
who stayed at home and kept their faith
   and who betrayed the city.[6]

AGAMEMNON   First,
with justice I salute my Argos and my gods,   795
my accomplices who brought me home and won
my rights from Priam's Troy—the just gods.
No need to hear our pleas. Once for all
they consigned their lots to the urn of blood,[7]
they pitched on death for men, annihilation   800
for the city. Hope's hand, hovering
over the urn of mercy, left it empty.
Look for the smoke—it is the city's seamark,
building even now.
              The storms of ruin live!
Her last dying breath, rising up from the ashes   805
sends us gales of incense rich in gold.

---

6. The chorus tries to warn Agamemnon against flatterers and dissemblers, but he misses its drift.   7. In an Athenian law court there were two urns—one for acquittal, one for condemnation—into which the jurors dropped their pebbles. (The audience will see them on stage in the final play of the trilogy.)

For that we must thank the gods with a sacrifice
our sons will long remember. For their mad outrage
of a queen we raped their city—we were right.
The beast of Argos, foals of the wild mare,[8]   810
thousands massed in armor rose on the night
the Pleiades went down,[9] and crashing through
their walls our bloody lion lapped its fill,
gorging on the blood of kings.

                        Our thanks to the gods,
long drawn out, but it is just the prelude.   815
      [CLYTAEMNESTRA *approaches with her women; they are carrying*
        dark red tapestries. AGAMEMNON *turns to the* LEADER.]
And your concern, old man, is on my mind.
I hear you and agree, I will support you.
How rare, men with the character to praise
a friend's success without a trace of envy,
poison to the heart—it deals a double blow.   820
Your own losses weigh you down but then,
look at your neighbor's fortune and you weep.
Well I know. I understand society,
the fawning mirror of the proud.

                       My comrades . . .
they're shadows, I tell you, ghosts of men   825
who swore they'd die for me. Only Odysseus:
I dragged that man to the wars[1] but once in harness
he was a trace-horse, he gave his all for me.
Dead or alive, no matter, I can praise him.

And now this cause involving men and gods.   830
We must summon the city for a trial,
found a national tribunal. Whatever's healthy,
shore it up with law and help it flourish.
Wherever something calls for drastic cures
we make our noblest effort: amputate or wield   835
the healing iron, burn the cancer at the roots.

Now I go to my father's house—
I give the gods my right hand, my first salute.
The ones who sent me forth have brought me home.
      [*He starts down from the chariot, looks at* CLYTAEMNESTRA, *stops,*
        and offers up a prayer.]
Victory, you have sped my way before,   840
now speed me to the last.
      [CLYTAEMNESTRA *turns from the king to the* CHORUS.]
CLYTAEMNESTRA   Old nobility of Argos
gathered here, I am not ashamed to tell you

---

8. The wooden horse, the stratagem with which the Greeks captured the city.   9. The setting of the constellation Pleiades, late in the fall.   1. Feigning madness to escape going to Troy, Odysseus was tricked into demonstrating his sanity. Agamemnon's remark shows that the truth is far from his mind; he has no thought that his danger comes from a woman.

how I love the man. I am older,
and the fear dies away . . . I am human.
Nothing I say was learned from others.   845
This is my life, my ordeal, long as the siege
he laid at Troy and more demanding.
                              First,
when a woman sits at home and the man is gone,
the loneliness is terrible,
unconscionable . . .   850
and the rumors spread and fester,
a runner comes with something dreadful,
close on his heels the next and his news worse,
and they shout it out and the whole house can hear;
and wounds—if he took one wound for each report   855
to penetrate these walls, he's gashed like a dragnet,
more, if he had only died . . .
for each death that swelled his record, he could boast
like a triple-bodied Geryon[2] risen from the grave,
"Three shrouds I dug from the earth, one for every body   860
that went down!"
                    The rumors broke like fever,
broke and then rose higher. There were times
they cut me down and eased my throat from the noose.
I wavered between the living and the dead.
          [*Turning to* AGAMEMNON.]
                                        And so
our child is gone, not standing by our side,   865
the bond of our dearest pledges, mine and yours;
by all rights our child should be here . . .
Orestes. You seem startled.
You needn't be. Our loyal brother-in-arms
will take good care of him, Strophios[3] the Phocian.   870
He warned from the start we court two griefs in one.
You risk all on the wars—and what if the people
rise up howling for the king, and anarchy
should dash our plans?
                    Men, it is their nature,
trampling on the fighter once he's down.   875
Our child is gone. That is my self-defense
and it is true.
                    For me, the tears that welled
like springs are dry. I have no tears to spare.
I'd watch till late at night, my eyes still burn,
I sobbed by the torch I lit for you alone.   880
          [*Glancing towards the palace.*]
I never let it die . . . but in my dreams
the high thin wail of a gnat would rouse me,

---

2. A monster (eventually killed by Heracles) who had three bodies and three heads.   3. King of Phocis,
a mountainous region near Delphi. His son, Pylades, accompanies Orestes when he returns to avenge
Agamemnon's death.

piercing like a trumpet—I could see you
suffer more than all
the hours that slept with me could ever bear.   885

I endured it all. And now, free of grief,
I would salute that man the watchdog of the fold,
the mainroyal,[4] saving stay of the vessel,
rooted oak that thrusts the roof sky-high,
the father's one true heir.   890
Land at dawn to the shipwrecked past all hope,
light of the morning burning off the night of storm,
the cold clear spring to the parched horseman—
O the ecstasy, to flee the yoke of Fate!

It is right to use the titles he deserves.   895
Let envy keep her distance. We have suffered
long enough.
          [Reaching toward AGAMEMNON.]
                    Come to me now, my dearest,
down from the car of war, but never set the foot
that stamped out Troy on earth again, my great one.

Women, why delay? You have your orders.   900
Pave his way with tapestries.[5]
          [They begin to spread the crimson tapestries between the king and
          the palace doors.]
                              Quickly.
Let the red stream flow and bear him home
to the home he never hoped to see—Justice,
lead him in!
               Leave all the rest to me.
The spirit within me never yields to sleep.   905
We will set things right, with the god's help.
We will do whatever Fate requires.
AGAMEMNON   There
is Leda's daughter,[6] the keeper of my house.
And the speech to suit my absence, much too long.
But the praise that does us justice,   910
let it come from others, then we prize it.
                              This—
You treat me like a woman. Groveling, gaping up at me!
What am I, some barbarian[7] peacocking out of Asia?
Never cross my path with robes and draw the lightning.
Never—only the gods deserve the pomps of honor   915
and the stiff brocades of fame. To walk on them . . .

4. Upper section of the mainmast.   5. To walk on those tapestries, wall hangings dyed with the expensive
crimson, would be an act of extravagant pride. Pride is the keynote of Agamemnon's character, and it suits
Clytaemnestra's sense of fitness that he should go into his death in godlike state, *trampling royal crimson*
(line 957), the color of blood.   6. Clytaemnestra. Helen is also a daughter of Leda.   7. Foreigner,
especially Asiatic. Aeschylus is thinking of the pomp and servility of the contemporary Persian court.

I am human, and it makes my pulses stir
with dread.
        Give me the tributes of a man
and not a god, a little earth to walk on,
not this gorgeous work.   920
There is no need to sound my reputation.
I have a sense of right and wrong, what's more—
heaven's proudest gift. Call no man blest
until he ends his life in peace, fulfilled.
If I can live by what I say, I have no fear.   925
CLYTAEMNESTRA   One thing more. Be true to your ideals and tell me—
AGAMEMNON   True to my ideals? Once I violate them I am lost.
CLYTAEMNESTRA   Would you have sworn this act to god in a time of terror?
AGAMEMNON   Yes, if a prophet called for a last, drastic rite.
CLYTAEMNESTRA   But Priam—can you see him if he had your
    success?   930
AGAMEMNON   Striding on the tapestries of God, I see him now.
CLYTAEMNESTRA   And *you* fear the reproach of common men?
AGAMEMNON   The voice of the people—aye, they have enormous power.
CLYTAEMNESTRA   Perhaps, but where's the glory without a little gall?
AGAMEMNON   And where's the woman in all this lust for glory?   935
CLYTAEMNESTRA   But the great victor—it becomes him to give way.
AGAMEMNON   Victory in this . . . war of ours, it means so much to you?
CLYTAEMNESTRA   O give way! The power is yours if you surrender
    all of your own free will to me.
AGAMEMNON   Enough.
If you are so determined—   940
    [*Turning to the women, pointing to his boots.*]
Let someone help me off with these at least.
Old slaves, they've stood me well.
                          Hurry,
and while I tread his splendors dyed red in the sea,[8]
may no god watch and strike me down with envy
from on high. I feel such shame—   945
to tread the life of the house, a kingdom's worth
of silver in the weaving.
    [*He steps down from the chariot to the tapestries and reveals* CAS-
    SANDRA, *dressed in the sacred regalia, the fillets, robes and scepter
    of Apollo.*]
                     Done is done.
Escort this stranger[9] in, be gentle.
Conquer with compassion. Then the gods
shine down upon you, gently. No one chooses   950
the yoke of slavery, not of one's free will—
and she least of all. The gift of the armies,

---

8. The dye was made from shellfish.   9. Cassandra, daughter of Priam, Agamemnon's share of the
human booty of the sack of Troy. She was loved by Apollo, who gave her the gift of prophecy, but when
she refused her love to the god, he saw to it that her prophecies, though true, would never be believed until
it was too late.

flower and pride of all the wealth we won,
she follows me from Troy.
              And now,
since you have brought me down with your insistence,   955
just this once I enter my father's house,
trampling royal crimson as I go.
      [*He takes his first steps and pauses.*]
CLYTAEMNESTRA   There is the sea
and who will drain it dry? Precious as silver,
inexhaustible, ever-new, it breeds the more we reap it—
tides on tides of crimson dye our robes blood-red.   960
Our lives are based on wealth, my king,
the gods have seen to that.
Destitution, our house has never heard the word.
I would have sworn to tread on legacies of robes,
at one command from an oracle, deplete the house—   965
suffer the worst to bring that dear life back!
      [*Encouraged*, AGAMEMNON *strides to the entrance.*]
When the root lives on, the new leaves come back,
spreading a dense shroud of shade across the house
to thwart the Dog Star's[1] fury. So you return
to the father's hearth, you bring us warmth in winter   970
like the sun—
           And you are Zeus when Zeus
tramples the bitter virgin grape for new wine
and the welcome chill steals through the halls, at last
the master moves among the shadows of his house, fulfilled.
      [AGAMEMNON *goes over the threshold; the women gather up the*
      tapestries while CLYTAEMNESTRA *prays.*]
Zeus, Zeus, master of all fullfillment, now fulfill our prayers—   975
speed our rites to their fulfillment once for all!
      [*She enters the palace, the doors close, the old men huddle in terror.*]
CHORUS   Why, why does it rock me, never stops,
this terror beating down my heart,
   this seer that sees it all—
it beats its wings, uncalled unpaid   980
thrust on the lungs
the mercenary song beats on and on
singing a prophet's strain—
   and I can't throw it off
like dreams that make no sense,   985
and the strength drains
that filled the mind with trust,
and the years drift by and the driven sand
      has buried the mooring lines
that churned when the armored squadrons cut for Troy . . .   990

1. Sirius; its appearance in the summer sky marked the beginning of the hot season (the "dog days" of summer).

and now I believe it, I can prove he's home,
    my own clear eyes for witness—
                          Agamemnon!
Still it's chanting, beating deep so deep in the heart
this dirge of the Furies, oh dear god,
not fit for the lyre,[2] its own master   995
    it kills our spirit
kills our hopes
and it's real, true, no fantasy—
        stark terror whirls the brain
        and the end is coming   1000
              Justice comes to birth—
I pray my fears prove false and fall
and die and never come to birth!
Even exultant health, well we know,
    exceeds its limits,[3] comes so near disease   1005
it can breach the wall between them.

Even a man's fate, held true on course,
    in a blinding flash rams some hidden reef;
but if caution only casts the pick of the cargo—
one well-balanced cast—   1010
the house will not go down, not outright;[4]
laboring under its wealth of grief
the ship of state rides on.

Yes, and the great green bounty of god,
sown in the furrows year by year and reaped each fall   1015
can end the plague of famine.

But a man's lifeblood
    is dark and mortal.
Once it wets the earth
what song can sing it back?   1020
Not even the master-healer[5]
    who brought the dead to life—
Zeus stopped the man before he did more harm.

Oh, if only the gods had never forged
the chain that curbs our excess,   1025
    one man's fate curbing the next man's fate,
my heart would outrace my song, I'd pour out all I feel—
        but no, I choke with anguish,
        mutter through the nights.
Never to ravel out a hope in time   1030

2. A stringed instrument played on joyful occasions (hence "lyric" poetry).   3. Excess, even in blessings
like health, is always dangerous. The chorus fears that Agamemnon's triumphant success may threaten his
safety.   4. These lines refer to a traditional Greek belief that the fortunate person could avert the envy
of heaven by deliberately getting rid of some precious possession.   5. Asclepius, the great physician who
was so skilled that he finally succeeded in restoring a dead man to life. Zeus struck him with a thunderbolt
for going too far.

and the brain is swarming, burning—
  [CLYTAEMNESTRA *emerges from the palace and goes to* CASSANDRA,
  impassive in the chariot.]
CLYTAEMNESTRA   Won't you come inside? I mean you, Cassandra.
Zeus in all his mercy wants you to share
some victory libations with the house.
The slaves are flocking. Come, lead them   1035
up to the altar of the god who guards
our dearest treasures.
                    Down from the chariot,
no time for pride. Why even Heracles,[6]
they say, was sold into bondage long ago,
he had to endure the bitter bread of slaves.   1040
But if the yoke descends on you, be grateful
for a master born and reared in ancient wealth.
Those who reap a harvest past their hopes
are merciless to their slaves.
                    From us
you will receive what custom says is right.   1045
  [CASSANDRA *remains impassive.*]
LEADER   It's *you* she is speaking to, it's all too clear.
You're caught in the nets of doom—obey
if you can obey, unless you cannot bear to.
CLYTAEMNESTRA   Unless she's like a swallow, possessed
of her own barbaric song,[7] strange, dark.   1050
I speak directly as I can—she must obey.
LEADER   Go with her. Make the best of it, she's right.
Step down from the seat, obey her.
CLYTAEMNESTRA   Do it *now*—
I have no time to spend outside. Already
the victims crowd the hearth, the Navelstone,[8]   1055
to bless this day of joy I never hoped to see!—
our victims waiting for the fire and the knife,
and you,
if you want to taste our mystic rites, come now.
If my words can't reach you—
  [*Turning to the* LEADER.]
                    Give her a sign,   1060
one of her exotic handsigns.
LEADER   I think
the stranger needs an interpreter, someone clear.
She's like a wild creature, fresh caught.
CLYTAEMNESTRA   She's mad,
her evil genius murmuring in her ears.
She comes from a *city* fresh caught.   1065
She must learn to take the cutting bridle

---

6. The Greek hero, famous for his twelve labors that rid the Earth of monsters, was at one time forced to
be the slave to Omphale, an Eastern queen.   7. The comparison of foreign speech to the twittering of a
swallow was a Greek commonplace.   8. An altar of Zeus Herkeios, guardian of the hearth, which was
the religious center of the home.

before she foams her spirit off in blood—
and that's the last I waste on her contempt!

[*Wheeling, re-entering the palace. The* LEADER *turns to* CASSANDRA, *who remains transfixed.*]

LEADER Not I, I pity her. I will be gentle.
Come, poor thing. Leave the empty chariot—   1070
Of your own free will try on the yoke of Fate.

CASSANDRA Aieeeeee! Earth—Mother—
Curse of the Earth—Apollo Apollo!

LEADER Why cry to Apollo?
He's not the god to call with sounds of mourning.

CASSANDRA Aieeeeee! Earth—Mother—   1075
Rape of the Earth—Apollo Apollo!

LEADER Again, it's a bad omen.
She cries for the god who wants no part of grief.[9]

[CASSANDRA *steps from the chariot, looks slowly towards the rooftops of the palace.*]

CASSANDRA God of the long road,
Apollo *Apollo* my destroyer—
you destroy me once,[1] destroy me twice—   1080

LEADER She's about to sense her own ordeal, I think.
Slave that she is, the god lives on inside her.

CASSANDRA God of the iron marches,
Apollo *Apollo* my destroyer—
where, where have you led[2] me now? what house—   1085

LEADER The house of Atreus and his sons. Really—
don't you know? It's true, see for yourself.

CASSANDRA No . . . the house that hates god,
an echoing womb of guilt, kinsmen
torturing kinsmen, severed heads,   1090
slaughterhouse of heroes, soil streaming blood—

LEADER A keen hound, this stranger.
Trailing murder, and murder she will find.

CASSANDRA See, my witnesses—
I trust to them, to the babies   1095
wailing, skewered on the sword,
their flesh charred, the father gorging on their parts[3]—

LEADER We'd heard your fame as a seer,
but no one looks for seers in Argos.

CASSANDRA Oh no, what horror, what new plot,[4]   1100
new agony this?—
it's growing, massing, deep in the house,
a plot, a monstrous—*thing*
to crush the loved ones, no,

9. Apollo (and the Olympian gods in general) was not invoked in mourning or lamentation.   1. The name *Apollo* suggests the Greek word *apollumi*, "destroy." He destroyed her the first time when he saw to it that no one would believe her prophecies. *God of the long road*: Apollo Agyieus. This statue, a conical pillar, was set up outside the door of the house; no doubt there was one onstage.   2. The Greek word (a form of the verb *ago*) suggests the god's title Agyieus.   3. The feast of Thyestes, who was tricked by his brother, Atreus, into eating his children. The story is told by Aegisthus below (lines 1606–43).   4. Clytaemnestra's murder of Agamemnon.

there is no cure, and rescue's far away[5] and— 1105
LEADER   I can't read these signs; I knew the first,
  the city rings with them.
CASSANDRA   You, you godforsaken—you'd do *this*?
  The lord of your bed,
  you bathe him . . . his body glistens, then— 1110
    how to tell the climax?—
      comes so quickly, see,
  hand over hand shoots out, hauling ropes—
                                then lunge!
LEADER   Still lost. Her riddles, her dark words of god—
  I'm groping, helpless.
CASSANDRA   No no, look *there*!— 1115
  what's that? some net flung out of hell—
    No, *she* is the snare,
  the bedmate, deathmate, murder's strong right arm!
      Let the insatiate discord in the race
  rear up and shriek "Avenge the victim—stone them dead!" 1120
LEADER   What Fury is this? Why rouse it, lift its wailing
  through the house? I hear you and lose hope.
CHORUS   Drop by drop at the heart, the gold of life ebbs out.
    We are the old soldiers . . . wounds will come
  with the crushing sunset of our lives. 1125
  Death is close, and quick.
CASSANDRA   Look out! *look out!*—
  Ai, drag the great bull from the mate!—
    a thrash of robes, she traps him—
  writhing—
      black horn glints, twists—
                  she gores him through!
      And now he buckles, look, the bath swirls red— 1130
  There's stealth and murder in the cauldron, do you hear?
LEADER   I'm no judge, I've little skill with the oracles,
  but even I know danger when I hear it.
CHORUS   What good are the oracles to men? Words, more words,
    and the hurt comes on us, endless words 1135
  and a seer's techniques have brought us
  terror and the truth.
CASSANDRA   The agony—O I am breaking!—Fate's so hard,
    and the pain that floods my voice is mine alone.
  Why have you brought me here, tormented as I am? 1140
  Why, unless to die with him, why else?
LEADER AND CHORUS   Mad with the rapture—god speeds you on
    to the song, the deathsong,
  like the nightingale[6] that broods on sorrow,

---

5. A reference to Menelaus (distant in space) and Orestes (distant in time).   **6.** Philomela was raped by Tereus, the husband of her sister Procne. The two sisters avenged themselves by killing Tereus's son, Itys, and serving up his flesh to Tereus to eat. Procne was changed into a nightingale mourning for Itys (the name is an imitation of the sound of the nightingale's song).

mourns her son, her son, 1145
her life inspired with grief for him,
she lilts and shrills, dark bird that lives for night.
CASSANDRA   The nightingale—O for a song, a fate like hers!
The gods gave her a life of ease, swathed her in wings,
no tears, no wailing. The knife waits for me. 1150
They'll splay me on the iron's double edge.
LEADER AND CHORUS   Why?—what god hurls you on, stroke on
stroke
to the long dying fall?
Why the horror clashing through your music,
terror struck to song?— 1155
why the anguish, the wild dance?
Where do your words of god and grief begin?
CASSANDRA   Ai, the wedding, wedding of Paris,
death to the loved ones. Oh Scamander,[7]
you nursed my father . . . once at your banks 1160
I nursed and grew, and now at the banks
of Acheron,[8] the stream that carries sorrow,
it seems I'll chant my prophecies too soon.
LEADER AND CHORUS   What are you saying? Wait, it's clear,
a child could see the truth, it wounds within, 1165
Like a bloody fang it tears—
I hear your destiny—breaking sobs,
cries that stab the ears.
CASSANDRA   Oh the grief, the grief of the city
ripped to oblivion. Oh the victims, 1170
the flocks my father burned at the wall,
rich herds in flames . . . no cure for the doom
that took the city after all, and I,
her last ember, I go down with her.
LEADER AND CHORUS   You cannot stop, your song goes on— 1175
some spirit drops from the heights and treads you down
and the brutal strain grows—
your death-throes come and come and
I cannot see the end!
CASSANDRA   Then off with the veils that hid the fresh young
bride[9]— 1180
we will see the truth.
Flare up once more, my oracle! Clear and sharp
as the wind that blows toward the rising sun,
I can feel a deeper swell now, gathering head
to break at last and bring the dawn of grief. 1185

No more riddles. I will teach you.
Come, bear witness, run and hunt with me.
We trail the old barbaric works of slaughter.

---

7. A Trojan river.   8. One of the rivers of the underworld.   9. At this point, as the meter indicates,
Cassandra changes from lyric song, the medium of emotion, to spoken iambic lines, the medium of rational
discourse.

These roofs—look up—there is a dancing troupe
that never leaves. And they have their harmony   1190
but it is harsh, their words are harsh, they drink
beyond the limit. Flushed on the blood of men
their spirit grows and none can turn away
their revel breeding in the veins—the Furies!
They cling to the house for life. They sing,   1195
sing of the frenzy that began it all,
strain rising on strain, showering curses
on the man who tramples on his brother's bed.[1]

There. Have I hit the mark or not? Am I a fraud,
a fortune-teller babbling lies from door to door?   1200
Swear how well I know the ancient crimes
that live within this house.

LEADER   And if I did?
Would an oath bind the wounds and heal us?
But you amaze me. Bred across the sea,
your language strange, and still you sense the truth   1205
as if you had been here.

CASSANDRA   Apollo the Prophet
introduced me to his gift.

LEADER   A *god*—and moved with love?

CASSANDRA   I was ashamed to tell this once,
but now . . .

LEADER   We spoil ourselves with scruples,   1210
long as things go well.

CASSANDRA   He came like a wrestler,
magnificent, took me down and breathed his fire
through me and—

LEADER   You bore him a child?

CASSANDRA   I yielded,
then at the climax I recoiled—I deceived Apollo!

LEADER   But the god's skills—they seized you even then?   1215

CASSANDRA   Even then I told my people all the grief to come.

LEADER   And Apollo's anger never touched you?—is it possible?

CASSANDRA   Once I betrayed him I could never be believed.

LEADER   We believe you. Your visions seem so true.

CASSANDRA   Aieeeee!—
the pain, the terror! the birth-pang of the seer   1220
who tells the truth—
                        it whirls me, oh,
the storm comes again, the crashing chords!
Look, you see them nestling at the threshold?
Young, young in the darkness like a dream,
like children really, yes, and their loved ones   1225
brought them down . . .
                        their hands, they fill their hands

---

1. Thyestes, who seduced the wife of his brother, Atreus.

with their own flesh, they are serving it like food,
holding out their entrails . . . now it's clear,
I can see the armfuls of compassion, see the father
reach to taste and—

                      For so much suffering,   1230
I tell you, someone plots revenge.
A lion[2] who lacks a lion's heart,
he sprawled at home in the royal lair
and set a trap for the lord on his return.
My lord . . . I must wear his yoke, I am his slave.   1235
The lord of the men-of-war, he obliterated Troy—
he is so blind, so lost to that detestable hellhound
who pricks her ears and fawns and her tongue draws out
her glittering words of welcome—

                                  No, he cannot see
the stroke that Fury's hiding, stealth, murder.   1240
What outrage—the woman kills the man!

                               What to call
that . . . monster of Greece, and bring my quarry down?
Viper coiling back and forth?

                         Some sea-witch?—
Scylla[3] crouched in her rocky nest—nightmare of sailors?
Raging mother of death, storming deathless war against   1245
the ones she loves!

                     And how she howled in triumph,
boundless outrage. Just as the tide of battle
broke her way, she seems to rejoice that he
is safe at home from war, saved for her.

Believe me if you will. What will it matter   1250
if you won't? It comes when it comes,
and soon you'll see it face to face
and say the seer was all too true.
You will be moved with pity.

LEADER   Thyestes' feast,
the children's flesh—that I know,   1255
and the fear shudders through me. It's true,
real, no dark signs about it. I hear the rest
but it throws me off the scent.

CASSANDRA   Agamemnon.
You will see him dead.

LEADER   Peace, poor girl!
Put those words to sleep.

CASSANDRA   No use,   1260
the Healer[4] has no hand in this affair.

LEADER Not if it's true—but god forbid it is!

CASSANDRA You pray, and they close in to kill!

LEADER What man prepares this, this dreadful—

---

2. Aegisthus.   3. A human-eating sea monster (see *Odyssey* 12, pp. 354–55).   4. Apollo.

CASSANDRA   Man?
  You *are* lost, to every word I've said.
LEADER   Yes—   1265
  I don't see who can bring the evil off.
CASSANDRA   And yet I know my Greek, too well.
LEADER   So does the Delphic oracle,[5]
  but he's hard to understand.
CASSANDRA   His *fire!*—
  sears me, sweeps me again—the torture!   1270
  Apollo Lord of the Light, you burn,
  you blind me—
          Agony!
               She is the lioness,
  she rears on her hind legs, she beds with the wolf
  when her lion king goes ranging—
                    she will kill me—
  Ai, the torture!
            She is mixing her drugs,   1275
  adding a measure more of hate for me.
  She gloats as she whets the sword for him.
  He brought me home and we will pay in carnage.

  Why mock yourself with these—trappings, the rod,
  the god's wreath, his yoke around my throat?   1280
  Before I die I'll tread you—
    [*Ripping off her regalia, stamping it into the ground.*]
                Down, out,
  die die die!
  Now you're down. I've paid you back.
  Look for another victim—I am free at last—
  make her rich in all your curse and doom.
    [*Staggering backwards as if wrestling with a spirit tearing at her robes.*]
                  See,   1285
  Apollo himself, his fiery hands—I feel him again,
  he's stripping off my robes, the Seer's robes!
  And after he looked down and saw me mocked,
  even in these, his glories, mortified by friends
  I loved, and they hated me, they were so blind   1290
  to their own demise—
              I went from door to door,
  I was wild with the god, I heard them call me
  "Beggar! Wretch! Starve for bread in hell!'

  And I endured it all, and now he will
  extort me as his due. A seer for the Seer.   1295
  He brings me here to die like this,
  not to serve at my father's altar. No,

5. Its replies were celebrated for their obscurity and ambiguity.

the block is waiting. The cleaver steams
with my life blood, the first blood drawn
for the king's last rites.
    [*Regaining her composure and moving to the altar.*]
                 We will die,   1300
but not without some honor from the gods.
There will come another[6] to avenge us,
born to kill his mother, born
his father's champion. A wanderer, a fugitive
driven off his native land, he will come home   1305
to cope the stones of hate that menace all he loves.
The gods have sworn a monumental oath: as his father lies
upon the ground he draws him home with power like a prayer.

Then why so pitiful, why so many tears?
I have seen my city faring as she fared,   1310
and those who took her, judged by the gods,
faring as they fare. I must be brave.
It is my turn to die.
    [*Approaching the doors.*]
I address you as the Gates of Death.
I pray it comes with one clear stroke,   1315
no convulsions, the pulses ebbing out
in gentle death. I'll close my eyes and sleep.
LEADER   So much pain, poor girl, and so much truth,
    you've told so much. But if you *see* it coming,
    clearly—how can you go to your own death,   1320
    like a beast to the altar driven on by god,
    and hold your head so high?
CASSANDRA   No escape, my friends,
    not now.
LEADER   But the last hour should be savored.
CASSANDRA   My time has come. Little to gain from flight.
LEADER   You're brave, believe me, full of gallant heart.   1325
CASSANDRA   Only the wretched go with praise like that.
LEADER   But to go nobly lends a man some grace.
CASSANDRA   My noble father—you and your noble children.
    [*She nears the threshold and recoils, groaning in revulsion.*]
LEADER   What now? what terror flings you back?
    Why? Unless some horror in the brain—
CASSANDRA   Murder.   1330
    The house breathes with murder—bloody shambles![7]
LEADER   No, no, only the victims at the hearth.
CASSANDRA   I know that odor. I smell the open grave.
LEADER   But the Syrian myrrh,[8] it fills the halls with splendor,
    can't you sense it?
CASSANDRA   Well, I must go in now,   1335

6. Orestes.   7. A slaughterhouse.   8. Incense burned at the sacrifice. Another interpretation of this
line runs, "What you speak of (that is, the smell of the open grave) is no Syrian incense, giving splendor to
the palace."

mourning Agamemnon's death and mine.
Enough of life!
    [*Approaching the doors again and crying out.*]
         Friends—I cried out,
not from fear like a bird fresh caught,
but that you will testify to *how* I died.
When the queen, woman for woman, dies for me,   1340
and a man falls for the man who married grief.
That's all I ask, my friends. A stranger's gift
for one about to die.
LEADER   Poor creature, you
and the end you see so clearly. I pity you.
CASSANDRA   I'd like a few words more, a kind of dirge,   1345
it is my own. I pray to the sun,
the last light I'll see,
that when the avengers cut the assassins down
they will avenge me too, a slave who died,
an easy conquest.
           Oh men, your destiny.   1350
When all is well a shadow can overturn it.
When trouble comes a stroke of the wet sponge,
and the picture's blotted out. And that,
I think that breaks the heart.
    [*She goes through the doors.*]
CHORUS   But the lust for power never dies—   1355
    men cannot have enough.
No one will lift a hand to send it
from his door, to give it warning,
"Power, never come again!"
Take this man: the gods in glory   1360
gave him Priam's city to plunder,
brought him home in splendor like a god.
But now if he must pay for the blood
his fathers shed, and die for the deaths
he brought to pass, and bring more death   1365
to avenge his dying, show us one
    who boasts himself born free
of the raging angel, once he hears—
    [*Cries break out within the palace.*]

AGAMEMNON   Aagh!
Struck deep—the death-blow, deep—
LEADER   Quiet. Cries,
but who? Someone's stabbed—
AGAMEMNON   Aaagh, again . . .   1370
second blow—struck home.
LEADER   The work is done,
you can feel it. The king, and the great cries—
Close ranks now, find the right way out.
    [*But the old men scatter, each speaks singly.*]

CHORUS   —I say send out heralds, muster the guard,
they'll save the house.

                         —And I say rush in now,   1375
catch them red-handed—butchery running on their blades.

—Right with you, do something—now or never!

—Look at them, beating the drum for insurrection.

                                      —Yes,
we're wasting time. They rape the name of caution,
their hands will never sleep.

                         —Not a plan in sight.   1380
Let men of action do the planning, too.

—I'm helpless. Who can raise the dead with words?

—What, drag out our lives? bow down to the tyrants,
the ruin of the house?

                —Never, better to die
on your feet than live on your knees.

                              —Wait,   1385
do we take the cries for signs, prophesy like seers
and give him up for dead?

                    —No more suspicions,
not another word till we have proof.

                         —Confusion
on all sides—one thing to do. See how it stands
with Agamemnon, once and for all we'll see—   1390
[*He rushes at the doors. They open and reveal a silver cauldron that
holds the body of* AGAMEMNON *shrouded in bloody robes, with the
body of* CASSANDRA *to his left and* CLYTAEMNESTRA *standing to his
right, sword in hand. She strides towards the* CHORUS.]
CLYTAEMNESTRA   Words, endless words I've said to serve the
      moment—
Now it makes me proud to tell the truth.
How else to prepare a death for deadly men
who seem to love you? How to rig the nets
of pain so high no man can overleap them?   1395

I brooded on this trial, this ancient blood feud
year by year. At last my hour came.
Here I stand and here I struck
and here my work is done.
I did it all. I don't deny it, no.   1400

He had no way to flee or fight his destiny—
    [*Unwinding the robes from* AGAMEMNON's *body, spreading them
    before the altar where the old men cluster around them, unified as
    a chorus once again.*]
our never-ending, all embracing net, I cast it
wide for the royal haul, I coil him round and round
in the wealth, the robes of doom, and then I strike him
once, twice, and at each stroke he cries in agony—   1405
he buckles at the knees and crashes here!
And when he's down I add the third, last blow,
to the Zeus who saves the dead beneath the ground
I send that third blow home in homage like a prayer.[9]

So he goes down, and the life is bursting out of him—   1410
great sprays of blood, and the murderous shower
wounds me, dyes me black and I, I revel
like the Earth when the spring rains come down,
the blessed gifts of god, and the new green spear
splits the sheath and rips to birth in glory!   1415

So it stands, elders of Argos gathered here.
Rejoice if you can rejoice—I glory.
And if I'd pour upon his body the libation
it deserves, what wine could match my words?
It is right and more than right. He flooded   1420
the vessel of our proud house with misery,
with the vintage of the curse and now
he drains the dregs. My lord is home at last.
LEADER   You appall me, you, your brazen words—
exulting over your fallen king.
CLYTAEMNESTRA   And you,   1425
you try me like some desperate woman.
My heart is steel, well you know. Praise me,
blame me as you choose. It's all one.
Here is Agamemnon, my husband made a corpse
by this right hand—a masterpiece of Justice.   1430
Done is done.
CHORUS   Woman!—what poison cropped from the soil
or strained from the heaving sea, what nursed you,
drove you insane? You brave the curse of Greece.
    You have cut away and flung away and now
the people cast you off to exile,   1435
broken with our hate.
CLYTAEMNESTRA   And now you sentence me?—
you banish *me* from the city, curses breathing
down my neck? But *he*—
name one charge you brought against him then.
He thought no more of it than killing a beast,   1440

9. Like the third libation to Zeus (see n. 7, p. 528).

and his flocks were rich, teeming in their fleece,
but he sacrificed his own child, our daughter,
the agony I labored into love,
to charm away the savage winds of Thrace.[1]

Didn't the law demand you banish him?— 1445
hunt him from the land for all his guilt?
But now you witness what I've done
and you are ruthless judges.

                  Threaten away!
I'll meet you blow for blow. And if I fall
the throne is yours. If god decrees the reverse, 1450
late as it is, old men, you'll learn your place.

CHORUS   Mad with ambition,
      shrilling pride!—some Fury
crazed with the carnage rages through your brain—
    I can see the flecks of blood inflame your eyes! 1455
But vengeance comes—you'll lose your loved ones,
stroke for painful stroke.

CLYTAEMNESTRA   Then learn this, too, the power of my oaths.
By the child's Rights I brought to birth,
by Ruin, by Fury—the three gods to whom 1460
I sacrificed this man—I swear my hopes
will never walk the halls of fear so long
as Aegisthus lights the fire on my hearth.
Loyal to me as always, no small shield
to buttress my defiance.

                  Here he lies. 1465
He brutalized me. The darling of all
the golden girls[2] who spread the gates of Troy.
And here his spearprize . . . what wonders she beheld!—
the seer of Apollo shared my husband's bed,
his faithful mate who knelt at the rowing-benches, 1470
worked by every hand.

              They have their rewards.
He as you know. And she, the swan of the gods
who lived to sing her latest, dying song—
his lover lies beside him.
She brings a fresh, voluptuous relish to my bed! 1475

CHORUS   Oh quickly, let me die—
no bed of labor, no, no wasting illness . . .
bear me off in the sleep that never ends,
    now that he has fallen,
now that our dearest shield lies battered— 1480
    Woman made him suffer,
      woman struck him down.

---

1. Winds from the North (at Aulis).   2. In Greek *chryseidon*, which recalls the girl in the first book of the *Iliad* (1.130–33), Chryseis, whom Agamemnon said he preferred to Clytaemnestra.

Helen the wild, maddening Helen,
one for the many, the thousand lives
you murdered under Troy. Now you are crowned   1485
with this consummate wreath, the blood
that lives in memory, glistens age to age.
Once in the halls she walked and she was war,
angel of war, angel of agony, lighting men to death.

CLYTAEMNESTRA   Pray no more for death, broken   1490
    as you are. And never turn
        your wrath on her, call her
    the scourge of men, the one alone
    who destroyed a myriad Greek lives—
    Helen the grief that never heals.   1495
CHORUS   The *spirit!*—you who tread
    the house and the twinborn sons of Tantalus[3]—
    you empower the sisters, Fury's twins
        whose power tears the heart!
    Perched on the corpse your carrion raven   1500
        glories in her hymn,
            her screaming hymn of pride.
CLYTAEMNESTRA   Now you set your judgment straight,
    you summon *him!* Three generations
        feed the spirit in the race.   1505
    Deep in the veins he feeds our bloodlust—
    aye, before the old wound dies
    it ripens in another flow of blood.
CHORUS   The great curse of the house, the spirit,
        dead weight wrath—and you can praise it!   1510
    Praise the insatiate doom that feeds
    relentless on our future and our sons.
    Oh all through the will of Zeus,
    the cause of all, the one who works it all.
        What comes to birth that is not Zeus?   1515
    Our lives are pain, what part not come from god?

        Oh, my king, my captain,
        how to salute you, how to mourn you?
        What can I say with all my warmth and love?
        Here in the black widow's web you lie,   1520
        gasping out your life
        in a sacrilegious death, dear god,
        reduced to a slave's bed,
        my king of men, yoked by stealth and Fate,
        by the wife's hand that thrust the two-edged sword.   1525

CLYTAEMNESTRA   You claim the work is mine, call me
    Agamemnon's wife—you are so wrong.

---

3. Father of Pelops, grandfather of Atreus. *Sons:* descendants—that is, Agamemnon and Menelaus.

Fleshed in the wife of this dead man,
   the spirit lives within me,
our savage ancient spirit of revenge.   1530
In return for Atreus' brutal feast
he kills his perfect son—for every
murdered child, a crowning sacrifice.

CHORUS   And *you*, innocent of his murder?
   And who could swear to that? and how? . . .   1535
and still an avenger could arise,
bred by the fathers' crimes, and lend a hand.
He wades in the blood of brothers,
stream on mounting stream—black war erupts
   and where he strides revenge will stride,   1540
clots will mass for the young who were devoured.

         Oh my king, my captain,
         how to salute you, how to mourn you?
         What can I say with all my warmth and love?
         Here in the black widow's web you lie,   1545
         gasping out your life
         in a sacrilegious death, dear god,
         reduced to a slave's bed,
         my king of men, yoked by stealth and Fate,
         by the wife's hand that thrust the two-edged sword.   1550

CLYTAEMNESTRA   No slave's death, I think—
no stealthier than the death he dealt
our house and the offspring of our loins,
   Iphigeneia, girl of tears.
Act for act, wound for wound!   1555
Never exult in Hades, swordsman,
here you are repaid. By the sword
you did your work and by the sword you die.

CHORUS   The mind reels—where to turn?
         All plans dashed, all hope! I cannot think . . .   1560
      the roofs are toppling, I dread the drumbeat thunder
         the heavy rains of blood will crush the house
               the first light rains are over—
               Justice brings new acts of agony, yes,
      on new grindstones Fate is grinding sharp the sword of Justice. 1565

Earth, dear Earth,
if only you'd drawn me under
long before I saw him huddled
in the beaten silver bath.
Who will bury him, lift his dirge?   1570
      [*Turning to* CLYTAEMNESTRA.]
You, can you dare *this*?
To kill your lord with your own hand
then mourn his soul with tributes, terrible tributes—

do his enormous works a great dishonor.
This godlike man, this hero. Who at the grave   1575
will sing his praises, pour the wine of tears?
Who will labor there with truth of heart?

CLYTAEMNESTRA   This is no concern of yours.
The hand that bore and cut him down
will hand him down to Mother Earth.   1580
This house will never mourn for him.
    Only our daughter Iphigeneia,
by all rights, will rush to meet him
first at the churning straits,[4]
the ferry over tears—   1585
she'll fling her arms around her father,
pierce him with her love.

CHORUS   Each charge meets counter-charge.
          None can judge between them. Justice.
      The plunderer plundered, the killer pays the price.   1590
    The truth still holds while Zeus still holds the throne:
              the one who acts must suffer—
      that is law. Who, who can tear from the veins
      the bad seed, the curse? The race is welded to its ruin.

CLYTAEMNESTRA   At last you see the future and the truth!   1595
But I will swear a pact with the spirit
born within us. I embrace his works,
cruel as they are but done at last,
    if he will leave our house
in the future, bleed another line   1600
with kinsmen murdering kinsmen.
Whatever he may ask. A few things
are all I need, once I have purged
our fury to destroy each other—
    purged it from our halls.
    [AEGISTHUS *has emerged from the palace with his bodyguard and*
    stands triumphant over the body of AGAMEMNON.]

AEGISTHUS   O what a brilliant day   1605
it is for vengeance! Now I can say once more
there are gods in heaven avenging men,
blazing down on all the crimes of earth.
Now at last I see this man brought down
in the Furies' tangling robes. It feasts my eyes—   1610
he pays for the plot his father's hand contrived.

Atreus, this man's father, was king of Argos.
My father, Thyestes—let me make this clear—
Atreus' brother challenged him for the crown,
and Atreus drove him out of house and home   1615

---

4. The river of the underworld over which the dead were ferried.

then lured him back, and home Thyestes came,
poor man, a suppliant to his own hearth,
to pray that Fate might save him.
                           So it did.
There was no dying, no staining our native ground
with *his* blood. Thyestes was the guest,   1620
and this man's godless father—
        [*Pointing to* AGAMEMNON.]
the zeal of the host outstripping a brother's love,
made my father a feast that seemed a feast for gods,
a love feast of his children's flesh.
                           He cuts
the extremities, feet and delicate hands   1625
into small pieces, scatters them over the dish
and serves it to Thyestes throned on high.
He picks at the flesh he cannot recognize,
the soul of innocence eating the food of ruin—
look,
        [*Pointing to the bodies at his feet.*]
        that feeds upon the house! And then,   1630
when he sees the monstrous thing he's done, he shrieks,
he reels back head first and vomits up that butchery,
tramples the feast—brings down the curse of Justice:
"Crash to ruin, all the race of Pleisthenes,[5] crash down!"

So you see him, down. And I, the weaver of Justice,   1635
plotted out the kill. Atreus drove us into exile,
my struggling father and I, a babe-in-arms,
his last son, but I became a man
and Justice brought me home. I was abroad
but I reached out and seized my man,   1640
link by link I clamped the fatal scheme
together. Now I could die gladly, even I—
now I see this monster in the nets of Justice.

LEADER   Aegisthus, you revel in pain—you sicken me.
You say you killed the king in cold blood,   1645
singlehanded planned his pitiful death?
I say there's no escape. In the hour of judgment,
trust to this, your head will meet the people's
rocks and curses.

AEGISTHUS   You say! you slaves at the oars—
while the master of the benches cracks the whip?   1650
You'll learn, in your late age, how much it hurts
to teach old bones their place. We have techniques—
chains and the pangs of hunger,
two effective teachers, excellent healers.
They can even cure old men of pride and gall.   1655
Look—can't you see? The more you kick

─────────────
5. A name sometimes inserted into the genealogy of the house of Tantalus.

against the pricks, the more you suffer.
LEADER   You, pathetic—
    the king had just returned from battle.
    You waited out the war and fouled his lair,   1660
    you planned my great commander's fall.
AEGISTHUS   Talk on—
    you'll scream for every word, my little Orpheus.[6]
    We'll see if the world comes dancing to your song,
    your absurd barking—snarl your breath away!
    I'll make you dance, I'll bring you all to heel.   1665
LEADER   *You* rule Argos? You who schemed his death
    but cringed to cut him down with your own hand?
AEGISTHUS   The treachery was the woman's work, clearly.
    I was a marked man, his enemy for ages.
    But I will use his riches, stop at nothing   1670
    to civilize his people. All but the rebel:
    him I'll yoke and break—
    no cornfed colt, running free in the traces.
    Hunger, ruthless mate of the dark torture-chamber,
    trains her eyes upon him till he drops!   1675
LEADER   Coward, why not kill the man yourself?
    Why did the woman, the corruption of Greece
    and the gods of Greece, have to bring him down?
    Orestes—If he still sees the light of day,
    bring him home, good Fates, home to kill   1680
    this pair at last. Our champion in slaughter!
AEGISTHUS   Bent on insolence? Well, you'll learn, quickly.
    At them, men—you have your work at hand!
        [*His men draw swords; the old men take up their sticks.*]
LEADER   At them, fist at the hilt, to the last man—
AEGISTHUS   Fist at the hilt, I'm not afraid to die.   1685
LEADER   It's death you want and death you'll have—
    we'll make that word your last.
        [CLYTAEMNESTRA *moves between them, restraining* AEGISTHUS.]
CLYTAEMNESTRA   No more, my dearest,
    no more grief. We have too much to reap
    right here, our mighty harvest of despair.
    Our lives are based on pain. No bloodshed now.   1690

    Fathers of Argos, turn for home before you act
    and suffer for it. What we did was destiny.
    If we could end the suffering, how we would rejoice.
    The spirit's brutal hoof has struck our heart.
    And that is what a woman has to say.   1695
    Can you accept the truth?
        [CLYTAEMNESTRA *turns to leave.*]
AEGISTHUS   But these . . . mouths
    that bloom in filth—spitting insults in my teeth.

6. A mythical singer who charmed all nature with his music.

You tempt your fates, you insubordinate dogs—
to hurl abuse at me, your master!
LEADER   No Greek
   worth his salt would grovel at your feet.   1700
AEGISTHUS   I—I'll stalk you all your days!
LEADER   Not if the spirit brings Orestes home.
AEGISTHUS   Exiles feed on hope—well I know.
LEADER   More,
   gorge yourself to bursting—soil justice, while you can.
AEGISTHUS   I promise you, you'll pay, old fools—in good time, too!   1705
LEADER   Strut on your own dunghill, you cock beside your mate.
CLYTAEMNESTRA   Let them howl—they're impotent. You and I have
   power now.
We will set the house in order once for all.
   [*They enter the palace; the great doors close behind them; the old
   men disband and wander off.*]

The Libation Bearers

Summary   In the final scene of *Agamemnon* the chorus leader, confronted with
Aegisthus's threats, cries out in desperation, "*Orestes*—If he still sees the light of day,
/ bring him home, good Fates." In the second play of the the trilogy, *The Libation
Bearers*, Orestes, now grown to manhood, comes home, accompanied by his friend
Pylades, to avenge his father. On stage is the grave of Agamemnon, on which Orestes
lays two locks of his hair as an offering. But this homage to the dead man is interrupted by the arrival of a procession of black-robed women, the chorus of the play;
they carry libations, liquid offerings to be poured on the grave. With them is Electra,
Orestes' sister. The two men retire out of sight, to watch and listen. They learn from
the chorus's song that it was Clytaemnestra who sent the libations; she has been
terrified by a nightmare that, according to her dream interpreters, signals the rage of
the dead king against his murderers. Electra, who loved her father as much as she
now hates her mother (who lives with the man who helped to murder him), prays, as
she pours the libations, for the return of Orestes and for vengeance on the killers of
Agamemnon.

   The chorus leader meanwhile has noticed the locks of hair on the grave; the hair
is like Electra's, and the footprints around the grave are like hers—can Orestes have
returned? He comes out of hiding and brother and sister embrace. He tells her of his
visit to Delphi to consult Apollo and the command he received: to avenge his father
or suffer a life of torment and a shameful death. Brother and sister and the chorus
now join in a long series of appeals to the spirit of Agamemnon to help them in their
enterprise. Orestes then learns from Electra the nature of Clytaemnestra's dream:
she gave birth to a serpent and nursed it, offering it her breast, only to have it bite
and draw blood. "I turn serpent," says Orestes, "I kill her. So the vision says."

   He proceeds to explain his plans. Electra is to go into the house; he and Pylades,
pretending to be travelers from Phocis (the place to which Clytaemnestra sent the
young Orestes for safekeeping), will knock at the door, and once inside, Orestes will
kill Aegisthus. But it is Clytaemnestra who comes to the door, and it is to her that he
tells the story that he claims to have heard on his journey: Orestes is dead. Clytaemnestra greets the news with what seems like genuine grief, then takes Orestes and
Pylades into the house. But we are told later by an old nurse who comes out that
"deep down her eyes are laughing." The nurse, who cared for Orestes when he was a
baby, has been sent to tell Aegisthus to come home, so that he can hear the news in

person and question the messengers. "Is he to come alone?" the chorus asks. "No," it is told, he is to come with his bodyguard. The chorus persuades the nurse to tell him to come alone, which she does. When Aegisthus arrives, exultant at the news of Orestes' death, he walks into a trap. We hear his death cry inside the house, and a distraught servant comes onstage, shouting for Clytaemnestra as he pounds at the door of the women's quarters. Clytaemnestra comes out and sends the servant to fetch her a battle-ax—too late. Orestes and Pylades appear at the central door. Orestes, sword in hand, moves toward his mother; he intends to kill her so that she will lie next to the man she loved. But she makes a desperate move; she bares the breast that suckled him. He lowers his sword, his resolution gone, and turns to Pylades. "What will I do, Pylades?—I dread to kill my mother!" Pylades has not spoken so far in the play and will not speak again; the three lines he speaks now are decisive. He reminds Orestes of the god Apollo's command and of the oath he swore. Orestes turns back to Clytaemnestra and forces her to stand by the body of Aegisthus. She still defends her action but finally recognizes in him the serpent of her dream. But as she accepts her fate, she warns him: "the hounds of a mother's curse will hunt you down." Orestes pulls her inside; the chorus celebrates the victory—"Lift the cry of triumph!"—and the fulfillment of the god's command—"the pure god came down and healed our ancient wounds." But as the doors open and we see the same tableau we saw in *Agamemnon*—the killer standing over his victims, man and woman—we realize that this cannot be the end. This is the repetitive pattern of the curse on the house of Atreus.

Orestes displays the net in which Agamemnon was trapped as he justifies his action by recalling Clytaemnestra's treachery. But there is a hysterical note to his passionate denunciation, and the chorus feels that all is not well: "She is gone. But oh, for you the survivor / suffering is just about to bloom." Orestes recognizes the truth of what they say. He now speaks of "my victory" as "my guilt / my curse" and soon fears that he is losing control of his words and feelings. He is a "charioteer—the reins flying back, look / the mares plunge off the track." He appeals to the authority of Apollo, to whose sanctuary at Delphi he now prepares to go as a suppliant. The chorus protests: "You have done well . . . don't lash yourself with guilt. You've set us free." But Orestes does not hear them. He screams in terror as he sees a vision: "women—look—like Gorgons, / shrouded in black, their heads wreathed, / swarming serpents! . . . Here they come, thick and fast, / their eyes dripping hate—" And in answer to the chorus's attempt to comfort him he shouts, "You can't see them—/ I can, and they drive me on! I must move on—" as, followed by Pylades, he rushes offstage.

The chorus cannot see them, nor can we. But we shall see them in the next play; they are its chorus. They are "the hounds of a mother's curse" that Clytaemnestra told Orestes would hunt him down. In *The Eumenides* we shall see them in pursuit of Orestes at Delphi and then at Athens, where they will, in the end, serve as prosecutors (the Greek legal term, like the English, has the literal meaning "pursuers") at his trial before the court of the Areopagus.

The Eumenides

CHARACTERS

The PYTHIA, *the priestess of Apollo*
APOLLO
HERMES
ORESTES
THE GHOST OF CLYTAEMNESTRA

CHORUS OF FURIES *and their* LEADER
ATHENA
Escorting CHORUS *of Athenian*
women
Men of the jury, herald, citizens

[Time and Scene: *The* Furies *have pursued* Orestes *to the temple of* Apollo *at Delphi. It is morning. The priestess of the god appears at the great doors and offers up her prayer.*]

PYTHIA   First of the gods I honor in my prayer is Mother Earth,
the first of the gods to prophesy,[1] and next I praise
Tradition, second to hold her Mother's mantic seat,
so legend says, and third by the lots of destiny,
by Tradition's free will—no force to bear her down—   5
another Titan, child of the Earth, took her seat
and Phoebe passed it on as a birthday gift to Phoebus,
Phoebus a name for clear pure light derived from hers.
Leaving the marsh and razorback of Delos, landing
at Pallas' headlands flocked by ships, here he came   10
to make his home Parnassus and the heights.[2]
And an escort filled with reverence brought him on,
the highway-builders, sons of the god of fire[3] who tamed
the savage country, civilized the wilds—on he marched
and the people lined his way to cover him with praise,   15
led by Delphos, lord, helm of the land, and Zeus
inspired his mind with the prophet's skill, with godhead,
made him fourth in the dynasty of seers to mount this throne,
but it is Zeus that Apollo speaks for, Father Zeus.
These I honor in the prelude of my prayers—these gods.   20
But Athena at the Forefront of the Temple crowns our legends.
I revere the nymphs who keep the Corycian rock's deep hollows,[4]
loving haunt of birds where the spirits drift and hover.
And Great Dionysus rules the land. I never forget that day
he marshaled his wild women in arms—he was all god,   25
he ripped Pentheus[5] down like a hare in the nets of doom.
And the rushing springs of Pleistos,[6] Poseidon's force I call,
and the king of the sky, the king of all fulfillment, Zeus.
Now the prophet goes to take her seat. God speed me—
grant me a vision greater than all my embarkations past!   30
        [*Turning to the audience.*]
Where are the Greeks among you? Draw your lots and enter.
It is the custom here. I will tell the future
only as the god will lead the way.
        [*She goes through the doors and reappears in a moment, shaken, thrown to her knees by some terrific force.*]

1. The priestess of Apollo's oracle (Pythia) traces the peaceful succession of powers that controlled the great prophetic site of Delphi. First Mother Earth; then Tradition (*Themis* in the Greek); and then Phoebe, grandmother of Apollo, who handed it over to him as a birthday gift. This is a succession myth that stresses orderly, peaceful succession; in other versions Apollo fights and kills the great serpent Pytho to gain possession.   2. The oracular site is situated on the lower slopes of the Parnassus mountain range (2,457 meters at its summit). Delos is a small rocky island in the Cyclades and Apollo's birthplace. *Pallas' headlands*: the coast of Attica.   3. Athenians, whose legendary ancestor Erichthonios was a son of Hephaestus, the smith god.   4. A capacious cave high above the site of Delphi, sacred to Pan and the nymphs. *The Temple*: Pronaia, the temple of Athena situated at the entrance to the sacred precinct.   5. A king of Thebes who resisted the establishment of Dionysiac rites in his domains. Dionysus, giver of wine and ecstasy, was thought to inhabit Delphi in the winter months, when Apollo left for the land of the Hyperboreans (the happy people who lived, as their name indicates, beyond the North Wind). Dionysiac festivals at which women danced on the hills at night were held at Delphi in historical times.   6. The river (dry in summer) in the bottom of the deep gorge below Delphi.

               Terrors—
terrors to tell, terrors all can see!—
they send me reeling back from Apollo's house.   35
The strength drains, it's very hard to stand,
crawling on all fours, no spring in the legs . . .
an old woman, gripped by fear, is nothing,
a child, nothing more.
       [*Struggling to her feet, trying to compose herself.*]
I'm on my way to the vault,   40
it's green with wreaths, and there at the Navelstone[7]
I see a man—an abomination to god—
he holds the seat where suppliants sit for purging;
his hands dripping blood, and his sword just drawn,
and he holds a branch (it must have topped an olive)   45
wreathed with a fine tuft of wool,[8] all piety,
fleece gleaming white. So far it's clear, I tell you.
But there in a ring around the man, an amazing company—
women, sleeping, nestling against the benches . . .
women? No,   50
Gorgons I'd call them; but then with Gorgons
you'd see the grim, inhuman . . .
              I saw a picture
years ago, the creatures tearing the feast
away from Phineus[9]—
             These have no wings,
I looked. But black they are, and so repulsive.   55
Their heavy, rasping breathing makes me cringe.
And their eyes ooze a discharge, sickening,
and what they wear[1]—to flaunt *that* at the gods,
the idols, sacrilege! even in the homes of men.
The tribe that produced that brood I never saw,   60
or a plot of ground to boast it nursed their kind
without some tears, some pain for all its labor.

Now for the outcome. This is his concern,
Apollo the master of this house, the mighty power.
Healer, prophet, diviner of signs, he purges   65
the halls of others—He must purge his own.
       [*She leaves. The doors of the temple open and reveal* APOLLO *rising
       over* ORESTES; *he kneels in prayer at the Navelstone, surrounded by
       the* FURIES *who are sleeping.* HERMES *waits in the background.*]
APOLLO   No, I will never fail you, through to the end
   your guardian standing by your side or worlds away!
I will show no mercy to your enemies! Now
look at these—
       [*Pointing to the* FURIES.]
            these obscenities!—I've caught them,   70

---

7. A sacred stone that was supposed to mark the center of the Earth.   8. Suppliants usually carried a branch of olive, hung with small woolen wreaths.   9. Whenever he spread the table for a meal, the food was carried off by loathsome creatures—half bird, half woman—called Harpies. The Pythia first thinks the Furies (Erinyes) are Gorgons, but then rejects that theory (we are not told why); her next guess, Harpies, has to be abandoned because the Furies have no wings.   1. Long black robes.

beaten them down with sleep.
                                    They disgust me.
These gray, ancient children never touched
by god, man, or beast—the eternal virgins.
Born for destruction only, the dark pit,
they range the bowels of Earth, the world of death,   75
loathed by men and the gods who hold Olympus.

Nevertheless keep racing on and never yield.
Deep in the endless heartland they will drive you,
striding horizons, feet pounding the earth forever,
on, on over seas and cities swept by tides!   80
Never surrender, never brood on the labor.
And once you reach the citadel of Pallas, kneel
and embrace her ancient idol[2] in your arms and there,
with judges of your case, with a magic spell—
with words—we will devise the master-stroke   85
that sets you free from torment once for all.
I persuaded you to take your mother's life.
ORESTES   Lord Apollo, you know the rules of justice,
know them well. Now learn compassion, too.
No one doubts your power to do great things.   90
APOLLO   Remember that. No fear will overcome you.
        [*Summoning* HERMES *from the shadows.*]
You, my brother, blood of our common Father,
Hermes, guard him well. Live up to your name,
good Escort. Shepherd him well, he is my suppliant,
and outlaws have their rights that Zeus reveres.   95
Lead him back to the world of men with all good speed.
        [APOLLO *withdraws to his inner sanctuary;* ORESTES *leaves with*
        HERMES *in the lead.* THE GHOST[3] OF CLYTAEMNESTRA *appears at the*
        Navelstone, *hovering over the* FURIES *as they sleep.*]
THE GHOST OF CLYTAEMNESTRA   You—how can you *sleep?*
Awake, awake—what use are sleepers now?
I go stripped of honor, thanks to you,
alone among the dead. And for those I killed   100
the charges of the dead will never cease, never—
I wander in disgrace, I feel the guilt, I tell you,
withering guilt from all the outraged dead!

But I suffered too, terribly, from dear ones,
and none of my spirits rages to avenge me.   105
I was slaughtered by his matricidal hand.
See these gashes—
        [*Seizing one of the* FURIES *weak with sleep.*]
                    Carve them in your heart!

2. In a temple on the Acropolis at Athens there was an ancient wooden statue of Athena. *Citadel of Pallas:*
Athens.   3. She is not really a ghost. In line 121 she tells us that she is a dream in the head of the Furies.

The sleeping brain has eyes that give us light;
we can never see our destiny by day.

And after all my libations . . . how you lapped   110
the honey, the sober offerings poured to soothe you,
awesome midnight feasts[4] I burned at the hearthfire,
your dread hour never shared with gods.
All those rites, I see them trampled down.
And he springs free like a fawn, one light leap   115
at that—he's through the thick of your nets,
he breaks away!
Mocking laughter twists across his face.
Hear me, I am pleading for my life.
Awake, my Furies, goddesses of the Earth!   120
A dream is calling—Clytaemnestra calls you now.
    [*The* FURIES *mutter in their sleep.*]
Mutter on. Your man is gone, fled far away.
My son has friends to defend him, not like mine.
    [*They mutter again.*]
You sleep too much, no pity for my ordeal.
Orestes murdered his mother—he is gone.   125
    [*They begin to moan.*]
Moaning, sleeping—onto your feet, quickly.
What is your work? What but causing pain?
Sleep and toil, the two strong conspirators,
they sap the mother dragon's deadly fury—
    [*The* FURIES *utter a sharp moan and moan again, but they are still
    asleep.*]
FURIES   Get him, get him, get him, get him—   130
there he goes.
THE GHOST OF CLYTAEMNESTRA   The prey you hunt is just a dream—
like hounds mad for the sport you bay him on,
you never leave the kill.
                 But what are you *doing?*
Up! don't yield to the labor, limp with sleep.
Never forget my anguish.   135
Let my charges hurt you, they are just;
deep in the righteous heart they prod like spurs.

You, blast him on with your gory breath,
the fire of your vitals—wither him, after him,
one last foray—waste him, burn him out!
    [*She vanishes. The lead* FURY *urges on the pack.*]
LEADER   Wake up!   140
I rouse you, you rouse her. Still asleep?
Onto your feet, kick off your stupor.
See if this prelude has some grain of truth.

---

4. Offerings to the Furies were made only at night. *Sober offerings:* no wine was included in offerings to
them.

[*The* FURIES *circle, pursuing the scent with hunting calls, and cry
out singly when they find* ORESTES *gone.*]
FURIES   —Aieeeeee—no, no, *no*, they do us wrong, dear sisters.

—The miles of pain, the pain I suffer . . .   145
and all for nothing, all for pain, more pain,
        the anguish, oh, the grief too much to bear.

—The quarry's slipped from the nets, our quarry lost and gone.

        —Sleep defeats me . . . I have lost the prey.

—You—child of Zeus[5]—*you*, a common thief!   150

—Young god, you have ridden down the powers
proud with age. You worship the suppliant,
        the godless man who tears his parent's heart—

—The matricide, you steal him away, and you a god!

        —Guilt both ways, and who can call it justice?   155

—Not I: her charges stalk my dreams,
    yes, the charioteer rides hard,
            her spurs digging the vitals,
        under the heart, under the heaving breast—

—I can feel the executioner's lash, it's searing   160
        deeper, sharper, the knives of burning ice—

—Such is your triumph, you young gods,
    world dominion past all rights.
            Your throne is streaming blood,
        blood at the foot, blood at the crowning head—   165

—I can see the Navelstone of the Earth, it's bleeding,
        bristling corruption, oh, the guilt it has to bear—

Stains on the hearth! The Prophet stains the vault,
    he cries it on, drives on the crime himself.
        Breaking the god's first law, he rates men first,   170
            destroys the old dominions of the Fates.

He wounds me too, yet *him* he'll never free,
    plunging under the earth, no freedom then:
        curst as he comes for purging, at his neck
            he feels new murder springing from his blood.   175

5. Apollo.

[APOLLO *strides from his sanctuary in full armor, brandishing his bow and driving back the* FURIES.]

APOLLO   Out, I tell you, out of these halls—fast!—
set the Prophet's chamber free!
    [*Seizing one of the* FURIES, *shaking an arrow across her face.*]
                        Or take
the flash and stab of this, this flying viper
whipped from the golden cord that strings my bow!

Heave in torment, black froth erupting from your lungs,   180
vomit the clots of all the murders you have drained.
But never touch my halls, you have no right.

Go where heads are severed, eyes gouged out,
where Justice and bloody slaughter are the same . . .
castrations, wasted seed, young men's glories butchered,   185
extremities maimed, and huge stones at the chest,
and the victims wail for pity—
spikes inching up the spine, torsos stuck on spikes.⁶
    [*The* FURIES *close in on him.*]
So, you hear your love feast, yearn to have it all?
You revolt the gods. Your look,   190
your whole regalia gives you away—your kind
should infest a lion's cavern reeking blood.
But never rub your filth on the Prophet's shrine.
Out, you flock without a herdsman—out!
No god will ever shepherd you with love.   195
LEADER   Lord Apollo, now it is your turn to listen.
You are no mere accomplice in this crime.
You did it all, and all the guilt is yours.
APOLLO   No, how? Enlarge on that, and only that.
LEADER   You commanded the guest to kill his mother.   200
APOLLO   —Commanded him to avenge his father, what of it?
LEADER   And then you dared embrace him, fresh from bloodshed.
APOLLO   Yes, I ordered him on, to my house, for purging.⁷
LEADER   And we sped him on, and you revile us?
APOLLO   Indeed, you are not fit to approach this house.   205
LEADER   And yet we have our mission and our—
APOLLO   Authority—you? Sound out your splendid power.
LEADER   Matricides: we drive them from their houses.
APOLLO   And what of the wife who strikes her husband down?
LEADER   That murder would not destroy one's flesh and blood.⁸   210

6. The methods of torture and execution listed by Apollo are what the Greeks saw as typically Eastern, and indeed, castration and impalement were Persian, not Greek, customs. But Apollo's dismissal of the Furies as non-Greek has no basis in fact; the Furies are not only Greek but much older than he is.   7. Ritual purification.   8. Crimes of blood relations against each other are the most heinous kind. But husband and wife are, and must be, of different blood. The Furies would have pursued Orestes if he had not avenged his father, and they pursue him now because he killed his mother, but the killing of a husband by a wife seems to them a lesser crime. They think and feel in tribal terms, those of a society that has not yet developed the city-state, the *polis*, in which the institution of marriage (which Apollo champions in his reply, lines 215ff.) was the guarantee of the legitimacy of male heirs for the transmittal of property from generation to generation.

APOLLO   Why, you'd disgrace—obliterate the bonds of Zeus
and Hera queen of brides! And the queen of love[9]
you'd throw to the winds at a word, disgrace love,
the source of mankind's nearest, dearest ties.
Marriage of man and wife is Fate itself,   215
stronger than oaths, and Justice guards its life.
But if one destroys the other and you relent—
no revenge, not a glance in anger—then
I say your manhunt of Orestes is unjust.
Some things stir your rage, I see. Others,   220
atrocious crimes, lull your will to act.
                                                     Pallas
will oversee this trial. She is one of us.
LEADER   I will never let that man go free, never.
APOLLO   Hound him then, and multiply your pains.
LEADER   Never try to cut my power with your logic.   225
APOLLO   I'd never touch it, not as a gift—your power.
LEADER   Of course,
great as you are, they say, throned on high with Zeus.
But blood of the mother draws me on—must hunt
the man for Justice. Now I'm on his trail!
        [*Rushing out, with the* FURIES *in full cry.*]
APOLLO   And I will defend my suppliant and save him.   230
A terror to gods and men, the outcast's anger,
once I fail him, all of my own free will.
        [APOLLO *leaves. The scene changes to the Acropolis in Athens.
        Escorted by* HERMES, ORESTES *enters and kneels, exhausted, before
        the ancient shrine and idol of* ATHENA.]
ORESTES   Queen Athena,
under Apollo's orders I have come.
Receive me kindly. Curst and an outcast,
no suppliant for purging . . . my hands are clean.   235
My murderous edge is blunted now, worn down at last
on the outland homesteads, beaten paths of men.[1]
On and out over seas and dry frontiers,
I kept alive the Prophet's strong commands.
Struggling toward your house, your idol—
        [*Taking the knees of* ATHENA's *idol in his arms.*]
                                                     Goddess,   240
here I keep my watch,
I await the consummation of my trial.
        [*The* FURIES *enter in pursuit but cannot find* ORESTES *who is
        entwined around* ATHENA's *idol. The* LEADER *sees the footprints.*]
LEADER   At last!
The clear trail of the man. After it, silent
but it tracks his guilt to light. He's wounded—

---

9. Aphrodite. The marriage of Zeus and Hera was the divine model of earthly marriages, and Hera was the
goddess who presided over marriage ceremonies.   1. Orestes has been given ritual purification by Apollo,
but he also claims that the blood guilt is now "worn down" by his travels and contacts with men (compare
lines 278–82).

go for the fawn, my hounds, the splash of blood,   245
hunt him, rake him down.
                        Oh, the labor,
the man-killing labor. My lungs are bursting . . .
over the wide rolling earth we've ranged in flock,
hurdling the waves in wingless flight and now we come,
all hot pursuit, outracing ships astern—and now   250
he's here, somewhere, cowering like a hare . . .
the reek of human blood[2]—it's laughter to my heart!
      [*Inciting a pair of* FURIES.]
Look, look again, you two,
scour the ground before he escapes—one dodge
and the matricide slips free.
      [*Seeing* ORESTES, *one by one they press around him and* ATHENA *'s
      idol.*]

FURIES   —There he is!   255
Clutching the knees of power once again,
    twined in the deathless goddess' idol,[3] look,
he wants to go on trial for his crimes.

                        —Never . . .
    the mother's blood that wets the ground,
you can never bring it back, dear god,   260
the Earth drinks, and the running life is gone.

                         —No,
you'll give me blood for blood, you must!
    Out of your living marrow I will drain
    my red libation, out of your veins I suck my food,
    my raw, brutal cups—

                  —Wither you alive,   265
    drag you down and there you pay, agony
for mother-killing agony!

                —And there you will see them all.
Every mortal who outraged god or guest or loving parent:
each receives the pain his pains exact.

—A mighty god is Hades. There   270
at the last reckoning underneath the earth
    he scans all, he squares all men's accounts
and graves them on the tablets of his mind.
      [ORESTES *remains impassive.*]
ORESTES   I have suffered into truth. Well I know
    the countless arts of purging, where to speak,   275
    where silence is the rule. In this ordeal

---

2. The Furies track him down by scent of the blood he shed, as if he were a wounded animal leaving a
trace behind him.   3. Orestes is still clinging to the statue of Pallas Athena.

a compelling master urges me to speak.
  [*Looking at his hands.*]
The blood sleeps, it is fading on my hands,
the stain of mother's murder washing clean.
It was still fresh at the god's hearth. Apollo   280
killed the swine and the purges drove it off.
Mine is a long story
if I'd start with the many hosts I met,
I lived with, and I left them all unharmed.
Time refines all things that age with time.   285

And now with pure, reverent lips I call
the queen of the land. Athena, help me!
Come without your spear—without a battle
you will win myself, my land, the Argive people[4]
true and just, your friends-in-arms forever.   290
Where are you now? The scorching wilds of Libya,
bathed by the Triton pool where you were born?[5]
Robes shrouding your feet
or shod and on the march to aid allies?
Or striding the Giants' Plain, marshal of armies,[6]   295
hero scanning, flashing through the ranks?
                              Come—
you can hear me from afar, you are a god.
Set me free from this!
LEADER   Never—neither
Apollo's nor Athena's strength can save you.
Down you go, abandoned,   300
searching your soul for joy but joy is gone.
Bled white, gnawed by demons, a husk, a wraith—
  [*She breaks off, waiting for reply, but* ORESTES *prays in silence.*]
No reply? you spit my challenge back?
You'll feast me alive, my fatted calf,
not cut on the altar first. Now hear my spell,   305
the chains of song I sing to bind you tight.
FURIES   Come, Furies, dance!—
link arms for the dancing hand-to-hand,
now we long to reveal our art,
our terror, now to declare our right
    to steer the lives of men,   310
we all conspire, we dance! we are
the just and upright, we maintain.
Hold out your hands, if they are clean
    no fury of ours will stalk you,
    you will go through life unscathed.   315

---

4. This is the first clear reference to the alliance that Athens had concluded with Argos in 459 B.C., the year before the production of the trilogy.   5. One of Athena's titles, Tritogeneia, was thought to derive from Lake Tritonis, in Libya, where some said she was born. There may be a contemporary allusion here; Athens was backing, with ships and troops, the Libyan ruler Inaros, who was fighting the Persian rulers of Egypt.   6. Athena, a warrior goddess, took a prominent part in the battle between the gods and the giants, in which Zeus and the Olympians won a decisive victory.

But show us the guilty—one like this
   who hides his reeking hands,
and up from the outraged dead we rise,
witness bound to avenge their blood
we rise in flames against him to the end!   320

Mother who bore me,
   O dear Mother Night,
to avenge the blinded dead
and those who see by day,
   now hear me! The whelp Apollo   325
spurns my rights, he tears this trembling victim
       from my grasp—the one to bleed,
      to atone away the mother-blood at last.

     Over the victim's burning head
this chant this frenzy striking frenzy   330
     lightning crazing the mind
       this hymn of Fury
chaining the senses, ripping cross the lyre,[7]
     withering lives of men!

This, this is our right,   335
   spun for us by the Fates,
the ones who bind the world,
and none can shake our hold.
   Show us the mortals overcome,
insane to murder kin—we track them down   340
      till they go beneath the earth,
and the dead find little freedom in the end.

     Over the victim's burning head
this chant this frenzy striking frenzy
     lightning crazing the mind   345
       this hymn of Fury
chaining the senses, ripping cross the lyre,
     withering lives of men!

Even at birth, I say, our rights were so ordained.
   The deathless gods must keep their hands far off—   350
no god may share our cups, our solemn feasts.
We want no part of their pious white robes—
   the Fates who gave us power made us free.

     Mine is the overthrow of houses, yes,
when warlust reared like a tame beast   355
     seizes near and dear—
       down on the man we swoop, aie!

---

7. Not accompanied by the lyre, an instrument associated with joyous occasions.

for all his power black him out!—
for the blood still fresh from slaughter on his hands.

So now, striving to wrench our mandate from the gods,   360
    we make ourselves exempt from their control,
we brook no trial—no god can be our judge.
        [*Reaching toward* ORESTES.]
His breed, worthy of loathing, streaked with blood,
    Zeus slights, unworthy his contempt.

    Mine is the overthrow of houses, yes,   365
    when warlust reared like a tame beast
        seizes near and dear—
            down on the man we swoop, aie!
                for all his power black him out!—
for the blood still fresh from slaughter on his hands.   370

And all men's dreams of grandeur,
        tempting the heavens,
all melt down, under earth their pride goes down—
        lost in our onslaught, black robes swarming,
            Furies throbbing, dancing out our rage.   375

Yes! leaping down from the heights,
    dead weight in the crashing footfall
        down we hurl on the runner
            breakneck for the finish—
cut him down, our fury stamps him down!   380

Down he goes, sensing nothing,
        blind with defilement . . .
darkness hovers over the man, dark guilt,
    and a dense pall overhangs his house,
        legend tells the story through her tears.   385

Yes! leaping down from the heights,
    dead weight in the crashing footfall
        down we hurl on the runner
            breakneck for the finish—
cut him down, our fury stamps him down!   390

            So the center holds.
        We are the skilled, the masterful,
            we the great fulfillers,
        memories of grief, we awesome spirits
            stern, unappeasable to man,   395
    disgraced, degraded, drive our powers through;
    banished far from god to a sunless, torchlit dusk,
        we drive men through their rugged passage,
            blinded dead and those who see by day.

Then where is the man 400
not stirred with awe, not gripped by fear
to hear us tell the law that
Fate ordains, the gods concede the Furies,
absolute till the end of time?
And so it holds, our ancient power still holds. 405
We are not without our pride, though beneath the earth
our strict battalions form their lines,
groping through the mist and sunstarved night.

[Enter ATHENA, armed for combat with her aegis and her spear.]

ATHENA From another world I heard a call for help.
I was on the Scamander's banks, just claiming Troy. 410
The Achaean warlords chose the hero's share
of what their spear had won—they decreed that land,
root and branch all mine, for all time to be,
for Theseus' sons[8] a rare, matchless gift.

Home from the wars I come, my pace unflagging, 415
wingless, flown on the whirring, breasting cape[9]
that yokes my racing spirit in her prime.

[Unfurling the aegis, seeing ORESTES and the FURIES at her shrine.]

And I see some new companions on the land.
Not fear, a sense of wonder fills my eyes.

Who are you? I address you all as one: 420
you, the stranger seated at my idol,
and you, like no one born of the sown seed,
no goddess watched by the gods, no mortal either,
not to judge by your look at least, your features . . .
Wait, I call my neighbors into question. 425
They've done nothing wrong. It offends the rights,
it violates tradition.

LEADER   You will learn it all,
young daughter of Zeus, cut to a few words.
We are the everlasting children of the Night.
Deep in the halls of Earth they call us Curses. 430

ATHENA   Now I know your birth, your rightful name—

LEADER   But not our powers, and you will learn them quickly.

ATHENA   I can accept the facts, just tell them clearly.

LEADER   Destroyers of life: we drive them from their houses.

ATHENA   And the murderer's flight, where does it all end? 435

LEADER   Where there is no joy, the word is never used.

---

8. Homer does not mention it, but in later Athenian tradition, the two sons of Theseus, the national hero who unified the whole of Attica under Athens, fought at Troy. This reference to Athenian participation in the war may be another reference to contemporary reality; Athenians had won a foothold in the Troad, the region around Troy, under the tyrant Pisistratus at the end of the sixth century B.C., and in Aeschylus's day cities in and near the Troad, along the vital route for grain of the Black Sea area, were part of the Athenian empire. But there is another reason for introducing the subject of the Trojan War. In Agamemnon the audience is given an almost unrelievedly critical view of the war. But now Orestes is to be tried and acquitted, and Agamemnon's good name restored. The war has now to be presented in a favorable light (compare lines 470ff.).   9. The aegis, a cloak worn by Athena: it has the face of the Gorgon Medusa on it. Here Athena uses it to fly; at other times it is used as a shield to produce terror, as in Odyssey 22.

ATHENA   Such flight for him? You shriek him on to that?
LEADER   Yes,
  he murdered his mother—called that murder just.
ATHENA   And nothing forced him on, no fear of someone's anger?
LEADER   What spur would force a man to kill his mother?   440
ATHENA   Two sides are here, and only half is heard.
LEADER   But the oath—he will neither take the oath nor give it,
  no, his will is set.
ATHENA   And you are set
  on the name of justice rather than the act.
LEADER   How? Teach us. You have a genius for refinements.   445
ATHENA   Injustice, I mean, should never triumph thanks to oaths.
LEADER   Then examine him yourself, judge him fairly.
ATHENA   you would turn over responsibility to me,
  to reach the final verdict?
LEADER   Certainly.
  We respect you. You show us respect.   450
     [ATHENA *turns to* ORESTES.]
ATHENA   Your turn, stranger. What do you say to this?
  Tell us your land, your birth, your fortunes.
  Then defend yourself against their charge,
  if trust in your rights has brought you here to guard
  my hearth and idol, a suppliant for purging   455
  like Ixion,[1] sacred. Speak to all this clearly,
  speak to me.
ORESTES   Queen Athena, first,
  the misgiving in your final words is strong.
  Let me remove it. I haven't come for purging.
  Look, not a stain on the hands that touch your idol.   460
  I have proof for all I say, and it is strong.

  The law condemns the man of the violent hand
  to silence, till a master trained at purging
  slits the throat of a young suckling victim,
  blood absolves his blood. Long ago   465
  at the halls of others I was fully cleansed
  in the cleansing springs, the blood of many victims.
  Threat of pollution—sweep it from your mind.
  Now for my birth. You will know at once.
  I am from Argos. My father, well you ask,   470
  was Agamemnon, sea-lord of the men-of-war,
  your partisan when you made the city Troy
  a city of the dead.
             What an ignoble death he died
  when he came home—Ai! my blackhearted mother
  cut him down, enveloped him in her handsome net—   475
  it still attests his murder in the bath.

---

1. The Greek Cain, the first murderer. He killed his father-in-law; coming to Zeus as a suppliant, he was purified by the great god himself.

But I came back, my years of exile weathered—
killed the one who bore me, I won't deny it,
killed her in revenge. I loved my father,
fiercely.
       And Apollo shares the guilt—   480
he spurred me on, he warned of the pains I'd feel
unless I acted, brought the guilty down.
But were we just or not? Judge us now.
My fate is in your hands. Stand or fall
I shall accept your verdict.

ATHENA   Too large a matter,   485
some may think, for mortal men to judge.
But by all rights not even I should decide
a case of murder—murder whets the passions.
Above all, the rites have tamed your wildness.
A suppliant, cleansed, you bring my house no harm.   490
If you are innocent, I'd adopt you for my city.
    [*Turning to the* FURIES.]
But they have their destiny too, hard to dismiss,
and if they fail to win their day in court—
how it will spread, the venom of their pride,
plague everlasting blights our land, our future . . .   495

So it stands. A crisis either way.
    [*Looking back and forth from* ORESTES *to the* FURIES.]
Embrace the one? expel the other? It defeats me.

But since the matter comes to rest on us,
I will appoint the judges of manslaughter,
swear them in, and found a tribunal here   500
for all time to come.[2]
    [*To* ORESTES *and the* FURIES.]
              My contestants,
summon your trusted witnesses and proofs,
your defenders under oath to help your cause.
And I will pick the finest men of Athens,
return and decide the issue fairly, truly—   505
bound to our oaths, our spirits bent on justice.
    [ATHENA *leaves. The* FURIES *form their chorus.*]

FURIES   Here, now, is the overthrow
of every binding law—once his appeal,
    his outrage wins the day,
his matricide! One act links all mankind,   510
hand to desperate hand in bloody license.
    Over and over deathstrokes
        dealt by children wait their parents,
    mortal generations still unborn.

---

2. The Areopagus, which in Aeschylus's lifetime was the court that tried homicide cases.

We are the Furies still, yes,   515
but now our rage that patrolled the crimes of men,
    that stalked their rage dissolves—
we loose a lethal tide to sweep the world!
Man to man foresees his neighbor's torments,
    groping to cure his own—   520
        poor wretch, there is no cure, no use,
    the drugs that ease him speed the next attack.

Now when the sudden blows come down,
let no one sound the call that once brought help,
"Justice, hear me—Furies throned in power!"   525
    Oh I can hear the father now
    or the mother sob with pain
        at the pain's onset . . . hopeless now,
    the house of Justice falls.[3]

There is a time when terror helps,   530
the watchman must stand guard upon the heart.
It helps, at times, to suffer into truth.
    Is there a man who knows no fear
    in the brightness of his heart,
        or a man's city, both are one,   535
    that still reveres the rights?

            Neither the life of anarchy
            nor the life enslaved by tyrants, no,
                worship neither.
    Strike the balance all in all and god will give you power;   540
        the laws of god may veer from north to south—
            we Furies plead for Measure.
        Violence is Impiety's child, true to its roots,
    but the spirit's great good health breeds all we love
        and all our prayers call down,   545
            prosperity and peace.

            All in all I tell you people,
            bow before the altar of the rights,
                revere it well.
    Never trample it underfoot, your eyes set on spoils;   550
        revenge will hunt the godless day and night—
            the destined end awaits.
    So honor your parents first with reverence, I say,
        and the stranger guest you welcome to your house,
            turn to attend his needs,   555
            respect his sacred rights.

---

3. The Furies argue that the acquittal of Orestes will be a precedent for universal crime. Furthermore, they will no longer, in that case, continue to see that vengeance is exacted; appeals to the Furies for justice will be disregarded (lines 523ff.).

All of your own free will, all uncompelled,
  be just and you will never want for joy,
you and your kin can never be uprooted from the earth.
  But the reckless one—I warn the marauder   560
dragging plunder, chaotic, rich beyond all rights:
    he'll strike his sails,
      harried at long last,
  stunned when the squalls of torment break his spars to bits.

He cries to the deaf, he wrestles walls of sea   565
  sheer whirlpools down, down, with the gods' laughter
breaking over the man's hot heart—they see him flailing, crushed.
  The one who boasted never to shipwreck
now will never clear the cape and steer for home;
    who lived for wealth,   570
      golden his life long—
he rams on the reef of law and drowns unwept, unseen.

    [*The scene has shifted to the Areopagus, the tribunal on the Crag of
    Ares.*[4] ATHENA *enters in procession with a herald and ten Citizens
    she has chosen to be judges.*]

ATHENA   Call for order, herald, marshal our good people.
Lift the Etruscan battle-trumpet,[5]
strain it to full pitch with human breath,   575
crash out a stabbing blast along the ranks.

    [*The trumpet sounds. The judges take up positions between the audi-
    ence and the actors.* ATHENA *separates the* FURIES *and* ORESTES,
    directing him to the Stone of Outrage and the LEADER *to the Stone
    of Unmercifulness,*[6] *where the* FURIES *form their chorus. Then*
    ATHENA *takes her stand between two urns that will receive the
    ballots.*]

And while this court of judgment fills, my city,
silence will be best. So that you can learn
my everlasting laws. And you too,

    [*To* ORESTES *and the* FURIES.]

that our verdict may be well observed by all.   580

    [APOLLO *enters suddenly and looms behind* ORESTES.]

Lord Apollo—rule it over your own sphere!
What part have you in this? Tell us.[7]

APOLLO   I come
as a witness. This man, according to custom,
this suppliant sought out my house and hearth.
I am the one who purged his bloody hands.   585
His champion too, I share responsibility
for his mother's execution.
            Bring on the trial.

---

4. A literal translation of the word *Areopagus*.   **5.** The Etruscans, a people living in central Italy, were
supposed to have invented the trumpet.   **6.** Though Aeschylus does not mention them, we know that
there were two stone bases on the Areopagus where prosecutor and defendant took their places for the
trial; naturally, the Stone of Unmercifulness was reserved for the prosecutor.   **7.** The manuscripts assign
lines 581–82 to the leader of the chorus; the peremptory tone certainly sounds more suitable to the Furies
than to Athena.

You know the rules, now turn them into justice.

[ATHENA *turns to the* FURIES.]

ATHENA   The trial begins! Yours is the first word—
the prosecution opens. Start to finish,   590
set the facts before us, make them clear.

LEADER   Numerous as we are, we will be brief.

[*To* ORESTES.]

Answer count for count, charge for charge.
First, tell us, did you kill your mother?

ORESTES   I killed her. There's no denying that.   595

LEADER   Three falls in the match.[8] One is ours already.

ORESTES   You exult before your man is on his back.

LEADER   But *how* did you kill her? You must tell us that.

ORESTES   I will. I drew my sword—more, I cut her throat.

LEADER   And who persuaded you? who led you on?   600

ORESTES   This god and his command.

[*Indicating* APOLLO.]

He bears me witness.

LEADER   The Seer? He drove you on to matricide?

ORESTES   Yes,
and to this hour I have no regrets.

LEADER   If the verdict
brings you down, you'll change your story quickly.

ORESTES   I have my trust; my father will help me from the grave.   605

LEADER   Trust to corpses now! You made your mother one.

ORESTES   I do. She had two counts against her, deadly crimes.

LEADER   How? Explain that to your judges.

ORESTES   She killed her husband—killed my father too.

LEADER   But murder set her free, and you live on for trial.   610

ORESTES   She lived on. You never drove *her* into exile—why?

LEADER   The blood of the man she killed was not her own.

ORESTES   And I? Does mother's blood run in my veins?

LEADER   How could she breed you in her body, murderer?
Disclaim your mother's blood? She gave you life.   615

[ORESTES *turns to* APOLLO.]

ORESTES   Bear me witness—show me the way, Apollo!
Did I strike her down with justice?
Strike I did, I don't deny it, no.
But how does our bloody work impress you now?—
Just or not? Decide.   620
I must make my case to them.

APOLLO [*Looking to the judges.*]   *Just*,
I say, to you and your high court, Athena.
Seer that I am, I never lie. Not once
from the Prophet's thrones have I declared
a word that bears on man, woman or city   625
that Zeus did not command, the Olympian Father.
This is *his* justice—omnipotent, I warn you.

8. As in a Greek wrestling match.

Bend to the will of Zeus. No oath can match
the power of the Father.
LEADER   Zeus, you say,
   gave that command to your oracle? He charged   630
   Orestes here to avenge his father's death
   and spurn his mother's rights?[9]
APOLLO   —Not the same
   for a noble man to die, covered with praise,
   his scepter the gift of god—murdered, at that,
   by a woman's hand, no arrows whipping in   635
   from a distance as an Amazon[1] would fight.
   But as you will hear, Athena, and your people
   poised to cast their lots and judge the case.

   Home from the long campaign he came, more won
   than lost on balance, home to her loyal, waiting arms,   640
   the welcome bath . . .
                              he was just emerging at the edge,
   and there she pitched her tent, her circling shroud—
   she shackled her man in robes,
   in her gorgeous never-ending web she chopped him down!

   Such was the outrage of his death, I tell you,   645
   the lord of the squadrons, that magnificent man.
   Her I draw to the life to lash your people,
   marshaled to reach a verdict.
LEADER   Zeus, you say,
   sets more store by a father's death? He shackled
   his own father, Kronos proud with age.   650
   Doesn't that contradict you?
          [*To the judges.*]
   Mark it well. I call you all to witness.
APOLLO   You grotesque, loathsome—the gods detest you!
   Zeus can break chains, we've cures for that,
   countless ingenious ways to set us free.   655
   But once the dust drinks down a man's blood,
   he is gone, once for all. No rising back,
   no spell sung over the grave can sing him back—
   not even Father can. Though all things else
   he can overturn and never strain for breath.[2]
LEADER   So   660
   you'd force this man's acquittal? Behold, Justice!
          [*Exhibiting* APOLLO *and* ORESTES.]
   Can a son spill his mother's blood on the ground,
   then settle into his father's halls in Argos?

---

9. The chorus wants Apollo to state clearly that Zeus gave him the specific instructions for Orestes to kill his mother. When they have that assurance, they will face Apollo with a flagrant contradiction of his claim that Zeus is the champion of the father's rights (lines 648–51).   **1.** A member of a mythical tribe of female warriors, skilled archers, who were thought to have lived in Asia Minor on the Black Sea and to have once invaded Attica.   **2.** Apollo walks into the trap. Zeus only bound Kronos, he did not kill him, says Apollo. But Orestes did kill his mother.

Where are the public altars he can use?
Can the kinsmen's holy water touch his hands?   665
APOLLO   Here is the truth, I tell you—see how right I am.
The woman you call the mother of the child
is not the parent, just a nurse to the seed,
the new-sown seed that grows and swells inside her.
The *man* is the source of life—the one who mounts.   670
She, like a stranger for a stranger, keeps
the shoot alive unless god hurts the roots.

I give you proof that all I say is true.
The father can father forth without a mother.
Here she stands, our living witness. Look—   675
    [*Exhibiting* ATHENA.]
Child sprung full-blown from Olympian Zeus,
never bred in the darkness of the womb
but such a stock no goddess could conceive![3]

And I, Pallas, with all my strong techniques
will rear your host and battlements to glory.   680
So I dispatched this suppliant to your hearth
that he might be your trusted friend forever,
that you might win a new ally, dear goddess.
He and his generations arm-in-arm with yours,
your bonds stand firm for all posterity[4]—
ATHENA   Now   685
have we heard enough? May I have them cast
their honest lots as conscience may decide?
LEADER   For us, we have shot our arrows, every one.
I wait to hear how this ordeal will end.
ATHENA   Of course.
And what can I do to merit your respect?   690
APOLLO   You have heard what you have heard.
    [*To the judges.*]
Cast your lots, my friends,
strict to the oath that you have sworn.
ATHENA   And now
if you would hear my law, you men of Greece,
you who will judge the first trial of bloodshed.   695

Now and forever more, for Aegeus' people[5]
this will be the court where judges reign.
This is the Crag of Ares, where the Amazons
pitched their tents when they came marching down
on Theseus, full tilt in their fury, erecting   700

---

3. The doctrine that the woman is not really a parent of the child but merely a sort of receptacle and nurse also appears elsewhere in Greek literature. It was a comforting formula for a society that, like the goddess Athena (see line 753), honored the male. Apollo appeals for confirmation to the birth of the goddess herself; she had no mother but was born from the head of Zeus.   4. Another reference to the Athenian alliance with Argos.   5. The Athenians. Aegeus was the father of Theseus.

a new city to overarch his city, towers thrust
against his towers—they sacrificed to Ares,
named this rock from that day onward Ares' Crag.

Here from the heights, terror and reverence,
my people's kindred powers   705
will hold them from injustice through the day
and through the mild night. Never pollute
our law with innovations. No, my citizens,
foul a clear well and you will suffer thirst.

Neither anarchy nor tyranny,[6] my people.   710
Worship the Mean, I urge you,
shore it up with reverence and never
banish terror from the gates, not outright.
Where is the righteous man who knows no fear?
The stronger your fear, your reverence for the just,   715
the stronger your country's wall and city's safety,
stronger by far than all men else possess
in Scythia's rugged steppes or Pelops' level plain.[7]
Untouched by lust for spoil, this court of law
majestic, swift to fury, rising above you   720
as you sleep, our night watch always wakeful,
guardian of our land—I found it here and now.

So I urge you, Athens. I have drawn this out
to rouse you to your future. You must rise,
each man must cast his lot and judge the case,   725
reverent to his oath. Now I have finished.
        [*The judges come forward, pass between the urns and cast their lots.*]
LEADER   Beware. Our united force can break your land.
Never wound our pride, I tell you, never.
APOLLO   The oracles, not mine alone but Zeus', too—
dread them, I warn you, never spoil their fruit.   730
        [*The* LEADER *turns to* APOLLO.]
LEADER   You dabble in works of blood beyond your depth.
Oracles, your oracles will be stained forever.
APOLLO   Oh, so the Father's judgment faltered when Ixion,
the first man-slayer, came to him for purging?
LEADER   Talk on, talk on. But if I lose this trial   735
I will return in force to crush the land.
APOLLO   Never—among the gods, young and old,
you go disgraced. I will triumph over you!
LEADER   Just as you triumphed in the house of Pheres,
luring the Fates to set men free from death.   740
APOLLO   What?—is it a crime to help the pious man,

6. Athena repeats the advice and even the words of the Furies in lines 537ff.   7. The Peloponnese in central Greece. Scythia is in southern Russia. The expression may signify just geographical expanse, but there is possibly also an appropriateness in the choice of the two locations. The Scythians were famous for their good laws, and the Peloponnese was the territory of Sparta, famous for its stable constitution.

above all, when his hour of need has come?[8]

LEADER   You brought them down, the oldest realms of order,
seduced the ancient goddesses with wine.[9]

APOLLO   *You* will fail this trial—in just a moment   745
spew your venom and never harm your enemies.

LEADER   You'd ride me down, young god, for all my years?
Well here I stand, waiting to learn the verdict.
Torn with doubt . . . to rage against the city or—

ATHENA   My work is here, to render the final judgment.   750
Orestes,
> [*Raising her arm, her hand clenched as if holding a ballot-stone.*]
     I will cast my lot for you.
No mother gave me birth.
I honor the male, in all things but marriage.
Yes, with all my heart I am my Father's child.
I cannot set more store by the woman's death—   755
she killed her husband, guardian of their house.
Even if the vote is equal, Orestes wins.[1]

Shake the lots from the urns. Quickly,
you of the jury charged to make the count.
> [*Judges come forward, empty the urns, and count the ballot-stones.*]

ORESTES   O God of the Light, Apollo, how will the verdict go?   760

LEADER   O Night, dark mother, are you watching now?

ORESTES   Now for the goal—the noose, or the new day!

LEADER   Now we go down, or forge ahead in power.

APOLLO   Shake out the lots and count them fairly, friends
Honor Justice. An error in judgment now   765
can mean disaster. The cast of a single lot
restores a house to greatness.
> [*Receiving the judges' count,* ATHENA *lifts her arm once more.*]

ATHENA   The man goes free,
cleared of the charge of blood. The lots are equal.

ORESTES   O Pallas Athena—you, you save my house!
I was shorn of the fatherland but you   770
reclaim it for me. Now any Greek will say,
"He lives again, the man of Argos lives
on his fathers' great estates. Thanks to Pallas,
Apollo, and Zeus, the lord of all fulfillment,
Third, Saving Zeus." He respected father's death,   775
looked down on mother's advocates—
> [*Indicating the* FURIES.]
                          he saved me.
And now I journey home. But first I swear
to you, your land and assembled host, I swear

8. Father of Admetus, king of Thessaly. Apollo repaid kindness shown him by Admetus by persuading the fates to let Admetus avoid an early death if he could find someone willing to die in his stead. (His wife, Alcestis, was willing; this is the subject of Euripides' famous play *Alcestis*.)   9. According to the Furies, Apollo got the Fates drunk.   1. So, in Athenian courts, a split jury meant acquittal. Athena announces that if the votes are equal, she will give a casting vote for acquittal. (At the real court of the Areopagus, if the votes were equal, the defendant was declared acquitted by "the vote of Athena.")

by the future years that bring their growing yield
that no man, no helmsman of Argos wars on Athens,   780
spears in the vanguard moving out for conquest.
We ourselves, even if we must rise up from the grave,
will deal with those who break the oath I take[2]—
baffle them with disasters, curse their marches,
send them hawks aloft on the left[3] at every crossing—   785
make their pains recoil upon their heads.
But all who keep our oath, who uphold your rights
and citadel forever, comrades spear to spear,
we bless with all the kindness of our heart.

Now farewell, you and the people of your city.   790
Good wrestling—a grip no foe can break.
A saving hope, a spear to bring you triumph!
    [*Exit* ORESTES, *followed by* APOLLO. *The* FURIES *reel in wild con-
    fusion around* ATHENA.]

FURIES   You, you younger gods!—you have ridden down
    the ancient laws, wrenched them from my grasp—
and I, robbed of my birthright, suffering, great with wrath,   795
    I loose my poison over the soil, aieee!—
poison to match my grief comes pouring out my heart,
    cursing the land to burn it sterile and now
rising up from its roots a cancer blasting leaf and child,
    now for Justice, Justice!—cross the face of the earth   800
the bloody tide comes hurling, all mankind destroyed.
. . . Moaning, only moaning? What will I do?
    The mockery of it, Oh unbearable,
mortified by Athens,
we the daughters of Night,   805
our power stripped, cast down.

ATHENA   Yield to me.
No more heavy spirits. You were not defeated—
the vote was tied, a verdict fairly reached
with no disgrace to you, no, Zeus brought
luminous proof before us. He who spoke   810
god's oracle, he bore witness that Orestes
did the work but should not suffer harm.

And now you'd vent your anger, hurt the land?
Consider a moment. Calm yourself. Never
render us barren, raining your potent showers   815
down like spears, consuming every seed.
By all my rights I promise you your seat
in the depths of earth, yours by all rights—
stationed at hearths equipped with glistening thrones,
covered with praise! My people will revere you.   820

2. Orestes will be a "hero" in the Greek sense: a protecting spirit for the land.   3. Birds seen on the left
were a portent of an evil to come.

FURIES   You, you younger gods!—you have ridden down
    the ancient laws, wrenched them from my grasp—
  and I, robbed of my birthright, suffering, great with wrath,
    I loose my poison over the soil, aieee!—
poison to match my grief comes pouring out my heart,   825
      cursing the land to burn it sterile and now
rising up from its roots a cancer blasting leaf and child,
      now for Justice, Justice!—cross the face of the earth
the bloody tide comes hurling, all mankind destroyed.
   . . . Moaning, only moaning? What will I do?   830
    The mockery of it, Oh unbearable,
mortified by Athens,
we the daughters of Night,
our power stripped, cast down.
ATHENA   You have your power,
  you are goddesses—but not to turn   835
on the world of men and ravage it past cure.
I put my trust in Zeus and . . . must I add this?
I am the only god who knows the keys
to the armory where his lightning-bolt is sealed.
No need of that, not here.
                    Let me persuade you.   840
The lethal spell of your voice, never cast it
down on the land and blight its harvest home.
Lull asleep that salt black wave of anger—
awesome, proud with reverence, live with me.
The land is rich, and more, when its first fruits,   845
offered for heirs and the marriage rites, are yours[4]
to hold forever, you will praise my words.
FURIES   But for me to suffer such disgrace . . . I,
the proud heart of the past, driven under the earth,
condemned, like so much filth,   850
   and the fury in me breathing hatred—
O good Earth,
    what is this stealing under the breast,
what agony racks the spirit? . . . Night, dear Mother Night!
All's lost, our ancient powers torn away by their cunning,   855
ruthless hands, the gods so hard to wrestle down
obliterate us all.
ATHENA   I will bear with your anger.
You are older. The years have taught you more,
much more than I can know. But Zeus, I think,
gave me some insight too, that has its merits.   860
If you leave for an alien land and alien people,
you will come to love this land, I promise you.
As time flows on, the honors flow through all

---

4. The Furies, as spirits of the Earth, did in fact receive in Athens offerings for children born and marriages
made.

my citizens, and you, throned in honor
before the house of Erechtheus,[5] will harvest   865
more from men and women moving in solemn file
than you can win throughout the mortal world.

Here in our homeland never cast the stones
that whet our bloodlust. Never waste our youth,
inflaming them with the burning wine of strife.   870
Never pluck the heart of the battle cock
and plant it in our people—intestine war
seething against themselves. Let our wars
rage on abroad,[6] with all their force, to satisfy
our powerful lust for fame. But as for the bird   875
that fights at home—my curse on civil war.

This is the life I offer, it is yours to take.
Do great things, feel greatness, greatly honored.
Share this country cherished by the gods.
FURIES   But for me to suffer such disgrace . . . I,   880
the proud heart of the past, driven under the earth,
condemned, like so much filth,
   and the fury in me breathing hatred—
O good Earth,
      what is this stealing under the breast,   885
what agony racks the spirit? . . . Night, dear Mother Night!
All's lost, our ancient powers torn away by their cunning,
ruthless hands, the gods so hard to wrestle down
obliterate us all.
ATHENA   No, I will never tire
of telling you your gifts. So that you,   890
the older gods, can never say that I,
a young god and the mortals of my city
drove you outcast, outlawed from the land.

But if you have any reverence for Persuasion,
the majesty of Persuasion,   895
the spell of my voice that would appease your fury—
Oh please stay . . .
                  and if you refuse to stay,
it would be wrong, unjust to afflict this city
with wrath, hatred, populations routed. Look,
it is all yours, a royal share of our land—   900
justly entitled, glorified forever.
LEADER   Queen Athena,
where is the home you say is mine to hold?

5. The old shrine of Erechtheus on the Acropolis had been destroyed by the Persians in 480 B.C.; in 421
B.C. the Athenians began the construction of the new Erechtheum, which, much damaged, still
stands.   6. Athens was at this time at war with Sparta, and its forces may still have been engaged in
Egypt.

ATHENA   Where all the pain and anguish end. Accept it.
LEADER   And if I do, what honor waits for me?
ATHENA   No house can thrive without you.
LEADER   You would do that—   905
grant me that much power?
ATHENA   Whoever reveres us—
we will raise the fortunes of their lives.
LEADER   And you will pledge me that, for all time to come?
ATHENA   Yes—I must never promise things I cannot do.
LEADER   Your magic is working . . . I can feel the hate,   910
the fury slip away.
ATHENA   At last! And now take root
in the land and win yourself new friends.
LEADER   A spell—
what spell to sing? to bind the land forever? Tell us.
ATHENA   Nothing that strikes a note of brutal conquest. Only peace—
blessings, rising up from the earth and the heaving sea,   915
and down the vaulting sky let the wind-gods breathe
a wash of sunlight streaming through the land,
and the yield of soil and grazing cattle flood
our city's life with power and never flag
with time. Make the seed of men live on,   920
the more they worship you the more they thrive.
I love them as a gardener loves his plants,
these upright men, this breed fought free of grief.
All that is yours to give.
                                    And I,
in the trials of war where fighters burn for fame,   925
will never endure the overthrow of Athens—
all will praise her, victor city, pride of man.
        [The FURIES assemble, dancing around ATHENA, who becomes their
        leader.]
FURIES   I will embrace
                        one home with you, Athena,
                                never fail the city   930
                you and Zeus almighty, you and Ares
                hold as the fortress of the gods, the shield
        of the high Greek altars, glory of the powers.
        Spirit of Athens, hear my words, my prayer
                        like a prophet's warm and kind,   935
                        that the rare good things of life
                                come rising crest on crest,
                        sprung from the rich black earth and
                        gleaming with the bursting flash of sun.
ATHENA   These blessings I bestow on you, my people, gladly.   940
I enthrone these strong, implacable spirits here
and root them in our soil.
                                    Theirs,
        theirs to rule the lives of men,
                it is their fated power.

But he who has never felt their weight,   945
or known the blows of life and how they fall,
the crimes of his fathers hale him toward their bar,
and there for all his boasts—destruction,
   silent, majestic in anger,
crushes him to dust.

FURIES   Yes and I ban   950
        the winds that rock the olive—
          hear my love, my blessing—
   thwart their scorching heat that blinds the buds,
      hold from our shores the killing icy gales,
   and I ban the blight that creeps on fruit and withers—   955
    God of creation, Pan, make flocks increase
      and the ewes drop fine twin lambs
        when the hour of labor falls.
        And silver,[7] child of Earth,
          secret treasure of Hermes,   960
    come to light and praise the gifts of god.

ATHENA   Blessings—now do you hear, you guards of Athens,
   all that she will do?
Fury the mighty queen, the dread
of the deathless gods and those beneath the earth,   965
deals with mortals clearly, once for all.
She delivers songs to some, to others
   a blinding life of tears—
Fury works her will.

FURIES   And the lightning stroke
      that cuts men down before their prime, I curse,   970
       but the lovely girl who finds a mate's embrace,
   the deep joy of wedded life—O grant that gift, that prize,
      you gods of wedlock, grant it, goddesses of Fate!
      Sisters born of the Night our mother,
          spirits steering law,   975
        sharing at all our hearths,
       at all times bearing down
        to make our lives more just,
    all realms exalt you highest of the gods.

ATHENA   Behold, my land, what blessings Fury kindly,   980
   gladly brings to pass—
I am in my glory! Yes, I love Persuasion;
she watched my words, she met their wild refusals.
Thanks to Zeus of the Councils who can turn
dispute to peace—he won the day.   985
   [*To the* FURIES.]
Thanks to our duel for blessings;
we win through it all.

FURIES   And the brutal strife,

---

7. At Laurion (in southeast Attica) silver had been mined for many years when, sometime before 480 B.C., rich new veins were discovered. The Athenians used the money to build the fleet that fought at Salamis.

the civil war devouring men, I pray
that it never rages through our city, no,
that the good Greek soil never drinks the blood of Greeks,   990
shed in an orgy of reprisal life for life—
that Fury like a beast will never
rampage through the land.
Give joy in return for joy,
one common will for love,   995
and hate with one strong heart:
such union heals a thousand ills of man.

ATHENA   Do you *hear* how Fury sounds her blessings forth,
how Fury finds the way?
Shining out of the terror of their faces   1000
I can see great gains for you, my people.
Hold them kindly, kind as they are to you.
Exalt them always, you exalt your land,
your city straight and just—
its light goes through the world.

FURIES   Rejoice,   1005
rejoice in destined wealth,
rejoice, Athena's people—
poised by the side of Zeus,
loved by the loving virgin girl,
achieve humanity at last,   1010
nestling under Pallas' wings
and blessed with Father's love.

ATHENA   You too rejoice! and I must lead the way
to your chambers by the holy light of these,
your escorts bearing fire.   1015
[*Enter* ATHENA's *entourage of women, bearing offerings and victims
and torches still unlit.*]
Come, and sped beneath the earth
by our awesome sacrifices,
keep destruction from the country,
bring prosperity home to Athens,
triumph sailing in its wake.
And you,   1020
my people born of the Rock King,[8]
lead on our guests for life, my city—
May they treat you with compassion,
compassionate as you will be to them.

FURIES   Rejoice!—
rejoice—the joy resounds—   1025
all those who dwell in Athens,
spirits and mortals, come,
govern Athena's city well,
revere us well, we are your guests;
you will learn to praise your Furies,   1030

8. The legendary ancestor Cranaos, whose name means "rocky." The soil of Attica is not rich.

        you will praise the fortunes of your lives.
ATHENA   My thanks! And I will speed your prayers, your blessings—
  lit by the torches breaking into flame
  I send you home, home to the core of Earth,
  escorted by these friends who guard my idol   1035
  duty-bound.
       [ATHENA's *entourage comes forward, bearing crimson robes.*]
          Bright eye of the land of Theseus,
  come forth, my splendid troupe. Girls and mothers,
  trains of aged women grave in movement,
  dress our Furies now in blood-red robes.[9]
  Praise them—let the torch move on!   1040
  So the love this family bears toward our land
  will bloom in human strength from age to age.
       [*The women invest the* FURIES *and sing the final chorus. Torches
       blaze; a procession forms, including the actors and the judges.*
       ATHENA *leads them from the theater and escorts them through the
       city.*]
THE WOMEN OF THE CITY   On, on, good spirits born for glory,
  Daughters of Night, her children always young,
      now under loyal escort—   1045
  Blessings, people of Athens, sing your blessings out.

    Deep, deep in the first dark vaults of Earth,
  sped by the praise and victims we will bring,
      reverence will attend you—
  Blessings now, all people, sing your blessings out.   1050

  You great good Furies, bless the land with kindly hearts,
  you Awesome Spirits,[1] come—exult in the blazing torch,
      exultant in our fires, journey on.
  Cry, cry in triumph, carry on the dancing on and on!

  This peace between Athena's people and their guests   1055
  must never end. All-seeing Zeus and Fate embrace,
      down they come to urge our union on—
  Cry, cry in triumph, carry on the dancing on and on!

---

9. At the Great Panathenea, the principal festival of Athens, resident aliens as well as full citizens took part in the procession to the Acropolis. The resident aliens, *metics* as they were called, wore crimson cloaks on this occasion. The Furies are thus given residential status in Attic soil.   1. *Semnai* in Greek, a favorable formula for the Furies, like *Eumenides* (kindly ones), the title of the play.

SOPHOCLES

ca. 496–406 B.C.

Aeschylus belonged to the generation that fought at Marathon; his manhood and his old age were passed in the heroic period of the Persian defeat on Greek soil and the war that Athens fought to liberate its kin in the islands of the Aegean and on the Asiatic coast. Sophocles, his younger contemporary, lived to see an Athens that had advanced in power and prosperity far beyond the city that Aeschylus knew. The league of free Greek cities against Persia that Athens had led to victory in the Aegean had become an empire, in which Athens taxed and coerced the subject cities that had once been its free allies. Sophocles, born around 496 B.C., played his part—a prominent one—in the city's affairs. In 443 B.C. he served as one of the treasurers of the imperial league and, with Pericles, as one of the ten generals elected for the war against the island of Samos, which tried to secede from the Athenian league a few years later. When the Athenian expedition to Sicily ended in disaster, Sophocles was appointed to a special committee set up in 411 B.C. to deal with the emergency. He died two years before Athens surrendered to Sparta.

His career as a brilliantly successful dramatist began in 468; in that year he won first prize at the Dionysia, competing against Aeschylus. Over the next sixty-two years he produced more than 120 plays. He won first prize no fewer than twenty-four times, and when he was not first, he came in second, never third.

Aeschylus had been an actor as well as a playwright and director, but Sophocles, early in his career, gave up acting. It was he who added a third actor to the team; the early Aeschylean plays (*Persians, Seven Against Thebes,* and *Suppliants*) can be played by two actors (who of course can change masks to extend the range of *dramatis personae*). In the *Oresteia,* Aeschylus has taken advantage of the Sophoclean third actor; this makes possible the role of Cassandra, the one three-line speech of Pylades in *The Libation Bearers,* and the trial scene in *The Eumenides.* But Sophocles used his third actor to create complex triangular scenes like the dialogue between Oedipus and the Corinthian messenger, which reveals to a listening Jocasta the ghastly truth that Oedipus will not discover until the next scene.

We have only seven of his plays, and not many of them can be accurately dated. *Ajax* (which deals with the suicide of the hero whose shade turns silently away from Odysseus in the *Odyssey)* and *Trachiniae* (the story of the death of Heracles) are both generally thought to be early productions. *Antigone* is fairly securely fixed in the late 440s, and *Oedipus the King* was probably staged during the early years of the Peloponnesian War (431–404 B.C.). For *Electra* we have no date, but it is probably later than *Oedipus the King. Philoctetes,* a tale of the Trojan War, was staged in 409 B.C. and *Oedipus at Colonus,* which presents Oedipus's strangely triumphant death on Athenian soil, was produced after Sophocles' death.

Most of these plays date from the last half of the fifth century B.C.; they were written in and for an Athens that, since the days of Aeschylus, had undergone an intellectual revolution. It was in a time of critical reevaluation of accepted standards and traditions that Sophocles produced his masterpiece, *Oedipus the King,* and the problems of the time are reflected in the play.

Oedipus the King, which deals with a man of high principles and probing intelligence who follows the prompting of that intelligence to the final consequence of true self-knowledge—which makes him put out his eyes—was as full of significance for Sophocles' contemporaries as it is for us. Unlike a modern dramatist, Sophocles used for his tragedy a story well known to the audience and as old as their own history, a legend told by parent to child, handed down from generation to generation because of its implicit wealth of meaning, learned in childhood, and rooted deep in the consciousness of every member of the community. Such a story the Greeks called a myth, and the use of it presented Sophocles, as it did Aeschylus in his trilogy, with material that, apart from its great inherent dramatic potential, already possessed the significance and authority that modern dramatists must create for themselves. It had the authority of history, for the history of ages that leave no records is myth—that is to say, the significant event of the past, stripped of irrelevancies and imaginatively shaped by the oral tradition. It had a religious authority, for the Oedipus story, like the story of the house of Atreus, is concerned with the relation between humanity and gods. Last, and this is especially true of the Oedipus myth, it had the power, because of its subject matter, to arouse the irrational hopes and fears that lie deep and secret in the human consciousness.

The use of the familiar myth enabled the dramatist to draw on all its wealth of unformulated meaning, but it did not prevent him from striking a contemporary note. Oedipus, in Sophocles' play, is at one and the same time the mysterious figure of the past who broke the most fundamental human taboos and a typical fifth-century Athenian. His character contains all the virtues for which the Athenians were famous and the vices for which they were notorious. The best commentary on Oedipus's character is the speech that Thucydides, the contemporary historian of the Peloponnesian War, attributed to a Corinthian spokesman at Sparta; it is a hostile but admiring assessment of the Athenian genius. "Athenians . . . [are] equally quick in the conception and in the execution of every new plan"—so Oedipus has already sent to Delphi when the priest advises him to do so and has already sent for Tiresias when the chorus suggests this course of action. "They are bold beyond their strength; they run risks which prudence would condemn"—as Oedipus risked his life to answer the riddle of the Sphinx and later, in spite of the oracle about his marriage, accepted the hand of the queen. "In the midst of misfortune they are full of hope"—so Oedipus, when he is told that he is not the son of Polybus and Merope, and Jocasta has already realized whose son he is, claims that he is the "child of Fortune." "When they do not carry out an intention that they have formed, they seem to have sustained a personal bereavement"—so Oedipus, shamed by Jocasta and the chorus into sparing Creon's life, yields sullenly and petulantly.

The Athenian devotion to the city, which received the main emphasis in Pericles' praise of Athens, is strong in Oedipus; his answer to the priest at the beginning of the play shows that he is a conscientious and patriotic ruler. His quick rage is the characteristic fault of Athenian democracy, which in 406 B.C., to give only one instance, condemned and executed the generals who had failed, in the stress of weather and battle, to pick up the drowned bodies of their own men killed in the naval engagement at Arginusae. Oedipus is like the fifth-century Athenian most of all in his confidence in the human intelligence, especially his own. This confidence takes him in the play through the whole cycle of the critical, rationalist movement of the century, from the piety and orthodoxy he displays in the opening scene, through his taunts at oracles when he hears that Polybus is dead, to the despairing courage with which he accepts the consequences when he sees the abyss opening at his feet. "I'm right at the edge, the horrible truth—I've got to say it!" says the herdsman from whom he is dragging the truth. "And I'm right at the edge of hearing horrors, yes," Oedipus replies, "but I must hear!" And hear he does. He learns that the oracle he had first fought against and then laughed at has been fulfilled, that every step his intelligence prompted was one step nearer to disaster, that his knowledge was ignorance and his clear vision blindness. Faced with the reality that his determined probing finally reveals, he puts out his eyes.

The relation of Oedipus's character to the development of the action is the basis of the most famous attempt to define the nature of the tragic process. Aristotle, writing his *Poetics* in the next century, developed the theory that pity and terror are aroused most effectively by the spectacle of a man who is "not pre-eminent in virtue and justice, and yet on the other hand does not fall into misfortune through vice or depravity, but falls because of some mistake, one among the number of the highly renowned and prosperous, such as Oedipus." Other references by Aristotle to this play make it clear that this influential doctrine of the fall of the tragic hero was based particularly on Sophocles' masterpiece, and it has been universally applied to the play. But the great influence (and validity) of the Aristotelian theory should not be allowed to obscure the fact that Sophocles' *Oedipus the King* is more highly organized and economical than Aristotle implies. The fact that the critics have differed about the nature of Oedipus's mistake or frailty (his errors are many, and his frailties include anger, impiety, and self-confidence) is a clue to the real situation. Oedipus falls not through "some vicious mole of nature" or some "particular fault" (to use Hamlet's terms) but because he is the man he is, because of all aspects of his character, good and bad alike; and the development of the action right through to the catastrophe shows us every aspect of his character at work in the process of self-revelation and self-destruction. His first decision in the play, to hear Creon's message from Delphi in public rather than, as Creon suggests, in private, is evidence of his kingly solicitude for his people and his trust in them, but it makes certain the full publication of the truth. His proclamation of a curse on the murderer of Laius, although prompted by his civic zeal, makes his final situation worse than it otherwise would have been. His anger at Tiresias forces a revelation that drives him on to accuse Creon; this in turn provokes Jocasta's revelations. And throughout the play his confidence in the efficacy of his own action, his hopefulness as the situation darkens, and his passion for discovering the truth guide the steps of the investigation that is to reveal the detective as the criminal. All aspects of his character, good and bad alike, are equally involved; it is no frailty or error that leads him to the terrible truth, but his total personality.

The character of Oedipus as revealed in the play does something more than explain the present action; it also explains his past. In Oedipus's speeches and actions on stage we can see the man who, given the circumstances in which Oedipus was involved, would inevitably do just what Oedipus has done. Each action on stage shows us the mood in which he committed some action in the past; his angry death sentence on Creon reveals the man who killed Laius because of an insult on the highway; his proclamation of total excommunication for the unknown murderer shows us the man who, without forethought, accepted the hand of Jocasta; his intelligent, persistent search for the truth shows us the brain and the courage that solved the riddle of the Sphinx. The revelation of his character in the play is at once a re-creation of his past and an interpretation of the oracle that predicted his future.

This organization of the material is what makes it possible for us to accept the story as tragedy at all, for it emphasizes Oedipus's independence of the oracle. When we first see Oedipus, he has already committed the actions for which he is to suffer— actions prophesied, before his birth, by Apollo. But the dramatist's emphasis on Oedipus's character suggests that although Apollo has predicted what Oedipus will do, he does not determine it; Oedipus determines his own conduct, by being the man he is. The relationship between Apollo's prophecy and Oedipus's actions is not that of cause and effect. It is the relationship of two independent entities that are equated.

This correspondence between his character and his fate removes the obstacle to our full acceptance of the play that an external fate governing his action would set up. Nevertheless, we feel that he suffers more than he deserves. He has served as an example of the inadequacy of the human intellect and a warning that there is a power in the universe that humanity cannot control or even fully understand, but Oedipus the man still has our sympathy. Sophocles felt this too, and in his last play, *Oedipus at Colonus,* he dealt with the reward that finally balanced Oedipus's suffering. In *Oedipus the King* itself there is a foreshadowing of this final development; the last scene shows us a man already beginning to recover from the shock of the catastrophe and reasserting a natural superiority.

"I am going—you know on what condition?" he says to Creon when ordered back into the house, and a few lines later Creon has to say bluntly to him: "Still the king, the master of all things? / No more: here your power ends." This renewed imperiousness is the first expression of a feeling on his part that he is not entirely guilty, a beginning of the reconstitution of the magnificent man of the opening scenes; it reaches its fulfillment in the final Oedipus play, *Oedipus at Colonus*, in which he is a titanic figure, confident of his innocence and more masterful than he has ever been.

For a short, general survey of Sophoclean drama, see P. E. Easterling in *The Cambridge History of Classical Literature* (1985), pp. 295–316. B. M. W. Knox, *Oedipus at Thebes* (1957), is a detailed examination of the play in the context of its age; Knox's *The Heroic Temper* (1964) concentrates on the characters of Oedipus, Antigone, Electra, and Philoctetes. Sophocles, *The Three Theban Plays* (1982), contains a substantial introduction to *Oedipus the King*. Harold Bloom, *Sophocles's Oedipus Rex* (1988), is a well-chosen collection of essays on the play. See also R. P. Winnington-Ingram, *Sophocles: An Interpretation* (1980), pp. 150–204, and Charles Segal, *Oedipus Tyrannus: Tragic Heroism and the Limits of Knowledge* (1993). David Seale, *Vision and Stagecraft in Sophocles* (1982), is a stimulating discussion of the themes of sight, blindness, and knowledge in relation to the experience of watching a play.

PRONOUNCING GLOSSARY

The following list uses common English syllables and stress accents to provide rough equivalents of selected words whose pronunciation may be unfamiliar to the general reader.

Antigone: *an-ti'-go-nee*

Oedipus: *ee'-di-pus* or *é-di-pus*

Eteocles: *ee-tee'-ok-leez*

Polynices: *po-li-nai'-seez*

Ismene: *iz-mee'-nee*

Tiresias: *tai-ree'-see-uhs*

Oedipus the King[1]

CHARACTERS

OEDIPUS, *king of Thebes*

A PRIEST *of Zeus*

CREON, *brother of Jocasta*

A CHORUS *of Theban citizens and their* LEADER

TIRESIAS, *a blind prophet*

JOCASTA, *the queen, wife of Oedipus*

A MESSENGER *from Corinth*

A SHEPHERD

A MESSENGER *from inside the palace*

ANTIGONE, ISMENE, *daughters of Oedipus and Jocasta*

GUARDS *and attendants*

PRIESTS *of Thebes*

[TIME AND SCENE: *The royal house of Thebes. Double doors dominate the façade; a stone altar stands at the center of the stage.*

Many years have passed since OEDIPUS *solved the riddle of the Sphinx and ascended the throne of Thebes, and now a plague has struck the city. A procession of priests enters; suppliants, broken and despondent, they carry branches wound in wool and lay them on the altar.*

The doors open. Guards assemble. OEDIPUS *comes forward, majestic but for a telltale limp, and slowly views the condition of his people.*]

OEDIPUS   Oh my children, the new blood of ancient Thebes,
    why are you here? Huddling at my altar,
    praying before me, your branches wound in wool.[2]
    Our city reeks with the smoke of burning incense,

---

1. Translated by Robert Fagles.   2. The insignia of suppliants, laid on the altar and left there until the suppliant's request was granted. At the end of the scene, when Oedipus promises action, he will tell them to take the branches away.

rings with cries for the Healer[3] and wailing for the dead.   5
I thought it wrong, my children, to hear the truth
from others, messengers. Here I am myself—
you all know me, the world knows my fame:
I am Oedipus.
      [*Helping a* PRIEST *to his feet.*]
                Speak up, old man. Your years,
your dignity—you should speak for the others.   10
Why here and kneeling, what preys upon you so?
Some sudden fear? some strong desire?
You can trust me. I am ready to help,
I'll do anything. I would be blind to misery
not to pity my people kneeling at my feet.   15
PRIEST   Oh Oedipus, king of the land, our greatest power!
You see us before you now, men of all ages
clinging to your altars. Here are boys,
still too weak to fly from the nest,
and here the old, bowed down with the years,   20
the holy ones—a priest of Zeus myself—and here
the picked, unmarried men, the young hope of Thebes.
And all the rest, your great family gathers now,
branches wreathed, massing in the squares,
kneeling before the two temples of queen Athena   25
or the river-shrine where the embers glow and die
and Apollo sees the future in the ashes.[4]
                          Our city—
look around you, see with your own eyes—
our ship pitches wildly, cannot lift her head
from the depths, the red waves of death . . .   30
Thebes is dying. A blight on the fresh crops
and the rich pastures, cattle sicken and die,
and the women die in labor, children stillborn,
and the plague, the fiery god of fever hurls down
on the city, his lightning slashing through us—   35
raging plague in all its vengeance, devastating
the house of Cadmus![5] And black Death luxuriates
in the raw, wailing miseries of Thebes.
Now we pray to you. You cannot equal the gods,
your children know that, bending at your altar.   40
But we do rate you first of men,
both in the common crises of our lives
and face-to-face encounters with the gods.
You freed us from the Sphinx, you came to Thebes
and cut us loose from the bloody tribute we had paid   45
that harsh, brutal singer.[6] We taught you nothing,

---

3. Apollo.   4. At a temple of Apollo in Thebes the priests foretold the future according to patterns they saw in the ashes of the burned flesh of sacrificial victims.   5. Mythical founder of Thebes and its first king.   6. The sphinx was the winged female monster that terrorized the city of Thebes until her riddle was finally answered by Oedipus. The riddle was "What is it that walks on four feet and two feet and three feet and has only one voice; when it walks on most feet, it is weakest?" Oedipus's answer was "Man." (We have four feet as children crawling on all fours and three feet in old age when we walk with the aid of a stick.) Many young men of Thebes had tried to answer the riddle, failed, and been killed.

no skill, no extra knowledge, still you triumphed.
A god was with you, so they say, and we believe it—
you lifted up our lives.
                              So now again,
Oedipus, king, we bend to you, your power—   50
we implore you, all of us on our knees:
find us strength, rescue! Perhaps you've heard
the voice of a god or something from other men,
Oedipus . . . what do you know?
The man of experience—you see it every day—   55
his plans will work in a crisis, his first of all.

Act now—we beg you, best of men, raise up our city!
Act, defend yourself, your former glory!
Your country calls you savior now
for your zeal, your action years ago.   60
Never let us remember of your reign:
you helped us stand, only to fall once more.
Oh raise up our city, set us on our feet.
The omens were good that day you brought us joy—
be the same man today!   65
Rule our land, you know you have the power,
but rule a land of the living, not a wasteland.
Ship and towered city are nothing, stripped of men
alive within it, living all as one.

OEDIPUS   My children,
I pity you. I see—how could I fail to see   70
what longings bring you here? Well I know
you are sick to death, all of you,
but sick as you are, not one is sick as I.
Your pain strikes each of you alone, each
in the confines of himself, no other. But my spirit   75
grieves for the city, for myself and all of you.
I wasn't asleep, dreaming. You haven't wakened me—
I've wept through the nights, you must know that,
groping, laboring over many paths of thought.
After a painful search I found one cure: 80
I acted at once. I sent Creon,
my wife's own brother, to Delphi—
Apollo the Prophet's oracle[7]—to learn
what I might do or say to save our city.

Today's the day. When I count the days gone by   85
it torments me . . . what is he doing?
Strange, he's late, he's gone too long.
But once he returns, then, then I'll be a traitor
if I do not do all the god makes clear.

PRIEST   Timely words. The men over there   90
are signaling—Creon's just arriving.

7. Below Mount Parnassus in central Greece.

OEDIPUS [*Sighting* CREON, *then turning to the altar.*]
                                    Lord Apollo,
   let him come with a lucky word of rescue,
   shining like his eyes!
PRIEST Welcome news, I think—he's crowned, look,
   and the laurel wreath is bright with berries.[8]   95
OEDIPUS We'll soon see. He's close enough to hear—
   [*Enter* CREON *from the side; his face is shaded with a wreath.*]
   Creon, prince, my kinsman, what do you bring us?
   What message from the god?
CREON   Good news.
   I tell you even the hardest things to bear,
   if they should turn out well, all would be well.   100
OEDIPUS Of course, but what were the god's *words*? There's no hope
   and nothing to fear in what you've said so far.
CREON If you want my report in the presence of these . . .
   [*Pointing to the priests while drawing* OEDIPUS *toward the palace.*]
   I'm ready now, or we might go inside.
OEDIPUS   Speak out,
   speak to us all. I grieve for these, my people,   105
   far more than I fear for my own life.
CREON   Very well,
   I will tell you what I heard from the god.
   Apollo commands us—he was quite clear—
   "Drive the corruption from the land,
   don't harbor it any longer, past all cure,   110
   don't nurse it in your soil—root it out!"
OEDIPUS How can we cleanse ourselves—what rites?
   What's the source of the trouble?
CREON Banish the man, or pay back blood with blood.
   Murder sets the plague-storm on the city.
OEDIPUS   Whose murder?   115
   Whose fate does Apollo bring to light?
CREON   Our leader,
   my lord, was once a man named Laius,
   before you came and put us straight on course.
OEDIPUS   I know—
   or so I've heard. I never saw the man myself.
CREON Well, he was killed, and Apollo commands us now—   120
   he could not be more clear,
   "Pay the killers back—whoever is responsible."
OEDIPUS Where on earth are they? Where to find it now,
   the trail of the ancient guilt so hard to trace?
CREON: "Here in Thebes," he said.   125
   Whatever is sought for can be caught, you know,
   whatever is neglected slips away.
OEDIPUS   But where,
   in the palace, the fields or foreign soil,

---

8. Creon is wearing a crown of laurel as a sign that he brings good news.

where did Laius meet his bloody death?
CREON   He went to consult an oracle, Apollo said,   130
    and he set out and never came home again.
OEDIPUS   No messenger, no fellow-traveler saw what happened?
    Someone to cross-examine?
CREON   No,
    they were all killed but one. He escaped,
    terrified, he could tell us nothing clearly,   135
    nothing of what he saw—just one thing.
OEDIPUS   What's that?
    one thing could hold the key to it all,
    a small beginning give us grounds for hope.
CREON   He said thieves attacked them—a whole band,
    not single-handed, cut King Laius down.
OEDIPUS   A thief,   140
    so daring, so wild, he'd kill a king? Impossible,
    unless conspirators paid him off in Thebes.
CREON   We suspected as much. But with Laius dead
    no leader appeared to help us in our troubles.
OEDIPUS   Trouble? Your *king* was murdered—royal blood!   145
    What stopped you from tracking down the killer
    then and there?
CREON   The singing, riddling Sphinx.
    She . . . persuaded us to let the mystery go
    and concentrate on what lay at our feet.
OEDIPUS   No,
    I'll start again—I'll bring it all to light myself!   150
    Apollo is right, and so are you, Creon,
    to turn our attention back to the murdered man.
    Now you have *me* to fight for you, you'll see:
    I am the land's avenger by all rights,
    and Apollo's champion too.   155
    But not to assist some distant kinsman, no,
    for my own sake I'll rid us of this corruption.
    Whoever killed the king may decide to kill me too,
    with the same violent hand—by avenging Laius
    I defend myself.
        [*To the priests.*]
                    Quickly, my children.   160
    Up from the steps, take up your branches now.
        [*To the guards.*]
    One of you summon the city[9] here before us,
    tell them I'll do everything. God help us,
    we will see our triumph—or our fall.
        [OEDIPUS *and* CREON *enter the palace, followed by the guards.*]
PRIEST   Rise, my sons. The kindness we came for   165
    Oedipus volunteers himself.
    Apollo has sent his word, his oracle—

---

9. Represented by the chorus, which comes on to the circular dancing floor immediately after this scene.

Come down, Apollo, save us, stop the plague.

[*The priests rise, remove their branches and exit to the side. Enter a* CHORUS, *the citizens of Thebes, who have not heard the news that* CREON *brings. They march around the altar, chanting.*]

CHORUS   Zeus!
Great welcome voice of Zeus,[1] what do you bring?
What word from the gold vaults of Delphi   170
comes to brilliant Thebes? Racked with terror—
      terror shakes my heart
and I cry your wild cries, Apollo, Healer of Delos[2]
I worship you in dread . . . what now, what is your price?
some new sacrifice? some ancient rite from the past   175
come round again each spring?—
      what will you bring to birth?
Tell me, child of golden Hope
      warm voice that never dies!

You are the first I call, daughter of Zeus   180
deathless Athena—I call your sister Artemis,[3]
heart of the market place enthroned in glory,
      guardian of our earth—
I call Apollo, Archer astride the thunderheads of heaven—
O triple shield against death, shine before me now!   185
If ever, once in the past, you stopped some ruin
launched against our walls
      you hurled the flame of pain
far, far from Thebes—you gods
      come now, come down once more!
                                                    No, no   190
the miseries numberless, grief on grief, no end—
too much to bear, we are all dying
O my people . . .
      Thebes like a great army dying
and there is no sword of thought to save us, no   195
and the fruits of our famous earth, they will not ripen
no and the women cannot scream their pangs to birth—
screams for the Healer, children dead in the womb
      and life on life goes down
            you can watch them go   200
      like seabirds winging west, outracing the day's fire
down the horizon, irresistibly
      streaking on to the shores of Evening
                                                    Death
so many deaths, numberless deaths on deaths, no end—
Thebes is dying, look, her children   205
stripped of pity . . .
      generations strewn on the ground

---

1. Apollo was his son and spoke for him.   2. A sacred island, Apollo's birthplace.   3. Apollo's sister, a goddess associated with hunting and also a protector of women in childbirth.

unburied, unwept, the dead spreading death
and the young wives and gray-haired mothers with them
cling to the altars, trailing in from all over the city—   210
Thebes, city of death, one long cortege
       and the suffering rises
             wails for mercy rise
       and the wild hymn for the Healer blazes out
clashing with our sobs our cries of mourning—   215
       O golden daughter of god,[4] send rescue
       radiant as the kindness in your eyes!

Drive him back!—the fever, the god of death
       that raging god of war
not armored in bronze, not shielded now, he burns me,[5]   220
battle cries in the onslaught burning on—
O rout him from our borders!
Sail him, blast him out to the Sea-queen's chamber
       the black Atlantic gulfs
       or the northern harbor, death to all   225
where the Thracian[6] surf comes crashing.
Now what the night spares he comes by day and kills—
the god of death.

                    O lord of the stormcloud,
you who twirl the lightning, Zeus, Father,
thunder Death to nothing!   230

Apollo, lord of the light, I beg you—
       whip your longbow's golden cord
showering arrows on our enemies—shafts of power
champions strong before us rushing on!

Artemis, Huntress,   235
torches flaring over the eastern ridges—
       ride Death down in pain!

God of the headdress gleaming gold, I cry to you—
your name and ours are one, Dionysus—
       come with your face aflame with wine   240
             your raving women's[7] cries
       your army on the march! Come with the lightning
come with torches blazing, eyes ablaze with glory!
Burn that god of death that all gods hate!
       [OEDIPUS *enters from the palace to address the* CHORUS, *as if address-
       ing the entire city of Thebes.*]

---

4. Athena, daughter of Zeus.   5. The plague is identified with Ares, the war god, though he comes now
without armor and shield. Ares is not elsewhere connected with plague; this passage may be an allusion to
the early years of the Peloponnesian War, when Spartan troops threatened the city from outside and the
plague raged inside the walls.   6. Ares was thought to be at home among the savages of Thrace, to the
northeast of Greece proper.   7. The Bacchanals, nymphs or human female votaries of the god Dionysus
(Bacchus) who celebrated him with wild dancing rites.

OEDIPUS   You pray to the gods? Let me grant your prayers.   245
   Come, listen to me—do what the plague demands:
   you'll find relief and lift your head from the depths.
   I will speak out now as a stranger to the story,
   a stranger to the crime. If I'd been present then,
   there would have been no mystery, no long hunt   250
   without a clue in hand. So now, counted
   a native Theban years after the murder,
   to all of Thebes I make this proclamation:
   if any one of you knows who murdered Laius,
   the son of Labdacus, I order him to reveal   255
   the whole truth to me. Nothing to fear,
   even if he must denounce himself,
   let him speak up
   and so escape the brunt of the charge—
   he will suffer no unbearable punishment,   260
   nothing worse than exile, totally unharmed.
      [OEDIPUS *pauses, waiting for a reply.*]
                              Next,
   if anyone knows the murderer is a stranger,
   a man from alien soil, come, speak up.
   I will give him a handsome reward, and lay up
   gratitude in my heart for him besides.   265
      [*Silence again, no reply.*]
   But if you keep silent, if anyone panicking,
   trying to shield himself or friend or kin,
   rejects my offer, then hear what I will do.
   I order you, every citizen of the state
   where I hold throne and power: banish this man—   270
   whoever he may be—never shelter him, never
   speak a word to him, never make him partner
   to your prayers, your victims burned to the gods.
   Never let the holy water touch his hands
   Drive him out, each of you, from every home.   275
   He is the plague, the heart of our corruption,
   as Apollo's oracle has just revealed to me.
   So I honor my obligations:
   I fight for the god and for the murdered man.

   Now my curse on the murderer. Whoever he is,   280
   a lone man unknown in his crime
   or one among many, let that man drag out
   his life in agony, step by painful step—
   I curse myself as well . . . if by any chance
   he proves to be an intimate of our house,   285
   here at my hearth, with my full knowledge,
   may the curse I just called down on him strike me!

   These are your orders: perform them to the last.
   I command you, for my sake, for Apollo's, for this country

blasted root and branch by the angry heavens.   290
Even if god had never urged you on to act,
how could you leave the crime uncleansed so long?
A man so noble—your king, brought down in blood—
you should have searched. But I am the king now,
I hold the throne that he held then, possess his bed   295
and a wife who shares our seed . . . why, our seed
might be the same, children born of the same mother
might have created blood-bonds between us
if his hope of offspring hadn't met disaster—
but fate swooped at his head and cut him short.   300
So I will fight for him as if he were my father,
stop at nothing, search the world
to lay my hands on the man who shed his blood,
the son of Labdacus descended of Polydorus,
Cadmus of old and Agenor, founder of the line: 305
their power and mine are one.
                     Oh dear gods,
my curse on those who disobey these orders!
Let no crops grow out of the earth for them—
shrivel their women, kill their sons,
burn them to nothing in this plague   310
that hits us now, or something even worse.
But you, loyal men of Thebes who approve my actions,
may our champion, Justice, may all the gods
be with us, fight beside us to the end!

LEADER   In the grip of your curse, my king, I swear   315
I'm not the murderer, I cannot point him out.
As for the search, Apollo pressed it on us—
he should name the killer.

OEDIPUS   Quite right,
but to force the gods to act against their will—
no man has the power.

LEADER   Then if I might mention   320
the next best thing . . .

OEDIPUS   The third best too—
don't hold back, say it.

LEADER   I still believe . . .
Lord Tiresias[8] sees with the eyes of Lord Apollo.
Anyone searching for the truth, my king,
might learn it from the prophet, clear as day.   325

OEDIPUS   I've not been slow with that. On Creon's cue
I sent the escorts, twice, within the hour.
I'm surprised he isn't here.

LEADER   We need him—
without him we have nothing but old, useless rumors.

OEDIPUS   Which rumors? I'll search out every word.   330

LEADER   Laius was killed, they say, by certain travelers.

---

8. The blind prophet of Thebes (whose ghost Odysseus goes to consult in Hades in *Odyssey* 11).

OEDIPUS   I know—but no one can find the murderer.

LEADER   If the man has a trace of fear in him
he won't stay silent long,
not with your curses ringing in his ears.   335

OEDIPUS   He didn't flinch at murder,
he'll never flinch at words.

[*Enter* TIRESIAS, *the blind prophet, led by a boy with escorts in atten-*
dance. He remains at a distance.]

LEADER   Here is the one who will convict him, look,
they bring him on at last, the seer, the man of god.
The truth lives inside him, him alone.

OEDIPUS   O Tiresias,   340
master of all the mysteries of our life,
all you teach and all you dare not tell,
signs in the heavens, signs that walk the earth!
Blind as you are, you can feel all the more
what sickness haunts our city. You, my lord,   345
are the one shield, the one savior we can find.

We asked Apollo—perhaps the messengers
haven't told you—he sent his answer back:
"Relief from the plague can only come one way.
Uncover the murderers of Laius,   350
put them to death or drive them into exile."
So I beg you, grudge us nothing now, no voice,
no message plucked from the birds, the embers
or the other mantic ways within your grasp.
Rescue yourself, your city, rescue me—   355
rescue everything infected by the dead.
We are in your hands. For a man to help others
with all his gifts and native strength:
that is the noblest work.

TIRESIAS   How terrible—to see the truth
when the truth is only pain to him who sees!   360
I knew it well, but I put it from my mind,
else I never would have come.

OEDIPUS   What's this? Why so grim, so dire?

TIRESIAS   Just send me home. You bear your burdens,
I'll bear mine. It's better that way,   365
please believe me.

OEDIPUS   Strange response . . . unlawful,
unfriendly too to the state that bred and reared you—
you withhold the word of god.

TIRESIAS   I fail to see
that your own words are so well-timed.
I'd rather not have the same thing said of me . . .   370

OEDIPUS   For the love of god, don't turn away,
not if you know something. We beg you,
all of us on our knees.

TIRESIAS   None of you knows—

and I will never reveal my dreadful secrets,
not to say your own.   375

OEDIPUS   What? You know and you won't tell?
You're bent on betraying us, destroying Thebes?

TIRESIAS   I'd rather not cause pain for you or me.
So why this . . . useless interrogation?
You'll get nothing from me.

OEDIPUS   Nothing! You,   380
you scum of the earth, you'd enrage a heart of stone!
You won't talk? Nothing moves you?
Out with it, once and for all!

TIRESIAS   You criticize my temper . . . unaware
of the one[9] *you* live with, you revile me.   385

OEDIPUS   Who could restrain his anger hearing you?
What outrage—you spurn the city!

TIRESIAS   What will come will come.
Even if I shroud it all in silence.

OEDIPUS   What will come? You're bound to *tell* me that.   390

TIRESIAS   I'll say no more. Do as you like, build your anger
to whatever pitch you please, rage your worst—

OEDIPUS   Oh I'll let loose, I have such fury in me—
now I see it all. You helped hatch the plot,
you did the work, yes, short of killing him   395
with your own hands—and given eyes I'd say
you did the killing single-handed!

TIRESIAS   Is that so!
I charge you, then, submit to that decree
you just laid down: from this day onward
speak to no one, not these citizens, not myself.   400
You are the curse, the corruption of the land!

OEDIPUS   You, shameless—
aren't you appalled to start up such a story?
You think you can get away with this?

TIRESIAS   I have already.
The truth with all its power lives inside me.   405

OEDIPUS   Who primed you for this? Not your prophet's trade.

TIRESIAS   You did, you forced me, twisted it out of me.

OEDIPUS   What? Say it again—I'll understand it better.

TIRESIAS   Didn't you understand, just now?
Or are you tempting me to talk?   410

OEDIPUS   No, I can't say I grasped your meaning.
Out with it, again!

TIRESIAS   I say you are the murderer you hunt.

OEDIPUS   That obscenity, twice—by god, you'll pay.

TIRESIAS   Shall I say more, so you can really rage?   415

OEDIPUS   Much as you want. Your words are nothing—futile.

TIRESIAS   You cannot imagine . . . I tell you,

9. In the Greek the veiled reference to Jocasta is more forceful, because the word translated "the one" has
a feminine ending (agreeing with the feminine noun *orgê*, "temper").

you and your loved ones live together in infamy,
you cannot see how far you've gone in guilt.
OEDIPUS   You think you can keep this up and never suffer?   420
TIRESIAS   Indeed, if the truth has any power.
OEDIPUS   It does
but not for you, old man. You've lost your power,
stone-blind, stone-deaf—senses, eyes blind as stone!
TIRESIAS   I pity you, flinging at me the very insults
each man here will fling at you so soon.
OEDIPUS   Blind,   425
lost in the night, endless night that cursed you!
You can't hurt me or anyone else who sees the light—
you can never touch me.
TIRESIAS   True, it is not your fate
to fall at my hands. Apollo is quite enough,
and he will take some pains to work this out.   430
OEDIPUS   Creon! Is this conspiracy his or yours?
TIRESIAS   Creon is not your downfall, no, you are your own.
OEDIPUS   O power—
wealth and empire, skill outstripping skill
in the heady rivalries of life,
what envy lurks inside you! Just for this,   435
the crown the city gave me—I never sought it,
they laid it in my hands—for this alone, Creon,
the soul of trust, my loyal friend from the start
steals against me . . . so hungry to overthrow me
he sets this wizard on me, this scheming quack,   440
this fortune-teller peddling lies, eyes peeled
for his own profit—seer blind in his craft!

Come here, you pious fraud. Tell me,
when did you ever prove yourself a prophet?
When the Sphinx, that chanting Fury kept her deathwatch here,   445
why silent then, not a word to set our people free?
There was a riddle, not for some passer-by to solve—
it cried out for a prophet. Where were you?
Did you rise to the crisis? Not a word,
you and your birds, your gods—nothing.   450
No, but I came by, Oedipus the ignorant,
I stopped the Sphinx! With no help from the birds,
the flight of my own intelligence hit the mark.

And this is the man you'd try to overthrow?
You think you'll stand by Creon when he's king?   455
You and the great mastermind—
you'll pay in tears, I promise you, for this,
this witch-hunt. If you didn't look so senile
the lash would teach you what your scheming means!
LEADER   I would suggest his words were spoken in anger,   460
Oedipus . . . yours too, and it isn't what we need.

The best solution to the oracle, the riddle
posed by god—we should look for that.

TIRESIAS   You are the king no doubt, but in one respect,
    at least, I am your equal: the right to reply.   465
    I claim that privilege too.
    I am not your slave. I serve Apollo.
    I don't need Creon to speak for me in public.

                      So,
you mock my blindness? Let me tell you this.
You with your precious eyes,   470
you're blind to the corruption of your life,
to the house you live in, those you live with—
who *are* your parents? Do you know? All unknowing
you are the scourge of your own flesh and blood,
the dead below the earth and the living here above,   475
and the double lash of your mother and your father's curse
will whip you from this land one day, their footfall
treading you down in terror, darkness shrouding
your eyes that now can see the light!

                 Soon, soon
you'll scream aloud—what haven won't reverberate?   480
What rock of Cithaeron[1] won't scream back in echo?
That day you learn the truth about your marriage,
the wedding-march that sang you into your halls,
the lusty voyage home to the fatal harbor!
And a crowd of other horrors you'd never dream   485
will level you with yourself and all your children.

There. Now smear us with insults—Creon, myself,
and every word I've said. No man will ever
be rooted from the earth as brutally as you.

OEDIPUS   Enough! Such filth from him? Insufferable—   490
what, still alive? Get out—
faster, back where you came from—vanish!

TIRESIAS   I would never have come if you hadn't called me here.

OEDIPUS   If I thought you would blurt out such absurdities,
    you'd have died waiting before I'd had you summoned.   495

TIRESIAS   Absurd, am I! To you, not to your parents:
    the ones who bore you found me sane enough.

OEDIPUS   Parents—who? Wait . . . who is my father?

TIRESIAS   This day will bring your birth and your destruction.

OEDIPUS   Riddles—all you can say are riddles, murk and darkness.   500

TIRESIAS   Ah, but aren't you the best man alive at solving riddles?

OEDIPUS   Mock me for that, go on, and you'll reveal my greatness.

TIRESIAS   Your great good fortune, true, it was your ruin.

OEDIPUS   Not if I saved the city—what do I care?

TIRESIAS   Well then, I'll be going.
    [*To his attendant.*]

---

1. The mountain range near Thebes, on which Oedipus was left to die when an infant.

                                    Take me home, boy.   505
OEDIPUS   Yes, take him away. You're a nuisance here.
    Out of the way, the irritation's gone.
            [*Turning his back on* TIRESIAS, *moving toward the palace.*]²
TIRESIAS   I will go,
    once I have said what I came here to say.
    I'll never shrink from the anger in your eyes—
    you can't destroy me. Listen to me closely: 510
    the man you've sought so long, proclaiming,
    cursing up and down, the murderer of Laius—
    he is here. A stranger,
    you may think, who lives among you,
    he soon will be revealed a native Theban   515
    but he will take no joy in the revelation.
    Blind who now has eyes, beggar who now is rich,
    he will grope his way toward a foreign soil,
    a stick tapping before him step by step.
            [OEDIPUS *enters the palace.*]
    Revealed at last, brother and father both   520
    to the children he embraces, to his mother
    son and husband both—he sowed the loins
    his father sowed, he spilled his father's blood!

    Go in and reflect on that, solve that.
    And if you find I've lied   525
    from this day onward call the prophet blind.
            [TIRESIAS *and the boy exit to the side.*]
CHORUS   Who—
    who is the man the voice of god denounces
    resounding out of the rocky gorge of Delphi?
        The horror too dark to tell,
    whose ruthless bloody hands have done the work?   530
    His time has come to fly
        to outrace the stallions of the storm
            his feet a streak of speed—
    Cased in armor, Apollo son of the Father
    lunges on him, lightning-bolts afire!   535
    And the grim unerring Furies³
            closing for the kill.
                        Look,
    the word of god has just come blazing
    flashing off Parnassus' snowy heights!
    That man who left no trace—   540
    after him, hunt him down with all our strength!
    Now under bristling timber

---

2. There are no stage directions in the texts. It is suggested here that Oedipus moves off stage and does not hear the critical section of Tiresias's speech (lines 520ff.), which he could hardly fail to connect with the prophecy made to him by Apollo many years ago.   3. Avenging spirits who pursued a murderer when no earthly avenger was at hand.

up through rocks and caves he stalks
  like the wild mountain bull—
cut off from men, each step an agony, frenzied, racing blind   545
but he cannot outrace the dread voices of Delphi
ringing out of the heart of Earth,
  the dark wings beating around him shrieking doom
   the doom that never dies, the terror—
The skilled prophet scans the birds and shatters me with terror!   550
I can't accept him, can't deny him, don't know what to say,
I'm lost, and the wings of dark foreboding beating—
I cannot see what's come, what's still to come . . .
and what could breed a blood feud between
  Laius' house and the son of Polybus?[4]   555
I know of nothing, not in the past and not now,
no charge to bring against our king, no cause
to attack his fame that rings throughout Thebes—
  not without proof—not for the ghost of Laius,
  not to avenge a murder gone without a trace.   560

Zeus and Apollo know, they know, the great masters
  of all the dark and depth of human life.
But whether a mere man can know the truth,
whether a seer can fathom more than I—
there is no test, no certain proof   565
  though matching skill for skill
a man can outstrip a rival. No, not till I see
these charges proved will I side with his accusers.
We saw him then, when the she-hawk[5] swept against him,
saw with our own eyes his skill, his brilliant triumph—   570
  there was the test—he was the joy of Thebes!
  Never will I convict my king, never in my heart.
   [Enter CREON from the side.]
CREON   My fellow-citizens, I hear King Oedipus
levels terrible charges at me. I had to come.
I resent it deeply. If, in the present crisis   575
he thinks he suffers any abuse from me,
anything I've done or said that offers him
the slightest injury, why, I've no desire
to linger out this life, my reputation in ruins.
The damage I'd face from such an accusation   580
is nothing simple. No, there's nothing worse:
branded a traitor in the city, a traitor
to all of you and my good friends.
LEADER   True,
but a slur might have been forced out of him,
by anger perhaps, not any firm conviction.   585
CREON   The charge was made in public, wasn't it?
  I put the prophet up to spreading lies?

---

4. King of Corinth and, so far as anyone except Tiresias knows, the father of Oedipus.   5. The Sphinx.

LEADER   Such things were said . . .
    I don't know with what intent, if any.
CREON   Was his glance steady, his mind right   590
    when the charge was brought against me?
LEADER   I really couldn't say. I never look
    to judge the ones in power.
        [*The doors open.* OEDIPUS *enters.*]
                           Wait,
  here's Oedipus now.
OEDIPUS   You—here? You have the gall
    to show your face before the palace gates?   595
    You, plotting to kill me, kill the king—
    I see it all, the marauding thief himself
    scheming to steal my crown and power!
                          Tell me,
  in god's name, what did you take me for,
  coward or fool, when you spun out your plot?   600
  Your treachery—you think I'd never detect it
  creeping against me in the dark? Or sensing it,
  not defend myself? Aren't you the fool,
  you and your high adventure. Lacking numbers,
  powerful friends, out for the big game of empire—   605
  you need riches, armies to bring that quarry down!
CREON   Are you quite finished? It's your turn to listen
    for just as long as you've . . . instructed me.
    Hear me out, then judge me on the facts.
OEDIPUS   You've a wicked way with words, Creon,   610
    but I'll be slow to learn—from you.
    I find you a menace, a great burden to me.
CREON   Just one thing, hear me out in this.
OEDIPUS   Just one thing,
  don't tell *me* you're not the enemy, the traitor.
CREON   Look, if you think crude, mindless stubbornness   615
    such a gift, you've lost your sense of balance.
OEDIPUS   If you think you can abuse a kinsman,
    then escape the penalty, you're insane.
CREON   Fair enough, I grant you. But this injury
    you say I've done you, what is it?   620
OEDIPUS   Did you induce me, yes or no,
    to send for that sanctimonious prophet?
CREON   I did. And I'd do the same again.
OEDIPUS   All right then, tell me, how long is it now
    since Laius . . .
CREON   Laius—what did *he* do?
OEDIPUS   Vanished,   625
  swept from sight, murdered in his tracks.
CREON   The count of the years would run you far back . . .
OEDIPUS   And that far back, was the prophet at his trade?
CREON   Skilled as he is today, and just as honored.

OEDIPUS   Did he ever refer to me then, at that time?
CREON   No,   630
    never, at least, when I was in his presence.
OEDIPUS   But you did investigate the murder, didn't you?
CREON   We did our best, of course, discovered nothing.
OEDIPUS   But the great seer never accused me then—why not?
CREON   I don't know. And when I don't, I keep quiet.   635
OEDIPUS   You do know this, you'd tell it too—
    if you had a shred of decency.
CREON   What?
    If I know, I won't hold back.
OEDIPUS   Simply this:
    if the two of you had never put heads together,
    we would never have heard about *my* killing Laius.   640
CREON   If that's what he says . . . well, you know best.
    But now I have a right to learn from you
    as you just learned from me.
OEDIPUS   Learn your fill,
    you never will convict me of the murder.
CREON   Tell me, you're married to my sister, aren't you?   645
OEDIPUS   A genuine discovery—there's no denying that.
CREON   And you rule the land with her, with equal power?
OEDIPUS   She receives from me whatever she desires.
CREON   And I am the third, all of us are equals?
OEDIPUS   Yes, and it's there you show your stripes—   650
    you betray a kinsman.
CREON   Not at all.
    Not if you see things calmly, rationally,
    as I do. Look at it this way first:
    who in his right mind would rather rule
    and live in anxiety than sleep in peace?   655
    Particularly if he enjoys the same authority.
    Not I, I'm not the man to yearn for kingship,
    not with a king's power in my hands. Who would?
    No one with any sense of self-control.
    Now, as it is, you offer me all I need,   660
    not a fear in the world. But if I wore the crown . . .
    there'd be many painful duties to perform,
    hardly to my taste.
                        How could kingship
    please me more than influence, power
    without a qualm? I'm not that deluded yet,   665
    to reach for anything but privilege outright,
    profit free and clear.
    Now all men sing my praises, all salute me,
    now all who request your favors curry mine.
    I am their best hope: success rests in me.   670
    Why give up that, I ask you, and borrow trouble?
    A man of sense, someone who sees things clearly

would never resort to treason.
No, I've no lust for conspiracy in me,
nor could I ever suffer one who does.

Do you want proof? Go to Delphi yourself,
examine the oracle and see if I've reported
the message word-for-word. This too:
if you detect that I and the clairvoyant
have plotted anything in common, arrest me, 680
execute me. Not on the strength of one vote,
two in this case, mine as well as yours.
But don't convict me on sheer unverified surmise.
How wrong it is to take the good for bad,
purely at random, or take the bad for good. 685
But reject a friend, a kinsman? I would as soon
tear out the life within us, priceless life itself.
You'll learn this well, without fail, in time.
Time alone can bring the just man to light—
the criminal you can spot in one short day.

LEADER   Good advice, 690
my lord, for anyone who wants to avoid disaster.
Those who jump to conclusions may go wrong.

OEDIPUS   When my enemy moves against me quickly,
plots in secret, I move quickly too, I must,
I plot and pay him back. Relax my guard a moment, 695
waiting his next move—he wins his objective,
I lose mine.

CREON   What do you want?
You want me banished?

OEDIPUS   No, I want you dead.

CREON   Just to show how ugly a grudge can . . .

OEDIPUS   So,
still stubborn? you don't think I'm serious? 700

CREON   I think you're insane.

OEDIPUS   Quite sane—in my behalf.

CREON   Not just as much in mine?

OEDIPUS   You—my mortal enemy?

CREON   What if you're wholly wrong?

OEDIPUS   No matter—I must rule.

CREON   Not if you rule unjustly.

OEDIPUS   Hear him, Thebes, my city!

CREON   My city too, not yours alone! 705

LEADER   Please, my lords.

            [Enter JOCASTA from the palace.]
                          Look, Jocasta's coming,
and just in time too. With her help
you must put this fighting of yours to rest.

JOCASTA   Have you no sense? Poor misguided men,
such shouting—why this public outburst?
Aren't you ashamed, with the land so sick, 710

to stir up private quarrels?
    [*To* OEDIPUS.]
Into the palace now. And Creon, you go home.
Why make such a furor over nothing?

CREON   My sister, it's dreadful . . . Oedipus, your husband,   715
he's bent on a choice of punishments for me,
banishment from the fatherland or death.

OEDIPUS   Precisely. I caught him in the act, Jocasta,
plotting, about to stab me in the back.

CREON   Never—curse me, let me die and be damned   720
if I've done you any wrong you charge me with.

JOCASTA   Oh god, believe it, Oedipus,
honor the solemn oath he swears to heaven.
Do it for me, for the sake of all your people.
    [*The* CHORUS *begins to chant.*]

CHORUS   Believe it, be sensible   725
give way, my king, I beg you!

OEDIPUS   What do you want from me, concessions?

CHORUS   Respect him—he's been no fool in the past
and now he's strong with the oath he swears to god.

OEDIPUS   You know what you're asking?

CHORUS   I do.

OEDIPUS   Then out with it!   730

CHORUS   The man's your friend, your kin, he's under oath—
don't cast him out, disgraced
branded with guilt on the strength of hearsay only.

OEDIPUS   Know full well, if that is what you want
you want me dead or banished from the land.

CHORUS   Never—   735
no, by the blazing Sun, first god of the heavens!
   Stripped of the gods, stripped of loved ones,
let me die by inches if that ever crossed my mind.
But the heart inside me sickens, dies as the land dies
and now on top of the old griefs you pile this,   740
your fury—both of you!

OEDIPUS   Then let him go,
even if it does lead to my ruin, my death
or my disgrace, driven from Thebes for life.
It's you, not him I pity—your words move me.
He, wherever he goes, my hate goes with him.   745

CREON   Look at you, sullen in yielding, brutal in your rage—
you'll go too far. It's perfect justice:
natures like yours are hardest on themselves.

OEDIPUS   Then leave me alone—get out!

CREON   I'm going.
You're wrong, so wrong. These men know I'm right.   750
    [*Exit to the side. The* CHORUS *turns to* JOCASTA.]

CHORUS   Why do you hesitate, my lady
why not help him in?

JOCASTA   Tell me what's happened first.

CHORUS   Loose, ignorant talk started dark suspicions
and a sense of injustice cut deeply too.   755
JOCASTA   On both sides?
CHORUS   Oh yes.
JOCASTA   What did they say?
CHORUS   Enough, please, enough! The land's so racked already
or so it seems to me . . .
End the trouble here, just where they left it.
OEDIPUS   You see what comes of your good intentions now?   760
And all because you tried to blunt my anger.
CHORUS   My king,
I've said it once, I'll say it time and again—
I'd be insane, you know it,
senseless, ever to turn my back on you.
You who set our beloved land—storm-tossed, shattered—   765
straight on course. Now again, good helmsman,
steer us through the storm!
       [*The* CHORUS *draws away, leaving* OEDIPUS *and* JOCASTA *side by side.*]
JOCASTA   For the love of god,
Oedipus, tell me too, what is it?
Why this rage? You're so unbending.
OEDIPUS   I will tell you. I respect you, Jocasta,
much more than these . . .   770
       [*Glancing at the* CHORUS.]
Creon's to blame, Creon schemes against me.
JOCASTA   Tell me clearly, how did the quarrel start?
OEDIPUS   He says *I* murdered Laius—I am guilty.
JOCASTA   How does he know? Some secret knowledge   775
or simple hearsay?
OEDIPUS   Oh, he sent his prophet in
to do his dirty work. You know Creon,
Creon keeps his own lips clean.
JOCASTA   A prophet?
Well then, free yourself of every charge!
Listen to me and learn some peace of mind: 780
no skill in the world,
nothing human can penetrate the future.
Here is proof, quick and to the point.

An oracle came to Laius one fine day
(I won't say from Apollo himself   785
but his underlings, his priests) and it said
that doom would strike him down at the hands of a son,
our son, to be born of our own flesh and blood. But Laius,
so the report goes at least, was killed by strangers,
thieves, at a place where three roads meet . . . my son—   790
he wasn't three days old and the boy's father
fastened his ankles, had a henchman fling him away
on a barren, trackless mountain.

There, you see?
Apollo brought neither thing to pass. My baby
no more murdered his father than Laius suffered—   795
his wildest fear—death at his own son's hands.
That's how the seers and all their revelations
mapped out the future. Brush them from your mind.
Whatever the god needs and seeks
he'll bring to light himself, with ease.

OEDIPUS   Strange,   800
hearing you just now . . . my mind wandered,
my thoughts racing back and forth.

JOCASTA   What do you mean? Why so anxious, startled?

OEDIPUS   I thought I heard you say that Laius
was cut down at a place where three roads meet.   805

JOCASTA   That was the story. It hasn't died out yet.

OEDIPUS   Where did this thing happen? Be precise.

JOCASTA   A place called Phocis, where two branching roads,
one from Daulia, one from Delphi,
come together—a crossroads.   810

OEDIPUS   When? How long ago?

JOCASTA   The heralds no sooner reported Laius dead
than you appeared and they hailed you king of Thebes.

OEDIPUS   My god, my god—what have you planned to do to me?

JOCASTA   What, Oedipus? What haunts you so?

OEDIPUS   Not yet.   815
Laius—how did he look? Describe him.
Had he reached his prime?

JOCASTA   He was swarthy,
and the gray had just begun to streak his temples,
and his build . . . wasn't far from yours.

OEDIPUS   Oh no no,
I think I've just called down a dreadful curse   820
upon myself—I simply didn't know!

JOCASTA   What are you saying? I shudder to look at you.

OEDIPUS   I have a terrible fear the blind seer can see.
I'll know in a moment. One thing more—

JOCASTA   Anything,
afraid as I am—ask, I'll answer, all I can.   825

OEDIPUS   Did he go with a light or heavy escort,
several men-at-arms, like a lord, a king?

JOCASTA   There were five in the party, a herald among them,
and a single wagon carrying Laius.

OEDIPUS   Ai—
now I can see it all, clear as day.   830
Who told you all this at the time, Jocasta?

JOCASTA   A servant who reached home, the lone survivor.

OEDIPUS   So, could he still be in the palace—even now?

JOCASTA   No indeed. Soon as he returned from the scene
and saw you on the throne with Laius dead and gone,   835
he knelt and clutched my hand, pleading with me

to send him into the hinterlands, to pasture,
far as possible, out of sight of Thebes.
I sent him away. Slave though he was,
he'd earned that favor—and much more.   840

OEDIPUS   Can we bring him back, quickly?

JOCASTA   Easily. Why do you want him so?

OEDIPUS   I'm afraid,
Jocasta, I have said too much already.
That man—I've got to see him.

JOCASTA   Then he'll come.
But even I have a right, I'd like to think,   845
to know what's torturing you, my lord.

OEDIPUS   And so you shall—I can hold nothing back from you,
now I've reached this pitch of dark foreboding.
Who means more to me than you? Tell me,
whom would I turn toward but you   850
as I go through all this?

My father was Polybus, king of Corinth.
My mother, a Dorian, Merope. And I was held
the prince of the realm among the people there,
till something struck me out of nowhere,   855
something strange . . . worth remarking perhaps,
hardly worth the anxiety I gave it.
Some man at a banquet who had drunk too much
shouted out—he was far gone, mind you—
that I am not my father's son. Fighting words!   860
I barely restrained myself that day
but early the next I went to mother and father,
questioned them closely, and they were enraged
at the accusation and the fool who let it fly.
So as for my parents I was satisfied,   865
but still this thing kept gnawing at me,
the slander spread—I had to make my move.
                                    And so,
unknown to mother and father I set out for Delphi,
and the god Apollo spurned me, sent me away
denied the facts I came for,   870
but first he flashed before my eyes a future
great with pain, terror, disaster—I can hear him cry,
"You are fated to couple with your mother, you will bring
a breed of children into the light no man can bear to see—
you will kill your father, the one who gave you life!"   875
I heard all that and ran. I abandoned Corinth,
from that day on I gauged its landfall only
by the stars, running, always running
toward some place where I would never see
the shame of all those oracles come true.   880
And as I fled I reached that very spot
where the great king, you say, met his death.

Now, Jocasta, I will tell you all.
Making my way toward this triple crossroad
I began to see a herald, then a brace of colts   885
drawing a wagon, and mounted on the bench . . . a man,
just as you've described him, coming face-to-face,
and the one in the lead and the old man himself
were about to thrust me off the road—brute force—
and the one shouldering me aside, the driver,   890
I strike him in anger!—and the old man, watching me
coming up along his wheels—he brings down
his prod, two prongs straight at my head!
I paid him back with interest!
Short work, by god—with one blow of the staff   895
in this right hand I knock him out of his high seat,
roll him out of the wagon, sprawling headlong—
I killed them all—every mother's son!

Oh, but if there is any blood-tie
between Laius and this stranger . . .   900
what man alive more miserable than I?
More hated by the gods? I am the man
no alien, no citizen welcomes to his house,
law forbids it—not a word to me in public,
driven out of every hearth and home.   905
And all these curses I—no one but I
brought down these piling curses on myself!
And you, his wife, I've touched your body with these,
the hands that killed your husband cover you with blood.

Wasn't I born for torment? Look me in the eyes!   910
I am abomination—heart and soul!
I must be exiled, and even in exile
never see my parents, never set foot
on native ground again. Else I am doomed
to couple with my mother and cut my father down . . .   915
Polybus who reared me, gave me life.
                              But why, why?
Wouldn't a man of judgment say—and wouldn't he be right—
some savage power has brought this down upon my head?

Oh no, not that, you pure and awesome gods,
never let me see that day! Let me slip   920
from the world of men, vanish without a trace
before I see myself stained with such corruption,
stained to the heart.
LEADER   My lord, you fill our hearts with fear.
    But at least until you question the witness,   925
    do take hope.
OEDIPUS   Exactly. He is my last hope—
    I am waiting for the shepherd. He is crucial.

JOCASTA   And once he appears, what then? Why so urgent?
OEDIPUS   I will tell you. If it turns out that his story
    matches yours, I've escaped the worst.   930
JOCASTA   What did I say? What struck you so?
OEDIPUS   You said *thieves*—
    he told you a whole band of them murdered Laius.
    So, if he still holds to the same number,
    I cannot be the killer. One can't equal many.
    But if he refers to one man, one alone,   935
    clearly the scales come down on me:
    I am guilty.
JOCASTA   Impossible. Trust me,
    I told you precisely what he said,
    and he can't retract it now;
    the whole city heard it, not just I.   940
    And even if he should vary his first report
    by one man more or less, still, my lord,
    he could never make the murder of Laius
    truly fit the prophecy. Apollo was explicit:
    my son was doomed to kill my husband . . . my son,   945
    poor defenseless thing, he never had a chance
    to kill his father. They destroyed him first.

    So much for prophecy. It's neither here nor there.
    From this day on, I wouldn't look right or left.
OEDIPUS   True, true. Still, that shepherd,   950
    someone fetch him—now!
JOCASTA   I'll send at once. But do let's go inside.
    I'd never displease you, least of all in this.
       [OEDIPUS *and* JOCASTA *enter the palace.*]
CHORUS   Destiny guide me always
    Destiny find me filled with reverence   955
        pure in word and deed.
    Great laws tower above us, reared on high
    born for the brilliant vault of heaven—
        Olympian Sky their only father,
    nothing mortal, no man gave them birth,   960
    their memory deathless, never lost in sleep:
    within them lives a mighty god, the god does not grow old.

    Pride breeds the tyrant
    violent pride, gorging, crammed to bursting
        with all that is overripe and rich with ruin—   965
    clawing up to the heights, headlong pride
    crashes down the abyss—sheer doom!
        No footing helps, all foothold lost and gone.
    But the healthy strife that makes the city strong—
    I pray that god will never end that wrestling: 970
    god, my champion, I will never let you go.

But if any man comes striding, high and mighty
   in all he says and does,
no fear of justice, no reverence
for the temples of the gods— 975
   let a rough doom tear him down,
repay his pride, breakneck, ruinous pride!
If he cannot reap his profits fairly
   cannot restrain himself from outrage—
mad, laying hands on the holy things untouchable! 980

     Can such a man, so desperate, still boast
      he can save his life from the flashing bolts of god?
        If all such violence goes with honor now
          why join the sacred dance?

Never again will I go reverent to Delphi, 985
   the inviolate heart of Earth
or Apollo's ancient oracle at Abae
or Olympia[6] of the fires—
   unless these prophecies all come true
for all mankind to point toward in wonder. 990
King of kings, if you deserve your titles
   Zeus, remember, never forget!
You and your deathless, everlasting reign.

     They are dying, the old oracles sent to Laius,
     now our masters strike them off the rolls. 995
        Nowhere Apollo's golden glory now—
        the gods, the gods go down.
     [*Enter* JOCASTA *from the palace, carrying a suppliant's branch
     wound in wool.*]
JOCASTA   Lords of the realm,[7] it occurred to me,
   just now, to visit the temples of the gods,
so I have my branch in hand and incense too. 1000

Oedipus is beside himself. Racked with anguish,
no longer a man of sense, he won't admit
the latest prophecies are hollow as the old—
he's at the mercy of every passing voice
if the voice tells of terror. 1005
I urge him gently, nothing seems to help,
so I turn to you, Apollo, you are nearest.
     [*Placing her branch on the altar, while an old herdsman enters from
     the side, not the one just summoned by the King but an unexpected
     * MESSENGER *from Corinth.*]
I come with prayers and offerings . . . I beg you,

---

6. In the western Peloponnese, a site of an oracle of Zeus. Abae is a city in central Greece.   7. The
chorus.

cleanse us, set us free of defilement!
Look at us, passengers in the grip of fear,   1010
watching the pilot of the vessel go to pieces.

MESSENGER   [Approaching JOCASTA and the CHORUS.]
Strangers, please, I wonder if you could lead us
to the palace of the king . . . I think it's Oedipus.
Better, the man himself—you know where he is?

LEADER   This is his palace, stranger. He's inside.   1015
But here is his queen, his wife and mother
of his children.

MESSENGER   Blessings on you, noble queen,
queen of Oedipus crowned with all your family—
blessings on you always!

JOCASTA   And the same to you, stranger, you deserve it . . .   1020
such a greeting. But what have you come for?
Have you brought us news?

MESSENGER   Wonderful news—
for the house, my lady, for your husband too.

JOCASTA   Really, what? Who sent you?

MESSENGER   Corinth.
I'll give you the message in a moment.   1025
You'll be glad of it—how could you help it?—
though it costs a little sorrow in the bargain.

JOCASTA   What can it be, with such a double edge?

MESSENGER   The people there, they want to make your Oedipus
king of Corinth, so they're saying now.   1030

JOCASTA   Why? Isn't old Polybus still in power?

MESSENGER   No more. Death has got him in the tomb.

JOCASTA   What are you saying? Polybus, dead?—dead?

MESSENGER   If not,
if I'm not telling the truth, strike me dead too.

JOCASTA   [To a servant.] Quickly, go to your master, tell him this!   1035
You prophecies of the gods, where are you now?
This is the man that Oedipus feared for years,
he fled him, not to kill him—and now he's dead,
quite by chance, a normal, natural death,
not murdered by his son.

OEDIPUS   [Emerging from the palace.]
                          Dearest,   1040
what now? Why call me from the palace?

JOCASTA   [Bringing the MESSENGER closer.]
Listen to him, see for yourself what all
those awful prophecies of god have come to.

OEDIPUS   And who is he? What can he have for me?

JOCASTA   He's from Corinth, he's come to tell you   1045
your father is no more—Polybus—he's dead!

OEDIPUS   [Wheeling on the MESSENGER.]
What? Let me have it from your lips.

MESSENGER: Well,
if that's what you want first, then here it is:

make no mistake, Polybus is dead and gone.

OEDIPUS   How—murder? sickness?—what? what killed him?   1050

MESSENGER   A light tip of the scales can put old bones to rest.

OEDIPUS   Sickness then—poor man, it wore him down.

MESSENGER   That,
   and the long count of years he'd measured out.

OEDIPUS   So!
   Jocasta, why, why look to the Prophet's hearth,
   the fires of the future? Why scan the birds   1055
   that scream above our heads? They winged me on
   to the murder of my father, did they? That was my doom?
   Well look, he's dead and buried, hidden under the earth,
   and here I am in Thebes, I never put hand to sword—
   unless some longing for me wasted him away,   1060
   then in a sense you'd say I caused his death.
   But now, all those prophecies I feared—Polybus
   packs them off to sleep with him in hell!
   They're nothing, worthless.

JOCASTA   There.
   Didn't I tell you from the start?   1065

OEDIPUS   So you did. I was lost in fear.

JOCASTA   No more, sweep it from your mind forever.

OEDIPUS   But my mother's bed, surely I must fear—

JOCASTA   Fear?
   What should a man fear? It's all chance,
   chance rules our lives. Not a man on earth   1070
   can see a day ahead, groping through the dark.
   Better to live at random, best we can.
   And as for this marriage with your mother—
   have no fear. Many a man before you,
   in his dreams, has shared his mother's bed.   1075
   Take such things for shadows, nothing at all—
   Live, Oedipus,
   as if there's no tomorrow!

OEDIPUS   Brave words,
   and you'd persuade me if mother weren't alive.
   But mother lives, so for all your reassurances   1080
   I live in fear, I must.

JOCASTA   But your father's death,
   that, at least, is a great blessing, joy to the eyes!

OEDIPUS   Great, I know . . . but I fear *her*—she's still alive.

MESSENGER   Wait, who is this woman, makes you so afraid?

OEDIPUS   Merope, old man. The wife of Polybus.   1085

MESSENGER   The queen? What's there to fear in her?

OEDIPUS   A dreadful prophecy, stranger, sent by the gods.

MESSENGER   Tell me, could you? Unless it's forbidden
   other ears to hear.

OEDIPUS   Not at all.
   Apollo told me once—it is my fate—   1090
   I must make love with my own mother,

shed my father's blood with my own hands.
So for years I've given Corinth a wide berth,
and it's been my good fortune too. But still,
to see one's parents and look into their eyes   1095
is the greatest joy I know.

MESSENGER   You're afraid of that?
That kept you out of Corinth?

OEDIPUS   My *father*, old man—
so I wouldn't kill my father.

MESSENGER   So that's it.
Well then, seeing I came with such good will, my king,
why don't I rid you of that old worry now?   1100

OEDIPUS   What a rich reward you'd have for that!

MESSENGER   What do you think I came for, majesty?
So you'd come home and I'd be better off.

OEDIPUS   Never, I will never go near my parents.

MESSENGER   My boy, it's clear, you don't know what you're doing.   1105

OEDIPUS   What do you mean, old man? For god's sake, explain.

MESSENGER   If you ran from *them*, always dodging home . . .

OEDIPUS   Always, terrified Apollo's oracle might come true—

MESSENGER   And you'd be covered with guilt, from both your parents.

OEDIPUS   That's right, old man, that fear is always with me.   1110

MESSENGER   Don't you know? You've really nothing to fear.

OEDIPUS   But why? If I'm their son—Merope, Polybus?

MESSENGER   Polybus was nothing to you, that's why, not in blood.

OEDIPUS   What are you saying—Polybus was not my father?

MESSENGER   No more than I am. He and I are equals.

OEDIPUS   My father—   1115
how can my father equal nothing? You're nothing to me!

MESSENGER   Neither was he, no more your father than I am.

OEDIPUS   Then why did he call me his son?

MESSENGER   You were a gift,
years ago—know for a fact he took you
from my hands.

OEDIPUS   No, from another's hands?   1120
Then how could he love me so? He loved me, deeply . . .

MESSENGER   True, and his early years without a child
made him love you all the more.

OEDIPUS   And you, did you . . .
buy me? find me by accident?

MESSENGER   I stumbled on you,
down the woody flanks of Mount Cithaeron.

OEDIPUS   So close,   1125
what were you doing here, just passing through?

MESSENGER   Watching over my flocks, grazing them on the slopes.

OEDIPUS   A herdsman, were you? A vagabond, scraping for wages?

MESSENGER   Your savior too, my son, in your worst hour.

OEDIPUS   Oh—
when you picked me up, was I in pain? What exactly?   1130

MESSENGER   Your ankles . . . they tell the story. Look at them.

OEDIPUS   Why remind me of that, that old affliction?

MESSENGER   Your ankles were pinned together. I set you free.

OEDIPUS   That dreadful mark—I've had it from the cradle.

MESSENGER   And you got your name[8] from that misfortune too,   1135
   the name's still with you.

OEDIPUS   Dear god, who did it?—
   mother? father? Tell me.

MESSENGER   I don't know.
   The one who gave you to me, he'd know more.

OEDIPUS   What? You took me from someone else?
   You didn't find me yourself?

MESSENGER   No sir,   1140
   another shepherd passed you on to me.

OEDIPUS   Who? Do you know? Describe him.

MESSENGER   He called himself a servant of . . .
   if I remember rightly—Laius.
          [JOCASTA *turns sharply.*]

OEDIPUS   The king of the land who ruled here long ago?   1145

MESSENGER   That's the one. That herdsman was *his* man.

OEDIPUS   Is he still alive? Can I see him?

MESSENGER   They'd know best, the people of these parts.
       [OEDIPUS *and the* MESSENGER *turn to the* CHORUS.]

OEDIPUS   Does anyone know that herdsman,
   the one he mentioned? Anyone seen him   1150
   in the fields, in the city? Out with it!
   The time has come to reveal this once for all.

LEADER   I think he's the very shepherd you wanted to see,
   a moment ago. But the queen, Jocasta,
   she's the one to say.

OEDIPUS   Jocasta,   1155
   you remember the man we just sent for?
   Is *that* the one he means?

JOCASTA   That man . . .
   why ask? Old shepherd, talk, empty nonsense,
   don't give it another thought, don't even think—

OEDIPUS   What—give up now, with a clue like this?   1160
   Fail to solve the mystery of my birth?
   Not for all the world!

JOCASTA   Stop—in the name of god,
   if you love your own life, call off this search!
   My suffering is enough.

OEDIPUS   Courage!
   Even if my mother turns out to be a slave,   1165
   and I a slave, three generations back,
   you would not seem common.

JOCASTA   Oh no,
   listen to me, I beg you, don't do this.

OEDIPUS   Listen to you? No more. I must know it all,

---

8. In Greek the name *Oidipous* suggests "swollen foot."

must see the truth at last.

JOCASTA　　　　　　　　No, please— 1170
for your sake—I want the best for you!

OEDIPUS Your best is more than I can bear.

JOCASTA　　　　　　　　　　　You're doomed—
may you never fathom who you are!

OEDIPUS [To a servant.] Hurry, fetch me the herdsman, now!
Leave her to glory in her royal birth. 1175

JOCASTA Aieeeeee—
　　　　　　　man of agony—
that is the only name I have for you,
that, no other—ever, ever, ever!

[Flinging through the palace doors. A long, tense silence follows.]

LEADER Where's she gone, Oedipus?
Rushing off, such wild grief . . . 1180
I'm afraid that from this silence
something monstrous may come bursting forth.

OEDIPUS Let it burst! Whatever will, whatever must!
I must know my birth, no matter how common
it may be—I must see my origins face-to-face. 1185
She perhaps, she with her woman's pride
may well be mortified by my birth,
but I, I count myself the son of Chance,
the great goddess, giver of all good things—
I'll never see myself disgraced. She is my mother! 1190
And the moons have marked me out, my blood-brothers,
one moon on the wane, the next moon great with power.
That is my blood, my nature—I will never betray it,
never fail to search and learn my birth!

CHORUS Yes—if I am a true prophet 1195
　　　if I can grasp the truth,
　　by the boundless skies of Olympus,
at the full moon of tomorrow, Mount Cithaeron
you will know how Oedipus glories in you—
you, his birthplace, nurse, his mountain-mother! 1200
And we will sing you, dancing out your praise—
you lift our monarch's heart!
　　　Apollo, Apollo, god of the wild cry
　　　　may our dancing please you!
　　　　　　　　　Oedipus—
　　　son, dear child, who bore you? 1205
Who of the nymphs who seem to live forever[9]
mated with Pan,[1] the mountain-striding Father?
Who was your mother? who, some bride of Apollo
the god who loves the pastures spreading toward the sun?
　　Or was it Hermes, king of the lightning ridges?
Or Dionysus,[2] lord of frenzy, lord of the barren peaks— 1210
did he seize you in his hands, dearest of all his lucky finds?—

9. Nymphs were not immortal, like the gods, but lived much longer than mortals.　1. A woodland god,
patron of shepherds and flocks.　2. Dionysus, like Pan and Hermes, haunted the wild country, woods,
and mountains. Hermes was born on Mount Kyllene in Arcadia.

found by the nymphs, their warm eyes dancing, gift
  to the lord who loves them dancing out his joy!

> [OEDIPUS *strains to see a figure coming from the distance. Attended
> by palace guards, an old* SHEPHERD *enters slowly, reluctant to
> approach the king.*]

OEDIPUS I never met the man, my friends . . . still,   1215
  if I had to guess, I'd say that's the shepherd,
  the very one we've looked for all along.
  Brothers in old age, two of a kind,
  he and our guest here. At any rate
  the ones who bring him in are my own men,   1220
  I recognize them.

> [*Turning to the* LEADER.]

                 But you know more than I,
  you should, you've seen the man before.
LEADER I know him, definitely. One of Laius' men,
  a trusty shepherd, if there ever was one.
OEDIPUS You, I ask you first, stranger,   1225
  you from Corinth—is this the one you mean?
MESSENGER You're looking at him. He's your man.
OEDIPUS [*To the* SHEPHERD.]
  You, old man, come over here—
  look at me. Answer all my questions.
  Did you ever serve King Laius?
SHEPHERD   So I did . . .   1230
  a slave, not bought on the block though,
  born and reared in the palace.
OEDIPUS Your duties, your kind of work?
SHEPHERD Herding the flocks, the better part of my life.
OEDIPUS Where, mostly? Where did you do your grazing?
SHEPHERD   Well,   1235
  Cithaeron sometimes, or the foothills round about.
OEDIPUS This man—you know him? ever see him there?
SHEPHERD [*Confused, glancing from the* MESSENGER *to the King.*]
  Doing what?—what man do you mean?
OEDIPUS [*Pointing to the* MESSENGER.]
  This one here—ever have dealings with him?
SHEPHERD Not so I could say, but give me a chance,   1240
  my memory's bad . . .
MESSENGER No wonder he doesn't know me, master.
  But let me refresh his memory for him.
  I'm sure he recalls old times we had
  on the slopes of Mount Cithaeron;   1245
  he and I, grazing our flocks, he with two
  and I with one—we both struck up together,
  three whole seasons, six months at a stretch
  from spring to the rising of Arcturus[3] in the fall,

---

3. The principal star in the constellation Boötes; its appearance in the sky *(rising)* just before dawn in September signals the end of summer.

then with winter coming on I'd drive my herds   1250
to my own pens, and back he'd go with his
to Laius' folds.

    [*To the* SHEPHERD.]

               Now that's how it was,
wasn't it—yes or no?

SHEPHERD   Yes, I suppose . . .
it's all so long ago.

MESSENGER   Come, tell me,
you gave me a child back then, a boy, remember?   1255
A little fellow to rear, my very own.

SHEPHERD   What? Why rake up that again?

MESSENGER   Look, here he is, my fine old friend—
the same man who was just a baby then.

SHEPHERD   Damn you, shut your mouth—quiet!   1260

OEDIPUS   Don't lash out at him, old man—
you need lashing more than he does.

SHEPHERD   Why,
master, majesty—what have I done wrong?

OEDIPUS   You won't answer his question about the boy.

SHEPHERD   He's talking nonsense, wasting his breath.   1265

OEDIPUS   So, you won't talk willingly—
then you'll talk with pain.

    [*The guards seize the* SHEPHERD.]

SHEPHERD   No, dear god, don't torture an old man!

OEDIPUS   Twist his arms back, quickly!

SHEPHERD   God help us, why?—
what more do you need to know?   1270

OEDIPUS   Did you give him that child? He's asking.

SHEPHERD   I did . . . I wish to god I'd died that day.

OEDIPUS   You've got your wish if you don't tell the truth.

SHEPHERD   The more I tell, the worse the death I'll die.

OEDIPUS   Our friend here wants to stretch things out, does he?   1275

    [*Motioning to his men for torture.*]

SHEPHERD   No, no, I gave it to him—I just said so.

OEDIPUS   Where did you get it? Your house? Someone else's?

SHEPHERD   It wasn't mine, no, I got it from . . . someone.

OEDIPUS   Which one of them?

    [*Looking at the citizens.*]

                          Whose house?

SHEPHERD   No—
god's sake, master, no more questions!   1280

OEDIPUS   You're a dead man if I have to ask again.

SHEPHERD   Then—the child came from the house . . . of Laius.

OEDIPUS   A slave? or born of his own blood?

SHEPHERD   Oh no,
I'm right at the edge, the horrible truth—I've got to say it!

OEDIPUS   And I'm at the edge of hearing horrors, yes, but I must
    hear!   1285

SHEPHERD   All right! His son, they said it was—his son!
But the one inside, your wife,

she'd tell it best.
OEDIPUS   My wife—
    she gave it to you?   1290
SHEPHERD   Yes, yes, my king.
OEDIPUS   Why, what for?
SHEPHERD   To kill it.
OEDIPUS   Her own child,
    how could she?   1295
SHEPHERD   She was afraid—
    frightening prophecies.
OEDIPUS   What?
SHEPHERD   They said—
    he'd kill his parents.   1300
OEDIPUS   But you gave him to this old man—why?
SHEPHERD   I pitied the little baby, master,
    hoped he'd take him off to his own country,
    far away, but he saved him for this, this fate.
    If you are the man he says you are, believe me,   1305
    you were born for pain.
OEDIPUS   O god—
    all come true, all burst to light!
    O light—now let me look my last on you!
    I stand revealed at last—
    cursed in my birth, cursed in marriage,   1310
    cursed in the lives I cut down with these hands!
       [*Rushing through the doors with a great cry. The Corinthian* MES-
       SENGER, *the* SHEPHERD *and attendants exit slowly to the side.*]
CHORUS   O the generations of men
    the dying generations—adding the total
    of all your lives I find they come to nothing . . .
          does there exist, is there a man on earth   1315
    who seizes more joy than just a dream, a vision?
    And the vision no sooner dawns than dies
    blazing into oblivion.
    You are my great example, you, your life
    your destiny, Oedipus, man of misery—   1320
    I count no man blest.

                    You outranged all men!
          Bending your bow to the breaking-point
    you captured priceless glory, O dear god,
    and the Sphinx came crashing down,
          the virgin, claws hooked   1325
    like a bird of omen singing, shrieking death—
    like a fortress reared in the face of death
    you rose and saved our land.

    From that day on we called you king
    we crowned you with honors, Oedipus, towering over all—   1330
    mighty king of the seven gates of Thebes.

But now to hear your story—is there a man more agonized?
More wed to pain and frenzy? Not a man on earth,
the joy of your life ground down to nothing
O Oedipus, name for the ages— 1335
    one and the same wide harbor served you
        son and father both
son and father came to rest in the same bridal chamber.
How, how could the furrows your father plowed
bear you, your agony, harrowing on 1340
in silence O so long?

                    But now for all your power
Time, all-seeing Time has dragged you to the light,
judged your marriage monstrous from the start—
the son and the father tangling, both one—
O child of Laius, would to god 1345
    I'd never seen you, never never!
    Now I weep like a man who wails the dead
and the dirge comes pouring forth with all my heart!
I tell you the truth, you gave me life
my breath leapt up in you 1350
and now you bring down night upon my eyes.

            [*Enter a* MESSENGER *from the palace.*]
MESSENGER: Men of Thebes, always first in honor,
    what horrors you will hear, what you will see,
    what a heavy weight of sorrow you will shoulder . . .
    if you are true to your birth, if you still have 1355
    some feeling for the royal house of Thebes.
    I tell you neither the waters of the Danube
    nor the Nile[4] can wash this palace clean.
    Such things it hides, it soon will bring to light—
    terrible things, and none done blindly now, 1360
    all done with a will. The pains
    we inflict upon ourselves hurt most of all.
LEADER   God knows we have pains enough already.
    What can you add to them?
MESSENGER   The queen is dead.
LEADER   Poor lady—how? 1365
MESSENGER   By her own hand. But you are spared the worst,
    you never had to watch . . . I saw it all,
    and with all the memory that's in me
    you will learn what that poor woman suffered.

    Once she'd broken in through the gates, 1370
    dashing past us, frantic, whipped to fury,
    ripping her hair out with both hands—
    straight to her rooms she rushed, flinging herself

---

4. The Greek reads "Phasis," a river in Asia Minor. The translator has substituted a big river more familiar
to modern readers.

across the bridal-bed, doors slamming behind her—
once inside, she wailed for Laius, dead so long,   1375
remembering how she bore his child long ago,
the life that rose up to destroy him, leaving
its mother to mother living creatures
with the very son she'd borne.
Oh how she wept, mourning the marriage-bed   1380
where she let loose that double brood—monsters—
husband by her husband, children by her child.

                        And then—
but how she died is more than I can say. Suddenly
Oedipus burst in, screaming, he stunned us so
we couldn't watch her agony to the end,   1385
our eyes were fixed on him. Circling
like a maddened beast, stalking, here, there,
crying out to us—

                    Give him a sword![5] His wife,
no wife, his mother, where can he find the mother earth
that cropped two crops at once, himself and all his children?   1390
He was raging—one of the dark powers pointing the way,
none of us mortals crowding around him, no,
with a great shattering cry—someone, something leading him on—
he hurled at the twin doors and bending the bolts back
out of their sockets, crashed through the chamber.   1395
And there we saw the woman hanging by the neck,
cradled high in a woven noose, spinning,
swinging back and forth. And when he saw her,
giving a low, wrenching sob that broke our hearts,
slipping the halter from her throat, he eased her down,   1400
in a slow embrace he laid her down, poor thing . . .
then, what came next, what horror we beheld!

He rips off her brooches, the long gold pins
holding her robes—and lifting them high,
looking straight up into the points,   1405
he digs them down the sockets of his eyes, crying, "You,
you'll see no more the pain I suffered, all the pain I caused!
Too long you looked on the ones you never should have seen,
blind to the ones you longed to see, to know! Blind
from this hour on! Blind in the darkness—blind!"   1410
His voice like a dirge, rising, over and over
raising the pins, raking them down his eyes.
And at each stroke blood spurts from the roots,
splashing his beard, a swirl of it, nerves and clots—
black hail of blood pulsing, gushing down.   1415

These are the griefs that burst upon them both,
coupling man and woman. The joy they had so lately,

---

5. Presumably so that he could kill himself.

the fortune of their old ancestral house
was deep joy indeed. Now, in this one day,
wailing, madness and doom, death, disgrace   1420
all the griefs in the world that you can name,
all are theirs forever.

LEADER   Oh poor man, the misery—
has he any rest from pain now?
        [A voice within, in torment.]

MESSENGER   He's shouting,
"Loose the bolts, someone, show me to all of Thebes!
My father's murderer, my mother's—"   1425
No, I can't repeat it, it's unholy.
Now he'll tear himself from his native earth,
not linger, curse the house with his own curse.
But he needs strength, and a guide to lead him on.
This is sickness more than he can bear.
        [The palace doors open.]
                                    Look,   1430
he'll show you himself. The great doors are opening—
you are about to see a sight, a horror
even his mortal enemy would pity.
        [Enter OEDIPUS, blinded, led by a boy. He stands at the palace steps,
        as if surveying his people once again.]

CHORUS   O the terror—
the suffering, for all the world to see,
the worst terror that ever met my eyes.
What madness swept over you? What god,   1435
what dark power leapt beyond all bounds,
beyond belief, to crush your wretched life?—
godforsaken, cursed by the gods!
I pity you but I can't bear to look.   1440
I've much to ask, so much to learn,
so much fascinates my eyes,
but you . . . I shudder at the sight.

OEDIPUS   Oh, Ohh—
the agony! I am agony—
where am I going? where on earth?   1445
        where does all this agony hurl me?
where's my voice?—
        winging, swept away on a dark tide—
        My destiny, my dark power, what a leap you made!

CHORUS   To the depths of terror, too dark to hear, to see. 1450

OEDIPUS   Dark, horror of darkness
        my darkness, drowning, swirling around me
        crashing wave on wave—unspeakable, irresistible
            headwind, fatal harbor! Oh again,
        the misery, all at once, over and over   1455
            the stabbing daggers, stab of memory
        raking me insane.

CHORUS   No wonder you suffer

twice over, the pain of your wounds,
the lasting grief of pain.

OEDIPUS   Dear friend, still here?
   Standing by me, still with a care for me,   1460
      the blind man? Such compassion,
         loyal to the last. Oh it's you,
      I know you're here, dark as it is
      I'd know you anywhere, your voice—
   it's yours, clearly yours.

CHORUS   Dreadful, what you've done . . .   1465
   how could you bear it, gouging out your eyes?
What superhuman power drove you on?

OEDIPUS   Apollo, friends, Apollo—
   he ordained my agonies—these, my pains on pains!
      But the hand that struck my eyes was mine,   1470
      mine alone—no one else—
         I did it all myself!
      What good were eyes to me?
      Nothing I could see could bring me joy.

CHORUS   No, no, exactly as you say.

OEDIPUS   What can I ever see?   1475
      What love, what call of the heart
   can touch my ears with joy? Nothing, friends.
      Take me away, far, far from Thebes,
         quickly, cast me away, my friends—
   this great murderous ruin, this man cursed to heaven,   1480
   the man the deathless gods hate most of all!

CHORUS   Pitiful, you suffer so, you understand so much . . .
   I wish you'd never known.

OEDIPUS   Die, die—
   whoever he was that day in the wilds
who cut my ankles free of the ruthless pins,   1485
   he pulled me clear of death, he saved my life
   for this, this kindness—
      Curse him, kill him!
   If I'd died then, I'd never have dragged myself,
   my loved ones through such hell.   1490

CHORUS   Oh if only . . . would to god.

OEDIPUS   I'd never have come to this,
      my father's murderer—never been branded
   mother's husband, all men see me now! Now,
      loathed by the gods, son of the mother I defiled
      coupling in my father's bed, spawning lives in the loins 1495
   that spawned my wretched life. What grief can crown this grief?
      It's mine alone, my destiny—I am Oedipus!

CHORUS   How can I say you've chosen for the best?
   Better to die than be alive and blind.

OEDIPUS   What I did was best—don't lecture me,   1500
   no more advice. I, with *my* eyes,
   how could I look my father in the eyes

when I go down to death? Or mother, so abused . . .
I have done such things to the two of them,
crimes too huge for hanging.
                                        Worse yet,   1505
the sight of my children, born as they were born,
how could I long to look into their eyes?
No, not with these eyes of mine, never.
Not this city either, her high towers,
the sacred glittering images of her gods—   1510
I am misery! I, her best son, reared
as no other son of Thebes was ever reared,
I've stripped myself, I gave the command myself.
All men must cast away the great blasphemer,
the curse now brought to light by the gods,   1515
the son of Laius—I, my father's son!

Now I've exposed my guilt, horrendous guilt,
could I train a level glance on you, my countrymen?
Impossible! No, if I could just block off my ears,
the springs of hearing, I would stop at nothing—   1520
I'd wall up my loathsome body like a prison,
blind to the sound of life, not just the sight.
Oblivion—what a blessing . . .
for the mind to dwell a world away from pain.

O Cithaeron, why did you give me shelter?   1525
Why didn't you take me, crush my life out on the spot?
I'd never have revealed my birth to all mankind.

O Polybus, Corinth, the old house of my fathers,
so I believed—what a handsome prince you raised—
under the skin, what sickness to the core.   1530
Look at me! Born of outrage, outrage to the core.
O triple roads—it all comes back, the secret,
dark ravine, and the oaks closing in
where the three roads join . . .
You drank my father's blood, my own blood   1535
spilled by my own hands—you still remember me?
What things you saw me do? Then I came here
and did them all once more!
                                        Marriages! O marriage,
you gave me birth, and once you brought me into the world
you brought my sperm rising back, springing to light   1540
fathers, brothers, sons—one murderous breed—
brides, wives, mothers. The blackest things
a man can do, I have done them all!
                                        No more—
it's wrong to name what's wrong to do. Quickly,
for the love of god, hide me somewhere,   1545
kill me, hurl me into the sea

where you can never look on me again.
    [*Beckoning to the* CHORUS *as they shrink away.*]
                              Closer,
it's all right. Touch the man of grief.
Do. Don't be afraid. My troubles are mine
and I am the only man alive who can sustain them.   1550
    [*Enter* CREON *from the palace, attended by palace guards.*]
LEADER   Put your requests to Creon. Here he is,
just when we need him. He'll have a plan, he'll act.
Now that he's the sole defense of the country
in your place.
OEDIPUS   Oh no, what can I say to him?
How can I ever hope to win his trust?   1555
I wronged him so, just now, in every way.
You must see that—I was so wrong, so wrong.
CREON   I haven't come to mock you, Oedipus,
or to criticize your former failings.
    [*Turning to the guards.*]
                          You there,
have you lost all respect for human feelings?   1560
At least revere the Sun, the holy fire
that keeps us all alive. Never expose a thing
of guilt and holy dread so great it appalls
the earth, the rain from heaven, the light of day!
Get him into the halls—quickly as you can.   1565
Piety demands no less. Kindred alone
should see a kinsman's shame. This is obscene.
OEDIPUS   Please, in god's name . . . you wipe my fears away,
coming so generously to me, the worst of men.
Do one thing more, for your sake, not mine.   1570
CREON   What do you want? Why so insistent?
OEDIPUS   Drive me out of the land at once, far from sight,
where I can never hear a human voice.
CREON   I'd have done that already, I promise you.
First I wanted the god to clarify my duties.   1575
OEDIPUS   The god? His command was clear, every word:
death for the father-killer, the curse—
he said destroy me!
CREON   So he did. Still, in such a crisis
it's better to ask precisely what to do.
OEDIPUS   So miserable—   1580
you'd consult the god about a man like me?
CREON   By all means. And this time, I assume,
even you will obey the god's decrees.
OEDIPUS   I will,
I will. And you, I command you—I beg you . . .
the woman inside, bury her as you see fit.   1585
It's the only decent thing,
to give your own the last rites. As for me,
never condemn the city of my fathers

to house my body, not while I'm alive, no,
let me live on the mountains, on Cithaeron,   1590
my favorite haunt, I have made it famous.
Mother and father marked out that rock
to be my everlasting tomb—buried alive.
Let me die there, where they tried to kill me.

Oh but this I know: no sickness can destroy me,   1595
nothing can. I would never have been saved
from death—I have been saved
for something great and terrible, something strange.
Well let my destiny come and take me on its way!
About my children, Creon, the boys at least,   1600
don't burden yourself. They're men,
wherever they go, they'll find the means to live.
But my two daughters, my poor helpless girls,
clustering at our table, never without me
hovering near them . . . whatever I touched,   1605
they always had their share. Take care of them,
I beg you. Wait, better—permit me, would you?
Just to touch them with my hands and take
our fill of tears. Please . . . my king.
Grant it, with all your noble heart.   1610
If I could hold them, just once, I'd think
I had them with me, like the early days
when I could see their eyes.
            [ANTIGONE and ISMENE, *two small children, are led in from the
            palace by a nurse.*]
                              What's that
O god! Do I really hear you sobbing?—
my two children. Creon, you've pitied me?   1615
Sent me my darling girls, my own flesh and blood!
Am I right?
CREON   Yes, it's my doing.
    I know the joy they gave you all these years,
    the joy you must feel now.
OEDIPUS   Bless you, Creon!
    May god watch over you for this kindness,   1620
    better than he ever guarded me.
                              Children, where are you?
Here, come quickly—
            [*Groping for* ANTIGONE *and* ISMENE, *who approach their father cau-
            tiously, then embrace him.*]
                              Come to these hands of mine,
your brother's hands, your own father's hands
that served his once bright eyes so well—
that made them blind. Seeing nothing, children,   1625
knowing nothing, I became your father,
I fathered you in the soil that gave me life.

How I weep for you—I cannot see you now . . .
just thinking of all your days to come, the bitterness,
the life that rough mankind will thrust upon you.   1630
Where are the public gatherings you can join,
the banquets of the clans? Home you'll come,
in tears, cut off from the sight of it all,
the brilliant rites unfinished.
And when you reach perfection, ripe for marriage,   1635
who will he be, my dear ones? Risking all
to shoulder the curse that weighs down my parents,
yes and you too—that wounds us all together.
What more misery could you want?
Your father killed his father, sowed his mother,   1640
one, one and the selfsame womb sprang you—
he cropped the very roots of his existence.

Such disgrace, and you must bear it all!
Who will marry you then? Not a man on earth.
Your doom is clear: you'll wither away to nothing,   1645
single, without a child.
          [*Turning to* CREON.]
                    Oh Creon,
you are the only father they have now . . .
we who brought them into the world
are gone, both gone at a stroke—
Don't let them go begging, abandoned,   1650
men without men. Your own flesh and blood!
Never bring them down to the level of my pains.
Pity them. Look at them, so young, so vulnerable,
shorn of everything—you're their only hope.
Promise me, noble Creon, touch my hand!   1655
          [*Reaching toward* CREON, *who draws back.*]
You, little ones, if you were old enough
to understand, there is much I'd tell you.
Now, as it is, I'd have you say a prayer.
Pray for life, my children,
live where you are free to grow and season.   1660
Pray god you find a better life than mine,
the father who begot you.
CREON   Enough.
You've wept enough. Into the palace now.
OEDIPUS   I must, but I find it very hard.
CREON   Time is the great healer, you will see.   1665
OEDIPUS   I am going—you know on what condition?
CREON   Tell me. I'm listening.
OEDIPUS   Drive me out of Thebes, in exile.
CREON   Not I. Only the gods can give you that.
OEDIPUS   Surely the gods hate me so much—   1670
CREON   You'll get your wish at once.

OEDIPUS   You consent?
CREON   I try to say what I mean; it's my habit.
OEDIPUS   Then take me away. It's time.
CREON   Come along, let go of the children.
OEDIPUS   No—
    don't take them away from me, not now! No no no!   1675
        [*Clutching his daughters as the guards wrench them loose and take
        them through the palace doors.*]
CREON   Still the king, the master of all things?
    No more: here your power ends.
    None of your power follows you through life.
        [*Exit* OEDIPUS *and* CREON *to the palace. The* CHORUS *comes forward
        to address the audience directly.*]
CHORUS   People of Thebes, my countrymen, look on Oedipus.
    He solved the famous riddle with his brilliance,   1680
    he rose to power, a man beyond all power.
    Who could behold his greatness without envy?
    Now what a black sea of terror has overwhelmed him.
    Now as we keep our watch and wait the final day,
    count no man happy till he dies, free of pain at last.   1685
        [*Exit in procession.*]

EURIPIDES
480–406 B.C.

Euripides' *Medea*, produced in 431 B.C., the year that brought the beginning of the
Peloponnesian War, appeared earlier than Sophocles' *Oedipus the King*, but it has a
bitterness that is more in keeping with the spirit of a later age. If *Oedipus* is, in one
sense, a warning to a generation that has embarked on an intellectual revolution,
Medea is the ironic expression of the disillusion that comes after the shipwreck. In
this play we are conscious for the first time of an attitude characteristic of modern
literature, the artist's feeling of separation from the audience, the isolation of the
poet. "Often previously," says Medea to the king,

> Through being considered clever I have suffered much. . . .
> If you put new ideas before the eyes of fools
> They'll think you foolish and worthless into the bargain;
> And if you are thought superior to those who have
> Some reputation for learning, you will become hated.

The common background of audience and poet is disappearing, the old certainties
are being undermined, the city divided. Euripides is the first Greek poet to suffer the
fate of so many of the great modern writers: rejected by most of his contemporaries
(he rarely won first prize and was the favorite target for the scurrilous humor of the
comic poets), he was universally admired and revered by the Greeks of the centuries
that followed his death.

   It is significant that what little biographical information we have for Euripides
makes no mention of military service or political office; unlike Aeschylus, who fought
in the ranks at Marathon, and Sophocles, who took an active part in public affairs

from youth to advanced old age, Euripides seems to have lived a private, an intellectual life. Younger than Sophocles (though they died in the same year), he was more receptive to the critical theories and the rhetorical techniques offered by the Sophist teachers; his plays often subject received ideas to fundamental questioning, expressed in vivid dramatic debate. His *Medea* is typical of his iconoclastic approach; his choice of subject and central characters is in itself a challenge to established canons. He still dramatizes myth, but the myth he chooses is exotic and disturbing, and the protagonist is not a man but a woman. Medea is both woman and foreigner—that is, in terms of the audience's prejudice and practice she is a representative of the two free-born groups in Athenian society that had almost no rights at all (though the male foreign resident had more rights than the native woman). The tragic hero is no longer a king, "one who is highly renowned and prosperous such as Oedipus," but a woman who, because she finds no redress for her wrongs in society, is driven by her passion to violate that society's most sacred laws in a rebellion against its typical representative, Jason, her husband. She is not just a woman and a foreigner, she is also a person of great intellectual power. Compared with her the credulous king and her complacent husband are children, and once her mind is made up, she moves them like pawns to their proper places in her barbaric game. The myth is used for new purposes, to shock the members of the audience, attack their deepest prejudices, and shake them out of their complacent pride in the superiority of Greek masculinity.

But the play is more compelling than that. Before it is over, our sympathies have come full circle; the contempt with which we regard the Jason of the opening scenes turns to pity as we feel the measure of his loss and the ferocity of Medea's revenge. Medea's passion has carried her too far; the death of Kreon (Creon) and his daughter we might have accepted, but the murder of the children is too much. It was, of course, meant to be. Euripides' theme, like Homer's, is violence, but this is the unspeakable violence of the oppressed, which is greater than the violence of the oppressor and which, because it has been long pent up, cannot be controlled.

In this, as in the other Greek plays, the gods have their place. In *Oresteia* the will of Zeus is manifested in every action and implied in every word; in *Oedipus the King* the gods bide their time and watch Oedipus fulfill the truth of their prophecy, but in *Medea*, the divine will, which is revealed at the end, is enigmatic and, far from bringing harmony, concludes the play with a terrifying discord. All through *Medea* the human beings involved call on the gods; two especially are singled out for attention: Earth and Sun. It is by these two gods that Medea makes Aegeus swear to give her refuge in Athens, the chorus invokes them to prevent Medea's violence against her sons, and Jason wonders how Medea can look on Earth and Sun after she has killed her own children. These emphatic appeals clearly raise the question of the attitude of the gods, and the answer to the question is a shock. We are not told what Earth does, but Sun sends the magic chariot on which Medea makes her escape. His reason, too, is stated: it is not any concern for justice but the fact that Medea is his granddaughter. Euripides is here using the letter of the myth for his own purposes. This jarring detail emphasizes the significance of the whole. The play creates a world in which there is no relation whatsoever between the powers that rule the universe and the fundamental laws of human morality. It dramatizes disorder, not just the disorder of the family of Jason and Medea but the disorder of the universe as a whole. It is the nightmare in which the dream of the fifth century B.C. was to end, the senseless fury and degradation of permanent violence. "Flow backward to your sources, sacred rivers," the chorus sings. "And let the world's great order be reversed."

For a short, general survey of Euripidean drama, see B. M. W. Knox in *The Cambridge History of Classical Literature* (1985), pp. 316–39. Perceptive analyses of *Medea* can be found in Emily A. McDermott, *Euripides' Medea: The Incarnation of Disorder* (1989), and E. Segal, ed., *Euripides, A Collection of Critical Essays* (1968). Knox, "The *Medea* of Euripides," and P. E. Easterling, "The Infanticide in Euripides' *Medea*," both in *Yale Classical Studies* 24 (1977), will also be helpful to students.

PRONOUNCING GLOSSARY

The following list uses common English syllables and stress accents to provide rough equivalents of selected words whose pronunciation may be unfamiliar to the general reader.

Aigeus: *ai'-jioos*　　　　　　　　Medea: *me-dee'-uh*

Aphrodite: *a-froh-dai'-tee*　　　　Pelias: *pee'-lee-as*

Hecate: *he'-kah-tee*　　　　　　　Pieria: *pai-ee'-ree-uh*

Iolcos: *yol'-kuhs*

Medea[1]

CHARACTERS

MEDEA, *princess of Colchis and wife*　　　AIGEUS, *king of Athens*
　of Jason　　　　　　　　　　　　　　NURSE *to Medea*
JASON, *son of Aeson, king of Iolcos*　　　　TUTOR *to Medea's children*
Two CHILDREN *of Medea and Jason*　　　　MESSENGER
KREON, *king of Corinth*　　　　　　　　　CHORUS OF CORINTHIAN WOMEN

[SCENE—*In front of* MEDEA's *house in Corinth. Enter from the house*
MEDEA's NURSE.]

NURSE　How I wish the Argo[2] never had reached the land
　Of Colchis, skimming through the blue Symplegades,
　Nor ever had fallen in the glades of Pelion[3]
　The smitten fir-tree to furnish oars for the hands
　Of heroes who in Pelias'[4] name attempted　　　　　　　　　　　　5
　The Golden Fleece! For then my mistress Medea[5]
　Would not have sailed for the towers of the land of Iolcos,
　Her heart on fire with passionate love for Jason;
　Nor would she have persuaded the daughters of Pelias
　To kill their father,[6] and now be living here　　　　　　　　　　　10
　In Corinth[7] with her husband and children. She gave
　Pleasure to the people of her land of exile,
　And she herself helped Jason in every way.
　This is indeed the greatest salvation of all,—
　For the wife not to stand apart from the husband.　　　　　　　　15
　But now there's hatred everywhere. Love is diseased.
　For, deserting his own children and my mistress,
　Jason has taken a royal wife to his bed,

1. Translated by Rex Warner.　2. The ship in which Jason and his companions sailed on the quest for the Golden Fleece.　3. A mountain in northern Greece near Iolcos, the place from which Jason sailed. The Symplegades were clashing rocks that crushed ships endeavoring to pass between them. They were supposed to be located at the Hellespont, the passage between the Mediterranean and Black Seas.　4. He seized the kingdom of Iolcos, expelling Aeson, Jason's father. When Jason came to claim his rights, Pelias sent him to get the Golden Fleece.　5. Daughter of the king of Colchis who fell in love with Jason and helped him take the Golden Fleece away from her own country.　6. After Jason and Medea returned to Iolcos, Medea (who had a reputation as a sorceress) persuaded Pelias's daughters to cut Pelias up and boil the pieces, which would restore him to youth. The experiment was, of course, unsuccessful, and Pelias's son banished Jason and Medea from the kingdom.　7. On the isthmus between the Peloponnese and Attica, where they took refuge. In Euripides' time it was a wealthy trading city, a commercial rival of Athens.

The daughter of the ruler of this land, Kreon.
And poor Medea is slighted, and cries aloud on the   20
Vows they made to each other, the right hands clasped
In eternal promise. She calls upon the gods to witness
What sort of return Jason has made to her love.
She lies without food and gives herself up to suffering,
Wasting away every moment of the day in tears.   25
So it has gone since she knew herself slighted by him.
Not stirring an eye, not moving her face from the ground,
No more than either a rock or surging sea water
She listens when she is given friendly advice.
Except that sometimes she twists back her white neck and   30
Moans to herself, calling out on her father's name,
And her land, and her home betrayed when she came away with
A man who now is determined to dishonor her.
Poor creature, she has discovered by her sufferings
What it means to one not to have lost one's own country.   35
She has turned from the children and does not like to see them.
I am afraid she may think of some dreadful thing,
For her heart is violent. She will never put up with
The treatment she is getting. I know and fear her
Lest she may sharpen a sword and thrust to the heart,   40
Stealing into the palace where the bed is made,
Or even kill the king and the new-wedded groom,
And thus bring a greater misfortune on herself.
She's a strange woman. I know it won't be easy
To make an enemy of her and come off best.   45
But here the children come. They have finished playing.
They have no thought at all of their mother's trouble.
Indeed it is not usual for the young to grieve.

> [*Enter from the right the slave who is the* TUTOR *to* MEDEA's *two
> small* CHILDREN. *The* CHILDREN *follow him.*]

TUTOR   You old retainer of my mistress's household,
Why are you standing here all alone in front of the   50
Gates and moaning to yourself over your misfortune?
Medea could not wish you to leave her alone.
NURSE   Old man, and guardian of the children of Jason,
If one is a good servant, it's a terrible thing
When one's master's luck is out; it goes to one's heart.   55
So I myself have got into such a state of grief
That a longing stole over me to come outside here
And tell the earth and air of my mistress's sorrows.
TUTOR   Has the poor lady not yet given up her crying?
NURSE   Given up? She's at the start, not halfway through her tears.   60
TUTOR   Poor fool,—if I may call my mistress such a name,—
How ignorant she is of trouble more to come.
NURSE   What do you mean, old man? You needn't fear to speak.
TUTOR   Nothing. I take back the words which I used just now.
NURSE   Don't, by your beard, hide this from me, your fellow-servant.   65
If need be, I'll keep quiet about what you tell me.

TUTOR   I heard a person saying, while I myself seemed
   Not to be paying attention, when I was at the place
   Where the old draught-players[8] sit, by the holy fountain,
   That Kreon, ruler of the land, intends to drive   70
   These children and their mother in exile from Corinth.
   But whether what he said is really true or not
   I do not know. I pray that it may not be true.
NURSE   And will Jason put up with it that his children
   Should suffer so, though he's no friend to their mother?   75
TUTOR   Old ties give place to new ones. As for Jason, he
   No longer has a feeling for this house of ours.
NURSE   It's black indeed for us, when we add new to old
   Sorrows before even the present sky has cleared.
TUTOR   But you be silent, and keep all this to yourself.   80
   It is not the right time to tell our mistress of it.
NURSE   Do you hear, children, what a father he is to you?
   I wish he were dead,—but no, he is still my master.
   Yet certainly he has proved unkind to his dear ones.
TUTOR   What's strange in that? Have you only just discovered   85
   That everyone loves himself more than his neighbor?
   Some have good reason, others get something out of it.
   So Jason neglects his children for the new bride.
NURSE   Go indoors, children. That will be the best thing.
   And you, keep them to themselves as much as possible.   90
   Don't bring them near their mother in her angry mood.
   For I've seen her already blazing her eyes at them
   As though she meant some mischief and I am sure that
   She'll not stop raging until she has struck at someone.
   May it be an enemy and not a friend she hurts!   95
   [MEDEA *is heard inside the house.*]
MEDEA   Ah, wretch! Ah, lost in my sufferings,
   I wish, I wish I might die.
NURSE   What did I say, dear children? Your mother
   Frets her heart and frets it to anger.
   Run away quickly into the house,   100
   And keep well out of her sight.
   Don't go anywhere near, but be careful
   Of the wildness and bitter nature
   Of that proud mind.
   Go now! Run quickly indoors.   105
   It is clear that she soon will put lightning
   In that cloud of her cries that is rising
   With a passion increasing. Oh, what will she do,
   Proud-hearted and not to be checked on her course,
   A soul bitten into with wrong?   110
   [*The* TUTOR *takes the* CHILDREN *into the house.*]
MEDEA   Ah, I have suffered
   What should be wept for bitterly. I hate you,
   Children of a hateful mother. I curse you

---

8. Checker players.

And your father. Let the whole house crash.
NURSE   Ah, I pity you, you poor creature.   115
How can your children share in their father's
Wickedness? Why do you hate them? Oh children,
How much I fear that something may happen!
Great people's tempers are terrible, always
Having their own way, seldom checked,   120
Dangerous they shift from mood to mood.
How much better to have been accustomed
To live on equal terms with one's neighbors.
I would like to be safe and grow old in a
Humble way. What is moderate sounds best,   125
Also in practice is best for everyone.
Greatness brings no profit to people.
God indeed, when in anger, brings
Greater ruin to great men's houses.

[Enter, on the right, a CHORUS OF CORINTHIAN WOMEN. They have
come to inquire about MEDEA and to attempt to console her.]

CHORUS   I heard the voice, I heard the cry   130
Of Colchis' wretched daughter.
Tell me, mother, is she not yet
At rest? Within the double gates
Of the court I heard her cry. I am sorry
For the sorrow of this home. O, say, what has happened?   135
NURSE   There is no home. It's over and done with.
Her husband holds fast to his royal wedding,
While she, my mistress, cries out her eyes
There in her room, and takes no warmth from
Any word of any friend.   140
MEDEA   Oh, I wish
That lightning from heaven would split my head open.
Oh, what use have I now for life?
I would find my release in death
And leave hateful existence behind me.   145
CHORUS   O God and Earth and Heaven!
Did you hear what a cry was that
Which the sad wife sings?
Poor foolish one, why should you long
For that appalling rest?   150
The final end of death comes fast.
No need to pray for that.
Suppose your man gives honor
To another woman's bed.
It often happens. Don't be hurt.   155
God will be your friend in this.
You must not waste away
Grieving too much for him who shared your bed.
MEDEA   Great Themis, lady Artemis,[9] behold
The things I suffer, though I made him promise,   160

9. The protector of women in pain and distress. Themis, a Titan, was justice personified.

My hateful husband. I pray that I may see him,
Him and his bride and all their palace shattered
For the wrong they dare to do me without cause.
Oh, my father! Oh, my country! In what dishonor
I left you, killing my own brother for it.[1]   165

NURSE   Do you hear what she says, and how she cries
On Themis, the goddess of Promises, and on Zeus,
Whom we believe to be the Keeper of Oaths?
Of this I am sure, that no small thing
Will appease my mistress's anger.   170

CHORUS   Will she come into our presence?
Will she listen when we are speaking
To the words we say?
I wish she might relax her rage
And temper of her heart.   175
My willingness to help will never
Be wanting to my friends.
But go inside and bring her
Out of the house to us,
And speak kindly to her: hurry,   180
Before she wrongs her own.
This passion of hers moves to something great.

NURSE   I will, but I doubt if I'll manage
To win my mistress over.
But still I'll attempt it to please you.   185
Such a look she will flash on her servants
If any comes near with a message,
Like a lioness guarding her cubs.
It is right, I think, to consider
Both stupid and lacking in foresight   190
Those poets of old who wrote songs
For revels and dinners and banquets,
Pleasant sounds for men living at ease;
But none of them all has discovered
How to put an end with their singing   195
Or musical instruments grief,
Bitter grief, from which death and disaster
Cheat the hopes of a house. Yet how good
If music could cure men of this! But why raise
To no purpose the voice at a banquet? For *there* is   200
Already abundance of pleasure for men
With a joy of its own.
          [*The* NURSE *goes into the house.*]

CHORUS   I heard a shriek that is laden with sorrow.
Shrilling out her hard grief she cries out
Upon him who betrayed both her bed and her marriage.   205
Wronged, she calls on the gods,
On the justice of Zeus, the oath sworn,

---

1. Medea killed him to delay the pursuit when she escaped with Jason.

Which brought her away
To the opposite shore of the Greeks
Through the gloomy salt straits to the gateway   210
Of the salty unlimited sea.
    [MEDEA, *attended by servants, comes out of the house.*]
MEDEA   Women of Corinth, I have come outside to you
Lest you should be indignant with me; for I know
That many people are overproud, some when alone,
And others when in company. And those who live   215
Quietly, as I do, get a bad reputation.
For a just judgment is not evident in the eyes
When a man at first sight hates another, before
Learning his character, being in no way injured;
And a foreigner[2] especially must adapt himself.   220
I'd not approve of even a fellow-countryman
Who by pride and want of manners offends his neighbors.
But on me this thing has fallen so unexpectedly,
It has broken my heart. I am finished. I let go
All my life's joy. My friends, I only want to die.   225
It was everything to me to think well of one man,
And he, my own husband, has turned out wholly vile.
Of all things which are living and can form a judgment
We women are the most unfortunate creatures.[3]
Firstly, with an excess of wealth it is required   230
For us to buy a husband and take for our bodies
A master; for not to take one is even worse.
And now the question is serious whether we take
A good or bad one; for there is no easy escape
For a woman, nor can she say no to her marriage.   235
She arrives among new modes of behavior and manners,
And needs prophetic power, unless she has learnt at home,
How best to manage him who shares the bed with her.
And if we work out all this well and carefully,
And the husband lives with us and lightly bears his yoke,   240
Then life is enviable. If not, I'd rather die.
A man, when he's tired of the company in his home,
Goes out of the house and puts an end to his boredom
And turns to a friend or companion of his own age.
But we are forced to keep our eyes on one alone.   245
What they say of us is that we have a peaceful time
Living at home, while they do the fighting in war.
How wrong they are! I would very much rather stand
Three times in the front of battle than bear one child.
Yet what applies to me does not apply to you.   250
You have a country. Your family home is here.
You enjoy life and the company of your friends.

2. Foreign residents were encouraged to come to Athens but were rarely admitted to the rights of full citizenship, which was a jealously guarded privilege.   3. Athenian rights and institutions were made for men; the women had few privileges and almost no legal rights. Lines 230–31 refer to the dowry that had to be provided for the bride.

But I am deserted, a refugee, thought nothing of
By my husband,—something he won in a foreign land.
I have no mother or brother, nor any relation   255
With whom I can take refuge in this sea of woe.
This much then is the service I would beg from you:
If I can find the means or devise any scheme
To pay my husband back for what he has done to me,—
Him and his father-in-law and the girl who married him,—   260
Just to keep silent. For in other ways a woman
Is full of fear, defenseless, dreads the sight of cold
Steel; but, when once she is wronged in the matter of love,
No other soul can hold so many thoughts of blood.
CHORUS   This I will promise. You are in the right, Medea,   265
In paying your husband back. I am not surprised at you
For being sad. But look! I see our king Kreon
Approaching. He will tell us of some new plan.
          [*Enter, from the right,* KREON, *with attendants.*]
KREON   You, with that angry look, so set against your husband,
Medea, I order you to leave my territories   270
An exile, and take along with you your two children,
And not to waste time doing it. It is my decree,
And I will see it done. I will not return home
Until you are cast from the boundaries of my land.
MEDEA   Oh, this is the end for me. I am utterly lost.   275
Now I am in the full force of the storm of hate
And have no harbor from ruin to reach easily.
Yet still, in spite of it all, I'll ask the question:
What is your reason, Kreon, for banishing me?
KREON   I am afraid of you,—why should I dissemble it?—   280
Afraid that you may injure my daughter mortally.
Many things accumulate to support my feeling.
You are a clever woman, versed in evil arts,
And are angry at having lost your husband's love.
I hear that you are threatening, so they tell me,   285
To do something against my daughter and Jason
And me, too. I shall take my precautions first.
I tell you, I prefer to earn your hatred now
Than to be soft-hearted and afterwards regret it.
MEDEA   This is not the first time, Kreon. Often previously   290
Through being considered clever I have suffered much.
A person of sense ought never to have his children
Brought up to be more clever than the average.
For, apart from cleverness bringing them no profit,
It will make them objects of envy and ill-will.   295
If you put new ideas before the eyes of fools
They'll think you foolish and worthless into the bargain;
And if you are thought superior to those who have
Some reputation for learning, you will become hated.
I have some knowledge myself of how this happens;   300
For being clever, I find that some will envy me,

Others object to me. Yet all my cleverness
Is not so much. Well, then, are you frightened, Kreon,
That I should harm you? There is no need. It is not
My way to transgress the authority of a king.   305
How have you injured me? You gave your daughter away
To the man you wanted. O, certainly I hate
My husband, but you, I think, have acted wisely;
Nor do I grudge it you that your affairs go well.
May the marriage be a lucky one! Only let me   310
Live in this land. For even though I have been wronged,
I will not raise my voice, but submit to my betters.

KREON   What you say sounds gentle enough. Still in my heart
  I greatly dread that you are plotting some evil,
  And therefore I trust you even less than before.   315
  A sharp-tempered woman, or for that matter a man,
  Is easier to deal with than the clever type
  Who holds her tongue. No. You must go. No need for more
  Speeches. The thing is fixed. By no manner of means
  Shall you, an enemy of mine, stay in my country.   320

MEDEA   I beg you. By your knees, by your new-wedded girl.
KREON   Your words are wasted. You will never persuade me.
MEDEA   Will you drive me out, and give no heed to my prayers?
KREON   I will, for I love my family more than you.
MEDEA   O my country! How bitterly now I remember you!   325
KREON   I love my country too,—next after my children.
MEDEA   O what an evil to men is passionate love!
KREON   That would depend on the luck that goes along with it.
MEDEA   O God, do not forget who is the cause of this!
KREON   Go. It is no use. Spare me the pain of forcing you.   330
MEDEA   I'm spared no pain. I lack no pain to be spared me.
KREON   Then you'll be removed by force by one of my men.
MEDEA   No, Kreon, not that! But do listen, I beg you.
KREON   Woman, you seem to want to create a disturbance.
MEDEA   I *will* go into exile. *This* is not what I beg for.   335
KREON   Why then this violence and clinging to my hand?
MEDEA   Allow me to remain here just for this one day,
  So I may consider where to live in my exile,
  And look for support for my children, since their father
  Chooses to make no kind of provision for them.   340
  Have pity on them! You have children of your own.
  It is natural for you to look kindly on them.
  For myself I do not mind if I go into exile.
  It is the children being in trouble that I mind.

KREON   There is nothing tyrannical about my nature,   345
  And by showing mercy I have often been the loser.
  Even now I know that I am making a mistake.
  All the same you shall have your will. But this I tell you,
  That if the light of heaven tomorrow shall see you,
  You and your children in the confines of my land,   350
  You die. This word I have spoken is firmly fixed.

But now, if you must stay, stay for this day alone.
For in it you can do none of the things I fear.
　　[*Exit* KREON *with his attendants.*]

CHORUS　Oh, unfortunate one! Oh, cruel!
　　Where will you turn? Who will help you?　　　　　　355
　　What house or what land to preserve you
　　From ill can you find?
　　Medea, a god has thrown suffering
　　Upon you in waves of despair.

MEDEA　Things have gone badly every way. No doubt of that.　360
　　But not these things this far, and don't imagine so.
　　There are still trials to come for the new-wedded pair,
　　And for their relations pain that will mean something.
　　Do you think that I would ever have fawned on that man
　　Unless I had some end to gain or profit in it?　　　　365
　　I would not even have spoken or touched him with my hands.
　　But he has got to such a pitch of foolishness
　　That, though he could have made nothing of all my plans
　　By exiling me, he has given me this one day
　　To stay here, and in this I will make dead bodies　　　370
　　Of three of my enemies,—father, the girl and my husband.
　　I have many ways of death which I might suit to them,
　　And do not know, friends, which one to take in hand;
　　Whether to set fire underneath their bridal mansion,
　　Or sharpen a sword and thrust it to the heart,　　　　375
　　Stealing into the palace where the bed is made.
　　There is just one obstacle to this. If I am caught
　　Breaking into the house and scheming against it,
　　I shall die, and give my enemies cause for laughter.
　　It is best to go by the straight road, the one in which　380
　　I am most skilled, and make away with them by poison.
　　So be it then.
　　And now suppose them dead. What town will receive me?
　　What friend will offer me a refuge in his land,
　　Or the guarantee of his house and save my own life?　　385
　　There is none. So I must wait a little time yet,
　　And if some sure defense should then appear for me,
　　In craft and silence I will set about this murder.
　　But if my fate should drive me on without help,
　　Even though death is certain, I will take the sword　　390
　　Myself and kill, and steadfastly advance to crime.
　　It shall not be,—I swear it by her, my mistress,
　　Whom most I honor and have chosen as partner,
　　Hecate,[4] who dwells in the recesses of my hearth,—
　　That any man shall be glad to have injured me.　　　　395
　　Bitter I will make their marriage for them and mournful,
　　Bitter the alliance and the driving me out of the land.

---

4. The patron of witchcraft, sometimes identified with Artemis; Medea has a statue and shrine of her in
the house.

Ah, come, Medea, in your plotting and scheming
Leave nothing untried of all those things which you know.
Go forward to the dreadful act. The test has come   400
For resolution. You see how you are treated. Never
Shall you be mocked by Jason's Corinthian wedding,
Whose father was noble, whose grandfather Helios.[5]
You have the skill. What is more, you were born a woman,
And women, though most helpless in doing good deeds,   405
Are of every evil the cleverest of contrivers.

CHORUS   Flow backward to your sources, sacred rivers,
And let the world's great order be reversed.
It is the thoughts of *men* that are deceitful,
Their pledges that are loose.   410
Story shall now turn my condition to a fair one,
Women are paid their due.
No more shall evil-sounding fame be theirs.

Cease now, you muses of the ancient singers,
To tell the tale of my unfaithfulness;   415
For not on us did Phoebus,[6] lord of music,
Bestow the lyre's divine
Power, for otherwise I should have sung an answer
To the other sex. Long time
Has much to tell of us, and much of them.   420

You sailed away from your father's home,
With a heart on fire you passed
The double rocks of the sea.
And now in a foreign country
You have lost your rest in a widowed bed,   425
And are driven forth, a refugee
In dishonor from the land.

Good faith has gone, and no more remains
In great Greece a sense of shame.
It has flown away to the sky.   430
No father's house for a haven
Is at hand for you now, and another queen
Of your bed has dispossessed you and
Is mistress of your home.
        [*Enter* JASON, *with attendants.*]

JASON   This is not the first occasion that I have noticed 435
How hopeless it is to deal with a stubborn temper.
For, with reasonable submission to our ruler's will,
You might have lived in this land and kept your home.
As it is you are going to be exiled for your loose speaking.
Not that I mind myself. You are free to continue   440
Telling everyone that Jason is a worthless man.

---

5. The sun, father of Medea's father, Aeëtes.   6. Apollo.

But as to your talk about the king, consider
Yourself most lucky that exile is your punishment.
I, for my part, have always tried to calm down
The anger of the king, and wished you to remain.   445
But you will not give up your folly, continually
Speaking ill of him, and so you are going to be banished.
All the same, and in spite of your conduct, I'll not desert
My friends, but have come to make some provision for you,
So that you and the children may not be penniless   450
Or in need of anything in exile. Certainly
Exile brings many troubles with it. And even
If you hate me, I cannot think badly of you.

MEDEA O coward in every way,—that is what I call you,
With bitterest reproach for your lack of manliness,   455
You have come, you, my worst enemy, have come to me!
It is not an example of over-confidence
Or of boldness thus to look your friends in the face,
Friends you have injured,—no, it is the worst of all
Human diseases, shamelessness. But you did well   460
To come, for I can speak ill of you and lighten
My heart, and you will suffer while you are listening.
And first I will begin from what happened first.
I saved your life, and every Greek knows I saved it
Who was a ship-mate of yours aboard the Argo,   465
When you were sent to control the bulls that breathed fire
And yoke them, and when you would sow that deadly field.
Also that snake, who encircled with his many folds
The Golden Fleece and guarded it and never slept,[7]
I killed, and so gave you the safety of the light.   470
And I myself betrayed my father and my home,
And came with you to Pelias' land of Iolcos.
And then, showing more willingness to help than wisdom,
I killed him, Pelias, with a most dreadful death
At his own daughters' hands, and took away your fear.   475
This is how I behaved to you, you wretched man,
And you forsook me, took another bride to bed
Though you had children; for, if that had not been,
You would have had an excuse for another wedding.
Faith in your word has gone. Indeed I cannot tell   480
Whether you think the gods whose names you swore by then
Have ceased to rule and that new standards are set up,
Since you must know you have broken your word to me.
O my right hand, and the knees which you often clasped
In supplication, how senselessly I am treated   485
By this bad man, and how my hopes have missed their mark!
Come, I will share my thoughts as though you were a friend,—
You! Can I think that you would ever treat me well?

7. These lines refer to ordeals through which Jason had to pass to win the fleece and in which Medea
helped him. He had to yoke a team of fire-breathing bulls, then sow a field that immediately sprouted armed
warriors, and then deal with the snake that guarded the fleece.

But I will do it, and these questions will make you
Appear the baser. Where am I to go? To my father's? 490
Him I betrayed and his land when I came with you.
To Pelias' wretched daughters? What a fine welcome
They would prepare for me who murdered their father!
For this is my position,—hated by my friends
At home, I have, in kindness to you, made enemies 495
Of others whom there was no need to have injured.
And how happy among Greek women you have made me
On your side for all this! A distinguished husband
I have,—for breaking promises. When in misery
I am cast out of the land and go into exile, 500
Quite without friends and all alone with my children,
That will be a fine shame for the new-wedded groom,
For his children to wander as beggars and she who saved him.
O God, you have given to mortals a sure method
Of telling the gold that is pure from the counterfeit; 505
Why is there no mark engraved upon men's bodies,
By which we could know the true ones from the false ones?
CHORUS   It is a strange form of anger, difficult to cure
When two friends turn upon each other in hatred.
JASON   As for me, it seems I must be no bad speaker. 510
But, like a man who has a good grip of the tiller,
Reef up his sail, and so run away from under
This mouthing tempest, woman, of your bitter tongue.
Since you insist on building up your kindness to me,
My view is that Cypris8 was alone responsible 515
Of men and gods for the preserving of my life.
You are clever enough,—but really I need not enter
Into the story of how it was love's inescapable
Power that compelled you to keep my person safe.
On this I will not go into too much detail. 520
In so far as you helped me, you did well enough.
But on this question of saving me, I can prove
You have certainly got from me more than you gave.
Firstly, instead of living among barbarians,
You inhabit a Greek land and understand our ways, 525
How to live by law instead of the sweet will of force.
And all the Greeks considered you a clever woman.
You were honored for it; while, if you were living at
The ends of the earth, nobody would have heard of you.
For my part, rather than stores of gold in my house 530
Or power to sing even sweeter songs than Orpheus,
I'd choose the fate that made me a distinguished man.
There is my reply to your story of my labors.
Remember it was you who started the argument.
Next for your attack on my wedding with the princess: 535
Here I will prove that, first, it was a clever move,

8. Aphrodite, goddess of love.

Secondly, a wise one, and, finally, that I made it
In your best interests and the children's. Please keep calm.
When I arrived here from the land of Iolcos,
Involved, as I was, in every kind of difficulty,   540
What luckier chance could I have come across than this,
An exile to marry the daughter of the king?
It was not,—the point that seems to upset you—that I
Grew tired of your bed and felt the need of a new bride;
Nor with any wish to outdo your number of children.   545
We have enough already. I am quite content.
But,—this was the main reason—that we might live well,
And not be short of anything. I know that all
A man's friends leave him stone-cold if he becomes poor.
Also that I might bring my children up worthy   550
Of my position, and, by producing more of them
To be brothers of yours, we would draw the families
Together and all be happy. You need no children.
And it pays me to do good to those I have now
By having others. Do you think this a bad plan?   555
You wouldn't if the love question hadn't upset you.
But you women have got into such a state of mind
That, if your life at night is good, you think you have
Everything; but, if in that quarter things go wrong,
You will consider your best and truest interests   560
Most hateful. It would have been better far for men
To have got their children in some other way, and women
Not to have existed. Then life would have been good.

CHORUS   Jason, though you have made this speech of yours look well,
Still I think, even though others do not agree,   565
You have betrayed your wife and are acting badly.

MEDEA   Surely in many ways I hold different views
From others, for I think that the plausible speaker
Who is a villain deserves the greatest punishment.
Confident in his tongue's power to adorn evil,   570
He stops at nothing. Yet he is not really wise.
As in your case. There is no need to put on the airs
Of a clever speaker, for one word will lay you flat.
If you were not a coward, you would not have married
Behind my back, but discussed it with me first.   575

JASON   And you, no doubt, would have furthered the proposal,
If I had told you of it, you who even now
Are incapable of controlling your bitter temper.

MEDEA   It was not that. No, you thought it was not respectable
As you got on in years to have a foreign wife.   580

JASON   Make sure of this: it was not because of a woman
I made the royal alliance in which I now live,
But, as I said before, I wished to preserve you
And breed a royal progeny to be brothers
To the children I have now, a sure defense to us.   585

MEDEA   Let me have no happy fortune that brings pain with it,

Or prosperity which is upsetting to the mind!

JASON   Change your ideas of what you want, and show more sense.
   Do not consider painful what is good for you,
   Nor, when you are lucky, think yourself unfortunate.   590

MEDEA   You can insult me. You have somewhere to turn to.
   But I shall go from this land into exile, friendless.

JASON   It was what you chose yourself. Don't blame others for it.

MEDEA   And how did I choose it? Did I betray my husband?

JASON   You called down wicked curses on the king's family.   595

MEDEA   A curse, that is what I am become to your house too.

JASON   I do not propose to go into all the rest of it;
   But, if you wish for the children or for yourself
   In exile to have some of my money to help you,
   Say so, for I am prepared to give with open hand,   600
   Or to provide you with introductions to my friends
   Who will treat you well. You are a fool if you do not
   Accept this. Cease your anger and you will profit.

MEDEA   I shall never accept the favors of friends of yours,
   Nor take a thing from you, so you need not offer it.   605
   There is no benefit in the gifts of a bad man.

JASON   Then, in any case, I call the gods to witness that
   I wish to help you and the children in every way,
   But you refuse what is good for you. Obstinately
   You push away your friends. You are sure to suffer for it.   610

MEDEA   Go! No doubt you hanker for your virginal bride,
   And are guilty of lingering too long out of her house.
   Enjoy your wedding. But perhaps,—with the help of God—
   You will make the kind of marriage that you will regret.

   [JASON *goes out with his attendants.*]

CHORUS   When love is in excess   615
   It brings a man no honor
   Nor any worthiness.
   But if in moderation Cypris comes,
   There is no other power at all so gracious.
   O goddess, never on me let loose the unerring   620
   Shaft of your bow in the poison of desire.

   Let my heart be wise.
   It is the gods' best gift.
   On me let mighty Cypris
   Inflict no wordy wars or restless anger   625
   To urge my passion to a different love.
   But with discernment may she guide women's weddings,
   Honoring most what is peaceful in the bed.

   O country and home,
   Never, never may I be without you,   630
   Living the hopeless life,
   Hard to pass through and painful,
   Most pitiable of all.

Let death first lay me low and death
Free me from this daylight. 635
There is no sorrow above
The loss of a native land.

I have seen it myself,
Do not tell of a secondhand story.
Neither city nor friend 640
Pitied you when you suffered
The worst of sufferings.
O let him die ungraced whose heart
Will not reward his friends,
Who cannot open an honest mind 645
No friend will he be of mine.

[*Enter* AIGEUS, *king of Athens, an old friend of* MEDEA.]

AIGEUS   Medea, greeting! This is the best introduction
Of which men know for conversation between friends.

MEDEA   Greeting to you too, Aigeus, son of King Pandion,
Where have you come from to visit this country's soil? 650

AIGEUS   I have just left the ancient oracle of Phoebus.

MEDEA   And why did you go to earth's prophetic center?

AIGEUS   I went to inquire how children might be born to me.

MEDEA   Is it so? Your life still up to this point childless?

AIGEUS   Yes. By the fate of some power we have no children. 655

MEDEA   Have you a wife, or is there none to share your bed?

AIGEUS   There is. Yes, I am joined to my wife in marriage.

MEDEA   And what did Phoebus say to you about children?

AIGEUS   Words too wise for a mere man to guess their meaning.

MEDEA   Is it proper for me to be told the God's reply? 660

AIGEUS   It is. For sure what is needed is cleverness.

MEDEA   Then what was his message? Tell me, if I may hear.

AIGEUS   I am not to loosen the hanging foot of the wine-skin[9] . . .

MEDEA   Until you have done something, or reached some country?

AIGEUS   Until I return again to my hearth and house. 665

MEDEA   And for what purpose have you journeyed to this land?

AIGEUS   There is a man called Pittheus, king of Troezen.[1]

MEDEA   A son of Pelops, they say, a most righteous man.

AIGEUS   With him I wish to discuss the reply of the god.

MEDEA   Yes. He is wise and experienced in such matters. 670

AIGEUS   And to me also the dearest of all my spear-friends.[2]

MEDEA   Well, I hope you have good luck, and achieve your will.

AIGEUS   But why this downcast eye of yours, and this pale cheek?

MEDEA   O Aigeus, my husband has been the worst of all to me.

AIGEUS   What do you mean? Say clearly what has caused this grief. 675

MEDEA   Jason wrongs me, though I have never injured him.

AIGEUS   What has he done? Tell me about it in clearer words.

MEDEA   He has taken a wife to his house, supplanting me.

---

9. Cryptic; probably not to have intercourse.   1. In the Peloponnese. Pittheus was Aigeus's father-in-law. Corinth was on the way from Delphi to Troezen.   2. Allies in war, companions in fighting.

AIGEUS   Surely he would not dare to do a thing like that.

MEDEA   Be sure he has. Once dear, I now am slighted by him.   680

AIGEUS   Did he fall in love? Or is he tired of your love?

MEDEA   He was greatly in love, this traitor to his friends.

AIGEUS   Then let him go, if, as you say, he is so bad.

MEDEA   A passionate love,—for an alliance with the king.

AIGEUS   And who gave him his wife? Tell me the rest of it.   685

MEDEA   It was Kreon, he who rules this land of Corinth.

AIGEUS   Indeed, Medea, your grief was understandable.

MEDEA   I am ruined. And there is more to come: I am banished.

AIGEUS   Banished? By whom? Here you tell me of a new wrong.

MEDEA   Kreon drives me an exile from the land of Corinth.   690

AIGEUS   Does Jason consent? I cannot approve of this.

MEDEA   He pretends not to, but he will put up with it.
    Ah, Aigeus, I beg and beseech you, by your beard
    And by your knees I am making myself your suppliant,
    Have pity on me, have pity on your poor friend,   695
    And do not let me go into exile desolate,
    But receive me in your land and at your very hearth.
    So may your love, with God's help, lead to the bearing
    Of children, and so may you yourself die happy.
    You do not know what a chance you have come on here.   700
    I will end your childlessness, and I will make you able
    To beget children. The drugs I know can do this.

AIGEUS   For many reasons, woman, I am anxious to do
    This favor for you. First, for the sake of the gods,
    And then for the birth of children which you promise,   705
    For in that respect I am entirely at my wits' end.
    But this is my position: if you reach my land,
    I, being in my rights, will try to befriend you.
    But this much I must warn you of beforehand:
    I shall not agree to take you out of this country;   710
    But if you by yourself can reach my house, then you
    Shall stay there safely. To none will I give you up.
    But from this land you must make your escape yourself,
    For I do not wish to incur blame from my friends.

MEDEA   It shall be so. But, if I might have a pledge from you   715
    For this, then I would have from you all I desire.

AIGEUS   Do you not trust me? What is it rankles with you?

MEDEA   I trust you, yes. But the house of Pelias hates me,
    And so does Kreon. If you are bound by this oath,
    When they try to drag me from your land, you will not   720
    Abandon me; but if our pact is only words,
    With no oath to the gods, you will be lightly armed,
    Unable to resist their summons. I am weak,
    While they have wealth to help them and a royal house.

AIGEUS   You show much foresight for such negotiations.   725
    Well, if you will have it so, I will not refuse.
    For, both on my side this will be the safest way
    To have some excuse to put forward to your enemies,

And for you it is more certain. You may name the gods.

MEDEA   Swear by the plain of Earth, and Helios, father   730
   Of my father, and name together all the gods. . . .

AIGEUS   That I will act or not act in what way? Speak.

MEDEA   That you yourself will never cast me from your land,
   Nor, if any of my enemies should demand me,
   Will you, in your life, willingly hand me over.   735

AIGEUS   I swear by the Earth, by the holy light of Helios,
   By all the gods, I will abide by this you say.

MEDEA   Enough. And, if you fail, what shall happen to you?

AIGEUS   What comes to those who have no regard for heaven.

MEDEA   Go on your way. Farewell. For I am satisfied,   740
   And I will reach your city as soon as I can,
   Having done the deed I have to do and gained my end.
       [AIGEUS goes out.]

CHORUS   May Hermes, god of travelers,
   Escort you, Aigeus, to your home!
   And may you have the things you wish   745
   So eagerly; for you
   Appear to me to be a generous man.

MEDEA   God, and God's daughter, justice, and light of Helios!
   Now, friends, has come the time of my triumph over
   My enemies, and now my foot is on the road.   750
   Now I am confident they will pay the penalty.
   For this man, Aigeus, has been like a harbor to me
   In all my plans just where I was most distressed.
   To him I can fasten the cable of my safety
   When I have reached the town and fortress of Pallas.[3]   755
   And now I shall tell to you the whole of my plan.
   Listen to these words that are not spoken idly.
   I shall send one of my servants to find Jason
   And request him to come once more into my sight.
   And when he comes, the words I'll say will be soft ones.   760
   I'll say that I agree with him, that I approve
   The royal wedding he has made, betraying me.
   I'll say it was profitable, an excellent idea.
   But I shall beg that my children may remain here:
   Not that I would leave in a country that hates me   765
   Children of mine to feel their enemies' insults,
   But that by a trick I may kill the king's daughter.
   For I will send the children with gifts in their hands
   To carry to the bride, so as not to be banished,—
   A finely woven dress and a golden diadem.   770
   And if she takes them and wears them upon her skin
   She and all who touch the girl will die in agony;
   Such poison will I lay upon the gifts I send.
   But there, however, I must leave that account paid.
   I weep to think of what a deed I have to do   775

---

3. Athens, city of Pallas Athene.

Next after that; for I shall kill my own children.
My children, there is none who can give them safety.
And when I have ruined the whole of Jason's house,
I shall leave the land and flee from the murder of my
Dear children, and I shall have done a dreadful deed.   780
For it is not bearable to be mocked by enemies.
So it must happen. What profit have I in life?
I have no land, no home, no refuge from my pain.
My mistake was made the time I left behind me
My father's house, and trusted the words of a Greek,   785
Who, with heaven's help, will pay me the price for that.
For those children he had from me he will never
See alive again, nor will he on his new bride
Beget another child, for she is to be forced
To die a most terrible death by these my poisons.   790
Let no one think me a weak one, feeble-spirited,
A stay-at-home, but rather just the opposite,
One who can hurt my enemies and help my friends;
For the lives of such persons are most remembered.
CHORUS   Since you have shared the knowledge of your plan with us,   795
I both wish to help you and support the normal
Ways of mankind, and tell you not to do this thing.
MEDEA   I can do no other thing. It is understandable
For you to speak thus. You have not suffered as I have.
CHORUS   But can you have the heart to kill your flesh and blood?   800
MEDEA   Yes, for this is the best way to wound my husband.
CHORUS   And you too. Of women you will be most unhappy.
MEDEA   So it must be. No compromise is possible.
        [*She turns to the* NURSE.]
Go, you, at once, and tell Jason to come to me.
You I employ on all affairs of greatest trust.   805
Say nothing of these decisions which I have made,
If you love your mistress, if you were born a woman.
CHORUS   From of old the children of Erechtheus[4] are
Splendid, the sons of blessed gods. They dwell
In Athens' holy and unconquered land,[5]   810
Where famous Wisdom feeds them and they pass gaily
Always through that most brilliant air where once, they say,
That golden Harmony gave birth to the nine
Pure Muses of Pieria.[6]

And beside the sweet flow of Cephisos' stream,   815
Where Cypris[7] sailed, they say, to draw the water,
And mild soft breezes breathed along her path,
And on her hair were flung the sweet-smelling garlands

---

4. An early king of Athens, a son of Hephaestus.   5. It was the Athenians' boast that their descent from
the original settlers was uninterrupted by an invasion. There is a topical reference here, for the play was
produced in 431 B.C., in a time of imminent war.   6. A fountain in Boeotia where the Muses were
supposed to live. The sentence means that the fortunate balance (*Harmony*) of the elements and the genius
of the people produced the cultivation of the arts (*the nine Pure Muses*).   7. The goddess of love and,
therefore, of the principle of fertility. Cephisos is an Athenian river.

Of flowers of roses by the Lovers, the companions
Of Wisdom, her escort, the helpers of men   820
In every kind of excellence.

How then can these holy rivers
Or this holy land love you,
Or the city find you a home,
You, who will kill your children,   825
You, not pure with the rest?
O think of the blow at your children
And think of the blood that you shed.
O, over and over I beg you,
By your knees I beg you do not   830
Be the murderess of your babes!
O where will you find the courage
Or the skill of hand and heart,
When you set yourself to attempt
A deed so dreadful to do?   835
How, when you look upon them,
Can you tearlessly hold the decision
For murder? You will not be able,
When your children fall down and implore you,
You will not be able to dip   840
Steadfast your hand in their blood.

    [*Enter* JASON *with attendants.*]

JASON   I have come at your request. Indeed, although you are
   Bitter against me, this you shall have: I will listen
   To what new thing you want, woman, to get from me.

MEDEA   Jason, I beg you to be forgiving towards me   845
   For what I said. It is natural for you to bear with
   My temper, since we have had much love together.
   I have talked with myself about this and I have
   Reproached myself. "Fool" I said, "why am I so mad?
   Why am I set against those who have planned wisely?   850
   Why make myself an enemy of the authorities
   And of my husband, who does the best thing for me
   By marrying royalty and having children who
   Will be as brothers to my own? What is wrong with me?
   Let me give up anger, for the gods are kind to me.   855
   Have I not children, and do I not know that we
   In exile from our country must be short of friends?"
   When I considered this I saw that I had shown
   Great lack of sense, and that my anger was foolish.
   Now I agree with you. I think that you are wise   860
   In having this other wife as well as me, and I
   Was mad. I should have helped you in these plans of yours,
   Have joined in the wedding, stood by the marriage bed,
   Have taken pleasure in attendance on your bride.
   But we women are what we are,—perhaps a little   865
   Worthless; and you men must not be like us in this,

Nor be foolish in return when we are foolish.
Now I give in, and admit that then I was wrong.
I have come to a better understanding now.
    [*She turns towards the house.*]
Children, come here, my children, come outdoors to us!   870
Welcome your father with me, and say goodbye to him,
And with your mother, who just now was his enemy,
Join again in making friends with him who loves us.
    [*Enter the* CHILDREN, *attended by the* TUTOR.]
We have made peace, and all our anger is over.
Take hold of his right hand,—O God, I am thinking   875
Of something which may happen in the secret future.
O children, will you just so, after a long life,
Hold out your loving arms at the grave? O children,
How ready to cry I am, how full of foreboding!
I am ending at last this quarrel with your father,   880
And, look, my soft eyes have suddenly filled with tears.
CHORUS   And the pale tears have started also in my eyes.
O may the trouble not grow worse than now it is!
JASON   I approve of what you say. And I cannot blame you
Even for what you said before. It is natural   885
For a woman to be wild with her husband when he
Goes in for secret love. But now your mind has turned
To better reasoning. In the end you have come to
The right decision, like the clever woman you are.
And of you, children, your father is taking care.   890
He has made, with God's help, ample provision for you.
For I think that a time will come when you will be
The leading people in Corinth with your brothers.
You must grow up. As to the future, your father
And those of the gods who love him will deal with that.   895
I want to see you, when you have become young men,
Healthy and strong, better men than my enemies.
Medea, why are your eyes all wet with pale tears?
Why is your cheek so white and turned away from me?
Are not these words of mine pleasing for you to hear?   900
MEDEA   It is nothing. I was thinking about these children.
JASON   You must be cheerful. I shall look after them well.
MEDEA   I will be. It is not that I distrust your words,
But a woman is a frail thing, prone to crying.
JASON   But why then should you grieve so much for these children?   905
MEDEA   I am their mother. When you prayed that they might live
I felt unhappy to think that these things will be.
But come, I have said something of the things I meant
To say to you, and now I will tell you the rest.
Since it is the king's will to banish me from here,—   910
And for me too I know that this is the best thing,
Not to be in your way by living here or in
The king's way, since they think me ill-disposed to them,—
I then am going into exile from this land;

But do you, so that you may have the care of them,   915
Beg Kreon that the children may not be banished.
JASON   I doubt if I'll succeed, but still I'll attempt it.
MEDEA   Then you must tell your wife to beg from her father
That the children may be reprieved from banishment.
JASON   I will, and with her I shall certainly succeed.   920
MEDEA   If she is like the rest of us women, you will.
And I too will take a hand with you in this business,
For I will send her some gifts which are far fairer,
I am sure of it, than those which now are in fashion,
A finely-woven dress and a golden diadem,   925
And the children shall present them. Quick, let one of you
Servants bring here to me that beautiful dress.
          [One of her attendants goes into the house.]
She will be happy not in one way, but in a hundred,
Having so fine a man as you to share her bed,
And with this beautiful dress which Helios of old,   930
My father's father, bestowed on his descendants.
          [Enter attendant carrying the poisoned dress and diadem.]
There, children, take these wedding presents in your hands.
Take them to the royal princess, the happy bride,
And give them to her. She will not think little of them.
JASON   No, don't be foolish, and empty your hands of these.   935
Do you think the palace is short of dresses to wear?
Do you think there is no gold there? Keep them, don't give them
Away. If my wife considers me of any value,
She will think more of me than money, I am sure of it.
MEDEA   No, let me have my way. They say the gods themselves   940
Are moved by gifts, and gold does more with men than words.
Hers is the luck, her fortune that which god blesses;
She is young and a princess; but for my children's reprieve
I would give my very life, and not gold only.
Go children, go together to that rich palace,   945
Be suppliants to the new wife of your father,
My lady, beg her not to let you be banished.
And give her the dress,—for this is of great importance,
That she should take the gift into her hand from yours.
Go, quick as you can. And bring your mother good news   950
By your success of those things which she longs to gain.
          [JASON goes out with his attendants, followed by the TUTOR and the
          CHILDREN carrying the poisoned gifts.]
CHORUS   Now there is no hope left for the children's lives.
Now there is none. They are walking already to murder.
The bride, poor bride, will accept the curse of the gold,
Will accept the bright diadem.   955
Around her yellow hair she will set that dress
Of death with her own hands.
The grace and the perfume and glow of the golden robe
Will charm her to put them upon her and wear the wreath,
And now her wedding will be with the dead below,   960

Into such a trap she will fall,
Poor thing, into such a fate of death and never
Escape from under that curse.
You too, O wretched bridegroom, making your match with kings,
You do not see that you bring   965
Destruction on your children and on her,
Your wife, a fearful death.
Poor soul, what a fall is yours!

In your grief too I weep, mother of little children,
You who will murder your own,   970
In vengeance for the loss of married love
Which Jason has betrayed
As he lives with another wife.
          [*Enter the* TUTOR *with the* CHILDREN.]
TUTOR   Mistress, I tell you that these children are reprieved,
     And the royal bride has been pleased to take in her hands   975
     Your gifts. In that quarter the children are secure.
     But come,
     Why do you stand confused when you are fortunate?
     Why have you turned round with your cheek away from me?
     Are not these words of mine pleasing for you to hear?   980
MEDEA   Oh! I am lost!
TUTOR   That word is not in harmony with my tidings.
MEDEA   I am lost, I am lost!
TUTOR   Am I in ignorance telling you
     Of some disaster, and not the good news I thought?
MEDEA   You have told what you have told. I do not blame you.   985
TUTOR   Why then this downcast eye, and this weeping of tears?
MEDEA   Oh, I am forced to weep, old man. The gods and I,
     I in a kind of madness have contrived all this.
TUTOR   Courage! You too will be brought home by your children.
MEDEA   Ah, before that happens I shall bring others home.   990
TUTOR   Others before you have been parted from their children.
     Mortals must bear in resignation their ill luck.
MEDEA   That is what I shall do. But go inside the house,
     And do for the children your usual daily work.
          [*The* TUTOR *goes into the house.* MEDEA *turns to her* CHILDREN.]
O children, O my children, you have a city,   995
You have a home, and you can leave me behind you,
And without your mother you may live there for ever.
But I am going in exile to another land
Before I have seen you happy and taken pleasure in you,
Before I have dressed your brides and made your marriage beds   1000
And held up the torch at the ceremony of wedding.
Oh, what a wretch I am in this my self-willed thought!
What was the purpose, children, for which I reared you?
For all my travail and wearing myself away?
They were sterile, those pains I had in the bearing of you.   1005
O surely once the hopes in you I had, poor me,

Were high ones: you would look after me in old age,
And when I died would deck me well with your own hands;
A thing which all would have done. O but now it is gone,
That lovely thought. For, once I am left without you,   1010
Sad will be the life I'll lead and sorrowful for me.
And you will never see your mother again with
Your dear eyes, gone to another mode of living.
Why, children, do you look upon me with your eyes?
Why do you smile so sweetly that last smile of all?   1015
Oh, Oh, what can I do? My spirit has gone from me,
Friends, when I saw that bright look in the children's eyes.
I cannot bear to do it. I renounce my plans
I had before. I'll take my children away from
This land. Why should I hurt their father with the pain   1020
They feel, and suffer twice as much of pain myself?
No, no, I will not do it. I renounce my plans.
Ah, what is wrong with me? Do I want to let go
My enemies unhurt and be laughed at for it?
I must face this thing. Oh, but what a weak woman   1025
Even to admit to my mind these soft arguments.
Children, go into the house. And he whom law forbids
To stand in attendance at my sacrifices,
Let him see to it. I shall not mar my handiwork.
Oh! Oh!   1030
Do not, O my heart, you must not do these things!
Poor heart, let them go, have pity upon the children.
If they live with you in Athens they will cheer you.
No! By Hell's avenging furies it shall not be,—
This shall never be, that I should suffer my children   1035
To be the prey of my enemies' insolence.
Every way is it fixed. The bride will not escape.
No, the diadem is now upon her head, and she,
The royal princess, is dying in the dress, I know it.
But,—for it is the most dreadful of roads for me   1040
To tread, and them I shall send on a more dreadful still—
I wish to speak to the children.
      [*She calls the* CHILDREN *to her.*]
                                    Come, children, give
Me your hands, give your mother your hands to kiss them.
O the dear hands, and O how dear are these lips to me,
And the generous eyes and the bearing of my children!   1045
I wish you happiness, but not here in this world.
What is here your father took. O how good to hold you!
How delicate the skin, how sweet the breath of children!
Go, go! I am no longer able, no longer
To look upon you. I am overcome by sorrow.   1050
      [*The* CHILDREN *go into the house.*]
I know indeed what evil I intend to do,
But stronger than all my afterthoughts is my fury,
Fury that brings upon mortals the greatest evils.

[*She goes out to the right, towards the royal palace.*]

CHORUS   Often before
    I have gone through more subtle reasons,
    And have come upon questionings greater
    Than a woman should strive to search out.
    But we too have a goddess to help us
    And accompany us into wisdom.
    Not all of us. Still you will find
    Among many women a few,
    And our sex is not without learning.
    This I say, that those who have never
    Had children, who know nothing of it,
    In happiness have the advantage
    Over those who are parents.
    The childless, who never discover
    Whether children turn out as a good thing
    Or as something to cause pain, are spared
    Many troubles in lacking this knowledge.
    And those who have in their homes
    The sweet presence of children, I see that their lives
    Are all wasted away by their worries.
    First they must think how to bring them up well and
    How to leave them something to live on.
    And then after this whether all their toil
    Is for those who will turn out good or bad,
    Is still an unanswered question.
    And of one more trouble, the last of all,
    That is common to mortals I tell.
    For suppose you have found them enough for their living,
    Suppose that the children have grown into youth
    And have turned out good, still, if God so wills it,
    Death will away with your children's bodies,
    And carry them off into Hades.
    What is our profit, then, that for the sake of
    Children the gods should pile upon mortals
    After all else
    This most terrible grief of all?

    [*Enter* MEDEA, *from the spectators' right.*]

MEDEA   Friends, I can tell you that for long I have waited
    For the event. I stare towards the place from where
    The news will come. And now, see one of Jason's servants
    Is on his way here, and that labored breath of his
    Shows he has tidings for us, and evil tidings.

    [*Enter, also from the right, the* MESSENGER.]

MESSENGER   Medea, you who have done such a dreadful thing,
    So outrageous, run for your life, take what you can,
    A ship to bear you hence or chariot on land.

MEDEA   And what is the reason deserves such flight as this?

MESSENGER   She is dead, only just now, the royal princess,
    And Kreon dead too, her father, by your poisons.

MEDEA   The finest words you have spoken. Now and hereafter
  I shall count you among my benefactors and friends.
MESSENGER   What! Are you right in the mind? Are you not mad,
  Woman? The house of the king is outraged by you.
  Do you enjoy it? Not afraid of such doings?   1105
MEDEA   To what you say I on my side have something too
  To say in answer. Do not be in a hurry, friend,
  But speak. How did they die? You will delight me twice
  As much again if you say they died in agony.
MESSENGER   When those two children, born of you, had entered in, 1110
  Their father with them, and passed into the bride's house,
  We were pleased, we slaves who were distressed by your wrongs.
  All through the house we were talking of but one thing,
  How you and your husband had made up your quarrel.
  Some kissed the children's hands and some their yellow hair,   1115
  And I myself was so full of my joy that I
  Followed the children into the women's quarters.
  Our mistress, whom we honor now instead of you,
  Before she noticed that your two children were there,
  Was keeping her eye fixed eagerly on Jason.   1120
  Afterwards however she covered up her eyes,
  Her cheek paled and she turned herself away from him,
  So disgusted was she at the children's coming there.
  But your husband tried to end the girl's bad temper,
  And said "You must not look unkindly on your friends.   1125
  Cease to be angry. Turn your head to me again.
  Have as your friends the same ones as your husband has.
  And take these gifts, and beg your father to reprieve
  These children from their exile. Do it for my sake."
  She, when she saw the dress, could not restrain herself.   1130
  She agreed with all her husband said, and before
  He and the children had gone far from the palace,
  She took the gorgeous robe and dressed herself in it,
  And put the golden crown around her curly locks,
  And arranged the set of the hair in a shining mirror,   1135
  And smiled at the lifeless image of herself in it.
  Then she rose from her chair and walked about the room,
  With her gleaming feet stepping most soft and delicate,
  All overjoyed with the present. Often and often
  She would stretch her foot out straight and look along it.   1140
  But after that it was a fearful thing to see.
  The color of her face changed, and she staggered back,
  She ran, and her legs trembled, and she only just
  Managed to reach a chair without falling flat down.
  An aged woman servant who, I take it, thought   1145
  This was some seizure of Pan[8] or another god,

---

8. As the god of wild nature he was supposed to be the source of the sudden, apparently causeless terror that solitude in wild surroundings may produce and hence of all kinds of sudden madness (compare the English word *panic*).

Cried out "God bless us," but that was before she saw
The white foam breaking through her lips and her rolling
The pupils of her eyes and her face all bloodless.
Then she raised a different cry from that "God bless us,"   1150
A huge shriek, and the women ran, one to the king,
One to the newly wedded husband to tell him
What had happened to his bride; and with frequent sound
The whole of the palace rang as they went running.
One walking quickly round the course of a race-track   1155
Would now have turned the bend and be close to the goal,
When she, poor girl, opened her shut and speechless eye,
And with a terrible groan she came to herself.
For a two-fold pain was moving up against her.
The wreath of gold that was resting around her head   1160
Let forth a fearful stream of all-devouring fire,
And the finely-woven dress your children gave to her,
Was fastening on the unhappy girl's fine flesh.
She leapt up from the chair, and all on fire she ran,
Shaking her hair now this way and now that, trying   1165
To hurl the diadem away; but fixedly
The gold preserved its grip, and, when she shook her hair,
Then more and twice as fiercely the fire blazed out.
Till, beaten by her fate, she fell down to the ground,
Hard to be recognized except by a parent.   1170
Neither the setting of her eyes was plain to see,
Nor the shapeliness of her face. From the top of
Her head there oozed out blood and fire mixed together.
Like the drops on pine-bark, so the flesh from her bones
Dropped away, torn by the hidden fang of the poison.   1175
It was a fearful sight; and terror held us all
From touching the corpse. We had learned from what had happened.
But her wretched father, knowing nothing of the event,
Came suddenly to the house, and fell upon the corpse,
And at once cried out and folded his arms about her,   1180
And kissed her and spoke to her, saying, "O my poor child,
What heavenly power has so shamefully destroyed you?
And who has set me here like an ancient sepulchre,
Deprived of you? O let me die with you, my child!"
And when he had made an end of his wailing and crying,   1185
Then the old man wished to raise himself to his feet;
But, as the ivy clings to the twigs of the laurel,
So he stuck to the fine dress, and he struggled fearfully.
For he was trying to lift himself to his knee,
And she was pulling him down, and when he tugged hard   1190
He would be ripping his aged flesh from his bones.
At last his life was quenched and the unhappy man
Gave up the ghost, no longer could hold up his head.
There they lie close, the daughter and the old father,
Dead bodies, an event he prayed for in his tears.   1195
As for your interests, I will say nothing of them,

For you will find your own escape from punishment.
Our human life I think and have thought a shadow,
And I do not fear to say that those who are held
Wise amongst men and who search the reasons of things   1200
Are those who bring the most sorrow on themselves.
For of mortals there is no one who is happy.
If wealth flows in upon one, one may be perhaps
Luckier than one's neighbor, but still not happy.
    [*Exit.*]

CHORUS   Heaven, it seems, on this day has fastened many   1205
   Evils on Jason, and Jason has deserved them.
   Poor girl, the daughter of Kreon, how I pity you
   And your misfortunes, you who have gone quite away
   To the house of Hades because of marrying Jason.

MEDEA   Women, my task is fixed: as quickly as I may   1210
To kill my children, and start away from this land,
And not, by wasting time, to suffer my children
To be slain by another hand less kindly to them.
Force every way will have it they must die, and since
This must be so, then I, their mother, shall kill them.   1215
O arm yourself in steel, my heart! Do not hang back
From doing this fearful and necessary wrong.
O come, my hand, poor wretched hand, and take the sword,
Take it, step forward to this bitter starting point,
And do not be a coward, do not think of them,   1220
How sweet they are, and how you are their mother. Just for
This one short day be forgetful of your children,
Afterwards weep; for even though you will kill them,
They were very dear,—O, I am an unhappy woman!
    [*With a cry she rushes into the house.*]

CHORUS   O Earth, and the far shining   1225
   Ray of the sun, look down, look down upon
   This poor lost woman, look, before she raises
   The hand of murder against her flesh and blood.
   Yours was the golden birth from which
   She sprang, and now I fear divine   1230
   Blood may be shed by men.
   O heavenly light, hold back her hand,
   Check her, and drive from out the house
   The bloody Fury raised by fiends of Hell.

   Vain waste, your care of children;   1235
   Was it in vain you bore the babes you loved,
   After you passed the inhospitable strait
   Between the dark blue rocks, Symplegades?
   O wretched one, how has it come,
   This heavy anger on your heart,   1240
   This cruel bloody mind?
   For God from mortals asks a stern
   Price for the stain of kindred blood

In like disaster falling on their homes.

[*A cry from one of the* CHILDREN *is heard.*]

CHORUS   Do you hear the cry, do you hear the children's cry?   1245
O you hard heart, O woman fated for evil!

ONE OF THE CHILDREN   [*From within.*] What can I do and how escape
my mother's hands?

ONE OF THE CHILDREN   [*From within.*] O my dear brother, I cannot tell.
We are lost.

CHORUS   Shall I enter the house? O surely I should   1250
Defend the children from murder.

A CHILD   [*From within.*] O help us, in God's name, for now we need
your help.
Now, now we are close to it. We are trapped by the sword.

CHORUS   O your heart must have been made of rock or steel,
You who can kill   1255
With your own hand the fruit of your own womb.
Of one alone I have heard, one woman alone
Of those of old who laid her hands on her children,
Ino, sent mad by heaven when the wife of Zeus
Drove her out from her home and made her wander;   1260
And because of the wicked shedding of blood
Of her own children she threw
Herself, poor wretch, into the sea and stepped away
Over the sea-cliff to die with her two children.
What horror more can be? O women's love,   1265
So full of trouble,
How many evils have you caused already!

[*Enter* JASON, *with attendants.*]

JASON   You women, standing close in front of this dwelling,
Is she, Medea, she who did this dreadful deed,
Still in the house, or has she run away in flight?   1270
For she will have to hide herself beneath the earth,
Or raise herself on wings into the height of air,
If she wishes to escape the royal vengeance.
Does she imagine that, having killed our rulers,
She will herself escape uninjured from this house?   1275
But I am thinking not so much of her as for
The children,—her the king's friends will make to suffer
For what she did. So I have come to save the lives
Of my boys, in case the royal house should harm them
While taking vengeance for their mother's wicked deed.   1280

CHORUS   Jason, if you but knew how deeply you are
Involved in sorrow, you would not have spoken so.

JASON   What is it? That she is planning to kill me also?

CHORUS   Your children are dead, and by their own mother's hand.

JASON   What! This is it? O woman, you have destroyed me.   1285

CHORUS   You must make up your mind your children are no more.

JASON   Where did she kill them? Was it here or in the house?

CHORUS   Open the gates and there you will see them murdered.

JASON   Quick as you can unlock the doors, men, and undo

The fastenings and let me see this double evil,   1290
My children dead and her,—O her I will repay.

> [*His attendants rush to the door.* MEDEA *appears above the house in
> a chariot drawn by dragons. She has the dead bodies of the* CHILDREN
> *with her.*]

MEDEA   Why do you batter these gates and try to unbar them,
Seeking the corpses and for me who did the deed?
You may cease your trouble, and, if you have need of me,
Speak, if you wish. You will never touch me with your hand,   1295
Such a chariot has Helios, my father's father,
Given me to defend me from my enemies.

JASON   You hateful thing, you woman most utterly loathed
By the gods and me and by all the race of mankind,
You who have had the heart to raise a sword against   1300
Your children, you, their mother, and left me childless,—
You have done this, and do you still look at the sun
And at the earth, after these most fearful doings?
I wish you dead. Now I see it plain, though at that time
I did not, when I took you from your foreign home   1305
And brought you to a Greek house, you, an evil thing,
A traitress to your father and your native land.
The gods hurled the avenging curse of yours on me.
For your own brother you slew at your own hearthside,
And then came aboard that beautiful ship, the Argo.   1310
And that was your beginning. When you were married
To me, your husband, and had borne children to me,
For the sake of pleasure in the bed you killed them.
There is no Greek woman who would have dared such deeds,
Out of all those whom I passed over and chose you   1315
To marry instead, a bitter destructive match,
A monster not a woman, having a nature
Wilder than that of Scylla[9] in the Tuscan sea.
Ah! no, not if I had ten thousand words of shame
Could I sting you. You are naturally so brazen.   1320
Go, worker in evil, stained with your children's blood.
For me remains to cry aloud upon my fate,
Who will get no pleasure from my newly-wedded love,
And the boys whom I begot and brought up, never
Shall I speak to them alive. Oh, my life is over!   1325

MEDEA   Long would be the answer which I might have made to
These words of yours, if Zeus the father did not know
How I have treated you and what you did to me.
No, it was not to be that you should scorn my love,
And pleasantly live your life through, laughing at me;   1330
Nor would the princess, nor he who offered the match,
Kreon, drive me away without paying for it.
So now you may call me a monster, if you wish,

---

9. A monster located in the straits between Italy and Sicily, who snatched sailors off passing ships and
devoured them. See *Odyssey* 12.

Or Scylla housed in the caves of the Tuscan sea
I too, as I had to, have taken hold of your heart.   1335
JASON   You feel the pain yourself. You share in my sorrow.
MEDEA   Yes, and my grief is gain when you cannot mock it.
JASON   O children, what a wicked mother she was to you!
MEDEA   They died from a disease they caught from their father.
JASON   I tell you it was not my hand that destroyed them.   1340
MEDEA   But it was your insolence, and your virgin wedding.
JASON   And just for the sake of that you chose to kill them.
MEDEA   Is love so small a pain, do you think, for a woman?
JASON   For a wise one, certainly. But you are wholly evil.
MEDEA   The children are dead. I say this to make you suffer.   1345
JASON   The children, I think, will bring down curses on you.
MEDEA   The gods know who was the author of this sorrow.
JASON   Yes, the gods know indeed, they know your loathsome heart.
MEDEA   Hate me. But I tire of your barking bitterness.
JASON   And I of yours. It is easier to leave you.   1350
MEDEA   How then? What shall I do? I long to leave you too.
JASON   Give me the bodies to bury and to mourn them.
MEDEA   No, that I will not. I will bury them myself,
Bearing them to Hera's temple on the promontory;
So that no enemy may evilly treat them   1355
By tearing up their grave. In this land of Corinth
I shall establish a holy feast and sacrifice[1]
Each year for ever to atone for the blood guilt.
And I myself go to the land of Erechtheus
To dwell in Aigeus' house, the son of Pandion.   1360
While you, as is right, will die without distinction,
Struck on the head by a piece of the Argo's timber,
And you will have seen the bitter end of my love.
JASON   May a Fury for the children's sake destroy you,
And justice, requitor of blood.   1365
MEDEA   What heavenly power lends an ear
To a breaker of oaths, a deceiver?
JASON   O, I hate you, murderess of children.
MEDEA   Go to your palace. Bury your bride.
JASON   I go, with two children to mourn for.   1370
MEDEA   Not yet do you feel it. Wait for the future.
JASON   Oh, children I loved!
MEDEA   I loved them, you did not.
JASON   You loved them, and killed them.
MEDEA   To make you feel pain.
JASON   Oh, wretch that I am, how I long
To kiss the dear lips of my children!   1375
MEDEA   Now you would speak to them, now you would kiss them.
Then you rejected them.
JASON   Let me, I beg you,
Touch my boys' delicate flesh.

---

1. Some such ceremony was still performed at Corinth in Euripides' time.

MEDEA I will not. Your words are all wasted.

JASON O God, do you hear it, this persecution, 1380
These my sufferings from this hateful
Woman, this monster, murderess of children?
Still what I can do that I will do:
I will lament and cry upon heaven,
Calling the gods to bear me witness 1385
How you have killed my boys and prevent me from
Touching their bodies or giving them burial.
I wish I had never begot them to see them
Afterwards slaughtered by you.

CHORUS Zeus in Olympus is the overseer 1390
Of many doings. Many things the gods
Achieve beyond our judgment. What we thought
Is not confirmed and what we thought not god
Contrives. And so it happens in this story.

ARISTOPHANES
450?–385? B.C.

By the fifth century B.C. both tragedy and comedy were regularly produced at the winter festivals of the god Dionysus in Athens. Comedy, like tragedy, employed a chorus, that is to say, a group of dancers (who also sang) and actors, who wore masks; its tone was burlesque and parodic, though there was often a serious theme emphasized by the crude clowning and the free play of wit. The only comic poet of the fifth century whose work has survived is Aristophanes; in his thirteen extant comedies, produced over the years 425–388 B.C., the institutions and personalities of his time are caricatured and criticized in a brilliant combination of poetry and obscenity, of farce and wit that can be described only in terms of itself, by the adjective *Aristophanic*.

He was born sometime in the middle of the fifth century and died in the next, around 385 B.C. The earliest of his plays to survive, *The Acharnians,* was produced in 425 B.C., and the bulk of his extant work dates from the years of the Peloponnesian War (431–404 B.C.). The war, in fact, is one of his comic targets; in *The Acharnians,* an Athenian citizen, fed up with the privations caused by the Spartan invasions that shut the Athenians inside their walls, makes a separate peace for himself and his family, defends his decision against an irate chorus of patriots (the Acharnians of the title), and proceeds to enjoy all the benefits of peace while his fellow citizens suffer as before. In *Peace* (421 B.C.) another Athenian flies up to heaven on a gigantic dung beetle (a parody of a Euripidean play in which a hero flew up on a winged horse); once arrived, he petitions Zeus to stop the war. Euripides is another favorite target and was held up to ridicule in play after play; and Socrates was the "hero" of a play, *Clouds* (423 B.C.), that held him up to ridicule as a Sophistic charlatan. (Socrates refers to this play in his speech in court, p. 728.) In *Birds* (414 B.C.), two Athenians, tired of the war and taxes, go off to found a new city; they organize the birds, who cut off the smoke of sacrifice that the gods live on, and force Zeus to surrender the government of the universe to the birds. These plays are all very funny, with plenty of sexual and scatological wit. But coarse humor and exquisite wit combine with lyric poetry of a high quality and comic plots of startling audacity to produce a mixture unlike anything that went before or has come after it.

Lysistrata, which is outstanding among the Aristophanic comedies in its coherence of structure and broad humor, was first produced in 411 B.C. In 413 the news of the total destruction of the Athenian fleet in Sicily had reached Athens, and though heroic efforts to carry on the war were under way, the confidence in victory with which Athens had begun the war had disappeared forever. It is a recurring feature of Aristophanic comedy that the comic hero upsets the status quo to produce a series of extraordinary results that are exploited to the full for their comic potential. In this play the Athenian women, who have no political rights, seize the Acropolis, repository of the city's treasury, and leave the men without women or money to carry on the war. At the same time similar revolutions take place in all the Greek cities according to a coordinated plan. The men are eventually "starved" into submission, and the Spartans come to Athens to end the war.

Aristophanes does not miss a trick in his exploitation of the possibilities for ribald humor inherent in this female sex-strike against war; Myrrhine's teasing game with her husband, Cinesias, for example, is rare fooling, and the final appearance of the uncomfortably rigid Spartan ambassadors and their equally tense Athenian hosts is a visual and verbal climax of astonishing brilliance. But underneath all the fooling, real issues are pursued, and they come to the surface with telling effect in the argument between Lysistrata and the commissioner who has been sent to suppress the revolt. Reversing the words of Hector to Andromache, which had become proverbial, Lysistrata claims that "war shall be the concern of Women!" (or in the translation given here, which in this line imitates the archaic nature of Homer's Greek, "ye women must wive ye warre!")—it is too important a matter to be left to men, for women are its real victims. When asked what the women will do, she explains that they will treat politics just as they do wool in their household tasks: "when a hank's in a tangle, we . . . work out the snarls by winding it up on spindles. . . . That's how we'll wind up the war."

Women, who spent a great deal of their time weaving indoors, might be expected to express themselves this way, if they ever got a chance to talk politics. The Commissioner replies, "Spruce up the world's disasters with spindles—typically woolly female logic." These words, of course, say as much about his own prejudices as they do about women's supposed incapacities. Aristophanes can scarcely have meant Lysistrata's words as a serious formula for peace, and yet there is a lucid simplicity to them. Men have botched affairs, as the prolonged war shows. *Why not* simply declare peace and work out the snarls amicably? As this example shows, Aristophanes works through gender stereotypes in this play, both inviting us to see the world through them and holding them up to good-natured ridicule. Women are addicted to wine and sex. They are tricky and deceitful, always probing for men's weaknesses, and an obstacle to the conduct of serious political business. So men say, and the women in this play admit it. But these characteristics are here enlisted in the service of peace (to see them viewed as destructive, compare Euripides' *Medea*.) As for men, Aristophanes suggests that the dirty secret of imperialism is that war and territorial aggression are a substitute for sex, and vice versa. The great expression of this diagnosis is the scene in which the Athenian and Spartan ambassadors divide up the naked body of Peace, personified as a beautiful woman, relating her various anatomical features to territories of Greece over which their cities were fighting. This suggestion is at once devastatingly accurate and an oversimplification. But this sort of reductiveness is characteristic of comedy, which offers us the reassurance that the world is not always as complicated as our daily experience and the rival genre, tragedy, would seem to suggest, that there is room in the world for wish-fulfilling fantasies—in this case, that a sex-strike might actually end war. Well, why not?

We do not know how the Athenians welcomed the play. All we know is that they were not impressed by its serious undertone; the war continued for seven more exhausting years, until Athens's last fleet was defeated, the city laid open to the enemy, the empire lost.

K. J. Dover, *Aristophanic Comedy* (1972), is a general survey of the whole range of Aristophanic comedy. Helpful introductions to the *Lysistrata* are given by Jeffrey Henderson, *Aristophanes' Lysistrata* (1987), pp. xv–xli, and Douglas M. MacDowell, *Aristophanes and Athens: An Introduction to the Plays* (1996), pp. 229–50. Erich Segal, *Oxford Readings in Aristophanes* (1996), includes an excellent selection of essays on various aspects of Aristophanes' drama. See also Kenneth J. Reckford, *Aristophanes' Old-and-New Comedy* (1987), pp. 301–11.

PRONOUNCING GLOSSARY

The following list uses common English syllables and stress accents to provide rough equivalents of selected words whose pronunciation may be unfamiliar to the general reader.

Andromache: *an-dro'-ma-kee*

Aristophanes: *a-ri-sto'-fa-neez*

Kleonike: *klee-oh-neé'-kay*

Kinesias: *kin-ay'-see-as*

Koryphaios: *ko-ree-fai'-os*

Lysistrata: *lai-sis'-trah-tuh*

Myrrhine: *meer-ree'-nee*

Lysistrata[1]

CHARACTERS[2]

LYSISTRATA ⎫	FOUR POLICEMEN
KLEONIKE ⎬ *Athenian women*	KINESIAS, *Myrrhine's husband*
MYRRHINE ⎭	CHILD *of Kinesias and Myrrhine*
LAMPITO, *a Spartan woman*	SLAVE
ISMENIA, *a Boiotian girl*	SPARTAN HERALD
KORINTHIAN GIRL	SPARTAN AMBASSADOR
POLICEWOMAN	DELEGATION OF SPARTANS
KORYPHAIOS OF THE MEN	FLUTE-PLAYER
CHORUS OF OLD MEN *of Athens*	ATHENIAN WOMEN
SWIFTY	PELOPONNESIAN WOMEN
CHIPPER	PELOPONNESIAN MEN
KORYPHAIOS OF THE WOMEN	*Athenian men*
CHORUS OF OLD WOMEN *of Athens*	PEACE
COMMISSIONER *of Public Safety*	

[SCENE: *A street in Athens. In the background, the Akropolis; center, its gateway, the Propylaia. The time is early morning.* LYSISTRATA *is discovered alone, pacing back and forth in furious impatience.*]

LYSISTRATA   *Women!*
> Announce a debauch in honor of Bacchos,
> a spree for Pan, some footling fertility fieldday,
> and traffic stops—the streets are absolutely clogged

---

1. Translated by Douglass Parker.   2. The leading characters have significant names. *Lysistrata:* "she who disbands the armies." *Lampito:* a typical Spartan name. *Kinesias:* suggests the Greek verb *kinein,* "to move," then "to copulate."

with frantic females banging on tambourines. No urging 5
for an orgy!

But *today*—there's not one woman here.
[*Enter* KLEONIKE.]
Correction: one. Here comes my next door neighbor.
—Hello, Kleonike.

KLEONIKE   Hello to *you*, Lysistrata.
—But what's the fuss? Don't look so barbarous, baby;
knitted brows just aren't your style.

LYSISTRATA   It doesn't 10
matter, Kleonike—I'm on fire right down to the bone.
I'm positively ashamed to be a woman—a member
of a sex which can't even live up to male slanders!
To hear our husbands talk, we're *sly*: deceitful,
always plotting, monsters of intrigue. . . .

KLEONIKE [*Proudly*.]   That's us! 15

LYSISTRATA   And so we agreed to meet today and plot
an intrigue that really deserves the name of monstrous . . .
and WHERE are the women?

                          Slyly asleep at home—
they won't get up for anything!

KLEONIKE   Relax, honey.
They'll be here. You know a woman's way is hard— 20
mainly the way out of the house: fuss over hubby,
wake the maid up, put the baby down, bathe him,
feed him . . .

LYSISTRATA   Trivia. They have more fundamental business to engage in.

KLEONIKE   Incidentally, Lysistrata, just why are
you calling this meeting? Nothing teeny, I trust? 25

LYSISTRATA   Immense.

KLEONIKE   Hmmm. And pressing?

LYSISTRATA   Unthinkably tense.

KLEONIKE   Then where IS everybody?

LYSISTRATA   Nothing like that. If it were,
we'd already be in session. Seconding motions.
—No, *this* came to hand some time ago. I've spent
my nights kneading it, mulling it, filing it down. . . . 30

KLEONIKE   Too bad. There can't be very much left.

LYSISTRATA   Only this:
the hope and salvation of Hellas lies with the WOMEN!

KLEONIKE   Lies with the women? Now *there's* a last resort.

LYSISTRATA   It lies with us to decide affairs of state
and foreign policy.

                    The Spartan Question: Peace 35
or Extirpation?

KLEONIKE   How *fun*!

                          I cast an Aye for Extirpation!

LYSISTRATA   The utter Annihilation of every last Boiotian?

KLEONIKE   AYE!—I mean Nay. Clemency, please, for those
    scrumptious eels.³

LYSISTRATA   And as for Athens . . . I'd rather not put
    the thought into words. Just fill in the blanks, if you will.   40
    —To the point: If we can meet and reach agreement
    here and now with the girls from Thebes and the Peloponnese,
    we'll form an alliance and save the States of Greece!

KLEONIKE   Us? Be practical. Wisdom for women? There's nothing
    cosmic about cosmetics—and Glamor is our only talent.   45
    All we can do is *sit,* primped and painted,
    made up and dressed up,
        [*Getting carried away in spite of her argument.*]
                        ravishing in saffron wrappers,
    peekaboo peignoirs, exquisite negligees, those chic,
    expensive little slippers that come from the East. . . .

LYSISTRATA   Exactly. You've hit it. I see our way to salvation   50
    in just such ornamentation—in slippers and slips, rouge
    and perfumes, negligees and décolletage. . . .

KLEONIKE   How so?

LYSISTRATA   So effectively that not one husband will take up his spear
    against another . . .

KLEONIKE   Peachy!
                I'll have that kimono
    dyed . . .

LYSISTRATA   . . . or shoulder his shield . . .

KLEONIKE   . . . squeeze into that   55
    daring negligee . . .

LYSISTRATA   . . . or unsheathe his sword!

KLEONIKE   . . . and buy those slippers!

LYSISTRATA   Well, now. Don't you think the girls should be here?

KLEONIKE   *Be* here? Ages ago—they should have flown!
        [*She stops.*]
    But no. You'll find out. These are authentic Athenians:
    no matter what they do, they do it late.   60

LYSISTRATA   But what about the out-of-town delegations? There isn't
    a woman here from the Shore; none from Salamis . . .

KLEONIKE   *That's* quite a trip. They usually get on board
    at sunup. Probably riding at anchor now.

LYSISTRATA   I thought the girls from Acharnai would be here first.   65
    I'm especially counting on them. And they're not here.

KLEONIKE   I think Theogenes' wife is under way.
    When I went by, she was hoisting her sandals . . .
    [*Looking off right.*]   But look!
    Some of the girls are coming!
        [*Women enter from the right.* LYSISTRATA *looks off to the left where
        more—a ragged lot—are straggling in.*]

LYSISTRATA   And more over here!

KLEONIKE   Where did you find *that* group?

---

3. Eels from Lake Copais in Boeotia, a delicacy, were now under embargo because Boeotia was enemy
territory.

LYSISTRATA   They're from the outskirts.   70
KLEONIKE   Well, that's something. If you haven't done anything
    else, you've really ruffled up the outskirts.
        [MYRRHINE *enters guiltily from the right.*]
MYRRHINE   Oh, Lysistrata,
    we aren't late, are we?
                            Well, *are* we?
                                    Speak to me!
LYSISTRATA   What is it, Myrrhine? Do you want a medal for tardiness?
    Honestly, such behavior, with so much at stake . . .   75
MYRRHINE   I'm sorry. I couldn't find my girdle in the dark.
    And anyway, we're here now. So tell us all about it,
    whatever it is.
KLEONIKE   No, wait a minute. Don't
    begin just yet. Let's wait for those girls from Thebes
    and the Peloponnese.
LYSISTRATA   Now *there* speaks the proper attitude.   80
        [LAMPITO, *a strapping Spartan woman, enters left, leading a pretty*
        Boiotian girl (ISMENIA) *and a huge, steatopygous Korinthian.*]
    And here's our lovely Spartan.
                            Hel*lo*, Lampito
    dear.
            Why darling, you're simply ravishing! Such
    a blemishless complexion—so clean, so out-of-doors![4]
    And will you look at that figure—the pink of perfection!
KLEONIKE   I'll bet you could strangle a bull.
LAMPITO   I calklate so.[5]   85
    Hit's fitness whut done it, fitness and dancin'. You know
    the step?
            [*Demonstrating.*] Foot it out back'ards an' toe yore twitchet.
            [*The women crowd around* LAMPITO.]
KLEONIKE   What unbelievably beautiful bosoms!
LAMPITO   Shuckins,
    whut fer you tweedlin' me up so? I feel like a heifer
    come fair-time.
LYSISTRATA [*Turning to* ISMENIA.]
                    And who is this young lady here?   90
LAMPITO   Her kin's purt-near the bluebloodiest folk in Thebes—
    the First Fam'lies of Boiotia.
LYSISTRATA [*As they inspect* ISMENIA.]   Ah, picturesque Boiotia:
    her verdant meadows, her fruited plain . . .
KLEONIKE [*Peering more closely.*]   Her sunken
    garden where no grass grows. A cultivated country.
LYSISTRATA [*Gaping at the gawking Korinthian.*]
    And who is *this*—er—little thing?
LAMPITO   She hails   95

---

4. Spartan women took part in athletics and were in other ways less restricted than their counterparts in
other Greek cities.   5. Lampito and the other Spartans speak a version of the Doric dialect of Greek, as
actual Spartans did. It could be mocked as boorish by Athenians, who spoke Attic-Ionic. The translator has
tried to reproduce this stereotyping effect.

from over by Korinth, but her kinfolk's quality—mighty
big back there.
KLEONIKE [*On her tour of inspection.*]
             She's mighty big back *here*.
LAMPITO   The womenfolk's all assemblied. Who-all's notion
was this-hyer confabulation?
LYSISTRATA   Mine.
LAMPITO   Git on with the give-out.
I'm hankerin' to hear.
MYRRHINE   Me, too! I can't imagine   100
what could be so important. Tell us about it!
LYSISTRATA   Right away.
           —But first, a question. It's not
an involved one. Answer yes or no.
      [*A pause.*]
MYRRHINE   Well, ASK, it!
LYSISTRATA   It concerns the fathers of your children—your husbands.
absent on active service. I know you all have men   105
abroad.
       —Wouldn't you like to have them home?
KLEONIKE   My husband's been gone for the last five months! Way up
to Thrace,[6] watchdogging military waste. It's horrible!
MYRRHINE   Mine's been posted to Pylos[7] for seven whole months!
LAMPITO   My man's no sooner rotated out of the line   110
than he's plugged back in. Hain't no discharge in this war!
KLEONIKE   And lovers can't be had for love or money,
not even synthetics. Why, since those beastly Milesians
revolted and cut off the leather trade, that handy
do-it-yourself kit's *vanished* from the open market![8]   115
LYSISTRATA   If I can devise a scheme for ending the war,
I gather I have your support?
KLEONIKE   You can count on me!
If you need money, I'll pawn the shift off my back—
[*Aside.*] and drink up the cash before the sun goes down.
MYRRHINE   Me, too! I'm ready to split myself right up   120
the middle like a mackerel, and give you half!
LAMPITO   Me, too! I'd climb Taygetos[9] Mountain plumb
to the top to git the leastes' peek at Peace!
LYSISTRATA   Very well, I'll tell you. No reason to keep a secret.
[*Importantly, as the women cluster around her.*] We can force our
      husbands to negotiate Peace,   125
Ladies, by exercising steadfast Self-Control—
By Total Abstinence.
      [*A pause.*]
KLEONIKE   From WHAT?

6. Region of northeastern Greece, the scene of considerable fighting during the war.   7. Located in the southern Peloponnesus and strategically important against Sparta, Pylos had been occupied by the Athenians since 425 B.C.   8. Leather dildos were evidently a manufacturing specialty of Miletus, a city on the coast of Asia Minor that had recently revolted from the Athenian alliance and had become an important base of Spartan naval operations.   9. The massive range that towers over Sparta.

MYRRHINE   Yes, what?
LYSISTRATA   You'll do it?
KLEONIKE   Of course we'll do it! We'd even *die*!
LYSISTRATA   Very well,
  then here's the program:
                                    Total Abstinence
                                        from SEX!
      [*The cluster of women dissolves.*]
  —Why are you turning away? Where are you going?   130
  [*Moving among the women.*] —What's this? Such stricken expressions!
      Such gloomy gestures!
  —Why so pale?
                    —Whence these tears?
                                    —What IS this?
  Will you do it or won't you?
                            Cat got your tongue?
KLEONIKE   Afraid I can't make it. Sorry.
                                On with the War!
MYRRHINE   Me neither. Sorry.
                            On with the War!
LYSISTRATA   *This* from   135
  my little mackerel? The girl who was ready, a minute
  ago, to split herself right up the middle?
KLEONIKE [*Breaking in between* LYSISTRATA *and* MYRRHINE.]   Try
      something else. Try anything. If you say so,
  I'm willing to walk through fire barefoot
                                    But not
  to give up SEX—there's nothing like it, Lysistrata!   140
LYSISTRATA [*To* MYRRHINE.]   And you?
MYRRHINE   Me, too! I'll walk through fire.
LYSISTRATA   *Women!*
  Utter sluts, the entire sex! Will-power,
  nil. We're perfect raw material for Tragedy,
  the stuff of heroic lays. "Go to bed with a god
  and then get rid of the baby"—that sums us up!   145
  [*Turning to* LAMPITO.] —Oh, Spartan, be a dear. If *you* stick by me,
  just you, we still may have a chance to win.
  Give me your vote.
LAMPITO   Hit's right onsettlin' fer gals
  to sleep all lonely-like, withouten no humpin'.
  But I'm on your side. We shore need Peace, too.   150
LYSISTRATA   You're a darling—the only woman here
  worthy of the name!
KLEONIKE   Well, just suppose we *did*,
  as much as possible, abstain from . . . what you said,
  you know—not that we *would*—could something like
  that bring Peace any sooner?
LYSISTRATA   Certainly. Here's how it works: 155
  We'll paint, powder, and pluck ourselves to the last

detail, and stay inside, wearing those filmy
tunics that set off everything we *have*—
and then
slink up to the men. They'll snap to attention, go
absolutely *mad* to love us—
but we won't let them. We'll Abstain.   160
—I imagine they'll conclude a treaty rather quickly.

LAMPITO [*Nodding.*]   Menelaos he tuck one squint at Helen's bubbies
all nekkid, and plumb throwed up.
[*Pause for thought.*]   Throwed up his sword.[1]

KLEONIKE   Suppose the men just leave us flat?

LYSISTRATA   In that case,
we'll have to take things into our own hands.   165

KLEONIKE   There simply isn't any reasonable facsimile!
—Suppose they take us by force and drag us off
to the bedroom against our wills?

LYSISTRATA   Hang on to the door.

KLEONIKE   Suppose they beat us!

LYSISTRATA   Give in—but be bad sports.
Be nasty about it—they don't enjoy these forced   170
affairs. So make them suffer.
Don't worry; they'll stop
soon enough. A married man wants harmony—
cooperation, not rape.

KLEONIKE   Well, I suppose so.
[*Looking from* LYSISTRATA *to* LAMPITO.] If *both* of you approve this, then
so do we.

LAMPITO   Hain't worried over our menfolk none. We'll bring 'em   175
round to makin' a fair, straightfor'ard Peace
withouten no nonsense about it. But take this rackety
passel in Athens: I misdoubt no one could make 'em
give over thet blabber of theirn.[2]

LYSISTRATA   They're our concern.
Don't worry. We'll bring them around.

LAMPITO   Not likely.   180
Not long as they got ships kin still sail straight,
an' thet fountain of money up thar in Athene's temple.[3]

LYSISTRATA   That point is quite well covered:
We're taking over
the Akropolis, including Athene's temple, today.
It's set: Our oldest women have their orders.   185
They're up there now, pretending to sacrifice, waiting
for us to reach an agreement. As soon as we do,
they seize the Akropolis.

LAMPITO   The way you put them thengs,

---

1. As Troy was being sacked, Menelaus was about to kill Helen in revenge for her adultery but dropped his sword, dazzled by her beauty, when she bared her breast.   **2.** A jab at the Athenian democracy.   **3.** Athenian power was based on its navy and on the money that flowed from the annual tribute of the "allies." It was stored in Athena's temple, the Parthenon, on the Acropolis.

I swear I can't see how we kin possibly lose!

LYSISTRATA   Well, now that it's settled, Lampito, let's not lose   190
any time. Let's take the Oath to make this binding.

LAMPITO   Just trot out thet-thar Oath. We'll swear it.

LYSISTRATA   Excellent.
—Where's a policewoman?

[*A huge girl, dressed as a Skythian archer (the Athenian police) with
bow and circular shield, lumbers up and gawks.*]
                              —What are *you* looking for?

[*Pointing to a spot in front of the women.*]
Put your shield down here.

        [*The girl obeys.*]
                              No, hollow *up!*

[*The girl reverses the shield.* LYSISTRATA *looks about brightly.*]
—Someone give me the entrails.

        [*A dubious silence.*]

KLEONIKE   Lysistrata, what kind   195
of an Oath are we supposed to swear?

LYSISTRATA   The Standard.
Aischylos used it in a play,[4] they say—the one where
you slaughter a sheep and swear on a shield.

KLEONIKE   Lysistrata,
you *do not* swear an Oath for *Peace* on a *shield!*

LYSISTRATA   What Oath do you want?

[*Exasperated.*]   Something bizarre and
        expensive?   200
A fancier victim—"Take one white horse and disembowel"?

KLEONIKE   *White horse?* The symbolism's too obscure.

LYSISTRATA   *Then how*
do we swear this oath?

KLEONIKE   Oh, *I* can tell you
that, if you'll let me.
                          First, we put an enormous
black cup right here—hollow up, of course.   205
Next, into the cup we slaughter a jar of Thasian
wine, and swear a mighty Oath that we won't . . .
dilute it with water.[5]

LAMPITO [*To* KLEONIKE.]   Let me corngratulate you—
that were the beatenes' Oath I ever heerd on!

LYSISTRATA [*Calling inside.*]   Bring out a cup and jug of wine!

        [*Two women emerge, the first staggering under the weight of a huge
        black cup, the second even more burdened with a tremendous wine
        jar.* KLEONIKE *addresses them.*]

KLEONIKE   You darlings!   210
What a tremendous display of pottery!

[*Fingering the cup.*]   A girl
could get a glow just *holding* a cup like this!

---

4. *The Seven Against Thebes.*   5. Wine from the northern Aegean island of Thasos was especially strong;
to drink any wine neat was considered a sign of intemperance.

[*She grabs it away from the first woman, who exits.*]

LYSISTRATA [*Taking the wine jar from the second serving woman (who exits), she barks at* KLEONIKE.] Put that down and help me butcher this boar! [KLEONIKE *puts down the cup, over which she and* LYSISTRATA *together hold the jar of wine (the "boar"). LYSISTRATA prays.*[6]]

> O Mistress Persuasion,
> O Cup of Devotion,   215
> Attend our invocation:
> Accept this oblation,
> Grant our petition,
> Favor our mission.

[LYSISTRATA *and* KLEONIKE *tip up the jar and pour the gurgling wine into the cup.* MYRRHINE, LAMPITO, *and the others watch closely.*]

MYRRHINE Such an attractive shade of blood. And the spurt—   220
pure Art!

LAMPITO Hit shore do smell mighty purty!

[LYSISTRATA *and* KLEONIKE *put down the empty wine jar.*]

KLEONIKE Girls, let me be the first
[*Launching herself at the cup.*]   to take the Oath!

LYSISTRATA [*Hauling* KLEONIKE *back.*]   You'll have to wait your turn like
everyone else.
—Lampito, how do we manage with this mob?

Cumbersome.

—Everyone place her right hand on the cup.   225
[*The women surround the cup and obey.*]
I need a spokeswoman. One of you to take
the Oath in behalf of the rest.
[*The women edge away from* KLEONIKE, *who reluctantly finds herself elected.*]

The rite will conclude
with a General Pledge of Assent by all of you, thus
confirming the Oath. Understood?
[*Nods from the women.* LYSISTRATA *addresses* KLEONIKE.]

Repeat after me:

LYSISTRATA I will withhold all rights of access or entrance   230
KLEONIKE I will withhold all rights of access or entrance
LYSISTRATA From every husband, lover, or casual acquaintance
KLEONIKE from every husband, lover, or casual acquaintance
LYSISTRATA Who moves in my direction in erection.

—Go on

KLEONIKE who m-moves in my direction in erection.

Ohhhhh!   235

—Lysistrata, my knees are shaky. Maybe I'd better . . .

LYSISTRATA I will create, imperforate in cloistered chastity,
KLEONIKE I will create, imperforate in cloistered chastity,
LYSISTRATA A newer, more glamorous, supremely seductive me
KLEONIKE a newer, more glamorous, supremely, seductive me   240
LYSISTRATA And fire my husband's desire with my molten allure—

---

6. A parody of sacrifice, in which an animal victim's throat was slit above an altar.

KLEONIKE   and fire my husband's desire with my molten allure—
LYSISTRATA   But remain, to his panting advances, icily pure.
KLEONIKE   but remain, to his panting advances, icily pure.
LYSISTRATA   If he should force me to share the connubial couch,   245
KLEONIKE   If he should force me to share the connubial couch,
LYSISTRATA   I refuse to return his stroke with the teeniest twitch.
KLEONIKE   I refuse to return his stroke with the teeniest twitch.
LYSISTRATA   I will not lift my slippers to touch the thatch
KLEONIKE   I will not lift my slippers to touch the thatch   250
LYSISTRATA   Or submit sloping prone in a hangdog crouch.
KLEONIKE   or submit sloping prone in a hangdog crouch.
LYSISTRATA   If I this oath maintain,
      may I drink this glorious wine.
KLEONIKE   If I this oath maintain,   255
      may I drink this glorious wine.
LYSISTRATA   But if I slip or falter,
      let me drink water.
KLEONIKE   But if I slip or falter,
      let me drink water.   260
LYSISTRATA   —And now the General Pledge of Assent:
WOMEN   A-MEN!
LYSISTRATA   Good. I'll dedicate the oblation.
      [*She drinks deeply.*]
KLEONIKE   Not too much,
   darling. You know how anxious we are to become
   allies and friends.
                  Not to mention *staying* friends.
      [*She pushes* LYSISTRATA *away and drinks. As the women take their
      turns at the cup, loud cries and alarums are heard offstage.*]
LAMPITO   What-all's that bodacious ruckus?
LYSISTRATA   Just what I told you: 265
   It means the women have taken the Akropolis. Athene's
   Citadel is ours!
                  It's time for you to go,
   Lampito, and set your affairs in order in Sparta.
   [*Indicating the other women in Lampito's group.*] Leave these girls here
      as hostages.
            [LAMPITO *exits left.* LYSISTRATA *turns to the others.*]
                  Let's hurry inside
   the Akropolis and help the others shoot the bolts.   270
KLEONIKE   Don't you think the men will send reinforcements
   against us as soon as they can?
LYSISTRATA   So where's the worry?
   The men can't burn their way in or frighten us out.
   The Gates are ours—they're proof against fire and fear—
   and they open only on our conditions.
KLEONIKE   Yes!   275
   That's the spirit—let's deserve our reputations:
      [*As the women hurry off into the Akropolis.*]
   UP THE SLUTS!

WAY FOR THE OLD IMPREGNABLES!

[*The door shuts behind the women, and the stage is empty. A pause,
and the* CHORUS OF MEN *shuffles on from the left in two groups, led
by their* KORYPHAIOS.[7] *They are incredibly aged Athenians; though
they may acquire spryness later in the play, at this point they are
sheer decrepitude. Their normally shaky progress is impeded by their
burdens: each man not only staggers under a load of wood across his
shoulders, but has his hands full as well—in one, an earthen pot
containing fire (which is in constant danger of going out); in the
other, a dried vinewood torch, not yet lit. Their progress toward the
Akropolis is very slow.*]

KORYPHAIOS OF MEN [*To the right guide of the First Semichorus, who is
stumbling along in mild agony.*] Forward, Swiftly, keep 'em in step!
Forget your shoulder.
I know these logs are green and heavy—but duty, boy, duty!

SWIFTY [*Somewhat inspired, he quavers into slow song to set a pace for his
group.*]

> I'm never surprised. At my age, life   280
> is just one damned thing after another.
> And yet, I never thought my wife
> was anything more than a home-grown bother.
> But now, dadblast her,
> she's a National Disaster!   285

FIRST SEMICHORUS OF MEN

> What a catastrophe—
> MATRIARCHY!
> They've brought Athene's statue to heel,
> they've put the Akropolis under a seal,
> they've copped the whole damned commonweal . . .   290
> What is there left for them to steal?

KORYPHAIOS OF MEN [*To the right guide of the Second Semichorus—a slower
soul, if possible, than* SWIFTY.] Now, Chipper, speed's the word. The Akropolis, on the double!
Once we're there, we'll pile these logs around them, and convene
a circuit court for a truncated trial. Strictly impartial:
With a show of hands, we'll light a spark of justice under   295
every woman who brewed this scheme. We'll burn them all
on the first ballot—and the first to go is Ly . . .
[*Pause for thought.*]   is Ly . . .
[*Remembering and pointing at a spot in the audience.*] Is *Lykon's* wife[8]—
and there she is, right over there!

CHIPPER [*Taking up the song again.*]

> I won't be twitted, I won't be guyed,
> I'll teach these women not to trouble us!   300
> Kleomenes the Spartan tried
> expropriating our Akropolis[9]

---

7. Leader of the chorus.   8. Notorious for her loose morals.   9. In 508 B.C. the Spartans under Cleo-
menes tried to intervene in Athens on behalf of the aristocratic resistance to the democratic reforms of
Cleisthenes. They seized the Acropolis, were besieged there by the Athenians, and withdrew from the city
after two days.

some time ago—
ninety-five years or so—

SECOND SEMICHORUS OF MEN
but he suffered damaging losses   305
when he ran across US!
He breathed defiance—and more as well:
No bath for six years—you could tell.
We fished him out of the Citadel
and quelled his spirit—but not his smell.   310

KORYPHAIOS OF MEN   That's how I took him. A savage siege:
Seventeen
ranks
of shields were massed at that gate, with blanket infantry cover.
I slept like a baby.
So when mere women (who gall the gods
and make Euripides sick)[1] try the same trick, should I
sit idly by?
Then demolish the monument, I won at Marathon![2]   315

FIRST SEMICHORUS OF MEN [*Singly.*]
—The last lap of our journey!
—I greet it with some dismay.
—The danger doesn't deter me.
—but
it's uphill
—all the way.
—Please, somebody,
—find a jackass   320
to drag these logs
—to the top.
—I ache to join the fracas,
—but
my shoulder's aching
—to stop.

SWIFTY   Backward there's no turning.
Upward and onward, men!   325
And keep those firepots burning, or
we make this trip again.

CHORUS OF MEN [*Blowing into their firepots, which promptly send forth
clouds of smoke.*]   With a puff (pfffff). . . .
and a cough (hhhhh). . . .
The smoke! I'll choke! Turn it off!   330

SECOND SEMICHORUS OF MEN [*Singly.*]
—Damned embers.
—Should be muzzled.
—There oughta be a law.
—They jumped me

1. Aristophanes always presents Euripides, improbably, as a misogynist and hence hated by women in
return.   2. Town on the north coast of Attica, site of the Athenians' great victory when in 490 B.C. a
small Athenian army repelled a large Persian expedition. The commemorative mound covering the Athenian
dead is still in place.

                              —when I whistled
                                                —and then
          they gnawed my eyeballs
                              —raw.
          —There's lava in my lashes.   335
          —My lids are oxidized.
          —My brows are braised.
                              —These ashes are
          volcanoes
                    —in disguise.

CHIPPER   This way, men. And remember.
               The Goddess needs our aid.   340
               So don't be stopped by cinders. Let's
               press on to the stockade!

CHORUS OF MEN [*Bowing again into their firepots, which erupt as before.*]
               With a huff (hfffff).
               and a chuff (chffff).
               Drat that smoke. Enough is enough!   345

KORYPHAIOS OF MEN [*Signalling the* CHORUS (OF MEN), *which has now
tottered into position before the Akropolis gate, to stop, and peering into
his firepot.*]   Praise be to the gods, it's awake. There's fire in the old fire
    yet.
—Now the directions. See how they strike you:
                                        First, we deposit
these logs at the entrance and light our torches. Next, we crash
the gate. When that doesn't work, we request admission politely.
When *that* doesn't work, we burn the damned door down, and
    smoke   350
these women into submission.
                              That seem acceptable? Good
Down with the load . . . ouch, that smoke! Sonofabitch!
          [*A horrible tangle results as the* CHORUS (OF MEN) *attempts to
          deposit the logs. The* KORYPHAIOS *turns to the audience.*]
Is there a general in the house? We have a logistical problem.
          [*No answer. He shrugs.*]
Same old story. Still at loggerheads over in Samos.[3]
          [*With great confusion, the logs are placed somehow.*]
That's better. The pressure's off. I've got my backbone back.   355
[*To his firepot.*] What, pot? You forgot your part in the plot?
                                                  Urge that
          smudge
to be hot on the dot and scorch my torch.
                              Got it, pot?
[*Praying.*]
               Queen Athene, let these strumpets
               crumple before our attack.

_____

3. Most of the Athenian fleet was at the moment based in Samos, practically the only Ionian ally left to
Athens, in order to make ready moves against those states who had defected to Sparta in 412 after the
Sicilian fiasco [Translator's note].

Grant us victory, male supremacy   360
and a testimonial plaque.

[*The* (CHORUS OF) MEN *plunge their torches into firepots and
arrange themselves purposefully before the gate. Engaged in their
preparations, they do not see the sudden entrance, from the right, of
the* CHORUS OF WOMEN, *led by their* KORYPHAIOS. *These wear long
cloaks and carry pitchers of water. They are very old—though not so
old as the* (CHORUS OF) MEN—*but quite spry. In their turn, they do
not perceive the* CHORUS OF MEN.]

KORYPHAIOS OF WOMEN [*Stopping suddenly.*]   What's this—soot? And
smoke as well? I may be all wet,
but this might mean fire. Things look dark, girls; we'll have to dash.

[*They move ahead, at a considerably faster pace than the* (CHORUS
OF) MEN.]

FIRST SEMICHORUS OF WOMEN [*Singly.*]

Speed! Celerity!   Save our sorority
from arson   Combustion   And heat exhaustion   365
Don't let our sisterhood   shrivel to blisterhood.
Fanned into slag by hoary typhoons.
By flatulent, nasty, gusty baboons.
We're late! Run!
The girls might be done!   370

[*Tutte.*] Filling my pitcher   was absolute torture:
The fountains in town   are so *crowded* at dawn,
glutted with masses   of the lower classes
blatting and battering,   shoving, and shattering
jugs. But I juggled   my burden, and wriggled   375
away to extinguish   the igneous anguish
of neighbor, and sister, and daughter—
Here's Water!

SECOND SEMICHORUS OF WOMEN [*Singly.*]

Get wind of the news?   The gaffers are loose.
The blowhards are off   with fuel enough   380
to furnish a bathhouse.   But the finish is pathos:
They're scaling the heights with a horrid proposal
They're threatening women with rubbish disposal!
How ghastly—how gauche!
burned up with the trash!   385

[*Tutte.*] Preserve me, Athene,   from gazing on any
matron or maid   auto-da fé'd.
Cover with grace   these redeemers of Greece
from battles, insanity,   Man's inhumanity.
Gold-browed goddess,   hither to aid us!   390
Fight as our ally,   join in our sally
against pyromaniac slaughter—
Haul Water!

KORYPHAIOS OF WOMEN [*Noticing for the first time the* CHORUS OF MEN,
still busy at their firepots, she cuts off a member of her CHORUS *who seems
about to continue the song.*]   Hold it. What have we here? You don't
catch true-blue

patriots red-handed. These are authentic degenerates,   395
male, taken *in flagrante*.
KORYPHAIOS OF MEN   Oops. Female troops. This could be upsetting.
I didn't expect such a flood of reserves.
KORYPHAIOS OF WOMEN   Merely a spearhead.
If our numbers stun you, watch that yellow streak
spread. We represent just one percent of one percent of This Woman's
    Army.
KORYPHAIOS OF MEN   Never been confronted with such backtalk. Can't
    allow   400
it. Somebody pick up a log and pulverize that brass.
                                            Any Volunteers?
    [*There are none among the* CHORUS (OF MEN).]
KORYPHAIOS OF WOMEN   Put down the pitchers, girls. If they start waving
    that lumber,
we don't want to be encumbered.
KORYPHAIOS OF MEN   Look, men, a few sharp jabs
will stop that jawing. It never fails.
                              The poet Hipponax
swears by it.[4]
    [*Still no volunteers. The* KORYPHAIOS OF WOMEN *advances.*]
KORYPHAIOS OF WOMEN   Then step right up. Have a jab at me.   405
Free shot.
KORYPHAIOS OF MEN [*Advancing reluctantly to meet her.*]
                  Shut up! I'll peel your pelt. I'll pit your pod.
KORYPHAIOS OF WOMEN   The name is Stratyllis. I dare you to lay one finger
    on me.
KORYPHAIOS OF MEN   I'll lay on you with a fistful. Er—any specific threats?
KORYPHAIOS OF WOMEN [*Earnestly.*]   I'll crop your lungs and reap your
    bowels, bite by bite,
and leave no balls on the body for other bitches to gnaw.   410
KORYPHAIOS OF MEN [*Retreating hurriedly.*] Can't beat Euripides for
    insight. And I quote:
                  No creature's found
so lost to shame as Woman.
                  Talk about realist playwrights!
KORYPHAIOS OF WOMEN   Up with the water, ladies. Pitchers at the ready,
    place!
KORYPHAIOS OF MEN   Why the water, you sink of iniquity? More sedition?
KORYPHAIOS OF WOMEN   Why the fire, you walking boneyard? Self-
    cremation?   415
KORYPHAIOS OF MEN   I brought this fire to ignite a pyre and fricassee your
    friends.
KORYPHAIOS OF WOMEN   I brought this water to douse your pyre. Tit for
    tat.
KORYPHAIOS OF MEN   *You'll* douse my fire? Nonsense!
KORYPHAIOS OF WOMEN   You'll see, when the
    facts soak in.

---

4. The Greek refers to the sculptor Boupalus, who was said to have been driven to suicide by the scurrilous
abuse of the poet Hipponax (sixth century B.C.).

KORYPHAIOS OF MEN   I have the torch right here. Perhaps I should bar-
　　becue *you*.
KORYPHAIOS OF WOMEN   If you have any soap, I could give you a bath.
KORYPHAIOS OF MEN   A
　　bath from those   420
polluted hands?
KORYPHAIOS OF WOMEN   Pure enough for a blushing young bridegroom.
KORYPHAIOS OF MEN   Enough of that insolent lip.
KORYPHAIOS OF WOMEN   It's merely freedom of
　　speech.
KORYPHAIOS OF MEN   I'll stop that screeching!
KORYPHAIOS OF WOMEN   You're helpless outside the
　　jury-box.[5]
KORYPHAIOS OF MEN [*Urging his men, torches at the ready, into a
charge.*]   Burn, fire, burn!
KORYPHAIOS OF WOMEN [*As the women empty their pitchers over the men.*]
　　And cauldron bubble.
KORYPHAIOS OF MEN [*Like his troops, soaked and routed.*]   Arrrgh!
KORYPHAIOS OF WOMEN   Goodness.
What seems to be the trouble? Too hot?
KORYPHAIOS OF MEN   Hot, hell! Stop it!   425
What do you think you're doing?
KORYPHAIOS OF WOMEN   If you must know, I'm gardening.
Perhaps you'll bloom.
KORYPHAIOS OF MEN   Perhaps I'll fall right off the vine!
I'm withered, frozen, shaking . . .
KORYPHAIOS OF WOMEN   Of course. But, providentially,
you brought along your smudgepot.
　　　　　　　　　　　The sap should rise eventually.
[*Shivering, the* CHORUS OF MEN *retreats in utter defeat.*]

A COMMISSIONER *of Public Safety*[6] *enters from the left, followed
quite reluctantly by a squad of police—four Skythian archers. He
surveys the situation with disapproval.*]
COMMISSIONER   Fire, eh? Females again—spontaneous combustion   430
of lust. Suspected as much.
　　　　　　　　　　Rubadubdubbing, incessant
incontinent keening for wine, damnable funeral
foofaraw for Adonis resounding from roof to roof[7]—
heard it all before . . .
　　　[*Savagely, as the* KORYPHAIOS OF MEN *tries to interpose a remark.*]
　　　　　　　　　　and WHERE?
　　　　　　　　　　The ASSEMBLY!
Recall, if you can, the debate on the Sicilian Question: 435
That bullbrained demagogue Demostratos[8] (who will rot, I trust)

---

5. Pericles had instituted pay for jury service, and the poor and the aged made something of a living this
way.   6. One prominent citizen on a board of ten chosen in the wake of the Sicilian disaster to restrain
possible legislative excesses by the Assembly.   7. The Asiatic cult of the vegetation god Adonis (Tammuz)
was celebrated by women, who lamented the god's death each year on the roofs of their houses. In male
eyes, the cult, as both Oriental and female, threatened the Greek ideal of self-restraint.   8. One of the
supporters of the Sicilian Expedition, who proposed to enroll heavily armed infantry from the island of
Zakynthos, off the west coast of Greece, on the way to Sicily.

rose to propose a naval task force.
                                        His wife,
writhing with religion on a handy roof, bleated
a dirge:
            "BEREFT! OH WOE OH WOE FOR ADONIS!"
And so of course Demostratos, taking his cue   440
outblatted her:
            "A DRAFT! ENROLL THE WHOLE OF ZAKYNTHOS!"
His wife, a smidgin stewed, renewed her yowling:
"OH GNASH YOUR TEETH AND BEAT YOUR
BREASTS FOR ADONIS!"
And so of course Demostratos (that god-detested blot,   445
that foul-lunged son of an ulcer) gnashed tooth and nail
and voice, and bashed and rammed his program through.
And THERE is the Gift of Women:
                                MORAL CHAOS!
KORYPHAIOS OF MEN   Save your breath for actual felonies, Commissioner;
see what's happened to us! Insolence, insults,   450
these we pass over, but not lese-majesty:
                                We're flooded
with indignity from those bitches' pitchers—like a bunch
of weak-bladdered brats. Our cloaks are sopped. We'll sue!
COMMISSIONER   Useless. Your suit won't hold water. Right's on their
        side.
For female depravity, gentlemen, WE stand guilty—   455
we, their teachers, preceptors of prurience, accomplices
before the fact of fornication. We sowed them in sexual
license, and now we reap rebellion.
                                The proof?
Consider. Off we trip to the goldsmith's to leave
an order:
            "That bangle you fashioned last spring for my wife   460
is sprung. She was thrashing around last night, and the prong
popped out of the bracket. I'll be tied up all day—I'm
boarding the ferry right now—but my wife'll be home.
If you get the time, please stop by the house in a bit
and see if you can't do something—anything—to fit   465
a new prong into the bracket of her bangle."
                                And bang.
Another one ups to a cobbler—young, but no apprentice,
full kit of tools, ready to give his awl—
and delivers this gem:
            "My wife's new sandals are tight.
The cinch pinches her pinkie right where she's sensitive.   470
Drop in at noon with something to stretch her cinch
and give it a little play."
                                And a cinch it is.
Such hanky-panky we have to thank for today's
Utter Anarchy: I, a Commissioner of Public
Safety, duly invested with extraordinary powers   475

to protect the State in the Present Emergency, have secured
a source of timber to outfit our fleet and solve
the shortage of oarage. I need the money immediately . . .
the WOMEN, no less, have locked me out of the Treasury!
[*Pulling himself together.*] —Well, no profit in standing around.
[*To one of the archers.*]   Bring   480
the crowbars. I'll jack these women back on their
pedestals!
            —WELL, you slack-jawed jackass? What's the
attraction? Wipe that thirst off your face. I said *crow*bar,
not saloon!—All right, men, all together. Shove those
bars underneath the gate and HEAVE!
[*Grabbing up a crowbar*]   I'll take this side.   485
And now let's root them out, men, ROOT them out.
One, Two . . .
            [*The gates to the Akropolis burst open suddenly, disclosing* LYSIS-
            TRATA. *She is perfectly composed and bears a large spindle. The*
            COMMISSIONER *and the* (FOUR) POLICE(MEN) *fall back in con-*
            sternation.]
LYSISTRATA   Why the moving equipment?
I'm quite well motivated, thank you, and here I am.
Frankly, you don't need crowbars nearly so much as brains.
COMMISSIONER   Brains? O name of infamy! Where's a policeman?   490
            [*He grabs wildly for the First Archer and shoves him toward*
            LYSISTRATA.]
Arrest that woman!
                  Better tie her hands behind her.
LYSISTRATA   By Artemis, goddess of the hunt, if he lays a finger
on me, he'll rue the day he joined the force!
            [*She jabs the spindle viciously at the First Archer, who leaps, terri-*
            fied, back to his comrades.]
COMMISSIONER   What's this—retreat? Never! Take her on the flank.
            [*The First Archer hangs back. The* COMMISSIONER *grabs the Second*
            Archer.]
—Help him.
            —Will the two of you kindly TIE HER UP?   495
            [*He shoves them toward* LYSISTRATA. KLEONIKE *carrying a large*
            chamber pot, springs out of the entrance and advances on the Second
            Archer.]
KLEONIKE   By Artemis, goddess of the dew, if you so much
as touch her, I'll stomp the shit right out of you!
            [*The two Archers run back to their group.*]
COMMISSIONER   *Shit?* Shameless! Where's another policeman?
            [*He grabs the Third Archer and propels him toward* KLEONIKE.]
Handcuff *her* first. Can't stand a foul-mouthed female.
            [MYRRHINE, *carrying a large, blazing lamp, appears at the entrance*
            and advances on the Third Archer.]
MYRRHINE   By Artemis, bringer of light, if you lay a finger   500
on her, you won't be able to stop the swelling!
            [*The Third Archer dodges her swing and runs back to the group.*]

COMMISSIONER Now what? Where's an officer?
  [*Pushing the Fourth Archer toward Myrrhine.*] Apprehend that woman!
I'll see that *somebody* stays to take the blame!
    [ISMENIA *the Boiotian, carrying a huge pair of pincers, appears at
    the entrance and advances on the Fourth Archer.*]
ISMENIA By Artemis, goddess of Tauris, if you go near
that girl, I'll rip the hair right out of your head!   505
  [*The Fourth Archer retreats hurriedly.*]
COMMISSIONER What a colossal mess: Athens' Finest—
finished!
  [*Arranging the Archers.*] —Now, men, a little *esprit de corps*. Worsted
by women? Drubbed by drabs?
                    Never!
                              Regroup,
reform that thin red line.
                  Ready?
                  CHARGE!
  [*He pushes them ahead of him.*]
LYSISTRATA I warn you. We have four battalions behind us—   510
full-armed combat infantrywomen, trained
from the cradle . . .
COMMISSIONER   Disarm them, Officers! Go for the hands!
LYSISTRATA [*Calling inside the Akropolis.*]   MOBILIZE THE RESERVES!
  [*A horde of women, armed with household articles, begins to pour
  from the Akropolis.*]
                Onward, you ladies from hell!
Forward, you market militia, you battle-hardened
bargain hunters, old sales campaigners, grocery   515
grenadiers, veterans never bested by an overcharge!
You troops of the breadline, doughgirls—
                  INTO THE FRAY!
Show them no mercy!
          Push!
              Jostle!
                Shove!
Call them nasty names!
          Don't be ladylike.
  [*The women charge and rout the Archers in short order.*]
Fall back—don't strip the enemy![9] The day is ours!   520
  [*The women obey, and the Archers run off left. The COMMISSIONER,
  dazed, is left muttering to himself.*]
COMMISSIONER Gross ineptitude. A sorry day for the Force.
LYSISTRATA Of course. What did you expect? We're not slaves;
we're freeborn Women, and when we're scorned, we're
full of fury. Never underestimate the Power of a Woman.
COMMISSIONER Power? You mean Capacity. I should have remem-
bered   525
the proverb: *The lower the tavern, the higher the dudgeon.*
KORYPHAIOS OF MEN Why cast your pearls before swine, Commissioner?

---

9. Victorious soldiers after a battle commonly stripped the armor from enemy corpses.

I know you're a civil
servant, but don't overdo it. Have you forgotten the bath
they gave us—in public,
                              fully dressed,
                                                       totally soapless?
Keep rational discourse for *people!*
    [*He aims a blow at the* KORYPHAIOS OF WOMEN, *who dodges and
raises her pitcher.*]

KORYPHAIOS OF WOMEN   I might point out that lifting   530
one's hand against a neighbor is scarcely civilized
behavior—and entails, for the lifter, a black eye.
                                 I'm really peaceful by
    nature,
compulsively inoffensive—a perfect doll. My ideal is a
well-bred repose that doesn't even stir up dust . . .
    [*Swinging at the Koryphaios of Men with the pitcher.*] unless some no-
    good lowlife
tries to rifle my hive and gets my dander up!   535
    [*The* KORYPHAIOS OF MEN *backs hurriedly away, and the* CHORUS
OF MEN *goes into a worried dance.*]

CHORUS OF MEN [*Singly.*]
          O Zeus, what's the use of this constant abuse?
          How do we deal with this female zoo?
          Is there no solution to Total Immersion?
             What can a poor man DO?
    [*Tutti.*]   Query the Adversary!   540
                Ferret out their story!
                What end did they have in view,
                to seize the city's sanctuary,
                snatch its legendary eyrie,
                snare an area so very   545
              terribly taboo?

KORYPHAIOS OF MEN [*To the* COMMISSIONER.]   Scrutinize those women!
Scour their depositions—assess their rebuttals!
Masculine honor demands this affair be probed to the bottom!

COMMISSIONER [*Turning to the women from the Akropolis.*]   All right, you.
Kindly inform me, dammit, in your own words:
What possible object could you have had in blockading the
    Treasury?   550

LYSISTRATA   We thought we'd deposit the money in escrow and withdraw
    you men
from the war.

COMMISSIONER   The money's the cause of the war?

LYSISTRATA   And all our internal
disorders—the Body Politic's chronic bellyaches: What causes
Peisandros' frantic rantings, or the raucous caucuses of the Friends
of Oligarchy?[1] The chance for graft.

1. One of several political clubs formed to gain offices and power. A few months after this play was
performed, Peisandros and an oligarchic faction overthrew the democratic constitution, with widespread
assassinations and confiscations for a short time. By the following year (410 B.C.) the democracy was
restored.

But now, with the money up
there,   555
they can't upset the City's equilibrium—or lower its balance.
COMMISSIONER   And what's your next step?
LYSISTRATA   Stupid question. We'll budget
the money.
COMMISSIONER   *You'll budget the money?*
LYSISTRATA   Why should you find that so
shocking?
We budget the household accounts, and you don't object at all.
COMMISSIONER   That's different.
LYSISTRATA   Different? How?
COMMISSIONER   The War Effort needs
this money!   560
LYSISTRATA   Who needs the War Effort?
COMMISSIONER   Every patriot who pulses to save
all that Athens holds near and dear.
LYSISTRATA   Oh, *that*. Don't worry.
We'll save you.
COMMISSIONER   *You* will save us?
LYSISTRATA   Who else?
COMMISSIONER   But this is unscrupulous!
LYSISTRATA   We'll save you. You can't deter us.
COMMISSIONER   Scurrilous!
LYSISTRATA   You seem disturbed,
This makes it difficult. But, still—we'll save you.
COMMISSIONER   Doubtless illegal!   565
LYSISTRATA   We deem it a duty. For friendship's sake.
COMMISSIONER   Well, forsake this
friend.
I DO NOT WANT TO BE SAVED. DAMMIT!
LYSISTRATA   All the more reason.
It's not only Sparta; now we'll have to save you from you.
COMMISSIONER   Might I ask where you women conceived this concern
about War and Peace?
LYSISTRATA [*Loftily.*]   We shall explain.
COMMISSIONER [*Making a fist*]   Hurry up, and you won't   570
get hurt.
LYSISTRATA   Then *listen*. And do try to keep your hands to yourself.
COMMISSIONER [*Moving threateningly toward her.*]   I can't. Righteous
anger forbids restraint and decrees . . .
KLEONIKE [*Brandishing her chamber pot.*]   Multiple fractures?
COMMISSIONER [*Retreating.*]   Keep those
croaks for yourself, you old crow!
[*To Lysistrata.*] All right, lady, I'm ready. Speak.
LYSISTRATA   I shall proceed:
When the War began, like the prudent, dutiful wives that   575
we are, we tolerated you men, and endured your actions in silence.
   (Small wonder—
you wouldn't let us say boo.)

You were not precisely the answer
to a matron's prayer—we knew you too well, and found out more.
Too many times, as we sat in the house, we'd hear that
you'd done it again—manhandled another affair of   580
state with your usual staggering incompetence. Then,
masking our worry with a nervous laugh,
we'd ask you, brightly, "How was the Assembly today, dear? Anything
in the minutes about Peace?" And my husband would
give his stock reply.   585
"What's that to you? Shut up!" And I did.

KLEONIKE [*Proudly.*]   *I* never shut up!

COMMISSIONER   I trust you were shut up. Soundly.

LYSISTRATA   Regardless, *I* shut up.
And then we'd learn that you'd passed another decree,
fouler than the first, and we'd ask again: "Darling, how
did you manage anything so idiotic?" And my   590
husband, with his customary glare, would tell me to spin
my thread, or else get a clout on the head.
And of course he'd quote from Homer:
                              Yᵉ menne must husband yᵉ warre.[2]

COMMISSIONER   Apt and irrefutably right.

LYSISTRATA   *Right,* you miserable misfit?
To keep us from giving advice while you fumbled the   595
City away in the Senate? Right, indeed!
                              But this time was really too
     much.
Wherever we went, we'd hear you engaged in the same conversation:
"What Athens needs is a Man."
                              "But there isn't a Man in the country."
"You can say that again."
                    There was obviously no time to lose.
We women met in immediate convention and passed a   600
unanimous resolution: To work in concert for safety and
Peace in Greece. We have valuable advice to impart,
and, if you can possibly deign to emulate our silence,
and take your turn as audience, we'll rectify you—
we'll straighten you out and set you right.   605

COMMISSIONER   *You'll* set *us* right? You go too far. I cannot permit
     such a statement to . . .

LYSISTRATA   Shush.

COMMISSIONER   I categorically decline to shush
for some confounded woman, who wears—as a constant
reminder of congenital inferiority, an injunction to
public silence—a veil!   610
Death before such dishonor!

LYSISTRATA [*Removing her veil.*]   If that's the only obstacle . . .
          I feel you need a new panache,
          so take the veil, my dear Commis-

---

2. *Iliad* 6.492. Homer's Greek would have sounded similarly archaic.

sioner, and drape it thus—
                              and SHUSH!
[*As she winds the veil around the startled* COMMISSIONER's *head,*
KLEONIKE *and* MYRRHINE, *with carding-comb and wool-basket, rush
forward and assist in transforming him into a woman.*]

KLEONIKE   Accept, I pray, this humble comb.   615
MYRRHINE   Receive this basket of fleece as well.
LYSISTRATA   Hike up your skirts, and card your wool,
                and gnaw your beans—and stay at home!
                        While we rewrite Homer:
                        Y^e WOMEN must WIVE ye warre!   620
[*To the* CHORUS OF WOMEN, *the* COMMISSIONER *struggles to re-
move his new outfit.*]
Women, weaker vessels, arise!
                                Put down your pitchers.
It's our turn, now. Let's supply our friends with some moral support.
[*The* CHORUS OF WOMEN *dances to the same tune as the (*CHORUS
OF*)* MEN *but with much more confidence.*]

CHORUS OF WOMEN [*Singly.*]
                Oh, yes! I'll dance to bless their success.
                Fatigue won't weaken my will. Or my knees
                I'm ready to join in any jeopardy.   625
                        with girls as good as *these!*
[*Tutte.*]
                        A tally of their talents
                        convinces me they're giants
                        of excellence. To commence:
                        there's Beauty, Duty, Prudence, Science,   630
                        Self-Reliance, Compliance, Defiance,
                        and Love of Athens in balanced alliance
                                with Common Sense!

KORYPHAIOS OF WOMEN   [*To the women from the Akropolis.*]
Autochthonous daughters of Attika, sprung from the
soil that bore your mothers, the spiniest, spikiest   635
nettles known to man, prove your mettle and attack!
Now is no time to dilute your anger. You're
running ahead of the wind!

LYSISTRATA   We'll wait for the wind
from heaven. The gentle breath of Love and his Kyprian
mother will imbue our bodies with desire, and raise a   640
storm to tense and tauten these blasted men until they
crack. And soon we'll be on every tongue in
Greece—the *Pacifiers.*

COMMISSIONER   That's quite
a mouthful. How will you win it?

LYSISTRATA   First, we intend to withdraw
that crazy Army of Occupation from the downtown shopping
        section.   645

KLEONIKE   Aphrodite be praised!

LYSISTRATA   The pottery shop and the grocery stall

are overstocked with soldiers, clanking around like those maniac
    Korybants,[3]
armed to the teeth for a battle.
COMMISSIONER   A Hero is Always Prepared!
LYSISTRATA   I suppose he is. But it does look silly to shop for sardines
    from behind a shield.
KLEONIKE   I'll second that. I saw   650
    a cavalry captain buy vegetable soup on horseback. He
    carried the whole mess home in his helmet.
                                 And then that fellow from
    Thrace,
shaking his buckler and spear—a menace straight from the stage.
The saleslady was stiff with fright. He was hogging her ripe figs—free.
COMMISSIONER   I admit, for the moment, that Hellas' affairs are in
    one   655
hell of a snarl. But how can you set them straight?
LYSISTRATA   Simplicity itself.
COMMISSIONER   Pray demonstrate.
LYSISTRATA   It's rather like yarn. When a hank's in
    a tangle,
we lift it—so—and work out the snarls by winding it up
on spindles, now this way, now that way.
                              That's how we'll wind up the
    War,
if allowed: We'll work out the snarls by sending Special Commis-
    sions—   660
back and forth, now this way, now that way—to ravel
these tense international kinks.
COMMISSIONER   I lost your thread, but I know there's a
    hitch.
Spruce up the world's disasters with spindles—typically
woolly female logic.
LYSISTRATA   If *you* had a scrap of logic, you'd adopt
our wool as a master plan for Athens.
COMMISSIONER   What course of action   665
    does the wool advise?
LYSISTRATA   Consider the City as fleece, recently
shorn. The first step is Cleansing: Scrub it in a public
bath, and remove all corruption, offal, and sheepdip.
                                 Next, to the couch
for Scutching and Plucking: Cudgel the leeches and
similar vermin loose with a club, then pick the prickles   670
and cockleburs out. As for the clots—those lumps
that clump and cluster in knots and snarls to snag
important posts—you comb these out,
twist off their heads, and discard.
                      Next, to raise the City's
nap, you card the citizens together in a single basket   675

---

3. The armed priests of the goddess Cybele.

of common weal and general welfare. Fold in our loyal
Resident Aliens, all Foreigners of proven and tested
friendship, and any Disenfranchised Debtors. Combine these closely
    with the rest.
Lastly, cull the colonies settled by our own people:
these are nothing but flocks of wool from the City's   680
fleece, scattered throughout the world. So gather home
these far-flung flocks, amalgamate them with the others.

                                        Then, drawing
    this blend
of stable fibers into one fine staple, you spin a mighty
bobbin of yarn—and weave, without bias or seam, a
cloak to clothe the City of Athens!

COMMISSIONER   This is too much! The City's   685
died in the wool, worsted by the distaff side—by women
who bore no share in the War. . . .

LYSISTRATA   None, you hopeless hypocrite?
The quota we bear is double. First, we delivered our
sons to fill out the front lines in Sicily . . .

COMMISSIONER   Don't tax me with that mem-
    ory.

LYSISTRATA   Next, the best years of our lives were levied. Top-level   690
strategy attached our joy, and we sleep alone.

                              But it's not the matrons
like us who matter. I mourn for the virgins, bedded in
single blessedness, with nothing to do, but grow old.

COMMISSIONER   Men *have* been
    known
to age, as well as women.

LYSISTRATA   No, not as well as—better.
A man, an absolute antique, comes back from the war, and he's
    barely   695
doddered into town before he's married the veriest nymphet.
But a woman's season is brief; it slips, and she'll have
no husband, but sit out her life groping at omens—and finding no men.

COMMISSIONER   Lamentable state of affairs. Perhaps we can rectify mat-
    ters:
    [*To the audience.*] TO EVERY MAN JACK, A CHALLENGE:
                                          ARISE!   700
Provided you can . . .

LYSISTRATA   Instead, Commissioner, why not simply curl up and *die?*
    Just buy a coffin; here's the place.
    [*Banging him on the head with her spindle.*]
    I'll knead you a cake for the wake[4]—and *these*
    [*Winding the threads from the spindle around him.*]
    make excellent wreaths. So Rest In Peace.   705

KLEONIKE [*Emptying the chamber pot over him.*]

---

4. The dead were provided with a honey cake to throw to Cerberus, the three-headed dog that guarded
the entry to the underworld.

Accept these tokens of deepest grief.
MYRRHINE [*Breaking her lamp over his head.*]
A final garland for the dear deceased.
LYSISTRATA
May I supply any last request?
Then run along. You're due at the wharf:
Charon's[5] anxious to sail—   710
you're holding up the boat for Hell!
COMMISSIONER   This is monstrous—maltreatment of a public official—
maltreatment of ME!
I must repair directly
to the Board of Commissioners, and present my
colleagues concrete evidence of the sorry specifics of this shocking
attack!   715
[*He staggers off left.* LYSISTRATA *calls after him.*]
LYSISTRATA   You won't haul us into court on a charge of neglecting
the dead, will you? (How like a man to insist
on his rights—even his last ones.) Two days between
death and funeral, that's the rule.
Come back here early
day after tomorrow, Commissioner:
We'll lay you out.   720
[LYSISTRATA *and her women re-enter the Akropolis. The* KORY-
PHAIOS OF MEN *advances to address the audience.*]
KORYPHAIOS OF MEN   Wake up, Athenians! Preserve your freedom—the
time is Now!
[*To the* CHORUS OF MEN.] Strip for action, men. Let's cope with the
current mess.
[*The* (CHORUS OF) MEN *put off their long mantles, disclosing short
tunics underneath, and advance toward the audience.*]
CHORUS OF MEN   This trouble may be terminal; it has a loaded odor, an
ominous aroma of constitutional rot.
My nose gives a prognosis of radical disorder—it's just the first install-
ment of an absolutist plot!
The Spartans are behind it: 725
they must have masterminded
some morbid local contacts (engineered by Kleisthenes).[6]
Predictably infected,
these women straightway acted
to commandeer the City's cash. They're feverish to freeze   730
my be-all,
my end-all . . .
my *payroll!*[7]
KORYPHAIOS OF MEN   The symptoms are clear. Our birthright's already
nibbled. And oh, so
daintily: WOMEN ticking off troops for improper etiquette.   735

5. The ferryman of the dead over the river Styx.   6. Not the great reformer who set up the democracy,
but a contemporary of Aristophanes and notorious as a homosexual. Pederasty may have been fashionable,
at least among the upper classes, but the Athenians considered a man who allowed himself to be penetrated
effeminate.   7. The jury pay, which came from the funds stored on the Acropolis.

WOMEN propounding their featherweight views on the fashionable use
and abuse of the shield. And (if any more proof were needed) WOMEN
nagging us to trust the Nice Spartan, and put our heads
in his toothy maw—to make a dessert and call it Peace.
They've woven the City a seamless shroud, bedecked with the
    legend   740
DICTATORSHIP.
                       But I won't be hemmed in. I'll use
their weapon against them, and uphold the right by sneakiness.
                                           With
    knyf under cloke,
gauntlet in glove, sword in olive branch,
[*Slipping slowly toward the* KORYPHAIOS OF WOMEN.] I'll take up my post
in Statuary Row, beside our honored National Heroes,
the natural foes of tyranny: Harmodios,
                             Aristogeiton,[8]
                                  and Me.   745
[*Next to her.*] Striking an epic pose, so, with the full approval
of the immortal gods,
                      I'll bash this loathsome hag in the jaw!
    [*He does, and runs cackling back to the* (CHORUS OF) MEN. *She
    shakes a fist after him.*]
KORYPHAIOS OF WOMEN Mama won't know her little boy when he gets
    home!
    [*To the* (CHORUS OF) WOMEN, *who are eager to launch a full-scale attack.*]
Let's not be hasty, fellow . . . hags. Cloaks off first.
    [*The* (CHORUS OF) WOMEN *remove their mantles, disclosing tunics
    very like those of the* (CHORUS OF) MEN, *and advance toward the
    audience.*]
CHORUS OF WOMEN We'll address you, citizens, in beneficial, can-
    did,   750
    patriotic accents, as our breeding says we must,
since, from the age of seven, Athens graced me with a
    splendid string of civic triumphs to signalize her
        trust:
        I was Relic-Girl quite early,[9]   755
        then advanced to Maid of Barley;
in Artemis' "Pageant of the Bear" I played the lead.
        To cap this proud progression,
        I led the whole procession
at Athene's Celebration, certified and pedigreed   760
        —that cachet
        so distingué—
        a *Lady!*
KORYPHAIOS OF WOMEN [*To the audience.*] I trust this establishes my
    qualifications. I may, I take it,

---

8. The two men who assassinated Hipparchus, brother of the tyrant Hippias, and became heroes of the
democracy. In the preceding lines, Aristophanes alludes to a popular Athenian drinking song: "In a branch
of myrtle, I'll hide my sword, like Harmodius and Aristogeiton, who killed the tyrant, and made Athens
free."   9. Lines 755–63 describe the religious duties of a well-born Athenian girl.

address the City to its profit? Thank you
                                        I admit to being a woman— 765
but don't sell my contribution short on that account.
It's better than the present panic. And my word is as
good as my bond, because I hold stock in Athens—stock I paid for in
    sons.
[*To the* CHORUS OF MEN.] —But you, you doddering bankrupts, where
    are your shares in the State?
[*Slipping slowly toward the* KORYPHAIOS OF MEN.] Your grandfathers
    willed you the Mutual Funds from the Persian War[1]— 770
and where are they?
[*Nearer.*]   You dipped into capital, then lost interest . . .
and now a pool of your assets won't fill a hole in the ground.
All that remains is one last potential killing—Athens.
Is there any rebuttal?
        [*The* KORYPHAIOS OF MEN *gestures menacingly. She ducks down, as*
        if to ward off a blow, and removes a slipper.]
                        Force is a footing resort. I'll take
my very sensible shoe, and paste you in the jaw! 775
[*She does so, and runs back to the women.*]
CHORUS OF MEN   Their native respect for our manhood is small,
        and keeps getting smaller. Let's bottle their gall.
        The man who won't battle has no balls at all!
KORYPHAIOS OF MEN   All right, men, skin out the skivvies. Let's give them
    a whiff of Man, full strength. No point in muffling the essential Us. 780
        [*The* (CHORUS OF) MEN *remove their tunics.*]
CHORUS OF MEN   A century back, we soared to the Heights[2]
        and beat down Tyranny there.
        Now's the time to shed our moults
        and fledge our wings once more,
        to rise to the skies in our reborn force, 785
        and beat back Tyranny here!
KORYPHAIOS OF MEN   No fancy grappling with these grannies; straightfor-
    ward strength. The tiniest
toehold, and those nimble, fiddling fingers will have their
foot in the door, and we're done for.
                        No amount of know-how can lick
a woman's knack.
                        They'll want to build ships   next thing
    we know, 790
we're all at sea, fending off female boarding parties.
(Artemisia[3] fought us at Salamis. Tell me, has anyone
caught her yet?)
                        But we're *really* sunk if they take up horses. Scratch
    the Cavalry:
                        A woman is an easy rider with a natural seat.

1. The treasury of the Delian League, which was formed as a defensive alliance against Persia in the wake
of Xerxes' invasion of 480–79 B.C. but became Athens's empire.   2. The base of the aristocratic family
of the Alcmaeonidae in their first attempt to overthrow the tyrant Hippias in 513 B.C.   3. Queen of
Halicarnassus in Asia Minor who fought prominently on Xerxes' side at Salamis.

Take her over the jumps bareback, and she'll never slip   795
her mount. (That's how the Amazons nearly took Athens. On horseback.[4]
Check on Mikon's mural down in the Stoa.)
                                          Anyway,
the solution is obvious. Put every woman in her place—
stick her in the stocks.
                          To do this, first
snare your woman around the neck.
        [*He attempts to demonstrate on the* KORYPHAIOS OF WOMEN. *After
        a brief tussle, she works loose and chases him back to the* (CHORUS
        OF) MEN.]
CHORUS OF WOMEN   The beast in me's eager and fit for
    a brawl.   800
        Just rile me a bit and she'll kick down the wall.
        You'll bawl to your friends that you've no balls at all.
KORYPHAIOS OF WOMEN   All right, ladies, strip for action. Let's give them
    a whiff
of *Femme Enragée*—piercing and pungent, but not at all tart.
        [*The* (CHORUS OF) WOMEN *remove their tunics.*]
CHORUS OF WOMEN   We're angry. The brainless bird who tangles   805
        with *us* has gummed his last mush.
        In fact, the coot who even heckles
          is being daringly rash.
        So look to your nests, you reclaimed eagles—
          whatever you lay, we'll squash!   810
KORYPHAIOS OF WOMEN   Frankly, you don't faze me. *With* me, I have my
    friends—
Lampito from Sparta; that genteel girl from Thebes, Ismenia—
committed to me forever. *Against* me, *you*—permanently
out of commission. So do your damnedest.
                                    Pass a law.
Pass seven. Continue the winning ways that have made   815
your name a short and ugly household word.
                             Like yesterday:
I was giving a little party, nothing fussy, to honor
the goddess Hekate. Simply to please my daughters,
I'd invited a sweet little thing from the neighborhood—flawless pedigree,
    perfect
taste, a credit to any gathering—a Boiotian eel.   820
But she had to decline. Couldn't pass the border. You'd passed a law.
Not that you care for my party. You'll overwork your right of passage
till your august body is overturned,
                         and you break your silly neck!
        [*She deftly grabs the* KORYPHAIOS OF MEN *by the ankle and upsets
        him. He scuttles back to the* (CHORUS OF) MEN, *who retire in
        confusion.*

        LYSISTRATA *emerges from the citadel, obviously distraught.*]

---

4. The painter Mikon had lately decorated several public buildings with frescoes. The battles of the Greeks and Amazons were favorite subjects of sculptors and painters.

KORYPHAIOS OF WOMEN [*Mock-tragic.*]   *Mistress, queen of this our subtle
    scheme,*
why burst you from the hall with brangled brow?   825
LYSISTRATA   *Oh, wickedness of woman! The female mind*
does sap my soul and set my wits a-totter.
KORYPHAIOS OF WOMEN   *What drear accents are these?*
LYSISTRATA   *The merest truth.*
KORYPHAIOS OF WOMEN   *Be nothing loath to tell the tale to friends.*
LYSISTRATA   *'Twere shame to utter, pain to hold unsaid.*   830
KORYPHAIOS OF WOMEN   *Hide not from me affliction which we share.*
LYSISTRATA   *In briefest compass,*
    [*Dropping the paratragedy.*]   We want to get laid.
KORYPHAIOS OF WOMEN   By Zeus!
LYSISTRATA   No, no, not HIM!
                              Well, that's the way things are.
I've lost my grip on the girls—they're mad for men!
But sly—they slip out in droves.
                          A minute ago,   835
I caught one scooping out the little hole
that breaks through just below Pan's grotto.
                                        One
had jerry-rigged some block-and-tackle business
and was wriggling away on a rope.
                          Another just flat
deserted.
            Last night I spied one mounting a sparrow,   840
all set to take off for the nearest bawdyhouse. I hauled
her back by the hair.
                  And excuses, pretexts for overnight
passes? I've heard them all.
                          Here comes one. Watch.
        [*To the* FIRST WOMAN, *as she runs out of the Akropolis.*]
—You there! What's your hurry?
FIRST WOMAN   I have to get home.
I've got all this lovely Milesian wool in the house,   845
and the moths will simply batter it to bits!
LYSISTRATA   I'll bet.
Get back inside.
FIRST WOMAN   I swear I'll hurry right back!
—Just time enough to spread it out on the couch?
LYSISTRATA   Your wool will stay unspread. And you'll stay here.
FIRST WOMAN   Do I have to let my piecework *rot*?
LYSISTRATA   Possibly.   850
        [*The* SECOND WOMAN *runs on.*]
SECOND WOMAN   Oh dear, oh goodness, what shall I do—my flax!
I left and forgot to peel it!
LYSISTRATA   Another one.
She suffers from unpeeled flax.
                          —Get back inside!
SECOND WOMAN   I'll be right back. I just have to pluck the fibers.

LYSISTRATA   No. No plucking. You start it, and everyone else   855
will want to go and do their plucking, too.
[*The* THIRD WOMAN, *swelling conspicuously, hurries on, praying
loudly.*]

THIRD WOMAN   *O Goddess of Childbirth, grant that I not deliver
until I get me from out this sacred precinct!*

LYSISTRATA   What sort of nonsense is *this?*

THIRD WOMAN   I'm due—any second!

LYSISTRATA   You weren't pregnant yesterday.

THIRD WOMAN   Today I am—   860
a miracle!
                Let me go home for a midwife, *please!*
I may not make it!

LYSISTRATA [*Restraining her.*]   You can do better than that.
[*Tapping the woman's stomach and receiving a metallic clang.*] What's
this? It's hard.

THIRD WOMAN   I'm going to have a boy.

LYSISTRATA   Not unless he's made of bronze. Let's see.
[*She throws open the* THIRD WOMAN'S *cloak, exposing a huge bronze
helmet.*]
Of all the brazen . . . You've stolen the helmet from   865
Athene's statue! Pregnant, indeed!

THIRD WOMAN   I am *so* pregnant!

LYSISTRATA   Then why the helmet?

THIRD WOMAN   I thought my time might come
while I was still on forbidden ground.[5] If it did,
I could climb inside Athene's helmet and have
my baby there.
                The pigeons do it all the time.   870

LYSISTRATA   Nothing but excuses!
[*Taking the helmet.*]   *This* is your baby. I'm afraid
you'll have to stay until we give it a name.

THIRD WOMAN   But the Akropolis is *awful.* I can't even sleep! I saw
the snake that guards the temple.

LYSISTRATA   That snake's a fabrication.[6]

THIRD WOMAN   I don't care *what* kind it is—I'm *scared!*   875
[*The other* WOMEN, *who have emerged from the citadel, crowd
around.*]

KLEONIKE   And those goddamned holy owls.[7] All night long,
tu-wit, tu-wu—they're hooting me into my grave!

LYSISTRATA   Darlings, let's call a halt to this hocus-pocus.
You miss your men—now isn't that the trouble?
[*Shamefaced nods from the group.*]
Don't you think they miss you just as much?   880
I can assure you, their nights are every bit
as hard as yours. So be good girls; endure!
Persist a few days more, and Victory is ours.

---

5. As sacred ground, the Acropolis would be polluted by either birth or death.   6. No one had ever seen
the sacred snake that lived in the Erechtheum.   7. Athena's sacred birds.

It's fated: a current prophecy declares that the men
will go down to defeat before us, provided that *we*   885
maintain a United Front.
[*Producing a scroll.*]   I happen to have
a copy of the prophecy.
KLEONIKE   Read it!
LYSISTRATA   Silence, *please*.
    [*Reading from the scroll.*]
But when the swallows, in flight from the
    hoopoes, have flocked to a hole
on high, and stoutly eschew their   890
    accustomed perch on the pole,
yea, then shall Thunderer Zeus to
    their suff'ring establish a stop,
by making the lower the upper . . .
KLEONIKE   Then *we'll* be lying on top?   895
LYSISTRATA
But should these swallows, indulging their
    lust for the perch, lose heart,
dissolve their flocks in winged dissension,
    and singly depart
the sacred stronghold, breaking the   900
    bands that bind them together—
then know them as lewd, the pervertedest
    birds that ever wore feather.
KLEONIKE   There's nothing obscure about *that* oracle. Ye gods!
LYSISTRATA   Sorely beset as we are, we must not flag   905
or falter. So back to the citadel!
[*As the women troop inside.*] And if we fail
that oracle, darlings, our image is absolutely *mud!*
    [*She follows them in. A pause, and the* CHORUSES *assemble.*]
CHORUS OF MEN   I have a simple
                    tale to relate you.
                    a sterling example   910
                    of masculine virtue:

            The huntsman bold Melanion
                was once a harried quarry.
            The women in town tracked him down
                and badgered him to marry.   915

            Melanion knew the cornered male
                eventually cohabits.
            Assessing the odds, he took to the woods
                and lived trapping rabbits.

            He stuck to the virgin stand, sustained   920
                by rabbit meat and hate,
            and never returned, but ever remained
                an alfresco celibate.

Melanion is our ideal;
　　his loathing makes us free.　　　　　　　925
Our dearest aim is the gemlike flame
　　of his misogyny.[8]

OLD MAN　Let me kiss that wizened cheek.
OLD WOMAN [*Threatening with a fist.*]
　　A wish too rash for that withered flesh.

OLD MAN
　　and lay you low with a highflying kick.　　930
　　[*He tries one and misses.*]
OLD WOMAN
　　Exposing an overgrown underbrush.
OLD MAN　A hairy behind, historically, means
　　masculine force: Myronides
harassed the foe with his mighty mane,
　　and furry Phormion[9] swept the seas　　　935
　　of enemy ships, never meeting his match—
　　such was the nature of his thatch.

CHORUS OF WOMEN　　I offer an anecdote
　　　　　　　　　for your opinion,
　　　　　　　　an adequate antidote　　　　940
　　　　　　　　for your Melanion:

Timon,[1] the noted local grouch,
　　put rusticating hermits
out of style by building his wilds
　　inside the city limits　　　　　　　　945

He shooed away society
　　with natural battlements:
his tongue was edgèd; his shoulder, frigid;
　　his beard, a picket fence.

When random contacts overtaxed him,　　　950
　　he didn't stop to pack,
but loaded curses on the male of the species,
　　left town, and never came back.

Timon, you see, was a misanthrope
　　in a properly narrow sense:　　　　　　955
his spleen was vented only on men . . .
　　we were his dearest friends.
OLD WOMAN [*Making a fist.*]
　　Enjoy a chop to that juiceless chin?

---

8. The chorus of men here recasts a well-known myth for their own purposes. In the myth, it was Atalanta who avoided marriage, challenging her suitors to a footrace that she always won. Melanion threw a golden apple in front of her; when she stopped to pick it up, she lost the race to him.　　9. Like Myronides, a famous Athenian general.　　1. A famous misanthrope, and the subject of Shakespeare's play *Timon of Athens*. There is no evidence that he hated women any less than he hated men.

OLD MAN [*Backing away.*]
> I'm jolted already. Thank you, no.
OLD WOMAN
> Perhaps a trip from a well-turned shin?   960
> [*She tries a kick and misses.*]
OLD MAN
> Brazenly baring the mantrap below.
OLD WOMAN   At least it's *neat*. I'm not too sorry
> to have you see my daintiness.
My habits are still depilatory;
> age hasn't made me a bristly mess.   965
> > Secure in my smoothness, I'm never in doubt—
> > > though even down is out.
> > [LYSISTRATA *mounts the platform and scans the horizon. When her gaze reaches the left, she stops suddenly.*]
LYSISTRATA   Ladies, attention! Battle stations, please!
> And quickly!
> > [*A general rush of women to the battlements.*]
KLEONIKE   What is it?
MYRRHINE   What's all the shouting for?
LYSISTRATA   A MAN!
> [*Consternation.*]   Yes, it's a man. And he's coming this way!   970
Hmm. Seems to have suffered a seizure. Broken out
with a nasty attack of love.
> [*Prayer, aside.*]   O Aphrodite,
> > Mistress all-victorious,
> > mysterious, voluptuous,
> > you who make the crooked straight . . .   975
> > don't let this happen to US!
KLEONIKE   I don't care who he is—*where is he?*
LYSISTRATA [*Pointing.*]   Down there—
> just flanking that temple—Demeter the Fruitful.
KLEONIKE   My.
> Definitely a man.
MYRRHINE [*Craning for a look.*]   I wonder who it can be?
LYSISTRATA   See for yourselves.—Can anyone identify him?   980
MYRRHINE   Oh lord, I can.
> That is my husband—Kinesias.
LYSISTRATA [*To* MYRRHINE.]   Your duty is clear.
> Pop him on the griddle,
> twist
the spit, braize him, baste him, stew him in his own
juice, do him to a turn. Sear him with kisses,
coyness, caresses, *everything*—
> but stop where Our Oath   985
> begins.
MYRRHINE   Relax. I can take care of this.
LYSISTRATA   Of course
> you can, dear. Still, a little help can't hurt, now

can it? I'll just stay around for a bit
and—er—poke up the fire.
                                        —Everyone else inside!
                [*Exit all the women but* LYSISTRATA, *on the platform, and* MYR-
                RHINE, *who stands near the Akropolis entrance, hidden from her
                husband's view.* KINESIAS *staggers on, in erection and considerable
                pain, followed by a male slave who carries a baby boy.*]
KINESIAS   OUCH!!
                        Omigod.   990
        Hypertension, twinges. . . . I can't hold out much more.
        I'd rather be dismembered.
                                How long, ye gods, how long?
LYSISTRATA [*Officially.*]   WHO GOES THERE?
                                                        WHO PENETRATES
        OUR POSITIONS?
KINESIAS   Me.
LYSISTRATA   A Man?
KINESIAS   Every inch.
LYSISTRATA   Then inch yourself out
        of here. Off Limits to Men.
KINESIAS   This *is* the limit.   995
        Just who are *you* to throw me out?
LYSISTRATA   The Lookout.
KINESIAS   Well, look here, Lookout. I'd like to see Myrrhine.
        How's the outlook?
LYSISTRATA   Unlikely. Bring Myrrhine
        to you? The idea!
                        Just by the by, who are you?
KINESIAS   A private citizen. Her husband, Kinesias.
LYSISTRATA   No!   1000
        Meeting you—I'm overcome!
                                Your name, you know,
        is not without its fame among us girls.
        [*Aside.*] —Matter of fact, we have a name for *it.*—
        I swear, you're never out of Myrrhine's mouth.
        She won't even nibble a quince, or swallow an egg,   1005
        without reciting, "Here's to Kinesias!"
KINESIAS   For god's sake.
        will you . . .
LYSISTRATA [*Sweeping on over his agony.*]   Word of honor, it's true. Why,
            when
        we discuss our husbands (you know how women are),
        Myrrhine refuses to argue. She simply insists:
        "Compared with Kinesias, the rest have *nothing!*"   1010
        Imagine!
KINESIAS   *Bring her out here!*
LYSISTRATA   Really? And what would I
        get out of this?
KINESIAS   You see my situation. I'll raise

whatever I can. This can all be yours.
LYSISTRATA   Goodness.
  It's really her place. I'll go and get her.
      [*She descends from the platform and moves to* MYRRHINE, *out of
      Kinesias's sight.*]
KINESIAS   Speed!   1015
—Life is a husk. She left our home, and happiness
went with her. Now pain is the tenant. Oh, to enter
that wifeless house, to sense that awful emptiness,
to eat that tasteless, joyless food—it makes
it hard, I tell you.
                    Harder all the time.   1020
MYRRHINE [*Still out of his sight, in a voice to be overhead.*]   Oh, I *do* love
      him! I'm mad about him! But he
  doesn't want my love. Please don't make me see him
KINESIAS   Myrrhine darling, why do you *act* this way?
  Come down here!
MYRRHINE [*Appearing at the wall.*]   Down there? Certainly not!
KINESIAS   It's me, Myrrhine. I'm begging you. Please come down.   1025
MYRRHINE   I don't see why you're begging me. You don't need me.
KINESIAS   I don't need you? I'm at the end of my rope!
MYRRHINE   I'm leaving.
      [*She turns.* KINESIAS *grabs the boy from the slave.*]
KINESIAS   No! Wait! At least you'll have to listen
  to the voice of your child.
  [*To the boy, in a fierce undertone.*] —(Call your mother!)
  [*Silence.*]   . . . to the voice
  of your very own child . . .
                    —(Call your mother, brat!)   1030
CHILD   MOMMYMOMMYMOMMY!
KINESIAS   Where's your maternal instinct? He hasn't been washed
  or fed for a week. How can you be so pitiless?
MYRRHINE   *Him* I pity. Of all the pitiful excuses
  for a father. . . .
KINESIAS   Come down here, dear. For the baby's sake.   1035
MYRRHINE   Motherhood! I'll have to come. I've got no choice.
KINESIAS [*Soliloquizing as she descends.*]   It may be me, but I'll swear she
      looks years younger—
  and gentler—her eyes caress me. And then they flash:
  that anger, that verve, the high-and-mighty air!
  She's fire, she's ice—and I'm stuck right in the middle.   1040
MYRRHINE [*Taking the baby.*]   Sweet babykins with such a nasty daddy!
  Here, let Mummy kissums. Mummy's little darling.
KINESIAS [*The injured husband.*]   You should be ashamed of yourself, let-
      ting those women
  lead you around. Why do you DO these things?
  You only make me suffer and hurt your poor,   1045
  sweet self.
MYRRHINE   Keep your hands away from me!

KINESIAS But the house, the furniture, everything we own—you're
letting it go to hell!

MYRRHINE   Frankly, I couldn't care less.

KINESIAS But your weaving's unraveled—the loom is full of
chickens! You couldn't care less about *that*?

MYRRHINE   I certainly couldn't. 1050

KINESIAS And the holy rites of Aphrodite? Think how long
that's been.
                   Come on, darling, let's go home.

MYRRHINE I absolutely refuse!
                         Unless you agree to a truce
to stop the war.

KINESIAS   Well, then, if that's your decision.
we'll STOP the war!

MYRRHINE   Well, then, if that's your decision. 1055
I'll come back—*after* it's done.
                         But, for the present.
I've sworn off.

KINESIAS   At least lie down for a minute.
We'll talk.

MYRRHINE I know what you're up to—NO!
—And yet. . . . I really can't say I don't love you . . .

KINESIAS   You love me?
So what's the trouble? *Lie down.*

MYRRHINE   Don't be disgusting. 1060
In front of the baby?

KINESIAS   Er . . . no. Heaven Forfend.
[*Taking the baby and pushing it at the slave.*] —Take this home.
     [*The slave obeys.*]
                    —Well, darling, we're rid of the kid . . .
let's go to bed!

MYRRHINE   Poor dear.
                    But where does one do
this sort of thing?

KINESIAS   Where? All we need is a little
nook. . . . We'll try Pan's grotto. Excellent spot. 1065

MYRRHINE [*With a nod at the Akropolis.*] I'll have to be pure to get back
in *there*. How can I
expunge my pollution?

KINESIAS   Sponge off in the pool next door.

MYRRHINE I did swear an Oath. I'm supposed to perjure myself?

KINESIAS Bother the Oath. Forget it—I'll take the blame.
     [*A pause.*]

MYRRHINE Now I'll go get us a cot.

KINESIAS   No! Not a cot! 1070
The ground's enough for us.

MYRRHINE   *I'll get the cot.*
For all your faults, I refuse to put you to bed
in the dirt.
     [*She exists into the Akropolis.*]

KINESIAS   She certainly loves me. That's nice to know.

MYRRHINE [*Returning with a rope-tied cot.*]   Here. You hurry to bed while
I undress.

[KINESIAS *lies down.*]

Gracious me—I forgot. We need a mattress.   1075

KINESIAS   Who wants a mattress? Not me!

MYRRHINE   Oh, yes, you do.
It's perfectly squalid on the ropes.

KINESIAS   Well, give me a kiss
to tide me over.

MYRRHINE   *Voilà.*

[*She pecks at him and leaves.*]

KINESIAS   OoolaLAlala!
—Make it a quick trip, dear.

MYRRHINE [*Entering with the mattress, she waves* KINESIAS *off the cot and
lays the mattress on it.*]   Here we are.
Our mattress. Now hurry to bed while I undress.   1080

[KINESIAS *lies down again.*]

Gracious me—I forgot. You don't have a pillow.

KINESIAS   I do *not* need a pillow.

MYRRHINE   I know, but *I* do.

[*She leaves.*]

KINESIAS   What a lovefeast! Only the table gets laid.

MYRRHINE [*Returning with a pillow.*]   Rise and shine!

[KINESIAS *jumps up. She places the pillow.*]

And now I have
everything I need.

KINESIAS [*Lying down again.*]   You certainly do.

Come here, my little
jewelbox!   1085

MYRRHINE   Just taking off my bra.

Don't break your promise:
no cheating about the Peace.

KINESIAS   I swear to god,
I'll die first!

MYRRHINE [*Coming to him.*]   Just look. You don't have a blanket.

KINESIAS   I didn't plan to go camping—I want to make love!

MYRRHINE   Relax. You'll get your love. I'll be right back.   1090

[*She leaves.*]

KINESIAS   Relax? I'm dying a slow death by dry goods!

MYRRHINE [*Returning with the blanket.*]   Get up!

KINESIAS [*Getting out of bed.*]   I've been up for hours. I was up before I
was up.

[MYRRHINE *spreads the blanket on the mattress, and he lies down
again.*]

MYRRHINE   I presume you want perfume?

KINESIAS   Positively NO!

MYRRHINE   Absolutely *yes*—whether you want it or not.

[*She leaves.*]

KINESIAS   Dear Zeus, I don't ask for much—but please let her spill it.   1095

MYRRHINE [*Returning with a bottle.*]
  Hold out your hand like a good boy.
                            Now rub it in.

KINESIAS [*Obeying and sniffing.*]   *This* is to quicken desire? Too strong. It grabs
  your nose and bawls out: *Try again tomorrow.*

MYRRHINE I'm *awful!* I brought you that rancid Rhodian brand.
    [*She starts off with the bottle.*]

KINESIAS This is just *lovely.* Leave it, woman!

MYRRHINE   Silly!   1100
    [*She leaves.*]

KINESIAS God damn the clod who first concocted perfume!

MYRRHINE [*Returning with another bottle.*] Here, try this flask.

KINESIAS   Thanks—
  but you try mine.
  Come to bed, you witch—
                    and please stop bringing things!

MYRRHINE *That* is exactly what I'll do.
  There go my shoes.
                Incidentally, darling, you *will*   1105
  remember to vote for the truce?

KINESIAS   I'LL THINK IT OVER!
    [MYRRHINE *runs off for good.*]
  That woman's laid me waste—destroyed me, root
  and branch!
          I'm scuttled,
                gutted,
                     up the spout!
  And Myrrhine's gone!
  [*In a parody of a tragic kommos.*[2]]
          Out upon't! But how? But where?   1110
  Now I have lost the fairest fair,
  how screw my courage to yet another
  sticking-place? Aye, there's the rub—
  And yet, this wagging, wanton babe
  must soon be laid to rest, or else...   1115
  Ho, Pandar!
             Pandar!
                 I'd hire a nurse.

KORYPHAIOS OF MEN
          Grievous your bereavement, cruel
  the slow tabescence of your soul.
  I bid my liquid pity mingle.

          Oh, where the soul, and where, alack!   1120
  the cod to stand the taut attack

2. Lament.

of swollen prides, the scorching tensions
that ravine up the lumbar regions?
    His morning lay
    has gone astray.   1125

KINESIAS [*In agony.*]
    O Zeus, reduce the throbs, the throes!

KORYPHAIOS OF MEN
    I turn my tongue to curse the cause
of your affliction—that jade, that slut,
that hag, that ogress . . .

KINESIAS   No! Slight not
my light-o'-love, my dove, my sweet!   1130

KORYPHAIOS OF MEN
    Sweet!
        O Zeus who rul'st the sky,
snatch that slattern up on high,
crack thy winds, unleash thy thunder,
tumble her over, trundle her under,
juggle her from hand to hand;   1135
twirl her ever near the ground—
drop her in a well-aimed fall
on our comrade's tool! That's all.

[KINESIAS *exits left.*

A SPARTAN HERALD *enters from the right, holding his cloak together
in a futile attempt to conceal his condition.*]

HERALD   This Athens? Where-all kin I find the Council of Elders
or else the Executive Board? I brung some news.   1140
    [*The* COMMISSIONER, *swathed in his cloak, enters from the left.*]

COMMISSIONER   And what are you—a man? a signpost? a joint-stock
company?

HERALD   A herald, sonny, an honest-to-Kastor
herald. I come to chat 'bout thet-there truce.

COMMISSIONER   . . . carrying a concealed weapon? Pretty underhanded.

HERALD [*Twisting to avoid the* COMMISSIONER's *direct gaze.*]   Hain't done
no sech a thang!

COMMISSIONER   Very well, stand still.   1145
Your cloak's out of crease—hernia? Are the roads that bad?

HERALD   I swear this feller's plumb tetched in the haid!

COMMISSIONER [*Throwing open the* SPARTAN (HERALD)'s *cloak, exposing the
phallus.*]
                           You clown,
you've got an erection!

HERALD [*Wildly embarrassed.*]   Hain't got no sech a thang!
You stop this-hyer foolishment!

COMMISSIONER   What *have* you got there, then?

HERALD   Thet-thur's a Spartan *epistle.*[3] In code.

COMMISSIONER   I have the key.   1150

---

3. An encoding device. Papyrus was wrapped around a wooden staff on a spiral, and a message was written on it. The message could be read only when the papyrus was wrapped around an exactly similar staff.

[*Throwing open his cloak.*] Behold another Spartan epistle. In code.
[*Tiring of teasing.*] Let's get down to cases. I know the score,
so tell me the truth.

                    How are things with you in Sparta?

HERALD   Thangs is up in the air. The whole Alliance
is purt-near 'bout to explode. We-uns'll need barrels,   1155
'stead of women.

COMMISSIONER   What was the cause of this outburst?
The great god Pan?

HERALD   Nope. I'll lay 'twere Lampito,
most likely. She begun, and then they was off
and runnin' at the post in a bunch, every last little gal
in Sparta, drivin' their menfolk away from the winner's   1160
circle.

COMMISSIONER   How are you taking this?

HERALD   Painful-like.
Everyone's doubled up worse as a midget nursin'
a wick in a midnight wind come moon-dark time.
Cain't even tetch them little old gals on the moosey
without we all agree to a Greece-wide Peace.   1165

COMMISSIONER   Of course!

                  A universal female plot—all Hellas
risen in rebellion—I should have known!

                             Return
to Sparta with this request:

                  Have them despatch us
a Plenipotentiary Commission, fully empowered
to conclude an armistice. I have full confidence   1170
that I can persuade our Senate to do the same,
without extending myself. The evidence is at hand.

HERALD   I'm a-flyin'. Sir! I hev never heered your equal!

      [*Exeunt hurriedly, the* COMMISSIONER *to the left, the* (SPARTAN)
      HERALD *to the right.*]

KORYPHAIOS OF MEN
   The most unnerving work of nature,
   the pride of applied immorality,   1175
   is the common female human.
   No fire can match, no beast can best her.
   O Unsurmountability,
   thy name—worse luck—is Woman.

KORYPHAIOS OF WOMEN
   After such knowledge, why persist   1180
   in wearing out this feckless
   war between the sexes?
   When can I apply for the post
   of ally, partner, and general friend?

KORYPHAIOS OF MEN
   I won't be ployed to revise, re-do,   1185
   amend, extend, or bring to an end

my irreversible credo:
Misogyny Forever!
—The answer's never.

KORYPHAIOS OF WOMEN

 All right. Whenever you choose.   1190
 But, for the present, I refuse
 to let you look your absolute worst,
 parading around like an unfrocked freak:
 I'm coming over and get you dressed.
  [*She dresses him in his tunic, an action (like others in this scene)
  imitated by the members of the* CHORUS OF WOMEN *toward their
  opposite numbers in the* CHORUS OF MEN.]

KORYPHAIOS OF MEN

 This seems sincere. It's not a trick.   1195
 Recalling the rancor with which I stripped,
 I'm overlaid with chagrin.

KORYPHAIOS OF WOMEN

 Now you resemble a man,
 not some ghastly practical joke.
 And if you show me a little respect   1200
 (and promise not to kick), I'll extract
 the beast in you.

KORYPHAIOS OF MEN [*Searching himself.*] What beast in me?

KORYPHAIOS OF WOMEN

 That insect. There. The bug that's stuck
 in your eye.

KORYPHAIOS OF MEN [*Playing along dubiously.*] This gnat?

KORYPHAIOS OF WOMEN   Yes, nitwit!

KORYPHAIOS OF MEN   Of
  course.
 That steady, festering agony. . . .   1205
 You've put your finger on the source
 of all my lousy troubles. Please
 roll back the lid and scoop it out.
 I'd like to see it.

KORYPHAIOS OF WOMEN All right, I'll do it.
  [*Removing the imaginary insect.*]
 Although, of all the impossible cranks. . . .   1210
 Do you sleep in a swamp? Just look at this.
 I've never seen a bigger chigger.

KORYPHAIOS OF MEN   Thanks.
 Your kindness touches me deeply. For years,
 that thing's been sinking wells in my eye.
 Now you've unplugged me. Here come the tears.   1215

KORYPHAIOS OF WOMEN

 I'll dry your tears, though I can't say why.
  [*Wiping away the tears.*]
 Of all the irresponsible boys. . . .
 And I'll kiss you.

KORYPHAIOS OF MEN   Don't you kiss me!

KORYPHAIOS OF WOMEN
    What made you think you had a choice?
        [*She kisses him.*]

KORYPHAIOS OF MEN   All right, damn you, that's enough of that ingrained
    palaver.   1220
    I can't dispute the truth or logic of the pithy old proverb:
            Life with women is hell.
            Life without women is hell, too.
    And so we conclude a truce with you, on the following terms:
    in future, a mutual moratorium on mischief in all its forms.   1225
    Agreed?—Let's make a single chorus and start our song.
        [*The two* CHORUSES *unite and face the audience.*]

CHORUS OF MEN
            We're not about to introduce
            the standard personal abuse—
                the Choral Smear
            Of Present Persons (usually,   1230
            in every well-made comedy,
                inserted here).
            Instead, in deed and utterance, we
            shall now indulge in philanthropy
                because we feel   1235
            that members of the audience
            endure, in the course of current events,
                sufficient hell.
            Therefore, friends, be rich! Be flush!
            Apply to us, and borrow cash   1240
                in large amounts.
            The Treasury stands behind us—there—
            and we can personally take care
                of small accounts.
            Drop up today. Your credit's good.   1245
            Your loan won't have to be repaid
                in full until
            the war is over. And then, your debt
            is only the money you actually get—
                nothing at all.   1250

CHORUS OF WOMEN
            Just when we meant to entertain
            some madcap gourmets from out of town
                —such flawless taste!—
            the present unpleasantness intervened,
            and now we fear the feast we planned   1255
                will go to waste.
            The soup is waiting, rich and thick:
            I've sacrificed at a suckling pig
                —the pièce de résistance—
            whose toothsome cracklings should amaze   1260
            the most fastidious gourmets—

      you, for instance.
To everybody here, I say
take potluck at my house today
      with me and mine.   1265
Bathe and change as fast as you can,
bring the children, hurry down,
      and walk right in.
Don't bother to knock. No need at all.
My house is yours. Liberty Hall.   1270
      What are friends for?
Act self-possessed when you come over:
it may help out when you discover
      I've locked the door.
      [A DELEGATION OF SPARTANS *enters from the right, with difficulty.*
      They have removed their cloaks, but hold them before themselves in
      an effort to conceal their condition.]
KORYPHAIOS OF MEN   What's this? Behold the Spartan ambassadors, drag-
      ging their beards,   1275
pussy-footing along. It appears they've developed a hitch in the crotch.
[*Advancing to greet them.*] Men of Sparta, I bid you welcome!
                                                             And now
to the point: What predicament brings you among us?
SPARTAN   We-uns is up a stump. Hain't fit fer chatter.
      [*Flipping aside his cloak.*] Here's our predicament. Take a look for
      yourselfs.   1280
KORYPHAIOS OF MEN   Well, I'll be damned—a regular disaster area.
      Inflamed. I imagine the temperature's rather intense?
SPARTAN   Hit ain't the heat, hit's the tumidity.
                                                    But words
won't help what ails us. We-uns come after Peace.
Peace from any person, at any price.   1285
      [*Enter the Athenian (men) from the left, led by Kinesias. They are*
      wearing cloaks, but are obviously in as much travail as the
      SPARTANS.]
KORYPHAIOS OF MEN   Behold our local Sons of the Soil, stretching
      their garments away from their groins, like wrestlers
Grappling with their plight. Some sort of athlete's disease, no doubt.
An outbreak of epic proportions.
                                        Athlete's foot?
No. Could it be athlete's . . . ?
KINESIAS   Who can tell us   1290
how to get hold of Lysistrata? We've come as delegates
to the Sexual Congress.
      [*Opening his cloak.*]   Here are our credentials.
KORYPHAIOS OF MEN [*Ever the scientist, looking from the Athenians to the*
      SPARTANS *and back again.*]   The words are different, but the malady
      seems the same.
      [*To* KINESIAS.] Dreadful disease. When the crisis reaches its height,
what do you take for it?
KINESIAS   Whatever comes to hand.   1295

But now we've reached the bitter end. It's Peace
or we fall back on Kleisthenes.
                                    And he's got a waiting list.
KORPHAIOS OF MEN [*To the* SPARTANS.]   Take my advice and put your
    clothes on. If someone
from that self-appointed Purity League comes by, you
may be docked. They do it to the statues of Hermes,[4]   1300
they'll do it to you.
KINESIAS [*Since he has not yet noticed the* SPARTANS, *he interprets the warn-
    ing as meant for him, and hurriedly pulls his cloak together, as do the other
    Athenians.*]   Excellent advice.
SPARTAN   Hit shorely is.
Hain't nothing to argue after. Let's git dressed.
        [*As they put on their cloaks, the* SPARTANS *are finally noticed by*
        KINESIAS.]
KINESIAS   Welcome, men of Sparta! This is a shameful
    disgrace to masculine honor.
SPARTAN   Hit could be worser.
Ef them Herm-choppers seed us all fired up,   1305
they'd *really* take us down a peg or two.
KINESIAS   Gentlemen, let's descend to details. Specifically,
    why are you here?
SPARTAN   Ambassadors. We come to dicker
'bout thet-thur Peace.
KINESIAS   Perfect! Precisely our purpose.
Let's send for Lysistrata. Only she can reconcile   1310
our differences. There'll be no Peace for us without her.
SPARTAN   We-uns ain't fussy. Call Lysistratos, too, if you want.
        [*The gates to the Akropolis open, and Lysistrata emerges, accompa-
        nied by her handmaid,* PEACE—*a beautiful girl without a stitch on.*
        PEACE *remains out of sight by the gates until summoned.*]
KORYPHAIOS OF MEN   Hail, most virile of women! Summon up all your
    experience:
Be terrible and tender,
                    lofty and lowbrow,
                                    severe and demure.
Here stand the Leaders of Greece, enthralled by your charm.   1315
They yield the floor to you and submit their claims for your arbitration.
LYSISTRATA   Really, it shouldn't be difficult, if I can catch them
    all bothered, before they start to solicit each other.
    I'll find out soon enough. Where's Peace?
                                    —Come here.
        [PEACE *moves from her place by the gates to* LYSISTRATA. *The dele-
        gations goggle at her.*]
Now, dear, first get those Spartans and bring them to me.   1320
Take them by the hand, but don't be pushy about it,
not like our husbands (no savoir-faire at all!).

---

4. Just before the great expedition left for Sicily, rioters (probably oligarchic conspirators opposed to the
expedition) broke the erect phalluses off many of the statues of the god Hermes that stood at the doors of
most Athenian houses.

Be a lady, be proper, do just what you'd do at home:
if hands are refused, conduct them by the handle.
    [PEACE *leads the* SPARTANS *to a position near* LYSISTRATA.]
And now a hand to the Athenians—it doesn't matter   1325
where; accept any offer—and bring *them* over.
    [PEACE *conducts the Athenians to a position near* LYSISTRATA, *oppo-
    site the* SPARTANS.]
You Spartans move up closer—right *here*—
[*To the Athenians.*]   and *you*
stand over *here.*
                —And now attend my speech.
    [*This the delegations do with some difficulty, because of the conflict-
    ing attractions of* PEACE, *who is standing beside her mistress.*]
I am a woman—but not without some wisdom:
my native wit is not completely negligible,   1330
and I've listened long and hard to the discourse of my
elders—my education is not entirely despicable.
                                            Well,
now that I've got you, I intend to give you hell,
and I'm perfectly right. Consider your actions:
                                    At festivals,
in Pan-Hellenic harmony, like true blood-brothers, you share   1335
the selfsame basin of holy water, and sprinkle
altars all over Greece—Olympia, Delphoi,
Thermopylai . . . (I could go on and on, if length
were my only object.)
                    But now, when the Persians sit by
and wait, in the very presence of your enemies, you fight   1340
each other, destroy *Greek* men, destroy *Greek* cities!
—Point One of my address is now concluded.
KINESIAS [*Gazing at* PEACE.]   *I'm* destroyed, if this is drawn out much
        longer!
LYSISTRATA [*Serenely unconscious of the interruption.*]   —Men of Sparta,
        I direct these remarks to you.
Have you forgotten that a Spartan suppliant once came   1345
to beg assistance from Athens? Recall Perikleidas:
Fifty years ago, he clung to our altar,
his face dead-white above his crimson robe, and pleaded
for an army.[5] Messene was pressing you hard in revolt,
and to this upheaval, Poseidon, the Earthshaker, added   1350
another.
        But Kimon took four thousand troops
from Athens—an army which saved the state of Sparta.
Such treatment have you received at the hands of Athens,
you who devastate the country that came to your aid!
KINESIAS [*Stoutly; the condemnation of his enemy has made him forget the
        girl momentarily.*]   You're right, Lysistrata. The Spartans are clearly in
        the wrong!   1355

5. After a disastrous earthquake the Spartans were in great danger as a result of a rebellion of their serfs,
the Messenian Helots. The Athenians under Cimon sent a large military force to help them (464 B.C.).

SPARTAN [*Guiltily backing away from* PEACE, *whom he has attempted to pat.*] Hit's wrong, I reckon, but that's the purtiest behind . . .

LYSISTRATA [*Turning to the Athenians.*] —Men of Athens, do you think I'll let you off?

Have you forgotten the Tyrant's days, when you wore
the smock of slavery,[6] when the Spartans turned to the
spear, cut down the pride of Thessaly, despatched the   1360
friends of tyranny, and dispossessed your oppressors?

Recall:

On that great day, your only allies were Spartans;
your liberty came at their hands, which stripped away
your servile garb and clothed you again in Freedom!

SPARTAN [*Indicating* LYSISTRATA.] Hain't never seed no higher type of
woman.   1365

KINESIAS [*Indicating* PEACE.] Never saw one I wanted so much to top.

LYSISTRATA [*Oblivious to the byplay, addressing both groups.*] With such a
history of mutual benefits conferred
and received, why are you fighting? Stop this wickedness!
Come to terms with each other! What prevents you?

SPARTAN We'd a heap sight druther make Peace, if we was   1370
indemnified with a plumb strategic location.

[*Pointing at* PEACE's *Rear.*]   We'll take thet butte.

LYSISTRATA Butte?

SPARTAN   The Promontory of Pylos—Sparta's Back Door.[7]
We've missed it fer a turrible spell.

[*Reaching.*]   Hev to keep our
hand in.

KINESIAS [*Pushing him away.*] The price is too high—you'll never take
that!

LYSISTRATA Oh, let them have it.

KINESIAS   What room will we have left   1375
for maneuvers?

LYSISTRATA   Demand another spot in exchange.

KINESIAS [*Surveying* PEACE *like a map as he addresses the* SPARTAN.] Then
you hand over to us—uh, let me see—
let's try Thessaly—
[*Indicating the relevant portions of* PEACE.] First of all, Easy
Mountain . . .
then the Maniac Gulf behind it . . .

and down to Megara
for the legs . . .

SPARTAN   You cain't take all of thet! Yore plumb   1380
out of yore mind!

LYSISTRATA [*To* KINESIAS.] Don't argue. Let the legs go.

[KINESIAS *nods. A pause. General smiles of agreement.*]

6. Hippias the tyrant had allowed exiled democrats to return to Attica, but they had to stay outside the
city and wear sheepskins so that they could readily be identified. With the help of Spartan soldiers the
exiles and the people of Attica finally defeated the Thessalian troops of Hippias.   7. The stock Athenian
joke about Spartan men's supposed predilection for anal intercourse with either women or other men. As
with Pylos here, the next lines contain double-barreled references to territories in dispute in the war and
salient portions of Peace's anatomy.

KINESIAS [*Doffing his cloak.*]   I feel an urgent desire to plow a few furrows.
SPARTAN [*Doffing his cloak.*]   Hit's time to work a few loads of fertilizer
    in.
LYSISTRATA   Conclude the treaty and the simple life is yours,
  If such is your decision convene your councils,   1385
  and then deliberate the matter with your allies.
KINESIAS   *Deliberate? Allies?*
                            We're over-extended already!
  Wouldn't every ally approve our position—
  Union Now?
SPARTAN   I know I kin speak for ourn.
KINESIAS   And I for ours.
                    They're just a bunch of gigolos.   1390
LYSISTRATA   I heartily approve.
                  Now first attend to your purification,
  then we, the women, will welcome you to the Citadel
  and treat you to all the delights of a home-cooked
  banquet. Then you'll exchange your oaths and pledge
  your faith, and every man of you will take his wife and   1395
  depart for home.
      [LYSISTRATA *and* PEACE *enter the Akropolis.*]
KINESIAS   Let's hurry!
SPARTAN   Lead on, everwhich
  way's yore pleasure.
KINESIAS   This way, then—and HURRY!
    [*The delegations exeunt at a run.*]
CHORUS OF WOMEN   I'd never stint on anybody.
  And now I include, in my boundless bounty,
        the younger set.   1400
  Attention, you parents of teenage girls
  about to debut in the social whirl.
      Here's what you get:
  Embroidered linens, lush brocades,
  a huge assortment of ready-mades,   1405
      from mantles to shifts;
  plus bracelets and bangles of solid gold—
  every item my wardrobe holds—
      absolute gifts!
  Don't miss this offer. Come to my place,   1410
  barge right in, and make your choice.
      You can't refuse
  Everything there must go today.
  Finders keepers—cart it away!
      How can you lose?   1415
  Don't spare me. Open all the locks.
  Break every seal. Empty every box.
      Keep ferreting—
  And your sight's considerably better than mine
  if you should possibly chance to find   1420
      a single thing.

CHORUS OF MEN   Troubles, friend? Too many mouths
   to feed, and not a scrap in the house
      to see you through?
   Faced with starvation? Don't give it a thought.   1425
   Pay attention; I'll tell you what
      I'm gonna do.
   I overbought. I'm overstocked.
   Every room in my house is clogged
      with flour (best ever),   1430
   glutted with luscious loaves whose size
   you wouldn't believe. I need the space;
      do me a favor:
   Bring gripsacks, knapsacks, duffle bags,
   pitchers, cisterns, buckets, and kegs   1435
      around to me.
   A courteous servant will see to your needs;
   he'll fill them up with A-1 wheat—
      and all for free!
   —Oh. Just one final word before   1440
   you turn your steps to my front door:
      I happen to own
   a dog. Tremendous animal.
   Can't stand a leash. And bites like hell—
      better stay home.   1445
      [*The united* CHORUS *flocks to the door of the Akropolis.*]
KORYPHAIOS OF MEN [*Banging at the door.*]   Hey, open up in there!
      [*The door opens, and the* COMMISSIONER *appears. He wears a*
      wreath, carries a torch, and is slightly drunk. He addresses the
      KORYPHAIOS.]
COMMISSIONER   You
   know the Regulations.
  Move along!
      [*He sees the entire* CHORUS.]
      —And why are YOU lounging around?
  I'll wield my trusty torch and scorch the lot!
      [*The* CHORUS *backs away in mock horror. He stops and looks at his*
      torch.]
  —*This* is the bottom of the barrel. A cheap burlesque bit.
  I refuse to do it. I have my pride.
      [*With a start, he looks at the audience, as though hearing a protest.*
      He shrugs and addresses the audience.]
                —No, choice, eh?   1450
  Well, if that's the way it is, we'll take the trouble.
  Anything to keep you happy.
      [*The* CHORUS *advances eagerly.*]
KORYPHAIOS OF MEN   Don't forget us!
  We're in this, too. Your trouble is ours!
COMMISSIONER [*Resuming his character and jabbing with his torch at the*
  CHORUS.]   Keep moving!
  Last man out of the way goes home without hair!
  Don't block the exit. Give the Spartans some room.   1455

They've dined in comfort; let them go home in peace.

[*The* CHORUS *shrinks back from the door.* KINESIAS, *wreathed and quite drunk, appears at the door. He speaks his first speech in Spartan.*]

KINESIAS   Hain't never seed sech a spread! Hit were splendiferous!

COMMISSIONER   I gather the Spartans won friends and influenced people?

KINESIAS   And *we've* never been so brilliant. It was the wine.

COMMISSIONER   Precisely.

The reason? A sober Athenian is just   1460
non compos. If I can carry a little proposal
I have in mind, our Foreign Service will flourish,
guided by this rational rule:

No Ambassador

Without a Skinful.

Reflect on our past performance:
Down to a Spartan parley we troop, in a state   1465
of disgusting sobriety, looking for trouble. It muddles
our senses: we read between the lines; we hear,
not what the Spartans say, but what we suspect
they might have been about to be going to say.
We bring back paranoid reports—cheap fiction, the fruit   1470
of temperance. Cold-water diplomacy, pah!

Contrast

this evening's total pleasure, the free-and-easy
give-and-take of friendship: If we were singing,

Just Kleitagora and me,

Alone in Thessaly,   1475

and someone missed his cue and cut in loudly,

Ajax, son of Telamon,

He was one hell of a man—

no one took it amiss, or started a war;
we clapped him on the back and gave three cheers.   1480

[*During this recital, the* CHORUS *has sidled up to the door.*]

—Dammit, are you back here again?

[*Waving his torch.*]   Scatter!
Get out of the road! Gangway, you gallowsbait!

KINESIAS   Yes, everyone out of the way. They're coming out.

[*Through the door emerge the* DELEGATION (OF SPARTANS), *a* (FLUTE-PLAYER), *the Athenian* (men), LYSISTRATA, KLEONIKE, MYR-RHINE, *and the rest of the women from the citadel, both Athenian and Peloponnesian. The Chorus splits into its male and female components and draws to the sides to give the procession room.*]

SPARTAN [*To the* (FLUTE-PLAYER).]   Friend and kinsman, take up them pipes a yourn.
I'd like fer to shuffle a bit and sing a right sweet   1485
song in honor of Athens and us'uns, too.

COMMISSIONER [*To the* (FLUTE-PLAYER).]   Marvelous, marvelous—come, take up your pipes!

[*To the* SPARTAN.] I certainly love to see you Spartans dance.

[*The* (FLUTE-PLAYER.) *plays, and the* SPARTAN *begins a slow dance.*]

SPARTAN   Memory,

send me   1490
your Muse,
who knows
our glory,
knows Athens'—
Tell the story: 1495
At Artemision[8]
like gods, they stampeded
the hulks of the Medes, and
beat them.

And Leonidas   1500
leading us—
the wild boars
whetting their tusks.
And the foam flowered,
flowered and flowed,   1505
down our cheeks
to our knees below.
The Persians there
like the sands of the sea—

Hither, huntress,[9]   1510
virgin, goddess,
tracker, slayer,
to our truce!
Hold us ever
fast together;   1515
bring our pledges
love and increase;
wean us from the
fox's wiles—

Hither, huntress!   1520
Virgin, hither!

LYSISTRATA [*Surveying the assemblage with a proprietary air.*] Well, the
preliminaries are over—very nicely, too.
So, Spartans,
[*Indicating the* PELOPONNESIAN WOMEN *who have been hostages.*]
Take these girls back home. And *you*
[*To the* ATHENIAN (*men*), *indicating the women from the Akropolis.*]
take *these* girls. Each man stand by his wife, each wife
by her husband. Dance to the gods' glory, and thank   1525
them for the happy ending. And, from now on, please be
careful. Let's not make the same mistakes again.
[*The* DELEGATIONS (OF SPARTANS *and the Athenian men*) *obey; the
men and women of the* CHORUS *join again for a rapid ode.*]

---

8. Site of an indecisive naval battle that took place off the coast while the Spartan king Leonidas held the
pass at Thermopylae against the Persians in 480 B.C.   9. Artemis.

CHORUS   Start the chorus dancing,
             Summon all the Graces,
        Send a shout to Artemis in invocation.   1530
             Call upon her brother,[1]
             healer, chorus master,
        Call the blazing Bacchus, with his maddened muster.

        Call the flashing, fiery Zeus, and
        call his mighty, blessed spouse,[2] and   1535
        call the gods, call all the gods,
        to witness now and not forget
        our gentle, blissful Peace—the gift,
             the deed of Aphrodite.

               Ai!   1540
          Alalai!   Paion!
          Leap you!   Paion!
          Victory!   Alalai!
       Hail!   Hail!   Hail!

LYSISTRATA   Spartan, let's have another song from you, a new one.   1545
SPARTAN   Leave darlin' Taygetos,
                      Spartan Muse! Come to us
                      once more, flyin'
                      and glorifyin'
                      Spartan themes: 1550
                      the god at Amyklai,
                      bronze-house Athene.[3]
                      Tyndaros' twins,[4]
                      the valiant ones,
                      playin' still by Eurotas' streams.[5]   1555

                      Up! Advance!
                      Leap to the dance!

                      Help us hymn Sparta,
                      lover of dancin',
                      lover of foot-pats,   1560
                      where girls go prancin'
                  like fillies along Eurotas' banks,
                whirlin' the dust, twinklin' their shanks,
                    shakin' their hair
                    like Maenads[6] playin'   1565
                    and jugglin' the thyrsis,
                    in frenzy obeyin'
                Leda's daughter, the fair, the pure
                Helen, the mistress of the choir.

                        Here, Muse, here!   1570
                        Bind up your hair!

---

1. Apollo.   **2.** Hera.   **3.** Athena had a bronze-plated temple in Sparta.   **4.** Castor and Pollux, Helen's brothers.   **5.** The river that runs by Sparta.   **6.** Female devotees of Dionysus.

Stamp like a deer! Pound your feet!
Clap your hands! Give us a beat!

Sing the greatest,
sing the mightiest,
sing the conqueror,
sing to honor her—

Athene of the Bronze House!
Sing Athene!
[*Exeunt omnes, dancing and singing.*]

1575

PLATO

429–347 B.C.

Socrates himself (see pp. 7–8) wrote nothing; we know what we do about him mainly from the writings of his pupil Plato, a philosophical and literary genius of the first rank. It is very difficult to distinguish between what Socrates actually said and what Plato put into his mouth, but there is general agreement that the *Apology*, which Plato wrote as a representation of what Socrates said at his trial, is the clearest picture we have of the historical Socrates. He is on trial for impiety and "corrupting the youth." He deals with these charges, but he also takes the opportunity to present a defense and explanation of the mission to which his life has been devoted.

The *Apology* is a defiant speech; Socrates rides roughshod over legal forms and seems to neglect no opportunity of outraging his listeners. But this defiance is not stupidity (as he hints himself, he could, if he had wished, have made a speech to please the court), nor is it a deliberate courting of martyrdom. It is the only course possible for him in the circumstances if he is not to betray his life's work, for Socrates knows as well as his accusers that what the Athenians really want is to silence him without having to take his life. What Socrates is making clear is that there is no such easy way out; he will have no part of any compromise that would restrict his freedom of speech or undermine his moral position. The speech is a sample of what the Athenians will have to put up with if they allow him to live; he will continue to be the gadfly that stings the sluggish horse. He will go on persuading them not to be concerned for their persons or their property but first and chiefly to care about the improvement of the soul. He has spent his life denying the validity of worldly standards, and he will not accept them now.

He was declared guilty and condemned to death. Though influential friends offered means of escape (and there is reason to think the Athenians would have been glad to see him go), Socrates refused to disobey the laws; in any case he had already, in his court speech, rejected the possibility of living in some foreign city.

The sentence was duly carried out. And in Plato's account of the execution we can see the calmness and kindness of a man who has led a useful life and who is secure in his faith that, contrary to appearances, "no evil can happen to a good man, either in life or after death."

The form of the *Apology* is dramatic: Plato re-creates the personality of his beloved teacher by presenting him as speaking directly to the reader. In most of the many books that he wrote in the course of a long life, Plato continued to feature Socrates as the principal speaker in philosophical dialogues that explored the ethical and political problems of the age. These dialogues (the *Republic* the most famous) were preserved in their entirety and have exerted an enormous influence on Western thought ever since. Plato also founded a philosophical school, the Academy, in 385 B.C., and it remained active as a center of philosophical training and research until it was suppressed by the Roman emperor Justinian in A.D. 529. Plato came from an aristocratic Athenian family and as a young man thought of a political career; the execution of Socrates by the courts of democratic Athens disgusted him with politics and prompted his famous remark that there was no hope for the cities until the rulers became philosophers or the philosophers, rulers. His attempts, however, to influence real rulers—the tyrant Dionysius of Syracuse in Sicily and, later, his son—ended in failure.

A. E. Taylor, *Plato, The Man and His Work* (1927), is a detailed analysis of the whole corpus of Platonic dialogues. G. M. A. Grube, *Plato's Thought* (1935), studies six principal themes of Platonic philosophy. R. S. Brumbaugh, *Plato for the Modern Age* (1962), presents a general introduction with stress on the historical background and an emphasis on the scientific and mathematical aspects of Plato's thought. On the importance of Socrates, see W. K. C. Guthrie, *A History of Greek Philosophy,* vol. 3 (1969), pp. 378–567.

PRONOUNCING GLOSSARY

The following list uses common English syllables and stress accents to provide rough equivalents of selected words whose pronunciation may be unfamiliar to the general reader.

Adeimantus: *ad-ee-mant'-us*

Aeacus: *ee'-ak-us*

Aeantodorus: *ai-ant-o-dor'-us*

Aeschines: *es'-kin-eez*

Amphipolis: *am-fip'-o-lis*

Anytus: *an'-i-tus*

Arginusae: *ar-gin-yoo'-sai*

Asclepius: *as-klee'-pee-us*

Cebes: *see'-beez*

Ceos: *ke'-os*

Cephisus: *ke'-fi-sus*

Chaerephon: *kai'-re-fon*

Crito: *crai'-toh*

Critobulus: *cri-to'-boo-luhs*

Demodocus: *dee-mod'-o-kus*

Echecrates: *ek-ek'-rat-eez*

Epigenes: *e-pig'-en-eez*

Evenus: *ee-vee'-nus*

Gorgias: *gor'-jee-as*

Leontium: *le-ont'-ee-um*

Lysanias: *lai-san'-ee-as*

Meletus: *mee-lee'-tus*

Minos: *mai'-nos*

Musaeus: *myoo-zee'-us*

Nicostratus: *ni-kos'-tra-tus*

Palamedes: *pal-am-ee'-deez*

Phaedo: *fee'-doh*

Potidaea: *pot-i-dee'-ah*

Prodicus: *pro'-dik-us*

Prytanes: *pri'-tan-eez*

Prytaneum: *pri-tan-ee'-um*

Rhadamanthus: *rad-am-anth'-us*

Simmias: *sim'-ee-as*

Theages: *thee-ah'-jeez*

Theosdotides: *thee-os-dot'-id-eez*

Triptolemus: *trip-to'-le-muhs*

The Apology of Socrates[1]

How you, O Athenians, have been affected by my accusers, I cannot tell; but I know that they almost made me forget who I was—so persuasively did

1. Translated by Benjamin Jowett. *Apology* here means "defense."

they speak; and yet they have hardly uttered a word of truth. But of the many falsehoods told by them, there was one which quite amazed me;—I mean when they said that you should be upon your guard and not allow yourselves to be deceived by the force of my eloquence. To say this, when they were certain to be detected as soon as I opened my lips and proved myself to be anything but a great speaker, did indeed appear to me most shameless—unless by the force of eloquence they mean the force of truth; for if such is their meaning, I admit that I am eloquent. But in how different a way from theirs! Well, as I was saying, they have scarcely spoken the truth at all; but from me you shall hear the whole truth: not, however, delivered after their manner in a set oration duly ornamented with words and phrases. No, by heaven! but I shall use the words and arguments which occur to me at the moment; for I am confident in the justice of my cause: at my time of life I ought not to be appearing before you, O men of Athens, in the character of a juvenile orator—let no one expect it of me. And I must beg of you to grant me a favor:—If I defend myself in my accustomed manner, and you hear me using the words which I have been in the habit of using in the agora,[2] at the tables of the money-changers, or anywhere else, I would ask you not to be surprised, and not to interrupt me on this account. For I am more than seventy years of age, and appearing now for the first time in a court of law, I am quite a stranger to the language of the place; and therefore I would have you regard me as if I were really a stranger, whom you would excuse if he spoke in his native tongue, and after the fashion of his country:—Am I making an unfair request of you? Never mind the manner, which may or may not be good; but think only of the truth of my words, and give heed to that: let the speaker speak truly and the judge decide justly.

And first, I have to reply to the older charges and to my first accusers, and then I will go on to the later ones.[3] For of old I have had many accusers, who have accused me falsely to you during many years; and I am more afraid of them than of Anytus and his associates, who are dangerous, too, in their own way. But far more dangerous are the others, who began when you were children, and took possession of your minds with their falsehoods, telling of one Socrates, a wise man, who speculated about the heaven above, and searched into the earth beneath, and made the worse appear the better cause.[4] The disseminators of this tale are the accusers whom I dread; for their hearers are apt to fancy that such enquirers do not believe in the existence of the gods. And they are many, and their charges against me are of ancient date, and they were made by them in the days when you were more impressible than you are now—in childhood, or it may have been in youth—and the cause when heard went by default, for there was none to answer. And hardest of all, I do not know and cannot tell the names of my accusers; unless in the chance case of a Comic poet.[5] All who from envy and malice have persuaded you—some of them having first convinced themselves—all

2. The marketplace.   3. Socrates had been the object of much criticism and satire for many years before the trial. He here disregards legal forms and announces that he will deal first with the prejudices that lie behind the formal charge that has been brought against him.   4. He was accused by some of his enemies of being a materialist philosopher who speculated about the physical nature of the universe and by others of being one of the Sophists, professional teachers of rhetoric and other subjects, many of whom taught methods that were more effective than honest.   5. He is referring to the poet Aristophanes, whose play *Clouds* (produced in 423 B.C.) is a broad satire on Socrates and his associates and a good example of the prejudice Socrates is dealing with, for it presents him propounding fantastic theories about matter and religion and teaching students how to avoid payment of debts.

this class of men are most difficult to deal with; for I cannot have them up here, and cross-examine them, and therefore I must simply fight with shadows in my own defence, and argue when there is no one who answers. I will ask you then to assume with me, as I was saying, that my opponents are of two kinds; one recent, the other ancient: and I hope that you will see the propriety[6] of my answering the latter first, for these accusations you heard long before the others, and much oftener.

Well, then, I must make my defence, and endeavor to clear away, in a short time, a slander which has lasted a long time. May I succeed, if to succeed be for my good and yours, or likely to avail me in my cause! The task is not an easy one; I quite understand the nature of it. And so leaving the event with God, in obedience to the law I will now make my defence.

I will begin at the beginning, and ask what is the accusation which has given rise to the slander of me, and in fact has encouraged Meletus to prefer this charge against me. Well, what do the slanderers say? They shall be my prosecutors, and I will sum up their words in an affidavit: 'Socrates is an evildoer, and a curious person, who searches into things under the earth, and in heaven, and he makes the worse appear the better cause; and he teaches the aforesaid doctrines to others.' Such is the nature of the accusation: it is just what you have yourselves seen in the comedy of Aristophanes, who has introduced a man whom he calls Socrates, going about and saying that he walks in air, and talking a deal of nonsense concerning matters of which I do not pretend to know either much or little—not that I mean to speak disparagingly of any one who is a student of natural philosophy.[7] I should be very sorry if Meletus could bring so grave a charge against me. But the simple truth is, O Athenians, that I have nothing to do with physical speculations. Very many of those here present are witnesses to the truth of this, and to them I appeal. Speak then, you who have heard me, and tell your neighbors whether any of you have ever known me hold forth in few words or in many upon such matters. . . . You hear their answer. And from what they say of this part of the charge you will be able to judge of the truth of the rest.

As little foundation is there for the report that I am a teacher, and take money;[8] this accusation has no more truth in it than the other. Although, if a man were really able to instruct mankind, to receive money for giving instruction would, in my opinion, be an honor to him. There is Gorgias of Leontium, and Prodicus of Ceos, and Hippias of Elis,[9] who go the round of the cities, and are able to persuade the young men to leave their own citizens by whom they might be taught for nothing, and come to them whom they not only pay, but are thankful if they may be allowed to pay them. There is at this time a Parian[1] philosopher residing in Athens, of whom I have heard; and I came to hear of him in this way:—I came across a man who has spent

6. He says this tongue in cheek, for he is actually paying no attention to legal propriety. This becomes clearer below, where he goes so far as to paraphrase the actual terms of the indictment and put into the mouths of his accusers the prejudice he claims is the basis of their action. 7. In Aristophanes' comedy Socrates first appears suspended in a basket; when asked what he is doing, he replies, "I walk in air and contemplate the sun." He explains that only by suspending his intelligence can he investigate celestial matters. 8. Unlike Socrates, who beggared himself in the quest for truth, the professional teachers made great fortunes. The wealth of Protagoras, the first of the Sophists who demanded fees, was proverbial. 9. In the Peloponnese. Hippias claimed to be able to teach any and all subjects, including handicrafts. Gorgias was famous as the originator of an antithetical, ornate prose style that had great influence. Leontium is in Sicily. Prodicus taught rhetoric and was well known for his pioneering grammatical studies. Ceos is an island in the Aegean. 1. From Paros, a small island in the Aegean.

a world of money on the Sophists, Callias, the son of Hipponicus, and knowing that he had sons, I asked him: 'Callias,' I said, 'if your two sons were foals or calves, there would be no difficulty in finding some one to put over them; we should hire a trainer of horses, or a farmer probably, who would improve and perfect them in their own proper virtue and excellence; but as they are human beings, whom are you thinking of placing over them? Is there any one who understands human and political virtue? You must have thought about the matter, for you have sons; is there any one?' 'There is,' he said. 'Who is he?' said I; 'and of what country? and what does he charge?' 'Evenus the Parian,' he replied; 'he is the man, and his charge is five minae.'[2] Happy is Evenus, I said to myself; if he really has this wisdom, and teaches at such a moderate charge. Had I the same, I should have been very proud and conceited; but the truth is that I have no knowledge of the kind.

I dare say, Athenians, that some one among you will reply, 'Yes, Socrates, but what is the origin of these accusations which are brought against you; there must have been something strange which you have been doing? All these rumors and this talk about you would never have arisen if you had been like other men: tell us, then, what is the cause of them, for we should be sorry to judge hastily of you.' Now I regard this as a fair challenge, and I will endeavor to explain to you the reason why I am called wise and have such an evil fame. Please to attend then. And although some of you may think that I am joking, I declare that I will tell you the entire truth. Men of Athens, this reputation of mine has come of a certain sort of wisdom which I possess. If you ask me what kind of wisdom, I reply, wisdom such as may perhaps be attained by man, for to that extent I am inclined to believe that I am wise; whereas the persons of whom I was speaking have a superhuman wisdom, which I may fail to describe, because I have it not myself; and he who says that I have, speaks falsely, and is taking away my character. And here, O men of Athens, I must beg you not to interrupt me, even if I seem to say something extravagant. For the word which I will speak is not mine. I will refer you to a witness who is worthy of credit; that witness shall be the God of Delphi[3]—he will tell you about my wisdom, if I have any, and of what sort it is. You must have known Chaerephon;[4] he was early a friend of mine, and also a friend of yours, for he shared in the recent exile of the people,[5] and returned with you. Well, Chaerephon, as you know, was very impetuous in all his doings, and he went to Delphi and boldly asked the oracle to tell him whether—as I was saying, I must beg you not to interrupt—he asked the oracle to tell him whether any one was wiser than I was, and the Pythian prophetess answered, that there was no man wiser. Chaerephon is dead himself; but his brother, who is in court, will confirm the truth of what I am saying.

Why do I mention this? Because I am going to explain to you why I have such an evil name. When I heard the answer, I said to myself, What can the god mean? and what is the interpretation of his riddle? for I know that I have no wisdom, small or great. What then can he mean when he says that I am

---

2. A relatively moderate sum; Protagoras is said to have charged one hundred minae for a course of instruction.   3. Apollo.   4. One of Socrates' closest associates (he appears in Aristophanes' comedy); he was an enthusiastic enough partisan of the democratic regime to have to go into exile in 404 B.C. when the Thirty Tyrants carried on an oligarchic reign of terror.   5. This refers to the exile into which all known champions of democracy were forced until the democracy was restored.

the wisest of men? And yet he is a god, and cannot lie; that would be against his nature. After long consideration, I thought of a method of trying the question. I reflected that if I could only find a man wiser than myself, then I might go to the god with a refutation in my hand. I should say to him, 'Here is a man who is wiser than I am; but you said that I was the wisest.' Accordingly I went to one who had the reputation of wisdom, and observed him— his name I need not mention; he was a politician whom I selected for examination—and the result was as follows: When I began to talk with him, I could not help thinking that he was not really wise, although he was thought wise by many, and still wiser by himself; and thereupon I tried to explain to him that he thought himself wise, but was not really wise; and the consequence was that he hated me, and his enmity was shared by several who were present and heard me. So I left him, saying to myself, as I went away: Well, although I do not suppose that either of us knows anything really beautiful and good, I am better off than he is,—for he knows nothing, and thinks that he knows; I neither know nor think that I know. In this latter particular, then, I seem to have slightly the advantage of him. Then I went to another who had still higher pretensions to wisdom, and my conclusion was exactly the same. Whereupon I made another enemy of him, and of many others besides him.

Then I went to one man after another, being not unconscious of the enmity which I provoked, and I lamented and feared this: But necessity was laid upon me,—the word of God, I thought, ought to be considered first. And I said to myself, Go I must to all who appear to know, and find out the meaning of the oracle. And I swear to you, Athenians, by the dog I swear![6]—for I must tell you the truth—the result of my mission was just this: I found that the men most in repute were all but the most foolish; and that others less esteemed were really wiser and better. I will tell you the tale of my wanderings and of the 'Herculean' labors, as I may call them, which I endured only to find at last the oracle irrefutable. After the politicians, I went to the poets; tragic, dithyrambic,[7] and all sorts. And there, I said to myself, you will be instantly detected; now you will find out that you are more ignorant than they are. Accordingly, I took them some of the most elaborate passages in their own writings, and asked what was the meaning of them—thinking that they would teach me something. Will you believe me? I am almost ashamed to confess the truth, but I must say that there is hardly a person present who would not have talked better about their poetry than they did themselves. Then I knew that not by wisdom do poets write poetry, but by a sort of genius and inspiration; they are like diviners or soothsayers who also say many fine things, but do not understand the meaning of them.[8] The poets appeared to me to be much in the same case; and I further observed that upon the strength of their poetry they believed themselves to be the wisest of men in other things in which they were not wise. So I departed, conceiving myself to be superior to them for the same reason that I was superior to the politicians.

At last I went to the artisans, for I was conscious that I knew nothing at all, as I may say, and I was sure that they knew many fine things; and here

6. A euphemistic oath (compare "by George").   7. The dithyramb was a short performance by a chorus, produced, like tragedy, at state expense and at a public festival.   8. For a fuller exposition of this famous theory of poetic inspiration see Plato's *Ion*.

I was not mistaken, for they did know many things of which I was ignorant, and in this they certainly were wiser than I was. But I observed that even the good artisans fell into the same error as the poets;—because they were good workmen they thought that they also knew all sorts of high matters, and this defect in them overshadowed their wisdom; and therefore I asked myself on behalf of the oracle, whether I would like to be as I was, neither having their knowledge nor their ignorance, or like them in both; and I made answer to myself and to the oracle that I was better off as I was.

This inquisition has led to my having many enemies of the worst and most dangerous kind, and has given occasion also to many calumnies. And I am called wise, for my hearers always imagine that I myself possess the wisdom which I find wanting in others: but the truth is, O men of Athens, that God only is wise; and by his answer he intends to show that the wisdom of men is worth little or nothing; he is not speaking of Socrates, he is only using my name by way of illustration, as if he said, He, O men, is the wisest, who, like Socrates, knows that his wisdom is in truth worth nothing. And so I go about the world, obedient to the god, and search and make enquiry into the wisdom of any one, whether citizen or stranger, who appears to be wise; and if he is not wise, then in vindication of the oracle I show him that he is not wise; and my occupation quite absorbs me, and I have no time to give either to any public matter of interest or to any concern of my own, but I am in utter poverty by reason of my devotion to the god.

There is another thing:—young men of the richer classes, who have not much to do, come about me of their own accord; they like to hear the pretenders examined, and they often imitate me, and proceed to examine others; there are plenty of persons, as they quickly discover, who think that they know something, but really know little or nothing; and then those who are examined by them instead of being angry with themselves are angry with me: This confounded Socrates, they say; this villainous misleader of youth!—and then if somebody asks them, Why, what evil does he practice or teach? they do not know, and cannot tell; but in order that they may not appear to be at a loss, they repeat the ready-made charges which are used against all philosophers about teaching things up in the clouds and under the earth, and having no gods, and making the worse appear the better cause; for they do not like to confess that their pretence of knowledge has been detected—which is the truth; and as they are numerous and ambitious and energetic, and are drawn up in battle array and have persuasive tongues, they have filled your ears with their loud and inveterate calumnies. And this is the reason why my three accusers, Meletus and Anytus and Lycon, have set upon me; Meletus, who has a quarrel with me on behalf of the poets; Anytus, on behalf of the craftsmen and politicians; Lycon, on behalf of the rhetoricians:[9] and as I said at the beginning, I cannot expect to get rid of such a mass of calumny all in a moment. And this, O men of Athens, is the truth and the whole truth; I have concealed nothing, I have dissembled nothing. And yet, I know that my plainness of speech makes them hate me, and what is their hatred but a proof that I am speaking the truth?—Hence has arisen the prejudice against me; and this is the reason of it, as you will find out either in this or in any future enquiry.

9. The connection of Meletus with poetry and of Lycon with rhetoric is known only from this passage.

I have said enough in my defence against the first class of my accusers; I turn to the second class. They are headed by Meletus, that good man and true lover of his country, as he calls himself. Against these, too, I must try to make a defence:—Let their affidavit be read: it contains something of this kind: It says that Socrates is a doer of evil, who corrupts the youth; and who does not believe in the gods of the state, but has other new divinities of his own.[1] Such is the charge; and now let us examine the particular counts. He says that I am a doer of evil, and corrupt the youth; but I say, O men of Athens, that Meletus is a doer of evil, in that he pretends to be in earnest when he is only in jest, and is so eager to bring men to trial from a pretended zeal and interest about matters in which he really never had the smallest interest. And the truth of this I will endeavor to prove to you.

Come hither, Meletus, and let me ask a question of you.[2] You think a great deal about the improvement of youth?

Yes, I do.

Tell the judges, then, who is their improver; for you must know, as you have taken the pains to discover their corrupter, and are citing and accusing me before them. Speak, then, and tell the judges who their improver is.—Observe, Meletus, that you are silent, and have nothing to say. But is not this rather disgraceful, and a very considerable proof of what I was saying, that you have no interest in the matter? Speak up, friend, and tell us who their improver is.

The laws.

But that, my good sir, is not my meaning. I want to know who the person is, who, in the first place, knows the laws.

The judges,[3] Socrates, who are present in court.

What, do you mean to say, Meletus, that they are able to instruct and improve youth?

Certainly they are.

What, all of them, or some only and not others?

All of them.

By the goddess Here,[4] that is good news! There are plenty of improvers, then. And what do you say of the audience,—do they improve them?

Yes, they do.

And the senators?[5]

Yes, the senators improve them.

But perhaps the members of the assembly[6] corrupt them?—or do they too improve them?

1. The precise meaning of the charge is not clear. As this translation indicates, the Greek words may mean "new divinities," with a reference to Socrates' famous inner voice, which from time to time warned him against action on which he had decided. Or the words may mean "practicing strange rites," though this charge is difficult to understand. In any case, the importance of the phrase is that it implies religious belief of some sort and can later be used against Meletus when he loses his head and accuses Socrates of atheism.   2. Socrates avails himself of his right to interrogate the accuser. He is, of course, a master in this type of examination, for he has spent his life in the practice of puncturing inflated pretensions and exposing logical contradictions in the arguments of his adversaries. He is here fulfilling his earlier promise to defend himself in the manner to which he has been accustomed and use the words that he has been in the habit of using in the agora (p. 728).   3. The jury; there was no judge in the Athenian law court. The Athenian jury was large; in this trial it probably consisted of five hundred citizens. In the following questions Socrates forces Meletus to extend the capacity to improve the youth to successively greater numbers, until it appears that the entire citizen body is a good influence and Socrates the only bad one. Meletus is caught in the trap of his own demagogic appeal.   4. Hera.   5. The five hundred members of the standing council of the assembly.   6. The sovereign body in the Athenian constitution, theoretically an assembly of the whole citizen body.

They improve them.

Then every Athenian improves and elevates them; all with the exception of myself; and I alone am their corrupter? Is that what you affirm?

That is what I stoutly affirm.

I am very unfortunate if you are right. But suppose I ask you a question: How about horses?[7] Does one man do them harm and all the world good? Is not the exact opposite the truth? One man is able to do them good, or at least not many;—the trainer of horses, that is to say, does them good, and others who have to do with them rather injure them? Is not that true, Meletus, of horses, or any other animals? Most assuredly it is; whether you and Anytus say yes or no. Happy indeed would be the condition of youth if they had one corrupter only, and all the rest of the world were their improvers. But you, Meletus, have sufficiently shown that you never had a thought about the young: your carelessness is seen in your not caring about the very things which you bring against me.

And now, Meletus, I will ask you another question—by Zeus I will: Which is better, to live among bad citizens, or among good ones? Answer, friend, I say; the question is one which may be easily answered. Do not the good do their neighbors good, and the bad do them evil?

Certainly.

And is there any one who would rather be injured than benefited by those who live with him? Answer, my good friend, the law requires you to answer—does any one like to be injured?

Certainly not.

And when you accuse me of corrupting and deteriorating the youth, do you allege that I corrupt them intentionally or unintentionally?

Intentionally, I say.

But you have just admitted that the good do their neighbors good, and evil do them evil. Now, is that a truth which your superior wisdom has recognized thus early in life, and am I, at my age, in such darkness and ignorance as not to know that if a man with whom I have to live is corrupted by me, I am very likely to be harmed by him; and yet I corrupt him, and intentionally, too—so you say, although neither I nor any other human being is ever likely to be convinced by you. But either I do not corrupt them, or I corrupt them unintentionally; and on either view of the case you lie. If my offence is unintentional, the law has no cognizance of unintentional offences: you ought to have taken me privately, and warned and admonished me; for if I had been better advised, I should have left off doing what I only did unintentionally—no doubt I should; but you would have nothing to say to me and refused to teach me. And now you bring me up in this court, which is not a place of instruction, but of punishment.

It will be very clear to you, Athenians, as I was saying, that Meletus has no care at all, great or small, about the matter. But still I should like to know, Meletus, in what I am affirmed to corrupt the young. I suppose you mean, as I infer from your indictment, that I teach them not to acknowledge the gods which the state acknowledges, but some other new divinities or spiritual agencies in their stead. These are the lessons by which I corrupt the youth, as you say.

---

7. This simple analogy is typical of the Socratic method; he is still defending himself in his accustomed manner.

Yes, that I say emphatically.

Then, by the gods, Meletus, of whom we are speaking, tell me and the court, in somewhat plainer terms, what you mean! for I do not as yet understand whether you affirm that I teach other men to acknowledge some gods, and therefore that I do believe in gods, and am not an entire atheist—this you do not lay to my charge,—but only you say that they are not the same gods which the city recognizes—the charge is that they are different gods. Or, do you mean that I am an atheist simply, and a teacher of atheism?

I mean the latter—that you are a complete atheist.[8]

What an extraordinary statement! Why do you think so, Meletus? Do you mean that I do not believe in the godhead of the sun or moon, like other men?

I assure you, judges, that he does not: for he says that the sun is stone, and the moon earth.[9]

Friend Meletus, you think that you are accusing Anaxagoras: and you have but a bad opinion of the judges, if you fancy them illiterate to such a degree as not to know that these doctrines are found in the books of Anaxagoras the Clazomenian,[1] which are full of them. And so, forsooth, the youth are said to be taught them by Socrates, when [they can buy the book in the theater district for one drachma at most][2] and laugh at Socrates if he pretends to father these extraordinary views. And so, Meletus, you really think that I do not believe in any god?

I swear by Zeus that you believe absolutely in none at all.

Nobody will believe you, Meletus, and I am pretty sure that you do not believe yourself. I cannot help thinking, men of Athens, that Meletus is reckless and impudent, and that he has written this indictment in a spirit of mere wantonness and youthful bravado. Has he not compounded a riddle, thinking to try me? He said to himself:—I shall see whether the wise Socrates will discover my facetious contradiction, or whether I shall be able to deceive him and the rest of them. For he certainly does appear to me to contradict himself in the indictment as much as if he said that Socrates is guilty of not believing in the gods, and yet of believing in them—but this is not like a person who is in earnest.

I should like you, O men of Athens, to join me in examining what I conceive to be his inconsistency; and do you, Meletus, answer. And I must remind the audience of my request that they would not make a disturbance[3] if I speak in my accustomed manner:

Did ever man, Meletus, believe in the existence of human things, and not of human beings? . . . I wish, men of Athens, that he would answer, and not be always trying to get up an interruption. Did ever any man believe in horsemanship, and not in horses? or in flute-playing, and not in flute-players? No, my friend; I will answer to you and to the court, as you refuse to answer

8. Meletus jumps at the most damaging charge and falls into the trap (see n. 1, p. 733).   9. Meletus falls back on the old prejudices that Socrates claims are the real indictment against him.   1. Clazomenae is in Asia Minor. Anaxagoras was a fifth-century philosopher and an intimate friend of Pericles, but this did not save him from indictment for impiety. He was condemned and forced to leave Athens. He is famous for his doctrine that matter was set in motion and ordered by Intelligence (*Nous*), which, however, did not create it. He also declared that the sun was a mass of red-hot metal larger than the Peloponnese and that there were hills and ravines on the moon.   2. The translator took this to mean that the doctrines of Anaxagoras were reflected in the works of the tragic poets; the bracketed passage reflects what is now the generally accepted interpretation.   3. Presumably due to the frustration of the enemies of Socrates, who see him assuming complete control of the proceedings and turning them into a streetcorner argument of the type in which he is invincible.

for yourself. There is no man who ever did. But now please to answer the next question: Can a man believe in spiritual and divine agencies, and not in spirits or demigods?

He cannot.

How lucky I am to have extracted that answer, by the assistance of the court! But then you swear in the indictment that I teach and believe in divine or spiritual agencies (new or old, no matter for that); at any rate, I believe in spiritual agencies,—so you say and swear in the affidavit; and yet if I believe in divine beings, how can I help believing in spirits or demigods;— must I not? To be sure I must; and therefore I may assume that your silence gives consent. Now what are spirits or demigods? are they not either gods or the sons of gods?

Certainly they are.

But this is what I call the facetious riddle invented by you: the demigods or spirits are gods, and you say first that I do not believe in gods, and then again that I do believe in gods; that is, if I believe in demigods. For if the demigods are the illegitimate sons of gods, whether by the nymphs or by any other mothers, of whom they are said to be the sons—what human being will ever believe that there are no gods if they are the sons of gods? You might as well affirm the existence of mules, and deny that of horses and asses. Such nonsense, Meletus, could only have been intended by you to make trial of me. You have put this into the indictment because you had nothing real of which to accuse me. But no one who has a particle of understanding will ever be convinced by you that the same men can believe in divine and super-human things, and yet not believe that there are gods and demigods and heroes.

I have said enough in answer to the charge of Meletus: any elaborate defence is unnecessary; but I know only too well how many are the enmities which I have incurred, and this is what will be my destruction if I am destroyed;—not Meletus, nor yet Anytus, but the envy and detraction of the world, which has been the death of many good men, and will probably be the death of many more; there is no danger of my being the last of them.

Some one will say: And are you not ashamed, Socrates, of a course of life which is likely to bring you to an untimely end? To him I may fairly answer: There you are mistaken: a man who is good for anything ought not to cal- culate the chance of living or dying; he ought only to consider whether in doing anything he is doing right or wrong—acting the part of a good man or of a bad. Whereas, upon your view, the heroes who fell at Troy were not good for much, and the son of Thetis[4] above all, who altogether despised danger in comparison with disgrace; and when he was so eager to slay Hector, his goddess mother said to him, that if he avenged his companion Patroclus, and slew Hector, he would die himself—'Fate,' she said, in these or the like words, 'waits for you next after Hector'; he, receiving this warning, utterly despised danger and death, and instead of fearing them, feared rather to live in dishonor, and not to avenge his friend. 'Let me die forthwith,' he replies, 'and be avenged of my enemy, rather than abide here by the beaked ships, a laughing-stock and a burden of the earth.' Had Achilles any thought of death and danger? For wherever a man's place is, whether the place which he has

---

4. Achilles (see *Iliad* 18.110ff.).

chosen or that in which he has been placed by a commander, there he ought to remain in hour of danger; he should not think of death or of anything but of disgrace. And this, O men of Athens, is a true saying.

Strange, indeed, would be my conduct, O men of Athens, if I who, when I was ordered by the generals whom you chose to command me at Potidaea and Amphipolis and Delium,[5] remained where they placed me, like any other man, facing death—if now, when, as I conceive and imagine, God orders me to fulfil the philosopher's mission of searching into myself and other men, I were to desert my post through fear of death, or any other fear; that would indeed be strange, and I might justly be arraigned in court for denying the existence of the gods, if I disobeyed the oracle because I was afraid of death, fancying that I was wise when I was not wise. For the fear of death is indeed the pretence of wisdom, and not real wisdom, being a pretence of knowing the unknown; and no one knows whether death, which men in their fear apprehend to be the greatest evil, may not be the greatest good. Is not this ignorance of a disgraceful sort, the ignorance which is the conceit that man knows what he does not know? And in this respect only I believe myself to differ from men in general, and may perhaps claim to be wiser than they are: —that whereas I know but little of the world below,[6] I do not suppose that I know: but I do know that injustice and disobedience to a better, whether God or man, is evil and dishonorable, and I will never fear or avoid a possible good rather than a certain evil. And therefore if you let me go now, and are not convinced by Anytus, who said that since I had been prosecuted I must be put to death (or if not that I ought never to have been prosecuted at all); and that if I escape now, your sons will all be utterly ruined by listening to my words—if you say to me, Socrates, this time we will not mind Anytus, and you shall be let off, but upon one condition, that you are not to enquire and speculate in this way any more, and that if you are caught doing so again you shall die:—if this was the condition on which you let me go, I should reply: Men of Athens, I honor and love you; but I shall obey God rather than you, and while I have life and strength I shall never cease from the practice and teaching of philosophy, exhorting any one whom I meet and saying to him after my manner: You, my friend,—a citizen of the great and mighty and wise city of Athens,—are you not ashamed of heaping up the greatest amount of money and honor and reputation, and caring so little about wisdom and truth and the greatest improvement of the soul, which you never regard or heed at all? And if the person with whom I am arguing, says: Yes, but I do care; then I do not leave him or let him go at once; but I proceed to inter-rogate and examine and cross-examine him, and if I think that he has no virtue in him, but only says that he has, I reproach him with undervaluing the greater, and overvaluing the less. And I shall repeat the same words to every one whom I meet, young and old, citizen and alien, but especially to the citizens, inasmuch as they are my brethren. For know that this is the command of God; and I believe that no greater good has ever happened in the state than my service to the God. For I do nothing but go about per-

---

5. Three battles of the Peloponnesian War in which Socrates had fought as an infantryman. The battle at Potidaea (in northern Greece) occurred in 432 B.C. (for a fuller account of Socrates' conduct there see Plato's *Symposium*). The date of the battle at Amphipolis (in northern Greece) is uncertain. The battle at Delium (in central Greece) took place in 424 B.C.   **6.** The next world (that is, the underworld); the dead were supposed to carry on a sort of existence below the Earth.

suading you all, old and young alike, not to take thought for your persons or your properties, but first and chiefly to care about the greatest improvement of the soul. I tell you that virtue is not given by money, but that from virtue comes money and every other good of man, public as well as private. This is my teaching, and if this is the doctrine which corrupts the youth, I am a mischievous person. But if any one says that this is not my teaching, he is speaking an untruth. Wherefore, O men of Athens, I say to you, do as Anytus bids or not as Anytus bids, and either acquit me or not; but whichever you do, understand that I shall never alter my ways, not even if I have to die many times.

Men of Athens, do not interrupt,[7] but hear me; there was an understanding between us that you should hear me to the end: I have something more to say, at which you may be inclined to cry out; but I believe that to hear me will be good for you, and therefore I beg that you will not cry out. I would have you know, that if you kill such an one as I am, you will injure yourselves more than you will injure me. Nothing will injure me, not Meletus nor yet Anytus—they cannot, for a bad man is not permitted to injure a better than himself. I do not deny that Anytus may, perhaps, kill him, or drive him into exile, or deprive him of civil rights; and he may imagine, and others may imagine, that he is inflicting a great injury upon him: but there I do not agree. For the evil of doing as he is doing—the evil of unjustly taking away the life of another—is greater far.

And now, Athenians, I am not going to argue for my own sake, as you may think, but for yours, that you may not sin against the God by condemning me, who am his gift to you. For if you kill me you will not easily find a successor to me, who, if I may use such a ludicrous figure of speech, am a sort of gadfly, given to the state by God; and the state is a great and noble steed who is tardy in his motions owing to his very size, and requires to be stirred into life. I am that gadfly which God has attached to the state, and all day long and in all places am always fastening upon you, arousing and persuading and reproaching you. You will not easily find another like me, and therefore I would advise you to spare me. I dare say that you may feel out of temper (like a person who is suddenly awakened from sleep), and you think that you might easily strike me dead as Anytus advises, and then you would sleep on for the remainder of your lives, unless God in his care of you sent you another gadfly. When I say that I am given to you by God, the proof of my mission is this:—if I had been like other men, I should not have neglected all my own concerns or patiently seen the neglect of them during all these years, and have been doing yours, coming to you individually like a father or elder brother, exhorting you to regard virtue; such conduct, I say, would be unlike human nature. If I had gained anything, or if my exhortations had been paid, there would have been some sense in my doing so; but now, as you will perceive, not even the impudence of my accusers dares to say that I have ever exacted or sought pay of any one; of that they have no witness. And I have a sufficient witness to the truth of what I say—my poverty.

Some one may wonder why I go about in private giving advice and busying myself with the concerns of others, but do not venture to come forward in

---

7. The disturbance this time is presumably more general, for Socrates is defying the court and the people.

public and advise the state. I will tell you why. You have heard me speak at sundry times and in divers places of an oracle or sign which comes to me, and is the divinity which Meletus ridicules in the indictment. This sign, which is a kind of voice, first began to come to me when I was a child; it always forbids but never commands me to do anything which I am going to do. This is what deters me from being a politician. And rightly, as I think. For I am certain, O men of Athens, that if I had engaged in politics, I should have perished long ago, and done no good either to you or to myself. And do not be offended at my telling you the truth: for the truth is, that no man who goes to war with you or any other multitude, honestly striving against the many lawless and unrighteous deeds which are done in a state, will save his life; he who will fight for the right, if he would live even for a brief space, must have a private station and not a public one.

I can give you convincing evidence of what I say, not words only, but what you value far more—actions. Let me relate to you a passage of my own life which will prove to you that I should never have yielded to injustice from any fear of death, and that 'as I should have refused to yield' I must have died at once. I will tell you a tale of the courts, not very interesting perhaps, but nevertheless true. The only office of state which I ever held, O men of Athens, was that of senator: the tribe Antiochis,[8] which is my tribe, had the presidency at the trial of the generals who had not taken up the bodies of the slain after the battle of Arginusae;[9] and you proposed to try them in a body, contrary to law, as you all thought afterwards; but at the time I was the only one of the Prytanes who was opposed to the illegality, and I gave my vote against you; and when the orators threatened to impeach and arrest me, and you called and shouted, I made up my mind that I would run the risk, having law and justice with me, rather than take part in your injustice because I feared imprisonment and death. This happened in the days of the democracy. But when the oligarchy of the Thirty was in power,[1] they sent for me and four others into the rotunda, and bade us bring Leon the Sal-aminian from Salamis,[2] as they wanted to put him to death. This was a specimen of the sort of commands which they were always giving with the view of implicating as many as possible in their crimes; and then I showed, not in word only but in deed, that, if I may be allowed to use such an expression, I cared not a straw for death, and that my great and only care was lest I should do an unrighteous or unholy thing. For the strong arm of that oppressive power did not frighten me into doing wrong; and when we came out of the rotunda the other four went to Salamis and fetched Leon, but I

8. The Council of the Five Hundred consisted of fifty members of each of the ten tribes into which the population was divided. Socrates' tribe, like the other nine, was named after a mythical hero, in this case Antiochus. Each tribal delegation acted as a standing committee of the whole body for a part of the year. The members of this standing committee were called Prytanes. In acting as a member of the council Socrates was not "engaging in politics" but simply fulfilling his duty as a citizen when called on.   9. An Athenian naval victory over Sparta, in 406 B.C. The Athenian commanders failed to pick up the bodies of a large number of Athenians whose ships had been destroyed. Whether they were prevented from doing so by the wind or simply neglected this duty in the excitement of victory is not known; in any case, the Athenian population suspected the worst and put all ten generals on trial, not in a court of law but before the assembly. The generals were tried not individually, but in a group, and condemned to death. The six who had returned to Athens were executed, among them a son of Pericles.   1. Socrates gives two instances of his political actions, one under the democracy and one under the Thirty Tyrants. In both cases, he was in opposition to the government. In 404 B.C., with Spartan backing, the Thirty Tyrants (as they were known to their enemies) ruled for eight months over a defeated Athens. Prominent among them was Critias, who had been one of the rich young men who listened eagerly to Socrates.   2. Athenian territory, an island off Piraeus, the port of Athens. Rotunda: the circular building in which the Prytanes held their meetings.

went quietly home. For which I might have lost my life, had not the power of the Thirty shortly afterwards come to an end. And many will witness to my words.

Now do you really imagine that I could have survived all these years, if I had led a public life, supposing that like a good man I had always maintained the right and had made justice, as I ought, the first thing? No indeed, men of Athens, neither I nor any other man. But I have been always the same in all my actions, public as well as private, and never have I yielded any base compliance to those who are slanderously termed my disciples, or to any other. Not that I have any regular disciples. But if any one likes to come and hear me while I am pursuing my mission, whether he be young or old, he is not excluded. Nor do I converse only with those who pay; but any one, whether he be rich or poor, may ask and answer me and listen to my words; and whether he turns out to be a bad man or a good one, neither result can be justly imputed to me; for I never taught or professed to teach him anything. And if any one says that he has ever learned or heard anything from me in private which all the world has not heard, let me tell you that he is lying.

But I shall be asked, Why do people delight in continually conversing with you? I have told you already, Athenians, the whole truth about this matter: they like to hear the cross-examination of the pretenders to wisdom; there is amusement in it. Now this duty of cross-examining other men has been imposed upon me by God; and has been signified to me by oracles, visions, and in every way in which the will of divine power was ever intimated to any one. This is true, O Athenians; or, if not true, would be soon refuted. If I am or have been corrupting the youth, those of them who are now grown up and become sensible that I gave them bad advice in the days of their youth should come forward as accusers, and take their revenge; or if they do not like to come themselves, some of their relatives, fathers, brothers, or other kinsmen, should say what evil their families have suffered at my hands. Now is their time. Many of them I see in the court. There is Crito, who is of the same age and of the same deme[3] with myself, and there is Critobulus his son, whom I also see. Then again there is Lysanias of Sphettus, who is the father of Aeschines—he is present; and also there is Antiphon of Cephisus, who is the father of Epigenes; and there are the brothers of several who have associated with me. There is Nicostratus the son of Theosdotides, and the brother of Theodotus (now Theodotus himself is dead, and therefore he, at any rate, will not seek to stop him); and there is Paralus the son of Demodocus, who had a brother Theages; and Adeimantus the son of Ariston, whose brother Plato[4] is present; and Aeantodorus, who is the brother of Apollodorus, whom I also see. I might mention a great many others, some of whom Meletus should have produced as witnesses in the course of his speech; and let him still produce them, if he has forgotten—I will make way for him. And let him say, if he has any testimony of the sort which he can produce. Nay, Athenians, the very opposite is the truth. For all these are ready to witness on behalf of the corrupter, of the injurer of their kindred, as Meletus and Anytus call me; not the corrupted youth only—there might

---

3. Precinct; the local unit of Athenian administration. Crito was a friend of Socrates who later tried to persuade him to escape from prison.   4. The writer of the *Apology*.

have been a motive for that—but their uncorrupted elder relatives. Why should they too support me with their testimony? Why, indeed, except for the sake of truth and justice, and because they know that I am speaking the truth, and that Meletus is a liar.

Well, Athenians, this and the like of this is all the defence which I have to offer. Yet a word more. Perhaps there may be some one who is offended at me, when he calls to mind how he himself on a similar, or even a less serious occasion, prayed and entreated the judges with many tears, and how he produced his children in court, which was a moving spectacle, together with a host of relations and friends; whereas I, who am probably in danger of my life, will do none of these things. The contrast may occur to his mind, and he may be set against me, and vote in anger because he is displeased at me on this account.[5] Now if there be such a person among you,—mind, I do not say that there is,—to him I may fairly reply: My friend, I am a man, and like other men, a creature of flesh and blood, and not 'of wood or stone,' as Homer says;[6] and I have a family, yes, and sons, O Athenians, three in number, one almost a man, and two others who are still young; and yet I will not bring any of them hither in order to petition you for an acquittal. And why not? Not from any self-assertion or want of respect for you. Whether I am or am not afraid of death is another question, of which I will not now speak. But, having regard to public opinion, I feel that such conduct would be discreditable to myself, and to you, and to the whole state. One who has reached my years, and who has a name for wisdom, ought not to demean himself. Whether this opinion of me be deserved or not, at any rate the world has decided that Socrates is in some way superior to other men. And if those among you who are said to be superior in wisdom and courage, and any other virtue, demean themselves in this way, how shameful is their conduct! I have seen men of reputation, when they have been condemned, behaving in the strangest manner: they seemed to fancy that they were going to suffer something dreadful if they died, and that they could be immortal if you only allowed them to live; and I think that such are a dishonor to the state, and that any stranger coming in would have said of them that the most eminent men of Athens, to whom the Athenians themselves give honor and command, are no better than women. And I say that these things ought not to be done by those of us who have a reputation; and if they are done, you ought not to permit them; you ought rather to show that you are far more disposed to condemn the man who gets up a doleful scene and makes the city ridiculous, than him who holds his peace.

But, setting aside the question of public opinion, there seems to be something wrong in asking a favor of a judge, and thus procuring an acquittal, instead of informing and convincing him. For his duty is, not to make a present of justice, but to give judgment; and he has sworn that he will judge according to the laws, and not according to his own good pleasure; and we ought not to encourage you, nor should you allow yourself to be encouraged, in this habit of perjury—there can be no piety in that. Do not then require me to do what I consider dishonorable and impious and wrong, especially

---

5. The accepted ending of the speech for the defense was an unrestrained appeal to the pity of the jury. Socrates' refusal to make it is another shock for the prejudices of the audience. **6.** In the *Odyssey* (19.173–74) Penelope says to her husband, Odysseus (who is disguised as a beggar), "Tell me of your family and where you come from. For you did not spring from an oak or a rock, as the old saying goes."

now, when I am being tried for impiety on the indictment of Meletus. For if, O men of Athens, by force of persuasion and entreaty I could overpower your oaths, then I should be teaching you to believe that there are no gods, and in defending should simply convict myself of the charge of not believing in them. But that is not so—far otherwise. For I do believe that there are gods, and in a sense higher than that in which any of my accusers believe in them. And to you and to God I commit my cause, to be determined by you as is best for you and me.[7]

There are many reasons why I am not grieved, O men of Athens, at the vote of condemnation. I expected it, and am only surprised that the votes are so nearly equal; for I had thought that the majority against me would have been far larger; but now, had thirty votes gone over to the other side, I should have been acquitted. And I may say, I think, that I have escaped Meletus. I may say more; for without the assistance of Anytus and Lycon, any one may see that he would not have had a fifth part of the votes,[8] as the law requires, in which case he would have incurred a fine of a thousand drachmae.

And so he proposes death as the penalty. And what shall I propose on my part, O men of Athens? Clearly that which is my due. And what is my due? What return shall be made to the man who has never had the wit to be idle during his whole life; but has been careless of what the many care for— wealth, and family interests, and military offices, and speaking in the assembly, and magistracies, and plots, and parties. Reflecting that I was really too honest a man to be a politician and live, I did not go where I could do no good to you or to myself; but where I could do the greatest good privately to every one of you, thither I went, and sought to persuade every man among you that he must look to himself, and seek virtue and wisdom before he looks to his private interests, and look to the state before he looks to the interests of the state; and that this should be the order which he observes in all his actions. What shall be done to such an one? Doubtless some good thing, O men of Athens, if he has his reward; and the good should be of a kind suitable to him. What would be a reward suitable to a poor man who is your bene-factor, and who desires leisure that he may instruct you? There can be no reward so fitting as maintenance in the Prytaneum,[9] O men of Athens, a reward which he deserves far more than the citizen who has won the prize at Olympia in the horse or chariot race, whether the chariots were drawn by two horses or by many. For I am in want, and he has enough; and he only gives you the appearance of happiness, and I give you the reality. And if I am to estimate the penalty fairly, I should say that maintenance in the Pry-taneum is the just return.

Perhaps you think that I am braving you in what I am saying now, as in what I said before about the tears and prayers. But this is not so. I speak rather because I am convinced that I never intentionally wronged any one,

7. The jury reaches a verdict of guilty. It appears from what Socrates says later that the jury was split: 280 for this verdict and 220 against it. The penalty is to be settled by the jury's choice between the penalty proposed by the prosecution and that offered by the defense. The jury itself cannot propose a penalty. Meletus demands death. Socrates must propose the lightest sentence he thinks he can get away with, but one heavy enough to satisfy the majority of the jury who voted him guilty. The prosecution probably expects him to propose exile from Athens, but Socrates surprises them.   8. Socrates jokingly divides the votes against him into three parts, one for each of his three accusers, and points out that Meletus's votes fall below the minimum necessary to justify the trial.   9. The place in which the Prytanes, as representatives of the city, entertained distinguished visitors and winners at the athletic contests at Olympia.

although I cannot convince you—the time has been too short; if there were a law at Athens, as there is in other cities, that a capital cause should not be decided in one day,[1] then I believe that I should have convinced you. But I cannot in a moment refute great slander; and, as I am convinced that I never wronged another, I will assuredly not wrong myself. I will not say of myself that I deserve any evil, or propose any penalty. Why should I? Because I am afraid of the penalty of death which Meletus proposes? When I do not know whether death is a good or an evil, why should I propose a penalty which would certainly be an evil? Shall I say imprisonment? And why should I live in prison, and be the slave of the magistrates of the year—of the Eleven?[2] Or shall the penalty be a fine, and imprisonment until the fine is paid? There is the same objection. I should have to lie in prison, for money I have none, and cannot pay. And if I say exile (and this may possibly be the penalty which you will affix), I must indeed be blinded by the love of life, if I am so irrational as to expect that when you, who are my own citizens, cannot endure my discourses and words, and have found them so grievous and odious that you will have no more of them, others are likely to endure me. No indeed, men of Athens, that is not very likely. And what a life should I lead, at my age, wandering from city to city, ever changing my place of exile, and always being driven out! For I am quite sure that wherever I go, there, as here, the young men will flock to me; and if I drive them away, their elders will drive me out at their request; and if I let them come, their fathers and friends will drive me out for their sakes.

Some one will say: Yes, Socrates, but cannot you hold your tongue, and then you may go into a foreign city, and no one will interfere with you? Now I have great difficulty in making you understand my answer to this. For if I tell you that to do as you say would be a disobedience to the God, and therefore that I cannot hold my tongue, you will not believe that I am serious; and if I say again that daily to discourse about virtue, and of those other things about which you hear me examining myself and others, is the greatest good of man, and that the unexamined life is not worth living, you are still less likely to believe me. Yet I say what is true, although a thing of which it is hard for me to persuade you. Also, I have never been accustomed to think that I deserve to suffer any harm. Had I money I might have estimated the offence at what I was able to pay, and not have been much the worse. But I have none, and therefore I must ask you to proportion the fine to my means. Well, perhaps I could afford a mina,[3] and therefore I propose that penalty: Plato, Crito, Critobulus, and Apollodorus, my friends here, bid me say thirty minae, and they will be the sureties. Let thirty minae be the penalty; for which sum they will be ample security to you.[4]

Not much time will be gained, O Athenians, in return for the evil name which you will get from the detractors of the city, who will say that you killed Socrates, a wise man; for they will call me wise, even although I am not wise, when they want to reproach you. If you had waited a little while, your desire

---

1. There was such a law in Sparta.   2. A committee that had charge of prisons and public executions.   3. It is almost impossible to express the value of ancient money in modern terms. A mina was a considerable sum; in Aristotle's time (fourth century B.C.) one mina was recognized as a fair ransom for a prisoner of war.   4. The jury decides for death (according to a much later source, the vote this time was three hundred to two hundred). The decision is not surprising in view of Socrates' intransigence. Socrates now makes a final statement to the court.

would have been fulfilled in the course of nature. For I am far advanced in years, as you may perceive, and not far from death. I am speaking now not to all of you, but only to those who have condemned me to death. And I have another thing to say to them: You think that I was convicted because I had no words of the sort which would have procured my acquittal—I mean, if I had thought fit to leave nothing undone or unsaid. Not so; the deficiency which led to my conviction was not of words—certainly not. But I had not the boldness or impudence or inclination to address you as you would have liked me to do, weeping and wailing and lamenting, and saying and doing many things which you have been accustomed to hear from others, and which, as I maintain, are unworthy of me. I thought at the time that I ought not to do anything common or mean when in danger: nor do I now repent of the style of my defence; I would rather die having spoken after my manner, than speak in your manner and live. For neither in war nor yet at law ought I or any man to use every way of escaping death. Often in battle there can be no doubt that if a man will throw away his arms, and fall on his knees before his pursuers, he may escape death; and in other dangers there are other ways of escaping death, if a man is willing to say and do anything. The difficulty, my friends, is not to avoid death, but to avoid unrighteousness; for that runs faster than death. I am old and move slowly, and the slower runner has overtaken me, and my accusers are keen and quick, and the faster runner, who is unrighteousness, has overtaken them. And now I depart hence condemned by you to suffer the penalty of death,—they too go their ways condemned by the truth to suffer the penalty of villainy and wrong; and I must abide by my award—let them abide by theirs. I suppose that these things may be regarded as fated,—and I think that they are well.

And now, O men who have condemned me, I would fain prophesy to you; for I am about to die, and in the hour of death men are gifted with prophetic power.[5] And I prophesy to you who are my murderers, that immediately after my departure punishment far heavier than you have inflicted on me will surely await you. Me you have killed because you wanted to escape the accuser, and not to give an account of your lives. But that will not be as you suppose: far otherwise. For I say that there will be more accusers of you than there are now; accusers whom hitherto I have restrained:[6] and as they are younger they will be more inconsiderate with you, and you will be more offended at them. If you think that by killing men you can prevent some one from censuring your evil lives, you are mistaken; that is not a way of escape which is either possible or honorable; the easiest and the noblest way is not to be disabling others, but to be improving yourselves. This is the prophecy which I utter before my departure to the judges who have condemned me.

Friends, who would have acquitted me, I would like also to talk with you about the thing which has come to pass, while the magistrates are busy, and before I go to the place at which I must die. Stay then a little, for we may as well talk with one another while there is time. You are my friends, and I should like to show you the meaning of this event which has happened to me. O my judges—for you I may truly call judges—I should like to tell you of a wonderful circumstance. Hitherto the divine faculty of which the inter-

---

5. As the dying Hector foretells the death of Achilles (see *Iliad* 22.418–24). 6. Socrates' prophecy was fulfilled, for all of the many different philosophical schools of the early fourth century B.C. claimed descent from Socrates and developed one or another aspect of his teachings.

nal oracle is the source has constantly been in the habit of opposing me even about trifles, if I was going to make a slip or error in any matter; and now as you see there has come upon me that which may be thought, and is generally believed to be, the last and worst evil. But the oracle made no sign of opposition, either when I was leaving my house in the morning, or when I was on my way to the court, or while I was speaking, at anything which I was going to say; and yet I have often been stopped in the middle of a speech, but now in nothing I either said or did touching the matter in hand has the oracle opposed me. What do I take to be the explanation of this silence? I will tell you. It is an intimation that what has happened to me is a good, and that those of us who think that death is an evil are in error. For the customary sign would surely have opposed me had I been going to evil and not to good.

Let us reflect in another way, and we shall see that there is great reason to hope that death is a good; for one of two things—either death is a state of nothingness and utter unconsciousness, or, as men say, there is a change and migration of the soul from this world to another. Now if you suppose that there is no consciousness, but a sleep like the sleep of him who is undisturbed even by dreams, death will be an unspeakable gain. For if a person were to select the night in which his sleep was undisturbed even by dreams, and were to compare with this the other days and nights of his life, and then were to tell us how many days and nights he had passed in the course of his life better and more pleasantly than this one, I think that any man, I will not say a private man, but even the great king will not find many such days or nights, when compared with the others. Now if death be of such a nature, I say that to die is gain; for eternity is then only a single night. But if death is the journey to another place, and there, as men say, all the dead abide, what good, O my friends and judges, can be greater than this? If indeed when the pilgrim arrives in the world below, he is delivered from the professors of justice in this world, and finds the true judges who are said to give judgment there, Minos and Rhadamanthus and Aeacus and Triptolemus,[7] and other sons of God who were righteous in their own life, that pilgrimage will be worth making. What would not a man give if he might converse with Orpheus and Musaeus and Hesiod[8] and Homer? Nay, if this be true, let me die again and again. I myself, too, shall have a wonderful interest in there meeting and conversing with Palamedes, and Ajax the son of Telamon,[9] and any other ancient hero who has suffered death through an unjust judgment; and there will be no small pleasure, as I think, in comparing my own sufferings with theirs. Above all, I shall then be able to continue my search into true and false knowledge; as in this world, so also in the next and I shall find out who is wise, and who pretends to be wise, and is not. What would not a man give, O judges, to be able to examine the leader of the great Trojan expedition; or Odysseus or Sisyphus,[1] or numberless others, men and

---

7. The mythical inventor of agriculture, who is associated with judgment in the next world only in this passage. Minos appears as a judge of the dead in Homer's *Odyssey* 11; Rhadamanthus and Aeacus, like Minos, were models of just judges in life and after death. The first three named by Socrates are sons of Zeus.   8. Greek poet (eighth century B.C.?) who wrote *The Works and Days,* a didactic poem containing precepts for the farmer. Orpheus and Musaeus are legendary poets and religious teachers.   9. Both victims of unjust trials. Palamedes, one of the Greek chieftains at Troy, was unjustly executed for treason on the false evidence of Odysseus. Ajax committed suicide after the arms of the dead Achilles were adjudged to Odysseus as the bravest warrior on the Greek side.   1. Famous for his unscrupulousness and cunning. Odysseus was the most cunning of the Greek chieftains at Troy and the hero of Homer's *Odyssey.* Each is presumably an example of the man who "pretends to be wise and is not."

women too! What infinite delight would there be in conversing with them and asking them questions! In another world they do not put a man to death for asking questions: assuredly not. For besides being happier than we are, they will be immortal, if what is said is true.

Wherefore, O judges, be of good cheer about death, and know of a certainty, that no evil can happen to a good man, either in life or after death. He and his are not neglected by the gods; nor has my own approaching end happened by mere chance. But I see clearly that the time had arrived when it was better for me to die and be released from trouble; wherefore the oracle gave no sign. For which reason, also, I am not angry with my condemners, or with my accusers; they have done me no harm, although they did not mean to do me any good; and for this I may gently blame them.

Still I have a favor to ask of them. When my sons are grown up, I would ask you, O my friends, to punish them; and I would have you trouble them, as I have troubled you, if they seem to care about riches, or anything more than about virtue; or if they pretend to be something when they are really nothing,—then reprove them, as I have reproved you, for not caring about that for which they ought to care, and thinking that they are something when they are really nothing. And if you do this, both I and my sons will have received justice at your hands.

The hour of departure has arrived, and we go our ways—I to die, and you to live. Which is better God only knows.

ARISTOTLE
384–322 B.C.

One member of Plato's Academy, Aristotle, was to become as celebrated and influential as his teacher. He was not, like Plato, a native Athenian; he was born in northern Greece, at Stagira, close to the kingdom of Macedonia, which was eventually to become the dominant power in the Greek world. Aristotle entered the Academy at the age of seventeen but left it when Plato died (347 B.C.). He carried on his researches (he was especially interested in zoology) at various places on the Aegean; served as tutor to the young Alexander, son of Philip II of Macedon; and returned to Athens in 335, to found his own philosophical school, the Lyceum, where he established the world's first research library. At the Lyceum he and his pupils carried on research in zoology, botany, biology, physics, political science, ethics, logic, music, and mathematics. He left Athens when Alexander died in Babylon (323 B.C.) and the Athenians, for a while, were able to demonstrate their hatred of Macedon and everything connected with it; he died a year later.

The scope of his written work, philosophical and scientific, is immense; he is represented here by some excerpts from the *Poetics,* the first systematic work of literary criticism in our tradition.

Aristotle's Poetics, translated by James Hutton (1982), is the best source for the student.

From Poetics[1]

* * * Thus, Tragedy is an imitation of an action that is serious, complete, and possessing magnitude; in embellished language, each kind of which is used separately in the different parts; in the mode of action and not narrated; and effecting through pity and fear [what we call] the *catharsis*[2] of such emotions. By "embellished language" I mean language having rhythm and melody, and by "separately in different parts" I mean that some parts of a play are carried on solely in metrical speech while others again are sung.

The constituent parts of tragedy. Since the imitation is carried out in the dramatic mode by the personages themselves, it necessarily follows, first, that the arrangement of Spectacle will be a part of tragedy, and next, that Melody and Language will be parts, since these are the media in which they effect the imitation. By "language" I mean precisely the composition of the verses, by "melody" only that which is perfectly obvious. And since tragedy is the imitation of an action and is enacted by men in action, these persons must necessarily possess certain qualities of Character and Thought, since these are the basis for our ascribing qualities to the actions themselves— character and thought are two natural causes of actions—and it is in their actions that men universally meet with success or failure. The imitation of the action is the Plot. By plot I here mean the combination of the events; Character is that in virtue of which we say that the personages are of such and such a quality; and Thought is present in everything in their utterances that aims to prove a point or that expresses an opinion. Necessarily, therefore, there are in tragedy as a whole, considered as a special form, six constituent elements, viz. Plot, Character, Language, Thought, Spectacle, and Melody. Of these elements, two [Language and Melody] are the *media* in which they effect the imitation, one [Spectacle] is the *manner,* and three [Plot, Character, Thought] are the *objects* they imitate; and besides these there are no other parts. So then they employ these six forms, not just some of them so to speak; for every drama has spectacle, character, plot, language, melody, and thought in the same sense, but the most important of them is the organization of the events [the plot].

Plot and character. For tragedy is not an imitation of men but of actions and of life. It is in action that happiness and unhappiness are found, and the end[3] we aim at is a kind of activity, not a quality; in accordance with their characters men are of such and such a quality, in accordance with their actions they are fortunate or the reverse. Consequently, it is not for the purpose of presenting their characters that the agents engage in action, but

---

1. Translated by James Hutton. Bracketed text has been added for clarity.   2. This is probably the most disputed passage in the Western critical tradition. There are two main schools of interpretation, which differ in their understanding of the metaphor implied in the word *catharsis.* Some critics take the word to mean "purification," implying a metaphor from the religious process of purification from guilt; the passions are "purified" by the tragic performance because the excitement of these passions by the performance weakens them and reduces them to just proportions in the individual. This theory was supported by the German critic Lessing. Others take the metaphor to be medical, reading the word as "purging" and interpreting the phrase to mean that the tragic performance excites the emotions only to allay them, thus ridding the spectator of the disquieting emotions from which he or she suffers in everyday life. Tragedy thus has a therapeutic effect.   3. Purpose.

rather it is for the sake of their actions that they take on the characters they have. Thus, what happens—that is, the plot—is the end for which a tragedy exists, and the end or purpose is the most important thing of all. What is more, without action there could not be a tragedy, but there could be without characterization. * * *

Now that the parts are established, let us next discuss what qualities the plot should have, since plot is the primary and most important part of tragedy. I have posited that tragedy is an imitation of an action that is a whole and complete in itself and of a certain magnitude—for a thing may be a whole, and yet have no magnitude to speak of. Now a thing is a whole if it has a beginning, a middle, and an end. A beginning is that which does not come necessarily after something else, but after which it is natural for another thing to exist or come to be. An end, on the contrary, is that which naturally comes after something else, either as its necessary sequel or as its usual [and hence probable] sequel, but itself has nothing after it. A middle is that which both comes after something else and has another thing following it. A well-constructed plot, therefore, will neither begin at some chance point nor end at some chance point, but will observe the principles here stated. * * *

Contrary to what some people think, a plot is not ipso facto a unity if it revolves about one man. Many things, indeed an endless number of things, happen to any one man some of which do not go together to form a unity, and similarly among the actions one man performs there are many that do not go together to produce a single unified action. Those poets seem all to have erred, therefore, who have composed a *Heracleid*, a *Theseid*, and other such poems, it being their idea evidently that since Heracles was one man, their plot was bound to be unified. * * *

From what has already been said, it will be evident that the poet's function is not to report things that have happened, but rather to tell of such things as might happen, things that are possibilities by virtue of being in themselves inevitable or probable. Thus the difference between the historian and the poet is not that the historian employs prose and the poet verse—the work of Herodotus[4] could be put into verse, and it would be no less a history with verses than without them; rather the difference is that the one tells of things that have been and the other of such things as might be. Poetry, therefore, is a more philosophical and a higher thing than history, in that poetry tends rather to express the universal, history rather the particular fact. A universal is: The sort of thing that (in the circumstances) a certain kind of person will say or do either probably or necessarily, which in fact is the universal that poetry aims for (with the addition of names for the persons); a particular, on the other hand is: What Alcibiades[5] did or had done to him. * * *

Among plots and actions of the simple type, the episodic form is the worst. I call episodic a plot in which the episodes follow one another in no probable or inevitable sequence. Plots of this kind are constructed by bad poets on their own account, and by good poets on account of the actors; since they are composing entries for a competitive exhibition, they stretch the plot beyond what it can bear and are often compelled, therefore, to dislocate the natural order. * * *

---

4. Historian of the Persian Wars, a contemporary of Sophocles.   5. A brilliant but unscrupulous Athenian statesman (fifth century B.C.).

Some plots are simple, others complex; indeed the actions of which the plots are imitation are at once so differentiated to begin with. Assuming the action to be continuous and unified, as already defined, I call that action simple in which the change of fortune takes place without a reversal or recognition, and that action complex in which the change of fortune involves a recognition or a reversal or both. These events [recognitions and reversals] ought to be so rooted in the very structure of the plot that they follow from the preceding events as their inevitable or probable outcome; for there is a vast difference between following from and merely following after. * * *

Reversal (Peripety) is, as aforesaid, a change from one state of affairs to its exact opposite, and this, too, as I say, should be in conformance with probability or necessity. For example, in *Oedipus,* the messenger[6] comes to cheer Oedipus by relieving him of fear with regard to his mother, but by revealing his true identity, does just the opposite of this. * * *

Recognition, as the word itself indicates, is a change from ignorance to knowledge, leading either to friendship or to hostility on the part of those persons who are marked for good fortune or bad. The best form of recognition is that which is accompanied by a reversal, as in the example from *Oedipus.* * * *

Next in order after the points I have just dealt with, it would seem necessary to specify what one should aim at and what avoid in the construction of plots, and what it is that will produce the effect proper to tragedy.

Now since in the finest kind of tragedy the structure should be complex and not simple, and since it should also be a representation of terrible and piteous events (that being the special mark of this type of imitation), in the first place, it is evident that good men ought not to be shown passing from prosperity to misfortune, for this does not inspire either pity or fear, but only revulsion; nor evil men rising from ill fortune to prosperity, for this is the most untragic plot of all—it lacks every requirement, in that it neither elicits human sympathy nor stirs pity or fear. And again, neither should an extremely wicked man be seen falling from prosperity into misfortune, for a plot so constructed might indeed call forth human sympathy, but would not excite pity or fear, since the first is felt for a person whose misfortune is undeserved and the second for someone like ourselves—pity for the man suffering undeservedly, fear for the man like ourselves—and hence neither pity nor fear would be aroused in this case. We are left with the man whose place is between these extremes. Such is the man who on the one hand is not pre-eminent in virtue and justice, and yet on the other hand does not fall into misfortune through vice or depravity, but falls because of some mistake;[7] one among the number of the highly renowned and prosperous, such as Oedipus and Thyestes and other famous men from families like theirs.

It follows that the plot which achieves excellence will necessarily be single in outcome and not, as some contend, double, and will consist in a change of fortune, not from misfortune to prosperity, but the opposite from prosperity to misfortune, occasioned not by depravity, but by some great mistake on the part of one who is either such as I have described or better than this rather than worse. (What actually has taken place confirms this; for though

---

6. The Corinthian herdsman.   7. The Greek word is *hamartia.* It has sometimes been translated as "flaw" (hence the expression "tragic flaw") and thought of as a moral defect, but comparison with Aristotle's use of the word in other contexts suggests strongly that he means by it "mistake" or "error" (of judgment).

at first the poets accepted whatever myths came to hand, today the finest trag-edies are founded upon the stories of only a few houses, being concerned, for example, with Alcmeon, Oedipus, Orestes, Meleager, Thyestes, Telephus, and such others as have chanced to suffer terrible things or to do them.) So, then, tragedy having this construction is the finest kind of tragedy from an artistic point of view. And consequently, those persons fall into the same error who bring it as a charge against Euripides that this is what he does in his tragedies and that most of his plays have unhappy endings. For this is in fact the right procedure, as I have said; and the best proof is that on the stage and in the dramatic contests, plays of this kind seem the most tragic, provided they are successfully worked out, and Euripides, even if in every-thing else his management is faulty, seems at any rate the most tragic of the poets. * * *

In the characters and the plot construction alike, one must strive for that which is either necessary or probable, so that whatever a character of any kind says or does may be the sort of thing such a character will inevitably or probably say or do and the events of the plot may follow one after another either inevitably or with probability. (Obviously, then, the denouement of the plot should arise from the plot itself and not be brought about "from the machine,' as it is in *Medea* and in the embarkation scene in the *Iliad*.[8] The machine is to be used for matters lying outside the drama, either antecedents of the action which a human being cannot know, or things subsequent to the action that have to be prophesied and announced; for we accept it that the gods see everything. Within the events of the plot itself, however, there should be nothing unreasonable, or if there is, it should be kept outside the play proper, as is done in the *Oedipus* of Sophocles.) * * *

The chorus in tragedy. The chorus ought to be regarded as one of the actors, and as being part of the whole and integrated into performance, not in Eurip-ides' way but in that of Sophocles. In the other poets, the choral songs have no more relevance to the plot than if they belonged to some other play. And so nowadays, following the practice introduced by Agathon,[9] the chorus merely sings interludes. But what difference is there between the singing of interludes and taking a speech or even an entire episode from one play and inserting it into another?

---

8. The reference is to an incident in the second book of the *Iliad*: an attempt of the Greek rank and file to return home and abandon the siege is arrested by the intervention of Athena. If it were a drama she would appear *on the machine*, literally the machine that was employed in the theater to show the gods flying in space. It has come to mean any implausible way of solving complications of the plot. Medea escapes from Corinth "on the machine" in her magic chariot.   9. A younger contemporary of Euripides; most of his plays were produced in the fourth century B.C.

PLAUTUS
254?–184? B.C.

The comedies of Plautus are the earliest Roman literature that survives, and they make an exuberant beginning. With their drawing of human character types, their extravagant puns and wordplay, their ingenious plot twists, and their impeccable timing of jokes and pacing of action, they are gems of dramatic art, and their broad farce and physical humor have delighted audiences of all periods. Plautus helped to shape the later European comic tradition, bequeathing to it not only plot elements and typical characters (the braggart, the grouch, the clever servant) but also whole plays. Shakespeare and Molière based comedies on Plautus's plays, and twentieth-century playwrights such as Friedrich Dürrenmatt and Jean Giraudoux have continued to borrow from him. The Broadway hit and film *A Funny Thing Happened on the Way to the Forum* is a recreation of Plautus's comedy that draws mainly on the play printed here, the *Pseudolus*.

Titus Maccius Plautus was born in the town of Sarsina in Umbria (northeastern Italy). Information about his life, as for many classical authors, is sparse. The traditional date of his birth is probably accurate to within a year or two. The date of his death is a mere guess, based on his apparent survival to a ripe old age. A much later writer says that Plautus made money in theatrical production as a young man but lost it in bad trading investments and was reduced to working in a mill, where he wrote three of his plays, but these details are probably fictitious. He certainly wrote and produced his plays in Rome, and their theatrical brilliance suggests practical experience as an actor before he began to write—a supposition strengthened if his name means what it seems to ("Titus the Flatfoot Clown"?). The twenty comedies that survive complete (out of perhaps 130) probably date from the last decades of his life, from around 210 to 184 B.C.

ROMAN COMEDY

The kind of comedy that Plautus wrote represents the convergence of several traditions, such as the burlesques on myth that were performed in the Greek areas of southern Italy and Sicily or native Italian farces improvised around stock situations and typical characters from daily life. The most important influence, however, was Greek New Comedy. The Old Comedy of Aristophanes—for example, *Lysistrata* (see p. 674)—which centered on extravagant fantasy, uninhibited obscenity, and pungent political and personal commentary, was a product of Athenian democracy. But the conquests of Alexander (died 323 B.C.), which ushered in the Hellenistic period, wrought huge changes in political conditions and in outlook. The New Comedy of this period, known to us mainly through substantial fragments and one complete play of the Greek poet Menander (344?–292? B.C.), reflects these altered conditions. Gone are fantasy, politics, and the chorus as an integral part of the drama. Instead, New Comedy portrays daily life centered on the family, with stereotyped situations and a repertoire of characters so typical that a conventional mask evolved for the actor playing each role and the audience could identify the character on sight (the slave, the young lovers, the old man, and so on). Much of the art of New Comedy was to combine and recombine stock characters and plot elements into new mixtures—a process that was infinitely extendable and, it seems, endlessly enjoyable to its audiences. Roman comic writers not only used these conventions; they also based each of their plays on a Greek comedy (or sometimes conflated two Greek models). They did more than translate or imitate, however. They rearranged freely, omitting some scenes and adding new ones, emphasizing certain themes at the expense of others, expanding and contracting various characters' roles. Plautus also recast as songs some scenes or passages that were spoken in the Greek plays, producing the metrically brilliant *cantica*, or lyric sections, that are a distinctive feature of his style.

Like his Greek models, Plautus presents typical characters responding in fairly predictable ways to stereotyped situations. An astonishing range of characters populates his plays: affluent citizens, respectable matrons, impecunious sons, parasites (professional meal-cadgers), slaves of both sexes, mercenary soldiers, prostitutes, pimps, cooks, quack doctors, and so on. These are caricatures of people who could be found filling well-defined social roles in any Hellenistic Greek city or in Rome itself. Many of these character types were to enjoy a long life on the European stage. Plautus's clever slaves, for example, are the ancestors of the irrepressible servant Dorine in Molière's *Tartuffe* (vol. 2, p. 13) and of the clever valets in Beaumarchais's eighteenth-century plays *The Marriage of Figaro* and *The Barber of Seville*. From such earlier examples as these to modern television sitcoms, stereotyped characters and situations have been used to reflect contemporary social concerns, just as they are in Greek New Comedy and Roman comedy.

One of the pleasures of comedy is that the sympathetic characters manage to overcome various obstacles to get what they want and achieve a happy ending. A common plot of this type in the ancient comedies revolves around a love intrigue. A young man of good family, dependent on his father for money and under his authority, is in love with a girl, but there is a social and/or economic impediment to their union. The girl is apparently lowborn and a foreigner, and so the boy's father opposes the match (or would if he knew about it); someone else is in love with her and has the money to procure her; she is in the power of someone else (usually disreputable and greedy)— any or all of these conditions may obtain. The young man, usually despairing and ineffectual, is aided by a clever slave, who improvises a stratagem, often involving impersonation, to get the girl for his master. The blocking characters—those who stand in the way of the young couple's desires and often represent the repressive aspects of society—are punished or absorbed into the festivities that mark the wish-fulfilling end of the play, in which the girl often is discovered to be wellborn and a citizen, mislaid in infancy, and therefore marriageable. Thus erotic desire and the demands of society, whose conflict underlies many a tragic situation, are harmonized in the end, and youth succeeds in pressing its claims against old age. On the way to this happy conclusion, the play explores such issues as intergenerational relations (particularly those between fathers and sons), the social roles defined by gender and class, money and economic relations, marriage and the structure of the family, the distinction between slavery and freedom, and the question of who does and does not belong in the community.

Such issues must have been important for the ancient city-state at any time, but a form of drama that explored them and harmoniously reconciled them was especially pertinent to Rome in the opening decades of the second century B.C. The power and economic prosperity brought about by the defeat of Carthage and a number of subsequent military successes caused rapid social and cultural changes that were beginning to strain the traditional fabric of Roman society. The comedy of Plautus puts us in Rome at the historical moment of transition from city-state to world empire, just when the social and economic tensions it reflects were becoming urgent.

Rome had clear class divisions and a strict, traditional code of public and private morality, which was now challenged by the temptations of prosperity. Within the family, hierarchical authority was, if anything, more rigid still. The father controlled the property and had the power of life and death over his children as well as his slaves. Married women of any social standing were expected to behave beyond hint of reproach, especially where marital fidelity was concerned. And yet the Romans seem to have enjoyed the spectacle, offered in one comedy after another, of upstanding citizens tricked and made ridiculous, of low-life pimps and soldiers wielding economic power over the supposedly respectable, of sons successfully eluding paternal authority, and of slaves much smarter than their owners. (Only the matronly ideal seems to have been off-limits to comedy, although the stage wife, more often than not, is a tiresome shrew.) Plautus, in fact, seems to have invented, or at least greatly expanded, the role of the clever slave, just at a time when slaves, captured in the Romans' many wars, were becoming more than ever a fact of Roman life. This systematic inversion of conventional social relations may have been permitted because comedy was performed at festivals, whose number had been growing in the late third century B.C. and continued to expand. The Romans had a well-developed sense of the distinction between business and leisure, and they were very good at enjoying themselves. The festival was a holiday from the business of daily life, and the normal rules could, while it lasted, be relaxed and even mocked. Comedy was part of this festive atmosphere; and if anyone thought that it allowed un-Roman behavior to go too far, it was always possible to reply that the characters and the plots were, after all, Greek. Although a bit of satire was possible and even expected, however, these plays did not mount any serious challenge to the social order. The festival, by providing a *temporary* relaxation of hierarchies and rules, ultimately strengthened them: when the festival was over, people went back to business-as-usual. In the same way, comedy did not seriously challenge the customary order of things but if anything affirmed it, for the plays usually end with an accommodation between social requirements and individual desire rather than the complete triumph of misrule.

Performances at these festivals were relatively informal, and because the plays had to compete with other events, such as gladiatorial shows, rope dancing, and boxing matches, they had to grab and keep the audience's attention. Temporary wooden scenery and seating were evidently erected for each festival and dismantled at its end (no permanent stone theater existed in Rome until the middle of the first century B.C.). The background scenery generally represented the facades of two, sometimes three, houses, each with a front door perhaps set within a roofed and columned porch. The setting was usually, though not always, in a town. The raised stage represented a street in front of the houses, and it was here, in the open, that the play's action occurred. Characters frequently engaged in asides to the audience, or could deliver soliloquies without seeing or being heard by others on stage. Conversely, one character or group of characters could spy on others from hiding. The side entrance on the audience's right (stage left) was imagined to lead to the forum; that on the left (stage right), to the harbor or outside the city. Seating was available to at least some of the audience. A portion of it was reserved for senators, and rank may have determined who got the rest as well, with the poor and slaves standing at the back. Social hierarchy therefore operated inside as well as outside the theater. It is fairly certain, in any case, that people from all levels of society could attend the plays, women and children as well as men, slaves as well as their masters. The actors were probably all men and wore masks. Many, if not all, may have been slaves themselves.

THE PSEUDOLUS

The *Pseudolus*, produced in 191 B.C., is a glorious example of Roman comedy. In adjacent houses represented by the background scenery, Simo and the pimp Ballio— types emblematic of social propriety and sleaze—live side by side. Their proximity illustrates the penetration of respectability by sordidness, and the hold Ballio has on his social superiors through their lust, their need for money, and his own shamelessness provides some pointed commentary on social pretensions. What unites these two worlds in the play's action is a typical amatory intrigue. Simo's penniless son Calidorus is in love with Phoenicium, a girl in Ballio's establishment, who has been all but sold to a soldier. Calidorus plays the helpless lover to the hilt but gets Phoenicium through the machinations of his slave, the title character. Pseudolus—the name means "liar"—is Roman comedy's greatest portrait of the clever slave. His deceit and his zest for carrying it out provide the driving force of the play. Not only does he improvise a plot out of thin air, thinking at lightning speed to take advantage of every opportunity (and everyone else's stupidity), but he also tells his opponents Simo and Ballio exactly what he intends to do—and then, having maximized the challenge, he proceeds to demolish their defenses. Calidorus may get his girl, but the triumph belongs to Pseudolus.

One unusual feature of the love intrigue is that the girl, Phoenicium, appears only twice, both times briefly, and never speaks. In addition, there is never any suggestion that Calidorus will marry her, and she does not rise in status. The only female character (except for other prostitutes working for Ballio), she is the object of transactions among men, and her role reflects a view of women as a means to male ends common in patriarchal societies such as Rome's. This treatment of her also means that love itself is relatively unimportant as a theme of the play, outside of Calidorus's sentimental posturing, and the emphasis shifts to Pseudolus's plot and the obstacles he must overcome. As a blocking character, the father, Simo, is not very formidable, although he keeps his son on a short leash where money is concerned. He represents paternal severity, and his more tolerant contemporary and neighbor Callipho is there to serve as a foil to him and remind him that he had his share of fun in his youth. He does embody the obstacle to desire that the family structure poses, but he pales beside Ballio. In the pimp, and in the soldier who can afford to buy Phoenicium, we see economic power at its repressive worst. It is typical of comedy's life-affirming triumph of desire over economics that Pseudolus turns this weapon against Ballio, leveraging five *minas* (Greek coins) into twenty and making imaginary sums circulate as bets in a dizzying process. Fittingly, it is ultimately Pseudolus himself who gets twenty *minas*, which materialize in the money Simo has to pay him as a result of their wager.

In the end, the slave emerges paramount and rewarded, the young lovers are united, and the father must give way with what grace he can muster. But these inversions are not the play's last word. The *Pseudolus* ends, as so many comedies do, with a feast emblematic of the continuity of life and its energies, represented on stage by the drunken Pseudolus himself. In the play's last lines, Simo is invited to join the celebration and is included in the general merrymaking: his claims too are acknowledged. Only Ballio and the challenge to social order that he represents are rejected.

The *Pseudolus* represents a further important aspect of Plautus's art. It is one of the best examples among his plays of theatrical self-consciousness, or *metatheater*. Especially through Pseudolus's words, we are often reminded that we are watching a play in which the characters are filling roles—an effect of which modern playwrights such as Pirandello, Brecht, and Beckett are especially fond. Not only is the dramatic illusion broken in small ways ("I don't want to repeat myself: that's how plays become too long"), but the improvisation of Pseudolus's plot and the charade he stages with Simia's help to trick Ballio are compared to the way a poet creates plot and action out of nothing but fantasy. This emphasis on fiction-making provides another link with the festival atmosphere surrounding the play and points explicitly to its removal from daily life. Through this device as well as in other ways, Plautine comedy offers a detached perspective from which Roman society could laugh at itself.

George Duckworth, *The Nature of Roman Comedy: A Study in Popular Entertainment* (1952), is a mine of information about the origins, conventions, style, and influence of Roman comedy. The performance and social context of Roman comedy are well discussed by Richard Beacham, *The Roman Theatre and its Audience* (1992). Erich Segal, *Roman Laughter: The Comedy of Plautus*, 2 ed. (1987), is a classic interpretation with particular reference to the festival setting. David Konstan, *Roman Comedy* (1983), discusses the ideology of the city-state in various plays by Plautus and Terence. On metatheater in Plautus, see Niall Slater, *Plautus in Performance: The Theatre of the Mind* (1985).

PRONOUNCING GLOSSARY

The following list uses common English syllables and stress accents to provide rough equivalents of selected words whose pronunciation may be unfamiliar to the general readers.

Ballio: *bahl'-ee-oh*

Calidorus: *kahl-i-doh'-rus*

Callipho: *kahl'-i-foh*

Charinus: *kahr-ee'-nus*

Plautus: *plaw'-tus*

Pseudolus: *soo'-doh-lus*

Pseudolus[1]

CHARACTERS

PSEUDOLUS, *a cunning slave*
CALIDORUS, *his master's teenaged son*
BALLIO, *a slave dealer and pimp*
SIMO, *Calidorus' father, a stern old man*
CALLIPHO, *Simo's friend, a tolerant old man*
HARPAX, *an officer's slave*
CHARINUS, *a young man, Calidorus' friend*
SIMIA, *a cunning slave*

YOUNG SLAVE, *an unnamed slave of Ballio's*
COOK, *anonymous, but not reticent*
COURTESANS, *Ballio's female slaves; silent roles*
    Delectium
    Obscenium
    Gymnasium
    Phoenicium
ATTENDANT SLAVES, *minor or silent roles*

Prologue[2]

You'd better rise and stretch your legs,
    Walk up and down the aisle;
Here comes a Plautine comedy,
    It's bound to last a while.

Act I

[*The stage depicts three adjacent houses on a street in Athens. In the center is Simo's residence, flanked by the houses of his wealthy neighbor Callipho (stage right) and the disreputable pimp Ballio (stage left). As the play opens, the slave* PSEUDOLUS *and his young master,* CALIDORUS, *emerge from Simo's front door.*

PSEUDOLUS *wears the bizarre stock costume of the cunning slave—his physical appearance will be graphically described later in the play.* CALIDORUS *is a typical lovesick adolescent—a handsome, well-dressed, well-mannered, and appealing youth. Though he is not unintelligent, he is predictably unresourceful and naive. He is now preoccupied with the scrutiny of folding wooden letter-tablets, a standard form of ancient correspondence.*]

ACT I, SCENE 1

PSEUDOLUS   Master, if only I could read your mind
    And learn the torture that's tormenting you,
    I'd gladly spare two men a lot of bother:
    I wouldn't need to ask, or you to answer.
    Now, since that's impossible, necessity   5
    Compels me to question you. Answer me this:
    Why have you been acting half-alive
    These last few days, toting letter-tablets

---

1. Translated by Peter L. Smith, who uses a five-beat line for the spoken passages of the original, two four-beat lines for each of Plautus's lines in chanted passages, and lyric stanzas for the parts that were sung.   2. This short prologue (two lines of Latin) may be a later addition replacing a longer prologue by Plautus that explained the situation and plot to the audience.

Everywhere and drenching them with tears,
Taking no one into your confidence?   10
[*Heroically.*] Give voice, that I may know what I know not.
CALIDORUS   Oh, Pseudolus, I'm suffering!
PSEUDOLUS   Jupiter forbid!
CALIDORUS   It's out of Jupiter's control;
Venus rules the region of my pain.
PSEUDOLUS   Am I allowed some knowledge? In the past,   15
You've made me privy-partner of your plans.
CALIDORUS   My attitude's unchanged.
PSEUDOLUS   Then state your problem.
I can offer cash, concern, or kind advice.
CALIDORUS [*Handing him the tablets.*]   Take this message; learn for yourself
Why I am quite consumptified with gloom and worry.   20
PSEUDOLUS   As you wish.
[*Examining tablets.*]   But oh! what's this?
CALIDORUS   What is it?
PSEUDOLUS   I think these letters must be sexy characters:
They're climbing all over each other.
CALIDORUS   Very funny.
PSEUDOLUS   Holy Pol, unless the Sibyl[3] reads this first,
No one else could ever decipher it.   25
CALIDORUS   Why are you so rude to charming letters,
Charming tablets, traced with a charming hand?
PSEUDOLUS   Excuse me, sir; do chickens now have hands?
These are hen-tracts.
CALIDORUS   Oh, you make me sick.
Read it or hand it back.
PSEUDOLUS   All right, I'll read.   30
Take heart.
CALIDORUS   My heart is lost.
PSEUDOLUS   Well, find it again!
CALIDORUS   No, I'll keep quiet; find it yourself in the wax.
That's where my heart resides—my breast is vacant now.
PSEUDOLUS [*Suddenly.*]   I see your girl friend, Calidorus.
CALIDORUS [*Startled.*]   Where is she?
Where?
PSEUDOLUS [*Pointing to her name.*]   Here, stretched out upon the boards,
relaxed in wax.[4]   35
CALIDORUS [*Furious.*]   May the gods all smother you—
PSEUDOLUS   —with happiness.
CALIDORUS [*Tragically.*]   My life's been brief, like a blade of summer grass:
Sudden was my birth, and suddenly I'm gone.
PSEUDOLUS   Shut up, I'm trying to read.
CALIDORUS   Why not begin?
PSEUDOLUS [*Reading.*]   "Phoenicium to her darling Calidorus: 40
With wax and string[5] and these appealing characters

---

3. Prophetess of Apollo. *Holy Pol*: a mild oath by Pollux (one of the Dioscuri, twin sons of
Zeus).   4. Wood tablets were coated with wax, on which letters were incised with a stylus.   5. To tie
together the wooden tablets when they were folded face to face.

I wish you love and health; your healing love I beg.
My eyes are moist, my heart and soul are faltering."
CALIDORUS   I'm sunk, Pseudolus! I can't find the healing love
To send her back.
PSEUDOLUS   What healing love?
CALIDORUS   The silver kind.   45
PSEUDOLUS [*Waving the tablets.*]   You're willing to repay her wooden love
With silver? Keep your wits about you, please!
CALIDORUS   Read on, and soon the letter will explain
How urgently that silver must be found.
PSEUDOLUS   "My pimp has sold me to a foreigner   50
(A Macedonian military man)
For twenty silver minas,[6] dearest love.
Before that soldier left, he paid out fifteen
In advance. Now there's a balance of only five.
Therefore the soldier left a token here,   55
A portrait wax impression from his ring,[7]
And so, when someone brings a token like it,
I'm to be sent with him at once. A day is set
For the transaction: next Dionysia."
CALIDORUS   And that's tomorrow! I'm on the brink of doom,   60
Unless you've help to offer.
PSEUDOLUS   Let me finish.
CALIDORUS   Yes! I feel as though I'm talking with her.
Read—you give me bittersweet delight.
PSEUDOLUS [*Reading again, with increasing fervor.*]   "Now our loves, our
lives, our passionate embraces,
Laughter, fun, sweet talk, and sexy face-to-faces,   65
Slender little hips and thighs a-jiggle,
Tender little lips and tongues a-wiggle,
Juicy jousts of bouncy-boob and titty-tickle—
All our hopes of orgiastic consummation
Face dismemberment, disaster, desolation,   70
If we fail to find some mutual salvation.
Everything I know I've tried to tell you clearly:
Now I'll put you to the test. One question, merely:
Are you in love or just pretending?
                                        Yours sincerely."
CALIDORUS   An awful letter, Pseudolus.
PSEUDOLUS   Absolutely awful!   75
CALIDORUS   Why aren't you crying?
PSEUDOLUS   I've got stony eyes; I can't
Implore them to spit out a single tear.
CALIDORUS   How's that?
PSEUDOLUS   Hereditary dry-eye-itis.
CALIDORUS   Won't you help me just a little?
PSEUDOLUS   What should I do?

---

6. Athenian coins.   7. His seal ring, the impression of which in wax had the same function in antiquity as our signatures do today.

CALIDORUS   *Oh, dear!*

PSEUDOLUS   "Oh, dear"? Great Herc,[8] no need to scrimp   80
In that department; go ahead.

CALIDORUS   I'm so depressed, I can't find any cash to borrow—

PSEUDOLUS   *Oh, dear!*

CALIDORUS   There's not a penny in the house—

PSEUDOLUS   *Oh, dear!*

CALIDORUS   He's going to carry off my girl tomorrow—

PSEUDOLUS   *Oh, dear!*

CALIDORUS   Do you really think that helps?

PSEUDOLUS   I give what I've got: 85
I have an inexhaustible supply of groans.

CALIDORUS   It's all over for me today. But can you lend me
A single drachma[9] I'd pay back tomorrow?

PSEUDOLUS   Hardly—not if my life were on the line.
What will you do with a drachma?

CALIDORUS   Buy a rope.   90

PSEUDOLUS   What for?

CALIDORUS   To help me learn to swing. [*Tragically.*] I plan,
Ere shadows fall, to fall among the shades.

PSEUDOLUS   Then who'll pay back the drachma that I gave you?
Is that why you want to hang yourself, you sneak,
To dun me out of the drachma I've donated?   95

CALIDORUS   There's just no way that I can go on living
If she is grabbed from me and granted to another.
            [*Bursts into tears.*]

PSEUDOLUS   Why cry, you cuckoo? You'll survive.

CALIDORUS   I've got to cry:
I haven't any money of my own,
No hope on earth of scraping up a scrap.   100

PSEUDOLUS   If I caught the drift of the lady's billet-doux,[1]
Your eyes have got to shower silver tears,
Or this pretentious crying act will help
As much as catching raindrops in a sieve.
Don't fear, my lovesick dear, I won't desert you.   105
Somewhere, somehow, some way (maybe) today
I'll find you silvery succor and salvation.
Where, oh where will it come from? I don't know,
But I know it will: I've got a twitching brow.

CALIDORUS   I only hope your deeds can match your words!   110

PSEUDOLUS   Holy Herc! If once I bang my holy gong,[2]
You know the holy rumpus I can raise!

CALIDORUS   You're now the repository of all my hopes.

PSEUDOLUS   Is it enough if I get this girl for you today
As your very own, or if I give you twenty minas?   115

CALIDORUS   It's enough—if it happens.

PSEUDOLUS   Demand your twenty minas,

---

8. Oath by Hercules.   9. Another Athenian coin.   1. Love letter.   2. Literally, "set the sacred implements in motion," as if beginning a religious ritual.

So you'll know I'll carry out my promise to you.
 Make it all quite legal: I'm itching to take the oath.
CALIDORUS [*Formally.*] Sir, this day will you give me twenty minas?
PSEUDOLUS Sir, I will. And now don't be a nuisance.   120
 Listen to this, if you still have any doubts:
 If all else fails, I'll pinch it from your papa.
CALIDORUS God save you, I love you! But look: if possible,
 For goodness' sake, put the pinch on Mother, too.
PSEUDOLUS Dispel these worries from your fevered nose.   125
CALIDORUS My fevered brain, do you mean?
PSEUDOLUS   I hate clichés.
 [*Hailing the audience.*] Now hear ye, hear ye! Lend an ear, ye!
 These are my solemn words of public warning
 For the throng assembled here this morning,
 All the citizens by tribe enrolled,   130
 All my acquaintances and friends of old:
 If you should meet me, be on guard today,
 And don't believe a single word I say.
CALIDORUS [*Startled by a noise from Ballio's house.*] Shh!
                 Sweet
   Hercules, keep quiet!
PSEUDOLUS   Why, what's up?
CALIDORUS The pimp's front door just gave a squeaking noise. 135
PSEUDOLUS I'd rather twist his legs[3] to make *him* squeak.
CALIDORUS He's coming out in person: Lord of Lies!

ACT I, SCENE 2

[*As* PSEUDOLUS *and* CALIDORUS *make themselves inconspicuous,* BALLIO *emerges from his house, wielding a whip; the villainous slave dealer is berating a number of cowering male* SLAVES, *who are his household servants and personal attendants.*]

BALLIO Get out! Come on, get out, you slugs!
  As merchandise you're rotten;
 You never do no good nohow:
  There's naught you've not forgotten!
 Unless I whip you up this way,   5
  You aren't the least bit useful;
 You're more like donkeys than like men,
  With ribs all striped and bruiseful.

 [*To audience.*] Flog 'em, you'll be the one to cry;
 These whipper-slappers always try,   10
 If given the chance, to have their fun:
 Grab, swipe, snitch, snatch, eat, drink, and run!
 That's just their nature; that's their way.
 And so, believe me when I say

---

3. Criminals were often punished by having their shins broken.

You'd rather wolves control your flock   15
Than have these thugs patrol your block.

It isn't always true, you know,
    That seeing is believing;
Though their appearances aren't bad,
    Their actions are deceiving.   20

[*Turning back to the* SLAVES.] Now unless you obey my command, all
        you guys,
If you don't wipe the sleepiness out of your eyes,
    I'll embroider your hips
    With such colorful strips
        You'll resemble bright linen embroidered for feasts,   25
Alexandrian coverlets covered with beasts.

I issued orders yesterday,
Your provinces were all assigned;
But you're such crooked characters,
So careless, so devoid of mind,   30
You can't remember any job
Without a swift kick from behind.
    Perhaps you hope to get so tough
    That my whip won't be hard enough.

[*To audience.*] Just look at that! No concentration.   35
[*Cracking his whip at the* SLAVES.] Pay attention, look this way!
Make sure you point your ears at me,
You whip-lashed human specimens!
Your backsides can't get any harder
Than this rawhide whip of mine.   40
[*Flicking his whip at various victims.*] How now? That hurt? There! That's
        what's done
If any slave shows disrespect.

Now form a line in front of me
And pay attention to my words.
[*Pointing to a* SLAVE.] You with the jug: go fetch some water;   45
Fill the kettle for the cook.
[*To another.*] You with the axe: you'll oversee
The Province of Woodsplittia.
SLAVE   This axe is dull.
BALLIO   What if it is?
You're not so very sharp yourself.
Do I enjoy your service less   50
Because you're blunted with my blows?
[*To another.*] Your task is cleaning up the house.
You know the job. Hurry up! Go in!
[*To another.*] Be thou the Keeper of the Couch.   55
[*To another.*] You get to wash the silver plate.

Make sure these jobs are done when I
Return from town; I want to find
That everything's been swept and sprinkled,
Cleaned and leveled, washed and shined.   60
Today's my birthday, don't you see?
You all must celebrate with me.

Throw ham and pork-rind in the pot,
Get sweetbreads, sow-tits boiling hot!
I want to throw a banquet which   65
Will make the powerful think I'm rich.
Go in and quickly work away;
When cook comes, we want no delay.
    [*Except for one personal* ATTENDANT, *Ballio's male* SLAVES *now
    enter the house.*]
I'm off to market, where I wish
To buy the market out of fish.   70
Lead on, my boy, and guard your back:
Let no one grab my money sack.

Just wait! It nearly slipped my mind
There's something else I've got to do.
You women! Listen to me please: 75
My next announcement is for you.
    [*Ballio's contingent of lovely* ladies (COURTESANS) *files out of his
    house in response to his call.*]
All you who live the languid life
Of dissipation and decay,
Famed mistresses of mighty men,
I'll learn your preference today: 80
Choose gluttony or liberty;
Siestas or self-interest.
Which girls I free and which I sell
I'll find out by a simple test.
Make sure I'm loaded down with loot   85
From lover-boys that you delight.
Bring in a full year's keep today
Or work the street tomorrow night.

Today's my birthday, as you know.
Bring on the lads who find you fun,   90
Who call you "sweetheart," "dearest darling,"
"Smoochie-pooch" or "honey-bun."
    Make sure they march up by platoon,
    Each bearing a beautiful birthday boon.

Why do I give you clothing, jewelry,   95
    Everything you need,
When you repay me with obnoxious

    Drunkenness and greed?
    You soak and guzzle, getting high,
    While I sit soberly and cry.   100

    So now I'm going to call your names,
        Proceeding one by one;
    Don't try to tell me, by and by,
        If any job's undone,
    That tasks have not been all assigned.   105
        Attention, everyone!

    I'll start with you, Delectium,
    The darling of the grain suppliers.
    All your lovers own vast stores
    Of golden wheat piled mountain high.   110
    Get grain delivered to us, please,
    For me and all my household staff—
    Enough to see us through the year.
    Bring me such wheaty affluence
    The citizens will change my name   115
    From Ballio, the pauper pimp,
    To Jason, prince of opulence.
        [*Exit Delectium.*]
CALIDORUS [*To* PSEUDOLUS.]   You hear this jailbird chattering?
    He's quite a loudmouth, don't you think?
PSEUDOLUS   Dear Pollux, yes! A foulmouth, too.   120
    Be quiet, though, and listen on!
BALLIO   Obscenium, your patrons are
    The butchers, rivals of the pimps:
    They make their living, just like us,
    By selling poor and tainted meat.   125
    Unless I get three meat-racks jammed
    With juicy carcasses today,
    Tomorrow I'll copy what was done
    To Dirce by the sons of Jove:[4]
    They bound her to a raging bull;   130
    I'll stretch you on an empty meat-rack.
        [*Exit Obscenium.*]
PSEUDOLUS [*To* CALIDORUS.]   This person makes me blazing mad!
    To think the manly youth of Athens
    Let him go on living here!
    Where do they hide, those lusty lads   135
    Who get their loving from a pimp?
    Why don't they meet and all combine
    To rid our public of these pests?
    But hey, no way!
    I've been too simple, too naive.   140
    Where would they get the nerve to hurt

---

4. Amphion and Zethus. In revenge for their stepmother Dirce's harsh treatment of their mother, Antiope, they bound Dirce to the horns of a bull.

The men their love enslaves them to?
Their passion keeps them all from doing
Things their pimps would not approve.
CALIDORUS   Be quiet!
PSEUDOLUS   Why?
CALIDORUS   You bother me   145
When you drown out this fellow's words.
PSEUDOLUS   Then I'll shut up.
CALIDORUS   I wish you would,
Instead of saying that you will.
BALLIO   It's your turn now, Gymnasium,
All of whose lover-boys possess   150
Untold reserves of olive oil.
If oil's not dumped in leather sacks
And carried here to me forthwith,
I'll have *you* dumped in a leather sack
And carried to the whorehouse shed.   155
There you'll be issued with a couch
Where you will get no sleep, but where,
To the point of sheer exhaustion. . . . Do you
Get the drift of my remarks?
[See here, you snake! When you've so many   160
Boyfriends oozing olive oil,
Do any of your fellow slaves
Have hair a wee bit glossier?
Do I enjoy a salad that's
A smidgen tastier? I know,   165
You don't care very much for oil;
You like to drench yourself in wine.
I'll check your faults in one fell swoop
If my commands aren't all obeyed.][5]
        [*Exit Gymnasium.*]
But you, who are always on the point   170
Of paying cash for liberty,
So skilled in promising, less skilled
In having promises fulfilled:
Phoenicium, it's you I mean,
You plaything of the upper class!   175
Unless your boyfriends' grand estates
Provide me all your keep today,
Tomorrow, dear Phoenicium,
I'll tan your hide Phoenician red
And pack you off to the whorehouse shed.   180
        [*Exit Phoenicium.*]

ACT I, SCENE 3

CALIDORUS   Pseudolus, don't you hear what he's saying?
PSEUDOLUS   Sir, my attention's undivided.

5. The bracketed passage is thought to be a later addition to the original text.

CALIDORUS Help me: what should I send this man
    To stop my girl from going on sale?
PSEUDOLUS Don't worry! Keep your mind unclouded; 5
    I'll look after you and me.
    This fellow and I've been friends for years;
    We've traded favors back and forth.
    I'll send him a great big birthday gift:
    A bulging bundle of misery. 10
CALIDORUS What's the use?
PSEUDOLUS   Can't you change the subject?
CALIDORUS But—
PSEUDOLUS   Tut!
CALIDORUS   I'm tortured!
PSEUDOLUS   Toughen up!
CALIDORUS I can't.
PSEUDOLUS   Well, force yourself!
CALIDORUS   How can I?
PSEUDOLUS Try to control your emotions, man!
    Concentrate on constructive thoughts; 15
    When things go wrong, don't pander to passion.
CALIDORUS That's all nonsense; there's no pleasure
    In love unless you can play the fool.
PSEUDOLUS Must you?
CALIDORUS   Pseudolus, let me be silly. Please!
PSEUDOLUS I'll let you, if you let me leave. 20
CALIDORUS Wait! Wait! I'll be just the way you want me.
PSEUDOLUS Now you're sounding sensible.
BALLIO It's late; time's wasting. Move, slave, move!
      [BALLIO *and his* SLAVE *start to move offstage.*]
CALIDORUS Hey, he's leaving. Why not call him?
PSEUDOLUS [*Restraining* CALIDORUS.] Slow down! Easy does it.
CALIDORUS   He
    mustn't leave. 25
BALLIO Dammit, move, you lazy slave!
PSEUDOLUS [*Aloud to* BALLIO.] Birthday boy! Hey, birthday boy!
    I'm calling you. Hey, birthday boy!
    Come on back, take a look at us.
    Though you're such a busy person, 30
    We'll detain you. Wait! See,
    People want to talk to you!
BALLIO What's this? Who'd hold up
    A very busy man like me?
PSEUDOLUS A friend and helpmate from your past. 35
BALLIO The past is dead; I live right now.
PSEUDOLUS You blasted boor!
BALLIO   You blasted bother!
CALIDORUS Seize the fellow; chase him!
BALLIO [*To his* SLAVE.]   Move on, boy.
PSEUDOLUS Let's go round and block his way.
BALLIO Jupiter damn you, whoever you are! 40

PSEUDOLUS   I wish you—

BALLIO   —the same to you both!
   Come on, forward march, my boy.

PSEUDOLUS   May we not have a word with you?

BALLIO   No, you may not when I'm not in the mood.

PSEUDOLUS   Not even something advantageous?   45

BALLIO   Will you or won't you let me leave?

PSEUDOLUS   No, wait!

BALLIO   Let go.

CALIDORUS   Ballio, listen! Are you deaf?

BALLIO   Yes, to empty words and wallets.

CALIDORUS   I always gave you cash in the past.

BALLIO   Cash in the past is not what I'm after.   50

CALIDORUS   I'll give when I get it.

BALLIO   You'll have when you've got it.

CALIDORUS   Oh, how foolishly I've wasted
   All my presents and payments to you!

BALLIO   Now that your account's defunct   55
   You want to pay me off in words.
   Stupid boy! Your books are closed.

PSEUDOLUS   Just realize who this boy is!

BALLIO   I've known for ages who he *was*;
   He should discover who he *is*.   60
   [*To his* SLAVE.] Let's get walking.

PSEUDOLUS   Ballio, could you
   Grant us just a single glance?
   There may be filthy lucre.

BALLIO   *Lucre!*
   That's a word that's worth a glance.
   If I were involved in sacrifice   65
   To mighty Jupiter on high,
   Holding sacred vessels in my hands,
   And there and then I saw a chance
   Of finding filthy lucre—well,
   I'd ditch the whole divine affair.   70
   All else aside, lucre's one
   Religious force I can't resist.

PSEUDOLUS [*To* CALIDORUS.]   The gods we honor and revere
   This fellow holds in total scorn.

BALLIO [*Aside.*]   I'll speak to him. [*To* PSEUDOLUS.] My kindest
      greetings,   75
   Most egregious slave in Athens!

PSEUDOLUS   This lad and I would like the gods
   To shower blessings on your head;
   But, if you get your just deserts,
   The gods are bound to cut you dead.   80

BALLIO [*Ignoring* PSEUDOLUS.]   What's the trouble, Calidorus?

CALIDORUS   Love and cruel lack of cash.

BALLIO   "What a pity!" I might say—
   If pity kept my stomach full.

PSEUDOLUS   O.K. We know the type you are: 85
   No need at all to advertise.
   But do you know what we want?
BALLIO   Oh, Pollux! Pretty well: trouble for me!
PSEUDOLUS   That, too; but there is something else.
   Come on, pay attention.
BALLIO   I'm listening.   90
   Since you see I'm very busy,
   Keep your story cut and dried.
PSEUDOLUS   My man's ashamed, because he promised
   On the appointed day to give you
   Twenty minas for his girl,   95
   And hasn't arranged delivery.
BALLIO   If you've got to bear some burden,
   Shame's far easier than disgust.
   He hasn't delivered: he's feeling down;
   I haven't collected: I'm fed up!   100
PSEUDOLUS   He'll come across, he'll raise the money;
   Just you wait a few more days.
   You see, he's terribly afraid
   You'll sell his girl friend out of spite.
BALLIO   If he wanted, he had a chance   105
   To pay me the money long ago.
CALIDORUS   What if I didn't have the cash?
BALLIO   If you were in love, you'd have floated a loan.
   You could have gone to a financier;
   You could have carried a carrying charge;   110
   You could have defrauded dear old Dad.
PSEUDOLUS   This boy defraud his dad? Outrageous!
   No danger you would ever suggest
   A moral act!
BALLIO   That would be un-pimp-ly.
CALIDORUS   How could I defraud my father,   115
   When he's such a sly old man?
   And even if I had the chance,
   Filial love forbids!
BALLIO   I see.
   Then hug that filial love of yours
   At night instead of Phoenicium.   120
   But since you apparently prefer
   To put filial love before romance,
   Is every man alive your father?
   Is there no one you could ask
   To lend you money?
CALIDORUS   Lend? Oh, no: 125
   The word itself is dead and buried.
PSEUDOLUS   Holy Herc, no lending these days!
   Bloated bankers leave the table
   Gorged on debts that they've recalled,

And let their creditors go starving;[6]   130
  All the world is far too cagey
  Ever to credit another man.
CALIDORUS   I'm most unhappy. I can't find
  A solitary silver piece;
  And so, unhappily I die   135
  Of love and lack of currency.
BALLIO   Corner the market in olive oil!
  Speculate and sell for cash.
  By Herc, I'm sure that you could put
  At least two hundred in your pocket.   140
CALIDORUS   Fat chance! The wretched law declares
  I'm underage.[7] Everyone's scared
  To give me credit.
BALLIO   That's my kind
  Of law: I'm scared to give you credit.
PSEUDOLUS   Credit! Hey, aren't you satisfied   145
  To know how useful he's been to you?
BALLIO   There's no such thing as a useful lover
  Unless he gives perpetually.
  Let him give, give; and when there's
  Nothing left, then let him cease to love.   150
CALIDORUS   Have you no pity?
BALLIO   Look: you're coming
  Empty-handed. Words don't clink.
  Yet I sincerely hope you'll live
  And thrive.
PSEUDOLUS   You speak as if he's dying.
BALLIO   Dead, as far as I'm concerned—   155
  If he keeps on talking the way he has.
  A lover's given up the ghost
  When he starts pleading with a pimp.
  Learn to sing a loud lament
  That has a silvery, tinkling tune;   160
  Toward your present woeful dirge
  About your lack of cash, I feel
  A stepmother's sympathy.
PSEUDOLUS   What?
  Were you once married to his father?
BALLIO   God forbid!
PSEUDOLUS   Do as we ask you, Ballio.   165
  Give *me* credit, if you're afraid
  To trust this boy. Within three days
  By land or sea (or somewhere else)
  I'll scrape this money up for you.
BALLIO   Give *you* credit?

---

6. A year before the play was produced, bankers (who did their business at tables in the forum) were punished for cheating their own creditors.   7. I.e., under twenty-five and so legally prohibited from borrowing or engaging in business.

PSEUDOLUS   Why not?

BALLIO   Well,   170
  To give you credit would be much
  Like tying up a hungry dog
  With twisted strips of mutton tripe.

CALIDORUS   How, when I'm so deserving, can you
  Show this kind of gratitude?   175

BALLIO   Well, what do you want?

CALIDORUS   I want you to wait,
  Six days only, more or less,
  And don't sell her or destroy me,
  The man who loves her.

BALLIO   Oh, cheer up!
  I'm prepared to wait six months.   180

CALIDORUS   Hurray! You dear, delightful man!

BALLIO   Hang on—do you want me to increase
  Your happiness a hundredfold?

CALIDORUS   How so?

BALLIO   By telling you, right now
  Phoenicium is not for sale.   185

CALIDORUS   She isn't?

BALLIO   That's a fact, by Herc!

CALIDORUS [*Ecstatically.*]   Pseudolus, go, get holy victims,
  Beasts and butchers; I would pay
  This Jove a sacrifice divine.
  I now regard our friend right here   190
  As a mightier Jove than Jupiter.

BALLIO   No victims, please. I much prefer
  To be appeased with chunks of lamb.

CALIDORUS   Hurry! Move! Go get the lambs!
  Do you hear what Jupiter has said?   195

PSEUDOLUS   I'll soon be back; but first I've got
  To run outside the city gate.

CALIDORUS   Why there?

PSEUDOLUS   I'll find two human butchers,[8]
  Armed with deadly warning bells;
  And while I'm there, I'll bring two flocks   200
  Of weeping-willow flogging whips:
  Today there'll be a sweet supply
  Of offerings for this Jupiter.

BALLIO   Go hang yourself!

PSEUDOLUS   No, hanging's what
  They do to a pimp-ly Jupiter.   205

BALLIO   You wouldn't stand to gain a thing
  If I should die.

PSEUDOLUS   Why not?

BALLIO   Well, look:
  If I were dead, in all of Athens

---

8. Public executioners.

There'd be no one worse than you.
CALIDORUS   Holy Herc, you've got to tell me—   210
Answer seriously, please:
You haven't got my girl for sale,
My lovely, dear Phoenicium?
BALLIO   She's not for sale; by Pollux, no.
You see, I sold her long ago.   215
CALIDORUS   You sold her? How?
BALLIO   Right off the stall:
Neck and gizzard, guts and all.[9]
CALIDORUS   You sold my girl?
BALLIO   Precisely so;
For twenty minas.
CALIDORUS   Twenty?
BALLIO   Yes.
Or four times five, if you prefer.   220
I sold her to a soldier boy,
A captain out of Macedon.
He paid me fifteen in advance.
CALIDORUS   What am I hearing?
BALLIO   That your girl's
Converted into currency.   225
CALIDORUS   How could you?
BALLIO   Well, I felt like it;
And she was mine.
CALIDORUS   Ho! Pseudolus:
Run, fetch a sword!
PSEUDOLUS   Why do I need
A sword?
CALIDORUS   To kill this man—and me!
PSEUDOLUS   Why not just destroy yourself?   230
This fellow soon will starve to death.
CALIDORUS [To BALLIO.]   What do you say, you ultimate
Extreme of human perjury?
Did you swear that you would never
Sell her to anyone but me?   235
BALLIO   I did, and I admit it.
CALIDORUS   Well, then.
Hadn't you pledged, and formally, too?
BALLIO   Yes, but I fudged; I normally do.
CALIDORUS   Perjury! You criminal!
BALLIO   I put some money in my pocket.   240
If that's criminal, don't knock it.
You've got virtue and family fame—
But not a penny to your name.
CALIDORUS   Pseudolus, stand on the other side
And pile the curses on him.
PSEUDOLUS   Fine.   245

9. Like cattle, who were sold either gutted or with their entrails.

I wouldn't be more keen to run
To the praetor for my liberty.[1]

CALIDORUS   Bring on the insults!

PSEUDOLUS   Here we go;
My tongue will tear you limb from limb.
Shameless!

BALLIO   All right.

PSEUDOLUS   *Criminal!*   250

BALLIO   That's true enough.

PSEUDOLUS   *You whipping-boy!*

BALLIO   Why not?

PSEUDOLUS   *Grave-robber!*

BALLIO   Certainly.

PSEUDOLUS   *Filthy jailbird!*

BALLIO   Excellent!

PSEUDOLUS   *Treacherous swindler!*

BALLIO   That's my style.

PSEUDOLUS   *Foul assassin!*

BALLIO   Yes. Continue.   255

CALIDORUS   *Sacrilegious!*

BALLIO   I admit it.

CALIDORUS   *Perjurer!*

BALLIO   An old refrain.

CALIDORUS   *Lawbreaker!*

BALLIO   Most emphatically.

PSEUDOLUS   *Youth-corrupter!*

BALLIO   Ouch! That stings.

CALIDORUS   *Thief!*

BALLIO   Touché!

PSEUDOLUS   *Deserter!*

BALLIO   Bravo!   260

CALIDORUS   *Public fraud!*

BALLIO   Too obvious.

PSEUDOLUS   *Crooked cheater!*

CALIDORUS   *Dirty pimp!*

PSEUDOLUS   *You crud!*

BALLIO   Your voices are divine.

CALIDORUS   *You beat your father and your mother!*

BALLIO   And what's more, I killed them both   265
Rather than provide them food;[2]
Was that an awful thing to do?

PSEUDOLUS   We're pouring all our juicy words
In a bottomless pot—a waste of time.

BALLIO   Is there nothing else you'd like to say?   270

CALIDORUS   Are you incapable of shame?

BALLIO   Or you—a lover who's been found
As empty as a rotten nut?

---

1. One of the procedures for legally setting a slave free involved the master and slave appearing before a magistrate such as a praetor, whose functions included administration of the law.   2. Mistreatment of parents was particularly horrifying to the Romans, with their deeply traditional notions of paternal authority.

[*Reconsidering.*] And yet, although you've shouted many
Nasty noises at my head,   275
If that captain doesn't bring
The other five he owes me still
By today, the final deadline
Formally agreed for payment—
Well, if he can't deliver, then   280
I think I can act in character.
CALIDORUS How's that?
BALLIO   If *you* bring me the money,
Then I'll break my word with *him*:
I'm that kind of character. I'd gladly
Chat with you, but it's not worthwhile.   285
If you're broke, it's a hopeless effort
Pleading with me to pity you.
Here's my final word on the subject:
Focus on the job at hand.
CALIDORUS You're leaving?
BALLIO   I've got many worries   290
On my mind.
         [BALLIO *and his* SLAVE *leave for the marketplace, stage left.*]
PSEUDOLUS   You'll soon have more!
[*To audience.*] I own that fellow now, unless
All gods and men abandon me.
I'll bone and fillet him, the way
A cook prepares a slippery eel.   295
Now, Calidorus, give me your
Attention.
CALIDORUS What is your command?
PSEUDOLUS I want this town[3] placed under siege;
I've got to capture it today.
To do that, I'll require a man   300
Who's wily, clever, cunning, crafty,
Able to execute commands,
Not fall asleep when he's on watch.
CALIDORUS What do you intend to do?
PSEUDOLUS When the time is ripe, I'll let you know.   305
I don't want to repeat myself:
That's how plays become too long.
CALIDORUS Very good and very fair.
PSEUDOLUS Hurry! Bring him right away.
CALIDORUS Of all our friends, there are so few   310
A man can really depend upon.
PSEUDOLUS I know that. You've a double job:
Prepare a prime selection drawn from
All our friends; then pick out one
That we can really count on.   315

3. Ballio. From here on, Pseudolus repeatedly refers to his plot against the pimp as if it were the siege of a city.

CALIDORUS   I'll have him here at once.
PSEUDOLUS   Get moving,
    Won't you? Talking means delay.

ACT I, SCENE 4

[As CALIDORUS leaves (stage right) to find an accomplice, PSEUDOLUS moves
downstage to address the audience.]

PSEUDOLUS   He's gone; you're on your own now, Pseudolus.
    Now what'll you do? You've loaded master's son
    With precious promises; can you get the goods?
    If you haven't a particle of a proper plan
    You can't begin to weave a cunning cloth   5
    Or execute a definite design.
    But look at the poet: when he starts to write,
    He seeks what doesn't exist, and then he finds it;
    He makes invented fiction look like truth.
    All right, I'll be a poet! Twenty coins,   10
    Which don't exist on the face of earth, I'll find.
    Ages ago I said I'd give him the money,
    Hoping to lay a snare for our old man;
    But somehow "Dad" got wind of what I wanted.
            [SIMO and CALLIPHO appear from the forum, stage left.]
    I must control my voice and hold my tongue;   15
    Look! Here's my master Simo coming this way,
    Strolling with his neighbor Callipho.
    Out of this old tomb today I'll dig up
    Twenty coins to give to master's son.
    I'll step aside and hear their conversation.   20

ACT I, SCENE 5

[Enter the two old men and neighbors, SIMO and CALLIPHO. SIMO, who is Calidorus' father and Pseudolus' master, is severe in temperament; CALLIPHO is more
tolerant and urbane.]

SIMO   If all the spendthrifts and the lovesick boys
    In Athens met to elect a president,
    I'm sure that no one would defeat my son.
    He's the only topic of the town—
    How he wants to free his girl by scrounging   5
    Money to save her. People tell me this;
    In fact, I sniffed the truth a while back
    But pretended not to know.
PSEUDOLUS [Aside.]   His son must stink.
    The plot is killed; the whole affair is jammed.
    I meant to take this route to silver city;   10
    Now I find the road's completely blocked.
    He's on to us: no spoils for the despoilers!
CALLIPHO   People who blab or listen to slanderous gossip,

If I were in charge of things, would all be hanged:
Blabbers by the tongue, listeners by the ears.   15
These stories that they tell you—that your son
Is so in love he'd swindle you of silver—
Chances are that these reports are lies.
But even if they're absolutely true,
In the light of present morals, what did he do   20
Remarkable? What's new if a young man
Loves or frees a mistress?
PSEUDOLUS [*Aside.*]   Charming fellow!
SIMO   As an old man I object.
CALLIPHO   But that's no use.
   You shouldn't have done these things when you were young.
   A father must be pure if he insists   25
   That his son be purer than he's been himself.
   When you were young, the damage that you caused
   Was enough to share with every man alive!
   "A chip off the old block": what's the big surprise?
PSEUDOLUS [*Aside.*]   O Zeus, how few obliging men there are.   30
   Hey! That's the kind of father a son should have.
SIMO   Who's talking here? It's my slave Pseudolus.
   He's the corrupter of my son, the crook!
   He's the leader, he's the teacher, he's the one
   That I want crucified.
CALLIPHO   Now that's just silly,   35
   Flying off the handle. How much better
   To go up and ask him diplomatically
   Whether those reports are true or false.
   When times are tough, good heart is half the battle.
SIMO   I'll take your advice.
PSEUDOLUS [*Aside.*]   Here they come, Pseudolus.   40
   Prepare your speech to take the old man on.
   [*Aloud.*] Good health to master first, that's only fair;
   What health is left can be his neighbor's share.
SIMO   Good day. What are you doing?
PSEUDOLUS   Standing here like this.
SIMO   See his attitude, Callipho? King of the roost!   45
CALLIPHO   I think he displays a fine self-confidence.
PSEUDOLUS   A slave who's free of crime and free of cunning
   Should stand tall in his master's company.
CALLIPHO   We want to question you about some news
   That's reached us, sort of drifting through a cloud.   50
SIMO   His words will now convince you that you've taken on
   Not Pseudolus, but Socrates.
PSEUDOLUS   All right. I realize you've always put me down;
   I know you've got no confidence in me.
   You'd like me worthless; still, I'll be first-class.   55
SIMO   Keep your ear space vacant, Pseudolus;
   Admit my words as tenants for a while.
PSEUDOLUS   Speak your mind, though I'm furious at you.

SIMO   A slave, furious at me, your master?
PSEUDOLUS   Does that
  Seem so strange?
SIMO   Great Herc! According to you,   60
  I've got to guard against your rage. You plan
  To batter me the way I batter you.
  [*To* CALLIPHO.] What do you think?
CALLIPHO   I feel his anger's justified,
  When you place no confidence in him.
SIMO   All right,
  Let him rage! I'll stop him doing any damage.   65
  [*To* PSEUDOLUS.] Well? What about my question?
PSEUDOLUS   Go head and ask.
  Treat my knowledge as your Delphic oracle.
SIMO   Pay attention, then, and remember your promise.
  What do you say? Do you know my son's in love
  With a music-girl?
PSEUDOLUS [*In oracular tones.*]   Yea, yea, forsooth.
SIMO   And he wants her
    freed?   70
PSEUDOLUS   In truth, forsooth.
SIMO   And twenty silver minas,
  Through skulduggery and dirty tricks,
  You're planning to snatch from me?
PSEUDOLUS   I? Snatch from you?
SIMO   Yes. To give my son, to free his girl.
  Confess it! Speak: in truth, forsooth?
PSEUDOLUS   In truth, forsooth.   75
SIMO   He admits it! Didn't I tell you, Callipho?
CALLIPHO   I remember.
SIMO   The moment you knew this, why was it
  Concealed from me? Why didn't I hear?
PSEUDOLUS   I'll tell you.
  I didn't want to breed a wicked custom
  By denouncing master A to master B.   80
SIMO   This fellow's fit for service in the mill!
CALLIPHO   But Simo, has he sinned?
SIMO   You bet he has!
PSEUDOLUS   Please stop. I keep my own books, Callipho;
  My sins belong to me. Just listen; I'll
  Explain why I shut you out of the love affair.   85
  I knew I'd land in the gristmill,[4] if I spoke.
SIMO   Didn't you know the mill would be your lot
  If you kept mum?
PSEUDOLUS   I knew.
SIMO   Why wasn't I told?
PSEUDOLUS   One fate was instant; one was more remote.

---

4. Hard labor often threatened to slaves in comedy. The huge stones that ground the wheat were turned by animals or slaves.

Silence gained me a day or two of grace.   90
SIMO   What'll you do now? There's no hope of pinching
   Money out of me; I'm wide awake.
   I'll pass a law: *"Don't lend to Pseudolus!"*
PSEUDOLUS   Ye gods! I'll never beg from another man
   While you're alive. You'll give the cash yourself.   95
   I'll wheedle it from you.
SIMO   From me?
PSEUDOLUS   Precisely.
SIMO   Holy Herc, knock out my eye, if I give.
PSEUDOLUS   You'll give.
   Watch out; you've got fair warning.
CALLIPHO   One thing's sure:
   If you succeed, you'll stage a stunning coup!
PSEUDOLUS   I will.
SIMO   And if you don't?
PSEUDOLUS   Then flog me with canes.   100
   But what if I pull it off?
SIMO   So help me Jove,
   You'll live your life unpunished.
PSEUDOLUS   Don't forget!
SIMO   You think I can't take care, when I'm forewarned?
PSEUDOLUS   You're warned: take care! You're told: take care! *Take care!*
   Those hands will bestow the cash on me today.   105
CALLIPHO   He's a living masterpiece if he keeps his word.
PSEUDOLUS   Haul me off into slavery if I fail.
SIMO   Very generous! You're mine already.
PSEUDOLUS   Do you want to hear a more amazing story?
CALLIPHO   Gladly! I love to listen to you talk.   110
PSEUDOLUS [*To* SIMO.]   Before I tackle you, I'll first engage
   Another foe in a memorable match.
SIMO   What other foe?
PSEUDOLUS   This pimp, your neighbor here.
   Through trickery and dirty double-dealing,
   I'll deprive our precious pandering pimp   115
   Of the music-girl your son adores.
SIMO   You will?
PSEUDOLUS   The two campaigns will be finished by this evening.
SIMO   If you carry out these tasks, as you declare,
   You'll be mightier than King Agathocles.[5]
   But if you fail, won't I be justified   120
   In sending you to the mill?
PSEUDOLUS   Not just for a day,
   But for all eternity! If I succeed,
   Will you give me the cash to pay the pimp,
   Of your own free will?
CALLIPHO [*To* SIMO.]   That's reasonable and fair;
   Say yes.

5. Rose from humble origins to become tyrant and then king of Syracuse in Sicily, 316–289 B.C.

SIMO   But something's just occurred to me.   125
   What if there's collusion, Callipho,
   Or they've arranged some underhanded deal
   To dupe me of my wealth?
PSEUDOLUS   Not even I
   Would have the nerve to stoop so low! Look here:
   If there's collusion, Simo, or if we   130
   Have ever wheeled and dealed in such a way,
   Then use your whip like a writing instrument
   And scratch red letters all across my back.
SIMO   Your comedy can start now, any time.
PSEUDOLUS   Help me out today, please, Callipho;   135
   Don't get involved in any other scheme.
CALLIPHO   I had set up a visit to the country.
PSEUDOLUS   Un-set it then; upset your settled plans.
CALLIPHO   All right, I'll choose to stay on your account;
   I yearn to watch you in action, Pseudolus.   140
   And if I see him holding back the cash
   He promised, I'll come through with it myself.
SIMO   I won't renege.
PSEUDOLUS   By Pollux, if you do,
   You'll be dunned to death with a devastating din.
   Come on now, move along inside, you two,   145
   And give my tricks some room: it's their turn now.
CALLIPHO   All right; you'll get your way,
PSEUDOLUS   Remember, don't
   Leave home today.
CALLIPHO   I promise you my help.
        [CALLIPHO *enters his house.*]
SIMO   Well, I'm off to the forum. I'll be back here.
PSEUDOLUS   Make it soon!
       [EXIT SIMO, *stage left.* PSEUDOLUS *moves downstage again to address
       the audience.*]
   I suspect that you're suspicious of me now.   150
   You think I'm making these grand promises
   To entertain you, till our play is done.
   You don't expect me to do what I said I would.
   Well, I won't back down. One fact I know for sure:
   I don't quite know just how I'll pull it off . . .   155
   And yet I'll manage! Somehow every actor ought
   To bring some novel innovation to the stage.
   If he can't, he should give way to one who can.

   I think I'll step inside here for a while
   To drill my regiment of roguery.   160

   I'll hurry back; expect a brief delay.
   Here's music[6] that will charm the time away.
       [*Exit into house.*]

---

6. An interlude of instrumental music often marked major divisions in the action of Roman comedy.

Act II

[*A very short time has elapsed.* PSEUDOLUS *emerges from Simo's house, in obvious good spirits.*]

ACT II, SCENE 1

PSEUDOLUS   Great Jupiter! How sweet to find
   That everything is working out!
   I've chased anxiety and doubt
   From this grand scheme I have in mind.
   It's stupid to entrust a plan   5
   To a weak or wishy-washy man;
   For all endeavors must depend
   On how much effort you expend.

   Inside my brain I've so prepared
   My tricky troops, my sneaky squad   10
   Of flimflam, fakery, and fraud,
   That, after war has been declared,
   My ancestral fortitude, combined
   With hard work and a nasty mind,
   Will snare my enemies with ease,   15
   And falsely force them to their knees.

   This adversary that I share
   With all you lusty men out there,
   This Ballio I'll bash and break:
   Just pay attention, for my sake.   20

   Today I will besiege this town,
   Draw up my legions, tear it down;
   And when I've stormed and scaled that wall
   (My men won't find it hard at all),
   I'll lead my army straightaway   25
   To a second town, all old and gray.
   This will provide my friends and me
   With loads of booty, duty-free.
   My destiny, the world will know,
   Is striking panic in the foe.   30
   It's in my blood: I feel the need
   To carry out some doughty deed—
   A hero's act, enshrined in fame,
   That will perpetuate my name.

   But who's this fellow striding up?   35
     He's quite unknown to me;
   And why's he coming with that sword?
     I'll step aside and see.

ACT II, SCENE 2

[*From the harbor (stage right) there appears a figure dressed in the conventional traveler's outfit of cloak, broad-brimmed hat, and conspicuous sword. It is* HAR-PAX, *the somewhat dim-witted messenger slave of the Macedonian captain.*]

HARPAX   Here we are, the neighborhood
My master carefully described.
Everything seems to correspond
With my instructions from the captain:
Seventh block beyond the gate,   5
The home of Ballio the pimp,
The fellow I'm supposed to give
This token and this moneybag.
But I could use some guidance now.
Which one's the pimp's establishment?   10
PSEUDOLUS [*Aside.*]   Quiet! Shh! I've got this man,
If heaven and earth approve my plan.
But I'll require a new invention:
Here's a sudden, new dimension.
Let's proceed with all dispatch;   15
Scrap the old scheme, start from scratch!
I'll pulverize and quite destroy
This regimental errand-boy.
HARPAX   I'll knock on the door and see if I
Can rouse up anyone inside.   20
    [*He knocks loudly on Ballio's door.*]
PSEUDOLUS [*Rushing up to* HARPAX.]   Knock it off, whoever you are;
Please save your knocks and spare these doors.
I'm here to plead on their behalf
As guardian patron of the portals.
HARPAX   Are you Ballio?
PSEUDOLUS   Not quite,   25
But I'm Assistant Ballio.
HARPAX   What's that supposed to mean?
PSEUDOLUS   It means
I'm Exchequer, In-checker, Prince of the Pantry.
HARPAX   Sort of majordomo?
PSEUDOLUS   Higher up
In rank: I'm General Factotum.   30
HARPAX   What's your status, slave or free?
PSEUDOLUS   Right at the moment, I'm a slave.
HARPAX   You look the part. You don't appear
A candidate for liberty.
PSEUDOLUS   Shouldn't you check the looking glass   35
When you've got insults to unload?
HARPAX [*Aside*]   This fellow's just a troublemaker.
PSEUDOLUS [*Aside.*]   Gods be gracious, here's an anvil
For my craft! I'll hammer out
A brazen masterpiece today.   40

HARPAX [*Aside.*]   Why's he talking to himself?
PSEUDOLUS   Look here, you youngster!
HARPAX   What do you want?
PSEUDOLUS   Do you or don't you represent
  That Macedonian officer
  Who bought a beauty from our stock,   45
  Who paid my master, Mister Pimp,
  A cash advance of fifteen minas,
  Five still owing?
HARPAX   I'm your man.
  But how in the world do you know me?
  Where have you seen or talked to me?   50
  I've never made a trip to Athens
  In the past, and till today,
  I'd never laid an eye on you.
PSEUDOLUS   It's just because you look the part.
  When he left town, we all agreed   55
  The balance would fall due today,
  But no cold comfort has arrived.
HARPAX   Well, here it is.
PSEUDOLUS   You've brought it?
HARPAX   Yes.
PSEUDOLUS   Then why so slow to hand it over?
HARPAX   Give it to you?
PSEUDOLUS   Yes, Herc, to me!   60
  I'm Ballio's financial wizard:
  Bursar, purser, debt-disperser.
HARPAX   Holy Herc, if you controlled
  The treasure of almighty Jove,
  I'd never trust you with a single   65
  Silver sliver!
PSEUDOLUS [*Reaching for the bag.*]   Quick as a wink
  We'll see your debt discharged.
HARPAX [*Protecting the bag.*]   I'd rather keep these funds tied up.
PSEUDOLUS   Damn you! It's very obvious   70
  You're smearing my integrity—
  As though I'd never handled trust
  Accounts a thousand times as large.
HARPAX   Well, maybe others have more faith;
  You don't inspire my confidence.   75
PSEUDOLUS   Are you suggesting I might want
  To con the silver out of you?
HARPAX   No. You're the source of that suggestion;
  My suspicions are my own.
  But what's your name?   80
PSEUDOLUS [*Aside.*]   This pimp has a slave called Syrus.
  I'll pretend that's me. [*Aloud.*] I'm Syrus.
HARPAX   Syrus?
PSEUDOLUS   Yessir, that's my name.
HARPAX   We're wasting time. If your master's home,

Why don't you call him to the door,   85
So I can get my business finished
Here, whatever your name may be.
PSEUDOLUS   If he were home, I'd summon him.
But trusting me with all the cash
Would be a more conclusive act   90
Than paying him.
HARPAX   Conclusive? Sure!
I'd close the deal and kiss it sweet
Goodbye! Of course, I realize
You're hot and bothered when you see
The money slipping through your claws.   95
I won't negotiate with anyone
But Ballio in person.
PSEUDOLUS   He's occupied and busy now:
He's got a case before the judge.
HARPAX   Good luck to him! I'll just return   100
Another time, when he's at home.
But take this letter from me, please,
And give it to him. Inside he'll find
The token our masters both agreed
To use in dealing with the girl.   105
PSEUDOLUS   I understand. Your captain wanted
Her released to anyone
Who brought the cash, together with
His portrait image, stamped in wax.
He left a specimen with us.   110
HARPAX   You know about the whole affair.
PSEUDOLUS   Why shouldn't I?
HARPAX   Then give him the token.
PSEUDOLUS   O.K. But what's your name?
HARPAX   Harpax.[7]
PSEUDOLUS   Harp off, Harpax! You're not welcome.
You won't get inside our house   115
To play your snatching harpy acts.
HARPAX   I snatch great foes right off the battlefield:
That's how I got my name.
PSEUDOLUS   I'm more inclined to think
You snatch great pots right off the pantry shelf.   120
HARPAX   Not true! But Syrus, do you know
What I would like?
PSEUDOLUS   I'll know if you tell me.
HARPAX   I've got a room beyond the gate,
The third tavern on the right;
My hostess is a tubby, chubby,   125
Gimpy grandma, name of Chrysis.
PSEUDOLUS   What do you want from me?
HARPAX   Please reach me there, when your master comes.

---

7. Connected with a Greek verb for "seize" or "plunder."

PSEUDOLUS   As you would have it, certainly.

HARPAX   I'm now so weary from my travels,   130
    I must rest and freshen up.

PSEUDOLUS   A wise and admirable plan.
    But please make sure you don't go missing
    When I need to summon you.

HARPAX   No fear. I'll have a delicious meal,   135
    And then an after-dinner nap.

PSEUDOLUS   I quite approve.

HARPAX   And is that all?

PSEUDOLUS   Go off to slumberland.

HARPAX   I'm going.

      [*Exit* HARPAX, *stage right.*]

PSEUDOLUS   Just you listen, Harpy-boy:
    Bundle up in lots of blankets;   140
    Sweating makes a person sweet.

ACT II, SCENE 3

PSEUDOLUS [*Moving downstage to confide in the audience.*]   Immortal
      gods! I think this fellow
    Saved my skin by coming here.
    He's paid the ticket for my trip
    From Way-off-course to Journey's-end.
    Father Nick-of-Time himself   5
    Couldn't have made a timelier entrance
    Than this timeliest of letters
    That has landed in my lap.

    Here I've found my horn of plenty—
    Plenty of everything I need: 10
    A horn of hoax and hocus-pocus,
    Sleight of hand, bamboozlement;
    Plenty of cash, and a horny girl
    To hug my master's horny son.

    How I'm going to swagger now,   15
    When I've got cause for confidence!
    Already I'd laid out a plan
    Of action, scheming how to snatch
    The little lady from the pimp;
    It all took shape inside my mind,   20
    Well ordered, beautifully arranged.

    But this will often be the case:
    The plans of a hundred clever men
    Can be overturned by a single goddess—
    Luck. And isn't it the truth?   25
    Depending on how a person uses Luck
    He may succeed, and everyone of course

Will then pronounce him sensible and wise.
If a scheme should turn out well, then all the world
Declares him shrewd; but if disaster strikes,   30
We look upon him as an utter fool.

Well, we're the fools; we just can't see our folly!
All of us pursue our greedy goals,
Grasping at gain, as if we possibly
Could judge what serves our real interest.   35
We sacrifice the real world
By chasing unreality.
The outcome is predictable:
We groan and moan our lives away,
While death creeps closer all the while.   40

Enough profound philosophy!
My lectures always last too long.

Immortal gods! My little fib
Was worth its weight in platinum—
That sudden, spur-of-the-moment claim   45
That I belonged to Ballio.
Now I'll use this letter here
To dupe three victims: master, pimp,
And military messenger.

What's this? Oh bliss! I think another   50
Wish I made is coming true.
Look: Calidorus is approaching,
Leading someone by the hand.

ACT II, SCENE 4

[As PSEUDOLUS steps aside to watch and listen, CALIDORUS returns (stage right) with CHARINUS, a bright and appealing youth of about his own age.]

CALIDORUS   Sweet and bitter, I've revealed
    The truth in its entirety.
    You know my passion and my pain;
    You know my abject poverty.
CHARINUS   I remember everything;   5
    Just let me know what I should do.
CALIDORUS   Pseudolus commanded me
    To find a strong and sympathetic
    Friend, and then to bring him here.
CHARINUS   You've followed orders to the letter: 10
    Here's a friend and sympathy.
    But that man Pseudolus of yours
    Is new to me.
CALIDORUS   A living masterpiece!

He's my inventive genius.
He told me he could carry out   15
The project I discussed with you.
PSEUDOLUS [*Aside.*]   I'll try the grand, heroic style.
CALIDORUS   Is that a voice?
PSEUDOLUS   Oh yea, rejoice!
Dire despot, unto thee I bow;
Pseudolus' sovereign lord art thou.   20
A threefold pleasure, thrice prepared,
Three victims cunningly ensnared
Thou shalt possess: a triple treat;
A triform triumph of deceit.
Judge not this letter by its size: 25
It holds a vast and precious prize.
CALIDORUS   That's him.
CHARINUS   A bold, bombastic beggar!
PSEUDOLUS   Forward march, extend your arm,
And greet the answer to your prayer.
CALIDORUS   Pray, how should I greet you, Pseudolus?   30
As Wishful Hope or Wish Fulfilled?
PSEUDOLUS   As both, I'd say.
CALIDORUS   As both, good day!
But what's the news?
PSEUDOLUS   Dispel your fear!
CALIDORUS [*Identifying* CHARINUS *for* PSEUDOLUS.]   I packed this
      man out.
PSEUDOLUS   Come again?
CALIDORUS   I picked him out, I meant to say.   35
PSEUDOLUS   Who is he?
CALIDORUS   Charinus.
PSEUDOLUS   Gracious me!
A graceful name! My gratitude.[8]
CHARINUS   Look, if I can be of service,
Say the word.
PSEUDOLUS   Thanks just the same.
Bless you, Charinus, I don't want   40
The two of us to bother you.
CHARINUS   Could you two be a bother? Nothing
Bothers me.
PSEUDOLUS   Then wait a while.
CALIDORUS   What's that you've got?
PSEUDOLUS   A letter
I waylaid just now; a token, too.   45
CALIDORUS   A token? What do you mean, a token?
PSEUDOLUS   One the captain sent this way.
His flunky was delivering it,
Along with five bright silver coins;
He'd come to fetch your ladylove,   50

8. A pun: *Charinus* suggests the Greek word *charis,* "thanks" or "favor."

But I threw dust into his eyes.
CALIDORUS   How?
PSEUDOLUS   This audience has paid
    To see us act our comedy.
    They know precisely how it happened;
    You'll get caught up later on.   55
CALIDORUS   What's our next move?
PSEUDOLUS   Today your girl
    Will be free to take you in her arms.
CALIDORUS   Me?
PSEUDOLUS   Yes you, yourself, in person,
    If yours truly lives so long;
    And if you can find a man to help me—   60
    Quickly!
CHARINUS   What should he be like?
PSEUDOLUS   Immoral, clever, cunning, one
    Who quickly gets the hang of things
    And then relies on native wit
    To see what action he should take.   65
    Someone unknown in these parts.
CHARINUS   If he's a slave, could that create
    A problem?
PSEUDOLUS   Not at all; I much
    Prefer the slave to the freeborn.[9]
CHARINUS   Well, I think I can provide your man: 70
    Quick-witted, rotten to the core.
    My father sent him from Carystus;[1]
    So far, he hasn't ventured from
    Our house, and never until yesterday
    Had he set foot in Athens.   75
PSEUDOLUS   Wonderful! But I'll still need
    To float a loan—five silver minas,
    Which I'll pay back today; you see,
    His father [Pointing to CALIDORUS.] owes a debt to me.
CHARINUS   I'll lend you the money; look no farther.   80
PSEUDOLUS   What a dear, obliging man!
    I'll also need a cloak, a dagger,
    And a broad-brimmed hat.
CHARINUS   Can do.
PSEUDOLUS   Immortal gods! This fellow's not
    Charinus, he's sweet Charity!   85
    Tell me about your father's slave:
    Has he any sense about him?
CHARINUS   Armpit scents: he stinks to heaven.
PSEUDOLUS   Phew! We'll get him longer sleeves.
    Can he be sanguine, sharp, and keen?   90
CHARINUS   His blood is two parts vinegar.

---

9. A slave could be unscrupulous in ways thought beneath a free man.   1. A city on Euboea, the long island stretching along the north coast of the Athenian territory.

PSEUDOLUS   But what if he has to tap his veins
  For sweeter fluids?
CHARINUS   Sweeter? He'll drip
  Spiced liqueur and raisin brandy,
  Muscatel and honey-mead;   95
  In fact, he had a notion once
  To start a walking winery.
PSEUDOLUS   Touché, Charinus! You're a treat;
  You fleece me at my favorite game.
  But how shall I address your flunky?   100
CHARINUS   Simia, alias Mister Monkey.[2]
PSEUDOLUS   When it's windy, can he whirl?
CHARINUS   He'd teach a twister how to twirl.
PSEUDOLUS   Is he cautious?
CHARINUS   Maybe not:
  He's often cautioned, never caught.   105
PSEUDOLUS   What if they nail him fast and firm?
CHARINUS   He's just an eel: away he'll squirm.
PSEUDOLUS   And is he sharp at dirty tricks?
CHARINUS   Sharp enough for politics.
PSEUDOLUS   The man's an ideal choice, to judge   110
  From your account.
CHARINUS   If you only knew!
  He'll glance at you, and straightaway
  He'll tell you what you want him for.
  But what's your proposal?
PSEUDOLUS   I'll explain.
  When I have got him all dressed up,   115
  I want this fellow to become
  A counterfeit of the captain's slave;
  He'll take the token to the pimp,
  Along with the sack of silver coins,
  Then whisk the woman off to safety.   120

  Help! I've given the plot[3] away!

  Any instructions that remain
  I'll tell the fellow face to face.
CALIDORUS   Then what are we doing standing here?
PSEUDOLUS   Get the man and all the trappings,   125
  Bring him right away to meet me
  At the countinghouse of Aeschinus.
  Be quick about it!
CALIDORUS   We'll be there
  Ahead of you.
        [*Exeunt* CALIDORUS AND CHARINUS, *stage left*.]
PSEUDOLUS   More haste, less speed!

2. The name suggests the Greek *simos*, "snub-nosed."   3. I.e., of the play: a metatheatrical comment
directed to the audience.

[*Addressing the audience.*] All my plans that earlier   130
Were clouded and obscure have now
Become transparent, and my vision's
Crystal clear. The road's wide open:
All my legions now are marshaled,
Standards proudly raised on high.   135
The birds are soaring overhead;
The auspices all point my way.
My heart's abrim with confidence
That I can rout the enemy.
Off to the forum, where I'll load   140
My orders on this Simia:

    He mustn't trip, his leadership
    Is crucial in my grand design;
    I'll sound the call, we'll storm the wall,
    And then Fort Pimp will all be mine.   145
        [*Exit stage left.*]

Act III

[*From Ballio's doorway there emerges a* YOUNG SLAVE, *a wretched and timid boy in his early teens.*]

ACT III, SCENE 1

SLAVE When the gods assign a boy the job of slaving
    For a pimp, and then they grant him ugliness,
    That boy has been assigned, if you ask me,
    A lousy load, a low-down dirty deal.
    Just look at me slaving here, where I'm obliged   5
    To shore up every shape and size of misery;
    And I can't find a single lover-boy
    To give me even a smidgen of tenderness.

    Today's the birthday of our boss the pimp;
    He's threatened the household, high and low alike: 10
    Whoever fails to give him a gift today
    Will die tomorrow in cruel agony.
    Hey! I don't know what I'm supposed to do;
    I lack the wherewithal all do it with.
    If I don't find a present for our pimp,   15
    I'm bound to get the long end of the stick.
    That's awful for a little kid like me!

    Gosh! I'm so scared of catching holy heck
    That if some fellow lays a load on me,
    Though people say that really makes you groan,   20
    I guess I'll somehow learn to clench my teeth.

    I'd better learn to clench my lips. Just look!
    My master's coming home; he's brought a cook.

ACT III, SCENE 2

[*As the* (YOUNG) SLAVE *tries to become invisible, enter (stage left)* BALLIO *and a*
COOK, *accompanied by apprentice cooks and other* ATTENDANT (SLAVES).]

BALLIO "Cook's Marketplace"—that's such a stupid name:
 Not cooks but crooks go on the market there.
 Upon my oath, I couldn't hope to find
 A worse type than this cook I've got in tow—
 A loud-mouthed, swaggering, useless nincompoop.   5

 The King of Hell refused to let him in:
 He's needed here to cater to the dead,
 Since he alone can satisfy their taste.
COOK If you hold that opinion of me,
 Why did you hire me?
BALLIO   Scarcity: no choice!   10
 If you're a cook, why were you sitting there,
 Left out in the market all alone?
COOK   I'll tell you:
 Human greed's the cause of my decline,
 Not lack of talent.
BALLIO   How so?
COOK   Let me explain:
 As soon as people come to hire a cook,   15
 Nobody wants the best and highest priced;
 They'd rather hire the cheapest one around.
 That's why I sat alone in the marketplace.
 No drachma-per-diem dope am I; no one
 Gets me off my butt for less than double that.   20

 My dinner menu's not like other cooks',
 Who spice up mounds of mouldy meadow grass,
 Converting guests to cattle (greens galore!),
 Then lace that fodder with more foliage.
 They toss in coriander, fennel, garlic,   25
 Parsley, sorrel, cabbage, spinach, beet,
 Dissolve a pound of asafetida,
 Then grind in murderous mustard, guaranteed
 To make you howl before you touch the stuff.
 When these boys cook, their seasonings do not   30
 Consist of spices, but of vampire bats,
 To gnaw the living entrails from their guests.
 So that's why people here live such short lives,
 Their bellies bloated with this kind of fodder,
 Scary to mention, let alone to munch on.   35
 Humans choose the greens that cows refuse.
BALLIO And you? Do you use heavenly seasoning
 That can extend the span of human life,
 Since you attack those spices?
COOK   Shout it aloud!

People can aspire to live two hundred years   40
By sticking to the spicy diets I've designed.
When I've put scorchilender in the pan,
Or torridopsis or inflammagon,
The dish becomes red hot upon the spot.
Those are my seasonings for Neptune's creatures;[4]   45
Earth-born beasts I spice with yummiander,
Smackalyptus, or delectamom.

BALLIO   May Jupiter and all the gods destroy you
With your spices and your pack of lies!

COOK   Please let me speak.

BALLIO   Speak on, and go to hell!   50

COOK   When the pans are boiling, I remove their lids:
The savor flies to heaven on soaring feet.

BALLIO   A savor with sore feet?

COOK   A careless slip.

BALLIO   How so?

COOK   I meant to say, "on soaring wings."
Jupiter dines daily on that scent.   55

BALLIO   On your day off, what's Jupiter to eat?

COOK   He goes to bed on an empty stomach.

BALLIO   Damn you!
Is it for this I'm shelling out hard cash?

COOK   Though I admit I'm an expensive cook,
I promise that my hiring price is matched   60
By service rendered.

BALLIO   Larceny, no doubt.[5]

COOK   Do you expect to find a single cook
Who's not equipped with grasping eagle talons?

BALLIO   Do you expect to cook a single meal
Without those grasping talons tightly tied?   65
[Catching sight of the lurking (YOUNG) SLAVE.]   Hey, boy, look lively!
Here's a job for you!
Get all my valuables locked away.
Don't let this fellow's face out of your sight:
If he looks sideways, you look sideways, too.
If he steps forward, match him step for step.   70
If he sticks out his hand, you do the same.
If he should grab what's his, just let him grab it;
But if he grabs what's mine, then hold him fast.
He starts: you start. He stops: you stop likewise.
He squats upon the ground: just squat away!   75
And each apprentice cook gets a private guard.

COOK   Come on, cheer up!

BALLIO   Will you explain how I
Can be cheerful when I'm going home with you?

COOK   Because today I'll dip you in my broth

_____

4. Fish (*Neptune*: god of the sea).   5. Cooks in comedy are proverbial thieves.

The way Medea cooked old Pelias.   80
  Her poisons and her magic drugs, they tell us,
  Made the old man a little lad again;[6]
  I'll do the same for you.
BALLIO   So you're also a poisoner?
COOK   Heavens, no! I'm a man-preserver.
BALLIO   Ha!
  How much to teach me that single recipe?   85
COOK   Which one?
BALLIO   Preserving you from fleecing me.
COOK   Base price, if you trust me; otherwise, no deal.
  But is it your friends or enemies you're going
  To feast today?
BALLIO   Why, they're my friends, of course.
COOK   Why don't you call your enemies instead?   90
  Today I'll give your guests a banquet so bespiced,
  So sprinkled with sweet seasoning,
  The instant someone samples my delights
  He'll want to nibble off his fingertips.
BALLIO   By Herc, before you serve a single guest,   95
  Be sure that you and your henchmen have a taste,
  To make you nibble off your pilfering paws.
COOK   Perhaps you don't believe what I'm telling you.
BALLIO   Don't be a nuisance! Too much nagging! Shush!
  Look: here's my house. Go in and cook your meal.   100
  Hurry!
SLAVE:[7]   Why not sit down and call your guests?
  The dinner's already a mess.
          [*The* COOK *and his retinue go into Ballio's house, leaving* BALLIO
          alone on stage.]
BALLIO   Just look at the sprig!
  That rascal is the cook's assistant tongue.
  Really, I don't know where to watch out first,
  With thieves inside my house and a thug next door.   105
  You see, my neighbor here (Calidorus' dad),
  As he left for the forum, warned me specially
  To be on guard against Pseudolus, his slave,
  And not to trust him; for he's on the prowl today,
  Hoping somehow to swindle the girl from me.   110
  The old man said he'd promised solemnly
  That he would filch away Phoenicium.

  So now I'll go inside and tell my household staff
  On no account to trust this Pseudolus riffraff.
          [*Goes into his house.*]

6. In fact, Medea persuaded Pelias's daughters to chop him up by promising that he would emerge from
the cooking pot a young man, but when they did so nothing happened.   7. Either Ballio's slave-boy or
the cook's assistant.

Act IV

[PSEUDOLUS *enters from the forum (stage left), singing exultantly to his newly found assistant, the slave* SIMIA. SIMIA, *who does not appear immediately, is disguised as the messenger-slave Harpax, with cloak, broad hat, and conspicuous sword; in guile and virtuosity, he can rival Pseudolus.*]

ACT IV, SCENE 1

PSEUDOLUS If ever immortal benevolent gods
    Get involved in our human condition,
They must want Calidorus and me to be saved,
    And the pimp to go down to perdition.
What a godsent support they've provided in you: 5
    You're a fellow so cunning and clever!
[*Looking back, and failing to see* SIMIA.] Where's he gone? If I've started to talk to myself,
    I'm becoming more loony than ever.

    By Herc, I'm tricked, it's plain to see:
    I failed to check a cheat like me.   10

Holy Pollux, I'm ruined if he's taken off,
    My design won't unfold as expected.
Look at that! There's my whipping-post strutting along,
    With his arrogant manner perfected.
[*To* SIMIA.] Hello, there, I was hunting all over for you;   15
    I was frightened that you had defected.
SIMIA I confess I'm a frightfully flighty type.
PSEUDOLUS Where were you dawdling?
SIMIA   Wherever I pleased.
PSEUDOLUS I know that already.
SIMIA   Then why do you ask?
PSEUDOLUS I want to school you in this scheme.   20
SIMIA You need the school; don't scholar me.
PSEUDOLUS You're treating me with cool contempt.
SIMIA Don't you deserve contempt from me,
    A legendary legionary?
PSEUDOLUS Concentrate on the job at hand.   25
SIMIA Do you see my attention wandering?
PSEUDOLUS Then walk along more quickly.
SIMIA No, I like to take my time.
PSEUDOLUS Here's our chance: while he's asleep,
    I want you to get the jump on him.   30
SIMIA Why such a rush? Relax! No fear!
    If only Jupiter would place
    That soldier's emissary here
    To meet my challenge, face to face:
    There's no way he could ever be   35
    A Harpax half as good as me.
    Cheer up! I'll fix your fine affair,

Untangling it with tender care.
My tricks and lies will so dismay
This foreign army type, he'll say   40
He isn't who he seems to be;
He'll calmly claim that I am he.
PSEUDOLUS   How come?
SIMIA   How dumb a question! I'm going to die!
PSEUDOLUS [*Aside*.]   A really charming sort of guy!   45
SIMIA   I'll outclass even you in lying,
Master snitch, without half trying.
PSEUDOLUS   Jupiter watch over you
For my sake!
SIMIA   And for my sake, too.
Does this outfit suit me, would you say?   50
PSEUDOLUS   It's quite magnificent!
SIMIA   O.K.
PSEUDOLUS   I pray the kindly gods may grant you
Everything for which you yearn;
If I prayed them to grant what you were worth,
You'd get less than nothing in return.   55
[*Aside*.] He's so downright sly and sneaky;
I've never seen a man more cheeky.
SIMIA   What's that I heard?
PSEUDOLUS   Hey, mum's the word.
But what rewards you'll get from me
If you manage this business properly!   60
SIMIA   Won't you shut up?
Reminding the mindful is mindless and mad:
The rememberer's memory may become bad.
I've absorbed all the facts and I've learned them by heart;
I've religiously practiced my fraudulent part.   65
PSEUDOLUS   An upright man!
SIMIA [*Aside*.]   Not he nor I.
PSEUDOLUS   Don't falter now!
SIMIA   Won't you shut up?
PSEUDOLUS   So help me heaven—
SIMIA   But heaven won't;
You're spouting undiluted lies.
PSEUDOLUS   For your treachery, Simia, you have earned   70
My love, my fear, my high esteem.
SIMIA   I've learned to hand out guff like that;
You can't pat me upon the head.
PSEUDOLUS   What a lovely reception you'll get from me
When you've done this job today!
SIMIA   Ha, ha!   75
PSEUDOLUS   With lovely food and wine and perfume,
Succulent morsels and drinks galore.
A lovely girl will be there as well,
To lavish kisses upon you.
SIMIA   You're a lovely host.

PSEUDOLUS   I'll cause you to say 80
 Much more, if you pull off this job.
SIMIA If I don't, may the crucifixioner
 Give me a cross reception!
 Now get a move on! Show me the mouth
 Of the pimp's establishment. Which door? 85
PSEUDOLUS Third along here.
SIMIA   Shh! That mouth just
 Yawned.
PSEUDOLUS The house has a bellyache,
 I'd say.
SIMIA Why?
PSEUDOLUS Because, so help me
 Pollux, it's vomiting the pimp!
    [PSEUDOLUS *and* SIMIA *make themselves inconspicuous, as* BALLIO
    emerges from his house in an odd, furtive manner.]
SIMIA Is that the man?
PSEUDOLUS   That's him.
SIMIA   What measly 90
 Merchandise! Just take a look:
 Forward motion's not for him;
 He skitters sideways like a crab.

ACT IV, SCENE 2

BALLIO I'll admit this cook's less foul
 A character than I supposed;
 So far he's pilfered nothing but
 A ladle and a little mug.
PSEUDOLUS [*To* SIMIA, *sotto voce.*]
 Here you go now, this is the perfect 5
 Moment.
SIMIA I agree with you.
PSEUDOLUS Step out into the street. Be tricky!
 I'll be waiting in ambush here.
SIMIA [*in a loud "soliloquy," moving toward* BALLIO.] I've been counting
   carefully:
 Sixth lane from the city gate. 10
 Here we are; this must be the alley
 Where he told me to turn aside.
 But how many houses down the alley,
 That I really couldn't say.
BALLIO [*Aside.*] Who's this fellow in the cloak? 15
 Where's he come from? Who does he want?
 He's got a sort of foreign look, and
 I don't recognize his face.
SIMIA Here's a man who's sure to know
 The matter I'm unsure about. 20
BALLIO [*Aside.*] He's heading straight for me. I wonder
 Where in the world the fellow's from.

SIMIA   Hey there! You with the wild goatee,
   I've got a question; answer me.
BALLIO   Well, well! You've no "good day" to share?   25
SIMIA   No, I have no good days to spare.
BALLIO   You'll get from me as good as you give.
PSEUDOLUS [*Aside.*]   A fine beginning: superlative!
SIMIA   Tell me, then, do you know any
   Person living on this lane?   30
BALLIO   I know myself.
SIMIA   Few human beings
   Reach the condition you describe.
   Down in the forum I doubt you'd find
   One man in ten who knows himself.
PSEUDOLUS [*Aside.*]   I'm safe; he's turned philosopher.   35
SIMIA   I'm looking for a nasty fellow—
   Scofflaw, low-life, perjurer,
   Degenerate.
BALLIO [*Aside.*]   It's me he wants.
   Those are my nicknames, sure enough.
   I hope he gets my surname right.   40
   [*Aloud.*] What is this fellow's name?
SIMIA   Pimp Ballio.
BALLIO   Do I know myself?
   I am the object of your search,
   Young man.
SIMIA   You're Ballio?
BALLIO   Me, yours truly.
SIMIA   The way you're dressed,   45
   You look like a second-story man.
BALLIO   If you spotted me on some dark street,
   I think you'd treat me with respect.
SIMIA   My master asked me to express
   His warmest compliments to you.   50
   Take this letter from me now;
   He told me to deliver it.
BALLIO   Just who issued the command?
PSEUD. [*Aside.*]   We're sunk! My man is all mucked up.
   Names weren't mentioned; what a mess!   55
BALLIO   Who do you say sent me this letter?
SIMIA   Look at his picture on the seal;
   Then, sir, *you* tell *me* his name,
   Proving to me that you are really
   Ballio.
BALLIO   Give me the letter.   60
SIMIA [*Handing it over.*]   Here: identify the seal.
BALLIO [*Aside, as he studies the seal.*]   Ah! Polymachaeroplagides:[8]
   Pure and simple recognition.
   [*To* SIMIA.] Hey! Polymachaeroplagides

8. "Son-of-many-sword-wounds."

Is his name.

SIMIA   Now I know how right   65
I was in giving you the letter,
Seeing how you spoke the name
Of Polymachaeroplagides.

BALLIO   What's he doing?

SIMIA   Playing the role
Of brave heroic warrior.   70
But hurry up and scrutinize
This letter, please—I'm very rushed—
Take the cash immediately
And give the woman her release.
I must be in Sicyon today   75
Or else tomorrow I die.
Master's very domineering.

BALLIO   Don't tell me; I know him too.

SIMIA   Come on, read the letter through, then.

BALLIO   Well, I will, if you'll shut up.   80
[Reads.] "Captain Polymachaeroplagides
Dispatches to the pimp named Ballio
This letter sealed with a portrait mutually
Agreed upon."

SIMIA   The token's in the letter.

BALLIO   I see; I'm satisfied. But does he never   85
Start a letter with a friendly wish?

SIMIA   No; that would violate army protocol.
By action he confers good health on friends
And likewise deals destruction to his foes.
But keep on reading, let experience teach you   90
What this letter says.

BALLIO   Just listen, then:
"Harpax, my aide, is on his way to you—"
You're Harpax?

SIMIA   I'm your man, [Aside.] and harp I can.

BALLIO   "—Bearing this letter. He'll convey the cash;
I want the woman sent with him at once.   95
It's right to wish the righteous 'Best of health':
I'd do so, if I thought you qualified."

SIMIA   What next?

BALLIO   Pay up and take away the girl.

SIMIA   What are we waiting for?

BALLIO   Follow inside, then.

SIMIA   Here I come.

ACT IV, SCENE 3

[As BALLIO and SIMIA disappear into Ballio's house, PSEUDOLUS
comes downstage to address the audience yet again.]

PSEUDOLUS   I swear to Pollux I've never seen a man
More devious or deceitful than this Simia.

I'm frightened of the fellow. I'm really scared
I'll face the gory treatment Ballio got:
My man may turn his lucky horns on me,   5
If any chance of mischief should arise.
Heavens! I hope not, for I wish him well.
Now I'm feeling triply terrified.
First, I'm nervous that my pal here could
Desert me and defect to the enemy;   10
Next, master might arrive back anytime,
To snatch the loot and catch the looters, too;
Finally, Harpax the First could reappear
Before this Harpax gets the girl away.

Oh Herc, I'm doomed! They've been inside too long.   15
My heart is waiting with its suitcase packed;
It plans to fly away to distant realms,
Unless he brings the girl out right away.

[*Seeing Ballio's door open.*] I've won! I've overthrown my overseers!

ACT IV, SCENE 4

[SIMIA *reappears from Ballio's house, leading the girl Phoenicium.*]

SIMIA   Don't cry, you don't understand, Phoenicium.
You'll get the picture soon, at dinner time.
You're not being led to the fellow with the fangs,
That Macedonian who provokes your tears;
I'm taking you to your dearest sweet desire: 5
In a twinkling you'll be in Calidorus' arms.
PSEUDOLUS   Why did you loiter so long inside the house?
My heart's been battered, bruised, and beaten flat.
SIMIA   You jailbird, how can you find the luxury
Of grilling me when the enemy's everywhere?   10
I'd say, "Forward march, in double time!"
PSEUDOLUS   By Pollux, good advice from such a no-good thug!
Advance! Let's crown our win with a triumphant jug!
[*They leave with Phoenicium, stage right.*]

ACT IV, SCENE 5

[BALLIO *comes out of his house, obviously pleased at the success of his transaction.*]

BALLIO   Ha, ha! At last my mind's been set at rest:
That fellow's gone; he's led the girl away.
Let Pseudolus come now, the dirty crook,
And try to snatch the girl by trickery!
By Herc, I'm positive I'd rather swear   5
An oath, commit a thousand perjuries,
Than let that swindler get the laugh on me.

Now when we meet, he'll be my laughingstock.
He's bound for the gristmill soon—that was the deal.

I'd love to meet old Simo, I confess;   10
How happily he'd share my happiness!

ACT IV, SCENE 6

[SIMO *enters from the forum, stage left.*]

SIMO   I'll see if my Ulysses has achieved
      The sack of Ballio's sacred citadel.[9]
BALLIO   Give me your lucky hand, you lucky fellow,
      Simo.
SIMO   What's up?
BALLIO   Now—
SIMO   What now?
BALLIO   No problem!
SIMO   Why?
      Did my man come here?
BALLIO   No.
SIMO   Then what's so good?   5
BALLIO   Your twenty mina coins are safe and sound—
      The bet you made today with Pseudolus.
SIMO   I'd like to think so.
BALLIO   I'll pay up myself,
      If your slave gets possession of that girl
      Or else conveys her to your son, as pledged.   10
      Oh, Herc! Please bet me! I'm itching to give my word,
      To reassure you that your money's safe.
      You can even keep the woman as a gift.
SIMO   I see no risk in closing out the deal
      On those conditions. [*Formally.*] Twenty minas do you   15
      Swear to give?
BALLIO   I do.
SIMO   That's not so bad!
      But have you ever met Pseudolus?
BALLIO   Sure, with your son.
SIMO   What did he say to you? What words did he use?
BALLIO   Theater rubbish, standard pimp abuse
      From the comic stage, well known to every child: 20
      He called me a dirty double-crossing crook.
SIMO   He didn't tell a lie.
BALLIO   So I wasn't angry.
      How can it matter if you bad-mouth a man
      Who doesn't care and doesn't contradict?
SIMO   All right, I'd like to hear why he's no problem.   25
BALLIO   Because he'll never nab the girl from me:

9. Troy could not be captured as long as it possessed the Palladium, a statue of Athena. Ulysses (Odysseus) stole it and guaranteed the Greek victory.

He can't! Remember I told you she was sold,
  Some time back, to a captain from Macedon?
SIMO I do.
BALLIO   Well, sir, his slave brought me the cash,
  With a sign in sealing wax—
SIMO   Go on.   30
BALLIO —As prearranged by the officer and me.
  He took away the girl a while ago.
SIMO Is that the honest truth?
BALLIO   The what? From me?
SIMO Watch out it's not some fabricated scheme.
BALLIO The seal and the letter make me positive.   35
  He took her and left for Sicyon just now.
SIMO Great Herc! Great work! I can hardly wait to appoint
  Pseudolus Mayor of Millstone Colony.[1]
  [*Looking offstage, left.*] But who's this in the cloak?
BALLIO   I've no idea.
  Let's watch to see where he goes and what he does.   40

ACT IV, SCENE 7

[*The real* HARPAX *enters (stage right) singing a self-congratulatory solo.* BALLIO
and SIMO *are not quite close enough to understand his words; at first,* BALLIO
will take him to be a young client, ripe for the plucking.]

HARPAX I find corrupt those slaves who flout
    Or disregard their master's rules.
  Some can't perform a task without
    A blunt reminder: stupid fools!
  No sooner out of master's sight   5
      They think they're free,
      At liberty
      To wench and brawl
      And squander all
  They have; but they're still slaves, all right!   10
  The only talent they possess
  Is getting by on craftiness.
  I've had no contact with that mob:
  I've kept my distance, done my job.
  In master's absence, I assume   15
  My master's standing in the room.
  I'm frightened when he's nowhere near;
  When he's around I feel no fear.

  And now for this assignment here!

  I remained in the tavern for Syrus' call—   20
    He had taken the letter and told me to wait;
    I expected some word when the pimp arrived home,

---

1. The gristmill, here ironically called a colony (which would be settled only by free citizens).

But the man hasn't come and it's now getting late.
So I'm here to discover just what's going on;
   Did he take me, perhaps, for a bit of a ride?   25
Now my sensible move is to knock on the door
   And to summon somebody who may be inside.
    [*Waving the purse, as he moves toward Ballio's door.*]
   I want the pimp to take this fee
   And send the girl away with me.

BALLIO [*Whispering to* SIMO.]   Hey there!
SIMO   What is it?
BALLIO   The man is mine.   30
SIMO   How so?
BALLIO   Because this catch looks fine.
   He's got the dough, he wants a doll;
   I'm going to crunch him, bones and all.
SIMO   Will you devour him on the spot?
BALLIO   Yes, while he's fresh and piping hot.   35
   For while he's in a giving mood,
   Not to eat him would be rude.
     Upstanding fellows make me poor,
       And sinners make me fat;
     The public likes the hero type,   40
       But I prefer the rat.
SIMO [*Aside.*]   The gods will give you living hell
   For wickedness like that!
HARPAX [*Aside.*]   I'm wasting time; I'll give these doors a swat,
   To see if Ballio's at home or not.   45
BALLIO [*To* SIMO.]   It's Venus who confers these joys,
    Who sends me all these good-time boys,
   These damn-the-cost, let's-go-for-brokers,
    Self-indulgent, carefree jokers.
   Lads who eat and drink and screw,   50
    In temperament they're not like you:
   A pleasure-hater so repressed
    You spoil all pleasure for the rest.
HARPAX [*Shouting at the door.*]   Hey, anybody home?
BALLIO [*Aside.*]   I think
   He's heading straight toward my house.   55
   I'll get a load of loot from him;
   I recognize my lucky charm.
HARPAX [*Knocking loudly.*]   Will no one open?
BALLIO   You in the cloak!
   What debt are you collecting here?
HARPAX   I'm after Ballio the pimp,   60
   The master of this residence.
BALLIO   Whoever you may be, young fellow,
   Spare the effort of that search.
HARPAX   Why so?
BALLIO   Because he's here before you,
   Face to face and large as life.   65

HARPAX [*Pointing to* SIMO.]   You're him?
SIMO [*Outraged.*]   Watch out, you dressed-up lout,
  Beware my crooked walking stick
  And point your filthy finger this way:
  [*Indicating* BALLIO.] Here's the pimp.   70
BALLIO [*Indicating* SIMO.]   And here's the gent.
  But gentle sir, you've often heard
  The howls of raging creditors,
  When you've been penniless except
  For what this pimp's provided you.   75
HARPAX   Why don't you talk to me?
BALLIO   O.K.,
  I'm talking. What do you want?
HARPAX   For you to take some money.
BALLIO   Give!
  My hand is constantly outstretched.
HARPAX   Here, then. Take these silver minas—   80
  Five, all counted and correct.
  My master, Polymachaeroplagides,
  Said I should bring them here to you,
  The sum he owed, and you should send
  Phoenicium away with me.   85
BALLIO   Your master?
HARPAX   That's correct.
BALLIO   The soldier?
HARPAX   Yes, that's right.
BALLIO   From Macedon?
HARPAX   Exactly so.
BALLIO   Sent you to me?
  Polymachaeroplagides?
HARPAX   You speak the truth.
BALLIO   Instructing you   90
  To give me this cash?
HARPAX   If you're in fact
  Pimp Ballio.
BALLIO   And told you then
  To take the woman away from me?
HARPAX   Yes.
BALLIO   Did he say Phoenicium?
HARPAX   Your memory is excellent!
BALLIO   Wait here!   95
  I'll soon be back.
HARPAX   Well, hurry up;
  Be quick! I'm in a rush. You see
  How late in the day it is.
BALLIO   I do;
  But still I want this man's advice.
  Just wait right here, I'll soon   100
  Be back to see you.
  [*Taking* SIMO *aside.*] What now, Simo?

What'll we do? He's caught in the act,
This man who brought the moneybag.
SIMO How so?
BALLIO   Don't you understand?   105
SIMO My ignorance is absolute.
BALLIO Your Pseudolus has hired this man
    To play the role of messenger
    From Macedon.
SIMO   Have you received
    His moneybag?
BALLIO   Is seeing believing?   110
SIMO Say! In dealing with those spoils,
    Remember to give half to me:
    Friends should share and share alike.
BALLIO Good grief! The whole amount is yours.
HARPAX [*Impatiently.*] How soon will you attend to me?
BALLIO [*Aloud.*]   Hang on!   115
    [*Sotto voce.*] What do you suggest now, Simo?
SIMO Let's have a little fun and games
    With this fictitious courier;
    We'll keep it up until he comes
    To realize the joke's on him.   120
BALLIO [*To* SIMO.] Just follow me.
    [*To* HARPAX.]   Well, well! So you're
    His slave, you say?
HARPAX   Most certainly.
BALLIO What was your purchase price?
HARPAX   His valor
    Won me on the battlefield.
    I was commanding officer   125
    In the place where I was born, back home.
SIMO Did he ransack the city jail,
    The place where you were born, back home?
HARPAX If you speak insulting words to me,
    You'll get them back.
BALLIO   How long a time   130
    Did it take to come from Sicyon?
HARPAX I arrived the second day, at noon.[2]
BALLIO Holy Herc! You made good time!
SIMO The man's as speedy as can be:
    When you look at his calves, you know he's fit—   135
    To wear great thumping ankle-chains.
BALLIO Tell me, were you accustomed to sleep
    In a cradle as a little boy?
SIMO Of course he was.
BALLIO   And had you the habit
    Of doing (tut, tut!) . . . you know what I mean?   140

2. Noon of the day after he set out (the ancients counted inclusively). Sicyon, a city in the northern Peloponnesus, is about fifty miles southwest of Athens as the crow flies, and longer by road through the rugged mountains of the Isthmus of Corinth—an impressive distance to cover in a day and a half.

SIMO   Tut, tut! Of course he had.
HARPAX   Are you both
   Quite sane?
BALLIO   A probing question now:
   At night, when the captain took the watch
   And you stood guard along with him,
   Did his sword-blade always fit   145
   Inside your scabbard perfectly?
HARPAX   Go hang yourself!
BALLIO   You'll get your chance
   At hanging soon enough today.
HARPAX   Either bring me out the girl
   Or else return the money.
BALLIO   Wait!   150
HARPAX   Why wait?
BALLIO   Tell us about this cloak:
   How much was the rental fee?
HARPAX   The which?
SIMO   What does it cost to hire a sword?
HARPAX [*Aside.*]   These men need their heads examined!
BALLIO   Don't leave—
HARPAX   Let go!
BALLIO   That hat: what price   155
   Will it fetch its owner for the day?
HARPAX   What "owner"? Are you raving mad?
   I own these clothes; I bought them as
   My private things.
BALLIO   You've got your only
   Private things between your legs.   160
HARPAX [*Aside.*]   These gents are smeared with oil; they need
   A good old-fashioned rubbing down.
BALLIO   Answer this question, in the name
   Of Herc (I'm very serious!):
   What are your wages? At what pittance   165
   Were you hired by Pseudolus?
HARPAX   Who is that Pseudolus?
BALLIO   Your coach,
   Who trained you in this stratagem,
   So you could use more stratagems
   To snatch the girl away from me.   170
HARPAX   What Pseudolus? What stratagems
   Do you keep going on about?
   I haven't the faintest notion who
   He is.
BALLIO   Come on, away with you!
   Today there'll be no profit here   175
   For swindlers. Just tell Pseudolus
   Another fellow snatched the spoils,
   The first Harpax who came along.
HARPAX   Honest to Pol, I'm really Harpax.

BALLIO   Honest to Pol, you want to be.   180
   This is a swindle, pure and simple.
HARPAX   I've handed you the moneybag;
   When I first came some time ago,
   I gave the token to your slave,
   Right here before your door—the letter   185
   Signed with the portrait of my master.
BALLIO   You gave a letter to my slave?
   Which slave?
HARPAX   Syrus was his name.
BALLIO [To SIMO.]   This swindle's based on more than nonsense:
   It's been thought out wickedly.   190
   That scoundrel of a Pseudolus!
   How cleverly he's planned it all!
   He gave him the exact amount
   Of money that the captain owed,
   And dressed the fellow up like this   195
   So he could take away the girl.
   [Aloud.] The real Harpax personally
   Brought that letter to me here.
HARPAX   My name is Harpax, and I am
   The Macedonian captain's slave.   200
   I've not been guilty of a single
   Wicked or deceitful deed,
   And I've no knowledge or awareness
   Of your precious Pseudolus.
SIMO   Barring a miracle, old pimp,   205
   You've forfeited the girl for good.
BALLIO   Ye gods, I'm getting really scared,
   The more I listen to his words.
   Ye gods, that Syrus fellow, too,
   Has left my heart frigidified—   210
   The one who took the token in.
   It's a wonder if he's not Pseudolus.
   [To HARPAX.] Hey, you, what did he look like, then,
   The man you gave the token to?
HARPAX   Bright red hair, protruding belly,   215
   Rather swarthy, chubby calves,
   With large head, ruddy face, sharp eyes,
   And utterly enormous feet.
BALLIO   You killed me when you reached those feet!
   It was Pseudolus himself.   220
   I'm done for! Now I'm dying, Simo.
HARPAX   I won't let you die, by Herc,
   Unless the money's paid me back—
   All twenty minas.
SIMO   In addition,
   Twenty minas more for me.   225
BALLIO [To SIMO.]   So will you take away the prize
   That I put forward as a joke?
SIMO   From wicked men it's right to take

All loot and lucre that they make.

BALLIO   At least hand over Pseudolus.   230

SIMO   Hand over Pseudolus to you?
What harm's he done? Did I not tell you
A hundred times to watch for him?

BALLIO   He ruined me.

SIMO   He sentenced me
To pay a twenty-mina fine.   235

BALLIO   What shall I do now?

HARPAX   Give me
The money, then go hang yourself.

BALLIO   Damn you! Follow me this way, please,
To the forum; I'll pay up.

HARPAX   I follow.

SIMO   What about me?

BALLIO   All foreigners get paid   240
Today; but citizens, tomorrow.
Pseudolus convened a court
That put me on trial for life or death,
When he dispatched that other man
To steal the girl from me today.   245
[To HARPAX.] Follow me. [To audience.] But don't you wait
For me to take this road back home.
The way life's gone, I've now decided
Alley travel's best for me.

HARPAX   If you only walked at the rate you talked,   250
We'd have reached the forum long ago.
     [Exit stage left.]

BALLIO   My happy birthday soon will be
My gloomy death-day. Woe is me!
     [Exit.]

ACT IV, SCENE 8

SIMO   I've hit him up just fine, the way
My slave has hit his enemy.
Now I intend to lie in wait
For Pseudolus—not the way it's done
In other plays, where people lurk   5
With whips and prods; I'll go inside
To find the twenty minas that
I promised if he did the job.
I'll pay him of my own free will.
The creature is so very clever,   10
Very cunning, very sly.
Pseudolus has quite surpassed
The Trojan horse, Ulysses too.

I'll get the money all prepared;
     Then Pseudolus will be ensnared.   15
     [Exit into his own house.]

Act V

[*Enter* PSEUDOLUS, *stage right, in wild disarray; he is wearing a garland and has obviously been drinking nonstop since he was last seen.*]

ACT V, SCENE 1

PSEUDOLUS   What's up, feet? My word, feet!
   You're acting absurd, feet.
Do you really suppose I'll be offered a hand
When I wobble because you're unable to stand?
     If I stumble and fall,   5
     My tumble is all
       Your fault!
Well, moving at last? Hey, foot, I feel
You need your backside kicked, you heel.
That's the trouble with wine: it always knows   10
Like a sneaky wrestler, to tackle the toes.

So help me Pollux, I do declare
I've gone on a simply spectacular tear!

Such an elegant spread, good taste sublime,
A marvellous host and a marvellous time.   15
No need for a rambling rhetorical style:
Parties like this make life worthwhile!
All forms of pleasure, all manner of love;
The next best thing to heaven above.

Two lovers locked in love's embrace,   20
   With lips engaged and tongues entwined;
Two partners snuggling breast to breast,
   A couple with coupling on their mind.

A snow-white hand, a toast, a sip,
Sweet cup of love and fellowship.   25

No hateful or obnoxious guest,
   No idiotic bore;
Just perfumes, unguents, pretty ribbons,
   Floral wreaths galore,
Provided in profusion there—   30
   Don't ask me any more.

    That's the way
    We spent the day,
Young master and I, getting happy and tight,
    After I   35
    Accomplished my
Objective by putting the foe to flight.

There I left them wining and dining,
　　Reclining and fondling their ladies of leisure;
My sweetheart was acting the life of the party,　　　　　40
　　Indulging herself with the utmost of pleasure.

I rose to leave; "Come, dance!" they cried.
　　I gave a sort of jiggle,
This way; with expert skill I tried
　　The Asiatic[3] wiggle.　　　　　45
All bundled in my frilly cloak,
I did these steps (a silly joke);
They clapped, they shouted out "Encore!"
"Come back, we want a little more!"
I had my doubts, but just the same　　　　　50
Continued with my foolish game:
Parading for my girl, like this,
So she would offer me a kiss,
I pirouetted—and I fell!
That was my frolic's sad farewell;　　　　　55
For while I struggled, *oops!* Watch out!
I shit my cloak (or just about).
Sweet Pollux, how they roared at me
For such a loss of dignity!

I'm given a jug: I take a quaff.　　　　　60
I change my cloak, get that one off;
I head for home, and home I'll stay
Till this hangover goes away.

So long, young boss! Old boss must learn
　　The bargain's satisfied.　　　　　65
[*Knocking on his own door.*] Hey, open up, somebody, hey!
　　Tell Simo I'm outside.

ACT V, SCENE 2

SIMO [*Cautiously opening his door.*]　　Some wretch at the door is calling
　　me.
What's this? How come? What do I see?
PSEUDOLUS　Your Pseudolus, garlanded and stewed.
SIMO [*Aside.*]　That's frank, at least. Some attitude!
Is he scared on my account? No, sir!　　　　　5
I wonder, should I growl or purr?
[*Pointing to a purse that he is carrying.*] This moneybag rules out brute
　　force;
I hope to save it still, of course.
PSEUDOLUS [*Approaching* SIMO.]　Good man, meet bad man: how do you
　　do.

---

3. Literally, "Ionic"—a reference to Greeks who lived on the Aegean Islands and on the coast of Asia Minor. Ionic dancing was known for its lasciviousness.

SIMO God bless you, Pseudolus! [*Recoiling.*] Phew!   10
    Get lost!

PSEUDOLUS Hey, why am I rejected?

SIMO What the hell had you expected,
    Drunk and belching in my face?

PSEUDOLUS Just hold me gently, please, in case
    I crash. How can you fail to see   15
    That I am smashed quite smashingly?

SIMO What gall is this, to come here tight,
    A wreath on your head, in broad daylight?

PSEUDOLUS It gives me pleasure. [*Belches again.*]

SIMO   Pleasure, sure!
    You're pleased to belch in my face once more.   20

PSEUDOLUS Belching's beautiful. Don't be a pain!

SIMO I think, you rascal, you've the power
    To guzzle Massic wine and drain
    Four harvests in a single hour.

PSEUDOLUS   "In winter," add.[4]   25

SIMO   All right, not bad!
    From where exactly should I say
    You steered your loaded barge this way?

PSEUDOLUS   From a bash with your son.
    Oh, Simo, what fun   30
    To cheat Ballio!
    My mission's accomplished
    According to plan.

SIMO   You're a terrible man!

PSEUDOLUS   The girl's doing this. [*A lewd gesture.*]   35
    She's in bed with your boy
    And she's actually free.

SIMO   I know the whole story;
    No need to tell me.

PSEUDOLUS   Then where is my money   40
    And why the delay?

SIMO   You've got right on your side.
    I admit; I'll pay.

        [SIMO *hands the purse to* PSEUDOLUS.]

PSEUDOLUS You said I'd never get it, yet it's mine.
    [*Pointing to his own shoulder*]. Just load this fellow up and fall in
    line.   45

SIMO [*To audience.*] Load him up?

PSEUDOLUS That's what I said.

SIMO [*To audience.*] May I beat him up instead?
    Will he pinch my purse and laugh at me, the swine?

PSEUDOLUS Woe to the vanquished!

SIMO   All right, turn your shoulder.   50

---

4. Because the Romans divided the daylight period into twelve hours, regardless of season, winter hours were of shorter duration [Translator's note].

[*Humiliated,* SIMO *places the purse over* PSEUDOLUS' *shoulder, and falls to his knees to beg for mercy.*]

PSEUDOLUS Ah!

SIMO I never thought I would become
A suppliant at your feet. Oh dear! Oh dear!

PSEUDOLUS Oh, stop it!

SIMO I hurt!

PSEUDOLUS If you didn't hurt, I would.

SIMO Will you take this purse from master, Pseudolus, friend?

PSEUDOLUS With all the feeling in my heart and soul! 55

SIMO Please give me a tiny refund; you agree?

PSEUDOLUS A greedy fellow: you can call me that,
For you won't get a penny richer from this purse.
You'd feel no pity for my wretched back,
If I had not achieved my goal today. 60

SIMO Someday, sure as I live, I'll get even with you!

PSEUDOLUS Why do you threaten me? My skin is tough.

SIMO Then go ahead. [*Starting to leave.*]

PSEUDOLUS All right, come back.

SIMO What for?

PSEUDOLUS Come back, that's all; no trick involved.

SIMO I'm here.

PSEUDOLUS Come, join me for a drink together.

SIMO *Me?* 65

PSEUDOLUS Just do as I tell you. If you come, I'll give you
Half or even more of your money back.

SIMO I'll come; conduct me where you will.

PSEUDOLUS Well, then. This business hasn't made you cross
At me or my young master, has it, boss? 70

SIMO Of course not!

PSEUDOLUS Step this way; I'll follow you.

SIMO Perhaps you should invite the audience, too.

PSEUDOLUS Those cheapskates never have invited me;
Why offer them our hospitality?
[*To audience.*]
But if you say 75
You liked our play,
And cheer our company before you go,
Then I'll invite you—to tomorrow's show.
[*Exeunt omnes.*]

CATULLUS
84?–54? B.C.

Gaius Valerius Catullus, born in the northern Italian city of Verona, lived out his short life in the last violent century of the Roman republic, but his poetry gives little hint that it was produced amid political upheaval. The 116 poems by him that have come down to us present a rich variety: imitations of Greek poets, long poems on Greek mythological themes, scurrilous personal attacks on contemporary politicians and private individuals, lighthearted verses designed to amuse his friends, and a magnificent marriage hymn. He also wrote a series of poems about his love affair with a Roman woman he calls Lesbia but who may have been Clodia, the enchanting but complex sister of one of Rome's most violent aristocrats turned political gangster. These poems, from which our selection is taken, present all the phases of the liaison, from the unalloyed happiness of the first encounters through doubt and hesitation to despair and virulent accusation, ending in heartbroken resignation to the bitter fact of Lesbia's betrayal.

Their tone ranges from the heights of joy at passionate love requited through the torments of simultaneous love and hate to the depths of morbid self-pity. Their direct and simple language seems to give readers immediate access to the experience of desire and betrayal and the feelings it arouses. In one sense, this impression is surely correct. But the poems are exceedingly complex. The passion is joined with considerable learning, and it is one of the remarkable characteristics of Catullus's poetry that strong emotion and sophistication are not at odds with each other but complementary. Poem 51, for example, powerfully describes the physical symptoms of love in the speaker; it is a translation into Latin of one of Sappho's most passionate Greek lyrics. Or consider poem 2, on Lesbia's pet sparrow: scholars have long suspected, probably correctly, an obscene double meaning in this pet.

There are further complexities. Many of the poems are addressed to someone—Lesbia, Catullus himself, or some third party—and the reader is a privileged audience to this communication. Who the addressee is and the relation between that person and the poet subtly shape the reader's view of the situation described in each poem. In poem 83, for example, when Lesbia seems to abuse "Catullus" in the presence of her husband, the speaker interprets this as a sign of love to which the husband is obtusely oblivious. Perhaps. Or is this a wishful interpretation? Who really is the dupe? Does the reader ever get access to Lesbia's feelings? Catullus's poetry is not simply a spontaneous outpouring of emotion but a carefully meditated portrayal of a love affair in which the poet's persona as well as his mistress is a character; and that gives depth and range to its passion.

The best general introduction to Catullus, with essential background and perceptive discussion of the poetry, is Charles Martin, *Catullus* (1992). For more detailed but highly readable discussions of contemporary culture and society, Clodia and her circle, and the poems' relation to this context, T. P. Wiseman, *Catullus and His World: A Reappraisal* (1985), is excellent. Two older books are still valuable: A. L. Wheeler, *Catullus and the Traditions of Ancient Poetry* (1934), and E. A. Havelock, *The Lyric Genius of Catullus* (1964). The first puts Catullus in his cultural and literary context; the second translates selected poems and offers a sensitive appreciation of them. Kenneth Quinn, *Catullus: An Interpretation* (1973), gives an interesting if idiosyncratic view of the poetry. For a depiction of Catullus as well as Lesbia/Clodia and her circle in a carefully researched historical detective novel, see Steven Saylor, *The Venus Throw* (1995).

5[1]

Lesbia, let us live only for loving,
and let us value at a single penny
all the loose flap of senile busybodies!
Suns when they set are capable of rising,
but at the setting of our own brief light   5
night is one sleep from which we never waken.
Give me a thousand kisses, then a hundred,
another thousand next, another hundred,
a thousand without pause & then a hundred,
until when we have run up our thousands   10
we will cry bankrupt, hiding our assets
from ourselves & any who would harm us,
knowing the volume of our trade in kisses.

2

Sparrow, you darling pet of my beloved,
which she caresses, presses to her body
or teases with the tip of one sly finger
until you peck at it in tiny outrage!
—for there are times when my desired, shining   5
lady is moved to turn to you for comfort,
to find (as I imagine) ease for ardor,
solace, a little respite from her sorrow—
if I could only play with you as she does,
and be relieved of my tormenting passion!   10

51[2]

To me that man seems like a god in heaven,
seems—may I say it?—greater than all gods are,
who sits by you & without interruption
      watches you, listens

1. All selections translated by Charles Martin.   2. A translation into Latin of Sappho's Greek poem *Like the very gods in my sight is he* (see above, p. 516), that reproduces Sappho's metrical scheme (imitated in the English translation).

to your light laughter, which casts such confusion   5
onto my senses, Lesbia, that when I
gaze at you merely, all of my well-chosen
    words are forgotten[3]

as my tongue thickens & a subtle fire
runs through my body while my ears are deafened   10
by their own ringing & at once my eyes are
    covered in darkness!

Leisure, Catullus. More than just a nuisance,
leisure: you riot, overmuch enthusing.
Fabulous cities & their sometime kings have   15
    died of such leisure.[4]

86

Many find Quintia stunning. I find her attractive:
    tall, "regal," fair in complexion—these points are granted.
But stunning? No, I deny it: the woman is scarcely venerious,
    there's no spice at all in all the length of her body!
Now Lesbia is stunning, for Lesbia's beauty is total: 5
    and by that sum all other women are diminished.

87

No other woman can truthfully say she was cherished
    as much as Lesbia was when I was her lover.
Never, in any such bond, was fidelity greater
    than mine, in my love for you, ever discovered.

109

Darling, we'll both have equal shares in the sweet love you offer,
    and it will endure forever—you assure me.
O heaven, see to it that she can truly keep this promise,
    that it came from her heart & was sincerely given,
so that we may spend the rest of our days in this lifelong   5
    union, this undying compact of holy friendship.

---

3. *All . . . forgotten* is a guess at the sense of a line missing in the original.   4. The final stanza may not
belong to this poem; if it does, it is Catullus's addition to his Sapphic original.

83

Lesbia hurls abuse at me in front of her husband:
    that fatuous person finds it highly amusing!
Nothing gets through to you, jackass—for silence would signal
    that she'd been cured of me, but her barking & bitching
show that not only [have][5] I not been forgotten,   5
    —but that this burns her: and so she rants & rages.

70

My woman says there is no one whom she'd rather marry
    than me, not even Jupiter,[6] if he came courting.
That's what she says—but what a woman says to a passionate lover
    ought to be scribbled on wind, on running water.

72

You used to say that you wished to know only Catullus,
    Lesbia, and wouldn't take even Jove before me!
I didn't regard you just as my mistress then: I cherished you
    as a father does his sons or his daughters' husbands.
Now that I know you, I burn for you even more fiercely,   5
    though I regard you as almost utterly worthless.
How can that be, you ask? It's because such cruelty forces
    lust to assume the shrunken place of affection.

85

I hate & love. And if you should ask how I can do both,
    I couldn't say; but I feel it, and it shivers me.

75

To such a state have I been brought by your mischief, my Lesbia,
    and so completely ruined by my devotion,
that I couldn't think kindly of you if you did the best only,
    nor cease to love, even if you should do—everything.

---

5. Editorial substitution for the translator's *haven't*.   **6.** Jupiter (or Jove) was the supreme god of the Roman pantheon, corresponding to the Greek Zeus.

8

Wretched Catullus! You have to stop this nonsense,
admit that what you see has ended is over!
Once there were days which shone for you with rare brightness,
when you would follow wherever your lady led you,
the one we once loved as we will love no other;   5
there was no end in those days to our pleasures,
when what you wished for was what she also wanted.
Yes, there were days which shone for you with rare brightness.
Now she no longer wishes; you mustn't want it,
you've got to stop chasing her now—cut your losses,   10
harden your heart & hold out firmly against her.
Goodbye now, lady. Catullus' heart is hardened,
he will not look to you nor call against your wishes—
how you'll regret it when nobody comes calling!
So much for you, bitch—your life is all behind you!   15
Now who will come to see you, thinking you lovely?
Whom will you love now, and whom will you belong to?
Whom will you kiss? And whose lips will you nibble?
But *you*, Catullus! *You* must hold out now, firmly!

58

Lesbia, Caelius[7]—yes, our darling,
yes, *Lesbia*, the Lesbia Catullus
once loved uniquely, more than any other!
—now on streetcorners & in wretched alleys
she shucks the offspring of greathearted Remus.[8]   5

11[9]

Aurelius & Furius, true comrades,
whether Catullus penetrates to where in
outermost India booms the eastern ocean's
    wonderful thunder;

whether he stops with Arabs or Hyrcani,   5
Parthian bowmen or nomadic Sagae;[1]
or goes to Egypt, which the Nile so richly
    dyes, overflowing;

even if he should scale the lofty Alps, or
summon to mind the mightiness of Caesar   10

---

7. Perhaps the Marcus Caelius Rufus who was one of Clodia's lovers and whom the statesman and orator Cicero defended when she sued him for trying to poison her.   8. Brother of Romulus, founder of Rome; symbol of Rome's greatness.   9. Like poem 51, also in Sapphic meter.   1. These are all peoples on the fringes of the Roman empire (and so in Roman eyes exotic and menacing).

    viewing the Gallic Rhine, the dreadful Britons[2]
      at the world's far end—

    you're both prepared to share in my adventures,
    and any others which the gods may send me.
    Back to my girl then, carry her this bitter   15
      message, these spare words:

    May she have joy & profit from her cocksmen,
    go down embracing hundreds all together,
    never with love, but without interruption
      wringing their balls dry;   20

    nor look to my affection as she used to,
    for she has left it broken, like a flower
    at the edge of a field after the plowshare
      brushes it, passing.

76

If any pleasure can come to a man through recalling
    decent behavior in his relations with others,
not breaking his word, and never, in any agreement,
    deceiving men by abusing vows sworn to heaven,
then countless joys will await you in old age, Catullus,   5
    as a reward for this unrequited passion!
For all of those things which a man could possibly say or
    do have all been said & done by you already,
and none of them counted for anything, thanks to her vileness!
    Then why endure your self-torment any longer?   10
Why not abandon this wretched affair altogether,
    spare yourself pain the gods don't intend you to suffer!
It's hard to break off with someone you've loved such a long time:
    it's hard, but you have to do it, somehow or other.
Your only chance is to get out from under this sickness,   15
    no matter whether or not you think you're able.
O gods, if pity is yours, or if ever to any
    who lay near death you offered the gift of your mercy,
look on my suffering: if my life seems to you decent,
    then tear from within me this devouring cancer,   20
this heavy dullness wasting the joints of my body,
    completely driving every joy from my spirit!
Now I no longer ask that she love me as I love her,
    or—even less likely—that she give up the others:
all that I ask for is health, an end to this foul sickness!   25
    O gods, grant me this in exchange for my worship.

---

2. Julius Caesar (100–44 B.C.) began the conquest of Gaul in 58 B.C. and in 55 B.C. made an expedition
to Britain.

VIRGIL
70–19 B.C.

Publius Virgilius Maro was born in northern Italy, and very little is known about his life. The earliest work that is certainly his is the *Bucolics,* a collection of poems in the pastoral genre that have had enormous influence. These were followed by the *Georgics,* a didactic poem on farming, in four books, which many critics consider his finest work. The *Aeneid,* the Roman epic, was left unfinished at his death.

Like all the Latin poets, Virgil built on the solid foundations of his Greek predecessors. The story of Aeneas, the Trojan prince who came to Italy and whose descendants founded Rome, combines the themes of the *Odyssey* (the wanderer in search of home) and the *Iliad* (the hero in battle). Virgil borrows Homeric turns of phrase, similes, sentiments, and whole incidents; his Aeneas, like Achilles, sacrifices prisoners to the shade of a friend and, like Odysseus, descends alive to the world of the dead. But unlike Achilles, Aeneas does not satisfy the great passion of his life, nor, like Odysseus, does he find a home and peace. The personal objectives of both of Homer's heroes are sacrificed by Aeneas for a greater objective. His mission, imposed on him by the gods, is to found a city, from which, in the fullness of time, will spring the Roman state.

Homer presents us in the *Iliad* with the tragic pattern of the individual will, Achilles' wrath. But Aeneas is more than an individual. He is the prototype of the ideal Roman ruler; his qualities are the devotion to duty and the seriousness of purpose that were to give the Mediterranean world two centuries of ordered government after Augustus. Aeneas's mission begins in disorder in the burning city of Troy, but he leaves it, carrying his father on his shoulders and leading his little son by the hand. This famous picture emphasizes the fact that, unlike Achilles, he is securely set in a continuity of generations, the immortality of the family group, just as his mission to found a city, a home for the gods of Troy whose statues he carries with him, places him in a political and religious continuity. Achilles has no future. When he mentions his father and son, neither of whom he will see again, he emphasizes for us the loneliness of his short career. Odysseus has a father, wife, and son, and his heroic efforts are directed toward reestablishing himself in his proper context, that home in which he will be no longer a man in a world of magic and terror but a man in an organized and continuous community. But he fights for himself. Aeneas, on the other hand, suffers and fights, not for himself but for the future; his own life is unhappy, and his death miserable. Yet he can console himself with the glory of his sons to come, the pageant of Roman achievement that he is shown by his father in the world below and that he carries on his shield. Aeneas's future is Virgil's present; the consolidation of the Roman peace under Augustus is the reward of Aeneas's unhappy life of effort and suffering.

Summarized like this, the *Aeneid* sounds like propaganda, which, in one sense of the word, it is. What saves it from the besetting fault of even the best propaganda—the partial concealment of the truth—is the fact that Virgil maintains an independence of the power that he is celebrating and sees his hero in the round. He knows that the Roman ideal of devotion to duty has another side, the suppression of many aspects of the personality, and that the man who wins and uses power must sacrifice much of himself, must live a life that, compared with that of Achilles or Odysseus, is constricted. In Virgil's poem Aeneas betrays the great passion of his life, his love for Dido, queen of Carthage. He does it reluctantly, but nevertheless he leaves her, and the full realization of what he has lost comes to him only when he meets her ghost in the world below. He weeps (as he did not at Carthage) and he pleads, in stronger terms than he did then, the overriding power that forced him to depart: "I left your land against my will, my queen." She leaves him without a word, her silence as impervious to pleas and tears as his was once at Carthage, and she goes back to join her first love, her husband, Sychaeus. Aeneas has sacrificed his love to something greater, but this does not insulate him from unhappiness. The limitations on the dedicated individual are emphasized by the contrasting figure of Dido, who follows her own impulse always, even in death. By her death, Virgil tells us expressly, she forestalls fate, breaks loose from the pattern in which Aeneas remains to the bitter end.

The angry reactions that this part of the poem has produced in many critics are the true measure of Virgil's success. Aeneas does act in such a way that he forfeits much of our sympathy, but this is surely exactly what Virgil intended. The Dido episode is not, as many critics have supposed, a flaw in the great design, a case of Virgil's sympathy outrunning his admiration for Aeneas; it is Virgil's emphatic statement of the sacrifice that the Roman ideal of duty demands. Aeneas's sacrifice is so great that few of us could make it ourselves, and none of us can contemplate it in another without a feeling of loss. It is an expression of the famous Virgilian sadness that informs every line of the *Aeneid* and that makes a poem that was in its historical context a command performance into the great epic that has dominated Western literature ever since.

VIRGIL IN LATIN

Conticuere omnes intentique ora tenebant;
inde toro pater Aeneas sic orsus ab alto:
　　Infandum, regina, iubes renovare dolorem,
Troianas ut opes et lamentabile regnum
eruerint Danai, quaeque ipse miserrima uidi　　　　　　　　5
et quorum pars magna fui. quis talia fando
Myrmidonum Dolopomue aut duri miles Ulixi
temperet a lacrimis? et iam nox umida caelo
praecipitat suadentque cadentia sidera somnos.
　　sed si tantus amor casus cognoscere nostros　　　　　　10
et breviter Troiae supremum audire laborem,
quamquam animus meminisse horret luctuque refugit,
incipiam.

This is the beginning of book 2 of the *Aeneid*; Aeneas, at the banquet in Carthage, tells the story of the fall of Troy. The long lines do not employ rhyme but they have a regular rhythmic pattern based not on stress, as in English verse, but on length of syllable—that is, the time taken to pronounce it. Some vowels are naturally long, and others naturally short, but a short vowel may be made long by position (if it is followed by two consonants, it takes just as much time to pronounce as if it were naturally long). The line consists of six feet, either dactyl ($-\smile\smile$) or spondee ($--$). In the first four feet various combinations are employed, but the last two feet, except in cases where a special effect is sought, are always dactyl plus spondee.

This hexameter (six-foot) line is capable of great variety, contained always in the formal pattern. Unfortunately, attempts to reproduce its disciplined variety in English stressed verse (Longfellow's "This is the forest primeval," for example) have not proved successful, and the translator has used a modern adaptation of the basic English line, the iambic pentameter of Shakespeare and Milton.

The subtle variation of the rhythm is not the only problem faced by translators; they must also try to compensate for the loss of effects that depend on the flexibility of Latin word order. In English, syntactical relationship is determined by that order: "man bites dog" means the opposite of "dog bites man." In Latin, because the terminations of the nouns show who does what to whom, "man bites dog" is *vir mordet canem,* and "dog bites man" *canis mordet virum.* Consequently, the words can be arranged in any order with no change of meaning. *Virum canis mordet, canis virum mordet,* and any other combination of these three elements all mean the same thing: "dog bites man." But the word order is not without its force; it can indicate emphasis. Normal order—subject, object, verb (for the Latin verb tends toward the end of the sentence)—would be *canis virum mordet*. But putting *virum*, the object, first—*virum canis mordet*—would draw attention to that word: "it was a *man* the dog bit."

This is a simple example; much more complicated effects are available to a poet in extended sentences. Line 3 of the passage quoted above, for example, uses the flexibility of word order not only for emphasis but also for exploring the possibilities of ambiguity and surprise offered by a highly inflected language. *Infandum* ("unspeakable, something that cannot be said") is the first word, and we do not know from its termination whether it is subject or object or whether it is to be understood as a noun ("an unspeakable thing") or an adjective for which a noun will be supplied later. *Regina* ("queen") could, according to its termination, be the subject of the sentence, but the context, Aeneas's reply to the queen's request for his story, suggests strongly that it is a form of address: "Unspeakable, oh Queen." The subject comes with the next word, the verb *iubes*; its termination shows that this is the second person, the "you" form—"you command." She has commanded something unspeakable. Is the reader being prepared for a refusal on the part of Aeneas to tell his story? *Renovare* defines the queen's order—"to renew"—and *dolorem* tells us what he is to renew— "sorrow." And the termination of this word suggests that the first word of the line, *infandum*, is in fact an adjective defining *dolorem*. The line, when one reaches this last word, re-forms itself into an unexpected pattern: "Unspeakable, oh Queen, is the sorrow you command me to renew." The line is enclosed between the two most important words in Aeneas's statement, *infandum* and *dolorem*; its last word imposes on us a slight change in our understanding of its first and so redirects attention to that solemn opening word of Aeneas's evocation of the fall of Troy, three long syllables heavy with grief for the lost splendor of a city that is now ash and rubble.

Useful and accessible discussions of basic aspects of the *Aeneid* and of its historical and literary context are W. A. Camps, *An Introduction to Virgil's Aeneid* (1969); Jasper Griffin, *Virgil* (1986); and K. W. Gransden, *Virgil, the Aeneid* (1990). R. D. Williams, *The Aeneid of Virgil: A Companion to the Translation of C. Day Lewis* (1985), gives a summary and outline of the poem, with brief notes on specific passages. W. S. Anderson, *The Art of the Aeneid* (1969), is a sensible book-by-book reading of the poem. Brooks Otis, *Virgil: A Study in Civilized Poetry* (1963, 1985), and R. O. A. M. Lyne, *Further Voices in Virgil's Aeneid* (1987), are more detailed but readable and influential works of criticism. Valuable collections of essays by various authors are Steele Commager, ed., *Virgil: A Collection of Critical Essays* (1966); Harold Bloom, ed., *Virgil* (1986), and Harold Bloom, ed., *Virgil's Aeneid* (1987).

PRONOUNCING GLOSSARY

The following list uses common English syllables and stress accents to provide rough equivalents of selected words whose pronunciation may be unfamiliar to the general reader.

Aeneas: *i-nee'-uhs*	Deiphobus: *day-i'-fo-bus*
Aeneid: *i-nee'-id*	Dido: *dai'-doh*
Anchisēs: *an-kai'-seez*	Dionysus: *dai-oh-nai'-sus*
Andromachë: *an-dro'-ma-kee*	Eumenidēs: *yoo-me'-ni-deez*
Aurora: *aw-roh'-rah*	Hecate: *he'-kat-ee*
Automedon: *aw-to'-me-don*	Lethe: *lee'-thee*
Charon: *kah'-ron*	Musaeus: *moo-see'-us*
Cyllenē: *si-lee'-nee*	Peneleus: *pee-ne'-lyoos*
Chimaera: *kai-meer'-uh*	Phrygian: *fri'-jun*
Cytherëa: *si-the-ree'-uh*	Pirithoüs: *pi-ri'-thoh-us*
Danaans: *da'-nay-unz*	Scaean: *see'-an*

Teucer: *tyoo'-ser*   Tisiphone: *ti-si'-fo-nee*
Thymoetes: *thee-moy'-teez*   Xanthus: *zan'-thus*

The Aeneid[1]

FROM BOOK I

[Prologue]

I sing of warfare and a man at war.[2]
From the sea-coast of Troy in early days
He came to Italy by destiny,
To our Lavinian[3] western shore,
A fugitive, this captain, buffeted   5
Cruelly on land as on the sea
By blows from powers of the air—behind them
Baleful Juno[4] in her sleepless rage.
And cruel losses were his lot in war,
Till he could found a city and bring home   10
His gods to Latium, land of the Latin race,
The Alban[5] lords, and the high walls of Rome.
Tell me the causes now, O Muse, how galled
In her divine pride, and how sore at heart
From her old wound, the queen of gods compelled him—   15
A man apart, devoted to his mission—
To undergo so many perilous days
And enter on so many trials. Can anger
Black as this prey on the minds of heaven?
Tyrian[6] settlers in that ancient time   20
Held Carthage,[7] on the far shore of the sea,
Set against Italy and Tiber's[8] mouth,
A rich new town, warlike and trained for war.
And Juno, we are told, cared more for Carthage
Than for any walled city of the earth,   25
More than for Samos,[9] even. There her armor
And chariot were kept, and, fate permitting,
Carthage would be the ruler of the world.
So she intended, and so nursed that power.
But she had heard long since   30
That generations born of Trojan blood
Would one day overthrow her Tyrian walls,

1. Translated by Robert Fitzgerald.   2. Aeneas, a Trojan champion in the fight for Troy, son of Venus (or Aphrodite, the goddess of love) and Anchisēs, and a member of the royal house of Troy.   3. Near Rome, named after the city of Lavinium. After the fall of Troy, Aeneas went in search of a new home, eventually settling here.   4. Wife of the ruler of the gods (Hera in Greek). As in the *Iliad*, she is a bitter enemy of the Trojans.   5. The city of Alba Longa was founded by Aeneas's son Ascanius. Romulus and Remus, the builders of Rome, were also from Alba. Latium is the coastal plain on which Rome is situated.   6. From Tyre, on the coast of Palestine, the principal city of the Phoenicians, a seafaring people.   7. On the coast of North Africa, opposite Sicily. Originally a Tyrian colony, it became a rich commercial center, controlling traffic in the western Mediterranean.   8. The river that flows through Rome.   9. A large island off the coast of Asia Minor, famous for its cult of Hera (Juno).

And from that blood a race would come in time
With ample kingdoms, arrogant in war,
For Libya's ruin: so the Parcae[1] spun.   35
In fear of this, and holding in memory
The old war she had carried on at Troy
For Argos'[2] sake (the origins of that anger,
That suffering, still rankled: deep within her,
Hidden away, the judgment Paris[3] gave,   40
Snubbing her loveliness; the race she hated;
The honors given ravished Ganymede),
Saturnian Juno,[4] burning for it all,
Buffeted on the waste of sea those Trojans
Left by the Greeks and pitiless Achilles,   45
Keeping them far from Latium. For years
They wandered as their destiny drove them on
From one sea to the next: so hard and huge
A task it was to found the Roman people.

[Aeneas Arrives in Carthage]

Summary   The story opens with a storm, provoked by Juno's agency, which scatters Aeneas's fleet off Sicily and separates him from his companions. He lands on the African coast near Carthage. Setting out with his friend Achatës to explore the country, he meets his mother, Venus (Aphrodite), who tells him that the rest of his ships are safe and directs him to the city just founded by Dido, the queen of Carthage. Venus surrounds Aeneas and Achatës with a cloud so that they can see without being seen.

Meanwhile

The two men pressed on where the pathway led,
Soon climbing a long ridge that gave a view
Down over the city and facing towers.
Aeneas found, where lately huts had been,   5
Marvelous buildings, gateways, cobbled ways,
And din of wagons. There the Tyrians[5]
Were hard at work: laying courses for walls,
Rolling up stones to build the citadel,
While others picked out building sites and plowed   10
A boundary furrow. Laws were being enacted,
Magistrates and a sacred senate chosen.
Here men were dredging harbors, there they laid
The deep foundation of a theater,
And quarried massive pillars to enhance   15
The future stage—as bees in early summer
In sunlight in the flowering fields

---

1. The Fates, who were imagined as female divinities who spun human destinies. Rome captured and destroyed Carthage in 146 B.C. Libya is used as an inclusive name for the North African Coast.   2. Home city of the Achaean (Greek) kings Agamemnon and Menelaus. Juno was on their side when they went to Troy to retrieve Helen, Menelaus's wife.   3. Son of King Priam of Troy. He was asked to judge which goddess—Venus, Juno, or Minerva (Athena)—was most beautiful. All three offered bribes, but Venus's promise (of Helen's love) prevailed, and Paris awarded her the prize.   4. Her father was Saturn, a Titan. Ganymede was a Trojan boy of extreme beauty who was taken up into heaven by Jupiter (Zeus), ruler of the gods.   5. See p. 817, n.6.

Hum at their work, and bring along the young
Full-grown to beehood; as they cram their combs
With honey, brimming all the cells with nectar,   20
Or take newcomers' plunder, or like troops
Alerted, drive away the lazy drones,
And labor thrives and sweet thyme scents the honey.
Aeneas said: "How fortunate these are
Whose city walls are rising here and now!"   25

He looked up at the roofs, for he had entered,
Swathed in cloud—strange to relate—among them,
Mingling with men, yet visible to none.
In mid-town stood a grove that cast sweet shade
Where the Phoenicians, shaken by wind and sea,   30
Had first dug up that symbol Juno showed them,
A proud warhorse's head: this meant for Carthage
Prowess in war and ease of life[6] through ages.
Here being built by the Sidonian[7] queen
Was a great temple planned in Juno's honor,   35
Rich in offerings and the godhead there.
Steps led up to a sill of bronze, with brazen
Lintel, and bronze doors on groaning pins.
Here in this grove new things that met his eyes
Calmed Aeneas' fear for the first time.   40
Here for the first time he took heart to hope
For safety, and to trust his destiny more
Even in affliction. It was while he walked
From one to another wall of the great temple
And waited for the queen, staring amazed   45
At Carthaginian promise, at the handiwork
Of artificers and the toil they spent upon it:
He found before his eyes the Trojan battles
In the old war, now known throughout the world—
The great Atridae, Priam, and Achilles,   50
Fierce in his rage at both sides.[8] Here Aeneas
Halted, and tears came.
                         "What spot on earth,"
He said, "what region of the earth, Achatës,
Is not full of the story of our sorrow?
Look, here is Priam. Even so far away   55
Great valor has due honor; they weep here
For how the world goes, and our life that passes
Touches their hearts. Throw off your fear. This fame
Insures some kind of refuge."
                         He broke off
To feast his eyes and mind on a mere image,   60
Sighing often, cheeks grown wet with tears,

6. Because they would have a land fertile enough to support horses.   7. From Sidon, a Phoenician city.   8. Because Achilles, the greatest warrior on the Achaean side, quarreled with Agamemnon. *Atridae*: sons of Atreus: Agamemnon and Menelaus.

To see again how, fighting around Troy,
The Greeks broke here, and ran before the Trojans,
And there the Phrygians[9] ran, as plumed Achilles
Harried them in his warcar. Nearby, then,   65
He recognized the snowy canvas tents
Of Rhesus,[1] and more tears came: these, betrayed
In first sleep, Diomedes devastated,
Swording many, till he reeked with blood,
Then turned the mettlesome horses toward the beachhead   70
Before they tasted Trojan grass or drank
At Xanthus ford.[2]
                And on another panel
Troilus,[3] without his armor, luckless boy,
No match for his antagonist, Achilles,
Appeared pulled onward by his team: he clung   75
To his warcar, though fallen backward, hanging
On to the reins still, head dragged on the ground,
His javelin scribbling S's in the dust.
Meanwhile to hostile Pallas'[4] shrine
The Trojan women walked with hair unbound,   80
Bearing the robe of offering, in sorrow,
Entreating her, beating their breasts. But she,
Her face averted, would not raise her eyes.
And there was Hector, dragged around Troy walls
Three times, and there for gold Achilles sold him,   85
Bloodless and lifeless. Now indeed Aeneas
Heaved a mighty sigh from deep within him,
Seeing the spoils, the chariot, and the corpse
Of his great friend, and Priam, all unarmed,
Stretching his hands out.
              He himself he saw   90
In combat with the first of the Achaeans,
And saw the ranks of Dawn, black Memnon's[5] arms;
Then, leading the battalion of Amazons
With half-moon shields, he saw Penthesilëa[6]
Fiery amid her host, buckling a golden   95
Girdle beneath her bare and arrogant breast,
A girl who dared fight men, a warrior queen.
Now, while these wonders were being surveyed
By Aeneas of Dardania,[7] while he stood
Enthralled, devouring all in one long gaze,   100
The queen paced toward the temple in her beauty,
Dido, with a throng of men behind.

---

9. Trojans.   1. King of Thrace, who came to the aid of Troy just before the end of the war.   2. An oracle proclaimed that if Rhesus's horses ate Trojan grass and drank the water of the river Xanthus, Troy would not fall. Odysseus and Diomedes went into the Trojan lines at night, killed the king, and stole the horses.   3. A young son of Priam.   4. Athena (see *Iliad* 6.218ff.).   5. King of the Ethiopians, who fought on the Trojan side.   6. Queen of the Amazons, killed by Achilles.   7. The kingdom of Troy.

As on Eurotas bank or Cynthus ridge
Diana[8] trains her dancers, and behind her
On every hand the mountain nymphs appear,   105
A myriad converging; with her quiver
Slung on her shoulders, in her stride she seems
The tallest, taller by a head than any,
And joy pervades Latona's[9] quiet heart:
So Dido seemed, in such delight she moved   110
Amid her people, cheering on the toil
Of a kingdom in the making. At the door
Of the goddess' shrine, under the temple dome,
All hedged about with guards on her high throne,
She took her seat. Then she began to give them   115
Judgments and rulings, to apportion work
With fairness, or assign some tasks by lot,
When suddenly Aeneas saw approaching,
Accompanied by a crowd, Antheus and Sergestus
And brave Cloanthus,[1] with a few companions,   120
Whom the black hurricane had driven far
Over the sea and brought to other coasts.
He was astounded, and Achatës too
Felt thrilled by joy and fear: both of them longed
To take their friends' hands, but uncertainty   125
Hampered them. So, in their cloudy mantle,
They hid their eagerness, waiting to learn
What luck these men had had, where on the coast
They left their ships, and why they came. It seemed
Spokesmen for all the ships were now arriving,   130
Entering the hall, calling for leave to speak.
When all were in, and full permission given
To make their plea before the queen, their eldest,
Ilioneus, with composure said:
                             "Your majesty,
Granted by great Jupiter freedom to found   135
Your new town here and govern fighting tribes
With justice—we poor Trojans, worn by winds
On every sea, entreat you: keep away
Calamity of fire from our ships!
Let a godfearing people live, and look   140
More closely at our troubles. Not to ravage
Libyan hearths or turn with plunder seaward
Have we come; that force and that audacity
Are not for beaten men.
                    There is a country
Called by the Greeks Hesperia, very old,   145
Potent in warfare and in wealth of earth;
Oenotrians farmed it; younger settlers now,

---

8. Virgin goddess of the hunt (Artemis in Greek). Eurotas is a river near Sparta where Diana was worshiped. Cynthus is a mountain on the island of Delos, Diana's birthplace. 9. Diana's mother (Leto in Greek). 1. Ship captains of Aeneas's fleet from whom he had been separated in the storm.

The tale goes, call it by their chief's[2] name, Italy.
We laid our course for this.
But stormy Orion[3] and a high sea rising   150
Deflected us on shoals and drove us far,
With winds against us, into whelming waters,
Unchanneled reefs. We kept afloat, we few,
To reach your coast. What race of men is this?
What primitive state could sanction this behavior?   155
Even on beaches we are denied a landing,
Harried by outcry and attack, forbidden
To set foot on the outskirts of your country.
If you care nothing for humanity
And merely mortal arms, respect the gods   160
Who are mindful of good actions and of evil!

We had a king, Aeneas—none more just,
More zealous, greater in warfare and in arms.
If fate preserves him, if he does not yet
Lie spent amid the insensible shades but still   165
Takes nourishment of air, we need fear nothing;
Neither need you repent of being first
In courtesy, to outdo us. Sicily too
Has towns and plowlands and a famous king
Of Trojan blood, Acestës.[4] May we be   170
Permitted here to beach our damaged ships,
Hew timbers in your forest, cut new oars,
And either sail again for Latium, happily,
If we recover shipmates and our king,
Or else, if that security is lost,   175
If Libyan waters hold you, Lord Aeneas,
Best of Trojans, hope of Iulus[5] gone,
We may at least cross over to Sicily
From which we came, to homesteads ready there,
And take Acestës for our king."
                                    Ilioneus   180
Finished, and all the sons of Dardanus[6]
Murmured assent. Dido with eyes downcast
Replied in a brief speech:
                    "Cast off your fear,
You Teucrians, put anxiety aside.
Severe conditions and the kingdom's youth   185
Constrain me to these measures, to protect
Our long frontiers with guards.
                            Who has not heard
Of the people of Aeneas, of Troy city,
Her valors and her heroes, and the fires

2. Italus. *Hesperia*: the western country. The Oenotrians were the original inhabitants of Italy. 3. The
setting of this constellation in November signaled the onset of stormy weather at sea. 4. His mother
was Trojan; he had offered Aeneas and his people a home in his dominions. 5. Ascanius, Aeneas's
son. 6. Ancestor of the Trojans.

Of the great war? We are not so oblivious, 190
We Phoenicians. The sun yokes his team
Within our range[7] at Carthage. Whether you choose
Hesperia Magna and the land of Saturn
Or Eryx[8] in the west and King Acestës,
I shall dispatch you safely with an escort, 195
Provisioned from my stores. Or would you care
To join us in this realm on equal terms?
The city I build is yours; haul up your ships;
Trojan and Tyrian will be all one to me.
If only he were here, your king himself, 200
Caught by the same easterly, Aeneas!
Indeed, let me send out trustworthy men
Along the coast, with orders to comb it all
From one end of Libya to the other,
In case the sea cast the man up and now 205
He wanders lost, in town or wilderness."

Elated at Dido's words, both staunch Achatës
And father Aeneas had by this time longed
To break out of the cloud. Achatës spoke
With urgency:
                    "My lord, born to the goddess, 210
What do you feel, what is your judgment now?
You see all safe, our ships and friends recovered.
One is lost;[9] we saw that one go down
Ourselves, amid the waves. Everything else
Bears out your mother's own account of it." 215

He barely finished when the cloud around them
Parted suddenly and thinned away
Into transparent air. Princely Aeneas
Stood and shone in the bright light, head and shoulders
Noble as a god's. For she who bore him[1] 220
Breathed upon him beauty of hair and bloom
Of youth and kindled brilliance in his eyes,
As an artist's hand gives style to ivory,
Or sets pure silver, or white stone of Paros,[2]
In framing yellow gold. Then to the queen 225
He spoke as suddenly as, to them all,
He had just appeared:
                    "Before your eyes I stand,
Aeneas the Trojan, that same one you look for,
Saved from the sea off Libya.
                    You alone,
Moved by the untold ordeals of old Troy, 230

7. I.e., we are not outside the circuit of the sun; we are part of the civilized world and hear the news.   8. On the west coast of Sicily. *Land of Saturn*: an old legend connected Italy with Saturn, the father of Jupiter.   9. One ship, captained by Orontes, sank in the storm.   1. Venus.   2. The marble of the island of Paros was famous.

Seeing us few whom the Greeks left alive,
Worn out by faring ill on land and sea,
Needy of everything—you'd give these few
A home and city, allied with yourselves.
Fit thanks for this are not within our power,   235
Not to be had from Trojans anywhere
Dispersed in the great world.
             May the gods—
And surely there are powers that care for goodness,
Surely somewhere justice counts—may they
And your own consciousness of acting well   240
Reward you as they should. What age so happy
Brought you to birth? How splendid were your parents
To have conceived a being like yourself!
So long as brooks flow seaward, and the shadows
Play over mountain slopes, and highest heaven   245
Feeds the stars, your name and your distinction
Go with me, whatever lands may call me."

With this he gave his right hand to his friend
Ilioneus, greeting Serestus with his left,
Then took the hands of those brave men, Cloanthus,   250
Gyas, and the rest.
            Sidonian Dido
Stood in astonishment, first at the sight
Of such a captain, then at his misfortune,
Presently saying:
           "Born of an immortal
Mother though you are, what adverse destiny   255
Dogs you through these many kinds of danger?
What rough power brings you from sea to land
In savage places? Are you truly he,
Aeneas, whom kind Venus bore
To the Dardanian, the young Anchisës,   260
Near to the stream of Phrygian Simoïs?
I remember the Greek, Teucer,[3] came to Sidon,
Exiled, and in search of a new kingdom.
Belus, my father, helped him. In those days
Belus campaigned with fire and sword on Cyprus   265
And won that island's wealth. Since then, the fall
Of Troy, your name, and the Pelasgian kings
Have been familiar to me. Teucer, your enemy,
Spoke often with admiration of the Teucrians
And traced his own descent from Teucrian stock.   270
Come, then, soldiers, be our guests. My life
Was one of hardship and forced wandering
Like your own, till in this land at length
Fortune would have me rest. Through pain I've learned

---

3. A warrior who fought at Troy and was later exiled from his home. He founded a city on the island of
Cyprus. He is not the Trojan king Teucer.

To comfort suffering men."

She led Aeneas   275

Into the royal house, but not before
Declaring a festal day in the gods' temples.
As for the ships' companies, she sent
Twenty bulls to the shore, a hundred swine,
Huge ones, with bristling backs, and fatted lambs,   280
A hundred of them, and their mother ewes—
All gifts for happy feasting on that day.

Now the queen's household made her great hall glow
As they prepared a banquet in the kitchens.
Embroidered table cloths, proud crimson-dyed,   285
Were spread, and set with massive silver plate,
Or gold, engraved with brave deeds of her fathers,
A sequence carried down through many captains
In a long line from the founding of the race.

BOOK II

[How They Took the City]⁴

The room fell silent, and all eyes were on him,
As Father Aeneas from his high couch began:

"Sorrow too deep to tell, your majesty,
You order me to feel and tell once more:
How the Danaans⁵ leveled in the dust   5
The splendor of our mourned-forever kingdom—
Heartbreaking things I saw with my own eyes
And was myself a part of. Who could tell them,
Even a Myrmidon or Dolopian
Or ruffian of Ulysses,⁶ without tears?   10
Now, too, the night is well along, with dewfall
Out of heaven, and setting stars weigh down
Our heads toward sleep. But if so great desire
Moves you to hear the tale of our disasters,
Briefly recalled, the final throes of Troy,   15
However I may shudder at the memory
And shrink again in grief, let me begin.

Knowing their strength broken in warfare, turned
Back by the fates, and years—so many years—
Already slipped away, the Danaan captains   20
By the divine handicraft of Pallas built
A horse of timber, tall as a hill,
And sheathed its ribs with planking of cut pine.
This they gave out to be an offering
For a safe return by sea, and the word went round.   25
But on the sly they shut inside a company

4. At the banquet that Dido gives for Aeneas, he relates, at her request, the story of the fall of Troy.   5. The Greeks.   6. Odysseus in Greek. Myrmidons and Dolopians were Achilles' soldiers.

Chosen from their picked soldiery by lot,
Crowding the vaulted caverns in the dark—
The horse's belly—with men fully armed.

Offshore there's a long island, Tenedos, 30
Famous and rich while Priam's kingdom lasted,
A treacherous anchorage now, and nothing more.
They crossed to this and hid their ships behind it
On the bare shore beyond. We thought they'd gone,
Sailing home to Mycenae before the wind, 35
So Teucer's town is freed of her long anguish,
Gates thrown wide! And out we go in joy
To see the Dorian⁷ campsites, all deserted,
The beach they left behind. Here the Dolopians
Pitched their tents, here cruel Achilles lodged, 40
There lay the ships, and there, formed up in ranks,
They came inland to fight us. Of our men
One group stood marveling, gaping up to see
The dire gift of the cold unbedded goddess,⁸
The sheer mass of the horse.

                     Thymoetes shouts 45
It should be hauled inside the walls and moored
High on the citadel—whether by treason
Or just because Troy's fate went that way now.
Capys opposed him; so did the wiser heads:
'Into the sea with it,' they said, 'or burn it, 50
Build up a bonfire under it,
This trick of the Greeks, a gift no one can trust,
Or cut it open, search the hollow belly!'

Contrary notions pulled the crowd apart.
Next thing we knew, in front of everyone, 55
Laocoön with a great company
Came furiously running from the Height,⁹
And still far off cried out: 'O my poor people,
Men of Troy, what madness has come over you?
Can you believe the enemy truly gone? 60
A gift from the Danaans, and no ruse?
Is that Ulysses' way, as you have known him?
Achaeans must be hiding in this timber,
Or it was built to butt against our walls,
Peer over them into our houses, pelt 65
The city from the sky. Some crookedness
Is in this thing. Have no faith in the horse!
Whatever it is, even when Greeks bring gifts
I fear them, gifts and all.'

                     He broke off then
And rifled his big spear with all his might 70
Against the horse's flank, the curve of belly.
It stuck there trembling, and the rounded hull

7. Greek. 8. Athena. 9. The citadel, the acropolis.

Reverberated groaning at the blow.
If the gods' will had not been sinister,
If our own minds had not been crazed, 75
He would have made us foul that Argive den
With bloody steel, and Troy would stand today—
O citadel of Priam, towering still!

But now look: hillmen, shepherds of Dardania,
Raising a shout, dragged in before the king 80
An unknown fellow with hands tied behind—
This all as he himself had planned,
Volunteering, letting them come across him,
So he could open Troy to the Achaeans.
Sure of himself this man was, braced for it 85
Either way, to work his trick or die.
From every quarter Trojans run to see him,
Ring the prisoner round, and make a game
Of jeering at him. Be instructed now
In Greek deceptive arts: one barefaced deed 90
Can tell you of them all.
As the man stood there, shaken and defenceless,
Looking around at ranks of Phrygians,
'Oh god,' he said, 'what land on earth, what seas
Can take me in? What's left me in the end, 95
Outcast that I am from the Danaans,
Now the Dardanians will have my blood?'

The whimpering speech brought us up short; we felt
A twinge for him. Let him speak up, we said,
Tell us where he was born, what news he brought, 100
What he could hope for as a prisoner.
Taking his time, slow to discard his fright,
He said:
         'I'll tell you the whole truth, my lord,
No matter what may come of it. Argive
I am by birth, and will not say I'm not. 105
That first of all: Fortune has made a derelict
Of Sinon, but the bitch
Won't make an empty liar of him, too.
Report of Palamedes[1] may have reached you,
Scion of Belus' line, a famous man 110
Who gave commands against the war. For this,
On a trumped-up charge, on perjured testimony,
The Greeks put him to death—but now they mourn him,
Now he has lost the light. Being kin to him,
In my first years I joined him as companion, 115
Sent by my poor old father on this campaign,
And while he held high rank and influence
In royal councils, we did well, with honor.

---

1. A Greek warrior who advised Agamemnon to abandon the war against Troy; his downfall was engineered by Ulysses, who planted forged proofs of dealings with the enemy in his tent.

Then by the guile and envy of Ulysses—
Nothing unheard of there!—he left this world,   120
And I lived on, but under a cloud, in sorrow,
Raging for my blameless friend's downfall.
Demented, too, I could not hold my peace
But said if I had luck, if I won through
Again to Argos, I'd avenge him there.   125
And I roused hatred with my talk; I fell
Afoul now of that man. From that time on,
Day in, day out, Ulysses
Found new ways to bait and terrify me,
Putting out shady rumors among the troops,   130
Looking for weapons he could use against me.
He could not rest till Calchas[2] served his turn—
But why go on? The tale's unwelcome, useless,
If Achaeans are all one,
And it's enough I'm called Achaean, then   135
Exact the punishment, long overdue;
The Ithacan[3] desires it; the Atridae
Would pay well for it.'
                          Burning with curiosity,
We questioned him, called on him to explain—
Unable to conceive such a performance,   140
The art of the Pelasgian. He went on,
Atremble, as though he feared us:
                                    'Many times
The Danaans wished to organize retreat,
To leave Troy and the long war, tired out.
If only they had done it! Heavy weather   145
At sea closed down on them, or a fresh gale
From the Southwest would keep them from embarking,
Most of all after this figure here,
This horse they put together with maple beams,
Reached its full height. Then wind and thunderstorms   150
Rumbled in heaven. So in our quandary
We sent Eurypylus to Phoebus'[4] oracle,
And he brought back this grim reply:

'Blood and a virgin slain[5]
You gave to appease the winds, for your first voyage   155
Troyward, O Danaans. Blood again
And Argive blood, one life, wins your return.'

When this got round among the soldiers, gloom
Came over them, and a cold chill that ran
To the very marrow. Who had death in store?   160
Whom did Apollo call for? Now the man
Of Ithaca haled Calchas out among us
In tumult, calling on the seer to tell

---

2. The prophet of the Greek army.   3. Ulysses.   4. Apollo. Eurypylus was a minor Greek chieftain.   5. Iphigenia, Agamemnon's daughter.

The true will of the gods. Ah, there were many
Able to divine the crookedness   165
And cruelty afoot for me, but they
Looked on in silence. For ten days the seer
Kept still, kept under cover, would not speak
Of anyone, or name a man for death,
Till driven to it at last by Ulysses' cries—   170
By prearrangement—he broke silence, barely
Enough to designate me for the altar.[6]
Every last man agreed. The torments each
Had feared for himself, now shifted to another,
All could endure. And the infamous day came,   175
The ritual, the salted meal, the fillets[7] . . .
I broke free, I confess it, broke my chains,
Hid myself all night in a muddy marsh,
Concealed by reeds, waiting for them to sail
If they were going to.
           Now no hope is left me   180
Of seeing my home country ever again,
My sweet children, my father, missed for years.
Perhaps the army will demand they pay
For my escape, my crime here, and their death,
Poor things, will be my punishment. Ah, sir,   185
I beg you by the gods above, the powers
In whom truth lives, and by what faith remains
Uncontaminated to men, take pity
On pain so great and so unmerited!'

For tears we gave him life, and pity, too.   190
Priam himself ordered the gyves removed
And the tight chain between. In kindness then
He said to him:
           'Whoever you may be,
The Greeks are gone; forget them from now on;
You shall be ours. And answer me these questions: 195
Who put this huge thing up, this horse?
Who designed it? What do they want with it?
Is it religious or a means of war?'

These were his questions. Then the captive, trained
In trickery, in the stagecraft of Achaea,   200
Lifted his hands unfettered to the stars.
'Eternal fires of heaven,' he began,
'Powers inviolable, I swear by thee,
As by the altars and blaspheming swords
I got away from, and the gods' white bands[8]   205
I wore as one chosen for sacrifice,
This is justice, I am justified
In dropping all allegiance to the Greeks—
As I had cause to hate them; I may bring

6. The altar of sacrifice.   7. Tufts of wool attached to the victim.   8. The fillets.

Into the open what they would keep dark. 210
No laws of my own country bind me now.
Only be sure you keep your promises
And keep faith, Troy, as you are kept from harm
If what I say proves true, if what I give
Is great and valuable.
      The whole hope 215
Of the Danaans, and their confidence
In the war they started, rested all along
In help from Pallas. Then the night came
When Diomedes and that criminal,
Ulysses, dared to raid her holy shrine. 220
They killed the guards on the high citadel
And ripped away the statue, the Palladium,[9]
Desecrating with bloody hands the virginal
Chaplets of the goddess. After that,
Danaan hopes waned and were undermined, 225
Ebbing away, their strength in battle broken,
The goddess now against them. This she made
Evident to them all with signs and portents.
Just as they set her statue up in camp,
The eyes, cast upward, glowed with crackling flames, 230
And salty sweat ran down the body. Then—
I say it in awe—three times, up from the ground,
The apparition of the goddess rose
In a lightning flash, with shield and spear atremble.
Calchas divined at once that the sea crossing 235
Must be attempted in retreat—that Pergamum[1]
Cannot be torn apart by Argive swords
Unless at Argos first they beg new omens,
Carrying homeward the divine power
Brought overseas in ships. Now they are gone 240
Before the wind to the fatherland, Mycenae,
Gone to enlist new troops and gods. They'll cross
The water again and be here, unforeseen.
So Calchas read the portents. Warned by him,
They set this figure up in reparation 245
For the Palladium stolen, to appease
The offended power and expiate the crime.
Enormous, though, he made them build the thing
With timber braces, towering to the sky,
Too big for the gates, not to be hauled inside 250
And give the people back their ancient guardian.
If any hand here violates this gift
To great Minerva,[2] then extinction waits,
Not for one only—would god it were so—
But for the realm of Priam and all Phrygians. 255
If this proud offering, drawn by your hands,

---

9. The statue of Pallas Athena. An oracle stated that Troy could not be captured as long as the Palladium remained in place in the shrine. 1. The citadel of Troy. 2. Athena.

Should mount into your city, then so far
As the walls of Pelops' town[3] the tide of Asia
Surges in war: that doom awaits our children.'

This fraud of Sinon, his accomplished lying,   260
Won us over; a tall tale and fake tears
Had captured us, whom neither Diomedes
Nor Larisaean[4] Achilles overpowered,
Nor ten long years, nor all their thousand ships.

And now another sign, more fearful still,   265
Broke on our blind miserable people,
Filling us all with dread. Laocoön,
Acting as Neptune's[5] priest that day by lot,
Was on the point of putting to the knife
A massive bull before the appointed altar,   270
When ah—look there!
From Tenedos, on the calm sea, twin snakes—
I shiver to recall it—endlessly
Coiling, uncoiling, swam abreast for shore,
Their underbellies showing as their crests   275
Reared red as blood above the swell; behind
They glided with great undulating backs.
Now came the sound of thrashed seawater foaming;
Now they were on dry land, and we could see
Their burning eyes, fiery and suffused with blood,   280
Their tongues a-flicker out of hissing maws.
We scattered, pale with fright. But straight ahead
They slid until they reached Laocoön.
Each snake enveloped one of his two boys,
Twining about and feeding on the body.   285
Next they ensnared the man as he ran up
With weapons: coils like cables looped and bound him
Twice round the middle; twice about his throat
They whipped their back-scales, and their heads towered,
While with both hands he fought to break the knots,   290
Drenched in slime, his head-bands black with venom,
Sending to heaven his appalling cries
Like a slashed bull escaping from an altar,
The fumbled axe shrugged off. The pair of snakes
Now flowed away and made for the highest shrines,   295
The citadel of pitiless Minerva,
Where coiling they took cover at her feet
Under the rondure of her shield. New terrors
Ran in the shaken crowd: the word went round
Laocoön had paid, and rightfully,   300
For profanation of the sacred hulk
With his offending spear hurled at its flank.

---

3. Argos. Pelops was Atreus's father.   4. After Larissa, a town in Achilles' homeland of Thessaly.
5. Poseidon in Greek.

'The offering must be hauled to its true home,'
They clamored. 'Votive prayers to the goddess
Must be said there!'
         So we breached the walls   305
And laid the city open. Everyone
Pitched in to get the figure underpinned
With rollers, hempen lines around the neck.
Deadly, pregnant with enemies, the horse
Crawled upward to the breach. And boys and girls   310
Sang hymns around the towrope as for joy
They touched it. Rolling on, it cast a shadow
Over the city's heart. O Fatherland,
O Ilium, home of gods! Defensive wall
Renowned in war for Dardanus's people!   315
There on the very threshold of the breach
It jarred to a halt four times, four times the arms
In the belly thrown together made a sound—
Yet on we strove unmindful, deaf and blind,
To place the monster on our blessed height.   320
Then, even then, Cassandra's[6] lips unsealed
The doom to come: lips by a god's command
Never believed or heeded by the Trojans.
So pitiably we, for whom that day
Would be the last, made all our temples green   325
With leafy festal boughs throughout the city.

As heaven turned, Night from the Ocean stream
Came on, profound in gloom on earth and sky
And Myrmidons in hiding. In their homes
The Teucrians lay silent, wearied out,   330
And sleep enfolded them. The Argive fleet,
Drawn up in line abreast, left Tenedos
Through the aloof moon's friendly stillnesses
And made for the familiar shore. Flame signals
Shone from the command ship. Sinon, favored   335
By what the gods unjustly had decreed,
Stole out to tap the pine walls and set free
The Danaans in the belly. Opened wide,
The horse emitted men; gladly they dropped
Out of the cavern, captains first, Thessandrus,   340
Sthenelus and the man of iron, Ulysses;
Hand over hand upon the rope, Acamas, Thoas,
Neoptolemus[7] and Prince Machaon,
Menelaus and then the master builder,
Epeos, who designed the horse decoy.   345
Into the darkened city, buried deep
In sleep and wine, they made their way,
Cut the few sentries down,
Let in their fellow soldiers at the gate,
And joined their combat companies as planned.   350

6. Daughter of King Priam of Troy. She was able to foretell the future correctly, but because of a curse, no one believed her prophecies (see Aeschylus's *Agamemnon* 1202ff.).   7. Son of Achilles.

That time of night it was when the first sleep,
Gift of the gods, begins for all mankind,
Arriving gradually, delicious rest.
In sleep, in dream, Hector appeared to me,
Gaunt with sorrow, streaming tears, all torn—   355
As by the violent car on his death day—
And black with bloody dust,
His puffed-out feet cut by the rawhide thongs.
Ah god, the look of him! How changed
From that proud Hector who returned to Troy   360
Wearing Achilles' armor,[8] or that one
Who pitched the torches on Danaan ships;
His beard all filth, his hair matted with blood,
Showing the wounds, the many wounds, received
Outside his father's city walls. I seemed   365
Myself to weep and call upon the man
In grieving speech, brought from the depth of me:

'Light of Dardania, best hope of Troy,
What kept you from us for so long, and where?
From what far place, O Hector, have you come,   370
Long, long awaited? After so many deaths
Of friends and brothers, after a world of pain
For all our folk and all our town, at last,
Boneweary, we behold you! What has happened
To ravage your serene face? Why these wounds?'   375

He wasted no reply on my poor questions
But heaved a great sigh from his chest and said:
'Ai! Give up and go, child of the goddess,
Save yourself, out of these flames. The enemy
Holds the city walls, and from her height   380
Troy falls in ruin. Fatherland and Priam
Have their due; if by one hand our towers
Could be defended, by this hand, my own,
They would have been. Her holy things, her gods
Of hearth and household[9] Troy commends to you.   385
Accept them as companions of your days;
Go find for them the great walls that one day
You'll dedicate, when you have roamed the sea.'

As he said this, he brought out from the sanctuary
Chaplets and Vesta,[1] Lady of the Hearth,   390
With her eternal fire.
                    While I dreamed,
The turmoil rose, with anguish, in the city.
More and more, although Anchises' house
Lay in seclusion, muffled among trees,

8. Hector stripped it from the corpse of Patroclus, Achilles' close friend, whom Hector killed in battle.
Achilles avenged Patroclus by killing Hector.   9. The Romans kept images of household gods, the Penatës, in a shrine in their homes; the custom is here transferred, unhistorically, to Troy.   1. The goddess
of the hearth and fire, which, in the temple, was never allowed to go out.

The din at the grim onset grew; and now   395
I shook off sleep, I climbed to the roof top
To cup my ears and listen. And the sound
Was like the sound a grassfire makes in grain,
Whipped by a Southwind, or a torrent foaming
Out of a mountainside to strew in ruin   400
Fields, happy crops, the yield of plowing teams,
Or woodlands borne off in the flood; in wonder
The shepherd listens on a rocky peak.
I knew then what our trust had won for us,
Knew the Danaan fraud: Deïphobus'[2]   405
Great house in flames, already caving in
Under the overpowering god of fire;
Ucalegon's already caught nearby;
The glare lighting the straits beyond Sigeum;[3]
The cries of men, the wild calls of the trumpets.   410

To arm was my first maddened impulse—not
That anyone had a fighting chance in arms;
Only I burned to gather up some force
For combat, and to man some high redoubt.
So fury drove me, and it came to me   415
That meeting death was beautiful in arms.
Then here, eluding the Achaean spears,
Came Panthus, Orthrys' son, priest of Apollo,
Carrying holy things, our conquered gods,
And pulling a small grandchild along: he ran   420
Despairing to my doorway.
                                    'Where's the crux,
Panthus,' I said. 'What strongpoint shall we hold?'

Before I could say more, he groaned and answered:
'The last day for Dardania has come,
The hour not to be fought off any longer.   425
Trojans we have been; Ilium has been;
The glory of the Teucrians is no more;
Black Jupiter has passed it on to Argos.
Greeks are the masters in our burning city.
Tall as a cliff, set in the heart of town,   430
Their horse pours out armed men. The conqueror,
Gloating Sinon, brews new conflagrations.
Troops hold the gates—as many thousand men
As ever came from great Mycenae; others
Block the lanes with crossed spears; glittering   435
In a combat line, swordblades are drawn for slaughter.
Even the first guards at the gates can barely
Offer battle, or blindly make a stand.'

Impelled by these words, by the powers of heaven,
Into the flames I go, into the fight,   440
Where the harsh Fury, and the din and shouting,

---

2. A son of Priam.   3. A promontory overlooking the strait that connects the Aegean with the Black Sea.

Skyward rising, calls. Crossing my path
In moonlight, five fell in with me, companions:
Ripheus, and Epytus, a great soldier,
Hypanis, Dymas, cleaving to my side   445
With young Coroebus, Mygdon's son. It happened
That in those very days this man had come
To Troy, aflame with passion for Cassandra,
Bringing to Priam and the Phrygians
A son-in-law's right hand. Unlucky one,   450
To have been deaf to what his bride foretold!
Now when I saw them grouped, on edge for battle,
I took it all in and said briefly,
                              'Soldiers,
Brave as you are to no end, if you crave
To face the last fight with me, and no doubt of it,   455
How matters stand for us each one can see.
The gods by whom this kingdom stood are gone,
Gone from the shrines and altars. You defend
A city lost in flames. Come, let us die,
We'll make a rush into the thick of it.   460
The conquered have one safety: hope for none.'

The desperate odds doubled their fighting spirit:
From that time on, like predatory wolves
In fog and darkness, when a savage hunger
Drives them blindly on, and cubs in lairs   465
Lie waiting with dry famished jaws—just so
Through arrow flights and enemies we ran
Toward our sure death, straight for the city's heart,
Cavernous black night over and around us.
Who can describe the havoc of that night   470
Or tell the deaths, or tally wounds with tears?
The ancient city falls, after dominion
Many long years. In windows, on the streets,
In homes, on solemn porches of the gods,
Dead bodies lie. And not alone the Trojans   475
Pay the price with their heart's blood; at times
Manhood returns to fire even the conquered
And Danaan conquerors fall. Grief everywhere,
Everywhere terror, and all shapes of death.

Androgeos was the first to cross our path   480
Leading a crowd of Greeks; he took for granted
That we were friends, and hailed us cheerfully:

'Men, get a move on! Are you made of lead
To be so late and slow? The rest are busy
Carrying plunder from the fires and towers.   485
Are you just landed from the ships?'
                              His words
Were barely out, and no reply forthcoming
Credible to him, when he knew himself
Fallen among enemies. Thunderstruck,
He halted, foot and voice, and then recoiled   490

Like one who steps down on a lurking snake
In a briar patch and jerks back, terrified,
As the angry thing rears up, all puffed and blue.
So backward went Androgeos in panic.
We were all over them in a moment, cut 495
And thrust, and as they fought on unknown ground,
Startled, unnerved, we killed them everywhere.
So Fortune filled our sails at first. Coroebus,
Elated at our feat and his own courage,
Said:
      'Friends, come follow Fortune. She has shown 500
The way to safety, shown she's on our side.
We'll take their shields and put on their insignia!
Trickery, bravery: who asks, in war?
The enemy will arm us.'
              He put on
The plumed helm of Androgeos, took the shield 505
With blazon and the Greek sword to his side.
Ripheus, Dymas—all were pleased to do it,
Making the still fresh trophies our equipment.
Then we went on, passing among the Greeks,
Protected by our own gods now no longer; 510
Many a combat, hand to hand, we fought
In the black night, and many a Greek we sent
To Orcus.[4] There were some who turned and ran
Back to the ships and shore; some shamefully
Clambered again into the horse, to hide 515
In the familiar paunch.
          When gods are contrary
They stand by no one. Here before us came
Cassandra, Priam's virgin daughter, dragged
By her long hair out of Minerva's shrine,
Lifting her brilliant eyes in vain to heaven— 520
Her eyes alone, as her white hands were bound.
Coroebus, infuriated, could not bear it,
But plunged into the midst to find his death.
We all went after him, our swords at play,
But here, here first, from the temple gable's height, 525
We met a hail of missiles from our friends,
Pitiful execution, by their error,
Who thought us Greek from our Greek plumes and shields.
Then with a groan of anger, seeing the virgin
Wrested from them, Danaans from all sides 530
Rallied and attacked us: fiery Ajax,[5]
Atreus' sons, Dolopians in a mass—
As, when a cyclone breaks, conflicting winds
Will come together, Westwind, Southwind, Eastwind
Riding high out of the Dawnland; forests 535
Bend and roar, and raging all in spume

---

4. The abode of the dead.   5. The lesser Ajax, son of Oileus, who raped Cassandra after dragging her
away from the shrine; as punishment, he was drowned on his way back to Greece. This is not the great
Greek warrior Ajax; he had committed suicide before Troy fell (see *Odyssey* 11).

Nereus[6] with his trident churns the deep.
Then some whom we had taken by surprise
Under cover of night throughout the city
And driven off, came back again: they knew   540
Our shields and arms for liars now, our speech
Alien to their own. They overwhelmed us.
Coroebus fell at the warrior goddess' altar,
Killed by Peneleus; and Ripheus fell,
A man uniquely just among the Trojans,   545
The soul of equity; but the gods would have it
Differently. Hypanis, Dymas died,
Shot down by friends; nor did your piety,
Panthus, nor Apollo's fillets shield you
As you went down.   550
             Ashes of Ilium!
Flames that consumed my people! Here I swear
That in your downfall I did not avoid
One weapon, one exchange with the Danaans,
And if it had been fated, my own hand
Had earned my death. But we were torn away   555
From that place—Iphitus and Pelias too,
One slow with age, one wounded by Ulysses,
Called by a clamor at the hall of Priam.
Truly we found here a prodigious fight,
As though there were none elsewhere, not a death   560
In the whole city: Mars[7] gone berserk, Danaans
In a rush to scale the roof; the gate besieged
By a tortoise shell of overlapping shields.[8]
Ladders clung to the wall, and men strove upward
Before the very doorposts, on the rungs,   565
Left hand putting the shield up, and the right
Reaching for the cornice. The defenders
Wrenched out upperworks and rooftiles: these
For missiles, as they saw the end, preparing
To fight back even on the edge of death.   570
And gilded beams, ancestral ornaments,
They rolled down on the heads below. In hall
Others with swords drawn held the entrance way,
Packed there, waiting. Now we plucked up heart
To help the royal house, to give our men   575
A respite, and to add our strength to theirs,
Though all were beaten. And we had for entrance
A rear door, secret, giving on a passage
Between the palace halls; in other days
Andromachë, poor lady, often used it,   580
Going alone to see her husband's parents
Or taking Astyanax[9] to his grandfather.
I climbed high on the roof, where hopeless men

6. An old sea god and father of the Nereids, the sea nymphs.   7. The war god (Ares in Greek).
8. When attacking a walled position, Roman soldiers protected themselves from overhead missiles by
holding their shields above their heads, forming a "roof," which looked like the plates of a tortoiseshell.
9. Son of Andromachë and Hector.

Were picking up and throwing futile missiles.
Here was a tower like a promontory   585
Rising toward the stars above the roof:
All Troy, the Danaan ships, the Achaean camp,
Were visible from this. Now close beside it
With crowbars, where the flooring made loose joints,
We pried it from its bed and pushed it over.   590
Down with a rending crash in sudden ruin
Wide over the Danaan lines it fell;
But fresh troops moved up, and the rain of stones
With every kind of missile never ceased.

Just at the outer doors of the vestibule   595
Sprang Pyrrhus,[1] all in bronze and glittering,
As a serpent, hidden swollen underground
By a cold winter, writhes into the light,
On vile grass fed, his old skin cast away,
Renewed and glossy, rolling slippery coils,   600
With lifted underbelly rearing sunward
And triple tongue a-flicker. Close beside him
Giant Periphas and Automedon,
His armor-bearer, once Achilles' driver,
Besieged the place with all the young of Scyros,[2]   605
Hurling their torches at the palace roof.
Pyrrhus shouldering forward with an axe
Broke down the stony threshold, forced apart
Hinges and brazen door-jambs, and chopped through
One panel of the door, splitting the oak,   610
To make a window, a great breach. And there
Before their eyes the inner halls lay open,
The courts of Priam and the ancient kings,
With men-at-arms ranked in the vestibule.
From the interior came sounds of weeping,   615
Pitiful commotion, wails of women
High-pitched, rising in the formal chambers
To ring against the silent golden stars;
And, through the palace, mothers wild with fright
Ran to and fro or clung to doors and kissed them.   620
Pyrrhus with his father's brawn stormed on,
No bolts or bars or men availed to stop him:
Under his battering the double doors
Were torn out of their sockets and fell inward.
Sheer force cleared the way: the Greeks broke through   625
Into the vestibule, cut down the guards,
And made the wide hall seethe with men-at-arms—
A tumult greater than when dykes are burst
And a foaming river, swirling out in flood,
Whelms every parapet and races on   630
Through fields and over all the lowland plains,
Bearing off pens and cattle. I myself

1. Neoptolemus.   2. Island in the north Aegean where Neoptolemus grew up.

Saw Neoptolemus furious with blood
In the entrance way, and saw the two Atridae;
Hecuba[3] I saw, and her hundred daughters,   635
Priam before the altars, with his blood
Drenching the fires that he himself had blessed.
Those fifty bridal chambers, hope of a line
So flourishing; those doorways high and proud,
Adorned with takings of barbaric gold,   640
Were all brought low: fire had them, or the Greeks.

What was the fate of Priam, you may ask.
Seeing his city captive, seeing his own
Royal portals rent apart, his enemies
In the inner rooms, the old man uselessly   645
Put on his shoulders, shaking with old age,
Armor unused for years, belted a sword on,
And made for the massed enemy to die.
Under the open sky in a central court
Stood a big altar; near it, a laurel tree   650
Of great age, leaning over, in deep shade
Embowered the Penatës. At this altar
Hecuba and her daughters, like white doves
Blown down in a black storm, clung together,
Enfolding holy images in their arms.   655
Now, seeing Priam in a young man's gear,
She called out:
              'My poor husband, what mad thought
Drove you to buckle on these weapons?
Where are you trying to go? The time is past
For help like this, for this kind of defending,   660
Even if my own Hector could be here.
Come to me now: the altar will protect us,
Or else you'll die with us.'
                        She drew him close,
Heavy with years, and made a place for him
To rest on the consecrated stone.
                              Now see   665
Politës, one of Priam's sons, escaped
From Pyrrhus' butchery and on the run
Through enemies and spears, down colonnades,
Through empty courtyards, wounded. Close behind
Comes Pyrrhus burning for the death-stroke: has him,   670
Catches him now, and lunges with the spear.
The boy has reached his parents, and before them
Goes down, pouring out his life with blood.
Now Priam, in the very midst of death,
Would neither hold his peace nor spare his anger.   675

'For what you've done, for what you've dared,' he said,
'If there is care in heaven for atrocity,

3. Wife of Priam and mother of Hector.

May the gods render fitting thanks, reward you
As you deserve. You forced me to look on
At the destruction of my son: defiled   680
A father's eyes with death. That great Achilles
You claim to be the son of—and you lie—
Was not like you to Priam, his enemy;
To me who threw myself upon his mercy
He showed compunction, gave me back for burial   685
The bloodless corpse of Hector, and returned me
To my own realm.'
              The old man threw his spear
With feeble impact; blocked by the ringing bronze,
It hung there harmless from the jutting boss.
Then Pyrrhus answered:
                 'You'll report the news   690
To Pelidës,[4] my father; don't forget
My sad behavior, the degeneracy
Of Neoptolemus. Now die.'
                With this,
To the altar step itself he dragged him trembling,
Slipping in the pooled blood of his son,   695
And took him by the hair with his left hand.
The sword flashed in his right; up to the hilt
He thrust it in his body.
            That was the end
Of Priam's age, the doom that took him off,
With Troy in flames before his eyes, his towers   700
Headlong fallen—he that in other days
Had ruled in pride so many lands and peoples,
The power of Asia.
            On the distant shore
The vast trunk headless lies without a name.

For the first time that night, inhuman shuddering   705
Took me, head to foot. I stood unmanned,
And my dear father's image came to mind
As our king, just his age, mortally wounded,
Gasped his life away before my eyes.
Creusa[5] came to mind, too, left alone;   710
The house plundered; danger to little Iulus.
I looked around to take stock of my men,
But all had left me, utterly played out,
Giving their beaten bodies to the fire
Or plunging from the roof.
              It came to this,   715
That I stood there alone. And then I saw
Lurking beyond the doorsill of the Vesta,
In hiding, silent, in that place reserved,
The daughter of Tyndareus.[6] Glare of fires
Lighted my steps this way and that, my eyes   720

---

4. Achilles, son of Peleus.   5. Aeneas's wife.   6. Helen.

Glancing over the whole scene, everywhere.
That woman, terrified of the Trojans' hate
For the city overthrown, terrified too
Of Danaan vengeance, her abandoned husband's
Anger after years—Helen, that Fury   725
Both to her own homeland and Troy, had gone
To earth, a hated thing, before the altars.
Now fires blazed up in my own spirit—
A passion to avenge my fallen town
And punish Helen's whorishness.
                                    'Shall this one   730
Look untouched on Sparta and Mycenae
After her triumph, going like a queen,
And see her home and husband, kin and children,
With Trojan girls for escort, Phrygian slaves?
Must Priam perish by the sword for this?   735
Troy burn, for this? Dardania's littoral
Be soaked in blood, so many times, for this?
Not by my leave. I know
No glory comes of punishing a woman,
The feat can bring no honor. Still, I'll be   740
Approved for snuffing out a monstrous life,
For a just sentence carried out. My heart
Will teem with joy in this avenging fire,
And the ashes of my kin will be appeased.'

So ran my thoughts. I turned wildly upon her,   745
But at that moment, clear, before my eyes—
Never before so clear—in a pure light
Stepping before me, radiant through the night,
My loving mother came: immortal, tall,
And lovely as the lords of heaven know her.   750
Catching me by the hand, she held me back,
Then with her rose-red mouth reproved me:
                                              'Son,
Why let such suffering goad you on to fury
Past control? Where is your thoughtfulness
For me, for us? Will you not first revisit   755
The place you left your father, worn and old,
Or find out if your wife, Creusa, lives,
And the young boy, Ascanius—all these
Cut off by Greek troops foraging everywhere?
Had I not cared for them, fire would by now   760
Have taken them, their blood glutted the sword.
You must not hold the woman of Laconia,[7]
That hated face, the cause of this, nor Paris.
The harsh will of the gods it is, the gods,
That overthrows the splendor of this place   765
And brings Troy from her height into the dust.
Look over there: I'll tear away the cloud

7. Helen.

That curtains you, and films your mortal sight,
The fog around you.—Have no fear of doing
Your mother's will, or balk at obeying her.— 770
Look: where you see high masonry thrown down,
Stone torn from stone, with billowing smoke and dust,
Neptune is shaking from their beds the walls
That his great trident pried up, undermining,
Toppling the whole city down. And look: 775
Juno in all her savagery holds
The Scaean Gates,[8] and raging in steel armor
Calls her allied army from the ships.
Up on the citadel—turn, look—Pallas Tritonia[9]
Couched in a stormcloud, lightening, with her Gorgon![1] 780
The Father himself empowers the Danaans,
Urges assaulting gods on the defenders.
Away, child; put an end to toiling so.
I shall be near, to see you safely home.'

She hid herself in the deep gloom of night, 785
And now the dire forms appeared to me
Of great immortals, enemies of Troy.
I knew the end then: Ilium was going down
In fire, the Troy of Neptune[2] going down,
As in high mountains when the countrymen 790
Have notched an ancient ash, then make their axes
Ring with might and main, chopping away
To fell the tree—ever on the point of falling,
Shaken through all its foliage, and the treetop
Nodding; bit by bit the strokes prevail 795
Until it gives a final groan at last
And crashes down in ruin from the height.

Now I descended where the goddess guided,
Clear of the flames, and clear of enemies,
For both retired; so gained my father's door, 800
My ancient home. I looked for him at once,
My first wish being to help him to the mountains;
But with Troy gone he set his face against it,
Not to prolong his life, or suffer exile.

'The rest of you, all in your prime,' he said, 805
'Make your escape; you are still hale and strong.
If heaven's lords had wished me a longer span
They would have saved this home for me. I call it
More than enough that once before I saw
My city taken and wrecked,[3] and went on living. 810
Here is my death bed, here. Take leave of me.
Depart now. I'll find death with my sword arm.

8. One of the principal entrances to Troy.   9. The significance of this adjective is not known; perhaps a reference to her birthplace, Lake Tritonis, in North Africa. But the birthplace legend may have been invented to explain the title.   1. Monster whose appearance turned people to stone; Athena had a Gorgon face on her shield.   2. Neptune was hostile to Troy, although he had helped build the city.   3. By the hero Heracles.

The enemy will oblige; they'll come for spoils.
Burial can be dispensed with. All these years
I've lingered in my impotence, at odds   815
With heaven, since the Father of gods and men
Breathed high winds of thunderbolt upon me
And touched me with his fire.'4
                     He spoke on
In the same vein, inflexible. The rest of us,
Creusa and Ascanius and the servants,   820
Begged him in tears not to pull down with him
Our lives as well, adding his own dead weight
To the fates' pressure. But he would not budge,
He held to his resolve and to his chair.
I felt swept off again to fight, in misery   825
Longing for death. What choices now were open,
What chance had I?
                'Did you suppose, my father,
That I could tear myself away and leave you?
Unthinkable; how could a father say it?
Now if it please the powers above that nothing   830
Stand of this great city; if your heart
Is set on adding your own death and ours
To that of Troy, the door's wide open for it:
Pyrrhus will be here, splashed with Priam's blood;
He kills the son before his father's eyes,   835
The father at the altars.
              My dear mother,
Was it for this, through spears and fire, you brought me,
To see the enemy deep in my house,
To see my son, Ascanius, my father,
And near them both, Creusa,   840
Butchered in one another's blood? My gear,
Men, bring my gear. The last light calls the conquered.
Give me back to the Greeks. Let me take up
The combat once again. We shall not all
Die this day unavenged.'
             I buckled on   845
Swordbelt and blade and slid my left forearm
Into the shield-strap, turning to go out,
But at the door Creusa hugged my knees,
Then held up little Iulus to his father.

'If you are going out to die, take us   850
To face the whole thing with you. If experience
Leads you to put some hope in weaponry
Such as you now take, guard your own house here.
When you have gone, to whom is Iulus left?
Your father? Wife?—one called that long ago.'   855

She went on, and her wailing filled the house,
But then a sudden portent came, a marvel:

4. Anchisës was struck by a thunderbolt and crippled as punishment by Jupiter for being the lover of
Venus.

Amid his parents' hands and their sad faces
A point on Iulus' head seemed to cast light,
A tongue of flame that touched but did not burn him,   860
Licking his fine hair, playing round his temples.
We, in panic, beat at the flaming hair
And put the sacred fire out with water;
Father Anchises lifted his eyes to heaven
And lifted up his hands, his voice, in joy: 865

'Omnipotent Jupiter, if prayers affect you,
Look down upon us, that is all I ask,
If by devotion to the gods we earn it,
Grant us a new sign, and confirm this portent!'
The old man barely finished when it thundered   870
A loud crack on the left. Out of the sky
Through depths of night a star fell trailing flame
And glided on, turning the night to day.
We watched it pass above the roof and go
To hide its glare, its trace, in Ida's⁵ wood;   875
But still, behind, the luminous furrow shone
And wide zones fumed with sulphur.
                        Now indeed
My father, overcome, addressed the gods,
And rose in worship of the blessed star.

'Now, now, no more delay. I'll follow you.   880
Where you conduct me, there I'll be.
                      Gods of my fathers,
Preserve this house, preserve my grandson. Yours
This portent was. Troy's life is in your power.
I yield. I go as your companion, son.'
Then he was still. We heard the blazing town   885
Crackle more loudly, felt the scorching heat.

'Then come, dear father. Arms around my neck:
I'll take you on my shoulders, no great weight.
Whatever happens, both will face one danger,
Find one safety. Iulus will come with me,   890
My wife at a good interval behind.
Servants, give your attention to what I say.
At the gate inland there's a funeral mound
And an old shrine of Ceres the Bereft;⁶
Near it an ancient cypress, kept alive   895
For many years by our fathers' piety.
By various routes we'll come to that one place.
Father, carry our hearthgods, our Penatës.
It would be wrong for me to handle them—
Just come from such hard fighting, bloody work—   900
Until I wash myself in running water.'

---

5. The mountain range near Troy.   6. So called because she mourns the loss of her daughter, Proserpina (Persephone in Greek). Her Greek name is Demeter.

When I had said this, over my breadth of shoulder
And bent neck, I spread out a lion skin
For tawny cloak and stooped to take his weight.
Then little Iulus put his hand in mine   905
And came with shorter steps beside his father.
My wife fell in behind. Through shadowed places
On we went, and I, lately unmoved
By any spears thrown, any squads of Greeks,
Felt terror now at every eddy of wind,   910
Alarm at every sound, alert and worried
Alike for my companion and my burden.
I had got near the gate, and now I thought
We had made it all the way, when suddenly
A noise of running feet came near at hand,   915
And peering through the gloom ahead, my father
Cried out:

       'Run, boy; here they come; I see
Flame light on shields, bronze shining.'

                      I took fright,
And some unfriendly power, I know not what,
Stole all my addled wits—for as I turned   920
Aside from the known way, entering a maze
Of pathless places on the run—

                     Alas,
Creusa, taken from us by grim fate, did she
Linger, or stray, or sink in weariness?
There is no telling. Never would she be   925
Restored to us. Never did I look back
Or think to look for her, lost as she was,
Until we reached the funeral mound and shrine
Of venerable Ceres. Here at last
All came together, but she was not there;   930
She alone failed[7] her friends, her child, her husband.
Out of my mind, whom did I not accuse,
What man or god? What crueller loss had I
Beheld, that night the city fell? Ascanius,
My father, and the Teucrian Penatës,   935
I left in my friends' charge, and hid them well
In a hollow valley.

            I turned back alone
Into the city, cinching my bright harness.
Nothing for it but to run the risks
Again, go back again, comb all of Troy,   940
And put my life in danger as before:
First by the town wall, then the gate, all gloom,
Through which I had come out—and so on backward,
Tracing my own footsteps through the night;
And everywhere my heart misgave me: even   945
Stillness had its terror. Then to our house,

---

7. The original Latin does not imply fault and is better read "was not to be found" (literally, "was lacking
to").

Thinking she might, just might, have wandered there.
Danaans had got in and filled the place,
And at that instant fire they had set,
Consuming it, went roofward in a blast; 950
Flames leaped and seethed in heat to the night sky.
I pressed on, to see Priam's hall and tower.
In the bare colonnades of Juno's shrine
Two chosen guards, Phoenix and hard Ulysses,
Kept watch over the plunder. Piled up here 955
Were treasures of old Troy from every quarter,
Torn out of burning temples: altar tables,
Robes, and golden bowls. Drawn up around them,
Boys and frightened mothers stood in line.
I even dared to call out in the night; 960
I filled the streets with calling; in my grief
Time after time I groaned and called Creusa,
Frantic, in endless quest from door to door.
Then to my vision her sad wraith appeared—
Creusa's ghost, larger than life, before me. 965
Chilled to the marrow, I could feel the hair
On my head rise, the voice clot in my throat;
But she spoke out to ease me of my fear:

'What's to be gained by giving way to grief
So madly, my sweet husband? Nothing here 970
Has come to pass except as heaven willed.
You may not take Creusa with you now;
It was not so ordained, nor does the lord
Of high Olympus give you leave. For you
Long exile waits, and long sea miles to plough. 975
You shall make landfall on Hesperia
Where Lydian Tiber[8] flows, with gentle pace,
Between rich farmlands, and the years will bear
Glad peace, a kingdom, and a queen for you.
Dismiss these tears for your beloved Creusa. 980
I shall not see the proud homelands of Myrmidons
Or of Dolopians, or go to serve
Greek ladies, Dardan lady that I am
And daughter-in-law of Venus the divine.
No: the great mother of the gods[9] detains me 985
Here on these shores. Farewell now; cherish still
Your son and mine.'
　　　　　　　　　With this she left me weeping,
Wishing that I could say so many things,
And faded on the tenuous air. Three times
I tried to put my arms around her neck, 990
Three times enfolded nothing, as the wraith
Slipped through my fingers, bodiless as wind,
Or like a flitting dream.
　　　　　　　　　So in the end
As night waned I rejoined my company.

8. The river was the center of many settlements of Etruscans, who were supposed to be immigrants from Lydia, in Asia Minor.   9. Cybele, an Asiatic mother goddess worshiped (according to Virgil) at Troy.

And there to my astonishment I found   995
New refugees in a great crowd: men and women
Gathered for exile, young—pitiful people
Coming from every quarter, minds made up,
With their belongings, for whatever lands
I'd lead them to by sea.
                          The morning star   1000
Now rose on Ida's ridges, bringing day.
Greeks had secured the city gates. No help
Or hope of help existed.
So I resigned myself, picked up my father,
And turned my face toward the mountain range.'   1005

Summary   Aeneas goes on to tell the story of his wanderings in search of a new home. By the end of the evening, Dido, who began to fall in love with him before the banquet (through the intervention of Venus and Juno, who both promote the affair, each for different reasons), now feels the full force of her passion for Aeneas.

BOOK IV

[The Passion of the Queen]

The queen, for her part, all that evening ached
With longing that her heart's blood fed, a wound
Or inward fire eating her away.
The manhood of the man, his pride of birth,
Came home to her time and again; his looks,   5
His words remained with her to haunt her mind,
And desire for him gave her no rest.
                          When Dawn
Swept earth with Phoebus' torch and burned away
Night-gloom and damp, this queen, far gone and ill,
Confided to the sister of her heart: 10
"My sister Anna, quandaries and dreams
Have come to frighten me—such dreams!
                          Think what a stranger
Yesterday found lodging in our house:
How princely, how courageous, what a soldier.
I can believe him in the line of gods,   15
And this is no delusion. Tell-tale fear
Betrays inferior souls. What scenes of war
Fought to the bitter end he pictured for us!
What buffetings awaited him at sea!
Had I not set my face against remarriage   20
After my first love died and failed me, left me
Barren and bereaved—and sick to death
At the mere thought of torch and bridal bed—
I could perhaps give way in this one case
To frailty. I shall say it: since that time   25
Sychaeus, my poor husband, met his fate,
And blood my brother[1] shed stained our hearth gods,

---

1. Pygmalion, king of Tyre who killed Sychaeus, Dido's *first love* (line 21). Sychaeus's ghost warned her in a dream to leave Tyre and seek a new home.

This man alone has wrought upon me so
And moved my soul to yield. I recognize
The signs of the old flame, of old desire.   30
But O chaste life, before I break your laws,
I pray that Earth may open, gape for me
Down to its depth, or the omnipotent
With one stroke blast me to the shades, pale shades
Of Erebus[2] and the deep world of night!   35
That man who took me to himself in youth
Has taken all my love; may that man keep it,
Hold it forever with him in the tomb.''

At this she wept and wet her breast with tears.
But Anna answered:
                    ''Dearer to your sister   40
Than daylight is, will you wear out your life,
Young as you are, in solitary mourning,
Never to know sweet children, or the crown
Of joy that Venus brings? Do you believe
This matters to the dust, to ghosts in tombs?   45
Granted no suitors up to now have moved you,
Neither in Libya nor before, in Tyre—
Iarbas[3] you rejected, and the others,
Chieftains bred by the land of Africa
Their triumphs have enriched—will you contend   50
Even against a welcome love? Have you
Considered in whose lands you settled here?
On one frontier the Gaetulans, their cities,
People invincible in war—with wild
Numidian horsemen, and the offshore banks,   55
The Syrtës; on the other, desert sands,
Bone-dry, where fierce Barcaean[4] nomads range.
Or need I speak of future wars brought on
From Tyre, and the menace of your brother?
Surely by dispensation of the gods   60
And backed by Juno's will, the ships from Ilium
Held their course this way on the wind.
                                        Sister,
What a great city you'll see rising here,
And what a kingdom, from this royal match!
With Trojan soldiers as companions in arms   65
By what exploits will Punic[5] glory grow!
Only ask the indulgence of the gods,
Win them with offerings, give your guests ease,
And contrive reasons for delay, while winter
Gales rage, drenched Orion storms at sea,   70
And their ships, damaged still, face iron skies.'

This counsel fanned the flame, already kindled,
Giving her hesitant sister hope, and set her

2. The lower depths of Hades, the underworld.   3. The most prominent of Dido's African suitors.   4. African groups that lived near Carthage. The Gaetulans, a savage people, lived to the southwest.
The Numidians were the most powerful group. The Syrtes lived on the coast to the west. The Barcaeans
lived to the east.   5. Carthaginian.

Free of scruple. Visiting the shrines
They begged for grace at every altar first, 75
Then put choice rams and ewes to ritual death
For Ceres Giver of Laws, Father Lyaeus,
Phoebus, and for Juno most of all
Who has the bonds of marriage in her keeping.[6]
Dido herself, splendidly beautiful, 80
Holding a shallow cup, tips out the wine
On a white shining heifer, between the horns,
Or gravely in the shadow of the gods
Approaches opulent altars. Through the day
She brings new gifts, and when the breasts are opened 85
Pores over organs, living still, for signs.[7]
Alas, what darkened minds have soothsayers!
What good are shrines and vows to maddened lovers?
The inward fire eats the soft marrow away,
And the internal wound bleeds on in silence. 90

Unlucky Dido, burning, in her madness
Roamed through all the city, like a doe
Hit by an arrow shot from far away
By a shepherd hunting in the Cretan woods—
Hit by surprise, nor could the hunter see 95
His flying steel had fixed itself in her;
But though she runs for life through copse and glade
The fatal shaft clings to her side.
                                    Now Dido
Took Aeneas with her among her buildings,
Showed her Sidonian wealth, her walls prepared, 100
And tried to speak, but in mid-speech grew still.
When the day waned she wanted to repeat
The banquet as before, to hear once more
In her wild need the throes of Ilium,
And once more hung on the narrator's words. 105
Afterward, when all the guests were gone,
And the dim moon in turn had quenched her light,
And setting stars weighed weariness to sleep,
Alone she mourned in the great empty hall
And pressed her body on the couch he left: 110
She heard him still, though absent—heard and saw him.
Or she would hold Ascanius in her lap,
Enthralled by him, the image of his father,
As though by this ruse to appease a love
Beyond all telling.
                      Towers, half-built, rose 115
No farther; men no longer trained in arms

<hr>

6. Ceres, the goddess who guarantees the growth of crops; Lyaeus (Dionysus or Bacchus), the wine god; and Phoebus (Apollo) are selected as deities especially connected with the founding of cities. One of Apollo's titles is "founder," and Ceres and Lyaeus control the essential crops that will enable the colonists to live. Dido prays to these gods at the moment when she is about to abandon her responsibilities as founder of a city. A similar irony is present in her prayer to Juno, who oversees the marriage bond, at the moment when she is about to break her long fidelity to the memory of Sychaeus.   7. An Etruscan and Roman practice was to inspect the entrails of the sacrificial victim and interpret irregular or unusual features as signs of the future.

Or toiled to make harbors and battlements
Impregnable. Projects were broken off,
Laid over, and the menacing huge walls
With cranes unmoving stood against the sky.   120

As soon as Jove's[8] dear consort saw the lady
Prey to such illness, and her reputation
Standing no longer in the way of passion,
Saturn's daughter said to Venus:
                        "Wondrous!
Covered yourself with glory, have you not,   125
You and your boy, and won such prizes, too.
Divine power is something to remember
If by collusion of two gods one mortal
Woman is brought low.
                    I am not blind.
Your fear of our new walls has not escaped me,   130
Fear and mistrust of Carthage at her height.
But how far will it go? What do you hope for,
Being so contentious? Why do we not
Arrange eternal peace and formal marriage?
You have your heart's desire: Dido in love,   135
Dido consumed with passion to her core.
Why not, then, rule this people side by side
With equal authority? And let the queen
Wait on her Phrygian lord, let her consign
Into your hand her Tyrians as a dowry."   140

Now Venus knew this talk was all pretence,
All to divert the future power from Italy
To Libya; and she answered:
                      "Who would be
So mad, so foolish as to shun that prospect
Or prefer war with you? That is, provided   145
Fortune is on the side of your proposal.
The fates here are perplexing: would one city
Satisfy Jupiter's will for Tyrians
And Trojan exiles? Does he approve
A union and a mingling of these races?   150
You are his consort: you have every right
To sound him out. Go on, and I'll come, too."

But regal Juno pointedly replied:
"That task will rest with me. Just now, as to
The need of the moment and the way to meet it,   155
Listen, and I'll explain in a few words.
Aeneas and Dido in her misery
Plan hunting in the forest, when the Titan
Sun comes up with rays to light the world.
While beaters in excitement ring the glens   160

8. Jupiter's.

My gift will be a black raincloud, and hail,
A downpour, and I'll shake heaven with thunder.
The company will scatter, lost in gloom,
As Dido and the Trojan captain come
To one same cavern. I shall be on hand,   165
And if I can be certain you are willing,
There I shall marry them and call her his.
A wedding, this will be."
                Then Cytherëa,[9]
Not disinclined, nodded to Juno's plea,
And smiled at the stratagem now given away.   170

Dawn came up meanwhile from the Ocean stream,
And in the early sunshine from the gates
Picked huntsmen issued: wide-meshed nets and snares,
Broad spearheads for big game, Massylian[1] horsemen
Trooping with hounds in packs keen on the scent.   175
But Dido lingered in her hall, as Punic
Nobles waited, and her mettlesome hunter
Stood nearby, cavorting in gold and scarlet,
Champing his foam-flecked bridle. At long last
The queen appeared with courtiers in a crowd,   180
A short Sidonian cloak edged in embroidery
Caught about her, at her back a quiver
Sheathed in gold, her hair tied up in gold,
And a brooch of gold pinning her scarlet dress.
Phrygians came in her company as well,   185
And Iulus, joyous at the scene. Resplendent
Above the rest, Aeneas walked to meet her,
To join his retinue with hers. He seemed—
Think of the lord Apollo in the spring
When he leaves wintering in Lycia   190
By Xanthus torrent, for his mother's isle
Of Delos, to renew the festival;
Around his altars Cretans, Dryopës,
And painted Agathyrsans[2] raise a shout,
But the god walks the Cynthian ridge alone   195
And smooths his hair, binds it in fronded laurel,
Braids it in gold; and shafts ring on his shoulders.
So elated and swift, Aeneas walked
With sunlit grace upon him.
                Soon the hunters,
Riding in company to high pathless hills,   200
Saw mountain goats shoot down from a rocky peak
And scamper on the ridges; toward the plain
Deer left the slopes, herding in clouds of dust
In flight across the open lands. Alone,
The boy Ascanius, delightedly riding   205
His eager horse amid the lowland vales,
Outran both goats and deer. Could he only meet

---

9. Venus.   1. After Massilia (Marseilles), in southern France.   2. Pilgrims from various regions.

Amid the harmless game some foaming boar,
Or a tawny lion down from the mountainside!

Meanwhile in heaven began a rolling thunder,   210
And soon the storm broke, pouring rain and hail.
Then Tyrians and Trojans in alarm—
With Venus' Dardan grandson[3]—ran for cover
Here and there in the wilderness, as freshets
Coursed from the high hills.
                  Now to the self-same cave   215
Came Dido and the captain of the Trojans.
Primal Earth herself and Nuptial Juno
Opened the ritual, torches of lightning blazed,
High Heaven became witness to the marriage,
And nymphs cried out wild hymns from a mountain top.   220
    That day was the first cause of death, and first
Of sorrow. Dido had no further qualms
As to impressions given and set abroad;
She thought no longer of a secret love
But called it marriage. Thus, under that name,   225
She hid her fault.
                Now in no time at all
Through all the African cities Rumor goes—
Nimble as quicksilver among evils. Rumor
Thrives on motion, stronger for the running,
Lowly at first through fear, then rearing high,   230
She treads the land and hides her head in cloud.
As people fable it, the Earth, her mother,
Furious against the gods, bore a late sister
To the giants Coeus and Enceladus,
Giving her speed on foot and on the wing: 235
Monstrous, deformed, titanic. Pinioned, with
An eye beneath for every body feather,
And, strange to say, as many tongues and buzzing
Mouths as eyes, as many pricked-up ears,
By night she flies between the earth and heaven   240
Shrieking through darkness, and she never turns
Her eye-lids down to sleep. By day she broods,
On the alert, on rooftops or on towers,
Bringing great cities fear, harping on lies
And slander evenhandedly with truth.   245
In those days Rumor took an evil joy
At filling countrysides with whispers, whispers,
Gossip of what was done, and never done:
How this Aeneas landed, Trojan born,
How Dido in her beauty graced his company,   250
Then how they reveled all the winter long
Unmindful of the realm, prisoners of lust.

These tales the scabrous goddess put about
On men's lips everywhere. Her twisting course

3. Ascanius.

Took her to King Iarbas, whom she set   255
Ablaze with anger piled on top of anger.
Son of Jupiter Hammon by a nymph,
A ravished Garamantean, this prince
Had built the god a hundred giant shrines,
A hundred altars, each with holy fires.   260
Alight by night and day, sentries on watch,
The ground enriched by victims' blood, the doors
Festooned with flowering wreaths. Before his altars
King Iarbas, crazed by the raw story,
Stood, they say, amid the Presences,   265
With supplicating hands, pouring out prayer:

"All powerful Jove, to whom the feasting Moors
At ease on colored couches tip their wine,
Do you see this? Are we then fools to fear you
Throwing down your bolts? Those dazzling fires   270
Of lightning, are they aimless in the clouds
And rumbling thunder meaningless? This woman
Who turned up in our country and laid down
A tiny city at a price, to whom
I gave a beach to plow—and on my terms—   275
After refusing to marry me has taken
Aeneas to be master in her realm.
And now Sir Paris with his men, half-men,
His chin and perfumed hair tied up
In a Maeonian bonnet, takes possession.   280
As for ourselves, here we are bringing gifts
Into these shrines—supposedly your shrines—
Hugging that empty fable."
                  Pleas like this
From the man clinging to his altars reached
The ears of the Almighty. Now he turned   285
His eyes upon the queen's town and the lovers
Careless of their good name; then spoke to Mercury,[4]
Assigning him a mission:
                    "Son, bestir yourself,
Call up the Zephyrs,[5] take to your wings and glide.
Approach the Dardan captain where he tarries   290
Rapt in Tyrian Carthage, losing sight
Of future towns the fates ordain. Correct him,
Carry my speech to him on the running winds:
No son like this did his enchanting mother
Promise to us, nor such did she deliver   295
Twice from peril at the hands of Greeks.
He was to be the ruler of Italy,
Potential empire, armorer of war;
To father men from Teucer's[6] noble blood
And bring the whole world under law's dominion.   300
If glories to be won by deeds like these
Cannot arouse him, if he will not strive

---

4. The messenger god; Hermes in Greek.   **5.** The west winds.   **6.** The first Trojan king.

For his own honor, does he begrudge his son,
Ascanius, the high strongholds of Rome?
What has he in mind? What hope, to make him stay   305
Amid a hostile race, and lose from view
Ausonian progeny, Lavinian lands?[7]
The man should sail: that is the whole point.
Let this be what you tell him, as from me."

He finished and fell silent. Mercury   310
Made ready to obey the great command
Of his great father, and he first tied on
The golden sandals, winged, that high in air
Transport him over seas or over land
Abreast of gale winds; then he took the wand   315
With which he summons pale souls out of Orcus
And ushers others to the undergloom,
Lulls men to slumber or awakens them,
And opens dead men's eyes. This wand in hand,
He can drive winds before him, swimming down   320
Along the stormcloud. Now aloft, he saw
The craggy flanks and crown of patient Atlas,
Giant Atlas, balancing the sky
Upon his peak[8]—his pine-forested head
In vapor cowled, beaten by wind and rain.   325
Snow lay upon his shoulders, rills cascaded
Down his ancient chin and beard a-bristle,
Caked with ice. Here Mercury of Cyllenë[9]
Hovered first on even wings, then down
He plummeted to sea-level and flew on   330
Like a low-flying gull that skims the shallows
And rocky coasts where fish ply close inshore.
So, like a gull between the earth and sky,
The progeny of Cyllenë, on the wing
From his maternal grandsire, split the winds   335
To the sand bars of Libya.
                  Alighting tiptoe
On the first hutments, there he found Aeneas
Laying foundations for new towers and homes.
He noted well the swordhilt the man wore,
Adorned with yellow jasper; and the cloak   340
Aglow with Tyrian dye upon his shoulders—
Gifts of the wealthy queen, who had inwoven
Gold thread in the fabric. Mercury
Took him to task at once:
                  "Is it for you
To lay the stones for Carthage's high walls,   345
Tame husband that you are, and build their city?
Oblivious of your own world, your own kingdom!

7. The dowry of Lavinia, daughter of Latinus, whom Aeneas marries. *Ausonian:* Italian.   8. The Atlas Mountains are in western North Africa; the reference here is also to the Titan Atlas, who, as punishment for his part in the revolt against Jupiter, must hold up the heavens on his shoulders.   9. A mountain in Arcadia and Mercury's birthplace.

From bright Olympus he that rules the gods
And turns the earth and heaven by his power—
He and no other sent me to you, told me   350
To bring this message on the running winds:
What have you in mind? What hope, wasting your days
In Libya? If future history's glories
Do not affect you, if you will not strive
For your own honor, think of Ascanius,   355
Think of the expectations of your heir,
Iulus, to whom the Italian realm, the land
Of Rome, are due."
                  And Mercury, as he spoke,
Departed from the visual field of mortals
To a great distance, ebbed in subtle air.   360
Amazed, and shocked to the bottom of his soul
By what his eyes had seen, Aeneas felt
His hackles rise, his voice choke in his throat.
As the sharp admonition and command
From heaven had shaken him awake, he now   365
Burned only to be gone, to leave that land
Of the sweet life behind. What can he do? How tell
The impassioned queen and hope to win her over?
What opening shall he choose? This way and that
He let his mind dart, testing alternatives,   370
Running through every one. And as he pondered
This seemed the better tactic: he called in
Mnestheus, Sergestus and stalwart Serestus,
Telling them:
             "Get the fleet ready for sea,
But quietly, and collect the men on shore.   375
Lay in ship stores and gear."
                     As to the cause
For a change of plan, they were to keep it secret,
Seeing the excellent Dido had no notion,
No warning that such love could be cut short;
He would himself look for the right occasion,   380
The easiest time to speak, the way to do it.
The Trojans to a man gladly obeyed.

The queen, for her part, felt some plot afoot
Quite soon—for who deceives a woman in love?
She caught wind of a change, being in fear   385
Of what had seemed her safety. Evil Rumor,
Shameless as before,[1] brought word to her
In her distracted state of ships being rigged
In trim for sailing. Furious, at her wits' end,
She traversed the whole city, all aflame   390
With rage, like a Bacchanté[2] driven wild
By emblems shaken, when the mountain revels

---

1. Earlier, Rumor (a semidivine being) had spread the report of Dido's "marriage," which had incited Iarbas to make his indignant prayer to Jupiter.   2. A female devotee of the god Bacchus, in an ecstatic trance at the festival held every other year in the god's honor.

Of the odd year possess her, when the cry
Of Bacchus rises and Cithaeron[3] calls
All through the shouting night. Thus it turned out   395
She was the first to speak and charge Aeneas:

"You even hoped to keep me in the dark
As to this outrage, did you, two-faced man,
And slip away in silence? Can our love
Not hold you, can the pledge we gave not hold you,   400
Can Dido not, now sure to die in pain?
Even in winter weather must you toil
With ships, and fret to launch against high winds
For the open sea? Oh, heartless!
                              Tell me now,
If you were not in search of alien lands   405
And new strange homes, if ancient Troy remained,
Would ships put out for Troy on these big seas?
Do you go to get away from me? I beg you,
By these tears, by your own right hand,[4] since I
Have left my wretched self nothing but that—   410
Yes, by the marriage that we entered on,
If ever I did well and you were grateful
Or found some sweetness in a gift from me,
Have pity now on a declining house!
Put this plan by, I beg you, if a prayer   415
Is not yet out of place.
Because of you, Libyans and nomad kings
Detest me, my own Tyrians are hostile;
Because of you, I lost my integrity
And that admired name by which alone   420
I made my way once toward the stars.
                              To whom
Do you abandon me, a dying woman,
Guest that you are—the only name now left
From that of husband? Why do I live on?
Shall I, until my brother Pygmalion comes   425
To pull my walls down? Or the Gaetulan
Iarbas leads me captive? If at least
There were a child by you for me to care for,
A little one to play in my courtyard
And give me back Aeneas, in spite of all,   430
I should not feel so utterly defeated,
Utterly bereft."
                              She ended there.
The man by Jove's command held fast his eyes
And fought down the emotion in his heart.
At length he answered:
                              "As for myself, be sure   435
I never shall deny all you can say,

---

3. Mountain near Thebes, sacred to Bacchus.   4. The handclasp with which he pledged his love and
that Dido took as an earnest of marriage.

Your majesty, of what you meant to me.
Never will the memory of Elissa[5]
Stale for me, while I can still remember
My own life, and the spirit rules my body. 440
As to the event, a few words. Do not think
I meant to be deceitful and slip away.
I never held the torches of a bridegroom,
Never entered upon the pact of marriage.
If Fate permitted me to spend my days 445
By my own lights, and make the best of things
According to my wishes, first of all
I should look after Troy and the loved relics
Left me of my people. Priam's great hall
Should stand again; I should have restored the tower 450
Of Pergamum for Trojans in defeat.
But now it is the rich Italian land
Apollo tells me I must make for: Italy,
Named by his oracles. There is my love;
There is my country. If, as a Phoenician, 455
You are so given to the charms of Carthage,
Libyan city that it is, then tell me,
Why begrudge the Teucrian new lands
For homesteads in Ausonia? Are we not
Entitled, too, to look for realms abroad? 460
Night never veils the earth in damp and darkness,
Fiery stars never ascend the east,
But in my dreams my father's troubled ghost[6]
Admonishes and frightens me. Then, too,
Each night thoughts come of young Ascanius, 465
My dear boy wronged, defrauded of his kingdom,
Hesperian lands of destiny. And now
The gods' interpreter, sent by Jove himself—
I swear it by your head and mine—has brought
Commands down through the racing winds! I say 470
With my own eyes in full daylight I saw him
Entering the building! With my very ears
I drank his message in! So please, no more
Of these appeals that set us both afire.
I sail for Italy not of my own free will." 475

During all this she had been watching him
With face averted, looking him up and down
In silence, and she burst out raging now:

"No goddess was your mother. Dardanus
Was not the founder of your family. 480
Liar and cheat! Some rough Caucasian cliff
Begot you on flint. Hyrcanian[7] tigresses
Tendered their teats to you. Why should I palter?

5. Dido.   6. Anchisës had died in Sicily just before Aeneas, leaving for Italy, was blown by the storm winds to Carthage.   7. Near the Caspian Sea. *Caucasian:* after Caucasus Mountains, also near the Caspian Sea. The adjective connoted outlandishness and cruelty.

Why still hold back for more indignity?
Sigh, did he, while I wept? Or look at me?   485
Or yield a tear, or pity her who loved him?
What shall I say first, with so much to say?
The time is past when either supreme Juno
Or the Saturnian father[8] viewed these things
With justice. Faith can never be secure.   490
I took the man in, thrown up on this coast
In dire need, and in my madness then
Contrived a place for him in my domain,
Rescued his lost fleet, saved his shipmates' lives.
Oh, I am swept away burning by furies!   495
Now the prophet Apollo, now his oracles,
Now the gods' interpreter, if you please,
Sent down by Jove himself, brings through the air
His formidable commands! What fit employment
For heaven's high powers! What anxieties   500
To plague serene immortals![9] I shall not
Detain you or dispute your story. Go,
Go after Italy on the sailing winds,
Look for your kingdom, cross the deepsea swell!
If divine justice counts for anything,   505
I hope and pray that on some grinding reef
Midway at sea you'll drink your punishment
And call and call on Dido's name!
From far away I shall come after you
With my black fires, and when cold death has parted   510
Body from soul I shall be everywhere
A shade to haunt you! You will pay for this,
Unconscionable! I shall hear! The news will reach me
Even among the lowest of the dead!"

At this abruptly she broke off and ran   515
In sickness from his sight and the light of day,
Leaving him at a loss, alarmed, and mute
With all he meant to say. The maids in waiting
Caught her as she swooned and carried her
To bed in her marble chamber.
                          Duty-bound,   520
Aeneas, though he struggled with desire
To calm and comfort her in all her pain,
To speak to her and turn her mind from grief,
And though he sighed his heart out, shaken still
With love of her, yet took the course heaven gave him   525
And went back to the fleet. Then with a will
The Teucrians fell to work and launched ships
Along the whole shore: slick with tar each hull
Took to the water. Eager to get away,
The sailors brought oar-boughs out of the woods   530
With leaves still on, and oaken logs unhewn.
Now you could see them issuing from the town

8. Jupiter.   9. A reference to the Epicurean idea that the gods are unaffected by human events.

To the water's edge in streams, as when, aware
Of winter, ants will pillage a mound of spelt
To store it in their granary; over fields   535
The black battalion moves, and through the grass
On a narrow trail they carry off the spoil;
Some put their shoulders to the enormous weight
Of a trundled grain, while some pull stragglers in
And castigate delay; their to-and-fro   540
Of labor makes the whole track come alive.
At that sight, what were your emotions, Dido?
Sighing how deeply, looking out and down
From your high tower on the seething shore
Where all the harbor filled before your eyes   545
With bustle and shouts! Unconscionable Love,
To what extremes will you not drive our hearts!
She now felt driven to weep again, again
To move him, if she could, by supplication,
Humbling her pride before her love—to leave   550
Nothing untried, not to die needlessly.

"Anna, you see the arc of waterfront
All in commotion: they come crowding in
From everywhere. Spread canvas calls for wind,
The happy crews have garlanded the sterns.   555
If I could brace myself for this great sorrow,
Sister, I can endure it, too. One favor,
Even so, you may perform for me.
Since that deserter chose you for his friend
And trusted you, even with private thoughts,   560
Since you alone know when he may be reached,
Go, intercede with our proud enemy.
Remind him that I took no oath at Aulis[1]
With Danaans to destroy the Trojan race;
I sent no ship to Pergamum. Never did I   565
Profane his father Anchisës' dust and shade.
Why will he not allow my prayers to fall
On his unpitying ears? Where is he racing?
Let him bestow one last gift on his mistress:
This, to await fair winds and easier flight.   570
Now I no longer plead the bond he broke
Of our old marriage, nor do I ask that he
Should live without his dear love, Latium,
Or yield his kingdom. Time is all I beg,
Mere time, a respite and a breathing space   575
For madness to subside in, while my fortune
Teaches me how to take defeat and grieve.
Pity your sister. This is the end, this favor—
To be repaid with interest when I die."

She pleaded in such terms, and such, in tears,   580
Her sorrowing sister brought him, time and again.

---

1. Alluding to Agamemnon's oath when departing from Aulis for Troy.

But no tears moved him, no one's voice would he
Attend to tractably. The fates opposed it;
God's will blocked the man's once kindly ears.
And just as when the north winds from the Alps 585
This way and that contend among themselves
To tear away an oaktree hale with age,
The wind and tree cry, and the buffeted trunk
Showers high foliage to earth, but holds
On bedrock, for the roots go down as far 590
Into the underworld as cresting boughs
Go up in heaven's air: just so this captain,
Buffeted by a gale of pleas
This way and that way, dinned all the day long,
Felt their moving power in his great heart, 595
And yet his will stood fast; tears fell in vain.

On Dido in her desolation now
Terror grew at her fate. She prayed for death,
Being heartsick at the mere sight of heaven.
That she more surely would perform the act 600
And leave the daylight, now she saw before her
A thing one shudders to recall: on altars
Fuming with incense where she placed her gifts,
The holy water blackened, the spilt wine
Turned into blood and mire. Of this she spoke 605
To no one, not to her sister even. Then, too,
Within the palace was a marble shrine
Devoted to her onetime lord, a place
She held in wondrous honor, all festooned
With snowy fleeces and green festive boughs. 610
From this she now thought voices could be heard
And words could be made out, her husband's words,
Calling her, when midnight hushed the earth;
And lonely on the rooftops the night owl
Seemed to lament, in melancholy notes, 615
Prolonged to a doleful cry. And then, besides,
The riddling words of seers in ancient days,
Foreboding sayings, made her thrill with fear.
In nightmare, fevered, she was hunted down
By pitiless Aeneas, and she seemed 620
Deserted always, uncompanioned always,
On a long journey, looking for her Tyrians
In desolate landscapes—
                              as Pentheus gone mad
Sees the oncoming Eumenidés[2] and sees
A double sun and double Thebes appear, 625
Or as when, hounded on the stage, Orestës[3]

---

2. Pentheus, king of Thebes, persecuted the worshipers of Bacchus and imprisoned the god himself. He
was later mocked by the god, who inspired him with the Dionysiac spirit (and perhaps with wine) so that
he saw double. In this state he was led off to his death on Cithaeron. These events are dramatized in
Euripides' play *The Bacchanals* (*Bacchae*) but the Eumenidés (Furies) are not mentioned there. Perhaps
Virgil is using them simply as a symbol for madness.   3. Another reference to Greek tragedy; in Aeschylus's *Choephoroe* (*The Libation Bearers*), Orestës kills his mother, Clytaemnestra, and is pursued by the
Furies. In other tragic contexts he is represented as pursued by the ghost of his mother.

Runs from a mother armed with burning brands,
With serpents hellish black,
And in the doorway squat the Avenging Ones.

So broken in mind by suffering, Dido caught   630
Her fatal madness and resolved to die.
She pondered time and means, then visiting
Her mournful sister, covered up her plan
With a calm look, a clear and hopeful brow.

"Sister, be glad for me! I've found a way   635
To bring him back or free me of desire.
Near to the Ocean boundary, near sundown,
The Aethiops' farthest territory lies,
Where giant Atlas turns the sphere of heaven
Studded with burning stars. From there   640
A priestess of Massylian[4] stock has come;
She had been pointed out to me: custodian
Of that shrine named for daughters of the west,
Hesperidës;[5] and it is she who fed
The dragon, guarding well the holy boughs   645
With honey dripping slow and drowsy poppy.
Chanting her spells she undertakes to free
What hearts she wills, but to inflict on others
Duress of sad desires; to arrest
The flow of rivers, make the stars move backward,   650
Call up the spirits of deep Night. You'll see
Earth shift and rumble underfoot and ash trees
Walk down mountainsides. Dearest, I swear
Before the gods and by your own sweet self,
It is against my will that I resort   655
For weaponry to magic powers. In secret
Build up a pyre in the inner court
Under the open sky, and place upon it
The arms that faithless man left in my chamber,
All his clothing, and the marriage bed   660
On which I came to grief—solace for me
To annihilate all vestige of the man,
Vile as he is: my priestess shows me this."

While she was speaking, cheek and brow grew pale.
But Anna could not think her sister cloaked   665
A suicide in these unheard-of rites;
She failed to see how great her madness was
And feared no consequence more grave
Than at Sychaeus' death. So, as commanded,
She made the preparations. For her part,   670
The queen, seeing the pyre in her inmost court
Erected huge with pitch-pine and sawn ilex,

---

4. From the African tribe. 5. The daughters of Hesperus, who lived in a garden that contained golden
apples and was guarded by a dragon.

Hung all the place under the sky with wreaths
And crowned it with funereal cypress boughs.
On the pyre's top she put a sword he left   675
With clothing, and an effigy on a couch,
Her mind fixed now ahead on what would come.
Around the pyre stood altars, and the priestess,
Hair unbound, called in a voice of thunder
Upon three hundred gods, on Erebus,   680
On Chaos, and on triple Hecatë,[6]
Three-faced Diana. Then she sprinkled drops
Purportedly from the fountain of Avernus.[7]
Rare herbs were brought out, reaped at the new moon
By scythes of bronze, and juicy with a milk   685
Of dusky venom; then the rare love-charm
Or caul torn from the brow of a birthing foal
And snatched away before the mother found it.
Dido herself with consecrated grain
In her pure hands, as she went near the altars,   690
Freed one foot from sandal straps, let fall
Her dress ungirdled, and, now sworn to death,
Called on the gods and stars that knew her fate.
She prayed then to whatever power may care
In comprehending justice for the grief   695
Of lovers bound unequally by love.

The night had come, and weary in every land
Men's bodies took the boon of peaceful sleep.
The woods and the wild seas had quieted
At that hour when the stars are in mid-course   700
And every field is still; cattle and birds
With vivid wings that haunt the limpid lakes
Or nest in thickets in the country places
All were asleep under the silent night.
Not, though, the agonized Phoenician queen: 705
She never slackened into sleep and never
Allowed the tranquil night to rest
Upon her eyelids or within her heart.
Her pain redoubled; love came on again,
Devouring her, and on her bed she tossed   710
In a great surge of anger.
                        So awake,
She pressed these questions, musing to herself:

"Look now, what can I do? Turn once again
To the old suitors, only to be laughed at—
Begging a marriage with Numidians   715
Whom I disdained so often? Then what? Trail
The Ilian ships and follow like a slave
Commands of Trojans? Seeing them so agreeable,

---

6. Diana as goddess of sorcery and the moon. *Erebus:* the lowest depth of the underworld. *Chaos:* the Greek personification of the disorder that preceded the creation of the universe. 7. A lake in southern Italy that was supposed to be the entrance to the lower world.

In view of past assistance and relief,
So thoughtful their unshaken gratitude? 720
Suppose I wished it, who permits or takes
Aboard their proud ships one they so dislike?
Poor lost soul, do you not yet grasp or feel
The treachery of the line of Laömedon?[8]
What then? Am I to go alone, companion 725
Of the exultant sailors in their flight?
Or shall I set out in their wake, with Tyrians,
With all my crew close at my side, and send
The men I barely tore away from Tyre
To sea again, making them hoist their sails 730
To more sea-winds? No: die as you deserve,
Give pain quietus with a steel blade.
                              Sister,
You are the one who gave way to my tears
In the beginning, burdened a mad queen
With sufferings, and thrust me on my enemy. 735
It was not given me to lead my life
Without new passion, innocently, the way
Wild creatures live, and not to touch these depths.
The vow I took to the ashes of Sychaeus
Was not kept."
                    So she broke out afresh 740
In bitter mourning. On his high stern deck
Aeneas, now quite certain of departure,
Everything ready, took the boon of sleep.
In dream the figure of the god returned
With looks reproachful as before: he seemed 745
Again to warn him, being like Mercury
In every way, in voice, in golden hair,
And in the bloom of youth.
                              "Son of the goddess,
Sleep away this crisis, can you still?
Do you not see the dangers growing round you, 750
Madman, from now on? Can you not hear
The offshore westwind blow? The woman hatches
Plots and drastic actions in her heart,
Resolved on death now, whipping herself on
To heights of anger. Will you not be gone 755
In flight, while flight is still within your power?
Soon you will see the offing boil with ships
And glare with torches; soon again
The waterfront will be alive with fires,
If Dawn comes while you linger in this country. 760
Ha! Come, break the spell! Woman's a thing
Forever fitful and forever changing."

At this he merged into the darkness. Then
As the abrupt phantom filled him with fear,
Aeneas broke from sleep and roused his crewmen: 765

8. A king of Troy who twice broke his promise, once to Heracles and once to Apollo and Poseidon.

"Up, turn out now! Oarsmen, take your thwarts!
Shake out sail! Look here, for the second time
A god from heaven's high air is goading me
To hasten our break away, to cut the cables.
Holy one, whatever god you are,   770
We go with you, we act on your command
Most happily! Be near, graciously help us,
Make the stars in heaven propitious ones!"

He pulled his sword aflash out of its sheath
And struck at the stern hawser. All the men   775
Were gripped by his excitement to be gone,
And hauled and hustled. Ships cast off their moorings,
And an array of hulls hid inshore water
As oarsmen churned up foam and swept to sea.

Soon early Dawn, quitting the saffron bed   780
Of old Tithonus,[9] cast new light on earth,
And as air grew transparent, from her tower
The queen caught sight of ships on the seaward reach
With sails full and the wind astern. She knew
The waterfront now empty, bare of oarsmen.   785
Beating her lovely breast three times, four times,
And tearing her golden hair,
                    "O Jupiter,"
She said, "will this man go, will he have mocked
My kingdom, stranger that he was and is?
Will they not snatch up arms and follow him   790
From every quarter of the town? and dockhands
Tear our ships from moorings? On! Be quick
With torches! Give out arms! Unship the oars!
What am I saying? Where am I? What madness
Takes me out of myself? Dido, poor soul,   795
Your evil doing has come home to you.
Then was the right time, when you offered him
A royal scepter. See the good faith and honor
Of one they say bears with him everywhere
The hearthgods of his country! One who bore   800
His father, spent with age, upon his shoulders!
Could I not then have torn him limb from limb
And flung the pieces on the sea? His company,
Even Ascanius could I not have minced
And served up to his father at a feast?   805
The luck of battle might have been in doubt—
So let it have been! Whom had I to fear,
Being sure to die? I could have carried torches
Into his camp, filled passage ways with flame,
Annihilated father and son and followers   810
And given my own life on top of all!

---

9. Human consort of Aurora (Eos in Greek), the dawn goddess. He is old because, although she made him immortal when she took him to her bed, she forgot to obtain for him the gift of eternal youth.

O Sun, scanning with flame all works of earth,
And thou, O Juno, witness and go-between
Of my long miseries; and Hecatë,
Screeched for at night at crossroads in the cities; 815
And thou, avenging Furies, and all gods
On whom Elissa dying may call: take notice,
Overshadow this hell with your high power,
As I deserve, and hear my prayer!
If by necessity that impious wretch 820
Must find his haven and come safe to land,
If so Jove's destinies require, and this,
His end in view, must stand, yet all the same
When hard beset in war by a brave people,
Forced to go outside his boundaries 825
And torn from Iulus, let him beg assistance,
Let him see the unmerited deaths of those
Around and with him, and accepting peace
On unjust terms, let him not, even so,
Enjoy his kingdom or the life he longs for, 830
But fall in battle before his time and lie
Unburied on the sand![1] This I implore,
This is my last cry, as my last blood flows.
Then, O my Tyrians, besiege with hate
His progeny and all his race to come: 835
Make this your offering to my dust. No love,
No pact must be between our peoples; No,
But rise up from my bones, avenging spirit!
Harry with fire and sword the Dardan countrymen
Now, or hereafter, at whatever time 840
The strength will be afforded. Coast with coast
In conflict, I implore, and sea with sea,
And arms with arms: may they contend in war,
Themselves and all the children of their children!"[2]

Now she took thought of one way or another, 845
At the first chance, to end her hated life,
And briefly spoke to Barcë, who had been
Sychaeus' nurse; her own an urn of ash
Long held in her ancient fatherland.

                              "Dear nurse,
Tell Sister Anna to come here, and have her 850
Quickly bedew herself with running water
Before she brings out victims for atonement.
Let her come that way. And you, too, put on
Pure wool around your brows. I have a mind
To carry out that rite to Stygian[3] Jove 855

1. Dido's prophecy-wish does come true. Aeneas meets resistance in Italy, and at one point in the war he must leave Ascanius behind and beg aid from King Evander. One of the conditions of peace is that his people call themselves Latins (not Trojans). He is eventually drowned in an Italian river, never to see the glory of his descendants.   2. These prophecies also come true. The Romans and Carthaginians fought three wars (the Punic Wars); Rome won them all, razing Carthage after the third. In the third century B.C. Hannibal invaded Italy, winning many battles, although he failed to take Rome.   3. After the river Styx, which flowed in the underworld.

That I have readied here, and put an end
To my distress, committing to the flames
The pyre of that miserable Dardan."

At this with an old woman's eagerness
Barcë hurried away. And Dido's heart   860
Beat wildly at the enormous thing afoot.
She rolled her bloodshot eyes, her quivering cheeks
Were flecked with red as her sick pallor grew
Before her coming death. Into the court
She burst her way, then at her passion's height   865
She climbed the pyre and bared the Dardan sword—
A gift desired once, for no such need.
Her eyes now on the Trojan clothing there
And the familiar bed, she paused a little,
Weeping a little, mindful, then lay down   870
And spoke her last words:
                          "Remnants dear to me
While god and fate allowed it, take this breath
And give me respite from these agonies.
I lived my life out to the very end
And passed the stages Fortune had appointed.   875
Now my tall shade goes to the under world.
I built a famous town, saw my great walls,
Avenged my husband, made my hostile brother
Pay for his crime. Happy, alas, too happy,
If only the Dardanian keels had never   880
Beached on our coast." And here she kissed the bed.
"I die unavenged," she said, "but let me die.
This way, this way,[4] a blessed relief to go
Into the undergloom. Let the cold Trojan,
Far at sea, drink in this conflagration   885
And take with him the omen of my death!"

Amid these words her household people saw her
Crumpled over the steel blade, and the blade
Aflush with red blood, drenched her hands. A scream
Pierced the high chambers. Now through the shocked city   890
Rumor went rioting, as wails and sobs
With women's outcry echoed in the palace
And heaven's high air gave back the beating din,
As though all Carthage or old Tyre fell
To storming enemies, and, out of hand,   895
Flames billowed on the roofs of men and gods.
Her sister heard the trembling, faint with terror,
Lacerating her face, beating her breast,
Ran through the crowd to call the dying queen:

"It came to this, then, sister? You deceived me?   900
The pyre meant this, altars and fires meant this?

4. In Latin *sic, sic*; the repetition represents two thrusts of the sword.

What shall I mourn first, being abandoned? Did you
Scorn your sister's company in death?
You should have called me out to the same fate!
The same blade's edge and hurt, at the same hour,   905
Should have taken us off. With my own hands
Had I to build this pyre, and had I to call
Upon our country's gods, that in the end
With you placed on it there, O heartless one,
I should be absent? You have put to death   910
Yourself and me, the people and the fathers
Bred in Sidon, and your own new city.
Give me fresh water, let me bathe her wound
And catch upon my lips any last breath
Hovering over hers."
                   Now she had climbed   915
The topmost steps and took her dying sister
Into her arms to cherish, with a sob,
Using her dress to stanch the dark blood flow.
But Dido trying to lift her heavy eyes
Fainted again. Her chest-wound whistled air.   920
Three times she struggled up on one elbow
And each time fell back on the bed. Her gaze
Went wavering as she looked for heaven's light
And groaned at finding it. Almighty Juno,
Filled with pity for this long ordeal   925
And difficult passage, now sent Iris[5] down
Out of Olympus to set free
The wrestling spirit from the body's hold.
For since she died, not at her fated span
Nor as she merited, but before her time   930
Enflamed and driven mad, Proserpina
Had not yet plucked from her the golden hair,[6]
Delivering her to Orcus of the Styx.
So humid Iris through bright heaven flew
On saffron-yellow wings, and in her train   935
A thousand hues shimmered before the sun.
At Dido's head she came to rest.
                        "This token
Sacred to Dis[7] I bear away as bidden
And free you from your body."
                      Saying this,
She cut a lock of hair. Along with it   940
Her body's warmth fell into dissolution,
And out into the winds her life withdrew.

Summary   After his hurried departure from Carthage, Aeneas goes to Sicily, to the kingdom of his friend Acestës. There he organizes funeral games in honor of his father, Anchisës (who had died in Sicily on their first visit there), and leaves behind

---

5. As in Homer, a divine messenger; sometimes identified with the rainbow. 6. Queen of the underworld. Before a human died she was thought to cut a lock of his or her hair as an offering to Dis, god of the underworld. Dido (by suicide) dies unexpectedly; thus Juno sends Iris to cut the lock. 7. Hades in Greek.

those of his following who are unwilling to go on to the uncertainty of a settlement in Italy. Once on Italian soil, Aeneas, obeying instructions from his dead father, who had appeared to him in a dream, consults the Sibyl, who guides him down to the world of the dead. There he is to see his father and the vision of his race, which is to be his only reward, for he will die before his people are settled in their new home.

FROM BOOK VI

[Aeneas in the Underworld]

Gods who rule the ghosts; all silent shades;
And Chaos and infernal Fiery Stream,[8]
And regions of wide night without a sound,
May it be right to tell what I have heard,
May it be right, and fitting, by your will,   5
That I describe the deep world sunk in darkness
Under the earth.
             Now dim to one another
In desolate night they[9] walked on through the gloom,
Through Dis's homes all void, and empty realms,
As one goes through a wood by a faint moon's   10
Treacherous light, when Jupiter veils the sky
And black night blots the colors of the world.
Before the entrance, in the jaws of Orcus,
Grief and avenging Cares have made their beds,
And pale Diseases and sad Age are there,   15
And Dread, and Hunger that sways men to crime,
And sordid Want—in shapes to affright the eyes—
And Death and Toil and Death's own brother, Sleep,
And the mind's evil joys; on the door sill
Death-bringing War, and iron cubicles   20
Of the Eumenidës, and raving Discord,
Viperish hair bound up in gory bands.
In the courtyard a shadowy giant elm
Spreads ancient boughs, her ancient arms where dreams,
False dreams, the old tale goes, beneath each leaf   25
Cling and are numberless. There, too,
About the doorway forms of monsters crowd—
Centaurs, twiformed Scyllas, hundred-armed
Briareus, and the Lernaean hydra
Hissing horribly, and the Chimaera   30
Breathing dangerous flames, and Gorgons, Harpies,[1]
Huge Geryon, triple-bodied ghost.
Here, swept by sudden fear, drawing his sword,
Aeneas stood on guard with naked edge
Against them as they came. If his companion,   35
Knowing the truth, had not admonished him
How faint these lives were—empty images

8. A translation of *Phlegethon*, the name of one of the underworld rivers.   9. Aeneas and the Sibyl.   1. All mythical creatures. Centaurs were half human and half horse. Scyllas have many heads. Briareus had fifty heads. The Hydra had nine heads; but if one were cut off, two would grow in its place. The Chimaera was one-third lion, one-third goat, and one-third snake. Here the Harpies are spirits of the storm wind that carry souls to Hades.

Hovering bodiless—he had attacked
And cut his way through phantoms, empty air.

The path goes on from that place to the waves   40
Of Tartarus's Acheron. Thick with mud,
A whirlpool out of a vast abyss
Boils up and belches all the silt it carries
Into Cocytus.² Here the ferryman,
A figure of fright, keeper of waters and streams,   45
Is Charon, foul and terrible, his beard
Grown wild and hoar, his staring eyes all flame,
His sordid cloak hung from a shoulder knot.
Alone he poles his craft and trims the sails
And in his rusty hull ferries the dead,   50
Old now—but old age in the gods is green.³

Here a whole crowd came streaming to the banks,
Mothers and men, the forms with all life spent
Of heroes great in valor, boys and girls
Unmarried, and young sons laid on the pyre   55
Before their parents' eyes—as many souls
As leaves that yield their hold on boughs and fall
Through forests in the early frost of autumn,
Or as migrating birds from the open sea
That darken heaven when the cold season comes   60
And drives them overseas to sunlit lands.
There all stood begging to be first across
And reached out longing hands to the far shore.

But the grim boatman now took these aboard,
Now those, waving the rest back from the strand.   65
In wonder at this and touched by the commotion,
Aeneas said:
            "Tell me, Sister, what this means,
The crowd at the stream. Where are the souls bound?
How are they tested, so that these turn back,
While those take oars to cross the dead-black water?"   70

Briefly the ancient priestess answered him:

"Cocytus is the deep pool that you see,
The swamp of Styx beyond, infernal power
By which the gods take oath and fear to break it.
All in the nearby crowd you notice here   75
Are pauper souls, the souls of the unburied.
Charon's the boatman. Those the water bears
Are souls of buried men. He may not take them
Shore to dread shore on the hoarse currents there
Until their bones rest in the grave, or till   80

2. A river of the underworld; the name suggests "mourning" or "lamentation." Tartarus is in the lower depths of the underworld. Acheron is another river.   3. I.e., age in gods does not affect their vitality or strength. Thus Charon, although old, is still able to ferry the souls of the dead over the river Styx.

They flutter and roam this side a hundred years;
They may have passage then, and may return
To cross the deeps they long for."

                                 Anchisës' son
Had halted, pondering on so much, and stood
In pity for the souls' hard lot. Among them   85
He saw two sad ones of unhonored death,
Leucaspis and the Lycian fleet's commander,
Orontës,[4] who had sailed the windy sea
From Troy together, till the Southern gale
Had swamped and whirled them down, both ship and men.   90
Of a sudden he saw his helmsman, Palinurus,
Going by, who but a few nights before
On course from Libya, as he watched the stars,
Had been pitched overboard astern. As soon
As he made sure of the disconsolate one   95
In all the gloom, Aeneas called:

                             "Which god
Took you away from us and put you under,
Palinurus? Tell me. In this one prophecy
Apollo, who had never played me false,
Falsely foretold you'd be unharmed at sea   100
And would arrive at the Ausonian coast.
Is the promise kept?"

                      But the shade said:

                                 "Phoebus' caldron[5]
Told you no lie, my captain, and no god
Drowned me at sea. The helm that I hung on to,
Duty bound to keep our ship on course,   105
By some great shock chanced to be torn away,
And I went with it overboard. I swear
By the rough sea, I feared less for myself
Than for your ship: with rudder gone and steersman
Knocked overboard, it might well come to grief   110
In big seas running. Three nights, heavy weather
Out of the South on the vast water tossed me.
On the fourth dawn, I sighted Italy
Dimly ahead, as a wave-crest lifted me.
By turns I swam and rested, swam again   115
And got my footing on the beach, but savages
Attacked me as I clutched at a cliff-top,
Weighted down by my wet clothes. Poor fools,
They took me for a prize and ran me through.
Surf has me now, and sea winds, washing me   120
Close inshore.

                By heaven's happy light
And the sweet air, I beg you, by your father,
And by your hopes of Iulus' rising star,
Deliver me from this captivity,

---

4. Trojans lost at sea in the storm that took Aeneas to Carthage.   **5.** The Pythia, priestess of Apollo at Delphi, delivered the god's prophecies seated on a tripod, a three-legged shallow caldron.

Unconquered friend! Throw earth on me—you can— 125
Put in to Velia⁶ port! Or if there be
Some way to do it, if your goddess mother
Shows a way—and I feel sure you pass
These streams and Stygian marsh by heaven's will—
Give this poor soul your hand, take me across, 130
Let me at least in death find quiet haven."
When he had made his plea, the Sibyl said:
"From what source comes this craving, Palinurus?
Would you though still unburied see the Styx
And the grim river of the Eumenidës, 135
Or even the river bank, without a summons?
Abandon hope by prayer to make the gods
Change their decrees. Hold fast to what I say
To comfort your hard lot: neighboring folk
In cities up and down the coast will be 140
Induced by portents to appease your bones,
Building a tomb and making offerings there
On a cape forever named for Palinurus."

The Sibyl's words relieved him, and the pain
Was for a while dispelled from his sad heart, 145
Pleased at the place-name. So the two walked on
Down to the stream. Now from the Stygian water
The boatman, seeing them in the silent wood
And headed for the bank, cried out to them
A rough uncalled-for challenge:
                      "Who are you 150
In armor, visiting our rivers? Speak
From where you are, stop there, say why you come.
This is the region of the Shades, and Sleep,
And drowsy Night. It breaks eternal law
For the Stygian craft to carry living bodies. 155
Never did I rejoice, I tell you, letting
Alcidës cross, or Theseus and Pirithous,⁷
Demigods by paternity though they were,
Invincible in power. One forced in chains
From the king's own seat the watchdog of the dead 160
And dragged him away trembling. The other two
Were bent on carrying our lady off
From Dis's chamber."
                    This the prophetess
And servant of Amphrysian Apollo⁸
Briefly answered:
                "Here are no such plots, 165
So fret no more. These weapons threaten nothing.
Let the great watchdog at the door howl on

6. South of the Bay of Naples, near Cape Palinuro (named after Aeneas's pilot). 7. They came to kidnap Proserpina, failed, and were imprisoned. *Alcidës*: Heracles, who, as one of his labors, was to bring Cerberus, the watchdog of Hades, up from the lower world. He also managed to rescue Theseus. 8. An elaborate learned allusion; Apollo had once served as herdsman to King Admetus on the banks of the river Amphrysus in Thessaly.

Forever terrifying the bloodless shades.
Let chaste Proserpina remain at home
In her uncle's house. The man of Troy, Aeneas,   170
Remarkable for loyalty, great in arms,
Goes through the deepest shades of Erebus
To see his father.
                    If the very image
Of so much goodness moves you not at all,
Here is a bough"⁹—at this she showed the bough   175
That had been hidden, held beneath her dress—
"You'll recognize it."
                       Then his heart, puffed up
With rage, subsided. They had no more words.
His eyes fixed on the ancient gift, the bough,
The destined gift, so long unseen, now seen,   180
He turned his dusky craft and made for shore.
There from the long thwarts where they sat he cleared
The other souls and made the gangway wide,
Letting the massive man step in the bilge.
The leaky coracle groaned at the weight   185
And took a flood of swampy water in.
At length, on the other side, he put ashore
The prophetess and hero in the mire,
A formless ooze amid the grey-green sedge.
Great Cerberus barking with his triple throat   190
Makes all that shoreline ring, as he lies huge
In a facing cave. Seeing his neck begin
To come alive with snakes, the prophetess
Tossed him a lump of honey and drugged meal
To make him drowse. Three ravenous gullets gaped   195
And he snapped up the sop. Then his great bulk
Subsided and lay down through all the cave.
Now seeing the watchdog deep in sleep, Aeneas
Took the opening: swiftly he turned away
From the river over which no soul returns.   200

Now voices crying loud were heard at once—
The souls of infants wailing. At the door
Of the sweet life they were to have no part in,
Torn from the breast, a black day took them off
And drowned them all in bitter death. Near these   205
Were souls falsely accused, condemned to die.
But not without a judge, or jurymen,
Had these souls got their places: Minos reigned
As the presiding judge, moving the urn,
And called a jury of the silent ones¹   210
To learn of lives and accusations. Next
Were those sad souls, benighted, who contrived
Their own destruction, and as they hated daylight,

9. The golden bough that Aeneas had been ordered to take as tribute to Proserpina.   1. The dead. Minos,
once king of Crete, is now judge of the dead. The magistrate of a Roman court decided the order in which
cases were heard by drawing lots from an urn.

Cast their lives away. How they would wish
In the upper air now to endure the pain   215
Of poverty and toil! But iron law
Stands in the way, since the drear hateful swamp
Has pinned them down here, and the Styx that winds
Nine times around exerts imprisoning power.
Not far away, spreading on every side,   220
The Fields of Mourning came in view, so called
Since here are those whom pitiless love consumed
With cruel wasting, hidden on paths apart
By myrtle woodland growing overhead.
In death itself, pain will not let them be.   225
He saw here Phaedra, Procris, Eriphylë
Sadly showing the wounds her hard son gave;
Evadnë and Pasiphaë, at whose side
Laodamia walked, and Caeneus,[2]
A young man once, a woman now, and turned   230
Again by fate into the older form.
Among them, with her fatal wound still fresh,
Phoenician Dido wandered the deep wood.
The Trojan captain paused nearby and knew
Her dim form in the dark, as one who sees,   235
Early in the month, or thinks to have seen, the moon
Rising through cloud, all dim. He wept and spoke
Tenderly to her:
                     "Dido, so forlorn,
The story then that came to me was true,
That you were out of life, had met your end   240
By your own hand. Was I, was I the cause?
I swear by heaven's stars, by the high gods,
By any certainty below the earth,
I left your land against my will, my queen.
The gods' commands drove me to do their will,   245
As now they drive me through this world of shades,
These mouldy waste lands and these depths of night.
And I could not believe that I would hurt you
So terribly by going. Wait a little.
Do not leave my sight.   250
Am I someone to flee from? The last word
Destiny lets me say to you is this."

Aeneas with such pleas tried to placate
The burning soul, savagely glaring back,

---

2. Virgil's words in the original are ambiguous (perhaps to reflect the ambiguity of the sex of Caeneus).
The usual explanation of the passage is that Caenis (a woman) was changed by Neptune into a man
(Caeneus) but returned to her original sex after death. Because the name occurs here in a list of women,
this seems the most likely explanation. Phaedra was the wife of Theseus, king of Athens, who fell in love
with Hippolytus, her husband's son by another woman; the result was her death by suicide and Hippolytus's
death through his father's curse. Procris was killed by her husband in an accident that was brought about
by her own jealousy. Eriphylë betrayed her husband for gold and was killed by her own son. Evadnë threw
herself on the pyre of her husband, who was killed by Jupiter for impiety. Pasiphaë was the wife of Minos;
she was made to fall in love with a bull, and their union produced the Minotaur. Laodamia begged to be
allowed to talk with her dead husband; the request was granted by the gods, and when his time came to
return she went with him to the underworld.

And tears came to his eyes. But she had turned   255
With gaze fixed on the ground as he spoke on,
Her face no more affected than if she were
Immobile granite or Marpesian[3] stone.
At length she flung away from him and fled,
His enemy still, into the shadowy grove   260
Where he whose bride she once had been, Sychaeus,
Joined in her sorrows and returned her love.
Aeneas still gazed after her in tears,
Shaken by her ill fate and pitying her.

With effort then he took the given way,   265
And they went on, reaching the farthest lands
Where men famous in war gather apart.
Here Tydeus came to meet him, and then came
Parthenopaeus, glorious in arms,
Adrastus[4] then, a pallid shade. Here too   270
Were Dardans long bewept in the upper air,
Men who died in the great war. And he groaned
To pick these figures out, in a long file,
Glaucus, Medon, Thersilochus, besides
Antenor's three sons, then the priest of Ceres   275
Polyboetës, then Idaeus, holding
Still to his warcar, holding his old gear.
To right and left they crowd the path and stay
And will not have enough of seeing him,
But love to hold him back, to walk beside him,   280
And hear the story of why he came.

                        Not so
Agamemnon's phalanx, chiefs of the Danaans:
Seeing the living man in bronze that glowed
Through the dark air, they shrank in fear. Some turned
And ran, as once, when routed, to the ships,   285
While others raised a battle shout, or tried to,
Mouths agape, mocked by the whispering cry.
Here next he saw Deïphobus, Priam's son,
Mutilated from head to foot, his face
And both hands cruelly torn, ears shorn away,   290
Nose to the noseholes lopped by a shameful stroke.
Barely knowing the shade who quailed before him
Covering up his tortured face, Aeneas
Spoke out to him in his known voice:

                                "Deïphobus,
Gallant officer in high Teucer's line,   295
Who chose this brutal punishment, who had
So much the upper hand of you? I heard
On that last night that you had fallen, spent
After a slaughter of Pelasgians—
Fallen on piled-up carnage. It was I   300
Who built on Rhoeteum Point an empty tomb

---

3. From the island of Paros.   4. Three of the seven Argive attackers of Thebes in the generation before
the Trojan War. Tydeus was father of Diomedes.

And sent a high call to your soul three times.
Your name, your armor, marks the place. I could not
Find you, friend, to put your bones in earth
In the old country as I came away."   305

And Priam's son replied:
                               "You left undone
Nothing, my friend, but gave all ritual due
Deïphobus, due a dead man's shade. My lot
And the Laconian woman's[5] ghastly doing
Sank me in this hell. These are the marks   310
She left me as her memorial. You know
How between one false gladness and another
We spent that last night—no need to remind you.
When the tall deadly horse came at one bound,
With troops crammed in its paunch, above our towers,   315
She made a show of choral dance and led
Our Phrygian women crying out on Bacchus
Here and there—but held a torch amid them,
Signalling to Danaans from the Height.
Worn by the long day, heavily asleep,   320
I lay in my unlucky bridal chamber,
And rest, profound and sweet, most like the rest
Of death, weighed on me as I lay. Meanwhile
She, my distinguished wife,[6] moved all my arms
Out of the house—as she had slipped my sword,   325
My faithful sword, out from beneath my pillow—
Opened the door and called in Menelaus,
Hoping no doubt by this great gift to him,
Her lover, to blot old infamy out. Why hold back
From telling it? The two burst in the bedroom,   330
Joined by that ringleader of atrocity,
Ulysses, of the windking's[7] line. O gods,
If with pure lips I pray, requite the Greeks
With equal suffering! But you, now tell me
What in the world has brought you here alive: 335
Have you come from your sea wandering, and did heaven
Direct you? How could harrying fortune send you
To these sad sunless homes, disordered places?"

At this point in their talk Aurora,[8] borne
Through high air on her glowing rosy car   340
Had crossed the meridian: should they linger now
With stories they might spend the allotted time.
But at Aeneas' side the Sibyl spoke,
Warning him briefly:
                        "Night comes on, Aeneas,
We use up hours grieving. Here is the place   345
Where the road forks: on the right hand it goes

5. Helen's.   6. Deïphobus had married Helen after the death of Paris.   7. Aeolus's. His son was Sisyphus, one of the great tricksters of Greek legend, who was reputed to be Ulysses' actual father, rather than Laertes.   8. Dawn goddess.

Past mighty Dis's walls, Elysium way,
Our way; but the leftward road will punish
Malefactors, taking them to Tartarus."
Deïphobus answered her:

                "No need for anger,   350
Reverend lady. I'll depart and make
The tally in the darkness full again.
Go on, sir, glory of us all! Go on,
Enjoy a better destiny."

                      He spoke,
And even as he spoke he turned away.   355
Now of a sudden Aeneas looked and saw
To the left, under a cliff, wide buildings girt
By a triple wall round which a torrent rushed
With scorching flames and boulders tossed in thunder,
The abyss's Fiery River. A massive gate   360
With adamantine pillars faced the stream,
So strong no force of men or gods in war
May ever avail to crack and bring it down,
And high in air an iron tower stands
On which Tisiphonë,[9] her bloody robe   365
Pulled up about her, has her seat and keeps
Unsleeping watch over the entrance way
By day and night. From the interior, groans
Are heard, and thud of lashes, clanking iron,
Dragging chains. Arrested in his tracks,   370
Appalled by what he heard, Aeneas stood.

"What are the forms of evil here? O Sister,
Tell me. And the punishments dealt out:
Why such a lamentation?"

                  Said the Sibyl:
"Light of the Teucrians, it is decreed   375
That no pure soul may cross the sill of evil.
When, however, Hecatë[1] appointed me
Caretaker of Avernus wood, she led me
Through heaven's punishments and taught me all.
This realm is under Cretan Rhadamanthus'[2]   380
Iron rule. He sentences. He listens
And makes the souls confess their crooked ways,
How they put off atonements in the world
With foolish satisfaction, thieves of time,
Until too late, until the hour of death.   385
At once the avenger girdled with her whip,
Tisiphonë, leaps down to lash the guilty,
Vile writhing snakes held out on her left hand,
And calls her savage sisterhood. The awaited
Time has come, hell gates will shudder wide   390
On shrieking hinges. Can you see her now,
Her shape, as doorkeeper, upon the sill?
More bestial, just inside, the giant Hydra

---

9. One of the Furies.   1. Goddess of witchcraft, often identified with Diana by the Romans.
2. Brother of Minos, king of Crete, and like him a judge of the dead.

Lurks with fifty black and yawning throats.
Then Tartarus itself goes plunging down   395
In darkness twice as deep as heaven is high
For eyes fixed on etherial Olympus.
Here is Earth's ancient race, the brood of Titans,[3]
Hurled by the lightning down to roll forever
In the abyss. Here, too, I saw those giant   400
Twins of Aloeus[4] who laid their hands
Upon great heaven to rend it and to topple
Jove from his high seat, and I saw, too,
Salmoneus paying dearly for the jape
Of mimicking Jove's fire, Olympus' thunder: 405
Shaking a bright torch from a four-horse car
He rode through Greece and his home town in Elis,
Glorying, claiming honor as a god—
Out of his mind, to feign with horses' hoofs
On bronze the blast and inimitable bolt.   410
The father almighty amid heavy cloud
Let fly his missile—no firebrand for him
Nor smoky pitchpine light—and spun the man
Headlong in a huge whirlwind.
                                            One had sight
Of Tityos,[5] too, child of all-mothering Earth,   415
His body stretched out over nine whole acres
While an enormous vulture with hooked beak
Forages forever in his liver,
His vitals rife with agonies. The bird,
Lodged in the chest cavity, tears at his feast,   420
And tissues growing again get no relief.
As for the Lapiths, need I tell: Ixion,
Pirithoüs,[6] and the black crag overhead
So sure to fall it seems already falling.
Golden legs gleam on the feasters' couches,   425
Dishes in royal luxury prepared
Are laid before them—but the oldest Fury
Crouches near and springs out with her torch.
Her outcry, if they try to touch the meal.
Here come those who as long as life remained   430
Held brothers hateful, beat their parents, cheated
Poor men dependent on them; also those
Who hugged their newfound riches to themselves
And put nothing aside for relatives—
A great crowd, this—then men killed for adultery,   435
Men who took arms in war against the right,
Not scrupling to betray their lords. All these
Are hemmed in here, awaiting punishment.
Best not inquire what punishment, what form
Of suffering at their last end overwhelms them.   440

3. The second generation of gods, offspring of Earth and Sky, overthrown by the Olympians under Jupiter
(Zeus).   4. Otus and Ephialtes, who piled Mt. Pelion on top of Mt. Ossa in order to scale heaven and
attack Jupiter.   5. Punished for trying to rape Leto (Latona). Odysseus sees him in the land of the dead
also (*Odyssey* 11.646–54).   6. Ixion tried to rape Juno, and Pirithoüs aided Theseus in his unsuccessful
attempt to carry off Proserpina from the underworld. The punishment described here, however, was traditionally assigned to Tantalus, another of the great sinners.

Some heave at a great boulder, or revolve,
Spreadeagled, hung on wheel-spokes. Theseus
Cleaves to his chair and cleaves to it forever.
Phlegyas in his misery teaches all souls
His lesson, thundering out amid the gloom: 445
'Be warned and study justice, not to scorn
The immortal gods.' Here's one who sold his country,
Foisted a tyrant on her, set up laws
Or nullified them for a price; another
Entered his daughter's room to take a bride   450
Forbidden him. All these dared monstrous wrong
And took what they dared try for. If I had
A hundred tongues, a hundred mouths, a voice
Of iron, I could not tell of all the shapes
Their crimes had taken, or their punishments."   455

All this he heard from her who for long years
Had served Apollo. Then she said:
                              "Come now,
Be on your way, and carry out your mission.
Let us go faster. I can see the walls
The Cyclops' forges built and, facing us,   460
The portico and gate[7] where they command us
To leave the gifts required."
                              On this the two
In haste strode on abreast down the dark paths
Over the space between, and neared the doors.
Aeneas gained the entrance, halted there,   465
Asperged his body with fresh water drops,
And on the sill before him fixed the bough.

Now that at last this ritual was performed,
His duty to the goddess done, they came
To places of delight, to green park land,   470
Where souls take ease amid the Blessed Groves.
Wider expanses of high air endow
Each vista with a wealth of light. Souls here
Possess their own familiar sun and stars.
Some train on grassy rings, others compete   475
In field games, others grapple on the sand.
Feet moving to a rhythmic beat, the dancers
Group in a choral pattern as they sing.
Orpheus, the priest of Thrace, in his long robe
Accompanies, plucking his seven notes   480
Now with his fingers, now with his ivory quill.
Here is the ancient dynasty of Teucer,
Heroes high of heart, beautiful scions,
Born in greater days: Ilus, Assaracus,
And Dardanus,[8] who founded Troy. Aeneas   485

---

7. The entrance to Elysium, the paradise of the souls of the blessed. This gate can be passed only with the
token of the golden bough.   8. Trojan ancestors.

Marvels to see their chariots and gear
Far off, all phantom: lances fixed in earth,
And teams unyoked, at graze on the wide plain.
All joy they took, alive, in cars and weapons,
As in the care and pasturing of horses, 490
Remained with them when they were laid in earth.
He saw, how vividly! along the grass
To right and left, others who feasted there
And chorused out a hymn praising Apollo,
Within a fragrant laurel grove, where Po[9] 495
Sprang up and took his course to the world above,
The broad stream flowing on amid the forest.
This was the company of those who suffered
Wounds in battle for their country; those
Who in their lives were holy men and chaste 500
Or worthy of Phoebus in prophetic song;
Or those who bettered life, by finding out
New truths and skills; or those who to some folk
By benefactions made themselves remembered.
They all wore snowy chaplets on their brows. 505
To these souls, mingling on all sides, the Sibyl
Spoke now, and especially to Musaeus,[1]
The central figure, toward whose towering shoulders
All the crowd gazed:
              "Tell us, happy souls,
And you, great seer, what region holds Anchises, 510
Where is his resting place? For him we came
By ferry across the rivers of Erebus."
And the great soul answered briefly:
                    "None of us
Has one fixed home. We walk in shady groves
And bed on riverbanks and occupy 515
Green meadows fresh with streams. But if your hearts
Are set on it, first cross this ridge; and soon
I shall point out an easy path."
                       So saying,
He walked ahead and showed them from the height
The sweep of shining plain. Then down they went 520
And left the hilltops.
             Now Aeneas' father
Anchises, deep in the lush green of a valley,
Had given all his mind to a survey
Of souls, till then confined there, who were bound
For daylight in the upper world.[2] By chance 525
His own were those he scanned now, all his own
Descendants, with their futures and their fates,
Their characters and acts. But when he saw
Aeneas advancing toward him on the grass,

---

9. An Italian river.   1. A legendary singer, like Orpheus.   2. I.e., destined to be reincarnated, as Anchisës will explain.

He stretched out both his hands in eagerness   530
As tears wetted his cheeks. He said in welcome:

"Have you at last come, has that loyalty
Your father counted on conquered the journey?
Am I to see your face, my son, and hear
Our voices in communion as before?   535
I thought so, surely; counting the months I thought
The time would come. My longing has not tricked me.
I greet you now, how many lands behind you,
How many seas, what blows and dangers, son!
How much I feared the land of Libya   540
Might do you harm."
                          Aeneas said:
                                        "Your ghost,
Your sad ghost, father, often before my mind,
Impelled me to the threshold of this place.
My ships ride anchored in the Tuscan sea.
But let me have your hand, let me embrace you,   545
Do not draw back."
                          At this his tears brimmed over
And down his cheeks. And there he tried three times
To throw his arms around his father's neck,
Three times the shade untouched slipped through his hands,
Weightless as wind and fugitive as dream.   550
Aeneas now saw at the valley's end
A grove standing apart, with stems and boughs
Of woodland rustling, and the stream of Lethe[3]
Running past those peaceful glades. Around it
Souls of a thousand nations filled the air,   555
As bees in meadows at the height of summer
Hover and home on flowers and thickly swarm
On snow-white lilies, and the countryside
Is loud with humming. At the sudden vision
Shivering, at a loss, Aeneas asked   560
What river flowed there and what men were those
In such a throng along the riverside.
His father Anchises told him:
                                  "Souls for whom
A second body is in store: their drink
Is water of Lethe, and it frees from care   565
In long forgetfulness. For all this time
I have so much desired to show you these
And tell you of them face to face—to take
The roster of my children's children here,
So you may feel with me more happiness   570
At finding Italy."
                          "Must we imagine,
Father, there are souls that go from here
Aloft to upper heaven, and once more
Return to bodies' dead weight? The poor souls,

3. River of forgetfulness.

How can they crave our daylight so?"
                                                    "My son,   575
I'll tell you, not to leave you mystified,"
Anchisës said, and took each point in order:

First, then, the sky and lands and sheets of water,
The bright moon's globe, the Titan sun and stars,
Are fed within by Spirit, and a Mind   580
Infused through all the members of the world
Makes one great living body of the mass.
From Spirit come the races of man and beast,
The life of birds, odd creatures the deep sea
Contains beneath her sparkling surfaces,   585
And fiery energy from a heavenly source
Belongs to the generative seeds of these,
So far as they are not poisoned or clogged
By mortal bodies, their free essence dimmed
By earthiness and deathliness of flesh.   590
This makes them fear and crave, rejoice and grieve.
Imprisoned in the darkness of the body
They cannot clearly see heaven's air;[4] in fact
Even when life departs on the last day
Not all the scourges of the body pass   595
From the poor souls, not all distress of life.
Inevitably, many malformations,
Growing together in mysterious ways,
Become inveterate. Therefore they undergo
The discipline of punishments and pay   600
In penance for old sins: some hang full length
To the empty winds, for some the stain of wrong
Is washed by floods or burned away by fire.
We suffer each his own shade. We are sent
Through wide Elysium, where a few abide   605
In happy lands, till the long day, the round
Of Time fulfilled, has worn our stains away,
Leaving the soul's heaven-sent perception clear,
The fire from heaven pure.[5] These other souls,
When they have turned Time's wheel a thousand years,   610
The god calls in a crowd to Lethe stream,
That there unmemoried they may see again
The heavens and wish re-entry into bodies."
Anchises paused. He drew both son and Sibyl
Into the middle of the murmuring throng,   615
Then picked out a green mound from which to view
The souls as they came forward, one by one,
And to take note of faces.
                              "Come," he said,
"What glories follow Dardan generations

---

4. The idea that the body is the tomb of the soul is found also in Plato. Like a number of other ideas in Anchisës' speech (such as reincarnation), it was characteristic of Orphism, a set of beliefs that underlay various mystery rituals outside the state religions of Greece and Rome.   5. These souls, having successfully purged the impurities of the body, are now ready to return to the company of the gods. The other souls whom Anchisës goes on to mention must undergo further rebirths before they are purified. They include the souls of the future Romans, whom Aeneas now surveys.

In after years, and from Italian blood 620
What famous children in your line will come,
Souls of the future, living in our name,
I shall tell clearly now, and in the telling
Teach you your destiny. That one you see,
The young man leaning on a spear unarmed, 625
Has his allotted place nearest the light.
He will be first to take the upper air,
Silvius, a child with half Italian blood
And an Alban name, your last born, whom your wife,
Lavinia,[6] late in your great age will rear 630
In forests to be king and father of kings.
Through him our race will rule in Alba Longa.
Next him is Procas, pride of the Trojan line,
And Capys, too, then Numitor, then one
Whose name restores you: Silvius Aeneas,[7] 635
Both in arms and piety your peer,
If ever he shall come to reign in Alba.
What men they are! And see their rugged forms
With oakleaf crowns shadowing their brows. I tell you,
These are to found Nomentum, Gabii, 640
Fidenae town, Collatia's hilltop towers,
Pometii, Fort Inuus, Bola, Cora[8]—
Names to be heard for places nameless now.
Then Romulus, fathered by Mars, will come
To make himself his grandfather's companion, 645
Romulus, reared by his mother, Ilia,
In the blood-line of Assaracus. Do you see
The double plume of Mars fixed on his crest,
See how the father of the gods himself
Now marks him out with his own sign of honor? 650
Look now, my son: under his auspices
Illustrious Rome will bound her power with earth,
Her spirit with Olympus. She'll enclose
Her seven hills with one great city wall,
Fortunate in the men she breeds. Just so 655
Cybelë Mother,[9] honored on Berecynthus,
Wearing her crown of towers, onward rides
By chariot through the towns of Phrygia,
In joy at having given birth to gods,
And cherishing a hundred grandsons, heaven 660
Dwellers with homes on high.
                                Turn your two eyes
This way and see this people, your own Romans.
Here is Caesar, and all the line of Iulus,
All who shall one day pass under the dome
Of the great sky: this is the man, this one, 665

---

6. The bride Aeneas will win by war in the second half of the poem.   7. Kings of Alba Longa, the city
(Rome's forerunner) founded in Italy by Ascanius. Silvius Aeneas was son of the Silvius mentioned in line
628 and grandson of Aeneas. Numitor was father of Ilia (or Rhea Silvia), the mother by Mars of Romulus
and Remus (see lines 644–50).   8. Towns near Rome.   9. The great mother goddess of Asia Minor,
whose cult was important in Rome from an early period. Mt. Berecynthus, near Troy, was a center of her
Asian cult. One of her attributes was a crown that resembled a city wall with turrets.

Of whom so often you have heard the promise,
Caesar Augustus, son of the deified,
Who shall bring once again an Age of Gold
To Latium, to the land where Saturn reigned
In early times. He will extend his power   670
Beyond the Garamants[1] and Indians,
Over far territories north and south
Of the zodiacal stars, the solar way,
Where Atlas, heaven-bearing, on his shoulder
Turns the night-sphere, studded with burning stars.   675
At that man's coming even now the realms
Of Caspia and Maeotia tremble, warned
By oracles, and the seven mouths of Nile
Go dark with fear. The truth is, even Alcidës[2]
Never traversed so much of earth—I grant   680
That he could shoot the hind with brazen hoofs
Or bring peace to the groves of Erymanthus,
Or leave Lerna affrighted by his bow.[3]
Neither did he who guides his triumphal car
With reins of vine-shoots twisted, Bacchus, driving   685
Down from Nysa's height his tiger team.
Do we lag still at carrying our valor
Into action? Can our fear prevent
Our settling in Ausonia?
                              Who is he
So set apart there, olive-crowned, who holds   690
The sacred vessels in his hands? I know
That snowy mane and beard: Numa,[4] the king,
Who will build early Rome on a base of laws,
A man sent from the small-town poverty
Of Curës to high sovereignty. After him   695
Comes Tullus, breaker of his country's peace,
Arousing men who have lost victorious ways,
Malingering men, to war. Near him is Ancus,
Given to boasting, even now too pleased
With veering popularity's heady air.   700
Do you care to see now, too, the Tarquin kings
And the proud soul of the avenger, Brutus,[5]
By whom the bundled *fasces* are regained?
Consular power will first be his, and his
The pitiless axes.[6] When his own two sons   705
Plot war against the city, he will call
For the death penalty in freedom's name—
Unhappy man, no matter how posterity
May see these matters. Love of the fatherland
Will sway him—and unmeasured lust for fame.   710
Now see the Decii and the Drusi there,

1. A people of Africa. 2. Hercules. 3. Three of Hercules' labors: killing the Cerynaian stag, the Erymanthian boar, and the hydra of Lerna. 4. The second king of Rome. His successors are mentioned in the next ten lines. 5. Avenger of the rape of Lucretia by Sextus, son of Tarquin the Proud; after Tarquin was expelled from Rome, the kingship was abolished. This Brutus (claimed as ancestor by the assassin of Julius Caesar) was the first consul, chief magistrate of the republic that succeeded the monarchy at Rome. 6. Rods (*fasces*) wrapped around an axe were the symbol of the consul's power.

And stern Torquatus, with his axe, and see
Camillus[7] bringing the lost standards home.
That pair,[8] however, matched in brilliant armor,
Matched in their hearts' desire now, while night   715
Still holds them fast, once they attain life's light
What war, what grief, will they provoke between them—
Battle-lines and bloodshed—as the father
Marches from the Alpine ramparts, down
From Monaco's walled height, and the son-in-law,   720
Drawn up with armies of the East, awaits him.
Sons, refrain! You must not blind your hearts
To that enormity of civil war,
Turning against your country's very heart
Her own vigor of manhood. You above all   725
Who trace your line from the immortals, you
Be first to spare us. Child of my own blood,[9]
Throw away your sword!
                          Mummius[1] there,
When Corinth is brought low, will drive his car
As victor and as killer of Achaeans   730
To our high Capitol. Paulus will conquer
Argos and Agamemnon's old Mycenae,
Defeating Perseus,[2] the Aeacid,
Heir to the master of war, Achilles—thus
Avenging his own Trojan ancestors   735
And the defilement of Minerva's shrine.
Great Cato![3] Who would leave you unremarked,
Or, Cossus, you, or the family of Gracchi,
Or the twin Scipios, bright bolts of war,
The bane of Libya, or you, Fabricius,   740
In poverty yet powerful, or you,
Serranus, at the furrow, casting seed?
Where, though I weary, do you hurry me,
You Fabii? Fabius Maximus,
You are the only soul who shall restore   745
Our wounded state by waiting out the enemy.
Others will cast more tenderly in bronze
Their breathing figures, I can well believe,
And bring more lifelike portraits out of marble;
Argue more eloquently, use the pointer   750
To trace the paths of heaven accurately
And accurately foretell the rising stars.
Roman, remember by your strength to rule
Earth's peoples—for your arts are to be these:
To pacify, to impose the rule of law,   755

7. All heroic figures from Rome's past.   8. Julius Caesar and his opponent in the Civil War, Pompey.
The war was provoked when Caesar crossed the Alps from Gaul and entered Italy with an army. Pompey
had married Caesar's daughter, Julia.   9. Caesar's family, the Julii, traced their ancestry back through
Ascanius (Iulus) to Aeneas and Anchisës.   1. Roman general, one of the conquerors of Greece, who
sacked the city of Corinth in 167 B.C.   2. Macedonian king defeated by the Roman general Aemilius
Paulus in 168 B.C. He claimed descent from Achilles.   3. Statesman and orator of the early second
century B.C., known for his sternness and rigid morals (and so an embodiment of Romanness). He begins
a list of illustrious figures out of Rome's past, almost all of them famous generals.

To spare the conquered, battle down the proud."
Anchises paused here as they gazed in awe,
Then added:
                    "See there, how Marcellus[4] comes
With spoils of the commander that he killed:
How the man towers over everyone.   760
Cavalry leader, he'll sustain the realm
Of Rome in hours of tumult, bringing to heel
The Carthaginians and rebellious Gaul,
And for the third time in our history
He'll dedicate an enemy general's arms   765
To Father Romulus."
                        But here Aeneas
Broke in, seeing at Marcellus' side
A young man[5] beautifully formed and tall
In shining armor, but with clouded brow
And downcast eyes:
                    "And who is that one, Father   770
Walking beside the captain as he comes:
A son, or grandchild from the same great stock?
The others murmur, all astir. How strong
His presence is! But night like a black cloud
About his head whirls down in awful gloom."   775

His father Anchisës answered, and the tears
Welled up as he began:
                    "Oh, do not ask
About this huge grief of your people, son.
Fate will give earth only a glimpse of him,
Not let the boy live on. Lords of the sky,   780
You thought the majesty of Rome too great
If it had kept these gifts. How many groans
Will be sent up from that great Field of Mars
To Mars' proud city, and what sad rites you'll see,
Tiber, as you flow past the new-built tomb.   785
Never will any boy of Ilian race
Exalt his Latin forefathers with promise
Equal to his; never will Romulus' land
Take pride like this in any of her sons.
Weep for his faithful heart, his old-world honor,   790
His sword arm never beaten down! No enemy
Could have come through a clash with him unhurt,
Whether this soldier went on foot or rode,
Digging his spurs into a lathered mount.
Child of our mourning, if only in some way   795
You could break through your bitter fate. For you
Will be Marcellus. Let me scatter lilies,
All I can hold, and scarlet flowers as well,

---

4. A Roman general famous for killing the leader of Gauls from northern Italy in 222 B.C. in single combat and for leading the war against Hannibal in the Second Punic War.   5. Another Marcellus, Augustus's nephew and presumptive heir, who died in 23 B.C. at the age of nineteen.

To heap these for my grandson's shade at least,
Frail gifts and ritual of no avail."   800

So raptly, everywhere, father and son
Wandered the airy plain and viewed it all.
After Anchises had conducted him
To every region and had fired his love
Of glory in the years to come, he spoke   805
Of wars that he must fight, of Laurentines,
And of Latinus' city, then of how
He might avoid or bear each toil to come.

There are two gates of Sleep, one said to be
Of horn, whereby the true shades pass with ease,   810
The other all white ivory agleam
Without a flaw, and yet false dreams are sent
Through this one by the ghosts to the upper world.
Anchises now, his last instructions given,
Took son and Sibyl there and let them go   815
By the Ivory Gate.
                    Aeneas made his way
Straight to the ships to see his crews again,
Then sailed directly to Caieta's port.
Bow anchors out, the sterns rest on the beach.

Summary   After returning from the underworld to the upper air, Aeneas begins his settlement in Italy. He is offered the hand of the princess Lavinia by her father Latinus, but this provokes a war against the Trojans, led by King Turnus of Laurentum. While Aeneas is on an embassy to seek help from the Etruscans, his mother, Venus, comes to him at night with the armor made for him by Vulcan (Hephaestus in Greek), her husband and guardian of fire. On the shield is carved a representation of the future glories of Rome.

FROM BOOK VIII

[*The Shield of Aeneas*]

                            Venus the gleaming goddess,
Bearing her gifts, came down amid high clouds
And far away still, in a vale apart,
Sighted her son beside the ice-cold stream.
Then making her appearance as she willed   5
She said to him:
                "Here are the gifts I promised,
Forged to perfection by my husband's craft,
So that you need not hesitate to challenge
Arrogant Laurentines or savage Turnus,
However soon, in battle."
                        As she spoke   10
Cytherëa[6] swept to her son's embrace
And placed the shining arms before his eyes

6. So called because she was born from the sea foam off the Greek island Cythera.

Under an oak tree. Now the man in joy
At a goddess' gifts, at being so greatly honored,
Could not be satisfied, but scanned each piece   15
In wonder and turned over in his hands
The helmet with its terrifying plumes
And gushing flames, the sword-blade edged with fate,
The cuirass of hard bronze, blood-red and huge—
Like a dark cloud burning with sunset light   20
That sends a glow for miles—the polished greaves[7]
Of gold and silver alloy, the great spear,
And finally the fabric of the shield
Beyond description.
                    There the Lord of Fire,
Knowing the prophets, knowing the age to come,   25
Had wrought the future story of Italy,
The triumphs of the Romans: there one found
The generations of Ascanius' heirs,
The wars they fought, each one. Vulcan had made
The mother wolf, lying in Mars' green grotto;   30
Made the twin boys at play about her teats,[8]
Nursing the mother without fear, while she
Bent round her smooth neck fondling them in turn
And shaped their bodies with her tongue.[9]
                              Nearby,
Rome had been added by the artisan,   35
And Sabine women roughly carried off
Out of the audience at the Circus games;
Then suddenly a new war coming on
To pit the sons of Romulus against
Old Tatius[1] and his austere town of Curës.   40
Later the same kings, warfare laid aside,
In arms before Jove's altar stood and held
Libation dishes as they made a pact
With offering of wine. Not far from this
Two four-horse war-cars, whipped on, back to back,   45
Had torn Mettus apart (still, man of Alba,
You should have kept your word) and Roman Tullus[2]
Dragged the liar's rags of flesh away
Through woods where brambles dripped a bloody dew.
There, too, Porsenna stood, ordering Rome   50
To take the exiled Tarquin back,[3] then bringing
The whole city under massive siege.
There for their liberty Aeneas' sons
Threw themselves forward on the enemy spears.
You might have seen Porsenna imaged there   55

7. Leg pieces.   8. The twins who were to build Rome, Romulus and Remus, sons of Mars the war god, were cast out into the woods and there suckled by a she-wolf.   9. See Ovid's *Metamorphoses* 15.330–33.   1. A Sabine king. Because the new city of Rome consisted mostly of men, the Romans decided to steal women from the Sabines. The Romans invited them to an athletic festival, and at a given signal every Roman carried off a Sabine bride. The war that followed ended in the amalgamation of the Roman and Sabine peoples.   2. The king who punished Mettus for breaking an agreement made during the early wars of Rome. Mettus was torn apart by two chariots moving in opposite directions.   3. The Etruscan king Porsenna attempted to restore Tarquin, the last of the Roman kings, to the throne from which he had been expelled.

To the life, a menacing man, a man in anger
At Roman daring: Cocles who downed the bridge,
Cloelia[4] who broke her bonds and swam the river.

On the shield's upper quarter Manlius,
guard of the Tarpeian Rock, stood fast   60
Before the temple and held the Capitol,[5]
Where Romulus' house[6] was newly thatched and rough.
Here fluttering through gilded porticos
At night, the silvery goose warned of the Gauls
Approaching: under cover of the darkness   65
Gauls amid the bushes had crept near
And now lay hold upon the citadel.
Golden locks they had and golden dress,
Glimmering with striped cloaks, their milky necks
Entwined with gold. They hefted Alpine spears,   70
Two each, and had long body shields for cover.
Vulcan had fashioned naked Luperci
And Salii[7] leaping there with woolen caps
And fallen-from-heaven shields, and put chaste ladies
Riding in cushioned carriages through Rome   75
With sacred images. At a distance then
He pictured the deep hell of Tartarus,
Dis's high gate, crime's punishments, and, yes,
You, Catiline,[8] on a precarious cliff
Hanging and trembling at the Furies' glare.   80
Then, far away from this, were virtuous souls
And Cato[9] giving laws to them. Mid-shield,
The pictured sea flowed surging, all of gold,
As whitecaps foamed on the blue waves, and dolphins
Shining in silver round and round the scene   85
Propelled themselves with flukes and cut through billows.
Vivid in the center were the bronze-beaked
Ships and the fight at sea off Actium.
Here you could see Leucata[1] all alive
With ships maneuvering, sea glowing gold,   90
Augustus Caesar leading into battle
Italians, with both senators and people,
Household gods and great gods: there he stood

---

4. A Roman hostage held by Porsenna. Horatius Cocles, with two companions, defended the bridge across the Tiber to give the Romans time to destroy it.   5. In 392 B.C. Manlius was in charge of the citadel (*Tarpeian Rock*) at a time when the Gauls from the north held all the rest of the city. They made a night attack on the citadel, but Manlius, awakened by the cackling of the sacred geese, beat it off, and saved Rome.   6. In Virgil's time there was still preserved at Rome a rustic building that was supposed to have been the dwelling place of Romulus.   7. The twelve priests of Mars, who danced in his honor carrying shields that had fallen from heaven. *Luperci*: priests of Lupercus, a Roman god corresponding to the Greek Pan.   8. Leader of a conspiracy to overthrow the republic; it was halted mainly through the efforts of Cicero, consul in 63 B.C. Catiline connotes the type of discord, represented by the civil war that almost destroyed the Roman state, to which Augustus later put an end.   9. The noblest of the republicans who had fought Julius Caesar; he stood for honesty and the seriousness that the Romans most admired. He committed suicide in 47 B.C. after Caesar's victory in Africa. Before taking his life he read through Plato's *Phaedo*, a dialogue concerned with the immortality of the soul, which ends with an account of the death of Socrates.   1. A promontory near Actium, on the west coast of Greece, which had a temple of Apollo on it. The naval battle fought here in 31 B.C. was the decisive engagement of the civil war. Augustus, the master of the western half of the empire, defeated Antony, who held the eastern half and was supported by Cleopatra, queen of Egypt.

High on the stern, and from his blessed brow
Twin flames gushed upward, while his crest revealed   95
His father's star. Apart from him, Agrippa,[2]
Favored by winds and gods, led ships in column,
A towering figure, wearing on his brows
The coronet adorned with warships' beaks,
Highest distinction for command at sea.   100
Then came Antonius with barbaric wealth
And a diversity of arms, victorious
From races of the Dawnlands and Red Sea,
Leading the power of the East, of Egypt,
Even of distant Bactra[3] of the steppes   105
And in his wake the Egyptian consort came
So shamefully. The ships all kept together
Racing ahead, the water torn by oar-strokes,
Torn by the triple beaks, in spume and foam.
All made for the open sea. You might believe   110
The Cyclades[4] uprooted were afloat
Or mountains running against mountain heights
When seamen in those hulks pressed the attack
Upon the other turreted ships. They hurled
Broadsides of burning flax on flying steel,   115
And fresh blood reddened Neptune's fields. The queen
Amidst the battle called her flotilla on
With a sistrum's[5] beat, a frenzy out of Egypt,
Never turning her head as yet to see
Twin snakes of death behind, while monster forms   120
Of gods of every race, and the dog-god
Anubis[6] barking, held their weapons up
Against our Neptune, Venus, and Minerva.
Mars, engraved in steel, raged in the fight
As from high air the dire Furies came   125
With Discord, taking joy in a torn robe,
And on her heels, with bloody scourge, Bellona.[7]

Overlooking it all, Actian[8] Apollo
Began to pull his bow. Wild at this sight,
All Egypt, Indians, Arabians, all   130
Sabaeans[9] put about in flight, and she,
The queen, appeared crying for winds to shift
Just as she hauled up sail and slackened sheets.
The Lord of Fire had portrayed her there,
Amid the slaughter, pallid with death to come,   135
Then borne by waves and wind from the northwest,
While the great length of mourning Nile awaited her
With open bays, calling the conquered home
To his blue bosom and his hidden streams.

2. Augustus's admiral at Actium.   3. On the borders of India.   4. The islands of the southern Aegean Sea.   5. An Oriental rattle, used in the worship of Isis.   6. The Egyptian death god, depicted with the head of a jackal.   7. A Roman war goddess.   8. So called because of his temple at Actium; the temple (and its cult statue) overlooked the sea battle.   9. Arabs from the Yemen.

But Caesar then in triple triumph[1] rode   140
Within the walls of Rome, making immortal
Offerings to the gods of Italy—
Three hundred princely shrines throughout the city.
There were the streets, humming with festal joy
And games and cheers, an altar to every shrine,   145
To every one a mothers' choir, and bullocks
Knifed before the altars strewed the ground.
The man himself, enthroned before the snow-white
Threshold of sunny Phoebus, viewed the gifts
The nations of the earth made, and he fitted them   150
To the tall portals. Conquered races passed
In long procession, varied in languages
As in their dress and arms. Here Mulciber,[2]
Divine smith, had portrayed the Nomad tribes
And Afri with ungirdled flowing robes,   155
Here Leleges and Carians, and here
Gelonians[3] with quivers. Here Euphrates,
Milder in his floods now, there Morini,[4]
Northernmost of men; here bull-horned Rhine,
And there the still unconquered Scythian Dahae;   160
Here, vexed at being bridged, the rough Araxes.[5]
All these images on Vulcan's shield,
His mother's gift, were wonders to Aeneas.
Knowing nothing of the events themselves,
He felt joy in their pictures, taking up   165
Upon his shoulder all the destined acts
And fame of his descendants.

Summary   In the course of the desperate battles that follow, the young Pallas,
entrusted to Aeneas's care by his father, is killed by the Italian champion Turnus,
who takes and wears the belt of Pallas as the spoil of victory. The fortunes of the war
later change in favor of the Trojans, and Aeneas kills the Etruscan king Mezentius,
Turnus's ally. Eventually, as the Italians prepare to accept the generous peace terms
offered by Aeneas, Turnus forestalls them by accepting Aeneas's challenge to single
combat to decide the issue. But this solution is frustrated by the intervention of Juno,
who foresees Aeneas's victory. She prompts Turnus's sister, the river nymph Juturna,
to intervene in an attempt to save Turnus's life. Juturna stirs up the Italians, who are
watching the champions prepare for the duel; the truce is broken, and in the subsequent fighting Aeneas is wounded by an arrow. Healed by Venus, he returns to the
fight, and the Italians are driven back. Turnus finally faces his adversary. His sword
breaks on the armor forged by Vulcan, and he runs from Aeneas. He is saved by
Juturna, who, assuming the shape of his charioteer, hands him a fresh sword. At this
point Jupiter intervenes to stop the vain attempts of Juno and Juturna to save Turnus.

FROM BOOK XII

[The Death of Turnus]

Omnipotent Olympus' king meanwhile
Had words for Juno, as she watched the combat

---

1. For victories in Dalmatia and at Actium and Alexandria.   2. Vulcan.   3. Peoples from Scythia (in
the Balkans). The Leleges and Carians were from Asia Minor.   4. A Belgian tribe.   5. A turbulent
river in Armenia. Augustus built a new bridge over it.

Out of a golden cloud. He said:
"My consort,
What will the end be? What is left for you?
You yourself know, and say you know, Aeneas   5
Born for heaven, tutelary of this land,
By fate to be translated to the stars.[6]
What do you plan? What are you hoping for,
Keeping your seat apart in the cold clouds?
Fitting, was it, that a mortal archer   10
Wound an immortal? That a blade let slip
Should be restored to Turnus, and new force
Accrue to a beaten man? Without your help
What could Juturna do? Come now, at last
Have done, and heed our pleading, and give way.   15
Let yourself no longer be consumed
Without relief by all that inward burning;
Let care and trouble not forever come to me
From your sweet lips. The finish is at hand.
You had the power to harry men of Troy   20
By land and sea, to light the fires of war
Beyond belief, to scar a family
With mourning before marriage.[7] I forbid
Your going further."
So spoke Jupiter,
And with a downcast look Juno replied: 25

"Because I know that is your will indeed,
Great Jupiter, I left the earth below,
Though sore at heart, and left the side of Turnus.
Were it not so, you would not see me here
Suffering all that passes, here alone,   30
Resting on air. I should be armed in flames
At the very battle-line, dragging the Trojans
Into a deadly action. I persuaded
Juturna—I confess—to help her brother
In his hard lot, and I approved her daring   35
Greater difficulties to save his life,
But not that she should fight with bow and arrow.
This I swear by Styx' great fountainhead
Inexorable, which high gods hold in awe.
I yield now and for all my hatred leave   40
This battlefield. But one thing not retained
By fate I beg for Latium, for the future
Greatness of your kin: when presently
They crown peace with a happy wedding day—
So let it be—and merge their laws and treaties,   45
Never command the land's own Latin folk
To change their old name, to become new Trojans,
Known as Teucrians; never make them alter
Dialect or dress. Let Latium be.
Let there be Alban kings for generations,   50

6. Aeneas is destined for immortality, because after his death he will be worshiped as a local god.   7. A
reference not only to the Italian losses but also to the suicide of Amata, wife of King Latinus, who hanged
herself when the Trojans assaulted the city just before the duel between Aeneas and Turnus began.

And let Italian valor be the strength
Of Rome in after times. Once and for all
Troy fell, and with her name let her lie fallen."

The author of men and of the world replied
With a half-smile:
                    "Sister of Jupiter[8]   55
Indeed you are, and Saturn's other child,
To feel such anger, stormy in your breast.
But come, no need; put down this fit of rage.
I grant your wish. I yield, I am won over
Willingly. Ausonian folk will keep   60
Their fathers' language and their way of life,
And, that being so, their name. The Teucrians
Will mingle and be submerged, incorporated.
Rituals and observances of theirs
I'll add, but make them Latin, one in speech.   65
The race to come, mixed with Ausonian blood,
Will outdo men and gods in its devotion,
You shall see—and no nation on earth
Will honor and worship you so faithfully."

To all this Juno nodded in assent   70
And, gladdened by his promise, changed her mind.
Then she withdrew from sky and cloud.
                                    That done,
The Father set about a second plan—
To take Juturna from her warring brother.
Stories are told of twin fiends, called the Dirae,   75
Whom, with Hell's Megaera,[9] deep Night bore
In one birth. She entwined their heads with coils
Of snakes and gave them wings to race the wind.
Before Jove's throne, a step from the cruel king,
These twins attend him and give piercing fear   80
To ill mankind, when he who rules the gods
Deals out appalling death and pestilence,
Or war to terrify our wicked cities.
Jove now dispatched one of these, swift from heaven,
Bidding her be an omen to Juturna.   85
Down she flew, in a whirlwind borne to earth,
Just like an arrow driven through a cloud
From a taut string, an arrow armed with gall
Of deadly poison, shot by a Parthian[1]—
A Parthian or a Cretan[2]—for a wound   90
Immedicable; whizzing unforeseen
It goes through racing shadows: so the spawn
Of Night went diving downward to the earth.

On seeing Trojan troops drawn up in face
Of Turnus' army, she took on at once   95

8. Jupiter and Juno (like the Greek Zeus and Hera) are brother and sister as well as husband and
wife.   9. One of the Dirae, literally "dreadful ones."   1. Parthia was the most dangerous neighbor of
the Roman Empire in the east.   2. Parthian mounted archers were famous, as were Cretan archers.

The shape of that small bird[3] that perches late
At night on tombs or desolate roof-tops
And troubles darkness with a gruesome song.
Shrunk to that form, the fiend in Turnus' face
Went screeching, flitting, flitting to and fro   100
And beating with her wings against his shield.
Unstrung by numbness, faint and strange, he felt
His hackles rise, his voice choke in his throat.
As for Juturna, when she knew the wings,
The shriek to be the fiend's, she tore her hair,   105
Despairing, then she fell upon her cheeks
With nails, upon her breast with clenched hands.

"Turnus, how can your sister help you now?
What action is still open to me, soldierly
Though I have been? Can I by any skill   110
Hold daylight for you? Can I meet and turn
This deathliness away? Now I withdraw,
Now leave this war. Indecent birds, I fear you;
Spare me your terror. Whip-lash of your wings
I recognize, that ghastly sound, and guess   115
Great-hearted Jupiter's high cruel commands.
Returns for my virginity, are they?
He gave me life eternal[4]—to what end?
Why has mortality been taken from me?
Now beyond question I could put a term   120
To all my pain, and go with my poor brother
Into the darkness, his companion there.
Never to die? Will any brook of mine
Without you, brother, still be sweet to me?
If only earth's abyss were wide enough   125
To take me downward, goddess though I am,
To join the shades below!"
                              So she lamented,
Then with a long sigh, covering up her head
In her grey mantle, sank to the river's depth.

Aeneas moved against his enemy   130
And shook his heavy pine-tree spear. He called
From his hot heart:
                    "Rearmed now, why so slow?
Why, even now, fall back? The contest here
Is not a race, but fighting to the death
With spear and sword. Take on all shapes there are,   135
Summon up all your nerve and skill, choose any
Footing, fly among the stars, or hide
In caverned earth—"
                    The other shook his head,
Saying:
        "I do not fear your taunting fury,

3. The owl.   4. Jupiter had been the lover of Juturna and had rewarded her with immortality.

Arrogant prince. It is the gods I fear 140
And Jove my enemy."
               He said no more,
But looked around him. Then he saw a stone,
Enormous, ancient, set up there to prevent
Landowners' quarrels. Even a dozen picked men
Such as the earth produces in our day 145
Could barely lift and shoulder it. He swooped
And wrenched it free, in one hand, then rose up
To his heroic height, ran a few steps,
And tried to hurl the stone against his foe—
But as he bent and as he ran 150
And as he hefted and propelled the weight
He did not know himself. His knees gave way,
His blood ran cold and froze. The stone itself,
Tumbling through space, fell short and had no impact.

Just as in dreams when the night-swoon of sleep 155
Weighs on our eyes, it seems we try in vain
To keep on running, try with all our might,
But in the midst of effort faint and fail;
Our tongue is powerless, familiar strength
Will not hold up our body, not a sound 160
Or word will come: just so with Turnus now:
However bravely he made shift to fight
The immortal fiend blocked and frustrated him.
Flurrying images passed through his mind.
He gazed at the Rutulians,[5] and beyond them, 165
Gazed at the city, hesitant, in dread.
He trembled now before the poised spear-shaft
And saw no way to escape; he had no force
With which to close, or reach his foe, no chariot
And no sign of the charioteer, his sister. 170
At a dead loss he stood. Aeneas made
His deadly spear flash in the sun and aimed it,
Narrowing his eyes for a lucky hit.
Then, distant still, he put his body's might
Into the cast. Never a stone that soared 175
From a wall-battering catapult went humming
Loud as this, nor with so great a crack
Burst ever a bolt of lightning. It flew on
Like a black whirlwind bringing devastation,
Pierced with a crash the rim of sevenfold shield, 180
Cleared the cuirass' edge, and passed clean through
The middle of Turnus' thigh. Force of the blow
Brought the huge man to earth, his knees buckling,
And a groan swept the Rutulians as they rose,
A groan heard echoing on all sides from all 185
The mountain range, and echoed by the forests.

---

5. The Italian troops watching the combat between Turnus and Aeneas.

The man brought down, brought low, lifted his eyes
And held his right hand out to make his plea:

"Clearly I earned this, and I ask no quarter.
Make the most of your good fortune here.   190
If you can feel a father's grief—and you, too,
Had such a father in Anchisës—then
Let me bespeak your mercy for old age
In Daunus,[6] and return me, or my body,
Stripped, if you will, of life, to my own kin.   195
You have defeated me. The Ausonians
Have seen me in defeat, spreading my hands.
Lavinia is your bride. But go no further
Out of hatred."
                    Fierce under arms, Aeneas
Looked to and fro, and towered, and stayed his hand   200
Upon the sword-hilt. Moment by moment now
What Turnus said began to bring him round
From indecision. Then to his glance appeared
The accurst swordbelt surmounting Turnus' shoulder,
Shining with its familiar studs—the strap   205
Young Pallas wore when Turnus wounded him
And left him dead upon the field; now Turnus
Bore that enemy token on his shoulder—
Enemy still. For when the sight came home to, him,
Aeneas raged at the relic of his anguish   210
Worn by this man as trophy. Blazing up
And terrible in his anger, he called out:

"You in your plunder, torn from one of mine,
Shall I be robbed of you? This wound will come
From Pallas: Pallas makes this offering   215
And from your criminal blood exacts his due."

He sank his blade in fury in Turnus' chest.
Then all the body slackened in death's chill,
And with a groan for that indignity
His spirit fled into the gloom below.   220

6. Father of Turnus.

OVID

43 B.C.–A.D. 17

Born in the year after Julius Caesar's assassination, Ovid did not know the time of
civil war, when no one's property, or life, was safe. He was twenty-four when Virgil
died, and he turned to different themes: the sophisticated and somewhat racy life of

the urban elite in Rome, love in its manifold social and psychological guises, Greco-Roman myth and local Italian legend. Like Catullus and Virgil, he was profoundly influenced by the learned and polished works of the Greek Alexandrian period, but like his predecessors he translated their example into his personal idiom and used it for his own purposes. He was a versifier of genius. "Whatever I tried to say," he wrote, "came out in verse," and Alexander Pope adapted the line for his own case: "I lisped in numbers for the numbers came." Elegance, wit, and precision remained the hallmarks of Ovid's poetry throughout his long and productive career, and his way of telling stories was extraordinary for its subtlety and its depth of psychological understanding. His influence on the poets and artists of the Middle Ages, the Renaissance, and beyond was massive, second only, if at all, to Virgil's.

The early years of Ovid's manhood were marked by rapid literary and social success in the brilliant society of a capital intent on enjoying the peace and prosperity inaugurated by Augustus. The *Amores*, or "Love Affairs," unabashed chronicles of a Roman Don Juan, was his first publication. It was soon followed by the *Art of Love*, a handbook of seduction (originally circulated as books 1 and 2, for men; book 3, for women, was added by popular request). Not content with teaching his readers how to start a love affair, Ovid then advised them how to end it, in the *Remedies of Love*. At some point he wrote a poem on women's cosmetics; another, the *Fasti* (never finished), on the Roman calendar; and a collection of poetic letters, the *Heroides*, purporting to have been written by heroines of legend, such as Helen, to their lovers. In A.D. 8 Ovid was banished by imperial decree to the town of Tomi, in what is now Romania. It was on the fringe of the empire, and to a devotee of Roman high life it was a grim place indeed. He remained there until his death, sending back to Rome poetic epistles, collected as the *Sorrows* and the *Letters from Pontus*, that asked for pardon—to no effect. The reason for his banishment is not known. Involvement in some scandal concerning Augustus's daughter Julia is a possibility, but the ultimate cause was probably the love poetry, which ran afoul of Augustus's political and social program. Augustus was trying hard, by propaganda and legislation, to revive old Roman standards of morality and cannot have found Ovid's *Art of Love*, with its suggestion that Rome was a prime location for seduction, amusing. He correctly read the poem as political critique, a mode of resistance to the authoritarian imposition of moral reform. Ovid's greatest work, the *Metamorphoses*, suggests a similar critique. It was still unfinished at the time of his exile.

THE METAMORPHOSES

Virgil had written what Augustus wanted to be the "official" epic of the new order, which was to be seen as the fulfillment of a history that began with Aeneas's journey from Troy to Italy. The *Aeneid*, for all its innovations, was an epic in the traditional style: it focused on the deeds of a single hero, and it exemplified and transmitted its culture's dominant values. The *Metamorphoses* is recognizably epic; it is the only poem Ovid wrote in the epic meter, dactylic hexameter. But it can be seen as a critical response to Virgil, even an anti-*Aeneid*. Ovid produced a series of stories using the Alexandrian form of the *epyllion*, or "miniature epic," and he strung these together into a long narrative of fifteen books. The transitions between them, and the connections drawn by the narrator, are often transparently contrived—perhaps in mockery of the idea of narrative unity. There is no single hero, and one would have to seek hard for representative national values presented without irony. There is, however, a common element to these stories: all in one way or another involve changes of shape. And despite its leisurely and roundabout course, the narrative has a discernible direction—as Ovid says in his introduction, "from the world's beginning to our day." Starting with the creation of the world, the transformation of matter into living bodies (the first great metamorphosis), Ovid regales his readers with tales of human beings changed into animals, flowers, and trees. He proceeds through Greek myth to stories of early Rome and so to his own time, including, as the final metamorphoses, the ascension of the murdered Julius Caesar to the heavens in the form of a star and the divine promise that Augustus too, far in the future, will become a god.

Fluidity, then, is a key concept of the *Metamorphoses*. It underlies both the narrative style and the vision of the world the poem projects. Virgil also told of a transformation, the new (Roman) order arising from the ruins of the old (Troy). But once the transformation was completed by the Augustan order, there was to be stability, permanence. Ovid tells of a world ceaselessly coming to be in a process that never ends. To Virgil's story of national origins he opposes creation itself, which sets the pattern of instability, the fleetingness of form, and constant transformation. Ambivalence and ambiguity there may be in the *Aeneid*—but within a single set of Roman values summed up in Aeneas himself. Ovid's epic without a hero presents shifting perspectives and offers the reader no single point of view or end point from which to judge his very complex narratives. Virgil responded to the chaos of civil war with a vision of political stability; Ovid responds in turn to the new order. To the forced imposition of political and moral unity he opposes fluidity itself.

The political implications do not exhaust the richness of the *Metamorphoses*, though they are never far to seek. Within the poem's large-scale framework, each story in turn engages and delights the reader with its verbal wit, the cunningly calculated emphasis on this or that telling detail, the shifts between pathos and ironic distance, and the brilliant psychological insights suggested by the narrative or the characters' words and actions. Ovid constantly plays with narrative technique. A story will be told partly from one character's perspective, and then, with a sudden shift, partly from another's. One story will be embedded in another, with a consequent imposition of one narrative voice on top of another, as when, in the excerpt from book 10 printed below, Venus tells Adonis the story of Atalanta. This story is set within the tale of the goddess's love for Adonis and of his death, which is one of a series of stories sung by Orpheus within the poem's main narrative. In such cases, both the immediate and the larger contexts give the same story different shades of meaning. And there are thematic connections between stories. Daphne and Syrinx are turned into plants (the laurel and the reed) that are henceforth attributes of the gods who tried to rape them: a form of appropriation that substitutes for sexual violence. Just as Jupiter turns Io, the girl *he* has raped, into a cow, so he tricks Europa, in order to possess her, by becoming a seductively handsome bull. Europa offers the god-bull flowers; the terrified Proserpina, victim of a far more direct and brutal rape, drops the flowers she has been collecting when the god of Death carries her on his chariot beneath the Earth.

As these examples indicate, a common element of many stories in books 1 and 2 is the portrayal of important male gods as both destructive and ridiculous in their lust. "Slow your pace," Apollo calls to the fleeing Daphne in fear that she will fall and disfigure herself, "I pray you, stay your flight. I'll slow down too." Or, as the narrator comments on Jupiter-as-bull, "Majesty and love do not go hand in glove." As the examples also show, the poem contains a number of stories of rape. Ovid gives different perspectives on what is essentially the same situation in order to emphasize the variety of possible responses to it by different readers, and he leaves it to those readers to evaluate their own responses. That is, fluidity not only is a theme of the poem but also characterizes the multiple positions open to the reader. In addition, one of the possible implications of these stories of rape is, again, political, for rape is the ultimate imposition of control. When powerful gods, however ridiculous they may appear, force themselves on defenseless women, imposed authority is held up to questioning. After all, as Ovid points out gleefully in the *Art of Love*, a rape was at the heart of Rome's foundation legend: it was through the rape of the Sabine women that the male inhabitants of the new city acquired wives and were able to supply Rome with future citizens.

The stories selected here from later in the *Metamorphoses* bring out other aspects of gender and sexuality. From the story of Iphis and Ianthe we learn that the instability of gender is not a modern discovery; nor is the recognition that the roles it determines for women and men in society are more or less arbitrary. That episode, the last in book 9, ends with the triumph of heterosexual love. The tales from book 10 all have to do, in one way or another, with the psychopathology of love. The case of Pygmalion may seem an exception, but we should remember that it begins with his hatred of women for their loose morals, and that the story as a whole, whatever it may say about the power of art, can also be read as a fable of the male fabrication of woman—her person and her functions—according to his desires. In the same way, Atalanta's conquest by Hippomenes represents, in the Greek and Roman cultural code, the "taming" of the "wild" virgin into marriage; but the story ends as a tale of divine wrath against this couple, and it is told by Venus to a lover whom she is about to lose to death. These stories, and others, including Myrrha's consummated love for her own father, are narrated by Orpheus, the archetypal poet, after his failure to bring Eurydice back from the underworld. Ovid tells us—and it seems to be his invention—that in reaction to his loss Orpheus had turned to pederasty, and that he was torn to pieces in his native Thrace by Maenads, female worshipers of Dionysus.

The Italian Baroque sculptor Giovanni Bernini carved statue groups of Apollo and Daphne and of Hades and Proserpina—stunning translations of Ovid's poetry into marble. Among their many allusions to the *Metamorphoses*, Milton and Dante both used Ovid's version of the Proserpina story: the former in book 9 of *Paradise Lost* as an image of the entry of death into the world, the latter in the *Purgatorio* to emphasize redemption from death. It was surely not only the fact that the *Metamorphoses* draws into itself most of the major classical myths (and a number of lesser-known stories as well) that has made the poem a source of subjects for artists and poets ever since but also the memorable ways these stories are told and their rich potential for meaning. The poem has many themes, but it also tells about itself: the irresistible power of a well-told narrative to hold the attention and shape the imagination of those who read or listen to it.

Sara Mack, *Ovid* (1988), provides an excellent introduction to all of Ovid's poems for the general reader, with a long chapter on the *Metamorphoses*. A classic treatment of this poem is Brooks Otis, *Ovid as an Epic Poet* (1966, 1970). G. K. Galinsky, *Ovid's Metamorphoses: An Introduction to the Basic Aspects*, is also a useful guide. L. P. Wilkinson, *Ovid Recalled* (1955), abridged as *Ovid Surveyed* (1962), gives a comprehensive overview of various aspects of Ovid's poetry. For later poets' and artists' uses of Ovid, see the essays collected in Charles Martindale, *Ovid Renewed: Ovidian Influences on Literature and Art from the Middle Ages to the Twentieth Century* (1988).

PRONOUNCING GLOSSARY

The following list uses common English syllables and stress accents to provide rough equivalents of selected words whose pronunciation may be unfamiliar to the general reader.

Achelous: *a-kel-oh'-us*

Alpheus: *al'-fyoos*

Anapos: *a-nap'-os*

Arethusa: *a-reth-oos'-a*

Calliope: *kal-lai'-o-pee*

Cenchreis: *ken-kray'-is*

Ceres: *see'-reez*

Cinyras: *kin-ee'-ras*

Cyane: *see-ah'-nee*

Daedalus: *dee'-dal-us/dai'-dal-us*

Epaphus: *e-paf'-us*

Erigone: *e-rig'-o-nee*

Europa: *yoo-roh'-pa*

Hippomenes: *hip-po'-men-eez*

Icarus: *i'-kar-us*

Inachus: *i'-na-kus*

Iphis: *i'-fis*

Isis: *ai'-sis*

Naiads: *nai'-adz*

Osiris: *oh-sai'-ris*

Pasiphae: *pa-sif'-ay-ee*

Peneus: *pen'-yoos/pen-ay'-us*

Phoebus: *fee'-bus*

Proserpina: *pros-ehr'-pi-na*

Pygmalion: *pig-may'-lyon*

Satyr: *say'-ter*

Telethusa: *tel-e-thoo'-sa*

Typhoeus: *ti-foy'-oos*

Tenedos: *ten'-e-dos*

Metamorphoses[1]

FROM BOOK I

[Prologue]

My soul would sing of metamorphoses.
But since, o gods, you were the source of these
bodies becoming other bodies, breathe
your breath into my book of changes: may
the song I sing be seamless as its way   5
weaves from the world's beginning to our day.

*   *   *

[Apollo and Daphne]

Now Daphne[2]—daughter of the river-god,
Peneus—was the first of Phoebus'[3] loves.
This love was not the fruit of random chance:
what fostered it was Cupid's cruel wrath.
For now, while Phoebus still was taking pride   10
in his defeat of Python,[4] he caught sight
of Cupid as he bent his bow to tie
the string at the two ends. He said: "Lewd boy,
what are you doing with that heavy bow?[5]
My shoulders surely are more fit for it;   15
for I can strike wild beasts—I never miss.
I can fell enemies; just recently
I even hit—my shafts were infinite—
that swollen serpent, Python, sprawled across   20
whole acres with his pestilential paunch.
Be glad your torch can spark a bit of love;
don't try to vie with me for praise and wreaths!"
And Venus' son replied: "Your shafts may pierce
all things, o Phoebus, but you'll be transfixed   25
by mine; and even as all earthly things
can never equal any deity,
so shall your glory be no match for mine."

That said, he hurried off; he beat his wings
until he reached Parnassus' shady peak;   30

1. All selections translated by Allen Mandelbaum.   2. The name means "laurel" in Greek.
3. Apollo's.   4. The enormous snake that Apollo had to kill in order to found his oracle at Delphi.
5. The bow was one of Apollo's attributes.

there, from his quiver, Cupid drew two shafts
of opposite effect: the first rejects,
the second kindles love. This last is golden,
its tip is sharp and glittering; the first
is blunt, its tip is leaden—and with this   35
blunt shaft the god pierced Daphne. With the tip
of gold he hit Apollo; and the arrow
pierced to the bones and marrow.

                      And at once
the god of Delos[6] is aflame with love;
but Daphne hates its very name; she wants   40
deep woods and spoils of animals she hunts;
it is Diana, Phoebus' virgin sister,
whom she would emulate. Around her hair—
in disarray—she wears a simple band.
Though many suitors seek her, she spurns all;   45
she wants to roam uncurbed; she needs no man;
she pays no heed to marriage, love, or husbands.
Her father often said: "You're in my debt:
a son-in-law is owed me." And he said:
"You owe me grandsons." But his daughter scorns,   50
as things quite criminal, the marriage torch
and matrimony; with a modest blush
on her fair face, she twines her arms around
her father's neck: "Allow me to enjoy
perpetual virginity," she pleads;   55
"o dear, dear father, surely you'll concede
to me the gift Diana has received
from her dear father."[7] And in fact, Peneus
would have agreed. O Daphne, it's your beauty
that will prevent your getting that dear gift.   60
Your fair form contradicts your deepest wish.

Phoebus is lovestruck; having seen the girl,
he longs to wed her and, in longing, hopes;
but though he is the god of oracles,
he reads the future wrongly. Even as,   65
when grain is harvested, the stubble left
will burn, or as the hedges burn when chance
has led some traveler to bring his torch
too close, or to forget it on the road
when he went off at dawn, so Phoebus burns,   70
so is his heart aflame; with hope he feeds
a fruitless love. He looks at Daphne's hair
as, unadorned, it hangs down her fair neck,
and says: "Just think, if she should comb her locks!"
He sees her lips and never tires of them;   75
her fingers, hands, and wrists are unsurpassed;
her arms—more than half-bare—cannot be matched;
whatever he can't see he can imagine;

6. Island in the Aegean Sea where Apollo was born.   7. Jove.

he conjures it as even more inviting.
But swifter than the lightest breeze, she flees
and does not halt—not even when he pleads: 80
"O, daughter of Peneus, stay! Dear Daphne,
I don't pursue you as an enemy!
Wait, nymph! You flee as would the lamb before
the wolf, the deer before the lion, or   85
the trembling dove before the eagle; thus
all flee from hostile things, but it is love
for which I seek you now! What misery!
I fear you'll stumble, fall, be scratched by brambles
and harm your faultless legs—and I'm to blame.   90
You're crossing trackless places. Slow your pace;
I pray you, stay your flight. I'll slow down, too.
But do consider who your lover is.
I'm not a mountain dweller, not a shepherd,
no scraggly guardian of flocks and herds.   95
Too rash, you don't know whom you're fleeing from;
in fact, that's why you run. I am the lord
of Delphi's land, and Claros, Tenedos,
and regal Patara.[8] Jove is my father.
Through me, all is revealed: what's yet to be,   100
what was, and what now is. The harmony
of song and lyre is achieved through me.
My shaft is sure in flight; but then there's he
whose arrow aimed still more infallibly,
the one who wounded me when I was free   105
of any love within my heart. I am
the one who has invented medicine,[9]
but now there is no herb to cure my passion;
my art, which helps all men, can't heal its master."

He'd have said more, but Daphne did not halt;   110
afraid, she left him there, with half-done words.
But even then, the sight of her was striking.
The wind laid bare her limbs; against the nymph
it blew; her dress was fluttering; her hair
streamed in the breeze; in flight she was more fair.   115

But now the young god can't waste time: he's lost
his patience; his beguiling words are done;
and so—with love as spur—he races on;
he closes in. Just as a Gallic hound[1]
surveys the open field and sights a hare,   120
and both the hunter and the hunted race
more swiftly—one to catch, one to escape
(he seems about to leap on his prey's back;
he's almost sure he's won; his muzzle now
is at her heels; the other, still in doubt—   125

8. All centers of Apollo's cult.   9. Apollo was, among other functions, god of healing.   1. A hunting breed famous for speed.

not sure if she is caught—slips from his mouth;
at the last instant, she escapes his jaws):
such were the god and girl; while he is swift
because of hope, what urges her is fear.
But love has given wings to the pursuer;   130
he's faster—and his pace will not relent.
He's at her shoulders now; she feels his breath
upon the hair that streams down to her neck.
Exhausted, wayworn, pale, and terrified,
she sees Peneus' stream nearby; she cries: 135
"Help me, dear father; if the river-gods
have any power, then transform, dissolve
my gracious shape, the form that pleased too well!"
As soon as she is finished with her prayer,
a heavy numbness grips her limbs; thin bark   140
begins to gird her tender frame, her hair
is changed to leaves, her arms to boughs; her feet—
so keen to race before—are now held fast
by sluggish roots; the girl's head vanishes,
becoming a treetop. All that is left   145
of Daphne is her radiance.
                              And yet
Apollo loves her still; he leans against
the trunk; he feels the heart that beats beneath
the new-made bark; within his arms he clasps
the branches as if they were human limbs;   150
and his lips kiss the wood, but still it shrinks
from his embrace, at which he cries: "But since
you cannot be my wife, you'll be my tree.
O laurel, I shall always wear your leaves
to wreathe my hair, my lyre, and my quiver.   155
When Roman chieftains crown their heads with garlands
as chants of gladness greet their victory,
you will be there. And you will also be
the faithful guardian who stands beside
the portals of Augustus' house and keeps   160
a close watch on the Roman crown of oak leaves.[2]
And even as my head is ever young,
and my hair ever long, may you, unshorn,
wear your leaves, too, forever: never lose
that loveliness, o laurel, which is yours!"   165

Apollo's words were done. With new-made boughs
the laurel nodded; and she shook her crown,
as if her head had meant to show consent.

[Io and Jove]

In Thessaly[3] there is a deep-set valley
surrounded on all sides by wooded slopes   170

---

2. The laurel tree, sacred to Apollo, was the symbol of victory in athletic contests or in war. The oak was sacred to Jupiter.   3. A region of central Greece.

that tower high. They call that valley Tempe.
And the Peneus River, as it flows
down from Mount Pindus' base—waves flecked with foam—
runs through that valley. In its steep descent,
a heavy fall, the stream gives rise to clouds   175
and slender threads of mist—like curling smoke;
and from on high, the river sprays treetops;
its roar resounds through places near and far.
This is the home, the seat, the sanctuary
of that great stream. And here, within a cave   180
carved out of rock, sat Daphne's father, god
and ruler of these waters and of all
the nymphs who made their home within his waves.
And it was here that—though they were unsure
if they should compliment or comfort him—   185
first came the river-gods of his own region:
Enipeus, restless river; poplar-rich
Sperchios; veteran Apidanus
and gentle Aeas and Amphrysus; then
the other, distant rivers came—all those   190
who, on whatever course their currents flow,
lead down their wayworn waters to the sea.

The only missing god was Inachus.[4]
He had retreated to his deepest cave,
and as he wept, his tears increased his waves;   195
the disappearance of his daughter, Io,
had left him desperate. He did not know
if she was still alive or with the Shades;
he could not find her anywhere, and so
he thought that she was nowhere; in his heart   200
his fears foresaw things devious and dark.

Now it was Jove who had caught sight of Io;
she was returning from her father's stream,
and Jove had said: "O virgin, you indeed
would merit Jove and will make any man   205
you wed—whoever he may be—most glad.
But now it's time for you to seek the shade
of those deep woods" (and here he pointed toward
a nearby forest); "for the sun is high—
at its midcourse; such heat can't be defied.   210
And do not be afraid to find yourself
alone among the haunts of savage beasts:
within the forest depths you can be sure
of safety, for your guardian is a god—
and I am not a common deity: 215
for I am he who holds within his hand
the heavens' scepter: I am he who hurls
the roaming thunderbolts. So do not flee!"
But even as he spoke, she'd left behind

4. A river near Argos.

the pasturelands of Lerna, and the plains   220
around Lyrceus' peak,[5] fields thick with trees.
Then with a veil of heavy fog, the god
concealed a vast expanse of land; Jove stopped
her flight; he raped chaste Io.

                              Meanwhile Juno,
from heaven's height, had chanced to cast her eyes   225
on Argus' center; she was stupefied
to see that hovering clouds, in full daylight,
had brought about a darkness deep as night;
she knew that this could not be river mist
or fog that rises up from the damp soil.   230
So Saturn's daughter[6] looked around to see
just where her Jove might be—so frequently
she'd caught him sneaking or, more flagrantly,
at play. And since he wasn't in the sky,
she said: "I am mistaken or betrayed";   235
and then, descending from the heavens' height,
she stood upon the ground and told the clouds
that they must now recede.
                              Jove had foreseen
his wife's arrival; he had changed the daughter
of Inachus: she now was a white heifer.   240
And even as a heifer she was lovely.
Great Juno—grudgingly—praised the cow's beauty,
then asked who was her owner, where did she
come from, what herd did she belong to—all
as if she were aware of nothing. Jove,   245
contriving, said the earth had given birth
to this fine heifer—hoping that would stop
his wife's barrage. And Juno asked to have
the heifer as a gift. What should he do?
It would be cruel to consign his love;   250
but if he kept her, he would just raise doubts.
On one side, shame keeps urging: Give her up.
Love, on the other side, insists: Do not.

Love could have overcome his shame, but if
he should refuse so slight, so poor a gift   255
to one who was his sister and his wife,
he'd have to run a disconcerting risk,
since Juno could conclude that, after all,
this heifer was no cow. So, in the end,
the goddess got her rival as a present.   260
Yet Juno still suspected treachery;
to ward off any wiles, she now entrusted
the heifer to Arestor's son; for Argus
was gifted with a hundred eyes, and he

---

5. *Lyrceus:* a mountain on the border between Argos and Arcadia to the west. *Lerna:* a marsh in the territory of Argos, near the coast.   6. Juno.

would sleep with only two of these eyes shut   265
at any time, in turn—the rest he left
awake and watchful. He was Io's guardian;
no matter where he turned, he always kept
some eyes on her; though he might turn his back,
he still had her in view. By day he let   270
the heifer graze; but when the sun had set,
he locked her in and tied, around her neck,
a shameful halter. She was always fed
on leaves from trees and bitter herbs, and slept
upon the ground—and it was often bare   275
of grass; poor Io drank from muddy streams
and, when she tried to lift her arms to plead
with Argus, found she had no arms to stretch;
and when she tried to utter some lament,
nothing but lowings issued from her lips,   280
a sound that she was frightened to emit—
her own voice frightened her.
                    And Io reached
the shores on which she had so often played,
the river banks of Inachus; she stared
at her strange horns reflected in the waves,   285
and at her muzzle; and she fled, dismayed
and terrified. Not even Inachus
and all his Naiads knew just who she was;
but she would trail her father and her sisters
and let them touch her as she sidled up   290
to be admired. Once, old Inachus
had plucked some grass and held it out to her:
she licked her father's hands, and tried to kiss
his palms, and then began to weep; and if
she could have uttered words, she would have told   295
her name and wretched fate and begged for aid.
Instead of words, it's letters that she traced
in sand—she used her hoof: so she revealed
her transformation—all of her sad tale.
"What misery!" cried Inachus; he clasped   300
her horns and neck; and snow-white Io moaned.
"What misery!" he wailed. "Are you my daughter,
the one whom I have sought through all the world?
My sorrow at the loss of you was less
than in my finding you; and now there's silence;   305
my words receive no answer, only sighs
and lowing—these must serve as your reply.
To think that—unaware, oblivious—
I was intent on all your wedding rites,
your marriage torch, and I was hoping for   310
a son-in-law and then grandsons. But now
it is a bull whom you must wed; you'll bear
a bull as son. And I can't kill myself,
however deep my grief: sad fate indeed
to be a god: the gate of death is closed   315

against me; I am doomed to bear this sorrow
eternally."

           And while her father mourned,
Argus, the many-eyed, came up, and drove
old Inachus away; her guardian grabbed
poor Io; and to other pasturelands,   320
he thrust her. Then he sat upon a peak
and, from that height, kept all the fields in sight.

But now the ruler of the gods cannot
endure his Io's suffering so much;
he summons Mercury, the son that Jove   325
had by the shining Pleiad;[7] he instructs
his son to murder Argus. And at once,
with his winged sandals, Mercury flies off;
within his hand, he grasps the potent wand
that can bring sleep; his cap is on his head.   330
And so arrayed, the son of Jove descends—
down from his father's fortress high in heaven
to earth. He sets aside his cap, his wings;
the wand is all he keeps but makes it seem
a shepherd's crook; and then, in rural guise,   335
along stray paths, the son of Maia drives
some goats he'd rustled from the countryside;
and as he goes, upon the reeds he'd tied
together—rustic pipes—he plays a song.

And Argus is entranced by those strange sounds: 340
"Whoever you may be," he says, "sit down
beside me on this rock; no other spot
can offer richer grass to all your flock;
and there is perfect shade for shepherds here."

So Mercury joins Argus on the rock   345
and whiles away the time with varied talk;
he plays upon the reeds—with that he hopes
that Argus' watchful eyes will drop their guard.
But Argus tries to ward off languid sleep;
and though some of his eyes have shut, he keeps   350
the rest awake and watchful. And indeed,
since pipes had been invented recently,
he asks how that invention came about.

The god replied: "On the cool mountainside
of Arcady, among the woodland nymphs   355
whose home was in the forest of Nonacris,
one was most famous—she whom they called Syrinx.[8]
And more than once that nymph had been pursued
but had eluded all the guile and wiles
of Satyrs[9] and the many gods who dwell   360

---

7. Maia.   8. The name means "shepherd's pipe," which is a musical instrument made of reeds.
9. Woodland creatures, half man, bald, bearded, and highly sexed.

in shaded woods or on the fertile fields.
For like Diana, goddess of Ortygia,[1]
she was a devotee of chastity;
and she dressed like Diana, so that one
might well have thought she was Latona's daughter[2]—   365
except for this: Diana bore a bow
of gold, while Syrinx' was of cornel wood.
Despite that difference, she was often taken
to be Diana. And one day, as she
was coming back from Mount Lycaeus, Pan[3]   370
caught sight of Syrinx. He—whose head was wreathed
with sharp pine needles—said . . ."
                                        And much was left
to tell: how Syrinx, scorning all his pleas,
fled through the barren waste until she reached
the placid, sandy stream of Ladon: here   375
the river blocked her flight, and so she begged
her sister water nymphs to change her shape.
And Pan, who thought that he had caught the nymph,
did not clutch her fair body but marsh reeds;
and he began to sigh; and then the air,   380
vibrating in the reeds, produced a sound
most delicate, like a lament. And Pan,
enchanted by the sweetness of a sound
that none had ever heard before, cried out:
"And this is how I shall converse with you!"   385
He took unequal lengths of reeds, and these
Pan joined with wax: this instrument still keeps
the name Pan gave it then, the nymph's name—Syrinx.

When Mercury was just about to tell
these things, he saw that Argus' hundred eyes   390
had given in to sleep; they all were closed.
At once he checks his talk; and to abet
the power of sleep, with his enchanted wand
he touches lightly Argus' drowsing eyes;
and then, unhesitatingly, he strikes   395
the watchman with a sword curved like a scythe;
he strikes the nodding head just where the neck
and body join; he knocks it off the rock
and sends it tumbling, bleeding, down the steep
descent, and stains the cliffside with that blood.   400

O Argus, you lie low; the light that glowed
in many pupils now is spent; one night
alone now holds in sway your hundred eyes.

And Juno took the hundred eyes of Argus
and set them on her sacred bird: she filled   405

1. An old name of Delos.   2. Diana (her mother was Leto or Latona).   3. A god of the wild mountain
pastures and woods, with goat's feet and horns. *Mount Lycaeus:* high mountain in Arcadia.

the feathers of the peacock's tail with jewels
that glittered like the stars. And then the goddess
unleashed her rage; she struck her Grecian rival
at once: she sent a Fury to harass
poor Io's eyes and mind; she pierced her breast   410
with an invisible, relentless goad;
she drove the frightened girl across the world—
a fugitive.
          And nothing else was left
for way-worn Io on her endless path
but to seek refuge on your banks, o Nile.   415
And there she knelt and, drawing back her head,
lifted her eyes—she had no other way
to plead or pray—up to the stars, with moans
and tears and wretched lowings, as if she,
beseeching Jove, asked him to end her grief.   420
At that, Jove threw his arms round Juno's neck;
he begged his wife to end this punishment.
"You need not fear the future," so he pledged;
"she'll never cause you harm or grief again—"
and as his witness for the oath he'd sworn,   425
it was the Stygian marsh he called upon.[4]
Now Io, with the goddess' rage appeased,
regains the form she had before: she sheds
the rough hairs on her body, and her horns
recede; her round eyes shrink, her mouth retracts,   430
her arms and hands appear again; and each
of Io's hoofs is changed into five nails.
There's no trace of the heifer that is left,
except the lovely whiteness of her flesh.
Content that just two feet now meet her needs,   435
the nymph stands up but hesitates to speak
for fear that, like a heifer, she will low;
then, timidly, she once again employs
the power of speech she had—for so long—lost.
And now she is a celebrated goddess,   440
revered by crowds clothed in white linen: Isis.

Her son was Epaphus, and it's believed
that she gave birth to him from great Jove's seed;
he shares his mother's shrines in many cities.

*   *   *

FROM BOOK II

[Europa and Jove]

And when he[5] was in heaven once again,
his father, Jove, draws him apart and says

---

4. Gods swore solemn oaths by the Styx, one of the rivers of the underworld.   5. Mercury, son of Jove and messenger of the gods. He has been in Athens, where he tried to have a love affair with Herse, daughter of King Cecrops, was promised help and then foiled by her sister Aglauros, and took his revenge on Aglauros by turning her into a statue.

(though not revealing to his son the cause
for all of this—that is, the call of love):
"My son, who always faithfully fulfill   5
whatever I may ask, do not waste time;
glide down to earth—be swift as usual—
and find the land from which your mother's star[6]
is seen on high along the left-hand skies
(the men who live there call that country Sidon).[7]   10
You'll see a herd (the king's own cattle) grazing
far off, on a green hillside; drive that herd
down to the shore."
                    He spoke—at once his words
were acted on: the herd was headed shoreward.
That beach was where the daughter of the king,   15
Europa, always played with her companions.

Now, majesty and love do not go hand
in glove—they don't mix well. And so, great Jove
renounced his solemn sceptre: he—the lord
and father of the gods—whose right hand holds   20
his massive weapons, three-pronged lightning bolts,
the king whose simple nod can shake the world—
takes on the semblance of a bull; among
the herd he lows; he mingles with the heifers;
he roams the tender grass—a handsome presence.   25
He's white—precisely like untrodden snow,
like snow intact, untouched by rainy Auster.[8]
His neck has robust muscles; from his shoulders,
his dewlap[9] hangs. His horns, it's true, are small,
but so well wrought, one would have thought a craftsman   30
had made them; they were more translucent than
pure gems. His brow has nothing menacing;
his gaze inspires no fear. He seems so calm.

Agenor's daughter[1] stares at him in wonder:
he is so shapely, so unthreatening.   35
At first, however, though he is not fierce,
she is afraid to touch him. Then she nears,
draws closer, and her hand holds flowers out
to his white face. Delighted, as he waits—
a lover—for still other, greater joys,   40
he kisses her fair hands—no easy test
to check his eagerness, delay the rest.
And now the great bull sports along the grass,
and now he stretches snow-white flanks along
the golden sands. Her fear has disappeared,   45
and now he offers to the girl his chest,
that she might stroke him with her virgin hand;
and now his horns, that she might twine them round

6. Maia, Mercury's mother, had been transformed into a star in the constellation Pleiades.   7. One of
the principal cities of Phoenicia (the modern Lebanon).   8. The south wind, bringer of rain.   9. A
fold of loose skin hanging from the neck.   1. Europa. Agenor was the Phoenician king.

with garlands. At a certain point, Europa
dares to sit down upon his back: the girl 50
is not aware of what he is in truth.
And then, as casually as he can,
the god moves off, away from the dry sands;
with his feigned hooves, he probes the shallows, then
advances even farther; soon he bears 55
his prey out to the waves, the open sea.

Europa now is terrified; she clasps
one horn with her right hand; meanwhile the left
rests on the bull's great croup.[2] She turns to glance
back at the shore, so distant now. Her robes 60
are fluttering—they swell in the sea breeze.

FROM BOOK V

[Ceres and Proserpina]

The Muse
was still not finished with her words,[3] when through
the air, there came the sound of whirring wings
and, from the high boughs, voices offered greetings.
Minerva looked on high: she tried to find 5
what tongues had voiced those sounds, which seemed so like
the speech of humans—but it was magpies
she saw upon those branches. There were nine
who, all aligned, lamented their sad fate;
whatever sounds they like, they imitate. 10
And as Minerva wondered, even as
a goddess speaks to goddess, one Muse said:

"Those whom you see have only recently
been added to the many families
of birds; they faced a contest, and they lost. 15
Their father was rich Pierus, the lord
of Pella; and they had Paeonian[4]
Evippe as their mother. Nine times she
had called upon the powerful Lucina[5]
for help, and nine times she had given birth. 20
Those stupid sisters—proud that they were nine
in number—traveled through Haemonia
and through Achaia,[6] touching every town,
until at last they came to Helicon
and challenged us to match their art of song: 25
'O goddesses of Thespia,[7] it's time
you stop beguiling the untutored mob

2. Rump.   3. Minerva (equivalent of the Greek Athena) has come to Mount Helicon in central Greece,
the home of the nine Muses (daughters of Zeus and Memory, patronesses of poetry and the other arts).
One of the Muses has told her of an attempt recently made to trap and rape them by the wicked Pyre-
neus.   4. *Pella:* city of Macedonia, in northern Greece. The Paeonians were a tribe living north of Macedonia.   5. Goddess of childbirth.   6. Regions of central Greece. The sisters are traveling south toward
Helicon.   7. Largest city near Mt. Helicon.

with counterfeited songs; for you are frauds.
If you are confident, compete with us!
Neither your voice nor art can match our own, 30
and we can match your numbers. If you lose,
then yield to us the spring of Pegasus[8]
and Aganippe, too, your other fount;
and if you win, we will concede to you
the plains of all our broad Emathia[9] 35
as far as our snow-clad Paeonia.
And let the nymphs be judges of this test!'

"Though it was shameful to contend with them,
there was more shame—we thought—in turning down
their challenge. So the Nymphs were called to judge: 40
they swore upon their streams and then sat down
on benches that were formed of porous stone.

"Now all was ready; without drawing lots,
the one who'd been the first to challenge us
began. She sang the battle of the gods 45
and Giants; she—unjustly—glorified
the Giants and belittled the great gods.
She said that, when Typhoeus[1] bounded up
from Earth's abyss, the gods on high were so
afraid that they ran off and did not stop 50
until, exhausted, they were taken in
by Egypt, at the point where seven mouths
divide the flow of Nile. And then she dared
to tell us that Typhoeus, son of Earth,
had reached their refuge; and to hide, the gods 55
took on deceitful shapes as camouflage:[2]
'So Jove became a ram, the lord of flocks;
that's why the Libyan Ammon[3] still is shown
with curving horns. The god of Delos hid
within a crow's shape, Bacchus in a kid, 60
and Phoebus' sister in a cat; the daughter
of Saturn took the form of a white heifer;
and just as Venus hid herself as fish,
Cyllene's god[4] became a winged ibis.'

"With that, her song was done; her voice had been 65
accompanied by chords upon the strings.

"Now we—the Muses of Aonia—
were challenged to reply. But if your time
is short, and other cares call you away,

8. Hippocrene ("horse fountain"), said to have been created on Mt. Helicon by a blow of the winged horse Pegasus's hoof. 9. A region of Macedonia. 1. Monstrous son of Earth. Like the Earth-born Giants, he challenged Jove and the Olympian gods and was defeated—a detail omitted in this song, which ridicules the gods. 2. An "explanation" of the Egyptian gods' animal forms. 3. Chief Egyptian god, identified by the Greeks and Romans with Zeus/Jove, who had an important oracular cult in the Libyan desert (west of the Nile Valley and part of Egypt under Roman rule). 4. Mercury, born on Mount Cyllene in the Greek Peloponnesus.

you may not want to hear the song we sang."
"No, no; you can be sure," Minerva said;
"I'll listen from the start until you end."
She sat down in the woodland's pleasant shade.
The Muse replied: "We chose Calliope;[5]
for all of us, she would—as one—compete.
Our sister rose; her flowing tresses wreathed
with ivy, she began to pluck the strings;
and their vibrations joined her mournful chant:

" 'The first to furrow earth with the curved plow,
the first to harvest wheat, the first to feed
the world with food men cultivate in peace,
the first to bless the earth with laws—was Ceres;[6]
all things are gifts she gave. I want to sing
of Ceres: may my offering be worthy—
this goddess surely merits poetry.

" 'The island mass of Sicily is heaped
upon a giant's body: underneath
its soil and stones Typhoeus lies—the one
who dared to hope for heaven as his kingdom.
He writhes; he often tries to rise again.
But Mount Pelorus (closest to the land
of the Italians) crushes his right hand;
his left is in Pachynus' grip, just as
his legs are in Mount Lilybaeum's grasp;[7]
his head is pressed—vast Etna[8] holds it fast.
Beneath this mountain, on his back, in rage,
Typhoeus' mouth spits ashes, vomits flames.
He often strives to heave aside the ground—
the towns and heavy peaks that pin him down.
Then earth quakes. As it trembles, even he
who rules the kingdom of the silent dead
is anxious, for the crust of Sicily
may split and a wide crack reveal things secret:
daylight might penetrate so deep that it
would terrify the trembling Shades. His fear
of such disaster led that lord of darkness
to leave his sunless kingdom. Mounted on
his chariot—it was drawn by two black stallions—
he carefully assessed the island mass.
When he was sure that there were no vast cracks.
that Sicily was everywhere intact,
his fears were ended. Then, as Pluto rode
from site to site, down from her mountain slopes
of Eryx,[9] Venus saw him. As she clasped
her winged son, Cupid, this is what she asked:

70

75

80

85

90

95

100

105

110

115

---

5. "Lovely Voice": Muse of epic poetry.   6. The Greek Demeter, goddess of grain.   7. Mountains on the northeast, southeast, and western promontories of Sicily, respectively.   8. The great (and still active) volcano approximately in the center of the east coast of Sicily.   9. Mountain in western Sicily with an important cult of Venus.

" ' "O you, my son, my weapon and my armor,
dear Cupid—you, my power—take those shafts
to which both gods and mortals must submit;
with one of your swift arrows pierce the chest
of Pluto—god who, when the lots were cast,   120
assigning the three realms, received the last.
You conquer and command sky-deities—
not even Jove is free from your decrees;
sea-gods are governed by your rule—and he
who is the god of gods who rule the sea.   125
And why should Tartarus[1] elude our laws?
Why not extend your mother's power—and yours?
One-third of all the world is still not ours.
We have been slow to act, but indecision
has earned us nothing more than scorn in heaven.   130
And—son—if my authority should weaken,
then yours would suffer, too. Do you not see
how both Athena and the hunting goddess,
Diana, would defy me? And the daughter
of Ceres, if we let her choose, will be   135
like them: she is so bent on chastity.
But for the sake of all I share with you,
please join that goddess-girl, Proserpina,
to her great uncle, Pluto." This, she asked.
Love, opening his quiver—he respects   140
his mother—from his thousand shafts selects
the sharpest, surest shaft—the arrow most
responsive to the pressure of his bow.
Across his knee, the pliant bow is bent;
Love's hooked barb pierces Pluto through the chest.   145

" 'Not far from Enna's[2] walls there are deep waters.
That lake—called Pergus—hears a music richer,
more songs of swans, than even the Cayster[3]
hears as its current courses. Tall hills circle
that lake. Woods crown the slopes—and like a veil,   150
the forest boughs abate the flames of Phoebus.
Beneath those leaves, the air is cool, the soil
is damp—with many flowers, many colors.
There spring is never-ending. In that grove
Proserpina was playing, gathering   155
violets and white lilies. She had filled
her basket and, within her tunic's folds,
had tucked fresh flowers, vying with her friends
to see which girl could gather more of them.
There Pluto—almost in one instant—saw,   160
was struck with longing, carried that girl off—
so quick—unhesitating—was his love.

" 'The goddess-girl was terrified. She called—
in grief—upon her mother and companions,

1. The underworld.   2. A city in central Sicily.   3. River in Lydia in Asia Minor, proverbial for its many swans.

but more upon her mother. She had ripped
her tunic at its upper edge, and since
the folds were loosened now, the flowers fell.
So simple is the heart of a young girl
that, at that loss, new grief is what she felt.
Her captor urged his chariot, incited   170
his horses, calling each by name and shaking
the dark-rust reins upon their necks and manes.
He galloped over the deep lake and through
the pools of the Palici, where the soil
spews fumes of sulfur and the waters boil.   175
He reached that place where the Bacchiadae—
a race that came from Corinth, which is bathed
by seas upon two sides—had built their city[4]
between two harbors of unequal size.

" 'Between the spring of Cyane and the spring   180
of Arethusa (which had flowed from Greece),
there is a stretch of sea that is hemmed in,
confined between two narrow horns of land.
Among those waves lived Cyane, Sicily's
most celebrated nymph, and she had given   185
her name to that lagoon. Above the eddies,
just at the center, Cyane rose, waist-high.
She recognized Proserpina and cried:
"Pluto, you cannot pass. You cannot be
the son-in-law of Ceres unless she   190
gives her consent. To ask is not to rape.
And if I may compare small things to great,
I, too, was wooed—by Anapis[5]—but I
wed him in answer to his prayers and pleas—
he never used the terror you abuse."   195
That said, she stretched her arms upon both sides
to block his chariot. But Saturn's son
could not contain his anger any longer:
he spurred his terrifying stallions, whirled
his royal scepter with his sturdy arm.   200
He struck the very depths of Cyane's pool.
The blow was such that, down to Tartarus,
earth opened up a crater: on that path
he plunged to darkness in his chariot.

" 'But Cyane nursed an inconsolable—   205
a silent—wound that was incurable:
a sadness for the rape of Ceres' daughter
and for the violation of the waters
of her own pool—for Pluto's scorn and anger.
She gave herself to tears and then dissolved   210
into the very pool of which she had—
till now—been the presiding deity.

4. Syracuse, on the southeastern coast of Sicily.   5. River that empties into the sea near Syracuse.

You could have seen the softening of her limbs,
the bones and nails that lost solidity.
Her slender hairs, her fingers, legs, and feet—   215
these were the first to join the waves. In fact,
the slenderest parts can sooner turn into
cool waters. Shoulders, back, and sides, and breasts
were next to vanish in thin streams. At last,
clear water flows through Cyane's weakened veins,   220
and there is nothing left that one can grasp.

" 'Meanwhile, the heartsick Ceres seeks her daughter:
she searches every land, all waves and waters.
No one—not Dawn with her dew-laden hair,
nor Hesperus[6]—saw Ceres pause. She kindled   225
two pinewood torches in the flames of Etna.
Through nights of frost, a torch in either hand,
she wandered. Ceres never rested. When
the gracious day had dimmed the stars, again
the goddess searched from west to east, from where   230
the sun would set to where the sun ascends.

" 'Worn out and racked by thirst—she had not wet
her lips at any spring along her path—
she chanced to see a hut whose roof was thatched
with straw. And Ceres knocked at that poor door,   235
which an old woman opened. When she saw
the goddess there and heard her ask for water,
she gave her a sweet drink in which she'd soaked
roast barley. While the goddess drank this brew,
a boy came up to her; and scornful, rude,   240
he laughed and said she drank too greedily.
Offended, Ceres stopped her sipping, threw
the brew and all of its pearl-barley grains
full in his face. So—soaked—his face soon showed
those grains as spots; his arms were changed to claws;   245
a tail was added to his altered limbs.
And that his form might not inflict much harm,
the goddess shrank him, left him small—much like
a lizard, and yet tinier in size.
This wondrous change was watched by the old woman,   250
who wept to see it, even as she tried
to touch the transformed shape: he scurried off
to find a place to hide. The name he got
is suited to his skin: the starry newt—
a beast that glitters with his starlike spots.   255

" 'To tell the lands and seas that Ceres crossed
would take too long: the world was not enough
to satisfy the searching mother. She
returned to Sicily, explored again

6. The evening star.

each part. She reached the pool of Cyane. 260
If Cyane had not been changed, she now
would have told Ceres all she knew; but while
she longs to speak, she lacks a tongue to tell.

" 'Yet Cyane transmitted one sure clue:
upon the surface of her waters floats 265
the girdle that Proserpina had worn;
that girdle—one that Ceres knew so well—
had chanced to fall into the sacred pool.
No sooner had she recognized that sign,
than Ceres—as if now, for the first time, 270
she knew her daughter had been stolen—tore
her unkempt hair; her hands beat at her breast
again, again. She did not know as yet
just where her daughter was, but she condemned
all lands. She said they were ungrateful and 275
unworthy of the gift of harvests she
had given them—above all, Sicily,
the place that showed the trace of the misdeed.
And there, in Sicily, she—without pity—
shattered the plows that turned the soil; her fury 280
brought death to both the farmers and their cattle.
She spoiled the seeds; she ordered the plowed fields
to fail; she foiled the hope and trust of mortals.
Now Sicily's fertility—renowned
throughout the world—appears to be a lie: 285
as soon as grass is in the blade, it dies,
undone by too much rain or too much sun.
The stars and winds bring blight; the greedy birds
devour the seed as soon as it is sown;
the crop is blocked by chokeweeds, tares, and thorns. 290
Then Arethusa, whom Alpheus[7] loved,
lifted her head above her waters—these
had flowed to Sicily from Grecian Elis.
She brushed her dripping hair back from her brow
and said: "O Ceres, mother of the girl 295
you seek throughout the world, you, mother of
earth's fruits and grain, forgo your fury, end
your devastating violence. This land
does not deserve your scourging: it was forced
to yield before the bandit's brutal course. 300
And I do not beseech you on behalf
of my own homeland. I was not born here:
I come from Pisa,[8] in the land of Elis.
My origins were there—yet Sicily
is dearer to me than all other countries. 305
I, Arethusa, have a newfound home:
sweet Sicily is now my country—and,
kind Ceres, may your mercy save this island.

7. River that flows past Olympia in Elis, a region of the western Peloponnesus in mainland Greece.
8. The Greek district in which Olympia is located.

" ' "Why I have left my homeland, why I crossed
so vast a stretch of sea until I touched
Ortygia[9]—there will yet be time enough   310
to speak of that, a time when you are free
of cares, a moment of tranquillity.
But I can tell you now my journey's path:
earth, opening a chasm, let me pass.
I flowed through caverns deep below the surface,   315
then—here—I lifted up my head again,
again I saw the stars I had forgotten.
But in my passage underneath the earth
among the eddies of the Styx, I saw   320
Proserpina with my own eyes: she was
downcast, still somewhat touched by fear—and yet
she was a queen within that world of darkness,
the powerful companion—mighty mistress—
of Pluto, tyrant of the underworld." '   325

" 'Hearing these things, the mother, Ceres, stood
as motionless as stone. Long moments passed:
her mind seemed lost. When that paralysis
of fear had given way to grief no less
oppressive, Ceres, on her chariot,   330
rode toward the upper air. With shadowed eyes,
her hair disheveled, hate-inflamed, she cried:
"For one who is of both your blood and mine,
o Jupiter, I come to plead with you.
Though I, her mother, do not matter, you   335
at least can care to save your daughter—I
should hope your care will not be any less
because she owes her birth to me. Our daughter,
after so long a search, is found—if one
can speak of finding when it just confirms   340
the loss more certainly, when finding means
no more than merely knowing where she is.
As for his theft of her—that I can bear—
he only has to give her back! My daughter
is mine no longer, but you cannot let   345
a robber win her as his wife—through theft." '

" 'Then Jupiter replied: "We share the care
and tenderness we owe to our dear daughter.
But if we would have things named properly,
then we must speak of love, not injury   350
or robbery. We should not be ashamed
of Pluto as a son-in-law—if only
you, goddess, would consent to that. Were he
to lack all else, it is no meager thing
to be the brother of a Jupiter!   355
But he, in fact, has many other splendors:

9. The island on which Syracuse was founded.

the portion of the world assigned to him
is, after all, a kingdom, only less
than what my portion is—and only chance
assigned this part to me and that to him.   360
In any case, if you are so intent
on separating them, Proserpina
can see the sky again—on one condition:
that in the world below, she has not taken
food to her lips. This is the Fates' edict."   365

" 'These were his words. And yet, though Ceres wanted
to bring her daughter back, the Fates prevented
Proserpina's return, for she had broken
her fast: the girl, in all her innocence,
while she was wandering through a well-kept garden   370
within the underworld, from a bent branch
had plucked a pomegranate. She had taken—
peeling away its pale rind—seven seeds
and pressed them to her lips. No one had seen
that act of hers—except Ascalaphus   375
(the son, they say, that Orphne—not the least
famous among Avernus' nymphs—conceived
out of her love for Acheron,[1] and bore
within the dark groves of the underworld).
He saw her taste those seeds: denouncing her,   380
he thwarted her return to earth. She moaned—
the queen of Erebus.[2] Then, in revenge,
she changed that witness. He was made a bird
of evil omen: on his head she poured
waters of Phlegethon.[3] Enormous eyes   385
and beak and feathers now are his. Deprived
of what he was, he now wears tawny wings;
his head is swollen, and his nails grow long
and hook back, forming claws; and it is hard
for him to move the feathers that now sprout   390
upon his sluggish arms. He has become
the bird that men detest—that would announce
calamities. He is the lazy screech-owl,
bringer of bitter auguries to mortals.

" 'Ascalaphus indeed seems to have earned   395
his punishment—his tongue was indiscreet.
But, Achelous'[4] daughters, why do you,
as Sirens, have birds' feathers and birds' feet—
and features like a girl's? Is it because
you, Sirens skilled in song, had been among   400
the band of friends who joined Proserpina
when she was gathering spring flowers near Enna?
For after you—in vain—had searched all lands

---

1. Acheron ("Woe") is one of the rivers, and Avernus a lake, in the underworld. *Orphne*: the name means
"darkness" in Greek.   2. The underworld.   3. Fiery river of the underworld.   4. Large river in northwest Greece.

for her, so that the waves might also witness
that search for one you loved, you voiced a plea   405
to be allowed to glide above the sea,
using your arms as oars to beat the air.
You found the gods were well disposed to answer:
your limbs were wrapped—at once—in golden feathers.
But you were mesmerizing, suasive singers,   410
born to entrance the ears; and that your lips
not lose that gift, each one of you was left
with young girl's features and a human voice.

" 'And what did Jupiter do then? Between
his brother Pluto and his grieving sister,   415
he has to strike a balance: he divides
the turning year into two equal portions.
Proserpina is shared by the two kingdoms:
the goddess is to spend six months beside
her husband, and six months beside her mother.   420
At once, the goddess' face and spirit alter:
her brow, which until then seemed overcast
even to somber Pluto, now is glad,
just as, when it defeats the dark rainclouds,
the sun appears—victorious and proud.   425

" 'Generous Ceres, now at peace—at last
she has her daughter back—returns to ask
you, Arethusa, why you fled from Greece
and why you have become a sacred spring.
The waves fall still. Their tutelary goddess   430
raises her head above the depths; and after
her hands have twisted dry her damp green tresses,
she tells the tale of how—long since—Alpheus,
the river-god of Elis, longed for her.

" ' "I was," she says, "one of the nymphs who live   435
in the Achaean woods. I was intent
on tracks and trails and setting hunting nets—
no nymph had greater passion for such tasks.
I never wanted to be known for beauty—
I thought my courage was conspicuous,   440
but all my fame was for mere loveliness.
One day—no day that I forget—I made
my way back from the forest of Stymphalus.
That day was hot—but twice as hot for me:
the hunting had been hard, and I was weary.   445
I came upon a stream. Unmurmuring
and unperturbed it glided, crystalline—
so clear down to the riverbed that one
could count each pebble there. That stream was so
transparent that it did not seem to flow.   450
Along the riverbanks the slopes received
the shadows cast by gray-white willow trees

and poplars nourished by those waters—shade
that was the gift of nature. I drew near
And first I bathed my feet, then I went in   455
up to my knees. But now I wanted more
cool water: I undid my dress. I left
my soft gown draped on a bent willow branch;
naked, I plunged into the stream; and while
I strike those waters in a thousand ways,   460
dividing, joining, splashing as I play,
my arms withdrawing, plunging in—I hear
the strangest murmur rising from the depths.
I seek the nearest riverbank—in fear.
'Where do you flee so quickly, Arethusa?'   465
Alpheus, from his waters, called to me.
'Where do you flee so quickly?'—so did he
again speak hoarsely. I could only flee
without my dress—left on the other shore.
My nakedness only inflames him more.   470
He hurries after me; naked, I seem
to him that much more ready for the taking.
I race; he—fiercely—presses after me:
even as doves with trembling wings will flee
the hawk, and hawk pursue the frightened doves.   475

" ' "I passed Orchomenus, Psophis, Cyllene,
the vales of Maenalus, chill Erymanthus,[5]
and Elis; I sustained my pace; Alpheus
did not outrace me. But I could not match
his strength: my speed was spent—it could not last   480
as long as his. Yet, over level fields
and wooded hills, across the spurs and rocks
no path had ever marked, I did not stop.
The sun was at my back, and I could see
a giant shadow stretch ahead of me—   485
perhaps a phantom fashioned by my fear;
but I could surely hear his dread footsteps,
and I could feel his massive panting breath
upon the band that clasped my hair. As I
collapsed, exhausted by that course, I cried: 490
'Diana, save me! He is at my side!
I was your weapons' faithful guardian,
the huntress whom you chose to bear your bow,
the keeper of your quiver and your arrows.'

" ' "The goddess had been touched. And she detached   495
one cloud from a thick cloudbank, and she cast
that cloud around me.[6] And when I was wrapped
in darkness, then Alpheus, ignorant
of where I was, searched in the mist—vainly.

---

5. Cities and mountains of Arcadia, the region of the central Peloponnesus.   6. Conventional means in
ancient epic of making someone invisible.

Around the spot where she had hidden me,500
he circled twice, and twice—unknowing—cried:
'O Arethusa, Arethusa!' I
was in the grip of what great misery!
Was I not like the lamb when it can hear
wolves howl around the fold? Or like the hare505
that, hidden by a hedge, can see the dread
muzzles of the dogs and dares not stir?

" ' "And yet Alpheus does not leave; aware
that I have stopped—no footprints trail beyond—
Alpheus probes the cloud that cloaks the ground.510
I am beset. Cold sweat runs down my flesh;
My body rains dark drops, my hair drips dew,
and where I move my feet a pool is born.
In less time than it takes to tell you now
all that was happening, I am a spring.515

" ' "But in those waters, he, the river-god
Alpheus, recognizes me, his love;
leaving the human likeness he had worn,
he once again takes on his river form,
that he might mingle with me. And the goddess520
of Delos⁷ cracked a chasm through earth's crust:
I plunged into deep caverns, then was brought
here to Ortygia, dear to me because
its name is like the other name of Delos,⁸
the island of Diana—and because525
Ortygia is the place where, from below
the earth, up toward the air and sky, I flowed."

" 'When Arethusa's tale had reached its end,
the goddess of fertility prepared
her chariot; she yoked her sacred pair530
of dragons. With their bits held tight, she rides
upon the air, between the earth and sky.
Once at Athena's town,⁹ on touching ground,
she gives her chariot as well as seeds
of grain to young Triptolemus,¹ and these535
she'd have him scatter wide in many lands.
The youth flies over Europe and the breadth
of Asia; reaching Scythia, he descends.
The ruler of that land is Lyncus, and
he enters the king's palace. When he's asked540
to tell how he had come, and what and why
might be his name and country, he replies:
"My home is famous Athens; and my name,
Triptolemus. No ship has brought me here
across the waves; my feet did not cross land:545

7. Diana.   8. Also called Ortygia.   9. Athens.   1. Son of the King of Elevsis, Demeter's great cult center near Athens.

the air disclosed its roads to me; I bring
the gifts of Ceres; if you scatter these
across your spacious fields, they're sure to yield
rich harvests—cultivated, peaceful food."
And Lyncus, that barbarian, was struck   550
by envy; but that he might come to be
far-famed as a great benefactor, he
received his guest with hospitality.

" 'Yet when his guest was fast asleep, the king
attacked; his blade was just about to pierce   555
the chest of the Athenian when Ceres
transformed the Scythian king into a lynx,
then had Triptolemus ride off; across
the air, he drove her sacred dragon pair.'

"Calliope was done: her learned song,   560
sung with such skill, stopped here. The Nymphs, as one,
agreed: we goddesses of Helicon
had won. The losers could not stand their loss.
They shouted insults at us. As they scoffed,
Calliope replied: 'You challenged us: 565
for that alone, you merit punishment.
But now you dare to add your rude abuse.
Our patience is not endless: you would test
our anger, and our wrath will rage—unchecked.'
The sisters jeer and fleer; they scorn our threats;   570
but even as we warned them, when they lift
their hands to mock us, they now notice this:
the feathers sprouting from their fingers and
the plumage covering their arms. And each
can see a sister's face with rigid beak   575
protruding now, and see new birds retreat
into the trees. And when they try to beat
their breasts, they all are borne by flapping wings;
they fly into the air as insolent
magpies, the mocking dwellers in the woods.   580
Yet, though they now are winged, their endless need
for sharp, impulsive, harsh, derisive speech
remains: their old loquacity—they keep."

FROM BOOK IX

[Iphis and Ianthe]

Word of this prodigy² might well have stirred
all Crete—its hundred towns--if Crete itself
had not—so recently—produced its own
great miracle: when Iphis changed her form.

In Phaestus, close to Gnossus' royal city,   5
there lived a man called Ligdus. Though the son

---

2. The transformation of Byblis, who loved her brother Caunus, into a fountain.

of humble parents, Ligdus was freeborn.
And like his lineage, his property
was modest; but he'd lived most honestly—
he bore no stain, no blame. And when his wife　　10
was just about to have their child, he turned
to her with these admonitory words:
"There are two things for which I pray: the first,
that you may suffer little in childbirth;
the second, that your child may be a boy.　　15
Our means are meager—girls require more.[3]
So, if by chance (I pray it not be so)
you bear a female, I would have you know
that (hateful as it is—and may the gods
forgive me) I shall have her put to death."　　20
Such were his words. They both were bathed in tears:
he who had ordered this, and she who must
obey. Though Telethusa, his dear wife,
entreated Ligdus not to set such limits
upon the birth they both had longed for so,　　25
she prayed in vain. He would not change his course.

And now the hour of birth drew close; her womb
was full—a burden she could hardly bear—
when at midnight she saw—or thought she saw—
an image in her dreams: before her bed　　30
stood Isis[4] and her train of deities.
Upon her forehead she bore lunar horns
and, round her head, a yellow garland—stalks
of wheat that had been wrought in gleaming gold;
and she had other signs of royalty.　　35
Beside her stood the barking god, Anubis;
sacred Bubastis; Apis, in his cloak
of many colors; and Osiris' son,[5]
who checks his voice and, with his finger on
his lips, urges our silence. There were sistrums;[6]　　40
and there, at Isis' side, Osiris,[7] he
who always is longed for; and the Egyptian
snake swollen with his soporific venom.[8]
And Telethusa, who saw all of this
as if she were awake, heard Isis say:　　45
"O Telethusa, you, who worship me
so faithfully, can set aside despair:
there is no need to heed your husband's order.
And once Lucina has delivered you,
don't hesitate to let your newborn live.　　50
I am the goddess who, when called upon
for help and hope, bring comfort: I respond.
No, I am not a thankless deity."
Her counsel ended here. The goddess left.

---

3. They had to be provided with a dowry when they reached marriageable age.　　4. Egyptian goddess of fertility, marriage, and maternity, whose cult was widespread in the Roman world.　　5. Horus, or Harpocrates.　　6. Sacred rattles used in Isis's cult.　　7. Husband of Isis, killed by his brother Set and restored to life by Isis, and so a figure of rebirth.　　8. Set, whom the Greeks identified with the snaky Typhoeus.

The Cretan woman rose up from her bed,   55
rejoicing; stretching out her blameless hands
unto the stars, she prayed—a suppliant—
that what she'd seen in dreams would be confirmed.
Her labor pains grew more intense, and soon
she'd given easy birth: a girl was born.   60
Now, to deceive her husband, Telethusa
gave orders to the nurse (for she alone
knew of this guile) to feed the newborn child
and to tell everyone it was a son.
And Ligdus thanked the gods, and to the child   65
he gave the name of Ligdus' father: Iphis.
And Telethusa was most pleased with this:
it was a name that suited male or female—
a neutral name, whose use involved no tricks.
No one unmasked the pious lie. She dressed   70
her Iphis as a boy—and whether one
assigned them to a daughter or a son,
the features of the child were surely handsome.

Some thirteen years had come; thirteen had gone.
O Iphis, now, for you, your father found   75
a bride, the blond Ianthe—there was none
among the girls of Phaestus who had won
more praise for the perfection of her form.
Her father was a man of Crete, Telestes.

Iphis and she were equal in their age,   80
their beauty; and the two of them were trained
by the same tutors; they had learned—together—
the basic rudiments of arts and letters.
In sum, they had shared much; and so when love
had struck their unsuspecting hearts, they both   85
shared one same wound—but not with equal hopes.
Ianthe waits impatiently to wed;
she longs for what was promised and accepted,
her wedding one she takes to be a man;
while Iphis is in love with one she knows   90
is never to be hers; and just for this,
the flame is still more fierce; and now she burns—
a virgin for a virgin. It is hard
to check her tears.
                    "What end awaits me now?"
she says. "I am possessed by love so strange   95
that none has ever known its monstrous pangs.
If heaven meant to spare me, then the gods
should have done so; and if the gods' intent
was to destroy me, then the means they chose
could have been natural—a normal woe.   100
Cows don't love cows, and mares do not love mares;
but sheep desire rams, and does are drawn
by stags. And birds, too, follow that same norm;
among the animals, no female wants

a female! Would I could annul myself!   105
Yes, it is true that all monstrosities
occur in Crete; and here Pasiphae⁹
has loved a bull. But even that is less
insane than what I feel; for, after all,
she was a female longing for a male.   110
Yet she was able to attain her goal:
when she appeared in heifer's guise, then he—
deceived—appeased her with adultery.
But how can I be helped? For even if
the world's most cunning minds were gathered here,   115
if Daedalus¹ himself flew back to Crete
on waxen wings, what could he do? Nothing—
no learned art—can ever make of me
a boy. And it cannot change you, Ianthe.

"Why then not summon all your mettle, Iphis?   120
Return to your own self; extinguish this
flame that is hopeless, heedless, surely foolish.
For you were born a girl; and now, unless
you would deceive yourself, acknowledge that:
accept it; long for what is lawful; love   125
as should a woman love! What gives most life
to love is hope; it's hope that lets love thrive—
but it is hope of which you are deprived.
No guardian keeps you from her loving touch;
no jealous husband keeps a sleepless watch,   130
and no harsh father; nor would she herself
deny you what you seek; yet you cannot
possess her. Though all things may favor you,
though men and gods may help in your pursuit,
you can't be happy. Even now there's no   135
desire of mine that's been denied; the gods
have been benevolent—they've given me
as much as they could give; and what I want
is what my father and Ianthe want,
and what my future father-in-law wants.   140
It's nature, with more power than all of these,
that does not want it: my sole enemy
is nature! Now the longed-for moment nears,
my wedding day is close at hand: Ianthe
will soon be mine—but won't belong to me.   145
With all that water, we shall thirst indeed.
Why do you, Juno, guardian of brides,
and you, too, Hymen,² come to grace these rites
at which there is no husband—just two brides?"

9. Wife of King Minos of Crete, and mother by the bull of the Minotaur.   1. Fabled craftsman, who
devised the heifer disguise for Pasiphae and, later, the labyrinth for the Minotaur. Forced to flee Crete, he
made waxen wings for himself and his son Icarus.   2. God of marriage, whose presence was invoked at
weddings.

Her words were done. Meanwhile the other virgin, 150
whose passion matches Iphis', prays, o Hymen,
that you be quick to come. But Telethusa,
who fears the very thing Ianthe seeks,
delays the date; at times she feigns some illness
and often uses omens seen in dreams 155
as an excuse. But no pretext is left,
and now the wedding day is imminent—
indeed it looms tomorrow. She removes
the bands that circle her and Iphis' heads;
with hair unbound, she holds the altar fast 160
and pleads: "O Isis, you who make your home
in Mareota's fields and Paraetonium
and Pharos and the Nile, whose waters flow
to seven mouths, I pray you, help us now
and heal the fear we feel. O goddess, I 165
have seen you: yes, I saw and recognized
you and your regal signs—your mighty band
of gods, the torches, and the sistrums' sounds—
and I can still remember your commands.
If my dear daughter is alive, if I 170
have not been punished, we owe all of this
to your advice, your gift. Take pity, Isis:
we two indeed have need of you." Her words
were followed by her tears.
                    The goddess seemed
to shake her altar (and Osiris had 175
in fact done that): her temple doors had trembled;
one saw the glitter of her crescent horns;
one heard the clash and clatter of her sistrums.
Still not completely sure, yet glad to have
such hopeful auguries, the mother left 180
the temple. Iphis walked behind her, but
her stride was longer than it was before,
and her complexion darker; she was more
robust; her features had grown sharper, and
her hair was shorter, without ornaments. 185
You are more vigorous than you had been,
o Iphis, when you still were feminine—
for you who were a girl so recently
are now a boy! So, bring your offerings
unto the shrines; set fear aside—rejoice! 190

They bring their offerings, and then they add
a votive tablet, one on which they had
inscribed these words: "These gifts, which Iphis pledged
as girl, are paid by him as man." And when
the first rays of the next day's sun again 195
revealed the wide world, Venus, Juno, and
Hymen assembled: marriage flames were lit,
and the boy Iphis made Ianthe his.

FROM BOOK X[3]

[Pygmalion]

"Pygmalion had seen the shameless lives
of Cyprus' women;[4] and disgusted by
the many sins to which the female mind
had been inclined by nature, he resigned
himself: for years he lived alone, without   5
a spouse: he chose no wife to share his couch.

"Meanwhile, Pygmalion began to carve
in snow-white ivory, with wondrous art,
a female figure more exquisite than
a woman who was born could ever match.   10
That done, he falls in love with his own work.
The image seems, in truth, to be a girl;
one could have thought she was alive and keen
to stir, to move her limbs, had she not been
too timid: with his art, he's hidden art.   15
He is enchanted and, within his heart,
the likeness of a body now ignites
a flame. He often lifts his hand to try
his work, to see if it indeed is flesh
or ivory; he still will not admit   20
it is but ivory. He kisses it:
it seems to him that, in return, he's kissed.
He speaks to it, embraces it; at each
caress, the image seems to yield beneath
his fingers: and he is afraid he'll leave   25
some sign, some bruise. And now he murmurs words
of love, and now he offers gifts that girls
find pleasing: shells, smooth pebbles, little birds,
and many-colored flowers, painted balls,
and amber tears that the Heliades[5]   30
let drop from trees. He—after draping it
with robes—adorns its fingers with fine gems,
its neck with a long necklace; light beads hang
down from its ears, and ribbons grace its breast.
All this is fair enough, but it's not less   35
appealing in its nakedness. He rests
the statue on the covers of his bed,
on fabric dyed with hues of Sidon's shells;[6]
he calls that form the maid that shares his couch
and sets its head on cushions—downy, soft—   40
delicately, as if it could respond.

---

3. This selection of stories is part of the song sung by Orpheus after he has failed to redeem his wife, Eurydice, from the underworld. His theme, announced in the prologue of his song, is "boys the gods have loved, and girls / incited by unlawful lust and passions, / who paid the penalty for their transgressions."   **4.** Orpheus has just told of the Propoetides of Cyprus, who became the first women to prostitute themselves as punishment for having denied Venus's divinity.   **5.** Daughters of the Sun, turned to pine trees in mourning for their brother Phaethon. Their tears were the source of amber (actually fossilized pine resin).   **6.** Purple or red, a costly dye from shellfish found off the coast of Phoenicia.

"The day of Venus' festival had come—
the day when, from all Cyprus, people thronged;
and now—their curving horns are sheathed with gold—
the heifers fall beneath the fatal blows   45
that strike their snow-white necks; the incense smokes.
Pygmalion, having paid the honors owed
to Venus, stopped before the altar: there
the sculptor offered—timidly—this prayer:
'O gods, if you indeed can grant all things,   50
then let me have the wife I want'—and here
he did not dare to say 'my ivory girl'
but said instead, 'one like my ivory girl.'
And golden Venus (she indeed was there
at her own feast-day) understood his prayer: 55
three times the flame upon her altar flared
more brightly, darting high into the air—
an omen of the goddess' kindly care.
At once, Pygmalion, at home again,
seeks out the image of the girl; he bends   60
over his couch; he kisses her. And when
it seems her lips are warm, he leans again
to kiss her; and he reaches with his hands
to touch her breasts. The ivory had lost
its hardness; now his fingers probe; grown soft,   65
the statue yields beneath the sculptor's touch,
just as Hymettian[7] wax beneath the sun
grows soft and, molded by the thumb, takes on
so many varied shapes—in fact, becomes
more pliant as one plies it. Stupefied,   70
delighted yet in doubt, afraid that he
may be deceived, the lover tests his dream:
it is a body! Now the veins—beneath
his anxious fingers—pulse. Pygmalion
pours out rich thanks to Venus; finally,   75
his lips press lips that are not forgeries.
The young girl feels these kisses; blushing, she
lifts up her timid eyes; she seeks the light;
and even as she sees the sky, she sees
her lover. Venus graces with her presence   80
the wedding she has brought about. And when
the moon shows not as crescent but as orb
for the ninth time, Pygmalion's wife gives birth
to Paphos—and in honor of that child,
Cyprus has since been called the Paphian isle.   85

[*Myrrha and Cinyras*]

"And Paphos' son was Cinyras, a man
who, if he'd not had children, might have found
some happiness. The tale I now would sing

7. Of Hymettos, a mountain near Athens famous for its honey.

is dread indeed: o daughters, fathers, leave;
or if your minds delight in listening,   90
do not put trust in me, do not believe
the truth that I will tell; or if you must
believe it, then believe the penalty
that punishes such acts. In any case,
if nature can permit so foul a sin   95
to see the light, I do congratulate
this region of the world, my Thracian race;[8]
I'm grateful that we are so far away
from lands where such obscenities take place.

"Panchaea's land[9] is rich in balsam and   100
in cinnamon and unguents; and its trees
drip incense, and its soil has many flowers.
What need had it for myrrh? Did it deserve
so sad a plant? O Myrrha, Cupid had
no part in your undoing—for he says   105
his arrow did not strike you; he declares
his torches innocent. The firebrand
and venom-swollen snakes were brought from Styx
by one of the three Sisters:[1] she did this
to crush you. Yes, to hate a father is   110
a crime, but love like yours is worse than hate.

"Young lords from every land, the noblest men
from all the Orient, have sought your hand;
among all these, choose one as your dear husband.
But, Myrrha, there is one who can't belong   115
to those from whom you choose.
                              "And she, in truth,
knows that; she strives; she tries; she would subdue
her obscene love: 'Where has my mind led me?
What am I plotting? Gods, I do beseech,
and, too, I call upon the piety   120
I owe my parents: check my sacrilege,
prevent my sinning—if it is a sin.
Parental piety does not exclude
such love: the other animals pursue
delight and mate without such niceties.   125
There's nothing execrable when a heifer
is mounted by her father; stallions, too,
mate with their daughters; and a goat can choose
to couple with his child; the female bird
conceives from that same seed which fathered her.   130
Blessed are those who have that privilege.
It's human scruples that have stifled us
with jealous edicts; law is envious—
what nature would permit, the law forbids.

8. A reminder that these stories form Orpheus's song in Thrace.   9. An imaginary island near Arabia,
rich in spices.   1. The Furies.

And yet they say that there are tribes in which   135
the mother mates with her own son, the daughter
with her own father, and the loving bonds,
so reinforced, make families more fond.
But I—to my misfortune—was not born
among those tribes; instead I am—forlorn—   140
denied the very man for whom I long.
But why do I keep coming back again,
again, to this? I must dismiss such thoughts:
blot out my lust. Yes, Cinyras deserves
much love—but as a father. Were I not   145
his daughter, I could lie with him; but since
I'm his, he can't be mine; and that close link
dictates my loss. If I were but a stranger,
I would have had some chance. But now I want
to leave my native land: nothing but flight   150
can save me from so foul a flaw. And yet
I stay: this evil ardor holds me here,
that I may gaze at Cinyras, and touch
and speak to him, and give him kisses if
I cannot hope for more. Would you transgress   155
beyond that? Can you let such sacrilege
incite you? Do you know what holy ties
and names would be confronted by your crimes?
Would you be your own mother's rival and
your father's mistress? Would you want to be   160
a sister to your son? Your brother's mother?
And those three Sisters, don't they make you fear?
Their hair is wreathed with serpents, and they bear
barbaric brands when they appear before
the eyes and faces of unholy souls.   165
Come now, your body's still unstained: do not
debauch your soul with lust, defile the code
of nature with a lawless mating. Though
you will it, nature will not have it so;
for Cinyras is pious in his ways,   170
a man of virtue. Would that he were prey
to my same frenzy, to that passion's sway!'

"These were her words. Now Cinyras, confused,
does not know what to do: the suitors crowd—
so many worthy men. He calls upon   175
his daughter to select the one she wants,
and he lists all their names. At first, the girl
is silent: staring at him, she's in doubt;
and warm tears veil her eyes. Her father thinks
these tears are simply signs of modesty,   180
forbids her weeping, dries her cheeks; and then
he kisses her. She takes too much delight
in this; and when he asks what kind of man
she'll have her husband be, she answers: 'One

like you.' Not understanding what is hid 185
beneath her words, he praises her for this:
'And may you always be so filial.'
When she hears him say 'filial,' the girl
lowers her eyes: she knows she's criminal.

"Midnight: now sleep sets cares and flesh to rest. 190
But Myrrha does not sleep: she cannot check
the fire that feeds on her; she is held fast—
her madness does not slack; first she despairs
and then is set to try; she is ashamed;
but though she longs, she cannot find a plan. 195
As, when the axes strike the massive trunk,
the tree will waver at the moment just
before the final blow: one does not know
which way it is to fall; upon all sides
men now rush off—so, too, enfeebled by 200
so many blows from many sides, the mind
of Myrrha leans this way, then that. At last
it seems no thing can check her love, bring rest,
except for death. On death she now is set.
She rises from her bed: she ties her belt 205
around a ceiling beam—to hang herself.

" 'Dear Cinyras, farewell,' his daughter moans,
'I hope you come to know why I would die.'
Then she begins to run the cord around
her pallid neck. They say her murmurs reached 210
the ears of her old nurse, who faithfully
stood watch before the door of her dear charge.
The nurse leaps up at once; on opening
the door, she sees her Myrrha readying
the tools of death; in one same moment, she 215
cries out and beats her breast and tears her dress
and snatches off the rope from Myrrha's neck.
And only after that, the nurse takes time
to weep, to clasp her Myrrha, and to ask
why she was driven to the noose. The girl 220
is silent, speechless; staring at the ground,
she's sorry her attempt at death was foiled—
she was too slow. But her old nurse insists:
she bares her white hairs and her withered breasts;
she calls on all the days and nights she'd spend 225
on Myrrha in the cradle, and she begs:
what grief had brought her Myrrha to this pass?
But Myrrha turns aside those pleas; she groans.
The nurse is set on finding out, and so
she promises not only to hold close 230
the secret but to help her: 'I am old,
but I'm not useless. If it is a stroke
of madness that afflicts you, my dear girl,

I know a woman who has charms and herbs
to heal you; and if anyone has cast   235
an evil spell upon you, magic rites
can purify you; and to cure your plight,
you can bring offerings, a sacrifice
unto the gods, and so appease their wrath
if they, in anger, led you to this pass.   240
I've thought of all that could have brought distress.
This house can only bring you happiness:
yes, all things here go well; your mother and
your father are alive and prosperous.'
As soon as she has heard those words, 'your father,'   245
the girl sighs deeply; but the nurse—although
she has begun to sense that Myrrha's soul
is sick with love—does not as yet suspect
a passion so profane. And stubbornly,
she probes: she wants to hear in full the cause   250
of Myrrha's pain—whatever it might be.
She hugs the tearful girl to her old breast
and, holding Myrrha in her frail arms, says:
'I know, I know: you are in love. But set
your fears aside; you'll find that I can help;   255
and I shall keep your secret; Cinyras
won't hear a word of this. But, come, confess.'
The frenzied girl breaks loose and, on her bed,
collapses, helpless; as she sinks her head
into the cushions, Myrrha cries: 'Don't seek   260
the source of this! Stop probing, I beseech!
The thing you want to find is my foul crime!'

"At that, the girl's old nurse is horrified.
And as she stretches out her hands that shake
with years and fears, the old nurse falls; prostrate   265
before the feet of her dear girl, she pleads
and menaces: she threatens to reveal
the noose, the try at suicide—but then
she promises to help if Myrrha will
just tell the truth about her secret love.   270
The young girl lifts her head; against the breast
of her old nurse, it's many tears she sheds.
Again, again, she tries—she would confess—
but checks her voice; ashamed, she hides her face
within her robes and sighs: 'How happy you,   275
my mother, are beside the mate you chose.'
And Myrrha says no more; she only moans.
Then through the nurse's body, to the bone,
a shudder lances, sharp and cold (she knows,
she knows); her white hair stiffens on her head;   280
she tries with warning word on word to rid
the girl from that dread love; and Myrrha knows
the nurse's pleas are just; but she is set

on death if what she wants cannot be had.
At this, the nurse says: 'Live, for you will have   285
your . . . ' Daring not to utter 'father,' she
falls still; but then—before the gods on high—
she vows to keep the promise she had made.

"And now, their bodies clothed in snow-white robes,
all pious wives were honoring the feast   290
of Ceres; her first fruits, the ears of wheat,
were bound in garlands as an offering
on these, the days they celebrate each year.
This was the time when women, for nine nights,
shun union with their husbands; any touch   295
of man is banned. Cenchreis, the king's wife,
has joined the throng; she shares these secret rites.
When, in her wretched zeal, the old nurse finds
that Cinyras is drunk with wine, deprived,
without his lawful wife, she tells the king   300
that a young girl is now in love with him;
but she does not reveal the girl's true name—
the girl whose beauty she is quick to praise.
And when he wants to know the young girl's age,
she says, 'the same as Myrrha's.' When he tells   305
the nurse to fetch that girl, she runs to find
her Myrrha and, 'My dear, we've won,' she cries;
'you can rejoice!' The wretched girl is stirred,
and yet her joy is not complete; a sad
foreboding grips her heart, but she is glad: 310
the virgin's mind is torn by such discord.

"The hour when all is silent now is here.
And, seen between the stars of the two Bears,
Boötes,[2] veering downward with his wain,
inclines his guide-pole. Myrrha makes her way   315
to her misdeed. The golden moon now flees
the sky; black clouds conceal the stars; the night
has lost its flaring lights. The first to hide
their faces at the shameless sight were you,
o Icarus,[3] and dear Erigone,   320
your daughter, she whose holy love for you
won her a starry place—her sacred due.
Three times young Myrrha stumbles on her path,
an omen telling her she should turn back;
three times the screech-owl, with his eerie chant,   325
warns her. But still the longing daughter moves
ahead; her shame is muted by the black

2. The Ox-herder, a constellation, thought to drive Ursa Major, the Great Bear (also called the Wagon
[Wain]).   3. More properly Ikarios, a mythic Athenian. He received Dionysus into the city, and the god
rewarded him with wine, which he shared with his countrymen. Feeling its effect, they thought they had
been poisoned and killed him. His daughter Erigone hanged herself in grief, and both were changed into
constellations.

of night. Her left hand grips her nurse hard fast,
and with her right she gropes and probes. At last
she's at the threshold, opening the door;   330
and now she is inside the room. Her knees
are trembling; and as blood and color flee,
her face is pale; her courage leaves; as she
draws closer to her crime, her fears increase;
the girl repents of her audacity: 335
she would turn back if she could go unseen.
As Myrrha hesitates, her old nurse takes
her hand; she draws her toward the high bed's side—
consigns her to the king and says: 'Take her,
o Cinyras; she's yours.' And she unites   340
those two in dark damnation. Cinyras
obscenely welcomes to his bed the flesh
of his own flesh; he helps her to defeat
her virgin's shame; he sets her fears at ease.
Perhaps because she is so young, the king   345
calls timid Myrrha 'daughter,' even as
she calls him 'father'; so do they complete
their sacrilege; they name their guilt in speech.

"Filled with her father, Myrrha leaves that room;
she bears his impious seed within her womb.   350
And on the second night, again they lie
together; so it went, time after time,
until the father, keen to recognize
the girl he'd held so often, carried in
a lamp—and saw his daughter and his sin.   355
Struck dumb by grief, he pulls his gleaming sword
out from its sheath, which hung along the wall.

"And Myrrha fled. The night was kind; the shades
and darkness favored her; the girl escaped
her death; she crossed the open fields; she left   360
palm-rich Arabia and Panchaea's lands.
Nine times the moon had shown its crescent horns,
and still she wandered on. At last she stayed
her weary steps in the Sabaeans' land.[4]
Her womb was heavy now—so hard to carry.   365
Not knowing what to hope for—torn between
her fear of death and the fatigue of living—
she gathered up her wishes and beseeched:
'Oh, if there is some god to hear the plea
of one who knows that she is guilty, I   370
accept the death that I deserve. But lest
I, in my life, profane the living and,
in death, profane the dead, do banish me
from both these realms; transform me, and deny

4. Arabia Felix, the southern tip of the Arabian peninsula.

both life and death to me.'
                    "And some god heard   375
the girl confess her guilt: her final plea
was answered. As she spoke, the earth enclosed
her legs; roots slanted outward from her toes;
supported by those roots, a tall trunk rose.
Her bones became tough wood (although her marrow   380
remained unchanged); her blood was turned to sap;
her arms became long boughs; her fingers, twigs;
her skin was now dark bark. And as it grew,
the tree had soon enveloped her full womb;
then it submerged her breasts and was about   385
to wrap itself around her neck; but she—
impatient—met the rising bark: she sank
down, down, until her face was also bark.
Her flesh had lost the senses it once had,
but she still wept—and, trickling down the tree,   390
tears fell. But even tears can gain long fame:
myrrh, dripping from that trunk, preserves the name
of Myrrha, mistress of that tree; and she
will be remembered through the centuries.

[Venus and Adonis]

"But when the misbegotten child had grown   395
inside the wood, it wanted to come forth
to leave its mother. Halfway up the trunk,
the pregnant tree was swollen; all the bark
was taut with that full burden. But the pain
and pangs could not find words; though this is birth, 400
there is no speech that can beseech Lucina.
And yet the tree trunk bends and moans in labor;
the bark is wet with fallen tears. Lucina
takes pity: standing near the groaning boughs
she lays her hands upon them, even as   405
she speaks that spell which shepherds safe childbirth.
At that, the tree trunk cracked, the bark was torn;
the tree delivered what had weighed it down;
a living thing, a wailing boy was born:
Adonis. And the Naiads[5] set him on   410
the tender meadow and anointed him
with myrrh, his mother's tears. And even Envy
would praise his beauty, for indeed his body
is like the naked Cupid artists paint.
And to remove the only difference,   415
just add a quiver to Adonis or
remove the quiver from the Cupid's form.

"The flight of time eludes our eyes, it glides
unseen; no thing is swifter than the years.

5. Water nymphs.

Yes, he who is the son of his own sister   420
and his grandfather, was but recently
enclosed within a tree. But recently
a newborn, then a handsome baby boy,
Adonis has become a youth, a man;
his beauty now surpasses what he was,   425
inflaming even Venus' love, and thus
avenging that dread fire—incestuous—
which Venus made his mother, Myrrha, suffer.
And this is how that vengeance came about.

"One day, as Cupid, son of Venus, kissed   430
his mother, unaware, he scratched her breast:
an arrow jutting from his quiver chanced
to graze her. Though the goddess felt the prick
and pushed her son aside, the wound was far
more deep than it had seemed to her at first.   435

"And Venus now is taken by the mortal
Adonis' beauty: she no longer cares
for her Cythera's[6] shores; she cannot spare
the time to visit sea-encircled Paphos
and Cnidos, rich with fish; and she neglects   440
her Amathus,[7] the city rich with ores.
She even finds the skies too tedious:
she much prefers Adonis. She stays close
to him; it is with him she always goes;
and she, who always used to seek the shade—   445
there she could rest at ease and cultivate
her beauty—now frequents the mountain slopes,
the woods, the rocks beset by spiny thorns;
as if she were Diana,[8] Venus keeps
her tunic tied above her knees. She spurs   450
the hounds and chases after game: that is,
those beasts whom it is safe to hunt—the hares
that leap headlong, the stags with branching horns,
or does. But she is careful to avoid
stout boars, rapacious wolves, bears armed with claws,   455
and lions stained with blood of slaughtered herds.
Adonis, she would warn you, too, to stay
away from those fierce beasts: 'Be bold,' she says,
'when you approach the timid animals,
those who are quick to flee: but do not be   460
audacious when you face courageous beasts.
Dear boy, do not be reckless when the risk
involves me, too; don't let me lose you just
because you wanted glory; don't provoke
those animals whom nature has armed well.   465
Your youth, your loveliness—the many things

6. Island south of the Peloponnesus, and like Cyprus sacred to Venus.   7. Cities on Cyprus and (Cnidos)
in Asia Minor, important centers of Venus's cult.   8. Virgin and huntress, the antithesis of Venus.

with which you have enchanted even me—
don't move the lion or the bristling boar,
don't touch the eyes and hearts of those fierce beasts.
Those boars have lightning in their curving claws;   470
the tawny lion's wrath is wild and raw—
I do indeed detest that race.' At this,
he asked her why, and she replied: 'Adonis,
you'll hear the answer now: an ancient crime—
which had a monstrous outcome. But since I   475
am weary now—you see, I'm not quite used
to such hard labors—let us profit by
the poplar, here at hand; its shade invites,
and here, along the grass, we can recline.
I want to rest beside you.' She stretched out   480
along the ground and held him close—for he
had stretched out, too. And pillowing her head
upon his chest, the goddess—even as
she mingled kisses with her words—began:

" 'You may have heard of Atalanta: one   485
who, when she ran, would beat the fastest men.
That was no idle rumor, for she won
in truth. And, too, you would have found it hard
to say if she was worthier of praise
for her amazing speed or splendid grace.   490

" 'Now she had gone to ask the oracle
about a husband: "No, you have no need
of any husband"—so the god replied—
"you must shun any marriage. This advice
will not be taken; though you stay alive,   495
you will have lost yourself." Then, terrified
by what the god had said, she lived unwed
within the shadowed forests; to hold off
the crowd of her insistent suitors, she
set harsh conditions for her matrimony: 500
"Whoever hopes to have me," so she said,
"must first defeat me in a footrace; bed
and wife are what await the man who wins;
for all of those who are too slow, it's death
they'll get. These are the terms of this contest."   505
Yes, she showed little pity; but her beauty
was so entrancing that, despite the terms
that Atalanta set, a reckless crowd
of suitors came to race that fateful course.

" 'Of those who took their seats to watch the race,   510
one was Hippomenes. He had exclaimed:
"Can anyone be fool enough to risk
his life to gain a wife?" So he condemned
those young fanatics' love. But when she sheds
her clothes and shows her splendid form (much like   515

my own, or what your beauty, too, would be
were you a woman), then Hippomenes,
astonished, lifts his hands and cries: "Forgive me,
you whom I just rebuked! I did not know
the value of the prize you wanted so." 520
And even as he praises her, love grows:
his hope, that none would outrace Atalanta;
his fear, that some young suitor now may win—
and this spurs jealousy in him. "But why
don't I risk, too? Why not compete?" he cries; 525
"the god helps those who dare." Hippomenes
is pondering this course, when she flies by
as if her feet were wings. She seems to speed
as swiftly as a Scythian arrow, but
the young Aonian[9] is even more 530
astonished by the splendor of her form—
a grace that is enhanced as she competes.
She wears gold sandals on her rapid feet;
her hair is fluttering over her white shoulders
as, at her knees, the ribbons with white borders 535
are fluttering; and all her young, fair body
is flushed with rose, just as a purple awning
within a marble hall will lend white walls
a darker hint, a veil, a shadowed tint.
The stranger notices all this; and now 540
they cross the finish line; and she has won;
a victor, she receives the festal crown
of garlands. The defeated suitors go
with heavy groans, to pay the deaths they owe.

" 'And yet Hippomenes is not dismayed 545
and not delayed by their sad fate. He makes
his way to her; eyes fixed upon her face;
"Why seek such easy glory, why outrace
such sluggish men?" he says. "Contend with me,
for then, if fortune gives me victory, 550
your losing to so grand an enemy
would not bring shame to you. For I can claim
Megareus of Onchestus as my father,
and he had Neptune as grandfather: thus,
I am the great-grandson of one who rules 555
the waters; and my worth does not belie
my lineage. And if I meet defeat,
for having outraced me, Hippomenes,
you'll gain unending fame." And as he speaks,
the eyes of Atalanta take him in 560
most tenderly. Oh, does she want to win
or does the virgin long to lose to him?

" 'So Atalanta wonders, inwardly:
"Is there some god who, wishing to destroy

---

9. From Boeotia, a region in central Greece.

fair youths, has willed the ruin of this boy 565
and prods him now to seek me out as wife
and risk his own dear life? Were I to judge,
I'd hardly say that I was worth that much.
It's not his self that stirs me—it's his years:
he's young—and yet he's bold, a fearless soul! 570
He's young, yet he can claim that he is fourth
within the line of sons descended from
the monarch of the seas! And he loves me
and wants so much to marry me that if
an evil fate should foil him, he will live 575
no more! No, stranger, leave while you still can;
forget this savage marriage; wedding me
means sure fatality. No woman would
refuse to marry you; you'll surely find
a wiser girl to welcome you. But why 580
must I, who've sent so many to their deaths,
feel such distress for you? He can take care
of his own self. Then let him perish, too,
since, after all, the death of those who wooed
was not enough to warn him off; he must 585
be weary of this life. But that would mean
he died because he wished to live with me;
is that a just, a seemly penalty
to pay for having loved? My victory—
if I should win—is not a thing to envy. 590
Yet that is not my fault. Can't you renounce?
But if you're mad enough to try, I would
that you might be more swift than me. Yes, yes,
his gaze, his face have charm and tenderness.
Ah, poor Hippomenes, I would that you 595
had not set eyes on me. You were so worthy
of life. If I were just more fortunate,
if wretched fate had not forbidden me
to marry, you would be the only one
with whom I'd ever want to share my couch." 600
Such were her troubled words; a neophyte
whom Cupid now has touched for the first time,
indeed she loves—but knows not that she does.

" 'But now the people and her father—all
call for another trial—as usual. 605
Hippomenes, a son of Neptune's race,
prays urgently to me: "O Venus, may
I count upon your favor as I dare
to face this test; and may you treat with care
the love that she has stirred in me." His plea 610
was gentle, and it was a gentle breeze
that bore that prayer to me. And I confess,
it moved me—but so little time was left.

" 'There is a field the Cypriots have called
the field of Tamasus; within that isle 615

there is no place more fair. In ancient times
that field was set aside as sacred site:
a holy place they added to my shrines.
Within that field there grows a tree with leaves
of gold; its crackling branches also gleam   620
with tawny gold. And when his gentle plea
reached me, I was, by chance, returning from
that sacred site—my hands were carrying
three golden apples gathered from that tree.
Invisible to all but him, I drew   625
close to Hippomenes; I taught him how
to use the apples. Blaring trumpets now
announce the race's start: and from their crouch,
those two flash out; they skim the sandy course
with flying feet. Indeed, one might have thought   630
that she and he could even graze the sea
yet leave their feet still dry; or speed across
a field of standing grain and leave the stalks
untouched. Applause and shouts are loud; the crowd
cheers on Hippomenes, and some cry out: 635
"Go, go; this is the time to take the lead,
to give it all you have, Hippomenes!
Don't spare your speed! Don't slack—and you will win!"
It's hard to say if this applause brought more
delight to Megareus' heroic son   640
or Scheneus' virgin daughter. As they sped,
how many times did she, about to pass
Hippomenes, relent and gaze at length
upon his face until, at last, she raced
ahead—reluctantly? And now his throat   645
is weary: he is parched; he pants, and yet
the run is long, the goal is still far off.
And finally, he drops the first of those
three golden apples. Even as it rolls,
she is enchanted by the gleaming gold;   650
she veers off course to pick it up. The crowd
applauds Hippomenes, who takes the lead.
But she recoups her loss; a surge of speed—
once more the girl has gained the lead. And when
he throws the second apple, she retrieves   655
that apple, too, but passes him again.
The final stretch is all that's left. He pleads:
"O goddess, giver of this gift to me,
do stand beside me now." With all the force
of youth he throws the gleaming golden fruit—   660
obliquely, distantly—off course. The girl
seemed hesitant—uncertain of her choice:
to let it lie or pick it up. But I
compelled her: she went off; she picked it up.
So she lost time—and, too, the weight of three   665
gold apples hampered her. So that my story
not take much longer than that race, I say

she was outstripped; the winner led away
his prize, his wife.
          " 'But now, Adonis, I
must ask you this: did I not merit thanks   670
for all I did? Did I not earn sweet incense
to honor me? But he forgot completely:
I had no incense and no thanks from him.
At that offense, my wrath was spurred; and lest
in time to come I ever suffer such   675
a slight again, I saw that I would have
to make them serve as an example: I
incited my own self against that pair.
One day, they chanced to pass before the shrine
that, to fulfill a vow that he had pledged,   680
Echion built: a temple for Cybele,
the Mother of the gods, a shrine that stood
concealed within the shadows of deep woods.
The pair had journeyed long; they needed rest;
and I ignited him: Hippomenes—   685
such is my power as a deity—
was struck with an indecent, sudden need
for Atalanta's body. Near that shrine,
there was a cavelike cell where little light
could filter; it was vaulted by soft rock,   690
the pumice of that place—a sacred cave,
where men had venerated deities
for age on age, beyond all memory:
indeed a priest had set within that cell
the wooden statues of the ancient gods.   695
Hippomenes, on entering that cave,
was quick to desecrate the sacred place
with lust. The hallowed statues turned away
their eyes; the Mother goddess,[1] turret-crowned,
was set to plunge the obscene lovers down   700
into the waves of Styx. But then that seemed
too slight a penalty: instead, she wraps
their necks in tawny manes; their fingers take
the shape of cunning claws; their arms are changed
to legs; their weight moves forward to their chests;   705
and they grow tails that sweep along the ground;
their faces harden now; they speak in growls,
not words; the wild woods are their mating place.
As lions, they strike terror into all;
but they indeed are tame when, yoked, they draw   710
Cybele's chariot: they champ tight bits.

    " 'Avoid those beasts, dear boy, and any sort
of animal that will not turn its back
and flee from you but, ready to attack,

---

1. Cybele, a fertility goddess of Asia Minor known as the Great Mother. She was often pictured wearing a crown that resembled a city wall with towers, and flanked by lions or riding in a cart drawn by them.

stands firm, chest forward; no, I would not have 715
your daring damage you and ruin me.'

"So did the goddess warn Adonis; then
she yoked her swans, rode off across the air.
But daring is not keen to heed such warnings.
By chance, Adonis' hounds had caught a scent 720
that led them to a wild boar's hidden den;
the trail was sure. The boar was roused
out of the woods: Adonis' spearhead caught
the boar—a slanting thrust. With his curved snout,
the savage beast worked free—he had torn out 725
the spearhead stained with his own blood. The chase
is on: he charges at Adonis now.
The youth, in fear of his own life, runs hard,
but he is caught: the boar sinks his long tusks
into Adonis' groin; he fells him—and 730
the boy lies prone along the yellow sands.

"On her light chariot, Venus, who was drawn
across the middle air by her winged swans,
had not reached Cyprus yet; she heard, far off,
the dying boy—his moans. She turned around 735
her white swans and rode back. When, from the heights,
she saw him lifeless there, a bleeding corpse,
she leaped down to the ground. And Venus tore
her hair, and—much unlike a goddess[2]—beat
her hands against her breast. She challenged fate: 740
'But destiny does not rule all. Adonis,
your memory will live eternally:
each year they will repeat this final scene—
your day of death, my day of grief, will be
enacted in a feast that bears your name. 745

" 'I shall transform your blood into a flower.
If you, Proserpina, were once allowed
the metamorphosis of Mentha,[3] when
you changed that nymph into a fragrant plant—
the mint—can anyone begrudge me if 750
I change the form of Cinyras' dear son?'
That said, she sprinkled scented nectar on
his blood, which then fermented, even as
bright bubbles form when raindrops fall on mud.
One hour had yet to pass when, from that gore, 755
a bloodred flower sprang, the very color
of pomegranates when that fruit is ripe
and hides sweet seeds beneath its pliant rind.
And yet Adonis' blossoms have brief life:
his flower is light and delicate; it clings 760

2. Because these gestures are typical of women mourning the dead, as goddesses usually do not have to
do.   3. Hades' mistress, trampled by the jealous Proserpina and transformed into the mint (the meaning
of her name).

too loosely to the stem and thus is called
Anemone—'born of the wind'—because
winds shake its fragile petals, and they fall."

PETRONIUS
died A.D. 66

It is not certain that Titus Petronius (Arbiter) was the author of the *Satyricon*, but he is the best candidate. A friend of Nero's, he committed suicide at the imperial order after becoming involved in the Pisonian conspiracy against the emperor in A.D. 65. A brilliant account of Petronius's character and death is given by Tacitus in the *Annals* (book 16, chapters 18 and 19).

It is in the satiric masterpiece of this Roman aristocrat that the pragmatic, materialistic attitude Christianity was to supplant is most clearly displayed. It was probably written during the principate of Nero (A.D. 54–68), a period in which the material benefits and the spiritual weakness of the new order had already become apparent. The *Satyricon* itself has survived only in fragments; we know nothing certain about the scope of the work as a whole, but from the fragments it is clear that this book is the work of a satiric genius, perhaps the most original genius of Latin literature.

Dinner with Trimalchio, one of the longer fragments (printed here), shows us a tradesman's world. The narrator, a student of literature, and his cronies may have an aristocratic disdain for the businessmen at whose tables they eat, but they know that Trimalchio and his kind have inherited the Earth. Trimalchio began life as a foreign slave, but he is now a multimillionaire. The representative of culture, Agamemnon the teacher, drinks his wine and praises his fatuous remarks; he is content to be the court jester, the butt of Trimalchio's witticisms. Trimalchio knows no god but Mercury, the patron of business operations, but the gold bracelet, which represents a percentage of his income that he has dedicated to Mercury, he wears on his own arm rather than depositing it in a shrine of the god. He identifies himself with the god, and worships himself, the living embodiment of the power of money. The conversation at his table is a sardonic revelation of the temper of a whole civilization. Written in brilliantly humorous and colloquial style, it exposes mercilessly a blindness to spiritual values of any kind, a distrust of the intellect, and a ferocious preoccupation with the art of cheating one's neighbor. The point is made more effective by the conscious evocation of the epic tradition throughout the work: the names alone of the teacher, Agamemnon, and his assistant in instruction, Menelaus; the wall paintings that show "the *Iliad* and *Odyssey,* and the gladiatorial show given by Laenas"; Trimalchio's exhibition of monstrous ignorance of Homer (which nobody dares to correct); the Nestorian tone of Ganymedes, who regrets the old days when men were men (he is talking of the time when Safinius forced the bakers to lower the price of bread)—one touch after another reminds us that these figures are the final product of a tradition that began with Achilles and Odysseus.

The satire is witty, but it is nonetheless profound. Trimalchio and his friends all live for the moment, in material enjoyment, but they know that it cannot last. "Let us remember the living" is their watchword, but they cannot forget the dead. And as the banquet goes on, the thought of death, suppressed beneath the debased Epicureanism of Trimalchio and his associates, emerges slowly to the surface of their consciousness and comes to dominate it completely. The last arrival at the banquet is Habinnas the undertaker, and his coming coincides with the last stage of Trimalchio's drunkenness, the maudlin exhibition of his funeral clothes and the description of his tomb. "I want to die," says the Sibyl in the story Trimalchio tells early in the evening; at its end Trimalchio himself acts out his own funeral, complete with ointment, robes, wine, and trumpet players. The fact of death, the one fact that the practical materialism of Trimalchio and his circle can neither deny nor assimilate, asserts itself triumphantly as the supreme fact in the emptiness of Trimalchio's mind.

The introduction to *Petronius: The Satyricon* (1977), translated by J. P. Sullivan, will be helpful to the student, as will William Arrowsmith's introduction to his *The Satyricon of Petronius* (1959) and the introduction and notes to *Satyrica* (1996), translated by Bracht Branham and Daniel Kinney. J. P. Sullivan, *The 'Satyricon' of Petronius: A Literary Study* (1969), and Niall Slater, *Reading Petronius* (1990), are full-length critical discussions of the work.

PRONOUNCING GLOSSARY

The following list uses common English syllables and stress accents to provide rough equivalents of selected words whose pronunciation may be unfamiliar to the general reader.

Encolpius: *en-kol'-pi-us*   Scintilla: *sin-til'-lah*

Gaius: *gai'-us*   Trimalchio: *tri-mal'-ki-oh*

The Satyricon

[Dinner with Trimalchio[1]]

Summary   The narrator, Encolpius, is a penniless vagabond who is a student of rhetoric under a master named Agamemnon. His close associates are Ascyltus, a fellow student, and Giton, a handsome boy who has no particular occupation. After some disreputable and very tiring adventures they are invited, as pupils of Agamemnon, to a banquet. The scene of the story is an unidentified city in southern Italy, the time probably about A.D. 50.

The next day but one finally arrived. But we were so knocked about that we wanted to run rather than rest. We were mournfully discussing how to avoid the approaching storm,[2] when one of Agamemnon's slaves broke in on our frantic debate.

"Here," said he, "don't you know who's your host today? It's Trimalchio—he's terribly elegant. . . . He has a clock in the dining-room and a trumpeter[3] all dressed up to tell him how much longer he's got to live."

This made us forget all our troubles. We dressed carefully and told Giton, who was very kindly acting as our servant, to attend us at the baths.[4]

We did not take our clothes off but began wandering around, or rather exchanging jokes while circulating among the little groups. Suddenly we saw a bald old man in a reddish shirt, playing ball with some long-haired boys. It was not so much the boys that made us watch, although they alone were worth the trouble, but the old gentleman himself. He was taking his exercise in slippers and throwing a green ball around. But he didn't pick it up if it

---

1. Translated by J. P. Sullivan.   2. A repetition of the unsavory incidents they have just experienced.   3. To sound off every hour on the hour. A clock was a rare and expensive item. The name Trimalchio suggests "triply blessed" or "triply powerful."   4. A public institution; they were magnificent buildings, containing not only baths of many types and temperatures but places for conversation and games and even libraries.

touched the ground; instead there was a slave holding a bagful, and he supplied them to the players. We noticed other novelties. Two eunuchs stood around at different points: one of them carried a silver chamber pot, the other counted the balls, not those flying from hand to hand according to the rules, but those that fell to the ground. We were still admiring these elegant arrangements when Menelaus[5] hurried up to us.

"This is the man you'll be dining with," he said. "In fact, you are now watching the beginning of the dinner."

No sooner had Menelaus spoken than Trimalchio snapped his fingers. At the signal the eunuch brought up the chamber pot for him, while he went on playing. With the weight off his bladder, he demanded water for his hands, splashed a few drops on his fingers and wiped them on a boy's head.

It would take too long to pick out isolated incidents. Anyway, we entered the baths where we began sweating at once and we went immediately into the cold water. Trimalchio had been smothered in perfume and was already being rubbed down, not with linen towels, but with bath-robes of the finest wool. As this was going on, three masseurs sat drinking Falernian[6] in front of him. Through quarreling they spilled most of it and Trimalchio said they were drinking his health.[7] Wrapped in thick scarlet felt he was put into a litter. Four couriers with lots of medals went in front, as well as a go-cart in which his favourite boy was riding—a wizened, bleary-eyed youngster, uglier than his master. As he was carried off, a musician with a tiny set of pipes took his place by Trimalchio's head and whispered a tune in his ear the whole way.

We followed on, choking with amazement by now, and arrived at the door with Agamemnon at our side. On the doorpost a notice was fastened which read:

ANY SLAVE LEAVING THE HOUSE WITHOUT HIS MASTER'S
PERMISSION WILL RECEIVE ONE HUNDRED LASHES

Just at the entrance stood the hall-porter, dressed in a green uniform with a belt of cherry red. He was shelling peas into a silver basin. Over the doorway hung—of all things—a golden cage from which a spotted magpie greeted visitors.

As I was gaping at all this, I almost fell over backwards and broke a leg. There on the left as one entered, not far from the porter's cubbyhole, was a huge dog with a chain round its neck. It was painted on the wall and over it, in big capitals, was written:

BEWARE OF THE DOG

My colleagues laughed at me, but when I got my breath back I went to examine the whole wall. There was a mural of a slave market, price tags and all. Then Trimalchio himself, holding a wand of Mercury and being led into Rome by Minerva.[8] After this a picture of how he learned accounting and, finally how he became a steward. The painstaking artist had drawn it all in great detail with descriptions underneath. Just where the colonnade ended Mercury hauled him up by the chin and rushed him to a high platform. . . .

5. Appropriately enough, Agamemnon's assistant in instruction.   6. A famous wine from Campania, south of Rome.   7. He claims they are pouring a libation.   8. Patron goddess of arts and skills (Athena in Greek). Mercury (Hermes in Greek), as a trickster, is the patron god of thieves and business.

I began asking the porter what were the pictures they had in the middle. "The *Iliad*, and *Odyssey*, and the gladiatorial show given by Laenas," he told me.

Time did not allow us to look at many things there . . . by now we had reached the dining-room. . . .

Finally we took our places. Boys from Alexandria poured iced water over our hands. Others followed them and attended to our feet, removing any hangnails with great skill. But they were not quiet even during this troublesome operation: they sang away at their work. I wanted to find out if the whole staff were singers, so I asked for a drink. In a flash a boy was there, singing in a shrill voice while he attended to me—and anyone else who was asked to bring something did the same. It was more like a musical comedy than a respectable dinner party.

Some extremely elegant hors d'oeuvre were served at this point—by now everyone had taken his place with the exception of Trimalchio, for whom, strangely enough, the place at the top was reserved. The dishes for the first course included an ass of Corinthian bronze with two panniers, white olives on one side and black on the other. Over the ass were two pieces of plate, with Trimalchio's name and the weight of the silver inscribed on the rims. There were some small iron frames shaped like bridges supporting dormice sprinkled with honey and poppy seed. There were steaming hot sausages too, on a silver gridiron with damsons and pomegranate seeds underneath.

We were in the middle of these elegant dishes when Trimalchio himself was carried in to the sound of music and set down on a pile of tightly stuffed cushions. The sight of him drew an astonished laugh from the guests. His cropped head stuck out from a scarlet coat; his neck was well muffled up and he had put round it a napkin with a broad purple stripe and tassels dangling here and there. On the little finger of his left hand he wore a heavy gilt ring and a smaller one on the last joint of the next finger. This I thought was solid gold, but actually it was studded with little iron stars. And to show off even more of his jewellery, he had his right arm bare and set off by a gold armlet and an ivory circlet fastened with a gleaming metal plate.

After picking his teeth with a silver toothpick, he began: "My friends, I wasn't keen to come into the dining room yet. But if I stayed away any more, I would have kept you back, so I've deprived myself of all my little pleasures for you. However, you'll allow me to finish my game."

A boy was at his heels with a board of terebinth wood[9] with glass squares, and I noticed the very last word in luxury—instead of white and black pieces he had gold and silver coins. While he was swearing away like a trooper over his game and we were still on the hors d'oeuvre, a tray was brought in with a basket on it. There sat a wooden hen, its wings spread round it the way hens are when they are broody. Two slaves hurried up and as the orchestra played a tune they began searching through the straw and dug out peahens' eggs, which they distributed to the guests.

Trimalchio turned to look at this little scene and said: "My friends, I gave orders for that bird to sit on some peahens' eggs. I hope to goodness they are not starting to hatch. However, let's try them and see if they are still soft."

9. A very hard wood that takes a high polish and is very expensive (like everything Trimalchio has).

We took up our spoons (weighing at least half a pound each) and cracked the eggs, which were made of rich pastry. To tell the truth, I nearly threw away my share, as the chicken seemed already formed. But I heard a guest who was an old hand say: "There should be something good here." So I searched the shell with my fingers and found the plumpest little figpecker, all covered with yolk and seasoned with pepper.

At this point Trimalchio became tired of his game and demanded that all the previous dishes be brought to him. He gave permission in a loud voice for any of us to have another glass of mead if we wanted it. Suddenly there was a crash from the orchestra and a troop of waiters—still singing—snatched away the hors d'oeuvre. However in the confusion one of the side-dishes happened to fall and a slave picked it up from the floor. Trimalchio noticed this, had the boy's ears boxed and told him to throw it down again. A cleaner came in with a broom and began to sweep up the silver plate along with the rest of the rubbish. Two long-haired Ethiopians followed him, carrying small skin bottles like those they use for scattering sand in the circus, and they poured wine over our hands—no one ever offered us water.

Our host was complimented on these elegant arrangements. "You've got to fight fair," he replied. "That is why I gave orders for each guest to have his own table. At the same time these smelly slaves won't crowd so."

Carefully sealed wine bottles were immediately brought, their necks labelled:

FALERNIAN
CONSUL OPIMIUS[1]
ONE HUNDRED YEARS OLD

While we were examining the labels, Trimalchio clapped his hands and said with a sigh:

"Wine has a longer life than us poor folks. So let's wet our whistles. Wine is life. I'm giving you real Opimian. I didn't put out such good stuff yesterday, though the company was much better class."

Naturally we drank and missed no opportunity of admiring his elegant hospitality. In the middle of this a slave brought in a silver skeleton, put together in such a way that its joints and backbone could be pulled out and twisted in all directions. After he had flung it about on the table once or twice, its flexible joints falling into various postures, Trimalchio recited:

> "Man's life alas! is but a span,
> So let us live it while we can,
> We'll be like this when dead."

After our applause the next course was brought in. Actually it was not as grand as we expected, but it was so novel that everyone stared. It was a deep circular tray with the twelve signs of the Zodiac arranged round the edge. . . .

After this course Trimalchio got up and went to the toilet. Free of his domineering presence, we began to strike up a general conversation. Dama[2] started off by calling for bigger glasses.

---

1. The wine was labeled with the name of the man who was consul in the year it was bottled. Opimius was consul in 121 B.C.; because it was in this year that the custom of dating the wine by the consul's name began, Trimalchio's wine was the oldest possible. If genuine, it would have been undrinkable.   2. One of Trimalchio's friends. Like those of Seleucus and Phileros, who join the conversation later, his name is Greek.

"The day's nothin'," he said, "It's night 'fore y'can turn around. So the best thing's get out of bed and go straight to dinner. Lovely cold weather we've had too. M'bath hardly thawed me out. Still, a hot drink's as good as an overcoat. I've been throwin' it back neat, and I'm pretty tight—the wine's gone to m'head."

This started Seleucus off.

"Me now," he said, "I don't have a bath every day. It's like gettin' rubbed with fuller's earth,[3] havin' a bath. The water bites into you, and as the days go by, your heart turns to water. But when I've knocked back a hot glass of wine and honey, kiss-my-arse I say to the cold weather. Mind you, I couldn't have a bath—I was at a funeral today. Poor old Chrysanthus has just given up the ghost—nice man he was! It was only the other day he stopped me in the street. I still seem to hear his voice. Dear, dear! We're just so many walking bags of wind. We're worse than flies—at least flies have got some strength in them, but we're no more than empty bubbles.

"And what would he have been like if he hadn't been on a diet? For five days he didn't take a drop of water or a crumb of bread into his mouth. But he's gone to join the majority. The doctors finished him—well, hard luck, more like. After all, a doctor is just to put your mind at rest. Still, he got a good sendoff—he had a bier and all beautifully draped. His mourners—several of his slaves were left their freedom—did him proud, even though his widow was a bit mean with her tears. Suppose now he hadn't been so good to her! But women as a sex are real vultures. It's no good doing them a favour, you might as well throw it down a well. An old passion is just an ulcer."

He was being a bore and Phileros said loudly:

"Let's think of the living. He's got what he deserved. He lived an honest life and he died an honest death. What has he got to complain about? He started out in life with just a penny and he was ready to pick up less than that from a muck-heap, if he had to use his teeth. He went up in the world. He got bigger and bigger till he got where you see, like a honeycomb. I honestly think he left a solid hundred thousand and he had the lot in hard cash. But I'll be honest about it—seeing I'm a bit of a cynic—he had a foul mouth and too much lip. He wasn't a man, he was just murder.

"Now his brother was a fine man, a real friend to his friends, always ready with a helping hand or a decent meal.

"Chrysanthus had bad luck at first, but the first vintage set him on his feet. He fixed his own price when he sold the wine. And what properly kept his head above water was a legacy he came in for, when he pocketed more than was left to him. And the blockhead, when he had a quarrel with his brother, cut him out of his will in favour of some sod we've never heard of. You're leaving a lot behind when you leave your own flesh and blood. But he took advice from his slaves and they really fixed him. It's never right to believe all you're told, especially for a business man. But it's true he enjoyed himself while he lived. You got it, you keep it. He was certainly Fortune's favourite—lead turned to gold in his hand. Mind you, it's easy when everything runs smoothly.

"And how old do you think he was? Seventy or more! But he was hard as

---

3. A strong solvent used by cleaners.

nails and carried his age well. His hair was black as a raven's wing. I knew the man for ages and ages and he was still an old lecher. I honestly don't think he left the dog alone. What's more, he liked little boys—he could turn his hand to anything. Well, I don't blame him—after all, he couldn't take anything else with him."

This was Phileros, then Ganymedes said:

"You're all talking about things that don't concern heaven or earth. Meanwhile, no one gives a damn the way we're hit by the corn situation. Honest to God, I couldn't get hold of a mouthful of bread today. And look how there's still no rain. It's been absolute starvation for a whole year now. To hell with the food officers! They're in with the bakers—'You be nice to me and I'll be nice to you.' So the little man suffers, while those grinders of the poor never stop celebrating. Oh, if only we still had the sort of men I found here when I first arrived from Asia. Like lions they were. That was the life! Come one, come all! If white flour was inferior to the very finest, they'd thrash those bogeymen till they thought God Almighty was after them.

"I remember Safinius—he used to live by the old arch then; I was a boy at the time. He wasn't a man, he was all pepper. He used to scorch the ground wherever he went. But he was dead straight—don't let him down and he wouldn't let you down. You'd be ready to play *morra*[4] with him in the dark. But on the city council, how he used to wade into some of them—no beating about the bush, straight from the shoulder! And when he was in court, his voice got louder and louder like a trumpet. He never sweated or spat—I think there was a touch of the old acid about him. And very affable he was when you met him, calling everyone by name just like one of us. Naturally at the time corn was dirt cheap. You could buy a penny loaf that two of you couldn't get through. Today—I've seen bigger bull's-eyes.

"Ah me! It's getting worse every day. This place is going down like a calf's tail. But why do we have a third-rate food officer who wouldn't lose a penny to save our lives? He sits at home laughing and rakes in more money a day than anyone else's whole fortune. I happen to know he's just made a thousand in gold. But if we had any balls at all, he wouldn't be feeling so pleased with himself. People today are lions at home and foxes outside.

"Take me, I've already sold the rags off my back for food and if this shortage continues, I'll be selling my bit of a house. What's going to happen to this place if neither god nor man will help us? As I hope to go home tonight, I'm sure all this is heaven's doing.

"Nobody believes in heaven, see, nobody fasts, nobody gives a damn for the Almighty. No, people only bow their heads to count their money. In the old days high-class ladies used to climb up the hill barefoot, their hair loose and their hearts pure, and ask God for rain. And he'd send it down in bucketfuls right away—it was then or never—and everyone went home like drowned rats. Since we've given up religion the gods nowadays keep their feet well wrapped up. The fields just lie . . . ."

"Please, please," broke in Echion the rag merchant, "be a bit more cheerful. 'First it's one thing, then another,' as the yokel said when he lost his spotted pig. What we haven't got today, we'll have tomorrow. That's the way

---

4. A game (still played in southern Italy) that requires the players to match the number of fingers held out by the opponent.

life goes. Believe me, you couldn't name a better country, if it had the people. As things are, I admit, it's having a hard time, but it isn't the only place. We mustn't be soft. The sky don't get no nearer wherever you are. If you were somewhere else, you'd be talking about the pigs walking round ready roasted back here.

"And another thing, we'll be having a holiday with a three-day show that's the best ever—and not just a hack troupe of gladiators but freedmen for the most part. My old friend Titus has a big heart and a hot head. Maybe this, maybe that, but something at all events. I'm a close friend of his and he does nothing by halves. He'll give us cold steel, no quarter and the slaughterhouse right in the middle where all the stands can see it. And he's got the wherewithal—he was left thirty million when his poor father died. Even if he spent four hundred thousand, his pocket won't feel it and he'll go down in history. He's got some big brutes already, and a woman who fights in a chariot and Glyco's steward, who was caught having fun with his mistress. You'll see quite a quarrel in the crowd between jealous husbands and romantic lovers. But that half-pint Glyco threw his steward to the lions,[5] which is just giving himself away. How is it the servant's fault when he's forced into it? It's that old pisspot who really deserves to be tossed by a bull. But if you can't beat the ass you beat the saddle. But how did Glyco imagine the poisonous daughter of Hermogenes[6] would ever turn out well? The old man could cut the claws off a flying kite, and a snake don't hatch old rope. Glyco—well, Glyco's got his. He's branded for as long as he lives and only the grave will get rid of it. But everyone pays for their mistakes.

"But I can almost smell the dinner Mammaea is going to give us[7]—two denarii apiece for me and the family. If he really does it, he'll make off with all Norbanus's votes, I tell you he'll win at a canter. After all, what good has Nobanus done us? He put on some half-pint gladiators, so done in already that they'd have dropped if you blew at them. I've seen animal-killers[8] fight better. As for the horsemen killed, he got them off a lamp[9]—they ran round like cocks in a backyard. One was just a carthorse, the other couldn't stand up, and the reserve was just one corpse instead of another—he was practically hamstrung. One boy did have a bit of spirit—he was in Thracian armour,[1] and even he didn't show any initiative. In fact, they were all flogged afterwards, there were so many shouts of 'Give 'em what for!' from the crowd. Pure yellow, that's all. " 'Well, I've put on a show for you,' he says. 'And I'm clapping you,' says I. 'Reckon it up—I'm giving more than I got. So we're quits.'

"Hey, Agamemnon! I suppose you're saying 'What is that bore going on and on about?' It's because a good talker like you don't talk. You're a cut above us, and so you laugh at what us poor people say. We all know you're off your head with all that reading. But never mind! Some day I'll get you to come down to my place in the country and have a look at our little cottage. We'll find something to eat—a chicken, some eggs. It'll be nice, even though the unreliable weather this year has made off with everything. Anyway, we'll find enough to fill our bellies.

5. Glyco was permitted by law to punish his slave by forcing him to fight wild beasts in the arena. 6. Presumably Glyco's father-in-law. 7. A public banquet given by Mammaea as part of his electoral campaign. His rival, Norbanus, has been giving gladiatorial shows. 8. Professional fighters of wild animals, considered inferior to gladiators. 9. I.e., they were as small as the horsemen depicted on a lamp. 1. Light armor, such as that worn by soldiers from Thrace, a savage country northeast of Greece.

"And my kid is growing up to be a pupil of yours. He can divide by four already. If God spares him, you'll have him ready to do anything for you. In his spare time, he won't take his head out of his exercise book. He's clever and there's good stuff in him, even if he is crazy about birds. Only yesterday I killed his three goldfinches and told him a weasel ate them. But he's found some other silly hobbies, and he's having a fine time painting. Still, he's already well ahead with his Greek, and he's starting to take to his Latin, though his tutor is too pleased with himself and unreliable—he just comes and goes. He knows his stuff but doesn't want to work. There is another one as well, not so clever but he is conscientious—he teaches the boy more than he knows himself. In fact, he makes a habit of coming around on holidays, and whatever you give him, he's happy.

"Anyway, I've just bought the boy some law books, as I want him to pick up some legal training for home use. There's a living in that sort of thing. He's done enough dabbling in poetry and such like. If he objects, I've decided he'll learn a trade—barber, auctioneer, or at least a barrister—something he can't lose till he dies. Well, yesterday I gave it to him straight: 'Believe me, my lad, any studying you do will be for your own good. You see Phileros the solicitor—if he hadn't studied, he'd be starving today. It's not so long since he was humping round loads on his back. Now he can even look Norbanus in the face. An education is an investment, and a proper profession never goes dead on you.'"

This was the sort of conversation flying round when Trimalchio came in, dabbed his forehead and washed his hands in perfume. There was a short pause, then he said:

"Excuse me, dear people, my inside has not been answering the call for several days now. The doctors are puzzled. But some pomegranate rind and resin in vinegar has done me good. But I hope now it will be back on its good behaviour. Otherwise my stomach rumbles like a bull. So if any of you wants to go out, there's no need for him to be embarrassed. None of us was born solid. I think there's nothing so tormenting as holding yourself in. This is the one thing even God Almighty can't object to. Yes, laugh, Fortunata,[2] but you generally keep me up all night with this sort of thing.

"Anyway, I don't object to people doing what suits them even in the middle of dinner—and the doctors forbid you to hold yourself in. Even if it's a longer business, everything is there just outside—water, bowls, and all the other little comforts. Believe me, if the wind goes to your brain it starts flooding your whole body too. I've known a lot of people die from this because they wouldn't be honest with themselves."

We thanked him for being so generous and considerate and promptly proceeded to bury our amusement in our glasses. Up to this point we'd not realized we were only in mid-stream, as you might say.

The orchestra played, the tables were cleared, and then three white pigs were brought into the dining-room, all decked out in muzzles and bells. The first, the master of ceremonies announced, was two years old, the second three, and the third six. I was under the impression that some acrobats were on their way in and the pigs were going to do some tricks, the way they do in street shows. But Trimalchio dispelled this impression by asking:

"Which of these would you like for the next course? Any clodhopper can

2. Trimalchio's wife.

do you a barnyard cock or a stew and trifles like that, but my cooks are used to boiling whole calves."

He immediately sent for the chef and without waiting for us to choose he told him to kill the oldest pig.

He then said to the man in a loud voice:

"Which division are you from?"

When he replied he was from number forty, Trimalchio asked:

"Were you bought or were you born here?"

"Neither," said the chef, "I was left to you in Pansa's will."

"Well, then," said Trimalchio, "see you serve it up carefully—otherwise I'll have you thrown into the messenger's division."

So the chef, duly reminded of his master's magnificence, went back to his kitchen, the next course leading the way.

Trimalchio looked around at us with a gentle smile: "If you don't like the wine, I'll have it changed. It is up to you to do it justice. I don't buy it, thank heaven. In fact, whatever wine really tickles your palate this evening, it comes from an estate of mine which as yet I haven't seen. It's said to join my estates at Tarracina and Tarentum. What I'd like to do now is add Sicily to my little bit of land, so that when I want to go to Africa, I could sail there without leaving my own property.

"But tell me, Agamemnon, what was your debate about today? Even though I don't go in for the law, still I've picked up enough education for home consumption. And don't you think I turn my nose up at studying, because I have two libraries, one Greek, one Latin. So tell us, just as a favour, what was the topic of your debate?"

Agamemnon was just beginning, "A poor man and a rich man were enemies . . ." when Trimalchio said: "What's a poor man?" "Oh, witty!" said Agamemnon, and then told us about some fictitious case or other. Like lightning Trimalchio said: "If this happened, it's not a fictitious case—if it didn't happen, then it's nothing at all."

We greeted this witticism and several more like it with the greatest enthusiasm.

"Tell me, my dear Agamemnon," continued Trimalchio, "do you remember the twelve labours of Hercules and the story of Ulysses—how the Cyclops tore out his thumb with a pair of pincers.[3] I used to read about them in Homer, when I was a boy. In fact, I actually saw the Sibyl at Cumae with my own eyes dangling in a bottle, and when the children asked her in Greek: 'What do you want, Sybil?' she used to answer: 'I want to die.' "

Summary   Presents for the guests are distributed, with a slave announcing the nature of each gift and making in each case an atrocious pun on the name of the guest.

We laughed for ages. There were hundreds of things like this but they've slipped my mind now.

Ascyltus, with his usual lack of restraint, found everything extremely funny, lifting up his hands and laughing till the tears came. Eventually one

3. Trimalchio refers to Ulysses' (Odysseus's) adventures in the cave of the Cyclops (*Odyssey* 9); despite what he goes on to say, he has obviously not read Homer.

of Trimalchio's freedman[4] friends flared up at him—the one sitting above me, in fact.

"You with the sheep's eyes," he said, "what's so funny? Isn't our host elegant enough for you? You're better off, I suppose, and used to a bigger dinner. Holy guardian here preserve me! If I was sitting by him, I'd make him bleat! A fine pippin he is to be laughing at other people! Some fly-by-night from god knows where—not worth his own piss. In fact, if I pissed round him, he wouldn't know where to turn.

"By god, it takes a lot to make me boil, but if you're too soft, worms like this only come to the top. Look at him laughing! What's he got to laugh at? Did his father pay cash for him? You're a Roman knight,[5] are you? Well, my father was a king.

" 'Why are you only a freedman?' did you say? Because I went into service voluntarily. I wanted to be a Roman citizen, not a subject with taxes to pay. And today, I hope no one can laugh at the way I live. I'm a man among men, and I walk with my head up. I don't owe anybody a penny—there's never been a court-order out for me. No one's said 'Pay up!' to me in the street.

"I've bought a bit of land and some tiny pieces of plate. I've twenty bellies to feed, as well as a dog. I bought my old woman's freedom so nobody could wipe his dirty hands on her hair. Four thousand I paid for myself. I was elected to the Augustan College[6] and it cost me nothing. I hope when I die I won't have to blush in my coffin.

"But you now, you're such a busybody you don't look behind you. You see a louse on somebody else, but not the fleas on your own back. You're the only one who finds us funny. Look at the professor now—he's an older man than you and we get along with him. But you're still wet from your mother's milk and not up to your ABC yet. Just a crackpot—you're like a piece of wash-leather in soak, softer but no better! You're grander than us—well, have two dinners and two suppers! I'd rather have my good name than any amount of money. When all's said and done, who's ever asked me for money twice? For forty years I slaved but nobody ever knew if I was a slave or a free man. I came to this colony when I was a lad with long hair—the town-hall hadn't been built then. But I worked hard to please my master—there was a real gentleman, with more in his little finger-nail than there is in your whole body. And I had people in the house who tried to trip me up one way or another, but still—thanks be to his guardian spirit!—I kept my head above water. That's real success: being born free is as easy as all get-out. Now what are you gawping at, like a goat in a vetch field?"

At this remark, Giton, who was waiting on me, could not suppress his laughter and let out a filthy guffaw, which did not pass unnoticed by Ascyltus's opponent. He turned his abuse on the boy.

"So!" he said, "you're amused too, are you, you curly-headed onion? A merry Saturnalia[7] to you! Is it December, I'd like to know? When did you pay your liberation tax?[8] Look, he doesn't know what to do, the gallow's bird, the crow's meat.

---

4. A former slave who had bought his freedom.   5. A Roman class including all who had property above a certain amount.   6. The state religion was the worship of Augustus, the emperor; the office of priest might be sold or conferred.   7. A December festival in honor of an ancient Italian deity at which the normal order of everyday life was reversed and the slaves and children made fun of their masters.   8. As a freed slave he had to pay 5 percent of his value to the treasury.

"God's curse on you, and your master too, for not keeping you under control! As sure as I get my bellyful, it's only because of Trimalchio that I don't take it out of you here and now. He's a freedman like myself. We're doing all right, but those good-for-nothings, well—. It's easy to see, like master, like man. I can hardly hold myself back, and I'm not naturally hot-headed— but once I start, I don't give a penny for my own mother.

"All right! I'll see you when we get outside, you rat, you excrescence. I'll knock your master in the dirt before I'm an inch taller or shorter. And I won't let you off either, by heaven, even if you scream down God Almighty. Your cheap curls and your no-good master won't be much use to you then—I'll see to that. I'll get my teeth into you, all right. Either I'm much mistaken about myself or you won't be laughing at us behind your golden beard. Athena's curse on you and the man who first made you such a forward brat.

"I didn't learn no geometry or criticism and such silly rubbish, but I can read the letters on a notice board and I can do my percentages in metal, weights, and money. In fact, if you like, we'll have a bet. Come on, here's my cash. Now you'll see how your father wasted his money, even though you do know how to make a speech.

"Try this:

> Something we all have.
> Long I come, broad I come. What am I?

"I'll give you it: something we all have that runs and doesn't move from its place: something we all have that grows and gets smaller.[9]

"You're running round in circles, you've had enough, like the mouse in the pisspot. So either keep quiet or keep out of the way of your betters, they don't even know you're alive—unless you think I care about your box-wood rings that you swiped from your girl friend! Lord make me lucky! Let's go into town and borrow some money. You'll soon see they trust this iron one.

"Pah! a drownded fox makes a nice sight, I must say. As I hope to make my pile and die so famous that people swear by my dead body, I'll hound you to death. And he's a nice thing too—the one who taught you all these tricks— a muttonhead, not a master. We learned different. Our teacher used to say: 'Are your things in order? Go straight home. No looking around. And be polite to your elders.' Nowadays it's all an absolute muck-heap. They turn out nobody worth a penny. I'm like you see me and I thank God for the way I was learnt.'' . . .

In the middle of all this, a lictor[1] knocked at the double doors and a drunken guest entered wearing white, followed by a large crowd of people. I was terrified by this lordly apparition and thought it was the chief magistrate arriving. So I tried to rise and get my bare feet on the floor. Agamemnon laughed at this panic and said:

"Get hold of yourself, you silly fool. This is Habinnas—Augustan College and monumental mason."

Relieved by this information I resumed my position and watched Habinnas' entry with huge admiration. Being already drunk, he had his hands on

---

9. There is no agreement about the correct answer to these riddles. Suggested answers are, to the first, the foot; the second, the eye; the third, hair.   1. A magistrate's attendant.

his wife's shoulders; loaded with several garlands, oil pouring down his forehead and into his eyes, he settled himself into the place of honour and immediately demanded some wine and hot water. Trimalchio, delighted by these high spirits, demanded a larger cup for himself and asked how he had enjoyed it all.

"The only thing we missed," replied Habinnas, "was yourself—the apple of my eye was here. Still, it was damn good. Scissa was giving a ninth-day dinner[2] in honour of a poor slave of hers she'd freed on his death-bed. And I think she'll have a pretty penny to pay in liberation tax because they reckon he was worth fifty thousand. Still, it was pleasant enough, even if we did have to pour half our drinks over his wretched bones."

"Well," said Trimalchio, "what did you have for dinner?"

"I'll tell you if I can—I've such a good memory that I often forget my own name. For the first course we had a pig crowned with sausages and served with blood-puddings and very nicely done giblets, and of course beetroot and pure wholemeal bread—which I prefer to white myself: it's very strengthening and I don't regret it when I do my business. The next course was cold tart and a concoction of first-class Spanish wine poured over hot honey. I didn't eat anything at all of the actual tart, but I dived right into the honey. Scattered round were chickpeas, lupines, a choice of nuts and an apple apiece—though I took two. And look, I've got them tied up in a napkin, because if I don't take something in the way of a present to my youngster, I'll have a row on my hands.

"Oh, yes, my good lady reminds me. We had a hunk of bearmeat set before us, which Scintilla was foolish enough to try, and she practically spewed up her guts; but I ate more than a pound of it, as it tasted like real wild-boar. And I say if bears can eat us poor people, it's all the more reason why us poor people should eat bears.

"To finish up with, we had some cheese basted with new wine, snails all round, chitterlings, plates of liver, eggs in pastry hoods, turnips, mustard, and some filthy concoction—good riddance to that. There were pickled cumin seeds too, passed round in a bowl and some people were that bad-mannered they took three handfuls. You see, we sent the ham away.

"But tell me something, Gaius, now I ask—why isn't Fortunata at the table?"

"You know her," replied Trimalchio, "unless she's put the silver away and shared out the left-overs among the slaves, she won't put a drop of water to her mouth."

"All the same," retorted Habinnas, "unless she sits down, I'm shagging off."

And he was starting to get up, when at a given signal all the servants shouted "Fortunata" four or five times. So in she came with her skirt tucked up under a yellow sash to show her cerise petticoat underneath, as well as her twisted anklets and gold-embroidered slippers. Wiping her hands on a handkerchief which she carried round her neck, she took her place on the couch where Habbinas' wife was reclining. She kissed her. "Is it really you?" she said, clapping her hands together.

It soon got to the point where Fortunata took the bracelets from her great

---

2. On the last day of the mourning period.

fat arms and showed them to the admiring Scintilla. In the end she even undid her anklets and her gold hair net, which she said was pure gold. Trimalchio noticed this and had it all brought to him and commented:

"A woman's chains, you see. This is the way us poor fools get robbed. She must have six and a half pounds on her. Still, I've got a bracelet myself, made up from one-tenth per cent to Mercury[3]—and it weighs not an ounce less than ten pounds."

Finally, for fear he looked like a liar, he even had some scales brought in and had them passed round to test the weight.

Scintilla was no better. From round her neck she took a little gold locket, which she called her "lucky box." From it she extracted two earrings and in her turn gave them to Fortunata to look at.

"A present from my good husband," she said, "and no one has a finer set."

"Hey!" said Habinnas, "you cleaned me out to buy you a glass bean. Honestly, if I had a daughter, I'd cut her little ears off. If there weren't any women, everything would be dirt cheap. As it is, we've got to drink cold water and piss it out hot."

Meanwhile, the women giggled tipsily between themselves and kissed each other drunkenly, one crying up her merits as a housewife, the other crying about her husband's demerits and boy friends. While they had their heads together like this, Habinnas rose stealthily and taking Fortunata's feet, flung them up over the couch.

"Oh, oh!" she shrieked, as her underskirt wandered up over her knees. So she settled herself in Scintilla's lap and hid her disgusting red face in her handkerchief.

Then came an interval, after which Trimalchio called for dessert. . . .

Fortunata was now wanting to dance, and Scintilla was doing more clapping than talking, when Trimalchio said:

"Philargyrus—even though you are such a terrible fan of the Greens[4]— you have my permission to join us. And tell your dear Menophila to sit down as well."

Need I say more? We were almost thrown out of our places, so completely did the household fill the dining-room. I even noticed that the chef was actually given a place above me, and he was reeking of pickles and sauce. And he wasn't satisfied with just having a place, but he had to start straight off on an imitation of the tragedian Ephesus, and then challenge his master to bet against the Greens winning at the next races.

Trimalchio became expansive after this argument.

"My dear people," he said, "slaves are human beings too. They drink the same milk as anybody else, even though luck's been agin 'em. Still, if nothing happens to me, they'll have their taste of freedom soon. In fact, I'm setting them all free in my will. I'm giving Philargyrus a farm, what's more, and the woman he lives with. As for Cario, I'm leaving him a block of flats, his five per cent manumission tax, and a bed with all the trimmings. I'm making Fortunata my heir, and I want all my friends to look after her.

"The reason I'm telling everyone all this is so my household will love me now as much as if I was dead."

---

3. Trimalchio sets aside a percentage of his profits to offer to his patron deity. 4. One of the teams in the chariot races.

Everyone began thanking his lordship for his kindness, when he became very serious and had a copy of his will brought in. Amid the sobs of his household he read out the whole thing from beginning to end.

Then looking at Habinnas, he said:

"What have you to say, my dear old friend? Are you building my monument the way I told you? I particularly want you to keep a place at the foot of my statue and put a picture of my pup there, as well as paintings of wreaths, scent-bottles, and all the contests of Petraites,[5] and thanks to you I'll be able to live on after I'm dead. And another thing! See that it's a hundred feet facing the road and two hundred back into the field. I want all the various sorts of fruit round my ashes and lots and lots of vines. After all, it's a big mistake to have nice houses just for when you're alive and not worry about the one we have to live in for much longer. And that's why I want this written up before anything else:

THIS MONUMENT DOES NOT GO TO THE HEIR

"But I'll make sure in my will that I don't get done down once I'm dead. I'll put one of my freedmen in charge of my tomb to look after it and not let people run up and shit on my monument. I'd like you to put some ships there too, sailing under full canvas, and me sitting on a high platform in my robes of office, wearing five gold rings and pouring out a bagful of money for the people. You know I gave them all a dinner and two denarii apiece. Let's have in a banqueting hall as well, if you think it's a good idea, and show the whole town having a good time. Put up a statue of Fortunata on my right, holding a dove, and have her leading her little dog tied to her belt—and this dear little chap as well, and great big wine jars sealed up so the wine won't spill. And perhaps you could carve me a broken wine jar and boy crying over it. A clock in the middle, so that anybody who looks at the time, like it or not, has got to read my name. As for the inscription now, take a good look and see if this seems suitable enough:

HERE SLEEPS
GAIUS POMPEIUS TRIMALCHIO
MAECENATIANUS
ELECTED TO THE AUGUSTAN COLLEGE IN HIS ABSENCE
HE COULD HAVE BEEN ON EVERY BOARD IN ROME
BUT HE REFUSED
GOD-FEARING BRAVE AND TRUE
A SELF-MADE MAN
HE LEFT AN ESTATE OF 30,000,000
AND HE NEVER HEARD A PHILOSOPHER
FAREWELL
AND YOU FARE WELL, TRIMALCHIO."

Summary   After a visit to the baths, where Encolpius and his friends make an unsuccessful attempt to escape, the dinner is resumed.

After this dish Trimalchio looked at the servants and said:

"Why haven't you had dinner yet? Off you go and let some others come on duty."

5. A popular gladiator.

Up came another squad and as the first set called out: "Good night, Gaius!" the new arrivals shouted: "Good evening, Gaius!"

This led to the first incident that damped the general high spirits. Not a bad-looking boy entered with the newcomers and Trimalchio jumped at him and began kissing him at some length. Fortunata, asserting her just and legal rights, began hurling insults at Trimalchio, calling him a low scum and a disgrace, who couldn't control his beastly desires. "You dirty dog!' she finally added.

Trimalchio took offence at this abuse and flung his glass into Fortunata's face. She screamed as though she'd lost an eye and put her trembling hands across her face. Scintilla was terrified too and hugged the quaking woman to her breast. An obliging slave pressed a little jug of cold water to her cheek, while Fortunata rested her head on it and began weeping. Trimalchio just said:

"Well, well, forgotten her chorus days, has she? She doesn't remember, but she was bought and sold, and I took her away from it all and made her as good as the next. Yet she puffs herself up like a frog and doesn't even spit for luck. Just a great hunk, not a woman. But those as are born over a shop don't dream of a house. May I never have a day's good luck again, if I don't teach that Cassandra in clogs some manners!

"There was I, not worth twopence, and I could have had ten million. And you know I'm not lying about it. Agatho, who ran a perfume shop for the lady next door, he took me on one side and said: 'You don't want to let your family die out, you know!' But me, trying to do the right thing and not wanting to look changeable, I cut my own throat.

"All right! I'll make you want to dig me up with your bare nails. Just so you'll know on the spot what you've done for yourself—Habinnas! I don't want you to put her statue on my tomb, so at least when I'm dead I won't have any more squabbles. And another thing! just to show I can get my own back—when I'm dead I don't want her to kiss me."

After this thunderbolt, Habinnas began asking him to calm down: "None of us are without faults," he said, "we're not gods, we're human!" Scintilla said the same, calling him Gaius, and she began asking him, in the name of his guardian spirit, to give in.

Trimalchio held back his tears no longer. "I ask you, Habinnas," he said, "as you hope to enjoy your bit of savings—if I did anything wrong, spit in my face. I kissed this very careful little fellow, not for his pretty face, but because he's careful with money—he says his ten times table, he reads a book at sight, he's got himself some Thracian kit out of his daily allowance, and he's bought himself an easy chair and two cups out of his own pocket. Doesn't he deserve to be the apple of my eye? But Fortunata won't have it.

"Is that the way you feel, high heels? I'll give you a piece of advice: don't let your good luck turn your head, you kite, and don't make me show my teeth, my little darling—otherwise you'll feel my temper. You know me: once I've decided on something, it's fixed with a twelve-inch nail.

"But to come back to earth—I want you to enjoy yourselves, my dear people. After all, I was once like you are, but being the right sort, I got where I am. It's the old headpiece that makes a man, the rest is all rubbish. 'Buy right—sell right!'—that's me! Different people will give you a different line. I'm just on top of the world, I'm that lucky.

"But you, you snoring thing, are you still moaning? I'll give you something to moan about in a minute.

"However, as I'd started to say, it was my shrewd way with money that got me to my present position. I came from Asia as big as this candlestick. In fact, every day I used to measure myself against it, and to get some whiskers round my beak quicker, I used to oil my lips from the lamp. Still, for fourteen years I was the old boy's fancy. And there's nothing wrong if the boss wants it. But I did all right by the old girl too. You know what I mean—I don't say anything because I'm not the boasting sort.

"Well, as heaven will have it, I became boss in the house, and the old boy, you see, couldn't think of anything but me. That's about it—he made me co-heir with the Emperor[6] and I got a senator's fortune. But nobody gets enough, never. I wanted to go into business. Not to make a long story of it, I built five ships, I loaded them with wine—it was absolute gold at the time—and I sent them to Rome. You'd have thought I ordered it—every single ship was wrecked. That's fact, not fable! In one single day Neptune swallowed up thirty million. Do you think I gave up? This loss honestly wasn't more than a flea-bite to me—it was as if nothing had happened. I built more boats, bigger and better and luckier, so nobody could say I wasn't a man of courage. You know, the greater the ship, the greater the confidence. I loaded them again—with wine, bacon, beans, perfumes and slaves. At this point Fortunata did the decent thing, because she sold off all her gold trinkets, all her clothes, and put ten thousand in gold pieces in my hand. This was the yeast my fortune needed to rise. What heaven wants, soon happens. In one voyage I carved out a round ten million. I immediately bought back all my old master's estates. I built a house, I invested in slaves, and I bought up the horse trade. Whatever I touched grew like a honeycomb. Once I had more than the whole country, then down tools! I retired from business and began advancing loans through freedmen.

"Actually I was tired of trading on my own account, but it was an astrologer who convinced me. He happened to come to our colony, a sort of Greek, Serapa by name, and he could have told heaven itself what to do. He even told me things I'd forgotten. He went through everything for me from A to Z. He knew me inside out—the only thing he didn't tell me was what I ate for dinner the day before. You'd have thought he'd never left my side.

"Wasn't there that thing, Habinnas?—I think you were there: 'You got your lady wife out of those *certain circumstances*. You are not lucky in your friends. Nobody thanks you enough for your trouble. You have large estates. You are nursing a viper in your bosom.'

"And he said—though I shouldn't tell you—I have thirty years, four months, two days to live. What's more, I shall soon receive a legacy. My horoscope tells me this. If I'm allowed to join my estates to Apulia,[7] I'll have lived enough.

"Meantime, under the protection of Mercury, I built this house. As you know, it was still a shack, now it's a shrine. It has four dining-rooms, twenty bedrooms, two marble colonnades, a row of boxrooms up above, a bedroom

---

6. An honor that Trimalchio shared with many others, for it was customary (as a prudent measure, to avoid confiscation on some pretext or other) to include a bequest to the emperor in one's will.   7. The southeastern extremity of Italy.

porter. The guest apartment takes a hundred guests. In fact, when Scaurus[8] came here, he didn't want to stay anywhere else, even though he's got his father's guest house down by the sea. And there are a lot of other things I'll show you in a second.

"Believe me: have a penny, and you're worth a penny. You got something, you'll be thought something. Like your old friend—first a frog, now a king.

"Meantime, Stichus, bring out the shroud and the things I want to be buried in. Bring some cosmetic cream too, and a sample from that jar of wine I want my bones washed in."

Stichus did not delay over it, but brought his white shroud and his formal dress into the dining-room. . . . Trimalchio told us to examine them and see if they were made of good wool. Then he said with a smile:

"Now you, Stichus, see no mice or moths get at those—otherwise I'll burn you alive. I want to be buried in style, so the whole town will pray for my rest.'

He opened a bottle of nard on the spot, rubbed some on all of us and said: "I hope this'll be as nice when I'm dead as when I'm alive.' The wine he had poured into a big decanter and he said:

"I want you to think you've been invited to my wake."

The thing was becoming absolutely sickening, when Trimalchio, showing the effects of his disgusting drunkenness, had a fresh entertainment brought into the dining-room, some cornet players. Propped up on a lot of cushions, he stretched out along the edge of the couch and said: "Pretend I'm dead and say something nice."

The cornet players struck up a dead march. One man in particular, the slave of his undertaker (who was the most respectable person present) blew so loudly that he roused the neighbourhood. As a result, the fire brigade, thinking Trimalchio's house was on fire, suddenly broke down the front door and began kicking up their own sort of din with their water and axes.

Seizing this perfect chance, we gave Agamemnon the slip and escaped as rapidly as if there really were a fire.

THE BIBLE: THE NEW TESTAMENT
ca. first century

When Jesus was born in the Roman province of Judea, there were four languages spoken in the area, a consequence of its complicated history. Classical Hebrew, the language of the sacred books of the Jews, was understood by educated people, especially the priestly caste, but the general population spoke Aramaic. This was a Semitic language close to classical Hebrew—the relationship has been compared with that between Portuguese and Spanish—but different enough to necessitate an Aramaic paraphrase of the sacred texts for use in the synagogue. Aramaic was the language in which Jesus preached to crowds and conversed with his disciples; the last words he

---

8. Unidentified. The name is aristocratic, but it may be a reference to a well-known manufacturer of fish sauce from Pompeii.

spoke in agony on the cross were Aramaic: *Eli, eli, lama sabachthani?* ("My God, my God, why hast thou forsaken me?").

But Judea, like all of the territory conquered by Alexander the Great, had come under Macedonian-Greek rule by the beginning of the second century B.C., and many Jews, especially those of the upper and educated classes, had learned Greek, an entry to the new administrative, commercial, and cultural milieux of the Hellenistic empires. Finally, in the last half of the first century B.C. Judea became a Roman province, and Latin (the language of the Roman governor and the military establishment) became the language of government. Most cultured Romans, however, knew Greek, and Greek remained the lingua franca of the educated classes all over the huge territory now called the Middle East.

If the disciples of Jesus were to obey his command—"Go into all the world and preach the good news to all creation"—they would have to use Greek outside the Aramaic-speaking world. And it is in Greek that the four Gospels (the word is an Old English translation of the Greek for "good news") were written, probably some forty to sixty years after Jesus' death. They must have been based on the oral teaching of the original disciples, and the first three (selections from which are printed here) were clearly designed with an eye to different readerships. The Gospel according to Matthew, for example, has a Jewish public in mind; one of its main concerns is to convince its readers not only that Jesus was the legitimate heir to the throne of the royal house of David but also that Jesus was the king, the Messiah, announced by the Hebrew prophets. Mark, on the other hand, is clearly written with a Gentile audience in mind and pays particular attention to the needs of the Roman reader, translating Aramaic words and even explaining that the courtyard into which the Roman soldiers took Jesus after he was condemned was the place the Romans called the *praetorium*. And the Gospel according to Luke is obviously addressed to cultured Greek readers; it makes very few references to the Hebrew prophecies and is in fact dedicated to a Greek called Theophilos.

These three Gospels contain a central core of identical material that must come from an earlier source now lost (it is known as the Q document). The fourth Gospel, that of John, draws on different sources and also has greater theological density than the other three. The collection known to Christians as the New Testament was formed by combining the four Gospels with another book by Luke, The Acts of the Apostles, which is an account of Paul's missionary journeys to the cities of Greece and Asia Minor. Added to this were letters of Paul and others to the Christian communities in such cities as Corinth, Thessalonica, and Rome and the book called Revelation, a vision of the end of the world and the second coming of Jesus.

There were, of course, many other documents that gave accounts of the life and teaching of Jesus, but this particular collection contained those judged most reliable by the Church authorities and was declared canonical some time in the third century. Latin translations of the Greek texts were made for the use of the Churches of the Western Roman Empire, but there was no official version until in 382 Pope Damasus commissioned a scholar called Jerome to produce a correct translation. It soon became known as the Vulgate—the "common" or "popular" version. This was the text used and quoted by Augustine, and with some revisions over the centuries, the one that remained in use in the Christian churches of the west through the Middle Ages.

Recommended reading is Bruce M. Metzger, *The New Testament, Its Background, Growth, and Content* (1965), and the relevant chapters in Robert Alter and Frank Kermode, eds., *The Literary Guide to the Bible* (1987). For a translation in modern English, with commentary, see *The New Oxford Annotated Bible* (1975), edited by Herbert E. May and Bruce Metzger.

THE BIBLE: THE NEW TESTAMENT[1]

Luke 2

[The Birth and Youth of Jesus]

2. And it came to pass in those days, that there went out a decree from Cæsar Augustus, that all the world[2] should be taxed. (And this taxing was first made when Cyrenius was governor of Syria.) And all went to be taxed, every one unto his own city. And Joseph also went up from Galilee, out of the city of Nazareth, into Judæa, unto the city of David, which is called Bethlehem; (because he was of the house and lineage of David:) to be taxed with Mary his espoused wife, being great with child. And so it was, that, while they were there, the days were accomplished that she should be delivered. And she brought forth her firstborn son, and wrapped him in swaddling clothes, and laid him in a manger; because there was no room for them in the inn. And there were in the same country shepherds abiding in the field, keeping watch over their flock by night. And, lo, the angel of the Lord came upon them, and the glory of the Lord shone round about them: and they were sore afraid. And the angel said unto them, Fear not: for, behold, I bring you good tidings of great joy, which shall be to all people. For unto you is born this day in the city of David a Saviour, which is Christ[3] the Lord. And this shall be a sign unto you; ye shall find the babe wrapped in swaddling clothes, lying in a manger. And suddenly there was with the angel a multitude of the heavenly host praising God, and saying, Glory to God in the highest, and on earth peace, good will toward men. And it came to pass, as the angels were gone away from them into heaven, the shepherds said one to another, Let us now go even unto Bethlehem, and see this thing which is come to pass, which the Lord hath made known unto us. And they came with haste, and found Mary, and Joseph, and the babe lying in a manger. And when they had seen it, they made known abroad the saying which was told them concerning this child. And all they that heard it wondered at those things which were told them by the shepherds. But Mary kept all these things, and pondered them in her heart. And the shepherds returned, glorifying and praising God for all the things that they had heard and seen, as it was told unto them. And when eight days were accomplished for the circumcising of the child, his name was called JESUS, which was so named of the angel[4] before he was conceived in the womb. And when the days of her purification according to the law of Moses were accomplished, they brought him to Jerusalem, to present him to the Lord; (as it is written in the law of the Lord, Every male that openeth the womb[5] shall be called holy to the Lord;) and to offer a sacrifice according to that which is said in the law of the Lord, A pair of turtledoves, or two young pigeons. And, behold, there was a man in Jerusalem, whose name was Simeon; and the same man was just and devout, waiting for the consolation of Israel: and the Holy Ghost was upon him. And it was revealed unto him by the Holy Ghost, that he should not see death,

---

1. The King James Version.   2. The Roman Empire.   3. Anointed (Greek); used of kings, priests, and the deliverer promised by the prophets.   4. In the Annunciation to Mary (Luke 1.31). *Jesus* is a form of the name Joshua, which means "he shall save."   5. The firstborn son is believed to belong to God (Exodus 13.2). The purification laws are given in Leviticus 12.

before he had seen the Lord's Christ. And he came by the Spirit into the temple: and when the parents brought in the child Jesus, to do for him after the custom of the law, then took he him up in his arms, and blessed God, and said, Lord, now lettest thou thy servant depart in peace, according to thy word: for mine eyes have seen thy salvation, which thou hast prepared before the face of all people; a light to lighten the Gentiles,[6] and the glory of thy people Israel. And Joseph and his mother marvelled at those things which were spoken of him. And Simeon blessed them, and said unto Mary his mother, Behold, this child is set for the fall and rising again[7] of many in Israel; and for a sign which shall be spoken against; (yea, a sword shall pierce through thy own soul also,) that the thoughts of many hearts may be revealed. And there was one Anna, a prophetess, the daughter of Phanuel, of the tribe of Aser: she was of a great age, and had lived with an husband seven years from her virginity; and she was a widow of about fourscore and four years, which departed not from the temple, but served God with fastings and prayers night and day. And she coming in that instant gave thanks likewise unto the Lord, and spoke of him to all them that looked for redemption in Jerusalem. And when they had performed all things according to the law of the Lord, they returned into Galilee, to their own city Nazareth. And the child grew, and waxed strong in spirit, filled with wisdom: and the grace of God was upon him. Now his parents went to Jerusalem every year at the feast of the passover. And when he was twelve years old, they went up to Jerusalem after the custom of the feast. And when they had fulfilled the days, as they returned, the child Jesus tarried behind in Jerusalem; and Joseph and his mother knew not of it. But they, supposing him to have been in the company, went a day's journey; and they sought him among their kinsfolk and acquaintance. And when they found him not, they turned back again to Jerusalem, seeking him. And it came to pass that after three days they found him in the temple, sitting in the midst of the doctors,[8] both hearing them, and asking them questions. And all that heard him were astonished at his understanding and answers. And when they saw him, they were amazed: and his mother said unto him, Son, why hast thou thus dealt with us? behold, thy father and I have sought thee sorrowing. And he said unto them, How is it that ye sought me? wist ye not that I must be about my Father's business? And they understood not the saying which he spake unto them. And he went down with them, and came to Nazareth, and was subject unto them: but his mother kept all these sayings in her heart. And Jesus increased in wisdom and stature, and in favour with God and man.

Matthew 5–7

[The Teaching of Jesus: The Sermon on the Mount]

5. And seeing the multitudes, he went up into a mountain: and when he was set, his disciples came unto him: and he opened his mouth, and taught them, saying, Blessed are the poor in spirit: for theirs is the kingdom of

6. Non-Jews. 7. The Greek word is the one always used for the resurrection of the dead.
8. Teachers, rabbis.

heaven. Blessed are they that mourn: for they shall be comforted. Blessed are the meek: for they shall inherit the earth. Blessed are they which do hunger and thirst after righteousness: for they shall be filled. Blessed are the merciful: for they shall obtain mercy. Blessed are the pure in heart: for they shall see God. Blessed are the peacemakers: for they shall be called the children of God. Blessed are they which are persecuted for righteousness' sake: for theirs is the kingdom of heaven. Blessed are ye, when men shall revile you, and persecute you, and shall say all manner of evil against you falsely, for my sake. Rejoice, and be exceeding glad: for great is your reward in heaven: for so persecuted they the prophets which were before you.

Ye are the salt of the earth: but if the salt have lost his savour, wherewith shall it be salted?[1] it is thenceforth good for nothing, but to be cast out, and to be trodden under foot of men. Ye are the light of the world. A city that is set on a hill cannot be hid. Neither do men light a candle, and put it under a bushel,[2] but on a candlestick; and it giveth light unto all that are in the house. Let your light so shine before men, that they may see your good works, and glorify your Father which is in heaven.

Think not that I am come to destroy the law, or the prophets: I am not come to destroy, but to fulfil. For verily I say unto you, Till heaven and earth pass, one jot or one tittle shall in no wise pass from the law, till all be fulfilled. Whosoever therefore shall break one of these least commandments, and shall teach men so, he shall be called the least in the kingdom of heaven: but whosoever shall do and teach them, the same shall be called great in the kingdom of heaven. For I say unto you, That except your righteousness shall exceed the righteousness of the scribes and Pharisees,[3] ye shall in no case enter into the kingdom of heaven.

Ye have heard that it was said by them of old time, Thou shalt not kill; and whosoever shall kill shall be in danger of the judgment: but I say unto you, That whosoever is angry with his brother without a cause shall be in danger of the judgment: and whosoever shall say to his brother, Raca,[4] shall be in danger of the council: but whosoever shall say, Thou fool, shall be in danger of hell fire.[5] Therefore if thou bring thy gift to the altar, and there rememberest that thy brother hath ought against thee; leave there thy gift before the altar, and go thy way; first be reconciled to thy brother, and then come and offer thy gift. Agree with thine adversary quickly, whiles thou art in the way with him; lest at any time the adversary deliver thee to the judge, and the judge deliver thee to the officer, and thou be cast into prison. Verily I say unto thee, Thou shalt by no means come out thence, till thou hast paid the uttermost farthing.

Ye have heard that it was said by them of old time, Thou shalt not commit adultery: but I say unto you, That whosoever looketh on a woman to lust after her hath committed adultery with her already in his heart. And if thy right eye offend thee, pluck it out, and cast it from thee: for it is profitable

---

1. How can it regain its savor?   2. A household vessel with the capacity of a bushel.   3. A sect that insisted on strict observance of the Mosaic law. *Scribes:* the official interpreters of the sacred Scriptures.   4. Empty (Aramaic?).   5. The reference is to Jewish legal institutions. The penalties that might be inflicted for murder were death by the sword (a sentence of a local court, *the judgment*), death by stoning (the sentence of a higher court, *the council*), and the burning of the criminal's body in the place where refuse was thrown, Gehenna, which is hence used as a name for hell. Jesus compares the different degrees of punishment (administered by God) for the new sins, which he here lists, with the degrees of punishment recognized by Jewish law.

for thee that one of thy members should perish, and not that thy whole body should be cast into hell. And if thy right hand offend thee, cut it off, and cast it from thee: for it is profitable for thee that one of thy members should perish, and not that thy whole body should be cast into hell. It hath been said, Whosoever shall put away his wife, let him give her a writing of divorcement: but I say unto you, That whosoever shall put away his wife, saving for the cause of fornication, causeth her to commit adultery: and whosoever shall marry her that is divorced committeth adultery.

Again, ye have heard that it hath been said by them of old time, Thou shalt not forswear thyself, but shalt perform unto the Lord thine oaths: but I say unto you, Swear not at all; neither by heaven; for it is God's throne: nor by the earth; for it is his footstool: neither by Jerusalem; for it is the city of the great King. Neither shalt thou swear by thy head, because thou canst not make one hair white or black. But let your communication be, Yea, yea; Nay, nay: for whatsoever is more than these cometh of evil.

Ye have heard that it hath been said, An eye for an eye, and a tooth for a tooth: but I say unto you, That ye resist not evil: but whosoever shall smite thee on thy right cheek, turn to him the other also. And if any man will sue thee at the law, and take away thy coat, let him have thy cloak also. And whosoever shall compel thee to go a mile, go with him twain. Give to him that asketh thee, and from him that would borrow of thee turn not thou away.

Ye have heard that it hath been said, Thou shalt love thy neighbour, and hate thine enemy. But I say unto you, Love your enemies, bless them that curse you, do good to them that hate you, and pray for them which despitefully use you, and persecute you; that ye may be the children of your Father which is in heaven: for he maketh his sun to rise on the evil and on the good, and sendeth rain on the just and on the unjust. For if ye love them which love you, what reward have ye? do not even the publicans[6] the same? And if ye salute your brethren only, what do ye more than others? do not even the publicans so? Be ye therefore perfect, even as your Father which is in heaven is perfect.

6. Take heed that ye do not your alms before men, to be seen of them: otherwise ye have no reward of your Father which is in heaven. Therefore when thou doest thine alms, do not sound a trumpet before thee, as the hypocrites do in the synagogues and in the streets, that they may have glory of men. Verily I say unto you, They have their reward. But when thou doest alms, let not thy left hand know what thy right hand doeth: that thine alms may be in secret: and thy Father which seeth in secret himself shall reward thee openly.

And when thou prayest, thou shalt not be as the hypocrites are: for they love to pray standing in the synagogues and in the corners of the streets, that they may be seen of men. Verily I say unto you, They have their reward. But thou, when thou prayest, enter into thy closet, and when thou hast shut thy door, pray to thy Father which is in secret; and thy Father which seeth in secret shall reward thee openly. But when ye pray, use not vain repetitions,

---

6. The men who collected the taxes for the Roman tax-farming corporations; they were, naturally, universally despised and hated.

as the heathen do; for they think that they shall be heard for their much speaking. Be not ye therefore like unto them: for your Father knoweth what things ye have need of, before ye ask him. After this manner therefore pray ye: Our Father which art in heaven, Hallowed be thy name. Thy kingdom come. Thy will be done in earth, as it is in heaven. Give us this day our daily bread. And forgive us our debts, as we forgive our debtors. And lead us not into temptation, but deliver us from evil: For thine is the kingdom, and the power, and the glory, for ever. Amen. For if ye forgive men their trespasses, your heavenly Father will also forgive you: but if ye forgive not men their trespasses, neither will your Father forgive your trespasses.

Moreover when ye fast, be not, as the hypocrites, of a sad countenance: for they disfigure their faces, that they may appear unto men to fast. Verily I say unto you, They have their reward. But thou, when thou fastest, anoint thine head, and wash thy face; that thou appear not unto men to fast, but unto thy Father which is in secret: and thy Father, which seeth in secret shall reward thee openly.

Lay not up for yourselves treasures upon earth, where moth and rust doth corrupt, and where thieves break through and steal: but lay up for yourselves treasures in heaven, where neither moth nor rust doth corrupt, and where thieves do not break through nor steal: for where your treasure is, there will your heart be also. The light of the body is the eye: if therefore thine eye be single,[7] thy whole body shall be full of light. But if thine eye be evil, thy whole body shall be full of darkness. If therefore the light that is in thee be darkness, how great is that darkness!

No man can serve two masters: for either he will hate the one, and love the other; or else he will hold to the one, and despise the other. Ye cannot serve God and Mammon. Therefore I say unto you, Take no thought for your life, what ye shall eat, or what ye shall drink; nor yet for your body, what ye shall put on. Is not the life more than meat, and the body than raiment? Behold the fowls of the air: for they sow not, neither do they reap, nor gather into barns; yet your heavenly Father feedeth them. Are ye not much better than they? Which of you by taking thought can add one cubit unto his stature? And why take ye thought for raiment? Consider the lilies of the field, how they grow; they toil not, neither do they spin. And yet I say unto you, That even Solomon in all his glory was not arrayed like one of these. Wherefore, if God so clothe the grass of the field, which today is, and tomorrow is cast into the oven, shall he not much more clothe you, O ye of little faith? Therefore take no thought, saying, What shall we eat? or, What shall we drink? or, Wherewithal shall we be clothed? (For after all these things do the Gentiles seek:) for your heavenly Father knoweth that ye have need of all these things. But seek ye first the kingdom of God, and his righteousness; and all these things shall be added unto you. Take therefore no thought for the morrow: for the morrow shall take thought for the things of itself. Sufficient unto the day is the evil thereof.

7. Judge not, that ye be not judged. For with what judgment ye judged, ye shall be judged: and with what measure ye mete, it shall be measured to you again. And why beholdest thou the mote that is in thy brother's eye, but considerest not the beam[8] that is in thine own eye? Or how wilt thou say to

7. Clear. 8. A long piece of heavy timber, in contrast to a *mote,* a particle or speck.

thy brother, Let me pull out the mote out of thine eye; and, behold, a beam is in thine own eye? Thou hypocrite, first cast out the beam out of thine own eye; and then shalt thou see clearly to cast out the mote out of thy brother's eye.

Give not that which is holy unto the dogs, neither cast ye your pearls before swine, lest they trample them under their feet, and turn again and rend you.

Ask, and it shall be given you; seek, and ye shall find; knock, and it shall be opened unto you: for every one that asketh receiveth; and he that seeketh findeth; and to him that knocketh it shall be opened. Or what man is there of you, whom if his son ask bread, will he give him a stone? Or if he ask a fish, will he give him a serpent? If ye then, being evil, know how to give good gifts unto your children, how much more shall your Father which is in heaven give good things to them that ask him? Therefore all things whatsoever ye would that men should do to you, do ye even so to them: for this is the law and the prophets.

Enter ye in at the strait gate: for wide is the gate, and broad is the way, that leadeth to destruction, and many there be which go in thereat: because strait is the gate, and narrow is the way, which leadeth unto life, and few there be that find it.

Beware of false prophets, which come to you in sheep's clothing, but inwardly they are ravening wolves. Ye shall know them by their fruits. Do men gather grapes of thorns, or figs of thistles? Even so every good tree bringeth forth good fruit; but a corrupt tree bringeth forth evil fruit. A good tree cannot bring forth evil fruit, neither can a corrupt tree bring forth good fruit. Every tree that bringeth not forth good fruit is hewn down, and cast into the fire. Wherefore by their fruits ye shall know them.

Not every one that saith unto me, Lord, Lord, shall enter into the kingdom of heaven; but he that doeth the will of my Father which is in heaven. Many will say to me in that day, Lord, Lord, have we not prophesied in thy name? and in thy name have cast out devils? and in thy name done many wonderful works? And then will I profess unto them, I never knew you: depart from me, ye that work iniquity.

Therefore whosoever heareth these sayings of mine, and doeth them, I will liken him unto a wise man, which built his house upon a rock; and the rain descended, and the floods came and the winds blew, and beat upon that house; and it fell not: for it was founded upon a rock. And every one that heareth these sayings of mine, and doeth them not, shall be likened unto a foolish man, which built his house upon the sand: and the rain descended, and the floods came, and the winds blew, and beat upon that house; and it fell: and great was the fall of it. And it came to pass, when Jesus had ended these sayings, the people were astonished at his doctrine: for he taught them as one having authority, and not as the scribes.

Luke 15

[The Teaching of Jesus: Parables]

15. Then drew near unto him all the publicans and sinners for to hear him. And the Pharisees and scribes murmured, saying, This man receiveth sinners, and eateth with them.

And he spoke this parable unto them, saying, What man of you, having a hundred sheep, if he lose one of them, doth not leave the ninety and nine in the wilderness, and go after that which is lost, until he find it? And when he hath found it, he layeth it on his shoulders, rejoicing. And when he cometh home, he calleth together his friends and neighbours, saying unto them, Rejoice with me; for I have found my sheep which was lost. I say unto you that likewise joy shall be in heaven over one sinner that repenteth, more than over ninety and nine just persons, which need no repentance.

Either what woman having ten pieces of silver, if she lose one piece, doth not light a candle, and sweep the house, and seek diligently till she find it? And when she hath found it, she calleth her friends and her neighbours together, saying, Rejoice with me; for I have found the piece which I had lost. Likewise, I say unto you, there is joy in the presence of the angels of God over one sinner that repenteth.

And he said, A certain man had two sons: and the younger of them said to his father, Father, give me the portion of goods that falleth to me. And he divided unto them his living. And not many days after the younger son gathered all together, and took his journey into a far country, and there wasted his substance with riotous living. And when he had spent all, there arose a mighty famine in that land; and he began to be in want. And he went and joined himself to a citizen of that country; and he sent him into his fields to feed swine. And he would fain have filled his belly with the husks that the swine did eat: and no man gave unto him. And when he came to himself, he said, How many hired servants of my father's have bread enough and to spare, and I perish with hunger! I will arise and go to my father, and will say unto him, Father, I have sinned against heaven, and before thee, and am no more worthy to be called thy son: make me as one of thy hired servants. And he arose, and came to his father. But when he was yet a great way off, his father saw him, and had compassion, and ran, and fell on his neck, and kissed him. And the son said unto him, Father, I have sinned against heaven, and in thy sight, and am no more worthy to be called thy son. But the father said to his servants, Bring forth the best robe, and put it on him; and put a ring on his hand, and shoes on his feet: and bring hither the fatted calf, and kill it; and let us eat, and be merry: for this my son was dead, and is alive again; he was lost, and is found. And they began to be merry. Now his elder son was in the field: and as he came and drew nigh to the house, he heard musick and dancing. And he called one of the servants, and asked what these things meant. And he said unto him, Thy brother is come; and thy father hath killed the fatted calf, because he hath received him safe and sound. And he was angry, and would not go in: therefore came his father out, and intreated him. And he answering said to his father, Lo, these many years do I serve thee, neither transgressed I at any time thy commandment: and yet thou never gavest me a kid, that I might make merry with my friends: but as soon as this thy son was come, which hath devoured thy living with harlots, thou hast killed for him the fatted calf. And he said unto him, Son, thou art ever with me, and all that I have is thine. It was meet that we should make merry, and be glad: for this thy brother was dead, and is alive again; and was lost, and is found.

Matthew 13[1]

[Why Jesus Teaches in Parables]

13. The same day went Jesus out of the house, and sat by the sea side. And great multitudes were gathered together unto him, so that he went into a ship, and sat; and the whole multitude stood on the shore. And he spake many things unto them in parables, saying, Behold, a sower went forth to sow; and when he sowed, some seeds fell by the wayside, and the fowls came and devoured them up: some fell upon stony places, where they had not much earth: and forthwith they sprung up, because they had no deepness of earth: and when the sun was up, they were scorched; and because they had no root, they withered away. And some fell among thorns; and the thorns sprung up, and choked them: but other fell into good ground, and brought forth fruit, some a hundredfold, some sixtyfold, some thirtyfold. Who hath ears to hear, let him hear.

And the disciples came, and said unto him, Why speakest thou unto them in parables? He answered and said unto them, Because it is given unto you to know the mysteries of the kingdom of heaven, but to them it is not given. For whosoever hath, to him shall be given, and he shall have more abundance: but whosoever hath not, from him shall be taken away even that he hath. Therefore speak I to them in parables: because they seeing see not; and hearing they hear not, neither do they understand. And in them is fulfilled the prophecy of Esaias, which saith, By hearing ye shall hear, and shall not understand; and seeing ye shall see, and shall not perceive: for this people's heart is waxed gross, and their ears are dull of hearing, and their eyes they have closed; lest at any time they should see with their eyes, and hear with their ears, and should understand with their heart, and should be converted, and I should heal them. But blessed are your eyes, for they see: and your ears, for they hear. For verily I say unto you, That many prophets and righteous men have desired to see those things which ye see, and have not seen them; and to hear those things which ye hear, and have not heard them.

Hear ye therefore the parable of the sower. When any one heareth the word of the kingdom, and understandeth it not, then cometh the wicked one, and catcheth away that which was sown in his heart. This is he which received seed by the wayside. But he that received the seed into stony places, the same is he that heareth the word, and anon with joy receiveth it; yet hath he not root in himself, but dureth for a while: for when tribulation or persecution ariseth because of the word, by and by he is offended. He also that received seed among the thorns is he that heareth the word; and the care of this world, and the deceitfulness of riches, choke the word, and he becometh unfruitful. But he that received seed into the good ground is he that heareth the word, and understandeth it; which also beareth fruit, and bringeth forth, some a hundredfold, some sixty, some thirty.

Another parable put he forth unto them, saying, The kingdom of heaven is likened unto a man which sowed good seed in his field: but while men slept, his enemy came and sowed tares among the wheat, and went his way. But when the blade was sprung up, and brought forth fruit, then appeared

1. Verses 1–35.

the tares also. So the servants of the householder came and said unto him, Sir, didst not thou sow good seed in thy field? from whence then hath it tares? He said unto them, An enemy hath done this. The servants said unto him, Wilt thou then that we go and gather them up? But he said, Nay; lest while ye gather up the tares, ye root up also the wheat with them. Let both grow together until the harvest: and in the time of harvest I will say to the reapers, Gather ye together first the tares, and bind them in bundles to burn them: but gather the wheat into my barn.

Another parable put he forth unto them, saying, The kingdom of heaven is like to a grain of mustard seed, which a man took, and sowed in his field: which indeed is the least of all seeds: but when it is grown, it is the greatest among herbs, and becometh a tree, so that the birds of the air come and lodge in the branches thereof.

Another parable spake he unto them; The kingdom of heaven is like unto leaven, which a woman took, and hid in three measures of meal, till the whole was leavened.

All these things spake Jesus unto the multitude in parables; and without a parable spake he not unto them: that it might be fulfilled which was spoken by the prophet, saying, I will open my mouth in parables; I will utter things which have been kept secret from the foundation of the world.

Matthew 26[1]

[The Betrayal of Jesus]

26. * * * Then one of the twelve, called Judas Iscariot, went unto the chief priests, and said unto them, What will ye give me, and I will deliver him unto you? And they covenanted with him for thirty pieces of silver. And from that time he sought opportunity to betray him.

Now the first day of the feast of unleavened bread[2] the disciples came to Jesus, saying unto him, Where wilt thou that we prepare for thee to eat the passover? And he said, Go into the city to such a man, and say unto him, The Master saith, My time is at hand; I will keep the passover at thy house with my disciples. And the disciples did as Jesus had appointed them; and they made ready the passover. Now when the even was come, he sat down with the twelve. And as they did eat, he said, Verily I say unto you, that one of you shall betray me. And they were exceeding sorrowful, and began every one of them to say unto him, Lord, is it I? And he answered and said, He that dippeth his hand with me in the dish, the same shall betray me. The Son of man goeth as it is written of him: but woe unto that man by whom the Son of man is betrayed! it had been good for that man if he had not been born. Then Judas, which betrayed him, answered and said, Master, is it I? He said unto him, Thou hast said.

And as they were eating, Jesus took bread, and blessed it, and brake it, and gave it to the disciples, and said, Take, eat; this is my body. And he took

1. Verses 14–75. 2. Passover, held in remembrance of the delivery of the Jews from captivity in Egypt (Exodus 12).

the cup, and gave thanks, and gave it to them, saying, Drink ye all of it; for this is my blood of the new testament,[3] which is shed for many for the remission of sins. But I say unto you, I will not drink henceforth of this fruit of the vine, until that day when I drink it new with you in my Father's kingdom. And when they had sung an hymn, they went out into the mount of Olives. Then saith Jesus unto them, All ye shall be offended because of me this night: for it is written,[4] I will smite the shepherd, and the sheep of the flock shall be scattered abroad. But after I am risen again, I will go before you into Galilee. Peter answered and said unto him, Though all men shall be offended because of thee, yet will I never be offended. Jesus said unto him, Verily I say unto thee, That this night, before the cock crow, thou shalt deny me thrice. Peter said unto him, Though I should die with thee, yet will I not deny thee. Likewise also said all the disciples.

Then cometh Jesus with them unto a place called Gethsemane, and saith unto the disciples, Sit ye here, while I go and pray yonder. And he took with him Peter and the two sons of Zebedee,[5] and began to be sorrowful and very heavy. Then saith he unto them, My soul is exceeding sorrowful, even unto death: tarry ye here, and watch[6] with me. And he went a little farther, and fell on his face, and prayed, saying, O my Father, if it be possible, let this cup pass from me: nevertheless, not as I will, but as thou wilt. And he cometh unto the disciples, and findeth them asleep, and saith unto Peter, What, could ye not watch with me one hour? Watch and pray, that ye enter not into temptation: the spirit indeed is willing, but the flesh is weak. He went away again the second time, and prayed, saying, O my Father, if this cup may not pass away from me, except I drink it, thy will be done. And he came and found them asleep again: for their eyes were heavy. And he left them, and went away again, and prayed the third time, saying the same words. Then cometh he to his disciples, and saith unto them, Sleep on now, and take your rest: behold, the hour is at hand, and the Son of man is betrayed into the hands of sinners. Rise, let us be going: behold, he is at hand that doth betray me.

And while he yet spake, lo, Judas, one of the twelve, came, and with him a great multitude with swords and staves, from the chief priests and elders of the people. Now he that betrayed him gave them a sign, saying, Whomsoever I shall kiss, that same is he: hold him fast. And forthwith he came to Jesus and said, Hail, master; and kissed him. And Jesus said unto him, Friend, wherefore art thou come? Then came they and laid hands on Jesus, and took him. And behold, one of them[7] which were with Jesus stretched out his hand, and drew his sword, and struck a servant of the high priest's, and smote off his ear. Then said Jesus unto him, Put up again thy sword into his place: for all they that take the sword shall perish with the sword. Thinkest thou that I cannot now pray to my Father, and he shall presently give me more than twelve legions[8] of angels? But how then shall the scriptures be fulfilled, that thus it must be? In that same hour said Jesus to the multitudes, Are ye come out as against a thief with swords and staves for to take

---

3. I.e., of the new covenant, or agreement. Jesus compares himself to the lamb that was killed at the Passover as a sign of the covenant between God and the Jews.　4. In Zechariah 13.7. *Be offended*: be made to stumble (literal trans. of the Greek).　5. James and John.　6. Stay awake.　7. Peter. 8. A legion was a Roman military formation; its full complement was six thousand men.

me? I sat daily with you teaching in the temple, and ye laid no hold on me. But all this was done that the scriptures of the prophets might be fulfilled. Then all the disciples forsook him, and fled.

And they that had laid hold on Jesus led him away to Caiaphas the high priest, where the scribes and the elders were assembled. But Peter followed him afar off unto the high priest's palace, and went in, and sat with the servants, to see the end. Now the chief priests, and elders, and all the council, sought false witness against Jesus, to put him to death; but found none: yea, though many false witnesses came, yet found they none. At the last came two false witnesses, and said, This fellow said, I am able to destroy the temple of God, and to build it in three days. And the high priest arose, and said unto him, Answerest thou nothing? What is it which these witness against thee? But Jesus held his peace. And the high priest answered and said unto him, I adjure thee by the living God, that thou tell us whether thou be the Christ, the Son of God. Jesus saith unto him, Thou hast said: nevertheless I say unto you, Hereafter shall ye see the Son of man sitting on the right hand of power, and coming in the clouds of heaven. Then the high priest rent his clothes, saying, He hath spoken blasphemy; what further need have we of witnesses? behold, now ye have heard his blasphemy. What think ye? They answered and said, He is guilty of death.[9] Then did they spit in his face, and buffeted him; and others smote him with the palms of their hands, saying, Prophesy unto us, thou Christ, Who is he that smote thee?

Now Peter sat without in the palace: and a damsel came unto him, saying, Thou also wast with Jesus of Galilee. But he denied before them all, saying, I know not what thou sayest. And when he was gone out into the porch, another maid saw him and said unto them that were there, This fellow was also with Jesus of Nazareth. And again he denied with an oath, I do not know the man. And after a while came unto him they that stood by, and said to Peter, Surely thou also art one of them; for thy speech betrayeth thee.[1] Then began he to curse and to swear, saying, I know not the man. And immediately the cock crew. And Peter remembered the word of Jesus, which said unto him, Before the cock crow thou shalt deny me thrice. And he went out, and wept bitterly.

Matthew 27

[The Trial and Crucifixion of Jesus]

27. When the morning was come, all the chief priests and elders of the people took counsel against Jesus to put him to death: and when they had bound him, they led him away, and delivered him to Pontius Pilate the governor.[1]

Then Judas, which had betrayed him, when he saw that he was condemned, repented himself, and brought again the thirty pieces of silver to

---

9. Liable to the death penalty.   1. In other words, Peter's speech revealed his Galilean origin.   1. His official title was procurator of the province of Judea. Roman policy was to allow the Jews as much independence as possible (especially in religious matters), but only the Roman authorities could impose a death sentence.

the chief priests and elders, saying, I have sinned in that I have betrayed the innocent blood. And they said, What is that to us? see thou to that. And he cast down the pieces of silver in the temple, and departed, and went and hanged himself. And the chief priests took the silver pieces, and said, It is not lawful for to put them into the treasury, because it is the price of blood. And they took counsel, and bought with them the potter's field,[2] to bury strangers in. Wherefore that field was called, The field of blood, unto this day. Then was fulfilled that which was spoken by Jeremy the prophet,[3] saying, And they took the thirty pieces of silver, the price of him that was valued, whom they of the children of Israel did value; and gave them for the potter's field, as the Lord appointed me.[4] And Jesus stood before the governor: and the governor asked him, saying, Art thou the King of the Jews? And Jesus said unto him, Thou sayest.

And when he was accused of the chief priests and elders, he answered nothing. Then said Pilate unto him, Hearest thou not how many things they witness against thee? And he answered him to never a word; insomuch that the governor marvelled greatly. Now at that feast the governor was wont to release unto the people a prisoner, whom they would. And they had then a notable prisoner, called Barabbas.[5] Therefore when they were gathered together, Pilate said unto them, Whom will ye that I release unto you? Barabbas, or Jesus which is called Christ? For he knew that for envy they had delivered him.[6]

When he was set down on the judgment seat, his wife sent unto him, saying, Have thou nothing to do with that just man: for I have suffered many things this day in a dream because of him. But the chief priests and elders persuaded the multitude that they should ask Barabbas, and destroy Jesus. The governor answered and said unto them, Whether of the twain will ye that I release unto you? They said, Barabbas. Pilate saith unto them, What shall I do then with Jesus which is called Christ? They all say unto him, Let him be crucified.[7] And the governor said, Why, what evil hath he done? But they cried out the more, saying, Let him be crucified.

When Pilate saw that he could prevail nothing, but that rather a tumult was made, he took water, and washed his hands before the multitude, saying, I am innocent of the blood of this just person: see ye to it. Then answered all the people, and said, His blood be on us, and on our children.

Then released he Barabbas unto them: and when he had scourged[8] Jesus, he delivered him to be crucified. Then the soldiers of the governor took Jesus into the common hall, and gathered unto him the whole band of soldiers. And they stripped him, and put on him a scarlet robe.

And when they had platted a crown of thorns, they put it upon his head, and a reed[9] in his right hand: and they bowed the knee before him, and mocked him, saying, Hail, King of the Jews! And they spit upon him, and took the reed, and smote him on the head. And after that they had mocked him, they took the robe off from him, and put his own raiment on him, and

---

2. A field that had been dug for potter's clay and thus was not worth very much as land.
3. Jeremiah.   4. Compare Zechariah 11.13: "And the Lord said unto me, Cast it unto the potter: a goodly price that I was prised at of them."   5. Under sentence of death for sedition and murder.   6. Delivered him to the Roman authorities.   7. The regular Roman punishment for sedition.   8. Whipped, a routine part of the punishment.   9. To represent the king's scepter.

led him away to crucify him. And as they came out, they found a man of Cyrene,[1] Simon by name: him they compelled to bear his cross. And when they were come unto a place called Golgotha, that is to say, a place of a skull,

They gave him vinegar to drink mingled with gall:[2] and when he had tasted thereof, he would not drink. And they crucified him, and parted his garments, casting lots: that it might be fulfilled which was spoken by the prophet, They parted my garments among them, and upon my vesture did they cast lots.[3] And sitting down they watched him there; and set up over his head his accusation written, THIS IS JESUS THE KING OF THE JEWS. Then were there two thieves crucified with him, one on the right hand, and another on the left.

And they that passed by reviled him, wagging their heads, and saying, Thou that destroyest the temple, and buildest it in three days, save thyself. If thou be the Son of God, come down from the cross. Likewise also the chief priests mocking him, with the scribes and elders, said, He saved others; himself he cannot save. If he be the King of Israel, let him now come down from the cross, and we will believe him. He trusted in God; let him deliver him now, if he will have him: for he said, I am the Son of God. The thieves also, which were crucified with him, cast the same in his teeth. Now from the sixth hour there was darkness over all the land unto the ninth hour. And about the ninth hour Jesus cried with a loud voice, saying, Eli, Eli, lama sabachthani? that is to say, My God, my God, why hast thou forsaken me?[4] Some of them that stood there, when they heard that, said, This man calleth for Elias.[5] And straightway one of them ran, and took a sponge, and filled it with vinegar, and put it on a reed, and gave him to drink. The rest said, Let be, let us see whether Elias will come to save him.

Jesus, when he had cried again with a loud voice, yielded up the ghost. And, behold, the veil of the temple[6] was rent in twain from the top to the bottom; and the earth did quake, and the rocks rent; and the graves were opened; and many bodies of the saints which slept arose, and came out of the graves after his resurrection, and went into the holy city, and appeared unto many. Now when the centurion,[7] and they that were with him, watching Jesus, saw the earthquake, and those things that were done, they feared greatly, saying, Truly this was the Son of God. And many women were there beholding afar off, which followed Jesus from Galilee, ministering unto him: among which was Mary Magdalene, and Mary the mother of James and Joseph, and the mother of Zebedee's children. When the even was come, there came a rich man of Arimathæa, named Joseph, who also himself was Jesus' disciple. He went to Pilate, and begged the body of Jesus. Then Pilate commanded the body to be delivered. And when Joseph had taken the body, he wrapped it in clean linen cloth, and laid it in his own new tomb, which he had hewn out in the rock: and he rolled a great stone to the door of the sepulchre, and departed. And there was Mary Magdalene, and the other Mary, sitting over against the sepulchre.

Now the next day, that followed the day of the preparation, the chief

---

1. On the coast of North Africa.   2. The Greek word translated *vinegar* describes a sour wine that was the regular drink of the Roman soldiery; the addition of bitter gall is further mockery.   3. It is generally agreed that this sentence is a late addition to the text.   4. The opening words of Psalm 22. Jesus spoke Aramaic, a language closely related to Hebrew.   5. The prophet Elijah.   6. The curtain that screened off the holy of holies.   7. The Roman officer in charge of the execution.

priests and Pharisees came together unto Pilate, saying, Sir, we remember that that deceiver said, while he was yet alive, After three days I will rise again. Command therefore that the sepulchre be made sure[8] until the third day, lest his disciples come by night, and steal him away, and say unto the people, He is risen from the dead: so the last error shall be worse than the first. Pilate said unto them, Ye have a watch:[9] go your way, make it as sure as ye can. So they went, and made the sepulchre sure, sealing the stone, and setting a watch.

Matthew 28

[The Resurrection]

28. In the end of the sabbath, as it began to dawn toward the first day of the week, came Mary Magdalene and the other Mary to see the sepulchre. And, behold, there was a great earthquake: for the angel of the Lord descended from heaven, and came and rolled back the stone from the door, and sat upon it. His countenance was like lightning, and his raiment white as snow: and for fear of him the keepers did shake, and became as dead men. And the angel answered and said unto the women, Fear not ye: for I know that ye seek Jesus, which was crucified. He is not here: for he is risen, as he said. Come, see the place where the Lord lay. And go quickly, and tell his disciples that he is risen from the dead; and, behold, he goeth before you into Galilee; there shall ye see him: lo, I have told you. And they departed quickly from the sepulchre with fear and great joy; and did run to bring his disciples word.

And as they went to tell his disciples, behold, Jesus met them, saying, All hail! And they came and held him by the feet, and worshipped him. Then said Jesus unto them, Be not afraid: go tell my brethren that they go into Galilee, and there shall they see me.

Now when they were going, behold, some of the watch came into the city, and shewed unto the chief priests all the things that were done. And when they were assembled with the elders, and had taken counsel, they gave large money unto the soldiers, saying, Say ye, His disciples came by night, and stole him away while we slept. And if this come to the governor's ears, we will persuade him, and secure you. So they took the money, and did as they were taught: and this saying is commonly reported among the Jews until this day.

Then the eleven disciples went away into Galilee, unto a mountain where Jesus had appointed them. And when they saw him, they worshipped him: but some doubted. And Jesus came and spake unto them, saying, All power is given unto me in heaven and in earth.

Go ye therefore, and teach all nations, baptizing them in the name of the Father, and of the Son, and of the Holy Ghost: teaching them to observe all things whatsoever I have commanded you: and, lo, I am with you always, even unto the end of the world. Amen.

---

8. Guarded.   9. Police force.

LUCIAN

A.D. 120?–190?

Satirist, rhetorician, parodist, creator of memorable fiction, Lucian brought his ironic sensibility to bear on the pretensions of people in his contemporary world and equally on the Greek traditions—historical, philosophic, religious, and literary—extending all the way back to Homer. Neither the gods on Olympus nor philosophers disputing the nature of reality were immune to his biting wit. Mixing together prose and poetry, dialogue and narrative, bits from all the established genres (that is, epic, tragedy, comedy, rhetoric, history, the philosophic dialogue), Lucian created new forms and renewed Greek literature in a late age even while he made affectionate fun of it. The eighty or so works that have survived under his name exerted a considerable influence in the Renaissance and after, both as vehicles for the transmission of Greek culture and as literary creations in their own right. The great Renaissance humanist Erasmus taught himself Greek by reading Lucian, and his *The Praise of Folly* is a virtual re-creation of a Lucianic rhetorical satire. There is a direct line from Lucian's fictional travel tale *A True Story* to Thomas More's *Utopia*, Ariosto's *Orlando Furioso*, and Jonathan Swift's *Gulliver's Travels*. With its account of a trip to the moon, *A True Story* also looks ahead to modern science fiction. In more recent times, however, Lucian has been relegated to the margins of literature or considered outside the canon. He has often been ignored as late and therefore decadent, too trivial to be included in the company of the giants of classical literature and thought, and beneath the established forms of "high" literature. These judgments are unfair. Modern solemnizers have just been fooled by the broadness of Lucian's grin into thinking that there is nothing behind it.

Lucian lived when the Roman Empire was at its height, but he wrote in Greek, not Latin. Although the empire unified a vast area politically, it remained culturally diverse. As the official language of government, Latin overrode local linguistic differences, especially in the western half of the Empire, and in Italy itself a strong Latin literary tradition had developed. In the east, the situation was more complicated. From mainland Greece across the Aegean Sea to the coast and inland of Asia Minor, the great cities had a proud Greek heritage, which had been strengthened and spread through the Hellenistic culture inaugurated by the conquests of Alexander the Great (356–323 B.C.). Thus, in the eastern empire Greek was the language of the educated and political elite, and to write and speak in Greek was a mark of cultural prestige. It was here that important works—particularly rhetoric and prose narrative—were composed in Greek during the resurgence of Greek culture known as the Second Sophistic (late first to early third century A.D.; the name connects it to the Sophists of the fifth and fourth centuries B.C.). Lucian was one of the most remarkable writers in this movement.

What we can infer of Lucian's life (mainly from what he says in his fictions) illustrates the complexity of cultural identity in an Asia ruled by Rome. He was born in the Syrian city of Samosata, on the west bank of the Euphrates River. He probably grew up speaking not Greek but a Semitic language, Aramaic, most likely the dialect of it known as Syriac. For a man of his talents, however, the way to riches and high standing led through the Greek language and rhetoric. So Lucian indicates elaborately in a work entitled *The Dream, or Lucian's Biography*. On the night after a disastrous first day of apprenticeship to his sculptor uncle, he says, two women appeared to him in a dream and disputed over him. Each urged him to become her disciple. The one named Sculpture—mannish, with unkempt hair and calloused hands, covered with marble dust, and speaking with bad grammar—offered him strong muscles, artistic fame, and a settled life with no need to travel outside his native land. The more patrician Education promised him the full range of knowledge, the admiration of the rich and well born, clothing as fine as her own, instant recognition when he traveled abroad, and political influence at home through his eloquence. Lucian, of course, chose Education and the career as a professional rhetorician that she offered. But the dream captures nicely the class distinction between the two careers, and the social and political prestige that access to Greek culture entailed.

So Lucian the barbarian (in the Hellenic sense of one who did not know Greek) learned Greek and somehow absorbed the whole of its literature. He then set about fitting into the established structures supported by Roman rule, first putting his oratorical skills to practical use in the law courts and then becoming a professional rhetorician. Being a professional meant joining the circuit of traveling orators and giving public declamations, which consisted of a short prelude, or rhetorical show-piece, followed by a speech on a more weighty topic. Lucian's works include a number of such preludes, such as his speech in praise of a housefly, and the *Dream*, evidently composed for a performance when Lucian visited his home town of Samosata as a local boy who had made good. The widespread interest in rhetoric and the public adulation it attracted are suggested in the *Dream* when Education promises Lucian, "If you give a speech, the common people will listen with their mouths agape, marveling and congratulating you on the power of your words and your father on his good fortune." Lucian's professional travels took him through the Ionian cities of Asia Minor, to mainland Greece, to Italy, and as far as Gaul, where he settled for some time in a (by his account) highly paid post as teacher of rhetoric. Around 160 A.D., however, at the age of forty, he shifted his career and probably went to live in Athens, which still, under Roman domination, enjoyed enormous prestige as the cradle of Greek culture. It is to this period that his great satirical and parodic works, including *A True Story*, belong. We last hear of him as holding an administrative position in the retinue of the Roman governor of Egypt—the kind of job given as patronage by influential officials. The post marks how far this provincial had moved, from the cultural margins into the center of imperial power, by means of Greek learning.

A TRUE STORY

Lucian's most famous and influential work, *A True Story* brilliantly parodies several kinds of narrative, such as earlier travel stories that purported to be true but retailed all kinds of fanciful descriptions and anecdotes. Another target is Herodotus, the "Father of History" (fifth century B.C.), who traveled around the eastern Mediterranean gathering information about the past and about contemporary geography. His descriptions of places at or beyond the fringes of the known world often include exotic giant or hybrid animals. Lucian condemns him for lying even while imitating such accounts as well as Herodotus's ethnographic descriptions of foreign peoples. The accounts of the fighting between the Moonmen and the Sunmen and between the giants on their warship islands caricature descriptions of land and naval fighting by other historians such as Thucydides (ca. 460–ca. 400 B.C.) and Xenophon (ca. 430–ca. 354 B.C.). Furthermore, in the prologue of *A True Story* Lucian's narrator condemns Odysseus as a liar for the famous tales of his deep-sea adventures that he tells to the Phaeacians in books 9–12 of the *Odyssey*, which in that poem purport to be true. As we might expect, several incidents in *A True Story* allude to those tales. The narrator himself visits Calypso, bringing her a love note from Odysseus; the account of the islands of the Blest and the Damned recalls the visit to the dead in book 11 of the *Odyssey*; the island with streams of wine evokes the Lotus Eaters; and so on. And finally there must have been sea yarns and other travel tales circulating orally and in writing. The episode in the belly of the whale raises a strong suspicion that Lucian knew the Biblical story of Jonah (above, p. 95), perhaps in oral form.

Here and in many of Lucian's works, such parodies and recombinations of traditional forms challenge the authority of the Greek literary and cultural tradition, identified as it was with the values and outlook of the elite in the Greek east. In this way they imply an alternative, more popular sensibility. At the same time, they also renew and reproduce the works of which they make fun; in this way, Lucian helped to keep his Hellenized culture in touch with the past with which it proudly identified and to transmit that past to future ages. Another effect of the parody in *A True Story* is to raise the question of truth and fiction in narrative—even in those narratives that pretend to be true. Lucian's narrator-hero raises this issue right at the beginning when he claims that he will be engaging in "honest lying: The one and only truth you'll hear from me is that I *am* lying." This is, of course, a self-undermining statement; if he says that he is lying, can we be sure that he really is? Or is this statement too a lie? If we take him at his word, when he condemns Herodotus to the islands of the Damned for his falsehoods, can we trust him that Herodotus really was a liar—especially when he goes out of his way to defend as true Aristophanes' extravagant fantasy of a bird republic in his *Birds*? The title, *A True Story*, by itself raises these complicated ironies; and by presenting us with a thoroughly unreliable narrator, Lucian suggests that the fictions we enjoy, such as this work and all the works it parodies, escape our normal categories of truth and falsehood.

A True Story taps into the human impulse to wonder about what lies beyond the known world. Nowadays scientists are rapidly accumulating an enormous quantity of factual knowledge about what lies beyond Earth and beyond this solar system. This information will bring us into contact with what is truly other, what exists without any reference to human beings. But traditionally—and this is as true of Homer as it is of Lucian—works that imagine worlds beyond our own arrange them with reference to human institutions and experience. Such worlds may contrast with our own, by being either utopian (such as the Isle of the Blest) or savage (the sexually predatory women called Asslegs). Or, like the island in the whale's belly, they may reproduce human civilization both in its productive aspects (farming) and in its evil impulses (power disputes and warfare), and thereby clarify our own culture for us. Or they may show alien beings engaged in similar activities to those of humans, but with implements adapted to the foreign setting. The giants, for example, row islands instead of ships, the Moonmen's helmets are made of beans, and the plain on which they fight the Sunmen is woven from spiderwebs. In the royal palace on the moon is a well with a giant mirror suspended over it, through which life on Earth can be viewed in minutest detail. This arrangement is Lucian's image for what *A True Story* does: it presents our own world reflected in distant, imaginary ones.

An excellent discussion of Lucian's satire and his relation to tradition is R. Bracht Branham, *Unruly Eloquence: Lucian and the Comedy of Traditions* (1989). C. P. Jones, *Culture and Society in Lucian* (1986), examines the question of whether Lucian's art is connected to its surrounding culture or only to the Greek past, and Christopher Robinson, *Lucian and His Influence in Europe* (1979), surveys his effects on later European literature and thought. On the complexities of Lucian's cultural identity, see Simon Swain, *Hellenism and Empire: Language, Classicism, and Power in the Greek World A.D. 50–250* (1996), pp. 298–329.

PRONOUNCING GLOSSARY

The following list uses common English syllables and stress accents to provide rough equivalents of selected words whose pronunciation may be unfamiliar to the general reader.

Cinyras: *kin-ee'-ras*

Cnidus: *k-nee'-dus*

Ctesias: *ktay'-sias*

Ctesiochus: *ktay-see'-o-kus*

Diogenes: *dai-o'-jen-eez*

Empedocles: *em-ped'-o-kleez*

Endymion: *en-di'-mee-on*

Hippocrates: *hip-po'-cra-teez*

Nauplius: *now'-plee-us*

Palamedes: *pal-a-mee'-deez*

Phaëthon: *fa-ee'-thon*

Rhadamanthus: *ra-da-man'-thus*

Salmoneus: *sal-mon-ews'* Zenodotus: *ze-no'-do-tus*
Scintharus: *skin'-tha-rus*

A True Story[1]

PART I

No athlete or body-building enthusiast thinks only of exercising and being in condition. He thinks also of relaxing when the occasion calls for it and, as a matter of fact, he considers this the most important part of training. In my opinion the same holds for book enthusiasts: after poring over a lot of serious works, they ought give the mind a rest to get it into even better shape for the next workout. The most suitable way for them to spend the interval is with light, pleasant reading which, instead of merely entertaining, furnishes some intellectual fare as well—and this I think they'll agree is true of the present work.

It is a work that will appeal to them not only because of the exotic subject matter, the amusing plot, and the way I've told all sorts of lies with an absolutely straight face, but because I've included comic allusions to all our noted poets, historians, and philosophers of old who have written so many fabulous tall stories. I don't need to name names: you'll recognize them yourselves as you read along. Ctesias of Cnidus, the son of Ctesiochus, has written things about India and the Indians that he neither saw himself nor heard from anyone who had any respect for the truth. Iambulus[2] has written a lot of unbelievable stuff about the ocean; everyone knows he made it all up, yet, for all that, he has put together an amusing account. Lots of other writers have shown a preference for the same technique: under the guise of reporting their travels abroad they spin yarns of huge monsters, savage tribes, and strange ways of life. The arch-exponent of, and model for, this sort of tomfoolery is Homer's Odysseus telling the court of Alcinous about a bag with the winds in it, one-eyed giants, cannibals, savages, even many-headed monsters and magic drugs that change shipmates into swine—with one such story after another he had those simple-minded Phaeacians goggle-eyed.[3]

Now, I've read all the practitioners of this art and I've never been very hard on them for not telling the truth—not when I see how common this failing is even among those who profess to be writing philosophy. What I have wondered at, though, is the way they're convinced they can write pure fable and get away with it. Since I'm vain enough myself to want to leave something behind to posterity and since I have nothing true to record—I never had any experiences worth talking about—in order not to be the only writer without a stake in the right to make up tall tales, I, too, have turned to lying—but a much more honest lying than all the others. The one and

---

1. Translated by Lionel Casson. 2. Lucian here alludes to two of his predecessors in the kind of narrative he is writing. Ctesias (fifth century B.C.) wrote the earliest known account of India, a romantic history of Persia, and a work on geography. Iambulus (probably third century B.C.) wrote a fantastic description of a journey to the island of the sun (in the ocean) and of its inhabitants' idyllic existence. 3. In books 9–12 of the *Odyssey*.

only truth you'll hear from me is that I *am* lying; by frankly admitting that there isn't a word of truth in what I say, I feel I'm avoiding the possibility of attack from any quarter.

Well, then, I'm writing about things I neither saw nor heard of from another soul, things which don't exist and couldn't possibly exist. So all readers beware: don't believe any of it.

Some time ago I set out on a voyage from the Straits of Gibraltar. A favorable breeze carried me into the Atlantic Ocean, and I was on my way. The basic reasons for the trip were my intellectual curiosity, my thirst for novelty, and the desire to find out what formed the farther border of the ocean and what peoples lived there. I had consequently put aboard a large stock of provisions and plenty of water and had taken on as crew fifty acquaintances who shared my interests; I had also laid in a good supply of weapons, induced—by the offer of a handsome salary—the best navigator available to go along, and had our vessel, a fast brig, made shipshape for a long and hard stay at sea.

For a day and a night we sailed before a wind that was favorable but not strong enough to carry us out of sight of land. At dawn of the following day, however, the wind made up, the sea began to run, and the sky grew dark. There wasn't even time to take in sail; we gave up and let the ship scud before the gale. For the next seventy-nine days we were driven along by a furious storm. Suddenly, on the eightieth, the sun broke through and we saw, fairly near, a hilly island covered with forest. The sound of the surf was not too loud; by now the storm had mostly subsided. We made for the shore, disembarked, and for hours just lay on the ground, a natural thing to do after such a long ordeal.

Finally we got up and decided that thirty of us would stand by to guard the ship while I took the other twenty to reconnoiter the island. We had advanced about a third of a mile through thick forest when we came upon a bronze shaft. It was inscribed in Greek, and the legend, dim and worn, read: "This marks the spot reached by Heracles and Dionysus."[4] And, pressed in the rock nearby, were two sets of footprints, one a hundred feet long, the other somewhat less. I figured the smaller were Dionysus' and the larger Heracles'. We paid our respects and pushed on.

We hadn't proceeded very far when we came upon a river, not of water, but of wine, which had the very same taste as our vintage Chian. The stream was so wide and deep that in places it was actually navigable. In view of such tangible evidence of a visit from Dionysus I was now much more inclined to believe the inscription on the shaft. I decided to track down the source of the river and walked upstream. Here I found no signs of any spring but, instead, a large number of enormous vines full of grapes. The roots of each were oozing drops of clear white wine, and these formed the river. Under the surface we could see a good many wine-colored fish which, it turned out, also tasted like wine; in fact, we got drunk on some that we caught and ate. (Naturally, when we cut them open we found them full of dregs.) Later,

---

4. Son of Zeus and god of the vine, who traveled to spread his own cult. *Heracles:* also son of Zeus, famous for the labors that took him all over the world.

having given the matter some thought, we mixed them with fresh-water fish and thus made our sea-food cocktails less potent.[5]

After fording the river at a narrow point, we came upon vines of a fabulous type. The part growing out of the ground, the stalk proper, was well set up and thick. But the part above that was a perfect replica of a female body from hips to head, looking somewhat like Daphne in those paintings where she's shown turning into a tree as Apollo lays his hands on her.[6] The women had branches bearing clusters of grapes growing out of the tips of their fingers and, instead of hair, actual shoots with leaves and grapes. They called out to welcome us as we came up, some in Lydian, some in Indian, but most in Greek. They also started kissing us on the lips, and everyone they did this to immediately became drunk and began to reel. We weren't able to pick the grapes because, as we pulled them off, the women would cry out in pain. They were burning with desire to have intercourse with us. Two of my men tried it—and couldn't be pried loose: they were held fast by the penis; it had grown into, become grafted onto, the vines. Soon the pair became entwined in a network of tendrils, sprouted shoots from their fingers, and looked as if even they were ready to bear fruit. We abandoned them and fled back to the ship where we gave the men who had stayed behind a report of everything, including the vinous intercourse of their two shipmates.

We then broke out the water jars, watered up—and also wined up from the river—and, after spending the night on the beach, sailed off at dawn before a moderate wind. Around noon, when the island had dropped out of sight, a typhoon suddenly hit us. It spun the ship around and lifted it about thirty miles high in the air. But, before it could let us drop back into the water, as we hung suspended in the sky, a wind filled our sails and carried us along. For seven days and nights we sailed the air. On the eighth we sighted a large land mass like an island in the sky. It was round and, illuminated by some immense light, shone brightly. We put in there, anchored, and disembarked, and, upon reconnoitering the countryside, found it was inhabited and under cultivation. During the day we could see no other land about but, when night came on, we saw a good many other islands the color of fire, some bigger than ours and some smaller. Below was another land mass with cities, rivers, seas, forests, and mountains; we guessed it was our own earth.

I decided to push farther inland. En route we ran into what is called locally the Buzzard Cavalry and were taken captive. Now the Buzzard Cavalry is made up of men who ride on buzzard back; they use birds the way we do horses. Their buzzards, you see, are enormous creatures, mostly three-headed; to give you an idea of their size I need only point out that any one of their wing feathers is longer and thicker than the mast on a big cargo vessel. This Buzzard Cavalry has orders to run patrol flights over the countryside and bring before the king any aliens they find. So we were arrested and brought before him. He looked us over and, guessing from the way we were dressed, said, "You are Greek, gentlemen?" We nodded. Then he said, "How did you get here with all that air to cross?" We told him our whole story and he, in turn, told us all about himself. His name was Endymion[7]

---

5. An allusion to the Greek habit of mixing wine with water. 6. The story is told in Ovid, *Metamorphoses* 1 (above, p. 899), although this was not necessarily Lucian's source or that of the painters he mentions. 7. Handsome mortal beloved by Selene, the moon.

and he, too, had come from earth: some time in the past he had been snatched up in his sleep, brought here, and made king of the place.

He explained to us that the land we were in was what appeared to people on earth as the moon. He told us, however, not to worry or be apprehensive, that we were in no danger, and that we would be given everything we needed. "Once I win this war I'm involved in against the people living on the sun," he added, "you can stay here with me and live happily ever after." We asked him who his enemies were and how the disagreement had come about. "Phaëthon,"[8] he told us, "is king of the people living on the sun—the sun, you see, is inhabited just like the moon—and he's been at war with us for a long while. It all started this way. Some time ago I got the idea of collecting the poorest among my subjects and sending them out to found a colony on the Morning Star, which is completely bare and uninhabited. Phaëthon out of spite called out his Ant Cavalry and intercepted the expedition before it had gone halfway. We were beaten—we were no match for his forces at the time—and turned back. Now I want to take the offensive again and establish my colony. If you're willing, come, join our army. I'll supply each of your men with one buzzard from the royal stables plus a complete outfit. We leave tomorrow."

"If that's what you want, why, of course," I replied.

We stayed the night with him as his guests. At the crack of dawn his lookouts reported that the enemy was approaching, and we rose and took our positions. Endymion had 100,000 troops, not counting supply corps, engineers, infantry, and contingents from foreign allies. Of the 100,000, 80,000 were Buzzard Cavalry and 20,000 Saladbird Cavalry. The saladbird is an enormous bird covered all over with salad greens instead of feathers; its wings look exactly like lettuce leaves. Alongside these were units of Peashooters and Garlickeers. He also had some allied forces from the Big Dipper: 30,000 Fleaborne Bowmen and 50,000 Windrunners. The Fleaborne Bowmen are mounted on huge fleas—hence the name—each as big as twelve elephants. The Windrunners, though ground forces, are able to fly through the air without wings. This is the way they do it: they wear shirts that go down to their feet; by pulling these up through the belt and letting them belly before the wind like sails, they're carried along the way a boat would be. In battle they serve for the most part as mobile infantry. There was talk that 70,000 Ostrich-Acorns and 50,000 Crane Cavalry were expected from the stars over Cappadocia, but they never showed up so I didn't see them and, consequently, haven't dared to describe what they're like—the fabulous things I heard about them are unbelievable.

So much for the make-up of Endymion's army. The equipment was standard throughout: a helmet made from a bean (enormous, tough beans are grown there), a breastplate of overlapping lupine husks (since the husks of the local lupines are very hard, like horn, they are made into armor by being stitched together), and a sword and shield of the Greek type.

At the appropriate moment Endymion drew up his forces for battle. The Buzzard Cavalry together with the king and his elite guard (including us) were on the right, the Saladbird Cavalry on the left, and, in the center, the

---

8. His father was the sun, or Apollo. The famous story of how he drove the sun's chariot too close to Earth and plunged to his death is ignored here.

cavalry units from the foreign allies, each disposed as it chose. The infantry, numbering about 60,000,000, he positioned as follows. He ordered the local spiders—they are numerous and big, any one of them larger by far than the average Aegean island—to span the air between the moon and the Morning Star with a web; as soon as they finished he stationed the infantry on the plain so formed, with General Nightly Goodday and two others in command.

On the enemy side the Ant Cavalry with Phaëthon in command formed the left wing. This arm uses enormous winged beasts similar to our ants in every respect except size, for the largest can run upwards of two hundred feet in length. The mount as well as the rider fights, principally by using its feelers. Their number was reportedly 50,000. On the right wing were the Aerognats, bowmen astride huge gnats, also 50,000 in number, and, behind them, the Aerojumpers. These, although light-armed infantrymen, are especially dangerous because they have slings that fire elephantine radishes capable of inflicting in whomever they hit a gangrenous wound which spells instant death; rumor has it these missiles are tipped with mallow juice. On the Aerojumpers' flank were 10,000 Stalk-and-Mushroomeers, heavy-armed troops for hand-to-hand combat, so called because they use mushrooms for shields and asparagus stalks for spears. Nearby were 5000 Dog-Acorns, dog-faced men who fought mounted on winged acorns; they had been sent by the inhabitants of Sirius. According to reports, Phaëthon had other allies who were late—the Cloud-Centaurs[9] and a detachment of slingers he had summoned from the Milky Way. The Cloud-Centaurs arrived after the battle had been decided. (How I wish they hadn't gotten there at all!) The slingers never showed up, and I've heard say that Phaëthon was so angry he subsequently laid their country waste with fire.

Such was the make-up of the force attacking us.[1] The standards were raised; donkeys—the substitute in these armies for trumpeters—brayed the charge on both sides; the lines clashed, and the battle was on. The sun's left immediately fled without waiting to engage our Buzzard Cavalry; we pursued, slaughtering as we galloped. Their right, however, overpowered our left, and the Aerognats gave chase all the way to where our infantry was drawn up. The infantry came to the rescue, and the Aerognats, well aware that their left had been defeated, gave way and ran. The retreat turned into a full-scale rout: our men killed or captured huge numbers. Streams of blood spilled over the clouds, drenching them and turning them the scarlet color they take on at sunset. Quite a lot dripped down on earth—which makes me wonder whether something similar hadn't occurred centuries ago and Homer simply jumped to the conclusion it was Zeus sending down a shower of blood to honor Sarpedon's death.[2]

As soon as we returned from the pursuit we erected two monuments, one on the cobwebs to commemorate the infantry battle, the other on the clouds for the air battle. Before we had finished, our lookouts reported the approach of the Cloud-Centaurs, the forces which were to have joined Phaëthon before the battle. Sure enough, they came into view, an absolutely incredible sight: each was a combination of man and winged horse, the human part as

---

9. Half human, half horse. When the legendary sinner Ixion tried to rape Hera, Zeus replaced her with an image made from a cloud. The Centaurs were born from this union.   1. This description of the battle lines of both sides parodies the battle narratives in Greek historians such as Thucydides.   2. *Iliad* 16.458–61.

tall as the upper half of the Colossus of Rhodes[3] and the equine as big as a large cargo vessel. I won't put down their number; it was so great I'm afraid no one will believe it. Sagittarius, the archer from the Zodiac, was in command. When they realized their allies had been defeated, they sent word to Phaëthon to return to the attack and, lining up in battle formation, charged. The Moonmen who, because of the chase and subsequent search for plunder, had broken ranks and scattered all over, were routed to a man; the king himself was pursued to the walls of his capital, and most of his birds were killed. After tearing down our two monuments, the Cloud-Centaurs overran the entire plain woven by the spiders and, in the process, took me and two of my shipmates prisoner. When Phaëthon arrived on the scene, monuments were again erected—this time for his side.

The very same day we were carried off to the sun, our hands tied behind our backs with a strip of cobweb. The enemy decided against laying siege; instead, on the way back they set up a barricade in mid-air, a double wall of cloud, which cut the moon off completely from the sun's light. The moon consequently went into total eclipse and remained in the grip of perpetual night. Greatly upset, Endymion sent a message to the Sunmen imploring them to tear down the structure and not force his subjects to live their lives in pitch-darkness. He said he was ready to submit to taxation, furnish military aid when required, and enter into a nonaggression pact, and he volunteered to supply hostages to guarantee performance. Phaëthon and his people held two referendums: in the first they were as bitter as ever, but in the second they changed their minds and agreed to a treaty of peace worded thus:[4]

The Sunmen and their allies hereby agree to a treaty of peace with the Moonmen and their allies on the following terms:

The Sunmen shall tear down the barricade they erected, shall hereafter never make war on the moon, and shall return all prisoners at a ransom to be determined for each;

the Moonmen shall grant autonomy to all other stars and shall not bear arms against the sun;

each party shall render aid to the other in the event of aggression by a third party;

the king of the Moonmen shall pay to the king of the Sunmen an annual levy of 10,000 jars of dew and provide 10,000 hostages from his own subjects;

both parties shall co-operate in founding the colony on the Morning Star; interested nationals of any other country may take part;

this treaty shall be inscribed on a tablet of silver and gold to be erected in mid-air at the common frontier.

Sworn to by

Firestone
Heater
Burns
for the sun;

---

3. Bronze statue of Helios, the sun god, over one hundred feet tall; one of the seven wonders of the ancient world.   4. What follows is a parody of treaties quoted by Thucydides.

> Nighting
> Moony
> Allbright
> for the moon.

Peace was made on these terms, and the moment it took effect the wall was torn down and the prisoners, including us, released. When we arrived back on the moon, our shipmates and Endymion himself came out a little way to meet us and welcomed us with tears in their eyes. Endymion asked us to stay on and take part in founding the colony, promising to give me his own son in marriage (there are no women on the moon). I was not to be persuaded and requested instead to be sent back down to the ocean. When he realized my mind was made up he let us go after a week's entertainment as his guests.

I want to describe the strange, new phenomena I observed during this stay on the moon.

The first is that males and not females do the childbearing. Marriage is with males, and there isn't even a word for "woman." Men under twenty-five are the wives, men over, the husbands. The embryo is carried not in the belly but in the calf. Once conception takes place, the calf swells up; after a due period of time it is cut open and the child, not yet alive, extracted. Life is induced by placing the child, mouth wide open, toward the wind. It's my opinion that the Greek word for calf, which literally means "belly of the leg," came to us from the moon, since there the calf and not the belly serves as the region of gestation.[5]

I shall now describe a second phenomenon which is even stranger, namely the race called "tree people." The procreation of tree people is as follows. A man's right testicle is cut off and planted in the ground. This produces a huge tree of flesh with a trunk like a penis. It has branches and leaves and, as fruit, bears eighteen-inch acorns. When ripe, these are gathered, the shells cracked open, and men are hatched from them.

Moonmen have artificial penises, generally of ivory but, in the case of the poor, of wood; these enable them to have intercourse when they mount their mates.

They never die of old age but dissolve and turn into air, like smoke.

The diet is the same for everyone: frog. Every time they light a fire they grill frogs on the coals because there's such a plentiful supply of these creatures flying about. While the cooking goes on, people seat themselves in a circle around the fire as if at a table and have a banquet sniffing in the smoke that's given off. Frogs provide their food; for drink they compress air in a cup to produce a liquid resembling dew.

They don't urinate or defecate. They have no rectal orifice so, instead of the anus, boys offer for intercourse the hollow of the knee above the calf, since there's an opening there. A bald pate or no hair at all is considered a mark of beauty; they can't stand men who wear their hair long. (Among the inhabitants

---

5. A Greek word for "calf" literally meant "shin's belly." It referred to the curved outline of the calf of the leg.

of the comets, on the other hand, the opposite is true, as some natives who were visiting the moon informed me.)[6] They do, however, wear beards which grow a little above the knee. Their feet terminate in a single toe, and they have no toenails. Above the rump grows a cabbage which hangs down like a tail; it's always ripe and doesn't break off even when they fall on their backs.

Their nasal discharge is a very bitter honey. When they work or exercise they sweat milk from every pore; by adding a few drops of the honey, they can curdle this into cheese. They make oil not from olives but onions, a rich grade that smells as sweet as myrrh. Their vines, which are plentiful, are a water-producing variety since the grapes are a form of hailstone; it's my theory that, when the wind blows and shakes the vines, the clusters burst and this produces hail on earth.

They use the belly as a pocket, putting into it whatever they need to carry with them, for it can be opened and closed. No liver is visible inside, only a rough, furry lining; infants consequently snuggle in there during cold weather.

The wealthy wear clothes of flexible glass and the poor of woven copper. The country is rich in copper; it's worked the way we work wool, by being soaked in water.

I am going to describe the kind of eyes they have, though I hesitate to do so since you're sure to think I'm lying. They have removable eyes: whenever they want they take them out and keep them safe until they need them; then they put them back and have sight again. Many who have lost their own borrow other people's, and some men, all well-to-do of course, own a good supply of spares. Everybody has ears of plane-tree leaves except the men hatched from acorns; theirs are of wood.

Another marvel I saw was in the royal palace. Here there is an enormous mirror suspended over a rather shallow well. If you stand in the well, you hear everything said on earth; if you look at the mirror, you see each city and nation as clearly as if you were standing over it. When I took a look, I saw my own homeland and my house and family; I can't say for sure whether they saw me.

Any person who doesn't believe that all this is so need only go there himself. He'll quickly discover I'm telling the truth.

When the time came, we bid farewell to the king and his court, embarked, and set off. Endymion gave me as a good-by gift two glass and five copper shirts and a suit of lupine-husk armor, all of which I left behind in the whale. He also sent a thousand of the Buzzard Cavalry to escort us for the first fifty miles. On the way we passed a number of other countries but didn't stop till we came to the Morning Star, which we found in the course of being colonized. Here we disembarked and took on water. Boarding ship again, we entered the Zodiac and passed the sun close to port, almost touching the shore. We didn't land, although my men were very anxious to, because the wind was foul. We could see, however, that the countryside was green and fertile, well-watered, and full of good things. The Cloud-Centaurs, who are in Phaëthon's pay, spotted us and came after our ship but, on learning we were protected by the treaty, turned back. Our Buzzard Cavalry escort had left us earlier.

---

6. The Greek word *komêtês*, "comet," means "long-haired." Citing the information of natives is in the manner of Herodotus.

We continued sailing that night and the next day and, toward evening, when we had already begun the slant down to earth, arrived at Lampville. This city is located in mid-air halfway between the Pleiades and the Hyades, at a much lower altitude than the Zodiac. On going ashore, we found no humans but only great numbers of lamps scurrying about or lounging around the main square and the water front. Most were small, the lower classes as it were; a few, the rich and influential, were conspicuously bright. The lamps had each their own house and bracket, bore names the way we do, and were capable of speech (we heard them talking). They did us no harm but actually offered hospitality; we, however, were afraid, and not one of us had the courage to accept their invitations to dine or spend the night. Downtown they have a city hall where the mayor, sitting in judgment all night, calls up each lamp by name. Those who don't answer are considered deserters and receive the death penalty, namely snuffing out. We stood around watching the proceedings, listening to the lamps defend themselves and submit their reasons for being late. At one point I recognized my own lamp. I spoke to it and asked how things were back home, and it gave me a full account.

We stayed the night there and the following day raised sail and set off again. By this time we were down among the clouds. We sighted Cloudcuckooland[7] and wondered about it but couldn't put in because of an unfavorable wind. We did receive word, however, that Jay Crow was on the throne. I was minded how people had foolishly been skeptical of what the playwright Aristophanes had written; he was a wise man who told the truth. Two days later we could see the ocean clearly. No land was visible except, of course, the islands in the air, and these now had a fiery bright aspect. On the third day, toward noon, the wind slackened off to a gentle breeze, and we landed on the surface of the sea. The moment we touched water we went hysterical with joy; we celebrated as best we could under the circumstances and then jumped overboard for a swim since the day was calm and the sea smooth.

But the prelude to worse trouble often wears the guise of a change for the better. We sailed along under ideal conditions for just two days. Toward sunrise of the third we suddenly sighted a host of sea monsters and whales, one of which, the biggest there, was over a hundred and fifty miles long. It came at us, churning up the sea far in front and making the water foam along its sides; the gaping jaws revealed a set of ivory-white teeth, each one of which was sharp as a stake and longer than our large phallic poles. We bid each other farewell, embraced, and waited for the end. By now the monster was on top of us and drank us in with a gulp, ship and all. But, before it could grind us to bits, the ship slipped through one of the gaps between the teeth and tumbled safely into its insides. There it was pitch-dark at first and we could see nothing; later, however, when the creature opened its mouth, we made out a vast cavity, big enough on all four sides, and high enough, to accommodate a town of ten thousand people. Lying about were the mangled remains of all sorts of fish and other sea creatures, large and small, as well as of anchors and spars, items of cargo, and human bones. Toward the center was a hilly land mass, the result, I imagine, of the settling of silt the monster had swallowed. As a matter of fact, a forest with all kinds of trees had taken

---

7. The city in the air built by the birds to usurp the gods' power in Aristophanes' comedy *The Birds*.

root in it, garden truck[8] had come up, and the whole expanse looked like a farm area. The coast was twenty-seven miles around. Sea birds—gulls and kingfishers—could be seen nesting in the trees.

At first we did nothing but weep. After a while I got my comrades on their feet and we took care of the ship by propping it up and of ourselves by rubbing sticks together to make a fire and cooking a meal out of what was available. There was all we wanted of every kind of sea food scattered about, and we still had some of the water we had taken on at the Morning Star. The following day, after getting up, whenever the monster opened its mouth we would catch sight sometimes of mountains, sometimes of sky alone, often of islands; this made us realize that the creature was rushing along into every part of the ocean.

By now we had become used to our new mode of life so, since I was curious to investigate everything, I took seven of my comrades and made my way into the forest. Before we had gone half a mile we came upon a shrine dedicated, as its inscription showed, to Poseidon; a little further on was a spring of clear water and a number of graves marked by tombstones. In addition we heard a dog barking, and smoke was visible in the distance. We guessed there was some sort of habitation about. We quickened our pace and came upon an old man and a young man hard at work tilling a garden plot and irrigating it with water piped from the spring. We stopped in our tracks, delighted, yet at the same time frightened. They, reacting probably in the same way, stood there speechless. Finally the old man spoke. "Who are you?" he said. "Seagods or men who have had the same bad luck as we? Though we two are human beings, born and bred on land, we've turned into marine life: we swim along with this beast that envelops us, and we're not at all sure just what we're experiencing—our guess is it's death, though we're convinced we're alive."

"We're human beings too," I replied. "New arrivals swallowed just yesterday, boat and all. We're here right now because we wanted to find out what was going on in this forest which looked so deep and thick. Apparently some god led us here to lay eyes on you and discover that we're not the only ones imprisoned in this monster. But tell us your story. Who are you? How did you get here?" He answered that he would neither talk about himself nor inquire about us until he had shared whatever hospitality he had available. He took us into his house—a building just big enough, furnished with beds and fitted out with everything else necessary—put before us greens, nuts, and fish, and poured out some wine. When we had eaten all we wanted, he asked about our experiences. I told him all our adventures in order: the storm, the island and what we had found there, the voyage in air, the war, and everything else up to our descent into the whale. After expressing amazement he, in turn, told us his story.

"Gentlemen," he said, "I am a Cypriot.[9] I left my homeland along with my son here and a large number of servants to go on a trading voyage. I headed for Italy with a general cargo aboard a big ship; you perhaps noticed the wreckage near the whale's mouth. We had a good voyage as far as Sicily. But at that point a gale caught us and, within three days, we were swept out into the Atlantic Ocean. There we met up with this whale and were gulped down,

8. Vegetables.   9. From Cyprus, island in the eastern Mediterranean.

ship and all. Only we two were saved; everyone else perished. After burying our shipmates, we erected a shrine to Poseidon and began the life you see us living—growing vegetables and existing on fish and nuts. The forest, as you can see, is extensive, but you can actually find inside it a good many vines which produce a very sweet wine. And you may have observed the spring; its water is delicious and ice-cold. We have leaves for bedding, burn all the wood we want, trap the birds that fly in, and catch live fish by going up to the monster's gills—where we can also bathe whenever we feel like it. What's more, not far away is a lake two miles around, full of all sorts of fish, and there we swim or sail in a little boat I built. It's been twenty-seven years since we were swallowed up. We can cope with just about everything except the people living around us; they're wild savages, hard to get along with, and they cause serious trouble."

"You mean to say," I broke in, "that there are others besides us in this whale?"

"Lots," he replied. "Hostile creatures with weird features. In the western part of the forest, that is, toward the tail, live the Kipperites who have an eel's eyes and a lobster's face; they're a bold, warlike people who eat their food raw. As for the sides, along the starboard flank live the Mermencats, human from the waist up and polecat below; they, however, have a somewhat less primitive sense of justice than the others. Along the port flank are the Crabhands and the Tunaheads, bound to each other by a military pact as well as emotional ties. In the central sector are the Lobstertails and Flounderfoots, belligerent and fast as a flash on their feet. The eastern sector, near the mouth proper, suffers from flooding and is, consequently, mostly uninhabited. In spite of this I live in it and pay the Flounderfoots an annual levy of five hundred oysters. That's the kind of country we're in. What you people have to do now is figure out how to stay alive in it and how to contend with so many enemies."

"How many are there all told?" I asked.

"Over a thousand," he said.

"How are they armed?" I asked.

"Nothing but fishbones," he replied.

"Then," I said, "since we're armed and they're unarmed, the best plan would be to fight it out with them. If we win, we'll live in peace for the rest of our lives."

Everybody agreed, so we went back to the ship and started our preparations. The provocation to war was to be a refusal to pay the tax. The due date was already at hand, and sure enough, messengers from the Flounderfoots arrived, demanding payment. The old man gave them a contemptuous answer and chased them away. The first to react were the Flounderfoots and Lobstertails; in a rage at Scintharus—to give the old man his name—they raised a great uproar and advanced to attack us. We had anticipated this and were ready for them: we were armed to the teeth, and twenty-five of our number were posted on the road in ambush. The ambuscade's orders were to lie low until they saw the enemy go by and then strike. They did precisely that. While they hit the enemy from behind and cut down his rear, the twenty-five of us—for Scintharus and his son fought, too—advanced on the enemy's front and, coming to grips with them, put up a desperate struggle with all the strength and courage we could command. Finally we put them to flight and chased them to the mouths of their caves. They had 170 casualties and we only one—our navigator, stabbed in the back with a mullet rib. The rest of the day and that night we spent on the battlefield. As a commemorative monument we planted in the ground the dried-out backbone of a dolphin.

By the next day the rest of the tribes had gotten the word and were on hand. On the right were the Kipperites under the command of General Tunny, on the left the Tunaheads, and in the center the Crabhands. The Mermencats stayed out, preferring to remain neutral. We advanced to meet the throng and, near the shrine of Poseidon, joined battle with a great war whoop that made the monster's insides re-echo like a cave. Since they were fighting unarmed, we forced them to break and run and, chasing them into the forest, made ourselves masters of the land once and for all. Pretty soon messengers arrived to parley about burying the dead and concluding a truce. It was not our intention to come to terms with them, so the next day we took the offensive and cut them down to a man—all except the Mermencats, that is. When they saw what was happening they made for the gills where they threw themselves into the sea. We advanced over the countryside, now wiped clean of enemies, and settled down to a life of peace from that moment on. Most of the time we spent in sports, hunting, raising vines, and gathering fruit from the trees—it was, in a word, like living a luxurious and untrammeled life in a vast prison from which there was no escape.

For twenty months we lived like this. On the fifth day of the twenty-first, toward the second opening of the mouth—the monster opened its mouth once every hour, and we used this as a way of reckoning time—toward the second opening of the mouth, as I was saying, we suddenly heard a great shouting and commotion plus what sounded like rowers at the oars and coxswains giving the stroke. In great excitement we crept right up to the mouth and, standing just back of the teeth, witnessed the strangest sight I have ever seen in my whole life: giants, three hundred feet tall, were sailing about on vast islands the way we do on war galleys. I know that what I'm going to describe will sound incredible, but I shall tell it anyway.

The islands, though not very high, were long, approximately ten miles around. Aboard each were about one hundred and twenty of these giants. Some, seated one behind the other along the two long sides of each island, were manipulating large cypress trees, leaves, branches, and all, like oars; aft, on the part that would be the poop, the helmsman stood atop a lofty hill, holding a bronze steering oar a thousand yards long. On the foredeck were about forty giants under arms to do the fighting; they resembled men in every feature except their hair, which was flaming fire, thereby doing away with the need for a helmet. There were no sails; instead, the wind struck the trees which grew all over, bellied them out, and so drove the island wherever the helmsman steered it. There was a rowing officer on each, and they had the oarsmen moving the islands at a smart pace just as on war galleys.

At first we saw only two or three but, after a while, about six hundred were visible. They split into two lines, clashed—and a naval battle was in full swing. Many of them met prow to prow and dashed each other to bits; many were sunk by a ram-thrust in the side; some were grappled and managed to break loose only after a long and hard struggle, for the marines on the foredecks boarded and fought gallantly, giving no quarter. Instead of grappling irons, they hurled huge octopuses tied to the end of a line; these wound their tentacles about the trees on an island and held it fast. For missiles they used, and very effectively, wagon-sized oysters and hundred-foot sponges. Fastcentaur commanded one side, Seadrink the other. The reason for the fight, apparently, was dolphin-rustling: Seadrink, it was alleged, had stolen great numbers from Fastcentaur's herds. All this we gathered from the shouting as they called to their leaders by name or hurled accusations at each other.

Finally Fastcentaur's forces won the day. They put about a hundred and fifty enemy islands out of action and captured three with crews and all; the rest backed water and fled. For a time the victors gave chase; then, since night was falling, they turned back to the disabled ships, took most of the enemy's as prizes, and salvaged all of their own—they had themselves suffered no less than eighty islands put out of action. To commemorate the naval victory they planted a monument on the whale's head, an enemy island nailed to a stake.

The victors moored their fleet for the night just off the beast, the sterns held by lines made fast to its flanks and the prows by anchors (they use big, powerful ones made of glass). The following day, after making a burnt offering on the whale's back and burying their dead there, they sailed off in the best spirits, singing some sort of song of victory.

And so ended the battle of the islands.

PART II

Fed up with our stay in the whale and unable to bear the life there any longer, I cast about for some way to escape. My first thought was to get out by tunneling through the starboard flank, and we began to hack away. However, after penetrating over half a mile without getting anywhere, we stopped digging and decided to start a forest fire instead. This, we figured, would kill the whale and, once that happened, a way out would be simple. So, beginning at the tail, we set a raging fire going. For seven days and nights the beast showed no reaction to the heat. On the eighth and ninth we could tell it was getting sick: it opened its mouth very slowly and each time quickly shut it again. On the tenth and eleventh necrosis finally set in and the body began to putrefy. On the twelfth we realized just in time that, unless we took advantage of a mouth-opening to prop the jaws apart so they couldn't be closed again, we were in danger of being locked up inside and dying along with the beast. So we braced the mouth open with huge beams and made our vessel ready for sea, putting aboard all the water and provisions it could carry. Scintharus was to be our navigator and helmsman.

The next day the whale was dead. We hauled the ship forward and worked it through a gap between the teeth. There, by slacking off on lines made fast to the teeth, we slowly lowered it into the sea. Then we climbed on the whale's back and, near where the giants' monument stood, offered up a sacrifice to Poseidon. Since there was no wind we camped there for three days. On the fourth we set off and en route ran into a great many corpses from the naval battle and kept going aground on them. We took the measurements of the bodies and were astonished.

A moderate wind carried us along for a few days. Then a strong northerly began to blow, bringing bitter cold and freezing the sea solid, not only on the surface but three hundred fathoms deep as well, so that we were able to leave the boat and run about on the ice. When the wind persisted and we could no longer bear it, we solved the problem by following a suggestion of Scintharus': we excavated a large cave in the ice and stayed in it for a month, keeping a fire going and eating the fish we had found while digging. Eventually our food ran out, so we emerged, pulled the ship free from where it had been frozen in, and, raising sail, glided easily and smoothly over the ice just as if we were traveling over water. Four days later the weather turned warm, the ice thawed, and all was water again.

After covering somewhat over thirty miles we put in at a small deserted island. Here we replenished our water supply, which had run out, and shot down two wild bulls. These had horns, not on the head, but under the eyes, just where Momus[1] had argued horns ought to be. We sailed away and before long left salt water and entered a sea of milk. In it was visible a white, vine-covered island which proved to be, as we found out later when we ate some of it, an enormous solid piece of cheese three miles around. The vines were full of clusters; we pressed some and got milk to drink instead of wine. In the center of the island was a shrine dedicated, as its inscription indicated, to Galatea,[2] the sea nymph. During the whole of our stay there the ground furnished our bread and meat and the vine-milk our drink. We heard that Salmoneus' daughter Tyro[3] was queen of the place; Poseidon had given her the appointment after he let her go.

We spent five days on the island and then sailed away before a light breeze over a gentle sea. Two days later we were out of the milk and back in blue salt water. Here we caught sight of a great number of men running about on the surface of the sea. They were like us in body, size, and every other respect except feet: theirs were of cork, and I presume this is why they were called "Corkfoots." We were amazed at the way they traveled fearlessly over the tops of the waves without going under. They came toward us and, greeting us in Greek, told us they were hurrying to their homeland, Cork. For a while they ran alongside and kept us company; then, after wishing us bon voyage, they turned off to head in their own direction.

Soon a great many islands came into view. Nearby, to port, was the Cork our friends were hurrying to, a town built on a large dome-shaped piece of cork. Farther on, and more to starboard, five enormous islands towered upward; huge flames were spurting from their summits. Dead ahead, over fifty miles away, was a low, flat island. When we finally came within range, we were caressed by a marvelous offshore wind, sweetly scented like the breeze the historian Herodotus tells us carries the perfume of southern Araby. For it was like a blend of the fragrance of roses, narcissuses, hyacinths, lilies, and violets, plus myrrh, laurel, and wild-grape blooms. Soon we drew near, breathing in the aroma joyfully and looking forward to a respite from our long succession of hardships. We could see any number of harbors, all capacious and sheltered on every side, crystal-clear rivers flowing placidly toward the sea, meadows, woods, and a multitude of songbirds, some warbling on the shore and many in the trees. An atmosphere rare and pure pervaded the place. Sweet, gently blowing breezes stirred the trees, and the

---

1. Personification of reproach and carping.   2. Her name would suggest the Greek *gala*, "milk."   3. Mother by Poseidon of Pelias, father of Jason the Argonaut, and Neleus, father of Nestor. She is at home in this milky landscape because her name suggests the Greek word for "cheese."

movement of the leaves produced a continuous melodic whistling like the sound from a shepherd's pipe in some deserted spot. And we could hear the mingled noises of a crowd, not a confused babel, but as at a banquet when some are playing music, some singing, and others beating time to the flute or lyre.

Entranced by it all, we headed for shore, moored, and disembarked, leaving Scintharus and two others in the boat. Advancing through a meadow filled with flowers, we ran into the local guards and sentries who bound us with rose garlands—the strongest fetters used there—and took us to their ruler. On the way we learned from them that the place was called the Isle of the Blest and that Rhadamanthus of Crete[4] ruled it. Sure enough, we were brought before him, and our hearing was put fourth on his docket. In the first case the defendant was Ajax the Greater: charged with having gone mad and committed suicide,[5] he was being tried to determine whether he should be allowed to associate with the Heroes. After a good deal of debate Rhadamanthus finally handed down his verdict: for the present Ajax was to take a dose of hellebore[6] and be turned over to Dr. Hippocrates;[7] later, when he had regained his sanity, he could attend the daily Heroes' banquet. The second involved the eternal triangle: a wrangle between Theseus and Menelaus over which of them Helen should live with.[8] Rhadamanthus decided in favor of Menelaus because of all the trouble and danger he had gone through on behalf of his marriage, plus the fact that Theseus had a number of other wives, the Amazon girl[9] and Minos' daughters.[1] The third was an argument between Alexander the Great and Hannibal of Carthage over precedence; judgment was in favor of Alexander, and a throne was set up for him alongside Cyrus the Elder of Persia.

The fourth case was ours. We were brought before Rhadamanthus; he asked us how it was we had set foot on hallowed soil while still alive, and we gave him a complete account of our adventures. He then had us removed and deliberated for a long time with his associate justices—quite a few shared the bench with him, including Athens' Aristides the Just.[2] He closed the discussion, and they handed down their verdict: after death we were to stand trial for leaving home and meddling; for the present, however, we could remain a specified time on the island, attend the Heroes' banquet, and then leave. Our departure date was set at not more than seven months hence.

The next thing we knew, our fetters of flowers had fallen from us of their own accord and we were being led toward the city and the banquet of the blest. Now this city is all of gold and encircled by walls of emerald. There are seven gates, each made from a solid piece of cinnamonwood. The city rests on foundations of ivory, and the entire area within the walls is paved with ivory. All the gods have temples built of beryl; inside each is an altar made of a huge single block of amethyst, on which the hecatombs[3] are

---

4. Traditionally, along with his brother Minos, one of the judges of the dead; he also appears in book 6 of Virgil's *Aeneid* (above, p. 876) as judge of the wicked in Tartarus. But he was also ruler of extraordinary souls in Elysium, or the Isle of the Blest.   5. Because the Greeks awarded the dead Achilles' armor to Odysseus and not to him. See *Odyssey* 11.605–36.   6. An emetic used to cure madness.   7. Traditionally the founder of medicine.   8. Long before she married Menelaus, Helen was carried off by Theseus but was rescued by her brothers Castor and Pollux.   9. Hippolyta (or Antiope), who bore Hippolytus to him.   1. Ariadne and Phaedra. The first he abandoned on the island of Naxos. Phaedra tricked Theseus into fatally cursing his son Hippolytus, by committing suicide and leaving a note falsely claiming that Hippolytus had raped her.   2. Athenian statesman (fifth century B.C.) and rival of Themistocles. His uprightness was proverbial.   3. Groups of one hundred animals for sacrifice.

offered up. Around the city flows a river of the finest myrrh, almost two hundred feet wide and deep enough to swim in comfortably. The baths are large chambers of glass heated by cinnamonwood fires; instead of water the tubs are filled with warm dew. All clothing is made of finespun purple cobwebs.

The inhabitants are disembodied, i.e., they are without flesh or substance. They do have a discernible outline and form but no more than this. In spite of having no body, they stand and move, think and talk; in short, it's as if their naked souls were walking about clad in the semblance of their bodies. Without testing them by touch, you would never know you weren't looking at actual bodies; they're like shadows but shadows that stand erect and have color. They never grow old but remain the age they were when they arrived.

The island experiences neither night nor the full light of day. Something like the bright gray we see preceding the dawn, when the sun hasn't yet risen, illuminates the place at all times. There is only one season of the year, an eternal spring, and only one wind blows, the Zephyr.[4] The countryside is lush with every variety of flower and of fruit and shade tree. The vines bear twelve times a year and are harvested monthly. The pomegranate, apple, and other fruit trees bear, we were told, thirteen times a year since they bear twice during Minosmonth, as it's called in the local calendar. Instead of wheat the grain stalks are tipped with loaves of bread like mushrooms. Around the city are 365 springs of water, 365 of honey, and 500 of myrrh (smaller, however, than the others), plus seven rivers of milk and eight of wine.

The Heroes' banquet is held on the outskirts of town in what is called the Elysian Field, a lovely meadow in the center of a thick stand of trees of every kind which shade the diners. The couches are mounds of flowers. The winds wait on table and serve everything except wine. There's no need to serve this—the banqueting area is surrounded by large glass trees of the finest crystal whose fruit is wineglasses of all sizes and shapes; as each Hero takes his place at table, he harvests one or two, puts them by his setting, and they immediately fill themselves up. This takes care of the wine; for garlands the nightingales and other songbirds gather in their bills flowers from the nearby meadows and, hovering overhead and warbling sweetly, let them flutter down like snowflakes. And perfume is provided as follows: thick clouds suck up myrrh from the five hundred springs and the river, float over the banqueters, and, squeezed gently by the wind, send it down in a fine rain like the dew.

At table ample time is given over to music and singing. The songs are mostly from the epics of Homer (who is there in person, taking part in the festivities; his seat is just above Odysseus'). There's a boys' and a girls' chorus. The leaders, who also provide the musical accompaniment, are Locris' Eunomus, Lesbos' Arion, Anacreon, and Stesichorus (I actually saw him: since Helen had by this time forgiven him, he was one of the company).[5] When these choruses finish, a relief chorus of swans, swallows, and nightingales takes over and sings to a musical accompaniment supplied by the whole forest under the leadership of the wind. What chiefly ensures a good time for all, however, is this: right beside the banquet area are two springs, one of laughter and the other of joy; inasmuch as all the guests begin the feast

4. The west wind, typically gentle and associated with fertility.   5. Eunomos and Arion were legendary singers. Anacreon and Stesichorus were lyric poets of the sixth century B.C. Stesichorus is said to have gone blind after writing a poem condemning Helen for her infidelity but to have regained his sight when he wrote another poem that absolved her guilt.

with a drink from each, they spend the rest of the time laughing and enjoying themselves.

I want to mention some of the celebrities I saw there. All the demigods were present, plus all the veterans of the Trojan War except Ajax the Lesser;[6] he, we were told, was the only one from either army undergoing punishment in the Land of the Damned. Of the non-Greeks, there were Cyrus the Elder and Younger, Scythia's Anacharsis, Thrace's Zamolxis, and Italy's Numa.[7] Also present were Sparta's Lycurgus, Athens' Phocion and Tellus, and all the Sages except Periander.[8] I saw Socrates chatting with Nestor and Palamedes[9] amid a circle of good-looking boys, among whom were Hyacinth, Narcissus, and Hylas.[1] I got the impression Hylas was the one he was in love with; at least it was mostly Hylas he was refuting. We heard that Rhadamanthus was annoyed with him and had threatened a number of times to throw him off the island if he kept on with his nonsense and refused to give up his Socratic irony and have fun. Plato wasn't there—the only one missing; they told us he was living in the republic he had invented, running it with the constitution and laws he had written. Aristippus[2] and Epicurus[3] were not only there but were the island's favorites—they were such nice, pleasant fellows and such good company at parties. I saw Aesop, who's assigned the role of buffoon at the banquets, and Diogenes,[4] so changed in his ways that he had married Lais the courtesan and gone in for drink; he was always getting up from the table to go into a dance or other alcoholic carryings-on. None of the Stoics was there: we were told that Chrysippus[5] had been denied permission to enter the island until he had had his fourth dose of hellebore, and all the others were still toiling up the straight and narrow path to virtue. We heard that the people of the Academy[6] wanted to come but were still holding off and arguing; the one point they couldn't come to any conclusion about was whether an island such as this existed. Besides, I imagine they were afraid to stand judgment before Rhadamanthus; after all, they were the ones who denied all standards of judgment. Rumor had it that a big group of them once did follow the people who were heading here but, being dawdlers and lacking the courage of conviction, fell behind and turned back at the halfway point.

These were the chief celebrities. Of them all the most respected was Achilles and, after him, Theseus.

Their attitude on sex and making love is as follows. They have intercourse

6. Greek hero of the Trojan War who was shipwrecked and drowned on the voyage home for defying the gods.   7. Second king of Rome; was thought to have established a framework of laws and religious cults in the city. The elder Cyrus founded the Persian Empire in the sixth century B.C. The younger Cyrus was a Persian prince who died trying to depose his older brother from the throne at the end of the fifth century B.C.; the Greek writer Xenophon gives a favorable portrait of him. Anacharsis, a Scythian prince, was said to have traveled in Greece in the sixth century B.C. and was celebrated for his wisdom. Zamolxis was supposed to be either a Thracian god or a former slave of Pythagoras who successfully passed himself off as a god.   8. *Lycurgus:* legendary lawgiver of Sparta. *Phocion:* a leading Athenian general and statesman of the fourth century B.C. and a student of Plato. *Tellus:* an Athenian described as the embodiment of happiness by Solon to the Lydian king Croesus, according to Herodotus. *Sages:* seven statesmen and practical thinkers of the early sixth century in Greece, whose sayings were widely quoted. The list sometimes included Periander, the bloodthirsty tyrant of Corinth.   9. Hero known for his cleverness, whose condemnation and death by the Greek army at Troy his rival Odysseus was said to have contrived.   1. Boy loved by Heracles who was pulled into a pool and drowned by amorous nymphs. *Hyacinth:* mortal boy loved by Apollo. *Narcissus:* handsome youth who fell in love with his own image reflected in a pool, to the nymph Echo's chagrin.   2. Follower of Socrates known for his luxurious style of living.   3. Founder of the Epicurean school of philosophy, which depended on the atomic theory of Democritus and based the happy life on pleasure and the absence of disturbance.   4. Famous Cynic philosopher known for the exceptional austerity of his life and his acerbic attacks on all forms of social and civic life.   5. Greek philosopher of the third century B.C. who established Stoic thought on a systematic basis.   6. A school established by Plato that lasted until the first century B.C. A rigorous skepticism became characteristic of its thought.

with both males and females, and in public with everybody looking on; this doesn't strike them as anything to be the least bit ashamed of. Socrates is an exception. He swore up and down that his relations with young men were of the purest—and everybody there accused him of perjuring himself; as a matter of fact, he still insisted on it even after Hyacinth and Narcissus had a number of times confessed the truth. They all share women in common ungrudgingly;[7] on this point they're perfect Platonists. And young boys offer themselves without hesitation to whoever wants them.

I didn't let more than two or three days go by before I went to see Homer at a time when neither of us was busy and quizzed him at length. I made a point of asking him where his birthplace was, explaining that it was a matter people were still trying hard to settle at this late date. He told me he was aware that some thought it was Chios, others Smyrna, and most Colophon, but actually he was a Babylonian; his real name was Tigranes and he only changed it to Homer when he was later sent as a hostage (*homeros*) to Greece. Next I asked him about the verses marked by editors as spurious: had he written them? His answer was yes, every one; this made me realize what a lot of nonsense Professors Zenodotus and Aristarchus[8] had written. Since he had satisfied me on these points, I then asked why he had started the *Iliad* with the words "Sing of the wrath." For no particular reason, he replied; it had just come into his head that way. I also wanted to know whether he had written the *Odyssey* before the *Iliad* as is generally held, and the answer was no. And he's not blind, as is also generally believed; I knew that immediately—I didn't have to ask; I could see it with my own eyes. I quizzed him like this on a number of occasions later on as well, whenever I saw he had time to spare, and he answered all my questions readily— particularly after his success in the lawsuit. This was an action for criminal assault brought by Thersites[9] on the grounds that the poet had jeered at him in the *Iliad*; Homer retained Odysseus as attorney and won the case.

About this time Pythagoras[1] arrived; having gone through his seventh metamorphosis and seventh mortal existence, he was finally finished with the transmigrations of his soul. The whole right side of his body was of gold. He was judged qualified to join the company, although even when I left there was still uncertainty under what name, whether Pythagoras or Euphorbus. Then Empedocles[2] showed up, cooked through and through, his whole body roasted. In spite of all his begging he was denied admission.

Time passed, and the date came around for the athletic contests they call the Mortuaric Games. The board of commissioners consisted of Achilles, serving his fifth consecutive term, and Theseus, serving his seventh. To go through the whole program would take too long, so I'll report on only the most important events. In wrestling Carus, one of Heracles' descendants, threw Odysseus to take the championship. In boxing Areus, the Egyptian whose grave is in Corinth, was paired with Epeus, and the match ended in

7. A characteristic of the ideal state in Plato's *Republic*.   8. Heads of the great library at Alexandria in the third and second centuries B.C., whose work on Homer established texts of his poems that are the ancestors of our own. Both were concerned to identify interpolated lines and passages.   9. A common soldier, described as ugly and misshapen, who defies Agamemnon in book 2 of the *Iliad* and is beaten by Odysseus, to the Greek army's amusement.   1. Philosopher of the sixth century B.C. who believed in reincarnation and claimed, it was said, that he had been the Trojan warrior Euphorbus.   2. Philosopher of the fifth century B.C. rumored to have committed suicide by throwing himself into the volcanic crater of Mt. Aetna.

a draw.[3] Combined boxing and wrestling wasn't on the program; they don't go in for it. I can't remember any longer who was the winner in track. In the poets' contest Hesiod[4] was awarded the victory, although Homer actually won by a wide margin. The prizes for all events were crowns made of plaited peacock feathers.

The games had scarcely ended when word came that the condemned in the Land of the Damned had broken their chains and overpowered the guards and were advancing on the island; the ringleaders were the Sicilian dictator Phalaris, the Egyptian despot Busiris, the Thracian despot Diomed, plus Sciron and Pityocamptes.[5] On receiving the news, Rhadamanthus mobilized the Heroes, and they formed up on the shore; the commanding officers were Theseus, Achilles, and Ajax, who had by now recovered his sanity. Battle was joined and the Heroes won, with most of the credit going to Achilles. Socrates also distinguished himself in action, much more than he had at Delium[6] during his lifetime. He was stationed on the right wing and, when four of the enemy charged him, he didn't retreat; he never once turned his back. For this he was afterward awarded a lovely, spacious estate in the suburbs where he would gather his disciples and hold dialogues with them; he named the place Post Mortem Academy. The defeated forces were rounded up and sent back in irons to serve even stiffer sentences. Homer wrote an epic about the fight and, when I left, gave me the manuscript to bring to the people on earth, but I subsequently lost it along with everything else. The first line went:

Sing to me this time, O Muse, of the war fought by ghosts of the Heroes.

After the battle they declared a holiday and, as is the custom whenever they win a war, cooked up beans for a great victory feast. Everyone took part except Pythagoras, who sat by himself and went hungry since he can't stand bean food.[7]

Six months had passed and we were in the middle of the seventh when an unexpected situation arose. For some time Scintharus' son Cinyras, a big, handsome boy, had been in love with Helen, and it wasn't hard to see that she was madly in love with him. In fact, time and again during the banqueting they would exchange signals or drink to each other or get up, just the two of them, and go wandering in the forest. The boy was so much in love that the moment came when he lost his head and made plans to abduct her—she was perfectly agreeable—and escape to one of the surrounding islands, either Cork or the Isle of Cheese. Well in advance they swore in the three most reckless men in my crew as accomplices. To his father Cinyras didn't mention a word; he knew the old man would have put a stop to the whole business. When the time seemed right they put their plan into action. After nightfall—I wasn't there; I was still at the banquet where I happened to have

---

3. Areus was a philosopher at the court of Augustus and presumably a scrawny specimen. Epeus won the boxing crown at the funeral games for Patroclus (*Iliad* 23.664–99) [Translator's note].   4. Seventh century B.C. poet whose works, especially the *Theogony* and the *Works and Days*, were often ranked with Homer's. According to an ancient story, Hesiod defeated Homer in a poetry contest by a decision of the judge that overrode the popular will.   5. Mythical rulers, all masters at particularly gruesome ways of killing people [Translator's note].   6. Site of an Athenian defeat in the Peloponnesian War at which Socrates distinguished himself for courage.   7. Pythagoreans, though vegetarians, were not supposed to eat beans.

dozed off—giving everybody the slip, Cinyras smuggled Helen aboard our ship and quickly got under way. Toward midnight Menelaus woke up and, seeing his wife's bed empty, raised a hue and cry, routed out his brother,[8] and hurried to the chief authority, Rhadamanthus. When day dawned the lookouts reported they could see the ship well out to sea. So Rhadamanthus ordered fifty Heroes to take one of their men-of-war (galleys hewn from a single stalk of asphodel) and give chase. By rowing hard they caught up around noon, just as the runaways were about to enter the sea of milk near the Isle of Cheese; that's how close they had come to making their escape. The ship was taken in tow with a hawser of roses, and everybody returned. Helen was in tears and hid her face in shame. Cinyras and his accomplices were brought to Rhadamanthus who, before passing sentence, asked them whether there were any more in on the scheme; when they said no, he had them bound by the penis, flogged with mallow, and sent off to the Land of the Damned. The Assembly of Heroes then voted to expel us from the island before our time was up; we could stay the next day and no longer.

This filled me with dismay; I broke into tears at the thought of leaving such a good life and becoming a wanderer again. They consoled me with the assurance that I would be back before many years had passed, and even pointed out my future assembly seat and banquet couch, both in choice locations. I called on Rhadamanthus and begged him to tell me my future and show me my route. He vouchsafed that, after a good deal of wandering and danger, I would eventually return home, but he refused to add how long it would take. However, he did point to the surrounding islands—five were visible nearby and a sixth in the distance—and say, "These five, the ones you see spurting great flames, are where the damned are. That sixth is the City of Dreams. Beyond it is Calypso's island, but you can't make it out from here. After sailing past all these you will come to the vast continent that lies across the sea from Europe. There you will have many adventures, pass through various lands, and live among hostile peoples before you finally reach your own continent."

This was all he would tell. But he plucked a mallow root[9] from the ground and, handing it to me, told me to pray to it when we were in mortal danger. And he warned me, when I did reach the land across the sea, not to poke fires with a sword, eat beans, or make love to boys over eighteen; if I kept these rules in mind, I could look forward to making my return to his island.

So I made the ship ready for sea and, when it was banquet time, had my final feast with the Heroes. The following day I went to see Homer and asked him to compose a two-line memorial for me. He did so, and I had it inscribed on a slab of beryl which I set up on the water front. The inscription read:

Lucian, a man who is dear to the blessed immortals in heaven,
Witnessed the things that are here, then returned to his dearly loved
homeland.

We stayed that day as well and the following morning, with all the Heroes on hand to see us off, sailed away. At the last minute, while Penelope wasn't looking, Odysseus came up to me and handed me a letter to deliver to

8. Agamemnon.   9. An edible plant, proverbially food for paupers.

Calypso in Ogygia. Rhadamanthus had Nauplius the ferryman go along with us so that, in case we stopped off at the islands of the damned, we wouldn't be mistaken for the usual callers and arrested.

We passed out of range of the island's breeze, and the fragrance was suddenly replaced by a stink like burning asphalt, sulphur, and pitch combined. In addition there was an unbearable odor of human flesh roasting. The air was murky and misty, and a pitchy dew dripped steadily down. We could hear the crack of whips and the screams of a great many men.

Of these islands I will describe only the one we went ashore on; we didn't go near the others. It was a parched expanse of jagged stone without a tree or spring on it, girdled by sheer rock walls. We managed to creep up along ledges and made our way inland by a path full of prickles and thorns over a revoltingly ugly countryside. We came up to the prison and punishmentarium, and the first thing to astonish us was the nature of the place. The very ground was carpeted with knife points and thorns. Three rivers ringed the area: the outer of slime, the middle of blood, and the inner of fire. This last was a vast and impassable body that flowed like water, had waves like the sea, and was full of fish, some of which looked like torches and others, a smaller variety called candlefish, like glowing coals. There was only one narrow entrance way across all three, and the man on guard at the gate was Timon of Athens.[1] With Nauplius in the lead, however, we got through and witnessed the condemned undergoing punishment. There were plenty of kings as well as ordinary people; we even recognized some faces among the latter. We also spotted Cinyras hanging by the penis and smoldering over a slow fire. Guides took us around and, for each case, filled in the biographical data and reasons for punishment. The stiffest sentences of all were being served by those who, in life, had been liars or had written books that didn't tell the truth; Ctesias, Herodotus, and a good many others were in this group. The sight of them gave me high hopes for my own future: I knew in my heart that I had never told a lie. But I couldn't take any more of the sight, so I rushed back to the ship, said good-by to Nauplius, and sailed away.

Soon we sighted, not far off, the Isle of Dreams, dim and hard to make out. It behaved very much the way dreams do: as we approached, it receded, moving further away and eluding us. Eventually we caught up and sailed into what is called Sleepy Harbor, situated near the ivory gates and the spot where the Shrine of the Holy Rooster stands. Late in the afternoon we went ashore, entered the city, and were confronted by hosts of dreams of all kinds.

I want first to describe the city itself, since no one else has ever written about it except Homer,[2] who does little more than mention it and not very accurately at that. It's completely surrounded by a forest of lofty poppy and mandrake trees where hordes of bats, the only species of bird on the island, roost. Alongside flows Nightway River, as it's named, and by the gates are two springs called Sleepytime and Allnight. The city wall is high and gaily painted the colors of the rainbow. There are four gates, not two as Homer says. One of iron and one of ceramic lead to Drowsy Meadow; we were told that nightmares and dreams of murder and violence leave by these. Then two others lead to the water front and the sea, one of horn and the one we

---

1. The proverbial misanthrope.   2. In book 19 of the *Odyssey,* where Penelope describes the ivory gate of false dreams and the horn gate of true ones.

came through, of ivory. As you enter the city, on the right is the Temple of Night—Night is one of the two chief local deities; the other is the Holy Rooster whose shrine is near the water front—and, on the left, the palace of Sleep. Sleep is king of the place along with two subordinates chosen by him, Prince A. Confusing Revery and Prince I. Dreamof Wealth. In the middle of the main square is a spring called Fount Snoreful. Nearby are the twin temples of Trick and Truth as well as the holy of holies and the local seat of prophecy. This last is in the hands of Antiphon, the interpreter of dreams, who also delivers the oracles; he received his appointment from Sleep.

As for the dreams, no two are alike in either character or appearance. Some are tall, with good figures and good looks, others short and ugly; some are golden (that was my impression, at least), others plain and cheap. There were dreams with wings, freakish dreams, and dreams which, dressed up like kings, queens, gods, and the like, looked as if they were going to a carnival. Many we recognized because we had seen them long ago. These actually came up and greeted us like old friends, then invited us to their homes and, putting us to sleep, extended us the warmest and most generous hospitality, including lavish entertainment of every sort plus a promise to make us kings and princes. Some of them even led us to our homelands, gave us a look at our families, and brought us back, all the same day. We stayed a month among them, regaling ourselves with slumber. Then a sudden clap of thunder awoke us; we sprang up, provisioned the ship, and sailed off.

Three days later we put in at Ogygia[3] and disembarked. The first thing I did was to open Odysseus' letter and read it. Here is what it said:

> Dear Calypso,
>   Let me tell you what happened to me. Right after I finished the raft and sailed away from you, I was shipwrecked, and Leucothea barely managed to rescue me and bring me to Phaeacia. The Phaeacians escorted me home and there I found a mob of my wife's suitors living high, wide, and handsome at my expense. I killed them all, and Telegonus, the son I had by Circe, later on killed me. Now I'm on the Isle of the Blest full of regrets at having given up my life with you and the immortality you offered me. If I ever get the chance, I'll run away and come to you.

This is how the letter read, except for a postscript about us, a request to furnish us hospitality. I went a short distance in from the beach and came upon the cave—it was just as Homer had described it—and the lady herself busy with her spinning. She took the letter, read it, and had a good long cry. But then she invited us to be her guests and, in the course of serving us a fine dinner, quizzed us about Penelope as well as Odysseus: What did she look like? Was she as discreet as Odysseus used to brag she was? We gave her the answers we imagined she wanted to hear.

Afterward we went back to the ship and camped for the night alongside it on the beach. At dawn we set off with a strong wind driving us on. For two days we were buffeted about and then, on the third, ran into the Pumpkin-

---

3. The home of the sea nymph Calypso, with whom Odysseus spent seven years before making his way to the Phaeacians and then home to Ithaca.

pirates. These are savages from the neighboring islands who prey upon all passing traffic. Their ships are enormous pumpkins, ninety feet long, which they make into boats by removing the pulp to leave just a hollow shell, drying thoroughly, and stepping a reed mast with a pumpkin leaf for a sail instead of a piece of canvas. They attacked with two detachments of marines who, by firing pumpkin seeds instead of stones, wounded quite a few of us. The battle went on with neither side gaining until, about noon, we noticed the Sailingnuts coming up on the Pumpkinpirates' rear. The next moment made clear that the two were enemies. For, as soon as our opponents realized who were heading their way, they forgot all about us, put about, and engaged the new foe. We seized the occasion to raise sail and flee, leaving the two of them to fight it out. The Sailingnuts were sure to win since there were more of them—they had five detachments of marines—and they were fighting from stronger ships. These, made from the shells of nuts cracked in half and scooped out, were each thirty yards long.

As soon as they were out of sight we attended to our wounded. From that moment on we generally kept ourselves fully armed in the constant expectation of attack—and not for nothing; just before sunset, from the shore of a barren island a second band of pirates dashed out at us, this time twenty or so men riding big dolphins. The dolphins, rearing and neighing just like horses, carried them in perfect safety. When they came within range they divided their forces and, from both sides at once, peppered us with dried cuttlefish and crabs' eyes. We replied with a volley of arrows and javelins which they couldn't stand up to; they fled back to their island, most of them nursing wounds.

About midnight, in a calm sea, before we realized what was happening we ran aground on an immense kingfisher's nest, no less than seven miles around.[4] The kingfisher, not much smaller than the nest, was sailing along on it, hatching her eggs. She flew away in fright with a mournful cry, and the stream from her wings as she took off nearly capsized our ship. When day dawned we climbed into the nest and saw that it was constructed of huge logs, very much like a raft. There were five hundred eggs, each larger than a seven-gallon jug. The chicks inside were already alive and croaking away. As a matter of fact, we hacked one of the eggs open with axes and hatched out a chick that, even without feathers, was twenty times as big as a buzzard.

We had sailed a little over twenty miles from the nest when a series of tremendous miracles left their mark on us. The figurehead of the goose on our stern suddenly flapped its wings and honked; our helmsman Scintharus, who had been bald for years, grew a shock of hair; and, strangest of all, the mast burst into bloom, sprouting branches at its sides and bearing fruit at its tip, figs and a cluster of dark grapes not quite ripe. The sight naturally left us in consternation; we prayed to the gods at these singular apparitions.

A little over fifty miles further on we sighted a vast and thick forest of pine and cypress. We figured it was land, but it turned out to be a bottomless sea overgrown with rootless trees. In spite of this the trees stood firm and erect, as if floating upright. When we drew near and sized up the situation, we were in a quandary as to what to do: to sail through the trees was impossi-

---

4. It was popularly believed that the kingfisher (*halcyon*) built its nest on the water and that during the days the eggs were hatching—the "halcyon days"—the sea remained perfectly calm [Translator's note].

ble—they were too thickly massed—nor did it seem any easier to go back the way we had come. I climbed to the top of the tallest tree and took a look at what lay beyond. I could see that the forest stretched for only five miles or a bit more, and after that was more ocean. So we decided to set the ship on the solidly matted foliage of the treetops and see if we couldn't transport it that way to the water on the other side. And so we did: we made a heavy cable fast to the vessel, heaved and hauled until we had swayed it up, set it on the treetops, and, hoisting sail, were drawn along by the force of the wind just as on water. At this point I was minded of a line by Antimachus;[5] somewhere he writes of

Those who arrived after setting a course through the shadowy forest.

Having forced our way through the forest, we arrived at open water and, using the same technique, lowered the ship into it. We sailed on over a crystal-clear sea until we came to a point where the water had parted to form a vast chasm like the fissures, caused by earthquake, that we so often see on land. We doused sail and the ship lost way just inches short of going over the brink. Leaning over, we peered down to a depth of more than a hundred miles. It was a weird and frightening sight—the sea stood fixed on each side as if split apart. We then looked about us and noticed that, not too far off on the right, the chasm was spanned by a bridge of water which, joining the surface of the sea on either side, flowed from the one into the other. So we ran out the oars, drove the ship over the bridge, and, after a grueling struggle, completed a crossing we had never expected to make.

On the other side we were met by a calm sea and an island of no great size, inhabited and easy to approach. The natives, a race of savages called Bullheads, had horns and looked like the mental image we have of the Minotaur. We disembarked and headed inland to see if we could secure water and provisions somewhere, for we had run out of both. We found water nearby but nothing else. However, we did hear not far off a great bellowing. Thinking it was a herd of bulls, we inched forward and came upon the Bullheads. The minute they saw us they charged and managed to snatch three of my men; the rest of us made it back to the sea. We armed ourselves—we had no intention of leaving our comrades go unavenged—and then fell on the Bullheads as they were dividing up the flesh of the men they had killed. They scattered in fear, and we went after them. After cutting down about fifty and taking two alive, we returned to the shore with our prisoners.

We still hadn't found any food. All my shipmates were in favor of slaughtering the two captives, but I didn't approve. Instead, I tied the pair up and kept them under guard until a delegation arrived from the Bullheads bringing an offer of ransom. We could make out what they were after from the way they nodded their heads and bellowed mournfully, as if pleading. The ransom consisted of a big batch of cheeses, dried fish, onions, and four deer of a species which had only three feet—two in back but in front, where the forelegs had fused, only one. We accepted these terms, surrendered our prisoners, and, after spending a day on the island, sailed off.

By now we were seeing fish, birds were flying by, and many other signs that we were nearing land kept appearing. A little farther along we saw men

5. An epic poet who flourished around 400 B.C.

using a novel method to travel over water, one in which they were boat and passenger at one and the same time. This is the way it was done: a man would lie on his back in the water, induce an erection, hoist a sail on it (their penises were enormous), and, holding the sheets in his hands, bowl along before the wind. Behind these came others sitting on pieces of cork and driving, reins in hand, teams of dolphins; these plunged ahead, pulling the corks behind them. None of these people harmed us or fled from us; they continued fearlessly and peaceably on their way after looking our ship over from all sides and registering astonishment at its shape.

Toward evening we arrived at an island of middling size. It was inhabited by women—at least so we thought. They spoke Greek, as we discovered when they came up to greet us and bid us welcome. They were all beautiful and young, heavily made up the way courtesans are, and dressed in flowing gowns that swept the ground. The place was called Nag Island and the city Waterburg. Each of the women paired off with one of my men and, leading him to her house, made him her guest. I held back a bit—I had a premonition all was not well. Looking about me more closely, I caught sight of piles of human bones and skulls lying about. But to raise an alarm, gather my men, and make a rush for our arms didn't seem the thing to do. Instead I took out my mallow and prayed to it long and hard to rescue us from the tight spot we were in. A little while later, as my hostess was serving me, I got a glimpse of her legs—and they weren't a woman's limbs but a donkey's shanks. Drawing my sword, I seized her and tied her up. Then I interrogated her thoroughly. Very reluctantly she admitted to me that she and the others were women of the sea called Asslegs and that their food was the strangers who came to the island. "We get them drunk," she explained, "go to bed with them, and then attack them in their sleep." The minute I heard this I left her there trussed up and, climbing on the roof, summoned my shipmates with a shout. When I had gotten them together, I told them the whole story, pointed out the bones, and led them inside to my prisoner. She dissolved into water on the spot and disappeared. However, just as a test, I thrust my sword into it—and it turned into blood.

We rushed back to the ship and sailed off. When day dawned we sighted a continent that we took to be the one across the ocean from Europe. After falling on our knees and praying, we held a council about the future. Some of us felt we should merely step ashore and then turn right around and sail back; others held we should leave the ship and proceed into the interior to see what the natives were like. In the midst of the discussion a violent storm broke which dashed our ship on the beach and smashed it to pieces. We barely managed to swim to safety, each of us clutching his weapons and anything else he could carry.

You now know our story up to the moment we reached this new continent: our adventures on the sea, during our trip around the islands, in the air, and, after that, inside the whale; then, after escaping from there, our further adventures among the Heroes, the dreams, and, finally, the Bullheads and Asslegs. What happened to us on the new continent I will tell in the subsequent volumes.[6]

---

6. The biggest lie of all, as a disappointed ancient scribe noted in the margin of his copy [Translator's note].

AUGUSTINE

A.D. 354–430

Aurelius Augustine was born in 354 in Tagaste, in North Africa. He was baptized as a Christian in 387 and ordained bishop of Hippo, in North Africa, in 395. When he died there in 430, the city was besieged by Gothic invaders. Besides the *Confessions* (begun in 397) he wrote *The City of God* (finished in 426) and many polemical works against schismatics and heretics.

He was born into a world that no longer enjoyed the "Roman peace." Invading barbarians had pierced the empire's defenses and were increasing their pressure every year. The economic basis of the empire was cracking under the strain of the enormous taxation needed to support the army; the land was exhausted. The empire was Christian, but the Church was split, beset by heresies and organized heretical sects. The empire was on the verge of ruin, and there was every prospect that the Church would go down with it.

Augustine, one of the men responsible for the consolidation of the Church in the West, especially for the systematization of its doctrine and policy, did not convert to Christianity until he had reached middle life. "Late have I loved Thee, O Beauty so ancient and so new," he says in his *Confessions*, written long after his conversion. The lateness of his conversion and his regret for his wasted youth were among the sources of the energy that drove him to assume the intellectual leadership of the Western church and to guarantee, by combating heresy on the one hand and laying new ideological foundations for Christianity on the other, the Church's survival through the dark centuries to come. Augustine had been brought up in the literary and philosophical tradition of the classical world, and it is partly because of his assimilation of classical literature and method to Christian training and teaching that the literature of the ancient world survived at all when Roman power collapsed in a welter of bloodshed and destruction that lasted for generations.

In his *Confessions* he set down, for the benefit of others, the story of his early life and his conversion to Christianity. This is, as far as we know, the first authentic ancient autobiography, and that fact itself is a significant expression of the Christian spirit, which proclaims the value of the individual soul and the importance of its relation with God. Throughout the *Confessions* Augustine talks directly to God, in humility, yet conscious that God is concerned for him personally. At the same time he comes to an understanding of his own feelings and development as a human being that marks his *Confessions* as one of the great literary documents of the Western world. His description of his childhood is the only detailed account of the childhood of a great man that antiquity has left us, and his accurate observation and keen perception are informed by the Hebrew and Christian idea of the sense of sin. "So small a boy and so great a sinner"—from the beginning of his narrative to the end Augustine sees individuals not as the Greeks at their most optimistic tended to see humanity, the center and potential masters of the universe, but as children, wandering in ignorance, capable of reclamation only through the divine mercy that waits eternally for them to turn to it.

In Augustine are combined the intellectual tradition of the ancient world and the religious feeling that was characteristic of the Middle Ages. The transition from the old world to the new can be seen in his pages; his analytical intellect pursues its odyssey through strange and scattered islands—the mysticism of the Manichees, the skepticism of the academic philosophers, the fatalism of the astrologers—until he finds his home in the Church, to which he was to render such great service. His account of his conversion in the garden at Milan records the true moment of transition from the ancient to the medieval world. The innumerable defeats and victories, the burning towns and ravaged farms, the bloodshed, dates, and statistics of the end of an era are all illuminated and ordered by this moment in the history of the human spirit. Here is the point of change itself.

Peter Brown, *Augustine of Hippo* (1967), is an authoritative and engrossing account of Augustine's career and major works. Warren Thomas Smith, *Augustine, His Life and Thought* (1980), gives a brief and readable overview of his biography, his times, and his intellectual development. Another introduction to Augustine's life and thought, with a substantial discussion of the *Confessions*, is James J. O'Donnell, *Augustine* (1985). Gillian Clark, *Augustine, the Confessions* (1993), is an excellent short guide to this work, with discussions of various literary and intellectual issues that it raises and particular attention to the historical context.

From Confessions[1]

FROM BOOK I

[*Childhood*]

What have I to say to Thee, God, save that I know not where I came from, when I came into this life-in-death—or should I call it death-in-life? I do not know. I only know that the gifts Your mercy had provided sustained me from the first moment: not that I remember it but so I have heard from the parents of my flesh, the father from whom, and the mother in whom, You fashioned me in time.

Thus for my sustenance and my delight I had woman's milk: yet it was not my mother or my nurses who stored their breasts for me: it was Yourself, using them to give me the food of my infancy, according to Your ordinance and the riches set by You at every level of creation. It was by Your gift that I desired what You gave and no more, by Your gift that those who suckled me willed to give me what You had given them: for it was by the love implanted in them by You that they gave so willingly that milk which by Your gift flowed in the breasts. It was a good for them that I received good from them, though I received it not *from* them but only through them: since all good things are from You, O God, and *from God is all my health.*[2] But this I have learnt since: You have made it abundantly clear by all that I have seen You give, within me and about me. For at that time I knew how to suck, to lie quiet when I was content, to cry when I was in pain: and that was all I knew.

Later I added smiling to the things I could do, first in sleep, then awake. This again I have on the word of others, for naturally I do not remember; in any event, I believe it, for I have seen other infants do the same. And gradually I began to notice where I was, and the will grew in me to make my wants known to those who might satisfy them; but I could not, for my wants were within me and those others were outside: nor had they any faculty enabling them to enter into my mind. So I would fling my arms and legs about and utter sounds, making the few gestures in my power—these being as apt to express my wishes as I could make them: but they were not very apt. And when I did not get what I wanted, either because my wishes were not clear or the things not good for me, I was in a rage—with my parents as though I had a right to their submission, with free human beings as though they had been bound to serve me; and I took my revenge in screams. That

---

1. Translated by F. J. Sheed.   2. Throughout the *Confessions* Augustine quotes liberally from the Bible; the quotations are set off in italics. When a quotation bears on Augustine's situation, it is annotated.

infants are like this, I have learnt from watching other infants; and that I was like it myself I have learnt more clearly from these other infants, who did not know me, than from my nurses who did.

* * *

From infancy I came to boyhood, or rather it came to me, taking the place of infancy. Yet infancy did not go: for where was it to go to? Simply it was no longer there. For now I was not an infant, without speech, but a boy, speaking. This I remember; and I have since discovered by observation how I learned to speak. I did not learn by elders teaching me words in any systematic way, as I was soon after taught to read and write. But of my own motion, using the mind which You, my God, gave me, I strove with cries and various sounds and much moving of my limbs to utter the feelings of my heart—all this in order to get my own way. Now I did not always manage to express the right meanings to the right people. So I began to reflect [I observed that][3] my elders would make some particular sound, and as they made it would point at or move towards some particular thing: and from this I came to realize that the thing was called by the sound they made when they wished to draw my attention to it. That they intended this was clear from the motions of their body, by a kind of natural language common to all races which consists in facial expressions, glances of the eye, gestures, and the tones by which the voice expresses the mind's state—for example whether things are to be sought, kept, thrown away, or avoided. So, as I heard the same words again and again properly used in different phrases, I came gradually to grasp what things they signified; and forcing my mouth to the same sounds, I began to use them to express my own wishes. Thus I learnt to convey what I meant to those about me; and so took another long step along the stormy way of human life in society, while I was still subject to the authority of my parents and at the beck and call of my elders.

O God, my God, what emptiness and mockeries did I now experience: for it was impressed upon me as right and proper in a boy to obey those who taught me, that I might get on in the world and excel in the handling of words[4] to gain honor among men and deceitful riches. I, poor wretch, could not see the use of the things I was sent to school to learn; but if I proved idle in learning, I was soundly beaten. For this procedure seemed wise to our ancestors: and many, passing the same way in days past, had built a sorrowful road by which we too must go, with multiplication of grief and toil upon the sons of Adam.

Yet, Lord, I observed men praying to You: and I learnt to do likewise, thinking of You (to the best of my understanding) as some great being who, though unseen, could hear and help me. As a boy I fell into the way of calling upon You, my Help and my Refuge; and in those prayers I broke the strings of my tongue—praying to You, small as I was but with no small energy, that I might not be beaten at school.[5] And when You did not hear me (*not as giving me over to folly*), my elders and even my parents, who certainly wished me no harm, treated my stripes as a huge joke, which they were very far from

---

3. Words in brackets are the translator's.   4. The study of rhetoric, which was the passport to eminence in public life.   5. Augustine recognizes the necessity of this rigorous training; that he never forgot its harshness is clear from his remark in the *City of God* (21.14): "If a choice were given him between suffering death and living his early years over again, who would not shudder and choose death?"

being to me. Surely, Lord, there is no one so steeled in mind or cleaving to You so close—or even so insensitive, for that might have the same effect— as to make light of the racks and hooks and other torture instruments[6] (from which in all lands men pray so fervently to be saved) while truly loving those who are in such bitter fear of them. Yet my parents seemed to be amused at the torments inflicted upon me as a boy by my masters, though I was no less afraid of my punishments or zealous in my prayers to You for deliverance. But in spite of my terrors I still did wrong, by writing or reading or studying less than my set tasks. It was not, Lord, that I lacked mind or memory, for You had given me as much of these as my age required; but the one thing I revelled in was play; and for this I was punished by men who after all were doing exactly the same things themselves. But the idling of men is called business; the idling of boys, though exactly like, is punished by those same men: and no one pities either boys or men. Perhaps an unbiased observer would hold that I was rightly punished as a boy for playing with a ball: because this hindered my progress in studies—studies which would give me the opportunity as a man to play at things more degraded. And what differ- ence was there between me and the master who flogged me? For if on some trifling point he had the worst of the argument with some fellow-master, he was more torn with angry vanity than I when I was beaten in a game of ball.

* * *

But to continue with my boyhood, which was in less peril of sin than my adolescence. I disliked learning and hated to be forced to it. But I *was* forced to it, so that good was done to me though it was not my doing. Short of being driven to it, I certainly would not have learned. But no one does well against his will, even if the thing he does is a good thing to do. Nor did those who forced me do well: it was by You, O God, that well was done. Those others had no deeper vision of the use to which I might put all they forced me to learn, but to sate the insatiable desire of man for wealth that is but penury and glory that is but shame. But You, Lord, *by Whom the very hairs of our head are numbered*,[7] used for my good the error of those who urged me to study; but my own error, in that I had no will to learn, you used for my punishment—a punishment richly deserved by one so small a boy and so great a sinner. Thus, You brought good for me out of those who did ill, and justly punished me for the ill I did myself. So You have ordained and so it is: that every disorder of the soul is its own punishment.

To this day I do not quite see why I so hated the Greek tongue[8] that I was made to learn as a small boy. For I really liked Latin—not the rudiments that we got from our first teachers but the literature that we came to be taught later. For the rudiments—reading and writing and figuring—I found as hard and hateful as Greek. Yet this too could come only from sin and the vanity of life, because I *was flesh, and a wind that goes away and returns not.* For those first lessons were the surer. I acquired the power I still have to read what I find written and to write what I want to express; whereas in the

---

6. The instruments of public execution.   7. Who knows and attends to the smallest detail of each life (compare Matthew 10.30).   8. Important not only for gaining knowledge of Greek literature but also because it was the official language of the Eastern Roman Empire. Augustine never really mastered Greek, though his remark elsewhere that he had acquired so little Greek that it amounted to practically none is overmodest.

studies that came later I was forced to memorize the wanderings of Aeneas[9]—whoever *he* was—while forgetting my own wanderings; and to weep for the death of Dido who killed herself for love,[1] while bearing dry-eyed my own pitiful state, in that among these studies I was becoming dead to You, O God, my life.

Nothing could be more pitiful than a pitiable creature who does not see to pity himself, and weeps for the death that Dido suffered through love of Aeneas and not for the death he suffers himself through not loving You, O God, Light of my heart, Bread of my soul, Power wedded to my mind and the depths of my thought. I did not love You and I went away from You in fornication:[2] and all around me in my fornication echoed applauding cries "Well done! Well done!" *For the friendship of this world is fornication against Thee:* and the world cries "Well done" so loudly that one is ashamed of unmanliness not to do it. And for this I did not grieve; but I grieved for Dido, slain as she sought by the sword an end to her woe, while I too followed after the lowest of Your creatures, forsaking You, earth going unto earth. And if I were kept from reading, I grieved at not reading the tales that caused me such grief. This sort of folly is held nobler and richer than the studies by which we learn to read and write!

But now let my God cry aloud in my soul, and let Your truth assure me that it is not so: the earlier study is the better. I would more willingly forget the wanderings of Aeneas and all such things than how to write and read. Over the entrance of these grammar schools hangs a curtain:[3] but this should be seen not as lending honor to the mysteries, but as a cloak to the errors taught within. Let not those masters—who have now lost their terrors for me—cry out against me, because I confess to You, my God, the desire of my soul, and find soul's rest in blaming my evil ways that I may love Your holy ways. Let not the buyers or sellers of book-learning cry out against me. If I ask them whether it is true, as the poet says, that Aeneas ever went to Carthage, the more ignorant will have to answer that they do not know, the more scholarly that he certainly did not. But if I ask with what letters the name Aeneas is spelt, all whose schooling has gone so far will answer correctly, according to the convention men have agreed upon for the use of letters. Or again, were I to ask which loss would be more damaging to human life—the loss from men's memory of reading and writing or the loss of these poetic imaginings—there can be no question what anyone would answer who had not lost his own memory. Therefore as a boy I did wrong in liking the empty studies more than the useful—or rather in loving the empty and hating the useful. For one and one make two, two and two make four, I found a loathsome refrain; but such empty unrealities as the Wooden Horse with its armed men, and Troy on fire, and Creusa's Ghost, were sheer delight.[4]

Give me leave, O my God, to speak of my mind, Your gift, and of the follies in which I wasted it. It chanced that a task was set me, a task which I did not like but had to do. There was the promise of glory if I won, the fear of ignominy, and a flogging as well, if I lost. It was to declaim the words uttered by Juno in her rage and grief when she could not keep the Trojan prince

---

9. Virgil's *Aeneid* 3.   1. *Aeneid* 4.   2. Here, metaphorically.   3. School was often held in a building open on one side and curtained off from the street.   4. *Aeneid* 2.

from coming to Italy.[5] I had learnt that Juno had never said these words, but we were compelled to err in the footsteps of the poet who had invented them: and it was our duty to paraphrase in prose what he had said in verse. In this exercise that boy won most applause in whom the passions of grief and rage were expressed most powerfully and in the language most adequate to the majesty of the personage represented.

What could all this mean to me, O My true Life, My God? Why was there more applause for the performance I gave than for so many classmates of my own age? Was not the whole business so much smoke and wind? Surely some other matter could have been found to exercise mind and tongue. Thy praises, Lord, might have upheld the fresh young shoot of my heart, so that it might not have been whirled away by empty trifles, defiled, a prey to the spirits of the air. For there is more than one way of sacrificing to the fallen angels. * * *

FROM BOOK II

[The Pear Tree]

I propose now to set down my past wickedness and the carnal corruptions of my soul, not for love of them but that I may love Thee, O my God. I do it for love of Thy love, passing again in the bitterness of remembrance over my most evil ways that Thou mayest thereby grow ever lovelier to me, O Loveliness that dost not deceive, Loveliness happy and abiding: and I collect myself out of that broken state in which my very being was torn asunder because I was turned away from Thee, the One, and wasted myself upon the many.

Arrived now at adolescence I burned for all the satisfactions of hell, and I sank to the animal in a succession of dark lusts: *my beauty consumed away,* and I stank in Thine eyes, yet was pleasing in my own and anxious to please the eyes of men.

My one delight was to love and to be loved. But in this I did not keep the measure of mind to mind, which is the luminous line of friendship; but from the muddy concupiscence of the flesh and the hot imagination of puberty mists steamed up to becloud and darken my heart so that I could not distinguish the white light of love from the fog of lust. Both love and lust boiled within me, and swept my youthful immaturity over the precipice of evil desires to leave me half drowned in a whirlpool of abominable sins. Your wrath had grown mighty against me and I knew it not. I had grown deaf from the clanking of the chain of my mortality, the punishment for the pride of my soul: and I departed further from You, and You left me to myself: and I was tossed about and wasted and poured out and boiling over in my fornications: and You were silent, O my late-won Joy. You were silent, and I, arrogant and depressed, weary and restless, wandered further and further from You into more and more sins which could bear no fruit save sorrows.

* * *

---

5. Augustine was assigned the task of delivering a prose paraphrase of Juno's angry speech in *Aeneid* 1. In it she complains that her enemies, the Trojans under Aeneas, are on their way to their destined goal in Italy in spite of her resolution to prevent them. Rhetorical exercises such as this were common in the schools, because they served the double purpose of teaching both literature and rhetorical composition.

Where then was I, and how far from the delights of Your house, in that sixteenth year of my life in this world, when the madness of lust—needing no licence from human shamelessness, receiving no licence from Your laws—took complete control of me, and I surrendered wholly to it? My family took no care to save me from this moral destruction by marriage: their only concern was that I should learn to make as fine and persuasive speeches as possible.

* * *

Your law, O Lord, punishes theft; and this law is so written in the hearts of men that not even the breaking of it blots it out: for no thief bears calmly being stolen from—not even if he is rich and the other steals through want. Yet I chose to steal, and not because want drove me to it—unless a want of justice and contempt for it and an excess for iniquity. For I stole things which I already had in plenty and of better quality. Nor had I any desire to enjoy the things I stole, but only the stealing of them and the sin. There was a pear tree near our vineyard, heavy with fruit, but fruit that was not particularly tempting either to look at or to taste. A group of young blackguards, and I among them, went out to knock down the pears and carry them off late one night, for it was our bad habit to carry on our games in the streets till very late. We carried off an immense load of pears, not to eat—for we barely tasted them before throwing them to the hogs. Our only pleasure in doing it was that it was forbidden. Such was my heart, O God, such was my heart: yet in the depth of the abyss You had pity on it. Let that heart now tell You what it sought when I was thus evil for no object, having no cause for wrong-doing save my wrongness. The malice of the act was base and I loved it—that is to say I loved my own undoing, I loved the evil in me—not the thing for which I did the evil, simply the evil: my soul was depraved, and hurled itself down from security in You into utter destruction, seeking no profit from wickedness but only to be wicked.

There is an appeal to the eye in beautiful things, in gold and silver and all such; the sense of touch has its own powerful pleasures; and the other senses find qualities in things suited to them. Worldly success has its glory, and the power to command and to overcome: and from this springs the thirst for revenge. But in our quest of all these things, we must not depart from You, Lord, or deviate from Your Law. This life we live here below has its own attractiveness, grounded in the measure of beauty it has and its harmony with the beauty of all lesser things. The bond of human friendship is admirable, holding many souls as one. Yet in the enjoyment of all such things we commit sin if through immoderate inclination to them—for though they are good, they are of the lowest order of good—things higher and better are forgotten, even You, O Lord our God, and Your Truth and Your Law. These lower things have their delights but not such as my God has, for He made them all: *and in Him doth the righteous delight, and He is the joy of the upright of heart.*

Now when we ask why this or that particular evil act was done, it is normal to assume that it could not have been done save through the desire of gaining or the fear of losing some one of these lower goods. For they have their own charm and their own beauty, though compared with the higher values of heaven they are poor and mean enough. Such a man has committed a murder. Why? He wanted the other man's wife or his property; or he had chosen robbery as a means of livelihood; or he feared to lose this or that through his victim's act; or he had been wronged and was aflame for vengeance. Would any man commit a murder for no cause, for the sheer delight of murdering? The thing would be incredible. There is of course the case of the man [Catiline] who was said to be so stupidly and savagely cruel that he practised cruelty and evil even when he had nothing to gain by them. But even there a cause was stated—he did it, he said, lest through idleness his hand or his resolution should grow slack. And why did he want to prevent that? So that one day by the multiplication of his crimes the city should be his, and he would have gained honors and authority and riches, and would no longer be in fear of the law or in the difficulties that want of money and the awareness of his crimes had brought him. So that not even Catiline loved his crimes as crimes: he loved some other thing which was his reason for committing them.

What was it then that in my wretched folly I loved in you, O theft of mine, deed wrought in that dark night when I was sixteen? For you were not lovely: you were a theft. Or are you anything at all, that I should talk with you? The pears that we stole were beautiful for they were created by Thee, Thou most Beautiful of all, Creator of all, Thou good God, my Sovereign and true Good. The pears were beautiful but it was not pears that my empty soul desired. For I had any number of better pears of my own, and plucked those only that I might steal. For once I had gathered them I threw them away, tasting only my own sin and savouring that with delight; for if I took so much as a bite of any one of those pears, it was the sin that sweetened it. And now, Lord my God, I ask what was it that attracted me in that theft, for there was no beauty in it to attract. I do not mean merely that it lacked the beauty that there is in justice and prudence, or in the mind of man or his senses and vegetative life: or even so much as the beauty and glory of the stars in the heavens, or of earth and sea with their oncoming of new life to replace the generations that pass. It had not even that false show or shadow of beauty by which sin tempts us.

[For there *is* a certain show of beauty in sin.] Thus pride wears the mask of loftiness of spirit, although You alone, O God, are high over all. Ambition seeks honor and glory, although You alone are to be honored before all and glorious forever. By cruelty the great seek to be feared, yet who is to be feared but God alone: from His power what can be wrested away, or when or where or how or by whom? The caresses by which the lustful seduce are a seeking for love: but nothing is more caressing than Your charity, nor is anything more healthfully loved than Your supremely lovely, supremely luminous Truth. Curiosity may be regarded as a desire for knowledge, whereas You supremely know all things. Ignorance and sheer stupidity hide under the names of simplicity and innocence: yet no being has simplicity like to Yours: and none is more innocent than You, for it is their own deeds that harm the wicked. Sloth pretends that it wants quietude: but what sure rest is there save the Lord? Luxuriousness would be called abundance and completeness; but You are the fullness and inexhaustible abundance of incorruptible delight. Wastefulness is a parody of generosity: but You are the infinitely generous giver of all good. Avarice wants to possess overmuch: but You possess all. Enviousness claims that it strives to excel: but what can excel before You? Anger clamors for just vengeance: but whose vengeance is so just as

Yours? Fear is the recoil from a new and sudden threat to something one holds dear, and a cautious regard for one's own safety: but nothing new or sudden can happen to You, nothing can threaten Your hold upon things loved, and where is safety secure save in You? Grief pines at the loss of things in which desire delighted: for it wills to be like to You from whom nothing can be taken away.

Thus the soul is guilty of fornication when she turns from You and seeks from any other source what she will nowhere find pure and without taint unless she returns to You. Thus even those who go from You and stand up against You are still perversely imitating You. But by the mere fact of their imitation, they declare that You are the creator of all that is, and that there is nowhere for them to go where You are not.

So once again what did I enjoy in that theft of mine? Of what excellence of my Lord was I making perverse and vicious imitation? Perhaps it was the thrill of acting against Your law—at least in appearance, since I had no power to do so in fact, the delight a prisoner might have in making some small gesture of liberty—getting a deceptive sense of omnipotence from doing something forbidden without immediate punishment. I was that slave, who fled from his Lord and pursued his Lord's shadow. O rottenness, O monstrousness of life and abyss of death! Could you find pleasure only in what was forbidden, and only because it was forbidden? * * *

FROM BOOK III

[*Student at Carthage*]

I came to Carthage[6] where a cauldron of illicit loves leapt and boiled about me. I was not yet in love, but I was in love with love, and from the very depth of my need hated myself for not more keenly feeling the need. I sought some object to love, since I was thus in love with loving; and I hated security and a life with no snares for my feet. For within I was hungry, all for the want of that spiritual food which is Thyself, my God; yet [though I was hungry for want of it] I did not hunger for it: I had no desire whatever for incorruptible food, not because I had it in abundance but the emptier I was, the more I hated the thought of it. Because of all this my soul was sick, and broke out in sores, whose itch I agonized to scratch with the rub of carnal things— carnal, yet if there were no soul in them, they would not be objects of love. My longing then was to love and to be loved, but most when I obtained the enjoyment of the body of the person who loved me.

Thus I polluted the stream of friendship with the filth of unclean desire and sullied its limpidity with the hell of lust. And vile and unclean as I was, so great was my vanity that I was bent upon passing for clean and courtly. And I did fall in love, simply from wanting to. O my God, my Mercy, with how much bitterness didst Thou in Thy goodness sprinkle the delights of that time! I was loved, and our love came to the bond of consummation: I wore my chains with bliss but with torment too, for I was scourged with the red hot rods of jealousy, with suspicions and fears and tempers and quarrels.

I developed a passion for stage plays, with the mirror they held up to my

6. The capital city of the province, where Augustine went to study rhetoric.

own miseries and the fuel they poured on my flame. How is it that a man wants to be made sad by the sight of tragic sufferings that he could not bear in his own person? Yet the spectator does want to feel sorrow, and it is actually his feeling of sorrow that he enjoys. Surely this is the most wretched lunacy? For the more a man feels such sufferings in himself, the more he is moved by the sight of them on the stage. Now when a man suffers himself, it is called misery; when he suffers in the suffering of another, it is called pity. But how can the unreal sufferings of the stage possibly move pity? The spectator is not moved to aid the sufferer but merely to be sorry for him; and the more the author of these fictions makes the audience grieve, the better they like him. If the tragic sorrows of the characters—whether historical or entirely fictitious—be so poorly represented that the spectator is not moved to tears, he leaves the theatre unsatisfied and full of complaints; if he *is* moved to tears, he stays to the end, fascinated and revelling in it.

* * *

Those of my occupations at that time which were held as reputable[7] were directed towards the study of the law, in which I meant to excel—and the less honest I was, the more famous I should be. The very limit of human blindness is to glory in being blind. By this time I was a leader in the School of Rhetoric and I enjoyed this high station and was arrogant and swollen with importance: though You know, O Lord, that I was far quieter in my behavior and had no share in the riotousness of the *eversores*—the Overturners[8]—for this blackguardly diabolical name they wore as the very badge of sophistication. Yet I was much in their company and much ashamed of the sense of shame that kept me from being like them. I was with them and I did for the most part enjoy their companionship, though I abominated the acts that were their specialty—as when they made a butt of some hapless newcomer, assailing him with really cruel mockery for no reason whatever, save the malicious pleasure they got from it. There was something very like the action of devils in their behavior. They were rightly called Overturners, since they had themselves been first overturned and perverted, tricked by those same devils who were secretly mocking them in the very acts by which they amused themselves in mocking and making fools of others.

With these men as companions of my immaturity, I was studying the books of eloquence; for in eloquence it was my ambition to shine, all from a damnable vaingloriousness and for the satisfaction of human vanity. Following the normal order of study I had come to a book of one Cicero, whose tongue[9] practically everyone admires, though not his heart. That particular book is called *Hortensius*[1] and contains an exhortation to philosophy. Quite definitely it changed the direction of my mind, altered my prayers to You, O Lord, and gave me a new purpose and ambition. Suddenly all the vanity I had hoped in I saw as worthless, and with an incredible intensity of desire I longed after immortal wisdom. I had begun that journey upwards by which I was to return to You. My father was now dead two years; I was eighteen

---

7. I.e., his rhetorical studies.   8. *Eversores* is the Latin word that means "overturners": a group of students who prided themselves on their wild actions and lack of discipline.   9. Style.   1. Only fragments of this dialogue remain. In it Cicero replies to an opponent of philosophy with an impassioned defense of the intellectual life.

and was receiving money from my mother for the continuance of my study of eloquence. But I used that book not for the sharpening of my tongue; what won me in it was what it said, not the excellence of its phrasing.

* * *

So I resolved to make some study of the Sacred Scriptures and find what kind of books they were. But what I came upon was something not grasped by the proud, not revealed either to children, something utterly humble in the hearing but sublime in the doing, and shrouded deep in mystery. And I was not of the nature to enter into it or bend my neck to follow it. When I first read those Scriptures, I did not feel in the least what I have just said; they seemed to me unworthy to be compared with the majesty of Cicero. My conceit was repelled by their simplicity, and I had not the mind to penetrate into their depths. They were indeed of a nature to grow in Your little ones.[2] But I could not bear to be a little one; I was only swollen with pride, but to myself I seemed a very big man. * * *

FROM BOOK V

[Augustine Leaves Carthage for Rome]

It was by Your action upon me that I was moved to go to Rome and teach there what I had taught in Carthage. How I was persuaded to this, I shall not omit to confess to you, because therein Your most profound depths and Your mercy ever present towards us are to be meditated upon and uttered forth. My reason for going to Rome was not the greater earnings and higher dignity promised by the friends who urged me to go—though at that time, these considerations certainly influenced my mind: the principal and practically conclusive reason, was that I had heard that youths there pursued their studies more quietly and were kept within a stricter limit of discipline. For instance, they were not allowed to come rushing insolently and at will into the school of one who was not their own master, nor indeed to enter it at all unless he permitted.

At Carthage the licence of the students is gross and beyond all measure. They break in impudently and like a pack of madmen play havoc with the order which the master has established for the good of his pupils. They commit many outrages, extraordinarily stupid acts, deserving the punishment of the law if custom did not protect them. Their state is the more hopeless because what they do is supposed to be sanctioned, though by Your eternal law it could never be sanctioned; and they think they do these things unpunished, when the very blindness in which they do them is their punishment, so that they suffer things incomparably worse than they do. When I was a student I would not have such habits in myself, but when I became a teacher I had to endure them in others; and so I decided to go to a place where, as I had been told by all who knew, such things were not done. But You, O my Hope and my Portion in the land of the living, forced me to change countries for my soul's salvation: You pricked me with such goads at Carthage as drove me out of it, and You set before me certain attractions by

---

2. Refers not only to the rhetorical simplicity of Jesus' teachings but also to his interest in teaching children; compare Matthew 19.14: "For of such is the kingdom of heaven."

which I might be drawn to Rome—in either case using men who loved this
life of death, one set doing lunatic things, the other promising vain things:
and to reform my ways You secretly used their perversity and my own. For
those who had disturbed my peace were blind in the frenzy of their viciousness, and those who urged me to go elsewhere savoured of earth. While I,
detesting my real misery in the one place, hoped for an unreal happiness in
the other.

Why I left the one country and went to the other, You Knew, O God, but
You did not tell either me or my mother. She indeed was in dreadful grief at
my going and followed me right to the seacoast. There she clung to me
passionately, determined that I should either go back home with her or take
her to Rome with me, but I deceived her with the pretence that I had a friend
whom I did not want to leave until he had sailed off with a fair wind. Thus
I lied to my mother, and such a mother; and so got away from her. But this
also You have mercifully forgiven me, bringing me from the waters of that
sea, filled as I was with execrable uncleanness, unto the water of Your grace;
so that when I was washed clean, the floods that poured from my mother's
eyes, the tears with which daily she watered the ground towards which she
bent her face in prayer for me, should cease to flow. She would not return
home without me, but I managed with some difficulty to persuade her to
spend the night in a place near the ship where there was an oratory in memory of St. Cyprian, That night I stole away without her: she remained praying
and weeping. And what was she praying for, O my God, with all those tears
but that You should not allow me to sail! But You saw deeper and granted
the essential of her prayer: You did not do what she was at that moment
asking, that You might do the thing she was always asking. The wind blew
and filled our sails and the shore dropped from our sight. And the next morning she was frantic with grief and filled Your ears with her moaning and
complaints because You seemed to treat her tears so lightly, when in fact
You were using my own desires to snatch me away for the healing of those
desires, and were justly punishing her own too earthly affection for me with
the scourge of grief. For she loved to have me with her, as is the way of
mothers but far more than most mothers; and she did not realize what joys
you would bring her from my going away. She did not realize it, and so
she wept and lamented, and by the torments she suffered showed the
heritage of Eve in her, seeking with sorrow what in sorrow she had brought
forth. But when she had poured out all her accusation at my cruel deception,
she turned once more to prayer to You for me. She went home and I to
Rome. * * *

FROM BOOK VI

[Worldly Ambitions]

By this time my mother had come to me, following me over sea and land
with the courage of piety and relying upon You in all perils. For they were
in danger from a storm, and she reassured even the sailors—by whom travelers newly ventured upon the deep are ordinarily reassured—promising
them safe arrival because thus You had promised her in a vision. She found
me in a perilous state through my deep despair of ever discovering the truth.
But even when I told her that if I was not yet a Catholic Christian, I was no

longer a Manichean,[3] she was not greatly exultant as at some unlooked-for good news, because she had already received assurance upon that part of my misery; she bewailed me as one dead certainly, but certainly to be raised again by You, offering me in her mind as one stretched out dead, that You might say to the widow's son: *"Young man, I say to thee arise"*:[4] and he should sit up and begin to speak and You should give him to his mother.

* * *

Nor did I then groan in prayer for Your help. My mind was intent upon inquiry and unquiet for argumentation. I regarded Ambrose[5] as a lucky man by worldly standards to be held in honor by such important people: only his celibacy seemed to me a heavy burden. I had no means of guessing, and no experience of my own to learn from, what hope he bore within him, what struggles he might have against the temptations that went with his high place, what was his consolation in adversity, and on what joys of Your bread the hidden mouth of his heart fed. Nor did he know how I was inflamed nor the depth of my peril. I could not ask of him what I wished as I wished, for I was kept from any face to face conversation with him by the throng of men with their own troubles, whose infirmities he served. The very little time he was not with these he was refreshing either his body with necessary food or his mind with reading. When he read, his eyes traveled across the page and his heart sought into the sense, but voice and tongue were silent. No one was forbidden to approach him nor was it his custom to require that visitors should be announced: but when we came into him we often saw him reading and always to himself; and after we had sat long in silence, unwilling to interrupt a work on which he was so intent, we would depart again. We guessed that in the small time he could find for the refreshment of his mind, he would wish to be free from the distraction of other men's affairs and not called away from what he was doing. Perhaps he was on his guard lest [if he read aloud] someone listening should be troubled and want an explanation if the author he was reading expressed some idea over-obscurely, and it might be necessary to expound or discuss some of the more difficult questions. And if he had to spend time on this, he would get through less reading than he wished. Or it may be that his real reason for reading to himself was to preserve his voice, which did in fact readily grow tired. But whatever his reason for doing it, that man certainly had a good reason.

* * *

I was all hot for honors, money, marriage: and You made mock of my hotness. In my pursuit of these, I suffered most bitter disappointments, but in this You were good to me since I was thus prevented from taking delight in anything not Yourself. Look now into my heart, Lord, by whose will I remember all this and confess it to You. Let my soul cleave to You now that You have freed it from the tenacious hold of death. At that time my soul was in misery,

---

3. Augustine had for nine years been a member of this religious sect, which followed the teaching of the Babylonian mystic Mani (216–277). The Manicheans believed that the world was a battleground for the forces of good and evil; redemption in a future life would come to the elect, who renounced worldly occupations and possessions and practiced a severe asceticism (including abstention from meat). Augustine's mother, Monica, was a Christian, and lamented her son's Manichean beliefs. **4.** Luke 7.14, recounting one of Christ's miracles. **5.** The leading personality among the Christians of the West; not many years after this he defied the power of Emperor Theodosius and forced him to beg for God's pardon in the church at Milan for having put the inhabitants of Thessalonica to the sword.

and You pricked the soreness of its wound, that leaving all things it might turn to You, who are over all and without whom all would return to nothing, that it might turn to You and be healed. I was in utter misery and there was one day especially on which You acted to bring home to me the realization of my misery. I was preparing an oration in praise of the Emperor[6] in which I was to utter any number of lies to win the applause of people who knew they were lies. My heart was much wrought upon by the shame of this and inflamed with the fever of the thoughts that consumed it. I was passing along a certain street in Milan when I noticed a beggar. He was jesting and laughing and I imagine more than a little drunk. I fell into gloom and spoke to the friends who were with me about the endless sorrows that our own insanity brings us: for here was I striving away, dragging the load of my unhappiness under the spurring of my desires, and making it worse by dragging it: and with all our striving, our one aim was to arrive at some sort of happiness without care: the beggar had reached the same goal before us, and we might quite well never reach it at all. The very thing that he had attained by means of a few pennies begged from passers-by—namely the pleasure of a temporary happiness—I was plotting for with so many a weary twist and turn.

Certainly his joy was no true joy; but the joy I sought in my ambition was emptier still. In any event he was cheerful and I worried, he had no cares and I nothing but cares. Now if anyone had asked me whether I would rather be cheerful or fearful, I would answer: "Cheerful"; but if he had gone on to ask whether I would rather be like that beggar or as I actually was, I would certainly have chosen my own state though so troubled and anxious. Now this was surely absurd. It could not be for any true reason. I ought not to have preferred my own state rather than his merely because I was the more learned, since I got no joy from my learning, but sought only to please men by it—not even to teach them, only to please them. Therefore did You break my bones with the rod of Your discipline.

* * *

Great effort was made to get me married. I proposed, the girl was promised me. My mother played a great part in the matter for she wanted to have me married and then cleansed with the saving waters of baptism,[7] rejoicing to see me grow every day more fitted for baptism and feeling that her prayers and Your promises were to be fulfilled in my faith. By my request and her own desire she begged You daily with the uttermost intensity of her heart to show her in a vision something of my future marriage, but You would never do it. She did indeed see certain vain fantasies, under the pressure of her mind's preoccupation with the matter; and she told them to me, not, however, with the confidence she always had when You had shown things to her, but as if she set small store by them; for she said that there was a certain unanalyzable savor, not to be expressed in words, by which she could distinguish between what You revealed and the dreams of her own spirit. Still she pushed on with the matter of my marriage, and the girl was asked for. She was still two years short of the age for marriage[8] but I liked her and agreed to wait.

There was a group of us friends who had much serious discussion together,

---

6. Probably the young Valentinian, whose court was at Milan.   7. He could not be baptized while living in sin with his mistress, a liaison that resulted in the birth of a son, Adeodatus, who later accompanied Augustine to Italy.   8. The legal age was twelve years; Augustine was in his early thirties.

concerning the cares and troubles of human life which we found so hard to endure. We had almost decided to seek a life of peace, away from the throng of men. This peace we hoped to attain by putting together whatever we could manage to get, and making one common household for all of us: so that in the clear trust of friendship, things should not belong to this or that individual, but one thing should be made of all our possessions, and belong wholly to each one of us, and everybody own everything. It seemed that there might be perhaps ten men in this fellowship. Among us there were some very rich men, especially Romanianus, our fellow townsman, who had been a close friend of mine from childhood and had been brought to the court in Milan by the press of some very urgent business. He was strongest of all for the idea and he had considerable influence in persuasion because his wealth was much greater than anyone else's. We agreed that two officers should be chosen every year to handle the details of our life together, leaving the rest undisturbed. But then we began to wonder whether our wives would agree, for some of us already had wives and I meant to have one. So the whole plan, which we had built up so neatly, fell to pieces in our hands and was simply dropped. We returned to our old sighing and groaning and treading of this world's broad and beaten ways:[9] for many thoughts were in our hearts, but *Thy counsel standeth forever.* And out of Thy counsel didst Thou deride ours and didst prepare Thine own things for us, meaning to *give us meat in due season and to open Thy hands and fill our souls with Thy blessing.*

Meanwhile my sins were multiplied. She with whom I had lived so long was torn from my side as a hindrance to my forthcoming marriage. My heart which had held her very dear was broken and wounded and shed blood. She went back to Africa, swearing that she would never know another man, and left with me the natural son I had had of her. But I in my unhappiness could not, for all my manhood, imitate her resolve. I was unable to bear the delay of two years which must pass before I was to get the girl I had asked for in marriage. In fact it was not really marriage that I wanted. I was simply a slave to lust. So I took another woman, not of course as a wife; and thus my soul's disease was nourished and kept alive as vigorously as ever, indeed worse than ever, that it might reach the realm of matrimony in the company of its ancient habit. Nor was the wound healed that had been made by the cutting off of my former mistress. For there was first burning and bitter grief; and after that it festered, and as the pain grew duller it only grew more hopeless. * * *

FROM BOOK VIII

[Conversion]

* * * Thus I was sick at heart and in torment, accusing myself with a new intensity of bitterness, twisting and turning in my chain in the hope that it might be utterly broken, for what held me was so small a thing! But it still held me. And You stood in the secret places of my soul, O Lord, in the harshness of Your mercy redoubling the scourges of fear and shame lest I should give way again and that small slight tie which remained should not be broken but should grow again to full strength and bind me closer even

---

9. Compare Matthew 7.13: "Broad is the way that leadeth to destruction," that is, to damnation.

than before. For I kept saying within myself: "Let it be now, let it be now," and by the mere words I had begun to move toward the resolution. I almost made it, yet I did not quite make it. But I did not fall back into my original state, but as it were stood near to get my breath. And I tried again and I was almost there, and now I could all but touch it and hold it: yet I was not quite there, I did not touch it or hold it. I still shrank from dying unto death and living unto life. The lower condition which had grown habitual was more powerful than the better condition which I had not tried. The nearer the point of time came in which I was to become different, the more it struck me with horror; but it did not force me utterly back nor turn me utterly away, but held me there between the two.

Those trifles of all trifles, and vanities of vanities, my one-time mistresses, held me back, plucking at my garment of flesh and murmuring softly: "Are you sending us away?" And "From this moment shall we not be with you, now or forever?" And "From this moment shall this or that not be allowed you, now or forever?" What were they suggesting to me in the phrase I have written "this or that," what were they suggesting to me, O my God? Do you in your mercy keep from the soul of Your servant the vileness and unclean- ness they were suggesting. And now I began to hear them not half so loud; they no longer stood against me face to face, but were softly muttering behind my back and, as I tried to depart, plucking stealthily at me to make me look behind. Yet even that was enough, so hesitating was I, to keep me from snatching myself free, from shaking them off and leaping upwards on the way I was called: for the strong force of habit said to me: "Do you think you can live without them?"

But by this time its voice was growing fainter. In the direction toward which I had turned my face and was quivering in fear of going, I could see the austere beauty of Continence, serene and indeed joyous but not evilly, honorably soliciting me to come to her and not linger, stretching forth loving hands to receive and embrace me, hands full of multitudes of good examples. With her I saw such hosts of young men and maidens, a multitude of youth and of every age, gray widows and women grown old in virginity, and in them all Continence herself, not barren but the fruitful mother of children, her joys, by You, Lord, her Spouse. And she smiled upon me and her smile gave courage as if she were saying: "Can you not do what these men have done, what these women have done? Or could men or women have done such in themselves, and not in the Lord their God? The Lord their God gave me to them. Why do you stand upon yourself and so not stand at all? Cast yourself upon Him and be not afraid; He will not draw away and let you fall. Cast yourself without fear, He will receive you and heal you."

Yet I was still ashamed, for I could still hear the murmuring of those vanities, and I still hung hesitant. And again it was as if she said: "Stop your ears against your unclean members, that they may be mortified. They tell you of delights, but not of such delights as the law of the Lord your God tells." This was the controversy raging in my heart, a controversy about myself against myself. And Alypius[1] stayed by my side and awaited in silence the issue of such agitation as he had never seen in me.

---

1. A student of Augustine's at Carthage; he had joined the Manichees with Augustine, followed him to Rome and Milan, and now shared his desires and doubts. Alypius finally became a bishop in North Africa.

When my most searching scrutiny had drawn up all my vileness from the secret depths of my soul and heaped it in my heart's sight, a mighty storm arose in me, bringing a mighty rain of tears. That I might give way to my tears and lamentations, I rose from Alypius: for it struck me that solitude was more suited to the business of weeping. I went far enough from him to prevent his presence from being an embarrassment to me. So I felt, and he realized it. I suppose I had said something and the sound of my voice was heavy with tears. I arose, but he remained where we had been sitting, still in utter amazement. I flung myself down somehow under a certain fig tree and no longer tried to check my tears, which poured forth from my eyes in a flood, *an acceptable sacrifice to Thee.* And much I said not in these words but to this effect: *"And Thou, O Lord, how long? How long, Lord; wilt Thou be angry forever? Remember not our former iniquities."*[2] For I felt that I was still bound by them. And I continued my miserable complaining: "How long, how long shall I go on saying tomorrow and again tomorrow? Why not now, why not have an end to my uncleanness this very hour?"

Such things I said, weeping in the most bitter sorrow of my heart. And suddenly I heard a voice from some nearby house, a boy's voice or a girl's voice, I do not know: but it was a sort of singsong, repeated again and again. "Take and read, take and read." I ceased weeping and immediately began to search my mind most carefully as to whether children were accustomed to chant these words in any kind of game, and I could not remember that I had ever heard any such thing. Damming back the flood of my tears I arose, interpreting the incident as quite certainly a divine command to open my book of Scripture and read the passage at which I should open. For it was part of what I had been told about Anthony,[3] that from the Gospel which he happened to be reading he had felt that he was being admonished as though what he read was spoken directly to himself: *Go, sell what thou hast and give to the poor and thou shalt have treasure in heaven; and come follow Me.*[4] By this experience he had been in that instant converted to You. So I was moved to return to the place where Alypius was sitting, for I had put down the Apostle's[5] book there when I arose. I snatched it up, opened it and in silence read the passage upon which my eyes first fell: *Not in rioting and drunkenness, not in chambering and impurities, not in contention and envy, but put ye on the Lord Jesus Christ and make not provision for the flesh in its concupiscences.* [Romans 13.13.] I had no wish to read further, and no need. For in that instant, with the very ending of the sentence, it was as though a light of utter confidence shone in all my heart, and all the darkness of uncertainty vanished away. Then leaving my finger in the place or marking it by some other sign, I closed the book and in complete calm told the whole thing to Alypius and he similarly told me what had been going on in himself, of which I knew nothing. He asked to see what I had read. I showed him, and he looked further than I had read. I had not known what followed. And this is what followed: *"Now him that is weak in faith, take unto you."* He applied this to himself and told me so. And he was confirmed by this message, and with no troubled wavering gave himself to God's goodwill and purpose—a purpose indeed most suited to his character, for in these matters he had been immeasurably better than I.

---

2. Compare Psalm 79.5–8; Augustine compares his spiritual despair with that of captive and subjected Israel.   3. The Egyptian saint whose abstinence and self-control are still proverbial; he was one of the founders of the system of monastic life.   4. Luke 18.22.   5. Paul.

Then we went in to my mother and told her, to her great joy. We related how it had come about: she was filled with triumphant exultation, and praised You who are mighty beyond what we ask or conceive: for she saw that You had given her more than with all her pitiful weeping she had ever asked. For You converted me to Yourself so that I no longer sought a wife nor any of this world's promises, but stood upon that same rule of faith in which You had shown me to her so many years before.[6] Thus You changed her mourning into joy, a joy far richer than she had thought to wish, a joy much dearer and purer than she had thought to find in grandchildren of my flesh.

FROM BOOK IX

[Death of His Mother]

* * * And I thought it would be good in Your sight if I did not dramatically snatch my tongue's service from the speech-market but quietly withdrew; but that in any event withdraw I must, so that youths—not students of Your law or Your peace but of lying follies and the conflicts of the law—should no longer buy at my mouth the tools of their madness. Fortunately it happened that there were only a few days left before the Vintage Vacation,[7] and I decided to endure them so that I might leave with due deliberation, seeing that I had been redeemed by You and was not going to put myself up for sale again. Our purpose therefore was known to You, but not to men other than our own friends. We had agreed among ourselves not to spread the news abroad at all, although, in our ascent from *the valley of tears and our singing of the song of degrees,* You had given us *sharp arrows* and *burning coals* against *cunning tongues* that might argue against us with pretended care for our interest, might destroy us saying that they loved us: as men consume food saying that they love it.

*   *   *

Furthermore that very summer, under the too heavy labor of teaching, my lungs had begun to give way and I breathed with difficulty,[8] the pain in my breast showed that they were affected and they no longer let me talk with any strength for too long at a time. At first this had disturbed me, because it made it practically a matter of necessity that I should lay down the burden of teaching, or at least give it up for the time if I was to be cured and grow well again. But when the full purpose of giving myself leisure to meditate on how You are the Lord arose in me and became a settled resolve—as you know, O my God—I actually found myself glad to have this perfectly truthful excuse to offer parents who might be offended and for their children's sake would never willingly have let me give up teaching. So I was full of joy, and I put up with the space of time that still had to run—I fancy it was about twenty days. But to bear the time took considerable fortitude. Desire for money, which formerly had helped me to bear the heavy labor of teaching, was quite gone; so that I should have [had nothing to help me bear it and

---

6. At Carthage, when Augustine was still a Manichee, Monica had dreamed that she was standing on a wooden ruler weeping for her son and then saw that he was standing on the same ruler as herself.   7. This grape-harvesting and wine-making holiday lasted from the end of August to the middle of October.   8. Because he not only lectured but also read aloud, as is suggested by his comments on Ambrose's silent reading (book 6).

so] found it altogether crushing if patience had not taken the place of covetousness. Some of Your servants, my brethren, may think that I sinned in this, since having enrolled with all my heart in Your service, I allowed myself to sit for so much as an hour in the chair of untruthfulness. It may be so. But, most merciful Lord, have You not pardoned and remitted this sin, along with others most horrible and deadly, in the holy water of baptism?

* * *

And now the day was come on which I was to be set free from the teaching of Rhetoric in fact, as I was already free in mind. And so it came about. You delivered my tongue as You had already delivered my heart, and I rejoiced and praised You, and so went off with my friends to the countryhouse.[9] The amount of writing I did there—the writing was now in your service but during this breathing-space still smacked of the school of pride—my books[1] exist to witness, with the record they give of discussions either with my friends there present or with Yourself when I was alone with You; and there are my letters to show what correspondence I had with Nebridius[2] while he was away.

* * *

When the Vintage Vacation was over I gave the people of Milan notice that they must find someone else to sell the art of words to their students, because I had chosen to serve You, and because owing to my difficulty in breathing and the pain in my lungs I could not continue my teaching. And in a letter I told Your bishop, the holy Ambrose, of my past errors and my present purpose, that he might advise me which of Your Scriptures I should especially read to prepare me and make me more fit to receive so great a grace. He told me to read Isaiah the prophet, I imagine because he more clearly foretells the gospel and the calling of the gentiles[3] than the other Old Testament writers; but I did not understand the first part of this book, and thinking that it would be all of the same kind, put it aside meaning to return to it when I should be more practised in the Lord's way of speech.

When the time had come to give in my name for baptism, we left the country and returned to Milan. Alypius had decided to be born again in You at the same time, for he was already endowed with the humility that Your sacraments require, and had brought his body so powerfully under control that he could tread the icy soil of Italy with bare feet, which required unusual fortitude. We also took with us the boy Adeodatus, carnally begotten by me in my sin. You had made him well. He was barely fifteen, yet he was more intelligent than many a grave and learned man. In this I am but acknowledging to You Your own gifts, O Lord my God, Creator of all and powerful to reshape our shapelessness: for I had no part in that boy but the sin. That he had been brought up by us in Your way was because You had inspired us, no other. I do but acknowledge to You Your own gifts. There is a book of

9. At Cassiciacum, placed at his disposal by a friend.   1. While at Cassiciacum, Augustine wrote a book attacking the academic philosophers; a book on the happy life; and another titled *De ordine*, a treatise on divine providence.   2. Nebridius came from Carthage to Milan with Augustine, shared his spiritual pilgrimage through the pagan philosophies and Manichean doctrines to become a Christian, and returned to Africa, where he died. Augustine's letters to Nebridius are still extant.   3. The appeal of Christ's apostles to peoples outside the Hebrew nation: "I am sought of them that asked not for me; I am found of them that sought me not" (Isaiah 65.1).

mine called *De Magistro:*[4] it is a dialogue between him and me. You know, O God, that all the ideas which are put into the mouth of the other party to the dialogue were truly his, though he was but sixteen. I had experience of many other remarkable qualities in him. His great intelligence filled me with a kind of awe: and who but You could be the maker of things so wonderful? But You took him early from this earth, and I think of him utterly without anxiety, for there is nothing in his boyhood or youth or anywhere in him to cause me to fear. We took him along with us, the same age as ourselves in Your grace, to be brought up in Your discipline: and we were baptized, and all anxiety as to our past life fled away. The days were not long enough as I meditated, and found wonderful delight in meditating, upon the depth of Your design for the salvation of the human race. I wept at the beauty of Your hymns and canticles, and was powerfully moved at the sweet sound of Your Church's singing. Those sounds flowed into my ears, and the truth streamed into my heart: so that my feeling of devotion overflowed, and the tears ran from my eyes, and I was happy in them.

It was only a little while before that the church of Milan had begun to practice this kind of consolation and exultation, to the great joy of the brethen singing together with heart and voice. For it was only about a year, or not much more, since Justina, the mother of the boy emperor Valentinian, was persecuting Your servant Ambrose in the interests of her own heresy: for she had been seduced by the Arians.[5] The devoted people had stayed day and night in the church, ready to die with their bishop, Your servant. And my mother, Your handmaid, bearing a great part of the trouble and vigil, had lived in prayer. I also, though still not warmed by the fire of Your Spirit, was stirred to excitement by the disturbed and wrought-up state of the city. It was at this time that the practice was instituted of singing hymns and psalms after the manner of the Eastern churches,[6] to keep the people from being altogether worn out with anxiety and want of sleep. The custom has been retained from that day to this, and has been imitated by many, indeed in almost all congregations throughout the world.

At this time You revealed to Your bishop Ambrose in a vision the place where the bodies of the martyrs Protasius and Gervasius[7] lay hid, which You had for so many years kept incorrupt in the treasury of Your secret knowledge that You might bring them forth at the proper moment to check a woman's fury—the woman[8] being the ruler of the Empire! For when they were discovered and dug up and with due honor brought to Ambrose's basilica, not only were people cured who had been tormented by evil spirits—and the devils themselves forced to confess it—but also there was a man, a citizen well known to the city, who had been blind for many years: he asked what was the cause of the tumultuous joy of the people, and when he heard, he sprang up and asked his guide to lead him into the place. When he arrived

---

4. *The Teacher,* written in Tagaste, Africa, two years after Augustine's baptism and shortly after his return from Italy; it concerns teaching and the thesis that only God is the cause for humankind's acquisition of learning and truth.   5. Members of a sect who followed the doctrine of Arius (250–336) that the Son had not existed from all eternity and was, therefore, inferior to the Father. At the Council of Nicaea (325) Arius and his followers were declared heretical, but the Arian heresy remained a serious problem for the Church for many years. Justina demanded that Ambrose allow the Arians to hold public services inside the walls of Milan.   6. The Greek-speaking churches of the Eastern Roman Empire; they split off from the Catholic Church in the ninth century.   7. Two beheaded skeletons discovered by Ambrose at Milan were identified as the relics of these saints; nothing certain is known about them, but they were said to have been martyred in the second century.   8. Justina.

there he asked to be allowed to touch with his handkerchief the place on which lay the saints, whose death is precious in Your sight. He did so, put the handkerchief to his eyes, and immediately they were opened. The news spread abroad, Your praises glowed and shone, and if the mind of that angry woman was not brought to the sanity of belief, it was at least brought back from the madness of persecution. Thanks be to my God! From what and towards what have You led my memory, that it should confess to You these great things which I had altogether forgotten? Yet even then, *when the odor of Thy ointments was so sweet smelling,* I did *not run after Thee:* and for this I wept all the more now when I heard Your hymns and canticles, as one who had then sighed for You and now breathed in You, breathed so far as the air allows in this our house of grass.[9]

You, Lord, who make men of one mind to dwell in one house brought to our company a young man of our own town, Evodius. He had held office in the civil service, had been converted and baptized before us, had resigned from the state's service, and given himself to Yours. We kept together, meaning to live together in our devout purpose. We thought deeply as to the place in which we might serve You most usefully. As a result we started back for Africa. And when we had come as far as Ostia[1] on the Tiber, my mother died. I pass over many things, for I must make haste. Do You, O my God, accept my confessions and my gratitude for countless things of which I say nothing. But I will not omit anything my mind brings forth concerning her, Your servant, who brought me forth—brought me forth in the flesh to this temporal light, and in her heart to light eternal. Not of her gifts do I speak but of Your gifts in her. For she did not bring herself into the world or educate herself in the world: it was You who created her, nor did her father or mother know what kind of being was to come forth from them. It was the scepter of Your Christ, the discipline of your Only-Begotten, that brought her up in holy fear, in a Catholic family which was a worthy member of Your church. Yet it was not the devotion of her mother in her upbringing that she talked most of, but of a certain aged servant, who had indeed carried my mother's father on her back when he was a baby, as little ones are accustomed to be carried on the backs of older girls. Because of this, because also of her age and her admirable character, she was very much respected by her master and mistress in their Christian household. As a result she was given charge of her master's daughters. This charge she fulfilled most conscientiously, checking them sharply when necessary with holy severity and teaching them soberly and prudently. Thus, except at the times when they ate—and that most temperately—at their parents' table, she would not let them even drink water, no matter how tormenting their thirst. By this she prevented the forming of a bad habit, and she used to remark very sensibly: "Now you drink water because you are not allowed to have wine: but when you are married, and thus mistresses of food-stores and wine-cellars, you will despise water, but the habit of drinking will still remain." By this kind of teaching and the authority of her commands she moderated the greediness that goes with childhood and brought the little girls' thirst to such a control that they no longer wanted what they ought not to have.

9. Compare Isaiah 40.6–8: "All flesh is grass. . . . The grass withereth, the flower fadeth: but the word of our God will stand forever."   1. On the southwest coast of Italy; it was the port of Rome and the point of departure for Africa.

Yet, as Your servant told me, her son, there did steal upon my mother an inclination to wine. For when, in the usual way, she was sent by her parents, as a well-behaved child, to draw wine from the barrel, she would dip the cup in, but before pouring the wine from the cup into the flagon, she would sip a little with the very tip of her lips, only a little because she did not yet like the taste sufficiently to take more. Indeed she did it not out of any craving for wine, but rather from the excess of childhood's high spirits, which tend to boil over in absurdities, and are usually kept in check by the authority of elders. And so, adding to that daily drop a little more from day to day—for he that despises small things, falls little by little—she fell into the habit, so that she would drink off greedily cups almost full of wine. Where then was that wise old woman with her forceful prohibitions? Could anything avail against the evil in us, unless Your healing, O Lord, watched over us? When our father and mother and nurses are absent, You are present, who created us, who call us, who can use those placed over us for some good unto the salvation of our souls. What did You do then, O my God? How did You cure her, and bring her to health? From another soul you drew a harsh and cutting sarcasm, as though bringing forth a surgeon's knife from Your secret store, and with one blow amputated that sore place. A maidservant with whom she was accustomed to go to the cellar, one day fell into a quarrel with her small mistress when no one else chanced to be about, and hurled at her the most biting insult possible, calling her a drunkard. My mother was pierced to the quick, saw her fault in its true wickedness, and instantly condemned it and gave it up. Just as the flattery of a friend can pervert, so the insult of an enemy can sometimes correct. Nor do You, O God, reward men according to what You do by means of them, but according to what they themselves intended. For the girl being in a temper wanted to enrage her young mistress, not to amend her, for she did it when no one else was there, either because the time and place happened to be thus when the quarrel arose, or because she was afraid that elders[2] would be angry because she had not told it sooner. But You, O Lord, Ruler of heavenly things and earthly, who turn to Your own purposes the very depths of rivers as they run and order the turbulence of the flow of time, did by the folly of one mind bring sanity to another; thus reminding us not to attribute it to our own power if another is amended by our word, even if we meant to amend him.

My mother, then, was modestly and soberly brought up, being rather made obedient to her parents by You than to You by her parents. When she reached the age for marriage, and was bestowed upon a husband, she served him as her lord. She used all her effort to win him to You, preaching You to him by her character, by which You made her beautiful to her husband, respected and loved by him and admirable in his sight. For she bore his acts of unfaithfulness quietly, and never had any jealous scene with her husband about them. She awaited Your mercy upon him, that he might grow chaste through faith in You. And as a matter of fact, though generous beyond measure, he had a very hot temper. But she knew that a woman must not resist a husband in anger, by deed or even by word. Only, when she saw him calm again and quiet, she would take the opportunity to give him an explanation of her actions, if it happened that he had been roused to anger unreasonably. The

2. Leaders of the Church.

result was that whereas many matrons with much milder husbands carried the marks of blows to disfigure their faces, and would all get together to complain of the way their husbands behaved, my mother—talking lightly but meaning it seriously—advised them against their tongues: saying that from the day they heard the matrimonial contract read to them they should regard it as an instrument by which they became servants; and from that time they should be mindful of their condition and not set themselves up against their masters. And they often expressed amazement—for they knew how violent a husband she had to live with—that it had never been heard, and there was no mark to show, that Patricius[3] had beaten his wife or that there had been any family quarrel between them for so much as a single day. And when her friends asked her the reason, she taught them her rule, which was as I have just said. Those who followed it, found it good and thanked her; those who did not, went on being bullied and beaten.

Her mother-in-law began by being angry with her because of the whispers of malicious servants. But my mother won her completely by the respect she showed, and her unfailing patience and mildness. She ended by going to her son, telling him of the tales the servants had bandied about to the destruction of peace in the family between herself and her daughter-in-law, and asking him to punish them for it. So he, out of obedience to his mother and in the interests of order in the household and peace among his womenfolk, had the servants beaten whose names he had been given, as she had asked when giving them. To which she added the promise that anyone must expect a similar reward from her own hands who should think to please her by speaking ill of her daughter-in-law. And as no one had the courage to do so, they lived together with the most notable degree of kindness and harmony.

This great gift also, O my God, my Mercy, You gave to Your good servant, in whose womb You created me, that she showed herself, wherever possible, a peacemaker between people quarreling and minds at discord. For swelling and undigested discord often belches forth bitter words when in the venom of intimate conversation with a present friend hatred at its rawest is breathed out upon an absent enemy. But when my mother heard bitter things said by each of the other, she never said anything to either about the other save what would help to reconcile them. This might seem a small virtue, if I had not had the sorrow of seeing for myself so many people who—as if by some horrible widespreading infection of sin—not only tell angry people the things their enemies said in anger, but even add things that were never said at all. Whereas, on the contrary, ordinary humanity would seem to require not merely that we refrain from exciting or increasing wrath among men by evil speaking, but that we study to extinguish wrath by kind speaking. Such a one was she: and You were the master who taught her most secretly in the school of her heart.

The upshot was that toward the very end of his life she won her husband to You; and once he was a Christian she no longer had to complain of the things she had had to bear with before he was a Christian. Further, she was a servant of Your servants. Such of them as knew her praised and honored and loved You, O God, in her; for they felt Your presence in her heart, showing itself in the fruit of her holy conversation. She had been *the wife of*

---

3. Augustine's father.

one husband, had requited her parents, had governed her house piously, *was well reported of for good works. She had brought up her children,*[4] being in labor of them as often as she saw them swerving away from You. Finally of all of us Your servants, O Lord—since by Your gift You suffer us to speak— who before her death were living together[5] after receiving the grace of baptism, she took as much care as if she had been the mother of us all, and served us as if she had been the daughter of us all.

When the day was approaching on which she was to depart this life—a day that You knew though we did not—it came about, as I believe by Your secret arrangement, that she and I stood alone leaning in a window, which looked inwards to the garden within the house where we were staying, at Ostia on the Tiber; for there we were away from everybody, resting for the sea voyage from the weariness of our long journey by land. There we talked together, she and I alone, in deep joy; and *forgetting the things that were behind and looking forward to those that were before,* we were discussing in the presence of Truth, which You are, what the eternal life of the saints could be like, *which eye has not seen nor ear heard, nor has it entered into the heart of man.* But with the mouth of our heart we panted for the high waters of Your fountain, the fountain of the life which is with You: that being sprinkled from that fountain according to our capacity, we might in some sense meditate upon so great a matter.

And our conversation had brought us to this point, that any pleasure whatsoever of the bodily senses, in any brightness whatsoever of corporeal light, seemed to us not worthy of comparison with the pleasure of that eternal Light, not worthy even of mention. Rising as our love flamed upward towards that Selfsame,[6] we passed in review the various levels of bodily things, up to the heavens themselves, whence sun and moon and stars shine upon this earth. And higher still we soared, thinking in our minds and speaking and marveling at Your works: and so we came to our own souls, and went beyond them to come at last to that region of richness unending, where You feed Israel forever with the food of truth: and there life is that Wisdom by which all things are made, both the things that have been and the things that are yet to be. But this Wisdom itself is not made: it is as it has ever been, and so it shall be forever: indeed "has ever been" and "shall be forever" have no place in it, but it simply is, for it is eternal: whereas "to have been" and "to be going to be" are not eternal. And while we were thus talking of His Wisdom and panting for it, with all the effort of our heart we did for one instant attain to touch it; then sighing, and leaving the first fruits of our spirit bound to it, we returned to the sound of our own tongue, in which a word has both beginning and ending. For what is like to your Word, Our Lord, who abides in Himself forever, yet grows not old and makes all things new!

So we said: If to any man the tumult of the flesh grew silent, silent the images of earth and sea and air: and if the heavens grew silent, and the very soul grew silent to herself and by not thinking of self mounted beyond self: if all dreams and imagined visions grew silent, and every tongue and every sign and whatsoever is transient—for indeed if any man could hear them, he should hear them saying with one voice: We did not make ourselves, but

---

4. Augustine is paraphrasing Paul's description of the duties of a widow, given in I Timothy 5.   **5.** Augustine and his fellow converts.   **6.** Reality, the divine principle. This ecstasy of Augustine and Monica is throughout described in philosophical terms, in which God is Wisdom.

He made us who abides forever: but if, having uttered this and so set us to listening to Him who made them, they all grew silent, and in their silence He alone spoke to us, not by them but by Himself: so that we should hear His word, not by any tongue of flesh nor the voice of an angel nor the sound of thunder nor in the darkness of a parable,[7] but that we should hear Himself whom in all these things we love, should hear Himself and not them: just as we two had but now reached forth and in a flash of the mind attained to touch the eternal Wisdom which abides over all: and if this could continue, and all other visions so different be quite taken away, and this one should so ravish and absorb and wrap the beholder in inward joys that his life should eternally be such as that one moment of understanding for which we had been sighing—would not this be: *Enter Thou into the joy of Thy Lord?* But when shall it be? Shall it be when *we shall all rise again* and *shall not all be changed?*[8]

Such thoughts I uttered, though not in that order or in those actual words; but You know, O Lord, that on that day when we talked of these things the world with all its delights seemed cheap to us in comparison with what we talked of. And my mother said: "Son, for my own part I no longer find joy in anything in this world. What I am still to do here and why I am here I know not, now that I no longer hope for anything from this world. One thing there was, for which I desired to remain still a little longer in this life, that I should see you a Catholic Christian before I died. This God has granted me in superabundance, in that I now see you His servant to the contempt of all worldly happiness. What then am I doing here?"

What answer I made, I do not clearly remember; within five days or not much longer she fell into a fever. And in her sickness, she one day fainted away and for the moment lost consciousness. We ran to her but she quickly returned to consciousness, and seeing my brother and me standing by her she said as one wondering: "Where was I?" Then looking closely upon us as we stood wordless in our grief, she said: "Here you will bury your mother." I stayed silent and checked my weeping. But my brother said something to the effect that he would be happier if she were to die in her own land and not in a strange country. But as she heard this she looked at him anxiously, restraining him with her eye because he savored of earthly things, and then she looked at me and said: "See the way he talks." And then she said to us both: "Lay this body wherever it may be. Let no care of it disturb you: this only I ask of you that you should remember me at the altar of the Lord wherever you may be." And when she had uttered this wish in such words as she could manage, she fell silent as her sickness took hold of her more strongly.

But as I considered Your gifts, O unseen God, which You send into the hearts of Your faithful to the springing up of such wonderful fruits, I was glad and gave thanks to You, remembering what I had previously known of the care as to her burial which had always troubled her: for she had arranged to be buried by the body of her husband. Because they had lived together in such harmony, she had wished—so little is the human mind capable of rising

---

7. Compare Luke 8.10: "Unto you it is given to know the mysteries of the kingdom of God: but to others in parables; that seeing they might not see, and hearing they might not understand." 8. Compare 1 Corinthians 15.52: "the trumpet shall sound, and the dead shall be raised incorruptible, and we shall be changed," referring to the Last Judgment.

to the divine—that it should be granted her, as an addition to her happiness and as something to be spoken of among men, that after her pilgrimage beyond the sea the earthly part of man and wife should lie together under the same earth. Just when this vain desire had begun to vanish from her heart through the fullness of Your goodness, I did not know; but I was pleased and surprised that it had now so clearly vanished: though indeed in the conversation we had had together at the window, when she said: "What am I still doing here?" there had appeared no desire to die in her own land. Further I heard afterwards that in the time we were at Ostia, she had talked one day to some of my friends, as a mother talking to her children, of the contempt of this life and of the attraction of death. I was not there at the time. They marveled at such courage in a woman—but it was You who had given it to her—and asked if she was not afraid to leave her body so far from her own city. But she said: "Nothing is far from God, and I have no fear that He will not know at the end of the world from what place He is to raise me up." And so on the ninth day of her illness, in the fifty-sixth year of her life and the thirty-third of mine, that devout and holy soul was released from the body.

I closed her eyes; and an immeasurable sorrow flowed into my heart and would have overflowed in tears. But my eyes under the mind's strong constraint held back their flow and I stood dry-eyed. In that struggle it went very ill with me. As she breathed her last, the child Adeodatus broke out into lamentation and we all checked him and brought him to silence. But in this very fact the childish element in me, which was breaking out into tears, was checked and brought to silence by the manlier voice of my mind. For we felt that it was not fitting that her funeral should be solemnized with moaning and weeping and lamentation, for so it is normal to weep when death is seen as sheer misery or as complete extinction. But she had not died miserably, nor did she wholly die. Of the one thing we were sure by reason of her character, of the other by the reality of our faith.

What then was it that grieved my heart so deeply? Only the newness of the wound, in finding the custom I had so loved of living with her suddenly snapped short. It was a joy to me to have this one testimony from her: when her illness was close to its end, meeting with expressions of endearment such services as I rendered, she called me a dutiful loving son, and said in the great affection of her love that she had never heard from my mouth any harsh or reproachful word addressed to herself. But what possible comparison was there, O my God who made us, between the honor I showed her and the service she had rendered me?

Because I had now lost the great comfort of her, my soul was wounded and my very life torn asunder, for it had been one life made of hers and mine together. When the boy had been quieted and ceased weeping, Evodius took up the psalter and began to chant—with the whole house making the responses—the psalm *Mercy and judgment I will sing to Thee, O Lord.*[9] And when they heard what was being done, many of the brethren and religious women came to us; those whose office it was were making arrangement for the burial, while, in another part of the house where it could properly be done I discoursed, with friends who did not wish to leave me by myself, upon

9. Compare Psalm 101.1.

matters suitable for that time. Thus I used truth as a kind of fomentation[1] to bring relief to my torment, a torment known to You, but not known to those others: so that listening closely to me they thought that I lacked all feeling of grief. But in Your ears, where none of them could hear, I accused the emotion in me as weakness; and I held in the flood of my grief. It was for the moment a little diminished, but returned with fresh violence, not with any pouring of tears or change of countenance: but I knew what I was crushing down in my heart. I was very much ashamed that these human emotions could have such power over me—though it belongs to the due order and the lot of our earthly condition that they should come to us—and I felt a new grief at my grief and so was afflicted with a twofold sorrow.

When the body was taken to burial, I went and returned without tears. During the prayers which we poured forth to you when the sacrifice of our redemption[2] was offered for her—while the body, as the custom there is, lay by the grave before it was actually buried—during those prayers I did not weep. Yet all that day I was heavy with grief within and in the trouble of my mind I begged of You in my own fashion to heal my pain; but You would not—I imagine because You meant to impress upon my memory by this proof how strongly the bond of habit holds the mind even when it no longer feeds upon deception. The idea came to me to go and bathe, for I had heard that the bath—which the Greeks call βαλανειον[3]—is so called because it drives anxiety from the mind. And this also I acknowledge to Your mercy, O Father of orphans, that I bathed and was the same man after as before. The bitterness of grief had not sweated out of my heart. Then I fell asleep, and woke again to find my grief not a little relieved. And as I was in bed and no one about, I said over those true verses that Your servant Ambrose wrote of You:

> Deus creator omnium
> polique rector vestiens
> diem decoro lumine,
> noctem sopora gratia,
>
> artus solutos ut quies
> reddat laboris usui
> mentesque fessas allevet
> luctusque solvat anxios.[4]

And then little by little I began to recover my former feeling about Your handmaid, remembering how loving and devout was her conversation with You, how pleasant and considerate her conversation with me, of which I was thus suddenly deprived. And I found solace in weeping in Your sight both about her and for her, about myself and for myself. I no longer tried to check my tears, but let them flow as they would, making them a pillow for my heart: and it rested upon them, for it was Your ears that heard my weeping, and not the ears of a man, who would have misunderstood my tears and despised them. But now, O Lord, I confess it to You in writing, let him read it who

---

1. Soothing dressing for a wound.   2. Perhaps a communion service.   3. Augustine evidently derives *balaneion* ("bath") from the words *ballo* ("cast away") and *ania* ("sorrow").   4. God, the creator of all things / and ruler of the heavens / you who clothe the day with the glory of light, / and the night with the gift of sleep, / so that rest may relax the limbs / and restore them for the day's work / relieve the fatigue of the mind / and dispel anxiety and grief (Latin).

will and interpret it as he will: and if he sees it as sin that for so small a portion of an hour I wept for my mother, now dead and departed from my sight, who had wept so many years for me that I should live ever in Your sight—let him not scorn me but rather, if he is a man of great charity, let him weep for my sins to You, the Father of all the brethren of Your Christ.

Now that my heart is healed of that wound, in which there was perhaps too much of earthly affection, I pour forth to You, O our God, tears of a very different sort for Your handmaid—tears that flow from a spirit shaken by the thought of the perils there are for every soul that dies in Adam.[5] For though she had been made alive in Christ, and while still in the body had so lived that Your name was glorified in her faith and her character, yet I dare not say that from the moment of her regeneration in baptism no word issued from her mouth contrary to Your Command. Your Son, who is Truth, has said: *Whosoever shall say to his brother, Thou fool, shall be in danger of hell fire;*[6] and it would go ill with the most praiseworthy life lived by men, if You were to examine it with Your mercy laid aside! But because You do not enquire too fiercely into our sins, we have hope and confidence of a place with You. Yet if a man reckons up before You the merits he truly has, what is he reckoning except Your own gifts? If only men would know themselves to be but men, so that he that glories would glory in the Lord!

Thus, my Glory and my Life, God of my heart, leaving aside for this time her good deeds, for which I give thanks to Thee in joy, I now pray to Thee for my mother's sins. Grant my prayer through the true Medicine of our wounds,[7] who hung upon the cross and who now sitting at Thy right hand makes intercession for us. I know that she dealt mercifully, and from her heart forgave those who trespassed against her: do Thou also forgive such trespasses as she may have been guilty of in all the years since her baptism, forgive them, Lord, forgive them, I beseech Thee: enter not into judgment with her. Let Thy mercy be exalted above Thy justice for Thy words are true and Thou hast promised that the merciful shall obtain mercy. That they should be merciful is Thy gift who *hast mercy on whom Thou wilt, and wilt have compassion on whom Thou wilt.*

And I believe that Thou hast already done what I am now asking; but be not offended, Lord, at the things my mouth would utter. For on that day when her death was so close, she was not concerned that her body should be sumptuously wrapped or embalmed with spices, nor with any thought of choosing a monument or even for burial in her own country. Of such things she gave us no command, but only desired to be remembered at Thy altar, which she had served without ever missing so much as a day, on which she knew that the holy Victim was offered; *by whom the handwriting is blotted out of the decree that was contrary to us,*[8] by which offering too the enemy was overcome who, reckoning our sins and seeking what may be laid to our charge, found nothing in Him, in whom we are conquerors. Who shall restore to Him his innocent blood? Who shall give Him back the price by which He purchased us and so take us from Him? To this sacrament of our

---

5. That is, with the curse of Adam not nullified through baptism in Jesus Christ and conformity with his teachings.　**6.** From Matthew 5.22, Jesus' Sermon on the Mount. He is preaching a more severe moral code than the traditional one that whoever kills shall be liable to judgment.　**7.** Jesus.　**8.** Alludes to Christ's redemption of humanity from the curse of Adam through the Crucifixion.

redemption Thy handmaid had bound her soul by the bond of faith. Let none wrest her from Thy protection; let neither the lion nor the dragon[9] bar her way by force or craft. For she will not answer that she owes nothing, lest she should be contradicted and confuted by that cunning accuser: but she will answer that her debts have been remitted by Him, to whom no one can hand back the price which He paid for us, though He owed it not.

So let her rest in peace, together with her husband, for she had no other before nor after him, but served him, in patience bringing forth fruit for Thee, and winning him likewise for Thee. And inspire, O my Lord my God, inspire Thy servants my brethren, Thy sons my masters, whom I serve with heart and voice and pen, that as many of them as read this may remember at Thy altar Thy servant Monica, with Patricius, her husband, by whose bodies Thou didst bring me into this life, though how I know not.[1] May they with loving mind remember these who were my parents in this transitory light, my brethren who serve Thee as our Father in our Catholic mother, and those who are to be fellow citizens with me in the eternal Jerusalem,[2] which Thy people sigh for in their pilgrimage from birth until they come there: so that what my mother at her end asked of me may be fulfilled more richly in the prayers of so many gained for her by my Confessions than by my prayers alone.

*　　*　　*

9. Compare Psalm 91.13: "Thou shalt tread upon the lion and the adder: the young lion and the dragon shalt thou trample under feet, which invokes God's protection of the godly."　1. Augustine does not understand the seemingly miraculous process by which the fetus grows in the womb.　2. I.e., heaven.

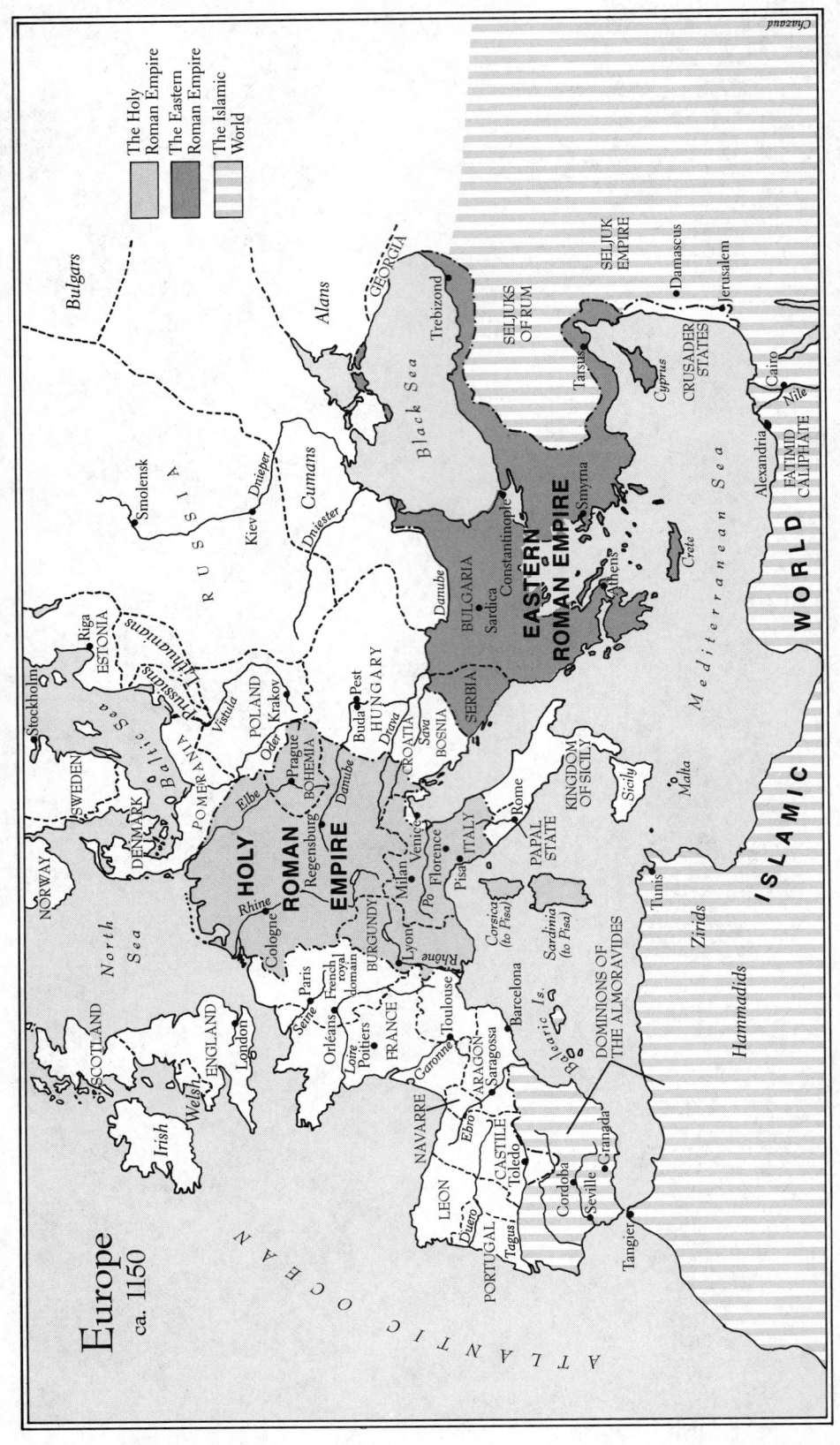

Europe
ca. 1150

The Holy
Roman Empire

The Eastern
Roman Empire

The Islamic
World

Chazaud

ATLANTIC OCEAN

North Sea

Irish

Welsh

SCOTLAND

ENGLAND

London

Seine

Paris

Orléans

French
royal
domain

Loire

Poitiers

FRANCE

Toulouse

Garonne

NAVARRE

ARAGON

Ebro

Saragossa

Barcelona

Balearic Is.

LEON

PORTUGAL

Duero

Tagus

CASTILE

Toledo

Córdoba

Seville

Granada

Tangier

DOMINIONS OF
THE ALMORAVIDES

NORWAY

SWEDEN

Stockholm

DENMARK

Baltic Sea

Riga

ESTONIA

Prussians

Lithuanians

POMERANIA

Vistula

Oder

POLAND

Krakow

Elbe

Rhine

Cologne

Regensburg

BOHEMIA

Prague

HOLY
ROMAN
EMPIRE

BURGUNDY

Lyon

Rhône

Po

Milan

Venice

Florence

Pisa

Corsica
(to Pisa)

Sardinia
(to Pisa)

ITALY

Rome

PAPAL
STATE

KINGDOM
OF SICILY

Sicily

Malta

Tunis

Zirids

Hammadids

Danube

Buda

Pest

HUNGARY

Drava

Sava

CROATIA

BOSNIA

SERBIA

Danube

BULGARIA

Sardica

Smolensk

Kiev

Dnieper

Dniester

R U S S I A

Cumans

Bulgars

Alans

GEORGIA

Black Sea

Trebizond

Constantinople

EASTERN
ROMAN EMPIRE

Athens

Crete

Smyrna

Tarsus

Cyprus

Mediterranean Sea

SELJUKS
OF RUM

SELJUK
EMPIRE

Damascus

Jerusalem

CRUSADER
STATES

Cairo

Nile

Alexandria

FATIMID
CALIPHATE

ISLAMIC WORLD

Masterpieces of the Middle Ages

The Middle Ages—approximately the thousand years from 500 to 1500—saw the classical civilization of Greece and Rome transformed by contact with three very different cultures. One was the Germanic culture of the tribes who invaded and, by the fifth century, had effectively conquered the western half of the Roman Empire. The second was the Christianity that began in Palestine and then quickly spread throughout the empire until almost all of Western Europe was thoroughly Christianized by the eleventh century (as early as 325 the Emperor Constantine had established Christianity as virtually the official religion of the empire). The third influence—less pronounced but still important—was Islam, which arose in the Arabian peninsula in the seventh century and quickly spread throughout North Africa and into the Iberian peninsula, where it remained a powerful force until the fifteenth century. Because it was an amalgam of these vastly different cultural forces, medieval Europe displayed an unusually wide range of values, ideas, and social forms. But for all this variety there emerged at the end of the process a recognizable culture. In the year 500 "the West" could hardly be characterized either politically or culturally, but by 1500 the map of Europe looked very much as it does today, and many of the values we think of as characteristically Western—individualism, consensual government, a recognition of religious difference, even the idea of Europe itself—were emergent realities. Another central event within Western culture during this period was the emergence of vernacular literatures. The great national literatures of Europe took form during the Middle Ages, and here we find both individual literary masterpieces and traditions of writing that have continued to define what counts as literature.

Because it is the period during which the cultural identities of the European nations took shape, the Middle Ages has always generated both fascination and controversy. Take, for example, its distinctly odd name: the *middle* of what? The answer is that the period was named by the people who came immediately after it, who called their own age the Renaissance because they saw it as the time in which the cultural achievements of antiquity were being reborn. For them the immediately preceding period was a time of middleness, a space of cultural emptiness that separated them from the classical past they so admired: hence, the Middle Ages (or, in Latin, *medium aevum*, from which we get our term *medieval*). That this narrow view of cultural history is still in force today is shown by the way in which "medieval" continues to be used to mean antiquated, or quaint, or barbaric. It is also evident in the widespread notion that the Middle Ages was unusually homogeneous, a time in which all men and women thought and felt more or less the same things and behaved in much the same way. Yet in fact this period contains not one but many different kinds of people with many different cultures.

These cultures were oral and literate; Germanic and Latin; Arabic, Jewish, and Christian; secular and religious; tolerant and repressive; vernacular and learned; rural and urban; skeptical and pious; popular and aristocratic. For every example of one kind of cultural product we can find an example of another, and most significant literary works incorporated elements and values drawn from different and often conflicting traditions. *The Song of Roland*, for instance, composed in the eleventh century, promotes with unabashed enthusiasm the superiority of Christianity to Islam. Yet already in the ninth century, Islamic scholars had translated much of Greek science and philosophy into Arabic, preserving and enriching this tradition at the very time it was in decline in Western Europe. And beginning in the twelfth century, Muslim centers of learning in Spain, Sicily, and southern Italy made it possible for European scholars to regain access to these Greek originals and to study their Muslim commentators. Similarly complex is the way *The Song of Roland* struggles with internal contradictions of its own. A poem that exalts a great warrior according to Germanic traditions of military heroism, it also affirms the necessity of subordinating individual accomplishment to the needs of a unified Christian community. Another example of the clash of competing interests can be found in the work of Geoffrey Chaucer, the founding poet of English literature. For the first two-thirds of his career he was a court poet who catered almost exclusively to the narrow tastes of an aristocratic readership, and yet in *The Canterbury Tales* he recorded with remarkable sensitivity the discontents and desires of men and women from almost every social class. These complexities and contradictions are everywhere in medieval writing, and if they frustrate modern attempts to define the period in simple terms they also make reading its literature a process of continuing surprise.

The most familiar description of the Middle Ages is as "an age of faith," by which is meant the notion that medieval people shared a uniform commitment to Catholic Christianity. The Roman Empire had provided political unity, law, and order, but beyond that it had pretty much left moral and spiritual issues to be handled by the individual, either singly or in voluntary or ethnic groups. As the Middle Ages developed, however, the Church gradually extended its spiritual and institutional authority across most of Europe. By 1200, with the exception of beleaguered Jewish communities, the area of the Iberian peninsula under Muslim control, and frontier lands in the Slavic east, Europe had become virtually identical with Christendom. But this acknowledgment of the primacy of Christian doctrine and the ritual practices that went with it (such as baptism, communion, and confession), meant neither that religious values were universally recognized as primary nor that one single form of Christianity was placidly accepted by all medieval people. On the contrary, as the literature of the period makes clear, many people took the central doctrines of Christianity so much for granted that their daily lives seem largely untroubled by the moral and spiritual demands of religion. In the *Lais* of Marie de France, for example, and the vernacular love lyrics, men and women lead their romantic lives without giving much if any thought to Christian standards of behavior. In a more satiric vein, the French fabliaux and the tales from Boccaccio's *Decameron* provide an often acerbic and always witty puncturing of the pretensions of individual churchmen. The lecherous priest and the greedy friar are stock characters of medieval satire, as are the wayward nun and the gluttonous monk. Another pressure point at which Christian doctrine is tested is the Germanic epic *Beowulf,* a poem written by a believer who nonetheless deeply admires the pagan past that he knows must be left behind. Even in *The Divine Comedy,* the work that seems most securely and unproblematically located within the Christian worldview, Dante is poignantly aware of the gulf that separates him from the classical past, represented in the *Inferno* and *Purgatorio* by the man he calls "my author and my father," the pagan poet Virgil. The Middle Ages *is* an age of faith, but one that at its best is alert to the complexities and dilemmas that any faith poses to its adherents.

Another familiar description of the Middle Ages is as "an age of chivalry." Medieval literature for the most part expresses the values of the most powerful members of society, the aristocracy. These people achieved their domination through military might, both by imposing their will upon their neighbors and, more benevolently, by providing them with protection from invaders like the Vikings from the north, the Magyars and Mongols from the east, and the various Islamic peoples from the south.

At times, indeed, they became themselves the invaders, most notably in the various crusading expeditions that began in the eleventh century against Islam in the Iberian peninsula and the Levant and, later, against the Slavs in what is now Eastern Europe. Not surprisingly, throughout its medieval history, from the time of *Beowulf* (eighth to tenth century) to that of Malory's Arthurian tales (late fifteenth century), the European nobility—and the writers they supported—celebrated the values that sustained these military practices. These values included unwavering valor in the face of danger, loyalty to one's leader and companions, and an intense concern with personal honor. They also came to include a more or less explicit code of chivalry that stressed gentility of demeanor, generosity of both spirit and material goods, concern for the well-being of the powerless, and—above all—a capacity for experiencing a romantic love that was at once selfless and passionate. Whether or not medieval men actually lived up to these chivalric ideals is impossible to say, but that many believed in them—and believed that they achieved them—is undeniable. Yet many other members of medieval society, especially non-nobles like churchmen, urban dwellers, and peasants, were more likely than not to think that chivalry was just a fancy name for the heavy-handed imposition of force upon those least able to resist. More important for the writing of the time is the fact that chivalric values are never entirely consistent with each other. Where does personal bravery give way to the needs of the group?—this is a question at the heart of both *Beowulf* and *The Song of Roland*. Can one be both a full-hearted lover and a loyal warrior?—this is the dilemma that motivates many of the Arthurian tales that the medieval nobility loved to read. And can the same people perform both the deeds of war and those of civilization?—this is a question central to Western literature since the time of Homer and still challenging to us today.

The busy millennium we call, in the absence of a more precise term, the Middle Ages is thus dominated by certain leading concerns—the demands of religious faith and the appropriate use of physical force—that remain current. What continues to make its literature compelling to us is the skill with which individual writers dealt with these themes through the creation of unforgettable literary characters. For all its accomplishments in the arts of governing and the skills of commerce, in philosophy and theology, and in art and architecture, the most vivid legacy of the Middle Ages is the roster of characters it has contributed to world literature. Lancelot and Guinevere, Roland and Charlemagne, Renard the Fox and Robin Hood, Sir Gawain and Beowulf, the pilgrims of *The Canterbury Tales* and the lost souls of the *Inferno*: whether searching for the road to salvation or killing monsters, whether battling pagan enemies or hoodwinking unwary dupes, the protagonists of medieval literature continue to intrigue readers and inspire writers. In the last analysis the central concern of medieval literature is neither religious truth nor codes of conduct, important as these may be, but individual human beings working out their individual destinies.

FURTHER READING

An excellent reference work that contains articles on virtually all medieval topics, with bibliographies, is *The Dictionary of the Middle Ages*, 13 vols. (1987). Specific questions about medieval Christian doctrines can be answered by consulting Jaroslav Pelikan, *The Christian Tradition: A History of the Development of Doctrine*, vols. 1–4 (1971–84). C. W. Previté-Orton, *Shorter Cambridge Medieval History*, 2 vols. (1952), provides useful information on the relevant historical context of each literary work. An authoritative and readable introduction to social and economic conditions is M. M. Postan, *The Medieval Economy and Society* (1975). Two classic accounts well worth reading are R. W. Southern, *The Making of the Middle Ages* (1953), and J. W. Huizinga, *The Autumn of the Middle Ages* (first published in 1919, newly translated in 1996).

THE MIDDLE AGES

TEXTS	CONTEXTS
	529 Foundation of Monte Cassino, the first Benedictine monastery
610–32 *The Koran* **8th–10th centuries** *Beowulf* • Latin lyrics, saints' lives, and histories	**8th–10th centuries** Invasions of Western Europe by Arabs, Norsemen, and Magyars
	800 Charlemagne crowned Holy Roman Emperor
	899 Alfred the Great, king of Wessex in England, dies
11th century Hispano-Arabic and Provençal lyrics	**11th century** Consolidation of feudal social structure
	1066 Norman invasion of England
	1099 Knights of the First Crusade capture Jerusalem
12th century *The Song of Roland* • Marie de France, *Lais* • Arthurian romances • *Romance of Renard*, which includes *The Trial of Renard*	**12th century** Establishment of the universities of Paris, Oxford, and Bologna • Recovery of Aristotelian philosophy • Period of religious reform
	1187 Arabs recover Jerusalem permanently
13th century Fabliaux • *Romance of the Rose* • *Thorstein the Staff-Struck*	**13th century** Age of the great cathedrals and of scholastic philosophy
	1226 Francis of Assisi, founder of the first order of friars, dies
	1274 Thomas Aquinas, leading scholastic philosopher, dies
1301–1321 Dante, *The Divine Comedy*	**1337** War begins between France and England (The Hundred Years' War), ending only in 1453
	1348–1350 Bubonic plague sweeps through Europe, killing almost half the population
1353 Boccaccio, *The Decameron* **1380?** *Sir Gawain and the Green Knight*	
	1384 John Wyclif, promoter of religious views that prepare for the Reformation, dies
1390–1400 Chaucer, *The Canterbury Tales* **14th century** *The Thousand and One Nights*	**14th century** Peasant risings in England, France, Flanders, and Italy

Boldface titles indicate works in the anthology.

THE MIDDLE AGES

TEXTS	CONTEXTS
	15th century Growing centralization of state power throughout Europe
	1453 Fall of Constantinople to the Muslim Turks
	1455 Gutenberg prints the Bible, the first printed book
ca. 1470 Malory, *Morte Darthur* • Villon, *The Testament*	
	1492 Christopher Columbus's first voyage to the western hemisphere
1495? *Everyman*	

THE KORAN
610–632

For Muslims the Koran is something greater than prophetic revelation. It is an earthly duplicate of a divine Koran that exists in paradise, engraved in figures of gold on tablets of marble. Like God, it was not created but exists for all eternity—a complete and sufficient guide to our conduct on Earth. It is God's final revelation to humanity and was sent by Him to complete and correct all prior revelations. In its divinity it is greater than any prophet or any prophecy. It stands to Muslims as Christ does to Christians. To the glory of Muhammad's community, God chose to make this, His final revelation, in Arabic and through an Arab prophet. Because the Koran is, literally, God's word and is, like Him, miraculous and eternal, it cannot be translated. Interpretive renderings into other languages have been made and used for teaching purposes since the earliest period of Islam, but Muslims do not accept them as the Koran in the sense that Christians accept the Bible in English, or any of the other languages into which it has been translated, as still the Bible.

The Koran's revelations were received by Muhammad, known to Muslims as the Prophet of God, during the last two decades of his life—from roughly 610, when the angel Gabriel first appeared to him, to his death on June 8, 632. During his lifetime these revelations were recorded by various of his followers, but they were gathered together into a comprehensive volume only after his death. The title given this collection is the Koran (al-qur'ân), or The Recitation, and as its title suggests, the Koran is a work to be heard and recited, an oral work with a music and rhythm of its own that does not appear to best advantage on the printed page. The revelations came to Muhammad in verses (âya) of varying length and number. These were gathered into larger divisions (Suras) that were organized roughly by subject. These gatherings often appear arbitrary, and there are abrupt transitions in the longer Suras. Only the shortest are thematically unified and only Sura 12, Yusuf, tells a complete narrative. The Suras were then arranged by length, with the longer Suras preceding the shorter. Each Sura was given a name taken from some striking image or theme that appears in it. They are also identified as having been received in either Mecca or Medina, the two communities in which Muhammad lived. It is an article of faith with Muslims that the Koran we now have is a complete and accurate record of God's revelations to Muhammad and an exact copy of the divine Koran that exists in the seventh heaven.

Although the Koran was revealed over a relatively brief period, its style varies enormously. The earliest and shortest Suras sound like charms or incantations, evoking the wonder and glory of God, while the later and longer ones are filled with legal prescriptions. And many, perhaps most, of the Suras have the quality of sermons delivered in a highly charged and poetic language, often enriched by parables and brief narratives that exhort us to remember God and live pious lives.

The style of the individual Suras reflects in general terms the moments in Muhammad's life when they were revealed. In the early Meccan period of his mission, his concerns were those of an embattled prophet exhorting his community to believe in God and fear Him and defending himself against the hostility and skepticism of those who doubted both him and his God. The Suras from this period are filled with fierce and eloquent exhortations promising paradise to those who believe in God and eternal damnation to those who deny Him. These Suras are also marked by calls for social justice, expressed principally in concern for the plight of widows and orphans. It was in Mecca, too, that the accounts of earlier prophets from Noah (Nuh) to Jesus (Isâ)— who, like Muhammad, had to defend themselves against a hostile and unbelieving community—were revealed to him.

Eventually, Muhammad's success in creating a community of believers made him so unwelcome in his home that the Meccans forced him and his followers to emigrate to the nearby oasis of Medina. There he established his community among the tribes already settled around the oasis. While Muhammad continued to be the Prophet of Islam, the legal and political demands of his community now demanded most of his attention. He also had to cope with the growing number of believers who flocked to him and, eventually, to manage a war with the Meccans. The Suras revealed in Medina reflect these concerns in setting forth an extensive and detailed legal code that addresses the demands of the day-to-day life of the community as well as its spiritual needs.

These stylistic differences point out an obvious distinction between the Koran and the Bible. The essence of the Koran is admonition and guidance. No narrative thread runs through it, nor is it embedded in the history of a single people. The Koran's coherence is a product of the themes that are reiterated throughout its many Suras. For all the importance it gives to one language, Arabic, its message is a more general one. The many allusions to Moses (Musa), for example, stress that God may choose even an ordinary, flawed man to be His prophet, and as in the story of Joseph, say nothing of Moses' role as the leader of his people. The meaning of the Koran, as it often asserts, is for all humanity.

The Exordium, the opening Sura of the Koran, has an exceptional resonance in the life of Muslims. Muslims recite it at the beginning of every formal address and inscribe it at the head of every written document from works of scholarship to the stones that mark a grave. It begins every prayer.

Joseph (Sura 12) is, of course, not a prophet in Judaism or Christianity, but he is in Islam. He is also the only one whose tale is told continuously, and the only one to be mentioned exclusively in a single Sura. The Koranic version of this story includes most of the key events of Genesis 36–38, but excludes virtually everything that links Joseph to the Hebrew nation. In Genesis, Joseph is a divinely guided young man who is first tested severely and then becomes the leader of his nation, guiding them to prosperity in Egypt. In the Koran he is a divinely guided young man but not the leader of any nation. Although God tests Joseph, it is to prove that only those who follow divine guidance prosper. In the most famous scene, the temptation by his master's wife, he is not more righteous than she, but God gives him a sign that he should not succumb. Islam does not believe in original sin, and is more accepting of human error than Genesis. Joseph's innocence in this encounter is also explicitly established in Sura 12, while in Genesis only we and God see that Joseph is blameless. His master's wife, identified as Zuleikha in the commentaries, is also treated in a more tolerant fashion than Potiphar's wife. In a remarkable scene she shows the women of the city that they, too, would have been seduced by Joseph's angelic beauty. In the Koran, in short, the story of Joseph has nothing of the epic dimensions it has in Genesis but focuses instead on the smaller and more general theme of the importance of trusting in God.

The most informative general introduction to the Koran is the revised edition of *Bell's Introduction to the Qur'ân* (1970). Michael Cook, *Muhammad* (1983), is an excellent brief biography of the Prophet of Islam. Fazlur Rahman, *Major Themes of the Qur'ân* (1980), is a lucid presentation, by a Muslim scholar who has taught in the United States for many years, of the principal beliefs of Islam as they appear in the Koran. Marilyn R. Waldman, "New Approaches to 'Biblical' Materials in the Qur'ân," *The Muslim World* 75, no. 1 (January 1985), 1–16, gives a good comparison of Joseph in the Koran and the Bible.

PRONOUNCING GLOSSARY

The following list uses common English syllables and stress accents to provide rough equivalents of selected words whose pronunciation may be unfamiliar to the general reader.

al-qur'ân: *al-ko-ran'*   âya: *eye'-yuh*

bahirah: *buh-hee'-ruh*
Idris: *ee-drees'*
Isâ: *ee'-suh*
Ka'ba: *ka'-buh*
Nuh: *nooh*
Potiphar: *poh'-tee-far*
saibah: *saw'-ee-buh*

Suwâ: *soo-wah'*
wasilah: *wuh-see'-luh*
Ya'uq: *yah-ook'*
Yaghuth: *yah-gooth'*
Yusuf: *you'-suff*
Zuleikha: *zoo-lay'-kuh*

FROM THE KORAN[1]

Sura 1. The Exordium

[MECCA]

In the Name of God the Compassionate the Merciful[2]

Praise be to God, Lord of the Creation,
The Compassionate, the Merciful,
King of the Last Judgement!
You alone we worship, and to You alone
we pray for help.
Guide us to the straight path,
The path of those whom You have favoured,
Not of those who have incurred Your wrath,
Nor of those who have gone astray.

Sura 5. The Table

[MEDINA]

In the Name of God, the Compassionate, the Merciful

Believers, be true to your obligations. It is lawful for you to eat the flesh of all beasts other than that which is hereby announced to you. Game is forbidden while you are on pilgrimage. God decrees what He will.

Believers, do not violate the rites of God, or the sacred month, or the offerings or their ornaments, or those that repair to the Sacred House seeking God's grace and pleasure. Once your pilgrimage is ended, you shall be free to go hunting.

Do not allow your hatred for those who would debar you from the Holy Mosque to lead you into sin. Help one another in what is good and pious, not in what is wicked and sinful. Have fear of God, for He is stern in retribution.

---

1. Translated by N. J. Dawood.   2. According to Islamic law, this phrase, spoken or written, must precede all written work; it is also used by Muslims at the beginning of most formal tasks.

You are forbidden carrion, blood, and the flesh of swine; also any flesh dedicated to any other than God. You are forbidden the flesh of strangled animals and of those beaten or gored to death; of those killed by a fall or mangled by beasts of prey (unless you make it clean by giving the death-stroke yourselves); also of animals sacrificed to idols.

You are forbidden to settle disputes by consulting the Arrows.[3] That is a pernicious practice.

The unbelievers have this day abandoned all hope of vanquishing your religion. Have no fear of them: fear Me.

This day I have perfected your religion for you and completed My favour to you. I have chosen Islam to be your faith.

He that is constrained by hunger to eat of what is forbidden, not intending to commit sin, will find God forgiving and merciful.

They ask you what is lawful to them. Say: "All good things are lawful to you, as well as that which you have taught the birds and beasts of prey to catch, training them as God has taught you. Eat of what they catch for you, pronouncing upon it the name of God. And have fear of God: swift is God's reckoning."

All good things have this day been made lawful to you. The food of those to whom the Book was given[4] is lawful to you, and yours to them.

Lawful to you are the believing women and the free women from among those who were given the Book before you, provided that you give them their dowries and live in honour with them, neither committing fornication nor taking them as mistresses.

He that denies the Faith shall gain nothing from his labours. In the world to come he shall have much to lose.

Believers, when you rise to pray wash your faces and your hands as far as the elbow, and wipe your heads and your feet to the ankle. If you are polluted cleanse yourselves. But if you are sick or travelling the road; or if, when you have just relieved yourselves or had intercourse with women, you can find no water, take some clean sand and rub your hands and faces with it. God does not wish to burden you; He seeks only to purify you and to perfect His favour to you, so that you may give thanks.

Remember God's favour to you, and the covenant with which He bound you when you said: "We hear and obey." Have fear of God. God knows the innermost thoughts of men.

Believers, fulfil your duties to God and bear true witness. Do not allow your hatred for other men to turn you away from justice. Deal justly; that is nearer to true piety. Have fear of God; God is cognizant of all your actions.

God has promised those that have faith and do good works forgiveness and a rich reward. As for those who disbelieve and deny Our revelations, they are the heirs of Hell.

Believers, remember the favour which God bestowed upon you when He restrained the hands of those who sought to harm you. Have fear of God. In God let the faithful put their trust.

God made a covenant with the Israelites and raised among them twelve chieftains. God said: "I shall be with you. If you attend to your prayers and render the alms levy; if you believe in My apostles and assist them and give

---

3. A form of casting lots.   4. The Jews.

God a generous loan, I shall forgive you your sins and admit you to gardens watered by running streams. But he that hereafter denies Me shall stray from the right path."

But because they broke their covenant We laid on them Our curse and hardened their hearts. They have tampered with words out of their context and forgotten much of what they were enjoined. You will ever find them deceitful, except for a few of them. But pardon them and bear with them. God loves those who do good.

With those who said they were Christians We made a covenant also, but they too have forgotten much of what they were enjoined. Therefore We stirred among them enmity and hatred, which shall endure till the Day of Resurrection, when God will declare to them all that they have done.

People of the Book![5] Our aspostle has come to reveal to you much of what you have hidden of the Scriptures, and to forgive you much. A light has come to you from God and a glorious Book, with which God will guide to the paths of peace those that seek to please Him; He will lead them by His will from darkness to the light; He will guide them to a straight path.

Unbelievers are those who declare: "God is the Messiah, the son of Mary." Say: "Who could prevent God, if He so willed, from destroying the Messiah, the son of Mary, his mother, and all the people of the earth? God has sovereignty over the heavens and the earth and all that lies between them. He creates what He will and God has power over all things."

The Jews and the Christians say: "We are the children of God and His loved ones." Say: "Why then does He punish you for your sins? Surely you are mortals of His own creation. He forgives whom He will and punishes whom He pleases. God has sovereignty over the heavens and the earth and all that lies between them. All shall return to Him."

People of the Book! Our apostle has come to you with revelations after an interval during which there were no apostles, lest you say: "No one has come to give us good news or to warn us." Now someone has come to give you good news and to warn you. God has power over all things.

Bear in mind the words of Moses to his people. He said: "Remember, my people, the favours which God has bestowed upon you. He has raised up prophets among you, made you kings, and given you that which He has given to no other nation. Enter, my people, the holy land which God has assigned for you. Do not turn back, or you shall be ruined."

"Moses," they replied, "a race of giants dwells in this land. We will not set foot in it till they are gone. As soon as they are gone we will enter."

Thereupon two God-fearing men whom God had favoured, said: "Go in to them through the gates, and when you have entered you shall surely be victorious. In God put your trust, if you are true believers."

But they replied: "Moses, we will not go in so long as *they* are in it. Go, you and your Lord, and fight. Here we will stay."

"Lord," cried Moses, "I have none but myself and my brother. Do not confound us with these wicked people."

He replied: "They shall be forbidden this land for forty years, during which time they shall wander homeless on the earth. Do not grieve for these wicked people."

---

5. Here, Jews and Christians.

Recount to them in all truth the story of Adam's two sons: how they each made an offering, and how the offering of the one was accepted while that of the other was not. One said: "I will surely kill you." The other replied: "God accepts offerings only from the righteous. If you stretch your hand to kill me, I shall not lift mine to slay you; for I fear God, Lord of the Universe. I would rather you should add your sin against me to your other sins and thus become an inmate of the Fire. Such is the reward of the wicked."

His soul prompted him to slay his brother; he slew him and thus became one of the lost. Then God sent down a raven, which dug the earth to show him how to bury the naked corpse of his brother. "Alas!" he cried. "Have I not strength enough to do as this raven has done and so bury my brother's naked corpse?" And he repented.

That was why We laid it down for the Israelites that whoever killed a human being, except as a punishment for murder or other villainy in the land, shall be looked upon as though he had killed all mankind; and that whoever saved a human life should be regarded as though he had saved all mankind.

Our apostles brought them veritable proofs: yet it was not long before many of them committed great evils in the land.

Those that make war against God and His apostle and spread disorder in the land shall be put to death or crucified or have their hands and feet cut off on alternate sides, or be banished from the country. They shall be held up to shame in this world and sternly punished in the hereafter: except those that repent before you reduce them. For you must know that God is forgiving and merciful.

Believers, have fear of God and seek the right path to Him. Fight valiantly for His cause, so that you may triumph.

As for the unbelievers, if they offered all that the earth contains and as much besides to redeem themselves from the torment of the Day of Resurrection, it shall not be accepted from them. Theirs shall be a woeful punishment.

They will strive to get out of Hell, but they shall not: theirs shall be a lasting punishment.

As for the man or woman who is guilty of theft, cut off their hands to punish them for their crimes. That is the punishment enjoined by God. God is mighty and wise. But whoever repents after committing evil, and mends his ways, shall be pardoned by God. God is forgiving and merciful.

Do you not know that God has sovereignty over the heavens and the earth? He punishes whom He will and forgives whom He pleases. God has power over all things.

Apostle, do not grieve for those who plunge headlong into unbelief; those who say with their tongues: "We believe," but have no faith in their hearts, and those Jews who listen to the lies of others and pay no heed to you. They tamper with the words out of their context and say: "If this be given you, accept it; if not, then beware!"

You cannot help a man if God seeks to confound him. Those whose hearts He does not please to purify shall be rewarded with disgrace in this world and a grievous punishment in the hereafter.

They listen to falsehoods and practise what is unlawful. If they come to you, give them your judgement or avoid them. If you avoid them they can in no way harm you; but if you do act as their judge, judge them with fairness. God loves those that deal justly.

But how will they come to you for judgement, when they already have the Torah which enshrines God's own judgement? Soon after, they will turn their backs: they are no true believers.

We have revealed the Torah, in which there is guidance and light. By it the prophets who surrendered themselves judged the Jews, and so did the rabbis and the divines, according to God's Book which had been committed to their keeping and to which they themselves were witnesses.

Have no fear of man; fear Me, and do not sell My revelations for a paltry end. Unbelievers are those who do not judge according to God's revelations.

We decreed for them a life for a life, an eye for an eye, a nose for a nose, an ear for an ear, a tooth for a tooth, and a wound for a wound. But if a man charitably forbears from retaliation, his remission shall atone for him. Transgressors are those that do not judge according to God's revelations.

After them We sent forth Jesus, the son of Mary, confirming the Torah already revealed, and gave him the Gospel, in which there is guidance and light, corroborating what was revealed before it in the Torah, a guide and an admonition to the righteous. Therefore let the followers of the Gospel judge according to what God has revealed therein. Evil-doers are those that do not base their judgements on God's revelations.

And to you We have revealed the Book with the truth. It confirms the Scriptures which came before it and stands as a guardian over them. Therefore give judgement among men according to God's revelations and do not yield to their fancies or swerve from the truth made known to you.

We have ordained a law and assigned a path for each of you. Had God pleased, He could have made you one nation: but it is His wish to prove you by that which He has bestowed upon you. Vie with each other in good works, for to God you shall all return and He will resolve for you your differences.

Pronounce judgement among them according to God's revelations and do not be led by their desires. Take heed lest they should turn you away from a part of that which God has revealed to you. If they reject your judgement, know that it is God's wish to scourge them for their sins. A great many of mankind are evil-doers.

Is it pagan laws that they wish to be judged by? Who is a better judge than God for men whose faith is firm?

Believers, take neither Jews nor Christians for your friends. They are friends with one another. Whoever of you seeks their friendship shall become one of their number. God does not guide the wrongdoers.

You see the faint-hearted hastening to woo them. They say: "We fear lest a change of fortune should befall us." But when God grants you victory or makes known His will, they shall regret their secret plans. Then will the faithful say: "Are these the men who solemnly swore by God that they would stand with you?" Their works will come to nothing and they will lose all.

Believers, if any of you renounce the faith, God will replace them by others who love Him and are loved by Him, who are humble towards the faithful and stern towards the unbelievers, zealous for God's cause and fearless of man's censure. Such is the grace of God: He bestows it on whom He will. God is munificent and all-knowing.

Your only protectors are God, His apostle, and the faithful: those who attend to their prayers, render the alms levy, and kneel down in worship. Those who seek the protection of God, His apostle, and the faithful must know that God's followers are sure to triumph.

Believers, do not seek the friendship of the infidels and those who were given the Book before you, who have made of your religion a jest and a pastime. Have fear of God, if you are true believers. When you call them to pray, they treat their prayers as a jest and a pastime. This is because they are devoid of understanding.

Say: "People of the Book, is it not that you hate us only because we believe in God and in what has been revealed to us and to others before us, and that most of you are evil-doers?"

Say: "Shall I tell you who will receive the worse reward from God? Those whom God has cursed and with whom He has been angry, transforming them into apes and swine, and those who serve the devil. Worse is the plight of these, and they have strayed farther from the right path."

When they came to you they said: "We are believers." Indeed, infidels they came and infidels they departed. God knew best what they concealed.

You see many among them vie with one another in sin and wickedness and practice what is unlawful. Evil is what they do.

Why do their rabbis and divines not forbid them to blaspheme or to practise what is unlawful? Evil indeed are their doings.

The Jews say: "God's hand is chained." May their own hands be chained! May they be cursed for what they say! By no means. His hands are both outstretched: He bestows as He will.

That which is revealed to you from your Lord will surely increase the wickedness and unbelief of many of them. We have stirred among them enmity and hatred, which will endure till the Day of Resurrection. Whenever they kindle the fire of war, God puts it out. They spread evil in the land, but God does not love the evil-doers.

If the People of the Book accept the true faith and keep from evil, We will pardon them their sins and admit them to the gardens of delight. If they observe the Torah and the Gospel and what is revealed to them from their Lord, they shall enjoy abundance from above and from beneath.

There are some among them who are righteous men; but many among them who do nothing but evil.

Apostle, proclaim what is revealed to you from your Lord; if you do not, you will surely fail to convey His message. God will protect you from all men. He does not guide the unbelievers.

Say: "People of the Book, you will attain nothing until you observe the Torah and the Gospel and that which is revealed to you from your Lord."

That which is revealed to you from your Lord will surely increase the wickedness and unbelief of many of them. But do not grieve for the unbelievers.

Believers, Jews, Sabaeans, or Christians—whoever believes in God and the Last Day and does what is right—shall have nothing to fear or to regret.

We made a covenant with the Israelites and sent forth apostles among them. But whenever an apostle came to them with a message that did not suit their fancies, some they accused of lying and some they put to death. They thought no harm would come to them: they were blind and deaf. God turned to them in mercy, but many of them again became blind and deaf. God is ever watching over their actions.

Unbelievers are those that say: "God is the Messiah, the son of Mary." For the Messiah himself said: "Children of Israel, serve God, my Lord and your Lord." He that worships other gods besides God, God will deny him Paradise and Hell shall be his home. None shall help the evil-doers.

Unbelievers are those that say: "God is one of three." There is but one God. If they do not desist from so saying, those of them that disbelieve shall be sternly punished.

Will they not turn to God in repentance and seek forgiveness of Him? He is forgiving and merciful.

The Messiah, the son of Mary, was no more than an apostle: other apostles passed away before him. His mother was a saintly woman. They both ate earthly food.

See how We make plain to them Our revelations. See how they ignore the truth.

Say: "Will you serve instead of God that which can neither harm nor help you? God hears all and knows all."

Say: "People of the Book! Do not transgress the bounds of truth in your religion. Do not yield to the desires of those who have erred before; who have led many astray and have themselves strayed from the even path."

Those of the Israelites who disbelieved were cursed by David and Jesus, the son of Mary: they cursed them because they rebelled and committed evil. Nor did they censure themselves for any wrong they did. Evil were their deeds.

You see many of them making friends with unbelievers. Evil is that to which their souls prompt them. They have incurred the wrath of God and shall endure eternal torment. Had they believed in God and the Prophet and that which is revealed to him, they would not have befriended them. But many of them are evil-doers.

You will find that the most implacable of men in their enmity to the faithful are the Jews and the pagans, and that the nearest in affection to them are those who say: "We are Christians." That is because there are priests and monks among them; and because they are free from pride.

When they listen to that which was revealed to the Apostle, you will see their eyes fill with tears as they recognize its truth. They say: "Lord, we believe. Count us among Your witnesses. Why should we not believe in God and in the truth that has come down to us? Why should we not hope our Lord will admit us among the righteous?" And for their words God has rewarded them with gardens watered by running streams, where they shall dwell for ever. Such is the recompense of the righteous. But those that disbelieve and deny Our revelations shall be the inmates of Hell.

Believers, do not forbid the wholesome things which God has made lawful to you. Do not transgress; God does not love the transgressors. Eat of the lawful and wholesome things which God has given you. Have fear of God, in whom you believe.

God will not punish you for that which is inadvertent in your oaths. But He will take you to task for the oaths which you solemnly swear. The penalty for a broken oath is the feeding of ten needy men with such food as you normally offer to your own people; or the clothing of ten needy men; or the freeing of one slave. He that cannot afford any of these must fast three days. In this way you shall expiate your broken oaths. Therefore be true to that which you have sworn. Thus God makes plain to you His revelations, so that you may give thanks.

Believers, wine and games of chance, idols and divining arrows, are abominations devised by Satan. Avoid them, so that you may prosper. Satan seeks to stir up enmity and hatred among you by means of wine and gambling, and to keep you from the remembrance of God and from your prayers. Will you not abstain from them?

Obey God, and obey the Apostle. Beware; if you give no heed, know that Our apostle's duty is only to give plain warning.

No blame shall be attached to those that have embraced the faith and done good works in regard to any food they may have eaten, so long as they fear God and believe in Him and do good works; so long as they fear God and believe in Him; so long as they fear God and do good works. God loves the charitable.

Believers, God will put you to the proof by means of the game which you can catch with your hands or with your spears, so that He may know those who fear Him in their hearts. He that transgresses hereafter shall be sternly punished.

Believers, kill no game whilst on pilgrimage. He that kills game by design, shall present, as an offering to the Ka'ba, an animal equivalent to that which he has killed, to be determined by two just men among you; or he shall, in expiation, either feed the poor or fast, so that he may taste the evil consequences of his deed. God has forgiven what is past; but if any one relapses into wrongdoing He will avenge Himself on him: He is mighty and capable of revenge.

Lawful to you is what you catch from the sea and the sustenance it provides; a wholesome food for you and for the seafarer. But you are forbidden the game of the land while you are on pilgrimage. Have fear of God, before whom you shall all be assembled.

God has made the Ka'ba, the Sacred House, the sacred month, and the sacrificial offerings with their ornaments, eternal values for mankind; so that you may know that God has knowledge of all that the heavens and the earth contain; that God has knowledge of all things.

Know that God is stern in retribution, and that God is forgiving and merciful.

The duty of the Apostle is only to give warning. God knows all that you hide and all that you reveal.

Say: "Good and evil are not alike, even though the abundance of evil may tempt you. Have fear of God, you men of understanding, so that you may triumph."

Believers, do not ask questions about things which, if made known to you, would only pain you; but if you ask them when the Koran is being revealed, they shall be made plain to you. God will pardon you for this; God is forgiving and gracious. Other men inquired about them before you, only to disbelieve them afterwards.

God demands neither a *bahirah*, nor a *saibah*, nor a *wasilah*, nor a *hami*.[6]

---

6. Names given by pagan Arabs to sacred animals offered at the Ka'ba.

The unbelievers invent falsehoods about God. Most of them are lacking in judgement.

When it is said to them: "Come to that which God has revealed, and to the Apostle," they reply: "Sufficient for us is the faith we have inherited from our fathers," even though their fathers knew nothing and were not rightly guided.

Believers, you are accountable for none but yourselves; he that goes astray cannot harm you if you are on the right path. To God you shall all return, and He will declare to you what you have done.

Believers, when death approaches you, let two just men from among you act as witnesses when you make your testaments; or two men from another tribe if the calamity of death overtakes you while you are travelling the land. Detain them after prayers, and if you doubt their honesty ask them to swear by God: "We will not sell our testimony for any price even to a kinsman. We will not hide the testimony of God; for we should then be evil-doers." If both prove dishonest, replace them by another pair from among those immediately concerned, and let them both swear by God, saying: "Our testimony is truer than theirs. We have told no lies, for we should then be wrongdoers." Thus they will be more likely to bear true witness or to fear that the oaths of others may contradict theirs. Have fear of God and be obedient. God does not guide the evil-doers.

One day God will gather all the apostles and ask them: "How were you received?" They will reply: "We have no knowledge. You alone know what is hidden." God will say: "Jesus, son of Mary, remember the favour I have bestowed on you and on your mother: how I strengthened you with the Holy Spirit, so that you preached to men in your cradle and in the prime of manhood; how I instructed you in the Book and in wisdom, in the Torah and in the Gospel; how by My leave you fashioned from clay the likeness of a bird and breathed into it so that, by My leave, it became a living bird; how, by My leave, you healed the blind man and the leper, and by My leave restored the dead to life; how I protected you from the Israelites when you had come to them with clear signs: when those of them who disbelieved declared: 'This is but plain sorcery'; how when I enjoined the disciples to believe in Me and in My apostle they replied: 'We believe; bear witness that we submit.'"

"Jesus, son of Mary," said the disciples, "can your Lord send down to us from heaven a table spread with food?"

He replied: "Have fear of God, if you are true believers."

"We wish to eat of it," they said, "so that we may reassure our hearts and know that what you said to us is true, and that we may be witnesses of it."

"Lord," said Jesus, the son of Mary, "send to us from heaven a table spread with food, that it may mark a feast for us and for those that will come after us: a sign from You. Give us our sustenance; You are the best Giver."

God replied: "I am sending one to you. But whoever of you disbelieves hereafter shall be punished as no man has ever been punished."

Then God will say: "Jesus, son of Mary, did you ever say to mankind: 'Worship me and my mother as gods beside God?'"

"Glory to You," he will answer, "how could I ever say that to which I have no right? If I had ever said so, You would have surely known it. You know what is in my mind, but I know not what is in Yours. You alone know what is hidden. I told them only what You bade me. I said: 'Serve God, my Lord and your Lord.' I watched over them while living in their midst, and ever since You took me to Yourself, You have been watching over them. You are the witness of all things. If You punish them, they surely are Your servants; and if You forgive them, surely You are mighty and wise."

God will say: "This is the day when their truthfulness will benefit the truthful. They shall for ever dwell in gardens watered by running streams. God is pleased with them and they are pleased with Him. That is the supreme triumph."

God has sovereignty over the heavens and the earth and all that they contain. He has power over all things.

Sura 12. Joseph

[MECCA]

In the Name of God, the Compassionate, the Merciful

Alif lām rā. These are the verses of the Glorious Book. We have revealed the Koran in the Arabic tongue so that you may grow in understanding.

In revealing this Koran We will recount to you the best of narratives, though before it you were heedless.

Joseph said to his father: "Father, I dreamt of eleven stars and the sun and the moon; I saw them prostrate themselves before me."

"My son," he replied, "say nothing of this dream to your brothers, lest they plot evil against you: Satan is the sworn enemy of man. You shall be chosen by your Lord. He will teach you to interpret visions, and will perfect His favour to you and to the house of Jacob, as He perfected it to your forefathers Abraham and Isaac before you. Your Lord is wise and all-knowing."

Surely in Joseph and his brothers there are signs for doubting men.

They said to each other: "Joseph and his brother are dearer to our father than ourselves, though we are many. Truly, our father is much mistaken. Let us slay Joseph, or cast him away in some far-off land, so that we may have no rivals in our father's love, and after that be honourable men."

One of them said: "Do not slay Joseph; but if you must, rather cast him into a dark pit. Some caravan will take him up."

They said to their father: "Why do you not trust us with Joseph? Surely we wish him well. Send him with us tomorrow, that he may play and enjoy himself. We will take good care of him."

He replied: "It would much grieve me to let him go with you; for I fear lest the wolf should eat him when you are off your guard."

They said: "If the wolf could eat him despite our numbers, then we should surely be lost!"

And when they took Joseph with them, they decided to cast him into a dark pit. We revealed to him, saying: "You shall tell them of all this when they will not know you."

At nightfall they returned weeping to their father. They said: "We went off to compete together and left Joseph with our packs. The wolf devoured him. But you will not believe us, though we speak the truth." And they showed him their brother's shirt, stained with false blood.

"No!" he cried. "Your souls have tempted you to evil. Sweet patience! God alone can help me bear the loss you speak of."

And a caravan passed by, who sent their water-bearer to the pit. And when he had let down his pail, he cried: "Rejoice! A boy!"

They concealed him as part of their merchandise. But God knew what they did. They sold him for a trifling price, for a few pieces of silver. They cared nothing for him.

The Egyptian who bought him said to his wife:[7] "Be kind to him. He may prove useful to us, or we may adopt him as our son."

Thus We established Joseph in the land, and taught him to interpret dreams. God has power over all things, though most men may not know it. And when he reached maturity We bestowed on him wisdom and knowledge. Thus We reward the righteous.

His master's wife sought to seduce him. She bolted the doors and said: "Come!"

"God forbid!" he replied. "My lord has treated me with kindness. Wrong-doers never prosper."

She made for him, and he himself would have succumbed to her had he not been shown a sign from his Lord. Thus did We shield him from wantonness, for he was one of Our faithful servants.

They both rushed to the door. She tore his shirt from behind. And at the door they met her husband.

She cried: "Shall not the man who wished to violate your wife be thrown into prison or sternly punished?"

Joseph said: "It was she who attempted to seduce me."

"If his shirt is torn from the front," said one of her people, "she is speaking the truth and he is lying. If it is torn from behind, then he is speaking the truth and she is lying."

And when her husband saw Joseph's shirt rent from behind, he said to her: "This is but one of your tricks. Your cunning is great indeed! Joseph, say no more about this. Woman, ask pardon for your sin. You have done wrong."

In the city women were saying: "The Prince's wife has sought to seduce her servant. She has conceived a passion for him. It is clear that she has gone astray."

When she heard of their intrigues, she invited them to a banquet at her house. To each she gave a knife, and ordered Joseph to present himself before them. When they saw him, they were amazed at him and cut their hands, exclaiming: "God preserve us! This is no mortal, but a gracious angel."

"This is the man," she said, "on whose account you blamed me. I sought to seduce him, but he was unyielding. If he declines to do my bidding, he shall be thrown into prison and shall be held in scorn."

"Lord," said Joseph, "sooner would I go to prison than give in to their advances. Shield me from their cunning, or I shall yield to them and lapse into folly."

His Lord heard his prayer and warded off their wiles from him. He hears all and knows all.

Yet for all the evidence they had seen, they thought it right to jail him for a time.

---

7. Traditionally given the name Zuleikha.

Two young men entered the prison with him. One of them said: "I dreamt that I was pressing grapes." And the other said: "I dreamt that I was carrying a loaf upon my head, and that the birds came and ate of it. Tell us the meaning of these dreams, for we can see you are a virtuous man."

Joseph replied: "I can interpret them long before they are fulfilled. Whatever food you are provided with, I can divine for you its meaning, even before it reaches you. This knowledge my Lord has given me, for I have left the faith of those that disbelieve in God and deny the life to come. I follow the faith of my forefathers, Abraham, Isaac, and Jacob. We will serve no idols besides God. Such is the grace which God has bestowed on us and on all mankind. Yet most men do not give thanks.

"Fellow-prisoners! Are sundry gods better than God, the One, the One who conquers all? Those you serve besides Him are nothing but names which you and your fathers have devised and for which God has revealed no sanction. Judgement rests only with God. He has commanded you to worship none but Him. That is the true faith: yet most men do not know it.

"Fellow-prisoners, one of you will serve his lord with wine. The other will be crucified, and the birds will peck at his head. This is the answer to your question."

And Joseph said to the prisoner who he knew would be freed: "Remember me in the presence of your lord."

But Satan made him forget to mention Joseph to his lord, so that he stayed in prison for several years.

The king said: "I saw seven fatted cows which seven lean ones devoured; also seven green ears of corn and seven others dry. Tell me the meaning of this vision, my nobles, if you can interpret visions."

They replied: "It is but a medley of dream; nor are we skilled in the interpretation of dreams."

Thereupon the man who had been freed remembered Joseph after all that time. He said: "I shall tell you what it means. Give me leave to go."

He said to Joseph: "Tell us, man of truth, of the seven fatted cows which seven lean ones devoured; also of the seven green ears of corn and the other seven which were dry: so that I may go back to my masters and inform them."

He replied: "You shall sow for seven consecutive years. Leave in the ear the corn you reap, except a little which you may eat. Then there shall follow seven hungry years which will consume all but little of what you have stored. Then there will come a year of abundant rain, in which the people will press the grape."

The king said: "Bring this man before me."

But when the envoy came to him, Joseph said: "Go back to your master and ask him about the women who cut their hands. My master knows their cunning."

The king questioned the women, saying: "What made you attempt to seduce Joseph?"

"God forbid!" they replied. "We know no evil of him."

"Now the truth must come to light," said the Prince's wife. "It was I who sought to seduce him. He has told the truth."

"From this," said Joseph, "my lord will know that I did not betray him in his absence, and that God does not guide the work of the treacherous. Not that I am free from sin: man's soul is prone to evil, except his to whom God has shown mercy. My Lord is forgiving and merciful."

The king said: "Bring him before me. I will choose him for my own."

And when he had spoken with him, the king said: "You shall henceforth dwell with us, honoured and trusted."

Joseph said: "Give me charge of the granaries of the realm. I shall husband them wisely."

Thus did We establish Joseph in the land, and he dwelt there as he pleased. We bestow Our mercy on whom We will, and never deny the righteous their reward. Better is the reward of the life to come for those who believe in God and keep from evil.

Joseph's brothers arrived and presented themselves before him. He recognized them, but they knew him not. And when he had given them their provisions, he said: "Bring me your other brother from your father. Do you not see that I give just measure and am the best of hosts? If you do not bring him, you shall have no corn, nor shall you come near me again."

They replied: "We will endeavour to fetch him from his father. This we will surely do."

Joseph said to his servants: "Put their money into their packs, so that they may find it when they return to their people. Perchance they will come back."

When they returned to their father, they said: "Father, corn is henceforth denied us. Send our brother with us and we shall have our measure. We will take good care of him."

He replied: "Am I to trust you with him as I once trusted you with his brother? But God is the best of guardians: and of all those that show mercy He is the most merciful."

When they opened their packs, they discovered that their money had been returned to them. "Father," they said, "what more can we desire? Here is our money paid back to us. We will buy provisions for our people and take good care of our brother. We shall receive an extra camel-load; a camel-load should be easy enough."

He replied: "I will not let him go with you until you promise in God's name to bring him back to me, unless the worst befall you."

And when they had given him their pledge, he said: "God is the witness of your oath. My sons, enter the town by different gates. If you do wrong, I cannot ward off from you the wrath of God: judgement is His alone. In Him I have put my trust. In Him alone let the faithful put their trust."

And when they entered as their father had bade them, his counsel availed them nothing against the decree of God. It was but a wish in Jacob's soul which he had thus fulfilled. He was possessed of knowledge which We had given him, though most men have no knowledge.

When they went in to Joseph, he embraced his brother, and said: "I am your brother. Do not grieve at what they did."

And when he had given them their provisions, he hid a drinking-cup in his brother's pack.

Then a crier called out after them: "Travellers, you are thieves!"

They turned back and asked: "What have you lost?"

"We miss the king's drinking-cup," he replied. "He that brings it shall have a camel-load of corn. I pledge my word for it."

"In God's name," they cried, "you know we did not come to do evil in this land. We are no thieves."

The Egyptians said: "What penalty shall be his who stole it, if you prove to be lying?"

They replied: "He in whose pack the cup is found shall be your bondsman. Thus we punish the wrongdoers."

Joseph searched their bags before his brother's, and then took out the cup from his brother's bag.

Thus We directed Joseph. By the king's law he had no right to seize his brother: but God willed otherwise. We exalt in knowledge whom We will: but above those that have knowledge there is One more knowing.

They said: "If he has stolen—know then that a brother of his has committed theft before him."[8]

But Joseph kept his secret and revealed nothing to them. He said: "Your deed was worse. God best knows the things you speak of."

They said: "Noble prince, this boy has an aged father. Take one of us, instead of him. We can see you are a generous man."

He replied: "God forbid that we should take any but the man with whom our property was found: for then we should be unjust."

When they despaired of him, they went aside to confer in private. The eldest said: "Have you forgotten that your father took from you a pledge in God's name, and that long ago you did your worst with Joseph. I will not stir from this land until my father gives me leave or God makes known to me His judgement: He is the best of judges. Return to your father and say to him: 'Father, your son has committed a theft. We testify only to what we know. How could we guard against the unforeseen? Inquire at the city where we lodged, and from the caravan with which we travelled. We speak the truth.'"

"No!" cried their father. "Your souls have tempted you to evil. But I will have sweet patience. God may bring them all to me. He alone is all-knowing and wise." And he turned away from them, crying: "Alas for Joseph!" His eyes went white with grief and he was oppressed with silent sorrow.

His sons exclaimed: "In God's name, will you not cease to think of Joseph until you ruin your health and die?"

He replied: "I complain to God of my sorrow and sadness. He has made known to me things that you know not. Go, my sons, and seek news of Joseph and his brother. Do not despair of God's spirit; none but unbelievers despair of God's spirit."

And when they went in to him, they said: "Noble prince, we and our people are scourged with famine. We have brought but little money. Give us some corn, and be charitable to us: God rewards the charitable."

"Do you know," he replied, "what you did to Joseph and his brother? You are surely unaware."

They cried: "Can you indeed be Joseph?"

"I am Joseph," he answered, "and this is my brother. God has been gracious to us. Those that keep from evil and endure with fortitude, God will not deny them their reward."

"By the Lord," they said, "God has exalted you above us all. We have indeed been guilty."

---

8. Commentators say that Joseph had stolen an idol of his maternal grandfather's and broken it, so that he might not worship it.

He replied: "None shall reproach you this day. May God forgive you: Of all those who show mercy, He is the most merciful. Take this shirt of mine and throw it over my father's face: he will recover his sight. Then return to me with all your people."

When the caravan departed their father said: "I feel the breath of Joseph, though you will not believe me."

"In God's name," said those who heard him, "it is but your old illusion."

And when the bearer of good news arrived, he threw Joseph's shirt over the old man's face, and he regained his sight. He said: "Did I not tell you that God has made known to me what you know not?"

His sons said: "Father, implore forgiveness for our sins. We have indeed done wrong."

He replied: "I shall implore my Lord to forgive you. He is forgiving and merciful."

And when they went in to Joseph, he embraced his parents and said: "Welcome to Egypt, safe, if God wills!"

He helped his parents to a couch, and they all fell on their knees and prostrated themselves before him.

"This," said Joseph to his father, "is the meaning of my old vision: my Lord has fulfilled it. He has been gracious to me. He has released me from prison and brought you out of the desert after Satan had stirred up strife between me and my brothers. My lord is gracious to whom He will. He alone is all-knowing and wise.

"Lord, You have given me authority and taught me to interpret dreams. Creator of the heavens and the earth, my Guardian in this world and in the hereafter. Allow me to die in submission, and admit me among the righteous."

That which We have now revealed to you[9] is a tale of the unknown. You were not present when Joseph's brothers conceived their plans and schemed against him. Yet strive as you may, most men will not believe.

You shall demand of them no recompense for this. It is an admonition to all mankind.

Many are the marvels of the heavens and the earth; yet they pass them by and pay no heed to them. The greater part of them believe in God only if they can worship other gods besides Him.

Are they confident that God's scourge will not fall upon them, or that the Hour of Doom will not overtake them unawares, without warning?

Say: "This is my path. With sure knowledge I call on you to have faith in God, I and all my followers. Glory be to God! I am no idolater."

Nor were the apostles whom We sent before you other than mortals inspired by Our will and chosen from among their people.

Have they not travelled in the land and seen what was the end of those who disbelieved before them? Better is the world to come for those that keep from evil. Can you not understand?

And when at length Our apostles despaired and thought they were denied, Our help came down to them, delivering whom We pleased. The evil-doers could not be saved from Our scourge. Their annals point to a moral to men of understanding.

9. Muhammad.

This[10] is no invented tale, but a confirmation of previous scriptures, an explanation of all things, a guide and a blessing to true believers.

10. The Koran.

BEOWULF
ca. ninth century

Beowulf, composed perhaps (but not certainly) about 850 in the Anglo-Saxon language then current in England, is both a heroic poem of dark magnificence and the most vivid account left to us of the social world and life experiences of the Germanic and Scandinavian peoples who overran the Roman Empire. In its bare narrative outline the poem is a fairy-tale story of how the hero Beowulf conquered three monsters: first a man-eating, troll-like creature named Grendel, then Grendel's vengeance-seeking mother, and finally—when Beowulf has become an old man—a fire-breathing dragon. From these unlikely events the poet has fashioned a poem that represents with great power and specificity not merely the details of the warrior life of the Germanic tribes but its meaning to the people who lived it. Although himself a Christian, the poet provides us with a unique insight into a pagan world that had passed away by the time he was writing, but one whose legends and values he knows well. Like those of the Homeric poems and *The Song of Roland,* the historical period of the action of *Beowulf* is many centuries prior to the poem's date of composition: the one event in the poem that can be dated—the death of Beowulf's lord, Hygelac, in a raid on the Franks—occurred around 520. The protagonists of the poem are not the English who were its audience but two of their forebears, the Germanic tribes of the South Danes, who lived in Denmark, and their neighbors to the east, the Geats, who lived in southern Sweden. In addition to these two groups the poem alludes to the history of other northern European peoples, especially the Swedes, the Frisians, and the Franks, and it mentions as well more-obscure tribal groupings like the Heatho-Bards, the Wylfings, and the Waegmundings. In reading the poem, we enter into a pre-Christian Germanic world that is both mysterious and fascinating. And that world is also, as Beowulf himself comes to understand, doomed.

The most important fact about Germanic tribal society is its violence, which is why the poet describes that society by means of a narrative of monster-killing. Each of the various tribes is in competition with the others for land and plunder, and even within tribes there are constant struggles for power. The central bond that holds the society together at all is the loyalty between a lord and his warriors, or thanes. The lord is a "ring-giver," which means that he distributes to his thanes objects of value that include bracelets and necklaces ("rings"), armor and weapons, and even land and political authority. In return the thane is expected to provide unswerving loyalty on the battlefield and good counsel during times of peace. More important, this bond of loyalty establishes the community within which individuals find meaning.

In the Germanic world the worst condition into which a man can fall is to be an outlaw or wanderer, someone who has no home. This is, in fact, the situation of the monster Grendel, described in the poem as "a rover of borders, one who held the moors, fen and fastness." The Christian poet interprets Grendel and his mother as deriving from the race of Cain, who was condemned by God to wander the Earth after his murder of Abel. The poem begins with Grendel's attack upon the great hall Heorot, built as a place to celebrate community solidarity and the beneficence of the deity by Hrothgar, the old Danish king. What motivates Grendel's attack is his sense of exclusion and singularity: in this world, to be an independent individual is to be isolated and rejected. Appropriately, Grendel's slayer, Beowulf, is himself something of an individual, who, by this act, achieves inclusion within his own social world. Almost two-thirds of the way through the poem we learn that Beowulf "had long been despised" by his people, the Geats: "they strongly suspected that he was slack, a young man unbold." But the victory over Grendel and his mother, and the gifts he receives from the Danes and gives in turn to his own lord, Hygelac, change all that. Hygelac gives him a sword that had belonged to his own father, Hrethel, and grants him land and lordship: "a hall and a throne." After the deaths of Hygelac and his son Heardred, the Geats then turn to Beowulf to become their king, and he rules for fifty years until his fatal battle with a dragon.

Given that martial prowess is the primary means by which a man earns the respect of his fellows—Beowulf is recognized as worthy not because he is thoughtful or self-controlled (although he is both) but because he is fierce in battle—we should not be surprised that the poet presents a tribal world constantly engulfed in violence. The monster-killing that constitutes the main action of the poem is located within a dense historical context of tribal feuding. These feuds are mentioned so allusively and indirectly that we can assume the poet's English audience was fully informed about the early history of their Germanic ancestors. But the modern reader does not know this history, and it will be helpful to outline it here. (The genealogical table will help to keep the characters straight.)

The poem tells us of five primary feuds. The most important, between the Geats and the Swedes, takes place in two phases. The first phase—which we learn about only at the end of the poem (pp. 1094–95)—begins when the Swedes, under their king Ongentheow, defeat the Geats in a battle at Hreosnabeorh (or Sorrow Hill) in which great slaughter is committed by Ongentheow's sons, Ohthere and Onela. This slaughter is then avenged by the killing of Ongentheow by the Geat Eofer in a battle in which the Geatish king Haethcyn also dies. The second phase of the Swedish-Geatish feud is initiated by a civil war within the Swedish royal family. After the death of his elder brother Ohthere, Onela seizes the throne and drives out the rightful heirs, Ohthere's sons Eanmund and Eadgils. They find refuge with the Geats, then being led by Hygelac's son Heardred. Onela attacks the Geats, killing both Heardred and one of the brothers, Eanmund. (The warrior who actually kills Eanmund is named Weohstan and is the father of Wiglaf, who at the end of the poem is the only one of Beowulf's thanes to stand by him in the attack on the dragon. How Wiglaf—who like Beowulf is referred to as a Waegmunding—came to be accepted among the Geats is never explained.) Heardred's death leaves Beowulf king of the Geats, and he later supports Eadgils, who kills Onela and regains the Swedish throne. Yet despite this apparent alliance, after the death of Beowulf we are told that "the feud and the enmity" between the Swedes and Geats will now lead to renewed Swedish attacks on the leaderless Geats (possibly because Wiglaf, the presumptive heir to the Geatish throne, is the son of the slayer of Eadgil's brother).

The second feud mentioned in the poem is that between the Heatho-Bards and the Danes. While Beowulf is visiting Hrothgar in order to deal with the monsters, there are several cryptic references to a deadly fire that awaits the great hall Heorot. When Beowulf returns from his adventure and describes the trip to Hygelac, he explains that Hrothgar's daughter Freawaru is promised to Ingeld, the son of the murdered Heatho-Bard king Froda. Yet Beowulf predicts, in a sinister description of the way that enmity will be stirred up when a Heatho-Bard warrior sees a Dane wearing Froda's armor, that the peace will not hold: "Yet most often after the fall of a prince in any nation the deadly spear rests but a little while, even though the bride is good."

The third feud, predicted but not described, is within the Danish royal house. The old king Hrothgar has two young sons, Hrethric and Hrothmund, and his queen, Wealtheow, asks Beowulf to protect them from their uncle Hrothulf after the death of Hrothgar—protection Beowulf will be unable to provide.

As to the fourth feud: Hrothgar tells Beowulf that Beowulf's father, Ecgtheow, started a feud with the Wylfings by killing a man called Heatholaf, and that the Geats exiled him in order to protect themselves from retaliation. Hrothgar, however, not only provided Ecgtheow with asylum but also settled the feud by paying compensation to the Wylfings for Heatholaf, a compensation known among the Germanic tribes as *wergild*, or "man-money."

The fifth feud is that between the Geats and three tribes to the south of them, the Frisians, the Hetware, and the Franks (or Hugas, as they are occasionally called). This feud started when the Geatish king Hygelac raided the other tribes' territory— as mentioned, there is an independent record of this raid, which took place about 520—and was killed in the process. As he prepares to fight the dragon, Beowulf tells us that he avenged Hygelac's death: "I became Daeghrefn's slayer in the press—the warrior of the Hugas." After Beowulf's death the Geats are told that they face harsh battle at the hands of the Franks.

In addition to these feuds, which occur within the historical world of the poem, one other is mentioned in detail in a song sung by a *scop*, or bard, during the celebrations after the death of Grendel. This is known as the fight at Finnsburg. A Dane named Hnaef and his entourage of warriors, while visiting the Jute Finn at the fortress of Finnsburg, are attacked by the Jutes despite the fact that Finn is married to Hnaef's sister Hildeburh (doubtless as part of an effort to patch up a previous feud). Hnaef is killed, along with the son of Finn and Hildeburh. Neither party is powerful enough to finish off the other, and they agree to a truce: they will winter together in Finnsburg, and the Danes will sail home in the spring. Not surprisingly, with the coming of spring "breast might not contain the restless heart," and the Danes slaughter Finn and the other Jutes in their hall, returning home with plunder and with the bereft Hildeburh, whose son and husband are now dead.

The poet makes clear that the awful cost of their violence is not lost on these people. The description of the future that awaits the leaderless Geats now that Beowulf is dead—delivered to the waiting people by a messenger sent from the battle with the dragon—is only one of several chilling passages that acknowledge the effect of tribal warfare: "Therefore many a spear, cold in the morning, shall be grasped with fingers, raised by hands; no sound of the harp shall waken warriors, but the dark raven, low over the doomed, shall tell many tales, say to the eagle how he fared at the feast when with the wolf he spoiled the slain bodies." Nor will things go better for the women of the tribe: "mournful-hearted, stripped of gold, they shall walk, often, not once, in strange countries—now that [Beowulf] has laid aside laughter, his game and his mirth." Yet the poem also argues that it is only by violence that civilization can be maintained. The attacks by both Grendel and his mother are themselves a feud, in the first instance against God (hence the monsters' descent from the race of Cain), more immediately against the peaceful society that Hrothgar has established in Heorot. As Hrothgar says of Heorot, "Here is each earl true to other, mild of heart, loyal to the lord; the thanes are at one, the people are obedient, the retainers cheered with drink do as I bid." Grendel wants to destroy this social harmony, and his mother is an avenging spirit who seeks retaliation. Similarly, the dragon is roused to rage by the need to avenge the theft of a drinking cup from the hoard he guards: "he took joy in the thought of war, in the work of fighting." Thus the monsters can be understood, at least in part, as embodiments of the feuding principle that is inevitably destroying Germanic society. Yet in killing them Beowulf is involved in a paradox: violence can be controlled only by violence, a circle from which no one in the poem is able to escape.

Violence is thus part and parcel of this civilization. After Grendel's mother has killed one of Hrothgar's men, Beowulf advises the Danish king, in a succinct sentence that could stand as a motto for the poem, "It is better for a man to avenge his friend than much mourn." The miserable condition of the man who cannot avenge the death of a kinsman is vividly described in the story Beowulf tells about Hygelac's father, Hrethel. Hrethel had three sons, Herebeald, Haethcyn, and Hygelac. In an accident,

Haethcyn killed Herebeald; because it was an accident, and because the perpetrator was his own son, Hrethel could not compensate himself for his loss with either *wergild* or vengeance. As Beowulf arms himself for the battle with the dragon he tells this grim story, and he draws a parallel between Hrethel's unassuageable grief and the sorrow of the father who sees his son die on the gallows as an outlaw. The grieving father looks at his son's empty dwelling-place, the silent winehall, and he goes then to his bed, chanting grief-songs. "To him," Beowulf concludes, "all too wide seemed the land and the dwelling." This sense of emptiness is an effect of more than simply the technical problem of how to find satisfaction for certain kinds of injury. By having Beowulf tell this story as he prepares for what he knows will be his final battle, the poet shows us that the hero understands at some level the futility of the entire world of Germanic heroism that he himself so fully represents. Trolls and dragons can be killed, but how does one eradicate the violence that serves to constitute society itself? The monsters are, finally, instances of a social sickness that infects the culture as a whole: they may be killed, but the violence they represent will continue unabated. Perhaps Beowulf's greatest act of heroism is found not in the physical courage he displays in his battles against human and superhuman foes but in his spiritual capacity to persevere despite his dark realization of the futility of his efforts.

The poem survives in only a single manuscript written about 1000, but it was composed earlier, probably over a period of many years. Like the Homeric poems and *The Song of Roland, Beowulf* emerged from an oral tradition of composition (for a discussion of oral composition, see above, p. 98). It was put into its final form by a Christian, but one who is both careful to preserve the distinction between his Christian present and the pagan past and unusually tolerant of the culture of his forebears. For one thing, he avoids putting Christian sentiments in the mouths of pre-Christian characters. The terms with which the characters refer to the deity—God, the Lord of All, All-Wielding Father, the King of Glory, the Eternal Prince, the Ruler of the Heavens, and so forth—are, in their original Anglo-Saxon forms, the same terms as appear in explicitly non-Christian writings. We should also remember that the habit of capitalizing sacred names is a modern convention: in the manuscript they are, like all proper names, lowercase. For example, when the Geats arrive in Denmark they are described in the translation as having "thanked God" that the trip was successful. But the Anglo-Saxon could just as accurately be translated "thanked a god," which has a very different implication. Another example is the way in which the translator has Hrothgar say that Beowulf was sent to the Danes by "Holy God of His grace"; again, one could just as accurately, and more consistently, translate this as "by a divine god of his kindness." Hrothgar's speech of advice to Beowulf is certainly consistent with Christianity, but it contains nothing out of character with the values of the Germanic, pagan world in which Hrothgar and Beowulf live. Perhaps most important, the poet refrains from criticizing his pagan characters for their paganism. While he makes it clear that the Danes are wrong to offer sacrifices to their heathen gods in an effort to fend off Grendels' attacks, he is more sorrowful than judgmental or moralistic. They commit this error because they do not yet know of the true, Christian God whom the poet himself worships, just as they cannot know that the monsters are of the race of Cain. They do indeed live in a world ruled over by the Christian God: as the poet says, "the truth has been made known that mighty God has always ruled mankind." But while the audience knows this truth, their pagan forebears cannot. Moreover, the poet shows remarkable restraint in not criticizing pagan practices—such as cremation—that were strictly forbidden by Christian doctrine. Indeed, in its respect for the past the poem participates in its own central theme. Feuding, after all, is caused by an inability to make peace with the past, an unwillingness to put aside what has happened and move into a new future. *Beowulf* confronts this dilemma by asking, How can one celebrate one's own cultural past while admitting that it must be left behind?

A good introduction to the Anglo-Saxon period, and to the techniques of Anglo-Saxon poetry, can be found in the essays collected by Malcolm Godden and Michael

Lapidge, eds., *The Cambridge Companion to Old English Literature* (1991). *A Beowulf Handbook* (1997), ed. Robert E. Bjork and John D. Niles, provides useful essays about the poem, its context, and its criticism. Other useful collections of essays are R. D. Fulk, ed., *Interpretations of Beowulf* (1991), and Peter S. Baker, ed., *Beowulf: Basic Readings* (1995). An excellent account of the relation of pagan to Christian in the poem is Fred C. Robinson, *Beowulf and the Appositive Style* (1985), and a good treatment of other issues is Edward B. Irving, *Rereading Beowulf* (1989).

PRONOUNCING GLOSSARY

The following list uses common English syllables and stress accents to provide rough equivalents of selected words whose pronunciation may be unfamiliar to the general reader.

Aeschere: *ash'-hair-uh*

Daeghrefn: *dayh'-hrefn*

Eadgils: *ay'ud-yils*

Eanmund: *ay'un-mund*

Ecglaf: *edge'-lahf*

Ecgtheow: *edge'-thay-oh*

Eofer: *e'o-ver*

Freawaru: *fray'a-wa-ru*

Geats: *yay'-ats*

Haethcyn: *hath'-kin*

Healfdene: *hay'alf-den-uh*

Heardred: *hey'ard-red*

Heatho-Bards: *hay'ath-o-bards*

Heatholaf: *hay'ath-o-lahf*

Heorogar: *hay'o-ro-gahr*

Heorot: *hay'o-rot*

Herebeald: *her'uh-bay-ald*

Hildeburh: *hil'de-burhk*

Hnaef: *hnaf*

Hondscioh: *hond'-shee-o*

Hreosnabeorh: *hray-os'-na-beorgh*

Hrethel: *hray'-thuhl*

Hrethric: *hreth'-rik*

Hrothgar: *hroth'-gahr*

Hrothmund: *hroth'-mund*

Hrothulf: *hroth'-ulf*

Hygd: *higd*

Hygelac: *hee'-uh-lahk*

Ohthere: *ohkt'-her-uh*

Onela: *on'-el-a*

Ongentheow: *on-gen'-thay-oh*

Scyld: *shuld*

Waegmundings: *wey'-mun-dings*

Wealtheow: *way'al-thay-oh*

Weohstan: *way'oh-stahn*

Wiglaf: *wee'-lahf*

Wylfings: *wilf'-ings*

TRIBES AND GENEALOGIES

1. *The Danes (Bright-, Half-, Ring-, Spear-, North-, East-, South-, West-Danes; Scyldings, Honor-, Victor-, War-Scyldings: Ing's friends).*

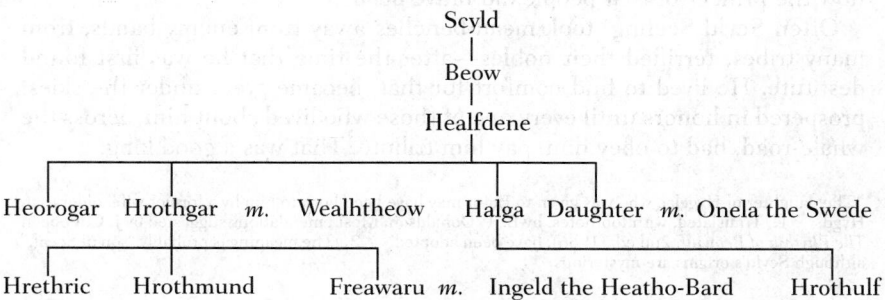

2. *The Geats (Sea-, War-, Weather-Geats).*

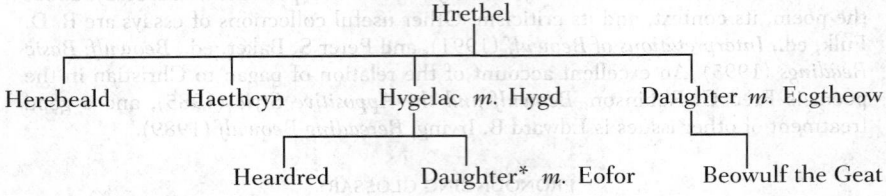

3. *The Swedes*

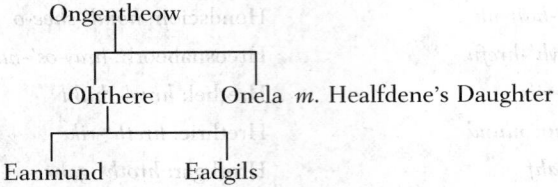

4. *Miscellaneous.*

A. The Half-Danes (also called Scyldings) involved in the fight at Finnsburg may represent a different tribe from the Danes described above. Their king Hoc had a son, Hnaef, who succeeded him, and a daughter Hildeburh, who married Finn, king of the Jutes.

B. The Jutes, or Frisians, are represented as enemies of the Danes in the fight at Finnsburg and as allies of the Franks, or Hugas, at the time Hygelac the Geat made the attack in which he lost his life and from which Beowulf swam home. Also allied with the Franks at this time were the Hetware.

C. The Heatho-Bards (i.e., "Battle-Bards") are represented as inveterate enemies of the Danes. Their king Froda had been killed in an attack on the Danes, and Hrothgar's attempt to make peace with them by marrying his daughter Freawaru to Froda's son Ingeld failed when the latter attacked Heorot. The attack was repulsed, although Heorot was burned.

Beowulf[1]

PROLOGUE: THE EARLIER HISTORY OF THE DANES

Yes, we have heard of the glory of the Spear-Danes' kings in the old days—how the princes of that people did brave deeds.

Often Scyld Scefing[2] took mead-benches away from enemy bands, from many tribes, terrified their nobles—after the time that he was first found destitute. He lived to find comfort for that, became great under the skies, prospered in honors until every one of those who lived about him, across the whale-road, had to obey him, pay him tribute. That was a good king.

---

*The daughter of Hygelac who was given to Eofor may have been born to him by a former wife, older than Hygd.   **1.** Translated, with footnotes, by E. T. Donaldson. Most emendations suggested by J. C. Pope in *The Rhythm of Beowulf*, 2nd ed. (1966), have been adopted.   **2.** The meaning is probably "son of Sceaf," although Scyld's origins are mysterious.

Afterwards a son was born to him, a young boy in his house, whom God sent to comfort the people: He had seen the sore need they had suffered during the long time they lacked a king. Therefore the Lord of Life, the Ruler of Heaven, gave him honor in the world: Beow was famous, the glory of the son of Scyld spread widely in the Northlands. In this way a young man ought by his good deeds, by giving splendid gifts while still in his father's house, to make sure that later in life beloved companions will stand by him, that people will serve him when war comes. Through deeds that bring praise, a man shall prosper in every country.

Then at the fated time Scyld the courageous went away into the protection of the Lord. His dear companions carried him down to the sea-currents, just as he himself had bidden them do when, as protector of the Scyldings,[3] he had ruled them with his words—long had the beloved prince governed the land. There in the harbor stood the ring-prowed ship, ice-covered and ready to sail, a prince's vessel. Then they laid down the ruler they had loved, the ring-giver, in the hollow of the ship, the glorious man beside the mast. There was brought great store of treasure, wealth from lands far away. I have not heard of a ship more splendidly furnished with war-weapons and battle-dress, swords and mail-shirts. On his breast lay a great many treasures that should voyage with him far out into the sea's possession. They provided him with no lesser gifts, treasure of the people, than those had done who at his beginning first sent him forth on the waves, a child alone. Then also they set a golden standard high over his head, let the water take him, gave him to the sea. Sad was their spirit, mournful their mind. Men cannot truthfully say who received that cargo, neither counsellors in the hall nor warriors under the skies.

Then in the cities was Beow of the Scyldings beloved king of the people, long famous among nations (his father had gone elsewhere, the king from his land), until later great Healfdene was born to him. As long as he lived, old and fierce in battle, he upheld the glorious Scyldings. To him all told were four children born into the world, to the leader of the armies: Heorogar and Hrothgar and the good Halga. I have heard tell that [. . . was On]ela's queen,[4] beloved bed-companion of the Battle-Scylfing.

BEOWULF AND GRENDEL

[The Hall Heorot Is Attacked by Grendel]

Then Hrothgar was given success in warfare, glory in battle, so that his retainers gladly obeyed him and their company grew into a great band of warriors. It came to his mind that he would command men to construct a hall, a great mead-building that the children of men should hear of forever, and therein he would give to young and old all that God had given him, except for common land and men's bodies.[5] Then I have heard that the work was laid upon many nations, wide through this middle-earth, that they should adorn the folk-hall. In time it came to pass—quickly, as men count it—that it was finished, the largest of hall-dwellings. He gave it the name of Heorot,[6]

---

3. I.e., the Danes ("descendants of Scyld"). 4. The text is faulty, so that the name of Healfdene's daughter has been lost; her husband, Onela, was a Swedish (Scylfing) king. 5. Or "men's lives." Apparently slaves, along with public land, were not in the king's power to give away. 6. I.e., "Hart."

he who ruled wide with his words. He did not forget his promise: at the feast he gave out rings, treasure. The hall stood tall, high and wide-gabled: it would wait for the fierce flames of vengeful fire;[7] the time was not yet at hand for sword-hate between son-in-law and father-in-law to awaken after murderous rage.

Then the fierce spirit[8] painfully endured hardship for a time, he who dwelt in the darkness, for every day he heard loud mirth in the hall; there was the sound of the harp, the clear song of the scop.[9] There he spoke who could relate the beginning of men far back in time, said that the Almighty made earth, a bright field fair in the water that surrounds it, set up in triumph the lights of the sun and the moon to lighten land-dwellers, and adorned the surfaces of the earth with branches and leaves, created also life for each of the kinds that move and breathe.—Thus these warriors lived in joy, blessed, until one began to do evil deeds, a hellish enemy. The grim spirit was called Grendel, known as a rover of the borders, one who held the moors, fen and fastness. Unhappy creature, he lived for a time in the home of the monsters' race, after God had condemned them as kin of Cain. The Eternal Lord avenged the murder in which he slew Abel. Cain had no pleasure in that feud, but He banished him far from mankind, the Ruler, for that misdeed. From him sprang all bad breeds, trolls and elves and monsters—likewise the giants who for a long time strove with God: He paid them their reward for that.

Then, after night came, Grendel went to survey the tall house—how, after their beer-drinking, the Ring-Danes had disposed themselves in it. Then he found therein a band of nobles asleep after the feast: they felt no sorrow, no misery of men. The creature of evil, grim and fierce, was quickly ready, savage and cruel, and seized from their rest thirty thanes. From there he turned, to go back to his home, proud of his plunder, sought his dwelling with that store of slaughter.

Then in the first light of dawning day Grendel's war-strength was revealed to men: then after the feast weeping arose, great cry in the morning. The famous king, hero of old days, sat joyless; the mighty one suffered, felt sorrow for his thanes, when they saw the track of the foe, of the cursed spirit: that hardship was too strong, too loathsome and long-lasting. Nor was there a longer interval, but after one night Grendel again did greater slaughter—and had no remorse for it—vengeful acts and wicked: he was too intent on them. There after it was easy to find the man who sought rest for himself elsewhere, farther away, a bed among the outlying buildings—after it was made clear to him, told by clear proof, the hatred of him who now controlled the hall.[1] Whoever escaped the foe held himself afterwards farther off and more safely. Thus Grendel held sway and fought against right, one against all, until the best of houses stood empty. It was a long time, the length of twelve winters, that the lord of the Scyldings suffered grief, all woes, great sorrows. Therefore, sadly in songs, it became well-known to the children of men that Grendel had fought a long time with Hrothgar, for many half-years maintained mortal spite, feud, and enmity—constant war. He wanted no peace

---

7. The destruction by fire of Heorot occurred at a later time than that of the poem's action, probably during the otherwise unsuccessful attack of the Heatho-Bard Ingeld on his father-in-law, Hrothgar, mentioned in the next clause.   8. I.e., Grendel.   9. The Anglo-Saxon minstrel, who recited poetic stories to the accompaniment of a harp.   1. I.e., Grendel.

with any of the men of the Danish host, would not withdraw his deadly rancor, or pay compensation: no counselor there had any reason to expect splendid repayment at the hands of the slayer.[2] For the monster was relentless, the dark death-shadow, against warriors old and young, lay in wait and ambushed them. In the perpetual darkness he held to the misty moors: men do not know where hell-demons direct their footsteps.

Thus many crimes the enemy of mankind committed, the terrible walker-alone, cruel injuries one after another. In the dark nights he dwelt in Heorot, the richly adorned hall. He might not approach the throne, [receive] treasure, because of the Lord; He had no love for him.[3]

This was great misery to the lord of the Scyldings, a breaking of spirit. Many a noble sat often in council, sought a plan, what would be best for strong-hearted men to do against the awful attacks. At times they vowed sacrifices at heathen temples, with their words prayed that the soul-slayer[4] would give help for the distress of the people. Such was their custom, the hope of heathens; in their spirits they thought of Hell, they knew not the Ruler, the Judge of Deeds, they recognized not the Lord God, nor indeed did they know how to praise the Protector of Heaven, the glorious King. Woe is him who in terrible trouble must thrust his soul into the fire's embrace, hope for no comfort, not expect change. Well is the man who after his death-day may seek the Lord and find peace in the embrace of the Father.

[The Coming of Beowulf to Heorot]

So in the cares of his times the son of Healfdene constantly brooded, nor might the wise warrior set aside his woe. Too harsh, hateful and long-lasting was the hardship that had come upon the people, distress dire and inexorable, worst of night-horrors.

A thane of Hygelac,[5] a good man among the Geats, heard in his homeland of Grendel's deeds: of mankind he was the strongest of might in the time of this life, noble and great. He bade that a good ship be made ready for him, said he would seek the war-king over the swan's road, the famous prince, since he had need of men. Very little did wise men blame him for that adventure, though he was dear to them; they urged the brave one on, examined the omens. From the folk of the Geats the good man had chosen warriors of the bravest that he could find; one of fifteen he led the way, the warrior sought the wooden ship, the sea-skilled one the land's edge. The time had come: the ship was on the waves, the boat under the cliff. The warriors eagerly climbed on the prow—the sea-currents eddied, sea against sand; men bore bright weapons into the ship's bosom, splendid armor. Men pushed the well-braced ship from shore, warriors on a well-wished voyage. Then over the sea-waves, blown by the wind, the foam-necked boat traveled, most like a bird, until at good time on the second day the curved prow had come to where the seafarers could see land, the sea-cliffs shine, towering hills, great headlands. Then was the sea crossed, the journey at end. Then quickly the

---

2. According to old Germanic law, a slayer could achieve peace with his victim's kinsmen only by paying them *wergild*, i.e., compensation for the life of the slain man.   **3.** Behind this obscure passage seems to lie the idea that Grendel, unlike Hrothgar's thanes, could not approach the throne to receive gifts from the king, having been condemned by God as an outlaw.   **4.** I.e., the devil.   **5.** I.e., Beowulf the Geat, whose king was Hygelac.

men of the Geats climbed upon the shore, moored the wooden ship; mail-shirts rattled, dress for battle. They thanked God that the wave-way had been easy for them.

Then from the wall the Scyldings' guard who should watch over the sea-cliffs saw bright shields borne over the gangway, armor ready for battle; strong desire stirred him in mind to learn what the men were. He went riding on his horse to the shore, thane of Hrothgar, forcefully brandished a great spear in his hands, with formal words questioned them: "What are you, bearers of armor, dressed in mail-coats, who thus have come bringing a tall ship over the sea-road, over the water to this place? Lo, for a long time I have been guard of the coast, held watch by the sea so that no foe with a force of ships might work harm on the Danes' land: never have shieldbearers more openly undertaken to come ashore here; nor did you know for sure of a word of leave from our warriors, consent from my kinsmen. I have never seen a mightier warrior on earth than is one of you, a man in battle-dress. That is no retainer made to seem good by his weapons—may his appearance, his unequalled form, never belie him. Now I must learn your lineage before you go any farther from here, spies on the Danes' land. Now you far-dwellers, sea-voyagers, hear what I think: you must straightway say where you have come from."

To him replied the leader, the chief of the band unlocked his word-hoard: "We are men of the Geatish nation and Hygelac's hearth-companions. My father was well-known among the tribes, a noble leader named Ecgtheow. He lived many winters before he went on his way, an old man, from men's dwellings. Every wise man wide over the earth readily remembers him. Through friendly heart we have come to seek your lord, the son of Healfdene, protector of the people. Be good to us and tell us what to do: we have a great errand to the famous one, the king of the Danes. And I too do not think that anything ought to be kept secret: you know whether it is so, as we have indeed heard, that among the Scyldings I know not what foe, what dark doer of hateful deeds in the black nights, shows in terrible manner strange malice, injury and slaughter. In openness of heart I may teach Hrothgar remedy for that, how he, wise and good, shall overpower the foe—if change is ever to come to him, relief from evil's distress—and how his surging cares may be made to cool. Or else ever after he will suffer tribulations, constraint, while the best of houses remains there on its high place."

The guard spoke from where he sat on his horse, brave officer: "A sharp-witted shield-warrior who thinks well must be able to judge each of the two things, words and works. I understand this: that here is a troop friendly to the Scyldings' king. Go forward, bearing weapons and war-gear. I will show you the way; I shall also bid my fellow-thanes honorably to hold your boat against all enemies, your new-tarred ship on the sand, until again over the sea-streams it bears its beloved men to the Geatish shore, the wooden vessel with curved prow. May it be granted by fate that one who behaves so bravely pass whole through the battle-storm."

Then they set off. The boat lay fixed, rested on the rope, the deep-bosomed ship, fast at anchor. Boar-images[6] shone over cheek-guards gold-adorned, gleaming and fire-hardened—the war-minded boar held guard over fierce

---

6. Carved images of boars (sometimes represented as clothed like human warriors) were placed on helmets in the belief that they would protect the wearer in battle.

men. The warriors hastened, marched together until they might see the timbered hall, stately and shining with gold; for earth-dwellers under the skies that was the most famous of buildings in which the mighty one waited—its light gleamed over many lands. The battle-brave guide pointed out to them the shining house of the brave ones so that they might go straight to it. Warrior-like he turned his horse, then spoke words: "It is time for me to go back. The All-Wielding Father in His grace keep you safe in your undertakings. I shall go back to the sea to keep watch against hostile hosts."

The road was stone-paved, the path showed the way to the men in ranks. War-corselet shone, hard and hand-wrought, bright iron rings sang on their armor when they first came walking to the hall in their grim gear. Sea-weary they set down their broad shields, marvelously strong protections, against the wall of the building. Then they sat down on the bench—mail-shirts, warrior's clothing, rang out. Spears stood together, seamen's weapons, ash steel-gray at the top. The armed band was worthy of its weapons.

Then a proud-spirited man[7] asked the warriors there about their lineage: "Where do you bring those gold-covered shields from, gray mail-shirts and visored helmets, this multitude of battle-shafts? I am Hrothgar's herald and officer. I have not seen strangers—so many men—more bold. I think that it is for daring—not for refuge, but for greatness of heart—that you have sought Hrothgar." The man known for his courage replied to him; the proud man of the Geats, hardy under helmet, spoke words in return: "We are Hygelac's table-companions. Beowulf is my name. I will tell my errand to Healfdene's son, the great prince your lord, if, good as he is, he will grant that we might address him." Wulfgar spoke—he was a man of the Wendels, his bold spirit known to many, his valor and wisdom: "I will ask the lord of the Danes about this, the Scyldings' king, the ring-giver, just as you request—will ask the glorious ruler about your voyage, and will quickly make known to you the answer the good man thinks best to give me."

He returned at once to where Hrothgar sat, old and hoary, with his company of earls. The man known for his valor went forward till he stood squarely before the Danes' king: he knew the custom of tried retainers. Wulfgar spoke to his lord and friend: "Here have journeyed men of the Geats, come far over the sea's expanse. The warriors call their chief Beowulf. They ask that they, my prince, might exchange words with you. Do not refuse them your answer, gracious Hrothgar. From their wargear they seem worthy of earls' esteem. Strong indeed is the chief who has led the warriors here."

Hrothgar spoke, protector of the Scyldings: "I knew him when he was a boy. His father was called Ecgtheow: Hrethel of the Geats[8] gave him his only daughter for his home. Now has his hardy offspring come here, sought a fast friend. Then, too, seafarers who took gifts there to please the Geats used to say that he has in his handgrip the strength of thirty men, a man famous in battle. Holy God of His grace has sent him to us West-Danes, as I hope, against the terror of Grendel. I shall offer the good man treasures for his daring. Now make haste, bid them come in together to see my company of kinsmen. In your speech say to them also that they are welcome to the Danish people."

Then Wulfgar went to the hall's door, gave the message from within: "The

---

7. Identified below as Wulfgar.   8. Hrethel was the father of Hygelac and Beowulf's grandfather and guardian.

lord of the East-Danes, my victorious prince, has bidden me say to you that he knows your noble ancestry, and that you brave-hearted men are welcome to him over the sea-swells. Now you may come in your war-dress, under your battle helmets, to see Hrothgar. Let your war-shields, your wooden spears, await here the outcome of the talk."

Then the mighty one rose, many a warrior about him, a company of strong thanes. Some waited there, kept watch over the weapons as the brave one bade them. Together they hastened, as the warrior directed them, under Heorot's roof. The war-leader, hardy under helmet, advanced till he stood on the hearth. Beowulf spoke, his mail-shirt glistened, armor-net woven by the blacksmith's skill: "Hail, Hrothgar! I am kinsman and thane of Hygelac. In my youth I have set about many brave deeds. The affair of Grendel was made known to me on my native soil: sea-travelers say that this hall, best of buildings, stands empty and useless to all warriors after the evening-light becomes hidden beneath the cover of the sky. Therefore my people, the best wise earls, advised me thus, lord Hrothgar, that I should seek you because they know what my strength can accomplish. They themselves looked on when, bloody from my foes, I came from the fight where I had bound five, destroyed a family of giants, and at night in the waves slain water-monsters, suffered great pain, avenged an affliction of the Weather-Geats on those who had asked for trouble—ground enemies to bits. And now alone I shall settle affairs with Grendel, the monster, the demon. Therefore, lord of the Bright-Danes, protector of the Scyldings, I will make a request of you, refuge of warriors, fair friend of nations, that you refuse me not, now that I have come so far, that alone with my company of earls, this band of hardy men, I may cleanse Heorot. I have also heard say that the monster in his recklessness cares not for weapons. Therefore, so that my liege lord Hygelac may be glad of me in his heart, I scorn to bear sword or broad shield, yellow wood, to the battle, but with my grasp I shall grapple with the enemy and fight for life, foe against foe. The one whom death takes can trust the Lord's judgment. I think that if he may accomplish it, unafraid he will feed on the folk of the Geats in the war-hall as he has often done on the flower of men. You will not need to hide my head[9] if death takes me, for he will have me blood-smeared; he will bear away my bloody flesh meaning to savor it, he will eat ruthlessly, the walker alone, will stain his retreat in the moor; no longer will you need trouble yourself to take care of my body. If battle takes me, send to Hygelac the best of war-clothes that protects my breast, finest of mail-shirts. It is a legacy of Hrethel, the work of Weland.[1] Fate always goes as it must."

Hrothgar spoke, protector of the Scyldings: "For deeds done, my friend Beowulf, and for past favors you have sought us. A fight of your father's brought on the greatest of feuds. With his own hands he became the slayer of Heatholaf among the Wylfings. After that the country of the Weather-Geats might not keep him, for fear of war. From there he sought the folk of the South-Danes, the Honor-Scyldings, over the sea-swell. At that time I was first ruling the Danish people and, still in my youth, held the wide kingdom, hoard-city of heroes. Heorogar had died then, gone from life, my older brother, son of Healfdene—he was better than I. Afterwards I paid blood-

---

9. I.e. bury my body.   1. The blacksmith of the Norse gods.

money to end the feud; over the sea's back I sent to the Wylfings old treasures; he[2] swore oaths to me.

"It is a sorrow to me in spirit to say to any man what Grendel has brought me with his hatred—humiliation in Heorot, terrible violence. My hall-troop, warrior-band, has shrunk; fate has swept them away into Grendel's horror. (God may easily put an end to the wild ravager's deeds!) Full often over the ale-cups warriors made bold with beer have boasted that they would await with grim swords Grendel's attack in the beer-hall. Then in the morning this mead-hall was a hall shining with blood, when the day lightened, all the bench-floor blood-wet, a gore-hall. I had fewer faithful men, beloved retainers, for death had destroyed them. Now sit down to the feast and unbind your thoughts, your famous victories, as heart inclines."

[The Feast at Heorot]

Then was a bench cleared in the beer-hall for the men of the Geats all together. Then the stout-hearted ones went to sit down, proud in their might. A thane did his work who bore in his hands an embellished ale-cup, poured the bright drink. At times a scop sang, clear-voiced in Heorot. There was joy of brave men, no little company of Danes and Weather-Geats.

Unferth spoke, son of Ecglaf, who sat at the feet of the king of the Scyldings, unbound words of contention—to him was Beowulf's undertaking, the brave seafarer, a great vexation, for he would not allow that any other man of middle-earth should ever achieve more glory under the heavens than himself: "Are you that Beowulf who contended with Breca, competed in swimming on the broad sea, where for pride you explored the water, and for foolish boast ventured your lives in the deep? Nor might any man, friend nor enemy, keep you from the perilous venture of swimming in the sea. There you embraced the sea-streams with your arms, measured the sea-ways, flung forward your hands, glided over the ocean; the sea boiled with waves, with winter's swell. Seven nights you toiled in the water's power. He overcame you at swimming, had more strength. Then in the morning the sea bore him up among the Heathoraemas; from there he sought his own home, dear to his people, the land of the Brondings, the fair stronghold, where he had folk, castle, and treasures. All his boast against you the son of Beanstan carried out in deed. Therefore I expect the worse results for you—though you have prevailed everywhere in battles, in grim war—if you dare wait near Grendel a night-long space."

Beowulf spoke, the son of Ecgtheow: "Well, my friend Unferth, drunk with beer you have spoken a great many things about Breca—told about his adventures. I maintain the truth that I had more strength in the sea, hardship on the waves, than any other man. Like boys we agreed together and boasted—we were both in our first youth—that we would risk our lives in the salt sea, and that we did even so. We had naked swords, strong in our hands, when we went swimming; we thought to guard ourselves against whale-fishes. He could not swim at all far from me in the flood-waves, be quicker in the water, nor would I move away from him. Thus we were together on the sea for the time of five nights until the flood drove us apart,

---

2. Ecgtheow, whose feud with the Wylfings Hrothgar had settled.

the swelling sea, coldest of weathers, darkening night, and the north wind battle-grim turned against us: rough were the waves. The anger of the sea-fishes was roused. Then my body-mail, hard and hand-linked, gave me help against my foes; the woven war-garment, gold-adorned, covered my breast. A fierce cruel attacker dragged me to the bottom, held me grim in his grasp, but it was granted me to reach the monster with my sword-point, my battle-blade. The war-stroke destroyed the mighty sea-beast—through my hand.

"Thus often loathsome assailants pressed me hard. I served them with my good sword, as the right was. They had no joy at all of the feast, the malice-workers, that they should eat me, sit around a banquet near the sea-bottom. But in the morning, sword-wounded they lay on the shore, left behind by the waves, put to sleep by the blade, so that thereafter they would never hinder the passage of sea-voyagers over the deep water. Light came from the east, bright signal of God, the sea became still so that I might see the headlands, the windy walls of the sea. Fate often saves an undoomed man when his courage is good. In any case it befell me that I slew with my sword nine sea-monsters. I have not heard tell of a harder fight by night under heaven's arch, nor of a man more hard-pressed in the sea-streams. Yet I came out of the enemies' grasp alive, weary of my adventure. Then the sea bore me onto the lands of the Finns, the flood with its current, the surging waters.

"I have not heard say of you any such hard matching of might, such sword-terror. Breca never yet in the games of war—neither he nor you—achieved so bold a deed with bright swords (I do not much boast of it), though you became your brothers' slayer, your close kin; for that you will suffer punishment in hell, even though your wit is keen. I tell you truly, son of Ecglaf, that Grendel, awful monster, would never have performed so many terrible deeds against your chief, humiliation in Heorot, if your spirit, your heart, were so fierce in fight as you claim. But he has noticed that he need not much fear the hostility, not much dread the terrible sword-storm of your people, the Victory-Scyldings. He exacts forced levy, shows mercy to none of the Danish people; but he is glad, kills, carves for feasting, expects no fight from the Spear-Danes. But I shall show him soon now the strength and courage of the Geats, their warfare. Afterwards he will walk who may, glad to the mead, when the morning light of another day, the bright-clothed sun, shines from the south on the children of men."

Then was the giver of treasure in gladness, gray-haired and battle-brave. The lord of the Bright-Danes could count on help. The folk's guardian had heard from Beowulf a fast-resolved thought.

There was laughter of warriors, voices rang pleasant, words were cheerful. Wealhtheow came forth, Hrothgar's queen, mindful of customs, gold-adorned, greeted the men in the hall; and the noble woman offered the cup first to the keeper of the land of the East-Danes, bade him be glad at the beer-drinking, beloved of the people. In joy he partook of feast and hall-cup, king famous for victories. Then the woman of the Helmings went about to each one of the retainers, young and old, offered them the costly cup, until the time came that she brought the mead-bowl to Beowulf, the ring-adorned queen, mature of mind. Sure of speech she greeted the man of the Geats, thanked God that her wish was fulfilled, that she might trust in some man for help against deadly deeds. He took the cup, the warrior fierce in battle, from Wealhtheow, and then spoke, one ready for fight—Beowulf spoke, the son of Ecgtheow: "I resolved, when I set out on the sea, sat down in the sea-boat with my band of men, that I should altogether fulfill the will of your people or else fall in slaughter, fast in the foe's grasp. I shall achieve a deed of manly courage or else have lived to see in this mead-hall my ending day." These words were well-pleasing to the woman, the boast of the Geat. Gold-adorned, the noble folk-queen went to sit by her lord.

Then there were again as at first strong words spoken in the hall, the people in gladness, the sound of a victorious folk, until, in a little while, the son of Healfdene wished to seek his evening rest. He knew of the battle in the high hall that had been plotted by the monster, plotted from the time that they might see the light of the sun until the night, growing dark over all things, the shadowy shapes of darkness, should come gliding, black under the clouds. The company all arose. Then they saluted each other, Hrothgar and Beowulf, and Hrothgar wished him good luck, control of the wine-hall, and spoke these words: "Never before, since I could raise hand and shield, have I entrusted to any man the great hall of the Danes, except now to you. Hold now and guard the best of houses: remember your fame, show your great courage, keep watch against the fierce foe. You will not lack what you wish if you survive that deed of valor."

[The Fight with Grendel]

Then Hrothgar went out of the hall with his company of warriors, the protector of the Scyldings. The war-chief would seek the bed of Wealhtheow the queen. The King of Glory—as men had learned—had appointed a hall-guard against Grendel; he had a special mission to the prince of the Danes: he kept watch against monsters.

And the man of the Geats had sure trust in his great might, the favor of the Ruler. Then he took off his shirt of armor, the helmet from his head, handed his embellished sword, best of irons, to an attendant, bade him keep guard over his war-gear. Then the good warrior spoke some boast-words before he went to his bed, Beowulf of the Geats: "I claim myself no poorer in war-strength, war works, than Grendel claims himself. Therefore I will not put him to sleep with a sword, so take away his life, though surely I might. He knows no good tools with which he might strike against me, cut my shield in pieces, though he is strong in fight. But we shall forgo the sword in the night—if he dare seek war without weapon—and then may wise God, Holy Lord, assign glory on whichever hand seems good to Him."

The battle-brave one laid himself down, the pillow received the earl's head, and about him many a brave seaman lay down to hall-rest. None of them thought that he would ever again seek from there his dear home, people or town where he had been brought up; for they knew that bloody death had carried off far too many men in the wine-hall, folk of the Danes. But the Lord granted to weave for them good fortune in war, for the folk of the Weather-Geats, comfort and help that they should quite overcome their foe through the might of one man, through his sole strength: the truth has been made known that mighty God has always ruled mankind.

There came gliding in the black night the walker in darkness. The warriors slept who should hold the horned house—all but one. It was known to men that when the Ruler did not wish it the hostile creature might not drag them away beneath the shadows. But he, lying awake for the fierce foe, with heart swollen in anger awaited the outcome of the fight.

Then from the moor under the mist-hills Grendel came walking, wearing God's anger. The foul ravager thought to catch some one of mankind there in the high hall. Under the clouds he moved until he could see most clearly the wine-hall, treasure-house of men, shining with gold. That was not the first time that he had sought Hrothgar's home. Never before or since in his life-days did he find harder luck, hardier hall-thanes. The creature deprived of joy came walking to the hall. Quickly the door gave way, fastened with fire-forged bands, when he touched it with his hands. Driven by evil desire, swollen with rage, he tore it open, the hall's mouth. After that the foe at once stepped onto the shining floor, advanced angrily. From his eyes came a light not fair, most like a flame. He saw many men in the hall, a band of kinsmen all asleep together, a company of war-men. Then his heart laughed: dreadful monster, he thought that before the day came he would divide the life from the body of every one of them, for there had come to him a hope of full-feasting. It was not his fate that when that night was over he should feast on more of mankind.

The kinsman of Hygelac, mighty man, watched how the evil-doer would make his quick onslaught. Nor did the monster mean to delay it, but, starting his work, he suddenly seized a sleeping man, tore at him ravenously, bit into his bone-locks, drank the blood from his veins, swallowed huge morsels; quickly he had eaten all of the lifeless one, feet and hands. He stepped closer, then felt with his arm for the brave-hearted man on the bed, reached out toward him, the foe with his hand; at once in fierce response Beowulf seized it and sat up, leaning on his own arm. Straightway the fosterer of crimes knew that he had not encountered on middle-earth, anywhere in this world, a harder handgrip from another man. In mind he became frightened, in his spirit: not for that might he escape the sooner. His heart was eager to get away, he would flee to his hiding-place, seek his rabble of devils. What he met there was not such as he had ever before met in the days of his life. Then the kinsman of Hygelac, the good man, thought of his evening's speech, stood upright and laid firm hold on him: his fingers cracked. The giant was pulling away, the earl stepped forward. The notorious one thought to move farther away, wherever he could, and flee his way from there to his fen-retreat; he knew his fingers' power to be in a hateful grip. That was a painful journey that the loathsome despoiler had made to Heorot. The retainers' hall rang with the noise—terrible drink[3] for all the Danes, the house-dwellers, every brave man, the earls. Both were enraged, fury-filled, the two who meant to control the hall. The building resounded. Then was it much wonder that the wine-hall withstood them joined in fierce fight, that it did not fall to the ground, the fair earth-dwelling; but it was so firmly made fast with iron bands, both inside and outside, joined by skillful smith-craft. There started from the floor—as I have heard say—many a mead-bench, gold-adorned, when the furious ones fought. No wise men of the Scyldings ever before thought that any men in any manner might break it down, splendid with bright horns, have skill to destroy it, unless flame should embrace it, swallow

---

3. The metaphor reflects the idea that the chief purpose of a hall such as Heorot was as a place for men to feast in.

it in fire. Noise rose up, sound strange enough. Horrible fear came upon the North-Danes, upon every one of those who heard the weeping from the wall, God's enemy sing his terrible song, song without triumph—the hell-slave bewail his pain. There held him fast he who of men was strongest of might in the days of this life.

Not for anything would the protector of warriors let the murderous guest go off alive: he did not consider his life-days of use to any of the nations. There more than enough of Beowulf's earls drew swords, old heirlooms, wished to protect the life of their dear lord, famous prince, however they might. They did not know when they entered the fight, hardy-spirited warriors, and when they thought to hew him on every side, to seek his soul, that not any of the best of irons on earth, no war-sword, would touch the evildoer: for with a charm he had made victory-weapons useless, every swordedge. His departure to death from the time of this life was to be wretched; and the alien spirit was to travel far off into the power of fiends. Then he who before had brought trouble of heart to mankind, committed many crimes—he was at war with God—found that his body would do him no good, for the great-hearted kinsman of Hygelac had him by the hand. Each was hateful to the other alive. The awful monster had lived to feel pain in his body, a huge wound in his shoulder was exposed, his sinews sprang apart, his bone-locks broke. Glory in battle was given to Beowulf. Grendel must flee from there, mortally sick, seek his joyless home in the fen-slopes. He knew the more surely that his life's end had come, the full number of his days. For all the Danes was their wish fulfilled after the bloody fight. Thus he who had lately come from far off, wise and stout-hearted, had purged Heorot, saved Hrothgar's house from affliction. He rejoiced in his night's work, a deed to make famous his courage. The man of the Geats had fulfilled his boast to the East-Danes; so too he had remedied all the grief, the malice-caused sorrow that they had endured before, and had had to suffer from harsh necessity, no small distress. That was clearly proved when the battle-brave man set the hand up under the curved roof—the arm and the shoulder: there all together was Grendel's grasp.

[Celebration at Heorot]

Then in the morning, as I have heard, there was many a warrior about the gift-hall. Folk-chiefs came from far and near over the wide-stretching ways to look on the wonder, the footprints of the foe. Nor did his going from life seem sad to any of the men who saw the tracks of the one without glory—how, weary-hearted, overcome with injuries, he moved on his way from there to the mere[4] of the water-monsters with life-failing footsteps, death-doomed and in flight. There the water was boiling with blood, the horrid surge of waves swirling, all mixed with hot gore, sword-blood. Doomed to die he had hidden, then, bereft of joys, had laid down his life in his fen-refuge, his heathen soul: there hell took him.

From there old retainers—and many a young man, too—turned back in their glad journey to ride from the mere, high-spirited on horseback, warriors on steeds. There was Beowulf's fame spoken of; many a man said—and not

4. Lake.

only once—that, south nor north, between the seas, over the wide earth, no other man under the sky's expanse was better of those who bear shields, more worthy of ruling. Yet they found no fault with their own dear lord, gracious Hrothgar, for he was a good king. At times battle-famed men let their brown horses gallop, let them race where the paths seemed fair, known for their excellence. At times a thane of the king, a man skilled at telling adventures, songs stored in his memory, who could recall many of the stories of the old days, wrought a new tale in well-joined words; this man undertook with his art to recite in turn Beowulf's exploit, and skillfully to tell an apt tale, to lend words to it.

He spoke everything that he had heard tell of Sigemund's valorous deeds, many a strange thing, the strife of Waels's son,[5] his far journeys, feuds and crimes, of which the children of men knew nothing—except for Fitela with him, to whom he would tell everything, the uncle to his nephew, for they were always friends in need in every fight. Many were the tribes of giants that they had laid low with their swords. For Sigemund there sprang up after his death-day no little glory—after he, hardy in war, had killed the dragon, keeper of the treasure-hoard: under the hoary stone the prince's son had ventured alone, a daring deed, nor was Fitela with him. Yet it turned out well for him, so that his sword went through the gleaming worm and stood fixed in the wall, splendid weapon: the dragon lay dead of the murdering stroke. Through his courage the great warrior had brought it about that he might at his own wish enjoy the ring-hoard. He loaded the sea-boat, bore into the ship's bosom the bright treasure, offspring of Waels. The hot dragon melted.

He was adventurer most famous, far and wide through the nations, for deeds of courage—he had prospered from that before, the protector of warriors—after the war-making of Heremod had came to an end, his strength and his courage.[6] Among the Jutes Heremod came into the power of his enemies, was betrayed, quickly dispatched. Surging sorrows had oppressed him too long: he had become a great care to his people, to all his princes; for many a wise man in former times had bewailed the journey of the fierce-hearted one—people who had counted on him as a relief from affliction—that that king's son should prosper, take the rank of his father, keep guard over the folk, the treasure and stronghold, the kingdom of heroes, the home of the Scyldings. The kinsman of Hygelac became dearer to his friends, to all mankind: crime took possession of Heremod.

Sometimes racing their horses they passed over the sand-covered ways. By then the morning light was far advanced, hastening on. Many a stout-hearted warrior went to the high hall to see the strange wonder. The king himself walked forth from the women's apartment, the guardian of the ring-hoards, secure in his fame, known for his excellence, with much company; and his queen with him passed over the path to the mead-hall with a troop of attendant women.

Hrothgar spoke—he had gone to the hall, taken his stand on the steps, looked at the high roof shining with gold, and at Grendel's hand: "For this sight may thanks be made quickly to the Almighty: I endured much from the foe, many griefs from Grendel: God may always work wonder upon wonder,

---

5. Waels was Sigemund's father.   **6.** Heremod was an unsuccessful king of the Danes, one who began brilliantly but became cruel and avaricious, ultimately having to take refuge among the Jutes, who put him to death. His reputation was thus overshadowed by that of Sigemund.

the Guardian of Heaven. It was not long ago that I did not expect ever to live to see relief from any of my woes—when the best of houses stood shining with blood, stained with slaughter, a far-reaching woe for each of my counselors, for every one, since none thought he could ever defend the people's stronghold from its enemies, from demons and evil spirits. Now through the Lord's might a warrior has accomplished the deed that all of us with our skill could not perform. Yes, she may say, whatever woman brought forth this son among mankind—if she still lives—that the God of Old was kind to her in her child-bearing. Now, Beowulf, best of men, in my heart I will love you as a son: keep well this new kinship. To you will there be no lack of the good things of the world that I have in my possession. Full often I have made reward for less, done honor with gifts to a lesser warrior, weaker in fighting. With your deeds you yourself have made sure that your glory will be ever alive. May the Almighty reward you with good—as just now he has done."

Beowulf spoke, the son of Ecgtheow: "With much good will we have achieved this work of courage, that fight, have ventured boldly against the strength of the unknown one. I should have wished rather that you might have seen him, your enemy brought low among your furnishings. I thought quickly to bind him on his deathbed with hard grasp, so that because of my hand-grip he should lie struggling for life—unless his body should escape. I could not stop his going, since the Lord did not wish it, nor did I hold him firmly enough for that, my life-enemy: he was too strong, the foe in his going. Yet to save his life he has left his hand behind to show that he was here— his arm and shoulder; nor by that has the wretched creature bought any comfort; none the longer will the loathsome ravager live, hard-pressed by his crimes, for a wound has clutched him hard in its strong grip, in deadly bonds. There, like a man outlawed for guilt, he shall await the great judgment, how the bright Lord will decree for him."

Then was the warrior more silent in boasting speech of warlike deeds, the son of Ecglaf,[7] after the nobles had looked at the hand, now high on the roof through the strength of a man, the foe's fingers. The end of each one, each of the nail-places, was most like steel; the hand-spurs of the heathen warrior were monstrous spikes. Everyone said that no hard thing would hurt him, no iron good from old times would harm the bloody battle-hand of the monster.

Then it was ordered that Heorot be within quickly adorned by hands. Many there were, both men and women, who made ready the wine-hall, the guest-building. The hangings on the walls shone with gold, many a wondrous sight for each man who looks on such things. That bright building was much damaged, though made fast within by iron bonds, and its door-hinges sprung; the roof alone came through unharmed when the monster, outlawed for his crimes, turned in flight, in despair of his life. That is not easy to flee from— let him try it who will—but driven by need one must seek the place prepared for earth-dwellers, soul-bearers, the sons of men, the place where, after its feasting, one's body will sleep fast in its death-bed.

Then had the proper time come that Healfdene's son should go to the hall; the king himself would share in the feast. I have never heard that a people in a larger company bore themselves better about their treasure-giver. Men

---

7. I.e., Unferth, who had taunted Beowulf the night before.

who were known for courage sat at the benches, rejoiced in the feast. Their kinsmen, stout-hearted Hrothgar and Hrothulf, partook fairly of many a mead-cup in the high hall. Heorot within was filled with friends: the Scylding-people had not then known treason's web.[8]

Then the son of Healfdene gave Beowulf a golden standard to reward his victory—a decorated battle-banner—a helmet and mail-shirt: many saw the glorious, costly sword borne before the warrior. Beowulf drank of the cup in the mead-hall. He had no need to be ashamed before fighting men of those rich gifts. I have not heard of many men who gave four precious, gold-adorned things to another on the ale-bench in a more friendly way. The rim around the helmet's crown had a head-protection, wound of wire, so that no battle-hard sharp sword might badly hurt him when the shield-warrior should go against his foe. Then the people's protector commanded eight horses with golden bridles to be led into the hall, within the walls. The saddle of one of them stood shining with hand-ornaments, adorned with jewels: that had been the war-seat of the high king when the son of Healfdene would join sword-play: never did the warfare of the wide-known one fail when men died in battle. And then the prince of Ing's friends[9] yielded possession of both, horses and weapons, to Beowulf: he bade him use them well. So generously the famous prince, guardian of the hoard, repaid the warrior's battle-deeds with horses and treasure that no man will ever find fault with them—not he that will speak truth according to what is right.

Then further the lord gave treasure to each of the men on the mead-bench who had made the sea-voyage with Beowulf, gave heirlooms; and he commanded that gold be paid for the one whom in his malice Grendel had killed—as he would have killed more if wise God and the man's courage had not forestalled that fate. The Lord guided all the race of men then, as he does now. Yet is discernment everywhere best, fore-thought of mind. Many a thing dear and loath he shall live to see who here in the days of trouble long makes use of the world.

There was song and music together before Healfdene's battle-leader, the wooden harp touched, tale oft told, when Hrothgar's scop should speak hall-pastime among the mead-benches . . . [of] Finn's retainers when the sudden disaster fell upon them.[1] . . .

The hero of the Half-Danes, Hnaef of the Scyldings, was fated to fall on Frisian battlefield. And no need had Hildeburh[2] to praise the good faith of the Jutes: blameless she was deprived of her dear ones at the shield-play, of son and brother; wounded by spears they fell to their fate. That was a mournful woman. Not without cause did Hoc's daughter lament the decree of destiny when morning came and she might see, under the sky, the slaughter of kinsmen—where before she had the greatest of world's joy. The fight took

8. A reference to the later history of the Danes, when, after Hrothgar's death, his nephew Hrothulf apparently drove his son and successor Hrethric from the throne. 9. Ing was a Germanic deity, and his "friends" are the Danes. 1. The lines introducing the scop's song seem faulty. The story itself is recounted in a highly allusive way and many of its details are obscure, although some help is offered by an independent version of the story given in a fragmentary Old English lay called *The Fight at Finnsburg*. 2. Hildeburh, daughter of the former Danish king Hoc and sister of the ruling Danish king Hnaef, was married to Finn, king of the Jutes (Frisians). Hnaef, with a party of Danes, made what was presumably a friendly visit to Hildeburh and Finn at their home, Finnsburg, but during a feast a quarrel broke out between the Jutes and the Danes (because the scop's sympathies are with the Danes, he ascribes the cause to the bad faith of the Jutes), and in the ensuing fight, Hnaef and his nephew, the son of Finn and Hildeburh, were killed along with many other Danes and Jutes.

away all Finn's thanes except for only a few, so that he could in no way continue the battle on the field against Hengest, nor protect the survivors by fighting against the prince's thane. But they offered them peace-terms,[3] that they should clear another building for them, hall and high sea, that they might have control of half of it with the sons of the Jutes; and at givings of treasure the son of Folcwalda[4] should honor the Danes each day, should give Hengest's company rings, such gold-plated treasure as that with which he would cheer the Frisians' kin in the high hall. Then on both sides they confirmed the fast peace-compact. Finn declared to Hengest, with oaths deep-sworn, unfeigned, that he would hold those who were left from the battle in honor in accordance with the judgment of his counselors, so that by words or by works no man should break the treaty nor because of malice should ever mention that, priceless, the Danes followed the slayer of their own ring-giver, since necessity forced them. If with rash speech any of the Frisians should insist upon calling to mind the cause of murderous hate, then the sword's edge should settle it.

The funeral pyre was made ready and gold brought up from the hoard. The best of the warriors of the War-Scyldings[5] was ready on the pyre. At the fire it was easy to see many a blood-stained battle-shirt, boar-image all golden—iron-hard swine—many a noble destroyed by wounds: more than one had died in battle. Then Hildeburh bade give her own son to the flames on Hnaef's pyre, burn his body, put him in the fire at the shoulder of his uncle. The woman mourned, sang her lament. The warrior took his place.[6] The greatest of death-fires wound to the skies, roared before the barrow. Heads melted as blood sprang out—wounds opened wide, hate-bites of the body. Fire swallowed them—greediest of spirits—all of those whom war had taken away from both peoples: their strength had departed.

Then warriors went to seek their dwellings, bereft of friends, to behold Friesland, their homes and high city.[7] Yet Hengest stayed on with Finn for a winter darkened with the thought of slaughter, all desolate. He thought of his land, though he might not drive his ring-prowed ship over the water—the sea boiled with storms, strove with the wind, winter locked the waves in ice-bonds—until another year came to men's dwellings, just as it does still, glorious bright weather always watching for its time. Then winter was gone, earth's lap fair, the exile was eager to go, the guest from the dwelling: [yet] more he thought of revenge for his wrongs than of the sea-journey—if he might bring about a fight where he could take account of the sons of the Jutes with his iron. So he made no refusal of the world's custom when the son of Hunlaf[8] placed on his lap Battle-Bright, best of swords: its edges were known to the Jutes. Thus also to war-minded Finn in his turn cruel sword-evil came in his own home, after Guthlaf and Oslaf complained of the grim

3. It is not clear who proposed the peace terms, but in view of the teller's Danish sympathies, it was probably the Jutes that sought the uneasy truce from Hengest, who became the Danes' leader after Hnaef's death. The truce imposed on Hengest and the Danes the intolerable condition of having to dwell in peace with the Jutish king who was responsible for the death of their own king.   4. I.e., Finn.   5. I.e., Hnaef.   6. The line is obscure, but it perhaps means that the body of Hildeburh's son was placed on the pyre.   7. This seems to refer to the few survivors on the Jutish side.   8. The text is open to various interpretations. The one adopted here assumes that the Dane Hunlaf, brother of Guthlaf and Oslaf, had been killed in the fight, and that ultimately Hunlaf's son demanded vengeance by the symbolic act of placing his father's sword in Hengest's lap, while at the same time Guthlaf and Oslaf reminded Hengest of the Jutes' treachery. It is not clear whether the subsequent fight in which Finn was killed was waged by the Danish survivors alone or whether the party first went back to Denmark and then returned to Finnsburg with reinforcements.

attack, the injury after the sea-journey, assigned blame for their lot of woes: breast might not contain the restless heart. Then was the hall reddened from foes' bodies, and thus Finn slain, the king in his company, and the queen taken. The warriors of the Scyldings bore to ship all the hall-furnishings of the land's king, whatever of necklaces, skillfully wrought treasures, they might find at Finn's home. They brought the noble woman on the sea-journey to the Danes, led her to her people.

The lay was sung to the end, the song of the scop. Joy mounted again, bench-noise brightened, cup-bearers poured wine from wonderful vessels. Then Wealhtheow came forth to walk under gold crown to where all good men sat, nephew and uncle: their friendship was then still unbroken, each true to the other.[9] There too Unferth the spokesman sat at the feet of the prince of the Scyldings: each of them trusted his spirit, that he had much courage, though he was not honorable to his kinsmen at sword-play. Then the woman of the Scyldings spoke:

"Take this cup, my noble lord, giver of treasure. Be glad, gold-friend of warriors, and speak to the Geats with mild words, as a man ought to do. Be gracious to the Geats, mindful of gifts [which][1] you now have from near and far. They have told me that you would have the warrior for your son. Heorot is purged, the bright ring-hall. Enjoy while you may many rewards, and leave to your kinsmen folk and kingdom when you must go forth to look on the Ruler's decree. I know my gracious Hrothulf, that he will hold the young warriors in honor if you, friend of Scyldings, leave the world before him. I think he will repay our sons with good if he remembers all the favors we did to his pleasure and honor when he was a child."

Then she turned to the bench where her sons were, Hrethric and Hrothmund, and the sons of the warriors, young men together. There sat the good man Beowulf of the Geats beside the two brothers.

The cup was borne to him and welcome offered in friendly words to him, and twisted gold courteously bestowed on him, two arm-ornaments, a mail-shirt and rings, the largest of necklaces of those that I have heard spoken of on earth. I have heard of no better hoard-treasure under the heavens since Hama carried away to his bright city the necklace of the Brosings,[2] chain and rich setting: he fled the treacherous hatred of Eormenric, got eternal favor. This ring Hygelac of the Geats,[3] grandson of Swerting, had on his last venture, when beneath his battle-banner he defended his treasure, protected the spoils of war: fate took him when for pride he sought trouble, feud with the Frisians. Over the cup of the waves the mighty prince wore that treasure, precious stone. He fell beneath his shield; the body of the king came into the grasp of the Franks, his beast-armor and the neck-ring together. Lesser warriors plundered the fallen after the war-harvest: people of the Geats held the place of corpses.

The hall was filled with noise. Wealhtheow spoke, before the company she said to him: "Wear this ring, beloved Beowulf, young man, with good luck, and make use of this mail-shirt from the people's treasure, and prosper well;

---

9. See n. 8, p. 1076.   1. The text seems corrupt.   2. The Brisings' ("Brosings") necklace had been worn by the goddess Freya. Nothing more is known of this story of Hama, who seems to have stolen the necklace from the famous Gothic king Eormenric.   3. Beowulf is later said to have presented the necklace to Hygelac's queen, Hygd, although here Hygelac is said to have been wearing it on his ill-fated expedition against the Franks and Frisians, into whose hands it fell at his death.

make yourself known with your might, and be kind of counsel to these boys:
I shall remember to reward you for that. You have brought it about that, far
and near, for a long time all men shall praise you, as wide as the sea surrounds the shores, home of the winds. While you live, prince, be prosperous.
I wish you well of your treasure. Much favored one, be kind of deeds to my
son. Here is each earl true to other, mild of heart, loyal to his lord; the thanes
are at one, the people obedient, the retainers cheered with drink do as I bid."

Then she walked to her seat. There was the best of feasts, men drank wine.
They did not know the fate, the grim decree made long before, as it came to
pass to many of the earls after evening had come and Hrothgar had gone to
his chambers, the noble one to his rest. A great number of men remained in
the hall, just as they had often done before. They cleared the benches from
the floor. It was spread over with beds and pillows. One of the beer-drinkers,
ripe and fated to die, lay down to his hall-rest. They set at their heads their
battle-shields, bright wood; there on the bench it was easy to see above each
man his helmet that towered in battle, his ringed mail-shirt, his great spear-
wood. It was their custom to be always ready for war whether at home or in
the field, in any case at any time that need should befall their liege lord: that
was a good nation.

[Grendel's Mother's Attack]

Then they sank to sleep. One paid sorely for his evening rest, just as had
often befallen them when Grendel guarded the gold-hall, wrought wrong
until the end came, death after misdeeds. It came to be seen, wide-known
to men, that after the bitter battle an avenger still lived for an evil space:
Grendel's mother, woman, monster-wife, was mindful of her misery, she who
had to dwell in the terrible water, the cold currents, after Cain became
sword-slayer of his only brother, his own father's son. Then Cain went as an
outlaw to flee the cheerful life of men, marked for his murder, held to the
wasteland. From him sprang many a devil sent by fate. Grendel was one of
them, hateful outcast who at Heorot found a waking man waiting his warfare.
There the monster had laid hold upon him, but he was mindful of the great
strength, the large gift God had given him, and relied on the Almighty for
favor, comfort and help. By that he overcame the foe, subdued the hell-spirit.
Then he went off wretched, bereft of joy, to seek his dying-place, enemy of
mankind. And his mother, still greedy and gallows-grim, would go on a sorrowful venture, avenge her son's death.

Then she came to Heorot where the Ring-Danes slept throughout the hall.
Then change came quickly to the earls there, when Grendel's mother made
her way in. The attack was the less terrible by just so much as is the strength
of women, the war-terror of a wife, less than an armed man's when a hard
blade, forge-hammered, a sword shining with blood, good of its edges, cuts
the stout boar on a helmet opposite. Then in the hall was hard-edged sword
raised from the seat, many a broad shield lifted firmly in hand: none thought
of helmet, of wide mail-shirt, when the terror seized him. She was in haste,
would be gone out from there, protect her life after she was discovered.
Swiftly she had taken fast hold on one of the nobles, then she went to the
fen. He was one of the men between the seas most beloved of Hrothgar in
the rank of retainer, a noble shield-warrior whom she destroyed at his rest,

a man of great repute. Beowulf was not there, for earlier, after the treasure-giving, another lodging had been appointed for the renowned Geat. Outcry arose in Heorot: she had taken, in its gore, the famed hand. Care was renewed, come again on the dwelling. That was not a good bargain, that on both sides they had to pay with the lives of friends.

Then was the old king, the hoary warrior, of bitter mind when he learned that his chief thane was lifeless, his dearest man dead. Quickly Beowulf was fetched to the bed-chamber, man happy in victory. At daybreak together with his earls he went, the noble champion himself with his retainers, to where the wise one was, waiting to know whether after tidings of woe the All-Wielder would ever bring about change for him. The worthy warrior walked over the floor with his retainers—hall-wood resounded—that he might address words to the wise prince of Ing's friends, asked if the night had been pleasant according to his desires.

Hrothgar spoke, protector of the Scyldings: "Ask not about pleasure. Sorrow is renewed to the people of the Danes: Aeschere is dead, Yrmen-laf's elder brother, my speaker of wisdom and my bearer of counsel, my shoulder-companion when we used to defend our heads in battle, when troops clashed, beat on boar-images. Whatever an earl should be, a man good from old times, such was Aeschere. Now a wandering murderous spirit has slain him with its hands in Heorot. I do not know by what way the awful creature, glorying in its prey, has made its retreat, gladdened by its feast. She has avenged the feud—that last night you killed Grendel with hard hand-grips, savagely, because too long he had diminished and destroyed my people. He fell in the fight, his life forfeited, and now the other has come, a mighty worker of wrong, would avenge her kinsman, and has carried far her revenge—as many a thane may think who weeps in his spirit for his treasure-giver, bitter sorrow in heart. Now the hand lies lifeless that was strong in support of all your desires.

"I have heard landsmen, my people, hall-counselors, say this, that they have seen two such huge walkers in the wasteland holding to the moors, alien spirits. One of them, so far as they could clearly discern, was the likeness of a woman. The other wretched shape trod the tracks of exile in the form of a man, except that he was bigger than any other man. Land-dwellers in the old days named him Grendel. They know of no father, whether in earlier times any was begotten for them among the dark spirits. They hold to the secret land, the wolf-slopes, the windy headlands, the dangerous fen-paths where the mountain stream goes down under the darkness of the hills, the flood under the earth. It is not far from here, measured in miles, that the mere stands; over it hang frost-covered woods, trees fast of root close over the water. There each night may be seen fire on the flood, a fearful wonder. Of the sons of men there lives none, old of wisdom, who knows the bottom. Though the heath-stalker, the strong-horned hart, harassed by hounds makes for the forest after long flight, rather will he give his life, his being, on the bank than save his head by entering. That is no pleasant place. From it the surging waves rise up black to the heavens when the wind stirs up awful storms, until the air becomes gloomy, the skies weep. Now once again is the cure in you alone. You do not yet know the land, the perilous place, where you might find the seldom-seen creature: seek if you dare. I will give you wealth for the feud, old treasure, as I did before, twisted gold—if you come away."

Beowulf spoke, the son of Ecgtheow: "Sorrow not, wise warrior. It is better for a man to avenge his friend than much mourn. Each of us must await his end of the world's life. Let him who may get glory before death: that is best for the warrior after he has gone from life. Arise, guardian of the kingdom, let us go at once to look on the track of Grendel's kin. I promise you this: she will not be lost under cover, not in the earth's bosom nor in the mountain woods nor at the bottom of the sea, go where she will. This day have patience in every woe—as I expect you to."

Then the old man leapt up, thanked God, the mighty Lord, that the man had so spoken. Then was a horse bridled for Hrothgar, a curly-maned mount. The wise king moved in state; the band of shield-bearers marched on foot. The tracks were seen wide over the wood-paths where she had gone on the ground, made her way forward over the dark moor, borne lifeless the best of retainers of those who watched over their home with Hrothgar. The son of noble forebears[4] moved over the steep rocky slopes, narrow paths where only one could go at a time, an unfamiliar trail, steep hills, many a lair of water-monsters. He went before with a few wise men to spy out the country, until suddenly he found mountain trees leaning out over hoary stone, a joyless wood: water lay beneath, bloody and troubled. It was pain of heart for all the Danes to suffer, for the friends of the Scyldings, for many a thane, grief to each earl when on the cliff over the water they came upon Aeschere's head. The flood boiled with blood—the men looked upon it—with hot gore. Again and again the horn sang its urgent war-song. The whole troop sat down to rest. Then they saw on the water many a snake-shape, strong sea-serpents exploring the mere, and water-monsters lying on the slopes of the shore such as those that in the morning often attend a perilous journey on the paths of the sea, serpents and wild beasts.

These fell away from the shore, fierce and rage-swollen: they had heard the bright sound, the war-horn sing. One of them a man of the Geats with his bow cut off from his life, his water-warring, after the hard war-arrow stuck in his heart: he was weaker in swimming the lake when death took him. Straightway he was hard beset on the waves with barbed boar-spears, strongly surrounded, pulled up on the shore, strange spawn of the waves. The men looked on the terrible alien thing.

Beowulf put on his warrior's dress, had no fear for his life. His war-shirt, hand-fashioned, broad and well-worked, was to explore the mere: it knew how to cover his body-cave so that foe's grip might not harm his heart, or grasp of angry enemy his life. But the bright helmet guarded his head, one which was to stir up the lake-bottom, seek out the troubled water—made rich with gold, surrounded with splendid bands, as the weapon-smith had made it in far-off days, fashioned it wonderfully, set it about with boar-images so that thereafter no sword or battle-blade might bite into it. And of his strong supports that was not the least which Hrothgar's spokesman[5] lent to his need: Hrunting was the name of the hilted sword; it was one of the oldest of ancient treasures; its edge was iron, decorated with poison-stripes, hardened with battle-sweat. Never had it failed in war any man of those who grasped it in their hands, who dared enter on dangerous enterprises, onto the common meeting place of foes: this was not the first time that it should do work of courage. Surely the son of Ecglaf, great of strength, did not have in mind

---

4. I.e., Hrothgar.   5. I.e., Unferth.

what, drunk with wine, he had spoken, when he lent that weapon to a better swordfighter. He did not himself dare to risk his life under the warring waves, to engage his courage: there he lost his glory, his name for valor. It was not so with the other when he had armed himself for battle.

[Beowulf Attacks Grendel's Mother]

Beowulf spoke, the son of Ecgtheow: "Think now, renowned son of Healf-dene, wise king, now that I am ready for the venture, gold-friend of warriors, of what we said before, that, if at your need I should go from life, you would always be in a father's place for me when I am gone: be guardian of my young retainers, my companions, if battle should take me. The treasure you gave me, beloved Hrothgar, send to Hygelac. The lord of the Geats may know from the gold, the son of Hrethel may see when he looks on that wealth, that I found a ring-giver good in his gifts, enjoyed him while I might. And let Unferth have the old heirloom, the wide-known man my splendid-waved sword, hard-edged: with Hrunting I shall get glory, or death will take me."

After these words the man of the Weather-Geats turned away boldly, would wait for no answer: the surging water took the warrior. Then was it a part of a day before he might see the bottom's floor. Straightway that which had held the flood's tract a hundred half-years, ravenous for prey, grim and greedy, saw that some man from above was exploring the dwelling of monsters. Then she groped toward him, took the warrior in her awful grip. Yet not the more for that did she hurt his hale body within: his ring-armor shielded him about on the outside so that she could not pierce the war-dress, the linked body-mail, with hateful fingers. Then as she came to the bottom the sea-wolf bore the ring-prince to her house so that—no matter how brave he was—he might not wield weapons; but many monsters attacked him in the water, many a sea-beast tore at his mail-shirt with war-tusks, strange creatures afflicted him. Then the earl saw that he was in some hostile hall where no water harmed him at all, and the flood's onrush might not touch him because of the hall-roof. He saw firelight, a clear blaze shine bright.

Then the good man saw the accursed dweller in the deep, the mighty mere-woman. He gave a great thrust to his sword—his hand did not withhold the stroke—so that the etched blade sang at her head a fierce war-song. Then the stranger found that the battle-lightning would not bite, harm her life, but the edge failed the prince in his need: many a hand-battle had it endured before, often sheared helmet, war-coat of man fated to die: this was the first time for the rare treasure that its glory had failed.

But still he was resolute, not slow of his courage, mindful of fame, the kinsman of Hygelac. Then, angry warrior, he threw away the sword, wavy-patterned, bound with ornaments, so that it lay on the ground, hard and steel-edged: he trusted in his strength, his mighty hand-grip. So ought a man to do when he thinks to get long-lasting praise in battle: he cares not for his life. Then he seized by the hair Grendel's mother—the man of the War-Geats did not shrink from the fight. Battle-hardened, now swollen with rage, he pulled his deadly foe so that she fell to the floor. Quickly in her turn she repaid him his gift with her grim claws and clutched at him: then weary-hearted, the strongest of warriors, of foot-soldiers, stumbled so that he fell. Then she sat upon the hall-guest and drew her knife, broad and bright-edged.

She would avenge her child, her only son. The woven breast-armor lay on his shoulder: that protected his life, withstood entry of point or of edge. Then the son of Ecgtheow would have fared amiss under the wide ground, the champion of the Geats, if the battle-shirt had not brought help, the hard war-net—and holy God brought about victory in war; the wise Lord, Ruler of the Heavens, decided it with right, easily, when Beowulf had stood up again.

Then he saw among the armor a victory-blessed blade, an old sword made by the giants, strong of its edges, glory of warriors: it was the best of weapons, except that it was larger than any other man might bear to war-sport, good and adorned, the work of giants. He seized the linked hilt, he who fought for the Scyldings, savage and slaughter-bent, drew the patterned-blade; desperate of life, he struck angrily so that it bit her hard on the neck, broke the bone-rings. The blade went through all the doomed body. She fell to the floor, the sword was sweating, the man rejoiced in his work.

The blaze brightened, light shone within, just as from the sky heaven's candle shines clear. He looked about the building; then he moved along the wall, raised his weapon hard by the hilt, Hygelac's thane, angry and resolute: the edge was not useless to the warrior, for he would quickly repay Grendel for the many attacks he had made on the West-Danes—many more than the one time when he slew in their sleep fifteen hearth-companions of Hrothgar, devoured men of the Danish people while they slept, and another such number bore away, a hateful prey. He had paid him his reward for that, the fierce champion, for there he saw Grendel, weary of war, lying at rest, lifeless with the wounds he had got in the fight at Heorot. The body bounded wide when it suffered the blow after death, the hard sword-swing; and thus he cut off his head.

At once the wise men who were watching the water with Hrothgar saw that the surging waves were troubled, the lake stained with blood. Gray-haired, old, they spoke together of the good warrior, that they did not again expect of the chief that he would come victorious to seek their great king; for many agreed on it, that the sea-wolf had destroyed him.

Then came the ninth hour of the day. The brave Scyldings left the hill. The gold-friend of warriors went back to his home. The strangers sat sick at heart and stared at the mere. They wished—and did not expect—that they would see their beloved lord himself.

Then the blade began to waste away from the battle-sweat, the war-sword into battle-icicles. That was a wondrous thing, that it should all melt, most like the ice when the Father loosens the frost's fetters, undoes the water-bonds—He Who has power over seasons and times: He is the true Ruler. Beowulf did not take from the dwelling, the man of the Weather-Geats, more treasures—though he saw many there—but only the head and the hilt, bright with jewels. The sword itself had already melted, its patterned blade burned away: the blood was too hot for it, the spirit that had died there too poisonous. Quickly he was swimming, he who had lived to see the fall of his foes; he plunged up through the water. The currents were all cleansed, the great tracts of the water, when the dire spirit left her life-days and this loaned world.

Then the protector of seafarers came toward the land, swimming stout-hearted; he had joy of his sea-booty, the great burden he had with him. They went to meet him, thanked God, the strong band of thanes, rejoiced in their chief that they might see him again sound. Then the helmet and war-shirt of the mighty one were quickly loosened. The lake drowsed, the water beneath the skies, stained with blood. They went forth on the foot-tracks, glad in their hearts, measured the path back, the known ways, men bold as kings. They bore the head from the mere's cliff, toilsomely for each of the great-hearted ones: four of them had trouble in carrying Grendel's head on spear-shafts to the goldhall—until at last they came striding to the hall, fourteen bold warriors of the Geats; their lord, high-spirited, walked in their company over the fields to the mead-hall.

Then the chief of the thanes, man daring in deeds, enriched by new glory, warrior dear to battle, came in to greet Hrothgar. Then Grendel's head was dragged by the hair over the floor to where men drank, a terrible thing to the earls and the woman with them, an awful sight: the men looked upon it.

[Further Celebration at Heorot]

Beowulf spoke, the son of Ecgtheow: "Yes, we have brought you this sea-booty, son of Healfdene, man of the Scyldings, gladly, as evidence of glory—what you look on here. Not easily did I come through it with my life, the war under water, not without trouble carried out the task. The fight would have been ended straightway if God had not guarded me. With Hrunting I might not do anything in the fight, though that is a good weapon. But the Wielder of Men granted me that I should see hanging on the wall a fair, ancient great-sword—most often He has guided the man without friends—that I should wield the weapon. Then in the fight when the time became right for me I hewed the house-guardians. Then that war-sword, wavy-patterned, burnt away as their blood sprang forth, hottest of battle-sweats. I have brought the hilt away from the foes. I have avenged the evil deeds, the slaughter of Danes, as it was right to do. I promise you that you may sleep in Heorot without care with your band of retainers, and that for none of the thanes of your people, old or young, need you have fear, prince of the Scyldings—for no life-injury to your men on that account, as you did before."

Then the golden hilt was given into the hand of the old man, the hoary war-chief—the ancient work of giants. There came into the possession of the prince of the Danes, after the fall of devils, the work of wonder-smiths. And when the hostile-hearted creature, God's enemy, guilty of murder, gave up this world, and his mother too, it passed into the control of the best of worldly kings between the seas, of those who gave treasure in the Northlands.

Hrothgar spoke—he looked on the hilt, the old heirloom, on which was written the origin of ancient strife, when the flood, rushing water, slew the race of giants—they suffered terribly: that was a people alien to the Everlasting Lord. The Ruler made them a last payment through water's welling. On the sword-guard of bright gold there was also rightly marked through rune-staves, set down and told, for whom that sword, best of irons, had first been made, its hilt twisted and ornamented with snakes. Then the wise man spoke, the son of Healfdene—all were silent: "Lo, this may one say who works truth and right for the folk, recalls all things far distant, an old guardian of the land: that this earl was born the better man. Glory is raised up over the far ways—your glory over every people, Beowulf my friend. All of it, all your strength, you govern steadily in the wisdom of your heart. I shall fulfill my friendship to you, just as we spoke before. You shall become a comfort, whole and long-lasting, to your people, a help to warriors.

"So was not Heremod to the sons of Ecgwela, the Honor-Scyldings. He grew great not for their joy, but for their slaughter, for the destruction of Danish people. With swollen heart he killed his table-companions, shoulder-comrades, until he turned away from the joys of men, alone, notorious king, although mighty God had raised him in power, in the joys of strength, had set him up over all men. Yet in his breast his heart's thought grew blood-thirsty: no rings did he give to the Danes for glory. He lived joyless to suffer the pain of that strife, the long-lasting harm of the people. Teach yourself by him, be mindful of munificence. Old of winters, I tell this tale for you.

"It is a wonder to say how in His great spirit mighty God gives wisdom to mankind, land and earlship—He possesses power over all things. At times He lets the thought of a man of high lineage move in delight, gives him joy of earth in his homeland, a stronghold of men to rule over, makes regions of the world so subject to him, wide kingdoms, that in his unwisdom he may not himself have mind of his end. He lives in plenty; illness and age in no way grieve him, neither does dread care darken his heart, nor does enmity bare sword-hate, for the whole world turns to his will—he knows nothing worse—until his portion of pride increases and flourishes within him; then the watcher sleeps, the soul's guardian; that sleep is too sound, bound in its own cares, and the slayer most near whose bow shoots treacherously. Then is he hit in the heart, beneath his armor, with the bitter arrow—he cannot protect himself—with the crooked dark commands of the accursed spirit. What he has long held seems to him too little, angry-hearted he covets, no plated rings does he give in men's honor, and then he forgets and regards not his destiny because of what God, Wielder of Heaven, has given him before, his portion of glories. In the end it happens in turn that the loaned body weakens, falls doomed; another takes the earl's ancient treasure, one who recklessly gives precious gifts, does not fearfully guard them.

"Keep yourself against that wickedness, beloved Beowulf, best of men, and choose better—eternal gains. Have no care for pride, great warrior. Now for a time there is glory in your might: yet soon it shall be that sickness or sword will diminish your strength, or fire's fangs, or flood's surge, or sword's swing, or spear's flight, or appalling age; brightness of eyes will fail and grow dark; then it shall be that death will overcome you, warrior.

"Thus I ruled the Ring-Danes for a hundred half-years under the skies, and protected them in war with spear and sword against many nations over middle-earth, so that I counted no one as my adversary underneath the sky's expanse. Well, disproof of that came to me in my own land, grief after my joys, when Grendel, ancient adversary, came to invade my home. Great sorrow of heart I have always suffered for his persecution. Thanks be to the Ruler, the Eternal Lord, that after old strife I have come to see in my lifetime, with my own eyes, his blood-stained head. Go now to your seat, have joy of the glad feast, made famous in battle. Many of our treasures will be shared when morning comes."

The Geat was glad at heart, went at once to seek his seat as the wise one bade. Then was a feast fairly served again, for a second time, just as before, for those famed for courage, sitting about the hall.

Night's cover lowered, dark over the warriors. The retainers all arose. The gray-haired one would seek his bed, the old Scylding. It pleased the Geat, the brave shield-warrior, immensely that he should have rest. Straightway a hall-thane led the way on for the weary one, come from far country, and showed every courtesy to the thane's need, such as in those days seafarers might expect as their due.

Then the great-hearted one rested; the hall stood high, vaulted and gold-adorned; the guest slept within until the black raven, blithe-hearted, announced heaven's joy. Then the bright light came passing over the shadows. The warriors hastened, the nobles were eager to set out again for their people. Bold of spirit, the visitor would seek his ship far thence.

Then the hardy one bade that Hrunting be brought to the son of Ecglaf,[6] that he take back his sword, precious iron. He spoke thanks for that loan, said that he accounted it a good war-friend, strong in battle; in his words he found no fault at all with the sword's edge; he was a thoughtful man. And then they were eager to depart, the warriors ready in their armor. The prince who had earned honor of the Danes went to the high seat where the other was: the man dear to war greeted Hrothgar.

[BEOWULF RETURNS HOME]

Beowulf spoke, the son of Ecgtheow: "Now we sea-travelers come from afar wish to say that we desire to seek Hygelac. Here we have been entertained splendidly according to our desire: you have dealt well with us. If on earth I might in any way earn more of your heart's love, prince of warriors, than I have done before with warlike deeds, I should be ready at once. If beyond the sea's expanse I hear that men dwelling near threaten you with terrors, as those who hated you did before, I shall bring you a thousand thanes, warriors to your aid. I know of Hygelac, lord of the Geats, though he is young as a guardian of the people, that he will further me with words and works so that I may do you honor and bring spears to help you, strong support where you have need of men. If Hrethric, king's son, decides to come to the court of the Geats, he can find many friends there; far countries are well sought by him who is himself strong."

Hrothgar spoke to him in answer: "The All-Knowing Lord sent those words into your mind: I have not heard a man of so young age speak more wisely. You are great of strength, mature of mind, wise of words. I think it likely if the spear, sword-grim war, takes the son of Hrethel, sickness or weapon your prince, the people's ruler, and you have your life, that the Sea-Geats will not have a better to choose as their king, as guardian of their treasure, if you wish to hold the kingdom of your kinsmen. So well your heart's temper has long pleased me, beloved Beowulf. You have brought it about that peace shall be shared by the peoples, the folk of the Geats and the Spear-Danes, and enmity shall sleep, acts of malice which they practiced before; and there shall be, as long as I rule the wide kingdom, sharing of treasures, many a man shall greet his fellow with good gifts over the sea-bird's baths; the ring-prowed ship will bring gifts and tokens of friendship over the sea. I know your people, blameless in every respect, set firm after the old way both as to foe and to friend."

6. I.e., Unferth.

Then the protector of earls, the kinsman of Healfdene, gave him there in the hall twelve precious things; he bade him with these gifts seek his own dear people in safety, quickly come back. Then the king noble of race, the prince of the Scyldings, kissed the best of thanes and took him by his neck: tears fell from the gray-haired one. He had two thoughts of the future, the old and wise man, one more strongly than the other—that they would not see each other again, bold men at council. The man was so dear to him that he might not restrain his breast's welling, for fixed in his heartstrings a deep-felt longing for the beloved man burned in his blood. Away from him Beowulf, warrior glorious with gold, walked over the grassy ground, proud of his treasure. The seagoer awaited its owner, riding at anchor. Then on the journey the gift of Hrothgar was oft-praised: that was a king blameless in all things until age took from him the joys of his strength—old age that has often harmed many.

There came to the flood the band of brave-hearted ones, of young men. They wore mail-coats, locked limb-shirts. The guard of the coast saw the coming of the earls, just as he had done before. He did not greet the guests with taunts from the cliff's top, but rode to meet them, said that the return of the warriors in bright armor in their ship would be welcome to the people of the Weather-Geats. There on the sand the broad sea-boat was loaded with armor, the ring-prowed ship with horses and rich things. The mast stood high over Hrothgar's hoard-gifts. He gave the boat-guard a sword wound with gold, so that thereafter on the mead-bench he was held the worthier for the treasure, the heirloom. The boat moved out to furrow the deep water, left the land of the Danes. Then on the mast a sea-cloth, a sail, was made fast by a rope. The boat's beams creaked: wind did not keep the sea-floater from its way over the waves. The sea-goer moved, foamy-necked floated forth over the swell, the ship with bound prow over the sea-currents until they might see the cliffs of the Geats, the well-known headlands. The ship pressed ahead, borne by the wind, stood still at the land. Quickly the harbor-guard was at the sea-side, he who had gazed for a long time far out over the currents, eager to see the beloved men. He[7] moored the deep ship in the sand, fast by its anchor ropes, lest the force of the waves should drive away the fair wooden vessel. Then he bade that the prince's wealth be borne ashore, armor and plated gold. It was not far for them to seek the giver of treasure, Hygelac son of Hrethel, where he dwelt at home near the sea-wall, himself with his retainers.

The building was splendid, its king most valiant, set high in the hall, Hygd[8] most youthful, wise and well-taught, though she had lived within the castle walls few winters, daughter of Haereth. For she was not niggardly, nor too sparing of gifts to the men of the Geats, of treasures. Modthryth,[9] good folk-queen, did dreadful deeds [in her youth]: no bold one among her retainers dared venture—except her great lord—to set his eyes on her in daylight, but [if he did] he should reckon deadly bonds prepared for him, arresting hands: that straightway after his seizure the sword awaited him, that the patterned

---

7. Beowulf.   8. Hygd is Hygelac's young queen. The suddenness of her introduction here is perhaps due to a faulty text.   9. A transitional passage introducing the contrast between Hygd's good behavior and Modthryth's bad behavior as young women of royal blood seems to have been lost. Modthryth's practice of having those who looked into her face put to death may reflect the folk motif of the princess whose unsuccessful suitors are executed, although the text does not say that Modthryth's victims were suitors. Modthryth's "great lord" was probably her father.

blade must settle it, make known its death-evil. Such is no queenly custom for a woman to practice, though she is peerless—that one who weaves peace[1] should take away the life of a beloved man after pretended injury. However the kinsman of Hemming stopped that:[2] ale-drinkers gave another account, said that she did less harm to the people, fewer injuries, after she was given, gold-adorned, to the young warrior, the beloved noble, when by her father's teaching she sought Offa's hall in a voyage over the pale sea. There on the throne she was afterwards famous for generosity, while living made use of her life, held high love toward the lord of warriors, [who was] of all mankind the best, as I have heard, between the seas of the races of men. Since Offa was a man brave of wars and gifts, wide-honored, he held his native land in wisdom. From him sprang Eomer to the help of warriors, kinsman of Hemming, grandson of Garmund, strong in battle.

Then the hardy one came walking with his troop over the sand on the sea-plain, the wide shores. The world-candle shone, the sun moved quickly from the south. They made their way, strode swiftly to where they heard that the protector of earls, the slayer of Ongentheow,[3] the good young war-king, was dispensing rings in the stronghold. The coming of Beowulf was straightway made known to Hygelac, that there in his home the defender of warriors, his comrade in battle, came walking alive to the court, sound from the battle-play. Quickly the way within was made clear for the foot-guests, as the mighty one bade.

Then he sat down with him, he who had come safe through the fight, kinsman with kinsman, after he had greeted his liege lord with formal speech, loyal, with vigorous words. Haereth's daughter moved through the hall-building with mead-cups, cared lovingly for the people, bore the cup of strong drink to the hands of the warriors. Hygelac began fairly to question his companion in the high hall, curiosity pressed him, what the adventures of the Sea-Geats had been. "How did you fare on your journey, beloved Beowulf, when you suddenly resolved to seek distant combat over the salt water, battle in Heorot? Did you at all help the wide-known woes of Hrothgar, the famous prince? Because of you I burned with seething sorrows, care of heart—had no trust in the venture of my beloved man. I entreated you long that you should in no way approach the murderous spirit, should let the South-Danes themselves settle the war with Grendel. I say thanks to God that I may see you sound."

Beowulf spoke, the son of Ecgtheow: "To many among men it is not hidden, lord Hygelac, the great encounter—what a fight we had, Grendel and I, in the place where he made many sorrows for the Victory-Scyldings, constant misery. All that I avenged, so that none of Grendel's kin over the earth need boast of that clash at night—whoever lives longest of the loathsome kind, wrapped in malice. There I went forth to the ring-hall to greet Hrothgar. At once the famous son of Healfdene, when he knew my purpose, gave me a seat with his own sons. The company was in joy: I have not seen in the time of my life under heaven's arch more mead-mirth of hall-sitters. At times

---

1. Daughters of kings were frequently given in marriage to the king of a hostile nation to bring about peace; hence Modthryth may be called *one who weaves peace*.   2. I.e., Offa I, a legendary king of the Angles; who Hemming was—besides being Offa's forebear—is not known.   3. Ongentheow was a Scylfing (Swedish) king, whose story is fully told below. In fact Hygelac was not his slayer, but is called so because he led the attack on the Scylfings in which Ongentheow was killed.

the famous queen, peace-pledge of the people, went through all the hall, cheered the young men; often she would give a man a ring-band before she went to her seat. At times Hrothgar's daughter bore the ale-cup to the retainers, to the earls throughout the hall. I heard hall-sitters name her Freawaru when she offered the studded cup to warriors. Young and gold-adorned, she is promised to the fair son of Froda.[4] That has seemed good to the lord of the Scyldings, the guardian of the kingdom, and he believes of this plan that he may, with this woman, settle their portion of deadly feuds, of quarrels.[5] Yet most often after the fall of a prince in any nation the deadly spear rests but a little while, even though the bride is good.

"It may displease the lord of the Heatho-Bards and each thane of that people when he goes in the hall with the woman, [that while] the noble sons of the Danes, her retainers, [are] feasted,[6] the heirlooms of their ancestors will be shining on them—the hard and wave-adorned treasure of the Heatho-Bards, [which was theirs] so long as they might wield those weapons, until they led to the shield-play, to destruction, their dear companions and their own lives.[7] Then at the beer he[8] who sees the treasure, an old ash-warrior who remembers it all, the spear-death of warriors—grim is his heart—begins, sad of mind, to tempt a young fighter in the thoughts of his spirit, to awaken war-evil, and speaks this word:

" 'Can you, my friend, recognize that sword, the rare iron-blade, that your father, beloved man, bore to battle his last time in armor, where the Danes slew him, the fierce Scyldings, got possession of the battle-field, when Withergeld[9] lay dead, after the fall of warriors? Now here some son of his murderers walks in the hall, proud of the weapon, boasts of the murder, and wears the treasure that you should rightly possess.' So he will provoke and remind at every chance with wounding words until that moment comes that the woman's thane,[1] forfeiting life, shall lie dead, blood-smeared from the sword-bite, for his father's deeds. The other escapes with his life, knows the land well. Then on both sides the oath of the earls will be broken; then deadly hate will well up in Ingeld, and his wife-love after the surging of sorrows will become cooler. Therefore I do not think the loyalty of the Heatho-Bards, their part in the alliance with the Danes, to be without deceit—do not think their friendship fast.

"I shall speak still more of Grendel, that you may readily know, giver of treasure, what the hand-fight of warriors came to in the end. After heaven's jewel had glided over the earth, the angry spirit came, awful in the evening, to visit us where, unharmed, we watched over the hall. There the fight was fatal to Hondscioh, deadly to one who was doomed. He was dead first of all, armed warrior. Grendel came to devour him, good young retainer, swallowed all the body of the beloved man. Yet not for this would the bloody-toothed slayer, bent on destruction, go from the gold-hall empty-handed; but, strong of might, he made trial of me, grasped me with eager hand. His glove[2] hung huge and wonderful, made fast with cunning clasps: it had been made all

4. I.e., Ingeld, who succeeded his father as king of the Heatho-Bards.   5. I.e., the feud between the Danes and Heatho-Bards.   6. The text is faulty here.   7. I.e., the weapons and armor that had once belonged to the Heatho-Bards and were captured by the Danes will be worn by the Danish attendants of Hrothgar's daughter Freawaru when she goes to the Heatho-Bards to marry King Ingeld.   8. I.e., some old Heatho-Bard warrior.   9. Apparently a leader of the Heatho-Bards in their unsuccessful war with the Danes.   1. I.e., the Danish attendant of Freawaru who is wearing the sword of his Heatho-Bard attacker's father.   2. Apparently a large glove that could be used as a pouch.

with craft; with devil's devices and dragon's skins. The fell doer of evils would put me therein, guiltless, one of many. He might not do so after I had stood up in anger. It is too long to tell how I repaid the people's foe his due for every crime. My prince, there with my deeds I did honor to your people. He slipped away, for a little while had use of life's joy. Yet his right hand remained as his spoor in Heorot, and he went from there abject, mournful of heart sank to the mere's bottom.

"The lord of the Scyldings repaid me for that bloody combat with much plated gold, many treasures, after morning came and we sat down to the feast. There was song and mirth. The old Scylding, who has learned many things, spoke of times far-off. At times a brave one in battle touched the glad wood, the harp's joy; at times he told tales, true and sad; at times he related strange stories according to right custom; at times, again, the great-hearted king, bound with age, the old warrior, would begin to speak of his youth, his battle-strength. His heart welled within when, old and wise, he thought of his many winters. Thus we took pleasure there the livelong day until another night came to men.

"Then in her turn Grendel's mother swiftly made ready to take revenge for his injuries, made a sorrowful journey. Death had taken her son, war-hate of the Weather-Geats. The direful woman avenged her son, fiercely killed a warrior: there the life of Aeschere departed, a wise old counselor. And when morning came the folk of the Danes might not burn him, death-weary, in the fire, nor place him on the pyre, beloved man: she had borne his body away in fiend's embrace beneath the mountain stream. That was the bitterest of Hrothgar's sorrows, of those that had long come upon the people's prince. Then the king, sore-hearted, implored me by your life[3] that I should do a man's work in the tumult of the waters, venture my life, finish a glorious deed. He promised me reward. Then I found the guardian of the deep pool, the grim horror, as is now known wide. For a time there we were locked hand in hand. Then the flood boiled with blood, and in the war-hall I cut off the head of Grendel's mother with a mighty sword. Not without trouble I came from there with my life. I was not fated to die then, but the protector of earls again gave me many treasures, the son of Healfdene.

"Thus the king of that people lived with good customs. I had lost none of the rewards, the meed of my might, but he gave me treasures, the son of Healfdene, at my own choice. I will bring these to you, great king, show my good will. On your kindnesses all still depends: I have few close kinsmen besides you, Hygelac."

Then he bade bring in the boar-banner—the head-sign—the helmet towering in battle, the gray battle-shirt, the splendid sword—afterwards spoke words: "Hrothgar, wise king, gave me this armor; in his words he bade that I should first tell you about his gift: he said that king Heorogar,[4] lord of the Scyldings, had had it for a long time; not for that would he give it, the breast-armor, to his son, bold Heoroweard, though he was loyal to him. Use it all well!"

I have heard that four horses, swift and alike, followed that treasure, fallow as apples. He gave him the gift of both horses and treasure. So ought kinsmen do, not weave malice-nets for each other with secret craft, prepare death for comrades. To Hygelac his nephew was most true in hard fights, and each

---

3. I.e., in your name.   4. Hrothgar's elder brother, whom Hrothgar succeeded as king.

one mindful of helping the other. I have heard that he gave Hygd the neck-ring, the wonderfully wrought treasure, that Wealhtheow had given him—gave to the king's daughter as well three horses, supple and saddle-bright. After the gift of the necklace, her breast was adorned with it.

Thus Beowulf showed himself brave, a man known in battles, of good deeds, bore himself according to discretion. Drunk, he slew no hearth-companions. His heart was not savage, but he held the great gift that God had given him, the most strength of all mankind, like one brave in battle. He had long been despised,[5] so that the sons of the Geats did not reckon him brave, nor would the lord of the Weather-Geats do him much gift-honor on the mead-bench. They strongly suspected that he was slack, a young man unbold. Change came to the famous man for each of his troubles.

Then the protector of earls bade fetch in the heirloom of Hrethel,[6] king famed in battle, adorned with gold. There was not then among the Geats a better treasure in sword's kind. He laid that in Beowulf's lap, and gave him seven thousand [hides of land], a hall and a throne. To both of them alike land had been left in the nation, home and native soil: to the other more especially wide was the realm, to him who was higher in rank.

[BEOWULF AND THE DRAGON]

Afterwards it happened, in later days, in the crashes of battle, when Hyge-lac lay dead and war-swords came to slay Heardred[7] behind the shield-cover, when the Battle-Scylfings, hard fighters, sought him among his victorious nation, attacked bitterly the nephew of Hereric—then the broad kingdom came into Beowulf's hand. He held it well fifty winters—he was a wise king, an old guardian of the land—until in the dark nights a certain one, a dragon, began to hold sway, which on the high heath kept watch over a hoard, a steep stone-barrow. Beneath lay a path unknown to men. By this there went inside a certain man [who made his way near to the heathen hoard; his hand took a cup, large, a shining treasure. The dragon did not afterwards conceal it though in his sleep he was tricked by the craft of the thief. That the people discovered, the neighboring folk—that he was swollen with rage].[8]

Not of his own accord did he who had sorely harmed him[9] break into the worm's hoard, not by his own desire, but for hard constraint; the slave of some son of men fled hostile blows, lacking a shelter, and came there, a man guilty of wrong-doing. As soon as he saw him,[1] great horror arose in the stranger; [yet the wretched fugitive escaped the terrible worm . . . When the sudden shock came upon him, he carried off a precious cup].[2] There were many such ancient treasures in the earth-house, as in the old days some one of mankind had prudently hidden there the huge legacy of a noble race, rare treasures. Death had taken them all in earlier times, and the only one of the nation of people who still survived, who walked there longest, a guardian mourning his friends, supposed the same of himself as of them—that he might little while enjoy the long-got treasure. A barrow stood all ready on the shore near the sea-waves, newly placed on the headland, made fast by

5. Beowulf's poor reputation as a young man is mentioned only here.   6. Hygelac's father.
7. Hygelac's son Heardred, who succeeded Hygelac as king, was killed by the Swedes (Battle-Scylfings) in his own land (see n. 6, p. 1093). His uncle Hereric was perhaps Hygd's brother.   8. This part of the manuscript is badly damaged, and the text within brackets is highly conjectural.   9. The dragon.
1. The dragon.   2. Several lines of the text have been lost.

having its entrances skillfully hidden. The keeper of the rings carried in the part of his riches worthy of hoarding, plated gold; he spoke few words:

"Hold now, you earth, now that men may not, the possession of earls. What, from you good men got it first! War-death has taken each man of my people, evil dreadful and deadly, each of those who has given up this life, the hall-joys of men. I have none who wears sword or cleans the plated cup, rich drinking vessel. The company of retainers has gone elsewhere. The hard helmet must be stripped of its fair-wrought gold, of its plating. The polishers are asleep who should make the war-mask shine. And even so the coat of mail, which withstood the bite of swords after the crashing of the shields, decays like its warrior. Nor may the ring-mail travel wide on the war-chief beside his warriors. There is no harp-delight, no mirth of the singing wood, no good hawk flies through the hall, no swift horse stamps in the castle court. Baleful death has sent away many races of men."

So, sad of mind, he spoke his sorrow, alone of them all, moved joyless through day and night until death's flood reached his heart. The ancient night-ravager found the hoard-joy standing open, he who burning seeks barrows, the smooth hateful dragon who flies at night wrapped in flame. Earth-dwellers much dread him. He it is who must seek a hoard in the earth where he will guard heathen gold, wise for his winters: he is none the better for it.

So for three hundred winters the harmer of folk held in the earth one of its treasure-houses, huge and mighty, until one man angered his heart. He bore to his master a plated cup, asked his lord for a compact of peace: thus was the hoard searched, the store of treasures diminished. His requests were granted the wretched man: the lord for the first time looked on the ancient work of men. Then the worm woke; cause of strife was renewed: for then he moved over the stones, hard-hearted beheld his foe's footprints—with secret stealth he had stepped forth too near the dragon's head. (So may an undoomed man who holds favor from the Ruler easily come through his woes and misery.) The hoard-guard sought him eagerly over the ground, would find the man who had done him injury while he slept. Hot and fierce-hearted, often he moved all about the outside of the barrow. No man at all was in the emptiness. Yet he took joy in the thought of war, in the work of fighting. At times he turned back into the barrow, sought his rich cup. Straightway he found that some man had tampered with his gold, his splendid treasure. The hoard-guard waited restless until evening came; then the barrow-keeper was in rage: he would requite that precious drinking cup with vengeful fire. Then the day was gone—to the joy of the worm. He would not wait long on the sea-wall, but set out with fire, ready with flame. The beginning was terrible to the folk on the land, as the ending was soon to be sore to their giver of treasure.

Then the evil spirit began to vomit flames, burn bright dwellings; blaze of fire rose, to the horror of men; there the deadly flying thing would leave nothing alive. The worm's warfare was wide-seen, his cruel malice, near and far—how the destroyer hated and hurt the people of the Geats. He winged back to the hoard, his hidden hall, before the time of day. He had circled the land-dwellers with flame, with fire and burning. He had trust in his barrow, in his war and his wall: his expectation deceived him.

Then the terror was made known to Beowulf, quickly in its truth, that his own home, best of buildings, had melted in surging flames, the throne-seat of the Geats. That was anguish of spirit to the good man, the greatest of heart-sorrows. The wise one supposed that he had bitterly offended the Ruler, the Eternal Lord, against old law. His breast within boiled with dark thoughts—as was not for him customary. The fiery dragon with his flames had destroyed the people's stronghold, the land along the sea, the heart of the country. Because of that the war-king, the lord of the Weather-Geats, devised punishment for him. The protector of fighting men, lord of earls, commanded that a wonderful battle-shield be made all of iron. Well he knew that the wood of the forest might not help him—linden against flame. The prince good from old times was to come to the end of the days that had been lent him, life in the world, and the worm with him, though he had long held the hoarded wealth. Then the ring-prince scorned to seek the far-flier with a troop, a large army. He had no fear for himself of the combat, nor did he think the worm's war-power anything great, his strength and his courage, because he himself had come through many battles before, dared perilous straits, clashes of war, after he had purged Hrothgar's hall, victorious warrior, and in combat crushed to death Grendel's kin, loathsome race.

Nor was that the least of his hand-combats where Hygelac was slain, when the king of the Geats, the noble lord of the people, the son of Hrethel, died of sword-strokes in the war-storm among the Frisians, laid low by the blade. From there Beowulf came away by means of his own strength, performed a feat of swimming; he had on his arm the armor of thirty earls when he turned back to the sea. There was no need for the Hetware[3] to exult in the foot-battle when they bore their shields against him: few came again from that warrior to seek their homes. Then the son of Ecgtheow swam over the water's expanse, forlorn and alone, back to his people. There Hygd offered him hoard and kingdom, rings and a prince's throne. She had no trust in her son, that he could hold his native throne against foreigners now that Hygelac was dead. By no means the sooner might the lordless ones get consent from the noble that he would become lord of Heardred or that he would accept royal power.[4] Yet he held him up among the people by friendly counsel, kindly with honor, until he became older,[5] ruled the Weather-Geats.

Outcasts from over the sea sought him, sons of Ohthere.[6] They had rebelled against the protector of the Scylfings, the best of the sea-kings of those who gave treasure in Sweden, a famous lord. For Heardred that became his life's limit: because of his hospitality there the son of Hygelac got his life's wound from the strokes of a sword. And the son of Ongentheow went back to seek his home after Heardred lay dead, let Beowulf hold the royal throne, rule the Geats: that was a good king.

In later days he was mindful of repaying the prince's fall, became the friend of the destitute Eadgils,[7] with folk he supported the son of Ohthere over the wide sea, with warriors and weapons. Afterwards he got vengeance by forays that brought with them cold care: he took the king's life.

Thus he had survived every combat, every dangerous battle, every deed of

---

3. I.e., a tribe, with whom the Frisians were allied.   4. I.e., Beowulf refused to take the throne from the rightful heir, Heardred.   5. I.e., Beowulf supported the young Heardred.   6. Ohthere succeeded his father, Ongentheow, as king of the Scylfings (Swedes), but after his death his brother, Onela, seized the throne, driving out Ohthere's sons Eanmund and Eadgils. They were given refuge at the Geatish court by Heardred, whom Onela attacked for this act of hospitality. In the fight, Eanmund and Heardred were killed, and Onela left the kingdom in Beowulf's charge.   7. The surviving son of Ohthere was befriended by Beowulf, who supported him in his successful attempt to gain the Swedish throne and who killed the usurper Onela.

courage, the son of Ecgtheow, until that one day when he should fight with the worm. Then, one of twelve, the lord of the Geats, swollen with anger, went to look on the dragon. He had learned then from what the feud arose, the fierce malice to men: the glorious cup had come to his possession from the hand of the finder: he was the thirteenth of that company, the man who had brought on the beginning of the war, the sad-hearted slave—wretched, he must direct them to the place. Against his will he went to where he knew of an earth-hall, a barrow beneath the ground close to the sea-surge, to the struggling waves: within, it was full of ornaments and gold chains. The terrible guardian, ready for combat, held the gold treasure, old under the earth. It was no easy bargain for any man to obtain. Then the king, hardy in fight, sat down on the headland; there he saluted his hearth-companions, gold-friend of the Geats. His mind was mournful, restless and ripe for death: very close was the fate which should come to the old man, seek his soul's hoard, divide life from his body; not for long then was the life of the noble one wound in his flesh.

Beowulf spoke, the son of Ecgtheow: "In youth I lived through many battle-storms; times of war. I remember all that. I was seven winters old when the lord of treasure, the beloved king of the folk, received me from my father: King Hrethel had me and kept me, gave me treasure and feast, mindful of kinship. During his life I was no more hated by him as a man in his castle than any of his own sons, Herebeald and Haethcyn, or my own Hygelac. For the eldest a murder-bed was wrongfully spread through the deed of a kinsman, when Haethcyn struck him down with an arrow from his horned bow— his friend and his lord—missed the mark and shot his kinsman dead, one brother the other, with the bloody arrowhead. That was a fatal fight, without hope of recompense, a deed wrongly done, baffling to the heart; yet it had happened that a prince had to lose life unavenged.

"So it is sad for an old man to endure that his son should ride young on the gallows. Then he may speak a story, a sorrowful song, when his son hangs for the joy of the raven, and, old in years and knowing, he can find no help for him. Always with every morning he is reminded of his son's journey elsewhere. He cares not to wait for another heir in his hall, when the first through death's force has come to the end of his deeds. Sorrowful he sees in his son's dwelling the empty wine-hall, the windy resting place without joy—the riders sleep, the warriors in the grave. There is no sound of the harp, no joy in the dwelling, as there was of old. Then he goes to his couch, sings a song of sorrow, one alone for one gone. To him all too wide has seemed the land and the dwelling.

"So the protector of the Weather-Geats bore in his heart swelling sorrow for Herebeald. In no way could he settle his feud with the life-slayer; not the sooner could he wound the warrior with deeds of hatred, though he was not dear to him. Then for the sorrow that had too bitterly befallen him he gave up the joys of men, chose God's light. To his sons he left—as a happy man does—his land and his town when he went from life.

"Then there was battle and strife of Swedes and Geats, over the wide water a quarrel shared, hatred between hardy ones, after Hrethel died. And the sons of Ongentheow[8] were bold and active in war, wanted to have no peace

---

8. I.e., the Swedes Onela and Ohthere: the reference is, of course, to a time earlier than that referred to in n. 6, p. 1093.

over the seas, but about Hreosnabeorh often devised awful slaughter. That my friends and kinsmen avenged, both the feud and the crime, as is well-known, though one of them bought it with his life, a hard bargain: the war was mortal to Haethcyn, lord of the Geats.[9] Then in the morning, I have heard, one kinsman avenged the other on his slayer with the sword's edge, when Ongentheow attacked Eofor: the war-helm split, the old Scylfing fell mortally wounded: his hand remembered feuds enough, did not withstand the life-blow.

"I repaid in war the treasures that he[1] gave me—with my bright sword, as was granted me by fate: he had given me land, a pleasant dwelling. There was not any need for him, any reason, that he should have to seek among the Gifthas or the Spear-Danes or in Sweden in order to buy with treasure a worse warrior. I would always go before him in the troop, alone in the front. And so all my life I shall wage battle while this sword endures that has served me early and late ever since I became Daeghrefn's slayer in the press—the warrior of the Hugas.[2] He could not bring armor to the king of the Frisians, breast ornament, but fell in the fight, keeper of the standard, a noble man. Nor was my sword's edge his slayer, but my warlike grip broke open his heart-streams, his bone-house. Now shall the sword's edge, the hand and hard blade, fight for the hoard."

[Beowulf Attacks the Dragon]

Beowulf spoke, for the last time spoke words in boast: "In my youth I engaged in many wars. Old guardian of the people, I shall still seek battle, perform a deed of fame, if the evil-doer will come to me out of the earth-hall."

Then he saluted each of the warriors, the bold helmet-bearers, for the last time—his own dear companions. "I would not bear sword, weapon, to the worm, if I knew how else according to my boast I might grapple with the monster, as I did of old with Grendel. But I expect here hot battle-fire, steam and poison. Therefore I have on me shield and mail-shirt. I will not flee a foot-step from the barrow-ward, but it shall be with us at the wall as fate allots, the ruler of every man. I am confident in heart, so I forgo help against the war-flier. Wait on the barrow, safe in your mail-shirts, men in armor—which of us two may better bear wounds after our bloody meeting. This is not your venture, nor is it right for any man except me alone that he should spend his strength against the monster, do this man's deed. By my courage I shall get gold, or war will take your king, dire life-evil."

Then the brave warrior arose by his shield; hardy under helmet he went in his mail-shirt beneath the stone-cliffs, had trust in his strength—that of one man: such is not the the way of the cowardly. Then he saw by the wall—he who had come through many wars, good in his great-heartedness, many clashes in battle when troops meet together—a stone arch standing, through it a stream bursting out of the barrow: there was welling of a current hot with killing fires, and he might not endure any while unburnt by the dragon's flame the hollow near the hoard. Then the man of the Weather-Geats,

9. Haethcyn had succeeded his father, Hrethel, as king of the Geats after his accidental killing of his brother Herebeald. When Haethcyn was killed while attacking the Swedes, he was succeeded by Hygelac, who, as the next sentence relates, avenged Haethcyn's death on Ongentheow. The death of Ongentheow is described below.   1. Hygelac.   2. I.e., the Franks.

enraged as he was, let a word break from his breast. Stout-hearted he shouted; his voice went roaring, clear in battle, in under the gray stone. Hate was stirred up, the hoard's guard knew the voice of a man. No more time was there to ask for peace. First the monster's breath came out of the stone, the hot war-steam. The earth resounded. The man below the barrow, the lord of the Geats, swung his shield against the dreadful visitor. Then the heart of the coiled thing was aroused to seek combat. The good war-king had drawn his sword, the old heirloom, not blunt of edge. To each of them as they threatened destruction there was terror of the other. Firm-hearted he stood with his shield high, the lord of friends, while quickly the worm coiled itself; he waited in his armor. Then, coiling in flames, he came gliding on, hastening to his fate. The good shield protected the life and body of the famous prince, but for a shorter while than his wish was. There for the first time, the first day in his life, he might not prevail, since fate did not assign him such glory in battle. The lord of the Geats raised his hand, struck the shining horror so with his forged blade that the edge failed, bright on the bone, bit less surely than its folk-king had need, hard-pressed in perils. Then because of the battle-stroke the barrow-ward's heart was savage, he exhaled death-fire—the war-flames sprang wide. The gold-friend of the Geats boasted of no great victories: the war blade had failed, naked at need, as it ought not to have done, iron good from old times. That was no pleasant journey, not one on which the famous son of Ecgtheow would wish to leave his land; against his will he must take up a dwelling-place elsewhere—as every man must give up the days that are lent him.

It was not long until they came together again, dreadful foes. The hoard-guard took heart, once more his breast swelled with his breathing. Encircled with flames, he who before had ruled a folk felt harsh pain. Nor did his companions, sons of nobles, take up their stand in a troop about him with the courage of fighting men, but they crept to the wood, protected their lives. In only one of them the heart surged with sorrows: nothing can ever set aside kinship in him who means well.

He was called Wiglaf, son of Weohstan, a rare shield-warrior, a man of the Scylfings,[3] kinsman of Aelfhere. He saw his liege lord under his war-mask suffer the heat. Then he was mindful of the honors he had given him before, the rich dwelling-place of the Waegmundings, every folk-right such as his father possessed. He might not then hold back, his hand seized his shield, the yellow linden-wood; he drew his ancient sword. Among men it was the heirloom of Eanmund, the son of Ohthere:[4] Weohstan had become his slayer in battle with sword's edge—an exile without friends; and he bore off to his kin the bright-shining helmet, the ringed mail-armor, the old sword made by giants that Onela had given him,[5] his kinsman's war-armor, ready battle-gear: he did not speak of the feud, though he had killed his brother's

3. Although in the next sentence Wiglaf is said to belong to the family of the Waegmundings, the Geatish family to which Beowulf belonged, he is here called a Scylfing (Swede), and immediately below, his father, Weohstan, is represented as having fought for the Swede Onela in his attack on the Geats. But for a man to change his nation was not unusual, and Weohstan, who may have had both Swedish and Geatish blood, had evidently become a Geat long enough before to have brought up his son Wiglaf as one. The identity of Aelfhere is not known.   4. Weohstan not only supported Onela's attack on Geat King Heardred but actually killed Eanmund, whom Heardred was supporting, and it is Eanmund's sword that Wiglaf is now wielding (see n. 6, p. 1093).   5. The spoils of war belonged to the victorious king, who apportioned them among his fighters; thus Onela gave Weohstan the armor of Eanmund, whom Weohstan had killed.

son.[6] He[7] held the armor many half-years, the blade and the battle-dress, until his son might do manly deeds like his old father. Then he gave him among the Geats war-armor of every kind, numberless, when, old, he went forth on the way from life. For the young warrior this was the first time that he should enter the war-storm with his dear lord. His heart's courage did not slacken, nor did the heirloom of his kinsman fail in the battle. That the worm found when they had come together.

Wiglaf spoke, said many fit words to his companions—his mind was mournful: "I remember that time we drank mead, when we promised our lord in the beer-hall—him who gave us these rings—that we would repay him for the war-arms if a need like this befell him—the helmets and the hard swords. Of his own will he chose us among the host for this venture, thought us worthy of fame—and gave me these treasures—because he counted us good war-makers, brave helm-bearers, though our lord intended to do this work of courage alone, as keeper of the folk, because among men he had performed the greater deeds of glory, daring actions. Now the day has come that our liege lord has need of the strength of good fighters. Let us go to him, help our war-chief while the grim terrible fire persists. God knows of me that I should rather that the flame enfold my body with my gold-giver. It does not seem right to me for us to bear our shields home again unless we can first fell the foe, defend the life of the prince of the Weather-Geats. I know well that it would be no recompense for past deeds that he alone of the company of the Geats should suffer pain, fall in the fight. For us both shall there be a part in the work of sword and helmet, of battle-shirt and war-clothing."

Then he waded through the deadly smoke, bore his war-helmet to the aid of his king, spoke in few words: "Beloved Beowulf, do all well, for, long since in your youth, you said that you would not let your glory fail while you lived. Now, great-spirited noble, brave of deeds, you must protect your life with all your might. I shall help you."

After these words, the worm came on, angry, the terrible malice-filled foe, shining with surging flames, to seek for the second time his enemies, hated men. Fire advanced in waves; shield burned to the boss; mail-shirt might give no help to the young spear-warrior; but the young man went quickly under his kinsman's shield when his own was consumed with flames. Then the war-king was again mindful of fame, struck with his war-sword with great strength so that it stuck in the head-bone, driven with force: Naegling broke, the sword of Beowulf failed in the fight, old and steel-gray. It was not ordained for him that iron edges might help in the combat. Too strong was the hand that I have heard strained every sword with its stroke, when he bore wound-hardened weapon to battle: he was none the better for it.

Then for the third time the folk-harmer, the fearful fire-dragon, was mindful of feuds, set upon the brave one when the chance came, hot and battle-grim seized all his neck with his sharp fangs: he was smeared with life-blood, gore welled out in waves.

Then, I have heard, at the need of the folk-king the earl at his side made his courage known, his might and his keenness—as was natural to him. He

6. This ironic remark points out that Onela did not claim *wergild* or seek vengeance from Weohstan, as in other circumstances he ought to have done inasmuch as Weohstan had killed Onela's close kinsman, his nephew Eanmund, but Onela was himself trying to kill Eanmund.   7. Weohstan.

took no heed for that head,[8] but the hand of the brave man was burned as he helped his kinsman, as the man in armor struck the hateful foe a little lower down, so that the sword sank in, shining and engraved; and then the fire began to subside. The king himself then still controlled his senses, drew the battle-knife, biting and war-sharp, that he wore on his mail-shirt: the protector of the Weather-Geats cut the worm through the middle. They felled the foe, courage drove his life out, and they had destroyed him together, the two noble kinsmen. So ought a man be, a thane at need. To the prince that was the last moment of victory for his own deeds, of work in the world.

Then the wound that the earth-dragon had caused began to burn and to swell; at once he felt dire evil boil in his breast, poison within him. Then the prince, wise of thought, went to where he might sit on a seat near the wall. He looked on the work of giants, how the timeless earth-hall held within it stone-arches fast on pillars. Then with his hands the thane, good without limit, washed him with water, blood-besmeared, the famous prince, his beloved lord, sated with battle; and he unfastened his helmet.

Beowulf spoke—despite his wounds spoke, his mortal hurts. He knew well he had lived out his days' time, joy on earth; all passed was the number of his days, death very near. "Now I would wish to give my son my war-clothing, if any heir after me, part of my flesh, were granted. I held this people fifty winters. There was no folk-king of those dwelling about who dared approach me with swords, threaten me with fears. In my land I awaited what fate brought me, held my own well, sought no treacherous quarrels, nor did I swear many oaths unrightfully. Sick with life-wounds, I may have joy of all this, for the Ruler of Men need not blame me for the slaughter of kinsmen when life goes from my body. Now quickly go to look at the hoard under the gray stone, beloved Wiglaf, now that the worm lies sleeping from sore wounds, bereft of his treasure. Be quick now, so that I may see the ancient wealth, the golden things, may clearly look on the bright curious gems, so that for that, because of the treasure's richness, I may the more easily leave life and nation I have long held."

Then I have heard that the son of Weohstan straightway obeyed his lord, sick with battle-wounds, according to the words he had spoken, went wearing his ring-armor, woven battle-shirt, under the barrow's roof. Then he saw, as he went by the seat, the brave young retainer, triumphant in heart, many precious jewels, glittering gold lying on the ground, wonders on the wall, and the worm's lair, the old night-flier's—cups standing there, vessels of men of old, with none to polish them, stripped of their ornaments. There was many a helmet old and rusty, many an arm-ring skillfully twisted. (Easily may treasure, gold in the ground, betray each one of the race of men; hide it who will.) Also he saw a standard all gold hang high over the hoard, the greatest of hand-wonders, linked with fingers' skill. From it came a light so that he might see the ground, look on the works of craft. There was no trace of the worm, for the blade had taken him. Then I have heard that one man in the mound pillaged the hoard, the old work of giants, loaded in his bosom cups and plates at his own desire. He took also the standard, brightest of banners. The sword of the old lord—its edge was iron—had already wounded the one who

8. I.e., the dragon's flame-breathing head.

for a long time had been guardian of the treasure, waged his fire-terror, hot for the hoard, rising up fiercely at midnight, till he died in the slaughter.

The messenger was in haste, eager to return, urged on by the treasures. Curiosity tormented him, whether eagerly seeking he should find the lord of the Weather-Geats, strength gone, alive in the place where he had left him before. Then with the treasures he found the great prince, his lord, bleeding, at the end of his life. Again he began to sprinkle him with water until this word's point broke through his breast-hoard—he spoke, the king, old man in sorrow, looked on the gold: "I speak with my words thanks to the Lord of All for these treasures, to the King of Glory, Eternal Prince, for what I gaze on here, that I might get such for my people before my death-day. Now that I have bought the hoard of treasures with my old life, you attend to the people's needs hereafter: I can be here no longer. Bid the battle-renowned make a mound, bright after the funeral fire, on the sea's cape. It shall stand high on Hronesness as a reminder to my people, so that sea-travelers later will call it Beowulf's barrow, when they drive their ships far over the darkness of the seas."

He took off his neck the golden necklace, bold-hearted prince, gave it to the thane, to the young spear-warrior—gold-gleaming helmet, ring, and mail-shirt, bade him use them well. "You are the last left of our race, of the Waegmundings. Fate has swept away all my kinsmen, earls in their strength, to destined death. I have to go after." That was the last word of the old man, of the thoughts of his heart, before he should taste the funeral pyre, hot hostile flames. The soul went from his breast to seek the doom of those fast in truth.

[BEOWULF'S FUNERAL]

Then sorrow came to the young man that he saw him whom he most loved on the earth, at the end of his life, suffering piteously. His slayer likewise lay dead, the awful earth-dragon bereft of life, overtaken by evil. No longer should the coiled worm rule the ring-hoard, for iron edges had taken him, hard and battle-sharp work of the hammers, so that the wide-flier, stilled by wounds, had fallen on the earth near the treasure-house. He did not go flying through the air at midnight, proud of his property, showing his aspect, but he fell to earth through the work of the chief's hands. Yet I have heard of no man of might on land, though he was bold of every deed, whom it should prosper to rush against the breath of the venomous foe or disturb with hands the ring-hall, if he found the guard awake who lived in the barrow. The share of the rich treasures became Beowulf's, paid for by death: each of the two had journeyed to the end of life's loan.

Then it was not long before the battle-slack ones left the woods, ten weak troth-breakers together, who had not dared fight with their spears in their liege lord's great need. But they bore their shields, ashamed, their war-clothes, to where the old man lay, looked on Wiglaf. He sat wearied, the foot-soldier near the shoulders of his lord, would waken him with water: it gained him nothing. He might not, though he much wished it, hold life in his chieftain on earth nor change anything of the Ruler's: the judgment of God would control the deeds of every man, just as it still does now. Then it was easy to get from the young man a grim answer to him who before had lost courage. Wiglaf spoke, the son of Weohstan, a man sad at heart, looked on the unloved ones:

"Yes, he who will speak truth may say that the liege lord who gave you treasure, the war-gear that you stand in there, when he used often to hand out to hall-sitters on the ale-benches, a prince to his thanes, helmets and war-shirts such as he could find mightiest anywhere, both far and near— that he quite threw away the war-gear, to his distress when war came upon him. The folk-king had no need to boast of his war-comrades. Yet God, Ruler of Victories, granted him that he might avenge himself, alone with his sword, when there was need for his courage. I was able to give him little life-protection in the fight, and yet beyond my power I did begin to help my kinsman. The deadly foe was ever the weaker after I struck him with my sword, fire poured less strongly from his head. Too few defenders thronged about the prince when the hard time came upon him. Now there shall cease for your race the receiving of treasure and the giving of swords, all enjoyment of pleasant homes, comfort. Each man of your kindred must go deprived of his land-right when nobles from afar learn of your flight, your inglorious deed. Death is better for any earl than a life of blame."

Then he bade that the battle-deed be announced in the city, up over the cliff-edge, where the band of warriors sat the whole morning of the day, sad-hearted, shield-bearers in doubt whether it was the beloved man's last day or whether he would come again. Little did he fail to speak of new tidings, he who rode up the hill, but spoke to them all truthfully: "Now the joy-giver of the people of the Weathers, the lord of the Geats, is fast on his death-bed, lies on his slaughter-couch through deeds of the worm. Beside him lies his life-enemy, struck down with dagger-wounds—with his sword he might not work wounds of any kind on the monster. Wiglaf son of Weohstan sits over Beowulf, one earl by the lifeless other, in weariness of heart holds death-watch over the loved and the hated.

"Now may the people expect a time of war, when the king's fall becomes wide-known to the Franks and the Frisians. A harsh quarrel was begun with the Hugas when Hygelac came traveling with his sea-army to the land of the Frisians, where the Hetware assailed him in battle, quickly, with stronger forces, made the mailed warrior bow; he fell in the ranks: that chief gave no treasure to his retainers. Ever since then the good will of the Merewioing king has been denied us.

"Nor do I expect any peace or trust from the Swedish people, for it is wide-known that Ongentheow took the life of Haethcyn, Hrethel's son, near Ravenswood when in their over-pride the people of the Geats first went against the War-Scylfings. Straightway the wary father of Ohthere,[9] old and terrible, gave a blow in return, cut down the sea-king,[1] rescued his wife, old woman of times past, bereft of her gold, mother of Onela and Ohthere, and then he followed his life-foes until they escaped, lordless, painfully, to Ravenswood. Then with a great army he besieged those whom the sword had left, weary with wounds, often vowed woes to the wretched band the livelong night, said that in the morning he would cut them apart with sword-blades, [hang] some on gallows-trees as sport for birds. Relief came in turn to the sorry-hearted

---

9. I.e., Ongentheow.   1. I.e., Haethcyn, king of the Geats. Haethcyn's brother Hygelac, who succeeded him, was not present at this battle but arrived after the death of Haethcyn with reinforcements to relieve the survivors and to pursue Ongentheow in his retreat to his city.

together with dawn when they heard Hygelac's horn and trumpet, his sound as the good man came on their track with a body of retainers. Wide-seen was the bloody track of Swedes and Geats, the slaughter-strife of men, how the peoples stirred up the feud between them. Then the good man went with his kinsmen, old and much-mourning, to seek his stronghold: the earl Ongentheow moved further away. He had heard of the warring of Hygelac, of the war-power of the proud one. He did not trust in resistance, that he might fight off the sea-men, defend his hoard against the war-sailors, his children and wife. Instead he drew back, the old man behind his earth-wall.

"Then pursuit was offered to the people of the Swedes, the standards of Hygelac overran the stronghold as Hrethel's people pressed forward to the citadel. There Ongentheow the gray-haired was brought to bay by sword-blades, and the people's king had to submit to the judgment of Eofor alone. Wulf[2] son of Wonred had struck him angrily with his weapon so that for the blow the blood sprang forth in streams beneath his hair. Yet not for that was he afraid, the old Scylfing, but he quickly repaid the assault with worse exchange, the folk-king, when he turned toward him. The strong son of Won-red could not give the old man a return blow, for Ongentheow had first cut through the helmet of his head so that he had to sink down, smeared with blood—fell on the earth: he was not yet doomed, for he recovered, though the wound hurt him. The hardy thane of Hygelac,[3] when his brother lay low, let his broad sword, old blade made by giants, break the great helmet across the shield-wall; then the king bowed, the keeper of the folk was hit to the quick.

"Then there were many who bound up the brother, quickly raised him up after it was granted them to control the battle-field. Then one warrior stripped the other, took from Ongentheow his iron-mail, hard-hilted sword, and his helmet, too; he bore the arms of the hoary one to Hygelac. He accepted that treasure and fairly promised him rewards among the people, and he stood by it thus: the lord of the Geats, the son of Hrethel, when he came home, repaid Wulf and Eofor for their battle-assault with much trea-sure, gave each of them a hundred thousand [units] of land and linked rings: there was no need for any man on middle-earth to blame him for the rewards, since they had performed great deeds. And then he gave Eofor his only daughter as a pledge of friendship—a fair thing for his home.

"That is the feud and the enmity, the death-hatred of men, for which I expect that the people of the Swedes, bold shield-warriors after the fall of princes, will set upon us after they learn that our prince has gone from life, he who before held hoard and kingdom against our enemies, did good to the people, and further still, did what a man should. Now haste is best, that we look on the people's king there and bring him who gave us rings on his way to the funeral pyre. Nor shall only a small share melt with the great-hearted one, but there is a hoard of treasure, gold uncounted, grimly purchased, and rings bought at the last now with his own life. These shall the fire devour, flames enfold—no earl to wear ornament in remembrance, nor any bright maiden add to her beauty with neck-ring; but mournful-hearted, stripped of gold, they shall walk, often, not once, in strange countries—now that the

---

2. The two sons of Wonred, Wulf and Eofor, attacked Ongentheow in turn. Wulf was struck down but not killed by the old Swedish king, who was then slain by Eofor.　　3. I.e., Eofor.

army-leader has laid aside laughter, his game and his mirth. Therefore many a spear, cold in the morning, shall be grasped with fingers, raised by hands; no sound of harp shall waken the warriors, but the dark raven, low over the doomed, shall tell many tales, say to the eagle how he fared at the feast when with the wolf he spoiled the slain bodies."

Thus the bold man was a speaker of hateful news, nor did he much lie in his words or his prophecies. The company all arose. Without joy they went below Earnaness[4] to look on the wonder with welling tears. Then they found on the sand, soulless, keeping his bed of rest, him who in former times had given them rings. Then the last day of the good man had come, when the war-king, prince of the Weather-Geats, died a wonderful death. First they saw the stranger creature, the worm lying loathsome, opposite him in the place. The fire-dragon was grimly terrible with his many colors, burned by the flames; he was fifty feet long in the place where he lay. Once he had joy of the air at night, came back down to seek his den. Then he was made fast by death, had made use of the last of his earth-caves. Beside him stood cups and pitchers, plates and rich swords lay eaten through by rust, just as they had been there in the bosom of the earth for a thousand winters. Then that huge heritage, gold of men of old, was wound in a spell, so that no one of men must touch the ring-hall unless God himself, the True King of Victories—He is men's protection—should grant to whom He wished to open the hoard—whatever man seemed fit to Him.

Then it was seen that the act did not profit him who wrongly kept hidden the handiworks under the wall. The keeper had first slain a man like few others, then the feud had been fiercely avenged. It is a wonder where an earl famed for courage may reach the end of his allotted life—then may dwell no longer in the mead-hall, man with his kin. So it was with Beowulf when he sought quarrels, the barrow's ward: he himself did not then know in what way his parting with the world should come. The great princes who had put it[5] there had laid on it so deep a curse until doomsday that the man who should plunder the place should be guilty of sins, imprisoned in idol-shrines, fixed with hell-bonds, punished with evils—unless the Possessor's favor were first shown the more clearly to him who desired the gold.

Wiglaf spoke, the son of Weohstan: "Often many a man must suffer distress for the will of one man, as has happened to us. We might by no counsel persuade our dear prince, keeper of the kingdom, not to approach the gold-guardian, let him lie where he long was, live in his dwelling to the world's end. He held to his high destiny. The hoard has been made visible, grimly got. What drove the folk-king thither was too powerfully fated. I have been therein and looked at it all, the rare things of the chamber, when it was granted me—not at all friendly was the journey that I was permitted beneath the earth-wall. In haste I seized with my hands a huge burden of hoard-treasures, of great size, bore it out here to my king. He was then still alive, sound-minded and aware. He spoke many things, old man in sorrow, and bade greet you, commanded that for your lord's deeds you make a high barrow in the place of his pyre, large and conspicuous, since he was of men the worthiest warrior through the wide earth, while he might enjoy wealth in his castle.

---

4. The headland near where Beowulf had fought the dragon. 5. The treasure.

"Let us now hasten to see and visit for the second time the heap of precious jewels, the wonder under the walls. I shall direct you so that you may look on enough of them from near at hand—rings and broad gold. Let the bier be made ready, speedily prepared, when we come out, and then let us carry our prince, beloved man, where he shall long dwell in the Ruler's protection."

Then the son of Weohstan, man brave in battle, bade command many warriors, men who owned houses, leaders of the people, that they carry wood from afar for the pyre for the good man. "Now shall flame eat the chief of warriors—the fire shall grow dark—who often survived the iron-shower when the storm of arrows driven from bow-strings passed over the shield-wall—the shaft did its task, made eager by feather-gear served the arrowhead."

And then the wise son of Weohstan summoned from the host thanes of the king, seven together, the best; one of eight warriors, he went beneath the evil roof. One who walked before bore a torch in his hands. Then there was no lot to decide who should plunder that hoard, since the men could see that every part of it rested in the hall without guardian, lay wasting. Little did any man mourn that hastily they should bear out the rare treasure. Also they pushed the dragon, the worm, over the cliff-wall, let the wave take him, the flood enfold the keeper of the treasure. Then twisted gold was loaded on a wagon, an uncounted number of things, and the prince, hoary warrior, borne to Hronesness.

Then the people of the Geats made ready for him a funeral pyre on the earth, no small one, hung with helmets, battle-shields, bright mail-shirts, just as he had asked. Then in the midst they laid the great prince, lamenting their hero, their beloved lord. Then warriors began to awaken on the barrow the greatest of funeral-fires; the wood-smoke climbed, black over the fire; the roaring flame mixed with weeping—the wind-surge died down—until it had broken the bone-house, hot at its heart. Sad in spirit they lamented their heart-care, the death of their liege lord. [And the Geatish woman, wavy-haired, sang a sorrowful song about Beowulf, said][6] again and again that she sorely feared for herself invasions of armies, many slaughters, terror of troops, humiliation, and captivity. Heaven swallowed the smoke.

Then the people of the Weather-Geats built a mound on the promontory, one that was high and broad, wide-seen by seafarers, and in ten days completed a monument for the bold in battle, surrounded the remains of the fire with a wall, the most splendid that men most skilled might devise. In the barrow they placed rings and jewels, all such ornaments as troubled men had earlier taken from the hoard. They let the earth hold the wealth of earls, gold in the ground, where now it still dwells, as useless to men as it was before. Then the brave in battle rode round the mound, children of nobles, twelve in all, would bewail their sorrow and mourn their king, recite dirges and speak of the man. They praised his great deeds and his acts of courage, judged well of his prowess. So it is fitting that man honor his liege lord with words, love him in heart when he must be led forth from the body. Thus the people of the Geats, his hearth-companions, lamented the death of their lord. They said that he was of world-kings the mildest of men and the gentlest, kindest to his people, and most eager for fame.

---

6. The manuscript is badly damaged and the interpretation conjectural.

THE SONG OF ROLAND
ca. 1100

The Song of Roland is the foundational text of the French literary tradition. One of the earliest poems written in French, it describes the process by which France left behind its Germanic past as a loose confederation of powerful families and accepted its future as a Christian nation united by loyalties to king and country. This story is told as a clash of powerful personalities who are together engaged in a holy war against the Muslims in Spain. The central protagonist is the great warrior Roland, who embodies in an especially pure form the spirit of feudal loyalty to one's overlord. The Emperor Charlemagne is the object of this loyalty, but his commitments are split: he owes to Roland a reciprocal loyalty, but he is also the head of the Holy Roman Empire, the institutional heir to classical Rome that is endowed with the mission not merely to defend but to expand Christendom. Opposed to Roland is his uncle Ganelon, a member of Charlemagne's Frankish nobility who believes he can settle a feud with Roland without compromising his loyalty to the king. And surrounding these three main characters are men who provide further perspectives on the central issue of what kind of loyalty is valid. Oliver, Roland's closest companion in arms, criticizes Roland's narrow conception of his duty; Turpin, a warrior archbishop, provides justifications for Roland's actions that may be merely rationalizations; Pinabel, one of Ganelon's kinsmen, comes to his defense when he is charged with treason for his part in Roland's death; and Tierri, a warrior, challenges Pinabel not merely to defend Roland or even Charlemagne but to promote national and supranational loyalties that transcend Ganelon's tribal conception.

Many modern readers have been tempted to read the poem as a kind of medieval *Iliad*, with the heroic yet arrogantly intransigent Roland as a French Achilles. Yet in the manuscript the poem is untitled, Roland dies less than two-thirds of the way through, and the beginning and ending of the poem focus on "Charles the King, our Emperor, the Great." The poem could with equal justice be entitled—as indeed it was in some of its medieval translations—*The Song of Charlemagne*. In fact, the relation of Roland's story to Charles's—the relation, that is, of the heroic acts of one man to the historically transcendent mission of establishing a universal Christian empire—is the poem's overriding theme. Roland embodies the unswerving and reciprocal allegiance that bound together lord and vassal into a stable unit, a relationship that made possible the establishment of the feudal system that, from the tenth through twelfth centuries, came to dominate Europe. From his first appearance in the poem, at the council scene in which the Franks debate whether to accept the offer of the Saracen leader Marsilion to submit to Charles if the Franks will leave Spain, Roland both promotes and himself displays this fidelity. He argues against accepting the offer for three reasons, all of them having to do with loyalty. First, Marsilion has already been proven untrustworthy in fulfilling his sworn oath; second, Basan and Basile, the ambassadors whom Marsilion killed during the previous negotiations, must be avenged (they were, Roland reminds Charles, "*your* men"); and third, Charles must also be true to his commitment to conquer Spain ("Fight the war you came to fight!"), an obligation he owes to God, who has sanctioned this Holy War. Again, the poem's climactic scene, in which the members of the rear guard are ambushed and Roland refuses to blow his horn to call back the army to help them, has often been read as expressing Roland's intemperate and unjustified reliance upon his own prowess. Yet another interpretation, centered on loyalty, is also possible. As the leader of the rear guard, Roland has sworn to protect the army: to call it back now, in the face of overwhelming enemy forces, would be to place it in danger and to betray his commitment. Indeed, when he accepted this dangerous assignment—dangerous because everyone, including Roland, suspected that Ganelon had conspired with the Saracens to set a trap—he promised Charles not victory over any

Saracen attack but rather that he would not lose any part of his baggage train "that has not first been bought and paid for with swords." In other words, Roland swore an oath to fight to the utmost to protect the army, and this he must now do. At this point in the poem he explicitly describes the values that guide his life:

> We know our duty: to stand here for our King.
> A man must bear some hardships for his lord,
> stand everything, the great heat, the great cold,
> lose the hide and hair on him for his good lord.
> Now let each man make sure to strike hard here:
> let them not sing a bad song about us!

Certainly Roland is concerned with personal honor, but this depends above all not on valor but on loyalty: he fights not for himself but "for his good lord." Surprisingly, however, when it is clear that the Saracens have been defeated at the cost of the whole of the rear guard, Roland does blow the horn. Is this an admission that he was wrong before, as his companion Oliver implies? Perhaps; yet Turpin says that Roland should blow the horn to summon Charles so that he may, as is required of a good lord, avenge the deaths of the men who died for him. Moreover, it is this final act of feudal loyalty, and not the wounds inflicted by the Saracens, that kills Roland: the force of the horn blast bursts his temples. As the battle nears its end the poet describes Roland as "a brave man keeping faith," and the religious imagery with which his passing is surrounded makes it clear that, whatever the modern reader may think, the poet wants his audience to approve of Roland's choices. Yet we also cannot forget that Roland has said that his companions died "for me," which could mean simply that they performed their feudal duty to him but could also mean that they died "because of him."

If loyalty is the theme of the poem, it is analyzed rather than simply celebrated. The poem provides three other perspectives from which to make an assessment. One is provided by Oliver. In a famous line, we are told that "Roland is good [*proz*], and Oliver is wise [*sages*]." It is not easy to know exactly what the poet means by these terms. Is Roland primarily a fighter, a man of prowess, while Oliver is a strategist, a man of thought? While the poem is unwilling to criticize Roland's decisions about the horn, it also presents Oliver as capable of a larger, more pragmatic view than his companion. As Oliver urges him to look at the surrounding pagan hordes, Roland gazes instead at his sword, Durendal; as Oliver argues for Charles's need for the twelve peers and the warriors of the rear guard, Roland focuses only on the immediate challenge posed by the Saracen ambush. Roland's intensity and narrow commitment may be necessary for the functioning of the feudal system, but the poet also wants us to know that it is bought at a fearful price, that there are other ways of understanding one's duty.

The same could be said of Ganelon. He is no petty traitor: as the poet says of him at his trial, he would have been "a great man, had he been loyal." His behavior as an ambassador at Marsilion's camp is both shrewd and courageous. In order to accomplish Roland's downfall he must first provoke the now peacefully inclined Marsilion to wrath and then turn his anger against Roland. To this end he takes a calculated risk for the sake of a calculated—but far from guaranteed—result. Insulting Marsilion deliberately, in the name of the emperor, he makes himself the first target of the Saracen king's fury and certainly endangers his own life. Luckily for him, the king's hand is stayed, and the Saracens applaud Ganelon's magnificent courage. We are never told, however, why this otherwise admirable man so loathes Roland that he betrays both his companions and his lord—and himself—in order to bring about his death. Ganelon is Roland's stepfather, and the poet may have known of the legend that made Roland the offspring of an incestuous relationship between Charlemagne and his sister and thus (as with Arthur and Mordred) both his uncle and his father.

But nothing is made of these family relationships, and we are probably on firmer ground to think that Ganelon simply cannot bear Roland's utter self-confidence in his own virtue and prowess. The story—perhaps true, perhaps not—that he tells the Saracen Blancandrin of Roland's plundering expedition, and of his haughty offer to Charles of a bright red apple as a sign that he can deliver to him "the crowns of all earth's kings," is a more reliable indicator of Ganelon's abhorrence than of Roland's character. At his trial Ganelon claims that his betrayal of the rear guard was justified by his formal defiance of Roland: this was a private matter, a feud, and no business of Charles's. But we get no sense that this argument carries much weight with either the Franks or the poet. The reluctance of Charles's council to punish Ganelon comes not from sympathy with his self-justification but from fear of his champion Pinabel. The danger Ganelon presents, then, is that he will return the Franks to a world of private vengeance where might makes right and where the larger interests of the community can be sacrificed to the impulses of its individual members. If Oliver sees the largest view, Ganelon sees the narrowest.

The final perspective we are offered is Charles's. He is in some ways the most complex character in the poem. On the one hand, he is the great Christian emperor, the agent of God in bringing about the unification of the world under the cross. As Roland lies dying, he recites a list of the lands he has brought under Charles's rule—a list that includes not just France but most of Europe, exceeding the boundaries of even the huge empire ruled over by the historical Charlemagne (742–814). This idea of a single Christendom under a divinely authorized emperor was one of the persistent dreams of medieval Christians. It was part of the justification for the crusades, and we will meet it again in Dante's *Divine Comedy*. It also contributed to the incapacity of most medieval Christians to recognize cultural differences as anything other than either threatening or contemptible, an affront to the cultural unity that God desired. In this poem Islamic religion and culture are presented in a degrading travesty: the Saracens are shown as idolaters and worshipers of Muhammad and Apollo, when in fact Islam rejects religious images, regards Muhammad as a prophet, not a god, and is monotheistic. (This ill-informed picture was produced, ironically, at the very time that Christian scholars were beginning to benefit from contact with their far more sophisticated Arab contemporaries, who had direct access to Greek texts, especially those of Aristotle, that were lost to the Latin West.) In any case, the fullest expression of Charles's role as God's agent in spreading Christian rule comes in the battle against Marsilion's overlord Baligant. Omitted in this selection, this battle is presented as an apocalyptic confrontation between good and evil, and Charles's victory is capped by the conversion of Marsilion's queen Bramimonde and her renaming as Juliana.

Yet Charles is also a human being, in some ways the most human in the poem. He is the only character whose inner life is made visible to us, partly in his dreams, partly in the single, sad line he speaks when informed by the angel Gabriel that further campaigns await him: " 'God!' said the King, 'the pains, the labors of my life!' " Charles embodies the weariness that made the Franks vulnerable to Marsilion's and Ganelon's deceptions at the outset, and that led them to want to avoid confronting Ganelon and Pinabel at the end. This is a weariness that is utterly foreign to Roland, that he seems not even to notice much less sympathize with. That the poet allows it so much room in his poem, while acknowledging that it must not be allowed to prevail, is testimony to the breadth of his own sympathies.

The Song of Roland derives ultimately from a historical event. In the year 778 the thirty-six-year-old Charles, then king of the Franks (he did not become the Emperor Charlemagne until 800), entered Spain at the request of an Arabic ruler in revolt against his overlord. But Charles's self-interested intervention in this Muslim civil war went awry, and by the end of July he had decided to return to France. On August 15, as the army made its way through the narrow valleys of the Pyrenees, the rear guard protecting its retreat was annihilated in an ambush set by the native Basques. Among those killed was one Hruodlandus, governor of the marches (or borders) of

Brittany. About 350 years later, between 1125 and 1150, someone wrote out the manuscript that contains the poem that we now call *The Song of Roland*. This manuscript was written in the French spoken at the time in England, a dialect known as Anglo-Norman, but the poem itself was composed in continental French around the year 1100. This date fits well with two contemporary conditions. One is the struggle then under way between the French king Philip I and the powerful barons who were technically subordinate to him but controlled much of what now constitutes France— a struggle that finds a parallel in the poem in the confrontation between Charles and Ganelon. The other is the growing interest in crusading. Throughout the eleventh century French knights fought against the Arab rulers of Spain, and in 1095 Pope Urban urged the nobility of Europe, and especially of France, to direct their martial energies away from their internal wrangling and toward the Holy Land, at the time governed by Muslim "infidels" (although governed in fact in a spirit of religious tolerance). The result was the First Crusade, which succeeded in capturing Jerusalem in 1099, in massacring most of the non-Christian population, and in establishing the French-controlled Kingdom of Jerusalem. *The Song of Roland* is steeped in this crusading spirit: as Roland says, and as the poem continually insists, "Pagans are wrong and Christians are right!"

Although there have been a number of theories, no one really knows how—or why—the story of the ill-fated Hruodlandus survived. It was a traditional story by at least the eleventh century: one later medieval chronicler even tells us that a minstrel called Taillefer sang about Roland to the Norman army of William the Conqueror before the battle of Hastings in 1066. The poem shows unmistakable signs of having emerged from a period of oral composition. As in the Homeric poems and *Beowulf,* many of its phrases are metrical formulas originally combined by an oral poet into complete lines and then larger passages as he re-created the poem anew at each performance (for a fuller account of oral composition, see above, p. 98). As testimony to its oral prehistory, the vocabulary of the whole of *The Song of Roland* comprises only some eighteen hundred words. In its written form the poem is comprised of 291 stanzas, or *laisses* (from the Latin *lectio,* or "reading"); the number of lines in each *laisse* varies widely, but it averages about fourteen. Each line contains ten or eleven syllables, with a strong caesura, or break, in the middle; the lines are then linked by assonance, which means that their final stressed vowels are identical (the final words of lines 1240–42, for example, are *vil, guarit,* and *murir,* the *i* being pronounced the same in each case). Even when written, the poem was almost certainly presented orally by a minstrel, or *jongleur* (like Taillefer), who would accompany himself with a simple stringed instrument. Like *Beowulf,* the poem would be chanted rather than sung, producing an effect of cadenced, ritualistic ceremony. This effect was doubtless enhanced by the so-called *laisses similaires,* groups of *laisses* that repeat, with variations, an especially significant scene or act (see, for example, lines 1049–92). These groups of *laisses* endow such moments with an unavoidable sense of solemnity and consequence.

A scholarly edition, with translation and commentary, is Gerald S. Brault, *The Song of Roland: An Analytical Edition,* 2 vols. (1978). Useful critical discussions are Eugene Vance, *Reading the Song of Roland* (1970), and Robert Francis Cook, *The Sense of the Song of Roland* (1987).

PRONOUNCING GLOSSARY

The following list uses common English syllables to provide rough equivalents of selected words whose pronunciation may be unfamiliar to the general reader.

Aquitaine: *ah-kee-ten*   Durendal: *dur-ahn-dahl*

Blancandrin: *blanh-cahn-drinh*   Geret: *zhehr-ay*

Gerin: *zhehr-inh*

Halteclere: *ahlt-clehr*

Haltille: *ahl-tee*

Malduit: *mahl-dwee*

Marsilion: *mah-seel-yonh*

Munjoie: *munh-zhwah*

Ogier: *oh-zhyay*

Rencesvals: *rahnc-vahl*

Roland: *roh-lanh*

Rousillon: *roo-see-yonh*

Veillantif: *ve-yanh-teef*

From The Song of Roland[1]

1

Charles the King, our Emperor, the Great,
has been in Spain for seven full years,
has conquered the high land down to the sea.
There is no castle that stands against him now,
no wall, no citadel left to break down—   5
except Saragossa, high on a mountain.[2]
King Marsilion holds it, who does not love God,
who serves Mahumet and prays to Apollin.[3]
He cannot save himself: his ruin will find him there. AOI.[4]

2

King Marsilion was in Saragossa.   10
He has gone forth into a grove, beneath its shade,
and he lies down on a block of blue marble,
twenty thousand men, and more, all around him.
He calls aloud to his dukes and his counts:
"Listen, my lords, to the troubles we have.   15
The Emperor Charles of the sweet land of France
has come into this country to destroy us.
I have no army able to give him battle,
I do not have the force to break his force.
Now act like my wise men: give me counsel,   20
save me, save me from death, save me from shame!"
No pagan there has one word to say to him
except Blancandrin, of the castle of Valfunde.

3

One of the wisest pagans was Blancandrin,
brave and loyal, a great mounted warrior,   25
a useful man, the man to aid his lord;

---

1. Translated by Frederick Goldin. Many of Goldin's notes have been adapted for use here.
2. Saragossa, in northeastern Spain, is not actually on a mountaintop. The poet's geography is not always accurate.   3. The Greek god Apollo; but the poet is mistaken, for these people worship only one god, Allah. *Mahumet*: Muhammad, founder of the Islamic religion.   4. These three mysterious letters appear at certain moments throughout the text, 180 times in all. No one has ever adequately explained them, though every reader feels their effect.

said to the King: "Do not give way to panic.
Do this: send Charles, that wild, terrible man,
tokens of loyal service and great friendship:
you will give him bears and lions and dogs,   30
seven hundred camels, a thousand molted hawks,
four hundred mules weighed down with gold and silver,
and fifty carts, to cart it all away:
he'll have good wages for his men who fight for pay.
Say he's made war long enough in this land: 35
let him go home, to France, to Aix, at last—
come Michaelmas[5] you will follow him there,
say you will take their faith, become a Christian,
and be his man with honor, with all you have.
If he wants hostages, why, you'll send them,   40
ten, or twenty, to give him security.
Let us send him the sons our wives have borne.
I'll send my son with all the others named to die.
It is better that they should lose their heads[6]
than that we, Lord, should lose our dignity   45
and our honors—and be turned into beggars!" AOI.

4

Said Blancandrin: "By this right hand of mine
and by this beard that flutters on my chest,
you will soon see the French army disband,
the Franks will go to their own land, to France.   50
When each of them is in his dearest home,
King Charles will be in Aix, in his chapel.
At Michaelmas he will hold a great feast—
that day will come, and then our time runs out,
he'll hear no news, he'll get no word from us.   55
This King is wild, the heart in him is cruel:
he'll take the heads of the hostages we gave.
It is better, Lord, that they lose their heads
than that we lose our bright, our beautiful Spain—
and nothing more for us but misery and pain!"   60
The pagans say: "It may be as he says."

5

King Marsilion brought his counsel to end,
then he summoned Clarin of Balaguét,
Estramarin and Eudropin, his peer,
And Priamun, Guarlan, that bearded one,   65
and Machiner and his uncle Maheu,
and Joüner, Malbien from over-sea,
and Blancandrin, to tell what was proposed.
From the worst of criminals he called these ten.

---

5. The feast of St. Michael, September 29. *Aix:* Aix-la-Chapelle, or Aachen, was the capital of Charlemagne's empire.   6. The speaker expects that the hostages will be killed by the French when the deception becomes clear. Sometime before, hostages sent by the French had been similarly slain (see lines 207–9).

"Barons, my lords, you're to go to Charlemagne;   70
he's at the siege of Cordres,[7] the citadel.
Olive branches are to be in your hands—
that signifies peace and humility.
If you've the skill to get me an agreement,
I will give you a mass of gold and silver   75
and lands and fiefs, as much as you could want."
Say the pagans: "We'll benefit from this!" AOI.

6

Marsilion brought his council to an end,
said to his men: "Lords, you will go on now,
and remember: olive branches in your hands;   80
and in my name tell Charlemagne the King
for his god's sake to have pity on me—
he will not see a month from this day pass
before I come with a thousand faithful;
say I will take that Christian religion   85
and be his man in love and loyalty.
If he wants hostages, why, he'll have them."
Said Blancandrin: "Now you will get good terms." AOI.

7

King Marsilion had ten white mules led out,
sent to him once by the King of Suatilie,[8]   90
with golden bits and saddles wrought with silver.
The men are mounted, the men who brought the message,
and in their hands they carry olive branches.
They came to Charles, who has France in his keeping.
He cannot prevent it: they will fool him. AOI.   95

8

The Emperor is secure and jubilant:
he has taken Cordres, broken the walls,
knocked down the towers with his catapults.
And what tremendous spoils his knights have won—
gold and silver, precious arms, equipment.   100
In the city not one pagan remained
who is not killed or turned into a Christian.
The Emperor is in an ample grove,
Roland and Oliver are with him there,
Samson the Duke and Ansëis the fierce,   105
Geoffrey d'Anjou, the King's own standard-bearer;
and Gerin and Gerer, these two together always,
and the others, the simple knights, in force:
fifteen thousand from the sweet land of France.
The warriors sit on bright brocaded silk;   110
they are playing at tables to pass the time,
the old and the wisest men sitting at chess,

7. Córdoba, in southern Spain, at that time part of the Muslim empire.   8. A subordinate king, owing
allegiance to Marsilion.

the young light-footed men fencing with swords.
Beneath a pine, beside a wild sweet-briar,
there was a throne, every inch of pure gold.   115
There sits the King, who rules over sweet France.
His beard is white, his hair flowering white.
That lordly body! the proud fierce look of him!—
If someone should come here asking for him,
     there'd be no need to point out the King of France.
The messengers dismounted, and on their feet   120
they greeted him in all love and good faith.

9

Blancandrin spoke, he was the first to speak,
said to the King: "Greetings, and God save you,
that glorious God whom we all must adore.
Here is the word of the great king Marsilion: 125
he has looked into this law of salvation,
wants to give you a great part of his wealth,
bears and lions and hunting dogs on chains,
seven hundred camels, a thousand molted hawks,
four hundred mules packed tight with gold and silver,   130
and fifty carts, to cart it all away;
and there will be so many fine gold bezants,[9]
you'll have good wages for the men in your pay.
You have stayed long—long enough!—in this land,
it is time to go home, to France, to Aix.   135
My master swears he will follow you there."
The Emperor holds out his hands toward God,
bows down his head, begins to meditate. AOI.

10

The Emperor held his head bowed down;
never was he too hasty with his words: 140
his custom is to speak in his good time.
When his head rises, how fierce the look of him;
he said to them: "You have spoken quite well.
King Marsilion is my great enemy.
Now all these words that you have spoken here—   145
how far can I trust them? How can I be sure?"
The Saracen: "He wants to give you hostages.
How many will you want? ten? fifteen? twenty?
I'll put my son with the others named to die.[1]
You will get some, I think, still better born.   150
When you are at home in your high royal palace,
at the great feast of Saint Michael-in-Peril,[2]
the lord who nurtures me will follow you,
and in those baths[3]—the baths God made for you—

9. Gold coins; the name is derived from Byzantium.   1. I.e., if the promise is broken. *Saracen:* the usual
term for the enemy.   2. The epithet *in peril of the sea* was applied to the famous sanctuary Mont-St.-
Michel off the Normandy coast because it could be reached on foot only at low tide, and pilgrims were
endangered by the incoming tide. Eventually, the phrase was applied to the saint himself.   3. Famous
healing springs at Aix-la-Chapelle.

my lord will come and want to be made Christian." 155
King Charles replies: "He may yet save his soul." AOI.

11

Late in the day it was fair, the sun was bright.
Charles has them put the ten mules into stables.
The King commands a tent pitched in the broad grove,
and there he has the ten messengers lodged; 160
twelve serving men took splendid care of them.
There they remained that night till the bright day.
The Emperor rose early in the morning,
the King of France, and heard the mass and matins.
And then the King went forth beneath a pine, 165
calls for his barons to complete his council:
he will proceed only with the men of France. AOI.

12

The Emperor goes forth beneath a pine,
calls for his barons to complete his council:
Ogier the Duke, and Archbishop Turpin, 170
Richard the Old, and his nephew Henri;
from Gascony, the brave Count Acelin,
Thibaut of Reims, and his cousin Milun;
and Gerer and Gerin, they were both there,
and there was Count Roland, he came with them, 175
and Oliver, the valiant and well-born;
a thousand Franks of France, and more, were there.
Ganelon came, who committed the treason.
Now here begins the council that went wrong.[4] AOI.

13

"Barons, my lords," said Charles the Emperor, 180
"King Marsilion has sent me messengers,
wants to give me a great mass of his wealth,
bears and lions and hunting dogs on chains,
seven hundred camels, a thousand molting hawks,
four hundred mules packed with gold of Araby, 185
and with all that, more than fifty great carts;
but also asks that I go back to France:
he'll follow me to Aix, my residence,
and take our faith, the one redeeming faith,
become a Christian, hold his march[5] lands from me. 190
But what lies in his heart? I do not know."
And the French say: "We must be on our guard!" AOI.

14

The Emperor has told them what was proposed.
Roland the Count will never assent to that,
gets to his feet, comes forth to speak against it; 195

---

4. The poet anticipates that the plan adopted at the council will prove to be a mistake and that Ganelon will commit treason.   5. A frontier province or territory.

says to the King: "Trust Marsilion—and suffer!
We came to Spain seven long years ago,
I won Noples for you, I won Commibles,
I took Valterne and all the land of Pine,
and Balaguer and Tudela and Seville.   200
And then this king, Marsilion, played the traitor:
he sent you men, fifteen of his pagans—
and sure enough, each held an olive branch;
and they recited just these same words to you.
You took counsel with all your men of France;   205
they counseled you to a bit of madness:
you sent two Counts across to the Pagans,
one was Basan, the other was Basile.
On the hills below Haltille, he took their heads.
They were your men. Fight the war you came to fight!   210
Lead the army you summoned on to Saragossa!
Lay siege to it all the rest of your life!
Avenge the men that this criminal murdered!" AOI.

15

The Emperor held his head bowed down with this,
and stroked his beard, and smoothed his mustache down,   215
and speaks no word, good or bad, to his nephew.
The French keep still, all except Ganelon:
he gets to his feet and, come before King Charles,
how fierce he is as he begins his speech;
said to the King: "Believe a fool—me or   220
another—and suffer! Protect your interest!
When Marsilion the King sends you his word
that he will join his hands[6] and be your man,
and hold all Spain as a gift from your hands
and then receive the faith that we uphold—   225
whoever urges that we refuse this peace,
that man does not care, Lord, what death we die.
That wild man's counsel must not win the day here—
let us leave fools, let us hold with wise men!" AOI.

16

And after that there came Naimon the Duke—   230
no greater vassal in that court than Naimon—
said to the King: "You've heard it clearly now,
Count Ganelon has given you your answer:
let it be heeded, there is wisdom in it.
King Marsilion is beaten in this war,   235
you have taken every one of his castles,
broken his walls with your catapults,
burnt his cities and defeated his men.
Now when he sends to ask you to have mercy,
it would be a sin to do still more to him.   240
Since he'll give you hostages as guarantee,

6. Part of the gesture of homage; the lord enclosed the joined hands of his vassal with his own.

this great war must not go on, it is not right."
And the French say: "The Duke has spoken well." AOI.

17

"Barons, my lords, whom shall we send down there,
to Saragossa, to King Marsilion?"   245
Naimon replies, "I'll go, if you grant it!
At once, my lord! give me the glove and the staff."[7]
The King replies: "You're a man of great wisdom:
now by my beard, now by this mustache of mine,
you will not go so far from me this year; or ever.   250
Go take your seat when no one calls on you."

18

"Barons, my lords, whom can we send down there,
to this Saracen who holds Saragossa?"
Roland replies: "I can go there! No trouble!"
"No, no, not you!" said Oliver the Count,   255
"that heart in you is wild, spoils for a fight,
how I would worry—you'd fight with them, I know.
Now I myself could go, if the King wishes."
The King replies: "Be still, the two of you!
Not you, not he—neither will set foot there.   260
Now by this beard, as sure as you see white,
let no man here name one of the Twelve Peers!"
The French keep still, see how he silenced them.

19

Turpin of Reims has come forth from the ranks,
said to the King: "Let your Franks have a rest.   265
You have been in this land for seven years,
the many pains, the struggles they've endured!
I'm the one, Lord, give me the glove and the staff,
and I'll go down to this Saracen of Spain
and then I'll see what kind of man we have."   270
The Emperor replies to him in anger:
"Now you go back and sit on that white silk
and say no more unless I command it!" AOI.

20

"My noble knights," said the Emperor Charles,
"choose me one man: a baron from my march,[8]   275
to bring my message to King Marsilion."
And Roland said: "Ganelon, my stepfather."
The French respond: "Why, that's the very man!
pass this man by and you won't send a wiser."
And hearing this Count Ganelon began to choke,   280
pulls from his neck the great furs of marten
and stands there now, in his silken tunic,

---

7. Symbols of his commission from the Emperor Charles.   8. Charlemagne wants them to choose a
baron from an outlying region and not one of the Twelve Peers, the circle of his dearest men.

eyes full of lights, the look on him of fury,
he has the body, the great chest of a lord;
stood there so fair, all his peers gazed on him;   285
said to Roland: "Madman, what makes you rave?
Every man knows I am your stepfather,
yet you named me to go to Marsilion.
Now if God grants that I come back from there,
you will have trouble: I'll start a feud with you,   290
it will go on till the end of your life."
Roland replies: "What wild words—all that blustering!
Every man knows that threats don't worry me.
But we need a wise man to bring the message:
if the King wills, I'll gladly go in your place."   295

21

Ganelon answers: "You will not go for me. AOI.
You're not my man, and I am not your lord.
Charles commands me to perform this service:
I'll go to Marsilion in Saragossa.
And I tell you, I'll play a few wild tricks   300
before I cool the anger in me now."
When he heard that, Roland began to laugh. AOI.

22

Ganelon sees: *Roland laughing at him!*
and feels such pain he almost bursts with rage,
needs little more to go out of his mind;   305
says to the Count: "I have no love for you,
you *made* this choice fall on me, and that was wrong.
Just Emperor, here I am, before you.
I have one will: to fulfill your command."

23

"I know now I must go to Saragossa. AOI.   310
Any man who goes there cannot return.
And there is this: I am your sister's husband,
have a son by her, the finest boy there can be,
Baldewin," says he, "who will be a good man.
To him I leave my honors, fiefs, and lands.   315
Protect my son: these eyes will never see him."
Charles answers him: "That tender heart of yours!
You have to go, I have commanded it."

24

And the King said: "Ganelon, come forward, AOI.
come and receive the staff and the glove.   320
You have heard it: the Franks have chosen you."
Said Ganelon: "Lord, it's Roland who did this.
In all my days I'll have no love for him,
or Oliver, because he's his companion,
or the Twelve Peers, because they love him so.   325

I defy them, here in your presence, Lord."
And the King said: "What hate there is in you!
You will go there, for I command you to."
"I can go there, but I'll have no protector. AOI.
Basile had none, nor did Basan his brother." 330

25

The Emperor offers him his right glove.
But Ganelon would have liked not to be there.
When he had to take it, it fell to the ground.
"God!" say the French, "What's that going to mean?
What disaster will this message bring us!" 335
Said Ganelon: "Lords, you'll be hearing news."

26

Said Ganelon: "Lord, give me leave to go,
since go I must, there's no reason to linger."
And the King said: "In Jesus' name and mine,"
absolved him and blessed him with his right hand. 340
Then he gave him the letter and the staff.

27

Count Ganelon goes away to his camp.
He chooses, with great care, his battle-gear,
picks the most precious arms that he can find.
The spurs he fastened on were golden spurs; 345
he girds his sword, Murgleis, upon his side;
he has mounted Tachebrun, his battle horse,
his uncle, Guinemer, held the stirrup.
And there you would have seen brave men in tears,
his men, who say: "Baron, what bad luck for you! 350
All your long years in the court of the King,
always proclaimed a great and noble vassal!
Whoever it was doomed you to go down there—
Charlemagne himself will not protect that man.
Roland the Count should not have thought of this— 355
and you the living issue of a mighty line!"
And then they say: "Lord, take us there with you!"
Ganelon answers: "May the Lord God forbid!
It is better that I alone should die
    than so many good men and noble knights.
You will be going back, Lords, to sweet France: 360
go to my wife and greet her in my name,
and Pinabel, my dear friend and peer,
and Baldewin, my son, whom you all know:
give him your aid, and hold him as your lord."
And he starts down the road; he is on his way. AOI. 365

28

Ganelon rides to a tall olive tree,
there he has joined the pagan messengers.

And here is Blancandrin, who slows down for him:
and what great art they speak to one another.
Said Blancandrin: "An amazing man, Charles!   370
conquered Apulia, conquered all of Calabria,
crossed the salt sea on his way into England,
won its tribute,[9] got Peter's pence[1] for Rome:
what does he want from us here in our march?"
Ganelon answers: "That is the heart in him.   375
There'll never be a man the like of him." AOI.

29

Said Blancandrin: "The Franks are a great people.
Now what great harm all those dukes and counts do
to their own lord when they give him such counsel:
they torment him, they'll destroy him, and others."   380
Ganelon answers: "Well, now, I know no such man
except Roland, who'll suffer for it yet.
One day the Emperor was sitting in the shade:
his nephew came, still wearing his hauberk,
he had gone plundering near Carcassonne;   385
and in his hand he held a bright red apple:
'Dear Lord, here, take,' said Roland to his uncle;
'I offer you the crowns of all earth's kings.'
Yes, Lord, that pride of his will destroy him,
for every day he goes riding at death.   390
And *should* someone kill him, we would have peace." AOI.

30

Said Blancandrin: "A wild man, this Roland!
wants to make every nation beg for his mercy
and claims a right to every land on earth!
But what men support him, if that is his aim?"   395
Ganelon answers: "Why, Lord, the men of France.
They love him so, they will never fail him.
He gives them gifts, masses of gold and silver,
mules, battle horses, brocaded silks, supplies.
And it is all as the Emperor desires: 400
he'll win the lands from here to the Orient." AOI.

31

Ganelon and Blancandrin rode on until
each pledged his faith to the other and swore
they'd find a way to have Count Roland killed.
They rode along the paths and ways until,   405
in Saragossa, they dismount beneath a yew.
There was a throne in the shade of a pine,
covered with silk from Alexandria.
There sat the king who held the land of Spain,

9. Although begun perhaps as early as the eighth century, the tribute was not the result of any effort of Charlemagne, who did not in fact visit England.   1. A tribute of one penny per house "for the use of Saint Peter," i.e., for the pope in Rome.

and around him twenty thousand Saracens.   410
There is no man who speaks or breathes a word,
poised for the news that all would like to hear.
Now here they are: Ganelon and Blancandrin.

32

Blancandrin came before Marsilion,
his hand around the fist of Ganelon,   415
said to the King: "May Mahumet save you,
and Apollin, whose sacred laws we keep!
We delivered your message to Charlemagne:
when we finished, he raised up both his hands
and praised his god. He made no other answer.   420
Here he sends you one of his noble barons,
a man of France, and very powerful.
You'll learn from him whether or not you'll have peace."
"Let him speak, we shall hear him," Marsilion answers. AOI.

33

But Ganelon had it all well thought out.   425
With what great art he commences his speech,
a man who knows his way about these things;
said to the King: "May the Lord God save you,
that glorious God, whom we must all adore.
Here is the word of Charlemagne the King: 430
you are to take the holy Christian faith;
he will give you one half of Spain in fief.
If you refuse, if you reject this peace,
you will be taken by force, put into chains,
and then led forth to the King's seat at Aix;   435
you will be tried; you will be put to death:
you will die there, in shame, vilely, degraded."
King Marsilion, hearing this, was much shaken.
In his hand was a spear, with golden feathers.
He would have struck, had they not held him back. AOI.   440

34

Marsilion the King—his color changed!
He shook his spear, waved the shaft to and fro.
When he saw that, Ganelon laid hand to sword,
he drew it out two fingers from its sheath;
and spoke to it: "How beautiful and bright!   445
How long did I bear you in the King's court
before I died! The Emperor will not say
I died alone in that foreign country:
they'll buy you first, with the best men they have!"
The pagans say: "Let us break up this quarrel!"   450

35

The pagan chiefs pleaded with Marsilion
till he sat down once again on his throne.

The Caliph[2] spoke: "You did us harm just now,
served us badly, trying to strike this Frenchman.
You should have listened, you should have heard him out."   455
Said Ganelon: "Lord, I must endure it.
I shall not fail, for all the gold God made,
for all the wealth there may be in this land,
to tell him, as long as I have breath, all
that Charlemagne—that great and mighty King!—   460
has sent through me to his mortal enemy."
He is buckled in a great cloak of sable,
covered with silk from Alexandria:
he throws it down. Blancandrin picks it up.
But his great sword he will never throw down!   465
In his right fist he grasps its golden pommel.
Say the pagans: "That's a great man! A noble!" AOI.

36

Now Ganelon drew closer to the King
and said to him: "You are wrong to get angry,
for Charles, who rules all France, sends you this word: 470
you are to take the Christian people's faith;
he will give you one half of Spain in fief,
the other half goes to his nephew: Roland—
quite a partner you will be getting there!
If you refuse, if you reject this peace,   475
he will come and lay siege to Saragossa;
you will be taken by force, put into chains,
and brought straight on to Aix, the capital.
No saddle horse, no war horse for you then,
no he-mule, no she-mule for you to ride: 480
you will be thrown on some miserable dray;
you will be tried, and you will lose your head.
Our Emperor sends you this letter."
He put the letter in the pagan's right fist.

37

Marsilion turned white; he was enraged;   485
he breaks the seal, he's knocked away the wax,
runs through the letter, sees what is written there:
"Charles sends me word, this king who rules in France:
I'm to think of his anger and his grief—
he means Basan and his brother Basile,   490
I took their heads in the hills below Haltille;
if I want to redeem the life of my body,
I must send him my uncle: the Algalife.[3]
And otherwise he'll have no love for me."
Then his son came and spoke to Marsilion,   495
said to the King: 'Ganelon has spoken madness.
He crossed the line, he has no right to live.
Give him to me, I will do justice on him."

2. A high official of King Marsilion.   3. The Caliph.

When he heard that, Ganelon brandished his sword;
he runs to the pine, set his back against the trunk.   500

38

King Marsilion went forth into the orchard,
he takes with him the greatest of his men;
Blancandrin came, that gray-haired counselor,
and Jurfaleu, Marsilion's son and heir,
the Algalife, uncle and faithful friend.   505
Said Blancandrin: "Lord, call the Frenchman back.
He swore to me to keep faith with our cause."
And the King said: "Go, bring him back here, then."
He took Ganelon's right hand by the fingers,
leads him into the orchard before the King.   510
And there they plotted that criminal treason. AOI.

39

Said Marsilion: "My dear Lord Ganelon,
that was foolish, what I just did to you,
I showed my anger, even tried to strike you.
Here's a pledge of good faith, these sable furs,   515
the gold alone worth over five hundred pounds:
I'll make it all up before tomorrow night."
Ganelon answers: "I will not refuse it.
May it please God to reward you for it." AOI.

40

Said Marsilion: "I tell you, Ganelon,   520
I have a great desire to love you dearly.
I want to hear you speak of Charlemagne.
He is so old, he's used up all his time—
from what I hear, he is past two hundred!
He has pushed his old body through so many lands,   525
taken so many blows on his buckled shield,
made beggars of so many mighty kings:
when will he lose the heart for making war?"
Ganelon answers: "Charles is not one to lose heart.
No man sees him, no man learns to know him   530
who does not say: the Emperor is great.
I do not know how to praise him so highly
that his great merit would not surpass my praise.
Who could recount his glory and his valor?
God put the light in him of such lordliness,   535
he would choose death before he failed his barons."

41

Said the pagan: "I have reason to marvel
at Charlemagne, a man so old and gray—
he's two hundred years old, I hear, and more;
he has tortured his body through so many lands,   540
and borne so many blows from lance and spear,

made beggars of so many mighty kings:
when will he lose the heart for making war?"
"Never," said Ganelon, "while his nephew lives,
he's a fighter, there's no vassal like him
   under the vault of heaven. And he has friends.   545
There's Oliver, a good man, his companion.
And the Twelve Peers, whom Charles holds very dear,
form the vanguard, with twenty thousand knights.
Charles is secure, he fears no man on earth." AOI.

42

Said the pagan: "Truly, how I must marvel   550
at Charlemagne, who is so gray and white—
over two hundred years, from what I hear;
gone through so many lands a conqueror,
and borne so many blows from strong sharp spears,
killed and conquered so many mighty kings: 555
when will he lose the heart for making war?"
"Never," said Ganelon, "while one man lives: Roland!
no man like him from here to the Orient!
There's his companion, Oliver, a brave man.
And the Twelve Peers, whom Charles holds very dear,   560
form the vanguard, with twenty thousand Franks.
Charles is secure, he fears no man alive." AOI.

43

"Dear Lord Ganelon," said Marsilion the King,
"I have my army, you won't find one more handsome:
I can muster four hundred thousand knights!   565
With this host, now, can I fight Charles and the French?"
Ganelon answers: "No, no, don't try that now,
you'd take a loss: thousands of your pagans!
Forget such foolishness, listen to wisdom:
send the Emperor so many gifts   570
there'll be no Frenchman there who does not marvel.
For twenty hostages—those you'll be sending—
he will go home: home again to sweet France!
And he will leave his rear-guard behind him.
There will be Roland, I do believe, his nephew,   575
and Oliver, brave man, born to the court.
These Counts are dead, if anyone trusts me.
Then Charles will see that great pride of his go down,
he'll have no heart to make war on you again." AOI.

44

"Dear Lord Ganelon," said Marsilion the King,   580
"What must I do to kill Roland the Count?"
Ganelon answers: "Now I can tell you that.
The King will be at Cize,[4] in the great passes,

---

4. The pass through the Pyrenees.

he will have placed his rear-guard at his back:
there'll be his nephew, Count Roland, that great man,   585
and Oliver, in whom he puts such faith,
and twenty thousand Franks in their company.
Now send one hundred thousand of your pagans
against the French—let them give the first battle.
The French army will be hit hard and shaken.   590
I must tell you: your men will be martyred.
Give them a second battle, then, like the first.
One will get him, Roland will not escape.
Then you'll have done a deed, a noble deed,
and no more war for the rest of your life!" AOI.   595

45

"If someone can bring about the death of Roland,
then Charles would lose the right arm of his body,
that marvelous army would disappear—
never again could Charles gather such forces.
Then peace at last for the Land of Fathers!"[5]   600
When Marsilion heard that, he kissed his neck.
Then he begins to open up his treasures. AOI.

46

Marsilion said, "Why talk. . . .
No plan has any worth which one. . . . [6]
Now swear to me that you will betray Roland."   605
Ganelon answers: "Let it be as you wish."
On the relics in his great sword Murgleis
he swore treason and became a criminal. AOI.

47

There stood a throne made all of ivory.
Marsilion commands them bring forth a book: 610
it was the law of Mahum and Tervagant.[7]
This is the vow sworn by the Saracen of Spain:
if he shall find Roland in the rear-guard,
he shall fight him, all his men shall fight him,
and once he finds Roland, Roland will die.   615
Says Ganelon: "May it be as you will." AOI.

48

And now there came a pagan, Valdabrun,
he was the man who raised Marsilion.
And, all bright smiles, he said to Ganelon:
"You take my sword, there's no man has one better: 620
a thousand coins, and more, are in the hilt.
It is a gift, dear lord, made in friendship,
only help us to Roland, that great baron,

---

5. *Tere Major,* in the original; it can mean either "the great land" or "the land of fathers, ancestors." It always refers to France.   6. Parts of lines 603–4 are unintelligible in the manuscript.   7. A fictitious deity whom the poet mistakenly says the Saracens worshiped.

let us find him standing in the rear-guard."
"It shall be done," replies Count Ganelon.   625
And then they kissed, on the face, on the chin.

49

And there came then a pagan, Climborin,
and, all bright smiles, he said to Ganelon:
"You take my helmet, I never saw one better,
only help us to Roland, lord of the march,   630
show us the way to put Roland to shame."
"It shall be done," replied Count Ganelon.
And then they kissed, on the face, on the mouth. AOI.

50

And then there came the Queen, Bramimunde;
said to the Count: "Lord, I love you well,   635
for my lord and all his men esteem you so.
I wish to send your wife two necklaces,
they are all gold, jacinths, and amethysts,
they are worth more than all the wealth of Rome.
Your Emperor has never seen their like."   640
He has taken them, thrusts them into his boot. AOI.

51

The King calls for Malduit, his treasurer:
"The gifts for Charles—is everything prepared?"
And he replies: "Yes, Lord, and well prepared:
seven hundred camels, packed with gold and silver,   645
and twenty hostages, the noblest under heaven." AOI.

52

Marsilion took Ganelon by the shoulder
and said to him: "You're a brave man, a wise man.
Now by that faith you think will save your soul,
take care you do not turn your heart from us.   650
I will give you a great mass of my wealth,
ten mules weighed down with fine Arabian gold;
and come each year, I'll do the same again.
Now you take these, the keys to this vast city:
present King Charles with all of its great treasure;   655
then get me Roland picked for the rear-guard.
Let me find him in some defile or pass,
I will fight him, a battle to the death."
Ganelon answers: "It's high time that I go."
Now he is mounted, and he is on his way. AOI.   660

53

The Emperor moves homeward, he's drawing near.
Now he has reached the city of Valterne:
Roland had stormed it, destroyed it, and it stood
from that day forth a hundred years laid waste.

Charles is waiting for news of Ganelon   665
and the tribute from Spain, from that great land.
In the morning, at dawn, with the first light,
Count Ganelon came to the Christian camp. AOI.

54

The Emperor rose early in the morning,
the King of France, and has heard mass and matins.   670
On the green grass he stood before his tent.
Roland was there, and Oliver, brave man,
Naimon the Duke, and many other knights.
Ganelon came, the traitor, the foresworn.
With what great cunning he commences his speech;   675
said to the King: "May the Lord God save you!
Here I bring you the keys to Saragossa.
And I bring you great treasure from that city,
and twenty hostages, have them well guarded.
And good King Marsilion sends you this word: 680
Do not blame him concerning the Algalife:
I saw it all myself, with my own eyes:
      four hundred thousand men, and all in arms,
their hauberks on, some with their helms laced on,
swords on their belts, the hilts enameled gold,
who went with him to the edge of the sea.   685
They are in flight: it is the Christian faith—
they do not want it, they will not keep its law.
They had not sailed four full leagues out to sea
when a high wind, a tempest swept them up.
They were all drowned; you will never see them;   690
if he were still alive, I'd have brought him.
As for the pagan King, Lord, believe this:
before you see one month from this day pass,
he'll follow you to the Kingdom of France
and take the faith—he will take your faith, Lord,   695
and join his hands and become your vassal.
He will hold Spain as a fief from your hand."
Then the King said: "May God be thanked for this.
You have done well, you will be well rewarded."
Throughout the host they sound a thousand trumpets.   700
The French break camp, strap their gear on their pack-horses.
They take the road to the sweet land of France. AOI.

55

King Charlemagne laid waste the land of Spain,
stormed its castles, ravaged its citadels.
The King declares his war is at an end.   705
The Emperor rides toward the land of sweet France.
Roland the Count affixed the gonfanon,[8]
raised it toward heaven on the height of a hill;

8. Pennant.

the men of France make camp across that country.
Pagans are riding up through these great valleys, 710
their hauberks on, their tunics of double mail,
their helms laced on, their swords fixed on their belts,
shields on their necks, lances trimmed with their banners.
In a forest high in the hills they gathered:
four hundred thousand men waiting for dawn. 715
God, the pity of it! the French do not know! AOI.

56

The day goes by; now the darkness of night.
Charlemagne sleeps, the mighty Emperor.
He dreamt he was at Cize, in the great passes,
and in his fists held his great ashen lance. 720
Count Ganelon tore it away from him
and brandished it, shook it with such fury
the splinters of the shaft fly up toward heaven.
Charlemagne sleeps, his dream does not wake him.

57

And after that he dreamed another vision: 725
he was in France, in his chapel at Aix,
a cruel wild boar was biting his right arm;
saw coming at him—from the Ardennes—a leopard,
it attacked him, fell wildly on his body.
And a swift hound running down from the hall 730
came galloping, bounding over to Charles,
tore the right ear off that first beast, the boar,
turns, in fury, to fight against the leopard.
And the French say: It is a mighty battle,
but cannot tell which one of them will win. 735
Charlemagne sleeps, his dream does not wake him. AOI.

58

The day goes by, and the bright dawn arises.
Throughout that host. . . . [9]
The Emperor rides forth with such fierce pride.
"Barons, my lords," said the Emperor Charles, 740
"look at those passes, at those narrow defiles—
pick me a man to command the rear-guard."
Ganelon answers: "Roland, here, my stepson.
You have no baron as great and brave as Roland."
When he hears that, the King stares at him in fury; 745
and said to him: "You are the living devil,
a mad dog—the murderous rage in you!
And who will precede me, in the vanguard?"
Ganelon answers, "Why, Ogier of Denmark,
you have no baron who could lead it so well." 750

9. Rest of line unintelligible in the manuscript.

59

Roland the Count, when he heard himself named,
knew what to say, and spoke as a knight must speak:
"Lord Stepfather, I have to cherish you!
You have had the rear-guard assigned to me.
Charles will not lose, this great King who rules France,   755
I swear it now, one palfrey, one war horse—
    while I'm alive and know what's happening—
one he-mule, one she-mule that he might ride,
Charles will not lose one sumpter, not one pack horse
that has not first been bought and paid for with swords."
Ganelon answers: "You speak the truth, I know." AOI.   760

60

When Roland hears he will lead the rear-guard,
he spoke in great fury to his stepfather:
"Hah! you nobody, you base-born little fellow,
and did you think the glove would fall from my hands
as the staff fell[1] from yours before King Charles?" AOI.   765

61

"Just Emperor," said Roland, that great man,
"give me the bow that you hold in your hand.
And no man here, I think, will say in reproach
I let it drop, as Ganelon let the staff drop[2]
from his right hand, when he should have taken it."   770
The Emperor bowed down his head with this,
he pulled his beard, he twisted his mustache,
cannot hold back, tears fill his eyes, he weeps.

62

And after that there came Naimon the Duke,
no greater vassal in the court than Naimon,   775
said to the King: "You've heard it clearly now:
it is Count Roland. How furious he is.
He is the one to whom the rear-guard falls,
no baron here can ever change that now.
Give him the bow that you have stretched and bent,   780
and then find him good men to stand with him."
The King gives him the bow; Roland has it now.

63

The Emperor calls forth Roland the Count:
"My lord, my dear nephew, of course you know
I will give you half my men, they are yours.   785
Let them serve you, it is your salvation."
"None of that!" said the Count. "May God strike me
if I discredit the history of my line.

---

1. Ganelon had let fall a glove, not a staff (line 333). For this and other less objective reasons, some editors have questioned the authenticity of this *laisse*.   2. In this *laisse* a reviser tried to make the text more consistent by adding the reference to the staff.

I'll keep twenty thousand Franks—they are good men.
Go your way through the passes, you will be safe. 790
You must not fear any man while I live."

64

Roland the Count mounted his battle horse. AOI.
Oliver came to him, his companion.
And Gerin came, and the brave Count Gerer,
and Aton came, and there came Berenger, 795
and Astor came, and Anseïs, fierce and proud,
and the old man Gerard of Roussillon,
and Gaifier, that great and mighty duke.
Said the Archbishop: "I'm going, by my head!"
"And I with you," said Gautier the Count, 800
"I am Count Roland's man and must not fail him."
And together they choose twenty thousand men. AOI.

65

Roland the Count summons Gautier de l'Hum:
"Now take a thousand Franks from our land, France,
and occupy those passes and the heights there. 805
The Emperor must not lose a single man." AOI.
Gautier replies: "Lord, I'll fight well for you."
And with a thousand French of France, their land,
Gautier rides out to the hills and defiles;
will not come down, for all the bad news, again, 810
till seven hundred swords have been drawn out.
King Almaris of the Kingdom of Belferne
gave them battle that day, and it was bitter.

66

High are the hills, the valleys tenebrous,
the cliffs are dark, the defiles mysterious. 815
That day, and with much pain, the French passed through.
For fifteen leagues around one heard their clamor.
When they reach Tere Majur, the Land of Fathers,
they beheld Gascony, their lord's domain.
Then they remembered: their fiefs, their realms, their honors, 820
remembered their young girls, their gentle wives:
not one who does not weep for what he feels.
Beyond these others King Charles is in bad straits:
his nephew left in the defiles of Spain!
feels the pity of it; tears break through. AOI. 825

67

And the Twelve Peers are left behind in Spain,
and twenty thousand Franks are left with them.
They have no fear, they have no dread of death.
The Emperor is going home to France.
Beneath his cloak, his face shows all he feels. 830
Naimon the Duke is riding beside him;

and he said to the King: "What is this grief?"
And Charles replies: "Whoever asks me, wrongs me.
I feel such pain, I cannot keep from wailing.
France will be destroyed by Ganelon.   835
Last night I saw a vision brought by angels:
the one who named my nephew for the rear-guard
shattered the lance between my fists to pieces.
I have left him in a march among strangers.
If I lose him, God! I won't find his like." AOI.   840

68

King Charles the Great cannot keep from weeping.
A hundred thousand Franks feel pity for him;
and for Roland, an amazing fear.
Ganelon the criminal has betrayed him;
got gifts for it from the pagan king,   845
gold and silver, cloths of silk, gold brocade,
mules and horses and camels and lions.
Marsilion sends for the barons of Spain,
counts and viscounts and dukes and almaçurs,
and the emirs,[3] and the sons of great lords: 850
four hundred thousand assembled in three days.
In Saragossa he has them beat the drums,
they raise Mahumet upon the highest tower:
no pagan now who does not worship him
and adore him. Then they ride, racing each other,   855
search through the land, the valleys, the mountains;
and then they saw the banners of the French.
The rear-guard of the Twelve Companions
will not fail now, they'll give the pagans battle.

69

Marsilion's nephew has come forward   860
riding a mule that he goads with a stick;
said—a warrior's laugh on him—to his uncle:
"Dear Lord and King, how long I have served you,
and all the troubles, the pains I have endured,
so many battles fought and won on the field   865
Give me a fief, the first blow at Roland.
I will kill him, here's the spear I'll do it with.
If Mahumet will only stand by me,
I will set free every strip of land in Spain,
from the passes of Aspre to Durestant.   870
Charles will be weary, his Franks will give it up:
and no more war for the rest of your life!"
King Marsilion gave him his glove, as sign. AOI.

70

The King's nephew holds the glove in his fist,
speaks these proud words to Marsilion his uncle: 875
"You've given me, dear Lord, King, a great gift!

3. All lords of high rank.

Choose me twelve men, twelve of your noble barons,
and I will fight against the Twelve Companions."
And Falsaron was the first to respond—
he was the brother of King Marsilion: 880
"Dear Lord, Nephew, it's you and I together!
We'll fight, that's sure! We'll battle the rear-guard
of Charlemagne's grand army! We are the ones!
We have been chosen. We'll kill them all! It is fated." AOI.

71

And now again: there comes King Corsablis,   885
a Berber, a bad man, a man of cunning;
and now he spoke as a brave vassal speaks:
for all God's gold he would not be a coward.
Now rushing up: Malprimis de Brigal,
faster on his two feet than any horse;   890
and cries great-voiced before Marsilion:
"I'm on my way to Rencesvals to fight!
Let me find Roland, I won't stop till I kill him!"

[Lines 894–993 continue the roll call of volunteers.]

79

They arm themselves in Saracen hauberks,
all but a few are lined with triple mail;   995
they lace on their good helms of Saragossa,
gird on their swords, the steel forged in Vienne;
they have rich shields, spears of Valencia,
and gonfanons of white and blue and red.
They leave the mules and riding horses now,   1000
mount their war horses and ride in close array.
The day was fair, the sun was shining bright,
all their armor was aflame with the light;
a thousand trumpets blow: that was to make it finer.
That made a great noise, and the men of France heard.   1005
Said Oliver: "Companion, I believe
we may yet have a battle with the pagans."
Roland replies: "Now may God grant us that.
We know our duty: to stand here for our King.
A man must bear some hardships for his lord,   1010
stand everything, the great heat, the great cold,
lose the hide and hair on him for his good lord.
Now let each man make sure to strike hard here:
let them not sing a bad song about us!
Pagans are wrong and Christians are right!   1015
They'll make no bad example of me this day!" AOI.

80

Oliver climbs to the top of a hill,
looks to his right, across a grassy vale,
sees the pagan army on its way there;
and called down to Roland, his companion: 1020

"That way, toward Spain: the uproar I see coming!
All their hauberks, all blazing, helmets like flames!
It will be a bitter thing for our French.
Ganelon knew, that criminal, that traitor,
when he marked us out before the Emperor."   1025
"Be still, Oliver," Roland the Count replies.
"He is my stepfather—my stepfather.
      I won't have you speak one word against him."

81

Oliver has gone up upon a hill,
sees clearly now: the kingdom of Spain,
and the Saracens assembled in such numbers: 1030
helmets blazing, bedecked with gems in gold,
those shields of theirs, those hauberks sewn with brass,
and all their spears, the gonfanons affixed;
cannot begin to count their battle corps,
there are too many, he cannot take their number.   1035
And he is deeply troubled by what he sees.
He made his way quickly down from the hill,
came to the French, told them all he had seen.

82

Said Oliver: "I saw the Saracens,
no man on earth ever saw more of them—   1040
one hundred thousand, with their shields, up in front,
helmets laced on, hauberks blazing on them,
the shafts straight up, the iron heads like flames—
you'll get a battle, nothing like it before.
My lords, my French, may God give you the strength.   1045
Hold your ground now! Let them not defeat us!"
And the French say: "God hate the man who runs!
We may die here, but no man will fail you." AOI.

83

Said Oliver: "The pagan force is great;
from what I see, our French here are too few.   1050
Roland, my companion, sound your horn then,
Charles will hear it, the army will come back."
Roland replies: "I'd be a fool to do it.
I would lose my good name all through sweet France.
I will strike now, I'll strike with Durendal,   1055
the blade will be bloody to the gold from striking!
These pagan traitors came to these passes doomed!
I promise you, they are marked men, they'll die." AOI.

84

"Roland, Companion, now sound the olifant,[4]
Charles will hear it, he will bring the army,   1060

4. A form of *elephant*, which means "ivory" or "a horn made of ivory." It is used specifically, almost as a proper name, to denote Roland's horn, made of an elephant's tusk and adorned with gold and jewels about the rim.

the King will come with all his barons to help us."
Roland replies: "May it never please God
that my kin should be shamed because of me,
or that sweet France should fall into disgrace.
Never! Never! I'll strike with Durendal,   1065
I'll strike with this good sword strapped to my side,
you'll see this blade running its whole length with blood.
These pagan traitors have gathered here to die.
I promise you, they are all bound for death." AOI.

85

"Roland, Companion, sound your olifant now,   1070
Charles will hear it, marching through those passes.
I promise you, the Franks will come at once."
Roland replies: "May it never please God
that any man alive should come to say
that pagans—pagans!—once made me sound this horn: 1075
no kin of mine will ever bear that shame.
Once I enter this great battle coming
and strike my thousand seven hundred blows,
you'll see the bloody steel of Durendal.
These French are good—they will strike like brave men.   1080
Nothing can save the men of Spain from death."

86

Said Oliver: "I see no blame in it—
I watched the Saracens coming from Spain,
the valleys and mountains covered with them,
every hillside and every plain all covered,   1085
hosts and hosts everywhere of those strange men—
and here we have a little company."
Roland replies: "That whets my appetite.
May it not please God and his angels and saints
to let France lose its glory because of me—   1090
let me not end in shame, let me die first.
The Emperor loves us when we fight well."

87

Roland is good, and Oliver is wise,
both these vassals men of amazing courage:
once they are armed and mounted on their horses,   1095
they will not run, though they die for it, from battle.
Good men, these Counts, and their words full of spirit.
Traitor pagans are riding up in fury.
Said Oliver: "Roland, look—the first ones,
on top of us—and Charles is far away.   1100
You did not think it right to sound your olifant:
if the King were here, we'd come out without losses.
Now look up there, toward the passes of Aspre—
you can see the rear-guard: it will suffer.
No man in that detail will be in another."   1105
Roland replies: "Don't speak such foolishness—

shame on the heart gone coward in the chest.
We'll hold our ground, we'll stand firm—we're the ones!
We'll fight with spears, we'll fight them hand to hand!" AOI.

88

When Roland sees that there will be a battle,   1110
it makes him fiercer than a lion or leopard;
shouts to the French, calls out to Oliver:
"Lord, companion: friend, do not say such things.
The Emperor, who left us these good French,
had set apart these twenty thousand men: 1115
he knew there was no coward in their ranks.
A man must meet great troubles for his lord,
stand up to the great heat and the great cold,
give up some flesh and blood—it is his duty.
Strike with the lance, I'll strike with Durendal—   1120
it was the King who gave me this good sword!
If I die here, the man who gets it can say:
it was a noble's, a vassal's, a good man's sword."

89

And now there comes the Archbishop Turpin.
He spurs his horse, goes up into a mountain,   1125
summons the French; and he preached them a sermon:
"Barons, my lords, Charles left us in this place.
We know our duty: to die like good men for our King.
Fight to defend the holy Christian faith.
Now you will have a battle, you know it now,   1130
you see the Saracens with your own eyes.
Confess your sins, pray to the Lord for mercy.
I will absolve you all, to save your souls.
If you die here, you will stand up holy martyrs,
you will have seats in highest Paradise."   1135
The French dismount, cast themselves on the ground;
the Archbishop blesses them in God's name.
He commands them to do one penance: strike.

90

The French arise, stand on their feet again;
they are absolved, released from all their sins: 1140
the Archbishop has blessed them in God's name.
Now they are mounted on their swift battle horses,
bearing their arms like faithful warriors;
and every man stands ready for the battle.
Roland the Count calls out to Oliver: 1145
"Lord, Companion, you knew it, you were right,
Ganelon watched for his chance to betray us,
got gold for it, got goods for it, and money.
The Emperor will have to avenge us now.
King Marsilion made a bargain for our lives,   1150
but still must pay, and that must be with swords." AOI.

91

Roland went forth into the Spanish passes
on Veillantif, his good swift-running horse.
He bears his arms—how they become this man!—
grips his lance now, hefting it, working it,   1155
now swings the iron point up toward the sky,
the gonfanon all white laced on above—
the golden streamers beat down upon his hands:
a noble's body, the face aglow and smiling.
Close behind him his good companion follows;   1160
the men of France hail him: their protector!
He looks wildly toward the Saracens,
and humbly and gently to the men of France;
and spoke a word to them, in all courtesy:
"Barons, my lords, easy now, keep at a walk.   1165
These pagans are searching for martyrdom.
We'll get good spoils before this day is over,
no king of France ever got such treasure!"
And with these words, the hosts are at each other. AOI.

92

Said Oliver: "I will waste no more words.   1170
You did not think it right to sound your olifant,
there'll be no Charles coming to your aid now.
He knows nothing, brave man, he's done no wrong;
those men down there—they have no blame in this.
Well, then, ride now, and ride with all your might!   1175
Lords, you brave men, stand your ground, hold the field!
Make up your minds, I beg you in God's name,
to strike some blows, take them and give them back!
Here we must not forget Charlemagne's war cry."
And with that word the men of France cried out.   1180
A man who heard that shout: Munjoie! Munjoie![5]
would always remember what manhood is.
Then they ride, God! Look at their pride and spirit!
and they spur hard, to ride with all their speed,
come on to strike—what else would these men do?   1185
The Saracens kept coming, never fearing them.
Franks and pagans, here they are, at each other.

93

Marsilion's nephew is named Aëlroth.
He rides in front, at the head of the army,
comes on shouting insults against our French: 1190
"French criminals, today you fight our men.
One man should have saved you: he betrayed you.
A fool, your King, to leave you in these passes.
This is the day sweet France will lose its name,
and Charlemagne the right arm of his body."   1195
When he hears that—God!—Roland is outraged!

5. For the poet's derivation of this war cry, see *laisse* 183 below.

He spurs his horse, gives Veillantif its head.
The Count comes on to strike with all his might,
smashes his shield, breaks his hauberk apart,
and drives: rips through his chest, shatters the bones,   1200
knocks the whole backbone out of his back,
casts out the soul of Aëlroth with his lance;
which he thrusts deep, makes the whole body shake,
throws him down dead, lance straight out,[6] from his horse;
he has broken his neck; broken it in two.   1205
There is something, he says, he must tell him:
"Clown! Nobody! Now you know Charles is no fool,
he never was the man to love treason.
It took his valor to leave us in these passes!
France will not lose its name, sweet France! today.   1210
Brave men of France, strike hard! The first blow is ours!
We're in the right, and these swine in the wrong!" AOI.

94

A duke is there whose name is Falsaron,
he was the brother of King Marsilion,
held the wild land of Dathan and Abiram;[7]   1215
under heaven, no criminal more vile;
a tremendous forehead between his eyes—
a good half-foot long, if you had measured it.
His pain is bitter to see his nephew dead;
rides out alone, baits the foe with his body,   1220
and riding shouts the war cry of the pagans,
full of hate and insults against the French:
"This is the day sweet France will lose its honor!"
Oliver hears, and it fills him with fury,
digs with his golden spurs into his horse,   1225
comes on to strike the blow a baron strikes,
smashes his shield, breaks his hauberk apart,
thrusts into him the long streamers of his gonfalon,
knocks him down, dead, lance straight out, from the saddle;
looks to the ground and sees the swine stretched out,   1230
and spoke these words—proud words, terrible words:
"You nobody, what are your threats to me!
Men of France, strike! Strike and we will beat them!"
Munjoie! he shouts—the war cry of King Charles. AOI.

95

A king is there whose name is Corsablis,   1235
a Berber, come from that far country.
He spoke these words to all his Saracens:
"Now here's one battle we'll have no trouble with,
look at that little troop of Frenchmen there,
a few odd men—they're not worth noticing!   1240

---

6. The lance is held, not thrown, and used to knock the enemy from his horse. To throw one's weapons is savage and ignoble. See *laisses* 154 and 160 and the outlandish names of the things the pagans throw at Roland, Gautier, and Turpin.   7. See Numbers 16.1–35.

King Charles won't save a single one of them.
Their day has come, they must all die today."
And Archbishop Turpin heard every word:
no man on earth he wants so much to hate!
digs with spurs of fine gold into his horse,   1245
comes on to strike with all his awful might;
smashed through his shield, burst the rings of his hauberk,
sent his great lance into the body's center,
drove it in deep, he made the dead man shake,
knocked him down, dead, lance straight out, on the road;   1250
looks to the ground and sees the swine stretched out;
there is something, he says, he must tell him:
"You pagan! You nobody! You told lies there:
King Charles my lord is our safeguard forever!
Our men of France have no heart for running.   1255
As for your companions—we'll nail them to the ground;
and then you must all die the second death.[8]
At them, you French! No man forget what he is!
Thanks be to God, now the first blow is ours";
and shouts Munjoie! Munjoie! to hold the field.   1260

[Lines 1261–319 narrate a series of single combats, many of them quite similar.]

104

The battle is fearful and wonderful   1320
and everywhere. Roland never spares himself,
strikes with his lance as long as the wood lasts:
the fifteenth blow he struck, it broke, was lost.
Then he draws Durendal, his good sword, bare,
and spurs his horse, comes on to strike Chernuble,   1325
smashes his helmet, carbuncles shed their light,
cuts through the coif, through the hair on his head,
cut through his eyes, through his face, through that look,
the bright, shining hauberk with its fine rings,
down through the trunk to the fork of his legs,   1330
through the saddle, adorned with beaten gold,
into the horse; and the sword came to rest:
cut through the spine, never felt for the joint;
knocks him down, dead, on the rich grass of the meadow;
then said to him: "You were doomed when you started,   1335
Clown! Nobody! Let Mahum help you now.
No pagan swine will win this field today."

105

Roland the Count comes riding through the field,
holds Durendal, that sword! it carves its way!
and brings terrible slaughter down on the pagans.   1340
To have seen him cast one man dead on another,
the bright red blood pouring out on the ground,
his hauberk, his two arms, running with blood,
his good horse—neck and shoulders running with blood!

8. The death of the soul, eternal damnation (see Revelation 20.14 and 21.8).

And Oliver does not linger, he strikes! 1345
and the Twelve Peers, no man could reproach them;
and the brave French, they fight with lance and sword.
The pagans die, some simply faint away!
Said the Archbishop: "Bless our band of brave men!"
Munjoie! he shouts—the war cry of King Charles. AOI. 1350

106

Oliver rides into that battle-storm,
his lance is broken, he holds only the stump;
comes on to strike a pagan, Malsarun;
and he smashes his shield, all flowers and gold,
sends his two eyes flying out of his head, 1355
and his brains come pouring down to his feet;
casts him down, dead, with seven hundred others.
Now he has killed Turgis and Esturguz,
and the shaft bursts, shivers down to his fists.
Count Roland said: "Companion, what are you doing? 1360
Why bother with a stick in such a battle?
Iron and steel will do much better work!
Where is your sword, your Halteclere—that name!
Where is that crystal hilt, that golden guard?"
"Haven't had any time to draw it out, 1365
been so busy fighting," said Oliver. AOI.

107

Lord Oliver has drawn out his good sword—
that sword his companion had longed to see—
and showed him how a good man uses it:
strikes a pagan, Justin of Val Ferrée, 1370
and comes down through his head, cuts through the center,
through his body, his hauberk sewn with brass,
the good saddle beset with gems in gold,
into the horse, the backbone cut in two;
knocks him down, dead, before him on the meadow. 1375
Count Roland said: "Now I know it's you, Brother.
The Emperor loves us for blows like that."
Munjoie! that cry! goes up on every side. AOI.

108

Gerin the Count sits on his bay Sorél
and Gerer his companion on Passe-Cerf; 1380
and they ride, spurring hard, let loose their reins,
come on to strike a pagan, Timozel,
one on his shield, the other on his hauberk.
They broke their two lances in his body;
turn him over, dead, in a fallow field. 1385
I do not know and have never heard tell
which of these two was swifter, though both were swift.
Esperveris: he was the son of Borel
and now struck dead by Engeler of Bordeaux.

Turpin the Archbishop killed Siglorel,   1390
the enchanter, who had been in Hell before:
Jupiter brought him there, with that strange magic.
Then Turpin said: "That swine owed us his life!
Roland replies: "And now the scoundrel's dead.
Oliver, Brother, those were blows! I approve!"   1395

109

In the meantime, the fighting grew bitter.
Franks and pagans, the fearful blows they strike—
those who attack, those who defend themselves;
so many lances broken, running with blood,
the gonfanons in shreds, the ensigns torn,   1400
so many good French fallen, their young lives lost:
they will not see their mothers or wives again,
or the men of France who wait for them at the passes. AOI.
Charlemagne waits and weeps and wails for them.
What does that matter? They'll get no help from him.   1405
Ganelon served him ill that day he sold,
in Saragossa, the barons of his house.
He lost his life and limbs for what he did:
was doomed to hang in the great trial at Aix,
and thirty of his kin were doomed with him,   1410
who never expected to die that death. AOI.

110

The battle is fearful and full of grief.
Oliver and Roland strike like good men,
the Archbishop, more than a thousand blows,
and the Twelve Peers do not hang back, they strike!   1415
the French fight side by side, all as one man.
The pagans die by hundreds, by thousands:
whoever does not flee finds no refuge from death,
like it or not, there he ends all his days.
And there the men of France lose their greatest arms;   1420
they will not see their fathers, their kin again,
or Charlemagne, who looks for them in the passes.
Tremendous torment now comes forth in France,
a mighty whirlwind, tempests of wind and thunder,
rains and hailstones, great and immeasurable,   1425
bolts of lightning hurtling and hurtling down:
it is, in truth, a trembling of the earth.
From Saint Michael-in-Peril to the Saints,
from Besançon to the port of Wissant,
there is no house whose veil of walls does not crumble.   1430
A great darkness at noon falls on the land,
there is no light but when the heavens crack.
No man sees this who is not terrified,
and many say: "The Last Day! Judgment Day!
The end! The end of the world is upon us!"   1435
They do not know, they do not speak the truth:
it is the worldwide grief for the death of Roland.

111

The French have fought with all their hearts and strength,
pagans are dead by the thousands, in droves:
of one hundred thousand, not two are saved.   1440
Said the Archbishop: "Our men! What valiant fighters!
No king under heaven could have better.
It is written in the Gesta Francorum:[9]
our Emperor's vassals were all good men."
They walk over the field to seek their dead,   1445
they weep, tears fill their eyes, in grief and pity
for their kindred, with love, with all their hearts.
Marsilion the King, with all his men
    in that great host, rises up before them. AOI.

112

King Marsilion comes along a valley
with all his men, the great host he assembled:
twenty divisions, formed and numbered by the King,   1450
helmets ablaze with gems beset in gold,
and those bright shields, those hauberks sewn with brass.
Seven thousand clarions sound the pursuit,
and the great noise resounds across that country.
Said Roland then: "Oliver, Companion, Brother,   1455
that traitor Ganelon has sworn our deaths:
it is treason, it cannot stay hidden,
the Emperor will take his terrible revenge.
We have this battle now, it will be bitter,   1460
no man has ever seen the like of it.
I will fight here with Durendal, this sword,
and you, my companion, with Halteclere—
we've fought with them before, in many lands!
how many battles have we won with these two!   1465
Let no one sing a bad song of our swords." AOI.

113

When the French see the pagans so numerous,
the fields swarming with them on every side,
they call the names of Oliver, and Roland,
and the Twelve Peers: protect them, be their warranter.   1470
The Archbishop told them how he saw things:
"Barons, my lords, do not think shameful thoughts,
do not, I beg you all in God's name, run.
Let no brave man sing shameful songs of us:
let us all die here fighting: that is far better.   1475
We are promised: we shall soon find our deaths,
after today we won't be living here.
But here's one thing, and I am your witness:
Holy Paradise lies open to you,
you will take seats among the Innocents."[1]   1480

---

9. The Deeds of the French (Latin), title of an account of these events that has not survived.   1. The
infants slain by King Herod (see Matthew 2.16).

And with these words the Franks are filled with joy,
there is no man who does not shout Munjoie! AOI.

114

A Saracen was there of Saragossa,
half that city was in this pagan's keeping,
this Climborin, who fled before no man,   1485
who took the word of Ganelon the Count,
kissed in friendship the mouth that spoke that word,
gave him a gift: his helmet and its carbuncle.
Now he will shame, says he, the Land of Fathers,
he will tear off the crown of the Emperor;   1490
sits on the horse that he calls Barbamusche,
swifter than the sparrowhawk, than the swallow;
digs in his spurs, gives that war horse its head,
comes on to strike Engeler of Gascony,
whose shield and fine hauberk cannot save him;   1495
gets the head of his spear into his body,
drives it in deep, gets all the iron through,
throws him back, dead, lance straight out, on the field.
And then he cries: "It's good to kill these swine!
At them, Pagans! At them and break their ranks!"   1500
"God!" say the French, "the loss of that good man!" AOI.

115

Roland the Count calls out to Oliver:
"Lord, Companion, there is Engeler dead,
we never had a braver man on horse."
The Count replies: "God let me avenge him";   1505
and digs with golden spurs into his horse,
grips—the steel running with blood—Halteclere,
comes on to strike with all his mighty power:
the blow comes flashing down; the pagan falls.
Devils take away the soul of Climborin.   1510
And then he killed Alphaïen the duke,
cut off the head of Escababi,
struck from their horses seven great Arrabites:
they'll be no use for fighting any more!
And Roland said: "My companion is enraged!   1515
Why, he compares with me! he earns his praise!
Fighting like that makes us dearer to Charles";
lifts up his voice and shouts: "Strike! you are warriors!" AOI.

[Lines 1519–627 narrate another series of single combats.]

125

Marsilion sees his people's martyrdom.
He commands them: sound his horns and trumpets;
and he rides now with the great host he has gathered.   1630
At their head rides the Saracen Abisme:
no worse criminal rides in that company,

stained with the marks of his crimes and great treasons,
lacking the faith in God, Saint Mary's son.
And he is black, as black as melted pitch,   1635
a man who loves murder and treason more
than all the gold of rich Galicia,
no living man ever saw him play or laugh;
a great fighter, a wild man, mad with pride,
and therefore dear to that criminal king;   1640
holds high his dragon,[2] where all his people gather.
The Archbishop will never love that man,
no sooner saw than wanted to strike him;
considered quietly, said to himself:
"That Saracen—a heretic, I'll wager.   1645
Now let me die if I do not kill him—
I never loved cowards or cowards' ways." AOI.

126

Turpin the Archbishop begins the battle.
He rides the horse that he took from Grossaille,
who was a king this priest once killed in Denmark.   1650
Now this war horse is quick and spirited,
his hooves high-arched, the quick legs long and flat,
short in the thigh, wide in the rump, long in the flanks,
and the backbone so high, a battle horse!
and that white tail, the yellow mane on him,   1655
the little ears on him, the tawny head!
No beast on earth could ever run with him.
The Archbishop—that valiant man!—spurs hard,
he will attack Abisme, he will not falter,
strikes on his shield, a miraculous blow: 1660
a shield of stones, of amethysts, topazes,
esterminals,[3] carbuncles all on fire—
a gift from a devil, in Val Metas,
sent on to him by the Amiral Galafre.
There Turpin strikes, he does not treat it gently—   1665
after that blow, I'd not give one cent for it;
cut through his body, from one side to the other,
and casts him down dead in a barren place.
And the French say: "A fighter, that Archbishop!
Look at him there, saving souls with that crozier!"   1670

127

Roland the Count calls out to Oliver:
"Lord, Companion, now you have to agree
the Archbishop is a good man on horse,
there's none better on earth or under heaven,
he knows his way with a lance and a spear."   1675
The Count replies: "Right! Let us help him then."
And with these words the Franks began anew,
the blows strike hard, and the fighting is bitter;
there is a painful loss of Christian men.

2. Banner.   3. Precious ornaments.

To have seen them, Roland and Oliver,   1680
these fighting men, striking down with their swords,
the Archbishop with them, striking with his lance!
One can recount the number these three killed:
it is written—in charters, in documents;
the Geste tells it: it was more than four thousand.   1685
Through four assaults all went well with our men;
then comes the fifth, and that one crushes them.
They are all killed, all these warriors of France,
all but sixty, whom the Lord God has spared:
they will die too, but first sell themselves dear. AOI.   1690

128

Count Roland sees the great loss of his men,
calls on his companion, on Oliver:
"Lord, Companion, in God's name, what would you do?
All these good men you see stretched on the ground.
We can mourn for sweet France, fair land of France!   1695
a desert now, stripped of such great vassals.
Oh King, and friend, if only you were here!
Oliver, Brother, how shall we manage it?
What shall we do to get word to the King?"
Said Oliver: "I don't see any way.   1700
I would rather die now than hear us shamed." AOI.

129

And Roland said: "I'll sound the olifant,
Charles will hear it, drawing through the passes,
I promise you, the Franks will return at once."
Said Oliver: "That would be a great disgrace,   1705
a dishonor and reproach to all your kin,
the shame of it would last them all their lives.
When I urged it, you would not hear of it;
you will not do it now with my consent.
It is not acting bravely to sound it now—   1710
look at your arms, they are covered with blood."
The Count replies: "I've fought here like a lord."[4] AOI.

130

And Roland says: "We are in a rough battle.
I'll sound the olifant, Charles will hear it."
Said Oliver: "No good vassal would do it.   1715
When I urged it, friend, you did not think it right.
If Charles were here, we'd come out with no losses.
Those men down there—no blame can fall on them."
Oliver said: "Now by this beard of mine,
If I can see my noble sister, Aude,   1720
once more, you will never lie in her arms!"[5] AOI.

---

4. Some have found lines 1710–12 difficult. Oliver means, "We have fought this far—look at the enemy's blood on your arms: It is too late, it would be a disgrace to summon help when there is no longer any chance of being saved." But Roland thinks that that is the one time when it is not a disgrace.   5. Aude had been betrothed to Roland.

131

And Roland said: "Why are you angry at me?"
Oliver answers: "Companion, it is your doing.
I will tell you what makes a vassal good:
    it is judgment, it is never madness;
restraint is worth more than the raw nerve of a fool.   1725
Frenchmen are dead because of your wildness.
And what service will Charles ever have from us?
If you had trusted me, my lord would be here,
we would have fought this battle through to the end,
Marsilion would be dead, or our prisoner.   1730
Roland, your prowess—had we never seen it!
    And now, dear friend, we've seen the last of it.
No more aid from us now for Charlemagne,
a man without equal till Judgment Day,
you will die here, and your death will shame France.
We kept faith, you and I, we were companions;
    and everything we were will end today.   1735
We part before evening, and it will be hard." AOI.

132

Turpin the Archbishop hears their bitter words,
digs hard into his horse with golden spurs
and rides to them; begins to set them right:
"You, Lord Roland, and you, Lord Oliver,   1740
I beg you in God's name do not quarrel.
To sound the horn could not help us now, true,
but still it is far better that you do it:
let the King come, he can avenge us then—
these men of Spain must not go home exulting!   1745
Our French will come, they'll get down on their feet,
and find us here—we'll be dead, cut to pieces.
They will lift us into coffins on the backs of mules,
and weep for us, in rage and pain and grief,
and bury us in the courts of churches;   1750
and we will not be eaten by wolves or pigs or dogs."
Roland replies, "Lord, you have spoken well." AOI.

133

Roland has put the olifant to his mouth,
he sets it well, sounds it with all his strength.
The hills are high, and that voice ranges far,   1755
they heard it echo thirty great leagues away.
King Charles heard it, and all his faithful men.
And the King says: "Our men are in a battle."
And Ganelon disputed him and said:
"Had someone else said that, I'd call him liar!" AOI.   1760

134

And now the mighty effort of Roland the Count:
he sounds his olifant; his pain is great,

and from his mouth the bright blood comes leaping out,
and the temple bursts in his forehead.
That horn, in Roland's hands, has a mighty voice: 1765
King Charles hears it drawing through the passes.
Naimon heard it, the Franks listen to it.
And the King said: "I hear Count Roland's horn;
he'd never sound it unless he had a battle."
Says Ganelon: "Now no more talk of battles!   1770
You are old now, your hair is white as snow,
the things you say make you sound like a child.
You know Roland and that wild pride of his—
what a wonder God has suffered it so long!
Remember? he took Noples without your command: 1775
the Saracens rode out, to break the siege;
they fought with him, the great vassal Roland.
Afterwards he used the streams to wash the blood
from the meadows: so that nothing would show.
He blasts his horn all day to catch a rabbit,   1780
he's strutting now before his peers and bragging—
who under heaven would dare meet him on the field?
So now: ride on! Why do you keep on stopping?
The Land of Fathers lies far ahead of us." AOI.

135

The blood leaping from Count Roland's mouth,   1785
the temple broken with effort in his forehead,
he sounds his horn in great travail and pain.
King Charles heard it, and his French listen hard.
And the King said: "That horn has a long breath!"
Naimon answers: "It is a baron's breath.   1790
There is a battle there, I know there is.
He betrayed him! and now asks you to fail him!
Put on your armor! Lord, shout your battle cry,
and save the noble barons of your house!
You hear Roland's call. He is in trouble."   1795

136

The Emperor commanded the horns to sound,
the French dismount, and they put on their armor:
their hauberks, their helmets, their gold-dressed swords,
their handsome shields; and take up their great lances,
the gonfalons of white and red and blue.   1800
The barons of that host mount their war horses
and spur them hard the whole length of the pass;
and every man of them says to the other:
"If only we find Roland before he's killed,
we'll stand with him, and then we'll do some fighting!"   1805
What does it matter what they say? They are too late.

137

It is the end of day, and full of light,
arms and armor are ablaze in the sun,

and fire flashes from hauberks and helmets,
and from those shields, painted fair with flowers,
and from those lances, those gold-dressed gonfanons.   1810
The Emperor rides on in rage and sorrow,
the men of France indignant and full of grief.
There is no man of them who does not weep,
they are in fear for the life of Roland.   1815
The King commands: seize Ganelon the Count!
and gave him over to the cooks of his house;
summons the master cook, their chief, Besgun:
"Guard him for me like the traitor he is:
he has betrayed the barons of my house."   1820
Besgun takes him, sets his kitchen comrades,
a hundred men, the best, the worst, on him;
and they tear out his beard and his mustache,
each one strikes him four good blows with his fist;
and they lay into him with cudgels and sticks,   1825
put an iron collar around his neck
and chain him up, as they would chain a bear;
dumped him, in dishonor, on a packhorse,
and guard him well till they give him back to Charles.

138

High are the hills, and tenebrous, and vast, AOI.   1830
the valleys deep, the raging waters swift;
to the rear, to the front, the trumpets sound:
they answer the lone voice of the olifant.
The Emperor rides on, rides on in fury,
the men of France in grief and indignation.   1835
There is no man who does not weep and wail,
and they pray God: protect the life of Roland
till they come, one great host, into the field
and fight at Roland's side like true men all.
What does it matter what they pray? It does no good.   1840
They are too late, they cannot come in time. AOI.

139

King Charles the Great rides on, a man in wrath,
his great white beard spread out upon his hauberk.[6]
All the barons of France ride spurring hard,
there is no man who does not wail, furious   1845
not to be with Roland, the captain count,
who stands and fights the Saracens of Spain,
so set upon, I cannot think his soul abides.
God! those sixty men who stand with him, what men!
No king, no captain ever stood with better. AOI.   1850

140

Roland looks up on the mountains and slopes,
sees the French dead, so many good men fallen,

6. A gesture of defiance toward the enemy.

and weeps for them, as a great warrior weeps:
"Barons, my lords, may God give you his grace,
may he grant Paradise to all your souls,   1855
make them lie down among the holy flowers.
I never saw better vassals than you.
All the years you've served me, and all the times,
the mighty lands you conquered for Charles our King!
The Emperor raised you for this terrible hour!   1860
Land of France, how sweet you are, native land,
laid waste this day, ravaged, made a desert.
Barons of France, I see you die for me,
and I, your lord—I cannot protect you.
May *God* come to your aid, that God who never failed.   1865
Oliver, brother, now I will not fail *you*.
I will die here—of grief, if no man kills me.
Lord, Companion, let us return and fight."

141

Roland returned to his place on the field,
strikes—a brave man keeping faith—with Durendal,   1870
struck through Faldrun de Pui, cut him to pieces,
and twenty-four of the men they valued most;
no man will ever want his vengeance more!
As when the deer turns tail before the dogs,
so the pagans flee before Roland the Count.   1875
Said the Archbishop: "You! Roland! What a fighter!
Now that's what every knight must have in him
who carries arms and rides on a fine horse:
he must be strong, a savage, when he's in battle;
for otherwise, what's he worth? Not four cents!   1880
Let that four-cent man be a monk in some minster,
and he can pray all day long for our sins."
Roland replies: "Attack, do not spare them!"
And with that word the Franks began again.
There was a heavy loss of Christian men.   1885

142

When a man knows there'll be no prisoners,
what will that man not do to defend himself!
And so the Franks fight with the fury of lions.
Now Marsilion, the image of a baron,
mounted on that war horse he calls Gaignun,   1890
digs in his spurs, comes on to strike Bevon,
who was the lord of Beaune and of Dijon;
smashes his shield, rips apart his hauberk,
knocks him down, dead, no need to wound him more.
And then he killed Yvorie and Yvon,   1895
and more: he killed Gerard of Rousillon.
Roland the Count is not far away now,
said to the pagan: "The Lord God's curse on you!
You kill my companions, how you wrong me!
You'll feel the pain of it before we part,   1900

you will learn my sword's name by heart today";
comes on to strike—the image of a baron.
He has cut off Marsilion's right fist;
now takes the head of Jurfaleu the blond—
the head of Jurfaleu! Marsilion's son.   1905
The pagans cry: "Help, Mahumet! Help us!
Vengeance, our gods, on Charles! the man who set
these criminals on us in our own land,
they will not quit the field, they'll stand and die!"
And one said to the other: "Let *us* run then."   1910
And with that word, some hundred thousand flee.
Now try to call them back: they won't return. AOI.

143

What does it matter? If Marsilion has fled,
his uncle has remained: the Algalife,[7]
who holds Carthage, Alfrere, and Garmalie,   1915
and Ethiopia: a land accursed;
holds its immense black race under his power,
the huge noses, the enormous ears on them;
and they number more than fifty thousand.
These are the men who come riding in fury,   1920
and now they shout that pagan battle cry.
And Roland said: "Here comes our martyrdom;
I see it now: we have not long to live.
But let the world call any man a traitor
        who does not make them pay before he dies!
My lords, attack! Use those bright shining swords!   1925
Fight a good fight for your deaths and your lives,
let no shame touch sweet France because of us!
When Charles my lord comes to this battlefield
and sees how well we punished these Saracens,
finds fifteen of their dead for one of ours,   1930
I'll tell you what he will do: he will bless us." AOI.

144

When Roland sees that unbelieving race,
those hordes and hordes blacker than blackest ink—
no shred of white on them except their teeth—
then said the Count: "I see it clearly now,   1935
we die today: it is there before us.
Men of France, strike! I will start it once more."
Said Oliver: "God curse the slowest man."
And with that word, the French strike into battle.

145

The Saracens, when they saw these few French,   1940
looked at each other, took courage, and presumed,

---

7. The Caliph, Marsilion's uncle, whom Ganelon lied about to Charlemagne (see lines 680–91).

telling themselves: "The Emperor is wrong!"
The Algalife rides a great sorrel horse,
digs into it with his spurs of fine gold,
strikes Oliver, from behind, in the back,   1945
shattered the white hauberk upon his flesh,
drove his spear through the middle of his chest;
and speaks to him: "Now you feel you've been struck!
Your great Charles doomed you when he left you in this pass.
That man wronged us, he must not boast of it.   1950
I've avenged all our dead in you alone!"

146

Oliver feels: he has been struck to death;
grips Halteclere, that steel blade shining, strikes
on the gold-dressed pointed helm of the Algalife,
sends jewels and flowers crackling down to the earth,   1955
into the head, into the little teeth;
draws up his flashing sword, casts him down, dead,
and then he says: "Pagan, a curse on you!
If only I could say Charles has lost nothing—
but no woman, no lady you ever knew   1960
will hear you boast, in the land you came from,
that you could take one thing worth a cent from me,
or do me harm, or do any man harm";
then cries out to Roland to come to his aid. AOI.

147

Oliver feels he is wounded to death,   1965
will never have his fill of vengeance, strikes,
as a baron strikes, where they are thickest,
cuts through their lances, cuts through those buckled shields,
through feet, through fists, through saddles, and through flanks.
Had you seen him, cutting the pagans limb   1970
from limb, casting one corpse down on another,
you would remember a brave man keeping faith.
Never would he forget Charles' battle-cry,
Munjoie! he shouts, that mighty voice ringing;
calls to Roland, to his friend and his peer: 1975
"Lord, Companion, come stand beside me now.
We must part from each other in pain today." AOI.

148

Roland looks hard into Oliver's face,
it is ashen, all its color is gone,
the bright red blood streams down upon his body,   1980
Oliver's blood spattering on the earth.
"God!" said the Count, "I don't know what to do,
Lord, Companion, your fight is finished now.
There'll never be a man the like of you.
Sweet land of France, today you will be stripped   1985
of good vassals, laid low, a fallen land!

The Emperor will suffer the great loss";
faints with that word, mounted upon his horse. AOI.

149

Here is Roland, lords, fainted on his horse,
and Oliver the Count, wounded to death: 1990
he has lost so much blood, his eyes are darkened—
he cannot see, near or far, well enough
to recognize a friend or enemy:
struck when he came upon his companion,
strikes on his helm, adorned with gems in gold,   1995
cuts down straight through, from the point to the nasal,[8]
but never harmed him, he never touched his head.
Under this blow, Count Roland looked at him;
and gently, softly now, he asks of him:
"Lord, Companion, do you mean to do this?   2000
It is Roland, who always loved you greatly.
You never declared that we were enemies."
Said Oliver: "Now I hear it is you—
I don't see you, may the Lord God see you.
Was it you that I struck? Forgive me then."   2005
Roland replies: "I am not harmed, not harmed,
I forgive you, Friend, here and before God."
And with that word, each bowed to the other.
And this is the love, lords, in which they parted.

150

Oliver feels: death pressing hard on him;   2010
his two eyes turn, roll up into his head,
all hearing is lost now, all sight is gone;
gets down on foot, stretches out on the ground,
cries out now and again: *mea culpa!*[9]
his two hands joined, raised aloft toward heaven,   2015
he prays to God: grant him His Paradise;
and blesses Charles, and the sweet land of France,
his companion, Roland, above all men.
The heart fails him, his helmet falls away,
the great body settles upon the earth.   2020
The Count is dead, he stands with us no longer.
Roland, brave man, weeps for him, mourns for him,
you will not hear a man of greater sorrow.

151

Roland the Count, when he sees his friend dead,
lying stretched out, his face against the earth,
softly, gently, begins to speak the regret:[1]   2025
"Lord, Companion, you were brave and died for it.
We have stood side by side through days and years,
you never caused me harm, I never wronged you;

8. The nosepiece protruding down from the cone-shaped helmet. 9. My guilt (Latin); a formula used
in the confession of one's sins. 1. What follows is a formal and customary lament for the dead.

when you are dead, to be alive pains me." 2030
And with that word the lord of marches faints
upon his horse, which he calls Veillantif.
He is held firm by his spurs of fine gold,
whichever way he leans, he cannot fall.

152

Before Roland could recover his senses
and come out of his faint, and be aware, 2035
a great disaster had come forth before him:
the French are dead, he has lost every man
except the Archbishop, and Gautier de l'Hum,
who has come back, down from that high mountain: 2040
he has fought well, he fought those men of Spain.
His men are dead, the pagans finished them;
flees now down to these valleys, he has no choice,
and calls on Count Roland to come to his aid:
"My noble Count, my brave lord, where are you? 2045
I never feared whenever you were there.
It is Walter: I conquered Maëlgut,
my uncle is Droün, old and gray: your Walter
and always dear to you for the way I fought;
and I have fought this time: my lance is shattered, 2050
my good shield pierced, my hauberk's meshes broken;
and I am wounded, a lance struck through my body.
I will die soon, but I sold myself dear."
And with that word, Count Roland has heard him,
he spurs his horse, rides spurring to his man. AOI. 2055

153

Roland in pain, maddened with grief and rage:
rushes where they are thickest and strikes again,
strikes twenty men of Spain, strikes twenty dead,
and Walter six, and the Archbishop five.
The pagans say: "Look at those criminals! 2060
Now take care, Lords, they don't get out alive,
only a traitor will not attack them now!
Only a coward will let them save their skins!"
And then they raise their hue and cry once more,
rush in on them, once more, from every side. AOI. 2065

154

Count Roland was always a noble warrior,
Gautier de l'Hum is a fine mounted man,
the Archbishop, a good man tried and proved:
not one of them will ever leave the others;
strike, where they are thickest, at the pagans. 2070
A thousand Saracens get down on foot,
and forty thousand more are on their mounts:
and I tell you, not one will dare come close,
they throw, and from afar, lances and spears,

wigars and darts, mizraks, javelins, pikes.   2075
With the first blows they killed Gautier de l'Hum
and struck Turpin of Reims, pierced through his shield,
broke the helmet on him, wounded his head;
ripped his hauberk, shattered its rings of mail,
and pierced him with four spears in his body,   2080
the war horse killed under him; and now there comes
great pain and rage when the Archbishop falls. AOI.

155

Turpin of Reims, when he feels he is unhorsed,
struck to the earth with four spears in his body,
quickly, brave man, leaps to his feet again;   2085
his eyes find Roland now, he runs to him
and says one word: "See! I'm not finished yet!
What good vassal ever gives up alive!";
and draws Almace, his sword, that shining steel!
and strikes, where they are thickest, a thousand blows, and more.   2090
Later, Charles said: Turpin had spared no one;
he found four hundred men prostrate around him,
some of them wounded, some pierced from front to back,
some with their heads hacked off. So says the Geste,
and so says one who was there, on that field,   2095
the baron Saint Gilles,[2] for whom God performs miracles,
who made the charter setting forth these great things
      in the Church of Laon. Now any man
who does not know this much understands nothing.

156

Roland the Count fights well and with great skill,
but he is hot, his body soaked with sweat;   2100
has a great wound in his head, and much pain,
his temple broken because he blew the horn.
But he must know whether King Charles will come;
draws out the olifant, sounds it, so feebly.
The Emperor drew to a halt, listened.   2105
"Seigneurs," he said, "it goes badly for us—
My nephew Roland falls from our ranks today.
I hear it in the horn's voice: he hasn't long.
Let every man who wants to be with Roland
ride fast! Sound trumpets! Every trumpet in this host!"   2110
Sixty thousand, on these words, sound, so high
the mountains sound, and the valleys resound.
The pagans hear: it is no joke to them;
cry to each other: "We're getting Charles on us!"

157

The pagans say: "The Emperor is coming, AOI.   2115
listen to their trumpets—it is the French!

---

2. St. Gilles of Provence. These lines explain how the story of Rencesvals could be told after all who had
fought there died.

If Charles comes back, it's all over for us,
if Roland lives, this war begins again
and we have lost our land, we have lost Spain."
Some four hundred, helmets laced on, assemble,   2120
some of the best, as they think, on that field.
They storm Roland, in one fierce, bitter attack.
And now Count Roland has some work on his hands. AOI.

158

Roland the Count, when he sees them coming,
how strong and fierce and alert he becomes!   2125
He will not yield to them, not while he lives.
He rides the horse they call Veillantif, spurs,
digs into it with his spurs of fine gold,
and rushes at them all where they are thickest,
the Archbishop—that Turpin!—at his side.   2130
Said one man to the other: "Go at it, friend.
The horns we heard were the horns of the French,
King Charles is coming back with all his strength."[3]

159

Roland the Count never loved a coward,
a blusterer, an evil-natured man,   2135
a man on horse who was not a good vassal.
And now he called to Archbishop Turpin:
"You are on foot, Lord, and here I am mounted,
and so, here I take my stand: for love of you.
We'll take whatever comes, the good and bad,   2140
together, Lord: no one can make me leave you.
They will learn our swords' names today in battle,
the name of Almace, the name of Durendal!"
Said the Archbishop: "Let us strike or be shamed!
Charles is returning, and he brings our revenge."   2145

160

Say the pagans: "We were all born unlucky!
The evil day that dawned for us today!
We have lost our lords and peers, and now comes Charles—
that Charlemagne!—with his great host. Those trumpets!
that shrill sound on us—the trumpets of the French!   2150
And the loud roar of that Munjoie! This Roland
is a wild man, he is too great a fighter—
What man of flesh and blood can ever hope
to bring him down? Let us cast at him, and leave him there."
And so they did: arrows, wigars, darts,   2155
lances and spears, javelots dressed with feathers;
struck Roland's shield, pierced it, broke it to pieces,
ripped his hauberk, shattered its rings of mail,
but never touched his body, never his flesh.

3. The lines could be spoken either by Roland and the archbishop or by the pagans.

They wounded Veillantif in thirty places, 2160
struck him dead, from afar, under the Count.
The pagans flee, they leave the field to him.
Roland the Count stood alone, on his feet. AOI.

161

The pagans flee, in bitterness and rage,
strain every nerve running headlong toward Spain, 2165
and Count Roland has no way to chase them,
he has lost Veillantif, his battle horse;
he has no choice, left alone there on foot.
He went to the aid of Archbishop Turpin,
unlaced the gold-dressed helmet, raised it from his head, 2170
lifted away his bright, light coat of mail,
cut his under tunic into some lengths,
stilled his great wounds with thrusting on the strips;
then held him in his arms, against his chest,
and laid him down, gently, on the green grass; 2175
and softly now Roland entreated him:
"My noble lord, I beg you, give me leave:
our companions, whom we have loved so dearly,
are all dead now, we must not abandon them.
I want to look for them, know them once more, 2180
and set them in ranks, side by side, before you."
Said the Archbishop: "Go then, go and come back.
The field is ours, thanks be to God, yours and mine."

162

So Roland leaves him, walks the field all alone,
seeks in the valleys, and seeks in the mountains. 2185
He found Gerin, and Gerer his companion,
and then he found Berenger and Otun,
Anseïs and Sansun, and on that field
he found Gerard the old of Roussillon;
and carried them, brave man, all, one by one, 2190
came back to the Archbishop with these French dead,
and set them down in ranks before his knees.
The Archbishop cannot keep from weeping,
raises his hand and makes his benediction;
and said: "Lords, Lords, it was your terrible hour. 2195
May the Glorious God set all your souls
among the holy flowers of Paradise!
Here is my own death, Lords, pressing on me,
I shall not see our mighty Emperor."

163

And Roland leaves, seeks in the field again; 2200
he has found Oliver, his companion,
held him tight in his arms against his chest;
came back to the Archbishop, laid Oliver
down on a shield among the other dead.

The Archbishop absolved him, signed him with the Cross.   2205
And pity now and rage and grief increase;
and Roland says: "Oliver, dear companion,
you were the son of the great duke Renier,
who held the march of the vale of Runers.
Lord, for shattering lances, for breaking shields,   2210
for making men great with presumption weak with fright,
for giving life and counsel to good men,
for striking fear in that unbelieving race,
no warrior on earth surpasses you."

164

Roland the Count, when he sees his peers dead,   2215
and Oliver, whom he had good cause to love,
felt such grief and pity, he begins to weep;
and his face lost its color with what he felt:
a pain so great he cannot keep on standing,
he has no choice, falls fainting to the ground.   2220
Said the Archbishop: "Baron, what grief for you."

165

The Archbishop, when he saw Roland faint,
felt such pain then as he had never felt;
stretched out his hand and grasped the olifant.
At Rencesvals there is a running stream: 2225
he will go there and fetch some water for Roland;
and turns that way, with small steps, staggering;
he is too weak, he cannot go ahead,
he has no strength: all the blood he has lost.
In less time than a man takes to cross a little field   2230
that great heart fails, he falls forward, falls down;
and Turpin's death comes crushing down on him.

166

Roland the Count recovers from his faint,
gets to his feet, but stands with pain and grief;
looks down the valley, looks up the mountain, sees: 2235
on the green grass, beyond his companions,
that great and noble man down on the ground,
the Archbishop, whom God sent in His name;
who confesses his sins, lifts up his eyes,
holds up his hands joined together to heaven,   2240
and prays to God: grant him that Paradise.
Turpin is dead, King Charles' good warrior.
In great battles, in beautiful sermons
he was ever a champion against the pagans.
Now God grant Turpin's soul His holy blessing. AOI.   2245

167

Roland the Count sees the Archbishop down,
sees the bowels fallen out of his body,

and the brain boiling down from his forehead.
Turpin has crossed his hands upon his chest
beneath the collarbone, those fine white hands.   2250
Roland speaks the lament, after the custom
followed in his land: aloud, with all his heart:
"My noble lord, you great and well-born warrior,
I commend you today to the God of Glory,
whom none will ever serve with a sweeter will.   2255
Since the Apostles no prophet the like of you[4]
arose to keep the faith and draw men to it.
May your soul know no suffering or want,
and behold the gate open to Paradise."

168

Now Roland feels that death is very near.   2260
His brain comes spilling out through his two ears;
prays to God for his peers: let them be called;
and for himself, to the angel Gabriel;
took the olifant: there must be no reproach!
took Durendal his sword in his other hand,   2265
and farther than a crossbow's farthest shot
he walks toward Spain, into a fallow land,
and climbs a hill: there beneath two fine trees
stand four great blocks of stone, all are of marble;
and he fell back, to earth, on the green grass,   2270
has fainted there, for death is very near.

169

High are the hills, and high, high are the trees;
there stand four blocks of stone, gleaming of marble.
Count Roland falls fainting on the green grass,
and is watched, all this time, by a Saracen: 2275
who has feigned death and lies now with the others,
has smeared blood on his face and on his body;
and quickly now gets to his feet and runs—
a handsome man, strong, brave, and so crazed with pride
that he does something mad and dies for it: 2280
laid hands on Roland, and on the arms of Roland,
and cried: "Conquered! Charles's nephew conquered!
I'll carry this sword home to Arabia!"
As he draws it, the Count begins to come round.

170

Now Roland feels: *someone taking his sword!*   2285
opened his eyes, and had one word for him:
"I don't know you, you aren't one of ours";
grasps that olifant that he will never lose,
strikes on the helm beset with gems in gold,

---

4. Cf. Deuteronomy 34.10, on the death of Moses: "And there arose not a prophet since in Israel like unto Moses, whom the Lord knew face to face."

shatters the steel, and the head, and the bones,   2290
sent his two eyes flying out of his head,
dumped him over stretched out at his feet dead;
and said: "You nobody! how could you dare
lay hands on me—rightly or wrongly: how?
Who'll hear of this and not call you a fool?   2295
Ah! the bell-mouth of the olifant is smashed,
the crystal and the gold fallen away."

171

Now Roland the Count feels: his sight is gone;
gets on his feet, draws on his final strength,
the color on his face lost now for good.   2300
Before him stands a rock; and on that dark rock
in rage and bitterness he strikes ten blows:
the steel blade grates, it will not break, it stands unmarked.
"Ah!" said the Count, "Blessed Mary, your help!
Ah Durendal, good sword, your unlucky day,   2305
for I am lost and cannot keep you in my care.
The battles I have won, fighting with you,
the mighty lands that holding you I conquered,
that Charles rules now, our King, whose beard is white!
Now you fall to another: it must not be
    a man who'd run before another man!   2310
For a long while a good vassal held you:
there'll never be the like in France's holy land."

172

Roland strikes down on that rock of Cerritania:
the steel blade grates, will not break, stands unmarked.
Now when he sees he can never break that sword,   2315
Roland speaks the lament, in his own presence:
"Ah Durendal, how beautiful and bright!
so full of light, all on fire in the sun!
King Charles was in the vales of Moriane
when God sent his angel and commanded him,   2320
from heaven, to give you to a captain count.
That great and noble King girded it on me.
And with this sword I won Anjou and Brittany,
I won Poitou, I won Le Maine for Charles,
and Normandy, that land where men are free,   2325
I won Provence and Aquitaine with this,
and Lombardy, and every field of Romagna,
I won Bavaria, and all of Flanders,
all of Poland, and Bulgaria, for Charles,
Constantinople, which pledged him loyalty,   2330
and Saxony, where he does as he wills;
and with this sword I won Scotland and Ireland,
and England, his chamber, his own domain—
the lands, the nations I conquered with this sword,
for Charles, who rules them now, whose beard is white!   2335

Now, for this sword, I am pained with grief and rage:
Let it not fall to pagans! Let me die first!
Our Father God, save France from that dishonor."

173

Roland the Count strikes down on a dark rock,
and the rock breaks, breaks more than I can tell,   2340
and the blade grates, but Durendal will not break,
the sword leaped up, rebounded toward the sky.
The Count, when he sees that sword will not be broken,
softly, in his own presence, speaks the lament:
"Ah Durendal, beautiful, and most sacred,   2345
the holy relics in this golden pommel!
Saint Peter's tooth and blood of Saint Basile,
a lock of hair of my lord Saint Denis,
and a fragment of blessed Mary's robe:
your power must not fall to the pagans,   2350
you must be served by Christian warriors.
May no coward ever come to hold you!
It was with you I conquered those great lands
that Charles has in his keeping, whose beard is white,
the Emperor's lands, that make him rich and strong."   2355

174

Now Roland feels: death coming over him,
death descending from his temples to his heart.
He came running underneath a pine tree
and there stretched out, face down, on the green grass,
lays beneath him his sword and the olifant.   2360
He turned his head toward the Saracen hosts,
and this is why: with all his heart he wants
King Charles the Great and all his men to say,
he died, that noble Count, a conqueror;
makes confession, beats his breast often, so feebly,   2365
offers his glove, for all his sins, to God. AOI.

175

Now Roland feels that his time has run out;
he lies on a steep hill, his face toward Spain;
and with one of his hands he beat his breast:
"Almighty God, *mea culpa* in thy sight,[5]   2370
forgive my sins, both the great and the small,
sins I committed from the hour I was born
until this day, in which I lie struck down."
And then he held his right glove out to God.
Angels descend from heaven and stand by him. AOI.   2375

176

Count Roland lay stretched out beneath a pine;
he turned his face toward the land of Spain,

---

5. See Psalm 51.4: "Against thee, thee only, have I sinned, and done this evil in thy sight."

began to remember many things now:
how many lands, brave man, he had conquered;
and he remembered: sweet France, the men of his line,   2380
remembered Charles, his lord, who fostered him:
cannot keep, remembering, from weeping, sighing;
but would not be unmindful of himself:
he confesses his sins, prays God for mercy:
"Loyal Father, you who never failed us,   2385
who resurrected Saint Lazarus from the dead,
and saved your servant Daniel from the lions:[6]
now save the soul of me from every peril
for the sins I committed while I still lived."
Then he held out his right glove to his Lord: 2390
Saint Gabriel took the glove from his hand.
He held his head bowed down upon his arm,
he is gone, his two hands joined, to his end.
Then God sent him his angel Cherubin[7]
and Saint Michael, angel of the sea's Peril;   2395
and with these two there came Saint Gabriel:
they bear Count Roland's soul to Paradise.

177

Roland is dead, God has his soul in heaven.
The Emperor rides into Rencesvals;
there is no passage there, there is no track,   2400
no empty ground, not an elle, not one foot,
that does not bear French dead or pagan dead.
King Charles cries out: "Dear Nephew, where are you?
Where is the Archbishop? Count Oliver?
Where is Gerin, his companion Gerer?   2405
Where is Otun, where is Count Berenger,
Yves and Yvoire, men I have loved so dearly?
What has become of Engeler the Gascon,
Sansun the Duke, and Anseïs, that fighter?
Where is Gerard the Old of Roussillon,   2410
and the Twelve Peers, whom I left in these passes?"
And so forth—what's the difference? No one answered.
"God!" said the King, "how much I must regret
I was not here when the battle began";
pulls his great beard, a man in grief and rage.   2415
His brave knights weep, their eyes are filled with tears,
twenty thousand fall fainting to the ground;
Duke Naimon feels the great pity of it.

178

There is no knight or baron on that field
who does not weep in bitterness and grief;   2420
for they all weep: for their sons, brothers, nephew,
weep for their friends, for their sworn men and lords;

6. See Daniel 6.12–23. For the raising of Lazarus, see John 11.1–44.   7. The poet seems to have regarded this as the name of a single angel.

the mass of them fall fainting to the ground.
Here Naimon proved a brave and useful man:
he was the first to urge the Emperor: 2425
"Look ahead there, two leagues in front of us,
you can see the dust rising on those wide roads:
the pagan host—and how many they are!
After them now! Ride! Avenge this outrage!"
"Oh! God!" said Charles, "look how far they have gotten!   2430
Lord, let me have my right, let me have honor,
they tore from me the flower of sweet France."
The King commands Gebuïn and Othon,
Thibaut of Reims and Count Milun his cousin:
"Now guard this field, the valleys, the mountains,   2435
let the dead lie, all of them, as they are,
let no lion, let no beast come near them,
let no servant, let no groom come near them,
I command you, let no man come near these dead
until God wills we come back to this field."   2440
And they reply, gently, and in great love:
"Just Emperor, dear Lord, we shall do that."
They keep with them a thousand of their knights. AOI.

179

The Emperor has his high-pitched trumpets sound,
and then he rides, brave man, with his great host.   2445
They made the men of Spain show them their heels,
and they keep after them, all as one man.
When the King sees the twilight faltering,
he gets down in a meadow on the green grass,
lies on the ground, prays to the Lord his God   2450
to make the sun stand still for him in heaven,
hold back the night, let the day linger on.
Now comes the angel[8] always sent to speak with Charles;
and the angel at once commanded him:
"Charles, ride: God knows. The light will not fail you.   2455
God knows that you have lost the flower of France.
You can take vengeance now on that criminal race."
The Emperor, on that word, mounts his horse. AOI.

180

God made great miracles for Charlemagne,
for on that day in heaven the sun stood still.   2460
The pagans flee, the Franks keep at their heels,
catch up with them in the Vale Tenebrous,
chase them on spurring hard to Saragossa,
and always killing them, striking with fury;
cut off their paths, the widest roads away: 2465
the waters of the Ebro lie before them,
very deep, an amazing sight, and swift;
and there is no boat, no barge, no dromond, no galley.
They call on Tervagant, one of their gods.

8. Gabriel. Cf. *laisses* 185, 291, and others.

Then they jump in, but no god is with them:
those in full armor, the ones who weigh the most,
sank down, and they were many, to the bottom;
the others float downstream: the luckiest ones,
who fare best in those waters, have drunk so much,
they all drown there, struggling, it is amazing.
The French cry out: "Curse the day you saw Roland!" AOI.

181

When Charlemagne sees all the pagans dead,
many struck down, the great mass of them drowned—
the immense spoils his knights win from that battle!—
the mighty King at once gets down on foot,
lies on the ground, and gives thanks to the Lord.
When he stands up again, the sun has set.
Said the Emperor: "It is time to make camp.
It is late now to return to Rencesvals;
our horses are worn out, they have no strength—
take off their saddles, the bridles on their heads,
let them cool down and rest in these meadows."
The Franks reply: "Yes, as you well say, Lord." AOI.

182

The Emperor commands them to make camp.
The French dismount into that wilderness;
they have removed the saddles from their horses,
and the bridles, dressed in gold, from their heads,
free them to the meadows and the good grass;
and that is all the care they can give them.
Those who are weary sleep on the naked earth;
and all sleep, they set no watch that night.

183

The Emperor lay down in a meadow,
puts his great spear, brave man, beside his head;
he does not wish, on this night, to disarm:
he has put on his bright, brass-sewn hauberk,
laced on his helm, adorned with gems in gold,
and girded on Joiuse, there never was its like:
each day it shines with thirty different lights.
There are great things that we can say about the lance
with which Our Lord was wounded on the Cross:
thanks be to God, Charles has its iron point,
he had it mounted in that sword's golden pommel.
For this honor, and for this mighty grace,
the name Joiuse was given to that sword.
Brave men of France must never forget this:
from this sword's name they get their cry Munjoie!
This is why no nation can withstand them.

184

The night is clear, the moon is shining bright,
Charles lies down in grief and pain for Roland,

and for Oliver, it weighs down on him hard,   2515
for the Twelve Peers, for all the men of France
whom he left dead, covered with blood, at Rencesvals;
and cannot keep from weeping, wailing aloud,
and prays to God: lead their souls to safety.
His weariness is great, for his pain is great;   2520
he has fallen asleep, he cannot go on.
Through all the meadows now the Franks are sleeping.
There is no horse that has the strength to stand:
if one wants grass, he grazes lying down.
He has learned much who knows much suffering.   2525

185

Charlemagne sleeps, a man worn out with pain.
God sent Saint Gabriel to him that night
with this command: watch over the Emperor.
All through the night the angel stands at his head;
and in a vision he brought the King dread tidings   2530
of a great battle soon to come against him:
revealed to him its grave signification:
Charles raised his eyes and looked up to the sky,
he sees the thunder, the winds, the blasts of ice,
the hurricanes, the dreadful tempests,   2535
the fires and flames made ready in the sky.
And suddenly all things fall on his men.
Their lances burn, the wood of ash and apple,
and their shields burn down to their golden bosses,
the shafts of their sharp spears burst into pieces,   2540
then the grating of hauberks, helmets of steel.
He sees his warriors in great distress—
leopards and bears furious to devour them,
serpents, vipers, dragons, demons of hell,
swarms of griffins, thirty thousand and more,   2545
and all come swooping down upon the French;
and the French cry: "Charlemagne, come help us!"
The King is filled with rage and pain and pity,
wants to go there, but something blocks his way:
out of a wood a great lion coming at him,   2550
it is tremendous, wild, and great with pride:
seeks the King's very body, attacks the King!
and they lock arms, King and lion, to fight,
and still he cannot tell who strikes, who falls.
The Emperor sleeps, his dream does not wake him.   2555

186

And after this he was shown another vision:
he was in France, at Aix, on a stone step,
and two chains in his hands holding a bear;
from the Ardennes he saw thirty bears coming,
and each of them was speaking like a man;   2560
they said to him: "Lord, give him back to us,
you must not keep him longer, it is not right;

he is our kin, we must deliver him."
From his palace a greyhound now, running,
leaps on the greatest bear among them all,   2565
on the green grass beyond his companions,
there the King sees an amazing struggle
but cannot tell who conquers, who goes down.
These are the things God's angel showed this baron.
Charles sleeps until the morning and the bright day.   2570

[Lines 2571–3675 describe the death of Marsilion and Charlemagne's defeat of the
army of Baligant, the emir of Cairo and Marsilion's overlord.]

267

Night passes on, and the bright day appears.
Charles fortified the towers of Saragossa,
left a thousand knights there, fighting men all;
they guard the city in the Emperor's name.
Now the King mounts his horse, all his men mount,   3680
and Bramimunde, whom he leads prisoner,
though he has but one will: to do her good.
They turn toward home, in joy, in jubilation,
and pass in force, a mighty host, through Nerbone;
and Charles came to Bordeaux, that . . . city, sets⁹   3685
on the altar of the baron saint Sevrin
the olifant, filled with gold and pagan coins—
pilgrims passing can see it there today;
crosses the Gironde in great ships that lie there;
he has escorted as far as Blaye his nephew   3690
and Oliver, his noble companion,
and the Archbishop, who was so wise and brave;
and bids these lords be laid in white stone coffins:
at Saint-Romain the brave men lie there still;
the Franks leave them to the Lord and His Names.¹   3695
And Charles rides over the valleys and the mountains,
would take no rest all the long way to Aix,
and rode until he dismounts at the steps.
When he is in his sovereign high palace,
he summons all his judges, sends messengers: 3700
Saxons, Bavarians, Frisians, men of Lorraine,
the Alemans, the men of Burgundy,
the Poitevins, the Normans, the Bretons,
the wisest men among the men of France.
And now begins the trial of Ganelon.   3705

268

The Emperor is home again from Spain,
and comes to Aix, best residence of France,
ascends to the palace; entered the hall.
And now comes Aude, fair maid, before the King;

9. The line is incomplete in the manuscript.   1. A reference to prayers containing some of the many
names (Adonai, Emmanuel, Yehovah, and so on) by which God is called in sacred writings. These prayers
were considered effective in times of danger.

and said to him: "Where is Roland the captain,   3710
who swore to me to take me for his wife?"
And Charlemagne feels the weight and grief of this,
tears fill his eyes, he weeps, pulls his white beard:
"Sweet friend, dear sister, you ask for a dead man.
I will give you a good man in his place,   3715
it is Louis, I cannot name a better—
he is my son, he will possess my marches."
And Aude replies: "How strange these words sound to me.
May it never please God or his angels or saints
that I should go on living after Roland";   3720
loses color, falls at Charlemagne's feet,
already dead, God take pity on her soul.
Brave men of France weep and lament for Aude.

269

Aude the fair maid is gone now to her end;
the King believes that she has only fainted;   3725
and he is moved, the Emperor weeps for Aude,
takes her two hands; now he has raised her up,
her head sinks down, fallen upon her shoulders;
when Charlemagne sees she is dead in his arms,
he has four countesses sent for at once,   3730
and Aude is borne to a minster of nuns;
all through the night till dawn they wake beside her,
then nobly buried her by an altar.
The King gave Aude great honors, the church great gifts. AOI.

270

The Emperor has come home again to Aix.   3735
In iron chains, the traitor Ganelon
stands before the palace, within the city.
He has been bound, and by serfs, to a stake;
they tie his hands with deerhide straps and thongs,
and beat him hard, with butcher's hooks, with clubs—   3740
for what better reward has this man earned?
There he stands, in pain and rage, awaiting his trial.

271

It is written in the ancient Geste
that Charles summons his vassals from many lands;
they are gathered in the chapel at Aix,   3745
a high day this, a very solemn feast,
the feast, some say, of the baron saint Sylvester.[2]
Now here begin the trial and the pleadings
of Ganelon, who committed treason.
The Emperor has had this man brought forth. AOI.   3750

272

"Barons, my lords," said Charlemagne the King,
"judge what is right concerning Ganelon.

2. The feast of Saint Sylvester: December 31.

He was with me, came in my army to Spain,
and took from me twenty thousand of my French,
and my nephew, whom you'll not see again,   3755
and Oliver, brave man, born to the court,
and the Twelve Peers—betrayed them all for money."
Said Ganelon: "Let me be called a traitor
    if I hide what I did. It was Roland
who cheated me of gold and goods; and so I wanted
to make him suffer and die; and found the way.   3760
But treason, no—I'll grant no treason there!"
The Franks reply: "We shall take counsel now."

273

And there Ganelon stood, before the King,
breathing power—that lordly color on his face:
the image of a great man, had he been loyal.   3765
He sees his judges, he sees the men of France,
and his kinsmen, the thirty with him there;
then he cried out, with that great ringing voice:
"Barons, hear me, hear me for the love of God!
I was in that army with the Emperor   3770
and served him well, in love and loyalty.
Then his nephew Roland began to hate me,
and he doomed me to die an outrageous death:
I was sent as messenger to King Marsilion.
I used my wits, and I came back alive.   3775
Now I had challenged Roland, that great fighter,
and Oliver, and all of their companions:
King Charles heard it, and all his noble barons.
I took *revenge*, but there's no treason there."
The Franks reply: "We shall go into council."   3780

274

When Ganelon sees that his great trial commences,
he got his thirty kinsmen all around him.
There is one man the others listen to:
it is Pinabel of the castle of Sorence,
a man who counsels well and judges well,   3785
a valiant fighter—no man can win his arms. AOI.
Said Ganelon: "In you, friend . . . ³
free me from death and from this accusation!"
Said Pinabel: "You will soon be out of this.
Let one Frenchman dare sentence you to hang: 3790
once the Emperor sets us down man to man,
I will give him the lie with this steel sword."
And Ganelon, the Count, falls at his feet.

275

Bavarians, Saxons have gone into council,
Poitevins and Normans and men of France,   3795

---

3. The line is incomplete in the manuscript.

the Alemans, the Germans from the North,
men of Auvergne, the courtliest of all.
They keep their voices low, because of Pinabel;
said to each other: "Best to let it stop here—
let's leave this trial and then entreat the King   3800
to let Count Ganelon go free this time
and serve henceforth in love and loyalty.
Roland is dead: you won't see him again,
he will not come for gold or goods again:
only a fool would fight over this now."   3805
All go along, no one there disagrees
except one man, Lord Gefrei's brother: Tierri. AOI.

276

The barons now come back to Charlemagne,
say to the King: "Lord, this we beg of you:
let Ganelon go free, renounce your claim,   3810
then let him serve you in love and loyalty:
let this man live, for his family is great.
Roland is dead: we'll not see a hair of him,
    though we die for it, not a shred of his garment,
or get him back for gold or goods again."   3815
And the King said: "You are all my traitors." AOI.

277

When Charles perceives all have abandoned him,
he bowed his head with that and hid his face,
and in such pain calls himself wretched man.
But now we see: a warrior before him,
Tierri, brother of Gefrei, a duke of Anjou—   3820
the meager body on him, such a slight man!
his hair all black, and his face rather dark;
hardly a giant, but at least not too small;
said to the Emperor, as one born to the court:
"Dear Lord and King, do not lament before us.   3825
You know I have served you well: I have the right,
my forebears' right! to give this judgment here:
Whatever wrong Count Roland may have done
to Ganelon, he was in your service,
    and serving you should have protected him,
Ganelon is a traitor: he betrayed Roland.   3830
It's you he wronged when he perjured himself,
and broke faith. Therefore, I sentence him
to die, to hang . . . his body cast . . . ⁴
like a traitor, a man who committed treason.
If his kinsman wants to give me the lie,   3835
here is my sword, girded on: and with this sword
I am ready to make my judgment good."
The Franks reply: "Now you have spoken well."

4. The line is incomplete in manuscript.

278

Now Pinabel has come before the King:
a huge man of swift grace, a valiant man—   3840
time has run out for the poor wretch he strikes!—
said to the King: "Lord, is this not your court?
Give orders then, tell them to stop this noise.
Here I see Tierri, who has given his judgment:
I declare it is false; I shall fight with him";   3845
places his deerhide glove in Charles's fist.
Said the Emperor: "I must have good surety."
Thirty kinsmen go hostage for his loyalty.
Then the King said: "I shall release him then";
and has them guarded until justice is done. AOI.   3850

279

When Tierri sees the battle will take place
he gave to Charles his own right glove as gage.
The Emperor sets him free, for hostages;
then has four benches set round that battle ground:
there they will sit: the two men pledged to fight.   3855
The others judge they have been duly summoned,
Oger of Denmark had settled every question.
And then they call for their horses and arms.

280

Now since both men have been brought forth for battle, AOI.
they make confession and are absolved and blessed;   3860
they hear their mass, receive the Sacrament,
lay down great offerings in these minsters.
Now the two men have come back before Charles.
They have fastened their spurs upon their feet,
and they put on white hauberks, strong and light,   3865
and laced their bright helmets glowing upon their heads,
gird on their swords, the hilts of purest gold;
hang their great quartered shields upon their necks,
take hold of their sharp spears in their right fists;
now they are mounted upon their swift war horses.   3870
And then a hundred thousand warriors wept,
moved for love of Roland to pity Tierri.
The Lord well knows how this battle will end.

281

Down below Aix there is a broad meadow;
there the battle is joined between these barons.   3875
They are brave men, great warriors keeping faith,
and their horses are swift and spirited.
They spur them hard, reins loosened all the way,
come on to strike, the great strength that is theirs!
their two shields burst in that attack to pieces,   3880
their hauberks tear, their saddle girths rip open,
the bosses turn, the saddles fall to earth.
A hundred thousand men, who watch them, weep.

282

Now the two warriors are on the ground, AOI.
now on their feet, and with what speed! again—   3885
the grace and lightness, the strength of Pinabel!—
fall on each other, they have no horses now,
strike with their swords, the hilts of purest gold,
and strike again on these helmets of steel
tremendous blows—blows that cut through helms of steel!   3890
The knights of France are wild with grief and worry.
"Oh, God," said Charles, "make the right between
      them clear!"

283

Said Pinabel: "Tierri, now give it up!
I'll be your man, in love and loyalty,
I'll give you all I own, take what you please,   3895
only make peace with the King for Ganelon."
Tierri replies: "I cannot hear of that,
call me traitor if I consent to that!
May God do right between us two today." AOI.

284

Now Tierri spoke: "Pinabel, you are good,   3900
the great body on you formed like a lord's;
your peers know you: all that a vassal should be;
let this battle go then, let it end here,
I will make peace for you with Charlemagne.
But justice will be done on Ganelon,
      such justice will be done on his body,   3905
no day will pass that men do not speak of it."
Said Pinabel: "May the Lord God forbid!
I will stand up for all my kin, I'll fight,
no man alive will make me quit my kin
      and cry defeat and beg for his mercy,
I'd sooner die than be reproached for that."   3910
And they begin to beat down with their swords
on these helmets beset with gems in gold,
and the bright fires fly from that fight toward heaven;
and no chance now that these two can be parted:
it cannot end without one of them dead. AOI.   3915

285

Pinabel of Sorence, that valiant man,
strikes Tierri now on that helm of Provence:
the fire shoots out and sets the grass aflame;
and shows Tierri the point of that steel sword:
he brought it down. Pinabel brought it down   3920
on his forehead, and down across his face,
the whole right cheek is bloody from that blow,
his hauberk runs with blood down to his waist.
God protects him, he is not struck down dead. AOI.

286

And Tierri sees: he is struck on the face— 3925
the bright blood falling on the grass in the meadow;
strikes Pinabel on his helm of bright steel,
and shattered it, split it to the nosepiece,
struck his brain out spattering from his head;
and raised his sword; he has cast him down, dead. 3930
That was the blow, and the battle is won.
The Franks cry out: "God has made a miracle!
Now Ganelon must hang, it is right now,
and all his kin who stood for him in court." AOI.

287

Now when Tierri had won his great battle, 3935
there came to him the Emperor Charlemagne,
and forty of his barons along with him,
Naimon the Duke, and Oger of Denmark,
William of Blaye, and Gefrei of Anjou.
The King has taken Tierri into his arms, 3940
he wipes his face with his great furs of marten,
throws them aside; they clasp new furs round him.
Very gently, they disarm the warrior,
then they mount him on a mule of Araby,
and he comes home in joy among brave men. 3945
They come to Aix, it is there they dismount.
It is the time now for the executions.

288

Now Charlemagne summons his counts and dukes:
"What is your counsel regarding those I have held?
They came to court to stand for Ganelon, 3950
bound themselves hostages for Pinabel."
The Franks reply: "Not one of them must live."
The King commands his officer, Basbrun:
"Go, hang them all on the accursed tree,
and by this beard, by the white hairs in this beard, 3955
if one escapes, you are lost, a dead man."
Basbrun replies: "What should I do but hang them?";
leads them, by force, with a hundred sergeants.
They are thirty men, and thirty men are hanged.
A traitor brings death, on himself and on others. AOI. 3960

289

Bavarians and Alemans returned,
and Poitevins, and Bretons, and Normans,
and all agreed, the Franks before the others,
Ganelon must die, and in amazing pain.
Four war horses are led out and brought forward; 3965
then they attach his two feet, his two hands.
These battle horses are swift and spirited,
four sergeants come and drive them on ahead

toward a river in the midst of a field.
Ganelon is brought to terrible perdition,   3970
all his mighty sinews are pulled to pieces,
and the limbs of his body burst apart;
on the green grass flows that bright and famous blood.
Ganelon died a traitor's and recreant's death.
Now when one man betrays another,
    it is not right that he should live to boast of it.   3975

290

When the Emperor had taken his revenge,
he called to him his bishops of France,
Bavaria, Germany: "In my household
there is a noble captive, and she has heard,
for so long now, such sermons and examples,   3980
she longs for faith in God, the Christian faith.
Baptize this Queen, that God may have her soul."
And they reply: "Let her be baptized now
by godmothers, ladies of noble birth."
At the baths of Aix there is a great crowd gathered,   3985
there they baptized the noble Queen of Spain,
and they found her the name Juliana;
she is Christian, by knowledge of the Truth.

291

When the Emperor had brought his justice to pass
and peace comes now to that great wrath of his,   3990
he put the Christian faith in Bramimunde;
the day passes, the soft night has gathered,
the King lay down in his vaulted chamber.
Saint Gabriel! come in God's name to say:
"Charles, gather the great hosts of your Empire!   3995
Go to the land of Bire, with all your force,
you must relieve King Vivien at Imphe,
the citadel, pagans have besieged it:
Christians are calling you, they cry your name!"
The Emperor would have wished not to go.   4000
"God!" said the King, "the pains, the labors of my life!";
weeps from his eyes, pulls his white beard.

Here ends the song   that Turold composes, paraphrases, amplifies,[5] 4003
                    that Turold completes, relates,
Here ends the tale   that Turold declaims, recounts, narrates,
                    that Turold copies, transcribes,
Here ends the geste   for Turold grows weak, grows weary, declines,
Here ends the written history,
Here ends the source   that Turold turns into poetry.

---

5. The last line of the poem reads *Ci falt la geste que Turoldus declinet.* The meaning of the words *geste* and *declinet* and the syntax of *que* have never been finally settled, and no line in the poem contains so many possible meanings as the last one. Some of the interpretations that have been proposed are given here, and every one is plausible.

MARIE DE FRANCE
twelfth century

The first woman writer in French (at least so far as we know), Marie de France created her work at a crucial time in the history of literature, a history to which she made a central contribution. For it was in the twelfth century that most of the major forms and themes that have shaped Western literature emerged in the vernacular languages of Europe. Primary among them were the works we now call romances, novelistic narratives that dealt with adventure and—above all—love. The most familiar of these narratives are the stories of King Arthur and his knights, stories that in the twelfth century received the literary treatment, and enjoyed the enormous popularity, they still have today. The Arthurian legends were part of a vast mythology developed by the Celts of Western Europe, peoples who were driven from their lands by the Germanic invaders of the fourth and fifth centuries and took refuge on the Atlantic fringe of the continent in what are now Ireland, Wales, and Brittany. Yet if they were conquered as a people, the Celts triumphed through their stories. There is hardly a work of medieval literature that does not reveal the influence of Celtic mythology.

Less popular than the long Arthurian narratives but more finely crafted as works of art were the short narratives of love, adventure, and the supernatural, also of Celtic origin, known as *lais* or, in English, lays. As a form of literature, the lay first appears in a collection composed about 1165 by a woman who identifies herself only as "Marie." In another work she tells us that she is "from France," and ever since the Renaissance she has been given the designation "Marie de France." From the evidence of her writing, we know that she was a noblewoman, that she could read French, English, and Latin, and that she was familiar with a royal household, probably that of Henry II, king of England (reigned 1154–89). She may well have been a nun or even an abbess, since many noble daughters were placed in the elegant aristocratic nunneries of Europe. All of her work, including the twelve lays that survive, is written in octosyllabic verse in Anglo-Norman, a French dialect spoken by the nobility of postconquest England. The sources for her lays, she tells us, were stories that she heard, and while she provides us with several Breton terms—like the word *laüstic* for nightingale—we cannot know if she heard these stories in English, French, or Breton.

The two lays presented here deal with a topic that is central to the collection as a whole. These are stories in which love serves as an alternative—in one case successfully, in the other not—to an uncaring or unjust society. In both stories Marie combines an acute awareness of contemporary social conditions with sympathy for individuals who seek personal fulfillment. In the lay that bears his name, Lanval is a young foreigner who has come to the Arthurian court to seek his fortune. He is the son of a king, but his "inheritance"—by which Marie means his ancestral domain—is far away. The implication is that Lanval is like many noble young men in twelfth-century France and England who, as younger sons, were largely excluded from inheriting the family land under the recently established system of primogeniture, by which only the eldest son inherited. Thus when at the beginning of the story Arthur hands out lands and wives to his knights but neglects the deserving Lanval, he is dooming Lanval to a life of continued obscurity and lonely service. Rescue comes to him in the form of the fairy lover, who is not merely beautiful and loving but—as Marie is careful to stress—rich. Now that Lanval can comport himself with the confidence and liberality that befits a nobleman, he becomes attractive to the queen (presumably Guinevere, although she is not named). And in rejecting her advances he asserts not simply the superior beauty of his lady but the superiority of her handmaiden, making it clear that he is attached to a court that surpasses in its grandeur that of Arthur himself. This is why Arthur so quickly supports his queen in her false accusation, and why Lanval is accused not just of a social gaffe but of felony and treason. For as

Arthur's barons say, Lanval ought to honor his lord at all times, while he is acting (rightly, as it turns out) as if he is obligated to a different sovereign entirely. Yet the power of Marie's story derives from the fact that, despite this emphasis on social and material benefits, Lanval is primarily distressed because he has lost not the fairy queen's financial support but her love. And when the two pairs of damsels appear, he remains true to her by refusing to claim either of them as warrant for his rash words to the queen. Perhaps it is because he passes this test that his lover then herself appears and takes him away with her to Avalon, a world in which the petty jealousies and unfulfilled ambitions of the Arthurian court can be forgotten. Here love seems to conquer all, but no reader can ignore that its triumph is possible only in the fantasy world of fiction.

Laüstic, on the other hand, is a story of unfulfilled love. In this case the social reality to which the story is addressed is the aristocratic custom of arranged marriages. In Lanval Arthur gives away wives, yet there is no indication that the women involved have any say in their marital fate. Yet at the same time as the European nobility was treating marriage as a financial and political matter, the Church was teaching that marriage was above all a matter of free consent, that what made two people husband and wife was their agreement to enter into marriage with each other. Marie's lays are filled with unhappy wives—unhappy not only because they were forced into marriages against their will but because they know they deserve better (indeed, perhaps we should understand Guinevere's misbehavior in Lanval as caused by such knowledge). The young wife in Laüstic can only dream of escape as she gazes out her confining room at her would-be lover. The nightingale that she invokes to quiet her jealous husband becomes a symbol of this yearning to escape, and when her husband brutally kills it and throws its bleeding corpse at her, we can understand that the stain it leaves on the breast of her tunic is the outward sign of a broken heart. Yet this is not the end, for the golden casket in which her lover entombs the nightingale serves to celebrate a love that may not have found earthly fulfillment but has achieved another, higher permanence. In its exquisite concision, Laüstic is itself a literary version of that golden casket, a verbal equivalent to the jeweled reliquaries in which medieval people encased the bodies of their saints.

A complete translation of the Lais, with a helpful introduction and full bibliography, can be found in Glyn S. Burgess and Keith Busby, trans., The Lais of Marie de France (1986). A verse translation with commentary is provided by Robert Hanning and Joan Ferrante, The Lais of Marie de France (1978).

Lanval[1]

Just as it happened, I shall relate to you the story of another lay, which tells of a very noble young man whose name in Breton is Lanval.

Arthur, the worthy and courtly king, was at Carlisle[2] on account of the Scots and the Picts who were ravaging the country, penetrating into the land of Logres[3] and frequently laying it waste.

The king was there during the summer, at Pentecost,[4] and he gave many rich gifts to counts and barons and to those of the Round Table: there was no such company in the whole world. He apportioned wives and lands to all, save to one who had served him: this was Lanval, whom he did not remember, and for whom no one put in a good word. Because of his valor, generosity,

---

1. Translated by Glyn S. Burgess and Keith Busby.   2. City near the Scottish border.   3. The Arthurian name for England.   4. A feast day celebrated on the seventh Sunday after Easter.

beauty and prowess, many were envious of him. There were those who pretended to hold him in esteem, but who would not have uttered a single regret if misfortune had befallen him. He was the son of a king of noble birth, but far from his inheritance, and although he belonged to Arthur's household he had spent all his wealth, for the king gave him nothing and Lanval asked for nothing. Now he was in a plight, very sad and forlorn. Lords, do not be surprised: a stranger bereft of advice can be very downcast in another land when he does not know where to seek help.

This knight whose tale I am telling you had served the king well. One day he mounted his horse and went to take his ease. He left the town and came alone to a meadow, dismounting by a stream; but there his horse trembled violently, so he loosened its saddlegirth and left it, allowing it to enter the meadow to roll over on its back. He folded his cloak, which he placed beneath his head, very disconsolate because of his troubles, and nothing could please him. Lying thus, he looked downriver and saw two damsels coming, more beautiful than any he had ever seen: they were richly dressed in closely fitting tunics of dark purple and their faces were very beautiful. The older one carried dishes of gold, well and finely made—I will not fail to tell you the truth—and the other carried a towel. They went straight to where the knight lay and Lanval, who was very well-mannered, stood up to meet them. They first greeted him and then delivered their message: "Sir Lanval, my damsel, who is very worthy, wise and fair, has sent us for you. Come with us, for we will conduct you safely. Look, her tent is near." The knight went with them, disregarding his horse which was grazing before him in the meadow. They led him to the tent, which was so beautiful and well-appointed that neither Queen Semiramis at the height of her wealth, power and knowledge, nor the Emperor Octavian,[5] could have afforded even the right-hand side of it. There was a golden eagle placed on the top, the value of which I cannot tell, nor of the ropes or the poles which supported the walls of the tent. There is no king under the sun who could afford it, however much he might give. Inside this tent was the maiden who surpassed in beauty the lily and the new rose when it appears in summer. She lay on a very beautiful bed—the coverlets cost as much as a castle—clad only in her shift. Her body was well formed and handsome, and in order to protect herself from the heat of the sun, she had cast about her a costly mantle of white ermine covered with Alexandrian purple. Her side, though, was uncovered, as well as her face, neck and breast; she was whiter than the hawthorn blossom.

The maiden called the knight, who came forward and sat before the bed. "Lanval," she said, "fair friend, for you I came from my country. I have come far in search of you and if you are worthy and courtly, no emperor, count or king will have felt as much joy or happiness as you, for I love you above all else." He looked at her and saw that she was beautiful. Love's spark pricked him so that his heart was set alight, and he replied to her in seemly manner: "Fair lady, if it were to please you to grant me the joy of wanting to love me, you could ask nothing that I would not do as best I could, be it foolish or wise. I shall do as you bid and abandon all others for you. I never want to leave you and this is what I most desire." When the girl heard these words from the man who loved her so, she granted him her love and her body. Now

---

5. Roman emperor Caesar Augustus (63 B.C.–A.D. 14); *Semiramis:* a legendary queen of Assyria.

Lanval was on the right path! She gave him a boon, that henceforth he could wish for nothing which he would not have, and however generously he gave or spent, she would still find enough for him. Lanval was very well lodged, for the more he spent, the more gold and silver he would have. "Beloved," she said, "I admonish, order, and beg you not to reveal this secret to anyone! I shall tell you the long and the short of it: you would lose me forever if this love were to become known. You would never be able to see me or possess me." He replied that he would do what she commanded. He lay down beside her on the bed: now Lanval was well lodged. That afternoon he remained with her until evening and would have done so longer had he been able and had his love allowed him. "Beloved," she said, "arise! You can stay no longer. Go from here and I shall remain, but I shall tell you one thing: whenever you wish to speak with me, you will not be able to think of a place where a man may enjoy his love without reproach or wickedness, that I shall not be there with you to do your bidding. No man save you will see me or hear my voice." When he heard this, Lanval was well pleased and, kissing her, he arose. The damsels who had led him to the tent dressed him in rich garments, and in his new clothes there was no more handsome young man on earth. He was neither foolish nor ill-mannered. The damsels gave him water to wash his hands and a towel to dry them and then brought him food. He took his supper, which was not to be disdained, with his beloved. He was very courteously served and dined joyfully. There was one dish in abundance that pleased the knight particularly, for he often kissed his beloved and embraced her closely.

When they had risen from table, his horse was brought to him, well saddled. Lanval was richly served there. He took his leave, mounted, and went towards the city, often looking behind him, for he was greatly disturbed, thinking of his adventure and uneasy in his heart. He was at a loss to know what to think, for he could not believe it was true. When he came to his lodgings, he found his men finely dressed. That night he offered lavish hospitality but no one knew how this came to be. There was no knight in the town in sore need of shelter whom he did not summon and serve richly and well. Lanval gave costly gifts, Lanval freed prisoners, Lanval clothed the jongleurs,[6] Lanval performed many honorable acts. There was no one, stranger or friend, to whom he would not have given gifts. He experienced great joy and pleasure, for day or night he could see his beloved often and she was entirely at his command.

In the same year, I believe, after St John's day,[7] as many as thirty knights had gone to relax in a garden beneath the tower where the queen was staying. Gawain was with them and his cousin, the fair Ywain. Gawain, the noble and the worthy, who endeared himself to all, said: "In God's name, lords, we treat our companion Lanval ill, for he is so generous and courtly, and his father is a rich king, yet we have not brought him with us." So they returned, went to his lodgings and persuaded him to come with them.

The queen, in the company of three ladies, was reclining by a window cut out of the stone when she caught sight of the king's household and recognized Lanval. She called one of her ladies to summon her most elegant and beautiful damsels to relax with her in the garden where the others were. She

6. Minstrels.   7. June 24.

took more than thirty with her, and they went down the steps where the knights, glad of their coming, came to meet them. They took the girls by the hand and the conversation was not uncourtly. Lanval withdrew to one side, far from the others, for he was impatient to hold his beloved, to kiss, embrace and touch her. He cared little for other people's joy when he could not have his own pleasure. When the queen saw the knight alone, she approached him straightaway. Sitting down beside him, she spoke to him and opened her heart. "Lanval, I have honored, cherished and loved you much. You may have all my love: just tell me what you desire! I grant you my love and you should be glad to have me." "Lady," he said, "leave me be! I have no desire to love you, for I have long served the king and do not want to betray my faith. Neither you nor your love will ever lead me to wrong my lord!" The queen became angry and distressed, and spoke unwisely: "Lanval," she said, "I well believe that you do not like this kind of pleasure. I have been told often enough that you have no desire for women. You have well-trained young men and enjoy yourself with them. Base coward, wicked recreant, my lord is extremely unfortunate to have suffered you near him. I think he may have lost his salvation because of it!"

When he heard her, he was distressed, but not slow to reply. He said something in spite that he was often to regret. "Lady, I am not skilled in the profession you mention, but I love and am loved by a lady who should be prized above all others I know. And I will tell you one thing: you can be sure that one of her servants, even the very poorest girl, is worth more than you, my lady the Queen, in body, face and beauty, wisdom and goodness." Thereupon the queen left and went in tears to her chamber, very distressed and angry that he had humiliated her in this way. She took to her bed ill and said that she would never again get up, unless the king saw that justice was done her in respect of her complaint.

The king had returned from the woods after an extremely happy day. He entered the queen's apartments and when she saw him, she complained aloud, fell at his feet, cried for mercy and said that Lanval had shamed her. He had requested her love and because she had refused him, had insulted and deeply humiliated her. He had boasted of a beloved who was so well-bred, noble and proud that her chambermaid, the poorest servant she had, was worthier than the queen. The king grew very angry and swore on oath that, if Lanval could not defend himself in court, he would have him burned or hanged. The king left the room, summoned three of his barons and sent them for Lanval, who was suffering great pain. He had returned to his lodgings, well aware of having lost his beloved by revealing their love. Alone in his chamber, distraught and anguished, he called his beloved repeatedly, but to no avail. He lamented and sighed, fainting from time to time; a hundred times he cried to her to have mercy, to come and speak with her beloved. He cursed his heart and his mouth and it was a wonder he did not kill himself. His cries and moans were not loud enough nor his agitation and torment such that she would have mercy on him, or even permit him to see her. Alas, what will he do?

The king's men arrived and told Lanval to go to court without delay: the king had summoned him through them, for the queen had accused him. Lanval went sorrowfully and would have been happy for them to kill him. He came before the king, sad, subdued and silent, betraying his great sorrow.

The king said to him angrily: "Vassal, you have wronged me greatly! You were extremely ill-advised to shame and vilify me, and to slander the queen. You boasted out of folly, for your beloved must be very noble for her handmaiden to be more beautiful and more worthy than the queen."

Lanval denied point by point having offended and shamed his lord, and maintained that he had not sought the queen's love, but he acknowledged the truth of his words about the love of which he had boasted. He now regretted this, for as a result he had lost her. He told them he would do whatever the court decreed in this matter, but the king was very angry and sent for all his men to tell him exactly what he should do, so that his action would not be unfavourably interpreted. Whether they liked it or not, they obeyed his command and assembled to make a judgement, deciding that a day should be fixed for the trial, but that Lanval should provide his lord with pledges that he would await his judgement and return later to his presence. Then the court would be larger, for at that moment only the king's household itself was present. The barons returned to the king and explained their reasoning. The king asked for pledges, but Lanval was alone and forlorn, having no relation or friend there. Then Gawain approached and offered to stand bail, and all his companions did likewise. The king said to them: "I entrust him to you on surety of all that you hold from me, lands and fiefs, each man separately." When this had been pledged, there was no more to be done, and Lanval returned to his lodging with the knights escorting him. They chastised him and urged him strongly not to be so sorrowful, and cursed such foolish love. They went to see him every day, as they wished to know whether he was drinking and eating properly, being very much afraid that he might harm himself.

On the appointed day the barons assembled. The king and queen were there and the guarantors brought Lanval to court. They were all very sad on his account and I think there were a hundred who would have done all in their power to have him released without a trial because he had been wrongly accused. The king demanded the verdict according to the charge and the rebuttal, and now everything lay in the hands of the barons. They considered their judgement, very troubled and concerned on account of this noble man from abroad, who was in such a plight in their midst. Some of them wanted to harm him in conformity with their lord's will. Thus spoke the count of Cornwall: "There shall be no default on our part. Like it or not, right must prevail. The king accused his vassal, whom I heard you call Lanval, of a felony and charged him with a crime, about a love he boasted of which angered my lady. Only the king is accusing him, so by the faith I owe you, there ought, to tell the truth, to be no case to answer, were it not that one should honour one's lord in all things. An oath will bind Lanval and the king will put the matter in our hands. If he can provide proof and his beloved comes forward, and if what he said to incur the queen's displeasure is true, then he will be pardoned, since he did not say it to spite her. And if he cannot furnish proof, then we must inform him that he will lose the king's service and that the king must banish him." They sent word to the knight and informed him that he should send for his beloved to defend and protect him. He told them that this was not possible and that he would receive no help from her. The messengers returned to the judges, expecting no help to be forthcoming for Lanval. The king pressed them hard because the queen was waiting for them.

When they were about to give their verdict, they saw two maidens approaching on two fine ambling palfreys. They were extremely comely and dressed only in purple taffeta, next to their bare skin; the knights were pleased to see them. Gawain and three other knights went to Lanval, told him about this, and pointed the two maidens out to him. Gawain was very glad and strongly urged Lanval to tell him if this was his beloved, but he told them that he did not know who they were, whence they came or where they were going. The maidens continued to approach, still on horseback, and then dismounted before the dais where King Arthur was seated. They were of great beauty and spoke in courtly fashion: "King, make your chambers available and hang them with silken curtains so that my lady may stay here, for she wishes to lodge with you." This he granted them willingly and summoned two knights who led them to the upper chambers. For the moment they said no more.

The king asked his barons for the judgement and the responses, and said that they had greatly angered him by the long delay. "Lord," they said, "we are deliberating, but because of the ladies we saw, we have not reached a verdict. Let us continue with the trial." So they assembled in some anxiety, and there was a good deal of commotion and contention.

While they were in this troubled state, they saw two finely accoutred maidens coming along the street, dressed in garments of Phrygian[8] silk and riding on Spanish mules. The vassals were glad of this and they said to each other that Lanval, the worthy and brave, was now saved. Ywain went up to him with his companions, and said: "Lord, rejoice! For the love of God, speak to us! Two damsels are approaching, very comely and beautiful. It is surely your beloved." Lanval quickly replied that he did not recognize them, nor did he know or love them. When they had arrived, they dismounted before the king and many praised them highly for their bodies, faces, and complexions. They were both more worthy than the queen had ever been. The older of the two, who was courtly and wise, delivered her message fittingly: "King, place your chambers at our disposal for the purpose of lodging my lady. She is coming here to speak with you." He ordered them to be taken to the others who had arrived earlier. They paid no heed to their mules, and, as soon as they had left the king, he summoned all his barons so that they might deliver their verdict. This had taken up too much of the day and the queen, who had been waiting for them for such a long time, was getting angry.

Just as they were about to give their verdict, a maiden on horseback entered the town. There was none more beautiful in the whole world. She was riding a white palfrey which carried her well and gently; its neck and head were well-formed and there was no finer animal on earth. The palfrey was richly equipped, for no count or king on earth could have paid for it, save by selling or pledging his lands. The lady was dressed in a white tunic and shift, laced left and right so as to reveal her sides. Her body was comely, her lips low, her neck whiter than snow on a branch; her eyes were bright and her face white, her mouth fair and her nose well-placed; her eyebrows were brown and her brow fair, and her hair curly and rather blond. A golden thread does not shine as brightly as the rays reflected in the light from her hair. Her cloak was of dark silk and she had wrapped its skirts about her. She held a sparrowhawk on her wrist and behind her there followed a dog.

8. Phrygia is in modern Turkey, but here designates more generally the East.

There was no one in the town, humble or powerful, old or young, who did not watch her arrival, and no one jested about her beauty. She approached slowly and the judges who saw her thought it was a great wonder. No one who had looked at her could have failed to be inspired with real joy. Those who loved the knight went and told him about the maiden who was coming and who, please God, would deliver him. "Lord and friend, here comes a lady whose hair is neither tawny nor brown. She is the most beautiful of all women in the world." Lanval heard this and raised his head, for he knew her well, and sighed. His blood rushed to his face and he was quick to speak: "In faith," he said, "it is my beloved! If she shows me no mercy, I hardly care if anyone should kill me, for my cure is in seeing her." The lady entered the palace, where no one so beautiful had ever before been seen. She dismounted before the king, and in the sight of all, let her cloak fall so that they could see her better. The king, who was well-mannered, rose to meet her, and all the others honored her and offered themselves as her servants. When they had looked at her and praised her beauty greatly, she spoke thus, for she had no wish to remain: "King, I have loved one of your vassals, Lanval, whom you see there. Because of what he said, he was accused in your court, and I do not wish him to come to any harm. You should know that the queen was wrong, as he never sought her love. As regards the boast he made, if he can be acquitted by me, let your barons release him!" The king granted that it should be as the judges recommended, in accordance with justice. There was not one who did not consider that Lanval had successfully defended himself, and so he was freed by their decision. The maiden, who had many servants, then left, for the king could not retain her. Outside the hall there was a large block of dark marble on to which heavily armed men climbed when they left the king's court. Lanval mounted it and when the maiden came through the door, he leapt in a single bound on to the palfrey behind her. He went with her to Avalon,[9] so the Bretons tell us, to a very beautiful island. Thither the young man was borne and no one has heard any more about him, nor can I relate any more.

Laüstic[1]

I shall relate an adventure to you from which the Bretons composed a lay. *Laüstic* is its name, I believe, and that is what the Bretons call it in their land. In French the title is *Rossignol*, and Nightingale is the correct English word.

In the region of St Malo[2] was a famous town and two knights dwelt there, each with a fortified house. Because of the fine qualities of the two men the town acquired a good reputation. One of the knights had taken a wise, courtly and elegant wife who conducted herself, as custom dictated, with admirable propriety. The other knight was a young man who was well known amongst his peers for his prowess and great valour. He performed honorable deeds gladly and attended many tournaments, spending freely and giving gener-

9. The Celtic isle of the blessed.   1. Translated by Glyn S. Burgess and Keith Busby.   2. A town in Brittany.

ously whatever he had. He loved his neighbour's wife and so persistently did he request her love, so frequent were his entreaties and so many qualities did he possess that she loved him above all things, both for the good she had heard about him and because he lived close by. They loved each other prudently and well, concealing their love carefully to ensure that they were not seen, disturbed or suspected. This they could do because their dwellings were adjoining. Their houses, halls and keeps were close by each other and there was no barrier or division, apart from a high wall of dark-hued stone. When she stood at her bedroom window, the lady could talk to her beloved in the other house and he to her, and they could toss gifts to each other. There was scarcely anything to displease them and they were both very content except for the fact that they could not meet and take their pleasure with each other, for the lady was closely guarded when her husband was in the region. But they were so resourceful that day or night they managed to speak to each other and no one could prevent their coming to the window and seeing each other there. For a long time they loved each other, until one summer when the copses and meadows were green and the gardens in full bloom. On the flower-tops the birds sang joyfully and sweetly. If love is on anyone's mind, no wonder he turns his attention towards it. I shall tell you the truth about the knight. Both he and the lady made the greatest possible effort with their words and with their eyes. At night, when the moon was shining and her husband was asleep, she often rose from beside him and put on her mantle. Knowing her beloved would be doing the same, she would go and stand at the window and stay awake most of the night. They took delight in seeing each other, since they were denied anything more. But so frequently did she stand there and so frequently leave her bed that her husband became angry and asked her repeatedly why she got up and where she went. "Lord," replied the lady, "anyone who does not hear the song of the nightingale knows none of the joys of this world. This is why I come and stand here. So sweet is the song I hear by night that it brings me great pleasure. I take such delight in it and desire it so much that I can get no sleep at all." When the lord heard what she said, he gave a spiteful, angry laugh and devised a plan to ensnare the nightingale. Every single servant in his household constructed some trap, net or snare and then arranged them throughout the garden. There was no hazel tree or chestnut tree on which they did not place a snare or bird-lime, until they had captured and retained it. When they had taken the nightingale, it was handed over, still alive, to the lord, who was overjoyed to hold it in his hands. He entered the lady's chamber. "Lady," he said, "where are you? Come forward and speak to us. With bird-lime I have trapped the nightingale which has kept you awake so much. Now you can sleep in peace, for it will never awaken you again." When the lady heard him she was grief-stricken and distressed. She asked her husband for the bird, but he killed it out of spite, breaking its neck wickedly with his two hands. He threw the body at the lady, so that the front of her tunic was bespattered with blood, just on her breast. Thereupon he left the chamber. The lady took the tiny corpse, wept profusely and cursed those who had betrayed the nightingale by constructing the traps and snares, for they had taken so much joy from her. "Alas," she said, "misfortune is upon me. Never again can I get up at night or go to stand at the window where I used to see my beloved. I know one thing for certain. He will think I am faint-hearted, so I must take action. I shall send him the nightingale and let him know what has happened." She wrapped the little bird in a piece of samite, embroidered in gold and covered in designs. She called one of her servants, entrusted him with her message and sent him to her beloved. He went to the knight, greeted him on behalf of his lady, related the whole message to him and presented him with the nightingale. When the messenger had finished speaking, the knight, who had listened attentively, was distressed by what had happened. But he was not uncourtly or tardy. He had a small vessel prepared, not of iron or steel, but of pure gold with fine stones, very precious and valuable. On it he carefully placed a lid and put the nightingale in it. Then he had the casket sealed and carried it with him at all times.

This adventure was related and could not long be concealed. The Bretons composed a lay about it which is called *Laüstic*.

THORSTEIN THE STAFF-STRUCK
thirteenth century

Medieval Iceland produced not only a unique and highly interesting body of poetry but also some of the finest prose narratives in European literature. Some of these, like the *Saga of the Volsungs,* deal with figures of early Germanic tradition. But some thirty or forty, called sagas of Icelanders, are about men and women who lived in Iceland (and often in Norway in their youth) from the late ninth to the early eleventh centuries. Written mostly in the thirteenth century, they may remind us a bit of the historical novels of a later time. But in the historical novel, usually, the major characters are fictional, products of the author's invention, while those well known to history serve as framework or background. In the Icelandic saga the converse is true: the principal figures were actual people attested by documents and other evidence, as were also most of the events and acts attributed to them. Oral tradition bridged the interval between the tenth century and the thirteenth. Thus the author of an extant saga was free to shape characterization, motivation, mood, and tone as he saw fit. It is now believed that the milieu of thirteenth-century Iceland may have influenced features of some of these narratives. A few may have been entirely fictional, except for the use of the names of actual persons. Like the Eddic poems, the sagas are nearly always anonymous. Some of the most notable are of novel length, like the *Saga of the Laxdalers* or the Grettir saga, or the *Saga of Burnt Njal,* greatest of all.

As must be evident, the story of Thorstein the Staff-Struck is very short; in fact, it was not called a saga but a *thattr,* literally, a "thread." Nevertheless, it shows the characteristic features of a family saga. Although the action is "strong," to use a modern term—people kill and are killed—violence is not included for its own sake; instead, it interests the narrator chiefly as an expression of personality and character. The incidents of the story are conducted in such a way as to distinguish sharply nearly all of the participants; these are all members of one or the other of two families or households who live in northeast Iceland. The "fierce," now aged but still irascible Thorarin is contrasted with his husky and confident but even-tempered son, Thorstein; only when the insolent Thord willfully insults him does Thorstein take action. In prosecuting Thorstein for manslaughter, Bjarni, Thord's employer and also the district chieftain, fulfills a more or less automatic obligation. However, when Thorstein ignores the sentence of exile, Bjarni (whose responsibility it was to attack Thorstein) takes no action. We learn that he is unwilling to deprive the infirm, nearly blind

Thorarin of his son's support. Nevertheless, when Bjarni overhears the malicious gossip of Thorhall and Thorvald, he sends them out with instructions to kill Thorstein. We are not told what he expected would happen, but when he learns that Thorstein has slain the two brothers, once again he does nothing; when his wife Rannveig goads him, he remarks that "Thorstein has never killed anyone without a good reason." All the same, when she tells him of the taunts in circulation about him, he decides that he cannot avoid a confrontation with Thorstein.

Although the circumstances are different, Bjarni's motive in his (reluctant) challenge of Thorstein is the same as the latter's when he (at last) challenges Thord. Each man considers the respect of the community essential to his self-respect; hence they act as the code requires, regardless of their personal inclination or of the intrinsic merits of the case. The thirteenth-century Christian author faithfully presents this pre-Christian pattern; the ethical dilemma, unacknowledged by the protagonists, is implicit in the narration. Hence in the final encounter Bjarni and Thorstein carry out the *form* of conduct that tradition makes obligatory, while the *manner* in which they do so insures a morally satisfactory result.

Readers will enjoy this succinct narrative best if they ask themselves such questions—among others—as: What purposes are served by the dialogue? What is Thorarin's motive for each of his acts? How does the author make use of the two female characters?

A concise general account of the family sagas is Peter Hallberg, trans. Paul Schach, *The Icelandic Saga* (1962). A critical study of structure and organization, with plot summaries, is Theodore M. Anderson, *The Icelandic Family Saga* (1967). Admirable translations of several of the principal sagas are available in the Penguin paperback series. Jesse Byock, *Feud in the Icelandic Saga* (1982), is a recent scholarly study. Jacqueline Simpson, *Icelandic Folktales and Legends* (1972), paperback printing (1979), provides a modern translation of short narratives (not sagas) collected especially from oral sources.

PRONOUNCING GLOSSARY

The following list uses common English syllables to provide rough equivalents of selected words whose pronunciation may be unfamiliar to the general reader.

Bjorni: *b-yorn'-ee*   Thorstein: *thor'-stain*

Thorstein the Staff-Struck[1]

There was a man called Thorarin who lived at Sunnudale; he was old and nearly blind. He had been a fierce viking in his younger years, and even in his old age he was very hard to deal with. He had an only son, Thorstein, who was a tall man, powerful but even-tempered; he worked so hard on his father's farm that three other men could hardly have done any better. Thorarin had little money, but a good many weapons. He and his son owned some breeding horses and that was their main source of income, for the young colts they sold never failed in spirit or strength.

Bjarni of Hof[2] had a servant called Thord who looked after his riding horses and was considered very good at the job. Thord was an arrogant man and would never let anyone forget the fact that he was in the service of a chieftain. But this didn't make him a better man and added nothing to his pop-

---

1. Translated, with footnotes, by Hermann Pálsson.   2. Bjarni of Hof was the local chieftain, and the wealthiest and most powerful farmer in the district.

ularity. Bjarni also had two brothers working for him who were called Thorhall and Thorvald, both great scandalmongers about any gossip they heard in the district.

Thorstein and Thord arranged a horse-fight for their young stallions.[3] During the fight, Thord's horse started giving way, and when Thord realized he was losing, he struck Thorstein's horse a hard blow on the jaw. Thorstein saw this and hit back with an even heavier blow at Thord's horse, forcing it to back away. This got the spectators shouting with excitement. Then Thord aimed a blow at Thornstein with his horse-goad, hitting him so hard on the eye-brow that the skin broke and the lid fell hanging down over the eye. Thorstein tore a piece off his shirt and bandaged his head. He said nothing about what had happened, apart from asking people to keep this from his father. That should have been the end of the incident, but Thorvald and Thorhall kept jeering at Thorstein and gave him the nickname Staff-Struck.

One morning that winter just before Christmas, when the women at Sunnudale were getting up for their work, Thorstein went out to feed the cattle. He soon came back and lay down on a bench. His father, old Thorarin, came into the room and asked who was lying there. Thorstein told him.

"Why are you up so early, son?" said Thorarin.

Thorstein answered, "It seems to me there aren't many men about to share the work with me."

"Have you got a head-ache, son?" said Thorarin.

"Not that I've noticed," said Thorstein.

"What can you tell me about the horse-fight last summer, son?" said Thorarin. "Weren't you beaten senseless like a dog?"

"It's no credit to me if you call it a deliberate blow, not an accident," said Thorstein.

Thorarin said, "I'd never have thought I could have a coward for a son."

"Father," said Thorstein, "Don't say anything now that you'll live to regret later."

"I'm not going to say as much as I've a mind to," said Thorarin.

Thorstein got to his feet, seized his weapons and set off. He came to the stable where Thord was grooming Bjarni's horses, and when he saw Thord he said, "I'd like to know, friend Thord, whether it was accidental when you hit me in the horse-fight last summer, or deliberate. If it was deliberate, you'll be willing to pay me compensation."

"If only you were double-tongued," said Thord, "then you could easily speak with two voices and call the blow accidental with one and deliberate with the other. That's all the compensation you're getting from me."

"In that case don't expect me to make this claim a second time," said Thorstein.

With that he rushed at Thord and dealt him his death-blow. Then he went up to the house at Hof where he saw a woman standing outside the door. "Tell Bjarni that a bull has gored Thord, his horse-boy," he said to her, "and also that Thord will be waiting for him at the stable."

"Go back home, man," she said. "I'll tell Bjarni in my own good time."

Thorstein went back home, and the woman carried on with her work.

---

3. Horse-fights used to be a favourite sport in Iceland. Two stallions were pitted against one another, and behind each of them there was a man equipped with a goad to prod them on. At these horse fights tempers would often run high.

After Bjarni had got up that morning and was sitting at table, he asked where Thord could be, and was told he had gone to see to the horses.

"I'd have thought he'd be back by now, unless something has happened to him," said Bjarni.

The woman Thorstein had spoken to broke in. "It's true what we women are often told, we're not very clever. Thorstein the Staff-Struck came here this morning and he said Thord had been gored by a bull and couldn't look after himself. I didn't want to wake you, and then I forgot all about it."

Bjarni left the table, went over to the stable and found Thord lying there, dead. Bjarni had him buried, then brought a court action against Thorstein and had him sentenced to outlawry for manslaughter. But Thorstein stayed on at Sunnudale and worked for his father, and Bjarni did nothing more about it.

One day in the autumn when the men of Hof were busy singeing sheep's heads,[4] Bjarni lay down on top of the kitchen wall to listen to their talk. Now the brothers Thorhall and Thorvald started gossiping; "It never occurred to us when we came to live here with Killer-Bjarni[5] that we'd be singeing lambs' heads while his outlaw Thorstein is singeing the heads of wethers. It would have been better for Bjarni to have been more lenient with his kinsmen at Bodvarsdale and not to let his outlaw at Sunnudale act just like his own equal. But 'A wounded coward lies low,' and it's not likely that he'll ever wipe away this stain on his honour."

One of the men said, "Those words were better left unsaid, the trolls must have twisted your tongue. I think Bjarni simply isn't prepared to take the only breadwinner at Sunnudale away from Thorstein's blind father and other dependents there. I'll be more than surprised if you singe many more lambs' heads here, or tattle on much longer about the fight at Bodvarsdale."

Then they went inside to have their meal, and after that to bed. Bjarni gave no sign that he had heard anything of what had been said. But early next morning he roused Thorhall and Thorvald and told them to ride over to Sunnudale and bring him Thorstein's severed head before mid-morning. "I think you're more likely than anyone else to wipe away that stain from my honour, since I haven't the courage to do it for myself," he said.

The brothers realized they had said too much, but they set off and went over to Sunnudale. Thorstein was standing in the doorway, sharpening a short sword. He asked them where they were going, and they told him they were looking for some horses. Thorstein said they didn't have very far to go. "The horses are down by the fence."

"We're not sure we'll be able to find them unless you tell us more precisely," they said.

Thorstein came outside, and as they were walking together across the meadow, Thorvald raised his axe and rushed at him. But Thorstein pushed him back so hard that he fell, then ran him through with the short sword. Thorhall tried to attack Thorstein and went the same way as his brother. Thorstein tied them to their saddles, fixed the reins to the horses' manes, and drove them off.

---

4. In Iceland, as in some other sheep-raising countries, sheep's heads were (and still are) considered a great delicacy. The heads are singed over a fire to remove all traces of wool before they are cleaned and cooked.   5. The name Killer-Bjarni is an allusion to the fact that Bjarni fought and killed some of his own kinsmen in the battle of Bodvarsdale which is mentioned in the following sentence.

The horses went back to Hof. Some of the servants there were out of doors and went inside to tell Bjarni that Thorvald and Thorhall had come back and their journey hadn't been wasted. Bjarni went outside and saw what had happened. He said nothing and had the two men buried. Then everything was quiet till after Christmas.

One evening after Bjarni and his wife Rannveig had gone to bed, she said to him, "What do you think everyone in the district is talking about these days?"

"I couldn't say," said Bjarni. "In my opinion most people talk a lot of rubbish."

"This is what people are mainly talking about now," she continued: "They're wondering how far Thorstein the Staff-Struck can go before you bother to take revenge. He's killed three of your servants, and your supporters are beginning to doubt whether you can protect them, seeing that you've failed to avenge this. You often take action when you shouldn't and hold back when you should."

"It's the same old story," said Bjarni, "no one seems willing to learn from another man's lesson. Thorstein has never killed anyone without a good reason—but still, I'll think about your suggestion."

With that they dropped the subject and slept through the night. In the morning Rannveig woke up as Bjarni was taking down his sword and shield. She asked him where he was going.

"The time has come for me to settle that matter of honour between Thorstein of Sunnudale and myself," he said.

"How many men are you taking with you?" she asked.

"I'm not taking a whole army to attack Thorstein," he said. "I'm going alone."

"You mustn't do that," she said, "risking your life against the weapons of that killer."

"You're a typical woman," said Bjarni, "arguing against the very thing you were urging just a few hours ago! There's a limit to my patience, I can only stand so much taunting from you and others. And once my mind's made up, there's no point in trying to hold me back."

Bjarni went over to Sunnudale. He saw Thorstein standing in the doorway, and they exchanged some words.

"You'll fight me in single combat," said Bjarni, "on that hillock over there in the home-meadow."

"I'm in no way good enough to fight you," said Thorstein. "I give you my promise to leave the country with the first ship that sails abroad. I know a generous man like you will provide my father with labour to run the farm if I go away."

"You can't talk yourself out of this now," said Bjarni.

"You'll surely let me go and see my father first," said Thorstein.

"Certainly," said Bjarni.

Thorstein went inside and told his father that Bjarni had come and challenged him to a duel.

The old man said, "Anybody who offends a more powerful man in his own district can hardly expect to wear out many more new shirts. In my opinion your offences are so serious, I can't find any excuse for you. So you'd better take your weapons and defend yourself the best you can. In my younger days

I'd never have given way before someone like Bjarni, great fighting-man though he may be. I'd much rather lose you than have a coward for a son."

Thorstein went outside and walked with Bjarni up the hillock. They started fighting with determination and destroyed each other's shield. When they had been fighting for a long time, Bjarni said to Thorstein, "I'm getting very thirsty now, I'm not so used to hard work as you are."

"Go down to the stream then and drink," said Thorstein.

Bjarni did so, and laid the sword down beside him. Thorstein picked it up, examined it and said, "You can't have been using this sword at Bodvarsdale."

Bjarni said nothing, and they went back to the hillock. After they'd been fighting for a time, it became obvious to Bjarni that Thorstein was a highly skilled fighter, and the outcome seemed less certain than he'd expected.

"Everything seems to go wrong for me today," he said. "Now my shoe-thong's loose."

"Tie it up then," said Thorstein.

When Bjarni bent down to tie it, Thorstein went into the house and brought back two shields and a sword. He joined Bjarni on the hillock and said, "Here's a sword and shield my father sends you. The sword shouldn't get so easily blunted as the one you've been using. And I don't want to stand here any longer with no shield to protect me against your blows. I'd very much like us to stop this game now, for I'm afraid your good luck will prove stronger than my bad luck. Every man wants to save his life, and I would too, if I could."

"There's no point in your trying to talk yourself out of this," said Bjarni. "The fight must go on."

"I wouldn't like to be the first to strike," said Thorstein.

Then Bjarni struck at Thorstein, destroying his shield, and Thorstein hacked down Bjarni's shield in return.

"That was a blow," said Bjarni.

Thorstein replied, "Yours wasn't any lighter."

Bjarni said, "Your sword seems to be biting much better now than it was earlier."

"I want to save myself from the foulest of luck if I possibly can," said Thorstein. "It scares me to have to fight you, so I want you yourself to settle the matter between us."

It was Bjarni's turn to strike. Both men had lost their shields. Bjarni said, "It would be a great mistake in one stroke both to throw away good fortune and do wrong. In my opinion I'd be fully paid for my three servants if you took their place and served me faithfully."

Thorstein said, "I've had plenty of opportunity today to take advantage of you, if my bad luck had been stronger than your good luck. I'll never deceive you."

"Now I can see what a remarkable man you must be," said Bjarni. "You'll allow me to go inside to see your father and tell him about this in my own words?"

"You can go if you want as far as I'm concerned," said Thorstein, "but be on your guard."

Bjarni went up to the bed-closet where Old Thorarin was lying. Thorarin asked who was there, and Bjarni told him.

"What's your news, friend Bjarni?" said Thorarin.

"The killing of Thorstein, your son," said Bjarni.

"Did he put up any defence at all?" asked Thorarin.

"I don't think there's ever been a better fighter than your son, Thorarin," said Bjarni.

"It's no wonder your opponents at Bodvarsdale found you so hard to deal with," said Thorarin, "seeing that you've overcome my son."

Bjarni said, "I want to invite you to come over to Hof and take the seat of honour there for the rest of your life. I'll be just like a son to you."

"I'm in the same position now as any other pauper," said Thorarin. "Only a fool accepts a promise gladly, and promises of chieftains like yourself aren't usually honoured for more than a month after the event, while you're trying to console us. After that we're treated as ordinary paupers, though our grief doesn't grow any the less for that. Still, anyone who shakes hands on a bargain with a man of your character should be satisfied, in spite of other men's lessons. So I'd like to shake hands with you, and you'd better come into the bed-closet to me. Come closer now, for I'm an old man and trembling on my feet because of ill-health and old age. And I must admit, the loss of my son has upset me a bit."

Bjarni went into the bed-closet and shook Thorarin by the hand. Then he realized the old man was groping for a short sword with the idea of thrusting it at him. Bjarni pulled back his hand and said, "You merciless old rascal! I can promise you now you'll get what you deserve. Your son Thorstein is alive and well, and he'll come with me over to Hof, but you'll be given slaves to run the farm for you, and never suffer any want for the rest of your life."

Thorstein went with Bjarni over to Hof, and stayed in his service for the rest of his life. He was considered a man of great courage and integrity. Bjarni kept his standing and became better-liked and more self-controlled the older he grew. He was a very trustworthy man. In the last years of his life he became a devout Christian and went to Rome on pilgrimage. He died on that journey, and is buried at a town called Sutri,[6] just north of Rome.[7]

* * *

6. The MSS have Vateri, which is probably a scribal error. The town Sutri is mentioned elsewhere in early Icelandic records.   7. The story concludes with a long account of Bjarni's descendants, extending into the thirteenth century [Editor's note].

MEDIEVAL LYRICS: A SELECTION

While in classical Greece the term *lyric* referred to poems sung to the lyre, the short poems of Rome, such as those by Catullus, were composed to be read silently. The medieval period saw a return to the tradition of poetry as performance. Most medieval lyrics, including many written in Latin, were verses sung to an accompanying tune. One major reason for this return to performance was the influence of the vernacular traditions of song brought into prominence by the various cultures that reshaped Europe after the fall of Rome. All the peoples that together created the Middle Ages— the multifarious nations of the Roman Empire (from the Persians in the east to the Celts in the west), the tribes (Germanic, Scandinavian, Slavic, and Eurasian) that divided the fallen Roman Empire, and the inhabitants (both Arabic and non-Arabic)

of the Islamic world—had traditions of song that stretched back into time immemorial. By their very nature most of these songs were ephemeral. Arabic and
Anglo-Saxon songs do survive from as early as the seventh and eighth centuries, and
early Latin lyrics show the influence of vernacular forms. But we lack all but a very
few of the vernacular songs composed prior to about the year 1100. The reason is
not just that it is less likely for a vernacular text to be preserved in an expensive
manuscript than one in Latin, but that virtually all medieval lyrics were performed in
public rather than read in private. Those that were written down and survived thus
represent only a small fraction of the lyrics that actually circulated throughout the
Middle Ages.

The medieval lyrics selected here represent the most important linguistic communities and demonstrate both the range of topics treated by medieval lyricists and
their extraordinary skill. While the poems are printed in chronological order, regardless of their original language of composition, readers will notice that certain topics
recur with some frequency. Unsurprisingly, the most common is love. Most important
here are the lyrics written beginning around 1100 in Provençal, a literary language
derived from the various dialects spoken in the southern half of France and the
bordering regions of Italy and Spain. Here we find expressed, if not for the first time
in Western literature, then in terms that became decisive, our modern form of romantic love. Often called *courtly love*, a term coined by French scholars in the nineteenth
century, it was in the Middle Ages known as *fin'amors* (Provençal), *fine amour*
(French), or *minne* (German). Its central elements are that love is an overwhelming
emotion that promises ecstatic bliss but also causes painful yearning; that the beloved
is an embodiment of all virtue and yet often remains cool and distant, even unaware
of the lover's sufferings; and that love is an ennobling emotion, in the sense both that
it can be fully experienced only by gentlemen and ladies and that it causes them to
behave in exalted and selfless ways. Various aspects of this emotional complex are
certainly present in earlier writing. In the *Phaedrus* and the *Symposium*, for instance,
Plato (429–347 B.C.) described erotic love between men as providing a means for
philosophical and moral improvement, and the Roman poet Ovid (43 B.C.–A.D. 17)
described passionate, unrequited love between men and women in terms that medieval poets knew and imitated. So too, as early as the Umayyad period (A.D. 650–750)
Arabic poets described a love—known as ʿUdhrite love—that was ardent, chaste, and
incapacitating to the point of death. Indeed, it is likely that the Provençal poets were
influenced by singers and composers from the Iberian peninsula who continued to
celebrate this kind of love. One of these Arabic lyrics is *The Singing Lute*, written by
a poet of whom we know only his name, Ibn Arfaʿ Raʾsuh. (In the manuscripts medieval lyrics are untitled, so that all titles are supplied by the editor or translator.) The
poem was composed in Spain—or al-Andalus, as it was known to its Arab rulers—in
the mid-eleventh century to celebrate the poet's patron, known as al-Maʾmūn or
Yahya ibn Dhī n-Nūn, the ruler of Toledo. Written according to a strict scheme of
meter and rhyme, and deploying the delicate natural imagery characteristic of medieval Arabic poetry, it compares the disdain of the beautiful lady to the haughtiness
of the great warrior, a comparison that implies that because he is "the terrorizer of
armies" al-Maʾmūn is able to sustain a sophisticated culture that supports both poetry
and love. Other love poems from al-Andalus included here are the beautiful *Summer,*
written in Hebrew by Judah Halevi, perhaps the most distinguished of the many
Jewish scholars and poets who flourished under Arab rule, and the compact *In Battle,*
by the Arabic poet Abu-l-Hasan ibn Al-Qabturnuh, a poem that combines love and
war in a surprisingly effective way.

Quite apart from its originality or sources, the influence of the Provençal celebration of *fin'amors* was enormous. Like the poets of al-Andalus, those of Provence drew
connections between the virtuosity and elegance of their lyrics, the exalted delicacy
of the emotion they celebrated, and the aristocratic courts in which they lived and
composed. In this way the love lyric became not merely a private statement but an

expression of a way of life that was elegantly mannered and knowingly sophisticated. As the French term *courtoisie*, or "courtliness," suggests, the love lyric described values that derived from noble society: intensity of feeling matched elevation of social standing. In this way the poetry combined private and public concerns, and the relation of lover to beloved is often phrased in the same terms as the feudal relation of a lord to his vassal (the beloved was, in Provençal poetry, referred to as *midons*, "my lord"). It is hardly surprising, then, that many of the poems that survive are written by noble authors. The ability to compose both lyrics and music was one that every well-bred aristocrat wanted to possess. Certainly there were professional composers and performers, but they often served as mouthpieces or instructors to their noble patrons. The oldest datable Provençal lyrics are by William IX, duke of Aquitaine (ca. 1071–1127). He is represented here by his *Spring Song*, which includes in a few stanzas a remarkable range of amorous feelings, from a rather conventional statement about love in general through an anxious lover's doubt to a rousing celebration of mutual pleasure and a scornful rejection of mere braggarts. Another noble author is Beatrice, countess of Dia—one of a significant number of women troubadours—whose witty *A Lover's Prize* begins with resentment at her lover's betrayal and ends with a boldly explicit insistence on her own rights as a lover. On the other hand, the *Love Song* by Jaufré Rudel, who was probably not an aristocrat, begins by celebrating love, but the possibility of disappointment leads him to turn away from eroticism to religion: according to tradition, Jaufré died on crusade. In *The Art of Love* Arnaut Daniel, one of the most technically proficient of the troubadours, draws a connection between the control required for poetic virtuosity and the overwhelming ardor caused by love, a paradox that he triumphantly accepts in the poem's final lines.

Beginning in Provence around the year 1100, then, the love lyric spread throughout Europe to Sicily, Italy, France, Germany, and England. In each of these environments it took on slightly different characteristics. In Sicily and Italy there was a strong interest both in verbal and metrical virtuosity and in the way in which intense love could lead to religious truth. The great Italian poets of the late thirteenth century created what Dante called the *dolce stil nuovo*, or "sweet new style" (see below, p. 1422). By this Dante meant that poetic virtuosity was not opposed to but rather expressed the intensity and authenticity of the lover's feelings; and above all, that the lady opened her admirer to a love that was genuinely religious. As he said in his lyric autobiography, the *Vita nuova* or *New Life*, the lady "seems to be a creature come from Heaven to earth, to manifest a miracle." Dante and the other *stilnovisti*, as they are called, were thus the direct precursors of Petrarch. The earliest of the four Italian poems selected here is by Guido Guinizzelli, a Bolognese poet much admired by Dante. This famous poem, *Love and Nobility*, argues that true nobility is a function not of ancestry but of virtue, and that virtue is in turn a function of a love that is more philosophical and religious than emotional. The next poem, *An Encounter*, is by Guido Cavalcanti, a friend of Dante and the true founder of the *dolce stil nuovo*. Avoiding philosophical speculations about love, his poem celebrates instead a dream-like moment of amorous fulfillment. The sonnet that follows, *Love and Poetry*, is addressed by Dante to Guido Cavalcanti and another poet of their circle, Lapo Gianni. Here Dante invokes a company of poets "enchanted" by Merlin and devoted to a love that is simultaneously earthly and heavenly, a charmingly lighthearted treatment of a theme that in other places he expresses with greater seriousness. An example is the next sonnet, in which Dante provides his own version of Guinizzelli's equation of nobility, virtue, and love.

The two German love poems show how both the Provençal interest in the psychology of love and the Italian concern with its metaphysics were taken up by the poets of the north. *The Wound of Love*, by Heinrich von Morungen, one of the earliest of the *minnesingers*, combines the troubadour theme of unrequited love with an awareness that hostility often accompanies desire, a complexity of feeling intensified by the reduction of both lover and lady to two pairs of lips. Walther von der Vogelweide, generally regarded as the finest of the *minnesingers*, is represented here by *Dancing Girl*, which hides great depths beneath its apparently simple surface: vacillating between dreaming and waking, the poem ends with the poet searching for an ideal that is again more than simply amorous. Another poem that begins as a love poem but then develops into an enigmatic account of a natural creature that is more than natural is *The Fox*, by Dafydd ap Gwilym, the best-known representative of the rich poetic traditions of medieval Wales.

The two French love poems included here also show how the motifs of the Provençal lyric continued to provide poets with fresh inspiration until the very end of the Middle Ages. *Aubade* is an anonymous dawn song, a traditional poem in which lovers—in this case, the woman only—lament the coming of day because it will mean their parting. Charles d'Orleans, the author of the *Balade*, was captured at the battle of Agincourt in 1415 and spent twenty-five years as a prisoner in England. This delicate lyric, written in a traditional form, neatly combines the old feudal metaphors of the lady as lord and the lover as vassal with commercial imagery that derives from a new and very different world.

While medieval lyricists were preoccupied by love in its many manifestations, they also used the short poem to express and explore religious feelings. Many of these poems are in Latin, the language of the Church, and they are often written to serve as part of a religious service. The poems by Notker Balbulus, a monk in the great monastery at St. Gall in present-day Switzerland, and by Hildegard of Bingen, a German nun who became famous as a religious visionary, scientist, poet, musician, and reformer of Church abuses, are the words to a musical work known as a sequence, a chant sung during the Mass. Notker's *Hymn to Holy Women*, written to be sung on the feast days of holy women, is based on the traditional idea that Mary was the New Testament counterpart to Eve: where Eve had brought human beings into the grasp of Satan by her disobedience, it was through Mary that Christ came to free them. The other central idea of the poem is the harrowing of hell, when Christ, after his death on the cross, descended into hell and released the souls of the just held captive by the Devil, represented in the poem by the Ethiop and the dragon. Here the cross is symbolized both by the ladder that stretches up to heaven and by the hook that pierces the dragon's jaw, an image derived from the Book of Job. Hildegard's sequence, *A Hymn to St. Maximinus*, celebrates an early Christian saint. Using images derived from the Bible, and especially the Song of Songs, Hildegard describes a vision in which Maximinus is seen both as a priest celebrating the Mass and as a saint welcomed into heaven. He is both an embodiment of divine virtue and the means by which others can ascend to it. Other Latin poems drew upon the themes of secular poetry and turned them to religious purposes. *Song of Summer* is an anonymous work found in an anthology of various poems that were originally composed in Germany, France, and Italy and were copied together into a manuscript in eleventh-century England. By means of a catalog of birds and their songs it celebrates the fecundity, variety, and beauty of nature, invoking in its final stanza the Virgin Mary, who as the Mother of God is simultaneously the source of this goodness, a perfect instance of it, and—paradoxically—an alternative to it (hence she is represented by the bee rather than by a bird).

By no means were all religious poems in Latin, however, and vernacular poets were adept at expressing powerful religious feelings and complex thoughts. Two English examples are *Calvary*, which encapsulates the meaning of the Crucifixion in only four lines, and the late poem *Lament of the Virgin*, which describes the sufferings of the Virgin in a voice that reaches out to all men and women. Another example of the way secular and religious languages are brought together is *Strawberry Picking*, by the mysterious poet known as Alexander the Wild (i.e., the Vagabond), a poem that oscillates delicately between secular and religious meanings, between an observant realism and a suggestive symbolism. Finally, the woman writer Hadewijch of Antwerp (or Brabant), who composed in Flemish, is represented by *The Cult of Love*, a poem that begins within the conventions of troubadour verse but transforms them into a personal experience that is both intense and enigmatic: is it an earthly lover of whom she speaks, or—as we would expect of a religious writer like Hadewijch—Christ?

The subjects treated by medieval lyrics were by no means confined to love and religion. Then as now, one of the most common lyric themes was loss, and medieval poems are often elegiac. The first poem in our selection was written by a German monk named Walahfrid Strabo in 829, when he was about twenty: in order to further his education, he had been sent from Reichenau, a monastery on an island in Lake Constance where he had grown up, to Fulda, a monastery several hundred miles away. In the poem Walahfrid connects his own loneliness to the idea that all Christians are exiles from their true homeland, heaven, a heaven of which the island monastery is an earthly image; he defines himself as the child not of earthly parents—who no doubt committed him to the monastery at an early age—but as the son of his first teacher who was his spiritual father, of the monastery that is his spiritual mother, and finally of God Himself; and in the course of the poem he comes to understand that the "wisdom" he has come to Fulda to find can also be found in "the teaching of life" that his exile has forced upon him. Some ten years later Walahfrid did in fact return to Reichenau as its abbot. Another elegy, written almost six hundred years later, in the early 1400s, is *Alone in Martyrdom*, by Christine de Pizan, a remarkable writer who composed a wide range of works including treatises on moral, political, and feminist issues. Here she laments the early death of her husband in a graceful lyric whose elegance enhances its depth of feeling. A similar elegy, but one in which loss finds compensation in the thought of God's mercy, is *A Letter from the Grave*, by the Hebrew poet Meir Halevi Abulafia, written for his sister in 1212. Conversely, a poem that functions as an elegy for an entire civilization is the Anglo-Saxon *The Ruin*. Composed probably in the ninth or tenth century, it describes the wonder with which someone from the Germanic world—in which most building was done with timber—gazes on the mighty architectural achievements of the Romans (who preceded the Anglo-Saxons as rulers of England) while implicitly acknowledging the transience of all human accomplishment. Finally, *The Sacrifice of Isaac*, by Rabbi Ephraim ben Jacob of Bonn, combines elegy with prayer. Ephraim was a Hebrew scholar who witnessed and chronicled the massacres endured by the Jews of the Rhineland in 1146 during the Second Crusade, as they had endured similarly pitiless massacres in 1096 at the time of the First Crusade. His powerful poem memorializes these dreadful events—in which rather than abandon their religion Jews chose suicide or murder, often killing their own children—by locating them in the context of the biblical story of the sacrifice of Isaac. Ephraim here adopts an ancient Jewish tradition that interpreted the biblical story to mean that Isaac was actually killed by his father, Abraham, but resurrected, transported to Eden, and then returned to his father. Yet Ephraim's poem refuses to embrace any easy consolation, and it remains an unflinching affirmation of faith in the face of injustice and terrible suffering.

Last but not least, medieval poets often wrote poems simply about themselves—or, more accurately, about selves they pretended (or wanted) to be. A salient example is *The Archpoet's Confession*. The Archpoet is the name given to an anonymous writer who made popular the idea of the vagabond-poet, and while his vivid picture of the riotous life of the wandering scholar has been very influential, it now seems to have been composed as much of theatrical extravagance as hard fact. Similarly theatrical are two other "autobiographical" poems. *In Praise of War*, by Bertran de Born, a minor noble and notorious troublemaker, celebrates with unrestrained enthusiasm the warmaking that was so central a part of the life of the twelfth-century knight and brought misery to so many ordinary people (Bertran appears in Dante's *Inferno* among the sowers of discord [p. 1389]). And a selection from François Villon's *Testament* also moves us away from the aristocratic world of much medieval lyric to the harsher realities of economic and emotional necessity endured by the population at large. Villon, a man who knew both poverty and imprisonment, provides us with the dramatic monologue of an old woman who—like Chaucer's Wife of Bath—expresses the familiar medieval concern about mutability with a powerful sense of its personal meaning. These apparently personal poems are best read as dramatic monologues, virtually as theatrical performances. But that doesn't mean that they don't express, as do all of these lyrics, human feelings that were as real to medieval people as they are to us. Perhaps more immediate in its appeal, albeit deriving from the other end of the social scale, is *The Scorpions* by Alfonso X, thirteenth-century king of Castile and Léon, who created at his court an environment in which Christian, Jewish, and Muslim scholars and poets worked in harmony. In this poem Alfonso wistfully yearns to escape from the demands of kingship, and perhaps especially from the armed rebellions that characterized his reign, into the life of the merchant, which he romanticizes in an act of wistful imaginative freedom.

Accessible guides to the individual poets and to the development of the lyric within the various languages of medieval Europe can be found in the relevant articles in *The Dictionary of the Middle Ages*, 13 vols., ed. J. P. Strayer (1987). An excellent introduction, with commentary on a number of the poems printed here, is Peter Dronke, *The Medieval Lyric*, 3rd ed. (1996). Both these works contain suggestions for further reading. A brilliant study that locates Rabbi Ephraim's poem in the context of both Jewish tradition and the Christian massacres of Jews in the eleventh and twelfth centuries is Shalom Spiegel, *The Last Trial* (1979).

PRONOUNCING GLOSSARY

The following list uses common English syllables and stress accents to provide rough equivalents of selected words whose pronunciation may be unfamiliar to the general reader.

Abu-1-Hasan ibn Al-Qabturnuh: *a-boo-1-ha'san ibun al kwab-turn-uh*

al-Mamun: *al-ma-moon'*

Annwn: *an'-wun*

Arnaut Daniel: *ar-no'dan-yel'*

Dafydd ap Gwilem: *daff'-id ap gwil'-em*

François Villon: *frahn-swaw' vee-yonh'*

Guido Guinizzelli: *gwee'-do gween'-itz-elli*

Hadewijch: *had'-e-witch*

Ibn Arfaᶜ Raᵓsuh: *i'bun ar'-fah rah'-suh*

Jaufré Rudel: *jo-fray' ru-del'*

Meir Halevi Abulafia: *mey-er hal-ay-vee a-bool-a-fia'*

Reichenau: *raik'-en-ow*

Sulayma: *sul-ay'-ma*

Walther von der Vogelweide: *val'ter von der vo'-gel-vai'-duh*

Yahya ibn Dhi n-Nun: *ya'hya ibun thee' en-noon'*

Ya'rub: *yah'-roob*

WALAHFRID STRABO
808/9–849

Elegy on Reichenau[1]

Sister Muse, lament for my pain,
speak of my sad parting,

---

1. Translated from the Latin by Peter Godman. Reichenau is a monastery on an island in Lake Constance, which is located on what is now the Swiss-German border.

alas, from the land of my fathers, ceaselessly
harassed as I was by shameful penury.

Wretched, I seek heart-felt wisdom,   5
and so I leave my homeland,
stricken by many kinds of hardship, I lament,
loathed and in exile.

No kindly teacher consoles me,
nor does any good master hearten me;   10
the only thing that keeps my miserable body alive
is the food I eat.

Bitter cold assails my naked flesh,
there is no warmth in my hands,
goose-pimples stand out on my feet   15
and my face flinches before the harsh winter.

Indoors I suffer the icy cold,
the sight of my frozen bed gives no pleasure,
warm neither when I get up nor where I sleep,
I snatch what rest I can.   20

If only wisdom which I esteem
could take hold in my mind
even the smallest part of it, the warmth of my wits
would make me safer.

Alas, father,[2] if only you were there—   25
you whom I have followed to the ends of the earth—
I believe that no harm would have come
to the poor little heart of your pupil.

Look, tears burst forth as I recall
how good was the peace I long ago enjoyed,   30
when happy Reichenau gave me
a modest roof over my head.

May you always be my holy and dear, dear
mother, consecrated by your throngs of saints,
through praise-giving, the promotion of good deeds, and worship,   35
happy island.

Now too let us call that island holy
because there the mother of God is richly worshipped,
so that we joyously cry out as we should,
happy island!   40

Although you are surrounded by deep waters,
nonetheless your foundations are firm in love,

2. An older monk named Grimald.

and you spread its holy teachings among all men,
happy island.

Always wishing to see you,   45
I remember you day and night,
recalling all the kindness you bring me,
happy island.

Grow now and flourish, develop and prosper
so that, following the Lord's will,   50
with your children you may be called
happy Reichenau!

Let almighty Christ grant in His mercy
that I may return and rejoice on your site,
saying: "Hail, glorious mother,   55
forever!"

Christ, king of kings, lord of the mighty,
you who are called wisdom of the Father,
deign to refresh my heart
with the teaching of life.   60

Grant, redeemer, I pray, a span of years,
so that, on returning to the bosom of my fatherland[3]
for which I have longed, I may sing
to Christ in songs of praise.

We sing in thanks to the highest father,   65
joined to His son in all-embracing love
and to the Spirit ruling with equal power
forever and ever. Amen.

3. Could refer to either Reichenau or to heaven.

NOTKER BALBULUS

ca. 840–912

A Hymn to Holy Women[1]

1. A ladder stretching up to heaven,
      circled by torments—

2. At whose foot an attentive
      dragon
      stands on guard, forever
      awake,

3. So that no one can climb even
      to the first rung and not be
      torn—

1. Translated from the Latin by Peter Dronke.

4. The ascent of the ladder barred
   by an Ethiop,[2] brandishing
   a drawn sword, threatening
   death,

5. While over the topmost rung
   leans a young man, radiant,
   a golden bough in his hand—

6. This is the ladder the love of
   Christ
   made so free for women
   that, treading down the
   dragon
   and striding past the Ethiop's
   sword,

7. By way of torments of every kind
   they can reach heaven's
   summit
   and take the golden laurel
   from the hand of the strength-
   giving king.

8. What good did it do you,
   impious serpent,
   once to have a deceived a
   woman,

9. Since a virgin brought forth
   God incarnate,
   only-begotten of the Father:

10. He who took your spoils away
    and pierces your jaw with a hook[3]

11. To make of it an open gate
    for Eve's race, whom you long to
    hold.

12. So now you can see girls
    defeating you, envious one,

13. And married women now
    bearing sons who please
    God.

14. Now you groan at the loyalty
    of widows to their dead
    husbands,

15. You who once seduced a girl
    to disloyalty towards her
    creator.

16. Now you can see women made
    captains
    in the war that is waged against
    you,

17. Women who spur on their sons
    bravely to conquer all your
    tortures.

18. Even courtesans, your vessels,
    are purified by God,

19. Transmuted into a burnished
    temple for him alone.

20. For these graces let us now
    glorify him together,
    both the sinners and those who
    are just,

21. Him who strengthens those who
    stand
    and gives his right hand to
    the fallen,
    that at least after crimes we may
    rise.

2. I.e., the Devil.   3. See Job 40.20.

ANONYMOUS
ca. ninth or tenth century
The Ruin[1]

Marvelous is this wall-stone—but the fates broke,
smashed this city; this work of giants is decaying.
The roofs are fallen, the towers are in ruins,
the frosty gate is despoiled, frost is on the masonry,
damaged buildings are torn, collapsed,   5
undermined by age. The grasp of the earth holds
the master builder, he's dead and gone
into the hard grasp of the ground, until a hundred generations
of people shall have passed away. Often this wall,
red-stained and gray with lichen, one reign after another,   10
has withstood storms; high and wide, now it has fallen.
The wall-stone still survives, broken down by the weather . . .
. . . .
                                    . . . he put together a shrewd,
keen plan with rings, the clever man who bound
these wall braces together with wire, wonderfully!   20
Bright were the city halls, many the bath-houses,
high the crowd of gables, loud the noise of warriors,
many the mead-halls[2] full of people's joy—
until fate the powerful overturned all that.
Slaughtered men died everywhere, days of pestilence came,   25
death took away all the brave men.
Their sanctuaries became waste places,
their city decayed. The craftsmen died,
the warriors fell to the earth. So these halls decay,
and this red-curved roof of the vault splits off from   30
its tiles. The ruin fell to the ground,
broken into heaps, where once many a man,
happy of heart and bright with gold, adorned with splendor,
proud and flushed with wine, shone in his armor,
gazed on his treasure, on his silver, on jewels,   35
on wealth, on possessions, on valuable stone,
on this bright city and its broad kingdom.
Stone halls stood here, the streams gave off heat
in a great surge; the wall enclosed everything
in its bright bosom, there where the baths were.   40
hot to the core. That was elegant!
They let the hot streams gush . . .
over the gray stone . . .
. . . .
                                    . . . there the baths were . . .   46
. . . .
                                    . . . That is a kingly thing,
a house . . . . a city . . . .

1. Translated from the Anglo-Saxon by Lee Patterson. The poem survives in fragmentary form.   2. Mead
is an alcoholic drink made from honey.

ANONYMOUS
ca. eleventh century

Song of Summer[1]

The woodlands clothe the slender shoots
of boughs, laden with fruits;
from high perches wood pigeons sing
    songs to one and all.
Here the turtledove moans, here the thrush resounds,   5
here the age-old song of blackbirds rings out,
and the sparrow, not silent, with its chatter
    takes possession of the heights beneath the elms.
Here the nightingale sings, delighting in leafy boughs,
pours out a long warbling through the breeze,   10
solemnly, and with tremulous voice the kite
    causes the sky to echo.
The eagle as it soars starward sings, upon the breezes
the lark sings and produces sounds in melodies.
From above it swoops, with a different melody   15
    as it touches ground.
The swift swallow ever makes its call,
the quail sings, the jackdaw resounds:
thus birds everywhere celebrate for everyone
    the song of summer.   20
None among the birds is like the bee,
who represents the ideal of chastity,
if not she who bore Christ in her womb
    inviolate.

1. Translated from the Latin by Jan Ziolkowski.

IBN ARFAʿ RAʾSUH
eleventh century

The Singing Lute[1]

The lute trills the most wondrous melodies
And the watercourses cut through the flower beds of the gardens.
The birds sing on the branches of the *bān*,[2]
And joy enlivens the lions of the battlefield.
Every one of us is an Emir[3] and a sultan because of the wine.   5
The lute-strings speak with eloquent charm
While the birds respond to them from the myrtle branches.
Come, give me wine to drink for the garden exudes fragrance;

1. Translated from the Arabic by James T. Monroe. Bracketed words are the translator's interpolation.
2. The bonduc, or horse-radish tree, which has fragrant white flowers.   3. A ruler.

The Pleiads[4] have set and it is sweet to take the morning drink
Offered to me by a lovely gazelle   10
Who is like a tender branch enveloped in a cloak of eglantine,
Whose sides are covered in embroidered silks, who almost breaks
      because he is so tender.
Hold fast to the love and drink to the health of the Possessor of Dual Glory,[5]
Who supports the lands of the East and the West,
And who gives succor to believers, a descendant of Ya'rub,[6]   15
The lofty king, who humbles sultans,
Who leads cavalcades, and is the lion of the battlefields.
He is a king whose heart is braver than the lion's,
Just as his finger is more generous than the rain clouds.
Should Time ever appear frowning or with a severe face   20
He meets it smiling like the flowers in the gardens.
His deeds are stars [shining out over] this world and religion.
The beloved refuses to return the greeting
While the heart is aflame from the excess of love.
Thus the sorrowing one sings the song of one confused by love: 25
"You go by, yet you give no greeting as though you were al-Ma'mūn,[7]
The terrorizer of armies, Yahya ibn Dhī n-Nūn."[8]

4. A constellation.   5. The poet's patron, who is here presented as ruling over both the Islamic east (Persia, Arabia, and Egypt) and west (Spain).   6. The mythical ancestor of the patron's tribe.   7. One of the patron's names.   8. Another of the patron's names.

WILLIAM IX, DUKE OF AQUITAINE
1071–1127

Spring Song[1]

In the sweetness of new spring
the woods grow leafy, little birds,
each in their own language, sing,
rehearse new stanzas with new words,
and it is good that man should find   5
the joy that most enchants his mind.

I see no messenger or note
from her, my first source of delight;
my heart can neither sleep nor laugh,
I dare not make a further move,   10
till I know what the end will be—
is she what I would have her be?

Our love together goes the way
of the branch on the hawthorn-tree,
trembling in the night, a prey   15

1. Translated from the Provençal by Peter Dronke.

to the hoar-frost and the showers,
till next morning, when the sun
enfolds the green leaves and the boughs.

One morning I remember still
we put an end to skirmishing,   20
and she gave me so great a gift:
her loving body, and her ring.
May God keep me alive until
my hands again move in her mantle!

For I shun that strange talk which might pull   25
my Helpmeet and myself apart;
I know that words have their own life,
and swift discourses spread about—
let others vaunt love as they will,
we have love's food, we have the knife!   30

JUDAH HALEVI
ca. 1075–1141

Summer[1]

The earth, like a girl, sipped the rains
Of winter past, and those the ministering cloud distilled
Or perhaps, like a secluded bride in winter,
Whose soul longs for the coming of love's time
She waited, and sought the season ripe for love   5
Till summer came, and calmed her anxious heart
Wearing golden tunics and white embroidered flax.
Like a girl who delights in her finery and raiment,
Every day she renews the grace of her embroiderers
And provides all her neighbors with new garments.   10
Every day she changes the colors of her fields
Now with strings of pearls, now with emeralds or rubies,
Offering her meadows now white or green or gold
Or blushing like the sweetheart kissing her beloved.
Her trellises display such gorgeous flowers   15
It seems as if she stole the stars from heaven.
Here is paradise, whose sheltered buds are clustered
Among the vines, kindled with blushes that incite to love.
The grapes are cold as snow in the hand of him who plucks them.
But in his entrails, they burn as hot as fire.   20
From the whirling cask, the wine, like sun, is rising.
And we shall bring our onyx[2] cups to pour it.
In the love of wine we shall stroll beneath the bowers

1. Translated from the Hebrew by William M. Davis.   2. A semiprecious stone.

Around the garden, and smile with tears of rain,
Bright with shining drops spilled by the clouds   25
That scatter round like strings of pearls.
She finds joy in the song of the swallow, and in the song of the vintagers,
And in cooing pigeons tamed by love.
She twitters in the branches, as the maiden sings
Behind her zither, swaying as she dances.   30
My soul is attentive to the breeze of dawn,
For it fondles the breath of my beloved.
A wanton breeze it is, that steals the scent of myrtles
To waft it off to lovers apart.
The heads of the myrtle rise and nod in turn   35
While the tremulous fronds of the palm tree
Seem to applaud the singing of the birds.

ABU-L-HASAN IBN AL-QABTURNUH
twelfth century

In Battle[1]

I remembered Sulayma[2] when the passion
        of battle was as fierce
as the passion of my body when we parted.

I thought I saw, among the lances, the tall
        perfection of her body,   5
and when they bent toward me I embraced them.

1. Translated from the Arabic by Lysander Kemp.   2. The name of the beloved.

HILDEGARD OF BINGEN
1098–1179

A Hymn to St. Maximinus[1]

1A

The dove peered in
through the latticed window,
where before her gaze
raining, a balm rained down
from the brightness of Maximinus.[2]   5

1. Translated from the Latin by Peter Dronke.   2. A fourth-century saint, patron of the nuns at the
Benedictine Abbey at Trier for whom Hildegard probably wrote this sequence.

1B

The sun's heat blazed
and streamed into the darkness
from which blossomed the gem
—in the building of the temple—
of the purest generous heart.   10

2A

He, the sublime tower
made of Lebanon's tree,[3]
made of cypress,
is decked with jacinth and sardonyx,[4]
city that no architect's skill can match.   15

2B

He, the swift hart
ran up to the fountain
of purest water
bubbling from the mightiest stone
whose moisture made the sweet perfumes flow.   20

3A

You perfumers
who live in the gentlest greenness
of the king's gardens,
you who mount into the heights
when you have consummated   25
the only sacrifice among the rams,

3B

Lucent[5] among you
is this architect, wall of the temple,
he who longed
for an eagle's wings as he kissed   30
his foster-mother, Wisdom,
in Ekklesia's[6] glorious fecundity!

4A

Maximinus, you are mountain and valley,
and in both you appear, a pinnacle,
where the mountain-goat walked, and the elephant,   35
and Wisdom played in her delight.

4B

You are both brave and gentle;
in the rites and in the sparkling of the altar
you mount as a smoke of fragrant spices
to the column of praise   40

---

3. The cypress.   4. Precious stones.   5. I.e., glowing.   6. The Church.

5

Where you plead the cause of your people
who aspire to the mirror of light
for which there is praise on high.

THE ARCHPOET[1]
d. 1165?

His Confession

Seething over inwardly
  With fierce indignation,
In my bitterness of soul,
  Hear my declaration.
I am of one element,   5
  Levity my matter,
Like enough a withered leaf
  For the winds to scatter.

Since it is the property
  Of the sapient   10
To sit firm upon a rock,
  It is evident
That I am a fool, since I
  Am a flowing river,
Never under the same sky,   15
  Transient for ever.

Hither, thither, masterless
  Ship upon the sea,
Wandering through the ways of air,
  Go the birds like me.   20
Bound am I by ne'er a bond,
  Prisoner to no key,
Questing go I for my kind,
  Find depravity.

Never yet could I endure   25
  Soberness and sadness,
Jests I love and sweeter than
  Honey find I gladness.
Whatsoever Venus bids
  Is a joy excelling,   30
Never in an evil heart
  Did she make her dwelling.

1. Translated from the Latin by Helen Waddell.

Down the broad way do I go,
   Young and unregretting,
Wrap me in my vices up,   35
   Virtue all forgetting,
Greedier for all delight
   Than heaven to enter in:
Since the soul in me is dead,
   Better save the skin.   40

Pardon, pray you, good my lord,
   Master of discretion,
But this death I die is sweet,
   Most delicious poison.
Wounded to the quick am I   45
   By a young girl's beauty:
She's beyond my touching? Well,
   Can't the mind do duty?

Hard beyond all hardness, this
   Mastering of Nature: 50
Who shall say his heart is clean,
   Near so fair a creature?
Young are we, so hard a law,
   How should we obey it?
And our bodies, they are young,   55
   Shall they have no say in't?

Sit you down amid the fire,
   Will the fire not burn you?
To Pavia[2] come, will you
   Just as chaste return you?   60
Pavia, where Beauty draws
   Youth with finger-tips,
Youth entangled in her eyes,
   Ravished with her lips.

Let you bring Hippolytus,[3]   65
   In Pavia dine him,
Never more Hippolytus
   Will the morning find him.
In Pavia not a road
   But leads to venery,   70
Nor among its crowding towers
   One to chastity.

Yet a second charge they bring:
   I'm for ever gaming.
Yea, the dice hath many a time   75
   Stripped me to my shaming.

---

2. Italian city then known for its wild life.   3. Legendary figure of ancient Greece, noted for his vehement opposition to the pleasures of the flesh.

What an if the body's cold,
    If the mind is burning,
On the anvil hammering,
    Rhymes and verses turning?   80

Look again upon your list.
    Is the tavern on it?
Yea, and never have I scorned,
    Never shall I scorn it,
Till the holy angels come,   85
    And my eyes discern them,
Singing for the dying soul,
    Requiem aeternam.[4]

For on this my heart is set:
    When the hour is nigh me,   90
Let me in the tavern die,
    With a tankard by me,
While the angels looking down
    Joyously sing o'er me,
Deus sit propitius   95
    Huic potatori.[5]

'Tis the fire that's in the cup
    Kindles the soul's torches,
'Tis the heart that drenched in wine
    Flies to heaven's porches.   100
Sweeter tastes the wine to me
    In a tavern tankard
Than the watered stuff my Lord
    Bishop hath decanted.

Let them fast and water drink,   105
    All the poets' chorus,
Fly the market and the crowd
    Racketing uproarious:
Sit in quiet spots and think,
    Shun the tavern's portal,   110
Write, and never having lived,
    Die to be immortal.

Never hath the spirit of
    Poetry descended,
Till with food and drink my lean   115
    Belly was distended,
But when Bacchus lords it in
    My cerebral story,
Comes Apollo with a rush,
    Fills me with his glory.   120

4. Eternal rest (Latin), the opening words of the Catholic Mass for the dead.   5. May God be gracious to this drinker (Latin).

Unto every man his gift.
   Mine was not for fasting.
Never could I find a rhyme
   With my stomach wasting.
As the wine is, so the verse: 125
   'Tis a better chorus
When the landlord hath a good
   Vintage set before us.

Good my lord, the case is heard,
   I myself betray me,
And affirm myself to be   130
   All my fellows say me.
See, they in thy presence are:
   Let whoe'er hath known
His own heart and found it clean,   135
   Cast at me the stone.

JAUFRÉ RUDEL
twelfth century

Love Song[1]

When the nightingale in the leaves
Gives, seeks, and takes love,
And happily begins his song,
And gazes often at his mate,
And the streams are clear and the meadows fair,   5
Because of the new pleasure which prevails,
A great joy settles in my heart.

I am eager for a love affair—
For I know no more worthy enjoyment—
Which I pray for and desire, and it would be good   10
If she made me a gift of love;
For she has a full body, delicate and fair,
With nothing that could be unbecoming,
And her good, pleasurable love.

I am preoccupied with this love   15
Awake and then asleep in dreams,
For there I have amazing joy,
Because I enjoy her and am joyously happy;
But her beauty is worth nothing to me,
Because no friend will inform me   20
How I might obtain this pleasure.

1. Translated from the Provençal by George Wolf and Roy Rosenstein.

I am so anxious about this love
That when I go running towards her
It seems to me I'm turning
Backwards and that she's fleeing;   25
And my horse runs so slowly . . .
I do not think I shall ever get there,
Unless love makes her hold back.

Love, I leave you cheerfully,
For I seek what is best for me;   30
And I am so fortunate in this
That I am still rejoicing,
Thanks to my Good Protector
Who wants, calls, and approves me,
And has made me very hopeful.   35

And whoever stays here enjoying himself,
And does not follow God to Bethlehem,
I do not know how he will ever be worthy,
Or how he will ever reach salvation;
For I know and indeed believe   40
That whoever teaches of Jesus
Holds a good school.

RABBI EPHRAIM BEN JACOB
1132–1200

The Sacrifice of Isaac[1]

Let me recall my Fathers' (names)
   Today before Thee, examiner and knower (of hearts).
Oh grant the Fathers' merits to the sons,
   The father an old man, and the child, of his old age.[2]

You told your favorite[3] to offer up his only one,[4]   5
   On one of the mountains to enact the priest:
"Offer Me as sacrifice the soul of him you love,
   Get it for Me, for it pleases Me well."[5]

You called upon him to withstand the trial,
   As calls a king upon a seasoned warrior: 10
By this you shall be tested and prove victorious.
   The Lord trieth the righteous.[6]

---

1. Translated from the Hebrew by Judah Goldin; the parenthetical phrases are expansions of the original by the translator. For the biblical story of Abraham's obedience to God's command that he sacrifice his son Isaac, see Genesis 22.1–19.   2. Genesis 44.20; the last line of each stanza is a citation from the Bible.   3. Abraham.   4. Isaac.   5. Judges 14.3.   6. Psalms 11.5.

1204 / Rabbi Ephraim ben Jacob

The wild ass took pride in his bleeding and brayed:
    Drops of my blood I gave at the age of thirteen![7]
The beloved whispered: Oh that God would take me,   15
    Yea, let Him take all.[8]

Alert, (the father) ran to carry out a *mitsvah*,[9]
    And yearned to saddle his own ass himself,
(Bound to God) by a knot of love, that outweighed dignity.
    Behold, O Lord, Thou knowest it altogether.[1]   20

Then came the Satan, standing close by them,
    Murmuring, "Might one exchange a word with thee?"
Cried the perfect one, "I will walk in mine integrity,"
    For so the King has appointed.[2]

On the third day they arrived at Scopus,[3]   25
    Then to their Maker they looked:
The pillar of cloud shone in its splendor
    On the top of the mount, like devouring fire.[4]

The alert one piled on his son
    Faggots for the sacrifice, for the burnt offering.   30
Then the son opened his mouth to ask,
    Behold fire and wood, but where is the lamb for a burnt offering?[5]

In his reply, the saint spoke the rightful thing:
    The Lord will make it known who shall be His.
My son, the Master will look to His lamb   35
    And who is holy, He will draw to Him.[6]

The Pure One showed him the altar of the ancients.
    A male without blemish you shall offer of your own free will.
Whispered the soft-spoken dove:[7] Bind me as sacrifice
    With cords to the horns of the altar.[8]   40

Bind for me my hands and my feet
    Lest I be found wanting and profane the sacrifice.
I am afraid of panic; I am concerned to honor you,
    My will is to honor you greatly.[9]

When the one whose life was bound up in the lad's   45
    Heard this, he bound him hand and foot like the perpetual
        offering.
In their right order he prepared fire and wood,
    And offered upon them the burnt offering.[1]

---

7. *The Wild ass* refers to Ishmael, Isaac's half-brother; he was circumcised at thirteen (Genesis 17.25), and according to Jewish tradition he taunted Isaac that he was the more pious because he felt the pain of circumcision, while Isaac was circumcised when only eight days old. 8. 2 Samuel 19.30. 9. Sacrifice. 1. Psalms 139.4. 2. Esther 1.8. 3. A mountain near Jerusalem. 4. Exodus 24.17. 5. Genesis 22.7. 6. Numbers 16.5. 7. Isaac. 8. Psalms 118.28. 9. Numbers 24.11. 1. Exodus 40.29.

Then did the father and the son embrace,
    Mercy and Truth met and kissed each other.   50
Oh, my father, fill your mouth with praise,
    For He doth bless the sacrifice.[2]

I long to open my mouth to recite the Grace:
    Forever blessed be the Lord. Amen.
Gather my ashes, bring them to the city,   55
    Unto the tent, to Sarah.[3]

He made haste, he pinned him down with his knees,
    He made his two arms strong.
With steady hands he slaughtered him according to the rite,
    Full right was the slaughter.[4]   60

Down upon him fell the resurrecting dew, and he revived.
    (The father) seized him (then) to slaughter him once more.
Scripture, bear witness! Well-grounded is the fact:
    And the Lord called Abraham, even a second time from heaven.[5]

The ministering angels cried out, terrified: 65
    Even animal victims, were they ever slaughtered twice?
Instantly they made their outcry heard on high,
    Lo, Ariels cried out above the earth.[6]

We beg of Thee, have pity upon him!
    In his father's house, we were given hospitality.
He was swept by the flood of celestial tears   70
    Into Eden, the garden of God.[7]

The pure one thought: The child is free of guilt,
    Now I, whither shall I go?
Then he heard: Your son was found an acceptable sacrifice,   75
    By Myself have I sworn it, saith the Lord.[8]

In a nearby thicket did the Lord prepare
    A ram, meant for this *mitsvah*[9] even from Creation.
The proxy caught its leg in the skirts of his coat,
    And behold, he stood by his burnt offering.[1]   80

So he offered the ram, as he desired to do,
    Rather than his son, as a burnt offering.
Rejoicing, he beheld the ransom of his only one
    Which God delivered into his hand.[2]

This place he called Adonai-Yireh,[3]   85
    The place where light and the law are manifest.

---

2. Psalms 89.53.   3. Genesis 18.6. Sarah is Isaac's mother.   4. Genesis 43.16.   5. Genesis 22.15.
6. Isaiah 33.7.   7. Ezekiel 28.13.   8. Genesis 22.16.   9. Sacrifice.   1. Numbers 23.17.
2. Exodus 21.13. Isaac returns to his father from Eden.   3. Provision of the Lord.

He swore to bless it as the Temple site,
    For there the Lord commanded the blessing.[4]

Thus prayed the binder and the bound,
    That when their descendants commit a wrong   90
This act be recalled to save them from disaster,
    From all their transgressions and sins.[5]

O Righteous One, do us this grace!
    You promised our fathers mercy to Abraham.[6]
Let then their merit stand as our witness,   95
    And pardon our iniquity and our sin, and take us for Thine
        inheritance.[7]

Recall to our credit the many Akedahs,[8]
    The saints, men and women, slain for Thy sake.
Remember the righteous martyrs of Judah,
    Those that were bound of Jacob.[9]   100

Be Thou the shepherd of the surviving flock
    Scattered and dispersed among the nations.
Break the yoke and snap the bands
    Of the bound flock that yearns toward Thee[1]

O GOD! O KING. . .   105

---

4. Psalms 133.3.   5. Leviticus 16.16.   6. Abraham figures here as both an individual and Israel as a whole.   7. Exodus 34.9.   8. Sacrifices.   9. Genesis 30.42.   1. Genesis 30.41.

BEATRICE, COUNTESS OF DIA

ca. 1150–1200

A Lover's Prize[1]

I have been in great distress
for a knight for whom I longed;
I want all future times to know
how I loved him to excess
    Now I see I am betrayed—   5
he claims I did not give him love—
such was the mistake I made,
    naked in bed, and dressed.

How I'd long to hold him pressed
naked in my arms one night—   10
if I could be his pillow once,
would he not know the height of bliss?
    Floris was all to Blanchefleur,[2]

---

1. Translated from the Provençal by Peter Dronke.   2. Lovers in a well-known romance.

yet not so much as I am his:
I am giving my heart, my love, 15
   my mind, my life, my eyes.

Fair, gentle lover, gracious knight,
if once I held you as my prize
and lay with you a single night
and gave you a love-laden kiss— 20
   my greatest longing is for you
to lie there in my husband's place,
but only if you promise this:
   to do all I'd want to do.

BERTRAN DE BORN
ca. 1140–ca. 1215

In Praise of War[1]

I love the joyful time of Easter,
that makes the leaves and flowers come forth,
and it pleases me to hear the mirth
of the birds, who make their song
resound through the woods, 5
and it pleases me to see upon the meadows
tents and pavilions planted,
and I feel a great joy
when I see ranged along the field
knights and horses armed for war. 10

And it pleases me when the skirmishers
make the people and their baggage run away,
and it pleases me when I see behind them coming
a great mass of armed men together,
and I have pleasure in my heart 15
when I see strong castles besieged,
the broken ramparts caving in,
and I see the host on the water's edge,
closed in all around by ditches,
with palisades, strong stakes close together 20

And I am as well pleased by a lord
when he is first in the attack,
armed, upon his horse, unafraid,
so he makes his men take heart
by his own brave lordliness. 25
And when the armies mix in battle,

---

1. Translated from the Provençal by Frederick Goldin.

each man should be poised
to follow him, smiling,
for no man is worth a thing
till he has given and gotten blow on blow.   30

Maces and swords and painted helms,
the useless shields cut through,
we shall see as the fighting starts,
and many vassals together striking,
and wandering wildly,   35
the unreined horses of the wounded and dead.
And once entered into battle
let every man proud of his birth
think only of breaking arms and heads,
for a man is worth more dead than alive and beaten.   40

I tell you there is not so much savor
in eating or drinking or sleeping,
as when I hear them scream, "There they are! Let's get them!"
on both sides, and I hear riderless
horses in the shadows, neighing,   45
and I hear them scream, "Help! Help!"
and I see them fall among the ditches,
little men and great men on the grass,
and I see fixed in the flanks of the corpses
stumps of lances with silken streamers.   50

Barons, pawn your castles,
and your villages, and your cities
before you stop making war on one another.

Papiols,[2] gladly go
fast to my Lord Yes-and-No[3]   55
and tell him he has lived in peace too long.

---

2. Bertran's *joglar*, or minstrel, who will sing the lyric.   3. A mocking reference to Bertran's lord at the time, Richard the Lion-Hearted, whom he accuses of indecisiveness.

HEINRICH VON MORUNGEN
ca. 1150–1222

The Wound of Love[1]

She has wounded me
    in my innermost soul,
within the mortal core,
when I told her
    that I was raving and anguished   5
in desire for her glorious lips.

---

1. Translated from the German by Peter Dronke.

Once I bade my own lips
   to commend me to her service,
      and to steal me
a tender kiss of hers,   10
   that I might for ever be well.

How I begin to hate
   her rose-red lips,
which I never yet forgot!
It troubles me still,   15
   that they once refused me
with such vehemence.
Thus I have grown so weak
   that I would far rather—alive—
      burn in the abyss   20
of hell than serve her still,
   not knowing to what end.

ARNAUT DANIEL

twelfth century

The Art of Love[1]

To this sweet and pretty air
I set words that I plane and finish;
and every word will fit well,
once I have passed the file there,
for at once Love polishes and aureates   5
my song, which proceeds from her,
ruler and guardian of merit.

Each day I am a better man and purer,
for I serve the noblest lady in the world,
and I worship her, I tell you this in the open.   10
I belong to her from my foot to the top of my head;
and let the cold wind blow,
love raining in my heart
keeps me warm when it winters most.

I hear a thousand masses and pay to have them said,   15
I burn lights of wax and oil,
so may God give me good luck with her,
for no defense against her does me any good.
When I look at her golden hair,
her soft young spirited body,   20
if someone gave me Luserna,[2] I'd still love her more.

---

1. Translated from the Provençal by Frederick Goldin.   2. A city, probably in Spain.

I love her and seek her out with a heart so full,
I think I am stealing her out of my own hands by too much wanting,
if a man can lose a thing by loving it well.
For the heart of her submerges   25
mine and does not abate.
So usurious is her demand,
she gets craftsman and workshop together.

I do not want the empire of Rome,
do not make me pope of it   30
so that I could not turn back to her
for whom the heart in me burns and breaks apart.
If she does not cure me of this torment
with a kiss before new year's,
she murders me and sends herself to hell.   35

But this torment I endure
could not make me turn away from loving well,
though it holds me fast in loneliness,
for in this desert I cast my words in rhyme.
I labor in loving more than a man who works the earth,   40
for the Lord of Moncli did not love
N'Audierna an egg's worth more.[3]

I am Arnaut, who hoards the wind,
and chases the hare on an ox,
and swims against the tide.   45

3. Both the Lord of Moncli and his love, N'Audierna, have not been identified.

WALTHER VON DER VOGELWEIDE

ca. 1170–ca. 1230

Dancing Girl[1]

"Lady, accept this garland"—
these were the words I spoke to a pretty girl:
"then you will grace the dance
with the lovely flowers crowning you.
If I had priceless stones,   5
they would be for your hair—
indeed you must believe me,
by my faith, I mean it truly!"

She took my offering
as a gently nurtured child would take it.   10

1. Translated from the German by Peter Dronke.

Her cheeks became as red
as the rose that stands beside the lilies.
Her shining eyes were lowered then in shame,
yet she curtsied graciously.
That was my reward—   15
if any more becomes mine, I'll hold it secret.

"You are so fair,
that I want to give you my chaplet now,
the very best I have.
I know of many flowers, white and red,   20
so far away, on the heath over there,
where they spring up beautiful,
and where the birds are singing—
let us pluck them together there."

I thought that never yet   25
had I known such bliss as I knew then.
From the tree the flowers
rained on us endlessly as we lay in the grass.
Yes, I was filled with laughter in sheer joy.
Just then, when I was so gloriously   30
rich in my dreaming,
then day broke, and I was forced to wake.

She has stirred me so
that this summer, with every girl I meet,
I must gaze deep in her eyes: 35
perhaps one will be mine: then all my cares are gone.
What if she were dancing here?
Ladies, be so kind,
set your hats back a little.
Oh, if only, under a garland, I could see that face!   40

MEIR HALEVI ABULAFIA
ca. 1170–1244

A Letter from the Grave[1]

He wrote this when his sister—may God delight in her—died on
the Sabbath of 10 November 1212; he wrote to his father, in the
name of his sister, to inform him and to bring him comfort.

O clouds, bear these greetings to my father from my grave, in words not
spoken but written. Tell him, with the dumb lips of my disaster, what has
become of my lips and my voice. But take care that my distress should not

---

1. Translated from the Hebrew by T. Carmi.

overwhelm him, that my great sorrow should not oppress him. What good would it do to oppress him with my sorrow? Would his pain spare me mine? Would it be right to tear open his heart because of me? No, I would be wronging my father, whose loving wings were my bed, whose compassionate shoulders were my chariot. Once I shone like a sun in his house, but now I have set in the abyss.

Turn away from me! How much longer will you call to me? Know that the hand of God has touched me. Death, like a ravening lion, tore me out of the room of my beloved. No longer can I cast my fortunes on the dear friend of my youth; now I must commit my fortunes to the grave. They buried me, covering my face with the very dust which only yesterday I trampled underfoot. But I shall draw all men after me; both my loved ones and my rivals will join me. God summons all mortals to the house of the dead. Sinner and prophet perish alike. When He restores all souls to their bodies, then shall I come into your presence again.

Though He has made your heart—my heart's guardian—share my grief, though He has made a sea of tears flow over you and almost flooded you with weeping, He will now fill my grave with His dew of sparkling light, He will say to your welling tears: "Subside and dry!"

HADEWIJCH OF BRABANT
thirteenth century

The Cult of Love[1]

1

The birds have long been silent
that were blithe here before:
their blitheness has departed,
they have lost their summer now;
they would swiftly sing again   5
if that summer came again,
which they have chosen above all
and for which they were born:
one hears it in their voices then.

2

I'll say no more of birds' laments: 10
their joy, their pain, is quickly gone;
I have more grievous cause to moan:
Love, to whom we should aspire,
weighs us down with her noble cares,
so we chase after false delights   15

---

1. Translated from the Flemish by Peter Dronke.

and Love cannot enfold us then.
Ah, what has baseness done to us!
Who shall erase that faithlessness?

3

The mighty ones, whose hand is strong,
it is on them I still rely,   20
who work at all times in Love's bond,
heedless of pain, grief, tragedy;
they want to ride through all the land
that lovers loving by love have found,
so perfect is their noble heart;   25
they know what Love can teach by love,
how Love exalts lovers by love.

4

Why then should anyone refuse,
since by loving Love can be won?
Why not ride, longing, through the storm,   30
trusting in the power of Love,
aspiring to the cult of Love?
Love's peerlessness will then be seen—
there, in the brightness of Love's dawn,
where for Love's sake is shunned no pain   35
and no pain caused by Love weighs down.

5

Often I call for help as a lost one,
but then, when you come close, my dear one,
with new solace you bear me up
and with high spirit I ride on,   40
sport with my dear so joyously
as if north and south and east
and west all lands belonged to me!
Then suddenly I am dashed down.—
Oh, what use to tell my pain?   45

ALFONSO X
1221–1284

The Scorpions[1]

I cannot find such great delight
in the song
of birds, or in their twittering,

1. Translated from the Spanish by Peter Dronke.

in love or in ambition
or in arms—for I fear   5
that these indeed
are fraught with danger—
as in a good galleon
that can take me speedily
from this demonic landscape   10
where the scorpions dwell;
for within my heart
I have felt their sting!

And by the holy God I swear
I would wear   15
neither cloak nor beard,
nor would I involve myself in love
or arms, for injury
and lamentation
come from these at every season—   20
no, I'd pilot a merchant-ship
and sail across the ocean,
selling vinegar and flour,
and I would fly from the poison
of the scorpion, for I know   25
no other medicine against it.

I can take no pleasure here
in tilting,
nor, God save the mark,
in mock-tournaments;   30
as for going armed by night
or patrolling,
I do it without any joy—
for I find more enchantment in the sea
than in being a knight: 35
long ago I was a mariner,
and henceforth I long to guard
myself against the scorpion, and return
to what I was in the beginning.

I must try to explain to you: 40
the demon
will never be able to trick me
now into speaking the language
of arms, for this is not my role—
(useless   45
for me to reason thus,
I have not even arms to try)—
rather, I long to go alone
and in a merchant's guise
to find some land   50
where they cannot strike at me:
the black scorpion, and the mottled.

GUIDO GUINIZZELLI

thirteenth century

Love and Nobility[1]

Love always repairs to the noble heart
    Like a bird winging back into its grove:
Nor was love made before the noble heart,
    Nor did nature, before the heart, make love.
For they were there as long as was the Sun,   5
    Whose splendor's ever bright;
Never did love before that shining come.
Love nestles deep inside nobility
    Exactly the way
One sees the heart within the fiery blaze.   10

Fire of love in noble heart is caught
    Like power gleaming inside a precious stone.
The value does not come down from the stars
    Until the Sun has blenched the stone all pure.
Only after the might of the Sun   15
    Has drawn out all that's vile
Does the star bestow its noble power.
Just so a heart transformed by nature pure,
    Noble and elect,
A woman starlike with her love injects.   20

Love for this reason stays in noble heart
    Like a waving flame atop a burning brand,
Shining, its own delight, subtle and bright;
    It is so proud, it knows no other way.
Yet a nature which is still debased   25
    Greets love as water greets the fire,
With the cold hissing against the heat.
Love in noble heart will find a haven
    Like the shine
Of a diamond glinting in ore within the mine.   30

Sun beats against the mud the livelong day;
    Mud it remains; Sun does not lose its ray;
The haughty one says: "I am noble by my tribe."
    He is the mud; Sun is the noble power.
Man must never believe   35
    That nobility exists outside the heart
In the grandness of his ancestry,
For without virtue, heart has no noble worth;
    It's a ray through a wave;
The heavens retain the sparkle and splendor they gave.   40

1. Translated from the Italian by James J. Wilhelm.

Shines among the powers of heaven
   God the creator, more than Sun in our eye;
Each angel knows the Maker beyond its sphere,
   And turning its circle, obeys God's noble power.
And thus it follows at once: 45
   The blesséd tasks of the Master transpire.
In the same way, in all truth, the beautiful lady
Should behave, for in her eyes reflects the desire
   Of a noble man
Who will turn his every thought to her command.   50

Lady, God will ask me: "Why did you presume?"
   When my soul stands before his mighty throne.
"You passed the heavens, came all the way to me,
   And cheapened me in the light of profane love.
To me is due all the praise   55
   And to the Queen of the Royal Realm[2]
Who makes all fraudulence cease."
I'll tell him then: "She had an angel look—
   A heavenly face.
What harm occurred if my love in her was placed?"   60

2. The Virgin Mary.

GUIDO CAVALCANTI
ca. 1255–1300

An Encounter[1]

Once within a little grove a shepherdess I spied;
More than any star of sky beauteous did she prove.

Ringlets she had, blonde and curly locks,
Eyes filled with love, a face of rosy hue,
And with her staff she led her gentle flocks,   5
Barefoot, with their feet bathed by the dew.
She sang, indeed, as if she were enamored;
She had the glamour of every pleasing art.

I greeted her, and asked her then at once
If she had any company that day;   10
She answered sweetly: "For the nonce,
Alone throughout this grove I make my way."
And added: "Listen, but when the gentle bird is heard,
A friend should have my heart."

1. Translated from the Italian by James J. Wilhelm.

And when she told me of this state of mind,   15
Suddenly I heard birdsongs in the wood.
I said to myself: "This surely would be the time
To take from this shepherdess what joy I could."
Grace I requested—just to kiss her face—
And then embrace if she should feel like me.   20

She took my hand, seized with love's old power,
And said she'd give me her heart too;
She led me then into a fresh green bower,
And there I saw flowers of every hue.
And I was filled so full of sweetened joy   25
Love's godlike boy[2] there too I seemed to see.

2. Cupid.

DANTE ALIGHIERI
1265–1321

Love and Poetry[1]

Guido, I wish that you and Lapo[2] and I,
Spirited on the wings of a magic spell,
Could drift in a ship where every rising swell
Would sweep us at our will across the skies;
Then tempest never, or any weather dire   5
Could ever make our blissful living cease;
No, but abiding in a steady, blessèd peace
Together we'd share the increase of desire.

And Lady Vanna and Lady Lagia[3] then
And she[4] who looms above the thirty best[5]   10
Would join us at the good enchanter's[6] behest;
And there we'd talk of Love without an end
To make those ladies happy in the sky—
With Lapo enchanted too, and you and I.

Sonnet[1]

Love and the gentle heart are one thing,
    even as the sage[2] affirms in his poem,

---

1. Translated from the Italian by James J. Wilhelm.   2. Guido Cavalcanti and Lapo Gianni were poets in Dante's literary circle.   3. Giovanna and Lagia were Guido and Lapo's ladies.   4. Beatrice, Dante's beloved.   5. Dante wrote a poem naming the most beautiful ladies of Florence.   6. Merlin.
1. Translated from the Italian by Dino Cervigni and Edward Vasta.   2. Guido Guinizzelli; see above, p. 1215.

and so one can be without the other
as much as rational soul without reason.
Nature creates them when she is amorous: 5
Love as lord and the heart as his mansion,
in which, sleeping, he rests
sometimes a brief and sometimes a long season.
Beauty appears in a wise lady, then,
which so pleases the eyes that in the heart   10
is born a desire for that which pleases;
and so long it lasts sometimes therein
that it wakens the spirit of Love.
And the same to a lady does a worthy man.

ANONYMOUS
thirteenth century
Calvary

Now goeth sonne[1] under wood,
Me rueth, Mary, thy fair rood;[2]
Now goeth sonne under tree,
Me rueth, Mary, thy son and thee.

1. Both "sun" and "son."   2. Both "face" and "cross."

ALEXANDER THE WILD
thirteenth century
Strawberry Picking[1]

Long ago, when we were children,
in the time that spanned the years
when we ran across the meadows,
over from those, now back to these,
there, where we at times   5
found violets,
you now see cattle leap for flies.

I remember how we sat
deep in flowers, and decided
which girl was the prettiest.   10
Our young looks were radiant then
with the new garland

1. Translated from the German by Peter Dronke.

for the dance.
And so the time goes by.

Look, there we ran to find strawberries,   15
ran to the beech from the fir-tree,
over sticks and stones,
as long as the sun shone.
Then a forester called out
through the branches   20
"Come along, children, go home!"

All our hands were stained,
picking strawberries yesterday;
to us it was nothing but play.
Then, again and again, we heard   25
our shepherd calling
and moaning:
"Children, the forest is full of snakes!"

One child walked in the tall grass,
started, and cried aloud: 30
"Children, right here there was a snake!
He has bitten our pony—
it will never heal;
it must always
remain poisoned and unwell."   35

"Come along then, out of the forest!
If you do not now make haste
it will happen as I say:
if you are not sure to be gone
from the forest while there is day,   40
you will lose your way
and your joy will become a moan."

Do you know that five young women
loitered in the meadow-lands
till the king locked up his hall?   45
Great were their moans and their distress—
for the bailiffs tore
their clothes away,
so that they stood naked, without a dress.[2]

2. Probably an allusion to the parable of the five foolish virgins in the New Testament of the Bible: see
Matthew 25.1–13.

DAFYDD AP GWILYM
ca. 1310–1370

The Fox[1]

Yesterday was I, sure of purpose,
Under the trees (alas that the girl doesn't see it)
Standing under Ovid's[2] stems
And waiting for a pretty girl beneath the trees;
She made me weep on her way.   5
I saw when I looked there
(An ape's shape where I did not love)
A red fox (he doesn't love our hounds' place)
Sitting like a tame animal,
On his haunches near his den.   10

    I drew between my hands
A bow of yew there, it was brave,
About, like an armed man,
On the brow of the hill, a stirring of high spirits,
Weapon for coursing along a district,   15
To hit him with a long, stout bolt.
I drew for a try a shaft
Clear past the jaw.
My grief, my bow went
In three pieces, luckless disaster.   20

    I got mad (I did not dread him,
Unhappy bear) at the fox.
He's a lad who'd love a hen,
A silly bird, and bird flesh;
He doesn't follow the cry of horns,   25
Rough his voice and his carol.
Ruddy is he in front of a talus[3] slope,
Like an ape among green trees.
At both ends of a field there turns up
A dog-shape looking for a goose.   30
Crows' beacon near the brink of a hill,
Acre-strider, color of an ember,
Likeness of a lure for crows and magpies at a fair,
Portent looking like a dragon.
Lord of excitement, chewer of a fat hen,   35
Of acclaimed fleece, glowing flesh.
An awl of hollowed-out fine earth,
Fire-dish at the edge of a shuttered window.
Copper bow of light feet,
Tongs like a beak of blood.   40

1. Translated from the Welsh by Richard Morgan Loomis.   2. Roman love poet (43 B.C.–A.D. 17).
3. A pile of rock fragments.

Not easy for me to follow him,
And his dwelling toward Annwn.[4]
Red roamer, he was found to be too fierce,
He'd run ahead of a course of hounds.
Sharp his rushing, gorse-strider,   45
Leopard with a dart in his rump.

4. The otherworld of Welsh myth.

ANONYMOUS

fourteenth century

Aubade[1]

Deep in an orchard, under hawthorn leaves,
the lady holds her lover in her arms,
until the watcher cries, he sees the dawn.
Dear God, the daybreak! oh how soon it comes!

"If only God let night stay without end,   5
and my beloved never left my side,
and never again the guard saw day or dawn—
dear God, the daybreak! oh how soon it comes!"

"Let us kiss, sweet beloved, you and I,
down in the meadows where the birds now sing—   10
defy my jealous husband and do all!
Dear God, the daybreak! oh how soon it comes!

"Let us create new love-sports, sweet beloved,
down in the meadows where the birds now sing—
until the watcher plays his pipe again.   15
Dear God, the daybreak! oh how soon it comes!

"In the sweet wind that came to me from there
I drank a ray of my beloved's breath,
my fair and joyous, gracious lover's breath—
dear God, the daybreak! oh how soon it comes!"   20

The lady is delightful, lovable,
admired by many for her beauty's sake,
and holds her heart most loyally in love.
Dear God, the daybreak! oh how soon it comes!

1. Translated from the French by Peter Dronke.

CHRISTINE DE PIZAN
ca. 1364–ca. 1431

Alone in Martyrdom[1]

Alone in martyrdom I have been left
In the desert of this world, that's full of sadness,
By my sweet love, who held my heart
In sorrowless joy and in perfect gladness;
But he is dead, and such deep griefs oppress   5
Me, my weary heart such sorrows gnaw,
I shall bewail his death for evermore.

What can I ever do but weep and sigh for
My departed love, what wonder is this?
For when my heart profoundly ponders how   10
I lived secure and without bitterness,
Since childhood and early youthfulness
With him—at me such sufferings gnaw
I shall bewail his death for evermore.

As the turtledove without her mate does turn   15
To dry things only, nor cares more for greenness;
As the ewe that the wolf seeks to kill
Is terrified, by her shepherd left defenseless;
So am I left in great distress
By my dear love whose loss to me is sore;   20
I shall bewail his death for evermore.

1. Translated from the French by Muriel Kittel.

ANONYMOUS
fifteenth century

Lament of the Virgin

Of all women that ever were born,
That bear children, abide and see,
How my son lies me before,
Upon my knee, taken from the tree.
Your children ye dance upon your knee.   5
With laughing, kissing and merry cheer;
Behold my child, behold now me,
For now lies dead my dear son dear.

O woman, woman, well is thee,
Thy child's cap thee dotes upon;
Thou picks his hair, beholds his ble,[1]
Thou wost not well when thou hast done.
But ever, alas, I make my moan
To see my son's head as it is here;
I pick out thorns by one and one,
For now lies dead my dear son dear.

O woman, a chaplet chosen thou has
Thy child to wear, it does thee great liking;
Thou pins it on with great solace,
And I sit with my son sore weeping.
His chaplet is thorns' sore pricking,
His mouth I kiss with a careful[2] cheer;
I sit weeping and thou singing,
For now lies dead my dear son dear.

O woman, look to me again,
That plays and kisses your children's pappis.[3]
To see my son I have great pain,
In his breast so great a gap is.
And on his body so many swappis.[4]
With bloody lips I kiss him here,
Alas! full hard methink me happis,[5]
For now lies dead my dear son dear.

O woman, thou takes thy child by the hand
And says, "My son, give me a strake!"[6]
My son's hands are sorely bleeding;
To look on him me list not lake.[7]
His hands he suffered for thy sake
Thus to be bored with nail and spear;
When thou make mirth great sorrow I make,
For now lies dead my dear son dear.

Behold, women, when that ye play
And have your children on knees dansand;[8]
You feel their feet, so feat[9] are they,
And to your sight well likand,[1]
But the most[2] finger of any hand,
Through my son's feet I may put here,
And pull it out sorely bledand,[3]
For now lies dead my dear son dear.

10

15

20

25

30

35

40

45

---

1. Complexion.   2. Woeful.   3. Breasts.   4. Wounds.   5. I suffer.   6. Stroke, i.e., caress.
7. Is no pleasure to me.   8. Dancing.   9. Pretty.   1. Liking.   2. Largest.   3. Bleeding.

Therefore, women, by town and street,
Your children's hands when ye behold
Their breasts, their body, and their feet,   50
Then good it were on my son think you wolde,[4]
How care has made my heart full cold
To see my son, with nail and spear,
With scourge and thorns many-fold,   55
Wounded and dead, my dear son dear.

Thou hast thy son full whole and sound,
And mine is dead upon my knee;
Thy child is loose and mine is bound,
Thy child is alive and mine dead is he.   60
Why was this ought[5] but for thee?
For my child trespassed never here.
Me thinks ye be holden to weep with me,
For now lies dead my dear son dear.

Weep with me, both man and wife,   65
My child is yours and loves you well.
If your child had lost his life
You would weep at every mele.[6]
But for my son weep ye never a del.[7]
If you love yours, mine has no peer;   70
He sends yours both hap and hele[8]
And for you died my dear son dear.

Now all women that have your wit,[9]
And see my child on my knees dead,
Weep not for yours but weep for it,   75
And ye shall have full muchel mede.[1]
He would again for your love bleed
Rather than that ye damnéd were.
I pray you all to him take heed,
For now lies dead my dear son dear.   80

Farewell, woman, I may no more
For dread of death rehearse his pain.
Ye may laugh when ye list[2] and I weep sore,
That may ye see and ye look to me again.
To love my son and ye be fain,[3]   85
I will love yours with heart entere,[4]
And he shall bring your children and you, certain,
To bliss where is my dear son dear.

---

4. Would.   5. At all.   6. Occasion.   7. Not at all.   8. Both fortune and health.   9. I.e., wits.
1. A great reward.   2. Please.   3. If you be willing.   4. Entire.

CHARLES D'ORLEANS
ca. 1394–1465

Balade[1]

If you wish to sell your kisses,
I will gladly buy some,
And in return you will have my heart as deposit.
To use them as inheritance,
By the dozens, hundreds, or thousands.   5
Don't sell them to me at as high a price
As you would to a total stranger
For you are receiving me as your liegeman.
    If you wish to sell your kisses,
    I will gladly buy some.   10
    And in return you will have my heart as deposit.
My complete wish and desire
Are yours in spite of all suspicion;
Allow, as a faithful and wise woman,
That for my reward and share
I may be among the first served,   15
    If you wish to sell your kisses.

1. Translated from the French by Sarah Spence.

FRANÇOIS VILLON
1431–ca. 1470

From The Testament[1]

                    *   *   *

Now I think I hear the laments
Of the once-beautiful Helmet-seller[2]
Wishing she were a girl again   455
And saying something like this
"Ah, cruel, arrogant old age
Why have you beaten me down so soon?
What holds me back from striking myself
From killing myself with a blow?   460

"You have taken from me the high hand
That I had by right of beauty
Over clerics, merchants, men of the Church
For then there wasn't a man born
Who wouldn't have given me all he owned   465

1. Translated from the French by Galway Kinnell.   2. A woman who sells armor.

Repent though he might later on
If I'd just have let him have
What now tramps won't take for free.

"To many a man I refused it
Which wasn't exactly good sense   470
For the love of a smooth operator
Whom I gave free play with it
And what if I did fool around
I swear I loved him truly
But he just gave me a hard time   475
And loved me for my money.

"He could wipe the floor with me
Or kick me I loved him still
And even if he's broken my back
He could just ask for a kiss   480
And I'd forget my misery
The rascal rotten right through
Would take me in his arms (a lot I got for it)
What's left? The shame and sin.

"Dead he's been these thirty years   485
And here I am old and grizzled
When I think also of the happy times
What I was, what I've become
When I look at myself naked
And see how I've changed so much   490
Poor, dried-up, lean and bony
I nearly go off my head.

"What's become of the smooth forehead
The yellow hair, the arching eyebrows
The wide-set eyes, the fair gaze   495
That took in all the cleverest men
The straight nose neither large nor small
The little flattened ears
The dimpled chin, the bright rounded cheeks
And the lips beautiful and red?   500

"The delicate little shoulders
The long arms and slender hands
The small breasts, the full buttocks
High, broad, perfectly built
For holding the jousts of love   505
The wide loins and the sweet quim
Set over thick firm thighs
In its own little garden?

"The forehead lined, the hair gray
The eyebrows all fallen out, the eyes clouded   510
Which threw those bright glances

That felled many a poor devil
The nose hooked far from beauty
The ears hairy and lopping down
The cheeks washed out, dead and pasty   515
The chin furrowed, the lips just skin.

"This is what human beauty comes to
The arms short, the hands shriveled
The shoulders all hunched up
The breasts? Shrunk in again   520
The buttocks gone the way of the tits
The quim? aagh! As for the thighs
They aren't thighs now but sticks
Speckled all over like sausages.

"This is how we lament the good old days   525
Among ourselves, poor silly crones
Dumped down on our hunkers
In little heaps like so many skeins
Around a tiny hempstalk fire
That's soon lit and soon gone out   530
And once we were so adorable
So it goes for men and women.

"Now look here pretty Glover
Who used to study under me
And you too Blanche the Shoe-fitter   535
It's time you got it straight
Take what you can right and left
Don't spare a man I beg you
For there's no run on old crones
No more than cried-down money.   540

"And you sweet Sausage-filler
Such a born dancer
And Guillemette the Tapester[3]
Don't fall out with your man
Soon you'll have to close up shop   545
When you've gotten old and flabby
And good for no one but an old priest
No more than cried-down money.

"Jeanneton the Bonnet-maker
Don't let that one lover tie you down   550
And Catherine the Purse-seller
Stop putting men out to pasture
She who's lost her looks can ask them
To come back, she can flash her smile
But ugly old age can't buy love   555
No more than cried-down money.

3. Properly a maker or seller of rugs; her shop may have been headquarters for a prostitute.

"Girls, stop a moment
And let it sink in why I weep and cry
I can't get back in circulation
No more than cried-down money."   560

*   *   *

MEDIEVAL TALES: A SELECTION

Among the most popular forms of literature in the Middle Ages were brief narratives, some little more than anecdotes or jokes, some as ambitious as short stories. Indeed, as a glance at the table of contents of this anthology will show, some of the greatest medieval masterpieces—the *Lais* of Marie de France, Boccaccio's *Decameron*, Chaucer's *Canterbury Tales*, the *Arabian Nights*, and even Dante's *Divine Comedy*—are collections of stories. Yet these works derive from a vast network of largely anonymous stories that have their own kind of genius. If they are less carefully crafted works of art than their more illustrious literary progeny, they nonetheless display an uninhibited energy, a willingness to explore nonconformist attitudes, and a satiric vigor that the more official works tend to moderate. And these tales often seem to aim at no higher effect than to provide pleasure: wit and high spirits are, despite their moralizing claims to the contrary, the qualities these tales prize above all others.

While medieval audiences probably didn't much care what type of story they were listening to, many medieval writers did have a sense of the various genres available to them, even though the boundaries between them were often blurred. The most capacious of these generic types was the *exemplum*, by which is meant a story that provides an example of a general principle. From the time of the Gospels, Christian teachers had relied upon exemplary stories to drive home moral points. By the early twelfth century collections of these *exempla* began to appear, and in the thirteenth century, when public preaching had become a central aspect of religious life, these collections grew and became more carefully organized. A preacher looking for a story to illustrate a specific theme could now find in a handbook a number of stories located under various spiritual or moral categories. (A good instance of using an *exemplum* to enliven a sermon is found in Chaucer's *Pardoner's Tale*.) *Exempla* were also widely used in various kinds of didactic treatises, some secular and concerned with transmitting philosophical, political, or general moral truths, some religious and concerned with helping Christians understand both the elements of their faith and the nature of sin. Not surprisingly, some of the more severe moralists rejected *exempla* entirely, arguing that stories simply distracted the audience from the lesson being taught. Yet this moralizing severity had an unexpected literary benefit, for in the hands of skillful storytellers the relation of the story to the moral became itself a source of interest; and some storytellers actually challenged their listeners to find any moral at all while simultaneously making their stories irresistibly interesting.

In this small selection from the literally hundreds of medieval tales that survive we have included three *exempla*. The first two are from the earliest collection in Latin, made by Petrus Alfonsi in the first decades of the twelfth century. Petrus was born in 1062 as Moshe Sephardi, a member of the Jewish community in Huesca, Spain, a town at the time controlled by the Arabs. In 1096 the town was captured by the Christians, and on St. Peter's Day, June 29, 1106, Moshe himself converted to Christianity, taking his name from his patron saint Peter and from his godfather, King Alfonso I of Aragon. Well-educated in both Hebrew and Arabic science, Petrus served as a physician first for Alfonso and then for Henry I of England. It was probably in

England that he wrote the *Dialogue of Peter and Moses* justifying his conversion, as well as important astronomical works that for the first time made the sophisticated science then flourishing in Arabic Spain available to the Latin West. There is evidence that around 1125 Peter returned to Spain and took up residence in Toledo, where he continued his role as a transmitter of Arabic and Hebrew knowledge to the Latin West. The selection here is drawn from his work called the *Disciplina clericalis*. The title means literally *Rule for Clerics* but is more informatively translated as *The Scholar's Guide*: the book is meant to provide wisdom to those who can read Latin. In compiling his book Petrus drew upon Hebrew wisdom literature, Arabic proverbs, and tales drawn from the rich folklore of India, Byzantium, Persia, Israel, and Arabia. The *Disciplina* seems first to have been written in either Arabic or Hebrew and then translated into Latin prose, either by Petrus alone or with a collaborator. Its subsequent influence was enormous. Not only was it translated into most of the European languages, but its stories found their way, for the most part indirectly, into preachers' handbooks and vernacular collections like the *Decameron* and *The Canterbury Tales*. The two tales included here are based upon one of the most popular medieval narrative themes, the outwitting of the powerful by an apparently weaker opponent. In the first case we see peasant cunning vanquishing the arrogance of two city-dwellers; in the second it is Nehudi the apprentice who outsmarts his master. In both cases we are given morals that are acceptable but hardly exhaust the meanings of the narratives. For one thing, the tales are placed in the context of a conversation between a wise man and his son, and so we are encouraged to ask how they comment on that relationship. For another, the interest in the stories derives not simply from their moral significance but from an unexpected twist. While we think we know how the stories are going to turn out, each one ends with a verbal cleverness we had not anticipated. In a sense, the stories outwit the reader: we expect to be instructed but are instead charmed, an effect that forces us to examine our own scale of values.

Our second selection consists of four fabliaux. The fabliau (the term derives from the Northern French word for "little fable") is a short tale in rhyming couplets that must meet one criterion above all: humor. The earliest fabliaux date from the end of the twelfth century: *The Wild Dream* is ascribed in its final lines to Jean Bodel, author of a number of other works, who died in 1210. Of the 160 or so surviving fabliaux, almost all come from the north of France; there are a few English examples, but most—like Chaucer's *Miller's Tale*—have French sources. We know the names of only a few of the authors. Most of the authors seem to have been professional minstrels, and no doubt many of the fabliaux circulated orally before being written down. Although many fabliaux end with a hortatory statement, few actually claim to offer much moral improvement: as one poet says, fabliaux "are a great comfort to the frivolous and idle." The values the fabliaux promote are frankly hedonistic. They celebrate the pleasures of food and wine, comfortable lodgings, and—above all—sex. Many are unapologetically obscene, although it is difficult to know if medieval men and women had the same standards of verbal propriety as many modern readers. Fabliaux also celebrate specifically literary pleasures. They are written in a jaunty verse form (nicely replicated in this translation), they delight in witty rhymes and clever puns, and they often display playfully overelaborate plotting. Because of the nonaristocratic social status of most of their protagonists, and their raucous behavior, it used to be thought that the fabliaux were lower-class works. But we now know that they circulated in aristocratic circles as well, and the picture they present of the lower classes contains a strong element of the stereotype. Among the misdemeanors that the fabliaux most delight in punishing are social affectation and priestly misbehavior. But these affronts can offend members of every social class.

The Wild Dream and *The Ring That Controlled Erections* are two tales that display one of the most prominent characteristics of the fabliau, its capacity to give free rein to sexual fantasy. Yet in both cases the fantasy is located within a controlling context. In *The Wild Dream* that context is provided by the carefully detailed account of the genial domestic world of the husband and wife. The husband's good-humored acceptance of his wife's teasing, along with the wife's equally good-humored acceptance of her husband's physical limits, show how fantasy can actually serve to improve the workings of real life—a lesson that applies to the fabliau itself. *The Three Hunchbacks* is a much less cheerful story, in part because it expresses with shocking directness the medieval contempt for the deformed, in part because of the story's casual violence and complacent amoralism. Whether the price we have to pay for the story's wit is too high is a question readers will have to answer for themselves—bearing in mind, however, that this may well be the question that the fabliau means to pose. *The Butcher of Abbeville* is a good example of a number of central fabliau values: wit, as shown in the cleverness both of the protagonist and of the fabliau plot itself; realism, as in the careful rendering of the dialogue among the priest's household; hedonism, as in the butcher's loving description of the fine meal the purloined sheep will provide and his appreciation of the sexual pleasures he solicits from the household; and above all the pleasure of storytelling itself, as the narrative lovingly unfolds its deliciously inevitable denouement. It is, finally, this unabashed celebration of pleasure for its own sake that is the fabliau's greatest contribution to medieval culture.

Our third selection features one of the best-known and most beguiling characters in medieval literature, Renard the Fox. Far from being just a trickster, Renard in fact embodies a wide range of characteristics. He is always delightful in his witty inventiveness, and his lack of moral pretensions allows him to expose the hypocrisy—and appetitiveness—of others. Yet he is also frightening in his selfish concern for himself and in his utter lack of scruple in subjecting both friend and foe to violence and even death. Finally, he remains oddly impressive and even touching in his romantic role as a social outcast: for very good reason, none of his fellow animals—and certainly none of the humans who inhabit his world—trust or even much like him, an isolation that Renard sometimes treats as a mark of proud distinction and at other times clearly finds dispiriting.

Our selection consists of a self-contained part of the tale collection entitled the *Romance of Renard*. While brief animal fables had been popular throughout antiquity and the Middle Ages—they were, then as now, often used in schoolrooms to teach both language skills and ethics—it was not until 1148–49 that a fully formed and autonomous world of animal characters came into existence. It was then that an unidentified cleric from the city of Ghent, in modern Belgium, wrote a long Latin poem (entitled *Ysengrimus*) about the lion king and the animal "barons" who made up his court. Focusing on the animosity between the clever fox Renard and the brutish wolf Ysengrin, this poem inspired a French version written by another cleric, Pierre de Saint-Cloud, in the 1170s. For almost three hundred years other poets added new episodes and retold the old ones in various European languages. Indeed, even Chaucer includes a version of one of Renard's adventures in *The Canterbury Tales*, in a tale told (appropriately enough) by a priest. In fact, Renard and Ysengrin still live on, but now as Jerry the mouse and Tom the cat, Bugs Bunny and Elmer Fudd, and the Road Runner and Wile E. Coyote.

The selection printed here, *The Trial of Renard*, was composed around 1180 by one of the anonymous poets who added to Pierre's poem. It displays many of the characteristics that made the Renard stories so popular. The central premise is the concern of Noble the Lion King to maintain order among his barons, a pressing issue in a feudal world in which a weak monarchy attempted to control private feuding among a powerful nobility (the same situation we find, for instance, in *The Song of Roland* and Malory's *Morte Darthur*). The opening scene is set in Noble's court, where Ysengrin asks that Renard be brought to justice for raping his wife, Hersent, and urinating on his cubs. Immediately, however, the question is muddied by the suggestion—made by Grinbert the badger, the only friend Renard has at court—that Hersent in fact consented to Renard's advances, and eventually Hersent offers to suffer trial by ordeal, in this case to carry a piece of hot iron that will prove her innocence by creating a wound that will quickly heal. But Ysengrin objects for the obvious reason that Hersent may fail the test, proving that he is a cuckold. Just as Noble declares that a peace has been declared that Ysengrin must not violate, the absent Renard's fortunes take a turn for the worse with the arrival of the rooster Chantecler and an entourage of weeping chickens dragging in a bier on which lie the remains of Madame Copee, one of their sisters, who has been mauled by Renard. This hilarious scene—in which all the animals express grief and outrage that a fox should have eaten a chicken—is capped off by a derisive parody of a funeral service and then the "discovery" that Madame Copee is in fact a martyr at whose tomb miracles are now performed. Already we see the author's satiric mischief, as he presents king and nobility as foolishly squabbling over dubious questions of honor, religious rituals as hopelessly sentimental and self-interested, and above all the dignity that humans so carefully protect as a poor disguise for our essentially animal nature. As various members of the court try to bring Renard before the king to receive justice, the fox tricks his enemies by playing on their appetites. And when he does finally appear before the king and is condemned—without a trial—to be hung, he manages not only to escape by persuading his gullible opponents that he is (of all things) anxious for the fate of his soul but also to deride them in a particularly demeaning way. Utterly impenitent, equally scornful of aristocrat and peasant alike, and mocking the social and religious values that the official culture of the Middle Ages held so dear, the irrepressible Renard is an antihero who is simultaneously appealing and appalling. For if he gleefully punctures all pretensions, he also forces us to ask whether we want to—or in fact really do—live in a dog-eat-dog (or fox-eat-chicken) world.

With the final selection we return to the *exemplum,* in this case a tale found in a work called *Handling Sin,* written in the first two decades of the fourteenth century by Robert Mannyng, an English cleric. Composed in rough English couplets, the work is freely adapted from a French book called the *Manual of Sins.* As both the French and English titles imply, these works are meant to provide readers (or listeners, since Robert seems to have expected his work to have been read aloud) with information about sin. During the time they came into existence, the Church had decreed that every Christian was to go to confession at least once a year: these works—and many others like them—were designed to teach the laity how to "handle sin" by teaching them what acts were sinful and the remedies, especially confession, that could be marshaled against them. In the course of his exposition of various transgressions Robert includes a large number of illustrative *exempla.* The story of the dancers of Colbeck was widely known throughout Europe: Robert is correct when he says that it appears in many foreign chronicles. His source for the story is not in fact the French *Manual of Sins,* where a simpler, less interesting version appears. Instead Robert turned to a Latin saint's life written in the late eleventh century by a monk named Goscelin, a typical example of the complicated route by which these tales circulated throughout Europe. Within its context in *Handling Sin* Robert presents the story as illustrating the sin of sacrilege; he also wants his listeners to be respectful of priests. Yet he seems himself to realize that the story can hardly be contained by such a simple frame. He adds at the end that it is also about cursing, and readers will quickly see that other themes are involved. But what is most striking about the story is the contrast between its simple—even simplistic—form and its deeply mysterious content. Both dancers and priest are together caught up in an action they cannot themselves fully understand but that nonetheless reveals a complex and enigmatic purposiveness. God, we are led to believe, is the true author of this story, but exactly what is He telling us? The story's refusal to reveal its ultimate meaning leaves readers free to meditate on their own understanding of divine justice.

A good discussion of the *exempla* as a form can be found in F. A. C. Martello and A. G. Rigg, *Medieval Latin: An Introduction and Bibliographical Guide* (1996). Patricia Terry's translation of selections from the *Romance of Renard* (1983) can be supplemented by the fuller translation by D. D. R. Owen in *The Romance of Reynard the*

Fox (1994). Both books contain useful introductions and bibliographies. Charles Muscatine, *The Old French Fabliaux* (1986), is an informative account. Robert Mannyng's story is given a subtle and interesting interpretation by Mark Miller, "Displaced Souls, Idle Talk, Spectacular Scenes: *Handlyng Synne* and the Perspective of Agency," *Speculum* 71 (1996): 606–32.

PETRUS ALFONSI
1062–ca.1110

From The Scholar's Guide[1]

The Two City Dwellers and the Country Man

Once there were two city men and a country man who were going to Mecca on a pilgrimage. They ate together until they came near Mecca, where their provisions gave out, and they had nothing left but a little flour with which they could make one small loaf.

The city men, seeing this, said to each other, "We have little bread and our companion eats much; we should think how we can get his share of the bread and eat it by ourselves."

They all three agreed to the following plan: that they would make the loaf and bake it; and while it was cooking, they would go to sleep, and whoever had the most extraordinary dream should have the bread for himself. The city dwellers said this as a trick because they thought the country man was stupid enough to believe such ruses. They made the loaf, put it on the fire, and then lay down to sleep.

The country man, aware of the trick, took the half-baked loaf from the fire while his companions were sleeping, ate it, and lay down again.

One of the city dwellers, as if frightened by a dream, awoke and called to his companion. The second city dweller said, "What is the matter?"

And the first said, "I had a wonderful dream: it seemed that two angels opened the gates of heaven, took me up, and led me before God."

His companion said to him, "This dream is wonderful, but I dreamt that with two angels leading me and opening the earth, I was taken to hell."

The peasant heard all this and still pretended to be asleep; but the deceitful city men, who had already been deceived, called the country man to wake up. And he, slyly, as if he were frightened, answered, "Who is calling me?"

They said, "We, your companions."

And he said, "Have you returned already?"

And they said, "Where did we go, that we should return?"

And the rustic said, "I dreamed that two angels took one of you and opened the gates of heaven and took him before God; then two other angels took the other and opened the earth and took him to hell. When I saw these things, I thought that neither of you would ever return, and I got up and ate the bread."

The father: "So it happened, my son, that those who wanted to deceive their companion were tricked by their own ruse."

---

1. Translated from the Latin by J. R. Jones and J. E. Keller.

Then the son said, "It happened to them just as it says in the proverb: He who wanted all, lost all. These men resemble the dog, whose nature inclines him to take the food of the other dog. If they had imitated the camel, they would have imitated a more gentle nature. For the nature of the camel is such that when many are given feed at the same time, none of them eats until all eat at the same time. And if one is so sick that he is unable to eat, the others will not eat until it is led away. These two city men, when they decided to behave as animals, should have copied the nature of the gentlest animal. They deserved to lose their food."

"But I wish that they had been whipped, as the king's tailor was beaten through the cleverness of his pupil Nedui; I heard about it from my teacher some time ago."

The father: "Tell me, my boy, what you have heard. What happened to the pupil? Such a story should be very amusing!"

The son:

The King's Tailor's Apprentice

My teacher told me that a king had a tailor who cut different clothes for him suitable for different seasons, and the tailor had apprentices who sewed skillfully whatever the master tailor cut. Among the apprentices was one called Nedui, who was better than all his companions in the art of sewing.

Since a holiday was approaching, the king called his tailor and ordered him to prepare for him and his family expensive clothing for the occasion; and so that it could be done more quickly and without delay, he placed a eunuch, one of his chamberlains, as supervisor (for that was his task) over the men who sewed, and asked him to watch them closely and give them whatever was necessary.

One day the king's servants gave the tailor and his assistants hot bread and honey, with the other food, and those who were there began to eat.

The eunuch said to those eating, "Why do you eat when Nedui is not here and not wait for him?"

The master tailor said, "Because he would not eat honey even if he were here."

And they ate it all. Then Nedui came and said, "Why did you eat without me and not keep my share for me?"

The eunuch said to him, "Your master said that even if you were here you would not eat honey." Nedui said nothing, but he was thinking how he could get even with his master. He devised a plan, and later, the master being absent, in secrecy, he said to the eunuch:

"Sir, my master sometimes has spells of madness and loses his mind, and he beats and kills those who are near him without distinction."

The eunuch said to him, "If I knew when he was about to have a seizure, I would tie him up and whip him so that he would do nothing rash."

And Nedui said, "When you see him looking all around and feeling the floor with his hands and getting up from his seat and picking up the chair on which he is seated, then you will know that he is mad, and if you do not protect yourself and your servants, he will beat you on the head with a club."

"God bless you," said the eunuch, "I shall at once take precautions for myself and my servants."

The next day Nedui hid his master's shears, and when the master looked for his shears and did not find them, he began to feel around the floor with his hands and to look here and there and get up off his seat and to move the chair on which he was seated.

Seeing this, the eunuch immediately called his servants and ordered them to tie the tailor and beat him fiercely so that he could not beat the others.

The tailor screamed, "What harm have I done, that you torment me with this beating?"

But they, beating him more fiercely, said nothing; and when they were tired of beating him and he of being beaten they let him loose, half dead. When he came to after a long time, he asked the eunuch what crime he had committed, and the eunuch said to him:

"Nedui, your apprentice, told me that sometimes you went mad and that you did not stop until you were tied and beaten; therefore I had you tied and beaten."

The tailor, when he heard this, called Nedui and said to him, "Friend, when have you ever seen me crazy?"

The apprentice: "When have you ever seen me refuse to eat honey?"

The eunuch and the others, hearing this, laughed and judged that each one deserved the punishment he suffered.

To this the father answered: "The tailor deserved his punishment because if he had kept the precept of Moses, to love his brother as himself, this would not have happened to him."

FOUR FABLIAUX[1]
thirteenth century

The Butcher of Abbeville[2]

My lords, here's something marvelous—
you've never heard the like of this
which I am now about to tell,
so set your minds to listen well,
for words, when no one lends an ear,   5
in the end simply disappear.
   In Abbeville a butcher dwelt.
In high esteem the man was held:
he wasn't base or slanderous,
but wise, well-bred and virtuous;   10
he plied his trade with honesty
and often in adversity
helped out his neighbors who were needy;
he wasn't covetous or greedy.
   One All Saints' Day, as was his wont,   15
the butcher went to Oisemont[3]
to purchase livestock at the fair,

---

1. Translated from the French by Ned Dubin.   2. A town in northeastern France.   3. A nearby town.

but all his time was wasted there:
he found the animals too pricy,
the pigs looked dangerous and feisty,   20
a wretched and degraded breed;
nothing was there that met his need,
his whole trip was to no avail,
he'd keep his cash—forget the sale!
His meager marketing now done,   25
he quickly turned his steps toward home
with cape and sword, since day was ending
and twilight soon would be descending.
Listen, and you'll hear how he fared.
Night overtook him unprepared   30
when halfway home, there in Bailleul.[4]
The day was gone, the night was full;
it was so dark, he thought he'd stay
and go no further on his way,
because he feared the many robbers   35
the countryside around there harbors
might steal the money he had brought.
Before the entrance to a courtyard he caught sight of a poor woman.
He asked of her, calling her to him,   40
"Say, do you know some place nearby
where for a price a man can buy
the basic comforts for his body?
I'd not intrude on anybody."
The worthy woman in reply   45
said, "Sir, by all the world's saints, my
employer here, good Master Miles,
says there's no wine around for miles,
except Father Gautier, our priest,
has two casks at the very lease,   50
brought all the way from Nogentel.[5]
There's always wine there, I hear tell.
See if he'll put you up tonight."
The butcher said, "I'll go there right
away, good woman. God defend you."   55
"Sir, to His keeping I commend you."
   Before his doorstep he found seated
the deacon, who was most conceited.
The butcher greeted him and said,
"Father, as God may send you aid,   60
I ask your hospitality
in honor and in charity."
"Go seek your shelter with the Lord!
By Saint Hubert, I'll not accord
a layman lodgings for the night!   65
You'll find some other place, all right,
where you can stay somewhere in town—

---

4. A village between Oisement and Abbeville.   **5.** A town some 150 miles away, known for its fine wine.

just go on searching up and down
till someone offers you a bed.
I promise you, I'll not be led   70
to let you spend the night inside
this house of mine—it's occupied;
nor should a priest in any case
open his home to someone base."
"Base, father? Are you telling me   75
that you despise the laity?"
"Indeed I do, and I am right.
You've shown me disrespect and spite.
Now get off of my property!"
"What spite? It would be charity   80
for you to let me stay here, father,
for I'm not like to find another.
I spend my money willingly:
if you've something to sell to me,
I'll buy it of you, never fret,   85
and be in your eternal debt.
I'd never dream, sir, to impose."
"You'd do as well to knock, Lord knows,
against a stone wall with your head,
by Saint Peter!" the deacon said.   90
"I won't give you a place to rest."
"The devil come and be your guest,"
the butcher said, "dishonest priest!
You are a scoundrel and a beast!"
He went away—why waste his breath?—   95
but he was smouldering with wrath.
    What happened to him? Be it known
that just as he was leaving town,
before an old abandoned shelter
with rafters fallen helter-skelter   100
he met up with a flock of ewes.
Now you will hear a piece of news!
He gave the herding-man a call,
who'd had many a cow and bull
under his care back in his youth: 105
"God give you joy, shepherd. In truth,
whose beasts are these?" "Our priest's, in faith."
"God! can this really be the case?"
Hear what the butcher did next: he
purloined a sheep so cleverly   110
the shepherd didn't see the theft;
he was so tricky and so deft
it all escaped the shepherd's eyes.
The butcher quickly takes his prize
and hoists it up onto his back   115
and takes a detour to go back,
arriving at the deacon's manse
who's so puffed up with arrogance
as he's about to close the door,

and, saddled with a sheep, once more   120
he said, "May God, who rules mankind,
be good to you, father, and kind."
The deacon bid the man the same
and promptly asked from where he came.
"From Abbeville. Today I went   125
to market down in Oisemont.
This sheep is all I found to buy,
but it looks meaty in the thigh.
Will you not let me be your guest
tonight, for I'm in need of rest?   130
I'm not a stingy man, nor cheap.
Tonight we'll cook and eat the sheep
if you would like to, 'cause I've found
it quite a load to tote around.
It's big, and it has so much meat   135
we all will have enough to eat."
The priest approves—he has intense
desire to dine at his expense.
(He loves a funeral, which brings
him in more than four christenings.)   140
"Why certainly, sir, with a will!
If there were three of you here, still
I'd house you all and you would lack
for nothing. I'm not one to slack
on honor and consideration!   145
You seem to be a man of station,
and I would like to know your name."
"Father, by God, know that I came
to be called David by baptism
when I received the oil and chrism.[6]   150
May God not smile on in the least
the man who raised so large a beast!—
I'm tired from bearing such a load.
Your hearth means rest after the road."

    They went inside then. At that late   155
hour a fire sparkled in the grate.
He put the sheep down on the ground
and turned his head and looked around
requesting someone bring an axe,
which came as soon as he had asked.   160
He killed the beast and skinned it; after
he hung the skin up from a rafter
nearby for all of them to see.
"Father," he said, "what quality!
See for yourself, for love of God,   165
what first-class meat marbled with lard—
it's even better than I thought!
I must admit that having brought
it so far hurt my neck a bit.

6. Chrism is oil mixed with cream, used for anointing a baptized infant.

Now do with it as you see fit.   170
Make a roast of the shoulder quarter
and a pot full of boiling water
for stock for all the house to share
around. I think that it is fair
to say that this meat is the most   175
fine I've seen. Put it up to roast!
How tender and juicy it looks—
it will be done before the cooks
have even finished with the sauce!
I won't give orders. You're the boss,   180
good host—you've but to say the word,
so have them quickly lay the board:
it's ready! Let's wash up a bit
and have some candles brought and lit."
     Here's something now that's just for your   185
ears: the priest had a paramour
for whom he felt such jealousy
whenever he had company
he sent her to stay in her room,
but on this night he called her to him   190
to table to join their repast
in honor of his special guest.
When they had eaten royally,
the lady made especially
for their guest's comfort a fine bed   195
with white, fresh laundered sheets and spread.
The deacon called his serving-maid:
"I order you, sister," he said,
"that Master David here, our guest,
be waited on as he likes best.   200
Let nothing at all disagree
with him—he's been good company."
The deacon went off to his room
(his lady friend, too, I assume);
the butcher remained by the fire.   205
He'd everything to his desire:
good lodgings, also bonhomie.
He called the maid: "Come here to me—
a word with you, wench. Come on over,
grant me the favors of a lover,   210
and you will get a princely gift."
"How dare you? Hush!" she answered, miffed.
"Lord! men are such ill-mannered beasts!
Hands off! and let me be in peace!
What do I know of such a sin?"   215
"In faith, I'm sure that you'll give in
when you have heard my proposition."
"Come, out with it, and I will listen."
"If you will sleep with me tonight
and give me pleasure and delight,   220
I swear to God, I'll let you keep

in payment the skin of my sheep."
"Don't even think it! Stop your noise!
I see you don't go in for boys,
by God, to ask that thing of me!   225
Your mind is full of lechery,
you're such a crazy fool, I swear!
I'd do it, but I just don't dare:
tomorrow you would tell Madame."
"I'll keep it secret like a clam,   230
God bless my soul! I'd never use you,
then turn around, dear, and accuse you."
So she agreed to do his whim
and promptly gave herself to him.
    She lay with him until day broke.   235
She lit the fire when she awoke,
then did her chores and milked the cow.
The deacon, too, has woken now.
He leaves for church, where at the altar
he and his cleric sing the psalter,   240
and lets his concubine sleep late.
David the butcher doesn't wait
now that it's morning and time presses,
but quickly grabs his shoes and dresses;
to the room where his hostess lies   245
he now goes to say his goodbyes,
draws back the latch, opens the door.
To see her guest standing before
her bed when she opens her eyes,
the lovely lady shows surprise   250
and can't imagine to what ends
he's come there and what he intends.
"Let me express my gratitude,
lady," he says. "Nobody could
have shown more hospitality   255
and gracious generosity."
Having said this, he draws up closer
and lays his head down on the bolster,
pulls back the sheet and catches sight
of her breasts, beautiful and white.   260
"My God!" he says, "now here's a wonder!
Sweet blessed Virgin! Yes, by thunder,
this deacon really has it good
to lie with such a lady nude!
So help me Saint Honorius,[7]   265
a king would be content with less!
If it were given to me to
lie here at night in bed with you,
I'd be contented and made whole!"
"David, it's wrong, upon my soul,   270
for you to say the things you say!

---

7. Bishop of Amiens, a nearby city, in the sixth century.

Now leave me! Get your hands away!
My man won't be in church that long;
he'd think we'd done him grievous wrong
if he came in the room and saw.   275
He wouldn't love me anymore,
thanks to you. It would cost me dear."
He does his best to calm her fear:
"Lady," he tells her, "I will not,
for love of God, move from this spot   280
for any man alive. The same
holds for the deacon: if he came
and uttered so much as a word,
however prideful and absurd,
in protest like some uncouth villain,   285
I wouldn't hesitate to kill him.
But if you'll satisfy my wish,
sweet lady, I will make you rich:
that first-rate sheepskin will be yours."
"But what will people say?—because   290
I think that you're so indiscreet
you'll brag about it in the street."
"Will you not trust me when I've promised
that while I live I will be honest?
No one will know, woman or man,   295
by the saints in the Vatican."
He goes on urging and insists
until no longer she resists
and lets the butcher at his pleasure
enjoy her favors in full measure.   300
    After, he left,—why hang around?—
went to the church, and there he found
the priest, who had begun the readings
and never halted the proceedings.
Right at the *Jube Domine*[8]   305
the butcher came to him to say,
"Let me express my gratitude
for housing me; nobody could
have done so more hospitably,
but I would ask you to agree   310
to do something for me and buy
the skin of that fine sheep which I
brought you, for it would ease my road.
The wool must be a three-pound load
and first-rate. I'll sell it to you,   315
though it's worth three, for only two
shillings, and be grateful to boot."
"Most welcome guest, for you I'll do 't
gladly, if it's expedient.
Your company is excellent;   320

8. The beginning of a Latin phrase—"Father, do you wish to bless me?"—that the clerk directs to the priest before reading the lesson.

come back and visit frequently."
He sells him his own skin, then he
bids him farewell, and off he goes.
　　The deacon's lady friend arose,
who was so lovely and flirtatious;　　　　　　　　　325
her bluish-gray eyes were vivacious;
she chose to wear a bright green gown
with deep and large pleats hanging down
and tucked in tightly at the waist
(such vanity suited her taste);　　　　　　　　　　330
she was, in short, coquette and fair.
She went and sat down in a chair,
whereon without delay the maid
approached the skin and would have laid
her hands on it, had not her mistress　　　　　　　335
forbid her, saying, "Now what business
do you have with that sheepskin there?"
"Lady, I think that's my affair.
I mean to hang it up outside
in the bright sunshine till it's dried."　　　　　　340
"Oh no, you won't! You do your chores
and leave it hanging here indoors.
It's not disturbing anyone."
"But mistress, all my chores are done.
I got up earlier than you."　　　　　　　　　　　345
"I bet!" "Well, anyway, it's true,
while you slept late, so hold your peace."
"Be off! and don't dare touch that fleece!
Don't you so much as lay a hand
or fiddle with it—understand?"　　　　　　　　　350
"In God's name, lady, and why not?
I'll fiddle with it a whole lot.
I may, since it belongs to me."
"You say the skin's your property?"
"Indeed I do." "Oh, is that so?　　　　　　　　　355
You put that sheepskin down and go
hang yourself! Drown in a latrine!
I'm livid! Who has ever seen
a servant try to be so bossy?
You two-faced, stinking, brazen hussy!　　　　　360
Get out! Don't dare darken my door!"
"What do you carry on so for,
and why insult me for what's mine?
So what if you'd swear on divine
relics?—it's mine beyond a doubt."　　　　　　　365
"Get out before I throw you out!
Your service here is terminated!
You're shameless and you're self-inflated!
The priest himself may contradict it,
but all the same you are evicted,　　　　　　　　370
you fill me with such strong dislike!"
"I'm going,—may the black plague strike

who works for you a single day!—
but till the master comes I'll stay.
I mean to let him know completely,   375
in every detail, how you treat me."
"How *I* treat *you*? What cheek! You blasted
immoral bitch! You trull! You bastard!"
"Me? bastard? If you say so, that's
because the deacon sired your brats,   380
no doubt, in a more legal fashion?"
"Put down my sheepskin, by God's passion,
or you'll come to a sorry pass!
You'll wish that you were in Arras,[9]
or even in Cologne, by God!"   385
And then the woman struck her hard
using her distaff. The maid shouted,
"That skin will cost you, never doubt it!
My Saint Marie's pure reputation,
you hit me without provocation!   390
Although it kill me, you shall pay!"
She burst in tears and wailed away.
    Amid the ruckus and the fight
the priest returned and said, "All right,
who struck you? What's this argument?"   395
"My mistress, but I'm innocent!"
"She had some cause, and you know why,
so let me hear it, and don't lie."
"Indeed, sir, it was for the hide
that's hanging there by the fireside.   400
Remember, master, how you said
last evening when you went to bed
that I should do my level best
to entertain David, our guest?
I did as you commanded; he   405
in gratitude presented me
the sheepskin, and, by all that's holy,
I swear to you I earned it fully."
The deacon heard her and deduced
from what she said, she'd been seduced   410
and their guest had given his word
to make the sheepskin her reward.
It raised the hackles on his back,
but still he kept his true thoughts back
and said, "Now, lady, by our Savior,   415
I don't approve of your behavior.
You flaunt me and make a disturbance
and beat up on my household servants."
"What? Just because she wants our fleece?
I'm sure if you knew but a piece   420
of the shame she heaped on my head,
you'd pay her back for what she said.

---

9. A town about forty miles away.

The things she said about your children!
What kind of man are you, who're willing
to permit me to be the butt   425
of insults for this foul-mouthed slut?
Whatever else you may decide,
I will not let her have my hide.
I say the sheepskin isn't hers."
"Whose is it then?" "Why, mine, of course."   430
"It's yours?" "Why, yes." "Why should that be?"
"We showed him hospitality,
we gave him covers, sheets, a roof—
I'd think that was sufficient proof,
yet here I stand interrogated!"   435
"Dear lady, say, is what you've stated
true, by your promised honesty
when you first came to live with me?
Are you the owner of the pelt?"
"Saint Peter, yes! You heard me tell 't!"   440
Just then the serving-maid broke in:
"It was to me he gave the skin!
She's handing you a pack of lies!"
"Whore! what foul stars were in the skies
when you were born? He had his way   445
with you! Clear out of here today!
For shame! to boast of it aloud!"
The priest said, "By the sacred shroud
of Compiègne,[1] control yourself!
"I hate her more than death itself!   450
When she speaks there is no believing
her, and I've caught the baggage thieving!"
"What did I ever take from you?"
"My oats, my wheat, my barley, too,
my peas, my lard, my fresh-baked loaves!   455
How can you treat her with kid gloves
and let her so get on our nerves,
sir. Let her have what she deserves!
For God's sake, get rid of this menace!"
"Lady," he answered, "by Saint Dennis,[2]   460
listen to me. I want to know
to which of you the skin should go.
Now tell me who made you this gift."
"Our guest did, right before he left."
"How so?—for, by Saint Martin's maw,   465
this morning he got up before
the sun had risen in the sky!"
"How blasphemous! I can't think why
you need to swear with such élan.
When it was time to go the man   470
took fitting leave and was well-bred."

---

1. A town about eighty miles away, which claimed to possess the shroud in which Jesus had been wrapped after his death.   2. The patron saint of France.

"He saw you getting out of bed?"
"No way!" "Then when?" "I was reposing
and scarcely noticed in my dozing
when he came up to me. I fail   475
to see the need for such detail."
"With what words did he bid farewell?"
"You're out to trap me, I can tell!
He said: 'Lady, farewell. God bless!'
That's all he did or said—no less,   480
no more,—and so he took his leave.
He asked for nothing, I believe,
to cause you any harm or shame,
and now you're seeking to place blame!
You never did believe in me,   485
and yet there's nothing there to see
except great virtue, God be praised!,
still you accuse me as if crazed
and anger me in such a fashion
my flesh turns colors out of passion."   490
"Aha!" he cries, "deceitful shrew!
I went too far in coddling you!
I'll have you thrashed! I'll see you dead!
I know you fucked with him in bed!
You could have cried out—tell me why   495
you had to break our sacred tie?
I cast you out! Get out of here!
On the church altar I will swear
no more to lie beside you naked
in bed. You are repudiated!"   500
    The priest sat, overcome with choler,
sorrow, despondency and dolor.
On seeing him so irritated,
the lady heartily regretted
she'd been so headstrong and perverse   505
and, fearing he might yet do worse,
went to her room. Right then in sallied
the shepherd, who, it seems, had tallied
all of his sheep, and the count proved
that one of them had been removed.   510
He'd no idea what had become
of his sheep, and came at a run
to the priest's house, scratching his crotch.
The priest sat, taken down a notch,
angry and fuming, at his bible.   515
"The devil take you! What's the trouble,
you no good bum? What brings you here?
What's with this frown from ear to ear,
son of a bitch? You hick! You creep!
You should be out watching your sheep!   520
I ought to give you a good shaking."
"But one of your sheep has been taken,
master, the best of all the herd!

I can't think how or what occurred."
"So, now you've gone and lost a sheep—   525
that shows what kind of watch you keep!
You should be hanged or thrown in prison!"
The shepherd answered, "Master, listen!
Late in the evening yesterday
I met a stranger on the way   530
back into town, whom I had never
seen in the fields or road, wherever,
who eyed my flock most carefully
and made a point of asking me
who owned such admirable beasts,   535
and I said, 'Sir, they are our priest's.'
He, I imagine, was the thief."
"David, by my Christian belief!
Our guest last night!" exclaimed the priest.
"I've been outsmarted! I've been fleeced!   540
He's fucked all of the women in
my house and sold me my own skin!
He's wiped my nose on my own sleeve!
I must be a born fool to live
so long and still be caught off guard.   545
You're always learning, if you're smart.
With my own crust he bakes me pies!
The sheepskin, would you recognize
it?" "Master, what? If I've a chance
to look, I'll know it at a glance.   550
For seven years I've had that flock."
He takes the hide and has a look;
the ears and head identified
the sheep that had supplied the hide.
"Aha! Master," exclaimed the bilious   555
shepherd, "by God, why that's Cornelius,
my most favorite animal
and much the gentlest of them all!
By Saint Vincent,[3] whose faith I keep,
you couldn't find a fatter sheep,   560
and I know well of what I'm speaking."
"You come here, lady," said the deacon,
"and state your case, I order you;
and you, our servant, come here too
and speak, for I'll not be denied.   565
What claim do you have on the hide?"
"I swear that as I love you, sire,
it's mine alone, whole and entire."
"And you, fair lady, what's your claim?"
"Sir, God forgive me, all the same,   570
it should be mine, and for good cause."
"It will be neither hers nor yours.
I paid good money for the fleece

---

3. A third-century deacon, reputedly tortured to death for his faith.

and mean to keep the entire piece.
He asked I buy it at the altar   575
when I was reading from my psalter,
so, by God's true apostle Peter,
it won't be yours, no, nor hers either
unless a magistrate decides!"
    To you, my lords, who all are wise,   580
I, Eustace d'Amiens[4] submit
their case that you may settle it,
and ask you with due courtesy
to render judgment loyally.
Each one of you will speak his piece: 585
which of the three should have the fleece—
the deacon or his deaconess
or their maid (bless her sauciness).

The Three Hunchbacks

My lords, if you have time to spare,
though but a moment, you may hear
a little fabliau I wrote
in rhyme, based on an anecdote,
and not one word of it's a lie.   5
    In a walled town in days gone by
(but I've forgotten the town's name—
let's say Douay;[1] it's all the same)
there dwelt a worthy citizen
of decent means, the best of men,   10
who among his good friends could count
the foremost tradespeople around,
and, though he did not have great wealth,
who was respected for himself
and his good sense by all the city.   15
He had a daughter. She was pretty;
so pretty, she was a delight.
If I were to describe her right,
I doubt that Nature ever made
a creature fairer than this maid,   20
but I do not intend to dwell
on how she looked or try to tell
her beauty, because I'm afraid
you'd just discredit what I said,
so better leave the matter be   25
than understate reality.
    In that same town, not far from them,
a hunchback lived, a ruffian,
whose head was his outstanding feature.

---

4. Nothing is known of Eustace except that he came from Amiens, a city near Abbeville.   1. A town
located in northeastern France.

Nature, I think, who made this creature,   30
struggled immensely when she formed
him—nothing else was so deformed
and hideous beyond compare:
he'd a large head and shaggy hair,
a short neck and, as huge as boulders,   35
set too high up, enormous shoulders.
The man who'd foolishly detail
his ugliness is bound to fail.
His vicious way of life accorded
with how he looked, because he horded   40
all of his life to pile up gain.
To tell you truly and speak plain,
this hunchback was richer than Croesus[2]—
unless report of him deceives us,
none in town had more wealth than he.   45
What can I say? From A to Z,
that's how the hunchback's life was led.
Because of all the wealth he had,
his friends arranged to wed the lout
to the fair maid I told about,   50
but from the moment they were wed
he couldn't get out of his head
the beauty which she was endowed
with, and his jealousy allowed
him not a second of respite.   55
He always kept his doors shut tight
and let nobody in his home
who hadn't come there for a loan
or else had money to repay.
    Thus he sat keeping watch all day,   60
till once on Christmas there came three
strolling players, humpbacked as he,
where he was standing by the door
and said that they'd like nothing more
than to observe the holiday   65
with him—since he's humpbacked as they
and in the town there's no one else
as much like them as he himself,
they'd not do better anywheres.
He led the three of them upstairs   70
(for his house had a second floor),
where a repast was ready for
them all, and they sat down to dine.
Their meal was copious and fine,
to tell the truth, for this time he   75
was neither tight nor niggardly,
but offered his guests to partake in
a capon roast and peas with bacon,
and, when at length dinner was done,

_____

2. A mythological king of immense wealth.

distributed to every one   80
of the three hunchback minstrels plenty
of Paris pennies (I think, twenty).
Last of all, he forbade the men
that they ever appear again
inside his house or in his yard—   85
if caught there, then things would go hard:
they'd have a bath to make them shiver
in the cold water of the river.
(His house was set on the canal,
and it was wide, and deep as well).   90
The hunchbacks listened to their host
and left his house directly, most
willingly, in a festive mood,
because that day had been a good
one for them, of that they'd no doubt;   95
and then their host also went out
to the bridge and took up his station.
    His wife, who'd heard the celebration
and how the hunchbacks sang and played,
sent for them to come back and bade   100
them sing for her delight,
and had the household doors shut tight.
Now, while the hunchbacks sang their air
and entertained the lady there,
her husband, who had not been gone   105
too long, came back home thereupon.
He called in a commanding voice
from the door; when she heard the noise,
she recognized him in a wink.
For all the world she couldn't think   110
of any place where she could hide
the hunchbacks she had asked inside.
There was a bed beside the hearth
they used to carry back and forth
with three drawers built inside of it.   115
What can I say? Here's what she did:
she put one hunchback in each drawer
and let her husband in the door,
who went and sat by her since he
took pleasure in her company,   120
but not for too long did he stay
before he rose and went away,
climbed back downstairs and left the house.
It didn't incommode his spouse
her husband didn't hang about;   125
she wished to get the hunchbacks out,
the three she'd hidden in the drawers.
She had an awful shock, because,
when she had opened up the bed
and looked inside, she found them dead.   130
    When she saw all three had expired,

she ran to the door and required
a passing porter she waylaid
in God's name to come to her aid.
The young man, when he heard her call,   135
came running, didn't wait at all.
"My friend," she said, "I have a question.
Say, can I count on your discretion
and promise not to inculpate
me in the matter I'll relate?   140
I'll see to it it's worth your while,
for when you've done my errand I'll
reward you thirty pounds in cash."
The porter heard and in a flash
agreed to get her business done—he   145
wasn't a man to turn down money,
and so the job was to his taste.
He followed her upstairs in haste.
She opened one drawer in the bed;
"No need to be afraid," she said.   150
"Just dump this corpse in the canal
and I will say you've served me well."
She gave him a sack; in a minute
he'd packed away the hunchback in it,
and then he lifted up the sack,   155
went downstairs with it on his back,
ran straight down to the river's edge
and up onto the highest bridge
and tossed the hunchback in the drink.
Before you'd have had time to blink   160
he set off back home on the double.
The lady, with no end of trouble,
had taken out one hunchback more.
Lifting him up was quite a chore,
and, out of breath from her endeavor,   165
she drew aside from the cadaver.
The porter came back much elated:
"It's time that I were compensated,
lady. I got rid of your dwarf."
"What kind of joke would you pull off,   170
mister?" she said. "You dunce! you bounder!
The hunchback's back; he's still around here.
I don't think that you ever threw
him in. You brought him back with you.
If you don't trust me, look and see!"   175
"How in the name of Hell could he
have ever come back here, by thunder?
It baffles me, I'm filled with wonder.
Why, he was dead! I'd be surprised
if he were not the Antichrist!   180
I swear that it won't help him any!"
He grabbed the second hunchback, then he
shoved him into the sack and lifted

it on his shoulders, then he shifted
the weight for comfort and set out,   185
whereon the woman turned about,
opened the third drawer and drew forth
the hunchback, laid him by the hearth
and waited at the door. The porter
emptied the sack into the water,   190
letting the hunchback fall head first,
and told him, "May you be accursed
if you come back to me! Now go!"
and hurried back. He wasn't slow
to ask the lady for his fee,   195
which she accorded readily
and told him he would be well paid.
Then back to the fireplace she led
him, as if she were not aware
the third hunchback was lying there.   200
"What's this?" she said. "As God may strike
me dead, who's ever heard the like
of this? See where our hunchback's lying!"
The long-suffering porter, spying
him by the fire, was not amused   205
and cried, "Christ! Will my day be used
up lugging this damned dwarf around?
God's carcass! Was there ever found
a more persistent minstrel? Never!
I go and toss him in the river   210
only to find that he's come back!"
He stuffs the third one in the sack
and heaves it up onto his shoulders.
With anger and dismay he smolders,
irately turns and goes to trundle   215
back down the stairs toting his bundle,
and flings the final hunchback down
in the canal that flows through town.
"Good riddance, and the devil take you!
I've lugged you all day. I can't shake you,   220
but if again I catch you headed
back home, I tell you, you'll regret it!
You have bewitched me, I believe,
but, by God, by Whose grace I breathe,
if you come following behind,   225
with the first sword or stick I find
I'll strike your neck in such a manner
to leave you with a red bandanna!"
This said, he went straight back and strode
on up the steps of her abode.   230
    Now, well before he reached the top,
he glanced behind, came to a stop
to see her husband on his way
home again. In no mood for play,
he signed the cross thrice in succession   235

and prayed for divine intercession,
exclaiming, stricken to the quick,
"In God's name, is the creature sick
with rabies to tag after me
and dog me through eternity?   240
Now by the wheel that broke Saint Martin,[3]
he takes me for a hick, that's certain—
I just keep toting; when I'm done,
it's his idea of having fun
to come back for another ride!"   245
He grabbed a club which hung beside
the door with both fists, then he ran
back to the flight of stairs again.
The husband was close to the top.
"How, Mr. Hunchback? Go back! Stop!   250
How stubborn can a person be?
I promise you, by Saint Marie,
you'll rue having come back once more!
What kind of stooge d'you take me for?"
Without a pause he raised the club   255
and brought it down with such a thud
on the hunchback's enormous head
that on the stairs he struck him dead
with his brains spattered left and right,
then bagged him, tied the sack up tight   260
with a cord, then went at a run
the same way he had often gone
and pitched his burden in the river,
hunchback and sack, the two together,
for he was scared that for the fourth   265
time he'd be followed by the dwarf.
"Bad luck to you!" he said. "Now sink!
This time I can be sure, I think,
you won't return to give me grief
until the forests are in leaf!"   270
     He went right back to see the lady
and asked her if he might be paid—he
had done her errand to perfection.
The woman offered no objection,
but gave the young man his reward   275
of thirty pounds, not one cent short,
freely and generously paid,
the best bargain she'd ever made,
she said, delighted with her day,
because he'd got out of the way   280
her husband, who was so disfigured.
For the rest of her days, she figured,
she'd never suffer pain or strife
now her spouse is out of her life.
     Durant[4] says, rounding off his tale,   285

---

3. The meaning of this reference is unknown.   4. Nothing is known of Durant.

that everything on earth's for sale—
there's not a girl that can't be bought,
nor any treasure that God wrought,
however valuable and good,
that, if the truth be understood,   290
cannot be had for the right price.
The hunchback used wealth to entice
his marriage with a lady fair.
Shame on the man whose only care
is massing money for his purse!   295
And on who coined it first, a curse!

The Wild Dream

I'll tell as briefly as I can
about a woman and a man
and what befell them, if I may.
I heard about it in Douay.
I do not know his or her name,   5
but I can affirm all the same
what fine, upstanding folk they were
and that she loved him and he her.
    The good man had to leave one day
and go on business far away,   10
and thus for three full months he stayed
in foreign parts engaged in trade,
and he was so successful there
that he returned walking on air
to Douay on a Thursday evening.   15
Don't think that his wife felt like grieving
to have her husband back again;
the fuss she made over him then
gave proof of her wifely devotion
and of the strength of her emotion.   20
When she had hugged, kissed and embraced
him, so he could relax, she placed
a low-slung, comfortable chair
near her and then went to prepare
their meal. All in good time they ate   25
seated on cushions by the gate,
where a fire crackled warm and bright,
without smoke, but with lots of light.
They'd fish and meat, good, hearty fare,
and wine from Soissons and Auxerre,[1]   30
white linen, and fresh, healthful meat.
It pleased his wife to watch him eat;
she saw that he got all the fine,
choice morsels, and, with each bite, wine.

---

1. Two cities in northern France.

Eager to please her man, the lady   35
was more than willing, more than ready
to satisfy his every whim,
expecting in return from him
the welcome for which she was aching,
but it turned out she was mistaken   40
in plying him with all that drink,
for wine made his libido shrink,
and afterwards, when the man got in
their bed, that pleasure was forgotten.
Not by his wife—it filled her head   45
when she climbed next to him in bed,
nor would he have needed to ask,
for she was ready for the task.
He had no thought for his poor spouse,
who would have liked them to carouse   50
and stay awake a while still.
Don't think the lady just sits still
while her husband sleeps like a stone:
"Ha!" she protests, "he sure has shown
himself a stinking, oafish creep!   55
He should be up, but he's asleep!
My happy hopes have turned to pain.
Three months have passed since we have lain
together, and yet, sure enough,
the devil makes the man doze off.   60
Well, he can take him, if he will!"
She lies there quietly and still;
what's on her mind remains unspoken—
she doesn't wake him up or poke him,
though in her mind she sorely vexed,   65
lest he should think she's oversexed.
This reason makes her disregard her
thoughts of love-making and ardor
which she has entertained tonight.
She turns in, feeling wrath and spite.   70
      She dreamt a dream while she was lying
there fast asleep—don't think I'm lying!—
that she'd gone to a yearly fair,
the likes of which you have to hear,
for every stall and shop display   75
there, every house and place to stay,
every exchange and table was
not selling bolts of cloth or furs
or linen, wool or silks of price,
it seemed to her, or dyes, or spice,   80
or goods, or pharmaceuticals—
just penises and testicles
in wild profusion, for the sellers
had filled their houses, rooms and cellars
with the commodity, and porters   85
came toting them across the borders

upon their backs, while down the road
they rolled in by the wagonload.
Despite the massive inventory,
the merchants had no need to worry   90
of not exhausting their supplies.
The thirty-shilling merchandise
was awesome, good ones cost a pound,
and for the poor folk could be found
some smaller ones, which still could sate   95
a girl for ten or nine or eight.
They sold in gross and in detail.
The best and biggest ones for sale
were closely watched and very dear.
The wife went looking everywhere   100
and put much effort in her quest
till at one stall she came to rest
on seeing one so long and wide, it
just had to be hers, she decided.
The shaft was large and well-endowed   105
with a big head, cocky and proud,
and, if you want to hear the whole
truth, you could toss into the hole
with ease a round, ripe cherry, and it
would go on falling till it landed   110
down in the scrotum, which was made
like the shovel-end of a spade.
No man has ever seen its like.
The wife decided she would strike
a bargain, and she asked how much.   115
"If you were my own sister, such
as this would cost two marks of silver.
This penis is no scrawny sliver,
but of the finest Loheringian[2]
stock, both testicles and engine,   120
a worthy wand for a magician.
You would do well to take possession
of it. Do come give it a feel."
"Friend, why should we drag out the deal?
I'll buy it from you, if you're willing   125
to part with it for fifty shillings.
You won't get so much for it anywhere, and I'll throw in a penny
for God, that it may bring me bliss."
"A giveaway, that's what it is,   130
but I'm won over, and so suit your-
self, and I hope in the future
you'll try it out and praise the vendor.
I think from now on you'll remember
me when you pray or sing a psalm."   135
The woman lifted up her palm

---

2. From Lorraine, a province in northern France, where men were reputed to be sexually well-endowed.

to give him high five, well-disposed
on account of the deal she'd closed . . .
. . . and hits her husband in the jaw
with so much force, she feels her sore   140
hand turn bright red, tingle and burn,
and one can easily discern
the finger marks from chin to ear,
and he wakes up in startled fear
and sits bolt upright upon waking,   145
and his wife also wakens, shaking,
who'd sooner sleep on till tomorrow,
since now her joy has turned to sorrow.
She has no way to go on keeping
the joy she bought herself while sleeping,   150
so she'd prefer to stay asleep.
"Wife," the man says, "pray do not keep
from me the dream that made you go
just now and strike me such a blow.
Were you asleep then or awake?"   155
"Don't say such things, for goodness sake,"
she tells him, "sir. Hit you? Who, me?"
"In affection and harmony,
by the strength of your marriage vow,
what were you thinking of just now?   160
Don't keep it back for any cause."
I'll have you know, without a pause
the woman launched into her tale,
like it or not, and didn't fail
to lay all of the details bare   165
of her dream of the penis fair,
how some were good and some were bad,
and she bought the largest they had,
by far more impressive than any,
for fifty shillings and a penny.   170
"Sir," she explains, "here's what occurred.
To close the deal, I gave my word
and went to shake hands with good grace,
hitting you squarely in the face,
but only did it in my sleep.   175
For God's sake, dearest husband, keep
your temper, for as I admit
my error and sincere regret,
I beg your pardon for the blow."
"In faith, sweet wife," he says, "you know   180
I pardon you, and so should God!"
He embraces and hugs her hard
and kisses her sweet mouth as well,
and his penis begins to swell,
for she charms him and turns him on.   185
He lays his penis in her palm
as soon as he feels that it's ready,
and asks, "By your love for me, lady,

as God may keep you free from sin,
at that fair, what would it bring in,   190
the one you're holding on to now?"
"As I hope to survive, I vow
that someone selling a full coffer
of them would find no one who'd offer
a speck of money for the lot.   195
Why, even those the paupers bought
were such that one of them with ease
would equal at least two of these
the way it is now. Look here, sire!
There it would never find a buyer   200
who'd ask to see the thing up close."
"So what?" he says. "That's how it goes.
Take this one—the others don't matter!—
until you think you can do better."
(And so she did, if I am right).   205

    Together they thus passed the night,
but I think his judgment unsound,
for the next day he spread it round
till a rhymer of fabliaux,
Jean Bodel,[3] also came to know   210
of it, and for its merits he
put it in his anthology
neither embellished nor extended,
which means the lady's dream has ended.

The Ring That Controlled Erections

Haiseau[1] has yet another thing
to tell. A man once owned a ring
which, when worn, by a magic spell
at once would make his manhood swell.
It happened one day that he rode   5
across a field where a stream flowed.
He got off his horse when he saw it,
strode to the bank and crouched before it
and washed his hands, also his face
and ring, which he took from its case.   10
At length he got up and rode on,
but left the ring there on the lawn.

    A bishop soon came riding by.
As soon as the stream caught his eye,
he dismounted and found the ring,   15
and, enthralled by its glittering,
he picked it up and put it on.
His virile member thereupon
began to stiffen in due course.

---

3. The author of this and other fabliaux.   1. Either the author or the minstrel.

The bishop, now back on his horse,   20
was disconcerted to detect
his member had grown quite erect
and this growth didn't seem to end it,
for it grew ever more distended
and so enlarged, it burst the stitches   25
at the seams of the bishop's britches.
Ashamed, the bishop shows his servants
what hard luck mortifies and burdens
him, but they've no way of construing
this mischief is all the ring's doing.   30
  It grew till it dragged on the ground.
He sent his messengers around
to find someone who could advise
him how to bring it back to size.
The man who'd lost the ring got word   35
of what strange marvel had occurred,
and to the bishop straightaway
he went and asked how much he'd pay
him if he could effect a cure.
He said, unable to endure   40
such agony, "Just name your fee."
"Then I will ask you to agree
to give me those two rings you wear
and one hundred pounds as my share."
Without the rings on, his incessant   45
erection became detumescent.
Before the bishop paid his hundred-
pound fee, he was disencumbered,
and wasn't it a fair exchange
when each was glad to have the change?   50

THE TRIAL OF RENARD[1]
twelfth century

Though his wit and talent did not fail
When Perrot[2] set out to rhyme the tale
Of Renard and Ysengrin, his friend,
He left out the best part and the end:
The prosecution and defense   5
As to the guilt or innocence
Of Renard, dragged out, despite his guile,
To Noble's court where he stood trial
For having vilely fornicated
With Hersent, as her husband stated.   10

---

1. Translated from the French by Patricia Terry. 2. Pierre de Saint-Cloud, the author of the first Renard story in French.

The author tells us, in line one,[3]
That winter had passed, and in the sun
Roses were opening, and bright
Hawthorn flowers, shining white.
The king announced his firm intention,   15
Close to the Feast of the Ascension,[4]
That all the animals report
To the palace where he held his court.
Not one would dare let anything
Keep him from promptly answering   20
The lion's urgent proclamation,
Except for Sir Renard, damnation
Take him for a lying thief!
Whom the others said, in their belief,
The king should punish for his pride,   25
And for the crimes he hoped to hide.
Ysengrin had no objection,
Viewing Renard without affection;
Loudest of all he expressed his ire:
"Your majesty, dear gracious Sire,   30
Grant me justice! Madame Hersent,
Held by Renard with foul intent
In his domain at Maupertuis,[5]
Was forced to commit adultery,
And he pissed on my poor cubs as well!   35
That's the latest woe I have to tell."
All of this Renard denied,
And in order that the case be tried
He chose the day when he would swear
On holy relics, as is fair.   40
But somehow he was warned, and when
We came, retreated to his den.[6]
Why I'm so angry must be clear."
Then said the king, so all could hear:
"Forget about it, Ysengrin—   45
The only thing that you can win
Is more dishonor to your name.
Counts and kings will play that game,
And nowadays one sees all sorts
Of cuckolds, even ruling courts!   50
You have little cause, it seems to us,
For making such an awful fuss.
This woe you bring to our attention
Doesn't deserve the slightest mention."
"Most gracious Sire," said Bruin the bear,   55
"Is such an answer really fair?
Ysengrin is alive and free,
And if Renard's his enemy,
To seek revenge would not be wrong.

3. The poet is pretending to refer to an authoritative source, a typical gesture by medieval writers.
4. Forty days after Easter. 5. Renard's "castle." 6. Ysengrin had earlier tried to trick Renard by sub-
stituting for the relics a ferocious dog.

You know that Ysengrin is strong; 60
If Renard lived close to his domain,
And if your sworn peace did not restrain
All ruled by you from acts of war,
Renard would get what he's asking for!
Of all this kingdom you are lord— 65
Why don't you put an end to discord,
Put an end to your vassals' fray!
We will hate anyone you say.
Count on us to defend your side!
If Ysengrin's dissatisfied 70
About Renard, let the case be tried;
Let it be judged as you decide.
If one wronged the other, what is due
For that misdeed must be paid to you.
Send for Renard at Maupertuis; 75
If you'll entrust that task to me,
And I can find him, there's no doubt
He'll learn what a royal court's about."
As soon as he'd finished, Clamor[7] roared,
"Sir Bruin, a curse on any lord— 80
Saving your presence—who would say
That the king should let a fine repay
Adultery! Make Renard repent
The shame he inflicted on Hersent!
For other beasts so many times 85
Have suffered from his filthy crimes,
No one should help him in his need.
Why should Ysengrin have to plead
For justice when Renard attacked
His wife so openly the fact 90
Is known to all? Believe you me,
If he behaved so villainously
And it was my wife he molested,
However strongly she protested,
As far as Maupertuis let him run 95
But I would make him pay for his fun—
Deep in a muddy ditch he'd groan
Without a sex to call his own!
How could you dream of it, Hersent?
Surely it's something to lament 100
When Renard who lives without a care
Can boast of mounting you like a mare!"
The badger[8] said, "Before it's too late,
Sir Clamor, let us end this debate
Which will otherwise get worse and worse 105
And beyond our power to reverse.
A malicious tale will soon expand
Until it's entirely out of hand.
And since this case involves no use

7. A bull.   8. Grinbert, who is Renard's only real defender.

Of force, no broken door or truce,   110
And Renard was prompted by affection,
Why do you make such strong objection?
For a long time he has loved Hersent.
This complaint was never her intent,
And Ysengrin, with little wit,   115
Is making much too much of it.
Let King Noble and his lords decide
How Ysengrin should be satisfied!
If the baron really has good cause
To accuse Renard of breaking laws,   120
If he took a walnut not his own,
Then certainly he must atone—
But not until he is here to face
This court for judgment on his case.
However, I think Madame Hersent   125
Is very far from innocent.
Alas, it does you honor indeed
When your husband has to come and plead
His case where all of us can hear.
Truly, if you still hold him dear,   130
You have already lived too long!
He fears you not, and you were wrong
To let him give you a lover's name."
Hersent blushed; she felt such great shame
Her fur stood on end, as with a sigh   135
She made the badger this reply:
"My lord Grinbert, I can bear no more.
All my desire is to end the war
Between my husband and Renard
Whose conduct has in no way marred   140
My honor. Here and now I'd appeal
For the right to prove this by ordeal—
Boiling water, red iron would fail
To burn me—but truth would not prevail.
Alas! I'm doomed to a life of woe.   145
Why does my lord distrust me so?
I swear by the holy saints above,
And as I hope to deserve God's love,
Renard has had from me no other
Kindness than if I'd been his mother.   150
Don't think I say this to win support
For Sir Renard when he comes to court;
I care for him, and it's simply stated,
Whether he may be loved or hated,
Lose his case or win its dismissal,   155
As you care for a donkey's thistle.
But jealousy took my husband's wits,
And he thinks the name of cuckold fits!
On Easter day—April first, this year[9]—

9. This reference dates the poem to either 1179 or 1184.

As I hold Pinsard, my young son, dear,   160
For a decade I had lived my life
As Ysengrin's devoted wife.
Everyone came to celebrate
When we were married, a crowd so great,
Such a multitude in den and lair,   165
That truly you might look everywhere
And not find even so much space
As a goose needs for a nesting place.
Since Ysengrin took me for his own,
I have kept my love for him alone—   170
I'm wronged by this scandalous affair!
So, once again now, I will swear—
And if you don't take me at my word,
At least I will know that you have heard—
By the faith I owe to Saint Marie,   175
I'm guiltless of debauchery,
And there is nothing I've ever done
That would disgrace a holy nun."
    When they had listened to Hersent
Claiming that she was innocent,   180
Bernard the donkey took the floor.
He believed everything she swore,
Rejoicing to take as proven fact
That Ysengrin's honor was intact.
"Ah me!" he said, "most noble dame,   185
Would that my spouse were just the same
For loyalty—and everyone,
Dogs, wolves, and women, under the sun!
For, as I hope God will be kind,
Forgive my sins and let me find   190
Tender thistles where I graze,
So sure am I that it's not false praise
To say that you would in no measure
Care for Renard or give him pleasure,
Or to his love pay any heed.   195
But these are wicked times indeed;
The stink of slander fills the air
And people cheerfully will swear
To what was never in their sight,
And blame what they should say is right.   200
Wild Renard, you won't be believed!
In an evil hour were you conceived
And born. The entire world's persuaded
That you improperly invaded
Madame Hersent. And she'll appeal   205
For your acquittal by her ordeal.
Say, most noble, gracious king,
Why not put an end to this hateful thing?
On poor Renard bestow your grace!
Give me leave to go to his place   210
And bring him, by safe conduct, back

To answer Ysengrin's attack.
Renard will pay whatever fee
Your court in its wisdom may decree,
And if they find that lack of respect   215
Caused him to so long neglect
Your summons, for that too he'll pay
Before you let him go away."
"Sire!" the angry lords protest,
"May Saint Giles[1] deny your least request   220
If you favor Renard to that extent!
Don't have another message sent
To summon him! Let's wait right here
Two more days; if he doesn't appear,
Then have him brought back under guard,   225
And let his punishment be hard,
Something that he'll remember long."
Noble the king said, "You are wrong
To condemn Renard so out of hand.
I have forces at my command.   230
If I am threatened by your pride,
There will be nowhere you can hide!
Renard has a place in my heart still,
Whether you wish him well or ill.
I won't agree to your shameful plan,   235
If he still wants to be my man.
Ysengrin, as your wife suggested,
Let her innocence be tested,
Or else forget the whole affair."
"Don't say that, Sire! It isn't fair!   240
What if the red-hot iron is shown
To have burned her fingers to the bone?
Some will learn what they now don't know.
Joy will come to my every foe.
I'll hear their voices loud and clear   245
Shouting, 'The jealous cuckold's here!'
Let Renard think he's won the game.
I will live with my grief and shame
Until I can do what must be done.
But before the harvest has begun   250
He'll find himself in such a war
No wall or moat or bolted door
Will save him—I will strike him dead!"
"To Hell with that!" King Noble said;
"By Christ's bones, my lord Ysengrin,   255
Is that a war you think you'll win?
Can you really do as you have claimed?
Will Renard be either dead or maimed?
By the faith I owe to Saint Lenard,[2]
With all the tricks known to Renard,   260

1. According to legend, St. Giles was a hermit nourished by the milk of a doe. 2. Patron saint of prisoners.

It's much more likely he won't fail
To do you in than you prevail.
Anyway, what can be the use
Of discussing it? We've sworn a truce,
And all the land has been brought to peace.   265
Woe to the guilty if that should cease!"
    Ysengrin, when the king had spoken
Of his concern lest the truce be broken,
Was so upset and in such dismay
He didn't know to what saint to pray.   270
He sat near the benches on the ground;
Between his legs his tail was wound.
Renard would have much to celebrate
If God had meant him for that fate:
With the king determined to achieve   275
The peace whoever that might grieve,
Renard and Ysengrin could no more
Incite each other to make war.
But Chanteclere and Pinte his hen
Were arriving at the court just then   280
With three others all of whom
Want justice for their sister's doom.
Now the fat is in the fire,
For Chanteclere, that noble sire,
And Pinte, whose eggs have such a span,   285
And Blacky, Whitey, and Roseanne,
Had brought with them a little cart
With curtains that they drew apart.
The others saw, as they came near,
A litter on which, as on a bier,   290
A hen was lying. She'd been caught
By Renard whose cruel teeth had wrought
Such harm her leg was a splintered shred,
And one of her wings hung by a thread.
    King Noble felt that he had earned   295
A rest, and court should be adjourned;
But all at once the hens appear,
Wringing their hands, and Chanteclere.
First of all Pinte begins to plead,
And the others loudly take her lead: 300
"Most gracious beasts, for God's sweet sake,
You dogs and wolves, do not forsake
A poor creature so forlorn!
I curse the day that I was born!
Oh come, make haste and take me, Death,   305
Since Renard won't let me draw a breath
In peace. I had, on my father's side,
Five brothers—every one supplied
A dinner for Renard, the thief
Who has brought me to such bitter grief.   310
Not counting me, my mother gave birth
To five young virgin hens whose worth

For Gonbert del Frenne[3] would well repay
His fattening them to make them lay.
Oh! How I wish he'd kept his grain!   315
He fed them well, and yet the gain
Went to Renard, for all but one
Had passed through his throat when he was done.
And you who are lying in the bier,
My sister sweet, my friend so dear,   320
So tender and so plump, alas!
How wearily the days will pass
Without you—in sorrow I must dwell.
Renard, I hope you burn in Hell!
Not a moment can we turn our backs   325
Without the fear of your attacks—
Chased and mauled, your victim's pressed
Against the wall as you rip her vest!
I came out yesterday and found
My poor dead sister hurled to the ground,   330
And Renard so far away from the place
That Gonbert could not have given chase
On foot, and he has no swift horse.
That's why I've come here. But no force
Can bring to justice one who grins   335
At threats, and doesn't care two pins
For anyone's wrath." She said no more,
Poor Pinte, but fell straight down on the floor.
They saw she had fainted dead away,
And next to her the other three lay.   340
To get the ladies up on their feet,
Each dog and wolf rises from his seat,
And helped by the other beasts, they pour
Buckets of water on all four.

    Just as soon as they'd recovered,   345
As in my source book I discovered,[4]
They went where King Noble had his seat
And fell on their faces at his feet.
Meanwhile the kneeling Chanteclere
Wet the king's feet with many a tear.   350
When Noble saw Chanteclere, in truth
He felt such pity for the youth,
That nothing on earth could make him hide
His feelings; from his depths he sighed,
Then raging, lifted up his head.   355
The bravest beast could not have said—
Not even the mighty bear or boar—
He felt no fear at the lion's roar.
Coward the hare heard it and quivered,
Two whole days in a fever shivered.   360
All the courtiers shook as one.
By their terror they were quite undone.

---

3. The peasant who owns the chickens.   4. See note to line 11 above.

King Noble, lifting his tail up high,
In rage and anguish gave a cry
So loud that the house walls nearly broke,   365
And when the echoes died he spoke:
"My lady Pinte," the emperor said,
"I swear on my dead father's head—
His daily alms from me are still due[5]—
I feel great sympathy for you,   370
And wish somehow to relieve your woe.
Renard shall come if he will or no!
By what you shall see with your own eyes,
Hear with your ears, you'll realize
How truly justice has been done.   375
Vengeance I'll have on anyone
For breaking the peace and murdering!"
   Ysengrin, when he heard the king,
Leaped to his feet exclaiming, "Sire!
Actions of valor must inspire   380
Great praise. It will be a noble deed
If you can help poor Pinte in her need,
And get revenge for Madame Copee,
Mangled and butchered as we see.
I do not say it because I hate   385
Renard, but in sorrow for her fate;
Not out of hatred, but I resent
The slaughter of the innocent."
The emperor replied, "My friend,
My heart is heavy. Times without end   390
Renard's misdeeds have cost us dear.
To you and to the strangers here
I say the adulterer can't hide
From the consequences of his pride;
He broke the peace that I proclaimed,   395
And by his actions I am shamed.
But now there is another affair
We must attend to. Bruin the bear,
I ask you to put on your stole,[6]
Commend to God the poor hen's soul!   400
And you, Lord Clamor, by my command,
Shall dig a grave in that ploughed land."
"As you will, Sire," replied the bear,
And he went quickly to prepare
The several things that he would need.   405
Meanwhile, their ruler in the lead,
The other council members started
The vigil for the dear departed.
They heard Lord Slow the snail intone
Three whole lessons all on his own,   410
Bricemer the stag and the dog Roenel

---

5. Noble gives alms in his father's memory to the poor or, more likely, to a religious foundation.   6. Bruin here acts the priest.

Sang verse and responses very well.
   The service lasted through the night,
But when the sun gave its first light,
The burial could not be delayed.   415
First, in a casket that was made
Fit for a king, and all of lead,
They reverently placed the dead.
They buried her beneath a tree
With a marble stone in memory   420
Of Madame Copee and to extol
Her deeds and to God commend her soul.
Carved with a chisel or else a knife,
This epitaph summed up her life:
"Here on this plain, beneath this tree,   425
Lies Pinte's sister, Madame Copee.
Renard, who pursues his evil ways,
With cruel teeth cut short her days."
Whoever witnessed poor Pinte's crying,
Cursing Renard for her sister's dying,   430
And Chanteclere with his feet stretched out,
Would pity them, I have no doubt.
   When grief had lost its violence
And mourning was not quite so intense,
The lords cried, "Emperor, it's time   435
That you made that thief pay for his crime!
We're tired of his tricks, and it's no use
Hoping that he'll respect a truce."
"Yes," says the king, "that's all too true.
Brother Bruin, here's a task for you—   440
There's nothing at all for you to fear—
Tell Renard that I have been here
Waiting for him three whole days."
"Gladly," says Bruin. He delays
Not for a moment but mounts and rides   445
Toward the forest where Renard resides,
And, never stopping, on he went.
Meanwhile there was a great event,
As through the valley Bruin rode,
Back at the court, and it would bode   450
Ill for Renard. Sir Coward the hare,
Who'd caught such a fever from his scare
(Two days he was in a shivering fit),
Had now, thank God, been cured of it.
Here's how he found the remedy: 455
Not wanting to leave Madame Copee,
Above the martyr's grave he lay,
Fell fast asleep, and was cured that way.
Ysengrin, when he heard the story
Of the new martyr's proven glory,   460
Said that he had an awful earache,
And then, deciding he would take
Roenel's advice, he put his head

Upon the grave and was cured, he said.
Were it not good doctrine that about   465
A miracle one can have no doubt—
And there was Roenel to provide
A witness—they would have thought he lied.
    When they listened to this new report,
Some were happy at the court,   470
But Grinbert thought it bad indeed.
He and Tibert the cat, who plead
On Renard's behalf, fear that the news
Means that without a mighty ruse
Renard's in a bad way if he's caught.   475
And a shortcut had already brought
Lord Bruin through the depths of the wood
To where Renard's great fortress stood.
Bruin would have to shrink before
He found a way inside the door—   480
At the barbican[7] he has to stay.
Renard, who takes the world for his prey,
Had his inner lair dug very deep,
And just then he was fast asleep.
He had provisions in his den: 485
There was a beautiful plump hen;
And two chicken legs down to the feet
That morning had left him quite replete.
Now, as if he meant to ruin
Renard's sweet slumber, here comes Bruin!   490
"Renard," he says, "it's Bruin the bear,
Sent by the king. Come out of there!
Come out and talk to me where I stand,
And I will tell you the king's command."
Renard saw enough to recognize   495
Bruin the bear by his great size,
And, in an instant, he had planned
A way to get the upper hand.
"Good Bruin, as I hold you dear,
I'm sorry they sent you way down here   500
On a useless errand—it's a shame.
I would have left before you came
Except that I was disinclined
To leave a good French meal behind.
You know how a wealthy man is treated: 505
'Sir, will you wash?' is the way he's greeted
When he comes to court; everyone believes
It's an honor just to hold his sleeves.
They serve him beef cooked with vinegar,
Then ask him which he would prefer   510
Among the many other dishes.
Who listens to a poor man's wishes?
They think he's made of a devil's shit.

---

7. A fortified gate; Maupertuis is described as both a den and a castle.

Not by the fireside does he sit;
For a table he must use his lap
As the housedogs crowd around and snap, 515
Snatching the bread out of his fingers.
Over a single drink he lingers,
Knowing they won't refill his glass,
And once will the serving platter pass. 520
Boys will shower him with bones
Drier than red-hot burning stones.
Each holds his bread clutched in his hand.
The tables of the lords of the land
Miss what seneschals and cooks withhold, 525
All of them cut from the self-same mold.
Would they were burned and their ashes blown!
Whatever they want they take for their own;
Meat and bread from the master's stores
Go to make dinner for their whores. 530
All this is why I wouldn't have cared,
Good my lord, to travel unprepared,
And this noon I have not only dined
On good peas and bacon well combined,
But ate every bit I had at home 535
Of fresh new honey in the comb."
"*Nomini Dame, file Christom!*"[8]
The bear said, "Honeycomb! Where's it from?
By the bones of Giles the blessed saint,
My belly so craves it I feel faint! 540
God's heart! Dear gracious lord, please say,
Mea culpa![9] that you'll show the way!"
Renard sticks his tongue out with a look
That says the bear is on the hook,
And, all unknown to the poor Bruin, 545
Prepares to bring his victim in,
Carefully coiling his long line:
"Bruin, if you were a friend of mine,"
Renard said, "if I only knew
That I really could depend on you, 550
Then, by my son Rovel, I swear
This very day I'd take you there.
You'd be standing at the honeyed site,
Filling your belly with delight.
In Lanfroi the forester's domain, 555
Not far from here, rich combs remain.
But near or far, what does it matter?
All this is only idle chatter.
You, if I served you as a guide,
Would take it out of my poor hide." 560
"Renard, how can you distrust me so!"
"I do." "But why?" "What I know I know.

8. Confused Latin, meaning something like "By the name of our Lady, daughter of Christ."   9. I'm
guilty (Latin).

There's an evil purpose in your heart."
"Renard, it must be the devil's art
That makes you think I could be so vile."   565
"All right. I'll give your good faith a trial.
I would not wrong you, nor you me."
"That's the truth! For by the fealty
I swore to Noble, our gracious king,
Never would I do anything   570
To harm you; never do I intend
To treat you other than as my friend."
"Those are the words I wanted to hear,
Bruin, and now I have no fear."
When they had come to this agreement,   575
Happy for both, away they went
On their good chargers, the two abreast,
And galloped, never taking a rest,
So urgently did they wish to gain
Lanfroi's forest, where they drew rein.   580
There an enormous oak tree stood.
Lanfroi, who wanted to sell the wood,
Had driven in two mighty wedges,
Making a slit between their edges.
Renard said, "Bruin, my dear friend,   585
We have come to our journey's end.
The honey's inside there. Eat it first,
Then we will go and quench our thirst;
You shall have what you've always loved."
Standing on his hind legs, Bruin shoved   590
His muzzle and his two front paws
Into the hole. To help his cause,
Renard keeps pushing him from below,
Shouting he hasn't far to go:
"Open your mouth, you son of a whore!   595
You're almost there! Just a little more!
Only unlock your teeth, you scum!"
Now Renard's great moment has come;
For Bruin, though, it's not so funny—
He didn't find a drop of honey   600
However hard and long he tried,
And, while his mouth was opened wide,
Renard, damn his soul! with a mighty clout,
Suddenly knocked both wedges out!
In the space where the oak tree had been split,   605
A third of Bruin was tightly fit—
Not a good way to take a rest!
The poor bear really is hard-pressed,
Held a captive by the tree,
While Renard (not known for charity,   610
And let his confession not be made)[1]
Shouts that it's he who's been betrayed:

---

1. I.e., let him be damned.

"Bruin, I always did believe
That you had something up your sleeve!
You're at the honey and won't stop   615
Until you've left me not a drop!
Next time I'll beat you at your game!
But don't you feel the slightest shame
At eating all that lovely honey?
And then, I suppose, I'll get no money!   620
I can imagine the kind of trick
You'd have played on me had I fallen sick—
You'd have brought rotten pears for a treat!"
But Renard knew he had better retreat
When he looked up just in time to see   625
That Lanfroi was coming toward the tree.
The peasant could not believe his luck—
There was Bruin so tightly stuck!
Off to the village Lanfroi sped,
Shouting, "Come help and the bear is dead!   630
We've got him now but hurry! hurry!"
You should have seen the peasants scurry,
Swarm through the trees with bloodthirsty looks!
Some carry clubs, some pruning hooks,
Flails and axes raised to attack!   635
Bruin shivers, fears for his back.
    Hearing the mob's ferocious voice,
He knows in his heart he has no choice—
Better, no doubt, to sacrifice
His muzzle, held as in a vise,   640
Than to wait there for Lanfroi to seize.
So Bruin starts to push and squeeze
And pull, no matter how it hurts,
Stretching his skin while blood spurts
In bright streams from his broken veins.   645
His skin gives way—not enough remains
On his mangled head to make a purse—
Never did any beast look worse!
From all his dreadful wounds the blood
Comes pouring in a crimson flood;   650
There's no skin at all on his front feet.
Much has he suffered to retreat!
But now at last poor Bruin could
Run away through the depths of the wood.
And the shouting peasants are not slow: 655
The son of Lord Billin, called Bertot,
And with him Hardoin Hit and Run,
Gonbert and with him Gallon's son
(Falcon's nephew) and Count Ortrands
Who strangled his wife with his own hands;   660
Tygers, who baked the village's bread—
(Black Cornelia he took to bed).
And Aymery the Sickle Breaker,
And Rocelin the son of Shaker.

Ogier's son, not there to relax, 665
Held in his hand a battle-axe;
And there was my lord Hubert Grosset
And the son of Faucher Galopet.
The war party was increased
By the presence of the parish priest, 670
Father of Martin de la Tour.
He had just finished spreading manure
And took up the pitchfork he had plied
To plant it deep in Bruin's side
As the bear in pain and anguish fled— 675
A little deeper and he was dead.
Catching Bruin against an oak,
Another of those peasant folk,
A comb and lantern maker by trade,
Struck at him, not with a blade, 680
But with a steer's horn, wrenching his back.
Besides all these, there is no lack
Of peasants beating him with flails—
The wonder is that he prevails.
Renard, who knows his prospects are grim 685
If Bruin gets a chance at him,
Hears the bear at a distance, free,
And takes a shortcut to Maupertuis,
That mighty fortress where he knows
He'll be safe from his strongest foes. 690
Seeing Bruin close to his door,
Renard gibes at him once more:
"Bruin, I hope you're satisfied!
I know you never meant to divide
Lanfroi's honey. Those who pretend 695
Good faith will come to a bitter end,
And don't think a priest will see you through!
But tell me, are you aspiring to
A monastic order? What's this red
Hood-like thing that's on your head?"[2] 700
But Bruin, too far gone for banter,
Left at an energetic canter,
Still in terror at the thought
Of what would happen if he were caught.
    So he spurred on, so fast that soon, 705
Just as the bells were rung at noon,
The bear was riding through the gate
To where the lion sat in state.
Bruin fell fainting on the floor,
His face entirely covered with gore. 710
As his friends come running, it appears
The bear has arrived without his ears.
The king said, "Bruin, who did that?
Who so foully ripped off your hat

2. Renard jokes that Bruin's bloody head looks like the hood of a monastic order.

And left your legs in such a state?"   715
His loss of blood had been so great
That Bruin's voice was very weak:
"King," he said, "I went out to seek
Renard, and found him, as you can tell."
Then at King Noble's feet he fell.   720
   You should have heard the lion roar,
Tearing his mane out as he swore
On Christ's pure heart what he would do!
"Bruin," he says, "I think you're through.
You've been murdered, but it won't be long,   725
By the death of Christ, before this wrong
Is avenged. Renard will pay so dear
No one in France will fail to hear!
Where are you, Tibert? Be on your way
To Maupertuis, and with no delay!   730
Tell that red-haired bastard I command
That before the nobles of this land
He make the reparation due.
And that won't be accomplished through
Gold and silver, nor is there hope   735
That words will cut down the gallows rope
Waiting for the killer we accuse!"
Tibert, could he have dared refuse,
Would still not have come to Maupertuis,
But there's no way out; he must agree   740
With what the king and council decide.
So the cat, who doesn't ride astride,
Gallops along the valley floor,
Spurring his mule—and there's the door
Behind which he will find Renard.   745
He prays to God and to Saint Lenard,
Who oftentimes has captives freed,
That he, by his prayers, would intercede
And keep Tibert safe from his old friend,
For he is sure Renard would contend   750
With the devil to do an evil deed,
So dear to him is the holy creed!
Something increased his consternation
Just as he reached his destination:
Between an ash tree and a pine   755
He saw a buzzard. He made a sign,
And said to it, "Go right! Go right!"
But the bird kept on its left-hand flight.
For quite some moments Tibert paused.
It was most of all the bird that caused   760
The cat to think he'd be defeated,[3]
Shamed and very badly treated.
Tibert, by gloomy thoughts inspired,
Felt that he was not required

---

3. The flight of birds was sometimes interpreted as predicting the outcome of an enterprise.

To ask if he could go inside. 765
He went just up to the door and tried
To do his errand tactfully;
No good came of it, as you shall see.
"Renard," he said, "as I hold you dear,
Tell me, at least, if you are here." 770
Renard seemed not to reply at first;
Out of sight, between his teeth, he cursed:
"Tibert, my friend, you'll rue the day
You ever put yourself in my way!
I'll have your hide right down to the bone!" 775
Then he said, in a normal tone:
"*Welcomme*,[4] good Tibert, to my home!
If you were on your way from Rome
Or from Compostela,[5] I'd hold you dear
And be as glad to see you here 780
As to welcome the Pentecostal feast!"[6]
It doesn't hurt Renard in the least
To offer greetings of that sort.
Tibert's reply is rather short:
"Renard, please understand one thing: 785
I'm only here to speak for the king—
It's certainly not the way I feel—
And he condemns you without appeal.
Grinbert, your cousin, takes your side,
But with no one else are you allied— 790
What the others feel for you is hate."
Renard is not inclined to debate:
"How I deal with threats you shall see,
And those who'd sharpen their teeth on me.
While I can I will live my life! 795
I'll go to court and settle this strife,
If they dare accuse me to my face."
"That will be very wise, your Grace;
For this, as always, you have my praise.
But I've had nothing to eat for days— 800
My spine is bent just like a bow.
Haven't you something down below,
A hen or a rooster I could taste?"
Renard said, "That would be a waste.
Everyone knows the way you steal 805
Plump mice and rats to make a meal—
Poultry is not the thing for you!"
"Oh yes it is!" "That can't be true."
"I'll eat until the last hen's gone."
"All right. Tomorrow, before the dawn, 810
You'll be full where you now are hollow.
I'll go first, and you just follow."
  With that Renard came out of his lair.

---

4. In English in the original. 5. A pilgrimage site like Rome, located on the west coast of Spain. 6. A feast day seven weeks after Easter.

Tibert followed him, unaware
That he was already caught by guile.   815
They saw a village after a while
Where for sure you'd be hard-put to find
A coop where Renard had never dined.
"Tibert," he says, "you're in for a treat.
In one of the houses on that street,   820
Lucky for us, there lives a priest—
I know him well, to say the least.
His oats and barley would well suffice
Except that he is plagued by mice
Who take such pleasure in that fare   825
It was nearly gone when I was there.
I set out to capture a hen—
Before I knew it, I'd taken ten!
Five of them I ate today;
The others I put safely away.   830
Just inside is the hiding-place,
So go right in and stuff your face!"
That treacherous master of deceit
Was lying. Neither oats nor wheat
Were kept in the place where Tibert went,   835
A fact the priest did much lament.
The whole village used to deplore
The way the priest's light-fingered whore,
The mother of Martin de la Tour,
Took all he owned. I am quite sure   840
He had no oxen, not a cow—
His barnyard was reduced by now
To just two chickens and a cock.
Young Martin, who later wore the frock,[7]
And then would choose monkish robes to wear,   845
Had closed the entrance with a snare,
Hoping to catch the foxy beast.
God had most greatly blessed the priest
With a son to think of tricks like that,
And so outwit a fox or cat!   850
Renard says, "Tibert, my dear fellow,
Go help yourself, unless you're yellow!
I'll be waiting for you right outside."
Tibert sets forth in a running stride
And then his neck is in the noose—   855
There seems no way to get it loose!
He knows he's done a stupid thing—
The more he pulls, the tighter the string.
He struggles—surely something can be done!
But here comes Martin on the run   860
Yelling, "Father! Oh, make haste!
Help me, Mother! There's no time to waste!
Come to the hole and bring a light—

---

7. I.e., became village priest after his father.

We'll have some sport with the fox tonight!"
　　At this young Martin's mother awakes,　　　　865
Jumps up, lights a candle, and she takes
Her spindle with her. At Martin's calls
The priest, holding on to his balls,
Leaps out of bed, and runs still faster.
For Tibert it's a real disaster:　　　　　　　　870
He carries more than a hundred blows
Away with him when at last he goes.
The priest strikes, and his concubine,
And both of them are doing fine
When Tibert, in his struggle, spies　　　　　　875
What's dangling between the priest's thin thighs,
And grabs—this is told in all the books—
With teeth and claws like grappling hooks,
And hangs on until it is off for good.
As soon as the woman understood　　　　　　880
The full extent of the tragedy,
Three times she cried, "Alas for me!"
And when she would have made it four,
She swooned and fell down upon the floor.
This gave young Martin such a scare　　　　　885
That the cat, who'd bitten through the snare,
Could take advantage of the uproar
And run until he was safe once more.
Tibert has had some satisfaction—
Ah! could he now go into action　　　　　　　890
Against the cause of his rage and pain!
But Renard hadn't chosen to remain.
When he saw Tibert in the snare,
He was on his way right out of there,
Having no desire to come to harm;　　　　　　895
He heard young Martin sound the alarm
And went home—he didn't even wait
To see what would be poor Tibert's fate.
"Ah! Renard, Renard," Tibert said,
"May God not take you when you're dead!　　900
But I deserve to be badly treated,
Having so often been defeated
By that lying cheat, Renard the Red!
May the cuckold priest have little bread
And a wretched place to lay his head,　　　　905
He and the whore he takes to bed,
For what they've done to me today!
But at least he won't be able to play
The parish music very well
Since he'd been left with just one bell.　　　910
And as for Martin de la Tour,
I hope he'll be forever poor
And that, for giving me such blows,
His lifetime will not come to a close
Before he's a monk with no relief　　　　　　915

Until he's hanged for a proven thief!"
   So in a rage at his disgrace,
He came through the valley to the place
Where the king sat in his judgment seat.
Tibert saw him, fell at his feet,   920
And told him his fantastic tale.
"God!" said the king, "My powers fail.
My lords, I am extremely shocked
To find my dignity so mocked.
And where's the champion I need   925
To take revenge for Renard's foul deed?
My lord Grinbert, I'm half-inclined
To see your influence behind
The way Renard despises me."
"I swear, Sire, that could never be!"   930
"Then go and bring Renard to court.
If you fail, don't bother to report."
"Sire," said Grinbert, "it can't be done.
That bastard would just think it fun—
He'd never yield to my desire,   935
Unless I had a letter, Sire.
By Saint Israel,[8] no appeal
Would move him, but if he saw your seal,
He'd know, whatever pretext he used,
There's no way for him to be excused."   940
"My dear Sir, that makes very good sense."
Noble then dictated the contents
While Baucent[9] wrote down everything;
He sealed the letter for the king.
   Then Grinbert, with the king's permission, 945
Started out to perform his mission.
Through meadow and wood he went; no lack
Of sweat was pouring off his back,
And still he had far to go before
He would be close to Renard's front door. 950
At vespers he came upon a lane,
And at nightfall found Renard's domain.
The walls rose high above his head;
There were narrow passageways that led
To where he found a low-vaulted door   955
Into a courtyard. Then, still more
Afraid of what Renard would do
If he should hear him coming through,
He hugged the walls and waited to see—
That was Grinbert at Maupertuis.   960
As soon as his visitor had stepped
Onto the turning bridge and crept
Along the passageways—even then,
Before Grinbert came into his den,
Hindquarters first and head to the rear, 965

8. A fictitious saint.   9. A boar.

Renard knew who was coming near.
He welcomed Grinbert with warm delight,
Wrapped both arms around him tight,
And two soft pillows behind him pressed,
Because his cousin was his guest.   970
I think Grinbert was very wise
To keep his message for a surprise
Until he'd had enough to eat,
But after dinner, feeling replete,
"My lord," he said, "everyone knows   975
The way you lie and cheat—it shows.
I'm here to tell you the king demands,
No, no demands—the king commands
That at his palace you submit
To whatever sentence he deems fit.   980
Why wage a war you cannot win?
What did you want of Ysengrin?
Why harm Tibert? Why hurt Bruin?
You have betrayed them to your ruin.
I'd like to offer you some cheer,   985
But I think your time to die is near,
And all your children will share your fate.
Break this seal and you'll get it straight.
Just read the words that are written here."
Renard listens, and shakes with fear.   990
He trembles, as he breaks the seal,
For what that gesture may reveal.
He reads the first few words and sighs,
Well understanding what meets his eyes.
    "Noble the lion, whose majesty   995
Prevails throughout these lands where he
Over all the beasts is king and lord,
Promises Renard he cannot afford
To ignore this summons: he'll pay dear
If tomorrow he does not appear   1000
To make amends for his misdeeds.
Not silver and not gold he needs,
And let no champion give him hope;[1]
He'll pay his debt with a hangman's rope."
    A terrible message for Renard!   1005
Inside his chest his heart beat hard,
His face took on a somber hue.
"For God's sake, Grinbert, what shall I do?
Pity a poor defenseless captive!
Alas that I have this hour to live   1010
If I must hang until I'm dead
Tomorrow. I wish I'd been instead
A monk at Cluny or Citeaux![2]
But many of them are false, and so

---

1. I.e., there will be no judicial duel (as there is in *The Song of Roland*), in which Renard can be defended by someone else.   2. The two most famous monasteries in twelfth-century France.

I'd soon have wanted to depart;   1015
In that case better not to start."
"You've other things to worry about!"
Said Grinbert. "And while you're here without
People around you, I suggest
That it would be well if you confessed.   1020
Confess your sins to me at least—
Since I don't see any closer priest."[3]
"My lord Grinbert," Renard replies,
I think your counsel very wise;
I'm close to death for my transgression,   1025
And if you hear my true confession
I've nothing at all to lose thereby,
And I am saved if I have to die.
   Listen! I heartily repent
For what I did with Dame Hersent   1030
Who is the wife of Ysengrin.
She tried to cover up that sin
But no one believed her—that was shrewd
For she was well and truly screwed.
My God preserve my soul from Hell,   1035
So many times I rang her bell—
Mea culpa!—if I have to face
Ysengrin, I'll lose the case.
How to deny that he's been cheated,
Three times imprisoned and defeated!   1040
Now I will tell you all about it.
I made him fall into the pit
Just as he carried off a sheep.
Lucky for him he got to keep
Any skin at all, for it was shed   1045
In a hundred blows before he fled.
When I had trapped him as I planned,
There were three shepherds close at hand
Who beat him like a balky ass.
Another time I helped him to pass   1050
Through an entrance to a rich man's larder,
But getting out was a great deal harder,
For his belly swelled still more with each
Of three hams he found within his reach.
I set him to fishing through the ice;   1055
His tail was caught as in a vise.
I made him fish in a pool one night
When the full moon was very bright,
And its reflection, white and round,
Looked like a lovely cheese he'd found.   1060
So once again I had my wish—
He ended up on a load of fish.
A hundred times I took him in

---

3. Confession to a layman was permitted in extreme circumstances, but legitimate confessions were to be
made with a contrite heart. Renard recalls here tricks that are described elsewhere in the *Romance*.

With the guileful schemes my wits can spin.
Thanks to me he had a tonsured head.[4]   1065
Then he saw how well the canons[5] fed
And thought their life wouldn't be so hard;
Those fools gave him their sheep to guard!
I could talk all day and not be done
Telling you how I had my fun.   1070
There's not one beast in Noble's court
Who wouldn't give me a bad report.
When I led Tibert into the net
He thought that it was rats he'd get.
In all Pinte's family there lives   1075
One aunt; her other relatives,
Cocks and hens alike, were able
To fill a place at my dinner table.
When a cow and ox and the mighty boar
With other beasts stood at my door   1080
Well armed, Ysengrin, in the lead,
Was sure that he had all he'd need
To win. There were on his side as well,
With the watchdog, Loudmouth Roenel,
Seven times twenty dogs and bitches   1085
All of whom soon needed stitches,
Having most foully been betrayed—
I'd gotten to everyone they paid.
I certainly have no cause to boast
Of how I routed that great host—   1090
Only by guile were they defeated.
I watched as long as they retreated
And in salute stuck out my tongue.
God! What I did when I was young!
But now, *mea culpa!* true remorse   1095
Turns my life from its sinful course."
"Renard, Renard," Grinbert begins,
"I've heard the confession of your sins
And all the evil you have done.
Your trial, by God's will, may yet be won.   1100
Take care from now on to do no wrong."
"May God not let me live so long,"
Renard replied, "that all my ways
Are not deserving of His praise."
He shows a pious resolution,   1105
Kneels, and Grinbert gives absolution
In French and in the tongue of Rome.[6]
Next morning, before Renard left home,
He kissed his children and his wife,
All of them fearing for his life.   1110
When the time of separation came,
"My sons," he said, "defend our name!
However this misadventure goes,

---

4. He lost the hair on his head, so he looked like a monk. 5. Members of a religious order. 6. Latin.

Protect my castles against our foes.
Against a count, against a king,   1115
For months you won't need to fear a thing—
No count or baron, no lord would dare
Rob your head of a single hair.
You'll never be so much as grazed,
If you keep every drawbridge raised   1120
And are well provisioned—for seven years
You'll stand them off and have no fears.
What more is there for me to say?
I commend you now to God, and pray
That He will bring me back once more."   1125
With that he knelt down on the floor;
Because he would have to leave his lair,
Renard began to say a prayer.
    "God, King, in your omnipotence,
Let my craft and my common sense   1130
Not be lost to me out of fear
When before the king I must appear
To answer Ysengrin in court.
Whatever he chooses to report
Let me make it harmless to admit,   1135
Or find some way of denying it;
And let me come back to Maupertuis
Alive and well, so that I may be
Avenged on those who seek my disgrace."
Renard fell down upon his face,   1140
Then, beating his breast for what he'd done,
Made the sign against the evil one.
    And now the noble lords will go
To court; on their way swift rivers flow;
There are narrow trails to follow past   1145
High mountain ridges until at last
They ride across a level plain.
Renard is really feeling the strain;
That's why, in the woods, they go astray
And find no footpath, road or way   1150
Until, where farmland had been cleared,
A barn that belonged to nuns appeared.
Surely one would find inside
The best of what the world can provide:
Cheese and milk and lambs they keep,   1155
Geese and oxen, cows and sheep,
And young ones they fatten up to eat.
"Come on!" said Renard. "Don't drag your feet!
Now I can see where we went wrong.
There's underbrush to follow along   1160
To the henyard, then it's straight ahead."
"Renard, Renard," the badger said,
"Does God not know what you say that for?
Foul unbelieving son of a whore,
Stinking glutton—I thought you craved,   1165

Pleading for mercy, to be saved!
I heard your confession, did I not?"
Replied Renard, "I quite forgot.
I'm ready now. Let's go on like friends."
"Renard, Renard, it never ends!   1170
God himself you will try to trick!
On you repentance can never stick.
How you came to be so mad, God knows!
Your life may be coming to a close,
And scarcely have you confessed before   1175
You turn around and sin once more.
Evil has marked you out as prey.
Let's go now. A curse upon the day
When you were severed from your mother!"
"You do very well to say so, brother!   1180
But now let's go our way in peace."
To make his cousin's scolding cease
Renard was keeping very quiet
As to the farm—he dared not try it,
But he craned his neck a little when   1185
He caught a sight of a lovely hen,
Sadly thinking he'd rather have fed
And paid the price, though it were his head!
    As the two lords proceed with their ride,
Grinbert's mule has a mighty stride,   1190
But fear of his master's wrath so grips
Renard's horse that he constantly trips;
Beneath his skin the blood pounds hard,
So greatly does he fear Renard.
They run through fields, through woods they scramble,   1195
Galloping or at an amble,
Over the mountain pass they ride
To the valley on the other side
Where those accused are called to account;
In front of the great hall they dismount.   1200
    As soon as it's known Renard is there
Everyone hastens to prepare
An accusation or defense.
Renard's discomfort is intense.
He'll suffer whether or not he hangs;   1205
Ysengrin's sharpening his fangs,
Tibert the cat is thinking hard,
And Bruin whose face is red and scarred.
But regardless of their love or hate,
Renard's courage does not abate.   1210
He makes his speech with his head held high,
Looking the king straight in the eye.
    "Sire, I've come to meet you here
Knowing that you should hold me dear
Above all other lords of this land.   1215
You have been wronged by those who planned
To injure me. Perhaps it's just

My bad luck, but I could never trust
Your love, not for a single day—
That's about as long as I've been away.   1220
You know that there was no ill will
Between us, no dispute, and still,
When I left in peace and by your leave,
You were all ready to believe
Slander about me from my foes.   1225
That is the way a kingdom goes
To ruin—when the king will treat
Without suspicion those who cheat,
And loyalty cannot prevail:
He throws out the head and keeps the tail.   1230
Those who should be serfs by station
Don't know the wisdom of moderation.
They'll go to any lengths to gain
Favor by someone else's pain.
They'll do evil of any sort   1235
Providing they can rise at court,
Fleecing others as their hearts desire.
And now allow me to inquire
Why Tibert and Bruin complain of me.
Although, should it please Your Majesty,   1240
I can tell you what it's all about.
If I harmed them it was not without
Their help, as they both are well aware.
Who ate the honey if not the bear?
If Lanfroi defends his property,   1245
Should Bruin take it out on me?
Look what he has for legs and paws,
Enormous feet, with enormous claws.
And if Tibert here, my lord the cat,
Was eating a meal of mouse or rat   1250
When he was caught in nets and shamed,
God's heart! I don't see why I am blamed.
As for Ysengrin—what can I say?
His accusation's true, in a way,
For certainly I have loved Hersent.   1255
But that had to be with her consent—
Did she ever come here to protest?
Is it right, at a jealous fool's request,
That I be hanged until I'm dead?
God forbid, Sire! Recognize instead   1260
The good faith and true fidelity
I have always shown Your Majesty:
Your kingdom, so deserving praise,
Is what I've lived for all my days.
But now my muzzle has gone gray;   1265
There is no game left that I can play,
By God and Saint George, I'm much too weak.
It's a sin to drag me here to speak,
Old as I am, before this court.

When the king commands that I report,   1270
I do his will, as I hold him dear,
And now I stand in his presence here.
I could hang or perish at the stake;
There is no protest I can make
Against the king—I am not so strong.   1275
But to get revenge that way is wrong.
To hang me will be called a disgrace,
If there's no real judgment on my case."
"Renard," the emperor begins,
"May your father suffer for his sins!   1280
May the whore who bore you be accursed
Because she didn't abort your first!
Treacherous thief, can you explain
Why you have such a scheming brain?
You know how to argue and to plead,   1285
But to that my court will give no heed.
There's no way for you to leave this place;
You shall hear my verdict on your case!
Your bravado won't be any use;
Your scheming will find you no excuse.   1290
Though you are as slippery as an eel,
There's no escape and no appeal—
Your fate was predicted long ago,
And now its coming won't be slow.
My noble lords are in court to say   1295
Just what a thief who's caught must pay,
And to sentence a traitor for his crime.
You'll feel the weight of their wrath this time!
Unless you can find a hiding-place,
They'll say what they think right to your face."   1300
Then spoke Grinbert the badger: "Sire,
With the deference that you inspire,
We give you, and rightly, our full trust.
But that doesn't mean that you can just
Do what you want to—it is vile   1305
To deny a lord his rightful trial.
You may not like it, but it's clear
Renard had safe conduct to come here.
Let those who accuse him state their case,
And then allow him, by your grace,   1310
With your court as witness, to be tried
As justice and the law provide."
He could not say all he intended.
Before the badger's speech had ended,
Up on his feet was Ysengrin,   1315
And the sheep as well, my lord Belin,
And my lord Tiecelin, the crow,
Chanteclere, Dame Pinte, and also
The three other hens who support their claim.
The hedgehog, Spiky was his name,   1320
And the peacock, Petipas, step out,

And Frobert the cricket—he, no doubt,
Has the loudest voice of those who shout.
Then one with much to complain about:
The squirrel, called my lord Roxat,   1325
And Roenel and Tibert the cat.
Coward the hare, who's very fleet,
Hurries through courtyards, from street to street;
He has very good cause to pray
That justice should be done that day   1330
Renard is sure if he had to cope
With these he'd have very little hope.
But the king commands that they be still—
Vengeance is subject to his will.
    King Noble's voice, which is very loud,   1335
Carries through the assembled crowd:
"Hear me, my lords," he says in a roar,
"Renard can be trusted like a whore!
What punishment should I decree
To avenge what he has done to me?"   1340
"Sire," they answered, "as you said before,
Renard has the virtue of a whore.
The only thing that's of any use
To reform him is a hangman's noose."
The king replied, "I like what you say!   1345
Let's do it, and without delay!
He's a menace, and I don't know how
We'd get him back if we lost him now.
We'll suffer for it, should he leave:
Some who think they are safe will grieve."   1350
    On a hilltop, by the king's command,
In a rocky place, the gallows stand,
Set up to end the fox's career—
Death, it would seem, is very near.
A monkey, mocking Renard's disgrace,   1355
Is answered by a slap in the face.
Renard looks behind him; he can see
His foes approaching, more than three.
One gives him a kick and one a shove—
He has plenty to be fearful of.   1360
From a good distance—he wouldn't dare
Come any closer—Coward the hare
Did his part too: he threw a stone,
Hit Renard's head, and broke the bone.
But that gave Coward such a fright   1365
That henceforth he stayed out of sight.
One look from Renard put him on edge;
He ran to take shelter in a hedge.
From there, he thought, he could watch and wait
Till Renard had finally met his fate.   1370
But hiding was, I think, a mistake,
He'll have, this day, good cause to shake.
Renard, with stout ropes securing him,

Felt his prospects were growing dim,
He couldn't think of a thing that might   1375
Rescue him from his dreadful plight.
No doubt you'd have to be a master
To walk away from this disaster.
    When he saw the gallows standing there
Renard was reduced to real despair.   1380
He said, "Most gracious lord and king,
Allow me to mention just one thing:
You have had me brought out here and tied,
And want to hang me before I'm tried;
But there are sinful things I've done,   1385
And God's forgiveness could still be won,
Were I allowed, for my soul's defense,
To take the cross in penitence,
And obedient to God's command,
Cross the sea to the Holy Land.   1390
If I die there my soul will rise,
But if I'm hanged I'm the devil's prize—
More honor to you if you relent.
All I want now is to repent."
At the king's feet he lay his head.   1395
Noble was moved by what he'd said.
And then Grinbert came forward to plead
That Renard, repentant, should be freed:
"Before you answer, Sire, think twice!
For God's sake listen to my advice!   1400
Renard's not afraid of any foe.
If he stays away five months you'll know
That your kingdom really can't afford
To lose so fine and valiant a lord."
The king replied, "I'll be more than glad   1405
To lose him, and he'd be twice as bad
Should he return. The best ones trade
Virtue for evil on crusade.
If Renard survives, there is no doubt
That all of us had better look out!"   1410
"If he doesn't get his conscience clear,
Never again will you see him here."
"Then he shall be, by my command,
Forever in the Holy Land."
Renard hears that with a joyful heart.   1415
He may not do any more than start
His journey, so it's no great loss.
On his right shoulder he wears a cross;
They bring him a pilgrim's purse and staff.
Some do not feel inclined to laugh,   1420
Though they kicked and taunted him before;
They fear he will even up the score.
    Behold Renard, ashwood staff in hand,
A pilgrim bound for the Holy Land!
He must forgive them, says the king   1425

In the name of all, for everything;
And if he abandons tricks and lies,
He'll win salvation when he dies.
Whatever Renard may have in mind,
He seems not in the least inclined   1430
To turn away from piety.
He leaves, as he tells His Majesty,
With peace and forgiveness in his heart;
Just after noon he's ready to start.
To no else does he say farewell—   1435
He wishes each one of them in Hell!
He'd have revenge on that whole crowd
Except for the king and Fiere the proud,
His courteous and lovely queen
Whose parting words show her far from mean: 1440
"Renard," she says, "we'll pray for you,
And remember us in your prayers too."
"My lady, I will do my best
To show how I honor your request;
And who would not be joyful indeed   1445
To have your prayers in his soul's great need!
But even better would I fare
If I could have that ring you wear.
If you allow me that great boon,
You shall be well rewarded soon: 1450
I have jewels that I will bring
And they're worth a hundred times one ring."
Renard takes the ring that he is handed—
No need for him to be commanded!
Between his teeth he says very low: 1455
"If there is someone who doesn't know
This ring, I have only to appear
For that to cost him very dear."
Renard puts the ring upon his finger,
Bows to the king, and does not linger.   1460
His spurs strike at his horse's sides;
At a racing trot away he rides.
Presently, close at hand, he found
The hedge where Coward went to ground.
It was so long since Renard ate last   1465
He had a headache from his fast.
Coward, seeing Renard so near,
Is just about overcome with fear.
He jumps right up, and in his fright
Greets him, sounding very polite: 1470
"I can hardly tell you what delight
It gives me to see that you're all right!
I have felt weighed down by my dismay
At the way they treated you today."
Replies Renard from his crafty brain,   1475
"If my misfortune gives you pain,
And you see my person so disgraced,

Let's make sure that yours won't go to waste!"
Every word that Coward hears
Seems to justify his gravest fears. 1480
It would be better if he fled
(If he stays he thinks he'll soon be dead),
And he would have headed for the plain
Had Renard not grabbed his horse's rein.
"Ha! Coward, my lord, by God's heart 1485
I swear you shall not so soon depart!
Did you think your horse had so much speed
That you wouldn't be the one to feed
My hungry cubs at home today?"
With his staff he prods him on his way. 1490
   King Noble, his barons and their men
Were passing through a valley just then
Whose walls towered very high
To four huge rocks set against the sky.
At the top Renard pursues his course 1495
With Coward slung beneath his horse,
Face downward to his bitter shame.
Renard, well deserving his bad name,
Intends, and very soon, to greet
His cubs with a delicious treat. 1500
They'll have Coward for their dinner—
God save him from the crafty sinner!
Renard looks downward through the trees.
There, with the king and queen, he sees
So many beasts and barons swarm 1505
That the woods are shaking as in a storm.
They talk of Renard, quite unaware
Of what is happening to the hare,
Dragged off, like a convicted thief,
To a prison where he'll come to grief. 1510
Renard tears his cross off, holds it high,
And summons them with a mighty cry:
"My lord king, behold your flag!
I'm giving back the lousy rag!
Those who weighed me down with staff and purse 1515
May God in His own true wisdom curse!"
He wipes himself in a filthy place,
And throws the cross at Noble's face.
Then once again he shouts to the king,
"Listen to me, my lord! I bring 1520
The greetings Noradin[7] has sent
When I, as a worthy pilgrim, went
To where the pagans across the sea
At the very thought of you will flee."
Renard was so busy having fun 1525
That Coward got his ropes undone,
"With a mighty leap was on his horse,

7. Sultan who ruled the lands invaded by the crusaders.

And had set off on a headlong course
Before Renard could realize
That he was about to lose his prize.   1530
Soon Coward, going very fast,
Reached his friends and was safe at last.
His sides had lost quite a lot of skin
Where Renard had stuck his staff right in;
With both his hands and his feet stripped bare—   1535
He really needed a doctor's care.
Just barely able to complete
His journey, he fell at Noble's feet
And told how his life had been at stake.
"Help me, my lord, for God's sweet sake!"   1540
"Oh God, I'm betrayed!" King Noble mourned;
"How utterly is my power scorned!
It's all too easy now to see
How much Renard despises me.
But, my lords, make no mistake—   1545
We know what route Renard will take;
If he makes it home there's not a thing
Can save your necks—you all shall swing!
But whoever captures him shall win
Nobility for all his kin."   1550
     You should have seen the race begin!
There's Belin the sheep and Ysengrin,
Bruin the bear and Bald the rat,
As well as my lord Tibert the cat.
Dame Pinte and her three good friends appear   1555
And with them, of course, Lord Chanteclere,
Ferran, the horse who carries packs,
Roenel, the watchdog who attacks.
After him comes Frobert the cricket
And then the ferret, Little Sticket,   1560
Followed by the boar Baucent
Whose teeth can make a mighty dent,
And of course the raging bull won't lag,
Nor, at a gallop, Bricemer the stag.
The flag is carried by the snail   1565
Who's first in line as they take the trail.
Renard, looking back, can see their haste,
And knows he has little time to waste.
There, first in the field, goes Slow—
The wind is making his banner blow.   1570
What should he do? He can't decide;
Renard jumps out of the path to hide
In the underbrush, and finds a ditch—
But close behind is Short the bitch
With the others at her heels. They swear   1575
That Renard will never reach his lair,
That their attack will not be stayed
By castle wall or palisade;
The widest moat, the strongest tower,

Thickets, burrows, have no power   1580
To save Renard from the king this time—
On a rope he'll end his life of crime!
Renard feels that his strength has ended.
Flee or go on as he intended,
He knows he'll never reach his home.   1585
His mouth is dripping, white with foam.
And they've very nearly plucked him bare!
Tufts of his robe fly through the air.
His sides are totally abraded—
How can his capture be evaded?   1590
It's a miracle if, nearly in their grip
Renard gives his enemies the slip!
Yet twisting and turning he breaks free,
And is on his way to Maupertuis,
His palace, fortress, mighty tower,   1595
Home and citadel, seat of power,
The one place in all the world he knows
Will keep him safe from his strongest foes.
Let them love or hate him, once he's there
He will wait for them without a care.   1600
His wife embraced him even before
He had a foot inside the door.
Three sons had that noble lady,
One was Malebranche, one Shady,
The third was named Rovel, and he   1605
Was the handsomest among the three.
They all came running out in haste,
To clasp their arms around his waist,
And seeing his wounds—they were very deep—
Began to comfort him and weep.   1610
They washed his injuries with white wine,
Placed a pillow so that he'd recline;
Then they were ready to serve a meal.
But Renard was too worn out to feel
Like swallowing much of anything   1615
But a chicken leg and half a wing.
He lay in a bath his wife had filled,
And then she bled him. She was skilled
At leechcraft, and before too long
Renard, once again, was feeling strong   1620

ROBERT MANNYNG
early fourteenth century

The Cursed Dancers of Colbeck[1]

Carols,[2] wrestling, or summer games—whoever practices such disgraceful behavior in church or churchyard should be afraid of sacrilege. Interludes[3] or singing, beating the tabor[4] or piping—all these things are forbidden while the priest is conducting mass. These things are hateful to the good priest, and he'll be angry about them much sooner than will an ignorant man who doesn't understand Holy Writ, especially if people sing carols and read out rhymes[5] during feast days. In any holy place where the priest says his beads or is praying or performing any other devotion—it's all sacrilege, these and many other things.

But in order to persuade you not to dance in church I shall tell you about a remarkable event, most of which is the gospel truth. * * * It was upon a Christmas Eve that twelve fools made a carol—madly, as a kind of challenge—in a town called Colbeck.[6] The church in that town is dedicated to the martyr St. Magnus, and to his sister, St. Bukcester. The names of all of the carollers are written down, and you shall know them. Their leader, who made the music, was called Gerlew. The other twelve were as follows: Theodoric, Meinhold, Bovoline, Gerard, Edbert, Wenseline, Aceline, Folkward, Hildebrand, Aelward, Benne, and Odricus. There were also two maidens in their band, Mersewine and Wisbessine.[7] All of these people came because of the daughter of the town priest. The priest was called Robert, I believe, and his son was called Ayone. His daughter, whom these men wanted, was named Ave.

Together they agreed that both Wisbessine and Mersewine should go to entice Ave out. These women went and persuaded her to come and carol with them around the church. Benne organized the carol and Gerlew composed the song they should sing, as it says in the Latin:

> By the leafy wood rode Bovoline,
> With him he led the fair Mersewine.
> Why are we waiting? Why don't we go?[8]

This is the carol that Gerlew wrote, the song they sung in the church yard— they weren't afraid of being foolish—until matins[9] was finished and the priest robed himself to begin the Mass. Nevertheless they didn't leave off, but continued dancing as they had begun: despite the Mass, they didn't stop. The priest, who stood at the altar and heard their noise and their uproar, came down from the altar and went out to the church porch. "For God's sake," he said, "I prohibit you from continuing. But come in a seemly fashion to hear God's service, behave as Christians, and for reverence of Christ stop this carolling. With all your heart worship him who was born this night of

---

1. Translated from the Middle English by Lee Patterson.   2. Circle dances usually accompanied with singing.   3. Short plays or mimed performances.   4. A small drum.   5. I.e., tell rhyming tales, or sing ballads.   6. Kölbigk, in Saxony, an area in eastern Germany just north of the present-day Czech border.   7. A total of fifteen people are named, but presumably only the twelve men are actual dancers, Gerlew supplying the music and the two women being companions of dubious character.   8. Robert cites these lines in Latin and then translates them into Middle English.   9. The regular morning church service that did not usually include the Mass.

the Virgin." For all his asking they wouldn't stop, but continued dancing as they pleased.

Distressed by this, the priest prayed to the God of his faith that on behalf of St. Magnus, in whose honor the church was built, He would arrange it so that they would suffer such vengeance that they would continue in this way for a full year until they might depart. (In the Latin that I read he said not a year but forever.) He cursed them there all together as they carolled for fun. As soon as the priest had spoken, every hand was fast locked into the others so that no man might part them asunder for a twelvemonth. The priest went in then and commanded his son Ayone that he should go quickly after Ave, and bring her out of that carol. But all too late was that word said, for vengeance had been laid on all of them. Ayone expected to succeed, and he quickly went to the carol. He grabbed his sister by the arm but the arm separated from the body. All the people there wondered, but you will hear of a greater miracle: since he had the arm in his hand, the body went forth carolling, and neither body nor arm bled but was as dry, as was the shoulder, as if a branch were torn from a tree trunk.

Ayone went to his father and brought him a sad present. "Look, father," he said, "you have here the arm of your daughter, that was my own sister Ave whom I thought I might save. Your vengeance is now made manifest on your own flesh. Savagely and hastily you cursed: you asked for vengeance and you have your wish." You don't need to ask if there was grief for the priest and for many others. The priest that cursed because of that dance saw the harsh effect fall on his own.

He took his daughter's bereft arm and buried it the next morning. But the next day he found Ave's arm lying upon the grave. He buried it again, and again it appeared upon the grave. He buried it a third time, and again it was cast out of the pit. The priest wouldn't bury it again—he feared some vengeance. Instead he bore it into the church, for fear of more harm, and set it up so as to be visible to everyone.

These people who were carolling, all that year, hand in hand, never left that place nor might anyone lead them away. Where the cursing first began they continued to race about. Unlike many bodies, they felt no weariness, nor did they eat food or taste drink, nor sleep even a single wink. They knew nothing of either day nor night, when it was come, when it was gone. Frost nor snow, hail nor rain, of cold and heat they felt no pain. Their nails did not grow, their clothes did not get dirty, their complexions did not change. Thunder nor lightning gave them no fear: God's mercy warded it off them. But they sang the song that wrought their woe: "Why are we waiting? Why don't we go?"

What person alive would not journey to see this thing? Emperor Henry[1] came from Rome to see this harsh punishment. When he saw them he wept bitterly for the suffering he saw there. He arranged for carpenters to make a covering over them to protect them from storms, but whatever they made was in vain. Whatever they set up one day was down the next. Once, twice, thrice they built, and all their work was for nothing. No covering might protect the dancers from the cold until the time of mercy that Christ willed.

The time of grace arrived through His might and at the end of the twelve-

---

1. Henry II, Holy Roman Emperor from 1002 to 1024.

month, on Christmas Eve. The same hour that the priest bound them was the same hour when they came apart; the same hour that he cursed them was the same hour they separated. And in the twinkling of an eye they flew into the church, and on the pavement they all fell down as if they were dead or in a faint. For three days each lay still without stirring flesh or bone, and at the end of three days God granted that they should return to life. They stood up and spoke openly to the parish priest, sir Robert. "You are both an example and a cause of our long confusion; you are the maker of our travail that has been a marvel to so many. And you shall soon end your own travail, for to your eternal home you shall soon go." At that time they all rose except Ave: she lay dead beside them. Her father and brother had great sorrow; all the others felt wonder and fear. They feared, I believe, not that her soul was dead but of the pain that brought bodily death.[2]

The first man who died after the daughter was her father, the priest. For Ave's arm, that none might lay in a grave, the Emperor made a vessel to put it in and hang in the church, so that all men might see it and know and think on this event when they saw it. These people that had gone carolling all the year hand in hand, even though they were now apart everyone still spoke of this miracle. That same skipping that they first did—they continued that dance through lands and nations. But as they might not first be unbound, so might they now never again come together into one place. Four went to the court of Rome, and always skipping they went about. With many leaps they came there, but they never came together again. Their clothes didn't rot nor their nails grow; their hair didn't lengthen nor their complexions change. Nor did they ever have relief, so far as we have heard, at any shrine, except at that of the virgin saint Edith: there Theodoric was cured on Lady's Day in Lent as he slept beside her tomb. There he had his medicine from St. Edith, the holy virgin.[3]

Bruning, bishop of St. Toule, wrote this marvelous tale. Afterward his name was better known: men called him Pope Leo.[4] They know this story at the court of Rome, and it is written in chronicles in many places beyond the sea—more so than in this country.

Therefore people say and truly it is believed, "The nearer the church, the further from God." So people regard this tale: some hold it an idle story, while in other places it is held dearly and people take it for a great marvel. It is a tale of clear illustration, an example of and a warning against cursing. I told you this tale to make you afraid to carol in a church or churchyard, especially against the priest's will. Stop when he bids you to be still: jangling[5] is a form of sacrilege.

---

2. By the death of the soul the author means eternal damnation. 3. A tenth-century nun whose shrine was located at Wilton in England. 4. Goscelin, Robert's source, credits the story to Bruno, bishop of Toul (b. 1002), who presided as Pope Leo IX from 1048 until his death in 1054. 5. Chattering, babbling.

DANTE ALIGHIERI
1265–1321

Called by its author a comedy, and named by later ages—in recognition of both its subject matter and its achievement—*The Divine Comedy*, Dante's poem is one of the indisputably great works of world literature. It combines into an astonishingly coherent whole a remarkable range of disparate literary elements. Both structurally and thematically it is organized with the precision and harmony of the great philosophical systems and the vast Gothic cathedrals of its time; and yet it attends with extraordinary care to the tiniest detail. It celebrates with unqualified enthusiasm and at times even a dogmatic triumphalism the central doctrines of medieval Christianity; and yet it remains persistently alert to the complex sympathies of the human heart. It is epic in its scope and its central themes; and yet it sings with an exquisite lyricism. It is a poem that declares everywhere its commitment to the culture of medieval Christendom; and yet it celebrates the achievements of the classical world and extends its admiration even to Islamic philosophy. It is one of the most deeply serious works in world literature, concerned with nothing less than the relation of the Creator to His creatures and the ultimate destiny of the human soul; and yet it has room for not just grim irony but scenes of generous good humor and even vulgar horseplay. It does not shy away from episodes that the German writer Goethe accurately called "repulsive and often disgusting"; and yet it also includes moments of sublime beauty that have been rarely matched and never surpassed. Perhaps above all, it declares that a great work of literary art can be created in the vernacular, providing the declaration of independence that made possible the various national traditions of post-medieval literature. In this sense *The Divine Comedy* is the foundational text for the European literary imagination.

Dante was born in Florence in the spring of 1265. In his early years he wrote some ninety lyrics, thirty-one of which he collected and provided with a narrative commentary in a work he called the *Vita nuova* or *New Life* (completed between 1292 and 1295). This work recounted his love for a young woman he named Beatrice ("blessed" in Italian), who died in 1290. More than a love story, it described how Beatrice led him from a merely human love to something transcendental, almost divine. Dante realized that this transformation also required a new form of poetry, and it is from the *New Life* that *The Divine Comedy* was to spring as both a fulfillment and an alternative.

Meanwhile, however, political conflicts had decisively altered Dante's life. The Florentine political class, like that of much of northern Italy, was divided into two factions. The Guelphs, generally members of the urban elite and artisans, supported Florentine independence and resisted the claims of the Holy Roman Empire to sovereignty over the city or indeed any part of Italy, often by soliciting the support of the military power of the papacy. The Ghibellines, on the other hand, were drawn from the ancient feudal aristocracy and saw the empire as a means of furthering their own interests. After a series of bitter struggles, the Florentine Guelphs—of which Dante was a member—were triumphant. Around 1300, however, the Guelphs themselves broke into two parties, the Blacks and the Whites, and civil strife was renewed. The Whites, with Dante as a member, became associated with the Ghibellines in their resistance to the power of the pope. In 1301, while Dante was on a diplomatic mission for the city, the Blacks staged a coup with the help of Pope Boniface VII and his ally, the Frenchman Charles of Anjou. The next year Dante was condemned to exile, and he never returned to Florence. Dependent on the generosity of wealthy patrons throughout northern Italy, he was without a permanent home. This experience of exile is central to *The Divine Comedy*, which on the most literal level recounts the journey of a lost traveler back to his ultimate fatherland, Heaven. Also central is Dante's outrage at the internecine strife that tore northern Italy apart throughout his lifetime. Soon he came to believe that only the Holy Roman Emperor could bring order out of chaos, and he condemned the interference of the Church, and especially the pope, in political affairs, just as he condemned the Ghibellines' misuse of the empire's prestige for their own, self-seeking purposes. Dante's politics in *The Divine Comedy* are also religious and prophetic: he is concerned with restoring the conditions in which Christ first came—when Caesar Augustus presided over the "Roman peace" or *pax Romana*—so that He can come again and usher in the Final Judgment. Thus for Dante the Roman Empire is divinely ordained: it first provided the earthly unity and order appropriate to the birth of Christ, and only when it is restored will His second coming be possible.

As a sign of the availability of the divine, this unity and order are everywhere present in Dante's poem. The three parts or canticles—the *Inferno, Purgatorio,* and *Paradiso*—are of equal length. Each of the latter two has thirty-three cantos; the first, the *Inferno*, has thirty-four, but the first canto is a prologue to the whole. This threefold pattern serves to embody the Trinity within the very structure of the poem, as does the verse form. Dante created a verse known as *terza rima*, which rhymes in the Italian original according to the scheme *aba bcb cdc* and so on. The lines thus form groups of three (known in Italian as *terzine*, or tercets) interlocked by a repeated rhyme word—a verbal equivalent to the three-in-one of the Trinity. Moreover, since each line contains eleven syllables, the total number of syllables in each tercet is thirty-three, the same as the number of cantos in each canticle (again, if we take *Inferno* 1 as a prologue). Each canticle even ends with the same word, *stelle* (stars), objects that are for Dante the visible signs of God's providential oversight. Nine, the square of three, figures centrally in the interior structure of each canticle. In Hell, the lost souls are arranged in three main groups and occupy nine circles; Purgatory is divided into an Ante-Purgatory, seven terraces, and the Earthly Paradise, for a total of nine locations; and Heaven consists of nine embedded spheres beyond which lies the infinite Empyrean of the Trinity (see diagrams on pp. 1301–02).

In addition to these formal and cosmological structures, the poem is organized according to an ethical pattern. For Dante, as for medieval philosophy generally, the natural inclination of every human being is love, a movement toward something outside the self. The natural and proper object of love is God, either directly or as mediated through the created world. Sin occurs when love is immoderately directed to the wrong object, when the creature (including the self) is loved not *for* but *instead of* the Creator. In Hell, perverse love is represented in three forms, as incontinence, violence, and fraudulence. In Purgatory, it is also represented in three forms, as misdirected (pride, envy, and wrath), as defective (sloth), and as excessive (avarice, gluttony, and lust). In Paradise, the blessed are distinguished by the extent to which they enjoy the vision of God, and are again divided into three categories: those whose vision is limited by incomplete love, those who have fulfilled the four cardinal virtues (wisdom, fortitude, justice, and temperance), and finally those—like the angels—whose love comes nearest to perfection. Finally, Dante's geography is equally symmetrical. The globe is divided into a northern and southern hemisphere, but only the northern is inhabited. Its central point is Jerusalem, while to the east lies the Ganges and to the west the straits of Gibraltar. Hell is a huge funnel extending into the center of the Earth that was created when Lucifer fell from Heaven. The earth displaced by his fall rose into the southern hemisphere—which had previously been covered entirely with water—and formed Mount Purgatory. This mountain, organized into its three parts as described above, has at its top the Earthly Paradise, or Eden, the original home of the human race. After descending into Hell, climbing up through the Earth, and then mounting to the Earthly Paradise, Dante is transported through the nine spheres described by medieval astronomy—those of the moon, Mercury, Venus, the sun, Mars, Jupiter, Saturn, the fixed stars, and the *primum mobile*, or outermost sphere, which moves the others—until he reaches the Empyrean, which exists beyond time and space. This final vision is presented in our selection from the *Paradiso*.

There is, finally, one other organizing principle that governs the form of the poem as a whole. When Dante is told that he is to journey through Hell, Purgatory, and Paradise, he protests that he is not worthy by comparing himself to two previous otherworldly travelers: "I am not Aeneas, am not Paul." Aeneas visits the underworld in book 6 of Virgil's *Aeneid,* and Virgil plays a large role as both a literary influence and a character in Dante's poem. The reference to Paul is to a passage in 2 Corinthians 12.2: "I know a man in Christ who fourteen years ago was caught up to the third heaven—whether in the body or out of the body I do not know, God knows." Medieval readers understood Paul to be talking about himself, but their problem was to understand what he meant by the third heaven, since there is presumably only one kingdom of God. The solution was provided by Augustine in one of his commentaries on Genesis, in which he argued that the three Pauline "heavens" were really metaphors for three ways in which human beings can know. These three are, in ascending order of clarity, "corporeal vision," or knowledge by means of the senses; "spiritual" or "imaginative vision," or knowledge through images that have corporeal shape without corporeal substance, as in dreams; and finally "intellectual vision," which is the direct cognition of God and other realities, such as love, that have neither corporeal shape nor corporeal substance. God can be known in all three ways, which Augustine illustrated by passages from the Bible. He is known corporeally by Moses and the burning bush (Exodus 3–4); spiritually or imaginatively in the symbolic images of the Book of Revelation; and intellectually by Paul's vision, which he himself describes in 1 Corinthians 13.12: "For now we see in a mirror dimly but then face to face. Now I know in part; then I shall understand fully, even as I have been understood."

The important point for us is that the three canticles of *The Divine Comedy* are each constructed according to one of these modes of vision. The *Purgatorio,* for example, is a place of images that have corporeal shape but not corporeal substance. In *Purgatorio* 2 we have a vivid illustration of this in a scene that appears in both Homer's and Virgil's underworlds: Dante tries three times to embrace his old friend Casella and three times he fails. With the form of a human being but not the substance, Casella is not merely *seen* by the imagination; he *exists* as an image rather than a thing. He is dematerialized, which shows that he is on his way up to Paradise. For in the *Paradiso* we find that its inhabitants are neither bodies nor images but simply lights. Furthermore, Dante himself, as he ascends the paradisal ladder, becomes "enlightened" or "illuminated." But because he is still in this life rather than a pure spirit this happens to him not literally but metaphorically, as he is instructed by various people in the nature of ultimate truth. This is the reason that the *Paradiso* is so didactic, with characters talking little about themselves and instead explaining what are to us often abstruse points of theological or scholastic teaching. In the *Paradiso* Dante is "enlightened" or "illuminated" by this teaching. So what do we find in the *Inferno*? Not only are the inhabitants of Hell known corporeally but they *are* corporeal, and indeed become all the more so as Dante descends deeper into the pit. At the beginning of the journey, while Dante is in the upper levels, the characters flit about like the shades we expect them to be (as in canto 5), but very soon they become more and more substantial, so that—for example—Virgil and Dante can actually touch them, as in canto 8, where Virgil hurls Filippo Argenti back into the mud. Appropriately, the most corporeal place in Hell is the bottom circle, which is the most materialistic place in the universe. Dante calls it "the center / to which all weight is drawn," "the point / to which, from every part, all weights are drawn," because it is furthest from the pure spirituality and immateriality of Paradise (the Empyrean). At the bottom of Hell we find the heaviest thing in the universe, Satan: although originally Lucifer, the Angel of Light, he is now the being with the least amount of spirit. And with Satan we find not a wily tempter but a kind of idiot, a speechless creature from whose mouths—he has three heads, an infernal parody of the Trinity, to prove that God is present even here in the pit of Hell—flows a bloody drool, what Dante calls in Italian *bava,* a word that refers to infantile slaver.

If the least sinful people are spun round with wind, then, the worst are frozen into ice and utterly immobile. This is Dante's way of showing us that the perfect order of the universe includes the moral law that one's punishment is not merely appropriate to the crime but *is* the crime: these are the sinners who most fully denied the spirit, and so their spirit, which was created eternal by God, has come as close to pure matter as is possible. This moral law is called by one of the sinners a "counter-penalty," or *contrapasso*. It is clear from discussions by philosophers known to Dante—such as Thomas Aquinas—that the Latin term *contrapassum* meant "retribution" according to the law of retribution as defined in the Old Testament: an eye for an eye, a tooth for a tooth (see Exodus 21.23–24). But this is not really the principle that governs the distribution of punishment in Hell: this is what the sinners think, but they are oversimplifying. On the contrary, the moral economy of Hell is explained in a single sentence by another of the sinners (Capaneus): "That which I was in life, I am in death." The punishment of sin is the sin itself, as Augustine taught in the *Confessions* and as was the common understanding throughout the Middle Ages: "For [God has] ordered it, and so it is, that every disordered mind should be its own punishment." What this means is that in the *Inferno* every sinner commits his sin forever, for all of eternity: and it is this endless act of sinning that is the punishment.

Before exploring in more detail the workings of divine justice in the *Inferno*, we need to understand the role of Virgil, and of the *Aeneid*, in the poem. When Dante protests in *Inferno* 2 that he is neither Aeneas nor Paul, he is indicating that his poem will bring together, in a combination that will find its ultimate fulfillment in Milton's *Paradise Lost*, both the classical and the Christian traditions. This is a bold and largely unprecedented initiative in Western literature. In the *Confessions* Augustine struggles with and finally rejects the *Aeneid*: he describes how as a student he was seduced by the beauty of Virgil's poetry into weeping for the death of Dido while ignoring the spiritual death of his own soul. For Augustine the poem's poetic power was irresistible, but its meaning was worse than useless to the Christian; as another of the Church Fathers put it, the *Aeneid* was "a beautiful vase filled with vipers." For Virgil's poem celebrated the founding of an earthly empire and, worse, one that Jupiter prophesied would continue "without end" (book 1). In the *City of God*, written in part to defend Christians from the charge that it was their defection from Rome's traditional deities that had caused the sack of Rome by the Goths in 410, Augustine poured scorn on these words, "without end." For the Christian, nothing earthly can be eternal. For him there was only one city, the Heavenly Jerusalem, which was not a physical place at all but a condition of the soul—a vision of peace—available both in this life and in the life to come to those who have faith. The "eternal city" was not Rome but the City of God, populated by citizens faithful not to the emperor or the Roman deities but to the gospel of Jesus Christ.

But for Dante, as we have seen, Rome had a different meaning. For him, the establishment of the empire by Augustus, and the extension of Roman peace over the Western world, was the necessary precondition for the birth of Christ. It was not just one city among many but the source of an imperial order that was divinely sanctioned. For Dante, since Virgil was the prophet and celebrant of this empire, he was—although he could not know it—inspired in writing the *Aeneid* not by Jupiter but by the Christian God. This notion of Virgilian inspiration was furthered by a Christian interpretation of one of Virgil's early poems, the Fourth Eclogue. The poem begins in this way:

> Now comes the last age [prophesied] by the song of the Cumaean sybil; the great
> order of the ages is born anew; now the Virgin returns, now the reign of Saturn
> comes again; now a new child is sent down from heaven above.

It's easy enough to see how a devout reader could see in these words, and in the poem as a whole, a prophecy of the birth of Christ, although Virgil was in all likelihood actually thinking of a son born to some prominent Roman, perhaps even to Augustus. Dante believed that the second coming of Christ, and the fulfillment of history, was dependent upon the reestablishment of the imperial authority whose initial establishment Virgil had described in the *Aeneid*. This is why it is Virgil who in *Inferno* 1 prophesies the coming of the hound who will defeat the she-wolf and restore Italy by hunting her through all the cities of Italy—cities now torn by civil wars provoked by the *concupiscence* that the she-wolf represents, a sinfulness inherent in the flesh that Paul lamented (see Romans 5), and a quality that Augustine interpreted in political terms as the "the lust for domination." This hound will be the new Augustus (if Dante had anyone specific in mind it may have been either one of his patrons, Cangrande della Scala or, later, the Holy Roman Emperor, Henry VII). Apart from these details, however, the important point is that for Dante, Rome and its empire played a crucial role in history.

So part of the reason Virgil is chosen as the guide is that he is a poet who was divinely inspired to make known the meaning of history, a role that Dante assumes for himself as well—hence the political prophecies scattered throughout the poem. But Virgil is also chosen because he taught Dante what in *Inferno* 1 Dante calls "the noble style." What he means by this is that reading Virgil allowed him to move beyond the lyric love poetry that had characterized the early part of his career. This poetry was, as Dante's discussion in *Purgatorio* 24 and 26 makes clear, a necessary precondition to the writing of the *Comedy*. But it was Virgil who showed him that poetry might aspire to a vision of experience that dealt with the ultimate issues of life and death, and with a vision of the meaning of history. It was Virgil, in other words, who persuaded him that poetry could be a vehicle for moral and philosophical truth, and a means of self-fulfillment, as his final ratification of Dante's spiritual growth in *Purgatorio* 30 shows.

Yet despite the fact that Virgil is Dante's "master and author," there are important differences between them. Indeed, a central theme in both the *Inferno* and the *Purgatorio* is the fluctuation in the relationship between Dante and Virgil. Dante is usually submissive before Virgil, but there are moments when Virgil appears baffled and even inept. One of these occurs in canto 9 of the *Inferno,* when the devils in the City of Dis refuse Virgil entrance and he has to call upon a divine messenger sent from Heaven. In that canto the Furies threaten to bring Medusa in order to turn Dante to stone; Virgil makes Dante turn around and then covers up his eyes with both Dante's and his own hands. As soon as Virgil does this, Dante speaks—in the present tense— to the reader:

> O you possessed of sturdy intellects,
> observe the teaching that is hidden here
> beneath the veil of verses so obscure.

While Virgil the non-Christian covers up, Christian readers must *uncover:* they must interpret this action and this scene as a whole in order to understand the nature of the spiritual—not literal—threat posed by the Furies and Medusa. The answer has to do with the meaning of *petrification*, which in Christian terms means turning the heart to stone, being hard-hearted or *impenitent*; and the greatest source of impenitence is *despair*, which is the belief that you have committed sins so grave that they cannot be forgiven. The Furies are, for the Middle Ages, symbols of this despair, and despair is the condition of everyone in Hell, including Virgil: they have abandoned all hope of being saved. That is why in this very canto—canto 9—Dante mentions "the first circle, one whose only punishment is crippled hope" and Virgil mentions "Judas' circle," Judas representing the New Testament type of despair: according to medieval interpreters, Judas sinned more in hanging himself than in selling Christ. As a pagan, Virgil can *experience* this condition but cannot *understand* it: the despair or absence of hope at work here is Virgil's—he doesn't think they will get into the city of Dis—not Dante's; and the heavenly messenger who arrives is "full of high disdain" not only because of the useless resistance of the inhabitants of Dis but also because of Virgil's incapacity. To appreciate something of the subtlety of Dante's poetry, we should notice that this messenger opens the gate with a touch of his wand, or *verghetta*. In the Middle Ages the power of Virgil's poetry was such that there developed a tradition that he was a magician, perhaps even a soothsayer: we meet this tradition in canto 20, where Dante will have Virgil revise his own poem so as to distance himself from this accusation. But one of the effects of this connection between Virgil and magic was that the spelling of his name was revised from Vergil—in Latin his name is *Vergilius Maro*—to Virgil by assimilation with the Latin word for a magician's wand, which is *virga*. In other words, Virgil wields a *virga*. But here Virgil's powers fail him, and it is an angel of God—the God whom Virgil did not know—who wields the *verghetta*.

There are many examples of the way in which Dante marks the difference between Virgil's pre-Christian understanding and his own confident location within the context of Christian belief. The reader might want to compare, for instance, the description in *Aeneid* 6 of the souls awaiting their trip across the river Acheron with its rewriting in *Inferno* 3, or any of the other passages—indicated in the notes—where Dante draws directly upon the *Aeneid*. In addition to this indication of cultural and (for Dante) spiritual difference, Dante's relation to Virgil is not just literary but deeply emotional. Virgil may be a figure of authority, but he is also one of pathos, and nowhere more so than in the *Purgatorio*. There, in cantos 21 and 22, he meets his disciple Statius, the author of an epic poem that was, as Statius says, inspired by the *Aeneid*. More important is that Dante, quite unhistorically, presents Statius as having converted to Christianity by reading the lines from Virgil's Fourth Eclogue cited above. Statius says to Virgil,

> You did as he who goes by night and carries
> the lamp behind him—he is of no help
> to his own self but teaches those who follow.

Dante is here, even more anachronistically, having Statius apply to Virgil a description that in one of his treatises Augustine applied to the Jews: "O Jews, you carried in your hands the lamp of the law in order to show the way to others while you remained in the darkness." The point is twofold: Virgil is a classical version of Moses, who saw the promised land but could not himself enter; and Virgil is to Statius (and to Dante) as Moses is to Christ: he is the prefiguration, and they are the fulfillment. This sense of Virgil's exclusion from the ultimate reward of the righteous life is expressed with great poignancy in *Purgatorio* 30, where Virgil disappears from the poem to be replaced by Beatrice.

A further distinction between Dante and Virgil is generic: in canto 20, Virgil refers to his poem as "my high tragedy"; in the next canto, Dante calls his poem "my comedy" (the epithet "Divine" was not added until the sixteenth century). What are the differences between tragedy and comedy? In the Middle Ages, there are essentially four. First, *narrative structure*: a tragedy begins in happiness and ends in misery, while a comedy works in reverse, so that Dante begins in Hell and ends in Paradise. Second, *style*: tragedy is exalted in style, while comedy can indulge in a range of styles, and we see this in the *Inferno*, for example, where canto 21 provides a wonderful scene of a group of naughty devils who tease Virgil by pretending to be Roman soldiers but then, as they set off on their march, signal their departure with an obscene gesture—the leader "made a trumpet of his ass." Third, *character*: a tragedy deals with important historical figures (and for the Middle Ages the term *tragedy* indicated that the narrative was historically true), while a comedy deals with all sorts of people, the common as well as the high-born—and certainly this is true of Dante's poem. And fourth, *subject matter*: tragedy deals with events of grand historical importance while comedy deals with people's private or inward lives.

We can understand this last, most important difference in the way Dante manipulates the word "pity" (*pietà* in the Italian). This is the Italian version of the key Virgilian term *pietas*: for Virgil piety means essentially a dutiful or obedient compliance to a larger responsibility—one that in fact entails the abandonment of one's own personal or inner self. But for Dante *pietà* means pity or compassion. In Virgil *pietas* is always a moral good; but in Dante it is not. In canto 2, for instance, Virgil explains that Beatrice feels compassion or *pietà* for Dante, but that the sufferings of those in Hell, including Virgil himself, do not touch her. It would have been wrong for her to feel pity for Virgil: everyone in Hell is there as an effect not just of God's justice but of his love as well, as the inscription over the gate in canto 4 tells us. As Virgil says to Dante in one of the several times when he is misled into sympathizing with the sufferings of the damned, "Here pity only lives when it is dead." In a larger sense, one of the central concerns of the poem is precisely what the protagonist feels and the shifts of his personality—the turmoil within his inner self—throughout the course of the journey he undertakes. This is clearly not true, for example, of Aeneas, who is pretty much denied any but the most obvious emotions—and often not many of them. Indeed, Aeneas's piety is fully accomplished precisely when he has sacrificed his personality in the interest of founding Rome, whereas *The Divine Comedy* is concerned throughout with the spiritual development of its protagonist.

The Divine Comedy is concerned as well with the spiritual development of its readers. As Augustine's *Confessions* make clear, for the medieval Christian reading was itself a spiritual action with serious moral consequences. One of the greatest impediments to Augustine's conversion was his inability to understand how the Hebrew Bible—with what he thought its unsophisticated language and outlandish narratives—could compete with either the wisdom available in Greek philosophy or the beautiful style of Latin poetry, or how it could be reconciled to Christian doctrine. But he learned, with the help of Bishop Ambrose of Milan, to read the Bible not literally but, as he calls it, spiritually. He means by this what we would call an allegorical reading. For example, throughout the Middle Ages the Song of Songs in the Hebrew Bible was read not as a love poem but as an allegory about the love of God for the individual soul, or of Christ for the Church, or of the Holy Spirit for the Virgin Mary. Moses, Isaac, Noah, and the other patriarchs were seen not just as leaders of Israel but as prefigurations of Christ. And so on: virtually every passage in the Hebrew Bible was interpreted so as to render it consistent with both the New Testament and Christian doctrine as defined by the Church. In 2 Corinthians 3.6 Paul says that "the letter kills but the spirit gives life": to read the Bible only literally, simply as a series of historical narratives, is not merely to miss its deeper significance but to place oneself in spiritual danger, to risk one's very soul. As Augustine argues, to read literally is to read carnally or corporeally, with the eye of the flesh; but to interpret is to read spiritually, with the eye of the heart.

We have already seen how at a crucial moment in the *Inferno* (canto 9) Virgil seeks to cover Dante's eyes while Dante himself urges the reader to uncover the meaning of the events being portrayed. Throughout the *Comedy,* and especially in the *Inferno,* the most corporeal of the three canticles, both Dante the pilgrim and the reader are tempted to read carnally or corporeally, to be distracted from the need for interpretation by the visually powerful scenes presented to them. An example is the account in canto 5 of Paolo and Francesca, who are located in the third circle, where the lustful are punished. These young lovers are here because they committed adultery, and the winds that blow them about are an infernal version of the gusts of desire that drove them in life. But if we stop here we will make the same mistake as does the pilgrim Dante, who feels for them exactly the wrong sort of pity. For Francesca's punishment is not to whirl about endlessly, locked in the arms of her beloved: after all, is that really a punishment? No, her punishment is to repeat throughout eternity the act of seduction that brought about her damnation; and Paolo's punishment is to watch her as she works her wiles. It is no accident that in the conversation with Dante and Virgil Paolo says not a word but only sobs; indeed, Francesca refers to him only once, with the contemptuous demonstrative pronoun *questi*, "*this one*, who never shall be parted from me." And whom does Francesca seduce? After listening to her tell her carefully crafted tale of love—one that incorporates within it lines from the kind of lyric poetry that Dante himself had written as a youth—Dante falls to the ground with pity. Indeed, his description is painfully apt: "And then I fell as a dead body falls"—an act all too appropriate for a man in Hell. Nor does Francesca's power stop at Dante, for it has worked its magic on generations of readers. The challenge of this scene is to remember its deep significance—that this woman is in Hell, that she is currently repeating the very sin that put her there—while she does everything in her power to make you forget.

The interpretive drama acted out in this scene is repeated throughout the *Inferno*. The poem is peopled with brilliantly realized personalities who engage in rhetorical subtleties that simultaneously conceal and yet reveal their moral corruption. Farinata and Cavalcanti, Pier delle Vigne, Brunetto Latini, Vanni Fucci, Ulysses, Guido da Montefeltro, Bertran de Born, Geri del Bello, Ugolino—these and more provide a human drama that is unsurpassed in Western literature. Yet we are simultaneously never allowed to forget that they are all damned by a divine justice that is, for Dante, infallible. We are simultaneously intrigued and wary, powerfully drawn toward these men and women whose personalities have here, in eternity, achieved their full and at times glorious potential and yet also on the alert for the full meaning of their words. Of all the accomplishments of this great poem, perhaps its most enduring achievement is its capacity to provide the reader with a virtually limitless sense of the deep meaningfulness that literature can provide. For Dante this meaningfulness derived from God, but whatever its source, we can still agree with those readers who thought the poem divine.

The notes to this selection have been kept to a minimum. Of the many excellent commentaries in English, one of the most complete is in the edition and translation by Charles S. Singleton (1970–75). An excellent commentary on the *Inferno* can be found in the edition and translation by Robert M. Durling and Ronald L. Martinez (1996), who are preparing similar volumes for the rest of the poem. Useful commentaries on individual cantos can also be found in Ricardo Quinones, *Dante* (1979). A rightly celebrated essay on *Inferno* 10, with important comments on the *Comedy* as a whole, is by Erich Auerbach in his *Mimesis*, and illuminating and learned essays by one of the leading English-speaking Dantists are in John Freccero, *Dante: The Poetics of Conversion* (1986). *Dante Studies* is published annually and includes an annotated bibliography.

PRONOUNCING GLOSSARY

The following list uses common English syllables to provide rough equivalents of selected words whose pronunciation may be unfamiliar to the general reader.

Abbagliato: *ah-bahl-lee-ah'-toh*

Aghinolfo: *ah-gee-nol'-foh*

Alichino: *a-lee-kee'-noh*

Bacchiglione: *bahk-eel-lee-oh'-nay*

Barbariccia: *bar-bar-eetch'-yah*

Caccia: *cah'-chyah*

Capocchio: *ka-pawk'-yoh*

Ciacco: *chyah'-koh*

Draghignazzo: *drah-gee-nyah'-zoh*

Focaccia: *foh-cah'-chyah*

Gianfigliazzi: *jyahn'-feel-yah-tzee*

Gianni Schicchi: *jyahn'-ee skee'-kee*

Hypsipyle: *hip-sip'-il-ay*

Maghinardo: *mah-ghee-nard'-oh*

Malebolge: *mahl-uh-bowl'-jay*

Malebranche: *mahl-uh-branck'-eh*

Paolo: *powl'-oh*

Peschiera: *pes-kee-ehr'-ah*

Puccio: *poo'-chyoh*

Rinier: *ree-nyay*

Romagna: *row-mah'-nyah*

Ruggieri: *roo-jyehr'-ee*

Tagliacozzo: *tah-lyah-cot'-soh*

Tegghiaio: *teh-gyai'-oh*

Thibault: *tee'-bow*

Uguiccione: *oo-gwee-chyoh'-nay*

Verrucchio: *vehr-oo'-kyoh*

STRUCTURE OF DANTE'S HELL
(SEE CANTO 11.16–111)

	Dark Wood	cantos 1–2
Circle I	Neutrals	canto 3
Circle II	Virtuous Heathen	canto 4
Circle III	Lustful	canto 5
Circle IV	Gluttons	canto 6
Circle V	Avaricious and Prodigal	canto 7
Circle VI	Wrathful	canto 8
	Heretics	cantos 9–10
Circle VII	violent against others	canto 12
	violent against self	canto 13
	violent against God, nature, and art	cantos 14–17
Circle VIII	i. panderers and seducers	canto 18
	ii. flatterers	
	iii. simonists	canto 19
	iv. diviners	canto 20
	v. barrators	cantos 21–22
	vi. hypocrites	canto 23
	vii. thieves	cantos 24–25
	viii. false counsellors	cantos 26–27
	ix. makers of discord	canto 28
	x. impersonators	cantos 29–30
Circle IX	Treacherous	
	i. Caina: to kindred	canto 32
	ii. Antenora: to country	canto 33
	iii. Ptolomea: to guests	
	iv. Judecca: to benefactors	canto 34
	Satan	

(WOLF)

(LION)

(LEOPARD)

STRUCTURE OF DANTE'S PURGATORY

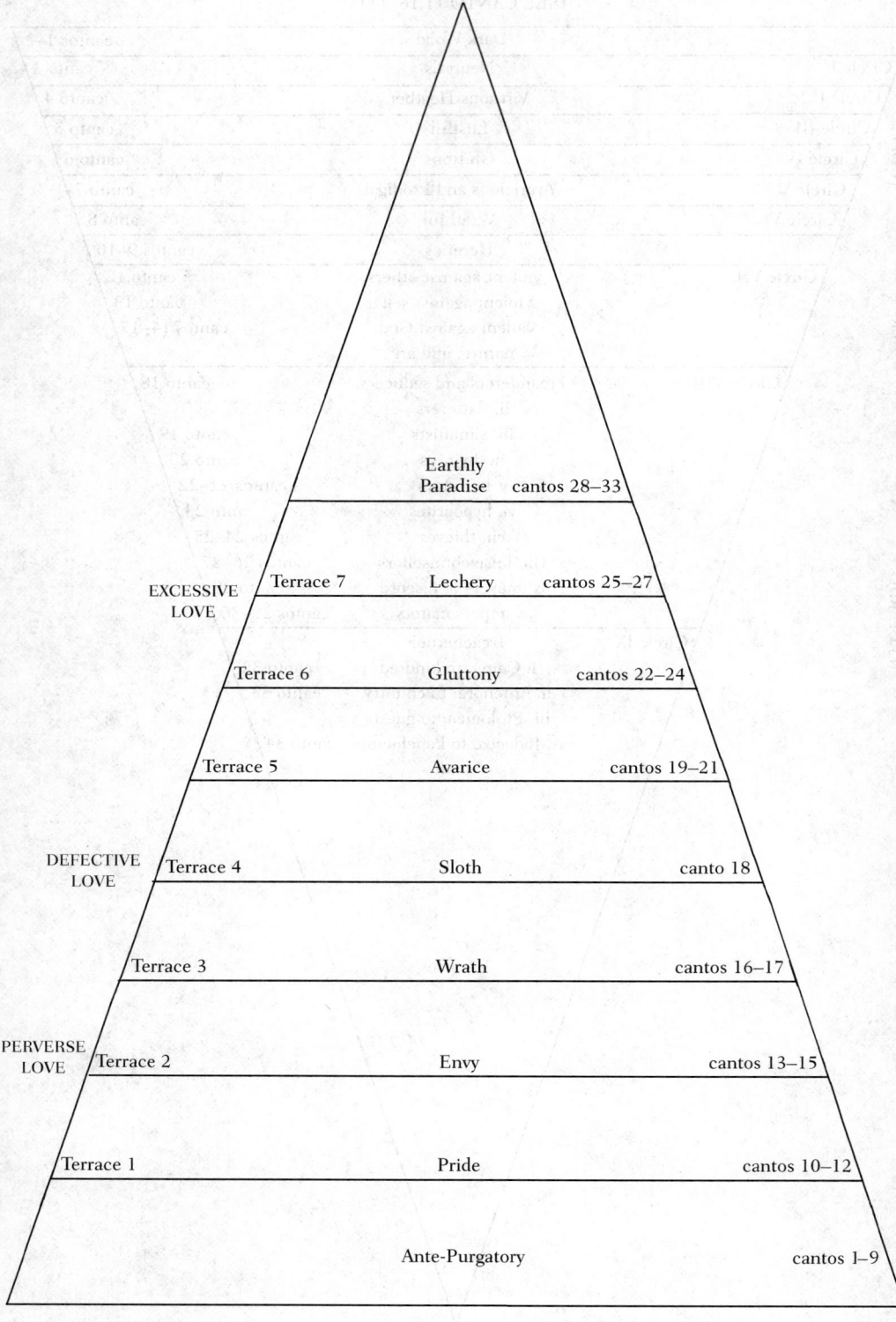

Earthly Paradise   cantos 28–33

EXCESSIVE LOVE

Terrace 7   Lechery   cantos 25–27

Terrace 6   Gluttony   cantos 22–24

Terrace 5   Avarice   cantos 19–21

DEFECTIVE LOVE

Terrace 4   Sloth   canto 18

Terrace 3   Wrath   cantos 16–17

PERVERSE LOVE

Terrace 2   Envy   cantos 13–15

Terrace 1   Pride   cantos 10–12

Ante-Purgatory   cantos 1–9

FROM THE DIVINE COMEDY[1]

Inferno

CANTO I

The voyager-narrator astray by night in a dark forest. Morning and the sunlit hill. Three beasts that impede his ascent. The encounter with Virgil, who offers his guidance and an alternative path through two of the three realms the voyager must visit.

When I had journeyed half of our life's way,[2]
I found myself within a shadowed forest,
for I had lost the path that does not stray.[3]
  Ah, it is hard to speak of what it was,
that savage forest, dense and difficult,   5
which even in recall renews my fear:
  so bitter—death is hardly more severe!
But to retell the good discovered there,
I'll also tell the other things I saw.
  I cannot clearly say how I had entered   10
the wood; I was so full of sleep[4] just at
the point where I abandoned the true path.[5]
  But when I'd reached the bottom of a hill—
it rose along the boundary of the valley
that had harassed my heart with so much fear—   15
  I looked on high and saw its shoulders clothed
already by the rays of that same planet[6]
which serves to lead men straight along all roads.
  At this my fear was somewhat quieted;
for through the night of sorrow I had spent,   20
the lake within my heart[7] felt terror present.
  And just as he who, with exhausted breath,
having escaped from sea to shore, turns back
to watch the dangerous waters he has quit,
  so did my spirit, still a fugitive,   25
turn back to look intently at the pass
that never has let any man survive.[8]
  I let my tired body rest awhile.
Moving again, I tried the lonely slope—
my firm foot always was the one below.   30
  And almost where the hillside starts to rise—
look there!—a leopard, very quick and lithe,

---

1. Translated by Allen Mandelbaum. The notes are by Mandelbaum and Lee Patterson.   2. Born in 1265, Dante was thirty-five in 1300, the fictional date of the poem. The biblical span of human life is seventy (see Psalms 90.10 and Isaiah 38.10).   3. See Proverbs 2.13–14 and 4.18–19, and also 2 Peter 2.15.   4. See Romans 13. 11–12.   5. See Psalms 23.3.   6. The sun, which in the astronomical system of Dante's time was a planet thought to revolve around the Earth.   7. This phrase referred to the inner chamber of the heart, a cavity that in the physiology of Dante's time was the physical location of fear. Not coincidentally, the *Inferno* ends at the lake of Cocytus (see 32.23).   8. This simile of Dante as the survivor of a passage through the sea invokes the story of the escape of the Israelites from Egypt through the Red Sea, a central metaphor throughout the *Comedy* (see *Purgatorio* 24. 46). See Exodus 14.

a leopard covered with a spotted hide.
   He did not disappear from sight, but stayed;
indeed, he so impeded my ascent
that I had often to turn back again.
   The time was the beginning of the morning;
the sun was rising now in fellowship
with the same stars that had escorted it
   when Divine Love first moved those things of beauty;[9]
so that the hour and the gentle season
gave me good cause for hopefulness on seeing
   that beast before me with his speckled skin;
but hope was hardly able to prevent
the fear I felt when I beheld a lion.
   His head held high and ravenous with hunger—
even the air around him seemed to shudder—
this lion seemed to make his way against me.
   And then a she-wolf showed herself; she seemed
to carry every craving in her leanness;
she had already brought despair to many.
   The very sight of her so weighted me
with fearfulness that I abandoned hope
of ever climbing up that mountain slope.[1]
   Even as he who glories while he gains
will, when the time has come to tally loss,
lament with every thought and turn despondent,
   so was I when I faced that restless beast,
which, even as she stalked me, step by step
had thrust me back to where the sun is speechless.
   While I retreated down to lower ground,
before my eyes there suddenly appeared
one who seemed faint because of the long silence.[2]
   When I saw him in that vast wilderness,
"Have pity on me," were the words I cried,
"whatever you may be—a shade, a man."
   He answered me: "Not man; I once was man.
Both of my parents came from Lombardy,
and both claimed Mantua as native city.[3]
   And I was born, though late, *sub Julio*,
and lived in Rome under the good Augustus—
the season of the false and lying gods.[4]
   I was a poet, and I sang the righteous
son of Anchises[5] who had come from Troy
when flames destroyed the pride of Ilium.
   But why do you return to wretchedness?
Why not climb up the mountain of delight,

35

40

45

50

55

60

65

70

75

---

9. The world was believed to have been created in spring, with the sun in the constellation of Aries.   **1.** The meaning of the leopard, lion, and she-wolf is open to a number of interpretations, the most plausible being that they represent the three major forms of sin found in Hell, respectively fraud, violence, and incontinence or immoderation (see 11. 78ff.). The structure of Hell indicates that the last is the least serious morally, but its role in this canto shows that it is the most difficult to overcome psychologically.   **2.** The Roman poet Virgil's voice has not been heard he died in 19 B.C.   **3.** Lombardy is the most northern area of Italy; Mantua is located to the east of Milan.   **4.** Virgil (70–19 B.C.) was born *sub Julio*, in the time of Julius Caesar (assassinated in 44 B.C.), who was regarded by Dante as the founder of the Roman Empire.   **5.** Aeneas, the hero of Virgil's *Aeneid*.

the origin and cause of every joy?"
    "And are you then that Virgil, you the fountain
that freely pours so rich a stream of speech?"   80
I answered him with shame upon my brow.
    "O light and honor of all other poets,
may my long study and the intense love
that made me search your volume serve me now.
You are my master and my author, you—   85
the only one from whom my writing drew
the noble style for which I have been honored.
    You see the beast that made me turn aside;
help me, o famous sage, to stand against her,
for she has made my blood and pulses shudder."   90
    "It is another path that you must take,"
he answered when he saw my tearfulness,
"if you would leave this savage wilderness;
    the beast that is the cause of your outcry
allows no man to pass along her track,   95
but blocks him even to the point of death;
    her nature is so squalid, so malicious
that she can never state her greedy will;
when she has fed, she's hungrier than ever.
    She mates with many living souls and shall   100
yet mate with many more, until the Greyhound[6]
arrives, inflicting painful death on her.
    That Hound will never feed on land or pewter,
but find his fare in wisdom, love, and virtue;
his place of birth shall be between two felts.[7]   105
    He will restore low-lying Italy
for which the maid Camilla died of wounds,
and Nisus, Turnus, and Euryalus.[8]
    And he will hunt that beast through every city
until he thrusts her back again to Hell,   110
from which she was first sent above by envy.
    Therefore, I think and judge it best for you
to follow me, and I shall guide you, taking
you from this place through an eternal place,
    where you shall hear the howls of desperation   115
and see the ancient spirits in their pain,
as each of them laments his second death;[9]
    and you shall see those souls who are content
within the fire,[1] for they hope to reach—
whenever that may be—the blessed people.[2]   120
    If you would then ascend as high as these,
a soul more worthy than I am[3] will guide you;
I'll leave you in her care when I depart,

6. Dante's prediction of a modern redeemer is so enigmatic that there can be no certainty of his identity.
Most commentators designate Cangrande (i.e., the great dog) della Scala of Verona, Dante's benefactor
after his exile from Florence.   7. Those who opt for Cangrande as the redeemer note that Feltre and
Montefeltro are towns that roughly mark the limits of Cangrande's domains. But other interpretations are
possible.   8. Characters in the *Aeneid* who die during Aeneas's conquest of Italy.   9. The second death
is damnation; see Revelation 21.8.   1. The souls in Purgatory.   2. The saved in Paradise.
3. Beatrice.

because that Emperor who reigns above,
since I have been rebellious to His law,
will not allow me entry to His city.   125
   He governs everywhere, but rules from there;
there is His city, His high capital:
o happy those He chooses to be there!"
   And I replied: "O poet—by that God   130
whom you had never come to know—I beg you,
that I may flee this evil and worse evils,
   to lead me to the place of which you spoke,
that I may see the gateway of Saint Peter
and those whom you describe as sorrowful."   135
   Then he set out, and I moved on behind him.

CANTO II

The following evening. Invocation to the Muses. The narrator's
questioning of his worthiness to visit the deathless world. Virgil's
comforting explanation that he has been sent to help Dante by three
Ladies of Heaven. The voyager heartened. Their setting out.

The day was now departing; the dark air
released the living beings of the earth
from work and weariness; and I myself
   alone prepared to undergo the battle
both of the journeying and of the pity,   5
which memory, mistaking not, shall show.
   O Muses, o high genius, help me now;
o memory that set down what I saw,
here shall your excellence reveal itself!
   I started: "Poet, you who are my guide,   10
see if the force in me is strong enough
before you let me face that rugged pass.
   You say that he who fathered Sylvius,[4]
while he was still corruptible, had journeyed
into the deathless world with his live body.   15
   For, if the Enemy of every evil
was courteous to him, considering
all he would cause and who and what he was,
   that does not seem incomprehensible,
since in the empyrean heaven he was chosen   20
to father honored Rome and her empire;
   and if the truth be told, Rome and her realm
were destined to became the sacred place,
the seat of the successor of great Peter.[5]
   And through the journey you ascribe to him,   25
he came to learn of things that were to bring
his victory and, too, the papal mantle.
   Later the Chosen Vessel[6] travelled there,
to bring us back assurance of that faith

---

4. Aeneas in *Aeneid* 6.   5 The apostle Peter is considered by the Catholic Church to be the first
pope.   6. St. Paul; see 2 Corinthians 12.2–4.

with which the way to our salvation starts.   30
    But why should I go there? Who sanctions it?
For I am not Aeneas, am not Paul;
nor I nor others think myself so worthy.
    Therefore, if I consent to start this journey,
I fear my venture may be wild and empty.   35
You're wise; you know far more than what I say."
    And just as he who unwills what he wills
and shifts what he intends to seek new ends
so that he's drawn from what he had begun,
    so was I in the midst of that dark land,   40
because, with all my thinking, I annulled
the task I had so quickly undertaken.
    "If I have understood what you have said,"
replied the shade of that great-hearted one,
"your soul has been assailed by cowardice,   45
    which often weighs so heavily on a man—
distracting him from honorable trials—
as phantoms frighten beasts when shadows fall.
    That you may be delivered from this fear,
I'll tell you why I came and what I heard   50
when I first felt compassion for your pain.
    I was among those souls who are suspended;[7]
a lady called to me, so blessed, so lovely
that I implored to serve at her command.
    Her eyes surpassed the splendor of the star's;   55
and she began to speak to me—so gently
and softly—with angelic voice. She said:
    'O spirit of the courteous Mantuan,
whose fame is still a presence in the world,
and shall endure as long as the world lasts,   60
    my friend, who has not been the friend of fortune,
is hindered in his path along that lonely
hillside; he has been turned aside by terror.
    From all that I have heard of him in Heaven,
he is, I fear, already so astray   65
that I have come to help him much too late.
    Go now; with your persuasive word, with all
that is required to see that he escapes,
bring help to him, that I may be consoled.
    For I am Beatrice who send you on;   70
I come from where I most long to return;[8]
Love prompted me, that Love which makes me speak.
    When once again I stand before my Lord,
then I shall often let Him hear your praises.'
Now Beatrice was silent. I began: 75
    'O Lady of virtue, the sole reason why
the human race surpasses all that lies
beneath the heaven with the smallest sphere,[9]
    so welcome is your wish, that even if

7. In Limbo, where the souls are "neither sad nor joyous" (4.84).   8. Paradise.   9. The moon.

it were already done, it would seem tardy;   80
all you need do is let me know your will.

But tell me why you have not been more prudent—
descending to this center, moving from
that spacious place where you long to return?'

'Because you want to fathom things so deeply,   85
I now shall tell you promptly,' she replied,
'why I am not afraid to enter here.

One ought to be afraid of nothing other
than things possessed of power to do us harm,
but things innocuous need not be feared.   90

God, in His graciousness, has made me so
that this, your misery, cannot touch me;
I can withstand the fires flaming here.

In Heaven there's a gentle lady[1]—one
who weeps for the distress toward which I send you,   95
so that stern judgment up above is shattered.

And it was she who called upon Lucia,[2]
requesting of her: "Now your faithful one
has need of you, and I commend him to you."

Lucia, enemy of every cruelty,   100
arose and made her way to where I was,
sitting beside the venerable Rachel.[3]

She said: "You, Beatrice, true praise of God,
why have you not helped him who loved you so
that—for your sake—he's left the vulgar crowd?   105

Do you not hear the anguish in his cry?
Do you not see the death he wars against
upon that river ruthless as the sea?"[4]

No one within this world has ever been
so quick to seek his good or flee his harm   110
as I—when she had finished speaking thus—

to come below, down from my blessed station;
I trusted in your honest utterance,
which honors you and those who've listened to you.'

When she had finished with her words to me,   115
she turned aside her gleaming, tearful eyes,
which only made me hurry all the more.

And, just as she had wished, I came to you:
I snatched you from the path of the fierce beast
that barred the shortest way up the fair mountain.   120

What is it then? Why, why do you resist?
Why does your heart host so much cowardice?
Where are your daring and your openness

as long as there are three such blessed women
concerned for you within the court of Heaven   125
and my words promise you so great a good?"

As little flowers, which the chill of night
has bent and huddled, when the white sun strikes,

---

1. The Virgin Mary.   2. St. Lucy, a third-century martyr and the patron saint of sight.   3. Rachel
signifies the contemplative life: see Genesis 29.16–17.   4. These are the waters of 1.22–24.

grow straight and open fully on their stems,
　so did I, too, with my exhausted force;　　　　　　　130
and such warm daring rushed into my heart
that I—as one who has been freed—began:
"O she, compassionate, who has helped me!
And you who, courteous, obeyed so quickly
　the true words that she had addressed to you!　　135
　You, with your words, have so disposed my heart
to longing for this journey—I return
to what I was at first prepared to do.
　Now go; a single will fills both of us:
you are my guide, my governor, my master."　　　140
These were my words to him; when he advanced,
　I entered on the steep and savage path.

CANTO III

The inscription above the Gate of Hell. The Ante-Inferno, where the
shades of those who lived without praise and without blame now
intermingle with the neutral angels. He who made the great refusal. The
River Acheron. Charon. Dante's loss of his senses as the earth trembles.

THROUGH ME THE WAY INTO THE SUFFERING CITY,
THROUGH ME THE WAY TO THE ETERNAL PAIN,
THROUGH ME THE WAY THAT RUNS AMONG THE LOST.
　JUSTICE URGED ON MY HIGH ARTIFICER;
MY MAKER WAS DIVINE AUTHORITY,　　　　　　　　5
THE HIGHEST WISDOM, AND THE PRIMAL LOVE.[5]
　BEFORE ME NOTHING BUT ETERNAL THINGS
WERE MADE, AND I ENDURE ETERNALLY.
ABANDON EVERY HOPE, WHO ENTER HERE.
　These words—their aspect was obscure—I read　　10
inscribed above a gateway, and I said:
"Master, their meaning is difficult for me."
　And he to me, as one who comprehends:
"Here one must leave behind all hesitation;
here every cowardice must meet its death.　　　　15
　For we have reached the place of which I spoke,
where you will see the miserable people,
those who have lost the good of the intellect."[6]
　And when, with gladness in his face, he placed
his hand upon my own, to comfort me,　　　　　　20
he drew me in among the hidden things.
　Here sighs and lamentations and loud cries
were echoing across the starless air,
so that, as soon as I set out, I wept.
　Strange utterances, horrible pronouncements,　　25
accents of anger, words of suffering,
and voices shrill and faint, and beating hands—
　all went to make a tumult that will whirl
forever through that turbid, timeless air,

---

5. God as Father, Son, and Holy Ghost.　6. *The good of the intellect:* i.e., God.

like sand that eddies when a whirlwind swirls.   30
    And I—my head oppressed by horror—said:
"Master, what is it that I hear? Who are
those people so defeated by their pain?"
    And he to me: "This miserable way
is taken by the sorry souls of those   35
who lived without disgrace and without praise.[7]
    They now commingle with the coward angels,
the company of those who were not rebels
nor faithful to their God, but stood apart.
    The heavens, that their beauty not be lessened,   40
have cast them out, nor will deep Hell receive them—
even the wicked cannot glory in them."
    And I: "What is it, master, that oppresses
these souls, compelling them to wail so loud?"
He answered: "I shall tell you in few words.   45
    Those who are here can place no hope in death,
and their blind life is so abject that they
are envious of every other fate.
    The world will let no fame of theirs endure;
both justice and compassion must disdain them;   50
let us not talk to them, but look and pass."
    And I, looking more closely, saw a banner
that, as it wheeled about, raced on—so quick
that any respite seemed unsuited to it.
    Behind that banner trailed so long a file   55
of people—I should never have believed
that death could have unmade so many souls.
    After I had identified a few,
I saw and recognized the shade of him[8]
who made, through cowardice, the great refusal.   60
    At once I understood with certainty:
this company contained the cowardly,
hateful to God and to His enemies.
    These wretched ones, who never were alive,
went naked and were stung again, again   65
by horseflies and by wasps that circled them.
    The insects streaked their faces with their blood,
which, mingled with their tears, fell at their feet,
where it was gathered up by sickening worms.
    And then, looking beyond them, I could see   70
a crowd along the bank of a great river;
at which I said: "Allow me now to know
    who are these people—master—and what law
has made them seem so eager for the crossing,
as I can see despite the feeble light."   75
    And he to me: "When we have stopped along
the melancholy shore of Acheron,[9]
then all these matters will be plain to you."

---

7. Those who declined to choose between good and evil.   8. Pope Celestine V, who was elected pope in July 1294 and then resigned five months later.   9. The first of the four rivers of Hell.

At that, with eyes ashamed, downcast, and fearing
that what I said had given him offense,
I did not speak until we reached the river.   80

And here, advancing toward us, in a boat,
an aged man[1]—his hair was white with years—
was shouting: "Woe to you, corrupted souls!

Forget your hope of ever seeing Heaven: 85
I come to lead you to the other shore,
to the eternal dark, to fire and frost.

And you approaching there, you living soul,
keep well away from these—they are the dead."
But when he saw I made no move to go,   90

he said: "Another way and other harbors—
not here—will bring you passage to your shore:
a lighter craft will have to carry you."

My guide then: "Charon, don't torment yourself:
our passage has been willed above, where One   95
can do what He has willed; and ask no more."

Now silence fell upon the wooly cheeks
of Charon, pilot of the livid marsh,
whose eyes were ringed about with wheels of flame.

But all those spirits, naked and exhausted,   100
had lost their color, and they gnashed their teeth
as soon as they heard Charon's cruel words;

they execrated God and their own parents
and humankind, and then the place and time
of their conception's seed and of their birth.   105

Then they forgathered, huddled in one throng,
weeping aloud along that wretched shore
which waits for all who have no fear of God.

The demon Charon, with his eyes like embers,
by signaling to them, has all embark;   110
his oar strikes anyone who stretches out.

As, in the autumn, leaves detach themselves,[2]
first one and then the other, till the bough
sees all its fallen garments on the ground,

similarly, the evil seed of Adam   115
descended form the shoreline one by one,
when signaled, as a falcon—called—will come.

So do they move across the darkened waters;
even before they reach the farther shore,
new ranks already gather on this bank.   120

"My son," the gracious master said to me,
"those who have died beneath the wrath of God,
all these assmeble here from every country;

and they are eager for the river crossing
because celestial justice spurs them on,   125
so that their fear is turned into desire.

No good soul ever takes its passage here;
therefore, if Charon has complained of you,

---

1. Charon; see *Aeneid* 6.   2. This simile is a rewriting of one in *Aeneid* 6.

by now you can be sure what his words mean."
    And after this was said, the darkened plain   130
quaked so tremendously—the memory
of terror then, bathes me in sweat again.
    A whirlwind burst out of the tear-drenched earth,[3]
a wind that crackled with a bloodred light,
a light that overcame all of my senses;   135
    and like a man whom sleep has seized, I fell.

CANTO IV

*Dante's awakening to the First Circle, or Limbo, inhabited by those who
were worthy but lived before Christianity and/or without baptism. The
welcoming of Virgil and Dante by Homer, Horace, Ovid, Lucan. The
catalogue of other great-hearted spirits in the noble castle of Limbo.*

The heavy sleep within my head was smashed
by an enormous thunderclap, so that
I started up as one whom force awakens;
    I stood erect and turned my rested eyes
from side to side, and I stared steadily   5
to learn what place it was surrounding me.
    In truth I found myself upon the brink
of an abyss, the melancholy valley
containing thundering, unending wailings.
    That valley, dark and deep and filled with mist,   10
is such that, though I gazed into its pit,
I was unable to discern a thing.
    "Let us descend into the blind world now,"
the poet, who was deathly pale, began;
"I shall go first and you will follow me."   15
    But I, who'd seen the change in his complexion,
said: "How shall I go on if you are frightened,
you who have always helped dispel my doubts?"
    And he to me: "The anguish of the people
whose place is here below, has touched my face   20
with the compassion you mistake for fear.
    Let us go on, the way that waits is long."
So he set out, and so he had me enter
on that first circle girdling the abyss.
    Here, for as much as hearing could discover,   25
there was no outcry louder than the sighs
that caused the everlasting air to tremble.
    The sighs arose from sorrow without torments,
out of the crowds—the many multitudes—
of infants and of women and of men.   30
    The kindly master said: "Do you not ask
who are these spirits whom you see before you?
I'd have you know, before you go ahead,
    they did not sin; and yet, though they have merits,

---

3. The science of Dante's time explained earthquakes as caused by the escape of pent-up vapors; it is while
he is unconscious that Dante crosses Acheron into Hell proper.

that's not enough, because they lacked baptism,   35
the portal of the faith that you embrace.
     And if they lived before Christianity,
they did not worship God in fitting ways;
and of such spirits I myself am one.
     For these defects, and for no other evil,   40
we now are lost and punished just with this:
we have no hope and yet we live in longing."
     Great sorrow seized my heart on hearing him,
for I had seen some estimable men
among the souls suspended in that limbo.[4]   45
     "Tell me, my master, tell me, lord," I then
began because I wanted to be certain
of that belief which vanquishes all errors,
     "did any ever go—by his own merit
or others'—from this place toward blessedness?"   50
And he, who understood my covert speech,
     replied:[5] "I was new-entered on this state
when I beheld a Great Lord enter here;
the crown he wore, a sign of victory.
     He carried off the shade of our first father,[6]   55
of his son Abel, and the shade of Noah,
of Moses, the obedient legislator,
     of father Abraham, David the king
of Israel, his father, and his sons,
and Rachel, she for whom he worked so long,   60
     and many others—and He made them blessed;
and I should have you know that, before them,
there were no human souls that had been saved."
     We did not stay our steps although he spoke;
we still continued onward through the wood—   65
the wood, I say, where many spirits thronged.
     Our path had not gone far beyond the point
where I had slept, when I beheld a fire
win out against a hemisphere of shadows.
     We still were at a little distance from it,   70
but not so far I could not see in part
that honorable men possessed that place.
     "O you who honor art and science both,
who are these souls whose dignity has kept
their way of being, separate from the rest?"   75
     And he to me: "The honor of their name,
which echoes up above within your life,
gains Heaven's grace, and that advances them."
     Meanwhile there was a voice that I could hear:
"Pay honor to the estimable poet;   80
his shadow, which had left us, now returns."
     After that voice was done, when there was silence,

---

4. Limbo is the location of unbaptized infants and virtuous pagans who lived before the birth of
Christic.   5. Virgil here describes the Harrowing of Hell, when after being crucified—according to the
Apocryphal Gospel of Nicodemus and confirmed by the medieval Church—Christ descended into Hell and
rescued the souls of the righteous of Israel; see also 12.44.   6. Adam.

I saw four giant shades approaching us;
in aspect, they were neither sad nor joyous.
    My kindly master then began by saying: 85
"Look well at him who holds that sword in hand,
who moves before the other three as lord.
    That shade is Homer, the consummate poet;
the other one is Horace, satirist;
the third is Ovid, and the last is Lucan.[7]   90
    Because each of these spirits shares with me
the name called out before by the lone voice,
they welcome me—and, doing that, do well."
    And so I saw that splendid school assembled,
led by the lord of song incomparable,   95
who like an eagle soars above the rest.
    Soon after they had talked a while together,
they turned to me, saluting cordially;
and having witnessed this, my master smiled;
    and even greater honor then was mine,   100
for they invited me to join their ranks—
I was the sixth among such intellects.
    So did we move along and toward the light,
talking of things about which silence here
is just as seemly as our speech was there.   105
    We reached the base of an exalted castle,[8]
encircled seven times by towering walls,
defended all around by a fair stream.
    We forded this as if upon hard ground;
I entered seven portals with these sages;   110
we reached a meadow of green flowering plants.[9]
    The people here had eyes both grave and slow;
their features carried great authority;
they spoke infrequently, with gentle voices.
    We drew aside to one part of the meadow,   115
an open place on both high and filled with light,
and we could see all those who were assembled.[1]
    Facing me there, on the enameled green,
great-hearted souls were shown to me and I
still glory in my having witnessed them.   120
    I saw Electra with her many comrades,
among whom I knew Hector and Aeneas,
and Caesar,[2] in his armor, falcon-eyed.
    I saw Camilla and Penthesilea
and, on the other side, saw King Latinus,   125
who sat beside Lavinia, his daughter.[3]
    I saw that Brutus who drove Tarquin out,

---

7. Horace, Ovid, and Lucan are famous Roman poets.   8. Commentators have suggested that this is a Castle of Fame, its seven walls symbolizing the seven liberal arts, a systemization of knowledge developed in the classical period.   9. A scene reminiscent of the classical Elysian fields (see *Aeneid* 6).   1. See *Aeneid* 6.   2. Julius Caesar (d. 44 B.C.) *Electra*: the mother of Dardanus, the founder of Troy. *Hector*: the leading warrior of the Trojans in the *Iliad*. *Aeneas*: the hero of the *Aeneid*.   3. Heiress to King Latinus who ruled the area of Italy where Rome was later located and who married Aeneas. *Camilla*: a female warrior in the *Aeneid*, where she is compared to Penthesilea, who fought for the Trojans against the Greeks.

Lucretia, Julia, Marcia, and Cornelia,
and, solitary, set apart, Saladin.[4]
    When I had raised my eyes a little higher,   30
I saw the master of the men who know,[5]
seated in philosophic family.
    There all look up to him, all do him honor:
there I beheld both Socrates and Plato,
closest to him, in front of all the rest;   135
    Democritus, who ascribes the world to chance,
Diogenes, Empedocles, and Zeno,
and Thales, Anaxagoras, Heraclitus;
    I saw the good collector of medicinals,
I mean Dioscorides; and I saw Orpheus,   140
and Tully, Linus, moral Seneca;[6]
    and Euclid the geometer, and Ptolemy,
Hippocrates and Galen, Avicenna,
Averroës,[7] of the great Commentary.
    I cannot here describe them all in full;   145
my ample theme impels me onward so:
what's told is often less than the event.
    The company of six divides in two;
my knowing guide leads me another way,
beyond the quiet, into trembling air.   150
And I have reached a part where no thing gleams.

CANTO V

*The Second Circle, where the Lustful are forever buffeted by violent
storm. Minos. The catalogue of carnal sinners. Francesca da Rimini and
her brother-in-law, Paolo Malatesta. Francesca's tale of their love and
death, at which Dante faints.*

So I descended from the first enclosure
down to the second circle, that which girdles
less space but grief more great, that goads to weeping.
    There dreadful Minos[8] stands, gnashing his teeth:
examining the sins of those who enter,   5
he judges and assigns as his tail twines.
    I mean that when the spirit born to evil
appears before him, it confesses all;
and he, the connoisseur of sin, can tell
the depth in Hell appropriate to it;   10

---

4. Admired for his chivalry in fighting against the crusaders, he was sultan of Egypt and Syria and died in 1193. *Brutus:* not the Brutus who killed Julius Caesar, but an earlier Roman who drove out the tyrant Tarquin. All four of the women mentioned were virtuous Roman matrons.   5. Aristotle (384–322 B.C.), Greek philosopher. The men mentioned in lines 132–38 are Greek philosophers of the seventh through the fourth centuries B.C.   6. Roman philosopher and dramatist (d. A.D. 65). *Dioscorides:* Greek physician (first century A.D.) *Orpheus:* mythical Greek poet. *Tully:* Cicero (d. 43 B.C.), Roman orator. *Seneca:* mythical Greek poet.   7. Avicenna (d. 1037) and Averroës (d. 1198) were Islamic philosophers who wrote commentaries on Aristotle's works that were highly influential in Christian Europe. *Euclid:* Greek mathematician (fourth century B.C.). *Ptolemy:* Greek astronomer and geographer (first century A.D.) credited with devising the cosomological system that was accepted until the time of Copernicus in the sixteenth century (hence the term *Ptolomaic universe*). *Hippocrates and Galen:* Greek physicians (fourth and second centuries B.C., respectively).   8. In *Aeneid* 6 Minos is described as judge of the underworld.

as many times as Minos wraps his tail
around himself, that marks the sinner's level.

    Always there is a crowd that stands before him:
each soul in turn advances toward that judgment;
they speak and hear, then they are cast below.   15

    Arresting his extraordinary task,
Minos, as soon as he had seen me, said:
"O you who reach this house of suffering,

    be careful how you enter, whom you trust;
the gate is wide,[9] but do not be deceived!"   20
To which my guide replied: "But why protest?

    Do not attempt to block his fated path:
our passage has been willed above, where One
can do what He has willed; and ask no more."

    Now notes of desperation have begun   25
to overtake my hearing; now I come
where mighty lamentation beats against me.

    I reached a place where every light is muted,
which bellows like the sea beneath a tempest,
when it is battered by opposing winds.   30

    The hellish hurricane, which never rests,
drives on the spirits with its violence:
wheeling and pounding, it harasses them.

    When they come up against the ruined slope,[1]
then there are cries and wailing and lament,   35
and there they curse the force of the divine.

    I learned that those who undergo this torment
are damned because they sinned within the flesh,
subjecting reason to the rule of lust.

    And as, in the cold season, starlings' wings   40
bear them along in broad and crowded ranks,
so does that blast bear on the guilty spirits:

    now here, now there, now down, now up, it drives them.
There is no hope that ever comforts them—
no hope for rest and none for lesser pain.   45

    And just as cranes in flight will chant their lays,
arraying their long file across the air,
so did the shades I saw approaching, borne

    by that assailing wind, lament and moan;
so that I asked him: "Master, who are those   50
who suffer punishment in this dark air?"

    "The first of those about whose history
you want to know," my master then told me,
"once ruled as empress over many nations.

    Her vice of lust became so customary   55
that she made license licit in her laws
to free her from the scandal she had caused.

    She is Semíramis,[2] of whom we read

---

9. Matthew 7.13.   1. A reference to the earthquake that occurred after the death of Christ (Matthew
27.51); see also 12.45.   2. Renowned for licentiousness, a mythical queen of Assyria. Because both the
capital of Assyria and Old Cairo were known as Babylon, her land is here confused with that ruled by the
sultan of Egypt.

that she was Ninus' wife and his successor:
she held the land the Sultan now commands.   60
    That other spirit killed herself for love,
and she betrayed the ashes of Sychaeus;
the wanton Cleopatra[3] follows next.
    See Helen, for whose sake so many years
of evil had to pass; see great Achilles,[4]   65
who finally met love—in his last battle.
    See Paris, Tristan[5] . . ."—and he pointed out
and named to me more than a thousand shades
departed from our life because of love.
    No sooner had I heard my teacher name   70
the ancient ladies and the knights, than pity
seized me, and I was like a man astray.
    My first words: "Poet, I should willingly
speak with those two[6] who go together there
and seem so lightly carried by the wind."   75
    And he to me: "You'll see when they draw closer
to us, and then you may appeal to them
by that love which impels them. They will come."
    No sooner had the wind bent them toward us
than I urged on my voice: "O battered souls,   80
if One does not forbid it, speak with us."
    Even as doves when summoned by desire,
borne forward by their will, move through the air
with wings uplifted, still, to their sweet nest,
    those spirits left the ranks where Dido suffers, 85
approaching us through the malignant air;
so powerful had been my loving cry.
    "O living being, gracious and benign,
who through the darkened air have come to visit
our souls that stained the world with blood, if He   90
    who rules the universe were friend to us,
then we should pray to Him to give you peace,
for you have pitied our atrocious state.
    Whatever pleases you to hear and speak
will please us, too, to hear and speak with you,   95
now while the wind is silent, in this place.
    The land where I was born lies on that shore
to which the Po[7] together with the waters
that follow it descends to final rest.
    Love,[8] that can quickly seize the gentle heart, 100
took hold of him because of the fair body
taken from me—how that was done still wounds me.
    Love, that releases no beloved from loving,

---

3. Who killed herself after the death of her lover, Marc Antony, in 30 B.C. *That other spirit*: Dido, widow of Sychaeus, whose suicide for love of Aeneas is described in *Aeneid* 4.   4. The medieval version of the Troy story described Achilles as enamored of a Trojan princess, Polyxena, and killed in an ambush set by Paris when he went to meet her. Helen's seduction by Paris (see line 67 below) was the cause of the Trojan War.   5. The lover of Iseult, wife of his lord King Mark.   6. Francesca da Rimini and her brother-in-law Paolo Malatesta.   7. A river in northern Italy. *The land*: Ravenna, a city on the Adriatic coast in northeastern Italy.   8. Cf. the next nine lines to the poems by Guido Guinizzelli and Dante included in *Medieval Lyrics: A Selection* (pp. 1215 and 1217).

took hold of me so strongly through his beauty
that, as you see, it has not left me yet.   105
    Love led the two of us unto one death.
Caïna waits for him[9] who took our life."
These words were borne across from them to us.
    When I had listened to those injured souls,
I bent my head and held it low until   110
the poet asked of me: "What are you thinking?"
    When I replied, my words began: "Alas,
how many gentle thoughts, how deep a longing,
had led them to the agonizing pass!"
    Then I addressed my speech again to them,   115
and I began: "Francesca, your afflictions
move me to tears of sorrow and of pity.
    But tell me, in the time of gentle sighs,
with what and in what way did Love allow you
to recognize your still uncertain longings?"   120
    And she to me: "There is no greater sorrow
than thinking back upon a happy time
in misery—and this your teacher knows.
    Yet if you long so much to understand
the first root of our love, then I shall tell   125
my tale to you as one who weeps and speaks.
    One day, to pass the time away, we read
of Lancelot[1]—how love had overcome him.
We were alone, and we suspected nothing.
    And time and time again that reading led   130
our eyes to meet, and made our faces pale,
and yet one point alone defeated us.
    When we had read how the desired smile
was kissed by one who was so true a lover,
this one, who never shall be parted from me,   135
while all his body trembled, kissed my mouth.
A Gallehault[2] indeed, that book and he
who wrote it, too; that day we read no more."
    And while one spirit said these words to me,
the other wept, so that—because of pity—   140
I fainted, as if I had met my death.
And then I fell as a dead body falls.

CANTO VI

*Dante's awakening to the Third Circle, where the Gluttonous, supine, are
flailed by cold and filthy rain and tormented by Cerberus. Ciacco and his
prophecy concerning Florence. The state of the damned after the
Resurrection.*

    Upon my mind's reviving—it had closed
on hearing the lament of those two kindred,

---

9. Gianciotto Malatesta, Francesca's husband and Paolo's brother. *Caïna:* The circle of Cain (described
in canto 32), where those who killed their kin are punished.   **1.** In Arthurian legend, the lover of Arthur's
wife, Guinevere.   **2.** The knight who, in the French romance being read by the lovers, acted as a go-
between for Lancelot and Guinevere.

since sorrow had confounded me completely—
    I see new sufferings, new sufferers
surrounding me on every side, wherever   5
I move or turn about or set my eyes.

    I am in the third circle, filled with cold,
unending, heavy, and accursèd rain;
its measure and its kind are never changed.

    Gross hailstones, water gray with filth, and snow   10
come streaking down across the shadowed air;
the earth, as it receives that shower, stinks.

    Over the souls of those submerged beneath
that mess, is an outlandish, vicious beast,
his three throats barking, doglike: Cerberus.[3]   15

    His eyes are bloodred; greasy, black, his beard;
his belly bulges, and his hands are claws;
his talons tear and flay and rend the shades.

    That downpour makes the sinners howl like dogs;
they use one of their sides to screen the other—   20
those miserable wretches turn and turn.

    When Cerberus, the great worm, noticed us,
he opened wide his mouths, showed us his fangs;
there was no part of him that did not twitch.

    My guide opened his hands to their full span,   25
plucked up some earth, and with his fists filled full
he hurled it straight into those famished jaws.

    Just as a dog that barks with greedy hunger
will then fall quiet when he gnaws his food,
intent and straining hard to cram it in,   30

    so were the filthy faces of the demon
Cerberus transformed—after he'd stunned
the spirits so, they wished that they were deaf.

    We walked across the shades on whom there thuds
that heavy rain, and set our soles upon   35
their empty images that seem like persons.

    And all those spirits lay upon the ground,
except for one[4] who sat erect as soon
as he caught sight of us in front of him.

    "O you who are conducted through this Hell,"   40
he said to me, "recall me, if you can;
for you, before I was unmade, were made."[5]

    And I to him: "It is perhaps your anguish
that snatches you out of my memory,
so that it seems that I have never seen you.   45

    But tell me who you are, you who are set
in such a dismal place, such punishment—
if other pains are more, none's more disgusting."

    And he to me: "Your city—one so full
of envy that its sack has always spilled—   50
that city held me in the sunlit life.

---

3. For this creature as one of the guardians of Hell, see *Aeneid* 6.   4. A Florentine named Ciacco, known only through his appearance here.   5. You were born before I died.

The name you citizens gave me was Ciacco;
and for the damning sin of gluttony,
as you can see, I languish in the rain.
And I, a wretched soul, am not alone, 55
for all of these have this same penalty
for this same sin." And he said nothing more.
I answered him: "Ciacco, your suffering
so weighs on me that I am forced to weep;
but tell me, if you know, what end awaits 60
the citizens of that divided city;
is any just man there? Tell me the reason
why it has been assailed by so much schism."
And he to me:[6] "After long controversy,
they'll come to blood; the party of the woods 65
will chase the other out with much offense.
But then, within three suns, they too must fall;
at which the other party will prevail,
using the power of one who tacks his sails.
This party will hold high its head for long 70
and heap great weights upon its enemies,
however much they weep indignantly.
Two men are just,[7] but no one listens to them.
Three sparks that set on fire every heart
are envy, pride, and avariciousness." 75
With this, his words, inciting tears, were done;
and I to him: "I would learn more from you;
I ask you for a gift of further speech:
Tegghiaio, Farinata, men so worthy,
Arrigo, Mosca, Jacopo Rusticucci, 80
and all the rest whose minds bent toward the good,
do tell me where they are and let me meet them;
for my great longing drives me on to learn
if Heaven sweetens or Hell poisons them."[8]
And he: "They are among the blackest souls; 85
a different sin has dragged them to the bottom;
if you descend so low, there you can see them.
But when you have returned to the sweet world,
I pray, recall me to men's memory:
I say no more to you, answer no more." 90
Then his straight gaze grew twisted and awry;
he looked at me awhile, then bent his head;
he fell as low as all his blind companions.
And my guide said to me: "He'll rise no more
until the blast of the angelic trumpet 95
upon the coming of the hostile Judge:
each one shall see his sorry tomb again
and once again take on his flesh and form,

---

6. This enigmatic "prophecy" refers first to the triumph of the Whites, or "the party of the woods" (to which Dante was allied), in 1300 and then their defeat by the Blacks, aided by Pope Boniface ("one who tacks his sails"), in 1302, at which time Dante was exiled.   7. The identity of these two is not known.   8. Dante asks about famous Florentines; he will find Farinata in canto 10, Tegghiaio and Rusticucci in canto 16, and Mosca in canto 28. Arrigo does not appear.

and hear what shall resound eternally."[9]
   So did we pass across that squalid mixture   100
of shadows and of rain, our steps slowed down,
talking awhile about the life to come.
   At which I said: "And after the great sentence—
o master—will these torments grow, or else
be less, or will they be just as intense?"   105
   And he to me: "Remember now your science,
which says that when a thing has more perfection,
so much the greater is its pain or pleasure.
   Though these accursed sinners never shall
attain the true perfection, yet they can   110
expect to be more perfect then than now."[1]
   We took the circling way traced by that road;
we said much more than I can here recount;
we reached the point that marks the downward slope.
   Here we found Plutus,[2] the great enemy.   115

CANTO VII

The demon Plutus. The Fourth Circle, where the Avaricious and the
Prodigal, in opposite directions, roll weights in semicircles. Fortune and
her ways. Descent into the Fifth Circle: the Wrathful and the Sullen, the
former besmirched by the muddy Styx, the latter immersed in it.

   "*Pape Satàn, pape Satàn aleppe!*"[3]
so Plutus, with his grating voice, began.
The gentle sage, aware of everything,
   said reassuringly, "Don't let your fear
defeat you; for whatever power he has,
he cannot stop our climbing down this crag."   5
   Then he turned back to Plutus' swollen face
and said to him: "Be quiet, cursed wolf!
Let your vindictiveness feed on yourself.
   His is no random journey to the deep: 10
it has been willed on high, where Michael[4] took
revenge upon the arrogant rebellion."
   As sails inflated by the wind collapse,
entangled in a heap, when the mast cracks,
so that ferocious beast fell to the ground.   15
   Thus we made our way down to the fourth ditch,
to take in more of that despondent shore
where all the universe's ill is stored.
   Justice of God! Who has amassed as many
strange tortures and travails as I have seen?   20
Why do we let our guilt consume us so?
   Even as waves that break above Charybdis,[5]

---

9. Virgil refers to the Last Judgment, when the dead will regain their bodies.   1. They will be more
perfect because body and soul will be reunited (a principle derived from Aristotelian science), which will
increase their pain.   2. Dante combines Pluto, the mythological god of the underworld, with Plutus, the
classical god of wealth.   3. Virgil apparently understands this mysterious outburst regarding Satan, but
commentators have remained baffled.   4. The angel Michael; see Revelation 12.7–9.   5. A famous
whirlpool in the Straits of Messina, between Sicily and Italy; see *Aeneid* 3.

each shattering the other when they meet,
so must the spirits here dance their round dance.

    Here, more than elsewhere, I saw multitudes   25
to every side of me; their howls were loud
while, wheeling weights, they used their chests to push.

    They struck against each other; at that point,
each turned around and, wheeling back those weights,
cried out: "Why do you hoard?" "Why do you squander?"[6]   25

    So did they move around the sorry circle
from left and right to the opposing point;
again, again they cried their chant of scorn;

    and so, when each of them had changed positions,
he circled halfway back to his next joust.   35
And I, who felt my heart almost pierced through,

    requested: "Master, show me now what shades
are these and tell me if they all were clerics—
those tonsured ones[7] who circle on our left."

    And he to me: "All these, to left and right   40
were so squint-eyed of mind in the first life—
no spending that they did was done with measure.

    Their voices bark this out with clarity
when they have reached the two points of the circle
where their opposing guilts divide their ranks.   45

    These to the left—their heads bereft of hair—
were clergymen, and popes and cardinals,
within whom avarice works its excess."

    And I to him: "Master, among this kind
I certainly might hope to recognize   50
some who have been bespattered by these crimes."

    And he to me: "That thought of yours is empty:
the undiscerning life that made them filthy
now renders them unrecognizable.

    For all eternity they'll come to blows: 55
these here will rise up from their sepulchers
with fists clenched tight; and these, with hair cropped close.

    Ill giving and ill keeping have robbed both
of the fair world and set them to this fracas—
what that is like, my words need not embellish.   60

    Now you can see, my son, how brief's the sport
of all those goods that are in Fortune's care,
for which the tribe of men contend and brawl;

    for all the gold that is or ever was
beneath the moon could never offer rest   65
to even one of these exhausted spirits."

    "Master," I asked of him, "now tell me too:
this Fortune whom you've touched upon just now—
what's she, who clutches so all the world's goods?"

    And he to me: "O unenlightened creatures,   70

---

6. Both misers and spendthrifts are punished here.   7. The tonsure—a shaving of part of the head—
was a mark of clerical status.

how deep—the ignorance that hampers you!
I want you to digest my words on this.[8]
    Who made the heavens and who gave them guides
was He whose wisdom transcends everything;
that every part may shine unto the other,   75
    He had the light apportioned equally;
similarly, for wordly splendors, He
ordained a general minister and guide
    to shift, from time to time, those empty goods
from nation unto nation, clan to clan,   80
in ways that human reason can't prevent;
    just so, one people rules, one languishes,
obeying the decision she has given,
which, like a serpent in the grass, is hidden.
    Your knowledge cannot stand against her force;   85
for she foresees and judges and maintains
her kingdom as the other gods do theirs.
    The changes that she brings are without respite:
it is necessity that makes her swift;
and for this reason, men change state so often.   90
    She is the one so frequently maligned
even by those who should give praise to her—
they blame her wrongfully with words of scorn.
    But she is blessed and does not hear these things;
for with the other primal beings, happy,   95
she turns her sphere and glories in her bliss.[9]
    But now let us descend to greater sorrow,
for every star that rose when I first moved
is setting now;[1] we cannot stay too long."
    We crossed the circle to the other shore;   100
we reached a foaming watercourse that spills
into a trench formed by its overflow.
    That stream was even darker than deep purple;
and we, together with those shadowed waves,
moved downward and along a strange pathway.   105
    When it has reached the foot of those malign
gray slopes, that melancholy stream descends,
forming a swamp that bears the name of Styx.[2]
    And I, who was intent on watching it,
could make out muddied people in that slime,   110
all naked and their faces furious.
    These struck each other not with hands alone,
but with their heads and chests and with their feet,
and tore each other piecemeal with their teeth.
    The kindly master told me: "Son, now see   115

8. Virgil now explains that each area of life is presided over by a *guide* or *intelligence,* a kind of angel,
under the ultimate authority of God. The classical goddess Fortune, thought to distribute the world's goods
capriciously, is here described to agree with this Christian conception.   9. Fortune was traditionally
depicted as turning a wheel, but here the term *sphere* is revised to refer to her area of authority in the
Christian scheme.   1. The stars that were rising at the start of the journey (1.37–40) are now setting:
Good Friday has passed, and the time is now the early hours of Holy Saturday.   2. The second river of
Hell.

the souls of those whom anger has defeated;
and I should also have you know for certain
    that underneath the water there are souls
who sigh and make this plain of water bubble,
as your eye, looking anywhere, can tell.   120
    Wedged in the slime, they say: 'We had been sullen
in the sweet air that's gladdened by the sun;
we bore the mist of sluggishness in us:
    now we are bitter in the blackened mud.'
This hymn they have to gurgle in their gullets,   125
because they cannot speak it in full words."
    And so, between the dry shore and the swamp,
we circled much of that disgusting pond,
our eyes upon the swallowers of slime.
We came at last upon a tower's base.   130

CANTO VIII

*Still the Fifth Circle: the Wrathful and the Sullen. The tall tower.
Phlegyas and the crossing of the Styx. Filippo Argenti and Dante's fury.
Approach to Dis, the lower part of Hell: its moat, its walls, its gate. The
demons, fallen angels, and their obstruction of the poets' entry into Dis.*

    I say, continuing, that long before
we two had reached the foot of that tall tower,[3]
    our eyes had risen upward, toward its summit,
because of two small flames that flickered there,
while still another flame returned their signal,   5
so far off it was scarcely visible.
    And I turned toward the sea of all good sense;
I said: "What does this mean? And what reply
comes from that other fire? Who kindled it?"
    And he to me: "Above the filthy waters   10
you can already see what waits for us,
if it's not hid by vapors from the marsh."
    Bowstring has not thrust from itself an arrow
that ever rushed as swiftly through the air
as did the little bark that at that moment   15
    I saw as it skimmed toward us on the water,
a solitary boatman at its helm.
I heard him howl: "Now you are caught, foul soul!"
    "O Phlegyas, Phlegyas,[4] such a shout is useless
this time," my master said; "we're yours no longer   20
than it will take to cross the muddy sluice."
    And just as one who hears some great deception
was done to him, and then resents it, so
was Phlegyas when he had to store his anger.
    My guide preceded me into the boat.   25
Once he was in, he had me follow him;

---

3. The watchtower that guards the entrance to lower Hell or the city of Dis, which is a name for the
classical god of the underworld, Pluto, that is applied to Satan (see 11.65, 12.39, and 34.20).   **4.** A
mythological figure condemned to Hell for setting fire to the temple of Apollo in revenge for the god's
seduction of his daughter; see *Aeneid* 6.

there seemed to be no weight until I boarded.
　No sooner were my guide and I embarked
than off that ancient prow went, cutting water
more deeply than it does when bearing others.[5]　　　　　30
　And while we steered across the stagnant channel,
before me stood a sinner thick with mud,
saying: "Who are you, come before your time?"
　And I to him: "I've come, but I don't stay;
but who are you, who have become so ugly?"　　　　　35
He answered: "You can see—I'm one who weeps."
　And I to him: "In weeping and in grieving,
accursèd spirit, may you long remain;
though you're disguised by filth, I know your name."
　Then he stretched both his hands out toward the boat,　40
at which my master quickly shoved him back,
saying: "Be off there with the other dogs!"
　That done, he threw his arms around my neck
and kissed my face and said: "Indignant soul,
blessèd is she who bore you in her womb![6]　　　　　45
　When in the world, he was presumptuous;
there is no good to gild his memory,
and so his shade down here is hot with fury.
　How many up above now count themselves
great kings, who'll wallow here like pigs in slime,　　　50
leaving behind foul memories of their crimes!"
　And I: "O master, I am very eager
to see that spirit soused within this broth
before we've made our way across the lake."
　And he to me: "Before the other shore　　　　　55
comes into view, you shall be satisfied;
to gratify so fine a wish is right."
　Soon after I had heard these words, I saw
the muddy sinners so dismember him
that even now I praise and thank God for it.　　　　　60
　They all were shouting: "At Filippo Argenti!"[7]
At this, the Florentine, gone wild with spleen,
began to turn his teeth against himself.
　We left him there; I tell no more of him.
But in my ears so loud a wailing pounded　　　　　65
that I lean forward, all intent to see.
　The kindly master said: "My son, the city
that bears the name of Dis is drawing near,
with its grave citizens, its great battalions."
　I said: "I can already see distinctly—　　　　　70
master—the mosques that gleam within the valley,
as crimson as if they had just been drawn
　out of the fire." He told me: "The eternal
flame burning there appears to make them red,
as you can see, within this lower Hell."　　　　　75

---

5. Because of the weight of the living Dante.　**6.** See Luke 11.27.　**7.** A Florentine contemporary of Dante.

So we arrived inside the deep-cut trenches
that are the moats of this despondent land:
the ramparts seemed to me to be of iron.

But not before we'd ranged in a wide circuit
did we approach a place where that shrill pilot   80
shouted: "Get out; the entrance way is here."

About the gates I saw more than a thousand[8]—
who once had rained from Heaven—and they cried
in anger: "Who is this who, without death,

can journey through the kingdom of the dead?"   85
And my wise master made a sign that said
he wanted to speak secretly to them.

Then they suppressed—somewhat—their great disdain
and said: "You come alone; let him be gone—
for he was reckless, entering this realm.   90

Let him return alone on his mad road—
or try to, if he can, since you, his guide
across so dark a land, you are to stay."

Consider, reader, my dismay before
the sound of those abominable words: 95
returning here seemed so impossible.

"O my dear guide, who more than seven times
has given back to me my confidence
and snatched me from deep danger that had menaced,

do not desert me when I'm so undone;   100
and if they will not let us pass beyond,
let us retrace our steps together, quickly."

These were my words; the lord who'd led me there
replied: "Forget your fear, no one can hinder
our passage; One so great has granted it.   105

But you wait here for me, and feed and comfort
your tired spirit with good hope, for I
will not abandon you in this low world."

So he goes on his way; that gentle father
has left me there to wait and hesitate,   110
for *yes* and *no* contend within my head.

I could not hear what he was telling them;
but he had not been long with them when each
ran back into the city, scrambling fast.

And these, our adversaries, slammed the gates   115
in my lord's face; and he remained outside,
then, with slow steps, turned back again to me.

His eyes turned to the ground, his brows deprived
of every confidence, he said with sighs:
"See who has kept me from the house of sorrow!"   120

To me he added: "You—though I am vexed—
must not be daunted; I shall win this contest,
whoever tries—within—to block our way.

This insolence of theirs is nothing new;

8. The rebel angels, cast out of Heaven; see Luke 10.18 and Revelation 12.9.

they used it once before and at a gate   125
less secret—it is still without its bolts[9]—
   the place where you made out the fatal text;
and now, already well within that gate,
across the circles—and alone—descends
   the one who will unlock this realm for us."   130

CANTO IX

*The gate of Dis. Dante's fear. The three Furies, invoking Medusa. Virgil's
warning to Dante lest he look at Gorgon, Medusa's head. A heavenly
messenger. The flight of the demons. Entry into Dis, where Virgil and
Dante reach the Sixth Circle and its Arch-Heretics, entombed in red-hot
sepulchers.*

The color cowardice displayed in me
when I saw that my guide was driven back,
made him more quickly mask his own new pallor.
   He stood alert, like an attentive listener,
because his eye could hardly journey far   5
across the black air and the heavy fog.
   "We have to win this battle," he began,
"if not . . . But one so great had offered aid.
But he seems slow in coming: I must wait
   But I saw well enough how he had covered   10
his first words with the words that followed after—
so different from what he had said before;
   nevertheless, his speech made me afraid,
because I drew out from his broken phrase
a meaning worse—perhaps—than he'd intended.   15
   "Does anyone from the first circle, one
whose only punishment is crippled hope,
ever descend so deep in this sad hollow?"[1]
   That was my question. And he answered so:
"It is quite rare for one of us to go   20
along the way that I have taken now.
   But I, in truth, have been here once before:
that savage witch Erichtho,[2] she who called
the shades back to their bodies, summoned me.
   My flesh had not been long stripped off when she   25
had me descend through all the rings of Hell,
to draw a spirit back from Judas' circle.[3]
   That is the deepest and the darkest place,
the farthest from the heaven that girds all:
so rest assured, I know the pathway well.   30
   This swamp that breeds and breathes the giant stench
surrounds the city of the sorrowing,

---

9. A reference to Christ's Harrowing of Hell; see 4.52, and Psalms 106.16 and Matthew 16.18.   1. I.e.,
has anyone from Limbo ever descended into lower Hell before?   2. A legendary sorceress. The story of
Virgil's descent into Hell is apparently Dante's own invention, although in the Middle Ages Virgil had the
reputation of being a magician.   3. Judecca, the last subdivision of the last circle of Hell, where Judas
is punished.

which now we cannot enter without anger."
   And he said more, but I cannot remember
because my eyes had wholly taken me   35
to that high tower with the glowing summit
   where, at one single point, there suddenly
stood three infernal Furies[4] flecked with blood,
who had the limbs of women and their ways
   but wore, as girdles, snakes of deepest green;   40
small serpents and horned vipers formed their hairs,
and these were used to bind their bestial temples.
   And he, who knew these handmaids well—they served
the Queen of never-ending lamentation[5]—
said: "Look at the ferocious Erinyes!   45
   That is Megaera on the left, and she
who weeps upon the right, that is Allecto;
Tisiphone's between them." He was done.
   Each Fury tore her breast with taloned nails;
each, with her palms, beat on herself and wailed   50
so loud that I, in fear, drew near the poet.
   "Just let Medusa[6] come; then we shall turn
him into stone," they all cried, looking down;
"we should have punished Theseus' assault."[7]
   "Turn round and keep your eyes shut fast, for should   55
the Gorgon show herself and you behold her,
never again would you return above,"
   my master said; and he himself turned me
around and, not content with just my hands,
used his as well to cover up my eyes.   60
   O you possessed of sturdy intellects,
observe the teaching that is hidden here
beneath the veil of verses so obscure.[8]
   And now, across the turbid waves, there passed
a reboantic[9] fracas—horrid sound,   65
enough to make both of the shorelines quake:
   a sound not other than a wind's when, wild
because it must contend with warmer currents,
it strikes against the forest without let,
   shattering, beating down, bearing off branches,   70
as it moves proudly, clouds of dust before it,
and puts to flight both animals and shepherds.
   He freed my eyes and said: "Now let your optic
nerve turn directly toward that ancient foam,
there where the mist is thickest and most acrid."   75
   As frogs confronted by their enemy,
the snake, will scatter underwater till
each hunches in a heap along the bottom,

---

4. Three mythological monsters who represent the spirit of vengeance, known in Greek as the Erinyes (see below, line 45, and lines 46–48 for their individual names); see *Aeneid* 6, 7, and 12.   5. Hecate, or Proserpina, the wife of Pluto.   6. A mythological figure known as a Gorgon (line 56), so frightful in appearance that she turned those who gazed on her into stone.   7. Theseus, a legendary Athenian hero, descended into the underworld in order to try to rescue Proserpina, whom Pluto had abducted.   8. Dante here reminds us of the need to interpret his poetry, although the lesson of this particular episode is far from self-evident.   9. Reverberating.

so did the thousand ruined souls I saw
take flight before a figure[1] crossing Styx   80
who walked as if on land and with dry soles.

He thrust away the thick air from his face,
waving his left hand frequently before him;
that seemed the only task that wearied him.

I knew well he was Heaven's messenger,   85
and I turned toward my master; and he made
a sign that I be still and bow before him.

How full of high disdain he seemed to me!
He came up to the gate, and with a wand,
he opened it, for there was no resistance.   90

"O you cast out of Heaven, hated crowd,"
were his first words upon that horrid threshold,
"why do you harbor this presumptuousness?

Why are you so reluctant to endure
that Will whose aim can never be cut short,   95
and which so often added to your hurts?

What good is it to thrust against the fates?
Your Cerberus, if you remember well,
for that, had both his throat and chin stripped clean."[2]

At that he turned and took the filthy road,   100
and did not speak to us, but had the look
of one who is obsessed by other cares

than those that press and gnaw at those before him;
and we moved forward, on into the city,
in safety, having heard his holy words.   105

We made our way inside without a struggle;
and I, who wanted so much to observe
the state of things that such a fortress guarded,

as soon as I had entered, looked about.
I saw, on every side, a spreading plain   110
of lamentation and atrocious pain.

Just as at Arles,[3] where Rhone becomes a marsh,
just as at Pola, near Quarnero's gulf,
that closes Italy and bathes its borders,

the sepulchers make all the plain uneven,   115
so they did here on every side, except
that here the sepulchers were much more harsh;

for flames were scattered through the tombs, and these
had kindled all of them to glowing heat;
no artisan could ask for hotter iron.   120

The lid of every tomb was lifted up,
and from each tomb such sorry cries arose
as could come only from the sad and hurt.

And I: "Master, who can these people be
who, buried in great chests of stone like these,   125
must speak by way of sighs in agony?"

---

1. An angel, here described in a way reminiscent of Mercury, the classical messenger of the gods.
2. Hercules dragged Cerberus into the daylight; see *Aeneid* 6.   3. Arles, located on the Rhone River in southern France, and Pola, located on the bay of Quarnero in what is now Yugoslavia, were the sites of Roman cemeteries.

And he to me: "Here are arch-heretics
and those who followed them, from every sect;
those tombs are much more crowded than you think.
Here, like has been ensepulchered with like;   130
some monuments are heated more, some less."
And then he turned around and to his right;
we passed between the torments and high walls.

CANTO X

*Still the Sixth Circle: the Heretics. The tombs of the Epicureans.
Farinata degli Uberti. Cavalcante dei Cavalcanti. Farinata's prediction of
Dante's difficulty in returning to Florence from exile. The inability of the
damned to see the present, although they can foresee the future.*

Now, by a narrow path that ran between
those torments and the ramparts of the city,
my master moves ahead, I following.
"O highest virtue, you who lead me through
these circles of transgression, at your will,   5
do speak to me, and satisfy my longings.
Can those who lie within the sepulchers
be seen? The lids—in fact—have all been lifted;
no guardian is watching over them."
And he to me: "They'll all be shuttered up   10
when they return here from Jehosaphat[4]
together with the flesh they left above.
Within this region is the cemetery
of Epicurus[5] and his followers,
all those who say the soul dies with the body.   15
And so the question you have asked of me
will soon find satisfaction while we're here,
as will the longing you have hid from me."[6]
And I: "Good guide, the only reason I
have hid my heart was that I might speak briefly,   20
and you, long since, encouraged me in this."
"O Tuscan, you who pass alive across
the fiery city with such seemly words,
be kind enough to stay your journey here.
Your accent makes it clear that you belong   25
among the natives of the noble city
I may have dealt with too vindictively."
This sound had burst so unexpectedly
out of one sepulcher that, trembling, I
then drew a little closer to my guide.   30
But he told me: "Turn round! What are you doing?
That's Farinata[7] who has risen there—
you will see all of him from the waist up."
My eyes already were intent on his;

---

4. According to the Bible, the Last Judgment will take place in the Valley of Jehosaphat: see Joel 3.2 and 3.12, and Matthew 25.31–32.   **5.** Greek philosopher (d. 270 B.C.) who rejected the idea of the immortality of the soul.   **6.** Presumably Dante's desire to see the Florentines who inhabit this circle. **7.** Farinata degli Uberti (d. 1264), a leader of the Ghibelline faction in Florence.

and up he rose—his forehead and his chest—   35
as if he had tremendous scorn for Hell.
    My guide—his hands encouraging and quick—
thrust me between the sepulchers toward him,
saying: "Your words must be appropriate."
    When I'd drawn closer to his sepulcher,   40
he glanced at me, and as if in disdain,
he asked of me: "Who were your ancestors?"
    Because I wanted so to be compliant,
I hid no thing from him: I told him all.
At this he lifted up his brows a bit,   45
    then said: "They were ferocious enemies
of mine and of my parents and my party,
so that I had to scatter them twice over."[8]
    "If they were driven out," I answered him,
"they still returned, both times, from every quarter;   50
but yours were never quick to learn that art."[9]
    At this there rose another shade alongside,[1]
uncovered to my sight down to his chin;
I think that he had risen on his knees.
    He looked around me, just as if he longed   55
to see if I had come with someone else;
but then, his expectation spent, he said
    in tears: "If it is your high intellect
that lets you journey here, through this blind prison,
where is my son? Why is he not with you?"   60
    I answered: "My own powers have not brought me;
he who awaits me there, leads me through here
perhaps to one[2] your Guido did disdain."
    His words, the nature of his punishment—
these had already let me read his name;   65
therefore, my answer was so fully made.
    Then suddenly erect, he cried: "What's that:
He 'did disdain'?[3] He is not still alive?
The sweet light does not strike against his eyes?"
    And when he noticed how I hesitated   70
a moment in my answer, he fell back—
supine—and did not show himself again.
    But that great-hearted one, the other shade
at whose request I'd stayed, did not change aspect
or turn aside his head or lean or bend;   75
    and taking up his words where he'd left off,
"If they were slow," he said, "to learn that art,

---

8. Dante's family were Guelphs, who were driven out of Florence twice, in 1248 and 1260.   9. The Ghibellines were exiled in 1280, never to return.   1. This is Cavalcante de Cavalcanti, father of Dante's friend and superb fellow poet Guido; a Guelph, Guido married the daughter of Farinata in an unsuccessful attempt to heal the feud. In June 1300—after the fictional date of this conversation—Guido was exiled to a part of Italy where he caught the malaria from which he died in August. Dante was at that time a member of the governing body that made the decision to exile Guido.   2. The passage is ambiguous in the original Italian: as translated here, the "one" refers to Beatrice; but the word can also be translated to refer to Virgil, so that these two lines would read: "he who awaits me there leads me through here, / him whom your Guido did perhaps disdain."   3. In lines 61–63 Dante uses a verbal form known in Italian as the remote past, which leads Cavalcante to believe, wrongly, that now, in April 1300, Guido is dead—although, ironically, in about four months he will die.

that is more torment to me than this bed.
And yet the Lady[4] who is ruler here
will not have her face kindled fifty times   80
before you learn how heavy is that art.[5]
And so may you return to the sweet world,
tell me: why are those citizens so cruel
against my kin in all of their decrees?"
To which I said: "The carnage, the great bloodshed   85
that stained the waters of the Arbia[6] red
have led us to such prayers in our temple."
He sighed and shook his head, then said: "In that,
I did not act alone, but certainly
I'd not have joined the others without cause.   90
But where I was alone was *there*[7] where all
the rest would have annihilated Florence,
had I not interceded forcefully."
"Ah, as I hope your seed may yet find peace,"
I asked, "so may you help me to undo   95
the knot that here has snarled my course of thought.
It seems, if I hear right, that you can see
beforehand that which time is carrying,
but you're denied the sight of present things."
"We see, even as men who are farsighted,   100
those things," he said, "that are remote from us;
the Highest Lord allots us that much light.
But when events draw near or are, our minds
are useless; were we not informed by others,
we should know nothing of your human state.   105
So you can understand how our awareness
will die completely at the moment when
the portal of the future has been shut."[8]
Then, as if penitent for my omission,
I said: "Will you now tell that fallen man   110
his son is still among the living ones;[9]
and if, a while ago, I held my tongue
before his question, let him know it was
because I had in mind the doubt you've answered."
And now my master was recalling me;   115
so that, more hurriedly, I asked the spirit
to name the others who were there with him.
He said: "More than a thousand lie with me:
the second Frederick[1] is but one among them,
as is the Cardinal;[2] I name no others."   120
With that, he hid himself; and pondering
the speech that seemed to me so menacing,
I turned my steps to meet the ancient poet.

---

4. Proserpina, who is also the goddess of the moon.   **5.** Farinata here predicts Dante's own exile.   **6.** A stream near the hill of Montaperti, where the Ghibellines defeated the Guelphs in 1260.   **7.** At Montaperti, where the other Ghibellines wanted to destroy Florence.   **8.** The damned can see the future but not the present; after the Last Judgment, when human time is abolished, they will know nothing.   **9.** See note to line 68 above.   **1.** Frederick II, Holy Roman Emperor from 1215 until his death in 1250; he reputedly denied life after death.   **2.** Ottaviano degli Ubaldini (d. 1273), who is reputed to have said, "If I have a soul, I have lost it for the Ghibellines."

He moved ahead, and as we made our way,
he said to me: "Why are you so dismayed?"   125
I satisfied him, answering him fully.[3]

And then that sage exhorted me: "Remember
the words that have been spoken here against you.
Now pay attention," and he raised his finger;

"when you shall stand before the gentle splendor   130
of one whose gracious eyes see everything,[4]
then you shall learn—from her—your lifetime's journey."

Following that, his steps turned to the left,
leaving the wall and moving toward the middle
along a path that strikes into a valley   135
whose stench, as it rose up, disgusted us.

CANTO XI

*Still the Sixth Circle. Pope Anastasius' tomb. Virgil on the parts of Dis
they now will visit, where the modes of malice are punished: violence in
the Seventh Circle's Three Rings; "ordinary" fraud in the Eighth Circle;
and treacherous fraud in the Ninth Circle. Hell's previous circles, Two
through Five, as circles of incontinence. Usury condemned.*

Along the upper rim of a high bank
formed by a ring of massive broken boulders,
we came above a crowd more cruelly pent.

And here, because of the outrageous stench
thrown up in excess by that deep abyss,   5
we drew back till we were behind the lid

of a great tomb, on which I made out this,
inscribed: "I hold Pope Anastasius,
enticed to leave the true path by Photinus."[5]

"It would be better to delay descent   10
so that our senses may grow somewhat used
to this foul stench; and then we can ignore it."

So said my master, and I answered him:
"Do find some compensation, lest this time
be lost." And he: "You see, I've thought of that."   15

"My son, within this ring of broken rocks,"
he then began, "there are three smaller circles;[6]
like those that you are leaving, they range down.

Those circles are all full of cursed spirits;
so that your seeing of them may suffice,   20
learn now the how and why of their confinement.

Of every malice that earns hate in Heaven,
injustice is the end; and each such end
by force or fraud brings harm to other men.

However, fraud is man's peculiar vice;   25

---

3. Dante is upset by Farinata's prediction of his exile.   4. Beatrice.   5. Pope Anastasius (d. 498) was
thought, wrongly, to have accepted a heresy promoted by the fifth-century theologian Photinus that Christ
was not divine but only human.   6. Virgil now describes the three remaining circles of Hell, the seventh,
eighth, and ninth. The seventh is for the violent and is divided into three parts; the eighth and ninth are
for the fraudulent, the eighth for those who deceive generally, the ninth for those who betray those who
love them. For the scheme of Hell as a whole, see the diagram on p. 1301.

God finds it more displeasing—and therefore,
the fraudulent are lower, suffering more.
    The violent take all of the first circle;
but since one uses force against three persons,
that circle's built of three divided rings.   30
    To God and to one's self and to one's neighbor—
I mean, to them or what is theirs—one can
do violence, as you shall now hear clearly.
    Violent death and painful wounds may be
inflicted on one's neighbor; his possessions   35
may suffer ruin, fire, and extortion;
    thus, murderers and those who strike in malice,
as well as plunderers and robbers—these,
in separated ranks, the first ring racks.
    A man can set violent hands against   40
himself or his belongings; so within
the second ring repents, though uselessly,
    whoever would deny himself your world,
gambling away, wasting his patrimony,
and weeping where he should instead be happy.   45
    One can be violent against the Godhead,
one's heart denying and blaspheming Him
and scorning nature and the good in her;
    so, with its sign, the smallest ring has sealed
both Sodom and Cahors[7] and all of those   50
who speak in passionate contempt of God.
    Now fraud, that eats away at every conscience,
is practiced by a man against another
who trusts in him, or one who has no trust.
    This latter way seems only to cut off   55
the bond of love that nature forges; thus,
nestled within the second circle are:
    hypocrisy and flattery, sorcerers,
and falsifiers, simony, and theft,
and barrators and panders and like trash.   60
    But in the former way of fraud, not only
the love that nature forges is forgotten,
but added love that builds a special trust;
    thus, in the tightest circle, where there is
the universe's center, seat of Dis,[8]   65
all traitors are consumed eternally."
    "Master, your reasoning is clear indeed,"
I said; "it has made plain for me the nature
of this pit and the population in it.
    But tell me: those the dense marsh holds, or those   70
driven before the wind, or those on whom
rain falls, or those who clash with such harsh tongues,
    why are they not all punished in the city

---

7. In the Middle Ages the names of Sodom (see Genesis 18.20–19.26) and Cahors, a city in southern France, became synonymous with sodomites and userers respectively. Usury, forbidden by the medieval Church, is charging interest on loans; the logic of this prohibition is explained in lines 97ff below.   8. Dis is Satan, who is found at the bottom of Hell (see canto 34).

of flaming red if God is angry with them?
And if He's not, why then are they tormented?"   75
    And then to me, "Why does your reason wander
so far from its accustomed course?" he said.
"Or of what other things are you now thinking?
    Have you forgotten, then, the words with which
your *Ethics*⁹ treats of those three dispositions   80
that strike at Heaven's will: incontinence
    and malice and mad bestiality?
And how the fault that is the least condemned
and least offends God is incontinence?
    If you consider carefully this judgment   85
and call to mind the souls of upper Hell,
who bear their penalties outside this city,
    you'll see why they have been set off from these
unrighteous ones, and why, when heaven's vengeance
hammers at them, it carries lesser anger."   90
    "O sun that heals all sight that is perplexed,
when I ask you, your answer so contents
that doubting pleases me as much as knowing.
    Go back a little to that point," I said,
"where you told me that usury offends   95
divine goodness; unravel now that knot."
    "Philosophy, for one who understands,
points out, and not in just one place," he said,
"how nature follows—as she takes her course—
    the Divine Intellect and Divine Art;¹   100
and if you read your *Physics*² carefully,
not many pages from the start, you'll see
    that when it can, your art would follow nature,
just as a pupil imitates his master;
so that your art is almost God's grandchild.   105
    From these two, art and nature, it is fitting,
if you recall how *Genesis* begins,³
for men to make their way, to gain their living;
    and since the usurer prefers another
pathway, he scorns both nature in herself   110
and art, her follower; his hope is elsewhere.⁴
    But follow me, for it is time to move;
the Fishes glitter now on the horizon
and all the Wain is spread out over Caurus;⁵
    only beyond, can one climb down the cliff."   115

---

9. Aristotle's *Nicomachean Ethics*.   1. The laws of nature are determined by God.   2. Aristotle's *Phys-ics*, which argues that human art should follow natural laws.   3. In Genesis 3.17–19, God decrees that because of the Fall people must toil, supporting themselves by the sweat of their brows.   4. The usurer makes money not from labor but from money itself, which is an unnatural and therefore illicit art.   5. The position of stars shows that it is now about 4 A.M. on Holy Saturday.

CANTO XII

The Seventh Circle, First Ring: the Violent against their Neighbors. The Minotaur. The Centaurs, led by Chiron, who assigns Nessus to guide Dante and Virgil across the boiling river of blood (Phlegethon). In that river, Tyrants and Murderers, immersed, watched over by the Centaurs.

The place that we had reached for our descent
along the bank was alpine; what reclined
upon that bank would, too, repel all eyes.

Just like the toppled mass of rock that struck—
because of earthquake or eroded props—   5
the Adige on its flank, this side of Trent,[6]

where from the mountain top from which it thrust
down to the plain, the rock is shattered so
that it permits a path for those above:

such was the passage down to that ravine.   10
And at the edge above the cracked abyss,
there lay outstretched the infamy of Crete,

conceived within the counterfeited cow;[7]
and, catching sight of us, he bit himself
like one whom fury devastates within.   15

Turning to him, my sage cried out: "Perhaps
you think this is the Duke of Athens here,[8]
who, in the world above, brought you your death.

Be off, you beast; this man who comes has not
been tutored by your sister;[9] all he wants   20
in coming here is to observe your torments."

Just as the bull that breaks loose from its halter
the moment it receives the fatal stroke,
and cannot run but plunges back and forth,

so did I see the Minotaur respond;   25
and my alert guide cried: "Run toward the pass;
it's better to descend while he's berserk."

And so we made our way across that heap
of stones, which often moved beneath my feet
because my weight was somewhat strange for them.   30

While climbing down, I thought. He said: "You wonder,
perhaps, about that fallen mass, watched over
by the inhuman rage I have just quenched.

Now I would have you know: the other time
that I descended into lower Hell,   35
this mass of boulders had not yet collapsed;

but if I reason rightly, it was just
before the coming of the One who took
from Dis the highest circle's splendid spoils

that, on all sides, the steep and filthy valley   40
had trembled so,[1] I thought the universe

6. A famous landslide on a mountain on the Adige River near Trent, a city in northern Italy. 7. The Minotaur, half man and half bull, was conceived when Pasiphaë, the wife of King Minos of Crete, had a wooden cow built within which she placed herself so as to have intercourse with a bull. The story of the Minotaur is told by Ovid, *Metamorphoses* 8. 8. Virgil is referring to Theseus, who killed the Minotaur in the labyrinth in which it was imprisoned. 9. Ariadne, daughter of Minos and Pasiphaë, who taught Theseus how to kill the Minotaur. 1. Because of the earthquake that accompanied Christ's death; see also 5.34.

felt love (by which, as some believe, the world
   has often been converted into chaos);[2]
and at that moment, here as well as elsewhere,
these ancient boulders toppled, in this way.   45
   But fix your eyes below, upon the valley,
for now we near the stream of blood, where those
who injure others violently, boil."
   O blind cupidity[3] and insane anger,
which goad us on so much in our short life,   50
then steep us in such grief eternally!
   I saw a broad ditch bent into an arc
so that it could embrace all of that plain,
precisely as my guide had said before;
   between it and the base of the embankment   55
raced files of Centaurs[4] who were armed with arrows,
as, in the world above, they used to hunt.
   On seeing us descend, they all reined in;
and, after they had chosen bows and shafts,
three of their number moved out from their ranks;   60
   and still far off, one cried: "What punishment
do you approach as you descend the slope?
But speak from there; if not, I draw my bow."
   My master told him: "We shall make reply
only to Chiron,[5] when we reach his side;   65
your hasty will has never served you well."
   Then he nudged me and said: "That one is Nessus,
who died because of lovely Deianira
and of himself wrought vengeance for himself.[6]
   And in the middle, gazing at his chest,   70
is mighty Chiron, tutor of Achilles;
the third is Pholus,[7] he who was so frenzied.
   And many thousands wheel around the moat,
their arrows aimed at any soul that thrusts
above the blood more than its guilt allots."   75
   By now we had drawn near those agile beasts;
Chiron drew out an arrow; with the notch,
he parted his beard back upon his jaws.
   When he'd uncovered his enormous mouth,
he said to his companions: "Have you noticed   80
how he who walks behind moves what he touches?
   Dead soles are not accustomed to do that."
And my good guide—now near the Centaur's chest,
the place where his two natures[8] met—replied:
   "He is indeed alive, and so alone   85
it falls to me to show him the dark valley.
Necessity has brought him here, not pleasure.

2. A reference to a theory of the Greek philosopher Empedocles that the universe is held together by alternating forces of love and hate, and that if either one predominates the result is chaos. This classical theory is not consistent with the Christian belief that the universe is created and organized by God's love.   **3.** Desire for wealth.   **4.** Mythological creatures that are half man and half horse.   **5.** A centaur renowned for wisdom who educated many legendary Greek heroes, including Achilles.   **6.** Nessus fell in love with Deianira, wife of Hercules, who killed him; while dying, Nessus poisoned with his own blood a robe that killed Hercules when he put it on.   **7.** Another centaur, whose rage seems typical of the race.   **8.** That is, of beast and man.

For she[9] who gave me this new task was one
who had just come from singing halleluiah:
he is no robber; I am not a thief.[1]   90
But by the Power that permits my steps
to journey on so wild a path, give us
one of your band, to serve as our companion;
    and let him show us where to ford the ditch,[2]
and let him bear this man upon his back,   95
for he's no spirit who can fly through air."
Then Chiron wheeled about and right and said
to Nessus: "Then, return and be their guide;
if other troops disturb you, fend them off."
    Now, with our faithful escort, we advanced   100
along the bloodred, boiling ditch's banks,
beside the piercing cries of those who boiled.
    I saw some who were sunk up to their brows,
and that huge Centaur said: "These are the tyrants
who plunged their hands in blood and plundering.   105
    Here they lament their ruthless crimes; here are
both Alexander and the fierce Dionysius,[3]
who brought such years of grief to Sicily.
    That brow with hair so black is Ezzelino;[4]
that other there, the blonde one, is Obizzo   110
of Este,[5] he who was indeed undone,
    within the world above, by his fierce son."
Then I turned to the poet, and he said:
"Now let him be your first guide, me your second."
    A little farther on, the Centaur stopped   115
above a group that seemed to rise above
the boiling blood as far up as their throats.
    He pointed out one shade,[6] alone, apart,
and said: "Within God's bosom, he impaled
the heart that still drips blood upon the Thames."   120
    Then I caught sight of some who kept their heads
and even their full chests above the tide;
among them—many whom I recognized.
    And so the blood grew always shallower
until it only scorched the feet; and here   125
we found a place where we could ford the ditch.
    "Just as you see that, on this side, the brook
continually thins," the Centaur said,
"so I should have you know the rivulet,
    along the other side, will slowly deepen   130
its bed, until it reaches once again
the depth where tyranny must make lament.

---

9. Beatrice   1. Virgil is answering the question asked in lines 61–62: we are here not because we are
condemned to this circle for cupidity (see line 49).   2. The river of blood, which we later learn is named
Phlegethon (see 14.116).   3. Dionysius of Syracuse in Sicily (d. 367 B.C.). *Alexander*: Alexander the
Great (d. 323 B.C.).   4. Ezzolino III (d. 1259), a brutal ruler in northern Italy.   5. Obizzo II d'Este (d.
1293), another northern Italian ruler, reputedly murdered by his son.   6. Guy de Montfort (d. 1298),
who killed his cousin Prince Henry of Cornwall during a church service ("within God's bosom") in the
Italian city of Viterbo. Nessus's image of the blood dripping from the victim's heart indicates his focus on
the fact that the murder is still unavenged.

And there divine justice torments Attila[7]
he who was such a scourge upon the earth,
and Pyrrhus, Sextus;[8] to eternity   135
it milks the tears that boiling brook unlocks
from Rinier of Corneto, Rinier Pazzo,[9]
those two who waged such war upon the highroads."
Then he turned round and crossed the ford again.

CANTO XIII

The Seventh Circle, Second Ring: the Violent against Themselves
(Suicides) or against their Possessions (Squanderers). The dreary wood ,
with the Suicides transformed into strange trees, and the Squanderers,
hounded and rent by bitches. Pier della Vigna. Lano and Jacopo da Santo
Andrea. The anonymous Florentine suicide.

Nessus had not yet reached the other bank
when we began to make our way across
a wood on which no path had left its mark.
No green leaves in that forest, only black;
no branches straight and smooth, but knotted, gnarled;   5
no fruits were there, but briers bearing poison.
Even those savage beasts that roam between
Cécina and Corneto,[1] beasts that hate
tilled lands, do not have holts so harsh and dense.
This is the nesting place of the foul Harpies,[2]   10
who chased the Trojans from the Strophades
with sad foretelling of their future trials.
Their wings are wide, their necks and faces human;
their feet are taloned, their great bellies feathered;
they utter their laments on the strange trees.   15
And my kind master then instructed me:
"Before you enter farther know that now
you are within the second ring and shall
be here until you reach the horrid sand;[3]
therefore look carefully; you'll see such things   20
as would deprive my speech of all belief."
From every side I heard the sound of cries,
but I could not see any source for them,
so that, in my bewilderment, I stopped.
I think that he was thinking that I thought   25
so many voices moaned among those trunks
from people who had been concealed from us.
Therefore my master said: "If you would tear
a little twig from any of these plants,
the thoughts you have will also be cut off."[4]   30

7. Attila the Hun (d. 453).   8. Roman pirate (first century B.C.). Pyrrhus, Achilles' son, killed the aged
Priam at the fall of Troy; see *Aeneid* 2.   9. Both Riniers were bandits of Dante's day; they are now weeping
from pain, whereas in life they never wept for their sins.   1. Two towns that mark the limits of the
Maremma, a desolate area in Tuscany.   2. Birds with the faces of women and clawed hands; in *Aeneid*
3 they drive the wandering Trojans from their refuge in the Strophades Islands and predict their future
suffering.   3. The third ring of the seventh circle.   4. Your thoughts that the moans come from people
concealed among the trees will be contradicted.

Then I stretched out my hand a little way[5]
and from a great thornbush snapped off a branch,
at which its trunk cried out: "Why do you tear me?"
    And then, when it had grown more dark with blood,
it asked again: "Why do you break me off?   35
Are you without all sentiment of pity?
    We once were men and now are arid stumps:
your hand might well have shown us greater mercy
had we been nothing more than souls of serpents."
    As from a sapling log that catches fire   40
along one of its ends, while at the other
it drips and hisses with escaping vapor,
    so from that broken stump issued together
both words and blood; at which I let the branch
fall, and I stood like one who is afraid.   45
    My sage said: "Wounded soul, if, earlier,
he had been able to believe what he
had only glimpsed within my poetry,[6]
    then he would not have set his hand against you;
but its incredibility made me   50
urge him to do a deed that grieves me deeply.
    But tell him who you were, so that he may,
to make amends, refresh your fame within
the world above, where he can still return."
    To which the trunk:[7] "Your sweet speech draws me so   55
that I cannot be still; and may it not
oppress you, if I linger now in talk.
    I am the one who guarded both the keys
of Frederick's heart and turned them, locking and
unlocking them with such dexterity   60
    that none but I could share his confidence;
and I was faithful to my splendid office,
so faithful that I lost both sleep and strength.
    The whore[8] who never turned her harlot's eyes
away from Caesar's dwelling,[9] she who is   65
the death of all and vice of every court,
    inflamed the minds of everyone against me;
and those inflamed, then so inflamed Augustus[1]
that my delighted honors turned to sadness.
    My mind, because of its disdainful temper,   70
believing it could flee disdain through death,
made me unjust against my own just self.[2]
    I swear to you by the peculiar roots
of this thornbush, I never broke my faith
with him who was so worthy—with my lord.   75

5. This episode derives from *Aeneid* 3, where Aeneas and his Trojan companions, stopping in their search for a new home, discover Polydorus transformed into a bush. Sent out by Priam during the war to solicit aid from the Thracians, Polydorus had been murdered by his hosts, and the javelins with which his body had been pierced had grown into the bush from which Aeneas breaks off a branch that bleeds. See also Ovid, *Metamorphoses* 2.   6. Had Dante been able to believe the story of Polydorus recounted in the *Aeneid*.   7. This is the soul of Pier della Vigna (ca. 1190–1249), who had risen to become minister to the Emperor Frederick II (on whom see the note to 10.119). His name means Peter of the Vine, probably because his father had been a simple worker in a vineyard.   8. Pier blames his fall from favor on Envy.   9. The imperial court.   1. Frederick.   2. I unjustly committed suicide.

If one of you returns into the world,
then let him help my memory, which still
lies prone beneath the battering of envy."
    The poet waited briefly, then he said
to me: "Since he is silent, do not lose   80
this chance, but speak and ask what you would know."
    And I: "Do you continue; ask of him
whatever you believe I should request;
I cannot, so much pity takes my heart."
    Then he began again: "Imprisoned spirit,   85
so may this man do freely what you ask,
may it please you to tell us something more
    of how the soul is bound into these knots;
and tell us, if you can, if any one
can ever find his freedom from these limbs."   90
    At this the trunk breathed violently, then
that wind became this voice: "You shall be answered
promptly. When the savage spirit quits
    the body from which it has torn itself,
then Minos sends it to the seventh maw.   95
It falls into the wood, and there's no place
    to which it is allotted, but wherever
fortune has flung that soul, that is the space
where, even as a grain of spelt,[3] it sprouts.
    It rises as a sapling, a wild plant;   100
and then the Harpies, feeding on its leaves,
cause pain and for that pain provide a vent.
    Like other souls, we shall seek out the flesh
that we have left,[4] but none of us shall wear it;
it is not right for any man to have   105
    what he himself has cast aside. We'll drag
our bodies here; they'll hang in this sad wood,
each on the stump of its vindictive shade."
    And we were still intent upon the trunk—
believing it had wanted to say more—   110
when we were overtaken by a roar,
    just as the hunter is aware of chase
and boar as they draw near his post—he hears
the beasts and then the branches as they crack.
    And there upon the left were two[5] who, scratched   115
and naked, fled so violently that
they tore away each forest bough they passed.
    The one in front: "Now come, death, quickly come!"
The other shade, who thought himself too slow,
was shouting after him: "Lano, your legs   120
    were not so nimble at the jousts of Toppo!"[6]
And then, perhaps because he'd lost his breath,
he fell into one tangle with a bush.
    Behind these two, black bitches filled the wood,

3. Wheat.   4. At the Last Judgment.   5. Lano of Siena and Jacopo da Santo Andrea of Padua, two
Italians of a generation earlier than Dante's; both were reputed to be spendthrifts.   6. Lano was killed
at a battle on the river Toppo in 1287.

and they were just as eager and as swift   125
as greyhounds that have been let off their leash.
    They set their teeth in him where he had crouched;
and, piece by piece, those dogs dismembered him
and carried off his miserable limbs.
    Then he who was my escort took my hand;   130
he led me to the lacerated thorn
that wept in vain where it was bleeding, broken.
    "O Jacopo," it[7] said, "da Santo Andrea,
what have you gained by using me as screen?
Am I to blame for your indecent life?"   135
    When my good master stood beside that bush,
he said: "Who were you, who through many wounds
must breathe with blood your melancholy words?"
    And he to us: "O spirits who have come
to witness the outrageous laceration   140
that leaves so many of my branches torn,
    collect them at the foot of this sad thorn.
My home was in the city[8] whose first patron
gave way to John the Baptist; for this reason,
    he'll always use his art to make it sorrow;   145
and if—along the crossing of the Arno[9]—
some effigy of Mars had not remained,
    those citizens who afterward rebuilt
their city on the ashes that Attila[1]
had left to them, would have travailed in vain.   150
    I made—of my own house—my gallows place."

CANTO XIV

*The Seventh Circle, Third Ring: the Violent against God. The First Zone:
Blasphemers, supine on fiery sands. Capaneus. Virgil on the Old Man of
Crete, whose streaming tears form the rivers of Hell: Acheron, Phlegethon,
Styx, and Cocytus. The sight of Lethe postponed.*

Love of our native city overcame me;
I gathered up the scattered boughs and gave
them back to him whose voice was spent already.
    From there we reached the boundary that divides
the second from the third ring—and the sight   5
of a dread work that justice had devised.
    To make these strange things clear, I must explain
that we had come upon an open plain
that banishes all green things from its bed.
    The wood of sorrow is a garland round it,   10
just as that wood is ringed by a sad channel;[2]
here, at the very edge, we stayed our steps.

7. Nothing is known about this suicide, who hung himself from his own house.   8. Florence; when
the Florentines converted to Christianity, John the Baptist replaced Mars as patron of the city, and therefore Mars will forever persecute the city with civil war.   9. The river that runs through Florence.   1. According to legend, Attila the Hun destroyed Florence when he invaded Italy in the fifth
century.   2. The third ring of the seventh circle is surrounded by the second ring of the woods through
which Dante has just passed and the first ring of the river of blood described in canto 12.

The ground was made of sand, dry and compact,
a sand not different in kind from that
on which the feet of Cato[3] had once tramped.   15

O vengeance of the Lord, how you should be
dreaded by everyone who now can read
whatever was made manifest to me!

I saw so many flocks of naked souls,
all weeping miserably, and it seemed   20
that they were ruled by different decrees.

Some lay upon the ground, flat on their backs;
some huddled in a crouch, and there they sat;
and others moved about incessantly.

The largest group was those who walked about,   25
the smallest, those supine in punishment;
but these had looser tongues to tell their torment.

Above that plain of sand, distended flakes
of fire showered down; their fall was slow—
as snow descends on alps when no wind blows.   30

Just like the flames that Alexander saw
in India's hot zones, when fires fell,
intact and to the ground, on his battalions,

for which—wisely—he had his soldiers tramp
the soil to see that every fire was spent   35
before new flames were added to the old;[4]

so did the never-ending heat descend;
with this, the sand was kindled just as tinder
on meeting flint will flame—doubling the pain.

The dance of wretched hands was never done;   40
now here, now there, they tried to beat aside
the fresh flames as they fell. And I began

to speak: "My master, you who can defeat
all things except for those tenacious demons
who tried to block us at the entryway,   45

who is that giant there,[5] who does not seem
to heed the singeing—he who lies and scorns
and scowls, he whom the rains can't seem to soften?"

And he himself, on noticing that I
was querying my guide about him, cried: 50
"That which I was in life, I am in death.

Though Jove wear out the smith[6] from whom he took,
in wrath, the keen-edged thunderbolt with which
on my last day I was to be transfixed;

or if he tire the others, one by one,   55
in Mongibello,[7] at the sooty forge,
while bellowing: 'O help, good Vulcan, help!'—

just as he did when there was war at Phlegra[8]—

---

3. Roman general (first century B.C.) who campaigned in Libya.   4. Dante is here following an account
by the German philosopher Albertus Magnus (d. 1280) of a legendary adventure that befell Alexander the
Great in his conquest of India.   5. Capaneus, one of the seven legendary kings who besieged Thebes as
described in the *Thebaid* by Statius (d. A.D. 95). He was struck with a thunderbolt when he boasted that
not even Jupiter could stop him.   6. Vulcan   7. The Sicilian name for Mt. Etna, thought to be Vulcan's
furnace. *The others:* The Cyclopes, Vulcan's helpers.   8. Capaneus refers to the battle of Phlegra, where
Jove defeated the rebellious Titans (see 31.43).

and casts his shafts at me with all his force,
not even then would he have happy vengeance."   60

  Then did my guide speak with such vehemence
as I had never heard him use before:
"O Capaneus, for your arrogance

  that is not quenched, you're punished all the more:
no torture other than your own madness   65
could offer pain enough to match your wrath."

  But then, with gentler face he turned to me
and said: "That man was one of seven kings
besieging Thebes; he held—and still, it seems,

  holds—God in great disdain, disprizing Him;   70
but as I told him now, his maledictions
sit well as ornaments upon his chest.

  Now follow me and—take care—do not set
your feet upon the sand that's burning hot,
but always keep them back, close to the forest."   75

  In silence we had reached a place where flowed
a slender watercourse out of the wood—
a stream whose redness makes me shudder still.

  As from the Bulicame[9] pours a brook
whose waters then are shared by prostitutes,   80
so did this stream run down across the sand.

  Its bed and both its banks were made of stone,
together with the slopes along its shores,
so that I saw our passageway lay there.

  "Among all other things that I have shown you   85
since we first made our way across the gate
whose threshold is forbidden to no one,

  no thing has yet been witnessed by your eyes
as notable as this red rivulet,
which quenches every flame that burns above it."   90

  These words were spoken by my guide; at this,
I begged him to bestow the food for which
he had already given me the craving.

  "A devastated land lies in midsea,
a land that is called Crete," he answered me.   95
"Under its king[1] the world once lived chastely.

  Within that land there was a mountain blessed
with leaves and waters, and they called it Ida;
but it is withered now like some old thing.

  It once was chosen as a trusted cradle   100
by Rhea for her son;[2] to hide him better,
when he cried out, she had her servants clamor.

  Within the mountain is a huge Old Man,
who stands erect—his back turned toward Damietta[3]—
and looks at Rome as if it were his mirror.   105

  The Old Man's head is fashioned of fine gold,

---

9. A hot sulphurous spring that supplied water to the houses of prostitutes in the region north of Viterbo. **1.** Saturn, mythical king of Crete during the golden age. **2.** Jupiter was hidden by his mother, Rhea, from his father, Saturn, who tried to devour all his children to thwart a prophecy that he would be dethroned by one of them. So that Saturn would not hear the infant's cries, Rhea had her servants cry out and beat their shields with their swords. **3.** A city in Egypt. The Old Man has been interpreted as an emblem of degenerating humankind.

the purest silver forms his arms and chest,
but he is made of brass down to the cleft;
  below that point he is of choicest iron
except for his right foot, made of baked clay; 110
and he rests more on this than on the left.[4]
  Each part of him, except the gold, is cracked;
and down that fissure there are tears that drip;
when gathered, they pierce through that cavern's floor
  and, crossing rocks into this valley, form 115
the Acheron and Styx and Phlegethon;
and then they make their way down this tight channel,
  and at the point past which there's no descent,
they form Cocytus;[5] since you are to see
what that pool is, I'll not describe it here." 120
  And I asked him: "But if the rivulet
must follow such a course down from our world,
why can we see it only at this boundary?"[6]
  And he to me: "You know this place is round;
and though the way that you have come is long, 125
and always toward the left and toward the bottom,
  you still have not completed all the circle:
so that, if something new appears to us,
it need not bring such wonder to your face."[7]
  And I again: "Master, where's Phlegethon 130
and where is Lethe? You omit the second
and say this rain of tears has formed the first."
  "I'm pleased indeed," he said, "with all your questions;
yet one of them might well have found its answer
already—when you saw the red stream boiling.[8] 135
  You shall see Lethe, but past this abyss,
there where the spirits go to cleanse themselves
when their repented guilt is set aside."[9]
  Then he declared: "The time has come to quit
this wood; see that you follow close behind me; 140
these margins form a path that does not scorch,
  and over them, all flaming vapor is quenched."

CANTO XV

Still the Seventh Circle, Third Ring: the Violent against God. Second
Zone: the Sodomites, endlessly crossing the fiery sands beneath the rain of
fire. Brunetto Latini, whom Dante treats as mentor. Priscian, Francesco
d'Accorso, and Andrea dei Mozzi, Bishop of Florence.

  Now one of the hard borders bears us forward;
the river mist forms shadows overhead
and shields the shores and water from the fire.
  Just as between Wissant and Bruges,[1] the Flemings,

---

4. The four metals and the clay represent the degeneration of history: see Daniel 2.31–35.   **5.** The frozen lake at the bottom of Hell: see 32.22–30 and 34.52.   **6.** Not entirely consistently, Dante seems to have thought of the four rivers of Hell as ponds or pools formed by a single river that flows from the tears of the Old Man of Crete.   **7.** Since Dante has not yet completed a full round of the circular pit that is Hell he should not be surprised to see something new.   **8.** See note to 12.94.   **9.** Lethe is crossed when Dante passes into the Earthly Paradise on the top of Mount Purgatory.   **1.** Cities that, for Dante, mark the two ends of the dike that protects Flanders from the sea.

in terror of the tide that floods toward them, 5
have built a wall of dykes to daunt the sea;
    and as the Paduans, along the Brenta,[2]
build bulwarks to defend their towns and castles
before the dog days fall on Carentana;
    just so were these embankments, even though 10
they were not built so high and not so broad,
whoever was the artisan who made them.
    By now we were so distant from the wood
that I should not have made out where it was—
not even if I'd turned around to look— 15
    when we came on a company of spirits
who made their way along the bank; and each
stared steadily at us, as in the dusk,
    beneath the new moon, men look at each other.
They knit their brows and squinted at us—just 20
as an old tailor at his needle's eye.
    And when that family looked harder, I
was recognized by one, who took me by
the hem and cried out: "This is marvelous!"
    That spirit having stretched his arm toward me, 25
I fixed my eyes upon his baked, brown features,
so that the scorching of his face could not
    prevent my mind from recognizing him;
and lowering my face to meet his face,
I answered him: "Are you here, Ser Brunetto?" 30
    And he: "My son, do not mind if Brunetto
Latino[3] lingers for a while with you
and lets the file he's with pass on ahead."
    I said: "With all my strength I pray you, stay;
and if you'd have me rest awhile with you, 35
I shall, if that please him with whom I go."
    "O son," he said, "whoever of this flock
stops but a moment, stays a hundred years
and cannot shield himself when fire strikes.
    Therefore move on; below—but close—I'll follow; 40
and then I shall rejoin my company,
who go lamenting their eternal sorrows."
    I did not dare to leave my path for his
own level; but I walked with head bent low
as does a man who goes in reverence. 45
    And he began: "What destiny or chance
has led you here below before your last
day came, and who is he who shows the way?"
    "There, in the sunlit life above," I answered,
"before my years were full, I went astray 50
within a valley. Only yesterday

<hr>

2. A river that flows through Padua, fed by the melting snows in the mountains of the province of Carentana (modern Carinthia in Austria).   3. Brunetto Latini (ca. 1220–1294), active in Florentine politics and the author of—among other works—two books: a prose encyclopedia in French called the *Tresor*, which emphasizes the qualities needed for civic duty, and a shorter allegorical poem in Italian called the *Tesoretto*, which combines autobiography with philosophy.

at dawn I turned my back upon it—but
when I was newly lost, he here appeared,
to guide me home again along this path."

And he to me: "If you pursue your star,   55
you cannot fail to reach a splendid harbor,
if in fair life, I judged you properly;

and if I had not died too soon for this,
on seeing Heaven was so kind to you,
I should have helped sustain you in your work.   60

But that malicious, that ungrateful people
come down, in ancient times, from Fiesole⁴—
still keeping something of the rock and mountain—

for your good deeds, will be your enemy:
and there is cause—among the sour sorbs,   65
the sweet fig is not meant to bear its fruit.⁵

The world has long since called them blind, a people
presumptuous, avaricious, envious;
be sure to cleanse yourself of their foul ways.

Your fortune holds in store such honor for you,   70
one party and the other will be hungry
for you—but keep the grass far from the goat.⁶

For let the beasts of Fiesole find forage
among themselves, and leave the plant alone—
if still, among their dung, it rises up—   75

in which there lives again the sacred seed
of those few Romans who remained in Florence
when such a nest of wickedness was built."

"If my desire were answered totally,"
I said to Ser Brunetto, "you'd still be   80
among, not banished from, humanity.

Within my memory is fixed—and now
moves me—your dear, your kind paternal image
when, in the world above, from time to time

you taught me how man makes himself eternal;⁷   85
and while I live, my gratitude for that
must always be apparent in my words.

What you have told me of my course, I write;
I keep it with another text, for comment
by one who'll understand, if I may reach her.⁸   90

One thing alone I'd have you plainly see:
so long as I am not rebuked by conscience,
I stand prepared for Fortune, come what may.

My ears find no new pledge in that prediction;
therefore, let Fortune turn her wheel as she   95
may please, and let the peasant turn his mattock."⁹

At this, my master turned his head around

---

4. A hill town north of Florence whose rustic inhabitants were supposed to have joined with noble Romans in the founding of Florence, creating an unstable mixture.   5. The *sour sorbs*—a sorb is a small fruit, edible only when overripe—are the Florentines descended from Fiesole; the *sweet fig* is Brunetto's term for the aristocratic Dante.   6. Either both parties will ask you to join them or both parties will want to devour you—but keep yourself apart.   7. In the *Tresor* Brunetto says that earthly glory gives man a second life through an enduring reputation.   8. Beatrice.   9. The traditional image of Fortune and her wheel is here compared to the rustic image of the peasant turning the soil with his hoe.

and toward the right, and looked at me and said:
"He who takes note of this has listened well."
But nonetheless, my talk with Ser Brunetto   100
continues, and I ask of him who are
his comrades of repute and excellence.
And he to me: "To know of some is good;
but for the rest, silence is to be praised;
the time we have is short for so much talk.   105
In brief, know that my company has clerics
and men of letters and of fame—and all
were stained by one same sin upon the earth.[1]
That sorry crowd holds Priscian and Francesco
d'Accorso;[2] and among them you can see,   110
if you have any longing for such scurf,
the one[3] the Servant of His Servants sent
from the Arno to the Bacchiglione's banks,[4]
and there he left his tendons strained by sin.
I would say more; but both my walk and words   115
must not be longer, for—beyond—I see
new smoke emerging from the sandy bed.
Now people come with whom I must not be.
Let my *Tesoro*, in which I still live,
be precious to you; and I ask no more."   120
And then he turned and seemed like one of those
who race across the fields to win the green
cloth at Verona;[5] of those runners, he
    appeared to be the winner, not the loser.

CANTO XVI

Still the Seventh Circle, Third Ring, Second Zone: other Sodomites.
Three Florentines, Guido Guerra, Tegghiaio Aldobrandi, Jacopo
Rusticucci. The decadence of Florence. Phlegethon, cascading into the
next zone. The cord of Dante, used by Virgil to summon a monstrous
figure from the waters.

No sooner had I reached the place where one
could hear a murmur, like a beehive's hum,
of waters as they fell to the next circle,
    when, setting out together, three shades ran,
    leaving another company that passed   5
    beneath the rain of bitter punishment.
They came toward us, and each of them cried out:
"Stop, you who by your clothing seem to be
someone who comes from our indecent country!"[6]
    Ah me, what wounds I saw upon their limbs,   10
    wounds new and old, wounds that the flames seared in!

---

1. Sodomy, condemned in the Middle Ages as unnatural.   2. A Florentine law professor (d. 1293).
Priscian: Greek-language grammarian (sixth century A.D.).   3. Andrea de' Mozzi, bishop of Florence
(1287–95), transferred by Pope Boniface (designated here by an official title for the pope, *the Servant of
His* [i.e., Christ's] *Servants*) from Florence to Vicenza.   4. The Arno runs through Florence, the Bacchiglione through Vicenza.   5. A footrace run at Verona on the first Sunday in Lent, the prize being a
piece of green cloth (the *palio*). For the race to be run by the Christian, see 1 Corinthians 9.24–25.
6. Florence.

It pains me still as I remember it.
　　When they cried out, my master paid attention;
he turned his face toward me and then he said:
"Now wait: to these one must show courtesy.　　　　　　15
　　And were it not the nature of this place
for shafts of fire to fall, I'd say that haste
was seemlier for you than for those three."[7]
　　As soon as we stood still, they started up
their ancient wail again; and when they reached us,　　20
they formed a wheel, all three of them together.
　　As champions, naked, oiled, will always do,
each studying the grip that serves him best
before the blows and wounds begin to fall,[8]
　　while wheeling so, each one made sure his face　　25
was turned to me, so that their necks opposed
their feet in one uninterrupted flow.
　　And, "If the squalor of this shifting sand,
together with our baked and barren features,
makes us and our requests contemptible,"　　　　　30
　　one said, "then may our fame incline your mind
to tell us who you are, whose living feet
can make their way through Hell with such assurance.
　　He in whose steps you see me tread, although
he now must wheel about both peeled and naked,　　35
was higher in degree than you believe:
　　he was a grandson of the good Gualdrada,
and Guido Guerra[9] was his name; in life
his sword and his good sense accomplished much.
　　The other who, behind me, tramples sand—　　　40
Tegghiaio Aldobrandi,[1] one whose voice
should have been heeded in the world above.
　　And I, who share this punishment with them,
was Jacopo Rusticucci;[2] certainly,
more than all else, my savage wife destroyed me."　　45
　　If I'd had shield and shelter from the fire,
I should have thrown myself down there among them—
I think my master would have sanctioned that;
　　but since that would have left me burned and baked,
my fear won out against the good intention　　　50
that made me so impatient to embrace them.
　　Then I began: "Your present state had fixed
not scorn but sorrow in me—and so deeply
that it will only disappear slowly—
　　as soon as my lord spoke to me with words　　　55
that made me understand what kind of men
were coming toward us, men of worth like yours.
　　For I am of your city; and with fondness,
I've always told and heard the others tell

---

7. To hurry was considered undignified.　　8. The three naked Florentines form a circle and are compared to oiled wrestlers (a sport practiced in Dante's time).　　9. A leading participant in the civil strife in Florence (d. 1272).　　1. An ally of Guido (see 6.79).　　2. An ally of Tegghiaio who blames his wife for his sodomy (see 6.80).

of both your actions and your honored names.   60
   I leave the gall and go for the sweet apples[3]
that I was promised by my truthful guide;
but first I must descend into the center."
   "So may your soul long lead your limbs and may
your fame shine after you," he answered then,   65
"tell us if courtesy and valor still
   abide within our city as they did
when we were there, or have they disappeared
completely; for Guiglielmo Borsiere,[4]
   who only recently has come to share   70
our torments, and goes there with our companions,
has caused us much affliction with his words."[5]
   "Newcomers to the city and quick gains
have brought excess and arrogance to you,
o Florence, and you weep for it already!"   75
   So I cried out with face upraised; the three
looked at each other when they heard my answer
as men will stare when they have heard the truth.
   "If you can always offer a reply
so readily to others," said all three,   80
"then happy you who speak, at will, so clearly.
   So, if you can escape these lands of darkness
and see the lovely stars on your return,
when you repeat with pleasure, 'I was there,'
   be sure that you remember us to men."   85
At this they broke their wheel; and as they fled,
their swift legs seemed to be no less than wings.
   The time it took for them to disappear—
more brief than time it takes to say "amen";
and so, my master thought it right to leave.   90
   I followed him. We'd only walked a little
when roaring water grew so near to us
we hardly could have heard each other speak.
   And even as the river[6] that is first
to take its own course eastward from Mount Viso,   95
along the left flank of the Apennines
   (which up above is called the Acquacheta,
before it spills into its valley bed
and flows without that name beyond Forlì),
   reverberates above San Benedetto   100
dell'Alpe as it cascades in one leap,
where there is space enough to house a thousand;
   so did we hear that blackened water roar
as it plunged down a steep and craggy bank,
enough to deafen us in a few hours.   105

---

3. Leave Hell and head for Paradise.　4. An elegant member of Florentine society.　5. An account of the recent dissension within the city, to which Dante himself was soon to fall victim.　6. Dante compares the roar of Phlegethon to the Montone River in northern Italy, whose course he traces in the next few lines.

Around my waist I had a cord[7] as girdle,
and with it once I thought I should be able
to catch the leopard with the painted hide.[8]

And after I had loosened it completely,
just as my guide commanded me to do,
I handed it to him, knotted and coiled.

At this, he wheeled around upon his right
and cast it, at some distance from the edge,
straight down into the depth of the ravine.

"And surely something strange must here reply,"
I said within myself, "to this strange sign—
the sign my master follows with his eye."

Ah, how much care men ought to exercise
with those whose penetrating intellect
can see our thoughts—not just our outer act![9]

He said to me: "Now there will soon emerge
what I await and what your thought has conjured:
it soon must be discovered to your sight."

Faced with that truth which seems a lie, a man
should always close his lips as long as he can—
to tell it shames him, even though he's blameless;

but here I can't be still; and by the lines
of this my Comedy, reader, I swear—
and may my verse find favor for long years—

that through the dense and darkened air I saw
a figure swimming, rising up, enough
to bring amazement to the firmest heart,

like one returning from the waves where he
went down to loose an anchor snagged upon
a reef or something else hid in the sea,

who stretches upward and draws in his feet.

110

115

120

125

130

135

CANTO XVII

*The monster Geryon. The Seventh Circle, Third Ring, Third Zone: the
Violent against Nature and Art (Usurers), each seated beneath the rain of
fire with a purse—bearing his family's heraldic emblem—around his neck.
Descent to the Eighth Circle on the back of Geryon.*

"Behold the beast who bears the pointed tail,
who crosses mountains, shatters weapons, walls!
Behold the one whose stench fills all the world!"[1]

So did my guide begin to speak to me,
and then he signaled him to come ashore
close to the end of those stone passageways.

5

---

7. While commentators disagree, it seems likely that this cord is a reference both to Job 41.1, where God
says He can draw Leviathan up with a hook and bind his tongue with a cord, and to Francis of Assisi, who
wore a cord as a sign of humility and obedience. As a layman, Dante may have had a connection with the
Franciscan friars, a common circumstance at the time.   8. The leopard of canto 1, representing
fraud.   9. Dante now realizes that Virgil can read his thoughts.   1. Geryon, the embodiment of fraud.
For this figure Dante drew upon classical literature, where he had not three natures—human, reptilian,
and bestial—combined into one, as here, but three bodies and three heads.

And he came on, that filthy effigy
of fraud, and landed with his head and torso
but did not draw his tail onto the bank.
    The face he wore was that of a just man,   10
so gracious was his features' outer semblance;
and all his trunk, the body of a serpent;
    he had two paws, with hair up to the armpits;
his back and chest as well as both his flanks
had been adorned with twining knots and circlets.   15
    No Turks or Tartars ever fashioned fabrics
more colorful in background and relief,
nor had Arachne[2] ever loomed such webs.
    As boats will sometimes lie along the shore,
with part of them on land and part in water,   20
and just as there, among the guzzling Germans,[3]
    the beaver[4] sets himself when he means war,
so did that squalid beast lie on the margin
of stone that serves as border for the sand.
    And all his tail was quivering in the void   25
while twisting upward its envenomed fork,
which had a tip just like a scorpion's.
    My guide said: "Now we'd better bend our path
a little, till we reach as far as that
malicious beast which crouches over there."   30
    Thus we descended on the right hand side
and moved ten paces on the stony brink
in order to avoid the sand and fire.
    When we had reached the sprawling beast, I saw—
a little farther on, upon the sand—   35
some sinners sitting near the fissured rock.
    And here my master said to me: "So that
you may experience this ring in full,
go now, and see the state in which they are.
    But keep your conversation with them brief;   40
till you return, I'll parley with this beast,
to see if he can lend us his strong shoulders."
    So I went on alone and even farther
along the seventh circle's outer margin,
to where the melancholy people sat.   45
    Despondency was bursting from their eyes;
this side, then that, their hands kept fending off,
at times the flames, at times the burning soil:
    not otherwise do dogs in summer—now
with muzzle, now with paw—when they are bitten   50
by fleas or gnats or by the sharp gadfly.
    When I had set my eyes upon the faces
of some on whom that painful fire falls,
I recognized no one; but I did notice
    that from the neck of each a purse was hung   55

2. A woman in classical literature famous for weaving, turned into a spider: see Ovid, *Metamorphoses* 6.
3. A tradition going back to the Romans accused the Germans of gluttony.   **4.** Which was thought to
catch fish by putting its tail into the water.

that had a special color and an emblem,
and their eyes seemed to feast upon these pouches.[5]

    Looking about—when I had come among them—
I saw a yellow purse with azure on it
that had the face and manner of a lion.   60

    Then, as I let my eyes move farther on,
I saw another purse that was bloodred,
and it displayed a goose more white than butter.

    And one who had an azure, pregnant sow
inscribed as emblem on his white pouch, said   65
to me: "What are you doing in this pit?

    Now you be off; and since you're still alive,
remember that my neighbor Vitaliano[6]
shall yet sit here, upon my left hand side.

    Among these Florentines, I'm Paduan;   70
I often hear them thunder in my ears,
shouting, 'Now let the sovereign cavalier,

    the one who'll bring the purse with three goats,[7] come!' "
At this he slewed his mouth, and then he stuck
his tongue out, like an ox that licks its nose.   75

    And I, afraid that any longer stay
might anger him who'd warned me to be brief,
made my way back from those exhausted souls.

    I found my guide, who had already climbed
upon the back of that brute animal,   80
and he told me: "Be strong and daring now,

    for our descent is by this kind of stairs:
you mount in front; I want to be between,
so that the tail can't do you any harm."[8]

    As one who feels the quartan fever near   85
and shivers, with his nails already blue,
the sight of shade enough to make him shudder,

    so I became when I had heard these words;
but then I felt the threat of shame, which makes
a servant—in his kind lord's presence—brave.   90

    I settled down on those enormous shoulders;
I wished to say (and yet my voice did not
come as I thought): "See that you hold me tight."

    But he who—other times, in other dangers—
sustained me, just as soon as I had mounted,   95
clasped me within his arms and propped me up,

    and said: "Now, Geryon, move on; take care
to keep your circles wide, your landing slow;
remember the new weight you're carrying."

    Just like a boat that, starting from its moorings,   100
moves backward, backward, so that beast took off;
and when he felt himself completely clear,

---

5. These are usurers, men who lent money for interest, which was forbidden by the Church in the Middle Ages (although often practiced). Each has a coat of arms on his purse by which he can be identified; all are Italians.   6. The speaker is from Padua and here maliciously identifies another Paduan who will soon be joining him.   7. A prominent Florentine banker.   8. Virgil protects Dante from Geryon's scorpion's tail.

he turned his tail to where his chest had been
and, having stretched it, moved it like an eel,
and with his paws he gathered in the air.   105

I do not think that there was greater fear
in Phaethon[9] when he let his reins go free—
for which the sky, as one still sees, was scorched—

nor in poor Icarus[1] when he could feel
his sides unwinged because the wax was melting,   110
his father shouting to him, "That way's wrong!"

than was in me when, on all sides, I saw
that I was in the air, and everything
had faded from my sight—except the beast.

Slowly, slowly, swimming, he moves on;   115
he wheels and he descends, but I feel only
the wind upon my face and the wind rising.

Already, on our right, I heard the torrent
resounding, there beneath us, horribly,
so that I stretched my neck and looked below.   120

Then I was more afraid of falling off,
for I saw fires and I heard laments,
at which I tremble, crouching, and hold fast.

And now I saw what I had missed before:
his wheeling and descent—because great torments   125
were drawing closer to us on all sides.

Just as a falcon long upon the wing—
who, seeing neither lure nor bird, compels
the falconer to cry, "Ah me, you fall!"—

descends, exhausted, in a hundred circles,   130
where he had once been swift, and sets himself,
embittered and enraged, far from his master;[2]

such, at the bottom of the jagged rock,
was Geryon, when he had set us down.
And once our weight was lifted from his back,   135
he vanished like an arrow from a bow.

CANTO XVIII

*The Eighth Circle, called Malebolge ("Evil-Pouches"), with its Ten
Pouches, where "ordinary" fraud is punished. The First Pouch, with
Panders and Seducers scourged by horned demons. Venèdico
Caccianemico. Jason. The Second Pouch, with Flatterers immersed in
excrement. Alessio Interminei. Thaïs.*

There is a place in Hell called Malebolge,[3]
made all of stone the color of crude iron,
as is the wall that makes its way around it.
Right in the middle of this evil field

---

9. Son of Apollo, Phaethon tried to drive the chariot of the sun, but when it got out of control it scorched both Earth and the heavens, creating the Milky Way (Ovid, *Metamorphoses* 2).   1. Who, flying with wings made of wax and feathers, went too near the sun and fell (Ovid, *Metamorphoses* 8).   2. Unless it sights prey or is called back with a lure by its master, a trained falcon will continue flying until exhaustion compels it to descend.   3. Evil-pouches (Italian), since the eighth circle is divided into ten *bolge*, pouches or ditches.

is an abyss, a broad and yawning pit,[4]   5
whose structure I shall tell in its due place.

The belt, then, that extends between the pit
and that hard, steep wall's base is circular;
its bottom has been split into ten valleys.

Just as, where moat on moat surrounds a castle   10
in order to keep guard upon the walls,
the ground they occupy will form a pattern,

so did the valleys here from a design;
and as such fortresses have bridges running
right from their thresholds toward the outer bank,   15

so here, across the banks and ditches, ridges
ran from the base of that rock wall until
the pit that cuts them short and joins them all.

This was the place in which we found ourselves
when Geryon had put us down; the poet   20
held to the left, and I walked at his back.

Upon the right I saw new misery,
I saw new tortures and new torturers,
filling the first of Malebolge's moats.

Along its bottom, naked sinners moved,   25
to our side of the middle, facing us;
beyond that, they moved with us, but more quickly—

as, in the year of Jubilee,[5] the Romans,
confronted by great crowds, contrived a plan
that let the people pass across the bridge,   30

for to one side went all who had their eyes
upon the Castle, heading toward St. Peter's,
and to the other, those who faced the Mount.

Both left and right, along the somber rock,
I saw horned demons with enormous whips,   35
who lashed those spirits cruelly from behind.

Ah, how their first strokes made those sinners lift
their heels! Indeed no sinner waited for
a second stroke to fall—or for a third.

And as I moved ahead, my eyes met those   40
of someone else, and suddenly I said:
"I was not spared the sight of him before."

And so I stayed my steps, to study him;
my gentle guide had stopped together with me
and gave me leave to take a few steps back.   45

That scourged soul thought that he could hide himself
by lowering his face; it helped him little,
for I said: "You, who cast your eyes upon

the ground, if these your features are not false,
must be Venèdico Caccianemico;[6]   50
but what brings you to sauces so piquant?"

And he to me: "I speak unwillingly;

---

4. The last, or ninth, circle of Hell, described in cantos 21–34.   **5.** Thirteen hundred was a Jubilee Year, and Dante here describes the crowd control on the bridge that ran between the Castle of St. Angelo and St. Peter's.   **6.** A man from Bologna (renowned for its good food) who was reputed to have turned his sister Gisobella over to the Marquis of Este.

but your plain speech, that brings the memory
of the old world to me, is what compels me;
　　For it was I who led Ghisolabella   55
to do as the Marquis would have her do—
however they retell that filthy tale.
　　I'm not the only Bolognese who weeps here;
indeed, this place is so crammed full of us
that not so many tongues have learned to say 60
　　sipa between the Sàvena and Reno;[7]
if you want faith and testament of that,
just call to mind our avaricious hearts."
　　And as he spoke, a demon cudgeled him
with his horsewhip and cried: "Be off, you pimp, 65
there are no women here for you to trick."
　　I joined my escort once again; and then
with but few steps, we came upon a place
where, from the bank, a rocky ridge ran out.
　　We climbed quite easily along that height; 70
and turning right upon its jagged back,
we took our leave of those eternal circlings.
　　When we had reached the point where that ridge opens
below to leave a passage for the lashed,
my guide said: "Stay, and make sure that the sight 75
　　of still more ill-born spirits strikes your eyes,
for you have not yet seen their faces, since
they have been moving in our own direction."
　　From the old bridge we looked down at the ranks
of those approaching from the other side; 80
they too were driven onward by the lash.
　　And my good master, though I had not asked,
urged me: "Look at that mighty one who comes
and does not seem to shed a tear of pain:
　　how he still keeps the image of a king! 85
That shade is Jason,[8] who with heart and head
deprived the men of Colchis of their ram.
　　He made a landfall on the isle of Lemnos
after its women, bold and pitiless,
had given all their island males to death. 90
　　With polished words and love signs he took in
Hypsipyle, the girl whose own deception
had earlier deceived the other women.
　　And he abandoned her, alone and pregnant;
such guilt condemns him to such punishment; 95
and for Medea, too, revenge is taken.
　　With him go those who cheated so: this is
enough for you to know of that first valley
and of the souls it clamps within its jaws."

---

7. *Sipa* is a word for "yes" in the dialect spoken in the territory between the rivers Sàvena and Reno, which comprise the boundaries of Bologna.　　8. Jason led the Argonauts on the voyage to the island of Colchis, where they stole the golden fleece. He seduced and abandoned Hypsipyle, who had hidden her father when the other women of Lemnos were killing all the males. He also abandoned Medea. For his story, see Ovid, *Metamorphoses* 7.

We were already where the narrow path   100
reaches and intersects the second bank
and serves as shoulder for another bridge.

We heard the people whine in the next pouch
and heard them as they snorted with their snouts;
we heard them use their palms to beat themselves.   105

And exhalations, rising from below,
stuck to the banks, encrusting them with mold,
and so waged war against both eyes and nose.

The bottom is so deep, we found no spot
to see it from, except by climbing up   110
the arch until the bridge's highest point.

This was the place we reached; the ditch beneath
held people plunged in excrement that seemed
as if it had been poured from human privies.

And while my eyes searched that abysmal sight,   115
I saw one with a head so smeared with shit,
one could not see if he were lay or cleric.

He howled: "Why do you stare more greedily
at me than at the others who are filthy?"
And I: "Because, if I remember right,   120

I have seen you before, with your hair dry;
and so I eye you more than all: you are
Alessio Interminei of Lucca."[9]

Then he continued, pounding on his pate:
"I am plunged here because of flatteries—   125
of which my tongue had such sufficiency."

At which my guide advised me: "See you thrust
your head a little farther to the front,
so that your eyes can clearly glimpse the face

of that besmirched, bedraggled harridan   130
who scratches at herself with shit-filled nails,
and now she crouches, now she stands upright.

That is Thaïs,[1] the harlot who returned
her lover's question, 'Are you very grateful
to me?' by saying, 'Yes, enormously.' "   135
And now our sight has had its fill of this."

CANTO XIX

*The Eighth Circle, Third Pouch, where the Simonists are set, heads
down, into holes in the rock, with their protruding feet tormented by
flames. Pope Nicholas III. Dante's invective against simoniacal popes.*

O Simon Magus![2] O his sad disciples!
Rapacious ones, who take the things of God,
that ought to be the brides of Righteousness,
      and make them fornicate for gold and silver!
The time has come to let the trumpet sound   5

9. A prominent citizen of Lucca, in northern Italy.   1. A character in a play by the Roman writer Terence
(186 or 185–159? B.C.)   2. Because in the Bible Simon Magus tried to buy spiritual power from the
apostles (Acts 8. 9–24), the selling of any spiritual good for material gain was known in the Middle Ages
as simony. The most common form of simony was the selling of Church offices.

for you; your place is here in this third pouch.

We had already reached the tomb beyond
and climbed onto the ridge, where its high point
hangs just above the middle of the ditch.

O Highest Wisdom, how much art you show   10
in heaven, earth, and this sad world below,
how just your power is when it allots!³

Along the sides and down along the bottom,
I saw that livid rock was perforated:
the openings were all one width and round.   15

They did not seem to me less broad or more
than those that in my handsome San Giovanni⁴
were made to serve as basins for baptizing;

and one of these, not many years ago,
I broke for someone who was drowning in it: 20
and let this be my seal to set men straight.

Out from the mouth of each hole there emerged
a sinner's feet and so much of his legs
up to the thigh; the rest remained within.

Both soles of every sinner were on fire;   25
their joints were writhing with such violence,
they would have severed withes⁵ and ropes of grass.

As flame on oily things will only stir
along the outer surface, so there, too,
that fire made its way from heels to toes.   30

"Master," I said, "who is that shade who suffers
and quivers more than all his other comrades,
that sinner who is licked by redder flames?"

And he to me: "If you would have me lead
you down along the steepest of the banks,   35
from him you'll learn about his self and sins."

And I: "What pleases you will please me too:
you are my lord; you know I do not swerve
from what you will; you know what is unspoken."

At this we came upon the fourth embankment;   40
we turned and, keeping to the left, descended
into the narrow, perforated bottom.

My good lord did not let me leave his side
until he'd brought me to the hole that held
that sinner who lamented with his legs.   45

"Whoever you may be, dejected soul,⁶
whose head is downward, planted like a pole,"
my words began, "do speak if you are able."

I stood as does the friar who confesses
the foul assassin who, fixed fast, head down,   50
calls back the friar, and so delays his death;

---

3. Dante is here applauding the artfulness of infernal justice because the simoniacs, who cared most for their purses, are here stuffed into fiery purses hewn into the rock; see line 72 below.   **4.** The baptistery in Florence where Dante was baptized. The subsequent personal reference has never been satisfactorily explained.   **5.** Ropes made of twisted vines.   **6.** Pope Nicholas III (pope 1277–80). He mistakenly believes that one of his successors, Boniface VIII, has come to be squeezed into the hole (line 53). Like all damned souls, Nicholas has foreknowledge, and because Boniface did not die until 1303 Nicholas is surprised at what he thinks is his appearance in 1300.

and he cried out: "Are you already standing,
already standing there, o Boniface?
The book has lied to me by several years.

Are you so quickly sated with the riches   55
for which you did not fear to take by guile
the Lovely Lady,[7] then to violate her?"

And I became like those who stand as if
they have been mocked, who cannot understand
what has been said to them and can't respond.   60

But Virgil said: "Tell this to him at once:
'I am not he—not whom you think I am.' "
And I replied as I was told to do.

At this the spirit twisted both his feet,
and sighing and with a despairing voice,   65
he said: "What is it, then, you want of me?

If you have crossed the bank and climbed so far
to find out who I am, then know that I
was one of those who wore the mighty mantle,

and surely was a son of the she-bear,[8]   70
so eager to advance the cubs that I
pursed wealth above while here I purse myself.

Below my head there is the place of those
who took the way of simony before me;
and they are stuffed within the clefts of stone.   75

I, too, shall yield my place and fall below
when he arrives, the one for whom I had
mistaken you when I was quick to question.

But I have baked my feet a longer time,
have stood like this, upon my head, than he   80
is to stand planted here with scarlet feet:

for after him, one uglier in deeds
will come, a lawless shepherd from the west,
worthy to cover him and cover me.[9]

He'll be a second Jason,[1] of whom we read   85
in *Maccabees*; and just as Jason's king
was soft to him, so shall the king of France

be soft to this one." And I do not know
if I was too rash here—I answered so:
"Then tell me now, how much gold did our Lord   90

ask that Saint Peter give to him before
he placed the keys within his care?[2] Surely
the only thing he said was: 'Follow me.'

And Peter and the others never asked
for gold or silver when they chose Matthias   95
to take the place of the transgressing soul.[3]

Stay as you are, for you are rightly punished;
and guard with care the money got by evil

---

7. The Church.   8. The arms of Nicholas's family (the Orsini) included a she-bear.   9. Clement V, who became pope in 1305 after agreeing with the French king to remove the papacy to Avignon in France.   1. Jason became high priest of the Jews by bribing the king: see 2 Maccabees 4.7–9.   2. See Matthew 16.18–19 and 4.18–19. The keys are the Church's power to bind (condemn) and to loose (absolve).   3. Matthias was chosen by lot to fill the place of Judas (Acts 1.23–26).

that made you so audacious against Charles.[4]

And were it not that I am still prevented   100
by reverence for those exalted keys
that you had held within the happy life,

I'd utter words much heavier than these,
because your avarice afflicts the world:
it tramples on the good, lifts up the wicked.   105

You, shepherds, the Evangelist[5] had noticed
when he saw her who sits upon the waters
and realized she fornicates with kings,

she who was born with seven heads and had
the power and support of the ten horns,   110
as long as virtue was her husband's pleasure.

You've made yourselves a god of gold and silver;
how are you different from idolaters,
save that they worship one and you a hundred?

Ah, Constantine,[6] what wickedness was born—   115
and not from your conversion—from the dower
that you bestowed upon the first rich father!"

And while I sang such notes to him—whether
it was his indignation or his conscience
that bit him—he kicked hard with both his soles.   120

I do indeed believe it pleased my guide:
he listened always with such satisfied
expression to the sound of those true words.

And then he gathered me in both his arms
and, when he had me fast against his chest,   125
where he climbed down before, climbed upward now;

nor did he tire of clasping me until
he brought me to the summit of the arch
that crosses from the fourth to the fifth rampart.

And here he gently set his burden down—   130
gently because the ridge was rough and steep,
and would have been a rugged pass for goats.

From there another valley lay before me.

CANTO XX

The Eighth Circle, Fourth Pouch, where Diviners, Astrologers, Magicians,
all have their heads turned backward. Amphiaraus. Tiresias. Aruns.
Manto. Virgil on the origin of Mantua, his native city. Eurypylus.
Michael Scot and other moderns adept at fraud.

I must make verses of new punishment
and offer matter now for Canto Twenty
of this first canticle—of the submerged.

I was already well prepared to stare

---

4. Nicholas was supposed to be involved in a plot against Charles of Anjou (1226–1285), ruler of Naples and Sicily.   **5.** John, author of Revelation: for this passage, which was originally interpreted as referring to pagan Rome but which Dante applies to the corrupt Church, see Revelation 17.1–108. The seven heads are the seven sacraments; the ten horns, the ten commandments; the husband, God.   **6.** Reputed author (d. 337) of a document—known as the Donation of Constantine—in which he granted temporal power and the right to acquire wealth to Pope Sylvester I, *the first rich father* of this passage. The document was proved to be a forgery in the fifteenth century.

below, into the depth that was disclosed,   5
where tears of anguished sorrow bathed the ground;
    and in the valley's circle I saw souls
advancing, mute and weeping, at the pace
that, in our world, holy processions take.
    As I inclined my head still more, I saw   10
that each, amazingly, appeared contorted
between the chin and where the chest begins;
    they had their faces twisted toward their haunches
and found it necessary to walk backward,
because they could not see ahead of them.   15
    Perhaps the force of palsy has so fully
distorted some, but that I've yet to see,
and I do not believe that that can be.
    May God so let you, reader, gather fruit
from what you read; and now think for yourself   20
how I could ever keep my own face dry
    when I beheld our image so nearby
and so awry that tears, down from the eyes,
bathed the buttocks, running down the cleft.
    Of course I wept, leaning against a rock   25
along that rugged ridge, so that my guide
told me: "Are you as foolish as the rest?
    Here pity only lives when it is dead:
for who can be more impious than he
who links God's judgment to passivity?[7]   30
    Lift, lift your head and see the one for whom
the earth was opened while the Thebans watched,
so that they all cried: 'Amphiaraus,[8]
    where are you rushing? Have you quit the fight?'
Nor did he interrupt his downward plunge   35
to Minos, who lays hands on every sinner.
    See how he's made a chest out of his shoulders;
and since he wanted so to see ahead,
he looks behind and walks a backward path.
    And see Tiresias,[9] who changed his mien   40
when from a man he turned into a woman,
so totally transforming all his limbs
    that then he had to strike once more upon
the two entwining serpents with his wand
before he had his manly plumes again.   45
    And Aruns[1] is the one who backs against
the belly of Tiresias—Aruns who,
in Luni's hills, tilled by the Carrarese,
    who live below, had as his home, a cave
among white marbles, from which he could gaze   50
at stars and sea with unimpeded view.

---

7. This is a rebuke to Dante, whose *passivity* is shown in his sympathy for the damned.   8. A Greek priest swallowed up by the Earth in a battle against the Thebans. For Minos, see 5.4.   9. A famous soothsayer of Thebes, he came upon two coupling serpents and, striking them with his rod, was transformed into a woman. Seven years later an identical encounter provoked the same action, and he was changed back into a man. See Ovid, *Metamorphoses* 3.   1. An Etruscan soothsayer from the city of Luni, in the area of Carrera where marble is quarried, is described by the Roman poet Lucan (d. A.D. 65) in his *Pharsalia*.

And she who covers up her breasts—which you
can't see—with her disheveled locks, who keeps
all of her hairy parts to the far side,
    was Manto,[2] who had searched through many lands,   55
then settled in the place where I was born;
on this, I'd have you hear me now a while.
    When Manto's father took his leave of life,
and Bacchus' city[3] found itself enslaved,
she wandered through the world for many years.   60
    High up, in lovely Italy, beneath
the Alps that shut in Germany above
Tirolo, lies a lake known as Benaco.[4]
    A thousand springs and more, I think, must flow
out of the waters of that lake to bathe   65
Pennino, Garda, Val Camonica.[5]
    And at its middle is a place where three—
the bishops of Verona, Brescia, Trento—
may bless if they should chance to come that way.
    Peschiera, strong and handsome fortress, built   70
to face the Brescians and the Bergamasques[6]
stands where the circling shore is at its lowest.
    There, all the waters that cannot be held
within the bosom of Benaco fall,
to form a river running through green meadows.   75
    No sooner has that stream begun to flow
than it is called the Mincio, not Benaco—
until Govèrnolo,[7] where it joins the Po.
    It's not flowed far before it finds flat land;
and there it stretches out to form a fen   80
that in the summer can at times be fetid.
    And when she passed that way, the savage virgin
saw land along the middle of the swamp,
untilled and stripped of its inhabitants.
    And there, to flee all human intercourse,   85
she halted with her slaves to ply her arts;
and there she lived, there left her empty body.
    And afterward, the people of those parts
collected at that place, because the marsh—
surrounding it on all sides—made it strong.   90
    They built a city over her dead bones;
and after her who first had picked that spot,
they called it Mantua—they cast no lots.
    There once were far more people in its walls,
before the foolishness of Casalodi   95
was tricked by the deceit of Pinamonte.[8]
    Therefore, I charge you, if you ever hear
a different tale of my town's origin,

---

2. A famous Theban soothsayer described by Roman poets.   **3.** Thebes.   **4.** The present-day Lake Garda, located in terms of an island where the boundaries of the three dioceses of Trent, Brescia, and Verona meet. *Tirolo:* a castle on the Adige River in the Italian Alps.   **5.** Two towns and a valley below the lake.   **6.** Inhabitants of two towns to the northwest of Peschiera, which is a town on the south shore of the lake.   **7.** A town some thirty miles south of Peschiera.   **8.** A reference to the internal intrigues of the rulers of Mantua in the thirteenth century.

do not let any falsehood gull the truth."[9]

And I: "O master, that which you have spoken   100
convinces me and so compels my trust
that others' words would only be spent coals.

But tell me if among the passing souls
you see some spirits worthy of our notice,
because my mind is bent on that alone."   105

Then he to me: "That shade who spreads his beard
down from his cheeks across his swarthy shoulders—
when Greece had been so emptied of its males

    that hardly any cradle held a son,
he was an augur; and at Aulis, he   110
and Calchas set the time to cut the cables.

    His name's Eurypylus;[1] a certain passage
of my high tragedy has sung it so;
you know that well enough, who know the whole.

That other there, his flanks extremely spare,   115
was Michael Scot,[2] a man who certainly
knew how the game of magic fraud was played.

See there Guido Bonatti; see Asdente,[3]
who now would wish he had attended to
his cord and leather, but repents too late.   120

See those sad women who had left their needle,
shuttle, and spindle to become diviners;[4]
they cast their spells with herbs and effigies.

But let us go; Cain with his thorns already
is at the border of both hemispheres   125
and there, below Seville, touches the sea.[5]

Last night the moon was at its full; you should
be well aware of this, for there were times
when it did you no harm in the deep wood."

These were his words to me; meanwhile we journeyed.   130

CANTO XXI

*The Eighth Circle, Fifth Pouch, with Barrators plunged into boiling pitch
and guarded by demons armed with prongs. A newly arrived magistrate
from Lucca. Ten demons assigned by Malacoda ("Evil-Tail"), the chief of
the Malebranche ("Evil-Claws"), to escort Dante and Virgil. The
remarkable signal for their march.*

We came along from one bridge to another,
talking of things my Comedy is not
concerned to sing. We held fast to the summit,
    then stayed our steps to spy the other cleft

---

9. Oddly enough, another account is given by Virgil in *Aeneid* 10.   **1.** Calchas and Eurypylus were prophets (or augurs) involved in the Trojan War; here Virgil says that they determined when the Greeks were to set out for the war from the island of Aulis, although *Aeneid* 2 gives a different account.   **2.** A famous scientist, philosopher, and astrologer from Scotland, he spent many years at the court of Frederick II (10.119) in Palermo and died in 1235.   **3.** A shoemaker famous as a soothsayer in thirteen-century Italy. *Guido Bonatti:* an astrologer at the court of Guido da Montefeltro (see canto 32).   **4.** Local soothsayers and potion makers.   **5.** Popular belief held that God placed Cain in the moon after the murder of Abel; *Cain with his thorns* means the moon with its spots, which is now setting at the western edge of the northern hemisphere. Overhead, in Jerusalem, it is the dawn of Holy Saturday.

of Malebolge and other vain laments.   5
I saw that it was wonderfully dark.
     As in the arsenal of the Venetians,[6]
all winter long a stew of sticky pitch
boils up to patch their sick and tattered ships
     that cannot sail (instead of voyaging,   10
some build new keels, some tow and tar the ribs
of hulls worn out by too much journeying;
     some hammer at the prow, some at the stern,
and some make oars, and some braid ropes and cords;
one mends the jib, another, the mainsail);   15
     so, not by fire but by the art of God,
below there boiled a thick and tarry mass
that covered all the banks and clamminess.
     I saw it, but I could not see within it;
no thing was visible but boiling bubbles,   20
the swelling of the pitch; and then it settled.
     And while I watched below attentively,
my guide called out to me: "Take care! Take care!"
And then, from where I stood, he drew me near.
     I turned around as one who is keen to see   25
a sight from which it would be wise to flee,
and then is horror-stricken suddenly—
     who does not stop his flight and yet looks back.
And then—behind us there—I saw a black
demon as he came racing up the crags.   30
     Ah, he was surely barbarous to see!
And how relentless seemed to me his acts!
His wings were open and his feet were lithe;
     across his shoulder, which was sharp and high,
he had slung a sinner, upward from the thighs;   35
in front, the demon gripped him by the ankles.
     Then from our bridge, he called: "O Malebranche,
I've got an elder of Saint Zita[7] for you!
Shove this one under—I'll go back for more—
     his city is well furnished with such stores;   40
there, everyone's a grafter but Bonturo;[8]
and there—for cash—they'll change a *no* to *yes*."
     He threw the sinner down, then wheeled along
the stony cliff: no mastiff's ever been
unleashed with so much haste to chase a thief.   45
     The sinner plunged, then surfaced, black with pitch;
but now the demons, from beneath the bridge,
shouted: "The Sacred Face[9] has no place here;
     here we swim differently than in the Serchio;[1]
if you don't want to feel our grappling hooks,   50
don't try to lift yourself above that ditch."

6. The Arsenal at Venice was one of the most important shipyards in Europe.   7. The elders of Saint
Zita in Lucca (a town near Florence) were ten citizens who ran the government. Malebranche (Evil-claws
[Italian]) is the generic name for the devils in this ditch, and each has a proper name as well (lines 76,
105, 118–26).   8. A current official in Lucca, Bonturo Dati was in fact known as the most corrupt of
all; the devil is being ironic.   9. The Sacred Face of Lucca, a venerated icon.   1. A river near Lucca.

They pricked him with a hundred prongs and more,
then taunted: "Here one dances under cover,
so try to grab your secret graft below."

The demons did the same as any cook   55
who has his urchins force the meat with hooks
deep down into the pot, that it not float.

Then my good master said to me: "Don't let
those demons see that you are here; take care
to crouch behind the cover of a crag.   60

No matter what offense they offer me,
don't be afraid; I know how these things go—
I've had to face such fracases before."[2]

When this was said, he moved beyond the bridgehead.
And on the sixth embankment, he had need   65
to show his imperturbability.

With the same frenzy, with the brouhaha
of dogs, when they beset a sorry wretch
who—startled—stops dead in his tracks and begs.

so, from beneath the bridge, the demons rushed   70
against my guide with all their prongs, but he
called out: "Can't you forget your savagery!

Before you try to maul me, just let one
of all your troop step forward. Hear me out,
and then decide if I am to be hooked."   75

At this they howled, "Let Malacoda[3] go!"
And one of them moved up—the others stayed—
and as he came, he asked: "How can he win?"

"O Malacoda, do you think I've come,"
my master answered him, "already armed—   80
as you can see—against your obstacles,

without the will of God and helpful fate?
Let us move on; it is the will of Heaven
for me to show this wild way to another."

At this the pride of Malacoda fell;   85
his prong dropped to his feet. He told his fellows:
"Since that's the way things stand, let us not wound him."

My guide then spoke to me: "O you, who crouch,
bent low among the bridge's splintered rocks,
you can feel safe—and now return to me."   90

At this I moved and quickly came to him.
The devils had edged forward, all of them;
I feared that they might fail to keep their word:

just so, I saw the infantry when they
marched out, under safe conduct, from Caprona;[4]   95
they trembled when they passed their enemies.

My body huddled closer to my guide;
I did not let the demons out of sight;
the looks they cast at us were less than kind.

They bent their hooks and shouted to each other: 100

2. Virgil may be referring to his difficulties with the devils in 8.82–130, when he and Dante tried to enter
the city of Dis.   3. Evil-tail (Italian).   4. A battle outside Florence in 1289, in which Dante may have
taken part.

"And shall I give it to him on the rump?"
And all of them replied, "yes, let him have it!"
    But Malacoda, still in conversation
with my good guide, turned quickly to his squadron
and said: "Be still, Scarmiglione, still!"   105
    To us he said: "There is no use in going
much farther on this ridge, because the sixth
bridge—at the bottom there—is smashed to bits.[5]
    Yet if you two still want to go ahead,
move up and walk along this rocky edge;   110
nearby, another ridge will form a path.[6]
    Five hours from this hour yesterday,
one thousand and two hundred sixty-six
years passed since that roadway was shattered here.[7]
    I'm sending ten of mine out there to see   115
if any sinner lifts his head for air;
go with my men—there is no malice in them."
    "Step forward, Alichino and Calcabrina,"
he then began to say, "and you, Cagnazzo;
and Barbariccia, who can lead the ten.   120
    Let Libicocco go, and Draghignazzo
and tusky Ciriatto and Graffiacane
and Farfarello and mad Rubicante.[8]
    Search all around the clammy stew of pitch;
keep these two safe and sound till the next ridge   125
that rises without break across the dens."
    "Ah me! What is this, master, that I see?"
I said. "Can't we do without company?
If you know how to go, I want no escort.
    If you are just as keen as usual,   130
can't you see how those demons grind their teeth?
Their brows are menacing, they promise trouble."
    And he to me: "I do not want you frightened:
just let them gnash away as they may wish;
they do it for the wretches boiled in pitch."   135
    They turned around along the left hand bank:
but first each pressed his tongue between his teeth
as signal for their leader, Barbariccia.
    And he had made a trumpet of his ass.

CANTO XXII

Still the Eighth Circle, Fifth Pouch: the Barrators. The Barrator from
Navarre. Fra Gomita and Michele Zanche, two Sardinians. The astuteness
of the Navarrese that leads two demons to fall into the pitch.

    Before this I've seen horsemen start to march
and open the assault and muster ranks

---

5. The bridge across the fifth ditch was smashed, as Malacoda soon explains, by the earthquake that occurred at the time of the Crucifixion.   6. As the travelers discover, this is a lie.   7. This account makes the current time 7 A.M. on Holy Saturday, April 9, 1300.   8. These names—like Scarmiglione in line 105—imply raffish irreverence in general, although some do have specific if ignoble meanings: Cagnazzo = "Big Dog," Barbariccia = "Curly Beard," Graffiacane = "Dog-Scratcher."

and seen them, too, at times beat their retreat;
    and on your land, o Aretines,⁹ I've seen
rangers and raiding parties galloping,   5
the clash of tournaments, the rush of jousts,
    now done with trumpets, now with bells, and now
with drums, and now with signs from castle walls,
with native things and with imported ware;
    but never yet have I seen horsemen or   10
seen infantry or ship that sails by signal
of land or star move to so strange a bugle!
    We made our way together with ten demons:
ah, what ferocious company! And yet
"in church with saints, with rotters in the tavern."   15
    But I was all intent upon the pitch,
to seek out every feature of the pouch
and of the people who were burning in it.
    Just as the dolphins do, when with arched back,
they signal to the seamen to prepare   20
for tempest, that their vessel may be spared,
    so here from time to time, to ease his torment,
some sinner showed his back above the surface,
then hid more quickly than a lightning flash.
    And just as on the margin of a ditch,   25
frogs crouch, their snouts alone above the water,
so as to hide their feet and their plump flesh,
    so here on every side these sinners crouched;
but faster than a flash, when Barbariccia
drew near, they plunged beneath the boiling pitch.   30
    I saw—my heart still shudders in recall—
one who delayed, just as at times a frog
is left behind while others dive below;
    and Graffiacane, who was closest to him,
then hooked him by his pitch-entangled locks   35
and hauled him up; he seemed to me an otter.
    By now I knew the names of all those demons—
I'd paid attention when the fiends were chosen;
I'd watched as they stepped forward one by one.
    "O Rubicante, see you set your talons   40
right into him, so you can flay his flesh!"
So did those cursed ones cry out together.
    And I: "My master, if you can, find out
what is the name of that unfortunate
who's fallen victim to his enemies."   45
    My guide, who then drew near that sinner's side,
asked him to tell his birthplace. He replied:
"My homeland was the kingdom of Navarre.
    My mother, who had had me by a wastrel,
destroyer of himself and his possessions,   50
had placed me in the service of a lord.
    Then I was in the household of the worthy

9. The people of Arezzo, a city south of Florence.

King Thibault; there I started taking graft;
with this heat I pay reckoning for that."[1]
    And Ciriatto, from whose mouth there bulged   55
to right and left two tusks like a wild hog's,
then let him feel how one of them could mangle.
    The mouse had fallen in with evil cats;
but Barbariccia clasped him in his arms
and said: "Stand off there, while I fork him fast."   60
    And turning toward my master then, he said:
"Ask on, if you would learn some more from him
before one of the others does him in."
    At which my guide: "Now tell: among the sinners
who hide beneath the pitch, are any others   65
Italian?" And he: "I have just left
    one who was nearby there; and would I were
still covered by the pitch as he is hidden,
for then I'd have no fear of hook or talon."
    And Libicocco said, "We've been too patient!"   70
and, with his grapple, grabbed him by the arm
and, ripping, carried off a hunk of flesh.
    But Draghignazzo also looked as if
to grab his legs; at which, their captain wheeled
and threatened all of them with raging looks.   75
    When they'd grown somewhat less tumultuous,
without delay my guide asked of that one
who had his eyes still fixed upon his wound:
    "Who was the one you left to come ashore—
unluckily—as you just said before?"   80
He answered: "Fra Gomita of Gallura,[2]
    who was a vessel fit for every fraud;
he had his master's enemies in hand,
but handled them in ways that pleased them all.
    He took their gold and smoothly let them off,   85
as he himself says; and in other matters,
he was a sovereign, not a petty, swindler.
    His comrade there is Don Michele Zanche[3]
of Logodoro; and their tongues are never
too tired to talk of their Sardinia.   90
    Ah me, see that one there who grinds his teeth!
If I were not afraid, I'd speak some more,
but he is getting set to scratch my scurf."
    And their great marshal, facing Farfarello—
who was so hot to strike he rolled his eyes,   95
said: "Get away from there, you filthy bird!"
    "If you perhaps would like to see or hear,"
that sinner, terrified, began again,
"Lombards or Tuscans, I can fetch you some;
but let the Malebranche stand aside   100

1. The identity of this sinner is not known, but he was employed in the household of Thibaut II of Champagne, a man renowned for his honesty who was also king of Navarre, the area of Spain that is now Basque country.   2. A friar who was chancellor of the Gallura district on the island of Sardinia. He was hanged by his master, a lord of Pisa, when it was discovered that he had sold prisoners their freedom.   3. Little is known of this sinner, except that he too was a Sardinian.

so that my comrades need not fear their vengeance.
Remaining in this very spot, I shall,
    although alone, make seven more appear
when I have whistled, as has been our custom
when one of us has managed to get out."   105
    At that, Cagnazzo lifted up his snout
and shook his head, and said: "Just listen to
that trick by which he thinks he can dive back!"
    To this, he who was rich in artifice
replied: "Then I must have too many tricks,   110
if I bring greater torment to my friends."
    This was too much for Alichino and,
despite the others, he cried out: "If you
dive back, I shall not gallop after you
    but beat my wings above the pitch; we'll leave   115
this height; with the embankment as a screen,
we'll see if you—alone—can handle us."
    O you who read, hear now of this new sport:
each turned his eyes upon the other shore,
he first who'd been most hesitant before.   120
    The Navarrese, in nick of time, had planted
his feet upon the ground; then in an instant
he jumped and freed himself from their commander.
    At this each demon felt the prick of guilt,
and most, he who had led his band to blunder;[4]   125
so he took off and shouted: "You are caught!"
    But this could help him little; wings were not
more fast than fear; the sinner plunged right under;
the other, flying up, lifted his chest:
    not otherwise the wild duck when it plunges   130
precipitously, when the falcon nears
and then—exhausted, thwarted—flies back up.
    But Calcabrina, raging at the trick,
flew after Alichino; he was keen
to see the sinner free and have a brawl;   135
    and once the Navarrese had disappeared,
he turned his talons on his fellow demon
and tangled with him just above the ditch.
    But Alichino clawed him well—he was
indeed a full-grown kestrel;[5] and both fell   140
into the middle of the boiling pond.
    The heat was quick to disentangle them,
but still there was no way they could get out;
their wings were stuck, enmeshed in glue-like pitch.
    And Barbariccia, grieving with the rest,   145
sent four to fly out toward the other shore
with all their forks, and speedily enough
    on this side and on that they took their posts;
and toward those two—stuck fast, already cooked
beneath that crust—they stretched their grappling hooks.   150
    We left them still contending with that mess.

4. Alichino. 5. A kind of falcon.

CANTO XXIII

Still the Eighth Circle, Fifth Pouch: the Barrators. Pursuit by the
demons, with Virgil snatching up Dante and sliding down to the Sixth
Pouch, where the Hypocrites file along slowly, clothed in caps of lead.
Two Jovial Friars of Bologna, Catalano and Loderingo. Caiaphas. Virgil's
distress at Malacoda's deceitfulness.

Silent, alone, no one escorting us,
we made our way—one went before, one after—
as Friars Minor[6] when they walk together.
The present fracas made me think of Aesop—
that fable where he tells about the mouse   5
and frog; for "near" and "nigh" are not more close
than are that fable and this incident,
if you compare with care how each begins
and then compare the endings that they share.[7]
And even as one thought springs from another,   10
so out of that was still another born,
which made the fear I felt before redouble.
I thought: "Because of us, they have been mocked,
and this inflicted so much hurt and scorn
that I am sure they feel deep indignation.   15
If anger's to be added to their malice,
they'll hunt us down with more ferocity
than any hound whose teeth have trapped a hare."
I could already feel my hair curl up
from fear, and I looked back attentively,   20
while saying: "Master, if you don't conceal
yourself and me at once—they terrify me,
those Malebranche; they are after us;
I so imagine them, I hear them now."
And he to me: "Were I a leaded mirror,   25
I could not gather in your outer image
more quickly than I have received your inner.
For even now your thoughts have joined my own;
in both our acts and aspects we are kin—
with both our minds I've come to one decision.   30
If that right bank is not extremely steep,
we can descend into the other moat
and so escape from the imagined chase."
He'd hardly finished telling me his plan
when I saw them approach with outstretched wings,   35
not too far off, and keen on taking us.
My guide snatched me up instantly, just as
the mother who is wakened by a roar
and catches sight of blazing flames beside her,

6. Franciscan friars.   7. The fable that Dante seems to be referring to tells how a frog offers to ferry a
mouse across a river, then halfway over tries to drown him, only to be seized by a kite (a hawklike bird)
while the mouse escapes.

will lift her son and run without a stop— 40
she cares more for the child than for herself—
not pausing even to throw on a shift;
    and down the hard embankment's edge—his back
lay flat along the sloping rock that closes
one side of the adjacent moat—he slid. 45
    No water ever ran so fast along
a sluice to turn the wheels of a land mill,[8]
not even when its flow approached the paddles,
    as did my master race down that embankment
while bearing me with him upon his chest, 50
just like a son, and not like a companion.
    His feet had scarcely reached the bed that lies
along the deep below, than those ten demons
were on the edge above us; but there was
    nothing to fear; for that High Providence 55
that willed them ministers of the fifth ditch,
denies to all of them the power to leave it.
    Below that point we found a painted people,
who moved about with lagging steps, in circles,
weeping, with features tired and defeated. 60
    And they were dressed in cloaks with cowls so low
they fell before their eyes, of that same cut
that's used to make the clothes for Cluny's[9] monks.
    Outside, these cloaks were gilded and they dazzled;
but inside they were all of lead, so heavy 65
that Frederick's capes were straw compared to them.[1]
    A tiring mantle for eternity!
We turned again, as always, to the left,
along with them, intent on their sad weeping;
    but with their weights that weary people paced 70
so slowly that we found ourselves among
new company each time we took a step.
    At which I told my guide: "Please try to find
someone whose name or deed I recognize;
and while we walk, be watchful with your eyes." 75
    And one who'd taken in my Tuscan speech
cried out behind us: "Stay your steps, o you
who hurry so along this darkened air!
    Perhaps you'll have from me that which you seek."
At which my guide turned to me, saying: "Wait, 80
and then continue, following his pace."
    I stopped, and I saw two whose faces showed
their minds were keen to be with me; but both
their load and the tight path forced them to slow.
    When they came up, they looked askance at me 85
a long while, and they uttered not a word
until they turned to one another, saying:

---

8. A mill built on the land while the water of the river turns its wheel.   **9.** One of the largest monasteries in Europe, located in Burgundy in France.   **1.** Frederick II (see note to 10.119) was reported to have punished traitors by encasing them in lead and throwing them into heated cauldrons.

"The throbbing of his throat makes this one seem
alive; and if they're dead, what privilege
lets them appear without the heavy mantle?" 90
Then they addressed me: "Tuscan, you who come
to this assembly of sad hypocrites,
do not disdain to tell us who you are."
I answered: "Where the lovely Arno flows,[2]
there I was born and raised, in the great city; 95
I'm with the body I have always had.
But who are you, upon whose cheeks I see
such tears distilled by grief? And let me know
what punishment it is that glitters so."
And one of them replied: "The yellow cloaks 100
are of a lead so thick, their heaviness
makes us, the balances beneath them, creak.
We both were Jovial Friars,[3] and Bolognese;
my name was Catalano, Loderingo[4]
was his, and we were chosen by your city 105
together, for the post that's usually
one man's, to keep the peace; and what we were
is still to be observed around Gardingo."
I then began, "O Friars, your misdeeds . . ."
but said no more, because my eyes had caught 110
one crucified by three stakes on the ground.[5]
When he saw me, that sinner writhed all over,
and he breathed hard into his beard with sighs;
observing that, Fra Catalano said
to me: "That one impaled there, whom you see, 115
counseled the Pharisees that it was prudent
to let one man—and not one nation—suffer.
Naked, he has been stretched across the path,
as you can see, and he must feel the weight
of anyone who passes over him. 120
Like torment, in this ditch, afflicts both his
father-in-law[6] and others in that council,
which for the Jews has seeded so much evil."
Then I saw Virgil stand amazed above
that one who lay stretched out upon a cross 125
so squalidly in his eternal exile.
And he addressed the friar in this way:
"If it does not displease you—if you may—
tell us if there's some passage on the right
that would allow the two of us to leave 130
without our having to compel black angels
to travel to this deep, to get us out."
He answered: "Closer than you hope, you'll find

---

2. Florence.   3. A military and religious order in Bologna called the Knights of the Blessed Virgin Mary,
or popularly the Jovial Friars because of the laxity of its rules. The members were meant to fight only in
order to protect the weak and enforce peace.   4. Two citizens of Bologna who were involved in founding
the Jovial Friars in 1261. They shared the office of governor in 1265 and 1267. Gardingo (line 108), a
district in Florence, was destroyed by a civil war incited by their meddling in Florentine affairs.   5. This
is Caiaphas, the high priest under Pontius Pilate who advised that Christ be crucified (John 11.45–
52).   6. Annas; see John 18.13.

a rocky ridge that stretches from the great
round wall and crosses all the savage valleys,   135
    except that here it's broken—not a bridge.
But where its ruins slope along the bank
and heap up at the bottom, you can climb."
    My leader stood a while with his head bent,
then said: "He who hooks sinners over there   140
gave us a false account of this affair."[7]
    At which the Friar: "In Bologna, I
once heard about the devil's many vices—
they said he was a liar and father of lies."
    And then my guide moved on with giant strides,   145
somewhat disturbed, with anger in his eyes;
at this I left those overburdened spirits,
    while following the prints of his dear feet.

CANTO XXIV

*Still the Eighth Circle, Sixth Pouch: the Hypocrites. Hard passage to the
Seventh Pouch: the Thieves. Bitten by a serpent, a thieving sinner who
turns to ashes and is then restored: Vanni Fucci. His prediction of the
defeat of the Whites—Dante's party—at Pistoia.*

In that part of the young year when the sun
begins to warm its locks beneath Aquarius[8]
and nights grow shorter, equaling the days,
    when hoarfrost mimes the image of his white
sister[9] upon the ground—but not for long,   5
because the pen he uses is not sharp—
    the farmer who is short of fodder rises
and looks and sees the fields all white, at which
he slaps his thigh, turns back into the house,
    and here and there complains like some poor wretch   10
who doesn't know what can be done, and then
goes out again and gathers up new hope
    on seeing that the world has changed its face
in so few hours, and he takes his staff
and hurries out his flock of sheep to pasture.   15
    So did my master fill me with dismay
when I saw how his brow was deeply troubled,
yet then the plaster soothed the sore as quickly:
    for soon as we were on the broken bridge,
my guide turned back to me with that sweet manner   20
I first had seen along the mountain's base.
    And he examined carefully the ruin;
then having picked the way we would ascend,
he opened up his arms and thrust me forward.
    And just as he who ponders as he labors,   25
who's always ready for the step ahead,
so, as he lifted me up toward the summit
    of one great crag, he'd see another spur,

7. See 21.111.   8. January 21–February 21.   9. Snow.

saying: "That is the one you will grip next,
but try it first to see if it is firm." 30

That was no path for those with cloaks of lead,
for he and I—he, light; I, with support—
could hardly make it up from spur to spur.

And were it not that, down from this enclosure,
the slope was shorter than the bank before, 35
I cannot speak for him, but I should surely

have been defeated. But since Malebolge
runs right into the mouth of its last well,
the placement of each valley means it must

have one bank high and have the other short;[1] 40
and so we reached, at length, the jutting where
the last stone of the ruined bridge breaks off.

The breath within my lungs was so exhausted
from climbing, I could not go on; in fact,
as soon as I had reached that stone, I sat. 45

"Now you must cast aside your laziness,"
my master said, "for he who rests on down
or under covers cannot come to fame;

and he who spends his life without renown
leaves such a vestige of himself on earth 50
as smoke bequeaths to air or foam to water.

Therefore, get up; defeat your breathlessness
with spirit that can win all battles if
the body's heaviness does not deter it.

A longer ladder still is to be climbed;[2] 55
it's not enough to have left them behind;
if you have understood, now profit from it."

Then I arose and showed myself far better
equipped with breath than I had been before:
"Go on, for I am strong and confident." 60

We took our upward way upon the ridge,
with crags more jagged, narrow, difficult,
and much more steep than we had crossed before.

I spoke as we went on, not to seem weak;
at this, a voice came from the ditch beyond— 65
a voice that was not suited to form words.

I know not what he said, although I was
already at the summit of the bridge
that crosses there; and yet he seemed to move.

I had bent downward, but my living eyes 70
could not see to the bottom through that dark;
at which I said: "O master, can we reach

the other belt? Let us descend the wall,[3]
for as I hear and cannot understand,
so I see down but can distinguish nothing." 75

"The only answer that I give to you
is doing it," he said. "A just request

---

1. Because the whole of the eighth circle is tilted downward, the downside wall of each ditch is lower than that on the upside.   2. Both the climb from the pit of Hell back to Earth and the climb up Mount Purgatory.   3. Of the seventh ditch.

is to be met in silence, by the act."
We then climbed down the bridge, just at the end
where it runs right into the eighth embankment,[4]   80
and now the moat was plain enough to me;
　　and there within I saw a dreadful swarm
of serpents so extravagant in form—
remembering them still drains my blood from me.
　　Let Libya boast no more about her sands;[5]   85
for if she breeds chelydri, jaculi,
cenchres with amphisbaena, pareae,
　　she never showed—with all of Ethiopia
or all the land that borders the Red Sea—
so many, such malignant, pestilences.   90
　　Among this cruel and depressing swarm,
ran people who were naked, terrified,
with no hope of a hole or heliotrope.[6]
　　Their hands were tied behind by serpents; these
had thrust their head and tail right through the loins,   95
and then were knotted on the other side.
　　And—there!—a serpent sprang with force at one
who stood upon our shore, transfixing him
just where the neck and shoulders form a knot.
　　No o or i has ever been transcribed   100
so quickly as that soul caught fire and burned
and, as he fell, completely turned to ashes;
　　and when he lay, undone, upon the ground,
the dust of him collected by itself
and instantly returned to what it was: 105
　　just so, it is asserted by great sages,
that, when it reaches its five-hundredth year,
the phoenix[7] dies and then is born again;
　　lifelong it never feeds on grass or grain,
only on drops of incense and amomum;   110
its final winding sheets are nard and myrrh.
　　And just as he who falls, and knows not how—
by demon's force that drags him to the ground
or by some other hindrance that binds man—
　　who, when he rises, stares about him, all   115
bewildered by the heavy anguish he
has suffered, sighing as he looks around;
　　so did this sinner stare when he arose.
Oh, how severe it is, the power of God
that, as its vengeance, showers down such blows!   120
　　My guide then asked that sinner who he was;
to this he answered: "Not long since, I rained
from Tuscany into this savage maw.

---

4. They cross the bridge over the seventh ditch and then climb down the wall between the seventh and eighth ditches.   5. The following list of exotic serpents derives from a description by the Roman poet Lucan (A.D. 39–65) of the plagues of Libya.   6. A fictitious stone that was supposed to make the bearer invisible.   7. The phoenix is a mythical bird that is supposed to burn to death in its own nest every five hundred years, after which either itself or its son is reborn from the ashes; for these details, including its diet of exotic herbs and its funeral preparations (lines 110–11), see Ovid, Metamorphoses 15. In medieval mythography the phoenix was often taken as an image of Christ.

Mule that I was, the bestial life pleased me
and not the human; I am Vanni Fucci,[8]   125
beast; and the den that suited me—Pistoia."
    And I to Virgil: "Tell him not to slip
away, and ask what sin has thrust him here;
I knew him as a man of blood and anger."
    The sinner heard and did not try to feign   130
but turned his mind and face, intent, toward me;
and coloring with miserable shame,
    he said: "I suffer more because you've caught me
in this, the misery you see, than I
suffered when taken from the other life.   135
    I can't refuse to answer what you ask:
I am set down so far because I robbed
the sacristy of its fair ornaments,
    and someone else was falsely blamed for that.
But lest this sight give you too much delight,   140
if you can ever leave these lands of darkness,
    open your ears to my announcement, hear:[9]
Pistoia first will strip herself of Blacks,
then Florence will renew her men and manners.
    From Val di Magra, Mars will draw a vapor   145
which turbid clouds will try to wrap; the clash
between them will be fierce, impetuous,
    a tempest, fought upon Campo Piceno,
until that vapor, vigorous, shall crack
the mist, and every White be struck by it.   150
    And I have told you this to make you grieve."

CANTO XXV

Still the Eighth Circle, Seventh Pouch: the Thieves. Vanni Fucci and his
obscene figs against God. The Centaur Cacus. Five Florentine Thieves,
three of them humans and two of them serpents. The astounding
metamorphoses undergone by four of them.

When he had finished with his words, the thief
raised high his fists with both figs[1] cocked and cried:
"Take that, o God; I square them off for you!"
    From that time on, those serpents were my friends,
for one of them coiled then around his neck,   5
as if to say, "I'll have you speak no more";
    another wound about his arms and bound him
again and wrapped itself in front so firmly,
he could not even make them budge an inch.
    Pistoia, ah, Pistoia, must you last: 10
why not decree your self-incineration,

8. The illegitimate son (*mule*) of a noble father of Pistoia, a town just north of Florence; known as "the beast" because of the extravagance of his misbehavior. He reputedly robbed a church in Pistoia, a crime for which a similarly named man was wrongly hanged.   9. Vanni Fucci now prophesies, in the enigmatic terms appropriate to the genre, that the party of the Blacks (of which he was a member) will first be expelled from Pistoia by the Whites, but that then the Whites of Florence (Dante's party) will be defeated. The prophecy refers to events that occurred in either 1302 or 1306.   1. An obscene gesture made by thrusting a protruding thumb between the first and second fingers of a closed fist.

since you surpass your seed[2] in wickedness?
    Throughout the shadowed circles of deep Hell,
I saw no soul against God so rebel,
not even he who fell from Theban walls.[3]   15
    He fled and could not say another word;
and then I saw a Centaur full of anger,
shouting: "Where is he, where's that bitter one?"
    I do not think Maremma[4] has the number
of snakes that Centaur carried on his haunch   20
until the part that takes our human form.
    Upon his shoulders and behind his nape
there lay a dragon with its wings outstretched;
it sets ablaze all those it intercepts.
    My master said: "That Centaur there is Cacus,[5]   25
who often made a lake of blood within
a grotto underneath Mount Aventine.
    He does not ride the same road as his brothers
because he stole—and most deceitfully—
from the great herd nearby; his crooked deeds   30
    ended beneath the club of Hercules,
who may have given him a hundred blows—
but he was not alive to feel the tenth."
    While he was talking so, Cacus ran by
and, just beneath our ledge, three souls arrived;   35
but neither I nor my guide noticed them
    until they had cried out: "And who are you?"
At this the words we shared were interrupted,
and we attended only to those spirits.
    I did not recognize them, but it happened,   40
as chance will usually bring about,
that one of them called out the other's name,
    exclaiming: "Where was Cianfa[6] left behind?"
At this, so that my guide might be alert,
I held my finger up from chin to nose.   45
    If, reader, you are slow now to believe
what I shall tell, that is no cause for wonder,
for I—who saw it—hardly can accept it.
    As I kept my eyes fixed upon those sinners,
a serpent with six feet springs out against   50
one of the three, and clutches him completely.
    It gripped his belly with its middle feet,
and with its forefeet grappled his two arms;
and then it sank its teeth in both his cheeks;
    it stretched its rear feet out along his thighs   55
and ran its tail along between the two,
then straightened it again behind his loins.
    No ivy ever gripped a tree so fast
as when that horrifying monster clasped

---

2. Its founder Catiline, who was a traitor against the Roman republic in the first century B.C.
3. Capaneus (see 14.46–75).   **4.** A region infested with snakes; see 13.8.   **5.** A monster who lived in
a cave on Mount Aventine in Rome and was killed by Hercules, from whom he stole cattle; see *Aeneid*
8.   **6.** A noble Florentine reputedly a thief.

and intertwined the other's limbs with its.   60
   Then—just as if their substance were warm wax—
they stuck together and they mixed their colors,
so neither seemed what he had been before;
   just as, when paper's kindled, where it still
has not caught flame in full, its color's dark   65
though not yet black, while white is dying off.
   The other two souls stared, and each one cried:
"Ah me, Agnello,[7] how you change! Just see,
you are already neither two nor one!"
   Then two heads were already joined in one,   70
when in one face where two had been dissolved,
two intermingled shapes appeared to us.
   Two arms came into being from four lengths;
the thighs and legs, the belly and the chest
became such limbs as never had been seen.   75
   And every former shape was canceled there:
that perverse image seemed to share in both—
and none; and so, and slowly, it moved on.
   Just as the lizard, when it darts from hedge
to hedge, beneath the dog days' giant lash,   80
seems, if it cross one's path, a lightning flash,
   so seemed a blazing little serpent moving
against the bellies of the other two,
as black and livid as a peppercorn.
   Attacking one of them, it pierced right through   85
the part where we first take our nourishment;
and then it fell before him at full length.
   The one it had transfixed stared but said nothing;
in fact he only stood his ground and yawned
as one whom sleep or fever has undone.   90
   The serpent stared at him, he at the serpent;
one through his wound, the other through his mouth
were smoking violently; their smoke met.
   Let Lucan now be silent, where he sings
of sad Sabellus and Nasidius,[8]   95
and wait to hear what flies off from my bow.
   Let Ovid now be silent, where he tells
of Cadmus, Arethusa;[9] if his verse
has made of one a serpent, one a fountain,
   I do not envy him; he never did   100
transmute two natures, face to face, so that
both forms were ready to exchange their matter.
   These were the ways they answered to each other:
the serpent split its tail into a fork;
the wounded sinner drew his steps together.   105
   The legs and then the thighs along with them
so fastened to each other that the juncture
soon left no sign that was discernible.

---

7. Another noble Florentine thief. 8. Two soldiers bitten by serpents in Lucan's *Pharsalia*. 9. See
Metamorphoses 4.

Meanwhile the cleft tail took upon itself
the form the other gradually lost;
its skin grew soft, the other's skin grew hard.   110
    I saw the arms that drew in at his armpits
and also saw the monster's two short feet
grow long for just as much as those were shortened.
    The serpent's hind feet, twisted up together,   115
became the member that man hides; just as
the wretch put out two hind paws from his member.
    And while the smoke veils each with a new color,
and now breeds hair upon the skin of one,
just as it strips the hair from off the other,   120
    the one rose up, the other fell; and yet
they never turned aside their impious eyelamps,
beneath which each of them transformed his snout:
    he who stood up drew his back toward the temples,
and from the excess matter growing there   125
came ears upon the cheeks that had been bare;
    whatever had not been pulled back but kept,
superfluous, then made his face a nose
and thickened out his lips appropriately.
    He who was lying down thrust out his snout;   130
and even as the snail hauls in its horns,
he drew his ears straight back into his head;
    his tongue, which had before been whole and fit
for speech, now cleaves; the other's tongue, which had
been forked, now closes up; and the smoke stops.   135
    The soul that had become an animal,
now hissing, hurried off along the valley;
the other one, behind him, speaks and spits.
    And then he turned aside his new-made shoulders
and told the third soul: "I'd have Buoso¹ run   140
on all fours down this road, as I have done."
    And so I saw the seventh ballast² change
and rechange; may the strangeness plead for me
if there's been some confusion in my pen.
    And though my eyes were somewhat blurred, my mind   145
bewildered, those three sinners did not flee
so secretly that I could not perceive
    Puccio Sciancato³ clearly, he who was
the only soul⁴ who'd not been changed among
the three companions we had met at first;   150
    the other one made you, Gaville, grieve.

---

1. The identity of this Buoso is uncertain.   2. The sinners of this ditch are here reduced to dead weight.   3. The third thief, also a noble Florentine.   4. The little serpent of line 82 above, identified as Francesco, a Florentine nobleman who lived in Gaville (line 151), a town south of Florence. When he was murdered by the townsmen, his kinsmen took brutal revenge.

CANTO XXVI

Still the Eighth Circle, Seventh Pouch: the Thieves. Dante's invective
against Florence. View of the Eighth Pouch, where Fraudulent
Counselors are clothed in the flames that burn them. Ulysses and
Diomedes in one shared flame. Ulysses' tale of his final voyage.

Be joyous, Florence, you are great indeed,
for over sea and land you beat your wings;
through every part of Hell your name extends!
    Among the thieves I found five citizens[5]
of yours—and such, that shame has taken me;   5
with them, you can ascend to no high honor.
    But if the dreams dreamt close to dawn are true,
then little time will pass before you feel
what Prato[6] and the others crave for you.
    Were that already come, it would not be   10
too soon—and let it come, since it must be!
As I grow older, it will be more heavy.
    We left that deep and, by protruding stones
that served as stairs for our descent before,
my guide climbed up again and drew me forward;   15
    and as we took our solitary path
among the ridge's jagged spurs and rocks,
our feet could not make way without our hands.
    It grieved me then and now grieves me again
when I direct my mind to what I saw;   20
and more than usual, I curb my talent,
    that it not run where virtue does not guide;
so that, if my kind star or something better
has given me that gift, I not abuse it.
    As many as the fireflies the peasant   25
(while resting on a hillside in the season
when he who lights the world least hides his face),
    just when the fly gives way to the mosquito,
sees glimmering below, down in the valley,
there where perhaps he gathers grapes and tills—   30
    so many were the flames that glittered in
the eighth abyss; I made this out as soon
as I had come to where one sees the bottom.
    Even as he[7] who was avenged by bears
saw, as it left, Elijah's chariot—   35
its horses rearing, rising right to heaven—
    when he could not keep track of it except
by watching one lone flame in its ascent,
just like a little cloud that climbs on high:
    so, through the gullet of that ditch, each flame   40
must make its way; no flame displays its prey,
though every flame has carried off a sinner.
    I stood upon the bridge and leaned straight out

---

5. Cianfa (25.43), Agnello (25.68), Francesco (25.82, 149), Buoso (25.140), and Puccio (25.148), all Florentines.   **6.** A town just north of Florence, on the way to Pistoia. The exact significance of this threat is unclear.   **7.** Elisha, an Old Testament prophet, was mocked by children, who were then attacked by bears. He saw the ascent to heaven of the prophet Elijah in his chariot and continued Elijah's mission: 2 Kings 2.1–25.

to see; and if I had not gripped a rock,
I should have fallen off—without a push.   45

   My guide, who noted how intent I was,
told me: "Within those fires there are souls;
each one is swathed in that which scorches him."

   "My master," I replied, "on hearing you,
I am more sure; but I'd already thought   50
that it was so, and I had meant to ask:

   Who is within the flame that comes so twinned
above that it would seem to rise out of
the pyre Eteocles shared with his brother?"[8]

   He answered me: "Within that flame, Ulysses   55
and Diomedes[9] suffer; they, who went
as one to rage, now share one punishment.

   And there, together in their flame, they grieve
over the horse's fraud that caused a breach—
the gate that let Rome's noble seed escape.[1]   60

   There they regret the guile that makes the dead
Deïdamia[2] still lament Achilles;
and there, for the Palladium, they pay."

   "If they can speak within those sparks," I said,
"I pray you and repray and, master, may   65
my prayer be worth a thousand pleas, do not

   forbid my waiting here until the flame
with horns approaches us; for you can see
how, out of my desire, I bend toward it."

   And he to me: "What you have asked is worthy   70
of every praise; therefore, I favor it.
I only ask you this: refrain from talking.

   Let me address them—I have understood
what you desire of them. Since they were Greek,
perhaps they'd be disdainful of your speech."[3]   75

   And when my guide adjudged the flame had reached
a point where time and place were opportune,
this was the form I heard his words assume:

   "You two who move as one within the flame,
if I deserved of you while I still lived,   80
if I deserved of you much or a little

   when in the world I wrote my noble lines,
do not move on; let one of you retell
where, having gone astray, he found his death."

   The greater horn within that ancient flame   85
began to sway and tremble, murmuring
just like a fire that struggles in the wind;

   and then he waved his flame-tip back and forth
as if it were a tongue that tried to speak,

---

8. Eteocles and his brother, Polynices, were the sons of Oedipus; cursed by their father for their imprisonment of him, they engaged in a civil war over Thebes, killed each other, and were cremated on the same
pyre, the flame of which divided into two as a sign of their enmity.   **9.** Two of the Greek leaders in the
Trojan War. They devised the trick of the Trojan horse and stole the Palladium, a statue of Pallas Athena
that protected the city. Their villainy is described by Aeneas in *Aeneid* 2.   **1.** The Trojan survivors, who
founded Rome.   **2.** Achilles' lover, who tried to prevent him from going to the Trojan War but was
thwarted by Ulysses.   **3.** Virgil may assume that Greeks would disdain anyone who, like Dante, did not
know Greek (and was therefore a "barbarian"); or that because he derives from the classical world he is the
more appropriate interlocutor.

and flung toward us a voice that answered: "When 90
  I sailed away from Circe,[4] who'd beguiled me
to stay more than a year there, near Gaeta—
before Aeneas gave that place a name[5]—
  neither my fondness for my son nor pity
for my old father nor the love I owed 95
Penelope,[6] which would have gladdened her,
  was able to defeat in me the longing
I had to gain experience of the world
and of the vices and the worth of men.
  Therefore, I set out on the open sea 100
with but one ship and that small company
of those who never had deserted me.
  I saw as far as Spain, far as Morocco,
along both shores; I saw Sardinia
and saw the other islands that sea bathes. 105
  And I and my companions were already
old and slow, when we approached the narrows
where Hercules set up his boundary stones
  that men might heed and never reach beyond:
upon my right, I had gone past Seville, 110
and on the left, already passed Ceüta.[7]
  'Brothers,' I said, 'o you, who having crossed
a hundred thousand dangers, reach the west,
to this brief waking-time that still is left
  unto your senses, you must not deny 115
experience of that which lies beyond
the sun, and of the world that is unpeopled.[8]
  Consider well the seed that gave you birth:
you were not made to live your lives as brutes,
but to be followers of worth and knowledge.' 120
  I spurred my comrades with this brief address
to meet the journey with such eagerness
that I could hardly, then, have held them back;
  and having turned our stern toward morning, we
made wings out of our oars in a wild flight 125
and always gained upon our left-hand side.
  At night I now could see the other pole
and all its stars; the stars of ours had fallen
and never rose above the plain of the ocean.[9]
  Five times the light beneath the moon had been 130
rekindled, and, as many times, was spent,
since that hard passage faced our first attempt,
  when there before us rose a mountain,[1] dark
because of distance, and it seemed to me

4. Who in this version lives near Gaeta, on the coast of Italy north of Naples; she transforms men into beasts. 5. Aeneas named it after his nurse Caieta, who died there: *Aeneid* 7. 6. Ulysses' faithful wife. 7. The straits of Gibraltar, with Seville on the European side and Ceüta on the African. According to myth, Hercules separated a single mountain into two to mark the point beyond which human beings should not venture. 8. According to the geography of Dante's day, the southern hemisphere was made up entirely of water, with the only land being Mount Purgatory. To go *beyond the sun* means to follow a westward course. 9. They had crossed the equator and could see only the stars of the southern hemisphere. 1. Mount Purgatory.

the highest mountain I had ever seen.   135
   And we were glad, but this soon turned to sorrow,
for out of that new land a whirlwind rose
and hammered at our ship, against her bow.
   Three times it turned her round with all the waters;
and at the fourth, it lifted up the stern   140
so that our prow plunged deep, as pleased an Other,[2]
until the sea again closed—over us."

CANTO XXVII

*Still the Eighth Circle, Eighth Pouch: the Fraudulent Counselors. Guido
da Montefeltro, for whom Dante provides a panorama of the state of
political affairs in Romagna. Guido's tale of the anticipatory—but
unavailing—absolution given him by Boniface VIII. The quarrel of a
demon and St Francis over Guido's soul.*

   The flame already was erect and silent—
it had no more to say. Now it had left us
with the permission of the gentle poet,
   when, just behind it, came another flame
that drew our eyes to watch its tip because   5
of the perplexing sound that it sent forth.
   Even as the Sicilian bull[3] (that first
had bellowed with the cry—and this was just—
of him who shaped it with his instruments)
   would always bellow with its victim's voice,   10
so that, although that bull was only brass,
it seemed as if it were pierced through by pain;
   so were the helpless words that, from the first,
had found no path or exit from the flame,
transformed into the language of the fire.   15
   But after they had found their way up toward
the tip, and given it that movement which
the tongue had given them along their passage,
   we heard: "O you to whom I turn my voice,[4]
who only now were talking Lombard,[5] saying,   20
'Now you may leave—I'll not provoke more speech,'
   though I have come perhaps a little late,
may it not trouble you to stop and speak
with me; see how I stay—and I am burning!
   If you have fallen into this blind world   25
but recently, out of the sweet Italian
country from which I carry all my guilt,
   do tell me if the Romagnoles[6] have peace

---

2. God.   **3.** According to classical legend, Phalaris, the tyrant of Agrigentum in Sicily, had an artisan
build a brazen bull in which he roasted his victims alive, their shrieks emerging as the sounds of a bull's
bellowing. His first victim was the artisan himself, Perillus.   **4.** The speaker is Guido da Montefeltro (d.
1298), a nobleman deeply involved in the constant warfare of thirteenth-century Italy but who became a
friar two years before his death (see line 67).   **5.** The dialect of northern Italy. Dante believed that since
Virgil came from Mantua, his spoken language would be not Latin but this dialect.   **6.** The people of
Romagna, an area northeast of Florence and bordering the Adriatic Sea; the city of Urbino marks its
southern limit, the Apennine mountains its northern. The subsequent passage describes the political conditions in the cities of Romagna.

or war; I was from there—the hills between
Urbino and the ridge where Tiber springs."   30
   I still was bent, attentive, over him,
when my guide nudged me lightly at the side
and said: "You speak; he is Italian."
   And I, who had my answer set already,
without delay began to speak to him: 35
"O soul that is concealed below in flame,
   Romagna is not now and never was
quite free of war inside its tyrants' hearts;
but when I left her, none had broken out.
   Ravenna[7] stands as it has stood for years;   40
the eagle of Polenta shelters it
and also covers Cervia with his wings.
   The city[8] that already stood long trial
and made a bloody heap out of the French,
now finds itself again beneath green paws.   45
   Both mastiffs of Verrucchio,[9] old and new,
who dealt so badly with Montagna, use
their teeth to bore where they have always gnawed.
   The cities on Lamone and Santerno[1]
are led by the young lion of the white lair;   50
from summer unto winter, he shifts factions.
   That city with its side bathed by the Savio,[2]
just as it lies between the plain and mountain,
lives somewhere between tyranny and freedom.
   And now, I pray you, tell me who you are: 55
do not be harder than I've been with you,
that in the world your name may still endure."
   After the flame, in customary fashion,
had roared awhile, it moved its pointed tip
this side and that and then set free this breath: 60
   "If I thought my reply were meant for one
who ever could return into the world,
this flame would stir no more; and yet, since none—
   if what I hear is true—ever returned
alive from this abyss, then without fear   65
of facing infamy, I answer you.
   I was a man of arms, then wore the cord,
believing that, so girt, I made amends;
and surely what I thought would have been true
   had not the Highest Priest[3]—may he be damned!—   70
made me fall back into my former sins;
and how and why, I'd have you hear from me.
   While I still had the form of bones and flesh
my mother gave to me, my deeds were not

---

7. The major city of Romagna, ruled at the time by the Polenta family, who also controlled the small city of Cervia.   8. Forlì, which defeated French invaders but then fell under the control of the tyrannical Ordelaffi family, which had green paws on its coat of arms.   9. The Verrucchio, Malatesta and his son Malatestino, were tyrants of Rimini who killed their enemy Montagna.   1. The cities of Faenza and Imola, on the Lamone and Santerno Rivers respectively, governed by an unreliable ruler who had a lion on a white ground on his coat of arms.   2. Cesena, located on the Savio River, was a free municipality although its politics were dominated by a single family.   3. Pope Boniface VIII.

those of the lion but those of the fox.   75

   The wiles and secret ways—I knew them all
and so employed their arts that my renown
had reached the very boundaries of earth.

   But when I saw myself come to that part
of life when it is fitting for all men   80
to lower sails and gather in their ropes,

   what once had been my joy was now dejection;
repenting and confessing, I became
a friar; and—poor me—it would have helped.

   The prince of the new Pharisees, who then   85
was waging war so near the Lateran[4]—
and not against the Jews or Saracens,

   for every enemy of his was Christian,
and none of them had gone to conquer Acre[5]
or been a trader in the Sultan's lands—   90

   took no care for the highest office or
the holy orders that were his, or for
my cord, which used to make its wearers leaner.

   But just as Constantine,[6] on Mount Soracte,
to cure his leprosy, sought out Sylvester,   95
so this one sought me out as his instructor,

   to ease the fever of his arrogance.
He asked me to give counsel. I was silent—
his words had seemed to me delirious.

   And then he said: 'Your heart must not mistrust: 100
I now absolve you in advance—teach me
to batter Penestrino[7] to the ground.

   You surely know that I posses the power
to lock and unlock Heaven; for the keys
my predecessor[8] did not prize are two.'   105

   Then his grave arguments compelled me so,
my silence seemed a worse offense than speech,
and I said: 'Since you cleanse me of the sin

   that I must now fall into, Father, know:
long promises and very brief fulfillments   110
will bring a victory to your high throne.'

   Then Francis[9] came, as soon as I was dead,
for me; but one of the black cherubim
told him: 'Don't bear him off; do not cheat me.

   He must come down among my menials;   115
the counsel that he gave was fraudulent;
since then, I've kept close track, to snatch his scalp;

   one can't absolve a man who's not repented,
and no one can repent and will at once;

---

4. Boniface was struggling to retain the papacy against the challenge of another Roman family, the Colonnas. **5.** City in the Holy Land, captured by the crusaders and then recaptured by the Saracens. **6.** According to legend, the Emperor Constantine (d. 337) was cured of his leprosy by Pope Sylvester, who was hiding on Mount Soracte, some twenty miles north of Rome; see 19.115. **7.** The fortress of the Colonnas. **8.** Celestine V, who resigned after five months (3.59–60). The keys are those of damnation and absolution, given by Christ to Peter: see 19.92. **9.** Francis of Assisi (1181 or 1182–1226), founder of the order of friars joined by Guido.

the law of contradiction won't allow it.'[1]   120
   O miserable me, for how I started
when he took hold of me and said: 'Perhaps
you did not think that I was a logician!'[2]
   He carried me to Minos;[3] and that monster
twisted his tail eight times around his hide   125
and then, when he had bit it in great anger,
   announced: 'This one is for the thieving fire';
for which—and where, you see—I now am lost,
and in this garb I move in bitterness."
   And when, with this, his words were at an end,   130
the flame departed, sorrowing and writhing
and tossing its sharp horn. We moved beyond;
   I went together with my guide, along
the ridge until the other arch that bridges
the ditch where payment is imposed on those   135
who, since they brought such discord, bear such loads.

CANTO XXVIII

*The Eighth Circle, Ninth Pouch, where the Sowers of Scandal and
Schism, perpetually circling, are wounded and—after each healing—
wounded again by a demon with a sword. Mohammed and Alì. Warning
to Fra Dolcino. Curio. Mosca. Bertran de Born.*

   Who, even with untrammeled words and many
attempts at telling, ever could recount
in full the blood and wounds that I now saw?
   Each tongue that tried would certainly fall short
because the shallowness of both our speech   5
and intellect cannot contain so much.
   Were you to reassemble all the men
who once, within Apulia's fateful land,
had mourned their blood, shed at the Trojans' hands,[4]
   as well as those who fell in the long war   10
where massive mounds of rings were battle spoils—
even as Livy[5] writes, who does not err—
   and those who felt the thrust of painful blows
when they fought hard against Robert Guiscard;[6]
with all the rest whose bones are still piled up   15
   at Ceperano[7]—each Apulian was
a traitor there—and, too, at Tagliacozzo,[8]
where old Alardo conquered without weapons;
   and then, were one to show his limb pierced through

---

1. The contradiction is that Guido wanted forgiveness for his sin of guile at the same time as he was committing it; in willing the sin he showed that he was not truly repentant, the precondition for forgiveness.   2. The devil is referring to the logical law of noncontradiction.   3. For Minos, see 5.4.
4. Those killed when the Trojans conquered Latium, in the *Aeneid* 7–12. *Apulia's . . . land:* Southern Italy.   5. Roman historian (d. A.D. 17). *Long war:* the Second Punic War (218–01 B.C.) between Rome and Carthage under Hannibal. After the Battle of Cannae (216) the victorious Carthaginians displayed rings taken from fallen Romans.   6. Norman adventurer (1015–1085) who fought the Greeks and Saracens.   7. A town that the barons of Apulia were pledged to defend for Manfred, the natural son of Frederick II (10.119), but whom they betrayed; he was then killed at the battle of Benevento in 1266.   8. A town where in 1268 Manfred's nephew Conradin was defeated by the strategy rather than the brute force of Erard (or Alardo) de Valery.

and one his limb hacked off, that would not match   20
the hideousness of the ninth abyss.

　　No barrel, even though it's lost a hoop
or end-piece, ever gapes as one whom I
saw ripped right from his chin to where we fart:

　　his bowels hung between his legs, one saw   25
his vitals and the miserable sack
that makes of what we swallow excrement.

　　While I was all intent on watching him,
he looked at me, and with his hands he spread
his chest and said: "See how I split myself!   30

　　See now how maimed Mohammed⁹ is! And he
who walks and weeps before me is Alì,
whose face is opened wide from chin to forelock.

　　And all the others here whom you can see
were, when alive, the sowers of dissension   35
and scandal, and for this they now are split.

　　Behind us here, a devil decks us out
so cruelly, re-placing every one
of this throng underneath the sword edge when

　　we've made our way around the road of pain,   40
because our wounds have closed again before
we have returned to meet his blade once more.

　　But who are you who dawdle on this ridge,
perhaps to slow your going to the verdict
that was pronounced on your self-accusations?"   45

　　"Death has not reached him yet," my master answered,
"nor is it guilt that summons him to torment;
but that he may gain full experience,

　　I, who am dead, must guide him here below,
to circle after circle, throughout Hell: 50
this is as true as that I speak to you."

　　More than a hundred, when they heard him, stopped
within the ditch and turned to look at me,
forgetful of their torture, wondering.

　　"Then you, who will perhaps soon see the sun,   55
tell Fra Dolcino¹ to provide himself
with food, if he has no desire to join me

　　here quickly, lest when snow besieges him,
it bring the Novarese the victory
that otherwise they would not find too easy."   60

　　When he had raised his heel, as if to go,
Mohammed said these words to me, and then
he set it on the ground and off he went.

　　Another sinner, with his throat slit through
and with his nose hacked off up to his eyebrows,   65
and no more than a single ear remaining,

---

9. Founder of Islam (570–632), regarded by some as a renegade Christian and a creator of religious disunity. Alì was his nephew and son-in-law, and his disputed claim to the rulership (or caliphate) divided Islam into Suni and Shia sects.　　1. In 1300 Fra Dolcino was head of a reformist order known as the Apostolic Brothers that was condemned as heretical by the pope. He and his followers escaped to the hills near the town of Novara, but starvation forced them out and many were executed.

had—with the others—stayed his steps in wonder;
he was the first, before the rest, to open
his windpipe—on the outside, all bloodred—
and said: "O you whom guilt does not condemn,   70
and whom, unless too close resemblance cheats me,
I've seen above upon Italian soil,
    remember Pier da Medicina if
you ever see again the gentle plain
that from Vercelli slopes to Marcabò.[2]   75
    And let the two best men of Fano[3] know—
I mean both Messer Guido and Angiolello—
that, if the foresight we have here's not vain,
    they will be cast out of their ship and drowned,
weighed down with stones, near La Cattolica,   80
because of a foul tyrant's treachery.
    Between the isles of Cyprus and Majorca,
Neptune has never seen so cruel a crime
committed by the pirates or the Argives.[4]
    That traitor who sees only with one eye   85
and rules the land which one who's here with me
would wish his sight had never seen, will call
    Guido and Angiolello to a parley,
and then will so arrange it that they'll need
no vow or prayer to Focara's wind!"   90
    And I to him: "If you would have me carry
some news of you above, then tell and show me
who so detests the sight of Rimini."
    And then he set his hand upon the jaw
of a companion, opening his mouth   95
and shouting: "This is he,[5] and he speaks not.
    A man cast out, he quenched the doubt in Caesar,
insisting that the one who is prepared
can only suffer harm if he delays."
    Oh, how dismayed and pained he seemed to me,   100
his tongue slit in his gullet: Curio,
who once was so audacious in his talk!
    And one who walked with both his hands hacked off,
while lifting up his stumps through the dark air,
so that his face was hideous with blood,   105
    cried out: "You will remember Mosca,[6] too,
who said—alas—'What's done is at an end,'
which was the seed of evil for the Tuscans."
    I added: "—and brought death to your own kinsmen";
then having heard me speak, grief heaped on grief,   110

---

2. The town of Medicina lies in the Po Valley between Vercelli and Marcabò. Nothing certain is known of Pier da Medicina. **3.** A town on the Adriatic coast of Italy; its two leaders—named in the next line— were drowned in 1312 by the one-eyed tyrant Malatestino of Rimini (27.46) near the promontory of Focara after he had invited them to the town of La Cattolica for a parley. **4.** Greeks. *Cyprus and Majorca:* islands at the western and eastern ends of the Mediterranean. *Neptune:* classical god of the sea. **5.** Caius Curio, a Roman of the first century B.C., was bribed by Julius Caesar to betray his friends; he urged Caesar to cross the Rubicon and invade the Roman republic, starting a civil war. **6.** A Florentine noble, who in 1215 started the disastrous civil strife by advising a father to avenge the slight to his daughter by killing the man who had broken his engagement to her. Mosca's own family was a victim of the strife some sixty years later.

he went his way as one gone mad with sadness.
　　But I stayed there to watch that company
and saw a thing that I should be afraid
to tell with no more proof than my own self—
　　except that I am reassured by conscience,　　　　　　115
that good companion, heartening a man
beneath the breastplate of its purity.
　　I surely saw, and it still seems I see,
a trunk without a head that walked just like
the others in that melancholy herd;　　　　　　　　　120
　　it carried by the hair its severed head,
which swayed within its hand just like a lantern;
and that head looked at us and said: "Ah me!"
　　Out of itself it made itself a lamp,
and they were two in one and one in two;　　　　　　125
how that can be, He knows who so decrees.
　　When it was just below the bridge, it lifted
its arm together with its head, so that
its words might be more near us, words that said:
　　"Now you can see atrocious punishment,　　　　　　130
you who, still breathing, go to view the dead:
see if there's any pain as great as this.
　　And so that you may carry news of me,
know that I am Bertran de Born,[7] the one
who gave bad counsel to the fledgling king.　　　　　135
　　I made the son and father enemies:
Achitophel with his malicious urgings
did not do worse with Absalom and David.
　　Because I severed those so joined, I carry—
alas—my brain dissevered from its source,　　　　　140
which is within my trunk. And thus, in me
one sees the law of counter-penalty."

CANTO XXIX

*Still the Eighth Circle, Ninth Pouch: the Sowers of Scandal and Schism.
Geri del Bello, an unavenged ancestor of Dante. The Tenth Pouch: the
Falsifiers. The First Group, Falsifiers of Metals (Alchemists), plagued by
scabs, lying on the earth, scratching furiously. Griffolino. Capocchio.*

　　So many souls and such outlandish wounds
had made my eyes inebriate—they longed
to stay and weep. But Virgil said to me:
　　"Why are you staring so insistently?
Why does your vision linger there below　　　　　　5
among the lost and mutilated shadows?
　　You did not do so at the other moats.
If you would count them all, consider: twenty-

---

7. A Provençal nobleman and poet, who reputedly advised the son of Henry II of England to rebel against
his father. For Achitophel's similar scheming between David and his son Absalom, see 2 Samuel 15–17. A
poem by Bertran is included in *Medieval Lyrics: A Selection* (p. 1207).

two miles[8] make up the circuit of the valley.
   The moon already is beneath our feet;[9]   10
the time alloted to us now is short,
and there is more to see than you see here."
   "Had you," I answered him without a pause,
"been able to consider why I looked,
you might have granted me a longer stay."   15
   Meanwhile my guide had moved ahead; I went
behind him, answering as I walked on,
and adding: "In that hollow upon which,
   just now, I kept my eyes intent, I think
a spirit born of my own blood laments   20
the guilt which, down below, costs one so much."
   At this my master said: "Don't let your thoughts
about him interrupt you from here on:
attend to other things, let him stay there;
   for I saw him below the little bridge,   25
his finger pointing at you, threatening,
and heard him called by name—Geri del Bello.[1]
   But at that moment you were occupied
with him who once was lord of Hautefort;[2]
you did not notice Geri—he moved off."   30
   "My guide, it was his death by violence,
for which he still is not avenged," I said,
"by anyone who shares his shame, that made
   him so disdainful now; and—I suppose—
for this he left without a word to me,   35
and this has made me pity him the more."
   And so we talked until we found the first
point of the ridge that, if there were more light,
would show the other valley to the bottom.
   When we had climbed above the final cloister   40
of Malebolge, so that its lay brothers
were able to appear before our eyes,
   I felt the force of strange laments, like arrows
whose shafts are barbed with pity; and at this,
I had to place my hands across my ears.   45
   Just like the sufferings that all the sick
of Val di Chiana's hospitals, Maremma's,
Sardinia's,[3] from July until September
   would muster if assembled in one ditch—
so was it here, and such a stench rose up   50
as usually comes from festering limbs.
   And keeping always to the left, we climbed
down to the final bank of the long ridge,

---

8. The reason for this exact measurement is not known. At 30.86 we are told that the circumference of the ninth circle is eleven miles, showing that Hell is shaped like a funnel.   9. This means that the sun (which they cannot see) is over their heads, and the time is about 2 P.M. The journey to the center of Hell lasts twenty-four hours, so only four hours are left.   1. First cousin to Dante's father; his death at the hands of a member of another Florentine family initiated a feud between the two families that lasted some fifty years.   2. Bertran de Born (see 28.134).   3. The river valley of Val di Chiana, the region of Maremma, and the island of Sardinia were all plagued by malaria.

and then my sight could see more vividly
    into the bottom, where unerring Justice,   55
the minister of the High Lord, punishes
the falsifiers she had registered.
    I do not think that there was greater grief
in seeing all Aegina's⁴ people sick
    (then, when the air was so infected that   60
all animals, down to the little worm,
collapsed; and afterward, as poets hold
    to be the certain truth, those ancient peoples
received their health again through seed of ants)
than I felt when I saw, in that dark valley,   65
    the spirits languishing in scattered heaps.
Some lay upon their bellies, some upon
the shoulders of another spirit, some
    crawled on all fours along that squalid road.
We journeyed step by step without a word,   70
watching and listening to those sick souls,
    who had not strength enough to lift themselves.
I saw two sitting propped against each other—
as pan is propped on pan to heat them up⁵—
    and each, from head to foot, spotted with scabs;   75
and I have never seen a stableboy
whose master waits for him, or one who stays
    awake reluctantly, so ply a horse
with currycomb, as they assailed themselves
with clawing nails—their itching had such force   80
    and fury, and there was no other help.
And so their nails kept scraping off the scabs,
just as a knife scrapes off the scales of carp
    or of another fish with scales more large.
"O you who use your nails to strip yourself,"   85
my guide began to say to one of them,
"and sometimes have to turn them into pincers,
    tell us if there are some Italians
among the sinners in this moat—so may
your nails hold out, eternal, at their work."   90
    "We two whom you see so disfigured here,
we are Italians," one said, in tears.
"But who are you who have inquired of us?"
    My guide replied: " From circle down to circle,
together with this living man, I am   95
one who descends; I mean to show him Hell."
    At this their mutual support broke off;
and, quivering, each spirit turned toward me
with others who, by chance, had heard his words.
    Then my good master drew more close to me,   100
saying: "Now tell them what it is you want."

---

4. A mythical island that was infected by Juno with a pestilence that killed all its inhabitants and was then repopulated when Jupiter turned ants into men: see Ovid, *Metamorphoses* 7.   **5.** The image is of pans leaned against one another on the stove.

And I began to speak, just as he wished:
  "So that your memory may never fade
within the first world from the minds of men,
but still live on—and under many suns—   105
  do tell me who you are and from what city,
and do not let your vile and filthy torment
make you afraid to let me know your names."
  One answered me: "My city was Arezzo
and Albero of Siena had me burned;[6]   110
but what I died for does not bring me here.
  It's true that I had told him—jestingly—
'I'd know enough to fly through air'; and he,
with curiosity, but little sense,
  wished me to show that art to him and, just   115
because I had not made him Daedalus,
had one who held him as a son burn me.
  But Minos, who cannot mistake, condemned
my spirit to the final pouch of ten
for alchemy[7] I practiced in the world."   120
  And then I asked the poet: "Was there ever
so vain a people as the Sienese?
Even the French can't match such vanity."
  At this, the other leper,[8] who had heard me,
replied to what I'd said: "Except for Stricca,   125
for he knew how to spend most frugally;
  and Niccolò, the first to make men see
that cloves can serve as luxury (such seed,
in gardens where it suits, can take fast root);
  and, too, Caccia d'Asciano's company,   130
with whom he squandered vineyards and tilled fields,
while Abbagliato showed such subtlety.
  But if you want to know who joins you so
against the Sienese, look hard at me—
that way, my face can also answer rightly—   135
  and see that I'm the shade of that Capocchio
whose alchemy could counterfeit fine metals.
And you, if I correctly take your measure,
  recall how apt I was at aping nature."

CANTO XXX

Still the Eighth Circle, Tenth Pouch: the Falsifiers. Gianni Schicchi and Myrrha in the Second Group, Counterfeiters of Others' Persons. Master Adam in the Third Group, Counterfeiters of Coins. Potiphar's wife and Sinon the Greek in the Fourth Group, Falsifiers of Words, Liars. The quarrel between Adam and Sinon.

---

6. Griffolino of Arezzo cheated Albero of Siena by promising to teach him the art of Daedalus—flying. The bishop of Siena, father of the illegitimate Albero, had Griffolino burned as a heretic.   **7.** A practice that sought to turn base metals like lead into gold.   **8.** Capocchio, a Florentine burned in 1293 for alchemy, which he here admits was mere counterfeiting. The people he lists were rich young noblemen of Siena who joined a "Spendthrifts' Club"—the *company* of line 130—and sought to outdo each other in profligacy. For another member of this club, Lano of Siena, see 13.115.

When Juno was incensed with Semele[9]
and, thus, against the Theban family
had shown her fury time and time again,
    then Athamas was driven so insane
that, seeing both his wife and their two sons,   5
as she bore one upon each arm, he cried:
    "Let's spread the nets, to take the lioness
together with her cubs along the pass";
and he stretched out his talons, pitiless,
    and snatched the son who bore the name Learchus,   10
whirled him around and dashed him on a rock;
she, with her other burden, drowned herself.
    And after fortune turned against the pride
of Troy,[1] which had dared all, so that the king
together with his kingdom, was destroyed,   15
    then Hecuba was wretched, sad, a captive;
and after she had seen Polyxena
dead and, in misery, had recognized
    her Polydorus lying on the shore,
she barked, out of her senses, like a dog—   20
her agony had so deformed her mind.
    But neither fury—Theban, Trojan—ever
was seen to be so cruel against another,
in rending beasts and even human limbs,
    as were two shades I saw, both pale and naked,   25
who, biting, ran berserk in just the way
a hog does when it's let loose from its sty.
    The one came at Capocchio and sank
his tusks into his neck so that, by dragging,
he made the hard ground scrape against his belly.   30
    And he who stayed behind, the Aretine,[2]
trembled and said: "That phantom's Gianni Schicchi,[3]
and he goes raging, rending others so."
    And, "Oh," I said to him, "so may the other
not sink its teeth in you, please tell me who   35
it is before it hurries off from here."
    And he to me: "That is the ancient soul
of the indecent Myrrha,[4] she who loved
her father past the limits of just love.
    She came to sin with him by falsely taking   40
another's shape upon herself, just as
the other phantom who goes there had done,
    that he might gain the lady of the herd,

9. Daughter of the king of Thebes, she was loved by Jupiter and therefore incited the wrath of Juno, who drove Semele's brother-in-law Athamas insane. While mad, Athamas thought his wife, Ino, and his two sons, Learchus and Melicertes, were a lioness and two cubs; he killed Learchus, and Ino drowned herself and Melicertes. See Ovid, *Metamorphoses* 4.   **1.** Parallel to the fate of Thebes is that of Troy, which is here represented by the madness into which Queen Hecuba fell when she saw her daughter Polyxena sacrificed on Achilles' tomb and the unburied body of her betrayed son Polydorus. See Ovid, *Metamorphoses* 13.   **2.** Griffolino (see 29.110).   **3.** A Florentine who impersonated Buoso Donati (line 44), who had just died, and dictated a new will that gave him Buoso's best beast (*the lady of the herd* of line 43).   **4.** Who impersonated another woman in order to sleep with her father: see Ovid, *Metamorphoses* 10.

when he disguised himself as Buoso Donati,
making a will as if most properly." 45

And when the pair of raging ones had passed,
those two on whom my eyes were fixed, I turned
around to see the rest of the ill-born.

I saw one who'd be fashioned like a lute
if he had only had his groin cut off 50
from that part of his body where it forks.

The heavy dropsy,[5] which so disproportions
the limbs with unassimilated humors
that there's no match between the face and belly,

had made him part his lips like a consumptive,[6] 55
who will, because of thirst, let one lip drop
down to his chin and lift the other up.

"O you exempt from every punishment
in this grim world, and I do not know why,"
he said to us, "look now and pay attention 60
to this, the misery of Master Adam:[7]
alive, I had enough of all I wanted;
alas, I now long for one drop of water.

The rivulets that fall into the Arno
down from the green hills of the Casentino 65
with channels cool and moist, are constantly

before me; I am racked by memory—
the image of their flow parches me more
than the disease that robs my face of flesh.

The rigid Justice that would torment me 70
uses, as most appropriate, the place
where I had sinned, to draw swift sighs from me.

There is Romena, there I counterfeited
the currency that bears the Baptist's seal;
for this I left my body, burned, above. 75

But could I see the miserable souls
of Guido, Alessandro, or their brother,
I'd not give up the sight for Fonte Branda.[8]

And one of them is in this moat already,
if what the angry shades report is true. 80
What use is that to me whose limbs are tied?

Were I so light that, in a hundred years,
I could advance an inch, I should already
be well upon the road to search for him

among the mutilated ones, although 85
this circuit measures some eleven miles
and is at least a half a mile across.

Because of them I'm in this family;
it was those three who had incited me
to coin the florins with three carats' dross." 90

---

5. A disease in which fluid (*humors* of line 53) gathers in the cells and the affected part becomes grotesquely swollen. 6. A person with a fever. 7. A counterfeiter, burned in 1281, who made coins stamped with the image of John the Baptist, the patron saint of Florence, that contained twenty-one rather than twenty-four carets of gold (see line 90); he worked for a noble family of Romena (individual members are mentioned in line 77), a town in the Florentine district of Casentino. 8. A fountain near Romena.

And I to him: "Who are those two poor sinners
who give off smoke like wet hands in the winter
and lie so close to you upon the right?"

"I found them here," he answered, "when I rained
down to this rocky slope; they've not stirred since   95
and will not move, I think, eternally.

One is the lying woman who blamed Joseph;
the other, lying Sinon,[9] Greek from Troy:
because of raging fever they reek so."

And one of them, who seemed to take offense,   100
perhaps at being named so squalidly,
struck with his fist at Adam's rigid belly.

It sounded as if it had been a drum;
and Master Adam struck him in the face,
using his arm, which did not seem less hard,   105

saying to him: "Although I cannot move
my limbs because they are too heavy, I
still have an arm that's free to serve that need."

And he replied: "But when you went to burning,
your arm was not as quick as it was now;   110
though when you coined, it was as quick and more."

To which the dropsied one: "Here you speak true;
but you were not so true a witness there,
when you were asked to tell the truth at Troy."

"If I spoke false, you falsified the coin,"   115
said Sinon; "I am here for just one crime—
but you've committed more than any demon."

"Do not forget the horse, you perjurer,"
replied the one who had the bloated belly,
"may you be plagued because the whole world knows it."   120

The Greek: "And you be plagued by thirst that cracks
your tongue, and putrid water that has made
your belly such a hedge before your eyes."

And then the coiner: "So, as usual,
your mouth, because of racking fever, gapes;   125
for if I thirst and if my humor bloats me,

you have both dryness and a head that aches;
few words would be sufficient invitation
to have you lick the mirror of Narcissus."[1]

I was intent on listening to them   130
when this was what my master said: "If you
insist on looking more, I'll quarrel with you!"

And when I heard him speak so angrily,
I turned around to him with shame so great
that it still stirs within my memory.   135

Even as one who dreams that he is harmed
and, dreaming, wishes he were dreaming, thus
desiring that which is, as if it were not,

so I became within my speechlessness:

9. A Greek priest who persuaded the Trojans to accept the wooden horse (*Aeneid* 2). *Lying woman:* Potiphar's wife, who falsely accused Joseph of trying to lie with her (Genesis 39.6–20).   1. Narcissus saw his reflection in a pool of water (Ovid, *Metamorphoses* 3).

I wanted to excuse myself and did   140
excuse myself, although I knew it not.
    "Less shame would wash away a greater fault
than was your fault," my master said to me;
"therefore release yourself from all remorse
    and see that I am always at your side,   145
should it so happen—once again—that fortune
brings you where men would quarrel in this fashion:
to want to hear such bickering is base."

CANTO XXXI

*Passage to the Ninth Circle. The central pit or well of Hell, where
Cocytus, the last river of Hell, freezes. The Giants: Nimrod, Ephialtes,
Briareus, Antaeus. Antaeus's compliance with Virgil's request to lower the
two poets into the pit.*

    The very tongue that first had wounded me,
sending the color up in both my cheeks,
was then to cure me with its medicine—
    as did Achilles' and his father's lance,[2]
even as I have heard, when it dispensed   5
a sad stroke first and then a healing one.
    We turned our backs upon that dismal valley
by climbing up the bank that girdles it;
we made our way across without a word.
    Here it was less than night and less than day,   10
so that my sight could only move ahead
slightly, but then I heard a bugle blast
    so strong, it would have made a thunder clap
seem faint; at this, my eyes—which doubled back
upon their path—turned fully toward one place.   15
    Not even Roland's horn,[3] which followed on
the sad defeat when Charlemagne had lost
his holy army, was as dread as this.
    I'd only turned my head there briefly when
I seemed to make out many high towers; then   20
I asked him: "Master, tell me, what's this city?"
    And he to me: "It is because you try
to penetrate from far into these shadows
that you have formed such faulty images.
    When you have reached that place, you shall see clearly   25
how much the distance has deceived your sense;
and, therefore, let this spur you on your way."
    Then lovingly he took me by the hand
and said: "Before we have moved farther on,
so that the fact may seem less strange to you,   30
    I'd have you know they are not towers, but giants,
and from the navel downward, all of them

---

2. Achilles' father, Peleus, gave him a lance that would heal any wound it inflicted.   **3.** In *The Song of
Roland* (see pp. 1142–43), Roland blows his horn to alert Charlemagne to the fact that the rear guard
Roland commands has been slaughtered.

are in the central pit, at the embankment."

    Just as, whenever mists begin to thin,
when, gradually, vision finds the form   35
that in the vapor-thickened air was hidden,

    so I pierced through the dense and darkened fog;
as I drew always nearer to the shore,
my error fled from me, my terror grew;

    for as, on its round wall, Montereggioni[4]   40
is crowned with towers, so there towered here,
above the bank that runs around the pit,

    with half their bulk, the terrifying giants,[5]
who still—whenever Jove hurls bolts from heaven—
remember how his thunder shattered them.   45

    And I could now make out the face of one,[6]
his shoulders and his chest, much of his belly,
and both his arms that hung along his sides.

    Surely when she gave up the art of making
such creatures, Nature acted well indeed,   50
depriving Mars of instruments like these.

    And if she still produces elephants
and whales, whoever sees with subtlety
holds her—for this—to be more just and prudent;

    for where the mind's acutest reasoning   55
is joined to evil will and evil power,
there human beings can't defend themselves.

    His face appeared to me as broad and long
as Rome can claim for its St. Peter's pine cone;[7]
his other bones shared in that same proportion;   60

    so that the bank, which served him as an apron
down from his middle, showed so much of him
above, that three Frieslanders[8] would in vain

    have boasted of their reaching to his hair;
for downward from the place where one would buckle   65
a mantle, I saw thirty spans[9] of him.

    "*Raphèl maì amècche zabì almi*,"[1]
began to bellow that brute mouth, for which
no sweeter psalms would be appropriate.

    And my guide turned to him: "O stupid soul,   70
keep to your horn[2] and use that as an outlet
when rage or other passion touches you!

    Look at your neck, and you will find the strap
that holds it fast; and see, bewildered spirit,
how it lies straight across your massive chest."   75

    And then to me: "He is his own accuser;
for this is Nimrod, through whose wicked thought

---

4. A castle surrounded by towers, built to protect Siena from attack by Florence.   **5.** According to classical mythology, Titans, giants born of the Earth, assaulted Olympus and were defeated and imprisoned by Jupiter.   **6.** Nimrod, described in Genesis as "the first on earth to be a mighty man" (10.8) and understood by medieval commentators to be a giant. He ruled over Babylon, where the tower of Babel was built (11.1–9).   **7.** This bronze pine cone, over twelve feet high, stood outside St. Peter's Cathedral in Dante's time; today it can be seen in the papal gardens in the Vatican.   **8.** Inhabitants of the northernmost province of what is now the Netherlands, considered the tallest men of the time.   **9.** About fifteen feet. **1.** Appropriately for the builder of Babel, he speaks an incomprehensible language.   **2.** Nimrod has a horn because in the Bible he is described as a hunter (Genesis 10.9).

one single language cannot serve the world.
　　Leave him alone—let's not waste time in talk;
for every language is to him the same　　　　　　　　　　　80
as his to others—no one knows his tongue."
　　So, turning to the left, we journeyed on
and, at the distance of a bow-shot, found
another giant, far more huge and fierce.
　　Who was the master who had tied him so,　　　　　　　85
I cannot say, but his left arm was bent
behind him and his right was bent in front,
　　both pinioned by a chain that held him tight
down from the neck; and round the part of him
that was exposed, it had been wound five times.　　　　　90
　　"This giant in his arrogance had tested
his force against the force of highest Jove,"
my guide said, "so he merits this reward.
　　His name is Ephialtes;[3] and he showed
tremendous power when the giants frightened　　　　　　95
the gods; the arms he moved now move no more."
　　And I to him: "If it is possible,
I'd like my eyes to have experience
of the enormous one, Briareus."[4]
　　At which he answered: "You shall see Antaeus[5]　　　100
nearby. He is unfettered and can speak;
he'll take us to the bottom of all evil.
　　The one you wish to see lies far beyond
and is bound up and just as huge as this one,
and even more ferocious in his gaze."　　　　　　　　　105
　　No earthquake ever was so violent
when called to shake a tower so robust,
as Ephialtes quick to shake himself.
　　Then I was more afraid of death than ever;
that fear would have been quite enough to kill me,　　　110
had I not seen how he was held by chains.
　　And we continued on until we reached
Antaeus, who, not reckoning his head,
stood out above the rock wall full five ells.[6]
　　"O you, who lived within the famous valley[7]　　　　115
(where Scipio became the heir of glory
when Hannibal retreated with his men),
　　who took a thousand lions as your prey—
and had you been together with your brothers
in their high war, it seems some still believe　　　　　120
　　the sons of earth would have become the victors—
do set us down below, where cold shuts in
Cocytus,[8] and do not disdain that task.
　　Don't send us on to Tityus or Typhon;[9]

3. Ephialtes and his twin brother, Otus, were Titans who tried to attack Olympus by piling Mount Ossa on Mount Pelion: see Virgil, *Aeneid* 6. 　4. Another Titan. 　5. A Titan born too late to participate in the rebellion against Jupiter and therefore not chained; he was known for eating lions (line 118) and was defeated by Hercules in a wrestling match (line 132). 　6. About fifteen feet. 　7. The valley of the Bagradas River in Tunisia, where the Roman Scipio defeated the Carthaginian Hannibal in 202 B.C. 　8. The frozen lake of Cocytus is in the ninth and last circle of Hell. 　9. Two more Titans.

this man can give you what is longed for here;   125
therefore bend down and do not curl your lip.
    He still can bring you fame within the world,
for he's alive and still expects long life,
unless grace summon him before his time."
    So said my master; and in haste Antaeus   130
stretched out his hands, whose massive grip had once
been felt by Hercules, and grasped my guide.
    And Virgil, when he felt himself caught up,
called out to me: "Come here, so I can hold you,"
then made one bundle of himself and me.   135
    Just as the Garisenda[1] seems when seen
beneath the leaning side, when clouds run past
and it hangs down as if about to crash,
    so did Antaeus seem to me as I
watched him bend over me—a moment when   140
I'd have preferred to take some other road.
    But gently—on the deep that swallows up
both Lucifer and Judas[2]—he placed us;
nor did he, so bent over, stay there long,
but, like a mast above a ship, he rose.   145

CANTO XXXII

*The Ninth Circle, First Ring, called Caïna, where Traitors to their Kin
are immersed in the ice, heads bent down. Camiscione dei Pazzi. The
Second Ring, called Antenora: the Traitors to their Homeland or Party.
Bocca degli Abati's provocation of Dante. Two traitors, one gnawing at
the other's head.*

    Had I the crude and scrannel rhymes to suit
the melancholy hole upon which all
the other circling crags converge and rest,
    the juice of my conception would be pressed
more fully; but because I feel their lack,   5
I bring myself to speak, yet speak in fear;
    for it is not a task to take in jest,
to show the base of all the universe—
nor for a tongue that cries out, "mama," "papa."
    But may those ladies[3] now sustain my verse   10
who helped Amphion when he walled up Thebes,
so that my tale not differ from the fact.
    O rabble, miscreated past all others,
there in the place of which it's hard to speak,
better if here you had been goats or sheep!   15
    When we were down below in the dark well,
beneath the giant's feet and lower yet,
with my eyes still upon the steep embankment,
    I heard this said to me: "Watch how you pass;

1. A leaning tower of Bologna; when a cloud passes over it, moving opposite to the tower's slant, it appears
to be falling away from the sky.   2. Two of the inhabitants of Cocytus.   3. The Muses who helped the
legendary musician Amphion raise the walls of Thebes with the music of his lyre.

walk so that you not trample with your soles   20
the heads of your exhausted, wretched brothers."

   At this I turned and saw in front of me,
beneath my feet, a lake[4] that, frozen fast,
had lost the look of water and seemed glass.

   The Danube where it flows in Austria,   25
the Don beneath its frozen sky, have never
made for their course so thick a veil in winter

   as there was here; for had Mount Tambernic[5]
or Pietrapana's mountain crashed upon it,
not even at the edge would it have creaked.   30

   And as the croaking frog sits with its muzzle
above the water, in the season when
the peasant woman often dreams of gleaning,[6]

   so, livid in the ice, up to the place
where shame can show itself, were those sad shades,   35
whose teeth were chattering with notes like storks'.[7]

   Each kept his face bent downward steadily;
their mouths bore witness to the cold they felt,
just as their eyes proclaimed their sorry hearts.

   When I had looked around a while, my eyes   40
turned toward my feet and saw two locked so close,
the hair upon their heads had intermingled.

   "Do tell me, you whose chests are pressed so tight,"
I said, "who are you?" They bent back their necks,
and when they'd lifted up their faces toward me,   45

   their eyes, which wept upon the ground before,
shed tears down on their lips until the cold
held fast the tears and locked their lids still more.

   No clamp has ever fastened plank to plank
so tightly; and because of this, they butted   50
each other like two rams, such was their fury.

   And one from whom the cold had taken both
his ears, who kept his face bent low, then said:
"Why do you keep on staring so at us?

   If you would like to know who these two are: 55
that valley where Bisenzio descends,
belonged to them and to their father Alberto.[8]

   They came out of one body; and you can
search all Caïna,[9] you will never find
a shade more fit to sit within this ice—   60

   not him who, at one blow, had chest and shadow
shattered by Arthur's hand; and not Focaccia;[1]
and not this sinner here who so impedes

---

4. The water for this lake derives from the crack in the Old Man of Crete (14.103). **5.** Probably Mt. Tambura, close to Mt. Pietrapana in the Italian Alps. **6.** Picking over harvested fields for bits of grain left behind, an activity for the early summer. **7.** A harsh, clacking sound. *The place . . . itself:* the face. **8.** When Count Alberto degli Alberti died (ca. 1280), his two sons killed each other over politics and their inheritance. *Bisenzio:* a river north of Florence. **9.** Named after Cain, the first of the four subdivisions of Cocytus is where those who betrayed their kin are imprisoned. **1.** A nobleman of Pistoia who killed his cousin. *Not him . . . hand:* Mordred, Arthur's nephew and son; when Arthur pierced him with a sword, he created a wound so large that the sun shone through, thus creating a hole in Mordred's shadow.

my vision with his head, I can't see past him;
his name was Sassol Mascheroni;[2] if 65
you're Tuscan, now you know who he has been.

And lest you keep me talking any longer,
know that I was Camiscion de' Pazzi;[3]
I'm waiting for Carlino[4] to absolve me."

And after that I saw a thousand faces 70
made doglike by the cold; for which I shudder—
and always will—when I face frozen fords.

And while we were advancing toward the center
to which all weight is drawn[5]—I, shivering
in that eternally cold shadow—I 75

know not if it was will or destiny
or chance, but as I walked among the heads,
I struck my foot hard in the face of one.[6]

Weeping, he chided then: "Why trample me?
If you've not come to add to the revenge 80
of Montaperti, why do you molest me?"

And I: "My master, now wait here for me,
that I may clear up just one doubt about him;
then you can make me hurry as you will."

My guide stood fast, and I went on to ask 85
of him who still was cursing bitterly:
"Who are you that rebukes another so?"

"And who are you who go through Antenora,[7]
striking the cheeks of others," he replied,
"too roughly—even if you were alive?" 90

"I am alive, and can be precious to you
if you want fame," was my reply, "for I
can set your name among my other notes."

And he to me: "I want the contrary;
so go away and do not harass me— 95
your flattery is useless in this valley."

At that I grabbed him by the scruff[8] and said:
"You'll have to name yourself to me or else
you won't have even one hair left up here."

And he to me: "Though you should strip me bald, 100
I shall not tell you who I am or show it,
not if you pound my head a thousand times."

His hairs were wound around my hand already,
and I had plucked from him more than one tuft
while he was barking and his eyes stared down, 105

when someone else cried out: "What is it, Bocca?
Isn't the music of your jaws enough
for you without your bark? What devil's at you?"

"And now," I said, "you traitor bent on evil,

2. A Florentine nobleman who murdered a relative.   3. A Florentine who killed his kinsman.   4. A Florentine who betrayed a castle belonging to his party. When he dies he will therefore be sent to the next subdivision, Antenora, for those who committed treachery against their country, city, or party—a harsher punishment, which Camiscion says will "absolve" him.   5. The *base of all the universe* (line 8) is where gravity is most strong and to which all material things are drawn.   6. Bocca degli Abati, who betrayed his party at the battle of Montaperti in 1260.   7. Named after Antenor, a Trojan who betrayed the city to the Greeks.   8. The hair at the nape of the neck.

I do not need your talk, for I shall carry   110
true news of you, and that will bring you shame."
    "Be off," he answered; "tell them what you like,
but don't be silent, if you make it back,
about the one whose tongue was now so quick.[9]
    Here he laments the silver of the Frenchmen;   115
'I saw,' you then can say, 'him of Duera,
down there, where all the sinners are kept cool.'
    And if you're asked who else was there in ice,
one of the Beccheria[1] is beside you—
he had his gullet sliced right through by Florence.   120
    Gianni de' Soldanieri, I believe,
lies there with Ganelon and Tebaldello,[2]
he who unlocked Faenza while it slept."
    We had already taken leave of him,
when I saw two shades frozen in one hole,   125
so that one's head served as the other's cap;
    and just as he who's hungry chews his bread,
one sinner dug his teeth into the other
right at the place where brain is joined to nape:
    no differently had Tydeus[3] gnawed the temples   130
of Menalippus, out of indignation,
than this one chewed the skull and other parts.
    "O you who show, with such a bestial sign,
your hatred for the one on whom you feed,
tell me the cause," I said; "we can agree   135
    that if your quarrel with him is justified,
then knowing who you are and what's his sin,
I shall repay you yet on earth above,
    if that with which I speak does not dry up."

CANTO XXXIII

Still the Ninth Circle, Second Ring. Ugolino's tale of his and his sons'
death in a Pisan prison. Dante's invective against Pisa. The Third Ring,
Ptolomea, where Traitors against their Guests jut out from ice, their eyes
sealed by frozen tears. Fra Alberigo and Branca Doria, still alive on earth
but already in Hell.

That sinner[4] raised his mouth from his fierce meal,
then used the head that he had ripped apart
in back: he wiped his lips upon its hair.
    Then he began: "You want me to renew
despairing pain that presses at my heart   5
even as I think back, before I speak.
    But if my words are seed from which the fruit
is infamy for this betrayer whom

9. Buoso da Duera, who betrayed the ruler of Naples, Manfred, to his enemy Charles of Anjou in 1265.   1. A churchman executed for treason in Florence in 1258.   2. A citizen of Faenza (a town east of Florence) who betrayed it to its enemies. *Gianni de' Soldanieri:* a Florentine nobleman who switched political parties. *Ganelon:* the betrayer of Roland in *The Song of Roland.*   3. In the war against Thebes, Tydeus was mortally wounded by Menalippus, whom he killed and whose skull he gnawed in fury while dying.   4. Ugolino, a governor of Pisa who was betrayed by his enemy Archbishop Ruggieri in 1289. His own crime is obliquely explained by his narrative.

I gnaw, you'll see me speak and weep at once.

I don't know who you are or in what way　　　　　　　10
you've come down here; and yet you surely seem—
from what I hear—to be a Florentine.

You are to know I was Count Ugolino,
and this one here, Archbishop Ruggieri;
and now I'll tell you why I am his neighbor.　　　　15

There is no need to tell you that, because
of his malicious tricks, I first was taken
and then was killed—since I had trusted him;

however, that which you cannot have heard—
that is, the cruel death devised for me—　　　　　20
you now shall hear and know if he has wronged me.

A narrow window in the Eagles' Tower,[5]
which now, through me, is called the Hunger Tower,
a cage in which still others will be locked,

had, through its opening, already showed me　　　25
several moons, when I dreamed that bad dream
which rent the curtain of the future for me.

This man appeared to me as lord and master;
he hunted down the wolf and its young whelps
upon the mountain[6] that prevents the Pisans　　　30

from seeing Lucca; and with lean and keen
and practiced hounds, he'd sent up front, before him,
Gualandi and Sismondi and Lanfranchi.[7]

But after a brief course, it seemed to me
that both the father and the sons were weary;　　　35
I seemed to see their flanks torn by sharp fangs.

When I awoke at daybreak, I could hear
my sons, who were together with me there,
weeping within their sleep, asking for bread.

You would be cruel indeed if, thinking what　　　40
my heart foresaw, you don't already grieve;
and if you don't weep now, when would you weep?

They were awake by now; the hour drew near
at which our food was usually brought,
and each, because of what he'd dreamed, was anxious;　　45

below, I heard them nailing up the door
of that appalling tower; without a word,
I looked into the faces of my sons.

I did not weep; within, I turned to stone.
They wept; and my poor little Anselm said:　　　50
'Father, you look so . . . What is wrong with you?'

At that I shed no tears and—all day long
and through the night that followed—did not answer
until another sun had touched the world.

As soon as a thin ray had made its way　　　55
into that sorry prison, and I saw,
reflected in four faces, my own gaze,

---

5. The prison in Pisa.　　6. Mt. San Giuliano lies between Pisa and Lucca. *Wolf and . . . whelps:* Ugolino and his four sons, each of whom he names in subsequent lines.　　7. Pisan families of the political party opposed to that of Ugolino.

out of my grief, I bit at both my hands;
and they, who thought I'd done that out of hunger,
immediately rose and told me: 'Father,   60
    it would be far less painful for us if
you ate of us; for you clothed us in this
sad flesh—it is for you to strip it off.'[8]
    Then I grew calm, to keep them from more sadness;
through that day and the next, we all were silent;   65
O hard earth, why did you not open up?
    But after we had reached the fourth day, Gaddo,
throwing himself, outstretched, down at my feet,
implored me: 'Father, why do you not help me?'[9]
    And there he died; and just as you see me,   70
I saw the other three fall one by one
between the fifth day and the sixth; at which,
    now blind, I started groping over each;
and after they were dead, I called them for
two days; then fasting had more force than grief."   75
    When he had spoken this, with eyes awry,
again he gripped the sad skull in his teeth,
which, like a dog's, were strong down to the bone.
    Ah, Pisa, you the scandal of the peoples
of that fair land where *si* is heard,[1] because   80
your neighbors are so slow to punish you,
    may, then, Caprara and Gorgona[2] move
and build a hedge across the Arno's mouth,
so that it may drown every soul in you!
    For if Count Ugolino was reputed   85
to have betrayed your fortresses, there was
no need to have his sons endure such torment.
    O Thebes renewed,[3] their years were innocent
and young—Brigata, Uguiccione, and
the other two my song has named above!   90
    We passed beyond,[4] where frozen water wraps—
a rugged covering—still other sinners,
who were not bent, but flat upon their backs.
    Their very weeping there won't let them weep,
and grief that finds a barrier in their eyes   95
turns inward to increase their agony;
    because their first tears freeze into a cluster,
and, like a crystal visor, fill up all
the hollow that is underneath the eyebrow.
    And though, because of cold, my every sense   100
had left its dwelling in my face, just as
a callus has no feeling, nonetheless,
    I seemed to feel some wind now, and I said:

8. See Job 1.21.   9. See Matthew 27.46.   1. I.e., Italy, where *si* means "yes."   2. Islands belonging
to Pisa that lie close to the mouth of the Arno, which flows through Pisa.   3. In classical mythology,
Thebes was notorious for its intergenerational horrors, such as the story of Oedipus; his father, Laius; and
his sons, Eteocles and Polynices (see 26.54).   4. They pass into the third division of Cocytus, called
Ptolomea (line 124) after Ptolemy, governor of Jericho, who killed his father-in-law, Simon, and two of his
sons while they were dining with him (1 Maccabees 16.11–17). In Ptolomea those who have betrayed their
guests are punished.

"My master, who has set this gust in motion?
For isn't every vapor quenched down here?"[5]   105
    And he to me: "You soon shall be where your
own eye will answer that, when you shall see
the reason why this wind blasts from above."
    And one of those sad sinners in the cold
crust, cried to us: "O souls who are so cruel   110
that this last place has been assigned to you,
    take off the hard veils from my face so that
I can release the suffering that fills
my heart before lament freezes again."
    To which I answered: "If you'd have me help you,   115
then tell me who you are; if I don't free you,
may I go to the bottom of the ice."
    He answered then: "I am Fra Alberigo,[6]
the one who tended fruits in a bad garden,
and here my figs have been repaid with dates."   120
    "But then," I said, "are you already dead?"
And he to me: "I have no knowledge of
my body's fate within the world above.
    For Ptolomea has this privilege:
quite frequently the soul falls here before   125
it has been thrust away by Atropos.[7]
    And that you may with much more willingness
scrape these glazed tears from off my face, know this:
as soon as any soul becomes a traitor,
    as I was, then a demon takes its body   130
away—and keeps that body in his power
until its years have run their course completely.
    The soul falls headlong, down into this cistern;
and up above, perhaps, there still appears
the body of the shade that winters here   135
    behind me; you must know him, if you've just
come down; he is Ser Branca Doria;[8]
for many years he has been thus pent up."
    I said to him: "I think that you deceive me,
for Branca Doria is not yet dead;   140
he eats and drinks and sleeps and puts on clothes."
    "There in the Malebranche's ditch above,
where sticky pitch boils up, Michele Zanche
had still not come," he said to me, "when this one—
    together with a kinsman, who had done   145
the treachery together with him—left
a devil in his stead inside his body.
    But now reach out your hand; open my eyes."
And yet I did not open them for him;

5. Since the sun's heat was thought to cause wind, Dante wonders why he feels wind in this cold place.   **6.** A member of the Jovial Friars (see 23.103), he killed two of his relatives during a banquet at his house, signaling the assassins with an order to bring the fruit. In saying that his figs have been repaid with dates, he is ironically complimenting God for His generosity, since a date would be more valuable than a fig.   **7.** One of the mythological figures known as the Fates; she is the one who cuts the thread of life.   **8.** A nobleman of Genoa, who with a kinsman (line 145) killed his father-in-law, Michel Zanche, at a banquet in 1275 or 1290.

and it was courtesy to show him rudeness.   150
   Ah, Genoese, a people strange to every
constraint of custom, full of all corruption,
why have you not been driven from the world?
   For with the foulest spirit of Romagna,[9]
I found one of you such that, for his acts,   155
in soul he bathes already in Cocytus
   and up above appears alive, in body.

CANTO XXXIV

*The Ninth Circle, Fourth Ring, called Judecca, where Tratiors against
their Benefactors are fully covered by ice. Dis, or Lucifer, emperor of that
kingdom, his three mouths rending Judas, Brutus, and Cassius. Descent of
Virgil and Dante down Lucifer's body to the other, southern hemisphere.
Their vision of the stars.*

   "*Vexilla regis prodeunt inferni*[1]
toward us; and therefore keep your eyes ahead,"
my master said, "to see if you can spy him."
   Just as, when night falls on our hemisphere
or when a heavy fog is blowing thick,   5
a windmill seems to wheel when seen far off,
   so then I seemed to see that sort of structure.
And next, because the wind was strong, I shrank
behind my guide; there was no other shelter.
   And now—with fear I set it down in meter—   10
I was where all the shades were fully covered
but visible as wisps of straw in glass.
   There some lie flat and others stand erect,
one on his head, and one upon his soles;
and some bend face to feet, just like a bow.   15
   But after we had made our way ahead,
my master felt he now should have me see
that creature who was once a handsome presence;[2]
   he stepped aside and made me stop, and said:
"Look! Here is Dis,[3] and this the place where you   20
will have to arm yourself with fortitude."
   O reader, do not ask of me how I
grew faint and frozen then—I cannot write it:
all words would fall far short of what it was.
   I did not die, and I was not alive;   25
think for yourself, if you have any wit,
what I became, deprived of life and death.
   The emperor of the despondent kingdom
so towered—from midchest—above the ice,
that I match better with a giant's height   30
   than giants match the measure of his arms;

---

9. Fra Alberigo.   **1.** The first three words—"the banners of the king advance"—are the opening lines of
a sixth-century Latin hymn traditionally sung during Holy Week to celebrate Christ's Passion. Dante has
added the last word, *inferni*—"the banners of the king of Hell advance"—in order to apply the words to
Satan.   **2.** Lucifer, the "light-bearer," was the most beautiful of angels before he rebelled and was re-
named Satan.   **3.** A classical name for Pluto, here applied to Satan (see also 11.65 and 12.39).

now you can gauge the size of all of him
if it is in proportion to such limbs.
    If he was once as handsome as he now
is ugly and, despite that, raised his brows   35
against his Maker, one can understand
    how every sorrow has its source in him!
I marveled when I saw that, on his head,
he had three faces:⁴ one—in front—bloodred;
    and then another two that, just above   40
the midpoint of each shoulder, joined the first;
and at the crown, all three were reattached;
    the right looked somewhat yellow, somewhat white;
the left in its appearance was like those⁵
who come from where the Nile, descending, flows.   45
    Beneath each face of his, two wings spread out,
as broad as suited so immense a bird:
I've never seen a ship with sails so wide.
    They had no feathers, but were fashioned like
a bat's; and he was agitating them,   50
so that three winds made their way out from him—
    and all Cocytus froze before those winds.
He wept out of six eyes; and down three chins,
tears gushed together with a bloody froth.
    Within each mouth—he used it like a grinder—   55
with gnashing teeth he tore to bits a sinner,
so that he brought much pain to three at once.
    The forward sinner found that biting nothing
when matched against the clawing, for at times
his back was stripped completely of its hide.   60
    "That soul up there who has to suffer most,"
my master said: "Judas Iscariot—
his head inside, he jerks his legs without.
    Of those two others, with their heads beneath,
the one who hangs from that black snout is Brutus⁶—   65
see how he writhes and does not say a word!
    That other, who seems so robust, is Cassius.⁷
But night is come again, and it is time
for us to leave; we have seen everything."
    Just as he asked, I clasped him round the neck;   70
and he watched for the chance of time and place,
and when the wings were open wide enough,
    he took fast hold upon the shaggy flanks
and then descended, down from tuft to tuft,
between the tangled hair and icy crusts.   75
    When we had reached the point at which the thigh
revolves, just at the swelling of the hip,
my guide, with heavy strain and rugged work,
    reversed his head to where his legs had been

4. Satan's three faces (and much else) make him an infernal parody of the Trinity.   5. I.e., Ethiopians. The significance of these three colors is not certain; it has been suggested that they represent hatred, impotence, and ignorance.   6. The murderer of Julius Caesar in 44 B.C., and thus for Dante a betrayer of the empire.   7. The other murderer of Caesar.

and grappled on the hair, as one who climbs—   80
I thought that we were going back to Hell.[8]
  "Hold tight," my master said—he panted like
a man exhausted—"it is by such stairs
that we must take our leave of so much evil."
  Then he slipped through a crevice in a rock   85
and placed me on the edge of it, to sit;
that done, he climbed toward me with steady steps.
  I raised my eyes, believing I should see
the half of Lucifer that I had left;
instead I saw him with his legs turned up;   90
  and if I then became perplexed, do let
the ignorant be judges—those who can
not understand what point I had just crossed.
  "Get up," my master said, "be on your feet:
the way is long, the path is difficult;   95
the sun's already back to middle tierce."[9]
  It was no palace hall, the place in which
we found ourselves, but with its rough-hewn floor
and scanty light, a dungeon built by nature.
  "Before I free myself from this abyss,   100
master," I said when I had stood up straight,
"tell me enough to see I don't mistake:
  Where is the ice? And how is he so placed
head downward? Tell me, too, how has the sun
in so few hours gone from night to morning?"   105
  And he to me: "You still believe you are
north of the center, where I grasped the hair
of the damned worm who pierces through the world.
  And you were there as long as I descended;
but when I turned, that's when you passed the point   110
to which, from every part, all weights are drawn.
  And now you stand beneath the hemisphere
opposing that which cloaks the great dry lands
and underneath whose zenith died the Man
  whose birth and life were sinless in this world.[1]   115
Your feet are placed upon a little sphere
that forms the other face of the Judecca.
  Here it is morning when it's evening there;[2]
and he whose hair has served us as a ladder
is still fixed, even as he was before.   120
  This was the side on which he fell from Heaven;[3]

---

8. Virgil's reversal marks the point at which the two travelers pass from the northern to the southern hemisphere. They began by climbing down Satan's body, but now reverse directions and climb up from the Earth's center (hence when they have passed through the center Dante sees Satan's legs sticking up (line 90). Note that the travelers pass through the glassy ice, a passage that probably echoes 1 Corinthians 13.12: "We see now through a glass in a dark manner; but then face to face."   9. About 7:30 A.M. on Holy Saturday. Dante has added twelve hours to his scheme so that the travelers will emerge from the Earth and arrive at the shore of Mount Purgatory just before sunrise on the next day, Easter Sunday.   1. I.e., under the southern hemisphere, exactly opposite Jerusalem, the center of the northern hemisphere (see Ezekiel 5.5), which is right over the cavity of Hell.   2. The sun is now over the southern hemisphere, and it is night in the northern.   3. The land that was in the southern hemisphere before Satan fell fled to the northern to avoid him, while the earth that he displaced rose up in the southern hemisphere to form Mount Purgatory. This geography is Dante's own poetic scheme.

for fear of him, the land that once loomed here
made of the sea a veil and rose into
   our hemisphere; and that land which appears
upon this side—perhaps to flee from him—   125
left here this hollow space and hurried upward."
   There is a place below, the limit of
that cave, its farthest point from Beelzebub,[4]
a place one cannot see: it is discovered
   by ear—there is a sounding stream[5] that flows   130
along the hollow of a rock eroded
by winding waters, and the slope is easy.
   My guide and I came on that hidden road
to make our way back into the bright world;
and with no care for any rest, we climbed—   135
   he first, I following—until I saw,
through a round opening, some of those things
of beauty Heaven bears. It was from there
   that we emerged, to see—once more—the stars.

From Purgatorio

CANTO I

Proem and Invocation. The skies of the Southern Pole before dawn. The
four stars. Cato of Utica, custodian of the island Mountain of Purgatory.
Cato's queries and Virgil's reply. Instructions by Cato. Virgil bathing
Dante's face and, on the shore, girding him with a rush.

To course across more kindly waters now
my talent's little vessel lifts her sails,
leaving behind herself a sea so cruel;[1]
   and what I sing will be that second kingdom,
in which the human soul is cleansed of sin,   5
becoming worthy of ascent to Heaven.
   But here, since I am yours, o holy Muses,
may this poem rise again from Hell's dead realm;
and may Calliope[2] rise somewhat here,
   accompanying my singing with that music   10
whose power struck the poor Pierides
so forcefully that they despaired of pardon.[3]
   The gentle hue of oriental sapphire
in which the sky's serenity was steeped[4]—
its aspect pure as far as the horizon—   15
   brought back my joy in seeing just as soon
as I had left behind the air of death
that had afflicted both my sight and breast.

---

4. Satan.   **5.** This stream must flow down from Purgatory, perhaps from Lethe.   **1.** The metaphor of
the poem as a ship is traditional; the *kindly waters* refer to Purgatory, while the cruel sea is Hell.   **2.** The
Muse of epic poetry.   **3.** The nine daughters of Pierus—the Pierides—challenged the Muses to a singing
contest and, having lost, were turned into magpies: see Ovid, *Metamorphoses* 5.   **4.** The time is meant
to be just before sunrise on Easter Sunday, 1300.

The lovely planet that is patroness
of love[5] made all the eastern heavens glad,   20
veiling the Pisces[6] in the train she led.
   Then I turned to the right, setting my mind
upon the other pole, and saw four stars
not seen before except by the first people.[7]
   Heaven appeared to revel in their flames: 25
o northern hemisphere, because you were
denied that sight, you are a widower![8]
   After my eyes took leave of those four stars,
turning a little toward the other pole,
from which the Wain[9] had disappeared by now,   30
   I saw a solitary patriarch[1]
near me—his aspect worthy of such reverence
that even son to father owes no more.
   His beard was long and mixed with white, as were
the hairs upon his head; and his hair spread   35
down to his chest in a divided tress.
   The rays of the four holy stars so framed
his face with light that in my sight he seemed
like one who is confronted by the sun.
   "Who are you—who, against the hidden river,[2]   40
were able to escape the eternal prison?"
he said, moving those venerable plumes.
   "Who was your guide? What served you both as lantern
when, from the deep night that will always keep
the hellish valley dark, you were set free?   45
   The laws of the abyss—have they been broken?
Or has a new, a changed decree in Heaven
let you, though damned, approach my rocky slopes?"
   My guide took hold of me decisively;
by way of words and hands and other signs,   50
he made my knees and brow show reverence.
   Then he replied: "I do not come through my
own self. There was a lady sent from Heaven;[3]
her pleas led me to help and guide this man.
   But since your will would have a far more full   55
and accurate account of our condition,
my will cannot withhold what you request.
   This man had yet to see his final evening;
but, through his folly, little time was left
before he did—he was so close to it.   60

5. Venus, the morning star, although in fact on this date Venus would have been visible only after sunrise.   6. The constellation in which Venus would be located if it had risen before the sun on this date.   7. Prior to their expulsion from Eden, Adam and Eve saw four stars above the South Pole, which is located on the summit of Mount Purgatory. These stars symbolize the four cardinal virtues: prudence, temperance, justice, and fortitude.   8. Dante is lamenting the corruption of his present time compared to the perfection of prelapsarian life.   9. The constellation Ursa Major, which never disappears from northern skies but is not visible to an observer in the southern hemisphere. *The other pole*: the North Pole.   1. Cato (95–46 B.C.), a Roman known for his uncompromising morality and love of liberty; rather than submit to what he saw as Julius Caesar's tyranny, he committed suicide in Utica, a city in North Africa. Dante is here influenced by Virgil's treatment of Cato in the underworld, where he is presented not as a suicide but as the lawgiver to the righteous (*Aeneid* 6).   2. Probably Lethe (see *Inferno* 34.130–32).   3. Beatrice.

As I have told you, I was sent to him
for his deliverance; the only road
I could have taken was the road I took.
    I showed him all the people of perdition;
now I intend to show to him those spirits   65
who, in your care, are bent on expiation.
    To tell you how I led him would take long;
it is a power descending from above
that helps me guide him here, to see and hear you.
    Now may it please you to approve his coming;   70
he goes in search of liberty—so precious,
as he who gives his life for it must know.
    You know it—who, in Utica, found death
for freedom was not bitter, when you left
the garb[4] that will be bright on the great day.   75
    Eternal edicts are not broken for us;
this man's alive, and I'm not bound by Minos;[5]
but I am from the circle where the chaste
    eyes of your Marcia[6] are; and she still prays
to you, o holy breast, to keep her as   80
your own: for her love, then, incline to us.
    Allow our journey through your seven realms.
I shall thank her for kindness you bestow—
if you would let your name be named below."
    "While I was there, within the other world,   85
Marcia so pleased my eyes," he then replied,
"each kindness she required, I satisfied.
    Now that she dwells beyond the evil river,
she has no power to move me any longer,
such was the law decreed when I was freed.[7]   90
    But if a lady come from Heaven speeds
and helps you, as you say, there is no need
of flattery; it is enough, indeed,
    to ask me for her sake. Go then; but first
wind a smooth rush[8] around his waist and bathe   95
his face, to wash away all of Hell's stains;
    for it would not be seemly to approach
with eyes still dimmed by any mists, the first
custodian angel, one from Paradise.
    This solitary island, all around   100
its very base, there where the breakers pound,
bears rushes on its soft and muddy ground.
    There is no other plant that lives below:
no plant with leaves or plant that, as it grows,
hardens—and breaks beneath the waves' harsh blows. 105
    That done, do not return by this same pass;
the sun, which rises now, will show you how

---

4. The body, which will be glorified in its resurrection on Judgment Day.   5. See *Inferno* 5.4.
6. Cato's wife, now in Limbo (see *Inferno* 4. 128); according to a story told by the Roman poet Lucan (A.D. 39–65), Cato ceded Marcia to his friend Hortensius, but on Hortensius's death Marcia's entreaty to Cato that he remarry her was granted.   7. Cato was freed during the Harrowing of Hell (see *Inferno* 4.52) and is now unmoved by the sufferings of those left behind. *The evil river*: Acheron.   8. The rush is a symbol of humility.

this hillside can be climbed more easily."
With that he vanished; and without a word,
I rose and drew in closer to my guide,   110
and it was on him that I set my eyes.
And he began: "Son, follow in my steps;
let us go back; this is the point at which
the plain slopes down to reach its lowest bounds."
Daybreak was vanquishing the dark's last hour,   115
which fled before it; in the distance, I
could recognize the trembling of the sea.
We made our way across the lonely plain,
like one returning to a lost pathway,
who, till he finds it, seems to move in vain.   120
When we had reached the point where dew contends
with sun and, under sea winds, in the shade,
wins out because it won't evaporate,
my master gently placed both of his hands—
outspread—upon the grass; therefore, aware   125
of what his gesture and intention were,
I reached and offered him my tear-stained cheeks;
and on my cheeks, he totally revealed
the color that Inferno had concealed.
Then we arrived at the deserted shore,   130
which never yet had seen its waters coursed
by any man who journeyed back again.
There, just as pleased another, he girt me.
O wonder! Where he plucked the humble plant
that he had chosen, there that plant sprang up   135
again, identical, immediately.

CANTO II

*Ante-Purgatory. Dawn on the shore of the island mountain. The sudden
light upon the sea. The helmsman angel and the boat full of arriving
souls. The encounter with Casella, Dante's friend. Casella's singing. Cato's
rebuke. The simile of the doves.*

By now[9] the sun was crossing the horizon
of the meridian whose highest point
covers Jerusalem; and from the Ganges,
night, circling opposite the sun, was moving
together with the Scales that, when the length   5
of dark defeats the day, desert night's hands;
so that, above the shore that I had reached,
the fair Aurora's white and scarlet cheeks
were, as Aurora aged, becoming orange.
We still were by the sea, like those who think   10
about the journey they will undertake,
who go in heart but in the body stay.

9. These opening nine lines designate the time by reference to Jerusalem (where the sun is setting), the
Ganges (where it is midnight, and where the constellation Libra—the scales—is in the sky), and Mount
Purgatory (where the dawn—Aurora—is gradually reddening).

And just as Mars, when it is overcome
by the invading mists of dawn, glows red
above the waters' plain, low in the west,   15
    so there appeared to me—and may I see it
again—a light that crossed the sea: so swift,
there is no flight of bird to equal it.
    When, for a moment, I'd withdrawn my eyes
that I might ask a question of my guide,   20
I saw that light again, larger, more bright.
    Then, to each side of it, I saw a whiteness,
though I did not know what that whiteness was;
below, another whiteness slowly showed.
    My master did not say a word before   25
the whitenesses first seen appeared as wings;
but then, when he had recognized the helmsman,
    he cried: "Bend, bend your knees: behold the angel
of God, and join your hands; from this point on,
this is the kind of minister you'll meet.   30
    See how much scorn he has for human means;
he'd have no other sail than his own wings
and use no oar between such distant shores.
    See how he holds his wings, pointing to Heaven,
piercing the air with his eternal pinions,   35
which do not change as mortal plumage does."
    Then he—that bird divine—as he drew closer
and closer to us, seemed to gain in brightness,
so that my eyes could not endure his nearness,
    and I was forced to lower them; and he   40
came on to shore with boat so light, so quick
that nowhere did the water swallow it.
    The helmsman sent from Heaven, at the stern,
seemed to have blessedness inscribed upon him;
more than a hundred spirits sat within.   45
    "In exitu Isräel de Aegypto,"[1]
with what is written after of that psalm,
all of those spirits sang as with one voice.
    Then over them he made the holy cross
as sign; they flung themselves down on the shore,   50
and he moved off as he had come—swiftly.
    The crowd that he had left along the beach
seemed not to know the place; they looked about
like those whose eyes try out things new to them.
    Upon all sides the sun shot forth the day;   55
and from mid-heaven its incisive arrows
already had chased Capricorn[2] away,
    when those who'd just arrived lifted their heads
toward us and said: "Do show us, if you know,
the way by which we can ascend this slope."   60
    And Virgil answered: "You may be convinced

---

1. When Israel went out of Egypt (Latin). The initial verse of Psalms 113 (114 in Protestant Bibles), which is a song of thanksgiving for the liberation of the Israelites in Exodus.   2. This constellation has now passed beyond the horizon.

that we are quite familiar with this shore;
but we are strangers here, just as you are;
    we came but now, a little while before you,
though by another path, so difficult   65
and dense that this ascent seems sport to us."
    The souls who, noticing my breathing, sensed
that I was still a living being, then,
out of astonishment, turned pale; and just
    as people crowd around a messenger   70
who bears an olive branch, to hear his news,
and no one hesitates to join that crush,
    so here those happy spirits—all of them—
stared hard at my face, just as if they had
forgotten to proceed to their perfection.   75
    I saw one of those spirits moving forward
in order to embrace me—his affection
so great that I was moved to mime his welcome.
    O shades—in all except appearance—empty!
Three times I clasped my hands behind him and   80
as often brought them back against my chest.[3]
    Dismay, I think, was painted on my face;
at this, that shadow smiled as he withdrew;
and I, still seeking him, again advanced.
    Gently, he said that I could now stand back;   85
then I knew who he was, and I beseeched
him to remain awhile and talk with me.
    He answered: "As I loved you when I was
within my mortal flesh, so, freed, I love you:
therefore I stay. But you, why do you journey?"   90
    "My own Casella, to return again
to where I am, I journey thus;[4] but why,"
I said, "were you deprived of so much time?"
    And he: "No injury is done to me
if he who takes up whom—and when—he pleases   95
has kept me from this crossing many times,
    for his own will derives from a just will.[5]
And yet, for three months now, he has accepted,
most tranquilly, all those who would embark.[6]
    Therefore, I, who had turned then to the shore   100
at which the Tiber's waters mix with salt,[7]
was gathered in by his benevolence.
    Straight to that river mouth, he set his wings:
that always is the place of gathering
for those who do not sink to Acheron."[8]   105
    And I: "If there's no new law that denies

---

3. On the thwarted embrace of Aeneas and Anchisës, see *Aeneid* 6.   4. He journeys now so that after death he may return to purgatory. Casella, a Florentine musician, was said to have set some of Dante's lyrics to music. The question that follows assumes that Casella died well before the present moment.   5. The angel who chooses the souls to cross in his boat is directed by God.   6. Pope Boniface proclaimed 1300—the year of the poem's action—a Jubilee or Holy Year, when those making pilgrimage to Rome were granted release from punishments for their sins (see *Inferno* 18, 28). Dante follows popular belief in assuming that this grant applies to the souls awaiting transport to Purgatory as well as to the living.   7. At Ostia, where the Tiber enters the sea.   8. Hell.

you memory or practice of the songs
of love that used to quiet all my longings,
   then may it please you with those songs to solace
my soul somewhat; for—having journeyed here   110
together with my body—it is weary."
   "Love that discourses to me in my mind"[9]
he then began to sing—and sang so sweetly
that I still hear that sweetness sound in me.
   My master, I, and all that company   115
around the singer seemed so satisfied,
as if no other thing might touch our minds.
   We all were motionless and fixed upon
the notes, when all at once the grave old man[1]
cried out: "What have we here, you laggard spirits?   120
   What negligence, what lingering is this?
Quick, to the mountain to cast off the slough
that will not let you see God show Himself!"
   Even as doves, assembled where they feed,
quietly gathering their grain or weeds,   125
forgetful of their customary strut,
   will, if some thing appears that makes them fear,
immediately leave their food behind
because they are assailed by greater care;
   so did I see that new-come company—   130
they left the song behind, turned toward the slope,
like those who go and yet do not know where.
   And we were no less hasty in departure.

CANTO XXI

The Fifth Terrace: the Avaricious and the Prodigal. The appearance of
Statius. Virgil's explanation of Dante's and his presence in Purgatory.
Statius' explanation of the earthquake and the exultation. Statius on
himself and on his love for the Aeneid. Dante's embarrassment, then his
introduction of Virgil to Statius. Statius' reverence for Virgil.

   The natural thirst that never can be quenched
except by water that gives grace—the draught
the simple woman of Samaria sought[2]—
   tormented me; haste spurred me on the path
crowded with souls, behind my guide; and I   5
felt pity, though their pain was justified.
   And here—even as Luke records for us
that Christ, new-risen from his burial cave,
appeared to two along his way[3]—a shade
   appeared; and he advanced behind our backs   10
while we were careful not to trample on
the outstretched crowd.[4] We did not notice him

9. The first line of a lyric that Dante included in his prose philosophical work, the *Convivio*, which he left incomplete, interrupted in 1307 or thereabouts.   1. Cato.   2. The thirst for knowledge can be quenched only by divine revelation. In the previous canto Dante has heard a cry of exultation and felt Mount Purgatory shake; it is the meaning of these events that he wishes to know. See John 4.5–15. 3. Luke 24.13–17.   4. The avaricious are punished by being bound prone to the Earth since they worshiped earthly things in life.

until he had addressed us with: "God give
you, o my brothers, peace!" We turned at once;
then, after offering suitable response,   15

Virgil began: "And may that just tribunal
which has consigned me to eternal exile
place you in peace within the blessed assembly!"

"What!" he exclaimed, as we moved forward quickly.
"If God's not deemed you worthy of ascent,   20
who's guided you so far along His stairs?"

"If you observe the signs the angel traced
upon this man,"5 my teacher said, "you'll see
plainly—he's meant to reign with all the righteous;

but since she who spins night and day had not   25
yet spun the spool that Clotho set upon
the distaff and adjusts for everyone,6

his soul, the sister of your soul and mine,
in its ascent, could not—alone—have climbed
here, for it does not see the way we see.   30

Therefore, I was brought forth from Hell's broad jaws
to guide him in his going; I shall lead
him just as far as where I teach can reach.

But tell me, if you can, why, just before,
the mountain shook and shouted, all of it—   35
for so it seemed—down to its sea-bathed shore."

His question threaded so the needle's eye
of my desire that just the hope alone
of knowing left my thirst more satisfied.

That other shade began: "The sanctity   40
of these slopes does not suffer anything
that's without order or uncustomary.

This place is free from every perturbation:7
what heaven from itself and in itself
receives may serve as cause here—no thing else.   45

Therefore, no rain, no hail, no snow, no dew,
no hoarfrost falls here any higher than
the stairs of entry with their three brief steps;8

neither thick clouds nor thin appear, nor flash
of lightning; Thaumas' daughter,9 who so often   50
shifts places in your world, is absent here.

Dry vapor cannot climb up any higher
than to the top of the three steps of which
I spoke—where Peter's vicar1 plants his feet.

Below that point, there may be small or ample   55
tremors; but here above, I know not why,
no wind concealed in earth has ever caused

---

5. Before Dante entered Purgatory proper, an angel traced seven Ps upon his forehead, one for each deadly sin (*peccatum* in Latin): see *Purgatorio* 9.112–14. The marks disappear one by one as he climbs the mountain and passes through each of the seven terraces appointed for the purgation of a sin.   6. According to classical mythology, the three Fates determine the span of a person's life: Clotho holds the spool, Lachesis spins the thread, and Atropos cuts it at the predestined time.   7. Purgatory is free from any earthly influence, and therefore any change must be caused by motion from above.   8. To reach the gate of Purgatory proper one must climb three steps, which represent the three stages of penance: contrition of heart, confession of mouth, and satisfaction by deeds (see *Purgatorio* 9.94–102).   9. Iris, goddess of the rainbow.   1. The angel who guards the entrance to Purgatory and who marked Dante's forehead.

a tremor; for it only trembles here
when some soul feels it's cleansed, so that it rises
or stirs to climb on high; and that shout follows.   60
    The will alone is proof of purity
and, fully free, surprises soul into
a change of dwelling place—effectively.
    Soul had the will to climb before, but that
will was opposed by longing to do penance   65
(as once, to sin), instilled by divine justice.
    And I, who have lain in this suffering
five hundred years and more, just now have felt
my free will for a better threshold: thus,
    you heard the earthquake and the pious spirits   70
throughout the mountain as they praised the Lord—
and may He send them speedily upward."
    So did he speak to us; and just as joy
is greater when we quench a greater thirst,
the joy he brought cannot be told in words.   75
    And my wise guide: "I now can see the net
impeding you, how one slips through, and why
it quakes here, and what makes you all rejoice.
    And now may it please you to tell me who
you were, and in your words may I find why   80
you've lain here for so many centuries."[2]
    "In that age when the worthy Titus, with
help from the Highest King, avenged the wounds
from which the blood that Judas sold had flowed,[3]
    I had sufficient fame beyond," that spirit   85
replied; "I bore the name that lasts the longest
and honors most—but faith was not yet mine.[4]
    So gentle was the spirit of my verse
that Rome drew me, son of Toulouse,[5] to her,
and there my brow deserved a crown of myrtle.   90
    On earth my name is still remembered—Statius:
I sang of Thebes and then of great Achilles;
I fell along the way of that last labor.
    The sparks that warmed me, the seeds of my ardor,
were from the holy fire—the same that gave   95
more than a thousand poets light and flame.
    I speak of the *Aeneid*; when I wrote
verse, it was mother to me, it was nurse;
my work, without it, would not weigh an ounce.
    And to have lived on earth when Virgil lived—   100
for that I would extend by one more year
the time I owe before my exile's end."
    These words made Virgil turn to me, and as
he turned, his face, through silence, said: "Be still"

---

2. The spirit reveals himself to be Statius (d. A.D. 96), a Roman poet who composed the *Thebaid* and the unfinished *Achilleid*.   3. The destruction of Jerusalem in A.D. 70 by the Roman Titus was understood by Christians to be a divine punishment for the crucifixion of Christ.   4. He was a poet but not yet a Christian.   5. A city in southern France; Statius actually came from Naples, but Dante is following a medieval tradition.

(and yet the power of will cannot do all,   105
    for tears and smiles are both so faithful to
the feelings that have prompted them that true
feeling escapes the will that would subdue).
    But I smiled like a man whose eyes would signal;
at this, the shade was silent, and he stared   110
where sentiment is clearest—at my eyes—
    and said: "So may your trying labor end
successfully, do tell me why—just now—
your face showed me the flashing of a smile."
    Now I am held by one side and the other: 115
one keeps me still, the other conjures me
to speak; but when, therefore, I sigh, my master
    knows why and tells me: "Do not be afraid
to speak, but speak and answer what he has
asked you to tell him with such earnestness."   120
    At this, I answered: "Ancient spirit, you
perhaps are wondering at the smile I smiled:
but I would have you feel still more surprise.
    He who is guide, who leads my eyes on high,
is that same Virgil from whom you derived   125
the power to sing of men and of the gods.
    Do not suppose my smile had any source
beyond the speech you spoke; be sure—it was
those words you said of him that were the cause."
    Now he had bent to kiss my teacher's feet,   130
but Virgil told him: "Brother, there's no need—
you are a shade, a shade is what you see."
    And, rising, he: "Now you can understand
how much love burns in me for you, when I
forget our insubstantiality,   135
    treating the shades as one treats solid things."

FROM CANTO XXII

*From the Fifth to the Sixth Terrace: the Gluttonous. The angel of justice.
First part of the Fourth Beatitude. Ascent to the Sixth Terrace. Statius:
his true sin, prodigality; his conversion. Virgil on the other souls in
Limbo.*

The angel now was left behind us, he
who had directed us to the sixth terrace,
having erased one *P* that scarred my face;[6]
    he had declared that those who longed for justice
are blessed, and his voice concluded that   5
message with *"sitiunt,"* without the rest.[7]
    And while I climbed behind the two swift spirits,
not laboring at all, for I was lighter

---

6. The erased *P* was for avarice, the sin cleansed on the fifth terrace.   7. The angel quotes the beginning
of the Fourth Beatitude from the Sermon on the Mount, "Blessed are they which do hunger and thirst after
righteousness: for they shall be filled" (Matthew 5.6). He mentions only "thirst" (*sitiunt* in Latin), omitting
hunger, which will appear at the end of the journey through the sixth terrace, where gluttony is purged.

than I had been along the other stairs,[8]

Virgil began: "Love that is kindled by   10
virtue, will, in another, find reply,
as long as that love's flame appears without;[9]

so, from the time when Juvenal,[1] descending
among us, in Hell's Limbo, had made plain
the fondness that you felt for me, my own   15

benevolence toward you has been much richer
than any ever given to a person
one has not seen; thus, now these stairs seem short.

But tell me (and, as friend, forgive me if
excessive candor lets my reins relax   20
and, as a friend, exchange your words with me):

how was it that you found within your breast
a place for avarice, when you possessed
the wisdom you had nurtured with such care?"

These words at first brought something of a smile   25
to Statius; then he answered: "Every word
you speak, to me is a dear sign of love.

Indeed, because true causes are concealed,
we often face deceptive reasoning
and things provoke perplexity in us.   30

Your question makes me sure that you're convinced—
perhaps because my circle was the fifth—
that, in the life I once lived, avarice

had been my sin. Know then that I was far
from avarice—it was my lack of measure[2]   35
thousands of months have punished. And if I

had not corrected my assessment by
my understanding what your verses meant
when you, as if enraged by human nature,

exclaimed: 'Why cannot you, o holy hunger   40
for gold, restrain the appetite of mortals?'[3]—
I'd now, while rolling weights, know sorry jousts.[4]

Then I became aware that hands might open
too wide, like wings, in spending; and of this,
as of my other sins, I did repent.   45

How many are to rise again with heads
cropped close,[5] whom ignorance prevents from reaching
repentance in—and at the end of—life!

And know that when a sin is countered by
another fault—directly opposite   50
to it—then, here, both sins see their green wither.[6]

Thus, I join those who pay for avarice
in my purgation, though what brought me here

8. Dante grows lighter as he is gradually relieved of the sins, symbolized by the Ps on his forehead, that weigh him down. 9. Virtuous love, such as Statius displayed at the end of canto 21, will elicit a similar response. 1. A Roman poet, contemporary with Statius but who outlived him (dying about A.D. 140), located with Virgil in Limbo, as described in *Inferno* 4. 2. Prodigality, a vice that is opposite to avarice but its counterpart as an excess in the use of money; in *Inferno* 7 the avaricious and the prodigal are punished together. 3. Statius is quoting *Aeneid* 3. 4. Be punished in the fourth circle of Hell, described in *Inferno* 7. 5. The close-cropped heads of the prodigal are described in *Inferno* 7.57. 6. Statius uses a vegetative metaphor: sin is green when vigorous, but it withers in Purgatory.

was prodigality—its opposite."

"Now, when you sang the savage wars of those   55
twin sorrows of Jocasta,"[7] said the singer
of the bucolic poems,[8] "it does not seem—
from those notes struck by you and Clio[9] there—
that you had yet turned faithful to the faith
without which righteous works do not suffice.   60

If that is so, then what sun or what candles
drew you from darkness so that, in their wake,
you set your sails behind the fisherman?"[1]

And he to him: "You were the first to send me
to drink within Parnassus'[2] caves and you,   65
the first who, after God, enlightened me.

You did as he who goes by night and carries
the lamp behind him—he is of no help
to his own self but teaches those who follow—

when you declared: 'The ages are renewed;   70
justice and man's first time on earth return;
from Heaven a new progeny descends.'[3]

Through you I was a poet and, through you,
a Christian; but that you may see more plainly,
I'll set my hand to color what I sketch.   75

Disseminated by the messengers
of the eternal kingdom,[4] the true faith
by then had penetrated all the world,

and the new preachers preached in such accord
with what you'd said (and I have just repeated),   80
that I was drawn into frequenting them.

Then they appeared to me to be so saintly
that, when Domitian[5] persecuted them,
my own laments accompanied their grief;

and while I could—as long as I had life—   85
I helped them, and their honest practices
made me disdainful of all other sects.

Before—within my poem—I'd led the Greeks
unto the streams of Thebes,[6] I was baptized;
but out of fear, I was a secret Christian   90

and, for a long time, showed myself as pagan;
for this halfheartedness, for more than four
centuries, I circled the fourth circle.[7]

And now may you, who lifted up the lid

---

7. Statius's *Thebaid* deals with the history of Thebes: Jocasta's husband, Laius, was unwittingly killed by their son, Oedipus, who then—again in ignorance—married Laius's widow, Oedipus's own mother. Their sons, Polynices and Eteocles, imprisoned their father in a dungeon and then fought over the throne of Thebes in a war in which they killed each other. It is this fratricidal war, in which Jocasta lost both her sons at once, to which Virgil refers.   **8.** Virgil is here identified not as the epic poet of the *Aeneid* but as the pastoral or bucolic poet of the *Eclogues* and the *Georgics*.   **9.** The Muse of history, whom Statius invokes in the *Thebaid*.   **1.** I.e., followed Peter, a fisherman who became a fisher of men (see Mark 1.17).   **2.** Dante follows a tradition that takes Parnassus, a mountain in Greece, as the home of the Muses.   **3.** A slightly altered citation from Virgil's *Fourth Eclogue*. A pastoral poem written about 40 B.C., it celebrated the birth of the son of an important Roman politician but was taken by medieval Christians as a prophecy of the birth of Christ.   **4.** The apostles.   **5.** Roman emperor, A.D. 81–91; thought by early Christian historians to have persecuted Christians, but there is little evidence for this.   **6.** The *Thebaid* describes how six Greek rulers joined with Polynices to invade Thebes and topple Eteocles from the throne.   **7.** Where sloth is purged.

that hid from me the good of which I speak,   95
while time is left us as we climb, tell me
    where is our ancient Terence, and Caecilius
and Plautus, where is Varius,[8] if you know;
tell me if they are damned, and in what quarter."
    "All these and Persius, I, and many others,"   100
my guide replied, "are with that Greek to whom
the Muses gave their gifts in greatest measure.
    Our place is the blind prison, its first circle;
and there we often talk about the mountain
where those who were our nurses always dwell.   105
    Euripides is with us, Antiphon,
Simonides, and Agathon,[9] as well
as many other Greeks who once wore laurel
    upon their brow; and there—of your own people—
one sees Antigone, Deiphyle,   110
Ismene, sad still, Argia as she was.
    There one can see the woman who showed Langia,
and there, Tiresias' daughter; there is Thetis;
and, with her sister, there, Deidamia."[1]
    Both poets now were silent, once again   115
intent on their surroundings—they were free
of stairs and walls; with day's first four handmaidens[2]
    already left behind, and with the fifth
guiding the chariot-pole and lifting it,
so that its horn of flame rose always higher,   120
    my master said: "I think it's time that we
turn our right shoulders toward the terrace edge,
circling the mountain in the way we're used to."[3]
    In this way habit served us as a banner;
and when we chose that path, our fear was less   125
because that worthy soul gave his assent.
    Those two were in the lead; I walked alone,
behind them, listening to their colloquy,
which taught me much concerning poetry.[4]

FROM CANTO XXIV

Summary   Dante is still on the sixth terrace, where gluttony is purged. He meets Bonagiunta Orbicciani, a poet of the second half of the thirteenth century who was evidently acquainted with Dante's early lyrics. (In a literary treatise written prior to *The Divine Comedy,* Dante criticized Bonagiunta's poetic language for being too specialized and therefore not contributing to the creation of an Italian literary language that would be accessible to all educated readers.) This selection begins with Bonagiunta speaking.

*   *   *

8. These men and Persius (line 100) are Roman poets now in Limbo with Homer (lines 101–2). **9.** Greek dramatists.   **1.** Characters from Statius's *Thebaid* and *Achilleid,* which Dante considered historical epics.   **2.** The hours, the fifth of which is guiding the chariot of the sun: it is between 10 and 11 A.M.   **3.** Mount Purgatory is climbed by turning to the right; the travelers descended into Hell by turning to the left.   **4.** The canto continues with a new episode, not relevant to the literary issues that have so far occupied it.

"But tell me if the man whom I see here
is he who brought the new rhymes forth, beginning: 50
'*Ladies who have intelligence of love*.' "[5]
I answered: "I am one who, when Love breathes
in me, takes note; what he, within, dictates,
I, in that way, without, would speak and shape."
"O brother, now I see," he said, "the knot   55
that kept the Notary, Guittone, and me
short of the sweet new manner[6] that I hear.
I clearly see how your pens follow closely
behind him who dictates,[7] and certainly
that did not happen with our pens; and he   60
who sets himself to ferreting profoundly
can find no other difference between
the two styles." He fell still, contentedly.

FROM CANTO XXVI

Summary   Dante is now on the seventh and final terrace, where lust is purged with fire. He speaks with one of the souls, who describes the rationale of the purgation and then responds to Dante's curiosity about the identities of these souls.

"But with regard to me, I'll satisfy
your wish to know: I'm Guido Guinizzelli,[8]
purged here because I grieved before my end."
As, after the sad raging of Lycurgus,
two sons, finding their mother, had embraced her,[9]   95
so I desired to do—but dared not to—
when I heard him declare his name: the father
of me and of the others—those, my betters—
who ever used sweet, gracious rhymes of love.
And without hearing, speaking, pensive I,   100
walked on, still gazing at him, a long time,
prevented by the fire from drawing closer.
When I had fed my sight on him, I offered
myself—with such a pledge that others must
believe—completely ready for his service.[1]   105
And he to me: "Because of what I hear,
you leave a trace within me—one so clear,
Lethe[2] itself can't blur or cancel it.
But if your words have now sworn truthfully,
do tell me why it is that you have shown   110
in speech and gaze that I am dear to you."
And I to him: "It's your sweet lines that, for
as long as modern usage lasts, will still
make dear their very inks." "Brother," he said,

---

5. The first line of the first lyric in Dante's *New Life*, which tells the story in poetry and prose of his transformation by his love for Beatrice.   **6.** The *dolce still novo* that Dante saw as characterizing his own poetry and that was first defined for him by Guido Guinizzelli, whom he will meet in canto 26. The Notary (Giacomo da Lentini) and Guittone d'Arezzo, like Bonagiunta, were Italian poets of the generation before Dante's.   **7.** Love.   **8.** Bolognese poet (d. ca. 1276), considered the greatest Italian poet prior to Dante. A poem by him is included in *Medieval Lyrics: A Selection* (p. 1215).   **9.** In an episode in Statius's *Thebaid*, a woman condemned to death by the warrior Lycurgus is saved at the last moment by the arrival of her twin sons.   **1.** Dante here swears an oath to Guinizzelli to which the reader is not given access.   **2.** The river of forgetfulness that the fully purged souls will pass through in order to renounce their earthly lives.

"he there, whom I point out to you"[3]—he showed   115
us one who walked ahead—"he was a better
artisan of the mother tongue, surpassing
     all those who wrote their poems of love or prose
romances—let the stupid ones contend,
who think that from Limoges there came the best.[4]   120
     They credit rumor rather than the truth,
allowing their opinion to be set
before they hear what art or reason says.
     So, many of our fathers once persisted,
voice after voice, in giving to Guittone[5]   125
the prize—but then, with most, the truth prevailed.
     Now if you are so amply privileged
that you will be admitted to the cloister
where Christ is abbot of the college, then
     pray say, for me, to Him, a Paternoster[6]—   130
that is, as much of it as those in this
place need, since we have lost the power to sin."
     Then, to make place, perhaps, for those behind him,
he disappeared into the fire, just as
a fish, through water, plunges toward the bottom.   135
     Saying that my desire was making ready
a place of welcome for his name, I moved
ahead a little, toward the one who had
     been pointed out to me. And he spoke freely:[7]
"So does your courteous request please me—   140
I neither could nor would conceal myself
     from you. I am Arnaut, who, going, weep
and sing; with grief, I see my former folly;
with joy, I see the hoped-for day draw near.
     Now, by the Power that conducts you to   145
the summit of the stairway, I pray you:
remember, at time opportune, my pain!"
     Then, in the fire that refines, he hid.

FROM CANTO XXVII

Summary   Dante, Virgil, and Statius pass through the refining fire. Dante then
sleeps.

     And now, with the reflected lights that glow
before the dawn[8] and, rising, are most welcome   110
to pilgrims as, returning, they near home,
     the shadows fled upon all sides; my sleep
fled with them; and at this, I woke and saw
that the great teachers had already risen.
     "Today your hungerings will find their peace   115
through that sweet fruit the care of mortals seeks

3. Guinizzelli is indicating Arnaut Daniel (d. ca. 1210), Provençal poet. A poem by him is included in *Medieval Lyrics: A Selection* (pp. 1209–10).   4. The reference is to Giraut de Borneil (d. ca. 1220), another Provençal poet.   5. See *Purgatorio* 24, 56.   6. The Lord's Prayer.   7. In the original, Arnaut speaks not in Italian but in Provençal.   8. The morning stars.

among so many branches."[9] This, the speech,
   the solemn words, that Virgil spoke to me;
and there were never tidings to compare,
in offering delight to me, with these.   120
   My will on will to climb above was such
that at each step I took I felt the force
within my wings was growing for the flight.
   When all the staircase lay beneath us and
we'd reached the highest step, then Virgil set   125
his eyes insistently on me and said:
   "My son, you've seen the temporary fire
and the eternal fire;[1] you have reached
the place past which my powers cannot see.
   I've brought you here through intellect and art;   130
from now on, let your pleasure be your guide;
you're past the steep and past the narrow paths.
   Look at the sun that shines upon your brow;
look at the grasses, flowers, and the shrubs
born here, spontaneously, of the earth.   135
   Among them, you can rest or walk until
the coming of the glad and lovely eyes—
those eyes that, weeping, sent me to your side.[2]
   Await no further word or sign from me:
your will is free, erect, and whole—to act   140
against that will would be to err: therefore
I crown and miter you over yourself."

FROM CANTO XXX

Summary   Dante has arrived at the earthly paradise on the top of Mount Purgatory and finally sees Beatrice, drawn in a chariot as the centerpiece of an elaborate pageant. These lines describe his first exchange with her.

*   *   *

   I have at times seen all the eastern sky
becoming rose as day began and seen,
adorned in lovely blue, the rest of heaven;
   and seen the sun's face rise so veiled that it   25
was tempered by the mist and could permit
the eye to look at length upon it; so,
   within a cloud of flowers that were cast
by the angelic hands[3] and then rose up
and then fell back, outside and in the chariot,   30
   a woman showed herself to me; above
a white veil, she was crowned with olive boughs;
her cape was green; her dress beneath, flame-red.[4]
   Within her presence, I had once been used
to feeling—trembling—wonder, dissolution;   35
but that was long ago.[5] Still, though my soul,

9. On this day Dante will enter the Earthly Paradise and find Beatrice, who will conduct him through Paradise.   **1.** Purgatory and Hell.   **2.** See *Inferno* 2.55–74.   **3.** The chariot is accompanied by messengers of eternal life.   **4.** The colors of her clothing are symbolic: white signifies hope; green, faith; and red, charity.   **5.** Beatrice died in 1290, so it has been ten years since Dante saw her.

now she was veiled, could not see her directly,
by way of hidden force that she could move,
I felt the mighty power of old love.

As soon as that deep force had struck my vision   40
(the power that, when I had not yet left
my boyhood,[6] had already transfixed me),

I turned around and to my left—just as
a little child, afraid or in distress,
will hurry to his mother—anxiously,   45

to say to Virgil: "I am left with less
than one drop of my blood that does not tremble:
I recognize the signs of the old flame."[7]

But Virgil had deprived us of himself,
Virgil, the gentlest father, Virgil, he   50
to whom I gave my self for my salvation;[8]

and even all our ancient mother[9] lost
was not enough to keep my cheeks, though washed
with dew, from darkening again with tears.

"Dante, though Virgil's leaving you, do not   55
yet weep, do not weep yet; you'll need your tears
for what another sword must yet inflict."[1]

Just like an admiral who goes to stern
and prow to see the officers who guide
the other ships, encouraging their tasks;   60

so, on the left side of the chariot
(I'd turned around when I had heard my name—
which, of necessity, I transcribe here),

I saw the lady who had first appeared
to me beneath the veils of the angelic   65
flowers look at me across the stream.

Although the veil she wore—down from her head,
which was encircled by Minerva's leaves—
did not allow her to be seen distinctly,

her stance still regal and disdainful, she   70
continued, just as one who speaks but keeps
until the end the fiercest parts of speech:

"Look here! For I am Beatrice, I am!
How were you able to ascend the mountain?
Did you not know that man is happy here?"   75

My lowered eyes caught sight of the clear stream,
but when I saw myself reflected there,
such shame weighed on my brow, my eyes drew back

and toward the grass; just as a mother seems
harsh to her child, so did she seem to me—   80
how bitter is the savor of stern pity!

Her words were done.

---

6. Dante was nine when he fell in love with Beatrice.   7. A quotation from Virgil's *Aeneid* 4; it is Dido's response upon first seeing Aeneas.   8. This tercet echoes Virgil's *Georgics* 4.525–27, in which Orpheus looks back and laments the loss of Eurydice.   9. Eve, who caused the loss of the Eden in which Dante is now located.   1. The sharp words Beatrice will now speak.

From Paradiso

FROM CANTO XXXIII

Summary Dante has been led by Beatrice and other guides to the highest point of the universe, the Empyrean. The final canto of the poem begins with a prayer by Bernard of Clairvaux (1091–1153), abbot of the monastery of Clairvaux in France and one of the great spiritual leaders and mystical writers of the Middle Ages. Bernard is present here both as a mystic and because of the role his writings played in developing the cult of the Virgin Mary.

> "Virgin mother, daughter of your Son,
> more humble and sublime than any creature,
> fixed goal decreed from all eternity,
>   you are the one who gave to human nature
> so much nobility that its Creator   5
> did not disdain His being made its creature.
>   That love whose warmth allowed this flower[2] to bloom
> within the everlasting peace—was love
> rekindled in your womb; for us above,
>   you are the noonday torch of charity,   10
> and there below, on earth, among the mortals,
> you are a living spring of hope. Lady,
>   you are so high, you can so intercede,
> that he who would have grace but does not seek
> your aid, may long to fly but has no wings.   15
>   Your loving-kindness does not only answer
> the one who asks, but it is often ready
> to answer freely long before the asking.
>   In you compassion is, in you is pity,
> in you is generosity, in you   20
> is every goodness found in any creature.
>   This man—who from the deepest hollow in
> the universe, up to this height, has seen
> the lives of spirits, one by one—now pleads
>   with you, through grace, to grant him so much virtue   25
> that he may lift his vision higher still—
> may lift it toward the ultimate salvation.
>   And I, who never burned for my own vision
> more than I burn for his, do offer you
> all of my prayers—and pray that they may not   30
>   fall short—that, with your prayers, you may disperse
> all of the clouds of his mortality
> so that the Highest Joy be his to see.
>   This, too, o Queen, who can do what you would,
> I ask of you: that after such a vision,   35
> his sentiments preserve their perseverance.
>   May your protection curb his mortal passions.
> See Beatrice—how many saints with her!
> They join my prayers! They clasp their hands to you!"
>   The eyes that are revered and loved by God,   40

---

2. In *Paradiso* 30 Dante saw the blessed souls arranged in a vast rose, to which Bernard now refers.

now fixed upon the supplicant, showed us
how welcome such devotions are to her;
 then her eyes turned to the Eternal Light—
there, do not think that any creature's eye
can find its way as clearly as her sight.   45

And I, who now was nearing Him who is
the end of all desires, as I ought,
lifted my longing to its ardent limit.

 Bernard was signaling—he smiled—to me
to turn my eyes on high; but I, already   50
was doing what he wanted me to do,

 because my sight, becoming pure, was able
to penetrate the ray of Light more deeply—
that Light, sublime, which in Itself is true.

 From that point on, what I could see was greater 55
than speech can show: at such a sight, it fails—
and memory fails when faced with such excess.

 As one who sees within a dream, and, later,
the passion that had been imprinted stays,
but nothing of the rest returns to mind,   60

 such am I, for my vision almost fades
completely, yet it still distills within
my heart the sweetness that was born of it.

 So is the snow, beneath the sun, unsealed;[3]
and so, on the light leaves, beneath the wind,   65
the oracles the Sibyl wrote were lost.[4]

 O Highest Light , You, raised so far above
the minds of mortals, to my memory
give back something of Your epiphany,

 and make my tongue so powerful that I   70
may leave to people of the future one
gleam of the glory that is Yours, for by

 returning somewhat to my memory
and echoing awhile within these lines,
Your victory will be more understood.   75

 The living ray that I endured was so
acute that I believe I should have gone
astray had my eyes turned away from it.

 I can recall that I, because of this,
was bolder in sustaining it until   80
my vision reached the Infinite Goodness.

 O grace abounding, through which I presumed
to set my eyes on the Eternal Light
so long that I spent all my sight on it!

 In its profundity I saw—ingathered   85
and bound by love into one single volume—
what, in the universe, seems separate, scattered:

 substances, accidents, and dispositions[5]
as if conjoined—in such a way that what

3. Melted. 4. In *Aeneid* 3 Virgil describes how the Sibyl of Cumae writes down the future on leaves that the wind then scatters. 5. In the philosophical tradition followed by Dante, a *substance* is that which subsists in and of itself, an *accident* exists only as a quality or an attribute of a substance, and their *disposition* is the way substances and accidents are bound together.

I tell is only rudimentary.   90
    I think I saw the universal shape
which that knot takes; for, speaking this, I feel
a joy that is more ample. That one moment
    brings more forgetfulness to me than twenty-
five centuries have brought to the endeavor   95
that startled Neptune with the *Argo*'s shadow![6]
    So was my mind—completely rapt, intent,
steadfast, and motionless—gazing; and it
grew ever more enkindled as it watched.
    Whoever sees that Light is soon made such   100
that it would be impossible for him
to set that Light aside for other sight;
    because the good, the object of the will,
is fully gathered in that Light; outside
that Light, what there is perfect is defective.   105
    what little I recall is to be told,
from this point on, in words more weak than those
of one whose infant tongue still bathes at the breast.
    And not because more than one simple semblance
was in the Living Light at which I gazed—   110
for It is always what It was before—
    but through my sight, which as I gazed grew stronger,
that sole appearance, even as I altered,
seemed to be changing. In the deep and bright
    essence of that exalted Light, three circles[7]   115
appeared to me; they had three different colors,
but all of them were of the same dimension;
    one circle seemed reflected by the second,
as rainbow is by rainbow, and the third
seemed fire breathed equally by those two circles.   120
    How incomplete is speech, how weak, when set
against my thought! And this, to what I saw
is such—to call it little is too much.
    Eternal Light, You only dwell within
Yourself, and only You know You; Self-knowing,   125
Self-known, You love and smile upon Yourself!
    That circle—which, begotten so, appeared
in You as light reflected—when my eyes
had watched it with attention for some time,
    within itself and colored like itself,   130
to me seemed painted with our effigy,[8]
so that my sight was set on it completely.
    As the geometer intently seeks
to square the circle, but he cannot reach,
through thought on thought, the principle he needs,[9]   135
    so I searched that strange sight: I wished to see
the way in which our human effigy

6. The voyage of Jason and the Argonauts after the golden fleece was thought to have occurred about 1300
B.C.; see *Inferno* 18.86–87.   7. Signifying the Trinity.   8. Dante seems to see a human image in the
center of the Godhead.   9. The problem of constructing a square equal in area to a circle is a proverbially
insoluble mathematical problem.

suited the circle and found place in it—
and my own wings were far too weak for that.
But then my mind was struck by light that flashed   140
and, with this light, received what it had asked.
   Here force failed my high fantasy;[1] but my
desire and will were moved already—like
a wheel revolving uniformly—by
the Love that moves the sun and the other stars.[2]   145

---

1. By *fantasy* Dante means the capacity of the mind to form images; it is *high* because it is capable of representing in visible form invisible truths.   2. As in the *Inferno* and the *Purgatorio*, the last word of the *Paradiso* is *stars*, returning us to the perspective of the human gazing up at that which is beyond the human.

GIOVANNI BOCCACCIO
1313–1375

The *Decameron* by Giovanni Boccaccio has a reputation as a ribald classic, and certainly many of its stories—including some selected here—deal with sexual misadventures. But it also gathers into its hundred stories the diversity and energy that made fourteenth-century Italy one of the great cultural resources of medieval Europe. With his predecessor Dante and his slightly older contemporary Petrarch, Boccaccio established Italy and specifically Florence as a center of literary production that influenced European writing for centuries.

Boccaccio was born in Tuscany, probably in Florence, to a merchant and banker who did not marry the child's mother until some five years later. At fourteen he was taken to Naples, where his father made him spend six years studying arithmetic and then, when it became clear that Boccaccio would not make a successful merchant, another six years preparing for a career as a lawyer. But this enterprise also failed, for Boccaccio was drawn to the sophisticated circle of writers and scholars that the ruler of southern Italy, Robert of Anjou, has assembled into a court that was the most advanced cultural center of its time. Although known to modern readers almost exclusively through the *Decameron*, Boccaccio wrote primarily either courtly tales of love in Italian verse or learned treatises on subjects such as history, classical mythology and geography in Latin prose. Along with Petrarch, Boccaccio was one of the many medieval writers who worked to revive the literary heritage of the classical world. In a poem called the *Teseida* he produced the first vernacular version of a classical epic, initiating a tradition that was to culminate in Milton's *Paradise Lost*, and he sponsored the first translation of Homer from Greek (in this case into Latin). The humanism that was to come to fruition in the Renaissance finds one of its most important medieval inspirations in the work of Boccaccio.

The *Decameron* represents another aspect of Boccaccio's literary personality. Locating the collection, written between 1350 and 1353, in a specific historical context, Boccaccio first describes the devastating effects of the bubonic plague of 1348–50 on Florence. Indeed, while the plague killed at least one-third of the European population (as well as millions elsewhere in the world), in Florence the death rate was as high as 70 percent. For Boccaccio the effect of this unprecedented disaster was the destruction of both the social fabric of the city and the moral restraints on individual behavior. In response, he posits an alternative society by describing how seven young ladies of good family are joined by three young men and retreat from the ravaged city to a beautiful country estate, where they restore themselves with well-regulated pleasures. Among their recreations is a tale-telling game: for ten days each member of the group tells a story, creating the hundred stories that comprise the *Decameron*. But if Boccaccio presents these tales as an alternative to the social and moral collapse of plague-stricken Florence, he also insists that their goal is above all to give pleasure. In this he sets his work in opposition to that of one of his own literary heroes, Dante. Much of Boccaccio's work is heavily influenced by Dante, and near the end of his life he both wrote a treatise celebrating Dante and delivered a set of lectures commenting in detail on the first twenty-eight cantos of the *Inferno*. Yet the *Decameron* is an implicitly anti-Dantean work. Its division into one hundred tales echoes Dante's division of his *Comedy* into one hundred cantos, and Boccaccio gives his work an alternative title—"Prince Galeotto"—that refers to a crucial moment in the *Inferno*. In canto 5 of the *Inferno* Francesca explains to Dante that she and her brother-in-law Paolo fell in love while reading the story of Lancelot and Guinevere. She blames the book for their fall, calling it a Galeotto: she is referring to the knight in the Arthurian court who served as a go-between for the lovers. Dante is implying here that reading, and especially reading for pleasure, can be morally dangerous. Yet Boccaccio insists by his subtitle, and throughout the *Decameron* as a whole, that literature can provide a pleasure that is not merely legitimate but restorative.

Many different kinds of pleasure are both described in and made available by the *Decameron*. The most obvious pleasure the characters enjoy is sexual, and the sixth story of the ninth day is a characteristic example of Boccaccio's frank celebration of the joys of sex. But the story—a version of a tale that also survives as a French fabliau, which may have been the form in which Boccaccio first heard it—is also typical in its cheerful insistence that no harm has been done, and even the duped father and husband is treated with genial warmth. The story is typical as well in its celebration of values associated with the vigorous merchant class from which Boccaccio derived and that was largely dominant in Italy. The story describes a world of bewildering fluctuation. One of the literary pleasures it provides its readers is the plotting out of movements from bed to bed that occur during the night. To do so is to see that the baby's cradle is both the narrative device that makes the amorous events of the night possible and a metaphor for the circulation of sexual favors, much as commodities circulate throughout the mercantile world. Indeed, to succeed in the world of this story, as in commerce, requires a quick wit, a flexible sense of propriety, and an alertness to one's own self-interest without a vengeful desire to harm others that might make permanent enemies. On the whole the *Decameron* celebrates just this pragmatic and relativistic value system, refusing to endow any single set of values with ultimate authority. If one story teaches one lesson, then the next will teach a contradictory one, and readers are allowed to decide for themselves where true value is to be found.

In this relativism Boccaccio's *Decameron* is very different from Dante's *Divine Comedy*. Dante is an absolutist: he insists throughout his great work that there *is* a single truth, and the multiplicitous details of the poem are controlled by the author-itative coherence of Christian doctrine. But without being in any sense unmindful of the claims of religion—Boccaccio was certainly a fully devout Christian—the *Decameron* describes a much more multifarious, much less easily judged world than does *The Divine Comedy*. The first story tells of a thoroughgoing rogue, Ser Cepperello, who provides an outrageously false deathbed confession to a credulous and self-seeking friar. But while Cepperello seems to damn himself by his impenitent mockery of the salvation offered by the Church, we are aware that he is acting out of charitable motives in trying to protect his Florentine friends. So it becomes difficult to know if the townspeople are entirely wrong in thinking he is a saint. And we are also aware that the good deed performed is itself an act of tale-telling, and a tale that is both an outrageous lie and a pleasure to read. On the other side, the story of Nastagio and the hunt of love (the eighth story of the fifth day) presents a scene straight out of the *Inferno*: a scornful lady is eternally hunted down and eviscerated by her suicidal lover. Are we to think that here divine justice is being done? The context in which the scene is placed might give us pause. Used by Nastagio to persuade his lady to accept him as a lover, this scene reveals both the emotional absolutism of the courtly lover—as does the ninth story of the fourth day, in which the noble lady commits suicide in order to remain magnificently true to her lover—but also its cruelty and violence. Finally, these complexities are brought together in the story of Griselda (the tenth story of the tenth day), which proved to be one of the most popular stories of the later Middle Ages (both Petrarch and Chaucer produced versions). Is Griselda a saint of patience who is finally rewarded for her virtue? Or is she an unreasonably passive creature who solicits her own victimization? Is Walter a monster, a tyrant both politically and domestically, and the story a psychological study of despotism? Or is he an agent of God who makes possible the revelation of Griselda's superhuman virtue, or perhaps even God himself? In this fascinating puzzle of a story, Boccaccio poses questions without providing any obvious answer, showing us that perhaps the deepest pleasure that literature can offer is the pleasure of interpretation.

Vittore Branca, *Boccaccio: The Man and His Works* (1975), is the standard biography with useful literary commentary; for guides to the *Decameron*, see Giuseppe Mazzotta, *The World at Play in Boccaccio's Decameron* (1986), and David Wallace, *Giovanni Boccaccio: Decameron* (1991).

PRONOUNCING GLOSSARY

The following list uses common English syllables to provide rough equivalents of selected words whose pronunciation may be unfamiliar to the general reader.

Cepperello Dietaiuti: *chep-er-el-lo dee-tie-yu-tee*

Giannùcole: *gee-an-ooh'-co-lay*

Gualtieri: *gwal-tee'-e-ree*

Guido degli Anastagi: *gwee'-do day'-lee an-as-ta'-jee*

Guillaume de Cabestanh: *ghee-ohm' de cab-es-stan'*

Guillaume de Rousillon: *ghee-ohm' de roo-see-yonh*

Musciatto: *mus-chee-at'-to*

Nastagio degli Onesti: *nas-taj'-io day'-lee on-es'-tee*

Paolo Traversari: *pow'-lo tra-ver-sa'-ree*

Pinuccio: *pin-ooch'-ee-o*

The Decameron[1]

[THE FIRST STORY OF THE FIRST DAY]

Ser Cepperello deceives a holy friar with a false confession, then he dies; and although in life he was a most wicked man, in death he is reputed to be a Saint, and is called Saint Ciappelletto.

It is proper, dearest ladies,[2] that everything made by man should begin with the sacred and admirable name of Him that was maker of all things. And therefore, since I[3] am the first and must make a beginning to our storytelling, I propose to begin by telling you of one of His marvellous works,

---

1. Translated by G. H. McWilliam.   2. The tale is addressed to the seven ladies of the group that has escaped the plague in Florence.   3. The speaker is Panfilo, one of the three young men in the group of ten.

so that, when we have heard it out, our hopes will rest in Him as in something immutable, and we shall forever praise His name. It is obvious that since all temporal things are transient and mortal, so they are filled and surrounded by troubles, trials and tribulations, and fraught with infinite dangers which we, who live with them and are part of them, could without a shadow of a doubt neither endure, nor defend ourselves against, if God's special grace did not lend us strength and discernment. Nor should we suppose that His grace descends upon and within us through any merit of our own, for it is set in motion by His own loving-kindness, and is obtained by the pleas of people who like ourselves were mortal, and who, by firmly doing His pleasure whilst they were in this life, have now joined Him in eternal blessedness. To these, as to advocates made aware, through experience, of our frailty (perhaps because we have not the courage to submit our pleas personally in the presence of so great a judge) we present whatever we think is relevant to our cause. And our regard for Him, who is so compassionate and generous towards us, is all the greater when, the human eye being quite unable to penetrate the secrets of divine intelligence, common opinion deceives us and perhaps we appoint as our advocate in His majestic presence one who has been cast by Him into eternal exile. Yet He from whom nothing is hidden, paying more attention to the purity of the supplicant's motives than to his ignorance or to the banishment of the intercessor, answers those who pray to Him exactly as if the advocate were blessed in His sight. All of which can clearly be seen in the tale I propose to relate; and I say clearly because it is concerned, not with the judgement of God, but with that of men.

It is said, then, that Musciatto Franzesi,[4] having become a fine gentleman after acquiring enormous wealth and fame as a merchant in France, was obliged to come to Tuscany with the brother of the French king, the Lord Charles Lackland,[5] who had been urged and encouraged to come by Pope Boniface. But finding that his affairs, as is usually the case with merchants, were entangled here, there, and everywhere, and being unable quickly or easily to unravel them, he decided to place them in the hands of a number of different people. All this he succeeded in arranging, except that he was left with the problem of finding someone capable of recovering certain loans which he had made to various people in Burgundy.[6] The reason for his dilemma was that he had been told the Burgundians were a quarrelsome, thoroughly bad and unprincipled set of people; and he was quite unable to think of anyone he could trust, who was at the same time sufficiently villainous to match the villainy of the Burgundians. After devoting much thought to this problem, he suddenly recalled a man known as Ser Cepperello, of Prato,[7] who had been a frequent visitor to his house in Paris. This man was short in stature and used to dress very neatly, and the French, who did not know the meaning of the word Cepperello, thinking that it signified *chapel*, which in their language means "garland," and because as we have said he was a little man, used to call him, not Ciappello, but Ciappelletto:

---

4. Like many other characters in the *Decameron*, those appearing in this first story are based on actual people. Musciatto was a Florentine financier who made a huge fortune in France by dubious means; Cepperello Dietaiuti was one of his associates. 5. Brother of King Philip of France, who invaded Italy in 1301. 6. A region of northeastern France. 7. A city just to the north of Florence.

and everywhere in that part of the world, where few people knew him as Ser Cepperello, he was known as Ciappelletto.[8]

This Ciappelletto was a man of the following sort: a notary by profession, he would have taken it as a slight upon his honor if one of his legal deeds (and he drew up very few of them) were discovered to be other than false. In fact, he would have drawn up free of charge as many false documents as were requested of him, and done it more willingly than one who was highly paid for his services. He would take great delight in giving false testimony, whether asked for it or not. In those days, great reliance was placed in France upon sworn declarations, and since he had no scruples about swearing falsely, he used to win, by these nefarious means, every case in which he was required to swear upon his faith to tell the truth. He would take particular pleasure, and a great amount of trouble, in stirring up enmity, discord and bad blood between friends, relatives and anybody else; and the more calamities that ensued, the greater would be his rapture. If he were invited to witness a murder or any other criminal act, he would never refuse, but willingly go along; and he often found himself cheerfully assaulting or killing people with his own hands. He was a mighty blasphemer of God and His Saints, losing his temper on the tiniest pretext, as if he were the most hot-blooded man alive. He never went to church, and he would use foul language to pour scorn on all of her sacraments, declaring them repugnant. On the other hand, he would make a point of visiting taverns and other places of ill repute, and supplying them with his custom. Of women he was as fond as dogs are fond of a good stout stick; in their opposite, he took greater pleasure than the most depraved man on earth. He would rob and pilfer as conscientiously as if he were a saintly man making an offering. He was such a prize glutton and heavy drinker, that he would occasionally suffer for his over-indulgence in a manner that was most unseemly. He was a gambler and a card-sharper of the first order. But why do I lavish so many words upon him? He was perhaps the worst man ever born. Yet for all his villainy, he had long been protected by the power and influence of Messer Musciatto, on whose account he was many a time treated with respect, both by private individuals, whom he frequently abused, and by the courts of law, which he was forever abusing.

So that when Musciatto, who was well acquainted with his way of living, called this Ser Ciappelletto to mind, he judged him to be the very man that the perverseness of the Burgundians required. He therefore sent for him and addressed him as follows:

"Ser Ciappelletto, as you know, I am about to go away from here altogether, but I have some business to settle, amongst others with the Burgundians. These people are full of tricks, and I know of no one better fitted than yourself to recover what they owe me. And so, since you are not otherwise engaged at present, if you will attend to this matter I propose to obtain favors for you at court, and allow you a reasonable portion of the money you recover."

Ser Ciappelletto, who was out of a job at the time and ill-supplied with worldly goods, seeing that the man who had long been his prop and stay was

---

8. This nickname assumes that Ciappello's name derives from the Italian word *ceppo* ("log" or "tree-stump"), and the suffix *-etto* is a diminutive. Hence the name means "little stump," which may have an obscene connotation.

about to depart, made up his mind without delay and said (for he really had no alternative) that he would do it willingly. So that when they had agreed on terms, Ser Ciappelletto received powers of attorney from Musciatto and letters of introduction from the King, and after Musciatto's departure he went to Burgundy, where scarcely anybody knew him. And there, in a gentle and amiable fashion that ran contrary to his nature, as though he were holding his anger in reserve as a last resort, he issued his first demands and began to do what he had gone there to do. Before long, however, while lodging in the house of two Florentine brothers who ran a money-lending business there and did him great honor out of their respect for Musciatto, he happened to fall ill; whereupon the two brothers promptly summoned doctors and servants to attend him, and provided him with everything he needed to recover his health. But all their assistance was unavailing, because the good man, who was already advanced in years and had lived a disordered existence, was reported by his doctors to be going each day from bad to worse, like one who was suffering from a fatal illness. The two brothers were filled with alarm, and one day, alongside the room in which Ser Ciappelletto was lying, they began talking together.

"What are we to do about the fellow?" said one to the other. "We've landed ourselves in a fine mess on his account, because to turn him away from our house in his present condition would arouse a lot of adverse comment and show us to be seriously lacking in common sense. What would people say if they suddenly saw us evicting a dying man after giving him hospitality in the first place, and taking so much trouble to have him nursed and waited upon, when he couldn't possibly have done anything to offend us? On the other hand, he has led such a wicked life that he will never be willing to make his confession or receive the sacraments of the Church; and if he dies unconfessed, no church will want to accept his body and he'll be flung into the moat like a dog. But even if he makes his confession, his sins are so many and so appalling that the same thing will happen, because there will be neither friar nor priest who is either willing or able to give him absolution; in which case, since he will not have been absolved, he will be flung into the moat just the same. And when the townspeople see what has happened, they'll create a commotion, not only because of our profession which they consider iniquitous and never cease to condemn, but also because they long to get their hands on our money, and they will go about shouting: 'Away with these Lombard dogs[9] that the Church refuses to accept'; and they'll come running to our lodgings and perhaps, not content with stealing our goods, they'll take away our lives into the bargain. So we shall be in a pretty fix either way, if this fellow dies."

Ser Ciappelletto, who as we have said was lying near the place where they were talking, heard everything they were saying about him, for he was sharp of hearing, as invalids invariably are. So he called them in to him, and said:

"I don't want you to worry in the slightest on my account, nor to fear that I will cause you to suffer any harm. I heard what you were saying about me and I agree entirely that what you predict will actually come to pass, if matters take the course you anticipate; but they will do nothing of the kind. I have done our good Lord so many injuries whilst I lived, that to do Him

---

9. Outside Italy, Italian bankers were known as Lombards, even if they came from a different province.

another now that I am dying will be neither here nor there. So go and bring me the holiest and ablest friar you can find, if there is such a one, and leave everything to me, for I shall set your affairs and my own neatly in order, so that all will be well and you'll have nothing to complain of."

Whilst deriving little comfort from all this, the two brothers nevertheless went off to a friary and asked for a wise and holy man to come and hear the confession of a Lombard who was lying ill in their house. They were given an ancient friar of good and holy ways who was an expert in the Scriptures and a most venerable man, towards whom all the townspeople were greatly and specially devoted, and they conducted him to their house.

On reaching the room where Ser Ciappelletto was lying, he sat down at his bedside, and first he began to comfort him with kindly words, then he asked him how long it was since he had last been to confession. Whereupon Ser Ciappelletto, who had never been to confession in his life, replied:

"Father, it has always been my custom to go to confession at least once every week, except that there are many weeks in which I go more often. But to tell the truth, since I fell ill, nearly a week ago, my illness has caused me so much discomfort that I haven't been to confession at all."

"My son," said the friar, "you have done well, and you should persevere in this habit of yours. Since you go so often to confession, I can see that there will be little for me to hear or to ask."

"Master friar," said Ser Ciappelletto, "do not speak thus, for however frequently or regularly I confess, it is always my wish that I should make a general confession of all the sins I can remember committing from the day I was born till the day of my confession. I therefore beg you, good father, to question me about everything, just as closely as if I had never been confessed. Do not spare me because I happen to be ill, for I would much rather mortify this flesh of mine than that, by treating it with lenience, I should do anything that could lead to the perdition of my soul, which my Saviour redeemed with His precious blood."

These words were greatly pleasing to the holy friar, and seemed to him proof of a well-disposed mind. Having warmly commended Ser Ciappelletto for this practice of his, he began by asking him whether he had ever committed the sin of lust with any woman. To which, heaving a sigh, Ser Ciappelletto replied:

"Father, I am loath to tell you the truth on this matter, in case I should sin by way of vainglory."

To which the holy friar replied:

"Speak out freely, for no man ever sinned by telling the truth, either in confession or otherwise."

"Since you assure me that this is so," said Ser Ciappelletto, "I will tell you. I am a virgin as pure as on the day I came forth from my mother's womb."

"Oh, may God give you His blessing!" said the friar. "How nobly you have lived! And your restraint is all the more deserving of praise in that, had you wished, you would have had greater liberty to do the opposite than those who, like ourselves, are expressly forbidden by rule."

Next he asked him whether he had displeased God by committing the sin of gluttony; to which, fetching a deep sigh, Ser Ciappelletto replied that he had, and on many occasions. For although, apart from the periods of fasting normally observed in the course of the year by the devout, he was accustomed to fasting on bread and water for at least three days every week, he had drunk the water as pleasurably and avidly (especially when he had been fatigued from praying or going on a pilgrimage) as any great bibber of wine; he had often experienced a craving for those dainty little wild herb salads that women eat when they go away to the country; and sometimes the thought of food had been more attractive to him than he considered proper in one who, like himself, was fasting out of piety. Whereupon the friar said:

"My son, these sins are natural and they are very trivial, and therefore I would not have you burden your conscience with them more than necessary. No matter how holy a man may be, he will be attracted by the thought of food after a long spell of fasting, and by the thought of drink when he is fatigued."

"Oh!" said Ser Ciappelletto. "Do not tell me this to console me, father. As you are aware, I know that things done in the service of God must all be done honestly and without any grudge; and if anyone should do otherwise, he is committing a sin."

The friar, delighted, said to him:

"I am contented to see you taking such a view, and it pleases me greatly that you should have such a good and pure conscience in this matter. But tell me, have you ever been guilty of avarice, by desiring to have more than was proper, or keeping what you should not have kept?"

To which Ser Ciappelletto replied:

"Father, I would not wish you to judge me ill because I am in the house of these money-lenders. I have nothing to do with their business; indeed I had come here with the express intention of warning and reproaching them, and dissuading them from this abominable form of money-making; and I think I would have succeeded, if God had not stricken me in this manner. However, I would have you know that my father left me a wealthy man, and when he was dead, I gave the greater part of his fortune to charity. Since then, in order to support myself and enable me to assist the Christian poor, I have done a small amount of trading, in the course of which I have desired to gain, and I have always shared what I have gained with the poor, allocating one half to my own needs and giving the other half to them. And in this I have had so much help from my Creator that I have continually gone from strength to strength in the management of my affairs."

"You have done well," said the friar, "but tell me, how often have you lost your temper?"

"Oh!" said Ser Ciappelletto, "I can assure you I have done that very often. But who is there who could restrain himself, when the whole day long he sees men doing disgusting things, and failing to observe God's command-ments, or to fear His terrible wrath? There have been many times in the space of a single day when I would rather have been dead than alive, looking about me and seeing young people frittering away their time, telling lies, going drinking in taverns, failing to go to church, and following the ways of the world rather than those of God."

"My son," said the friar, "this kind of anger is justified, and for my part I could not require you to do penance for it. But has it ever happened that your anger has led you to commit murder or to pour abuse on anyone or do them any other form of injury?"

To which Ser Ciappelletto replied:

"Oh, sir, however could you, that appear to be a man of God, say such a thing? If I had thought for a single moment of doing any of the things you mention, do you suppose I imagine that God would have treated me so generously? Those things are the business of cut-throats and evildoers, and whenever I have chanced upon one of their number, I have always sent him packing, and offered up a prayer for his conversion!"

"May God give you His blessing," said the friar, "but now, tell me, my son: have you ever borne false witness against any man, or spoken ill of people, or taken what belonged to others without seeking their permission?"

"Never, sir, except on one occasion," replied Ser Ciappelletto, "when I spoke ill of someone. For I once had a neighbor who, without the slightest cause, was forever beating his wife, so that on this one occasion I spoke ill of him to his wife's kinsfolk, for I felt extremely sorry for that unfortunate woman. Whenever the fellow had had too much to drink, God alone could tell you how he battered her."

Then the friar said:

"Let me see now, you tell me you were a merchant. Did you ever deceive anyone, as merchants do?"

"Faith, sir, I did," said Ser Ciappelletto. "But all I know about him is that he was a man who brought me some money that he owed me for a length of cloth I had sold him. I put the money away in a box without counting it, and a whole month passed before I discovered there were four pennies more than there should have been. I kept them for a year with the intention of giving them back, but I never saw him again, so I gave them away to a beggar."

"That was a trivial matter," said the friar, "and you did well to dispose of the money as you did."

The holy friar questioned him on many other matters, but always he answered in similar vein, and hence the friar was ready to proceed without further ado to give him absolution. But Ser Ciappelletto said:

"Sir, I still have one or two sins I have not yet told you about."

The friar asked him what they were, and he said:

"I recall that I once failed to show a proper respect for the Holy Sabbath, by making one of my servants sweep the house after nones[1] on a Saturday."

"Oh!" said the friar. "This, my son, is a trifling matter."

"No, father," said Ser Ciappelletto, "you must not call it trifling, for the Sabbath has to be greatly honored, seeing that this was the day on which our Lord rose from the dead."

Then the friar said:

"Have you done anything else?"

"Yes, sir," replied Ser Ciappelletto, "for I once, without thinking what I was doing, spat in the house of God."

The friar began to smile, and said:

"My son, this is not a thing to worry about. We members of religious orders spit there continually."

"That is very wicked of you," said Ser Ciappelletto, "for nothing should be kept more clean than the holy temple in which sacrifice is offered up to God."

In brief, he told the friar many things of this sort, and finally he began to sigh, and then to wail loudly, as he was well able to do whenever he pleased.

"My son," said the holy friar. "What is the matter?"

1. A church service held about 3 P.M.

"Oh alas, sir," replied Ser Ciappelletto, "I have one sin left to which I have never confessed, so great is my shame in having to reveal it; and whenever I remember it, I cry as you see me doing now, and feel quite certain that God will never have mercy on me for this terrible sin."

"Come now, my son," said the holy friar, "what are you saying? If all the sins that were ever committed by the whole of mankind, together with those that men will yet commit till the end of the world, were concentrated in one single man, and he was as truly repentant and contrite as I see you to be, God is so benign and merciful that He would freely remit them on their being confessed to Him; and therefore you may safely reveal it."

Then Ser Ciappelletto said, still weeping loudly:

"Alas, father, my sin is too great, and I can scarcely believe that God will ever forgive me for it, unless you intercede with your prayers."

To which the friar replied:

"You may safely reveal it, for I promise that I will pray to God on your behalf."

Ser Ciappelletto went on weeping, without saying anything, and the friar kept encouraging him to speak. But after Ser Ciappelletto, by weeping in this manner, had kept the friar for a very long time on tenterhooks, he heaved a great sigh, and said:

"Father, since you promise that you will pray to God for me, I will tell you. You are to know then that once, when I was a little boy, I cursed my mother." And having said this, he began to weep loudly all over again.

"There now, my son," said the friar, "does this seem so great a sin to you? Why, people curse God the whole day long, and yet He willingly forgives those who repent for having cursed Him. Why then should you suppose He will not forgive you for this? Take heart and do not weep, for even if you had been one of those who set Him on the cross, I can see that you have so much contrition that He would certainly forgive you."

"Oh alas, father," said Ser Ciappelletto, "what are you saying? My dear, sweet mother, who carried me day and night for nine months in her body, and held me more than a hundred times in her arms! It was too wicked of me to curse her, and the sin is too great; and if you do not pray to God for me, it will never be forgiven me.'

Perceiving that Ser Ciappelletto had nothing more to say, the friar absolved him and gave him his blessing. He took him for a very saintly man indeed, being fully convinced that what Ser Ciappelletto had said was true; but then, who is there who would not have been convinced, on hearing a dying man talk in this fashion? Finally, when all this was done, he said to him:

"Ser Ciappelletto, with God's help you will soon be well again. But in case it were to happen that God should summon your blessed and well-disposed soul to His presence, are you willing for your body to be buried in our convent?"

To which Ser Ciappelletto replied:

"Yes, father. In fact, I would not wish to be elsewhere, since you have promised that you will pray to God for me. Besides, I have always been especially devoted to your Order. So when you return to your convent, I beg you to see that I am sent that true body of Christ which you consecrate every morning on the altar. For although I am unworthy of it, I intend with your permission to take it, and afterwards to receive the holy Extreme Unction,[2] so that, having lived as a sinner, I shall at least die as a Christian."

The holy man said that he was greatly pleased, that the words were well spoken, and that he would see it was brought to him at once; and so it was.

The two brothers, who strongly suspected that Ser Ciappelletto was going to deceive them, had posted themselves behind a wooden partition which separated the room where Ser Ciappelletto was lying from another, and as they stood there listening they could easily follow what Ser Ciappelletto was saying to the friar. When they heard the things he confessed to having done, they were so amused that every so often they nearly exploded with mirth, and they said to each other:

"What manner of man is this, whom neither old age nor illness, nor fear of the death which he sees so close at hand, nor even the fear of God, before whose judgement he knows he must shortly appear, have managed to turn from his evil ways, or persuade to die any differently from the way he has lived?"

Seeing, however, that he had said all the right things to be received for burial in a church, they cared nothing for the rest.

Shortly thereafter Ser Ciappelletto made his communion, and, failing rapidly, he received Extreme Unction. Soon after vespers[3] on the very day that he had made his fine confession, he died. Whereupon the two brothers made all necessary arrangements, using his own money to see that he had an honorable funeral, and sending news of his death to the friars and asking them to come that evening to observe the customary vigil, and the following morning to take away the body.

On hearing that he had passed away, the holy friar who had received his confession arranged with the prior for the chapterhouse bell to be rung, and to the assembled friars he showed that Ser Ciappelletto had been a saintly man, as his confession had amply proved. He expressed the hope that through him the Lord God would work many miracles, and persuaded them that his body should be received with the utmost reverence and loving care. Credulous to a man, the prior and the other friars agreed to do so, and that evening they went to the place where Ser Ciappelletto's body lay, and celebrated a great and solemn vigil over it; and in the morning, dressed in albs and copes,[4] carrying books in their hands and bearing crosses before them, singing as they went, they all came for the body, which they then carried back to their church with tremendous pomp and ceremony, followed by nearly all the people of the town, men and women alike. And when it had been set down in the church, the holy friar who had confessed him climbed into the pulpit and began to preach marvellous things about Ser Ciappelletto's life, his fasts, his virginity, his simplicity and innocence and saintliness, relating among other things what he had tearfully confessed to him as his greatest sin, and describing how he had barely been able to convince him that God would forgive him, at which point he turned to reprimand his audience, saying:

"And yet you miserable sinners have only to catch your feet in a wisp of straw for you to curse God and the Virgin and all the Saints in heaven."

---

2. The sacrament in which a dying person is anointed by a priest.   3. A church service held at eventide.   4. Albs and copes are religious vestments worn by priests while performing a religious ritual.

Apart from this, he said much else about his loyalty and his purity of heart. And in brief, with a torrent of words that the people of the town believed implicitly, he fixed Ser Ciappelletto so firmly in the minds and affections of all those present that when the service was over, everyone thronged round the body to kiss his feet and his hands, all the clothes were torn from his back, and those who succeeded in grabbing so much as a tiny fragment felt they were in Paradise itself. He had to be kept lying there all day, so that everyone could come and gaze upon him, and on that same night he was buried with honor in a marble tomb in one of the chapels. From the next day forth, people began to go there to light candles and pray to him, and later they began to make votive offerings and to decorate the chapel with figures made of wax, in fulfilment of promises they had given.

The fame of his saintliness, and of the veneration in which he was held, grew to such proportions that there was hardly anyone who did not pray for his assistance in time of trouble, and they called him, and call him still, Saint Ciappelletto. Moreover it is claimed that through him God has wrought many miracles, and that He continues to work them on behalf of whoever commends himself devoutly to this particular Saint.

It was thus, then, that Ser Cepperello of Prato lived and died, becoming a Saint in the way you have heard. Nor would I wish to deny that perhaps God has blessed and admitted him to His presence. For albeit he led a wicked, sinful life, it is possible that at the eleventh hour he was so sincerely repentant that God had mercy upon him and received him into His kingdom. But since this is hidden from us, I speak only with regard to the outward appearance, and I say that the fellow should rather be in Hell, in the hands of the devil, than in Paradise. And if this is the case, we may recognize how very great is God's loving-kindness towards us, in that it takes account, not of our error, but of the purity of our faith, and grants our prayers even when we appoint as our emissary one who is His enemy, thinking him to be His friend, as though we were appealing to one who was truly holy as our intercessor for His favor. And therefore, so that we, the members of this joyful company, may be guided safely and securely by His grace through these present adversities, let us praise the name of Him with whom we began our storytelling, let us hold Him in reverence, and let us commend ourselves to Him in the hour of our need, in the certain knowledge that we shall be heard.

And there the narrator fell silent.

[THE NINTH STORY OF THE FOURTH DAY][5]

Guillaume de Roussillon causes his wife to eat the heart of her lover, Guillaume de Cabestanh,[6] whom he has secretly murdered. When she finds out, she kills herself by leaping from a lofty casement to the ground below, and is subsequently buried with the man she loved.

You must know, then, that according to the Provençals, there once lived in Provence two noble knights, each of whom owned several castles and had a number of dependants. The name of the first was Guillaume de Roussillon,

---

5. This story is told by Dioneo, one of the young men.   6. The story is based on a poetic account of the love affair between an early thirteenth-century Provençal poet of this name and the wife of his lord, Raimon de Castel-Rousillon.

whilst the other was called Guillaume de Cabestanh. Since both men excelled in feats of daring, they were bosom friends and made a point of accompanying one another to jousts and tournaments and other armed contests, each bearing the same device.[7]

Although[8] the castles in which they lived were some ten miles apart, Guillaume de Cabestanh chanced to fall hopelessly in love with the charming and very beautiful wife of Guillaume de Roussillon, and, notwithstanding the bonds of friendship and brotherhood that united the two men, he managed in various subtle ways to bring his love to the lady's notice. The lady, knowing him to be a most gallant knight, was deeply flattered, and began to regard him with so much affection that there was nothing she loved or desired more deeply. All that remained for him to do was to approach her directly, which he very soon did, and from then on they met at frequent intervals for the purpose of making passionate love to one another.

One day, however, they were incautious enough to be espied by the lady's husband, who was so incensed by the spectacle that his great love for Cabestanh was transformed into mortal hatred. He firmly resolved to do away with him, but concealed his intentions far more successfully than the lovers had been able to conceal their love.

His mind being thus made up, Roussillon happened to hear of a great tournament that was to be held in France. He promptly sent word of it to Cabestanh and asked him whether he would care to call upon him, so that they could talk it over together and decide whether or not to go and how they were to get there. Cabestanh was delighted to hear of it, and sent back word to say that he would come and sup with him next day without fail.

On receiving Cabestanh's message, Roussillon judged this to be his opportunity for killing him. Next day, he armed himself, took horse with a few of his men, and lay in ambush about a mile away from his castle, in a wood through which Cabestanh was bound to pass. After a long wait, he saw him approaching, unarmed, and followed by two of his men, who were likewise unarmed, for he never suspected for a moment that he was running into danger. Roussillon waited until Cabestanh was at close range, then he rushed out at him with murder and destruction in his heart, brandishing a lance above his head and shouting: "Traitor, you are dead!" And before the words were out of his mouth he had driven the lance through Cabestanh's breast.

Cabestanh was powerless to defend himself, or even to utter a word, and on being run through by the lance he fell to the ground. A moment later he was dead, and his men, without stopping to see who had perpetrated the deed, turned the heads of their horses and galloped away as fast as they could in the direction of their master's castle.

Dismounting from his horse, Roussillon cut open Cabestanh's chest with a knife, tore out the heart with his own hands, and, wrapping it up in a banderole,[8] told one of his men to take it away. Having given strict orders that no one was to breathe a word about what had happened, he then remounted and rode back to his castle, by which time it was already dark.

The lady had heard that Cabestanh was to be there that evening for supper and was eagerly waiting for him to arrive. When she saw her husband arriving without him she was greatly surprised, and said to him:

7. Coat of arms.   8. A long narrow flag or streamer.

"And how is it, my lord, that Cabestanh has not come?"

To which her husband replied:

"Madam, I have received word from him that he cannot be here until tomorrow."

Roussillon left her standing there, feeling somewhat perturbed, and when he had dismounted, he summoned the cook and said to him:

"You are to take this boar's heart and see to it that you prepare the finest and most succulent dish you can devise. When I am seated at table, send it in to me in a silver tureen."

The cook took the heart away, minced it, and added a goodly quantity of fine spices, employing all his skill and loving care and turning it into a dish that was too exquisite for words.

When it was time for dinner, Roussillon sat down at the table with his lady. Food was brought in, but he was unable to do more than nibble at it because his mind was dwelling upon the terrible deed he had committed. Then the cook sent in his special dish, which Roussillon told them to set before his lady, saying that he had no appetite that evening.

He remarked on how delicious it looked, and the lady, whose appetite was excellent, began to eat it, finding it so tasty a dish that she ate every scrap of it.

On observing that his lady had finished it down to the last morsel, the knight said:

"What did you think of that, madam?"

"In good faith, my lord," replied the lady, "I liked it very much."

"So help me God," exclaimed the knight, "I do believe you did. But I am not surprised to find that you liked it dead, because when it was alive you liked it better than anything else in the whole world."

On hearing this, the lady was silent for a while; then she said:

"How say you? What is this that you have caused me to eat?"

"That which you have eaten," replied the knight, "was in fact the heart of Guillaume de Cabestanh, with whom you, faithless woman that you are, were so infatuated. And you may rest assured that it was truly his, because I tore it from his breast myself, with these very hands, a little before I returned home."

You can all imagine the anguish suffered by the lady on hearing such tidings of Cabestanh, whom she loved more dearly than anything else in the world. But after a while, she said:

"This can only have been the work of an evil and treacherous knight, for if, of my own free will, I abused you by making him the master of my love, it was not he but I that should have paid the penalty for it. But God forbid that any other food should pass my lips now that I have partaken of such excellent fare as the heart of so gallant and courteous a knight as Guillaume de Cabestanh."

And rising to her feet, she retreated a few steps to an open window, through which without a second thought she allowed herself to fall.

The window was situated high above the ground, so that the lady was not only killed by her fall but almost completely disfigured.

The spectacle of his wife's fall threw Roussillon into a panic and made him repent the wickedness of his deed. And fearing the wrath of the local people and of the Count of Provence, he had his horses saddled and rode away.

By next morning the circumstances of the affair had become common knowledge throughout the whole of the district, and people were sent out from the castles of the lady's family and of Guillaume de Cabestanh to gather up the two bodies, which were later placed in a single tomb in the chapel of the lady's own castle amid widespread grief and mourning. And the tombstone bore an inscription, in verse, to indicate who was buried there and the manner and the cause of their deaths.

[THE EIGHTH STORY[9] OF THE FIFTH DAY]

In his love for a young lady of the Traversari family, Nastagio degli Onesti squanders his wealth without being loved in return. He is entreated by his friends to leave the city, and goes away to Classe, where he sees a girl being hunted down and killed by a horseman, and devoured by a brace of hounds. He then invites his kinsfolk and the lady he loves to a banquet, where this same girl is torn to pieces before the eyes of his beloved, who, fearing a similar fate, accepts Nastagio as her husband.

In Ravenna,[1] a city of great antiquity in Romagna, there once used to live a great many nobles and men of property, among them a young man called Nastagio degli Onesti, who had inherited an incredibly large fortune on the deaths of his father and one of his uncles. Being as yet unmarried, he fell in love, as is the way with young men, with a daughter of Messer Paolo Traversari, a girl of far more noble lineage than his own, whose love he hoped to win by dint of his accomplishments. But though these were very considerable, and splendid, and laudable, far from promoting his cause they appeared to damage it, inasmuch as the girl he loved was persistently cruel, harsh and unfriendly towards him. And on account possibly of her singular beauty, or perhaps because of her exalted rank, she became so haughty and contemptuous of him that she positively loathed him and everything he stood for.

All of this was so difficult for Nastagio to bear that he was frequently seized, after much weeping and gnashing of teeth, with the longing to kill himself out of sheer despair. But, having stayed his hand, he would then decide that he must give her up altogether, or learn if possible to hate her as she hated him. All such resolutions were unavailing, however, for the more his hopes dwindled, the greater his love seemed to grow.

As the young man persisted in wooing the girl and spending money like water, certain of his friends and relatives began to feel that he was in danger of exhausting both himself and his inheritance. They therefore implored and advised him to leave Ravenna and go to live for a while in some other place, with the object of curtailing both his wooing and his spending. Nastagio rejected this advice as often as it was offered, but they eventually pressed him so hard that he could not refuse them any longer, and agreed to do as they suggested. Having mustered an enormous baggage-train, as though he were intending to go to France or Spain or some other remote part of the world, he mounted his horse, rode forth from Ravenna with several of his friends, and repaired to a place which is known as Classe, some three miles distant from the city. Having sent for a number of tents and pavilions, he told his companions that this was where he intended to stay, and that they

9. The teller is Filomena, one of the young ladies.   1. On the west coast of Italy.

could all go back to Ravenna. So Nastagio pitched his camp in this place, and began to live in as fine and lordly a fashion as any man ever born, from time to time inviting various groups of friends to dine or breakfast with him, as had always been his custom.

Now, it so happened that one Friday morning towards the beginning of May, the weather being very fine, Nastagio fell to thinking about his cruel mistress. Having ordered his servants to leave him to his own devices so that he could meditate at greater leisure, he sauntered off, lost in thought, and his steps led him straight into the pinewoods. The fifth hour of the day was already spent, and he had advanced at least half a mile into the woods, oblivious of food and everything else, when suddenly he seemed to hear a woman giving vent to dreadful wailing and ear-splitting screams. His pleasant reverie being thus interrupted, he raised his head to investigate the cause, and discovered to his surprise that he was in the pinewoods. Furthermore, on looking straight ahead he caught sight of a naked woman, young and very beautiful, who was running through a dense thicket of shrubs and briars towards the very spot where he was standing. The woman's hair was dishevelled, her flesh was all torn by the briars and brambles, and she was sobbing and screaming for mercy. Nor was this all, for a pair of big, fierce mastiffs were running at the girl's heels, one on either side, and every so often they caught up with her and savaged her. Finally, bringing up the rear he saw a swarthy-looking knight, his face contorted with anger, who was riding a jet-black steed and brandishing a rapier, and who, in terms no less abusive than terrifying, was threatening to kill her.[2]

This spectacle struck both terror and amazement into Nastagio's breast, to say nothing of compassion for the hapless woman, a sentiment that in its turn engendered the desire to rescue her from such agony and save her life, if this were possible. But on finding that he was unarmed, he hastily took up a branch of a tree to serve as a cudgel, and prepared to ward off the dogs and do battle with the knight. When the latter saw what he was doing, he shouted to him from a distance:

"Keep out of this, Nastagio! Leave me and the dogs to give this wicked sinner her deserts!"

He had no sooner spoken than the dogs seized the girl firmly by the haunches and brought her to a halt. When the knight reached the spot he dismounted from his horse, and Nastagio went up to him saying:

"I do not know who you are, or how you come to know my name; but I can tell you that it is a gross outrage for an armed knight to try and kill a naked woman, and to set dogs upon her as though she were a savage beast. I shall do all in my power to defend her, of that you may be sure."

Whereupon the knight said:

"I was a fellow citizen of yours, Nastagio, my name was Guido degli Anastagi, and you were still a little child when I fell in love with this woman. I loved her far more deeply than you love that Traversari girl of yours, but her pride and cruelty led me to such a pass that, one day, I killed myself in sheer despair with this rapier that you see in my hand, and thus I am condemned to eternal punishment. My death pleased her beyond measure, but shortly thereafter she too died, and because she had sinned by her cruelty and by

---

2. Cf. the account of the punishment of the spendthrifts in Dante's *Inferno,* canto 13.

gloating over my sufferings, and was quite unrepentant, being convinced that she was more of a saint than a sinner, she too was condemned to the pains of Hell. No sooner was she cast into Hell than we were both given a special punishment, which consisted in her case of fleeing before me, and in my own of pursuing her as though she were my mortal enemy rather than the woman with whom I was once so deeply in love. Every time I catch up with her, I kill her with this same rapier by which I took my own life; then I slit her back open, and (as you will now observe for yourself) I tear from her body that hard, cold heart to which neither love nor pity could ever gain access, and together with the rest of her entrails I cast it to these dogs to feed upon.

"Within a short space of time, as ordained by the power and justice of God, she springs to her feet as though she had not been dead at all, and her agonizing flight begins all over again, with the dogs and myself in pursuit. Every Friday at this hour I overtake her in this part of the woods, and slaughter her in the manner you are about to observe; but you must not imagine that we are idle for the rest of the week, because on the remaining days I hunt her down in other places where she was cruel to me in thought and deed. As you can see for yourself, I am no longer her lover but her enemy, and in this guise I am obliged to pursue her for the same number of years as the months of her cruelty towards me. Stand aside, therefore, and let me carry out the judgement of God. Do not try to oppose what you cannot prevent."

On hearing these words, Nastagio was shaken to the core, there was scarcely a single hair on his head that was not standing on end, and he stepped back to fix his gaze on the unfortunate girl, waiting in fear and trembling to see what the knight would do to her. This latter, having finished speaking, pounced like a mad dog, rapier in hand, upon the girl, who was kneeling before him, held by the two mastiffs, and screaming for mercy at the top of her voice. Applying all his strength, the knight plunged his rapier into the middle of her breast and out again at the other side, whereupon the girl fell on her face, still sobbing and screaming, whilst the knight, having laid hold of a dagger, slashed open her back, extracted her heart and everything else around it, and hurled it to the two mastiffs, who devoured it greedily on the instant. But before very long the girl rose suddenly to her feet as though none of these things had happened, and sped off in the direction of the sea, being pursued by the dogs, who kept tearing away at her flesh as she ran. Remounting his horse, and seizing his rapier, the knight too began to give chase, and within a short space of time they were so far away that Nastagio could no longer see them.

For some time after bearing witness to these events, Nastagio stood rooted to the spot out of fear and compassion, but after a while it occurred to him that since this scene was enacted every Friday, it ought to prove very useful to him. So he marked the place and returned to his servants; and when the time seemed ripe, he sent for his friends and kinsfolk, and said to them:

"For some little time you have been urging me to desist from wooing this hostile mistress of mine and place a curb on my extravagance, and I am willing to do so on condition that you obtain for me a single favor, which is this: that on Friday next you arrange for Messer Paolo Traversari and his wife and daughter and all their womenfolk, together with any other lady you care to invite, to join me in this place for breakfast. My reason for wanting this will become apparent to you on the day itself."

They thought this a very trifling commission for them to undertake, and promised him they would do it. On their return to Ravenna, they invited all the people he had specified. And although they had a hard job, when the time came, in persuading Nastagio's beloved to go, she nevertheless went there along with the others.

Nastagio saw to it that a magnificent banquet was prepared, and had the tables placed beneath the pine-trees in such a way as to surround the place where he had witnessed the massacre of the cruel lady. Moreover, in seating the ladies and gentlemen at table, he so arranged matters that the girl he loved sat directly facing the spot where the scene would be enacted.

The last course had already been served, when they all began to hear the agonized yells of the fugitive girl. Everyone was greatly astonished and wanted to know what it was, but nobody was able to say. So they all stood up to see if they could find out what was going on, and caught sight of the wailing girl, together with the knight and the dogs. And shortly thereafter they came into the very midst of the company.

Everyone began shouting and bawling at the dogs and the knight, and several people rushed forward to the girl's assistance; but the knight, by repeating to them the story he had related to Nastagio, not only caused them to retreat but filled them all with terror and amazement. And when he dealt with the girl in the same way as before, all the ladies present (many of whom, being related either to the suffering girl or to the knight, still remembered his great love and the manner of his death) wept as plaintively as though what they had witnessed had been done to themselves.

When the spectacle was at an end, and the knight and the lady had gone, they all began to talk about what they had seen. But none was stricken with so much terror as the cruel maiden loved by Nastagio, for she had heard and seen everything distinctly and realized that these matters had more to do with herself than with any of the other guests, in view of the harshness she had always displayed towards Nastagio; consequently, she already had the sensation of fleeing before her enraged suitor, with the mastiffs tearing away at her haunches.

So great was the fear engendered within her by this episode, that in order to avoid a similar fate she converted her enmity into love; and, seizing the earliest opportunity (which came to her that very evening), she privily sent a trusted maidservant to Nastagio, requesting him to be good enough to call upon her, as she was ready to do anything he desired. Nastagio was overjoyed, and told her so in his reply, but added that if she had no objection he preferred to combine his pleasure with the preservation of her good name, by making her his lawful wedded wife.

Knowing that she alone was to blame for the fact that she and Nastagio were not already married, the girl readily sent him her consent. And so, acting as her own intermediary, she announced to her father and mother, to their enormous satisfaction, that she would be pleased to become Nastagio's wife. On the following Sunday Nastagio married her, and after celebrating their nuptials they settled down to a long and happy life together.

Their marriage was by no means the only good effect to be produced by this horrible apparition, for from that day forth the ladies of Ravenna in general were so frightened by it that they became much more tractable to men's pleasures than they had ever been in the past.

[THE SIXTH STORY OF THE NINTH DAY][3]

Two young men lodge overnight at a cottage, where one of them goes and sleeps with their host's daughter, whilst his wife inadvertently sleeps with the other. The one who was with the daughter clambers into bed beside her father, mistaking him for his companion, and tells him all about it. A great furor then ensues, and the wife, realizing her mistake, gets into her daughter's bed, whence with a timely explanation she restores the peace.

Not long ago, there lived in the valley of the Mugnone[4] a worthy man who earned an honest penny by supplying food and drink to wayfarers; and although he was poor, and his house was tiny, he would from time to time, in cases of urgent need, offer them a night's lodging, but only if they happened to be people he knew.

Now, this man had a most attractive wife, who had borne him two children, the first being a charming and beautiful girl of about fifteen or sixteen, as yet unmarried, whilst the second was an infant, not yet twelve months old, who was still being nursed at his mother's breast.

The daughter had caught the eye of a lively and handsome young Florentine gentleman who used to spend much of his time in the countryside, and he fell passionately in love with her. Nor was it long before the girl, being highly flattered to have won the affection of so noble a youth, which she strove hard to retain by displaying the greatest affability towards him, fell in love with him. And neither of the pair would have hesitated to consummate their love, but for the fact that Pinuccio (for such was the young man's name) was not prepared to expose the girl or himself to censure.

At length however, his ardor growing daily more intense, Pinuccio was seized with a longing to consort with her, come what may, and it occurred to him that he must find some excuse for lodging with her father overnight, since, being conversant with the layout of the premises, he had good reason to think that he and the girl could be together without anyone ever being any the wiser. And no sooner did this idea enter his head than he promptly took steps to carry it into effect.

Late one afternoon, he and a trusted companion of his called Adriano, who knew of his love for the girl, hired a couple of pack-horses, and having laden them with a pair of saddlebags, filled probably with straw, they set forth from Florence; and after riding round in a wide circle they came to the valley of the Mugnone, some time after nightfall. They then wheeled their horses round to make it look as though they were returning from Romagna, rode up to the cottage of our worthy friend, and knocked at the door. And since the man was well acquainted with both Pinuccio and his companion, he immediately came down to let them in.

"You'll have to put us up for the night," said Pinuccio. "We had intended

3. The teller is Panfilo, one of the young men. 4. This valley runs north from Florence into the Romagna.

to reach Florence before dark, but as you can see, we've made such slow progress that this is as far as we've come, and it's too late to enter the city at this hour."

"My dear Pinuccio," replied the host, "as you know, I can't exactly offer you a princely sort of lodging. But no matter: since night has fallen and you've nowhere else to go, I shall be glad to put you up as best I can."

So the two young men dismounted, and having seen that their nags were comfortably stabled, they went into the house, where, since they had brought plenty to eat with them, they made a hearty supper along with their host. Now, their host had only one bedroom, which was very tiny, and into this he had crammed three small beds, leaving so little space that it was almost impossible to move between them. Two of the beds stood alongside one of the bedroom walls, whilst the third was against the wall on the opposite side of the room; and having seen that the least uncomfortable of the three was made ready for his guests, the host invited them to sleep in that for the night. Shortly afterwards, when they appeared to be asleep, though in reality they were wide awake, he settled his daughter in one of the other two beds, whilst he and his wife got into the third; and beside the bed in which she was sleeping, his wife had placed the cradle containing her infant son.

Having made a mental note of all these arrangements, Pinuccio waited until he was sure that everyone was asleep, then quietly left his bed, stole across to the bed in which his lady-love was sleeping, and lay down beside her. Although she was somewhat alarmed, the girl received him joyously in her arms, and they then proceeded to take their fill of that sweet pleasure for which they yearned above all else.

Whilst Pinuccio and the girl were thus employed, a cat, somewhere in the house, happened to knock something over, causing the man's wife to wake up with a start. Being anxious to discover what it was, she got up and groped her way naked in the dark towards that part of the house from which the noise had come.

Meanwhile Adriano also happened to get up, not for the same reason, but in order to obey the call of nature, and as he was groping his way towards the door with this purpose in view, he came in contact with the cradle deposited there by the woman. Being unable to pass without moving it out of his way, he picked it up and set it down beside his own bed; and after doing what he had to do, he returned to his bed and forgot all about it.

Having discovered the cause of the noise and assured herself that nothing important had fallen, the woman swore at the cat, and, without bothering to light a lamp and explore the matter further, returned to the bedroom. Picking her way carefully through the darkness, she went straight to the bed where her husband was lying; but on finding no trace of the cradle, she said to herself: "How stupid I am! What a fine thing to do! Heavens above, I was just about to step into the bed where my guests are sleeping." So she walked a little further up the room, found the cradle, and got into bed beside Adriano, thinking him to be her husband.

On perceiving this, Adriano, who was still awake, gave her a most cordial reception; and without a murmur he tacked hard to windward over and over again, much to her delight and satisfaction.

This, then, was how matters stood when Pinuccio, who had gratified his longings to the full and was afraid of falling asleep in the young lady's arms, abandoned her so as to go back and sleep in his own bed. But on reaching the bed to find the cradle lying there, he moved on, thinking he had mistaken his host's bed for his own, and ended up by getting into bed with the host, who was awakened by his coming. And being under the impression that the man who lay beside him was Adriano, Pinuccio said:

"I swear to you that there was never anything so delicious as Niccolosa. By the body of God, no man ever had so much pleasure with any woman as I have been having with her. Since the time I left you, I assure you I've been to the bower of bliss half a dozen times at the very least."

The host was not exactly pleased to hear Pinuccio's tidings, and having first of all asked himself what the devil the fellow was doing in his bed, he allowed his anger to get the better of his prudence, and exclaimed:

"What villainy is this, Pinuccio? I can't think why you should have played me so scurvy a trick, but by all that's holy, I shall pay you back for it."

Now, Pinuccio was not the wisest of young men, and on perceiving his error, instead of doing all he could to remedy matters, he said:

"Pay me back? How? What could you do to me?"

Whereupon the host's wife, thinking she was with her husband, said to Adriano:

"Heavens! Just listen to the way those guests of ours are arguing with one another!"

Adriano laughed, and said:

"Let them get on with it, and to hell with them. They had far too much to drink last night."

The woman had already thought she could detect the angry tones of her husband, and on hearing Adriano's voice, she realized at once whose bed she was sharing. So being a person of some intelligence, she promptly got up without a word, seized her baby's cradle, and having picked her way across the room, which was in total darkness, she set the cradle down beside the bed in which her daughter was sleeping and scrambled in beside her. Then, pretending to have been aroused by the noise her husband was making, she called out to him and demanded to know what he was quarrelling with Pinuccio about. Whereupon her husband replied:

"Don't you hear what he says he has done to Niccolosa this night?"

"He's telling a pack of lies," said the woman. "He hasn't been anywhere near Niccolosa, for I've been lying beside her myself the whole time and I haven't managed to sleep a wink. You're a fool to take any notice of him. You men drink so much in the evening that you spend the night dreaming and wandering all over the place in your sleep, and imagine you've performed all sorts of miracles: it's a thousand pities you don't trip over and break your necks! What's Pinuccio doing there anyway? Why isn't he in his own bed?"

At which point, seeing how adroitly the woman was concealing both her own and her daughter's dishonor, Adriano came to her support by saying:

"How many times do I have to tell you, Pinuccio, not to wander about in the middle of the night? You'll land yourself in serious trouble one of these days, with this habit of walking in your sleep, and claiming to have actually done the fantastic things you dream about. Come back to bed, curse you!"

When he heard Adriano confirm what his wife had been saying, the host began to think that Pinuccio really had been dreaming after all; and seizing him by the shoulder, he shook him and yelled at him, saying:

"Wake up, Pinuccio! Go back to your own bed!"

Having taken all of this in, Pinuccio now began to thresh about as though he were dreaming again, causing his host to split his sides with laughter. But in the end, after a thorough shaking, he pretended to wake up; and calling to Adriano, he said:

"Why have you woken me up? Is it morning already?"

"Yes," said Adriano. "Come back here."

Pinuccio kept up the pretence, showing every sign of being extremely drowsy, but in the end he left his host's side and staggered back to bed with Adriano. When they got up next morning, their host began to laugh and make fun of Pinuccio and his dreams. And so, amid a constant stream of merry banter, the two young men saddled and loaded their horses, and after drinking the health of their host, they remounted and rode back to Florence, feeling no less delighted with the manner than with the outcome of the night's activities.

From then on, Pinuccio discovered other ways of consorting with Niccolosa, who meanwhile assured her mother that he had certainly been dreaming. And thus the woman, who retained a vivid memory of Adriano's embraces, was left with the firm conviction that she alone had been awake on the night in question.

[THE TENTH STORY OF THE TENTH DAY][5]

The Marquis of Saluzzo, obliged by the entreaties of his subjects to take a wife, follows his personal whims and marries the daughter of a peasant. She bears him two children, and he gives her the impression that he has put them to death. Later on, pretending that she has incurred his displeasure and that he has remarried, he arranges for his own daughter to return home and passes her off as his bride, having meanwhile turned his wife out of doors in no more than the shift she is wearing. But on finding that she endures it all with patience, he cherishes her all the more deeply, brings her back to his house, shows her their children, who have now grown up, and honors her as the Marchioness, causing others to honor her likewise.

A very long time ago, there succeeded to the marquisate of Saluzzo[6] a young man called Gualtieri, who, having neither wife nor children, spent the whole of his time hunting and hawking, and never even thought about marrying or raising a family, which says a great deal for his intelligence. His followers, however, disapproved of this, and repeatedly begged him to marry so that he should not be left without an heir nor they without a lord. Moreover, they offered to find him a wife whose parentage would be such as to strengthen their expectations and who would make him exceedingly happy.

So Gualtieri answered them as follows:

"My friends, you are pressing me to do something that I had always set my mind firmly against, seeing how difficult it is to find a person who will easily adapt to one's own way of living, how many thousands there are who will do precisely the opposite, and what a miserable life is in store for the

---

5. The teller is Dioneo, the young man who tells the last story of each day.   6. A town at the foot of the Alps about thirty miles south of Turin.

man who stumbles upon a woman ill-suited to his own temperament. More-over it is foolish of you to believe that you can judge the character of daughters from the ways of their fathers and mothers, hence claiming to provide me with a wife who will please me. For I cannot see how you are to know the fathers, or to discover the secrets of the mothers; and even if this were possible, daughters are very often different from either of their parents. Since, however, you are so determined to bind me in chains of this sort, I am ready to do as you ask; but so that I have only myself to blame if it should turn out badly, I must insist on marrying a wife of my own choosing. And I hereby declare that no matter who she may be, if you fail to honor her as your lady you will learn to your great cost how serious a matter it is for you to have urged me to marry against my will."

To this the gentlemen replied that if only he would bring himself to take a wife, they would be satisfied.

Now, for some little time, Gualtieri had been casting an appreciative eye on the manners of a poor girl from a neighboring village, and thinking her very beautiful, he considered that a life with her would have much to commend it. So without looking further afield, he resolved to marry the girl; and having summoned her father, who was very poor indeed, he arranged with him that he should take her as his wife.

This done, Gualtieri brought together all his friends from the various parts of his domain, and said to them:

"My friends, since you still persist in wanting me to take a wife, I am prepared to do it, not because I have any desire to marry, but rather in order to gratify your wishes. You will recall the promise you gave me, that no matter whom I should choose, you would rest content and honor her as your lady. The time has now come when I want you to keep that promise, and for me to honor the promise I gave to you. I have found a girl after my own heart, in this very district, and a few days hence I intend to marry her and convey her to my house. See to it, therefore, that the wedding-feast lacks nothing in splendor, and consider how you may honorably receive her, so that all of us may call ourselves contented—I with you for keeping your promise, and you with me for keeping mine."

As of one voice, the good folk joyously gave him their blessing, and said that whoever she happened to be, they would accept her as their lady and honor her as such in all respects. Then they all prepared to celebrate the wedding in a suitably grand and sumptuous manner, and Gualtieri did the same. A rich and splendid nuptial feast was arranged, to which he invited many of his friends, his kinsfolk, great nobles and other people of the locality; moreover he caused a quantity of fine, rich robes to be tailored to fit a girl whose figure appeared to match that of the young woman he intended to marry; and lastly he laid in a number of rings and ornamental belts, along with a precious and beautiful crown, and everything else that a bride could possibly need.

Early on the morning of the day he had fixed for the nuptials, Gualtieri, his preparations now complete, mounted his horse together with all the people who had come to do him honor, and said:

"Gentlemen, it is time for us to go and fetch the bride."

He then set forth with the whole of the company in train, and eventually they came to the village and made their way to the house of the girl's father, where they met her as she was returning with water from the fountain, making great haste so that she could go with other women to see Gualtieri's bride arriving. As soon as Gualtieri caught sight of her, he called to her by her name, which was Griselda, and asked her where her father was, to which she blushingly replied:

"My lord, he is at home."

So Gualtieri dismounted, and having ordered everyone to wait for him outside, he went alone into the humble dwelling, where he found the girl's father, whose name was Giannùcole, and said to him:

"I have come to marry Griselda, but first I want to ask her certain questions in your presence." He then asked her whether, if he were to marry her, she would always try to please him and never be upset by anything he said or did, whether she would obey him, and many other questions of this sort, to all of which she answered that she would.

Whereupon Gualtieri, having taken her by the hand, led her out of the house, and in the presence of his whole company and of all the other people there he caused her to be stripped naked. Then he called for the clothes and shoes which he had had specially made, and quickly got her to put them on, after which he caused a crown to be placed upon the dishevelled hair of her head. And just as everyone was wondering what this might signify, he said:

"Gentlemen, this is the woman I intend to marry, provided she will have me as her husband." Then, turning to Griselda, who was so embarrassed that she hardly knew where to look, he said: "Griselda, will you have me as your wedded husband?"

To which she replied:

"I will, my lord."

"And I will have you as my wedded wife," said Gualtieri, and he married her then and there before all the people present. He then helped her mount a palfrey, and led her back, honorably attended, to his house, where the nuptials were as splendid and as sumptuous, and the rejoicing as unrestrained, as if he had married the King of France's daughter.

Along with her new clothes, the young bride appeared to take on a new lease of life, and she seemed a different woman entirely. She was endowed, as we have said, with a fine figure and beautiful features, and lovely as she already was, she now acquired so confident, graceful and decorous a manner that she could have been taken for the daughter, not of the shepherd Giannùcole, but of some great nobleman, and consequently everyone who had known her before her marriage was filled with astonishment. But apart from this, she was so obedient to her husband, and so compliant to his wishes, that he thought himself the happiest and most contented man on earth. At the same time she was so gracious and benign towards her husband's subjects, that each and every one of them was glad to honor her, and accorded her his unselfish devotion, praying for her happiness, prosperity, and greater glory. And whereas they had been wont to say that Gualtieri had shown some lack of discretion in taking this woman as his wife, they now regarded him as the wisest and most discerning man on earth. For no one apart from Gualtieri could ever have perceived the noble qualities that lay concealed beneath her ragged and rustic attire.

In short, she comported herself in such a manner that she quickly earned widespread acclaim for her virtuous deeds and excellent character not only in her husband's domain but also in the world at large; and those who had formerly censured Gualtieri for choosing to marry her were now compelled to reverse their opinion.

Not long after she had gone to live with Gualtieri she conceived a child, and in the fullness of time, to her husband's enormous joy, she bore him a daughter. But shortly thereafter Gualtieri was seized with the strange desire to test Griselda's patience, by subjecting her to constant provocation and making her life unbearable.

At first he lashed her with his tongue, feigning to be angry and claiming that his subjects were thoroughly disgruntled with her on account of her lowly condition, especially now that they saw her bearing children; and he said they were greatly distressed about this infant daughter of theirs, of whom they did nothing but grumble.

The lady betrayed no sign of bitterness on hearing these words, and without changing her expression she said to him:

"My lord, deal with me as you think best[7] for your own good name and peace of mind, for I shall rest content whatever you decide, knowing myself to be their inferior and that I was unworthy of the honor which you so generously bestowed upon me."

This reply was much to Gualtieri's liking, for it showed him that she had not been puffed with pride by any honor that he or others had paid her.

A little while later, having told his wife in general terms that his subjects could not abide the daughter she had borne him, he gave certain instructions to one of his attendants, whom he sent to Griselda. The man looked very sorrowful, and said:

"My lady, if I do not wish to die, I must do as my lord commands me. He has ordered me to take this daughter of yours, and to . . ." And his voice trailed off into silence.

On hearing these words and perceiving the man's expression, Griselda, recalling what she had been told, concluded that he had been instructed to murder her child. So she quickly picked it up from its cradle, kissed it, gave it her blessing, and albeit she felt that her heart was about to break, placed the child in the arms of the servant without any trace of emotion, saying:

"There: do exactly as your lord, who is my lord too, has instructed you. But do not leave her to be devoured by the beasts and the birds, unless that is what he has ordered you to do."

The servant took away the little girl and reported Griselda's words to Gualtieri, who, marvelling at her constancy, sent him with the child to a kinswoman of his in Bologna,[8] requesting her to rear and educate her carefully, but without ever making it known whose daughter she was.

Then it came about that his wife once more became pregnant, and in due course she gave birth to a son, which pleased Gualtieri enormously. But not being content with the mischief he had done already, he abused her more viciously than ever, and one day he glowered at her angrily and said:

"Woman, from the day you produced this infant son, the people have made my life a complete misery, so bitterly do they resent the thought of a grandson of Giannùcole succeeding me as their lord. So unless I want to be deposed,

7. See Luke 1.38, where the Virgin Mary replies to the Angel Gabriel, "Be it unto me according to thy word." 8. A city in northern Italy, not far from Florence.

I'm afraid I shall be forced to do as I did before, and eventually to leave you and marry someone else."

His wife listened patiently, and all she replied was:

"My lord, look to your own comfort, see that you fulfil your wishes, and spare no thought for me, since nothing brings me pleasure unless it pleases you also."

Before many days had elapsed, Gualtieri sent for his son in the same way that he had sent for his daughter, and having likewise pretended to have had the child put to death, he sent him, like the little girl, to Bologna. To all of this his wife reacted no differently, either in her speech or in her looks, than she had on the previous occasion, much to the astonishment of Gualtieri, who told himself that no other woman could have remained so impassive. But for the fact that he had observed her doting upon the children for as long as he allowed her to do so, he would have assumed that she was glad to be rid of them, whereas he knew that she was too judicious to behave in any other way.

His subjects, thinking he had caused the children to be murdered, roundly condemned him and judged him a cruel tyrant, whilst his wife became the object of their deepest compassion. But to the women who offered her their sympathy in the loss of her children, all she ever said was that the decision of their father was good enough for her.

Many years after the birth of his daughter, Gualtieri decided that the time had come to put Griselda's patience to the final test. So he told a number of his men that in no circumstances could he put up with Griselda as his wife any longer, having now come to realize that his marriage was an aberration of his youth. He would therefore do everything in his power to obtain a dispensation from the Pope, enabling him to divorce Griselda and marry someone else. For this he was chided severely by many worthy men, but his only reply was that it had to be done.

On learning of her husband's intentions, from which it appeared she would have to return to her father's house, in order perhaps to look after the sheep as she had in the past, meanwhile seeing the man she adored being cherished by some other woman, Griselda was secretly filled with despair. But she prepared herself to endure this final blow as stoically as she had borne Fortune's earlier assaults.

Shortly thereafter, Gualtieri arranged for some counterfeit letters of his to arrive from Rome, and led his subjects to believe that in these, the Pope had granted him permission to abandon Griselda and remarry.

He accordingly sent for Griselda, and before a large number of people he said to her:

"Woman, I have had a dispensation from the Pope, allowing me to leave you and take another wife. Since my ancestors were great noblemen and rulers of these lands, whereas yours have always been peasants, I intend that you shall no longer be my wife, but return to Giannùcole's house with the dowry you brought me, after which I shall bring another lady here. I have already chosen her and she is far better suited to a man of my condition.'

On hearing these words, the lady, with an effort beyond the power of any normal woman's nature, suppressed her tears and replied:

"My lord, I have always known that my lowly condition was totally at odds with your nobility, and that it is to God and to yourself that I owe whatever standing I possess. Nor have I ever regarded this as a gift that I might keep and cherish as my own, but rather as something I have borrowed; and now that you want me to return it, I must give it back to you with good grace. Here is the ring with which you married me: take it. As to your ordering me to take away the dowry that I brought, you will require no accountant, nor will I need a purse or a pack-horse, for this to be done. For it has not escaped my memory that you took me naked as on the day I was born.[9] If you think it proper that the body in which I have borne your children should be seen by all the people, I shall go away naked. But in return for my virginity, which I brought to you and cannot retrieve, I trust you will at least allow me, in addition to my dowry, to take one shift away with me."

Gualtieri wanted above all else to burst into tears, but maintaining a stern expression he said:

"Very well, you may take a shift."

All the people present implored Gualtieri to let her have a dress, so that she who had been his wife for thirteen years and more would not have to suffer the indignity of leaving his house in a shift, like a pauper; but their pleas were unavailing. And so Griselda, wearing a shift, barefoot, and with nothing to cover her head, having bidden them farewell, set forth from Gualtieri's house and returned to her father amid the weeping and the wailing of all who set eyes upon her.

Giannùcole, who had never thought it possible that Gualtieri would keep his daughter as his wife, and was daily expecting this to happen, had preserved the clothes she discarded on the morning Gualtieri had married her. So he brought them to her, and Griselda, having put them on, applied herself as before to the menial chores in her father's house, bravely enduring the cruel assault of hostile Fortune.

No sooner did Gualtieri drive Griselda away, than he gave his subjects to understand that he was betrothed to a daughter of one of the Counts of Panago.[1] And having ordered that grandiose preparations were to be made for the nuptials, he sent for Griselda and said to her:

"I am about to fetch home this new bride of mine, and from the moment she sets foot inside the house, I intend to accord her an honorable welcome. As you know, I have no women here who can set the rooms in order for me, or attend to many of the things that a festive occasion of this sort requires. No one knows better than you how to handle these household affairs, so I want you to make all the necessary arrangements. Invite all the ladies you need, and receive them as though you were mistress of the house. And when the nuptials are over, you can go back home to your father."

Since Griselda was unable to lay aside her love for Gualtieri as readily as she had dispensed with her good fortune, his words pierced her heart like so many knives. But she replied:

"My lord, I am ready to do as you ask."[2]

And so, in her coarse, thick, woollen garments, Griselda returned to the house she had quitted shortly before in her shift, and started to sweep and tidy the various chambers. On her instructions, the beds were draped with hangings, the benches in the halls were suitably adorned, the kitchen was

9. See Job 1.21: "Naked came I out of my mother's womb, and naked shall I return thither: the Lord gave, and the Lord hath taken away." 1. An area near Bologna. 2. See again Luke 1.38: "Behold the handmaid of the Lord."

made ready; and she set her hand, as though she were a petty serving wench, to every conceivable household task, never stopping to draw breath until she had everything prepared and arranged as befitted the occasion.

Having done all this, she caused invitations to be sent, in Gualtieri's name, to all the ladies living in those parts, and began to await the event. And when at last the nuptial day arrived, heedless of her beggarly attire, she bade a cheerful welcome to each of the lady guests, displaying all the warmth and courtesy of a lady of the manor.

Gualtieri's children having meanwhile been carefully reared by his kinswoman in Bologna, who had married into the family of the Courts of Panago, the girl was now twelve years old, the loveliest creature ever seen, whilst the boy had reached the age of six. Gualtieri had sent word to his kinswoman's husband, asking him to do him the kindness of bringing this daughter of his to Saluzzo along with her little brother, to see that she was nobly and honorably escorted, and to tell everyone he met that he was taking her to marry Gualtieri, without revealing who she really was to a living soul.

In accordance with the Marquis's request, the gentleman set forth with the girl and her brother and a noble company, and a few days later, shortly before the hour of breakfast, he arrived at Saluzzo, where he found that all the folk thereabouts, and numerous others from neighboring parts, were waiting for Gualtieri's latest bride.

After being welcomed by the ladies, she made her way to the hall where the tables were set, and Griselda, just as we have described her, went cordially up to meet her, saying:

"My lady, you are welcome."

The ladies, who in vain had implored Gualtieri to see that Griselda remained in another room, or to lend her one of the dresses that had once been hers, so that she would not cut such a sorry figure in front of his guests, took their seats at table and addressed themselves to the meal. All eyes were fixed upon the girl, and everyone said that Gualtieri had made a good exchange. But Griselda praised her as warmly as anyone present, speaking no less admiringly of her little brother.

Gualtieri felt that he had now seen all he wished to see of the patience of his lady, for he perceived that no event, however singular, produced the slightest change in her demeanor, and he was certain that this was not because of her obtuseness, as he knew her to be very intelligent. He therefore considered that the time had come for him to free her from the rancor that he judged her to be hiding beneath her tranquil outward expression. And having summoned her to his table, before all the people present he smiled at her and said:

"What do you think of our new bride?"

"My lord," replied Griselda, "I think very well of her. And if, as I believe, her wisdom matches her beauty, I have no doubt whatever that your life with her will bring you greater happiness than any gentleman on earth has ever known. But with all my heart I beg you not to inflict those same wounds upon her that you imposed upon her predecessor, for I doubt whether she could withstand them, not only because she is younger, but also because she has had a refined upbringing, whereas the other had to face continual hardship from her infancy."

On observing that Griselda was firmly convinced that the young lady was to be his wife, and that even so she allowed no hint of resentment to escape her lips, Gualtieri got her to sit down beside him, and said:

"Griselda, the time has come for you to reap the reward of your unfailing patience, and for those who considered me a cruel and bestial tyrant, to know that whatever I have done was done of set purpose, for I wished to show you how to be a wife, to teach these people how to choose and keep a wife, and to guarantee my own peace and quiet for as long as we were living beneath the same roof. When I came to take a wife, I was greatly afraid that this peace would be denied me, and in order to prove otherwise I tormented and provoked you in the ways you have seen. But as I have never known you to oppose my wishes, I now intend, being persuaded that you can offer me all the happiness I desired, to restore to you in a single instant that which I took from you little by little, and delectably assuage the pains I have inflicted upon you. Receive with gladsome heart, then, this girl whom you believe to be my bride, and also her brother. These are our children, whom you and many others have long supposed that I caused to be cruelly murdered; and I am your husband, who loves you above all else, for I think I can boast that there is no other man on earth whose contentment in his wife exceeds my own."

Having spoken these words, he embraced and kissed Griselda, who by now was weeping with joy; then they both got up from table and made their way to the place where their daughter sat listening in utter amazement to these tidings. And after they had fondly embraced the girl and her brother, the mystery was unravelled to her, as well as to many of the others who were present.

The ladies rose from table in transports of joy, and escorted Griselda to a chamber, where, with greater assurance of her future happiness, they divested her of her tattered garments and clothed her anew in one of her stately robes. And as their lady and their mistress, a rôle which even in her rags had seemed to be hers, they led her back to the hall, where she and Gualtieri rejoiced with the children in a manner marvellous to behold.

Everyone being delighted with the turn that events had taken, the feasting and the merrymaking were redoubled, and continued unabated for the next few days. Gualtieri was acknowledged to be very wise, though the trials to which he had subjected his lady were regarded as harsh and intolerable, whilst Griselda was accounted the wisest of all.

The Count of Panago returned a few days later to Bologna, and Gualtieri, having removed Giannùcole from his drudgery, set him up in a style befitting his father-in-law, so that he lived in great comfort and honor for the rest of his days. As for Gualtieri himself, having married off his daughter to a gentleman of renown, he lived long and contentedly with Griselda, never failing to honor her to the best of his ability.

What more needs to be said, except that celestial spirits may sometimes descend even into the houses of the poor, whilst there are those in royal palaces who would be better employed as swineherds than as rulers of men? Who else but Griselda could have endured so cheerfully the cruel and unheard of trials that Gualtieri imposed upon her without shedding a tear? For perhaps it would have served him right if he had chanced upon a wife, who, being driven from the house in her shift, had found some other man to shake her skin-coat for her, earning herself a fine new dress in the process.

SIR GAWAIN AND THE GREEN KNIGHT
1380?

Although concerned with King Arthur and his knights, *Sir Gawain and the Green Knight* is far from a typical Arthurian romance. It focuses with unusual intensity on a single knight, it displays a remarkable economy and elegance of narrative form, and it deals not with the usual deeds of martial prowess but with an inner moral testing. In addition, it is written not only in verse, unlike the vast majority of late medieval romances, but in a verse of such subtlety and beauty that the work stands out as a masterpiece of literary craftsmanship. *Gawain* was composed sometime between 1370 and 1390 in the northwest midlands in England, in an area near the present city of Birmingham, and its anonymous author used alliteration for his primary poetic form. Each line has four stresses, at least two and usually three of which fall on words that begin with the same sound: "King Arthur was counted most courteous of all." The only exception to this pattern is the five-line verse that ends each stanza, known as a *bob and wheel*. The translation reproduces this pattern with great skill and fidelity, one result of which is the occasional use of unusual words or ordinary words in slightly unaccustomed senses: some of these have been glossed, while the meanings of others may be surmised from the context or, if necessary, found in a dictionary. This minor difficulty also replicates the experience of reading the original, which is written not only in a provincial dialect but with a deliberately artful vocabulary. The poem is, as the poet says, "linked in measures meetly / By letters tried and true," and much of its success derives from its verbal virtuosity.

In using this alliterative line the poet was harking back to the tradition of Anglo-Saxon verse, as represented in this anthology by *Beowulf* and by the lyric poem *The Ruin*. We do not know how this tradition survived from the middle of the twelfth century, when it disappeared from view under the influence of continental forms imported by the conquering Normans, until the second half of the fourteenth, when it burst forth in an impressive number of excellent poems. But the *Gawain*-poet seems to have been aware that he was using a native tradition, for one of the themes of his work is the contrast between Bercilak, who for all his sophistication is powerfully linked to a vividly described natural world, and Gawain, the representative of an elegant court that may be a bit too civilized. The poem is constructed from two originally separate narrative motifs, "The Beheading Game" and "The Exchange of Winnings." In both cases Gawain must meet a standard of behavior that is both courtly and more than courtly. He must show himself to be honorable both in submitting to the blow of an ax that must surely prove fatal and in exchanging with his host what each man has won that day. This second test then has an added challenge: each morning the host goes out hunting, while his wife offers *herself* to her husband's guest. Much of the comedy of the poem derives from the way in which Gawain refuses this attractive offer while avoiding any hint of discourtesy. But in both of the main tests the hero's resolve is weakened by the most natural of impulses: self-preservation. When he finally does accept from the lady what she says is a magic belt that will preserve his life, he violates his agreement with his host by not offering this gift in exchange for the pelt he receives. When his deception is discovered, Gawain is deeply humiliated and berates both himself and the lady, who has, he thinks, finally seduced him into disloyalty. But Bercilak is far less disturbed: he recognizes that Gawain is, after all, only a human being, not a paragon of perfect virtue. One way the poet stresses this theme is in the contrast between the pentangle that Gawain carries on his shield—a symbol of perfect fidelity—and the green baldrick that he comes to wear as a sign of his fallibility. When upon his return to the court Arthur and his household adopt the green baldrick as a sign of honor, Gawain is suddenly placed in the unusual—and difficult—position of knowing more about human nature, both his own and others, than does his sovereign. And oddly enough, not even the reader can be certain that Gawain's acceptance of the baldrick, which he sees as his failure, did not in fact save his life.

One of the most striking aspects of the poem is the symmetry it establishes between Bercilak's three days of hunting and the three wooing scenes between Gawain and his host's wife. The precise significance of this symmetry has never been satisfactorily explained, but every reader recognizes its instinctive fittingness. As Bercilak rushes through the wintry landscape in pursuit of his prey, Gawain uses his verbal dexterity to evade the lady's none too subtle advances. Gawain may be warmly tucked up in bed, but we can well imagine that he would prefer to be testing his mettle in a more active, less cerebral way. But his fate is to be denied the opportunity to act, and perhaps the most subtle aspect of the poet's genius is his ability to get us to admire a hero who must learn to succeed by doing nothing.

An accessible edition of the original poem is by J. A. Burrow (1972). Helpful articles, and a full bibliography, are available in Derek Brewer and Jonathan Gibson, eds., *A Companion to the Gawain-Poet* (1997).

PRONOUNCING GLOSSARY

The following list uses common English syllables and stress accents to provide rough equivalents of selected words whose pronunciation may be unfamiliar to the general reader.

Bercilak: *behr-see-lak'*   Sauvage: *soh-vazh'*

Sir Gawain and the Green Knight[1]

PART I

Since the siege and the assault was ceased at Troy,
The walls breached and burnt down to brands and ashes,
The knight that had knotted the nets of deceit
Was impeached for his perfidy,[2] proven most true,
It was high-born Aeneas and his haughty race   5
That since prevailed over provinces, and proudly reigned
Over well-nigh all the wealth of the West Isles.[3]
Great Romulus[4] to Rome repairs in haste;
With boast and with bravery builds he that city
And names it with his own name, that it now bears.   10
Ticius to Tuscany,[5] and towers raises,
Langobard[6] in Lombardy lays out homes,
And far over the French Sea, Felix Brutus[7]
On many broad hills and high Britain he sets,[8]
                    most fair.   15
          Where war and wrack and wonder
          By shifts have sojourned there,
          And bliss by turns with blunder
          In that land's lot had share.

1. Translated by Marie Borroff. Many of the notes are by E. Talbot Donaldson.   2. The treacherous knight is either Aeneas himself or Antenor, both of whom were, according to medieval tradition, traitors to their city, Troy; but Aeneas was actually tried ("impeached") by the Greeks for his refusal to hand over to them his sister Polyxena.   3. Perhaps western Europe.   4. The legendary founder of Rome is here given Trojan ancestry, like Aeneas.   5. A region north of Rome; modern Florence is located in it. *Ticius:* not otherwise known.   6. The reputed founder of Lombardy, a region in the north centered on modern Milan.   7. Great-grandson of Aeneas and legendary founder of Britain; not elsewhere given the name Felix (Latin "happy"). *French Sea:* The North Sea, including the English Channel.   8. Establishes.

And since this Britain was built by this baron great,   20
Bold boys bred there, in broils delighting,
That did in their day many a deed most dire.
More marvels have happened in this merry land
Than in any other I know, since that olden time,
But of those that here built, of British kings,   25
King Arthur was counted most courteous of all,
Wherefore an adventure I aim to unfold,
That a marvel of might some men think it,
And one unmatched among Arthur's wonders.
If you will listen to my lay but a little while,   30
As I heard it in hall, I shall hasten to tell
                              anew,
              As it was fashioned featly
              In tale of derring-do,
              And linked in measures meetly[9]   35
              By letters tried and true.

This king lay at Camelot[1] at Christmastide;
Many good knights and gay his guests were there,
Arrayed of the Round Table rightful brothers,[2]
With feasting and fellowship and carefree mirth.   40
There true men contended in tournaments many,
Joined there in jousting these gentle knights,
Then came to the court for carol-dancing,
For the feast was in force full fifteen days,
With all the meat and the mirth that men could devise,   45
Such gaiety and glee, glorious to hear,
Brave din by day, dancing by night.
High were their hearts in halls and chambers,
These lords and these ladies, for life was sweet.
In peerless pleasures passed they their days,   50
The most noble knights known under Christ,
And the loveliest ladies that lived on earth ever,
And he the comeliest king, that that court holds,
For all this fair folk in their first age
                              were still.   55
              Happiest of mortal kind,
              King noblest famed of will;
              You would now go far to find
              So hardy a host on hill.

While the New Year was new, but yesternight come,   60
This fair folk at feast two-fold was served,
When the king and his company were come in together,
The chanting in chapel achieved and ended.
Clerics and all the court acclaimed the glad season,
Cried Noel anew, good news to men;   65

9. Suitably.   1. Capital of Arthur's kingdom, presumably located in southwest England or southern Wales.   2. According to legend, the Round Table was made by Merlin, the wise magician who had helped Arthur become king after a dispute broke out among Arthur's knights about precedence: it seated one hundred knights. The table described in the poem is not round.

Then gallants gather gaily, hand-gifts to make,
Called them out clearly, claimed them by hand,
Bickered long and busily about those gifts.
Ladies laughed aloud, though losers they were,
And he that won was not angered, as well you will know.[3]   70
All this mirth they made until meat was served;
When they had washed them worthily, they went to their seats,
The best seated above, as best it beseemed,
Guenevere the goodly queen gay in the midst
On a dais well-decked and duly arrayed   75
With costly silk curtains, a canopy over,
Of Toulouse and Turkestan tapestries rich,
All broidered and bordered with the best gems
Ever brought into Britain, with bright pennies
                    to pay.   80
          Fair queen, without a flaw,
          She glanced with eyes of grey.
          A seemlier[4] that once he saw,
          In truth, no man could say.

But Arthur would not eat till all were served;   85
So light was his lordly heart, and a little boyish;
His life he liked lively—the less he cared
To be lying for long, or long to sit,
So busy his young blood, his brain so wild.
And also a point of pride pricked him in heart,   90
For he nobly had willed, he would never eat
On so high a holiday, till he had heard first
Of some fair feat or fray, some far-borne tale,
Of some marvel of might, that he might trust,
By champions of chivalry achieved in arms,   95
Or some suppliant came seeking some single knight
To join with him in jousting, in jeopardy each
To lay life for life, and leave it to fortune
To afford him on field fair hap[5] or other.
Such is the king's custom, when his court he holds   100
At each far-famed feast amid his fair host
                  so dear.
          The stout king stands in state
          Till a wonder shall appear;
          He leads, with heart elate,   105
          High mirth in the New Year.

So he stands there in state, the stout young king,
Talking before the high table[6] of trifles fair.
There Gawain the good knight by Guenevere sits,
With Agravain à la dure main[7] on her other side,   110
Both knights of renown, and nephews of the king.
Bishop Baldwin above begins the table,

3. The dispensing of New Year's gifts seems to have involved kissing.   **4.** More suitable and pleasing (queen).   **5.** Good luck.   **6.** The high table is on a dais; the side tables (lines 115) are on the main floor and run along the walls at a right angle to the high table.   **7.** Of the hard hand.

And Yvain, son of Urien, ate with him there.
These few with the fair queen were fittingly served;
At the side-tables sat many stalwart knights.   115
Then the first course comes, with clamor of trumpets
That were bravely bedecked with bannerets bright,
With noise of new drums and the noble pipes.
Wild were the warbles that wakened that day
In strains that stirred many strong men's hearts.   120
There dainties were dealt out, dishes rare,
Choice fare to choose, on chargers so many
That scarce was there space to set before the people
The service of silver, with sundry meats,
                                 on cloth.   125
              Each fair guest freely there
              Partakes, and nothing loth;[8]
              Twelve dishes before each pair;
              Good beer and bright wine both.

Of the service itself I need say no more,   130
For well you will know no tittle was wanting.
Another noise and a new was well-nigh at hand,
That the lord might have leave his life to nourish;
For scarce were the sweet strains still in the hall,
And the first course come to that company fair,   135
There hurtles in at the hall-door an unknown rider,
One the greatest on ground in growth of his frame:
From broad neck to buttocks so bulky and thick,
And his loins and his legs so long and so great,
Half a giant on earth I hold him to be,   140
But believe him no less than the largest of men,
And that the seemliest in his stature to see, as he rides,
For in back and in breast though his body was grim,
His waist in its width was worthily small,
And formed with every feature in fair accord   145
                                 was he.
              Great wonder grew in hall
              At his hue most strange to see,
              For man and gear and all
              Were green as green could be.   150

And in guise all of green, the gear and the man:
A coat cut close, that clung to his sides,
And a mantle to match, made with a lining
Of furs cut and fitted—the fabric was noble,
Embellished all with ermine, and his hood beside,   155
That was loosed from his locks, and laid on his shoulders.
With trim hose and tight, the same tint of green,
His great calves were girt, and gold spurs under
He bore on silk bands that embellished his heels,
And footgear well-fashioned, for riding most fit.   160

8. Not unwillingly.

And all his vesture verily was verdant green;
Both the bosses[9] on his belt and other bright gems
That were richly ranged on his raiment noble
About himself and his saddle, set upon silk,
That to tell half the trifles would tax my wits,   165
The butterflies and birds embroidered thereon
In green of the gayest, with many a gold thread.
The pendants of the breast-band, the princely crupper,[1]
And the bars of the bit were brightly enameled;
The stout stirrups were green, that steadied his feet,   170
And the bows of the saddle and the side-panels both,
That gleamed all and glinted with green gems about.
The steed he bestrides of that same green
               so bright.
          A green horse great and thick;   175
          A headstrong steed of might;
          In broidered bridle quick,
          Mount matched man aright.

Gay was this goodly man in guise all of green,
And the hair of his head to his horse suited;   180
Fair flowing tresses enfold his shoulders;
A beard big as a bush on his breast hangs,
That with his heavy hair, that from his head falls,
Was evened all about above both his elbows,
That half his arms thereunder were hid in the fashion   185
Of a king's cap-à-dos,[2] that covers his throat.
The mane of that mighty horse much to it like,
Well curled and becombed, and cunningly knotted
With filaments of fine gold amid the fair green,
Here a strand of the hair, here one of gold;   190
His tail and his foretop twin in their hue,
And bound both with a band of a bright green
That was decked adown the dock[3] with dazzling stones
And tied tight at the top with a triple knot
Where many bells well burnished rang bright and clear.   195
Such a mount in his might, nor man on him riding,
None had seen, I dare swear, with sight in that hall
               so grand.
          As lightning quick and light
          He looked to all at hand;   200
          It seemed that no man might
          His deadly dints withstand.

Yet had he no helm, nor hauberk[4] neither,
Nor plate, nor appurtenance appending to arms,
Nor shaft pointed sharp, nor shield for defense,   205
But in his one hand he had a holly bob
That is goodliest in green when groves are bare,

---

9. Ornamental knobs.   1. *Breast-band . . . crupper:* parts of the horse's harness.   2. Or *capados,* interpreted by the translator as a garment covering its wearer "from head to back."   3. The solid part of the tail.   4. Tunic of chain mail.

And an ax in his other, a huge and immense,
A wicked piece of work in words to expound:
The head on its haft was an ell[5] long;   210
The spike of green steel, resplendent with gold;
The blade burnished bright, with a broad edge,
As well shaped to shear as a sharp razor;
Stout was the stave in the strong man's gripe,
That was wound all with iron to the weapon's end,   215
With engravings in green of goodliest work.
A lace lightly about, that led to a knot,
Was looped in by lengths along the fair haft,
And tassels thereto attached in a row,
With buttons of bright green, brave to behold.   220
This horseman hurtles in, and the hall enters;
Riding to the high dais, recked he no danger;
Not a greeting he gave as the guests he o'erlooked,
Nor wasted his words, but "Where is," he said,
"The captain of this crowd? Keenly I wish   225
To see that sire with sight, and to himself say
          my say."
                   He swaggered all about
                   To scan the host so gay;
                   He halted, as if in doubt   230
                   Who in that hall held sway.

There were stares on all sides as the stranger spoke,
For much did they marvel what it might mean
That a horseman and a horse should have such a hue,
Grow green as the grass, and greener, it seemed,   235
Than green fused on gold more glorious by far.
All the onlookers eyed him, and edged nearer,
And awaited in wonder what he would do,
For many sights had they seen, but such a one never,
So that phantom and faerie the folk there deemed it,   240
Therefore chary of answer was many a champion bold,
And stunned at his strong words stone-still they sat
In a swooning silence in the stately hall.
As all were slipped into sleep, so slackened their speech
          apace   245
                   Not all, I think, for dread,
                   But some of courteous grace
                   Let him who was their head
                   Be spokesman in that place.

Then Arthur before the high dais that entrance beholds,   250
And hailed him, as behooved, for he had no fear,
And said "Fellow, in faith you have found fair welcome;
The head of this hostelry Arthur am I;
Leap lightly down, and linger, I pray,
And the tale of your intent you shall tell us after."   255

5. Three or four feet long.

"Nay, so help me," said the other, "He that on high sits,
To tarry here any time, 'twas not mine errand;
But as the praise of you, prince, is puffed up so high,
And your court and your company are counted the best,
Stoutest under steel-gear on steeds to ride,   260
Worthiest of their works the wide world over,
And peerless to prove in passages of arms,
And courtesy here is carried to its height,
And so at this season I have sought you out.
You may be certain by the branch that I bear in hand   265
That I pass here in peace, and would part friends,
For had I come to this court on combat bent,
I have a hauberk at home, and a helm beside,
A shield and a sharp spear, shining bright,
And other weapons to wield, I ween[6] well, to boot,   270
But as I willed no war, I wore no metal.
But if you be so bold as all men believe,
You will graciously grant the game that I ask
                by right."
                Arthur answer gave   275
                And said, "Sir courteous knight,
                If contest here you crave,
                You shall not fail to fight."

"Nay, to fight, in good faith, is far from my thought;
There are about on these benches but beardless children,   280
Were I here in full arms on a haughty steed,
For measured against mine, their might is puny.
And so I call in this court for a Christmas game,
For 'tis Yule and New Year, and many young bloods about;
If any in this house such hardihood claims,   285
Be so bold in his blood, his brain so wild,
As stoutly to strike one stroke for another,
I shall give him as my gift this gisarme[7] noble,
This ax, that is heavy enough, to handle as he likes,
And I shall bide[8] the first blow, as bare as I sit.   290
If there be one so wilful my words to assay,
Let him leap hither lightly, lay hold of this weapon;
I quitclaim it forever, keep it[9] as his own,
And I shall stand him a stroke, steady on this floor,
So you grant me the guerdon[1] to give him another,   295
                sans[2] blame.
                In a twelvemonth and a day
                He shall have of me the same;
                Now be it seen straightway
                Who dares take up the game."   300

If he astonished them at first, stiller were then
All that household in hall, the high and the low;
The stranger on his green steed stirred in the saddle,

6. Believe.   7. Weapon.   8. Endure.   9. I.e., let him keep it.   1. Reward.   2. Without.

And roisterously his red eyes he rolled all about,
Bent his bristling brows, that were bright green,   305
Wagged his beard as he watched who would arise.
When the court kept its counsel he coughed aloud,
And cleared his throat coolly, the clearer to speak:
"What, is this Arthur's house," said that horseman then,
"Whose fame is so fair in far realms and wide?   310
Where is now your arrogance and your awesome deeds,
Your valor and your victories and your vaunting words?
Now are the revel and renown of the Round Table
Overwhelmed with a word of one man's speech,
For all cower and quake, and no cut felt!"   315
With this he laughs so loud that the lord grieved;
The blood for sheer shame shot to his face,
                              and pride.
                    With rage his face flushed red,
                    And so did all beside.   320
                    Then the king as bold man bred
                    Toward the stranger took a stride.

And said "Sir, now we see you will say but folly,
Which whoso has sought, it suits that he find.
No guest here is aghast of your great words.   325
Give to me your gisarme, in God's own name,
And the boon you have begged shall straight be granted."
He leaps to him lightly, lays hold of his weapon;
The green fellow on foot fiercely alights.
Now has Arthur his ax, and the haft grips,   330
And sternly stirs it about, on striking bent.
The stranger before him stood there erect,
Higher than any in the house by a head and more;
With stern look as he stood, he stroked his beard,
And with undaunted countenance drew down his coat,   335
No more moved nor dismayed for his mighty dints
Than any bold man on bench had brought him a drink
                              of wine.
                    Gawain by Guenevere
                    Toward the king doth now incline: 340
                    "I beseech, before all here,
                    That this melee may be mine."

"Would you grant me the grace," said Gawain to the king,
"To be gone from this bench and stand by you there,
If I without discourtesy might quit this board,   345
And if my liege lady[3] misliked it not,
I would come to your counsel before your court noble.
For I find it not fit, as in faith it is known,
When such a boon is begged before all these knights,
Though you be tempted thereto, to take it on yourself   350
While so bold men about upon benches sit,

3. Lady entitled to the knight's feudal service.

That no host under heaven is hardier of will,
Nor better brothers-in-arms where battle is joined;
I am the weakest, well I know, and of wit feeblest;
And the loss of my life would be least of any;   355
That I have you for uncle is my only praise;
My body, but for your blood, is barren of worth;
And for that this folly befits not a king,
And 'tis I that have asked it, it ought to be mine,
And if my claim be not comely let all this court judge,   360
                              in sight."
          The court assays the claim,
          And in counsel all unite
          To give Gawain the game
          And release the king outright.   365

Then the king called the knight to come to his side,
And he rose up readily, and reached him with speed,
Bows low to his lord, lays hold of the weapon,
And he releases it lightly, and lifts up his hand,
And gives him God's blessing, and graciously prays   370
That his heart and his hand may be hardy both.
"Keep, cousin," said the king, "what you cut with this day,
And if you rule it aright, then readily, I know,
You shall stand the stroke it will strike after."
Gawain goes to the guest with gisarme in hand,   375
And boldly he bides there, abashed not a whit.
Then hails he Sir Gawain, the horseman in green:
"Recount we our contract, ere you come further.
First I ask and adjure you, how you are called
That you tell me true, so that trust it I may."   380
"In good faith," said the good knight, "Gawain am I
Whose buffet befalls you, whate'er betide after,
And at this time twelvemonth take from you another
With what weapon you will, and with no man else
                              alive."   385
          The other nods assent:
          "Sir Gawain, as I may thrive,
          I am wondrous well content
          That you this dint shall drive."

"Sir Gawain," said the Green Knight, "By God, I rejoice   390
That your fist shall fetch this favor I seek,
And you have readily rehearsed, and in right terms,
Each clause of my covenant with the king your lord,
Save that you shall assure me, sir, upon oath,
That you shall seek me yourself, wheresoever you deem   395
My lodgings may lie, and look for such wages
As you have offered me here before all this host."
"What is the way there?" said Gawain, "Where do you dwell?
I heard never of your house, by Him that made me,
Nor I know you not, knight, your name nor your court.   400
But tell me truly thereof, and teach me your name,

And I shall fare forth to find you, so far as I may,
And this I say in good certain, and swear upon oath."
"That is enough in New Year, you need say no more,"
Said the knight in the green to Gawain the noble,   405
"If I tell you true, when I have taken your knock,
And if you handily have hit, you shall hear straightway
Of my house and my home and my own name;
Then follow in my footsteps by faithful accord.
And if I spend no speech, you shall speed the better: 410
You can feast with your friends, nor further trace
                        my tracks.
                Now hold your grim tool steady
                And show us how it hacks."
                "Gladly, sir; all ready,"   415
                Says Gawain; he strokes the ax.

The Green Knight upon ground girds him with care:
Bows a bit with his head, and bares his flesh:
His long lovely locks he laid over his crown,
Let the naked nape for the need be shown.   420
Gawain grips to his ax and gathers it aloft—
The left foot on the floor before him he set—
Brought it down deftly upon the bare neck,
That the shock of the sharp blow shivered the bones
And cut the flesh cleanly and clove it in twain,   425
That the blade of bright steel bit into the ground.
The head was hewn off and fell to the floor;
Many found it at their feet, as forth it rolled;
The blood gushed from the body, bright on the green,
Yet fell not the fellow, nor faltered a whit,   430
But stoutly he starts forth upon stiff shanks,
And as all stood staring he stretched forth his hand,
Laid hold of his head and heaved it aloft,
Then goes to the green steed, grasps the bridle,
Steps into the stirrup, bestrides his mount,   435
And his head by the hair in his hand holds,
And as steady he sits in the stately saddle
As he had met with no mishap, nor missing were
                        his head.
                His bulk about he haled,[4]   440
                That fearsome body that bled;
                There were many in the court that quailed
                Before all his say was said.

For the head in his hand he holds right up;
Toward the first on the dais directs he the face,   445
And it lifted up its lids, and looked with wide eyes,
And said as much with its mouth as now you may hear:
"Sir Gawain, forget not to go as agreed,
And cease not to seek till me, sir, you find,

4. Hauled.

As you promised in the presence of these proud knights. 450
To the Green Chapel come, I charge you, to take
Such a dint as you have dealt—you have well deserved
That your neck should have a knock on New Year's morn.
The Knight of the Green Chapel I am well-known to many,
Wherefore you cannot fail to find me at last; 455
Therefore come, or be counted a recreant⁵ knight."
With a roisterous rush he flings round the reins,
Hurtles out at the hall-door, his head in his hand,
That the flint-fire flew from the flashing hooves.
Which way he went, not one of them knew 460
Nor whence he was come in the wide world
                so fair.
        The king and Gawain gay
        Make game of the Green Knight there,
        Yet all who saw it say
        'Twas a wonder past compare. 465

Though high-born Arthur at heart had wonder,
He let no sign be seen, but said aloud
To the comely queen, with courteous speech,
"Dear dame, on this day dismay you no whit; 470
Such crafts are becoming at Christmastide,
Laughing at interludes, light songs and mirth,
Amid dancing of damsels with doughty knights.
Nevertheless of my meat now let me partake,
For I have met with a marvel, I may not deny." 475
He glanced at Sir Gawain, and gaily he said,
"Now, sir, hang up your ax, that has hewn enough,"
And over the high dais it was hung on the wall
That men in amazement might on it look,
And tell in true terms the tale of the wonder. 480
Then they turned toward the table, these two together,
The good king and Gawain, and made great feast,
With all dainties double, dishes rare,
With all manner of meat and minstrelsy both,
Such happiness wholly had they that day 485
              in hold.
        Now take care, Sir Gawain,
        That your courage wax not cold
        When you must turn again
        To your enterprise foretold. 490

PART II

This adventure had Arthur of handsels⁶ first
When young was the year, for he yearned to hear tales;
Though they wanted for words when they went to sup,
Now are fierce deeds to follow, their fists stuffed full.
Gawain was glad to begin those games in hall, 495

5. Cowardly.   6. Gifts to mark the New Year.

But if the end be harsher, hold it no wonder,
For though men are merry in mind after much drink,
A year passes apace, and proves ever new:
First things and final conform but seldom.
And so this Yule to the young year yielded place,   500
And each season ensued at its set time;
After Christmas there came the cold cheer of Lent,
When with fish and plainer fare our flesh we reprove;
But then the world's weather with winter contends:
The keen cold lessens, the low clouds lift;   505
Fresh falls the rain in fostering showers
On the face of the fields; flowers appear.
The ground and the groves wear gowns of green;
Birds build their nests, and blithely sing
That solace of all sorrow with summer comes   510
              ere long.
          And blossoms day by day
          Bloom rich and rife in throng;
          Then every grove so gay
          Of the greenwood rings with song.   515

And then the season of summer with the soft winds,
When Zephyr sighs low over seeds and shoots;
Glad is the green plant growing abroad,
When the dew at dawn drops from the leaves,
To get a gracious glance from the golden sun.   520
But harvest with harsher winds follows hard after,
Warns him to ripen well ere winter comes;
Drives forth the dust in the droughty season,
From the face of the fields to fly high in air.
Wroth winds in the welkin[7] wrestle with the sun,   525
The leaves launch from the linden and light on the ground,
And the grass turns to gray, that once grew green.
Then all ripens and rots that rose up at first,
And so the year moves on in yesterdays many,
And winter once more, by the world's law,   530
              draws nigh.
          At Michaelmas[8] the moon
          Hangs wintry pale in sky;
          Sir Gawain girds him soon
          For travails yet to try.   535

Till All-Hallows' Day[9] with Arthur he dwells,
And he held a high feast to honor that knight
With great revels and rich, of the Round Table.
Then ladies lovely and lords debonair
With sorrow for Sir Gawain were sore at heart;   540
Yet they covered their care with countenance glad:
Many a mournful man made mirth for his sake.
So after supper soberly he speaks to his uncle

7. The heavens.   8. September 29.   9. November 1.

Of the hard hour at hand, and openly says,
"Now, liege lord of my life, my leave I take; 545
The terms of this task too well you know—
To count the cost over concerns me nothing.
But I am bound forth betimes[1] to bear a stroke
From the grim man in green, as God may direct."
Then the first and foremost came forth in throng: 550
Yvain and Eric and others of note,
Sir Dodinal le Sauvage, the Duke of Clarence,
Lionel and Lancelot and Lucan the good,
Sir Bors and Sir Bedivere, big men both,
And many manly knights more, with Mador de la Porte. 555
All this courtly company comes to the king
To counsel their comrade, with care in their hearts;
There was much secret sorrow suffered that day
That one so good as Gawain must go in such wise
To bear a bitter blow, and his bright sword 560
        lay by.
      He said, "Why should I tarry?"
      And smiled with tranquil eye;
      "In destinies sad or merry,
      True men can but try." 565

He dwelt there all that day, and dressed in the morning;
Asked early for his arms, and all were brought.
First a carpet of rare cost was cast on the floor
Where much goodly gear gleamed golden bright;
He takes his place promptly and picks up the steel, 570
Attired in a tight coat of Turkestan silk
And a kingly cap-à-dos, closed at the throat,
That was lavishly lined with a lustrous fur.
Then they set the steel shoes on his sturdy feet
And clad his calves about with comely greaves, 575
And plate well-polished protected his knees,
Affixed with fastenings of the finest gold.
Fair cuisses enclosed, that were cunningly wrought,
His thick-thewed thighs, with thongs bound fast,
And massy chain-mail of many a steel ring 580
He bore on his body, above the best cloth,
With brace burnished bright upon both his arms,
Good couters[2] and gay, and gloves of plate,
And all the goodly gear to grace him well
        that tide. 585
      His surcoat[3] blazoned bold;
      Sharp spurs to prick with pride;
      And a brave silk band to hold
      The broadsword at his side.

When he had on his arms, his harness was rich, 590
The least latchet or loop laden with gold;

---

1. Soon.   2. Armor for the elbows.   3. Cloth tunic worn over the armor.

So armored as he was, he heard a mass,
Honored God humbly at the high altar.
Then he comes to the king and his comrades-in-arms,
Takes his leave at last of lords and ladies, 595
And they clasped and kissed him, commending him to Christ.
By then Gringolet⁴ was girt with a great saddle
That was gaily agleam with fine gilt fringe,
New-furbished for the need with nail-heads bright;
The bridle and the bars bedecked all with gold; 600
The breast-plate, the saddlebow, the side-panels both,
The caparison and the crupper accorded in hue,
And all ranged on the red the resplendent studs
That glittered and glowed like the glorious sun.
His helm now he holds up and hastily kisses, 605
Well-closed with iron clinches, and cushioned within;
It was high on his head, with a hasp behind,
And a covering of cloth to encase the visor,
All bound and embroidered with the best gems
On broad bands of silk, and bordered with birds, 610
Parrots and popinjays preening their wings,
Lovebirds and love-knots as lavishly wrought
As many women had worked seven winters thereon,
                              entire.
             The diadem costlier yet 615
             That crowned that comely sire,
             With diamonds richly set,
             That flashed as if on fire.

Then they showed forth the shield, that shone all red,
With the pentangle⁵ portrayed in purest gold. 620
About his broad neck by the baldric⁶ he casts it,
That was meet for the man, and matched him well.
And why the pentangle is proper to that peerless prince
I intend now to tell, though detain me it must.
It is a sign by Solomon sagely devised 625
To be a token of truth, by its title of old,
For it is a figure formed of five points,
And each line is linked and locked with the next
For ever and ever, and hence it is called
In all England, as I hear, the endless knot. 630
And well may he wear it on his worthy arms,
For ever faithful five-fold in five-fold fashion
Was Gawain in good works, as gold unalloyed,
Devoid of all villainy, with virtues adorned
                              in sight. 635
             On shield and coat in view
             He bore that emblem bright,
             As to his word most true
             And in speech most courteous knight.

4. Gawain's horse.   5. A five-pointed star, formed by five lines drawn without lifting the pen, supposed
to have mystical significance; as Solomon's sign (line 625), it was enclosed in a circle.   6. Belt worn
diagonally across the chest.

And first, he was faultless in his five senses,   640
Nor found ever to fail in his five fingers,
And all his fealty was fixed upon the five wounds
That Christ got on the cross, as the creed tells;
And wherever this man in melee took part,
His one thought was of this, past all things else,   645
That all his force was founded on the five joys[7]
That the high Queen of heaven had in her child.
And therefore, as I find, he fittingly had
On the inner part of his shield her image portrayed,
That when his look on it lighted, he never lost heart.   650
The fifth of the five fives followed by this knight
Were beneficence boundless and brotherly love
And pure mind and manners, that none might impeach,
And compassion most precious—these peerless five
Were forged and made fast in him, foremost of men.   655
Now all these five fives were confirmed in this knight,
And each linked in other, that end there was none,
And fixed to five points, whose force never failed,
Nor assembled all on a side, nor asunder either,
Nor anywhere at an end, but whole and entire   660
However the pattern proceeded or played out its course.
And so on his shining shield shaped was the knot
Royally in red gold against red gules,[8]
That is the peerless pentangle, prized of old
                      in lore.   665
            Now armed is Gawain gay,
            And bears his lance before,
            And soberly said good day,
            He thought forevermore.

He struck his steed with the spurs and sped on his way   670
So fast that the flint-fire flashed from the stones.
When they saw him set forth they were sore aggrieved,
And all sighed softly, and said to each other,
Fearing for their fellow, "Ill fortune it is
That you, man, must be marred, that most are worthy!   675
His equal on this earth can hardly be found;
To have dealt more discreetly had done less harm,
And have dubbed him a duke, with all due honor.
A great leader of lords he was like to become,
And better so to have been than battered to bits,   680
Beheaded by an elf-man,[9] for empty pride!
Who would credit that a king could be counseled so,
And caught in a cavil in a Christmas game?"
Many were the warm tears they wept from their eyes
When goodly Sir Gawain was gone from the court   685
            that day.

---

7. These were the annunciation to Mary that she was to bear the Son of God, Christ's Nativity, Resurrection, and Ascension into heaven, and the "Assumption" or bodily taking up of Mary into heaven to join Him.   8. Background (*gules* is the heraldic name for red).   9. Supernatural being, in this case obviously not small.

No longer he abode,
But speedily went his way
Over many a wandering road,
As I heard my author say.   690

Now he rides in his array through the realm of Logres,[1]
Sir Gawain, God knows, though it gave him small joy!
All alone must he lodge through many a long night
Where the food that he fancied was far from his plate;
He had no mate but his mount, over mountain and plain,   695
Nor man to say his mind to but almighty God,
Till he had wandered well-nigh into North Wales.
All the islands of Anglesey he holds on his left,
And follows, as he fares, the fords by the coast,
Comes over at Holy Head, and enters next   700
The Wilderness of Wirral[2]—few were within
That had great good will toward God or man.
And earnestly he asked of each mortal he met
If he had ever heard aught of a knight all green,
Or of a Green Chapel, on ground thereabouts,   705
And all said the same, and solemnly swore
They saw no such knight all solely green
                                in hue.
            Over country wild and strange
            The knight sets off anew;
            Often his course must change   710
            Ere the Chapel comes in view.

Many a cliff must he climb in country wild;
Far off from all his friends, forlorn must he ride;
At each strand or stream where the stalwart passed   715
'Twere a marvel if he met not some monstrous foe,
And that so fierce and forbidding that fight he must.
So many were the wonders he wandered among
That to tell but the tenth part would tax my wits.
Now with serpents he wars, now with savage wolves,   720
Now with wild men of the woods, that watched from the rocks,
Both with bulls and with bears, and with boars besides,
And giants that came gibbering from the jagged steeps.
Had he not borne himself bravely, and been on God's side,
He had met with many mishaps and mortal harms.   725
And if the wars were unwelcome, the winter was worse,
When the cold clear rains rushed from the clouds
And froze before they could fall to the frosty earth.
Near slain by the sleet he sleeps in his irons
More nights than enough, among naked rocks,   730
Where clattering from the crest the cold stream ran
And hung in hard icicles high overhead.

---

1. Another name for Arthur's kingdom. 2. *North Wales . . . Wirral:* Gawain went from Camelot north to the northern coast of Wales, opposite the islands of Anglesey; there he turned east across the river Dee to the forest of Wirral, near what is now Liverpool.

Thus in peril and pain and predicaments dire
He rides across country till Christmas Eve,
                              our knight.   735
                    And at that holy tide
                    He prays with all his might
                    That Mary may be his guide
                    Till a dwelling comes in sight.

By a mountain next morning he makes his way   740
Into a forest fastness, fearsome and wild;
High hills on either hand, with hoar woods below,
Oaks old and huge by the hundred together.
The hazel and the hawthorn were all intertwined
With rough raveled moss, that raggedly hung,   745
With many birds unblithe upon bare twigs
That peeped most piteously for pain of the cold.
The good knight on Gringolet glides thereunder
Through many a marsh and mire, a man all alone;
He feared for his default, should he fail to see   750
The service of that Sire that on that same night
Was born of a bright maid, to bring us His peace.
And therefore sighing he said, "I beseech of Thee, Lord,
And Mary, thou mildest mother so dear,
Some harborage where haply I might hear mass   755
And Thy matins tomorrow—meekly I ask it,
And thereto proffer and pray my pater and ave[3]
                              and creed."
                    He said his prayer with sighs,
                    Lamenting his misdeed;   760
                    He crosses himself, and cries
                    On Christ in his great need.

No sooner had Sir Gawain signed himself[4] thrice
Than he was ware, in the wood, of a wondrous dwelling,
Within a moat, on a mound, bright amid boughs   765
Of many a tree great of girth that grew by the water—
A castle as comely as a knight could own,
On grounds fair and green, in a goodly park
With a palisade of palings planted about
For two miles and more, round many a fair tree.   770
The stout knight stared at that stronghold great
As it shimmered and shone amid shining leaves,
Then with helmet in hand he offers his thanks
To Jesus and Saint Julian,[5] that are gentle both,
That in courteous accord had inclined to his prayer;   775
"Now fair harbor," said he, "I humbly beseech!"
Then he pricks his proud steed with the plated spurs,

---

3. Two prayers, the Pater Noster ("Our Father," the Lord's Prayer) and Ave Maria ("Hail Mary").
4. Made the Sign of the Cross over his own chest.   5. Patron saint of hospitality.

And by chance he has chosen the chief path
That brought the bold knight to the bridge's end
                  in haste.   780
        The bridge hung high in air;
        The gates were bolted fast;
        The walls well-framed to bear
        The fury of the blast.

The man on his mount remained on the bank   785
Of the deep double moat that defended the place.
The wall went in the water wondrous deep,
And a long way aloft it loomed overhead.
It was built of stone blocks to the battlements' height,
With corbels under cornices[6] in comeliest style;   790
Watch-towers trusty protected the gate,
With many a lean loophole, to look from within:
A better-made barbican the knight beheld never.
And behind it there hoved a great hall and fair:
Turrets rising in tiers, with tines[7] at their tops,   795
Spires set beside them, splendidly long,
With finials well-fashioned, as filigree fine.
Chalk-white chimneys over chambers high
Gleamed in gay array upon gables and roofs;
The pinnacles in panoply, pointing in air,   800
So vied there for his view that verily it seemed
A castle cut of paper for a king's feast.
The good knight on Gringolet thought it great luck
If he could but contrive to come there within
To keep the Christmas feast in that castle fair   805
                and bright.
        There answered to his call
        A porter most polite;
        From his station on the wall
        He greets the errant knight.   810

"Good sir," said Gawain, "Wouldst go to inquire
If your lord would allow me to lodge here a space?"
"Peter!"[8] said the porter, "For my part, I think
So noble a knight will not want for a welcome!"
Then he bustles off briskly, and comes back straight,   815
And many servants beside, to receive him the better.
They let down the drawbridge and duly went forth
And kneeled down on their knees on the naked earth
To welcome this warrior as best they were able.
They proffered him passage—the portals stood wide—   820
And he beckoned them to rise, and rode over the bridge.
Men steadied his saddle as he stepped to the ground,
And there stabled his steed many stalwart folk.

6. Ornamental projections supporting the top courses of stone.   7. Sharp points. *Hoved:* arose.
8. I.e., "By Saint Peter!"

Now come the knights and the noble squires
To bring him with bliss into the bright hall.   825
When his high helm was off, there hied forth a throng
Of attendants to take it, and see to its care;
They bore away his brand[9] and his blazoned shield;
Then graciously he greeted those gallants each one,
And many a noble drew near, to do the knight honor.   830
All in his armor into hall he was led,
Where fire on a fair hearth fiercely blazed.
And soon the lord himself descends from his chamber
To meet with good manners the man on his floor.
He said, "To this house you are heartily welcome: 835
What is here is wholly yours, to have in your power
                          and sway."
                    "Many thanks," said Sir Gawain;
                    "May Christ your pains repay!"
                    The two embrace amain   840
                    As men well met that day.

Gawain gazed on the host that greeted him there,
And a lusty fellow he looked, the lord of that place:
A man of massive mold, and of middle age;
Broad, bright was his beard, of a beaver's hue,   845
Strong, steady his stance, upon stalwart shanks,
His face fierce as fire, fair-spoken withal,
And well-suited he seemed in Sir Gawain's sight
To be a master of men in a mighty keep.
They pass into a parlor, where promptly the host   850
Has a servant assigned him to see to his needs,
And there came upon his call many courteous folk
That brought him to a bower where bedding was noble,
With heavy silk hangings hemmed all in gold,
Coverlets and counterpanes curiously wrought,   855
A canopy over the couch, clad all with fur,
Curtains running on cords, caught to gold rings,
Woven rugs on the walls of eastern work,
And the floor, under foot, well-furnished with the same.
With light talk and laughter they loosed from him then   860
His war-dress of weight and his worthy clothes.
Robes richly wrought they brought him right soon,
To change there in chamber and choose what he would.
When he had found one he fancied, and flung it about,
Well-fashioned for his frame, with flowing skirts,   865
His face fair and fresh as the flowers of spring,
All the good folk agreed, that gazed on him then,
His limbs arrayed royally in radiant hues,
That so comely a mortal never Christ made
                          as he.   870
                    Whatever his place of birth,
                    It seemed he well might be

9. Sword.

Without a peer on earth
In martial rivalry.

A couch before the fire, where fresh coals burned,   875
They spread for Sir Gawain splendidly now
With quilts quaintly stitched, and cushions beside,
And then a costly cloak they cast on his shoulders
Of bright silk, embroidered on borders and hems,
With furs of the finest well-furnished within,   880
And bound about with ermine, both mantle and hood;
And he sat at that fireside in sumptuous estate
And warmed himself well, and soon he waxed merry.
Then attendants set a table upon trestles broad,
And lustrous white linen they laid thereupon,   885
A saltcellar of silver, spoons of the same.
He washed himself well and went to his place,
Men set his fare before him in fashion most fit.
There were soups of all sorts, seasoned with skill,
Double-sized servings, and sundry fish,   890
Some baked, some breaded, some broiled on the coals,
Some simmered, some in stews, steaming with spice,
And with sauces to sup that suited his taste.
He confesses it a feast with free words and fair;
They requite him as kindly with courteous jests,   895
well-sped.
"Tonight you fast and pray;
Tomorrow we'll see you fed."
The knight grows wondrous gay
As the wine goes to his head.   900

Then at times and by turns, as at table he sat,
They questioned him quietly, with queries discreet,
And he courteously confessed that he comes from the court,
And owns him of the brotherhood of high-famed Arthur,
The right royal ruler of the Round Table,   905
And the guest by their fireside is Gawain himself,
Who has happened on their house at that holy feast.
When the name of the knight was made known to the lord,
Then loudly he laughed, so elated he was,
And the men in that household made haste with joy   910
To appear in his presence promptly that day,
That of courage ever-constant, and customs pure,
Is pattern and paragon, and praised without end:
Of all knights on earth most honored is he.
Each said solemnly aside to his brother,   915
"Now displays of deportment shall dazzle our eyes
And the polished pearls of impeccable speech;
The high art of eloquence is ours to pursue
Since the father of fine manners is found in our midst.
Great is God's grace, and goodly indeed,   920
That a guest such as Gawain he guides to us here
When men sit and sing of their Savior's birth
in view.

> With command of manners pure
> He shall each heart imbue;   925
> Who shares his converse, sure,
> Shall learn love's language true."

When the knight had done dining and duly arose,
The dark was drawing on; the day nigh ended.
Chaplains in chapels and churches about   930
Rang the bells aright, reminding all men
Of the holy evensong of the high feast.
The lord attends alone; his fair lady sits
In a comely closet, secluded from sight.
Gawain in gay attire goes thither soon;   935
The lord catches his coat, and calls him by name,
And has him sit beside him, and says in good faith
No guest on God's earth would he gladlier greet.
For that Gawain thanked him; the two then embraced
And sat together soberly the service through.   940
Then the lady, that longed to look on the knight,
Came forth from her closet with her comely maids.
The fair hues of her flesh, her face and her hair
And her body and her bearing were beyond praise,
And excelled the queen herself, as Sir Gawain thought.   945
He goes forth to greet her with gracious intent;
Another lady led her by the left hand
That was older than she—an ancient, it seemed,
And held in high honor by all men about.
But unlike to look upon, those ladies were,   950
For if the one was fresh, the other was faded:
Bedecked in bright red was the body of one;
Flesh hung in folds on the face of the other;
On one a high headdress, hung all with pearls;
Her bright throat and bosom fair to behold,   955
Fresh as the first snow fallen upon hills;
A wimple[1] the other one wore round her throat;
Her swart chin well swaddled, swathed all in white;
Her forehead enfolded in flounces of silk
That framed a fair fillet,[2] of fashion ornate,   960
And nothing bare beneath save the black brows,
The two eyes and the nose, the naked lips,
And they unsightly to see, and sorrily bleared.
A beldame, by God, she may well be deemed,
           of pride!   965
> She was short and thick of waist,
> Her buttocks round and wide;
> More toothsome, to his taste,
> Was the beauty by her side.

When Gawain had gazed on that gay lady,   970
With leave of her lord, he politely approached;

---

1. A garment covering the neck and sides of the head.   2. Ornamental ribbon or headband.

To the elder in homage he humbly bows;
The lovelier he salutes with a light embrace.
He claims a comely kiss, and courteously he speaks;
They welcome him warmly, and straightway he asks   975
To be received as their servant, if they so desire.
They take him between them; with talking they bring him
Beside a bright fire; bade then that spices
Be freely fetched forth, to refresh them the better,
And the good wine therewith, to warm their hearts.   980
The lord leaps about in light-hearted mood;
Contrives entertainments and timely sports;
Takes his hood from his head and hangs it on a spear,
And offers him openly the honor thereof
Who should promote the most mirth at that Christmas feast;   985
"And I shall try for it, trust me—contend with the best,
Ere I go without my headgear by grace of my friends!"
Thus with light talk and laughter the lord makes merry
To gladden the guest he had greeted in hall
                              that day.   990
              At the last he called for light
              The company to convey;
              Gawain says goodnight
              And retires to bed straightway.

On the morn when each man is mindful in heart   995
That God's son was sent down to suffer our death,
No household but is blithe for His blessed sake;
So was it there on that day, with many delights.
Both at larger meals and less they were lavishly served
By doughty lads on dais, with delicate fare;   1000
The old ancient lady, highest she sits;
The lord at her left hand leaned, as I hear;
Sir Gawain in the center, beside the gay lady,
Where the food was brought first to that festive board,
And thence throughout the hall, as they held most fit,   1005
To each man was offered in order of rank.
There was meat, there was mirth, there was much joy,
That to tell all the tale would tax my wits,
Though I pained me, perchance, to paint it with care;
But yet I know that our knight and the noble lady   1010
Were accorded so closely in company there,
With the seemly solace of their secret words,
With speeches well-sped, spotless and pure,
That each prince's pastime their pleasures far
                              outshone.   1015
              Sweet pipes beguile their cares,
              And the trumpet of martial tone;
              Each tends his affairs
              And those two tend their own.

That day and all the next, their disport was noble,   1020
And the third day, I think, pleased them no less;

The joys of St. John's Day³ were justly praised,
And were the last of their like for those lords and ladies;
Then guests were to go in the gray morning,
Wherefore they whiled the night away with wine and with mirth,   1025
Moved to the measures of many a blithe carol;
At last, when it was late, took leave of each other,
Each one of those worthies, to wend his way.
Gawain bids goodbye to his goodly host
Who brings him to his chamber, the chimney beside,   1030
And detains him in talk, and tenders his thanks
And holds it an honor to him and his people
That he has harbored in his house at that holy time
And embellished his abode with his inborn grace.
"As long as I may live, my luck is the better   1035
That Gawain was my guest at God's own feast!"
"Noble sir," said the knight, "I cannot but think
All the honor is your own—may heaven requite it!
And your man to command I account myself here
As I am bound and beholden, and shall be, come   1040
            what may."
            The lord with all his might
            Entreats his guest to stay;
            Brief answer makes the knight:
            Next morning he must away.   1045

Then the lord of that land politely inquired
What dire affair had forced him, at that festive time,
So far from the king's court to fare forth alone
Ere the holidays wholly had ended in hall.
"In good faith," said Gawain, "you have guessed the truth: 1050
On a high errand and urgent I hastened away,
For I am summoned by myself to seek for a place—
I would I knew whither, or where it might be!
Far rather would I find it before the New Year
Than own the land of Logres, so help me our Lord!   1055
Wherefore, sir, in friendship this favor I ask,
That you say in sober earnest, if something you know
Of the Green Chapel, on ground far or near,
Or the lone knight that lives there, of like hue of green.
A certain day was set by assent of us both   1060
To meet at that landmark, if I might last,
And from now to the New Year is nothing too long,
And I would greet the Green Knight there, would God but allow,
More gladly, by God's Son, than gain the world's wealth!
And I must set forth to search, as soon as I may;   1065
To be about the business I have but three days
And would as soon sink down dead as desist from my errand."
Then smiling said the lord, "Your search, sir, is done,
For we shall see you to that site by the set time.
Let Gawain grieve no more over the Green Chapel;   1070

3. December 27.

You shall be in your own bed, in blissful ease,
All the forenoon, and fare forth the first of the year,
And make the goal by midmorn, to mind your affairs,
　　　　　　　　no fear!
　　　　　　　Tarry till the fourth day　　　　　　　　1075
　　　　　　　And ride on the first of the year.
　　　　　　　We shall set you on your way;
　　　　　　　It is not two miles from here."

Then Gawain was glad, and gleefully he laughed:
"Now I thank you for this, past all things else!　　　　1080
Now my goal is here at hand! With a glad heart I shall
Both tarry, and undertake any task you devise."
Then the host seized his arm and seated him there;
Let the ladies be brought, to delight them the better,
And in fellowship fair by the fireside they sit;　　　　1085
So gay waxed the good host, so giddy his words,
All waited in wonder what next he would say.
Then he stares on the stout knight, and sternly he speaks:
"You have bound yourself boldly my bidding to do—
Will you stand by that boast, and obey me this once?"　　1090
"I shall do so indeed," said the doughty knight;
"While I lie in your lodging, your laws will I follow."
"As you have had," said the host, "many hardships abroad
And little sleep of late, you are lacking, I judge,
Both in nourishment needful and nightly rest;　　　　1095
You shall lie abed late in your lofty chamber
Tomorrow until mass, and meet then to dine
When you will, with my wife, who will sit by your side
And talk with you at table, the better to cheer
　　　　　　　　our guest.　　　　　　　　1100
　　　　　　　A-hunting I will go
　　　　　　　While you lie late and rest."
　　　　　　　The knight, inclining low,
　　　　　　　Assents to each behest.

"And Gawain," said the good host, "agree now to this:　　1105
Whatever I win in the woods I will give you at eve,
And all you have earned you must offer to me;
Swear now, sweet friend, to swap as I say,
Whether hands, in the end, be empty or better."
"By God," said Sir Gawain, "I grant it forthwith!　　　1110
If you find the game good, I shall gladly take part."
"Let the bright wine be brought, and our bargain is done,"
Said the lord of that land—the two laughed together.
Then they drank and they dallied and doffed all constraint,
These lords and these ladies, as late as they chose,　　1115
And then with gaiety and gallantries and graceful adieux
They talked in low tones, and tarried at parting.
With compliments comely they kiss at the last;
There were brisk lads about with blazing torches
To see them safe to bed, for soft repose　　　　　　1120
　　　　　　　　long due.

Their covenants, yet awhile,
They repeat, and pledge anew;
That lord could well beguile
Men's hearts, with mirth in view.   1125

PART III

Long before daylight they left their beds;
Guests that wished to go gave word to their grooms,
And they set about briskly to bind on saddles,
Tend to their tackle, tie up trunks.
The proud lords appear, appareled to ride,   1130
Leap lightly astride, lay hold of their bridles,
Each one on his way to his worthy house.
The liege lord of the land was not the last
Arrayed there to ride, with retainers many;
He had a bite to eat when he had heard mass;   1135
With horn to the hills he hastens amain.
By the dawn of that day over the dim earth,
Master and men were mounted and ready.
Then they harnessed in couples the keen-scented hounds,
Cast wide the kennel-door and called them forth,   1140
Blew upon their bugles bold blasts three;
The dogs began to bay with a deafening din,
And they quieted them quickly and called them to heel,
A hundred brave huntsmen, as I have heard tell,
                              together.   1145
          Men at stations meet;
          From the hounds they slip the tether;
          The echoing horns repeat,
          Clear in the merry weather.

At the clamor of the quest, the quarry trembled;   1150
Deer dashed through the dale, dazed with dread;
Hastened to the high ground, only to be
Turned back by the beaters, who boldly shouted.
They harmed not the harts, with their high heads,
Let the bucks go by, with their broad antlers,   1155
For it was counted a crime, in the close[4] season,
If a man of that demesne should molest the male deer.
The hinds were headed up, with "Hey!" and "Ware!"
The does with great din were driven to the valleys.
Then you were ware, as they went, of the whistling of arrows;   1160
At each bend under boughs the bright shafts flew
That tore the tawny hide with their tapered heads.
Ah! They bray and they bleed, on banks they die,
And ever the pack pell-mell comes panting behind;
Hunters with shrill horns hot on their heels—   1165
Like the cracking of cliffs their cries resounded.
What game got away from the gallant archers
Was promptly picked off at the posts below

4. Or closed.

When they were harried on the heights and herded to the streams:
The watchers were so wary at the waiting-stations,   1170
And the greyhounds so huge, that eagerly snatched,
And finished them off as fast as folk could see
                              with sight.
                    The lord, now here, now there,
                    Spurs forth in sheer delight.   1175
                    And drives, with pleasures rare,
                    The day to the dark night.

So the lord in the linden-wood leads the hunt
And Gawain the good knight in gay bed lies,
Lingered late alone, till daylight gleamed,   1180
Under coverlet costly, curtained about.
And as he slips into slumber, slyly there comes
A little din at his door, and the latch lifted,
And he holds up his heavy head out of the clothes;
A corner of the curtain he caught back a little   1185
And waited there warily, to see what befell.
Lo! it was the lady, loveliest to behold,
That drew the door behind her deftly and still
And was bound for his bed—abashed was the knight,
And laid his head low again in likeness of sleep;   1190
And she stepped stealthily, and stole to his bed,
Cast aside the curtain and came within,
And set herself softly on the bedside there,
And lingered at her leisure, to look on his waking.
The fair knight lay feigning for a long while,   1195
Conning in his conscience what his case might
Mean or amount to—a marvel he thought it.
But yet he said within himself, "More seemly it were
To try her intent by talking a little."
So he started and stretched, as startled from sleep,   1200
Lifts wide his lids in likeness of wonder,
And signs himself swiftly, as safer to be,
                              with art.
                    Sweetly does she speak
                    And kindling glances dart,   1205
                    Blent white and red on cheek
                    And laughing lips apart.

"Good morning, Sir Gawain," said that gay lady,
"A slack sleeper you are, to let one slip in!
Now you are taken in a trice—a truce we must make,   1210
Or I shall bind you in your bed, of that be assured."
Thus laughing lightly that lady jested.
"Good morning, good lady," said Gawain the blithe,
"Be it with me as you will; I am well content!
For I surrender myself, and sue for your grace,   1215
And that is best, I believe, and behooves me now."
Thus jested in answer that gentle knight.
"But if, lovely lady, you misliked it not,

And were pleased to permit your prisoner to rise,
I should quit this couch and accoutre me better,   1220
And be clad in more comfort for converse here."
"Nay, not so, sweet sir," said the smiling lady;
"You shall not rise from your bed; I direct you better:
I shall hem and hold you on either hand,
And keep company awhile with my captive knight.   1225
For as certain as I sit here, Sir Gawain you are,
Whom all the world worships, whereso you ride;
Your honor, your courtesy are highest acclaimed
By lords and by ladies, by all living men;
And lo! we are alone here, and left to ourselves: 1230
My lord and his liegemen are long departed,
The household asleep, my handmaids too,
The door drawn, and held by a well-driven bolt,
And since I have in this house him whom all love,
I shall while the time away with mirthful speech   1235
                              at will.
                    My body is here at hand,
                    Your each wish to fulfill;
                    Your servant to command
                    I am, and shall be still."   1240

"In good faith," said Gawain, "my gain is the greater,
Though I am not he of whom you have heard;
To arrive at such reverence as you recount here
I am one all unworthy, and well do I know it.
By heaven, I would hold me the happiest of men   1245
If by word or by work I once might aspire
To the prize of your praise—'twere a pure joy!"
"In good faith, Sir Gawain," said that gay lady,
"The well-proven prowess that pleases all others,
Did I scant or scout[5] it, 'twere scarce becoming.   1250
But there are ladies, believe me, that had liefer far[6]
Have thee here in their hold, as I have today,
To pass an hour in pastime with pleasant words,
Assuage all their sorrows and solace their hearts,
Than much of the goodly gems and gold they possess.   1255
But laud be to the Lord of the lofty skies,
For here in my hands all hearts' desire
                              doth lie."
                    Great welcome got he there
                    From the lady who sat him by;   1260
                    With fitting speech and fair
                    The good knight makes reply.

"Madame," said the merry man, "Mary reward you!
For in good faith, I find your beneficence noble.
And the fame of fair deeds runs far and wide,   1265
But the praise you report pertains not to me,

5. Mock.   6. Would much rather.

But comes of your courtesy and kindness of heart."
"By the high Queen of heaven" (said she) "I count it not so,
For were I worth all the women in this world alive,
And all wealth and all worship were in my hands,   1270
And I should hunt high and low, a husband to take,
For the nurture I have noted in thee, knight, here,
The comeliness and courtesies and courtly mirth—
And so I had ever heard, and now hold it true—
No other on this earth should have me for wife."   1275
"You are bound to a better man," the bold knight said,
"Yet I prize the praise you have proffered me here,
And soberly your servant, my sovereign I hold you,
And acknowledge me your knight, in the name of Christ."
So they talked of this and that until 'twas nigh noon,   1280
And ever the lady languishing in likeness of love.
With feat[7] words and fair he framed his defence,
For were she never so winsome, the warrior had
The less will to woo, for the wound that his bane
                              must be.   1285
                    He must bear the blinding blow,
                    For such is fate's decree;
                    The lady asks leave to go;
                    He grants it full and free.

Then she gaily said goodbye, and glanced at him, laughing,   1290
And as she stood, she astonished him with a stern speech:
"Now may the Giver of all good words these glad hours repay!
But our guest is not Gawain—forgot is that thought."
"How so?" said the other, and asks in some haste,
For he feared he had been at fault in the forms of his speech.   1295
But she held up her hand, and made answer thus:
"So good a knight as Gawain is given out to be,
And the model of fair demeanor and manners pure,
Had he lain so long at a lady's side,
Would have claimed a kiss, by his courtesy,   1300
Through some touch or trick of phrase at some tale's end."
Said Gawain, "Good lady, I grant it at once!
I shall kiss at your command, as becomes a knight,
And more, lest you mislike, so let be, I pray."
With that she turns toward him, takes him in her arms,   1305
Leans down her lovely head, and lo! he is kissed.
They commend each other to Christ with comely words,
He sees her forth safely, in silence they part,
And then he lies no later in his lofty bed,
But calls to his chamberlain, chooses his clothes,   1310
Goes in those garments gladly to mass,
Then takes his way to table, where attendants wait,
And made merry all day, till the moon rose
                              in view

7. Fitting.

> Was never knight beset   1315
> 'Twixt worthier ladies two:
> The crone and the coquette;
> Fair pastimes they pursue.

And the lord of the land rides late and long,
Hunting the barren hind[8] over the broad heath.   1320
He had slain such a sum, when the sun sank low,
Of does and other deer, as would dizzy one's wits.
Then they trooped in together in triumph at last,
And the count of the quarry quickly they take.
The lords lent a hand with their liegemen many,   1325
Picked out the plumpest and put them together
And duly dressed the deer, as the deed requires.
Some were assigned the assay of the fat:
Two fingers'-width fully they found on the leanest.
Then they slit the slot[9] open and searched out the paunch,   1330
Trimmed it with trencher-knives and tied it up tight.
They flayed the fair hide from the legs and trunk,
Then broke open the belly and laid bare the bowels,
Deftly detaching and drawing them forth.
And next at the neck they neatly parted   1335
The weasand[1] from the windpipe, and cast away the guts.
At the shoulders with sharp blades they showed their skill,
Boning them from beneath, lest the sides be marred;
They breached the broad breast and broke it in twain,
And again at the gullet they begin with their knives,   1340
Cleave down the carcass clear to the breach;
Two tender morsels they take from the throat,
Then round the inner ribs they rid off a layer
And carve out the kidney-fat, close to the spine,
Hewing down to the haunch, that all hung together,   1345
And held it up whole, and hacked it free,
And this they named the numbles,[2] that knew such terms
                         of art.
> They divide the crotch in two,
> And straightway then they start   1350
> To cut the backbone through
> And cleave the trunk apart.

With hard strokes they hewed off the head and the neck,
Then swiftly from the sides they severed the chine,
And the corbie's bone[3] they cast on a branch.   1355
Then they pierced the plump sides, impaled either one
With the hock of the hind foot, and hung it aloft,
To each person his portion most proper and fit.
On a hide of a hind the hounds they fed
With the liver and the lights,[4] the leathery paunches, 1360

---

8. Female deer that are not pregnant.   9. The hollow above the breastbone.   1. Esophagus.
2. Other internal organs.   3. A bit of gristle for the ravens ("corbies").   4. Lungs.

And bread soaked in blood well blended therewith.
High horns and shrill set hounds a-baying,
Then merrily with their meat they make their way home,
Blowing on their bugles many a brave blast.
Ere dark had descended, that doughty and   1365
Was come within the walls where Gawain waits
                        at leisure.
            Bliss and hearth-fire bright
            Await the master's pleasure;
            When the two men met that night,   1370
            Joy surpassed all measure.

Then the host in the hall his household assembles,
With the dames of high degree and their damsels fair.
In the presence of the people, a party he sends
To convey him his venison in view of the knight.   1375
And in high good-humor he hails him then,
Counts over the kill, the cuts on the tallies,⁵
Holds high the hewn ribs, heavy with fat.
"What think you, sir, of this? Have I thriven well?
Have I won with my woodcraft a worthy prize?"   1380
"In good earnest," said Gawain, "this game is the finest
I have seen in seven years in the season of winter."
"And I give it to you, Gawain," said the goodly host,
"For according to our covenant, you claim it as your own."
"That is so," said Sir Gawain, "the same say I: 1385
What I worthily have won within these fair walls,
Herewith I as willingly award it to you."
He embraces his broad neck with both his arms,
And confers on him a kiss in the comeliest style.
"Have here my profit, it proved no better;   1390
Ungrudging do I grant it, were it greater far."
"Such a gift," said the good host, "I gladly accept—
Yet it might be all the better, would you but say
Where you won this same award, by your wits alone."
"That was no part of the pact; press me no further,   1395
For you have had what behooves; all other claims
                        forbear."
            With jest and compliment
            They conversed, and cast off care;
            To the table soon they went;   1400
            Fresh dainties wait them there.

And then by the chimney-side they chat at their ease;
The best wine was brought them, and bounteously served;
And after in their jesting they jointly accord
To do on the second day the deeds of the first: 1405
That the two men should trade, betide as it may,
What each had taken in, at eve when they met.

5. Notched sticks were used to count the animals taken in the hunt.

They seal the pact solemnly in sight of the court;
Their cups were filled afresh to confirm the jest;
Then at last they took their leave, for late was the hour,   1410
Each to his own bed hastening away.
Before the barnyard cock had crowed but thrice
The lord had leapt from his rest, his liegemen as well.
Both of mass and their meal they made short work:
By the dim light of dawn they were deep in the woods   1415
                away.
        With huntsmen and with horns
        Over plains they pass that day;
        They release, amid the thorns,
        Swift hounds that run and bay.   1420

Soon some were on a scent by the side of a marsh;
When the hounds opened cry, the head of the hunt
Rallied them with rough words, raised a great noise.
The hounds that had heard it came hurrying straight
And followed along with their fellows, forty together.   1425
Then such a clamor and cry of coursing hounds
Arose, that the rocks resounded again.
Hunters exhorted them with horn and with voice;
Then all in a body bore off together
Between a mere⁶ in the marsh and a menacing crag,   1430
To a rise where the rock stood rugged and steep,
And boulders lay about, that blocked their approach.
Then the company in consort closed on their prey:
They surrounded the rise and the rocks both,
For well they were aware that it waited within,   1435
The beast that the bloodhounds boldly proclaimed.
Then they beat on the bushes and bade him appear,
And he made a murderous rush in the midst of them all;
The best of all boars broke from his cover,
That had ranged long unrivaled, a renegade old,   1440
For of tough-brawned boars he was biggest far,
Most grim when he grunted—then grieved were many,
For three at the first thrust he threw to the earth,
And dashed away at once without more damage.
With "Hi!" "Hi!" and "Hey!" "Hey!" the others followed,   1445
Had horns at their lips, blew high and clear.
Merry was the music of men and of hounds
That were bound after this boar, his bloodthirsty heart
                to quell.
        Often he stands at bay,   1450
        Then scatters the pack pell-mell;
        He hurts the hounds, and they
        Most dolefully yowl and yell.

Men then with mighty bows moved in to shoot,
Aimed at him with their arrows and often hit,   1455

6. Pool.

But the points had no power to pierce through his hide,
And the barbs were brushed aside by his bristly brow;
Though the shank of the shaft shivered in pieces,
The head hopped away, wheresoever it struck.
But when their stubborn strokes had stung him at last,   1460
Then, foaming in his frenzy, fiercely he charges,
Hies at them headlong that hindered his flight,
And many feared for their lives, and fell back a little.
But the lord on a lively horse leads the chase;
As a high-mettled huntsman his horn he blows;   1465
He sounds the assembly and sweeps through the brush,
Pursuing this wild swine till the sunlight slanted.
All day with this deed they drive forth the time
While our lone knight so lovesome lies in his bed,
Sir Gawain safe at home, in silken bower   1470
            so gay.
            The lady, with guile in heart,
            Came early where he lay;
            She was at him with all her art
            To turn his mind her way.   1475

She comes to the curtain and coyly peeps in;
Gawain thought it good to greet her at once,
And she richly repays him with her ready words,
Settles softly at his side, and suddenly she laughs,
And with a gracious glance, she begins on him thus: 1480
"Sir, if you be Gawain, it seems a great wonder—
A man so well-meaning, and mannerly disposed,
And cannot act in company as courtesy bids,
And if one takes the trouble to teach him, 'tis all in vain.
That lesson learned lately is lightly forgot,   1485
Though I painted it as plain as my poor wit allowed."
"What lesson, dear lady?" he asked all alarmed;
"I have been much to blame, if your story be true."
"Yet my counsel was of kissing," came her answer then,
"Where favor has been found, freely to claim   1490
As accords with the conduct of courteous knights."
"My dear," said the doughty man," dismiss that thought;
Such freedom, I fear, might offend you much;
It were rude to request if the right were denied."
"But none can deny you," said the noble dame,   1495
"You are stout enough to constrain with strength, if you choose,
Were any so ungracious as to grudge you aught."
"By heaven," said he, "you have answered well,
But threats never throve among those of my land,
Nor any gift not freely given, good though it be.   1500
I am yours to command, to kiss when you please;
You may lay on as you like, and leave off at will."
            With this,
            The lady lightly bends
            And graciously gives him a kiss;   1505

The two converse as friends
Of true love's trials and bliss.

"I should like, by your leave," said the lovely lady,
"If it did not annoy you, to know for what cause
So brisk and so bold a young blood as you,   1510
And acclaimed for all courtesies becoming a knight—
And name what knight you will, they are noblest esteemed
For loyal faith in love, in life as in story;
For to tell the tribulations of these true hearts,
Why, 'tis the very title and text of their deeds,   1515
How bold knights for beauty have braved many a foe,
Suffered heavy sorrows out of secret love,
And then valorously avenged them on villainous churls
And made happy ever after the hearts of their ladies.
And you are the noblest knight known in your time;   1520
No household under heaven but has heard of your fame,
And here by your side I have sat for two days
Yet never has a fair phrase fallen from your lips
Of the language of love, not one little word!
And you, that with sweet vows sway women's hearts,   1525
Should show your winsome ways, and woo a young thing,
And teach by some tokens the craft of true love.
How! are you artless, whom all men praise?
Or do you deem me so dull, or deaf to such words?
                    Fie! Fie!   1530
        In hope of pastimes new
        I have come where none can spy;
        Instruct me a little, do,
        While my husband is not nearby."

"God love you, gracious lady!" said Gawain then;   1535
"It is a pleasure surpassing, and a peerless joy,
That one so worthy as you would willingly come
And take the time and trouble to talk with your knight
And content you with his company—it comforts my heart.
But to take to myself the task of telling of love,   1540
And touch upon its texts, and treat of its themes
To one that, I know well, wields more power
In that art, by a half, than a hundred such
As I am where I live, or am like to become,
It were folly, fair dame, in the first degree!   1545
In all that I am able, my aim is to please,
As in honor behooves me, and am evermore
Your servant heart and soul, so save me our Lord!"
Thus she tested his temper and tried many a time,
Whatever her true intent, to entice him to sin,   1550
But so fair was his defense that no fault appeared,
Nor evil on either hand, but only bliss
                    they knew.

> They linger and laugh awhile;
> She kisses the knight so true,   1555
> Takes leave in comeliest style
> And departs without more ado.

Then he rose from his rest and made ready for mass,
And then a meal was set and served, in sumptuous style;
He dallied at home all day with the dear ladies,   1560
But the lord lingered late at his lusty sport;
Pursued his sorry swine, that swerved as he fled,
And bit asunder the backs of the best of his hounds
When they brought him to bay, till the bowmen appeared
And soon forced him forth, though he fought for dear life,   1565
So sharp were the shafts they shot at him there.
But yet the boldest drew back from his battering head,
Till at last he was so tired he could travel no more,
But in as much haste as he might, he makes his retreat
To a rise on rocky ground, by a rushing stream.   1570
With the bank at his back he scrapes the bare earth,
The froth foams at his jaws, frightful to see.
He whets his white tusks—then weary were all
Those hunters so hardy that hoved⁷ round about
Of aiming from afar, but ever they mistrust   1575
> > his mood.
> > He had hurt so many by then
> > That none had hardihood
> > To be torn by his tusks again,
> > That was brainsick, and out for blood.   1580

Till the lord came at last on his lofty steed,
Beheld him there at bay before all his folk;
Lightly he leaps down, leaves his courser,
Bares his bright sword, and boldly advances;
Straight into the stream he strides towards his foe.   1585
The wild thing was wary of weapon and man;
His hackles rose high; so hotly he snorts
That many watched with alarm, lest the worst befall.
The boar makes for the man with a mighty bound
So that he and his hunter came headlong together   1590
Where the water ran wildest—the worse for the beast,
For the man, when they first met, marked him with care,
Sights well the slot, slips in the blade,
Shoves it home to the hilt, and the heart shattered,
And he falls in his fury and floats down the water,   1595
> > ill-sped.
> > Hounds hasten by the score
> > To maul him, hide and head;
> > Men drag him in to shore
> > And dogs pronounce him dead.   1600

7. Hovered.

With many a brave blast they boast of their prize,
All hallooed in high glee, that had their wind;
The hounds bayed their best, as the bold men bade
That were charged with chief rank in that chase of renown.
Then one wise in woodcraft, and worthily skilled,   1605
Began to dress the boar in becoming style:
He severs the savage head and sets it aloft,
Then rends the body roughly right down the spine;
Takes the bowels from the belly, broils them on coals,
Blends them well with bread to bestow on the hounds.   1610
Then he breaks out the brawn in fair broad flitches,
And the innards to be eaten in order he takes.
The two sides, attached to each other all whole,
He suspended from a spar that was springy and tough;
And so with this swine they set out for home;   1615
The boar's head was borne before the same man
That had stabbed him in the stream with his strong arm,
             right through.
        He thought it long indeed
        Till he had the knight in view;   1620
        At his call, he comes with speed
        To claim his payment due.

The lord laughed aloud, with many a light word,
When he greeted Sir Gawain—with good cheer he speaks.
They fetch the fair dames and the folk of the house;   1625
He brings forth the brawn, and begins the tale
Of the great length and girth, the grim rage as well,
Of the battle of the boar they beset in the wood.
The other men meetly commended his deeds
And praised well the prize of his princely sport,   1630
For the brawn of that boar, the bold knight said,
And the sides of that swine surpassed all others.
Then they handled the huge head; he owns it a wonder,
And eyes it with abhorrence, to heighten his praise.
"Now, Gawain," said the good man, "this game becomes yours   1635
By those fair terms we fixed, as you know full well."
"That is true," returned the knight, "and trust me, fair friend,
All my gains, as agreed, I shall give you forthwith."
He clasps him and kisses him in courteous style,
Then serves him with the same fare a second time.   1640
"Now we are even," said he, "at this evening feast,
And clear is every claim incurred here to date,
             and debt."
        "By Saint Giles!" the host replies,
        "You're the best I ever met!   1645
        If your profits are all this size,
        We'll see you wealthy yet!"

Then attendants set tables on trestles about,
And laid them with linen; light shone forth,

Wakened along the walls in waxen torches.   1650
The service was set and the supper brought;
Royal were the revels that rose then in hall
At that feast by the fire, with many fair sports:
Amid the meal and after, melody sweet,
Carol-dances comely and Christmas songs,   1655
With all the mannerly mirth my tongue may describe.
And ever our gallant knight beside the gay lady;
So uncommonly kind and complaisant was she,
With sweet stolen glances, that stirred his stout heart,
That he was at his wits' end, and wondrous vexed;   1660
But he could not in conscience her courtship repay,
Yet took pains to please her, though the plan might
                                             go wrong.
                    When they to heart's delight
                    Had reveled there in throng,   1665
                    To his chamber he calls the knight,
                    And thither they go along.

And there they dallied and drank, and deemed it good sport
To enact their play anew on New Year's Eve,
But Gawain asked again to go on the morrow,   1670
For the time until his tryst was not two days.
The host hindered that, and urged him to stay,
And said, "On my honor, my oath here I take
That you shall get to the Green Chapel to begin your chores
By dawn on New Year's Day, if you so desire.   1675
Wherefore lie at your leisure in your lofty bed,
And I shall hunt hereabouts, and hold to our terms,
And we shall trade winnings when once more we meet,
For I have tested you twice, and true have I found you;
Now think this tomorrow: the third pays for all;   1680
Be we merry while we may, and mindful of joy,
For heaviness of heart can be had for the asking."
This is gravely agreed on and Gawain will stay.
They drink a last draught and with torches depart
                                             to rest.   1685
                    To bed Sir Gawain went;
                    His sleep was of the best;
                    The lord, on his craft intent,
                    Was early up and dressed.

After mass, with his men, a morsel he takes;   1690
Clear and crisp the morning; he calls for his mount;
The folk that were to follow him afield that day
Were high astride their horses before the hall gates.
Wondrous fair were the fields, for the frost was light;
The sun rises red amid radiant clouds,   1695
Sails into the sky, and sends forth his beams.
They let loose the hounds by a leafy wood;

The rocks all around re-echo to their horns;
Soon some have set off in pursuit of the fox,
Cast about with craft for a clearer scent;   1700
A young dog yaps, and is yelled at in turn;
His fellows fall to sniffing, and follow his lead,
Running in a rabble on the right track,
And he scampers all before; they discover him soon,
And when they see him with sight they pursue him the faster, 1705
Railing at him rudely with a wrathful din.
Often he reverses over rough terrain,
Or loops back to listen in the lee of a hedge;
At last, by a little ditch, he leaps over the brush,
Comes into a clearing at a cautious pace,   1710
Then he thought through his wiles to have thrown off the hounds
Till he was ware, as he went, of a waiting-station
Where three athwart his path threatened him at once,
                            all gray.
                    Quick as a flash he wheels   1715
                    And darts off in dismay;
                    With hard luck at his heels
                    He is off to the wood away.

Then it was heaven on earth to hark to the hounds
When they had come on their quarry, coursing together!   1720
Such harsh cries and howls they hurled at his head
As all the cliffs with a crash had come down at once.
Here he was hailed, when huntsmen met him;
Yonder they yelled at him, yapping and snarling;
There they cried "Thief!" and threatened his life,   1725
And ever the harriers at his heels, that he had no rest.
Often he was menaced when he made for the open,
And often rushed in again, for Reynard was wily;
And so he leads them a merry chase, the lord and his men,
In this manner on the mountains, till midday or near,   1730
While our hero lies at home in wholesome sleep
Within the comely curtains on the cold morning.
But the lady, as love would allow her no rest,
And pursuing ever the purpose that pricked her heart,
Was awake with the dawn, and went to his chamber   1735
In a fair flowing mantle that fell to the earth,
All edged and embellished with ermines fine;
No hood on her head, but heavy with gems
Were her fillet and the fret[8] that confined her tresses;
Her face and her fair throat freely displayed;   1740
Her bosom all but bare, and her back as well.
She comes in at the chamber-door, and closes it with care,
Throws wide a window—then waits no longer,
But hails him thus airily with her artful words,
                            with cheer: 1745

8. Ornamental net.

"Ah, man, how can you sleep?
The morning is so clear!"
Though dreams have drowned him deep,
He cannot choose but hear.

Deep in his dreams he darkly mutters   1750
As a man may that mourns, with many grim thoughts
Of that day when destiny shall deal him his doom
When he greets his grim host at the Green Chapel
And must bow to his buffet, bating all strife.
But when he sees her at his side he summons his wits,   1755
Breaks from the black dreams, and blithely answers.
That lovely lady comes laughing sweet,
Sinks down at his side, and salutes him with a kiss.
He accords her fair welcome in courtliest style;
He sees her so glorious, so gaily attired,   1760
So faultless her features, so fair and so bright,
His heart swelled swiftly with surging joys.
They melt into mirth with many a fond smile,
And there was bliss beyond telling between those two,
                    at height.   1765
            Good were their words of greeting;
            Each joyed in other's sight;
            Great peril attends that meeting
            Should Mary forget her knight.

For that high-born beauty so hemmed him about,   1770
Made so plain her meaning, the man must needs
Either take her tendered love or distastefully refuse.
His courtesy concerned him, lest crass he appear,
But more his soul's mischief, should he commit sin
And belie his loyal oath to the lord of that house.   1775
"God forbid!" said the bold knight, "That shall not befall!"
With a little fond laughter he lightly let pass
All the words of special weight that were sped his way;
"I find you much at fault," the fair one said,
"Who can be cold toward a creature so close by your side,   1780
Of all women in this world most wounded in heart,
Unless you have a sweetheart, one you hold dearer,
And allegiance to that lady so loyally knit
That you will never love another, as now I believe.
And, sir, if it be so, then say it, I beg you;   1785
By all your heart holds dear, hide it no longer
                    with guile."
            "Lady, by Saint John,"
            He answers with a smile,
            "Lover have I none,   1790
            Nor will have, yet awhile."

"Those words," said the woman, "are the worst of all,
But I have had my answer, and hard do I find it!
Kiss me now kindly; I can but go hence

To lament my life long like a maid lovelorn."   1795
She inclines her head quickly and kisses the knight,
Then straightens with a sigh, and says as she stands,
"Now, dear, ere I depart, do me this pleasure:
Give me some little gift, your glove or the like,
That I may think on you, man, and mourn the less."   1800
"Now by heaven," said he, "I wish I had here
My most precious possession, to put it in your hands,
For your deeds, beyond doubt, have often deserved
A repayment far passing my power to bestow.
But a love-token, lady, were of little avail;   1805
It is not to your honor to have at this time
A glove as a guerdon from Gawain's hand,
And I am here on an errand in unknown realms
And have no bearers with baggage with becoming gifts,
Which distresses me, madame, for your dear sake.   1810
A man must keep within his compass: account it neither grief
                                        nor slight."
                        "Nay, noblest knight alive,"
                        Said that beauty of body white,
                        "Though you be loath to give,   1815
                        Yet you shall take, by right."

She reached out a rich ring, wrought all of gold,
With a splendid stone displayed on the band
That flashed before his eyes like a fiery sun;
It was worth a king's wealth, you may well believe.   1820
But he waved it away with these ready words:
"Before God, good lady, I forego all gifts;
None have I to offer, nor any will I take."
And she urged it on him eagerly, and ever he refused,
And vowed in very earnest, prevail she would not.   1825
And she sad to find it so, and said to him then,
"If my ring is refused for its rich cost—
You would not be my debtor for so dear a thing—
I shall give you my girdle;⁹ you gain less thereby."
She released a knot lightly, and loosened a belt   1830
That was caught about her kirtle, the bright cloak beneath,
Of a gay green silk, with gold overwrought,
And the borders all bound with embroidery fine,
And this she presses upon him, and pleads with a smile,
Unworthy though it were, that it would not be scorned.   1835
But the man still maintains that he means to accept
Neither gold nor any gift, till by God's grace
The fate that lay before him was fully achieved.
"And be not offended, fair lady, I beg,
And give over your offer, for ever I must   1840
                        decline.
                        I am grateful for favor shown
                        Past all deserts of mine,

9. Belt.

        And ever shall be your own
        True servant, rain or shine."   1845

"Now does my present displease you," she promptly inquired,
"Because it seems in your sight so simple a thing?
And belike, as it is little, it is less to praise,
But if the virtue that invests it were verily known,
It would be held, I hope, in higher esteem.   1850
For the man that possesses this piece of silk,
If he bore it on his body, belted about,
There is no hand under heaven that could hew him down,
For he could not be killed by any craft on earth."
Then the man began to muse, and mainly he thought   1855
It was a pearl for his plight, the peril to come
When he gains the Green Chapel to get his reward:
Could he escape unscathed, the scheme were noble!
Then he bore with her words and withstood them no more,
And she repeated her petition and pleaded anew,   1860
And he granted it, and gladly she gave him the belt,
And besought him for her sake to conceal it well,
Lest the noble lord should know—and the knight agrees
That not a soul save themselves shall see it thenceforth
                with sight.   1865
        He thanked her with fervent heart,
        As often as ever he might;
        Three times, before they part,
        She has kissed the stalwart knight.

Then the lady took her leave, and left him there,   1870
For more mirth with that man she might not have.
When she was gone, Sir Gawain got from his bed,
Arose and arrayed him in his rich attire;
Tucked away the token the temptress had left,
Laid it reliably where he looked for it after.   1875
And then with good cheer to the chapel he goes,
Approached a priest in private, and prayed to be taught
To lead a better life and lift up his mind,
Lest he be among the lost when he must leave this world.
And shamefaced at shrift[1] he showed his misdeeds   1880
From the largest to the least, and asked the Lord's mercy,
And called on his confessor to cleanse his soul,
And he absolved him of his sins as safe and as clean
As if the dread Day of Judgment should dawn on the morrow.
And then he made merry amid the fine ladies   1885
With deft-footed dances and dalliance light,
As never until now, while the afternoon wore
                away.
        He delighted all around him,
        And all agreed, that day,   1890

---

1. Confession.

        They never before had found him
        So gracious and so gay.

Now peaceful be his pasture, and love play him fair!
The host is on horseback, hunting afield;
He has finished off this fox that he followed so long: 1895
As he leapt a low hedge to look for the villain
Where he heard all the hounds in hot pursuit,
Reynard comes racing out of a rough thicket,
And all the rabble in a rush, right at his heels.
The man beholds the beast, and bides his time,   1900
And bares his bright sword, and brings it down hard,
And he blenches from the blade, and backward he starts;
A hound hurries up and hinders that move,
And before the horse's feet they fell on him at once
And ripped the rascal's throat with a wrathful din.   1905
The lord soon alighted and lifted him free,
Swiftly snatched him up from the snapping jaws,
Holds him over his head, halloos with a will,
And the dogs bayed the dirge, that had done him to death.
Hunters hastened thither with horns at their lips,   1910
Sounding the assembly till they saw him at last.
When that comely company was come in together,
All that bore bugles blew them at once,
And the others all hallooed, that had no horns.
It was the merriest medley that ever a man heard,   1915
The racket that they raised for Sir Reynard's soul
                that died.
        Their hounds they praised and fed,
        Fondling their heads with pride,
        And they took Reynard the Red   1920
        And stripped away his hide.

And then they headed homeward, for evening had come,
Blowing many a blast on their bugles bright.
The lord at long last alights at his house,
Finds fire on the hearth where the fair knight waits,   1925
Sir Gawain the good, that was glad in heart.
With the ladies, that loved him, he lingered at ease;
He wore a rich robe of blue, that reached to the earth
And a surcoat lined softly with sumptuous furs;
A hood of the same hue hung on his shoulders;   1930
With bands of bright ermine embellished were both.
He comes to meet the man amid all the folk,
And greets him good-humoredly, and gaily he says,
"I shall follow forthwith the form of our pledge
That we framed to good effect amid fresh-filled cups."   1935
He clasps him accordingly and kisses him thrice,
As amiably and as earnestly as ever he could.
"By heaven," said the host, "you have had some luck
Since you took up this trade, if the terms were good."

"Never trouble about the terms," he returned at once,   1940
"Since all that I owe here is openly paid."
"Marry!" said the other man, "mine is much less,
For I have hunted all day, and nought have I got
But this foul fox pelt, the fiend take the goods!
Which but poorly repays those precious things   1945
That you have cordially conferred, those kisses three
                    so good."
                    "Enough!" said Sir Gawain;
                    "I thank you, by the rood!"[2]
                    And how the fox was slain   1950
                    He told him, as they stood.

With minstrelsy and mirth, with all manner of meats,
They made as much merriment as any men might
(Amid laughing of ladies and light-hearted girls,
So gay grew Sir Gawain and the goodly host)   1955
Unless they had been besotted, or brainless fools.
The knight joined in jesting with that joyous folk,
Until at last it was late; ere long they must part,
And be off to their beds, as behooved them each one.
Then politely his leave of the lord of the house   1960
Our noble knight takes, and renews his thanks:
"The courtesies countless accorded me here,
Your kindness at this Christmas, may heaven's King repay!
Henceforth, if you will have me, I hold you my liege,
And so, as I have said, I must set forth tomorrow,   1965
If I may take some trusty man to teach, as you promised,
The way to the Green Chapel, that as God allows
I shall see my fate fulfilled on the first of the year."
"In good faith," said the good man, "with a good will
Every promise on my part shall be fully performed."   1970
He assigns him a servant to set him on the path,
To see him safe and sound over the snowy hills,
To follow the fastest way through forest green
                    and grove.
                    Gawain thanks him again,   1975
                    So kind his favors prove,
                    of the ladies then
                    He takes his leave, with love.

Courteously he kissed them, with care in his heart,
And often wished them well, with warmest thanks,   1980
Which they for their part were prompt to repay.
They commend him to Christ with disconsolate sighs;
And then in that hall with the household he parts—
Each man that he met, he remembered to thank
or his deeds of devotion and diligent pains,   1985
And the trouble he had taken to tend to his needs;
And each one as woeful, that watched him depart,

2. Cross.

As he had lived with him loyally all his life long.
By lads bearing lights he was led to his chamber
And blithely brought to his bed, to be at his rest.   1990
How soundly he slept, I presume not to say,
For there were matters of moment his thoughts might well
                              pursue.
                    Let him lie and wait;
                    He has little more to do,   1995
                    Then listen, while I relate
                    How they kept their rendezvous.

PART IV

Now the New Year draws near, and the night passes,
The day dispels the dark, by the Lord's decree;
But wild weather awoke in the world without: 2000
The clouds in the cold sky cast down their snow
With great gusts from the north, grievous to bear.
Sleet showered aslant upon shivering beasts;
The wind warbled wild as it whipped from aloft,
And drove the drifts deep in the dales below.   2005
Long and well he listens, that lies in his bed;
Though he lifts not his eyelids, little he sleeps;
Each crow of the cock he counts without fail.
Readily from his rest he rose before dawn,
For a lamp had been left him, that lighted his chamber.   2010
He called to his chamberlain, who quickly appeared,
And bade him get him his gear, and gird his good steed,
And he sets about briskly to bring in his arms,
And makes ready his master in manner most fit.
First he clad him in his clothes, to keep out the cold,   2015
And then his other harness, made handsome anew,
His plate-armor of proof, polished with pains,
The rings of his rich mail rid of their rust,
And all was fresh as at first, and for this he gave thanks
                              indeed.   2020
                    With pride he wears each piece,
                    New-furbished for his need:
                    No gayer from here to Greece;
                    He bids them bring his steed.

In his richest raiment he robed himself then: 2025
His crested coat-armor, close-stitched with craft,
With stones of strange virtue on silk velvet set;
All bound with embroidery on borders and seams
And lined warmly and well with furs of the best.
Yet he left not his love-gift, the lady's girdle;   2030
Gawain, for his own good, forgot not that:
When the bright sword was belted and bound on his haunches,
Then twice with that token he twined him about.
Sweetly did he swathe him in that swatch of silk,
That girdle of green so goodly to see,   2035

That against the gay red showed gorgeous bright.
Yet he wore not for its wealth that wondrous girdle,
Nor pride in its pendants, though polished they were,
Though glittering gold gleamed at the tips,
But to keep himself safe when consent he must   2040
To endure a deadly dint, and all defense
                                        denied.
                    And now the bold knight came
                    Into the courtyard wide;
                    That folk of worthy fame   2045
                    He thanks on every side.

Then was Gringolet girt, that was great and huge,
And had sojourned safe and sound, and savored his fare;
He pawed the earth in his pride, that princely steed.
The good knight draws near him and notes well his look,   2050
And says sagely to himself, and soberly swears,
"Here is a household in hall that upholds the right!
The man that maintains it, may happiness be his!
Likewise the dear lady, may love betide her!
If thus they in charity cherish a guest   2055
That are honored here on earth, may they have His reward
That reigns high in heaven—and also you all;
And were I to live in this land but a little while,
I should willingly reward you, and well, if I might."
Then he steps into the stirrup and bestrides his mount;   2060
His shield is shown forth; on his shoulder he casts it;
Strikes the side of his steed with his steel spurs,
And he starts across the stones, nor stands any longer
                                        to prance.
                    On horseback was the swain   2065
                    That bore his spear and lance;
                    "May Christ this house maintain
                    And guard it from mischance!"

The bridge was brought down, and the broad gates
Unbarred and carried back upon both sides;   2070
He commended him[3] to Christ, and crossed over the planks;
Praised the noble porter, who prayed on his knees
That God save Sir Gawain, and bade him good day,
And went on his way alone with the man
That was to lead him ere long to that luckless place   2075
Where the dolorous dint must be dealt him at last.
Under bare boughs they ride, where steep banks rise,
Over high cliffs they climb, where cold snow clings;
The heavens held aloof, but heavy thereunder
Mist mantled the moors, moved on the slopes.   2080
Each hill had a hat, a huge cape of cloud;
Brooks bubbled and broke over broken rocks,
Flashing in freshets that waterfalls fed.

3. I.e., himself.

Roundabout was the road that ran through the wood
Till the sun at that season was soon to rise,   2085
                    that day.
            They were on a hilltop high;
            The white snow round them lay;
            The man that rode nearby
            Now bade his master stay.   2090

"For I have seen you here safe at the set time,
And now you are not far from that notable place
That you have sought for so long with such special pains.
But this I say for certain, since I know you, sir knight,
And have your good at heart, and hold you dear—   2095
Would you heed well my words, it were worth your while—
You are rushing into risks that you reck not of:
There is a villain in yon valley, the veriest on earth,
For he is rugged and rude, and ready with fists,
And most immense in his mold of mortals alive,   2100
And his body bigger than the best four
That are in Arthur's house, Hector[4] or any.
He gets his grim way at the Green Chapel;
None passes by that place so proud in his arms
That he does not dash him down with his deadly blows,   2105
For he is heartless wholly, and heedless of right,
For be it chaplain or churl that by the Chapel rides,
Monk or mass-priest or any man else,
He would as soon strike him dead as stand on two feet.
Wherefore I say, just as certain as you sit there astride,   2110
You cannot but be killed, if his counsel holds,
For he would trounce you in a trice, had you twenty lives
                    for sale.
            He has lived long in this land
            And dealt out deadly bale;   2115
            Against his heavy hand
            Your power cannot prevail.

"And so, good Sir Gawain, let the grim man be;
Go off by some other road, in God's own name!
Leave by some other land, for the love of Christ,   2120
And I shall get me home again, and give you my word
That I shall swear by God's self and the saints above,
By heaven and by my halidom[5] and other oaths more,
To conceal this day's deed, nor say to a soul
That ever you fled for fear from any that I knew."   2125
"Many thanks!" said the other man—and demurring he speaks—
"Fair fortune befall you for your friendly words!
And conceal this day's deed I doubt not you would,
But though you never told the tale, if I turned back now,
Forsook this place for fear, and fled, as you say,   2130
I were a caitiff[6] coward; I could not be excused.

---

4. Either the Trojan hero or one of Arthur's knights.   5. Holiness or, more likely, patron saints.
6. Despicable.

But I must to the Chapel to chance my luck
And say to that same man such words as I please,
Befall what may befall through Fortune's will
                         or whim.   2135
                Though he be a quarrelsome knave
                With a cudgel great and grim,
                The Lord is strong to save:
                His servants trust in Him."

"Marry," said the man, "since you tell me so much,   2140
And I see you are set to seek your own harm,
If you crave a quick death, let me keep you no longer!
Put your helm on your head, your hand on your lance,
And ride the narrow road down yon rocky slope
Till it brings you to the bottom of the broad valley.   2145
Then look a little ahead, on your left hand,
And you will soon see before you that self-same Chapel,
And the man of great might that is master there.
Now goodbye in God's name, Gawain the noble!
For all the world's wealth I would not stay here,   2150
Or go with you in this wood one footstep further!"
He tarried no more to talk, but turned his bridle,
Hit his horse with his heels as hard as he might,
Leaves the knight alone, and off like the wind
                        goes leaping.   2155
                "By God," said Gawain then,
                "I shall not give way to weeping;
                God's will be done, amen!
                I commend me to His keeping."

He puts his heels to his horse, and picks up the path;   2160
Goes in beside a grove where the ground is steep,
Rides down the rough slope right to the valley;
And then he looked a little about him—the landscape was wild,
And not a soul to be seen, nor sign of a dwelling,
But high banks on either hand hemmed it about,   2165
With many a ragged rock and rough-hewn crag;
The skies seemed scored by the scowling peaks.
Then he halted his horse, and hoved there a space,
And sought on every side for a sight of the Chapel,
But no such place appeared, which puzzled him sore,   2170
Yet he saw some way off what seemed like a mound,
A hillock high and broad, hard by the water,
Where the stream fell in foam down the face of the steep
And bubbled as if it boiled on its bed below.
The knight urges his horse, and heads for the knoll;   2175
Leaps lightly to earth; loops well the rein
Of his steed to a stout branch, and stations him there.
He strides straight to the mound, and strolls all about,
Much wondering what it was, but no whit the wiser;
It had a hole at one end, and on either side,   2180

And was covered with coarse grass in clumps all without,
And hollow all within, like some old cave,
Or a crevice of an old crag—he could not discern
       aright.
     "Can this be the Chapel Green?   2185
     Alack!" said the man, "Here might
     The devil himself be seen
     Saying matins[7] at black midnight!"

"Now by heaven," said he, "it is bleak hereabouts;
This prayer-house is hideous, half-covered with grass!   2190
Well may the grim man mantled in green
Hold here his orisons, in hell's own style!
Now I feel it is the Fiend, in my five wits,
That has tempted me to this tryst, to take my life;
This is a Chapel of mischance, may the mischief take it!   2195
As accursed a country church as I came upon ever!"
With his helm on his head, his lance in his hand,
He stalks toward the steep wall of that strange house.
Then he heard, on the hill, behind a hard rock,
Beyond the brook, from the bank, a most barbarous din: 2200
Lord! it clattered in the cliff fit to cleave it in two,
As one upon a grindstone ground a great scythe!
Lord! it whirred like a mill-wheel whirling about!
Lord! it echoed loud and long, lamentable to hear!
Then "By heaven," said the bold knight, "That business up there   2205
Is arranged for my arrival, or else I am much
       misled.
     Let God work! Ah me!
     All hope of help has fled!
     Forfeit my life may be   2210
     But noise I do not dread."

Then he listened no longer, but loudly he called,
"Who has power in this place, high parley to hold?
For none greets Sir Gawain, or gives him good day;
If any would a word with him, let him walk forth   2215
And speak now or never, to speed his affairs."
"Abide," said one on the bank above over his head,
"And what I promised you once shall straightway be given."
Yet he stayed not his grindstone, nor stinted its noise,
But worked awhile at his whetting before he would rest,   2220
And then he comes around a crag, from a cave in the rocks,
Hurtling out of hiding with a hateful weapon,
A Danish ax devised for that day's deed,
With a broad blade and bright, bent in a curve,
Filed to a fine edge—four feet it measured   2225
By the length of the lace that was looped round the haft.
And in form as at first, the fellow all green,
His lordly face and his legs, his locks and his beard,

---

7. Morning prayers.

Save that firm upon two feet forward he strides,
Sets a hand on the ax-head, the haft to the earth;   2230
When he came to the cold stream, and cared not to wade,
He vaults over on his ax, and advances amain
On a broad bank of snow, overbearing and brisk
    of mood.
        Little did the knight incline   2235
        When face to face they stood;
        Said the other man, "Friend mine,
        It seems your word holds good!"

"God love you, Sir Gawain!" said the Green Knight then,
"And well met this morning, man, at my place!   2240
And you have followed me faithfully and found me betimes,[8]
And on the business between us we both are agreed:
Twelve months ago today you took what was yours,
And you at this New Year must yield me the same.
And we have met in these mountains, remote from all eyes: 2245
There is none here to halt us or hinder our sport;
Unhasp your high helm, and have here your wages;
Make no more demur than I did myself
When you hacked off my head with one hard blow."
"No, by God," said Sir Gawain, "that granted me life,   2250
I shall grudge not the guerdon, grim though it prove;
Bestow but one stroke, and I shall stand still,
And you may lay on as you like till the last of my part
        be paid."
        He proffered, with good grace,   2255
        His bare neck to the blade,
        And feigned a cheerful face:
        He scorned to seem afraid.

Then the grim man in green gathers his strength,
Heaves high the heavy ax to hit him the blow.   2260
With all the force in his frame he fetches it aloft,
With a grimace as grim as he would grind him to bits;
Had the blow he bestowed been as big as he threatened,
A good knight and gallant had gone to his grave.
But Gawain at the great ax glanced up aside   2265
As down it descended with death-dealing force,
And his shoulders shrank a little from the sharp iron.
Abruptly the brawny man breaks off the stroke,
And then reproved with proud words that prince among knights.
"You are not Gawain the glorious," the green man said,   2270
"That never fell back on field in the face of the foe,
And now you flee for fear, and have felt no harm:
Such news of that knight I never heard yet!
I moved not a muscle when you made to strike,
Nor caviled at the cut in King Arthur's house;   2275
My head fell to my feet, yet steadfast I stood,

8. In good time.

And you, all unharmed, are wholly dismayed—
Wherefore the better man I, by all odds,
           must be."
           Said Gawain, "Strike once more;   2280
           I shall neither flinch nor flee;
           But if my head falls to the floor
           There is no mending me!

"But go on, man, in God's name, and get to the point!
Deliver me my destiny, and do it out of hand,   2285
For I shall stand to the stroke and stir not an inch
Till your ax has hit home—on my honor I swear it!"
"Have at thee then!" said the other, and heaves it aloft,
And glares down as grimly as he had gone mad.
He made a mighty feint, but marred not his hide;   2290
Withdrew the ax adroitly before it did damage.
Gawain gave no ground, nor glanced up aside,
But stood still as a stone, or else a stout stump
That is held in hard earth by a hundred roots.
Then merrily does he mock him, the man all in green: 2295
"So now you have your nerve again, I needs must strike;
Uphold the high knighthood that Arthur bestowed,
And keep your neck-bone clear, if this cut allows!"
Then was Gawain gripped with rage, and grimly he said,
"Why, thrash away, tyrant, I tire of your threats;   2300
You make such a scene, you must frighten yourself."
Said the green fellow, "In faith, so fiercely you speak
That I shall finish this affair, nor further grace
           allow."
           He stands prepared to strike   2305
           And scowls with both lip and brow;
           No marvel if the man mislike
           Who can hope no rescue now.

He gathered up the grim ax and guided it well:
Let the barb at the blade's end brush the bare throat;   2310
He hammered down hard, yet harmed him no whit
Save a scratch on one side, that severed the skin;
The end of the hooked edge entered the flesh,
And a little blood lightly leapt to the earth.
And when the man beheld his own blood bright on the snow, 2315
He sprang a spear's length with feet spread wide,
Seized his high helm, and set it on his head,
Shoved before his shoulders the shield at his back,
Bares his trusty blade, and boldly he speaks—
Not since he was a babe born of his mother   2320
Was he once in this world one-half so blithe—
"Have done with your hacking—harry me no more!
I have borne, as behooved, one blow in this place;
If you make another move I shall meet it midway
And promptly, I promise you, pay back each blow   2325
           with brand.

> One stroke acquits me here;
> So did our covenant stand
> In Arthur's court last year—
> Wherefore, sir, hold your hand!"   2330

He lowers the long ax and leans on it there,
Sets his arms on the head, the haft on the earth,
And beholds the bold knight that bides there afoot,
How he faces him fearless, fierce in full arms,
And plies him with proud words—it pleases him well.   2335
Then once again gaily to Gawain he calls,
And in a loud voice and lusty, delivers these words:
"Bold fellow, on this field your anger forbear!
No man has made demands here in manner uncouth,
Nor done, save as duly determined at court.   2340
I owed you a hit and you have it; be happy therewith!
The rest of my rights here I freely resign.
Had I been a bit busier, a buffet, perhaps,
I could have dealt more directly, and done you some harm.
First I flourished with a feint, in frolicsome mood,   2345
And left your hide unhurt—and here I did well
By the fair terms we fixed on the first night;
And fully and faithfully you followed accord:
Gave over all your gains as a good man should.
A second feint, sir, I assigned for the morning   2350
You kissed my comely wife—each kiss you restored.
For both of these there behooved but two feigned blows
> by right.
> True men pay what they owe;
> No danger then in sight.   2355
> You failed at the third throw,
> So take my tap, sir knight.

"For that is my belt about you, that same braided girdle,
My wife it was that wore it; I know well the tale,
And the count of your kisses and your conduct too,   2360
And the wooing of my wife—it was all my scheme!
She made trial of a man most faultless by far
Of all that ever walked over the wide earth;
As pearls to white peas, more precious and prized,
So is Gawain, in good faith, to other gay knights.   2365
Yet you lacked, sir, a little in loyalty there,
But the cause was not cunning, nor courtship either,
But that you loved your own life; the less, then, to blame."
The other stout knight in a study stood a long while,
So gripped with grim rage that his great heart shook.   2370
All the blood of his body burned in his face
As he shrank back in shame from the man's sharp speech.
The first words that fell from the fair knight's lips:
"Accursed be a cowardly and covetous heart!
In you is villainy and vice, and virtue laid low!"   2375
Then he grasps the green girdle and lets go the knot,

Hands it over in haste, and hotly he says:
"Behold there my falsehood, ill hap betide it!
Your cut taught me cowardice, care for my life,
And coveting came after, contrary both   2380
To largesse and loyalty belonging to knights.
Now am I faulty and false, that fearful was ever
Of disloyalty and lies, bad luck to them both!
            and greed.
        I confess, knight, in this place,   2385
        Most dire is my misdeed;
        Let me gain back your good grace,
        And thereafter I shall take heed."

Then the other laughed aloud, and lightly he said,
"Such harm as I have had, I hold it quite healed.   2390
You are so fully confessed, your failings made known,
And bear the plain penance of the point of my blade,
I hold you polished as a pearl, as pure and as bright
As you had lived free of fault since first you were born.
And I give you, sir, this girdle that is gold-hemmed   2395
And green as my garments, that, Gawain, you may
Be mindful of this meeting when you mingle in throng
With nobles of renown—and known by this token
How it chanced at the Green Chapel, to chivalrous knights.
And you shall in this New Year come yet again   2400
And we shall finish out our feast in my fair hall,
            with cheer."
        He urged the knight to stay,
        And said, "With my wife so dear
        We shall see you friends this day,   2405
        Whose enmity touched you near."

"Indeed," said the doughty knight, and doffed his high helm,
And held it in his hands as he offered his thanks,
"I have lingered long enough—may good luck be yours,
And He reward you well that all worship bestows!   2410
And commend me to that comely one, your courteous wife,
Both herself and that other, my honoured ladies,
That have trapped their true knight in their trammels so quaint.
But if a dullard should dote, deem it no wonder,
And through the wiles of a woman be wooed into sorrow,   2415
For so was Adam by one, when the world began,
And Solomon by many more, and Samson the mighty—
Delilah was his doom, and David thereafter
Was beguiled by Bathsheba, and bore much distress;
Now these were vexed by their devices—'twere a very joy   2420
Could one but learn to love, and believe them not.
For these were proud princes, most prosperous of old,
Past all lovers lucky, that languished under heaven,
            bemused.
        And one and all fell prey   2425
        To women that they had used;

If I be led astray,
Methinks I may be excused.

"But your girdle, God love you! I gladly shall take
And be pleased to possess, not for the pure gold,   2430
Nor the bright belt itself, nor the beauteous pendants,
Nor for wealth, nor worldly state, nor workmanship fine,
But a sign of excess it shall seem oftentimes
When I ride in renown, and remember with shame
The faults and the frailty of the flesh perverse,   2435
How its tenderness entices the foul taint of sin;
And so when praise and high prowess have pleased my heart,
A look at this love-lace will lower my pride.
But one thing would I learn, if you were not loath,
Since you are lord of yonder land where I have long sojourned   2440
With honor in your house—may you have His reward
That upholds all the heavens, highest on throne!
How runs your right name?—and let the rest go."
"That shall I give you gladly," said the Green Knight then;
"Bercilak de Hautdesert this barony I hold,   2445
Through the might of Morgan le Fay,⁹ that lodges at my house,
By subtleties of science and sorcerers' arts,
The mistress of Merlin, she has caught many a man,
For sweet love in secret she shared sometime
With that wizard, that knows well each one of your knights   2450
                    and you.
            Morgan the Goddess, she,
            So styled by title true;
            None holds so high degree
            That her arts cannot subdue.   2455

"She guided me in this guise to your glorious hall,
To assay, if such it were, the surfeit of pride
That is rumored of the retinue of the Round Table.
She put this shape upon me to puzzle your wits,
To afflict the fair queen, and frighten her to death   2460
With awe of that elvish man that eerily spoke
With his head in his hand before the high table.
She was with my wife at home, that old withered lady,
Your own aunt is she,¹ Arthur's half-sister,
The Duchess' daughter of Tintagel, that dear King Uther   2465
Got Arthur on after, that honored is now.
And therefore, good friend, come feast with your aunt;
Make merry in my house; my men hold you dear,
And I wish you as well, sir, with all my heart,
As any mortal man, for your matchless faith."   2470
But the knight said him nay, that he might by no means.

9. Arthur's half-sister, an enchantress (*Faye*: fairy) who sometimes abetted him, sometimes made trouble for him.   1. Morgan was the daughter of Igraine, duchess of Tintagel, and her husband, the duke. Igraine conceived Arthur when his father, Uther, lay with her through one of Merlin's trickeries.

They clasped then and kissed, and commended each other
To the Prince of Paradise, and parted with one
                 assent.
         Gawain sets out anew;   2475
         Toward the court his course is bent;
         And the knight all green in hue,
         Wheresoever he wished, he went.

Wild ways in the world our worthy knight rides
On Gringolet, that by grace had been granted his life.   2480
He harbored often in houses, and often abroad,
And with many valiant adventures verily he met
That I shall not take time to tell in this story.
The hurt was whole that he had had in his neck,
And the bright green belt on his body he bore,   2485
Oblique, like a baldric, bound at his side,
Below his left shoulder, laced in a knot,
In betokening of the blame he had borne for his fault;
And so to court in due course he comes safe and sound.
Bliss abounded in hall when the high-born heard   2490
That good Gawain was come; glad tidings they thought it.
The king kisses the knight, and the queen as well,
And many a comrade came to clasp him in arms,
And eagerly they asked, and awesomely he told,
Confessed all his cares and discomfitures many,   2495
How it chanced at the Chapel, what cheer made the knight,
The love of the lady, the green lace at last.
The nick on his neck he naked displayed
That he got in his disgrace at the Green Knight's hands,
                 alone.   2500
         With rage in heart he speaks,
         And grieves with many a groan;
         The blood burns in his cheeks
         For shame at what must be shown.

"Behold, sir," said he, and handles the belt,   2505
"This is the blazon of the blemish that I bear on my neck;
This is the sign of sore loss that I have suffered there
For the cowardice and coveting that I came to there;
This is the badge of false faith that I was found in there,
And I must bear it on my body till I breathe my last.   2510
For one may keep a deed dark, but undo it no whit,
For where a fault is made fast, it is fixed evermore."
The king comforts the knight, and the court all together
Agree with gay laughter and gracious intent
That the lords and the ladies belonging to the Table,   2515
Each brother of that band, a baldric should have,
A belt borne oblique, of a bright green,
To be worn with one accord for that worthy's sake.
So that was taken as a token by the Table Round,
And he honored that had it, evermore after,   2520

As the best book of knighthood bids it be known.
In the old days of Arthur this happening befell;
The books of Brutus' deeds bear witness thereto
Since Brutus, the bold knight, embarked for this land
After the siege ceased at Troy and the city fared   2525
                        amiss.
            Many such, ere we were born,
            Have befallen here, ere this.
            May He that was crowned with thorn
            Bring all men to His bliss! Amen.   2530

GEOFFREY CHAUCER
1340?–1400

Chaucer is not only one of the earliest poets in the English literary tradition but also one of the greatest. Apart from the poetic virtuosity, psychological subtlety, and humane good humor of his writing, he is worthy of his place here because he is the poet who endowed English literature with a status equal to that of the other European vernaculars—who in effect showed that it could become a world literature. Ironically, the earliest important body of vernacular writing in the medieval period was that of Anglo-Saxon England (represented in this anthology by *Beowulf* and by the lyric poem *The Ruin*). With the Norman conquest of England in 1066 this rich tradition was soon extinguished, and cultural leadership was assumed by literature written in the languages of France—French, Provençal (the dialect of southern France), and Anglo-Norman (the dialect of Normandy and England)—and, to a lesser extent, Italy. Having undergone the break in cultural continuity caused by the Norman conquest, and hindered by the internal struggle for cultural dominance between French and English, English speakers did not develop their own national literature in their own language until the last third of the fourteenth century. This was when *Sir Gawain and the Green Knight* was written, and when other significant writers emerged, especially William Langland, the author of a brilliantly difficult long poem called *Piers Plowman*, and John Gower, who wrote in French and Latin but also composed a major English poem, the *Confessio amantis* (or *Lover's Confession*). Both Langland and Gower lived and worked in London, which was also Chaucer's home. But unlike these contemporaries, Chaucer was very much aware of the European literary traditions not just as collections of texts but as *traditions*, as ongoing cultural projects. This awareness gave to his poetry an artistic subtlety and cultural sophistication that has ensured his position in world literature. But just as important, it also allowed Chaucer to conceive of—and to accomplish—the establishment of an English literary tradition. For it was to his poetry that later English poets, including Shakespeare, Spenser, and Milton, turned to find the foundations of an English literary tradition upon which they could then build.

Chaucer was the son of a wealthy London merchant, and like many children in his position he was sent at an early age to serve as a page in a noble household, in his case that of the countess of Ulster, who was married to one of the sons of King Edward III. Although from a bourgeois background, Chaucer would there have been educated in the values of the aristocratic culture of the time, including its literary tastes, which were for the most part formed on French models. In 1359–60 Chaucer participated in one of the king's military expeditions against the French, was captured, and as was usual at the time, was ransomed by the king. By 1367 Chaucer was a squire in the king's household. This meant not that he resided with the king (although he may have), but that he was called upon to perform a number of services, primarily traveling abroad on the king's business. Chaucer undertook diplomatic journeys to Spain, to France, and—first in 1372–73, then again in 1378—to Italy. These last trips are particularly important because they suggest that Chaucer knew Italian (which he could have learned in London from dealings with the many Italian merchants and bankers who lived there). His poetry—virtually alone among his contemporaries—shows the strong influence of Dante, Petrarch, and Boccaccio, and it is in part their example that provided him with the model for a national literature. In 1374 Chaucer became the Controller of the Customs in London, and he leased a house there (he had already been married for some eight years). He kept this job until 1386, when—probably under political pressure—he resigned. By this time the king was the young Richard II, who had ascended the throne in 1377 at the age of ten. Richard was throughout his reign involved in dangerous struggles for power with the leading members of the aristocracy, and in 1386 he seemed on the verge of being deposed. Chaucer was probably a member of the king's party, and his resignation reflects the decline of Richard's power. By 1389 Richard had regained command, and Chaucer was given other posts and gifts, but ten years later Richard was first deposed and then murdered by Henry Bolingbroke, who became Henry IV. This made little financial difference to Chaucer, who had long maintained a relationship with Henry's father, John of Gaunt, and with Henry himself: his annuity was quickly renewed.

As even this brief account suggests, Chaucer lived in turbulent times. In addition to the struggles for power among the royal family, England was throughout this time at war with France and with the Scots, wars that went progressively badly. It was also during this time—in 1381—that England experienced the shock of the Peasants' Revolt, a violent rebellion that accomplished little substantively but made disturbingly clear the intense animosity that existed between the classes. Finally, this was a period of religious turmoil, when John Wyclif and his supporters were challenging the Church in terms of both its doctrine and its immense economic power—a challenge that would finally culminate in the Protestant Reformation of the sixteenth century. Oddly enough, most of these events find only the barest mention in Chaucer's poetry. Unlike Dante, he seems not to have held strong political convictions, and his religious commitments seem both generally orthodox and lacking in any special intensity. Finally, although Chaucer was generously rewarded by the great men of his day, there is no clear evidence that these rewards were given to him because he wrote poetry. He seems to have followed a career path much like that of other men of his background, and we do not know to what extent, if any, his extraordinary talent was appreciated in his own day. Indeed, two of the characteristics that make Chaucer such an appealing writer are a tolerant inquisitiveness toward all sorts of people and opinions and a self-effacing if sometimes disingenuous modesty. While he lacks Dante's learning, for example, and his intensity, he is a far more agreeable poet: one can hardly imagine Dante appreciating either the Miller's hilarious bawdy or the witty self-promotions of the Wife of Bath.

Chaucer's career as a poet can be usefully divided into three stages. The first stage comprises the poetry he wrote primarily under the influence of the fashionable French court poetry of the time. When Chaucer was a young man the literary language of the king's household was probably French, yet Chaucer seems to have written only in English. The earliest poem we can date with any certainty is an elegy, in English, for Blanche, duchess of Lancaster and the wife of John of Gaunt, who died in 1368. But while written in English, much of this poem is derived from the work of contemporary French court poets: Chaucer here accommodates the tastes of an elegant society hypersensitive to French fashions. This interest continues in all the poetry Chaucer wrote prior to *The Canterbury Tales,* even when his work begins to show the powerful influence of the Italian poets. This second phase begins as early as the late 1370s, when in a poem called the *House of Fame* Chaucer struggles to locate himself in relation to Dante, whose work he seems to have found both intimidating and pretentious. In the 1380s he wrote *Troilus and Criseyde,* a very beautiful narrative love poem based on a poem by Boccaccio, which explores the psychological depths and the ethical questions that are now treated by the novel. The third part of Chaucer's career is called the English period, and comprises *The Canterbury Tales,* a work begun about 1386 and left incomplete. The twenty-four tales that Chaucer completed in fact draw on a wide variety of sources, almost all of them Continental: Chaucer was never very interested in what native tradition of English writing there was. But *The Canterbury Tales* is still a very English work. It begins with a *General Prologue* that describes a group of about thirty pilgrims who meet by chance at an inn in a suburb of London prior to the trip to the shrine of St. Thomas à Becket at Canterbury cathedral. These pilgrims are drawn from almost every rank of fourteenth-century English society, with a decided emphasis on the middle strata, and the reader is left in no doubt that one of the purposes of the work as a whole is to provide a kind of portrait of the nation as a whole. Here Chaucer moves beyond the aristocratic circles to which all of his previous work had been addressed and writes for a larger, national audience. Whether he found such an audience in his own lifetime is very doubtful, but certainly his ambition has been amply rewarded by posterity.

The *Canterbury Tales,* like the *Decameron* and *The Thousand and One Nights,* is a collection of tales located within a frame. At the urging of their host, Harry Bailly, the pilgrims who have gathered at the Tabard Inn agree to tell two tales each, one while going to and one while returning from Canterbury. It seems doubtful that Chaucer himself meant to compose 120 tales, and there are clear indications that the tale-telling game is meant to end before the pilgrims reach Canterbury. Whether Chaucer decided that the twenty-four tales he did include were sufficient is not known, but he certainly did not complete all the links between the tales, and as a result the order in which many of the tales should be read is unclear. Yet this is not a serious impediment to understanding the individual tales, which together provide a brilliant anthology of virtually every medieval kind of writing. Chaucer offers us fabliaux, a mini-epic, romances, saints' lives, *exempla,* a lay, an animal fable, anecdotes, and even two prose treatises dealing with political and spiritual behavior. If he wants to show us almost every kind of person to be found in late medieval England, he also wants to survey almost the full range of medieval writing. Even the *General Prologue,* which describes with an air of casual spontaneity the pilgrims who gather at the Tabard Inn, is a recognizable kind of medieval writing. Medieval social theory held that society was divided into three *estates,* or classes: the nobility, who ruled; the clergy, who prayed; and the laborers, who worked. Much social criticism of the time was offered in the form of a critical commentary on the members of each of these estates. These works are known as *estates satires,* and the *General Prologue* fits the pattern. Chaucer begins with portraits of the knightly estate (the Knight, the Squire, and their servant, the Yeoman), then moves to the clergy (the Prioress, Monk, and Friar), and then to the largest group of all, the estate of those who work for a living. And if he doesn't keep strictly to this scheme—the Clerk, the Parson, the Summoner, and the Pardoner are all technically members of the clergy—he nonetheless includes two "ideal" portraits of each estate: the Knight and the Squire, the Clerk and the Parson, and the Yeoman and the Plowman. Yet, as is usual with Chaucer, he adopts a conventional form only in order to revise it in a new direction. The estates satire is a social form: its focus is on the ills of society and how they can be cured. But Chaucer's focus in the *General Prologue* is primarily on individuals and their psychological makeup. We are much less interested in the degree to which the Prioress fulfills her spiritual duties than we are in the needs she seeks to fulfill with her elegant dress, her love of pets, and her refined but avid dining. We know that the Friar violates his vows, but our attention is drawn to the sort of *person* he is. Striking in this regard is the fact that not until the final portraits does Chaucer pay much attention to the social effects of his characters' misbehavior: until we come to the out-and-out rogues (the Manciple, Miller, Reeve, Summoner and Pardoner—a group in which the narrator places himself!), there is remarkably little sense of anyone being seriously victimized by the pilgrims' foibles. This is not to say that Chaucer is uninterested in morality, but that the moralist's responsibility to judge seems often to conflict with the artist's desire to understand and to appreciate. This conflict corresponds to one within the *General Prologue* itself, between the duty of pilgrimage and the pleasure of tale-telling. In reading this vivid gallery of portraits, then, we do well to try to balance moral judgment with psychological analysis, and to seek to understand the many motivations and needs of these characters and the differing attitudes that the enthusiastic narrator—who is not to be identified with the historical Chaucer—takes toward them.

When the tale-telling game begins, the Knight—the highest representative of the aristocratic estate—is asked to tell the first story. He responds with a medievalized version of a classical epic: it deals with the fervent love of two knights for a fair maiden, and the inconclusive efforts of a wise ruler to bring order out of the chaos their passion creates. The Host then begins to call upon the highest representative of the clergy, the Monk, but is rudely interrupted by one of the lowest ranking members of the third estate, the Miller. The Miller says he will "pay off" the Knight, which means that he will both reward him and retaliate against him. But the social tensions of the time that for a moment burst into the tale-telling game are immediately displaced into *The Miller's Tale*, which is itself about reward and retaliation. Like the Knight, the Miller tells of two young men (Nicholas and Absalom) who desire a beautiful woman (Alison), and of an older man (John) who tries unsuccessfully to control events. But rather than the Knight's high seriousness the Miller presents ribald comedy; and rather than the courtly love the Knight celebrates the Miller presents sexual desire in much less exalted terms. *The Miller's Tale* is a fabliau— indeed, it is two fabliaux brought brilliantly together. One deals with the triangle of Nicholas, Alison, and John and ends with Nicholas's triumph and John's humiliation; the other is the triangle of Nicholas, Absalom and Alison and ends with both men humiliated and Alison cheerfully unscathed. Both these plots are brought together with a single word—"Water!"—that creates an almost metaphysical sense of harmonious resolution. Two stories have unfolded in apparently random ways, and yet suddenly we see that they are in fact one beautifully complex story. One is tempted to say that each story "pays off"—rewards and retaliates against—the other. But does the harmony of the plot extend to the theme as well? Is there moral as well as narrative order? To answer this question the reader must realize that what is being punished is not transgression against social or religious conventions but a presumptuous desire to overcontrol. All three men want to control Alison, but she not only has a mind of her own but also knows when a joke has gone far enough. It is this combination of frank self-gratification with prudent self-restraint that the Miller seems to admire, and that the three men lack.

The Wife of Bath is also called Alison, and it is not unreasonable to see her as Chaucer's idea of how the Miller's beautiful young woman might deal with growing old. But instead of being primarily an object that men desire, this Alison is endowed with a vivid personality and a complex inner life that she herself tells us all about. In her *Prologue* she sets her female experience against the misogynist stereotypes of women, as lawless, sexually voracious, and manipulative creatures, promoted by certain traditions of medieval religious thought. Yet the reader is forced to ask if the Wife's frank celebration of her own sexuality, and her account of the torment she has inflicted on her three old husbands, does not actually confirm those stereotypes. An answer is suggested by the Wife's claim that in her *Prologue* she is only playing: indeed, at one point she speaks as if she were showing her almost exclusively male audience how she would conduct a kind of school for wives. She seems, in other words, to be putting on a performance, pretending to reveal to her fascinated audience the secrets that women share among themselves and so letting men witness the intimate life of a woman. Yet as the *Prologue* proceeds we feel that her playful dramatics give way to a more serious, more authentic self-revelation. We learn that not only have her husbands suffered in marriage but that she has too, that she is unavoidably (if cheerfully) aware of the advancing years, and that what she seems most to value is neither money nor the sex she so aggressively celebrates but the companionship and love she comes finally to share with Jankin. In the same way her *Tale* gradually reveals itself to be more than simply a nostalgic wish fulfillment for the return of youth and beauty. When the criminal knight tries to learn what women most desire he is offered a series of misogynist answers, but when forced to marry he discovers, through the moral lecture his old wife delivers, that she possesses a wisdom he himself lacks. This is why he leaves the final decision about what form she will assume up to her, and in granting her mastery he is rewarded not merely with youth and beauty but with a marriage of mutual affection. It is through this experience, then, rather than by relying on the authority of time-honored opinions, that the knight comes to learn about the true nature of women.

The Pardoner provides a performance that is very similar to that of the Wife, but his subject is not marriage but religion. His function is to raise money for a charitable institution—in this case, a hospital—by selling papal indulgences. These were documents by which the Church remitted some of the punishment that awaited sinners in purgatory by virtue of their charitable gifts. On no account, despite what this Pardoner says, did indulgences remit the guilt of sin: only Christ could do that. In his *Prologue* the Pardoner admits that he is a thorough rogue—indeed, he trumpets his viciousness, and his impenitent lack of concern for his own spiritual future, so loudly and so brazenly that we may think he protests too much. Even in the *Prologue* we get hints that the Pardoner harbors somewhere in his tortured soul the thought that he is, despite himself, doing God's work. And in fact the story he tells is one of the most brilliantly effective religious stories in all medieval literature. Generically it is an exemplum, one of those tales with which preachers would enliven their sermons. It demonstrates with an almost mathematical efficiency that the wages of sin are death, and it also provides us with a startling insight into the Pardoner himself. For he too is seeking the spiritual death of damnation, and in the figure of the eerie old man he expresses with painful vividness the common medieval understanding of damnation as a condition of perpetual dying, a dying that never finds death. Just as the Wife of Bath is more than a stereotype, so too the Pardoner is more than an impenitent sinner. On the contrary, Chaucer allows us to see the deep suffering endured by a man who mocks religious truths while simultaneously yearning for them.

CHAUCER IN MIDDLE ENGLISH

Chaucer is presented here in a Modern English version by Theodore Morrison, which is remarkably clear, accurate, and easy to read. But, to get some idea of Chaucer's original language, we may profitably compare the first eighteen lines of the *General Prologue* in the two forms. It will be possible to point out only a few of the changes that have occurred in pronunciation, in grammatical forms, and sometimes in the use and meaning of words.

Whan that Aprille with his shoures sote
The droghte of Marche hath perced to the rote,
And bathed every veyne in swich licour,
Of which vertu engendred is the flour;
When Zephirus eek with his swete breeth   5
Inspired hath in every holt and heeth
The tendre croppes, and the yonge sonne
Hath in the Ram his halfe cours y-ronne,

And smale fowles maken melodye,
That slepen al the night with open yë,   10
So priketh hem nature in hir corages:
Than longen folk to goon on pilgrimages
And palmers for to seken straunge strandes
To ferne halwes, couthe in sondry landes;
And specially, from every shires ende   15
Of Engeland, to Caunterbury they wende,
The holy blisful martir for to seke,
That hem hath holpen, whan that they were seke.

In Middle English of the late fourteenth century, the letters representing the stressed vowels were pronounced about as they are in Spanish or Italian in our time. Thus the *A* of *Aprille* sounded like *a* in our *father;* the first *e* in *swete* (line 5) was like the *a* in modern English *late;* and the second *i* in *Inspired* (line 6) was like *i* in our *machine.* In verbs, the third person singular ended in *-th,* not *-s,* as in *hath* (line 2); and the plural ending, either *-en* or *-e,* formed a separate syllable, as in *maken* (line 9), *slepen* (line 10), and *wende* (line 16). Among the pronouns and pronominal adjectives, Chaucer's language did not have our *its, their,* or *them.* Instead, the corresponding forms were, respectively, *his* (line 1), *hir(e)* (line 11), and *hem* (line 18). Changes in the meaning or use of words may compel a substitution. Thus Chaucer's *couthe* (line 14) has become obsolete and hence is translated as *renowned* instead; so also *corages* (line 11) becomes *hearts,* and *ferne halwes* (line 14) becomes *foreign shrines.* Readers interested in hearing Chaucer's poetry read in its original language can order tapes from any good music store.

The standard edition of Chaucer's works is Larry Benson, ed., *The Riverside Chaucer,* 3rd. ed. (1987), which provides a fully annotated text in Middle English with a glossary and full introductions and notes. Useful guides to *The Canterbury Tales* are provided in accessible books by Derek A. Pearsall (1985) and Winthrop Wetherbee (1989). More detailed analyses of the three tales selected here may be found in Lee Patterson, *Chaucer and the Subject of History* (1991).

The Canterbury Tales[1]

General Prologue

As soon as April pierces to the root
The drought of March, and bathes each bud and shoot
Through every vein of sap with gentle showers
From whose engendering liquor spring the flowers;
When zephyrs[2] have breathed softly all about   5
Inspiring every wood and field to sprout,
And in the zodiac the youthful sun
His journey halfway through the Ram[3] has run;
When little birds are busy with their song
Who sleep with open eyes the whole night long   10
Life stirs their hearts and tingles in them so,
Then off as pilgrims people long to go,
And palmers[4] to set out for distant strands

---

1. Translated by Theodore Morrison.   2. The west wind.   3. A sign of the zodiac (Aries); the sun is in the Ram from March 12 to April 11.   4. Pilgrims, who, originally, brought back palm leaves from the Holy Land.

And foreign shrines renowned in many lands.
And specially in England people ride 15
To Canterbury from every countryside
To visit there the blessed martyred saint[5]
Who gave them strength when they were sick and faint.
   In Southwark at the Tabard[6] one spring day
It happened, as I stopped there on my way, 20
Myself a pilgrim with a heart devout
Ready for Canterbury to set out,
At night came all of twenty-nine assorted
Travelers, and to that same inn resorted,
Who by a turn of fortune chanced to fall 25
In fellowship together, and they were all
Pilgrims who had it in their minds to ride
Toward Canterbury. The stable doors were wide,
The rooms were large, and we enjoyed the best,
And shortly, when the sun had gone to rest, 30
I had so talked with each that presently
I was a member of their company
And promised to rise early the next day
To start, as I shall show, upon our way.
   But none the less, while I have time and space, 35
Before this tale has gone a further pace,
I should in reason tell you the condition
Of each of them, his rank and his position,
And also what array they all were in;
And so then, with a knight I will begin. 40
   A Knight was with us, and an excellent man,
Who from the earliest moment he began
To follow his career loved chivalry,
Truth, openhandedness, and courtesy.
He was a stout man in his lord's campaigns 45
And in that cause had gripped his horse's reins
In Christian lands and pagan through the earth,
None farther, and always honored for his worth.
He was on hand at Alexandria's[7] fall.
He had often sat in precedence to all 50
The nations at the banquet board in Prussia.[8]
He had fought in Lithuania and in Russia,
No Christian knight more often; he had been
In Moorish Africa at Benmarin,
At the siege of Algeciras in Granada, 55
And sailed in many a glorious armada
In the Mediterranean, and fought as well
At Ayas and Attalia when they fell
In Armenia and on Asia Minor's coast.
Of fifteen deadly battles he could boast, 60
And in Algeria, at Tremessen,
Fought for the faith and killed three separate men

5. St. Thomas à Becket, slain in Canterbury cathedral in 1170. 6. An inn at Southwark, across the
river Thames from London. 7. In Egypt, captured in 1365 by King Peter of Cyprus. 8. A reference
to crusades against the still-pagan Slavs.

In single combat. He had done good work
Joining against another pagan Turk
With the king of Palathia.⁹ And he was wise,   65
Despite his prowess, honored in men's eyes,
Meek as a girl and gentle in his ways.
He had never spoken ignobly all his days
To any man by even a rude inflection.
He was a knight in all things to perfection.   70
He rode a good horse, but his gear was plain,
For he had lately served on a campaign.
His tunic was still spattered by the rust
Left by his coat of mail, for he had just
Returned and set out on his pilgrimage.   75
    His son was with him, a young Squire, in age
Some twenty years as near as I could guess.
His hair curled as if taken from a press.
He was a lover and would become a knight.
In stature he was of a moderate height   80
But powerful and wonderfully quick.
He had been in Flanders, riding in the thick
Of forays in Artois and Picardy,¹
And bore up well for one so young as he,
Still hoping by his exploits in such places   85
To stand the better in his lady's graces.
He wore embroidered flowers, red and white,
And blazed like a spring meadow to the sight.
He sang or played his flute the livelong day.
He was as lusty as the month of May.   90
His coat was short, its sleeves were long and wide.
He sat his horse well, and knew how to ride,
And how to make a song and use his lance,
And he could write and draw well, too, and dance.
So hot his love that when the moon rose pale   95
He got no more sleep than a nightingale.
He was modest, and helped whomever he was able,
And carved as his father's squire at the table.
    But one more servant had the Knight beside,
Choosing thus simply for the time to ride: 100
A Yeoman, in a coat and hood of green.
His peacock-feathered arrows, bright and keen,
He carried under his belt in tidy fashion.
For well-kept gear he had a yeoman's passion,
No draggled feather might his arrows show,   105
And in his hand he held a mighty bow.
He kept his hair close-cropped, his face was brown.
He knew the lore of woodcraft up and down.
His arm was guarded from the bowstring's whip
By a bracer, gaily trimmed. He had at hip   110
A sword and buckler, and at his other side

---

9. An independent emirate on the southwest coast of Turkey.   1. Provinces in the north of France and
in Flanders.

A dagger whose fine mounting was his pride,
Sharp-pointed as a spear. His horn he bore
In a sling of green, and on his chest he wore
A silver image of St. Christopher,   115
His patron, since he was a forester.
    There was also a Nun, a Prioress,
Whose smile was gentle and full of guilelessness.
"By St. Loy!"[2] was the worst oath she would say.
She sang mass well, in a becoming way,   120
Intoning through her nose the words divine,
And she was known as Madame Eglantine.
She spoke good French, as taught at Stratford-Bow[3]
For the Parisian French she did not know.
She was schooled to eat so primly and so well   125
That from her lips no morsel ever fell.
She wet her fingers lightly in the dish
Of sauce, for courtesy was her first wish.
With every bite she did her skillful best
To see that no drop fell upon her breast.   130
She always wiped her upper lip so clean
That in her cup was never to be seen
A hint of grease when she had drunk her share.
She reached out for her meat with comely air.
She was a great delight, and always tried   135
To imitate court ways, and had her pride,
Both amiable and gracious in her dealings.
As for her charity and tender feelings,
She melted at whatever was piteous.
She would weep if she but came upon a mouse   140
Caught in a trap, if it were dead or bleeding.
Some little dogs that she took pleasure feeding
On roasted meat or milk or good wheat bread
She had, but how she wept to find one dead
Or yelping from a blow that made it smart,   145
And all was sympathy and loving heart.
Neat was her wimple in its every plait,
Her nose well formed, her eyes as gray as slate.
Her mouth was very small and soft and red.
She had so wide a brow I think her head   150
Was nearly a span broad, for certainly
She was not undergrown, as all could see.
She wore her cloak with dignity and charm,
And had her rosary about her arm,
The small beads coral and the larger green,   155
And from them hung a brooch of golden sheen,
On it a large A and a crown above;[4]
Beneath, "All things are subject unto love."
    A Priest accompanied her toward Canterbury,
And an attendant Nun, her secretary.   160

2. Perhaps St. Eligius, apparently a popular saint at this time.   3. In Middlesex, near London, where there was a nunnery.   4. The *A* stands for *Amor*, Latin for "love"; in the original the motto is *Amor vincit omnia*, "Love conquers all."

There was a Monk, and nowhere was his peer,
A hunter, and a roving overseer.[5]
He was a manly man, and fully able
To be an abbot. He kept a hunting stable,
And when he rode the neighborhood could hear   165
His bridle jingling in the wind as clear
And loud as if it were a chapel bell.
Wherever he was master of a cell
The principles of good St. Benedict,[6]
For being a little old and somewhat strict,   170
Were honored in the breach, as past their prime.
He lived by the fashion of a newer time.
He would have swapped that text for a plucked hen
Which says that hunters are not holy men,
Or a monk outside his discipline and rule   175
Is too much like a fish outside his pool;
That is to say, a monk outside his cloister.
But such a text he deemed not worth an oyster.
I told him his opinion made me glad.
Why should he study always and go mad,   180
Mewed in his cell with only a book for neighbor?
Or why, as Augustine[7] commanded, labor
And sweat his hands? How shall the world be served?
To Augustine be all such toil reserved!
And so he hunted, as was only right.   185
He had greyhounds as swift as birds in flight.
His taste was all for tracking down the hare,
And what his sport might cost he did not care.
His sleeves I noticed, where they met his hand,
Trimmed with gray fur, the finest in the land.   190
His hood was fastened with a curious pin
Made of wrought gold and clasped beneath his chin,
A love knot at the tip. His head might pass,
Bald as it was, for a lump of shining glass,
And his face was glistening as if anointed.   195
Fat as a lord he was, and well appointed.
His eyes were large, and rolled inside his head
As if they gleamed from a furnace of hot lead.
His boots were supple, his horse superbly kept.
He was a prelate to dream of while you slept.   200
He was not pale nor peaked like a ghost.
He relished a plump swan as his favorite roast.
He rode a palfrey brown as a ripe berry.
    A Friar was with us, a gay dog and a merry,
Who begged his district with a jolly air.   205
No friar in all four orders[8] could compare
With him for gallantry; his tongue was wooing.
Many a girl was married by his doing,
And at his own cost it was often done.

---

5. He is responsible for the monastery's outlying properties.   6. Monastic rules authored by St. Benedict
in the sixth century.   7. St. Augustine (A.D. 354–430) argued that monks should perform manual
labor.   8. Most friars belonged to one of four groups, or orders.

He was a pillar, and a noble one,   210
To his whole order. In his neighborhood
Rich franklins[9] knew him well, who served good food,
And worthy women welcomed him to town;
For the license that his order handed down,
He said himself, conferred on him possession   215
Of more than a curate's[1] power of confession.
Sweetly the list of frailties he heard,
Assigning penance with a pleasant word.
He was an easy man for absolution
Where he looked forward to a contribution,   220
For if to a poor order a man has given
It signifies that he has been well shriven,[2]
And if a sinner let his purse be dented
The Friar would stake his oath he had repented.
For many men become so hard of heart   225
They cannot weep, though conscience makes them smart.
Instead of tears and prayers, then, let the sinner
Supply the poor friars with the price of dinner.
For pretty women he had more than shrift.[3]
His cape was stuffed with many a little gift,   230
As knives and pins and suchlike. He could sing
A merry note, and pluck a tender string,
And had no rival at all in balladry.
His neck was whiter than a fleur-de-lis,[4]
And yet he could have knocked a strong man down.   235
He knew the taverns well in every town.
The barmaids and innkeepers pleased his mind
Better than beggars and lepers and their kind.
In his position it was unbecoming
Among the wretched lepers to go slumming.   240
It mocks all decency, it sews no stitch
To deal with such riffraff, but with the rich,
With sellers of victuals, that's another thing.
Wherever he saw some hope of profiting,
None so polite, so humble. He was good,   245
The champion beggar of his brotherhood.
Should a woman have no shoes against the snow,
So pleasant was his "In principio"[5]
He would have her widow's mite before he went.
He took in far more than he paid in rent   250
For his right of begging within certain bounds.[6]
None of his brethren trespassed on his grounds!
He loved as freely as a half-grown whelp.
On arbitration-days[7] he gave great help,
For his cloak was never shiny nor threadbare   255
Like a poor cloistered scholar's. He had an air

9. Landowners or country squires, not belonging to the nobility.   1. A parish priest.   2. Confessed.   3. Confession.   4. Lily.   5. In the beginning (Latin); the opening phrase of a famous passage in the New Testament of the Bible (John 1.1–16).   6. The territory in which he could beg, for which he paid a fee.   7. Days appointed for settling disputes.

As if he were a doctor or a pope.
It took stout wool to make his semicope[8]
That plumped out like a bell for portliness.
He lisped a little in his rakishness   260
To make his English sweeter on his tongue,
And twanging his harp to end some song he'd sung
His eyes would twinkle in his head as bright
As the stars twinkle on a frosty night.
Hubert this gallant Friar was by name.   265
    Among the rest a Merchant also came.
He wore a forked beard and a beaver hat
From Flanders. High up in the saddle he sat,
In figured cloth,[9] his boots clasped handsomely,
Delivering his opinions pompously,   270
Always on how his gains might be increased.
At all costs he desired the sea policed[1]
From Middleburg in Holland to Orwell.[2]
He knew the exchange rates, and the time to sell
French currency, and there was never yet   275
A man who could have told he was in debt
So grave he seemed and hid so well his feelings
With all his shrewd engagements and close dealings.
You'd find no better man at any turn;
But what his name was I could never learn.   280
    There was an Oxford Student too, it chanced,
Already in his logic well advanced.
He rode a mount as skinny as a rake,
And he was hardly fat. For learning's sake
He let himself look hollow and sober enough.   285
He wore an outer coat of threadbare stuff,
For he had no benefice[3] for his enjoyment
And was too unworldly for some lay employment.
He much preferred to have beside his bed
His twenty volumes bound in black or red   290
All packed with Aristotle from end to middle
Than a sumptuous wardrobe or a merry fiddle.
For though he knew what learning had to offer
There was little coin to jingle in his coffer.
Whatever he got by touching up a friend   295
On books and learning he would promptly spend
And busily pray for the soul of anybody
Who furnished him the wherewithal for study.
His scholarship was what he truly heeded.
He never spoke a word more than was needed,   300
And that was said with dignity and force,
And quick and brief. He was of grave discourse
Giving new weight to virtue by his speech,
And gladly would he learn and gladly teach.

8. A short cape.   9. Cloth of mixed color.   1. For protection from piracy.   2. An English port near
Harwich.   3. A paid position in the Church.

There was a Lawyer, cunning and discreet,   305
Who had often been to St. Paul's porch[4] to meet
His clients. He was a Sergeant of the Law,[5]
A man deserving to be held in awe,
Or so he seemed, his manner was so wise.
He had often served as Justice of Assize[6]   310
By the king's appointment, with a broad commission,
For his knowledge and his eminent position.
He had many a handsome gift by way of fee.
There was no buyer of land as shrewd as he.
All ownership to him became fee simple.[7]   315
His titles were never faulty by a pimple.
None was so busy as he with case and cause,
And yet he seemed much busier than he was.
In all cases and decisions he was schooled
That were of record since King William[8] ruled.   320
No one could pick a loophole or a flaw
In any lease or contract he might draw.
Each statute on the books he knew by rote.
He traveled in a plain, silk-belted coat.
     A Franklin traveled in his company.   325
Whiter could never daisy petal be
Than was his beard. His ruddy face gave sign
He liked his morning sop of toast in wine.
He lived in comfort, as he would assure us,
For he was a true son of Epicurus[9]   330
Who held the opinion that the only measure
Of perfect happiness was simply pleasure.
Such hospitality did he provide,
He was St. Julian[1] to his countryside.
His bread and ale were always up to scratch.   335
He had a cellar none on earth could match.
There was no lack of pasties in his house,
Both fish and flesh, and that so plenteous
That where he lived it snowed of meat and drink.
With every dish of which a man can think,   340
After the various seasons of the year,
He changed his diet for his better cheer.
He had coops of partridges as fat as cream,
He had a fishpond stocked with pike and bream.
Woe to his cook for an unready pot   345
Or a sauce that wasn't seasoned and spiced hot!
A table in his hall stood on display
Prepared and covered through the livelong day.
He presided at court sessions for his bounty
And sat in Parliament often for his county.   350
A well-wrought dagger and a purse of silk

---

4. A meeting place for lawyers and their clients in the porch of St. Paul's Cathedral, London.
5. Sergeants of the Law were the most prestigious and powerful lawyers of the time.   6. A judge in the
circuit court.   7. Owned outright without legal impediments.   8. The Conqueror (reigned 1066–
1087).   9. Greek philosopher whose teaching (presented here in a somewhat debased form) is believed
to make pleasure the goal of life.   1. Patron saint of hospitality.

Hung at his belt, as white as morning milk.
He had been a sheriff and county auditor.
On earth was no such rich proprietor!
   There were five Guildsmen, in the livery   355
Of one august and great fraternity,[2]
A Weaver, a Dyer, and a Carpenter,
A Tapestry-maker and a Haberdasher.
Their gear was furbished new and clean as glass.
The mountings of their knives were not of brass   360
But silver. Their pouches were well made and neat,
And each of them, it seemed, deserved a seat
On the platform at the Guildhall,[3] for each one
Was likely timber to make an alderman.
They had goods enough, and money to be spent,   365
Also their wives would willingly consent
And would have been at fault if they had not.
For to be "Madamed" is a pleasant lot,
And to march in first at feasts for being well married,
And royally to have their mantles carried.   370
   For the pilgrimage these Guildsmen brought their own
Cook to boil their chicken and marrow bone
With seasoning powder and capers and sharp spice.
In judging London ale his taste was nice.
He well knew how to roast and broil and fry,   375
To mix a stew, and bake a good meat pie,
Or capon creamed with almond, rice, and egg.
Pity he had an ulcer on his leg!
   A Skipper was with us, his home far in the west.
He came from the port of Dartmouth,[4] as I guessed.   380
He sat his carthorse pretty much at sea
In a coarse smock that joggled on his knee.
From his neck a dagger on a string hung down
Under his arm. His face was burnished brown
By the summer sun. He was a true good fellow.   385
Many a time he had tapped a wine cask mellow
Sailing from Bordeaux[5] while the owner slept.
Too nice a point of honor he never kept.
In a sea fight, if he got the upper hand,
Drowned prisoners floated home to every land.   390
But in navigation, whether reckoning tides,
Currents, or what might threaten him besides,
Harborage, pilotage, or the moon's demeanor,
None was his like from Hull to Cartagena.[6]
He knew each harbor and the anchorage there   395
From Gotland to the Cape of Finisterre[7]
And every creek in Brittany and Spain,
And he had called his ship the *Madeleine*.
   With us came also an astute Physician.

---

2. Members of a parish fraternity, an organization centered on the parish church that served both religious and social purposes.   **3.** London's city hall.   **4.** On the southwest coast.   **5.** On the southwest coast of France.   **6.** A Spanish port. *Hull:* an English port.   **7.** On the Spanish coast. *Gotland:* a Swedish island.

There was none like him for a disquisition   400
On the art of medicine or surgery,
For he was grounded in astrology.
He kept his patient long in observation,
Choosing the proper hour for application
Of charms and images by intuition   405
Of magic, and the planets' best position.
For he was one who understood the laws
That rule the humors, and could tell the cause
That brought on every human malady,
Whether of hot or cold, or moist or dry.   410
He was a perfect medico, for sure.
The cause once known, he would prescribe the cure
For he had his druggists ready at a motion
To provide the sick man with some pill or potion—
A game of mutual aid, with each one winning.   415
Their partnership was hardly just beginning!
He was well versed in his authorities,
Old Aesculapius, Dioscorides,
Rufus, and old Hippocrates, and Galen,
Haly, and Rhazes, and Serapion,   420
Averroës, Bernard, Johannes Damascenus,
Avicenna, Gilbert, Gaddesden, Constantinus.[8]
He urged a moderate fare on principle,
But rich in nourishment, digestible;
Of nothing in excess would he admit.   425
He gave but little heed to Holy Writ.
His clothes were lined with taffeta; their hue
Was all of blood red and of Persian blue,
Yet he was far from careless of expense.
He saved his fees from times of pestilence,   430
For gold is a cordial,[9] as physicians hold,
And so he had a special love for gold.
    A worthy woman there was from near the city
Of Bath,[1] but somewhat deaf, and more's the pity.
For weaving she possessed so great a bent   435
She outdid the people of Ypres and of Ghent.[2]
No other woman dreamed of such a thing
As to precede her at the offering,
Or if any did, she fell in such a wrath
She dried up all the charity in Bath.   440
She wore fine kerchiefs of old-fashioned air,
And on a Sunday morning, I could swear,
She had ten pounds of linen on her head.
Her stockings were of finest scarlet-red,
Laced tightly, and her shoes were soft and new.   445
Bold was her face, and fair, and red in hue.
She had been an excellent woman all her life
Five men in turn had taken her to wife,

8. Eminent medical authorities from ancient Greece, ancient and medieval Arabic civilization, and England in the thirteenth and fourteenth centuries.   9. Gold was thought to be a stimulant.   1. A town in southwest England.   2. Towns in Flanders famous for their cloth.

Omitting other youthful company—
But let that pass for now! Over the sea   450
She had traveled freely; many a distant stream
She crossed, and visited Jerusalem
Three times. She had been at Rome and at Boulogne,
At the shrine of Compostella, and at Cologne.[3]
She had wandered by the way through many a scene.   455
Her teeth were set with little gaps between.[4]
Easily on her ambling horse she sat.
She was well wimpled, and she wore a hat
As wide in circuit as a shield or targe.[5]
A skirt swathed up her hips, and they were large.   460
Upon her feet she wore sharp-roweled spurs.
She was a good fellow; a ready tongue was hers.
All remedies of love she knew by name,[6]
For she had all the tricks of that old game.
    There was a good man of the priests' vocation,   465
A poor town Parson of true consecration,
But he was rich in holy thought and work.
Learned he was, in the truest sense a clerk
Who meant Christ's gospel faithfully to preach
And truly his parishioners to teach.   470
He was a kind man, full of industry,
Many times tested by adversity
And always patient. If tithes[7] were in arrears,
He was loth to threaten any man with fears
Of excommunication; past a doubt   475
He would rather spread his offering about
To his poor flock, or spend his property.
To him a little meant sufficiency.
Wide was his parish, with houses far asunder,
But he would not be kept by rain or thunder,   480
If any had suffered a sickness or a blow,
From visiting the farthest, high or low
Plodding his way on foot, his staff in hand.
He was a model his flock could understand,
For first he did and afterward he taught.   485
That precept from the Gospel he had caught,
And he added as a metaphor thereto,
"If the gold rusts, what will the iron do?"
For if a priest is foul, in whom we trust,
No wonder a layman shows a little rust.   490
A priest should take to heart the shameful scene
Of shepherds filthy while the sheep are clean.
By his own purity a priest should give
The example to his sheep, how they should live.
He did not rent his benefice for hire,[8]   495
Leaving his flock to flounder in the mire,

3. Sites of shrines much visited by pilgrims.   4. I.e., gap-toothed; in a woman considered a sign of sexual prowess.   5. A small shield.   6. Chaucer has Ovid's *Love Cures* (*Remedia Amoris*) in mind.
7. Payments due to the priest, usually a tenth of annual income.   8. Rent out his appointment to a substitute.

And run to London, happiest of goals,
To sing paid masses in St. Paul's for souls,[9]
Or as chaplain from some rich guild take his keep,
But dwelt at home and guarded well his sheep   500
So that no wolf should make his flock miscarry.
He was a shepherd, and not a mercenary.
And though himself a man of strict vocation
He was not harsh to weak souls in temptation,
Not overbearing nor haughty in his speech,   505
But wise and kind in all he tried to teach.
By good example and just words to turn
Sinners to heaven was his whole concern.
But should a man in truth prove obstinate,
Whoever he was, of rich or mean estate,   510
The Parson would give him a snub to meet the case.
I doubt there was a priest in any place
His better. He did not stand on dignity
Nor affect in conscience too much nicety,
But Christ's and his disciples' words he sought   515
To teach, and first he followed what he taught.
    There was a Plowman with him on the road,
His brother, who had forked up many a load
Of good manure. A hearty worker he,
Living in peace and perfect charity.[1]   520
Whether his fortune made him smart or smile,
He loved God with his whole heart all the while
And his neighbor as himself. He would undertake,
For every luckless poor man, for the sake
Of Christ to thresh and ditch and dig by the hour   525
And with no wage, if it was in his power.
His tithes on goods and earnings he paid fair.
He wore a coarse, rough coat and rode a mare.
    There also were a Manciple, a Miller,
A Reeve, a Summoner, and a Pardoner,[2]   530
And I—this makes our company complete.
    As tough a yokel as you care to meet
The Miller was. His big-beefed arms and thighs
Took many a ram put up as wrestling prize.
He was a thick, squat-shouldered lump of sins.   535
No door but he could heave it off its pins
Or break it running at it with his head.
His beard was broader than a shovel, and red
As a fat sow or fox. A wart stood clear
Atop his nose, and red as a pig's ear   540
A tuft of bristles on it. Black and wide
His nostrils were. He carried at his side
A sword and buckler.[3] His mouth would open out

---

9. Many wealthy people endowed positions for priests, who would sing masses for the souls of their patrons after their deaths.   1. Ache.   2. A seller of indulgences that purported to release sinful souls from purgatory early. *Manciple:* an officer in charge of supplies. *Reeve:* farm overseer. *Summoner:* he summoned people to appear before the church court (presided over by the archdeacon) and in general acted as a kind of bailiff.   3. Shield.

Like a great furnace, and he would sing and shout
His ballads and jokes of harlotries and crimes.   545
He could steal corn and charge for it three times,
And yet was honest enough, as millers come,
For a miller, as they say, has a golden thumb.[4]
In white coat and blue hood this lusty clown,
Blowing his bagpipes, brought us out of town.   550
   The Manciple was of a lawyers' college,[5]
And other buyers might have used his knowledge
How to be shrewd provisioners, for whether
He bought on cash or credit, altogether
He managed that the end should be the same: 555
He came out more than even with the game.
Now isn't it an instance of God's grace
How a man of little knowledge can keep pace
In wit with a whole school of learned men?
He had masters to the number of three times ten   560
Who knew each twist of equity and tort;[6]
A dozen in that very Inn of Court
Were worthy to be steward of the estate
To any of England's lords, however great,
And keep him to his income well confined   565
And free from debt, unless he lost his mind,
Or let him scrimp, if he were mean in bounty;
They could have given help to a whole county
In any sort of case that might befall;
And yet this Manciple could cheat them all!   570
   The Reeve was a slender, fiery-tempered man.
He shaved as closely as a razor can.
His hair was cropped about his ears, and shorn
Above his forehead as a priest's is worn.[7]
His legs were very long and very lean.   575
No calf on his lank spindles could be seen.
But he knew how to keep a barn or bin,
He could play the game with auditors and win.
He knew well how to judge by drought and rain
The harvest of his seed and of his grain.   580
His master's cattle, swine, and poultry flock,
Horses and sheep and dairy, all his stock,
Were altogether in this Reeve's control.
And by agreement, he had given the sole
Accounting since his lord reached twenty years.   585
No man could ever catch him in arrears.
There wasn't a bailiff, shepherd, or farmer working
But the Reeve knew all his tricks of cheating and shirking.
He would not let him draw an easy breath.
They feared him as they feared the very death.   590
He lived in a good house on an open space,

---

4. A reference to the proverb "an honest miller has a golden thumb," i.e., there are no honest millers.   5. The Manciple manages the affairs of an Inn of Court (see line 562), an institution where young
men training to be lawyers lived and worked.   6. Different kinds of legal cases.   7. His head was
shaved in the form of the tonsure that indicated clerical status.

Well shaded by green trees, a pleasant place.
He was shrewder in acquisition than his lord.
With private riches he was amply stored.
He had learned a good trade young by work and will. 595
He was a carpenter of first-rate skill.
On a fine mount, a stallion, dappled gray.
Whose name was Scot, he rode along the way.
He wore a long blue coat hitched up and tied
As if it were a friar's, and at his side 600
A sword with rusty blade was hanging down.
He came from Norfolk, from nearby the town
That men call Bawdswell.[8] As we rode the while,
The Reeve kept always hindmost in our file.

    A Summoner in our company had his place. 605
Red as the fiery cherubim[9] his face.
He was pocked and pimpled, and his eyes were narrow.
He was lecherous and hot as a cock sparrow.
His brows were scabby and black, and thin his beard.
His was a face that little children feared. 610
Brimstone or litharge bought in any quarter,
Quicksilver, ceruse, borax, oil of tartar,
No salve nor ointment that will cleanse or bite
Could cure him of his blotches, livid white,
Or the nobs and nubbins sitting on his cheeks.[1] 615
He loved his garlic, his onions, and his leeks.
He loved to drink the strong wine down blood-red.
Then would he bellow as if he had lost his head.
And when he had drunk enough to parch his drouth,
Nothing but Latin issued from his mouth. 620
He had smattered up a few terms, two or three,
That he had gathered out of some decree—
No wonder; he heard law Latin all the day,
And everyone knows a parrot or a jay
Can cry out "Wat" or "Poll" as well as the pope; 625
But give him a strange term, he began to grope.
His little store of learning was paid out,
So "Questio quod juris"[2] he would shout.
He was a goodhearted bastard and a kind one.
If there were better, it was hard to find one. 630
He would let a good fellow, for a quart of wine,
The whole year round enjoy his concubine
Scot-free from summons, hearing, fine, or bail,
And on the sly he too could flush a quail.
If he liked a scoundrel, no matter for church law. 635
He would teach him that he need not stand in awe
If the archdeacon threatened with his curse—
That is, unless his soul was in his purse,
For in his purse he would be punished well.

---

8. A town in northern Norfolk, a county northwest of London.
seems to have thought (wrongly) were represented with red faces.
from a form of leprosy; these remedies were recommended by
tion.   2. The question is, what (part) of the law [applies] (Latin). 9. An order of angels that Chaucer
1. The Summoner seems to suffer
medieval physicians for his condi-

"The purse," he said, "is the archdeacon's hell."[3]   640
Of course I know he lied in what he said.
There is nothing a guilty man should so much dread
As the curse that damns his soul, when, without fail,
The church can save him, or send him off to jail.
He had the young men and girls in his control   645
Throughout the diocese; he knew the soul
Of youth, and heard their every last design.
A garland big enough to be the sign
Above an alehouse balanced on his head,
And he made a shield of a great round loaf of bread.   650
    There was a Pardoner of Rouncivalle
With him, of the blessed Mary's hospital,[4]
But now come straight from Rome (or so said he).
Loudly he sang, "Come hither, love, to me,"
While the Summoner's counterbass trolled out profound—   655
No trumpet blew with half so vast a sound.
This Pardoner had hair as yellow as wax,
But it hung as smoothly as a hank of flax.
His locks trailed down in bunches from his head,
And he let the ends about his shoulders spread,   660
But in thin clusters, lying one by one.
Of hood, for rakishness, he would have none,
For in his wallet he kept it safely stowed.
He traveled, as he thought, in the latest mode,
Disheveled. Save for his cap, his head was bare,   665
And in his eyes he glittered like a hare.
A Veronica[5] was stitched upon his cap
His wallet lay before him in his lap
Brimful of pardons from the very seat
In Rome. He had a voice like a goat's bleat.   670
He was beardless and would never have a beard.
His cheek was always smooth as if just sheared.
I think he was a gelding or a mare;
But in this trade, from Berwick down to Ware,[6]
No pardoner could beat him in the race,   675
For in his wallet he had a pillow case
Which he represented as Our Lady's veil;
He said he had a piece of the very sail
St. Peter, when he fished in Galilee
Before Christ caught him, used upon the sea.   680
He had a latten[7] cross embossed with stones
And in a glass he carried some pig's bones,
And with these holy relics, when he found
Some village parson grubbing his poor ground,
He would get more money in a single day   685

3. I.e., the archdeacon would punish sinners with a fine rather than send them to hell by excommunicating them, a view with which the narrator disagrees in the following lines.   4. The hospital of St. Mary of Rouncivalle was located at Charing Cross, now part of London. The money the Pardoner collects is supposed to go to the hospital.   5. A reproduction of the handkerchief bearing the miraculous impression of Christ's face, said to have been impressed on the handkerchief that St. Veronica gave Him to wipe His face with on the way to His Crucifixion.   6. Berwick was at the northern end of the Great North Road that traversed England; Ware, at the southern.   7. An alloy of copper and tin made to resemble brass.

Than in two months would come the parson's way.
Thus with his flattery and his trumped-up stock
He made dupes of the parson and his flock.
But though his conscience was a little plastic
He was in church a noble ecclesiastic. 690
Well could he read the Scripture or saint's story,
But best of all he sang the offertory,
For he understood that when this song was sung,
Then he must preach, and sharpen up his tongue
To rake in cash, as well he knew the art, 695
   And so he sang out gaily, with full heart.
   Now I have set down briefly, as it was,
Our rank, our dress, our number, and the cause
That made our sundry fellowship begin
In Southwark, at this hospitable inn 700
Known as the Tabard, nor far from the Bell.
But what we did that night I ought to tell,
And after that our journey, stage by stage,
And the whole story of our pilgrimage.
But first, in justice, do not look askance 705
I plead, nor lay it to my ignorance
If in this matter I should use plain speech
And tell you just the words and style of each,
Reporting all their language faithfully.
For it must be known to you as well as me 710
That whoever tells a story after a man
Must follow him as closely as he can.
If he takes the tale in charge, he must be true
To every word, unless he would find new
Or else invent a thing or falsify. 715
Better some breadth of language than a lie!
He may not spare the truth to save his brother.
He might as well use one word as another.
In Holy Writ Christ spoke in a broad sense
And surely his word is without offense. 720
Plato, if his pages you can read,
Says let the word be cousin to the deed.[8]
So I petition your indulgence for it
If I have cut the cloth just as men wore it,
Here in this tale, and shown its very weave. 725
My wits are none too sharp, you must believe.
   Our Host gave each of us a cheerful greeting
And promptly of our supper had us eating.
The victuals that he served us were his best.
The wine was potent, and we drank with zest. 730
Our Host cut such a figure, all in all,
He might have been a marshal in a hall.
He was a big man, and his eyes bulged wide.
No sturdier citizen lived in all Cheapside,[9]
Lacking no trace of manhood, bold in speech, 735

---

8. The Platonic text to which Chaucer refers is the *Timaeus*, but he knew it indirectly through references in Latin works.   9. A London district.

Prudent, and well versed in what life can teach,
And with all this he was a jovial man.
And so when supper ended he began
To jolly us, when all our debts were clear.
"Welcome," he said. "I have not seen this year   740
So merry a company in this tavern as now,
And I would give you pleasure if I knew how.
And just this very minute a plan has crossed
My mind that might amuse you at no cost.
    "You go to Canterbury—may the Lord   745
Speed you, and may the martyred saint reward
Your journey! And to while the time away
You mean to talk and pass the time of day,
For you would be as cheerful all alone
As riding on your journey dumb as stone.   750
Therefore, if you'll abide by what I say,
Tomorrow, when you ride off on your way,
Now, by my father's soul, and he is dead,
If you don't enjoy yourselves, cut off my head!
Hold up your hands, if you accept my speech."   755
    Our counsel did not take us long to reach.
We bade him give his orders at his will.
"Well, sirs," he said, "then do not take it ill,
But hear me in good part, and for your sport.
Each one of you, to make our journey short,   760
Shall tell two stories, as we ride, I mean,
Toward Canterbury; and coming home again
Shall tell two other tales he may have heard
Of happenings that some time have occurred.
And the one of you whose stories please us most,   765
Here in this tavern, sitting by this post
Shall sup at our expense while we make merry
When we come riding home from Canterbury.
And to cheer you still the more, I too will ride
With you at my own cost, and be your guide.   770
And if anyone my judgment shall gainsay
He must pay for all we spend along the way.
If you agree, no need to stand and reason.
Tell me, and I'll be stirring in good season."
    This thing was granted, and we swore our pledge   775
To take his judgment on our pilgrimage,
His verdict on our tales, and his advice.
He was to plan a supper at a price
Agreed upon; and so we all assented
To his command, and we were well contented.   780
The wine was fetched; we drank, and went to rest.
    Next morning, when the dawn was in the east,
Up spring our Host, who acted as our cock,
And gathered us together in a flock,
And off we rode, till presently our pace   785
Had brought us to St. Thomas' watering place.[1]

_____

1. A stream about a mile from London on the road to Canterbury.

And there our Host began to check his horse.
"Good sirs," he said, "you know your promise, of course.
Shall I remind you what it was about?
If evensong and matins don't fall out,[2]   790
We'll soon find who shall tell us the first tale.
But as I hope to drink my wine and ale,
Whoever won't accept what I decide
Pays everything we spend along the ride.
Draw lots, before we're farther from the Inn.   795
Whoever draws the shortest shall begin.
Sir Knight," said he, "my master, choose your straw.
Come here, my lady Prioress, and draw,
And you, Sir Scholar, don't look thoughtful, man!
Pitch in now, everyone!" So all began   800
To draw the lots, and as the luck would fall
The draw went to the Knight, which pleased us all.
And when this excellent man saw how it stood,
Ready to keep his promise, he said, "Good!
Since it appears that I must start the game,   805
Why then, the draw is welcome, in God's name.
Now let's ride on, and listen, what I say."
And with that word we rode forth on our way,
And he, with his courteous manner and good cheer,
Began to tell his tale, as you shall hear.   810

The Miller's Prologue and Tale

THE PROLOGUE

When the Knight had finished,[3] no one, young or old,
In the whole company, but said he had told
A noble story, one that ought to be
Preserved and kept alive in memory,
Especially the gentlefolk, each one.   5
Our good Host laughed, and swore, "The game's begun,
The ball is rolling! This is going well.
Let's see who has another tale to tell.
Come, match the Knight's tale if you can, Sir Monk!"
   The Miller, who by this time was so drunk   10
He looked quite bloodless, and who hardly sat
His horse, he was never one to doff his hat
Or stand on courtesy for any man.
Like Pilate in the Church plays[4] he began
To bellow. "Arms and blood and bones," he swore,   15
"I know a yarn that will even up the score,
A noble one, I'll pay off the Knight's tale!"
   Our Host could see that he was drunk on ale.
"Robin," he said, "hold on a minute, brother.
Some better man shall come first with another.   20

2. Evening and morning church services; the Host is asking if what was said in the evening is still acceptable in the morning.   3. *The Knight's Tale* is the first told, immediately following the *General Prologue*.   4. Mystery plays represented Pilate as a braggart and loudmouth.

Let's do this right. You tell yours by and by."
    "God's soul," the Miller told him, "that won't I!
Either I'll speak, or go on my own way."
    "The devil with you! Say what you have to say,"
Answered our Host. "You are a fool. Your head   25
Is overpowered."
                    "Now," the Miller said,
"Everyone listen! But first I will propound
That I am drunk, I know it by my sound.
If I can't get my words out, put the blame
On Southwark ale, I ask you, in God's name!   30
For I'll tell a golden legend and a life[5]
Both of a carpenter and of his wife,
How a student put horns on the fellow's head."
    "Shut up and stop your racket," the Reeve said.
"Forget your ignorant drunken bawdiness.   35
It is a sin and a great foolishness
To injure any man by defamation
And to give women such a reputation.
Tell us of other things; you'll find no lack."
    Promptly this drunken Miller answered back: 40
"Oswald, my brother, true as babes are suckled,
The man who has no wife, he is no cuckold.
I don't say for this reason that you are.
There are plenty of faithful wives, both near and far,
Always a thousand good for every bad,   45
And you know this yourself, unless you're mad.
I see you are angry with my tale, but why?
You have a wife; no less, by God, do I.
But I wouldn't, for the oxen in my plow,
Shoulder more than I need by thinking how   50
I may myself, for aught I know, be one.
I'll certainly believe that I am none.
A husband mustn't be curious, for his life,
About God's secrets or about his wife.
If she gives him plenty and he's in the clover,   55
No need to worry about what's left over."
    The Miller, to make the best of it I can,
Refused to hold his tongue for any man,
But told his tale like any low-born clown.
I am sorry that I have to set it down,   60
And all you people, for God's love, I pray,
Whose taste is higher, do not think I say
A word with evil purpose; I must rehearse
Their stories one and all, both better and worse,
Or play false with my matter, that is clear.   65
Whoever, therefore, may not wish to hear,
Turn over the page and choose another tale;
For small and great, he'll find enough, no fail,
Of things from history, touching courtliness,

5. A saint's life.

And virtue too, and also holiness.   70
If you choose wrong, don't lay it on my head.
You know the Miller couldn't be called well bred.
So with the Reeve, and many more as well,
And both of them had bawdy tales to tell.
Reflect a little, and don't hold me to blame.   75
There's no sense making earnest out of game.

THE TALE

There used to be a rich old oaf who made
His home at Oxford, a carpenter by trade,
And took in boarders. With him used to dwell
A student who had done his studies well,
But he was poor; for all that he had learned,   5
It was toward astrology his fancy turned.
He knew a number of figures and constructions
By which he could supply men with deductions
If they should ask him at a given hour
Whether to look for sunshine or for shower,   10
Or want to know whatever might befall,
Events of all sorts, I can't count them all.
     He was known as handy Nicholas,⁶ this student.
Well versed in love, he knew how to be prudent,
Going about unnoticed, sly, and sure.   15
In looks no girl was ever more demure.
Lodged at this carpenter's, he lived alone;
He had a room there that he made his own,
Festooned with herbs, and he was sweet himself
As licorice or ginger. On a shelf   20
Above his bed's head, neatly stowed apart,
He kept the trappings that went with his art,
His astrolabe,⁷ his books—among the rest,
Thick ones and thin ones, lay his *Almagest*⁸—
And the counters for his abacus as well.   25
Over his cupboard a red curtain fell
And up above a pretty zither lay
On which at night so sweetly would he play
That with the music the whole room would ring.
"Angelus to the Virgin"⁹ he would sing   30
And then the song that's known as "The King's Note."¹
Blessings were called down on his merry throat!
So this sweet scholar passed his time, his end
Being to eat and live upon his friend.²
     This carpenter had newly wed a wife   35
And loved her better than he loved his life.
He was jealous, for she was eighteen in age;
He tried to keep her close as in a cage,

6. Chaucer's word is hendë, implying both *ready to hand* and *ingratiating* [Translator's note].   7. An astronomical instrument for telling time.   8. A second-century treatise by Ptolemy, an astronomy textbook.   9. A song about the Annunciation, when the angel Gabriel tells Mary she is to bear Jesus.
1. Unidentified.   2. I.e., the friend who provided him with money for his education.

For she was wild and young, and old was he
And guessed that he might smack of cuckoldry.   40
His ignorant wits had never chanced to strike
On Cato's[3] word, that man should wed his like;
Men ought to wed where their conditions point,
For youth and age are often out of joint.
But now, since he had fallen in the snare,   45
He must, like other men, endure his care.
    Fair this young woman was, her body trim
As any mink, so graceful and so slim.
She wore a striped belt that was all of silk;
A piece-work apron, white as morning milk,   50
About her loins and down her lap she wore.
White was her smock, her collar both before
And on the back embroidered all about
In coal-black silk, inside as well as out.
And like her collar, her white-laundered bonnet   55
Had ribbons of the same embroidery on it.
Wide was her silken fillet, worn up high,
And for a fact she had a willing eye.
She plucked each brow into a little bow,
And each one was as black as any sloe.[4]   60
She was a prettier sight to see by far
Than the blossoms of the early pear tree are,
And softer than the wool of an old wether.
Down from her belt there hung a purse of leather
With silken tassels and with studs of brass.   65
No man so wise, wherever people pass,
Who could imagine in this world at all
A wench like her, the pretty little doll!
Far brighter was the dazzle of her hue
Than a coin struck in the Tower,[5] fresh and new.   70
As for her song, it twittered from her head
Sharp as a swallow perching on a shed.
And she could skip and sport as a young ram
Or calf will gambol, following his dam.
Her mouth was sweet as honey-ale or mead   75
Or apples in the hay, stored up for need.
She was as skittish as an untrained colt,
Slim as a mast and straighter than a bolt.
On her simple collar she wore a big brooch-pin
Wide as a shield's boss underneath her chin.   80
High up along her legs she laced her shoes.
She was a pigsney,[6] she was a primrose
For any lord to tumble in his bed
Or a good yeoman honestly to wed.
    Now sir, and again sir, this is how it was: 85
A day came round when handy Nicholas,
While her husband was at Oseney,[7] well away,

---

3. Dionysius Cato, the supposed author of a book of maxims employed in elementary education.   4. The
sloeberry.   5. Minted in the Tower of London.   6. *Pig's eye,* probably the name of a wild flower.
7. A town near Oxford.

Began to fool with this young wife, and play.
These students always have a wily head.
He caught her in between the legs, and said,   90
"Sweetheart, unless I have my will with you
I'll die for stifled love, by all that's true,"
And held her by the haunches, hard. "I vow
I'll die unless you love me here and now,
Sure as my soul," he said, "is God's to save."   95
    She shied just as a colt does in the trave,[8]
And turned her head hard from him, this young wife,
And said, "I will not kiss you, on my life.
Why, stop it now," she said, "stop, Nicholas,
Or I will cry out 'Help, help,' and 'Alas!'   100
Be good enough to take your hands away."
    "Mercy," this Nicholas began to pray,
And spoke so well and poured it on so fast
She promised she would be his love at last,
And swore by Thomas à Becket, saint of Kent,   105
That she would serve him when she could invent
Or spy out some good opportunity.
"My husband is so full of jealousy
You must be watchful and take care," she said,
"Or well I know I'll be as good as dead.   110
You must go secretly about this business."
    "Don't give a thought to that," said Nicholas.
"A student has been wasting time at school
If he can't make a carpenter a fool."
And so they were agreed, these two, and swore   115
To watch their chance, as I have said before.
When Nicholas had spanked her haunches neatly
And done all I have spoken of, he sweetly
Gave her a kiss, and then he took his zither
And loudly played, and sang his music with her.   120
    Now in her Christian duty, one saint's day,
To the parish church this good wife made her way,
And as she went her forehead cast a glow
As bright as noon, for she had washed it so
It glistened when she finished with her work.   125
    Serving this church there was a parish clerk
Whose name was Absolom, a ruddy man
With goose-gray eyes and curls like a great fan
That shone like gold on his neatly parted head.
His tunic was light blue and his nose red,   130
And he had patterns that had been cut through
Like the windows of St. Paul's in either shoe.[9]
He wore above his tunic, fresh and gay,
A surplice white as a blossom on a spray.
A merry devil, as true as God can save,   135
He knew how to let blood, trim hair, and shave,

---

8. A wooden frame confining a horse being shod.   9. The patterns cut in his shoes resembled the windows in St. Paul's Cathedral in London.

Or write a deed of land in proper phrase,
And he could dance in twenty different ways
In the Oxford fashion, and sometimes he would sing
A loud falsetto to his fiddle string   140
Or his guitar. No tavern anywhere
But he had furnished entertainment there.
Yet his speech was delicate, and for his part
He was a little squeamish toward a fart.
    This Absolom, so jolly and so gay,   145
With a censer[1] went about on the saint's day
Censing the parish women one and all.
Many the doting look that he let fall,
And specially on this carpenter's young wife.
To look at her, he thought, was a good life,   150
She was so trim, so sweetly lecherous.
I dare say that if she had been a mouse
And he a cat, he would have made short work
Of catching her. This jolly parish clerk
Had such a heartful of love-hankerings   155
He would not take the women's offerings;
No, no, he said, it would not be polite.
    The moon, when darkness fell, shone full and bright
And Absolom was ready for love's sake
With his guitar to be up and awake,   160
And toward the carpenter's, brisk and amorous,
He made his way until he reached the house
A little after the cocks began to crow.
Under a casement he sang sweet and low,
"Dear lady, by your will, be kind to me,"   165
And strummed on his guitar in harmony.
This lovelorn singing woke the carpenter
Who said to his wife, "What, Alison, don't you hear
Absolom singing under our bedroom wall?"
    "Yes, God knows, John," she answered, "I hear it all."   170
    What would you like? In this way things went on
Till jolly Absolom was woebegone
For wooing her, awake all night and day.
He combed his curls and made himself look gay.
He swore to be her slave and used all means   175
To court her with his gifts and go-betweens.
He sang and quavered like a nightingale.
He sent her sweet spiced wine and seasoned ale,
Cakes that were piping hot, mead sweet with honey,
And since she was town-bred, he proffered money.   180
For some are won by wealth, and some no less
By blows, and others yet by gentleness.
    Sometimes, to keep his talents in her gaze,
He acted Herod[2] in the mystery plays
High on the stage. But what can help his case?   185

1. A receptacle for incense with which to bless (or "cense") the wives of the parish as they made their offerings in church.   2. A role traditionally played as a bully in the mystery plays.

For she so loves this handy Nicholas
That Absolom is living in a bubble.
He has nothing but a laugh for all his trouble.
She leaves his earnestness for scorn to cool
And makes this Absolom her proper fool.   190
For this is a true proverb, and no lie;
"It always happens that the nigh and sly
Will let the absent suffer." So 'tis said,
And Absolom may rage or lose his head
But just because he was farther from her sight   195
This nearby Nicholas got in his light.
    Now hold your chin up, handy Nicholas,
For Absolom may wail and sing "Alas!"
One Saturday when the carpenter had gone
To Oseney, Nicholas and Alison   200
Agreed that he should use his wit and guile
This simple jealous husband to beguile.
And if it happened that the game went right
She would sleep in his arms the livelong night,
For this was his desire and hers as well.   205
At once, with no more words, this Nicholas fell
To working out his plan. He would not tarry,
But quietly to his room began to carry
Both food and drink to last him out a day,
Or more than one, and told her what to say   210
If her husband asked her about Nicholas.
She must say she had no notion where he was;
She hadn't laid eyes on him all day long;
He must be sick, or something must be wrong;
No matter how her maid had called and cried   215
He wouldn't answer, whatever might betide.
    This was the plan, and Nicholas kept away,
Shut in his room, for that whole Saturday.
He ate and slept or did as he thought best
Till Sunday, when the sun was going to rest,   220
This carpenter began to wonder greatly
Where Nicholas was and what might ail him lately,
"Now, by St. Thomas, I begin to dread
All isn't right with Nicholas," he said.
"He hasn't, God forbid, died suddenly!   225
The world is ticklish these days, certainly.
Today I saw a corpse to church go past,
A man that I saw working Monday last!
Go up," he told his chore-boy, "call and shout,
Knock with a stone, find what it's all about   230
And let me know."
                    The boy went up and pounded
And yelled as if his wits had been confounded.
"What, how, what's doing, Master Nicholas?
How can you sleep all day?" But all his fuss
Was wasted, for he could not hear a word.   235
He noticed at the bottom of a board

A hole the cat used when she wished to creep
Into the room, and through it looked in deep
And finally of Nicholas caught sight.
This Nicholas sat gaping there upright   240
As though his wits were addled by the moon
When it was new. The boy went down, and soon
Had told his master how he had seen the man.
    The carpenter, when he heard this news, began
To cross himself. "Help us, St. Frideswide![3]   245
Little can we foresee what may betide!
The man's astronomy has turned his wit,
Or else he's in some agonizing fit.
I always knew that it would turn out so.
What God has hidden is not for men to know.   250
Aye, blessed is the ignorant man indeed,
Blessed is he that only knows his creed!
So fared another scholar of the sky,
For walking in the meadows once to spy
Upon the stars and what they might foretell,   255
Down in a clay-pit suddenly he fell!
He overlooked that! By St. Thomas, though,
I'm sorry for handy Nicholas. I'll go
And scold him roundly for his studying
If so I may, by Jesus, heaven's king!   260
Give me a staff, I'll pry up from the floor
While you, Robin, are heaving at the door.
He'll quit his books, I think."
                      He took his stand
Outside the room. The boy had a strong hand
And by the hasp he heaved it off at once.   265
The door fell flat. With gaping countenance
This Nicholas sat studying the air
As still as stone. He was in black despair,
The carpenter believed, and hard about
The shoulders caught and shook him, and cried out   270
Rudely, "What, how! What is it? Look down at us!
Wake up, think of Christ's passion, Nicholas!
I'll sign you with the cross to keep away
These elves and things!" And he began to say,
Facing the quarters of the house, each side,   275
And on the threshold of the door outside,
The night-spell:[4] "Jesu and St. Benedict
From every wicked thing this house protect . . ."
    Choosing his time, this handy Nicholas
Produced a dreadful sigh, and said, "Alas,   280
This world, must it be all destroyed straightway?"
    "What," asked the carpenter, "what's that you say?
Do as we do, we working men, and think
Of God."

3. An eighth-century English saint noted for her ability to cast out devils. She was the patron saint of Oxford. 4. A magic charm said at night to protect a house from evil spirits.

Nicholas answered, "Get me a drink,
And afterwards I'll tell you privately   285
Of something that concerns us, you and me.
I'll tell you only, you among all men."
    This carpenter went down and came again
With a draught of mighty ale, a generous quart.
As soon as each of them had drunk his part   290
Nicholas shut the door and made it fast
And sat down by the carpenter at last
And spoke to him. "My host," he said, "John dear,
You must swear by all that you hold sacred here
That not to any man will you betray   295
My confidence. What I'm about to say
Is Christ's own secret. If you tell a soul
You are undone, and this will be the toll:
If you betray me, you shall go stark mad."
    "Now Christ forbid it, by His holy blood,"   300
Answered this simple man. "I don't go blabbing.
If I say it myself, I have no taste for gabbing.
Speak up just as you like, I'll never tell,
Not wife nor child, by Him that harrowed hell."[5]
    "Now, John," said Nicholas, "this is no lie.   305
I have discovered through astrology,
And studying the moon that shines so bright
That Monday next, a quarter through the night,
A rain will fall, and such a mad, wild spate
That Noah's flood was never half so great.   310
This world," he said, "in less time than an hour
Shall drown entirely in that hideous shower.
Yes, every man shall drown and lose his life."
    "Alas," the carpenter answered, "for my wife!
Alas, my Alison! And shall she drown?"   315
For grief at this he nearly tumbled down,
And said, "But is there nothing to be done?"
    "Why, happily there is, for anyone
Who will take advice," this handy Nicholas said.
"You mustn't expect to follow your own head.   320
For what said Solomon, whose words were true?
'Proceed by counsel, and you'll never rue.'
If you will act on good advice, no fail,
I'll promise, and without a mast or sail,
To see that she's preserved, and you and I.   325
Haven't you heard how Noah was kept dry
When, warned by Christ beforehand, he discovered
That the whole earth with water should be covered?"
    "Yes," said the carpenter, "long, long ago."
    "And then again," said Nicholas, "don't you know   330
The grief they all had trying to embark
Till Noah could get his wife into the Ark?[6]

---

5. I.e., Christ, who descended into hell and led away Adam, Eve, the Patriarchs, John the Baptist, and others, redeeming and releasing them.   6. A stock comedy scene in the mystery plays.

That was a time when Noah, I dare say,
Would gladly have given his best black wethers away
If she could have had a ship herself alone.   335
And therefore do you know what must be done?
This demands haste, and with a hasty thing
People can't stop for talk and tarrying.
    "Start out and get into the house right off
For each of us a tub or kneading-trough,   340
Above all making sure that they are large,
In which we'll float away as in a barge.
And put in food enough to last a day.
Beyond won't matter; the flood will fall away
Early next morning. Take care not to spill   345
A word to your boy Robin, nor to Jill
Your maid. I cannot save her, don't ask why.
I will not tell God's secrets, no, not I.
Let it be enough, unless your wits are mad,
To have as good a grace as Noah had.   350
I'll save your wife for certain, never doubt it.
Now go along, and make good time about it.
    "But when you have, for her and you and me,
Brought to the house these kneading-tubs, all three,
Then you must hang them under the roof, up high,   355
To keep our plans from any watchful eye.
When you have done exactly as I've said,
And put in snug our victuals and our bread,
Also an ax to cut the ropes apart
So when the rain comes we can make our start,   360
And when you've broken a hole high in the gable
Facing the garden plot, above the stable,
To give us a free passage out, each one,
Then, soon as the great fall of rain is done,
You'll swim as merrily, I undertake,   365
As the white duck paddles along behind her drake.
Then I shall call, 'How, Alison! How, John!
Be cheerful, for the flood will soon be gone.'
And 'Master Nicholas, what ho!' you'll say.
'Good morning, I see you clearly, for it's day.'   370
Then we shall lord it for the rest of life
Over the world, like Noah and his wife.
    "But one thing I must warn you of downright.
Use every care that on that selfsame night
When we have taken ship and climbed aboard,   375
No one of us must speak a single word,
Nor call, nor cry, but pray with all his heart.
It is God's will. You must hang far apart,
You and your wife, for there must be no sin
Between you, no more in a look than in   380
The very deed. Go now, the plans are drawn.
Go, set to work, and may God spur you on!
Tomorrow night when all men are asleep
Into our kneading-troughs we three shall creep

And sit there waiting, and abide God's grace.   385
Go along now, this isn't the time or place
For me to talk at length or sermonize.
The proverb says, 'Don't waste words on the wise.'
You are so wise there is no need to teach you.
Go, save our lives—that's all that I beseech you!"   390
    This simple carpenter went on his way.
Many a time he said, "Alack the day,"
And to his wife he laid the secret bare.
She knew it better than he; she was aware
What this quaint bargain was designed to buy.   395
She carried on as if about to die,
And said, "Alas, go get this business done.
Help us escape, or we are dead, each one.
I am your true, your faithful wedded wife.
Go, my dear husband, save us, limb and life!"   400
    Great things, in all truth, can the emotions be!
A man can perish through credulity
So deep the print imagination makes.
This simple carpenter, he quails and quakes.
He really sees, according to his notion,   405
Noah's flood come wallowing like an ocean
To drown his Alison, his pet, his dear.
He weeps and wails, and gone is his good cheer,
And wretchedly he sighs. But he goes off
And gets himself a tub, a kneading-trough,   410
Another tub, and has them on the sly
Sent home, and there in secret hangs them high
Beneath the roof. He made three ladders, these
With his own hands, and stowed in bread and cheese
And a jug of good ale, plenty for a day.   415
Before all this was done, he sent away
His chore-boy Robin and his wench likewise
To London on some trumped-up enterprise,
And so on Monday, when it drew toward night,
He shut the door without a candlelight   420
And saw that all was just as it should be,
And shortly they went clambering up, all three.
They sat there still, and let a moment pass.
    "Now then, 'Our Father,' mum!" said Nicholas,
And "Mum!" said John, and "Mum!" said Alison,   425
And piously this carpenter went on
Saying his prayers. He sat there still and straining,
Trying to make out whether he heard it raining.
    The dead of sleep, for very weariness,
Fell on this carpenter, as I should guess,   430
At about curfew time, or little more.
His head was twisted, and that made him snore.
His spirit groaned in its uneasiness.
Down from his ladder slipped this Nicholas,
And Alison too, downward she softly sped   435
And without further word they went to bed

Where the carpenter himself slept other nights.
There were the revels, there were the delights!
And so this Alison and Nicholas lay
Busy about their solace and their play
Until the bell for lauds[7] began to ring   440
And in the chancel friars began to sing.
   Now on this Monday, woebegone and glum
For love, this parish clerk, this Absolom
Was with some friends at Oseney, and while there   445
Inquired after John the carpenter.
A member of the cloister drew him away
Out of the church, and told him, "I can't say.
I haven't seen him working hereabout
Since Saturday. The abbot sent him out   450
For timber, I suppose. He'll often go
And stay at the granary a day or so.
Or else he's at his own house, possibly.
I can't for certain say where he may be."
   Absolom at once felt jolly and light,   455
And thought, "Time now to be awake all night,
For certainly I haven't seen him making
A stir about his door since day was breaking.
Don't call me a man if when I hear the cock
Begin to crow I don't slip up and knock   460
On the low window by his bedroom wall.
To Alison at last I'll pour out all
My love-pangs, for at this point I can't miss,
Whatever happens, at the least a kiss.
Some comfort, by my word, will come my way.   465
I've felt my mouth itch the whole livelong day,
And that's a sign of kissing at the least.
I dreamed all night that I was at a feast.
So now I'll go and sleep an hour or two,
And then I'll wake and play the whole night through."   470
   When the first cockcrow through the dark had come
Up rose this jolly lover Absolom
And dressed up smartly. He was not remiss
About the least point. He chewed licorice
And cardamom to smell sweet, even before   475
He combed his hair. Beneath his tongue he bore
A sprig of Paris[8] like a truelove knot.
He strolled off to the carpenter's house, and got
Beneath the window. It came so near the ground
It reached his chest. Softly, with half a sound,   480
He coughed, "My honeycomb, sweet Alison,
What are you doing, my sweet cinnamon?
Awake, my sweetheart and my pretty bird,
Awake, and give me from your lips a word!
Little enough you care for all my woe,   485

---

7. The second of the seven church services celebrated each day; it took place before sunrise.   8. A cloverlike plant.

How for your love I sweat wherever I go!
No wonder I sweat and faint and cannot eat
More than a girl; as a lamb does for the teat
I pine. Yes, truly, I so long for love
I mourn as if I were a turtledove." 490
    Said she, "You jack-fool, get away from here!
So help me God, I won't sing 'Kiss me, dear!'
I love another more than you. Get on,
For Christ's sake, Absolom, or I'll throw a stone.
The devil with you! Go and let me sleep." 495
    "Ah, that true love should ever have to reap
So evil a fortune," Absolom said. "A kiss,
At least, if it can be no more than this,
Give me, for love of Jesus and of me."
    "And will you go away for that?" said she. 500
    "Yes, truly, sweetheart," answered Absolom.
    "Get ready then," she said, "for here I come,"
And softly said to Nicholas, "Keep still,
And in a minute you can laugh your fill."
This Absolom got down upon his knee 505
And said, "I am a lord of pure degree,
For after this, I hope, comes more to savor.
Sweetheart, your grace, and pretty bird, your favor!"
    She undid the window quickly. "That will do,"
She said. "Be quick about it, and get through, 510
For fear the neighbors will look out and spy."
    Absolom wiped his mouth to make it dry.
The night was pitch dark, coal-black all about.
Her rear end through the window she thrust out.
He got no better or worse, did Absolom, 515
Than to kiss her with his mouth on the bare bum
Before he had caught on, a smacking kiss.
    He jumped back, thinking something was amiss.
A woman had no beard, he was well aware,
But what he felt was rough and had long hair. 520
    "Alas," he cried, "what have you made me do?"
    "Te-hee!" she said, and banged the window to.
    Absolom backed away a sorry pace.
    "You've bearded him!"[9] said handy Nicholas.
"God's body, this is going fair and fit!" 525
    This luckless Absolom heard every bit,
And gnawed his mouth, so angry he became.
He said to himself, "I'll square you, all the same."
    But who now scrubs and rubs, who chafes his lips
With dust, with sand, with straw, with cloth and chips 530
If not this Absolom? "The devil," says he,
"Welcome my soul if I wouldn't rather be
Revenged than have the whole town in a sack!
Alas," he cries, "if only I'd held back!"

9. "To beard" In Middle English means to trick, but Nicholas is also punning on the literal meaning of the word.

His hot love had become all cold and ashen. 535
He didn't have a curse to spare for passion
From the moment when he kissed her on the ass.
That was the cure to make his sickness pass!
He cried as a child does after being whipped;
He railed at love. Then quietly he slipped 540
Across the street to a smith who was forging out
Parts that the farmers needed round about.
He was busy sharpening colter[1] and plowshare
When Absolom knocked as though without a care.
"Undo the door, Jervice, and let me come." 545
"What? Who are you?"
                              "It is I, Absolom."
"Absolom, is it! By Christ's precious tree,
Why are you up so early? Lord bless me,
What's ailing you? Some gay girl has the power
To bring you out, God knows, at such an hour! 550
Yes, by St. Neot,[2] you know well what I mean!"
Absolom thought his jokes not worth a bean.
Without a word he let them all go by.
He had another kind of fish to fry
Than Jervice guessed. "Lend me this colter here 555
That's hot in the chimney, friend," he said. "Don't fear,
I'll bring it back right off when I am through.
I need it for a job I have to do."
"Of course," said Jervice. "Why, if it were gold
Or coins in a sack, uncounted and untold, 560
As I'm a rightful smith, I wouldn't refuse it.
But, Christ's foot! how on earth do you mean to use it?"
"Let that," said Absolom, "be as it may.
I'll let you know tomorrow or next day,"
And took the colter where the steel was cold 565
And slipped out with it safely in his hold
And softly over to the carpenter's wall.
He coughed and then he rapped the window, all
As he had done before.
                              "Who's knocking there?"
Said Alison. "It is a thief, I swear." 570
"No, no," said he. "God knows, my sugarplum,
My bird, my darling, it's your Absolom.
I've brought a golden ring my mother gave me,
Fine and well cut, as I hope that God will save me.
It's yours, if you will let me have a kiss." 575
Nicholas had got up to take a piss
And thought he would improve the whole affair.
This clerk, before he got away from there,
Should give *his* ass a smack; and hastily
He opened the window, and thrust out quietly, 580
Buttocks and haunches, all the way, his bum.
Up spoke this clerk, this jolly Absolom:

---

1. A turf cutter on a plow.   2. A ninth-century English saint.

"Speak, for I don't know where you are, sweetheart."
   Nicholas promptly let fly with a fart
As loud as if a clap of thunder broke, 585
So great he was nearly blinded by the stroke,
And ready with his hot iron to make a pass,
Absolom caught him fairly on the ass.
   Off flew the skin, a good handbreadth of fat
Lay bare, the iron so scorched him where he sat. 590
As for the pain, he thought that he would die,
And like a madman he began to cry.
"Help! Water! Water! Help, for God's own heart!"
   At this the carpenter came to with a start.
He heard a man cry "Water!" as if mad. 595
"It's coming now," was the first thought he had.
"It's Noah's flood, alas, God be our hope!"
He sat up with his ax and chopped the rope
And down at once the whole contraption fell.
He didn't take time out to buy or sell 600
Till he hit the floor and lay there in a swoon.
   Then up jumped Nicholas and Alison
And in the street began to cry, "Help, ho!"
The neighbors all came running, high and low,
And poured into the house to see the sight. 605
The man still lay there, passed out cold and white,
For in his tumble he had broken an arm.
But he himself brought on his greatest harm,
For when he spoke he was at once outdone
By handy Nicholas and Alison 610
Who told them one and all that he was mad.
So great a fear of Noah's flood he had,
By some delusion, that in his vanity
He had bought himself these kneading-troughs, all three.
And hung them from the roof there, up above, 615
And he had pleaded with them, for God's love,
To sit there in the loft for company.
   The neighbors laughed at such a fantasy,
And round the loft began to pry and poke
And turned his whole disaster to a joke. 620
He found it was no use to say a word.
Whatever reason he offered, no one heard.
With oaths and curses people swore him down
Until he passed for mad in the whole town.
Wit, clerk, and student all stood by each other. 625
They said, "It's clear the man is crazy, brother."
Everyone had his laugh about this feud.
So Alison, the carpenter's wife, got screwed
For all the jealous watching he could try,
And Absolom, he kissed her nether eye, 630
And Nicholas got his bottom roasted well.
God save this troop! That's all I have to tell.

The Wife of Bath's Prologue and Tale

THE PROLOGUE

"Experience, though all authority
Was lacking in the world, confers on me
The right to speak of marriage, and unfold
Its woes. For, lords, since I was twelve years old[3]
—Thanks to eternal God in heaven alive— 5
I've married at church door no less than five
Husbands, provided that I can have been
So often wed,[4] and all were worthy men.
But I was told, indeed, and not long since,
That Christ went to a wedding only once 10
At Cana, in the land of Galilee.[5]
By this example he instructed me
To wed once only—that's what I have heard!
Again, consider now what a sharp word,
Beside a well, Jesus, both God and man, 15
Spoke in reproving the Samaritan:
'Five husbands thou hast had'—this certainly
He said to her—'and the man that now hath thee
Is not thy husband.'[6] True, he spoke this way,
But what he meant is more than I can say 20
Except that I would ask why the fifth man
Was not a husband to the Samaritan?
To just how many could she be a wife?
I've never heard this number all my life
Determined up to now. For round and round 25
Scholars may gloze,[7] interpret, and expound,
But plainly, this I know without a lie,
God told us to increase and multiply.[8]
That noble text I can well understand.
My husband—this too I have well in hand— 30
Should leave both father and mother and cleave to me.[9]
Number God never mentioned, bigamy,
No, nor even octogamy; why do men
Talk of it as a sin and scandal, then?
    "Think of that monarch, wise King Solomon. 35
It strikes me that *he* had more wives than one![1]
To be refreshed, God willing, would please me
If I got it half as many times as he!
He had a gift, and one of God's own giving,
For all his wives! There isn't a man now living 40
Who has the like. By all that I make out
On the first night this king had many a bout
With each, he was so thoroughly alive.
Blessed be God that I have married five,

3. According to Church law, twelve was the earliest age at which a girl could be married; the Wife is probably bragging rather than telling the literal truth.   4. Assuming so many marriages are legitimate.   5. John 2.1–2.   6. John 4.6–19.   7. Gloss, or interpret.   8. Genesis 1.28.   9. Matthew 19.5–6.   1. 1 Kings 11.3 describes Solomon as having seven hundred wives and three hundred concubines.

And always, for the money in his chest   45
And for his nether purse, I picked the best.
In divers schools ripe scholarship is made,
And various practice in all kinds of trade
Makes perfect workmen, as the world can see.
Five husbands have had turns at schooling me.   50
Welcome the sixth, whenever I am faced
With yet another. I don't mean to be chaste
At all costs. When a spouse of mine is gone,
Some other Christian man shall take me on,
For then, says the Apostle, I'll be free   55
To wed, in God's name, where it pleases me.[2]
To marry is no sin, as we can learn
From him; better to marry than to burn,[3]
He says. Why should I care what obloquy
Men heap on Lamech and his bigamy?   60
Abraham was, by all that I can tell,
A holy man; so Jacob[4] was as well,
And each of them took more than two as brides,
And many another holy man besides.
Where, may I ask, in any period,   65
In plain words can you show Almighty God
Forbade us marriage? Point it out to me!
Or where did he command virginity?
The Apostle, when he speaks of maidenhood,
Lays down no law.[5] This I have understood   70
As well as you, milords, for it is plain.
Men may advise a woman to abstain
From marriage, but mere counsels aren't commands.
He left it to our judgment, where it stands.
Had God enjoined us all to maidenhood   75
Then marriage would have been condemned for good.
But truth is, if no seed were ever sown,
In what soil could virginity be grown?
Paul did not dare command a thing at best
On which his Master left us no behest.   80
    "But now the prize goes to virginity.
Seize it whoever can, and let us see
What manner of man shall run best in the race!
But not all men receive this form of grace
Except where God bestows it by his will.   85
The Apostle was a maid, I know; but still,
Although he wished all men were such as he,
It was only *counsel* toward virginity.[6]
To be a wife he gave me his permission,
And so it is no blot on my condition   90
Nor slander of bigamy upon my state
If when my husband dies I take a mate.

2. The Apostle is Paul, and the reference is to 1 Corinthians 7.39; throughout her *Prologue* the Wife returns to this chapter, sometimes using (or misusing) Paul to support her views, sometimes arguing against him.   3. 1 Cor. 7.9.   4. See Genesis 29.15–30. For Lamech, see Genesis 4.19–23. For Abraham, Genesis 16.1–6.   5. 1 Cor. 7.25.   6. 1 Cor. 7.8.

A man does virtuously, St. Paul has said,
To touch no woman[7]—meaning in his bed.
For fire and fat are dangerous friends at best. 95
You know what this example should suggest.
Here is the nub: he held virginity
Superior to wedded frailty,
And frailty I call it unless man
And woman both are chaste for their whole span. 100
    "I am not jealous if maidenhood outweighs
My marriages; I grant it all the praise.
It pleases, them, these virgins, flesh and soul
To be immaculate. I won't extol
My own condition. In a lord's household 105
You know that every vessel can't be gold.
Some are of wood, and serve their master still.
God calls us variously to do his will.
Each has his proper gift, of all who live,
Some this, some that, as it pleases God to give. 110
    "Virginity is a high and perfect course,
And continence is holy. But the source
Of all perfection, Jesus, never bade
Each one of us to go sell all he had
And give it to the poor; he did not say 115
That all should follow him in this one way.
He spoke to those who would live perfectly,[8]
And by your leave, lords, that is not for me!
The flower of my best years I find it suits
To spend on the acts of marriage and its fruits. 120
    "Tell me this also: why at our creation
Were organs given us for generation,
And for what profit were we creatures made?
Believe me, not for nothing! Ply his trade
Of twisting texts who will, and let him urge 125
That they were only given us to purge
Our urine; say without them we should fail
To tell a female rightly from a male
And that's their only object—say you so?
It won't work, as experience will show. 130
Without offense to scholars, I say this,
That they were made for both these purposes,
That we may both be cleansed, I mean, and eased
Through intercourse, where God is not displeased.
Why else in books is this opinion met, 135
That every man should pay his wife his debt?[9]
Tell me with what a man should hope to pay
Unless he put his instrument in play?
They were supplied us, then, for our purgation,
But they were also meant for generation. 140
    "But none the less I do not mean to say
That all those who are furnished in this way

7. 1 Cor. 7.1.   8. Matthew 9.16–22.   9. 1 Cor. 7.3.

Are bound to go and practice intercourse.
The world would then grant chastity no force.
Christ was a maid, yet he was formed a man,   145
And many a saint, too, since the world began,
And yet they lived in perfect chastity.
I am not spiteful toward virginity.
Let virgins be white bread of pure wheat-seed.
Barley we wives are called, and yet I read   150
In Mark, and tell the tale in truth he can,
That Christ with barley bread cheered many a man.[1]
In the state that God assigned to each of us
I'll persevere. I'm not fastidious.
In wifehood I will use my instrument   155
As freely by my Maker it was lent.
If I hold back with it, God give me sorrow!
My husband shall enjoy it night and morrow
Whenever it pleases him to pay his debt.
A husband, though—I've not been thwarted yet—   160
Shall always be my debtor and my slave.
From tribulation he shall never save
His flesh, not for as long as I'm his wife![2]
I have the power, during all my life,
Over his very body, and not he.   165
For so the Apostle has instructed me,
Who bade men love their wives for better or worse.
It pleases me from end to end, that verse!"[3]
    The Pardoner, before she could go on,
Jumped up and cried, "By God and by St. John,   170
Upon this topic you preach nobly, Dame!
I was about to wed, but now, for shame,
Why should my body pay a price so dear?
I'd rather not be married all this year!"
    "Hold on," she said. "I haven't yet begun.   175
You'll drink a keg of this before I'm done,
I promise you, and it won't taste like ale!
And after I have told you my whole tale
Of marriage, with its fund of tribulation—
And I'm the expert of my generation,   180
For I myself, I mean, have been the whip—
You can decide then if you want a sip
Out of the barrel that I mean to broach.
Before you come too close in your approach,
Think twice. I have examples, more than ten!   185
'The man who won't be warned by other men,
To other men a warning he shall be.'
These are the words we find in Ptolemy.
Go read them right there in his *Almagest*."[4]
    "Now, Madame, if you're willing, I suggest,"   190

---

1. The reference is actually found not in Mark but in John 6.9.   2. 1 Cor. 7.28; this verse, with its reference to the "tribulation of the flesh," is central to the Wife's *Prologue*.   3. 1 Cor. 7.4.   4. The *Almagest* is a second-century treatise on astronomy; this proverb appears in a preface that was later added to the work.

Answered the Pardoner, "as you began,
Continue with your tale, and spare no man.
Teach us young men your practice as our guide."
      "Gladly, if it will please you," she replied.
"But first I ask you, if I speak my mind,   195
That all this company may be well inclined,
And will not take offense at what I say.
I only mean it, after all, in play.
      "Now, sirs, I will get onward with my tale.
If ever I hope to drink good wine or ale,   200
I'm speaking truth: the husbands I have had,
Three of them have been good, and two were bad.
The three were kindly men, and rich, and old.
But they were hardly able to uphold
The statute which had made them fast to me.   205
You know well what I mean by this, I see!
So help me God, I can't help laughing yet
Thinking of how at night I made them sweat,
And I thought nothing of it, on my word!
Their land and wealth they had by then conferred   210
On me, and so I safely could neglect
Tending their love or showing them respect.
So well they loved me that by God above
I hardly set a value on their love.
A woman who is wise is never done   215
Busily winning love when she has none,
But since I had them wholly in my hand
And they had given me their wealth and land,
Why task myself to spoil them or to please
Unless for my own profit and my ease?   220
I set them working so that many a night
They sang a dirge, so grievous was their plight!
They never got the bacon, well I know,
Offered as prize to couples at Dunmow
Who live a year in peace, without repentance![5]   225
So well I ruled them, by my law and sentence,
They gladly brought me fine things from the fair,
Happy whenever I spoke with a mild air,
For God knows I could chide outrageously.
      "Now judge if I could do it properly!   230
You wives who understand and who are wise,
This is the way to throw dust in their eyes.
There isn't on the earth so bold a man
He can swear false or lie as a woman can.
I do not urge this course in every case,   235
Just when a prudent wife is caught off base;
Then she should swear the parrot's mad who tattled
Her indiscretions, and when she's once embattled
Should call her maid as witness, by collusion.
But listen, how I threw them in confusion: 240

5. At Dunmow, in Essex, a side of bacon was given to the couple who had lived a year without quarreling.

" 'Sir dotard, this is how you live?' I'd say.
'How can my neighbor's wife be dressed so gay?
She carries off the honors everywhere.
I sit at home. I've nothing fit to wear.
What were you doing at my neighbor's house?   245
Is she so handsome? Are you so amorous?
What do you whisper to our maid? God bless me,
Give up your jokes, old lecher. They depress me.
When I've a harmless friend myself, you balk
And scold me like a devil if I walk   250
For innocent amusement to his house.
You drink and come home reeling like a souse
And sit down on your bench, worse luck, and preach.
Taking a wife who's poor—this is the speech
That you regale me with—costs grievously,   255
And if she's rich and of good family,
It is a constant torment, you decide,
To suffer her ill humor and her pride.
And if she's fair, you scoundrel, you destroy her
By saying that every lecher will enjoy her;   260
For she can't long keep chastity intact
Who is from every side at once attacked.
    " 'Some want us for our wealth, so you declare,
Some for our figure, some think we are fair,
Some want a woman who can dance or sing,   265
Some want kindness, and some philandering,
Some look for hands and arms well turned and small.
Thus, by your tale, the devil may take us all!
Men cannot keep a castle or redoubt
Longer, you tell me, than it can hold out.   270
Or if a woman's plain, you say that she
Is one who covets each man she may see,
For at him like a spaniel she will fly
Until she finds some man that she can buy.
Down to the lake goes never a goose so gray   275
But it will have a mate, I've heard you say.
It's hard to fasten—this too I've been told—
A thing that no man willingly will hold.
Wise men, you tell me as you go to bed,
And those who hope for heaven should never wed.   280
I hope wild lightning and a thunderstroke
Will break your wizened neck! You say that smoke
And falling timbers and a railing wife
Drive a man from his house. Lord bless my life!
What ails an old man, so to make him chide?   285
We cover our vices till the knot is tied,
We wives, you say, and then we trot them out.
Here's a fit proverb for a doddering lout!
An ox or ass, you say, a hound or horse,
These we examine as a matter of course.   290
Basins and also bowls, before we buy them,
Spoons, spools, and such utensils, first we try them,

And so with pots and clothes, beyond denial;
But of their wives men never make a trial
Until they are married. After that, you say,   295
Old fool, we put our vices on display.
" 'I'm in a pique if you forget your duty
And aren't forever praising me for beauty
Or aren't at all hours doting on my face
And calling me "fair dame" in every place,   300
Or fail to give a feast on my birthday
To keep my spirits fresh and make me gay,
Or if all proper courtesies aren't paid
My nurse, and equally my chambermaid,
My father's kin with all his family ties—   305
You say so, you old barrelful of lies!
" 'Yet just because he has a head of hair
Like shining gold, and squires me everywhere,
You have a false suspicion in your heart
Of Jenkin, our apprentice. For my part   310
I wouldn't have him if you died tomorrow!
But tell me this, or go and live in sorrow:
That chest of yours, why do you hide the keys
Away from me? It's my wealth, if you please,
As much as yours. Will you make a fool of me,   315
The mistress of our house? You shall not be
Lord of my body and my wealth at once!
No, by St. James himself, you must renounce
One or the other, if it drives you mad!
What do you gain by spying? You'd be glad   320
To lock me up, I think, inside your chest.
"Enjoy yourself, and go where you think best,"
You ought to say; "I won't hear tales of malice.
I know you for a faithful wife, Dame Alice."
A woman loves no man who keeps close charge   325
Of where she goes. We want to be at large.
Blessed above all other men was he,
The wise astrologer, Don Ptolemy,
Who has this proverb in his *Almagest*:
"Of all wise men his wisdom is the best   330
Who does not care who has the world in hand."[6]
Now by this proverb you should understand,
Since you have plenty, it isn't yours to care
Or fret how richly other people fare,
For by your leave, old dotard, you for one   335
Can have all you can take when day is done.
The man's a niggard to the point of scandal
Who will not lend his lamp to light a candle;
His lamp won't lose although the candle gain.
If you've enough, you ought not to complain.   340
" 'You say, too, if we make ourselves look smart,
Put on expensive clothes and dress the part,

---

6. See note to line 189 above.

We lay our virtue open to disgrace.
And then you try to reinforce your case
By saying these words in the Apostle's name: 345
"In chaste apparel, with modesty and shame,
So shall you women clothe yourselves," said he,
"And not in rich coiffure or jewelry,
Pearls or the like, or gold, or costly wear."[7]
Now both your text and rubric,[8] I declare,   350
I will not follow as I would a gnat!
   " 'You told me once that I was like a cat,
For singe her skin and she will stay at home,
But if her skin is smooth, the cat will roam.
No dawn but finds her on the neighbors calling   355
To show her skin, and go off caterwauling.
If I am looking smart, you mean to say,
I'm off to put my finery on display.
   " 'What do you gain, old fool, by setting spies?
Though you beg Argus[9] with his hundred eyes   360
To be my bodyguard, for all his skill
He'll keep me only by my own free will.
I know enough to blind him, as I live!
   " 'There are three things, you also say, that give
Vexation to this world both south and north.   365
You add that no one can endure the fourth.
Of these catastrophes a hateful wife—
You precious wretch, may Christ cut short your life!—
Is always reckoned, as you say, for one.
Is this your whole stock of comparison,   370
And why from all your parables of contempt
Can luckless helpmates never be exempt?
You also liken woman's love to hell,
To barren land where water will not dwell.
I've heard you call it an unruly fire;   375
The more it burns, the hotter its desire
To burn up everything that burned will be.
You say that just as worms destroy a tree
A wife destroys her spouse, as they have found
Who get themselves in holy wedlock bound.'   380
   "By these devices, lords, as you perceive,
I got my three old husbands to believe
That in their cups they said things of this sort,
And all of it was false; but for support
Jenkin bore witness, and my niece did too.   385
These innocents, Lord, what I put them through!
God's precious pains! And they had no recourse,
For I could bite and whinny like a horse.
Though in the wrong, I kept them well annoyed,
Or oftentimes I would have been destroyed!   390
First to the mill is first to grind his grain.

---

7. 1 Timothy 2.9.   8. The rubric was a heading to the text written in red (*ruber* in Latin).   9. Argus
was a hundred-eyed creature set by Juno to watch over Io, whom Jove loved and had turned into a heifer;
see Ovid, *Metamorphoses* 1.

I was always the first one to complain,
And so our peace was made; they gladly bid
For terms to settle things they never did!
   "For wenching I would scold them out of hand   395
When they were hardly well enough to stand.
But this would tickle a man; it would restore him
To think I had so great a fondness for him!
I'd vow when darkness came and out I stepped,
It was to see the girls with whom he slept.   400
Under this pretext I had plenty of mirth!
Such wit as this is given us at our birth.
Lies, tears, and needlework the Lord will give
In kindness to us women while we live.
And thus in one point I can take just pride: 405
I showed myself in the end the stronger side.
By sleight or strength I kept them in restraint,
And chiefly by continual complaint.
In bed they met their grief in fullest measure.
There I would scold; I would not do their pleasure.   410
Bed was a place where I would not abide
Feeling my husband's arm across my side
Till he agreed to square accounts and pay,
And after that I'd let him have his way.
To every man, therefore, I tell this tale: 415
Win where you're able, all is up for sale.
No falcon by an empty hand is lured.
For victory their cravings I endured
And even feigned a show of appetite.
And yet in old meat I have no delight;   420
It made me always rail at them and chide them,
For though the pope himself sat down beside them
I would not give them peace at their own board.
No, on my honor, I paid them word for word.
Almighty God so help me, if right now   425
I had to make my last will, I can vow
For every word they said to me, we're quits.
For I so handled the contest by my wits
That they gave up, and took it for the best,
Or otherwise we should have had no rest.   430
Like a mad lion let my husband glare,
He finally got the worst of the affair.
   "Then I would say, 'My dear, you ought to keep
In mind how gentle Wilkin looks, our sheep.
Come here, my husband, let me kiss your cheek!   435
You should be patient, too; you should be meek.
Of Job and of his patience when you prate
Your conscience ought to show a cleaner slate.
He should be patient who so well can preach.
If not, then it will fall on me to teach   440
The beauty of a peaceful wedded life.
For one of us must give in, man or wife,
And since men are more reasonable creatures

Than women are, it follows that *your* features
Ought to exhibit patience. Why do you groan? 445
You want my body yours, and yours alone?
Why, take it all! Welcome to every bit!
But curse you, Peter,[1] unless you cherish it!
Were I inclined to peddle my *belle chose*,[2]
I could walk out dressed freshly as a rose. 450
But I will keep it for your own sweet tooth.
It's your fault if we fight. By God, that's truth!'
   "This was the way I talked when I had need.
But now to my fourth husband I'll proceed.
   "This fourth I married was a roisterer. 455
He had a mistress, and my passions were,
Although I say it, strong; and altogether
Stubborn and young I was, and pert in feather.
If anyone took up his harp to play,
How I could dance! I sang as merry a lay 460
As any nightingale when of sweet wine
I'd drunk my draft. Metellius,[3] the foul swine,
Who beat his spouse until he took her life
For drinking wine, if I had been his wife,
He'd never have frightened me away from drinking! 465
But after a drink, Venus gets in my thinking,
For just as true as cold engenders hail
A thirsty mouth goes with a thirsty tail.
Drinking destroys a woman's last defense
As lechers well know by experience. 470
   "But, Lord Christ, when it all comes back to me,
Remembering my youth and jollity,
It tickles me to the roots. It does me good
Down to this very day that while I could
I took my world, my time, and had my fling. 475
But age, alas, that poisons everything
Has robbed me of my beauty and my pith.
Well, let it go! Good-by! The devil with
What cannot last! There's only this to tell:
The flour is gone, I've only chaff to sell. 480
Yet I'll contrive to keep a merry cheek!
But now of my fourth husband I will speak.
   "My heart was, I can tell you, full of spite
That in another he should find delight.
I paid him for this debt; I made it good. 485
I furnished him a cross of the same wood,
By God and by St. Joce[4]—in no foul fashion,
Not with my flesh; but I put on such passion
And rendered him so jealous, I'll engage
I made him fry in his own grease for rage! 490
On earth, God knows, I was his purgatory;
I only hope his soul is now in glory.

---

1. This is not the husband's name but an oath by St. Peter.   **2.** Pretty thing (French).   **3.** A virtuous
Roman husband who reputedly killed his wife for drinking wine.   **4.** A seventh-century Breton saint,
whose relics were at an abbey near the Tabard Inn.

God knows it was a sad song that he sung
When the shoe pinched him; sorely was he wrung!
Only he knew, and God, the devious system,   495
By which outrageously I used to twist him.
He died when I came home from Jerusalem.
He's buried near the chancel,[5] under the beam
That holds the cross. His tomb is less ornate
Than that where King Darius lies in state   500
And which the paintings of Appelles graced
With subtle work.[6] It would have been a waste
To bury him lavishly. Farewell! God save
His soul and give him rest! He's in his grave.
    "And now of my fifth husband let me tell.   505
God never let his soul go down to hell
Though he of all five was my scourge and flail!
I feel it on my ribs, right down the scale,
And ever shall until my dying day.
And yet he was so full of life and gay   510
In bed, and could so melt me and cajole me
When on my back he had a mind to roll me,
What matter if on every bone he'd beaten me!
He'd have my love, so quickly he could sweeten me.
I loved him best, in fact; for as you see,   515
His love was a more arduous prize for me.
We women, if I'm not to tell a lie,
Are quaint in this regard. Put in our eye
A thing we cannot easily obtain,
All day we'll cry about it and complain.   520
Forbid a thing, we want it bitterly,
But urge it on us, then we turn and flee.
We're chary of what we hope that men will buy.
A throng at market makes the prices high;
Men set no value on cheap merchandise,   525
A truth all women know if they are wise.
    "My fifth, may God forgive his every sin,
I took for love, not money. He had been
An Oxford student once, but in our town
Was boarding with my good friend, Alison.   530
She knew each secret that I had to give
More than our parish priest did, as I live!
I told her my full mind, I shared it all.
For if my husband pissed against a wall
Or did a thing that might have cost his life,   535
To her, and to another neighbor's wife,
And to my niece, a girl whom I loved well,
His every thought I wouldn't blush to tell.
And often enough I told them, be it said.
God knows I made his face turn hot and red   540

5. The part of the church used by the officiating clergy; often a cross was placed on a beam that divided
it from the nave, where the congregation sat.   6. Darius, king of the Persians, reputedly had a tomb
decorated by the famous Jewish craftsman Appelles; Chaucer derived this fictional information from a
twelfth-century Latin poem.

For secrets he confided to his shame.
He knew he only had himself to blame.
  "And so it happened once that during Lent,
As I did often, to Alison's I went,
For I have loved my life long to be gay   545
And to walk out in April or in May
To hear the talk and seek a favorite haunt.
Jenkin the student, Alice, my confidante,
And I myself into the country went.
My husband was in London all that Lent.   550
I had the greater liberty to see
And to be seen by jolly company.
How could I tell beforehand in what place
Luck might be waiting with a stroke of grace?
And so I went to every merrymaking.   555
No pilgrimage was past my undertaking.
I was at festivals, and marriages,
Processions, preachings, and at miracle plays,
And in my scarlet clothes I made a sight.
Upon that costume neither moth nor mite   560
Nor any worm with ravening hunger fell.
And how so? It was kept in use too well.
  "Now for what happened. In the fields we walked,
The three of us, and gallantly we talked,
The student and I, until I told him he,   565
If I became a widow, should marry me.
For I can say, and not with empty pride,
I've never failed for marriage to provide
Or other things as well. Let mice be meek;
A mouse's heart I hold not worth a leek.   570
He has one hole to scurry to, just one,
And if that fails him, he is quite undone.
  "I let this student think he had bewitched me.
(My mother with this piece of guile enriched me!)
All night I dreamed of him—this too I said;   575
He was about to kill me flat in bed;
My very bed in fact was full of blood;
But still I hoped it would result in good,
For blood betokens gold, as I have heard.
It was a fiction, dream and every word,   580
But I was following my mother's lore
In all this matter, as in many more.
  "Sirs—let me see; what did I mean to say?
Aha! By God, I have it! When he lay,
My fourth, of whom I've spoken, on his bier,   585
I wept of course; I showed but little cheer,
As wives must do, since custom has its place,
And with my kerchief covered up my face.
But since I had provided for a mate,
I did not cry for long, I'll freely state.   590
And so to church my husband on the morrow
Was borne away by neighbors in their sorrow.

Jenkin, the student, was among the crowd,
And when I saw him walk, so help me God,
Behind the bier, I thought he had a pair   595
Of legs and feet so cleanly turned and fair
I put my heart completely in his hold.
He was in fact some twenty winters old
And I was forty, to confess the truth;
But all my life I've still had a colt's tooth.   600
My teeth were spaced apart; that was the seal
St. Venus printed, and became me well.
So help me God, I was a lusty one,
Pretty and young and rich, and full of fun.
And truly, as my husbands have all said,   605
I was the best thing there could be in bed.
For I belong to Venus in my feelings,
Yet have the heart of Mars in all my dealings.
From Venus come my lust and appetite,
From Mars I get my courage and my might,   610
Born under Taurus, while Mars stood therein.
Alas, alas, that ever love was sin!
I yielded to my every inclination
Through the predominance of my constellation;
This made me so I never could withhold   615
My chamber of Venus, if the truth be told,
From a good fellow; yet upon my face
Mars left his mark, and in another place.
Never, so may Christ grant me intercession,
Have I yet loved a fellow with discretion,   620
But always I have followed appetite,
Let him be long or short or dark or light.
I never cared, as long as he liked me,
What his rank was or how poor he might be.
     "What should I say, but when the month ran out,   625
This jolly student, always much about,
This Jenkin married me in solemn state.
To him I gave land, titles, the whole slate
Of goods that had been given me before;
But my repentance afterward was sore!   630
He wouldn't endure the pleasures I held dear.
By God, he gave me a lick once on the ear,
When from a book of his I tore a leaf,
So hard that from the blow my ear grew deaf.
Stubborn I was as a lioness with young,   635
And by the truth I had a rattling tongue,
And I would visit, as I'd done before,
No matter what forbidding oath he swore.
Against this habit he would sit and preach me
Sermons enough, and he would try to teach me   640
Old Roman stories,[7] how for his whole life

---

7. This and much of the following information is derived from a collection of Latin misogynist and anti-matrimonial literature popular in the Middle Ages; see note to line 667 below.

The man Sulpicius Gallus left his wife
Only because he saw her look one day
Bareheaded down the street from his doorway.
   "Another Roman he told me of by name   645
Who, since his wife was at a summer's game
Without his knowledge, thereupon forsook
The woman. In his Bible he would look
And find that proverb of the Ecclesiast[8]
Where he enjoins and makes the stricture fast   650
That men forbid their wives to rove about.
Then he would quote me this, you needn't doubt:
'Build a foundation over sands or shallows,
Or gallop a blind horse across the fallows,
Let a wife traipse to shrines that some saint hallows,   655
And you are fit to swing upon the gallows.'
Talk as he would, I didn't care two haws
About his proverbs or his stale old saws.
Set right by him I never meant to be.
I hate the man who tells my faults to me,   660
And more of us than I do, by your pleasure.
This made him mad with me beyond all measure.
Under his yoke in no case would I go.
   "No, by St. Thomas, I will let you know
Why from that book of his I tore a leaf,   665
For which I got the blow that made me deaf.
   "He had a book,[9] *Valerius*, he called it,
And *Theophrastus*, and he always hauled it
From where it lay to read both day and night
And laughed hard at it, such was his delight.   670
There was another scholar, too, at Rome,
A cardinal, whose name was St. Jerome;
He wrote a book against Jovinian.
The book included too Tertullian,
Chrysippus, Trotula, Abbess Héloïse   675
Who lived near Paris; it contained all these,
Bound in a single volume, and many a one
Besides; the Parables of Solomon
And Ovid's *Art of Love*. On such vacation
As he could snatch from worldly occupation   680
He dredged this book for tales of wicked wives.
He knew more stories of their wretched lives
Than those told of good women in the Bible.
No scholar ever lived who did not libel
Women, believe me; to speak well of wives   685
Is quite beyond them, unless it be in lives
Of holy saints; no woman else will do.

---

8. Ecclesiasticus 25.31.   9. Jenkin's book contains treatises called *Valerius* (written in the twelfth century) and *Theophrastus* (second century), Jerome's *Letter Against Jovinian* (fourth century), and works by
Tertullian (d. ca. 230), Crisippus (a writer mentioned in Jerome's *Letter*), Trotula (an eleventh-century
woman physician who wrote gynecological works), and Heloise (the lover of Abelard, who argued in her
letters that a philosopher should never marry). The *Parables of Solomon* is a reference to the biblical book
of Proverbs, ascribed to Solomon in the Middle Ages, while Ovid's *Art of Love* is a guidebook for seducers.

Who was it painted the lion, tell me who?[1]
By God, if women had only written stories
Like wits and scholars in their oratories,
They would have pinned on men more wickedness   690
Than the whole breed of Adam can redress.
Venus's children clash with Mercury's;[2]
The two work evermore by contraries.
Knowledge and wisdom are of Mercury's giving,   695
Venus loves revelry and riotous living,
And with these clashing dispositions gifted
Each of them sinks when the other is uplifted.
Thus Mercury falls, God knows, in desolation
In Pisces, which is Venus' exaltation.   700
And Venus falls when Mercury is raised.
Thus by a scholar no woman can be praised.
The scholar, when he's old and cannot do
The work of Venus more than his old shoe,
Then sits he down, and in his dotage fond   705
Writes that no woman keeps her marriage bond!
    "But now for the story that I undertook—
To tell how I was beaten for a book.
    "Jenkin, one night, who never seemed to tire
Of reading in his book, sat by the fire   710
And first he read of Eve, whose wickedness
Delivered all mankind to wretchedness
For which in his own person Christ was slain
Who with his heart's blood bought us all again.
'By this,' he said, 'expressly you may find   715
That woman was the loss of all mankind.'
    "He read me next how Samson lost his hair.
Sleeping, his mistress clipped it off for fair;
Through this betrayal he lost both his eyes.
He read me then—and I'm not telling lies—   720
How Deianeira, wife of Hercules,
Caused him to set himself on fire.[3] With these
He did not overlook the sad to-do
Of Socrates with *his* wives—he had two.[4]
Xantippe emptied the pisspot on his head.   725
This good man sat as patient as if dead.
He wiped his scalp; he did not dare complain
Except to say 'With thunder must come rain.'
    "Pasiphaë,[5] who was the queen of Crete,
For wickedness he thought her story sweet.   730
Ugh! That's enough, it was a grisly thing,
About her lust and filthy hankering!
And Clytemnestra[6] in her lechery
Who took her husband's life feloniously,

---

1. A reference to Aesop's fable in which a lion objects to a picture of a lion eating a man, arguing that if the lion had painted the picture it would have been quite different.   2. Mercury is the planet that rules over scholars, its "children."   3. Driven by jealousy, Hercules' wife, Deianeira, prepared for him a poisoned shirt that burned him to death.   4. This apocryphal story is derived from Jerome's *Letter*.   5. Pasiphaë made love with a bull and gave birth to the Minotaur.   6. She murdered her husband, Agamemnon, on his return from Troy.

He grew devout in reading of her treason. 735
And then he told me also for what reason
Unhappy Amphiaraus[7] lost his life.
My husband had the story of *his* wife,
Eriphyle, who for a clasp of gold
Went to his Grecian enemies and told 740
The secret of her husband's hiding place,
For which at Thebes he met an evil grace.
Livia and Lucilia,[8] he went through
Their tale as well; they killed their husbands, too.
One killed for love, the other killed for hate. 745
At evening Livia, when the hour was late,
Poisoned her husband, for she was his foe.
Lucilia doted on her husband so
That in her lust, hoping to make him think
Ever of her, she gave him a love-drink 750
Of such a sort he died before the morrow.
And so at all turns husbands come to sorrow!
  "He told me then how one Latumius,[9]
Complaining to a friend named Arrius,
Told him that in his garden grew a tree 755
On which his wives had hanged themselves, all three,
Merely for spite against their partnership.
'Brother,' said Arrius, 'let me have a slip
From this miraculous tree, for, begging pardon,
I want to go and plant it in my garden.' 760
  "Then about wives in recent times he read,
How some had murdered husbands lying abed
And all night long had let a paramour
Enjoy them with the corpse flat on the floor;
Or driven a nail into a husband's brain 765
While he was sleeping, and thus he had been slain;
And some had given them poison in their drink.
He told more harm than anyone can think,
And seasoned his wretched stories with proverbs
Outnumbering all the blades of grass and herbs 770
On earth. 'Better a dragon for a mate,
Better,' he said, 'on a lion's whims to wait
Than on a wife whose way it is to chide.
Better,' he said, 'high in the loft to bide
Than with a railing wife down in the house. 775
They always, they are so contrarious,
Hate what their husbands like,' so he would say.
'A woman,' he said, 'throws all her shame away
When she takes off her smock.' And on he'd go:
'A pretty woman, unless she's chaste also, 780
Is like a gold ring stuck in a sow's nose.'
Who could imagine, who would half suppose

---

7. The prophet Amphiaraus attempted to avoid joining a military expedition against Thebes that he knew to be doomed, but was betrayed by his wife. 8. Roman wives; Livia poisoned her husband at the instigation of her lover, while Lucilia poisoned hers with a love potion. 9. This unpleasant story appears in a collection of popular tales.

The gall my heart drank, raging at each drop?
    "And when I saw that he would never stop
Reading all night from his accursed book,   785
Suddenly, in the midst of it, I took
Three leaves and tore them out in a great pique,
And with my fist I caught him on the cheek
So hard he tumbled backward in the fire.
And up he jumped, he was as mad for ire   790
As a mad lion, and caught me on the head
With such a blow I fell down as if dead.
And seeing me on the floor, how still I lay,
He was aghast, and would have fled away,
Till I came to at length, and gave a cry.   795
'You'd kill me for my lands? Before I die,
False thief,' I said, 'I'll give you a last kiss!'
    "He came to me and knelt down close at this,
And said, 'So help me God, dear Alison,
I'll never strike you. For this thing I've done   800
You are to blame. Forgive me, I implore.'
So then I hit him on the cheek once more
And said, "Thus far I am avenged, you thief.
I cannot speak. Now I shall die for grief.'
But finally, with much care and ado,   805
We reconciled our differences, we two.
He let me have the bridle in my hand
For management of both our house and land.
To curb his tongue he also undertook,
And on the spot I made him burn his book.   810
And when I had secured in full degree
By right of triumph the whole sovereignty,
And he had said, 'My dear, my own true wife,
Do as you will as long as you have life;
Preserve your honor and keep my estate.'[1]   815
From that day on we'd settled our debate.
I was as kind, God help me, day and dark,
As any wife from India to Denmark,
And also true, and so he was to me.
I pray the Lord who sits in majesty   820
To bless his soul for Christ's own mercy dear.
And now I'll tell my tale, if you will hear."
"Dame," laughed the Friar, "as I hope for bliss,
It was a long preamble to a tale, all this!"
"God's arms!" the Summoner said, "it is a sin,   825
Good people, how friars are always butting in!
A fly and a friar will fall in every dish
And every question, whatever people wish.
What do you know, with your talk about 'preambling'?
Amble or trot or keep still or go scrambling,   830
You interrupt our pleasure."
                              "You think so,

1. Status.

Sir Summoner?" said the Friar. "Before I go,
I'll give the people here a chance or two
For laughs at summoners, I promise you."
"Curse on your face," the Summoner said, "curse me,   835
If I don't tell some stories, two or three,
On friars, before I get to Sittingborne,[2]
With which I'll twist your heart and make it mourn,
For you have lost your temper, I can see."
"Be quiet," cried our Host, "immediately,"   840
And ordered, "Let the woman tell her tale.
You act like people who've got drunk on ale.
Do, Madame, tell us. That is the best measure."
"All ready, sir," she answered, "at your pleasure,
With license from this worthy Friar here."   845
"Madame, tell on," he said. "You have my ear."

THE TALE

In the old days when King Arthur ruled the nation,
Whom Welshmen speak of with such veneration,
This realm we live in was a fairy land.
The fairy queen danced with her jolly band
On the green meadows where they held dominion.   5
This was, as I have read, the old opinion;
I speak of many hundred years ago.
But no one sees an elf now, as you know,
For in our time the charity and prayers
And all the begging of these holy friars   10
Who swarm through every nook and every stream
Thicker than motes of dust in a sunbeam,
Blessing our chambers, kitchens, halls, and bowers,
Our cities, towns, and castles, our high towers,
Our villages, our stables, barns, and dairies,   15
They keep us all from seeing any fairies,
For where you might have come upon an elf
There now you find the holy friar himself
Working his district on industrious legs
And saying his devotions while he begs.   20
Women are safe now under every tree.
No incubus[3] is there unless it's he,
And all they have to fear from him is shame.
    It chanced that Arthur had a knight who came
Lustily riding home one day from hawking,   25
And in his path he saw a maiden walking
Before him, stark alone, right in his course.
This young knight took her maidenhead by force,
A crime at which the outcry was so keen
It would have cost his neck, but that the queen,   30
With other ladies, begged the king so long
That Arthur spared his life, for right or wrong,

2. A town about two-thirds of the way to Canterbury.   3. A wicked spirit that fornicates with women.

And gave him to the queen, at her own will,
According to her choice, to save or kill.
    She thanked the king, and later told this knight,   35
Choosing her time, "You are still in such a plight
Your very life has no security.
I grant your life, if you can answer me
This question: what is the thing that most of all
Women desire? Think, or your neck will fall   40
Under the ax! If you cannot let me know
Immediately, I give you leave to go
A twelvemonth and a day, no more, in quest
Of such an answer as will meet the test.
But you must pledge your honor to return   45
And yield your body, whatever you may learn."
    The knight sighed; he was rueful beyond measure.
But what! He could not follow his own pleasure.
He chose at last upon his way to ride
And with such answer as God might provide   50
To come back when the year was at the close.
And so he takes his leave, and off he goes.
    He seeks out every house and every place
Where he has any hope, by luck or grace,
Of learning what thing women covet most.   55
But he could never light on any coast
Where on this point two people would agree,
For some said wealth and some said jollity,
Some said position, some said sport in bed
And often to be widowed, often wed.   60
Some said that to a woman's heart what mattered
Above all else was to be pleased and flattered.
That shaft, to tell the truth, was a close hit.
Men win us best by flattery, I admit,
And by attention. Some say our greatest ease   65
Is to be free and do just as we please,
And not to have our faults thrown in our eyes,
But always to be praised for being wise.
And true enough, there's not one of us all
Who will not kick if you rub us on a gall.   70
Whatever vices we may have within,
We won't be taxed with any fault or sin.
    Some say that women are delighted well
If it is thought that they will never tell
A secret they are trusted with, or scandal.   75
But that tale isn't worth an old rake handle!
We women, for a fact, can never hold
A secret. Will you hear a story told?
Then witness Midas![4] For it can be read
In Ovid that he had upon his head   80
Two ass's ears that he kept out of sight

4. The story of Midas and his ass's ears (given to him because he preferred Pan's songs to those of Apollo) is found in Ovid, *Metamorphoses* 11.174–93. In Ovid the secret is known not to Midas's wife but to his barber.

Beneath his long hair with such skill and sleight
That no one else besides his wife could guess.
He loved her well, and trusted her no less.
He begged her not to make his blemish known,   85
But keep her knowledge to herself alone.
She swore that never, though to save her skin,
Would she be guilty of so mean a sin,
And yet it seemed to her she nearly died
Keeping a secret locked so long inside.   90
It swelled about her heart so hard and deep
She was afraid some word was bound to leap
Out of her mouth, and since there was no man
She dared to tell, down to a swamp she ran—
Her heart, until she got there, all agog—   95
And like a bittern[5] booming in the bog
She put her mouth close to the watery ground:
"Water, do not betray me with your sound!
I speak to you, and you alone," she said.
"Two ass's ears grow on my husband's head!   100
And now my heart is whole, now it is out.
I'd burst if I held it longer, past all doubt."
Safely, you see, awhile you may confide
In us, but it will out; we cannot hide
A secret. Look in Ovid if you care   105
To learn what followed; the whole tale is there.

      This knight, when he perceived he could not find
What women covet most, was low in mind;
But the day came when homeward he must ride,
And as he crossed a wooded countryside   110
Some four and twenty ladies there by chance
He saw, all circling in a woodland dance,
And toward this dance he eagerly drew near
In hope of any counsel he might hear.
But the truth was, he had not reached the place   115
When dance and all, they vanished into space.
No living soul remained there to be seen
Save an old woman sitting on the green,
As ugly a witch as fancy could devise.
As he approached her she began to rise   120
And said, "Sir knight, here runs no thoroughfare.
What are you seeking with such anxious air?
Tell me! The better may your fortune be.
We old folk know a lot of things," said she.

      "Good mother," said the knight, "my life's to pay,   125
That's all too certain, if I cannot say
What women covet most. If you could tell
That secret to me, I'd requite you well."

      "Give me your hand," she answered. "Swear me true
That whatsoever I next ask of you,   130
You'll do it if it lies within your might

5. A kind of heron.

And I'll enlighten you before the night."
  "Granted, upon my honor," he replied.
  "Then I dare boast, and with no empty pride,
Your life is safe," she told him. "Let me die   135
If she, the queen, won't say the same as I.
Let's learn if the haughtiest of all who wear
A net or coverchief upon their hair
Will be so forward as to answer 'no'
To what I'll teach you. No more; let us go."   140
With that she whispered something in his ear,
And told him to be glad and have no fear.
  When they had reached the court, the knight declared
That he had kept his day, and was prepared
To give his answer, standing for his life.   145
Many the wise widow, many the wife,
Many the maid who rallied to the scene,
And at the head as justice sat the queen.
Then silence was enjoined; the knight was told
In open court to say what women hold   150
Precious above all else. He did not stand
Dumb like a beast, but spoke up at command
And plainly offered them his answering word
In manly voice, so that the whole court heard.
  "My liege and lady, most of all," said he,   155
"Women desire to have the sovereignty
And sit in rule and government above
Their husbands, and to have their way in love.
This is what most you want. Spare me or kill
As you may like; I stand here by your will."   160
  No widow, wife, or maid gave any token
Of contradicting what the knight had spoken.
He should not die; he should be spared instead;
He well deserved his life, the whole court said.
  The old woman whom the knight met on the grass   165
Sprang up at this. "My sovereign lady queen,
Before your court has risen, do me right!
I taught, myself, this answer to the knight,
For which he pledged his honor in my hand,
Solemnly, that the first thing I demand,   170
He'd do it, if it lay within his might.
Before the court I ask you, then, sir knight,
To take me," said the woman, "as your wife,
For well you know that I have saved your life.
Deny me, on your honor, if you can."   175
  "Alas," replied this miserable man,
"That was my promise, it must be confessed.
For the love of God, though, choose a new request!
Take all my wealth, and let my body be."
  "If that's your tune, then curse both you and me,"   180
She said. "Though I am ugly, old, and poor,
I'll have, for all the metal and the ore
That under earth is hidden or lies above,

Nothing, except to be your wife and love."
    "My love? No, my damnation, if you can!
Alas," he said, "that any of my clan   185
Should be so miserably misallied!"
    All to no good; force overruled his pride,
And in the end he is constrained to wed,
And marries his old wife and goes to bed.   190
    Now some will charge me with an oversight
In failing to describe the day's delight,
The merriment, the food, the dress at least.
But I reply, there was no joy nor feast;
Nothing but sorrow and sharp misery.   195
He married her in private, secretly,
And all day after, such was his distress,
Hid like an owl from his wife's ugliness.
    Great was the woe this knight had in his head
When in due time they both were brought to bed.   200
He shuddered, tossed, and turned, and all the while
His old wife lay and waited with a smile.
"Is every knight so backward with a spouse?
Is it," she said, "a law in Arthur's house?
I am your love, your own, your wedded wife.   205
I am the woman who has saved your life.
I've never done you anything but right.
Why do you treat me this way the first night?
You must be mad, the way that you behave!
Tell me my fault, and as God's love can save,   210
I will amend it, truly, if I can."
    "Amend it?" answered this unhappy man.
"It never can be amended, truth to tell.
You are so loathsome and so old as well,
And your low birth besides is such a cross   215
It is no wonder that I turn and toss.
God take my woeful spirit from my breast!"
    "Is this", she said, "the cause of your unrest?"
    "No wonder!" said the knight."It truly is."
    "Now sir," she said, "I could amend all this   220
Within three days, if it should please me to,
And if you deal with me as you should do.
    "But since you speak of that nobility
That comes from ancient wealth and pedigree,
As if *that* constituted gentlemen,   225
I hold such arrogance not worth a hen!
The man whose virtue is pre-eminent,
In public and alone, always intent
On doing every generous act he can,
Take him—he is the greatest gentleman!   230
Christ wills that we should claim nobility
From him, not from old wealth or family.
Our elders left us all that they were worth
And through their wealth and blood we claim high birth,
But never, since it was beyond their giving,   235

Could they bequeath to us their virtuous living;
Although it first conferred on them the name
Of gentlemen, they could not leave that claim!
    "Dante the Florentine on this was wise:
'Frail is the branch on which man's virtues rise'—   240
Thus runs his rhyme—'God's goodness wills that we
Should claim from him alone nobility.'[6]
Thus from our elders we can only claim
Such temporal things as men may hurt and maim.
    "It's plain enough that true nobility   245
Is not bequeathed along with property,
For many a lord's son does a deed of shame
And yet, God knows, enjoys his noble name.
But he, though scion of a noble house
And elders who were wise and virtuous,   250
Who will not follow his elders, who are dead,
But leads, himself, a shameful life instead,
He is not noble, be he duke or earl.
It is the churlish deed that makes the churl.
And therefore, my dear husband, I conclude   255
That though my ancestors were rough and rude,
Yet may Almighty God confer on me
The grace to live, as I hope, virtuously.
Call me of noble blood when I begin
To live in virtue and to cast out sin.   260
    "As for my poverty, at which you grieve,
Almighty God in whom we all believe
In willful poverty chose to lead his life,
And surely every man and maid and wife
Can understand that Jesus, heaven's king,   265
Would never choose a low or vicious thing.
A poor and cheerful life is nobly led;
So Seneca[7] and others have well said.
The man so poor he doesn't have a stitch
Who thinks himself repaid, I count as rich.   270
He that is covetous, he is the poor man,
Pining to have the things he never can.
It is of cheerful mind, true poverty.
Juvenal[8] says about it happily:
'The poor man as he goes along his way   275
And passes thieves is free to sing and play.'
Poverty is a good we loathe, a great
Reliever of our busy worldly state,
A great amender also of our minds
As he that patiently will bear it finds.   280
And poverty, for all it seems distressed,
Is a possession no one will contest.
Poverty, too, by bringing a man low,
Helps him the better God and self to know.

6. Chaucer's sources are Dante's *Convivio* and *Purgatorio* 7.121–23.   **7.** A Roman philosopher.   **8.** A
Roman poet.

Poverty is a glass where we can see   285
Which are our true friends, as it seems to me.
So, sir, I do not wrong you on this score;
Reproach me with my poverty no more.
   "Now, sir, you tax me with my age; but, sir,
You gentlemen of breeding all aver   290
That men should not despise old age, but rather
Grant an old man respect, and call him 'father.'
   "If I am old and ugly, as you have said,
You have less fear of being cuckolded,
For ugliness and age, as all agree,   295
Are notable guardians of chastity.
But since I know in what you take delight,
I'll gratify your worldly appetite.
   "Choose now, which of two courses you will try:
To have me old and ugly till I die   300
But evermore your true and humble wife,
Never displeasing you in all my life,
Or will you have me rather young and fair
And take your chances on who may repair
Either to your house on account of me   305
Or to some other place, it well may be.
Now make your choice, whichever you prefer."
   The knight took thought, and sighed, and said to her
At last, "My love and lady, my dear wife,
In your wise government I put my life.   310
Choose for yourself which course will best agree
With pleasure and honor, both for you and me.
I do not care, choose either of the two;
I am content, whatever pleases you."
   "Then have I won from you the sovereignty,   315
Since I may choose and rule at will?" said she.
   He answered, "That is best, I think, dear wife."
   "Kiss me," she said. "Now we are done with strife,
For on my word, I will be both to you,
That is to say, fair, yes, and faithful too.   320
May I die mad unless I am as true
As ever wife was since the world was new.
Unless I am as lovely to be seen
By morning as an empress or a queen
Or any lady between east and west,   325
Do with my life or death as you think best.
Lift up the curtain, see what you may see."
   And when the knight saw what had come to be
And knew her as she was, so young, so fair,
His joy was such that it was past compare.   330
He took her in his arms and gave her kisses
A thousand times on end; he bathed in blisses.
And she obeyed him also in full measure
In everything that tended to his pleasure.
   And so they lived in full joy to the end.   335
And now to all us women may Christ send

Submissive husbands, full of youth in bed,
And grace to outlive all the men we wed.
And I pray Jesus to cut short the lives
Of those who won't be governed by their wives;⁣   340
And old, ill-tempered niggards who hate expense,
God promptly bring them down with pestilence!

The Pardoner's Prologue and Tale

Now my fine friend," he⁹ said, "you Pardoner,
Be quick, tell us a tale of mirth or fun."
"St. Ninian!"¹ he said, "it shall be done,
But at this tavern here, before my tale,
I'll just go in and have some bread and ale."   5
The proper pilgrims in our company
Cried quickly, "Let him speak no ribaldry!
Tell us a moral tale, one to make clear
Some lesson to us, and we'll gladly hear."
"Just as you wish," he said. "I'll try to think   10
Of something edifying while I drink."

THE PROLOGUE

"In churches," said the Pardoner, "when I preach,
I use, milords, a lofty style of speech
And ring it out as roundly as a bell,
Knowing by rote all that I have to tell.
My text is ever the same, and ever was: 5
*Radix malorum est cupiditas.*²
"First I inform them whence I come; that done,
I then display my papal bulls,³ each one.
I show my license⁴ first, my body's warrant,
Sealed by the bishop, for it would be abhorrent   10
If any man made bold, though priest or clerk,
To interrupt me in Christ's holy work.
And after that I give myself full scope.
Bulls in the name of cardinal and pope,
Of bishops and of patriarchs I show.   15
I say in Latin some few words or so
To spice my sermon; it flavors my appeal
And stirs my listeners to greater zeal.
Then I display my cases made of glass
Crammed to the top with rags and bones. They pass   20
For relics with all the people in the place.
I have a shoulder bone in a metal case,
Part of a sheep owned by a holy Jew.
'Good men,' I say, 'heed what I'm telling you:
Just let this bone be dipped in any well   25

9. The Host; the Physician has just finished his tale.   1. A Scottish saint.   2. Avarice is the root of all evil (Latin).   3. Letters of indulgence, with the pope's seal (Latin *bulla*), which promise the purchaser release from some of the pains of purgatory.   4. A license from the bishop was required of all those who would preach in his diocese.

And if cow, calf, or sheep, or ox should swell
From eating a worm, or by a worm be stung,
Take water from this well and wash its tongue
And it is healed at once. And furthermore
Of scab and ulcers and of every sore   30
Shall every sheep be cured, and that straightway,
That drinks from the same well. Heed what I say:
If the good man who owns the beasts will go,
Fasting, each week, and drink before cockcrow
Out of this well, his cattle shall be brought   35
To multiply—that holy Jew so taught
Our elders—and his property increase.
    " 'Moreover, sirs, this bone cures jealousies.
Though into a jealous madness a man fell,
Let him cook his soup in water from this well,   40
He'll never, though for truth he knew her sin,
Suspect his wife again, though she took in
A priest, or even two of them or three.
    " 'Now here's a mitten that you all can see.
Whoever puts his hand in it shall gain,   45
When he sows his land, increasing crops of grain,
Be it wheat or oats, provided that he bring
His penny or so to make his offering.
    " 'There is one word of warning I must say,
Good men and women. If any here today   50
Has done a sin so horrible to name
He daren't be shriven[5] of it for the shame,
Or if any woman, young or old, is here
Who has cuckolded her husband, be it clear
They may not make an offering in that case   55
To these my relics; they have no power nor grace.
But any who is free of such dire blame,
Let him come up and offer in God's name
And I'll absolve him through the authority
That by the pope's bull has been granted me.'   60
    "By such hornswoggling I've won, year by year,
A hundred marks[6] since being a pardoner.
I stand in my pulpit like a true divine,
And when the people sit I preach my line
To ignorant souls, as you have heard before,   65
And tell skullduggeries by the hundred more.
Then I take care to stretch my neck well out
And over the people I nod and peer about
Just like a dove perching on a shed.
My hands fly and my tongue wags in my head   70
So busily that to watch me is a joy.
Avarice is the theme that I employ
In all my sermons, to make the people free
In giving pennies—especially to me.
My mind is fixed on what I stand to win   75

5. Confessed.   6. A very large sum; the Pardoner is almost certainly exaggerating.

And not at all upon correcting sin.
I do not care, when they are in the grave,
If souls go berry-picking that I could save.
Truth is that evil purposes determine,
And many a time, the origin of a sermon: 80
Some to please people and by flattery
To gain advancement through hypocrisy,
Some for vainglory, some again for hate.
For when I daren't fight otherwise, I wait
And give him a tongue-lashing when I preach. 85
No man escapes or gets beyond the reach
Of my defaming tongue, supposing he
Has done a wrong to my brethren or to me.
For though I do not tell his proper name,
People will recognize him all the same. 90
By sign and circumstance I let them learn.
Thus I serve those who have done us an ill turn.
Thus I spit out my venom under hue
Of sanctity, and seem devout and true!
     "But to put my purpose briefly, I confess 95
I preach for nothing but for covetousness.
That's why my text is still and ever was
Radix malorum est cupiditas.
For by this text I can denounce, indeed,
The very vice I practice, which is greed. 100
But though that sin is lodged in my own heart,
I am able to make other people part
From avarice, and sorely to repent,
Though that is not my principal intent.
     "Then I bring in examples, many a one, 105
And tell them many a tale of days long done.
Plain folk love tales that come down from of old.
Such things their minds can well report and hold.
Do you think that while I have the power to preach
And take in silver and gold for what I teach 110
I shall ever live in willful poverty?
No, no, that never was my thought, certainly.
I mean to preach and beg in sundry lands.
I won't do any labor with my hands,
Nor live by making baskets.[7] I don't intend 115
To beg for nothing; that is not my end.
I won't ape the apostles; I must eat,
I must have money, wool, and cheese, and wheat,
Though I took it from the meanest wretch's tillage
Or from the poorest widow in a village, 120
Yes, though her children starved for want. In fine,
I mean to drink the liquor of the vine
And have a jolly wench in every town.
But, in conclusion, lords, I will get down
To business: you would have me tell a tale. 125

---

7. A medieval tradition asserted that the apostle Paul was a basket maker.

Now that I've had a drink of corny ale,
By God, I hope the thing I'm going to tell
Is one that you'll have reason to like well.
For though myself a very sinful man,
I can tell a moral tale, indeed I can,   130
One that I use to bring the profits in
While preaching. Now be still, and I'll begin."

THE TALE

There was a company of young folk living
One time in Flanders, who were bent on giving
Their lives to follies and extravagances,
Brothels and taverns, where they held their dances
With lutes, harps, and guitars, diced at all hours,   5
And also ate and drank beyond their powers,
Through which they paid the devil sacrifice
In the devil's temple with their drink and dice,
Their abominable excess and dissipation.
They swore oaths that were worthy of damnation;   10
It was grisly to be listening when they swore.
The blessed body of our Lord they tore[8]—
The Jews, it seemed to them, had failed to rend
His body enough—and each laughed at his friend
And fellow in sin. To encourage their pursuits   15
Came comely dancing girls, peddlers of fruits,
Singers with harps, bawds and confectioners
Who are the very devil's officers
To kindle and blow the fire of lechery
That is the follower of gluttony.   20
    Witness the Bible, if licentiousness
Does not reside in wine and drunkenness!
Recall how drunken Lot, unnaturally,
With his two daughters lay unwittingly,
So drunk he had no notion what he did.[9]   25
    Herod, the stories tell us, God forbid,
When full of liquor at his banquet board
Right at his very table gave the word
To kill the Baptist, John, though guiltless he.[1]
    Seneca says a good word, certainly.   30
He says there is no difference he can find
Between a man who has gone out of his mind
And one who carries drinking to excess,
Only that madness outlasts drunkenness.[2]
O gluttony, first cause of mankind's fall,[3]   35
Of our damnation the cursed original
Until Christ bought us with his blood again!
How dearly paid for by the race of men
Was this detestable iniquity!

8. They swore by the various parts of Christ's body (see line 171 for examples). 9. Genesis 19.33–
35. 1. Matthew 14.1–11; Mark 6.14–28. 2. Seneca's *Epistles* 83. 3. Since the Fall was caused
by eating the forbidden fruit.

This whole world was destroyed through gluttony.   40
   Adam our father and his wife also
From paradise to labor and to woe
Were driven for that selfsame vice, indeed.
As long as Adam fasted—so I read—
He was in heaven; but as soon as he   45
Devoured the fruit of that forbidden tree
Then he was driven out in sorrow and pain.
Of gluttony well ought we to complain!
Could a man know how many maladies
Follow indulgences and gluttonies   50
He would keep his diet under stricter measure
And sit at table with more temperate pleasure.
The throat is short and tender is the mouth,
And hence men toil east, west, and north, and south,
In earth, and air, and water—alas to think—   55
Fetching a glutton dainty meat and drink.
   This is a theme, O Paul, that you well treat:
"Meat unto belly, and belly unto meat,
God shall destroy them both," as Paul has said.[5]
When a man drinks the white wine and the red—   60
This is a foul word, by my soul, to say,
And fouler is the deed in every way—
He makes his throat his privy through excess.
   The Apostle says, weeping for piteousness,
"There are many of whom I told you—at a loss   65
I say it, weeping—enemies of Christ's cross,
Whose belly is their god; their end is death."[6]
O cursed belly! Sack of stinking breath
In which corruption lodges, dung abounds!
At either end of you come forth foul sounds.   70
Great cost it is to fill you, and great pain!
These cooks, how they must grind and pound and strain
And transform substance into accident[7]
To please your cravings, though exorbitant!
From the hard bones they knock the marrow out.   75
They'll find a use for everything, past doubt,
That down the gullet sweet and soft will glide.
The spiceries of leaf and root provide
Sauces that are concocted for delight,
To give a man a second appetite.   80
But truly, he whom gluttonies entice
Is dead, while he continues in that vice.
   O drunken man, disfigured is your face,
Sour is your breath, foul are you to embrace!
You seem to mutter through your drunken nose   85
The sound of "Samson, Samson," yet God knows
That Samson never indulged himself in wine.[8]
Your tongue is lost, you fall like a stuck swine,

---

5. 1 Corinthians 6.13.   **6.** Philippians 3.18–19.   **7.** A distinction was made in philosophy between *substance*, the real nature of a thing, and *accident*, its merely sensory qualities, such as flavor.   **8.** Judges 13.4.

And all the self-respect that you possess
Is gone, for of man's judgment, drunkenness   90
Is the very sepulcher and annihilation.
A man whom drink has under domination
Can never keep a secret in his head.
Now steer away from both the white and red,
And most of all from that white wine keep wide   95
That comes from Lepe.[9] They sell it in Cheapside
And Fish Street.[1] It's a Spanish wine, and sly
To creep in other wines that grow nearby,
And such a vapor it has that with three drinks
It takes a man to Spain; although he thinks   100
He is home in Cheapside, he is far away
At Lepe. Then "Samson, Samson" will he say!
    By God himself, who is omnipotent,
All the great exploits in the Old Testament
Were done in abstinence, I say, and prayer.   105
Look in the Bible, you may learn it there.
    Attila,[2] conqueror of many a place,
Died in his sleep in shame and in disgrace
Bleeding out of his nose in drunkenness.
A captain ought to live in temperateness!   110
And more than this, I say, remember well
The injunction that was laid on Lemuel[3]—
Not Samuel, but Lemuel, I say!
Read in the Bible; in the plainest way
Wine is forbidden to judges and to kings.   115
This will suffice; no more upon these things.
    Now that I've shown what gluttony will do,
Now I will warn you against gambling, too;
Gambling, the very mother of low scheming,
Of lying and forswearing and blaspheming   120
Against Christ's name, of murder and waste as well
Alike of goods and time; and, truth to tell,
With honor and renown it cannot suit
To be held a common gambler by repute.
The higher a gambler stands in power and place,   125
The more his name is lowered in disgrace.
If a prince gambles, whatever his kingdom be,
In his whole government and policy
He is, in all the general estimation,
Considered so much less in reputation.   130
    Stilbon,[4] who was a wise ambassador,
From Lacedaemon once to Corinth bore
A mission of alliance. When he came
It happened that he found there at a game
Of hazard all the great ones of the land,   135
And so, as quickly as it could be planned,
He stole back, saying, "I will not lose my name

---

9. A town in Spain noted for strong wines.   1. London streets.   2. Leader of the Hun invasion of
Europe, fifth century.   3. Proverbs 31.4–7.   4. Chaucer adapted this and the next story—both fictitious—from a twelfth-century work.

Nor have my reputation put to shame
Allying you with gamblers. You may send
Other wise emissaries to gain your end,   140
For by my honor, rather than ally
My countrymen to gamblers, I will die.
For you that are so gloriously renowned
Shall never with this gambling race be bound
By will of mine or treaty I prepare."   145
Thus did this wise philosopher declare.
   Remember also how the Parthians' lord
Sent King Demetrius, as the books record,
A pair of golden dice, by this proclaiming
His scorn, because that king was known for gaming,   150
And the king of Parthia therefore held his crown
Devoid of glory, value, or renown.
Lords can discover other means of play
More suitable to while the time away.
   Now about oaths I'll say a word or two,   155
Great oaths and false oaths, as the old books do.
Great swearing is a thing abominable,
And false oaths yet more reprehensible.
Almighty God forbade swearing at all,
Matthew be witness;[5] but specially I call   160
The holy Jeremiah on this head.
"Swear thine oaths truly, do not lie," he said.
"Swear under judgment, and in righteousness."[6]
But idle swearing is a great wickedness.
Consult and see, and he that understands   165
In the first table of the Lord's commands
Will find the second of his commandments this:
"Take not the Lord's name idly or amiss."[7]
If a man's oaths and curses are extreme,
Vengeance shall find his house, both roof and beam.   170
"By the precious heart of God," and "By his nails"—
"My chance is seven,[8] by Christ's blood at Hailes,[9]
Yours five and three." "Cheat me, and if you do,
By God's arms, with this knife I'll run you through!"—
Such fruit comes from the bones,[1] that pair of bitches: 175
Oaths broken, treachery, murder. For the riches
Of Christ's love, give up curses, without fail,
Both great and small!—Now, sirs, I'll tell my tale.
   These three young roisterers of whom I tell
Long before prime had rung from any bell   180
Were seated in a tavern at their drinking,
And as they sat, they heard a bell go clinking
Before a corpse being carried to his grave.
One of these roisterers, when he heard it, gave
An order to his boy: "Go out and try   185
To learn whose corpse is being carried by.

5. Matthew 5.34.   6. Jeremiah 4.2.   7. Exodus 20.7.   8. I.e., "My number is seven."   9. An
abbey in Gloucestershire, where some of Christ's blood was believed to be preserved.   1. Dice.

Get me his name, and get it right. Take heed."
   "Sir," said the boy, "there isn't any need.
I learned before you came here, by two hours.
He was, it happens, an old friend of yours,   190
And all at once, there on his bench upright
As he was sitting drunk, he was killed last night.
A sly thief, Death men call him, who deprives
All the people in this country of their lives,
Came with his spear and smiting his heart in two   195
Went on his business with no more ado.
A thousand have been slaughtered by his hand
During this plague. And, sir, before you stand
Within his presence, it should be necessary,
It seems to me, to know your adversary.   200
Be evermore prepared to meet this foe.
My mother taught me thus; that's all I know."
   "Now by St. Mary," said the innkeeper,
"This child speaks truth. Man, woman, laborer,
Servant, and child the thief has slain this year   205
In a big village a mile or more from here.
I think it is his place of habitation.
It would be wise to make some preparation
Before he brought a man into disgrace."
   "God's arms!" this roisterer said. "So that's the case!   210
Is it so dangerous with this thief to meet?
I'll look for him by every path and street,
I vow it, by God's holy bones! Hear me,
Fellows of mine, we are all one, we three.
Let each of us hold up his hand to the other   215
And each of us become his fellow's brother.
We'll slay this Death, who slaughters and betrays.
He shall be slain whose hand so many slays,
By the dignity of God, before tonight!"
   The three together set about to plight   220
Their oaths to live and die each for the other
Just as though each had been to each born brother,
And in their drunken frenzy up they get
And toward the village off at once they set
Which the innkeeper had spoken of before,   225
And many were the grisly oaths they swore.
They rent Christ's precious body limb from limb—
Death shall be dead, if they lay hands on him!
   When they had hardly gone the first half mile,
Just as they were about to cross a stile,   230
An old man, poor and humble, met them there.
The old man greeted them with a meek air
And said, "God bless you, lords, and be your guide."
   "What's this?" the proudest of the three replied.
"Old beggar, I hope you meet with evil grace!   235
Why are you all wrapped up except your face?
What are you doing alive so many a year?"
   The old man at these words began to peer

Into this gambler's face. "Because I can,
Though I should walk to India, find no man,"   240
He said, "in any village or any town,
Who for my age is willing to lay down
His youth. So I must keep my old age still
For as long a time as it may be God's will.
Nor will Death take my life from me, alas!   245
Thus like a restless prisoner I pass
And on the ground, which is my mother's gate,
I walk and with my staff both early and late
I knock and say, 'Dear mother, let me in!
See how I vanish, flesh, and blood, and skin!   250
Alas, when shall my bones be laid to rest?
I would exchange with you my clothing chest,
Mother, that in my chamber long has been
For an old haircloth rag to wrap me in.'
And yet she still refuses me that grace.   255
All white, therefore, and withered is my face.
   "But, sirs, you do yourselves no courtesy
To speak to an old man so churlishly
Unless he had wronged you either in word or deed.
As you yourselves in Holy Writ may read,   260
'Before an aged man whose head is hoar
Men ought to rise.'[2] I counsel you, therefore,
No harm nor wrong here to an old man do,
No more than you would have men do to you
In your old age, if you so long abide.   265
And God be with you, whether you walk or ride!
I must go yonder where I have to go."
   "No, you old beggar, by St. John, not so,"
Said another of these gamblers. "As for me,
By God, you won't get off so easily!   270
You spoke just now of that false traitor, Death,
Who in this land robs all our friends of breath.
Tell where he is, since you must be his spy,
Or you will suffer for it, so say I
By God and by the holy sacrament.   275
You are in league with him, false thief, and bent
On killing us young folk, that's clear to my mind."
   "If you are so impatient, sirs, to find
Death," he replied, "turn up this crooked way,
For in that grove I left him, truth to say,   280
Beneath a tree, and there he will abide.
No boast of yours will make him run and hide.
Do you see that oak tree? Just there you will find
This Death, and God, who bought again mankind,
Save and amend you!" So said this old man;   285
And promptly each of these three gamblers ran
Until he reached the tree, and there they found
Florins of fine gold, minted bright and round,

2. Leviticus 19.32.

Nearly eight bushels of them, as they thought.
And after Death no longer then they sought.   290
Each of them was so ravished at the sight,
So fair the florins glittered and so bright,
That down they sat beside the precious hoard.
The worst of them, he uttered the first word.

  "Brothers," he told them, "listen to what I say.   295
My head is sharp, for all I joke and play.
Fortune has given us this pile of treasure
To set us up in lives of ease and pleasure.
Lightly it comes, lightly we'll make it go.
God's precious dignity! Who was to know   300
We'd ever tumble on such luck today?
If we could only carry this gold away,
Home to my house, or either one of yours—
For well you know that all this gold is ours—
We'd touch the summit of felicity.   305
But still, by daylight that can hardly be.
People would call us thieves, too bold for stealth,
And they would have us hanged for our own wealth.
It must be done by night, that's our best plan,
As prudently and slyly as we can.   310
Hence my proposal is that we should all
Draw lots, and let's see where the lot will fall,
And the one of us who draws the shortest stick
Shall run back to the town, and make it quick,
And bring us bread and wine here on the sly,   315
And two of us will keep a watchful eye
Over this gold; and if he doesn't stay
Too long in town, we'll carry this gold away
By night, wherever we all agree it's best."

  One of them held the cut out in his fist   320
And had them draw to see where it would fall,
And the cut fell on the youngest of them all.
At once he set off on his way to town,
And the very moment after he was gone
The one who urged this plan said to the other: 325
"You know that by sworn oath you are my brother.
I'll tell you something you can profit by.
Our friend has gone, that's clear to any eye,
And here is gold, abundant as can be,
That we propose to share alike, we three.   330
But if I worked it out, as I could do,
So that it could be shared between us two,
Wouldn't that be a favor, a friendly one?"

  The other answered, "How that can be done,
I don't quite see. He knows we have the gold.   335
What shall we do, or what shall he be told?"

  "Will you keep the secret tucked inside your head?
And in a few words," the first scoundrel said,
"I'll tell you how to bring this end about."

  "Granted," the other told him. "Never doubt,   340

I won't betray you, that you can believe."
    "Now," said the first, "we are two, as you perceive,
And two of us must have more strength than one.
When he sits down, get up as if in fun
And wrestle with him. While you play this game   345
I'll run him through the ribs. You do the same
With your dagger there, and then this gold shall be
Divided, dear friend, between you and me.
Then all that we desire we can fulfill,
And both of us can roll the dice at will."   350
Thus in agreement these two scoundrels fell
To slay the third, as you have heard me tell.
    The youngest, who had started off to town,
Within his heart kept rolling up and down
The beauty of those florins, new and bright.   355
"O Lord," he thought, "were there some way I might
Have all this treasure to myself alone,
There isn't a man who dwells beneath God's throne
Could live a life as merry as mine should be!"
And so at last the fiend, our enemy,   360
Put in his head that he could gain his ends
If he bought poison to kill off his friends.
Finding his life in such a sinful state,
The devil was allowed to seal his fate.
For it was altogether his intent   365
To kill his friends, and never to repent.
So off he set, no longer would he tarry,
Into the town, to an apothecary,
And begged for poison; he wanted it because
He meant to kill his rats; besides, there was   370
A polecat living in his hedge, he said,
Who killed his capons; and when he went to bed
He wanted to take vengeance, if he might,
On vermin that devoured him by night.
    The apothecary answered, "You shall have   375
A drug that as I hope the Lord will save
My soul, no living thing in all creation,
Eating or drinking of this preparation
A dose no bigger than a grain of wheat,
But promptly with his death-stroke he shall meet.   380
Die, that he will, and in a briefer while
Than you can walk the distance of a mile,
This poison is so strong and virulent."
    Taking the poison, off the scoundrel went,
Holding it in a box, and next he ran   385
To the neighboring street, and borrowed from a man
Three generous flagons. He emptied out his drug
In two of them, and kept the other jug
For his own drink; he let no poison lurk
In that! And so all night he meant to work   390
Carrying off the gold. Such was his plan,
And when he had filled them, this accursed man

Retraced his path, still following his design,
Back to his friends with his three jugs of wine.
   But why dilate upon it any more? 395
For just as they had planned his death before,
Just so they killed him, and with no delay.
When it was finished, one spoke up to say:
"Now let's sit down and drink, and we can bury
His body later on. First we'll be merry," 400
And as he said the words, he took the jug
That, as it happened, held the poisonous drug,
And drank, and gave his friend a drink as well,
And promptly they both died. But truth to tell,
In all that Avicenna[3] ever wrote 405
He never described in chapter, rule, or note
More marvelous signs of poisoning, I suppose,
Than appeared in these two wretches at the close.
Thus they both perished for their homicide,
And thus the traitorous poisoner also died. 410
   O sin accursed above all cursedness,
O treacherous murder, O foul wickedness,
O gambling, lustfulness, and gluttony,
Traducer of Christ's name by blasphemy
And monstrous oaths, through habit and through pride! 415
Alas, mankind! Ah, how may it betide
That you to your Creator, he that wrought you
And even with his precious heart's blood bought you,
So falsely and ungratefully can live?
   And now, good men, your sins may God forgive 420
And keep you specially from avarice!
My holy pardon will avail in this,
For it can heal each one of you that brings
His pennies, silver brooches, spoons, or rings.
Come, bow your head under this holy bull! 425
You wives, come offer up your cloth or wool!
I write your names here in my roll, just so.
Into the bliss of heaven you shall go!
I will absolve you here by my high power,[4]
You that will offer, as clean as in the hour 430
When you were born.—Sirs, thus I preach. And now
Christ Jesus, our souls' healer, show you how
Within his pardon evermore to rest,
For that, I will not lie to you, is best.
   But in my tale, sirs, I forgot one thing. 435
The relics and the pardons that I bring
Here in my pouch, no man in the whole land
Has finer, given me by the pope's own hand.
If any of you devoutly wants to offer
And have my absolution, come and proffer 440
Whatever you have to give. Kneel down right here,

---

3. An Arab physician.   4. The Pardoner is overstating the effect of his indulgences, which can promise relief only from punishment of sin, not from its guilt. According to medieval doctrine, full absolution can be provided only by Christ.

Humbly, and take my pardon, full and clear,
Or have a new, fresh pardon if you like
At the end of every mile of road we strike,
As long as you keep offering ever newly   445
Good coins, not counterfeit, but minted truly.
Indeed it is an honor I confer
On each of you, an authentic pardoner
Going along to absolve you as you ride.
For in the country mishaps may betide—   450
One or another of you in due course
May break his neck by falling from his horse.
Think what security it gives you all
That in this company I chanced to fall
Who can absolve you each, both low and high,   455
When the soul, alas, shall from the body fly!
By my advice, our Host here shall begin,
For he's the man enveloped most by sin.
Come, offer first, Sir Host, and once that's done,
Then you shall kiss the relics, every one,   460
Yes, for a penny! Come, undo your purse!"
     "No, no," said he. "Then I should have Christ's curse!
I'll do nothing of the sort, for love or riches!
You'd make me kiss a piece of your old britches
And for a saintly relic make it pass   465
Although it had the tincture of your ass.
By the cross St. Helen[5] found in the Holy Land,
I wish I had your balls here in my hand
For relics! Cut 'em off, and I'll be bound
If I don't help you carry them around.   470
I'll have the things enshrined in a hog's turd!"
     The Pardoner did not answer; not a word,
He was so angry, could he find to say.
     "Now," said our Host, "I will not try to play
With you, nor any other angry man."   475
     Immediately the worthy Knight began,
When he saw that all the people laughed, "No more,
This has gone far enough. Now as before,
Sir Pardoner, be gay, look cheerfully,
And you, Sir Host, who are so dear to me,   480
Come, kiss the Pardoner, I beg of you,
And Pardoner, draw near, and let us do
As we've been doing, let us laugh and play."
And so they kissed, and rode along their way.

---

5. Mother of Constantine the Great; believed to have found the True Cross.

THE THOUSAND AND ONE NIGHTS
fourteenth century

The Thousand and One Nights is rich in paradoxes. An anonymous work, it is nevertheless more widely known in the Arab world than any other work of Arabic literature. It is almost as well known in Europe, and so far is the only work of Arabic letters to become a permanent part of European and, indeed, of world literature. Despite this great popularity, and despite its shaping influence on modern literature, traditional Arabic literary scholars have never recognized it as a work of serious literature, and it is still occasionally banned as immoral by Arab governments—most recently by Egypt in 1989.

The history of *The Thousand and One Nights* is vague, and its shape as hard to pin down as a cloud's. The starting point of the work in Arabic was probably a collection of tales in Middle Persian called the "thousand stories" that had been translated or adapted from Sanskrit in the time of the Sassanids (226–652), the last pre-Islamic Iranian dynasty. During the ninth and tenth centuries a great deal of Persian literature, both popular and courtly, was translated into Arabic, particularly at the caliphal court in Baghdad. The tales that became the core of the *Nights* were probably among them. The Perso-Indian origins of the prologue and other tales are suggested by the Persian personal names (Shahrayar, Shahzaman, Shahrazad) and place-names (Indo-China, Samarkand) of the prologue. Stories set in the Baghdad of the late eighth century—those that mention the caliph Haroun al-Rashid and his vizier Ja'far the Barmakid, for instance—indicate that the original translator, or later copyists, felt free to add local tales to the originals. From Baghdad, manuscripts of this original translation circulated widely to other parts of the Islamic world, especially Syria and Egypt. The tales were also transmitted orally and adapted and translated into other languages of the region. Indeed, the initial translation into Arabic may have been an oral one—the work of a Persian storyteller who came to the great metropolis of Baghdad and adapted his wares to the language of his audience. What we know for certain is that written and oral transmissions of the tales have intermingled down to the present day. Oral versions were written down and written tales were memorized and added to oral repertories.

We can discern two quite distinct branches in the written transmission of the *Nights*. The earliest manuscript, which dates from thirteenth-century Syria, belongs to the more conservative branch. Later manuscripts derived from it adhere closely to it in substance, form, and style. Others, known collectively as the Egyptian branch, depart widely from it, deleting some of the original stories and adding others from Indian, Persian, Turkish, and Egyptian sources. The story of Sindbad is one of the earliest such additions, and that of Aladdin and the magic lamp one of the latest. At times it seems that the copyists were determined to expand the number of tales to fit the fanciful "one thousand and one" of the title. The first European translator of the *Nights*, the French scholar and traveler Jean Antoine Galland (1646–1715), followed the example of the copyists in the Egyptian branch, translating whatever stories he could find. The great success of his work encouraged other European translators, notably Sir Richard Burton (1821–1890), to do likewise. Some of the tales that Galland and Burton translated from oral sources were retranslated from French or English back into Arabic for new Arabic printings of the *Nights*, and the original character of the *Nights* was distorted almost beyond recognition. The first scholarly edition of *The Thousand and One Nights*, the first, that is, to be based on the thirteenth-century Syrian manuscript, was completed only in 1984, and the selection printed here was translated from it.

From the very beginning classical Arabic literature was unable to find a place for the *Nights*. It was a work neither of history nor of useful knowledge and moral instruction. It was not composed in an elegant, poetic style but in ordinary prose that was very close to common speech. It was filled with magical and fantastic stories that were clearly untrue. While such extravagant and improbable fabrications might be tolerated in poetry, they were unacceptable in a work of prose, since prose was expected to be more serious and substantial than poetry. The qualities that exclude the *Nights* from the canon of classical Arabic are, of course, the very ones that ensure its wide popular acceptance. It is a brilliantly entertaining work, and its stories vary from lighthearted and frivolous to touchingly romantic or terrifying and painful. The themes set forth in the prologue—lust, madness, violence, justice, retribution, and heroism—are weighty ones, and they are grounded in the stuff of everyday life. But they are told with great artistry and made magical by luxurious settings, fantastic adventures, magical turns of fortune, and the timely intervention of demons and sorcerers.

In the selections printed here, Shahrayar is a monarch driven mad by the infidelity of his wife. To ensure that another such humiliation will not occur, he has decided to marry a new young woman each night and murder her the next morning—before she has a chance to betray him. Three years pass in this way and Shahrayar has drastically depleted the number of marriageable young women in the kingdom. His chief vizier has been unable to think of a way to dissuade his monarch from this mad, self-destructive policy, but the vizier's elder daughter, Shahrazad, a young woman of exceptional learning and courage, has a plan. She will voluntarily marry Shahrayar and then use her skill as a storyteller to manipulate him into deferring her death endlessly. Her father tries, unsuccessfully, to dissuade her by telling her tales that are both irrelevant and unpersuasive, but she launches her scheme with the help of her sister, Dinarzad. Each night Shahrazad tells Shahrayar stories to while away the long hours, stopping each sunrise just before some crisis and counting on Shahrayar's eagerness to hear the end of the story to dissuade him from having her executed. In this way, she is able to hold his murderous impulses in check until he at last pardons her and and abandons his policy.

To Western readers, the *Nights* most resembles such other famous collections of tales as Chaucer's *Canterbury Tales,* Boccaccio's *Decameron,* and Marguerite de Navarre's *Heptameron.* Like these, its tales are set within the frame of another, larger tale. The prologue of the *Nights* does not surround or frame the tales it includes, however. There are examples of such framed collections within the *Nights,* starting with the first set that Shahrazad recites, but the *Prologue* is a frame tale with a difference. It has a single narrator, not many; and as a consequence there is none of the interplay between narrators, or between narrators and the tales they tell, that marks these other collections. That is, while there are many narrators, and tales within tales, all the stories are ultimately recounted by Shahrazad. Moreover, her motive throughout is the single and compelling one of preventing the destruction of herself and the other young women of her community. The formulaic exchange between Shahrazad, Shahrayar, and Dinarzad that is repeated each dawn and evening reminds us that Shahrazad is not telling tales simply to while away the time.

The image of Shahrazad deftly employing her skills as a narrator to buy her life a day at a time has captured the fancy of all who have read the *Nights,* but there may be more to her tales than an endlessly deferred conclusion. That is, her tales can also be read as a means of healing the wound inflicted on him by his wife's infidelity, and of teaching him that not all women wish him ill. That she may have cure in mind as much as delay is suggested by the neat fit between the first set of tales she tells and her own plight. In the first story, for example, a demon sets a precedent for allowing Shahrazad to purchase her life with her tales by allowing three old men to pay the merchant's blood price with theirs. This story also suggests that the demon is too harsh in threatening to kill the merchant for a crime that is at worst accidental. How much more innocent of any wrongdoing are the young women of Shahrayar's realm? In each of the tales a benign but powerful woman undoes the harm caused by an ill-intentioned one. The wicked characters are punished according to their crimes, and never by death. All this suggests that Shahrazad is not simply distracting Shahrayar with her tales, she is educating him or, better, attempting to cure him of his madness. Her choice of a cure may suggest that these tales were shaped by female narrators as well as male or at least by narrators who had an understanding and appreciation of women. A more characteristically male solution to the problem that Shahrayar poses might have been to depose or destroy him.

For those who wish to do more reading in the *Nights*, Husain Haddawy, *The Arabian Nights* (1990), is a complete translation of the text of Muhsin Mahdi's critical edition of the Syrian manuscript; Haddawy's *The Arabian Nights No. II: Sindbad and Other Popular Stories* includes material not in the Mahdi edition. The translations by Edward William Lane, *The Thousand and One Nights* (1838), and Richard Burton, *The Book of a Thousand Nights and a Night* (1885), are based on later, heterogeneous manuscripts. Burton's is the better known but Lane's is closer to the original (though it bowdlerizes the erotic scenes). N. J. Dawood, *Tales from the Thousand and One Nights* (1973), is more readable than either Lane or Burton and also includes stories not in the Mahdi edition. A useful literary commentary is Robert Irwin, *The Arabian Nights: A Companion* (1994).

PRONOUNCING GLOSSARY

The following list uses common English syllables and stress accents to provide rough equivalents of selected words whose pronunciation may be unfamiliar to the general reader.

Dinarzad: *dee-nar-zahd'*

Haroun al-Rashid: *ha-roon'ar–ra-sheed'*

Ja'far the Barmakid: *juh-far' the bar'- muh-kid*

Sa'd al-Din Mas'ud: *sad'ad–deen mass- ood'*

Shahrazad: *shah-ruh-zahd'*

Shahrayar: *shah-ruh-yahr'*

Shahzaman: *shah-zuh-mahn'*

From The Thousand and One Nights[1]

Prologue

[*The Story of King Shahrayar and Shahrazad, His Vizier's*[2] *Daughter*]

It is related—but God knows and sees best what lies hidden in the old accounts of bygone peoples and times—that long ago, during the time of the Sasanid dynasty,[3] in the peninsulas of India and Indochina, there lived two kings who were brothers. The older brother was named Shahrayar, the younger Shahzaman. The older, Shahrayar, was a towering knight and a daring champion, invincible, energetic, and implacable. His power reached the remotest corners of the land and its people, so that the country was loyal to him, and his subjects obeyed him. Shahrayar himself lived and ruled in India and Indochina, while to his brother he gave the land of Samarkand[4] to rule as king.

Ten years went by, when one day Shahrayar felt a longing for his brother the king, summoned his vizier (who had two daughters, one called Shahra-

---

1. All selections translated by Husian Huddawy except for *The Third Old Man's Tale*, translated by Jerome W. Clinton.   2. One who bears burdens (literal trans.); the highest state official or administrator under a caliph or shah.   3. The last pre-Islamic dynasty (ruled 226–652).   4. A city and province in central Asia, now in Uzbekistan.

zad, the other Dinarzad) and bade him go to his brother. Having made preparations, the vizier journeyed day and night until he reached Samarkand.
When Shahzaman heard of the vizier's arrival, he went out with his retainers
to meet him. He dismounted, embraced him, and asked him for news from
his older brother, Shahrayar. The vizier replied that he was well, and that he
had sent him to request his brother to visit him. Shahzaman complied with
his brother's request and proceeded to make preparations for the journey. In
the meantime, he had the vizier camp on the outskirts of the city, and took
care of his needs. He sent him what he required of food and fodder, slaughtered many sheep in his honor, and provided him with money and supplies,
as well as many horses and camels.

For ten full days he prepared himself for the journey; then he appointed
a chamberlain in his place, and left the city to spend the night in his tent,
near the vizier. At midnight he returned to his palace in the city, to bid his
wife good-bye. But when he entered the palace, he found his wife lying in
the arms of one of the kitchen boys. When he saw them, the world turned
dark before his eyes and, shaking his head, he said to himself, "I am still
here, and this is what she has done when I was barely outside the city. How
will it be and what will happen behind my back when I go to visit my brother
in India? No. Women are not to be trusted." He got exceedingly angry, adding, "By God, I am king and sovereign in Samarkand, yet my wife has
betrayed me and has inflicted this on me." As his anger boiled, he drew his
sword and struck both his wife and the cook. Then he dragged them by the
heels and threw them from the top of the palace to the trench below. He
then left the city and going to the vizier ordered that they depart that very
hour. The drum was struck, and they set out on their journey, while Shahzaman's heart was on fire because of what his wife had done to him and how
she had betrayed him with some cook, some kitchen boy. They journeyed
hurriedly, day and night, through deserts and wilds, until they reached the
land of King Shahrayar, who had gone out to receive them.

When Shahrayar met them, he embraced his brother, showed him favors,
and treated him generously. He offered him quarters in a palace adjoining
his own, for King Shahrayar had built two beautiful towering palaces in his
garden, one for the guests, the other for the women and members of his
household. He gave the guest house to his brother, Shahzaman, after the
attendants had gone to scrub it, dry it, furnish it, and open its windows,
which overlooked the garden. Thereafter, Shahzaman would spend the whole
day at his brother's, return at night to sleep at the palace, then go back to
his brother the next morning. But whenever he found himself alone and
thought of his ordeal with his wife, he would sigh deeply, then stifle his grief,
and say, "Alas, that this great misfortune should have happened to one in
my position!" Then he would fret with anxiety, his spirit would sag, and he
would say, "None has seen what I have seen." In his depression, he ate less
and less, grew pale, and his health deteriorated. He neglected everything,
wasted away, and looked ill.

When King Shahrayar looked at his brother and saw how day after day he
lost weight and grew thin, pale, ashen, and sickly, he thought that this was
because of his expatriation and homesickness for his country and his family,
and he said to himself, "My brother is not happy here. I should prepare a
goodly gift for him and send him home." For a month he gathered gifts for

his brother; then he invited him to see him and said, "Brother, I would like you to know that I intend to go hunting and pursue the roaming deer, for ten days. Then I shall return to prepare you for your journey home. Would you like to go hunting with me?" Shahzaman replied, "Brother, I feel distracted and depressed. Leave me here and go with God's blessing and help." When Shahrayar heard his brother, he thought that his dejection was because of his homesickness for his country. Not wishing to coerce him, he left him behind, and set out with his retainers and men. When they entered the wilderness, he deployed his men in a circle to begin trapping and hunting.

After his brother's departure, Shahzaman stayed in the palace and, from the window overlooking the garden, watched the birds and trees as he thought of his wife and what she had done to him, and sighed in sorrow. While he agonized over his misfortune, gazing at the heavens and turning a distracted eye on the garden, the private gate of his brother's palace opened, and there emerged, strutting like a dark-eyed deer, the lady, his brother's wife, with twenty slave-girls, ten white and ten black. While Shahzaman looked at them, without being seen, they continued to walk until they stopped below his window, without looking in his direction, thinking that he had gone to the hunt with his brother. Then they sat down, took off their clothes, and suddenly there were ten slave-girls and ten black slaves dressed in the same clothes as the girls. Then the ten black slaves mounted the ten girls, while the lady called, "Mas'ud, Mas'ud!" and a black slave jumped from the tree to the ground, rushed to her, and, raising her legs, went between her thighs and made love to her. Mas'ud topped the lady, while the ten slaves topped the ten girls, and they carried on till noon. When they were done with their business, they got up and washed themselves. Then the ten slaves put on the same clothes again, mingled with the girls, and once more there appeared to be twenty slave-girls. Mas'ud himself jumped over the garden wall and disappeared, while the slave-girls and the lady sauntered to the private gate, went in and, locking the gate behind them, went their way.

All of this happened under King Shahzaman's eyes. When he saw this spectacle of the wife and the women of his brother the great king—how ten slaves put on women's clothes and slept with his brother's paramours and concubines and what Mas'ud did with his brother's wife, in his very palace—and pondered over this calamity and great misfortune, his care and sorrow left him and he said to himself, "This is our common lot. Even though my brother is king and master of the whole world, he cannot protect what is his, his wife and his concubines, and suffers misfortune in his very home. What happened to me is little by comparison. I used to think that I was the only one who has suffered, but from what I have seen, everyone suffers. By God, my misfortune is lighter than that of my brother." He kept marveling and blaming life, whose trials none can escape, and he began to find consolation in his own affliction and forget his grief. When supper came, he ate and drank with relish and zest and, feeling better, kept eating and drinking, enjoying himself and feeling happy. He thought to himself, "I am no longer alone in my misery; I am well."

For ten days, he continued to enjoy his food and drink, and when his brother, King Shahrayar, came back from the hunt, he met him happily, treated him attentively, and greeted him cheerfully. His brother, King Shahrayar, who had missed him, said, "By God, brother, I missed you on this trip and wished you were with me." Shahzaman thanked him and sat down to carouse with him, and when night fell, and food was brought before them, the two ate and drank, and again Shahzaman ate and drank with zest. As time went by, he continued to eat and drink with appetite, and became lighthearted and carefree. His face regained color and became ruddy, and his body gained weight, as his blood circulated and he regained his energy; he was himself again, or even better. King Shahrayar noticed his brother's condition, how he used to be and how he had improved, but kept it to himself until he took him aside one day and said, "My brother Shahzaman, I would like you to do something for me, to satisfy a wish, to answer a question truthfully." Shahzaman asked, "What is it, brother?" He replied, "When you first came to stay with me, I noticed that you kept losing weight, day after day, until your looks changed, your health deteriorated, and your energy sagged. As you continued like this, I thought that what ailed you was your homesickness for your family and your country, but even though I kept noticing that you were wasting away and looking ill, I refrained from questioning you and hid my feelings from you. Then I went hunting, and when I came back, I found that you had recovered and had regained your health. Now I want you to tell me everything and to explain the cause of your deterioration and the cause of your subsequent recovery, without hiding anything from me." When Shahzaman heard what King Shahrayar said, he bowed his head, then said, "As for the cause of my recovery, that I cannot tell you, and I wish that you would excuse me from telling you." The king was greatly astonished at his brother's reply and, burning with curiosity, said, "You must tell me. For now, at least, explain the first cause."

Then Shahzaman related to his brother what happened to him with his own wife, on the night of his departure, from beginning to end, and concluded, "Thus all the while I was with you, great King, whenever I thought of the event and the misfortune that had befallen me, I felt troubled, careworn, and unhappy, and my health deteriorated. This then is the cause." Then he grew silent. When King Shahrayar heard his brother's explanation, he shook his head, greatly amazed at the deceit of women, and prayed to God to protect him from their wickedness, saying, "Brother, you were fortunate in killing your wife and her lover, who gave you good reason to feel troubled, careworn, and ill. In my opinion, what happened to you has never happened to anyone else. By God, had I been in your place, I would have killed at least a hundred or even a thousand women. I would have been furious; I would have gone mad. Now praise be to God who has delivered you from sorrow and distress. But tell me what has caused you to forget your sorrow and regain your health?" Shahzaman replied, "King, I wish that for God's sake you would excuse me from telling you." Shahrayar said, "You must." Shahzaman replied, "I fear that you will feel even more troubled and careworn than I." Shahrayar asked, "How could that be, brother? I insist on hearing your explanation."

Shahzaman then told him about what he had seen from the palace window and the calamity in his very home—how ten slaves, dressed like women, were sleeping with his women and concubines, day and night. He told him everything from beginning to end (but there is no point in repeating that). Then he concluded, "When I saw your own misfortune, I felt better—and said to myself, 'My brother is king of the world, yet such a misfortune has happened to him, and in his very home.' As a result I forgot my care and sorrow, relaxed, and began to eat and drink. This is the cause of my cheer and good spirits."

When King Shahrayar heard what his brother said and found out what had happened to him, he was furious and his blood boiled. He said, "Brother, I can't believe what you say unless I see it with my own eyes." When Shahzaman saw that his brother was in a rage, he said to him, "If you do not believe me, unless you see your misfortune with your own eyes, announce that you plan to go hunting. Then you and I shall set out with your troops, and when we get outside the city, we shall leave our tents and camp with the men behind, enter the city secretly, and go together to your palace. Then the next morning you can see with your own eyes."

King Shahrayar realized that his brother had a good plan and ordered his army to prepare for the trip. He spent the night with his brother, and when God's morning broke, the two rode out of the city with their army, preceded by the camp attendants, who had gone to drive the poles and pitch the tents where the king and his army were to camp. At nightfall King Shahrayar summoned his chief chamberlain and bade him take his place. He entrusted him with the army and ordered that for three days no one was to enter the city. Then he and his brother disguised themselves and entered the city in the dark. They went directly to the palace where Shahzaman resided and slept there till the morning. When they awoke, they sat at the palace window, watching the garden and chatting, until the light broke, the day dawned, and the sun rose. As they watched, the private gate opened, and there emerged as usual the wife of King Shahrayar, walking among twenty slave-girls. They made their way under the trees until they stood below the palace window where the two kings sat. Then they took off their women's clothes, and suddenly there were ten slaves, who mounted the ten girls and made love to them. As for the lady, she called, "Mas'ud, Mas'ud," and a black slave jumped from the tree to the ground, came to her, and said, "What do you want, you slut? Here is Sa'ad al-Din Mas'ud." She laughed and fell on her back, while the slave mounted her and like the others did his business with her. Then the black slaves got up, washed themselves, and, putting on the same clothes, mingled with the girls. Then they walked away, entered the palace, and locked the gate behind them. As for Mas'ud, he jumped over the fence to the road and went on his way.

When King Shahrayar saw the spectacle of his wife and the slave-girls, he went out of his mind, and when he and his brother came down from upstairs, he said, "No one is safe in this world. Such doings are going on in my kingdom, and in my very palace. Perish the world and perish life! This is a great calamity, indeed." Then he turned to his brother and asked, "Would you like to follow me in what I shall do?" Shahzaman answered, "Yes, I will." Shahrayar said, "Let us leave our royal state and roam the world for the love of the Supreme Lord. If we should find one whose misfortune is greater than ours, we shall return. Otherwise, we shall continue to journey through the land, without need for the trappings of royalty." Shahzaman replied, "This is an excellent idea. I shall follow you."

Then they left by the private gate, took a side road, and departed, journeying till nightfall. They slept over their sorrows, and in the morning resumed their day journey until they came to a meadow by the seashore.

While they sat in the meadow amid the thick plants and trees, discussing their misfortunes and the recent events, they suddenly heard a shout and a great cry coming from the middle of the sea. They trembled with fear, thinking that the sky had fallen on the earth. Then the sea parted, and there emerged a black pillar that, as it swayed forward, got taller and taller, until it touched the clouds. Shahrayar and Shahzaman were petrified; then they ran in terror and, climbing a very tall tree, sat hiding in its foliage. When they looked again, they saw that the black pillar was cleaving the sea, wading in the water toward the green meadow, until it touched the shore. When they looked again, they saw that it was a black demon, carrying on his head a large glass chest with four steel locks. He came out, walked into the meadow, and where should he stop but under the very tree where the two kings were hiding. The demon sat down and placed the glass chest on the ground. He took out four keys and, opening the locks of the chest, pulled out a full-grown woman. She had a beautiful figure, and a face like the full moon, and a lovely smile. He took her out, laid her under the tree, and looked at her, saying, "Mistress of all noble women, you whom I carried away on your wedding night, I would like to sleep a little." Then he placed his head on the young woman's lap, stretched his legs to the sea, sank into sleep, and began to snore.

Meanwhile, the woman looked up at the tree and, turning her head by chance, saw King Shahrayar and King Shahzaman. She lifted the demon's head from her lap and placed it on the ground. Then she came and stood under the tree and motioned to them with her hand, as if to say, "Come down slowly to me." When they realized that she had seen them, they were frightened, and they begged her and implored her, in the name of the Creator of the heavens, to excuse them from climbing down. She replied, "You must come down to me." They motioned to her, saying, "This sleeping demon is the enemy of mankind. For God's sake, leave us alone." She replied, "You must come down, and if you don't, I shall wake the demon and have him kill you." She kept gesturing and pressing, until they climbed down very slowly and stood before her. Then she lay on her back, raised her legs, and said, "Make love to me and satisfy my need, or else I shall wake the demon, and he will kill you." They replied, "For God's sake, mistress, don't do this to us, for at this moment we feel nothing but dismay and fear of this demon. Please, excuse us." She replied, "You must," and insisted, swearing, "By God who created the heavens, if you don't do it, I shall wake my husband the demon and ask him to kill you and throw you into the sea." As she persisted, they could no longer resist and they made love to her, first the older brother, then the younger. When they were done and withdrew from her, she said to them, "Give me your rings," and, pulling out from the folds of her dress a small purse, opened it, and shook out ninety-eight rings of different fashions and colors. Then she asked them, "Do you know what these rings are?" They answered, "No." She said, "All the owners of these rings slept with me, for whenever one of them made love to me, I took a ring from him. Since you two have slept with me, give me your rings, so that I may add them to the rest, and make a full hundred. A hundred men have known me under the very horns of this filthy, monstrous cuckold, who has imprisoned me in this chest, locked it with four locks, and kept me in the middle of this raging, roaring sea. He has guarded me and tried to keep me pure and chaste, not realizing that nothing can prevent or alter what is predestined and that when a woman desires something, no one can stop her." When Shahrayar and Shahzaman heard what the young woman said, they were greatly amazed, danced with joy, and said, "O God, O God! There is no power and no strength, save in God the Almighty, the Magnificent. Great is women's cunning." Then each of them took off his ring and handed it to her. She took them and put them with the rest in the purse. Then sitting again by the demon, she lifted his head, placed it back on her lap, and motioned to them, "Go on your way, or else I shall wake him."

They turned their backs and took to the road. Then Shahrayar turned to his brother and said, "My brother Shahzaman, look at this sorry plight. By God, it is worse than ours. This is no less than a demon who has carried a young woman away on her wedding night, imprisoned her in a glass chest, locked her up with four locks, and kept her in the middle of the sea, thinking that he could guard her from what God had foreordained, and you saw how she has managed to sleep with ninety-eight men, and added the two of us to make a hundred. Brother, let us go back to our kingdoms and our cities, never to marry a woman again. As for myself, I shall show you what I will do."

Then the two brothers headed home and journeyed till nightfall. On the morning of the third day, they reached their camp and men, entered their tent, and sat on their thrones. The chamberlains, deputies, princes, and viziers came to attend King Shahrayar, while he gave orders and bestowed robes of honor, as well as other gifts. Then at his command everyone returned to the city, and he went to his own palace and ordered his chief vizier, the father of the two girls Shahrazad and Dinarzad, who will be mentioned below, and said to him, "Take that wife of mine and put her to death." Then Shahrayar went to her himself, bound her, and handed her over to the vizier, who took her out and put her to death. Then King Shahrayar grabbed his sword, brandished it, and, entering the palace chambers, killed every one of his slave-girls and replaced them with others. He then swore to marry for one night only and kill the woman the next morning, in order to save himself from the wickedness and cunning of women, saying, "There is not a single chaste woman anywhere on the entire face of the earth." Shortly thereafter he provided his brother Shahzaman with supplies for his journey and sent him back to his own country with gifts, rarities, and money. The brother bade him good-bye and set out for home.

Shahrayar sat on his throne and ordered his vizier, the father of the two girls, to find him a wife from among the princes' daughters. The vizier found him one, and he slept with her and was done with her, and the next morning he ordered the vizier to put her to death. That very night he took one of his army officers' daughters, slept with her, and the next morning ordered the vizier to put her to death. The vizier, who could not disobey him, put her to death. The third night he took one of the merchants' daughters, slept with her till the morning, then ordered his vizier to put her to death, and the vizier did so. It became King Shahrayar's custom to take every night the daughter of a merchant or a commoner, spend the night with her, then have her put to death the next morning. He continued to do this until all the girls perished, their mothers mourned, and there arose a clamor among the fathers and mothers, who called the plague upon his head, complained to the Creator of the heavens, and called for help on Him who hears and answers prayers.

Now, as mentioned earlier, the vizier, who put the girls to death, had an older daughter called Shahrazad and a younger one called Dinarzad. The older daughter, Shahrazad, had read the books of literature, philosophy, and medicine. She knew poetry by heart, had studied historical reports, and was acquainted with the sayings of men and the maxims of sages and kings. She was intelligent, knowledgeable, wise, and refined. She had read and learned. One day she said to her father, "Father, I will tell you what is in my mind." He asked, "What is it?" She answered, "I would like you to marry me to King Shahrayar, so that I may either succeed in saving the people or perish and die like the rest." When the vizier heard what his daughter Shahrazad said, he got angry and said to her, "Foolish one, don't you know that King Shahrayar has sworn to spend but one night with a girl and have her put to death the next morning? If I give you to him, he will sleep with you for one night and will ask me to put you to death the next morning, and I shall have to do it, since I cannot disobey him." She said, "Father, you must give me to him, even if he kills me." He asked, "What has possessed you that you wish to imperil yourself?" She replied, "Father, you must give me to him. This is absolute and final." Her father the vizier became furious and said to her, "Daughter, 'He who misbehaves, ends up in trouble,' and 'He who considers not the end, the world is not his friend.' As the popular saying goes, 'I would be sitting pretty, but for my curiosity.' I am afraid that what happened to the donkey and the ox with the merchant will happen to you." She asked, "Father, what happened to the donkey, the ox, and the merchant?" He said:

[The Tale of the Ox and the Donkey]

There was a prosperous and wealthy merchant who lived in the countryside and labored on a farm. He owned many camels and herds of cattle and employed many men, and he had a wife and many grown-up as well as little children. This merchant was taught the language of the beasts, on condition that if he revealed his secret to anyone, he would die; therefore, even though he knew the language of every kind of animal, he did not let anyone know, for fear of death. One day, as he sat, with his wife beside him and his children playing before him, he glanced at an ox and a donkey he kept at the farmhouse, tied to adjacent troughs, and heard the ox say to the donkey, "Watchful one, I hope that you are enjoying the comfort and the service you are getting. Your ground is swept and watered, and they serve you, feed you sifted barley, and offer you clear, cool water to drink. I, on the contrary, am taken out to plow in the middle of the night. They clamp on my neck something they call yoke and plow, push me all day under the whip to plow the field, and drive me beyond my endurance until my sides are lacerated, and my neck is flayed. They work me from nighttime to nighttime, take me back in the dark, offer me beans soiled with mud and hay mixed with chaff, and let me spend the night lying in urine and dung. Meanwhile you rest on well-swept, watered, and smoothed ground, with a clean trough full of hay. You stand in comfort, save for the rare occasion when our master the merchant rides you to do a brief errand and returns. You are comfortable, while I am weary; you sleep, while I keep awake."

When the ox finished, the donkey turned to him and said, "Greenhorn, they were right in calling you ox, for you ox harbor no deceit, malice, or meanness. Being sincere, you exert and exhaust yourself to comfort others.

Have you not heard the saying 'Out of bad luck, they hastened on the road'? You go into the field from early morning to endure your torture at the plow to the point of exhaustion. When the plowman takes you back and ties you to the trough, you go on butting and beating with your horns, kicking with your hoofs, and bellowing for the beans, until they toss them to you; then you begin to eat. Next time, when they bring them to you, don't eat or even touch them, but smell them, then draw back and lie down on the hay and straw. If you do this, life will be better and kinder to you, and you will find relief."

As the ox listened, he was sure that the donkey had given him good advice. He thanked him, commended him to God, and invoked His blessing on him, and said, "May you stay safe from harm, watchful one." All of this conversation took place, daughter, while the merchant listened and understood. On the following day, the plowman came to the merchant's house and, taking the ox, placed the yoke upon his neck and worked him at the plow, but the ox lagged behind. The plowman hit him, but following the donkey's advice, the ox, dissembling, fell on his belly, and the plowman hit him again. Thus the ox kept getting up and falling until nightfall, when the plowman took him home and tied him to the trough. But this time the ox did not bellow or kick the ground with his hoofs. Instead, he withdrew, away from the trough. Astonished, the plowman brought him his beans and fodder, but the ox only smelled the fodder and pulled back and lay down at a distance with the hay and straw, complaining till the morning. When the plowman arrived, he found the trough as he had left it, full of beans and fodder, and saw the ox lying on his back, hardly breathing, his belly puffed, and his legs raised in the air. The plowman felt sorry for him and said to himself, "By God, he did seem weak and unable to work." Then he went to the merchant and said, "Master, last night, the ox refused to eat or touch his fodder."

The merchant, who knew what was going on, said to the plowman, "Go to the wily donkey, put him to the plow, and work him hard until he finishes the ox's task." The plowman left, took the donkey, and placed the yoke upon his neck. Then he took him out to the field and drove him with blows until he finished the ox's work, all the while driving him with blows and beating him until his sides were lacerated and his neck was flayed. At nightfall he took him home, barely able to drag his legs under his tired body and his drooping ears. Meanwhile the ox spent his day resting. He ate all his food, drank his water, and lay quietly, chewing his cud in comfort. All day long he kept praising the donkey's advice and invoking God's blessing on him. When the donkey came back at night, the ox stood up to greet him saying, "Good evening, watchful one! You have done me a favor beyond description, for I have been sitting in comfort. God bless you for my sake." Seething with anger, the donkey did not reply, but said to himself, "All this happened to me because of my miscalculation. 'I would be sitting pretty, but for my curiosity.' If I don't find a way to return this ox to his former situation, I will perish." Then he went to his trough and lay down, while the ox continued to chew his cud and invoke God's blessing on him.

"You, my daughter, will likewise perish because of your miscalculation. Desist, sit quietly, and don't expose yourself to peril. I advise you out of compassion for you." She replied, "Father, I must go to the king, and you must give me to him." He said, "Don't do it." She insisted, "I must." He replied, "If you don't desist, I will do to you what the merchant did to his wife." She asked, "Father, what did the merchant do to his wife?" He said:

[The Tale of the Merchant and His Wife]

After what had happened to the donkey and the ox, the merchant and his wife went out in the moonlight to the stable, and he heard the donkey ask the ox in his own language, "Listen, ox, what are you going to do tomorrow morning, and what will you do when the plowman brings you your fodder?" The ox replied, "What shall I do but follow your advice and stick to it? If he brings me my fodder, I will pretend to be ill, lie down, and puff my belly." The donkey shook his head, and said, "Don't do it. Do you know what I heard our master the merchant say to the plowman?" The ox asked, "What?" The donkey replied, "He said that if the ox failed to get up and eat his fodder, he would call the butcher to slaughter him and skin him and would distribute the meat for alms and use the skin for a mat. I am afraid for you, but good advice is a matter of faith; therefore, if he brings you your fodder, eat it and look alert lest they cut your throat and skin you." The ox farted and bellowed.

The merchant got up and laughed loudly at the conversation between the donkey and the ox, and his wife asked him, "What are you laughing at? Are you making fun of me?" He said, "No." She said, "Tell me what made you laugh." He replied, "I cannot tell you. I am afraid to disclose the secret conversation of the animals." She asked, "And what prevents you from telling me?" He answered, "The fear of death." His wife said, "By God, you are lying. This is nothing but an excuse. I swear by God, the Lord of heaven, that if you don't tell me and explain the cause of your laughter, I will leave you. You must tell me." Then she went back to the house crying, and she continued to cry till the morning. The merchant said, "Damn it! Tell me why you are crying. Ask for God's forgiveness, and stop questioning and leave me in peace." She said, "I insist and will not desist." Amazed at her, he replied, "You insist! If I tell you what the donkey said to the ox, which made me laugh, I shall die." She said, "Yes, I insist, even if you have to die." He replied, "Then call your family," and she called their two daughters, her parents and relatives, and some neighbors. The merchant told them that he was about to die, and everyone, young and old, his children, the farmhands, and the servants began to cry until the house became a place of mourning. Then he summoned legal witnesses, wrote a will, leaving his wife and children their due portions, freed his slave-girls, and bid his family good-bye, while everybody, even the witnesses, wept. Then the wife's parents approached her and said, "Desist, for if your husband had not known for certain that he would die if he revealed his secret, he wouldn't have gone through all this." She replied, "I will not change my mind," and everybody cried and prepared to mourn his death.

Well, my daughter Shahrazad, it happened that the farmer kept fifty hens and a rooster at home, and while he felt sad to depart this world and leave his children and relatives behind, pondering and about to reveal and utter his secret, he overheard a dog of his say something in dog language to the rooster, who, beating and clapping his wings, had jumped on a hen and, finishing with her, jumped down and jumped on another. The merchant heard and understood what the dog said in his own language to the rooster, "Shameless, no-good rooster. Aren't you ashamed to do such a thing on a day like this?" The rooster asked, "What is special about this day?" The dog replied, "Don't you know that our master and friend is in mourning today? His wife is demanding that he disclose his secret, and when he discloses it, he will surely die. He is in this predicament, about to interpret to her the language of the animals, and all of us are mourning for him, while you clap your wings and get off one hen and jump on another. Aren't you ashamed?" The merchant heard the rooster reply, "You fool, you lunatic! Our master and friend claims to be wise, but he is foolish, for he has only one wife, yet he does not know how to manage her." The dog asked, "What should he do with her?"

The rooster replied, "He should take an oak branch, push her into a room, lock the door, and fall on her with the stick, beating her mercilessly until he breaks her arms and legs and she cries out, 'I no longer want you to tell me or explain anything.' He should go on beating her until he cures her for life, and she will never oppose him in anything. If he does this, he will live, and live in peace, and there will be no more grief, but he does not know how to manage." Well, my daughter Shahrazad, when the merchant heard the conversation between the dog and the rooster, he jumped up and, taking an oak branch, pushed his wife into a room, got in with her, and locked the door. Then he began to beat her mercilessly on her chest and shoulders and kept beating her until she cried for mercy, screaming, "No, no, I don't want to know anything. Leave me alone, leave me alone. I don't want to know anything," until he got tired of hitting her and opened the door. The wife emerged penitent, the husband learned good management, and everybody was happy, and the mourning turned into a celebration.

"If you don't relent, I shall do to you what the merchant did to his wife." She said, "Such tales don't deter me from my request. If you wish, I can tell you many such tales. In the end, if you don't take me to King Shahrayar, I shall go to him by myself behind your back and tell him that you have refused to give me to one like him and that you have begrudged your master one like me." The vizier asked, "Must you really do this?" She replied, "Yes, I must."

Tired and exhausted, the vizier went to King Shahrayar and, kissing the ground before him, told him about his daughter, adding that he would give her to him that very night. The king was astonished and said to him, "Vizier, how is it that you have found it possible to give me your daughter, knowing that I will, by God, the Creator of heaven, ask you to put her to death the next morning and that if you refuse, I will have you put to death too?" He replied, "My King and Lord, I have told her everything and explained all this to her, but she refuses and insists on being with you tonight." The king was delighted and said, "Go to her, prepare her, and bring her to me early in the evening."

The vizier went down, repeated the king's message to his daughter, and said, "May God not deprive me of you." She was very happy and, after preparing herself and packing what she needed, went to her younger sister, Dinarzad, and said, "Sister, listen well to what I am telling you. When I go to the king, I will send for you, and when you come and see that the king has finished with me, say, 'Sister, if you are not sleepy, tell us a story.' Then

I will begin to tell a story, and it will cause the king to stop his practice, save myself, and deliver the people." Dinarzad replied, "Very well."

At nightfall the vizier took Shahrazad and went with her to the great King Shahrayar. But when Shahrayar took her to bed and began to fondle her, she wept, and when he asked her, "Why are you crying?" she replied, "I have a sister, and I wish to bid her good-bye before daybreak." Then the king sent for the sister, who came and went to sleep under the bed. When the night wore on, she woke up and waited until the king had satisfied himself with her sister Shahrazad and they were by now all fully awake. Then Dinarzad cleared her throat and said, "Sister, if you are not sleepy, tell us one of your lovely little tales to while away the night, before I bid you good-bye at daybreak, for I don't know what will happen to you tomorrow." Shahrazad turned to King Shahrayar and said, "May I have your permission to tell a story?" He replied, "Yes," and Shahrazad was very happy and said, "Listen":

[The Story of the Merchant and the Demon]

THE FIRST NIGHT

It is said, O wise and happy King, that once there was a prosperous merchant who had abundant wealth and investments and commitments in every country. He had many women and children and kept many servants and slaves. One day, having resolved to visit another country, he took provisions, filling his saddlebag with loaves of bread and with dates, mounted his horse, and set out on his journey. For many days and nights, he journeyed under God's care until he reached his destination. When he finished his business, he turned back to his home and family. He journeyed for three days, and on the fourth day, chancing to come to an orchard, went in to avoid the heat and shade himself from the sun of the open country. He came to a spring under a walnut tree and, tying his horse, sat by the spring, pulled out from the saddlebag some loaves of bread and a handful of dates, and began to eat, throwing the date pits right and left until he had had enough. Then he got up, performed his ablutions, and performed his prayers.

But hardly had he finished when he saw an old demon, with sword in hand, standing with his feet on the ground and his head in the clouds. The demon approached until he stood before him and screamed, saying, "Get up, so that I may kill you with this sword, just as you have killed my son." When the merchant saw and heard the demon, he was terrified and awestricken. He asked, "Master, for what crime do you wish to kill me?" The demon replied, "I wish to kill you because you have killed my son." The merchant asked, "Who has killed your son?" The demon replied, "You have killed my son." The merchant said, "By God, I did not kill your son. When and how could that have been?" The demon said, "Didn't you sit down, take out some dates from your saddlebag, and eat, throwing the pits right and left?" The merchant replied, "Yes, I did." The demon said, "You killed my son, for as you were throwing the stones right and left, my son happened to be walking by and was struck and killed by one of them, and I must now kill you." The merchant said, "O my lord, please don't kill me." The demon replied, "I must kill you as you killed him—blood for blood." The merchant said, "To God we belong and to God we turn. There is no power or strength, save in God the Almighty, the Magnificent. If I killed him, I did it by mistake. Please forgive me." The demon replied, "By God, I must kill you, as you killed my son." Then he seized him, and throwing him to the ground, raised the sword to strike him. The merchant began to weep and mourn his family and his wife and children. Again, the demon raised his sword to strike, while the merchant cried until he was drenched with tears, saying, "There is no power or strength, save in God the Almighty, the Magnificent." Then he began to recite the following verses:

> Life has two days: one peace, one wariness,
> And has two sides: worry and happiness.
> Ask him who taunts us with adversity,
> "Does fate, save those worthy of note, oppress?
> Don't you see that the blowing, raging storms   5
> Only the tallest of the trees beset,
> And of earth's many green and barren lots,
> Only the ones with fruits with stones are hit,
> And of the countless stars in heaven's vault
> None is eclipsed except the moon and sun?   10
> You thought well of the days, when they were good,
> Oblivious to the ills destined for one.
> You were deluded by the peaceful nights,
> Yet in the peace of night does sorrow stun."

When the merchant finished and stopped weeping, the demon said, "By God, I must kill you, as you killed my son, even if you weep blood." The merchant asked, "Must you?" The demon replied, "I must," and raised his sword to strike.

But morning overtook Shahrazad, and she lapsed into silence, leaving King Shahrayar burning with curiosity to hear the rest of the story. Then Dinarzad said to her sister Shahrazad, "What a strange and lovely story!" Shahrazad replied, "What is this compared with what I shall tell you tomorrow night if the king spares me and lets me live? It will be even better and more entertaining." The king thought to himself, "I will spare her until I hear the rest of the story; then I will have her put to death the next day." When morning broke, the day dawned, and the sun rose; the king left to attend to the affairs of the kingdom, and the vizier, Shahrazad's father, was amazed and delighted. King Shahrayar governed all day and returned home at night to his quarters and got into bed with Shahrazad. Then Dinarzad said to her sister Shahrazad, "Please, sister, if you are not sleepy, tell us one of your lovely little tales to while away the night." The king added, "Let it be the conclusion of the story of the demon and the merchant, for I would like to hear it." Shahrazad replied, "With the greatest pleasure, dear, happy King":

THE SECOND NIGHT

It is related, O wise and happy King, that when the demon raised his sword, the merchant asked the demon again, "Must you kill me?" and the demon replied, "Yes." Then the merchant said, "Please give me time to say good-bye to my family and my wife and children, divide my property among them, and appoint guardians. Then I shall come back, so that you may kill me." The demon replied, "I am afraid that if I release you and grant you time, you will go and do what you wish, but will not come back." The merchant said, "I swear to keep my pledge to come back, as the God of Heaven and earth is my witness." The demon asked, "How much time do you need?" The merchant replied, "One year, so that I may see enough of my children, bid my wife good-bye, discharge my obligations to people, and come back on New Year's Day." The demon asked, "Do you swear to God that if I let you go, you will come back on New Year's Day?" The merchant replied, "Yes, I swear to God."

After the merchant swore, the demon released him, and he mounted his horse sadly and went on his way. He journeyed until he reached his home and came to his wife and children. When he saw them, he wept bitterly, and when his family saw his sorrow and grief, they began to reproach him for his behavior, and his wife said, "Husband, what is the matter with you? Why do you mourn, when we are happy, celebrating your return?" He replied, "Why not mourn when I have only one year to live?" Then he told her of his encounter with the demon and informed her that he had sworn to return on New Year's Day, so that the demon might kill him.

When they heard what he said, everyone began to cry. His wife struck her face in lamentation and cut her hair, his daughters wailed, and his little children cried. It was a day of mourning, as all the children gathered around their father to weep and exchange good-byes. The next day he wrote his will, dividing his property, discharged his obligations to people, left bequests and gifts, distributed alms, and engaged reciters to read portions of the Quran in his house. Then he summoned legal witnesses and in their presence freed his slaves and slave-girls, divided among his elder children their shares of the property, appointed guardians for his little ones, and gave his wife her share, according to her marriage contract. He spent the rest of the time with his family, and when the year came to an end, save for the time needed for the journey, he performed his ablutions, performed his prayers, and, carrying his burial shroud, began to bid his family good-bye. His sons hung around his neck, his daughters wept, and his wife wailed. Their mourning scared him, and he began to weep, as he embraced and kissed his children good-bye. He said to them, "Children, this is God's will and decree, for man was created to die." Then he turned away and, mounting his horse, journeyed day and night until he reached the orchard on New Year's Day.

He sat at the place where he had eaten the dates, waiting for the demon, with a heavy heart and tearful eyes. As he waited, an old man, leading a deer on a leash, approached and greeted him, and he returned the greeting. The old man inquired, "Friend, why do you sit here in this place of demons and devils? For in this haunted orchard none come to good." The merchant replied by telling him what had happened to him and the demon, from beginning to end. The old man was amazed at the merchant's fidelity and said, "Yours is a magnificent pledge," adding, "By God, I shall not leave until I see what will happen to you with the demon." Then he sat down beside him and chatted with him. As they talked . . .

But morning overtook Shahrazad, and she lapsed into silence. As the day dawned, and it was light, her sister Dinarzad said, "What a strange and won-

*derful story!" Shahrazad replied, "Tomorrow night I shall tell something even
stranger and more wonderful than this."*

THE THIRD NIGHT

*When it was night and Shahrazad was in bed with the king, Dinarzad said
to her sister Shahrazad, "Please, if you are not sleepy, tell us one of your lovely
little tales to while away the night." The king added, "Let it be the conclusion
of the merchant's story." Shahrazad replied, "As you wish":*

I heard, O happy King, that as the merchant and the man with the deer
sat talking, another old man approached, with two black hounds, and when
he reached them, he greeted them, and they returned his greeting. Then he
asked them about themselves, and the man with the deer told him the story
of the merchant and the demon, how the merchant had sworn to return on
New Year's Day, and how the demon was waiting to kill him. He added that
when he himself heard the story, he swore never to leave until he saw what
would happen between the merchant and the demon. When the man with
the two dogs heard the story, he was amazed, and he too swore never to leave
them until he saw what would happen between them. Then he questioned
the merchant, and the merchant repeated to him what had happened to him
with the demon.

While they were engaged in conversation, a third old man approached and
greeted them, and they returned his greeting. He asked, "Why do I see the
two of you sitting here, with this merchant between you, looking abject, sad,
and dejected?" They told him the merchant's story and explained that they
were sitting and waiting to see what would happen to him with the demon.
When he heard the story, he sat down with them, saying, "By God, I too like
you will not leave, until I see what happens to this man with the demon." As
they sat, conversing with one another, they suddenly saw the dust rising from
the open country, and when it cleared, they saw the demon approaching,
with a drawn steel sword in his hand. He stood before them without greeting
them, yanked the merchant with his left hand, and, holding him fast before
him, said, "Get ready to die." The merchant and the three old men began to
weep and wail.

*But dawn broke and morning overtook Shahrazad, and she lapsed into
silence. Then Dinarzad said, "Sister, what a lovely story!" Shahrazad replied,
"What is this compared with what I shall tell you tomorrow night? It will be
even better; it will be more wonderful, delightful, entertaining, and delectable
if the king spares me and lets me live." The king was all curiosity to hear the
rest of the story and said to himself, "By God, I will not have her put to death
until I hear the rest of the story and find out what happened to the merchant
with the demon. Then I will have her put to death the next morning, as I did
with the others." Then he went out to attend to the affairs of his kingdom, and
when he saw Shahrazad's father, he treated him kindly and showed him favors,
and the vizier was amazed. When night came, the king went home, and when
he was in bed with Shahrazad, Dinarzad said, "Sister, if you are not sleepy, tell
us one of your lovely little tales to while away the night." Shahrazad replied,
"With the greatest pleasure":*

THE FOURTH NIGHT

It is related, O happy King, that the first old man with the deer approached the demon and, kissing his hands and feet, said, "Fiend and King of the demon kings, if I tell you what happened to me and that deer, and you find it strange and amazing, indeed stranger and more amazing than what happened to you and the merchant, will you grant me a third of your claim on him for his crime and guilt?" The demon replied, "I will." The old man said:

[*The First Old Man's Tale*]

Demon, this deer is my cousin, my flesh and blood. I married her when I was very young, and she a girl of twelve, who reached womanhood only afterward. For thirty years we lived together, but I was not blessed with children, for she bore neither boy nor girl. Yet I continued to be kind to her, to care for her, and to treat her generously. Then I took a mistress, and she bore me a son, who grew up to look like a slice of the moon.[5] Meanwhile, my wife grew jealous of my mistress and my son. One day, when he was ten, I had to go on a journey. I entrusted my wife, this one here, with my mistress and son, bade her take good care of them, and was gone for a whole year. In my absence my wife, this cousin of mine, learned soothsaying and magic and cast a spell on my son and turned him into a young bull. Then she summoned my shepherd, gave my son to him, and said, "Tend this bull with the rest of the cattle." The shepherd took him and tended him for a while. Then she cast a spell on the mother, turning her into a cow, and gave her also to the shepherd.

When I came back, after all this was done, and inquired about my mistress and my son, she answered, "Your mistress died, and your son ran away two months ago, and I have had no news from him ever since." When I heard her, I grieved for my mistress, and with an anguished heart I mourned for my son for nearly a year. When the Great Feast of the Immolation[6] drew near, I summoned the shepherd and ordered him to bring me a fat cow for the sacrifice. The cow he brought me was in reality my enchanted mistress. When I bound her and pressed against her to cut her throat, she wept and cried, as if saying, "My son, my son," and her tears coursed down her cheeks. Astonished and seized with pity, I turned away and asked the shepherd to bring me a different cow. But my wife shouted, "Go on. Butcher her, for he has none better or fatter. Let us enjoy her meat at feast time." I approached the cow to cut her throat, and again she cried, as if saying, "My son, my son." Then I turned away from her and said to the shepherd, "Butcher her for me." The shepherd butchered her, and when he skinned her, he found neither meat nor fat but only skin and bone. I regretted having her butchered and said to the shepherd, "Take her all for yourself, or give her as alms to whomever you wish, and find me a fat young bull from among the flock." The shepherd took her away and disappeared, and I never knew what he did with her.

Then he brought me my son, my heartblood, in the guise of a fat young

---

5. The moon is a symbol of beauty for men and women.   6. Celebrates the pilgrimage of Mecca; it lasts four days, during which sheep and cattle are sacrificed to God.

bull. Then my son saw me, he shook his head loose from the rope, ran toward me, and, throwing himself at my feet, kept rubbing his head against me. I was astonished and touched with sympathy, pity, and mercy, for the blood hearkened to the blood and the divine bond, and my heart throbbed within me when I saw the tears coursing over the cheeks of my son the young bull, as he dug the earth with his hoofs. I turned away and said to the shepherd, "Let him go with the rest of the flock, and be kind to him, for I have decided to spare him. Bring me another one instead of him." My wife, this very deer, shouted, "You shall sacrifice none but this bull." I got angry and replied, "I listened to you and butchered the cow uselessly. I will not listen to you and kill this bull, for I have decided to spare him." But she pressed me, saying, "You must butcher this bull," and I bound him and took the knife . . .

But dawn broke, and morning overtook Shahrazad, and she lapsed into silence, leaving the king all curiosity for the rest of the story. Then her sister Dinarzad said, "What an entertaining story!" Shahrazad replied, "Tomorrow night I shall tell you something even stranger, more wonderful, and more entertaining if the king spares me and lets me live."

THE FIFTH NIGHT

The following night, Dinarzad said to her sister Shahrazad, "Please, sister, if you are not sleepy, tell us one of your little tales." Shahrazad replied, "With the greatest pleasure":

I heard, dear King, that the old man with the deer said to the demon and to his companions:

I took the knife and as I turned to slaughter my son, he wept, bellowed, rolled at my feet, and motioned toward me with his tongue. I suspected something, began to waver with trepidation and pity, and finally released him, saying to my wife, "I have decided to spare him, and I commit him to your care." Then I tried to appease and please my wife, this very deer, by slaughtering another bull, promising her to slaughter this one next season. We slept that night, and when God's dawn broke, the shepherd came to me without letting my wife know, and said, "Give me credit for bringing you good news." I replied, "Tell me, and the credit is yours." He said, "Master, I have a daughter who is fond of soothsaying and magic and who is adept at the art of oaths and spells. Yesterday I took home with me the bull you had spared, to let him graze with the cattle, and when my daughter saw him, she laughed and cried at the same time. When I asked her why she laughed and cried, she answered that she laughed because the bull was in reality the son of our master the cattle owner, put under a spell by his step-mother, and that she cried because his father had slaughtered the son's mother. I could hardly wait till daybreak to bring you the good news about your son."

Demon, when I heard that, I uttered a cry and fainted, and when I came to myself, I accompanied the shepherd to his home, went to my son, and threw myself at him, kissing him and crying. He turned his head toward me, his tears coursing over his cheeks, and dangled his tongue, as if to say, "Look at my plight." Then I turned to the shepherd's daughter and asked, "Can you release him from the spell? If you do, I will give you all my cattle and all my possessions." She smiled and replied, "Master, I have no desire for your wealth, cattle, or possessions. I will deliver him, but on two conditions: first, that you let me marry him; second, that you let me cast a spell on her who had cast a spell on him, in order to control her and guard against her evil power." I replied, "Do whatever you wish and more. My possessions are for you and my son. As for my wife, who has done this to my son and made me slaughter his mother, her life is forfeit to you." She said, "No, but I will let her taste what she has inflicted on others." Then the shepherd's daughter filled a bowl of water, uttered an incantation and an oath, and said to my son, "Bull, if you have been created in this image by the All-Conquering, Almighty Lord, stay as you are, but if you have been treacherously put under a spell, change back to your human form, by the will of God, Creator of the wide world." Then she sprinkled him with the water, and he shook himself and changed from a bull back to his human form.

As I rushed to him, I fainted, and when I came to myself, he told me what my wife, this very deer, had done to him and to his mother. I said to him, "Son, God has sent us someone who will pay her back for what you and your mother and I have suffered at her hands." Then, O demon, I gave my son in marriage to the shepherd's daughter, who turned my wife into this very deer, saying to me, "To me this is a pretty form, for she will be with us day and night, and it is better to turn her into a pretty deer than to suffer her sinister looks." Thus she stayed with us, while the days and nights followed one another, and the months and years went by. Then one day the shepherd's daughter died, and my son went to the country of this very man with whom you have had your encounter. Some time later I took my wife, this very deer, with me, set out to find out what had happened to my son, and chanced to stop here. This is my story, my strange and amazing story.

The demon assented, saying, "I grant you one-third of this man's life."

Then, O King Shahrayar, the second old man with the two black dogs approached the demon and said, "I too shall tell you what happened to me and to these two dogs, and if I tell it to you and you find it stranger and more amazing than this man's story will you grant me one-third of this man's life?" The demon replied, "I will." Then the old man began to tell his story, saying . . .

But dawn broke, and morning overtook Shahrazad, and she lapsed into silence. Then Dinarzad said, "This is an amazing story," and Shahrazad replied, "What is this compared with what I shall tell you tomorrow night if the king spares me and lets me live!" The king said to himself, "By God, I will not have her put to death until I find out what happened to the man with the two black dogs. Then I will have her put to death, God the Almighty willing."

THE SIXTH NIGHT

When the following night arrived and Shahrazad was in bed with King Shahrayar, her sister Dinarzad said, "Sister, if you are not sleepy, tell us a little tale. Finish the one you started." Shahrazad replied, "With the greatest pleasure":

I heard, O happy King, that the second old man with the two dogs said:

[The Second Old Man's Tale]

Demon, as for my story, these are the details. These two dogs are my brothers. When our father died, he left behind three sons, and left us three thousand dinars,[7] with which each of us opened a shop and became a shop-keeper. Soon my older brother, one of these very dogs, went and sold the contents of his shop for a thousand dinars, bought trading goods, and, having prepared himself for his trading trip, left us. A full year went by, when one day, as I sat in my shop, a beggar stopped by to beg. When I refused him, he tearfully asked, "Don't you recognize me?" and when I looked at him closely, I recognized my brother. I embraced him and took him into the shop, and when I asked him about his plight, he replied, "The money is gone, and the situation is bad." Then I took him to the public bath, clothed him in one of my robes, and took him home with me. Then I examined my books and checked my balance, and found out that I had made a thousand dinars and that my net worth was two thousand dinars. I divided the amount between my brother and myself, and said to him, "Think as if you have never been away." He gladly took the money and opened another shop.

Soon afterward my second brother, this other dog, went and sold his merchandise and collected his money, intending to go on a trading trip. We tried to dissuade him, but he did not listen. Instead, he bought merchandise and trading goods, joined a group of travelers, and was gone for a full year. Then he came back, just like his older brother. I said to him, "Brother, didn't I advise you not to go?" He replied tearfully, "Brother, it was foreordained. Now I am poor and penniless, without even a shirt on my back." Demon, I took him to the public bath, clothed him in one of my new robes, and took him back to the shop. After we had something to eat, I said to him, "Brother, I shall do my business accounts, calculate my net worth for the year, and after subtracting the capital, whatever the profit happens to be, I shall divide it equally between you and myself. When I examined my books and subtracted the capital, I found out that my profit was two thousand dinars, and I thanked God and felt very happy. Then I divided the money, giving him a thousand dinars and keeping a thousand for myself. With that money he opened another shop, and the three of us stayed together for a while. Then my two brothers asked me to go on a trading journey with them, but I refused, saying, "What did you gain from your ventures that I can gain?"

They dropped the matter, and for six years we worked in our stores, buying and selling. Yet every year they asked me to go on a trading journey with them, but I refused, until I finally gave in. I said, "Brothers, I am ready to go with you. How much money do you have?" I found out that they had eaten and drunk and squandered everything they had, but I said nothing to them and did not reproach them. Then I took inventory, gathered all I had together, and sold everything. I was pleased to discover that the sale netted six thousand dinars. Then I divided the money into two parts, and said to my brothers, "The sum of three thousand dinars is for you and myself to use on our trading journey. The other three thousand I shall bury in the ground, in

7. Gold coins; the basic Muslim money units [Translator's note].

case what happened to you happens to me, so that when we return, we will find three thousand dinars to reopen our shops." They replied, "This is an excellent idea." Then, demon, I divided my money and buried three thousand dinars. Of the remaining three I gave each of my brothers a thousand and kept a thousand for myself. After I closed my shop, we bought merchandise and trading goods, rented a large seafaring boat, and after loading it with our goods and provisions, sailed day and night, for a month.

But morning overtook Shahrazad, and she lapsed into silence. Then her sister Dinarzad said, "Sister, what a lovely story!" Shahrazad replied, "Tomorrow night I shall tell you something even lovelier, stranger, and more wonderful if I live, the Almighty God willing."

THE SEVENTH NIGHT

The following night Dinarzad said to her sister Shahrazad, "For God's sake, sister, if you are not sleepy, tell us a little tale." The king added, "Let it be the completion of the story of the merchant and the demon." Shahrazad replied, "With the greatest pleasure":

I heard, O happy King, that the second old man said to the demon:

For a month my brothers, these very dogs, and I sailed the salty sea, until we came to a port city. We entered the city and sold our goods, earning ten dinars for every dinar. Then we bought other goods, and when we got to the seashore to embark, I met a girl who was dressed in tatters. She kissed my hands and said, "O my lord, be charitable and do me a favor, and I believe that I shall be able to reward you for it." I replied, "I am willing to do you a favor regardless of any reward." She said, "O my lord, marry me, clothe me, and take me home with you on this boat, as your wife, for I wish to give myself to you. I, in turn, will reward you for your kindness and charity, the Almighty God willing. Don't be misled by my poverty and present condition." When I heard her words, I felt pity for her, and guided by what God the Most High had intended for me, I consented. I clothed her with an expensive dress and married her. Then I took her to the boat, spread the bed for her, and consummated our marriage. We sailed many days and nights, and I, feeling love for her, stayed with her day and night, neglecting my brothers. In the meantime they, these very dogs, grew jealous of me, envied me for my increasing merchandise and wealth, and coveted all our possessions. At last they decided to betray me and, tempted by the Devil, plotted to kill me. One night they waited until I was asleep beside my wife; then they carried the two of us and threw us into the sea.

When we awoke, my wife turned into a she-demon and carried me out of the sea to an island. When it was morning, she said, "Husband, I have rewarded you by saving you from drowning, for I am one of the demons who believe in God.[8] When I saw you by the seashore, I felt love for you and came to you in the guise in which you saw me, and when I expressed my love for you, you accepted me. Now I must kill your brothers." When I heard

8. According to the Koran, God created both humans and demons (jinns), some of whom accepted Islam.

what she said, I was amazed and I thanked her and said, "As for destroying my brothers, this I do not wish, for I will not behave like them." Then I related to her what had happened to me and them, from beginning to end. When she heard my story, she got very angry at them, and said, "I shall fly to them now, drown their boat, and let them all perish." I entreated her, saying, "For God's sake, don't. The proverb advises 'Be kind to those who hurt you.' No matter what, they are my brothers after all." In this manner, I entreated her and pacified her. Afterward, she took me and flew away with me until she brought me home and put me down on the roof of my house. I climbed down, threw the doors open, and dug up the money I had buried. Then I went out and, greeting the people in the market, reopened my shop. When I came home in the evening, I found these two dogs tied up, and when they saw me, they came to me, wept, and rubbed themselves against me. I started, when I suddenly heard my wife say, "O my lord, these are your brothers." I asked, "Who has done this to them?" She replied, "I sent to my sister and asked her to do it. They will stay in this condition for ten years, after which they may be delivered." Then she told me where to find her and departed. The ten years have passed, and I was with my brothers on my way to her to have the spell lifted, when I met this man, together with this old man with the deer. When I asked him about himself, he told me about his encounter with you, and I resolved not to leave until I found out what would happen between you and him. This is my story. Isn't it amazing?

The demon replied, "By God, it is strange and amazing. I grant you one-third of my claim on him for his crime."

Then the third old man said, "Demon, don't disappoint me. If I told you a story that is stranger and more amazing than the first two would you grant me one-third of your claim on him for his crime?" The demon replied, "I will." Then the old man said, "Demon, listen":

But morning overtook Shahrazad, and she lapsed into silence. Then her sister said, "What an amazing story!" Shahrazad replied, "The rest is even more amazing." The king said to himself, "I will not have her put to death until I hear what happened to the old man and the demon; then I will have her put to death, as is my custom with the others."

THE EIGHTH NIGHT

The following night Dinarzad said to her sister Shahrazad, "For God's sake, sister, if you are not sleepy, tell us one of your lovely little tales to while away the night." Shahrazad replied, "With the greatest pleasure":

[The Third Old Man's Tale][9]

The demon said, "This is a wonderful story, and I grant you a third of my claim on the merchant's life."

The third sheikh approached and said to the demon, "I will tell you a story

---

9. Because the earliest manuscript does not include a story for the third sheikh, later narrators supplied one. This brief anecdote comes from a manuscript found in the library of the Royal Academy in Madrid.

more wonderful than these two if you will grant me a third of your claim on his life, O demon!"

To which the demon agreed.

So the sheikh began:

O sultan and chief of the demons, this mule was my wife. I had gone off on a journey and was absent from her for a whole year. At last I came to the end of my journey and returned home late one night. When I entered the house I saw a black slave lying in bed with her. They were chatting and dallying and laughing and kissing and quarreling together. When she saw me my wife leaped out of bed, ran to the water jug, recited a spell over it, then splashed me with some of the water and said, "Leave this form for the form of a dog."

Immediately I became a dog and she chased me out of the house. I ran out of the gate and didn't stop running until I reached a butcher's shop. I entered it and fell to eating the bones lying about. When the owner of the shop saw me, he grabbed me and carried me into his house. When his daughter saw me, she hid her face and said, "Why are you bringing this strange man in with you?"

"What man?" her father asked.

"This dog is a man whose wife has put a spell on him," she said, "but I can set him free again." She took a jug of water, recited a spell over it, then splashed a little water from it on me, and said, "Leave this shape for your original one."

And I became myself again. I kissed her hand and said, "I want to cast a spell on my wife as she did on me. Please give me a little of that water."

"Gladly," she said, "if you find her asleep, sprinkle a few drops on her and she will become whatever you wish."

Well, I did find her asleep, and I sprinkled some water on her and said, "Leave this shape for the shape of a she mule." She at once became the very mule you see here, oh sultan and chief of the demons."

The demon then turned to him and asked, "Is this really true?"

"Yes," he answered, nodding his head vigorously, "it's all true."

When the sheikh had finished his story, the demon shook with laughter and granted him a third of his claim on the merchant's blood.

Then the demon released the merchant and departed. The merchant turned to the three old men and thanked them, and they congratulated him on his deliverance and bade him good-bye. Then they separated, and each of them went on his way. The merchant himself went back home to his family, his wife, and his children, and he lived with them until the day he died. But this story is not as strange or as amazing as the story of the fisherman.

Dinarzad asked, "Please, sister, what is the story of the fisherman?" Shahrazad said: . . .

SIR THOMAS MALORY
ca. 1405–1471

The fullest and most influential version of the Arthurian legends in English was compiled in the 1460s by Sir Thomas Malory and published by England's first printer, William Caxton, in 1485. Malory's *Morte Darthur*, or "Death of Arthur," as Caxton somewhat misleadingly entitled it, has subsequently influenced writers and enthralled readers to a degree probably unparalleled by any other work of medieval literature. The success of Malory's work is all the more remarkable since despite his great skill he was far from being a professional writer. Socially he was a member of the gentry, that group of nobles that ranked below the great aristocrats—the king and peerage—but were still set apart from both the merchants and artisans of the city and the farmers of the country. Malory's public career had three dimensions. To begin with, he was a typical medieval country gentleman, serving as a Member of Parliament and filling various county offices. Then he participated in the Wars of the Roses, the internecine struggle among the ruling elite that raged for some thirty-five years until the consolidation of power by Henry VII in 1485. Malory seems to have fought on both sides of these civil wars, changing his allegiance for reasons we can only imagine but ending up backing the wrong party. Finally, the records tell us that Malory committed a series of violent acts—including extortion, theft, and rape—that marked him as an outlaw. Whether because of his political misjudgments or his violent behavior, or both, he spent much of the last decade of his life in prison, where he probably died.

It was in prison that Malory had the enforced leisure to compose the series of tales that trace the full history of the career of Arthur and his knights. In all but a very few cases he drew upon French or, occasionally, English originals. But he is more than a translator. He freely revises his material, radically abbreviating his sources by focusing almost exclusively upon action and abandoning most moralizing commentary. The result is a fast-paced narrative in which one episode follows another at sometimes bewildering speed and in which the responsibility for interpretation is left to the reader. Malory also untangles the complex plots of the original tales in order to place primary emphasis on the careers of individual knights. Yet he still creates out of the great mass of stories that he inherited a coherent totality. Dividing Arthurian history into seven parts focused on specific knights (two on Arthur, two on Lancelot, and one each on Gareth, Tristram, and Galahad), he then arranges the parts into a coherent form. He begins with the story of how Arthur was conceived surreptitiously by Uther Pendragon upon the unknowing Igrayne (thanks to Merlin's machinations) and concludes, some eight hundred pages later, with the story of Arthur's death at the hands of his son Mordred, born from a brief assignation with a woman who turned out to be his own half-sister Morgause. Between these two actions Malory records a huge variety of knightly adventures. These include farcical comedy and bleak tragedy, the fatal passions of Tristram and Isolde and Lancelot and Guinevere, the religious aspirations of Galahad, and above all the fate of Arthurian chivalry itself. Chivalry—the knightly code of honor—was one of the great civilizing ideas of the Middle Ages, and was responsible in part for controlling the violence from which medieval society emerged in the tenth and eleventh centuries. Yet it was also itself conducive to violence, since a knight's honor could be demonstrated only, as Malory repeatedly puts it, "on his body." This paradox, of a form of life that simultaneously creates and destroys social harmony, is Malory's central subject—as we might expect of a man whose own life was full of contradictions.

The selections printed here, drawn from the final part of the book, describe the final dissolution of the Round Table and the death of Arthur (Caxton applied the title of this section to the book as a whole). The narrative provides us with so many explanations for the final debacle that there is more than enough responsibility to go around. Lancelot and Guinevere are enthralled by their adulterous passion; Agravain and Mordred are consumed with envy of Lancelot; Gawain becomes murderously vengeful after Lancelot inadvertently kills his brothers Gaheris and Gareth (the latter one of Lancelot's favorites); Arthur is both strangely passive as events spin out of control and resolute in his unwillingness to make peace; and behind it all stands the malevolent figure of Mordred—himself the product of Arthur's illicit indiscretion. And then there is the "accident" of the adder. Here as throughout his great book, Malory provides so many explanations that readers are uncertain whether any or all of them is in fact fully adequate. We are left instead with the knowledge that something unique has been destroyed by malign forces and yet a simultaneous awareness that the victims are themselves, in ways that are difficult to specify, responsible. In the final pages of Malory's book we experience a powerful sense of fin-de-siècle pathos, and we realize that not just Arthurian society but the Middle Ages as a whole is drawing to a close.

Helpful commentary can be found in Larry Benson, *Malory's Morte Darthur* (1976), and Elizabeth Archibald and A. S. G. Edwards, eds., *A Companion to Malory* (1996).

From Morte Darthur[1]

[*The Conspiracy against Lancelot and Guinevere*]

In May, when every lusty[2] heart flourisheth and burgeoneth, for as the season is lusty to behold and comfortable,[3] so man and woman rejoiceth and gladdeth of summer coming with his fresh flowers, for winter with his rough winds and blasts causeth lusty men and women to cower and to sit fast by the fire—so this season it befell in the month of May a great anger and unhap that stinted not[4] till the flower of chivalry of all the world was destroyed and slain. And all was long upon two unhappy[5] knights which were named Sir Agravain and Sir Mordred that were brethren unto Sir Gawain.[6] For this Sir Agravain and Sir Mordred had ever a privy[7] hate unto the Queen, Dame Guinevere, and to Sir Lancelot, and daily and nightly they ever watched upon Sir Lancelot.

So it misfortuned Sir Gawain and all his brethren were in King Arthur's chamber, and then Sir Agravain said thus openly, and not in no counsel,[8] that many knights might hear: "I marvel that we all be not ashamed both to see and to know how Sir Lancelot lieth daily and nightly by the Queen. And all we know well that it is so, and it is shamefully suffered of us all[9] that we should suffer so noble a king as King Arthur is to be shamed."

Then spoke Sir Gawain and said, "Brother, Sir Agravain, I pray you and charge you, move no such matters no more afore[1] me, for wit you well, I will not be of your counsel."[2]

---

1. Translated by Alfred David. The selections given here are from the section that Caxton called book 20, chaps. 1–4, 8–10, and book 21, chaps. 3–7, 10–12, with omissions. In the Winchester manuscript this section is titled *The Most Piteous Tale of the Morte Arthur Saunz Guerdon* (i.e., the death of Arthur without reward or compensation). The text has been based on Winchester, with some readings introduced from the Caxton edition; spelling has been modernized and modern punctuation added. 2. Merry. 3. Pleasant. 4. Misfortune that ceased not. 5. On account of two ill-fated. 6. Gawain and Agravain are sons of King Lot of Orkney and his wife, Arthur's half-sister Morgause. Mordred is the illegitimate son of Arthur and Morgause. 7. Secret. 8. Secret manner. 9. Put up with by all of us. 1. Before. *Move*: propose. 2. On your side. *Wit you well*: know well, i.e., give you to understand.

"So God me help," said Sir Gaheris and Sir Gareth,[3] "we will not be known of your deeds."[4]

"Then will I!" said Sir Mordred.

"I lieve[5] you well," said Sir Gawain, "for ever unto all unhappiness, sir, ye will grant.[6] And I would that ye left all this and make you not so busy, for I know," said Sir Gawain, "what will fall of it."[7]

"Fall whatsoever fall may," said Sir Agravain, "I will disclose it to the King."

"Not by my counsel," said Sir Gawain, "for and[8] there arise war and wrack betwixt[9] Sir Lancelot and us, wit you well, brother, there will many kings and great lords hold with Sir Lancelot. Also, brother, Sir Agravain," said Sir Gawain, "ye must remember how often times Sir Lancelot hath rescued the King and the Queen. And the best of us all had been full cold at the heart-root[1] had not Sir Lancelot been better than we, and that has he proved himself full oft. And as for my part," said Sir Gawain, "I will never be against Sir Lancelot for[2] one day's deed, when he rescued me from King Carados of the Dolorous Tower and slew him and saved my life. Also, brother, Sir Agravain and Sir Mordred, in like wise Sir Lancelot rescued you both and three score and two[3] from Sir Tarquin. And therefore, brother, methinks such noble deeds and kindness should be remembered."

"Do as ye list,"[4] said Sir Agravain, "for I will layne[5] it no longer."

So with these words came in Sir Arthur.

"Now, brother," said Sir Gawain, "stint your noise."[6]

"That will I not," said Sir Agravain and Sir Mordred.

"Well, will ye so?" said Sir Gawain. "Then God speed you, for I will not hear of your tales, neither be of your counsel."

"No more will I," said Sir Gaheris.

"Neither I," said Sir Gareth, "for I shall never say evil by[7] that man that made me knight." And therewithal they three departed making great dole.[8]

"Alas!" said Sir Gawain and Sir Gareth, "now is this realm wholly destroyed and mischieved,[9] and the noble fellowship of the Round Table shall be disparbeled."[1]

So they departed, and then King Arthur asked them what noise they made. "My lord," said Sir Agravain, "I shall tell you, for I may keep[2] it no longer. Here is I and my brother Sir Mordred broke[3] unto my brother Sir Gawain, Sir Gaheris, and to Sir Gareth—for this is all, to make it short—how that we know all that Sir Lancelot holdeth your queen, and hath done long; and we be your sister[4] sons, we may suffer it no longer. And all we woot[5] that ye should be above Sir Lancelot, and ye are the king that made him knight, and therefore we will prove it that he is a traitor to your person."

"If it be so," said the King, "wit[6] you well, he is none other. But I would be loath to begin such a thing but[7] I might have proofs of it, for Sir Lancelot is an hardy knight, and all ye know that he is the best knight among us all. And but if he be taken with the deed,[8] he will fight with him that bringeth up the noise, and I know no knight that is able to match him. Therefore, and[9] it be sooth as ye say, I would that he were taken with the deed."

3. Sons of King Lot and Gawain's brothers.   4. A party to your doings.   5. Believe.   6. You will consent to all mischief.   7. Come of it.   8. If.   9. Strife between.   1. Would have been dead. 2. On account of.   3. I.e., sixty-two.   4. You please.   5. Conceal.   6. Stop making scandal. 7. About.   8. Lamentation.   9. Put to shame.   1. Dispersed.   2. Conceal.   3. Revealed. 4. Sister's.   5. Know.   6. Know.   7. Unless.   8. Unless he is caught in the act.   9. If.

For, as the French book saith, the King was full loath that such a noise should be upon Sir Lancelot and his queen. For the King had a deeming[1] of it, but he would not hear of it, for Sir Lancelot had done so much for him and for the Queen so many times that, wit you well, the King loved him passingly[2] well.

"My lord," said Sir Agravain, "ye shall ride tomorn[3] on hunting, and doubt ye not, Sir Lancelot will not go with you. And so when it draweth toward night, ye may send the Queen word that ye will lie out all that night, and so may ye send for your cooks. And then, upon pain of death, that night we shall take him with the Queen, and we shall bring him unto you, quick[4] or dead."

"I will well,"[5] said the King. "Then I counsel you to take with you sure fellowship."

"Sir," said Sir Agravain, "my brother, Sir Mordred, and I will take with us twelve knights of the Round Table."

"Beware," said King Arthur, "for I warn you, ye shall find him wight."[6]

"Let us deal!"[7] said Sir Agravain and Sir Mordred.

So on the morn King Arthur rode on hunting and sent word to the Queen that he would be out all that night. Then Sir Agravain and Sir Mordred got to them[8] twelve knights and hid themself in a chamber in the castle of Carlisle. And these were their names: Sir Colgrevance, Sir Mador de la Porte, Sir Guingalen, Sir Meliot de Logres, Sir Petipace of Winchelsea, Sir Galeron of Galway, Sir Melion de la Mountain, Sir Ascamore, Sir Gromore Somyr Jour, Sir Curselayne, Sir Florence, and Sir Lovell. So these twelve knights were with Sir Mordred and Sir Agravain, and all they were of Scotland, or else of Sir Gawain's kin, or well-willers[9] to his brother.

So when the night came, Sir Lancelot told Sir Bors[1] how he would go that night and speak with the Queen.

"Sir," said Sir Bors, "ye shall not go this night by my counsel."

"Why?" said Sir Lancelot.

"Sir," said Sir Bors, "I dread me[2] ever of Sir Agravain that waiteth upon[3] you daily to do you shame and us all. And never gave my heart against no going that ever ye went[4] to the queen so much as now, for I mistrust[5] that the King is out this night from the Queen because peradventure he hath lain[6] some watch for you and the Queen. Therefore, I dread me sore of some treason."

"Have ye no dread," said Sir Lancelot, "for I shall go and come again and make no tarrying."

"Sir," said Sir Bors, "that me repents,[7] for I dread me sore that your going this night shall wrath[8] us all."

"Fair nephew," said Sir Lancelot, "I marvel me much why ye say thus, sithen[9] the Queen hath sent for me. And wit you well, I will not be so much a coward, but she shall understand I will[1] see her good grace."

"God speed you well," said Sir Bors, "and send you sound and safe again!"

So Sir Lancelot departed and took his sword under his arm, and so he

---

1. Suspicion.   2. Exceedingly.   3. Tomorrow.   4. Alive.   5. Readily agree.   6. Strong.
7. Leave it to us.   8. Gathered to themselves.   9. Partisans.   1. Nephew and confidant of Sir Lancelot.   2. I am afraid.   3. Lies in wait.   4. Never misgave my heart against any visit you made.
5. Suspect.   6. Perhaps he has set.   7. I regret.   8. Cause injury to.   9. Since.   1. Wish to.

walked in his mantel,[2] that noble knight, and put himself in great jeopardy. And so he passed on till he came to the Queen's chamber, and so lightly he was had[3] into the chamber. And then, as the French book saith, the Queen and Sir Lancelot were together. And whether they were abed or at other manner of disports, me list[4] not thereof make no mention, for love that time[5] was not as love is nowadays.

But thus as they were together there came Sir Agravain and Sir Mordred with twelve knights with them of the Round Table, and they said with great crying and scaring[6] voice: "Thou traitor, Sir Lancelot, now are thou taken!" And thus they cried with a loud voice that all the court might hear it. And these fourteen knights all were armed at all points, as[7] they should fight in a battle.

"Alas!" said Queen Guinevere, "now are we mischieved[8] both!"

"Madam," said Sir Lancelot, "is there here any armor within your chamber that I might cover my body withal? And if there be any, give it me, and I shall soon stint[9] their malice, by the grace of God!"

"Now, truly," said the Queen, "I have none armor neither helm, shield, sword, neither spear, wherefore I dread me sore our long love is come to a mischievous end. For I hear by their noise there be many noble knights, and well I woot they be surely[1] armed, and against them ye may make no resistance. Wherefore ye are likely to be slain, and then shall I be burned! For and[2] ye might escape them," said the Queen, "I would not doubt but that ye would rescue me in what danger that ever I stood in."

"Alas!" said Sir Lancelot, "in all my life thus was I never bestead[3] that I should be thus shamefully slain for lack of mine armor."

But ever in one[4] Sir Agravain and Sir Mordred cried: "Traitor knight, come out of the Queen's chamber! For wit thou well thou art beset so that thou shalt not escape."

"Ah, Jesu mercy!" said Sir Lancelot, "this shameful cry and noise I may not suffer, for better were death at once than thus to endure this pain." Then he took the Queen in his arms and kissed her and said, "Most noblest Christian queen, I beseech you, as ye have been ever my special good lady, and I at all times your poor knight and true unto[5] my power, and as I never failed you in right nor in wrong sithen the first day King Arthur made me knight, that ye will pray for my soul if that I be slain. For well I am assured that Sir Bors, my nephew, and all the remnant of my kin, with Sir Lavain and Sir Urry,[6] that they will not fail you to rescue you from the fire. And therefore, mine own lady, recomfort yourself,[7] whatsoever come of me, that ye go with Sir Bors, my nephew, and Sir Urry and they all will do you all the pleasure that they may, and ye shall live like a queen upon my lands."

"Nay, Sir Lancelot, nay!" said the Queen. "Wit thou well that I will not live long after thy days. But and[8] ye be slain I will take my death as meekly as ever did martyr take his death for Jesu Christ's sake."

"Well, Madam," said Sir Lancelot, "sith it is so that the day is come that our love must depart,[9] wit you well I shall sell my life as dear as I may. And

---

2. Cloak. Lancelot goes unarmed. 3. Quickly he was received. 4. I care. *Disports:* pastimes.
5. At that time. 6. Terrifying. 7. Completely, as if. 8. Come to grief. 9. Stop.
1. Securely. 2. If. 3. Beset. 4. In unison. 5. To the utmost of. 6. The brother of Elaine,
the Fair Maid of Astolat, and a knight miraculously healed of his wound by Sir Lancelot. *Remnant:* rest.
7. Take heart again. 8. If. 9. Come to an end.

a thousandfold," said Sir Lancelot, "I am more heavier[1] for you than for myself! And now I had liefer[2] than to be lord of all Christendom that I had sure armor upon me, that men might speak of my deeds ere ever I were slain."

"Truly," said the Queen, "and[3] it might please God, I would that they would take me and slay me and suffer[4] you to escape."

"That shall never be," said Sir Lancelot. "God defend me from such a shame! But, Jesu Christ, be Thou my shield and mine armor!" And therewith Sir Lancelot wrapped his mantel about his arm well and surely; and by then they had gotten a great form[5] out of the hall, and therewith they all rushed at the door. "Now, fair lords," said Sir Lancelot, "leave[6] your noise and your rushing, and I shall set open this door, and then may ye do with me what it liketh you."[7]

"Come off,[8] then," said they all, "and do it, for it availeth thee not to strive against us all. And therefore let us into this chamber, and we shall save thy life until thou come to King Arthur."

Then Sir Lancelot unbarred the door, and with his left hand he held it open a little, that but one man might come in at once. And so there came striding a good knight, a much[9] man and a large, and his name was called Sir Colgrevance of Gore. And he with a sword struck at Sir Lancelot mightily. And he put aside[1] the stroke and gave him such a buffet[2] upon the helmet that he fell groveling dead within the chamber door. Then Sir Lancelot with great might drew the knight within[3] the chamber door. And then Sir Lancelot, with help of the Queen and her ladies, he was lightly[4] armed in Colgrevance's armor. And ever stood Sir Agravain and Sir Mordred, crying, "Traitor knight! Come forth out of the Queen's chamber!"

"Sirs, leave[5] your noise," said Sir Lancelot, "for wit you well, Sir Agravain, ye shall not prison me this night. And therefore, and[6] ye do by my counsel, go ye all from this chamber door and make you no such crying and such manner of slander as ye do. For I promise you by my knighthood, and ye will depart and make no more noise, I shall as tomorn appear afore you all and before the King, and then let it be seen which of you all, other else ye all,[7] that will deprove[8] me of treason. And there shall I answer you, as a knight should, that hither I came to the Queen for no manner of mal engine,[9] and that will I prove and make it good upon you with my hands."

"Fie upon thee, traitor," said Sir Agravain and Sir Mordred, "for we will have thee malgré thine head[1] and slay thee, and we list. For we let thee wit we have the choice of[2] King Arthur to save thee other slay thee."

"Ah, sirs," said Sir Lancelot, "is there none other grace with you? Then keep[3] yourself!" And then Sir Lancelot set all open the chamber door and mightily and knightly he strode in among them. And anon[4] at the first stroke he slew Sir Agravain, and after twelve of his fellows. Within a little while he had laid them down cold to the earth, for there was none of the twelve knights might stand Sir Lancelot one buffet.[5] And also he wounded Sir Mordred, and therewithal he fled with all his might.

And then Sir Lancelot returned again unto the Queen and said, "Madam,

1. More grieved. 2. Rather. 3. If. 4. Allow. 5. Bench. 6. Stop. 7. Pleases you.
8. Go ahead. 9. Big. 1. Fended off. 2. Blow. 3. Inside. 4. Quickly. 5. Stop. 6. If.
7. Or else all of you. 8. Accuse. 9. Evil design. 1. *Malgré thine head:* in spite of you.
2. From. 3. Defend. 4. Right away. 5. Withstand Sir Lancelot one blow.

now wit you well, all our true love is brought to an end, for now will King Arthur ever be my foe. And therefore, Madam, and it like you[6] that I may have you with me, I shall save you from all manner adventurous[7] dangers."

"Sir, that is not best," said the Queen, "me seemeth, for[8] now ye have done so much harm, it will be best that ye hold you still with this. And if ye see that as tomorn they will put me unto death, then may ye rescue me as ye think best."

"I will well,"[9] said Sir Lancelot, "for have ye no doubt, while I am a man living I shall rescue you." And then he kissed her, and either of them gave other a ring, and so there he left the Queen and went until[1] his lodging.

Summary Lancelot and Sir Bors mobilize their friends for the rescue of Guinevere. In the morning Mordred reports the events of the night to Arthur who, against Gawain's strong opposition, condemns the queen to be burned, for "the law was such in those days that whatsoever they were, of what estate or degree, if they were found guilty of treason there should be none other remedy but death."

[War Breaks Out between Arthur and Lancelot]

Then said King Arthur unto Sir Gawain, "Dear nephew, I pray you make ready in your best armor with your brethren, Sir Gaheris and Sir Gareth, to bring my Queen to the fire, there to have her judgment and receive the death."

"Nay, my most noble king," said Sir Gawain, "that will I never do, for wit you well I will never be in that place where so noble a queen as is my lady Dame Guinevere shall take such a shameful end. For wit you well," said Sir Gawain, "my heart will not serve me for to see her die, and it shall never be said that ever I was of your counsel for her death."

"Then," said the King unto Sir Gawain, "suffer[2] your brethren Sir Gaheris and Sir Gareth to be there."

"My lord," said Sir Gawain, "wit you well they will be loath to be there present because of many adventures[3] that is like to fall, but they are young and full unable to say you nay."

Then spake Sir Gaheris and the good knight Sir Gareth unto King Arthur: "Sir, ye may well command us to be there, but wit you well it shall be sore against our will. But and[4] we be there by your straight commandment, ye shall plainly[5] hold us there excused—we will be there in peaceable wise and bear none harness of war upon us."

"In the name of God," said the King, "then make you ready, for she shall have soon[6] her judgment."

"Alas," said Sir Gawain, "that ever I should endure[7] to see this woeful day." So Sir Gawain turned him and wept heartily, and so he went into his chamber.

And then the Queen was led forth without[8] Carlisle, and anon she was dispoiled into[9] her smock. And then her ghostly father[1] was brought to her to be shriven of her misdeeds.[2] Then was there weeping and wailing and

6. If it please you.   7. Perilous.   8. Because.   9. Agree.   1. To.   2. Allow.   3. Chance occurrences.   4. If.   5. Openly. *Straight*: strict.   6. Right away.   7. Live.   8. Outside. 9. Undressed down to.   1. Spiritual father, i.e., her priest.   2. For her to be confessed of her sins.

wringing of hands of many lords and ladies, but there were but few in comparison that would bear any armor for to strengthen[3] the death of the Queen.

Then was there one that Sir Lancelot had sent unto that place, which went to espy what time the Queen should go unto her death. And anon as[4] he saw the Queen dispoiled into her smock and shriven, then he gave Sir Lancelot warning. Then was there but spurring and plucking up[5] of horses, and right so they came unto the fire. And who[6] that stood against them, there were they slain—there might none withstand Sir Lancelot. So all that bore arms and withstood them, there were they slain, full many a noble knight.***And so in this rushing and hurling, as Sir Lancelot thrang[7] here and there, it misfortuned him[8] to slay Sir Gaheris and Sir Gareth, the noble knight, for they were unarmed and unwares.[9] As the French book saith, Sir Lancelot smote Sir Gaheris and Sir Gareth upon the brain-pans, wherethrough[1] that they were slain in the field, howbeit[2] Sir Lancelot saw them not. And so were they found dead among the thickest of the press.

Then when Sir Lancelot had thus done, and slain and put to flight all that would withstand him, then he rode straight unto Queen Guinevere and made a kirtle[3] and a gown to be cast upon her, and then he made her to be set behind him and prayed her to be of good cheer. Now wit you well the Queen was glad that she was escaped from death, and then she thanked God and Sir Lancelot.

And so he rode his way with the Queen, as the French book saith, unto Joyous Garde,[4] and there he kept her as a noble knight should. And many great lords and many good knights were sent him, and many full noble knights drew unto him. When they heard that King Arthur and Sir Lancelot were at debate,[5] many knights were glad, and many were sorry of their debate.

Now turn we again unto King Arthur, that when it was told him how and in what manner the Queen was taken away from the fire, and when he heard of the death of his noble knights, and in especial Sir Gaheris and Sir Gareth, then he swooned for very pure[6] sorrow. And when he awoke of his swoon, then he said: "Alas, that ever I bore crown upon my head! For now have I lost the fairest fellowship of noble knights that ever held Christian king[7] together. Alas, my good knights be slain and gone away from me. Now within these two days I have lost nigh forty knights and also the noble fellowship of Sir Lancelot and his blood,[8] for now I may nevermore hold them together with my worship.[9] Alas, that ever this war began!

"Now, fair fellows," said the King, "I charge you that no man tell Sir Gawain of the death of his two brethren, for I am sure," said the King, "when he heareth tell that Sir Gareth is dead, he will go nigh out of his mind. Mercy Jesu," said the King, "why slew he Sir Gaheris and Sir Gareth? For I dare say, as for Sir Gareth, he loved Sir Lancelot above all men earthly."[1]

"That is truth," said some knights, "but they were slain in the hurling,[2] as Sir Lancelot thrang in the thickest of the press. And as they were unarmed, he smote them and wist[3] not whom that he smote, and so unhappily[4] they were slain."

---

3. Secure.　　4. As soon as.　　5. Urging forward.　　6. Whoever.　　7. Pressed. *Hurling*: turmoil.
8. He had the misfortune.　　9. Unaware.　　1. Through which.　　2. Although.　　3. Petticoat.
4. Lancelot's castle in England.　　5. Strife.　　6. Sheer.　　7. That Christian king ever held.　　8. Kin.
9. Glory.　　1. Earthly men.　　2. Turmoil.　　3. Knew.　　4. Unluckily.

"Well," said Arthur, "the death of them will cause the greatest mortal war that ever was, for I am sure that when Sir Gawain knoweth hereof that Sir Gareth is slain, I shall never have rest of him[5] till I have destroyed Sir Lancelot's kin and himself both, other else he to destroy me. And therefore," said the King, "wit you well, my heart was never so heavy as it is now. And much more I am sorrier for my good knights' loss[6] than for the loss of my fair queen; for queens I might have enough, but such a fellowship of good knights shall never be together in no company. And now I dare say," said King Arthur, "there was never Christian king that ever held such a fellowship together. And alas, that ever Sir Lancelot and I should be at debate. Ah, Agravain, Agravain!" said the King, "Jesu forgive it thy soul, for thine evil will that thou and thy brother Sir Mordred haddest unto Sir Lancelot hath caused all this sorrow." And ever among these complaints the King wept and swooned.

Then came there one to Sir Gawain and told him how the Queen was led away with[7] Sir Lancelot, and nigh a four-and-twenty knights slain. "Ah, Jesu, save me my two brethren!" said Sir Gawain. "For full well wist I," said Sir Gawain, "that Sir Lancelot would rescue her, other else he would die in that field. And to say the truth he were not of worship but if he had[8] rescued the Queen, insomuch as she should have been burned for his sake. And as in that," said Sir Gawain, "he hath done but knightly, and as I would have done myself and I had stood in like case. But where are my brethren?" said Sir Gawain. "I marvel that I hear not of them."

Then said that man, "Truly, Sir Gaheris and Sir Gareth be slain."

"Jesu defend!"[9] said Sir Gawain. "For all this world I would not that they were slain, and in especial my good brother Sir Gareth."

"Sir," said the man, "he is slain, and that is great pity."

"Who slew him?" said Sir Gawain.

"Sir Lancelot," said the man, "slew them both."

"That may I not believe," said Sir Gawain, "that ever he slew my good brother Sir Gareth, for I dare say my brother loved him better than me and all his brethren and the King both. Also I dare say, an[1] Sir Lancelot had desired my brother Sir Gareth with him, he would have been with him against the King and us all. And therefore I may never believe that Sir Lancelot slew my brethren."

"Verily, sir," said the man, "it is noised[2] that he slew him."

"Alas," said Sir Gawain, "now is my joy gone." And then he fell down and swooned, and long he lay there as he had been dead. And when he arose out of his swoon, he cried out sorrowfully and said, "Alas!" And forthwith he ran unto the King, crying and weeping, and said, "Ah, mine uncle King Arthur! My good brother Sir Gareth is slain, and so is my brother Sir Gaheris, which were two noble knights."

Then the King wept and he both, and so they fell on swooning. And when they were revived, then spake Sir Gawain and said, "Sir, I will go and see my brother Sir Gareth."

"Sir, ye may not see him," said the King, "for I caused him to be interred and Sir Gaheris both, for I well understood that ye would make overmuch

---

5. He will never give me any peace.   6. The loss of my good knights.   7. By.   8. Of honor if he had not.   9. Forbid.   1. If.   2. Reported.

sorrow, and the sight of Sir Gareth should have caused your double sorrow."

"Alas, my lord," said Sir Gawain, "how slew he my brother Sir Gareth? Mine own good lord, I pray you tell me."

"Truly," said the King, "I shall tell you as it hath been told me—Sir Lancelot slew him and Sir Gaheris both."

"Alas," said Sir Gawain, "they bore none arms against him, neither of them both."

"I woot not how it was," said the King, "but as it is said, Sir Lancelot slew them in the thickest of the press and knew them not. And therefore let us shape a remedy for to revenge their deaths."

"My king, my lord, and mine uncle," said Sir Gawain, "wit you well, now I shall make you a promise which I shall hold by my knighthood, that from this day forward I shall never fail[3] Sir Lancelot until that one of us have slain the other. And therefore I require you, my lord and king, dress[4] you unto the wars, for wit you well, I will be revenged upon Sir Lancelot; and therefore, as ye will have my service and my love, now haste you thereto and assay[5] your friends. For I promise unto God," said Sir Gawain, "for the death of my brother Sir Gareth I shall seek Sir Lancelot throughout seven kings' realms, but I shall slay him, other else he shall slay me."

"Sir, ye shall not need to seek him so far," said the King, "for as I hear say, Sir Lancelot will abide me and us all within the castle of Joyous Garde. And much people draweth unto him, as I hear say."

"That may I right well believe," said Sir Gawain, "but my lord," he said, "assay your friends and I will assay mine."

"It shall be done," said the King, "and as I suppose I shall be big[6] enough to drive him out of the biggest tower of his castle."

So then the King sent letters and writs throughout all England, both the length and the breadth, for to summon all his knights. And so unto King Arthur drew many knights, dukes, and earls, that he had a great host, and when they were assembled the King informed them how Sir Lancelot had bereft him his Queen. Then the King and all his host made them ready to lay siege about Sir Lancelot where he lay within Joyous Garde.

Summary   The pope arranges a truce, Guinevere is returned to Arthur, and Lancelot and his kin leave England to become rulers of France. At Gawain's instigation Arthur invades France to resume the war against Lancelot.

Word comes to the king that Mordred has seized the kingdom, and Arthur leads his forces back to England. Mordred attacks them upon their landing, and Gawain is mortally wounded and dies, although not before he has repented for having insisted that Arthur fight Lancelot and has written Lancelot to come to the aid of his former lord.

[The Death of Arthur]

So upon Trinity Sunday at night King Arthur dreamed a wonderful dream, and in his dream him seemed that he saw upon a chafflet[7] a chair, and the chair was fast to a wheel, and thereupon sat King Arthur in the richest cloth

---

3. Give up the pursuit of.   4. Prepare.   5. Appeal to.   6. Strong.   7. Scaffold. *Him seemed:* it seemed to him.

of gold that might be made. And the King thought there was under him, far from him, an hideous deep black water, and therein was all manner of serpents, and worms, and wild beasts, foul and horrible. And suddenly the King thought that the wheel turned upside down, and he fell among the serpents, and every beast took him by a limb. And then the King cried as he lay in his bed, "Help, help!"

And then knights, squires, and yeomen awaked the King, and then he was so amazed that he wist[8] not where he was. And then so he awaked[9] until it was nigh day, and then he fell on slumbering again, not sleeping nor thoroughly waking. So the King seemed[1] verily that there came Sir Gawain unto him with a number of fair ladies with him. So when King Arthur saw him, he said, "Welcome, my sister's son. I weened ye had been dead. And now I see thee on-live, much am I beholden unto Almighty Jesu. Ah, fair nephew and my sister's son, what been these ladies that hither be come with you?"

"Sir," said Sir Gawain, "all these be ladies for whom I have foughten for when I was man living. And all these are tho[2] that I did battle for in righteous quarrels, and God hath given them that grace, at their great prayer, because I did battle for them for their right, that they should bring me hither unto you. Thus much hath given me leave God, for to warn you of your death. For and ye fight as tomorn[3] with Sir Mordred, as ye both have assigned,[4] doubt ye not ye must be slain, and the most party of your people on both parties. And for the great grace and goodness that Almighty Jesu hath unto you, and for pity of you and many mo other good men there[5] shall be slain, God hath sent me to you of his special grace to give you warning that in no wise ye do battle as tomorn, but that ye take a treatise for a month-day.[6] And proffer you largely,[7] so that tomorn ye put in a delay. For within a month shall come Sir Lancelot with all his noble knights and rescue you worshipfully and slay Sir Mordred and all that ever will hold with him."

Then Sir Gawain and all the ladies vanished. And anon the King called upon his knights, squires, and yeomen, and charged them wightly[8] to fetch his noble lords and wise bishops unto him. And when they were come the King told them of his avision,[9] that Sir Gawain had told him and warned him that, and he fought on the morn, he should be slain. Then the King commanded Sir Lucan the Butler[1] and his brother Sir Bedivere the Bold, with two bishops with them, and charged them in any wise to take a treatise for a month-day with Sir Mordred. "And spare not: proffer him lands and goods as much as ye think reasonable."

So then they departed and came to Sir Mordred where he had a grim host of an hundred thousand, and there they entreated[2] Sir Mordred long time. And at the last Sir Mordred was agreed for to have Cornwall and Kent by King Arthur's days,[3] and after that, all England, after the days of King Arthur.

Then were they condescended[4] that King Arthur and Sir Mordred should meet betwixt both their hosts, and everich[5] of them should bring fourteen persons. And so they came with this word unto Arthur. Then said he, "I am glad that this is done," and so he went into the field.

---

8. Knew.   9. Lay awake.   1. It seemed to the king.   2. Those.   3. If you fight tomorrow.
4. Decided.   5. I.e., who there. *Mo:* more.   6. For a month from today. *Treatise:* treaty, truce.
7. Make generous offers.   8. Quickly.   9. Dream.   1. *Butler* here is probably only a title of high rank, although it was originally used to designate the officer who had charge of wine for the king's table.
2. Dealt with.   3. During King Arthur's lifetime.   4. Agreed.   5. Each.

And when King Arthur should depart, he warned all his host that, and they see any sword drawn, "Look ye come on fiercely and slay that traitor Sir Mordred, for I in no wise trust him." In like wise Sir Mordred warned his host that "And ye see any manner of sword drawn, look that ye come on fiercely, and so slay all that ever before you standeth, for in no wise I will not trust for this treatise." And in the same wise said Sir Mordred unto his host, "For I know well my father will be avenged upon me."

And so they met as their pointment[6] was and were agreed and accorded thoroughly. And wine was fetched and they drank together. Right so came an adder out of a little heath-bush, and it stung a knight in the foot. And so when the knight felt him so stung, he looked down and saw the adder. And anon he drew his sword to slay the adder, and thought[7] none other harm. And when the host on both parties saw that sword drawn, then they blew beams,[8] trumpets, and horns, and shouted grimly. And so both hosts dressed them[9] together. And King Arthur took his horse and said, "Alas, this unhappy day!" and so rode to his party, and Sir Mordred in like wise.

And never since was there never seen a more dolefuller battle in no Christian land, for there was but rushing and riding, foining[1] and striking; and many a grim word was there spoken of either to other, and many a deadly stroke. But ever King Arthur rode throughout the battle[2] of Sir Mordred many times and did full nobly, as a noble king should do, and at all times he fainted never. And Sir Mordred did his devoir[3] that day and put himself in great peril.

And thus they fought all the long day, and never stinted[4] till the noble knights were laid to the cold earth. And ever they fought still till it was near night, and by then was there an hundred thousand laid dead upon the down. Then was King Arthur wood-wroth[5] out of measure when he saw his people so slain from him. And so he looked about him and could see no mo[6] of all his host, and good knights left no mo on-live, but two knights: the t'one[7] was Sir Lucan the Butler and [the other] his brother Sir Bedivere. And yet they were full sore wounded.

"Jesu, mercy," said the King, "where are all my noble knights become?[8] Alas that ever I should see this doleful day! For now," said King Arthur, "I am come to mine end. But would to God," said he, "that I wist[9] now where were that traitor Sir Mordred that has caused all this mischief."

Then King Arthur looked about and was ware where stood Sir Mordred leaning upon his sword among a great heap of dead men.

"Now give me my spear," said King Arthur unto Sir Lucan, "for yonder I have espied the traitor that all this woe hath wrought."

"Sir, let him be," said Sir Lucan, "for he is unhappy.[1] And if ye pass this unhappy day ye shall be right well revenged upon him. And, good lord, remember ye of your night's dream, and what the spirit of Sir Gawain told you tonight, and yet God of his great goodness hath preserved you hitherto. And for God's sake, my lord, leave off by this,[2] for, blessed be God, ye have won the field: for yet we been here three on-live, and with Sir Mordred is

6. Arrangement.   7. Meant.   8. A kind of trumpet.   9. Prepared to come.   1. Lunging.
2. Battalion.   3. Knightly duty.   4. Stopped.   5. Mad with rage.   6. Others.   7. That one, i.e., the first.   8. What has become of all my noble knights?   9. Knew.   1. I.e., unlucky for you.
2. I.e., with this much accomplished.

not one on-live. And therefore if ye leave off now, this wicked day of destiny is past."

"Now, tide[3] me death, tide me life," said the King, "now I see him yonder alone, he shall never escape mine hands. For at a better avail[4] shall I never have him."

"God speed you well!" said Sir Bedivere.

Then the King got his spear in both his hands and ran toward Sir Mordred, crying and saying, "Traitor, now is thy deathday come!"

And when Sir Mordred saw King Arthur he ran until him with his sword drawn in his hand, and there King Arthur smote Sir Mordred under the shield, with a foin[5] of his spear, throughout the body more than a fathom.[6] And when Sir Mordred felt that he had his death's wound, he thrust himself with the might that he had up to the burr[7] of King Arthur's spear, and right so he smote his father King Arthur with his sword holden in both his hands, upon the side of the head, that the sword pierced the helmet and the tay[8] of the brain. And therewith Sir Mordred dashed down stark dead to the earth.

And noble King Arthur fell in a swough[9] to the earth, and there he swooned oftentimes, and Sir Lucan and Sir Bedivere ofttimes heaved him up. And so, weakly betwixt them, they led him to a little chapel not far from the seaside, and when the King was there, him thought him reasonably eased. Then heard they people cry in the field. "Now go thou, Sir Lucan," said the King, "and do me to wit[1] what betokens that noise in the field."

So Sir Lucan departed, for he was grievously wounded in many places. And so as he yede[2] he saw and harkened by the moonlight how that pillers[3] and robbers were come into the field to pill and to rob many a full noble knight of brooches and bees[4] and of many a good ring and many a rich jewel. And who that were not dead all out there they slew them for their harness[5] and their riches. When Sir Lucan understood this work, he came to the King as soon as he might and told him all what he had heard and seen. "Therefore by my read,"[6] said Sir Lucan, "it is best that we bring you to some town."

"I would it were so," said the King, "but I may not stand, my head works[7] so. Ah, Sir Lancelot," said King Arthur, "this day have I sore missed thee. And alas that ever I was against thee, for now have I my death, whereof Sir Gawain me warned in my dream."

Then Sir Lucan took up the King the t'one party[8] and Sir Bedivere the other party; and in the lifting up the King swooned and in the lifting Sir Lucan fell in a swoon that part of his guts fell out of his body, and therewith the noble knight's heart burst. And when the King awoke he beheld Sir Lucan how he lay foaming at the mouth and part of his guts lay at his feet.

"Alas," said the King, "this is to me a full heavy[9] sight to see this noble duke so die for my sake, for he would have holpen[1] me that had more need of help than I. Alas that he would not complain him for[2] his heart was so set to help me. Now Jesu have mercy upon his soul."

Then Sir Bedivere wept for the death of his brother.

"Now leave this mourning and weeping, gentle knight," said the King, "for all this will not avail me. For wit thou well, and[3] I might live myself, the

---

3. Betide.　　4. Advantage.　　5. Thrust.　　6. I.e., six feet.　　7. Hand guard.　　8. Edge.
9. Swoon.　　1. Let me know.　　2. Walked.　　3. Plunderers.　　4. Bracelets.　　5. Armor. *All out:* entirely.　　6. Advice.　　7. Aches.　　8. On one side.　　9. Sorrowful.　　1. Helped.　　2. Because.
3. If.

death of Sir Lucan would grieve me evermore. But my time passeth on fast," said the King. "Therefore," said King Arthur unto Sir Bedivere, "take thou here Excalibur[4] my good sword and go with it to yonder water's side; and when thou comest there I charge thee throw my sword in that water and come again and tell me what thou sawest there."

"My lord," said Sir Bedivere, "your commandment shall be done, and [I shall] lightly[5] bring you word again."

So Sir Bedivere departed. And by the way he beheld that noble sword, that the pommel and the haft[6] was all precious stones. And then he said to himself, "If I throw this rich sword in the water, thereof shall never come good, but harm and loss." And then Sir Bedivere hid Excalibur under a tree. And so, as soon as he might, he came again unto the King and said he had been at the water and had thrown the sword into the water.

"What saw thou there?" said the King.

"Sir," he said, "I saw nothing but waves and winds."

"That is untruly said of thee," said the King. "And therefore go thou lightly again and do my commandment; as thou art to me lief[7] and dear, spare not, but throw it in."

Then Sir Bedivere returned again and took the sword in his hand. And yet him thought[8] sin and shame to throw away that noble sword. And so eft[9] he hid the sword and returned again and told the King that he had been at the water and done his commandment.

"What sawest thou there?" said the King.

"Sir," he said, "I saw nothing but waters wap and waves wan."[1]

"Ah, traitor unto me and untrue," said King Arthur, "now hast thou betrayed me twice. Who would have weened that thou that has been to me so lief and dear, and thou art named a noble knight, and would betray me for the riches of this sword. But now go again lightly, for thy long tarrying putteth me in great jeopardy of my life, for I have taken cold. And but if thou do now as I bid thee, if ever I may see thee I shall slay thee mine[2] own hands, for thou wouldest for my rich sword see me dead."

Then Sir Bedivere departed and went to the sword and lightly took it up, and so he went to the water's side; and there he bound the girdle[3] about the hilts, and threw the sword as far into the water as he might. And there came an arm and an hand above the water and took it and clutched it, and shook it thrice and brandished; and then vanished away the hand with the sword into the water. So Sir Bedivere came again to the King and told him what he saw.

"Alas," said the King, "help me hence, for I dread me I have tarried overlong."

Then Sir Bedivere took the King upon his back and so went with him to that water's side. And when they were at the water's side, even fast[4] by the bank hoved[5] little barge with many fair ladies in it; and among them all was a queen; and all they had black hoods, and all they wept and shrieked when they saw King Arthur.

---

4. The sword that Arthur had received as a young man from the Lady of the Lake; it is presumably she who catches it when Bedivere finally throws it into the water. 5. Quickly. 6. Handle. *Pommel*: rounded knob on the hilt. 7. Beloved. 8. It seemed to him. 9. Again. 1. The phrase seems to mean "waters wash the shore and waves grow dark." 2. I.e., with mine. 3. Sword belt. 4. Close. 5. Waited.

"Now put me into that barge," said the King; and so he did softly. And there received him three ladies with great mourning, and so they set them[6] down. And in one of their laps King Arthur laid his head, and then the queen said, "Ah, my dear brother, why have ye tarried so long from me? Alas, this wound on your head hath caught overmuch cold." And anon they rowed fromward the land, and Sir Bedivere beheld all tho ladies go froward him.

Then Sir Bedivere cried and said, "Ah, my lord Arthur, what shall become of me, now ye go from me and leave me here alone among mine enemies?"

"Comfort thyself," said the King, "and do as well as thou mayest, for in me is no trust for to trust in. For I must into the vale of Avilion[7] to heal me of my grievous wound. And if thou hear nevermore of me, pray for my soul."

But ever the queen and ladies wept and shrieked that it was pity to hear. And as soon as Sir Bedivere had lost the sight of the barge he wept and wailed and so took the forest, and went[8] all that night. And in the morning he was ware betwixt two holts hoar[9] of a chapel and an hermitage.

*   *   *

Summary   In the passage here omitted, Sir Bedivere meets the former bishop of Canterbury, now a hermit, who describes how on the previous night a company of ladies had brought to the chapel a dead body, asking that it be buried. Sir Bedivere exclaims that the dead man must have been King Arthur and vows to spend the rest of his life there in the chapel as a hermit.

Thus of Arthur I find no more written in books that been authorized,[1] neither more of the very certainty of his death heard I never read,[2] but thus was he led away in a ship wherein were three queens: that one was King Arthur's sister, Queen Morgan la Fée, the t'other[3] was the Queen of North Wales, and the third was the Queen of the Waste Lands.***

Now more of the death of King Arthur could I never find but that these ladies brought him to his burials,[4] and such one was buried there that the hermit bore witness that sometime was Bishop of Canterbury.[5] But yet the hermit knew not in certain that he was verily the body of King Arthur, for this tale Sir Bedivere, a Knight of the Table Round, made it to be written. Yet some men say in many parts of England that King Arthur is not dead, but had by the will of our Lord Jesu into another place. And men say that he shall come again and he shall win the Holy Cross. Yet I will not say that it shall be so, but rather I will say, Here in this world he changed his life. And many men say that there is written upon his tomb this verse: *Hic iacet Arthurus, rex quondam, rexque futurus.*[6]

Summary   Guinevere enters a convent at Amesbury, where Lancelot, returned with his companions to England, visits her, but she commands him never to see her again. Emulating her example, Lancelot joins the bishop of Canterbury and Bedivere in their hermitage, where he takes holy orders and is joined in turn by seven of his fellow knights.

6. I.e., they sat.   7. A legendary island, sometimes identified with the earthly paradise.   8. Walked. *Took:* took to.   9. Ancient copses.   1. That have authority.   2. Told.   3. The second. 4. Grave.   5. Of whom the hermit, who was formerly bishop of Canterbury, bore witness.   6. Here lies Arthur, who was once king and king will be again (Latin).

[*The Deaths of Lancelot and Guinevere*]

And thus upon a night there came a vision to Sir Lancelot and charged him, in remission[7] of his sins, to haste him unto Amesbury: "And by then[8] thou come there, thou shalt find Queen Guinevere dead. And therefore take thy fellows with thee, and purvey them of an horse-bier,[9] and fetch thou the corse[1] of her, and bury her by her husband, the noble King Arthur. So this avision[2] came to Lancelot thrice in one night. Then Sir Lancelot rose up ere day and told the hermit.

"It were well done," said the hermit, "that ye made you ready and that ye disobey not the avision."

Then Sir Lancelot took his eight fellows with him, and on foot they yede[3] from Glastonbury to Amesbury, the which is little more than thirty mile, and thither they came within two days, for they were weak and feeble to go. And when Sir Lancelot was come to Amesbury within the nunnery, Queen Guinevere died but half an hour afore. And the ladies told Sir Lancelot that Queen Guinevere told them all ere she passed that Sir Lancelot had been priest near a twelve-month:[4] "and hither he cometh as fast as he may to fetch my corse, and beside my lord King Arthur he shall bury me." Wherefore the Queen said in hearing of them all, "I beseech Almighty God that I may never have power to see Sir Lancelot with my worldly eyes."

"And thus," said all the ladies, "was ever her prayer these two days till she was dead."

Then Sir Lancelot saw her visage, but he wept not greatly, but sighed. And so he did all the observance of the service himself, both the *dirige*[5] and on the morn he sang mass. And there was ordained[6] an horse-bier, and so with an hundred torches ever burning about the corse of the Queen, and ever Sir Lancelot with his eight fellows went about[7] the horse-bier, singing and reading many an holy orison,[8] and frankincense upon the corse incensed.[9]

Thus Sir Lancelot and his eight fellows went on foot from Amesbury unto Glastonbury, and when they were come to the chapel and the hermitage, there she had a *dirige* with great devotion.[1] And on the morn the hermit that sometime[2] was Bishop of Canterbury sang the mass of requiem with great devotion, and Sir Lancelot was the first that offered, and then als[3] his eight fellows. And then she was wrapped in cered cloth of Rennes, from the top[4] to the toe, in thirty-fold, and after she was put in a web[5] of lead, and then in a coffin of marble.

And when she was put in the earth Sir Lancelot swooned and lay long still, while[6] the hermit came and awaked him, and said, "Ye be to blame, for ye displease God with such manner of sorrow-making."

"Truly," said Sir Lancelot, "I trust I do not displease God, for He knoweth mine intent—for my sorrow was not, nor is not, for any rejoicing of sin, but my sorrow may never have end. For when I remember of her beaulté and of her noblesse[7] that was both with her king and with her,[8] so when I saw his

7. For the remission. 8. By the time. 9. Provide them with a horse-drawn hearse. 1. Body.
2. Dream. 3. Went. 4. Nearly twelve months. 5. Funeral service. 6. Prepared.
7. Around. 8. Reciting many a prayer. 9. Burned frankincense over the body. 1. Solemnity. 2. Once. 3. Also. *Offered*: made his donation. 4. Head. *Cloth of Rennes*: a shroud made of fine linen smeared with wax, produced at Rennes. 5. Afterward she was put in a sheet.
6. Until. 7. Her beauty and nobility. 8. That she and her king both had.

corse and her corse so lie together, truly mine heart would not serve to sustain my careful[9] body. Also when I remember me how by my defaute and mine orgule[1] and my pride that they were both laid full low, that were peerless that ever was living of Christian people, wit you well," said Sir Lancelot, "this remembered, of their kindness and mine unkindness, sank so to mine heart that I might not sustain myself." So the French book maketh mention.

Then Sir Lancelot never after ate but little meat,[2] nor drank, till he was dead, for then he sickened more and more and dried and dwined[3] away. For the Bishop nor none of his fellows might not make him to eat, and little he drank, that he was waxen by a kibbet[4] shorter than he was, that the people could not know him. For evermore, day and night, he prayed, but sometime he slumbered a broken sleep. Ever he was lying groveling on the tomb of King Arthur and Queen Guinevere, and there was no comfort that the Bishop nor Sir Bors, nor none of his fellows could make him—it availed not.

So within six weeks after, Sir Lancelot fell sick and lay in his bed. And then he sent for the Bishop that there was hermit, and all his true fellows. Then Sir Lancelot said with dreary steven,[5] "Sir Bishop, I pray you give to me all my rights that longeth[6] to a Christian man."

"It shall not need you,"[7] said the hermit and all his fellows. "It is but heaviness of your blood. Ye shall be well mended by the grace of God tomorn."

"My fair lords," said Sir Lancelot, "wit you well my careful body will into the earth; I have warning more than now I will say. Therefore give me my rights."

So when he was houseled and annealed[8] and had all that a Christian man ought to have, he prayed the Bishop that his fellows might bear his body to Joyous Garde. (Some men say it was Alnwick, and some men say it was Bamborough.) "Howbeit," said Sir Lancelot, "me repenteth[9] sore, but I made mine avow sometime that in Joyous Garde I would be buried. And because of breaking[1] of mine avow, I pray you all, lead me thither." Then there was weeping and wringing of hands among his fellows.

So at a season of the night they all went to their beds, for they all lay in one chamber. And so after midnight, against[2] day, the Bishop that was hermit, as he lay in his bed asleep, he fell upon a great laughter. And therewith all the fellowship awoke and came to the Bishop and asked him what he ailed.[3]

"Ah, Jesu mercy," said the Bishop, "why did ye awake me? I was never in all my life so merry and so well at ease."

"Wherefore?" said Sir Bors.

"Truly," said the Bishop, "here was Sir Lancelot with me, with mo[4] angels than ever I saw men in one day. And I saw the angels heave[5] up Sir Lancelot unto heaven, and the gates of heaven opened against him."

"It is but dretching of swevens,"[6] said Sir Bors, "for I doubt not Sir Lancelot aileth nothing but good."[7]

"It may well be," said the Bishop. "Go ye to his bed and then shall ye prove the sooth."

---

9. Sorrowful.   1. My fault and my haughtiness.   2. Food.   3. Wasted.   4. Grown by a cubit.
5. Sad voice.   6. Pertains. *Rights*: last sacrament.   7. You shall not need it.   8. Given communion and extreme unction.   9. I am sorry.   1. In order not to break.   2. Toward.   3. Ailed him.
4 More.   5 Lift.   6. Illusion of dreams.   7. Has nothing wrong with him.

So when Sir Bors and his fellows came to his bed, they found him stark dead. And he lay as he had smiled, and the sweetest savor[8] about him that ever they felt. Then was there weeping and wringing of hands, and the greatest dole they made that ever made men. And on the morn the Bishop did his mass of Requiem, and after the Bishop and all the nine knights put Sir Lancelot in the same horse-bier that Queen Guinevere was laid in tofore that she was buried. And so the Bishop and they all together went with the body of Sir Lancelot daily, till they came to Joyous Garde. And ever they had an hundred torches burning about him.

And so within fifteen days they came to Joyous Garde. And there they laid his corse in the body of the choir,[9] and sang and read many psalters[1] and prayers over him and about him. And ever his visage was laid open and naked, that all folks might behold him; for such was the custom in tho[2] days that all men of worship should so lie with open visage till that they were buried.

And right thus as they were at their service, there came Sir Ector de Maris that had seven year sought all England, Scotland, and Wales, seeking his brother, Sir Lancelot. And when Sir Ector heard such noise and light in the choir of Joyous Garde, he alight and put his horse from him and came into the choir. And there he saw men sing and weep, and all they knew Sir Ector, but he knew not them. Then went Sir Bors unto Sir Ector and told him how there lay his brother, Sir Lancelot, dead. And then Sir Ector threw his shield, sword, and helm from him, and when he beheld Sir Lancelot's visage, he fell down in a swoon. And when he waked, it were hard any tongue to tell the doleful complaints that he made for his brother.

"Ah, Lancelot!" he said, "thou were head of all Christian knights. And now I dare say," said Sir Ector, "thou Sir Lancelot, there thou liest, that thou were never matched of earthly knight's hand. And thou were the courteoust[3] knight that ever bore shield. And thou were the truest friend to thy lover that ever bestrode horse, and thou were the truest lover, of a sinful man,[4] that ever loved woman, and thou were the kindest man that ever struck with sword. And thou were the goodliest person that ever came among press of knights, and thou was the meekest man and the gentlest that ever ate in hall among ladies, and thou were the sternest knight to thy mortal foe that ever put spear in the rest."[5]

Then there was weeping and dolor out of measure.

Thus they kept Sir Lancelot's corse aloft fifteen days, and then they buried it with great devotion. And then at leisure they went all with the Bishop of Canterbury to his hermitage, and there they were together more than a month.

Then Sir Constantine that was Sir Cador's son of Cornwall was chosen king of England, and he was a full noble knight, and worshipfully he ruled this realm. And then this King Constantine sent for the Bishop of Canterbury, for he heard say where he was. And so he was restored unto his bishopric and left that hermitage, and Sir Bedivere was there ever still hermit to his life's end.

Then Sir Bors de Ganis, Sir Ector de Maris, Sir Gahalantine, Sir Galihud, Sir Galihodin, Sir Blamour, Sir Bleoberis, Sir Villiars le Valiant, Sir Clarrus

---

8. Odor. A sweet scent is a conventional sign in saints' lives of a sanctified death.　　9. The center of the chancel, the place of honor.　　1. Psalms.　　2. Those.　　3. Most courteous.　　4. Of any man born in original sin.　　5. Support for the butt of the lance.

of Clermount, all these knights drew them to their countries. Howbeit[6] King Constantine would have had them with him, but they would not abide in this realm. And there they all lived in their countries as holy men.

And some English books make mention that they went never out of England after the death of Sir Lancelot—but that was but favor of makers.[7] For the French book maketh mention—and is authorized—that Sir Bors, Sir Ector, Sir Blamour, and Sir Bleoberis went into the Holy Land, thereas Jesu Christ was quick[8] and dead, and anon as they had stablished their lands;[9] for the book saith so Sir Lancelot commanded them for to do ere ever he passed out of this world. There these four knights did many battles upon the miscreaunts,[1] or Turks, and there they died upon a Good Friday for God's sake.

Here is the end of the whole book of King Arthur and of his noble knights of the Round Table, that when they were whole together there was ever an hundred and forty. And here is the end of *The Death of Arthur*.[2]

I pray you all gentlemen and gentlewomen that readeth this book of Arthur and his knights from the beginning to the ending, pray for me while I am alive that God send me good deliverance. And when I am dead, I pray you all pray for my soul.

For this book was ended the ninth year of the reign of King Edward the Fourth, by Sir Thomas Malory, knight, as Jesu help him for His great might, as he is the servant of Jesu both day and night.

6. However.   7. The authors' bias.   8. Living. *Thereas:* where.   9. As soon as they had put their lands in order.   1. Infidels.   2. By the "whole book" Malory refers to the entire work; the *Death of Arthur,* which Caxton made the title of the entire work, refers to the last part of Malory's book.

EVERYMAN
1495?

Although drama never attained the status of a dominant literary form in the Middle Ages, in the later centuries of the period it was popular, fairly abundant, and varied in character. It began with the impersonation or dramatization of passages from the liturgy of the Resurrection and the Nativity of Christ. Produced at first in the Latin language and inside a church, it was later moved outside and Latin was replaced with the vernacular languages of several European peoples. By the fourteenth century, if not earlier, whole "cycles" of short plays were performed on certain feast days of the Church, especially Corpus Christi. A complete sequence began with the revolt of Satan and his followers against God and ended with the Last Judgment; inside these limits, some forty "one-act" pieces presented the important events in the divine plan for human history. These plays were produced in the towns, with each of the various craft and trade guilds responsible for one of the plays. The carpenters, for example, would perform the story of Noah, while the "pinners," or nail-makers, would perform the Crucifixion. Because of their scriptural content, modern scholars sometimes called these works *miracle plays,* but the more current term is *mystery plays,* referring not to their content but to the guilds that mounted them: in Middle English a craft or trade is known as a *mystery.*

About the time when the mystery plays had reached their fullest development, another kind of dramatic composition emerged, also religious in nature and purpose. As the mystery plays dramatize biblical events, so the *morality* plays dramatize the content of a typical homily or sermon. By common consent, *Everyman* is regarded as the best of this kind of drama. We do not know the author's name, but the play belongs to the late fifteenth century; it almost certainly derives from a Dutch piece on the same theme. Whereas mystery plays were produced in a long sequence, with amateur casts, morality plays may have been acted by professional or semiprofessional companies. Nothing is actually known about the original productions of *Everyman*; it is well suited, however, to outdoor performance. Its comparative length, along with the large role of the title character, favors the possibility of some degree of professionalism in the cast.

The modern reader may find it profitable to compare *Everyman* with such different kinds of drama as Greek tragedy or Samuel Beckett's *Endgame*. In its brevity, simplicity, and concentration on a single theme and situation, it recalls especially the shorter plays of the ancient Greeks. Its topic has much in common with that of Beckett's play—facing death and coming to terms with life—but the choices involved and the consequent ending (or "ending," in Beckett's work) are different.

As in most morality plays, the characters are personifications of more-abstract concepts. Everyman himself, of course, represents all humanity. But we should not assume in advance that "abstract" characters make a dull play. In the first place, dramatizing the characters gives them actuality; the actors must be flesh and blood. Then, in *Everyman,* the situations, the speech, and the behavior of the various characters are thoroughly realistic as well as representative of their generalized significance. For example, Fellowship does and says what a single boon companion would be likely to say and do under the same circumstances. Good Deeds is not a static figure: we see her first bound to the Earth (the floor of the stage) by Everyman's sins; when he scourges himself in penance, she rises joyfully to accompany him. The author's ingenuity is notable in the character Goods (Riches): Goods is offstage when Everyman calls him; the audience hears but does not see him at first as he explains that he lies there in corners, trussed and piled up, locked in chests, stuffed in bags! Surely he must have got a laugh when he did come on stage. And of course God, who instigates the action by sending Death to call Everyman to his account, is no abstraction. He was probably a voice offstage rather than an actor—but a very effective character nonetheless.

Together with the lean and rapidly moving plot, it is the rightness of its words that makes *Everyman* a success. God speaks with an unfailing simplicity and directness:

> Charyte they do all clene forgete.
> I hoped well that every man
> In my glory shulde make his mansyon;
> And thereto I had them all electe. . . .
> They be so combred with worldly ryches
> That nedes on them I must do iustyce. . . .

Nor is humor absent from the play. Cousin, asked by Everyman to go with him at the summons of Death, exclaims: "No, by Our Lady! I have the crampe in my to[e]"; and later, Beauty replies to the same effect: "I crosse out all this! Adewe, by Saynt Iohan! / I take my cap in my lappe, and am gone." There is irony in Fellowship's farewell verse: "For you I wyll remember that partynge is mournynge." Best of all, perhaps, are the short speeches, scattered throughout the earlier parts of the play especially, which express Everyman's disappointment in his friends and consequent disillusion. One example must suffice. After a long colloquy with Goods, that character asks Everyman, "What! wenest thou that I am thyne?" Reversal, the necessary prelude to reorientation, is condensed in Everyman's brief reply: "I had weened [believed] so."

A good collection of medieval English plays, with commentary, is David Bevington, ed., *Medieval Drama* (1975). For discussions of *Everyman*, see Robert Potter, *The English Morality Play* (1975), and the edition, with bibliography, by A. C. Cawley, ed., *Everyman and Medieval Miracle Plays*, revised by Anne Rooney (1993). Guides to drama in the Middle Ages generally are provided by Glynne Wickham, *The Medieval Theatre,* 3rd. ed. (1987), and John W. Harris, *Medieval Theatre in Context* (1992).

Everyman[1]

DRAMATIS PERSONAE

MESSENGER	KNOWLEDGE
GOD	CONFESSION
DEATH	BEAUTY
EVERYMAN	STRENGTH
FELLOWSHIP	DISCRETION
KINDRED	FIVE-WITS
COUSIN	ANGEL
GOODS	DOCTOR
GOOD DEEDS	

Here Beginneth a Treatise How the High Father of
Heaven Sendeth Death to Summon Every Creature
to Come and Give Account of Their Lives in This
World, and is in Manner of a Moral Play

[*Enter* MESSENGER.]
MESSENGER   I pray you all give your audience,
   And hear this matter with reverence,
   By figure[2] a moral play,
   The Summoning of Everyman called it is,
   That of our lives and ending shows   5
   How transitory we be all day.[3]
   The matter is wonder precious,
   But the intent of it is more gracious
   And sweet to bear away.
   The story saith: Man, in the beginning   10
   Look well, and take good heed to the ending,
   Be you never so gay.
   You think sin in the beginning full sweet,
   Which in the end causeth the soul to weep,
   When the body lieth in clay.   15
   Here shall you see how fellowship and jollity,
   Both strength, pleasure, and beauty,
   Will fade from thee as flower in May.
   For ye shall hear how our Heaven-King

---

1. Modernized text by E. Talbot Donaldson, whose notes have been adapted here.   **2.** In form.
3. Always.

Calleth Everyman to a general reckoning. 20
Give audience and hear what he doth say.
    [*Exit* MESSENGER.—*Enter* GOD.]
GOD   I perceive, here in my majesty,
   How that all creatures be to me unkind,[4]
   Living without dread in worldly prosperity.
   Of ghostly[5] sight the people be so blind, 25
   Drowned in sin, they know me not for their God.
   In worldly riches is all their mind:
   They fear not of my righteousness the sharp rod;
   My law that I showed when I for them died
   They forget clean, and shedding of my blood red. 30
   I hanged between two,[6] it cannot be denied:
   To get them life I suffered to be dead.
   I healed their feet, with thorns hurt was my head.
   I could do no more than I did, truly—
   And now I see the people do clean forsake me. 35
   They use the seven deadly sins damnable,
   As pride, coveitise,[7] wrath, and lechery
   Now in the world be made commendable.
   And thus they leave of angels the heavenly company.
   Every man liveth so after his own pleasure, 40
   And yet of their life they be nothing sure.
   I see the more that I them forbear,
   The worse they be from year to year:
   All that liveth appaireth[8] fast.
   Therefore I will, in all the haste, 45
   Have a reckoning of every man's person.
   For, and[9] I leave the people thus alone
   In their life and wicked tempests,
   Verily they will become much worse than beasts;
   For now one would by envy another up eat. 50
   Charity do they all clean forgeet.
   I hoped well that every man
   In my glory should make his mansion,
   And thereto I had them all elect.[1]
   But now I see, like traitors deject,[2] 55
   They thank me not for the pleasure that I to them meant,
   Nor yet for their being that I them have lent.
   I proffered the people great multitude of mercy,
   And few there be that asketh it heartily.
   They be so cumbered with worldly riches 60
   That needs on them I must do justice—
   On every man living without fear.
   Where art thou, Death, thou mighty messenger?
       [*Enter* DEATH.]
DEATH   Almighty God, I am here at your will,

---

4. Thoughtless.   **5.** Spiritual.   **6.** The two thieves between whom Christ was crucified.   **7.** Avarice.
8. Degenerates.   **9.** If.   **1.** Chosen.   **2.** Abased.

Your commandment to fulfill.   65
GOD   Go thou to Everyman,
   And show him, in my name,
   A pilgrimage he must on him take,
   Which he in no wise may escape;
   And that he bring with him a sure reckoning   70
   Without delay or any tarrying.
DEATH   Lord, I will in the world go run over all,
   And cruelly out-search both great and small.
            [*Exit* GOD.]
   Everyman will I beset that liveth beastly
   Out of God's laws, and dreadeth not folly.   75
   He that loveth riches I will strike with my dart,
   His sight to blind, and from heaven to depart[3]—
   Except that Almsdeeds be his good friend—
   In hell for to dwell, world without end.
   Lo, yonder I see Everyman walking: 80
   Full little he thinketh on my coming;
   His mind is on fleshly lusts and his treasure,
   And great pain it shall cause him to endure
   Before the Lord, Heaven-King.
            [*Enter* EVERYMAN.]
   Everyman, stand still! Whither art thou going   85
   Thus gaily? Hast thou thy Maker forgeet?
EVERYMAN   Why askest thou?
   Why wouldest thou weet?[4]
DEATH   Yea, sir, I will show you:
   In great haste I am sent to thee   90
   From God out of his majesty.
EVERYMAN   What! sent to me?
DEATH   Yea, certainly.
   Though thou have forgot him here,
   He thinketh on thee in the heavenly sphere,
   As, ere we depart, thou shalt know.   95
EVERYMAN   What desireth God of me?
DEATH   That shall I show thee:
   A reckoning he will needs have
   Without any longer respite.   100
EVERYMAN   To give a reckoning longer leisure I crave.
   This blind[5] matter troubleth my wit.
DEATH   On thee thou must take a long journay:
   Therefore thy book of count with thee thou bring,
   For turn again thou cannot by no way.   105
   And look thou be sure of thy reckoning,
   For before God thou shalt answer and shew
   Thy many bad deeds and good but a few—
   How thou hast spent thy life and in what wise,
   Before the Chief Lord of Paradise.   110

3. Separate.   4. Know.   5. Unexpected.

Have ado that we were in that way,[6]
For weet thou well thou shalt make none attornay.[7]

EVERYMAN   Full unready I am such reckoning to give.
I know thee not. What messenger art thou?

DEATH   I am Death that no man dreadeth,[8]   115
For every man I 'rest, and no man spareth;
For it is God's commandment
That all to me should be obedient.

EVERYMAN   O Death, thou comest when I had thee least in mind.
In thy power it lieth me to save: 120
Yet of my good will I give thee, if thou will be kind,
Yea, a thousand pound shalt thou have—
And defer this matter till another day.

DEATH   Everyman, it may not be, by no way.
I set nought by gold, silver, nor riches,   125
Nor by pope, emperor, king, duke, nor princes,
For, and I would receive gifts great,
All the world I might get.
But my custom is clean contrary:
I give thee no respite. Come hence and not tarry!   130

EVERYMAN   Alas, shall I have no longer respite?
I may say Death giveth no warning.
To think on thee it maketh my heart sick,
For all unready is my book of reckoning.
But twelve year and I might have a biding,[9]   135
My counting-book I would make so clear
That my reckoning I should not need to fear.
Wherefore, Death, I pray thee, for God's mercy,
Spare me till I be provided of remedy.

DEATH   Thee availeth not to cry, weep, and pray;   140
But haste thee lightly[1] that thou were gone that journay,
And prove thy friends, if thou can.
For weet thou well the tide abideth no man,
And in the world each living creature
For Adam's sin must die of nature.[2]   145

EVERYMAN   Death, if I should this pilgrimage take
And my reckoning surely make,
Show me, for saint[3] charity,
Should I not come again shortly?

DEATH   No, Everyman. And thou be once there,   150
Thou mayst never more come here,
Trust me verily.

EVERYMAN   O gracious God in the high seat celestial,
Have mercy on me in this most need!
Shall I have no company from this vale terrestrial   155
Of mine acquaintance that way me to lead?

DEATH   Yea, if any be so hardy

---

6. Let's get started at once.   7. None to appear in your stead.   8. That fears nobody.   9. If I might
have a delay for just twelve years.   1. Quickly.   2. Naturally.   3. Holy.

That would go with thee and bear thee company.
Hie thee that thou were gone to God's magnificence,
Thy reckoning to give before his presence. 160
What, weenest[4] thou thy life is given thee,
And thy worldly goods also?

EVERYMAN   I had weened so, verily.

DEATH   Nay, nay, it was but lent thee.
For as soon as thou art go, 165
Another a while shall have it and then go therefro,
Even as thou hast done.
Everyman, thou art mad! Thou hast thy wits[5] five,
And here on earth will not amend thy life!
For suddenly I do come. 170

EVERYMAN   O wretched caitiff! Whither shall I flee
That I might 'scape this endless sorrow?
Now, gentle Death, spare me till tomorrow,
That I may amend me
With good advisement.[6] 175

DEATH   Nay, thereto I will not consent,
Nor no man will I respite,
But to the heart suddenly I shall smite,
Without any advisement.
And now out of thy sight I will me hie: 180
See thou make thee ready shortly,
For thou mayst say this is the day
That no man living may 'scape away.
        [Exit DEATH.]

EVERYMAN   Alas, I may well weep with sighs deep:
Now have I no manner of company 185
To help me in my journey and me to keep.
And also my writing[7] is full unready—
How shall I do now for to excuse me?
I would to God I had never be geet![8]
To my soul a full great profit it had be. 190
For now I fear pains huge and great.
The time passeth: Lord, help, that all wrought!
For though I mourn, it availeth nought.
The day passeth and is almost ago:
I wot[9] not well what for to do. 195
To whom were I best my complaint to make?
What and I to Fellowship thereof spake,
And showed him of this sudden chance?
For in him is all mine affiance,[1]
We have in the world so many a day 200
Be good friends in sport and play.
I see him yonder, certainly.
I trust that he will bear me company.
Therefore to him will I speak to ease my sorrow.

4. Suppose.   5. Senses.   6. Preparation.   7. Ledger.   8. Been begotten.   9. Know.   1. Trust.

[*Enter* FELLOWSHIP.]

Well met, good Fellowship, and good morrow!   205
FELLOWSHIP   Everyman, good morrow, by this day!
  Sir, why lookest thou so piteously?
  If anything be amiss, I pray thee me say,
  That I may help to remedy.
EVERYMAN   Yea, good Fellowship, yea: 210
  I am in great jeopardy.
FELLOWSHIP   My true friend, show to me your mind.
  I will not forsake thee to my life's end
  In the way of good company.
EVERYMAN   That was well spoken, and lovingly!   215
FELLOWSHIP   Sir, I must needs know your heaviness.
  I have pity to see you in any distress.
  If any have you wronged, ye shall revenged be,
  Though I on the ground be slain for thee,
  Though that I know before that I should die.   220
EVERYMAN   Verily, Fellowship, gramercy.[2]
FELLOWSHIP   Tush! by thy thanks I set not a stree.[3]
  Show me your grief and say no more.
EVERYMAN   If I my heart should to you break,[4]
  And then you to turn your mind fro me,   225
  And would not me comfort when ye hear me speak,
  Then should I ten times sorrier be.
FELLOWSHIP   Sir, I say as I will do, indeed.
EVERYMAN   Then be you a good friend at need.
  I have found you true herebefore.   230
FELLOWSHIP   And so ye shall evermore.
  For, in faith, and thou go to hell,
  I will not forsake thee by the way.
EVERYMAN   Ye speak like a good friend. I believe you well.
  I shall deserve[5] it, and I may.   235
FELLOWSHIP   I speak of no deserving, by this day!
  For he that will say and nothing do
  Is not worthy with good company to go.
  Therefore show me the grief of your mind,
  As to your friend most loving and kind.   240
EVERYMAN   I shall show you how it is:
  Commanded I am to go a journay,
  A long way, hard and dangerous,
  And give a strait[6] count, without delay,
  Before the high judge Adonai.[7]   245
  Wherefore I pray you bear me company,
  As ye have promised, in this journay.
FELLOWSHIP   This is matter indeed! Promise is duty—
  But, and I should take such a voyage on me,
  I know it well, it should be to my pain.   250
  Also it maketh me afeard, certain.

2. Many thanks.   3. Straw.   4. Disclose.   5. Repay.   6. Strict.   7. God.

But let us take counsel here, as well as we can—
For your words would fear a strong man.
EVERYMAN   Why, ye said if I had need,
   Ye would me never forsake, quick ne dead,   255
   Though it were to hell, truly.
FELLOWSHIP   So I said, certainly.
   But such pleasures[8] be set aside, the sooth to say.
   And also, if we took such a journay,
   When should we again come?   260
EVERYMAN   Nay, never again, till the day of doom.
FELLOWSHIP   In faith, then will not I come there!
   Who hath you these tidings brought?
EVERYMAN   Indeed, Death was with me here.
FELLOWSHIP   Now by God that all hath bought,[9]   265
   If Death were the messenger,
   For no man that is living today
   I will not go that loath journay—
   Not for the father that begat me!
EVERYMAN   Ye promised otherwise, pardie.[1]   270
FELLOWSHIP   I wot well I said so, truly.
   And yet, if thou wilt eat and drink and make good cheer,
   Or haunt to women the lusty company,
   I would not forsake you while the day is clear,
   Trust me verily!   275
EVERYMAN   Yea, thereto ye would be ready—
   To go to mirth, solace,[2] and play:
   Your mind to folly will sooner apply
   Than to bear me company in my long journay.
FELLOWSHIP   Now in good faith, I will not that way.   280
   But, and thou will murder or any man kill,
   In that I will help thee with a good will.
EVERYMAN   O that is simple[3] advice, indeed!
   Gentle fellow, help me in my necessity:
   We have loved long, and now I need—   285
   And now, gentle Fellowship, remember me!
FELLOWSHIP   Whether ye have loved me or no,
   By Saint John, I will not with thee go!
EVERYMAN   Yet I pray thee take the labor and do so much for me,
   To bring me forward,[4] for saint charity,   290
   And comfort me till I come without the town.
FELLOWSHIP   Nay, and thou would give me a new gown,
   I will not a foot with thee go.
   But, and thou had tarried, I would not have left thee so.
   And as now, God speed thee in thy journay!   295
   For from thee I will depart as fast as I may.
EVERYMAN   Whither away, Fellowship? Will thou forsake me?
FELLOWSHIP   Yea, by my fay! To God I betake[5] thee.
EVERYMAN   Farewell, good Fellowship! For thee my heart is sore.

---

8. Jokes.   9. Redeemed.   1. By God.   2. Pleasure.   3. Foolish.   4. Escort me.   5. Commend.

Adieu forever—I shall see thee no more   300
FELLOWSHIP   In faith, Everyman, farewell now at the ending:
  For you I will remember that parting is mourning.
        [*Exit* FELLOWSHIP.]
EVERYMAN   Alack, shall we thus depart[6] indeed—
  Ah, Lady, help!—without any more comfort?
  Lo, Fellowship forsaketh me in my most need!   305
  For help in this world whither shall I resort?
  Fellowship herebefore with me would merry make,
  And now little sorrow for me doth he take.
  It is said, "In prosperity men friends may find
  Which in adversity be full unkind."   310
  Now whither for succor shall I flee,
  Sith[7] that Fellowship hath forsaken me?
  To my kinsmen I will, truly,
  Praying them to help me in my necessity.
  I believe that they will do so,   315
  For kind will creep where it may not go.[8]
  I will go 'say[9]—for yonder I see them—
  Where[1] be ye now my friends and kinsmen.
        [*Enter* KINDRED *and* COUSIN.]
KINDRED   Here be we now at your commandment:
  Cousin, I pray you show us your intent   320
  In any wise, and not spare.
COUSIN   Yea, Everyman, and to us declare
  If ye be disposed to go anywhither.
  For, weet you well, we will live and die togither.
KINDRED   In wealth and woe we will with you hold,   325
  For over his kin a man may be bold.
EVERYMAN   Gramercy, my friends and kinsmen kind.
  Now shall I show you the grief of my mind.
  I was commanded by a messenger
  That is a high king's chief officer: 330
  He bade me go a pilgrimage, to my pain—
  And I know well I shall never come again.
  Also I must give a reckoning strait,
  For I have a great enemy that hath me in wait,[2]
  Which intendeth me to hinder.   335
KINDRED   What account is that which ye must render?
  That would I know.
EVERYMAN   Of all my works I must show
  How I have lived and my days spent;
  Also of ill deeds that I have used   340
  In my time sith life was me lent,
  And of all virtues that I have refused.
  Therefore I pray you go thither with me
  To help me make mine account, for saint charity.

---

6. Part.   7. Since.   8. For kinship will creep where it cannot walk (or kinsmen will suffer hardship for one another).   9. Assay.   1. Whether.   2. Satan lies in ambush for me.

COUSIN   What, to go thither? Is that the matter?   345
    Nay, Everyman, I had liefer fast³ bread and water
    All this five year and more!
EVERYMAN   Alas, that ever I was bore!
    For now shall I never be merry
    If that you forsake me.   350
KINDRED   Ah, sir, what? Ye be a merry man:
    Take good heart to you and make no moan.
    But one thing I warn you, by Saint Anne,
    As for me, ye shall go alone.
EVERYMAN   My Cousin, will you not with me go?   355
COUSIN   No, by Our Lady! I have the cramp in my toe:
    Trust not to me. For, so God me speed,
    I will deceive you in your most need.
KINDRED   It availeth you not us to 'tice.⁴
    Ye shall have my maid with all my heart: 360
    She loveth to go to feasts, there to be nice,⁵
    And to dance, and abroad to start.⁶
    I will give her leave to help you in that journey,
    If that you and she may agree.
EVERYMAN   Now show me the very effect of your mind: 365
    Will you go with me or abide behind?
KINDRED   Abide behind? Yea, that will I and I may!
    Therefore farewell till another day.
        [*Exit* KINDRED.]
EVERYMAN   How should I be merry or glad?
    For fair promises men to me make,   370
    But when I have most need they me forsake.
    I am deceived. That maketh me sad.
COUSIN   Cousin Everyman, farewell now,
    For verily I will not go with you;
    Also of mine own an unready reckoning   375
    I have to account—therefore I make tarrying.
    Now God keep thee, for now I go.
        [*Exit* COUSIN.]
EVERYMAN   Ah, Jesus, is all come hereto?
    Lo, fair words maketh fools fain:⁷
    They promise and nothing will do, certain.   380
    My kinsmen promised me faithfully
    For to abide with me steadfastly,
    And now fast away do they flee.
    Even so Fellowship promised me.
    What friend were best me of to provide?   385
    I lose my time here longer to abide.
    Yet in my mind a thing there is:
    All my life I have loved riches;
    If that my Good⁸ now help me might,
    He would make my heart full light.   390

---

3. Rather fast on.   4. Entice.   5. Wanton.   6. To go gadding about.   7. Glad.   8. Goods.

I will speak to him in this distress.
Where art thou, my Goods and riches?
GOODS [*Within.*]   Who calleth me? Everyman? What, hast thou haste?
I lie here in corners, trussed and piled so high,
And in chests I am locked so fast—   395
Also sacked in bags—thou mayst see with thine eye
I cannot stir, in packs low where I lie.
What would ye have? Lightly[9] me say.
EVERYMAN   Come hither, Good, in all the haste thou may,
For of counsel I must desire thee.   400
    [*Enter* GOODS.]
GOODS   Sir, and ye in the world have sorrow or adversity,
That can I help you to remedy shortly.
EVERYMAN   It is another disease[1] that grieveth me:
In this world it is not, I tell thee so.
I am sent for another way to go,   405
To give a strait count general
Before the highest Jupiter of all.
And all my life I have had joy and pleasure in thee:
Therefore I pray thee go with me,
For peradventure, thou mayst before God Almighty   410
My reckoning help to clean and purify.
For it is said ever among[2]
That money maketh all right that is wrong.
GOODS   Nay, Everyman, I sing another song:
I follow no man in such voyages.   415
For, and I went with thee,
Thou shouldest fare much the worse for me;
For because on me thou did set thy mind,
Thy reckoning I have made blotted and blind,[3]
That thine account thou cannot make truly—   420
And that hast thou for the love of me.
EVERYMAN   That would grieve me full sore,
When I should come to that fearful answer.
Up, let us go thither together.
GOODS   Nay, not so, I am too brittle, I may not endure.   425
I will follow no man one foot, be ye sure.
EVERYMAN   Alas, I have thee loved and had great pleasure
All my life-days on good and treasure.
GOODS   That is to thy damnation, without leasing,[4]
For my love is contrary to the love everlasting.   430
But if thou had me loved moderately during,
As to the poor to give part of me,
Then shouldest thou not in this dolor be,
Nor in this great sorrow and care.
EVERYMAN   Lo, now was I deceived ere I was ware,   435
And all I may wite[5] misspending of time.

---

9. Quickly.   1. Distress.   2. Now and then.   3. Illegible.   4. Lie.   5. Blame on.

GOODS   What, weenest⁶ thou that I am thine?

EVERYMAN   I had weened so.

GOODS   Nay, Everyman, I say no.
As for a while I was lent thee;   440
A season thou hast had me in prosperity.
My condition is man's soul to kill;
If I save one, a thousand I do spill.
Weenest thou that I will follow thee?
Nay, from this world, not verily.   445

EVERYMAN   I had weened otherwise.

GOODS   Therefore to thy soul Good is a thief;
For when thou art dead, this is my guise⁷—
Another to deceive in the same wise
As I have done thee, and all to his soul's repreef.⁸   450

EVERYMAN   O false Good, cursed thou be,
Thou traitor to God, that hast deceived me
And caught me in thy snare!

GOODS   Marry, thou brought thyself in care,⁹
Whereof I am glad;   455
I must needs laugh, I cannot be sad.

EVERYMAN   Ah, Good, thou hast had long my heartly¹ love;
I gave thee that which should be the Lord's above.
But wilt thou not go with me, indeed?
I pray thee truth to say.   460

GOODS   No, so God me speed!
Therefore farewell and have good day.
         [Exit GOODS.]

EVERYMAN   Oh, to whom shall I make my moan
For to go with me in that heavy journey?
First Fellowship said he would with me gone: 465
His words were very pleasant and gay,
But afterward he left me alone.
Then spake I to my kinsmen, all in despair,
And also they gave me words fair—
They lacked no fair speaking,   470
But all forsake me in the ending.
Then went I to my Goods that I loved best,
In hope to have comfort; but there had I least,
For my Goods sharply did me tell
That he bringeth many into hell.   475
Then of myself I was ashamed,
And so I am worthy to be blamed:
Thus may I well myself hate.
Of whom shall I now counsel take?
I think that I shall never speed   480
Till that I go to my Good Deed.
But alas, she is so weak
That she can neither go² nor speak.

---

6. Suppose.   7. Custom.   8. Shame.   9. Sorrow.   1. Sincere.   2. Walk.

Yet will I venture[3] on her now.
My Good Deeds, where be you?   485
GOOD DEEDS [*Speaking from the ground.*]   Here I lie, cold in the ground:
   Thy sins hath me sore bound
   That I cannot stear.[4]
EVERYMAN   O Good Deeds, I stand in fear:
   I must you pray of counsel,   490
   For help now should come right well.
GOOD DEEDS   Everyman, I have understanding
   That ye be summoned, account to make,
   Before Messiah of Jer'salem King.
   And you do by me, that journey with you will I take.   495
EVERYMAN   Therefore I come to you my moan to make.
   I pray you that ye will go with me.
GOOD DEEDS   I would full fain, but I cannot stand, verily.
EVERYMAN   Why, is there anything on you fall?
GOOD DEEDS   Yea, sir, I may thank you of all: 500
   If ye had perfectly cheered me,
   Your book of count full ready had be.
         [GOOD DEEDS *shows him the account book.*]
   Look, the books of your works and deeds eke,[5]
   As how they lie under the feet,
   To your soul's heaviness.   505
EVERYMAN   Our Lord Jesus help me!
   For one letter here I cannot see.
GOOD DEEDS   There is a blind reckoning in time of distress!
EVERYMAN   Good Deeds, I pray you help me in this need,
   Or else I am forever damned indeed.   510
   Therefore help me to make reckoning
   Before the Redeemer of all thing
   That King is and was and ever shall.
GOOD DEEDS   Everyman, I am sorry of your fall
   And fain would help you and I were able.   515
EVERYMAN   Good Deeds, your counsel I pray you give me.
GOOD DEEDS   That shall I do verily,
   Though that on my feet I may not go;
   I have a sister that shall with you also,
   Called Knowledge, which shall with you abide   520
   To help you to make that dreadful reckoning.
         [*Enter* KNOWLEDGE.]
KNOWLEDGE   Everyman, I will go with thee and be thy guide,
   In thy most need to go by thy side.
EVERYMAN   In good condition I am now in everything,
   And am whole content with this good thing,   525
   Thanked be God my Creator.
GOOD DEEDS   And when she hath brought you there
   Where thou shalt heal thee of thy smart,[6]
   Then go you with your reckoning and your Good Deeds together

---

3. Gamble.   4. Stir.   5. Also.   6. Pain.

For to make you joyful at heart 530
Before the blessed Trinity.

EVERYMAN   My Good Deeds, gramercy!
I am well content, certainly,
With your words sweet.

KNOWLEDGE   Now go we together lovingly 535
To Confession, that cleansing river.

EVERYMAN   For joy I weep—I would we were there!
But I pray you give me cognition,
Where dwelleth that holy man Confession?

KNOWLEDGE   In the House of Salvation: 540
We shall find him in that place
That shall us comfort, by God's grace.

[KNOWLEDGE *leads* EVERYMAN *to* CONFESSION.]

Lo, this is Confession: kneel down and ask mercy,
For he is in good conceit[7] with God Almighty.

EVERYMAN [*Kneeling.*]   O glorious fountain that all uncleanness doth
    clarify,[8] 545
Wash from me the spots of vice unclean,
That on me no sin may be seen.
I come with Knowledge for my redemption,
Redempt with heart and full contrition,
For I am commanded a pilgrimage to take 550
And great accounts before God to make.
Now I pray you, Shrift, mother of Salvation,
Help my Good Deeds for my piteous exclamation.

CONFESSION   I know your sorrow well, Everyman:
Because with Knowledge ye come to me, 555
I will you comfort as well as I can,
And a precious jewel I will give thee,
Called Penance, voider of adversity.
Therewith shall your body chastised be—
With abstinence and perseverance in God's service. 560
Here shall you receive that scourge of me,
Which is penance strong that ye must endure,
To remember thy Saviour was scourged for thee
With sharp scourges, and suffered it patiently.
So must thou ere thou 'scape that painful pilgrimage. 565
Knowledge, keep him in this voyage,
And by that time Good Deeds will be with thee.
But in any wise be secure of mercy—
For your time draweth fast—and ye will saved be.
Ask God mercy and he will grant, truly. 570
When with the scourge of penance man doth him bind,
The oil of forgiveness then shall he find.

EVERYMAN   Thanked be God for his gracious work,
For now I will my penance begin.
This hath rejoiced and lighted my heart, 575

7. Esteem.   8. Purify.

Though the knots be painful and hard within.[9]
KNOWLEDGE   Everyman, look your penance that ye fulfill,
    What pain that ever it to you be;
    And Knowledge shall give you counsel at will
    How your account ye shall make clearly.   580
EVERYMAN   O eternal God, O heavenly figure,
    O way of righteousness, O goodly vision,
    Which descended down in a virgin pure
    Because he would every man redeem,
    Which Adam forfeited by his disobedience;   585
    O blessed Godhead, elect and high Divine,
    Forgive my grievous offense!
    Here I cry thee mercy in this presence:
    O ghostly Treasure, O Ransomer and Redeemer,
    Of all the world Hope and Conduiter,[1]   590
    Mirror of joy, Foundator of mercy,
    Which enlumineth heaven and earth thereby,
    Hear my clamorous complaint, though it late be;
    Receive my prayers, of thy benignity.
    Though I be a sinner most abominable,   595
    Yet let my name be written in Moses' table.[2]
    O Mary, pray to the Maker of all thing
    Me for to help at my ending,
    And save me from the power of my enemy,
    For Death assaileth me strongly.   600
    And Lady, that I may by mean of thy prayer
    Of your Son's glory to be partner—
    By the means of his passion I it crave.
    I beseech you help my soul to save.
    Knowledge, give me the scourge of penance: 605
    My flesh therewith shall give acquittance.[3]
    I will now begin, if God give me grace.
KNOWLEDGE   Everyman, God give you time and space![4]
    Thus I bequeath you in the hands of our Saviour:
    Now may you make your reckoning sure.   610
EVERYMAN   In the name of the Holy Trinity
    My body sore punished shall be:
    Take this, body, for the sin of the flesh!
    Also[5] thou delightest to go gay and fresh,
    And in the way of damnation thou did me bring,   615
    Therefore suffer now strokes of punishing!
    Now of penance I will wade the water clear,
    To save me from purgatory, that sharp fire.
GOOD DEEDS   I thank God, now can I walk and go,
    And am delivered of my sickness and woe.   620
    Therefore with Everyman I will go, and not spare:
    His good works I will help him to declare.

9. To my senses. The knots are on the scourge (whip) of penance.   1. Guide.   2. Tablet on which
are recorded those who have been baptized and have done penance.   3. Satisfaction for sins.
4. Opportunity.   5. As.

KNOWLEDGE   Now Everyman, be merry and glad:
  Your Good Deeds cometh now, ye may not be sad.
  Now is your Good Deeds whole and sound,   625
  Going upright upon the ground.
EVERYMAN   My heart is light, and shall be evermore.
  Now will I smite faster than I did before.
GOOD DEEDS   Everyman, pilgrim, my special friend,
  Blessed be thou without end!   630
  For thee is preparate the eternal glory.
  Ye have me made whole and sound
  Therefore I will bide by thee in every stound.[6]
EVERYMAN   Welcome, my Good Deeds! Now I hear thy voice,
  I weep for very sweetness of love.   635
KNOWLEDGE   Be no more sad, but ever rejoice:
  God seeth thy living in his throne above.
  Put on this garment to thy behove,[7]
  Which is wet with your tears—
  Or else before God you may it miss   640
  When ye to your journey's end come shall.
EVERYMAN   Gentle Knowledge, what do ye it call?
KNOWLEDGE   It is a garment of sorrow;
  From pain it will you borrow:[8]
  Contrition it is   645
  That getteth forgiveness;
  It pleaseth God passing[9] well.
GOOD DEEDS   Everyman, will you wear it for your heal?[1]
EVERYMAN   Now blessed be Jesu, Mary's son,
  For now have I on true contrition.   650
  And let us go now without tarrying.
  Good Deeds, have we clear our reckoning?
GOOD DEEDS   Yea, indeed, I have it here.
EVERYMAN   Then I trust we need not fear.
  Now friends, let us not part in twain.   655
KNOWLEDGE   Nay, Everyman, that will we not, certain.
GOOD DEEDS   Yet must thou lead with thee
  Three persons of great might.
EVERYMAN   Who should they be?
GOOD DEEDS   Discretion and Strength they hight,[2]   660
  And thy Beauty may not abide behind.
KNOWLEDGE   Also ye must call to mind
  Your Five-Wits as for your counselors.
GOOD DEEDS   You must have them ready at all hours.
EVERYMAN   How shall I get them hither?   665
KNOWLEDGE   You must call them all togither,
  And they will be here incontinent.[3]
EVERYMAN   My friends, come hither and be present,
  Discretion, Strength, my Five-Wits, and Beauty!

---

6. Trial.   7. Advantage.   8. Redeem.   9. Surpassingly.   1. Welfare.   2. Are called.   3. At once.

[*They enter.*]

BEAUTY   Here at your will we be all ready.   670
  What will ye that we should do?
GOOD DEEDS   That ye would with Everyman go
  And help him in his pilgrimage.
  Advise you: will ye with him or not in that voyage?
STRENGTH   We will bring him all thither,   675
  To his help and comfort, ye may believe me.
DISCRETION   So will we go with him all togither.
EVERYMAN   Almighty God, loved might thou be!
  I give thee laud that I have hither brought
  Strength, Discretion, Beauty, and Five-Wits—lack I nought—   680
  And my Good Deeds, with Knowledge clear,
  All be in my company at my will here:
  I desire no more to my business.
STRENGTH   And I, Strength, will by you stand in distress,
  Though thou would in battle fight on the ground.   685
FIVE-WITS   And though it were through the world round,
  We will not depart for sweet ne sour.
BEAUTY   No more will I, until death's hour,
  Whatsoever thereof befall.
DISCRETION   Everyman, advise you first of all: 690
  Go with a good advisement[4] and deliberation.
  We all give you virtuous monition[5]
  That all shall be well.
EVERYMAN   My friends, hearken what I will tell;
  I pray God reward you in his heaven-sphere;   695
  Now hearken all that be here,
  For I will make my testament,
  Here before you all present:
  In alms half my good I will give with my hands twain,
  In the way of charity with good intent;   700
  And the other half, still[6] shall remain,
  I 'queath to be returned there it ought to be.
  This I do in despite of the fiend of hell,
  To go quit out of his perel,[7]
  Ever after and this day.   705
KNOWLEDGE   Everyman, hearken what I say:
  Go to Priesthood, I you advise,
  And receive of him, in any wise,
  The holy sacrament and ointment[8] togither;
  Then shortly see ye turn again hither: 710
  We will all abide you here.
FIVE-WITS   Yea, Everyman, hie you that ye ready were.
  There is no emperor, king, duke, ne baron,
  That of God hath commission
  As hath the least priest in the world being: 715

---

4. Preparation.   5. Confident prediction.   6. Which still.   7. To go free from danger from him.
8. Extreme unction.

For of the blessed sacraments pure and bening[9]
He beareth the keys, and thereof hath the cure[1]
For man's redemption—it is ever sure—
Which God for our souls' medicine
Gave us out of his heart with great pine,[2]   720
Here in this transitory life for thee and me.
The blessed sacraments seven there be:
Baptism, confirmation, with priesthood[3] good,
And the sacrament of God's precious flesh and blood,
Marriage, the holy extreme unction, and penance: 725
These seven be good to have in remembrance,
Gracious sacraments of high divinity.

EVERYMAN   Fain would I receive that holy body,
And meekly to my ghostly[4] father I will go.

FIVE-WITS   Everyman, that is the best that ye can do: 730
God will you to salvation bring.
For priesthood exceedeth all other thing:
To us Holy Scripture they do teach,
And converteth man from sin, heaven to reach;
God hath to them more power given   735
Than to any angel that is in heaven.
With five words[5] he may consecrate
God's body in flesh and blood to make,
And handleth his Maker between his hands.
The priest bindeth and unbindeth all bands,[6]   740
Both in earth and in heaven.
Thou ministers[7] all the sacraments seven;
Though we kiss thy feet, thou were worthy;
Thou art surgeon that cureth sin deadly;
No remedy we find under God   745
But all only priesthood.[8]
Everyman, God gave priests that dignity
And setteth them in his stead among us to be.
Thus be they above angels in degree.
     [Exit EVERYMAN.]

KNOWLEDGE   If priests be good, it is so, surely.   750
But when Jesu hanged on the cross with great smart,[9]
There he gave out of his blessed heart
The same sacrament in great torment,
He sold them not to us, that Lord omnipotent:
Therefore Saint Peter the Apostle doth say   755
That Jesu's curse hath all they
Which God their Saviour do buy or sell,[1]
Or they for any money do take or tell.[2]

9. Benign.   1. Care.   2. Torment.   3. Ordination.   4. Spiritual.   5. "For this is my body,"
spoken by the priest when he offers the wafer at communion.   6. A reference to the power of the keys,
inherited by the priesthood from St. Peter, who received it from Christ with the promise that whatever St.
Peter bound or loosed on Earth would be bound or loosed in heaven (Matthew 16.19).   7. Administers.   8. Except from priesthood alone.   9. Pain.   1. To give or receive money for the sacraments
is simony, named after Simon, who wished to buy the gift of the Holy Ghost and was cursed by St.
Peter.   2. Or who, for any sacrament, take or count out money.

Sinful priests giveth the sinners example bad:
  Their children sitteth by other men's fires, I have heard;   760
  And some haunteth women's company
  With unclean life, as lusts of lechery.
  These be with sin made blind.
FIVE-WITS   I trust to God no such may we find.
  Therefore let us priesthood honor,   765
  And follow their doctrine for our souls' succor.
  We be their sheep and they shepherds be
  By whom we all be kept in surety.
  Peace, for yonder I see Everyman come,
  Which hath made true satisfaction.   770
GOOD DEEDS   Methink it is he indeed.
     [Re-enter EVERYMAN.]
EVERYMAN   Now Jesu be your alder speed![3]
  I have received the sacrament for my redemption,
  And then mine extreme unction.
  Blessed be all they that counseled me to take it!   775
  And now, friends, let us go without longer respite.
  I thank God that ye have tarried so long.
  Now set each of you on this rood[4] your hond
  And shortly follow me:
  I go before there[5] I would be. God be our guide!   780
STRENGTH   Everyman, we will not from you go
  Till ye have done this voyage long.
DISCRETION   I, Discretion, will bide by you also.
KNOWLEDGE   And though this pilgrimage be never so strong,
  I will never part you fro.   785
STRENGTH   Everyman, I will be as sure by thee
  As ever I did by Judas Maccabee.[6]
EVERYMAN   Alas, I am so faint I may not stand—
  My limbs under me doth fold!
  Friends, let us not turn again to this land,   790
  Not for all the world's gold.
  For into this cave must I creep
  And turn to earth, and there to sleep.
BEAUTY   What, into this grave, alas?
EVERYMAN   Yea, there shall ye consume, more and lass.[7]   795
BEAUTY   And what, should I smother here?
EVERYMAN   Yea, by my faith, and nevermore appear.
  In this world live no more we shall,
  But in heaven before the highest Lord of all.
BEAUTY   I cross out all this! Adieu, by Saint John—   800
  I take my tape in my lap and am gone.[8]
EVERYMAN   What, Beauty, whither will ye?
BEAUTY   Peace, I am deaf—I look not behind me,
  Not and thou wouldest give me all the gold in thy chest.

---

3. The prosperer of you all.   4. Cross.   5. Where.   6. Judas Maccabaeus was an enormously powerful warrior in the defense of Israel against the Syrians in late Old Testament times.   7. Decay, all of you.   8. I tuck my skirts in my belt and am off.

[*Exit* BEAUTY.]

EVERYMAN   Alas, whereto may I trust?   805
Beauty goeth fast away fro me—
She promised with me to live and die!

STRENGTH   Everyman, I will thee also forsake and deny.
Thy game liketh me not at all.

EVERYMAN   Why then, ye will forsake me all?   810
Sweet Strength, tarry a little space.

STRENGTH   Nay, sir, by the rood of grace,
I will hie me from thee fast,
Though thou weep till thy heart tobrast.[9]

EVERYMAN   Ye would ever bide by me, ye said.   815

STRENGTH   Yea, I have you far enough conveyed!
Ye be old enough, I understand,
Your pilgrimage to take on hand:
I repent me that I hither came.

EVERYMAN   Strength, you to displease I am to blame,   820
Yet promise is debt, this ye well wot.[1]

STRENGTH   In faith, I care not:
Thou art but a fool to complain;
You spend your speech and waste your brain.
Go, thrust thee into the ground.   825
          [*Exit* STRENGTH.]

EVERYMAN   I had weened[2] surer I should you have found.
He that trusteth in his Strength
She him deceiveth at the length.
Both Strength and Beauty forsaketh me—
Yet they promised me fair and lovingly.   830

DISCRETION   Everyman, I will after Strength be gone:
As for me, I will leave you alone.

EVERYMAN   Why Discretion, will ye forsake me?

DISCRETION   Yea, in faith, I will go from thee.
For when Strength goeth before,   835
I follow after evermore.

EVERYMAN   Yet I pray thee, for the love of the Trinity,
Look in my grave once piteously.

DISCRETION   Nay, so nigh will I not come.
Farewell everyone!   840
          [*Exit* DISCRETION.]

EVERYMAN   Of all thing faileth save God alone—
Beauty, Strength, and Discretion.
For when Death bloweth his blast
They all run fro me full fast.

FIVE-WITS   Everyman, my leave now of thee I take.   845
I will follow the other, for here I thee forsake.

EVERYMAN   Alas, then may I wail and weep,
For I took you for my best friend.

FIVE-WITS   I will no longer thee keep.

9. Break.   1. Know.   2. Supposed.

Now farewell, and there an end!   850
    [*Exit* FIVE-WITS.]
EVERYMAN   O Jesu, help, all hath forsaken me!
GOOD DEEDS   Nay, Everyman, I will bide with thee:
  I will not forsake thee indeed;
  Thou shalt find me a good friend at need.
EVERYMAN   Gramercy, Good Deeds! Now may I true friends see.   855
  They have forsaken me every one—
  I loved them better than my Good Deeds alone.
  Knowledge, will ye forsake me also?
KNOWLEDGE   Yea, Everyman, when ye to Death shall go,
  But not yet, for no manner of danger.   860
EVERYMAN   Gramercy, Knowledge, with all my heart!
KNOWLEDGE   Nay, yet will I not from hence depart
  Till I see where ye shall become.
EVERYMAN   Methink, alas, that I must be gone
  To make my reckoning and my debts pay,   865
  For I see my time is nigh spent away.
  Take example, all ye that this do hear or see,
  How they that I best loved do forsake me,
  Except my Good Deeds that bideth truly.
GOOD DEEDS   All earthly things is but vanity.   870
  Beauty, Strength, and Discretion do man forsake,
  Foolish friends and kinsmen that fair spake—
  All fleeth save Good Deeds, and that am I.
EVERYMAN   Have mercy on me, God most mighty,
  And stand by me, thou mother and maid, holy Mary!   875
GOOD DEEDS   Fear not: I will speak for thee.
EVERYMAN   Here I cry God mercy!
GOOD DEEDS   Short our end, and 'minish our pain.[3]
  Let us go, and never come again.
EVERYMAN   Into thy hands, Lord, my soul I commend: 880
  Receive it, Lord, that it be not lost.
  As thou me boughtest,[4] so me defend,
  And save me from the fiend's boast,
  That I may appear with that blessed host
  That shall be saved at the day of doom.   885
  In manus tuas, of mights most,
  Forever *commendo spiritum meum.*[5]
    [EVERYMAN *and* GOOD DEEDS *descend into the grave.*]
KNOWLEDGE   Now hath he suffered that we all shall endure,
  The Good Deeds shall make all sure.
  Now hath he made ending,   890
  Methinketh that I hear angels sing
  And make great joy and melody
  Where Everyman's soul received shall be.
ANGEL [*Within.*]   Come, excellent elect spouse to Jesu![6]

---

3. Make our dying quick and diminish our pain.   4. Redeemed.   5. Into thy hands, O greatest of powers, I commend my spirit forever (Latin).   6. The soul is often referred to as the bride of Jesus.

Here above thou shalt go 895
Because of thy singular virtue.
Now the soul is taken the body fro,
Thy reckoning is crystal clear:
Now shalt thou into the heavenly sphere—
Unto the which all ye shall come 900
That liveth well before the day of doom.
　　　　[*Enter* DOCTOR.⁷]
DOCTOR　This memorial⁸ men may have in mind:
Ye hearers, take it of worth, old and young,
And forsake Pride, for he deceiveth you in the end.
And remember Beauty, Five-Wits, Strength, and Discretion, 905
They all at the last do Everyman forsake,
Save his Good Deeds there doth he take—
But beware, for and they be small,
Before God he hath no help at all—
None excuse may be there for Everyman. 910
Alas, how shall he do than?⁹
For after death amends may no man make,
For then mercy and pity doth him forsake.
If his reckoning be not clear when he doth come,
God will say, *"Ite, maledicti, in ignem eternum!"*¹ 915
And he that hath his account whole and sound,
High in heaven he shall be crowned,
Unto which place God bring us all thither,
That we may live body and soul togither.
Thereto help, the Trinity! 920
Amen, say ye, for saint charity.

7. The learned theologian who explains the meaning of the play.　8. Reminder.　9. Then.
1. Depart, ye cursed, into everlasting fire (Latin).

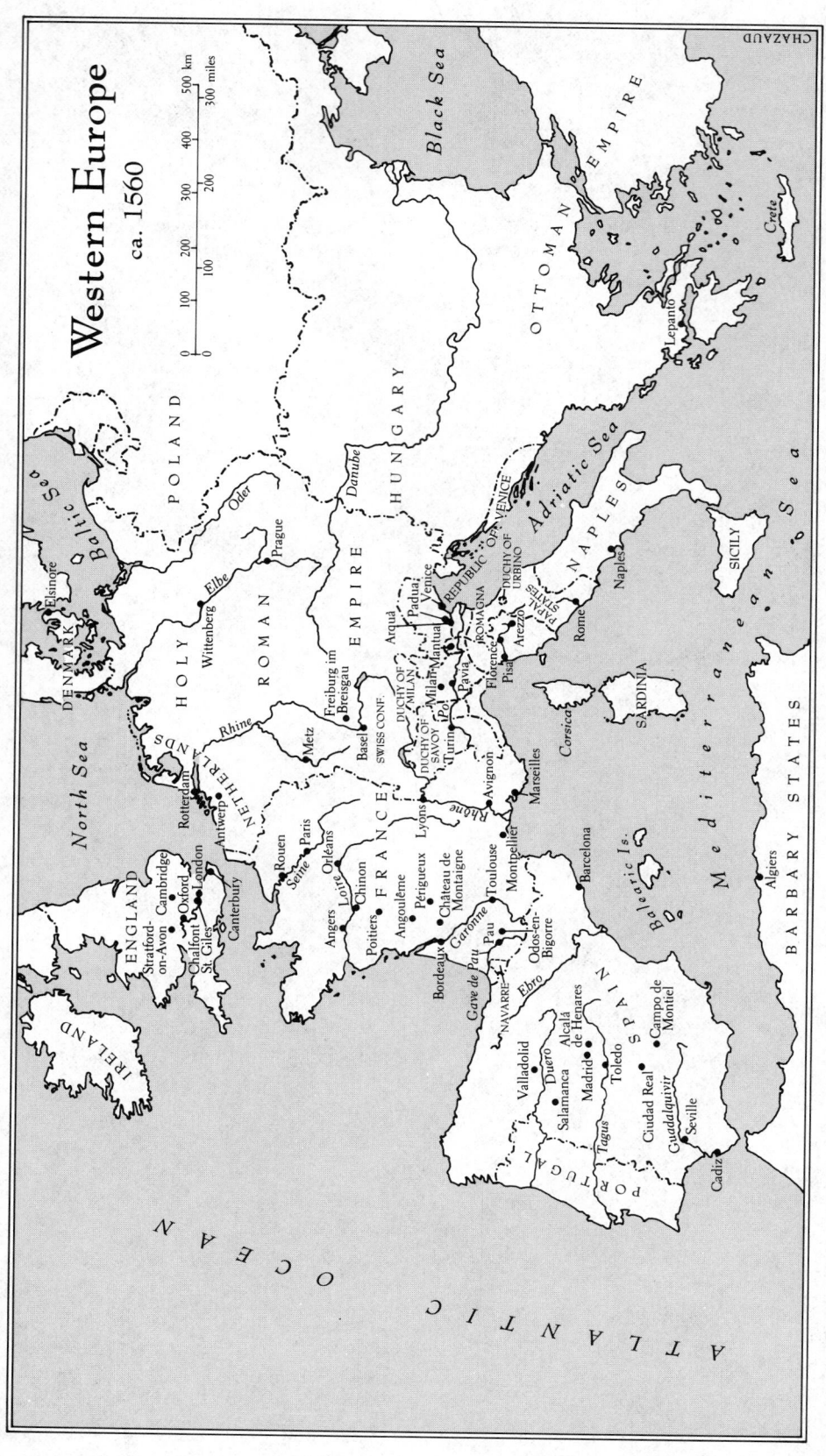

Western Europe
ca. 1560

500 km
300 miles

ATLANTIC OCEAN

IRELAND

North Sea

Baltic Sea

DENMARK
Elsinore

POLAND

Oder

Elbe
Prague

Wittenberg

HOLY
ROMAN
EMPIRE

Rhine

Metz

Freiburg im
Breisgau

Basel
SWISS CONF.

Danube

HUNGARY

Black Sea

OTTOMAN EMPIRE

Adriatic Sea

Arquà
Padua
Venice
REPUBLIC OF VENICE
DUCHY OF
URBINO
ROMAGNA
PAPAL
STATES

DUCHY OF
MILAN
Pavia
Mantua

DUCHY OF
SAVOY
Turin

Pau

Florence
Arezzo
Pisa

Rome

NAPLES
Naples

SICILY

SARDINIA

Corsica

Lepanto

Crete

ENGLAND
Stratford-
on-Avon
Chalfont
St. Giles
Cambridge
Oxford
London
Canterbury

Rotterdam
Antwerp
NETHERLANDS

Rouen
Seine
Paris
Orleans

Angers
Loire
Chinon
Poitiers
Angoulême
Périgueux
Château de
Montaigne
Bordeaux
Garonne

FRANCE

Lyons

Rhône

Avignon

Marseilles

Montpellier

Toulouse

Gave de Pau
Odos-en-
Bigorre
NAVARRE
Ebro

Barcelona

Balearic Is.

Mediterranean Sea

BARBARY STATES

Algiers

SPAIN

Valladolid
Duero
Salamanca
Alcalá
de Henares
Madrid
Toledo
Tagus
Ciudad Real
Campo de
Montiel
Guadalquivir
Seville
Cadiz

PORTUGAL

CHAZAUD

Masterpieces of the Renaissance

"All the world's a stage, / And all the men and women merely players": Shakespeare's famous comparison of human beings to actors playing their various roles in the great theater of the world conjures up the exhilarating liberty and mobility we associate with the memorable characters produced by the literary genius of the Renaissance. Since "merely" meant, in Shakespeare's day, "wholly" and "entirely," the line evokes a lively sense of the men and women of that world performing their roles with the gusto of actors. Their social roles as princes, clowns, thieves, or housewives appear, from one angle, exciting opportunities for the characters to explore. Yet such roles are also clearly confining: Renaissance men and women were born into societies that strictly regulated their actions and even their clothing—only actors had the right to vary their garb and dress above their station. Whether Renaissance subjects relished the pleasures of playing or resented the constraints of their social roles is a subject often taken up in the literature of the day.

When Renaissance writers explore the relationship of their characters to the social roles the characters play, they partly follow in the tradition exemplified in the Middle Ages by Chaucer's *Canterbury Tales*. Yet the most memorable characters of Renaissance literature enjoy greater autonomy and more fully realized personalities than Chaucer's pilgrims. Characters like Rabelais's broad-minded giant, Gargantua; Cervantes's idealistic but mad Quixote; Shakespeare's romantic but doomed Othello and Desdemona; and Milton's "domestic" Adam and "adventurous" Eve are frequently presented in acts of thought, fantasy, planning, doubt, and internal debate. Deliberating with others and themselves about what to do seems at least as important to these characters as putting their plans into action.

One reason for this shift toward internal, mental, and psychological portraiture is that Renaissance authors, like the characters they invent, inhabited a world of such widespread revolutionary change that they could not passively receive the traditional wisdom of previous ages. When Nicolaus Copernicus (1473–1543) discovered that the Earth moves around the sun and when Galileo Galilei (1564–1642) turned his telescope up to the heavens, the Renaissance mind had to reconceive the nature of the universe and Creation. When Christopher Columbus (1451–1506) sailed to what he thought were the Indies, he proved that the Earth was not flat and introduced a New World to Europe, which began for the first time to think of itself as the Old World. Around the time that Columbus was sailing to America, humanist scholars in Italy began to use new scholarly methods that gave them fuller access to the cultural legacy of the ancient world of Greece and Rome and a new sense of their own place in history. On scientific, geographical, and scholarly fronts, the world of Renaissance Europe was undergoing revolutionary change.

The new discoveries' challenge to European and human centrality in the world and in Creation met with fervent, if varied, responses. In 1633 the Inquisition forced Galileo to repudiate the Copernican theory that the Earth rotates around the sun. In his dialogue *The City of the Sun* (1602) Galileo's friend and supporter Tommasso Campanella (1568–1639) optimistically asserted that the three great inventions of his day—the compass, the printing press, and the gun—were "signs of the union of the entire world." François Rabelais, less sanguine about the idea of world union enforced by the gun and artillery, placed his hopes for peace only on the printing press, an instrument for intellectual deliberation and the dissemination of ideas. In *The First Anniversary*, John Donne (1572–1631), on the other hand, focused on the psychological threat of the new discoveries and theories to individuals unable to cope with so much uncertainty:

> The new philosophy calls all in doubt,
> The element of fire is quite put out;
> The sun is lost and the earth, and no man's wit
> Can well direct him where to look for it.
> And freely men confess that this world's spent,
> When in the planets and the firmament
> They seek so many new; they see that this
> Is crumbled out again to his atomies . . .

In Donne's poem, the new discoveries amount to a second creation, so radical is the new theory of the world's construction. For Renaissance intellectuals and for the literary characters they created, there was almost literally no firm ground to stand on as they moved through life in an increasingly complex and uncertain world. Although received wisdom appeared from one angle like an anchor in a sea of change, from another it seemed like a shackle to error: it is no wonder, then, that the reasoning and choices of the characters in Renaissance poetry and prose began to matter enormously.

As with other terms that have currency in cultural history (for instance, *Romanticism*), the usefulness of the term *Renaissance* depends on its keeping a certain degree of elasticity. The literal meaning of the word—"rebirth"—suggests that one impulse toward the great intellectual and artistic achievements of the period came from the example of ancient culture, or even better, from a certain vision that the artists and intellectuals of the Renaissance possessed of the world of antiquity, which was "reborn" through their work. Especially in the more mature phase of the Renaissance, these individuals were aware of having brought about a vigorous renewal, which they openly associated with the cult of antiquity. The restoration of ancient canons was regarded as a glorious achievement to be set beside the thrilling discoveries of their own age. "For now," Rabelais writes through his Gargantua,

> all courses of study have been restored, and the acquisition of languages has become supremely honorable: Greek, without which it is shameful for any man to be called a scholar; Hebrew; Chaldean; and Latin. And in my time we have learned how to produce wonderfully elegant and accurate printed books, just as, on the other hand, we have also learned (by diabolic suggestion) how to make cannon and other such fearful weapons.

Machiavelli, whose infatuation with antiquity is as typical a trait as his better-advertised political realism, suggests in the opening of his *Discourses on the First Ten Books of Livy* (1513–21) that rulers should be as keen on the imitation of ancient "virtues" as are artists, lawyers, and the scientists: "The civil laws are nothing but decisions given by the ancient jurisconsults. . . . And what is the science of medicine, but the experience of ancient physicians, which their successors have taken for their guide?"

Elasticity should likewise be maintained in regard to the chronological span of the Renaissance as a "movement" extending through varying periods of years and as including phases and traits of the epoch that is otherwise known as the Middle Ages (and vice versa). The peak of the Renaissance can be shown to have occurred at different times in different countries, the "movement" having had its inception in Italy, where its impact was at first most remarkable in the visual arts, while in England, for instance, it developed later and its main achievements were in literature, particularly the drama. The meaning of the term has also, in the course of time, widened considerably. Nowadays it conveys, to say the least, a general notion of artistic creativity, of extraordinary zest for life and knowledge, of sensory delight in opulence and magnificence, of spectacular individual achievement, thus extending far beyond the literal meaning of rebirth and the strict idea of a revival and imitation of antiquity.

Even in its stricter sense, however, the term continues to have its function. The degree to which European intellectuals of the period possessed and were possessed by the writings of the ancient world is difficult for the average modern reader to realize. For these writers references to classical mythology, philosophy, and literature are not ornaments or affectations. Along with references to the Scriptures they are part, and a major part, of their mental equipment and way of thinking. When Erasmus through his *The Praise of Folly* speaks in a cluster of classical allusions, or when Machiavelli writes to a friend: "I will get up before daylight, prepare my birdlime, and go out with a bundle of cages on my back, so that I look like Geta when he came back from the harbor with the books of Amphitryo" (p. 1708, n. 3), the words have by no means the sound of erudite self-gratification that they might have nowadays. They are wholly natural, familiar, unassuming.

When we are overcome by sudden emotion, our first exclamations are likely to be in the language most familiar to us—our dialect, if we happen to have one. Montaigne relates of himself that when once his father unexpectedly fell back in his arms in a swoon, the first words he uttered under the emotion of that experience were in Latin. Similarly Benvenuto Cellini, the Italian sculptor, goldsmith, and autobiographer, talking to his patron and expressing admiration of a Greek statue, establishes with the ancient artist an immediate contact, a proud familiarity:

> I cried to the Duke: "My lord, this is a statue in Greek marble, and it is a miracle of beauty. . . . If your Excellency permits, I should like to restore it—head and arms and feet. . . . It is certainly not my business to patch up statues, that being the trade of botchers, who do it in all conscience villainously ill; yet the art displayed by this great master of antiquity cries out to me to help him."

The people who, starting at about the middle of the fourteenth century, gave new impulse to this emulation of the classics are often referred to as humanists. The word in that sense is related to what we call the humanities, and the humanities at that time were Latin and Greek. Every cultivated person wrote and spoke Latin, with the result that a Western community of intellectuals could exist, a spiritual "republic of letters" above individual nations. There was also a considerable amount of individual contact among humanists. In glancing at the biographies of the authors included in this section, the extensiveness of their travels may strike us as a remarkable or even surprising fact, considering the hardships and slowness of traveling during those centuries.

The archetype of literature as a vocation is often said to be Petrarch—the first author in this section—who anticipated certain ideals of the high Renaissance: a lofty conception of the literary art, a taste for the good life, a basic pacifism, and a strong sense of the memories and glories of antiquity. In this last respect, what should be emphasized is the imaginative quality, the visionary impulse with which the writers of the period looked at those memories—the same vision and imagination with which they regarded such contemporary heroes as the great navigators and astronomers. The Renaissance view of the cultural monuments of antiquity was far from being that of the philologist and the antiquarian; indeed, familiarity was facilitated by the very lack of a scientific sense of history. We find the visionary and imaginative element not only in the creations of poets and dramatists (Shakespeare's Romans, to give an obvious example) but also in the works of political writers: as when Machiavelli describes himself entering, through his reading, the

> ancient courts of ancient men, where, being lovingly received, I feed on that food which alone is mine, and which I was born for; I am not ashamed to speak with them and to ask the reasons for their actions, and they courteously answer me.

> For . . . hours I feel no boredom and forget every worry; I do not fear poverty, and death does not terrify me. I give myself completely over to the ancients.

Imitation of antiquity acquires, in Machiavelli and many others, a special quality; whereas "academic" imitations transcribe, Machiavelli plunges into vital and reciprocal communication—even communion—with the ancients.

The vision of an ancient age of glorious intellectual achievement that is "now" brought to life again implies, of course, however roughly, the idea of an intervening "middle" time, by comparison ignorant and dark. The hackneyed, vastly inaccurate notion that the "light" of the Renaissance broke through a long "night" of the Middle Ages was not devised by subsequent "enlightened" centuries; it was held by the humanist scholars of the Renaissance themselves. In his genealogy of giants from Grangousier to Gargantua to Pantagruel, Rabelais conveniently represents the generations of modern learning with their varying degrees of enlightenment. Thus Gargantua writes to his son:

> Though my late father of worthy memory, Grandgousier, devoted all his energy to those things of which I might take the fullest advantage, and from which I might acquire the most sensible knowledge, and though my own effort matched his—or even surpassed it—still, as you know very well, it was neither so fit nor so right a time for learning as exists today, nor was there an abundance of such teachers as you have had. It was still a murky, dark time, oppressed by the misery, unhappiness, and disasters of the Goths, who destroyed all worthwhile literature of every sort. But divine goodness has let me live to see light and dignity returned to humanistic studies, and to see such an improvement, indeed, that it would be hard for me to qualify for the very first class of little schoolboys—I who, in my prime, had the reputation (and not in error) of the most learned man of my day.

The combination of self-deprecation, aspiration, and arrogance aptly characterizes the period's sense of its own achievements and its standing in relation to antiquity and the Middle Ages.

Definitions of the Renaissance must also take account of the period's preoccupation with this life rather than with the life beyond. The contrast of an ideal medieval man or woman, whose mode of action is basically oriented toward the thought of the afterlife (and who therefore conceives of life on Earth as transient and preparatory) with an ideal Renaissance man or woman, possessing and cherishing earthly interests so concrete and self-sufficient that the very realization of the ephemeral quality of life is to him or her nothing but an added spur to its immediate enjoyment—this is a useful contrast even though it represents an enormous oversimplification of the facts.

The same emphasis on the immediate and tangible is reflected in the earthly, amoral, and esthetic character of what we may call the Renaissance code of behavior. According to this "code," human action is judged not in terms of right and wrong, of good and evil (as it is judged when life is viewed as a moral "test," with reward or punishment in the afterlife), but in terms of its present concrete validity and effectiveness, of the delight it affords, of its memorability and its beauty. In that sense a good deal that is typical of the Renaissance, from architecture to poetry, from sculpture to rhetoric, may be related to a taste for the harmonious and the memorable, for the spectacular effect, for the successful striking of a pose. Individual human action, seeking as it were in itself its own reward, finds justification in its formal appropriateness; in its being a well-rounded achievement, perfect of its kind; in the zest and gusto with which it is, here and now, performed; and, finally, in its proving worthy of remaining as a testimony to the performer's power on Earth.

A convenient way to illustrate this emphasis is to consider certain words especially expressive of the interests of the period—"virtue," "fame," "glory." "Virtue," particularly in its Italian form, virtù, is to be understood in a wide sense. As we may see even now in some relics of its older meanings, the word (from the Latin vir, "man") connotes active power—the intrinsic force and ability of a person or thing (the "virtue" of a law or of a medicine)—and hence, also, technical skill (the capacity of the "virtuoso"). The Machiavellian prince's "virtues," therefore, are not necessarily goodness, temperance, clemency, and the like; they are whatever forces and skills may help him in the efficient management and preservation of his princely powers. The idealistic, intangible part of the prince's success is consigned to such concepts as "fame" and "glory," but even in this case the dimension within which human action is considered is still an earthly one. These concepts connote the hero's success and reputation with his contemporaries, or look forward to splendid recognition from posterity, on Earth.

In this sense (though completely pure examples of such an attitude are rare) the purpose of life is the unrestrained and self-sufficient practice of one's "virtue," the competent and delighted exercise of one's skill. At the same time, there is no reason to forget that such virtues and skills are God's gift. The worldview of even some of the most clearly earthbound Renaissance writers was hardly godless; Machiavelli, Rabelais, Cellini take for granted the presence of God in their own and in their heroes' lives:

> . . .we have before our eyes extraordinary and unexampled means prepared by God. The sea has been divided. A cloud has guided you on your way. The rock has given forth water. Manna has fallen. Everything has united to make you great. The rest is for you to do. God does not intend to do everything, lest he deprive us of our free will and the share of glory that belongs to us. (Machiavelli)

> And then Gargantua and Powerbrain would briefly recapitulate, according to the Pythagorean fashion, everything Gargantua had read and seen and understood, everything he had done and heard, all day long.
> They would both pray to God their Creator, worshiping, reaffirming their faith, glorifying Him for His immense goodness and thanking Him for all they had been given, and forever placing themselves in His hands.
> And then they would go to sleep. (Rabelais)

> I found that all the bronze my furnace contained had been exhausted in the head of this figure [of the statue of Perseus]. It was a miracle to observe that not one fragment remained in the orifice of the channel, and that nothing was wanting to the statue. In my great astonishment I seemed to see in this the hand of God arranging and controlling all. (Cellini)

Yet if we compare the attitudes of these authors with the view of the world and of the value of human action that emerges from the major literary work of the Middle Ages, *The Divine Comedy*, and with the manner in which human action is there seen within a grand extratemporal design, we see that the presence of God in the Renaissance writers cited above is conspicuously less dominating.

Renaissance intellectuals, artists, aristocrats, and princes did not lack in abiding religious faith or fervor. The most powerful lords of opulent Renaissance courts would unhesitatingly affirm John Calvin's starkly religious assessment of earthly life and gain:

> For if heaven is our country, what is earth but a place of exile! If the departure out of the world is an entrance into life, what is the world but a sepulchre? What is a continuance in it but an absorption in death? If deliverance from the body is an introduction into complete liberty, what is the body but a prison? Therefore, if the terrestrial life be compared with the celestial, it should undoubtedly be despised and accounted of no value.

These princes, however, sharply felt the conflict between the values of worldly goods and spiritual renunciation. The religious conviction in the transitory nature of earthly possessions, moreover, did not prevent princes and lords from seeking to expand their kingdoms. An anonymous Spanish writer was inspired to celebrate Spain's growing

empire as "the greatest event since the making of the world, apart from the incarnation and death of him who created it," a phrase that today rings with more patri-
otism than piety. At the time it was written, however, Church and state seemed
inextricably bound together. The Papacy was a political and military power as well as
a spiritual one; Charles V of Spain united most of Europe under his rule and declared
himself the Holy Roman Emperor; and Henry VIII of England broke with the Catholic
Church and declared himself head of the Church of England. Even movements originally intended to reform the Catholic Church—such as the Reformist movements
associated with Martin Luther (1483–1546), Ulrich Zwingli (1484–1531), and John
Calvin (1509–1564)—were rapidly adopted by Renaissance princes bridling under
papal authority. Given the political force of the Catholic Church and the Protestant
Reformation, it is no wonder that the Renaissance often appears to be more preoccupied with earthly princes and empires than with the heavenly King.

In a similar vein, religious convictions in no way hamper the capacity for Renaissance princes and poets to appreciate sensuous beauty and pleasure. Just as the
sensuous appraisal of a woman's beauties plays a large part in the Song of Songs from
the Hebrew Bible, for example, so Ludovico Ariosto rhapsodically describes the temptress Alcina as

> so beautifully modelled, no painter, however much he applied himself, could
> have achieved anything more perfect. Her long blonde tresses were gathered in
> a knot: pure gold itself could have no finer lustre. Roses and white privet blooms
> lent their colours to suffuse her delicate cheeks. Her serene brow was like pol-
> ished ivory, and in perfect proportion. / Beneath two of the thinnest black arches,
> two dark eyes—or rather, two bright suns; soft was their look, gentle their move-
> ment . . . down the midst of the face, the nose. . . . / Below this, the mouth, set
> between two dimples; it was imbued with native cinnabar. Here a beautiful soft
> pair of lips opened to disclose a double row of choicest pearls. . . . / Snow-white
> was her neck, milky her breast; the neck was round, the breast broad and full.
> A pair of apples, not yet ripe, fashioned in ivory, rose and fell like the sea-swell
> at times when a gentle breeze stirs the ocean. . . . You could easily judge that
> what lay hidden did not fall short of what was exposed to view.

Alcina is, evidently, at once a spiritual experience and "a paradise on earth" to conquer. The loving description of a woman's body often goes hand in glove with the
idea of conquest and world-discovery: when John Donne, for example, finally succeeds in stripping his beloved of all her clothing, he bursts out, "O my America, my
new-found land!"

Much about the religious temper of the age is expressed in its art, particularly in
Italian painting, where Renaissance Madonnas often make it difficult, as the saying
goes, to recite a properly devout Hail Mary—serving as celebrations of earthly beauty
rather than exhortations to contrite thoughts and mystical hopes of salvation. Castiglione in the first pages of the *Courtier* pays homage to the memory of the late lord
of Montefeltro, in whose palace at Urbino the book's personages hold their lofty
debate on the idea of a perfect gentleman (an earlier Montefeltro appears in Dante's
Hell, another in Dante's Purgatory); but Castiglione praises him only for his achievements as a man of arms and a promoter of the arts. There is no thought of either the
salvation or the damnation of his soul (though the general tone of the work would
seem to imply his salvation); he is exalted instead for military victories, and even more
warmly, for having built a splendid palace:

> He built on the rugged site of Urbino a palace thought by many the most beau-
> tiful to be found anywhere in all Italy and he furnished it so well with every
> suitable thing that it seemed not a palace but a city in the form of a palace; and
> furnished it not only with what is customary, such as silver vases, wall hangings
> of the richest cloth of gold, silk, and other like things, but for ornament he added

countless ancient statues of marble and bronze, rare paintings, and musical instruments of every sort; nor did he wish to have anything there that was not most rare and excellent. Then, at great expense, he collected many very excellent and rare books in Greek, Latin, and Hebrew, all of which he adorned with gold and silver, deeming these to be the supreme excellence of his great palace.

The almost legendary Duke Federico defines, through his life's history, the ideal prince as a heroic empire-builder, able to tame "rugged" terrain by force, amass luxurious wealth, and best of all, collect fine arts. The supreme testimony to his heroic virtue is his library of costly and sumptuous volumes, all collected to conserve the wisdom of antiquity and to promote the exchange of ideas at Urbino.

Thus the popular view that associates the idea of the Renaissance especially with the flourishing of the arts is correct. The leaders of the period saw in a work of art the clearest instance of beautiful, harmonious, and self-justified performance. To create such a work became the valuable occupation par excellence, the most satisfactory display of *virtù*. The Renaissance view of antiquity exemplifies this attitude. The artists and intellectuals of the period not only drew on antiquity for certain practices and forms but also found there a recognition of the place of the arts among outstanding modes of human action. In this way, the concepts of "fame" and "glory" became particularly associated with the art of poetry because the Renaissance drew from antiquity the idea of the poet as celebrator of high deeds, the "dispenser of glory."*

There is, then, an important part of the Renaissance mind that sees terrestrial life as positive fulfillment. This is especially clear where there is a close association between the practical and the intellectual, as in the exercise of political power, the act of scientific discovery, the creation of works of art. The Renaissance assumption is that there are things highly worth doing, within a strictly temporal pattern. By doing them, humanity proves its privileged position in Creation and therefore incidentally follows God's intent. The often cited phrase "the dignity of man" describes this positive, strongly affirmed awareness of the intellectual and physical "virtues" of the human being, and of the individual's place in Creation.

It is important, however, to see this fact about the Renaissance in the light of another phenomenon. Where there is a singularly high capacity for feeling the delight of earthly achievement, there is a possibility that its ultimate worth will also be questioned profoundly. What (the Renaissance mind usually seems to ask at some point) is the purpose of all this activity? What meaningful relation does it bear to any all-inclusive, cosmic pattern? The Renaissance coincided with, and perhaps to some extent occasioned, a loss of firm belief in the final unity and the final intelligibility of the universe, such belief as underlies, for example, *The Divine Comedy*, enabling Dante to say in Paradise:

> I saw within Its depth how It conceives
>   all things in a single volume bound by Love,
>   of which the universe is the scattered leaves;
> substance, accident, and their relation
>   so fused that all I say could do no more
>   than yield a glimpse of that bright revelation.

Once the notion of this grand unity of design has lost its authority, certainty about the final value of human actions is no longer to be found. For some minds, indeed, the sense of void becomes so strong as to paralyze all aspiration to power or thirst for knowledge or delight in beauty; the resulting attitude we may call Renaissance melancholy, whether it be openly shown (as by some characters in Elizabethan drama) or provide an undercurrent of sadness, or incite to ironical forms of compromise, to

*And of course, a typical guarantee of memorability was having oneself portrayed—perhaps at various stages in life—by some of the magnificent and highly honored painters of the period.

some sort of wise adjustment (as in Erasmus or Montaigne.) Thus while on one, and perhaps the better-known, side of the picture human intellect in Renaissance literature enthusiastically expatiates over the realms of knowledge and unveils the mysteries of the universe, on the other it is beset by puzzling doubts and a profound mistrust of its own powers.

Doubts about the value of human action within the scheme of eternity did not, however, diminish the outpouring of ideas about the ideal ordering of this world. Renaissance poets and intellectuals turned to the printing press as the means to disseminate and test ideas about the ideal prince, courtier, councilor, and humble subject as well as the ideal court and society. Renaissance epics, such as Ludovico Ariosto's *Orlando Furioso*, use the resources of comedy and tragedy (among other genres) to explore what is gained and lost in achieving that crystallization of the civilizing process, the imperial court. Niccolò Machiavelli turns to print in order to propose his amoral ideas about the effective (rather than ideal) prince; Baldesar Castiglione uses the dialogue form to define and expand the role of the courtier who would serve and, it is hoped, counsel the powerful prince. Other writers shift the focus from the court to the entire commonwealth. Marguerite de Navarre examines the strategies of individuals from the lower classes whose only resource against the abuses of powerful lords and clergymen is their own ingenuity. Lope de Vega transforms the historical case of a peasant uprising against a highly abusive military commander into a play, *Fuente Ovejuna*, which possesses the artistic charm of comedy and the weight of political ethics. Shakespeare's *Othello* investigates the social position—and its tragic consequences—of the title character, a military general, former slave, black man, Christian convert, object of wonder, and outsider in his adopted home of Venice. In all these works of imaginative scope and supreme artistic skill, Renaissance writers can be seen tirelessly examining the nature of their own world, the problem of power, and the vexed relations between the absolute authority of the prince and the rights and liberties of the people. Its zeal for defining the social contract partly explains why the Renaissance is often viewed as the "early modern" period; the "rebirth" and flourishing of antiquity also heralded ideas that we associate with the modern political world.

The joining of philosophical and imaginative thinking in literary expression is characteristic of the Renaissance, which cultivated the idea of "serious play." Throughout the literature of the period, we see the creative and restless mind of the Renaissance intellectual "freely ranging," as Sir Philip Sidney put it, "only in the zodiac of his own wit," creating fictional characters and worlds that might, if the poet is sufficiently persuasive, be put into practice and change the nature of the real world.

FURTHER READING

Richard L. DeMolen, ed., *The Meaning of Renaissance and Reformation* (1974), is a collection of essays by experts on the Renaissance and Reformation, with maps and illustrations. Eugene Rice with Anthony Grafton, *The Foundations of Early Modern Europe*, 2nd ed. (1994), is the finest introduction to the contexts in which Renaissance or early modern literature was produced. William Bouwsma, *A Usable Past: Essays in European Cultural History* (1990), especially the chapter on "Anxiety and the Formation of Early Modern Culture," also offers illuminating perspectives on the intellectual character of the period. Constance Jordan, *Renaissance Feminism: Literary Texts and Political Models* (1990), is a recommended study of the place of women in history and political thought. William Kerrigan and Gordon Braden, *The Idea of the Renaissance* (1989), offers a helpful and direct analysis of the critical construction of the Renaissance as a concept. Harry Berger Jr., *Second World and Green World: Studies in Renaissance Fiction-Making* (1988), especially the title essay, is a dense but recommended study of the aims of fiction-making.

THE RENAISSANCE

TEXTS	CONTEXTS
1335 Petrarch's poems to Laura, including *Sonnets,* underway (published 1360)	
	1338–1453 Hundred Years' War
	1348–1350 The Black Death: Petrarch's Laura dies in the plague
1349–1353 Boccaccio's *Decameron* in progress	
1387–1399 Chaucer's *The Canterbury Tales* in progress; he dies in 1400	
	1428 Joan of Arc liberates Orléans from the British; she is burned at the stake for heresy in 1431
	1453 Constantinople falls to the Turks, increasing dissemination of Greek culture in Western Europe
	1473 Printing comes to Spain
	1474 William Caxton prints the first book in English
	1492 Columbus discovers America • Expulsion of the Jews from Spain • Spanish reconquest of Granada • Expedition of Charles VIII of France
1494 Sebastian Brandt's *Ship of Fools*	
	1502 The "Nuremberg Egg," first portable timepiece
	1503 Leonardo da Vinci paints the *Mona Lisa*
1511 Erasmus's *The Praise of Folly* published	
	1512 Michelangelo completes the Sistine Chapel ceiling
1516 Erasmus's edition of the New Testament of the Bible • First publication of Ariosto's *Orlando Furioso*	
	1517 Luther's Ninety-five Theses denouncing abuses of the Roman Church
	1519 Charles I of Spain becomes Holy Roman Emperor, Charles V
1521 Second edition of *Orlando Furioso*	**1521** Luther is excommunicated
	1524 Francis I is captured in battle against the armies of Charles V

Boldface titles indicate works in the anthology.

THE RENAISSANCE

TEXTS	CONTEXTS
	1527 Rome sacked by the French • Castiglione, now bishop of Avila, is accused of treachery • Marguerite marries Henri d'Albret, king of Navarre
1528 Castiglione's *Book of the Courtier* published; he dies the following year	
1531 Erasmus publishes first complete edition of Aristotle's works	
1532 Rabelais's *Pantagruel* • Machiavelli's *The Prince* • Final publication of *Orlando Furioso*; Ariosto dies the following year	
	1533 Sorbonne accuses Marguerite's chaplain of heresy
1534 Rabelais's *Gargantua*	1534 Henry VIII breaks with Rome and becomes head of the Church of England
1536 John Calvin's *Institutes of the Christian Religion*	
1546 Rabelais's *Third Book*	
	1547 Francis I dies; Henry II accedes to the French throne
1549 Rabelais's *Fourth Book*	1549 England declares war on France
1551 First English translation of More's *Utopia*; More had been executed for high treason by Henry VIII in 1535	
	1555 Tobacco brought to Spain from America for the first time
1558 Marguerite de Navarre's *Heptameron* published	
	1559 Spain's most severe Index of banned books
	1563 Council of Trent concludes
	1571 Spain's battle of Lepanto against the Turks
1571? Montaigne's *Essays* in progress; books 1 and 2 published in 1580; complete publication in 1588	
1581 Tasso's *Jerusalem Delivered*	
	1586 El Greco paints the *Burial of Count Orgaz*
	1588 Spain's Invincible Armada defeated by England

THE RENAISSANCE

TEXTS	CONTEXTS
1590 Sir Philip Sidney's revised *Arcadia*	
1596 Edmund Spenser's *The Faerie Queene* 1–6 plus the "Mutabilitie Cantos"	
1597 Tasso's revised *Jerusalem Conquered*	
1597–1604 Cervantes's ***Don Quixote*** in progress; part 1 was published in 1605, part 2 in 1615	
	1598 Philip II of Spain dies; Philip III crowned • Literary quarrel between Lope de Vega and Luis de Gongora
1603–04 Shakespeare's ***Othello*** appears	
	1608 Dutch scientist Johann Lippershey invents the telescope
1611 King James version of the Bible published	
	1620 Colony founded by Pilgrims at Plymouth, Massachusetts
	1633 Galileo forced by the Inquisition to repudiate Copernican theory that Earth rotates around the sun
1641 René Descartes publishes his *Meditations on First Philosophy*	
	1643–1715 Reign of Louis XIV of France, "the Sun King"
	1645–1649 England's Charles I surrenders to antimonarchical forces of Oliver Cromwell and is executed; monarchy is abolished
1655? Milton's *Paradise Lost* in progress; published 1667	**1655** Velázquez paints *Las Meninas*
	1660 Charles II restores the English monarchy

FRANCIS PETRARCH
1304–1374

Although Petrarch, a contemporary of Dante and Boccaccio, lived and died in the Middle Ages, he did everything in his power to distinguish himself and his scholarship from the period he dismissed as the "Dark Ages." Frustrated with the corruption of scholarly Latin, Petrarch dedicated himself to the recovery of classical learning in a spirit commonly associated with a later period, in which humanist scholars zealously pursued the rebirth of antiquity. If Petrarch can be called a precursor of the Renaissance, it is not for his scholarly output in Latin or his derision of less elegant work. The credit is instead due to an aspect of Petrarch's work that neither he nor his contemporaries regarded as a lasting contribution to letters: Petrarch's 366 lyric poems in the vernacular, mostly dedicated to his frustrated desire for an elusive woman named Laura. Petrarch's art, experience of love, and sense of his own fragmented, fluid, and metamorphic self set the standard for the lyric expression of subjective and erotic experience in the Renaissance. His efforts to scrutinize himself intently and at times unflatteringly and to capture his own elusive inner workings in verse inspired a poetic tradition that has influenced lyric sequences from Shakespeare's sonnets to Walt Whitman's *Leaves of Grass* and to late twentieth-century pop lyrics.

Francesco Petrarca was born in Arezzo on July 20, 1304, three years after his father and Dante Alighieri were exiled from Florence. In 1314, Petrarch's father moved his family to Avignon, the new seat of the papacy (1309–77), where he became prosperous in the legal profession. Petrarch himself trained as a law student for ten years, but chose to pursue the study of classical culture and literature. He soon came to the attention of the powerful Colonna family, whose patronage launched his career as a diplomat-scholar and allowed him to travel widely and move in the intimate circles of European princes and scholars. He conducted diplomatic missions for popes and princes, but refused the offices of bishop and papal secretary, preferring instead to ground his growing prestige in his humanistic scholarship. He did not always manage to protect his scholarly independence from the manipulations of the powerful, such as the tyrannical Visconti family in Milan (as his usually admiring friend Boccaccio remarked). His politics are not easy to decipher: although he served as diplomat for the Visconti at one time, at another he supported the republican dream of the Roman tribune, Cola di Rienzo. Petrarch bequeathed to later humanists the hope that scholar-poets might one day be recognized as shaping forces of the nation-state; in practice, however, he established the humanist scholar's ambiguous position as counselor and exploited servant of powerful princes.

Petrarch expected that he would secure enduring fame through the *Africa,* his unfinished epic poem in Latin hexameters on the life of Scipio Africanus, who embodied the valiant and pious virtues that Petrarch admired in Roman heroism. Of greater importance were Petrarch's manuscript discoveries of Cicero's *Pro Archia* (For Archias), a Roman "defense of poetry," in 1333 and letters to Atticus in 1345. The discovery of Cicero's personal letters to friends inspired Petrarch to compose his own familiar letters, learned, intellectually exploratory, often moving, and profoundly dialogical. Addressed to his many friends and even to the ancients themselves, these letters illustrate how essential the dialogue was to Petrarch as a literary form and as a way of thinking about the past. Imaginative conversation with the ancients, like imitation of their poetry, brought him into volatile contact with the past: his research into classical history and arts profoundly influenced his sense of himself and his own cultural moment. He had discovered how faulty the medieval transmission of classical culture was, with a paradoxical result: he was convinced that he was at the cusp of a classical revival and tragically aware that the classical world was irretrievably lost, that its legacy was its ruins. By learning that the past was foreign and that the scholarly legacy of his own day was faulty, Petrarch discovered a modern sense of alienation. He understood, too, that the dislocations of history affect cultural and individual identity. This awareness ties Petrarch's thought and work to the aspects of the Renaissance that most anticipate modernity. In 1370, Petrarch retired to the Euganean hills at Arquà near Padua, where he lived with his daughter, Francesca (his estranged son, Giovanni, died of the plague in 1361). When Petrarch died on the night of July 18, 1374, his head was resting on an open volume of his beloved Virgil.

Petrarch's most famous work, the *Rime Sparse* (Scattered rhymes) or *Rerum Fragmenta Vulgarium* (Fragments in the vernacular), is a collection of 366 songs and sonnets (based on the calendar year associated with the liturgy) of extraordinary technical virtuosity and variety. Written in Italian and woven into a highly introspective narrative, the lyric collection takes the poet himself as its object of study; the poems painstakingly record how his thoughts and identity are scattered and transformed by the experience of love for a beautiful, unattainable woman named Laura. Even some of his friends suspected that Laura was merely the theme and emblem of his lyric poetry and not a historical woman; she appears to have been both. On the flyleaf of his magnificent copy of Virgil, Petrarch inscribed a note on her life:

> Laura, illustrious through her own virtues, and long famed through my verses, first appeared to my eyes in my youth, in the year of our Lord 1327, on the sixth day of April, in the church of St. Clare in Avignon, at matins; and in the same city, also on the sixth day of April, at the same first hour, but in the year 1348, the light of her life was withdrawn from the light of day, while I, as it chanced, was in Verona, unaware of my fate. * * * Her chaste and lovely form was laid to rest at vesper time, on the same day on which she died in the burial place of the Brothers Minor. I am persuaded that her soul returned to the heaven from which it came, as Seneca says of Africanus. I have thought to write this, in bitter memory, yet with a certain bitter sweetness, here in this place that is often before my eyes, so that I may be admonished, by the sight of these words and by the consideration of the swift flight of time, that there is nothing in this life in which I should find pleasure; and that it is time, now that the strongest tie is broken, to flee from Babylon; and this, by the prevenient grace of God, should be easy for me, if I meditate deeply and manfully on the futile cares, the empty hopes, and the unforeseen events of my past years. (Translated by E. H. Wilkins)

Petrarch's note illuminates the powerful role that Laura plays in his personal struggles between spiritual aspirations and earthly attachments. His thoughts of Laura habitually turn his mind to the problem of his own will, torn between spiritual and sensual desires, always delaying worldly renunciation. Even when he expresses disgust with earthly rewards and pleasures, his habitual ambivalence makes a last-minute entrance in the conditional "if" upon which his renunciation depends: he will choose the right course of action, Petrarch writes, *if* he meditates "deeply and manfully" on the disappointments and failures of his past and denies memory's seductively bittersweet pleasures.

In the *Rime Sparse*, Laura's ambiguous position between divine guide and earthly temptress contrasts sharply with the role that Beatrice played in Dante's spiritual pilgrimage. Whereas Dante's love finally leads him to paradise, it is never clear to Petrarch whether he is pursuing heavenly or earthly delights and whether his amorous and philosophical wanderings will lead him to any destination or "port" (in the nautical image of sonnet 189) at all. When Dante looks into Beatrice's eyes on Mt. Purgatory, he sees a reflection of the heavens; when Petrarch gazes into Laura's eyes, he sees himself. Not even his use of the liturgical year (especially the anniversaries of Christ's death and resurrection) to structure his account of their relationship guarantees that a spiritual conversion will follow Petrarch's self-analysis or "confession" of his life. It might instead represent a trap, as it does in sonnet 211, written on the eleventh anniversary of his first glimpse of Laura: "One thousand three hundred twenty seven, exactly at the first hour of the sixth day of April, I entered the labyrinth, nor do I see where I may get out of it." The image of the labyrinth evokes Petrarch's tortuous experience of love and mental wandering: apparently fresh paths turn into dead ends and avenues already traced in frustration. An allusion to the maze that the mythical Greek artist Daedalus created to contain the Minotaur, Petrarch's labyrinth also suggests that a threat lies at the center of the ingeniously crafted lyric collection. The metaphor of the self-enclosed and secretive labyrinth hints that love of the very classical figures that prompt philosophical discoveries may bar the poet from the less sensually appealing knowledge of Christian truths. For this reason, Dante must finally move beyond the guidance of his beloved Virgil. Petrarch is less confident: in a contrary and skeptical mood at the end of one of his most philosophical poems (song 264), Petrarch asserts, "I see the better, but choose the worse."

A haunting moral presence in the *Rime Sparse* is St. Augustine, who in his *Confessions* describes his conversion under a fig tree. In *The Secret*, his fictional dialogue with Augustine, Petrarch defends his adoration of Laura to an understanding but disapproving Augustine; finally, defeated by the saint who knows his pupil's arts of self-deception, Petrarch confesses that his love of her beauty is idolatrous, not idealistic. The lyric collection's first sonnet, in which Petrarch solicits compassion as well as pardon from his readers, establishes the *Rime Sparse*'s close relationship to confessional narrative. Its themes of conversion, memory, and forgetfulness (of God and oneself) evoke the model of Augustine and raise the question of whether Petrarch will follow suit: will he ultimately transcend his attachment to a woman's physical beauty, his love of language and poetic figures, and his narcissistic preoccupation with himself? In his final poem, a prayer to the Virgin Mary for her intercession, he confesses that "Medusa and my error have made of me a rock [*petra*, a play on his own name] dripping moisture."

The figure Petrarch puts in dramatic opposition to the transcendent model of Augustine is Ovid of the *Metamorphoses,* the classical counterepic that artfully uses fragmentation, fluid change, and scattering as principles of narrative composition and as motifs describing the effects of power—divine, political, or erotic—on bodies and on minds. Petrarch refers to a variety of Ovidian figures in the *Rime Sparse,* including Narcissus and Echo, Actaeon and Diana, Medusa, and Pygmalion. His chief Ovidian model, however, is the story of Apollo, the god who "invents" the genre of lyric during his amorous chase of the nymph Daphne. While running, Apollo describes her various beauties—eyes, figure, and hair—and imaginatively embellishes what he sees. When Daphne eludes him through her transformation into the laurel, Apollo claims her as his tree, if not his lover, and declares that the laurel will be the sign of triumph in letters and warfare.

The prominence of this tale in the *Rime Sparse* suggests that if Laura had not lived, Petrarch would have had to invent her. Her name interweaves key attributes of Petrarch's poetic imagination: *lauro* and *alloro* ("laurel"), *oro* ("gold," for her tresses and value), *l'aura* ("breeze" and "inspiration," which etymologically relates to "breath"), *laus* or *lauda* ("praise"). Such play on words suggests the selective, even obsessive character of Petrarch's poetic style. Like Apollo, Petrarch also "translates" his beloved's elusive body into the more tangible "figures" of rhetoric: her physical attributes reflect the style of his poetry and proclaim his triumphant glory. The Ovidian model poses the threat of the labyrinth, the trap of the artist's own making: the most significant and evocative words limit the poet to ranging within his well-defined obsessions. The Ovidian lover in Petrarch can expect no transcendence, only repeated and uncontrollable metamorphoses of the mind (e.g., despair, hope, ecstasy).

Petrarch's great legacy to Renaissance European literature is the *Rime Sparse*'s language of self-description. He absorbed the conventional use of hyperbole, antithesis, and oxymoron (rhetorical exaggeration and opposition) from troubadour songs, provençal lyric, and classical love elegy: *I freeze and burn, love is bitter and sweet, my sighs are tempests and my tears are floods, I am in ecstasy and agony, I am possessed by memories of her and I am in exile from myself.* Petrarch forged such rhetorical figures or tropes of love into a powerful language of introspection and self-fashioning that swept through European literature. Although it was often faddish and stylized, it had quite serious dimensions that helped articulate growing questions about the self: is it determined by God or flexible and in the shaping hands of men? Do culture, history, and force of will compose and transform it? The beloved does not fare as well: the eloquent expression of the male poet-lover's complex *interior* life depends, as Petrarchan successors noticed, on a correspondingly detailed description of the beloved's *exterior.* In *Paradise Lost,* for example, the angel Raphael chastises Adam for placing Eve's beauty above his own manly reason: "What admir'st thou," the angel chides, "what transports thee so, / An outside?" In the Petrarchan inventory of the beloved's adorable parts, from eyes to hair, cheeks, and hand, the poet converts her living body to ornaments, metal, and minerals, such as gold, topaz, and pearls. Although any one of her beauties is capable of scattering the poet's thoughts, the beloved herself has little independent coherence: as one critic puts it, "some of Laura's parts are greater than her whole person."

Petrarch's distinctive poetic style inspired countless imitations: whether the symptoms are found in a Shakespearean parody ("My mistress' eyes are nothing like the sun," sonnet 130) or in a twentieth-century Motown lyric ("Tracks of My Tears," Smokey Robinson and the Miracles), the lover who dies and is reborn a thousand times a day, who is mentally scattered and physically immobile, and who is never more alone than in a crowd has been tempered in the icy fire of Petrarchan love. He did not invent the idea of a divided, tormented lover, but his authoritative self-portrait defined a poetic tradition inseparable from the figure of Petrarch himself.

Ernest Hatch Wilkins' biography, *Life of Petrarch* (1961), is informative, but tends to take Petrarch's autobiographical writings at face value. In *The Poet as Philosopher* and *In Our Image and Likeness* (1970), Charles Trinkaus provides general studies of Petrarch and humanism. Robert Durling's introduction to *Petrarch's Lyric Poems* (1976) and Leonard Forster's essays in *The Icy Fire: Five Studies in European Petrarchism* (1969) are outstanding introductions to Petrarch's lyric poetry. Indispensable, if specialized, are Giuseppe Mazzotta, *The Worlds of Petrarch* (1993); Leonard Barkan, *The Gods Made Flesh: Metamorphosis and the Pursuit of Paganism* (1986); Thomas M. Greene, *The Light in Troy: Imitation and Discovery in Renaissance Poetry* (1982); Nancy Vickers, "Diana Described: Scattered Woman and Scattered Rhyme," *Writing and Sexual Difference*, ed. Elizabeth Abel (1982): 65–79; John Freccero, "The Fig Tree and the Laurel: Petrarch's Poetics," *Literary Theory / Renaissance Texts*, eds. Patricia Parker and David Quint (1986): 20–32; and Roland Greene, "Petrarchism among the Discourses of Imperialism," *America in European Consciousness, 1493–1750*, ed. Karen Ordahl Kupperman (1995): 130–65. Sara Sturm-Maddox, *Petrarch's Metamorphoses: Text and Subtext in the Rime Sparse* (1985), discusses the relationship of the lyric collection to St. Augustine and to Ovid.

PRONOUNCING GLOSSARY

The following list uses common English syllables and stress accents to provide rough equivalents of selected words whose pronunciation may be unfamiliar to the general reader.

Acheron: *ah'-ker-on*

Aigues Mortes: *eg mort*

Bologna: *bo-lon'-yah*

Dionisio: *dee-oh-nee'-zyoh*

Malaucène: *ma-loh-sen'*

Ventoux: *von-too'*

Letter to Dionisio da Borgo San Sepolcro[1]

[The Ascent of Mount Ventoux]

To-day[2] I made the ascent of the highest mountain in the region, which is not improperly called Ventosum.[3] My only motive was the wish to see what so great an elevation had to offer. I have had the expedition in mind for many years; for as you know, I have lived in this region from infancy, having been cast here by that fate which determines the affairs of men. Consequently the mountain, which is visible from a great distance, was ever before my eyes, and I conceived the plan of some time doing what I have at last accomplished to-day. The idea took hold upon me with especial force when, in re-reading Livy's *History of Rome,* yesterday, I happened upon the place where Philip of Macedon, the same who waged war against the Romans, ascended Mount Haemus in Thessaly, from whose summit he was able, it is said, to see two seas, the Adriatic and the Euxine.[4] Whether this be true or false I have not been able to determine, for the mountain is too far away, and writers disagree. Pomponius Mela, the cosmographer—not to mention others who have spoken of this occurrence—admits its truth without hesitation;[5] Titus Livius, on the other hand, considers it false. I, assuredly, should not have left the question long in doubt, had that mountain been as easy to explore as this one. Let us leave this matter to one side, however, and return to my mountain here,—it seems to me that a young man in private life may well be excused for attempting what an aged king could undertake without arousing criticism.

When I came to look about for a companion I found, strangely enough, that hardly one among my friends seemed suitable, so rarely do we meet with just the right combination of personal tastes and characteristics, even among those who are dearest to us. This one was too apathetic, that one over-anxious; this one too slow, that one too hasty; one was too sad, another over-cheerful; one more simple, another more sagacious, then I desired. I feared this one's taciturnity and that one's loquacity. The heavy deliberation of some repelled me as much as the lean incapacity of others. I rejected those who were likely to irritate me by a cold want of interest, as well as those who might weary me by their excessive enthusiasm. Such defects, however grave, could be borne with at home, for charity suffereth all things, and friendship accepts any burden; but it is quite otherwise on a journey, where every weakness becomes much more serious. So, as I was bent upon pleasure and anxious that my enjoyment should be unalloyed, I looked about me with unusual care, balanced against one another the various characteristics of my friends, and without committing any breach of friendship I silently condemned every trait which might prove disagreeable on the way. And—would you believe

1. Translated by James Harvey Robinson and Henry Winchester Rolfe. Letter 4.1 from *De Rebus Familiaribus.* Dionisio, or Dionigi, da Borgo San Sepolcro was an Augustinian monk whom Petrarch had probably met in Paris in 1333. A learned theologian, he taught at Paris and in 1339 was appointed bishop of Monopoli. He spent the last part of his life in Naples at the court of the learned king Robert d'Anjou and died there in 1342 (Petrarch wrote a verse epistle on his death). 2. April 26. From internal evidence the year should be 1336, ten years after Petrarch left Bologna, but the letter was probably revised and made into an "allegory" at a later date (see n. 8, p. 1669). 3. Windy. Mount Ventoux (six thousand feet) is near Malaucène, not far from Petrarch's home in Vaucluse. 4. Compare Livy's *Roman History* 40.21.2. 5. Pomponius Mela (A.D. first century), Roman geographer of Spanish birth. The passage referred to his *Corographia* 2.17.

it?—I finally turned homeward for aid, and proposed the ascent to my only brother, who is younger than I,[6] and with whom you are well acquainted. He was delighted and gratified beyond measure by the thought of holding the place of a friend as well as of a brother.

At the time fixed we left the house, and by evening reached Malaucène, which lies at the foot of the mountain, to the north. Having rested there a day, we finally made the ascent this morning, with no companions except two servants; and a most difficult task it was. The mountain is a very steep and almost inaccessible mass of stony soil. But, as the poet[7] has well said, "Remorseless toil conquers all." It was a long day, the air fine. We enjoyed the advantages of vigour of mind and strength and agility of body, and everything else essential to those engaged in such an undertaking, and so had no other difficulties to face than those of the region itself. We found an old shepherd in one of the mountain dales, who tried, at great length, to dissuade us from the ascent, saying that some fifty years before he had, in the same ardour of youth, reached the summit, but had gotten for his pains nothing except fatigue and regret, and clothes and body torn by the rocks and briars. No one, so far as he or his companions knew, had ever tried the ascent before or after him. But his counsels increased rather than diminished our desire to proceed, since youth is suspicious of warnings. So the old man, finding that his efforts were in vain, went a little way with us, and pointed out a rough path among the rocks, uttering many admonitions, which he continued to send after us even after we had left him behind. Surrendering to him all such garments or other possessions as might prove burdensome to us, we made ready for the ascent, and started off at a good pace. But, as usually happens, fatigue quickly followed upon our excessive exertion, and we soon came to a halt at the top of a certain cliff. Upon starting on again we went more slowly, and I especially advanced along the rocky way with a more deliberate step. While my brother chose a direct path straight up the ridge,[8] I weakly took an easier one which really descended. When I was called back, and the right road was shown me, I replied that I hoped to find a better way round on the other side, and that I did not mind going farther if the path were only less steep. This was just an excuse for my laziness; and when the others had already reached a considerable height I was still wandering in the valleys. I had failed to find an easier path, and had only increased the distance and difficulty of the ascent. At last I became disgusted with the intricate way I had chosen, and resolved to ascend without more ado. When I reached my brother, who, while waiting for me, had had ample opportunity for rest, I was tired and irritated. We walked along together for a time, but hardly had we passed the first spur when I forgot about the circuitous route which I had just tried, and took a lower one again. Once more I followed an easy, roundabout path through winding valleys, only to find myself soon in my old difficulty. I was simply trying to avoid the exertion of the ascent; but no human ingenuity can alter the nature of things, or cause anything to reach a height by going down. Suffice it to say that, much to my vexation and my brother's amusement, I made this same mistake three times or more during a few hours.

6. Gherardo, who was about three years younger.   7. Virgil in *Georgics* 1.145–46.   8. In the allegorical reading of the letter, this could be an allusion to Gherardo achieving God and salvation more directly (he became a monk in 1342, retiring into the monastery of Montrieux).

After being frequently misled in this way, I finally sat down in a valley and transferred my winged thoughts from things corporeal to the immaterial, addressing myself as follows:—"What thou hast repeatedly experienced to-day in the ascent of this mountain, happens to thee, as to many, in the journey toward the blessed life. But this is not so readily perceived by men, since the motions of the body are obvious and external while those of the soul are invisible and hidden. Yes, the life which we call blessed is to be sought for on a high eminence, and strait is the way that leads to it. Many, also, are the hills that lie between, and we must ascend, by a glorious stair-way, from strength to strength. At the top is at once the end of our struggles and the goal for which we are bound. All wish to reach this goal, but, as Ovid says, 'To wish is little; we must long with the utmost eagerness to gain our end.'[9] Thou certainly dost ardently desire, as well as simply wish, unless thou deceivest thyself in this matter, as in so many others. What, then, doth hold thee back? Nothing, assuredly, except that thou wouldst take a path which seems, at first thought, more easy, leading through low and worldly pleasures. But nevertheless in the end, after long wanderings, thou must perforce either climb the steeper path, under the burden of tasks foolishly deferred, to its blessed culmination, or lie down in the valley of thy sins, and (I shudder to think of it!), if the shadow of death overtake thee, spend an eternal night amid constant torments." These thoughts stimulated both body and mind in a wonderful degree for facing the difficulties which yet remained. Oh, that I might traverse in spirit that other road for which I long day and night, even as to-day I overcame material obstacles by my bodily exertions! And I know not why it should not be far easier, since the swift immortal soul can reach its goal in the twinkling of an eye, without passing through space, while my progress to-day was necessarily slow, dependent as I was upon a failing body weighed down by heavy members.

One peak of the mountain, the highest of all, the country people call "Sonny," why, I do not know, unless by antiphrasis,[1] as I have sometimes suspected in other instances; for the peak in question would seem to be the father of all the surrounding ones. On its top is a little level place, and here we could at least rest our tired bodies.

Now, my father, since you have followed the thoughts that spurred me on in my ascent, listen to the rest of the story, and devote one hour, I pray you, to reviewing the experiences of my entire day. At first, owing to the unaccustomed quality of the air and the effect of the great sweep of view spread out before me, I stood like one dazed. I beheld the clouds under our feet, and what I had read of Athos and Olympus seemed less incredible as I myself witnessed the same things from a mountain of less fame. I turned my eyes toward Italy, wither my heart most inclined. The Alps, rugged and snow-capped, seemed to rise close by, although they were really at a great distance; the very same Alps through which that fierce enemy of the Roman name once made his way, bursting the rocks, if we may believe the report, by the application of vinegar. I sighed, I must confess, for the skies of Italy, which I beheld rather with my mind than with my eyes. An inexpressible longing came over me to see once more my friend and my country. At the same time I reproached myself for this double weakness, springing, as it did, from a

<hr/>

9. *Ex Ponto* 3.1.35. 1. The rhetorical use of a word in a sense opposite to its actual meaning.

soul not yet steeled to manly resistance. And yet there were excuses for both of these cravings, and a number of distinguished writers might be summoned to support me.

Then a new idea took possession of me, and I shifted my thoughts to a consideration of time rather than place. "To-day it is ten years since, having completed thy youthful studies, thou didst leave Bologna. Eternal God! In the name of immutable wisdom, think what alterations in thy character this intervening period has beheld! I pass over a thousand instances. I am not yet in a safe harbour where I can calmly recall past storms. The time may come when I can review in due order all the experiences of the past, saying with St. Augustine, 'I desire to recall my foul actions and the carnal corruption of my soul, not because I love them, but that I may the more love thee, O my God.'[2] Much that is doubtful and evil still clings to me, but what I once loved, that I love no longer. And yet what am I saying? I still love it, but with shame, but with heaviness of heart. Now, at last, I have confessed the truth. So it is. I love, but love what I would not love, what I would that I might hate. Though loath to do so, though constrained, though sad and sorrowing, still I do love, and I feel in my miserable self the truth of the well known words, 'I will hate if I can; if not, I will love against my will.'[3] Three years have not yet passed since that perverse and wicked passion which had a firm grasp upon me and held undisputed sway in my heart began to discover a rebellious opponent, who was unwilling longer to yield obedience. These two adversaries have joined in close combat for the supremacy, and for a long time now a harassing and doubtful war has been waged in the field of my thoughts."

Thus I turned over the last ten years in my mind, and then, fixing my anxious gaze on the future, I asked myself, "If, perchance, thou shouldst prolong this uncertain life of thine for yet two lustres, and shouldst make an advance toward virtue proportionate to the distance to which thou hast departed from thine original infatuation during the past two years, since the new longing first encountered the old, couldst thou, on reaching thy fortieth year, face death, if not with complete assurance, at least with hopefulness, calmly dismissing from thy thoughts the residuum of life as it faded into old age?"

These and similar reflections occurred to me, my father. I rejoiced in my progress, mourned my weaknesses, and commiserated the universal instability of human conduct. I had well-nigh forgotten where I was and our object in coming; but at last I dismissed my anxieties, which were better suited to other surroundings, and resolved to look about me and see what we had come to see. The sinking sun and the lengthening shadows of the mountain were already warning us that the time was near at hand when we must go. As if suddenly wakened from sleep, I turned about and gazed toward the west. I was unable to discern the summits of the Pyrenees, which form the barrier between France and Spain; not because of any intervening obstacle that I know of but owing simply to the insufficiency of our mortal vision. But I could see with the utmost clearness, off to the right, the mountains of the region about Lyons, and to the left the bay of Marseilles and the waters that lash the shores of Aigues Mortes, altho' all these places were so distant that

2. *Confessions* 2.1.1.   3. Ovid's *Amores* 3.2.35.

it would require a journey of several days to reach them. Under our very eyes flowed the Rhone.

While I was thus dividing my thoughts, now turning my attention to some terrestial object that lay before me, now raising my soul, as I had done my body, to higher planes, it occurred to me to look into my copy of St. Augustine's *Confessions,* a gift that I owe to your love, and that I always have about me, in memory of both the author and the giver. I opened the compact little volume, small indeed in size, but of infinite charm, with the intention of reading whatever came to hand, for I could happen upon nothing that would be otherwise than edifying and devout. Now it chanced that the tenth book presented itself. My brother, waiting to hear something of St. Augustine's from my lips, stood attentively by. I call him, and God too, to witness that where I first fixed my eyes it was written: "And men go about to wonder at the heights of the mountains, and the mighty waves of the sea, and the wide sweep of rivers, and the circuit of the ocean, and the revolution of the stars, but themselves they consider not."[4] I was abashed, and asking my brother (who was anxious to hear more), not to annoy me, I closed the book, angry with myself that I should still be admiring earthly things who might long ago have learned from even the pagan philosophers that nothing is wonderful but the soul, which, when great itself, finds nothing great outside itself. Then, in truth, I was satisfied that I had seen enough of the mountain; I turned my inward eye upon myself, and from that time not a syllable fell from my lips until we had reached the bottom again. Those words had given me occupation enough, for I could not believe that it was by a mere accident that I happened upon them. What I had there read I believed to be addressed to me and to no other, remembering that St. Augustine had once suspected the same thing in his own case, when, on opening the book of the Apostle, as he himself tells us,[5] the first words that he saw there were, "Not in rioting and drunkenness, not in chambering and wantonness, not in strife and envying. But put ye on the Lord Jesus Christ, and make not provision for the flesh, to fulfil the lusts thereof."[6]

The same thing happened earlier to St. Anthony, when he was listening to the Gospel where it is written, "If thou wilt be perfect, go and sell that thou hast, and give to the poor, and thou shalt have treasure in heaven: and come and follow me."[7] Believing this scripture to have been read for his especial benefit, as his biographer Athanasius[8] says, he guided himself by its aid to the Kingdom of Heaven. And as Anthony on hearing these words waited for nothing more, and as Augustine upon reading the Apostle's admonition sought no farther, so I concluded my reading in the few words which I have given. I thought in silence of the lack of good counsel in us mortals, who neglect what is noblest in ourselves, scatter our energies in all directions, and waste ourselves in a vain show, because we look about us for what is to be found only within. I wondered at the natural nobility of our soul, save when it debases itself of its own free will, and deserts its original estate, turning what God has given it for its honour into dishonour. How many times, think you, did I turn back that day, to glance at the summit of the mountain, which seemed scarcely a cubit high compared with the range of

---

4. *Confessions* 10.8.15.   5. *Confessions* 8.12.29.   6. Romans 13.13–14.   7. Matthew 19.21.
8. A saint and doctor of the Church (ca. 295–373), in his *Vita Antonii* 2.

human contemplation,—when it is not immersed in the foul mire of earth? With every downward step I asked myself this: If we are ready to endure a little nearer heaven, how can a soul struggling toward God, up the steeps of human pride and human destiny, fear any cross or prison or sting of fortune? How few, I thought, but are diverted from their path by the fear of difficulties or the love of ease! How happy the lot of those few, if any such there be! It is to them, assuredly, that the poet was thinking, when he wrote:

> Happy the man who is skilled to understand
> Nature's hid causes; who beneath his feet
> All terrors casts, and death's relentless doom,
> And the loud roar of greedy Acheron.[9]

How earnestly should we strive, not to stand on mountain-tops, but to trample beneath us those appetites which spring from earthy impulses.

With no consciousness of the difficulties of the way, amidst these preoccupations which I have so frankly revealed, we came, long after dark, but with the full moon lending us its friendly light, to the little inn which we had left that morning before dawn. The time during which the servants have been occupied in preparing our supper, I have spent in a secluded part of the house, hurriedly jotting down these experiences on the spur of the moment, lest, in case my task were postponed, my mood should change on leaving the place, and so my interest in writing flag.

You will see, my dearest father, that I wish nothing to be concealed from you, for I am careful to describe to you not only my life in general but even my individual reflections. And I beseech you, in turn, to pray that these vague and wandering thoughts of mine may some time become firmly fixed, and, after having been vainly tossed about from one interest to another, may direct themselves at last toward the single, true, certain, and everlasting good.

MALAUCÈNE, April 26.

SONNETS

1[1]

You who hear in scattered rhymes the sound of those sighs with
which I nourished my heart during my first youthful error,[2] when
I was in part another man from what I am now:

for the varied style in which I weep and speak between vain
hopes and vain sorrow, where there is anyone who understands   5
love through experience, I hope to find pity, not only pardon.

---

9. Virgil's *Georgics* 2.490–92.   1. Translated by Robert M. Durling.   2. Mental and physical "wandering" as well as a moral "mistake." The *scattered rhymes* refer to the sonnet collection's title, *Rime Sparse*.

But now I see well how for a long time I was the talk of the crowd, for which often I am ashamed of myself within;[3]

and of my raving, shame is the fruit, and repentance, and the clear knowledge that whatever pleases in the world is a brief dream.   10

3[4]

It was the day when the sun's rays turned pale with grief for his Maker[5] when I was taken, and I did not defend myself against it, for your lovely eyes, Lady, bound me.

It did not seem to me a time for being on guard against Love's blows; therefore I went confident and without fear, and so my   5
misfortunes began in the midst of the universal woe.[6]

Love found me altogether disarmed, and the way open through my eyes to my heart, my eyes which are now the portal and passageway of tears.

Therefore, as it seems to me, it got him no honor to strike me   10
with an arrow in that state,[7] and not even to show his bow to you, who were armed.

34[8]

Apollo, if the sweet desire is still alive that inflamed you beside the Thessalian waves,[9] and if you have not forgotten, with the turning of the years, those beloved blond locks;

against the slow frost and the harsh and cruel time that lasts as long as your face is hidden, now defend the honored and holy   5
leaves where you first and then I were limed;

and by the power of the amorous hope that sustained you in your bitter life, disencumber the air of these impressions.[1]

Thus we shall then together see a marvel[2]—our lady sitting on the grass and with her arms making a shade for herself.   10

3. The Italian, *di me medesmo meco mi vergogno*, suggests intense self-consciousness.   4. Translated by Robert M. Durling.   5. The anniversary of Christ's crucifixion. Elsewhere (sonnet 211 and a note in Petrarch's copy of Virgil) given as April 6, 1327.   6. The communal Christian grief that contrasts with Petrarch's private woes.   7. State of grief over the crucifixion.   8. Translated by Robert M. Durling.   9. Petrarch links his love of Laura to the love of Apollo for Daphne in Ovid's *Metamorphoses*. Daphne, daughter of the god of the Peneus River in Thessaly, was pursued by Apollo, the god of poetry. She begged her father to change her form, which had "given too much pleasure," and was transformed into the laurel tree. Apollo, whom Petrarch associates with the sun god, claimed the laurel as his personal emblem.   1. Grief, cloudy weather, and aging.   2. Supernatural and highly meaningful spectacle.

61³

Blest be the day, and blest the month and year,
Season and hour⁴ and very moment blest,
The lovely land and place⁵ where first possessed
By two pure eyes I found me prisoner;

And blest the first sweet pain, the first most dear,   5
Which burnt my heart when Love came in as guest;
And blest the bow, the shafts which shook my breast,
And even the wounds which Love delivered there.

Blest be the words and voices which filled grove
And glen with echoes of my lady's name;   10
The sighs, the tears, the fierce despair of love;

And blest the sonnet-sources of my fame;
And blest that thought of thoughts which is her own,
Of her, her only, of herself alone!

62⁶

Father in heaven, after each lost day,
Each night spent raving with that fierce desire
Which in my heart has kindled into fire
Seeing your acts adorned for my dismay;

Grant henceforth that I turn, within your light⁷   5
To another life and deeds more truly fair,
So having spread to no avail the snare
My bitter foe⁸ might hold it in despite.

The eleventh year,⁹ my Lord, has now come round
Since I was yoked beneath the heavy trace   10
That on the meekest weighs most cruelly.

Pity the abject plight where I am found;
Return my straying thoughts to a nobler place;
Show them this day you were on Calvary.

78¹

When Simon² received the high idea which, for my sake, put his
hand to his stylus, if he had given to his noble work voice and
intellect along with form

3. Translated by Joseph Auslander.   4. Sunrise; April 6, 1327; spring.   5. The Church of Saint
Clare at Avignon.   6. Translated by Bernard Bergonzi.   7. Of grace.   8. Satan.   9. I.e., 1338.
1. Translated by Robert M. Durling.   2. Simone Martini (active 1315–44), a Sienese painter who lived
in Avignon during the last years of his life. His painting of Laura is the subject of the poem.

he would have lightened my breast of many sighs that make
what others prize most vile to me. For in appearance she seems   5
humble, and her expression promises peace;

then, when I come to speak to her, she seems to listen most
kindly: if she could only reply to my words!

Pygmalion,[3] how glad you should be of your statue, since you
received a thousand times what I yearn to have just once!   10

90[4]

She used to let her golden hair fly free
For the wind to toy and tangle and molest;
Her eyes were brighter than the radiant west.
(Seldom they shine so now.) I used to see

Pity look out of those deep eyes on me.   5
("It was false pity," you would now protest.)
I had love's tinder heaped within my breast;
What wonder that the flame burned furiously?

She did not walk in any mortal way,[5]
But with angelic progress; when she spoke,   10
Unearthly voices sang in unison.

She seemed divine among the dreary folk
Of earth. You say she is not so today?
Well, though the bow's unbent, the wound bleeds on.

126[6]

Clear, fresh, sweet waters,[7] where she who alone seems lady
to me rested her lovely body,
   gentle branch where it pleased her (with sighing I remember)
to make a column for her lovely side,
   grass and flowers that her rich garment covered along with   5
her angelic breast, sacred bright air where Love opened my heart
with her lovely eyes: listen all together to my sorrowful dying
words.

   If it is indeed my destiny and Heaven exerts itself that Love
close these eyes while they are still weeping,   10

---

3. Sculptor, from Ovid's *Metamorphoses* 10, who fell in love with his own ivory statue, which Venus brought
to life. Whereas Ovid's Pygmalion enjoys a thousand physical embraces, Petrarch yearns only for a reply to
his words, or poem.   **4.** Translated by Morris Bishop.   **5.** Like Venus in book 1 of Virgil's *Aeneid*,
when the goddess of love appears to Aeneas in the guise of a Spartan huntress. The image of Venus armed
conjured up an ideal synthesis of eroticism and chastity in the Renaissance.   **6.** Translated by Robert
M. Durling.   **7.** Of the river Sorgue.

let some grace bury my poor body among you and let my soul
return naked to this its own dwelling;
    death will be less harsh if I bear this hope to the fearful pass,
for my weary spirit could never in a more restful port or a more
tranquil grave flee my laboring flesh and my bones.   15

    There will come a time perhaps when to her accustomed
sojourn the lovely, gentle wild one will return
    and, seeking me, turn her desirous and happy eyes toward
where she saw me on that blessed day,
    and oh the pity! seeing me already dust amid the stones,   20
Love will inspire her to sigh so sweetly that she will win mercy
for me and force Heaven, drying her eyes with her lovely veil.

    From the lovely branches was descending (sweet in
memory) a rain of flowers over her bosom,
    and she was sitting humble in such a glory,[8] already covered   25
with the loving cloud;
    this flower was falling on her skirt, this one on her blond
braids, which were burnished gold and pearls to see that day;
this one was coming to rest on the ground, this one on the water,
this one, with a lovely wandering, turning about seemed to say: 30
"Here reigns Love."[9]

    How many times did I say to myself then, full of awe: "She was
surely born in Paradise!"
    Her divine bearing and her face and her words and her sweet
smile had so laden me with forgetfulness   35
    and so divided me from the true image, that I was sighing:
"How did I come here and when?" thinking I was in Heaven, not
there where I was. From then on this grass has pleased me so that
elsewhere I have no peace.

    If you had as many beauties as you have desire, you could   40
boldly leave the wood and go among people.[1]

189[2]

My ship laden with forgetfulness passes through a harsh sea, at
midnight, in winter, between Scylla and Charybdis, and at the
tiller sits my lord, rather my enemy;[3]

each oar is manned by a ready, cruel thought that seems to scorn
the tempest and the end; a wet, changeless wind of sighs, hopes,   5
and desires breaks the sail;

8. An image associated with the Virgin Mary.   9. Amor (Cupid) or Christ. The floral and bejeweled
images associate Laura's body with the bride of the Song of Songs, whose erotic chastity is celebrated
as an "enclosed garden" and "fountain sealed."   1. The last two lines are addressed to the
poem.   2. Translated by Robert M. Durling.   3. Love. Scylla and Charybdis are the twinned oceanic
dangers through which Odysseus, in Homer's *Odyssey*, and Aeneas, in Virgil's *Aeneid*, must chart a middle
course. Forgetfulness of oneself and of God is sinful in Augustinian terms. The ship, captained by Reason,
is a traditional figure for the embodied soul.

a rain of weeping, a mist of disdain wet and loosen the already
weary ropes, made of error twisted up with ignorance.

My two usual sweet stars[4] are hidden; dead among the waves are
reason and skill; so that I begin to despair of the port.   10

333[5]

Go, grieving rimes of mine, to that hard stone
Whereunder lies my darling, lies my dear,
And cry to her to speak from heaven's sphere.
Her mortal part with grass is overgrown.

Tell her, I'm sick of living; that I'm blown   5
By winds of grief from the course I ought to steer,
That praise of her is all my purpose here
And all my business; that of her alone

Do I go telling, that how she lived and died
And lives again in immortality,   10
All men may know, and love my Laura's grace.

Oh, may she deign to stand at my bedside
When I come to die; and may she call to me
And draw me to her in the blessèd place!

4. Laura's eyes.   5. Translated by Morris Bishop.

DESIDERIUS ERASMUS
1466?–1536

The importance of the scholarly model set by Desiderius Erasmus for the Christian
humanists of the later Renaissance can hardly be exaggerated. To this day, Erasmus
remains an ideal of the teacher-scholar: wise, experienced, and prodigiously learned,
yet personally modest, forbearing, and affectionate. His image as the Socrates of
Christian humanism is one that Erasmus himself had a hand in fashioning. If he
hoped for lasting influence over the conduct of intellectual labor, Erasmus knew, it
was not enough to draft treatises on moral behavior and annotate editions of important texts. He had to craft a persuasive persona for the new scholar (himself) that
would impart to the humanist enterprise the intellectual principle he most admired:
tireless, curious, nondogmatic pursuit of enlightenment over received wisdom.

His voluminous writings include such monumental works as *Adages* (sayings collected from classical sources), the popular *Handbook of the Christian Soldier* and
Education of a Christian Prince, and important editions of the New Testament and
collected works of St. Jerome. His most enduring work, however, is *The Praise of
Folly*, a mock assault on wisdom and a celebration of the mind in hedonistic play. Its
popularity is due partly to its dramatic and elegant literary form, partly to the fact

that it deals in a moderate and humorous way with concerns central to the intellectually ambitious Renaissance: the power (and arrogance) of the human intellect, the worth (and futility) of knowledge, and above all the folly (and wisdom) of human behavior. *The Praise of Folly* defines the Renaissance art of "serious play": the diverting exploration of philosophical and moral questions that were seen as essential both to the cultivation of erudition and to the direction of everyday life.

Erasmus was born at Rotterdam, probably in 1466. As a youth, he studied first at Gouda and then at Deventer until the deaths of his parents, when he and his brother, Peter, were urged by their guardians to enter into the monastic life. Erasmus, who had hoped for a university education, reluctantly joined the Augustinian canons at Steyn and was ordained in 1492. He gained the bishop's consent in 1495 to leave the monastery for Paris and the most famous of all universities. At the University of Paris, he became the tutor of William Blount, Lord Mountjoy, who arranged for Erasmus to visit England in 1499–1500. There he befriended Sir Thomas More and John Colet, who both profoundly influenced Erasmus's intellectual life. Colet, a passionate student of religion, turned Erasmus's mind from exclusively literary and classical interests to theological scholarship. Colet inspired in Erasmus a new dedication to religious morals (which culminated in his popular *Handbook of the Christian Soldier* of 1504) and scholarship: at a time when Greek was largely forgotten, Erasmus labored to teach himself Greek in order to study the New Testament in its original language.

Throughout his scholarly career, Erasmus had to search constantly for patronage to support his research and travels. He visited England again in 1505–06 and met the archbishop of Canterbury, William Warham, and influential members of the court. As tutor to the son of Henry VII's Italian physician (Giovanni Battista Boerio), he visited Italy, the original home of the humanist studies to which Erasmus devoted himself. He stayed at the Universities of Turin (where he received a doctorate of theology) and Bologna; he also visited Padua, Florence, Rome, and Venice, where he befriended Aldus Manutius, the great humanistic printer. He returned to England in 1509, following the coronation of Henry VIII, from whom Erasmus had hopes of financial support for his scholarly work. During his five-year stay, he lectured in Greek and divinity at Cambridge University and worked to edit, translate, and annotate the Greek New Testament. England lost its charms for Erasmus in 1514, however, when the country was swept up in a militaristic fervor following English victories over France and Scotland. Erasmus traveled to Basel, where he took his publishing ventures to a new level: he not only worked but lived in the publishing house of Johannes Froben, who produced Erasmus's editions of Jerome and the New Testament in 1516. This period of his life brings us the now familiar image of Erasmus, surrounded by disciples and the bustle of the printing house, producing some of his most demanding and influential work. His scholarly stature was recognized when he was made a councilor of the young Charles V, a post that prompted Erasmus to write his *Education of a Christian Prince*.

Despite his success, Erasmus found himself increasingly at odds with traditional Catholic scholars, who recognized that his editions of the New Testament and Jerome implicitly challenged the authority of the Church. His work also drew the favorable notice of Martin Luther, whose reformist zeal inspired both sympathy and anxiety in Erasmus. In October 1517, in the hope of generating debate about the system of papal indulgences, Luther nailed his Ninety-five Theses to the Castle Church door in Wittenberg. Erasmus at first hoped to negotiate a peaceful compromise between the Protestant reformers and the Catholic conservatives, but the differences between his temperament and intellectual qualities and those of Luther were ultimately insuperable. Shaking all Europe, Luther rejected the highest ecclesiastical authority, a challenge he summed up in his famous declaration "Here I stand." Erasmus, on the other hand, chose to explore all dimensions of intellectual problems. An old anecdote has it that Luther, annoyed at Erasmus's refusal to side with or against the reformers, demanded, "Where do you stand?" to which Erasmus responded, "I stand *here*. And here. And here." Reluctantly, Erasmus finally took issue with Luther in print. Their exchange, which focused on the necessity of free will (Erasmus) and God's uncircumscribed majesty (Luther), was bitter and led to their decisive break. Despite Erasmus's efforts to affirm his Christian faith and to seek peaceful reform, many of his works, including *The Praise of Folly*, were enrolled in the notorious Index of books banned by the Church. A victim of diatribes, he ruefully compared himself to Saint Cassianus, whose pupils stabbed him to death with their pencils. (Long after his death, such images of persecution became reality for Erasmian Christians in Spain, who were targets of Counter-Reformation persecution.) In 1535 Erasmus received the devastating news of Sir Thomas More's execution, and on July 12, 1536, following an illness, he died in Freiburg.

While crossing the Alps on his third visit to England, Erasmus conceived *The Praise of Folly*, his celebrated investigation of the relationship between wisdom and folly. He drafted the work at the home of Sir Thomas More, who inspired the work's playful style and serious theme (More's name, Erasmus noted gleefully, means "fool," *mora*). His speaker—a witty, sophistic, and ingratiating entertainer—is the feminine embodiment of Folly. The work opens dramatically when Folly appears and congratulates herself on her warm reception: "you immediately brightened up . . . and greeted me with happy congenial laughter—so much so that every last one of you here before me, wherever I look, seems to be high on the nectar of the Homeric gods." Having set the stage for the work's dramatic form, Folly begins her lecture, sermon, or comic monologue—she is equally at home at the lectern, behind the pulpit, or on the stage. Her subject is herself—particularly, her beneficent influence on the otherwise joyless lives human beings are condemned to lead. She remarks, in amazement, that no one has ever thought to deliver an oration on folly, although many have "spent sleepless nights burning the midnight oil to work out elaborate encomia [praiseful tributes]" to tyrants, the fever, flies, and baldness. Folly thus draws attention to the link between Erasmus's genre and the tradition of mock praise developed by Greek and Roman orators. Unlike the subjects chosen by classical orators for mock praise, folly turns out not to be utterly disagreeable: folly is pleasurable (a point on which Folly dwells at length) and cannot be eradicated even from the wisest person.

The major theme of Folly's three-part oration is that we owe all our joys to illusions, without which life would be unbearable. The Stoics are the chief targets of her satire in the first part of her speech. Such philosophers ignore the blessings of life: they pride themselves on their indifference to joy and pleasure (as well as pain), and lead their lives as an extended renunciation of life itself. When Folly points out that the wisdom of the Stoics imprisons rather than liberates, her perspective is "not altogether fool," as one of Shakespeare's characters remarks of King Lear's Fool. In the rhythm of Erasmus's text, Folly habitually mounts compelling arguments in favor of folly only to conclude them with classical quotations, lifted out of context, that undermine her own position. After demolishing the Stoics, for example, she borrows an improbable line from Sophocles: "Not to think, that is the good life." The great paradox of Erasmus's text is that Folly is both the object and source of praise, and her oration both celebrates and exposes its speaker's foolishness. In effect, Erasmus plays out an elaborate and sophisticated version of the liar's paradox beloved of Renaissance humanists: "All Cretans are liars. I am a Cretan." Like the (lying?) Cretan of the paradox, Folly cheerfully destabilizes our grounds for knowledge and judgment.

In the second part of Folly's speech, Erasmus turns to the abuse of power by religious and political authorities. In this section, Erasmus's own reformist voice often breaks through the fiction of Folly's self-presentation. The responsibilities of political and ecclesiastical office are heavy, Folly maintains, and were it not for her influence, no one would undertake such joyless work. When she describes the specific vices of administrators of the Church and State, she adopts a comically nonjudgmental approach: "Popes, however diligent in harvesting money, delegate their excessively apostolic labors to the bishops, the bishops to the pastors, the pastors to their vicars, the vicars to the mendicant friars, and they too foist off their charge on those who shear the fleece of the flock." Erasmus's satire of corruption is more heavy-handed than usual but still leavened with subtle touches: the images of harvest and sheep-shearing conjure up a lively sense of the victims—sheeplike manual laborers—and the predators, who have turned their pastoral care into the exploitation of an intricately organized financial enterprise.

The third and most radical part of her speech elaborates the assertion of the Apostle Paul that Christian evangelists, who neglect worldly interest and reputation, are "fools for Christ" (1 Corinthians 4.9–10). Folly regards this contingent of her following with wonder:

> they throw away their possessions, ignore injuries, allow themselves to be deceived, make no distinction between friend and foe, shudder at the thought of pleasure, find satisfaction in fasts, vigils, tears, and labors, shrink from life, desire death above all else—in short, they seem completely devoid of normal human responses, just as if their minds were living somewhere else, not in their bodies.

For Erasmus's Christian audiences, the responses to Folly's account of ideal Christian behavior could be legion: laughter at her ironic portrait of virtue; worry that self-negation seems possible only to Christians who reject the world; admiration for Folly's dexterous ability to cite and twist her authorities; revelation at the religious ecstasy she succinctly describes; and loss of equilibrium as they sway between the evangelical authorities she cites and her own exuberant, destabilizing text. Nowhere does Erasmus more radically question the sources and authorities with which people justify their actions.

Folly's goal throughout is to confuse the relationship between forms (religious, literary, or social) and their customary significances. At the end of her speech, she notices that her audience is waiting for a summary explanation. Instead of providing one, she facetiously asserts that she has no idea what she has just said and therefore has no epilogue—and she warmly recommends forgetfulness to her audience, too. An oration's epilogue, as Folly knows, encourages listeners to imitate the virtues singled out for praise. Folly, however, refuses to propose any relationship at all between her audience and her subject. To emulate Folly, evidently, we need only disregard the paradoxes she has unfolded and attempt no self-reform.

Understanding the structure of *The Praise of Folly* does not, of course, explain why Erasmus pursued reformist goals in a literary frolic. The spirit of fun that permeates *The Praise of Folly* comes from the popular tradition that flourished around the figure of the fool, dressed in cap and bells and carrying a bauble. Fools, who were figures of serious cultural play, presided over the popular carnivalesque festivities that took place during the liturgical year (e.g., May Day, Whitsuntide, Halloween, and Christmastide). During the festivals, common people and lower clergy were temporarily liberated from fixed social and ecclesiastical hierarchies: women were "on top" and from the ranks of servants people elected their Lord of Misrule. In the Feast of Fools, the lower clergy elected a bishop or even a pope of fools to lead a raucous parody of the ecclesiastical service. The French *sociétés joyeuses* ("joyous societies") featured a mock sermon on the life of a "saint" (e.g., St. Onion) and joked about love, women, and marriage, as well as taverns and drinkers.

The religious and political authorities of Erasmus's day were divided in their sense of the relationship between saturnalian rituals and civic order. The festivities were actively discouraged by the Church but generally tolerated by the Crown. The raucous play of saturnalian rituals seemed conservative to some and subversive to others: were the lower classes "letting off steam" or building up tensions destined to explode in rebellion? Like the ambiguous saturnalian rituals, Folly's performance and Erasmus's text are exuberant, recreative, and ambivalent about moral proprieties.

The figure of the fool also shielded Erasmus from a backlash against his biting social criticisms. Court fools, who lived in the palaces of kings and households of noblemen, enjoyed unique privileges: one of the most famous was Henry VIII's beloved Archie Armstrong, who not only joked, sang, and conversed with the king but also challenged his sovereign. The court fool might appeal to the king's magnanimity when he wished to invoke his royal prerogatives or felt disinclined to hear the concerns of the common people. Only the "all-licensed Fool," as Shakespeare calls him in *King Lear,* has the liberty to mock the king to his face and implicitly correct his abuses of power. It is to the fool's license that Erasmus refers in a public letter to a critic of the *Folly:* "Even the most savage tyrants put up with their buffoons and court fools, who sometimes taunt their masters with open insults." The prudent response to parody, he continues, is to laugh and admit or dissemble one's own faults. Erasmus makes his own radical aims when he appeals to the idea of the licensed fool in order to defend his text as innocuous. If his readers assume the privilege of fools, they will learn to challenge the arbitrary exercise of authority: this is the inspiring message that Erasmus has underscored throughout Folly's oration.

Lisa Jardine, *Erasmus, Man of Letters: The Construction of Charisma in Print* (1993), offers a stimulating analysis of Erasmus's career and scholarly image. Arthur F. Kinney, *Continental Humanist Poetics,* ch. 2, is recommended. Johan Huizinga, *Erasmus and the Age of Reformation* (1984), is an informative and interesting biography. Richard DeMolen, *Erasmus of Rotterdam: A Quintennial Symposium* (1971), and Kathleen Williams, ed., *Twentieth Century Interpretations of "The Praise of Folly"* (1969), contain useful essays.

The Praise of Folly[1]

Folly Herself Speaks:

Whatever mortals commonly say about me—and I am not unaware of how bad Folly's reputation is, even among the biggest fools of all—still it is quite clear that I myself, the very person now standing here before you, I and I alone pour forth joy into the hearts of gods and men alike. Hence it is that as soon as I came out to speak to this numerous gathering, the faces of all of you immediately brightened up with a strange, new expression of joy. You all suddenly perked up and greeted me with happy, congenial laughter—so much so that every last one of you here before me, wherever I look, seems to be high on the nectar of the Homeric gods, and on the drug nepenthe[2] too, whereas before you all sat there downcast and tense, as if you had just come back from the cave of Trophonius.[3] But when the sun first reveals his fair golden face to the earth, or when a harsh winter yields to the balmy breezes of early spring, everything suddenly takes on a new appearance, a new color, and a certain youthful freshness: so too, when you caught sight of me, your faces were transformed. Thus, what these eloquent orators can hardly accomplish in a long and carefully thought out speech—namely, to clear the mind of troubles and sorrows—that very goal I achieved in a flash simply by making an appearance.

* * * But since there are not very many who know my lineage, I will try (with the help of the Muses) to explain it. Neither Chaos, however, nor

---

1. Translated by Clarence Miller.   2. Legendary drug causing oblivion.   3. Seat of a particularly awesome oracle.

Orcus, nor Saturn, nor Japetus, nor any other of these worn-out, moldy old gods was my father. Rather, it was Plutus, the one and only father of men and gods alike, Hesiod and Homer and even Jupiter[4] himself to the contrary notwithstanding. Plutus alone, as it is now and ever has been, has everything and everyone, sacred and secular alike, at his beck and call: he keeps the whole pot boiling. His decision governs war, peace, kingdoms, counsels, judgments, agreements, marriages, pacts, treaties, laws, arts, recreations, serious business—I'm running out of breath—in short, all the affairs, public or private, in which mortals engage. Without his help that whole crew of poetic divinities—I will go further, even the so-called "select" gods—would either not exist at all or would eke out a miserable existence as homebodies. Whoever is frowned on by him can never find enough help even from Pallas[5] herself. Conversely, whoever is smiled on by Plutus can afford to tell Jupiter himself to go to hell, thunderbolt and all. Such is the father I can boast. And this great god certainly did not give birth to me from his brain, as Jupiter did to that sour stick-in-the-mud Pallas. Rather, he begot me on Neotes (Youth), the fairest, the most charming nymph of all. Moreover, he did not do it within the forbidding bonds of matrimony, like the progenitor of that limping black-smith,[6] but rather in a fashion not a little sweeter, "mingled together in passionate love," as my friend Homer says. But make no mistake, I was not begotten by Plutus[7] as Aristophanes represents him, his eyesight completely gone and one foot already in the grave, but rather when he was young, sound, and hot-blooded, inflamed not merely by youth but even more by nectar, which on that occasion he had drunk at the banquet of the gods, perhaps in larger, stronger drafts than usual.

But if anyone wants to know my birthplace—since nowadays people seem to think one of the most important points of nobility is the place where a person gives out his first wails—I was brought forth neither in wandering Delos, nor in the waves of the sea, nor in hollow-echoing caverns, but rather in the Isles of the Blest,[8] where everything grows without effort—they plough not, neither do they sow. In those isles there is no work, no old age, no disease. Nowhere in their fields do you see asphodel, mallows, sea onions, lupines, beans, or any such trash as that. Instead, both sight and smell are gratified by moly, panace, nepenthe, amaracus, ambrosia, lotus, roses, vio-lets, hyacinths, a veritable garden of Adonis. Born as I was among all these delights, I certainly did not begin my life by crying, but rather immediately smiled at my mother.

Far be it from me to envy the mighty son of Cronos the goat which gave him suck, since I was nursed at the breasts of two most elegant nymphs: Methe (Drunkenness), begotten by Bacchus, and Apaedia (Stupidity), the daughter of Pan. You can see them both here among my other attendants and handmaidens. If you want to know the names of the rest of them, you'll not get them from me in any language but Greek. This one—you see how

---

4. Sometimes called Jove (and Zeus in Greek), king of the gods. Plutus was the god of wealth and abun-dance. Hesiod (eighth century B.C.), Greek didactic poet, cited here because he was author of the *Theogony* (about the generation and genealogy of the gods). 5. Pallas Athena, daughter of Jove and goddess of wisdom. 6. Hephaestus (Vulcan), whose parents were Zeus and his wife, Hera (Juno). 7. Plutus was usually represented as a boy with a cornucopia. 8. The mythical and remote islands where, according to Greek tradition, some favorites of the gods dwelt in immortality and bliss. *Delos*: in Greek myth, once a floating island and birthplace of Apollo, god of sunlight, prophecy, music, and poetry. *Waves of the sea*: from which Venus (Aphrodite), goddess of love, emerged. *In hollow-echoing caverns*: a Homeric expression.

she raises her eyebrows—is obviously Philautia (Selflove). The one you see here, with smiling eyes and clapping hands, is named Kolakia (Flattery). This one, dosing and half asleep, is Lethe (Forgetfulness). This one, leaning on her elbows with her hands clasped, is Misoponia (Laziness). This one, wreathed with roses and drenched with sweet-smelling lotions, is Hedone (Pleasure). This one, with the restless glance and the rolling eyes, is Anoia (Madness). This one, with the smooth complexion and the plump, well-rounded figure, is Tryphe (Luxury). You also see two gods among the girls: one is called Comos (Rowdiness), the other Negreton Hypnon (Sweet Sleep). This, then, is the loyal retinue which helps me to subject the whole world to my dominion, lording it over the greatest lords.

You have heard about my birth, upbringing, and companions. Now, lest my claim to divinity should seem unsubstantiated, listen carefully and I will show you how many benefits I bestow on gods and men alike and how widely my divine power extends. Consider, if that author (whoever he was) was not far from the mark when he wrote that the essence of divinity is to give aid to mortals, and if the persons who taught mortals how to produce wine or grain or some other commodity have been justly elevated to the senate of the gods, why should I not rightly be considered and called the very *alpha*[9] of all the gods, since I alone bestow all things on all men?

First, what can be sweeter or more precious than life itself? But to whom should you attribute the origin of life if not to me? For it is not the spear of stern-fathered Pallas or the aegis of cloud-gathering Zeus which begets and propagates the human race. No, Jupiter himself, father of the gods and king over men, whose mere nod shakes all Olympus, even he must put aside that three-forked lightning bolt of his; he must dispense with that fierce Titanic countenance (with which he can, at his pleasure, terrify all the gods); clearly, he must change his role like an actor and play a humble part whenever he wants to do what in fact he is forever doing—that is, make a baby. To be sure, the Stoics[1] rank themselves only a little lower than the gods. But give me a man who is a Stoic three or four times over, a Stoic to the nth degree, and he too, though he may not have to shave off his beard—the sign of wisdom (though goats also have one)—he certainly will have to swallow his pride; he will have to smooth out his frowns, put aside his iron clad principles, and indulge just a bit in childish and fantastic trifles. In short, I am the one that wise man must come to—I repeat, he must come to me—if he ever wants to be a father.

But let me take you into my confidence even more candidly, as is my fashion. I ask you, is it the head, or the face, or the chest, or the hand, or the ear—all considered respectable parts of the body—is it any of these which generates gods and men? No, I think not. Rather, the human race is propagated by the part which is so foolish and funny that it cannot even be mentioned without a snicker. That is the sacred fount from which all things draw life, not the Pythagorean tetrad.[2] Come now, would any man ever sub-

---

9. First letter of the Greek alphabet, hence "beginning" or "origin." The author is Pliny.   1. Stoicism originated in the Stoa Poikile ("painted porch"), a building in the marketplace in Athens where the philosopher Zeno (fourth century B.C.) lectured; later it was perhaps the principal philosophy of the Roman elite. It became known during the Renaissance, especially through Seneca. Here the Stoics are the butt of Folly's irony because of their supposedly godlike disregard of the passions.   2. The first four numbers (which then added together equal the ideal number, ten); according to Pythagoras (sixth century B.C.), the tetrad signified the root of all being.

mit to the halter of matrimony if he followed the usual method of these wisemen and first considered the drawbacks of that state of life? Or what woman would ever yield to a man's advances if she either knew about or at least called to mind the perilous labor of childbirth, the trials and tribulations of raising children? So, if you owe your life to matrimony, and you owe matrimony to my handmaid Anoia, you can easily see how much you owe to me. Then again, what woman who has once had this experience would ever consent to go through it again if it were not for the divine influence of Lethe? Even Venus herself (in spite of what Lucretius[3] says) would never deny that her power is crippled and useless without the infusion of our divine influence. Thus, this game of ours, giddy and ridiculous as it is, is the source of supercilious philosophers (whose place has now been taken by so-called monks), and kings in their scarlet robes, and pious priests, and pope-holy pontiffs and, finally, even that assembly of poetic gods, so numerous that Olympus, large as it is, can hardly accommodate the crowd.

But it would be little enough for me to assert my role as the fountain and nursery of life, if I did not also show that all the benefits of life depend completely on my good offices. After all, what is this life itself—can you even call it life if you take away pleasure? . . . Your applause has answered for you. I was certain that none of you is so wise, or rather foolish—no, I mean wise— as to be of that opinion. In fact, even these Stoics do not scorn pleasure, however diligently they pretend to—ripping it to shreds in their public pronouncements for the very good reason that when they have driven others away from it they can enjoy it all the better by themselves. But for god's sake, I wish they would tell me, is there any part of life that is not sad, cheerless, dull, insipid, and wearisome unless you season it with pleasure, that is, with the spice of folly? To this fact Sophocles, a poet beyond all praise, offered ample testimony when he paid us that most elegant compliment: "Never to think, that is the good life."[4]

*   *   *

* * * If someone should try to strip away the costumes and makeup from the actors performing a play on the stage and to display them to the spectators in their own natural appearance, wouldn't he ruin the whole play? Wouldn't all the spectators be right to throw rocks at such a madman and drive him out of the theater? Everything would suddenly look different: the actor just now playing a woman would be seen to be a man; the one who had just now been playing a young man would look old; the man who played the king only a moment ago would become a pauper; the actor who played god would be revealed as a wretched human being. But to destroy the illusions in this fashion would spoil the whole play. This deception, this disguise, is the very thing that holds the attention of the spectators. Now the whole life of mortal men, what is it but a sort of play, in which various persons make their entrances in various costumes, and each one plays his own part until the director gives him his cue to leave the stage? Often he also orders one and the same actor to come on in different costumes, so that the actor who just now played the king in royal scarlet now comes on in rags to play

3. Poet (99?–55 B.C.) who, in *On the Nature of Things*, invokes Venus because "all living things" are conceived through her.   **4.** Compare Sophocles' *Ajax*, lines 554–55: "life is sweetest before the feelings are awake—until one learns to know joy and pain."

a miserable servant. True, all these images are unreal, but this play cannot be performed in any other way.

If at this point some wiseman, dropped down direct from heaven, should suddenly jump up and begin shouting that this figure whom everyone reverences as if he were the lord god is not even a man because he is controlled by his passions like an animal, that he is a servant of the lowest rank because he willingly serves so many filthy masters; or if he should turn to another man who is mourning the death of his parent and tell him to laugh instead because the dead man has at last really begun to live, whereas this life is really nothing but a sort of death; if he should see another man glorying in his noble lineage and call him a low-born bastard because he is so far removed from virtue, which is the only true source of nobility; and if he addressed everyone else in the same way, I ask you, what would he accomplish except to make everyone take him for a raving lunatic? Just as nothing is more foolish than misplaced wisdom, so too, nothing is more imprudent than perverse prudence. And surely it is perverse not to adapt yourself to the prevailing circumstances, to refuse "to do as the Romans do," to ignore the party-goer's maxim "take a drink or take your leave," to insist that the play should not be a play. True prudence, on the other hand, recognizes human limitations and does not strive to leap beyond them; it is willing to run with the herd, to overlook faults tolerantly or to share them in a friendly spirit. But, they say, that is exactly what we mean by folly. I will hardly deny it—as long as they will reciprocate by admitting that this is exactly what it means to perform the play of life.

Another point—by all the gods in heaven! Should I say it or keep still? But why keep still, since it is "truer than truth itself." But perhaps in such a weighty matter it would be well to summon the Muses from Helicon[5]—the poets often enough invoke them for the merest trifles. Be present, then, you daughters of Jove, for a bit, while I show that no one can reach the heights of wisdom and the very "inner sanctum," as they themselves say, "of happiness" except with the guidance of Folly.

First of all, everyone admits that the emotions all belong to Folly. Thus, the usual distinction between a wiseman and a fool is that the fool is governed by emotion, the wiseman by reason. That is why the Stoics eliminate from their wiseman all emotional perturbations, as if they were diseases. But actually the emotions not only function as guides to those who are hastening to the haven of wisdom, but also, in the whole range of virtuous action, they operate like spurs or goads, as it were, encouraging the performance of good deeds. I know that died-in-the-wool Stoic, Seneca, strenuously denies this, removing all emotion whatsoever from his wiseman. But by doing this he is left with something that cannot even be called human; he fabricates some new sort of divinity that has never existed and never will. Frankly, he sets up a marble statue of a man, utterly unfeeling and quite impervious to all human emotion. They can enjoy their wiseman all they like and have him all to themselves, or (if they prefer) they can live with him in Plato's republic, or in the realm of Platonic ideas, or in "the gardens of Tantalus."[6] Who would not flee in horror from such a man, as he would from a monster or a ghost—a

5. Mythical mountain, home of the Muses. 6. All are characterized by the presence of abstraction and figments. *Realm of Platonic ideas*: the celestial ideal models of which real things are only imperfect realizations. In Tantalus's garden in Hades, rich fruit is always just beyond his grasp.

man who is completely deaf to all human sentiment, who is untouched by emotion, no more moved by love or pity than "a chunk of flint or a mountain crag," who never misses anything, who never makes a mistake, who sees through everything as if he had "x-ray vision," measures everything "with plumb line and T square," never forgives anything, who is uniquely self-satisfied, who thinks he alone is rich, he alone is healthy, regal, free, in brief, he thinks that he alone is all things (but he is also alone in thinking so), who cares nothing about friendship, who makes friends with no one, who would not hesitate to tell the gods themselves to go hang, who can find nothing in all human life that he does not condemn and ridicule as madness? Yet just such a creature as this is that perfect wiseman of theirs. I ask you, if an office were to be awarded by election, what state would choose such a man for civic office, what army would select him for their general? Indeed, what woman would consent to marry him or put up with him as a husband? What host would want him (or tolerate him) as a guest? What servant would ever enter his service or continue in it? Who would not prefer someone chosen at random from the mob of out-and-out fools? Being a fool himself, he could either command fools or obey them, please his peers (who are clearly in the majority), be companionable with his wife, cheerful with his friends, a fine table companion, an easy-going messmate. In short, he considers nothing human foreign to him.[7] But for some time now I have been sick and tired of this wiseman. Therefore I shall proceed in my speech by returning to the remaining benefits.

Just think, if a person could look down from a watchtower, as Jupiter sometimes does according to the poets, and could see how many disasters human life is exposed to, how miserable and messy childbirth is, how toilsome it is to bring children up, how defenseless they are against injuries, how young men must make their way by the sweat of their brow, how burdensome old age is, how death comes cruel and ineluctable; and then too, if he could see during the course of life itself how man is besieged by a whole army of diseases, threatened by accidents, assailed by misfortunes, how everything everywhere is tinged with bitterness—to say nothing of the evils men inflict on each other, such as poverty, prison, disgrace, shame, torture, entrapment, betrayal, insults, quarrels, deception, but I might as well try "to number the sands of the seashore"—now, as for what crimes man committed to deserve all this or which god in his anger caused men to be born to all these miseries, those are things it is not proper for me to declare at the present time, but whoever gives these things serious consideration cannot but approve the example of the Milesian virgins,[8] however pitiable their case was. But in fact, who have been the most likely to commit suicide out of weariness with life? Isn't it those who have come closest to wisdom? Among these (to say nothing of such people as Diogenes, Xenocrates, Cato, Cassius, and Brutus) was Chiron,[9] who had an opportunity to be immortal but freely chose death instead. You can see, I imagine, what would happen if men

---

7. From a proverbial phrase in Terence's *Self-Tormentor*, line 77: "I am a man: nothing human do I consider alien to me."   8. From the city of Miletus, in Asia Minor; according to an ancient tale, most of them, seemingly gone insane, hanged themselves.   9. The centaur (half man, half horse) who, incurably wounded and suffering great pain, asked Zeus for relief from his own immortality [Editor's note]. Of the philosophers Diogenes and Xenocrates, the first killed himself, but the second died by accident (Diogenes Laertius 6.77–78, 4.14–15). Cato of Utica, Brutus, and Cassius committed suicide after being defeated in battle [Translator's note].

everywhere were wise: we would need another batch of clay, another potter like Prometheus.[1] But I, partly through ignorance, partly through thoughtlessness, sometimes through forgetfulness of past misfortunes, sometimes through hope of good things to come, now and then mixing some honey with their pleasures, I rescue men from such terrible sufferings—so effectively that they are even unwilling to leave this life behind when the thread is all unwound and life leaves them behind. The less cause they have to remain in this life, the more they want to stay alive—so little are they touched by the tedium of life.

It is my doing that you see everywhere men as old as Nestor,[2] who no longer even look like men: driveling, doting, toothless, whitehaired, bald, or (in the words of Aristophanes) "filthy, crookbacked, wretched, shriveled, bald, toothless, and lame of their best limb";[3] but yet they are so in love with life and "have such young ideas" that one of them will dye his hair, another will hide his baldness with a toupee, another will wear false teeth (borrowed perhaps from some hog), another will fall head over heels in love with some young girl and outdo any beardless youth in amorous idiocy. In fact, to see old codgers with one foot in the grave marry some sweet young thing—with no dowry at that, and of far more use to other men than to him—this sort of thing happens so often that people almost consider it praiseworthy.

But it is even more amusing to see these old women, so ancient they might as well be dead and so cadaverous they look as if they had returned from the grave, yet they are always mouthing the proverb "life is sweet." They are as hot as bitches in heat, or (as the Greeks say) they rut like goats. They pay a good price for the services of some handsome young Adonis. They never cease smearing their faces with makeup. They can't tear themselves away from the mirror. They pluck and thin their pubic bush. They show off their withered and flabby breasts. They whip up their languid lust with quavering whines and whimpers. They drink a lot. They mingle with the young girls on the dance floor. They write billets-doux. Everyone laughs at these things as utterly foolish (and indeed they are), but the old bags themselves are perfectly self-satisfied. They lead a life of the utmost pleasure. They swim in honey up to their ears. Through my blessing, they live in bliss. Now if anyone thinks such goings-on are absurd, I wish he would take the trouble to decide whether he thinks it better to live a life of perfect bliss by means of such folly or to look for a way to "end it all," as they say.

Now, the fact that such absurdities are generally considered disgraceful, that doesn't bother my fools at all: they are either unaware of their notoriety, or, if they are aware, they find it easy to ignore it. If a rock falls on your head, that is certainly bad for you. But shame, disgrace, reproaches, curses do harm only insofar as they are perceived. If they are not noticed, they are not harmful. "What harm if all the crowd should hiss and boo; you're safe as long as you can clap for you." But that is made possible only by Folly.

Even so, I can imagine the philosophers' objections: "But to be caught in the toils of such folly, to err, to be deceived, to be ignorant—such an existence is itself miserable." One thing is sure: such it is to be a man. But I don't see why they should call him miserable, since this is the way you are

---

1. He supposedly molded the human race out of clay.   2. The old, eloquent sage in the Homeric epic.   3. *Plutus*, lines 266–67.

born, this is the way you are formed and fashioned, this is the common lot of everyone. But nothing is miserable merely because it follows its own nature, unless perhaps someone thinks man's lot is deplorable because he cannot fly like the birds, or run on all fours like other animals, and is not armed with horns like a bull. But by the same token, he should argue that even a fine, thoroughbred horse is unhappy because he has never learned grammar and doesn't eat pancakes, or that a bull is miserable because he cannot work out in the gym. Therefore, just as a horse who is ignorant of grammar is not miserable, so too, a man who is a fool is not unhappy, because these things are inherent in their natures.

But these word-jugglers are back at it again: "The knowledge of various branches of learning," they say, "was especially added to human nature so that with their help he could use his mental skill to compensate for what Nature left out." As if it were the least bit likely that Nature, who was so alert in providing for gnats (and even for tiny flowers and blades of grass), should have nodded only in equipping mankind, so that there should be a need for the different branches of learning—which were actually thought up by Theutus,[4] a spirit quite hostile to mankind, as instruments of man's utter ruination. So little do they contribute to man's happiness, that they defeat the very purpose for which they were supposedly invented—as that most wise king in Plato cleverly argues concerning the invention of writing.[5] Thus, the branches of learning crept in along with the other plagues of man's life, and from the very same source from which all shameful crimes arise, namely, the demons—who also derive their name from this fact, since "demon" comes from δαήμονες ("scientes," knowing ones). Now the simple people of the golden age, who were not armed with any formal learning, lived their lives completely under the guidance of natural impulses. What need was there for grammar when everyone spoke the same language and when speech served no other purpose than to let one person understand another? What use was there for dialectic, when there was no disagreement among conflicting opinions? What room was there for rhetoric when there were no litigious troublemakers? What demand was there for legal learning when there was no such thing as bad morals—for good laws undoubtedly sprang from bad conduct. Then too, they had more reverence than to pry into the secrets of Nature with irreligious curiosity—to measure the stars, their motions and effects, to seek the causes of mysterious phenomena—for they considered it unlawful for mortals to seek knowledge beyond the limits of their lot. As for what is beyond the range of the furthest stars, the madness of exploring such things never even entered their minds. But when the purity of the golden age had gradually declined, then evil spirits, as I said, first began to invent the learned disciplines, but only a few at first and even those taken up only by a few. Afterwards, the superstition of the Chaldeans and the idle frivolity of the Greeks added hundreds more, all of them nothing but forms of mental torture, so painful that the grammar of even one language is more than enough to make life a perpetual agony.

Still, even among these disciplines, the ones held in highest esteem are those which come closest to the ordinary understanding—that is, the folly—

---

4. In Plato's *Phaedrus*, an Egyptian god who brought the art of writing to King Thamus.   5. King Thamus argued that the invention of writing would produce only false wisdom and destroy the power of people's memory.

of mankind. Theologians starve, physicists freeze, astronomers are ridiculed, logicians are ignored. "One physician alone is worth whole hosts of other men."[6] And even among physicians, the more ignorant, bold, and thoughtless one of them is, the more he is valued by these high and mighty princes. Besides, medicine (certainly as it is now practiced by most doctors) is nothing but a subdivision of flattery, just like rhetoric. The next rank beneath the doctors belongs to pettifogging lawyers; in fact, I wonder if they don't hold the highest rank of all, since their profession—not to speak of it myself—is universally ridiculed as asinine by the philosophers. Still, all business transactions, from the smallest to the greatest, are absolutely controlled by these asses. They acquire large estates, while a theologian who has carefully read through whole bookcases of divinity nibbles on dried peas, waging continual warfare with bedbugs and lice.

Moreover, just as those disciplines which are most closely related to Folly contribute most to happiness, so too, those men who have nothing whatever to do with any branch of learning and follow Nature as their only guide are by far the happiest of all. For she is completely adequate in every way, unless perhaps someone wants to leap over the bounds of human destiny. Nature hates disguises, and whatever has not been spoiled by artifice always produces the happiest results. After all, don't you see that, among all the other kinds of living creatures, those which remain at the furthest remove from any formal learning and take Nature for their only teacher lead the happiest lives? What could be happier or more marvelous than the bees? And yet they do not even have all the bodily senses. What architect has ever produced buildings like theirs? What philosopher has ever established a comparable republic? The horse, on the other hand, because his senses resemble those of man and because he left his original abode to dwell with men, has also become a sharer in the sufferings of men. Thus, often enough a horse that is ashamed to be defeated in a race becomes broken-winded, and a horse that strives for victory in warfare is stabbed and bites the dust with his rider. To say nothing of the sharp-toothed curb bits, the points of the spurs, the imprisonment of the stable, the whips, cudgels, fetters, the rider—in short, that whole miserable panorama of servitude that he willingly accepted when (like brave men of honor) he was overcome by a burning desire for revenge on his enemy. How much more attractive is the life of flies and little birds, who live for the moment purely by natural instinct, as long as they can avoid the snares of men. But if they should be put into cages and learn to speak human sounds, it is quite remarkable how they decline from their native sleekness and elegance. So certain is it that the creations of Nature are in every way more joyous than the fabrications of artifice.

Accordingly, I could never bestow sufficient praise on that cock embodying Pythagoras,[7] who had been, in his single person, a philosopher, a man, a woman, a king, a private citizen, a fish, a horse, a frog, even a sponge (I think), but who decided that no creature was more miserable than man because all the others were content to remain within the limits of Nature, while man alone tried to go beyond the bounds of his lot. Moreover, among men he places natural-born fools far above great and learned men; and Gryl-

---

6. Homer, *Iliad* 11.514.   7. In Lucian's *The Dream, or the Cock* (A.D. second century) the cock upholds the Pythagorean notion of transmigration of souls from one body to another by claiming that he is Pythagoras.

lus[8] was not a little wiser than wily Odysseus, since he preferred to grunt in the pigsty instead of being exposed with Odysseus to so many unexpected calamities. With Gryllus and the cock, Homer himself, the father of foolish fables, seems to be in agreement, since he repeatedly calls all mortals "miserable and wretched" and frequently applies the epithet "unhappy" to Ulysses, his model of wisdom, but never to Paris or Ajax or Achilles. And why this distinction? Wasn't it because the clever and cunning Ulysses never did anything without consulting Pallas Athene and was too smart for his own good, departing as far as possible from the guidance of Nature?

Therefore, just as among mortals those men who seek wisdom are furthest from happiness—indeed, they are fools twice over because, forgetting the human condition to which they were born, they aspire to the life of the immortal gods and (like the giants)[9] wage war against Nature with the engines of learning—so too, the least miserable among men are those who come closest to the level of intelligence (that is, the folly) of brute animals and never undertake anything beyond human nature. Come on, then, let us see if we can't show this, not with the fine-spun arguments of the Stoics, but with some plain, ordinary example. But by all the gods above! is anyone happier than the sort of men who are usually called fools, dolts, simpletons, nincompoops—actually very fine titles, as I see it? At first glance, what I am saying may perhaps seem foolish and absurd, but it is nevertheless true as can be.

First, they are spared all fear of death, a burden hardly to be taken lightly. They are not tortured by pangs of conscience. They are not frightened by silly tales about the underworld. They are not terrified by apparitions and ghosts. They are not tormented by the fear of impending evils, nor kept on tenterhooks by the hope of coming good. In brief, they are not harried by the thousands of cares to which this life is subject. They feel no shame, no fear, no ambition, no envy, no love. Finally, if they come close to the ignorance of brute animals, they do not even commit sins, according to theologians. Now at this point, most foolish wiseman, do me a favor: just consider how many ways your mind is tortured day and night—pile up all the troubles of your life into a single heap, and then you will finally understand how many evils I have spared my fools. On top of that, note that they not only rejoice continually themselves—playing, laughing, and singing little tunes—but also, wherever they turn, they provide everyone else with entertainment, jokes, fun and laughter, as if the gods in their goodness had granted them to men for the specific purpose of brightening up the gloominess of man's life. Hence, whereas various people react variously to other people, everyone agrees unanimously in claiming these fools as their own—they seek them out, maintain them, pamper them, coddle them, help them in time of need, freely allow them to do or say anything they like. So far is anyone from wishing to harm them that even savage beasts refrain from hurting them, out of a certain natural awareness of their innocence. As a matter of fact, they are sacred to the gods, especially to me, and therefore it is not without reason that everyone treats them with such respect.

In fact, even the mightiest monarchs are so delighted with them that with-

8. Character in a dialogue by Plutarch, changed into a pig by Circe. 9. Following the example of the giants, or Titans, of Greek mythology, who, inspired by their wronged mother, Gaea (Earth), fought the Olympian gods and were defeated.

out these fools some of them can neither eat breakfast, nor make their entry, nor even so much as survive for a single hour. And they value these simpletons far more then those sour wisemen, though it is true that they usually maintain some of them too, for the sake of appearances. The reason why they value them more is not far to seek, I think, and ought not to surprise anyone, since those wisemen normally offer princes nothing but melancholy—indeed, relying on their learning, they sometimes do not hesitate to make harsh truth grate upon their tender ears—whereas fools provide the very thing for which princes are always on the lookout: jokes, laughs, guffaws, fun. And don't forget another talent, by no means contemptible, that is peculiar to fools: they alone speak the plain, unvarnished truth. And what is more worthy of praise than truthfulness? True, Alcibiades' proverb in Plato attributes truthfulness to wine and children,[1] but actually the praise for that virtue is all mine and mine alone, as Euripides himself testifies in that famous saying about us which has come down from him: "a fool speaks like a fool."[2] Whatever a fool has in his heart, he reveals in his face and expresses in his speech. But wisemen have those two tongues, also mentioned by Euripides:[3] with one they speak the truth, with the other whatever they think convenient for the moment. They are the ones who turn black into white, who blow hot and cold in one breath, who profess to believe one thing in their speech but conceal quite another in their hearts. Princes, then, for all their great happiness, still seem to me most unhappy in one respect: there is no one from whom they can hear the truth, and they are forced to take flatterers for their friends.

But "a prince's ears tingle at the truth," someone will say, "and for that very reason they shun those wisemen: they are afraid that perhaps one of them might be so frank as to say what is true rather than pleasant." Quite right—kings do hate the truth. But my fools, on the other hand, have a marvelous faculty of giving pleasure not only when they speak the truth but even when they utter open reproaches, so that the very same statement which would have cost a wiseman his life causes unbelievable pleasure if spoken by a fool. For truthfulness has a certain inherent power of giving pleasure, if it contains nothing that gives offense. But the skill to manage this the gods have granted only to fools.

For almost the same reasons women, who naturally tend to be more inclined to pleasures and trifles, are extraordinarily fond of this kind of men. Accordingly, whatever they do with this sort of person (even though it is sometimes sufficiently serious), they explain away as mere entertainment and amusement—as indeed the fair sex is quite clever, especially in covering up their faux pas.

Therefore, to return to the happiness of simpletons, having lived their lives with great joy, with no fear or even awareness of death, they depart directly to the Elysian fields, where their antics continue to delight the leisurely souls of the blessed.

And now let us compare the lot of this fool with any wiseman whatsoever. Imagine, if you please, a model of wisdom to set over against the fool: a man who has wasted his whole childhood and youth in mastering the branches of learning and has lost the sweetest part of life in sleepless nights and

1. See Plato's *Symposium*. 2. *The Bacchanals (Bacchae)*, line 369. 3. *Rhesus*, lines 394–95; *Andromache*, lines 451–52.

endless painstaking labors, a man who even in the rest of his life has not tasted the tiniest crumb of pleasure, always frugal, poor, gloomy, surly, unfair and harsh to himself, severe and hateful to others, wasted away into a pale, thin, sickly, blear-eyed figure, old and gray long before his time, hastening to a premature grave—though what does it matter when such a person dies, since he never really lived at all? And there you have a fine picture of your wiseman.

But here the frogs of the Stoic ilk croak at me once again. "Nothing," they say, "is more miserable than madness. But extraordinary folly is either very close to madness or is actually identical with it. For what does it mean to be mad but to be of unsound mind?" But these cavilers are completely "on the wrong track." Come, let us demolish this syllogism also, with the help of the Muses. The argument is clever indeed, but just as Plato's Socrates taught when he divided one Venus into two and split one Cupid into two,[4] so, these dialecticians should have distinguished one kind of madness from the other if they ever intended to pass for sane themselves. For every sort of madness is not necessarily disastrous, in and of itself. Otherwise Horace would not have said "Or am I beguiled by a lovely madness"[5] nor would Plato have placed the frenzy of poets, prophets, and lovers among the chief goods of life; nor would the prophetess have called the labor of Aeneas mad.[6]

For there are two kinds of madness: one which is sent up from the underworld by the avenging Furies whenever they dart forth their serpents and inspire in the breasts of mortals a burning desire for war, or unquenchable thirst for gold, or disgraceful and wicked lust, or parricide, incest, sacrilege, or some other such plague, or when they afflict the guilty thoughts of some criminal with the maddening firebrands of terror. There is another kind far different from the first, namely the kind which takes its origin from me and is most desirable. It occurs whenever a certain pleasant mental distraction relieves the heart from its anxieties and cares and at the same time soothes it with the balm of manifold pleasures. Indeed, in a letter to Atticus, Cicero wishes for this mental distraction as a great gift from the gods, because it would have deprived him of all awareness of the great evils around him. Nor was there anything wrong with the judgment of the Greek who was so mad that he sat alone in the theater for whole days on end, laughing, applauding, enjoying himself, because he thought that wonderful tragedies were being acted there, whereas nothing at all was being performed. But in the other duties of life he conducted himself very well: he was cheerful with his friends, agreeable with his wife; he could overlook the faults of his servants and not fly into a mad rage when he found a winejar had been secretly tapped. Through the efforts of his friends he took some medicine which cured him of his disease, but when he was completely himself again, he took issue with his friends in this fashion: "Damn it all!" he said, "you have killed me, my friends, not cured me, by thus wresting my enjoyment from me and forcibly depriving me of a most pleasant delusion."[7] And rightly enough. For they were the ones who were deluded, and they had more need of hellebore than he did, since they thought such a felicitous and gratifying madness was some kind of evil that needed to be expelled by means of potions.

But in fact I haven't yet decided whether just any error of the senses or

---

4. I.e., in distinguishing heavenly love from other types of love. 5. *Odes* 3.4.5–6. 6. *Aeneid* 6.135. 7. This passage is a paraphrase of Horace's *Epistles* 2.128–40.

the mind ought to be designated by the name madness. Certainly, if a man with poor eyesight thinks a mule is an ass, or if someone takes a piece of doggerel for a very skillful poetic composition, he does not immediately strike everyone as mad. But if a person is deceived not only in the perceptions of his senses but also in the judgments of his mind, and if his deception is continual and beyond the usual share, only then will he be thought to verge on madness—as, for instance, if a person who hears an ass braying thinks he is listening to a marvelous choir, or if some poor beggar, born into the very lowest level of society, believes he is Croesus,[8] king of Lydia. But this kind of madness, if it errs in the direction of pleasure (as it usually does), brings no small share of delight both to those who experience it and to those who observe it without being mad to the same degree themselves. For this species of madness is far more widespread than most people realize. But one madman mocks another, and they maintain between them a mutual interchange of merriment. And not infrequently you see the greater madman laugh louder at the less. Still, everyone is all the happier the more ways he is deluded, as far as Folly can judge, as long as he remains within the category of madness that belongs peculiarly to us—a category which is in fact so widespread that I hardly know whether anyone at all can be found from the whole sum of mortals who is always impeccably wise and who is not subject to some kind of madness. The real difference is only this: the man who sees a cucumber and thinks it is a woman is labeled mad because this happens very rarely. But if a man who shares his wife in common with many other men nevertheless swears that she is more faithful than Penelope and warmly congratulates himself in his ignorant bliss, no one calls him mad because they see that this sort of thing happens to husbands everywhere.

This class of madness also includes those who look down on everything except hunting wild animals and whose spirits are incredibly exhilarated whenever they hear the nerve-shattering blasts on the horns or the baying of the hounds. I imagine that even the dung of the dogs smells like cinnamon to them. And then what exquisite pleasure they feel when the quarry is to be butchered! Lowly peasants may butcher bulls and rams, but only a nobleman may cut up wild animals. Baring his head and kneeling down, he takes a special blade set aside for that purpose (for it would hardly do to use just any knife) and exercises the most devout precision, in cutting up just these parts, with just these movements, in just this order. Meanwhile, the surrounding crowd stands in silent wonder, as if they were seeing some new religious ceremony, although they have beheld the same spectacle a thousand times before. Then, whoever gets a chance to taste some of the beast is quite convinced that he has gained no small share of added nobility. Thus, though these men have accomplished nothing more by constantly chasing and eating wild animals than to lower themselves almost to the level of the animals they hunt, still in the meantime they think they are living like kings.

Very like them is the sort of men who burn with an insatiable desire to build, replacing round structures with square and square with round. Nor is there an end to it, nor any limit, until they are reduced to such utter poverty that nothing at all is left—neither place to live nor food to eat. What of it? In the meantime they have passed several years with the greatest pleasure.

---

8. Proverbially wealthy man.

The group that comes closest to these builders, I think, consists of those who strive to change one substance into another by means of novel, occult arts, and move heaven and earth to track down a certain fifth element or "quintessence."[9] This honied hope entices them so powerfully that they spare no effort or expense. They are wonderfully clever in thinking up some new way to deceive themselves. They cheat themselves with a pleasing sort of fraud, until they have spent everything and don't even have enough left to fire their furnaces.[1] But still they never stop dreaming sweet dreams, and they also do everything they can to encourage others to pursue the same happiness. Even when they have been completely deprived of all hope whatsoever, there is still one saying left—a great comfort indeed: "in great affairs the intent alone's enough." And then they rail against the shortness of life, because it is inadequate for an enterprise of such great moment.

As to gamblers, I am in some doubt whether they should be admitted to our fellowship. But still it is a foolish and altogether absurd spectacle to see some of them so addicted to it that their hearts leap up and throb as soon as they hear the clatter of the dice. Finally, when the hope of winning has kept luring them onward until they suffer the shipwreck of all their resources, splitting the ship of their fortune against the dice-reef (hardly less fearful than the coast of Malea),[2] and when they have barely escaped from the sea with the shirts on their backs, they will cheat anyone rather than the winner of their money, lest anyone should think they are not men of honor. What shall we say when even old men who are already half-blind go on playing with the aid of eye-glasses? Or when they pay good money to hire a stand-in to roll the dice for them because their own finger-joints have been crippled by a well-earned attack of gout? A pleasant spectacle indeed, except that sometimes such gambling ends in violent quarrels and hence falls into the province of the Furies, not in mine.

But there can be no question at all that another group is entirely enlisted "under my banner": those who delight in hearing or telling miracles and monstrous lies. They can never get enough of such tales whenever strange horrors are told about apparitions, ghosts, specters, dead souls, and thousands of such marvels as these. And the further such tall tales are from the truth, the more easily they gain credence and the more delicately they tickle the ears of the listeners. Besides, they are not only wonderfully useful in relieving the boredom of the passing hours, but they also produce a fine profit, especially for priests and preachers.[3]

Closely related to such men are those who have adopted the very foolish (but nevertheless quite agreeable) belief that if they look at a painting or statue of that huge Polyphemus Christopher, they will not die on that day; or, if they address a statue of Barbara[4] with the prescribed words, they will return from battle unharmed; or, if they accost Erasmus on certain days, with certain wax tapers, and in certain little formulas of prayer, they will soon become rich. Moreover, in George they have discovered a new Hercules, just as they have found a new Hippolytus.[5] They all but worship

9. A substance (in addition to the four traditional elements—earth, water, air, and fire) of which the heavenly bodies were believed to be composed.   1. For alchemical experiments.   2. In Greece, proverbially dangerous.   3. Cf. Chaucer's *The Pardoner's Tale* (p. 1573).   4. St. Barbara is supposed to protect her worshipers against fire and artillery. Polyphemus is the Cyclops (one-eyed giant) in Homer's *Odyssey*. St. Christopher is also represented with only one eye.   5. In Greco-Roman mythology, both fought against monsters.

George's horse, most religiously decked out in breastplates and bosses, and from time to time oblige him with some little gift. To swear by his bronze helmet is thought to be an oath fit for a king.

Now what shall I say about those who find great comfort in soothing self-delusions about fictitious pardons for their sins, measuring out the times in purgatory down to the droplets of a waterclock, parceling out centuries, years, months, days, hours, as if they were using mathematical tables? Or what about those who rely on certain little magical tokens and prayers thought up by some pious impostor for his own amusement or profit? They promise themselves anything and everything: wealth, honor, pleasure, an abundance of everything, perpetual health, a long life, flourishing old age, and finally a seat next to Christ among the saints, though this last they don't want for quite a while yet—that is, when the pleasures of this life, to which they cling with all their might, have finally slipped through their fingers, then it will be soon enough to enter into the joys of the saints. Imagine here, if you please, some businessman or soldier or judge who thinks that if he throws into the collection basket one coin from all his plunder, the whole cesspool of his sinful life will be immediately wiped out. He thinks all his acts of perjury, lust, drunkenness, quarreling, murder, deception, dishonesty, betrayal are paid off like a mortgage, and paid off in such a way that he can start off once more on a whole new round of sinful pleasures.

Now who could be more foolish—rather, who could be happier—than those who assure themselves they will have the very ultimate felicity because they have recited daily those seven little verses from the holy psalms? A certain devil—certainly a merry one, but too loose-lipped to be very clever—is believed to have mentioned them to St. Bernard, but the poor devil was cheated by a clever trick.[6] Such absurdities are so foolish that even I am almost ashamed of them, but still they are approved not only by the common people but even by learned teachers of religion.

And then too, isn't it pretty much the same sort of nonsense when particular regions lay claim to a certain saint, when they parcel out particular functions to particular saints, and assign to particular saints certain modes of worship: one offers relief from a toothache, another helps women in labor, another restores stolen goods; one shines as a ray of hope in a shipwreck, another takes care of the flocks—and so on with the others, for it would take far too long to list all of them. Some saints have a variety of powers, especially the virgin mother of God, to whom the ordinary run of men attribute more almost than to her son.

But what do men end up asking from these saints except things that pertain to folly? Just think, among all the votive tablets that you see covering the walls and even the ceilings of some churches, have you ever seen anyone who escaped from folly or who became the least bit wiser? One saved his life by swimming. Another was stabbed by an enemy but recovered. Another, with no less luck than bravery, fled from the battle while the rest were fighting. Another who had been hung on the gallows fell down by the favor of some saint friendly to thieves, so that he could proceed in his career of disburdening those who are sadly overburdened by their riches. Another

---

6. A devil had told St. Bernard that repeating seven particular verses of the Psalms would bring him the certainty of salvation. The *clever trick* was that of proposing to recite all the Psalms.

escaped by breaking out of jail. Another, much to the chagrin of his physician, recovered from a fever. For another, a poisonous potion, because it worked as a purge, was curative rather than fatal, though his wife (who lost her effort and expense) was not exactly overjoyed at the result. Another, whose wagon had overturned, drove his horses home uninjured. Another, buried by the collapse of a building, was not killed. Another, caught by a husband, managed to get away. No one gives thanks for escaping from folly. To lack all wisdom is so very agreeable that mortals will pray to be delivered from anything rather than from folly.

But why have I embarked on this vast sea of superstitions?

> Not if I had a hundred tongues, a hundred mouths,
> A voice of iron, could I survey all kinds
> Of fools, or run through all the forms of folly.[7]

So rife, so teeming with such delusions is the entire life of all Christians everywhere. And yet priests are not unwilling to allow and even foster such delusions because they are not unaware of how many emoluments accumulate from this source. In the midst of all this, if some odious wiseman should stand up and sing out the true state of affairs: "You will not die badly if you live well. You redeem your sins if to the coin you add a hatred of evil deeds, then tears, vigils, prayers, fasts, and if you change your whole way of life. This saint will help you if you imitate his life"—if that wiseman were to growl out such assertions and more like them, look how much happiness he would immediately take away from the minds of mortals, look at the confusion he would throw them into!

Of the same stripe are those who prescribe in great detail, while they are still alive, how they wish to be buried, giving exact numbers for the torches, the people in mourning garments, the singers, the official mourners that they want in the funeral procession, as if they could have any awareness of this spectacle or as if the dead would be ashamed unless their corpses were grandly planted in the ground—they seem for all the world like political candidates staging a campaign dinner complete with entertainers.

Even though I am in a hurry, I can hardly pass over in silence those who preen themselves on the empty title of nobility, even though they are no different from the lowliest shoemaker. One traces his ancestry back to Aeneas, another to Brut,[8] another to Arthur. Everywhere they display statues and pictures of their ancestors, they count up their great-grandfathers and great-great-grandfathers, they rehearse their ancient family names, while they themselves are not much better than dumb statues, almost inferior to the very symbols they display. And yet this pleasant Selflove enables them to lead an altogether happy life. Nor is there any lack of others, equally foolish, who revere this class of beasts as if they were gods.

But why should I be talking about one group or another, as if such Selflove did not render almost everyone everywhere most happy in a variety of marvelous ways? One man who is uglier than any monkey is quite confident that he is as handsome as Nereus. Another, as soon as he can draw three lines with a compass, immediately thinks he is another Euclid. Another, who

---

7. A variation on a passage in the *Aeneid* (6.625–27) in which, however, Virgil is talking of "forms of crime," not folly. 8. The legendary founder of Britain.

sounds like an "ass playing a harp and who sings no better than the bird that gives the hen uxorious nips, still thinks he is another Hermogenes. But by far the most entertaining kind of madness is the sort which causes some people to boast of any talent among their servants as if it were their own. This was displayed by that twice-blessed rich man in Seneca[9] who always kept servants at hand when he intended to tell an anecdote so that they could prompt him with the names. He wouldn't have hesitated to engage in a fist fight (though he himself was so infirm he was just barely alive) because he relied on the many strapping servants he had at home.

As for professors of the arts, why bother to mention them?—since Selflove is the special prerogative of all of them, so much so that you will sooner find one who will admit that his father's farm is second-rate than one who will accept second rank in intelligence. But this is especially true of actors, singers, orators, and poets: the more ignorant anyone of them is, the more arrogant his self-complacence, conceit, and braggadocio. And "birds of a feather", or like will to like—in fact, the less skillful anything is, the more admirers it obtains, according to the rule that the worst things usually please most people, because the majority of men, as we said, are subject to folly. Therefore, if a man acquires more pleasure for himself and more admiration from others according to the depth of his ignorance, why on earth should he choose real learning? First of all it costs a great deal, and then it will make him more disagreeable and timid, and finally it will please far fewer people.

Then again, I see that Nature has not only given every mortal his own brand of Selflove but has also grafted a sort of communal form of it to particular nations and even cities. Hence it is that the British lay claim above all to good looks, music, and fine food. The Scots pride themselves on their nobility and close blood-ties to the royal house, not to mention dialectical subtlety. The French claim for themselves refinement of manners. The Parisians arrogate to themselves theological learning, to the exclusion of almost everyone else.[1] The Italians lay claim to literature and eloquence, and on one point they all preen themselves most complacently: that, of all mortals, they alone are not barbarians. In this sort of happiness the Romans lead the way, and still dream sweet dreams about that ancient Rome of theirs. The Venetians are happy in their reputation for nobility. The Greeks, as the founders of the various branches of learning, emblazon themselves with the ancient renown of their famous heroes. The Turks and all that scum of the real barbarians claim for themselves the praise due to religion, ridiculing Christians, precisely because of their superstitions. But the Jews have it even better, still waiting faithfully for their Messiah and clinging to their Moses tooth and nail even to this day. Spaniards yield to no one in military glory. The Germans pride themselves on their tallness and their knowledge of magic. But, not to run through all of them one by one, you see (I think) how much pleasure Selflove everywhere supplies to individual mortals and to mankind as a whole, and in this function her sister Flattery is almost her equal.

For Selflove is nothing but the soothing praise which a person bestows on himself. If he bestows it on someone else, then it is Kolakia. Nowadays flat-

---

9. *Epistles* 27.4–6.   1. The Sorbonne, the theological faculty in Paris, was the center of theological studies in Europe.

tery is thought of as disreputable, but only by people who are more concerned about words than about things themselves. They judge that flattery is inconsistent with good faith. That the fact is quite otherwise, we can learn even by examples drawn from dumb animals. Is there any animal more fawning than a dog? But then again, is there any more faithful? Is any creature more obsequious than a squirrel? But is any more friendly to man? Unless perhaps you think fierce lions or cruel tigers or treacherous panthers contribute more to man's life! True, there is a certain kind of flattery which is altogether destructive, the kind employed by some unprincipled cynics to ruin their wretched victims. But this Flattery of mine proceeds from a kind disposition and a certain frankness which is much closer to a virtue than the opposite qualities, "sourness" and peevishness, "jangling" (as Horace[2] says) "and dour." This kind of flattery gives a lift to those whose spirits are low, consoles those who mourn, stimulates the apathetic, rouses the dull, cheers the sick, tames the fierce, unites lovers and keeps them united. It entices children to learn their lessons, it cheers up old people, it advises and teaches princes under the cover of an encomium, without giving offense. In short, it makes everyone more agreeable and indulgent to himself—and this is surely the chief ingredient of happiness. What is more courteous than for one person to scratch another's back? Not to mention that this flattery plays a large part in that eloquence everyone praises, a larger in medicine, and the largest of all in poetry—in sum, it is the honey and spice of all human intercourse.

But to be deceived, they say, is miserable. Quite the contrary—not to be deceived is most miserable of all. For nothing could be further from the truth than the notion that man's happiness resides in things as they actually are. It depends on opinions. For human affairs are so manifold and obscure that nothing can be clearly known, as is rightly taught by my friends the Academics,[3] the least arrogant of the philosophers. Or, if anything can be known, it often detracts from the pleasures of life. Finally, the human mind is so constituted that it is far more taken with appearances than reality. If anyone wants clear and obvious evidence of this fact, he should go to church during sermons: if the preacher is explaining his subject seriously, they all doze, yawn, and are sick of it. But if that screacher—I beg your pardon, I meant to say preacher—tells some old wive's tale, as they often do, the whole congregation sits up and listens with open mouths. Likewise, if any saint is more legendary or poetic—for example, think of George or Christopher or Barbara—you will see that such a saint is worshiped with far more devotion than Peter or Paul or Christ himself. But such things are out of place here.

And then, how much less it costs to gain such happiness! Sometimes it requires a great deal of effort to acquire the real article, even if it is something quite trivial, such as grammar. But to think you have acquired it—nothing could be easier, and yet such an opinion contributes as much or more to happiness. Consider, if someone eats a rotten pickled fish, the mere smell of which would be unbearable to another person, and yet the one who eats it thinks it tastes like ambrosia, what difference does it make to his happiness? Conversely, if some delicacy like sturgeon turns another man's stomach, it will hardly add anything to his happiness. If someone who has an

2. *Epistles* 1.18.6.   3. Philosophers of Plato's school, the Academy, which later became a school of the skeptics.

extraordinarily ugly wife still thinks that she could compete with Venus herself, isn't it quite the same as if she were really beautiful? If someone values and admires a canvas daubed with red and yellow, quite convinced that it is by Apelles of Zeuxis, isn't he actually happier than the man who has paid a high price for the real work of those painters but who perhaps takes less pleasure in viewing them than the other man? I know a certain man named after me[4] who gave his bride some imitation gems, assuring her (and he is a clever jokester) that they were not only real and genuine but also that they were of unparalleled and inestimable value. I ask you, what difference did it make to the girl since she feasted her eyes and mind no less pleasantly on glass and kept them hidden among her things as if they were an extraordinary treasure? Meanwhile, the husband avoided expense and profited by his wife's mistake, nor was she any less grateful to him than if he had given her very costly gifts. Surely you don't believe that there is any difference between those who sit in Plato's cave[5] gazing in wonder at the images and likeness of various things—as long as they desire nothing more and are no less pleased— and that wiseman who left the cave and sees things as they really are? Now if Lucian's Mycillus[6] had been allowed to dream forever that rich, golden dream of his, he would have had no reason to wish for any other happiness.

Thus, there is either no difference, or if there is, the lot of fools is clearly preferable. First, because their happiness costs them so little—nothing more than a touch of persuasion. Then too, they enjoy it in common with most other men. And, of course, nothing is really enjoyable without someone to share it with. And who does not know how few wisemen there are—if, in fact, any at all can be found? True, out of so many centuries the Greeks count seven altogether,[7] but if you examine even those very carefully, may I drop dead on the spot if you can find so much as a semi-wiseman, or even a hemi-demi-semi-wiseman.

Now, among the many benefits for which Bacchus is praised, the chief one is held (and rightly so) to be that he clears the mind of its troubles— and that only for a short time, since as soon as you have slept off your little wine-drinking spree, all your anxieties come rushing back to your mind "posthaste," as they say. But how much more ample and lasting is the benefit I provide, a sort of continuous inebriation which fills the mind with joy, delight, and exquisite pleasure—and all with no effort from you. Nor do I ever refuse any mortal a share of my gifts, whereas other endowments of the gods are distributed some to one, some to another. It is not every vineyard that produces a noble, mellow wine, one that drives away care, one that enriches us with surging hope. Few have been endowed with delicate beauty, the gift of Venus; even fewer with eloquence, a benefit given by Mercury. Not so very many have received wealth through the good offices of Hercules. Homer's Jupiter has hardly granted everyone political supremacy. Very often Mars favors neither side. Many depart quite disappointed from the tripod of Apollo's oracle. The son of Saturn often hurls his lightning bolt. Phoebus sometimes throws down missiles armed with the plague. Neptune drowns

4. Sir Thomas More (1478–1535), a close friend of Erasmus. The pun is with *moria* (Latin for "folly").   5. In Plato's allegory in the *Republic* (book 7) he compares the soul in the body to a prisoner chained in a cave, his or her back against the light, able to see only the shadows of things outside.   6. A character in *The Dream, or the Cock* who dreams that he has taken the place of a rich man.
7. Philosophers in the sixth century B.C.; among them were Thales and Solon.

more than he saves. I might also mention in passing such powers as Vejovis, Pluto, Ate, the Poenae,[8] the god of Fever and the like—not really gods, but tormentors. I, Folly, am the only one who embraces everyone equally with such ready and easy generosity. I do not care for vows, nor do I grow angry and demand expiatory gifts if some point of ceremony is overlooked. Nor do I go on a rampage if someone invites the other gods and leaves me sitting at home with no share of the fragrant steam rising from the sacrificial victims. For the other gods are so touchy about such things that it is more advantageous, and even safer, to leave them alone than to follow their cult—just as there are some men who are so hard to please and quick to take offense that it is better to have nothing at all to do with them than to cultivate their friendship.

But no one sacrifices to Folly, they say, and no one has built a temple dedicated to her. Indeed, I myself, as I said, find this ingratitude somewhat surprising. Still, I am good-natured enough to take this also in good part, though I couldn't really want such things anyway. Why should I need a bit of incense or grain or a goat or a hog, when all mortals everywhere in the world worship me with the kind of homage that even the theologians rank highest of all? Unless perhaps I should envy Diana because human blood is sacrificed in her honor! I consider that I am being worshiped with the truest devotion when men everywhere do precisely what they now do: embrace me in their hearts, express me in their conduct, represent me in their lives. Clearly this sort of devotion to the saints, even among Christians, is not exactly common. What a huge flock of people light candles to the virgin mother of God—even at noon, when there is no need! But how few of them strive to imitate her chastity, her modesty, her love for the things of heaven! For, in the last analysis, that is true worship, the kind which is by far the most pleasing to the saints in heaven. Furthermore, why should I want a temple, since the whole world, unless I am badly mistaken, is a splendid temple dedicated to me? Nor will there ever be a lack of worshipers, as long as there is no lack of men. Moreover, I am not so foolish as to require stone statues decked out in gaudy colors. For sometimes these are a drawback to the worship of us gods—that is, when stupid numbskulls adore the figures instead of the divinities, and then we are left in the position of those who have been edged out of their jobs by substitutes. I consider that as many statues have been set up for me as there are men who display, sometimes even unwillingly, a living image of me. And so, there is no reason why I should envy the other gods because each is worshiped in his own corner of the world, and on set days too—as, for example, Phoebus is honored at Rhodes, Venus on Cyprus, Juno at Argos, Minerva at Athens, Jupiter on Olympus, Neptune at Terentum, Priapus[9] at Lampsacus—as long as the whole world in perfect unanimity never ceases to offer me far superior victims.

Now if anyone thinks my claims reveal more boldness than truth, come on, let's examine the actual lives of men for a bit, to make it clear just how much they owe me—throughout all society from top to bottom—and how highly they value me.

* * *

8. Poena was goddess of punishment. Vejovis was hostile to men. Pluto was god of the underworld. Ate was goddess of revenge and discord.   9. A god of procreation, son of Dionysus and Aphrodite.

But why should I fret uselessly, trying to establish these things through so much testimony from various witnesses,[1] when Christ himself in the mystical psalms openly says to the Father, "You know my folly"?[2] Nor is it merely an accident that fools are so extremely pleasing to God. I think the reason is simply this: just as great rulers suspect and despise those who are too intelligent (as Caesar did Brutus and Cassius, whereas he had no fear of the drunken Anthony, and as Nero did Seneca, and Dionysius[3] did Plato) but are delighted with crude and simple minds, so too Christ always despises and condemns those savants who rely on their own wisdom. Paul testifies very clearly on this point when he says "What is foolish to the world, God has chosen,"[4] and when he says that God was pleased to save the world through folly because it could not be redeemed by wisdom.[5] Indeed, God himself makes the same point clear enough when he cries out through the mouth of the prophet, "I will destroy the wisdom of the wise and the prudence of the prudent I will reject,"[6] and again when he gives thanks that the mystery of salvation has been hidden from the wise and revealed to the simple, that is, to fools.[7] For the Greek for "simple" is νηπίοις, which he contrasted with σοφοῖς (wise). Relevant here, too, are his attacks everywhere in the gospel against the scribes and pharisees and doctors of the law, whereas he carefully protected the ignorant populace. For isn't "Woe to you, scribes and pharisees"[8] equivalent to "Woe to you, wisemen"? But he seems to have taken the greatest delight in simple people, women, and fishermen. In fact, even on the level of animal creatures, Christ is most pleased with those who are farthest removed from the slyness of the fox. Hence he preferred to ride on an ass, when if he wished he could have mounted on a lion's back with impunity. And the Holy Spirit came down in the shape of a dove, not an eagle or a hawk. Moreover, throughout Holy Scripture, harts, young mules, and lambs are frequently mentioned. Consider also that he calls his own followers, destined for immortal life, sheep. No other animal is more stupid, as is quite clear from the Aristotelian proverb "a mind like a sheep's," which (as he informs us) is derived from that animal's stupidity and is frequently leveled at blockheads and dolts as an insult. But, of such a flock as this, Christ professes to be the shepherd. Even more, he himself delighted in the title "lamb," as when John pointed him out with, "Behold, the lamb of God,"[9] which is also frequently mentioned in the Apocalypse.

Do not all these witnesses cry out with one voice that all mortals are fools, even the pious? And that even Christ, though he was the wisdom of the Father,[1] became somehow foolish in order to relieve the folly of mortals when he took on human nature and appeared in the form of a man? Just as he became sin in order to heal sins.[2] Nor did he choose any other way to heal them but through the folly of the cross, through ignorant and doltish apostles. For them, too, he carefully prescribed folly, warning them against wisdom, when he set before them the example of children, lilies, mustard seed, and sparrows[3]—stupid creatures lacking all intelligence, leading their lives

---

1. I.e., of the relationship between Folly and Christianity.   2. Psalm 69.5. The speaker is not Christ but the psalmist.   3. Dionysius the Younger (fourth century B.C.), tyrant of Syracuse, in Sicily.   4. 1 Corinthians 1.27.   5. 1 Corinthians 1.21: "It pleased God by the foolishness of preaching to save them that believe."   6. 1 Corinthians 1.19.   7. Matthew 11.25: "I thank thee, O Father, Lord of heaven and earth, because thou hast hid these things from the wise and prudent, and hast revealed them unto babes."   8. Luke 11.44.   9. John 1.29.   1. 1 Corinthians 1.24: "But unto them which are called, both Jews and Greeks, Christ the power of God, and the wisdom of God."   2. 2 Corinthians 5.21.   3. Matthew 10.29. *Children:* Luke 18.17. *Lilies:* Matthew 6.28. *Mustard seed:* Luke 17.6.

according to the dictates of nature, artless and carefree—and also when he forbad them to be concerned about how they should speak before magistrates, and when he enjoined them not to examine dates and times, so as to keep them from relying on their own wisdom and make them depend on him heart and soul. To the same effect is the prohibition of God, the architect of the world, that they should not eat any fruit from the tree of knowledge, as if knowledge would poison their happiness. For that matter, Paul openly condemns knowledge as dangerous because it puffs men up.[4] St. Bernard, I imagine, was following Paul when he interpreted the mountain on which Lucifer established his throne as the mountain of knowledge.

Perhaps we ought not to omit the argument that folly is pleasing to the powers above because it alone can win pardon for mistakes, whereas a knowledgeable man is not forgiven. Hence, those who pray for forgiveness, even if they sinned knowingly, still employ folly as a pretext and defense. For this is the way Aaron prays to avert the punishment of his sister in The Book of Numbers, if I remember correctly: "I beg you, Lord, do not hold us responsible for this sin, which we have committed in our folly."[5] So too Saul begged David to forgive his offense, saying, "For it is clear that I acted in my folly."[6] Again, David himself coaxes the Lord in these words: "But I beg you, Lord, to take away the iniquity of your servant, because we have acted in our folly,"[7] as if he would not obtain pardon unless he pleaded folly and ignorance as excuses. But what is even more compelling, when Christ on the cross prayed for his enemies, "Father, forgive them," the only excuse he made for them was their ignorance: "for they do not know," he said, "what they are doing."[8] In the same way Paul, writing to Timothy: "For this reason I obtained mercy from God, because I acted ignorantly, as an unbeliever."[9] What does "I did it ignorantly" amount to but "I did it in my folly, not with malice?" What does "For this reason I obtained mercy" mean but that he would not have obtained it if he had not been recommended by the patronage of folly? Our case is also strengthened by that mystical psalmist, who did not occur to us in the proper place: "Do not remember the sins of my youth and my stupidities."[1] You hear the two excuses he makes: namely, youth, to whom I am a regular companion, and stupidities—and in the plural at that, so that we may understand the full force of his folly.

And now, to stop running through endless examples and to put it in a nutshell, it seems to me that the Christian religion taken all together has a certain affinity with some sort of folly and has little or nothing to do with wisdom. If you want some proof of this, notice first of all that children, old people, women, and retarded persons are more delighted than others with holy and religious matters and hence are always nearest to the altar, simply out of a natural inclination. Moreover, you see how those first founders of religion were remarkably devoted to simplicity and bitterly hostile to literature. Finally, no fools seem more senseless than those people who have been completely taken up, once and for all, with a burning devotion to Christian piety: they throw away their possessions, ignore injuries, allow themselves to be deceived, make no distinction between friend and foe, shudder at the

---

4. 1 Corinthians 8.1: "Knowledge puffeth up, but charity edifieth." 5. Numbers 12.11: "And Aaron said unto Moses, Alas, my lord, I beseech thee, lay not the sin upon us, wherein we have done foolishly, and wherein we have sinned." 6. 1 Samuel 26.21: "Behold, I have played the fool, and I have erred exceedingly." 7. 1 Chronicles 21.8. 8. Luke 23.34. 9. 1 Timothy 1.13: "But I obtained mercy, because I did it ignorantly in unbelief." 1. Psalm 25.7.

thought of pleasure, find satisfaction in fasts, vigils, tears, and labors, shrink from life, desire death above all else—in short, they seem completely devoid of normal human responses, just as if their minds were living somewhere else, not in their bodies. Can such a condition be called anything but insanity? In this light, it is not at all surprising that the apostles seemed to be intoxicated with new wine and that Paul seemed mad to the judge Festus.[2]

* * *

* * * In absolutely every activity of life, the pious man flees from whatever is related to the body and is carried away in the pursuit of the eternal and invisible things of the spirit. Hence, since these two groups[3] are in such utter disagreement on all matters, the result is that each thinks the other is insane—though that word applies more properly to the pious than to ordinary men, if you want my opinion. This will be much clearer if, according to my promise, I devote a few words to showing that their supreme reward is no more than a certain insanity.

First, therefore, consider that Plato had some glimmer of this notion when he wrote that the madness of lovers is the height of happiness.[4] For a person who loves intensely no longer lives in himself but rather in that which he loves, and the farther he gets from himself and the closer to it, the happier he is. Moreover, when the mind is set on leaving the body and no longer has perfect control over the bodily organs, no doubt you would rightly call this condition madness. Otherwise what is the meaning of such common expressions as "he is out of his wits," "come to your senses," and "he is himself once more." Also, the more perfect the love, the greater and happier is the madness. What, then, is that future life in heaven for which pious minds long so eagerly? I'll tell you: the spirit, stronger at last and victorious, will absorb the body. And it will do so all the more easily, partly because it is in its own kingdom now, partly because even in its former life it had purged and refined the body in preparation for such a transformation. Then the spirit will be absorbed by that highest mind of all, whose power is infinitely greater, in such a way that the whole man will be outside himself, and will be happy for no other reason than that he is located outside himself, and will receive unspeakable joy from that Highest Good which gathers all things to Himself.

Now, although this happiness is not absolutely perfect until the mind, having received its former body, is endowed with immortality, nevertheless it happens that, because the life of the pious is nothing but a meditation and a certain shadow (as it were) of that other life, they sometimes experience a certain flavor or odor of that reward. And this, even though it is like the tiniest droplet by comparison with that fountain of eternal happiness, nevertheless far surpasses all pleasures of the body, even if all the delights of all mortals were gathered into one. So much beyond the body are the things of the spirit; things unseen, beyond what can be seen. This, indeed, is what the prophet promises: "Eye has not seen, nor ear heard, nor has the heart of man conceived what things God has prepared for those who love him."[5] And this is Folly's part, which shall not be taken from her by the transformation of life, but shall be perfected. Those who have the privilege of experiencing

---

2. Acts 26.24: "Festus said with a loud voice, Paul, thou art beside thyself; much learning doth make thee mad." 3. The pious and the ordinary. 4. *Phaedrus*, line 245. 5. 1 Corinthians 2.9.

this (and it happens to very few) undergo something very like madness: they talk incoherently, not in a human fashion, making sounds without sense. Then the entire expression of their faces vacillates repeatedly: now happy, now sad; now crying, now laughing, now sighing—in short, they are completely beside themselves. Soon after, when they come to themselves, they say they do not know where they have been, whether in the body or out of it, whether waking or sleeping. They do not remember what they heard or saw or said or did except in a cloudy way, as if it were a dream. All they know is that they were never happier than while they were transported with such madness. Thus, they lament that they have come to their senses and want above all else to be forever mad with this kind of madness. And this is only a faint taste, as it were, of that future happiness.

But I have long since forgotten myself and "have gone beyond the pale." If you think my speech has been too pert or wordy, keep in mind that you've been listening to Folly and to a woman. But also remember that Greek proverb "Often a foolish man says something to the point"—unless, perhaps, you think it doesn't apply to women.

I see that you are waiting for an epilogue, but you are crazy if you think I still have in mind what I have said, after pouring forth such a torrent of jumbled words. The old saying was "I hate a drinking-companion with a memory." Updated, it is "I hate a listener with a memory." Therefore, farewell, clap your hands, live well, drink your fill, most illustrious initiates of Folly.

NICCOLÒ MACHIAVELLI
1469–1527

The most famous and controversial political writer and theorist of his time—indeed, possibly of all time—Niccolò Machiavelli was born in Florence on May 3, 1469. Little is known of his schooling, but it is obvious from his works that he knew the Latin and Italian writers well. He entered public life in 1494 as a clerk and from 1498 to 1512 was secretary to the second chancery of the commune of Florence, whose magistrates were in charge of internal and war affairs. During the conflict between Florence and Pisa, he dealt with military problems firsthand. Thus he had a direct experience of war as well as of diplomacy; he was entrusted with many missions—among others, to King Louis XII of France in 1500 and in 1502 to Cesare Borgia, duke of Valentinois or "il duca Valentino," the favorite son of Pope Alexander VI. Machiavelli described the duke's ruthless methods in crushing a conspiracy during his conquest of the Romagna region in a terse booklet *Of the Method Followed by Duke Valentino in Killing Vitellozzo Vitelli*, which already shows direct insight into the type of the amoral and technically efficient "prince." In 1506 Machiavelli went on a mission to Pope Julius II, whose expedition into Romagna (an old name for north-central Italy) he followed closely. From this and other missions—to Emperor Maximilian (1508) and again to the king of France (1509)—Machiavelli drew his two books of observations or *Portraits* of the affairs of those territories, written in 1508 and 1510.

Preeminently a student of politics and an acute observer of historical events, Machiavelli endeavored to apply his experience of other states to the strengthening of his own, the Florentine republic, and busied himself in 1507 with the establishment of a Florentine militia, encountering great difficulties. When the republican regime came to an end, he lost his post and was exiled from the city proper, though forbidden to leave Florentine territory. The new regime of the Medici accused him unjustly of conspiracy, and he was released only after a period of imprisonment and torture. To the period of his exile (spent near San Casciano, a few miles from Florence, where he retired with his wife, Marietta Corsini, and his five children), we owe his major works: the *Discourses on the First Ten Books of Livy* (1513–21) and *The Prince*, written in 1513 with the hope of obtaining public office from the Medici. In 1520 Machiavelli was commissioned to write a history of Florence, which he presented in 1525 to Pope Clement VII (Giulio de' Medici). The following year, conscious of imminent dangers, he took part in the work to improve the military fortifications of Florence. The fate of the city at this point depended on the outcome of the larger struggle between Francis I of France and the Holy Roman Emperor, Charles V. Pope Clement's siding with the king of France led to the disastrous "Sack of Rome" by Charles V in 1527, and the result for Florence was the collapse of Medici domination. Machiavelli's hopes, briefly raised by the reestablishment of the republic, came to naught, because he was now regarded as a Medici sympathizer. This last disappointment may have accelerated his end. He died on June 22, 1527, and was buried in the church of Santa Croce.

Though Machiavelli has a place in literary history for a short novel and two plays— one of which, *La mandragola* (The mandrake), first performed in the early 1520s, belongs in the upper rank of Italian comedies of intrigue—his world reputation is based on *The Prince*. This "handbook" on how to obtain and keep political power consists of twenty-six chapters. The first eleven deal with different types of dominions and the ways in which they are acquired and preserved—the early title of the whole book, in Latin, was *De principatibus* (Of princedoms)—and the twelfth to fourteenth chapters focus particularly on problems of military power. The book's astounding fame, however, is based on the final part (from chapter fifteen to the end), which deals primarily with the attributes and "virtues" of the prince himself. In other words, despite its reputation for cool, precise realism, the work presents a hypothetical type, the idealized portrait of a certain kind of person.

Manuals of this sort may be classified, in one sense, as pedagogical literature. Because of their merits of form and of vivid, if stylized, characterization they can be considered works of art, but their overt purpose is to codify a certain set of manners and rules of conduct; the authors, therefore, present themselves as especially wise, experts in the field, "minds" offering advice to the executive "arm." Machiavelli is a clear example of this approach. His fervor, the dramatic, oratorical way he confronts his reader, the wealth and pertinence of his illustrations are all essential qualities of his pedagogical *persona*: "Either you are already a prince, or you are on the way to become one. In the first case liberality is dangerous; in the second it is very necessary to be thought liberal. Caesar was one of those. . . . Somebody may answer. . . . I answer." Relying on his direct knowledge of politics, he uses examples he can personally vouch for:

> Men are so simple and so subject to present needs that he who deceives in this way will always find those who will let themselves be deceived.
>
> I do not wish to keep still about one of the recent instances. Alexander VI did nothing else than deceive men, and had no other intention.

The implied tone of *I know, I have seen such things myself* adds a special immediacy to Machiavelli's prose. His view of the practical world may have been an especially startling one, but the sensation caused by his work would have been far less without the rhetorical power, the drama of argumentation, that makes *The Prince* a unique example of "the art of persuasion."

The view of humanity in Machiavelli is not at all cheerful. Indeed, the pessimistic notion that humanity is evil is not so much Machiavelli's conclusion about human nature as his premise; it is the point of departure of all subsequent reasoning on the course for a ruler to follow. The very fact of its being given as a premise, however, tends to qualify it; it is not a firm philosophical judgment but a stratagem, dictated by the facts as they are seen by a lucid observer of the here and now. The author is committed to his view of the human being not as a philosopher or as a religious man but as a practical politician. He indicates the rules of the game as his experience shows it must, under the circumstances, be played.

> A prudent ruler . . . cannot and should not observe faith when such observance is to his disadvantage and the causes that made him give his promise have vanished. If men were all good, this advice would not be good, but since men are wicked and do not keep their promises to you, you likewise do not have to keep yours to them.

A basic question in the study of Machiavelli, therefore, is "How much of a realist is he?" His picture of the perfectly efficient ruler has something of the quality of an abstraction; it shows, though much less clearly than Castiglione's portrayal of the courtier, the well-known Renaissance tendency toward "perfected" form. Machiavelli's abandonment of complex actualities in favor of an ideal vision is shown most clearly at the conclusion of the book, particularly in the last chapter. This is where he offers what amounts to the greatest of his illustrations as the prince's preceptor and counselor: the ideal ruler, now technically equipped by his pedagogue, is to undertake a mission—the liberation of Machiavelli's Italy. If we regard the last chapter of *The Prince* as a culmination of Machiavelli's discussion rather than as a dissonant addition to it, we are likely to feel at that point not only that Machiavelli's realistic method is ultimately directed toward an ideal task but also that his conception of that task, far from being based on immediate realities, is founded on cultural and poetic myths. Machiavelli's method here becomes imaginative rather than scientific. His exhortation to liberate Italy, and his final prophecy, belong to the tradition of poetic visions in which a present state of decay is lamented and a hope of future redemption is expressed (as in Dante's *Purgatorio,* canto 6). And a very significant part of this hope is presented not in terms of technical political considerations (choice of the opportune moment, evaluation of military power) but in terms of a poetic justice for which precedents are sought in religious and ancient history and in mythology:

> . . . if it was necessary to make clear the ability of Moses that the people of Israel should be enslaved in Egypt, and to reveal Cyrus's greatness of mind that the Persians should be oppressed by the Medes, and to demonstrate the excellence of Theseus that the Athenians should be scattered, so at the present time. . . . Everything is now fully disposed for the work . . . if only your House adopts the methods of those I have set forth as examples. Moreover, we have before our eyes extraordinary and unexampled means prepared by God. The sea has been divided. . . . Manna has fallen.

Machiavelli's Italy, as he observes in chapter 25, is now a country "without dykes and without any wall of defence." It has suffered from "deluges," and its present rule, a "barbarian" one, "stinks in every nostril." Something is rotten in it, in short, as in Hamlet's Denmark. And we become more and more detached even from the particular example, Italy, as we recognize in the situation a pattern frequently exemplified in tragedy: the desire for communal regeneration, for the cleansing of the city-state, the *polis.* Of this cleansing, Italy on the one side and the imaginary prince on the other may be taken as symbols. The envisaged redemption is identified with antiquity and Roman virtue, while the realism of the political observer is here drowned out by the cry of the humanist dreaming of ancient glories.

Peter E. Bondanella focuses on the literary aspects of Machiavelli's works in *Machiavelli and the Art of Renaissance History* (1973). Sebastian De Grazia, *Machiavelli in Hell* (1989), on politics in *The Prince,* contains indexes and a bibliography. J. R.

Hale's biography, *Machiavelli and Renaissance Italy* (1972), places Machiavelli in a historical perspective. A political analysis is provided by Anthony Parel in *The Political Calculus: Essays on Machiavelli's Political Philosophy* (1972). Roberto Ridolfi, *The Life of Niccolò Machiavelli* (1963), is still considered the best and most accurate biography. Silvia Ruffo-Fiore, *Niccolò Machiavelli* (1982), is a useful comprehensive guide for the beginning student. Victoria Kahn, *Machiavellian Rhetoric: From the Counter-Reformation to Milton* (1994), and Wayne A. Rebhorn, *Foxes and Lions: Machiavelli's Confidence Men* (1988), are recommended.

PRONOUNCING GLOSSARY

The following list uses common English syllables and stress accents to provide rough equivalents of selected words whose pronunciation may be unfamiliar to the general reader.

Borgia: *bor'-juh* Pistoia: *pees-toh'-yah*

Chiron: *kai'-ron* San Casciano: *san ka-shah'-noh*

de' Medici: *day may'-dee-chee* Santa Croce: *san'-tuh croh'-chay*

Machiavelli: *ma-kee-ah-vel'-lee*

Letter to Francesco Vettori[1]

["That Food Which Alone Is Mine"]

I am living on my farm, and since my last troubles[2] I have not been in Florence twenty days, putting them all together. Up to now I have been setting snares for thrushes with my own hands; I get up before daylight, prepare my birdlime, and go out with a bundle of cages on my back, so that I look like Geta when he came back from the harbor with the books of Amphitryo,[3] and catch at the least two thrushes and at the most six. So I did all of September; then this trifling diversion, despicable and strange as it is, to my regret failed. What my life is now I shall tell you.

In the morning I get up with the sun and go out into a grove that I am having cut; there I remain a couple of hours to look over the work of the past day and kill some time with the woodmen, who always have on hand some dispute either among themselves or among their neighbors. . . .

When I leave the grove, I go to a spring, and from there into my aviary. I have a book in my pocket, either Dante or Petrarch or one of the minor poets, as Tibullus,[4] Ovid, and the like. I read about their tender passions and their loves, remember mine, and take pleasure for a while in thinking about them. Then I go along the road to the inn, talk with those who pass by, ask the news of their villages, learn various things, and note the varied tastes and different fancies of men. It gets to be dinner time, and with my troop I eat what food my poor farm and my little property permit. After dinner, I return to the inn; there I usually find the host, a butcher, a miller, and two furnace-tenders. With these fellows I sink into vulgarity for the rest of the day, playing

---

1. Translated by Allan H. Gilbert. From a letter dated December 10, 1513, to Vettori, ambassador in Rome. 2. Machiavelli had been suspected of participation in a conspiracy led by two young friends of his and had been imprisoned and subjected to torture before his innocence was recognized. 3. Allusion to a popular tale in which Amphitryo, returning to Thebes after having studied at Athens, sends forward from the harbor his servant Geta to announce his arrival to his wife, Alemene, and loads him with his books. 4. Albius Tibullus (first century B.C.), Roman elegiac poet.

at *cricca* and *tricche-trach*;[5] from these games come a thousand quarrels and numberless offensive and insulting words; we often dispute over a penny, and all the same are heard shouting as far as San Casciano.[6] So, involved in these trifles, I keep my brain from getting mouldy, and express the perversity of Fate, for I am willing to have her drive me along this path, to see if she will be ashamed of it.

In the evening, I return to my house, and go into my study. At the door I take off the clothes I have worn all day, mud spotted and dirty, and put on regal and courtly garments. Thus appropriately clothed, I enter into the ancient courts of ancient men,[7] where, being lovingly received, I feed on that food which alone is mine, and which I was born for; I am not ashamed to speak with them and to ask the reasons for their actions, and they courteously answer me. For four hours I feel no boredom and forget every worry; I do not fear poverty, and death does not terrify me. I give myself completely over to the ancients. And because Dante says that there is no knowledge unless one retains what one has read,[8] I have written down the profit I have gained from their conversation, and composed a little book *De principatibus*,[9] in which I go as deep as I can into reflections on this subject, debating what a principate is, what the species are, how they are gained, how they are kept, and why they are lost. If ever any of my trifles can please you, this one should not displease you; and to a prince, and especially a new prince, it ought to be welcome.

From The Prince[1]

New Princedoms Gained with Other Men's Forces and through Fortune

FROM CHAPTER 7

* * *

[Cesare Borgia][2]

* * * Cesare Borgia, called by the people Duke Valentino, gained his position through his father's Fortune and through her lost it, notwithstanding that he made use of every means and action possible to a prudent and vigorous man for putting down his roots in those states that another man's arms and Fortune bestowed on him. As I say above, he who does not lay his foundations beforehand can perhaps through great wisdom and energy lay them afterward, though he does so with trouble for the architect and danger to the building. So on examining all the steps taken by the Duke, we see that he himself laid mighty foundations for future power. To discuss these steps is not superfluous; indeed I for my part do not see what better precepts I

5. Two popular games, the first played with cards, the second with dice thrown to regulate the movements of pawns on a chessboard. 6. Nearby village, in the region around Florence. 7. Machiavelli here refers figuratively to his study of ancient history. 8. *Paradiso* 5.41–42: "For knowledge none can vaunt / Who retains not, although he have understood." 9. Of princedoms (Latin title of *The Prince*). All chapter headings are also in Latin in the original. 1. Translated by Allan H. Gilbert. 2. Son of Pope Alexander VI and duke of Valentinois and Romagna. His skillful and merciless subjugation of the local lords of Romagna occurred between 1499 and 1502.

can give a new prince than the example of Duke Valentino's actions. If his arrangements did not bring him success, the fault was not his, because his failure resulted from an unusual and utterly malicious stroke of Fortune.[3]

[Pope Alexander VI Attempts to Make Cesare a Prince]

Alexander VI,[4] in his attempt to give high position to the Duke his son, had before him many difficulties, present and future. First, he saw no way in which he could make him lord of any state that was not a state of the Church, yet if the Pope tried to take such a state from the Church, he knew that the Duke of Milan and the Venetians[5] would not allow it because both Faenza and Rimini were already under Venetian protection. He saw, besides, that the weapons of Italy, especially those of which he could make use, were in the hands of men who had reason to fear the Pope's greatness; therefore he could not rely on them, since they were all among the Orsini and the Colonnesi[6] and their allies. He therefore was under the necessity of disturbing the situation and embroiling the states of Italy so that he could safely master part of them. This he found easy since, luckily for him, the Venetians, influenced by other reasons, had set out to get the French to come again into Italy. He not merely did not oppose their coming; he made it easier by dissolving the early marriage of King Louis.[7] The King then marched into Italy with the Venetians' aid and Alexander's consent; and he was no sooner in Milan than the Pope got soldiers from him for an attempt on Romagna; these the King granted for the sake of his own reputation.[8]

[Borgia Determines to Depend on Himself]

Having taken Romagna, then, and suppressed the Colonnesi, the Duke, in attempting to keep the province and to go further, was hindered by two things: one, his own forces, which he thought disloyal; the other, France's intention. That is, he feared that the Orsini forces which he had been using would fail him and not merely would hinder his gaining but would take from him what he had gained, and that the King would treat him in the same way. With the Orsini, he had experience of this when after the capture of Faenza he attacked Bologna, for he saw that they turned cold over that attack. And as to the King's purpose, the Duke learned it when, after taking the dukedom of Urbino, he invaded Tuscany—an expedition that the King made him abandon. As a result, he determined not to depend further on another man's armies and Fortune.

[The Duke Destroys His Disloyal Generals]

The Duke's first act to that end was to weaken the Orsini and Colonnesi parties in Rome by winning over to himself all their adherents who were men of rank, making them his own men of rank and giving them large subsidies; and he honored them, according to their stations, with military and civil

---

3. Ill health.   4. Rodrigo Borgia (1431?–1503), pope (1492–1503), father of Cesare and Lucrezia Borgia.   5. The Venetian Republic opposed the expansion of the papal states. *Duke of Milan:* Ludovico Il Moro, the flamboyant duke of the Sforza family.   6. Powerful Roman families.   7. Louis XII, king of France (d. 1515).   8. According to his agreement with Pope Alexander VI.

offices, so that within a few months their hearts were emptied of all affection for the Roman parties, and it was wholly transferred to the Duke. After this, he waited for a good chance to wipe out the Orsini leaders, having scattered those of the Colonna family; such a chance came to him well and he used it better. When the Orsini found out, though late, that the Duke's and the Church's greatness was their ruin, they held a meeting at Magione, in Perugian territory. From that resulted the rebellion of Urbino, the insurrections in Romagna, and countless dangers for the Duke, all of which he overcame with the aid of the French. Thus having got back his reputation, but not trusting France or other outside forces, in order not to have to put them to a test, he turned to trickery. And he knew so well how to falsify his purpose that the Orsini themselves, by means of Lord Paulo,[9] were reconciled with him (as to Paulo the Duke did not omit any sort of gracious act to assure him, giving him money, clothing and horses) so completely that their folly took them to Sinigaglia into his hands. Having wiped out these leaders, then, and changed their partisans into his friends, the Duke had laid very good foundations for his power, holding all the Romagna along with the dukedom of Urbino, especially since he believed he had made the Romagna his friend and gained the support of all those people, through their getting a taste of well-being.

[Peace in Romagna; Remirro de Orco]

Because this matter is worthy of notice and of being copied by others, I shall not omit it. After the Duke had seized the Romagna and found it controlled by weak lords who had plundered their subjects rather than governed them, and had given them reason for disunion, not for union, so that the whole province was full of thefts, brawls, and every sort of excess, he judged that if he intended to make it peaceful and obedient to the ruler's arm, he must of necessity give it good government. Hence he put in charge there Messer Remirro de Orco, a man cruel and ready, to whom he gave the most complete authority. This man in a short time rendered the province peaceful and united, gaining enormous prestige. Then the Duke decided there was no further need for such boundless power, because he feared it would become a cause for hatred; so he set up a civil court in the midst of the province, with a distinguished presiding judge, where every city had its lawyer. And because he knew that past severities had made some men hate him, he determined to purge such men's minds and win them over entirely by showing that any cruelty which had gone on did not originate with himself but with the harsh nature of his agent. So getting an opportunity for it, one morning at Cesena he had Messer Remirro laid in two pieces in the public square with a block of wood and a bloody sword near him. The ferocity of this spectacle left those people at the same time gratified and awe-struck.

9. Member of the Orsini.

[*Princely Virtues*]

FROM CHAPTER 15

On the Things for Which Men, and Especially Princes, Are Praised or Censured

* * * Because I know that many have written on this topic, I fear that when I too write I shall be thought presumptuous, because, in discussing it, I break away completely from the principles laid down by my predecessors. But since it is my purpose to write something useful to an attentive reader, I think it more effective to go back to the practical truth of the subject than to depend on my fancies about it. And many have imagined republics and principalities that never have been seen or known to exist in reality. For there is such a difference between the way men live and the way they ought to live, that anybody who abandons what is for what ought to be will learn something that will ruin rather than preserve him, because anyone who determines to act in all circumstances the part of a good man must come to ruin among so many who are not good. Hence, if a prince wishes to maintain himself, he must learn how to be not good, and to use that ability or not as is required.

Leaving out of account, then, things about an imaginary prince, and considering things that are true, I say that all men, when they are spoken of, and especially princes, because they are set higher, are marked with some of the qualities that bring them either blame or praise. To wit, one man is thought liberal, another stingy (using a Tuscan word, because *avaricious* in our language is still applied to one who desires to get things through violence, but *stingy* we apply to him who refrains too much from using his own property); one is thought open-handed, another grasping; one cruel, the other compassionate; one is a breaker of faith, the other reliable; one is effeminate and cowardly, the other vigorous and spirited; one is philanthropic, the other egotistic; one is lascivious, the other chaste; one is straight-forward, the other crafty; one hard, the other easy to deal with; one is firm, the other unsettled; one is religious, the other unbelieving; and so on.

And I know that everybody will admit that it would be very praiseworthy for a prince to possess all of the above-mentioned qualities that are considered good. But since he is not able to have them or to observe them completely, because human conditions do not allow him to, it is necessary that he be prudent enough to understand how to avoid getting a bad name because he is given to those vices that will deprive him of his position. He should also, if he can, guard himself from those vices that will not take his place away from him, but if he cannot do it, he can with less anxiety let them go. Moreover, he should not be troubled if he gets a bad name because of vices without which it will be difficult for him to preserve his position. I say this because, if everything is considered, it will be seen that some things seem to be virtuous, but if they are put into practice will be ruinous to him; other things seem to be vices, yet if put into practice will bring the prince security and well-being.

FROM CHAPTER 16

On Liberality and Parsimony

Beginning, then, with the first of the above-mentioned qualities, I assert that it is good to be thought liberal.[1] Yet liberality, practiced in such a way that you get a reputation for it, is damaging to you, for the following reasons: If you use it wisely and as it ought to be used, it will not become known, and you will not escape being censured for the opposite vice. Hence, if you wish to have men call you liberal, it is necessary not to omit any sort of lavishness. A prince who does this will always be obliged to use up all his property in lavish actions; he will then, if he wishes to keep the name of liberal, be forced to lay heavy taxes on his people and exact money from them, and do everything he can to raise money. This will begin to make his subjects hate him, and as he grows poor he will be little esteemed by anybody. So it comes about that because of this liberality of his, with which he has damaged a large number and been of advantage to but a few, he is affected by every petty annoyance and is in peril from every slight danger. If he recognizes this and wishes to draw back, he quickly gets a bad name for stinginess.

Since, then, a prince cannot without harming himself practice this virtue of liberality to such an extent that it will be recognized, he will, if he is prudent, not care about being called stingy. As time goes on he will be thought more and more liberal, for the people will see that because of his economy his income is enough for him, that he can defend himself from those who make war against him, and that he can enter upon undertakings without burdening his people. Such a prince is in the end liberal to all those from whom he takes nothing, and they are numerous; he is stingy to those to whom he does not give, and they are few. In our times we have seen big things done only by those who have been looked on as stingy; the others have utterly failed. Pope Julius II,[2] though he made use of a reputation for liberality to attain the papacy, did not then try to maintain it, because he wished to be able to make war. The present King of France[3] has carried on great wars without laying unusually heavy taxes on his people, merely because his long economy has made provision for heavy expenditures. The present King of Spain,[4] if he had continued liberal, would not have carried on or completed so many undertakings.

Therefore a prince ought to care little about getting called stingy, if as a result he does not have to rob his subjects, is able to defend himself, does not become poor and contemptible, and is not obliged to become grasping. For this vice of stinginess is one of those that enables him to rule. Somebody may say: Caesar, by means of his liberality became emperor, and many others have come to high positions because they have been liberal and have been thought so. I answer: Either you are already prince, or you are on the way to become one. In the first case liberality is dangerous; in the second it is very necessary to be thought liberal. Caesar was one of those who wished to attain dominion over Rome. But if, when he had attained it, he had lived for a long

---

1. Generous, openhanded.　2. Giuliano della Rovere (1443–1513), elected to the papacy in 1503 at the death of Pius III, who had been successor to Alexander VI (Rodrigo Borgia). Alexander VI is discussed in chap. 18. Julius II's character is discussed in chap. 25.　3. Louis XII (1462–1515).　4. Ferdinand II, "the Catholic" (1452–1516).

time and had not moderated his expenses, he would have destroyed his authority. Somebody may answer: Many who have been thought very liberal have been princes and done great things with their armies. I answer: The prince spends either his own property and that of his subjects or that of others. In the first case he ought to be frugal; in the second he ought to abstain from no sort of liberality. When he marches with his army and lives on plunder, loot, and ransom, a prince controls the property of others. To him liberality is essential, for without it his soldiers would not follow him. You can be a free giver of what does not belong to you or your subjects, as were Cyrus, Caesar, and Alexander, because to spend the money of others does not decrease your reputation but adds to it. It is only the spending of your own money that hurts you.

There is nothing that eats itself up as fast as does liberality, for when you practice it you lose the power to practice it, and become poor and contemptible, or else to escape poverty you become rapacious and therefore are hated. And of all the things against which a prince must guard himself, the first is being an object of contempt and hatred. Liberality leads you to both of these. Hence there is more wisdom in keeping a name for stinginess, which produces a bad reputation without hatred, than in striving for the name of liberal, only to be forced to get the name of rapacious, which brings forth both bad reputation and hatred.

FROM CHAPTER 17

On Cruelty and Pity, and Whether It Is Better to Be Loved or to Be Feared, and Vice Versa

Coming then to the other qualities already mentioned, I say that every prince should wish to be thought compassionate and not cruel; still, he should be careful not to make a bad use of the pity he feels. Cesare Borgia[5] was considered cruel, yet this cruelty of his pacified the Romagna, united it, and changed its condition to that of peace and loyalty. If the matter is well considered, it will be seen that Cesare was much more compassionate than the people of Florence, for in order to escape the name of cruel they allowed Pistoia to be destroyed.[6] Hence a prince ought not to be troubled by the stigma of cruelty, acquired in keeping his subjects united and faithful. By giving a very few examples of cruelty he can be more truly compassionate than those who through too much compassion allow disturbances to continue, from which arise murders or acts of plunder. Lawless acts are injurious to a large group, but the executions ordered by the prince injure a single person. The new prince, above all other princes, cannot possibly avoid the name of cruel, because new states are full of perils. Dido in Vergil puts it thus: "Hard circumstances and the newness of my realm force me to do such things, and to keep watch and ward over all my lands."[7]

All the same, he should be slow in believing and acting, and should make no one afraid of him; his procedure should be so tempered with prudence and humanity that too much confidence does not make him incautious, and too much suspicion does not make him unbearable.

5. See n. 2, p. 1709.   6. By internal dissensions, because the Florentines, Machiavelli contends, failed to treat the leaders of the dissenting parties with an iron hand.   7. *Aeneid* 1.563–64.

All this gives rise to a question for debate: Is it better to be loved than to be feared, or the reverse? I answer that a prince should wish for both. But because it is difficult to reconcile them, I hold that it is much more secure to be feared than to be loved, if one of them must be given up. The reason for my answer is that one must say of men generally that they are ungrateful, mutable, pretenders and dissemblers, prone to avoid danger, thirsty for gain. So long as you benefit them they are all yours; as I said above, they offer you their blood, their property, their lives, their children, when the need for such things is remote. But when need comes upon you, they turn around. So if a prince has relied wholly on their words, and is lacking in other preparations, he falls. For friendships that are gained with money, and not with greatness and nobility of spirit, are deserved but not possessed, and in the nick of time one cannot avail himself of them. Men hesitate less to injure a man who makes himself loved than to injure one who makes himself feared, for their love is held by a chain of obligation, which, because of men's wickedness, is broken on every occasion for the sake of selfish profit; but their fear is secured by a dread of punishment which never fails you.

Nevertheless the prince should make himself feared in such a way that, if he does not win love, he escapes hatred. This is possible, for to be feared and not to be hated can easily coexist. In fact it is always possible, if the ruler abstains from the property of his citizens and subjects, and from their women. And if, as sometimes happens, he finds that he must inflict the penalty of death, he should do it when he has proper justification and evident reason. But above all he must refrain from taking property, for men forget the death of a father more quickly than the loss of their patrimony. Further, causes for taking property are never lacking, and he who begins to live on plunder is always finding cause to seize what belongs to others. But on the contrary, reasons for taking life are rare and fail sooner.

But when a prince is with his army and has a great number of soldiers under his command, then above all he must pay no heed to being called cruel, because if he does not have that name he cannot keep his army united or ready for duty. It should be numbered among the wonderful feats of Hannibal that he led to war in foreign lands a large army, made up of countless types of men, yet never suffered from dissension, either among the soldiers or against the general, in either bad or good fortune. His success resulted from nothing else than his inhuman cruelty, which, when added to his numerous other strong qualities, made him respected and terrible in the sight of his soldiers. Yet without his cruelty his other qualities would not have been adequate. So it seems that those writers have not thought very deeply who on one side admire his accomplishment and on the other condemn the chief cause for it.

The truth that his other qualities alone would not have been adequate may be learned from Scipio,[8] a man of the most unusual powers not only in his own times but in all ages we know of. When he was in Spain his armies mutinied. This resulted from nothing other than his compassion, which had allowed his soldiers more license than befits military discipline. This fault was censured before the Senate by Fabius Maximus, and Scipio was called

---

8. Publius Cornelius Scipio Africanus the Elder (235–183 B.C.). The episode of the mutiny occurred in 206 B.C.

by him the corrupter of the Roman soldiery. The Locrians[9] were destroyed by a lieutenant of Scipio's, yet he did not avenge them or punish the disobedience of that lieutenant. This all came from his easy nature, which was so well understood that one who wished to excuse him in the Senate said there were many men who knew better how not to err than how to punish errors. This easy nature would in time have overthrown the fame and glory of Scipio if, in spite of this weakness, he had kept on in independent command. But since he was under the orders of the Senate, this bad quality was not merely concealed but was a glory to him.

Returning, then, to the debate on being loved and feared, I conclude that since men love as they please and fear as the prince pleases, a wise prince will evidently rely on what is in his own power and not on what is in the power of another. As I have said, he need only take pains to avoid hatred.

FROM CHAPTER 18
In What Way Faith Should Be Kept by Princes

Everybody knows how laudable it is in a prince to keep his faith and to be an honest man and not a trickster. Nevertheless, the experience of our times shows that the princes who have done great things are the ones who have taken little account of their promises and who have known how to addle the brains of men with craft. In the end they have conquered those who have put their reliance on good faith.

You must realize, then, that there are two ways to fight. In one kind the laws are used, in the other, force. The first is suitable to man, the second to animals. But because the first often falls short, one has to turn to the second. Hence a prince must know perfectly how to act like a beast and like a man. This truth was covertly taught to princes by ancient authors, who write that Achilles and many other ancient princes[1] were turned over for their upbringing to Chiron the centaur, that he might keep them under his tuition. To have as teacher one who is half beast and half man means nothing else than that a prince needs to know how to use the qualities of both creatures. The one without the other will not last long.

Since, then, it is necessary for a prince to understand how to make good use of the conduct of the animals, he should select among them the fox and the lion, because the lion cannot protect himself from traps, and the fox cannot protect himself from the wolves. So the prince needs to be a fox that he may know how to deal with traps, and a lion that he may frighten the wolves. Those who act like the lion alone do not understand their business. A prudent ruler, therefore, cannot and should not observe faith when such observance is to his disadvantage and the causes that made him give his promise have vanished. If men were all good, this advice would not be good, but since men are wicked and do not keep their promises to you, you likewise do not have to keep yours to them. Lawful reasons to excuse his failure to keep them will never be lacking to a prince. It would be possible to give innumerable modern examples of this and to show many treaties and promises that have been made null and void by the faithlessness of princes. And the prince who has best known how to act as a fox has come out best. But

9. Citizens of Locri, in Sicily.   1. E.g., Theseus, Jason, and Hercules.

one who has this capacity must understand how to keep it covered, and be a skilful pretender and dissembler. Men are so simple and so subject to present needs that he who deceives in this way will always find those who will let themselves be deceived.

I do not wish to keep still about one of the recent instances. Alexander VI[2] did nothing else than deceive men, and had no other intention; yet he always found a subject to work on. There never was a man more effective in swearing that things were true, and the greater the oaths with which he made a promise, the less he observed it. Nonetheless his deceptions always succeeded to his wish, because he thoroughly understood this aspect of the world.

It is not necessary, then, for a prince really to have all the virtues mentioned above, but it is very necessary to seem to have them. I will even venture to say that they damage a prince who possesses them and always observes them, but if he seems to have them they are useful. I mean that he should seem compassionate, trustworthy, humane, honest, and religious, and actually be so; but yet he should have his mind so trained that, when it is necessary not to practice these virtues, he can change to the opposite, and do it skilfully. It is to be understood that a prince, especially a new prince, cannot observe all the things because of which men are considered good, because he is often obliged, if he wishes to maintain his government, to act contrary to faith, contrary to charity, contrary to humanity, contrary to religion. It is therefore necessary that he have a mind capable of turning in whatever direction the winds of Fortune and the variations of affairs require, and, as I said above, that he should not depart from what is morally right, if he can observe it, but should know how to adopt what is bad, when he is obliged to.

A prince, then, should be very careful that there does not issue from his mouth anything that is not full of the above-mentioned five qualities. To those who see and hear him he should seem all compassion, all faith, all honesty, all humanity, all religion. There is nothing more necessary to make a show of possessing than this last quality. For men in general judge more by their eyes than by their hands; everybody is fitted to see, few to understand. Everybody sees what you appear to be; few make out what you really are. And these few do not dare to oppose the opinion of the many, who have the majesty of the state to confirm their view. In the actions of all men, and especially those of princes, where there is no court to which to appeal, people think of the outcome. A prince needs only to conquer and to maintain his position. The means he has used will always be judged honorable and will be praised by everybody, because the crowd is always caught by appearance and by the outcome of events, and the crowd is all there is in the world; there is no place for the few when the many have room enough. A certain prince[3] of the present day, whom it is not good to name, preaches nothing else than peace and faith, and is wholly opposed to both of them, and both of them, if he had observed them, would many times have taken from him either his reputation or his throne.

---

2. Pope from 1492 to 1503; father of Cesare Borgia.   3. Ferdinand II. In refraining from mentioning him, Machiavelli apparently had in mind the good relations existing between Spain and the house of Medici.

["Fortune Is a Woman"]

FROM CHAPTER 25

The Power of Fortune in Human Affairs, and to What Extent She Should Be Relied On

It is not unknown to me that many have been and still are of the opinion that the affairs of this world are so under the direction of Fortune and of God that man's prudence cannot control them; in fact, that man has no resource against them. For this reason many think there is no use in sweating much over such matters, but that one might as well let Chance take control. This opinion has been the more accepted in our times, because of the great changes in the state of the world that have been and now are seen every day, beyond all human surmise. And I myself, when thinking on these things, have now and then in some measure inclined to their view. Nevertheless, because the freedom of the will should not be wholly annulled, I think it may be true that Fortune is arbiter of half of our actions, but that she still leaves the control of the other half, or about that, to us.

I liken her to one of those raging streams that, when they go mad, flood the plains, ruin the trees and the buildings, and take away the fields from one bank and put them down on the other. Everybody flees before them; everybody yields to their onrush without being able to resist anywhere. And though this is their nature, it does not cease to be true that, in calm weather, men can make some provisions against them with walls and dykes, so that, when the streams swell, their waters will go off through a canal, or their currents will not be so wild and do so much damage. The same is true of Fortune. She shows her power where there is no wise preparation for resisting her, and turns her fury where she knows that no walls and dykes have been made to hold her in. And if you consider Italy—the place where these variations occur and the cause that has set them in motion—you will see that she is a country without dykes and without any wall of defence. If, like Germany, Spain, and France, she had had a sufficient bulwark of military vigor, this flood would not have made the great changes it has, or would not have come at all.

And this, I think, is all I need to say on opposing oneself to Fortune, in general. But limiting myself more to particulars, I say that a prince may be seen prospering today and falling in ruin tomorrow, though it does not appear that he has changed in his nature or any of his qualities. I believe this comes, in the first place, from the causes that have been discussed at length in preceding chapters. That is, if a prince bases himself entirely on Fortune, he will fall when she varies. I also believe that a ruler will be successful who adapts his mode of procedure to the quality of the times, and likewise that he will be unsuccessful if the times are out of accord with his procedure. Because it may be seen that in things leading to the end each has before him, namely glory and riches, men proceed differently. One acts with caution, another rashly; one with violence, another with skill; one with patience, another with its opposite; yet with these different methods each one attains his end. Still further, two cautious men will be seen, of whom one comes to his goal, the other does not. Likewise you will see two who succeed with two different methods, one of them being cautious and the other rash. These results are caused by nothing else than the nature of the times, which is or is not in harmony with the procedure of men. It also accounts for what I have mentioned, namely, that two persons, working differently, chance to arrive at the same result; and that of two who work in the same way, one attains his end, but the other does not.

On the nature of the times also depends the variability of the best method. If a man conducts himself with caution and patience, times and affairs may come around in such a way that his procedure is good, and he goes on successfully. But if times and circumstances change, he is ruined, because he does not change his method of action. There is no man so prudent as to understand how to fit himself to this condition, either because he is unable to deviate from the course to which nature inclines him, or because, having always prospered by walking in one path, he cannot persuade himself to leave it. So the cautious man, when the time comes to go at a reckless pace, does not know how to do it. Hence he comes to ruin. Yet if he could change his nature with the times and with circumstances, his fortune would not be altered.

Pope Julius II proceeded rashly in all his actions, and found the times and circumstances so harmonious with his mode of procedure that he was always so lucky as to succeed. Consider the first enterprise he engaged in, that of Bologna, while messer Giovanni Bentivogli[4] was still alive. The Venetians were not pleased with it; the King of Spain felt the same way; the Pope was debating such an enterprise with the King of France. Nevertheless, in his courage and rashness Julius personally undertook that expedition. This movement made the King of Spain and the Venetians stand irresolute and motionless, the latter for fear, and the King because of his wish to recover the entire kingdom of Naples. On the other side, the King of France was dragged behind Julius, because the King, seeing that the Pope had moved and wishing to make him a friend in order to put down the Venetians, judged he could not refuse him soldiers without doing him open injury. Julius, then, with his rash movement, attained what no other pontiff, with the utmost human prudence, would have attained. If he had waited to leave Rome until the agreements were fixed and everything arranged, as any other pontiff would have done, he would never have succeeded, for the King of France would have had a thousand excuses, and the others would have raised a thousand fears. I wish to omit his other acts, which are all of the same sort, and all succeeded perfectly. The brevity of his life did not allow him to know anything different. Yet if times had come in which it was necessary to act with caution, they would have ruined him, for he would never have deviated from the methods to which nature inclined him.

I conclude, then, that since Fortune is variable and men are set in their ways, they are successful when they are in harmony with Fortune and unsuccessful when they disagree with her. Yet I am of the opinion that it is better to be rash than over-cautious, because Fortune is a woman and, if you wish to keep her down, you must beat her and pound her. It is evident that she allows herself to be overcome by men who treat her in that way rather than

4. Of the ruling family Bentivogli. The pope undertook to dislodge him from Bologna in 1506. *Messer:* my lord.

by those who proceed coldly. For that reason, like a woman, she is always the friend of young men, because they are less cautious, and more courageous, and command her with more boldness.

[The Roman Dream]

FROM CHAPTER 26

An Exhortation to Take Hold of Italy and Restore Her to Liberty from the Barbarians

Having considered all the things discussed above, I have been turning over in my own mind whether at present in Italy the time is ripe for a new prince to win prestige, and whether conditions there give a wise and vigorous ruler occasion to introduce methods that will do him honor, and bring good to the mass of the people of the land. It appears to me that so many things unite for the advantage of a new prince, that I do not know of any time that has ever been more suited for this. And, as I said, if it was necessary to make clear the ability of Moses that the people of Israel should be enslaved in Egypt, and to reveal Cyrus's greatness of mind that the Persians should be oppressed by the Medes, and to demonstrate the excellence of Theseus that the Athenians should be scattered, so at the present time, in order to make known the greatness of an Italian soul, Italy had to be brought down to her present position, to be more a slave than the Hebrews, more a servant than the Persians, more scattered than the Athenians; without head, without government; defeated, plundered, torn asunder, overrun; subject to every sort of disaster.

And though before this, certain persons[5] have showed signs from which it could be inferred that they were chosen by God for the redemption of Italy, nevertheless it has afterwards been seen that in the full current of action they have been cast off by Fortune. So Italy remains without life and awaits the man, whoever he may be, who is to heal her wounds, put an end to the plundering of Lombardy and the tribute laid on Tuscany and the kingdom of Naples, and cure her of those sores that have long been suppurating. She may be seen praying God to send some one to redeem her from these cruel and barbarous insults. She is evidently ready and willing to follow a banner, if only some one will raise it. Nor is there at present anyone to be seen in whom she can put more hope than in your illustrious House, because its fortune and vigor, and the favor of God and of the Church, which it now governs,[6] enable it to be the leader in such a redemption. This will not be very difficult, as you will see if you will bring to mind the actions and lives of those I have named above. And though these men were striking exceptions, yet they were men, and each of them had less opportunity than the present gives; their enterprises were not more just than this, nor easier, nor was God their friend more than he is yours. Here justice is complete. "A way is just

5. Possibly Cesare Borgia and Francesco Sforza, who were discussed earlier in the book.   6. Pope Leo X (1475–1521) was a Medici (Giovanni de' Medici). *House:* of Medici. *The Prince* was first meant for Giuliano de' Medici. After Giuliano's death it was dedicated to his nephew Lorenzo, later duke of Urbino.

to those to whom it is necessary, and arms are holy to him who has no hope save in arms."[7] Everything is now fully disposed for the work, and when that is true an undertaking cannot be difficult, if only your House adopts the methods of those I have set forth as examples. Moreover, we have before our eyes extraordinary and unexampled means prepared by God. The sea has been divided. A cloud has guided you on your way. The rock has given forth water. Manna has fallen.[8] Everything has united to make you great. The rest is for you to do. God does not intend to do everything, lest he deprive us of our free will and the share of glory that belongs to us.

It is no wonder if no one of the above-named Italians[9] has been able to do what we hope your illustrious House can. Nor is it strange if in the many revolutions and military enterprises of Italy, the martial vigor of the land always appears to be exhausted. This is because the old military customs were not good, and there has been nobody able to find new ones. Yet nothing brings so much honor to a man who rises to new power, as the new laws and new methods he discovers. These things, when they are well founded and have greatness in them, make him revered and worthy of admiration. And in Italy matter is not lacking on which to impress forms of every sort. There is great vigor in the limbs if only it is not lacking in the heads. You may see that in duels and combats between small numbers, the Italians have been much superior in force, skill, and intelligence. But when it is a matter of armies, Italians cannot be compared with foreigners. All this comes from the weakness of the heads, because those who know are not obeyed, and each man thinks he knows. Nor up to this time has there been a man able to raise himself so high, through both ability and fortune, that the others would yield to him. The result is that for the past twenty years, in all the wars that have been fought when there has been an army entirely Italian, it has always made a bad showing. Proof of this was given first at the Taro, and then at Alessandria, Capua, Genoa, Vailà, Bologna, and Mestri.[1]

If your illustrious House, then, wishes to imitate those excellent men who redeemed their countries, it is necessary, before everything else, to furnish yourself with your own army, as the true foundation of every enterprise. You cannot have more faithful, nor truer, nor better soldiers. And though every individual of these may be good, they become better as a body when they see that they are commanded by their prince, and honored and trusted by him. It is necessary, therefore, that your House should be prepared with such forces, in order that it may be able to defend itself against the foreigners with Italian courage.

And though the Swiss and the Spanish infantry are properly estimated as terribly effective, yet both have defects. Hence a third type would be able not merely to oppose them but to feel sure of overcoming them. The fact is that the Spaniards are not able to resist cavalry, and the Swiss have reason to fear infantry, when they meet any as determined in battle as themselves. For this reason it has been seen and will be seen in experience that the Spaniards are unable to resist the French cavalry, and the Swiss are over-

7. Livy's *History* 9.1, para. 10.　　8. Another allusion to Moses.　　9. Perhaps another reference to Borgia and Sforza.　　1. Sites of battles occurring between the end of the century and 1513.

thrown by Spanish infantry. And though of this last a clear instance has not been observed, yet an approach to it appeared in the battle of Ravenna,[2] when the Spanish infantry met the German battalions, who use the same methods as the Swiss. There the Spanish, through their ability and the assistance given by their shields, got within the points of the spears from below, and slew their enemies in security, while the Germans could find no means of resistance. If the cavalry had not charged the Spanish, they would have annihilated the Germans. It is possible, then, for one who realizes the defects of these two types, to equip infantry in a new manner, so that it can resist cavalry and not be afraid of foot-soldiers; but to gain this end they must have weapons of the right sorts, and adopt varied methods of combat. These are some of the things which, when they are put into service as novelties, give reputation and greatness to a new ruler.[3]

This opportunity, then, should not be allowed to pass, in order that after so long a time Italy may see her redeemer. I am unable to express with what love he would be received in all the provinces that have suffered from these foreign deluges; with what thirst for vengeance, what firm faith, what piety, what tears! What gates would be shut against him? what peoples would deny him obedience? what envy would oppose itself to him? what Italian would refuse to follow him? This barbarian rule stinks in every nostril. May your illustrious House, then, undertake this charge with the spirit and the hope with which all just enterprises are taken up, in order that, beneath its ensign, our native land may be ennobled, and, under its auspices, that saying of Petrarch may come true: "Manhood[4] will take arms against fury, and the combat will be short, because in Italian hearts the ancient valor is not yet dead."

2. Between Spain and France in April 1512.   3. Machiavelli was subsequently the author of the treatise *Art of War* (1521).   4. An etymological translation of the original *virtù* (from the Latin *vir*, "man"). The quotation is from the canzone "My Italy."

LUDOVICO ARIOSTO
1474–1533

The *Orlando Furioso* (Orlando gone crazy), Ludovico Ariosto's seriocomic romance epic, is as witty and playful in tone as it is philosophically and politically serious. The most important achievement of Renaissance Italy's greatest poet, it is also a study in contrasts, at once brilliantly original and self-consciously derivative. Ariosto, like many Renaissance writers, made use of literary "imitation," the method of allusion and adaptation by which writers simultaneously composed original works and competed with their contemporaries and predecessors. While the best "imitations" can be read independently of the literary traditions they engage, their full dimensions emerge only in comparison with the literature they imitate, parody, and honor. Such a poem is *Orlando Furioso*, which blithely recycles classical, medieval, and contemporary texts yet is not hampered by its web of allusions. In his title, which recalls a popular romance epic, *Orlando in Love* (the *Orlando Innamorato* of Count Matteo Maria Boiardo), Ariosto announces his plan to outstrip other poets in the romance epic tradition: he will show how Orlando, under the influence of desire, crosses the line from love to lunatic frenzy. As the shift in title indicates, much of Ariosto's humor comes from placing heroes of the past in new and unexpected situations. Readers of this anthology have at their fingertips a wide range of Ariosto's favorite models for his witty, subtle, and often irreverent imitations: the works of Homer, Virgil, Ovid, St. Augustine, Dante, Boccaccio, and Petrarch as well as *The Song of Roland*, from which Ariosto's title hero ultimately derives. The *Orlando Furioso* is, in turn, itself a source of inspiration to such writers of the later Renaissance as Rabelais, Cervantes, Shakespeare, and Milton.

Ludovico Ariosto's life as a poet and diplomat was inextricably woven into the dramatic political career of the Este family of Ferrara. In 1472 Niccolò Ariosti was made a count by Ercole d'Este, duke of Ferrara, for the dubious service of trying to assassinate Ercole's nephew and rival. Niccolò married in 1473, and his firstborn son, Ludovico, was born in Reggio Emilia in 1474. In 1485 Niccolò moved his family to Ferrara, where he prospered in the service of Duke Ercole and pressed his reluctant son to study law. Ludovico preferred poetry and drama, and an apocryphal story told by his affectionate younger brother describes young Ludovico listening humbly while his father severely chastised him for laziness, only to light up joyfully when his father left the room and adapt the lecture to the needs of a comedy he was writing. When Ludovico gained court notice by performing in festivities given for the Sforza family in 1494, Niccolò released his son from legal studies and found him a tutor, the humanist Gregorio da Spoleto. In 1502 Ludovico wrote a poem for the marriage of Alfonso d'Este and Lucrezia Borgia (whom he unblushingly praised as a virgin), and in 1503 he entered the service of Ippolito d'Este, the warlike and profligate cardinal. His most memorable adventure under Ippolito was a diplomatic mission to Pope Julius II: although the pope at first listened tolerantly to Ariosto's speech, he lost patience when a second diplomat arrived with the same message, and threatened to hang one and throw the other (Ariosto) in the Tiber River.

Ariosto assumed financial responsibility for his family when his father died in 1500, and his financial distresses at times interfered with his work on the *Orlando Furioso*. Cardinal Ippolito could be demanding, stingy, and unprincipled (for example, he had his servants put out the eyes of his half brother because they had attracted the interest of Angela Borgia, whom the Cardinal himself passionately desired); but he understood Ariosto's importance as a poet well enough to finance the publication of the first edition of the *Orlando Furioso* in 1516. When Ariosto refused to join him on a mission to Hungary in 1517, however, he fired the poet on the spot, and Ariosto transferred his services to the more cultured Duke Alfonso in 1518. In 1513 Ariosto had fallen in love with Alessandra Benucci, the great love of his remaining years. They married secretly, probably to protect the modest income that she received as a widow of the Strozzi family and that Ariosto, who had taken minor orders, received from his ecclesiastical benefices. The financial strains that threatened Ariosto's family worsened when one of his cousins died intestate: Duke Alfonso appropriated the inheritance and, despite litigation, refused to reconsider his action. Alfonso was himself strapped for cash in his constant negotiations with the Venetian Republic, King Francis I of France, and the Emperor Charles V to keep the pope from seizing Ferrara; his solution to Ariosto's financial woes was to make him governor of the bandit-infested Ganfagnana in 1522 (the year after the second edition of the *Orlando Furioso* appeared). In 1525, after begging for release from his onerous administrative duties, Ariosto returned to Ferrara, to Alessandra and his beloved son, Virginio, and to his poetic labors. He died in 1533 after seeing the final edition of the *Orlando Furioso* through publication in 1532.

Variety and broad scope are the hallmarks of the *Orlando Furioso*. The mood of the poem moves up and down the scale of genres, from epic fury to romance dalliance to pastoral repose, from tragedy to comedy, from panegyric (song of praise) to satire, and from the sublime to the grotesque. Characters within the poem also explore heights and depths: in a parody of Dante's pilgrimage through hell and purgatory to paradise in *The Divine Comedy,* the comic knight Astolfo visits hell but, finding the stench unbearable, heads upward to the earthly paradise at the highest point of the world (in Nubia) and finally leaves the terrestrial sphere to visit the moon. Range also characterizes the *Orlando Furioso*'s geography, which stretches from France, Italy, Spain, Holland, England, Scotland, India, Tunisia, Libya, Syria, and Nubia to Byzantium and beyond. From these diverse countries come Christian and pagan knights who mingle and clash as they try to make names for themselves. The breadth of the *Orlando Furioso*'s survey of Europe, the Levant, and the New World is matched by the depth of its scrutiny of human psychology and of the interior lives of its characters. During the course of the poem, its Christians and pagans, men and women, nobles and servants find themselves in wild adventures and compromising situations, which cause them to experience every passion dreamed of in the philosophy of Ariosto's day.

Wrath and desire are the passions Ariosto explores in greatest depth, and no character experiences them more violently than Orlando. For the first twenty-three cantos of the poem, he pursues his obsessive love for the beautiful Chinese princess, Angelica; at the poem's exact center, he enters into a frenzy of epic proportions (if not beyond). Although love-madness is considered sacred by the Neoplatonic philosophers of Renaissance Italy, Orlando's "great folly" turns out to be debasing and profane. We might consider Orlando's love-madness in light of Ariosto's many images of horsemen governing and giving way to impetuous horses that stand for the passions. In the allegory of the soul presented in Plato's dialogue the *Phaedrus,* Socrates describes the soul as three-part and compares it to a charioteer managing two contrasting horses, which represent the divine and physical dimensions of the charioteer's desire for a beautiful love object. Whereas one of the horses is easily restrained, well-formed, and noble, the other is willful, misshapen, and lustful. If the charioteer attains the Platonic ideal and masters the stubborn wrath of the lustful horse, his love becomes holy. For Ariosto, however, passion brings less insight into spiritual matters than it brings ethical blindness and psychological confusion. When Orlando discovers that Angelica loves another man and that the pair have consummated their mutual passion, he experiences a "deep, bitter hate" and a "burning wrath" that leave him motionless on the grass for three days and nights without food or sleep, after which

> his bitter agony grew and grew until it drove him out of his mind. On the fourth day, worked into a great frenzy, he stripped off his armour and chain-mail. / The helmet landed here, the shield there, more pieces of armour further off, the breastplate further still: arms and armor all found their resting-place here and there about the wood. Then he tore off his clothes and exposed his hairy belly and all his chest and back. Now began the great madness, so horrifying that none will ever know a worse instance. / He fell into a frenzy so violent that his every sense was darkened.

Abandoning his duty, his reason, and his very identity, Orlando is soon more bestial than human and, in fact, comes to behave exactly like the lustful and rebellious horse in Plato's allegory. When he comes across Angelica, he gallops after her in an attempt to rape her, kill her, or eat her (it is hard to say which), but he lands on her horse after Angelica has fallen off: "He followed the steed across the bare sand, constantly gaining on her; now he could touch her . . . he had her by the mane . . . now by the bridle . . . at last he held her. / He seized her as gleefully as another man would a maiden." Crazed Orlando rides the poor beast to death and drags it yet further; as Ariosto remarks, Angelica herself would have fared no better.

Orlando's story is not the sole, or even the most important, of Ariosto's tales; the poet weaves into a single tapestry an extraordinary range of story lines. In addition to Orlando's amorous search, his great madness, and the devastation they bring to his dearest friends, for example, Ariosto describes the trials of the woman Orlando pursues, following Angelica as she flees from a series of lecherous men (including some of Ariosto's redoubtable heroes) and discovers passion with Medor, the one man who demands nothing of her. Ariosto also presents the travails of the hero Rinaldo, an admirer of Angelica who eventually learns important lessons about marriage, trust, and jealousy. In further strands, the poet narrates the adventures of a woman warrior, Marfisa, who encounters a colony of man-hating women and a city governed by a woman-hating tyrant, and he traces the development of Rodomont, a proud and war-like follower of Islam, into the poem's antihero. As the description of even a few of the poem's story lines indicates, it is easy, while reading the *Orlando Furioso*, to become so engrossed in the pleasures of romance wandering and quests that one periodically "forgets" to notice how artfully Ariosto controls the design of his larger narrative.

What is more, readers swept up in the romance often fail to care about the moral purpose that, according to ancient and contemporary defenses of poetry, justifies pleasure in reading. When readers grow entranced by Ariosto's narrative digressions from and suspensions of the moral, they resemble Ariosto's own wandering and desiring characters. To this extent, Ariosto's poem mirrors his enchanted castle in which "the ladies and knights who venture" into it chase after various objects of desire:

> they all imagine they are espying the object of their quest, be it a lady, a page, a friend, or comrade—human desire differing in its objectives. So they search the palace through and through to no avail; and yet so great is their hope and their desire to find what they are searching for that they are unable to tear themselves away.

Prisoners of their own desires and illusions, characters in the labyrinthine castle seem caught in an eternal moment of pursuit. Much as Ariosto's readers suspend the educative purpose of reading for the sensual pleasures of romance, the characters run in circles both literally and figuratively.

As the design of the *Orlando Furioso* gradually takes shape, a larger purpose dominates the story lines. The main story, which comes from epic rather than romance, concerns the founding of the Este dynasty at Ferrara, the family and court that Ariosto served. Ariosto's premiere lady knight, Bradamant, undertakes an epic quest to rescue and marry her beloved Ruggiero, the young pagan knight destined to become the father of the Este family. Ruggiero's adventures in love, arms, and religious conversion form the theme of the "education of the prince" that is central to many Renaissance epics. Throughout the *Orlando Furioso*, Ruggiero faces ethical dilemmas: should he choose the seductive witch, Alcina, or his betrothed, Bradamant? After he rescues the gorgeous, naked Angelica from the virgin-eating sea monster, should he seize her for himself? Should he return to his liege lord, the pagan king Agrican, or conclude his personal quest? The pattern of evaluating moral alternatives casts Ruggiero as a new Hercules, the legendary hero of the Greco-Roman world who faced the choice between Virtue and Vice when he came to a crossroads. Ruggiero has a more complicated problem: if he has the power to know the good, does he also have the strength to choose the good? For Renaissance interpreters of Hercules' story, the difficulty lay not in recognizing but in choosing the better course of action: "I see the better, but choose the worse," Petrarch remarked in a line that might stand as an epigraph for Ariosto's poem. For Ariosto, the scene of Hercules-at-the-crossroads brings up the central question of the will: are human beings masters or slaves of their passions? Are moral deliberations doomed, for the most part, to end in the justification of acts one knows to be wrong? Ruggiero's final choice radically tests his heroic character: at the end of the poem, he must choose between his loyalty to his liege lord, who made Ruggiero a knight, and his newly plighted troth to Charlemagne, Christianity, and Bradamant. Since loyalty to one side means a betrayal of the other, he has no irreproachable choice between virtue and vice. Ruggiero must choose between two distinct models of faith and their systems of self-esteem; not until the end of the poem, when Rodomont challenges him as a "betrayer of the faith," is he in a position to prove, in combat, that his choice was the most virtuous. The epic component of the poem, dedicated to the loftier and directly political goals of Ariosto's poem, ultimately defines heroic identity as forceful yet cautious—qualities Ariosto views as appropriate to the court at Ferrara in fifteenth-century Italy.

The wandering, digressive nature of Ariostan romance comes to an ending of high seriousness when Ruggiero converts to Christianity, emerges as the poem's true hero (in place of Orlando), and founds the Este dynasty. At the poem's conclusion, Ariosto draws all of its populous world back to the Christian camp for a final battle between Ruggiero and Rodomont, the pagan antihero. Bradamant undergoes a social "conversion" when she discards her armor and independence before marrying Ruggiero. The fantastically resilient knights who once battled headless giants and sea monsters begin to confront tragic loss and death. The poem's vast geographical range and cultural mix shrink into a moralized opposition between East and West, pagan and Christian. By its ending, the *Orlando Furioso* shifts from an exploratory to a prescriptive mood: after enthusiastically testing authority and raising doubts during the vast bulk of the poem, Ariosto finally establishes fixed values and beliefs. With the move into epic seriousness, the *Orlando Furioso* acknowledges a certain loss of imaginative freedom that accompanies the triumph of civilized order; simultaneously, it confers on the Este family a memorable role in the cultural achievement of Renaissance Italy.

Important essays on Ariosto include Patricia Parker, *Inescapable Romance* (1970), A. Bartlett Giamatti, *The Earthly Paradise and the Renaissance Epic* (1966), and Robert M. Durling, *The Figure of the Poet in Renaissance Epic* (1965). A more specialized study can be found in Elizabeth J. Bellamy, *Translations of Power* (1992). Edmund Gardner, *Ariosto: King of Court Poets* (1906), remains the indispensable work on Ariosto's life and the Ferrarese court. Other useful readings are Elizabeth Chesney, *The Counter-Voyage of Rabelais and Ariosto* (1982), and Robert Griffin, *Ludovico Ariosto* (1974).

Orlando Furioso[1]

CANTO 1

I sing of knights and ladies, of love and arms, of courtly chivalry,[2] of courageous deeds—all from the time when the Moors crossed the sea from Africa and wrought havoc in France. I shall tell of the anger, the fiery rage of young Agramant their king, whose boast it was that he would avenge himself on Charles, Emperor of Rome, for King Trojan's[3] death. / I shall tell of Orlando,[4] setting down what has never before been recounted in prose or rhyme: of Orlando, driven raving mad by love—and he a man who had been always esteemed for his great prudence—if she,[5] who has reduced me almost to a like condition, and even now is eroding my last fragments of sanity, leaves me yet with sufficient to complete what I have undertaken. / Seed of Ercole, adornment and splendour of our age, Hippolytus,[6] great of heart, may it please you to accept this which your lowly servant would, and alone is able to, give you. My debt to you I can in part repay with words, with an outlay of ink; hold me not, though, a parsimonious giver, for all I have to give, I give you. / Among the most illustrious heroes to whose names I am

---

1. Translated by Guido Waldman.   2. Ariosto expands the opening line of Virgil's *Aeneid*, "I sing of arms and the man" (which Robert Fitzgerald expansively translates, "I sing of warfare and a man at war").   3. Agramant's father, killed by Orlando in Provence. *Moors*: Arabs who invaded France during the reign of Charles Martel.   4. Nephew of Charlemagne and hero of *The Song of Roland* and Boiardo's *Orlando Innamorato*.   5. Ariosto's great love was Alessandra Benucci.   6. Ippolito d'Este, son of Duke Ercole, and Ariosto's patron.

about to pay honour you will hear mention of Ruggiero,[7] your forefather, the founder of your noble line. I shall tell you of his pre-eminent valour, his splendid actions, if you will pay heed to me and make room in your mind, busied with matters of moment, for these my verses. /

Orlando, who had long been in love with the beautiful Angelica,[8] and who had for her sake left countless immortal trophies in India, in Media, in Tartary, had now returned with her to the West, to where, at the foot of the lofty Pyrenees, King Charlemagne and the hosts of France and Germany were assembled in their tented camp to / force Kings Agramant and Marsilius[9] once more to lament their rash stupidity—the one for leading from Africa as many men as could bear lance and sword; the other for inciting Spain to visit destruction upon the lovely realm of France. So Orlando arrived at a good moment; but he was quick to regret his return, / for his lady was taken from him. Such is the waywardness of human judgment! The damsel, whom he had defended so constantly all the way from the Hesperides to the shores of Sunrise, was taken from him now, now that he was surrounded by friends, in his own land, with not a blow struck. It was the wise emperor, anxious to extinguish a serious fire, who took her from him. / A quarrel had arisen a few days earlier between Count Orlando and his cousin Rinaldo, for both of them were aflame with love for this ravishing beauty. Charles, who could not abide this conflict, which rendered them questionable allies, gave this damsel, the cause of the quarrel, into the keeping of Namo, Duke of Bavaria; / and promised her as a prize to whichever of the two slaughtered the greater number of Infidels[1] and wrought him the worthiest assistance in the vital conflict of that day. The outcome, however, was not in keeping with their prayers: the ranks of the baptized were put to flight, and among the many captives was the duke, whose tent was abandoned. /

Here the damsel was left who was to have been the victor's prize; she had mounted her horse before the crucial moment and, when that came, foreseeing that Fortune was that day to turn traitor to those of the Christian faith, she turned and fled. Entering a wood and following a narrow path she came upon a knight who was approaching on foot. / He wore a breastplate, and on his head a helmet; his sword hung by his side, and on his arm he bore his shield; and he came running through the forest more fleet of foot than the lightly-clad athlete sprinting for the red mantle at the village games. Never did a timid shepherd-girl start back more violently from a horrid snake than did Angelica, jerking on the reins the moment she saw the armed man approach on foot. / The man was none other than Rinaldo, son of Aymon, lord of Montauban, and a doughty paladin, whose charger,[2] Bayard, had only a little earlier made off without him—a strange turn of affairs. When his eyes lit on the woman, he recognized her angel's countenance, even from a distance, and the lovely face which held him in amorous thraldom. / The damsel turned her palfrey's head and galloped off through the forest at full tilt. She made no attempt to choose the best and surest path, or to avoid the thickets and the underbrush: pale and trembling and quite unstrung, she left

---

7. Progenitor of the Este dynasty.   8. Daughter of the khan of Cathay and great Petrarchan beauty, as her "angelic" face suggests (cf. Petrarch's sonnet 126 above).   9. King of Spain and ally of Agramant.   1. Chivalric romances refer to all non-Christians as "infidels," "Saracens," and "pagans."   2. Horse.

it to her horse to find his own way through. High and low, on and on through the deep, grim forest she coursed, until she came to a river. /

On the river-bank stood Ferrau,[3] clothed in sweat and grime: a great need to slake his thirst and to rest had withdrawn him early from the battle. But here he was now forced to tarry, for in his greedy haste to drink he had dropped his helmet into the river, and was still trying to recover it. / The damsel, screaming with terror, came galloping in headlong flight. Hearing her voice, the Saracen leapt up the bank and peered at her face. As soon as she was close he recognized her: many a day though it was since he had last had news of her, and pale and distraught though she now appeared, she could be none other than the fair Angelica. / As he was chivalrous, and no less hot-headed than the two cousins, he hastened boldly to her rescue, reckless of his lost helmet. Drawing his sword, he ran full of menace towards Rinaldo, who feared him but little: many a time had they set eyes on each other, and indeed tested each other's valour at arms. / Both of them were on foot as they flung themselves upon each other with naked sword; no armour plate, no chain-mail could have resisted the blows they delivered—enough to split an anvil. Now, while the two warriors were hewing each other, the damsel's horse had perforce to pick his way with care, for as hard as she could dig her heels she spurred him faster and faster through the woods and fields. / For a long time the two champions strove in vain each to gain the upper hand, but neither was less skilled than the other in the use of arms.

The lord of Montauban it was who first broke silence and addressed the Spanish knight, and spoke like one whose heart is all consumed with fire. / "You are thinking," said he to the pagan, "that you will be doing injury to me alone, and yet you will hurt yourself as well as me: if all this is because the brilliant rays of the new Sun have set your heart afire, what do you win by delaying me here? Even if you were to take my life or capture me, the beautiful lady will not be yours for all that—see, while we tarry here, she is slipping away. / You would do far better, if you still love her, to go and stand in her path, make her stop, detain her before she goes any further. Once we have her in our keeping, then let us make trial with our swords to see whose she should be. Otherwise, after a weary struggle, I can see that we shall both be the losers." /

The pagan was not displeased with the proposal, and so they deferred their battle; indeed, the truce so drew them together, excluding from their thoughts both hatred and anger, that as they departed from the refreshing stream, the pagan would not suffer good Aymon's son to go on foot, but pressed him to come up and mount behind him; then they galloped away after Angelica. / Great was the goodness of the knights of old! Here they were, rivals, of different faiths, and they still ached all over from the cruel and vicious blows they had dealt each other; still, off they went together in mutual trust, through the dark woods and crooked paths. Goaded by four spurs, the charger came to a fork where the road divided. / Here, not knowing which path the damsel had taken (for in both there were fresh tracks which were not to be distinguished from each other), they left the decision to Fate: Rinaldo took the one path, the Saracen the other.

Ferrau thrust further and further through the wood, and in the end found

3. Nephew of Marsilius.

himself at the place whence he had started. / Back he was by the river's side, at the point where his helmet had fallen in. With no further hope of finding the damsel, he went down to the water's edge to recover his helmet where it lay buried in the river; but it was sunk so deep in sand that he was to have much work to do ere he set hands on it. / He had fashioned a long pole out of the branch of a tree, shorn of its foliage, and with this he searched the river bed, prodding and poking every inch of it. While he was thus passing the time with ill-contained impatience, he noticed a knight of fierce countenance emerging chest-deep from the middle of the river. / He was fully armed except for his head, and in his right hand he bore a helmet: the very helmet for which Ferraù had so long been searching in vain. He addressed Ferraù with angry words and said: "O vile deceiver,[4] why take you so ill the loss of your helmet when you should long ago have surrendered it to me? / Remember, pagan, when you killed Angelica's brother (I am he): you promised me that after a few days you would throw the helmet into the river, after the other arms. If Fortune now carries my wishes into effect (which you were unwilling to do), be not dismayed. Or rather, be dismayed, if you must, but at your faithlessness. / But if you still crave for a fine helmet, find yourself another one, and acquire it with greater honour. Orlando the paladin has such a one, and Rinaldo too—perhaps his is even better; the one belonged once to Almont, the other to Mambrino.[5] Bear off one of those two with your valour, for this you would do well to leave to me, as earlier you promised." /

When the phantom surged up out of the water, the Saracen's hair stood on end and he paled, and his voice died in his throat. Then, hearing Argalia[6] tax him with his broken pledge (Argalia was he called, whom he had slain here), he blazed inwardly with fury, and blushed for shame. / Having no time to invent an excuse, and well knowing that the phantom spoke true, he made no answer, but kept his lips sealed; his spirit, though, was so pierced with shame that he swore on Lanfusa's [7] life to set his heart on no helmet other than the prize one that Orlando had wrested once from proud Almont's head in Aspromont. / This oath he observed more faithfully than that which he had earlier sworn. He set off, then, in such a bitter mood that many days later he still fretted and fumed. His only thought was to seek out the paladin, searching wherever he thought he might be. Rinaldo, following another route from Ferraù's, encountered different adventures. / He had not gone far before his fiery charger leapt into view. "Stop, Bayard, oh stop! I cannot endure to be without you." Deaf to his words, the steed would not approach, but drew away from him, faster and faster. Rinaldo followed, consumed with anger. But let us pursue Angelica in her flight. /

Through fearful dark woods she fled, through wild, desolate and deserted places. The stirring of a branch, of a green leaf of oak, elm or beech would make her swerve in fright; at each shadow she espied, whether by hill or dale, she imagined that Rinaldo was still close behind her. / Like a baby fawn or kid, who has watched through the leaves of the wood where he was born, and has seen the leopard's fangs close on his mother's throat, seen her flank and breast torn open; he flees through the thickets to escape the monster,

---

4. Argalia's insult in full, "deceiver of your faith, *marano*," refers to the converted Jews in Spain and to the Spanish Moslems, who, after the fall of Granada in 1492, also fell under the surveillance of the Inquisition.   5. A king killed by Rinaldo; his helmet originally belonged to Hector of Troy. *Almont*: brother of Trojan, killed by Orlando in Aspromont.   6. Angelica's brother, killed by Ferraù.   7. Ferraù's mother.

trembling with terror and alarm; and every time he brushes against a twig he sees himself already in the cruel beast's jaws. / That day and night, and half the next day onward she pressed, and knew not whither. At last she came to a pleasant grove whose trees gently rustled in a delicious breeze; two limpid brooks murmured close by so that the grass was ever fresh and tender; the quiet waters, breaking as they flowed softly over the little pebbles, sounded musically. / Here she felt safe, and a thousand miles from Rinaldo, and she decided to rest a little from her weary journey and the summer's heat. She stepped down amid the flowers and, unbridling her horse, let him wander away to graze by the crystal waters whose verges were fresh with new grass. / Close by she noticed a beautiful thicket of flowering hawthorn and red roses mirrored in the limpid rippling water and sheltered from the sun by tall shady oaks. It was hollowed in the middle and offered a refreshing bower amid the deepest shade: the branches and leaves were so disposed that no sun—nor indeed any lesser observer—could peep in. / Soft young grass made an inviting bed for whoever ventured here. The lovely damsel stepped into the bower, lay down, and fell asleep. Not for long, however, for she thought she heard the trample of approaching feet. Silently she arose, and espied an armoured knight who had come to the water's edge. /

Whether he be friend or foe she could not tell; her doubting heart was assailed by hope and fear; as she waited to see how it would turn out, not so much as a sigh did she permit to escape her lips. The knight sat down on the bank of the stream and rested his cheek on his arm; so deeply did he lapse into thought that he might have been turned to unfeeling stone. / More than an hour, my Lord,[8] the sorrowing knight sat, his head bowed in thought. Then he began to lament, a mournful, weary sound, and yet so sweet that out of compassion the very rocks would have split, and a cruel tigress would have turned gentle.

He sighed and wept; tears streamed down his cheeks. His heart was a furnace. / He spoke: "You, thought, who set my heart afire and turn it to ice, and cause the pain which ever gnaws within me, what am I to do? For I have been late in coming, and another has been first to cull the fruit.[9] Little has fallen to me but words and looks while another has gathered the best of the crop. If I am to be denied both fruit and blossom, why does my heart keep aching for her? / A virgin is like a rose: while she remains on the thorn whence she sprang, alone and safe in a lovely garden, no flock, no shepherd approaches. The gentle breeze and the dewy dawn, water, and earth pay her homage; amorous youths and loving maidens like to deck their brows with her, and their breasts. / But no sooner is she plucked from her mother-stalk, severed from her green stem, than she loses all, all the favour, grace, and beauty wherewith heaven and men endowed her. The virgin who suffers one to cull her flower—of which she should be more jealous than of her own fair eyes, than of her life—loses the esteem she once enjoyed in the hearts of all her other wooers. / Let her be abhorred by those others, and loved only by him to whom she gave herself so abundantly. O cruel enemy, Fortune! The others triumph and I die of need. What then: am I to find her no longer pleasing? Am I to relinquish my own heart's life? Ah, let this day be my last, let me live no longer if I am no longer to love her." /

8. Ippolito d'Este.   9. Angelica's virginity.

Should anyone ask me who it is who was shedding such copious tears into the brook, well, he was the King of Circassia, the love-lorn Sacripant. Love, let me add, was the prime and only cause for his cruel sorrow: he was, indeed, one of the lovers of this damsel, who at once recognized him. / For love of her he had come out of the East to where the sun sets, for in India he had learned, to his great sorrow, that she had followed Orlando to the West; then in France he had learned how the emperor had set her apart, promising her as the prize to whichever of the two yielded greater assistance to the Golden Lilies.[1] He had been in the field of battle, had witnessed the rout of King Charlemagne. He had gone in search of fair Angelica, but so far he had been unable to find her. This, then, was the sad tale, this the plight which weighed so heavy on his love-lorn heart, provoking his grief to utterance in words which might have made even the sun pause for pity. /

While he was thus lamenting and shedding hot tears in copious streams, and uttering these words and many more which I think I need not relate, by a fortunate turn in his affairs, his words came to the ears of Angelica; and so in one hour he reached a point which otherwise he would never have reached, not in a thousand years. / The lovely woman paid the closest attention to the tears, the speech and behavior of this man who was so assiduous a lover, even though this was not the first time she had heard him. Hard, though, and cold as a stone pillar, she would not stoop to pity: it would seem she disdained all human kind, and believed that no man was worthy of her. / And yet, seeing herself all alone amid those woods, she conceived the idea of taking him as a guide—for when the water is up to your neck you must be truly stubborn not to cry for help. If she let this occasion slip she would never again find so trusty an escort: she had already long experience of the king's rare fidelity in love. / She had no mind, however, to alleviate the misery which rent her lover, or to heal the wounds he had suffered by affording him the pleasure which all lovers crave. No, she would spin a tale, devise a subterfuge to maintain him in hope for so long as she had need of him; afterwards, she would revert to her accustomed hardness. /

Forth she stepped from the blind concealment of the thicket, and made so radiant and unlooked-for an appearance, she might have been Diana, or Venus[2] issuing forth from a shady grove. Emerging, she said: "Peace be with you. God protect you and my good name: pray, do not entertain so false an opinion of me—it goes against all reason." / Never was such joy, such amazement to be seen in a mother's eyes when she lifted them to look on her son whom she had bewailed and lamented for dead as she heard the troops return without him: such, though, was the Saracen's joy, such his wonder on suddenly beholding her angel's face, her graceful movements, her overwhelming presence. / Brimful of gentle, loving thoughts he ran to his lady, his goddess, who threw her arms tightly about his neck—which she would perhaps not have done in her native Cathay. Now that she had his company, her thoughts turned to her father's kingdom, the cradle of her birth; hope suddenly revived in her of soon regaining her precious home. / She told him all that had befallen her since the day when she had sent him to the King of the Nabateans of Sericana to ask for help; and how Orlando had frequently saved her from death and outrage and all manner of evils; and how her virginal flower

1. Charlemagne's emblem.   2. Goddess of love. *Diana*: goddess of virginity and the hunt.

was still as intact as the day she had borne it from her mother's womb. / This may have been true, but scarcely plausible to anyone in his right mind; to him it seemed quite possible, however, lost as he was in a far deeper delusion. What a man sees, Love can make invisible—and what is invisible, that can Love make him see. This, then, was believed, for a poor wretch will readily believe whatever suits him. / "If the knight of Anglant[3] was so stupid as to neglect his opportunity, so much the worse for him: never again will Fortune offer him so rare a gift," remarked Sacripant to himself. "Far be it from me to imitate him, foregoing the offer of so great a good and then having only myself to blame. / I shall pluck the morning-fresh rose which I might lose were I to delay. Full well I know that there is nothing that a woman finds so delectable and pleasing, even when she pretends to resent it and will sometimes burst into tears. I shall not be put off by any repulse or show of anger, but shall carry into effect what I propose." /

Thus spoke he. But while he was preparing for his gentle assault, a terrible din from the wood close by resounded in his ears, so that he regretfully had to give up his enterprise, and put on his helmet—for it was his habit to go about fully armed. He approached his charger, bridled him, climbed into the saddle and grasped his lance. / Out of the wood a knight appeared. Stalwart and proud was his mien. His raiment was white as snow, and a white plume crested his helmet. King Sacripant could not endure this importunate fellow's arrival, just in time to interfere with the pleasure which lay in store, and the look he darted at him was fraught with menace. / When the other drew near he challenged him to battle, confident that he would sweep him from the saddle. But the other, who did not deem himself a jot inferior, and was ready to prove it, cut short his haughty threats, setting spurs to his steed and lowering his lance. Sacripant was off, too, like a hurricane, and they charged straight at each other. / No lions in the tall scrub, no bulls charging each other full tilt ever met with the impact of those two knights: each ran his lance through the other's shield. The clash reverberated all about, from the grassy valleys even to the summits of the barren hills. Lucky it was that the warriors wore good, sound breastplates, for these defended their chests. / Neither steed swerved from his course, indeed they butted each other head on, like rams. The pagan warrior's died almost instantly; alive, he had proved himself a champion. The other's fell also, but no sooner did he feel the prick of the spurs in his side than he rose to his feet. But the horse of the Saracen king lay inert, his full weight resting upon his master.[4]

The unknown champion, who had remained in the saddle and seen the other overthrown, horse and rider, decided he had had enough of this skirmish and felt no need to carry it further. So he pulled away and rode off at a fast gallop along the path which ran straight through the forest; and before the pagan had extricated himself, the other was little short of a mile away. / Just as a ploughman, dazed and stunned, gets up when the lightning has passed, from where the shattering thunderburst has thrown him down beside his dead oxen; he gets up and beholds the pine standing bereft of its leaves and of its dignity, the very pine he was accustomed to see in the distance. So it was with the pagan when he regained his feet. Angelica had been witness of this dire event. / He sighed and groaned, not because his

---

3. Orlando.   4. Horses traditionally depict passions that must be reined in.

arm or foot may have been broken or sprained, but simply for shame: never in his life, before or since, was his face so red. This was not only because of his fall, but all the more so in that his lady it was who had pulled the heavy weight off him. He would have remained dumb, I am convinced, were it not that she restored him to speech. / "Alas, good sir, take it not so hardly," she said, "for it was no fault of yours if you fell, but rather of the horse, who was less prepared for another fray than for rest and nourishment. Nor will this have added a jot to that warrior's glory, for he was quite clearly the loser: this is how I construe it, inasmuch as he was the first to leave the field." /

While she was thus consoling the Saracen, who should arrive at a gallop but a messenger, mounted on a palfrey; he carried his horn and his pouch at his side, and looked tired and dispirited. When he drew near to Sacripant he asked him whether he had seen a warrior come this way through the forest, with a white shield and crested with a white plume. / "As you see, he has overthrown me, and has only just departed," replied Sacripant. "Now tell me his name, so that I may know who it was who unseated me." "On that point," said the other, "I can satisfy you at once. You must know that the rare valour which swept you from the saddle was that of a gentle damsel. / She is brave, but, more than that, she is beautiful. Her name is famous and I shall keep it from you no longer: it is Bradamant[5] who has stripped you of all the honours you have won hitherto."

With these words he galloped off, leaving the Saracen far from pleased: he knew not what to do or say, and blushed crimson with shame. / After long and useless reflection on what had taken place, coming back always to his defeat by a woman—the more he thought about it, the more it hurt—he mounted the other horse without a word; and without a word he drew Angelica up behind him, and reserved her for happier entertainment in more tranquil surroundings. /

They had not gone two miles when a terrific noise filled the forest all about and seemed to send a shiver through it from end to end. Shortly after, a great war-horse came into view, richly caparisoned in cloth-of-gold; he came bounding over streams, over briars, and splintered trees and whatever else stood in his path. / "If the deep shade and the thickly meshed foliage do not impair my vision," said the damsel, "this charger forcing his boisterous passage through the choked wood is Bayard. Yes, this is certainly Bayard, I recognize him. Ah, how well he understands our need: one palfrey is quite unsuited to carry the two of us, and he is coming quickly to our assistance." / The Circassian dismounted and approached the horse, meaning to grasp his reins. But the charger pivoted round quick as a flash and presented his hindquarters; he did not reach the point, though, of unleashing a kick. A sad knight he would have been, had he been struck full on, for the horse had such power in his heels, he could have shattered a whole mountain of metal. / Then he meekly approached the damsel; he was almost human in his gesture of humility, like a dog dancing around his master who has just returned after a few days' absence. Bayard still remembered her, for she had tended him in Albracca in the days when she was so enamoured of Rinaldo, who was so cruel to her then, so unresponsing to her love. / She took his reins

---

5. Lady knight, Rinaldo's sister, and future mother of the Este dynasty, she is on her epic quest to find and marry her beloved Ruggiero.

in her left hand, and with the other hand she caressed his neck and chest. The horse, who was of remarkable intelligence, submitted to her as meekly as a lamb. Sacripant meanwhile seized his opportunity: he mounted Bayard and spurred him and reined him in. Now that her own steed was lightened of his burden, the damsel moved from his hindquarters and resumed her place in the saddle. / She happened then to look round, and her eyes fell upon a man of imposing stature advancing on foot, with much clanking of armour. She flared up with anger and vexation, for she recognized him as Rinaldo, Duke Aymon's son. He loved her, coveted her more than his life, but she loathed and avoided him, as a crane will flee from a falcon. Once upon a time it was he who hated her worse than death, while she loved him; now they had changed roles. / And the cause was to be found in two springs in the Ardennes,[6] not far apart, whose waters produce diverging effects: the one inclines the heart to love, whereas love loses place in the heart of whoever drinks from the other; what first is fire turns to ice. Rinaldo had tasted the one, and love held him in thrall: Angelica the other, and she hated and shunned him. / The effect of that liquid blended with secret venom, transforming love into loathing, was to cast a pall over the damsel's limpid eyes the moment she had set them upon Rinaldo. With tremulous voice and anxious face she begged and entreated Sacripant not to wait for the warrior to approach any nearer, but to turn with her and flee. /

"Am I," replied the Saracen, "am I held in so little esteem by you, that you reckon me of no use, of no avail to defend you against him? Have you already forgotten the battles at Albracca, and the night when I alone stood as your shield and refuge against Agrican and all his men?" / She made no answer, and knew not what to do, for Rinaldo was now too close at hand: he arrived threatening the Saracen from a distance once he saw and recognized the horse, and recognized the angel-face which had kindled a furnace in his heart. What passed between these two champions I mean to defer to the next canto.

Summary   Bradamant seeks Ruggiero, who has been captured and confined in an enchanted castle by his protector, the sorcerer Atlas. Pinabello, from the enemy house of Maganza, pushes Bradamant into an underground cavern that turns out to be the tomb of Merlin, wizard of the Arthurian legends. Merlin's spirit prophesies the coming Este dynasty, of which Bradamant and Ruggiero will be the progenitors, and the sorceress Melissa describes Bradamant's illustrious female descendants. Melissa also tells her how to destroy Atlas's spell and free Ruggiero. When Bradamant succeeds, the two lovers greet each other ecstatically, but they are swiftly separated when Ruggiero mounts Atlas's flying steed, the hippogryph (a cross between a horse and a gryphon), who takes to flight and carries Ruggiero away from the lamenting Bradamant.

---

6. In Boiardo's poem, Angelica loved Rinaldo, who hated her, until she drank from a stream that caused hatred at the very moment that he drank from another whose waters induced love.

FROM Canto 6; Canto 7

[*Ruggiero Visits the Isle of Alcina and Logistilla*]

* * *

But now it is time to return to Ruggiero, still coursing through the sky on the wind-borne beast. / Courageous man that he was, Ruggiero's face retained its normal hue; but I do believe that his heart within him was trembling like a leaf. He had left the European mainland far behind him, and had passed way out beyond the bounds which matchless Hercules had set for mariners.[7] / That great and wondrous bird, the hippogryph, bore him away so fast in winged flight that he far outpaced the eagle when it guides the falling thunderbolt. No creature sweeps through the air at a speed to equal his—I doubt whether thunder and lightning are more swift when they dart from the heavens. / The winged steed, after flying straight as an arrow for many a league, never once deflecting from his course, finally, as though sated with the air, began in lazy gyres to descend upon an island. After long hiding from her lover and taxing his constancy, the virgin Arethusa[8] came to just such an island by a dark, hollow passage beneath the sea. /

No lovelier, no happier land than this did he behold of any over which the steed had stretched his wings; were he to search the whole wide world, a more delightful land than this he would never find; here the great bird, after a broad circular sweep, descended with Ruggiero. Here were well-tilled plains and neat hills, limpid waters, shady banks, and soft meadows, / enticing thickets of cool laurel, of palms and loveliest myrtle, of cedar and orange-trees whose fruit and blossoms were disposed in sundry harmonious ways—these all afforded shade, with their thick spreading foliage, against the searing heat of the summer's day. And, safe amid their branches, flitted melodious nightingales. / Hares and rabbits were to be espied hopping among the deep-red roses and white lilies which a temperate breeze kept ever fresh; and deer, holding high their splendid heads, roamed about, stooping to crop the grass, quite unafraid that any might slay or capture them. Fawns and nimble goats skipped deftly—many was their number in these rustic parts. /

When the hippogryph was so close to the ground that to jump from his back would be less perilous, Ruggiero quickly slipped from the saddle and set foot on the green sward. He kept firm hold of the reins, though, lest the steed once more took wing, and tethered him to a green myrtle branch growing by the sea, by the water's edge, between a laurel and a pine. / And close by, where a spring bubbled up surrounded by cedars and fruitful palms, he set down his shield, drew off his helm and gauntlets, and turned his face now to the sea, now to the hills to capture the fresh vigorous breeze which, with a cheerful murmur, set the high tree-tops—the beeches and firs—a-rustling. / He dipped his parched lips in the fresh crystal pool and splashed himself to cool his veins, for he was overheated in his armour and little wonder if he found it burdensome, for not a solitary soul had presented himself for battle, and here he had travelled, all of three thousand miles at a stretch, armed to the teeth. /

7. Columns established by Hercules, marking the limits of the Western world: the straits of Gibraltar. 8. Ovidian nymph transformed into a spring as she tried to elude the river god, Alpheus; her stream took an underground course to an island, where his waters joined hers.

While Ruggiero was here, his steed, which he had left in the cool shade of a dense thicket, shied away, frightened by I know not what he had descried in the tangled wood. He so tore apart the myrtle to which he was tethered that he became ensnared in the branches strewn underfoot; he tugged at the myrtle, bringing down a shower of leaves, but was unable to pull free. / If a log with but a soft core of pith is placed in the fire, it starts to whine, because the intense heat consumes the vaporous air inside it, and it sizzles noisily so long as the vapour forces a way out. Just so, the damaged myrtle moaned and hissed in vexation, and finally a sad, tearful voice / issued from an open pore, and framed words pronounced with utmost clarity: "If you are good and kind, as your fair looks suggest, loose this animal from my branches. Let my own ill-fortune be sufficient torment without the addition of more evil, more pain inflicted upon me from without." / At the first sound of this voice Ruggiero turned his face and jumped up; when he realized that it issued from the tree, he was no little astonished.[9]

He hastened to untie the hippogryph and, blushing for shame, "Whatever you are," he said, "whether human spirit or woodland goddess, pardon me. / If I deranged your fair branches and wrought damage to your living myrtle, it was through not knowing that a human spirit was hidden beneath your rough bark. But do not deny me an answer: tell me who you are, who live and speak, a rational being in a spiky, contorted body—so may heaven's hailstones ever spare you! / And if now or in the future I can do you some favour by way of amends, I promise you, by the fair woman[1] in whose keeping lies the best part of me, that I shall so perform in word and action that you shall have just cause to thank me." Thus spoke Ruggiero, and the myrtle quivered from head to foot. / Perspiration now beaded through the tree's bark, like a faggot green from the forest which feels the flame overwhelm it after vainly trying to resist the heat.

"Your courtesy so prevails upon me that I must tell you both who I was and who it is who has changed me into this myrtle by the soft sea-shore. / Astolfo was my name; I was a paladin, much feared in battle; Orlando and Rinaldo were my cousins, whose fame has broken all bounds. I was heir, after my father Otho, to the crown of England. Handsome I was, and graceful, so that I was beloved by not a few ladies—yet in the end I proved my own undoing. /

"I was returning from those distant isles washed on the East by the Indian Sea, where with Rinaldo and others I had been shut away in a darkened vault until Orlando there displayed his utmost strength. We were journeying Westward, then, along the dunes which endure the wrath of the North winds. / Hard, spiteful Fate traced our path which brought us out, one morning, onto a lovely beach on which stood a castle of the potent Alcina.[2] She had come forth from it, and we found her standing alone at the edge of the sea: she was pulling ashore all the fishes she wanted, though she had neither net nor hook. / Swift-moving dolphins hastened to her, and ponderous tunny, open-mouthed; the sperm whales and the sea-lions were disturbed out of their indolent sleep; mullet and jelly-fish, salmon and black-fish came in shoals, as fast as they could swim; sea-wolves and cachalots, grampus and orcs rose

---

9. Ariosto imitates Virgil's Polidorus (*Aeneid* 3) and Dante's suicide, Pier delle Vigne (*Inferno* 13, 40), both turned into plants that bleed when torn.   **1.** Bradamant.   **2.** A sorceress and temptress like Homer's Circe.

out of the sea with their monstrous backs. / We descried a whale, the largest one ever to be seen in the ocean: its vast shoulders protruded eleven cubits and more above the briny waves. All of us fell into the same deception—we took it for an island, it lay so still with never even a ripple, and its two extremities were at so great a distance apart. / Alcina drew the fishes out of the water with simple words and magic charms. She and the witch Morgana were born of the same mother, but whether she was delivered first or last, or whether both at once I cannot say.

"Well, Alcina looked at me, and she liked what she saw, as was clear from her face; so she devised a crafty ruse to take me away from my companions; and here she succeeded. / With a cheerful smile she came to meet us, and showed easy courtesy as she addressed us: 'Good sirs, if you would like to abide with me today, I shall show you every manner of fish among those I have caught: some with scales, some all pulpy, some fur-clad, and more abundant than the stars in the sky. / And should you wish to see a siren, who can still the waves with her sweet singing, go with me to this further beach where she always comes at this hour.' She pointed to the vast whale which, as I said, looked like a small island. I, who have always (to my regret) been too impetuous, stepped onto that fish. / Rinaldo, and Dudone likewise, signalled to me not to go, but to no avail. Smiling, Alcina left them to themselves and stepped on behind me. The whale, faithful to its office, swam off through the salt waves. I was not long in regretting my folly, but by then I was too far from the shore. / Rinaldo flung himself into the sea to help me, but he almost sank, for a raging wind blew up from the South, drawing a dark veil over sky and sea. I know not what became of him. Alcina meanwhile addressed herself to reassuring me.

"All that day and through the night she kept me in the midst of the sea on the monster's back, / until we came to this beautiful island. Alcina owns a great part of it, having stolen a share from Logistilla, a sister of hers who, as the only legitimate daughter, had been left the whole of it by their father. Alcina and Morgana, as she fully avowed to me, were both born of incest. / A wicked, pernicious pair they make, surfeited with every sort of ugly infamy; not so Logistilla[3]—she is one who has steeped her heart in all that is virtuous, and lives in chastity. The two have conspired against her, and have recruited more than one army to drive her from the island; time and again they have seized castles from her—over a hundred of them; / indeed, Logistilla would be left with not so much as a parcel of land were it not that the island is narrowed on one side by a creek, and on the other by a deserted mountain— similar to the mountain and the firth which separate England from Scotland. Not that this deters Alcina and Morgana from trying to wrest from her what little is left. / The pair of them, being vicious to the core, cannot endure her, because she is chaste and good.

"But I was telling you how it came about that I was turned into a tree: Alcina entertained me in luxury, all ablaze as she was with love for me—and I burned for her no less ardently, seeing how beautiful she was, and how indulgent. / In her delicate body I found all my delight; every treasure was concentrated here, so it seemed to me, which is normally shared out among

---

3. Logistilla (from Greek *logos* "word" or "reason") represents virtue and reason, while Alcina, a figure of romance poetry, represents material pleasures with no transcendence.

human kind, some enjoying more, others less, and no one having a large share. Lost in contemplation of her looks, I quite forgot about France and all else—my every thought, my every good design ended in her, and never went beyond. / I was her beloved, too, as much as she was mine, or more. Alcina gave no further thought to anyone else: she had abandoned all her other lovers—for before me there had been a fair number. She made me her counsellor, kept me at her side day and night, set all the others under my command. Me she believed, to me she referred everything; night and day she would never address another, only me. / Alas! Why must I keep touching my wounds when I have no hope of a balm? Why must I recollect the good that was, now that I am suffering the most rigorous penitence? Whilst I counted myself happy, and whilst I believed I stood highest in Alcina's love, she took back from me the gift of her heart, and threw herself body and soul into a fresh infatuation.[4]

"I was late in discovering the fickleness of her nature, prone to falling in and out of love all at once. I had reigned in her affection for but two months when a new lover was assumed in my place. She drove me out disdainfully, and withdrew her favour from me. Later I learnt that she had meted similar treatment to a thousand lovers before me, and always without cause. / And, to prevent their spreading about the world the story of her wanton ways, she transforms them, every one, planting them here and there in the fertile soil, changing one into a fir-tree, another into an olive, another into a palm or cedar, or into the guise in which you see me on this verdant bank; yet others the proud enchantress changes into liquid springs, or into beasts, just as it suits her. /

"Now you, sir, have reached this enchanted island by an unusual way, and some lover shall, on your account, be turned into stone or water or something of the sort. A sceptre shall be yours, from Alcina's hand, and you shall reign, and you shall be the happiest of mortal men: but make no mistake—your time will soon come to be changed into a beast or a fountain, into wood or rock. / I have gladly given you warning, not that I imagine it will be of any use to you; and yet it is better that you should not go unprepared but rather knowing something of her ways. Perhaps, as faces differ, so do wit and skill, and you will devise some way to forestall the worst—some way which a thousand before you have not discovered." /

Ruggiero had heard that Astolfo was cousin to his lady, Bradamant, and he was deeply afflicted on seeing the change the knight had undergone from his true self into a scrawny, sterile shrub. And for the love he bore his lady, he would gladly have been of service to him (if only he had known how); but all he could do was to offer him consolation. / This he did as best he could; then he asked him if there was a way to reach the territory of Logistilla, whether by hill or by dale, so as to avoid passing through that of Alcina. There was indeed, returned the myrtle, a way studded with sheer rocks, if he went on a little towards the right, and climbed the hill towards the craggy peak. / But he was not to reckon on making much headway along that path, for he would come upon a whole band of pugnacious roughs, who would provide no easy passage. Alcina deployed them there to act as a wall or dyke

---

4. Like the medieval figure of Lady Fortune, she strikes down those at the height of happiness.

stopping whoever would seek to escape from her clutches. Ruggiero thanked the myrtle for everything, then left him, duly forewarned. /

He approached the hippogryph, untethered him, grasped his reins and walked him away instead of mounting him, as he had done before: he was not this time going to be carried off against his wishes. He pondered how best to reach Logistilla's realm in safety; he was firmly disposed to do whatever was necessary to avoid falling into Alcina's power. / He considered mounting his steed and spurring him on to a new flight through the air, but he feared this might prove a distinct mistake, seeing how little notice the beast took of the bridle. "I shall force my way through, if I go the right way about it," he told himself, but all in vain—he had not gone two miles from the shore when Alcina's splendid city came into view. / Off in the distance stood a wall which curved away, embracing a vast stretch of land; it was so high, its top seemed to merge with the heavens, and it looked as if it were solid gold from summit to foot. (There are some who part company with me here and maintain that it is an effect of alchemy;[5] they may know better than I, but, again, they may be quite mistaken. To me it looks like gold, the way it gleams.) / When he was close to these walls whose splendour is unmatched by any others in the world, the doughty knight left the road, which ran broad and straight across the plain to the massive gates, and veered off to the right along the safer path leading up to the mountain heights.

Soon, however, his journey was disturbed and interrupted by the onslaught of the band of ruffians. / Never did you set eyes on a more fantastic throng, or see faces so monstrous and misshapen.[6] Some of them were human from the neck down, but with the head of a monkey or of a cat; some stumped about on cloven hoofs; some were quick, agile centaurs. Some were young and pert, others old and stupid. Some were naked, others clad in strange pelts. / One galloped on an unbridled horse, another plodded along on a donkey or an ox, and yet another mounted a centaur; many rode on the backs of ostriches, eagles and cranes. Some set a horn to their lips, some their cup. They were male and female—some of them both at once. One carried a hook, the next a rope ladder, another a crowbar, yet another a stealthy file. / Their captain could be seen sitting astride a tortoise which shuffled stolidly along; he had a swollen paunch, the captain, and a fat face, and henchmen to support him on either side, as he was drunk and his head kept lolling forward. Some dabbed his forehead and chin while others flapped their garments to fan him. / A creature whose feet and belly were human, but whose neck, head, and ears were those of a dog, barked at Ruggiero to make him turn off towards the fair city which lay behind him. "Not I," retorted the knight, 'so long as I have strength to wield this'—and he flourished his sword, aiming its sharp point at the creature's face. /

The monster attacked him with a spear, but Ruggiero let fly at him and ran him through the paunch so that his sword stuck out through his back a palm's width. He grasped his shield and leapt in all directions, but the enemy thronged round him, pricking him here, clawing at him there. He whirled his sword and laid about him savagely, / splitting one open down to the jaw,

---

5. Pseudoscience and philosophy concerned with turning base metals into gold.　　6. Grotesque figures of vice.

the next right down to the chest, for this breed of scoundrels goes unarmoured (and besides, no helmet, shield, breastplate, or chain-mail can resist his sword). But he was so hemmed in on all sides that if he was to give himself room and hold this scum at bay, he would have needed more arms and hands than Briareus.[7] / Had he thought of bringing out the shield of Atlas[8]—the shield of the blinding light, which the magician had left suspended from the saddle—he would have overcome the ugly mob in a trice, and made them all fall down in a dazzle. It could be that he would not stoop to using it, preferring to rely on valour rather than on guile. / Be that as it may, he would sooner have died than fall a prisoner to so scurvy a crew.

Now who should sally forth from a gate in the walls (all gold and glitter, as I said), but two damsels. To judge by their bearing and apparel, they were clearly not of mean birth, brought up in poverty by shepherds, but reared amid the opulence of a royal palace. / They each rode on a unicorn whiter than the whitest ermine; both were of great beauty, and so exquisite in their dress and manners that a man would have needed the eyes of a god to look at their appearance and judge them for what they were. They could have passed for Beauty (had she a body) and Grace. / They both came to where Ruggiero was being hard pressed by the brutish throng. These all now melted away and the damsels held out their hand to the knight, who blushingly thanked them for their act of kindness. And, to do their pleasure, he was glad to go with them back to the golden gate. /

Above the gate, and jutting a little over it, the wall was ornamented, and there was not an inch but was encrusted in the rarest jewels from the Levant. Great columns made of solid diamond flanked the gate through the thickness of the walls. Whether they presented a true or false image to the eye, there was nothing like them for grace and felicity. / On the threshold and among the columns nymphs played and frolicked wantonly—their beauty might have been enhanced had they been more jealous of the respect which should have been their due as women. They were all dressed in green skirts and crowned with spring garlands. All smiles and charm, they welcomed Ruggiero into paradise. / The place could well be called by that name: I do believe it was the cradle of Love. Here it was all dancing and play-time, and the hours went by in one continuous festivity. Grey-headed Thought could not dwell here in a single heart, not even for a moment. There was no entrance here for Discomfort or Dearth, but Plenty was ever in attendance with her copious horn.[9] / This was the abode of youths and maidens, here where soft April, presenting a serene and merry face, seemed constantly to smile. By a spring, some there were who sang in sweet, melodious voice; in the shade of a tree or a cliff others played and danced and indulged in honest fun. Another had gone apart, and was communing with his true-love. / Round the tops of the pines and laurels, of the tall beeches and shaggy fir-trees the little cupids flitted and swooped merrily. Some of them were gloating contentedly over their victories; some were carefully aiming their heart-piercing arrows; others were spreading nets. Down by a stream one was honing darts, while another was sharpening his against a smooth stone. / Here Ruggiero was presented with a majestic bay charger; sturdy and robust he was, and his trappings were

---

7. A one-hundred-armed giant.   8. Uncovered, the shield belonging to Ruggiero's wizard mentor dazzles beholders and knocks them unconscious.   9. Horn of plenty, the cornucopia.

spangled with precious stones and embroidered with thread of gold. The winged horse, the same which used to do the old Moorish wizard's[1] bidding, was entrusted to a youth, who was to lead him after Ruggiero at a slower pace. /

The two lovesome maidens, the pretty pair who had protected Ruggiero from the band of knaves, the knaves who had forestalled him on the path he had taken off to the right, now addressed him: "Your valorous deeds, sir, of which we have heard tell, embolden us to avail ourselves of your assistance. / We shall soon be coming to a bog which divides this plain in two. The bridge across it is held by a savage woman called Erifilla,[2] who bullies and tricks and robs whoever would cross to the other side. She is built like a giant; her teeth are fangs and her bite venomous; her nails are pointed and she claws like a bear. / Not only does she keep molesting us on our path, which would be free of obstacle were it not for her, but also she often runs about the garden making a nuisance of herself in one way and another. Many of the murderous mob that attacked you outside the gate are spawn of hers— all of them are her followers, evil, like her, inhospitable and rapacious."/ Answered Ruggiero: "For you I shall gladly fight not merely one battle but a hundred! Command my person as you will, to the limits of its resources—if I wear plastron and coat of mail, it is not to win myself land or silver, but simply to serve and prosper others, the more so when they are lovely ladies like yourselves." /

The ladies replied with thanks as befitted a knight of his sort, and they continued in conversation until they came in sight of the bog and the bridge. Here they saw the insolent woman, armed—her arms were made of gold and adorned with emeralds and sapphires. The story of how Ruggiero risked her onslaught I shall defer to the next canto.[3]

• • •

He who travels far afield beholds things which lie beyond the bounds of belief; and when he returns to tell of them, he is not believed, but is dismissed as a liar, for the ignorant throng will refuse to accept his word, but needs must see with their own eyes, touch with their own hands. This being so, I realize that my words will gain scant credence where they outstrip the experience of my hearers. / Still, whatever degree of reliance is placed on my word, I shall not trouble myself about the ignorant and mindless rabble: I know that you, my sharp, clear-headed listeners, will see the shining truth of my tale. To convince you, and you alone, is all that I wish to strive for, the only reward I seek.

I left off at the point where they came in sight of the bog and the bridge over it which was guarded by proud Erifilla. / Her armour was of the finest metal, encrusted with gems of various colours—red rubies, yellow topaz, green emeralds, and golden hyacinth. She was mounted, but not upon a horse: she had saddled a wolf, instead, with a saddle of unusual splendour, and this beast she was urging onto the bridge. / I doubt whether in Apulia there would be found one of his size—he bulked even larger than an ox. She had thrust no bit into his mouth to bring the foam to his lips—in fact I have

---

1. Atlas, Ruggiero's boyhood protector.   2. Signifies avarice and betrayal (from Erifila, who betrayed her husband for jewels).   3. Three bullets (as below) mark the end of each canto.

no idea how she schooled him to her bidding. Her Pestilence wore a sand-coloured cape over her armour; apart from its colour, it was not unlike that which bishops and prelates wear at court. / On her shield and helmet she sported a bloated, poisonous toad. The damsels pointed her out to the knight: she had crossed to their side of the bridge to block his path, to joust with him and bring him to shame, as she was normally inclined to do. She shouted to Ruggiero to turn back, but he grasped a lance, and yelled defiance at her. / The massive Amazon did not hesitate: she straightway set spurs to her wolf, braced herself firmly in the saddle and charged, setting her lance in rest as she came; the ground shuddered. But, after the impact, she was left lying on the field—Ruggiero caught her under the helmet and tipped her from the saddle with such force, he carried her back some six lengths. / Now, drawing the sword he had buckled on, he was coming to sever her proud head from her shoulders, as well he could do, for Erifilla was lying prostrate amid the meadow-flowers. But the ladies called to him: "She is overthrown—that is enough: no need to wreak any starker vengeance upon her. Sheathe your sword, gentle knight; let us cross the bridge and continue on our way." /

Their path led through a wood; it was somewhat rough and hard-going, for it was narrow and stony, and climbed steeply. When they reached the top of the hill, though, they came out into broad, open fields, and here they set eyes on the most splendid and delightful palace to be seen in the whole wide world. / From the outer gates stepped forth beauteous Alcina, and came to meet Ruggiero; and, surrounded by a handsome and dignified retinue, she extended to him a regal welcome. The whole court now paid such honour and respect to the valiant knight, they could not have done more had God himself come down from Heaven. / What was remarkable about the splendid palace was not its opulence (unrivalled though it was) so much as its inhabitants—the most attractive, courteous people in the world.

For youth and comeliness there was little to judge between them all; only Alcina outstripped them every one in beauty, as the sun is more radiant than any star. / She was so beautifully modelled, no painter, however much he applied himself, could have achieved anything more perfect. Her long blonde tresses were gathered in a knot: pure gold itself could have no finer lustre. Roses and white privet blooms lent their colours to suffuse her delicate cheeks. Her serene brow was like polished ivory, and in perfect proportion. / Beneath two of the thinnest black arches, two dark eyes—or rather, two bright suns; soft was their look, gentle their movement. Love seemed to flit, frolicsome, about them; indeed, Love from this vantage point would let fly his full quiver and openly steal away all hearts. Down the midst of the face, the nose—Envy herself could find no way of bettering it. / Below this, the mouth, set between two dimples; it was imbued with native cinnabar.[4] Here a beautiful soft pair of lips opened to disclose a double row of choicest pearls. Here was the course of those winning words which could not but soften every heart, however rugged and uncouth. Here was formed the melodious laughter which made a paradise on earth. / Snow-white was her neck, milky her breast; the neck was round, the breast broad and full. A pair of apples, not yet ripe, fashioned in ivory, rose and fell like the sea-swell at times when

---

4. The language is from the biblical Song of Songs (see above, p. 91), the possibly allegorical love song between the bride and bridegroom.

a gentle breeze stirs the ocean. Argus[5] himself could not see them entire, but you could easily judge that what lay hidden did not fall short of what was exposed to view. / Her arms were justly proportioned, and her lily-white hands were often to be glimpsed: they were slender and tapering, and quite without a knot or swelling vein. A pair of small, neat, rounded feet completes the picture of this august person. Her looks were angelic, heaven-sent—no veil could have concealed them. / Everything about her was an enticement, whether she spoke or laughed or sang, whether she but moved a step.

Little wonder that Ruggiero was ensnared, finding her, as he did, so entrancing. Little did it profit him to have been warned by the myrtle of her evil, treacherous nature—it did not seem to him possible for deceit and perfidy to keep company with so charming a smile. / On the contrary, he preferred to believe that if she had changed Astolfo into a myrtle by the sandy shore, it was because he had treated her with stark ingratitude, and so deserved his fate and worse. Everything he had been told about her he dismissed as false, deeming rather that the wretch was moved by spite and envy and was a shameless liar. / Intensely though he loved fair Bradamant, she was here and now wrested from his heart, for by magic Alcina erased all trace of the pangs with which up till now his soul was smitten. She alone became the unique burden of his love, she alone was now engraved upon his heart. Good Ruggiero must be forgiven, then, for this show of inconstancy. /

Around the festive board zithers, harps, and lyres set the air vibrating with delightful sounds, with soft harmony and tuneful notes. There was song, too, song of love's joys and ecstasies, and recitals of pleasing fantasies framed in verse of happiest inspiration. / Which of the splendid and sumptuous banquets arranged by any of those who sat upon King Ninus' throne, which of the many celebrated feasts offered by Cleopatra to the victorious Roman, which of these can compare to the banquet that the loving sorceress prepared for the paladin? No such feast, I am sure, was ever set out on Olympus when Ganymede[6] ministered to imperial Jove. / When the food and the tables were cleared away, they all sat down in a circle to play a merry game which consisted in each whispering into his neighbour's ear to ask a secret—any secret. This gave the lovers ample occasion to disclose their passion without hindrance; the final outcome was an assignation for that very night. / This game was not continued for long—it was ended far sooner than was the normal custom.

The pages then led the way into the palace with torches, driving out the darkness with an abundance of light. Preceded and followed by elegant company, Ruggiero was escorted to his downy bed in a little bedroom: it was airy and pleasantly decorated, the first choice of all the rooms in the palace. / Once more he was pressed to partake of sweet delicacies and choice wines, after which the company bowed respectfully and withdrew to their own quarters. Ruggiero slipped between the perfumed sheets, which might well have been the handiwork of Arachne[7] herself; he strained his ears now to listen for the approach of lovely Alcina. / At the slightest movement he heard, he

---

5. A mythological creature with one hundred eyes.   6. A beautiful Trojan boy snatched by Jupiter, in the shape of an eagle, to be his cup-bearer. *Victorious Roman:* Pompey the Great, Julius Caesar, or Marc Antony. *Ninus:* king of Assyria, husband and son of Semiramis; his successor was the profligate Sardanapalus.   7. Ovid's master weaver, who challenged Minerva to a weaving contest and was transformed into a spider.

would raise his head, hoping it was she; often he heard sounds when in fact there was nothing to hear—and then he would realize his mistake and sigh. Now and then he would jump out of bed, open the door, and look outside, but there was nothing to be seen. Endlessly he cursed weary time for moving so sluggishly. / Often he would tell himself: "Now she has set out"—and he would start counting the steps which must separate Alcina's room from the one where he awaited her. These and other vain fancies occupied him in the interval before she came, and frequently he feared lest some obstacle be placed between his hand and the fruit. / Alcina all the while was steeping herself in precious perfumes; she put an end to these labours once all was at peace in the household and there was no need for further delay. Now she slipped out of her room and stole by a secret passage to where Ruggiero awaited her; in his heart all this time hope and fear had fought many a round. /

When Astolfo's successor looked up to see those joyful-twinkling stars, he felt as though hot sulphur were coursing through his veins, which threatened to start out from his skin. Now he was engulfed up to his eyes in sheer sweetness, in loveliness. He jumped out of bed and gathered her into his arms, quite unable to wait for her to undress—/ for all that she was wearing neither gown nor petticoat: she had come in a light mantle which she had thrown over a white nightgown of gossamer texture. The mantle she abandoned to Ruggiero as he embraced her; this left only the insubstantial gossamer-gown which, before and behind, concealed no more than would a pane of glass placed before a spray of roses or lilies. / Ivy never clung so tightly to the stem round which it was entwined as did the two lovers cling to each other, drawing from each other's lips pollen so fragrant that it will be found on no flower which grows in the scented Indian or Arabian sands. As for describing their pleasure, better to leave this to them—the more so as they frequently had a second tongue in their mouth. / Such matters were kept a secret, or, if no secret, at least they were not spoken of: a seal on the lips often merits praise, seldom blame.

The whole court, astute company that it was, offered Ruggiero its service and a cheerful welcome; everybody reverenced him, deferred to him, for such was the will of love-struck Alcina. / There was not a pleasure which was overlooked, for the love-pavilion afforded every one of them. Two and three times a day they would change their costume depending on the pastime they next intended. Banqueting often, festival ever was the order of the day, with tourneys and trials of strength, with masques, and dances and bathing. Beside a spring, on a shady hillside they would read what was written of love in olden times; / or else they would course through the wooded valleys and over the glad hills, chasing the timid hare; or with their cunning hounds they would flush the frantic, flapping partridge from her cover amid the stubble and the underbrush; they would snare the thrush amid the scented juniper, using a running noose or a soothing lure. Or else they would bait their hooks or cast their nets to disturb the fish out of their contented secrecy. /

Thus did Ruggiero bask in every sort of pleasure, while toil was the lot of Charles the Emperor and of Agramant the King: I should not wish to forget their story, nor to leave aside Bradamant, who for many days bitterly lamented the loss of her lover whom she had seen borne off along so strange a path, she knew not whither. / Before taking up the kings' story, I shall take up hers: for many a day she scoured the country in vain, searching the shady forests and sunny fields, searching farmsteads and cities, hills and plains; but she could glean nothing about her dearest love who was so far, far away. Often she visited the Saracen host, but not a trace could she pick up of her Ruggiero. / Each day she would question over a hundred souls, but not one of them could give her news of him. She would go from one encampment to the next, seeking for him in every tent and pavilion. This was not difficult, for she could go among the mounted troops and those on foot thanks to the ring which, against all human experience, made her vanish when she put it in her mouth. / She could not, nor would she, seek him among the dead: the mighty downfall of a man so great would have made itself heard from the Indus to the lands of the setting sun. She could not tell, she could not imagine where his path lay, on or above the earth, and yet pitifully she kept searching for him, with sighs and tears and every kind of sorrow for companions. /

Eventually she thought of returning to the cave which sheltered the prophet Merlin's bones;[8] she would scream so piercingly about his tomb that the cold marble would be moved to pity. And whether Ruggiero still lived, or whether Death—that ultimate necessity—had cut short his happy years, she would here discover. Then she would pursue whatever course was best proposed. /

Thus decided, she set off towards the forests neighbouring Ponthieu, where, in wild and hilly country, was concealed the tomb from which Merlin spoke. Now the enchantress who had ever followed Bradamant in her thoughts, I mean the one who had instructed her about her posterity in the gorgeous cavern—/ the good and wise enchantress, who had always taken care of her, knowing her destiny as mother of unconquerable men, indeed of demi-gods—sought daily to know what she was doing, what saying, and daily cast spells to favour her. Ruggiero's delivery from Atlas, his abduction, where now he was in India, all this was known to her. / She had seen him mounted on that unbridled horse which he could not control, sailing out into the distance along so perilous and strange a path. Full well she knew how he was passing his time now in amusements, in dancing and feasting, in soft, pampered indolence, forgetful of his Liege, of his beloved, of his own renown.[9] / And it might therefore have been the lot of so goodly a knight to pass the best years of his life in sustained idleness, only to lose his soul and body all at once. And that odour, which is all we leave behind once our frail carcass falls to dust, and saves us from the tomb and keeps us ever-living, that odour would be like a fragrant flower severed from its stem or plucked out from the grass. / But the kind sorceress, who took more care of him then he did of himself, thought how to bring him back to true virtue, despite himself, by a hard and rugged way—just like a skilled physician who treats a wound with iron and fire, and often with poison: even though at first he causes much pain, he ultimately does good, and receives thanks. /

She showed him no indulgence: a transcendent love made her so blind to all else that she had, like Atlas, set her heart upon restoring his life to him. Atlas, however, would have him enjoy long life bereft of honour and renown rather than forego one year of his carefree existence for all the praise the

8. Where she met the sorceress Melissa and heard Merlin's prophecy of the dynasty she and Ruggiero would found.   9. Agramant, Bradamant, and his reputation.

world could accord him. / He had sent Ruggiero to Alcina's island to make him, at her court, forget about arms. And, being a magician of consummate art, skilled in every kind of magic spell, he had bound that queen's[1] heart to his in so strong a bond that there was no question of her breaking free, though Ruggiero were to grow as old as Nestor.[2] /

But back to the enchantress who could see into the future: she set out and found the wandering Bradamant on her way to see her. Coming upon her friend the enchantress, Bradamant found new hope in place of the anguish which had hitherto been all her company. The prophetess disclosed the truth to her—that her Ruggiero had been carried off to Alcina. / The maiden was stunned to learn just how far away was her beloved—and worse, that without immediate and effective help, their very love for each other was imperilled. But the kind enchantress comforted her and was quick to apply a dressing to the throbbing wound: she gave her word that within a few days she would restore Ruggiero to her. /

"As you possess the ring,"[3] she said, "which is proof against every magic spell, I have not the least doubt that if I take it with me to the place where Alcina is purloining your treasure, I shall foil her designs and bring back to you your only-beloved. I shall set out this evening with the gathering dusk, and as dawn breaks I shall be in India." / She went on to explain to her the manner in which she intended to use the ring so as to rescue her loved one from the soft, womanly realm and bring him back to France. Bradamant drew the ring from her finger; not only this would she have handed over, but also her heart, her very life, if this might have procured help for her Ruggiero. / She gave her the ring, and commended herself to the enchantress; even more did she commend Ruggiero to her, bidding her convey to him all her fondest love. Then, by a different path, she set out towards Provence.

The enchantress went her own way, and, to put her plan into effect, she that evening conjured up a palfrey; he was black all over, except for a red foot. / I believe he must have been some spirit she had summoned in that shape from hell. Barefoot and ungirded, she mounted him; her hair, now hideously withered, fell loose about her. She took the ring off her finger lest it would inhibit her own magic. Then she left in such haste that the following morning found her on Alcina's island. / Here she underwent a remarkable transformation: she put on almost a foot in height, grew her limbs stouter, and ended up so proportioned that she passed for Atlas, the wizard who had brought up Ruggiero so dotingly. She clothed her chin in a long beard and induced wrinkles on her brow and all over. / In face, speech, and person she took him off so perfectly that she seemed none other than the sorcerer himself.

Then she concealed herself, and remained alert for the moment when at last Ruggiero did not have the love-sick Alcina at his side—this was a stroke of fortune, for, go or stay, she could not stand being parted from him for even an hour. / She found him all on his own, as she wanted, enjoying the freshness and peace of the morning beside a delightful stream which flowed down a hillside towards a pleasant, limpid lake. The delicious softness of his dress suggested sloth and sensuality; Alcina had woven the garment with her

---

1. Alcina, who now resembles Virgil's Queen Dido.   2. I.e., ancient: Nestor saw three generations, according to Homer.   3. A magical ring originally belonging to Angelica; worn on the finger, it protects wearers from magical deceptions; placed in the mouth, it grants invisibility.

own hands in silk and gold, a subtle work. / A glittering, richly jewelled necklace fastened round his neck and hung to his chest, while his two arms, hitherto so virile, were now each clasped by a lustrous bangle. Each ear was pierced by a fine gold ring from which a fat pearl hung, such as no Arabian or Indian ever boasted. / His curly locks were saturated in perfumes, the most precious and aromatic that exist. His every gesture was mincing, as though he were accustomed to waiting on ladies in Valencia. All about him was sickly, all but his name; the rest was but corruption and decay.[4] Thus was Ruggiero discovered, thus changed from his true self by sorcery. /

The enchantress, then, presented herself to Ruggiero in Atlas' likeness, with Atlas' grave, venerable face which had always commanded his respect; on his face he wore the look of angry menace which Ruggiero had feared from early childhood.

"Are these then the fruits," she exclaimed, "for which I have toiled so long? / Early I fed you on the marrow of bears and lions; I accustomed you as a child to strangle snakes in grottoes and wild ravines, to disarm the clawing panthers and tigers and draw the tusks off live boars—was all this schooling to no better purpose than to make you play Adonis, or Atys,[5] to Alcina? / Was this, then, the promise of your manhood, made to me when you were still but a child at the breast—this the promise of the stars I studied, and the sacral threads, the conjunctions, the dreams and auguries and omens which have been my all-too-assiduous study? It was in deeds of arms that you were to stand out, a matchless champion. / A goodly beginning, this, from which we can hope soon to see you become another Alexander, Scipio, or Caesar![6] Alas, who could ever have dreamed it possible that you of all people would become a bondsman to Alcina! To make this obvious to everyone, you wear about your neck and on your arms the chains with which she drags you to her bidding. /

"Though you care nothing for your own renown, and for the shining deeds for which Heaven has appointed you, why must you defraud your own posterity of all the good which I have a thousand times predicted to you? What of the womb in which—so Heaven has decreed—you're to conceive a glorious and god-like race, more radiant than the sun: why must you suffer it to remain eternally sealed? / The noblest spirits conceived in the Eternal Mind must at their appointed time take human form, springing from the stock rooted in you: prevent them not! Do not prevent the triumphant and victorious deeds whereby your children, and your children's children, shall heal Italy of her dread afflictions and dire injuries, and restore her to her pristine glory. / Many and many a gracious soul, brilliant, illustrious, eminent, peerless, and holy, is to be sprung as shoots from your fecund tree; even if all of these cannot weigh upon your decision, yet but one pair should be sufficient: Hippolytus and his brother,[7] the likes of whom have seldom been encountered in the world to this day, for sheer eminence of virtue. / I used to speak to you more often of these two than of all the others put together, for, among them all, they shall enjoy the lion's share of pre-eminent qualities; also, when I spoke of them, I saw you pay closer attention than when I spoke of other

---

4. Ruggiero outdoes Aeneas in being decorated and smothered by Dido (in *Aeneid* 4). *Valencia*: Spanish city notorious in the 1500s for dissolute behavior.   5. A youth who castrated himself for the mother goddess, Cybele. *Adonis*: boy loved by Venus.   6. Famed world-conquerors of Greece and Rome.
7. Alfonso d'Este, duke of Ferrara, and Ippolito d'Este, the cardinal and Ariosto's patron.

of your seed—I saw you rejoice that such illustrious heroes were to be descended from you. /

"This woman you have made your queen, what has she to distinguish her from a thousand other whores? This woman, she's the whole world's concubine: judge for yourself whether she can really satisfy! Now, that you may know who Alcina is, stripped of her artifices and deceits, put this ring on your finger and return to her, and you shall realize just how fair are her looks." /

Ruggiero stood shamefaced and silent, staring at the ground, not knowing what to say. The enchantress put the ring on his little finger, and brought him back to reality. Coming to himself, Ruggiero was so overwhelmed with shame that he wished himself a thousand feet below ground, so that no one could look him in the face. / After these words, the enchantress switched back into her own likeness, as she had no further need to borrow Atlas', her effect once achieved. What I neglected to tell you earlier was her name: Melissa. She now gave Ruggiero a true account of herself and of her mission. / She had been sent, she explained, by one who loved him and ever longed for him, by one who could not be without him; she had come to deliver him from the shackles which had been forced upon him by sorcery. And in order the better to gain his confidence, she had assumed Atlas' form. But now that she had restored him to his senses, she would set all the facts before him. /

"A most worthy lady who loves you, and who would be deserving of your love—and, unless you are forgetful, you must realize how much you owed your liberty to the service she rendered you—this lady sends you this ring, proof against all magic. Her very heart she would have sent, had her heart possessed the same virtues as this ring to procure your safety." / She went on to speak of the love which Bradamant bore him, and she commended her merits in terms which combined truth with warmth of feeling. Being a skilled messenger, she chose her words to the best advantage, and she implanted in Ruggiero an utter revulsion for Alcina, such as one would feel for any loathsome object. /

She made her an object of disgust to him, for all that he had loved her up till now; be not surprised, though—his love had been wrought out of enchantment, and, with the ring, the spell was broken. What else the ring showed up was that Alcina's beauty was in every detail an imposture: it was wholly fraudulent—nothing, from her soles up to her tresses, was natural to her. Her beauty evaporated, leaving nothing but dregs. / If a child sets aside a ripe fruit and then, forgetting where he put it, is brought to the very place many days later and happens upon his fruit, he is amazed to find it all rotten and putrid, and not at all as he had left it; and though he normally had a weakness for that sort of fruit, he throws this one away in loathing and revulsion—/ so it was with Ruggiero: once Melissa had made him set eyes again upon Alcina, but this time wearing the ring that makes the wearer, while he has it on his finger, totally immune to magic, he was astonished to find that in place of the beauty he had just parted from, he was confronted with a woman so hideous that her equal for sheer ugliness and decrepitude could be found nowhere on earth. / She was whey-faced, wrinkled, and hollow-cheeked; her hair was white and sparse; she was not four feet high; the last tooth had dropped out of her jaw; she had lived longer than anyone on earth, longer than Hecuba or the Cumaean Sibyl.[8] But she made such use of arts unknown in our day that she could pass for young and fair. / Young and fair she made herself by artifice, and deceived many as she deceived Ruggiero. But now, with the ring, he could read the cards[9] aright and see the truth which for so many years had been kept hidden. Small wonder, then, if Ruggiero could no longer find in himself the slightest inclination to love Alcina, now that he was so equipped when he came upon her that her deceit could no longer serve her. /

But, as Melissa advised him, he betrayed no change in his face until he had resumed his armour, from head to foot, which for so many days he had neglected. And, so as to avert Alcina's suspicions, he pretended to try it on just to see how easily he could manage it—he pretended to see if he could still squeeze into it after so many days since he last wore it. / Then he buckled on his sword, which was called Balisard, and took up the miraculous shield, which not merely dazzles the eyes but so clouds the spirit that, to all appearances, it takes leave of the body. He took up the shield, then, still sheathed in its silken drape, and slung it from his shoulder. / Next, he went to the stables and had a horse saddled and bridled—a black horse, black as pitch, chosen on Melissa's instructions, for she knew that he could run like the wind. Those who knew him called him Rabican—he was the very horse which was borne on whale-back to this place, together with the knight who is now the sport of the breeze by the edge of the sea. / He might have taken the hippogryph, who was tethered next to Rabican, but Melissa had told him, "Bear in mind that he is, as you know, too unruly." And she gave him to hope that the next day she would take out the hippogryph and help Ruggiero to learn little by little how to control him and make him go anywhere. / Leaving him alone, too, Ruggiero would not arouse suspicions about the secret escape he was contriving. He did as Melissa directed—she kept, unseen, by his ear the whole time.

Thus feigning, he slipped out of the ancient harlot's palace, all soft sensuality, and came to a gate which gave onto the road leading to Logistilla's domain. / He drove into the sentinels, sword in hand, and caught them unawares; some he left wounded, others slain, and then charged out across the bridge. Before Alcina had an inkling of what had befallen, Ruggiero was already well away. In the next canto I shall tell you what path he took, and how he came to the realm of Logistilla.

FROM CANTOS 8 AND 9

[Angelica Travels Alone and Orlando Has a Dream]

Sorcerers and sorceresses, we may not know it but you thrive among us! Artfully you disguise your faces and ensnare the hearts of the opposite sex. You work your magic not by virtue of obedient sprites nor by conning the stars for signs: by trickery, lies, and dissimulation you bind the hearts of others with knots that cannot be untied. / Those of us who possessed Angelica's ring—I mean the ring of Reason—could descry each person's true face, undisguised by cunning artifice. A man who passes for handsome and kind

---

8. Apollo gave her immortality but not eternal youth. *Hecuba:* queen of Troy and Priam's wife. 9. Italian *carte,* meaning maps and pages of a book.

may well, beneath his veneer, look like an ugly brute. Ruggiero, then, was most fortunate to have the ring which disclosed to him the truth. /

As I said, Ruggiero feigned his way out and came to the gates, armed and mounted on Rabican. He took the guards unawares and, as he drove into them, he did not leave his sword in its sheath. Some he left dead, others the worse for wear, before he rode out across the bridge and smashed his way through the palisade. He set out towards the woods, but after only a short way he came upon one of Alcina's minions. / On his wrist the man was carrying some bird of prey which he liked to take out with him daily into the fields or to a nearby pond where there was always plenty of game to be caught. At his side trotted his faithful hound, and he was riding a quite ordinary hack. Seeing how fast Ruggiero was approaching, he judged that he must be a fugitive. /

The fellow made towards him and in an arrogant tone enquired: "Why such haste?" Ruggiero did not see fit to reply, so the other, more certain than ever that he was a fugitive, decided he must be stopped. He extended his left hand and cried: "What will you say if I stop you in your tracks— you'll find no shelter from this bird of mine!" / The huntsman released his bird, which winged away so fast that Rabican could not outdistance it. Then he jumped off his horse and in a trice had unbridled him: the horse became like an arrow shot from a bow and arrived kicking and biting viciously. Right behind him came the huntsman, as though borne on a lick of flame, or on the very wind. / Now the hound did not wish to play the laggard, but was off after Rabican like a hunting-cat after a hare. Ruggiero would have deemed it cowardly not to stand his ground, so he turned to face the man approaching at such a dashing stride. For all weapons the fellow carried only a small stick—the kind used to teach a dog obedience—so Ruggiero did not deign to draw his sword. / The huntsman reached him and landed him a powerful blow, while the hound sunk his teeth into his left foot. The unbridled horse meanwhile kicked out repeatedly with his back legs, which thudded against Ruggiero's right side. The bird wheeled and circled, every so often ripping at him with its talons, and so terrifying the charger with its shrieks that he scarce answered to spur or rein. / Finally Ruggiero's sword flashed out: if he was to stop their molesting him, there was no other way. Cut and thrust, he threatened the beasts and their master in turn, but his assailants only pinned him down the more: together they had closed the whole width of the path to him. Ruggiero foresaw the shame and evil he must incur if they delayed him further. / He knew that if he tarried there longer, any moment would bring into view Alcina and her minions. Already the valleys were ringing to the sound of bells, trumpets, and drums. He could see that against an unarmed groom with a dog his sword was not the answer: he would obtain better and faster results if he disclosed the shield which Atlas had made. / He stripped off the scarlet cloth which had covered the shield these many days, and the dazzle achieved its well-proved effect the moment it caught the eye of the beholders. The huntsman was left senseless; horse and hound collapsed all of a heap, and the bird's pinions fell inert, powerless to sustain it in flight. Ruggiero was glad to leave them all a prey to sleep. /

Alcina, meanwhile, had been told how Ruggiero had stormed the gates and killed several of the guard. She could almost have died for grief; she rent her garments and flayed her cheeks, cursing herself for an idiot and a fool.

She raised the alarm at once and summoned her henchmen to her, every one. / She split them into two groups, sending one along the path Ruggiero had taken, and assembling the other at the harbour to board ship and put out from shore: in the shadow of the spreading sails the whole sea grew dark. Alcina embarked with these; such was her desperation, such her devouring lust for Ruggiero that she left her city unguarded. /

She left no one to guard her palace, which gave Melissa the opportunity for which she had been waiting, to steal into this sinister stronghold and liberate the unfortunates detained there. Here was her opportunity to find everything in its proper place and lay her hands on it—figurines to burn, seals to remove, knots, magic squares, and whorls to disarrange. / Then, hastening through the countryside in search of the discarded lovers whom Alcina had turned—a great host of them—into wood or stone, into springs or wild beasts, she restored them all to their proper selves. Finding themselves now able to move freely, they all set off in the footsteps of good Ruggiero, and so made their escape to Logistilla's kingdom, whence they returned each to his own land—Greece, Persia, Scythia, India. / Melissa sent them each back to his own land, laden with a debt of gratitude which could never be repaid.

The first to be restored to human form was Astolfo, the duke of the English, thanks to the kinship he enjoyed with Ruggiero, and to this knight's intercession for him; beside commending Astolfo to her, he gave Melissa the ring, the better to be able to help him. / At Ruggiero's behest, then, the paladin was restored to his true self. But Melissa felt she had accomplished nothing until she had restored to him his weapons and his golden lance which has only to touch a person to tip him from the saddle. This lance was Argalia's, but then fell to Astolfo; it brought high honour to both of them in France. / Melissa found the golden lance, which Alcina had put away in her palace, and all the rest of the duke's arms which had been taken from him in that haunt of evil. She mounted the charger which had belonged to Atlas, the Moorish wizard, and had Astolfo climb on behind; then, taking flight for Logistilla's, they arrived there an hour before Ruggiero. /

Ruggiero, meanwhile, was making his way to Logistilla, the kindly enchantress. His path lay amid hard boulders and bramble thickets, from one hill's crest to the next; one path he followed and another, ever steep and solitary, wild and inhospitable. Strained and weary, he came out upon a beach hemmed in between the mountains and the sea; it was in the heat of mid-afternoon, and the place was exposed to the South, arid and bare, sterile and desolate. / The blazing sun beat down upon the hill nearby, which reflected back a heat so intense that it set the air simmering, and the sand: it would have taken less heat to liquefy glass. Every bird sat silent in the soft shade; alone the cricket amid the thick, leafy shrubs shrilled his monotonous refrain, which filled, which deafened, the hills and valleys, the sea and sky. / Tedious and oppressive was the heat, the thirst and weariness which were all Ruggiero had for company as he pursued his sand-strewn way along the sun-drenched desert shore.[1]

* * *

1. Typologically a spiritual middle ground, based on the Israelites' passage through the desert from Egypt to the Promised Land and through idolatry to true worship.

But ought I not, my Lord, to do as the good musician playing his subtle instrument? He will select different strings, fresh harmonies, as he seeks effects, now muted, now strident. And I, intent on unfolding Rinaldo's story, have just remembered sweet Angelica: I left her fleeing from him,[2] and falling in with a hermit. / I shall pursue her story a little. I told you how earnestly she enquired how she might reach the sea-coast, for she was so terrified of Rinaldo that she felt certain of dying if she did not cross the sea, imagining herself unsafe anywhere in Europe. But the hermit took his time, for he enjoyed her company. / Such rare beauty inflamed his heart and warmed the chill marrow in his bones. But, seeing that she took little notice of him, and indeed showed no disposition to bide with him, he mercilessly goaded and spurred his little mule, without being able to rouse him from his lethargic gait; the mule would walk only a few paces, and quite refused to trot—as for a full canter, that was out of the question. /

Now, as he was dropping a long way behind, and in a while would completely lose her traces, the hermit had recourse to his dark cave, and summoned forth a host of demons. He selected one of them and told him what it was he wanted; after which, he bade him enter into Angelica's palfrey which was bearing away the lady—and his heart. / A cunning hound, well used to hunting the fox or the hare in the mountains, will see the prey going by one path, and will himself choose another, as though disdaining to follow the scent; but where the fugitive's path comes out, that is where he will station himself, and he will seize his prey in his jaws and rend open its flanks. Thus did the hermit, taking another path to come up with the damsel, whichever way she went. / What he planned to do is obvious to me, and I shall tell you—later on.

Angelica, all unsuspecting, rode on, covering unequal daily stages. But in her horse the demon lay concealed, as sometimes a fire is concealed only to blaze forth in a while so mightily that there is no putting it out, and to escape from it is difficult. / The damsel followed the path which lay beside the broad sea which washes the land of the Gascons; she rode close to the water's edge, picking her way where the ground was firmest. But her steed was drawn into the water by the powerful demon, and began to swim; the fearful maiden knew not what to do—she just clung tightly to the saddle. / She tugged and tugged on the reins, but could not turn her steed, who was swimming straight out into the deep. She drew up her skirts so as to keep them dry, and pulled her feet clear of the water. Her tresses hung loose about her shoulders, while the lascivious breeze caressed her. The great winds fell silent: perhaps they, like the sea, were arrested by so rare a vision of beauty. / In vain she turned her soft eyes towards the shore, and bathed her face and breast with tears; she saw the land ever receding and growing smaller and smaller.[3] After swimming in a great arc, ever to the right, the beast carried her back to the shore, where it was all dark rocks and dreadful caverns.

Night was falling. / Finding herself alone in this desolate spot—the very look of the place was enough to inspire dread—at the hour when Phoebus[4] sinks into the ocean, leaving a pall of darkness in the air and over the land, Angelica stood motionless: anyone descrying her there would have been in

2. In canto 1. Charlemagne then sent Rinaldo on a mission to Scotland.   3. The scene echoes Ovid's tale of Europa, abducted by Jupiter in the guise of a bull, in *Metamorphoses* 2.   4. The sun god.

some doubt whether she was a real, sentient woman, or simply a rock tinted to look like one. / She stood paralysed in the shifting sand, her hair dishevelled, her hands clasped, her lips motionless; her languorous eyes were raised to heaven, as though accusing the Great Mover of having set all the Fates against her. She stood awhile as though in a trance, then tears came welling up and her tongue found utterance for her grief. /

"Fortune, what more have you to do," she said, "before you are sated and replete with hounding me? What have I still left to give you, except for this wretched life of mine? But you do not want it, for you have been so prompt to save it from the sea where it might have found an end to its sorrows. You must have wanted to see me tormented still more before I die. / But I cannot see how you can hurt me more than you have done already. You have had me banished from my royal home, whither I have no hope of returning. I have lost my good name,[5] which is worse: for though I have committed no fault, yet I give everyone the excuse to hold that, being a wanderer, I must be a loose woman. / Deprive a woman of her virtue, and what other blessing can she enjoy in this world? I suffer for being young, alas, and for being accounted, whether rightly or wrongly, beautiful. I cannot thank Heaven for this gift, as it is the source of all my sorrows. It was on this account that Argalia my brother died—little good did his enchanted weapons do him. / It was on this account that Agrican, King of Tartary, defeated my father Galafron, Great Khan of Cathay and the Indies, which led to my present sorry state, shifting my dwelling from day to day. Now that you have taken from me all my possessions, my honour and those dear to me, and done your worst to me, for what further misery are you preparing me? / If drowning me in the sea did not seem to you a cruel enough death, I'll not recoil if you send a wild beast to devour me and put an end to my torments, if only that will satisfy you. Send me any affliction, any at all and, as long as I die of it, I'll not be able to thank you enough." Thus spoke the maiden through her tears. The next moment the hermit appeared. /

The hermit, from the top of a high rock, had been observing Angelica who, all bewildered and forlorn, had been set ashore at the base of it. He had come six days before, borne hither by a demon who took an untrodden route. Now he approached her, with a show of piety as profound as that of Paul or Hilarion.[6] / When the damsel noticed him, she took comfort, for she did not know him; her terror gradually abated, though her face still remained pale and drawn. When he was close by she said, "Mercy, good father! I've come to a pitiful pass!" And, her voice choked with sobs, she explained to him what he already knew full well. / The hermit offered her good, devout words of comfort, and as he spoke, he boldly placed his hands now on her breast, now on her tear-stained cheeks. Then, gaining confidence, he tried to embrace her, but she angrily struck at his chest and pushed him away, her face suffused with a modest blush. / Out of his pocket the hermit now drew a phial of liquid and lightly sprayed a drop of it onto the maiden's eyes—eyes which sparkled with the most blazing brand in Cupid's armoury. The liquid drops put her to sleep: she lay supine on the sand, now a prey to the lustful old lecher. / He hugged her and felt her at his pleasure: she was asleep and could

---

5. Reputation; compare with Ruggiero's loss of all but his name on Alcina's island.   6. First hermit of Palestine. *Paul:* the apostle to the Gentiles.

offer no resistance. He planted kisses on her lovely breast and on her lips; there was no one to see him in that wild, deserted spot. But when he came to the impact, his charger stumbled, for his wasted body would not answer to his desire—his was too elderly, unsuitable a jade, and the harder he forced him the worse his success. / He tried one way, then another, but could not get his flop-eared nag to jump; vainly he shook his reins and spurred him on, but there was no making him raise his head. Eventually he fell asleep beside the damsel, who was now to suffer a worse assault: when Fortune takes it into her head to make play with a mortal, she does nothing by halves. /

But, before I tell you what happened, I must make a slight digression. In the northern seas, over towards the setting sun, out beyond Ireland, there lies an island; its name is Ebuda. It has only a few inhabitants, the survivors of the destruction wrought upon it by the horrid orc and the other sea-beasts brought thither by Proteus, the vengeful god.[7]/

An old legend, possibly true, relates that once upon a time a powerful king ruled the island; he had a daughter of such entrancing beauty that, when she walked on the briny beach, she could without effort leave Proteus burning even in the middle of his watery realm. And Proteus, coming upon her alone one day, caught her in an embrace and left her pregnant. / Her father, who was of exceedingly harsh and severe disposition, regarded the matter as an intolerable injury, so much so that no excuse, no pity would stay him from ordering her beheaded—passionate anger ruled him. Nor would he defer the execution of his cruel command in view of her pregnant condition. And the little grandson who had committed no fault: he had him slain even before he was born. / Proteus, the sea-god who pastures the proud flocks of Neptune, ruler of the Ocean, heard the dreadful torment of his lady and broke all bounds in his seething wrath. At once he sent onshore his orcs and sea-lions and all his watery flock to ravage the sheep and cattle, yes, and the hamlets and farms and those who toiled there; / often, too, they surged up to the town walls and laid siege to them from all sides. The townsfolk had to stand armed guard day and night—a wearisome duty, and terrifying. Everyone had withdrawn from the open fields. Eventually, to find some remedy, they repaired to the oracle for a consultation, and this was its reply: / They must find a maiden as beautiful as the first and take her to the water's edge and offer her to the irate god to compensate for the one who was slain. If he was satisfied with her beauty he would keep her, and would harass them no further; but if he rejected her they must offer him another and yet another until he was content. / Thus among the comeliest of the fair sex a hard toll began to be exacted: each day one of them was offered to Proteus until one acceptable to him were found. The first met her death, and so did all who followed, for one and all were engulfed in the maw of a great orc who remained near the river's mouth after the rest of the terrible sea-herd was dispersed. /

Whether or not there is any truth in this story about Proteus, I really have no idea; at all events, a wicked, ancient law was there enforced against women, on the basis of such a story: the monstrous orc, who visits their shore every day, must be fed on their flesh. To be a woman is a hard enough lot at the best of times—but here particularly so. / Poor wretched damsels,

---

7. Shape-shifting sea god.

borne by injurious Fate to so inclement a shore where the islanders keep watch upon the sea to make a wicked holocaust of alien women: for the more damsels from abroad who are sacrificed, the smaller the inroads they have to make among their own womenfolk. But as the wind does not always blow the prey in their direction, they go out scavenging along every other shore. / They scour every sea in their galleys and brigs and other vessels and from near and far they fetch in what they need to relieve their torment. Many women they carry off by force, a few they lure and entice, others they buy with gold; they keep gathering them in from all quarters and pack them into their prisons and keeps. /

As one of their galleys was passing close inshore, coasting along the deserted strand where poor Angelica lay asleep on the grass amid the underbrush, a number of sailors landed to refurbish their supplies of wood and fresh water. So they came upon this, the flower of feminine beauty and grace, lying clasped in the venerable father's arms. / Alas, too precious, too exalted a prey for men so base, so barbarous! Oh cruel Fortune, who would ever imagine that you could exercise such power over human affairs! You would feed a monster with the fairest of the fair, who stirred King Agrican to leave the Caucasian gates with half of Scythia in his train, and invade India, there to meet his death; / the fairest beauty, whom Sacripant preferred to his own honour and goodly kingdom; she who made Orlando, Duke of Anglant, besmirch his name and sully his lofty genius; she for whom, in massive disarray, the entire Orient stood to arms: now so abandoned is she, there is not one she can turn to for so much as a word of help. /

Oppressed by sleep, beautiful Angelica was shackled before she could rouse herself. With her they carried off the hermit in the ship already crowded with grieving humanity. The sail was hoisted to the masthead and drew the ship back to the grim island, where they shut the maiden in a dungeon until her turn arrived. / But her beauty produced such an effect upon those hardened folk that out of pity they postponed her sacrifice for many days, reserving her till the last possible moment. So long as there was another alien damsel to replace her, she was saved by her angelic countenance.

Finally, though, she was brought to the sea-monster, with the whole population following, weeping, in her train. / Who shall describe the sobs and shrieks and wails which mounted to the heavens? I am amazed that the shore did not gape open when she was exposed on the cold rock, to wait, chained and abandoned by all, for a stark, dreadful death. I shall not tell you more—it is too painful, and sorrow drives me to turn my rhymes in some other direction, / and find less harrowing verses until my weary spirit recovers: the baleful viper, the jealous tiger whipped up into a frenzy of rage, and whatever venomous species creep through the hot sands between the Atlantic and the Red Sea shore—they could none of them behold or contemplate without compassion the sight of Angelica tied to the bare rock. / Ah, if her Orlando had known—he had gone to Paris in search of her—or the two knights who were tricked by the wily old hermit who sent them his infernal messenger! They would have risked a thousand deaths to follow Angelica's traces and bring her aid. And yet, even had they known where to find her, what could they have done, seeing the distance that separated them from her? /

Paris meanwhile lay besieged by Agramant, King Trojan's famous son; and the day came when the city was reduced to such straits that it almost fell to the enemy. Were it not that God accepted the Christians' prayers and flooded the plain in a murky downpour, the Sacred Empire and the mighty name of France would that day have fallen to the African spears. / The Almighty Creator turned His eyes to the just lament of the old emperor, and dowsed the fires in a sudden rainstorm; probably no human ingenuity would have been able to master them. Wise is the man who always turns to God: for no one else can give him better assistance. The pious monarch well recognized this, owing his rescue to divine intervention. /

That night, Orlando imparted his fleeting thoughts to his restless bed. This way and that he drove them, and herded them all together, but could never pen them in. They were like the tremulous gleam which a limpid pool gives off under the rays of the sun or moon—high and low, to right and left it fans out, and leaps over the broad roof-tops.[8] / His lady returned to haunt his mind—not that she had ever been absent from it—and stoked up to a new incandescence the fire which during the day seemed to have waned. She had come with him to the West from Cathay; and now, with Charles' defeat at Bordeaux, he had lost all trace of her. / Bitterly Orlando regretted this, and vainly brooded on his stupidity.

"What a coward's role I played, my love!" said he. "Alas, how sickened I am to think that I could have had you with me night and day, for of your own goodness you did not deny me this, but I let you be handed over to Namo's[9] keeping, and knew not how to forestall such an affront! / Did not I have reason to make a stand? Aye, and supposing Charles had stood his ground? Well, supposing he had—who could have forced my hand? Who was going to take you away in the teeth of my opposition? Could I not have fought, sword in hand, or made them first tear my heart out of my breast? Neither Charles nor all his henchmen together were capable of wresting you from me by force. / He might at least have left her well guarded in Paris or some / other stronghold. If he gave her into Namo's keeping, it must surely have been with a view to losing her. Who could have guarded her better than I? Who would have guarded her with his own life, more jealously than his own heart, his very eyes? I should and could have done so, but I did not. / Where are you now, my love, my pretty nursling, where are you without me? Are you not like the ewe lamb lost in the wood as the daylight wanes—hither and yon she wanders, bleating, and hopes the shepherd will hear her; it is the wolf, though, that hears from afar, and the poor shepherd weeps for his lamb in vain. / Where are you, hope of my heart? Are you still a-wandering all by yourself? Or have the wicked wolves found you unprotected by your faithful Orlando? And your flower,[1] which could set me among the heavenly gods, the flower which I preserved for you intact, so as not to sadden your chaste heart, will they, alas, have plucked and despoiled it? / O, woe upon me, what would I but to die if they have plucked my pretty flower! Almighty God, afflict me with any sorrow, any, but not this! If this has truly come to pass, I must with my own hands take my life and damn my despairing soul."

Thus cried Orlando, tormented knight, amid sighs and bitter tears. / Now

---

8. Echoes Virgil's simile from *Aeneid* 8.22; Aeneas leaves camp to find allies, whereas Orlando abandons his sovereign and uncle for love.   9. Duke of Bavaria, Charlemagne's trusted friend and advisor.
1. Angelica's virginity; compare Orlando's speech with Sacripant's in canto 1.

was the time when every living creature concedes rest to his careworn spirit—some lying in feather-beds, others on hard stones or on the grass, or in the branches of beech and myrtle-trees. But you, Orlando, you scarcely shut your eyelids, pricked as you are by sharp and jagged thoughts, which leave you no peace to enjoy even the briefest snatch of slumber. / Orlando dreamed of a green bank all scattered with fragrant flowers, and there he saw a vision of ivory-white blent with a flush of crimson painted by Love's own hand, and a pair of limpid stars whose light nourished his soul, caught in Love's toils—I mean he saw the lovely eyes and face which had plucked his heart from his breast. / He enjoyed a wonderful sense of happiness and well-being, as deep as a man can feel who is happy in love. But a sudden storm blew up, which ravaged the flowers and threw down the trees—a storm the like of which you will not see when Aquilo, Auster, and Levanter meet and contend. He dreamed that he wandered through a wilderness in vain search of shelter. / Meanwhile the hapless lover somehow or other loses his lady in the failing light, and searches here and there through the woods and moors calling her name. And while in vain he cries, "Woe is me! Who is it who has changed my solace into poison?" he hears his lady tearfully calling to him for help. / He runs to where he thinks the cries come from, and searches desperately high and low; imagine his searing grief when he can no longer descry his love's sweet radiance. Now he hears a voice from a different quarter, which cries: "Look no more to have joy from her here below."[2]

At this dreadful cry he woke, to find himself bathed in tears. / Unmindful that the pictures must be false that fear or hope projects in the dreaming mind, Orlando was so wrought up about his lady, believing that some danger or disgrace must have overtaken her, that he leapt, fulminating, out of bed, clad himself in armour and chain-mail and all else he needed, then fetched Brigliador;[3] but he dispensed with the services of a squire. / And to go anywhere at will without compromising his reputation, he wore not his distinguished emblem of red and white quarterings, but chose a black one— perhaps it was consonant with his sense of mourning. This sable emblem he had wrested from one Amostant whom he had slain a few years earlier. / He stole off in the depth of the night, greeting nobody and leaving no word for the emperor, his uncle; he did not bid farewell even to Brandimart,[4] his boon companion whom he loved so well. But when the golden-haired Sun set forth from Tithonus'[5] splendid halls and routed the dark shades of night, the emperor realized that the paladin was gone. / Charles was profoundly displeased to discover that his nephew had made off in the night, when he was most bound to stay with him and lend his assistance. And, unable to restrain his anger, he broke out in imprecations against him and heaped abuse upon him, uttering threats if he did not return, and promising to make him sorry for such a dereliction. /

Now Brandimart, who loved Orlando as much as his own self, was quick to act, whether in the hope of persuading the paladin to return, or simply from anger at hearing him the butt of such abuse and raillery. He scarcely waited for dusk to gather than he set out in his turn, without a word to his Fiordiligi for fear she try to oppose his decision. / She was a damsel he deeply

2. Orlando's dream is intensely Petrarchan; cf. especially Petrarch's sonnet 126 above.   3. Orlando's horse.   4. Orlando's closest friend.   5. Ancient husband of the dawn, Aurora.

loved, and he was seldom apart from her: she was comely, graceful, and of gentle manners; nor was she lacking in shrewdness and wisdom. If he did not take leave of her, it was because he planned to return to her within the day; but events so fell out that he was delayed beyond the expected time. / After vainly waiting for him, and finding him still not returned after nearly a month, her desire for him was so sharpened that she set off without guides or any company. She travelled through many lands searching for him, as at the proper time her story shall reveal.

But I shall not for the present say more about these two: I am more concerned about Orlando, the lord of Anglant. / Once he had altered the glorious emblem of Almont, he went to the gate and whispered into the ear of the captain of the guard, "I am the count." Immediately the drawbridge was lowered for him, and he took the road leading directly to the enemy camp. What followed you shall discover in the next canto.

• • •

Cruel, treacherous Love! See what it can do to a heart, once conquered! It can make Orlando forget the sovereign fealty that he owes his lord. Once upon a time he was a man of sound judgement, awake to his duty, a true defender of Holy Church. But now? Thanks to feckless Love, he pays no heed to his uncle, none to his self-respect, still less to God. / I can forgive him, though, with all my heart. Indeed, I am delighted to have such a partner in crime: for my own efforts at self-improvement are something short of zealous, but when it comes to harmful pursuits, I run with the foremost.

Off he went, dressed all in black, with no concern for the many friends he was forsaking, and passed amid the tented camp of the Africans and Spaniards: / or rather, not tented, for the rain had driven them to shelter under trees and roofs. There they were, then, bedded down in groups of ten, twenty, four, seven, eight, some further off, others closer in. They were all sleeping, haggard and exhausted, some spread-eagled on the ground, others with their heads pillowed on their hands. All asleep—and the count was free to slaughter all he wanted, but not once did he set his hand to Durindana.[6] / For Orlando is great of heart, and would not stoop to striking men who sleep. Hither and thither he moved, intent on picking up the traces of his lady. And every time he came upon someone awake, with many a sigh he would give a description of her and of her apparel, and entreat the man out of kindness to tell him which way she went. / When the day dawned bright and clear he continued his search throughout the Moorish camp; this he could safely do, dressed as he was in Arab costume. He was also aided by the fact that French was not his only tongue: he spoke African with such fluency that he could have passed for a native of Tripoli. / Here he stopped, then, for three days, wholly intent on making a thorough search. After this he started to explore every town and village around; he not only visited those of the Ile-de-France, but also passed again through the Auvergne and Gascony, searching every last hamlet. From Provence to Brittany he searched, and from Picardy to the confines of Spain. /

It was the end of October and the onset of November, the season when the trees can be seen shedding their leafy raiment until they stand stripped

6. Orlando's sword.

and shivering in their nakedness, and the birds fly together in tight flocks. This was when Orlando began his amorous quest; all that winter he continued it, and still on into the following spring. / In the course of these wanderings from village to village he came one day to a river which separates the Normans from the Bretons and flows softly to the sea close by. It was swollen at present, and streaked with froth from the melting snows and the rains up in the mountains. And the current had demolished the bridge and swept it away so there was no crossing. / The paladin looked closely at each shore in turn to see how he was to reach the other side (inasmuch as he was neither bird nor fish). And what did he see but a boat coming towards him with a damsel sitting in the stern. She signed to him that she was coming, but stopped a little short of the bank. / She did not put into the shore, as though fearing lest the passenger come on board uninvited.

Orlando besought her to take him in her boat and land him on the other side, but "No knight crosses here," she replied, "who has not first given me his word that he will do battle at my request—the most just and honourable battle in the world. / If then, sir, you wish me to help you set foot on the other side, promise me that, before this next month is out, you will go to the King of Hibernia and join the fine host assembling there to destroy the island of Ebuda, the most sinister of any island set in the sea. / You must know that beyond Ireland there are many islands and one of them is Ebuda, which sends out its thievish people with orders to plunder. And any women they capture they give as food to a voracious beast which comes in daily to the shore and finds each time a new woman or maiden to devour. / For merchants and pirates go about bringing them in, and the more beautiful the better— and counting one a day, you can readily imagine how many women and maidens have died. But if you have room for pity, and are not entirely closed to Love, be glad to be numbered with this host who will be setting forth on so bounteous an errand." /

Orlando could scarcely wait for the end of the story before he swore he would be the first at that enterprise, like a person who cannot endure to listen to an account of some wicked, loathsome deed. And he found himself thinking, then fearing, that those people had taken Angelica, for he had been seeking her high and low and still had found no trace of her. / This idea so perturbed him, quite sweeping out of his mind any previous plan, that without waiting a moment he decided to set sail for that evil land.

*　　*　　*

Summary   Searching for Angelica, Orlando meets and aids Olimpia, whose lover has been captured by Cimosco, a neighboring king whose son had loved Olimpia and been killed by her on their wedding night. Orlando reunites Olimpia with her beloved Bireno, defeats Cimosco, and casts his magical fire-spitting tube (the first gun) to the bottom of the ocean.

FROM CANTOS 10 AND 11

[*Ruggiero Learns from Logistilla and Takes a Grand Tour*]

I want to take up Ruggiero's story: he was riding along the shore, weary and exhausted under the intense midday heat. The sun beat down on the hill and reverberated off it, while under foot the fine white sand smouldered.

The armour he wore was well nigh glowing red-hot, as at its first making./ Thirst, the exhaustion of plodding through the deep sand, and the solitude of his journey kept him tedious, unwelcome company as he rode along the sun-blinded beach.[7] After a while he came to an old tower which stood out of the water at the beach's edge, and in its shadow he discovered three ladies from Alcina's court: he recognized them by their dress and manner. / Reclining on Egyptian rugs, they were enjoying the fresh shade and a wide choice of wines in various jugs and all sorts of delicacies to eat. They had a little boat waiting off the beach; it was playing with the rippling waves until a helpful breeze should spring up and fill its sails, for at the moment the air was utterly still. / The ladies saw Ruggiero pursuing his way along the shifting dunes. They noticed how thirst had left its imprint on his lips, and how his worn face was bathed in sweat, and they invited him, bidding him not to be so set upon his journey, but to relent awhile and seek the fresh, sweet shade and give solace to his weary body. /

One of them approached his horse to hold his stirrup and invite him to dismount; another came with a crystal goblet of sparkling wine, which only excited his thirst. But Ruggiero was not going to dance to their tune: any delay would favour Alcina, giving her time to catch him up—she was now close behind him. / Imagine fine saltpetre and pure sulphur touched with a flame and igniting; or the sea boiling up when a dark whirlwind descends upon it. Far worse was the anger, the rage into which the third damsel flared when she saw Ruggiero calmly trudging on across the sand, ignoring them— and they fancied themselves as beauties! /

"A fine gentleman you are!" she shrieked at him. "Those arms of yours— you stole them! And that horse would in no other wise be yours. I know what I'm talking about, which is why I'd like to see you properly punished—with death! You ought to be quartered, set on fire, hanged, you hideous thief, you scurvy, arrogant knave!" / The insolent woman heaped abuse on him, but Ruggiero answered her not a word, for he could expect little honour from so paltry a quarrel. With her sisters she straightway put out in the boat which awaited them on the water, and rowing frantically, they followed him along the shore, keeping him in view. / She kept intensifying her stream of abuse, ceaselessly inventive in finding new epithets.

Meanwhile Ruggiero came to the channel separating him from the land of Logistilla, the more engaging sorceress. Here he noticed an old boatman casting off from the further shore, as though he had already been told and was there ready waiting for Ruggiero's arrival. / On sight of him the boatman cast off and came gladly to fetch him over to a happier shore. If the face gives a true warrant for the heart, he was a kindly man, the soul of discretion. Ruggiero set foot upon the little skiff thanking God. He set forth across the tranquil reach, and enjoyed some conversation with the ferryman, a wise and experienced man, / who praised him for having contrived to tear himself free of Alcina in time, before she gave him the enchanted cup which she ultimately presented to all her lovers.[8] And as he was conveying him to Logistilla's, where he would be able to witness virtuous behaviour, perennial

---

7. Ariosto elaborates the idea of the desert as a middle ground between captivity (on Alcina's island) and understanding (under Logistilla's tutelage).   8. On the model of Homer's Circe, Alcina presents an enchanted cup to her former lovers that transforms them into beasts and plants; Alcina, however, is herself enchanted by Atlas so that she will always adore Ruggiero.

beauty, and infinite grace, which / nourishes but never cloys the heart, "At first sight," he explained, "wonder and reverence are the emotions that Logistilla excites; on further contemplation of her fathomless presence, all other good dwindles to little value. Her love is different to others': normally, hope or fear erodes the heart of a man in love. Now in her love, desire craves no more, but rests content on sight of her. / She will teach you more alluring preoccupations than music and dancing, perfumes, baths, and fine fare: rather, how your mind, better informed, can soar to the heights, loftier than the kite: and how the glory of the blessed can in part permeate the bodies of mortals." As he spoke the boatman made great progress towards the safer shore. /

Now he noticed a fleet of ships out at sea all heading in their direction: they were bearing the slighted Alcina and the host she had assembled to bring ruin upon herself and her realm, or else to recapture her ravished treasure. Love played no small part in her motives, but an equal part was taken by injured pride. / Never since she was born had she been eaten by so intense an anger. She so urged the oars through the water that they threw up great plumes of spray to either side of the bows. So great was the noise, both sea and shore echoed with it.

"Bring out your shield, Ruggiero, now you must: else you are a dead man, or shamefully captured." / So urged Logistilla's boatman; and, acting on his own words, he himself grasped the sheath, drew it off the shield and disclosed its light for all to see. The magic radiance it gave off so dazzled the eyes of the enemy that they were struck blind on the instant; some of them fell overboard from the stern, others from the bows. / A man keeping watch from the castle saw Alcina's fleet approaching and raised the alarm, hammering on the bell to summon the defenders to the harbour. The artillery rained missiles against the intruders who were contriving harm against good Ruggiero. So he received support from every side and was able to save his life and liberty. / Four ladies now came down to the beach, sent hither by Logistilla: stout-hearted Andronica, prudent Fronesia, Dicilla the just, and chaste Sophrosina[9] who, having more to do here than the others, blazed and sparkled. And the army, which was unrivalled throughout the world, sallied forth from the castle and spread out along the shore. / Beneath the castle in the quiet estuary rode many a large vessel—a whole fleet of them—ready at the trumpet's shrill, ready day or night at a spoken command to issue forth to battle. Thus by the sea and land the battle was engaged, fierce and terrible; and because of it the realm which Alcina had earlier seized from her sister was thrown into turmoil. / How many battles have ended in a way never predicted for them! Not only did Alcina fail to retrieve, as she expected, her fugitive lover; but her ships, which had been so numerous that the sea could barely find room for them all, were all consumed by the fires which broke out, till but one remained to her in which to make her sorry escape. /

Alcina fled, leaving her wretched followers in disarray, some burnt, others drowned or captured. Ruggiero's loss stung her far worse than any other of her afflictions. Night and day she would be given over to bitter lament and to abundant tears because of him, and often she regretted that she was unable to die and thus put an end to her cruel agony. / No fairy may ever

---

9. Their names mean strength, prudence, justice, and temperance.

die so long as the sun holds his course and the Heavens remain unchanged. Were it otherwise, Alcina's grief was such that Clotho might have spun out her life-thread faster: or she herself might, as Dido, have ended her misery with a dagger; she might have followed the majestic queen of the Nile[1] into a mortal sleep. But fairies never can die. /

Let us return to Ruggiero, the knight worthy of eternal glory, and leave Alcina to her sorrow. He stepped out of the boat and onto the safer shore, thanking God for the happy outcome of his enterprise. Then, turning his back to the sea, he hastened across the dry land up to the castle. / Never before or since has mortal eye beheld a mightier nor a more beautiful castle. Its walls could not have been more precious had they been made of diamond or garnet. Jewels such as those to be found in it are never spoken of here below: whoever would hear tell of them needs must make the journey there himself—I don't believe that he would come across them anywhere else, except perhaps in Paradise. / What in particular gives these jewels their supremacy over every other is this: on looking at them, a man sees right into his own soul; he sees there reflected his vices and virtues, so that he no longer believes in the compliments he is paid, nor does he heed blame when he is charged unfairly. Looking into these bright mirrors, he discovers himself, and learns wisdom. / They give off a light, too, brilliant as the sun and so abundant that whoever possesses one of them may, wherever he be, make broad daylight at will, in spite of Phoebus. Nor are the walls remarkable only for their gems: the materials and the refinement of construction vie with each other, so that between the two there is no deciding which perfection is the greater. / Above the soaring arches, which looked as though they supported the very dome of Heaven, gardens extended which were so spacious and magnificent that even at ground-level they would be hard to lay out. Through the luminous crenellations could be seen the verdure of the fragrant trees, which were a delight in the summer, and in winter remained a mass of blossom and ripe fruit. / Trees as noble do not grow outside these lovely gardens, nor do such roses, violets and lilies, amarants and jasmine. You will observe, anywhere else, how all in one day a flower will be born, live out its term and die, drooping its head on its bereaved stalk, for it is subject to the changing seasons. / Here, though, every thing remained verdant green; the flowers bloomed in perpetual radiance, not through any beneficent working of Nature, but through the studious care of Logistilla: with no need to depend upon the climate (impossible though this would seem to anyone else), she maintained perennial spring in her garden. /

Logistilla was visibly pleased that so worthy a knight should have come to her, and she gave orders that everyone should make much of him and study to do him reverence. Astolfo had arrived some time earlier, and Ruggiero was delighted to see him. A few days later all the others arrived whom Melissa had restored to their proper selves. /

After a day or two in which to rest, Ruggiero went to the wise enchantress accompanied by Astolfo who, no less than he, was anxious to see the West again. Melissa spoke to her on behalf of them both, humbly entreating her to give them counsel and assistance in making good their return to whence

---

1. Cleopatra, who killed herself by applying asps to her breasts. *Clotho:* one of the fates. *Dido:* Virgil's queen, who committed suicide when Aeneas abandoned her.

they came. / "I shall give the matter thought," replied Logistilla, "and two days hence I shall let you know what I have devised." She took counsel with herself how best to help Ruggiero and, after him, the duke. Her conclusion was that the winged horse would have to return the former to the shores of Aquitania; but first the beast would have to be fitted with a special bridle wherewith Ruggiero could turn him in flight and rein him in. / She showed him what to do if he wanted the steed to climb, what to do to make him descend, how to make him wheel in a circle, or go fast, or simply hover. And whatever the knight was accustomed to performing on a good earth-bound horse he soon became adept at achieving in the air on the feathered steed. / When Ruggiero was fully prepared he took leave of the kind enchantress, to whom he remained attached ever after by a strong bond of affection, and departed from that country. He set off, and first I shall tell of his adventures. Afterwards I shall relate how the English knight, on a longer and more arduous journey, made his way back to Charlemagne, and to the court where his friends were. /

Ruggiero departed, but did not retrace the path he had earlier taken against his will, when the hippogryph kept course out over the sea and he scarcely sighted land. This time, as he could make the beast fly hither and yon at his own whim, he chose to take a different way back, like the Wise Men when they avoided Herod.[2] / Coming hither, he had left Spain behind and made a direct line for India, where it is washed by the Eastern Sea— where Alcina was entertaining a quarrel with her fellow-sorceress. This time he was disposed to see other lands than those where Aeolus incites the winds, and to complete the circle[3] he had started, so as to girdle the earth, like the sun. / On his journey he saw Cathay to one side and to the other Mangiana, as he passed over great Quinsai. He flew over the Himavian range, and skirted Sericana to his right. From the hyperborean land of the Scythians, he turned in towards the Hyrcanian sea and reached Sarmatia; then, arriving at the point where Europe and Asia meet, he beheld the lands of the Russians and Prussians, and came to Pomerania. / For all his pressing desire to return to Bradamant, Ruggiero was unwilling to forgo the pleasure of discovering the world, but had perforce to pass by way of the Poles, Hungarians, and Germans and the rest of those bleak northern lands. Finally he arrived in far-off England. / You must not imagine, my Lord, that he was constantly on the wing; every evening he put up at some hostelry, avoiding poor accommodation as best he could. Days and months went by as he pursued his way, so eager was he to visit lands and seas. Then, arriving one morning at London, the hippogryph swooped down over the Thames.

*   *   *

After this he turned his steed South towards the sea that washes the Breton coast, and looking down, he espied Angelica chained to the bare rock. / Chained to the bare rock, she was, on the Isle of Tears—for this was the name given to the island inhabited by those cruel savages, those barbarous folk who, as I related in a previous canto, went marauding along many a shore abducting every comely damsel in order to feed her infamously to a monster. / That very morning she was chained there for the huge sea-

2. Biblical tyrant.   3. Ruggiero takes a world tour to complete his humanist education.

monster, the orc, to come and swallow her alive; for this, horrible to relate, was how he fed. I explained earlier that she was the prize of the corsairs who found her on the beach asleep beside the old hermit who had lured her there by magic. / The brutal, ruthless savages left the exquisitely beautiful damsel exposed on the shore to the cruel monster, and as naked as when Nature first fashioned her; not even a veil did she have to cover the lily-white, the rose-red, unfading in December as in July, which coloured her lustrous limbs. / Ruggiero would have taken her for a statue fashioned in alabaster or some lambent marble, and tethered thus to the rock by some diligent sculptor's artifice, were it not that he distinctly saw tears coursing down her rose-fresh, lily-white cheeks and bedewing her unripe apple-breasts, and her golden tresses flowing in the wind. /

As he looked into her lovely eyes Ruggiero was reminded of his Bradamant; he was pricked with compassion and love, and could scarcely refrain from weeping. Tenderly he addressed the maiden, after reining in his charger. "Gentle lady, the only fetter you merit is that with which love binds his votaries: / quite undeserving must you be of this plight or of any other. Who is the miscreant so perverted as to blemish the smooth ivory of your delicate hands with unwelcome bruising?" On hearing him speak she perforce became like white ivory sprinkled with carmine, seeing those parts of her exposed to view which, for all their beauty, modesty would conceal. / She would have covered her face with her hands were they not tied to the hard rock. But she bathed it in tears—this at least she was free to do—and tried to keep it bowed. After sobbing a little, she prepared to speak, in a sad, small voice; but the words did not come—they were thwarted by the loud noise now to be heard from the sea. /

The colossal monster now appeared, half submerged; like a long ship making port, driven before the wind from North or South, so was the terrible orc as it approached the morsel shown to it. Now the monster had almost reached her. The damsel was half-dead with fright—she was past comforting. / Ruggiero was holding his lance not in rest, but in free play, and he struck at the orc, a beast I can only describe as a great coiling, twisting mass, quite unlike an animal in shape, except for its head, with protruding eyes and teeth like a boar's. Ruggiero struck at it between the eyes, but he might as well have been striking at solid iron or stone. / His first thrust proving ineffectual, he returned to do better the second time. The orc, seeing the shadow cast by the spreading wings flitting here and there across the water, left its certain prey awaiting it on shore and started a furious chase, curving and coiling, after the elusive one instead. Ruggiero dropped down and struck many a blow, / like an eagle dropping from the sky when it has spotted a snake weaving through the grass, or lying on a bare stone in the sun, smoothing and titivating its golden scales: it does not attack so as to meet the hissing, venomous jaws head-on, but endeavours rather to sink its talons into the serpent's back, and aims its flight so as to avoid the snake's turning and biting it. / So Ruggiero wielded his sword and lance so as to avoid the monster's snout bristling with teeth, but aimed blows between its ears, on its back and at its tail.

If the beast turned, he swerved aside, choosing the right moment to descend and to gain height. But as what he struck was always adamantine he could not penetrate the rock-hard carapace. / Such a battle will be fought between an impudent fly and a mastiff in dusty August, or the months before and after—from the corn harvest to that of the grape. The fly will infest him and buzz around him, stinging him now on the eye, now on the snapping muzzle. And frequently the mastiff will snap his jaws shut on nothing—but the moment he catches the fly, that moment makes up for everything. / So powerfully did the orc thrash the water with its tail that the seas surged up to the skies, and Ruggiero could not tell whether his mount was beating the air with its wings or swimming in the waves. Many times he wished himself safely on dry land, fearing that if the hippogryph continued having to endure the flying spray, his wings would be so sodden that he would vainly wish for something floatable, be it only a cockle-shell. /

He hit on a new and better plan: to overcome the cruel monster with other weapons. He would dazzle it with the flash of the enchanted shield still in its cover. He flew to the shore and, as a precaution, took the ring which defied all magic and slipped it onto the little finger of the damsel chained to the bare rock. / This was the ring which Bradamant, to effect Ruggiero's release, had seized from Brunello,[4] and subsequently sent to him in India by Melissa, to rescue him from wicked Alcina's hands. Melissa, as I described to you earlier, had used the ring to the advantage of many; then she had returned it to Ruggiero, who thereafter had always worn it on his finger. / He gave it now to Angelica, lest she be harmed by the glint of the shield, and to protect her eyes, which had already ensnared him. The monstrous sea-beast was approaching the shore, his belly displacing half the ocean. Ruggiero took up his station and lifted the veil: and it was as though another sun had entered the sky. / The enchanted light struck the monster's eyes and wrought its wonted effect.[5] As a trout or perch floats down a river made turbid with lime by some hill-dweller, thus was the monster, a ghastly sight as it lay upturned in the foaming sea. Ruggiero thrust at it all over but could find no way to penetrate its hide. /

All this while the beautiful damsel besought him not to continue his vain onslaught against the horny scales. "Come back good sir, for God's sake," she begged, weeping; "unchain me before the orc revives. Take me with you, drown me in the depths of the sea, but let me not end in the belly of the ghastly fish." Moved by this just entreaty, Ruggiero united the damsel and carried her away from the shore. / Spurred, the steed thrust off the beach and launched into the air and galloped through the sky. On his back he carried the knight, with the damsel mounted right behind him. Thus did he deprive the monster of a feast which was far too dainty and delicious for it. He kept turning round, and in his breast, and in his lively eyes a thousand kisses were a-smouldering. / Instead of circling Spain, as he had earlier planned,[6] he put down at a neighbouring shore, where Brittany juts furthest out to sea.

By the shore there was a shady oak-wood, which forever resounded with Philomena's[7] lament; in the middle was a grassy clearing with a spring, and to either side, a solitary hill. / Here the eager knight drew rein and set foot

---

4. A clever thief.   5. Compare Perseus's use of Medusa's head, the sight of which turns men to stone, to conquer the sea monster and save Andromeda; the story is told in Ovid, *Metamorphoses* 4.663–803, where Perseus, unlike Ruggiero, kills the stunned orc.   6. Ruggiero breaks off his educational world tour just short of a perfect circle.   7. The nightingale, named after a mythical young woman who was raped by her brother-in-law, Tereus; Ovid tells the tale in *Metamorphoses* 6.424–674.

in the clearing; he had his charger fold his wings, (leaving at liberty, however, another steed, who had now spread his even wider). He dismounted, but could scarcely restrain himself from climbing onto a different mount; but his gear delayed him: it delayed him, for he had to pull it off; it obstructed the impetus of his desire. / With hasty fingers he fumbled confusedly at his armour, now this side, now the other. Never before had it seemed such a long business—for every thong unlaced, two seemed to become entangled. But this canto has gone on too long, my Lord, and perhaps you are growing a-weary with listening to it: I shall defer my story to another time when it may prove more welcome.

* * *

A mettlesome charger will often suffer himself to be reined in from a full gallop, however gentle the hand on the rein. Seldom, however, will the bridle of Reason check rabid Lust once it scents its quarry. It is like a bear: there is no distracting him from the honey once he has sniffed at it or tasted a drop left in the jar. /

What argument can there be to stop Ruggiero and change his mind about taking his pleasure with lovely Angelica, whom he holds naked there in the convenient solitude of the glade? Bradamant he has quite forgotten, though she had always reigned in his heart. Or, if her memory was indeed fresh as ever, well—he would still be a fool not to make the most of the maiden present. / In this situation Xenocrates[8] himself, that austere paragon, would have yielded to lechery. Ruggiero had thrown down his lance and shield and was feverishly pulling off his armour. The damsel had modestly lowered her eyes to her exquisite body when she noticed on her finger the precious ring which Brunello had earlier stolen from her at Albracca. / This was the ring she took with her to France the first time she made the journey with her brother, who brought the lance which passed to the paladin Astolfo. With this ring she neutralized the spells Maugis[9] cast on her at Merlin's tomb. With it she helped Orlando and others to escape one morning from Dragontina;[1] / with this ring she made herself invisible and escaped from the dungeon where a wicked old man had imprisoned her. But why should I enumerate all the instances when it had proved its virtues? You know them as well as I do. Brunello found his way into her castle and stole the ring from her, for Agramant wanted it. Ever since that moment Fortune had frowned upon her until she lost her kingdom. /

Noticing the ring on her finger, as I said, she was so stunned with joy and amazement, she thought she must be dreaming, and could scarcely believe her eyes. She slipped it off her finger and straight into her mouth, and in less than a twinkling had vanished from Ruggiero's sight as completely as the sun behind a cloud. / Ruggiero looked in every direction and searched frantically all over the place, until he remembered the ring. He stopped, thunderstruck, thwarted. Cursing himself for his carelessness, he inveighed against Angelica for her discourtesy, her ingratitude—a fine way to thank him for his help! / "Heartless damsel," he complained, "is this how you reward me? You would snatch the ring from me rather than allow me to offer it to you. Why will you not accept it from me? Not only the ring, but the shield,

8. Plato's unseducible disciple.　9. Christian wizard.　1. Boiardo's witch.

too, and the fleet-footed horse, and myself I would give to you, to use me as you will—only hide not your lovely face from me. I know, heartless one, that you hear me but will not answer." / As he spoke, he went groping round the spring like a blind man; many a time he hugged the empty air, hoping to clasp the damsel in the same embrace.

She meanwhile was already well on her way, and kept on walking until she came to a spacious cave beneath a hill; here she found some food. / This was the abode of an old herdsman with a large herd of mares, which were browsing on the tender grass along the fresh streams down in the valley. On either side of the cave there were stables where they could take refuge from the midday sun. That day Angelica stopped here at leisure, unseen by anybody. / When evening came and she felt sufficiently restored, she dressed herself in rustic garments, all too different from her normal gay apparel, made after every conceivable fashion and hue—in shades of green, yellow, purple, blue, and red. Even so humble attire, however, could not disguise her natural beauty and nobility. / You who praise Phyllis, Neiera, Amaryllis, or elusive Galatea, be silent! For beauty none of them can touch Angelica— saving your presence, Tityrus, and yours, Meliboeus.[2] The beautiful damsel selected from the herd of mares one which pleased her well, and the idea came to her there and then to make away back to the Orient. /

Ruggiero waited a long time to see if she would discover herself, but to no purpose; once it was clear to him that he was wasting his time and she was no longer there to listen to him, he turned back to remount the horse which was at home in the air as well as on the ground. But he saw that the hippogryph had worked free of the bit and was climbing unimpeded through the sky. / It was a sorry blow, coming on top of the last, to find himself deprived of the flying horse. The loss weighed heavily upon him, no less than the damsel's trick. But what hurt more than either was the loss of the precious ring—this grieved him most especially, less for its magical properties than for the fact that it had been a gift from his lady. / Utterly dejected, he put on his armour, slung his shield on his shoulder, turned his back to the sea and set off through the grassy glades towards a broad valley. Here, amid the deep shady woods he came upon a wider, more frequented path, which he pursued only a short way when to his right, where the forest was thicker, he heard a great din. /

A great din he heard, and the shock of arms, a terrifying sound. He hastened in amid the trees and came upon two antagonists hemmed in a narrow glade and locked in battle. I know not what their quarrel was, but they were exchanging savage blows without mercy. One of them was a fierce-looking giant; the other a bold, valiant knight. / The knight was defending himself with sword and shield, and side-stepping deftly to avoid being laid out by the club which the giant was wielding two-handed. The knight's steed lay dead on the path. Ruggiero stopped to watch the battle, and soon reached the conclusion that he would prefer to see the knight win, / though he did not interfere, but stood out of the way and continued to watch. Now the giant raised his massy club over the knight's helmet and brought it down with both hands. Under the impact the knight fell. The other saw him lying dazed and, in order to put an end to him, unloosed his helmet. This enabled Ruggiero

2. Pastoral shepherds and their shepherdesses.

to see the knight's face. / The face he set eyes on was that of sweet, lovely Bradamant, his heart's delight; and here was the wicked giant making ready to slay her. Ruggiero challenged him to battle and advanced with drawn sword, but the giant, not prepared for another combat, took the stunned woman in his arms, / and threw her over his shoulder and carried her off as a wolf seizes a lamb, or an eagle seizes in its hooked talons a dove or some such bird. Ruggiero could see how urgently his help was needed and ran after the giant as fast as he could; but the giant strode away so fast that Ruggiero could scarcely follow him with his eyes. / The giant ran off and Ruggiero pursued him down a path through the deep shade; the path gradually broadened out until it took them clear of the wood into a broad meadow.

Summary   Orlando, still searching for Angelica, kills the orc and liberates his beautiful and naked victim, who turns out to be none other than Olimpia. Embarrassed by her nakedness, Orlando finds clothes for her and learns how she was deserted by Bireno. In the meantime, a young knight, Uberto, gazes his fill at the naked Olimpia and falls in love with her. After uniting them, Orlando continues his search.

FROM CANTOS 12 and 22

[Orlando Finds an Enchanted Castle and Ruggiero and Bradamant Unite]

When Ceres,[3] after visiting her mother on Mount Ida, sped back to the secluded valley where Mount Etna straddles the shoulders of Encelades,[4] the stricken giant, she did not find her daughter where she had left her, away from the trodden paths. After her cheeks and eyes, her hair and breast had borne the brunt of her grief, she uprooted two pines; / she lit them in Vulcan's[5] fire, enduing them with a flame which could never be quenched; and taking one in each hand, she entered her chariot, drawn by a pair of dragons. Thus she set off to search woods, fields, hills and plains, valleys, streams, pools and torrents, the land and sea: when she had scoured all the daylight world, she plunged down into the infernal regions. / Had Orlando possessed not only the zeal but also the powers of the Eleusinian goddess,[6] he would not have left a single wood, field, pond, stream, valley, hill, plain, land, or sea unsearched, nor even the heavens or the pit of eternal oblivion, in his quest for Angelica. But since he did not have the chariot with the dragons, he sought her as best he could. / He had sought her throughout France; now he was preparing to search for her through Italy and Germany, through new and old Castille, and thence across the Spanish sea to Libya.

While he was thus deciding, a voice came to his ear, and what sounded like weeping. He darted forward, and saw a knight approaching at a trot upon a great charger; / seated in front of him on the saddle and pinioned forcibly by his arm was a damsel in deepest distress. She wept and fought and gave evidence of utter sorrow, and she kept crying out, invoking the help of Orlando, the valiant Prince of Anglant; as his gaze rested upon the beautiful

---

3. Goddess of the harvest, she goes into mourning and blights the Earth when Pluto, god of the underworld, abducts her daughter, Proserpine.   **4.** Giant struck by Jupiter's thunderbolt and buried under the volcanic Mount Etna.   **5.** God of fire   **6.** Ceres.

maiden, she looked just like the very one whom he had been seeking night and day through the length and breadth of France. / I do not say that she *was* sweet Angelica, his well-beloved—but she looked like her. Seeing his lady, his goddess being carried off in such a wretched, pitiful state, he was possessed by a frenzy of black rage, and with a terrible roar he hailed the knight; full of menace he hailed him, and drove Brigliador forward at full tilt. / The villain, wholly intent upon his prize, his booty, did not wait for him or answer, but shot away so swiftly through the trees that even the wind could scarcely have followed him. One fled, the other pursued, and a high lament could be heard sounding through the deep forest. They came galloping out into a broad meadow, in the middle of which stood a magnificent great palace. /

The stately edifice was built of many kinds of marble, a work of intricate design. In through the gate, wrought in gold, ran the knight with the lady in his arms, followed shortly after by Brigliador carrying fierce Orlando, fuming with indignation. Once inside, Orlando looked about him, but saw no sign of the knight nor of the damsel. / He jumped from his horse and stormed through into the living quarters. He dashed hither and thither, never stopping until he had looked into every room, every gallery; after vainly probing the secrets of all the ground-floor rooms, he climbed the stairs and wasted no less time and effort searching upstairs. / The beds, he noticed, were all adorned with silk and thread of gold; not a wall was to be seen, for they, and the floors were covered with tapestries and carpets. Upstairs and downstairs and all over again Orlando hunted, but there was no joy for him: never did he set eyes upon Angelica or the thief who had wafted her sweet delicate face away from his sight. / And while vainly pursuing his quest hither and thither, full of care and anxiety, he came across Ferrau, Brandimart, King Gradasso, and King Sacripant[7] and other knights who were also searching high and low, pursuing a quest as fruitless as his own. They all complained about the malicious invisible lord of that palace— / the invisible lord for whom they were all searching. All accused him of one theft or another; one was grieving over the loss of his horse, another was raging over the loss of his lady; others had other thefts to charge him with, and none of them could tear themselves away from this cage—some there were, the victims of his deception, who had been there for whole weeks and months. /

After combing through the weird palace five and six times, Orlando said to himself: "I could stay here wasting time and effort to no purpose; the thief could have borne her out through another gate and now be far away." Thus thinking, he sallied out into the green meadow in the middle of which the palace stood. / As he skirted the outside of the woodland abode, his eyes fixed on the ground in case he caught sight of fresh footprints to right or left, he heard his name called from a window, and raised his eyes; and he imagined he heard that divine voice, thought he beheld the very face which had so transformed him. / He thought he heard Angelica addressing him in tearful entreaty: "Help! Help! I commend my virginity to you more than my soul, more than my life. Am I to be ravished by this brigand in the presence of my dearest Orlando? Rather slay me by your own hand than let me come

---

7. Christian and Islamic knights all wandering in circles after their desires: the enchanted castle is one of Ariosto's figures for romance.

to so sorry a pass." / These words set Orlando on a diligent search of every room, over and over, in desperation but with hope renewed. Now and then he would stop, and he would hear a voice which sounded like Angelica's, begging for help. But wherever he was, it always came from somewhere else and he could never locate it. /

But to go back to Ruggiero: I left him pursuing his lady, borne off by a giant along a densely shaded path which emerged from the wood into a broad meadow. He came to this very spot where Orlando arrived earlier, if I recognize the place aright. The giant disappeared in through the door with Ruggiero on his heels in tireless pursuit. / As he set foot inside the threshold he looked round the great courtyard and loggias, but could not espy the giant or the lady; in vain did he turn his gaze this way and that; he looked upstairs and down many a time but all to no avail—nor could he imagine where the villain could so quickly have found a hiding-place with the damsel. / When he had gone through the bedrooms, galleries, and public rooms, upstairs and down four or five times, he searched yet again and did not give up before searching even beneath the stairs. Finally, in the hope that they might be in the neighbouring woods, he left; but a voice recalled him, just as it had recalled Orlando, and made him, too, return inside the palace. / The same voice, the same person whom Orlando took for Angelica, Ruggiero took for Bradamant, on whose account he was beside himself. Whether the voice spoke to Gradasso or to any other of those wandering about the palace, each one identified it with the object of his search. / This was a new and unusual piece of magic devised by the wizard Atlas, who meant thus to keep Ruggiero so preoccupied with this bitter-sweet love-quest of his that the evil influence would pass him by—the influence appointing him to an early death. The steel-girt castle had proved useless, so had Alcina; here he was, trying something else. / It was not only Ruggiero whom Atlas plotted to draw into this magic trap, but anyone else in France who enjoyed the highest reputation for valour—athese he lured in lest Ruggiero die at their hands. And while he condemned them to this enforced residence, he had left the palace so abundantly provided that knights and ladies could dwell there in comfort and eat their fill. /

* * *

Summary   Orlando rescues Isabel from brigands. Rodomont, the strongest of the Islamic knights, storms Paris. Meanwhile, Mandricard abducts Doralice, who is betrothed to Rodomont. In the great battle at Paris, Cloridan and Medor try to rescue the body of their captain, killed by Rinaldo. Cloridan dies trying to save Medor, who refuses to leave the body; Medor, left for dead, is found by Angelica, who cures and falls in love with him. In one of the many episodes to follow, Astolfo destroys Atlas's enchanted castle by using his magical horn, which emits a noise so terrifyingly disgusting that all who hear it run for their lives. After all the captives flee in terror, Astolfo is left in custody of the hippogryph.

* * *

But if I'm to tell you the rest of the story, I must first go after Ruggiero and Bradamant. When the horn fell silent and the handsome couple were well away from this place, Ruggiero was quick to recognize at a glance what Atlas had concealed from him: Atlas had seen to it that until this moment the pair had not recognized each other. / Ruggiero looked at Bradamant and she at him in utter amazement, for their mind and vision had been clouded for so many days by the magic illusion. Ruggiero embraced his fair one who blushed redder than a rose; then he culled from her lips the first blooms of their blissful love. / A thousand times the two happy lovers renewed their embraces and hugged each other; they were so blissful, their breasts could scarcely contain their joy. They were grieved beyond measure that the magic spell had prevented their recognizing each other while they were in that restless palace, and so had made them lose so many days of happiness. / Bradamant was ready to concede all the pleasures that an honest virgin may give to a lover in order to keep him from sadness without hurting her own honour. Now she suggested to Ruggiero that if he was not to find her forever restive and stubborn about giving him the ultimate fruits, he should ask her father Aymon, in due form, for her hand—after accepting baptism. / Ruggiero would have submitted not merely to turning Christian for love of her (like her father and grandfather and all her noble house), but would there and then have given her what life remained to him, to please her. "It would be a small thing," he told her, "to place my head in fire, let alone in water,[8] for love of you." / To receive baptism, and then to have Bradamant to wife, Ruggiero set out to escort the damsel to Vallombrosa—a fair, rich monastery, devout and hospitable to all comers.

On emerging from the forest they came upon a woman whose face betrayed deep sorrow. / Ruggiero, kind and courteous with everyone, but especially with women, was moved at the sight of the lovely tears streaking her delicate face, and burned to know the cause of her grief. He turned to her and, after greeting her politely, enquired why her face was thus wet with tears. / She raised her beautiful, brimming eyes and answered him with good grace, giving him a full account of the reason for her sadness, as he had asked her: "Gentle sir," she said, "these cheeks are thus tear-streaked out of pity for a young man who is to die in a castle here today. / He loves a beautiful maiden, gently born, daughter of Marsilius, the Spanish king; and, concealed beneath a white veil and in a woman's skirts, disguising his voice and countenance, without raising the suspicions of the household, every night he has been sleeping with her. But there is no secret but must eventually come to another's attention. / One man found out and told two others who related it to others still, until it came to the ears of the king. One of the king's henchmen came two days ago and had the pair seized in bed. They have both been shut in separate dungeon cells, and I don't believe that the young man will see today through before he dies under torture. / I have escaped to avoid witnessing such cruelty, for they will burn him alive; nothing can distress me more than the suffering to be inflicted upon so fine a young man. There is no pleasure so great but my enjoyment of it must turn at once to grief when I think of the cruel flames which have scorched those handsome and delicate limbs." /

As Bradamant listened she appeared to be much disturbed by this story, and greatly upset; she seemed as concerned over the condemned man's fate as if he were a brother of hers—and her fear was not wholly unfounded, as I shall explain. She turned to Ruggiero and, "It seems to me," she observed, "that our arms should favour this man." / And to the grieving woman she said: "Take heart, and see to introducing us into the castle; if they have not

8. Fire and water are the two forms of baptism.

yet slain the youth, they shall not, take my word!" Ruggiero, noticing his lady's kindly disposition, her pity and concern, was fired with eagerness to prevent the youth from dying. /

* * *

Summary   Ruggiero and Bradamant are separated when she recognizes and chases Pinabello, the enemy who tried to kill her by pushing her into a cavern. When she catches and kills him (her only victim in the entire poem), she gets lost in the woods and then finds herself back at the home of her parents. There she is trapped in the role of dutiful daughter. Meanwhile, Orlando rescues Zerbin, the beloved of Isabel, and continues his search for Angelica.

FROM CANTOS 23 AND 24

[Orlando's Great Madness]

* * *

He came to a stream which looked like crystal; a pleasant meadow bloomed on its banks, picked out with lovely pure colours and adorned with many beautiful trees.[9] / A welcome breeze tempered the noontide for the rugged flock and naked shepherd, and Orlando felt no discomfort, for all that he was wearing breastplate, helmet, and shield. Here he stopped, then, to rest— but his welcome proved to be harsh and painful, indeed quite unspeakably cruel, on this unhappy, ill-starred day. / Looking about him, he saw inscriptions on many of the trees by the shady bank; he had only to look closely at the letters to be sure that they were formed by the hand of his goddess. This was one of the spots described earlier, to which the beautiful damsel, Queen of Cathay, often resorted with Medor, from the shepherd's house close by. / He saw "Angelica" and "Medor" in a hundred places, united by a hundred love-knots. The letters were so many nails with which Love pierced and wounded his heart. He searched in his mind for any number of excuses to reject what he could not help believing; he tried to persuade himself that it was some other Angelica who had written her name on the bark. / "But I recognize these characters," he told himself; "I've seen and read so many just like them. Can she perhaps be inventing this Medor? Perhaps by this name she means me." Thus deceiving himself with far-fetched notions, disconsolate Orlando clung to hopes which he knew he was stretching out to grasp. / But the more he tried to smother his dark suspicions the more they flared up with new vigour: he was like an unwary bird caught in a web or in birdlime—the more he beats his wings and tries to free himself, the worse ensnared he becomes.

Orlando came to where a bow-shaped curve in the hillside made a cave overlooking the clear spring. / Twisting on their stems, ivy and rambling vines adorned the entrance. Here during the heat of the day the two happy lovers used to lie in each other's arms. Their names figured here more than elsewhere; they were inscribed within and without, sometimes in charcoal, sometimes in chalk, or scratched with the point of a knife. / The dejected count approached on foot. At the entrance he saw many words which Medor had written in his own hand; they seem to have been freshly inscribed. The inscription was written in verse and spoke of the great plea-

---

9. The scene resembles Orlando's dream.

sure he had enjoyed in this cave. I believe it was written in his native tongue; in ours this is how it reads: / "Happy plants, verdant grass, limpid waters, dark, shadowy cave, pleasant and cool, where fair Angelica, born of Galafron, and loved in vain by many, often lay naked in my arms. I, poor Medor, cannot repay you for your indulgence otherwise than by ever praising you, / and by entreating every lover, knight, or maiden, every person, native or alien, who happens upon this spot by accident or by design, to say to the grass, the shadows, the cave, stream, and plants: 'May sun and moon be kind to you, and the chorus of the nymphs, and may they see that shepherds never lead their flocks to you.' " / It was written in Arabic, which the count knew as well as he knew Latin. He knew many and many a tongue, but Arabic is one with which he was most familiar: his grasp of it had saved him on more than one occasion from injury and insult when he was among the Saracens. But he was not to boast if formerly his knowledge had helped him—the pain it now brought him quite discounted every former advantage. /

Five and six times the unfortunate man re-read the inscription, trying in vain to wish it away, but it was more plain and clear each time he read it. And each time, he felt a cold hand clutch his heart in his afflicted breast. Finally he fell to gazing fixedly at the stone—stonelike himself. / He was ready to go out of his mind, so complete was his surrender to grief. Believe one who has experienced it—this is a sorrow to surpass all others. His chin had dropped onto his chest, his head was bowed, his brow had lost its boldness. So possessed was he by sorrow that he had no voice for laments, no moisture for tears. / His impetuous grief, set upon erupting all too quickly, remained within. A broad-bellied, narrow-necked vase full of water has the same effect, as can be observed: when the vase is inverted, the liquid so surges to the neck that it blocks its own egress, and can scarcely do more than come out drop by drop. / Returning to himself a little, he considered how he might yet be mistaken about it: he hoped against hope that it might simply be someone trying to besmirch his lady's name this way, or to charge him with a burden of jealousy so unendurable that he would die of it; and that whoever it was who had done this had copied her hand most skilfully. / With such meagre, such puny hopes he roused his spirits and found a little courage.

He mounted Brigliador, now that the sun was giving place to his sister in the sky. Before he had gone far he saw smoke issuing from the housetops, and heard dogs barking and cows lowing; he came to a farmhouse and found lodging. / Listlessly he dismounted, and left Brigliador to the care of a discreet stable-boy. Others there were to help him off with his armour and his golden spurs, and to refurbish them. This was the house where Medor lay wounded, and met with his great good fortune. Orlando did not ask for supper but for a bed: he was replete with sadness, not with other fare. / The harder he sought for rest, the worse the misery and affliction he procured himself—every wall, every door, every window was covered with the hateful inscriptions. He wanted to make enquiries there, but chose to keep his lips sealed: he was afraid to establish too clearly the very question he wanted to cloud with mist so as to dull the pain. / Little good did it do him to deceive himself; somebody there was to speak of the matter unasked. The herdsman, who saw him so downcast and sad and wanted to cheer him up, embarked, without asking leave, upon the story of those two lovers: he knew it well, and often repeated it to those who would listen. There were many who enjoyed hearing it. / He told how at the prayer of beautiful Angelica he had brought Medor back to his house. Medor was gravely wounded, and she tended his wound, and in a few days had healed it—but Love inflicted upon her heart a wound far worse than his, and from a small spark kindled so blazing a fire that she was all aflame and quite beside herself; / and, forgetting that she was daughter of the greatest monarch of the East, driven by excessive passion, she chose to become wife to a poor simple soldier. The herdsman ended his story by having the bracelet brought in—the one Angelica had given him on her departure as a token of thanks for his hospitality. /

This evidence shown in conclusion proved to be the axe which took his head off his shoulders at one stroke, now that Love, that tormentor, was tired of raining blows upon him. Orlando tried to conceal his grief, but it so pressed him, he could not succeed: willy nilly the sighs and tears had to find a vent through his eyes and lips. / When he was free to give rein to his sorrow, once he was alone without others to consider, tears began to stream from his eyes and furrow his cheeks, running down onto his breast. He sighed and moaned, and made great circular sweeps of the bed with his arms: it felt harder than rock; it stung worse than a bed of nettles. / Amid such bitter anguish the thought occurred to him that on this very bed in which he was lying the thankless damsel must have lain down many a time with her lover. The downy bed sent a shudder through him and he leapt off it with all the alacrity of a yokel who has lain down in the grass for a nap and spies a snake aclose by. /

The bed, the house, the herdsman filled him on a sudden with such revulsion that, without waiting for moonrise, or for the first light preceding the new day, he fetched his arms and his steed and went out into the darkest, most tangled depths of the wood; when he felt he was quite alone, he gave vent to his grief with cries and howls. / There was no checking his cries and tears; night and day he allowed himself no respite. Towns and villages he avoided, and lay out in the open on the hard forest-floor. He wondered that his head could hold such an unquenchable source of water, and that he could sigh so much. Frequently as he wept he said to himself: / "These are no longer tears that drop from my eyes so copiously. The tears were not enough for my grief: they came to an end before my grief was half expressed. Urged by fire, my vital spirit is now escaping by the ducts which lead to the eyes: this is what is now spilling out, and with it my sorrow and my life will flow out at its last hour. / These sighs, which are a token of my anguish, are not truly sighs: sighs are not like this—now and then they will cease, but never do I feel a relaxing of my pain as my breast exhales it. Love, which burns my heart, makes this wind, beating his wings about the flames. By what miracle, Love, do you keep my heart ever burning but never consumed by fire? / I am not who my face proclaims me; the man who was Orlando is dead and buried, slain by his most thankless lady who assailed him by her betrayal. I am his spirit sundered from him, and wandering tormented in its own hell, so that his shade, all that remains of him, should serve as an example to any who place hope in Love." /

All night the count wandered in the wood; at sunrise, Fate brought him back to the spring where Medor had carved his inscription. To see his calamity written there in the hillside so inflamed him that he was drained of every drop that was not pure hate, fury, wrath, and violence. On impulse he drew his sword, / and slashed at the words and the rock-face, sending tiny splinters shooting skywards. Alas for the cave, and for every trunk on which the names of Medor and Angelica were written! They were left, that day, in such a state that never more would they afford cool shade to shepherd or flock. The spring, too, which had been so clear and pure, was scarcely safer from wrath such as his; / branches, stumps and boughs, stones and clods he kept hurling into the lovely waters until he so clouded them from surface to bottom that they were clear and pure never again. In the end, exhausted and sweat-soaked, his stamina given out and no longer answering to his deep, bitter hate, his burning wrath, he dropped onto the grass and sighed up at the heavens. / Weary and heart-stricken, he dropped onto the grass and gazed mutely up at the sky. Thus he remained, without food or sleep while the sun three times rose and set. His bitter agony grew and grew until it drove him out of his mind.

On the fourth day, worked into a great frenzy, he stripped off his armour and chain-mail. / The helmet landed here, the shield there, more pieces of armour further off, the breastplate further still: arms and armour all found their resting-place here and there about the wood. Then he tore off his clothes and exposed his hairy belly and all his chest and back.

Now began the great madness, so horrifying that none will ever know a worse instance. / He fell into a frenzy so violent that his every sense was darkened. He did not think to draw his sword, with which I expect he would have performed marvels. But in view of his colossal strength he had no need of it, nor of any hatchet or battle-axe. He now performed some truly astonishing feats: at one jerk he rooted up a tall pine, / after which he tore up several more as though they were so many celery-stalks. He did the same to oaks and ancient elms, to beech and ash-trees, to ilexes and firs. What a birdcatcher does when clearing the ground before he lays nets—rooting up rushes, brushwood, and nettles—Orlando did to oaks and other age-old timber. / The shepherds who heard the din left their flocks scattered through the woodland and hastened from all parts to this spot to see what was happening. But I have reached a point which I must not overstep for fear of boring you with my story; I should rather postpone it than annoy you by making it too long.

. . .

If you have put your foot in the birdlime spread by Cupid, try to pull it out, and take care not to catch your wing in it too: love, in the universal opinion of wise men, is nothing but madness. Though not everyone goes raving mad like Orlando, Love's folly shows itself in other ways; what clearer sign of lunacy than to lose your own self through pining for another? / The effects vary, but the madness which promotes them is always the same. It is like a great forest into which those who venture must perforce lose their way: one here, another there, one and all go off the track. Let me tell you this, to conclude: whoever grows old in love ought, in addition to Cupid's torments, to be chained and fettered. / "You, my friend, are preaching to others," someone will tell me, "but you overlook your own failing." The answer is that now, in an interval of lucidity, I understand a great deal. And I am taking pains (with imminent success, I hope) to find peace and withdraw from the dance—though I cannot do so as quickly as I should wish, for the disease has eaten me to the bone. /

In the last canto I was telling you, my Lord, how Orlando, crazed and demented, had torn off arms and armour and scattered them everywhere, ripped his clothes, tossed away his sword, rooted up trees, and made the hollow caves and deep woods re-echo. And some shepherds were attracted to the noise, whether by their stars, or for some wicked misdeed of theirs. / When they had a closer sight of the madman's incredible feats and his prodigious strength, they turned to flee, but without direction, as people do when suddenly scared. The madman was after them at once; he grabbed one and took off his head with all the ease of a person plucking an apple from a tree or a dainty bloom from a briar. / He picked up the heavy carcass by one leg and used it to club the rest; he laid out two, leaving them in a sleep from which perhaps they would awake on Judgement Day. The others cleared off at once: they were quickfooted and had their wits about them. The madman would not have been slow to pursue them, but he had now turned upon their flocks. /

In the fields the labourers, wise from the shepherds' example, left their ploughs, hoes, and sickles and scrambled onto the housetops or onto the church roofs—there being no safety up elm or willow tree. From here they contemplated the fearsome frenzy unleashed upon horse and oxen: they were shattered, battered, and destroyed by dint of punches, thumps, and bites, kicks and scratches. It was a fast mover who could escape him. / Now you could have heard the neighbouring farms resound with shouts, the shrill of horns, and rustic trumpets and, most persistently, the peal of clarions; you could have seen a thousand men streaming down from the hills, armed with pikes and bows, spears, and slings; as many more came up from the plain, ready to wage a peasant war against the madman. / Imagine waves, driven by the South Wind which earlier had been playful, breaking on the shore; the second wave is higher than the first, the third follows with greater force; and, each time, the water builds up more and seethes more widely across the beach. Thus did the pitiless mob increase, coming down from the hills and out of the valleys against Orlando. / Out of that disorderly throng ten he killed who came within his reach, and then another ten. This experiment made it clear that it was far safer to stand well away. No one was able to draw blood from his body; steel was powerless to strike and wound it—the King of Heaven had given him this endowment so as to make him guardian of His holy faith. / Had he been capable of dying, his life would have been in danger; he might have learned what it was to throw aside his sword and, unarmed, to overreach himself.[1]

Now having seen their every blow prove ineffective, the throng began to ebb. With no one left to confront him, Orlando made off and came to a hamlet. / Here he found not a soul, man or child, for everyone had abandoned the place in terror. There was plenty of food set out, humble fare of which shepherds partake. Spurred by hunger and frenzy, he made no distinction between bread and acorns but set to with his hands and teeth and devoured whatever came first within reach, whether raw or cooked. / After this he

---

1. Orlando's frenzy resembles that of Hercules, the strongest man in classical mythology.

roamed about the countryside, preying upon men and wild beasts. He would range through the woods catching fleet-footed goats and nimble fawns. Often he would fight with bears and boars, wrestling them to the ground bare-handed; often he filled his ravenous belly with their meat, carcass and all. / He roamed across the length and breadth of France, until one day he came to a bridge. Beneath it a broad, full river flowed between steep, craggy banks. Beside it there stood a tower commanding a sweeping view in all directions. What he did here you shall learn later on.

Summary   Zerbin and Isabel find Orlando's armor. Zerbin dies trying to protect the armor for Orlando when Mandricard appears and claims the helmet (Mambrino's helmet), which once belonged to Hector of Troy. Isabel meets a hermit, who teaches her Christian consolation and converts her. Zerbin's death marks the beginning of tragedy's influence over the world of the *Furioso*.

FROM CANTO 25

[*Fiordispina's Love for Bradamant*]

Oh what conflict there can be in a young man's mind between a thirst for glory and the impulses of Love! There is no telling which of the two motives is the stronger when now one, now the other predominates. * * * / He had not travelled a mile beyond the well before he saw a messenger approaching at a gallop; he was one of those sent by Agramant to the warriors from whom he was expecting help. He learnt that the Saracens were in such danger from Charlemagne's blockade that, short of immediate assistance, degradation or even death would be their lot. / Ruggiero was perplexed by many thoughts which all assailed him at once; but this was not the time or the place to decide on his best course. He let the messenger go, then turned his steed to follow the damsel who was guiding him; he kept urging her to hasten, as there was no time to lose. / They continued along their way until, as the sun was setting, they came to a stronghold of Marsilius in the middle of France, one which he had seized from Charlemagne in the course of the war. They did not stop at the drawbridge nor at the gate—nobody blocked or obstructed their entry, even though the palisade and fosse were thronged with armed men. / As the damsel accompanying him was recognized by the bystanders, they were allowed through unhindered without even being asked from where they had come. They reached the square which they found aglow with flames and teeming with a malicious throng.

In the middle he saw the young man condemned to death. His face was white; / it was tearful and downcast, and when Ruggiero looked up at it he imagined he was looking at Bradamant, so closely did the youth resemble her. The more he gazed at his face and figure the more the likeness struck him. "Either this is Bradamant," he told himself, "or else I'm no longer Ruggiero. / Perhaps she was over-hasty in taking up the condemned boy's defence: her intervention must have miscarried and she has been captured, as I see. Oh why such haste, why could I not have been with her on this venture? But I have arrived, thank God, and there's still time for me to save her." / And without further delay he grasped his sword—he had broken his lance at Pinabello's castle—and drove his steed into the unarmed throng, assailing them in the chest, sides, and belly. He whirled his sword, catching one man on the brow, the next at the throat, another on the cheek. The rabble fled screaming: the entire throng was left maimed, if not with cracked skulls. / Imagine a flock of birds by a lake, flitting about confidently as they grub for food, when suddenly a hawk plummets down upon them from the sky and strikes or snatches one of their number; the rest scatter, each deserting his companion to attend to his own escape. Thus you would have seen the crowd behave the moment Ruggiero drove into them. / Some half dozen who were slow in leaving had their heads lopped off clean; as many more he split down to the chest, while a countless number were cleft down to the eyes or the jaw.

I'll grant you that they were not wearing helmets, but merely head-pieces of shining metal; had they been properly helmeted, though, he would have slashed them with almost as much ease. / No knight of the present day could match him for sheer strength—nor could any bear or lion or more ferocious beast, whether native or foreign to our shores. An earthquake might have equalled him, or the mighty Devil: not the one in hell—it's my Lord's Devil[2] I mean, the one which spits fire and forces its way everywhere, by land, sea, and air. / At every stroke at least one man fell, and more often two; he killed four and even five at a stroke, which soon brought the total to a hundred. The sword he had unsheathed could cut through steel as though it were soft whey. Falerina the sorceress[3] had made this cruel sword in the garden of Orgagna, for the purpose of slaying Orlando; / much did she regret having made it when she saw it used to destroy her garden. Imagine, then, the havoc and devastation wrought by it in the hands of a champion such as Ruggiero! If ever he manifested his rage, his strength, his supreme valour it was here and now as he strove to rescue his lady. /

The mob stood up to him as well as hare to unleashed hounds. A good number were killed; those who fled were legion. Meanwhile the damsel guiding Ruggiero had released the youth from the bonds tying his wrists, and procured him arms as best she could, a sword for his hand, a shield to sling from his neck. / He now did his utmost to avenge himself on these folk who had done him grievous wrong; he laid about him to such effect that he left a reputation for prowess and valour. The sun had dipped his golden rays into the Western sea when victorious Ruggiero and the young man set out from the castle. /

When the youth was outside the gates with Ruggiero, he thanked him profusely and most gracefully: his benefactor had, after all, risked his life to save him without knowing who he was. He asked Ruggiero to divulge his name, as he wanted to know who it was to whom he owed such a debt of gratitude. / "I am looking at the comely face and beautiful figure of my Bradamant," Ruggiero mused, "but I do not hear the dulcet tones of her voice. And her words are not appropriate to thanking a faithful lover. If she really is Bradamant, how is it that she has so soon forgotten my name?" / To establish who it was, Ruggiero employed subtlety. "I have seen you somewhere before," he remarked, "but though I have pondered and racked my brains I cannot remember where it was. Will you remind me, then, if you can recollect? And do me the pleasure of telling me your name, so that I may know who it was whom I saved today from the pyre." /

2. Duke Alfonso's great cannon.   3. Boiardo's sorceress, who created the sword Balisardo to kill Orlando.

"It could be that you have seen me before," replied the other, "but I cannot say where or when. I too wander about the world seeking high adventure. Perhaps it was a sister of mine you saw, one who wears armour and carries a sword at her side; we are twins from birth and look so alike that even our family cannot tell us apart. / You are not the first, nor the second, nor even the fourth to have mistaken us; neither our father, nor our brothers, nor even our mother who bore us at one birth is able to tell us apart. True, our hair used to mark a sharp difference between us when I wore my hair short and loose in the male fashion, while she wore hers long and coiled in a plait. / But one day she was wounded in the head (it would take too long to tell the story) and to heal her a servant of God cut her hair till it only half covered her ears. After that there was nothing to distinguish us beyond our sex and name: mine is Richardet, hers is Bradamant; we are brother and sister to Rinaldo. / And if it would not bore you to listen, I would tell you a story to amuse you—something that happened to me on account of my resemblance to her: at first it was rapture, but it ended in agony." Ruggiero, in whose ears no song was sweeter, no story dearer than one in which his lady featured, begged him to tell his story. /

"My sister had been wounded by a party of Saracens who had come upon her without a helmet, so she had been obliged to cut her long tresses if her dangerous head-wound was to heal. Now recently she happened to be travelling through these woods, her head shorn as I have said. / On her way she came to a shady spring and, being weary and dejected, she dismounted, took off her helmet and fell asleep in the tender grass. (I don't believe there can be a story more beautiful than this one.) Who should come upon her but the Spanish Princess Fiordispina, who had come into the woods to hunt. / When she saw my sister clad in armour all except for her face, and with a sword in place of a distaff, she imagined she was looking at a knight. After gazing awhile at her face and her manly build she felt her heart stolen. So she invited my sister to join the hunt, and ended by eluding her retinue and disappearing with her among the shady boughs. /

"Once she had brought her into a solitary place where she felt unlikely to be disturbed, little by little, by words and gestures she revealed that she was love-struck. With burning looks and fiery sighs she showed how consumed she was with desire. She paled and blushed and, summoning her courage, gave her a kiss. / It was clear to my sister that the damsel had illusions about her; my sister could never have satisfied her need and was quite perplexed as to what to do. 'My best course is to undeceive her,' she decided, 'and to reveal myself as a member of the gentle sex rather than to have myself reckoned an ignoble man'. / And she was right. It would have been a sheer disgrace, the conduct of a man made of plaster, if he had kept up a conversation with a damsel as fair as Fiordispina, sweet as nectar, who had set her cap at him, while like a cuckoo, he just trailed his wings. So Bradamant tactfully had her know that she was a maiden. / She was in quest of glory at arms, like Hippolyta and Camilla[4] of old. Born in Africa, in the seaside city of Arzilla, she was accustomed from childhood to the use of lance and shield. These revelations did not abate love-struck Fiordispina's passion one jot; Cupid had thrust in his dart to make so deep a gash that this remedy was now too late. / To Fiordispina my sister's face seemed no less beautiful for

---

4. Virgil's Amazon warrior; *Hippolyta:* queen of the Amazons.

this, her eyes, her movements no less graceful; she did not on this account retrieve mastery over her heart, which had gone out to Bradamant to bask in her adorable eyes. Seeing her accoutred as a man, she had imagined that there would be no need for her passion to remain unassuaged; but now the thought that her beloved was also a woman made her sigh and weep and betray boundless sorrow. /

"Anyone who heard her tears and grieving that day would have wept with her. 'Never was any torment so cruel,' she lamented, 'but mine is crueller. Were it a question of any other love, evil or virtuous, I could hope to see it consummated, and I should know how to cull the rose from the briar. My desire alone can have no fulfilment. / If you wanted to torment me, Love, because my happy state offended you, why could you not rest content with those torments which other lovers experience? Neither among humans nor among beasts have I ever come across a woman loving a woman; to a woman another woman does not seem beautiful, nor does a hind to a hind, a ewe to a ewe. / By land, sea, and air I alone suffer thus cruelly at your hands—you have done this to make an example of my aberration, the ultimate one in your power. King Ninus' wife was evil and profane in her love for her son; so was Myrrha, in love with her father, and Pasiphae with the bull. But my love is greater folly than any of theirs. / These females made designs upon the males and achieved the desired consummation, so I am told. Pasiphae went inside the wooden cow, the others achieved their end by other means. But even if Daedalus came flying to me with every artifice at his command, he would be unable to untie the knot made by that all-too-diligent Maker, Nature, who is all-powerful.'[5] /

"Thus the fair damsel grieved and fretted and would not be assuaged. She struck her face and tore her hair and sought to vent her feelings against her own person. My sister wept for pity and felt embarrassed[6] as she listened to her grieving. She tried to deflect her from this insane and profitless craving, but her words were in vain and to no effect. / It was help, not consolation, that she required and her grief only continued to increase. The day was now drawing to a close and the sun was reddening in the West; rather than spending the night in the woods it was time now to withdraw to some lodging. So the damsel invited Bradamant to this castle of hers not far away. / My sister was unable to refuse, so they came to the very spot where the wicked mob would have burned me to death had you not appeared. Here Fiordispina made much of my sister; she dressed her once more in feminine attire and made it plain to one and all that her guest was a woman. / Realizing how little benefit she derived from Bradamant's apparent masculinity, Fiordispina did not want any blame to attach to herself on her guest's account. In addition, she nurtured the hope that the sickness already implanted in her as a result of Bradamant's male aspect might be dispelled by a dose of femininity to show how matters really stood. /

"That night they shared a bed but they did not rest equally well. The one slept, the other wept and moaned, her desire ever mounting. And if sleep did

---

5. The entire speech is based on the soliloquy of Ovid's Myrrha, who loved her father (*Metamorphoses* 10). *King Ninus' wife*: Semiramis, Syrian queen who married her son. Pasiphae, wife of King Minos, loved a bull; Daedalus created the labyrinth in which Minos kept the Minotaur, the monstrous offspring of Pasiphae.   6. The Italian verb for Bradamant's emotional response, *è costretta,* indicates that she feels obliged or compelled to help Fiordispina rather than "embarrassed," as the translator puts it.

occasionally press upon her eyelids, it was but a brief sleep charged with dreams in which it seemed to her that Heaven had allotted to her a Bradamant transformed into a preferable sex. / If a thirst-tormented invalid goes to sleep craving for water, in his turbid, fitful rest he calls to mind every drop of water he ever saw. Likewise her dreaming mind threw up images to requite her desires. Then she would wake and reach out, only to find that what she had seen was but an empty dream. / How many prayers and vows did she not offer that night to Mahomet and all the gods, asking them to change Bradamant's sex for the better by a clear and self-evident miracle! But she saw that all her prayers were vain; perhaps Heaven even mocked her. The night ended and Phoebus lifted his fair head out of the sea and gave light to the world. / With the new day they left their bed, and Fiordispina's pain was aggravated when Bradamant, anxious to be clear of her predicament, mentioned that she was leaving. As a parting gift, Fiordispina presented her with an excellent jennet, caparisoned in gold; also with a costly surcoat woven by her own hand. / Fiordispina accompanied her a step of the way then returned, weeping, to her castle, while my sister pressed on so hastily that she reached Montauban the same day. Our poor mother and we, her brothers, crowded round her, rejoicing—for lack of news of her, we had been gravely anxious for fear she were dead. /

"When she removed her helmet we all stared at her cropped hair which previously had fallen about her neck; and the new surcoat she was wearing also caught our attention. And she told us all that had befallen her, from start to finish just as I've told you: how after she was wounded in the wood she cut off her fair tresses in order to be healed; / and how the beautiful huntress came upon her as she was by the spring; and how she took to her deceptive appearance and segregated her from her party. She did not pass in silence over Fiordispina's grief, and we were all filled with pity at it. She described how she lodged with her, and all she did until her return to our castle. /

"Now I had heard a great deal about Fiordispina, whom I had seen in Saragossa and in France. I had been much allured by her lovely eyes and smooth cheeks, but had not let my thoughts dwell upon her; to love without hope is idle dreaming. But, brought again so fully to the fore, she reawakened my passion at once. / Out of this hope, Love prepared bonds for me, having no other cord with which to capture me. He showed me how to set about obtaining what I wanted of this damsel. A little deception would procure an easy success: the similarity between my sister and myself had often deceived others, so perhaps it would deceive her too. / Shall I, shan't I? My conclusion was that it is always good to go in pursuit of one's pleasure. I did not divulge my thought to a soul, nor seek anyone's advice on the matter. When it was night, I went to where my sister had left her armour; I put it on and away I went on her horse without waiting for dawn to break. / I set off by night, with Cupid for guide, to be with lovely Fiordispina, and I arrived before the Sun had hidden his radiance in the sea. Happy the man who outstripped his fellows in bringing the news to the princess: as bearer of good tidings he could expect thanks and a reward from her. /

"They all of them took me for Bradamant—just as you did—the more so in that I had both the attire and the horse with which she had left the previous day. Fiordispina lost no time in coming out to meet me; she was so jubilant and affectionate, she could not possibly have shown greater pleasure and joy. / Throwing her graceful arms around my neck, she softly hugged me and kissed me on the lips. You can imagine after this how Love guided his dart to pierce me at the heart of my heart! She took me by the hand and quickly led me into her bedroom; here she would suffer none but herself to undo my armour, from helmet to spurs; no one else was to take a hand. / Next she sent for a dress of hers, richly ornate, which she herself spread out and put on me as though I were a woman; and she caught my hair in a golden net. I studied modesty in my glances, and none of my gestures betrayed my not being a woman. My voice might have betrayed me, but I controlled it so well that it aroused no suspicions. / Then we went into a hall crowded with knights and ladies who received us with the sort of honour paid to queens and great ladies. Here several times I was amused when certain men, unaware that my skirts concealed something sturdy and robust, kept making eyes at me. / When the evening was further advanced and the meal had been over for some while—the fare had been an excellent choice of what was then in season—Fiordispina did not wait for me to ask the favour which was the object of my visit, but invited me hospitably to share her bed for the night. /

"When the waiting-women and maidens, the pages, and attendants had withdrawn, and we were both changed and in bed, while the flaming sconces left the room bright as day, I said to her: 'Do not be surprised, my lady, at my returning to you so soon—perhaps you thought that you would not see me again for God knows how long. / First I shall tell you why I left, then why I have returned. Had I been able to abate your ardour by staying, I should have wanted to live and die in your service, and never for an hour be without you. But seeing how much pain my presence occasioned you, as I could do you no better service, I chose to leave. / Fate drew me off my path into the thick of a tangled wood, where I heard a cry sound close by, as of a damsel calling for help. I came running and found myself at the edge of a crystal lake where a faun had hooked a naked maiden in the water and was cruelly preparing to eat her raw. / I went over, sword in hand—only this way could I help her—and slew the boorish fisherman. Straight away she dived into the water and said: "It is not for nothing that you have saved me. You shall be richly rewarded and given as much as you ask for: I am a nymph and I live in this limpid lake. / I have the power to perform miracles, to coerce nature and the elements. Ask to the limits of my capabilities, then just leave it to me: at my singing the moon comes down from the sky, fire turns to ice, the air turns brittle, and with mere words I have moved the earth and stopped the sun." /

" 'I did not ask her for a hoard of treasure, or for power over nations, or for greater valour or might, or for honourable victory in every war. My only request was that she would show me some way I could fulfil your desire; I did not ask to achieve this in one way or in another, but left the method up to her own discretion. / Scarcely had I disclosed my wish than I saw her dive a second time, and for all reply to my request she splashed the enchanted water at me. The moment it touched my face I was quite transformed, I know not how. I could see, I could feel—though I could scarcely believe my senses—that I was changing from woman to man.[7] / You would never believe

<hr />

7. Richardet invents a fictional metamorphosis, which he bases generally on Ovid's tales, with specific allusions to the famous tales of Actaeon (who sees the goddess Diana naked and is metamorphosed into a stag when she sprinkles him with water) and Salmacis and Hermaphroditus (who together become the hermaphrodite).

me, except that now, right away, you shall be able to see for yourself. In my new sex as in my old, my desire is to give you ready service. Command my faculties, then, and you shall find them now and ever more alert and bestirred for you.' Thus I spoke to her, and I guided her hand to test the truth for herself. /

"Imagine the case of a person who has given up hope of having something for which he craves; the more he bemoans his deprivation, the more he works himself into a state of despair; and if later he acquires it, he is so vexed over the time wasted sowing seed in the sand, and despair has so eroded him that he is dumbfounded and cannot believe his luck. / So it was with Fiordispina: she saw and touched the object she had so craved for, but she could not believe her eyes or her fingers or herself, and kept wondering whether she were awake or asleep. She needed solid proof to convince her that she was actually feeling what she thought she felt. 'O God, if this is a dream,' she cried, 'keep me asleep for good, and never wake me again!' /

"There was no roll of drums, no peal of trumpets to herald the amorous assault: but caresses like those of billing doves gave the signal to advance or to stand firm. We used arms other than arrows and slingstones; and I, without a ladder, leapt onto the battlements and planted my standard there at one jab, and thrust my enemy beneath me. / If on the previous night that bed had been laden with heavy sighs and laments, this night made up for it with as much laughter and merriment, pleasure and gentle playfulness. Never did twisting acanthus entwine pillars and beams with more knots than those which bound us together, our necks and sides, our arms, legs, and breasts in a close embrace. / It remained a secret between us, so our pleasure continued for a few months. But eventually someone found us out, so the matter became known to the king—to my undoing. You, who rescued me from his people who had lit the pyre in the square, you can understand the rest: but God knows what an ache I am left with." /

* * *

Summary   When Doralice chooses to stay with Mandricard, Rodomont leaves the Saracen camp in a furious gloom, complaining of the fickleness of women. He is consoled by a spectacularly misogynistic tale, which Ariosto recommends that his readers disregard. Continuing in his journey, he comes across Isabel, who is mourning for Zerbin, and instantly feels the flame of lust kindle in his breast.

CANTO 29; *FROM CANTO 30*

[Isabel Outwits Rodomont and Angelica Encounters Orlando]

Oh the weak, inconstant minds of men! How ready we are to vacillate, how ready to change our ideas, especially those born of lovers' spite. I had just seen Rodomont so incensed against women that he broke all bounds: I could never imagine him cooling his passion, let alone quenching it. / Gentle ladies, I am so offended by what he said against you without cause that until I have shown him, to his chagrin, just how wrong he has been I shall not forgive him. I shall so exert myself, with pen and ink, that it will be plain to everyone how much better he would have done to have remained silent, even to have bitten his tongue sooner than slander you. /

Now experience clearly reveals the crass ignorance of his speech. He brandished the dagger of his wrath against the whole sex indiscriminately: then

one glance of Isabel's so touched him that he changed his mind on the spot—
he wanted her, now, instead of Doralice, though he had scarcely set eyes on
her and did not yet know who she was. / Hot and tingling with this new love,
he reasoned with her (to little purpose) to break her total, steadfast dedication to the Creator of all things. But the hermit acted as her buckler, her
plate-armour; lest her chaste decision be destroyed, he shielded her as best
he could with the surest, most valid arguments. / After enduring a great deal
of tedious discourse from the valiant monk and vainly inviting him to take
himself off to his desert without the damsel, and after seeing himself brazenly
flouted by the uncompromising fellow, the Saracen angrily grasped him by
the beard and pulled out a whole fistful of hair. / Then, his rage redoubled,
he closed his fingers round the other's neck like pincers and, whirling him
about a couple of times, tossed him up into the sky, towards the sea. What
became of the monk I cannot tell—I do not know. Various and conflicting
stories exist: one claims that he was so shattered against a rock that there
was no telling his head from his foot; / another, that he landed in the sea,
three miles away, and died for not being able to swim, having vainly offered
up many a prayer and supplication; another, that a saint came to his aid,
carrying him ashore with visible hand. One of these may be the truth—at
any rate my story says no more about him. /

Once rid of the garrulous monk, cruel Rodomont turned back to the distressed, bewildered damsel with greater composure and, using the terms
employed between lovers, told her that she was his heart, his life, his consolation, his dearest hope, and all the rest of it. / He behaved towards her
most gallantly, without the slightest display of force: her gentle look which
captured his heart quenched and stifled his customary arrogance. And
although he might simply have seized the fruit, he chose not to attack the
bark, deeming that the fruit could not be good unless he received it from her
as a gift. / In this way he expected little by little to win Isabel to do his
pleasure. But she, finding herself in this strange, solitary place, like a mouse
at the feet of a cat, would sooner have found herself in the midst of a fire.
She kept pondering what to do, what path to take in order to escape unblemished and intact. / She was resolved to slay herself before the cruel savage
had his way with her and forced her to so grave a sin against Zerbin, the
knight whom harsh and pitiless Fate had allowed to expire in her arms: to
him she had privately vowed her chastity for all time. / She saw the pagan
king's blind appetite ever growing and could not think what to do, well realizing that his ultimate aim was the squalid act to which her opposition would
have scant effect. But as she considered one thing and another, she hit upon
a way to protect herself and save her chastity, as I shall relate to her enduring
fame. /

As the evil Saracen was now accosting her with language and actions quite
devoid of the courtesy he had originally shown, "If you leave my honour safe,"
she told him, "and I need not fear for it in your company, I, for my part,
shall give you something of far greater value to you than the depriving me of
it. / Do not despise a lasting contentment, a true joy second to none, for the
sake of a trifling pleasure so easily available the world over: you can find a
hundred, a thousand comely women any time, but no one in the world, or
very few, can give you what I can. / I know of a herb—I've seen it on my way
here and know where to find it—which, boiled with ivy and rue over a fire

of cypress-wood, and then pressed out between innocent hands, produces a juice: and whoever bathes himself with this juice three times so hardens his body that he becomes proof against fire and steel. / Truly, whoever applies the liquid three times is invulnerable for a month—every month it must be re-applied, for its virtue lasts no longer. I know how to make it and today I shall do so, and today you shall feel its effect: and, if I am not mistaken, you will be better pleased than by the conquest this day of all Europe. / In reward for this, here is what I ask of you: swear on your honour neither in word nor deed ever more to threaten my chastity."

With these words she recalled Rodomont to his honour, for he conceived such a craving to be invulnerable that he promised her even more than she asked. / He would keep his oath until he had tried the remarkable juice for himself; meanwhile he would refrain from any act or show of violence. Later, he decided, he would not keep his word, for he neither feared nor respected God and the saints—when it came to breaking faith, the whole of deceitful Africa yielded to him. / Rodomont swore a thousand oaths to Isabel not to molest her provided that she prepared the juice that could render him invulnerable as Cygnus and Achilles.[8]

Up cliffs and down dark ravines, remote from towns and villages, she went gathering herbs; the Saracen never left her side but stayed close to her. / After gathering here and there as many herbs (with and without roots) as were needed, they returned home late; here Isabel, that paragon of chastity, spent the rest of the night boiling the herbs most expertly. Throughout the whole mysterious operation Rodomont was present. / Now as he passed the night in games with his few attendants, the heat from the fire in that confined place produced in him such a thirst that, with a sip here, a gulp there, he emptied two whole casks of Greek wine which a day or two earlier his pages had taken from some travellers. / But Rodomont was unaccustomed to wine, which Moslem law forbids and condemns. And it tasted to him like the liquor of the gods, better than nectar or manna; so, repudiating Saracen custom, he drank it by the bumper-full, flasks at a time. The excellent wine was passed round many a time till all their heads were spinning like lathes. /

Meanwhile the damsel took off the boil the cauldron in which the herbs were cooking and said to Rodomont: "Lest you should think my words are just air, I shall give you what it takes to distinguish truth from deceit and convince the dullest mind—I shall give you proof, here and now, and on my own person, not upon another's. / I want to be the first to try the potency of the benignant juice in case you imagine it contains a deadly poison. I shall bathe myself with it from the crown of my head down my neck and over my breast. Then turn your might and your sword upon me to try the juice's power, the sword's sharpness." / She bathed herself as she said, then joyfully offered her bare neck to the unwary pagan: he was all unwary and perhaps befuddled by the wine, against which helmet and shield are unavailing. The brute believed her and used his hand and his cruel sword to such effect that he lopped her fair head, once the abode of love, clean from her shoulders. /

Her head bounced thrice: from it a voice could be clearly heard pronouncing the name of Zerbin, to follow whom she had found so novel a way to escape from the Saracen. Depart in peace, then, beautiful, blessed spirit,

8. Both invulnerable to the sword.

who preferred fidelity and a name for chastity (virtually alien and unknown in our day) to your life, your green years! / If only my verses had the power, how hard I should work to the limit of my poet's art, which so refines and enhances speech, so that for a thousand years and more the world would have knowledge of your illustrious name. Go in peace to the supernal seat, and leave to other women an example of your faith. / At this incomparable, this amazing act, the Creator looked down from Heaven and said: "I commend you more than Lucretia, whose death deprived Tarquin[9] of his realm. For this cause I mean to make a law, one such that time may never dissolve, and I swear by the inviolable waters of Styx that no future age shall alter it: / in future every woman bearing your name shall be sublime of spirit, beautiful, noble, kind, and wise; she shall achieve the mark of true virtue, and afford writers cause to celebrate the praiseworthy, illustrious name, so that Parnassus, Pindus, and Helicon[1] shall ever ring with the name of Isabel." / God spoke thus, and made the air serener, the sea calmer than ever before. The chaste soul returned to the third heaven, back into the arms of her Zerbin.

Shamed and flouted, merciless Rodomont, a second Brehus, remained on earth. Once he had digested his excess of wine, he cursed his mistake and regretted it, / and considered how to placate or in part to satisfy Isabel's blessed soul: though he had slain her body, at least he could give life to her memory. To this end he converted the chapel in which he was living—the site of her death—into a tomb for her. This is how he did it. / He assembled masons from the whole vicinity, some with blandishments, others with threats; when he had a good six thousand men, he alleviated the neighbouring hills of many a heavy rock and had these compacted as a great mound, ninety yards from top to bottom, which encased the chapel containing the pair of lovers. / It almost copied the imposing mound thrown up by Hadrian[2] on the Tiber's bank. Beside the tomb he had a tall tower built in which he planned to live awhile.

Over the nearby river he built a narrow bridge, but two yards wide. The bridge was long, but so narrow that it scarcely allowed room for two horses, / whether approaching it abreast or arriving from opposite ends. The bridge had no parapet of any kind: it was possible to fall off either side. He meant to exact a high toll from every knight who crossed the bridge, whether pagan or Christian—he promised their spoils as trophies for the couple's tomb. /

In less than ten days the bridge across the river was completed. The tomb was not so quickly built, nor was the tower yet carried to its summit, though it was raised high enough for a sentry to take up his post on it and alert Rodomont with his horn each time a knight approached the bridge. / Rodomont would arm and go to challenge him from whichever bank served his purpose—if the passing knight arrived from the tower-side, Rodomont would cross to the further bank. The bridge was the jousting-place, and any charger veering at all off centre would fall into the river, which was deep—there was no danger in the world to match it. / The Saracen imagined that by frequently incurring the risk of falling from the bridge headfirst into the river, where he would be bound to drink a great deal of water, he would be cleansed of

9. The Roman king who raped Lucretia, a chaste Roman matron who committed suicide rather than live with the shame.   1. Sites sacred to the Muses and therefore popular topics in poetry.   2. *Mound . . . Hadrian:* Castel Sant' Angelo. Originally the mausoleum of the Roman emperor Hadrian.

the fault to which he was induced by too much wine—as though the water would dilute not merely the wine he had drunk but also the evil which the wine had made his hand or tongue commit. / Many knights passed this way within a few days. Some arrived in the course of their journey, for this was the most frequented road leading to Italy and Spain. Others were attracted hither by adventure and by honour (dearer than life itself) to try their mettle. One and all, confident of winning the palm, forfeited their arms and many their life as well. / If those he overthrew were pagans, he contented himself with despoiling them and taking their arms on which, before hanging them on the marble of the tomb, he clearly inscribed the name of their erstwhile owner. The Christians he held prisoner, and I believe he later sent them all to Algiers. The building-work was not yet completed when who should arrive but mad Orlando. /

The raving count chanced to arrive at the wide river where Rodomont, as I've said, was urgently building the tower and the tomb; these were still unfinished, and the bridge barely completed. Except for his visor the pagan was fully armed at the moment when Orlando came to the river and the bridge. / Impelled by his madness, Orlando jumped over the barrier and ran onto the bridge. Rodomont glowered as he waited on foot in front of the great tower, and yelled threats at him from a distance: he would not deign to use his sword against him. "Stop, you rash, reckless peasant, you impudent, meddlesome oaf: / this bridge is for lords and knights, not for the like of you!" Now Orlando, who was in a day-dream, did not listen but simply kept on. "I'll have to punish the idiot," thought the pagan and, nothing loth, made to hurl him into the water, never imagining he would meet resistance. / At this point a gentle maiden arrived at the bridge to cross the river. She was dainty in her dress, her face comely and her manner studiedly modest. She was Fiordiligi, the damsel (you may remember, my Lord) who was looking for the traces of her lover Brandimart, in every place except where he actually was, in Paris. / She reached the bridge at the moment when Orlando came to grips with Rodomont, who wanted to throw him into the river. /

Now she was well acquainted with the count and recognized him at once. She was astonished at the folly that possessed him to go about naked. / She stopped to see what would result from the fury of two men as strong as these. Each was intent on putting all his might into heaving the other off the bridge. "How can a madman be so strong?" the pagan muttered between his teeth as he twisted and turned this way and that, full of bile, contempt, and rage. / He tried out new holds with either hand, looking for the best grip, and skilfully advanced his right foot or his left, now between the other's legs, now outside them. Rodomont at grips with Orlando looked like a sturdy bear expecting to uproot the tree out of which he has fallen—as though the tree were wholly to blame and he were furious with it. / Orlando, whose wits had foundered, I know not where, and who was relying solely on his brawn (which few, if any, could match), dropped backwards off the bridge still clasping the pagan. They fell into the river with a mighty splash and sank to the bottom together, while the banks groaned. / The water parted them at once. Orlando, who was naked and swam like a fish, struck out with his arms and legs and reached the bank; as soon as he was out of the river he ran off without waiting to consider whether what he had done redounded to his credit or not. The pagan, however, was hampered by his armour and made a slower, more laboured return to the shore. / Meanwhile Fiordiligi, having safely crossed the bridge and the river, explored the tomb in search of her Brandimart's insignia; finding here neither his arms nor his surcoat, she hoped to find him elsewhere.

But let us return to Orlando, who left the tower, river, and bridge behind him. / I should be mad if I undertook to relate each and every folly of Orlando, for they were so many, I wouldn't know when I should finish. But I shall select a few important ones, fit to be sung in verse and appropriate to my story. And I shall not pass in silence over his prodigious feat in the Pyrenees above Toulouse. / He had travelled a long way, prompted by his dire insanity; eventually he came up into the mountains which divide France from Spain. As he proceeded in the direction of the setting sun he came onto a narrow path overhanging a deep valley. / Here two young woodcutters found him on their path. They were driving before them a donkey laden with wood; one look at him told them that there were no brains in his head, so they shouted at him threateningly to go back or move aside and clear out of their way. / For all reply Orlando gave the donkey a petulant kick in the chest: there was nothing like it for sheer drive, and the beast rose into the air, so that to an observer he looked like a little bird on the wing, and landed on the top of a hill rearing up across the valley a mile or so away. Then he fell upon the two young men. /

One of them had better luck than sense: in a panic he hurled himself into the precipice which fell away twice a hundred feet. Half-way down he hit a soft, pliant, leafy bush, which, apart from some scratches to his face from its thorns, let him go safe and sound. / The other grasped a spur jutting from the rockface to scramble up it; he hoped, if he gained the top, to find safety from the madman—who did not, however, intend that he survive: he grabbed the fugitive by the feet as he was trying to climb up, and, extending his hands to arm's length, tore him in two, / the way one may see a man tear a heron or chicken apart to feed its warm entrails to a falcon or goshawk. How fortunate it was that the one who risked breaking his neck was not killed! He related this prodigy to others so that Turpin[3] came to hear of it and wrote it down for us. / This and many other fantastic feats he accomplished as he crossed the mountains.

After much wandering he finally descended Southwards towards Spain. He took his way along the sea-shore in the region of Tarragona and, as his compelling madness dictated, he chose to make his home on the beach; / to afford himself some protection from the sun he dug into the fine, dry sand. While he was here, fair Angelica and her husband chanced upon him. (As I told you earlier, they had come down to the Spanish shore from the mountains.) Now she came within an arm's length of him, not having yet noticed his presence. / It never crossed her mind that he might be Orlando: he had changed too much.

From the moment he was possessed by madness he had always gone naked, in the shade as in the sun. Had he been born in sunny Assuan or where the Libyan Garamants worship Ammon, or in the mountains at the source of the Nile his skin could not have been more deeply tanned. / His eyes were almost hidden in his face, which was lean and wizened; his hair was a matted,

---

3. Ariosto's fictional source.

bristling mass, his bushy beard looked appalling and hideous. Angelica had no sooner set eyes on him than she turned back, quaking; quaking, she filled heaven with shrieks and turned to her escort for help. / When crazed Orlando noticed her he started to his feet to grab her—he took a liking to her delicate face and immediately wanted her. That he had once so loved and worshipped her was a memory now totally destroyed in him. He ran after her the way a hound pursues game. / Young Medor, seeing the madman in pursuit of his lady, charged at him on horseback and struck at him, finding his back turned. He expected to strike the head off his shoulders but found his skin as hard as bone, indeed harder than steel—Orlando was born under a spell of invulnerability. /

As he felt himself struck from behind, Orlando turned, clenching his fist, and, with a force beyond measure, punched the Saracen's horse. The blow landed on the steed's head, smashing it like glass, and killing him. On the instant, he turned away and chased after the fleeing Angelica, / who was frantically whipping and spurring on her mare—even had she flown faster than an arrow from a bow, the beast would have seemed slow for her present need. Then she remembered the ring on her finger: this could save her, and she thrust it into her mouth. The ring, which had not lost its virtue, made her vanish like a flame puffed out. / Whether it was fright, or that she lost her seat while transferring the ring, or that the mare stumbled—I cannot say which was the reason—the moment that she put the ring into her mouth and hid her lovely face she pitched out of the saddle and landed on her back in the sand. / Had her fall landed her two inches closer, she would have collided with the madman and been slain by the impact alone. Great good fortune helped her at this point: as to the horse, she needs would have to help herself to another horse as she had done before—she was never to recover this one who was trampling the beach ahead of the paladin. / Do not fear: she will secure another.

Let us follow Orlando now, whose frenzied impetus was no whit dispelled with the vanishing of Angelica. He followed the steed across the bare sand, constantly gaining on her; now he could touch her . . . he had her by the mane . . . now by the bridle . . . . at last he held her. / He seized her as gleefully as another man would a maiden. He adjusted the reins and headstall then gained the saddle in one leap, only to drive her many a mile at a gallop restlessly hither and yon, never unharnessing her, never letting her taste grass or hay. / Wanting to jump a ditch, he landed in it upside down with the mare. He was unscathed—never felt a jolt—but the wretched beast threw out her shoulder. Seeing no way of pulling her out, he finally loaded her onto his shoulder, climbed out of the ditch and walked with his burden the length of three arrows' flights and more. / When she grew too heavy he set her down in order to lead her; she limped slowly after him. "Come on," he urged her, but he urged in vain: had the mare followed him at a gallop she would not have satisfied his crazy whim. In the end he slipped the halter from her head and tied it above her right hind hoof. / Thus he dragged her along, assuring her that this way she would be able to follow him more comfortably. The road was rough: one stone tore at her coat, the next at her skin, and finally the ill-used beast died from her lacerations and sufferings. Orlando spared her not a glance, not a thought: he pressed on at a run. /

Even when she was dead he did not stop dragging her as he continued his way Westward, sacking farms and houses as he went, whenever he felt the need for food. He seized fruit, meat, and bread which he guzzled, and overpowered everybody: some he left dead, others, maimed; he tarried little and kept pressing onwards. / He would have dealt scarcely more tenderly with his lady had she not hidden herself: he could not tell black from white and believed that his inflictions were a kindness.

A curse upon the ring, and upon the knight who gave it her—were it not for that, Orlando would at a stroke have been avenged on his own and on many another's account! / Would that not she alone but the whole surviving sex had fallen into Orlando's hands: they're a nasty tribe and not an ounce of good is to be found in any of them! But before my slackened strings produce a discordant note in this canto, I should do well to continue it later, lest it prove irksome to my listeners.

• • •

Allow your reason to be mastered by sheer pique, put up no defence against it, leave blind rage to force your hand (or tongue) into offending your friends: then well may you weep for it—the wrong is not so easily righted! Alas, in vain I regret and curse myself for what I said in anger at the end of the last canto. / But I am like a sick man who has endured all too much pain and, at the end of his tether, gives way to passion and starts to curse. This relieves the pain, and with it the impulse which has allowed his tongue such freedom. Then he comes to his senses and regrets his impulse: but what has been said cannot be unsaid. / I crave pardon, ladies, which I hope your kindness shall afford me. You must excuse me if, overwhelmed as I am by a strong passion, I babble deliriously. Blame it on my enemy—a lady[4] who has reduced me to the most abject condition, making me say things I regret. That she's at fault, God knows: that I love her, she knows. / I am no less divorced from myself than was Orlando. I have no worse an excuse than he does, as he wanders over hill and over dale, scouring great tracts of Marsilius' kingdom.

For many a day he dragged the dead mare after him without let or hindrance, until he came to where a broad river flowed into the sea: here he had to abandon the carcass. / As he swam like an otter, he entered the river and emerged on the further shore, where he met a shepherd riding his horse down to the river to water him. The shepherd did not avoid Orlando as he approached, seeing that he was naked and alone. "I should like to swap my mare for that jade of yours," the madman told him. / "I'll point her out from here, if you like: there she is, lying dead on the other shore. You can have her seen to by a doctor—that apart, I find no fault in her. Let's have your nag, then, with some makeweight. Come now, dismount please: I want him." The shepherd laughed and, without a word, drew away and made for the ford. / "Hey, can't you hear? I want your horse!" cried Orlando, going after him in a temper. Now the shepherd had a staff with good solid knots to it, which he used against the paladin, sending him into a blind fury—more savage than he had ever looked before. He let fly with a punch at the shepherd's head, smashing his skull and knocking him dead to the ground. / He jumped onto the hack and dashed off at

4. Alessandra Benucci, Ariosto's great love.

a venture, robbing many a man. The horse never tasted hay nor oats, so in a few days he collapsed. Did Orlando continue on foot? No—he meant to have horses a-plenty: as many as he found he purloined to his own use, after slaying their owners. /

Finally he came to Malaga, where he wrought greater havoc than anywhere previously. Not only did the fearsome lunatic rob everybody, leaving them in such straits that neither this year nor next would they have made up for their losses, but also he killed so many people and razed and burned so many houses that he laid waste more than a third of the city. / After this he came to a town called Algeciras, on the straits of Gibraltar (or Hibraltar as it is also called). Here he noticed a boat casting off. It was full of merrymakers setting off across the glassy-smooth waters for a pleasant sail in the morning breeze. / The madman started yelling: "Stop!" for he had a sudden urge to ride in a boat. But his shouts and yells were all in vain, for he was not a cargo they were ready to embark. Their vessel drove through the water as swiftly as a migrant swallow through the air. Orlando beat and belaboured his mount and forced him into the water with his crop, / until the beast had no choice but to plunge in, for all his efforts to resist were in vain. He went in up to his knees, to his belly and rump, so far that barely his head emerged from the water. He could not hope to turn back, for the crop kept drumming him between the ears. Poor wretch, he would have to make the crossing to Africa or else drown on the way. /

The boat that had put out from dry land was meanwhile lost to view: Orlando could not descry its hull from any angle—it was too far off and the billowing waves concealed it from his low vantage-point. He kept urging the horse through the waves, his mind made up on crossing the sea, until the steed, waterlogged and breathless, reached the end of his swim—and of his life: / he sank to the bottom, and would have taken his burden with him, but Orlando used his arms to stay afloat. He bestirred his legs and the palms of his hands as he blew the water from his face. The day was serene, the water calm; and he certainly needed the fairest weather, for with any sea running, he would have been left dead in the water. / But Fortune, who takes care of the insane, pulled him from the sea onto a beach at Ceuta, about two arrows' flights from the town walls. For many days he pursued his course at a venture, hastening Eastwards along the shore, until he came upon a countless horde of black soldiers camped by the sea. / Now let us leave the paladin to his travels: we shall revert to him when the time comes. As to what became of Angelica, my Lord, after her narrow escape from the madman, and how she found a good ship and better weather to return to her own country, and how she gave Medor the sceptre of the Indies: perhaps another will sing to a better accompaniment. / I have so many things I want to relate that I do not care to pursue her adventures any further.[5]

* * *

5. Angelica's last appearance in the poem.

FROM CANTOS 34 AND 35

[Astolfo's Voyage to the Moon]⁶

* * *

* * * / Then he mounted his flying horse and rose into the air to reach the summit of the mountain, for it was generally believed that the orb of the moon stood not far from its highest peak. His urge to explore directed his aspirations heavenwards, spurning the earth. More and more height he gained until he reached the summit. /

The flowers which the breeze had painted on these smiling slopes looked like so many coloured gems—sapphires, rubies, gold, topaz, and pearls, diamonds, chrysolites, and jacinth. And the grass was so green that were it to grow down here it would outdo emeralds. No less beautiful were the boughs of the trees, permanently in fruit and in blossom. / In the branches lovely little birds sang; they were of many hues, white, blue and green, red and yellow. The murmuring brooks and quiet lakes were more limpid than crystal. A soft breeze, which seemed never to falter or fail, kept the air constantly astir so as to temper the heat of the day. / And as it blew, it ravished each blossom, fruit, and leaf of its particular odour, blending them all into a sweetness which nourished the spirit. In the middle of the plain stood a palace which seemed to be ablaze with a living flame, it radiated such splendour and light, beyond all mortal experience. / The palace had a perimeter of over thirty miles. Astolfo on his steed ambled slowly towards it, admiring the beautiful scene on every side. As he compared what he saw with this rank world we live in, he dismissed our world as ugly and evil and loathed by Heaven and nature in comparison with the sweetness, light, and happiness up there. /

When he was close to the gleaming edifice he was stunned with amazement: its smooth wall was fashioned from a single stone which shone redder than a carbuncle. What a stupendous work, what ingenious architect! What structure in our world resembles it? Let him be silent who proposes any of our Seven Wonders⁷ for such glory. / In the luminous vestibule of that house of bliss Astolfo was approached by an old man in a carmine robe and milk-white cloak. He was white-haired and a thick white beard mantled his chin and fell to his chest. His face was so venerable, he looked like one of the elect of Paradise. / With a cheerful smile he addressed the paladin, who had respectfully dismounted: "O baron," he said, "who by God's will have ascended to the earthly paradise: as the cause of your journey and the object of your desire are equally hidden from you, your arrival here from the Northern hemisphere is, believe me, not without highly-placed help. / It is to discover how you are to help Charlemagne and rescue the Holy Faith from peril that you have made so long a journey to come, all unawares, to consult me. You are not to attribute your coming here to your intelligence or courage, my son: neither your horn nor the winged horse would be of any use to you had not God given them to you. / Later we shall converse at greater leisure

---

6. Astolfo mounts the hippogryph and travels to the moon to recover Orlando's wits.   7. The Pyramids, the gardens of Babylon, the statue of Jove at Olympia, the Colossus of Rhodes, the temple of Diana at Ephesus, the mausoleum at Halicarnassus, and the palace of Cyrus.

and I shall tell you how you are to proceed. But first come in and restore yourself—you must feel by now you have fasted long enough."

The old man had more to say, and much surprised Astolfo when he revealed himself as the Evangelist: / it was John, beloved of the Redeemer, on whose account the word went around the disciples that he was destined not to end his years in death.[8] The Son of God was induced, therefore, to tell Peter: "If I have him remain thus till I come, what is it to you?" Now although he did not say, "he is not to die," it is clear that this is what he meant. / John, upon his assumption here, found company, for the patriarch Enoch had arrived already, and also the great prophet Elias:[9] they were yet to see their last evening, and they are to enjoy eternal spring outside the foul, pestilential air until the angels' trumpets give the signal that Christ is returning on the white clouds. /

The saints gave the knight a good welcome and allotted him a room. In another his steed was provided with good forage a-plenty. They gave Astolfo some of the fruits of paradise; in view of their flavour he was inclined to think that Man's first parents might well have been excused if this is what made them fail in obedience. / The adventurous duke had partaken of food and sleep enough to give Nature her due, for every conceivable amenity was here available, and Aurora had left her aged consort (of whom she never tired, for all his years) when he too left his bed—to find that the disciple so beloved of God had come to fetch him. / He took him by the hand and told him many things which need to remain unspoken.

Then he said: "Perhaps you don't know what is happening in France, my son, though you've come from there. Your Orlando has misappropriated the standards committed to him, and God is punishing him—for He is harshest against those He most loves, when they offend Him. / At his birth God endowed him with strength and courage to the highest degree and—what was quite abnormal—made him invulnerable to steel of any sort, in order thus to constitute him defender of His holy Faith, just as He made Samson defender of the Hebrews against the Philistines. / But your Orlando has given his Lord a poor return for such great benefits: for the greater duty he had to foster the Faithful the worse has been his desertion of them; so blinded has he been by his lustful passion for a pagan woman, the Faithful have suffered twice and more from his ruthless attempts to slay Rinaldo, his faithful cousin. / Therefore God has sent him mad, to go about with bared chest and belly, and has so clouded his reason that he cannot recognize anyone, still less himself. We read that in this fashion God also punished Nebuchadnezzar,[1] driving him to folly for seven years, when he cropped grass and hay like an ox. / But since the paladin's wrongdoing has been far less serious than Nebuchadnezzar's, the divine will has imposed a period of only three months to purge his sin. And if our Redeemer has permitted you to arrive up here after so long a journey, it is quite simply so that you may learn from us the way to bring Orlando to his senses. / You shall, in fact, have to make a further journey with me and leave the earth altogether: I have to take you to the orb of the moon, this being the planet that travels closest to us, for the medicine

8. Christians thought that John, author of Revelation, would remain alive until the second coming of Christ for the universal judgment. 9. Enoch and Elias, or Elijah, ascended to the heavens. 1. Wicked Babylonian king.

to restore Orlando's sanity is kept there. Tonight when the moon arrives over us we shall set out." /

The apostle discoursed about this and that for the rest of the day. But when the sun had plunged into the sea and the sickle-moon had risen above them, a chariot was made ready, designed for travelling about those skies—it had once lifted Elias from mortal gaze in the mountains of Judaea.[2] / The holy Evangelist harnessed four horses (of the most fiery red) to the shafts, and when he and Astolfo were settled in the chariot he took the reins and urged the steeds skywards. The chariot made a circle before lifting into the air, and soon arrived in the midst of the eternal fire, but the old man wrought a miracle whereby it gave no heat. / They crossed the whole sphere of fire and thence continued to the realm of the moon, which looked to them for the most part like untarnished steel. They found it equal in size (or nearly) to this ultimate sphere of ours, the earth, including the ocean that girdles it. /

Here Astolfo had a double surprise: what a big place the moon was from close up, when to us, who look at it from down here, it seems but a little sphere! And how he had to screw up his eyes if from up there he wanted to descry the earth and the sea spread over it; the earth being unilluminated, its features can span but a short distance. / The rivers, lakes, and fields up there were not as they are down here. The plains, valleys, mountains, cities, and castles were different, and there were houses the like of which for sheer size the paladin had never seen before or since. And there were spacious, empty forests where nymphs were forever hunting game. /

Astolfo did not stop to explore everything, for that was not the object of his coming. He was led by the holy apostle into a valley shut in between two hills, where everything that is lost on earth (be the fault ours or that of time or fate) fetches up miraculously. What is lost here collects up there. / I do not mean only dominion and wealth, subject to the vagaries of fickle Fortune. I mean also what is beyond Fortune's power to give or take: there is many a reputation up there which, little by little, time has consumed down here like a moth. There, too, are countless prayers and vows made to God by us sinners. / The tears and sighs of lovers, the useless time lost in gaming, the chronic idleness of ignorant men, the empty plans which know no rest, the vain desires are in such numbers that they clutter almost the whole place. In short, no matter what you ever lost here you would find if you went up there. /

As Astolfo passed among these mounds he asked his guide about various of them. Noticing a lofty pile of tumid bladders from which seemed to emanate a hubbub of cries, he was told that these were the ancient crowns of the Assyrians and of Lydia, of the Persians and Greeks—once so illustrious, now forgotten almost to their very names. / Next he saw a heap of gold and silver hooks: gifts made in hope of reward to kings, to greedy princes, to patrons. He asked about garlands he saw which concealed a noose: all flattery, he was told. Verses written in praise of patrons wore the guise of exploded crickets. / Love affairs pursued to little purpose had the shape of gilded bonds, jewel-studded shackles. There were eagles' talons—and these were, I am told, the authority which lords vest in their servants. The bellows

2. Elijah was borne to heaven in a flaming chariot.

littering the hillside all around denoted the praise given by princes and the favours conferred upon their favourites, all wafted away with the flower of their years. /

Cities and castles and immense treasures lay here in a confused jumble of ruins. They were treaties, he was told, and ill-concealed plots. He saw snakes with maiden's faces: the works of coiners and thieves. Then he noticed an assortment of broken phials: service as wretched courtiers. / He came upon a great mess of pottage and asked his mentor about it. "That," he explained, "is the charity left by a person after his death." Then he skirted a great mound of sundry flowers once sweet-smelling but now reeking. This (begging your pardons) was the Donation of Constantine to good Sylvester.[3] He saw great quantities of bird-lime for ensnaring: your charms, good ladies. It would take an age if I were to describe in verse each thing that was pointed out to him—after countless thousands I should still not be finished, for every one of our needs is to be found up there. Folly, however, whatever its degree, is missing from there: it stays down here and never leaves us. / Astolfo had some lost days and other oddments of his own to look for; without his guide, he would never have recognized them in their different transformations.

Next he came upon the substance which, it seems, is so innate in us that never were prayers offered to God for its possession: I mean brains. There was a mountain of them here, only a far bigger one than of anything previously mentioned. / They took the form of a soft, tenuous liquid, apt to vaporize if not kept tightly sealed. It could be seen collected in various phials of greater or lesser size adapted for this purpose. The one containing the mighty brain of mad Orlando was the biggest of them all. It was also distinguished from the others by the inscription upon it: "The wits of Orlando." / All the rest were similarly inscribed with the name of the person to whom the wits belonged. The valiant duke discovered a good portion of his own; but what surprised him far more was how many belonged to people he had credited with having all their wits about them—there was abundant evidence of how witless they really were, to judge by the amount that was here to hand. / Some lose their wits in loving, some in seeking honours, some in scouring the seas in search of wealth, some in hopes placed in princes, some in cultivating magical baubles; some lose them over jewels, some over paintings, and some over other objects which they value above all else. Here the wits of sophists, astrologers, and poets abound. /

Astolfo collected his, for the author of the mysterious Apocalypse permitted him. He held to his nose the phial containing his wits and they just seemed to make their way back into place. Turpin asserts, it seems, that from there on Astolfo lived sensibly for a long time, until a subsequent caprice of his lost him his wits a second time. / Astolfo took the fullest, most capacious phial which contained the wherewithal to restore Orlando to his senses. It was not as light as he had imagined when it lay on the pile with the others.

Before he returned down to the lower spheres from this radiant one, he was led by the holy apostle into a palace built beside a river. / Each room was full of lengths of spun flax, silk, cotton, and wool, dyed in various colours, some pleasing, others hideous. In the first courtyard a white-haired woman

3. Deed of Rome to the popes, discredited by the humanist scholar Lorenza Valla, who proved on linguistic grounds that the deed was a forgery.

was winding them onto reels—the way in summer one sees peasant women drawing the moist cocoons off the silkworms as they harvest the new silk. / When one skein was finished, another was brought in its place, the first taken away; another woman would sort out the attractive from the ugly threads which the first left all in confusion. "What is going on here? I can't make it out," asked Astolfo. "The old women are the Fates," replied John; "with these threads they spin lives for you mortals. / As long as one of these threads is spun out, so long does a human life last, and not a moment longer. Here Death and Nature keep watch to know the hour when a person is to die. The other Fate is responsible for selecting the beautiful strands to be woven into an adornment for paradise; out of the ugliest ones tough bonds are fashioned for the damned." / The skeins already wound and requisitioned for further use were all given little plaques stamped with the relevant name, some in iron, others in silver or gold. / Then they were disposed in thick piles from which a tireless old man was seen taking them away with never a moment's pause, always returning for more. / The old man was so swift and expeditious, he seemed to have been born to run. He kept leaving that hillside with a load of these name-plates gathered in his lap. Where he went and why he did this will be explained to you in the next canto, if you signify with your usual kind attention that this would be agreeable to you.

· · ·

Who will ascend to heaven, mistress mine, to fetch me back my lost wits? They have been ebbing away ever since my heart was transfixed by the arrows shot from your fair eyes—not that I complain of my misfortune so long as it grows no worse than it is now: I fear that any further depletion of my wits shall reduce me to the very condition I have described in Orlando. / I do not imagine, however, that there is any need for me to take flight through the air to the orb of the moon or into paradise in order to recover my wits. I don't believe they inhabit those heights. Their haunts are your beautiful eyes, your radiant face, your ivory breasts, those alabastrine hillocks; and I shall sip them up with my lips if that proves the way to recover them.[4] /

Astolfo went through the spacious palace gazing at all those lives-to-be, after seeing those already spun reeled onto the fateful spools. And he noticed one life-thread which seemed to glitter more than fine gold. If jewels could be skilfully powdered and then spun out in a thread, such a thread[5] would not be remotely as splendid as this one. / The gorgeous thread delighted him beyond measure—it was unique—and there came to him a strong desire to know when this life was to be lived and whose it was to be. The Evangelist made no secret of it: its first year was to be twenty years before the ciphers M and D marked the interval since the birth of the Word Incarnate.[6] / And as this thread was resplendent and beautiful beyond compare, so also would be the uniquely fortunate era which was then to begin: it would derive as a perpetual and unfailing inheritance every one of those rare and eminent graces which man acquires by Nature's or Fortune's kindness, or by his own efforts. /

"Between the mighty branches of the king of rivers," he continued, "there now nestles a humble little village; before it flows the Po; behind it spreads

---

4. Another joking reference to the influence of Alessandra Benucci on the poet.   5. Woven by the Parcae, the Roman fates.   6. Ariosto's hyperbolic and Dantesque announcement of the birth of Ippolito d'Este in 1479.

a misty vortex of deep marsh. I see it becoming, with the passage of time, the fairest of all the cities[7] of Italy, not only for its walls and great regal piles, but also for the quality of its learning and manners. / Such high and sudden eminence will not result from random chance: Heaven has ordained it, so that the city may be a fitting birthplace for the man of whom I speak. A branch is grafted, and its growth carefully fostered when it is expected to fruit; and the jeweller refines his gold if he intends it as a setting for precious gems. / No soul in the realm of Earth was ever clothed in such beauty. Rare has been—and shall be—the spirit descending from these higher spheres who can match the excellence that the Eternal Mind intends to bestow upon Hippolytus of Este. Hippolytus of Este is the name of the one whom God has chosen to inherit so rich a gift. / Those accomplishments which, shared among many, would shed sufficient lustre on them all, will be all concentrated upon the adornment of the man of whom you have asked me to speak. He shall foster the pursuit of every virtue. Were I to give a full description of his eminent merits, I should be carried so far that Orlando would wait in vain for his lost wits." /

Thus did Christ's imitator[8] talk to Astolfo. And when they had seen every room in the great building from which human lives emanated, they emerged beside the river, whose sand-clouded waters ran turbid and repellent. Here they found the old man who kept coming to the river-bank with the name-plates. / I don't know if you remember—the old man we left at the end of the last canto (old in his features, that is, but so sprightly in his movements that he was faster than any deer). He kept endlessly reducing the pile of name-plates, filling his lap with them and dropping—or rather dispersing— his precious burden into the river, known as Lethe.[9] / When the old prodigal came to the river-bank, he shook out his brimming lap and tipped all his plaques into the turbid waters. A countless number sank to the bottom without any use being derived from them; and of the myriad sunk in the sand of the river-bed, scarcely one was preserved. / Crows of every species, greedy vultures and various other birds wheeled and scudded along that river in a strident discord of cries. They all fell on this plentiful bounty when they saw it being scattered; some grasped the plaques in their beaks, others in their hooked talons, but they carried them no distance: / when they tried to take wing, they lacked the strength to lift their burden, so that these magnificent names, too, were robbed by Lethe of their renown. Among so many birds there was but a pair of swans, as white, my Lord,[1] as your device; they, with serene assurance, brought back in their beaks the plaques which fell to them. / In this way those beneficent creatures recovered a few despite the evil designs of the mischievous old man, who would have consigned them all to the river; oblivion consumed the rest. Now swimming, now winging their way through the air, the sacred swans reached a hill beside the cruel river, and on the hill-top, a shrine. / The place was sacred to Immortality. Here a beautiful nymph[2] came down from the hill to the shore of Lethe's stream and took the names from the swans' beaks. And she affixed the names round a statue set upon a pillar in the middle of the shrine. Here she consecrated them and took such care of them that they remained on view for all time. /

Who was the old man, and why did he so fruitlessly impart all those fine

---

7. Ferrara.   8. The apostle John.   9. The river of oblivion separating the world of the living from that of the dead.   1. Ippolito.   2. Fame.

names to the river? And what of the birds, and the holy shrine from which the fair nymph came down to the river's edge? Astolfo wanted to know the latent meaning, to penetrate the mystery of all these things. He asked the man of God about them, and here was his reply: / "Understand that not a bough moves down on earth but its motion is remarked up here. There must be a correspondence, albeit under differing guise, between every effect on earth and in heaven. The old man, whose beard flows down his chest and who is so swift-footed that nothing ever stops him, achieves up here the same effects, the same work, that Time does on earth. / When the threads are fully wound upon the reel, human life comes to an end, down below. Down there fame would persist, up here the echo of it—immortality and divinity subsisting in both spheres—were it not for the bearded one here, and down there for Time constantly at work, ravaging. Our old man, as you can see, throws the names into the river; Time immerses them in eternal oblivion. / And just as up here the crows of various sorts, the vultures and other kinds of birds all strive to pick out of the water the names which catch their eye, so down on earth the same is done by the panders, sycophants, buffoons, pretty-boys, tale-bearers, those who infest the courts and are better welcomed there than men of integrity and worth, / those who are reputed gentlemen at court because they can emulate the donkey, the scavenging hog. Now when just Fate (or rather Venus and Bacchus) have wound up their master's life-thread, all these folk I mention, supine cravens that they are, born only to feed their bellies, carry his name on their lips for a day or two, only to let the burden fall into oblivion. / But as the swans with their glad song convey the plaques safely to the shrine, so it is that men of worth are rescued from oblivion—crueller than death—by poets. O shrewd and sagacious princes, if you follow Caesar's example and make writers your friends you need have no fear of Lethe's waters![3] /

"Poets too are rare as swans—poets worthy of the name—partly because God will not permit too many men of eminence to reign at a time, and partly through the fault of niggardly lords who leave the heaven-sent geniuses to beg. Suppressing good and exalting evil, they banish the fair arts. / Believe me, God has robbed these simpletons of their wits and clouded their judgement, making them shun Poetry so that death should consume them whole and entire. They would otherwise emerge living from the grave even if their lives had been a disgrace: had they only known how to cultivate her friendship, they would give off a fragrance better than spikenard or myrrh. / Aeneas was not as devoted, nor Achilles as strong, nor Hector as ferocious as their reputations suggest.[4] There have existed men in their thousands who could claim preference over them. What has brought them their sublime renown have been the writers honoured with gifts of palaces and great estates donated by these heroes' descendants. / Augustus was not as august and beneficent as Virgil makes him out in clarion tones—but his good taste in poetry compensates for the evil of his proscriptions. And no one would know whether Nero had been wicked—he might even, for all his enemies on earth and in heaven, have left a better name—had he known how to keep friendly with writers. / Homer made Agamemnon appear the victor and the Trojans

---

3. Augustus Caesar was patron of the poets Virgil and Horace, whose verse immortalized the Roman emperor.   4. Aeneas is the epic hero of Virgil's *Aeneid*, and Achilles and Hector are the chief warriors of Homer's *Iliad*.

mere poltroons; he made Penelope faithful to her husband, and victim of a thousand slights from her suitors. But if you want to know what really happened, invert the story: Greece was vanquished, Troy triumphant, and Penelope a whore. / Listen on the other hand to what reputation Dido left behind, whose heart was so chaste: she was reputed a strumpet purely because Virgil was no friend of hers.

"Don't be surprised if this embitters me and if I talk about it at some length—I like writers and am doing my duty by them, for in your world I was a writer too. / And I, above all others, acquired something which neither Time nor Death can take from me: I praised Christ and merited from Him the reward of so great a good fortune. I am sorry for those who live in an evil day when Courtesy has shut her door: pallid, lean, and wizened, they beat at it day and night in vain. / So, as I was saying, poets and scholars are few and far between. Where they are offered neither board nor lodging even the wild beasts desert the place." As the saintly old man said this his eyes blazed like two flames. Then he turned to Astolfo with a gentle smile and his overwrought face became once more serene. /

But let us leave Astolfo with the Gospel-maker, for I want to leap the distance between heaven and earth—my wings can no longer support me at such heights.

*   *   *

FROM CANTO 39

[Orlando Regains His Wits]

The fleet was still waiting off the Moorish coast for a more favourable wind when a ship put in there, laden with captive warriors.[5] / It was carrying those whom bold Rodomont had captured at the perilous bridge where the tilting-ground was so restricted, as I have several times mentioned earlier. Among these were Oliver (brother of Orlando's wife), loyal Brandimart, Samsonet, and others whom I need not name—Germans, Italians, and Gascons. / Here the master, unaware of the enemy's presence, brought in his galley, leaving the port of Algiers, his intended goal, many miles astern, for a strong wind had got up and driven him beyond it. Now he imagined he was putting into a safe refuge, like Procne[6] returning to her twittering nest. / But when he noticed the Imperial Eagle, the Golden Lilies, and the Leopards[7] close by, he blanched like a man suddenly aware that his incautious foot has trodden upon a horrid poisonous snake which has been slumbering torpidly in the grass: he recoils in a fright and flees from the angry, venomous reptile. / But the master could not escape, nor conceal his prisoners. With Brandimart, Oliver, Samsonet, and many others he was brought before Astolfo and Dudone, who showed delight on seeing their friends. These requested that their warder, to requite him for bringing them here, be condemned to the galley-benches. / The Christian knights, as I said, were welcomed by Astolfo, in whose pavilion a banquet was given in their honour, and they were provided with arms and all else of which they stood in need. For their sakes Dudone postponed his departure: no less was to be gained, he felt, from

5. Astolfo has joined the Christian warriors whom Rodomont defeated and sent into captivity.   6. Sister of Philomela and wife of Tereus, she was transformed into a swallow.   7. Insignia of the Christian armies.

conversing with barons such as these than from setting out a day or two earlier. / He received reliable information about France and Charlemagne—how they were faring—and about where a landing would be safest and most effective.

While he was listening to them, they became aware of a growing pandemonium, and the alarm was raised so frantically that they all fell to wondering. / Astolfo and his goodly company, all in a group conversing, were armed and mounted in a trice and hastened towards the centre of the commotion, questioning everyone along the way. And they reached a spot where they beheld a man so ferocious that, though naked and alone, he was ravaging the whole army. / He had a wooden staff which he swung before him, and it was so solid and heavy and so firmly clenched that at every swing a man fell to the ground in not the best of health. Already he had dispatched more than a hundred, and no one any longer tried to resist him unless by shooting arrows from a distance—certainly no one ventured to await his approach. /

Dudone, Astolfo, and Brandimart and Oliver, who had hastened towards the noise, were still marvelling at the savage's great strength and remarkable spirit when they saw a damsel dressed in black come galloping up on a palfrey; she greeted Brandimart and threw her arms about his neck. /

It was Fiordiligi, who was so inflamed with love for Brandimart that, when she left him captive at the narrow bridge, she almost went crazy with sorrow. She had crossed the sea after learning from Rodomont, his captor, that he had been sent prisoner to Algiers with many knights. / On the point of embarking at Marseilles, she had found a Levantine ship which had brought an old retainer of King Monodant, Brandimart's father. He had scoured many a province, wandering over land and sea in search of Brandimart; on the way he had received news that he was to be found in France. / Now she recognized him for Bardino, the man who had abducted Brandimart as a little boy from his father and taken him to be brought up at Rocca Silvana. When she learned the reason for his journey, she had induced him to set sail with her, telling him how Brandimart had come to cross over to Africa. / On landing, they heard that Bizerta was besieged by Astolfo, and it was rumoured that Brandimart was with him. At sight of him, Fiordiligi sped towards him, giving clear evidence of the joy which was all the greater for the sorrows that had preceded it. / The courteous knight was no less pleased to see his loyal true-love whom he adored above all else; he embraced and hugged her in a gentle welcome, and the first kiss did not sate his inflamed desire, nor did the second or third.

He looked up, however, and noticed Bardino, her companion. / He reached out, meaning to embrace him and ask what brought him here, but there was no time: the army was fleeing in disorder before the staff with which the naked madman was clearing himself a path. Fiordiligi scrutinized the naked man's face and cried to Brandimart, "It's the count!" / At the same time Astolfo, who was present, recognized him for Orlando by certain signs he had been advised of by the holy ancients in the Earthly Paradise. Otherwise they should none of them have recognized in him the noble baron: after so long disdaining his own body, in his folly, his face resembled a beast's more than a man's. / Stabbed to the heart with pity, Astolfo turned, weeping, to Dudone, who stood beside him, and then to Oliver: "Look!" he cried. "That's Orlando!" And they all gazed at him intently, wide-eyed; to find him thus reduced filled them with wonder and compassion. / Most of those lords were moved to tears of distress.

"Now is the time to discover the art of healing him," observed Astolfo, "not to weep over him." With this he jumped from his horse, and so did Brandimart, Samsonet, Oliver, and saintly Dudone, and all together they fell upon Charlemagne's nephew, to capture him. / Seeing himself encircled, Orlando swung his staff in frantic desperation, and taught Dudone the serious consequences of his rashness when he tried to venture within arm's length, his head protected by his shield. Were it not for Oliver absorbing part of the blow with his sword, Orlando's injudicious staff would have shattered Dudone's shield, helmet, head, and torso. / It broke only his shield, though landing such a thump on his helmet that he fell to the ground.

Meanwhile Samsonet swung his sword with such vigour that it caught the staff two arms' lengths from the top and cut it clean in two, while Brandimart grabbed him from behind, clinching him with both arms as tightly as he could, and Astolfo seized him round the legs. / Orlando gave a jerk which sent Astolfo flying off to land on his back ten feet away. But Brandimart, who had a tighter hold, he could not shake off. Oliver ventured too close and received a clout so severe that it felled him: he turned ashy pale and the blood gushed from his nose and eyes. / Had his helmet been less than perfect, Oliver would have been killed by that clout; as it was, he fell like one who has rendered up his soul to paradise. Back on their feet, Astolfo, Dudone (the latter's face swollen), and Samsonet, who had delivered the deft stroke, all jumped on Orlando together. / Dudone clasped him forcefully from behind and tried tripping him up. Astolfo and the rest clung onto his arms, but even so, their combined efforts could not hold him. Anyone who has seen a bull being baited—savage jaws snap at his ears, and as he runs off, bellowing, he drags the hounds along with him but cannot shake free of them—/ may imagine Orlando dragging all those warriors with him.

At this point Oliver got up from the ground where the great blow had felled him; and seeing that this was no way to achieve what Astolfo intended, he hit upon a plan to bring down Orlando, and put it into effect—successfully. / He called for ropes, quickly made a slipknot in one end of each, had some of them secured to the Count's arms and legs, the rest round his body. Then he distributed the other rope-ends to those present, and thus brought down Orlando, the way a farrier will bring down a horse or ox. / Once down, they were all on top of him, and bound his hands and feet yet more securely. Orlando jerked this way and that, but his efforts were all in vain. Astolfo now ordered him to be removed, saying that he was going to heal him. Dudone, a giant, loaded him onto his back and carried him down the beach to the water's edge. / Astolfo had him washed seven times, and seven times had him plunged beneath the water so as to cleanse his face and brutish limbs of the unsightly layers of grime. Then, with certain herbs gathered to this end, he had his mouth sealed, as it puffed and huffed, for he was not to draw breath other than through his nose. / Astolfo had prepared the phial which contained Orlando's wits. This he applied to the count's nose to such effect that, as he inhaled, he sucked it dry.

O wonder of wonders! He recovered his wits in their pristine condition—and intellect, brighter and more lucid than ever, once more informed his graceful speech. / As one who, in a heavy, oppressive sleep, has been seeing horrible shapes of monsters who do not and cannot exist, or has dreamt of having committed some gross enormity, lingers in wonderment when sleep is ended and he is once more master of his senses: so Orlando, recovered from his ravings, remained bemused and stupefied. / He stared at Brandimart, at Oliver (fair Aude's brother[8]), and at Astolfo who had restored his senses to him; and, as he looked at them in utter silence, he mused on how and since when he came to be here. He turned his gaze this way and that but could not conceive where he was. He wondered at finding himself naked, and bound with so many ropes from shoulders to feet. / Then, choosing the words uttered by sobered Silenus to those who had trussed him up in the cave, "Solvite me,"[9] he said; and his face was so serene, his eyes so much less crazy than before, that he was untied; and they supplied him with clothing which they had sent for. Bitterly he regretted his aberration, and they all consoled him. /

His old self once more, a paragon of wisdom and manliness, Orlando also found himself cured of love: the damsel who had seemed hitherto so beautiful and good in his eyes, and whom he had so adored, he now dismissed as utterly worthless. His only concern, his only wish now was to recover all that Love had stolen from him. /

* * *

FROM CANTO 41

[Ruggiero Is Baptized and Hears a Prophecy][1]

But would it not be unpardonable, my Lord, if in my urge to pursue their story, I left Ruggiero in the sea so long that he drowned? / The young man struck out through the formidable swell with his arms and legs. If there was menace in the wind and sea, he suffered worse anxiety from his conscience. He feared that Christ was taking vengeance upon him: he had made so light about obtaining baptism in clean water when the occasion offered, and now he was being baptized in this bitter, salt water. / He recalled the promises so often made to his lady, and the oath he had sworn before fighting Rinaldo, none of which he had honoured. Penitently he asked God time and again not to punish him now, and swore faithfully from the bottom of his heart to become a Christian if he set foot on shore, / and never more to take up sword or lance for the Moors against the Christians. He would return straight to France and render due honours to Charlemagne; he would no longer dally with Bradamant but would achieve the honourable consummation of his love. By a miracle, as he made his vow he felt an increase of strength and swam more buoyantly. / He gathered strength and, his spirit unflagging, he struck the waves and swept them aside. The waves followed hard upon each other; one raised him up, the next carried him forward. Thus, bobbing up and down, he struggled to the shore and finally emerged from the water, soaked through, at a point where the rock sloped most gently into the sea. /

All the others who had abandoned ship were overwhelmed by the waves and remained in the water; Ruggiero, however, climbed out onto the lone rock, as it pleased God in His great goodness. Once he was safe from the

8. First allusion to the fact that Orlando is married, to Aude (or Alda).   9. "Release me," the words spoken by Virgil's Silenus, father of the satyrs, when he awakens from a drunken stupor in eclogue 8.
1. On his way to rejoin his sovereign, Agramant, in Africa, Ruggiero is shipwrecked.

sea on the stark, barren rock, though, a new fear possessed him of being exiled within such narrow confines and of meeting his death here from privations. / Still, with indomitable heart and ready to endure whatever Heaven sent him, he set out boldly to climb the hard rock, making straight for the top of the cliff.

He had not gone a hundred steps when he saw a man ravaged by years and abstinence; his dress and manner proclaimed him a hermit worthy of all deference and respect. / When Ruggiero was close by the hermit called out to him, "Saul, Saul, why do you persecute my Faith?"[2] just as the Lord had spoken to Saint Paul when he struck him down, to his redemption. "You expected to cross the sea without paying your passage, and to defraud another of his due. See, God has a long reach and grasps you when you think you are furthest from Him!" / The holy man had that night been sent a vision by God of how with His help Ruggiero was to reach this rock. God had given him a complete revelation of Ruggiero: all his past life, his future, his atrocious death, his sons, and grandsons, too, and all his posterity. / The hermit went on first to upbraid Ruggiero, then to console him. He chided him for having delayed placing his neck in the gentle yoke, for doing grudgingly, when he saw Christ threaten him with a whip, what he should have done when he was under no compulsion and Christ had called him with entreaties. / Then he consoled him, saying that whether early or late, God does not deny Christ to those who seek Him; he told him the Gospel parable of the labourers in the vineyard who all received the same wage.[3]

With charity and devoted zeal the hermit instructed Ruggiero in the Faith as they walked slowly towards his cell, which was cut out of the hard rock. / Above the holy cell stood a chapel facing East; it was beautiful and convenient. Below it a wood stretched down to the water's edge, planted with laurel, juniper, myrtle, and fruitful palms; it was forever watered by a murmuring spring which cascaded down from the summit. / It was almost forty years since the hermit had come to this rock, a place chosen for him by the Lord as suitable for leading the holy life of a solitary. He lived off the fruit of one tree and another and off pure water. Now he had reached his eightieth year— a healthy, robust existence free of worries. / The old man lit a fire in the cell, and loaded the table with an assortment of fruit, so that Ruggiero could restore himself a little once he had dried his clothes and hair. He learned here at greater leisure all the great mysteries of our Faith and the next day the old man baptized him in the pure spring. / Ruggiero was most content to stay in this place, for the good servant of God declared his intention of sending him back in a few days to where he most wanted to go. Meanwhile they talked of many things—the kingdom of God, Ruggiero's own affairs, his posterity. /

The Lord, who knows and sees all, had revealed to the holy hermit that Ruggiero would live for seven years, no more, from the day he received the faith; the slaying of Pinabello by his lady Bradamant would be laid at his door, as well as Bertolai's death at his hands; and he would be killed by those evil Maganzas, a ruthless clan.[4] / This treachery would remain so hidden that

2. The Lord's words to Saul, or Paul, on the road to Damascus, which precipitate the great persecutor of the Christian faith's conversion. Acts 9.4. **3.** Matthew 20.1–16: all earn the same wages, regardless of the hour at which they begin to serve the master. **4.** Enemies of the house of Agolant, to which Orlando, Rinaldo, and Bradamant belong.

no news of it would leak out, for he would be buried at the very spot where he was killed by the wicked men. Therefore he would not be at once avenged by his sister[5] and his faithful wife who would, while heavy with child, make a long journey in search of him. /

Here, between the Adige and the Brenta, at the foot of the hills which so enchanted the Trojan Antenor[6]—with their sulphur springs and gentle brooks, their smiling ploughlands and pleasant meadows—that he gladly chose them in preference to his own Mount Ida, his lamented Lake Ascanius and beloved River Xanthus: here in the forest, not far from Phrygian Ateste,[7] she was to bear her child. / Her child, also called Ruggiero, would grow up handsome and valorous. Those Trojans would recognize him as of Trojan blood and elect him their lord. Then Charlemagne, whom he, as a young man, would help against the Lombards, would give him the right to rule over this fair land, and the honourable title of Marquis. / And as Charles in making this award, would say to him in Latin, "Este Signori qui,"[8] the land would, as a good omen, be known to future ages as Este: the first two letters of the earlier name Ateste would be dropped. God had also predicted to His servant the harsh vengeance obtained for Ruggiero. / A little before daybreak he would appear to his faithful wife in a dream and tell her who it was who had slain him, and show her the place where he lay. So she with her redoubtable sister-in-law Marfisa would destroy Ponthieu by fire and the sword; nor would the Maganzas suffer any less injury from her son Ruggiero, when he was old enough. / The holy old man spoke to Ruggiero about many an Azzo, Alberto and Obice and their fine posterity up to Niccolò, Leonello, and Borso, Ercole and Alfonso, Hippolytus and Isabel;[9] he restrained his tongue, however, and divulged less than he knew—he told Ruggiero what it was suitable to disclose and suppressed what required suppressing. /

*　　*　　*

FROM CANTO 46

[Rodomont Interrupts the Wedding of Ruggiero and Bradamant][1]

*　　*　　*

The ladies and knights scrutinized the embroideries[2] without understanding them, for they had no one to explain to them that they represented what lay in the future; but they took pleasure in admiring the beautifully-wrought faces and in reading the inscriptions. Alone Bradamant rejoiced in secret: instructed by Melissa, she knew their full history. / Although Ruggiero was not as well-versed as Bradamant, he still recalled how frequently Atlas had commended this Hippolytus among his descendants.

Who could recite in full the many courtesies bestowed by Charlemagne upon everyone? There was a constant variety of festive games, and the table was always laden with food. / Here it became evident who were the champion warriors, for each day a thousand lances were broken. Combats were fought,

---

5. Marfisa, the poem's other warrior-woman.　　6. Mythical Trojan founder of Padua.　　7. Castle of the Este, founded by Trojans (Phrygians). *Ida:* mountain at Troy. *Lake Ascanius and River Xanthus:* lake and river at Troy.　　8. Pun on the name of the Este family.　　9. Illustrious members of the Este family.　　1. After considerable opposition from Bradamant's parents, Ruggiero and Bradamant are at last to wed.　　2. The wedding party has been admiring a tapestry containing a prophecy of the future Este dynasty.

mounted and on foot, some paired off, others in a *mêlée*. Ruggiero showed greater prowess than the rest; he jousted day and night, and always won. In dancing, in wrestling, in everything he always emerged the honoured victor. /

On the final day, at the opening of the solemn festive banquet, while Charlemagne was sitting with Bradamant and Ruggiero on his right and left, a knight in armour appeared out of the landscape, riding full tilt towards the banqueters. Like his steed, the knight was all in black; he was of giant build and arrogant mien. / He was Rodomont, King of Algiers. After the humiliation inflicted on him at his bridge by Bradamant, he had sworn not to wear armour, hold sword or sit saddle until he had spent a year, a month and a day in a cell as a hermit. (Thus knights in those days used to punish themselves for such lapses.) / Although in this interval he heard of all that had happened to Charlemagne and to his own liege, Agramant, so as not to deny his oath, he still would not take up arms, as though none of this concerned him. But once he had seen out the year, the month, and the day, here he came to the French court with new arms, new steed, sword and lance. /

He did not dismount or bow or make any gesture of respect: he displayed only contempt for Charles and his paladins and the mighty lords here present. All were astonished that he took such liberties; they pushed aside their food, broke off their conversations and listened to what the warrior had to say. /

When he stood opposite Charles and Ruggiero he loftily cried out: "I am Rodomont, King of Sarthia, and I challenge you, Ruggiero, to battle. Before the sun sets I mean to prove to you that you have been disloyal to your liege and that, as a traitor, you deserve no place of honour amid these knights.[3] / Although your treason is transparent because, being a Christian, you cannot deny it, to make it clearer still I have come to prove it in these lists. If anyone here offers to fight for you, I shall accept him; and if one does not suffice, I shall accept half a dozen—to all I shall maintain what I have said to you." /

At these words Ruggiero stood up and, with Charlemagne's leave, retorted that he lied, as did anyone who called him a traitor. His behaviour towards his liege had always been such that no accusation could rightfully be made against him. He was ready to maintain that he had always done his duty to him. / He was capable of defending his cause, he affirmed, without invoking anybody's help: indeed, he expected to show Rodomont that a single opponent would be as much as—and possibly more than—he could handle. Rinaldo, Orlando, the Marquis Oliver, his sons Grifon the White and Aquilant the Black, Dudone, Marfisa, all rushed to defend Ruggiero against the fierce pagan / on the grounds that a new bridegroom should not upset his honeymoon. To all Ruggiero replied: "Stop fussing—these excuses are ignoble!"

The armour (once Mandricard the Tartar's)[4] was fetched and all delays were curtailed. Count Orlando fitted Ruggiero's spurs, Charlemagne slung the sword at his side, / Bradamant and Marfisa put on his breastplate and other armour. Astolfo held his thoroughbred, Dudone son of Ogier held his stirrup, Rinaldo, Namo, and Oliver promptly cleared the lists, driving everyone out of the arena kept ever-ready for combats. /

3. Rodomont accuses Ruggiero, a convert to Christianity, of being a traitor to the loyalties he owes to the Islamic religion and to Agramant.   4. In his final battle with Rodomont, Ruggiero wears the complete armor of Hector of Troy (pieces of which caused many of the battles between knights during the course of the poem).

Matrons and maids blanched with fear for Ruggiero, who seemed to them no match for the ferocious pagan. They were like doves driven from the cornfields back to their nests by raging winds in a storm of thunder and lightning, while the inky sky threatens rain and hail to cause havoc among the crops. / The common people and most of the knights and barons read the odds no differently, for they had not yet forgotten what the pagan had done to Paris: all alone he had destroyed a great part of it by fire and the sword—the evidence still remained and would for many a day. Nowhere else did the realm suffer greater damage. /

Bradamant's heart trembled more than any other's, not that she imputed to Rodomont the greater strength or the greater courage; not that she believed that Justice was on the pagan's side (She often commits the honours of battle to her allies). But she could not avoid being afraid, for anxiety is a natural product of love. / Oh how willingly would she have taken that uncertain battle upon herself, even had she been more than certain of losing her life in it! She would have chosen to die any number of deaths (if death may be endured more than once) rather than permit her spouse to run the risk. / But she could find no way of persuading him to leave the combat to her; all she could do was glumly to watch the battle, her heart in her mouth.

Ruggiero and the pagan hurtled towards each other, lances lowered. At the impact the lances seemed to turn into icicles, their shafts into birds which flew into the sky. / The pagan's lance struck Ruggiero's shield full in the middle, but to little effect, so perfect was the steel which Vulcan had tempered for glorious Hector.[5] Ruggiero equally attained the other's shield, but he pierced it through, for all that it was bone, plated inside and out with steel and five inches thick. / Ruggiero's lance could not withstand the heavy impact and failed him at the first assault, breaking into splinters which seemed to wing their way sky-high; were it not for this, it would in its savage onset have pierced the breastplate, even had it been coated with adamant, and the battle would have been over. But the lance broke, and both horses sank back onto their cruppers. /

With bridle and spur the knights forced the steeds back onto their feet; and, tossing aside their lances, they seized their swords and returned to strike each other with cruel savagery. With masterly skill they turned their spirited mounts (aptly light-footed) this way and that as they applied their pointed swords to testing each other's armour for flaws. / Today Rodomont did not have the tough dragon's-hide breastplate on his chest, nor did he have Nembrot's[6] sharp sword nor his usual helmet on his head: when he lost to Bradamant on the bridge, he left his usual arms appended to the shrine-wall, as I believe I related to you earlier. / He had other arms of highest quality but not as perfect as his usual ones—not that either the old nor the present arms, nor even stronger ones would have resisted Balisard, for no enchantment or spell, no steel however choice or finely tempered could withstand it. Ruggiero strove to such good effect that he pierced the pagan's armour in a number of places. /

Now the pagan, seeing his armour bloodied at so many points, and aware that he could not prevent most of the sword-strokes reaching his flesh, was

---

5. Like Achilles and Aeneas, Ruggiero bears a great shield forged by Vulcan.   6. Builder of the Tower of Babel, and Rodomont's ancestor.

goaded to a greater fury than the sea in a winter storm. He threw away his shield and with all his might brought his sword down two-handed on Ruggiero's helmet. / He put all his weight (and no weight was heavier) behind his two-handed blow as he struck Ruggiero: the force of it was similar to that of the pile-driver on twin pontoons in the Po which, after being raised by men with winches, drops onto the pointed stakes. The enchanted helmet saved Ruggiero—without it, the blow would have cleft rider and steed in two. / Twice he sagged; he slackened his arms and legs to fall. Before he had a chance to recover the Saracen repeated his savage blow. Then he made to strike a third time, but the fine sword could not withstand so intense a hammering—it flew into splinters, leaving the cruel pagan disarmed. / This did not stop Rodomont, who flung himself on his dazed opponent while his head was so benumbed, his brain so clouded. The Saracen shook him awake all right: he threw a powerful arm round his neck and put him in so tight a clinch as to root him out of the saddle, then flung him to the ground. /

The moment he hit the ground he was on his feet, more ashamed, even, than angry, for he glanced at Bradamant and saw the dismay on her lovely face: his fall had filled her with well-nigh mortal anxiety. Quickly to amend this disgrace, Ruggiero seized his sword and faced the pagan. / Rodomont drove his steed at him, but Ruggiero skilfully avoided him, stepping back, and as he passed, grabbed the horse's bridle in his left hand and slewed him round, while with his right he sought to wound the other in the side or the belly or chest. He hurt him in two places—in the flank and thigh. / Now Rodomont, who still held the pommel and hilt of his broken sword, struck Ruggiero such a blow on the helmet that one more would have knocked him senseless. But Ruggiero, to whom victory justly belonged, grasped him by the arm and, using both hands, tugged so hard that he finally dragged him from the saddle. /

Whether it was his strength or his agility, the pagan landed in such a way as to retain an equal footing with Ruggiero: he landed, that is, on his feet. Otherwise it was felt that Ruggiero, with his sword, was in the stronger position. Ruggiero tried to hold off the pagan and avoid a close grapple: he had no interest in permitting so large and thick-set a man to fall upon him. / Meanwhile he observed how the Saracen was bleeding from his side and thigh and other wounds: he hoped that he would weaken little by little until he had to concede victory. Rodomont, though, still held the sword-hilt and pommel and, gathering all his strength, he hurled it at Ruggiero. The impact stunned him worse than ever—/ it struck him on his helmeted cheek and on the shoulder, and the blow made him reel and stagger and almost collapse. The pagan now made for him, but his foot betrayed him, weak as he was from his thigh-wound: trying to move faster than he could, he fell onto one knee. /

Ruggiero was quick to strike him violently in the chest and face; he hammered him and, clasping him tightly, wrestled him to the ground. With an effort the pagan regained his feet and hugged Ruggiero in a body-clinch. Together they turned and shook and strained, uniting skill with extreme force. / Rodomont, however, had been drained of much of his strength through his opened thigh and flank, while Ruggiero, with his agility, skill, and experience as a wrestler, felt he possessed the advantage and meant to retain it. Where he saw the pagan's blood flowing most freely, where his wounds were the worst he attacked him, using his chest as also both hands and feet. / In a passion of rage, the pagan seized Ruggiero by the neck and shoulders; he tugged and heaved, he levered him off the ground on his chest, he spun him this way and that, clinched him, and strove to make him fall. But Ruggiero remained self-possessed and called upon all his prudence and valour in order to maintain the upper hand. /

After trying several different holds, the doughty champion put a lock on his opponent, heaved his chest over to the left and bent all his might to holding him there; at the same time he advanced his right leg, thrust it between the other's knees and strained: this lifted Rodomont clear of the ground. He flung him down on his head. / Rodomont dented the ground with his head and shoulders; such was the impact that a gush of blood from his wounds spurted high to dye the earth red. To prevent the Saracen from rising again, Ruggiero, who had Fortune by the mane, held a dagger over his eyes with one hand while the other clutched his throat as he knelt on his belly. / In the gold-mines of Hungary or Spain it sometimes happens that the roof suddenly caves in upon the miners lured in by base cupidity, and they are crushed to a point where they can scarcely draw breath; the Saracen, once he was floored, found the victor no less oppressive. /

Ruggiero had drawn his dagger and brandished it over Rodomont's visor as he tried with menaces to make him surrender, offering to spare his life in exchange. But Rodomont, less appalled by death than by the betrayal of the smallest sign of cowardice, jerked and twisted and applied all his strength to rolling on top of Ruggiero: but he answered not a word. / Imagine a mastiff beneath a ferocious wolfhound which has clamped its teeth on his throat: with blazing eye and frothing mouth the mastiff strives in vain to free himself of the predator's grip, but the latter surpasses him in strength if not in fury. Similarly any thought the pagan had of escaping from beneath victorious Ruggiero proved ineffectual. / He twisted and struggled nonetheless until he brought his right arm back into play; in his hand he clasped a dagger which he too had drawn in the fray, and now he tried to stab Ruggiero beneath his back-plate. The young man realized the trap[7] into which he might fall if he delayed dispatching the impious Saracen; / so two or three times he raised his arm to its full height and plunged the dagger to the hilt in Rodomont's forehead, thus assuring his own safety.

Released from its body, now ice-cold, the angry spirit which, among the living, had been so proud and insolent, fled cursing down to the dismal shores of Acheron.[8]

7. Italian, *errore*. When Ruggiero avoids "error" and "delay," he rejects the key words of the romance form, and the poem concludes with a revision of the end of Virgil's epic, the *Aeneid*. 8. Hell.

BALDESAR CASTIGLIONE
1478–1529

The cultivation of manners mattered enormously to the courts of sixteenth-century Europe, and no book shaped their ideal formulation more than Castiglione's *The*

Book of the Courtier (1528), a dialogue on the qualities of the perfect courtier. Although set in Urbino, Italy, the *Courtier* quickly became a European phenomenon. The Emperor Charles V was said to have especially loved three books: Machiavelli's *Discourses* on the Roman history of Titus Livy, the work of the ancient Greek historian Polybius, and Castiglione's *Courtier*. Henry VIII, Mary Queen of Scots, Catherine de Médicis, and Francis I owned copies in the Italian. Translations into Latin, then the universal language of diplomacy in Europe, allowed the *Courtier* to make a fully cosmopolitan appearance before the learned elite. More fascinating were the book's translations into the customs as well as the languages of different European states. In his 1561 English translation, Sir Thomas Hoby remarked that Castiglione's courtier "has a long time haunted all the courts of Christendom," and has now "become an Englishman . . . and willing to dwell in the Court of England." 1566 saw the appearance of a *Polish Courtier,* which carefully revised the Italian text to suit the customs of its new country. The *Courtier's* popularity was by no means confined to princes, aristocrats, and the educated elite from Roger Ascham and John Locke in England to the Inca Garcilaso in Peru: by the end of the century, Castiglione's behavior manual could be found in the libraries of lawyers, physicians, merchants, and their wives.

Baldesar Castiglione, a nobleman from the region of Mantua in northern Italy, was born in Casanatico. His parents—his father was a courtier and mother a Gonzaga, related to the powerful Mantuan lords—sent him to Milan to be brought up in the spectacular court of Ludovico Sforza, who compensated for his upstart status by flamboyantly displaying his wealth and power. Castiglione served Francesco Gonzaga, marquis of Mantua, from 1499 until 1503, when he requested a transfer to the service of Guidobaldo da Montefeltro, duke of Urbino. Infuriated by the request, Francesco Gonzaga barred Castiglione from entering Mantuan territory, even to visit his mother; he did not forgive Castiglione until 1516, when he once again employed him in diplomatic services and even arranged Castiglione's marriage to Ippolita, a member of the Torelli family. In the court of Urbino, Castiglione served as a diplomat for Guidobaldo and later for his adopted heir, Francesco Maria della Rovere, commander of the pope's army. In 1506 he traveled to England to accept the Order of the Garter from Henry VII on behalf of Duke Guidobaldo. He later fought in the siege of Mirandola under Pope Julius II (1511) and, in reward for this and other services, was given the title of count. During the time he lived in Rome, as the Gonzaga family's ambassador to Pope Leo X, Castiglione made many friends, including the artists Michelangelo and Raphael, who painted a splendid portrait of Castiglione for his wedding.

Castiglione worked on the first draft of his *Courtier* during the years 1513–18. The grasping Pope Leo X excommunicated Francesco Maria della Rovere in 1516 and appropriated the dukedom of Urbino for his nephew. While Castiglione worked on the second draft of the *Courtier* in the early 1520s, he experienced a series of losses, including the deaths of his friend Raphael in April of 1520 and of his wife, who died in childbirth in August of the same year. In 1524 Pope Clement VII sent him to Spain as papal ambassador, or *nuncio,* to the court of the Emperor Charles V. Castiglione was still jointly serving the pope and Charles V three years later when Charles marched through Italy and attacked and plundered Rome, to the horror of Europeans who venerated Rome as the eternal, unconquerable city. The shock and embarrassment to Castiglione, put in an impossible position between the pope and the emperor, cost him his health: despite receiving continued approval from both of his masters— he was even elected bishop of Ávila in Spain—Castiglione died in Toledo in 1529, one year after the *Courtier* appeared and two years after the sack of Rome. At his funeral, the Emperor Charles V famously declared, "I tell you that one of the best knights (*caballeros*) of the world is dead."

In his letter to the bishop of Viseu, Castiglione explains that he was moved to write *The Book of the Courtier* when Duke Guidobaldo died: he wished to repay an emotional debt to the man who had fostered a court unmatched for its grace and distinction. The *Courtier* is an idealized commemoration of the court at Urbino. Divided into four books, it takes the form of a dialogue that took place over the four nights following a papal visit to Urbino, an occasion that gathered many illustrious courtiers and statesmen at the tiny court. Castiglione modestly exempts himself from the dialogue, which discusses the ideal qualities of the courtier, by claiming that he was in England at the time. Presiding silently over the conversation is the duchess, whose virtue and authority draw the company into what Castiglione calls the "golden chain of concord" that is their often contentious, if stylistically genial, conversation. The dialogue's form, as Castiglione takes pains to point out, has classical roots in Plato's *Republic* (the utopian city), Xenophon's *Education of Cyrus* (the ideal prince), and Cicero's *Orator* (the best speaker). Although the classical models help locate Castiglione's dialogue within moral and political philosophy, his text differs in important respects. Whereas Plato's Socrates and Cicero's orator hold forth as teachers to raptly attentive students, Castiglione's speakers insist on their own insufficiency and the superior qualifications of others in the company and must be cajoled or ordered to speak. When they reluctantly take up the authoritative position of speaker, it becomes obvious that they use the elaborate displays of diffidence and deference as a form of social armor: their speeches are usually greeted with a challenge. The speakers express dissent either laughingly, in the approved style, or if the spirit of rivalry momentarily overpowers their social decorum, with uncontrolled aggression. In such cases, Emilia Pia, the duchess's representative, teasingly reprimands the tactless speaker and guides the conversation back from dangerous extremes. As the *Courtier* unfolds, it becomes clear that the community, however affectionate, must constantly negotiate the differences and antipathies of class (the count differs with his social inferior on the importance of nobility in the ideal courtier), sex (the women at one point laughingly assault the group's most outspoken misogynist, or condemner of women), city-state (the Genoese republican and the citizen of a monarchy disagree about the ideal form of government), and religious temperament.

"Forming in words a perfect Courtier" is the object of the dialogue, or "game." Because the *Courtier* expresses great faith in the power of words to educate readers and create the ideal courtier, it has sometimes been criticized for its idealism, especially by those who prefer the prudential thought of Machiavelli's *The Prince*. In fact, the *Courtier* touches on both idealistic and prudential thinking and is ambivalent about surrendering to either a wholly optimistic (and potentially escapist) mode or a cynically pragmatic one. When Castiglione investigates political ethics, he avoids reaching a final resolution. He seems more comfortable describing the technical aspects of the ideal courtier's performance before admiring spectators, and he devotes lavish attention to their description. The courtier must above all be outstanding in combat and horsemanship. The proportion of the dialogue devoted to amplifying the ideal courtier's physical prowess is entirely consistent with the emphases of Renaissance Italian courts: in the court of Ludovico Sforza, for example, the humanist education of children is secondary to preparation in the martial arts (Castiglione himself sought out sword-and-buckler lessons for his six-year-old son). Nonetheless, the dialogue's most memorable and distinctive contribution to ideal courtiership is its elaboration of the social arts, in which the only thing worse than affectation is artlessness. Grace and lack of affectation are key words for the perfect courtier. So is *mediocrità*, which is not "mediocrity" but "moderation": it is the ability to avoid embarrassing or transgressive extremes and is associated with the "golden mean" of classical antiquity. For the courtier's defining word, *sprezzatura*, there is no adequate translation: it is the fine art of apparently effortless performance, or nonchalance. Etymologically related to the verbs *disdain* and *deprecate*, *sprezzatura* suggests that the most effective way to make an awe-inspiring impression is to appear utterly unconcerned about the performance and its effect on beholders. An example of *sprezzatura* is the response of one character, Unico Aretino, to a challenge. After a reflective silence, he utters a complete sonnet in praise of the duchess, leaving everyone to wonder: was his performance spontaneous or premeditated? *Sprezzatura* aims to keep them guessing and wanting more.

In book 4, Signor Ottaviano defines a weightier aim of the courtier's arts: "to win for himself, by means of the accomplishments ascribed to him by these gentlemen, the favor and mind of the prince whom he serves that he may be able to tell him, and always will tell him, the truth about everything he needs to know, without fear or risk of displeasing him." The courtier's arts—his skill in music, arms and horsemanship, verse, and talk of love—are "enticements" that beguile the prince

> with salutary deception; like shrewd doctors who often spread the edge of the cup with some sweet cordial when they wish to give a bitter-tasting medicine to sick and over-delicate children. Thus, by using the veil of pleasure to such an end, the Courtier will reach his aim in every time and place and activity.

Through Ottaviano, Castiglione decorously inserts a defense of poetry into the political discourse of book 4: the images of the veil of pleasure and the honey-rimmed cup of bitter herbs come from traditional metaphors for poetic fiction. The courtier's gestural arts are indistinguishable from the writer's rhetorical arts, and both are requirements of the counselor to the prince. The courtier's aim to make his charms profitable, however, is at best a proposition that can be fulfilled only by the good, educable prince. Castiglione, who served in Francesco Maria delle Rovere a man capable of murdering his sister's lover and ordering his men to assassinate a cardinal over a minor annoyance, knew well that Italy's princes too often lacked the self-control that was the hallmark of his ideal courtier. To hope that the courtier's arts could attract and civilize the prince was ambitiously optimistic.

These directly political and pragmatic concerns are implicit in book 1, which is the selection primarily represented here. Its bright atmosphere is darkened by brooding questions about the prince who is capable of making the courtiers' ornamental graces meaningful in the social world. Duke Guidobaldo, ill and crippled from venereal disease, retires nightly after supper: although he is physically absent from the conversation, his blighted promise and his sterility (the duchess, Castiglione says, lives like a widow) cast a gloomy shadow over the dialogue's optimism. The prince most frequently on the speakers' lips is Alexander the Great, the legendary world-conqueror who did everything in extremes (especially fight and drink). Castiglione leaves ambiguous how the graceful courtier, trained in civil arts and *mediocrità*, relates to the immoderate, ambitious, bloodthirsty, and staggeringly successful Alexander. The courtier's precarious social position, especially in its contrasting relationship with Alexander, causes some of Castiglione's speakers to fret that his fine arts render him "effeminate." Throughout the dialogue, the courtier is framed between the imposing image of Alexander the Great and the vulnerable image of a woman. The courtier's grand achievement, his celebrated *mediocrità*, is also his social vulnerability.

Valuable and accessible studies of Castiglione are in Peter Burke, *The Fortunes of the Courtier: the European Reception of Castiglione's Cortegiano* (1995), and the essays in R. W. Hanning and David Rosand, eds., *Castiglione: the Ideal and the Real in Renaissance Culture* (1993). Of more specialized interest are Virginia Cox, *The Renaissance Dialogue: Literary Dialogue in its Social and Political Contexts, Castiglione to Galileo* (1992), and Wayne A. Rebhorn, *Courtly Performances* (1978). For an exciting, thorough discussion of Castiglione's broad historical context, see Lauro Martines, *Power and Imagination: City-States in Renaissance Italy* (1979).

PRONOUNCING GLOSSARY

The following list uses common English syllables and stress accents to provide rough equivalents of selected words whose pronunciation may be unfamiliar to the general reader.

Cesare Gonzaga: *chay'-zah-ray gon-zah'gah*

disinvoltura: *dees-een-vol-tuh'rah*

Gaspar Pallavicino: *gahs-pahr' pahl-lah-vee-chee'noh*

Giuliano de' Medici: *juh-lee-ah'noh day may'dee-chee*

roegarze: *roh-ay-gahr'tzay*

The Book of the Courtier[1]

[From *The Dedication*]

To The Reverend and Illustrious Signor Don Michel de Silva, Bishop of Viseu[2]

[1]

When signor Guidobaldo of Montefeltro, Duke of Urbino, departed this life, I, together with several other gentlemen who had served him, remained in the service of Duke Francesco Maria della Rovere,[3] his heir and successor in the state. And, as the savor of Duke Guido's virtues was fresh in my mind, and the delight that in those years I had felt in the loving company of such excellent persons as then frequented the Court of Urbino, I was moved by the memory thereof to write these books of the Courtier: which I did in but a few days, meaning in time to correct those errors which had resulted from my desire to pay this debt quickly. But Fortune for many years now has kept me ever oppressed by such constant travail that I could never find the leisure to bring these books to a point where my weak judgment was satisfied with them.

Now being in Spain, and being informed from Italy that signora Vittoria della Colonna, Marchioness of Pescara,[4] to whom I had already given a copy of the book, had, contrary to her promise, caused a large part of it to be transcribed, I could not but feel a certain annoyance, fearing the considerable mischief that can arise in such cases.[5] Nevertheless, I trusted that the wisdom and prudence of that lady (whose virtue I have always held in veneration as something divine) would avail to prevent any wrong from befalling me for having obeyed her commands. In the end I learned that that part of the book was in Naples, in the hands of many persons; and, as men are always avid of new things, it appeared that certain of these persons were trying to have it printed. Wherefore, alarmed at this danger, I decided to revise at once such small part of the book as time would permit, with the intention of publishing it, thinking it better to let it be seen even slightly corrected by my own hand than much mutilated by the hands of others.

And so, to carry out this thought, I started to reread it; and immediately, at the very outset, by reason of the dedication, I was seized by no little sadness (which greatly grew as I proceeded), when I remembered that the greater

---

1. Translated by Charles S. Singleton. 2. Dom Miguel de Silva (d. 1556), ambassador to Popes Leo X, Adrian VI, and Clement VII. 3. Nephew and heir (1490–1538) of Guidobaldo of Montefeltro (1472–1508), duke of Urbino. 4. Renowned poet (1492–1547) and wife of the marquess of Pescara. 5. Publication was considered undignified for gentlemen.

part of those persons who are introduced in the conversations were already dead; for, besides those who are mentioned in the proem of the last Book, even messer Alfonso Ariosto, to whom the book is dedicated, is dead: an affable youth, prudent, abounding in the gentlest manners, and apt in everything befitting a man who lives at court. Likewise Duke Giuliano de' Medici, whose goodness and noble courtesy deserved to be enjoyed longer by the world. Messer Bernardo, Cardinal of Santa Maria in Pòrtico, who for his keen and entertaining readiness of wit was the delight of all who knew him, he too is dead. Dead also is signor Ottaviano Fregoso,[6] a most rare man in our times: magnanimous, devout, full of goodness, talent, prudence, and courtesy, and truly a lover of honor and worth, and so deserving of praise that his very enemies were always obliged to praise him; and those misfortunes which he so firmly endured were indeed enough to prove that fortune, as she ever was, is, even in these days, the enemy of virtue. Dead, too, are many others named in the book, to whom nature seemed to promise very long life.

But what should not be told without tears is that the Duchess,[7] too, is dead. And if my mind is troubled at the loss of so many friends and lords, who have left me in this life as in a desert full of woes, it is understandable that I should feel sorrow far more bitter for the death of the Duchess than for any of the others, because she was worth more than the others, and I was much more bound to her than to all the rest. Therefore, in order not to delay paying what I owe to the memory of so excellent a lady, and to that of the others who are no more, and moved too by the threat to my book, I have had it printed and published in such form as the brevity of time permitted.

And since, while they lived, you did not know the Duchess or the others who are dead (except Duke Giuliano and the Cardinal of Santa Maria in Pòrtico), in order to make you acquainted with them, in so far as I can, after their death, I send you this book as a portrait of the Court of Urbino, not by the hand of Raphael or Michelangelo,[8] but by that of a lowly painter and one who only knows how to draw the main lines, without adorning the truth with pretty colors or making, by perspective art,[9] that which is not seem to be. And, although I have endeavored to show in these conversations the qualities and conditions of those who are named therein, I confess that I have not even suggested, let alone expressed, the virtues of the Duchess, because not only is my style incapable of expressing them, but my mind cannot even conceive them; and if I be censured for this or for any other thing deserving of censure (and well do I know that such things are not wanting in the book), I shall not be gainsaying the truth.

* * *

[3]

Others say that since it is so difficult, and well-nigh impossible, to find a man as perfect as I wish the Courtier to be, it was wasted effort to write of

6. Nephew (d. 1524) of Duke Guidobaldo and older brother of Federico (1480–1541). Alfonso Ariosto (1475–1525), distant cousin of the poet Ludovico Ariosto; he urged Castiglione to write the *Courtier* on the suggestion of Francis I of France. Giuliano de' Medici (1479–1516), youngest son of Lorenzo de' Medici; Il Magnifico; and brother of Pope Leo X. Messer Bernardo Dovizi da Bibbiena (1470–1520), a Tuscan, author of the comedy *The Foolish Woman*, friend of the Medici, made cardinal by Pope Leo X. 7. Elisabetta Gonzaga (1471–1526), daughter of the Marquess Federico Gonzaga of Mantua, married Duke Guidobaldo in 1489; due to the frequent illness and retired life of her husband, the Duchess was the central and presiding figure in the life of the court [Translator's note]. 8. Michelangelo Buonarroti (1475–1564), sculptor, painter, architect, and poet. Raffaello Sanzio (1483–1520), painter and native of Urbino. 9. Illusion of three-dimensional space in artwork.

him, because it is useless to try to teach what cannot be learned. To such as these I answer (without wishing to get into any dispute about the Intelligible World or the Ideas) that I am content to have erred with Plato, Xenophon, and Marcus Tullius;[1] and just as, according to these authors, there is the Idea of the perfect Republic, the perfect King, and the perfect Orator, so likewise there is that of the perfect Courtier. And if I have been unable to approach the image of the latter, in my style, then courtiers will find it so much the easier to approach in their deeds the end and goal which my writing sets before them. And if, for all that, they are unable to attain to that perfection, such as it is, that I have tried to express, the one who comes the nearest to it will be the most perfect; as when many archers shoot at a target and none of them hits the bull's eye, the one who comes the closest is surely better than all the rest.

Still others say I have thought to take myself as a model, on the persuasion that the qualities which I attribute to the Courtier are all in me. To these persons I will not deny having tried to set down everything that I could wish the Courtier to know; and I think that anyone who did not have some knowledge of the things that are spoken of in the book, however erudite he might be, could not well have written of them; but I am not so wanting in judgment and self-knowledge as to presume to know all that I could wish to know.

Thus all defense against these charges, and perhaps many others, I leave for the present to the tribunal of public opinion; because more often than not the many, even without perfect knowledge, know by natural instinct the certain savor of good and bad, and, without being able to give any reason for it, enjoy and love one thing and reject and detest another. Hence, if my book pleases in a general way, I shall take it to be good, and I shall think that it is to survive. If, instead, it should not please, I shall take it to be bad and shall at once believe that the memory of it must needs be lost. And if my censors be not yet satisfied with this verdict of public opinion, then let them be content at least with that of time, which reveals the hidden defects of all things, and, being the father of truth and a judge without passion, is wont to pronounce always, on all writing, a just sentence of life or death.

BALDESAR CASTIGLIONE

From *Book 1*

To Messer Alfonso Ariosto

[1]

I have long wondered, dearest messer Alfonso, which of two things was the more difficult for me: to deny you what you have repeatedly and so insistently asked of me, or to do it. For, on the one hand, it seemed very hard for me to deny a thing—especially when it was something praiseworthy—to one whom I love most dearly and by whom I feel I am most dearly loved; yet, on the other hand, to undertake a thing which I was not sure I could finish seemed unbecoming to one who esteems just censure as much as it ought to be esteemed. Finally, after much thought, I have resolved that I would try

1. Plato's *Republic*, Xenophon's *Education of Cyrus*, and Cicero's *Orator*.

in this to see how much aid to diligence might be had from affection and the intense desire that I have to please, which, in things generally, is so wont to increase men's industry.

Now, you have asked me to write my opinion as to what form of Courtiership most befits a gentleman living at the courts of princes, by which he can have both the knowledge and the ability to serve them in every reasonable thing, thereby winning favor from them and praise from others: in short, what manner of man he must be who deserves the name of perfect Courtier, without defect of any kind. Wherefore, considering this request, I say that, had it not seemed to me more blameworthy to be judged by you to be wanting in love than by others to be wanting in prudence, I should have eschewed this labor, out of fear of being thought rash by all who know what a difficult thing it is to choose, from among so great a variety of customs as are followed at the courts of Christendom, the most perfect form and, as it were, the flower of Courtiership. For custom often makes the same things pleasing and displeasing to us; whence it comes about sometimes that the customs, dress, ceremonies, and fashions that were once prized become despised; and, contrariwise, the despised become prized. Hence, it is clearly seen that usage is more powerful than reason in introducing new things among us and in blotting out old things; and anyone who tries to judge of perfection in such matters is often deceived. For which reason, since I am well aware of this and of many another difficulty in the matter whereof it is proposed that I should write, I am forced to excuse myself somewhat and to submit evidence that this is an error (if indeed it can be called error) which I share with you, so that, if I am to be blamed for it, that blame will be shared by you, because your having put upon me a burden beyond my powers must not be deemed a lesser fault than my own acceptance of it.

So let us now make a beginning of our subject, and, if that be possible, let us form such a Courtier that any prince worthy of being served by him, even though he have but small dominion, may still be called a very great lord.

In these books we shall not follow any set order or rule of distinct precepts, as is most often the custom in teaching anything whatever, but, following the manner of many ancient writers, and to revive a pleasant memory, we shall rehearse some discussions which took place among men singularly qualified in such matters. And even though I was not present and did not take part in them, being in England at the time when they occurred, I learned of them shortly thereafter from a person who gave me a faithful report of them;[2] and I shall attempt to recall them accurately, in so far as my memory permits, so that you may know what was judged and thought in this matter by men worthy of the highest praise, and in whose judgment on all things one may have unquestioned faith. Nor will it be beside the purpose to give some account of the occasion of the discussions that took place, so that in due order we may come to the end at which our discourse aims.

[2]

On the slopes of the Apennines toward the Adriatic, at almost the center of Italy, is situated, as everyone knows, the little city of Urbino. And although it sits among hills that are perhaps not as pleasant as those we see in many

---

2. Castiglione, who did not travel to England until after the events described, removes himself from the dialogue for modesty's sake.

other places, still it has been blessed by Heaven with a most fertile and bountiful countryside, so that, besides the wholesomeness of the air, it abounds in all the necessities of life. But among the greater blessings that can be claimed for it, this I believe to be the chief, that for a long time now it has been ruled by excellent lords (even though, in the universal calamity of the wars of Italy, it was deprived of them for a time).[3] But, to look no further, we can cite good proof thereof in the glorious memory of Duke Federico,[4] who in his day was the light of Italy. Nor are there wanting many true witnesses still living who can testify to his prudence, humanity, justice, generosity, undaunted spirit, to his military prowess, signally attested by his many victories, the capture of impregnable places, the sudden readiness of his expeditions, the many times when with but small forces he routed large and very powerful armies, and the fact that he never lost a single battle; so that not without reason may we compare him to many famous men among the ancients.

Among his other laudable deeds, he built on the rugged site of Urbino a palace thought by many the most beautiful to be found anywhere in all Italy and he furnished it so well with every suitable thing that it seemed not a palace but a city in the form of a palace; and furnished it not only with what is customary, such as silver vases, wall hangings of the richest cloth of gold, silk, and other like things, but for ornament he added countless ancient statues of marble and bronze, rare paintings, and musical instruments of every sort; nor did he wish to have anything there that was not most rare and excellent. Then, at great expense, he collected many very excellent and rare books in Greek, Latin, and Hebrew, all of which he adorned with gold and silver, deeming these to be the supreme excellence of his great palace.

[3]

Following then the course of nature and being already sixty-five years old,[5] he died as gloriously as he had lived, leaving as his successor his only son, a child ten years of age and motherless, named Guidobaldo. This boy, even as he was heir to the state, seemed to be heir to all his father's virtues as well, and in his remarkable nature began at once to promise more than it seemed right to expect of a mortal; so that men judged none of the notable deeds of Duke Federico to be greater than his begetting such a son. But Fortune, envious of so great a worth, set herself against this glorious beginning with all her might, so that, before Duke Guido had reached the age of twenty, he fell sick of the gout, which grew upon him with grievous pain, and in a short time so crippled all his members that he could not stand upon his feet or move. Thus, one of the fairest and ablest persons in the world was deformed and marred at a tender age.

And not even content with this, Fortune opposed him so in his every undertaking that he rarely brought to a successful issue anything he tried to do; and, although he was very wise in counsel and undaunted in spirit, it seemed that whatever he undertook always succeeded ill with him whether in arms or in anything, great or small; all of which is attested by his many

3. For a certain period of time, Duke Guidobaldo had to relinquish the duchy of Urbino to Cesare Borgia, who occupied it by force. 4. Federico II (1422–1482), of the house of Montefeltro, duke of Urbino. 5. Actually only sixty.

and diverse calamities, which he always bore with such strength of spirit that his virtue was never overcome by Fortune; nay, despising her storms with stanch heart, he lived in sickness as if in health, and in adversity as if most fortunate, with the greatest dignity and esteemed by all. So that, although he was infirm of body in this way, he campaigned with a most honorable rank[6] in the service of their Serene Highnesses Kings Alfonso and Ferdinand the Younger of Naples;[7] and later with Pope Alexander VI,[8] as well as the signories of Venice and Florence.

Then when Julius II became Pope,[9] the Duke was made Captain of the Church;[1] during which time, and following his usual style, he saw to it that his household was filled with very noble and worthy gentlemen, with whom he lived on the most familiar terms, delighting in their company; in which the pleasure he gave others was not less than that which he had from them, being well versed in both Latin and Greek and combining affability and wit with the knowledge of an infinitude of things. Besides this, so much did the greatness of his spirit spur him on that, even though he could not engage personally in chivalric activities as he had once done, he still took the greatest pleasure in seeing others so engaged; and by his words, now criticizing and now praising each man according to his deserts, he showed clearly how much judgment he had in such matters. Wherefore, in jousts and tournaments, in riding, in the handling of every sort of weapon, as well as in revelries, in games, in musical performances, in short, in all exercises befitting noble cavaliers, everyone strove to show himself such as to deserve to be thought worthy of his noble company.

[4]

Thus, all the hours of the day were given over to honorable and pleasant exercises both of the body and of the mind; but because, owing to his infirmity, the Duke always retired to sleep very early after supper, everyone usually repaired to the rooms of the Duchess, Elisabetta Gonzaga, at that hour; where also signora Emilia Pia[2] was always to be found, who being gifted with such a lively wit and judgment, as you know, seemed the mistress of all, and all appeared to take on wisdom and worth from her. Here, then, gentle discussions and innocent pleasantries were heard, and on everyone's face a jocund gaiety could be seen depicted, so much so that this house could be called the very abode of joyfulness. Nor do I believe that the sweetness that is had from a beloved company was ever savored in any other place as it once was there. For, not to speak of the great honor it was for each of us to serve such a lord as I have described above, we all felt a supreme happiness arise within us whenever we came into the presence of the Duchess. And it seemed that this was a chain that bound us all together in love, in such wise that never was there concord of will or cordial love between brothers greater than that which was there among us all.

The same was among the ladies, with whom one had very free and most honorable association, for to each it was permitted to speak, sit, jest, and

6. As a mercenary captain, or *condottiere*.   7. Alfonso II and Ferdinand II (both of the house of Aragon), kings of Naples in the late fifteenth century.   8. Rodrigo Borgia, pope from 1492–1503.   9. In 1503.   1. Captain in the pontiff's army.   2. Sister-in-law and companion of the duchess, she wittily directs much of the conversation.

laugh with whom he pleased; but the reverence that was paid to the wishes of the Duchess was such that this same liberty was a very great check; nor was there anyone who did not esteem it the greatest pleasure in the world to please her and the greatest grief to displease her. For which reason most decorous customs were there joined with the greatest liberty, and games and laughter in her presence were seasoned not only with witty jests but with a gracious and sober dignity; for that modesty and grandeur which ruled over all the acts, words, and gestures of the Duchess, in jest and laughter, caused anyone seeing her for the first time to recognize her as a very great lady. And, in impressing herself thus upon those about her, it seemed that she tempered us all to her own quality and fashion, wherefore each one strove to imitate her style, deriving, as it were, a rule of fine manners from the presence of so great and virtuous a lady; whose high qualities I do not now intend to recount, this being not to my purpose, because they are well known to all the world, and much more than I could express either with tongue or pen; and those which might have remained somewhat hidden, Fortune, as if admiring such rare virtues, chose to reveal through many adversities and stings of calamity, in order to prove that in the tender breast of a woman, and accompanied by singular beauty, there may dwell prudence and strength of spirit, and all those virtues which are very rare even in austere men.

[5]

But, passing over this, I say that the custom of all the gentlemen of the house was to betake themselves immediately after supper to the Duchess; where, amidst the pleasant pastimes, the music and dancing which were continually enjoyed, fine questions would sometimes be proposed, and sometimes ingenious games, now at the behest of one person and now of another, in which, under various concealments, those present revealed their thoughts allegorically to whomever they chose. Sometimes other discussions would turn on a variety of subjects, or there would be a sharp exchange of quick retorts; often "emblems,"[3] as we nowadays call them, were devised; in which discussions a marvelous pleasure was had, the house (as I have said) being full of very noble talents. * * * So that poets, musicians, and all sorts of buffoons, and the most excellent of every kind of talent that cold be found in Italy, were always gathered there.

[6]

Now Pope Julius II,[4] having, by his presence and with the help of the French, brought Bologna under the rule of the Apostolic See in the year 1506, and being on his way back to Rome, passed through Urbino, where he was received with all possible honor and with as magnificent and splendid a welcome as could have been offered in any of the noble cities of Italy: so that, besides the Pope, all the cardinals and other courtiers were highly gratified. And there were some who were so captivated by the charm of the company they found here that when the Pope and his court had departed, they stayed on for many days in Urbino; during which time not only was the

3. Figure ("body") and motto or verse ("soul"). 4. Giuliano della Rovere (1443–1513), elected pope in 1503, famous as a patron of arts and letters.

usual style of festivities and ordinary diversions kept up, but every man endeavored to contribute something more, and especially in the games that were played almost every evening. And the order of these was such that, as soon as anyone came into the presence of the Duchess, he would take a seat in a circle wherever he pleased or where chance would have it; and so seated, all were arranged alternately, a man, then a woman, as long as there were women (for almost always the number of men was much the larger); then, the company was governed as it pleased the Duchess, who most of the time left this charge to signora Emilia.

So, the day following the departure of the Pope, when the company had gathered at the usual hour and place, after many pleasant discussions, it was the Duchess's wish that signora Emilia should begin the games; and she, after having declined the task for a time, spoke thus: "Madam, since it is your pleasure that I should be the one to begin the games this evening, and since I cannot in reason fail to obey you, I will propose a game for which I think I can have little blame and even less labor: and this shall be that each propose some game after his own liking that we have never played; then we shall choose the one which seems the worthiest of being played in this company."

And, so saying, she turned to signor Gaspar Pallavicino,[5] bidding him to tell his choice; and he replied at once: "It is for you, Madam, to tell yours first."

"But I have already told it," said signora Emilia; "now do you, Duchess, bid him obey."

To this the Duchess said, laughing: "So that all shall be bound to obey you, I make you my deputy, and give you all my authority."

[7]

"It is indeed a remarkable thing," replied signor Gasparo, "that women are always permitted such exemption from labor, and it is only right to wish to understand why; but, in order not to be the first to disobey, I will leave that for another time, and will speak now as required"; and he began: "It seems to me that in love, as in everything else, our minds judge differently; and so it often happens that what is most pleasing to one is most odious to another; but, for all that, our minds do, however, agree in prizing highly what is loved; so that often the excessive affection of lovers beguiles their judgment, causing them to think that the person whom they love is the only one in the world who is adorned with every excellent quality and is wholly without defect. But, since human nature does not admit of such complete perfection, nor is anyone to be found in whom something is not wanting, it cannot be said that these lovers are not deceived, or that the lover is not blinded respecting the beloved. I would therefore have our game this evening be so: let each one say which virtue above all others he would wish the one he loves to be adorned with; and, since it is inevitable that everyone have some defect, let him say also which fault he would desire in the beloved: so that we may see who can think of the most praiseworthy and useful virtues and of the faults which are the most excusable and least harmful either to the lover or to the beloved."

5. A Lombard (1486–1511) and friend of Castiglione.

When signor Gasparo had spoken thus, signora Emilia made a sign to madam Costanza Fregosa,[6] as she sat next in order, that she should speak; and she was making ready to do so, when suddenly the Duchess said: "Since signora Emilia does not choose to go to the trouble of devising a game, it would be quite right for the other ladies to share in this ease, and thus be exempt from such a burden this evening, especially since there are so many men here that we risk no lack of games."

"So be it," replied signora Emilia; and, imposing silence on madam Costanza, she turned to messer Cesare Gonzaga[7] who sat next, and bade him speak; and he began thus:

[8]

"Whoever considers carefully all our actions will always find various defects in them; the reason being that, in this, nature is variable, as in other things, bestowing the light of reason on one man in one respect and on another man in another: wherefore it happens that as one man knows what another does not know, and is ignorant of what the other knows, each easily perceives his neighbor's error and not his own; and we all think that we are very wise and perhaps the more so in that wherein we are most foolish. Thus, we have seen it happen in this house that many who were at first held to be very wise have been known, in the course of time, to be full of folly, and this came about through nothing save the attention we gave to it. For, even as they say that in Apulia many musical instruments are used for those who are bitten by the tarantula, and various tunes are tried until the humor which is causing the malady is (through a certain affinity which it has with some one of those tunes) suddenly stirred by the sound of it and so agitates the sick man that he is restored to health by that agitation: so we, whenever we have detected some hidden trace of folly, have stimulated it so artfully and with such a variety of inducements and in so many different ways that finally we have understood what its tendency was; then, having recognized the humor, we agitated it so thoroughly that it was always brought to the perfection of an open folly. Thus, one turned out to be foolish in verse, another in music, another in love, another in dancing, another in morrises, another in riding, another in fencing—each one according to the native quality of his metal; wherein, as you know, we have had some wonderful entertainment. I hold this, then, to be certain: that in each of us there is some seed of folly which, once awakened, can grow almost without limitation.

"Hence, I wish that for this evening our game might be a discussion of this matter, and that each would say: 'In case I should openly reveal my folly, what sort mine would be and about what, judging such an eventuality by the sparks of folly which are seen to come forth from me every day'; and let the same be said of all the others, keeping to the order of our games, and let each one seek to base his opinion on some real sign and evidence. Thus, each of us will profit from this game of ours by knowing his faults, the better thereby to guard against them. And if the vein of folly which we discover chances to be so abundant that it seems beyond repair, we will encourage it

6. Sister of Ottaviano and Federico, companion of the duchess.   7. Cousin (1475–1512) and friend of Castiglione, a great warrior, a diplomat, and a pastoral poet.

and, according to the doctrine of fra Mariano,[8] we shall have saved a soul, which will be no small gain."

There was much laughter about this game, nor was there anyone who could keep from talking. One said: "My folly would be in thinking"; another "in looking"; and another said: "I am already a fool in love," and the like.

[9]

Then fra Serafino[9] said, laughing as usual: "That would take too long; but if you want a good game, let everyone say why he thinks it is that nearly all women hate rats and love snakes; and you will see that no one will hit upon the reason except myself, for I know this secret by a strange way." And already he was starting his usual stories. But signora Emilia bade him keep quiet, and, passing over the lady who sat next, she made a sign to the Unico Aretino,[1] whose turn it was. And he, without awaiting further bidding, said: "Would that I were a judge with the authority to use any sort of torture to extract the truth from criminals; and this in order to uncover the deceits of a certain ingrate who, with an angel's eyes and a serpent's heart, never speaks as she thinks, and with a deceitful, feigned compassion attends to nothing but dissecting hearts. Nor is there in sandy Libya a snake so venomous, so avid of human blood, as this false one; who not only with the sweetness of her voice and her honeyed words, but also with her eyes, her smiles, her looks, and in all her ways, is a veritable Siren.[2] However, since I am not allowed (as I could wish I were) to make use of chains, rope, or fire, in order to learn a certain truth, I wish to learn it with a game, which is this: let each one say what he thinks that letter s means that the Duchess is wearing on her forehead; because, though this is certainly but another artful veil to make deception possible, perchance some interpretation will be given of it such as she would not have expected; and it will be found that Fortune, compassionate spectator of the sufferings of men, has led her to reveal by this little sign, and in spite of herself, her secret desire to kill and bury alive in calamities anyone who looks upon her or serves her."

The Duchess laughed, and Aretino, seeing that she wished to exonerate herself from this imputation, said: "Nay, Madam, it is not now your turn to speak."

Then signora Emilia turned to him and said: "Signor Unico, there is no one among us here who does not yield to you in all things, but most of all in your knowledge of our Duchess's mind. And just as you know it better than the rest, even so do you love it more than the rest, who are like those weak-sighted birds that fix not their eyes upon the orb of the sun and thus cannot well know how perfect it is. Hence, any attempt to clear up this doubt would be in vain, save by your own judgment. Therefore, let this task be left to you alone, as to the only one who can perform it."

Aretino remained silent for a while; then, being urged to speak, he at last recited a sonnet[3] on the aforesaid subject, declaring what was meant by that letter s; which sonnet was thought by many to have been improvised; but

---

8. Fra Mariano (1460–1531), a Dominican friar and renowned buffoon who lived under the protection of Lorenzo, then at the papal court [Translator's note].   9. A Mantuan, servant of the Gonzagas, organizer of festivals [Translator's note].   1. Bernardo Accolti (1458–1535), known as the Unico Aretino because born in Arezzo and "unique" as an improviser of verse [Translator's note].   2. Songs of the Sirens lured sailors to their deaths.   3. Not included in Castiglione's text.

because it was more ingenious and polished than the brevity of time would seem to have allowed, some thought that it had been prepared.

[10]

Then, when the sonnet had been praised with merry applause, and after some further talk, signor Ottaviano Fregoso,[4] whose turn it was, began laughingly as follows: "Gentlemen, if I should affirm that I have never felt any passion of love, I am sure that the Duchess and signora Emilia, even if they did not believe it, would make a show of believing it, and would say that this is because I have mistrusted my own ability to induce any woman ever to love me: wherein, to speak the truth, up to now I have not made any such persistent effort as to have reason to despair of being able to succeed some day. Nor certainly have I refrained from making that effort because I esteem myself so much, or women so little, as to think that many are not worthy of being loved and served by me. But I have rather been frightened away by the continual laments of certain lovers who, pale, sad, and taciturn, seem always to wear their unhappiness depicted in their eyes; and whenever they speak, they accompany every word with tripled sighs and talk of nothing but tears, torments, despairs, and longings for death. So that even if at times any spark of love did kindle my heart, I have immediately made every effort to extinguish it, not out of any hate that I feel towards women, as these ladies may think, but for my own good.

"And then I have known other lovers utterly different from such lamenters, who not only take joy and satisfaction in the kind looks and tender words and gentle mien of their ladies, but flavor all woes with sweetness, so that they say that their ladies' quarrels, wrath, and scorn are things most sweet: wherefore such lovers as these strike me as being exceedingly happy. For if they find such sweetness in those amorous fits of temper which the others hold to be more bitter than death, I think that in the manifestations of love they must experience that final beatitude which we seek in vain in this world. I wish therefore that our game this evening might be that each one should say, in case she whom he loves must be angry with him, what he would wish the cause of that anger to be. For if there be some here who have experienced such sweet outbursts of anger, I am sure that out of courtesy they will elect one of those causes that make these so sweet; and perhaps I shall find the courage to venture a little further in love, in the hope that I too may find this sweetness where some find bitterness; and thus these ladies will no longer be able to defame me for not loving."

[11]

All liked this game and were already preparing to speak on such a topic; but, as signora Emilia said nothing about it, messer Pietro Bembo,[5] who sat next in order, spoke thus: "Gentlemen, the game proposed by signor Ottaviano has brought no little doubt to my mind, since he has spoken of the angers of love, which, even though they have variety, yet have always been

---

4. Ottaviano Fregoso (d. 1524), Genoese nobleman, nephew of Duke Guidobaldo, elected doge of Genoa in 1513 and later appointed governor of the city by Francis I [Translator's note].   5. Pietro Bembo (1470–1547), a Venetian nobleman, a famous man of letters of the Italian Renaissance, later papal secretary to Leo X; he corrected the proofs of *The Courtier* [Translator's note].

most bitter to me, nor do I think that there could be learned from me any flavoring sufficient to sweeten them; but it may be that they are more or less bitter according to the cause whereby they arise. For I remember having seen the lady whom I was serving angry with me, either out of an idle doubt as to my faithfulness which she herself had conceived, or out of some other false notion awakened in her by what someone had said to my detriment; so that I judged no suffering could be compared to mine, and it seemed to me that the greatest pain that I felt was in having to suffer when I had not deserved it and in having this affliction through no fault of mine but through her lack of love. At other times I saw her angry at some error of mine, and recognized that her wrath was caused by my fault; and at such a point I would judge that my former woe was light indeed compared with what I now felt. And it seemed to me that the fact of having displeased (and through my own fault) the sole person whom I desired and sought so to please was the torment that surpassed all others. I wish therefore that our game might be that each should tell, if she whom he loves must be angry with him, where he would wish the cause of her anger to lie, in her or in himself, so that we may know which is the greater suffering, to give displeasure to one's beloved, or to receive the same from her."

[12]

Everyone was awaiting signora Emilia's reply; but she, saying nothing more to Bembo, turned to messer Federico Fregoso[6] and signified that he should tell his game; and he began at once as follows: "Madam, I wish that, as sometimes happens, I might be allowed to defer to someone else's judgment, since I, for one, would gladly approve any of the games proposed by these gentlemen, because truly it seems to me that they would all be amusing. Still, so as not to upset our order, I will say that if anyone should wish to praise our court—apart from the merits of our Duchess which, together with her divine virtue, would suffice to uplift from earth to heaven the meanest souls of this world—he might well say, without suspicion of flattery, that in all Italy it would perhaps be hard to find an equal number of cavaliers as outstanding and as excellent in different things, quite beyond their principal profession of chivalry, as are found here: wherefore, if there are anywhere men who deserve to be called good courtiers and who can judge of what belongs to the perfection of Courtiership, we must rightfully think that they are here present. So, in order to put down the many fools who in their presumption and ineptitude think to gain the name of good courtiers, I would have our game this evening be this, that one of this company be chosen and given the task of forming in words a perfect Courtier, setting forth all the conditions and particular qualities that are required of anyone who deserves this name; and that everyone be allowed to speak out against those things which seem not right, as in the schools of the philosophers it is permitted to offer objections to anyone maintaining a thesis."

Messer Federico was going on in his discourse when signora Emilia interrupted him, saying: "This, should it please the Duchess, shall be our game for the present."

---

6. Federico Fregoso (1480–1541), younger brother of Ottaviano, nephew of Duke Guidobaldo, made Archbishop of Salerno by Julius II in 1507 [Translator's note].

"It does please me," the Duchess replied.

Whereupon nearly all of those present began to say, both to the Duchess and among themselves, that this was the finest game that could possibly be played. And no one waited for the other's answer, but all urged signora Emilia to decide who should begin. And she, turning to the Duchess, said: "Madam, will you command him who it most pleases you should have this task, for I do not wish, in choosing one rather than another, to appear to decide which I judge to be more capable than the others in this matter, and so offend anyone."

The Duchess replied: "Nay, make the choice yourself, and take care lest you set others an example of not obeying, prompting them to refuse obedience in their turn."

[13]

Then signora Emilia laughed and said to Count Ludovico da Canossa:[7] "So, in order not to lose more time, you, Count, shall be the one to undertake this task in the way messer Federico has said; not indeed because we think you so good a Courtier that you know what befits one, but because if you say everything contrariwise, as we hope you will do, the game will be the livelier since everyone will have something to answer you; whereas, if another with more knowledge than you had this task, nothing could be objected to him because he would speak the truth, and so the game would be tedious."

The Count answered at once: "Madam, there could be no danger that anyone who speaks the truth would lack someone to gainsay him, so long as you are present." And when the company had laughed a while at this retort, he went on: "But truly I should be very glad to escape from this labor, since it seems too difficult for me; and I recognize as true in myself what you have affirmed in jest, namely, that I do not know what befits a good Courtier. Nor do I seek to prove this by any other witness than by the fact that since I do not perform the deeds of one such, it can be concluded that I do not have the knowledge. I believe that I may be blamed less in this, for it is surely worse not to wish to perform well than not to know how. Still, since it is your pleasure that I should have this charge, I cannot and will not refuse it, for I would not contravene our rule and your judgment, which I esteem far more than my own."

Then messer Cesare Gonzaga said: "As it is already rather late in the evening and we have many other kinds of entertainment ready at hand, perhaps it may be well to postpone this discussion until tomorrow; and this will give the Count time to think about what he is going to say, for truly it is a difficult thing to improvise on such a subject."

The Count replied: "I do not wish to be like the man who stripped to his doublet and jumped less far than he had done in his greatcoat; wherefore it seems to me fortunate that the hour is late, for by the brevity of the time I shall be forced to say very little, and shall be excused by the fact that I have given no thought to this matter and so, free of censure, I shall be permitted to say whatever comes first to my lips. Therefore, in order not to bear this burden of obligation longer upon my shoulders, I will say that in all things

7. A relative (1476–1532) of Castiglione and friend of the painter Raphael, he was later a bishop and papal ambassador to England.

it is so difficult to know what true perfection is that it is well-nigh impossible; and this is due to the diversity of our judgments. Thus, there are many who will welcome a man who talks a great deal, and will call him pleasing. Others will prefer a modest man; others, an active and restless man; still others, someone who shows calm and deliberation in all things. And so everyone praises or blames according to his own opinion, always hiding a vice under the name of the corresponding virtue, or a virtue under the name of the corresponding vice: for example, calling a presumptuous man, frank; a modest man, dull; a simpleton, good; a rascal, discreet; and likewise throughout. Still I do think that there is a perfection for everything, even though it be hidden; and that this perfection can be determined by someone reasoning about it who has knowledge of the subject. And because, as I have said, the truth is often hidden, and I do not claim to have this knowledge, I can only praise the manner of Courtier that I most esteem, and can approve of what seems to me to be nearest the right, according to my poor judgment: which you may follow if it seems good to you; or you may hold to your own, should it differ from mine. Certainly I will not protest that mine is better than yours, for not only can you think one thing and I another, but I myself may sometimes think one thing and sometimes another.

[14]

"Thus, I would have our Courtier born of a noble and genteel family; because it is far less becoming for one of low birth to fail to do virtuous things than for one of noble birth, who, should he stray from the path of his forebears, stains the family name, and not only fails to achieve anything but loses what has been achieved already. For noble birth is like a bright lamp that makes manifest and visible deeds both good and bad, kindling and spurring on to virtue as much for fear of dishonor as for hope of praise. And since this luster of nobility does not shine forth in the deeds of the lowly born, they lack that spur, as well as that fear of dishonor, nor do they think themselves obliged to go beyond what was done by their forebears; whereas to the wellborn it seems a reproach not to attain at least to the mark set them by their ancestors. Hence, it almost always happens that, in the profession of arms as well as in other worthy pursuits, those who are most distinguished are men of noble birth, because nature has implanted in everything that hidden seed which gives a certain force and quality of its own essence to all that springs from it, making it like itself: as we can see not only in breeds of horses and other animals, but in trees as well, the shoots of which nearly always resemble the trunk; and if they sometimes degenerate, the fault lies with the husbandman. And so it happens with men, who, if they are tended in the right way, are almost always like those from whom they spring, and often are better; but if they lack someone to tend them properly, they grow wild and never attain their full growth.

"It is true that, whether favored by the stars or by nature, some men are born endowed with such graces that they seem not to have been born, but to have been fashioned by the hands of some god, and adorned with every excellence of mind and body; even as there are many others so inept and uncouth that we cannot but think that nature brought them into the world out of spite and mockery. And just as the latter, for the most part, yield little fruit even with constant diligence and good care, so the former with little labor attain to the summit of the highest excellence. And take, as an example, Don Ippolito d'Este, Cardinal of Ferrara,[8] who enjoyed such a happy birth that his person, his appearance, his words, and all his actions are so imbued and ruled by this grace that, although he is young, he evinces among the most aged prelates so grave an authority that he seems more fit to teach than to be taught. Similarly, in conversing with men and women of every station, in play, in laughter, in jest, he shows a special sweetness and such gracious manners that no one who speaks with him or even sees him can do otherwise than feel an enduring affection for him.

"But, to return to our subject, I say that there is a mean to be found between such supreme grace on the one hand and such stupid ineptitude on the other, and that those who are not so perfectly endowed by nature can, with care and effort, polish and in great part correct their natural defects. Therefore, besides his noble birth, I would wish the Courtier favored in this other respect, and endowed by nature not only with talent and with beauty of countenance and person, but with that certain grace which we call an 'air,' which shall make him at first sight pleasing and lovable to all who see him; and let this be an adornment informing and attending all his actions, giving the promise outwardly that such a one is worthy of the company and the favor of every great lord."

[15]

At this point, without waiting any longer, signor Gaspar Pallavicino said: "So that our game may have the form prescribed and that we may not appear to esteem little that privilege of opposing which has been allowed us, I say that to me this nobility of birth does not seem so essential. And if I thought I was uttering anything not already known to us all, I would adduce many instances of persons born of the noblest blood who have been ridden by vices; and, on the contrary, many persons of humble birth who, through their virtue, have made their posterity illustrious. And if what you said just now is true, that there is in all things that hidden force of the first seed, then we should all be of the same condition through having the same source, nor would one man be more noble than another. But I believe that there are many other causes of the differences and the various degrees of elevation and lowliness among us. Among which causes I judge Fortune to be foremost; because we see her hold sway over all the things of this world and, as it seems, amuse herself often in uplifting to the skies whom she pleases and in burying in the depths those most worthy of being exalted.

"I quite agree with what you call the good fortune of those who are endowed at birth with all goodness of mind and body; but this is seen to happen with those of humble as well as with those of noble birth, because nature observes no such subtle distinctions as these. Nay, as I said, the greatest gifts of nature are often to be seen in persons of the humblest origin. Hence, since this nobility of birth is not gained either by talents or by force or skill, and is rather due to the merit of one's ancestors than to one's own, I deem it passing strange to hold that if the parents of our Courtier be of humble birth, all his good qualities are ruined, and that those other qualities

---

8. Ippolito d'Este (1479–1520), patron of Ludovico Ariosto, friend of Leonardo da Vinci, made a cardinal by Pope Alexander VI.

which you have named would not suffice to bring him to the height of perfection; that is, talent, beauty of countenance, comeliness of person, and that grace which will make him at first sight lovable to all."

[16]

Then Count Ludovico replied: "I do not deny that the same virtues can rule in the lowborn as in the wellborn: but (in order not to repeat what we have said already, along with many further reasons which might be adduced in praise of noble birth, which is always honored by everyone, because it stands to reason that good should beget good), since it is our task to form a Courtier free of any defect whatsoever, and endowed with all that is praiseworthy, I deem it necessary to have him be of noble birth, not only for many other reasons, but also because of that public opinion which immediately sides with nobility. For, in the case of two courtiers who have not yet given any impression of themselves either through good or bad deeds, immediately when the one is known to be of gentle birth and the other not, the one who is lowborn will be held in far less esteem than the one who is of noble birth, and will need much time and effort in order to give to others that good impression of himself which the other will give in an instant and merely by being a gentleman. And everyone knows the importance of these impressions, for, to speak of ourselves, we have seen men come to this house who, though dull-witted and maladroit, had yet the reputation throughout Italy of being very great courtiers; and, even though they were at last discovered and known, still they fooled us for many days and maintained in our minds that opinion of themselves which they found already impressed thereon, even though their conduct was in keeping with their little worth. Others we have seen who at first enjoyed little esteem and who, in the end, achieved a great success.

"And there are various causes of such errors, one being the judgment of princes who, thinking to work miracles, sometimes decide to show favor to one who seems to them to deserve disfavor. And they too are often deceived; but, because they always have countless imitators, their favor engenders a great fame which on the whole our judgments will follow. And if we notice anything which seems contrary to the prevailing opinion, we suspect that we must be mistaken, and we continue to look for something hidden: because we think that such universal opinions must after all be founded on the truth and arise from reasonable causes. And also because our minds are quick to love and hate, as is seen in spectacles of combats and of games and in every sort of contest, where the spectators often side with one of the parties without any evident reason, showing the greatest desire that this one should win and the other should lose. Moreover, as for the general opinion concerning a man's qualities, it is good or ill repute that sways our minds at the outset to one of these two passions. Hence, it happens that, for the most part, we judge from love or hate. Consider, then, how important that first impression is, and how anyone who aspires to have the rank and name of good Courtier must strive from the beginning to make a good impression.

[17]

"But to come to some particulars: I hold that the principal and true profession of the Courtier must be that of arms; which I wish him to exercise with vigor; and let him be known among the others as bold, energetic, and faithful to whomever he serves. And the repute of these good qualities will be earned by exercising them in every time and place, inasmuch as one may not ever fail therein without great blame. And, just as among women the name of purity, once stained, is never restored, so the reputation of a gentleman whose profession is arms, if ever in the least way he sullies himself through cowardice or other disgrace, always remains defiled before the world and covered with ignominy. Therefore, the more our Courtier excels in this art, the more will he merit praise; although I do not deem it necessary that he have the perfect knowledge of things and other qualities that befit a commander, for since this would launch us on too great a sea, we shall be satisfied, as we have said, if he have complete loyalty and an undaunted spirit, and be always seen to have them. For oftentimes men are known for their courage in small things rather than in great. And often in important perils and where there are many witnesses, some men are found who, although their hearts sink within them, still, spurred on by fear of shame or by the company of those present, press forward with eyes shut, as it were, and do their duty, God knows how; and in things of little importance and when they think they can avoid the risk of danger, they are glad to play safe. But those men who, even when they think they will not be observed or seen or recognized by anyone, show courage and are not careless of anything, however slight, for which they could be blamed, such have the quality of spirit we are seeking in our Courtier.

"However, we do not wish him to make a show of being so fierce that he is forever swaggering in his speech, declaring that he has wedded his cuirass, and glowering with such dour looks as we have often seen Berto[9] do; for to such as these one may rightly say what in polite society a worthy lady jestingly said to a certain man (whom I do not now wish to name) whom she sought to honor by inviting him to dance, and who not only declined this but would not listen to music or take any part in the other entertainments offered him, but kept saying that such trifles were not his business. And when finally the lady said to him: 'What then is your business?' he answered with a scowl: 'Fighting.' Whereupon the lady replied at once: 'I should think it a good thing, now that you are not away at war or engaged in fighting, for you to have yourself greased all over and stowed away in a closet along with all your battle harness, so that you won't grow any rustier than you already are'; and so, amid much laughter from those present, she ridiculed him in his stupid presumption. Therefore, let the man we are seeking be exceedingly fierce, harsh, and always among the first, wherever the enemy is; and in every other place, humane, modest, reserved, avoiding ostentation above all things as well as that impudent praise of himself by which a man always arouses hatred and disgust in all who hear him."

[18]

Then signor Gasparo replied: "As for me, I have known few men excellent in anything whatsoever who did not praise themselves; and it seems to me that this can well be permitted them, because he who feels himself to be of

9. An otherwise unidentified character.

some worth, and sees that his works are ignored, is indignant that his own worth should lie buried; and he must make it known to someone, in order not to be cheated of the honor that is the true reward of all virtuous toil. Thus, among the ancients, seldom does anyone of any worth refrain from praising himself. To be sure, those persons who are of no merit, and yet praise themselves, are insufferable; but we do not assume that our Courtier will be of that sort."

Then the Count said: "If you took notice, I blamed impudent and indiscriminate praise of one's self: and truly, as you say, one must not conceive a bad opinion of a worthy man who praises himself modestly; nay, one must take that as surer evidence than if it came from another's mouth. I do say that whoever does not fall into error in praising himself and does not cause annoyance or envy in the person who listens to him is indeed a discreet man and, besides the praises he gives himself, deserves praises from others; for that is a very difficult thing."

Then signor Gasparo said: "This you must teach us."

The Count answered: "Among the ancients there is no lack of those who have taught this; but, in my opinion, the whole art consists in saying things in such a way that they do not appear to be spoken to that end, but are so very apropos that one cannot help saying them; and to seem always to avoid praising one's self, yet do so; but not in the manner of those boasters who open their mouths and let their words come out haphazardly. As one of our friends the other day who, when he had had his thigh run through by a spear at Pisa, said that he thought a fly had stung him; and another who said that he did not keep a mirror in his room because when he was angry he became so fearful of countenance that if he were to see himself, he would frighten himself too much."

Everyone laughed at this, but messer Cesare Gonzaga added: "What are you laughing at? Do you not know that Alexander the Great, upon hearing that in the opinion of one philosopher there were countless other worlds, began to weep, and when asked why, replied: 'Because I have not yet conquered one'—as if he felt able to conquer them all? Does that not seem to you a greater boast than that of the fly sting?"

Then said the Count: "And Alexander was a greater man than the one who spoke so. But truly one has to excuse excellent men when they presume much of themselves, because anyone who has great things to accomplish must have the daring to do those things, and confidence in himself. And let him not be abject and base, but modest rather in his words, making it clear that he presumes less of himself than he accomplishes, provided such presumption does not turn to rashness."

[19]

When the Count paused here briefly, messer Bernardo Bibbiena said, laughing: "I remember you said before that this Courtier of ours should be naturally endowed with beauty of countenance and person, and with a grace that would make him lovable. Now this grace and beauty of countenance I do believe that I have myself, wherefore it happens that so many ladies, as you know, are ardently in love with me; but, as to the beauty of my person, I am rather doubtful, and especially as to these legs of mine which in truth do not seem to me as well disposed as I could wish; as to my chest and the rest, I am quite well enough satisfied. Now do determine a little more in detail what this beauty of body should be, so that I can extricate myself from doubt and put my mind at ease."

After some laughter at this, the Count added: "Certainly such grace of countenance you can truly be said to have; nor will I adduce any other example in order to make clear what that grace is; because we do see beyond any doubt that your aspect is very agreeable and pleasant to all, although the features of it are not very delicate: it has something manly about it, and yet is full of grace. And this is a quality found in many different types of faces. I would have our Courtier's face be such, not so soft and feminine as many attempt to have who not only curl their hair and pluck their eyebrows, but preen themselves in all those ways that the most wanton and dissolute women in the world adopt; and in walking, in posture, and in every act, appear so tender and languid that their limbs seem to be on the verge of falling apart; and utter their words so limply that it seems they are about to expire on the spot; and the more they find themselves in the company of men of rank, the more they make a show of such manners. These, since nature did not make them women as they clearly wish to appear and be, should be treated not as good women, but as public harlots, and driven not only from the courts of great lords but from the society of all noble men.

[20]

"Then, coming to bodily frame, I say it is enough that it be neither extremely small nor big, because either of these conditions causes a certain contemptuous wonder, and men of either sort are gazed at in much the same way that we gaze at monstrous things. And yet, if one must sin in one or the other of these two extremes, it is less bad to be on the small side than to be excessively big; because men who are so huge of body are often not only obtuse of spirit, but are also unfit for every agile exercise, which is something I very much desire in the Courtier. And hence I would have him well built and shapely of limb, and would have him show strength and lightness and suppleness, and know all the bodily exercises that befit a warrior. And in this I judge it his first duty to know how to handle every kind of weapon, both on foot and on horse, and know the advantages of each kind; and be especially acquainted with those arms that are ordinarily used among gentlemen, because, apart from using them in war (where perhaps so many fine points are not necessary), there often arise differences between one gentleman and another, resulting in duels, and quite often those weapons are used which happen to be at hand. Hence, knowledge of them is a very safe thing. Nor am I one of those who say that skill is forgotten in the hour of need; for he who loses his skill at such times shows that out of fear he has already lost his heart and head.

[21]

"I deem it highly important, moreover, to know how to wrestle, because this frequently accompanies the use of weapons on foot. Then, both for his own sake and for his friends', he must understand the quarrels and differences that can arise, and must be alert to seize an advantage, and must show courage and prudence in all things. Nor should he be quick to enter into a fight, except in so far as his honor demands it of him; for, besides the great danger that an uncertain fate can bring, he who rushes into such things precipitately and without urgent cause deserves greatly to be censured, even though he should meet with success. But when he finds that he is so far involved that he cannot withdraw without approach, he must be very deliberate both in the preliminaries to the duel and in the duel itself, and always show readiness and daring. Nor must he do as some who spend their time in wrangling and arguing over points of honor; and, when they have the choice of weapons, select those which neither cut nor prick, and arm themselves as if they were expecting to stand against cannonades; and, thinking it enough not to be defeated, stand always on the defensive and give ground to such a degree that they show extreme cowardice. And so they make themselves the laughingstock of children, like those two men from Ancona who fought at Perugia recently and made everyone laugh who saw them."

"And who were they?" asked signor Gaspar Pallavicino.

"Two cousins," replied messer Cesare.

Then the Count said: "In their fighting they seemed true brothers." Then he went on: "Weapons are also often used in various exercises in time of peace, and gentlemen are seen in public spectacles before the people and before ladies and great lords. Therefore I wish our Courtier to be a perfect horseman in every kind of saddle; and, in addition to having a knowledge of horses and what pertains to riding, let him put every effort and diligence into outstripping others in everything a little, so that he may be always recognized as better than the rest. And even as we read that Alcibiades[1] surpassed all those peoples among whom he lived, and each in the respect wherein it claimed greatest excellence, so would I have this Courtier of ours excel all others in what is the special profession of each. And as it is the peculiar excellence of the Italians to ride well with the rein, to manage wild horses especially with great skill, to tilt and joust, let him be among the best of the Italians in this. In tourneys, in holding a pass, in attacking a fortified position, let him be among the best of the French. In stick-throwing, bull-fighting, in casting spears and darts, let him be outstanding among the Spaniards. But, above all, let him temper his every action with a certain good judgment and grace, if he would deserve that universal favor which is so greatly prized.

[22]

"There are also other exercises which, although not immediately dependent upon arms, still have much in common therewith and demand much manly vigor; and chief among these is the hunt, it seems to me, because it has a certain resemblance to war. It is a true pastime for great lords, it befits a Courtier, and one understands why it was so much practiced among the ancients. He should also know how to swim, jump, run, throw stones; for, besides their usefulness in war, it is frequently necessary to show one's prowess in such things, whereby a good name is to be won, especially with the crowd (with whom one must reckon after all). Another noble exercise and most suitable for a man at court is the game of tennis which shows off the

1. Athenian general and follower of Socrates.

disposition of body, the quickness and litheness of every member, and all the qualities that are brought out by almost every other exercise. Nor do I deem vaulting on horseback to be less worthy, which, though it is tiring and difficult, serves more than anything else to make a man agile and dextrous; and besides its usefulness, if such agility is accompanied by grace, in my opinion it makes a finer show than any other.

"If, then, our Courtier is more than fairly expert in such exercises, I think he ought to put aside all others, such as vaulting on the ground, rope-walking, and the like, which smack of the juggler's trade and little befit a gentleman.

"But since one cannot always engage in such strenuous activities (moreover, persistence causes satiety, and drives away the admiration we have for rare things), we must always give variety to our lives by changing our activities. Hence, I would have our Courtier descend sometimes to quieter and more peaceful exercises. And, in order to escape envy and to enter agreeably into the company of others, let him do all that others do, yet never depart from comely conduct, but behave himself with that good judgment which will not allow him to engage in any folly; let him laugh, jest, banter, frolic, and dance, yet in such a manner as to show always that he is genial and discreet; and let him be full of grace in all that he does or says."

[23]

Then messer Cesare Gonzaga said: "Certainly no one ought to interrupt the course of this discussion; but if I were to remain silent, I should neither be exercising the privilege I have of speaking nor satisfying the desire I have of learning something. And I may be pardoned if I ask a question when I ought to be speaking in opposition; for I think this can be allowed me, after the example set by our messer Bernardo who, in his excessive desire to be thought handsome, has violated the laws of our game by asking instead of gainsaying."

Then the Duchess said: "You see how from a single error a host of others can come. Therefore, he who transgresses and sets a bad example, as messer Bernardo has done, deserves to be punished not only for his own transgression but for that of the others as well."

To this messer Cesare replied: "And so, Madam, I shall be exempt from penalty, since messer Bernardo is to be punished both for his own error and for mine."

"Nay," said the Duchess, "you both must be doubly punished: he for his own transgression and for having brought you to yours, you for your transgression and for having imitated him."

"Madam," answered messer Cesare, "I have not transgressed as yet; however, in order to leave all this punishment to messer Bernardo alone, I will keep quiet."

And he was already silent, when signora Emilia laughed and said: "Say what you will, for, with the permission of the Duchess, I pardon both the one that has transgressed and the one that is about to do so ever so little."

"So be it," the Duchess went on, "but take care lest you make the mistake of thinking it more commendable to be clement than to be just; for the excessive pardon of a transgressor does wrong to those who do not transgress. Still, at the moment, I would not have my austerity in reproaching your indulgence cause us not to hear messer Cesare's question."

And so, at a sign from the Duchess and from signora Emilia, he began forthwith:

[24]

"If I well remember, Count, it seems to me you have repeated several times this evening that the Courtier must accompany his actions, his gestures, his habits, in short, his every movement, with grace. And it strikes me that you require this in everything as that seasoning without which all the other properties and good qualities would be of little worth. And truly I believe that everyone would easily let himself be persuaded of this, because, by the very meaning of the word, it can be said that he who has grace finds grace. But since you have said that this is often a gift of nature and the heavens, and that, even if it is not quite perfect, it can be much increased by care and industry, those men who are born as fortunate and as rich in such treasure as some we know have little need, it seems to be, of any teacher in this, because such benign favor from heaven lifts them, almost in spite of themselves, higher than they themselves had desired, and makes them not only pleasing but admirable to everyone. Therefore I do not discuss this, it not being in our power to acquire it of ourselves. But as for those who are less endowed by nature and are capable of acquiring grace only if they put forth labor, industry, and care, I would wish to know by what art, by what discipline, by what method, they can gain this grace, both in bodily exercises, in which you deem it to be so necessary, and in every other thing they do or say. Therefore, since by praising this quality so highly you have, as I believe, aroused in all of us an ardent desire, according to the task given you by signora Emilia, you are still bound to satisfy it."

[25]

"I am not bound," said the Count, "to teach you how to acquire grace or anything else, but only to show you what a perfect Courtier ought to be. Nor would I undertake to teach you such a perfection; especially when I have just now said that the Courtier must know how to wrestle, vault, and so many other things which, since I never learned them myself, you all know well enough how I should be able to teach them. Let it suffice that just as a good soldier knows how to tell the smith what shape, style, and quality his armor must have, and yet is not able to teach him to make it, nor how to hammer or temper it; just so I, perhaps, shall be able to tell you what a perfect Courtier should be, but not to teach you what you must do to become one. Still, in order to answer your question in so far as I can (although it is almost proverbial that grace is not learned), I say that if anyone is to acquire grace in bodily exercises (granting first of all that he is not by nature incapable), he must begin early and learn the principles from the best of teachers. And how important this seemed to King Philip of Macedon can be seen by the fact that he wished Aristotle, the famous philosopher and perhaps the greatest the world has ever known, to be the one who should teach his son Alexander the first elements of letters. And among men whom we know today, consider how well and gracefully signor Galeazzo Sanseverino, Grand Equerry of France,[2] performs all bodily exercises; and this because, besides

2. Of a famous Neapolitan family, he fought for Louis XII and Francis I of France and died at the battle of Pavia (1525).

the natural aptitude of person that he possesses, he has taken the greatest care to study with good masters and to have about him men who excel, taking from each the best of what they know. For just as in wrestling, vaulting, and in the handling of many kinds of weapons, he took our messer Pietro Monte[3] as his guide, who is (as you know) the only true master of every kind of acquired strength and agility—so in riding, jousting, and the rest he has ever had before his eyes those men who are known to be most perfect in these matters.

[26]

"Therefore, whoever would be a good pupil must not only do things well, but must always make every effort to resemble and, if that be possible, to transform himself into his master. And when he feels that he has made some progress, it is very profitable to observe different men of that profession; and, conducting himself with that good judgment which must always be his guide, go about choosing now this thing from one and that from another. And even as in green meadows the bee flits about among the grasses robbing the flowers, so our Courtier must steal this grace from those who seem to him to have it, taking from each the part that seems most worthy of praise; not doing as a friend of ours whom you all know, who thought he greatly resembled King Ferdinand the Younger of Aragon, but had not tried to imitate him in anything save in the way he had of raising his head and twisting one side of his mouth, which manner the King had contracted through some malady. And there are many such, who think they are doing a great thing if only they can resemble some great man in something; and often they seize upon that which is his only bad point.

"But, having thought many times already about how this grace is acquired (leaving aside those who have it from the stars), I have found quite a universal rule which in this matter seems to me valid above all others, and in all human affairs whether in word or deed: and that is to avoid affectation in every way possible as though it were some very rough and dangerous reef; and (to pronounce a new word perhaps) to practice in all things a certain *sprezzatura* [nonchalance], so as to conceal all art and make whatever is done or said appear to be without effort and almost without any thought about it. And I believe much grace comes of this: because everyone knows the difficulty of things that are rare and well done; wherefore facility in such things causes the greatest wonder; whereas, on the other hand, to labor and, as we say, drag forth by the hair of the head, shows an extreme want of grace, and causes everything, no matter how great it may be, to be held in little account.

"Therefore we may call that art true art which does not seem to be art; nor must one be more careful of anything than of concealing it, because if it is discovered, this robs a man of all credit and causes him to be held in slight esteem. And I remember having read of certain most excellent orators in ancient times who, among the other things they did, tried to make everyone believe that they had no knowledge whatever of letters; and, dissembling their knowledge, they made their orations appear to be composed in the simplest manner and according to the dictates of nature and truth rather

---

3. Fencing master at the court of Urbino.

than of effort and art; which fact, had it been known, would have inspired in the minds of the people the fear that they could be duped by it.

"So you see how art, or any intent effort, if it is disclosed, deprives everything of grace. Who among you fails to laugh when our messer Pierpaolo[4] dances after his own fashion, with those capers of his, his legs stiff on tiptoe, never moving his head, as if he were a stick of wood, and all this so studied that he really seems to be counting his steps? What eye is so blind as not to see in this the ungainliness of affectation; and not to see the grace of that cool *disinvoltura* [ease] (for when it is a matter of bodily movements many call it that) in many of the men and women here present, who seem in words, in laughter, in posture not to care; or seem to be thinking more of everything than of that, so as to cause all who are watching them to believe that they are almost incapable of making a mistake?"

[27]

Here messer Bernardo Bibbiena said, without waiting: "Now you see that our messer Roberto[5] has at last found someone to praise his style of dancing, as it seems that none of the rest of you esteem it at all. For if this excellence consists in nonchalance, in showing no concern, and in seeming to have one's thoughts elsewhere rather than on what one is doing, then in dancing messer Roberto has no peer on earth, because to make it quite plain that he is giving no thought to what he is doing, he lets his clothes fall from his back and his slippers from his feet, and goes right on dancing without picking them up."

Then the Count replied: "Since you are determined that I shall go on talking, I will say something more of our faults. Do you not see that what you are calling nonchalance in messer Roberto is really affectation, because we clearly see him making every effort to show that he takes no thought of what he is about, which means taking too much thought; and because it exceeds certain limits of moderation, such nonchalance is affected, is unbecoming, and results in the opposite of the desired effect, which is to conceal the art. Hence, I do not believe that the vice of affectation is any less present in a nonchalance (in itself a praiseworthy thing) wherein one lets his clothes fall off than in a studied concern for one's personal appearance (also, in itself, a praiseworthy thing), bearing the head so stiff for fear of spoiling one's coiffure, or carrying a mirror in the fold of one's cap and a comb in one's sleeve, and having one's page follow about through the streets with a sponge and brush; because such care for personal appearance and such nonchalance both tend too much to extremes, which is always a fault, and is contrary to that pure and charming simplicity which is so appealing to all. Consider how ungraceful that rider is who tries to sit so very stiff in his saddle (in the Venetian style, as we are wont to say), compared with one who appears to give no thought to the matter and sits his horse as free and easy as if he were on foot. How much more pleasing and how much more praised is a gentleman whose profession is arms, and who is modest, speaking little and boasting little, than another who is forever praising himself, swearing and blustering about as if to defy the whole world—which is simply the

4. Unidentified.   5. Young gentleman of the court of Urbino and close friend of Castiglione.

affectation of wanting to cut a bold figure. And the same holds true in every practice, indeed in everything that is said or done."

[28]

Then the Magnifico Giuliano said: "It holds true as well in music, wherein it is a great mistake to place two perfect consonances one after the other, for our sense of hearing abhors this, whereas it often enjoys a second or a seventh which in itself is a harsh and unbearable discord. And this is due to the fact that to continue in perfect consonances generates satiety and gives evidence of a too affected harmony, which is avoided when imperfect consonances are mixed in, establishing a kind of comparison, by which our ears are held in greater suspense, and more avidly wait upon and enjoy the perfect consonances, delighting in that discord of the second or seventh as in something that shows nonchalance."

"So, you see," replied the Count, "that affectation is detrimental in this as in other things. Moreover, it is said to have been proverbial with certain most excellent painters of antiquity that excessive care is harmful, and Protogenes is said to have been censured by Apelles[6] for not knowing when to take his hands from the board."

Then messer Cesare said: "It seems to me that our fra Serafino has this same fault of not knowing when to take his hands from the board, at least not before all of the food has been taken from it too."

The Count laughed and added: "Apelles meant that Protogenes did not know when to stop in painting, which was nothing if not a kind of reproach for his being affected in his work. Thus, this excellence (which is opposed to affectation, and which, at the moment, we are calling *nonchalance*), besides being the real source from which grace springs, brings with it another adornment which, when it accompanies any human action however small, not only reveals at once how much the person knows who does it, but often causes it to be judged much greater than it actually is, since it impresses upon the minds of the onlookers the opinion that he who performs well with so much facility must possess even greater skill than this, and that, if he were to devote care and effort to what he does, he could do it far better.

"And, to multiply such examples, take a man who is handling weapons and is about to throw a dart or is holding a sword or other weapon in his hand: if immediately he takes a position of readiness, with ease, and without thinking, with such facility that his body and all his members fall into that posture naturally and without any effort, then, even if he does nothing more, he shows himself to be perfectly accomplished in that exercise. Likewise in dancing, a single step, a single movement of the body that is graceful and not forced, reveals at once the skill of the dancer. A singer who utters a single word ending in a group of four notes with a sweet cadence, and with such facility that he appears to do it quite by chance, shows with that touch alone that he can do much more than he is doing. Often too in painting, a single line which is not labored, a single brush stroke made with ease and in such a manner that the hand seems of itself to complete the line desired by the painter, without being directed by care or skill of any kind, clearly reveals

6. Both legendary Greek painters.

that excellence of craftsmanship, which people will then proceed to judge, each by his own lights. And the same happens in almost every other thing.

"Therefore our Courtier will be judged excellent, and will show grace in all things and particularly in his speech, if he avoids affectation." * * *

[40]

"Madam," replied the Count,[7] "I think the thread is broken. Still, if I am not mistaken, I believe we were saying that the bane of affectation always produces extreme gracelessness in all things and that, on the other hand, the greatest grace is produced by simplicity and nonchalance: in praise of which, and in blame of affectation, many other things could be said; but I wish to add only one thing more. All women have a great desire to be—and when they cannot be, at least to seem—beautiful. Therefore, wherever nature has failed in this regard, they try to remedy it with artifice: whence that embellishing of the face with so much care and sometimes with pain, that plucking of the eyebrows and the forehead, and the use of all those methods and the enduring of those nuisances which you ladies think are hidden to men, but which are well known."

Here madam Costanza Fregosa laughed and said: "It would be much more courteous of you to go on with your discussion, and tell us what the source of grace is, and speak of Courtiership, instead of trying to uncover the defects of women, which is not to the purpose."

"On the contrary, it is much to the purpose," replied the Count, "for the defects that I am speaking of deprive you ladies of grace, since they are caused by nothing but affectation, through which you openly let everyone know your inordinate desire to be beautiful. Do you not see how much more grace a woman has who paints (if at all) so sparingly and so little that whoever sees her is uncertain whether she is painted or not; than another woman so plastered with it that she seems to have put a mask on her face and dares not laugh so as not to cause it to crack, and never changes color except in the morning when she dresses; and, then, for the rest of the entire day remains motionless like a wooden statue and shows herself only by torch-light, like wily merchants who display their cloth in a dark place. And how much more attractive than all the others is one (not ugly, I mean) who is plainly seen to have nothing on her face, it being neither too white nor too red, but has her own natural color, a bit pale, and tinged at times with an open blush from shame or other cause, with her hair artlessly unadorned and in disarray, with gestures simple and natural, without showing effort or care to be beautiful. Such is that careless purity which is so pleasing to the eyes and minds of men who are ever fearful of being deceived by art.

"Beautiful teeth are very attractive in a woman, for since they do not show as openly as the face, not being visible most of the time, we may believe that less care has been taken to make them beautiful than with the face: and yet whoever laughs without cause and solely to display the teeth would betray his art, and, no matter how beautiful they are, would seem most ungraceful to all, like Catullus' Egnatius.[8] The same is true of the hands which, if they

7. The speaker is Count Ludovico da Canossa, who picks up his thread after a long digression on the purity of the Italian dialect that comes from Tuscany.   8. See Catullus's poem 39, on the ever-smiling, white-toothed Egnatius, who brushes his teeth with urine.

are delicate and beautiful, and are uncovered at the proper time, when there is need to use them and not merely to make a show of their beauty, leave one with a great desire to see them more and especially when they are covered with gloves again; for whoever covers them seems to have little care or concern whether they are seen or not, and to have beautiful hands more by nature than by any effort or design.

"Have you ever noticed when a woman, in passing along the street to church or elsewhere, unwittingly happens (in play or through whatever cause) to raise just enough of her dress to show her foot and often a little of her leg? Does this not strike you as something full of grace, if she is seen in that moment, charmingly feminine, dressed in velvet shoes and dainty stockings. Certainly to me it is a pleasing sight, as I believe it is to all of you, because everyone thinks that such elegance of dress, when it is where it would be hidden and rarely seen, must be natural and instinctive with the lady rather than calculated, and that she has no thought of gaining any praise thereby.

[41]

"In such a way one avoids or hides affectation, and you may now see how opposed the latter is to grace, how it deprives of grace every act of the body and the soul: of which so far we have spoken but little, and yet this is not to be neglected; for, as the soul is far more worthy than the body, it deserves to be more cultivated and adorned. And as to what ought to be done in the case of our Courtier, we will lay aside the precepts of the many wise philosophers who have written on this subject to define the virtues of the soul and who discuss their worth with such subtlety; and, holding to our purpose, we will declare in a few words that it suffices if he is, as we say, a man of honor and integrity: for included in this are prudence, goodness, fortitude, and temperance of soul, and all the other qualities proper to such an honored name. And I maintain that he alone is a true moral philosopher who wishes to be good; and for this he has need of few precepts beyond that wish. Socrates was right, therefore, in saying that all his teachings seemed to him to bear good fruit when anyone was incited by them to wish to know and understand virtue: for those persons who have reached the point of desiring nothing more ardently than to be good manage easily to learn all that is needed for that. Hence, we will discuss this no further.

[42]

"But, besides goodness, for everyone the true and principal adornment of the mind is, I think, letters; although the French recognize only the nobility of arms and reckon all the rest as nought; and thus not only do they not esteem, but they abhor letters, and consider all men of letters to be very base; and they think that it is a great insult to call anyone a clerk."

Then the Magnifico Giuliano replied: "What you say is true; this error has prevailed among the French for a long time now. But if kind fate will have it that Monseigneur d'Angoulême[9] succeed to the crown, as is hoped, then I think that just as the glory of arms flourishes and shines in France, so must

---

9. Francis I, who succeeded Louis XII in 1515.

that of letters flourish there also with the greatest splendor. Because, when I was at that court not so long ago, I saw this prince; and, besides the disposition of his body and the beauty of his countenance, he appeared to me to have in his aspect such greatness (yet joined with a certain gracious humanity) that the realm of France must always seem a petty realm to him. Then later, from many gentlemen, both French and Italian, I heard much about his noble manners, the greatness of his spirit, his valor and liberality; and I was told, among other things, how he loved and esteemed letters and how he held all men of letters in the greatest honor; and how he condemned the French themselves for being so hostile to this profession, especially as they have in their midst a university such as that of Paris, frequented by the whole world."

Then the Count said: "It is a great wonder that, at such a tender age, and solely by natural instinct and against the custom of his country, he should of himself have chosen so worthy a path; and, since subjects always imitate the ways of their superiors, it could be, as you say, that the French will yet come to esteem letters at their true worth: which they can easily be persuaded to do if they will but listen to reason, since nothing is more naturally desired by men or more proper to them than knowledge, and it is great folly to say or believe that knowledge is not always a good thing.

[43]

"And if I could speak with them or with others who hold an opinion contrary to mine, I would try to show them how useful and necessary to our life and dignity letters are, being truly bestowed upon men by God as a crowning gift; nor should I lack instances of many excellent commanders in antiquity, who all added the ornament of letters to valor in arms. For, as you know, Alexander venerated Homer so much that he always kept the *Iliad* by his bed. And he gave the greatest attention not only to these studies but to philosophical speculations as well, under Aristotle's guidance. Alcibiades increased his own good qualities and made them greater through letters and the teachings of Socrates. Also the effort that Caesar[1] devoted to study is witnessed by the surviving works he so divinely wrote. Scipio Africanus, it is said, always kept in his hand the works of Xenophon, wherein, under the name of Cyrus, a perfect king is imagined. I could tell you of Lucullus, Sulla, Pompey, Brutus,[2] and many other Romans and Greeks; but I will only remind you that Hannibal,[3] so excellent a military commander, and yet fierce by nature and a stranger to all humanity, faithless and a despiser of men and the gods—had nonetheless some knowledge of letters and was conversant with Greek. And, if I am not mistaken, I think I once read that he even left a book written by him in Greek.

"But there is no need to tell you this, for I am sure you all know how mistaken the French are in thinking that letters are detrimental to arms. You know that the true stimulus to great and daring deeds in war is glory, and whosoever is moved thereto for gain or any other motive, apart from the fact that he never does anything good, deserves to be called not a gentleman, but a base merchant. And it is true glory that is entrusted to the sacred treasury

1. Julius Caesar, author of *The Gallic Wars*.   2. Ambitious Roman politicians.   3. Great Carthaginian general who crossed the Alps to fight Rome.

of letters, as all may understand except those unhappy ones who have never tasted them.

"What soul is so abject, timid, and humble that when he reads of the great deeds of Caesar, Alexander, Scipio, Hannibal, and many others, does not burn with a most ardent desire to resemble them, and does not reckon this transitory life of a few days' span as less important, in order to win to an almost eternal life of fame which, in spite of death, makes him live on in far greater glory than before. But he who does not taste the sweetness of letters cannot know how great the glory is that letters so long preserve, and measures it only by the life of one or two men, because his own memory extends no further. Hence, he cannot value so brief a glory as he would one that is almost eternal (if, to his misfortune, he were not denied knowledge of it); and since he does not much esteem it, we may with reason think that he will not risk such danger to win it as one would who knows of it.

"But I should not want some objector to cite me instances to the contrary in order to refute my opinion, alleging that for all their knowledge of letters the Italians have shown little worth in arms for some time now—which, alas, is only too true. But it must be said that the fault of a few men has brought not only serious harm but eternal blame upon all the rest, and that they have been the true cause of our ruin and of the prostrate (if not dead) virtue of our spirits. Yet it would be a greater shame if we made this fact public than it is to the French to be ignorant of letters. Hence, it is better to pass over in silence what cannot be remembered without pain: and, leaving this subject, upon which I entered against my will, to return to our Courtier.

[44]

"I would have him more than passably learned in letters, at least in those studies which we call the humanities. Let him be conversant not only with the Latin language, but with Greek as well, because of the abundance and variety of things that are so divinely written therein. Let him be versed in the poets, as well as in the orators and historians, and let him be practiced also in writing verse and prose, especially in our own vernacular; for, besides the personal satisfaction he will take in this, in this way he will never want for pleasant entertainment with the ladies, who are usually fond of such things. And if, because of other occupations or lack of study, he does not attain to such a perfection that his writings should merit great praise, let him take care to keep them under cover so that others will not laugh at him, and let him show them only to a friend who can be trusted; because at least they will be of profit to him in that, through such exercise, he will be capable of judging the writing of others. For it very rarely happens that a man who is unpracticed in writing, however learned he may be, can ever wholly understand the toils and industry of writers, or taste the sweetness and excellence of styles, and those intrinsic niceties that are often found in the ancients.

These studies, moreover, will make him fluent, and (as Aristippus[4] said to the tyrant) bold and self-confident in speaking with everyone. However, I would have our Courtier keep one precept firmly in mind, namely, in this as in everything else, to be cautious and reserved rather than forward, and take

4. Companion of Socrates.

care not to get the mistaken notion that he knows something he does not know. For we are all by nature more avid of praise than we ought to be and, more than any other sweet song or sound, our ears love the melody of words that praise us; and thus, like Sirens' voices, they are the cause of shipwreck to him who does not stop his ears to such beguiling harmony. This danger was recognized by the ancients, and books were written to show how the true friend is to be distinguished from the flatterer.[5] But to what avail is this, if many, indeed countless persons know full well when they are being flattered, yet love the one who flatters them and hate the one who tells them the truth? And finding him who praises them to be too sparing in his words, they even help him and proceed to say such things of themselves that they make the impudent flatterer himself feel ashamed.

"Let us leave these blind ones to their error, and let us have our Courtier be of such good judgment that he will not let himself be persuaded that black is white, or presume of himself more than he clearly knows to be true; and especially in those points which (if your memory serves you) messer Cesare said we had often used as the means of bringing to light the folly of many persons. Indeed, even if he knows that the praises bestowed upon him are true, let him avoid error by not assenting too openly to them, nor concede them without some protest; but let him rather disclaim them modestly, always showing and really esteeming arms as his chief profession, and the other good accomplishments as ornaments thereto; and do this especially when among soldiers, in order not to act like those who in studies wish to appear as soldiers, and, when in the company of warriors, wish to appear as men of letters. In this way, for the reasons we have stated, he will avoid affectation and even the ordinary things he does will appear to be very great things."

[45]

Messer Pietro Bembo replied: "Count, I do not see why you insist that this Courtier, who is lettered and who has so many other worthy qualities, should regard everything as an ornament of arms, and not regard arms and the rest as an ornament of letters; which, without any other accompaniment, are as superior to arms in worth as the soul is to the body, because the practice of them pertains properly to the soul, even as that of arms does to the body."

Then the Count replied: "Nay, the practice of arms pertains to both the soul and the body. But I would not have you be a judge in such a case, messer Pietro, because you would be too much suspected of bias by one of the parties. And as this is a debate that has long been waged by very wise men, there is no need to renew it; but I consider it decided in favor of arms; and since I may form our Courtier as I please, I would have him be of the same opinion. And if you are contrary-minded, wait until you can hear of a contest wherein the one who defends the cause of arms is permitted to use arms, just as those who defend letters make use of letters in defending their own cause; for if everyone avails himself of his own weapons, you will see that the men of letters will lose."

"Ah," said messer Pietro, "a while ago you damned the French for their

---

5. Plutarch's *Moralia* addresses the topic.

slight appreciation of letters, and you spoke of what a light of glory letters shed on a man, how they make him immortal; and now it appears that you have changed your mind. Do you not remember that

> *Giunto Alessandro alla famosa tomba*
> *del fero Achille, sospirando disse:*
> *"O fortunato, che sì chiara tromba*
> *trovasti, e chi di te sì alto scrisse!"*

When Alexander had come to the famous tomb of Achilles,[6] sighing, he said: "O fortunate man, to find so clear a trumpet and someone to write of you so loftily!"

And if Alexander envied Achilles, not for his exploits, but for the fortune which had granted him the blessing of having his deeds celebrated by Homer, we see that the esteemed Homer's letters above Achilles' arms. What other judge would you have, or what other sentence on the worthiness of arms and of letters than what has been pronounced by one of the greatest commanders that have ever been?"

[46]

Then the Count replied: "I blame the French for thinking that letters are detrimental to the profession of arms, and I hold that to no one is learning more suited than to a warrior; and I would have these two accomplishments conjoined in our Courtier, each an aid to the other, as is most fitting: nor do I think I have changed my opinion in this. But, as I said, I do not wish to argue as to which of the two is more deserving of praise. Let it suffice to say that men of letters almost never choose to praise any save great men and glorious deeds, which in themselves deserve praise because of the essential worthiness from which they derive; besides this, such men and deeds are very noble material for writers, and are in themselves a great ornament and partly the reason why such writing is perpetuated, which perhaps would not be so much read or prized if it lacked a noble subject, but would be empty and of little moment.

"And if Alexander envied Achilles for being praised by Homer, this does not prove that he esteemed letters more than arms; wherein if he had thought himself to be as far beneath Achilles as he deemed all those who were to write of him to be beneath Homer, I am certain that he would have much preferred fine deeds on his own part to fine talk on the part of others. Hence, I believe that what he said was tacit praise of himself, expressing a desire for what he thought he lacked, namely, the supreme excellence of some writer, and not for what he believed he had already attained, namely, prowess in arms, wherein he did not at all take Achilles to be his superior. Wherefore he called him fortunate, as though to suggest that if his own fame had hitherto not been so celebrated in the world as Achilles' had (which was made bright and illustrious by a poem so divine), this was not because his valor and merits were fewer or less deserving of praise, but because Fortune had granted Achilles such a miracle of nature to be the glorious trumpet for his

6. The great warrior of Homer's *Iliad*.

deeds. Perhaps he wished also to incite some noble talent to write about him, thereby showing that his pleasure in this would be as great as his love and veneration for the sacred monuments of letters: about which by now we have said quite enough."

"Nay, too much," replied signor Ludovico Pio,[7] "for I believe it is not possible in all the world to find a vessel large enough to contain all the things you would have be in our Courtier."

Then the Count said: "Wait a little, for there are yet many more to come."

"In that case," replied Pietro da Napoli, "Grasso de' Medici[8] will have much the advantage over Pietro Bembo!"

[47]

Here everyone laughed, and the Count began again: "Gentlemen, you must know that I am not satisfied with our Courtier unless he be also a musician, and unless, besides understanding and being able to read music, he can play various instruments. For, if we rightly consider, no rest from toil and no medicine for ailing spirits can be found more decorous or praiseworthy in time of leisure than this; and especially in courts where, besides the release from vexations which music gives to all, many things are done to please the ladies, whose tender and delicate spirits are readily penetrated with harmony and filled with sweetness. Hence, it is no wonder that in both ancient and modern times they have always been particularly fond of musicians, finding music a most welcome food for the spirit."

Then signor Gasparo said: "I think that music, along with many other vanities, is indeed well suited to women, and perhaps also to others who have the appearance of men, but not to real men; for the latter ought not to render their minds effeminate and afraid of death."

"Say not so," replied the Count, "or I shall launch upon a great sea of praise for music, reminding you how greatly music was always celebrated by the ancients and held to be a sacred thing; and how it was the opinion of very wise philosophers that the world is made up of music, that the heavens in their motion make harmony, and that even the human soul was formed on the same principle, and is therefore awakened and has its virtues brought to life, as it were, through music. Wherefore it is recorded that Alexander was sometimes so passionately excited by music that, almost in spite of himself, he was obliged to quit the banquet table and rush off to arms; whereupon the musician would change the kind of music, and he would then grow calm and return from arms to the banquet. And, I tell you, grave Socrates learned to play the cithara when he was very old. I remember also having heard once that both Plato and Aristotle wish a man who is well constituted to be a musician; and with innumerable reasons they show that music's power over us is very great; and (for many reasons which would be too long to tell now) that music must of necessity be learned from childhood, not so much for the sake of that outward melody which is heard, but because of the power it has to induce a good new habit of mind and an inclination to virtue, rendering the soul more capable of happiness, just as corporal

---

7. Brave military captain and distant cousin of Emilia Pia.   8. Nickname of a fat (*grasso*) servant of the Medici. Nothing is known of Pietro da Napoli.

exercise makes the body more robust; and that not only is music not harmful to the pursuits of peace and of war, but greatly to their advantage.

"Moreover, Lycurgus[9] approved of music in his harsh laws. And we read that the bellicose Lacedemonians and the Cretans used citharas and other delicate instruments in battle; that many very excellent commanders of antiquity, like Epaminondas, practiced music, and that those who were ignorant of it, like Themistocles,[1] were far less esteemed. Have you not read that music was among the first disciplines that the worthy old Chiron[2] taught the boy Achilles, whom he reared from the age of nurse and cradle; and that such a wise preceptor wished the hands that were to shed so much Trojan blood to busy themselves often at playing the cithara? Where, then, is the soldier who would be ashamed to imitate Achilles, not to speak of many another famous commander that I could cite? Therefore, do not wish to deprive our Courtier of music, which not only makes gentle the soul of man, but often tames wild beasts; and he who does not take pleasure in it can be sure that his spirit lacks harmony among its parts.

"Consider that its power is such that it once caused a fish to let itself be ridden by a man over the stormy sea. You find it used in sacred temples to give praise and thanks to God, and we must believe that it is pleasing to Him, and that He has given it to us as a sweet respite from our toils and vexations. Wherefrom rude laborers in the fields under the burning sun will often beguile their heavy time with crude and rustic song. With it the simple peasant lass, rising before dawn to spin or weave, wards off sleep and makes pleasant her toil. This is the happy pastime of poor sailors after the rains and the winds and the storms. This is the consolation of tired pilgrims in their long and weary journeys, and oftentimes of miserable prisoners in their chains and fetters.

"Thus, as stronger evidence that even rude melody provides the greatest relief from every human toil and care, nature seems to have taught it to the nurse as the chief remedy for the continual crying of tender babes who by the sound of her voice are lulled to restful and placid sleep, forgetting the tears which are so much their lot and at that age are given us by nature as a presage of our later life."

[48]

As the Count now remained silent for a little, the Magnifico Giuliano said: "I am not at all of signor Gasparo's opinion. Indeed I think, for the reasons given by you and for many others, that music is not only an ornament but a necessity to the Courtier. Yet I would have you state how this and the other accomplishments which you assign to him are to be practiced, and at what times and in what manner. For many things which are praiseworthy in themselves often become most unseemly when practiced at the wrong times; and, on the contrary, others which appear to be quite trivial are much prized when done in a proper way."

---

9. Traditional founder of the Spartan constitution.   1. Athenian democratic statesman. Epaminondas of Thebes was famous for a crushing defeat of Sparta.   2. Teacher of Achilles.

[49]

Then the Count said: "Before we enter upon that subject, I would discuss another matter which I consider to be of great importance and which I think must therefore in no way be neglected by our Courtier: and this is a knowledge of how to draw and an acquaintance with the art of painting itself.

"And do not marvel if I require this accomplishment, which perhaps nowadays may seem mechanical and ill-suited to a gentleman; for I recall reading that the ancients, especially throughout Greece, required boys of gentle birth to learn painting in school, as a decorous and necessary thing, and admitted it to first rank among the liberal arts; then by public edict they prohibited the teaching of it to slaves. Among the Romans, too, it was held in highest honor and from it the very noble house of the Fabii took its name; for the first Fabius was called *Pictor*; and he was in fact a most excellent painter, and so devoted to painting that, when he painted the walls of the Temple of Salus,[3] he inscribed his name thereon; for, even though he was born of a family illustrious and honored by so many consular titles, triumphs, and other dignities, and even though he was a man of letters and learned in law, and was numbered among the orators, still it seemed to him that he could add splendor and ornament to his fame by leaving a memorial that he had been a painter. Nor was there any lack of others too who were born of illustrious families and were celebrated in this art; which, besides being most noble and worthy in itself, proves useful in many ways, and especially in warfare, in drawing towns, sites, rivers, bridges, citadels, fortresses, and the like; for, however well they may be stored away in the memory (which is something that is very hard to do), we cannot show them to others so.

"And truly he who does not esteem this art strikes me as being quite lacking in reason; for this universal fabric which we behold, with its vast heaven so resplendent with bright stars, with the earth at the center girdled by the seas, varied with mountains, valleys, rivers, adorned with such a variety of trees, pretty flowers, and grasses—can be said to be a great and noble picture painted by nature's hand and God's; and whoever can imitate it deserves great praise, in my opinion: nor is such imitation achieved without the knowledge of many things, as anyone knows who attempts it. For this reason the ancients held art and artists in the greatest esteem, wherefore art attained to the pinnacle of the highest excellence, very sure proof of which is to be found in the antique statues of marble and bronze that can still be seen. And, although painting differs from sculpture, both spring from the same source, namely, good design. Therefore, since those statues are divine, we can believe that the paintings were divine too; and the more so in being susceptible of greater artistry."

[50]

Then signora Emilia turned to Giancristoforo Romano[4] who was sitting there with the others, and said: "What do you think of this opinion? Do you agree that painting is susceptible of greater artistry than sculpture?"

---

3. Temple of an old Roman goddess associated with hygiene and medicine.   4. Renowned sculptor (1465–1512), goldsmith, and architect, was at the Court of Urbino at the time of the dialogue of the *Courtier.*

Giancristoforo replied: "I think, Madam, that sculpture requires more labor and more skill and is of greater dignity than painting."

The Count rejoined: "Because statues are more durable, one might perhaps say they have a greater dignity; for, since they are made as memorials, they serve better than painting the purpose for which they are made. But, apart from this service to memory, both painting and sculpture are made to adorn, and in this painting is much superior; for if it is not so diuturnal, so to say, as sculpture, still it lasts a long time: and the while it lasts, it is much more beautiful."

Then Giancristoforo replied: "I truly believe that you are speaking contrary to your own persuasion, and that you do this entirely for your Raphael's sake; and you may also be thinking that the excellence in painting which you find in him is so supreme that sculpture in marble cannot attain to such a mark. But, take care, this is to praise an artist and not an art."

Then he went on: "I do indeed think that both the one and the other are artful imitations of nature; but I do not know how you can say that that which is real and is nature's own work is any less imitated by a marble or bronze figure, in which all the members are round, fashioned and proportioned just as nature makes them, than on a panel where one sees only a surface and colors that deceive the eyes; nor will you tell me, surely, that being is not nearer truth than seeming. Besides, I consider sculpture to be more difficult because, if you happen to make a mistake, you cannot correct it, since marble cannot be patched up again, but you have to execute another figure; which does not happen in painting wherein you can make a thousand changes, adding and taking away, improving it all the while."

[51]

The Count said, laughing: "I am not speaking for Raphael's sake, nor must you think me so ignorant as not to know Michelangelo's excellence in sculpture, your own, and that of others. But I am speaking of the art and not of the artists.

"What you say is quite true, that both the one and the other are imitations of nature; but it is not a matter of painting seeming and of sculpture being. For, although statues are in the round as in life and painting is seen only no the surface, statues lack many things which paintings do not lack, and especially light and shade (for the color of flesh is one thing and that of marble another). And this the painter imitates in a natural manner, with light and dark, less or more, according to the need—which the sculptor in marble cannot do. And even though the painter does not fashion his figure in the round, he does make muscles and members rounded in such a manner as to join up with the parts which are not so seen, whereby we see clearly that the painter knows and understands those parts as well. And in this an even greater skill is needed to depict those members that are foreshortened and that diminish in proportion to the distance, on the principle of perspective; which, by means of proportioned lines, colors, light, and shade, gives you foreground and distance on the surface of an upright wall, and as bold or as faint as he chooses. And do you think it a trifle to imitate nature's colors in doing flesh, clothing, and all the other things that have color? This the sculptor cannot do; neither can he render the grace of black eyes or blue eyes, shining with amorous rays. He cannot render the color of blond hair or the gleam of weapons, or the dark of night, or a storm at sea, or lightnings and thunderbolts, or the burning of a city, or the birth of rosy dawn with its rays of gold and red. In short, he cannot do sky, sea, land, mountains, woods, meadows, gardens, rivers, cities, or houses—all of which the painter can do.

[52]

"Therefore I deem painting more noble and more susceptible of artistry than sculpture, and I think that among the ancients it must have had that excellence which other things had; and this we can still see from certain slight remains, particularly in the grottoes of Rome;[5] but we can know it much more clearly from the writings of the ancients in which there is such frequent and honored mention both of the works and of the masters, from which we learn how much the latter were always honored by great lords and republics.

"So we read that Alexander loved Apelles of Ephesus dearly—so much so that once, when he had him paint one of his favorite women and heard that the worthy painter had conceived a most passionate love for her because of her great beauty, he made him an outright gift of her: a generosity truly worthy of Alexander, to give away not only treasures and states, but his own affections and desires; and a sign of a very great love for Apelles to care nothing if, in pleasing the artist, he displeased that woman whom he so dearly loved—whereas we may believe that the woman was sorely grieved to exchange so great a king for a painter. Many other instances are cited of Alexander's kindness to Apelles; but he showed his esteem for him most clearly in giving order by public edict that no other painter should be so bold as to paint his portrait.

"Here I could tell of the rivalry of many noble painters who were the praise and wonder of nearly the whole world; I could tell you with what majesty the ancient emperors adorned their triumphs with paintings, dedicated them in public places, bought them as cherished objects; how some painters have been known to make a gift of their works, deeming gold and silver insufficient to pay for them; and how a painting by Protogenes was so highly prized that when Demetrius[6] was laying siege to Rhodes and could have entered the city and set fire to the quarter where he knew the painting was, he refrained from giving battle and so did not take the city; how Metrodorus, a philosopher and very excellent painter, was sent by the Athenians to Lucius Paulus [7] to teach his children and to decorate the triumph which he had to make ready. And many noble authors have also written about this art, which is a great sign of the esteem it enjoyed: but I would not have us discuss it any further.

"So let it be enough simply to say that it is fitting for our Courtier to have knowledge of painting also, since it is decorous and useful and was prized in those times when men were of greater worth than now. And even if no other utility or pleasure were had from it, it helps in judging the excellence of statues both ancient and modern, vases, buildings, medallions, cameos, inta-glios, and the like, and it also brings one to know the beauty of living bodies, not only in the delicacy of the face but in the proportions of the other parts,

---

5. Famous caves.   6. Famous Macedonian general.   7. Roman general, defeated King Perseus of Macedon.

both in man and in all other creatures. And so you see how a knowledge of painting is the source of very great pleasure. And let those consider this who are so enraptured when they contemplate a woman's beauty that they believe themselves to be in paradise, and yet cannot paint; but if they could, they would gain much greater pleasure because they would more perfectly discern the beauty that engenders so much satisfaction in their hearts."

[53]

Here messer Cesare Gonzaga laughed and said: "I, of course, am no painter; still I am sure I take much greater pleasure in looking at a certain woman than would that most worthy Apelles whom you mentioned a moment ago, were he to return to life now."

The Count replied: "This pleasure of yours does not derive entirely from her beauty but from the affection that you perchance feel for her; and if you were to tell the truth, the first time you beheld that woman, you did not feel a thousandth part of the pleasure that you later felt, even though her beauty was the same. Thus, you can see how much greater a part affection had in your pleasure than did beauty."

"That I do not deny," said messer Cesare; "but just as my pleasure arises from affection, so my affection arises from beauty; hence, we can still say that beauty is the cause of my pleasure."

The Count replied: "Many other causes besides beauty inflame our souls: such as manners, knowledge, speech, gestures, and a thousand other things (which might, however, in some way be called beauties too); but, above all, the feeling that one is loved. Thus, it is possible to love most ardently even in the absence of that beauty of which you speak; but the love which arises solely from the outward beauty we see in bodies will surely give far greater pleasure to him who discerns that beauty more than to him who discerns it less. Therefore, to return to our subject, I think Apelles must have taken more pleasure in contemplating the beauty of Campaspe[8] than did Alexander, because we can readily believe that both men's love sprang solely from her beauty, and that for this reason, perhaps, Alexander decided to give her to Apelles who appeared to have the ability to discern it more perfectly.

"Have you not read that those five girls of Crotone, whom the painter Zeuxis chose from among the others of that city for the purpose of forming from all five a single figure of surpassing beauty, were celebrated by many poets for having been judged beautiful by one who must have been a consummate judge of beauty?"

[54]

Messer Cesare seemed not to be satisfied with this, and would not at all grant that anyone except himself could experience the pleasure he felt in contemplating a certain woman's beauty, and was starting to speak again. But in that moment a great tramping of feet was heard and the noise of loud talking; whereupon everyone turned to see a great light from torches appear at the door of the room; and immediately following there arrived, with a numerous and noble company, the Prefect,[9] who was just coming back from

8. Beautiful slave given by Alexander to Apelles.   9. Maria Francesco della Rovere.

accompanying the Pope part of his way. On entering the palace he had at once asked what the Duchess was doing and had learned what kind of game was being played that evening and the charge given to Count Ludovico to speak of Courtiership. Hence, he was hurrying as fast as he could in order to arrive in time to hear something. Thus, when he had at once made his reverence to the Duchess and had urged the others to be seated (all had stood when he came in), he too sat down in the circle along with some of his gentlemen, among whom were the Marquess Febus da Ceva and his brother Ghirardino, messer Ettore Romano, Vincenzo Calmeta, Orazio Florido,[1] and many others; and, as everyone remained silent, the Prefect said: "Gentlemen, my coming here would indeed do great harm if I were thus to put an obstacle in the way of such fine discussions as I believe those are that were taking place among you just now. But do not do me the wrong of depriving yourselves and me of such pleasure."

Then Count Ludovico said: "Nay, Sir, I think we all must find it far more pleasant to keep silent than to talk; for since this labor has fallen more to me this evening than to the others, I am weary now of speaking, as I think all the others must be of listening; for my talk was not worthy of this company nor equal to the great matter I was charged with; in which, having little satisfied myself, I think I have satisfied the others even less. Hence, you, Sir, were fortunate to come in at the end. And it is well now to give the charge of what remains to someone else who can take my place, because whoever he may be, I know he will do much better than I should if I tried to go on, tired as I now am."

[55]

"Certainly I," replied the Magnifico Giuliano, "shall in no way allow myself to be cheated of the promise you made me; and I am sure that the Prefect will not be displeased to hear this part of it."

"And what was the promise?" asked the Count.

"To tell us how the Courtier should put into effect those good qualities which you have said befit him," replied the Magnifico.

The Prefect, although a mere boy, was more wise and discreet than it seemed could be in such tender years, and in his every movement showed a greatness of spirit together with a certain vivacity of temper that gave true presage of the high mark of virtue to which he would attain. Wherefore he said quickly: "If all this is still to be told, it seems to me that I have arrived in very good time; for in hearing how the Courtier must put into effect those good qualities, I shall also hear what they are, and in this way I shall come to know all that has been said up to now. Therefore, do not refuse, Count, to pay the debt, a part of which you have already settled."

"I should not have such a heavy debt to pay," replied the Count, "if labors were more equally distributed; but the mistake was in giving the authority of command to a lady who is too partial." And thus, laughing, he turned to signora Emilia, who quickly said: "It is not you who should complain of my partiality; but since you do so without reason, we will give someone else a portion of this honor which you call a labor," and, turning to messer Federico

1. Attendants of the Prefect.

Fregoso, she said: "It was you who proposed this game of the Courtier; therefore it is only right that it should fall to you to carry on with part of it; and that part shall be to satisfy the request of the Magnifico Giuliano, declaring in what way, manner, and time, the Courtier is to put into effect his good qualities and practice those things which the Count said befitted him."

Then messer Federico said: "Madam, you are trying to separate what cannot be separated, for these are the very things that make his qualities good and his practice good. Therefore, since the Count has spoken so long and so well, and has also said something of such matters as these and has prepared in his mind the remainder of what he has to say, it was only right that he should continue up to the end."

"Consider yourself to be the Count," signora Emilia replied, "and say what you think he would say; and in this way all satisfaction will be done."

[56]

Then Calmeta[2] said: "Gentlemen, since the hour is late and in order that messer Federico may have no excuse for not telling what he knows, I think it would be well to put off the rest of this discussion until tomorrow, and let the brief time that remains be spent in some other more modest entertainment."

When everyone agreed, the Duchess desired that madonna Margherita[3] and madonna Costanza Fregosa should dance. Whereupon Barletta, a delightful musician and an excellent dancer, who always kept the court amused, began to play upon his instruments; and the two ladies, joining hands, danced first a *bassa*, and then a *roegarze*[4] with extreme grace, much to the delight of those who watched. Then, the night being already far spent, the Duchess rose to her feet, whereupon everyone reverently took leave and retired to sleep.

From *Book 4*

[5]

"Therefore,[5] I think that the aim of the perfect Courtier, which we have not spoken of up to now, is so to win for himself, by means of the accomplishments ascribed to him by these gentlemen, the favor and mind of the prince whom he serves that he may be able to tell him, and always will tell him, the truth about everything he needs to know, without fear or risk of displeasing him; and that when he sees the mind of his prince inclined to a wrong action, he may dare to oppose him and in a gentle manner avail himself of the favor acquired by his good accomplishments, so as to dissuade him of every evil intent and bring him to the path of virtue. And thus, having in himself the goodness which these gentlemen attributed to him, together with readiness of wit, charm, prudence, knowledge of letters and of many other things—the Courtier will in every instance be able adroitly to show the

2. Poet, improviser of verses, and prose writer.   3. Attendant on the duchess.   4. French dance, sometimes danced by four or eight persons. *Bassa*: a popular Spanish dance, often danced by two or three persons.   5. The speaker is Ottaviano Fregoso of the Genoese Republic.

prince how much honor and profit will come to him and to his from justice, liberality, magnanimity, gentleness, and the other virtues that befit a good prince; and, on the other hand, how much infamy and harm result from the vices opposed to these virtues. Hence, I think that even as music, festivals, games, and the other pleasant accomplishments are, as it were, the flower; so to bring or help one's prince toward what is right and to frighten him away from what is wrong are the true fruit of Courtiership. And because the real merit of good deeds consists chiefly in two things, one of which is to choose a truly good end to aim at, and the other is to know how to find means timely and fitting to attain that good end—it is certain that a man aims at the best end when he sees to it that his prince is deceived by no one, listens to no flatterers or slanderers or liars, and distinguishes good from evil, loving the one and hating the other.

[6]

"I think too that the accomplishments attributed to the Courtier by these gentlemen may be a good means of attaining that end—and this because, among the many faults that we see in many of our princes nowadays, the greatest are ignorance and self-conceit. And the root of these two evils is none other than falsehood: which vice is deservedly odious to God and to men, and more harmful to princes than any other; because they have the greatest lack of what they would most need to have in abundance—I mean, someone to tell them the truth and make them mindful of what is right: because their enemies are not moved by love to perform these offices, but are well pleased to have them live wickedly and never correct themselves; and, on the other hand, their enemies do not dare to speak ill of them in public for fear of being punished. Then among their friends there are few who have free access to them, and those few are wary of reprehending them for their faults as freely as they would private persons, and, in order to win grace and favor, often think of nothing save how to suggest things that can delight and please their fancy, although these things be evil and dishonorable; thus, from friends these men become flatterers, and, to gain profit from their close association, always speak and act in order to please, and for the most part make their way by dint of lies that beget ignorance in the prince's mind, not only of outward things but of himself; and this may be said to be the greatest and most monstrous falsehood of all, for an ignorant mind deceives itself and inwardly lies to itself.

[7]

"From this it results that, besides never hearing the truth about anything at all, princes are made drunk by the great license that rule gives; and by a profusion of delights are submerged in pleasures, and deceive themselves so and have their minds so corrupted—seeing themselves always obeyed and almost adored with so much reverence and praise, without ever the least contradiction, let alone censure—that from this ignorance they pass to an extreme self-conceit, so that then they become intolerant of any advice or opinion from others. And since they think that to know how to rule is a very easy thing, and that to succeed therein they need no other art or discipline save sheer force, they give their mind and all their thoughts to maintaining the power they have, deeming true happiness to lie in being able to do what one wishes. Therefore some princes hate reason or justice, thinking it would be a kind of bridle and a way of reducing them to servitude, and of lessening the pleasure and satisfaction they have in ruling if they chose to follow it, and that their rule would be neither perfect nor complete if they were obliged to obey duty and honor, because they think that one who obeys is not a true ruler.

"Therefore, following these principles and allowing themselves to be transported by self-conceit, they become arrogant, and with imperious countenance and stern manner, with pompous dress, gold, and gems, and by letting themselves be seen almost never in public, they think to gain authority among men and to be held almost as gods. And to my mind these princes are like the colossi that were made last year at Rome on the day of the festival in Piazza d'Agone,[6] which outwardly had the appearance of great men and horses in a triumph, and which within were full of tow and rags. But princes of this kind are much worse in that these colossi were held upright by their own great weight, whereas these princes, since they are ill-balanced within and are heedlessly placed on uneven bases, fall to their ruin by reason of their own weight, and pass from one error to a great many: for their ignorance, together with the false belief that they cannot make a mistake and that the power they have comes from their own wisdom, brings them to seize states boldly, by fair means or foul, whenever the possibility presents itself.

[8]

"But if they would take it upon themselves to know and do what they ought, they would then strive not to rule as they now strive to rule, because they would see how monstrous and pernicious a thing it is when subjects, who have to be governed, are wiser than the princes who have to govern. Take note that ignorance of music, of dancing, of horsemanship, does not harm to anyone; nevertheless, one who is not a musician is ashamed and dares not sing in the presence of others, or dance if he does not know how, or ride if he does not sit his horse well. But from not knowing how to govern peoples there come so many woes, deaths, destructions, burnings, ruins, that it may be said to be the deadliest plague that exists on earth. And yet some princes who are so very ignorant of government are not ashamed to attempt to govern, I will not say in the presence of four or six men, but before the whole world, for they hold such a high rank that all eyes gaze upon them and hence not only their great but their least defects are always seen. Thus, it is recorded that Cimon was blamed for loving wine, Scipio for loving sleep, Lucullus for loving feasts. But would to God that the princes of our day might accompany their sins with as many virtues as did those ancients; who, even though they erred in some things, yet did not flee from the promptings and teachings of anyone who seemed to them able to correct those errors; nay, they made every effort to order their lives on the model of excellent men: as Epaminondas on that of Lysias the Pythagorean, Agesilaus on that of Xenophon, Scipio on that of Panaetius,[7] and countless others. But if some of our princes should happen upon a strict philosopher, or anyone at all who

---

6. Modern Piazza Navono.   7. Greek Stoic philosopher of the second century B.C. *Lysias*: Athenian general. *Agesilaus*: king of Sparta and noted general.

might try openly and artlessly to reveal to them the harsh face of true virtue, and teach them what good conduct is and what a good prince's life ought to be, I am certain they would abhor him as they would an asp, or indeed would deride him as a thing most vile.

[9]

"I say, then, that, since the princes of today are so corrupted by evil customs and by ignorance and a false esteem of themselves, and since it is so difficult to show them the truth and lead them to virtue, and since men seek to gain their favor by means of lies and flatteries and such vicious ways— the Courtier, through those fair qualities that Count Ludovico and messer Federico have given him, can easily, and must, seek to gain the good will and captivate the mind of his prince that he may have free and sure access to speak to him of anything whatever without giving annoyance. And if he is such as he has been said to be, he will have little trouble in succeeding in this, and will thus be able always adroitly to tell him the truth about all things; and also, little by little, to inform his prince's mind with goodness, and teach him continence, fortitude, justice, and temperance, bringing him to taste how much sweetness lies hidden beneath the slight bitterness that is at first tasted by anyone who struggles against his vices; which are always noxious and offensive and attended by infamy and blame, just as the virtues are beneficial, smiling, and full of praise. And he will be able to incite his prince to these by the example of the famous captains and other excellent men to whom the ancients were wont to make statues of bronze, of marble, and sometimes of gold, and to erect these in public places, both to honor these men and to encourage others, so that through worthy emulation they may be led to strive to attain that glory too.

[10]

"In this way the Courtier will be able to lead his prince by the austere path of virtue, adorning it with shady fronds and strewing it with pretty flowers to lessen the tedium of the toilsome journey for one whose strength is slight; and now with music, now with arms and horses, now with verses, now with discourse of love, and with all those means whereof these gentlemen have spoken, to keep his mind continually occupied in worthy pleasures, yet always impressing upon him also some virtuous habit along with these enticements, as I have said, beguiling him with salutary deception; like shrewd doctors who often spread the edge of the cup with some sweet cordial when they wish to give a bitter-tasting medicine to sick and overdelicate children.

"Thus, by using the veil of pleasure to such an end, the Courtier will reach his aim in every time and place and activity, and for this will deserve much greater praise and reward than for any other good work that he could do in the world. For there is no good more universally beneficial than a good prince, nor any evil more universally pernicious than a bad prince: likewise, there is no punishment atrocious and cruel enough for those wicked courtiers who direct gentle and charming manners and good qualities of character to an evil end, namely to their own profit, and who thereby seek their prince's favor in order to corrupt him, turn him from the path of virtue, and bring him to vice; for such as these may be said to contaminate with a deadly poison, not a single cup from which one man alone must drink, but the public fountain that is used by all the people."

MARGUERITE DE NAVARRE
1492–1549

The French "discovered" Italy in the latter part of the fifteenth century, both through travel and, starting with the expedition of 1494 under King Charles VIII, through military invasions. Covetous of the fame and distinction enjoyed by the smaller and more sophisticated Italian city-states (such as Castiglione's Urbino), French rulers and aristocrats adapted Italian artistic, literary, and social values to their own culture. Marguerite de Navarre, one of the most influential members of French courtly society, played a significant part in bringing about this transformation of court culture. As a writer and a patron of artists, she also responded seriously to the spiritual and intellectual challenge to Christian faith brought about by the Reformation movements, including the Christian humanism associated with Erasmus.

Marguerite was born at Angoulême on April 11, 1492, the daughter of Charles of Orléans, count of Angoulême, and of Louise of Savoy. Her brother, the future King Francis I, was born two years later. From her earliest years, Marguerite received an exceptionally good education, including instruction in Latin, Italian, Spanish, and German; later in life she also studied Greek and Hebrew. Marriages in her class were at the time arrangements between ruling houses, dictated by political and social convenience; thus at seventeen she was married to Charles, duke of Alençon, a feudal lord who was culturally not her match. When her brother succeeded Louis XII to the French throne in 1515, Marguerite became one of the most influential women at the royal court, where she advised the king and received dignitaries and ambassadors as well as eminent men of letters. Under Francis I, the French court flourished culturally, bringing artists as famous as Leonardo da Vinci (1452–1519) and Benvenuto Cellini (1500–1571) to work in the court.

Francis I also inherited the military tradition of his predecessors in carrying on the Italian wars, the complicated conflicts fought on Italian soil between his forces and those of the Holy Roman Emperor, Charles V. His defeat in the crucial battle of Pavia in 1525 was a double blow for Marguerite: her brother was taken to Madrid as a prisoner and her husband, thought to be in part responsible for the defeat, died upon his return to France that same year. Marguerite went to Madrid to assist her sick brother and helped negotiate with Charles V for his release, which was sanctioned by the Treaty of Madrid in 1526.

The year following her husband's death, Marguerite became "Queen of Navarre" when she married Henri d'Albret, the king of Navarre in title only, since most of that domain had been annexed by Spain in 1516, limiting the possessions of the d'Albret dynasty to the lower, French section. This region contained important castles at such places as Pau and Nérac, where Marguerite held court and received visiting intellectuals and reformist religious thinkers. Eleven years younger than Marguerite, Henri d'Albret was a dashing, flighty, and intellectually disappointing husband—and is thought to be the prototype for the philandering and misogynistic character of Hircan in the *Heptameron*. Their only daughter, Jeanne, born in 1527, was the mother of the future King Henry IV of France.

Marguerite continued to be involved in her royal brother's activities: in 1529 she took part in the negotiations that led to the Treaty of Cambrai and she participated in diplomacy and peace talks in the years 1536–38. Her interest, however, was increasingly focused on intellectual and literary pursuits and on religious meditation and debate. Erasmus, John Calvin, and Pope Paul III were among her numerous correspondents. Throughout her life she was a protector of writers and thinkers accused or suspected of Protestant leanings, including Rabelais, who dedicated the third book of *Gargantua and Pantagruel* to her. Her first published work, *The Mirror of the Sinful Soul* (1531), was found by the theologians of the Sorbonne to contain elements of Protestant "heresy"; the edition of 1533, containing an additional "Dialogue in the Form of a Night Vision" written earlier and dealing with the theological problem of salvation, was condemned. The king had to intervene on behalf of his sister and her chaplain. Later it became more difficult for Francis I to maintain a lenient and conciliatory stance in the rivalry between Catholics and Protestants, which was a political and military matter as much as it was a religious dispute. Protestants and their sympathizers were persecuted, and several prominent intellectuals went into prudent exile or were burned at the stake. Marguerite, who had an intellectual and mystical faith, appears never to have abandoned Catholicism but to have hoped for internal reform.

During the last part of her life, Marguerite took several retreats to the convent at Tusson in the French region of Poitou. There in April of 1547 she received news of her brother's death. In the same year she published her *Marguerite de la Marguerite des Princesses* (with a play on the word *marguerite,* which in French means both "pearl" and "daisy"), a collection including long devotional poems and theatrical pieces ranging from allegory to farce. Both in the collection and in later poems she returns to the theme of her sorrow at her brother's death, tempered by the solace of religious faith. During the following year Marguerite returned only for short periods to the French court, where her relations with her nephew, the new king, Henry II, were uneasy. In 1549 she retired to Navarre and died in the castle of Odos on December 21.

Marguerite's name is preeminently associated with the *Heptameron*, a collection of seventy stories organized into a series of ten tales told over seven days and framed by a larger narrative that reveals the storytellers' characters and relationships with each other. In the prologue, five men and five women are brought together in the Pyrenees, when natural and criminal forces—including a flood, bandits, a bear, and murderers—prevent them from returning home. They arrive independently at an abbey, where, at the suggestion of Parlamente, thought to represent Marguerite herself, they agree to tell stories each day until they are able to return home. Within the fiction, the stories are presented as a collective enterprise by courtly storytellers. The fictional situation may parallel the authorship of the *Heptameron* itself. We do not know the exact circumstances of its production: possibly Marguerite composed, collected, or commissioned tales for the narrative; perhaps she composed only the frame, which is in many ways the work's most compelling account of social and courtly relations. Critics' historical preference for single authorship over collaboration should not, at any rate, affect the pleasure or complexity one finds in the tales, their sequence, or the narrative framing them.

The stories largely deal with love, sexuality, clerical abuse in the Church, moderate struggles between social classes, and above all, the antagonism between the sexes, particularly concerning issues of marital fidelity and the status of women. The *Heptameron* pays considerable attention to ideas of masculinity and to ideals and stereotypes about women. Class tensions are somewhat more muted, but the conflicts between social superiors and inferiors are the same as those that emerge from the war between the sexes: the prerogative of powerful lords and husbands to license and dominance in social and marital contracts is set in conflict with the rights of those victimized to avenge their compromised honor, usually by cleverness. On these subjects, the men and women who narrate and hear the stories are, to say the least, unafraid to disagree with each other about the tales' significances, both in the dialogues of the frame and in their stories, which implicitly debate such issues as the appropriate evaluation of the philandering husband or the clever wife. Ennasuite, for example, uses her tale to celebrate a high-spirited, intelligent princess who physically resists and humiliates a gentleman who assaults her in her bedchamber. Hircan, on the other hand, retorts that Ennasuite's gentleman should have raped the princess rather than suffer humiliation and uses his own tale to present manly dominance—which characters like Ennasuite have been disparaging—in an attractive and romantic light.

The *Heptameron* belongs to a tradition of storytelling that includes the *Arabian Nights*, Chaucer's *Canterbury Tales*, and Boccaccio's *Decameron*. In the prologue, Parlamente overtly ties the storytelling game to the *Decameron* and a recent translation into French (commissioned by Marguerite) that drew, she says, the admiration of the French court, including Francis I, the Dauphin (heir to the throne), Queen Catherine de Médicis, and Marguerite. When the two women, along with other members of the court, propose to write a French *Decameron,* they agree to one difference from Boccaccio's precedent: "they should not write any story that was not truthful." The Dauphin (the future Henry II), moreover, rules out literary scholars on the grounds that "rhetorical ornament would in part falsify the truth of the account." The stories are, in fact, mysterious in origin, and with one exception, which the group approves after debate, none is drawn from a literary source.

The stipulation to relate only truthful stories identifies a dominant thematic concern of the *Heptameron*: the relationship between language and truth. For this overarching concern, there are two broad and largely irreconcilable frames of reference—one religious and the other social. In the prologue, when the travelers are considering how they should pass the time until they may safely return home, they acknowledge that the only means to calm their restless and dissatisfied souls is to devote themselves to the holy word of God as the only source of truth and consolation. Even Hircan, who places the most faith in his social position and manly self-assertion, indicates that he finds moments of solace in reading God's word, although he goes on to hint that he would choose the temporary solace of an adulterous conquest (like Petrarch, he "sees the better but chooses the worst"). Conversely, Oisille, the oldest and most evangelical of the group, chooses her strict regimen of religious study and devotion as the one "remedy"—of the many she has tried—for "boredom and . . . sorrow." Unable to "become so mortified in the flesh" as Oisille, however, the group desires a "pastime, which, while not being prejudicial to the soul, will be agreeable to the body." The conversation between Oisille and Hircan darkly suggests that to devote oneself entirely to spiritual contemplation is threatening to the young because it is tantamount to preparing oneself for death. Storytelling, then, is the group's concession to their social and physical needs: it is a middle ground between physical pleasures such as the adulterous liaison that Hircan contemplates and the worldly renunciation recommended by Oisille. The choice of strictly "truthful" stories emphasizes the group's compromise.

Yet the "truthfulness" of stories has little to do with the transcendent truth of God: as nonfiction, the tales instead heighten the social tensions that are frequently the themes of the characters' narratives. When the characters comment—in the frame and in their own stories—on each others' tales and motives for particular narrative choices, they reveal how social factors influence the ways in which they evaluate and interpret the world. Divine "truth" gives way to individual and social perspective: age, gender, social standing, education, marital status, and religious disposition form the grounds for rivalry and dispute among the group members. In this way, the *Heptameron* philosophically explores the relationship between fiction-making and spiritual knowledge at the same time that it presents a lively and complex portrait of the broad social and religious concerns entertained by the brilliant, aristocratic court to which Marguerite de Navarre belonged.

P. A. Chilton's justly praised translation of the *Heptameron* (1984) has an excellent introduction. John D. Lyons and Mary B. McKinley, eds., *Critical Tales: New Studies of the Heptameron and Early Modern Culture* (1993), contains useful essays on the *Heptameron*. B. J. Davis, *The Storytellers in Marguerite de Navarre's Heptameron* (1978), presents detailed discussions of the narrators, and Glyn P. Norton, "Narrative Function in the *Heptaméron* Frame-Story," in *La Nouvelle française à la Renaissance* (1981), analyzes the framing narrative. Marcel Tetel, *Marguerite de Navarre's Heptameron: Themes, Language, and Structure* (1973), is meant for the more advanced student. Samuel Putnam, *Marguerite de Navarre* (1935), is an informative and readable biography.

PRONOUNCING GLOSSARY

The following list uses common English syllables and stress accents to provide rough equivalents of selected words whose pronunciation may be unfamiliar to the general reader.

Alençon: *ah-lon-sohnh'*

Angoulême: *ahn-goo-lem'*

Cordeliers: *cohr-del-yay'*

Coucer: *coo-say'*

Dagoucin: *da-goo-sanh'*

d'Albret: *dahl-bray*

Ennasuite: *aw-nah-sweet'*

Gave de Pau: *gav deu poh*

Geburon: *zhay-byew-ronh'*

Grand-Maître de Chaumont: *grahn–metr' deu shoh-mon'*

Hircan: *eer'-canh*

lever: *leu-vay'*

Longarine: *lohn-gah-reen'*

Monseigneur the Dauphin: *mohnh-sen-yeur' leu doh-fanh'*

de Navarre: *deu na-vahr'*

Nomerfide: *noh-mehr-feed'*

Oisille: *wah-zee'*

Parlamente: *pahr-lah-mehnt'*

Sendras: *sawnh-dra'*

serviteur: *sehr-vee-teur'*

Simontaut: *see-mohn-toh'*

The Heptameron[1]

From *Prologue*

*   *   *

* * * Parlamente, the wife of Hircan,[2] was not one to let herself become idle or melancholy, and having asked her husband for permission, she spoke to the old Lady Oisille.[3]

"Madame," she said, "you have had much experience of life, and you now occupy the position of mother in regard to the rest of us women, and it surprises me that you do not consider some pastime to alleviate the boredom and distress that we shall have to bear during our long stay here. Unless we

1. Translated by P. A. Chilton.   2. Hircan is variously described, in the book itself and by its commentators, as brilliant, flighty, sensual, capable of sarcasm and grossness. The name is related to Hircania, an imaginary and proverbially wild region in classical literature; the root is that of *hircus*, Latin for "goat" (cf. English *hircine*: libidinous). Parlamente probably represents Marguerite, whose name can be construed as *perle amante*, "loving pearl," or as *parlementer*, which refers to eloquent speaking.   3. The oldest, most authoritative, and most evangelical of the storytellers; she seems to be named for Louise—either Louise of Savoy, Marguerite's mother, or her lady-in-waiting, Louise de Daillon.

have some amusing and virtuous way of occupying ourselves, we run the risk of [falling][4] sick."

Longarine,[5] the young widow, added, "What is worse, we'll all become miserable and disagreeable—and that's an incurable disease. There isn't a man or woman amongst us who hasn't every cause to sink into despair, if we consider all that we have lost."

Ennasuite[6] laughed and rejoined, "Not everyone's lost a husband, like you, you know. And as for losing servants, no need to despair about that—there are plenty of men ready to do service! All the same, I do agree that we ought to have something to amuse us, so that we can pass the time as pleasantly as we can."

Her companion Nomerfide[7] said that this was a very good idea, and that if she had to spend a single day without some entertainment, she would be sure to die the next.

All the men supported this, and asked the Lady Oisille if she would kindly organize what they should do.

"My children," replied Oisille, "when you ask me to show you a pastime that is capable of delivering you from your boredom and your sorrow, you are asking me to do something that I find very difficult. All my life I have searched for a remedy, and I have found only one—the reading of holy Scripture, in which one may find true and perfect spiritual joy, from which proceed health and bodily repose. And if you ask what the prescription is that keeps me happy and healthy in my old age, I will tell you. As soon as I rise in the morning I take the Scriptures and read them. I see and contemplate the goodness of God, who for our sakes has sent His son to earth to declare the holy word and the good news by which He grants remission of all our sins, and payment of all our debts, through His gift to us of His love, His passion and His merits. And my contemplations give me such joy, that I take my psalter, and with the utmost humility, sing the beautiful psalms and hymns that the Holy Spirit has composed in the heart of David and the other authors. The contentment this affords me fills me with such well-being that whatever the evils of the day, they are to me so many blessings, for in my heart I have by faith Him who has borne these evils for me. Likewise, before supper, I withdraw to nourish my soul with readings and meditations. In the evening I ponder in my mind everything I have done during the day, so that I may ask God forgiveness of my sins, and give thanks to Him for His mercies. And so I lay myself to rest in His love, fear and peace, assured against all evils. And this, my children, is the pastime that long ago I adopted. All other ways have I tried, but none has given me spiritual contentment. I believe that if, each morning, you give one hour to reading, and then, during mass, say your prayers devoutly, you will find even in this wilderness all the beauty a city could afford. For, a person who knows God will find all things beautiful in Him, and without Him all things will seem ugly. So I say to you, if you would live in happiness, heed my advice."

---

4. Brackets indicate translator's interpolations.   5. A young and wisely talkative widow, often identified with one of Marguerite's ladies-in-waiting, who among her titles had that of lady of Langrai (hence her name, which is also interpreted as a play on *langue orine*, meaning "tongue of gold").   6. *Enna* may stand for "Anne," and *suite* means "retinue"; so the character is identifiable with Anne de Vivonne, one of the ladies in Marguerite's entourage who collaborated on the *Heptameron* project at court. Her attitude toward men can be bitter and sharply ironical.   7. The youngest member of the group, who generally views life with joyful optimism.

Then Hircan spoke: "Madame, anyone who has read the holy Scriptures—as indeed I think we all have here—will readily agree that what you have said is true. However, you must bear in mind that we have not yet become so mortified in the flesh that we are not in need of some sort of amusement and physical exercise in order to pass the time. After all, when we're at home, we've got our hunting and hawking to distract us from the thousand and one foolish thoughts that pass through one's mind. The ladies have their housework and their needlework. They have their dances, too, which provide a respectable way for them to get some exercise. All this leads me to suggest, on behalf of the men here, that you, Madame, since you are the oldest among us, should read to us every morning about the life of our Lord Jesus Christ, and the great and wonderful things He has done for us. Between dinner and vespers I think we should choose some pastime, which, while not being prejudicial to the soul, will be agreeable to the body. In that way we shall spend a very pleasant day."

Lady Oisille replied that she herself found it so difficult to put behind her the vanities of life, that she was afraid the pastime suggested by Hircan might not be a good choice. However, the question should, she thought, be judged after an open discussion, and she asked Hircan to put his point of view first.

"Well, my point of view wouldn't take long to give," he began, "if I thought that the pastime I would really like were as agreeable to a certain lady among us as it would be to me. So I'll keep quiet for now, and abide by what the others say."

Thinking he was intending this for her, his wife, Parlamente, began to blush. "It may be, Hircan," she said, half angrily and half laughing, "that the lady you think ought to be the most annoyed at what you say would have ways and means of getting her own back, if she so desired. But let's leave on one side all pastimes that require only two participants, and concentrate on those which everybody can join in."

Hircan turned to the ladies. "Since my wife has managed to put the right interpretation on my words," he said, "and since private pastimes don't appeal to her, I think she's in a better position than anyone to know which pastime all of us will be able to enjoy. Let me say right now that I accept her opinion as if it were my own."

They all concurred in this, and Parlamente, seeing that it had fallen to her to make the choice, addressed them all as follows.

"If I felt myself to be as capable as the ancients, by whom the arts were discovered, then I would invent some pastime myself that would meet the requirements you have laid down for me. However, I know what lies within the scope of my own knowledge and ability—I can hardly even remember the clever things other people have invented, let alone invent new things myself. So I shall be quite content to follow closely in the footsteps of other people who have already provided for your needs. For example, I don't think there's one of us who hasn't read the hundred tales by Boccaccio,[8] which have recently been translated from Italian into French, and which are so highly thought of by the [most Christian] King Francis I, by Monseigneur the Dauphin, Madame the Dauphine[9] and Madame Marguerite. If Boccaccio

8. The *Decameron*. 9. The future queen Catherine de Médicis. The Dauphin is the future Henry II, nephew of Marguerite.

could have heard how highly these illustrious people praised him, it would have been enough to raise him from the grave. As a matter of fact, the two ladies I've mentioned, along with other people at the court, made up their minds to do the same as Boccaccio. There was to be one difference—that they should not write any story that was not truthful. Together with Monseigneur the Dauphin the ladies promised to produce ten stories each, and to get together a party of ten people who were qualified to contribute something, excluding those who studied and were men of letters. Monseigneur the Dauphin didn't want their art brought in, and he was afraid that rhetorical ornament would in part falsify the truth of the account. A number of things led to the project being completely forgotten—the major affairs of state that subsequently overtook the King, the peace treaty between him and the King of England, the confinement of Madame the Dauphine and several other events of sufficient importance to keep the court otherwise occupied. However, it can now be completed in the ten days of leisure we have before us, while we wait for our bridge to be finished. If you so wished, we could go each afternoon between midday and four o'clock to the lovely meadow that borders the Gave de Pau, where the leaves on the trees are so thick that the hot sun cannot penetrate the shade and the cool beneath. There we can sit and rest, and each of us will tell a story which he has either witnessed himself, or which he has heard from somebody worthy of belief. At the end of our ten days we will have completed the whole hundred. And if, God willing, the lords and ladies I've mentioned find our endeavors worthy of their attention, we shall make them a present of them when we get back, instead of the usual statuettes and beads. I'm sure they would find that preferable. In spite of all this, if any of you is able to think of something more agreeable, I shall gladly bow to his or her opinion."

But every one of them replied that it would be impossible to think of anything better, and that they could hardly wait for the morrow. So the day came happily to a close with reminiscences of things they had all experienced in their time.

As soon as morning came they all went into Madame Oisille's room, where she was already at her prayers. When they had listened for a good hour to the lesson she had to read them, and then devoutly heard mass, they went, at ten o'clock, to dine, after which they retired to their separate rooms to attend to what they had to do. At midday they all went back as arranged to the meadow, which was looking so beautiful and fair that it would take a Boccaccio to describe it as it really was. Enough for us to say that a more beautiful meadow there never was seen. When they were all seated on the grass, so green and soft that there was no need for carpets or cushions, Simontaut[1] said: "Which of us shall be [the one in charge]?"

"Since you have spoken first," replied Hircan, "it should be you who give the orders. Where games are concerned everybody is equal."

"Would to God," sighed Simontaut, "that the one thing in all the world I had were the power to order everyone in our party to comply with my wishes!"

1. Identified with François de Bourdeille, the husband of Anne of Vivonne. He is the long-standing *serviteur* to Parlamente: "According to the *serviteur*'s practice, as the *Heptameron* presents it, a married aristocratic woman has the right to maintain several devoted knights in her service. . . . Since it is supposed to be chaste, the *serviteur*'s relationship, this remnant of courtly and chivalrous love, can coexist with faithful marriage. . . . Nevertheless, there is evidently considerable anxiety about the institution as such" [From the translator's introduction]. His name punningly alludes to masculinity (*monte haut*: rises high).

Parlamente knew very well what he meant by this remark, and started to cough. Hircan did not notice the colour rising in her cheeks, and simply went on to invite Simontaut to start, which he did at once.

"Ladies, I have been so ill rewarded for my long and devoted service, that, in order to avenge myself on Love and on the woman who is so cruel to me, I shall do my utmost to collect together all the accounts of foul deeds perpetrated by women on us poor men. And every single one will be the unadulterated truth."

From *Day One*

STORY THREE

I've often wished, Ladies, that I'd been able to share the good fortune of the man in the story I'm about to tell you.[2]

So here it is. In the town of Naples in the time of King Alfonso[3] (whose well-known lasciviousness was, one might say, the very sceptre by which he ruled) there lived a nobleman—a handsome, upright and likeable man, a man indeed whose qualities were so excellent that a certain old gentleman granted him the hand of his daughter. In beauty and charm she was in every way her husband's equal, and they lived in deep mutual affection until a carnival, in the course of which the King disguised himself and went round all the houses in the town, where the people vied with one another to give him a good reception. When he came to the house of the gentleman I have referred to, he was entertained more lavishly than in any of the other houses. Preserves, minstrels, music—all were laid before him, but above all there was the presence of the most beautiful lady that the King had ever seen. At the end of the banquet, the lady sang for the King with her husband, and so sweetly did she sing that her beauty was more than ever enhanced. Seeing such physical perfection, the King took less delight in contemplating the gentle harmony that existed between the lady and her husband, than he did in speculating as to how he might go about spoiling it. The great obstacle to his desires was the evident deep mutual love between them, and so, for the time being, he kept his passion hidden and as secret as he could. But in order to obtain at least some relief for his feelings, he held a series of banquets for the lords and ladies of Naples, to which he did not, of course, omit to invite the gentleman and his fair wife.

As everyone knows, men see and believe just what they want to, and the King thought he caught something in the lady's eyes which augured well— if only the husband were not in the way. To find out if his surmise was correct, therefore, he sent the husband off for two or three weeks to attend to some business in Rome. Up till then the wife had never had him out of her sight, and she was heartbroken the moment he walked out of the door. The King took the opportunity to console her as often as possible, showering blandishments and gifts of all kinds upon her, with the result that in the end she felt not only consoled, but even content in her husband's absence. Before

2. The narrator is Saffredent, one of the younger members of the party, fond of company and pleasure, and a devoted admirer of Parlamente. He is often identified with an Admiral Bonnivet whom Marguerite knew well and some of whose amorous adventures are the subject of other stories in the *Heptameron*. 3. Alfonso V of Aragon (1396–1458), the cultivated and unfaithful husband of Maria, daughter of King Henry III of Castile.

the three weeks were up she had fallen so much in love with the King that she was every bit as upset about her husband's imminent return as she had been about his departure. So, in order that she should not be deprived of the King after her husband's return, it was agreed that she would let her royal lover know whenever her husband was going to his estates in the country. He could then come to see her without running any risks, and in complete secrecy, so that her honour and reputation—which gave her more concern than her conscience—could not possibly be damaged in any way.

Dwelling on the prospect of the King's visits with considerable pleasure, the lady gave her husband such an affectionate reception that, although he had heard during his absence that the King had been paying her a lot of attention, he had not the slightest suspicion of how far things had gone. However, the fire of passion cannot be concealed for long, and as time went by its flames began to be somewhat obvious. He naturally began to guess at the truth, and kept a close watch on his wife until there was no longer any room for doubt. But he decided to keep quiet about it, because he was afraid that if he let on that he knew, he might suffer even worse things at the hands of the King than he had already. He considered, in short, that it was better to put up with the affront, than to risk his life for the sake of a woman who apparently no longer loved him. He was, all the same, angry and bitter, and determined to get his own back if at all possible.

Now he was well aware of the fact that bitterness and jealousy can drive women to do things that love alone will never make them do, and that this is particularly true of women with strong feelings and high principles of honour. So one day, while he was conversing with the Queen, he made so bold as to say that he felt very sorry for her when he saw how little the King really loved her. The Queen had heard all about the affair between the King and the gentleman's wife, and merely replied:

"I do not expect to be able to combine both honour and pleasure in my position. I am perfectly well aware that while I receive honour and respect, it is *she* who has all the pleasure. But then, I know too that while she may have the pleasure, she does not receive the honour and respect."

He knew, of course, to whom she was referring, and this was his reply: "Madame, you were born to honour and respect. You are after all of such high birth that, being queen or being empress could scarcely add to your nobility. But you are also beautiful, charming and refined, and you deserve to have your pleasures as well. The woman who is depriving you of those pleasures which are yours by right, is in fact doing herself more harm— because her moment of glory will eventually turn to shame and she will forfeit as much pleasure as she, you or any woman in the Kingdom of Naples could ever have. And if I may say so, Madame, if the King didn't have a crown on his head, he wouldn't have the slightest advantage over me as far as giving pleasure to ladies is concerned. What is more, I'm quite sure that in order to satisfy a refined person such as yourself, he really ought to be wishing he could exchange his constitution for one more like my own!"

The Queen laughed, and said: "The King may have a more delicate constitution than your own. Even so, the love which he bears me gives me so much satisfaction that I prefer it to all else."

"Madame, if that were the case, then I would not feel so sorry for you, because I know that you would derive great happiness from the pure love you feel within you, if it were matched by an equally pure love on the part of the King. But God has denied you this, in order that you should not find in this man the answer to all your wants and so make him your god on earth."

"I admit," said the Queen, "that my love for him is so deep that you will never find its like, wherever you may look."

"Forgive me," said the gentlemen, "but there are hearts whose love you've never sounded. May I be so bold as to tell you that there is a certain person who loves you, and loves you so deeply and so desperately, that in comparison your love for the King is as nothing? And his love grows and goes on growing in proportion as he sees the King's love for you diminishing. So, if it were, Madame, to please you, and you were to receive his love, you would be more than compensated for all that you have lost."

The Queen began to realize, both from what he was saying, and from the expression on his face, that he was speaking from the depths of his heart. She remembered that he had some time ago sought to do her service,[4] and that he had felt so deeply about it that he had become quite melancholy. At the time she had assumed the cause of his mood lay with his wife, but she was now quite convinced that the real reason was his love for her. Love is a powerful force, and will make itself felt whenever it is more than mere pretence, and it was this powerful force that now made her certain of what remained hidden from the rest of the world. She looked at him again. He was certainly more attractive than her husband. He had been left by his wife, too, just as she had been left by the King. Tormented by jealousy and bitterness, allured by the gentleman's passion, she sighed, tears came to her eyes, and she began: "Oh God! Must it take the desire for revenge to drive me to do what love alone would never have driven me to?"

Her words were not lost on the gentleman who replied: "Madame, vengeance is sweet indeed, when instead of taking one's enemy's life, one gives life to a lover who is true. It is time, I think, that the truth freed you from this foolish love for a man who certainly has no love for you. It is time that a just and reasonable love banished from you these fears that so ill become one whose spirit is so strong and so virtuous. Why hesitate, Madame? Let us set aside rank and station. Let us look upon ourselves as a man and a woman, as the two most wronged people in the world, as two people who have been betrayed and mocked by those whom we loved with all our hearts. Let us, Madame, take our revenge, not in order to punish them as they deserve, but in order to do justice to our love. My love for you is unbearable. If it is not requited I shall die. Unless your heart is as hard as diamond or as stone, it is impossible that you should not feel some spark from this fire that burns the more fiercely within me the more I try to stifle it. I am dying for love of you! And if that cannot move you to take pity on me and grant me your love, then at least your own love for yourself must surely force you to do so. For you, who are so perfect that you merit the devotion of all the honourable and worthy men in all the world, have been despised and deserted by the very man for whose sake you have disdained all others!"

At this speech the Queen was quite beside herself. Lest her face betray the turmoil of her mind, she took his arm and led him into the garden adjoining her room. For a long time she walked up and down with him saying

---

4. I.e., become her *serviteur*. See n. 1, p. 1860.

nothing. But he knew that the conquest was almost complete, and when they reached the end of the path, where no one could see them, he expressed in the clearest possible way the love that for so long he had kept concealed. At last they were of one mind. And so it was, one might say, that together they enacted a Vengeance, having found the Passion too much to bear.[5]

Before they parted they arranged that whenever the husband made his trips to his village, he would, if the King had gone off to the town, go straight to the castle to see the Queen. Thus they would fool the very people who were trying to fool them. Moreover, there would now be four people joining in the fun, instead of just two thinking they had it all to themselves. Once this was settled, the Queen retired to her room and the gentleman went home, both of them now sufficiently cheered up to forget all their previous troubles. No longer did the King's visits to the gentleman's lady distress either of them. Dread had now turned to desire, and the gentleman started to make trips to his village rather more often than he had in the past. It was, after all, only half a league out of the town. Whenever the King heard that the gentleman had gone to the country, he would make his way straight to his lady. Similarly, whenever the gentleman heard that the King had left his castle, he would wait till nightfall and then go straight to the Queen—to act, so to speak, as the King's viceroy. He managed to do this in such secrecy that no one had the slightest inkling of what was going on. They proceeded in this fashion for quite a while, but the King, being a public person, had much greater difficulty concealing his love-affair sufficiently to prevent any-one at all getting wind of it. In fact, there were a few unpleasant wags who started to make fun of the gentleman, saying he was a cuckold, and putting up their fingers like cuckold's horns whenever his back was turned. Anyone with any decency felt very sorry for the man. He knew what they were saying, of course, but derived a good deal of amusement from it, and reckoned his horns were surely as good as the King's crown.

One day when the King was visiting the gentleman and his wife at their home, he noticed a set of antlers mounted on the wall. He burst out laughing, and could not resist the temptation to remark that the horns went very well with the house. The gentleman was a match for the King, however. He had an inscription placed on the antlers which read as follows:

> *Io porto le corna, ciascun lo vede,*
> *Ma tal le porta, che no lo crede.*[6]

Next time the king was in the house, he saw the inscription, and asked what it meant.

The gentleman simply said: "If the King doesn't tell his secrets to his subjects, then there's no reason why his subjects should tell their secrets to the King. And so far as horns are concerned, you should bear in mind that they don't always stick up and push their wearers' hats off. Sometimes they're so soft that you can wear a hat on top of them, without being troubled by them, and even without knowing they're there at all!"

From these words the King realized that the gentleman knew about his affair with his wife. But he never suspected that the gentleman was having

---

5. An allusion to medieval mystery plays: after the Passion and Resurrection, the mystery of Vengeance depicted the punishment of Christ's slayers [Translator's note].   6. "I am wearing horns, everyone sees that, / But there is one who wears them who doesn't know it."

an affair with *his* wife. For her part, the Queen was careful to feign displeasure at her husband's behaviour, though secretly she was pleased, and the more she was pleased, the more displeasure she affected. This amicable arrangement permitted the continuation of their amours for many years to come, until at length old age brought them to order.

"Well, Ladies," concluded Saffredent, "let that story be a lesson to you. When your husbands give you little roe-deer horns, make sure that you give them great big stag's antlers!"

"Saffredent," said Ennasuite, laughing, "I'm quite sure that if you were still such an ardent lover as you used to be, you wouldn't mind putting up with horns as big as oaks, as long as you could give a pair back when the fancy took you. But you're starting to go grey, you know, and it really is time you began to give your appetites a rest!"

"Mademoiselle," he replied, "even if the lady I love gives me no hope, and even if age has dampened my ardour somewhat, my desires are as strong as ever. But seeing that you object to my harbouring such noble desires, let me invite you to tell the fourth story, and let's see if you can produce an example to refute what I say."

During this exchange one of the ladies had started to laugh. She knew that the lady who had just taken Saffredent's words to be aimed at her was not in fact so much the object of his affections that he would put up with cuckoldry, disgrace or injury of any kind for her sake. When Saffredent saw that she was laughing and that she had understood him, he was [highly] pleased, and let Ennasuite go on. This is what she said:

"I have a story to tell, Ladies, which will show Saffredent and everyone else here that not *all* women are like the Queen he has told us about, and that not all men who are rash enough to try their tricks get what they want. It's a story that ought not to be kept back, and it tells of a lady in whose eyes failure in love was worse than death itself. I shan't mention the real names of the people involved, because it's not long since it all happened, and I should be afraid of giving offence to their close relatives."

STORY FOUR

In Flanders there once lived a lady of high birth, of birth so high, indeed, that there was no one higher in the land. She had no children and had been twice widowed. After her second husband's death she had gone to live with her brother, who was very fond of her. He was himself a noble lord of high estate, married to the daughter of a King. This young Prince was much given to his pleasures, being fond of the ladies, of hunting and generally enjoying himself, just as one would expect of a young man. His wife, however, was rather difficult, and did not enjoy the same things as he did, so he always used to take his sister along as well, because she, while being a sensible and virtuous woman, was also the most cheerful and lively company one could imagine.

Now there was a certain gentleman attached to the household, an extremely tall man, whose charm and good looks made him stand out among his companions. Taking careful note of the fact that his master's sister was a very lively lady who liked to enjoy herself, it occurred to him that it might be worth seeing if an amorous overture from a well-bred gentleman might not be to her taste. So he approached her, only to find that her reply was not what he would have expected. Nevertheless, in spite of the fact that she had given him the sort of answer that becomes an honest woman and a princess, she had had no difficulty in forgiving this good-looking and well-bred man for having been so presumptuous. Indeed, she made it plain that she did not at all mind his talking to her, though she also frequently reminded him that he must be careful what he said. In order to continue to enjoy the honour and pleasure of her company, he was only too glad to promise not to return to his earlier overtures. But as time went by his passion grew stronger, until he forgot his promises altogether. Not that he dared risk opening the subject again verbally—he had already to his cost had a taste of her ability to answer him back with her words of wisdom. No, what he had in mind was this. If he could find the right time and place, then might she not relent and indulge him a little, and indulge herself at the same time? After all, she was a widow and young, healthy and vivacious. To this end he mentioned to his master that he had lands adjoining his home that offered excellent hunting, and assured him that if he came and hunted a stag or two in May he would have the time of his life. Partly because he liked the gentleman and partly because he was addicted to hunting, the Prince accepted this invitation, and went to stay at his house, which was, as one would expect of the richest man in the land, a very fine place and very well maintained. In one wing of the house the gentleman accommodated the Prince and his wife. In the other wing opposite he accommodated the lady whom by now he loved more than he loved life itself. Her room had been luxuriously decorated from top to bottom with tapestries, and the floor was thickly covered with matting—so that it was impossible to see the trap-door by the side of the bed which led down to the room beneath. The gentleman's mother, who normally slept in this room, was old, and her catarrh made her cough in the night, so, in order to avoid disturbing the Princess, she had exchanged rooms with her son. Every evening this old lady took preserves up to the Princess, accompanied by her son, who, being very close to the brother of the Princess, was naturally permitted to attend both her *coucher* and her *lever*.[7] Needless to say, these occasions constantly served to inflame his passion.

So it was that one evening he kept her up very late, and only left her room when he saw she was falling asleep. Back in his own room, he put on the most magnificent and most highly perfumed nightshirt he possessed, and on his head he placed the most beautifully decorated nightcap you ever saw. As he admired himself in his mirror, he was absolutely convinced that there was not a woman in the world who could possible resist such a handsome and elegant sight. He looked forward with satisfaction to the success of his little plan, and went off to his bed. Not that he expected to stay there long, burning with desire as he was, and quite confident that he was soon to win his place in a bed that was both more pleasurable and more honourable than his own. Once he had dismissed his attendants, he got up to lock the door, and listened carefully for noises in the Princess's room above. When he was sure all was quiet, he turned to the task. Bit by bit he gently lowered the trap-

7. Retiring and arising (French).

door. It had been well constructed and was so densely covered with cloth, that not a sound was made. He hoisted himself through the aperture and into the room above. The Princess was just falling asleep. Without more ado, without a thought for her rank and station, or for the duty and respect he owed her, without, indeed, so much as a by-your-leave, he jumped into bed with her. Before she knew where she was he was lying there between her arms. But she was a strong woman. Struggling out of his clutches, she demanded to know who he was, and proceeded to lash out, scratching and biting for all she was worth. He was terrified she would call for help, and felt obliged to stuff the bedclothes into her mouth in a vain attempt to prevent her doing so. She realized that he would use all his strength to dishonour her, and fought back with all *her* strength in order to stop him. She shouted at the top of her lungs for her lady-in-waiting, a respectable elderly lady, who was sleeping in the next room, and who, as soon as she heard the shout, rushed to her mistress's rescue, still wearing her night attire.

When the gentleman realized that he had been caught, terrified of being recognized by the Princess, he beat a hasty retreat down through his trap-door. He arrived back in his room in a very sorry state indeed. It was a shattering experience for a man who had set out burning with desire, fully confident that his lady was going to receive him with open arms. He picked up his mirror from the table and examined himself in the candlelight. His face was streaming with blood from the bites and scratches she had inflicted. His beautiful embroidered nightshirt had more streaks of blood in it than it had gold thread.

"So much for good looks!" he groaned. "I suppose you've got what you deserve. I shouldn't have expected so much from my appearance. Now it's made me attempt something that I should have realized was impossible from the start. It might even make my situation worse, instead of making it better! If she realizes that it was I who did this senseless thing, breaking all the promises I had made, I know I shall lose even my privilege of visiting her chastely and openly. That's what my vanity's done for me! To make the most of my charm and good looks, and win her heart and her love, I ought not to have kept it so dark. I ought not to have tried to take her chaste body by force! I ought to have devoted myself to her service, in humility and with patience, accepting that I must wait till love should triumph. For without love, what good to a man are prowess and physical strength?"

And so he sat the whole night through, weeping, gnashing his teeth and wishing the incident had never happened. In the morning he looked at himself again in the mirror, and seeing that his face was lacerated all over, he took to his bed, pretending he was desperately ill and could not bear to go out into the light. There he remained until his visitors had gone home.

Meanwhile, the Princess was triumphant. She knew that the only person at her brother's court who would dare to do such an extraordinary thing was the man who had already once made so bold as to declare his love. In other words, she knew perfectly well that the culprit was her host. With the help of her lady-in-waiting she looked round all the possible hiding-places in the room, without, of course, finding anybody. She was beside herself with rage. "I know very well who it is!" she fumed. "It's the master of the house himself! That's the only person it can be. And mark my words, I shall speak to my brother in the morning, and I'll have the man's head as proof of my chastity!"

Seeing how angry she was, her lady-in-waiting just said: "I am pleased to see that your honour means so much to you, Madame, and that in order to enhance it you have no intention of sparing this man's life—he has already taken too many risks with it because of his violent love for you. But it very often happens that when people try to enhance their honour, they only end up doing the opposite. I would therefore urge you, Madame, to tell me the plain truth about the whole affair."

When she had heard the whole story, she asked: "Do you assure me that all he got from you was blows and scratches?"

"I do assure you," came the reply, "that that was all he got, and unless he manages to find a very good doctor indeed, we'll see the marks on his face tomorrow."

"Well, that being so," the old lady went on, "it seems to me that you should be thinking about giving thanks to the Lord, rather than talking about revenge. It must have taken some courage, you know, to make such a daring attempt, and at this moment he must be feeling so mortified by his failure, that death would be a good deal easier for him to bear! If what you want is revenge, then you should just leave him to his passion and his humiliation—he'll torture himself much more than you could. And if you're concerned about your honour, then be careful not to fall into the same trap as he did. He promised himself all kinds of pleasures and delights, and what he actually got was the worst disappointment that any gentleman could ever suffer. So take care, Madame—if you try to make your honour even more impressive, you may only end up doing the opposite. If you make an official complaint against him, you will have to bring the whole thing into the open, whereas at the moment nobody knows anything, and he certainly won't go and tell anybody. What is more, just suppose you did go ahead, and Monseigneur, your brother, did bring the case to justice, and the poor man was put to death—people will say that he *must* have had his way with you. Most people will argue that it's not very easy to accept that a man can carry out such an act, unless he has been given a certain amount of encouragement by the lady concerned. You're young and attractive, you're very lively and sociable in all kinds of company. There isn't a single person at this court who hasn't seen the encouraging way you treat the man you are now suspecting. That could only make people conclude that if he did indeed do what you say, then it couldn't have been without some blame being due to you as well. Your honour, which up till now has been such that you've been able to hold your head high wherever you went, would be put in doubt wherever this story was heard."

As she listened to the wise reasonings of her lady-in-waiting, the Princess knew that what she was saying was true. She would indeed be criticized and blamed, in view of the encouraging and intimate way she had always treated the gentleman, so she asked her lady-in-waiting what she thought she ought to do.

"It is most gracious of you, Madame," the old lady replied, "to heed my advice. You know that I have great affection for you. Well, it seems to me that you should rejoice in your heart that this man—and he is the most handsome and best-bred gentleman I saw in my life—has been completely unable to turn you from the path of virtue, in spite of his love for you, and in spite of using physical violence against you. For this you should humble yourself before God, and acknowledge that it was not your virtue that saved you. For there have been many women, women who have led a far more austere life than you have, who have been humiliated by men far less worthy of affection than the man we are talking of. From now on you should be even more cautious when men make overtures to you, and bear in mind that there are plenty of women who have escaped from danger the first time, only to succumb the second. Never forget that Love is blind, Madame, and descends upon his victims at the very moment when they are treading a path which they think is safe, but which in reality is slippery and treacherous. I think also that you should never allude in any way to what has happened, either to him or anyone else, and even if *he* were to bring it up, I think you should pretend not to understand what he is talking about. In this way there are two dangers that you will be able to avoid. First of all, there's the danger of glorying in your triumph. And then there's the danger that you might enjoy being reminded of the pleasures of the flesh. Even the most chaste of women have a hard time preventing some spark of pleasure being aroused by such things, however much they strive to avoid them. Finally, Madame, so that he should not get it into his head that you in some way enjoyed what he tried to do, I would advise you to gradually stop seeing so much of him. In that way you will bring home to him what a low opinion you have of his foolish and wicked behaviour. At the same time he will be brought to see what a good person you are to have been satisfied with the triumph that God has already granted you, without seeking any further revenge. May God grant you the grace, Madame, to continue in the path of virtue wherein he has placed you, to continue to love and to serve Him even better than hitherto, in the knowledge that it is from Him alone that all goodness flows."

The Princess made up her mind to follow the wise counsel of her lady-in-waiting, and slept peacefully for the rest of the night, while the wretched gentleman below spent a night of sleepless torment.

The next day the Princess's brother was ready to depart, and asked if he could take his leave of the master of the house. He was astonished to hear that he was ill, could not tolerate the light of day and refused to be seen by anyone. He would have gone to see him, but was told that he was sleeping, and decided not to disturb him. So together with his wife and his sister he left the house without being able to say goodbye. When his sister, the Princess, heard about their host's excuses for not seeing them before they left, she knew for certain that he was the one who had caused her so much distress. Obviously he did not dare to show his face because of the scratches he had received. Indeed, he refused all subsequent invitations to attend court until all his wounds—except, that is, for those he had suffered to his heart and to his pride—had healed. When eventually he did go back to court to face his triumphant enemy, he could not do so without blushing. He, who was the boldest man at court, would completely lose his self-assurance in her presence, and would frequently go quite to pieces. This only made the Princess the more sure that her suspicions had been well-founded. Gently, and little by little, she withdrew her attentions—but not so gently that he failed to appreciate what she was doing. Scared lest anything worse befell him, he dared not breathe a word. He simply had to nurse his passion in the depths of his heart, and put up with a rebuff that had been justly deserved.

"And that, Ladies, is a story that should strike fear into the hearts of any man who thinks he can help himself to what doesn't belong to him. The Princess's virtue and the good sense of her lady-in-waiting should inspire courage in the hearts of all women. So if anything like this should ever happen to any of you, you now know what the remedy is!"

"In my opinion," said Hircan, "the tall lord of your story lacked nerve, and didn't deserve to have his memory preserved. What an opportunity he had! He should never have been content to eat or sleep till he'd succeeded. And one really can't say that his love was very great, if there was still room in his heart for the fear of death and dishonour."

"And what," asked Nomerfide, "could the poor man have done with two women against him?"

"He should have killed the old one, and when the young one realized there was no one to help her, he'd have been half-way there!"

"Kill her!" Nomerfide cried. "You wouldn't mind him being a murderer as well, then? If that's what you think, we'd better watch out we don't fall into *your* clutches!"

"If I'd gone that far," he replied, "I'd consider my honour ruined if I didn't go through with it!"

Then Geburon[8] spoke up: "So you find it strange that a princess of high birth who's been brought up in the strict school of honour should be too much for one man? In that case you'd find it even stranger that a woman of poor birth should manage to get away from *two* men!"

"I invite you to tell the fifth story, Geburon," said Ennasuite, "because it sounds as if you have one about some poor woman that will be far from dull."

"Since you've chosen me [to speak]," he began, "I shall tell a story that I know to be true because I conducted an inquiry into it at the very place where it happened. As you'll see, it isn't only princesses who've got good sense in their heads and virtue in their heart. And love and resourcefulness aren't always to be found where you'd expect them, either."

STORY FIVE

At the port of Coulon near Niort, there was once a woman whose job it was to ferry people night and day across the river. One day she found herself alone in her boat with two Franciscan friars from Niort. Now this is one of the longest crossings on any river in France, and the two friars took it into their heads that she would find it less boring if they made amorous proposals to her. But, as was only right and proper, she refused to listen. However, the two were not to be deterred. They had not exactly had their strength sapped by rowing, nor their ardours chilled by the chilly water nor, indeed, their consciences pricked by the woman's refusals. So they decided to rape her,

8. One of the older members of the group, notable for his sententious wisdom. Suggested identifications are with a military man, the lord of Burye, a captain in the Italian Wars; or with Nicolas Bourbon, a tutor of Jeanne d'Albret, Marguerite's daughter.

both of them, and if she resisted, to throw her into the river. But she was as sensible and shrewd as they were vicious and stupid.

"I'm not as ungracious as you might think," she said to them, "and if you'll just grant me two little things, you'll see I'm just as keen to do what you want as you are."

The Cordeliers[9] swore by the good Saint Francis that they'd let her have anything she asked for, if she'd just let them have what they wanted.

"First of all, you must promise on your oath that neither of you will tell a soul about it," she said.

To this they readily agreed.

"Secondly, you must do what you want with me one at a time—I'd be too embarrassed to have both of you looking at me. So decide between you who's to have me first."

They thought this too was a very reasonable request, and the younger of the two offered to let the older man go first. As they sailed past a small island in the river, the ferrywoman said to the younger one: "Now my good father, jump ashore and say your prayers while I take your friend here to another island. If he's satisfied with me when he gets back, we'll drop him off here, and then you can come with me."

So he jumped out of the boat to wait on the island till his companion came back. The ferrywoman then took the other one to another island in the river, and while she pretended to be making the boat fast to a tree, told him to go and find a convenient spot.

He jumped out, and went off to look for a good place. No sooner was he on dry land than the ferrywoman shoved off with a kick against the tree, and sailed off down the river, leaving the two good friars stranded.

"You can wait till God sends an angel to console you, Messieurs!" she bawled at them. "You're not going to get anything out of me today!"

The poor friars saw they had been hoodwinked. They ran to the water's edge and pleaded on bended knees that she would take them to the port. They promised not to ask her for any more favours. But she went on rowing, and called back: "I'd be even more stupid to let myself get caught again, now I've escaped!"

As soon as she landed on the other side, she went into the village, fetched her husband and called out the officers of the law to go and round up these two ravenous wolves, from whose jaws she had just by the grace of God been delivered. They had plenty of willing helpers. There was no one in the village, great or small, who was not anxious to join in the hunt and have his share of the fun. When the two good brothers, each on his own island, saw this huge band coming after them, they did their best to hide—even as Adam hid from the presence of the Lord God, when he saw that he was naked. They were half dead for shame at this exposure of their sins, and trembled in terror at the thought of the punishment that surely awaited them. But there was nothing they could do. They were seized and bound, and led through the village to the shouts and jeers of every man and woman in the place. Some people said: "There they go, those good fathers who preach chastity to us yet want to take it from our wives!" Others said: "They are whited sepulchres, outwardly beautiful, but within full of dead men's bones and all unclean-

---

9. Franciscan friars.

ness!" And someone else called out, "Every tree is known by his own fruit!" In fact, they hurled at the two captives every text in the Gospels that condemns hypocrites. In the end their Father Superior came to the rescue. He lost no time in requesting their custody, reassuring the officers of the law that he would punish them more severely than secular law could. By way of reparation, they would, he promised, be made to say as many prayers and masses as might be required! [The Father Superior was a worthy man, so the judge granted his request and sent the two prisoners back to their convent, where they were brought before the full Chapter and severely reprimanded.] Never again did they take a ferry across a river, without making the sign of the cross and commending their souls to God!

"Now consider this story carefully, Ladies. We have here a humble ferrywoman who had the sense to frustrate the evil intentions of two vicious men. What then ought we to expect from women who all their lives have seen nothing but good examples, read of nothing but good examples and, in short, had examples of feminine virtue constantly paraded before them?[1] If well-fed women are virtuous, is it not just as much a matter of custom as of virtue? But it's quite another matter if you're talking about women who have no education, who probably don't hear two decent sermons in a year, who have time for nothing but thinking how to make a meagre living, and who, in spite of all this, diligently resist all pressures in order to preserve their chastity. It is in the heart of such women as these that one finds pure virtue, for in the hearts of those we regard as inferior in body and mind the spirit of God performs his greatest works. Woe to those women who do not guard their treasure with the utmost care, for it is a treasure that brings them great honour if it is well guarded and great dishonour if it is squandered!"

"If you ask me, Geburon," observed Longarine, "there's nothing very virtuous in rejecting the advances of a friar. I don't know how anyone could possibly feel any affection at all for them."

"Longarine," he replied, "women who are not so used as you are to having refined gentlemen to serve them find friars far from unpleasant. They're often just as good-looking as we are, just as well-built and less worn out, because they've not been knocked about in battle. What is more, they talk like angels and are as persistent as devils. That's why I think that any woman who's seen nothing better than the coarse cloth of monks' habits should be considered extremely virtuous if she manages to escape their clutches."

"Good Heavens!" exclaimed Nomerfide loudly. "You may say what you like, but I'd rather be thrown in the river any day, than go to bed with a friar!"

"*So you're a strong swimmer, are you then!*"[2] said Oisille, laughing.

Nomerfide took this in bad part, thinking that Oisille did not give her as much credit as she would have liked, and said heatedly: "There *are* plenty of people who've refused better men than friars, without blowing their trumpets about it!"

"Yes, and they've been even more careful not to beat their drums about ones they've accepted and given in to!" retorted Oisille, amused to see that she was annoyed.

---

1. Manuals on virtuous behavior and exemplary lives were common reading for noblewomen of the period. 2. The verb *nouer* meant "to swim" and "to knot," which had sexual connotations.

"I can see that Nomerfide would like to speak," Geburon intervened, "so I invite her to take over from me, in order that she may unburden herself by telling us a good story."

"I couldn't care less about people's remarks," she snapped, "they neither please nor annoy me. But since you ask me to speak, will you listen carefully, because I want to tell a story to show you that women can exercise their [cleverness] for bad purposes as well as for good ones. As we've sworn to tell the truth, I have no desire to conceal it. After all, just as the ferrywoman's virtue does not redound to the honour of other women unless they actually follow in her footsteps, so the *vice* of one woman does not bring dishonour on all other women. So, if you will listen . . ."

STORY SIX

Charles, the last Duke of Alençon, had a valet de chambre who was blind in one eye, and who was married to a woman a good few years younger than himself. Now, of all the men of that rank in the household this man was particularly well-liked by his master and mistress. This meant that he could not get home to see his wife as often as he would have liked, which in turn led to her neglecting her honour and conscience to the extent that she fell for a young man. There was so much malicious gossip about this affair that the husband eventually got wind of it, although he found it difficult to believe, as his wife always seemed to be very affectionate with him. One day he decided to check up on her and, if he could, get his own back on her for disgracing him. So he told her that he had to go away for two or three days to some place not far off. No sooner was he out of the door than the wife invited her young man round. But he had not been there above half an hour when back comes the husband and hammers loudly on the front door. She recognized the knock and told her lover, who was so terrified he wished he had never been born. He cursed his mistress and the whole wretched love-affair for placing him in such a tight corner. But she told him not to worry, she would find some way of getting him out of it without injury either to himself or his honour, and instructed him to get his clothes on as fast as he could. The husband was still banging at the door, and shouting for his wife at the top of his voice. But she pretended not to recognize him, and called out, as if to [the servants]: "Why don't you get up, and tell whoever it is out there to be quiet? This is no time to be knocking at respectable people's doors! If my husband were here, he'd soon put a stop to it!"

Hearing his wife's voice, the husband called out as loud as he could: "Open up, wife. Are you going to keep me standing here till morning?"

Seeing that her lover was ready to be off, she opened the door, and said to her husband: "My dear husband, how glad I am to see you! I've just had a marvellous dream, and I've never felt so happy, because I dreamt that you'd got the sight back in your eye!"

She put her arms round him and kissed him, took his head in both hands, and covered up his good eye.

"Is it not true that you can see better than before?" she demanded. He could not see a thing, of course, and the wife gave her lover the sign to make his getaway.

Guessing what was going on, the husband said: "By Heavens, woman, I'm not going to spy on *you* any more! I thought I was going to catch you out, but in return you play me the most cunning trick anyone's ever thought of. May God give you the punishment you deserve! Because there's not a man alive can make a bad woman behave herself, short of murdering her! Since treating you kindly as I've done up till now, hasn't made you mend your ways, perhaps you'll be brought to heel if from now on I treat you with the contempt you deserve!"

So saying, he stormed off, leaving her quite distressed, though in the end, by dint of tears, excuses and the mediation of her friends, she managed to get him to come back to her.

"So you can see, Ladies, that women can be very cunning when they're in a scrape. And if they're clever enough to cover up something bad, I think they'd be even more ingenious in avoiding bad deeds or in doing good ones. A shrewd wit is always stronger in the end, as everybody always says."

"You can talk about your feminine cunning as much as you like," said Hircan, "but in my opinion, if anything like that happened to *you*, you would be incapable of covering it up!"

"I'd rather you thought I was the stupidest woman in the world!" replied Nomerfide.

"I don't say *that*," he went on, "but I do think you're the sort of woman who gets worked up over a rumour, instead of thinking of some clever way of putting an end to it."

"You think that everyone's like you," she replied, "quite ready to cover up one rumour with another. But there's always the risk that a cover-up will end up destroying the very thing it was meant to conceal, like a building that collapses because the roof's too heavy for the foundations. However if you think that [male] cunning—and everyone knows you've got your fair share of *that*—is superior to female cunning, then I'll make way for you, so that you can tell us the seventh story. And if you'd like to tell us about yourself by way of example, I'm sure you'd teach us all a good deal about wickedness and trickery!"

"I'm not here to give myself a worse reputation than I've already got. There are already enough people willing to say worse things about me than I care for!" said Hircan, glancing at his wife, who quickly replied:

"Don't be afraid to tell the truth because of me. It will be easier for me to hear about your little games than to have had to watch you playing them under my nose—though nothing you may do could diminish the love I bear you."

"Then I shan't complain about all the wrong opinions that you have held about me. So, since we know and understand one another, there is reason to feel more reassurance for the future. All the same I wouldn't be so foolish as to tell you a story about myself, when the facts might be hurtful to you— but I *will* tell one about a man who was a close friend of mine."

STORY SEVEN

In the town of Paris there was once a merchant who was in love with a young girl who was a neighbour of his. To be more accurate, it was the girl who was in love with him, rather than the other way round. He merely pretended to be devoted to her in order to cover up a more exalted and honourable passion for someone else. But she let herself be deceived, and was so infatuated that she had completely forgotten that it is the custom for women to reject men's advances. For a long while the merchant had taken the trouble of going to seek her out, but eventually he was able to persuade her to come to meet him where it suited him. Her mother, who was a most respectable person, realized what was going on, and forbade the girl ever to speak to the merchant again, or she would be sent straight to a convent. But the girl was more in love with her merchant than she was in awe of her mother, and only did her best to see him more often than ever.

One day the merchant happened to find her alone in her dressing-room. It was a convenient place for his purposes, so he proceeded to make overtures to her in the most intimate fashion. But some chambermaid or other who had seen him going in ran off and told the mother, who flew into a rage and immediately came along to catch them. The girl heard her coming and burst into tears.

"Alas! Alas! My love," she wailed to her merchant, "my hour is come and I shall pay the price for the love I bear you! Here's my mother coming. This is what she's feared and suspected all along, and now she'll discover that it's true!"

The merchant was not the sort of man to be upset by a situation of this kind. He jumped up and went to meet the mother, put his arms around her and hugged and kissed her as hard as he could. Already in a passionate mood after flirting with her daughter, he flung the poor old woman on to a couch. She found this so extraordinary that all she could manage to say was: "What do you want? Have you gone mad?"

But he was not deterred. Indeed, he went about it as if she had been the most attractive young girl he had ever seen. If her screams had not brought her servants and chambermaids running to her rescue, she would have gone the same way she feared her daughter was going! The servants extricated the poor old dear from the merchant's embraces without her having the vaguest idea why he had given her such a mauling. While all this was going on, the girl escaped to a neighbour's house, where there happened to be a wedding reception going on.

The merchant and the girl often had a good laugh together at the mother's expense, and the old woman never found them out.

"So, you can see, Ladies, how male cleverness succeeded in outwitting the old woman and in saving the young girl's honour. But anyone who knew the names of the people involved, or who saw the merchant's face or the old woman's astonishment, would have to be very afraid for his conscience if he refused to laugh. But I'll be quite satisfied if my story has proved to you that men are just as resourceful and quick-witted as women when they need to be. So, dear Ladies, you should have no fear of falling into their hands, because, should you be lost for a way out, they will always be able to cover up and save your honour!"

"Yes, Hircan, I agree that it's a very funny story," said Longarine, "and that the man was very clever. All the same, I don't think it's an example that young girls should follow. I suspect there are some you'd like to persuade to do so. But I don't think you're so stupid as to want your wife to play such games, or the lady whose honour is dearer to you than pleasure. I don't think there's anyone who would keep a closer watch on them than you, or anyone who would more promptly put a stop to such things."

"On my oath," replied Hircan, "if [the ones] you refer to *had* done anything like that, I wouldn't think any the less of them for it—provided I knew nothing about it! For all I know, someone might have played just as good a trick on me, but if so, I know nothing about it, so it doesn't worry me."

Parlamente could not resist commenting: "It's impossible for men who do wrong themselves not to be suspicious of others. But it's a happy man who gives no cause for others to be suspicious of him."

"Well, I've never seen fire without smoke," said Longarine, "but I have seen smoke without fire! Malicious people are often just as good at smelling something bad when it doesn't exist, as they are when it does."

"Since you speak so strongly in favour of women who get suspected wrongly, Longarine," said Hircan, "I choose you to tell us the eighth story, on condition that you don't make us all weep, like Madame Oisille did, with her excessive zeal for stories in praise of virtuous women."[3]

Longarine broke into a hearty laugh, and said: "Since you want me to make you laugh, in my usual fashion, it won't be at the expense of women. Yet I *shall* tell you something to show how easy they are to deceive when they fill their heads with jealous thoughts, and pride themselves on their good sense for wanting to deceive their husbands."

STORY EIGHT

In the county of Alès there was once a man by the name of Bornet, who had married a very decent and respectable woman. He held her honour and reputation very dear, as I am sure all husbands here hold the honour and reputation of *their* wives dear. He wanted her to be faithful to him, but was not so keen on having the rule applied to them both equally. He had become enamoured of his chambermaid, though the only benefit he got from transferring his affections in this way was the sort of pleasure one gets from varying one's diet. He had a neighbour called Sendras, who was of similar station and temperament to himself—he was a tailor and a drummer. These two were such close friends that, with the exception of the wife, there was nothing that they did not share between them. Naturally he told him that he had designs on the chambermaid.

Not only did his friend wholeheartedly approve of this, but did his best to help him, in the hope that he too might get a share in the spoils.

The chambermaid herself refused to have anything to do with him, although he was constantly pestering her, and in the end she went to tell her mistress about it. She told her that she could not stand being badgered by him any longer, and asked permission to go home to her parents. Now the good lady of the house, who was really very much in love with her husband, had often had occasion to suspect him, and was therefore rather pleased to be one up on him, and to be able to show him that she had found out what he was up to. So she said to her maid: "Be nice to him, dear, encourage him

3. Reference to an earlier story.

a little bit, and then make a date to go to bed with him in my dressing-room. Don't forget to tell me which night he's supposed to be coming, and make sure you don't tell anyone else."

The maid did exactly as her mistress had instructed. As for her master, he was so pleased with himself that he went off to tell his friend about his stroke of luck, whereupon the friend insisted on taking his share afterwards, since he had been in on the business from the beginning. When the appointed time came, off went the master, as had been agreed, to get into bed, as he thought, with his little chambermaid. But his wife, having abandoned her position of authority in order to serve in a more pleasurable one, had taken her maid's place in the bed. When he got in with her, she did not act like a wife, but like a bashful young girl, and he was not in the slightest suspicious. It would be impossible to say which of them enjoyed themselves more—the wife deceiving her husband, or the husband who thought he was deceiving his wife. He stayed in bed with her for some time, not as long as he might have wished (many years of marriage were beginning to tell on him), but as long as he could manage. Then he went out to rejoin his accomplice, and tell him what a good time he had had. The lustiest piece of goods he had ever come across, he declared. His friend, who was younger and more active than he was, said: "Remember what you promised?"

"Hurry up, then," replied the master, "in case she gets up, or my wife wants her for something."

Off he went and climbed into bed with the supposed chambermaid his friend had just failed to recognize as his wife. *She* thought it was her husband again, and did not refuse anything he asked for (I say "asked," but "took" would be nearer the mark, because he did not dare open his mouth). He made a much longer business of it than the husband, to the surprise of the wife, who was not used to these long nights of pleasure. However, she did not complain, and looked forward to what she was planning to say to him in the morning, and the fun she would have teasing him. When dawn came, the man got up, and fondling her as he got out of bed, pulled off a ring she wore on her finger, a ring that her husband had given her at their marriage. Now the women in this part of the world are very superstitious about such things. They have great respect for women who hang on to their wedding rings till the day they die, and if a woman loses her ring, she is dishonoured, and is looked upon as having given her faith to another man. But she did not mind him taking it, because she thought it would be sure evidence against her husband of the way she had hoodwinked him.

The husband was waiting outside for his friend, and asked him how he had got on. The man said he shared the husband's opinion, and added that he would have stayed longer, had he not been afraid of getting caught by the daylight. The pair of them then went off to get as much sleep as they could. When morning came, and they were getting dressed together, the husband noticed that his friend had on his finger a ring that was identical to the one he had given his wife on their wedding day. He asked him where he had got it, and when he was told it had come from the chambermaid the night before, he was aghast. He began banging his head against the wall, and shouted: "Oh my God! Have I gone and made myself a cuckold without my wife even knowing about it?"

His friend tried to calm him down. "Perhaps your wife had given the ring to the girl to look after before going to bed?" he suggested. The husband made no reply, but marched straight out and went back to his house.

There he found his wife looking unusually gay and attractive. Had she not saved her chambermaid from staining her conscience, and had she not put her husband to the ultimate test, without any more cost to herself than a night's sleep? Seeing her in such good spirits, the husband thought to himself: "She wouldn't be greeting me so cheerfully if she knew what I'd been up to."

As they chatted, he took hold of her hand and saw that the ring, which normally never left her finger, had disappeared. Horrified, he stammered: "What have you done with your ring?"

She was pleased that he was giving her the opportunity to say what she had to say.

"Oh! You're the most dreadful man I ever met! Who do you think you got it from? You think you got it from the chambermaid, don't you? You think you got it from that girl you're so much in love with, the girl who gets more out of you than I've ever had! The first time you got into bed you were so passionate that I thought you must be about as madly in love with her as it was possible for any man to be! But when you came back the *second* time, after getting up, you were an absolute devil! Completely uncontrolled you were, didn't know when to stop! You miserable man! You must have been blinded by desire to pay such tribute to my body—after all you've had me long enough without showing much appreciation for my figure. So it wasn't because that young girl is so pretty and so shapely that you were enjoying yourself so much. Oh no! You enjoyed it so much because you were seething with some depraved pent-up lust—in short the sin of concupiscence was raging within you, and your senses were dulled as a result. In fact you'd worked yourself up into such a state that I think any old nanny-goat would have done for you, pretty or otherwise! Well, my dear, it's time you mended your ways. It's high time you were content with me for what I am—your own wife and an honest woman, and it's high time that you found *that* just as satisfying as when you thought I was a poor little erring chambermaid. I did what I did in order to save you from your wicked ways, so that when you get old, we can live happily and peacefully together without anything on our consciences. Because if you go on in the way you have been, I'd rather leave you altogether than see you destroying your soul day by day, and at the same time destroying your physical health and squandering everything you have before my very eyes! But if you will acknowledge that you've been in the wrong, and make up your mind to live according to the ways of God and His commandments, then I'll overlook all your past misbehavior, even as I hope God will forgive me *my* ingratitude to Him, and failure to love Him as I ought."

If there was ever a man who was dumbfounded and despairing, it was this poor husband. There was his wife, looking so pretty, and yet so sensible and so chaste, and he had gone and left her for a girl who did not love him. What was worse, he had had the misfortune to have gone and made her do something wicked without her even realizing what was happening. He had gone and let another man share pleasures which, rightly, were his alone to enjoy. He had gone and given himself cuckold's horns and made himself look ridiculous for evermore. But he could see she was already angry enough about the chambermaid, and he did not dare tell her about the other dirty trick he had played. So he promised that he would leave his wicked ways behind him, asked her to forgive him and gave her the ring back. He told his friend not to breathe a word to anybody, but secrets of this sort nearly always end up being proclaimed from the [roof-tops,] and it was not long before the facts became public knowledge. The husband was branded as a cuckold without his wife having done a single thing to disgrace herself.

"Ladies, it strikes me that if all the men who offend their wives like that got a punishment like that, then Hircan and Saffredent ought to be feeling a bit nervous."

"Come now, Longarine," said Saffredent, "Hircan and I aren't the only married men here, you know."

"True," she replied, "but you're the only two who'd play a trick like that."

"And just when have you heard of us chasing our wives' maids?" he retorted.

"If the ladies in question were to tell us the facts," Longarine said, "then you'd soon find plenty of maids who'd been dismissed before their pay-day!"

"Really," intervened Geburon, "a fine one you are! You promise to make us all laugh, and you end up making these two gentlemen annoyed."

"It comes to the same thing," said Longarine. "As long as they don't get their swords out, their getting angry makes it all the more amusing."

"But the fact remains," said Hircan, "that if our wives were to listen to what this lady here has to say, she'd make trouble for every married couple here!"

"I know what I'm saying, and who I'm saying it to," Longarine replied. "Your wives are so good, and they love you so much, that even if you gave them horns like a stag's, they'd still convince themselves, and everybody else, that they were garlands of roses!"

Everyone found this remark highly amusing, even the people it was aimed at, and the subject was brought to a close. Dagoucin,[4] however, who had not yet said a word, could not resist saying: "When a man already has everything he needs in order to be contented, it is very unreasonable of him to go off and seek satisfaction elsewhere. It has often struck me that when people are not satisfied with what they already have, and think they can find something better, then they only make themselves worse off. And they do not get any sympathy, because inconstancy is one thing that is universally condemned."

"But what about people who have not yet found their other half?" asked Simontaut. "Would you still say it was inconstancy if they seek her wherever she may be found?"

"No man can know," replied Dagoucin, "where his other half is to be found, this other half with whom he may find a union so equal that between [the parts] there is no difference; which being so, a man must hold fast where Love constrains him and, whatever may befall him, he must remain steadfast in heart and will. For if she whom you love is your true likeness, if she is of the same will, then it will be your own self that you love, and not her alone."

---

4. The most philosophical member of the group, described elsewhere (story 11) as "so wise that he would rather die than say something foolish." He is also the saintliest; our translator indicates that his name is "a fairly obvious pun: de goûts saints (of saintly tastes)."

"Dagoucin, I think you're adopting a position that is completely wrong," said Hircan. "You make it sound as if we ought to love women without being loved in return!"

"What I mean, Hircan, is this. If love is based on a woman's beauty, charm and favours, and if our aim is merely pleasure, ambition or profit, then such love can never last. For if the whole foundation on which our love is based should collapse, then love will fly from us and there will be no love left in us. But I am utterly convinced that if a man loves with no other aim, no other desire, than to love truly, he will abandon his soul in death rather than allow his love to abandon his heart."

"Quite honestly, Dagoucin, I don't think you've ever really been in love," said Simontaut, "because if you had felt the fire of passion, as the rest of us have, you wouldn't have been doing what you've just been doing—describing Plato's republic, which sounds all very fine in writing, but is hardly true to experience."

"If I have loved," he replied, "I love still, and shall love till the day I die. But my love is a perfect love, and I fear lest showing it openly should betray it. So greatly do I fear this, that I shrink to make it known to the lady whose love and friendship I cannot but desire to be equal to my own. I scarcely dare think my own thoughts, lest something should be revealed in my eyes, for the longer I conceal the fire of my love, the stronger grows the pleasure in knowing that it is indeed a perfect love."

"Ah, but all the same," said Geburon, "I don't think you'd be sorry if she did return your love!"

"I do not deny it. But even if I were loved as deeply as I myself love, my love could not possibly increase, just as it could not possibly decrease if I were loved less deeply than I love."

At this point, Parlamente, who was suspicious of these flights of fancy, said: "Watch your step, Dagoucin. I've seen plenty of men who've died rather than speak what's in their minds."

"Such men as those," he replied, "I would count happy indeed."

"Indeed," said Saffredent, "and worthy to be placed among the ranks of the Innocents—of whom the Church chants '*Non loquendo, sed moriendo confessi sunt*'![5] I've heard a lot of talk about these languishing lovers, but I've never seen a single one actually die. I've suffered enough from such torture, but I got over it in the end, and that's why I've always assumed that nobody else ever really dies from it either."

"Ah! Saffredent, the trouble is that you desire your love to be returned," Dagoucin replied, "and men of your opinions never die for love. But I know of many who *have* died, and died for no other cause than that they have loved, and loved perfectly."

---

5. "Not by speaking but by dying they confessed," a line recited during the Feast of the Holy Innocents.

FRANÇOIS RABELAIS
1495?–1553

François Rabelais created a distinctive blend of broad, lusty, and unsqueamish humor so influential that it took its creator's name: to this day, humor that blends the lofty and low, elegant and grotesque, erudite and physical is called *Rabelaisian*. Rabelais displays great artistic control over his work, which never shies away from the body: without breaking decorum, he introduces elements that elsewhere might seem crude or obscene (even a hiccup is inconceivable in Castiglione's Urbino). He creates a capacious narrative in which one character (the giant Gargantua) uses his dandruff for cannonballs, another (Panurge) proposes to rebuild the city walls of Paris out of women's genitals, and yet another (Alcofribas Nasier, the narrator) ventures into the mouth of the giant Pantagruel, wherein he discovers another world and converses with a farmer who is planting cabbages in the giant's tongue. Although irreverent, these scenarios allude to the epic tasks of founding city walls and colonizing new worlds. With bawdy humor, Rabelais both imitates and parodies the grandest of all literary genres, the imperial epic.

Rabelais, the son of a successful lawyer, was in all likelihood born around 1495 in the province of Touraine. He trained as a Franciscan monk and priest, gained proficiency in Greek, and came to the attention of Guillaume Budé, secretary to the king of France, as a promising young scholar. Rabelais experienced in 1523 the first of many dispiriting brushes with the Sorbonne, the college of powerful and conservative theologians at the University of Paris, when it banned the study of Greek in France and his books were confiscated. Disturbed at these antihumanist actions, he sought and gained authorization from Pope Clement VII to transfer to the less strict Benedictine order. He immortalized his hatred of the Sorbonne, which in future years would condemn with depressing regularity each of his books as they appeared, in his grotesque inventory of "sophistes, Sorbillans, Sorbonagres, Sorbonigènes, Sorbonicoles, Sorboniformes, Sorbonisecques, Niborcisans, Borsonisans, Saniborsans. . . ." Around 1527 he decided to pursue a career in medicine and gave up the monk's habit, an act for which he was not to receive papal absolution until 1536. Rabelais received the degree of bachelor of medicine from the University of Montpellier in 1530 and was by 1532 a successful physician at the important hospital of the Pont-du-Rhône at Lyon.

Under the pseudonym Alcofribas Nasier, an anagram for François Rabelais, he published a book about Pantagruel, the son he created for Gargantua, a gigantic folk hero of French oral tradition. He seems to have published his *Gargantua* just before a political nightmare, called the Affair of the Placards, in 1534. In this event, Reformers plastered antipapal posters in the main squares of Paris and even on the door of the king's bedchamber, alienating King Francis I from all reformers, even the peaceful Evangelicals associated with Rabelais and Francis's sister, Marguerite de Navarre. The king had previously been sympathetic to reform and had taken the unprecedented step of founding a nontheological university in France (the College of Royal Lecturers) where scholars taught Hebrew and Greek. After the affair, Francis I retaliated with persecutions of French Protestants. Rabelais felt threatened enough to leave his post at the hospital and disappear until the persecutions eased (due to interventions by the German princes and Pope Paul III). In 1537 Rabelais received his doctorate of medicine at Montpellier, where he later gave lectures, using the original texts of ancient Greek physicians such as Hippocrates. In the following years he traveled widely as doctor to Jean du Bellay, bishop of Paris, and his important brother, Seigneur de Langey. Rabelais even came to hold a minor post in the retinue of Francis I, and in 1538 he attended the meeting between Francis I and Charles V, the Holy Roman Emperor, that led to increased persecution of Reformers. Prepared to hold his religious opinions "up to but excluding the stake," Rabelais conformed.

In his definitive edition of *Gargantua and Pantagruel* of 1541, Rabelais toned down his lampoons of the Sorbonne, which nonetheless condemned the book, preventing its sale or possession. In 1544 he gained Francis I's permission to publish his third book, less flamboyant and optimistic than the first two. His efforts to appease the Sorbonne were unsuccessful, and when the third book appeared two years later, it too was condemned; at the time, Rabelais himself was in flight at Metz in Alsace (or on a secret mission—we do not know which). Encouraged by Chastillon, his last great patron and protector, and by the new king, Henry II, Rabelais published his fourth book in 1551; all too predictably it was condemned by the Sorbonne until the king lifted the ban. A fifth book, attributed to Rabelais but of unknown authorship, appeared in 1562–64. Tradition has it that in 1553 Rabelais died in Paris, in the Rue de Jardins.

As inspiration for his giant humanist, the title hero of *Pantagruel*, Rabelais chose a little devil from a medieval mystery play who provoked thirst wherever he went and liked to pour salt down the throats of drunkards. Pantagruel's father, Gargantua, explains that his son was born in a drought and that his name means "dominator of thirsts." Although Pantagruel loves good wine, his chief thirsts are intellectual. In the book's first chapters, Pantagruel completes his prodigious education along the lines recommended by his father and is well on his way to becoming an ideal humanist prince. Once educated and matured into a rational and generous-minded young prince, however, Pantagruel becomes less suited for the adventurous and mischievous middle of Rabelais's narrative than for its comparatively high-minded and educational beginning and conclusion. *Gargantua and Pantagruel* follows other Renaissance epics, using its middle chapters to test, question, and toy with the ideals of heroism and civility that epic narratives ultimately sanctify in a final battle and the founding of a new imperial city.

The playful and exploratory character at the center of *Pantagruel* is Panurge (Greek *pan + ourgos*, "he who will do all things"), a trickster, bad boy, and shadow version of Pantagruel. Panurge knows much, invents more, and stops at nothing. When Pantagruel first spies the noble but bedraggled figure, Panurge inspires the young giant's compassionate interest. He and his companions offer their help, and Panurge answers in no fewer than thirteen languages—three imaginary, three ancient, and seven modern. In pompous German, the language of the Antipodes (who dwell at the opposite side of the world), Italian, Scottish, vulgar Basque, "Lanternese," Dutch, Spanish, Danish, Hebrew, ancient Greek, "Utopian," and Latin, Panurge repeatedly laments that Pantagruel and his friends cannot understand him and begs for the food and drink they wish to give him (although the idiom of the Antipodes implies a threat to sodomize Pantagruel if he does not comply). When his would-be benefactors finally ask if he knows any French, Panurge delightedly reveals that he is a native, "born and brought up in the garden of France, that is Touraine"—precisely the birthplace of Rabelais himself.

Although not exactly a double for Rabelais, Panurge vibrantly embodies his author's intellectual and narrative tactics. He is an inventive and imitative trickster, an extroverted entertainer, and a multilingual scholar. He loves games and practical jokes that create an expansive sense of community (for all except the butts of his jokes). Eloquence of word and gesture comes easily to him. His rhetorical virtuosity is akin to that of Erasmus's Folly, although he takes far greater liberties in diction, ascending to high Ciceronian expression or descending to earthy obscenity at will. He achieves similar feats in the language of bodily gesture, notably in his sign-language debate with the daunting English scholar Thaumaste: by making liberal use of his enormous codpiece, which ornaments and enlarges the appearance of his penis, Panurge vanquishes his opponent. Farts, displays of incontinence, and phallic play are as expressive to Panurge as a classical or biblical allusion, a neologism (made-up word), or a cheerful obscenity.

Like Panurge, Rabelais mingles the earthy and grotesque with the lofty and elegant in *Gargantua and Pantagruel:* he chooses Virgil's *Aeneid* and Old Testament stories as his dominant models. Both of Rabelais's books juxtapose and mingle the erudite and bawdy, classical and folk, and high and low ("head" and "bottom" better suit the books' corporeal spirit). As the Russian critic Mikhail Bakhtin noted, Rabelais's epic seriousness cannot be properly understood apart from his presentation of the body, marked by its yawning mouth, flared nostrils, and anus. The lower regions of the Rabelaisian body—belly, buttocks, and genitals—prevail over the head or reason. Eating, drinking, defecating, farting, sweating, and nose-blowing pervade Rabelais's narratives. The gaping orifices mark the grotesque body's openness to sexual, economic, and emotional exchange and its stark contrast with the classical body, which is well-proportioned, closed, and upwardly focused. To an extent, Rabelais compares the classical body with classical epic and contrasts them with the grotesque body and the vital folk traditions that broaden the scope of his text.

The episodes from *Gargantua and Pantagruel* represented in this anthology include the bawdy and the epic: they begin with the education of the gigantic heroes in the humanistic arts and conclude with the ethical, learned giants' battle against tyrannical forces that threaten their fathers' kingdoms. When Pantagruel learns that a nation called the Dipsodes has invaded Gargantua's kingdom, he is forced to leave his "Dido" (a Parisian lady) and, like Virgil's Aeneas, choose the fatherland over love. Giant though he is, Pantagruel becomes a second David set in unequal battle with a new Goliath, the gigantic Werewolf who captains King Anarchy's army. Pantagruel's enemies represent terrifying worldly evils: anarchy means lawlessness, and the werewolf is a traditional figure for a tyrant. Rabelais uses the biblical story of David and Goliath (1 Samuel 17.4–51) to celebrate the fight of humanist enlightenment against menacing political abuses.

Gargantua, too, has an epic destiny in the first book (composed second and in many ways a revision of the first): his father's lands are under attack by a former ally, King Picrochole (Greek for "bitter bile"), and Gargantua returns home to defend them. Bad counselors have turned Picrochole from a friendly neighbor into an imperial marauder bent on conquering the world. They urge him to sail through the straits of Gibraltar and—in a Renaissance image of transgressive audacity—to "erect two columns more magnificent than those of Hercules in perpetual memory of [his] name." The Strait of Gibraltar, they promise him, "shall be called the Picrocholine Sea." The columns that these warmongering counselors have in mind were erected by Hercules, the legendary Greco-Roman demigod, to mark the ends of the Western world, beyond which no man should go (although Dante's bold Ulysses did). These pillars were also the emblem of the Holy Roman Emperor, Charles V, with whom Rabelais implicitly compares Picrochole. In *Gargantua,* Rabelais compares recent European history with an imperial epic in which Charles V and Francis I struggle for dominion in Europe and the title of emperor.

Yet Rabelais does not celebrate imperial expansion: Gargantua and his friends resist the would-be conquerors of their books, which form an anti-imperialistic epic. In his commitment to pacifism, Rabelais does not follow Virgil, who accepts the sacrifices of empire, but instead Erasmus, who believes that the only wars Christians should fight are defensive, a position that leaves out crusades and conquests.

After Gargantua and his friends defeat Picrochole's armies, they found a city that will cultivate the values for which they fought. They establish a community that affirms pacifist, liberal, humanistic values and name it the Abbey of Thélème, derived from the Greek word for "will" or "desire." The abbey's rules forbid men to live without women, and vice versa; ban clocks; and decree that all entrances and exits be voluntary (monks needed a papal dispensation to leave the monastery). Moreover, since monks and nuns usually took vows of chastity, poverty, and obedience, it was decided that in Thélème all inhabitants could marry with honor, be rich, and live wherever they wanted. On the great gate of Thélème, the architects inscribed a poem about Christian life, restored to its pristine state: hypocrites, bigots, liars, frauds, lawyers, and judges are cordially asked to stay away: they are dogs, frogs, fleas, and plague sores! "Sportsmen, lovers, friends," on the other hand, know and love the holy Word of God and are joyfully welcomed within the abbey's walls. Like the idealized court of Castiglione's Urbino, the abbey is populated with beautiful, intelligent, and learned youths who dress, converse, play games, value communal harmony, and relish the goal of married, sexual love. Designed to promote the simultaneous fulfillment of individual and communal will, Rabelais's abbey cultivates marriages that are free from conflicts of will and then releases the couples into the larger community, where the blissful unions lay the foundation of an equally harmonious society—one based on consent and the exercise of liberties.

Rabelais's abbey is not, however, a completely imagined world. It begins as a fantasy *negating* undesirable aspects of social reality in Europe rather than *creating* an independent social model. As Rabelais describes the abbey, he grows increasingly interested in the material conditions that produce the splendor of his fantasy world. His utopia, for example, follows the laws of supply and demand: as it turns out, there is a wing of low-lying buildings outside the abbey walls, where craftsmen import the wealth of the West Indies and set about their bourgeois trade of manufacturing luxuries for the wealthy. The more interested Rabelais grows in his abbey, the more it develops into an alluring paradox, beginning and ending in criticism of imperialism and colonization.

Few works in the Renaissance are as artistically and intellectually expansive as Rabelais's *Gargantua and Pantagruel*. The books are outrageous and serious, entertaining and thought-provoking. Rabelais's work takes the idea of "serious play" to such extremes that readers caught up in its rollicking humor may enter fully into the hedonistic escape that a brilliantly conceived fiction can offer. The same readers, drawn into its weighty artistic, intellectual, and sociopolitical thought, may at other times "forget" to laugh. Both are appropriate responses to Rabelais's extraordinary books.

Donald M. Frame, *François Rabelais: A Study* (1977), provides an overview of Rabelais's life, narrative techniques, and themes. Mikhail Bakhtin, *Rabelais and His World* (1968, 1984), is a groundbreaking analysis of the popular festivities that Rabelais draws on in his work. Thomas M. Greene, *Rabelais: A Study in Comic Courage* (1970), provides a concise overview and introduction. Although not meant for the general reader, Edwin M. Duval, *The Design of Rabelais's Pantagruel* (1991), Carla Freccero, *Father Figures: Genealogy and Narrative Structure in Rabelais* (1991), and Walter Stephens, *Giants in Those Days: Folklore, Ancient History, and Nationalism* (1989), are rewarding recent studies. Elizabeth Chesney Zegura and Marcel Tetel, *Rabelais Revisited* (1990), offers a good general introduction.

PRONOUNCING GLOSSARY

The following list uses common English syllables and stress accents to provide rough equivalents of selected words whose pronunciation may be unfamiliar to the general reader.

Alcofribas Nasier: *ahl-coh-free-bah'*
    nah-zyay'
Almain: *ahl-manh'*
Anatole: *ahn-ah-tohl'*
Artice: *ahr-tees*
Basché: *bah-shay'*
Beauce: *bohs*
Bonnivet: *bon-ee-vay'*
Boulogne: *boo-lun'*

Calaer: *cah-lah-ehr'*
Chantilly: *shawn-tee-yee'*
Chastillon: *shah-tee-yohnh'*
Chinon: *shee-nohn'*
Cryere: *cree-yehr'*
Fontainebleau: *fohn-ten-bloh'*
Gentilly: *zhawn-tee-yee'*
Jean Thenaud: *zhawn tay-noh'*
Langeais: *lawnh-zhay'*

Langedoc: *lawnh-ge-dawk'*

Mesembriné: *may-zawn-bree-nay'*

Nantes: *nawnt*

Papeligosse: *pah-plee-gaws'*

Philippe des Marais: *fee-leep' day
    mahr-ay'*

Picrochole: *pee-craw-shol'*

Port-Huault: *por—yew-oh'*

rondelle: *rohn-del'*

Rouen: *roo-awnh'*

Rue de Jardins: *rew deu zhahr-danh'*

Saint Denis: *sanh deu-nee'*

Saint-Cloud: *sanh—cloo'*

Saint-Mars: *sanh—mahr'*

Saint-Martin d'Ainay: *sanh—mahr-tanh'
    den-ay'*

Seine: *sen*

Thaumaste: *toh-mahst'*

Thélème: *tay-lem'*

Touraine: *too-ren'*

Vanves: *vahnv*

FROM GARGANTUA AND PANTAGRUEL[1]

From Book I

[Education of a Giant Humanist]

CHAPTER 14

How Gargantua Was Taught Latin by a Terribly Learned Philosopher

This subject disposed of, that good man Grandgousier was ravished with admiration, thinking about the good sense and marvelous comprehension of his son Gargantua. And so he said to his governesses:

"Philip, king of Macedonia, understood the good sense of his son Alexander by his skill in handling a certain horse, which was so terrible, so completely wild, that no one could even get up on its back. He bucked and threw everyone who tried to ride him, breaking the neck of one, the legs of another, cracking one man's skull and shattering another's jawbone. When Alexander went down into the Hippodrome (which was where they trained and exercised their horses) and analyzed the problem, he saw that the horse's desperate fury came, simply enough, from being afraid of his own shadow. Having come to this understanding, he jumped up on the horse's back and forced him to run straight toward the sun, so that his shadow fell behind him, and by this procedure turned the horse gentle and obedient. And that showed his father what divine understanding his son possessed, and he arranged that the boy be thoroughly trained by Aristotle, who was at that time considered the best philosopher in Greece.

"But I tell you that from this one discussion, which my son and I have just had, right here in front of you, I too understand that his understanding has something divine about it—so acute, subtle, profound, and yet serene—and will attain to a singularly lofty degree of wisdom, provided he is well taught. Accordingly, I wish to put him in the hands of some scholarly man who will

1. Translated by Burton Raffel.

teach him everything he is capable of learning. And to this end I propose to open my purse as freely as need be."

So they sent for a great philosopher, Maître Tubalcain Holofernes, who taught him the alphabet so well that he could say it backward, by heart, at which point he was five years and three months old. Then he read with the boy a Latin grammar by Donatus, plus a dull and well-meaning treatise on courtesy, and a long book by Bishop Theodulus, in which he proves that ancient mythology is all a heap of nonsense, and finally an exceedingly long poem in dreadfully moral quatrains.[2] All this took thirteen years, six months, and two weeks to accomplish.

Of course, it's also true that he learned to write in Gothic letters, and wrote out all his own books that way, since this was before the art of printing had been invented.

Most of the time he carried a large writing desk, weighing more than thirty tons, with a pencil box as big and heavy as the four great pillars of Saint-Martin d'Ainay, the old church in Lyons. And the inkpot hung down on huge iron chains, capable of supporting barrels and barrels of merchandise.

And then they read *De modis significandi*, "The Methods of Reasoned Analysis," with the commentaries of Broken Biscuithead, Bouncing Rock, Talktoomuch, Galahad, John the Fatted Calf, Balogny, Cuntprober, and a pile of others. And this took more than eighteen years and six months. And by then Gargantua knew it all so well that, if you asked him, he could recite every single line, backward, proving to his mother that he had the whole thing at his fingertips and, most important of all, that *de modis significandi non erat scientia*, the methods of reasoned analysis were neither reasonable nor a science.

Then they read that great book *Calculation*, surely the longest almanac ever compiled: this took another sixteen years and two months. And then, suddenly, his teacher died, being four hundred and twenty years old: it was the pox that carried him off.

So they brought in another old cougher, Maître Blowhard Birdbrain, with whom he read Bishop Huguito of Ferrara, Eberhard de Bethune's *Greekishnessisms*, Alexander de Villedieu's barbarous Latin grammar, Remigius' *Petty Doctrines* and also his *What's What*, a charming discourse set in question-and-answer form, the *Supplement to All Supplements*, a fat glossary of saints' lives and the like, Sulpicius' long, long poem on the psalms and death, Seneca's *De quatuor virtutibus cardinalibus*, The Four Cardinal Virtues (which wasn't by Seneca at all), Passavantus' *Mirror of True Penitence*, and the same author's *Sleep in Peace*, a collection of sermons chosen to make happy days still happier—and he also read other tough birds of the same feather. And in reading all this he became quite as wise as any blackbird ever baked in a pie.

CHAPTER 15

How Gargantua Got to Study with Other Teachers

By that point his father could see that although he was studying as hard as he could, and spending all his time at it, he didn't seem to be learning

2. The books mentioned in this chapter were actually part of the educational curriculum that Rabelais is here satirizing.

much and, what's worse, he was becoming distinctly stupid, a real simpleton, all wishy-washy and driveling.

When he complained of this to Don Philippe des Marais, viceroy of Pape-ligosse,[3] he was told that it would be better for Gargantua to learn nothing at all than to study such books with such teachers, whose learning was nothing but stupidity and whose wisdom was nothing but gloves with no hands in them—empty. They were specialists in ruining good and noble spirits and nipping the flowering of youth in the bud.

"To show you what I mean," he said, "take some modern youngster, who has only been studying for two years. If he doesn't show better judgment, better use of words, better ability to analyze and discuss than your son, as well as greater ease and courtesy in dealing with the world, then call me a fat-head from Brenne."

Grandgousier was delighted and told him to do exactly that.

That night, at supper, des Marais introduced one of his young pages, a young fellow named Rightway (in Greek, Eudemon), who was from Ville-gongis, near Saint-Genou. And he was so well-groomed, so beautifully dressed, so clean and neat in every respect, so courteous in his bearing, that he more nearly resembled a little angel than a human being. And des Marais said to Grandgousier:

"See this child? He's only twelve years old. Shall we see, if you care to, what a difference there is between the learning of your bird-chirping old philosophers and modern youngsters like this?"

Grandgousier liked the idea, and told the page to give them a demonstration of what he knew. Then Rightway, after asking his master's permission to proceed, stood on his feet, his hat in his hands, his face open, his lips red, his eyes confident, his glance fixed on Gargantua with a modesty appropriate to his age, and began both to praise and to glorify Grandgousier's son, first for his virtue and his good manners, second for his knowledge, third for his nobility, fourth for his physical beauty, and then, fifth, sweetly urged him always to honor his father, who had taken such pains to have him well brought up, finally begging Gargantua to consider Master Rightway the most insignificant of his servants, for the boy asked no other gift from the heavens but the grace of pleasing Gargantua by some cheerfully rendered service. And all of this was spoken with such extraordinarily tactful gestures, with a pronunciation so clear, a voice so eloquent, and in language so elegant and such good Latin, that he more nearly resembled a kind of ancient Gracchus, or Cicero, or Ennius than a young person of his own time.

But all Gargantua could do was weep like a cow. He hid his face behind his hat, and it was no more possible to draw a word from him than to get a fart from a dead donkey.

All of which made his father so furious that he wanted to kill Maître Blowhard Birdbrain. But des Marais checked him with a well-turned word of warning, so neatly administered that it cooled his anger. But he ordered that Blowhard Birdbrain be paid what he was owed and allowed to guzzle like a philosopher. And when he'd drunk to his heart's content, he was to be told to go to the devil.

---

3. Probably an allusion to a real person. Rabelais's method is to take real people and introduce them into his fantastic world; he also mentions real places and draws on local lore.

"It won't cost me a thing," he said, "not today at least, if he gets so drunk that he dies of it, like an Englishman."

Maître Blowhard Birdbrain left the house. Grandgousier sought des Marais' advice about who might be available to be Gargantua's new teacher, and the two of them decided that Powerbrain (in Greek, Ponocrates), Rightway's teacher, would be the best man for the job. The three of them would then travel to Paris, the better to understand how the young men of France were pursuing their studies.

CHAPTER 16

How Gargantua Was Sent to Paris, Riding an Enormous Brood Mare,
Which Waged War against the Cow Flies of Beauce

Now, at this same time Fayoles, fourth king of Numidia, happened to send Grandgousier, all the way from Africa, the biggest, tallest brood mare anyone had ever seen. And the most monstrous, too (it being well known that Africa always brings forth new things), for it was the size of six elephants and it had toes, like Julius Caesar's horse; its ears hung down like a Languedoc goat, and it had a horn sticking out of its ass. For the rest, it had a kind of burned chestnut hide, mottled with gray. Most impressive of all was its ghastly tail, because—give a pound, take a pound—it was as big as the old ruin of Saint-Mars, near Langeais (which is forty feet high), and every bit as wide, with hair as closely woven as the tassels on an ear of corn.

And if that strikes you as astonishing, what do you think of those amazing Scythian rams, weighing in at more than thirty pounds apiece, and those Syrian sheep, which (if Jean Thenaud is telling the truth) have an ass so heavy, so long and massive, that they have to tie a supporting cart to its rear end so it can get about at all. You haven't got anything like it, you lowland ass bangers!

It came by sea, in three Genoan schooners and a man-of-war, to the port of Les Sables-d'Olonne, in Talmont.

When Grandgousier saw it:

"This is exactly the right thing," he said, "to carry my son to Paris. Now, God be thanked, everything will turn out all right. Someday he'll surely be a great scholar. If it weren't for our friends the animals, we'd all have to live like philosophers."

The next day, but of course only after having drunk their fill, Gargantua, his new teacher Powerbrain, and all his attendants, together with the young page Rightway, took to the road. And because the weather was calm and moderate, his father had them make soft laced boots for Gargantua. (That great bootmaker Babin tells me they go by the name of buskins.)

So they went merrily down the highway, laughing and singing, until they had almost reached Orleáns. There they entered a large forest, ninety miles long and forty miles wide. The place swarmed with horrible cow flies, millions of them, and wasps and hornets, too, the sort that were true highway robbers for all poor mares and mules and horses. But Gargantua's mare took an appropriate revenge for all the outrages her species had suffered, playing a trick that those insects had never expected. Suddenly, as they entered the wood and the flies and wasps began their assault, she whipped out her tail and swatted them so vigorously that in fact she knocked down the entire forest. Left, right, here, there, length and width, over and under, she smashed those trees like a mower cutting grass, until finally there were neither any trees nor any insects, but just a nice flat stretch of land, which is all you can see to this day.

Gargantua watched this performance with immense delight. But he didn't want to sound vainglorious, so all he said to his companions was, "This is fine, but I don't want to boast." And ever since that part of the country has been known as Beauce. But all they got to put in their open mouths was their own yawns—in memory of which the gentlemen of Beauce (and everyone knows how poor they've always been) still dine by yawning and opening and closing their empty mouths, which they've grown to like, especially since it helps them spit.

When at last they reached Paris, Gargantua spent two or three days resting and recovering from their journey, drinking and chatting with the townsfolk and asking what scholars happened to be in the city at that time and what wine Parisians liked to drink.

*   *   *

CHAPTER 21

[Gargantua's Studies, and His Way of Life, according to His Philosophical Teachers]

Some days after the bells had been put back, and in recognition of Gargantua's courtesy in thus restoring them, the citizens of Paris offered to feed and maintain his mare for as long as he might like, an offer which Gargantua found most acceptable. So the mare was put to pasture in Fontainebleau Forest. I don't think she is still there.

Gargantua was absolutely determined to study under Powerbrain. To begin with, however, Powerbrain directed his new pupil to proceed exactly as he always had, the better to understand how, over such a long period of time, his former teachers had turned him into such a fop, such a fool and ignoramus.

Accordingly, Gargantua lived just as he usually did, waking up between eight and nine (whether it was daylight or not), exactly as his old teachers had prescribed. And they cited the words of King David: *Vanum est vobis ante lucem surgere*, It does you no good to wake before day begins.[4]

So he fooled about, swaggering, wallowing away the time in his bed (the better to enliven his animal spirits), and then dressed himself as the season dictated. But what he really liked to put on was a great long gown of heavy wool, lined with fox fur. And then he combed his hair as that great Ockhamist philosopher Jacob Almain always did—that is, with four fingers and a thumb, because his teachers used to say that, in this world of ours, to pay any more attention than that to your hair—or to washing and keeping yourself clean— was simply a waste of time.

Then he shat, pissed, vomited, belched, farted, yawned, spat, coughed, sighed, sneezed, and blew his nose abundantly. Then he put away a good breakfast, the better to protect himself against the dew and the bad morning

---

4. Psalm 127.2: "It is vain for you to rise up early, to sit up late, to eat the bread of sorrows: for so he giveth his beloved sleep."

air: good fried tripe, some nice broiled steak, several cheerful hams, some good grilled beef, and several platters of bread soaked in bouillon.

Powerbrain objected, observing that, fresh out of bed and before he'd been exercising, he hardly needed to take in so much refreshment. Gargantua replied:

"What! Haven't I already done enough exercise? I turned over in bed six or seven times before I got up. Isn't that enough? That's exactly what Pope Alexander used to do, and he was following the advice of his great Jewish doctor and astrologer, Bonnet de Lates. And he lived until he died, too, in spite of those who did not wish him well. This is what my prior teachers got me used to doing, saying that breakfast helped you develop your memory: that was why they started drinking at breakfast, too. I think it's marvelous— and it starts me off so well that I eat an even better supper. And Maître Tubalcain Holofernes (who was right at the head of his class, here in Paris) used to say there was no point at all just to running well: the idea was to leave early enough. So true good health for all of us doesn't require, does it, that we gulp it down, cup after cup after cup, like ducks, but certainly that we start to drink in the morning—*unde versus,* as the little poem says:

> To wake up early in the morning isn't the point:
> You've got to wet your whistle and bend that joint."

And so, after a hearty breakfast, he went to church, where they brought him, in a huge basket, a great fat prayer book, all wrapped in velvet, so heavily oiled, with such heavy clasps, and on such luxurious parchment that it must have weighed at least twenty-five hundred pounds. And then they heard twenty-six or maybe thirty masses. And then his private chaplain would come, dressed like a society swell, and with his breath nicely fortified by wine. He and Gargantua would mumble through the litany, thumbing the rosary so carefully that not a single bead ever fell to the ground.

As he walked out of church, they brought in a heavy-wheeled log carrier and delivered for his personal use an entire cask of carved-wood rosaries, each of them as round around as the rim of a man's hat. And as he and his chaplain strolled through the cloister of the church, and its galleries and gardens, they worked at their beads, saying more prayers than sixteen hermits.

Then he put in a scant half-hour of studying, keeping his eyes on his book. But, like the character in Terence's play, his soul was in the kitchen.[5]

Then he pissed his urinal full, sat down to table, and—being naturally of a calm and imperturbable disposition—began his meal with several dozen hams, smoked beef tongues, caviar, fried tripe, and assorted other appetizers.

Meanwhile, four of his servants began to toss into his mouth, one after the other—but never stopping—shovelfuls of mustard, after which he drank an incredibly long draft of white wine, to make things easier for his kidneys. And then, eating whatever happened to be in season and he happened to like, he stopped only when his belly began to hang down.

His drinking was totally unregulated, without any limits or decorum. As he said, the time to restrict your drinking was only when the cork soles of your slippers absorb enough so they swell half a foot thick.

*   *   *

---

5. *The Eunuch,* line 816.

CHAPTER 23

How Gargantua Was So Well Taught by Powerbrain That He Never
Wasted a Single Hour of the Day

Once Powerbrain understood Gargantua's vicious way of life, he began to reflect on other—and better—ways of instructing him in humanistic matters. But for the first few days he did not make any changes, realizing that nature would not allow abrupt shifts without cataclysmic violence.

Accordingly, to begin his work in the best way possible, he sought the advice of a wise physician, Holygift, with whom he discussed how to set Gargantua on a better path. The learned doctor, proceeding according to his profession's canonical rules, first purged the young man with a sovereign remedy for madness, Anticyrian hellebore, which powerful herb quickly cleaned away all the deterioration and perverse habits to which his brain had succumbed. This procedure had the advantage, also, of making Gargantua forget everything he had learned from his early teachers, just as in ancient times Timotheus[6] did with disciples who'd studied under other musicians.

To help in the good work, Powerbrain introduced Gargantua to some of Paris's truly learned scholars. In trying to be like them, he came to understand their spirit, wanting to acquire knowledge and to make something of himself.

And then he got him into such a way of studying that no hour in the day was wasted: all his time was spent in pursuit of humanistic learning and honest knowledge.

Accordingly, Gargantua now woke up at four in the morning. He would be given a massage, while a portion of the holy Scriptures was read aloud to him, in a high, clear voice, with precise and accurate pronunciation. A young page named Reader, a native of Basché, was given this task. The subject, and also the argument, of this lesson often led Gargantua into reverence and adoration of God, the majesty and marvelous wisdom of whom had thus been exhibited to him, and into prayer and supplication.

Then he would go off and, in some private place, permit the natural result of his digestive process to be excreted. While he was thus occupied, his teacher would repeat what had been read to him, clarifying and explaining the more obscure and difficult points.

Coming back, they would examine and reflect on the state of the heavens: was everything as it had been when they'd seen the sky the night before? into what constellations had the sun newly entered, and likewise the moon?

And then he was dressed and combed, his hair was properly done, and he was equipped and perfumed, while all the time the lessons he'd been given the day before were repeated for him. He recited them by heart, showing by some practical and compassionate illustrations that he understood their meaning. This often lasted two or three hours, though ordinarily they stopped when he was fully dressed.

Then he was read to for three solid hours.

After which they went outdoors, always discussing the meaning of what had been read, and went to the park or somewhere near it, where they played various games, especially three-handed palm ball, giving their bodies the same elegant exercise they had earlier given their souls.

6. Of Miletus, famous musician of the time of Alexander the Great (356–323 B.C.).

Their games were entirely free: they stopped whenever they felt like stopping—usually when they'd worked up a sweat or when they grew tired. Then they had a vigorous massage, and were wiped clean; they'd change their shirts and, walking quietly, would go to see if dinner was ready. And as they waited they'd recite, clearly and eloquently, remembered portions of the lesson.

However, Sir Appetite arrived, and when they could they seated themselves at the table.

Some entertaining story of ancient heroism was read to them, at the start of the meal, until wine was poured in Gargantua's cup.

Then, if they liked the idea, the reading was resumed, or else they'd begin to chat happily. At the beginning of this new regime, they talked about virtue, proper behavior, the nature and effect of everything placed on their table that day: bread, wine, water, salt, meat, fish, fruit, herbs, roots, and about the preparation of these things. In so doing, Gargantua soon learned all the appropriate passages from Pliny, Athenaeus, Dioscorides, Julius Pollux, Galen, Porphyry, Oppian, Polybius, Heliodorus, Aristotle, Claudius Aelian,[7] and others. In order to be sure they had their authorities right, they'd often have the books brought right to the table. And what was said became so clearly and entirely fixed in Gargantua's memory that no doctor alive understood anything like as much as he did.

Then, talking about the lessons read that morning, and finishing their meal with some quinced sweet, Gargantua would clean his teeth with a bit of fresh green mastic twig. He'd wash his hands and his eyes with good fresh water, and give thanks to God with sweet hymns of praise for His munificence and divine kindness. And cards were brought, not for playing games of chance, but to learn a thousand gracious things and new inventions, all founded in arithmetic.

And in this way Gargantua developed a genuine liking for the numerical science. Every day, after both dinner and supper, he passed his time in arithmetical games just as pleasantly as when he'd been in the habit of playing at dice or cards. Indeed, he came to understand both the theory and the practice of arithmetic so well that Cuthbert Tunstal,[8] the Englishman who had written so much on the subject, was obliged to admit that, truly, in comparison to Gargantua, all he understood was a pack of nonsense.

But arithmetic wasn't the end of it, for they went on to other mathematical sciences, like geometry, astronomy, and music. While waiting for their meal to be digested and properly absorbed, they worked out a thousand pleasant geometrical figures, and shaped appropriate instruments, and practiced astronomical laws in the same way.

Later, they had a wonderful good time, singing four- and five-part rounds, and sometimes singing variations on some melody that was a delight to their throats.

As for musical instruments, Gargantua learned to play the lute, the clavier, the harp, the transverse flute as well as the recorder, the viol, and also the trombone.

As this hour passed, digestion was indeed accomplished, and so he proceeded to purge himself of his natural excrement. Then he at once returned

7. Some of the most famous scientific authors of antiquity. The new curriculum, exacting as it is, reflects a less "medieval" type of learning than was embodied in his earlier course of study. See also the enumeration of authors in chap. 14.   8. Author of the treatise *The Art of Computation* (*De arte supputandi*, 1522).

to his main studies for three hours or even more, in order to repeat the morning's lesson and also to continue with whatever book had been set for him. And he practiced writing in the Italian and the Gothic alphabets, and also drawing.

And then they'd go back to their rooms, and along with them went a young gentleman from Touraine, Squire Gymnast by name, who was teaching Gargantua the arts of knighthood.

After changing his clothes, Gargantua would mount a battle horse, a traveling steed, a Spanish stallion, an Arabian racehorse, and a light, quick horse, and ride a hundred laps, making his mount fairly fly through the air, jump ditches, leap over fences, make quick circular turns, both to the right and to the left.

Nor did he break his lance, for it is sheer nonsense to say, "I broke ten lances in battle." Any carpenter could do as much. Real glory comes from breaking ten of your enemies' with one of your own. So, with his steel-tipped, solid, firm lance he learned to break down a door, crack open a suit of armor, uproot a tree, strike right through the center of a hoop, knock a knight's saddle right off his horse, and carry away a coat of mail or a pair of armored gloves. And all the time he was himself in armor, from his head right down to his toes.

When it came to marching his horse in rhythm, or making the animal obey his commands, there was simply no one better. Even Cesare Fieschi, the famous equestrian acrobat, seemed no better than a monkey on horseback, in comparison. He was especially good at leaping from one horse to another, without ever setting foot on the ground—the horses were known as leapers— and he could do this from either side, lance erect, without stirrups. Without any reins or bridle he could make a horse do anything he wanted it to do. In short, he was accomplished at everything useful in military matters.

Some days he exercised with the battle-ax, which he could wield like a razor, swinging it so powerfully, slicing it around in a circle so deftly, that he was ranked a knight at arms, passing every sort of trial and declared fit for any battle.

And then he'd practice with the pickax, or at wielding the two-handed sword, or with the short sword (so perfect for thrusting and parrying), and the dagger—sometimes wearing armor, sometimes not, or using a shield, or wearing a cape, or carrying a small wrist shield, known as a *rondelle*.

He hunted deer—stag and doe and fallow buck—bears, wild boar, hares, partridge, pheasant, buzzards. He played with the big kickball, making it bound high in the air, sometimes with his foot, sometimes with his fist. He fought and ran and leaped and jumped—but not a mere three-foot hop and leap, or a high jump in the German style—because, as Gymnast said, jumps of that sort were useless and of no good whatever, when it came to real war— but he'd jump great wide ditches, go flying over a hedgerow, climb six paces up a wall, and thus get in through a window as high off the ground as a lance.

He swam in deep water, breaststroke, backstroke, sidestroke, using his entire body or only his legs, or with one hand high in the air and holding a book, crossing the Seine River without getting a page wet. He swam with his cloak in his teeth, as Julius Caesar did (says Plutarch). Then, pulling himself right into a boat with just one hand, he'd throw himself back into the water, head first, going all the way down to the bottom, sinking among the rocks and swimming to great depths, plunging down to all sorts of chasms and deep abysses. Then he'd turn the boat, and steer it, sometimes quickly, sometimes slowly, now downstream, now upstream, sometimes bringing it to a halt by pressing it against a milldam, guiding it with one hand, his other wielding a great oar or raising the sail. He'd climb up the guide ropes, right to the top of the mast, and run out along the spars. He'd adjust the compass, brace the bowlines, tighten the helm.

Leaving the water, he'd go directly up a mountain and then come right down again. He'd climb trees like a cat, jumping from one to the other like a squirrel, tearing down thick branches as if he were another Milo of Croton. With a pair of sharp-pointed daggers and a couple of good marlinespikes, he'd climb to the top of a house exactly like a rat, then leap down so expertly that the drop wouldn't cause him so much as a twinge.

He threw the javelin, and the iron bar, the millstone, the boar spear, the hunting spear, the spiked halberd. He drew the longbow like an archer, pulled crossbows taut (though this was usually done with a winch), sighted a rifle right against his eye (though usually it had to be rested against the shoulder), set up and mounted cannon, centering them right in on target, aimed them so they could knock a stuffed parrot off a pole, pointing them straight up a mountain or right down into a valley, directing their fire up ahead or to the side or, like the ancient Parthians, back behind him.

They would attach a rope cable to some high tower, hanging down to the ground, and he would climb this, hand over hand, then come down so strongly and with such confidence that he might just as well have been strolling along some nice, flat meadow.

They would rig up a long pole, supported on each side by a tree, and he'd hang from it by his hands, going this way and that without his feet ever touching the ground—and at such a speed that, even running on flat ground, it would have been impossible to catch him.

And in order to exercise his chest and lungs, he would shout like all the devils in hell. Once, I heard him call to Rightway, from the Saint Victor Gate all the way across Paris to Montmartre. Even bull-throated Stentor,[9] at the battle of Troy, could not shout so loud.

To toughen his nerves, they made him two huge molded lead weights, cast in the shape of salmon, each just over eighty thousand pounds: he called them his dumbbells. He'd lift one in each hand, starting from the ground, and hold them both high up over his head—and then he'd keep them there, not moving a muscle, for three-quarters of an hour or even more. This was literally unmatchable strength!

No one was stronger, not in barriers or tug-of-war or any of the games. When it was his turn, he stood his ground so firmly that he could afford to let the most adventurous try to move him a single inch from his place, exactly as Milo of Croton used to do—and in imitation of whom he would clasp a pomegranate in his hand and offer it to anyone who could take it from him. Nor would he permit the fruit to be damaged in the attempt.

Having thus spent his time, he'd have another massage, then clean himself and change his clothes, returning with a smile and, strolling through mead-

9. The loud-voiced herald in the *Iliad* 5.

ows and other grassy spots, he'd turn his attention to trees and plants, examining them in the light of what the ancients wrote—Theophrastus, Dioscorides, Marinus, Pliny, Nicander, Aemilius Macer, and Galen.[1] He and his companions would fill their hands with herbs and roots and flowers, then bring it all back to their lodgings, where a young page, Rootgatherer, was in charge of all such matters, including care of the hoes, picks, rakes, spades, shovels, and everything else needed for the proper care of growing things.

And once they were back at their lodgings, and while waiting for their supper, they would repeat selected passages from what they had read, earlier, and also what they had discussed at table.

Note, please, that although dinner was a sober and even frugal meal, at which Gargantua would eat only just enough to control the growling in his stomach, supper was a great abundant affair. He would consume everything he needed to sustain and properly nourish himself, which is exactly the sort of diet prescribed by any good, knowing doctor, though there are plenty of medical hacks (in constant dispute, of course, with learned academic philosophers) who advise exactly the opposite.

Gargantua continued his lessons all during supper, or for as long as he felt in the mood. And then he would turn to good solid discussion, literate, informed, useful.

After a final grace had been said, they would turn to music, singing, the harmonious playing of various instruments, or to pleasant card and dice games. And there they would stay, having a fine time, often amusing themselves until it was time to go to bed. And sometimes they would go visiting the houses of learned people, or perhaps those newly returned from foreign countries.

When night had truly arrived, but before they climbed into bed, they would stand in their lodgings, in the spot from which the sky could be most closely observed, and compare notes about any comets they might see, and the configuration of the stars, their location and aspect, their oppositions and conjunctions.

And then Gargantua and Powerbrain would briefly recapitulate, according to the Pythagorean fashion, everything Gargantua had read and seen and understood, everything he had done and heard, all day long.

They would both pray to God their Creator, worshiping, reaffirming their faith, glorifying Him for His immense goodness and thanking Him for all they had been given, and forever placing themselves in His hands.

And then they would go to sleep.

CHAPTER 24

[What Gargantua Did When It Was Rainy]

When the weather turned rainy and bad, the time before dinner went exactly as usual, except that Gargantua had a good bright fire lit, to help moderate the intemperate air. But after dinner, in place of exercise, they would stay indoors and, according to the best therapeutic approach, amuse themselves by baling hay, sawing and splitting wood, and threshing the grain stored in the barn. Then they would study the art of painting and sculpture,

1. Greek and Roman scientists.

or else (following ancient custom) play knucklebones, an entertainment about which Leonicus Thomaeus has written so well—and a game which Andreas Lascaris,[2] teacher and friend of Erasmus, and my good friend too, has played with such pleasure. And while they played they turned over in their mind all the passages from classical authors in which the game is either mentioned or used as a metaphor.

In the same way, they would either go to watch the work at metal foundries, or the casting of cannon, or go to observe jewelers, goldsmiths, and those who cut precious stones, or else alchemists and coin makers, or tapestry weavers, silk weavers, velvet makers, watchmakers, mirror makers, printers, organ manufacturers, dyers, and other craftsmen of that sort. And treating all of them to wine, they learned from the mouths of these masters what their various trades and inventions were all about.

They would go to hear public lectures, solemn convocations, and the careful orations, declamations, and pleadings of wellborn lawyers, or the sermons of evangelical preachers.

He went to all the places where swordsmanship was practiced and taught, and tested himself against those who taught it, in every aspect of fencing and with all the sorts of swords and foils known. And he demonstrated to them that he knew as much as they did, and more.

Instead of going off to collect herbs and examine plants and flowers, they would go to drugstores, herb sellers, and other apothecaries, and contemplate with great care the fruits, roots, leaves, gums, seeds, and all the exotic unguents, and then how they were prepared and diluted for more effective use.

He went to see the jugglers and clowns, the magicians and those who peddled wonderful, half-magical remedies, and contemplated their games and tricks, their somersaults and smooth patter, especially those famous mountebanks from Chauny, in Picardy—born with a silver tongue, every one of them, able to sell water to people swimming in a lake or firewood to those who live inside a volcano.

They would return for supper, and eat more sparingly than on other days—in particular, meats that tend to dry and tame the body. This was made necessary by the excessive humidity in the air, which under the circumstances there was no way to avoid. These simple dietary measures corrected that natural imbalance and saved them from being bothered by the loss of their usual exercise.

And this was how Gargantua's life was regulated. He kept to these rules every day, and he benefited—to be sure!—as a young man of his years can, a youth with good sense. All regular exercise, no matter how hard it may at first seem, becomes pleasant and easy and finally great good fun, more like a royal pastime than a scholar's plodding.

In spite of which, and in order to allow him some relief from such a whirlwind way of life, Powerbrain made sure that Gargantua took off at least one day a month, some day of great clarity and calm brightness. They would leave Paris early in the morning and go to one of the pleasant villages beloved of all Parisian students—Gentilly, perhaps, or Boulogne on the Seine, or Mon-

---

2. André-Jean de Lascaris (ca. 1445–ca. 1535), librarian to King Francis I and a friend of Rabelais's. Leonicus Thomaeus (d. 1531), a Venetian and professor at Padua.

trouge, or Pont-Charenton, or Vanves, or Saint-Cloud. And they would spent the entire day there, just as happily as they could manage, laughing, telling jokes, drinking gaily, playing, singing, dancing, lying on their backs in beautiful meadows, hunting for sparrows' nests, catching quail, and fishing for frogs and crayfish.

But even on this day spent without books and reading, they didn't completely neglect higher matters, because even lying there in the lovely meadows they would recite from memory cheerful verses from Virgil's *Georgics*, from Hesiod, from Politian's *Rusticus* (Farming), or some pleasant Latin epigrams, which they'd then turn into equally pleasant poems in their own language.

And when they feasted they would not simply mix their wine and water. Instead, as Cato advises in his *Country Matters*, and Pliny too, they would use a cup of ivy wood and wash the wine in a full basin of water, then pour it back out with a funnel.[3] And they would pour the water from one glass to another and construct tiny automatic engines that seemed to work of their own accord, like automatons.

[The Abbey of Thélème]

CHAPTER 52

How Gargantua Built the Abbey of Desire (Thélème) for Brother John

The only one still left to be provided for was the monk.[4] Gargantua wanted to make him abbot of Seuilly, but the monk refused. Gargantua also offered him the abbey of Bourgueil or that of Saint-Florent, whichever best pleased him—and said he could have both those rich, old Benedictine cloisters, if he preferred that.[5] But the monk answered him in no uncertain terms: he wanted neither to govern nor to be in charge of other monks:

"And how," he asked, "should I govern others, when I don't know how to govern myself? If you really think I've done something for you, and I might in the future do something to please you, grant me this: establish an abbey according to my plan."

The request pleased Gargantua, so he offered him the whole land of Thélème, alongside the river Loire, two leagues from the great forest of Port-Huault. And the monk then asked Gargantua to establish this abbey's rules and regulations completely differently from all the others.

"Obviously," said Gargantua, "it won't be necessary to build walls all around it, because all the other abbeys are brutally closed in."

"Indeed," said the monk, "and for good reason. Whenever you've got a whole load of stones in front and a whole load of stones in back, you've got a whole lot of grumbling and complaining, and jealousy, and all kinds of conspiracies."

Moreover, since some of the cloisters already built in this world are in the

---

3. Both Cato's *On Farming (De re rustica)* 109 and Pliny's *Natural History* 16.63 suggest an ivy-wood cup as a means to detect water in wine. **4.** Brother John of the Funnels, the muscular and highly unconventional monk who has had a major part in helping the party of Gargantua's father win the mock-heroic war against the arrogant Picrochole. **5.** A satiric allusion to the custom of accumulating church livings.

habit, whenever any woman enters them (I speak only of modest, virtuous women), of washing the ground where she walked, it was decreed that if either a monk or a nun happened to enter the abbey of Thélème, they would scrub the blazes out of the places where they'd been. And since everything is completely regulated, in all the other cloistered houses, tied in and bound down, hour by hour, according to a fierce schedule, it was decreed that in Thélème there would not be a single clock, or even a sundial, and that work would be distributed strictly according to what was needed and who was available to do it—because (said Gargantua) the worst waste of time he knew of was counting the hours—what good could possibly come of it?—and the biggest, fattest nonsense in the whole world was to be ruled by the tolling of a bell rather than by the dictates of common sense and understanding.

Item: because in these times of ours women don't go into convents unless they're blind in one eye, lame, humpbacked, ugly, misshapen, crazy, stupid, deformed, or pox-ridden, and men only if they're tubercular, low born, blessed with an ugly nose, simpletons, or a burden on their parents . . .

("Oh yes," said the monk, "speaking of which: if a woman isn't pretty and she isn't good, what sort of path can she cut for herself?"

"Straight into a convent," said Gargantua.

"To be sure," said the monk, "especially with a scissors and a needle.")

. . . it was decreed that, in Thélème, women would be allowed only if they were beautiful, well formed, and cheerful, and men only if they were handsome, well formed, and cheerful.

Item: since men were not allowed in convents, unless they sneaked in under cover of darkness, it was decreed that in Thélème there would never be any women unless there were men, nor any men unless there were women.

Item: because both men and women, after they'd entered a cloister and served their probationary year, were obliged to spend the entire rest of their lives there, it was decided that men and women who came to Thélème could leave whenever they wanted to, freely and without restriction.

Item: because monks and nuns usually took three vows—chastity, poverty, and obedience—it was decided that in Thélème one could perfectly honorably be married, that anyone could be rich, and that they could all live wherever they wanted to.

As an age limitation, women should be allowed in at any time from ten to fifteen, and men from twelve to eighteen.

CHAPTER 53

How the Abbey of Desire (Thélème) Was Built and Endowed

In order to build and equip the abbey, Gargantua gave two million seven hundred thousand eight hundred and thirty-one gold pieces. Further, until everything had been completed, he assigned the yearly sum of one million six hundred and sixty thousand gold pieces, from the tolls on the river Dive, payable in funds of an unimaginable astrological purity. To endow and perpetually maintain the abbey he gave two million three hundred thousand and sixty-nine English pounds in property rentals, tax-free, fully secured, and payable yearly at the abbey gate, to which effect he had written out all the appropriate deeds and grants.

The building was hexagonal, constructed so that at each angle there was a great round tower sixty feet in diameter, and each of the towers was exactly like all the others. The river Loire was on the north side. One of the towers, called Artice (meaning "Arctic," or "Northern"), ran down almost to the river-bank; another, called Calaer (meaning "Lovely Air"), was just to the east. Then came Anatole (meaning "Oriental," or "Eastern"), and Mesembriné (meaning "Southern"), and then Hesperia (meaning "Occidental," or "Western"), and finally Cryere (meaning "Glacial"). The distance between each of the towers was three hundred and twelve feet. The building had six floors, counting the subterranean cellars as the first. The second or ground floor had a high vault, shaped like a basket handle. The other floors were stuccoed in a circular pattern, the way they do such things in Flanders; the roof was of fine slate, the coping being lead-decorated with small figurines and animals, handsomely colored and gilded; and there were rainspouts jutting out from the walls, between the casement windows, painted all the way to the ground with blue and gold stripes and ending in great pipes which led down to the river, below the building.

This was all a hundred times more magnificent than the grand chateau at Bonnivet, or that at Chambord, or that at Chantilly,[6] because it had nine thousand three hundred and thirty-two suites, each furnished with an antechamber, a private reading room, a dressing room, and a small personal chapel, and also because each and every room adjoined its own huge hall. Between each tower, in the middle of the main building, was a spiral staircase, its stairs made of crystal porphyry and red Numidian marble and green marble struck through with red and white, all exactly twenty-two feet wide and three fingers thick, there being twelve stairs between each landing. Further: each landing had a beautiful double arch, in Greek style, thus allowing light to flood through and also framing an entryway into overhanging private rooms, each of them just as broad as the stairway itself. The stair wound all the way to the roof, ending there in a pavilion. Off the stair, on each side, one could come to a great hall; the stair also led the way to the private suites and rooms.

Between the tower called Artice and that called Cryere were great beautiful reading rooms, well stocked with books in Greek, Latin, Hebrew, French, Italian, and Spanish, carefully divided according to the languages in which they had been written.

In the center of the main building, entered through an arch thirty-six yards across, stood a marvelous circular ramp. It was fashioned so harmoniously, and built so large, that six men-at-arms, their lances at the ready, could ride clear up to the top of the building, side by side.

Between the tower called Anatole and that called Mesembriné were beautiful galleries, large and open, painted with scenes of ancient heroism, episodes drawn from history, and strange and fascinating plants and animals. Here, too, just as on the side facing the river, were a ramp and a gate. And on this gate was written, in large antique letters, the poem which follows:

6. Châteaux built in the early and middle years of the sixteenth century. Rabelais is again mixing realism with fantasy.

CHAPTER 54

[The Inscription on the Great Gate of Thélème]

Hypocrites, bigots, stay away!
Old humbugs, puffed-up liars, playful
Religious frauds, worse than Goths
Or Ostrogoths (or other sloths):
No hairshirts, here, no sexy monks,   5
No healthy beggars, no preaching skunks,
No cynics, bombasts ripe with abuse:
Go peddle them elsewhere, your filthy views.

    Your wicked talk
    Would clutter our walks   10
    Like clustering flies:
    But flies or lies,
    We've no room for your cries,
    Your wicked talk.

Hungry lawyers, stay away!   15
People eaters, who grab while praying,
Scribes and assessors, and gouty judges
Who beat good men with the law's thick cudgels
And tie old pots to their tails, like dogs,
We'll hop you up and down like frogs,   20
We'll hang you high from the nearest tree:
We're decent men, not legal fleas.

    Summons and complaints
    Don't strike us as quaint,
    And we haven't got time   25
    For your legal whine
    As you hang from the line
    Of your summons and complaints.

Money suckers, stay away!
Greedy gougers, spending your days   30
Gobbling up men, stuffing your guts
With gold, you black-faced crows, busting
Your butts for another load of change,
Though your cellar's bursting with rotten exchange.
O lazy scum, you'll pile up more,   35
Till smiling death knocks at your door.

    Inhuman faces
    With ghastly spaces
    That no heart can see,
    Find other places: 40
    Here you can't be,
    You inhuman faces.

Slobbering old dogs, stay away!
Old bitter faces, old sour ways,

We want you elsewhere—the jealous, the traitors,   45
The slime who live as danger creators,
Wherever you come from, you're worse than wolves:
Shove it, you mangy, scabby oafs!
None of your stinking, ugly sores:
We've seen enough, we want no more.   50

    Honor and praise
    Fill all our days:
    We sing delight
    All day, all night:
    These are our ways: 55
    Honor and praise.

But you, you, you can always come,
Noble knights and gentlemen,
For this is where you belong: there's money
Enough, and pleasure enough: honey   60
And milk for all, and all as one:
Come be my friends, come join our fun,
O gallants, sportsmen, lovers, friends,
Or better still: come, gentlemen.

    Gentle, noble,   65
    Serene and subtle,
    Eternally calm;
    Civility's balm
    To live without trouble,
    Gentle, noble.   70

And welcome, you who know the Word
And preach it wherever the Word should be heard:
Make this place your holy castle
Against the false religious rascals
Who poison the world with filthy lies: 75
Welcome, you with your eyes on the skies
And faith in your hearts: we can fight to the death
For truth, fight with our every breath.

    For the holy Word
    Can still be heard,   80
    That Word is not dead:
    It rings in our heads,
    And we rise from our beds
    For that holy Word.

And welcome, ladies of noble birth,   85
Live freely here, like nowhere on earth!
Flowers of loveliness, with heaven in your faces,
Who walk like angels, the wisdom of ages
In your hearts: welcome, live here in honor,
As the lord who made this refuge wanted: 90

He built it for you, he gave it gold
To keep it free: Enter, be bold!

Money's a gift
To give, to lift
The souls of others: 95
It makes men brothers
In eternal bliss:
For money's a gift.

CHAPTER 55

How They Lived at Thélème

In the middle of the inner court was a magnificent fountain of beautiful alabaster. Above it stood the three Graces, holding the symbolic horns of abundance: water gushed from their breasts, mouths, ears, eyes, and every other body opening.

The building which rose above this fountain stood on giant pillars of translucent quartz and porphyry, joined by archways of sweeping classical proportions. And inside there were handsome galleries, long and large, decorated with paintings and hung with antlers and the horns of the unicorn, rhinoceros, hippopotamus, as well as elephant teeth and tusks and other spectacular objects.

The women's quarters ran from the tower called Artice all the way to the gates of the tower called Mesembriné. The rest was for men. Right in front of the women's quarters was a kind of playing field, an arena-like space set just between the two first towers, on the outer side. Here too were the horse-riding circle, a theater, and the swimming pools, with attached baths at three different levels, all provided with everything one could need, as well as with an endless supply of myrtle water.

Next to the river was a beautiful pleasure garden, and in the middle of it stood a handsome labyrinth. Between the other two towers were fields for playing palm ball and tennis. Alongside the tower called Cryere were the orchards, full of fruit trees of every description, carefully arranged in groups of five, staggered by rows of three. At the end was a great stretch of pastures and forest, well stocked with all kinds of wild animals.

Between the third pair of towers were the target ranges for muskets, bows, and crossbows. The offices were in a separate building, only one story high, which stood just beside the tower called Hesperia, and the stables were just beyond there. The falcon house was situated in front of the offices, staffed with thoroughly expert falconers and hawk trainers: every year supplies of every sort of bird imaginable, all perfect specimens of their breed, were sent by the Cretans, the Venetians, and the Sarmatian-Poles: eagles, great falcons, goshawks, herons and cranes and wild geese, partridge, gyrfalcons, sparrow hawks, tiny but fierce merlins, and others, so well trained and domesticated that, when they left the chateau to fly about in the fields, they would catch everything they found and bring everything to their handlers. The kennels were a bit farther away, in the direction of the woods and pastures.

All the rooms in all the suites, as well as all the smaller private rooms, were hung with a wide variety of tapestries, which were regularly changed to suit the changing seasons. The floors were covered with green cloth, the beds with embroidery. Every dressing room had a mirror of Venetian crystal, framed in fine gold, decorated around with pearls, and so exceedingly large that one could in truth see oneself in it, complete and entire. Just outside the doorways, in the ladies' quarters, were perfumers and hairdressers, who also attended to the men who visited. Every morning, too, they brought rose-water to each of the ladies' rooms, and also orange and myrtle water—and brought each lady a stick of precious incense, saturated with all manner of aromatic balms.

CHAPTER 56

How the Men and Women Who Dwelled at Thélème Were Dressed

In the beginning, the ladies dressed themselves as they pleased. Later, of their own free will, they changed and styled themselves all as one, in the following way:

They wore scarlet or yellow stockings, bordered with pretty embroidery and fretwork, which reached exactly three fingers above the knee. Their garters were colored like their bracelets (gold, enameled with black, green, red, and white), fastened both above and below the knee. Their shoes, dancing pumps, and slippers were red or purple velvet, with edges jagged like lobsters' claws.

Over the chemise they wore a handsome corset, woven of rich silk shot through with goat hair. Over this they wore taffeta petticoats, in white, red, tan, gray, and so on, and on top of this petticoat a tunic of silver taffeta embroidered with gold thread, sewn in tight spirals—or if they were in the mood and the weather was right, their tunics might be of satin, or damask, or orange-colored velvet, or perhaps tan, green, mustard gray, blue, clear yellow, red, scarlet, white, gold, or silvered linen, with bordered spirals, or embroidery, according to what holiday was being celebrated.

Their dresses, again according to the season, were of golden linen waved with silver, or red satin decorated with gold thread, or taffeta in white, blue, black, or tan, or silk serge, or that same rich silk shot through with goat hair, or velvet slashed with silver, or silvered linen, or golden, or else velvet or satin laced with gold in a variety of patterns.

Sometimes, in the summer, they wore shorter gowns, more like cloaks, ornamented in the ways I have described, or else full-length capes in the Moorish style, of purple velvet waved with gold and embroidered with thin spirals of silver, or else with heavier gold thread, decorated at the seams with small pearls from India. They were never without beautiful feathers in their hair, colored to match the sleeves of their gowns and always spangled in gold. In the winter they wore taffeta dresses, colored as I have described, lined with lynx fur, or black skunk, or Calabrian marten, or sable, or some other precious pelt.

Their prayer beads, rings, neck chains, and collar pieces were made of fine gems—red garnets, rubies, orange-red spinels, diamonds, sapphires, emeralds, turquoises, garnets, agates, green beryls, pearls, and fat onion pearls of a rare excellence.

They covered their heads, once again, as the season demanded: in winter, in the French style, with a velvet hood hanging down in the back like a pigtail; in spring, in the Spanish style, with a lace veil; in summer, in the Italian mode, with bare ringed hair studded with jewels, except on Sundays and holidays, when they used the French fashion, which seemed to them both more appropriate and more modest.

And the men wore their fashions, too: their stockings were of light linen or serge, colored scarlet, yellow, white, or black; their breeches were velvet, in the same colors (or very nearly), embroidered and patterned however they pleased. Their jackets were of gold or silver cloth, in velvet, satin, damask, taffeta, once again in the same colors, impeccably patterned and decorated and worn. Their shoes were laced to the breeches with silken thread, colored as before, each lace closed with an enameled gold tip. Their undervests and cloaks were of golden cloth or linen, or silver cloth, or velvet embroidered however they liked. Their gowns were as costly and beautiful as the women's, with silk belts, colored to match their breeches. Each of them wore a handsome sword, with a decorated hilt, the scabbard of velvet (the color matching their stockings), its endpiece of gold and heavily worked jewelry—and their daggers were exactly the same. Their hats were of black velvet, thickly garnished with golden berries and buttons, and the feathered plumes were white, delicately spangled in gold rows and fringed with rubies, emeralds, and the like.

But there was such a close fellowship between the men and the women that they were dressed almost exactly alike, day after day. And to make sure that this happened, certain gentlemen were delegated to inform the others, each and every morning, what sort of clothing the women had chosen to wear that day—because of course the real decisions, in this matter, were made by the women.

Although they wore such well-chosen and rich clothing, don't think these women wasted a great deal of time on their gowns and cloaks and jewelry. There were wardrobe men who, each day, had everything prepared in advance, and their ladies' maids were so perfectly trained that everyone could be dressed from head to toe, and beautifully, in the twinkling of an eye. And to make sure that all of this was perpetually in good order, the wood of Thélème was surrounded by a vast block of houses, perhaps half a league long, good bright buildings well stocked and supplied, and here lived goldsmiths, jewelers, embroiderers, tailors, specialists in hammering and filamenting gold and silver, velvet makers, tapestry weavers, and upholsterers, and they all worked at their trades right there alongside Thélème, and only for the men and women who dwelled in that abbey. All their supplies, metals and minerals and cloths, came to them courtesy My Lord Shipmaster (Nausiclète, in Greek), who each year brought in seven boats from the Little Antilles, the Pearl and Cannibal islands, loaded down with gold ingots, raw silk, pearls, and all sorts of gemstones. And any of the fat pearls which began to lose their sparkle and their natural whiteness were restored by feeding them to handsome roosters (as Avicenna recommends), just as we give laxatives to hawks and falcons.

CHAPTER 57

How the Men and Women of Thélème Governed Their Lives

Their lives were not ordered and governed by laws and statutes and rules, but according to their own free will. They rose from their beds when it seemed to them the right time, drank, ate, worked, and slept when they felt like it. No one woke them or obliged them to drink, or to eat, or to do anything whatever. This was exactly how Gargantua had ordained it. The constitution of this abbey had only a single clause:

DO WHAT YOU WILL

—because free men and women, wellborn, well taught, finding themselves joined with other respectable people, are instinctively impelled to do virtuous things and avoid vice. They draw this instinct from nature itself, and they name it "honor." Such people, if they are subjected to vile constraints, brought down to a lower moral level, oppressed and enslaved and turned away from that noble passion toward which virtue pulls them, find themselves led by that same passion to throw off and break any such bondage, just as we always seek out forbidden things and long for whatever is denied us.

And their complete freedom set them nobly in competition, all of them seeking to do whatever they saw pleased any one among them. If he or she said, "Let's drink," everyone drank. If he or she said, "Let's play," they all played. If he or she said, "Let's go and have fun in the meadows," there they all went. If they were engaged in falconry or hunting, the women joined in, mounted on their good tame horses, light but proud, delicately sporting heavy leather gloves, a sparrow hawk perched on their wrists, or a small falcon, or a tiny but fierce merlin. (The other birds were carried by men.)

All of them had been so well educated that there wasn't one among them who could not read, write, sing, play on harmonious instruments, speak five or six languages, and write easy poetry and clear prose in any and all of them. There were never knights so courageous, so gallant, so light on their feet, and so easy on their horses, knights more vigorous, agile, or better able to handle any kind of weapon. There were never ladies so well bred, so delicate, less irritable, or better trained with their hands, sewing and doing anything that any free and worthy woman might be asked to do.

And for this reason, when the time came for anyone to leave the abbey, whether because his parents had summoned him or on any other account, he took one of the ladies with him, she having accepted him, and then they were married. And whatever devotion and friendship they had shown one another, when they lived at Thélème, they continued and even exceeded in their marriage, loving each other to the end of their days just as much as they did on the first day after their wedding. . . .

From Book II

[Pantagruel: Birth and Education]

CHAPTER 2

The Birth of the Very Formidable Pantagruel

When he was four hundred and ninety-four, plus four more, Gargantua begat his son Pantagruel on his wife, the daughter of the king of the Amaurotes, in Utopia. Her name was Bigmouth, or Babedec,[1] as we say in the provinces, and she died giving birth to the baby: he was so immensely big, and weighed so incredibly much, that it was impossible for him to see the light without snuffing out his mother.

Now, to truly understand how he got his name, which was bestowed on him at the baptismal font, you must be aware that in the year of his birth there had been such a fearful drought, all across the continent of Africa, that it had not rained for more than thirty-six months, three weeks, four days, thirteen hours, and a little bit over, and the sun had been so hot, and so fierce, that the whole earth had dried up. It wasn't any hotter even in the days of the prophet Elijah than in that year, for not a tree on earth had a leaf or a bud. Grass never turned green, rivers dried up, fountains went dry; the poor fish, deprived of their proper element, flopped about on the ground, crying horribly; since there was no dew to make the air dense enough, the birds could not fly; dead animals lay all over the fields and meadows, their mouths gaping wide—wolves, foxes, stags, wild boars, fallow does, hares, rabbits, weasels, martens, badgers, and many, many others. And it was no better for human beings, whose lives became pitiful things. You could see them with their tongues hanging out, like hares that have been running for six solid hours. Some of them threw themselves down into wells; others crawled into a cow's belly, to stay in the shade (Homer calls them *Alibantes,* desiccated people[2]). Everything everywhere stood still, like a ship at anchor. It was painful to see how hard men worked to protect themselves from this ghastly change in nature: it wasn't easy to keep even the holy water in churches from being used up, though the pope and the College of Cardinals expressly ordered that no one should dare to dip from these blessed basins more than once. All the same, when a priest entered his church you'd see dozens and dozens of these poor parched people come crowding around behind him, and if he blessed anyone the mouths would all gape open to snatch up every single drop, letting nothing fall wasted to the ground—just like the tormented rich man in Luke, who begged for the relief of cool water.[3] Oh, the fortunate ones, in that burning year, whose vaults were cool and well stocked!

The Philosopher tells us, asking why seawater is salty, that once, when Phoebus Apollo let his son Phaeton drive his gleaming chariot,[4] the boy had

---

1. Names taken from Sir Thomas More's *Utopia.* Literally, "no place," the word *utopia* has become synonymous with "ideal country."   2. The allusion to Homer is apparently mistaken, but *Alibantes*—possibly derived from Alibas, a dry river in hell—is used by other ancient writers with reference to the dead or the very old.   3. Luke 16.24: "And he cried and said, Father Abraham, have mercy on me, and send Lazarus, that he may dip the tip of his finger in water, and cool my tongue; for I am tormented in this flame."   4. The chariot of the sun.

no idea how to manage it, nor any notion how to follow the sun's proper orbit from tropic to tropic, and drove off the right road and came so close to the earth that he dried up all the countries over which he passed, and burned a great swath through heaven, called by the philosophers *Via Lactea,* the Milky Way, but known to drunkards and lazy louts as Saint John's Road. But the fancy-pants poets say it's really where Juno's milk fell, when she suckled Hercules. Then the earth got so hot that it developed an enormous sweat, which proceeded to sweat away the entire ocean, which thus became salty, because sweat is always salty. And you can see for yourself that this is perfectly true, because all you have to do is taste it—or the sweat of pox-ridden people when they're put in steam baths and work up a great sweat. Try whichever you like: it doesn't matter to me.

It was almost exactly like that, in this year of which I write. One Friday, when everyone was saying prayers and making a beautiful procession, and litanies were being said, and psalms chanted, and they were begging omnipotent God to look mercifully down on them in their desolation, they could suddenly see great drops of water coming out of the earth, exactly as if someone were sweating profusely. And the poor people began to rejoice, as if this were something truly useful, some of them saying that since there wasn't a drop of liquid in the air from which one could have expected rain, the very ground itself was making up for what they lacked. Others, more scholarly, said that this was rain from the opposite side of the earth, as Seneca explains in the fourth book of *Questionum naturalium,* in which he speaks of the source and origin of the river Nile. But they were deceived: once the procession was over, and they went back to collect this precious dew and drink down a full glass, they found that it was just pickle brine, even worse to drink, and even saltier, than seawater.

And it was precisely because Pantagruel was born that very day that his father named him as he did: *Panta* in Greek means "all," and *Gruel* in Arabic means "thirsty," thus indicating that at the hour of his birth the whole world was thirsty—and he saw, prophetically, that someday his son would be lord of the thirsty, for this was shown to him at that same time and by a sign even more obvious. For when the child's mother was in labor, and all the midwives were waiting to receive him, the first thing that came out of her womb was sixty-eight mule drivers, each one leading a pack mule loaded with salt by its halter, after which came nine one-humped camels loaded with hams and smoked beef tongue, and then seven two-humped camels loaded with pickled eels, followed by twenty-five carts all loaded with onions, garlic, leeks, and spring onions. The midwives were frightened out of their wits. But some of them said to the others:

"Here's God's plenty. It signifies that we shouldn't either hold back, when we drink, or, on the other hand, pour it down the way the Swiss do. It's a good sign: these are truly wining signs."

And while they were gabbling and cackling about such trivialities, out popped Pantagruel, as hairy as a bear, at which one of them pronounced prophetically:

"He's been born all covered with fur, so he'll do wonderful things, and if he lives he'll live to an immense age."

[Father's Letter from Home]

CHAPTER 8

How Pantagruel, at Paris, Received a Letter from His Father, Gargantua, with a Copy of That Letter

Pantagruel studied hard, of course, and learned a great deal, because his brain was twice normal size and his memory was as capacious as a dozen kegs of olive oil. While he was thus occupied in Paris,[5] one day he received a letter from his father, which read as follows:

"My very dear son,

"Among the gifts, the graces and the prerogatives with which from the very beginning our sovereign Creator and God has blessed and endowed human nature, that which seems to me uniquely wonderful is the power to acquire a kind of immortality while still in this our mortal state—that is, while passing through this transitory life a man may perpetuate both his name and his race, and this we accomplish through the legitimate issue of holy wedlock. And by that means we partially reestablish that which we lost through the sin of our first parents, Adam and Eve, to whom it was declared that, because they had not obeyed the commands of God their Creator, they would know death and in dying would utterly destroy the magnificent form in which mankind had been shaped.

"But this seminal propagation permits what the parents lose to live on in their children, and what dies in the children to live on in the grand-children, and so it will continue until the hour of the Last Judgment, when Jesus Christ will return to the hands of God the Father His purified and peaceful kingdom, now utterly beyond any possibility or danger of being soiled by sin. And then all the generations and all the corruptions will come to an end, and all the elements will be taken from their endless cycle of transformations, for the peace so devoutly desired will be achieved, and will be perfect, and all things will be brought to their fit and proper ending.

"So I have very fair and just cause to be thankful to God, my preserver, for having permitted me to see my hoary old age blossoming once again in your youth. Whenever, at His pleasure, He who rules and governs all things, my soul leaves this human dwelling place, I will not consider myself entirely dead, but simply transported from one place to another, for in you, and by you, my visible image lives in in this world, wholly alive, able to see and speak to all honorable men, and all my friends, just as I myself was able to do. I confess that my life on this earth, though I have had divine help and divine grace to show me the way, has not been sinless (for indeed we are all sinners and continually beg God to wash away our sins), and yet it has been beyond reproach.

"Just as the image of my flesh lives on in you, so too shine on the ways of my soul, or else no one would think you the true keeper and treasure

5. Like his father before him, Pantagruel has been sent to Paris to study. The letter, patterned after Ciceronian models of eloquence, summarizes Rabelais's view of an ideal education, and generally illustrates the attitude of the Renaissance intellectual elite toward culture.

of our immortal name, and I would take little pleasure in seeing that, because in that case the least part of me, my body, would live on, and the best part, my soul, in which our name lives and is blessed among men, would be decayed and debased. Nor do I say this because I have any doubt about your virtue, which I have long since tested and approved, but simply to encourage you to proceed from good to still better. And the reason I write to you now is not so much to ensure that you follow the pathways of virtue, but rather that you rejoice in thus living and having lived, and find new joys and fresh courage for the future.

"To consummate and perfect that task, it should be enough for you to remember that I have held back nothing, but have given help and assistance as if I had no other treasure in the world but to someday see you, while I still lived, accomplished and established in virtue, integrity, and wisdom, perfected in all noble and honorable learning, and to be able to thus leave you, after my death, as a mirror representing me, your father—perhaps in actual practice not so perfect an image as I might have wished, but certainly exactly that in both intention and desire.

"But though my late father of worthy memory, Grandgousier, devoted all his energy to those things of which I might take the fullest advantage, and from which I might acquire the most sensible knowledge, and though my own effort matched his—or even surpassed it—still, as you know very well, it was neither so fit nor so right a time for learning as exists today, nor was there an abundance of such teachers as you have had. It was still a murky, dark time, oppressed by the misery, unhappiness, and disasters of the Goths, who destroyed all worthwhile literature of every sort. But divine goodness has let me live to see light and dignity returned to humanistic studies, and to see such an improvement, indeed, that it would be hard for me to qualify for the very first class of little schoolboys—I who, in my prime, had the reputation (and not in error) of the most learned man of my day. Nor do I say this as an empty boast, though indeed I could honorably do so in writing to you—for which you have the authority of Cicero in his book *On Old Age*, and also the judgment of Plutarch, in his book *How a Man May Praise Himself without Fear of Reproach*. No, I say these things to make you wish to surpass me.

"For now all courses of study have been restored, and the acquisition of languages has become supremely honorable: Greek, without which it is shameful for any man to be called a scholar; Hebrew; Chaldean; Latin.[6] And in my time we have learned how to produce wonderfully elegant and accurate printed books,[7] just as, on the other hand, we have also learned (by diabolic suggestion) how to make cannon and other such fearful weapons. The world is full of scholars, of learned teachers, of well-stocked libraries, so that in my opinion study has never been easier, not in Plato's time, or Cicero's, or Papinian's.[8] From this day forward no one will dare to appear anywhere, or in any company, who has not

6. The languages that are the instruments of classical learning are listed along with those useful for the study of the Old Testament of the Bible.   7. Printing from movable type was invented in Europe about the middle of the fifteenth century.   8. Jurisconsult of the time of Emperor Septimius Severus (reigned A.D. 193–211).

been well and properly taught in the wisdom of Minerva. Thieves and highwaymen, hangmen and executioners, common foot soldiers, grooms and stableboys, are now more learned than the scholars and preachers of my day. What should I say? Even women and girls have come to aspire to this marvelous, this heavenly manna of solid learning. Old as I am, I have felt obliged to learn Greek, though I had not despised it, as Cato[9] did: I simply had no leisure for it, when I was young. And how exceedingly glad I am, as I await the hour when it may please God, my Creator, to call me to leave this earth, to read Plutarch's *Morals,* Plato's beautiful *Dialogues,* Pausanias' *Monuments,* and Athenaeus' *Antiquities.*[1]

"Which is why, my son, I strongly advise you not to waste your youth, but to make full use of it for the acquisition of knowledge and virtue. You are in Paris, you have your tutor, Epistemon: you can learn from them, by listening and speaking, by all the noble examples held up in front of your eyes.

"It is my clear desire that you learn languages perfectly, first Greek, as Quintilian decreed, and then Latin.[2] And after that Hebrew, for the Holy Bible, and similarly Chaldean and Arabic. I wish you to form your literary style both on the Greek, following Plato, and on the Latin, following Cicero. Let there be nothing in all of history that is not clear and vivid in your mind, a task in which geographical texts will be of much assistance.

"I gave you some awareness of the liberal arts—geometry, arithmetic, and music—when you were still a child of five and six. Follow them further, and learn all the rules of astronomy. Ignore astrology and its prophecies, and all the hunt for the philosopher's stone which occupied Ramon Lully[3]—leave all those errors and vanities alone.

"As for the civil law, I wish you to know by heart all the worthy texts: deal with them and philosophy side by side.

"I wish you to carefully devote yourself to the natural world. Let there be no sea, river, or brook whose fish you do not know. Nothing should be unknown to you—all the birds of the air, each and every tree and bush and shrub in the forests, every plant that grows from the earth, all the metals hidden deep in the abyss, all the gems of the Orient and the Middle East—nothing.

"Then carefully reread all the books of the Greek physicians, and the Arabs and Romans, without turning your back on the talmudic scholars or those who have written on the Cabala. Make free use of anatomical dissection and acquire a perfect knowledge of that other world which is man himself. Spend several hours each day considering the holy Gospels, first the New Testament and the Apostles' letters, in Greek, and then the Old Testament, in Hebrew.

"In short, plumb all knowledge to the very depths, because when you are a grown man you will be obliged to leave the peace and tranquillity of learning, and acquire the arts of chivalry and warfare, in order to defend my house and lands and come to the aid of our friends if in any way they are attacked by evildoers.

9. Plutarch's life of Cato is the source of the notion that he despised Greek.   1. The works of Pausanias and Athenaeus were standard sources of information on ancient geography, art, and everyday life.   2. In his *Institutio oratoria* 1.1.12 he recommends studying Greek before Latin.   3. Raymond Lully (thirteenth century), Spanish philosopher who dabbled in magic.

"And soon I shall ask you to demonstrate just how much you have learned, which you can do in no better way than by publicly defending, in front of the entire world and against all who may come to question you, a thesis of your own devising. And continue, as you have been doing, to frequent the company of those leaned men who are so numerous in Paris.

"But since, as the wise Solomon says, wisdom can find no way into a malicious heart, and knowledge without self-awareness is nothing but the soul's ruin, you should serve, and love, and fear God. Put all your thought in Him, and all your hopes, and by faith which has been shaped by love unite yourself with Him so firmly that sin will never separate you away. Be ever watchful of the world's wicked ways. Never put your heart in vanity, for ours is a transitory existence and the Word of God lives forever. Help your neighbors and love them as you love yourself. Honor your teachers. Avoid the company of those you do not desire to imitate; do not take in vain the blessings God has given you. And when, finally, you know that you have learned all that Paris can teach you, return to me, so that I may look on you and, before I die, give you my blessing.

"My son, may the peace and grace of our Lord be with you. *Amen.*

"Written from Utopia, this seventeenth day of the month of March.

Your father,
GARGANTUA"

After receiving and reading this letter, Pantagruel was filled with new zeal, positively on fire to learn more than ever before—so much so that, had you seen him at his studies, and observed how much he learned, you would have declared that he was to his books like a fire in dry grass, burning with such an intense and consuming flame.

[*The World in Pantagruel's Mouth*]

CHAPTER 18

How a Great English Scholar Wanted to Dispute with Pantagruel, But Was Beaten by Panurge

At about the same time, a scholar named Thaumaste (in Greek, "Wonderful"), hearing all the fuss over Pantagruel's incomparable learning, and seeing how famous he'd become, came from England with the sole intention of meeting Pantagruel and finding out if his knowledge matched his reputation. Arriving in Paris, he immediately went to Pantagruel's lodgings, which were at the abbey of Saint Denis.[4] At that moment, Pantagruel was in the garden with Panurge, walking up and down and philosophizing after the fashion of the ancient Peripatetics.[5] Thaumaste quivered with fear, seeing how huge Pantagruel was, but then he greeted him in customary style and said, with great courtesy:

"How true it is, as Plato, prince of philosophers, says, that if the image of wisdom and learning is a physical matter, visible to human eyes, it excites

---

4. A college for Benedictines.   5. Followers of the Greek philosopher Aristotle, who wandered about in the Lyceum of ancient Athens while lecturing.

the whole world with admiration. The very word of such accomplishments, spread through the air and received by the ears of those who study and love philosophy, prevents them from taking any further rest, stirring them, urging them to hurry to where they may find and see the person in whom knowledge has erected its temple and given forth its oracles. Which was clearly demonstrated for us by the queen of Sheba, who traveled from the farthest reaches of the Orient and the Persian Sea to visit the house of the wise Solomon and hear his sage words;[6]

"and by Anacharsis,[7] who came from Scythia only to see Solon;

"and by Pythagoras, who journeyed to the prophets of Memphis;[8]

"and by Plato, who visited the Egyptian magi, and also Archytas of Tarentum;[9]

"and by Apollonius of Tyana,[1] who went to the Caucasian mountains, who journeyed among the Scythians, the Massagetae, and the Indians, who sailed down the great river Physon, all the way to the land of the Brahmans, to see Hiarchos, and who traveled in Babylonia, Chaldea, the land of the Medes, Assyria, Parthia, Syria, Phoenicia, Arabia, Palestine, and Alexandria, and in Ethiopia, too, to see the Gymnosophists.[2]

"We have another example in Livy,[3] to see and hear whom certain studious folk came to Rome from the farthest boundaries of France and Spain.

"I am not so presumptuous as to include myself among the ranks of such illustrious men. But I deeply desire to be thought of as a student and lover not only of humanistic learning but also of men of such learning.

"And, in fact, hearing of your priceless learning, I have left my country, my parents, and my home and come here, indifferent to the weariness of the journey, the anxiety of a voyage by sea, the strangeness of different lands, solely for the purpose of seeing and conferring with you about certain passages of philosophy, and geometrical divination, and also of cabalistic knowledge,[4] passages of which I am myself unsure and, about which I cannot rest content. If you can resolve these difficulties for me, I will be your servant from this day forth, and not only me but all my posterity, for I command no other gifts sufficient to repay you.

"I will put all of this in writing, and tomorrow I shall notify all the learned men of this city, so that we can discuss these matters publicly and in their presence.

"But I intend that our discussions, and any disputes in which we may engage, shall be conducted as follows. I do not wish to argue any barebones *for* and *against*, as do the besotted sophistical minds[5] of this and other cities. Nor do I wish to dispute after the fashion of academics, by declamation, or by the use of numbers, as Pythagoras did and as Picodella Mirandola,[6] at Rome, wished to do. I wish to dispute simply by signs, without a word being spoken, for these are matters so intricate and difficult that, as far as I am concerned, mere human speech will not be adequate to deal with them.

6. 2 Chronicles 9.1–12; the Queen of Sheba came from southern Arabia to test Solomon's legendary wisdom.   7. Scythian prince, renowned for his travels and wisdom (sixth century B.C.).   8. Capital of ancient Egypt. *Pythagoras:* Greek philosopher of the sixth century B.C.   9. Said to be the founder of mathematics (fourth century B.C.).   1. An ascetic wandering teacher of the early Christian period. 2. Ancient sect of Hindu ascetics.   3. Titus Livius (59 B.C.–A.D. 17 or 64 B.C.–A.D. 12), Roman historian.   4. Lore from an occult system of mystical speculation of rabbinical origin.   5. Sophists, for Thaumaste, are specious, overly subtle rhetoricians.   6. Pico della Mirandola (1463–1494), Italian humanist scholar. Pythagoras (sixth century B.C.) discovered the mathematical basis of the musical intervals.

"May it please Your Magnificence to accept my invitation and join me, at seven in the morning, in the great hall of the College of Navarre."

When he had finished, Pantagruel said to him, courteously:

"My dear sir, how could I deny anyone the right to share in whatever blessings God has given me? All good things come from Him, and surely He wishes us to spread the celestial manna we have from Him among men both worthy and capable of receiving true learning—among whose number in our time, as I know very well, you belong in the very first rank. Let me say to you, therefore, that you will find me ready at any time to accede to any of your requests, to the extent that my poor powers may enable me, and well aware as I am that it is I who should be learning from you. And so, as you have declared, we will discuss these doubts of yours together, and hunt as hard as we can for their resolution, diving even as far as the bottom of that bottomless well in which, according to Heraclitus,[7] the truth is said to be hidden.

"And I highly commend the style of argument you have proposed, that is to say, by using signs, without any words, for thus you and I will truly understand one another, free from the sort of hand clapping and applause produced during their discussions by these puerile sophists, whenever one party has the better of the argument.

"So, then, tomorrow I shall appear without fail at the time and place you have requested. I ask of you only that, as between us, there may be no contentiousness and fuss, and that we seek neither honor nor men's applause, but only the truth."

To which Thaumaste replied:

"Sir, may God keep you in His grace. I thank Your High Magnificence for being so willing to condescend to my humble talents. Until tomorrow, I leave you in His hands."

"Farewell," said Pantagruel.

Gentlemen, you who may read this book, please don't imagine that anyone was ever more exalted, more transported, that whole night long, than Thaumaste and Pantagruel. Thaumaste told the concierge at his lodgings, in the abbey of Cluny, that in his entire life he had never been so incredibly thirsty:

"It feels to me," he said, "as if Pantagruel has me by the throat. Order me wine, if you please, and make sure that there's enough fresh water so I can lubricate the roof of my mouth."

And for his part, Pantagruel felt himself carried away, so that all that night he did nothing but tear through:

> The Venerable Bede's *De numeris et signis,* Numbers and Signs;
> Plotinus' *De inenarrabilibus,* Inexpressible Things;
> Proclus' *De sacrificio et magia,* Sacrifices and Magic;
> Artemidorus' *Per onirocriticon,* On the Interpretation of Dreams;
> Anaxagoras' *Peri semion,* On Signs;
> Dinarius' *Peri aphaton,* Unknowable Things;
> Philistion's books;
> Hipponax's *Peri anecphoneton,* Things Better Left Undiscussed;

And many, many others, so that finally Panurge said to him:

"My lord, stop all this intellectual groping and go to bed, for I can see

---

7. Greek philosopher of the sixth century B.C.

you're far too agitated—indeed, such an extravagance of thinking and straining may well make you feverish. But first, have twenty-five or thirty good
drinks, then go to bed and sleep comfortably—for tomorrow I will answer
our English friend, I will argue with him, and if I don't get him *ad metam
non loqui*,[8] to the point where he can't say a word, well, then you can say
anything you like about me."

"All right," said Pantagruel, "but Panurge, my good friend, he's a deeply
learned man. How will you deal with him?"

"Very easily," said Panurge. "Please: don't even speak about it. Just leave
the whole thing to me. Do you know any man as learned as the devils in
hell?"

"Not really," said Pantagruel, "unless blessed by some special divine
grace."

"You see?" said Panurge. "I've had many arguments with devils, and I've
made them look like idiots, I've knocked them on their asses. So tomorrow
you can be sure I'll make this glorious Englishman shit vinegar, right out in
public."

Then Panurge spent the night boozing with the servants and playing
games, at which he lost all the roses and ribbons from his breeches. And
then, when the agreed-upon hour came, he conducted his master Pantagruel
to the assigned meeting place, where as you can easily understand everyone
in Paris, from the most important to the least, had assembled, all of them
thinking:

"This devil of a Pantagruel, he's beaten all our clever fellows, and all those
naive theologians and philosophers. But now he'll get what's coming to him,
because this Englishman is a regular devil. We'll see who beats whom today."

Everyone was assembled; Thaumaste was waiting for them. And when
Pantagruel and Panurge arrived in the hall, all the students—elementary,
high school, and college—began to applaud, in their usual ridiculous way.
But Pantagruel shouted at them, his voice as loud as the sound of a double
cannon:

"Quiet! In the name of the devil, quiet! By God, you rascals, bother me
and I'll cut the heads off every last one of you!"

Which announcement struck them as dumb as ducks: they were afraid
even to cough, no matter if they'd swallowed fifteen pounds of feathers. And
the very sound of his voice left them so parched and dry that their tongues
hung half a foot out of their mouths, as if Pantagruel had roasted their
throats.

Then Panurge began to speak, saying to the Englishman:

"Sir, have you come here seeking a debate, a contest, about these propo-
sitions which you have posted, or are you here to learn, to honestly understand the truth?"

To which Thaumaste answered:

"Sir, the only thing which has brought me here is my deep desire to understand that which I have struggled all my life to understand, and which neither
books nor men have ever been able to resolve for me. As far as disputing and
arguing is concerned, I have no interest whatever in that. That is a vulgar
affair, and I leave it to villainous sophists, who never truly seek for truth
when they argue, but only contradict each other and emptily debate."

8. Translated in the next phrase, "to the point where he can't say a word."

"And so," said Panurge, "if I, who am no more than a minor disciple of my master Pantagruel, am able to satisfy you in all these matters, it would be an indignity and an imposition to trouble my master. Accordingly, it would be better if for now he simply presided over this discussion, judging what we say—and I need hardly say that he will himself satisfy you, should I be unable to fully quench your scholarly thirst."

"Indeed," said Thaumaste, "that's perfectly true."

"Then let us begin."

But note, please, that Panurge had hung a handsome tassel of red, white, green, and blue silk at the end of his long codpiece,[9] and inside it he had stuffed a fat, juicy orange.

CHAPTER 19

How Panurge Made the Englishman Who Argued by Signs Look Like an Idiot

Then, with everyone watching and listening in absolute silence, the Englishman raised his hands high in the air, first one and then the other, holding his fingertips in the shape called, in Chinon, the hen's asshole. He struck the nails of one hand against the nails of the other four times in a row, then opened his hands and slapped his palms together with a sharp crack. Joining his hands once again, as he had done at the start, he clapped them twice, then opened them out and clapped them four times more. Then he clasped them and extended one right over the other, as if praying devoutly to God.

Suddenly Panurge raised his right hand and stuck his thumb into his nose, keeping the other four fingers extended in a row straight out from the tip of his nose. He closed his left eye and winked the right one, making a deep hollow between eyebrow and eyelid. Then he lifted his left hand, the four fingers held rigidly extended, the thumb raised, and lined it up precisely with his right hand, keeping it perhaps half again the width of his nose distant. Then he lowered both hands, keeping them just as they were, and ended by raising them halfway and holding them there, as if aiming at the Englishman's nose.

"And yet if Mercury[1]—" the Englishman began.

But Panurge interrupted him:

"You have spoken. Be silent."

Then the Englishman made the following sign: With palm open, he raised his left hand high in the air, then closed its four fingers in a tight fist, with the thumb lying across the bridge of his nose. And then, suddenly, he raised his right hand, palm out, and lowered it again, placing the thumb against the little finger of his left hand, the four fingers of which he moved slowly up and down. Then, in reverse, he repeated with his right hand what he had just done with his left and with his left hand what he had done with his right.

Not a bit surprised, Panurge lifted his immense codpiece with his left hand, and with his right pulled from it a piece of white ox rib and two bits of wood in the same shape, one of black ebony, the other of rose-colored brazilwood. Arranging these objects symmetrically, in the fingers of his right

9. Ornamental pouch at the crotch of tightly fitting breeches, worn by men of the fifteenth and sixteenth centuries.   1. Thaumaste may be referring to the messenger god or to quicksilver, used in alchemy. Panurge reminds him of the rule of silent, gestural communication.

hand, he clapped them together, making a sound exactly like that produced by the lepers in Brittany, to warn people off—but a sound infinitely more resonant and harmonious. And then, pulling his tongue slowly back into his mouth, he stood there, humming happily, staring at the Englishman.

The theologians, physicians, and surgeons thought this sign meant that the Englishman was a leper.

The counselors, jurists, and canon lawyers, however, thought his meaning was that being a leper brought with it a certain sort of happiness, as once our Lord had declared.

Not at all frightened, the Englishman raised both hands, holding them with the three largest fingers balled into a fist, then placed both thumbs between the index and middle fingers, with the little fingers sticking straight out. He presented his hands to Panurge, then rearranged them so that the right thumb touched the left one, and his little fingers, too, were pressed against each other.

At this, without a word, Panurge raised his hands and made the following sign: he put the nail of his right index finger against the thumbnail, shaping a loop. He bent all the fingers of his right hand into a fist, except for the index finger, which he jabbed in and out of the space framed by his other hand. Then he extended both the index and the middle fingers of his right hand, separating them as widely as he possibly could and pointing them at Thaumaste. Then placing his left thumb in the corner of his left eye, he extended his entire hand like a bird's wing or a fish's backbone, and waved it very delicately up and down. Then he did the same thing with his right hand and his right eye.

Thaumaste began to turn pale and tremble, then made the following sign: he struck the middle finger of his right hand against the muscle of his palm, just below the thumb, then inserted the index finger of his right hand into a loop shaped exactly like that Panurge had made, except that Thaumaste inserted it from below, not from above.

Accordingly, Panurge clapped his hands together and breathed into his palms. Then, once again, he shaped a loop with his left hand and, over and over, inserted into it the index finger of his right hand. Then he thrust his chin forward and stood staring at Thaumaste.

And though no one there understood what these signs meant, they understood perfectly well that he was asking Thaumaste, without a word being spoken:

"Hey, what do you make of that, eh?"

And indeed Thaumaste began to sweat heavily, looking like a man swept away by high contemplation. Then he stared back at Panurge and put the nails of his left hand against those of his right, opening all the fingers into semicircles, then raised his hands as high as he could, exhibiting this sign.

At which Panurge suddenly put his right thumb under his jaw, and stuck the little finger into the loop fashioned by his left hand, and proceeded to vigorously snap his jaw, making his teeth crash harmoniously together.

In great anguish, Thaumaste stood up, but as he rose let fly a fat baker's fart, with the dung right after it. He pissed a good dose of vinegar, and stank like the devils in hell. All those in the hall began to hold their noses, because, clearly, it was anxiety that was obliging him to beshit himself. Then he raised his right hand, the ends of all the fingers clutched together, and spread out his left hand, flat against his chest.

At which Panurge pulled out his long codpiece with its waving tassel, stretching it a good foot and a half or more, holding it in the air with his left hand and with his right, taking the ripe orange, he threw it in the air seven times, the eighth time catching it in his right fist and then holding it quietly, calmly high in the air. Then he began to shake his handsome codpiece, as if displaying it to Thaumaste.

After this, Thaumaste began to puff out his cheeks like a bagpipe musician, blowing as hard as if he were inflating a pig's bladder.

At which Panurge stuck one finger of his left hand right up his ass, sucking in air with his mouth, as if eating oysters in the shell or inhaling soup. Then he opened his mouth a bit and slapped himself with the palm of his right hand, making an immensely loud sound which seemed to work its way up from the very depths of his diaphragm all along the trachial artery. And he did this sixteen times.

But all Thaumaste could do was snuffle like a goose.

So Panurge next stuck his right index finger into his mouth, clamping down hard on it. Then he pulled it out and, as he did so, made a loud noise, like little boys firing turnips from an elderwood cannon. And he did this nine times.

And Thaumaste cried:

"Ah ha, gentlemen! The great secret! He's got his hand in there up to the elbow."

And he pulled out a dagger, holding it with the point facing down.

At which Panurge grabbed his great codpiece and shook it against his breeches as hard as he could. Then he joined his hands like a comb and put them on top of his head, sticking out his tongue as far as he could and rolling his eyes like a dying goat.

"Ah ha, I understand," said Thaumaste. "But what?" And he set the handle of his dagger against his chest, and put his palm over the point, letting his fingertips turn lightly against it.

At which Panurge bent his head to the left and put his middle finger in his left ear, raising his thumb. Then he crossed his arms on his chest, coughed five times, and the fifth time banged his right foot on the ground. Then he raised his left arm and, tightening his fingers into a fist, held the thumb against his forehead, and with his right hand clapped himself six times on the chest.

But Thaumaste, as though still unsatisfied, put his left thumb to the end of his nose and closed the rest of that hand.

So Panurge put his forefingers on each side of his mouth, pulling back as hard as he could and showing all his teeth. His thumbs drew his lower eyelids as far down as they would go, making an exceedingly ugly face, or so it seemed to everyone watching.

CHAPTER 20

What Thaumaste Said about Panurge's Virtues and His Learning

Then Thaumaste stood up and, removing his hat, thanked Panurge graciously, then turned to the audience and said in a loud voice:

"Gentlemen, now I can truly speak the biblical words: *Et ecce plus quam Solomon hic,* And here is one who is greater than Solomon.[2] You see in front of you an incomparable treasure: and that is Monsieur Pantagruel, whose fame drew me from the farthest reaches of England in order to discuss with him certain insoluble problems, involving not only magic, academy, cabalistic learning, geometrical divination, and astrology but philosophy as well, which had long been troubling me. But now his fame bothers me, because it seems to be afflicted with jealousy—certainly, it hasn't granted him a thousandth part of what he deserves.

"You have seen for yourselves how his only disciple has satisfied my questions—has even told me more than I'd asked. Moreover, he has first shown and then solved for me other problems of inexpressible difficulty and importance, and in so doing he has opened for me, I can assure you, the deepest, purest well of encyclopedic learning, and in a fashion, indeed, that I had never thought any man could accomplish—not even begin to accomplish. I refer to our disputation by signs alone, without a word being spoken. But in due time I will record everything he has said and shown me, so no one will think that this has been more tomfoolery in which we have been engaged, and I will have that record put into print so others can learn from it as I have. Then you will be able to judge how little the master is truly esteemed, when the mere disciple can demonstrate such ability, for as it is written, *Non est discipulus super magistrum,* The disciple is not superior to his master.[3]

"And now let praise be given to God, and let me humbly thank you all for the honor you have shown us. May the good Lord repay you through all the eternity."

Pantagruel said similarly courteous things to all who were gathered there, and as he left took Thaumaste with him, to dine—and you will believe they drank until they had to open their breeches to let their bellies breathe. (In those days men buttoned up their bellies, the way they buttoned up their collars today.) They drank, indeed, until all they could say was, "Where do *you* come from?"

Holy Mother of God, how they guzzled, and how many bottles of wine they put away:

"Over here!"

"More, more!"

"Waiter, wine!"

"Pour it, in the name of the devil, pour it!"

No one drank fewer than twenty-five or thirty jugs, and do you know how? *Sicut terra sine aqua,* Like a dry land with no water—for it was warm weather and, besides, they were good and thirsty.

But as for Thaumaste's explanation of the signs they used, in their disputation, well, I'd be glad to explain them all myself, but I'm told that Thaumaste in fact wrote a huge book, printed in London, in which he sets out everything, omitting not a single item. In consideration of which, for now at least I'll just leave the subject.

---

2. Matthew 12.42 and Luke 11.31.   **3.** Matthew 10.24.

CHAPTER 32

How Pantagruel Shielded an Entire Army with His Tongue, and What the Author Saw in His Mouth

As Pantagruel and all his people entered the land of the Dipsodes,[4] the inhabitants were delighted and immediately surrendered to him, bringing him of their own free will the keys to every city to which he journeyed—all except the Almyrods, who intended to resist him and told his heralds that they refused to surrender, except on good terms.

"What!" said Pantagruel. "They want more than their hand in the pot and a cup in their fist? Let's go, so you can knock down their walls for me."

So they got themselves ready, as if about to launch their attack.

But as they marched past a huge field, they were struck by a huge downpour, which began to knock their lines about and break up their formation. Seeing this, Pantagruel ordered the captains to assure them that this was nothing and he could see, past the clouds, that it was only a bit of dew. Whatever happened, however, they should maintain military discipline and he would provide them with cover. And when they had restored good marching order, Pantagruel stuck out his tongue, but just barely halfway, and shielded them as a mother hen protects her chicks.

Now I,[5] who report these totally true tales to you, had hidden myself under the leaf of a burdock weed, which was at least as big as the Mantrible Bridge. But when I saw how well they had been shielded, I went to take cover alongside them, but I couldn't, since there were so many of them and (as they say) "all things come to an end." So I climbed up as best I could and walked along his tongue for a good six miles, until I got into his mouth.

But, O you gods and goddesses, what did I see there? May Jupiter blow me away with his three-pointed lightning if I tell you a lie. I walked along in there, as you might promenade around Saint Sophia's Cathedral in Constantinople, and I saw immense boulders, just like the mountains of Denmark (I think they were his teeth), and great meadows, and huge forests, with castles and large cities, no smaller than Lyons or Poitiers.

The first person I met was an old man planting cabbage. And quite astonished I asked him:

"My friend, what are you doing here?"

"I," he said, "am planting cabbage."

"But why, and how?" I said.

"Oh ho, sir," said he, "we can't all walk around with our balls hanging down like mortars, and we can't all be rich. This is how I earn my living. They take this to the city you see over there, and sell them."

"Jesus!" I said. "Is this a whole new world in here?"

"Not at all," he said, "it isn't completely new, no. But I've heard that there is a new world outside of here, and that there's a sun and a moon out there, and all kinds of things going on. But this world is older."

"Well, my friend," I said, "what's the name of that city where they sell your cabbage?"

4. Fictive peoples, led by King Anarche (Unrule), who invade Pantagruel's kingdom.   5. Alcofribas Nasier, the narrator.

"It's called Throattown," he said, "and the people are good Christians, and will be pleased to see you."

So, in a word, I decided to go there.

Now, as I walked I found a fellow setting pigeon snares, and I asked him:

"My friend, where do these pigeons of yours come from?"

"Sir," he said, "they come from the other world."

And then I realized that, when Pantagruel yawned, pigeons with fully extended wings flew right down his throat, thinking it was a great bird house.

Then I came to the city, which seemed extremely pleasant, well fortified, and nicely located, with a good climate. But at the gates the porters asked for my passport and my certificate of good health, which truly astonished me, so I said to them:

"Gentlemen, is there any danger of plague here?"

"Oh, sir," they said, "they're dying of it so rapidly, not very far from here, that the body wagon is always rattling through the streets."

"Good God!" I said. "And just where is this?"

So they informed me that it was in Larynx and Pharynx, which were two cities as big as Rouen and Nantes, rich and doing a fine business, and that the plague was due to a stinking, infectious odor recently flowing up to them from the abysses below. More than twenty-two hundred and seventy-six people had died of it in the last week. So I thought about this, and added up the days, and realized that this was a foul breath from Pantagruel's stomach, which had begun after he'd eaten so much garlic (at Anarch's wedding feast), as I've already explained.

Leaving there, I walked between the great boulders that were his teeth, and climbed up on one, and found it one of the loveliest places in the whole world, with fine tennis courts, handsome galleries, beautiful meadows, and many vineyards. And these delightful fields were dotted with more Italian-style summerhouses than I could count, so I stayed on there for four months and have never been happier.

Then I climbed down the back teeth, in order to get to his lips, but as I journeyed I was robbed by a band of highwaymen in the middle of a huge forest, somewhere in the neighborhood of his ears.

Then I found a little village on the slope (I forget its name), where I was happier than ever, and worked happily for my supper. Can you guess what I did? I slept: they hire day laborers to sleep, down there, and you can make five or six dollars a day. But those who snore really loud can make seven or even seven and a half. And I told the senators how I'd been robbed in the valley, and they told me that, truthfully, the people in that neighborhood were naturally bad, and thieves to boot, which made me realize that, just as we have the Right Side of the Alps and the Wrong Side of the Alps, so they have the Right Side of the Teeth and the Wrong Side of the Teeth, but it was better on the Right Side, and the air was better, too.

And I began to think how true it was that half the world has no idea how the other half lives, seeing that no one has ever written a thing about that world down there, although it's inhabited by more than twenty-five kingdoms, not to mention the deserts and a great bay. Indeed, I have written a fat book entitled *History of an Elegant Throat Land*, which is what I called that country, since they lived in the throat of my master Pantagruel.

Finally, I decided to go back, and going past his beard I dropped onto his shoulders, and from there I got down to the ground and fell right in front of him.

And seeing me, he asked:

"Where are you coming from, Alcofribas?"

And I answered him:

"From your throat, sir."

"And how long have you been down there?" he said.

"Since you marched against the Almyrods," I said.

"But that," he said, "is more than six months. How did you live? What did you drink?"

I answered:

"My lord, just as you did, and I took a tax of the freshest morsels that came down your throat."

"Indeed," he said. "But where did you shit?"

"In your throat, sir," I said.

"Ha, ha, but you're a fine fellow!" he said. "Now, with God's help, we've conquered the entire land of the Dipsodes. And you shall have the castle of Salmagundi."

"Many thanks, sir," I said. "You're far more generous than I deserve."

MICHEL DE MONTAIGNE
1533–1592

The stylistically rich and thematically varied essays of Michel Eyquem de Montaigne offer an unparalleled view into a single Renaissance mind exploring its own workings. The first writer to ask "Who am I?" and pursue the question with extraordinary honesty and rigor, Montaigne presents himself, in his essays, as an explorer of existential dilemmas and of cultural and psychological identity crises. If at times he appears surprisingly modern in his outlook, his habits of thought, and his theories of selfhood, he is, in fact, best viewed as at once a precursor of modernity, a representative of his time, and an avid student of the classical past. The ease with which his thought turns from classical antiquity to the emerging modern world underscores Montaigne's awareness of his own position in history: he knew the world he inhabited was undergoing dramatic cultural and geopolitical changes, and he understood that the idea of the self was transforming along with it.

Montaigne was born on February 28, 1533, in the castle of Montaigne, to a Catholic father and a Protestant mother of Spanish-Jewish descent. His father, Pierre Eyquem, was for two terms mayor of Bordeaux and had fought in Italy under Francis I. Though no man of learning, Pierre had unconventional ideas of upbringing: Michel was awakened in the morning by the sound of music and had Latin taught him as his mother tongue. At six Michel went to the famous Collège de Guienne at Bordeaux; later he studied law, probably at Toulouse; and in 1557 he was a member of the Bordeaux parliament. In 1565 he married Françoise de la Chassaigne, daughter of a man who, as one of Montaigne's colleagues in the Bordeaux parliament, was a member of the new legal nobility (noblesse de robe). Perhaps because of disappointed political ambitions, Montaigne retired from politics in 1570 at the age of thirty-eight: he sold his post as magistrate and retreated to his castle of Montaigne, which he had inherited two years earlier. There in his country estate, he devoted himself to meditation and writing. His famous *Essays*, which began as a collection of interesting quotations, observations, and recordings of remarkable events, slowly developed into its final form of three large books. Although Montaigne spent, as he put it, "most of his days, and most hours of the day" in his library on the third floor of a round tower, the demands of his health and France's tumultuous politics often drew him out of retirement. For the sake of his health (he suffered from gallstones), in 1580 he took a journey through Switzerland, Germany, and Italy. While in Italy he received news that he had been appointed mayor of Bordeaux, an office he held for two terms (1581–85).

His greatest political distractions, however, concerned the Catholic and Protestant factions that violently divided the court and France itself. French politics profoundly influenced the attitudes toward warfare, political resistance, and clemency expressed in Montaigne's *Essays*. When Henry II died in a jousting accident in 1559 and left the fifteen-year-old Francis II to succeed him, the Huguenots (French Reformers in the tradition of John Calvin), recognized the opportunity to influence the weakened royal government. Catherine de Médicis, the queen mother, seized power when Francis II died in 1560 (his successor, Charles IX, was only ten years old). Her policy of limited religious toleration satisfied neither the Catholic nor the Huguenot factions, and from 1562 to 1568 France fell into civil war three times. Struggles among France, Spain, and England over territorial rights in the Netherlands led to the dangerous possibility of a French war with Spain, which Catherine tried to avoid by planning the assassination of its most influential supporter, the Huguenot Coligny. When her plot failed, she persuaded the young Charles IX that the Huguenots were planning a coup. He is said to have shouted "Then kill them all," sanctioning the St. Bartholomew's Day Massacre of August 24, 1572: noblemen, municipal authorities, and the Parisian mobs indiscriminately slaughtered the Protestants in Paris. The slaughter was imitated in other French cities, and the civil wars once again broke out, with the house of Guise leading the Catholic party and the Bourbons leading the Huguenots.

A third party of *politiques,* including Montaigne, the political theorist Jean Bodin, and the duke of Alençon (Catherine's youngest son), arose. This party favored religious tolerance and sought a compromise to the old saying that had facilitated so much carnage in France on religious grounds: "one faith, one law, one king." Throughout his country's political struggles, Montaigne sympathized with the unfanatical Henry of Navarre, leader of the Protestants, but his attitude was neutral and conservative. He expressed his joy when Henry of Navarre became King Henry IV and turned Catholic to do so: "Paris," Henry memorably observed, "is well worth a Mass." Montaigne, who died on September 13, 1592, did not live to see Henry's triumphal entrance into Paris.

Montaigne's essays are at once highly personal and outward-looking; they present a curious mind in acts of investigating history, the complex and changing sociopolitical world, and the mind's own slightly mysterious workings. "I am a man," he says, quoting the Roman playwright Terence, and "I consider nothing human to be alien to me." As an ethnographer and historian, he studies the characteristics of geographically and historically distant cultures and insists that cultural norms are relative and should be free from judgment by sixteenth-century European standards. As a psychologist, he is drawn to the "alien" or disowned thoughts and experiences of himself and his countrymen. His method is not didactic, and his criticism, which he reserves for fellow Europeans, emerges largely through subtle ironies that he leaves readers to detect. He moves suddenly, for example, from introspection to an ethical challenge. "Authors communicate themselves to the world by some special and extrinsic mark," he comments in the essay *Of Repentance,* but "I am the first to do so by my general being, as Michel de Montaigne, not as a grammarian or a poet or a lawyer. If the world finds fault with me for speaking too much of myself, I find fault with the world for not even thinking of itself."

When Montaigne thinks of himself, he does not aggrandize or justify himself but seeks to enlarge knowledge of how the mind works. Far from prizing his capacity for reason and judgment, for example, he neutrally observes, "My judgment floats, it wanders." Montaigne is, in fact, disarmingly modest: "Reader, I am myself the subject of my book; it is not reasonable to expect you to waste your leisure on a matter so frivolous and empty." Although massively learned, he emphasizes not what he knows but rather, like Plato's Socrates, the ways that knowledge reveals how little he truly knows. Ultimately, his essays lead readers away from character study toward philosophical questions about the grounds for knowledge itself (the branch of philosophy called *epistemology*).

Montaigne's assertions of doubt and consciousness of human vanity have little to do with gloomy despair: his stance is skeptical, not cynical. Thus if he "essays" or probes the human capacity to act purposefully and coherently—as he does in the essay *Of the Inconsistency of Our Actions*—his implicit verdict is not that our action is absolutely futile. Instead, he refuses to attribute to the human mind a coherence it does not possess; to Montaigne, if a man were able to achieve the Stoic ideal of the "constant man," unmoved by circumstance or emotion (the butt of Folly's jokes in Erasmus), the result would be impoverishing. "Our actions are nothing but a patch-work," he remarks, and the insight into the fragmentary, inconsistent pattern of our personal lives leads him to a dramatic perception of the strangeness and instability of the self: "There is as much difference between us and ourselves as between us and others." This idea became highly influential in Renaissance thinking and shaped such haunting insights as John Donne's observation that "ourselves are what we know not." For Renaissance thinkers who embraced Montaigne's perception of psychological mysteriousness, the difficult philosophical imperative of Socrates, "know thyself," seemed endlessly intriguing but doomed.

Montaigne pursues his arguments about the elusive and unstable character of the "self" by considering a wide range of anecdotes, both contemporary and classical. A slippery or undefinable historical character intrigues him far more than a monolithic or single-minded one. Alexander the Great—the legendary warrior who also haunts the pages of Castiglione's *Courtier*—is rendered frighteningly transparent by his obsession with power and conquest: he wants nothing less than to be a god. Emperor Augustus, on the other hand, rewards study precisely because his character has "escaped" the willful reductions of historians bent on "fashioning a consistent and solid fabric" of his character. As Montaigne admiringly puts it in *Of the Inconsistency of Our Actions,* there is in the life of Augustus "such an obvious, abrupt, and continual variety of actions that even the boldest judges have had to let him go, intact and unsolved."

Why was Montaigne so unusually able to suspend the self-interest and bias he considered ingrained in human nature in order to analyze himself, his culture, and the place of humankind in the cosmos? As his life in politics indicates, the violent instability of French history taught him tolerance, skepticism about human self-interest, and hatred of dogmatic positions:

> It demands a great deal of self-love and presumption, to take one's own opinions so seriously as to disrupt the peace in order to establish them, introducing so many inevitable evils, and so terrible a corruption of manners as civil wars and political revolutions with them.

His hatred of political radicalism influenced much of what he saw in ancient history and in contemporary accounts of New World discovery and conquest. This alienation from his own political context suggests one cause of his celebrated doubleness of perspective, which is at once ethnographic (outward-looking and impartial) and self-critical (introspective and moral). As he reflects on the ancient and new worlds, he pays special attention to how human beings respond to adversity, oppression, and physical torture. If we keep in mind his impatience with the political and religious ideologues of his own country, we may understand why the heroic self-assertions of

Alexander the Great or Hernán Cortés hold no sway over his imagination and sympathies. Violent repression and implacable resistance alike repel Montaigne, who keenly scrutinizes displays of courage that camouflage less-than-noble motives.

In the most famous essay, *Of Cannibals* (which influenced Shakespeare's reflections in *The Tempest* on the ideal commonwealth, colonialism, and the nature of savages), Montaigne compares the behavioral codes of Brazilian cannibals and those of "ourselves" (Europeans) and concludes that "each man calls barbarism whatever is not his own practice." Once he has asserted the relativity of customs, Montaigne is able to praise elements of the savages' culture that he regards as superior to Europe's. He admires the savages' courage, for instance, in which "the honor of valor consists in combating, not in beating." Moreover, he finds in the positive example of the Brazilian cannibals an implicit criticism of violence by Europeans both at home and in the New World. Montaigne remarks, "I am not sorry that we notice the barbarous horror" of cannibal culture, and then continues,

> but I am heartily sorry that judging their faults rightly, we should be so blind to our own. I think there is more barbarity in eating a man alive than in eating him dead; and in tearing by tortures and the rack a body still full of feeling, in roasting a man bit by bit, in having him bitten and mangled by dogs and swine (as we have not only read but seen within fresh memory, not among ancient enemies, but among neighbors and fellow citizens and what is worse, on the pretext of piety and religion), than in roasting and eating him after he is dead.

As an ethnographer, Montaigne is able to grapple with the distinct and alien culture of the savages without passing judgment; but when he reflects on France, he becomes a moralist. Central to the entire essay is the invocation of the Catholics' torture and burning of fellow citizens (Huguenots) that Montaigne ironically tucks in parentheses. Montaigne here juxtaposes two kinds of savagery: that which appears foreign (cannibalism) and that which has grown too familiar (religious persecution).

Montaigne shows as much interest in the behavior of Brazilian and European victims as he does in their torturers. Montaigne writes of paintings that show a Brazilian prisoner-of-war "spitting in the face of his slayers and scowling at them. Indeed, to the last gasp they never stop braving and defying their enemies by word and look." He continues, "Truly, here are real savages by our standards; for either they must be thoroughly so, or we must be; there is an amazing distance between their character and ours." What Montaigne's example suggests is an unnerving *identity* between the defiant Brazilian natives and the Huguenots of France, who have become inured to the ideas of violent resistance and martyrdom. Like the Brazilian victims of cannibalism, the Huguenots are unwilling, even in the face of death, to moderate their dealings with their torturers, the Catholics who dominate French politics. Montaigne's cannibals, then, help make the entrenched behavior of France's religious factions seem foreign, strange, and savage: both sides are guilty (if not equally so) of "so terrible a corruption of manners as civil wars and political revolutions." His own country's civil strife inspires in Montaigne an unusual ability to transcend smug cultural bias, making him a powerful critic of European culture and an ethnographer able to imagine and study communities other than his own. Like the world of antiquity, which also riveted his imagination, the idea of America allowed Montaigne to explore alternate worlds for their own sake and for their illumination of his own.

Hugo Friedrich, *Montaigne* (1991), is a careful historical study of the author. David Quint, "A Reconsideration of Montaigne's *Des cannibales*," *Modern Language Quarterly* 51.4 (1990): 459–89, analyzes the rhetorical structure and political implications of Montaigne's famous essay. Judith Shklar, *Ordinary Vices* (1984), and Edwin Duval, "Lessons of the New World: Design and Meaning in Montaigne's 'Des Cannibales' (I:31) and 'Des coches' (III:6)," in *Montaigne: Essays in Reading*, ed. Gerard Defaux, *Yale French Studies* 64 (1983): 95–112, provide excellent studies of Montaigne that include, but are not limited to, his New World contexts. Marcel Tetel, *Montaigne*, updated ed. (1990), and Richard Sayce, *The Essays of Montaigne: A Critical Exploration* (1972), are excellent introductions designed for the general reader.

PRONOUNCING GLOSSARY

The following list uses common English syllables and stress accents to provide rough equivalents of selected words whose pronunciation may be unfamiliar to the general reader.

de la Chassaigne: *deu lah shah-sen'*   Soissons: *swah-sohnh'*

Dordogne: *dor-don'*   Suidas: *soo'-ee-dahs*

Guise: *geez*   Valois: *val-wah'*

Jacques Peletier: *zhahk pel-tyay'*   Villegaignon: *vil-gen-yon'*

Montaigne: *mon-ten'*   Vitry-le-François: *vee-tree leu frahn-swah'*

FROM ESSAYS[1]

To the Reader

This book was written in good faith, reader. It warns you from the outset that in it I have set myself no goal but a domestic and private one. I have had no thought of serving either you or my own glory. My powers are inadequate for such a purpose. I have dedicated it to the private convenience of my relatives and friends, so that when they have lost me (as soon they must), they may recover here some features of my habits and temperament, and by this means keep the knowledge they have had of me more complete and alive.

If I had written to seek the world's favor, I should have bedecked myself better, and should present myself in a studied posture. I want to be seen here in my simple, natural, ordinary fashion, without straining or artifice; for it is myself that I portray. My defects will here be read to the life, and also my natural form, as far as respect for the public has allowed. Had I been placed among those nations which are said to live still in the sweet freedom of nature's first laws, I assure you I should very gladly have portrayed myself here entire and wholly naked.

Thus, reader, I am myself the matter of my book; you would be unreasonable to spend your leisure on so frivolous and vain a subject.

So farewell. Montaigne, this first day of March, fifteen hundred and eighty.

Of the Power of the Imagination

A strong imagination creates the event, say the scholars. I am one of those who are very much influenced by the imagination. Everyone feels its impact, but some are overthrown by it. Its impression on me is piercing. And my art is to escape it, not to resist it. I would live solely in the presence of gay,

1. Translated by Donald Frame.

healthy people. The sight of other people's anguish causes very real anguish to me, and my feelings have often usurped the feelings of others. A continual cougher irritates my lungs and throat. I visit less willingly the sick toward whom duty directs me than those toward whom I am less attentive and concerned. I catch the disease that I study, and lodge it in me. I do not find it strange that imagination brings fevers and death to those who give it a free hand and encourage it.

Simon Thomas was a great doctor in his time. I remember that one day, when he met me at the house of a rich old consumptive with whom he was discussing ways to cure his illness, he told him that one of these would be to give me occasion to enjoy his company; and that by fixing his eyes on the freshness of my face and his thoughts on the blitheness and overflowing vigor of my youth, and filling all his senses with my flourishing condition, he might improve his constitution. But he forgot to say that mine might get worse at the same time.

Gallus Vibius[2] strained his mind so hard to understand the essence and impulses of insanity that he dragged his judgment off its seat and never could get it back again; and he could boast of having become mad through wisdom. There are some who through fear anticipate the hand of the executioner. And one man who was being unbound to have his pardon read him dropped stone dead on the scaffold, struck down by his mere imagination. We drip with sweat, we tremble, we turn pale and turn red at the blows of our imagination; reclining in our feather beds we feel our bodies agitated by their impact, sometimes to the point of expiring. And boiling youth, fast asleep, grows so hot in the harness that in dreams it satisfies its amorous desires:

> So that as though it were an actual affair,
> They pour out mighty streams, and stain the clothes they wear.
> LUCRETIUS[3]

And although it is nothing new to see horns grow overnight on someone who did not have them when he went to bed, nevertheless what happened to Cippus,[4] king of Italy, is memorable; having been in the daytime a very excited spectator at a bullfight and having all night in his dreams had horns on his head, he grew actual horns on his forehead by the power of his imagination. Passion gave the son of Croesus the voice that nature had refused him. And Antiochus took fever from the beauty of Stratonice too vividly imprinted in his soul. Pliny says he saw Lucius Cossitius changed from a woman into a man on his wedding day. Pontanus[5] and others report similar metamorphoses as having happened in Italy in these later ages. And through his and his mother's vehement desire,

> Iphis the man fulfilled vows made when he was a girl.
> OVID[6]

Passing through Vitry-le-François, I might have seen a man whom the bishop of Soissons had named Germain at confirmation, but whom all the

---

2. Roman orator. Montaigne illustrates his points with many examples from both antiquity and contemporary Europe; it is less important to know who these historical persons were than to follow Montaigne's presentation of telling moments of their lives. 3. Titus Lucretius Caro (94–55 B.C.), Roman poet and Epicurean philosopher; *On the Nature of Things* 4.1035–36. 4. The story of Cippus is told by Pliny (A.D. 23/24–79). 5. Johannes Pontanus (1426–1503), Renaissance scholar and philosopher. Croesus, last king of Lydia (ca. 560–546 B.C.). Antiochus I (324–261 B.C.), who ruled the eastern Seleucid territories from 293/2 B.C., took Seleucus's wife, Stratonice. 6. *Metamorphoses* 9.793.

inhabitants of that place had seen and known as a girl named Marie until the age of twenty-two. He was now heavily bearded, and old, and not married. Straining himself in some way in jumping, he says, his masculine organs came forth; and among the girls there a song is still current by which they warn each other not to take big strides for fear of becoming boys, like Marie Germain. It is not so great a marvel that this sort of accident is frequently met with. For if the imagination has power in such things, it is so continually and vigorously fixed on this subject that in order not to have to relapse so often into the same thought and sharpness of desire, it is better off if once and for all it incorporates this masculine member in girls.

Some attribute to the power of imagination the scars of King Dagobert and of Saint Francis. It is said that thereby bodies are sometimes removed from their places. And Celsus tells of a priest who used to fly with his soul into such ecstasy that his body would remain a long time without breath and without sensation. Saint Augustine[7] names another who whenever he heard lamentable and plaintive cries would suddenly go into a trance and get so carried away that it was no use to shake him and shout at him, to pinch him and burn him, until he had come to; then he would say that he had heard voices, but as if coming from afar, and he would notice his burns and bruises. And that this was no feigned resistance to his senses was shown by the fact that while in this state he had neither pulse nor breath.

It is probable that the principal credit of miracles, visions, enchantments, and such extraordinary occurrences comes from the power of imagination, acting principally upon the minds of the common people, which are softer. Their belief has been so strongly seized that they think they see what they do not see.

I am still of this opinion, that those comical inhibitions by which our society is so fettered that people talk of nothing else are for the most part the effects of apprehension and fear. For I know by experience that one man,[8] whom I can answer for as for myself, on whom there could fall no suspicion whatever of impotence and just as little of being enchanted, having heard a friend of his tell the story of an extraordinary impotence into which he had fallen at the moment when he needed it least, and finding himself in a similar situation, was all at once so struck in his imagination by the horror of this story that he incurred the same fate. And from then on he was subject to relapse, for the ugly memory of his mishap checked him and tyrannized him. He found some remedy for this fancy by another fancy: which was that by admitting this weakness and speaking about it in advance, he relieved the tension of his soul, for when the trouble had been presented as one to be expected, his sense of responsibility diminished and weighed upon him less. When he had a chance of his own choosing, with his mind unembroiled and relaxed and his body in good shape, to have his bodily powers first tested, then seized and taken by surprise, with the other party's full knowledge of his problem, he was completely cured in this respect. A man is never after incapable, unless from genuine impotence, with a woman with whom he has once been capable.

This mishap is to be feared only in enterprises where our soul is immoderately tense with desire and respect, and especially if the opportunity is unexpected and pressing; there is no way of recovering from this trouble. I

7. Early Christian Church father (A.D. 354–430).   8. Possibly Montaigne himself.

know one man who found it helpful to bring to it a body that had already begun to be sated elsewhere, so as to lull his frenzied ardor, and who with age finds himself less impotent through being less potent. And I know another who was helped when a friend assured him that he was supplied with a counterbattery of enchantments that were certain to save him. I had better tell how this happened.

A count, a member of a very distinguished family, with whom I was quite intimate, upon getting married to a beautiful lady who had been courted by a man who was present at the wedding feast, had his friends very worried and especially an old lady, a relative of his, who was presiding at the wedding and holding it at her house. She was fearful of these sorceries, and gave me to understand this. I asked her to rely on me. I had by chance in my coffers a certain little flat piece of gold on which were engraved some celestial figures, to protect against sunstroke and take away a headache by placing it precisely on the suture of the skull; and, to keep it there, it was sewed to a ribbon intended to be tied under the chin: a kindred fancy to the one we are speaking of. Jacques Peletier[9] had given me this singular present. I thought of making some use of it, and said to the count that he might incur the same fate as others, there being men present who would like to bring this about; but that he should boldly go to bed and I would do him a friendly turn and would not, if he needed it, spare a miracle which was in my power, provided that he promised me on his honor to keep it most faithfully secret; he was only to make a given signal to me, when they came to bring him the midnight meal, if things had gone badly with him. He had had his soul and his ears so battered that he did find himself fettered by the trouble of his imagination, and gave me his signal. I told him then that he should get up on the pretext of chasing us out, and playfully take the bathrobe that I had on (we were very close in height) and put it on him until he had carried out my prescription, which was this: when we had left, he should withdraw to pass water, say certain prayers three times and go through certain motions; each of these three times he should tie the ribbon I was putting in his hand around him and very carefully lay the medal that was attached to it on his kidneys, with the figure in such and such a position; this done, having tied this ribbon firmly so that it could neither come untied nor slip from its place, he should return to his business with complete assurance and not forget to spread my robe over his bed so that it should cover them both. These monkey tricks are the main part of the business, our mind being unable to get free of the idea that such strange means must come from some abstruse science. Their inanity gives them weight and reverence. All in all, it is certain that the characters on my medal proved themselves more venereal than solar, more useful for action than for prevention. It was a sudden and curious whim that led me to do such a thing, which was alien to my nature. I am an enemy of subtle and dissimulated acts and hate trickery in myself, not only for sport but also for someone's profit. If the action is not vicious, the road to it is.

Amasis,[1] king of Egypt, married Laodice, a very beautiful Greek girl; and he, who showed himself a gay companion everywhere else, fell short when it came to enjoying her, and threatened to kill her, thinking it was some sort

---

9. Renaissance mathematician (1517–1582).   1. Pharaoh ca. 569 B.C., known for his great public works and unconventional life.

of sorcery. As is usual in matters of fancy, she referred him to religion; and having made his vows and promises to Venus, he found himself divinely restored from the first night after his oblations and sacrifices.

Now women are wrong to greet us with those threatening, quarrelsome, and coy countenances, which put out our fires even as they light them. The daughter-in-law of Pythagoras used to say that the woman who goes to bed with a man should put off her modesty with her skirt and put it on again with her petticoat. The soul of the assailant, when troubled with many various alarms, is easily discouraged; and when imagination has once made a man suffer this shame—and it does so only at the first encounters, inasmuch as these are more boiling and violent, and also because in this first intimacy a man is much more afraid of failing—having begun badly, he gets from this accident a feverishness and vexation which lasts into subsequent occasions.

Married people, whose time is all their own, should neither press their undertaking nor even attempt it if they are not ready; it is better to fail unbecomingly to handsel the nuptial couch, which is full of agitation and feverishness, and wait for some other more private and less tense opportunity, than to fall into perpetual misery for having been stunned and made desperate by a first refusal. Before taking possession, the patient should try himself out and offer himself, lightly, by sallies at different times, without priding himself and obstinately insisting on convincing himself definitively. Those who know that their members are naturally obedient, let them take care only to counteract the tricks of their fancies.

People are right to notice the unruly liberty of this member, obtruding so importunately when we have no use for it, and failing so importunately when we have the most use for it, and struggling for mastery so imperiously with our will, refusing with so much pride and obstinacy our solicitations, both mental and manual.

If, however, in the matter of his rebellion being blamed and used as proof to condemn him, he had paid me to plead his cause, I should perhaps place our other members, his fellows, under suspicion of having framed this trumped-up charge out of sheer envy of the importance and pleasure of the use of him, and of having armed everyone against him by a conspiracy, malignantly charging him alone with their common fault. For I ask you to think whether there is a single one of the parts of our body that does not often refuse its function to our will and exercise it against our will. They each have passions of their own which rouse them and put them to sleep without our leave. How many times do the forced movements of our face bear witness to the thoughts that we were holding secret, and betray us to those present. The same cause that animates this member also animates, without our knowledge, the heart, the lungs, and the pulse; the sight of a pleasing object spreading in us imperceptibly the flame of a feverish emotion. Are there only these muscles and these veins that stand up and lie down without the consent, not only of our will, but even of our thoughts? We do not command our hair to stand on end or our skin to shiver with desire or fear. The hand often moves itself to where we do not send it. The tongue is paralyzed, and the voice congealed, at their own time. Even when, having nothing to put in to fry, we should like to forbid it, the appetite for eating and drinking does not fail to stir the parts that are subject to it, no more nor less than that other appetite; and it likewise abandons us inopportunely when it sees fit.

The organs that serve to discharge the stomach have their own dilatations and compressions, beyond and against our plans, just like those that are destined to discharge the kidneys. To vindicate the omnipotence of our will, Saint Augustine alleges that he knew a man who commanded his behind to produce as many farts as he wanted, and his commentator Vives[2] goes him one better with another example of his own time, of farts arranged to suit the tone of verses pronounced to their accompaniment; but all this does not really argue any pure obedience in this organ; for is there any that is ordinarily more indiscreet or tumultuous? Besides, I know one so turbulent and unruly, that for forty years it has kept its master farting with a constant and unremitting wind and compulsion, and is thus taking him to his death.

But as for our will, on behalf of whose rights we set forth this complaint, how much more plausibly may we charge it with rebellion and sedition for its disorderliness and disobedience! Does it always will what we would will it to will? Doesn't it often will what we forbid it to will, and that to our evident disadvantage? Is it any more amenable than our other parts to the decisions of our reason?

To conclude, I would say this in defense of the honorable member whom I represent: May it please the court to take into consideration that in this matter, although my client's case is inseparably and indistinguishably linked with that of an accessory, nevertheless he alone has been brought to trial; and that the arguments and charges against him are such as cannot—in view of the status of the parties—be in any manner pertinent or relevant to the aforesaid accessory. Whereby is revealed his accusers' manifest animosity and disrespect for law. However that may be, Nature will meanwhile go her way, protesting that the lawyers and judges quarrel and pass sentence in vain. Indeed, she would have done no more than is right if she had endowed with some particular privilege this member, author of the sole immortal work of mortals. Wherefore to Socrates generation is a divine act; and love, a desire for immortality and itself an immortal daemon.[3]

Perhaps it is by this effect of the imagination that one man here gets rid of the scrofula which his companion carries back to Spain.[4] This effect is the reason why, in such matters, it is customary to demand that the mind be prepared. Why do the doctors work on the credulity of their patient beforehand with so many false promises of a cure, if not so that the effect of the imagination may make up for the imposture of their decoction? They know that one of the masters of the trade left them this in writing, that there have been men for whom the mere sight of medicine did the job.

And this whole caprice[5] has just come to hand apropos of the story that an apothecary, a servant of my late father, used to tell me, a simple man and Swiss, of a nation little addicted to vanity and lying. He had long known a merchant at Toulouse,[6] sickly and subject to the stone, who often needed enemas, and ordered various kinds from his doctors according to the circumstances of his illness. Once they were brought to him, nothing was omitted

2. Juan Luis Vives (1492–1540), Renaissance philosopher and scholar.   3. Socrates (ca. 470–399 B.C.) describes love as a *daemon* in Plato's *Symposium*.   4. Scrofula, or king's evil, was supposed to be curable by the touch of the kings of France. In Montaigne's time great numbers of Spaniards came to France for this purpose [Translator's note].   5. Montaigne's "cure" for his impotent friend.   6. City of southwestern France.

of the accustomed formalities; often he tested them by hand to make sure they were not too hot. There he was, lying on his stomach, and all the motions were gone through—except that no injection was made. After this ceremony, the apothecary having retired and the patient being accommodated as if he had really taken the enema, he felt the same effect from it as those who do take them. And if the doctor did not find its operation sufficient, he would give him two or three more, of the same sort. My witness swears that when to save the expense (for he paid for them as if he had taken them) this sick man's wife sometimes tried to have just warm water used, the effect revealed the fraud; and having found that kind useless, they were obliged to return to the first method.

A woman, thinking she had swallowed a pin with her bread, was screaming in agony as though she had an unbearable pain in her throat, where she thought she felt it stuck; but because externally there was neither swelling nor alteration, a smart man, judging that it was only a fancy and notion derived from some bit of bread that had scratched her as it went down, made her vomit, and, on the sly, tossed a crooked pin into what she threw up. The woman, thinking she had thrown it up, felt herself suddenly relieved of her pain. I know that one gentleman, having entertained a goodly company at his house, three or four days later boasted, as a sort of joke (for there was nothing in it), that he had made them eat cat in a pie; at which one lady in the party was so horrified that she fell into a violent stomach disorder and fever, and it was impossible to save her. Even animals are subject like ourselves to the power of imagination. Witness dogs, who let themselves die out of grief for the loss of their masters. We also see them yap and twitch in their dreams, and horses whinny and writhe.

But all this may be attributed to the narrow seam between the soul and body, through which the experience of the one is communicated to the other. Sometimes, however, one's imagination acts not only against one's own body, but against someone else's. And just as a body passes on its sickness to its neighbor, as is seen in the plague, the pox, and soreness of the eyes, which are transmitted from one body to the other—

> By looking at sore eyes, eyes become sore:
> From body into body ills pass o'er
>
> OVID[7]

—likewise the imagination, when vehemently stirred, launches darts that can injure an external object. The ancients maintained that certain women of Scythia,[8] when animated and enraged against anyone, would kill him with their mere glance. Tortoises and ostriches hatch their eggs just by looking at them, a sign that their sight has some ejaculative virtue. And as for sorcerers, they are said to have baleful and harmful eyes:

> some evil eye bewitched my tender lambs.
>
> VIRGIL[9]

To me, magicians are poor authorities. Nevertheless, we know by experience that women transmit marks of their fancies to the bodies of the children

---

7. *The Cure for Love*, lines 615–16. 8. Scythians, the Greek name for Asian tribes who lived in what are now parts of Iran and Turkey, were legendary in the Renaissance for their "barbarity." 9. *Eclogue* 3.103.

they carry in their womb; witness the one who gave birth to the Moor.[1] And there was presented to Charles, king of Bohemia and Emperor, a girl from near Pisa, all hairy and bristly, who her mother said had been thus conceived because of a picture of Saint John the Baptist hanging by her bed.

With animals it is the same: witness Jacob's sheep,[2] and the partridges and hares that the snow turns white in the mountains. Recently at my house a cat was seen watching a bird on a treetop, and, after they had locked gazes for some time, the bird let itself fall as if dead between the cat's paws, either intoxicated by its own imagination or drawn by some attracting power of the cat. Those who like falconry have heard the story of the falconer who, setting his gaze obstinately upon a kite in the air, wagered that by the sole power of his gaze he would bring it down, and did. At least, so they say—for I refer the stories that I borrow to the conscience of those from whom I take them. The reflections are my own, and depend on the proofs of reason, not of experience; everyone can add his own examples to them; and he who has none, let him not fail to believe that there are plenty, in view of the number and variety of occurrences. If I do not apply them well, let another apply them for me.

So in the study that I am making of our behavior and motives, fabulous testimonies, provided they are possible, serve like true ones. Whether they have happened or no, in Paris or Rome, to John or Peter, they exemplify, at all events, some human potentiality, and thus their telling imparts useful information to me. I see it and profit from it just as well in shadow as in substance. And of the different readings that histories often give, I take for my use the one that is most rare and memorable. There are authors whose end is to tell what has happened. Mine, if I could attain it, would be to talk about what can happen. The schools are justly permitted to suppose similitudes when they have none at hand. I do not do so, however, and in that respect I surpass all historical fidelity, being scrupulous to the point of superstition. In the examples that I bring in here of what I have heard, done, or said, I have forbidden myself to dare to alter even the slightest and most inconsequential circumstances. My conscience does not falsify one iota; my knowledge, I don't know.

In this connection, I sometimes fall to thinking whether it befits a theologian, a philosopher, and such people of exquisite and exact conscience and prudence, to write history. How can they stake their fidelity on the fidelity of an ordinary person? How be responsible for the thoughts of persons unknown and give their conjectures as coin of the realm? Of complicated actions that happen in their presence they would refuse to give testimony if placed under oath by a judge; and they know no man so intimately that they would undertake to answer fully for his intentions. I consider it less hazardous to write of things past than present, inasmuch as the writer has only to give an account of a borrowed truth.

Some urge me to write the events of my time, believing that I see them with a view less distorted by passion than another man's, and from closer,

---

1. Saint Jerome tells of a woman who, accused of adultery for giving birth to a black child, was absolved when Hippocrates explained that she had a picture of a dark man hanging in her room by her bed [Translator's note]. 2. Genesis 30.37–42. After Laban agreed to give Jacob the striped sheep from his flocks, Jacob bred the sheep in front of rods (the visual stimulation was thought to cause the females to produce striped offspring).

because of the access that fortune has given me to the heads of different parties.[3] What they forget is that even for all the glory of Sallust,[4] I would not take the trouble, being a sworn enemy of obligation, assiduity, perseverance; and that there is nothing so contrary to my style as an extended narration. I cut myself off so often for lack of breath; I have neither composition nor development that is worth anything; I am more ignorant than a child of the phrases and terms that serve for the commonest things. And so I have chosen to say what I know how to say, accommodating the matter to my power. If I took a subject that would lead me along, I might not be able to measure up to it; and with my freedom being so very free, I might publish judgments which, even according to my own opinion and to reason, would be illegitimate and punishable. Plutarch[5] might well say to us, concerning his accomplishments in this line, that the credit belongs to others if his examples are wholly and everywhere true; but that their being useful to posterity, and presented with a luster which lights our way to virtue, that is his work. There is no danger—as there is in a medicinal drug—in an old story being this way or that.

Of Cannibals

When King Pyrrhus[6] passed over into Italy, after he had reconnoitered the formation of the army that the Romans were sending to meet him, he said: "I do not know what barbarians these are" (for so the Greeks called all foreign nations), "but the formation of this army that I see is not at all barbarous." The Greeks said as much of the army that Flaminius brought into their country, and so did Philip, seeing from a knoll the order and distribution of the Roman camp, in his kingdom, under Publius Sulpicius Galba.[7] Thus we should beware of clinging to vulgar opinions, and judge things by reason's way, not by popular say.

I had with me for a long time a man who had lived for ten or twelve years in that other world which has been discovered in our century, in the place where Villegaignon landed, and which he called Antarctic France.[8] This discovery of a boundless country seems worthy of consideration. I don't know if I can guarantee that some other such discovery will not be made in the future, so many personages greater than ourselves having been mistaken about this one. I am afraid we have eyes bigger than our stomachs, and more curiosity than capacity. We embrace everything, but we clasp only wind.

Plato brings in Solon,[9] telling how he had learned from the priests of the city of Saïs in Egypt that in days of old, before the Flood, there was a great island named Atlantis, right at the mouth of the Strait of Gibraltar, which contained more land than Africa and Asia put together, and that the kings of that country, who not only possessed that island but had stretched out so far on the mainland that they held the breadth of Africa as far as Egypt, and

---

3. A centrist, Montaigne knew leaders of the rivaling factions in France.   4. Roman historian (probably 86–35 B.C.).   5. Philosopher and biographer (ca. A.D. 50–120).   6. King of Epirus (in Greece) who fought the Romans in Italy in 280 B.C.   7. Both Titus Quinctius Flaminius and Publius Sulpicius Galba were Roman statesmen and generals who fought Philip V of Macedon in the early years of the second century B.C.   8. In Brazil. Villegaignon landed there in 1557.   9. In his *Timaeus*.

the length of Europe as far as Tuscany, undertook to step over into Asia and subjugate all the nations that border on the Mediterranean, as far as the Black Sea; and for this purpose crossed the Spains, Gaul, Italy, as far as Greece, where the Athenians checked them; but that some time after, both the Athenians and themselves and their island were swallowed up by the Flood.

It is quite likely that that extreme devastation of waters made amazing changes in the habitations of the earth, as people maintain that the sea cut off Sicily from Italy—

> 'Tis said an earthquake once asunder tore
> These lands with dreadful havoc, which before
> Formed but one land, one coast
> > VIRGIL[1]

—Cyprus from Syria, the island of Euboea from the mainland of Boeotia; and elsewhere joined lands that were divided, filling the channels between them with sand and mud:

> A sterile marsh, long fit for rowing, now
> Feeds neighbor towns, and feels the heavy plow.
> > HORACE[2]

But there is no great likelihood that that island was the new world which we have just discovered; for it almost touched Spain, and it would be an incredible result of a flood to have forced it away as far as it is, more than twelve hundred leagues; besides, the travels of the moderns have already almost revealed that it is not an island, but a mainland connected with the East Indies on one side, and elsewhere with the lands under the two poles; or, if it is separated from them, it is by so narrow a strait and interval that it does not deserve to be called an island on that account.

It seems that there are movements, some natural, others feverish, in these great bodies, just as in our own. When I consider the inroads that my river, the Dordogne, is making in my lifetime into the right bank in its descent, and that in twenty years it has gained so much ground and stolen away the foundations of several buildings, I clearly see that this is an extraordinary disturbance; for if it had always gone at this rate, or was to do so in the future, the face of the world would be turned topsy-turvy. But rivers are subject to changes: now they overflow in one direction, now in another, now they keep to their course. I am not speaking of the sudden inundations whose causes are manifest. In Médoc, along the seashore, my brother, the sieur d'Arsac, can see an estate of his buried under the sands that the sea spews forth; the tops of some buildings are still visible; his farms and domains have changed into very thin pasturage. The inhabitants say that for some time the sea has been pushing toward them so hard that they have lost four leagues of land. These sands are its harbingers; and we see great dunes of moving sand that march half a league ahead of it and keep conquering land.

The other testimony of antiquity with which some would connect this discovery is in Aristotle, at least if that little book Of Unheard-of Wonders is by him. He there relates that certain Carthaginians, after setting out upon

---

1. *Aeneid* 3.414–15.   2. Horatius Flaccus (65–68 B.C.), great poet of Augustan Rome; *Art of Poetry*, lines 65–66.

the Atlantic Ocean from the Strait of Gibraltar and sailing a long time, at last discovered a great fertile island, all clothed in woods and watered by great deep rivers, far remote from any mainland; and that they, and others since, attracted by the goodness and fertility of the soil, went there with their wives and children, and began to settle there. The lords of Carthage, seeing that their country was gradually becoming depopulated, expressly forbade anyone to go there any more, on pain of death, and drove out these new inhabitants, fearing, it is said, that in course of time they might come to multiply so greatly as to supplant their former masters and ruin their state. This story of Aristotle does not fit our new lands any better than the other.

This man I had was a simple, crude fellow—a character fit to bear true witness; for clever people observe more things and more curiously, but they interpret them; and to lend weight and conviction to their interpretation, they cannot help altering history a little. They never show you things as they are, but bend and disguise them according to the way they have seen them; and to give credence to their judgment and attract you to it, they are prone to add something to their matter, to stretch it out and amplify it. We need a man either very honest, or so simple that he has not the stuff to build up false inventions and give them plausibility; and wedded to no theory. Such was my man; and besides this, he at various times brought sailors and merchants, whom he had known on that trip, to see me. So I content myself with his information, without inquiring what the cosmographers say about it.

We ought to have topographers who would give us an exact account of the places where they have been. But because they have over us the advantage of having seen Palestine, they want to enjoy the privilege of telling us news about all the rest of the world. I would like everyone to write what he knows, and as much as he knows, not only in this, but in all other subjects; for a man may have some special knowledge and experience of the nature of a river or a fountain, who in other matters knows only what everybody knows. However, to circulate this little scrap of knowledge, he will undertake to write the whole of physics. From this vice spring many great abuses.

Now, to return to my subject, I think there is nothing barbarous and savage in that nation, from what I have been told, except that each man calls barbarism whatever is not his own practice; for indeed it seems we have no other test of truth and reason than the example and pattern of the opinions and customs of the country we live in. *There* is always the perfect religion, the perfect government, the perfect and accomplished manners in all things. Those people are wild, just as we call wild the fruits that Nature has produced by herself and in her normal course; whereas really it is those that we have changed artificially and led astray from the common order, that we should rather call wild. The former retain alive and vigorous their genuine, their most useful and natural, virtues and properties, which we have debased in the latter in adapting them to gratify our corrupted taste. And yet for all that, the savor and delicacy of some uncultivated fruits of those countries is quite as excellent, even to our taste, as that of our own. It is not reasonable that art should win the place of honor over our great and powerful mother Nature. We have so overloaded the beauty and richness of her works by our inventions that we have quite smothered her. Yet wherever her purity shines forth, she wonderfully puts to shame our vain and frivolous attempts:

> Ivy comes readier without our care;
> In lonely caves the arbutus grows more fair;
> No art with artless bird song can compare.
> PROPERTIUS[3]

All our efforts cannot even succeed in reproducing the nest of the tiniest little bird, its contexture, its beauty and convenience; or even the web of the puny spider. All things, says Plato,[4] are produced by nature, by fortune, or by art; the greatest and most beautiful by one or the other of the first two, the least and most imperfect by the last.

These nations, then, seem to me barbarous in this sense, that they have been fashioned very little by the human mind, and are still very close to their original naturalness. The laws of nature still rule them, very little corrupted by ours; and they are in such a state of purity that I am sometimes vexed that they were unknown earlier, in the days when there were men able to judge them better than we. I am sorry that Lycurgus[5] and Plato did not know of them; for it seems to me that what we actually see in these nations surpasses not only all the pictures in which poets have idealized the golden age and all their inventions in imagining a happy state of man, but also the conceptions and the very desire of philosophy. They could not imagine a naturalness so pure and simple as we see by experience; nor could they believe that our society could be maintained with so little artifice and human solder. This is a nation, I should say to Plato, in which there is no sort of traffic, no knowledge of letters, no science of numbers, no name for a magistrate or for political superiority, no custom of servitude, no riches or poverty, no contracts, no successions, no partitions, no occupations but leisure ones, no care for any but common kinship, no clothes, no agriculture, no metal, no use of wine or wheat.[6] The very words that signify lying, treachery, dissimulation, avarice, envy, belittling, pardon—unheard of. How far from this perfection would he find the republic that he imagined: *Men fresh sprung from the gods* [Seneca].[7]

> These manners nature first ordained.
> VIRGIL[8]

For the rest, they live in a country with a very pleasant and temperate climate, so that according to my witnesses it is rare to see a sick man there; and they have assured me that they never saw one palsied, bleary-eyed, toothless, or bent with age. They are settled along the sea and shut in on the land side by great high mountains, with a stretch about a hundred leagues wide in between. They have a great abundance of fish and flesh which bear no resemblance to ours, and they eat them with no other artifice than cooking. The first man who rode a horse there, though he had had dealings with them on several other trips, so horrified them in this posture that they shot him dead with arrows before they could recognize him.

Their buildings are very long, with a capacity of two or three hundred souls; they are covered with the bark of great trees, the strips reaching to the ground at one end and supporting and leaning on one another at the top,

---

3. *Elegies* 1.2.10–12.   4. See his *Laws*.   5. The half-legendary Spartan lawgiver (ninth century B.C.).   6. This passage is always compared with Shakespeare's *The Tempest* 2.1.147ff.   7. Roman tragedian (4? B.C.–A.D. 65), philosopher, and political leader; *Epistles* 90.   8. *Georgics* 2.20.

in the manner of some of our barns, whose covering hangs down to the ground and acts as a side. They have wood so hard that they cut with it and make of it their swords and grills to cook their food. Their beds are of a cotton weave, hung from the roof like those in our ships, each man having his own; for the wives sleep apart from their husbands.

They get up with the sun, and eat immediately upon rising, to last them through the day; for they take no other meal than that one. Like some other Eastern peoples, of whom Suidas[9] tells us, who drank apart from meals, they do not drink then; but they drink several times a day, and to capacity. Their drink is made of some root, and is of the color of our claret wines. They drink it only lukewarm. This beverage keeps only two or three days; it has a slightly sharp taste, is not at all heady, is good for the stomach, and has a laxative effect upon those who are not used to it; it is a very pleasant drink for anyone who is accustomed to it. In place of bread they use a certain white substance like preserved coriander. I have tried it; it tastes sweet and a little flat.

The whole day is spent in dancing. The younger men go to hunt animals with bows. Some of the women busy themselves meanwhile with warming their drink, which is their chief duty. Some one of the old men, in the morning before they begin to eat, preaches to the whole barnful in common, walking from one end to the other, and repeating one single sentence several times until he has completed the circuit (for the buildings are fully a hundred paces long). He recommends to them only two things: valor against the enemy and love for their wives. And they never fail to point out this obligation, as their refrain, that it is their wives who keep their drink warm and seasoned.

There may be seen in several places, including my own house, specimens of their beds, of their ropes, of their wooden swords and the bracelets with which they cover their wrists in combats, and of the big canes, open at one end, by whose sound they keep time in their dances. They are close shaven all over, and shave themselves much more cleanly than we, with nothing but a wooden or stone razor. They believe that souls are immortal, and that those who have deserved well of the gods are lodged in that part of heaven where the sun rises, and the damned in the west.

They have some sort of priests and prophets, but they rarely appear before the people, having their home in the mountains. On their arrival there is a great feast and solemn assembly of several villages—each barn, as I have described it, makes up a village, and they are about one French league[1] from each other. The prophet speaks to them in public, exhorting them to virtue and their duty; but their whole ethical science contains only these two articles: resoluteness in war and affection for their wives. He prophesies to them things to come and the results they are to expect from their undertakings, and urges them to war or holds them back from it; but this is on the condition that when he fails to prophesy correctly, and if things turn out otherwise than he has predicted, he is cut into a thousand pieces if they catch him, and condemned as a false prophet. For this reason, the prophet who has once been mistaken is never seen again.

Divination is a gift of God; that is why its abuse should be punished as

---

9. A Byzantine lexicographer.   1. About 2.49 miles.

imposture. Among the Scythians, when the soothsayers failed to hit the mark, they were laid, chained hand and foot, on carts full of heather and drawn by oxen, on which they were burned. Those who handle matters subject to the control of human capacity are excusable if they do the best they can. But these others who come and trick us with assurances of an extraordinary faculty that is beyond our ken, should they not be punished for not making good their promise, and for the temerity of their imposture?

They have their wars with the nations beyond the mountains, further inland, to which they go quite naked, with no other arms than bows or wooden swords ending in a sharp point, in the manner of the tongues of our boar spears. It is astonishing what firmness they show in their combats, which never end but in slaughter and bloodshed; for as to routs and terror, they know nothing of either.

Each man brings back his trophy the head of the enemy he has killed, and sets it up at the entrance to his dwelling. After they have treated their prisoners well for a long time with all the hospitality they can think of, each man who has a prisoner calls a great assembly of his acquaintances. He ties a rope to one of the prisoner's arms, by the end of which he holds him, a few steps away, for fear of being hurt, and gives his dearest friend the other arm to hold in the same way; and these two, in the presence of the whole assembly, kill him with their swords. This done, they roast him and eat him in common and send some pieces to their absent friends. This is not, as people think, for nourishment, as of old the Scythians used to do; it is to betoken an extreme revenge. And the proof of this came when they saw the Portuguese, who had joined forces with their adversaries, inflict a different kind of death on them when they took them prisoner, which was to bury them up to the waist, shoot the rest of their body full of arrows, and afterward hang them. They thought that these people from the other world, being men who had sown the knowledge of many vices among their neighbors and were much greater masters than themselves in every sort of wickedness, did not adopt this sort of vengeance without some reason, and that it must be more painful than their own; so they began to give up their old method and to follow this one.

I am not sorry that we notice the barbarous horror of such acts, but I am heartily sorry that, judging their faults rightly, we should be so blind to our own. I think there is more barbarity in eating a man alive than in eating him dead; and in tearing by tortures and the rack a body still full of feeling, in roasting a man bit by bit, in having him bitten and mangled by dogs and swine (as we have not only read but seen within fresh memory, not among ancient enemies, but among neighbors and fellow citizens, and what is worse, on the pretext of piety and religion),[2] than in roasting and eating him after he is dead.

Indeed, Chrysippus and Zeno, heads of the Stoic sect, thought there was nothing wrong in using our carcasses for any purpose in case of need, and getting nourishment from them; just as our ancestors,[3] when besieged by Caesar in the city of Alésia, resolved to relieve their famine by eating old men, women, and other people useless for fighting.

2. The allusion is to the spectacles of religious warfare that Montaigne himself had witnessed in his time and country.   3. The Gauls.

> The Gascons once, 'tis said, their life renewed
> By eating of such food.
>
> JUVENAL[4]

And physicians do not fear to use human flesh in all sorts of ways for our health, applying it either inwardly or outwardly. But there never was any opinion so disordered as to excuse treachery, disloyalty, tyranny, and cruelty, which are our ordinary vices.

So we may well call these people barbarians, in respect to the rules of reason, but not in respect to ourselves, who surpass them in every kind of barbarity.

Their warfare is wholly noble and generous, and as excusable and beautiful as this human disease can be; its only basis among them is their rivalry in valor. They are not fighting for the conquest of new lands, for they still enjoy that natural abundance that provides them without toil and trouble with all necessary things in such profusion that they have no wish to enlarge their boundaries. They are still in that happy state of desiring only as much as their natural needs demand; anything beyond that is superfluous to them.

They generally call those of the same age, brothers; those who are younger, children; and the old men are fathers to all the others. These leave to their heirs in common the full possession of their property, without division or any other title at all than just the one that Nature gives to her creatures in bringing them into the world.

If their neighbors cross the mountains to attack them and win a victory, the gain of the victor is glory, and the advantage of having proved the master in valor and virtue; for apart from this they have no use for the goods of the vanquished, and they return to their own country, where they lack neither anything necessary nor that great thing, the knowledge of how to enjoy their condition happily and be content with it. These men of ours do the same in their turn. They demand of their prisoners no other ransom than that they confess and acknowledge their defeat. But there is not one in a whole century who does not choose to die rather than to relax a single bit, by word or look, from the grandeur of an invincible courage; not one who would not rather be killed and eaten than so much as ask not to be. They treat them very freely, so that life may be all the dearer to them, and usually entertain them with threats of their coming death, of the torments they will have to suffer, the preparations that are being made for the purpose, the cutting up of their limbs, and the feast that will be made at their expense. All this is done for the sole purpose of extorting from their lips some weak or base word, or making them want to flee, so as to gain the advantage of having terrified them and broken down their firmness. For indeed, if you take it the right way, it is in this point alone that true victory lies:

> It is no victory
> Unless the vanquished foe admits your mastery.
>
> CLAUDIAN[5]

The Hungarians, very bellicose fighters, did not in olden times pursue their advantage beyond putting the enemy at their mercy. For having wrung a confession from him to this effect, they let him go unharmed and unran-

---

4. Decimus Junius Juvenal (fl. early second century A.D.), last great Roman satirist; *Satires* 15.93–94.
5. *Of the Sixth Consulate of Honorius*, lines 248–49.

somed, except, at most, for exacting his promise never again to take up arms against them.

We win enough advantages over our enemies that are borrowed advantages, not really our own. It is the quality of a porter, not of valor, to have sturdier arms and legs; agility is a dead and corporeal quality; it is a stroke of luck to make our enemy stumble, or dazzle his eyes by the sunlight; it is a trick of art and technique, which may be found in a worthless coward, to be an able fencer. The worth and value of a man is in his heart and his will; there lies his real honor. Valor is the strength, not of legs and arms, but of heart and soul; it consists not in the worth of our horse or our weapons, but in our own. He who falls obstinate in his courage, *if he has fallen, he fights on his knees* [Seneca].[6] He who relaxes none of his assurance, no matter how great the danger of imminent death; who, giving up his soul, still looks firmly and scornfully at his enemy—he is beaten not by us, but by fortune; he is killed, not conquered.

The most valiant are sometimes the most unfortunate. Thus there are triumphant defeats that rival victories. Nor did those four sister victories, the fairest that the sun ever set eyes on—Salamis, Plataea, Mycale, and Sicily[7]—ever dare match all their combined glory against the glory of the annihilation of King Leonidas and his men at the pass of Thermopylae.[8]

Who ever hastened with more glorious and ambitious desire to win a battle than Captain Ischolas to lose one? Who ever secured his safety more ingeniously and painstakingly than he did his destruction? He was charged to defend a certain pass in the Peloponnesus against the Arcadians. Finding himself wholly incapable of doing this, in view of the nature of the place and the inequality of the forces, he made up his mind that all who confronted the enemy would necessarily have to remain on the field. On the other hand, deeming it unworthy both of his own virtue and magnanimity and of the Lacedaemonian name to fail in his charge, he took a middle course between these two extremes, in this way. The youngest and fittest of his band he preserved for the defense and service of their country, and sent them home; and with those whose loss was less important, he determined to hold this pass, and by their death to make the enemy buy their entry as dearly as he could. And so it turned out. For he was presently surrounded on all sides by the Arcadians, and after slaughtering a large number of them, he and his men were all put to the sword. Is there a trophy dedicated to victors that would not be more due to these vanquished? The role of true victory is in fighting, not in coming off safely; and the honor of valor consists in combating, not in beating.

To return to our story. These prisoners are so far from giving in, in spite of all that is done to them, that on the contrary, during the two or three months that they are kept, they wear a gay expression; they urge their captors to hurry and put them to the test; they defy them, insult them, reproach them with their cowardice and the number of battles they have lost to the prisoners' own people.

I have a song composed by a prisoner which contains this challenge, that they should all come boldly and gather to dine off him, for they will be eating

---

6. *Of Providence* 2.   7. References to the famous Greek victories against the Persians and (at Himera, Sicily) against the Carthaginians in or about 480 B.C.   8. The Spartan king Leonidas's defense here also took place in 480 B.C., during the war against the Persians.

at the same time their own fathers and grandfathers, who have served to feed and nourish his body. "These muscles," he says, "this flesh and these veins are your own, poor fools that you are. You do not recognize that the substance of your ancestors' limbs is still contained in them. Savor them well; you will find in them the taste of your own flesh." An idea that certainly does not smack of barbarity. Those that paint these people dying, and who show the execution, portray the prisoner spitting in the face of his slayers and scowling at them. Indeed, to the last gasp they never stop braving and defying their enemies by word and look. Truly here are real savages by our standards; for either they must be thoroughly so, or we must be; there is an amazing distance between their character and ours.

The men there have several wives, and the higher their reputation for valor the more wives they have. It is a remarkably beautiful thing about their marriages that the same jealousy our wives have to keep us from the affection and kindness of other women, theirs have to win this for them. Being more concerned for their husbands' honor than for anything else, they strive and scheme to have as many companions as they can, since that is a sign of their husbands' valor.

Our wives will cry "Miracle!" but it is no miracle. It is a properly matrimonial virtue, but one of the highest order. In the Bible, Leah, Rachel, Sarah, and Jacob's wives gave their beautiful handmaids to their husbands; and Livia seconded the appetites of Augustus to her own disadvantage; and Stratonice, the wife of King Deiotarus,[9] not only lent her husband for his use a very beautiful young chambermaid in her service, but carefully brought up her children, and backed them up to succeed to their father's estates.

And lest it be thought that all this is done through a simple and servile bondage to usage and through the pressure of the authority of their ancient customs, without reasoning or judgment, and because their minds are so stupid that they cannot take any other course, I must cite some examples of their capacity. Besides the warlike song I have just quoted, I have another, a love song, which begins in this vein: "Adder, stay; stay, adder, that from the pattern of your coloring my sister may draw the fashion and the workmanship of a rich girdle that I may give to my love; so may your beauty and your pattern be forever preferred to all other serpents." This first couplet is the refrain of the song. Now I am familiar enough with poetry to be a judge of this: not only is there nothing barbarous in this fancy, but it is altogether Anacreontic.[1] Their language, moreover, is a soft language, with an agreeable sound, somewhat like Greek in its endings.

Three of these men, ignorant of the price they will pay some day, in loss of repose and happiness, for gaining knowledge of the corruptions of this side of the ocean; ignorant also of the fact that of this intercourse will come their ruin (which I suppose is already well advanced: poor wretches, to let themselves be tricked by the desire for new things, and to have left the serenity of their own sky to come and see ours!)—three of these men were at Rouen, at the time the late King Charles IX was there. The king talked to them for a long time; they were shown our ways, our splendor, the aspect of a fine city. After that, someone asked their opinion, and wanted to know

---

9. Tetrarch of Galatia, in Asia Minor.   1. Worthy of Anacreon (572?–488? B.C.), major Greek writer of amatory lyrics.

what they had found most amazing. They mentioned three things, of which I have forgotten the third, and I am very sorry for it; but I still remember two of them. They said that in the first place they thought it very strange that so many grown men, bearded, strong, and armed, who were around the king (it is likely that they were talking about the Swiss of his guard) should submit to obey a child, and that one of them was not chosen to command instead. Second (they have a way in their language of speaking of men as halves of one another), they had noticed that there were among us men full and gorged with all sorts of good things, and that their other halves were beggars at their doors, emaciated with hunger and poverty; and they thought it strange that these needy halves could endure such an injustice, and did not take the others by the throat, or set fire to their houses.

I had a very long talk with one of them; but I had an interpreter who followed my meaning so badly, and who was so hindered by his stupidity in taking in my ideas, that I could get hardly any satisfaction from the man. When I asked him what profit he gained from his superior position among his people (for he was a captain, and our sailors called him king), he told me that it was to march foremost in war. How many men followed him? He pointed to a piece of ground, to signify as many as such a space could hold; it might have been four or five thousand men. Did all this authority expire with the war? He said that this much remained, that when he visited the villages dependent on him, they made paths for him through the underbrush by which he might pass quite comfortably.

All this is not too bad—but what's the use? They don't wear breeches.

Of the Inconsistency of Our Actions

Those who make a practice of comparing human actions are never so perplexed as when they try to see them as a whole and in the same light; for they commonly contradict each other so strangely that it seems impossible that they have come from the same shop. One moment young Marius is a son of Mars, another moment a son of Venus.[2] Pope Boniface VIII, they say, entered office like a fox, behaved in it like a lion, and died like a dog. And who would believe that it was Nero, that living image of cruelty, who said, when they brought him in customary fashion the sentence of a condemned criminal to sign: "Would to God I had never learned to write!" So much his heart was wrung at condemning a man to death!

Everything is so full of such examples—each man, in fact, can supply himself with so many—that I find it strange to see intelligent men sometimes going to great pains to match these pieces; seeing that irresolution seems to me the most common and apparent defect of our nature, as witness that famous line of Publilius, the farce writer:

> Bad is the plan that never can be changed.
> PUBLILIUS SYRUS[3]

2. Goddess of love. Marius was the nephew of the older and better-known Marius. Montaigne's source is Plutarch's *Life of Marius*. Mars was the god of war.   3. *Apothegms (Sententiae)*, line 362.

There is some justification for basing a judgment of a man on the most ordinary acts of his life; but in view of the natural instability of our conduct and opinions, it has often seemed to me that even good authors are wrong to insist on fashioning a consistent and solid fabric out of us. They choose one general characteristic, and go and arrange and interpret all a man's actions to fit their picture; and if they cannot twist them enough, they go and set them down to dissimulation. Augustus has escaped them; for there is in this man throughout the course of his life such an obvious, abrupt, and continual variety of actions that even the boldest judges have had to let him go, intact and unsolved. Nothing is harder for me than to believe in men's consistency, nothing easier than to believe in their inconsistency. He who would judge them in detail and distinctly, bit by bit, would more often hit upon the truth.

In all antiquity it is hard to pick out a dozen men who set their lives to a certain and constant course, which is the principal goal of wisdom. For, to comprise all wisdom in a word, says an ancient [Seneca], and to embrace all the rules of our life in one, it is "always to will the same things, and always to oppose the same things."[4] I would not deign, he says, to add "provided the will is just"; for if it is not just, it cannot always be whole.

In truth, I once learned that vice is only unruliness and lack of moderation, and that consequently consistency cannot be attributed to it. It is a maxim of Demosthenes, they say, that the beginning of all virtue is consultation and deliberation; and the end and perfection, consistency. If it were by reasoning that we settled on a particular course of action, we would choose the fairest course—but no one has thought of that:

> He spurns the thing he sought, and seeks anew
> What he just spurned; he seethes, his life's askew.
>   HORACE[5]

Our ordinary practice is to follow the inclinations of our appetite, to the left, to the right, uphill and down, as the wind of circumstance carries us. We think of what we want only at the moment we want it, and we change like that animal which takes the color of the place you set it on. What we have just now planned, we presently change, and presently again we retrace our steps: nothing but oscillation and inconsistency:

> Like puppets we are moved by outside strings.
>   HORACE[6]

We do not go; we are carried away, like floating objects, now gently, now violently, according as the water is angry or calm:

> Do we not see all humans unaware
> Of what they want, and always searching everywhere,
> And changing place, as if to drop the load they bear?
>   LUCRETIUS[7]

Every day a new fancy, and our humors shift with the shifts in the weather:

---

4. *Epistles* 20.   5. *Epistles* 1.1.98–99.   6. *Satires* 2.7.82.   7. *On the Nature of Things* 3.1057–59.

> Such are the minds of men, as is the fertile light
> That Father Jove himself sends down to make earth bright.
>   HOMER[8]

We float between different states of mind; we wish nothing freely, nothing absolutely, nothing constantly. If any man could prescribe and establish definite laws and a definite organization in his head, we should see shining throughout his life an evenness of habits, an order, and an infallible relation between his principles and his practice.

Empedocles noticed this inconsistency in the Agrigentines, that they abandoned themselves to pleasures as if they were to die on the morrow, and built as if they were never to die.[9]

This man would be easy to understand, as is shown by the example of the younger Cato[1]: he who has touched one chord of him has touched all; he is a harmony of perfectly concordant sounds, which cannot conflict. With us, it is the opposite: for so many actions, we need so many individual judgments. The surest thing, in my opinion, would be to trace our actions to the neighboring circumstances, without getting into any further research and without drawing from them any other conclusions.

During the disorders of our poor country,[2] I was told that a girl, living near where I then was, had thrown herself out of a high window to avoid the violence of a knavish soldier quartered in her house. Not killed by the fall, she reasserted her purpose by trying to cut her throat with a knife. From this she was prevented, but only after wounding herself gravely. She herself confessed that the soldier had as yet pressed her only with requests, solicitations, and gifts; but she had been afraid, she said, that he would finally resort to force. And all this with such words, such expressions, not to mention the blood that testified to her virtue, as would have become another Lucrece.[3] Now, I learned that as a matter of fact, both before and since, she was a wench not so hard to come to terms with. As the story[4] says: Handsome and gentlemanly as you may be, when you have had no luck, do not promptly conclude that your mistress is inviolably chaste; for all you know, the mule driver may get his will with her.

Antigonus,[5] having taken a liking to one of his soldiers for his virtue and valor, ordered his physicians to treat the man for a persistent internal malady that had long tormented him. After his cure, his master noticed that he was going about his business much less warmly, and asked him what had changed him so and made him such a coward. "You yourself, Sire," he answered, "by delivering me from the ills that made my life indifferent to me." A soldier of Lucullus[6] who had been robbed of everything by the enemy made a bold attack on them to get revenge. When he had retrieved his loss, Lucullus, having formed a good opinion of him, urged him to some dangerous exploit with all the fine expostulations he could think of,

8. *Odyssey* 18.135–36, 152–53 in the Fitzgerald translation.   9. From Diogenes Laertius's life of the Greek philosopher Empedocles (fifth century).   1. Cato Uticensis (first century B.C.), a philosopher. He is traditionally considered the epitome of moral and intellectual integrity.   2. See n. 2, p. 1320.   3. The legendary virtuous Roman who stabbed herself after being raped by King Tarquinius Superbus's son.   4. A common folktale.   5. Macedonian king (382–301 B.C.).   6. Roman general (first century B.C.).

With words that might have stirred a coward's heart.
                                                    HORACE[7]

"Urge some poor soldier who has been robbed to do it," he replied;

Though but a rustic lout,
"That man will go who's lost his money," he called out;
                                                    HORACE[8]

and resolutely refused to go.

We read that Sultan Mohammed outrageously berated Hassan, leader of his Janissaries, because he saw his troops giving way to the Hungarians and Hassan himself behaving like a coward in the fight. Hassan's only reply was to go and hurl himself furiously—alone, just as he was, arms in hand—into the first body of enemies that he met, by whom he was promptly swallowed up; this was perhaps not so much self-justification as a change of mood, nor so much his natural valor as fresh spite.

That man whom you saw so adventurous yesterday, do not think it strange to find him just as cowardly today: either anger, or necessity, or company, or wine, or the sound of a trumpet, had put his heart in his belly. His was a courage formed not by reason, but by one of these circumstances; it is no wonder if he has now been made different by other, contrary circumstances.

These supple variations and contradictions that are seen in us have made some imagine that we have two souls, and others that two powers accompany us and drive us, each in its own way, one toward good, the other toward evil; for such sudden diversity cannot well be reconciled with a simple subject.

Not only does the wind of accident move me at will, but, besides, I am moved and disturbed as a result merely of my own unstable posture; and anyone who observes carefully can hardly find himself twice in the same state. I give my soul now one face, now another, according to which direction I turn it. If I speak of myself in different ways, that is because I look at myself in different ways. All contradictions may be found in me by some twist and in some fashion. Bashful, insolent; chaste, lascivious; talkative, taciturn; tough, delicate; clever, stupid; surly, affable; lying, truthful; learned, ignorant; liberal, miserly, and prodigal: all this I see in myself to some extent according to how I turn; and whoever studies himself really attentively finds in himself, yes, even in his judgment, this gyration and discord. I have nothing to say about myself absolutely, simply, and solidly, without confusion and without mixture, or in one word. *Distinguo*[9] is the most universal member of my logic.

Although I am always minded to say good of what is good, and inclined to interpret favorably anything that can be so interpreted, still it is true that the strangeness of our condition makes it happen that we are often driven to do good by vice itself—were it not that doing good is judged by intention alone.

Therefore one courageous deed must not be taken to prove a man valiant; a man who was really valiant would be so always and on all occasions. If valor were a habit of virtue, and not a sally, it would make a man equally

7. *Epistles* 2.2.36.   8. *Epistles* 2.2.39–40.   9. I distinguish (Latin)—that is, I separate into its components.

resolute in any contingency, the same alone as in company, the same in single combat as in battle; for, whatever they say, there is not one valor for the pavement and another for the camp. As bravely would he bear an illness in his bed as a wound in camp, and he would fear death no more in his home than in an assault. We would not see the same man charging into the breach with brave assurance, and later tormenting himself, like a woman, over the loss of a lawsuit or a son. When, though a coward against infamy, he is firm against poverty; when, though weak against the surgeons' knives, he is steadfast against the enemy's swords, the action is praiseworthy, not the man.

Many Greeks, says Cicero, cannot look at the enemy, and are brave in sickness; the Cimbrians and Celtiberians, just the opposite; *for nothing can be uniform that does not spring from a firm principle* [Cicero].[1]

There is no more extreme valor of its kind than Alexander's; but it is only of one kind, and not complete and universal enough. Incomparable though it is, it still has its blemishes; which is why we see him worry so frantically when he conceives the slightest suspicion that his men are plotting against his life, and why he behaves in such matters with such violent and indiscriminate injustice and with a fear that subverts his natural reason. Also superstition, with which he was so strongly tainted, bears some stamp of pusillanimity. And the excessiveness of the penance he did for the murder of Clytus[2] is also evidence of the unevenness of his temper.

Our actions are nothing but a patchwork—*they despise pleasure, but are too cowardly in pain; they are indifferent to glory, but infamy breaks their spirit* [Cicero][3]—and we want to gain honor under false colors. Virtue will not be followed except for her own sake; and if we sometimes borrow her mask for some other purpose, she promptly snatches it from our face. It is a strong and vivid dye, once the soul is steeped in it, and will not go without taking the fabric with it. That is why, to judge a man, we must follow his traces long and carefully. If he does not maintain consistency for its own sake, *with a way of life that has been well considered and preconcerted* [Cicero][4]; if changing circumstances makes him change his pace (I mean his path, for his pace may be hastened or slowed), let him go: that man goes before the wind, as the motto of our Talbot[5] says.

It is no wonder, says an ancient [Seneca], that chance has so much power over us, since we live by chance.[6] A man who has not directed his life as a whole toward a definite goal cannot possibly set his particular actions in order. A man who does not have a picture of the whole in his head cannot possibly arrange the pieces. What good does it do a man to lay in a supply of paints if he does not know what he is to paint? No one makes a definite plan of his life; we think about it only piecemeal. The archer must first know what he is aiming at, and then set his hand, his bow, his string, his arrow, and his movements for that goal. Our plans go astray because they have no direction and no aim. No wind works for the man who has no port of destination.

I do not agree with the judgment given in favor of Sophocles, on the strength of seeing one of his tragedies, that it proved him competent to

---

1. Marcus Tullius Cicero (106–43 B.C.), Roman orator; *Tusculan Disputations* 2.27.   2. A commander in Alexander's army who was killed by him during an argument, an act Alexander immediately and bitterly regretted, as related by Plutarch in his *Life of Alexander*, chaps. 50–52.   3. *On Duties* (*De officiis*) 1.21.   4. *Paradoxes* 5.   5. An English captain who fought in France and died there in 1453.   6. *Epistles* 71.

manage his domestic affairs, against the accusation of his son. Nor do I think that the conjecture of the Parians sent to reform the Milesians was sufficient ground for the conclusion they drew. Visiting the island, they noticed the best-cultivated lands and the best-run country houses, and noted down the names of their owners. Then they assembled the citizens in the town and appointed these owners the new governors and magistrates, judging that they, who were careful of their private affairs, would be careful of those of the public.

We are all patchwork, and so shapeless and diverse in composition that each bit, each moment, plays its own game. And there is as much difference between us and ourselves as between us and others. *Consider it a great thing to play the part of one single man* [Seneca].[7] Ambition can teach men valor, and temperance, and liberality, and even justice. Greed can implant in the heart of a shop apprentice, brought up in obscurity and idleness, the confidence to cast himself far from hearth and home, in a frail boat at the mercy of the waves and angry Neptune; it also teaches discretion and wisdom. Venus herself supplies resolution and boldness to boys still subject to discipline and the rod, and arms the tender hearts of virgins who are still in their mothers' laps:

> Furtively passing sleeping guards, with Love as guide,
> Alone by night the girl comes to the young man's side.
> TIBULLUS[8]

In view of this, a sound intellect will refuse to judge men simply by their outward actions; we must probe the inside and discover what springs set men in motion. But since this is an arduous and hazardous undertaking, I wish fewer people would meddle with it.

Of Coaches

It is very easy to demonstrate that great authors, when they write about causes, adduce not only those they think are true but also those they do not believe in, provided they have some originality and beauty. They speak truly and usefully enough if they speak ingeniously. We cannot make sure of the master cause; we pile up several of them, to see if by chance it will be found among them,

> For one cause will not do;
> We must state many, one of which is true.
> LUCRETIUS[9]

Do you ask me whence comes this custom of blessing those who sneeze? We produce three sorts of wind. That which issues from below is too foul; that which issues from the mouth carries some reproach of gluttony; the third is sneezing. And because it comes from the head and is blameless, we give it this civil reception. Do not laugh at this piece of subtlety; it is, they say, from Aristotle.

7. *Epistles* 120.   8. *Elegies* 2.1.75–76.   9. *On the Nature of Things* 6.704–5.

It seems to me I have read in Plutarch (who, of all the authors I know, is the one who best combined art with nature and judgment with knowledge) that he gives the reason for the heaving of the stomach that afflicts those who travel by sea, as fear, having found some reason by which he proves that fear can produce such an effect. I, who am very subject to seasickness, know very well that this cause does not affect me, and I know it, not by reasoning, but by necessary experience. Not to mention what I have been told, that the same thing often happens to animals, and especially to pigs, without any apprehension of danger; and what an acquaintance of mine has told me about himself, that though he was very subject to it, the desire to vomit had left him two or three times when he found himself oppressed with fright in a big storm. And hear this ancient: *I was too sick to think about the danger* [Seneca].[1] I was never afraid on the water, nor indeed anywhere else (and I have often enough had just occasions, if death is one), at least not to the point of being confused or bewildered.

Fear sometimes arises from want of judgment as well as from want of courage. All the dangers I have seen, I have seen with open eyes, with my sight free, sound, and entire; besides, it takes courage to be afraid. It once served me in good stead, compared with others, so to conduct my flight and keep it orderly, that it was carried out, if not without fear, at all events without terror and without dismay; it was excited, but not dazed or distracted.

Great souls go much further yet and offer us examples of flights not merely composed and healthy, but proud. Let us tell of the one that Alcibiades reports of Socrates, his comrade in arms:[2] "I found him," he says, "after the rout of our army, him and Laches, among the last of the fugitives; and I observed him at my leisure and in safety, for I was on a good horse and he on foot, and we had fought that way. I noticed first how much presence of mind and resolution he showed compared with Laches; and then the boldness of his walk, no different from his ordinary one, his firm and steady gaze, considering and judging what was going on around him, looking now at one side, now the other, friends and enemies, in a way that encouraged the former and signified to the latter that he was a man to sell his blood and his life very dear to anyone who should try to take them away. And thus they made their escape; for people are not inclined to attack such men; they run after the frightened ones." That is the testimony of that great captain, which teaches us what we experience every day, that there is nothing that throws us so much into dangers as an unthinking eagerness to get clear of them. *Where there is less fear, there is generally less danger* [Livy].[3]

Our common people are wrong to say that such-and-such a man fears death, when they mean to say that he thinks about it and foresees it. Foresight is equally suitable in whatever concerns us, whether for good or ill. To consider and judge the danger is in a way the opposite of being stunned by it.

I do not feel myself strong enough to sustain the impact and impetuosity of this passion of fear, or of any other vehement passion. If I were once conquered and thrown by it, I would never get up again quite intact. If anything made my soul lose its footing, it would never set it back upright in

1. *Moral Epistles* 53.3.   2. Plato, *Symposium*.   3. Titus Livius (59 B.C.–A.D. 17 or 64 B.C.–A.D. 12), Roman historian; *On the Founding of Rome* 22.5.

its place; it probes and searches itself too keenly and deeply, and therefore would never let the wound that had pierced it close up and heal. It has been well for me that no illness has yet laid it low. Each attack made on me I meet and fight off in my full armor; thus the first one that swept me off my feet would leave me without resources. I have no secondary defense: no matter where the torrent should break my dike, I would be helpless and be drowned for good.

Epicurus[4] says that the wise man can never pass into a contrary state. I have an opinion about the converse of this saying: that anyone who has once been very foolish will never at any other time be very wise.

God tempers the cold according to the cloak, and gives me passions according to my means of withstanding them. Nature, having uncovered me on one side, has covered me up on the other; having disarmed me of strength, she has armed me with insensibility and a controlled, or dull, apprehensiveness.

Now I cannot long endure (and I could endure them less easily in my youth) either coach, or litter, or boat; and I hate any other transportation than horseback, both in town and in the country. But I can endure a litter less than a coach, and for the same reason I can more easily bear a rough tossing on the water, whereby fear is produced, than the movement felt in calm weather. By that slight jolt given by the oars, stealing the vessel from under us, I somehow feel my head and stomach troubled, as I cannot bear a shaky seat under me. When the sail or the current carries us along evenly or when we are towed, this uniform movement does not bother me at all. It is an interrupted motion that annoys me, and most of all when it is languid. I cannot otherwise describe its nature. The doctors have ordered me to bind and swathe my abdomen with a towel to remedy this trouble; which I have not tried, being accustomed to wrestle with the weaknesses that are in me and overcome them by myself.

If my memory were sufficiently stored with them, I should not begrudge my time to tell here the infinite variety of examples that histories offer us of the use of coaches in the service of war, varying according to the nations and according to the age; of great effect, it seems to me, and very necessary, so that it is a wonder that we have lost all knowledge of them. I will say only this, that quite recently, in our fathers' time, the Hungarians put coaches very usefully to work against the Turks, there being in each one a targeteer and a musketeer and a number of harquebuses lined up, loaded and ready, the whole thing covered with a wall of shields, like a galiot. They formed their battlefront of three thousand such coaches, and after the cannon had played, had them advance and made the enemy swallow this salvo before tasting the rest; which was no slight advantage. Or they launched them into the enemy squadrons to break them and open them up; not to mention the advantage they could derive from them by flanking enemy troops on their march through open country where they were vulnerable, or by covering a camp in haste and fortifying it.

In my time a gentleman on one of our frontiers, who was unwieldy of person and found no horse capable of bearing his weight, having a feud on his hands, went about the country in a coach of this very description, and

---

4. Greek moral and natural philosopher (341–270 B.C.)

made out very well. But let us leave these war coaches. The kings of our first dynasty went about the country in a chariot drawn by four oxen.

Mark Antony[5] was the first who had himself drawn in Rome—and a minstrel girl beside him—by lions harnessed to a chariot. Heliogabalus did as much later, calling himself Cybele, the mother of the gods; and also by tigers, imitating the god Bacchus; he also sometimes harnessed two stags to his coach, and another time four dogs, and yet again four naked wenches, having himself, starked naked too, drawn by them in pomp. The Emperor Firmus had his chariot drawn by ostriches of marvelous size, so that it seemed rather to fly than to roll.

The strangeness of these inventions puts into my head this other notion: that it is a sort of pusillanimity in monarchs, and evidence of not sufficiently feeling what they are, to labor at showing off and making a display by excessive expense. It would be excusable in a foreign country; but among his own subjects, where he is all-powerful, he derives from his dignity the highest degree of honor he can attain. Just as, it seems to me, for a gentleman it is superfluous to dress with studied care at home: his house, his retinue, his cuisine, answer for him sufficiently.

The advice that Isocrates[6] gives his king seems to me not without reason: that he be splendid in furniture and plate, since that is a lasting investment which passes on to his successors; and that he avoid all magnificences that flow away immediately out of use and memory.

I liked to adorn myself when I was a youth, for lack of other adornments, and it was becoming to me; there are those on whom fine clothes weep. We have marvelous stories of the frugality of our kings about their own persons and in their gifts—kings great in prestige, in valor, and in fortune. Demosthenes[7] fights tooth and nail against the law of his city that allotted public monies to lavish games and feasts; he wants the greatness of the city to be manifest in its quantity of well-equipped ships and of good, well-supplied armies.

And Theophrastus[8] is rightly blamed for setting forth a contrary opinion in his book on riches, and maintaining that lavish expenditure was the true fruit of opulence. These are pleasures, says Aristotle, that touch only the lowest of the people, that vanish from memory as soon as people are sated with them, and that no judicious and serious man can esteem. The outlay would seem to me much more royal as well as more useful, just, and durable, if it were spent on ports, harbors, fortifications, and walls, on sumptuous buildings, churches, hospitals, colleges, and the improvement of streets and roads, for which Pope Gregory XIII is gratefully remembered in my time, and in which our Queen Catherine[9] would leave evidence for many years of her natural liberality and munificence, if her means were equal to her wish. Fortune has given me great displeasure by interrupting the construction of the handsome new bridge[1] of our great city, and depriving me of the hope of seeing it in full use before I die.

Besides, it seems to the subjects, spectators of these triumphs, that they

5. Marcus Antonius (83–31 B.C.), Roman general, libertine, and triumvir, whose associations with Eastern luxury and religious cults are invoked here.   **6.** Athenian orator (436–338 B.C.).   **7.** Greatest Athenian orator (384–322 B.C.).   **8.** Greek philosopher and botanist, follower of Aristotle (ca. 370–288 B.C.).   **9.** Catherine de Médicis (1519–1589).   **1.** The Pont Neuf, as it is still called, was completed in 1604 [Translator's note].

are given a display of their own riches, and entertained at their own expense. For peoples are apt to assume about kings, as we do about our servants, that they should take care to prepare for us in abundance all we need, but that they should not touch it at all for their own part. And therefore the Emperor Galba,[2] having taken pleasure in a musician's playing during his supper, sent for his money box and gave into his hand a handful of crowns that he fished out of it, with these words: "This is not the public money, this is my own." At all events, it most often happens that the people are right, and that their eyes are feasted with what should go to feed their bellies.

Liberality itself is not in its proper light in the hands of a sovereign; private people have more right to exercise it. For, to be precise about it, a king has nothing that is properly his own; he owes his very self to others.

The authority to judge is not given for the sake of the judge, but for the sake of the person judged. A superior is never appointed for his own benefit, but for the benefit of the inferior, and a doctor for the sick, not for himself. All authority, like all art, has its end outside of itself: *no art is directed to itself* [Cicero].[3]

Wherefore the tutors of young princes who make it a point to impress on them this virtue of liberality and preach to them not to know how to refuse anything, and to think nothing so well spent as what they give away (a lesson that I have seen in great favor in my time), either look more to their own profit than to their master's, or do not well understand to whom they speak. It is all too easy to impress liberality on a man who has the means to practice it all he wants at the expense of others. And since its value is reckoned not by the measure of the gift, but by the measure of the giver's means, it amounts to nothing in such powerful hands. They find themselves prodigal before they are liberal. Therefore liberality is little to be commended compared with other royal virtues, and it is the only one, as the tyrant Dionysius said, that goes with tyranny itself. I would rather teach him this verse of the ancient farmer: that whoever wants to reap a good crop must sow with the hand, not pour out of the sack; he must scatter the seed, not spill it; and that since he has to give, or, to put it better, pay and restore to so many people according to their deserts, he should be a fair and wise distributor. If the liberality of a prince is without discretion and without measure, I would rather he were a miser.

Royal virtue seems to consist most of all in justice; and of all the parts of justice, that one best marks kings which accompanies liberality; for they have particularly reserved it as their function, whereas they are prone to exercise all other justice through the intermediary of others. Immoderate largesse is a feeble means for them to acquire good will; for it alienates more people than it wins over: *The more you have already practiced it on, the fewer you will be able to practice it on. What is more foolish than to take pains so that you can no longer do what you enjoy doing?* [Cicero.][4] And if it is exercised without regard to merit, it puts to shame him who receives it, and is received ungraciously. Tyrants have been sacrificed to the hatred of the people by the hands of the very ones whom they have unjustly advanced; for such men think to assure their possession of undeserved goods by showing contempt

2. Roman emperor (ca. 3 B.C.–A.D. 69) after Nero.   3. *De finibus* 5.6.16.   4. *On Duties* 2.15.52–54.

and hatred for the man from whom they received them, and rallying to the judgment and opinion of the people in that respect.

The subjects of a prince who is excessive in gifts become excessive in requests; they adjust themselves not to reason but to example. Surely we often have reason to blush for our impudence; we are overpaid according to justice when the recompense equals our service; for do we owe no service to our prince by natural obligation? If he bears our expenses, he does too much; it is enough that he helps out. The surplus is called benefit, and it cannot be exacted, for the very name of liberality rings of liberty. By our method, it is never done; the receipts are no longer taken into account; people love only the future liberality. Wherefore the more a prince exhausts himself in giving, the poorer he makes himself in friends. How could he assuage desires that grow the more they are fulfilled? He who has his mind on taking, no longer has it on what he has taken. Covetousness has nothing so characteristic about it as ingratitude.

The example of Cyrus[5] will not be amiss here to serve the kings of our time as a touchstone for ascertaining whether their gifts are well or ill bestowed, and to make them see how much more happily that emperor dealt them out than they do. Whereby they are reduced to doing their borrowing from unknown subjects, and rather from those they have wronged than from those they have benefited; and from them they receive no aid that is gratuitous in anything but the name.

Croesus reproached Cyrus for his extravagance and calculated how much his treasure would amount to if he had been more close-fisted. Cyrus, wanting to justify his liberality, sent dispatches in all directions to the grandees of his state whose career he had particularly advanced, and asked each one to help him out with as much money as he could for an urgent need of his, and to send him a declaration of the amount. When all these statements were brought to him, since each of his friends, thinking it was not enough to offer him merely as much as he had received from his munificence, added much that was more properly his own, it turned out that the total amounted to much more than the savings estimated by Croesus. Whereupon Cyrus said to him: "I am no less in love with riches than other princes, and am rather a more careful manager of them. You see at how small a cost I have acquired the inestimable treasure of so many friends, and how much more faithful treasurers they are to me than mercenary men without obligation, without affection, would be; and how much better my wealth is lodged than in coffers, where it would call down upon me the hatred, envy, and contempt of other princes."

The emperors derived an excuse for the superfluity of their public games and spectacles from the fact that their authority depended somewhat (at least in appearance) on the will of the Roman people, who from time immemorial had been accustomed to being flattered by that sort of spectacle and extravagance. But it was private citizens who had nourished this custom of gratifying their fellow citizens and companions, chiefly out of their own purse, by such profusion and magnificence; this had an altogether different flavor when it was the masters who came to imitate it *The transfer of money from its rightful owners to strangers should not be regarded as liberality* [Cicero].[6]

Philip, because his son was trying to win the good will of the Macedonians

---

5. Ideal prince of Xenophon's *Education of Cyrus.*   6. *On Duties* 1.14.43.

by presents, scolded him for it in a letter in this manner: "What, do you want your subjects to regard you as their purser, not as their king? Do you want to win them over? Win them over with the benefits of your virtue, not the benefits of your coffers."[7]

It was, however, a fine thing to bring and plant in the amphitheater a great quantity of big trees, all branching and green, representing a great shady forest, arranged in beautiful symmetry, and on the first day to cast into it a thousand ostriches, a thousand stags, a thousand wild boars, and a thousand fallow deer, leaving them to be hunted down by the people; on the next day to have a hundred big lions, a hundred leopards, and three hundred bears slaughtered in their presence; and for the third day, to have three hundred pairs of gladiators fight it out to the death, as the Emperor Probus[8] did.

It was also a fine thing to see those great amphitheaters faced with marble on the outside, wrought with ornaments and statues, the inside sparkling with many rare enrichments—

> Here is the diamond circle, the golden portico
> CALPURNIUS[9]

—all the sides of this vast space filled and surrounded from top to bottom with three or four score tiers of seats, also of marble, covered with cushions—

> "Let him begone," he says,
> "And leave the cushioned seats of knights, seeing he pays
> None of the lawful tax"
> JUVENAL[1]

—where a hundred thousand men could sit at their ease. Also, first of all, to have the place at the bottom, where the games were played, open artificially and split into crevasses representing caverns that vomited forth the beasts destined for the spectacle; and then, second, to flood it with a deep sea, full of sea monsters and laden with armed vessels to represent a naval battle; and third, to level it and dry it off again for the combat of the gladiators; and for the fourth show to strew it with vermilion and storax instead of sand, in order to set up a stately banquet there for all that huge number of people—the final act of a single day:

> How often have we seen
> Part of the sandy floor sink down, wild beasts emerge
> Out of the open chasm, and from its depths upsurge
> Forests of golden growing trees with yellow bark.
> Not only forest monsters were for us to mark,
> But I saw sea-calves mingled in with fighting bears,
> And hippopotami, the shapeless herd that wears
> The name of river-horse.
> CALPURNIUS[2]

Sometimes they created a high mountain there, full of fruit trees and other trees in leaf, spouting a stream of water from its top as from the mouth of a living spring. Sometimes they brought in a great ship which opened and came

7. *On Duties* 2.15.53–54; Philip of Macedon was the father of Alexander the Great.   8. Marcus Aurelius Probus (A.D. 232–282), a stern disciplinarian, eventually killed by his own troops.   9. Calpurnius Siculus (first century A.D.), pastoral poet; *Bucolics* 7.47.   1. *Satires* 3.153–55.   2. *Bucolics* 7.64–75.

apart of itself and, after having spewed forth from its belly four or five hundred fighting beasts, closed up again and vanished without assistance. At other times, from the floor of the place, they made spouts and jets of water spring forth which shot upward to an infinite height, then sprinkled and perfumed that infinite multitude. To protect themselves against damage from the weather, they had that immense space hung with awnings, sometimes made of purple worked with the needle, sometimes of silk of one color or another, and they drew them forward or back in a moment, as they had a mind to:

> The awnings, though the sun scorches the skin,
> Are, when Hermogenes appears, drawn in.
> MARTIAL[3]

The nets, too, which they put in front of the people to protect them from the violence of the loosened beasts, were woven of gold:

> Even the woven nets
> Glitter with gold.
> CALPURNIUS[4]

If there is anything excusable in such extravagances, it is when the inventiveness and the novelty of them, not the expense, provide amazement.

Even in these vanities we discover how fertile those ages were in minds different from ours. It is with this sort of fertility as with all other productions of Nature. This is not to say that she then put forth her utmost effort. We do not go in a straight line; we rather ramble, and turn this way and that. We retrace our steps. I fear that our knowledge is weak in every direction; we do not see very far ahead or very far behind. It embraces little and has a short life, short in both extent of time and extent of matter:

> Ere Agamemnon, heroes were the same;
> Many there were, but no one knows their name;
> They all are hurried on unwept
> Into unending night.
> HORACE

> Before the Trojan War, before Troy fell,
> Were other bards with other tales to tell.
> LUCRETIUS[5]

And Solon's story of what he had heard from the priests of Egypt about the long life of their state, and their manner of learning and preserving the histories of other countries, does not seem to me a testimony to be rejected in this consideration. *If we could view that expanse of countries and ages, boundless in every direction, into which the mind, plunging and spreading itself, travels so far and wide that it can find no limit where it can stop, there would appear in that immensity an infinite capacity to produce innumerable forms* [adapted from Cicero].[6]

Even if all that has come down to us by report from the past should be

---

3. Marcus Valerius Martial (ca. A.D. 40–ca.104), famous for his witty epigrams; *Epigrams* 12.29.15–16. **4.** *Bucolics* 7.53–54. **5.** *On the Nature of Things* 5.327–28. Above, *Odes* 4.9.25–28. **6.** *On the Nature of the Gods* 1.20.54. Solon (ca. A.D. 200), geographer.

true and known by someone, it would be less than nothing compared with what is unknown. And of this very image of the world which glides along while we live on it, how puny and limited is the knowledge of even the most curious! Not only of particular events which fortune often renders exemplary and weighty, but of the state of great governments and nations, there escapes us a hundred times more than comes to our knowledge. We exclaim at the miracle of the invention of our artillery, of our printing; other men in another corner of the world, in China, enjoyed these a thousand years earlier. If we saw as much of the world as we do not see, we would perceive, it is likely, a perpetual multiplication and vicissitude of forms.

There is nothing unique and rare as regards nature, but there certainly is as regards our knowledge, which is a miserable foundation for our rules and which is apt to represent to us a very false picture of things. As vainly as we today infer the decline and decrepitude of the world from the arguments we draw from our own weakness and decay—

> This age is broken down, and broken down the earth
>
> LUCRETIUS[7]

—so vainly did this poet infer the world's birth and youth from the vigor he saw in the minds of his time, abounding in novelties and inventions in various arts:

> The universe, I think, is very new,
> The world is young, its birth not far behind;
> Hence certain arts grow more and more refined
> Even today; the naval art is one.
>
> LUCRETIUS[8]

Our world has just discovered another world (and who will guarantee us that it is the last of its brothers, since the daemons, the Sibyls,[9] and we ourselves have up to now been ignorant of this one?) no less great, full, and well-limbed than itself, yet so new and so infantile that it is still being taught its A B C; not fifty years ago it knew neither letters, nor weights and measures, nor clothes, nor wheat, nor vines. It was still quite naked at the breast, and lived only on what its nursing mother provided. If we are right to infer the end of our world, and that poet is right about the youth of his own age, this other world will only be coming into the light when ours is leaving it. The universe will fall into paralysis; one member will be crippled, the other in full vigor.

I am much afraid that we shall have very greatly hastened the decline and ruin of this new world by our contagion, and that we will have sold it our opinions and our arts very dear. It was an infant world; yet we have not whipped it and subjected it to our discipline by the advantage of our natural valor and strength, nor won it over by our justice and goodness, nor subjugated it by our magnanimity. Most of the responses of these people and most of our dealings with them show that they were not at all behind us in natural brightness of mind and pertinence.

The awesome magnificence of the cities of Cuzco[1] and Mexico (and, among many similar things, the garden of that king in which all the trees,

---

7. *On the Nature of Things* 2.1136.   8. *On the Nature of Things* 5.331–35.   9. Female prophets.
1. Former capital of the Inca Empire in southeastern Peru.

the fruits, and all the herbs were excellently fashioned in gold, and of such size and so arranged as they might be in an ordinary garden; and in his curio room were gold replicas of all the living creatures native to his country and its waters), and the beauty of their workmanship in jewelry, feathers, cotton, and painting, show that they were not behind us in industry either. But as for devoutness, observance of the laws, goodness, liberality, loyalty, and frankness, it served us well not to have as much as they: by their advantage in this they lost, sold, and betrayed themselves.

As for boldness and courage, as for firmness, constancy, resoluteness against pains and hunger and death, I would not fear to oppose the examples I could find among them to the most famous ancient examples that we have in the memories of our world on this side of the ocean. For as regards the men who subjugated them, take away the ruses and tricks that they used to deceive them, and the people's natural astonishment at seeing the unexpected arrival of bearded men, different in language, religion, shape, and countenance, from a part of the world so remote, where they had never imagined there was any sort of human habitation, mounted on great unknown monsters, opposed to men who had never seen not only a horse, but any sort of animal trained to carry and endure a man or any other burden; men equipped with a hard and shiny skin and a sharp and glittering weapon, against men who, for the miracle of a mirror or a knife, would exchange a great treasure in gold and pearls, and who had neither the knowledge nor the material by which, even in full leisure, they could pierce our steel; add to this the lightning and thunder of our cannon and harquebuses—capable of disturbing Caesar[2] himself, if he had been surprised by them with as little experience and in his time—against people who were naked (except in some regions where the invention of some cotton fabric had reached them), without other arms at the most than bows, stones, sticks, and wooden bucklers; people taken by surprise, under color of friendship and good faith, by curiosity to see strange and unknown things: eliminate this disparity, I say, and you take from the conquerors the whole basis of so many victories.

When I consider that indomitable ardor with which so many thousands of men, women, and children came forth and hurled themselves so many times into inevitable dangers for the defense of their gods and of their liberty, and that noble, stubborn readiness to suffer all extremities and hardships, even death, rather than submit to the domination of those by whom they had been so shamefully deceived (for some of them when captured chose rather to let themselves perish of hunger and fasting than to accept food from the hands of such basely victorious enemies), I conclude that if anyone had attacked them on equal terms, with equal arms, experience, and numbers, it would have been just as dangerous for him as in any other war we know of, and more so.

Why did not such a noble conquest fall to Alexander or to those ancient Greeks and Romans? Why did not such a great change and alteration of so many empires and peoples fall into hands that would have gently polished and cleared away whatever was barbarous in them, and would have strengthened and fostered the good seeds that nature had produced in them, not only adding to the cultivation of the earth and the adornment of cities the arts of our side of the ocean, in so far as they would have been necessary,

2. Julius Caesar (100–44 B.C.), the great Roman general and conqueror.

but also adding the Greek and Roman virtues to those originally in that region? What an improvement that would have been, and what an amelioration for the entire globe, if the first examples of our conduct that were offered over there had called those peoples to the admiration and imitation of virtue and had set up between them and us a brotherly fellowship and understanding! How easy it would have been to make good use of souls so fresh, so famished to learn, and having, for the most part, such fine natural beginnings! On the contrary, we took advantage of their ignorance and inexperience to incline them the more easily toward treachery, lewdness, avarice, and every sort of inhumanity and cruelty, after the example and pattern of our ways. Who ever set the utility of commerce and trading at such a price? So many cities razed, so many nations exterminated, so many millions of people put to the sword, and the richest and most beautiful part of the world turned upside down, for the traffic in pearls and pepper! Base and mechanical victories! Never did ambition, never did public enmities, drive men against one another to such horrible hostilities and such miserable calamities.

Coasting the sea in quest of their mines, certain Spaniards landed in a fertile, pleasant, well-populated country, and made their usual declarations to its people: that they were peaceable men, coming from distant voyages, sent on behalf of the king of Castile, the greatest prince of the habitable world, to whom the Pope, representing God on earth, had given the principality of all the Indies; that if these people would be tributaries to him, they would be very kindly treated. They demanded of them food to eat and gold to be used in a certain medicine, and expounded to them the belief in one single God and the truth of our religion, which they advised them to accept, adding a few threats.

The answer was this: As for being peaceable, they did not look like it, if they were. As for their king, since he was begging, he must be indigent and needy; and he who had awarded their country to him must be a man fond of dissension, to go and give another person something that was not his and thus set him at strife with its ancient possessors. As for food, they would supply them. Gold they had little of, and it was a thing they held in no esteem, since it was useless to the service of their life, their sole concern being with passing life happily and pleasantly; however, they might boldly take any they could find, except what was employed in the service of their gods. As for one single God, the account had pleased them, but they did not want to change their religion, having followed it so advantageously for so long, and they were not accustomed to take counsel except of their friends and acquaintances. As for the threats, it was a sign of lack of judgment to threaten people whose nature and means were unknown to them. Thus they should promptly hurry up and vacate their land, for they were not accustomed to take in good part the civilities and declarations of armed strangers; otherwise they would do to them as they had done to these others—showing them the heads of some executed men around their city.

There we have an example of the babbling of this infancy. But at all events, neither in that place nor in several others where the Spaniards did not find the merchandise they were looking for, did they make any stay or any attack, whatever other advantages there might be; witness my Cannibals.[3]

---

3. *Of Cannibals.*

Of the two most powerful monarchs of that world, and perhaps of this as well, kings of so many kings, the last two that they drove out, one, the king of Peru, was taken in a battle and put to so excessive a ransom that it surpasses all belief; and when this had been faithfully paid, and the king in his dealings had given signs of a frank, liberal, and steadfast spirit and a clear and well-ordered understanding, the conquerors, after having extracted from him one million three hundred and twenty-five thousand five hundred ounces of gold, besides silver and other things that amounted to no less, so that their horses thenceforth went shod with solid gold, were seized with the desire to see also, at the price of whatever treachery, what could be the remainder of this king's treasures, and to enjoy freely what he had reserved. They trumped up against him a false accusation and false evidence that he was planning to rouse his provinces in order to regain his freedom. Whereupon, in a beautiful sentence pronounced by those very men who had set afoot this treachery against him, he was condemned to be publicly hanged and strangled, after being permitted to buy his way out of the torment of being burned alive by submitting to baptism at the moment of the execution. A horrible and unheard-of calamity, which nevertheless he bore without belying himself either by look or word, with a truly royal bearing and gravity. And then, to lull the people, stunned and dazed by such a strange thing, they counterfeited great mourning over his death and ordered a sumptuous funeral for him.

The other one, the king of Mexico, had long defended his besieged city and shown in this siege all that endurance and perseverance can do, if ever prince and people did so, when his bad fortune put him in his enemies' hands alive, on their promise that they would treat him as a king; nor did he in his captivity show anything unworthy of this title. After this victory, his enemies, not finding all the gold they had promised themselves, first ransacked and searched everything, and then set about seeking information by inflicting the cruelest tortures they could think up on the prisoners they held. But having gained nothing by this, and finding their prisoners' courage stronger than their torments, they finally flew into such a rage that, against their word and against all law of nations, they condemned the king himself and one of the principal lords of his court to the torture in each other's presence. This lord, finding himself overcome with the pain, surrounded with burning braziers, in the end turned his gaze piteously toward his master, as if to ask his pardon because he could hold out no longer. The king, fixing his eyes proudly and severely on him in reproach for his cowardice and pusillanimity, said to him only these words, in a stern, firm voice: "And I, am I in a bath? Am I more comfortable than you?" The other immediately after succumbed to the pain and died on the spot. The king, half roasted, was carried away from there, not so much out of pity (for what pity ever touched souls who, for dubious information about some gold vase to pillage, had a man grilled before their eyes, and what is more, a king so great in fortune and merit?), but because his fortitude made their cruelty more and more shameful. They hanged him later for having courageously attempted to deliver himself by arms from such a long captivity and subjection, and he made an end worthy of a great-souled prince.

Another time they burned alive, all at once and in the same fire, four hundred and sixty men, the four hundred being of the common people, the sixty from among the chief lords of a province, all merely prisoners of war.

We have these narrations from themselves, for they not only admit them but boast of them and preach them. Would it be as a testimonial to their justice or their zeal for religion? Truly, those are ways too contrary and hostile to so holy an end. If they had proposed to extend our faith, they would have reflected that faith is not spread by possession of territory but by possession of men, and they would have been more than satisfied with the murders brought about by the necessity of war, without adding to these an indiscriminate butchery, as of wild animals, as universal as fire and sword could make it, after purposely sparing only as many as they wanted to make into miserable slaves for the working and service of their mines: with the result that many of the leaders were punished with death by order of the kings of Castile, who were justly shocked by the horror of their conduct; and almost all were disesteemed and loathed. God deservedly allowed this great plunder to be swallowed up by the sea in transit, or by the intestine wars in which they devoured one another; and most of them were buried on the spot without any profit from their victory.

As for the fact that the revenue from this, even in the hands of a thrifty and prudent prince,[4] corresponds so little to the expectation of it given to his predecessors and to the abundance of riches that was first encountered in these new lands (for although much is being gotten out, we see that it is nothing compared with what was to be expected), the reason is that the use of money was entirely unknown, and that consequently their gold was found all collected together, being of no other use than for show and parade, like a chattel preserved from father to son by many powerful kings who were constantly exhausting their mines to make that great heap of vases and statues for the adornment of their palaces and their temples; whereas our gold is all in circulation and in trade. We cut it up small and change it into a thousand forms; we scatter and disperse it. Imagine it if our kings thus accumulated all the gold they could find for many centuries and kept it idle.

The people of the kingdom of Mexico were somewhat more civilized and skilled in the arts than the other nations over there. Thus they judged, as we do, that the universe was near its end, and they took as a sign of this the desolation that we brought upon them. They believed that the existence of the world was divided into five ages and into the life of five successive suns, of which four had already run their time, and that the one which gave them light was the fifth. The first perished with all other creatures by a universal flood of water. The second, by the heavens falling on us, which suffocated every living thing; to which age they assign the giants, and they showed the Spaniards some of their bones, judging by the size of which these men must have stood twenty hands high. The third, by fire, which burned and consumed everything. The fourth, by a turbulence of air and wind which beat down even many mountains; the men did not die, but they were changed into baboons (to what notions will the laxness of human credulity not submit!). After the death of this fourth sun, the world was twenty-five years in perpetual darkness, in the fifteenth of which a man and a woman were created who remade the human race; ten years later, on a certain day of their

4. Philip II of Spain (1527–1598).

calendar, the sun appeared newly created, and since then they reckon their years from that day. The third day after its creation the old gods died; the new ones have been born since little by little. What they think about the manner in which this last sun will perish, my author[5] did not learn. But their calculation of this fourth change coincides with that great conjunction of stars which produced, some eight hundred years ago, according to the reckoning of the astrologers, many great alterations and innovations in the world.

As for pomp and magnificence, whereby I entered upon this subject, neither Greece nor Rome nor Egypt can compare any of its works, whether in utility or difficulty or nobility, with the road which is seen in Peru, laid out by the kings of the country, from the city of Quito as far as Cuzco (a distance of three hundred leagues), straight, even, twenty-five paces wide, paved, lined on both sides with fine high walls, and along these, on the inside, two ever-flowing streams, bordered by beautiful trees, which they call *molly*. Wherever they encountered mountains and rocks, they cut through and leveled them, and filled the hollows with stone and lime. At the end of each day's journey there are fine palaces furnished with provisions, clothes, and arms, for travelers as well as for the armies that have to pass that way.

In my estimate of this work I have counted the difficulty, which is particularly considerable in that place. They did not build with any stones less than ten feet square; they had no other means of carrying than by strength of arm, dragging their load along; and they had not even the art of scaffolding, knowing no other device than to raise an equal height of earth against their building as it rose, and remove it afterward.

Let us fall back to our coaches. Instead of these or any other form of transport, they had themselves carried by men, and on their shoulders. That last king of Peru, the day that he was taken, was thus carried on shafts of gold, seated in a chair of gold, in the midst of his army. As many of these carriers as they killed to make him fall—for they wanted to take him alive—so many others vied to take the place of the dead ones, so that they never could bring him down, however great a slaughter they made of those people, until a horseman seized him around the body and pulled him to the ground.

5. Lopez de Gomara (1511–1564), a Spanish contemporary of Montaigne, whose histories of Cortez and of the West Indies Montaigne read in translation [Translator's note].

MIGUEL DE CERVANTES
1547–1616

The author of Don Quixote's extravagant adventures himself had a most unusual and adventurous life. The son of an apothecary, Miguel de Cervantes Saavedra was born in Alcalá de Henares, a university town near Madrid. Almost nothing is known of his childhood and early education. Only in 1569 is he mentioned as a favorite pupil by a Madrid humanist, Juan López. Records indicate that by the end of that year he had left Spain and was living in Rome, for a time in the service of Giulio Acquaviva, who later became a cardinal. We know that he enlisted in the Spanish fleet under the command of Don John of Austria and that he took part in the struggle of the allied forces of Christendom against the Turks. He was at the crucial Battle of Lepanto (1571), where in spite of fever he fought valiantly and received three gunshot wounds, one of which permanently impaired the use of his left hand, "for the greater glory of the right." After further military action and garrison duty at Palermo and Naples, he and his brother Rodrigo, bearing testimonials from Don John and from the viceroy of Sicily, began the journey back to Spain, where Miguel hoped to obtain a captaincy. In September 1575 their ship was captured near the Marseille coast by Barbary pirates, and the two brothers were taken as prisoners to Algiers. Cervantes's captors, considering him a person of some consequence, held him as a slave for a high ransom. He repeatedly attempted to escape, and his daring and fortitude excited the admiration of Hassan Pasha, the viceroy of Algiers, who bought him for five hundred crowns after five years of captivity.

Cervantes was freed on September 15, 1580, and reached Madrid in December of that year. There his literary career began rather inauspiciously; he wrote twenty to thirty plays, with little success, and in 1585 published a pastoral romance, *Galatea*. At about this time he had a daughter with Ana Franca de Rojas, and during the same period married Catalina de Salazar, who was eighteen years his junior. Seeking non-literary employment, he obtained a position in the navy, requisitioning and collecting supplies for the "Invincible Armada." Irregularities in his administration, for which he was held responsible if not directly guilty, caused him to spend more time in prison. In 1590 he tried unsuccessfully to obtain colonial employment in the New World. Later he served as tax collector in the province of Granada but was dismissed from government service in 1597.

The following years of Cervantes's life are the most obscure; there is a legend that *Don Quixote* was first conceived and planned while its author was in prison in Seville. In 1604 he was in Valladolid, then the temporary capital of Spain, living in sordid surroundings with the numerous women of his family (his wife, daughter, niece, and two sisters). It was in Valladolid, in late 1604, that he obtained the official license for the publication of *Don Quixote* (Part I). The book appeared in 1605 and was a popular success. Cervantes followed the Spanish court when it returned to Madrid, where he continued to live poorly in spite of a popularity with readers that quickly made pro-verbial figures of his heroes. A false sequel to his book appeared, prompting him to write his own continuation, *Don Quixote,* Part II, published in 1615. His *Exemplary Tales* had appeared in 1613. He died on April 23, 1616, and was buried in the convent of the Barefooted Trinitarian nuns. *Persiles and Sigismunda,* his last novel, was published posthumously in 1617.

Although, as we have indicated, *The Ingenious Gentleman Don Quixote de la Mancha* was a popular success from the time Part I was published in 1605, it was only later recognized as an important work of literature. This delay was due partly to the fact that in a period of established and well-defined literary genres such as the epic, the tragedy, and the pastoral romance (Cervantes himself had tried his hand at some of these forms), the unconventional combination of elements in *Don Quixote* resulted in a work of considerable novelty, with the serious aspects hidden under a mocking surface.

The initial and overt purpose of the book was to satirize the romances of chivalry. In those long yarns—which had to do with the Carolingian and Arthurian legends and which were full of supernatural deeds of valor, implausible and complicated adventures, duels, and enchantments—the literature that had expressed the medieval spirit of chivalry and romance had degenerated to the same extent to which, in our day, certain conventions of romantic literature have degenerated in "pulp" fiction and film melodrama. Up to a point, then, what Cervantes set out to do was to produce a parody, a caricature of a literary type. But neither the nature of his genius nor the particular method he chose allowed him to limit himself to such a relatively simple and direct undertaking. The actual method he followed to expose the silliness of the romances of chivalry was to show to what extraordinary consequences they would lead a man insanely infatuated with them, once this man set out to live "now" according to their patterns of action and belief.

So what we have is not mere parody or caricature; for there is a great deal of difference between presenting a remote and more or less imaginary world and presenting an individual deciding to live by the standards of that world in a modern and realistic context. The first consequence is a mingling of genres. On the one hand much of the book has the color and intonation of the world of medieval chivalry as its poets had portrayed it. The fact that that vision and that tone depend for their existence in the book on the self-deception of the hero makes them no less operative artistically and adds, in fact, an important element of idealization. On the other hand the chivalric world is continuously jostled by elements of contemporary life evoked by the narrator—the realities of landscape and speech, peasants and nobles, inns and highways. So the author can draw on two sources, roughly the realistic and the romantic, truth and vision, practical facts and lofty values. In this respect—having found a way to bring together concrete actuality and highly ideal values—Cervantes can be said to have created the modern novel.

The consequences of Cervantes's invention are more apparent when we begin to analyze a little more closely the nature of these worlds, romantic and realistic, and the kind of impact the first exerts on the second. The hero embodying the world of the romances is not, as we know, a cavalier; he is an impoverished country gentleman who embraces that code in the "modern" world. Chivalry is not directly satirized; it is simply placed in a context different from its native one. The result of that new association is a new whole, a new unity. The "code" is renovated; it is put into a different perspective, given another chance.

We should remember at this point that in the process of deterioration that the romances of chivalry had undergone, certain basically attractive ideals had become empty conventions—for instance, the ideal of love as devoted "service." In this connection, it may be especially interesting to observe that the treatment of love and Don Quixote's conception of it are not limited to his well-known admiration for his purely fantastic lady Dulcinea but are also dealt with from a feminine point of view. See, as illustration, Marcela's elaborate, logical, and poetic speech (Part I, chapter 14, printed here) that Don Quixote warmly admires; in it the noble shepherdess defends herself against the accusation of being "a wild beast and a basilisk" for having caused Grisóstomo's death and proclaims her right to choose her particular kind of freedom in nature, where "these mountain trees are my company, the clear running waters in these brooks are my mirror."

No less relevant are Quixote's ideals of adventurousness, of loyalty to high concepts of valor and generosity. In the new context those values are reexamined. Cervantes may well have gained a practical sense of them in his own life while still a youth, for instance at the Battle of Lepanto (the great victory of the European coalition against the "infidels") and as a pirate's captive. Because he began writing Don Quixote in his late fifties, a vantage point from which the adventures of his youth must have appeared impossibly remote, a factor of nostalgia—which could hardly have been present in a pure satire—may well have entered into his work. Furthermore, had he undertaken a direct caricature of the romance genre, the serious and noble values of chivalry could not have been made apparent except negatively, whereas in the context devised by him in Don Quixote they find a way to assert themselves positively as well.

The book in its development is, to a considerable extent, the story of that assertion—of the impact that Don Quixote's revitalization of the chivalric code has on a contemporary world. We must remember, of course, that there is ambiguity in the way the assertion is made; it works slowly on the reader, as his or her own discovery rather than as the narrator's overt suggestion. Actually, whatever attraction the chivalric world of his hero's vision may have had for Cervantes, he does not openly support Don Quixote at all. He even seems at times to go further in repudiating him than he needs to, for the hero is officially insane, and the narrator never tires of reminding us of this. One critic has described the attitude Cervantes affects toward his creature as "animosity." Nevertheless, by the very magniloquence and, often, the extraordinary coherence and beauty that the narrator allows his hero to display in his speeches in defense of his vision and his code, we are gradually led to discover for ourselves the serious and important elements these contain. For instance, Don Quixote's speech evoking the lost Golden Age and justifying the institution of knight-errantry (in Part I, chapter 11, printed here) is described by the narrator—after Don Quixote has delivered it—as a "futile harangue" that "might very well have been dispensed with"; but there it is, in all of its fervor and effectiveness. Thus the narrator's so-called animosity ultimately does nothing but intensify our interest in Don Quixote and our sympathy for him. And in that process we are, as audience, simply repeating the experience many characters have on the "stage" of the book, in their relationships with him.

Generally speaking, the encounters between the ordinary world and Don Quixote are encounters between the world of reality and that of illusion, between reason and imagination, and ultimately between the world in which action is prompted by material considerations and interests and a world in which action is prompted by ideal motives. The selections printed here illustrate these aspects of the experience. Among the first adventures are some that have most contributed to the popularity of the Don Quixote legend: he sees windmills and decides they are giants, country inns become castles, and flocks of sheep become armies. Though the conclusions of such episodes often have the ludicrousness of slapstick comedy, there is a powerfully imposing quality about Don Quixote's insanity; his madness always has method, a commanding persistence and coherence. And there is perhaps an inevitable sense of moral grandeur in the spectacle of anyone remaining so unflinchingly faithful to his or her own vision. The world of "reason" may win in point of fact, but we come to wonder whether from a moral point of view Quixote is not the victor.

Furthermore, we increasingly realize that Quixote's own manner of action has greatness in itself, and not only the greatness of persistence: his purpose is to redress wrongs, to come to the aid of the afflicted, to offer generous help, to challenge danger, and to practice valor. And we finally feel the impact of the arguments that sustain his action—for example, in the episode of the lions in which he expounds "the meaning of valor." The ridiculousness of the situation is counterbalanced by the basic seriousness of Quixote's motives; his notion of courage for its own sake appears, and is recognized, as singularly noble, a sort of generous display of integrity in a world usually ruled by lower standards. Thus the distinction between reason and madness, truth and illusion, becomes, to say the least, ambiguous. The hero's delusions are indeed exposed when they come up against hard facts, but the authority of such facts is seen to be morally questionable.

The effectiveness of Don Quixote's conduct and vision is seen most clearly in his relationship with his "squire," Sancho Panza. It would be a crude oversimplification to say that Don Quixote and Sancho represent illusion and reality, the insane code of knight-errantry versus down-to-earth practicalities. Actually Sancho—though his nature is strongly defined by such elements as his common sense, his earthy speech, his simple phrases studded with proverbs set against the hero's magniloquence—is mainly characterized in his development by the degree to which he believes in his master. He is caught in the snare of Don Quixote's vision; the seeds of the imaginative life are successfully implanted in him.

The impact of Quixote's view of life on Sancho serves, therefore, to illustrate one of the important qualities of the protagonist and, we may finally say, one of the important aspects of Renaissance literature: the attempt, ultimately frustrated but extremely attractive as long as it lasts, of the individual mind to produce a vision and a system of its own in a world that often seems to have lost a universal frame of reference and a fully satisfactory sense of the value and meaning of action. What Don Quixote presents is a vision of a world that, for all its aberrant qualities, appears generally to be more colorful and more thrilling and also, incidentally, to be inspired by more honorable rules of conduct than the world of ordinary people, "realism," current affairs, private interests, easy jibes, and petty pranks. It is a world in which actions are performed out of a sense of their beauty and excitement, not for the sake of their usefulness. It is, again, the world as stage, animated by "folly"; in this case the lights go out at the end, an end that is "reasonable" and, therefore, gloomy. Sancho provides the main example of one who is exposed to that vision and absorbs that light while it lasts. How successfully he has done so is seen during Don Quixote's death scene, in which Sancho begs his master not to die but to continue the play, as has been suggested, in a new costume—that of shepherds in an Arcadian setting. But at that final point the hero is "cured" and killed, and Sancho is restored to the petty interests of the world as he can see it by his own lights, after the cord connecting him to his imaginative master is cut by the latter's "repentance" and death.

William Byron, *Cervantes: A Biography* (1978), is thorough. Ruth El Saffar, ed., *Critical Essays on Cervantes* (1986), offers interesting essays by eminent scholars. Vladimir Nabokov, *Lectures on Don Quixote* (1983), presents an elegant engagement with Cervantes's fiction. More-technical studies can be found in Henry Higuera, *Eros and Empire: Politics and Christianity in Don Quijote* (1995), Thomas R. Hart, *Cervantes and Ariosto: Renewing Fiction* (1989), Howard Mancing, *The Chivalric World of Don Quijote: Style, Structure, and Narrative Techniques* (1982), Stephen Gilman, *The Novel According to Cervantes* (1980), and Ruth El Saffar, *Distance and Control: A Study in Narrative Technique* (1975).

PRONOUNCING GLOSSARY

The following list uses common English syllables and stress accents to provide rough equivalents of selected words whose pronunciation may be unfamiliar to the general reader.

Acquaviva: *ahk-wah-vee'-vah*

Benengeli: *ben-en-hel'-ee*

Boiardo: *boy-ar'-doh*

Eugenio: *yoo-hen'-yoh*

Fonseca: *fon-say'kah*

Mondoñedo: *mon-don-yay'-thah*

Orbaneja: *or-bah-nay'hah*

Periquillo: *pehr-i-kee'-yoh*

Quejana: *kay-hah'-nah*

Quesada: *kay-sah'-dah*

Quijada: *kee-hah'-dah*

Quintanar: *kin-ta-nar'*

real: *ray-al'*

Requesenses: *re-ke-sen'-ses*

Rocque: *ro'kay*

Tordesillas: *tor-thay-see'yas*

FROM DON QUIXOTE[1]

From Part I

Prologue

Idling reader, you may believe me when I tell you that I should have liked this book, which is the child of my brain, to be the fairest, the sprightliest, and the cleverest that could be imagined; but I have not been able to contravene the law of nature which would have it that like begets like. And so, what was to be expected of a sterile and uncultivated wit such as that which I possess if not an offspring that was dried up, shriveled, and eccentric: a

---

1. Translated by Samuel Putnam.

story filled with thoughts that never occurred to anyone else, of a sort that might be engendered in a prison where every annoyance has its home and every mournful sound its habitation?[2] Peace and tranquility, the pleasures of the countryside, the serenity of the heavens, the murmur of fountains, and ease of mind can do much toward causing the most unproductive of muses to become fecund and bring forth progeny that will be the marvel and delight of mankind.

It sometimes happens that a father has an ugly son with no redeeming grace whatever, yet love will draw a veil over the parental eyes which then behold only cleverness and beauty in place of defects, and in speaking to his friends he will make those defects out to be the signs of comeliness and intellect. I, however, who am but Don Quixote's stepfather, have no desire to go with the current of custom, nor would I, dearest reader, beseech you with tears in my eyes as others do to pardon or overlook the faults you discover in this book; you are neither relative nor friend but may call your soul your own and exercise your free judgment. You are in your own house where you are master as the king is of his taxes, for you are familiar with the saying, "Under my cloak I kill the king."[3] All of which exempts and frees you from any kind of respect or obligation; you may say of this story whatever you choose without fear of being slandered for an ill opinion any more than you will be rewarded for a good one.

I should like to bring you the tale unadulterated and unadorned, stripped of the usual prologue and the endless string of sonnets, epigrams, and eulogies such as are commonly found at the beginning of books. For I may tell you that, although I expended no little labor upon the work itself, I have found no task more difficult than the composition of this preface which you are now reading. Many times I took up my pen and many times I laid it down again, not knowing what to write. On one occasion when I was thus in suspense, paper before me, pen over my ear, elbow on the table, and chin in hand, a very clever friend of mine came in. Seeing me lost in thought, he inquired as to the reason, and I made no effort to conceal from him the fact that my mind was on the preface which I had to write for the story of Don Quixote, and that it was giving me so much trouble that I had about decided not to write any at all and to abandon entirely the idea of publishing the exploits of so noble a knight.

"How," I said to him, "can you expect me not to be concerned over what that venerable legislator, the Public, will say when it sees me, at my age, after all these years of silent slumber, coming out with a tale that is as dried as a rush, a stranger to invention, paltry in style, impoverished in content, and wholly lacking in learning and wisdom, without marginal citations or notes at the end of the book when other works of this sort, even though they be fabulous and profane, are so packed with maxims from Aristotle and Plato and the whole crowd of philosophers as to fill the reader with admiration and lead him to regard the author as a well read, learned, and eloquent individual? Not to speak of the citations from Holy Writ! You would think they were at the very least so many St. Thomases[4] and other doctors of the Church; for they are so adroit at maintaining a solemn face that, having portrayed in one line a distracted lover, in the next they will give you a nice little Christian sermon that is a joy and a privilege to hear and read.

2. Cervantes was imprisoned in Seville in 1597 and 1602.   3. I.e., the king does not own your body.   4. Thomas Aquinas (1225–1274), Italian philosopher and theologian.

"All this my book will lack, for I have no citations for the margins, no notes for the end. To tell the truth, I do not even know who the authors are to whom I am indebted, and so am unable to follow the example of all the others by listing them alphabetically at the beginning, starting with Aristotle and closing with Xenophon, or, perhaps, with Zoilus or Zeuxis, notwithstanding the fact that the former was a snarling critic, the latter a painter. This work will also be found lacking in prefatory sonnets by dukes, marquises, counts, bishops, ladies, and poets of great renown; although if I were to ask two or three colleagues of mine, they would supply the deficiency by furnishing me with productions that could not be equaled by the authors of most repute in all Spain.

"In short, my friend," I went on, "I am resolved that Señor Don Quixote shall remain buried in the archives of La Mancha until Heaven shall provide him with someone to deck him out with all the ornaments that he lacks; for I find myself incapable of remedying the situation, being possessed of little learning or aptitude, and I am, moreover, extremely lazy when it comes to hunting up authors who will say for me what I am unable to say for myself. And if I am in a state of suspense and my thoughts are woolgathering, you will find a sufficient explanation in what I have just told you."

Hearing this, my friend struck his forehead with the palm of his hand and burst into a loud laugh.

"In the name of God, brother," he said, "you have just deprived me of an illusion. I have known you for a long time, and I have always taken you to be clever and prudent in all your actions; but I now perceive that you are as far from all that as Heaven from the earth. How is it that things of so little moment and so easily remedied can worry and perplex a mind as mature as yours and ordinarily so well adapted to break down and trample underfoot far greater obstacles? I give you my word, this does not come from any lack of cleverness on your part, but rather from excessive indolence and a lack of experience. Do you ask for proof of what I say? Then pay attention closely and in the blink of an eye you shall see how I am going to solve all your difficulties and supply all those things the want of which, so you tell me, is keeping you in suspense, as a result of which you hesitate to publish the history of that famous Don Quixote of yours, the light and mirror of all knight-errantry."

"Tell me, then," I replied, "how you propose to go about curing my diffidence and bringing clarity out of the chaos and confusion of my mind?"

"Take that first matter," he continued, "of the sonnets, epigrams, or eulogies, which should bear the names of grave and titled personages: you can remedy that by taking a little trouble and composing the pieces yourself, and afterward you can baptize them with any name you see fit, fathering them on Prester John of the Indies or the Emperor of Trebizond, for I have heard tell that they were famous poets; and supposing they were not and that a few pedants and bachelors of arts should go around muttering behind your back that it is not so, you should not give so much as a pair of maravedis[5] for all their carping, since even though they make you out to be a liar, they are not going to cut off the hand that put these things on paper.

5. Coin worth one–thirty-fourth of a *real*.

"As for marginal citations and authors in whom you may find maxims and sayings that you may put in your story, you have but to make use of those scraps of Latin that you know by heart or can look up without too much bother. Thus, when you come to treat of liberty and slavery, jot down:

> Non bene pro toto libertas venditur auro.[6]

And then in the margin you will cite Horace or whoever it was that said it. If the subject is death, come up with:

> Pallida mors aequo pulsat pede pauperum tabernas
> Regumque turres.[7]

If it is friendship or the love that God commands us to show our enemies, then is the time to fall back on the Scriptures, which you can do by putting yourself out very little; you have but to quote the words of God himself:

> Ego autem dico vobis: diligite inimicos vestros.[8]

If it is evil thoughts, lose no time in turning to the Gospels:

> De corde exeunt cogitationes malae.[9]

If it is the instability of friends, here is Cato for you with a distich:

> Donec eris felix multos numerabis amicos;
> Tempora si fuerint nubila, solus eris.[1]

With these odds and ends of Latin and others of the same sort, you can cause yourself to be taken for a grammarian, although I must say that is no great honor or advantage these days.

"So far as notes at the end of the book are concerned, you may safely go about it in this manner: let us suppose that you mentioned some giant, Goliath let us say; with this one allusion which costs you little or nothing, you have a fine note which you may set down as follows: *The giant Golias or Goliath. This was a Philistine whom the shepherd David slew with a mighty cast from his slingshot in the valley of Terebinth,*[2] according to what we read in the Book of Kings, chapter so-and-so where you find it written.

"In addition to this, by way of showing that you are a learned humanist and a cosmographer, contrive to bring into your story the name of the River Tagus, and there you are with another great little note: *The River Tagus was so called after a king of Spain; it rises in such and such a place and empties into the ocean, washing the walls of the famous city of Lisbon; it is supposed to have golden sands,* etc. If it is robbers, I will let you have the story of Cacus,[3] which I know by heart. If it is loose women, there is the Bishop of Mondoñedo,[4] who will lend you Lamia, Laïs, and Flora, an allusion that will do you great credit. If the subject is cruelty, Ovid will supply you with Medea; or if it is enchantresses and witches, Homer has Calypso and Vergil Circe. If it is valorous captains, Julius Caesar will lend you himself, in his *Commentaries,* and Plutarch will furnish a thousand Alexanders. If it is loves,

---

6. Freedom is not bought by gold (Latin); from the anonymous *Aesopian Fables* 3.14.   7. Pale death knocks at the cottages of the poor and the palaces of kings with equal foot (Latin); Horace, *Odes* 1.4.13–14.   8. But I say unto you, love your enemies (Latin); Matthew 5.44.   9. For out of the heart proceed evil thoughts (Latin); Matthew 15.19.   1. As long as you are happy, you will count many friends, but if times become clouded, you will be alone (Latin); Ovid, *Sorrows* 1.9.5–6.   2. 1 Samuel 17.48–49.   3. Gigantic thief in *Aeneid* 8, defeated by Hercules.   4. Father Anthony of Guevara.

with the ounce or two of Tuscan that you know you may make the acquaintance of Leon the Hebrew,[5] who will satisfy you to your heart's content. And in case you do not care to go abroad, here in your own house you have Fonseca's *Of the Love of God,*[6] where you will encounter in condensed form all that the most imaginative person could wish upon this subject. The short of the matter is, you have but to allude to these names or touch upon those stories that I have mentioned and leave to me the business of the notes and citations; I will guarantee you enough to fill the margins and four whole sheets at the back.

"And now we come to the list of authors cited, such as other works contain but in which your own is lacking. Here again the remedy is an easy one; you have but to look up some book that has them all, from A to Z as you were saying, and transfer the entire list as it stands. What if the imposition is plain for all to see? You have little need to refer to them, and so it does not matter; and some may be so simple-minded as to believe that you have drawn upon them all in your simple unpretentious little story. If it serves no other purpose, this imposing list of authors will at least give your book an unlooked-for air of authority. What is more, no one is going to put himself to the trouble of verifying your references to see whether or not you have followed all these authors, since it will not be worth his pains to do so.

"This is especially true in view of the fact that your book stands in no need of all these things whose absence you lament; for the entire work is an attack upon the books of chivalry of which Aristotle never dreamed, of which St. Basil has nothing to say, and of which Cicero had no knowledge; nor do the fine points of truth or the observations of astrology have anything to do with its fanciful absurdities; geometrical measurements, likewise, and rhetorical argumentations serve for nothing here; you have no sermon to preach to anyone by mingling the human with the divine, a kind of motley in which no Christian intellect should be willing to clothe itself.

"All that you have to do is to make proper use of imitation in what you write, and the more perfect the imitation the better will your writing be. Inasmuch as you have no other object in view than that of overthrowing the authority and prestige which books of chivalry enjoy in the world at large and among the vulgar, there is no reason why you should go begging maxims of the philosophers, counsels of Holy Writ, fables of the poets, orations of the rhetoricians, or miracles of the saints; see to it, rather, that your style flows along smoothly, pleasingly, and sonorously, and that your words are the proper ones, meaningful and well placed, expressive of your intention in setting them down and of what you wish to say, without any intricacy or obscurity.

"Let it be your aim that, by reading your story, the melancholy may be moved to laughter and the cheerful man made merrier still; let the simple not be bored, but may the clever admire your originality; let the grave ones not despise you, but let the prudent praise you. And keep in mind, above all, your purpose, which is that of undermining the ill-founded edifice that is constituted by those books of chivalry, so abhorred by many but admired by many more; if you succeed in attaining it, you will have accomplished no little."

---

5. Leone Ebreo, Neoplatonic author of the *Dialogues of Love* (1535).   6. Cristóbal de Fonseca, *Treatise of the Love of God* (1592)

Listening in profound silence to what my friend had to say, I was so impressed by his reasoning that, with no thought of questioning them, I decided to make use of his arguments in composing this prologue. Here, gentle reader, you will perceive my friend's cleverness, my own good fortune in coming upon such a counselor at a time when I needed him so badly, and the profit which you yourselves are to have in finding so sincere and straight-forward an account of the famous Don Quixote de la Mancha, who is held by the inhabitants of the Campo de Montiel region to have been the most chaste lover and the most valiant knight that had been seen in those parts for many a year. I have no desire to enlarge upon the service I am rendering you in bringing you the story of so notable and honored a gentleman; I merely would have you thank me for having made you acquainted with the famous Sancho Panza, his squire, in whom, to my mind, is to be found an epitome of all the squires and their drolleries scattered here and there throughout the pages of those vain and empty books of chivalry. And with this, may God give you health, and may He be not unmindful of me as well. VALE.[7]

["I Know Who I Am, and Who I May Be, If I Choose"]

CHAPTER 1

Which treats of the station in life and the pursuits of the famous gentleman, Don Quixote de la Mancha.

In a village of La Mancha[1] the name of which I have no desire to recall, there lived not so long ago one of those gentlemen who always have a lance in the rack, an ancient buckler, a skinny nag, and a greyhound for the chase. A stew with more beef than mutton in it, chopped meat for his evening meal, scraps for a Saturday, lentils on Friday, and a young pigeon as a special delicacy for Sunday, went to account for three-quarters of his income. The rest of it he laid out on a broadcloth greatcoat and velvet stockings for feast days, with slippers to match, while the other days of the week he cut a figure in a suit of the finest homespun. Living with him were a housekeeper in her forties, a niece who was not yet twenty, and a lad of the field and market place who saddled his horse for him and wielded the pruning knife.

This gentleman of ours was close on to fifty, of a robust constitution but with little flesh on his bones and a face that was lean and gaunt. He was noted for his early rising, being very fond of the hunt. They will try to tell you that his surname was Quijada or Quesada—there is some difference of opinion among those who have written on the subject—but according to the most likely conjectures we are to understand that it was really Quejana. But all this means very little so far as our story is concerned, providing that in the telling of it we do not depart one iota from the truth.

You may know, then, that the aforesaid gentleman, on those occasions when he was at leisure, which was most of the year around, was in the habit of reading books of chivalry with such pleasure and devotion as to lead him almost wholly to forget the life of a hunter and even the administration of his estate. So great was his curiosity and infatuation in this regard that he

---

7. Farewell (Latin).   1. Efforts at identifying the village have proved inconclusive. La Mancha is a section of Spain south of Madrid.

even sold many acres of tillable land in order to be able to buy and read the books that he loved, and he would carry home with him as many of them as he could obtain.

Of all those that he thus devoured none pleased him so well as the ones that had been composed by the famous Feliciano de Silva,[2] whose lucid prose style and involved conceits were as precious to him as pearls; especially when he came to read those tales of love and amorous challenges that are to be met with in many places, such a passage as the following, for example: "The reason of the unreason that afflicts my reason, in such a manner weakens my reason that I with reason lament me of your comeliness." And he was similarly affected when his eyes fell upon such lines as these: " . . . the high Heaven of your divinity divinely fortifies you with the stars and renders you deserving of that desert your greatness doth deserve."

The poor fellow used to lie awake nights in an effort to disentangle the meaning and make sense out of passages such as these, although Aristotle himself would not have been able to understand them, even if he had been resurrected for that sole purpose. He was not at ease in his mind over those wounds that Don Belianís[3] gave and received; for no matter how great the surgeons who treated him, the poor fellow must have been left with his face and his entire body covered with marks and scars. Nevertheless, he was grateful to the author for closing the book with the promise of an interminable adventure to come; many a time he was tempted to take up his pen and literally finish the tale as had been promised, and he undoubtedly would have done so, and would have succeeded at it very well, if his thoughts had not been constantly occupied with other things of greater moment.

He often talked it over with the village curate, who was a learned man, a graduate of Sigüenza,[4] and they would hold long discussions as to who had been the better knight, Palmerin of England or Amadis of Gaul; but Master Nicholas, the barber of the same village, was in the habit of saying that no one could come up to the Knight of Phoebus,[5] and that if anyone *could* compare with him it was Don Galaor, brother of Amadis of Gaul, for Galaor was ready for anything—he was none of your finical knights, who went around whimpering as his brother did, and in point of valor he did not lag behind him.

In short, our gentleman became so immersed in his reading that he spent whole nights from sundown to sunup and his days from dawn to dusk in poring over his books, until, finally, from so little sleeping and so much reading, his brain dried up and he went completely out of his mind. He had filled his imagination with everything that he had read, with enchantments, knightly encounters, battles, challenges, wounds, with tales of love and its torments, and all sorts of impossible things, and as a result had come to believe that all these fictitious happenings were true; they were more real to him than anything else in the world. He would remark that the Cid Ruy Díaz had been a very good knight, but there was no comparison between him and the Knight of the Flaming Sword, who with a single backward stroke had cut

---

2. Author of romances (sixteenth century); the lines that follow are from his *Don Florisel de Niguea*. 3. The allusion is to a romance by Jeronimo Fernández. 4. Ironical, for Sigüenza was the seat of a minor and discredited university. 5. Or Knight of Sun. Heroes of romances customarily adopted emblematic names and also changed them according to circumstances. *Palmerin . . . Amadis:* each a hero of a very famous romance of chivalry.

in half two fierce and monstrous giants. He preferred Bernardo del Carpio, who at Roncesvalles had slain Roland despite the charm the latter bore, availing himself of the stratagem which Hercules employed when he strangled Antaeus,[6] the son of Earth, in his arms.

He had much good to say for Morgante;[7] who, though he belonged to the haughty, overbearing race of giants, was of an affable disposition and well brought up. But, above all, he cherished an admiration for Rinaldo of Montalbán,[8] especially as he beheld him sallying forth from his castle to rob all those that crossed his path, or when he thought of him overseas stealing the image of Mohammed which, so the story has it, was all of gold. And he would have liked very well to have had his fill of kicking that traitor Galalón,[9] a privilege for which he would have given his housekeeper with his niece thrown into the bargain.

At last, when his wits were gone beyond repair, he came to conceive the strangest idea that ever occurred to any madman in this world. It now appeared to him fitting and necessary, in order to win a greater amount of honor for himself and serve his country at the same time, to become a knight-errant and roam the world on horseback, in a suit of armor; he would go in quest of adventures, by way of putting into practice all that he had read in his books; he would right every manner of wrong, placing himself in situations of the greatest peril such as would redound to the eternal glory of his name. As a reward for his valor and the might of his arm, the poor fellow could already see himself crowned Emperor of Trebizond at the very least; and so, carried away by the strange pleasure that he found in such thoughts as these, he at once set about putting his plan into effect.

The first thing he did was to burnish up some old pieces of armor, left him by his great-grandfather, which for ages had lain in a corner, moldering and forgotten. He polished and adjusted them as best he could, and then he noticed that one very important thing was lacking: there was no closed helmet, but only a morion, or visorless headpiece, with turned up brim of the kind foot soldiers wore. His ingenuity, however, enabled him to remedy this, and he proceeded to fashion out of cardboard a kind of half-helmet, which, when attached to the morion, gave the appearance of a whole one. True, when he went to see if it was strong enough to withstand a good slashing blow, he was somewhat disappointed; for when he drew his sword and gave it a couple of thrusts, he succeeded only in undoing a whole week's labor. The ease with which he had hewed it to bits disturbed him no little, and he decided to make it over. This time he placed a few strips of iron on the inside, and then, convinced that it was strong enough, refrained from putting it to any further test; instead, he adopted it then and there as the finest helmet ever made.

After this, he went out to have a look at his nag; and although the animal had more *cuartos,* or cracks, in its hoof than there are quarters in a real,[1] and more blemishes than Gonela's steed which *tantum pellis et ossa fuit,*[2] it

6. The mythological Antaeus was invulnerable as long as he maintained contact with his mother, Earth. Hercules killed him while holding him raised in his arms. *Charm:* the magic gift of invulnerability. 7. In Pulci's *Morgante maggiore,* a comic-epic poem of the Italian Renaissance. 8. Roland's cousin. In Boiardo's *Roland in Love (Orlando innamorato)* and Ariosto's *Roland Mad (Orlando furioso),* romantic and comic-epic poems of the Italian Renaissance. 9. Ganelón, the villain in the Charlemagne legend who betrayed the French at Roncesvalles. 1. A coin (about five cents). *Cuarto:* one-eighth of a *real.* 2. Was so much skin and bones (Latin).

nonetheless looked to its master like a far better horse than Alexander's Bucephalus or the Babieca of the Cid.[3] He spent all of four days in trying to think up a name for his mount; for—so he told himself—seeing that it belonged to so famous and worthy a knight, there was no reason why it should not have a name of equal renown. The kind of name he wanted was one that would at once indicate what the nag had been before it came to belong to a knight-errant and what its present status was; for it stood to reason that, when the master's worldly condition changed, his horse also ought to have a famous, high-sounding appellation, one suited to the new order of things and the new profession that it was to follow.

After he in his memory and imagination had made up, struck out, and discarded many names, now adding to and now subtracting from the list, he finally hit upon "Rocinante," a name that impressed him as being sonorous and at the same time indicative of what the steed had been when it was but a hack, whereas now it was nothing other than the first and foremost of all the hacks[4] in the world.

Having found a name for his horse that pleased his fancy, he then desired to do as much for himself, and this required another week, and by the end of that period he had made up his mind that he was henceforth to be known as Don Quixote, which, as has been stated, has led the authors of this veracious history to assume that his real name must undoubtedly have been Quijada, and not Quesada as others would have it. But remembering that the valiant Amadis was not content to call himself that and nothing more, but added the name of his kingdom and fatherland that he might make it famous also, and thus came to take the name Amadis of Gaul, so our good knight chose to add his place of origin and become "Don Quixote de la Mancha"; for by this means, as he saw it, he was making very plain his lineage and was conferring honor upon his country by taking its name as his own.

And so, having polished up his armor and made the morion over into a closed helmet, and having given himself and his horse a name, he naturally found but one thing lacking still: he must seek out a lady of whom he could become enamored; for a knight-errant without a lady-love was like a tree without leaves or fruit, a body without a soul.

"If," he said to himself, "as a punishment for my sins or by a stroke of fortune I should come upon some giant hereabouts, a thing that very commonly happens to knights-errant, and if I should slay him in a hand-to-hand encounter or perhaps cut him in two, or, finally, if I should vanquish and subdue him, would it not be well to have someone to whom I may send him as a present, in order that he, if he is living, may come in, fall upon his knees in front of my sweet lady, and say in a humble and submissive tone of voice, 'I, lady, am the giant Caraculiambro, lord of the island Malindrania, who has been overcome in single combat by that knight who never can be praised enough, Don Quixote de la Mancha, the same who sent me to present myself before your Grace that your Highness may dispose of me as you see fit'?"

Oh, how our good knight reveled in this speech, and more than ever when he came to think of the name that he should give his lady! As the story goes, there was a very good-looking farm girl who lived near by, with whom he had

---

3. The chief (Spanish)—that is, Ruy Díaz, celebrated hero of *Poema del Cid* (twelfth century).　　4. In Spanish, *rocín*.

once been smitten, although it is generally believed that she never knew or suspected it. Her name was Aldonza Lorenzo, and it seemed to him that she was the one upon whom he should bestow the title of mistress of his thoughts. For her he wished a name that should not be incongruous with his own and that would convey the suggestion of a princess or a great lady; and, accordingly, he resolved to call her "Dulcinea del Toboso," she being a native of that place. A musical name to his ears, out of the ordinary and significant, like the others he had chosen for himself and his appurtenances.

CHAPTER 2

Which treats of the first sally that the ingenious Don Quixote made from his native heath.

Having, then, made all these preparations, he did not wish to lose any time in putting his plan into effect, for he could not but blame himself for what the world was losing by his delay, so many were the wrongs that were to be righted, the grievances to be redressed, the abuses to be done away with, and the duties to be performed. Accordingly, without informing anyone of his intention and without letting anyone see him, he set out one morning before daybreak on one of those very hot days in July. Donning all his armor, mounting Rocinante, adjusting his ill-contrived helmet, bracing his shield on his arm, and taking up his lance, he sallied forth by the back gate of his stable yard into the open countryside. It was with great contentment and joy that he saw how easily he had made a beginning toward the fulfillment of his desire.

No sooner was he out on the plain, however, than a terrible thought assailed him, one that all but caused him to abandon the enterprise he had undertaken. This occurred when he suddenly remembered that he had never formally been dubbed a knight, and so, in accordance with the law of knighthood, was not permitted to bear arms against one who had a right to that title. And even if he had been, as a novice knight he would have had to wear white armor, without any device on his shield, until he should have earned one by his exploits. These thoughts led him to waver in his purpose, but, madness prevailing over reason, he resolved to have himself knighted by the first person he met, as many others had done if what he had read in those books that he had at home was true. And so far as white armor was concerned, he would scour his own the first chance that offered until it shone whiter than any ermine. With this he became more tranquil and continued on his way, letting his horse take whatever path it chose, for he believed that therein lay the very essence of adventures.

And so we find our newly fledged adventurer jogging along and talking to himself. "Undoubtedly," he is saying, "in the days to come, when the true history of my famous deeds is published, the learned chronicler who records them, when he comes to describe my first sally so early in the morning, will put down something like this: 'No sooner had the rubicund Apollo spread over the face of the broad and spacious earth the gilded filaments of his beauteous locks, and no sooner had the little singing birds of painted plumage greeted with their sweet and mellifluous harmony the coming of the Dawn, who, leaving the soft couch of her jealous spouse, now showed herself to mortals at all the doors and balconies of the horizon that bounds La

Mancha—no sooner had this happened than the famous knight, Don Quixote de la Mancha, forsaking his own downy bed and mounting his famous
steed, Rocinante, fared forth and began riding over the ancient and famous
Campo de Montiel." '5

And this was the truth, for he was indeed riding over that stretch of plain.

"O happy age and happy century," he went on, "in which my famous
exploits shall be published, exploits worthy of being engraved in bronze,
sculptured in marble, and depicted in paintings for the benefit of posterity.
O wise magician, whoever you be, to whom shall fall the task of chronicling
this extraordinary history of mine! I beg of you not to forget my good Rocinante, eternal companion of my wayfarings and my wanderings."

Then, as though he really had been in love: "O Princess Dulcinea, lady of
this captive heart! Much wrong have you done me in thus sending me forth
with your reproaches and sternly commanding me not to appear in your
beauteous presence. O lady, deign to be mindful of this your subject who
endures so many woes for the love of you."

And so he went on, stringing together absurdities, all of a kind that his
books had taught him, imitating insofar as he was able the language of their
authors. He rode slowly, and the sun came up so swiftly and with so much
heat that it would have been sufficient to melt his brains if he had had any.
He had been on the road almost the entire day without anything happening
that is worthy of being set down here; and he was on the verge of despair,
for he wished to meet someone at once with whom he might try the valor of
his good right arm. Certain authors say that his first adventure was that of
Puerto Lápice, while others state that it was that of the windmills; but in
this particular instance I am in a position to affirm what I have read in the
annals of La Mancha; and that is to the effect that he went all that day until
nightfall, when he and his hack found themselves tired to death and famished. Gazing all around him to see if he could discover some castle or shepherd's hut where he might take shelter and attend to his pressing needs, he
caught sight of an inn not far off the road along which they were traveling,
and this to him was like a star guiding him not merely to the gates, but rather,
let us say, to the palace of redemption. Quickening his pace, he came up to
it just as night was falling.

By chance there stood in the doorway two lasses of the sort known as "of
the district"; they were on their way to Seville in the company of some mule
drivers who were spending the night in the inn. Now, everything that this
adventurer of ours thought, saw, or imagined seemed to him to be directly
out of one of the storybooks he had read, and so, when he caught sight of
the inn, it at once became a castle with its four turrets and its pinnacles of
gleaming silver, not to speak of the drawbridge and moat and all the other
things that are commonly supposed to go with a castle. As he rode up to it,
he accordingly reined in Rocinante and sat there waiting for a dwarf to
appear upon the battlements and blow his trumpet by way of announcing
the arrival of a knight. The dwarf, however, was slow in coming, and as
Rocinante was anxious to reach the stable, Don Quixote drew up to the door
of the hostelry and surveyed the two merry maidens, who to him were a pair
of beauteous damsels or gracious ladies taking their ease at the castle gate.

5. The scene of a battle in 1369.

And then a swineherd came along, engaged in rounding up his drove of hogs—for, without any apology, that is what they were. He gave a blast on his horn to bring them together, and this at once became for Don Quixote just what he wished it to be: some dwarf who was heralding his coming; and so it was with a vast deal of satisfaction that he presented himself before the ladies in question, who, upon beholding a man in full armor like this, with lance and buckler, were filled with fright and made as if to flee indoors. Realizing that they were afraid, Don Quixote raised his pasteboard visor and revealed his withered, dust-covered face.

"Do not flee, your Ladyships," he said to them in a courteous manner and gentle voice. "You need not fear that any wrong will be done you, for it is not in accordance with the order of knighthood which I profess to wrong anyone, much less such highborn damsels as your appearance shows you to be."

The girls looked at him, endeavoring to scan his face, which was half hidden by his ill-made visor. Never having heard women of their profession called damsels before, they were unable to restrain their laughter, at which Don Quixote took offense.

"Modesty," he observed, "well becomes those with the dower of beauty, and, moreover, laughter that has not good cause is a very foolish thing. But I do not say this to be discourteous or to hurt your feelings; my only desire is to serve you."

The ladies did not understand what he was talking about, but felt more than ever like laughing at our knight's unprepossessing figure. This increased his annoyance, and there is no telling what would have happened if at that moment the innkeeper had not come out. He was very fat and very peaceably inclined; but upon sighting this grotesque personage clad in bits of armor that were quite as oddly matched as were his bridle, lance, buckler, and corselet, mine host was not at all indisposed to join the lasses in their merriment. He was suspicious, however, of all this paraphernalia and decided that it would be better to keep a civil tongue in his head.

"If, Sir Knight," he said, "your Grace desires a lodging, aside from a bed—for there is none to be had in this inn—you will find all else that you may want in great abundance."

When Don Quixote saw how humble the governor of the castle was—for he took the innkeeper and his inn to be no less than that—he replied, "For me, Sir Castellan,[6] anything will do, since

> Arms are my only ornament,
> My only rest the fight, etc."

The landlord thought that the knight had called him a castellan because he took him for one of those worthies of Castile, whereas the truth was, he was an Andalusian from the beach of Sanlúcar, no less a thief than Cacus[7] himself, and as full of tricks as a student or a page boy.

"In that case," he said,

---

6. The Spanish, *castellano*, means both "castellan" and "Castilian."   7. In Roman mythology he stole some of the cattle of Hercules, concealing the theft by having them walk backward into his cave; he was finally discovered and slain.

> "Your bed will be the solid rock,
> Your sleep: to watch all night.

This being so, you may be assured of finding beneath this roof enough to keep you awake for a whole year, to say nothing of a single night."

With this, he went up to hold the stirrup for Don Quixote, who encountered much difficulty in dismounting, not having broken his fast all day long. The knight then directed his host to take good care of his steed, as it was the best piece of horseflesh in all the world. The innkeeper looked it over, and it did not impress him as being half as good as Don Quixote had said it was. Having stabled the animal, he came back to see what his guest would have and found the latter being relieved of his armor by the damsels, who by now had made their peace with the new arrival. They had already removed his breastplate and backpiece but had no idea how they were going to open his gorget or get his improvised helmet off. That piece of armor had been tied on with green ribbons which it would be necessary to cut, since the knots could not be undone, but he would not hear of this, and so spent all the rest of that night with his headpiece in place, which gave him the weirdest, most laughable appearance that could be imagined.

Don Quixote fancied that these wenches who were assisting him must surely be the chatelaine and other ladies of the castle, and so proceeded to address them very gracefully and with much wit:

> Never was knight so served
> By any noble dame
> As was Don Quixote
> When from his village he came,
> With damsels to wait on his every need
> While princesses cared for his hack . . .

"By hack," he explained, "is meant my steed Rocinante, for that is his name, and mine is Don Quixote de la Mancha. I had no intention of revealing my identity until my exploits done in your service should have made me known to you; but the necessity of adapting to present circumstances that old ballad of Lancelot has led to your becoming acquainted with it prematurely. However, the time will come when your Ladyships shall command and I will obey and with the valor of my good right arm show you how eager I am to serve you."

The young women were not used to listening to speeches like this and had not a word to say, but merely asked him if he desired to eat anything.

"I could eat a bite of something, yes," replied Don Quixote. "Indeed, I feel that a little food would go very nicely just now."

He thereupon learned that, since it was Friday, there was nothing to be had in all the inn except a few portions of codfish, which in Castile is called *abadejo,* in Andalusia *bacalao,* in some places *curadillo,* and elsewhere *truchuella* or small trout. Would his Grace, then, have some small trout, seeing that was all there was that they could offer him?

"If there are enough of them," said Don Quixote, "they will take the place of a trout, for it is all one to me whether I am given in change eight reales or one piece of eight. What is more, those small trout may be like veal, which is better than beef, or like kid, which is better than goat. But however that may be, bring them on at once, for the weight and burden of arms is not to be borne without inner sustenance."

Placing the table at the door of the hostelry, in the open air, they brought the guest a portion of badly soaked and worse cooked codfish and a piece of bread as black and moldy as the suit of armor that he wore. It was a mirth-provoking sight to see him eat, for he still had his helmet on with his visor fastened, which made it impossible for him to put anything into his mouth with his hands, and so it was necessary for one of the girls to feed him. As for giving him anything to drink, that would have been out of the question if the innkeeper had not hollowed out a reed, placing one end in Don Quixote's mouth while through the other end he poured the wine. All this the knight bore very patiently rather than have them cut the ribbons of his helmet.

At this point a gelder of pigs approached the inn, announcing his arrival with four or five blasts on his horn, all of which confirmed Don Quixote in the belief that this was indeed a famous castle, for what was this if not music that they were playing for him? The fish was trout, the bread was the finest, the wenches were ladies, and the innkeeper was the castellan. He was convinced that he had been right in his resolve to sally forth and roam the world at large, but there was one thing that still distressed him greatly, and that was the fact that he had not as yet been dubbed a knight; as he saw it, he could not legitimately engage in any adventure until he had received the order of knighthood.

CHAPTER 3

Of the amusing manner in which Don Quixote had himself dubbed a knight.

Wearied of his thoughts, Don Quixote lost no time over the scanty repast which the inn afforded him. When he had finished, he summoned the landlord and, taking him out to the stable, closed the doors and fell on his knees in front of him.

"Never, valiant knight," he said, "shall I arise from here until you have courteously granted me the boon I seek, one which will redound to your praise and to the good of the human race."

Seeing his guest at his feet and hearing him utter such words as these, the innkeeper could only stare at him in bewilderment, not knowing what to say or do. It was in vain that he entreated him to rise, for Don Quixote refused to do so until his request had been granted.

"I expected nothing less of your great magnificence, my lord," the latter then continued, "and so I may tell you that the boon I asked and which you have so generously conceded me is that tomorrow morning you dub me a knight. Until that time, in the chapel of this your castle, I will watch over my armor, and when morning comes, as I have said, that which I so desire shall then be done, in order that I may lawfully go to the four corners of the earth in quest of adventures and to succor the needy, which is the chivalrous duty of all knights-errant such as I who long to engage in deeds of high emprise."

The innkeeper, as we have said, was a sharp fellow. He already had a suspicion that his guest was not quite right in the head, and he was now convinced of it as he listened to such remarks as these. However, just for the sport of it, he determined to humor him; and so he went on to assure Don Quixote that he was fully justified in his request and that such a desire and purpose was only natural on the part of so distinguished a knight as his gallant bearing plainly showed him to be.

He himself, the landlord added, when he was a young man, had followed the same honorable calling. He had gone through various parts of the world seeking adventures, among the places he had visited being the Percheles of Málaga, the Isles of Riarán, the District of Seville, the Little Market Place of Segovia, the Olivera of Valencia, the Rondilla of Granada, the beach of Sanlúcar, the Horse Fountain of Cordova, the Small Taverns of Toledo,[8] and numerous other localities where his nimble feet and light fingers had found much exercise. He had done many wrongs, cheated many widows, ruined many maidens, and swindled not a few minors until he had finally come to be known in almost all the courts and tribunals that are to be found in the whole of Spain.

At last he had retired to his castle here, where he lived upon his own income and the property of others; and here it was that he received all knights-errant of whatever quality and condition, simply out of the great affection that he bore them and that they might share with him their possessions in payment of his good will. Unfortunately, in this castle there was no chapel where Don Quixote might keep watch over his arms, for the old chapel had been torn down to make way for a new one; but in case of necessity, he felt quite sure that such a vigil could be maintained anywhere, and for the present occasion the courtyard of the castle would do; and then in the morning, please God, the requisite ceremony could be performed and his guest be duly dubbed a knight, as much a knight as anyone ever was.

He then inquired if Don Quixote had any money on his person, and the latter replied that he had not a cent, for in all the storybooks he had never read of knights-errant carrying any. But the innkeeper told him he was mistaken on this point: supposing the authors of those stories had not set down the fact in black and white, that was because they did not deem it necessary to speak of things as indispensable as money and a clean shirt, and one was not to assume for that reason that those knights-errant of whom the books were so full did not have any. He looked upon it as an absolute certainty that they all had well-stuffed purses, that they might be prepared for any emergency; and they also carried shirts and a little box of ointment for healing the wounds that they received.

For when they had been wounded in combat on the plains and in desert places, there was not always someone at hand to treat them, unless they had some skilled enchanter for a friend who then would succor them, bringing to them through the air, upon a cloud, some damsel or dwarf bearing a vial of water of such virtue that one had but to taste a drop of it and at once his wounds were healed and he was as sound as if he had never received any.

But even if this was not the case, knights in times past saw to it that their squires were well provided with money and other necessities, such as lint and ointment for healing purposes; and if they had no squires—which happened very rarely—they themselves carried these objects in a pair of saddle-

8. All reputed to be haunts of robbers and rogues.

bags very cleverly attached to their horses' croups in such a manner as to be scarcely noticeable, as if they held something of greater importance than that, for among the knights-errant saddlebags as a rule were not favored. Accordingly, he would advise the novice before him, and inasmuch as the latter was soon to be his godson, he might even command him, that henceforth he should not go without money and a supply of those things that have been mentioned, as he would find that they came in useful at a time when he least expected it.

Don Quixote promised to follow his host's advice punctiliously; and so it was arranged that he should watch his armor in a large barnyard at one side of the inn. He gathered up all the pieces, placed them in a horse trough that stood near the well, and, bracing his shield on his arm, took up his lance and with stately demeanor began pacing up and down in front of the trough even as night was closing in.

The innkeeper informed his other guests of what was going on, of Don Quixote's vigil and his expectation of being dubbed a knight; and, marveling greatly at so extraordinary a variety of madness, they all went out to see for themselves and stood there watching from a distance. For a while the knight-to-be, with tranquil mien, would merely walk up and down; then, leaning on his lance, he would pause to survey his armor, gazing fixedly at it for a considerable length of time. As has been said, it was night now, but the brightness of the moon, which well might rival that of Him who lent it, was such that everything the novice knight did was plainly visible to all.

At this point one of the mule drivers who were stopping at the inn came out to water his drove, and in order to do this it was necessary to remove the armor from the trough.

As he saw the man approaching, Don Quixote cried out to him, "O bold knight, whoever you may be, who thus would dare to lay hands upon the accouterments of the most valiant man of arms that ever girded on a sword, look well what you do and desist if you do not wish to pay with your life for your insolence!"

The muleteer gave no heed to these words—it would have been better for his own sake had he done so—but, taking it up by the straps, tossed the armor some distance from him. When he beheld this, Don Quixote rolled his eyes heavenward and with his thoughts apparently upon his Dulcinea exclaimed, "Succor, O lady mine, this vassal heart in this my first encounter; let not your favor and protection fail me in the peril in which for the first time I now find myself."

With these and other similar words, he loosed his buckler, grasped his lance in both his hands, and let the mule driver have such a blow on the head that the man fell to the ground stunned; and had it been followed by another one, he would have had no need of a surgeon to treat him. Having done this, Don Quixote gathered up his armor and resumed his pacing up and down with the same calm manner as before. Not long afterward, without knowing what had happened—for the first muleteer was still lying there unconscious—another came out with the same intention of watering his mules, and he too was about to remove the armor from the trough when the knight, without saying a word or asking favor of anyone, once more adjusted his buckler and raised his lance, and if he did not break the second mule driver's head to bits, he made more than three pieces of it by dividing it into quarters. At the sound of the fracas everybody in the inn came running out, among them the innkeeper; whereupon Don Quixote again lifted his buckler and laid his hand on his sword.

"O lady of beauty," he said, "strength and vigor of this fainting heart of mine! Now is the time to turn the eyes of your greatness upon this captive knight of yours who must face so formidable an adventure."

By this time he had worked himself up to such a pitch of anger that if all the mule drivers in the world had attacked him he would not have taken one step backward. The comrades of the wounded men, seeing the plight those two were in, now began showering stones on Don Quixote, who shielded himself as best he could with his buckler, although he did not dare stir from the trough for fear of leaving his armor unprotected. The landlord, meanwhile, kept calling for them to stop, for he had told them that this was a madman who would be sure to go free even though he killed them all. The knight was shouting louder than ever, calling them knaves and traitors. As for the lord of the castle, who allowed knights-errant to be treated in this fashion, he was a lowborn villain, and if he, Don Quixote, had but received the order of knighthood, he would make him pay for his treachery.

"As for you others, vile and filthy rabble, I take no account of you; you may stone me or come forward and attack me all you like; you shall see what the reward of your folly and insolence will be."

He spoke so vigorously and was so undaunted in bearing as to strike terror in those who would assail him; and for this reason, and owing also to the persuasions of the innkeeper, they ceased stoning him. He then permitted them to carry away the wounded, and went back to watching his armor with the same tranquil, unconcerned air that he had previously displayed.

The landlord was none too well pleased with these mad pranks on the part of his guest and determined to confer upon him that accursed order of knighthood before something else happened. Going up to him, he begged Don Quixote's pardon for the insolence which, without his knowledge, had been shown the knight by those of low degree. They, however, had been well punished for their impudence. As he had said, there was no chapel in this castle, but for that which remained to be done there was no need of any. According to what he had read of the ceremonial of the order, there was nothing to this business of being dubbed a knight except a slap on the neck and one across the shoulder, and that could be performed in the middle of a field as well as anywhere else. All that was required was for the knight-to-be to keep watch over his armor for a couple of hours, and Don Quixote had been at it more than four. The latter believed all this and announced that he was ready to obey and get the matter over with as speedily as possible. Once dubbed a knight, if he were attacked one more time, he did not think that he would leave a single person in the castle alive, save such as he might command be spared, at the bidding of his host and out of respect to him.

Thus warned, and fearful that it might occur, the castellan brought out the book in which he had jotted down the hay and barley for which the mule drivers owed him, and, accompanied by a lad bearing the butt of a candle and the two aforesaid damsels, he came up to where Don Quixote stood and commanded him to kneel. Reading from the account book—as if he had been saying a prayer—he raised his hand and, with the knight's own sword, gave him a good thwack upon the neck and another lusty one upon the shoulder, muttering all the while between his teeth. He then directed one of the ladies to gird on Don Quixote's sword, which she did with much gravity and composure; for it was all they could do to keep from laughing at every point of the ceremony, but the thought of the knight's prowess which they had already witnessed was sufficient to restrain their mirth.

"May God give your Grace much good fortune," said the worthy lady as she attached the blade, "and prosper you in battle."

Don Quixote thereupon inquired her name, for he desired to know to whom it was he was indebted for the favor he had just received, that he might share with her some of the honor which his strong right arm was sure to bring him. She replied very humbly that her name was Tolosa and that she was the daughter of a shoemaker, a native of Toledo who lived in the stalls of Sancho Bicnaya.[9] To this the knight replied that she would do him a very great favor if from then on she would call herself Doña Tolosa, and she promised to do so. The other girl then helped him on with his spurs, and practically the same conversation was repeated. When asked her name, she stated that it was La Molinera and added that she was the daughter of a respectable miller of Antequera. Don Quixote likewise requested her to assume the "don" and become Doña Molinera and offered to render her further services and favors.

These unheard-of ceremonies having been dispatched in great haste, Don Quixote could scarcely wait to be astride his horse and sally forth on his quest for adventures. Saddling and mounting Rocinante, he embraced his host, thanking him for the favor of having dubbed him a knight and saying such strange things that it would be quite impossible to record them here. The innkeeper, who was only too glad to be rid of him, answered with a speech that was no less flowery, though somewhat shorter, and he did not so much as ask him for the price of a lodging, so glad was he to see him go.

CHAPTER 4

Of what happened to our knight when he sallied forth from the inn.

Day was dawning when Don Quixote left the inn, so well satisfied with himself, so gay, so exhilarated, that the very girths of his steed all but burst with joy. But remembering the advice which his host had given him concerning the stock of necessary provisions that he should carry with him, especially money and shirts, he decided to turn back home and supply himself with whatever he needed, and with a squire as well; he had in mind a farmer who was a neighbor of his, a poor man and the father of a family but very well suited to fulfill the duties of squire to a man of arms. With this thought in mind he guided Rocinante toward the village once more, and that animal, realizing that he was homeward bound, began stepping out at so lively a gait that it seemed as if his feet barely touched the ground.

The knight had not gone far when from a hedge on his right hand he heard the sound of faint moans as of someone in distress.

"Thanks be to Heaven," he at once exclaimed, "for the favor it has shown me by providing me so soon with an opportunity to fulfill the obligations that I owe to my profession, a chance to pluck the fruit of my worthy desires.

9. An old square in Toledo.

Those, undoubtedly, are the cries of someone in distress, who stands in need of my favor and assistance."

Turning Rocinante's head, he rode back to the place from which the cries appeared to be coming. Entering the wood, he had gone but a few paces when he saw a mare attached to an oak, while bound to another tree was a lad of fifteen or thereabouts, naked from the waist up. It was he who was uttering the cries, and not without reason, for there in front of him was a lusty farmer with a girdle who was giving him many lashes, each one accompanied by a reproof and a command, "Hold your tongue and keep your eyes open"; and the lad was saying, "I won't do it again, sir; by God's Passion, I won't do it again. I promise you that after this I'll take better care of the flock."

When he saw what was going on, Don Quixote was very angry. "Discourteous knight," he said, "it ill becomes you to strike one who is powerless to defend himself. Mount your steed and take your lance in hand"—for there was a lance leaning against the oak to which the mare was tied—"and I will show you what a coward you are."

The farmer, seeing before him this figure all clad in armor and brandishing a lance, decided that he was as good as done for. "Sir Knight," he said, speaking very mildly, "this lad that I am punishing here is my servant; he tends a flock of sheep which I have in these parts and he is so careless that every day one of them shows up missing. And when I punish him for his carelessness or his roguery, he says it is just because I am a miser and do not want to pay him the wages that I owe him, but I swear to God and upon my soul that he lies."

"It is you who lie, base lout," said Don Quixote, "and in my presence; and by the sun that gives us light, I am minded to run you through with this lance. Pay him and say no more about it, or else, by the God who rules us, I will make an end of you and annihilate you here and now. Release him at once."

The farmer hung his head and without a word untied his servant. Don Quixote then asked the boy how much has master owed him. For nine months' work, the lad told him, at seven reales the month. The knight did a little reckoning and found that this came to sixty-three reales; whereupon he ordered the farmer to pay over the money immediately, as he valued his life. The cowardly bumpkin replied that, facing death as he was and by the oath that he had sworn—he had not sworn any oath as yet—it did not amount to as much as that; for there were three pairs of shoes which he had given the lad that were to be deducted and taken into account, and a real for two blood-lettings when his servant was ill.

"That," said Don Quixote, "is all very well; but let the shoes and the blood-lettings go for the undeserved lashings which you have given him; if he has worn out the leather of the shoes that you paid for, you have taken the hide off his body, and if the barber let a little blood for him when he was sick,[1] you have done the same when he was well; and so far as that goes, he owes you nothing."

"But the trouble is, Sir Knight, that I have no money with me. Come along home with me, Andrés, and I will pay you real for real."

---

1. Barbers were also surgeons.

"I go home with him!" cried the lad. "Never in the world! No, sir, I would not even think of it; for once he has me alone he'll flay me like a St. Bartholomew."

"He will do nothing of the sort," said Don Quixote. "It is sufficient for me to command, and he out of respect will obey. Since he has sworn to me by the order of knighthood which he has received, I shall let him go free and I will guarantee that you will be paid."

"But look, your Grace," the lad remonstrated, "my master is no knight; he has never received any order of knighthood whatsoever. He is Juan Haldudo, a rich man and a resident of Quintanar."

"That makes little difference," declared Don Quixote, "for there may well be knights among the Haldudos, all the more so in view of the fact that every man is the son of his works."

"That is true enough," said Andrés, "but this master of mine—of what works is he the son, seeing that he refuses me the pay for my sweat and labor?"

"I do not refuse you, brother Andrés," said the farmer. "Do me the favor of coming with me, and I swear to you by all the orders of knighthood that there are in this world to pay you, as I have said, real for real, and perfumed at that."

"You can dispense with the perfume," said Don Quixote; "just give him the reales and I shall be satisfied. And see to it that you keep your oath, or by the one that I myself have sworn I shall return to seek you out and chastise you, and I shall find you though you be as well hidden as a lizard. In case you would like to know who it is that is giving you this command in order that you may feel the more obliged to comply with it, I may tell you that I am the valorous Don Quixote de la Mancha, righter of wrongs and injustices; and so, God be with you, and do not fail to do as you have promised, under that penalty that I have pronounced."

As he said this, he put spurs to Rocinante and was off. The farmer watched him go, and when he saw that Don Quixote was out of the wood and out of sight, he turned to his servant, Andrés.

"Come here, my son," he said. "I want to pay you what I owe you as that righter of wrongs has commanded me."

"Take my word for it," replied Andrés, "your Grace would do well to observe the command of that good knight—may he live a thousand years; for as he is valorous and a righteous judge, if you don't pay me then, by Rocque,[2] he will come back and do just what he said!"

"And I will give you my word as well," said the farmer; "but seeing that I am so fond of you, I wish to increase the debt, that I may owe you all the more." And with this he seized the lad's arm and bound him to the tree again and flogged him within an inch of his life. "There, Master Andrés, you may call on that righter of wrongs if you like and you will see whether or not he rights this one. I do not think I have quite finished with you yet, for I have a good mind to flay you alive as you feared."

Finally, however, he unbound him and told him he might go look for that judge of his to carry out the sentence that had been pronounced. Andrés left, rather down in the mouth, swearing that he would indeed go look for

2. The origin of this oath is unknown.

the brave Don Quixote de la Mancha; he would relate to him everything that had happened, point by point, and the farmer would have to pay for it seven times over. But for all that, he went away weeping, and his master stood laughing at him.

Such was the manner in which the valorous knight righted this particular wrong. Don Quixote was quite content with the way everything had turned out; it seemed to him that he had made a very fortunate and noble beginning with his deeds of chivalry, and he was very well satisfied with himself as he jogged along in the direction of his native village, talking to himself in a low voice all the while.

"Well may'st thou call thyself fortunate today, above all other women on earth, O fairest of the fair, Dulcinea del Toboso! Seeing that it has fallen to thy lot to hold subject and submissive to thine every wish and pleasure so valiant and renowned a knight as Don Quixote de la Mancha is and shall be, who, as everyone knows, yesterday received the order of knighthood and this day has righted the greatest wrong and grievance that injustice ever conceived or cruelty ever perpetrated, by snatching the lash from the hand of the merciless foeman who was so unreasonably flogging that tender child."

At this point he came to a road that forked off in four directions, and at once he thought of those crossroads where knights-errant would pause to consider which path they should take. By way of imitating them, he halted there for a while; and when he had given the subject much thought, he slackened Rocinante's rein and let the hack follow its inclination. The animal's first impulse was to make straight for its own stable. After they had gone a couple of miles or so Don Quixote caught sight of what appeared to be a great throng of people, who, as was afterward learned, were certain merchants of Toledo on their way to purchase silk at Murcia. There were six of them altogether with their sunshades, accompanied by four attendants on horseback and three mule drivers on foot.

No sooner had he sighted them than Don Quixote imagined that he was on the brink of some fresh adventure. He was eager to imitate those passages at arms of which he had read in his books, and here, so it seemed to him, was one made to order. And so, with bold and knightly bearing, he settled himself firmly in the stirrups, couched his lance, covered himself with his shield, and took up a position in the middle of the road, where he paused to wait for those other knights-errant (for such he took them to be) to come up to him. When they were near enough to see and hear plainly, Don Quixote raised his voice and made a haughty gesture.

"Let everyone," he cried, "stand where he is, unless everyone will confess that there is not in all the world a more beauteous damsel than the Empress of La Mancha, the peerless Dulcinea del Toboso."

Upon hearing these words and beholding the weird figure who uttered them, the merchants stopped short. From the knight's appearance and his speech they knew at once that they had to deal with a madman; but they were curious to know what was meant by that confession that was demanded of them, and one of their number who was somewhat of a jester and a very clever fellow raised his voice.

"Sir Knight," he said, "we do not know who this beauteous lady is of whom you speak. Show her to us, and if she is as beautiful as you say, then we will right willingly and without any compulsion confess the truth as you have asked of us."

"If I were to show her to you," replied Don Quixote, "what merit would there be in your confessing a truth so self-evident? The important thing is for you, without seeing her, to believe, confess, affirm, swear, and defend that truth. Otherwise, monstrous and arrogant creatures that you are, you shall do battle with me. Come on, then, one by one, as the order of knighthood prescribes; or all of you together, if you will have it so, as is the sorry custom of those of your breed. Come on, and I will await you here, for I am confident that my cause is just."

"Sir Knight," responded the merchant, "I beg your Grace, in the name of all the princes here present, in order that we may not have upon our consciences the burden of confessing a thing which we have never seen nor heard, and one, moreover, so prejudicial to the empresses and queens of Alcarria and Estremadura,[3] that your Grace will show us some portrait of this lady, even though it be no larger than a grain of wheat, for by the thread one comes to the ball of yarn; and with this we shall remain satisfied and assured, and your Grace will likewise be content and satisfied. The truth is, I believe that we are already so much of your way of thinking that though it should show her to be blind of one eye and distilling vermilion and brimstone from the other, nevertheless, to please your Grace, we would say in her behalf all that you desire.'

"She distills nothing of the sort, infamous rabble!" shouted Don Quixote, for his wrath was kindling now. "I tell you, she does not distill what you say at all, but amber and civet[4] wrapped in cotton; and she is neither one-eyed nor hunchbacked but straighter than a spindle that comes from Guadarrama. You shall pay for the great blasphemy which you have uttered against such a beauty as is my lady!"

Saying this, he came on with lowered lance against the one who had spoken, charging with such wrath and fury that if fortune had not caused Rocinante to stumble and fall in mid-career, things would have gone badly with the merchant and he would have paid for his insolent gibe. As it was, Don Quixote went rolling over the plain for some little distance, and when he tried to get to his feet, found that he was unable to do so, being too encumbered with his lance, shield, spurs, helmet, and the weight of that ancient suit of armor.

"Do not flee, cowardly ones," he cried even as he struggled to rise. "Stay, cravens, for it is not my fault but that of my steed that I am stretched out here."

One of the muleteers, who must have been an ill-natured lad, upon hearing the poor fallen knight speak so arrogantly, could not refrain from giving him an answer in the ribs. Going up to him, he took the knight's lance and broke it into bits, and then with a companion proceeded to belabor him so mercilessly that in spite of his armor they milled him like a hopper of wheat. The merchants called to them not to lay on so hard, saying that was enough and they should desist, but the mule driver by this time had warmed up to the sport and would not stop until he had vented his wrath, and, snatching up the broken pieces of the lance, he began hurling them at the wretched victim as he lay there on the ground. And through all this tempest of sticks that rained upon him Don Quixote never once closed his mouth nor ceased

---

3. Ironical, because both were known as particularly backward regions.   4. A musky substance used in perfume, imported from Africa in cotton packings.

threatening Heaven and earth and these ruffians, for such he took them to be, who were thus mishandling him.

Finally the lad grew tired, and the merchants went their way with a good story to tell about the poor fellow who had had such a cudgeling. Finding himself alone, the knight endeavored to see if he could rise; but if this was a feat that he could not accomplish when he was sound and whole, how was he to achieve it when he had been thrashed and pounded to a pulp? Yet nonetheless he considered himself fortunate; for as he saw it, misfortunes such as this were common to knights-errant, and he put all the blame upon his horse; and if he was unable to rise, that was because his body was so bruised and battered all over.

CHAPTER 5

In which is continued the narrative of the misfortune that befell our knight.

Seeing, then, that he was indeed unable to stir, he decided to fall back upon a favorite remedy of his, which was to think of some passage or other in his books; and as it happened, the one that he in his madness now recalled was the story of Baldwin and the Marquis of Mantua, when Carloto left the former wounded upon the mountainside,[5] a tale that is known to children, not unknown to young men, celebrated and believed in by the old, and, for all of that, not any truer than the miracles of Mohammed. Moreover, it impressed him as being especially suited to the straits in which he found himself; and, accordingly, with a great show of feeling, he began rolling and tossing on the ground as he feebly gasped out the lines which the wounded knight of the wood is supposed to have uttered:

> "Where art thou, lady mine,
> That thou dost not grieve for my woe?
> Either thou art disloyal,
> Or my grief thou dost not know."

He went on reciting the old ballad until he came to the following verses:

> "O noble Marquis of Mantua,
> My uncle and liege lord true!"

He had reached this point when down the road came a farmer of the same village, a neighbor of his, who had been to the mill with a load of wheat. Seeing a man lying there stretched out like that, he went up to him and inquired who he was and what was the trouble that caused him to utter such mournful complaints. Thinking that this must undoubtedly be his uncle, the Marquis of Mantua, Don Quixote did not answer but went on with his recitation of the ballad, giving an account of the Marquis' misfortunes and the amours of his wife and the emperor's son, exactly as the ballad has it.

The farmer was astounded at hearing all these absurdities, and after removing the knight's visor which had been battered to pieces by the blows it had received, the good man bathed the victim's face, only to discover, once the dust was off, that he knew him very well.

5. The allusion is to an old ballad about Charlemagne's son Charlot (Carloto) wounding Baldwin, nephew of the marquis of Mantua.

"Señor Quejana," he said (for such must have been Don Quixote's real name when he was in his right senses and before he had given up the life of a quiet country gentleman to become a knight-errant), "who is responsible for your Grace's being in such a plight as this?"

But the knight merely went on with his ballad in response to all the questions asked of him. Perceiving that it was impossible to obtain any information from him, the farmer as best he could relieved him of his breastplate and backpiece to see if he had any wounds, but there was no blood and no mark of any sort. He then tried to lift him from the ground, and with a great deal of effort finally managed to get him astride the ass, which appeared to be the easier mount for him. Gathering up the armor, including even the splinters from the lance, he made a bundle and tied it on Rocinante's back, and, taking the horse by the reins and the ass by the halter, he started out for the village. He was worried in his mind at hearing all the foolish things that Don Quixote said, and that individual himself was far from being at ease. Unable by reason of his bruises and his soreness to sit upright on the donkey, our knight-errant kept sighing to Heaven, which led the farmer to ask him once more what it was that ailed him.

It must have been the devil himself who caused him to remember those tales that seemed to fit his own case; for at this point he forgot all about Baldwin and recalled Abindarráez, and how the governor of Antequera, Rodrigo de Narváez, had taken him prisoner and carried him off captive to his castle. Accordingly, when the countryman turned to inquire how he was and what was troubling him, Don Quixote replied with the very same words and phrases that the captive Abindarráez used in answering Rodrigo, just as he had read in the story *Diana* of Jorge de Montemayor,[6] where it is all written down, applying them very aptly to the present circumstances as the farmer went along cursing his luck for having to listen to such a lot of nonsense. Realizing that his neighbor was quite mad, he made haste to reach the village that he might not have to be annoyed any longer by Don Quixote's tiresome harangue.

"Señor Don Rodrigo de Narváez," the knight was saying, "I may inform your Grace that this beautiful Jarifa of whom I speak is not the lovely Dulcinea del Toboso, in whose behalf I have done, am doing, and shall do the most famous deeds of chivalry that ever have been or will be seen in all the world."

"But, sir," replied the farmer, "sinner that I am, cannot your Grace see that I am not Don Rodrigo de Narváez nor the Marquis of Mantua, but Pedro Alonso, your neighbor? And your Grace is neither Baldwin nor Abindarráez but a respectable gentleman by the name of Señor Quijana."

"I know who I am," said Don Quixote, "and who I may be, if I choose: not only those I have mentioned but all the Twelve Peers of France and the Nine Worthies[7] as well; for the exploits of all of them together, or separately, cannot compare with mine."

With such talk as this they reached their destination just as night was

6. The reference is to the tale of the love of Abindarráez, a captive Moor, for the beautiful Jarifa, included in the second edition of Jorge de Montemayor's *Diana,* a pastoral romance.   7. In French medieval epics, the Twelve Peers (Roland, Oliver, and so on) were warriors all equal in rank, forming a kind of guard of honor around Charlemagne. In a tradition originating in France, the Nine Worthies consisted of three biblical, three classical, and three Christian figures (David, Hector, Alexander, Charlemagne, and so on).

falling; but the farmer decided to wait until it was a little darker in order that the badly battered gentleman might not be seen arriving in such a condition and mounted on an ass. When he thought the proper time had come, they entered the village and proceeded to Don Quixote's house, where they found everything in confusion. The curate and the barber were there, for they were great friends of the knight, and the housekeeper was speaking to them.

"Señor Licentiate Pero Pérez," she was saying, for that was the manner in which she addressed the curate, "what does your Grace think could have happened to my master? Three days now, and not a word of him, nor the hack, nor the buckler, nor the lance, nor the suit of armor. Ah, poor me! I am as certain as I am that I was born to die that it is those cursed books of chivalry he is always reading that have turned his head; for now that I recall, I have often heard him muttering to himself that he must become a knight-errant and go through the world in search of adventures. May such books as those be consigned to Satan and Barabbas,[8] for they have sent to perdition the finest mind in all La Mancha."

The niece was of the same opinion. "I may tell you, Señor Master Nicholas," she said, for that was the barber's name, "that many times my uncle would sit reading those impious tales of misadventure for two whole days and nights at a stretch; and when he was through, he would toss the book aside, lay his hand on his sword, and begin slashing at the walls. When he was completely exhausted, he would tell us that he had just killed four giants as big as castle towers, while the sweat that poured off him was blood from the wounds that he had received in battle. He would then drink a big jug of cold water, after which he would be very calm and peaceful, saying that the water was the most precious liquid which the wise Esquife, a great magician and his friend, had brought to him. But I blame myself for everything. I should have advised your Worships of my uncle's nonsensical actions so that you could have done something about it by burning those damnable books of his before things came to such a pass; for he has many that ought to be burned as if they were heretics."

"I agree with you," said the curate, "and before tomorrow's sun has set there shall be a public *auto da fé,* and those works shall be condemned to the flames that they may not lead some other who reads them to follow the example of my good friend."

Don Quixote and the farmer overheard all this, and it was then that the latter came to understand the nature of his neighbor's affliction.

"Open the door, your Worships," the good man cried. "Open for Sir Baldwin and the Marquis of Mantua, who comes badly wounded, and for Señor Abindarráez the Moor whom the valiant Rodrigo de Narváez, governor of Antequera, brings captive."

At the sound of his voice they all ran out, recognizing at once friend, master, and uncle, who as yet was unable to get down off the donkey's back. They all ran up to embrace him.

"Wait, all of you," said Don Quixote, "for I am sorely wounded through fault of my steed. Bear me to my couch and summon, if it be possible, the wise Urganda to treat and care for my wounds."

---

8. The thief whose release, rather than that of Jesus, the crowd requested when Pilate, conforming to Passover custom, was ready to have one prisoner set free.

"There!" exclaimed the housekeeper. "Plague take it! Did not my heart tell me right as to which foot my master limped on? To bed with your Grace at once, and we will take care of you without sending for that Urganda of yours. A curse, I say, and a hundred other curses, on those books of chivalry that have brought your Grace to this."

And so they carried him off to bed, but when they went to look for his wounds, they found none at all. He told them it was all the result of a great fall he had taken with Rocinante, his horse, while engaged in combating ten giants, the hugest and most insolent that were ever heard of in all the world.

"Tut, tut," said the curate. "So there are giants in the dance now, are there? Then, by the sign of the cross, I'll have them burned before nightfall tomorrow."

They had a thousand questions to put to Don Quixote, but his only answer was that they should give him something to eat and let him sleep, for that was the most important thing of all; so they humored him in this. The curate then interrogated the farmer at great length concerning the conversation he had had with his neighbor. The peasant told him everything, all the absurd things their friend had said when he found him lying there and afterward on the way home, all of which made the licentiate more anxious than ever to do what he did the following day,[9] when he summoned Master Nicholas and went with him to Don Quixote's house.

[*Fighting the Windmills and a Choleric Biscayan*]

CHAPTER 7

Of the second sally of our good knight, Don Quixote de la Mancha.

* * * After that he remained at home very tranquilly for a couple of weeks, without giving sign of any desire to repeat his former madness. During that time he had the most pleasant conversations with his two old friends, the curate and the barber, on the point he had raised to the effect that what the world needed most was knights-errant and a revival of chivalry. The curate would occasionally contradict him and again would give in, for it was only by means of this artifice that he could carry on a conversation with him at all.

In the meanwhile Don Quixote was bringing his powers of persuasion to bear upon a farmer who lived near by, a good man—if this title may be applied to one who is poor—but with very few wits in his head. The short of it is, by pleas and promises, he got the hapless rustic to agree to ride forth with him and serve him as his squire. Among other things, Don Quixote told him that he ought to be more than willing to go, because no telling what adventure might occur which would win them an island, and then he (the farmer) would be left to be the governor of it. As a result of these and other similar assurances, Sancho Panza forsook his wife and children and consented to take upon himself the duties of squire to his neighbor.

Next, Don Quixote set out to raise some money, and by selling this thing and pawning that and getting the worst of the bargain always, he finally scraped together a reasonable amount. He also asked a friend of his for the loan of a buckler and patched up his broken helmet as well as he could. He

9. He and the barber burned most of Don Quixote's library.

advised his squire, Sancho, of the day and hour when they were to take to the road and told him to see to laying in a supply of those things that were most necessary, and, above all, not to forget the saddlebags. Sancho replied that he would see to all this and added that he was also thinking of taking along with him a very good ass that he had, as he was not much used to going on foot.

With regard to the ass, Don Quixote had to do a little thinking, trying to recall if any knight-errant had ever had a squire thus asininely mounted. He could not think of any, but nevertheless he decided to take Sancho with the intention of providing him with a nobler steed as soon as occasion offered; he had but to appropriate the horse of the first discourteous knight he met. Having furnished himself with shirts and all the other things that the innkeeper had recommended, he and Panza rode forth one night unseen by anyone and without taking leave of wife and children, housekeeper or niece. They went so far that by the time morning came they were safe from discovery had a hunt been started for them.

Mounted on his ass, Sancho Panza rode along like a patriarch, with saddlebags and flask, his mind set upon becoming governor of that island that his master had promised him. Don Quixote determined to take the same route and road over the Campo de Montiel that he had followed on his first journey; but he was not so uncomfortable this time, for it was early morning and the sun's rays fell upon them slantingly and accordingly did not tire them too much.

"Look, Sir Knight-errant," said Sancho, "your Grace should not forget that island you promised me; for no matter how big it is, I'll be able to govern it right enough."

"I would have you know, friend Sancho Panza," replied Don Quixote, "that among the knights-errant of old it was a very common custom to make their squires governors of the islands or the kingdoms that they won, and I am resolved that in my case so pleasing a usage shall not fall into desuetude. I even mean to go them one better; for they very often, perhaps most of the time, waited until their squires were old men who had had their fill of serving their masters during bad days and worse nights, whereupon they would give them the title of count, or marquis at most, of some valley or province more or less. But if you live and I live, it well may be that within a week I shall win some kingdom with others dependent upon it, and it will be the easiest thing in the world to crown you king of one of them. You need not marvel at this, for all sorts of unforeseen things happen to knights like me, and I may readily be able to give you even more than I have promised."

"In that case," said Sancho Panza, "if by one of those miracles of which your Grace was speaking I should become king, I would certainly send for Juana Gutiérrez, my old lady, to come and be my queen, and the young ones could be infantes."

"There is no doubt about it," Don Quixote assured him.

"Well, I doubt it," said Sancho, "for I think that even if God were to rain kingdoms upon the earth, no crown would sit well on the head of Mari Gutiérrez,[1] for I am telling you, sir, as a queen she is not worth two maravedis.[2] She would do better as a countess, God help her."

"Leave everything to God, Sancho," said Don Quixote, "and he will give

---

1. Sancho's wife, Juana Gutiérrez.   2. Coin worth one–thirty-fourth of a *real*.

you whatever is most fitting; but I trust you will not be so pusillanimous as to be content with anything less than the title of viceroy."

"That I will not," said Sancho Panza, "especially seeing that I have in your Grace so illustrious a master who can give me all that is suitable to me and all that I can manage."

CHAPTER 8

Of the good fortune which the valorous Don Quixote had in the terrifying and never-before-imagined adventure of the windmills, along with other events that deserve to be suitably recorded.

At this point they caught sight of thirty or forty windmills which were standing on the plain there, and no sooner had Don Quixote laid eyes upon them than he turned to his squire and said, "Fortune is guiding our affairs better than we could have wished; for you see there before you, friend Sancho Panza, some thirty or more lawless giants with whom I mean to do battle. I shall deprive them of their lives, and with the spoils from this encounter we shall begin to enrich ourselves; for this is righteous warfare, and it is a great service to God to remove so accursed a breed from the face of the earth."

"What giants?" said Sancho Panza.

"Those that you see there," replied his master, "those with the long arms some of which are as much as two leagues in length."

"But look, your Grace, those are not giants but windmills, and what appear to be arms are their wings which, when whirled in the breeze, cause the millstone to go."

"It is plain to be seen," said Don Quixote, "that you have had little experience in this matter of adventures. If you are afraid, go off to one side and say your prayers while I am engaging them in fierce, unequal combat."

Saying this, he gave spurs to his steed Rocinante, without paying any heed to Sancho's warning that these were truly windmills and not giants that he was riding forth to attack. Nor even when he was close upon them did he perceive what they really were, but shouted at the top of his lungs, "Do not seek to flee, cowards and vile creatures that you are, for it is but a single knight with whom you have to deal!"

At that moment a little wind came up and the big wings began turning.

"Though you flourish as many arms as did the giant Briareus,"[3] said Don Quixote when he perceived this, "you still shall have to answer to me."

He thereupon commended himself with all his heart to his lady Dulcinea, beseeching her to succor him in this peril; and, being well covered with his shield and with his lance at rest, he bore down upon them at a full gallop and fell upon the first mill that stood in his way, giving a thrust at the wing, which was whirling at such a speed that his lance was broken into bits and both horse and horseman went rolling over the plain, very much battered indeed. Sancho upon his donkey came hurrying to his master's assistance as fast as he could, but when he reached the spot, the knight was unable to move, so great was the shock with which he and Rocinante had hit the ground.

"God help us!" exclaimed Sancho, "did I not tell your Grace to look well,

3. Mythological giant with a hundred arms.

that those were nothing but windmills, a fact which no one could fail to see unless he had other mills of the same sort in his head?"

"Be quiet, friend Sancho," said Don Quixote. "Such are the fortunes of war, which more than any other are subject to constant change. What is more, when I come to think of it, I am sure that this must be the work of that magician Frestón, the one who robbed me of my study and my books,[4] and who has thus changed the giants into windmills in order to deprive me of the glory of overcoming them, so great is the enmity that he bears me; but in the end his evil arts shall not prevail against this trusty sword of mine."

"May God's will be done," was Sancho Panza's response. And with the aid of his squire the knight was once more mounted on Rocinante, who stood there with one shoulder half out of joint. And so, speaking of the adventure that had just befallen them, they continued along the Puerto Lápice highway; for there, Don Quixote said, they could not fail to find many and varied adventures, this being a much traveled thoroughfare. The only thing was, the knight was exceedingly downcast over the loss of his lance.

"I remember," he said to his squire, "having read of a Spanish knight by the name of Diego Pérez de Vargas, who, having broken his sword in battle, tore from an oak a heavy bough or branch and with it did such feats of valor that day, and pounded so many Moors, that he came to be known as Machuca,[5] and he and his descendants from that day forth have been called Vargas y Machuca. I tell you this because I too intend to provide myself with just such a bough as the one he wielded, and with it I propose to do such exploits that you shall deem yourself fortunate to have been found worthy to come with me and behold and witness things that are almost beyond belief."

"God's will be done," said Sancho. "I believe everything that your Grace says; but straighten yourself up in the saddle a little, for you seem to be slipping down on one side, owing, no doubt, to the shaking-up that you received in your fall."

"Ah, that is the truth," replied Don Quixote, "and if I do not speak of my sufferings, it is for the reason that it is not permitted knights-errant to complain of any wound whatsoever, even though their bowels may be dropping out."

"If that is the way it is," said Sancho, "I have nothing more to say; but, God knows, it would suit me better if your Grace did complain when something hurts him. I can assure you that I mean to do so, over the least little thing that ails me—that is, unless the same rule applies to squires as well."

Don Quixote laughed long and heartily over Sancho's simplicity, telling him that he might complain as much as he liked and where and when he liked, whether he had good cause or not; for he had read nothing to the contrary in the ordinances of chivalry. Sancho then called his master's attention to the fact that it was time to eat. The knight replied that he himself had no need of food at the moment, but his squire might eat whenever he chose. Having been granted this permission, Sancho seated himself as best he could upon his beast, and, taking out from his saddlebags the provisions that he had stored there, he rode along leisurely behind his master, munch-

4. Don Quixote had promptly attributed the ruin of his library to magical intervention (see n. 9. p. 1989). 5. "The Crusher," the hero of a folk ballad.

ing his victuals and taking a good, hearty swig now and then at the leather flask in a manner that might well have caused the biggest-bellied tavern-keeper of Málaga to envy him. Between draughts he gave not so much as a thought to any promise that his master might have made him, nor did he look upon it as any hardship, but rather as good sport, to go in quest of adventures however hazardous they might be.

The short of the matter is, they spent the night under some trees, from one of which Don Quixote tore off a withered bough to serve him as a lance, placing it in the lance head from which he had removed the broken one. He did not sleep all night long for thinking of his lady Dulcinea; for this was in accordance with what he had read in his books, of men of arms in the forest or desert places who kept a wakeful vigil, sustained by the memory of their ladies fair. Not so with Sancho, whose stomach was full, and not with chicory water. He fell into a dreamless slumber, and had not his master called him, he would not have been awakened either by the rays of the sun in his face or by the many birds who greeted the coming of the new day with their merry song.

Upon arising, he had another go at the flask, finding it somewhat more flaccid then it had been the night before, a circumstance which grieved his heart, for he could not see that they were on the way to remedying the deficiency within any very short space of time. Don Quixote did not wish any breakfast; for, as has been said, he was in the habit of nourishing himself on savorous memories. They then set out once more along the road to Puerto Lápice, and around three in the afternoon they came in sight of the pass that bears that name.

"There," said Don Quixote as his eyes fell upon it, "we may plunge our arms up to the elbow in what are known as adventures. But I must warn you that even though you see me in the greatest peril in the world, you are not to lay hand upon your sword to defend me, unless it be that those who attack me are rabble and men of low degree, in which case you may very well come to my aid; but if they be gentlemen, it is in no wise permitted by the laws of chivalry that you should assist me until you yourself shall have been dubbed a knight."

"Most certainly, sir," replied Sancho, "your Grace shall be very well obeyed in this; all the more so for the reason that I myself am of a peaceful disposition and not fond of meddling in the quarrels and feuds of others. However, when it comes to protecting my own person, I shall not take account of those laws of which you speak, seeing that all laws, human and divine, permit each one to defend himself whenever he is attacked."

"I am willing to grant you that," assented Don Quixote, "but in this matter of defending me against gentlemen you must restrain your natural impulses."

"I promise you I shall do so," said Sancho. "I will observe this precept as I would the Sabbath day."

As they were conversing in this manner, there appeared in the road in front of them two friars of the Order of St. Benedict, mounted upon dromedaries—for the she-mules they rode were certainly no smaller than that. The friars wore travelers' spectacles and carried sunshades, and behind them came a coach accompanied by four or five men on horseback and a couple of muleteers on foot. In the coach, as was afterwards learned, was a lady of Biscay, on her way to Seville to bid farewell to her husband, who had been appointed to some high post in the Indies. The religious were not of her company although they were going by the same road.

The instant Don Quixote laid eyes upon them he turned to his squire. "Either I am mistaken or this is going to be the most famous adventure that ever was seen; for those black-clad figures that you behold must be, and without any doubt are, certain enchanters who are bearing with them a captive princess in that coach, and I must do all I can to right this wrong."

"It will be worse than the windmills," declared Sancho. "Look you, sir, those are Benedictine friars and the coach must be that of some travelers. Mark well what I say and what you do, lest the devil lead you astray."

"I have already told you, Sancho," replied Don Quixote, "that you know little where the subject of adventures is concerned. What I am saying to you is the truth, as you shall now see."

With this, he rode forward and took up a position in the middle of the road along which the friars were coming, and as soon as they appeared to be within earshot he cried out to them in a loud voice, "O devilish and monstrous beings, set free at once the highborn princesses whom you bear captive in that coach, or else prepare at once to meet your death as the just punishment of your evil deeds."

The friars drew rein and sat there in astonishment, marveling as much at Don Quixote's appearance as at the words he spoke. "Sir Knight," they answered him, "we are neither devilish nor monstrous but religious of the Order of St. Benedict who are merely going our way. We know nothing of those who are in that coach, nor of any captive princesses either."

"Soft words," said Don Quixote, "have no effect on me. I know you for what you are, lying rabble!" And without waiting for any further parley he gave spur to Rocinante and, with lowered lance, bore down upon the first friar with such fury and intrepidity that, had not the fellow tumbled from his mule of his own accord, he would have been hurled to the ground and either killed or badly wounded. The second religious, seeing how his companion had been treated, dug his legs into his she-mule's flanks and scurried away over the countryside faster than the wind.

Seeing the friar upon the ground, Sancho Panza slipped lightly from his mount and, falling upon him, began stripping him of his habit. The two mule drivers accompanying the religious thereupon came running up and asked Sancho why he was doing this. The latter replied that the friar's garments belonged to him as legitimate spoils of the battle that his master Don Quixote had just won. The muleteers, however, were lads with no sense of humor, nor did they know what all this talk of spoils and battles was about; but, perceiving that Don Quixote had ridden off to one side to converse with those inside the coach, they pounced upon Sancho, threw him to the ground, and proceeded to pull out the hair of his beard and kick him to a pulp, after which they went off and left him stretched out there, bereft at once of breath and sense.

Without losing any time, they then assisted the friar to remount. The good brother was trembling all over from fright, and there was not a speck of color in his face, but when he found himself in the saddle once more, he quickly spurred his beast to where his companion, at some little distance, sat watching and waiting to see what the result of the encounter would be. Having no curiosity as to the final outcome of the fray, the two of them now resumed their journey, making more signs of the cross than the devil would be able to carry upon his back.

Meanwhile Don Quixote, as we have said, was speaking to the lady in the coach.

"Your beauty, my lady, may now dispose of your person as best may please you, for the arrogance of your abductors lies upon the ground, overthrown by this good arm of mine; and in order that you may not pine to know the name of your liberator, I may inform you that I am Don Quixote de la Mancha, knight-errant and adventurer and captive of the peerless and beauteous Doña Dulcinea del Toboso. In payment of the favor which you have received from me, I ask nothing other than that you return to El Toboso and on my behalf pay your respects to this lady, telling her that it was I who set you free."

One of the squires accompanying those in the coach, a Biscayan,[6] was listening to Don Quixote's words, and when he saw that the knight did not propose to let the coach proceed upon its way but was bent upon having it turn back to El Toboso, he promptly went up to him, seized his lance, and said to him in bad Castilian and worse Biscayan, "Go, *caballero,* and bad luck go with you; for by the God that created me, if you do not let this coach pass, me kill you or me no Biscayan."

Don Quixote heard him attentively enough and answered him very mildly, "If you were a *caballero,*[7] which you are not, I should already have chastised you, wretched creature, for your foolhardiness and your impudence."

"Me no *caballero.*" cried the Biscayan "Me swear to God, you lie like a Christian. If you will but lay aside your lance and unsheath your sword, you will soon see that you are carrying water to the cat![8] Biscayan on land, gentleman at sea, but a gentleman in spite of the devil, and you lie if you say otherwise."

" 'You shall see as to that presently,' said Agrajes,"[9] Don Quixote quoted. He cast his lance to the earth, drew his sword, and, taking his buckler on his arm, attacked the Biscayan with intent to slay him. The latter, when he saw his adversary approaching, would have liked to dismount from his mule, for she was one of the worthless sort that are let for hire and he had no confidence in her; but there was no time for this, and so he had no choice but to draw his own sword in turn and make the best of it. However, he was near enough to the coach to be able to snatch a cushion from it to serve him as a shield; and then they fell upon each other as though they were mortal enemies. The rest of those present sought to make peace between them but did not succeed, for the Biscayan with his disjointed phrases kept muttering that if they did not let him finish the battle then he himself would have to kill his mistress and anyone else who tried to stop him.

The lady inside the carriage, amazed by it all and trembling at what she saw, directed her coachman to drive on a little way; and there from a distance she watched the deadly combat, in the course of which the Biscayan came down with a great blow on Don Quixote's shoulder, over the top of the latter's shield, and had not the knight been clad in armor, it would have split him to the waist.

6. From the Basque region.   7. Knight, gentleman (Spanish).   8. An inversion of a proverbial phrase: "carrying the cat to the water."   9. A violent character in the romance *Amadis de Gaul.* His challenging phrase is the conventional opener of a fight.

Feeling the weight of this blow, Don Quixote cried out, "O lady of my soul, Dulcinea, flower of beauty, succor this your champion who out of gratitude for your many favors finds himself in so perilous a plight!" To utter these words, lay hold of his sword, cover himself with his buckler, and attack the Biscayan was but the work of a moment; for he was now resolved to risk everything upon a single stroke.

As he saw Don Quixote approaching with so dauntless a bearing, the Biscayan was well aware of his adversary's courage and forthwith determined to imitate the example thus set him. He kept himself protected with his cushion, but he was unable to get his she-mule to budge to one side or the other, for the beast, out of sheer exhaustion and being, moreover, unused to such childish play, was incapable of taking a single step. And so, then, as has been stated, Don Quixote was approaching the wary Biscayan, his sword raised on high and with the firm resolve of cleaving his enemy in two; and the Biscayan was awaiting the knight in the same posture, cushion in front of him and with uplifted sword. All the bystanders were trembling with suspense at what would happen as a result of the terrible blows that were threatened, and the lady in the coach and her maids were making a thousand vows and offerings to all the images and shrines in Spain, praying that God would save them all and the lady's squire from this great peril that confronted them.

But the unfortunate part of the matter is that at this very point the author of the history breaks off and leaves the battle pending, excusing himself upon the ground that he has been unable to find anything else in writing concerning the exploits of Don Quixote beyond those already set forth. It is true, on the other hand, that the second author[1] of this work could not bring himself to believe that so unusual a chronicle would have been consigned to oblivion, nor that the learned ones of La Mancha were possessed of so little curiosity as not to be able to discover in their archives or registry offices certain papers that have to do with this famous knight. Being convinced of this, he did not despair of coming upon the end of this pleasing story. * * *

CHAPTER 9

In which is concluded and brought to an end the stupendous battle between the gallant Biscayan and the valiant Knight of La Mancha.

* * * We left the valorous Biscayan and the famous Don Quixote with swords unsheathed and raised aloft, about to let fall furious slashing blows which, had they been delivered fairly and squarely, would at the very least have split them in two and laid them wide open from top to bottom like a pomegranate; and it was at this doubtful point that the pleasing chronicle came to a halt and broke off, without the author's informing us as to where the rest of it might be found.

I was deeply grieved by such a circumstance, and the pleasure I had had in reading so slight a portion was turned into annoyance as I thought of how difficult it would be to come upon the greater part which it seemed to me must still be missing. It appeared impossible and contrary to all good precedent that so worthy a knight should not have had some scribe to take upon

---

1. Cervantes himself, adopting here—with tongue in cheek—a device used in the romances of chivalry to create suspense.

himself the task of writing an account of these unheard-of exploits; for that was something that had happened to none of the knights-errant who, as the saying has it, had gone forth in quest of adventures, seeing that each of them had one or two chroniclers, as if ready at hand, who not only had set down their deeds, but had depicted their most trivial thoughts and amiable weaknesses, however well concealed they might be. The good knight of La Mancha surely could not have been so unfortunate as to have lacked what Platir and others like him had in abundance. And so I could not bring myself to believe that this gallant history could have remained thus lopped off and mutilated, and I could not but lay the blame upon the malignity of time, that devourer and consumer of all things, which must either have consumed it or kept it hidden.

On the other hand, I reflected that inasmuch as among the knight's books had been found such modern works as *The Disenchantments of Jealousy* and *The Nymphs and Shepherds of Henares,* his story likewise must be modern, and that even though it might not have been written down, it must remain in the memory of the good folk of his village and the surrounding ones. This thought left me somewhat confused and more than ever desirous of knowing the real and true story, the whole story, of the life and wondrous deeds of our famous Spaniard, Don Quixote, light and mirror of the chivalry of La Mancha, the first in our age and in these calamitous times to devote himself to the hardships and exercises of knight-errantry and to go about righting wrongs, succoring widows, and protecting damsels—damsels such as those who, mounted upon their palfreys and with riding-whip in hand, in full possession of their virginity, were in the habit of going from mountain to mountain and from valley to valley; for unless there were some villain, some rustic with an ax and hood, or some monstrous giant to force them, there were in times past maiden ladies who at the end of eighty years, during all which time they had not slept for a single day beneath a roof, would go to their graves as virginal as when their mothers had borne them.

If I speak of these things, it is for the reason that in this and in all other respects our gallant Quixote is deserving of constant memory and praise, and even I am not to be denied my share of it for my diligence and the labor to which I put myself in searching out the conclusion of this agreeable narrative; although if heaven, luck, and circumstance had not aided me, the world would have had to do without the pleasure and the pastime which anyone may enjoy who will read this work attentively for an hour or two. The manner in which it came about was as follows:

I was standing one day in the Alcaná, or market place, of Toledo when a lad came up to sell some old notebooks and other papers to a silk weaver who was there. As I am extremely fond of reading anything, even though it be but the scraps of paper in the streets, I followed my natural inclination and took one of the books, whereupon I at once perceived that it was written in characters which I recognized as Arabic. I recognized them, but reading them was another thing; and so I began looking around to see if there was any Spanish-speaking Moor near by who would be able to read them for me. It was not very hard to find such an interpreter, nor would it have been even if the tongue in question had been an older and a better one.[2] To make a

2. I.e., Hebrew.

long story short, chance brought a fellow my way; and when I told him what it was I wished and placed the book in his hands, he opened it in the middle and began reading and at once fell to laughing. When I asked him what the cause of his laughter was, he replied that it was a note which had been written in the margin.

I besought him to tell me the content of the note, and he, laughing still, went on, "As I told you, it is something in the margin here: 'This Dulcinea del Toboso, so often referred to, is said to have been the best hand at salting pigs of any woman in all La Mancha.'"

No sooner had I heard the name Dulcinea del Toboso than I was astonished and held in suspense, for at once the thought occurred to me that those notebooks must contain the history of Don Quixote. With this in mind I urged him to read me the title, and he proceeded to do so, turning the Arabic into Castilian upon the spot: *History of Don Quixote de la Mancha, Written by Cid Hamete Benengeli*[3] Arabic Historian. It was all I could do to conceal my satisfaction and, snatching them from the silk weaver, I bought from the lad all the papers and notebooks that he had for half a real; but if he had known or suspected how very much I wanted them, he might well have had more than six reales for them.

The Moor and I then betook ourselves to the cathedral cloister, where I requested him to translate for me into the Castilian tongue all the books that had to do with Don Quixote, adding nothing and subtracting nothing; and I offered him whatever payment he desired. He was content with two arrobas of raisins and two fanegas[4] of wheat and promised to translate them well and faithfully and with all dispatch. However, in order to facilitate matters, and also because I did not wish to let such a find as this out of my hands, I took the fellow home with me, where in a little more than a month and a half he translated the whole of the work just as you will find it set down here.

In the first of the books there was a very lifelike picture of the battle between Don Quixote and the Biscayan, the two being in precisely the same posture as described in the history, their swords upraised, the one covered by his buckler, the other with his cushion. As for the Biscayan's mule, you could see at the distance of a crossbow shot that it was one for hire. Beneath the Biscayan there was a rubric which read: "Don Sancho de Azpeitia," which must undoubtedly have been his name; while beneath the feet of Rocinante was another inscription: "Don Quixote." Rocinante was marvelously portrayed: so long and lank, so lean and flabby, so extremely consumptive-looking that one could well understand the justness and propriety with which the name of "hack" had been bestowed upon him.

Alongside Rocinante stood Sancho Panza, holding the halter of his ass, and below was the legend: "Sancho Zancas." The picture showed him with a big belly, a short body and long shanks, and that must have been where he got the names of Panza y Zancas[5] by which he is a number of times called in the course of the history. There are other small details that might be mentioned, but they are of little importance and have nothing to do with the truth of the story—and no story is bad so long as it is true.

If there is any objection to be raised against the veracity of the present

---

3. Citing some ancient chronicle as the author's source and authority is very much in the tradition of the romances. *Benengeli:* eggplant (Arabic).   4. About fifty pounds. *Two arrobas:* three bushels.   5. Paunch and Shanks (Spanish).

one, it can be only that the author was an Arab, and that nation is known for its lying propensities; but even though they be our enemies, it may readily be understood that they would more likely have detracted from, rather than added to, the chronicle. So it seems to me, at any rate; for whenever he might and should deploy the resources of his pen in praise of so worthy a knight, the author appears to take pains to pass over the matter in silence; all of which in my opinion is ill done and ill conceived, for it should be the duty of historians to be exact, truthful, and dispassionate, and neither interest nor fear nor rancor nor affection should swerve them from the path of truth, whose mother is history, rival of time, depository of deeds, witness of the past, exemplar and adviser to the present, and the future's counselor. In this work, I am sure, will be found all that could be desired in the way of pleasant reading; and if it is lacking in any way, I maintain that this is the fault of that hound of an author rather than of the subject.

But to come to the point, the second part, according to the translation, began as follows:

As the two valorous and enraged combatants stood there, swords upraised and poised on high, it seemed from their bold mien as if they must surely be threatening heaven, earth, and hell itself. The first to let fall a blow was the choleric Biscayan, and he came down with such force and fury that, had not his sword been deflected in mid-air, that single stroke would have sufficed to put an end to this fearful combat and to all our knight's adventures at the same time; but fortune, which was reserving him for greater things, turned aside his adversary's blade in such a manner that, even though it fell upon his left shoulder, it did him no other damage than to strip him completely of his armor on that side, carrying with it a good part of his helmet along with half an ear, the headpiece clattering to the ground with a dreadful din, leaving its wearer in a sorry state.

Heaven help me! Who could properly describe the rage that now entered the heart of our hero of La Mancha as he saw himself treated in this fashion? It may merely be said that he once more reared himself in the stirrups, laid hold of his sword with both hands, and dealt the Biscayan such a blow, over the cushion and upon the head, that, even so good a defense proving useless, it was as if a mountain had fallen upon his enemy. The latter now began bleeding through the mouth, nose, and ears; he seemed about to fall from his mule, and would have fallen, no doubt, if he had not grasped the beast about the neck, but at that moment his feet slipped from the stirrups and his arms let go, and the mule, frightened by the terrible blow, began running across the plain, hurling its rider to the earth with a few quick plunges.

Don Quixote stood watching all this very calmly. When he saw his enemy fall, he leaped from his horse, ran over very nimbly, and thrust the point of his sword into the Biscayan's eyes, calling upon him at the same time to surrender or otherwise he would cut off his head. The Biscayan was so bewildered that he was unable to utter a single word in reply, and things would have gone badly with him, so blind was Don Quixote in his rage, if the ladies of the coach, who up to then had watched the struggle in dismay, had not come up to him at this point and begged him with many blandishments to do them the very great favor of sparing their squire's life.

To which Don Quixote replied with much haughtiness and dignity, "Most certainly, lovely ladies, I shall be very happy to do that which you ask of me,

but upon one conditon and understanding, and that is that this knight promise me that he will go to El Toboso and present himself in my behalf before
Doña Dulcinea, in order that she may do with him as she may see fit."

Trembling and disconsolate, the ladies did not pause to discuss Don Quixote's request, but without so much as inquiring who Dulcinea might be they
promised him that the squire would fulfill that which was commanded of
him.

"Very well, then, trusting in your word, I will do him no further harm,
even though he has well deserved it."

CHAPTER 10

Of the pleasing conversation that took place between Don Quixote and
Sancho Panza, his squire.

By this time Sancho Panza had got to his feet, somewhat the worse for
wear as the result of the treatment he had received from the friars' lads. He
had been watching the battle attentively and praying God in his heart to give
the victory to his master, Don Quixote, in order that he, Sancho, might gain
some island where he could go to be governor as had been promised him.
Seeing now that the combat was over and the knight was returning to mount
Rocinante once more, he went up to hold the stirrup for him; but first he
fell on his knees in front of him and, taking his hand, kissed it and said,
"May your Grace be pleased, Señor Don Quixote, to grant me the governorship of that island which you have won in this deadly affray; for however
large it may be, I feel that I am indeed capable of governing it as well as any
man in this world has ever done."

To which Don Quixote replied, "Be advised, brother Sancho, that this
adventure and other similar ones have nothing to do with islands; they are
affairs of the crossroads in which one gains nothing more than a broken head
or an ear the less. Be patient, for there will be others which will not only
make you a governor, but more than that."

Sancho thanked him very much and, kissing his hand again and the skirt
of his cuirass, he assisted him up on Rocinante's back, after which the squire
bestraddled his own mount and started jogging along behind his master, who
was now going at a good clip. Without pausing for any further converse with
those in the coach, the knight made for a near-by wood, with Sancho following as fast as his beast could trot; but Rocinante was making such speed that
the ass and its rider were left behind, and it was necessary to call out to Don
Quixote to pull up and wait for them. He did so, reining in Rocinante until
the weary Sancho had drawn abreast of him.

"It strikes me, sir," said the squire as he reached his master's side, "that it
would be better for us to take refuge in some church; for in view of the way
you have treated that one with whom you were fighting, it would be small
wonder if they did not lay the matter before the Holy Brotherhood[6] and have
us arrested; and faith, if they do that, we shall have to sweat a-plenty before
we come out of jail."

"Be quiet," said Don Quixote. "And where have you ever seen, or read of,

---

6. A tribunal instituted by Ferdinand and Isabella at the end of the fifteenth century to punish highway
robbers.

a knight being brought to justice no matter how many homicides he might have committed?"

"I know nothing about omecils,"[7] replied Sancho, "nor ever in my life did I bear one to anybody; all I know is that the Holy Brotherhood has something to say about those who go around fighting on the highway, and I want nothing of it."

"Do not let it worry you," said Don Quixote, "for I will rescue you from the hands of the Chaldeans, not to speak of the Brotherhood. But answer me upon your life: have you ever seen a more valorous knight than I on all the known face of the earth? Have you ever read in the histories of any other who had more mettle in the attack, more perseverance in sustaining it, more dexterity in wounding his enemy, or more skill in overthrowing him?"

"The truth is," said Sancho, "I have never read any history whatsoever, for I do not know how to read or write; but what I would wager is that in all the days of my life I have never served a more courageous master than your Grace; I only hope your courage is not paid for in the place that I have mentioned. What I would suggest is that your Grace allow me to do something for that ear, for there is much blood coming from it, and I have here in my saddlebags some lint and a little white ointment."

"We could well dispense with all that," said Don Quixote, "if only I had remembered to bring along a vial of Fierabrás's[8] balm, a single drop of which saves time and medicines."

"What vial and what balm is that?" inquired Sancho Panza.

"It is a balm the receipt[9] for which I know by heart; with it one need have no fear of death nor think of dying from any wound. I shall make some of it and give it to you; and thereafter, whenever in any battle you see my body cut in two—as very often happens—all that is necessary is for you to take the part that lies on the ground, before the blood has congealed, and fit it very neatly and with great nicety upon the other part that remains in the saddle, taking care to adjust it evenly and exactly. Then you will give me but a couple of swallows of the balm of which I have told you, and you will see me sounder than an apple in no time at all."

"If that is so," said Panza, "I herewith renounce the governorship of the island you promised me and ask nothing other in payment of my many and faithful services than that your Grace give me the receipt for this wonderful potion, for I am sure that it would be worth more than two reales the ounce anywhere, and that is all I need for a life of ease and honor. But may I be so bold as to ask how much it costs to make it?"

"For less than three reales you can make something like six quarts," Don Quixote told him.

"Sinner that I am!" exclaimed Sancho. "Then why does your Grace not make some at once and teach me also?"

"Hush, my friend," said the knight, "I mean to teach you greater secrets than that and do you greater favors; but, for the present, let us look after this ear of mine, for it is hurting me more than I like."

Sancho thereupon took the lint and the ointment from his saddlebags; but when Don Quixote caught a glimpse of his helmet, he almost went out of

7. In Spanish a wordplay on *homecidio-omecillo.* Not to bear an *omecillo* to anybody means not to bear a grudge, and good-natured Sancho does not. 8. A giant Saracen healer in the medieval epics of the Twelve Peers (see n. 7, p. 1387). 9. Recipe.

his mind and, laying his hand upon his sword and lifting his eyes heavenward, he cried, "I make a vow to the Creator of all things and to the four holy Gospels in all their fullness of meaning that I will lead from now on the life that the great Marquis of Mantua did after he had sworn to avenge the death of his nephew Baldwin: not to eat bread of a tablecloth, not to embrace his wife, and other things which, although I am unable to recall them, we will look upon as understood—all this until I shall have wreaked an utter vengeance upon the one who has perpetrated such an outrage upon me."

"But let me remind your Grace," said Sancho when he heard these words, "that if the knight fulfills that which was commanded of him, by going to present himself before my lady Dulcinea del Toboso, then he will have paid his debt to you and merits no further punishment at your hands, unless it be for some fresh offense."

"You have spoken very well and to the point," said Don Quixote, "and so I annul the vow I have just made insofar as it has to do with any further vengeance, but I make it and confirm it anew so far as leading the life of which I have spoken is concerned, until such time as I shall have obtained by force of arms from some other knight another headpiece as good as this. And do not think, Sancho, that I am making smoke out of straw; there is one whom I well may imitate in this matter, for the same thing happened in all literalness in the case of Mambrino's helmet[1] which cost Sacripante so dear."

"I wish," said Sancho, "that your Grace would send all such oaths to the devil, for they are very bad for the health and harmful for the conscience as well. Tell me, please; supposing that for many days to come we meet no man wearing a helmet, then what are we to do? Must you still keep your vow in spite of all the inconveniences and discomforts, such as sleeping with your clothes on, not sleeping in any town, and a thousand other penances contained in the oath of that old madman of a Marquis of Mantua, an oath which you would now revive? Mark you, sir, along all these roads you meet no men of arms but only muleteers and carters, who not only do not wear helmets but quite likely have never heard tell of them in all their livelong days."

"In that you are wrong," said Don Quixote, "for we shall not be at these crossroads for the space of two hours before we shall see more men of arms than came to Albraca to win the fair Angélica."[2] "Very well, then," said Sancho, "so be it, and pray God that all turns out for the best so that I may at last win that island that is costing me so dearly, and then let me die."

"I have already told you, Sancho, that you are to give no thought to that; should the island fail, there is the kingdom of Denmark or that of Sobradisa, which would fit you like a ring on your finger, and you ought, moreover, to be happy to be on *terra firma.*[3] But let us leave all this for some other time, while you look and see if you have something in those saddlebags for us to eat, after which we will go in search of some castle where we may lodge for the night and prepare that balm of which I was telling you, for I swear to God that my ear is paining me greatly."

"I have here an onion, a little cheese, and a few crusts of bread," said Sancho, "but they are not victuals fit for a valiant knight like your grace."

---

1. The enchanted helmet of Mambrino, a Moorish king, is stolen by Rinaldo in Bioardo's *Roland in Love.* 2. Another allusion to *Roland in Love.* 3. Solid earth (Latin, literal trans.), here Firm Island, an imaginary final destination for the squires of knights-errant. Sobradisa is an imaginary realm.

"How little you know about it!" replied Don Quixote. "I would inform you, Sancho, that it is a point of honor with knights-errant to go for a month at a time without eating, and when they do eat, it is whatever may be at hand. You would certainly know that if you had read the histories as I have. There are many of them, and in none have I found any mention of knights eating unless it was by chance or at some sumptuous banquet that was tendered them; on other days they fasted. And even though it is well understood that, being men like us, they could not go without food entirely, any more than they could fail to satisfy the other necessities of nature, nevertheless, since they spent the greater part of their lives in forest and desert places without any cook to prepare their meals, their diet ordinarily consisted of rustic viands such as those that you now offer me. And so, Sancho my friend, do not be grieved at that which pleases me, nor seek to make the world over, nor to unhinge the institution of knight-errantry."

"Pardon me, your Grace," said Sancho, "but seeing that, as I have told you I do not know how to read or write, I am consequently not familiar with the rules of the knightly calling. Hereafter, I will stuff my saddlebags with all manner of dried fruit for your Grace, but inasmuch as I am not a knight, I shall lay in for myself a stock of fowls and other more substantial fare."

"I am not saying, Sancho, that it is incumbent upon knights-errant to eat only those fruits of which you speak; what I am saying is that their ordinary sustenance should consist of fruit and a few herbs such as are to be found in the fields and with which they are well acquainted, as am I myself."

"It is a good thing," said Sancho, "to know those herbs, for, so far as I can see, we are going to have need of that knowledge one of these days."

With this, he brought out the articles he had mentioned, and the two of them ate in peace, and most companionably. Being desirous, however, of seeking a lodging for the night, they did not tarry long over their humble and unsavory repast. They then mounted and made what haste they could that they might arrive at a shelter before nightfall but the sun failed them, and with it went the hope of attaining their wish. As the day ended they found themselves beside some goatherds' huts, and they accordingly decided to spend the night there. Sancho was as much disappointed at their not having reached a town as his master was content with sleeping under the open sky; for it seemed to Don Quixote that every time this happened it merely provided him with yet another opportunity to establish his claim to the title of knight-errant.

[Fighting the Sheep]

CHAPTER 18

In which is set forth the conversation that Sancho Panza had with his master, Don Quixote, along with other adventures deserving of record.

* * * Don Quixote caught sight down the road of a large cloud of dust that was drawing nearer.

"This, O Sancho," he said, turning to his squire, "is the day when you shall see the boon that fate has in store for me; this, I repeat, is the day when, as well as on any other, shall be displayed the valor of my good right arm. On this day I shall perform deeds that will be written down in the book of fame for all centuries to come. Do you see that dust cloud rising there, Sancho? That is the dust stirred up by a vast army marching in this direction and composed of many nations."

"At that rate," said Sancho, "there must be two of them, for there is another one just like it on the other side."

Don Quixote turned to look and saw that this was so. He was overjoyed by the thought that these were indeed two armies about to meet and clash in the middle of the broad plain; for at every hour and every moment his imagination was filled with battles, enchantments, nonsensical adventures, tales of love, amorous challenges, and the like, such as he had read of in the books of chivalry, and every word he uttered, every thought that crossed his mind, every act he performed, had to do with such things as these. The dust clouds he had sighted were raised by two large droves of sheep coming along the road in opposite directions, which by reason of the dust were not visible until they were close at hand, but Don Quixote insisted so earnestly that they were armies that Sancho came to believe it.

"Sir," he said, "what are we to do?"

"What are we to do?" echoed his master. "Favor and aid the weak and needy. I would inform you, Sancho, that the one coming toward us is led and commanded by the great emperor Alifanfarón, lord of the great isle of Trapobana. This other one at my back is that of his enemy, the king of the Garamantas, Pentapolín of the Rolled-up Sleeve, for he always goes into battle with his right arm bare."

"But why are they such enemies?" Sancho asked.

"Because," said Don Quixote, "this Alifanfarón is a terrible pagan and in love with Pentapolín's daughter, who is a very beautiful and gracious lady and a Christian, for which reason her father does not wish to give her to the pagan king unless the latter first abjures the law of the false prophet, Mohammed, and adopts the faith that is Pentapolín's own."

"Then, by my beard," said Sancho, "if Pentapolín isn't right, and I am going to aid him all I can."

"In that," said Don Quixote, "you will only be doing your duty; for to engage in battles of this sort you need not have been dubbed a knight."

"I can understand that," said Sancho, "but where are we going to put this ass so that we will be certain of finding him after the fray is over? As for going into battle on such a mount, I do not think that has been done up to now."

"That is true enough," said Don Quixote. "What you had best do with him is to turn him loose and run the risk of losing him; for after we emerge the victors we shall have so many horses that even Rocinante will be in danger of being exchanged for another. But listen closely to what I am about to tell you, for I wish to give you an account of the principal knights that are accompanying these two armies; and in order that you may be the better able to see and take note of them, let us retire to that hillock over there which will afford us a very good view."

They then stationed themselves upon a slight elevation from which they would have been able to see very well the two droves of sheep that Don Quixote took to be armies if it had not been for the blinding clouds of dust.

In spite of this, however, the worthy gentleman contrived to behold in his imagination what he did not see and what did not exist in reality.

Raising his voice, he went on to explain, "That knight in the gilded armor that you see there, bearing upon his shield a crowned lion crouched at the feet of a damsel, is the valiant Laurcalco, lord of the Silver Bridge; the other with the golden flowers on his armor, and on his shield three crowns argent on an azure field, is the dread Micocolembo, grand duke of Quirocia. And that one on Micocolembo's right hand, with the limbs of a giant, is the ever undaunted Brandabarbarán de Boliche, lord of the three Arabias. He goes armored in a serpent's skin and has for shield a door which, so report has it, is one of those from the temple that Samson pulled down, that time when he avenged himself on his enemies with his own death.

"But turn your eyes in this direction, and you will behold at the head of the other army the ever victorious, never vanquished Timonel de Carcajona, prince of New Biscay, who comes with quartered arms—azure, vert, argent, and or—and who has upon his shield a cat or on a field tawny, with the inscription *Miau,* which is the beginning of his lady's name; for she, so it is said, is the peerless Miulina, daughter of Alfeñquén, duke of Algarve. And that one over there, who weights down and presses the loins of that powerful charger, in a suit of snow-white armor with a white shield that bears no device whatever—he is a novice knight of the French nation, called Pierres Papin, lord of the baronies of Utrique. As for him you see digging his iron spurs into the flanks of that fleet-footed zebra courser and whose arms are vairs azure, he is the mighty duke of Nervia, Espartafilardo of the Wood, who has for device upon his shield an asparagus plant with a motto in Castilian that says 'Rastrea mi suerte.'"[1]

In this manner he went on naming any number of imaginary knights on either side, describing on the spur of the moment their arms, colors, devices, and mottoes; for he was completely carried away by his imagination and by this unheard-of madness that had laid hold of him.

Without pausing, he went on, "This squadron in front of us is composed of men of various nations. There are those who drink the sweet waters of the famous Xanthus; woodsmen who tread the Massilian plain; those that sift the fine gold nuggets of Arabia Felix; those that are so fortunate as to dwell on the banks of the clear-running Thermodon, famed for their coolness; those who in many and diverse ways drain the golden Pactolus; Numidians, whose word is never to be trusted; Persians, with their famous bows and arrows; Medes and Parthians, who fight as they flee; Scythians, as cruel as they are fair of skin; Ethiopians, with their pierced lips; and an infinite number of other nationalities whose visages I see and recognize although I cannot recall their names.

"In this other squadron come those that drink from the crystal currents of the olive-bearing Betis; those that smooth and polish their faces with the liquid of the ever rich and gilded Tagus; those that enjoy the beneficial waters of the divine Genil; those that roam the Tartessian plains with their abundant pasturage; those that disport themselves in the Elysian meadows of Jerez; the men of La Mancha, rich and crowned with golden ears of corn; others

---

1. Probably a pun on *rastrear*. The meaning of the motto may be either "On Fortunes's track" or "My Fortune creeps."

clad in iron garments, ancient relics of the Gothic race; those that bathe in the Pisuerga, noted for the mildness of its current; those that feed their herds in the wide-spreading pasture lands along the banks of the winding Guadiana, celebrated for its underground course;[2] those that shiver from the cold of the wooded Pyrenees or dwell amid the white peaks of the lofty Apennines—in short, all those whom Europe holds within its girth."

So help me God! How many provinces, how many nations did he not mention by name, giving to each one with marvelous readiness its proper attributes; for he was wholly absorbed and filled to the brim with what he had read in those lying books of his! Sancho Panza hung on his words, saying nothing, merely turning his head from time to time to have a look at those knights and giants that his master was pointing out to him; but he was unable to discover any of them.

"Sir," he said, "may I go to the devil if I see a single man, giant, or knight of all those that your Grace is talking about. Who knows? Maybe it is another spell, like last night."[3]

"How can you say that?" replied Don Quixote. "Can you not hear the neighing of the horses, the sound of trumpets, the roll of drums?"

"I hear nothing," said Sancho, "except the bleating of sheep."

And this, of course, was the truth; for the flocks were drawing near.

"The trouble is, Sancho," said Don Quixote, "you are so afraid that you cannot see or hear properly; for one of the effects of fear is to disturb the senses and cause things to appear other than what they are. If you are so craven as all that, go off to one side and leave me alone, and I without your help will assure the victory to that side to which I lend my aid."

Saying this, he put spurs to Rocinante and, with his lance at rest, darted down the hillside like a flash of lightning.

As he did so, Sancho called after him, "Come back, your Grace, Señor Don Quixote; I vow to God those are sheep that you are charging. Come back! O wretched father that bore me! What madness is this? Look you, there are no giants, nor knights, nor cats, nor shields either quartered or whole, nor vairs azure or bedeviled. What is this you are doing, O sinner that I am in God's sight?"

But all this did not cause Don Quixote to turn back. Instead, he rode on, crying out at the top of his voice, "Ho, knights, those of you who follow and fight under the banners of the valiant Pentapolín of the Rolled-up Sleeve; follow me, all of you, and you shall see how easily I give you revenge on your enemy, Alifanfarón of Trapobana."

With these words he charged into the middle of the flock of sheep and began spearing at them with as much courage and boldness as if they had been his mortal enemies. The shepherds and herdsmen who were with the animals called to him to stop; but seeing it was no use, they unloosed their slings and saluted his ears with stones as big as your fist.

Don Quixote paid no attention to the missiles and, dashing about here and there, kept crying, "Where are you, haughty Alifanfarón? Come out to me; for here is a solitary knight who desires in single combat to test your

2. The Guadiana does run underground part of the way through La Mancha.   3. The inn where they had spent the previous night had been pronounced by Don Quixote to be an enchanted castle.

strength and deprive you of your life, as a punishment for that which you have done to the valorous Pentapolín Garamanta."

At that instant a pebble from the brook struck him in the side and buried a couple of ribs in his body. Believing himself dead or badly wounded, and remembering his potion, he took out his vial, placed it to his mouth, and began to swallow the balm; but before he had had what he thought was enough, there came another almond, which struck him in the hand, crushing the tin vial and carrying away with it a couple of grinders from his mouth, as well as badly mashing two of his fingers. As a result of these blows the poor knight tumbled from his horse. Believing that they had killed him, the shepherds hastily collected their flock and, picking up the dead beasts, of which there were more than seven, they went off down the road without more ado.

Sancho all this time was standing on the slope observing the insane things that his master was doing; and as he plucked savagely at his beard he cursed the hour and minute when luck had brought them together. But when he saw him lying there on the ground and perceived that the shepherds were gone, he went down the hill and came up to him, finding him in very bad shape though not unconscious.

"Didn't I tell you, Señor Don Quixote," he said, "that you should come back, that those were not armies you were charging but flocks of sheep?"

"This," said Don Quixote, "is the work of that thieving magician, my enemy, who thus counterfeits things and causes them to disappear. You must know, Sancho, that it is very easy for them to make us assume any appearance that they choose; and so it is that malign one who persecutes me, envious of the glory he saw me about to achieve in this battle, changed the squadrons of the foe into flocks of sheep. If you do not believe me, I beseech you on my life to do one thing for me, that you may be undeceived and discover for yourself that what I say is true. Mount your ass and follow them quietly, and when you have gone a short way from here, you will see them become their former selves once more; they will no longer be sheep but men exactly as I described them to you in the first place. But do not go now, for I need your kind assistance; come over here and have a look and tell me how many grinders are missing, for it feels as if I did not have a single one left."

["To Right Wrongs and Come to the Aid of the Wretched"]

CHAPTER 22

Of how Don Quixote freed many unfortunate ones who, much against their will, were being taken where they did not wish to go.

Cid Hamete Benengeli, the Arabic and Manchegan;[1] author, in the course of this most grave, high-sounding, minute, delightful, and imaginative history, informs us that, following the remarks that were exchanged between Don Quixote de la Mancha and Sancho Panza, his squire, . . . the knight

---

1. Of La Mancha.

looked up and saw coming toward them down the road which they were following a dozen or so men on foot, strung together by their necks like beads on an iron chain and all of them wearing handcuffs. They were accompanied by two men on horseback and two on foot, the former carrying wheel-lock muskets while the other two were armed with swords and javelins.

"That," said Sancho as soon as he saw them, "is a chain of galley slaves, people on their way to the galleys where by order of the king they are forced to labor."

"What do you mean by 'forced'?" asked Don Quixote. "Is it possible that the king uses force on anyone?"

"I did not say that," replied Sancho. "What I did say was that these are folks who have been condemned for their crimes to forced labor in the galleys for his Majesty the King."

"The short of it is," said the knight, "whichever way you put it, these people are being taken there by force and not of their own free will."

"That is the way it is," said Sancho.

"Well, in that case," said his master, "now is the time for me to fulfill the duties of my calling, which is to right wrongs and come to the aid of the wretched."

"But take note, your Grace," said Sancho, "that justice, that is to say, the king himself, is not using any force upon, or doing any wrong to, people like these, but is merely punishing them for the crimes they have committed."

The chain of galley slaves had come up to them by this time, whereupon Don Quixote very courteously requested the guards to inform him of the reason or reasons why they were conducting these people in such a manner as this. One of the men on horseback then replied that the men were prisoners who had been condemned by his Majesty to serve in the galleys, whither they were bound, and that was all there was to be said about it and all that he, Don Quixote, need know.

"Nevertheless," said the latter, "I should like to inquire of each one of them, individually, the cause of his misfortune." And he went on speaking so very politely in an effort to persuade them to tell him what he wanted to know that the other mounted guard finally said, "Although we have here the record and certificate of sentence of each one of these wretches, we have not the time to get them out and read them to you; and so your Grace may come over and ask the prisoners themselves, and they will tell you if they choose, and you may be sure that they will, for these fellows take a delight in their knavish exploits and in boasting of them afterward."

With this permission, even though he would have done so if it had not been granted him, Don Quixote went up to the chain of prisoners and asked the first whom he encountered what sins had brought him to so sorry a plight. The man replied that it was for being a lover that he found himself in that line.

"For that and nothing more?" said Don Quixote. "And do they, then, send lovers to the galleys? If so, I should have been rowing there long ago."

"But it was not the kind of love that your Grace has in mind," the prisoner went on. "I loved a wash basket full of white linen so well and hugged it so tightly that, if they had not taken it away from me by force, I would never of my own choice have let go of it to this very minute. I was caught in the act, there was no need to torture me, the case was soon disposed of, and they supplied me with a hundred lashes across the shoulders and, in addition, a three-year stretch in the *gurapas,* and that's all there is to tell."

"What are *gurapas?"* asked Don Quixote.

"*Gurapas* are the galleys," replied the prisoner. He was a lad of around twenty-four and stated that he was a native of Piedrahita.

The knight then put the same question to a second man, who appeared to be very downcast and melancholy and did not have a word to say. The first man answered for him.

"This one, sir," he said, "is going as a canary—I mean, as a musician and singer."

"How is that?" Don Quixote wanted to know. "Do musicians and singers go to the galleys too?"

"Yes, sir; and there is nothing worse than singing when you're in trouble."

"On the contrary," said Don Quixote, "I have heard it said that he who sings frightens away his sorrows."

"It is just the opposite," said the prisoner; "for he who sings once weeps all his life long."

"I do not understand," said the knight.

One of the guards then explained. "Sir Knight, with this *non sancta*[2] tribe, to sing when you're in trouble means to confess under torture. This singer was put to the torture and confessed his crime, which was that of being a *cuatrero,* or cattle thief, and as a result of his confession he was condemned to six years in the galleys in addition to two hundred lashes which he took on his shoulders; and so it is he is always downcast and moody, for the other thieves, those back where he came from and the ones here, mistreat, snub, ridicule, and despise him for having confessed and for not having had the courage to deny his guilt. They are in the habit of saying that the word *no* has the same number of letters as the word *sí,* and that a culprit is in luck when his life or death depends on his own tongue and not that of witnesses or upon evidence; and, in my opinion, they are not very far wrong."

"And I," said Don Quixote, "feel the same way about it." He then went on to a third prisoner and repeated his question.

The fellow answered at once, quite unconcernedly. "I'm going to my ladies, the *gurapas,* for five years, for the lack of five ducats."

"I would gladly give twenty," said Don Quixote, "to get you out of this."

"That," said the prisoner, "reminds me of the man in the middle of the ocean who has money and is dying of hunger because there is no place to buy what he needs. I say this for the reason that if I had had, at the right time, those twenty ducats your Grace is now offering me, I'd have greased the notary's quill and freshened up the attorney's wit with them, and I'd now be living in the middle of Zocodover Square in Toledo instead of being here on this highway coupled like a greyhound. But God is great; patience, and that's enough of it."

Don Quixote went on to a fourth prisoner, a venerable-looking old fellow with a white beard that fell over his bosom. When asked how he came to be there, this one began weeping and made no reply, but a fifth comrade spoke up in his behalf.

2. Unholy (Latin).

"This worthy man," he said, "is on his way to the galleys after having made the usual rounds clad in a robe of state and on horseback."[3]

"That means, I take it," said Sancho, "that he has been put to shame in public."

"That is it," said the prisoner, "and the offense for which he is being punished is that of having been an ear broker, or, better, a body broker. By that I mean to say, in short, that the gentleman is a pimp, and besides, he has his points as a sorcerer."

"If that point had not been thrown in," said Don Quixote, "he would not deserve, for merely being a pimp, to have to row in the galleys, but rather should be the general and give orders there. For the office of pimp is not an indifferent one; it is a function to be performed by persons of discretion and is most necessary in a well-ordered state; it is a profession that should be followed only by the wellborn, and there should, moreover, be a supervisor or examiner as in the case of other offices, and the number of practitioners should be fixed by law as is done with brokers on the exchange. In that way many evils would be averted that arise when this office is filled and this calling practiced by stupid folk and those with little sense, such as silly women and pages or mountebanks with few years and less experience to their credit, who, on the most pressing occasions, when it is necessary to use one's wits, let the crumbs freeze between their hand and their mouth and do not know which is their right hand and which is the left.

"I would go on and give reasons why it is fitting to choose carefully those who are to fulfill so necessary a state function, but this is not the place for it. One of these days I will speak of the matter to someone who is able to do something about it. I will say here only that the pain I felt at seeing those white hairs and this venerable countenance in such a plight, and all for his having been a pimp, has been offset for me by the additional information you have given me, to the effect that he is a sorcerer as well; for I am convinced that there are no sorcerers in the world who can move and compel the will, as some simple-minded persons think, but that our will is free and no herb or charm can force it.[4] All that certain foolish women and cunning tricksters do is to compound a few mixtures and poisons with which they deprive men of their senses while pretending that they have the power to make them loved, although, as I have just said, one cannot affect another's will in that manner."

"That is so," said the worthy old man; "but the truth is, sir, I am not guilty on the sorcery charge. As for being a pimp, that is something I cannot deny. I never thought there was any harm in it, however, my only desire being that everyone should enjoy himself and live in peace and quiet, without any quarrels or troubles. But these good intentions on my part cannot prevent me from going where I do not want to go, to a place from which I do not expect to return; for my years are heavy upon me and an affection of the urine that I have will not give me a moment's rest."

With this, he began weeping once more, and Sancho was so touched by it that he took a four-real piece from his bosom and gave it to him as an act of charity.

---

3. After having been flogged in public, with all the ceremony that accompanied that punishment.
4. Here Don Quixote despises charms and love potions, although often elsewhere, in his own vision of himself as a knight-errant, he accepts enchantments and spells as part of his world of fantasy.

Don Quixote then went on and asked another what his offense was. The fellow answered him, not with less, but with much more, briskness than the preceding one had shown.

"I am here," he said, "for the reason that I carried a joke too far with a couple of cousins-german of mine and a couple of others who were not mine, and I ended by jesting with all of them to such an extent that the devil himself would never be able to straighten out the relationship. They proved everything on me, there was no one to show me favor, I had no money, I came near swinging for it, they sentenced me to the galleys for six years, and I accepted the sentence as the punishment that was due me. I am young yet, and if I live long enough, everything will come out all right. If, Sir Knight, your Grace has anything with which to aid these poor creatures that you see before you, God will reward you in Heaven, and we here on earth will make it a point to ask God in our prayers to grant you long life and good health, as long and as good as your amiable presence deserves."

This man was dressed as a student, and one of the guards told Don Quixote that he was a great talker and a very fine Latinist.

Back of these came a man around thirty years of age and of very good appearance, except that when he looked at you his eyes were seen to be a little crossed. He was shackled in a different manner from the others, for he dragged behind a chain so huge that it was wrapped all around his body, with two rings at the throat, one of which was attached to the chain while the other was fastened to what is known as a keep-friend or friend's foot, from which two irons hung down to his waist, ending in handcuffs secured by a heavy padlock in such a manner that he could neither raise his hands to his mouth nor lower his head to reach his hands.

When Don Quixote asked why this man was so much more heavily chained than the others, the guard replied that it was because he had more crimes against him than all the others put together, and he was so bold and cunning that, even though they had him chained like this, they were by no means sure of him but feared that he might escape from them.

"What crimes could he have committed," asked the knight, "if he has merited a punishment no greater than that of being sent to the galleys?"

"He is being sent there for ten years," replied the guard, "and that is equivalent to civil death. I need tell you no more than that this good man is the famous Ginés de Pasamonte, otherwise known as Ginesillo de Parapilla."

"Señor Commissary," spoke up the prisoner at this point, "go easy there and let us not be so free with names and surnames. My just name is Ginés and not Ginesillo; and Pasamonte, not Parapilla as you make it out to be, is my family name. Let each one mind his own affairs and he will have his hands full."

"Speak a little more respectfully, you big thief, you," said the commissary, "unless you want me to make you be quiet in a way you won't like."

"Man goes as God pleases, that is plain to be seen," replied the galley slave, "but someday someone will know whether my name is Ginesillo de Parapilla or not."

"But, you liar, isn't that what they call you?"

"Yes," said Ginés, "they do call me that; but I'll put a stop to it, or else I'll skin their you-know-what. And you, sir, if you have anything to give us, give it and may God go with you, for I am tired of all this prying into other people's lives. If you want to know anything about my life, know that I am Ginés de Pasamonte whose life story has been written down by these fingers that you see here."

"He speaks the truth," said the commissary, "for he has himself written his story, as big as you please, and has left the book in the prison, having pawned it for two hundred reales."

"And I mean to redeem it," said Ginés, "even if it costs me two hundred ducats."

"Is it as good as that?" inquired Don Quixote.

"It is so good," replied Ginés, "that it will cast into the shade *Lazarillo de Tormes*[5] and all others of that sort that have been or will be written. What I would tell you is that it deals with facts, and facts so interesting and amusing that no lies could equal them."

"And what is the title of the book?" asked Don Quixote.

The Life of Ginés de Pasamonte."

"Is it finished?"

"How could it be finished," said Ginés, "when my life is not finished as yet? What I have written thus far is an account of what happened to me from the time I was born up to the last time that they sent me to the galleys."

"Then you have been there before?"

"In the service of God and the king I was there four years, and I know what the biscuit and the cowhide are like. I don't mind going very much, for there I will have a chance to finish my book. I still have many things to say, and in the Spanish galleys I shall have all the leisure that I need, though I don't need much, since I know by heart what it is I want to write."

"You seem to be a clever fellow," said Don Quixote.

"And an unfortunate one," said Ginés; "for misfortunes always pursue men of genius."

"They pursue rogues," said the commissary.

"I have told you to go easy, Señor Commissary," said Pasamonte, "for their Lordships did not give you that staff in order that you might mistreat us poor devils with it, but they intended that you should guide and conduct us in accordance with his Majesty's command. Otherwise, by the life of—But enough. It may be that someday the stains made in the inn will come out in the wash. Meanwhile, let everyone hold his tongue, behave well, and speak better, and let us be on our way. We've had enough of this foolishness."

At this point the commissary raised his staff as if to let Pasamonte have it in answer to his threats, but Don Quixote placed himself between them and begged the officer not to abuse the man; for it was not to be wondered at if one who had his hands so bound should be a trifle free with his tongue. With this, he turned and addressed them all.

"From all that you have told me, my dearest brothers," he said, "one thing stands out clearly for me, and that is the fact that, even though it is a punishment for offenses which you have committed, the penalty you are about to pay is not greatly to your liking and you are going to the galleys very much against your own will and desire. It may be that the lack of spirit which one of you displayed under torture, the lack of money on the part of another, the lack of influential friends, or, finally, warped judgment on the part of the

5. A picaresque or rogue novel, published anonymously about the middle of the fifteenth century.

magistrate, was the thing that led to your downfall; and, as a result, justice was not done you. All of which presents itself to my mind in such a fashion that I am at this moment engaged in trying to persuade and even force myself to show you what the purpose was for which Heaven sent me into this world, why it was it led me to adopt the calling of knighthood which I profess and take the knightly vow to favor the needy and aid those who are oppressed by the powerful.

"However, knowing as I do that it is not the part of prudence to do by foul means what can be accomplished by fair ones, I propose to ask these gentlemen, your guards, and the commissary to be so good as to unshackle you and permit you to go in peace. There will be no dearth of others to serve his Majesty under more propitious circumstances; and it does not appear to me to be just to make slaves of those whom God created as free men. What is more, gentlemen of the guard, these poor fellows have committed no offense against you. Up there, each of us will have to answer for his own sins; for God in Heaven will not fail to punish the evil and reward the good; and it is not good for self-respecting men to be executioners of their fellow-men in something that does not concern them. And so, I ask this of you, gently and quietly, in order that, if you comply with my request, I shall have reason to thank you; and if you do not do so of your own accord, then this lance and this sword and the valor of my arm shall compel you to do it by force."

"A fine lot of foolishness!" exclaimed the commissary. "So he comes out at last with this nonsense! He would have us let the prisoners of the king go free, as if we had any authority to do so or he any right to command it! Be on your way, sir, at once; straighten that basin that you have on your head, and do not go looking for three feet on a cat."[6]

"You," replied Don Quixote, "are the cat and the rat and the rascal!" And, saying this, he charged the commissary so quickly that the latter had no chance to defend himself but fell to the ground badly wounded by the lance blow. The other guards were astounded by this unexpected occurrence; but, recovering their self-possession, those on horseback drew their swords, those on foot leveled their javelins, and all bore down on Don Quixote, who stood waiting for them very calmly. Things undoubtedly would have gone badly for him if the galley slaves, seeing an opportunity to gain their freedom, had not succeeded in breaking the chain that linked them together. Such was the confusion that the guards, now running to fall upon the prisoners and now attacking Don Quixote, who in turn was attacking them, accomplished nothing that was of any use.

Sancho for his part aided Ginés de Pasamonte to free himself, and that individual was the first to drop his chains and leap out onto the field, where, attacking the fallen commissary, he took away that officer's sword and musket; and as he stood there, aiming first at one and then at another, though without firing, the plain was soon cleared of guards, for they had taken to their heels, fleeing at once Pasamonte's weapon and the stones which the galley slaves, freed now, were hurling at them. Sancho, meanwhile, was very much disturbed over this unfortunate event, as he felt sure that the fugitives would report the matter to the Holy Brotherhood, which, to the ringing of the alarm bell, would come out to search for the guilty parties. He said as

6. Looking for the impossible ("five feet" is the more usual form of the proverb).

much to his master, telling him that they should leave at once and go into hiding in the near-by mountains.

"That is all very well," said Don Quixote, "but I know what had best be done now." He then summoned all the prisoners, who, running riot, had by this time despoiled the commissary of everything that he had, down to his skin, and as they gathered around to hear what he had to say, he addressed them as follows:

"It is fitting that those who are wellborn should give thanks for the benefits they have received, and one of the sins with which God is most offended is that of ingratitude. I say this, gentlemen, for the reason that you have seen and had manifest proof of what you owe to me; and now that you are free of the yoke which I have removed from about your necks, it is my will and desire that you should set out and proceed to the city of El Toboso and there present yourselves before the lady Dulcinea del Toboso and say to her that her champion, the Knight of the Mournful Countenance, has sent you; and then you will relate to her, point by point, the whole of this famous adventure which has won you your longed-for freedom. Having done that, you may go where you like, and may good luck go with you."

To this Ginés de Pasamonte replied in behalf of all of them, "It is absolutely impossible, your Grace, our liberator, for us to do what you have commanded. We cannot go down the highway all together but must separate and go singly, each in his own direction, endeavoring to hide ourselves in the bowels of the earth in order not to be found by the Holy Brotherhood, which undoubtedly will come out to search for us. What your Grace can do, and it is right that you should do so, is to change this service and toll that you require of us in connection with the lady Dulcinea del Toboso into a certain number of Credos and Hail Marys which we will say for your Grace's intention, as this is something that can be accomplished by day or night, fleeing or resting, in peace or in war. To imagine, on the other hand, that we are going to return to the fleshpots of Egypt, by which I mean, take up our chains again by setting out along the highway for El Toboso, is to believe that it is night now instead of ten o'clock in the morning and is to ask of us something that is the same as asking pears of the elm tree."

"Then by all that's holy!" exclaimed Don Quixote, whose wrath was now aroused, "you, Don Son of a Whore, Don Ginesillo de Parapilla, or whatever your name is, you shall go alone, your tail between your legs and the whole chain on your back."

Pasamonte, who was by no means a long-suffering individual, was by this time convinced that Don Quixote was not quite right in the head, seeing that he had been guilty of such a folly as that of desiring to free them; and so, when he heard himself insulted in this manner, he merely gave the wink to his companions and, going off to one side, began raining so many stones upon the knight that the latter was wholly unable to protect himself with his buckler, while poor Rocinante paid no more attention to the spur than if he had been made of brass. As for Sancho, he took refuge behind his donkey as a protection against the cloud and shower of rocks that was falling on both of them, but Don Quixote was not able to shield himself so well, and there is no telling how many struck his body, with such force as to unhorse and bring him to the ground.

No sooner had he fallen than the student was upon him. Seizing the basin from the knight's head, he struck him three or four blows with it across the shoulders and banged it against the ground an equal number of times until it was fairly shattered to bits. They then stripped Don Quixote of the doublet which he wore over his armor, and would have taken his hose as well, if his greaves had not prevented them from doing so, and made off with Sancho's greatcoat, leaving him naked; after which, dividing the rest of the battle spoils amongst themselves, each of them went his own way, being a good deal more concerned with eluding the dreaded Holy Brotherhood than they were with burdening themselves with a chain or going to present themselves before the lady Dulcinea del Toboso.

They were left alone now—the ass and Rocinante, Sancho and Don Quixote: the ass, crestfallen and pensive, wagging its ears now and then, being under the impression that the hurricane of stones that had raged about them was not yet over; Rocinante, stretched alongside his master, for the hack also had been felled by a stone; Sancho, naked and fearful of the Holy Brotherhood; and Don Quixote, making wry faces at seeing himself so mishandled by those to whom he had done so much good.

["Set Free at Once That Lovely Lady"]

CHAPTER 52

Of the quarrel that Don Quixote had with the goatherd, together with the rare adventure of the penitents, which the knight by the sweat of his brow brought to a happy conclusion.[1]

All those who had listened to it were greatly pleased with the goatherd's story, especially the canon,[2] who was more than usually interested in noting the manner in which it had been told. Far from being a mere rustic herdsman, the narrator seemed rather a cultured city dweller; and the canon accordingly remarked that the curate had been quite right in saying that the mountain groves bred men of learning. They all now offered their services to Eugenio, and Don Quixote was the most generous of any in this regard.

"Most assuredly, brother goatherd," he said, "if it were possible for me to undertake any adventure just now, I would set out at once to aid you and would take Leandra out of that convent, where she is undoubtedly being held against her will, in spite of the abbess and all the others who might try to prevent me, after which I would place her in your hands to do with as you liked, with due respect, however, for the laws of chivalry, which command that no violence be offered to any damsel. But I trust in God, Our Lord, that the power of one malicious enchanter is not so great that another magician

---

1. Last chapter of Part I. Through various devices, including the use of Don Quixote's own belief in enchantments and spells, the curate and the barber have persuaded the knight to let himself be taken home in an ox cart.　　2. A canon from Toledo who has joined Don Quixote and his guardians on the way; conversing about chivalry with the knight, he has had cause to be "astonished at Don Quixote's well-reasoned nonsense." Eugenio, a very literate goatherd met on the way, has just told them the story of his unhappy love for Leandra. The girl, instead of choosing one of her local suitors, had eloped with a flashy and crooked soldier; robbed and abandoned by him, she had been put by her father in a convent.

2016 / MIGUEL DE CERVANTES

may not prove still more powerful, and then I promise you my favor and my aid, as my calling obliges me to do, since it is none other than that of succoring the weak and those who are in distress."

The goatherd stared at him, observing in some astonishment the knight's unprepossessing appearance.

"Sir," he said, turning to the barber who sat beside him, "who is this man who looks so strange and talks in this way?"

"Who should it be," the barber replied, "if not the famous Don Quixote de la Mancha, righter of wrongs, avenger of injustices, protector of damsels, terror of giants, and champion of battles?"

"That," said the goatherd, "sounds to me like the sort of thing you read of in books of chivalry, where they do all those things that your Grace has mentioned in connection with this man. But if you ask me, either your Grace is joking or this worthy gentleman must have a number of rooms to let inside his head."

"You are the greatest villain that ever was!" cried Don Quixote when he heard this. "It is you who are the empty one; I am fuller than the bitch that bore you ever was." Saying this, he snatched up a loaf of bread that was lying beside him and hurled it straight in the goatherd's face with such force as to flatten the man's nose. Upon finding himself thus mistreated in earnest, Eugenio, who did not understand this kind of joke, forgot all about the carpet, the tablecloth, and the other diners and leaped upon Don Quixote. Seizing him by the throat with both hands, he would no doubt have strangled him if Sancho Panza, who now came running up, had not grasped him by the shoulders and flung him backward over the table, smashing plates and cups and spilling and scattering all the food and drink that was there. Thus freed of his assailant, Don Quixote then threw himself upon the shepherd, who, with bleeding face and very much battered by Sancho's feet, was creeping about on his hands and knees in search of a table knife with which to exact a sanguinary vengeance, a purpose which the canon and the curate prevented him from carrying out. The barber, however, so contrived it that the goatherd came down on top of his opponent, upon whom he now showered so many blows that the poor knight's countenance was soon as bloody as his own.

As all this went on, the canon and the curate were laughing fit to burst, the troopers[3] were dancing with glee, and they all hissed on the pair as men do at a dog fight. Sancho Panza alone was in despair, being unable to free himself of one of the canon's servants who held him back from going to his master's aid. And then, just as they were all enjoying themselves hugely, with the exception of the two who were mauling each other, the note of a trumpet fell upon their ears, a sound so mournful that it caused them all to turn their heads in the direction from which it came. The one who was most excited by it was Don Quixote; who, very much against his will and more than a little bruised, was lying pinned beneath the goatherd.

"Brother Demon," he now said to the shepherd, "for you could not possibly be anything but a demon, seeing that you have shown a strength and valor greater than mine, I request you to call a truce for no more than an hour;

---

3. Law officers from the Holy Brotherhood. They had wanted to arrest Don Quixote for his attempt to liberate the galley salves, but had been persuaded not to do so because of the knight's insanity.

for the doleful sound of that trumpet that we hear seems to me to be some new adventure that is calling me."

Tired of mauling and being mauled, the goatherd let him up at once. As he rose to his feet and turned his head in the direction of the sound, Don Quixote then saw, coming down the slope of a hill, a large number of persons clad in white after the fashion of penitents; for, as it happened, the clouds that year had denied their moisture to the earth, and in all the villages of that district processions for prayer and penance were being organized with the purpose of beseeching God to have mercy and send rain. With this object in view, the good folk from a near-by town were making a pilgrimage to a devout hermit who dwelt on these slopes. Upon beholding the strange costumes that the penitents wore, without pausing to think how many times he had seen them before, Don Quixote imagined that this must be some adventure or other, and that it was for him alone as a knight-errant to undertake it. He was strengthened in this belief by the sight of a covered image that they bore, as it seemed to him this must be some highborn lady whom these scoundrelly and discourteous brigands were forcibly carrying off; and no sooner did this idea occur to him than he made for Rocinante, who was grazing not far away.

Taking the bridle and his buckler from off the saddletree, he had the bridle adjusted in no time, and then, asking Sancho for his sword, he climbed into the saddle, braced his shield upon his arm, and cried out to those present, "And now, valorous company, you shall see how important it is to have in the world those who follow the profession of knight-errantry. You have but to watch how I shall set at liberty that worthy lady who there goes captive, and then you may tell me whether or not such knights are to be esteemed."

As he said this, he dug his legs into Rocinante's flanks, since he had no spurs, and at a fast trot (for nowhere in this veracious history are we ever told that the hack ran full speed) he bore down on the penitents in spite of all that the canon, the curate, and the barber could do to restrain him—their efforts were as vain as were the pleadings of his squire.

"Where are you bound for, Señor Don Quixote?" Sancho called after him. "What evil spirits in your bosom spur you on to go against our Catholic faith? Plague take me, can't you see that's a procession of penitents and that lady they're carrying on the litter is the most blessed image of the Immaculate Virgin? Look well what you're doing, my master, for this time it may be said that you really do not know."

His exertions were in vain, however, for his master was so bent upon having it out with the sheeted figures and freeing the lady clad in mourning that he did not hear a word, nor would he have turned back if he had, though the king himself might have commanded it. Having reached the procession, he reined in Rocinante, who by this time was wanting a little rest, and in a hoarse, excited voice he shouted, "You who go there with your faces covered, out of shame, it may be, listen well to what I have to say to you."

The first to come to a halt were those who carried the image; and then one of the four clerics who were intoning the litanies, upon beholding Don Quixote's weird figure, his bony nag, and other amusing appurtenances, spoke up in reply.

"Brother, if you have something to say to us, say it quickly, for these brethren are engaged in macerating their flesh, and we cannot stop to hear anything, nor is it fitting that we should, unless it is capable of being said in a couple of words."

"I will say it to you in one word," Don Quixote answered, "and that word is the following: 'Set free at once that lovely lady whose tears and mournful countenance show plainly that you are carrying her away against her will and that you have done her some shameful wrong. I will not consent to your going one step farther until you shall have given her the freedom that should be hers.'"

Hearing these words, they all thought that Don Quixote must be some madman or other and began laughing heartily; but their laughter proved to be gunpowder to his wrath, and without saying another word he drew his sword and fell upon the litter. One of those who bore the image, leaving his share of the burden to his companions, then sallied forth to meet the knight, flourishing a forked stick that he used to support the Virgin while he was resting; and upon this stick he now received a mighty slash that Don Quixote dealt him, one that shattered it in two, but with the piece about a third long that remained in his hand he came down on the shoulder of his opponent's sword arm, left unprotected by the buckler, with so much force that the poor fellow sank to the ground sorely battered and bruised.

Sancho Panza, who was puffing along close behind his master, upon seeing him fall cried out to the attacker not to deal another blow, as this was an unfortunate knight who was under a magic spell but who had never in all the days of his life done any harm to anyone. But the thing that stopped the rustic was not Sancho's words; it was, rather, the sight of Don Quixote lying there without moving hand or foot. And so, thinking that he had killed him, he hastily girded up his tunic and took to his heels across the countryside like a deer.

By this time all of Don Quixote's companions had come running up to where he lay; and the penitents, when they observed this, and especially when they caught sight of the officers of the Brotherhood with their cross-bows, at once rallied around the image, where they raised their hoods and grasped their whips as the priests raised their tapers aloft in expectations of an assault; for they were resolved to defend themselves and even, if possible, to take the offensive against their assailants, but, as luck would have it, things turned out better than they had hoped. Sancho, meanwhile, believing Don Quixote to be dead, had flung himself across his master's body and was weeping and wailing in the most lugubrious and, at the same time, the most laughable fashion that could be imagined; and the curate had discovered among those who marched in the procession another curate whom he knew, their recognition of each other serving to allay the fears of all parties concerned. The first curate then gave the second a very brief account of who Don Quixote was, whereupon all the penitents came up to see if the poor knight was dead. And as they did do, they heard Sancho Panza speaking with tears in his eyes.

"O flower of chivalry,"[4] he was saying, "the course of whose well-spent years has been brought to an end by a single blow of a club! O honor of your line, honor and glory of all La Mancha and of all the world, which, with you absent from it, will be full of evil-doers who will not fear being punished for their deeds! O master more generous than all the Alexanders, who after only

4. Note how Sancho has absorbed some of his master's speech mannerisms.

eight months of service presented me with the best island that the sea washes and surrounds! Humble with the proud, haughty with the humble, brave in facing dangers, long-suffering under outrages, in love without reason, imitator of the good, scourge of the wicked, enemy of the mean—in a word, a knight-errant, which is all there is to say."

At the sound of Sancho's cries and moans, Don Quixote revived, and the first thing he said was, "He who lives apart from thee, O fairest Dulcinea, is subject to greater woes than those I now endure. Friend Sancho, help me onto that enchanted cart, as I am in no condition to sit in Rocinante's saddle with this shoulder of mine knocked to pieces the way it is."

"That I will gladly do, my master," replied Sancho, "and we will go back to my village in the company of these gentlemen who are concerned for your welfare, and there we will arrange for another sally and one, let us hope, that will bring us more profit and fame than this one has."

"Well spoken, Sancho," said Don Quixote, "for it will be an act of great prudence to wait until the present evil influence of the stars has passed."

The canon, the curate, and the barber all assured him that he would be wise in doing this; and so, much amused by Sancho Panza's simplicity, they placed Don Quixote upon the cart as before, while the procession of penitents re-formed and continued on its way. The goatherd took leave of all of them, and the curate paid the troopers what was coming to them, since they did not wish to go any farther. The canon requested the priest to inform him of the outcome of Don Quixote's madness, as to whether it yielded to treatment or not; and with this he begged permission to resume his journey. In short, the party broke up and separated, leaving only the curate and the barber, Don Quixote and Panza, and the good Rocinante, who looked upon everything that he had seen with the same resignation as his master. Yoking his oxen, the carter made the knight comfortable upon a bale of hay, and then at his customary slow pace proceeded to follow the road that the curate directed him to take. At the end of the six days they reached Don Quixote's village, making their entrance at noon of a Sunday, when the square was filled with a crowd of people through which the cart had to pass.

They all came running to see who it was, and when they recognized their townsman, they were vastly astonished. One lad sped to bring the news to the knight's housekeeper and his niece, telling them that their master had returned lean and jaundiced and lying stretched out upon a bale of hay on an ox-cart. It was pitiful to hear the good ladies' screams, to behold the way in which they beat their breasts, and to listen to the curses which they once more heaped upon those damnable books of chivalry, and this demonstration increased as they saw Don Quixote coming through the doorway.

At news of the knight's return, Sancho Panza's wife had hurried to the scene, for she had some while since learned that her husband had accompanied him as his squire; and now, as soon as she laid eyes upon her man, the first question she asked was if all was well with the ass, to which Sancho replied that the beast was better off than his master.

"Thank God," she exclaimed, "for all his blessings! But tell me now, my dear, what have you brought me from all your squirings? A new cloak to wear? Or shoes for the young ones?"

"I've brought you nothing of the sort, good wife," said Sancho, "but other things of greater value and importance."

"I'm glad to hear that," she replied. "Show me those things of greater value and importance, my dear. I'd like a sight of them just to cheer this heart of mine which has been so sad and unhappy all the centuries that you've been gone."

"I will show them to you at home, wife," said Sancho. "For the present be satisfied that if, God willing, we set out on another journey in search of adventures, you will see me in no time a count or the governor of an island, and not one of those around here, but the best that is to be had."

"I hope to Heaven it's true, my husband, for we certainly need it. But tell me, what is all this about islands? I don't understand."

"Honey," replied Sancho, "is not for the mouth of an ass. You will find out in good time, woman; and you're going to be surprised to hear yourself called 'my Ladyship' by all your vassals."

"What's this you are saying, Sancho, about ladyships, islands, and vassals?" Juana Panza insisted on knowing—for such was the name of Sancho's wife, although they were not blood relatives, it being the custom in La Mancha for wives to take their husbands" surnames.

"Do not be in such a hurry to know all this, Juana," he said. "It is enough that I am telling you the truth. Sew up your mouth, then; for all I will say, in passing, is that there is nothing in the world that is more pleasant than being a respected man, squire to a knight-errant who goes in search of adventures. It is true that most of the adventures you meet with do not come out the way you'd like them to, for ninety-nine out of a hundred will prove to be all twisted and crosswise. I know that from experience, for I've come out of some of them blanketed and out of others beaten to a pulp. But, all the same, it's a fine thing to go along waiting for what will happen next, crossing mountains, making your way through woods, climbing over cliffs, visiting castles, and putting up at inns free of charge, and the devil take the maravedi that is to pay."

Such was the conversation that took place between Sancho Panza and Juana Panza, his wife, as Don Quixote's housekeeper and niece were taking him in, stripping him, and stretching him out on his old-time bed. He gazed at them blankly, being unable to make out where he was. The curate charged the niece to take great care to see that her uncle was comfortable and to keep close watch over him so that he would not slip away from them another time. He then told them of what it had been necessary to do in order to get him home, at which they once more screamed to Heaven and began cursing the books of chivalry all over again, praying God to plunge the authors of such lying nonsense into the center of the bottomless pit. In short, they scarcely knew what to do, for they were very much afraid that their master and uncle would give them the slip once more, the moment he was a little better, and it turned out just the way they feared it might.

From Part II
Prologue

TO THE READER

God bless me, gentle or, it may be, plebeian reader, how eagerly you must be awaiting this prologue, thinking to find in it vengeful scoldings and vituperations directed against the author of the second Don Quixote—I mean the one who, so it is said, was begotten in Tordesillas and born in Tarragona.[1] The truth is, however, that I am not going to be able to satisfy you in this regard; for granting that injuries are capable of awakening wrath in the humblest of bosoms, my own must be an exception to the rule. You would, perhaps, have me call him an ass, a crackbrain, and an upstart, but it is not my intention so to chastise him for his sin. Let him eat it with his bread and have done with it.

What I cannot but resent is the fact that he describes me as being old and one-handed, as if it were in my power to make time stand still for me, or as if I had lost my hand in some tavern instead of upon the greatest occasion that the past or present has ever known or the future may ever hope to see.[2] If my wounds are not resplendent in the eyes of the chance beholder, they are at least highly thought of by those who know where they were received. The soldier who lies dead in battle has a more impressive mien than the one who by flight attains his liberty. So strongly do I feel about this that even if it were possible to work a miracle in my case, I still would rather have taken part in that prodigious battle than be today free of my wounds without having been there. The scars that the soldier has to show on face and breast are stars that guide others to the Heaven of honor, inspiring them with a longing for well-merited praise. What is more, it may be noted that one does not write with gray hairs but with his understanding, which usually grows better with the years.

I likewise resent his calling me envious; and as though I were some ignorant person, he goes on to explain to me what is meant by envy; when the truth of the matter is that of the two kinds, I am acquainted only with that which is holy, noble, and right-intentioned.[3] And this being so, as indeed it is, it is not likely that I should attack any priest, above all, one that is a familiar of the Holy Office.[4] If he made this statement, as it appears that he did, on behalf of a certain person, then he is utterly mistaken; for the person in question is one whose genius I hold in veneration and whose works I admire, as well as his constant industry and powers of application. But when all is said, I wish to thank this gentlemanly author for observing that my Novels[5] are more satirical than exemplary, while admitting at the same time that they are good; for they could not be good unless they had in them a little of everything.

You will likely tell me that I am being too restrained and overmodest, but it is my belief that affliction is not to be heaped upon the afflicted, and this gentleman must be suffering greatly, seeing that he does not dare to come out into the open and show himself by the light of day, but must conceal his name and dissemble his place of origin, as if he had been guilty of some treason or act of lese majesty. If you by chance should come to know him, tell him on my behalf that I do not hold it against him; for I know what temptations the devil has to offer, one of the greatest of which consists in putting it into a man's head that he can write a book and have it printed and thereby achieve as much fame as he does money and acquire as much money

---

1. A continuation of *Don Quixote* was published by a writer who gave himself the name of Avellaneda and claimed to come from Tordesillas. The mood of the second prologue is grim in comparison to the optimistic and witty prologue to Part I. **2.** The Battle of Lepanto in 1571. **3.** *Jealousy* and *zealousness* are etymologically related. **4.** An allusion to the Spanish playwright Lope de Vega (see p. 2072), who had been made a priest and appointed an official of the Spanish Inquisition. Avellaneda accused Cervantes of envying Lope's enormous popularity. **5.** *Exemplary Tales.*

as he does fame; in confirmation of which I would have you, in your own witty and charming manner, tell him this tale.

There was in Seville a certain madman whose madness assumed one of the drollest forms that ever was seen in this world. Taking a hollow reed sharpened at one end, he would catch a dog in the street or somewhere else; and, holding one of the animal's legs with his foot and raising the other with his hand, he would fix his reed as best he could in a certain part, after which he would blow the dog up, round as a ball. When he had it in this condition he would give it a couple of slaps on the belly and let it go, remarking to the bystanders, of whom there were always plenty, "Do your Worships think, then, that it is so easy a thing to inflate a dog?" So you might ask, "Does your Grace think that it is so easy a thing to write a book?" And if this story does not set well with him, here is another one, dear reader, that you may tell him. This one, also, is about a madman and a dog.

The madman in this instance lived in Cordova. He was in the habit of carrying on his head a marble slab or stone of considerable weight, and when he met some stray cur he would go up alongside it and drop the weight full upon it, and the dog in a rage, barking and howling, would then scurry off down three whole streets without stopping. Now, it happened that among the dogs that he treated in this fashion was one belonging to a capmaker, who was very fond of the beast. Going up to it as usual, the madman let the stone fall on its head, whereupon the animal set up a great yowling, and its owner, hearing its moans and seeing what had been done to it, promptly snatched up a measuring rod and fell upon the dog's assailant, flaying him until there was not a sound bone left in the fellow's body; and with each blow that he gave him he cried, "You dog! You thief! Treat my greyhound like that, would you? You brute, couldn't you see it was a greyhound?" And repeating the word "greyhound" over and over, he sent the madman away beaten to a pulp.

Profiting by the lesson that had been taught him, the fellow disappeared and was not seen in public for more than a month, at the end of which time he returned, up to his old tricks and with a heavier stone than ever on his head. He would go up to a dog and stare at it, long and hard, and without daring to drop his stone, would say, "This is a greyhound; beware." And so with all the dogs that he encountered: whether they were mastiffs or curs, he would assert that they were greyhounds and let them go unharmed.

The same thing possibly may happen to our historian; it may be that he will not again venture to let fall the weight of his wit in the form of books which, being bad ones, are harder than rocks.

As for the threat he has made to the effect that through his book he will deprive me of the profits on my own,[6] you may tell him that I do not give a rap. Quoting from the famous interlude, *La Perendenga*,[7] I will say to him in reply, "Long live my master, the Four-and-twenty,[8] and Christ be with us all." Long live the great Count of Lemos, whose Christian spirit and well-known liberality have kept me on my feet despite all the blows an unkind fate has dealt me. Long life to his Eminence of Toledo, the supremely charitable Don Bernardo de Sandoval y Rojas.[9] Even though there were no print-

---

6. Avellaneda asserted that his second part would earn the profits Cervantes might have expected from a continuation of his own.   7. No interlude by this name has survived.   8. Council of the town hall at Andalucía.   9. Archbishop of Toledo, uncle of the duke of Lerma, and patron of Cervantes.

ing presses in all the world, or such as there are should print more books directed against me than there are letters in the verses of *Mingo Revulgo*,[1] what would it matter to me? These two princes, without any cringing flattery or adulation on my part but solely out of their own goodness of heart, have taken it upon themselves to grant me their favor and protection, in which respect I consider myself richer and more fortunate than if by ordinary means I had attained the peak of prosperity. The poor man may keep his honor, but not the vicious one. Poverty may cast a cloud over nobility but cannot wholly obscure it. Virtue of itself gives off a certain light, even though it be through the chinks and crevices and despite the obstacles of adversity, and so comes to be esteemed and as a consequence favored by high and noble minds.

Tell him no more than this, nor do I have anything more to say to you, except to ask you to bear in mind that this *Second Part of Don Quixote*, which I herewith present to you, is cut from the same cloth and by the same crafts- man as Part I. In this book I give you Don Quixote continued and, finally, dead and buried, in order that no one may dare testify any further concerning him, for there has been quite enough evidence as it is. It is sufficient that a reputable individual should have chronicled these ingenious acts of madness once and for all, without going into the matter again; for an abundance even of good things causes them to be little esteemed, while scarcity may lend a certain worth to those that are bad.

I almost forgot to tell you that you may look forward to the *Persiles*, on which I am now putting the finishing touches, as well as Part Second of the *Galatea*.[2]

["Put into a Book"]

CHAPTER 3

Of the laughable conversation that took place between Don Quixote, Sancho Panza, and the bachelor Sansón Carrasco.

Don Quixote remained in a thoughtful mood as he waited for the bachelor Carrasco,[1] from whom he hoped to hear the news as to how he had been put into a book, as Sancho had said. He could not bring himself to believe that any such history existed, since the blood of the enemies he had slain was not yet dry on the blade of his sword; and here they were trying to tell him that his high deeds of chivalry were already circulating in printed form. But, for that matter, he imagined that some sage, either friend or enemy, must have seen to the printing of them through the art of magic. If the chronicler was a friend, he must have undertaken the task in order to magnify and exalt Don Quixote's exploits above the most notable ones achieved by knights- errant of old. If an enemy, his purpose would have been to make them out as nothing at all, by debasing them below the meanest acts ever recorded of any mean squire. The only thing was, the knight reflected, the exploits of

---

1. Long verse satire.   2. Never published.   1. The bachelor of arts Sansón Carrasco, an important new character who appears at the beginning of Part II and will play a considerable role in the story with his attempts at "curing" Don Quixote. Just now he has been telling Sancho about a book relating the adventures of Don Quixote and his squire, by which the two have been made famous; the book is, of course, *Don Quixote*, Part I.

squires never were set down in writing. If it was true that such a history existed, being about a knight-errant, then it must be eloquent and lofty in tone, a splendid and distinguished piece of work and veracious in its details.

This consoled him somewhat, although he was a bit put out at the thought that the author was a Moor, if the appellation "Cid" was to be taken as an indication,[2] and from the Moors you could never hope for any word of truth, seeing that they are all of them cheats, forgers, and schemers. He feared lest his love should not have been treated with becoming modesty but rather in a way that would reflect upon the virtue of his lady Dulcinea del Toboso. He hoped that his fidelity had been made clear, and the respect he had always shown her, and that something had been said as to how he had spurned queens, empresses, and damsels of every rank while keeping a rein upon those impulses that are natural to a man. He was still wrapped up in these and many other similar thoughts when Sancho returned with Carrasco.

Don Quixote received the bachelor very amiably. The latter, although his name was Sansón, or Samson, was not very big so far as bodily size went, but he was a great joker, with a sallow complexion and a ready wit. He was going on twenty-four and had a round face, a snub nose, and a large mouth, all of which showed him to be of a mischievous disposition and fond of jests and witticisms. This became apparent when, as soon as he saw Don Quixote, he fell upon his knees and addressed the knight as follows:

"O mighty Don Quixote de la Mancha, give me your hands; for by the habit of St. Peter that I wear[3]—though I have received but the first four orders—your Grace is one of the most famous knights-errant that ever have been or ever will be anywhere on this earth. Blessings upon Cid Hamete Benengeli who wrote down the history of your great achievements, and upon that curious-minded one who was at pains to have it translated from the Arabic into our Castilian vulgate for the universal entertainment of the people."

Don Quixote bade him rise. "Is it true, then," he asked, "that there is a book about me and that it was some Moorish sage who composed it?"

"By way of showing you how true it is," replied Sansón, "I may tell you that it is my belief that there are in existence today more than twelve thousand copies of that history. If you do not believe me, you have but to make inquiries in Portugal, Barcelona, and Valencia, where editions have been brought out, and there is even a report to the effect that one edition was printed at Antwerp. In short, I feel certain that there will soon not be a nation that does not know it or a language into which it has not been translated."

"One of the things," remarked Don Quixote, "that should give most satisfaction to a virtuous and eminent man is to see his good name spread abroad during his own lifetime, by means of the printing press, through translations into the languages of the various peoples. I have said 'good name,' for if he has any other kind, his fate is worse than death."

"If it is a matter of good name and good reputation," said the bachelor, "your Grace bears off the palm from all the knights-errant in the world; for the Moor in his tongue and the Christian in his have most vividly depicted your Grace's gallantry, your courage in facing dangers, your patience in

---

2. The allusion is to Cid Hamete Benengeli (see n. 3, p. 1998). The word *cid* is of Arabic derivation. 3. The dress of one of the minor clerical orders.

adversity and suffering, whether the suffering be due to wounds or to misfortunes of another sort, and your virtue and continence in love, in connection with that platonic relationship that exists between your Grace and my lady Doña Dulcinea del Toboso."

At this point Sancho spoke up. "Never in my life," he said, "have I heard my lady Dulcinea called 'Doña,' but only 'la Señora Dulcinea del Toboso'; so on that point, already, the history is wrong."

"That is not important," said Carrasco.

"No, certainly not," Don Quixote agreed. "But tell me, Señor Bachelor, what adventures of mine as set down in this book have made the deepest impression?"

"As to that," the bachelor answered, "opinions differ, for it is a matter of individual taste. There are some who are very fond of the adventure of the windmills—those windmills which to your Grace appeared to be so many Briareuses and giants. Others like the episode at the fulling mill. One relishes the story of the two armies which took on the appearance of droves of sheep, while another fancies the tale of the dead man whom they were taking to Segovia for burial. One will assert that the freeing of the galley slaves is the best of all, and yet another will maintain that nothing can come up to the Benedictine giants and the encounter with the valiant Biscayan."

Again Sancho interrupted him. "Tell me, Señor Bachelor," he said, "does the book say anything about the adventure with the Yanguesans, that time our good Rocinante took it into his head to go looking for tidbits in the sea?"

"The sage," replied Sansón, "has left nothing in the inkwell. He has told everything and to the point, even to the capers which the worthy Sancho cut as they tossed him in the blanket."

"I cut no capers in the blanket," objected Sancho, "but I did in the air, and more than I liked."

"I imagine," said Don Quixote, "that there is no history in the world, dealing with humankind, that does not have its ups and downs, and this is particularly true of those that have to do with deeds of chivalry, for they can never be filled with happy incidents alone."

"Nevertheless," the bachelor went on, "there are some who have read the book who say that they would have been glad if the authors had forgotten a few of the innumerable cudgelings which Señor Don Quixote received in the course of his various encounters."

"But that is where the truth of the story comes in," Sancho protested.

"For all of that," observed Don Quixote, "they might well have said nothing about them; for there is no need of recording those events that do not alter the veracity of the chronicle, when they tend only to lessen the reader's respect for the hero. You may be sure that Aeneas was not as pious as Vergil would have us believe, nor was Ulysses as wise as Homer depicts him."

"That is true enough," replied Sansón, "but it is one thing to write as a poet and another as a historian. The former may narrate or sing of things not as they were but as they should have been; the latter must describe them not as they should have been but as they were, without adding to or detracting from the truth in any degree whatsoever."

"Well," said Sancho, "if this Moorish gentleman is bent upon telling the truth, I have no doubt that among my master's thrashings my own will be found; for they never took the measure of his Grace's shoulders without measuring my whole body. But I don't wonder at that; for as my master himself says, when there's an ache in the head the members have to share it."

"You are a sly fox, Sancho," said Don Quixote. "My word, but you can remember things well enough when you choose to do so!"

"Even if I wanted to forget the whacks they gave me," Sancho answered him, "the welts on my ribs wouldn't let me, for they are still fresh."

"Be quiet, Sancho," his master admonished him, "and do not interrupt the bachelor. I beg him to go on and tell me what is said of me in this book."

"And what it says about me, too," put in Sancho, "for I have heard that I am one of the main presonages in it—"

"*Personages,* not *presonages,* Sancho my friend," said Sansón.

"So we have another one who catches you up on everything you say," was Sancho's retort. "If we go on at this rate, we'll never be through in a lifetime."

"May God put a curse on *my* life," the bachelor told him, "if you are not the second most important person in the story; and there are some who would rather listen to you talk than to anyone else in the book. It is true, there are those who say that you are too gullible in believing it to be the truth that you could become the governor of that island that was offered you by Señor Don Quixote, here present."

"There is still sun on the top of the wall," said Don Quixote, "and when Sancho is a little older, with the experience that the years bring, he will be wiser and better fitted to be a governor than he is at the present time."

"By God, master," said Sancho, "the island that I couldn't govern right now I'd never be able to govern if I lived to be as old as Methuselah. The trouble is, I don't know where that island we are talking about is located; it is not due to any lack of noddle on my part."

"Leave it to God, Sancho," was Don Quixote's advice, "and everything will come out all right, perhaps even better than you think; for not a leaf on the tree stirs except by His will."

"Yes," said Sansón, "if it be God's will, Sancho will not lack a thousand islands to govern, not to speak of one island alone."

"I have seen governors around here," said Sancho, "that are not to be compared to the sole of my shoe, and yet they call them 'your Lordship' and serve them on silver plate."

"Those are not the same kind of governors," Sansón informed him. "Their task is a good deal easier. The ones that govern islands must at least know grammar."

"I could make out well enough with the *gram,*" replied Sancho, "but with the *mar* I want nothing to do, for I don't understand it at all. But leaving this business of the governorship in God's hands—for He will send me wherever I can best serve Him—I will tell you, Señor Bachelor Sansón Carrasco, that I am very much pleased that the author of the history should have spoken of me in such a way as does not offend me; for, upon the word of a faithful squire, if he had said anything about me that was not becoming to an old Christian, the deaf would have heard of it."

"That would be to work miracles," said Sansón.

"Miracles or no miracles," was the answer, "let everyone take care as to what he says or writes about people and not be setting down the first thing that pops into his head."

"One of the faults that is found with the book," continued the bachelor, "is that the author has inserted in it a story entitled *The One Who Was Too Curious for His Own Good*. It is not that the story in itself is a bad one or badly written; it is simply that it is out of place there, having nothing to do with the story of his Grace, Señor Don Quixote."[4]

"I will bet you," said Sancho, "that the son of a dog has mixed the cabbages with the baskets."[5]

"And I will say right now," declared Don Quixote, "that the author of this book was not a sage but some ignorant prattler who at haphazard and without any method set about the writing of it, being content to let things turn out as they might. In the same manner, Orbaneja,[6] the painter of Ubeda, when asked what he was painting would reply, 'Whatever it turns out to be.' Sometimes it would be a cock, in which case he would have to write alongside it, in Gothic letters, 'This is a cock.' And so it must be with my story, which will need a commentary to make it understandable."

"No," replied Sansón, "that it will not; for it is so clearly written that none can fail to understand it. Little children leaf through it, young people read it, adults appreciate it, and the aged sing its praises. In short, it is so thumbed and read and so well known to persons of every walk in life that no sooner do folks see some skinny nag than they at once cry, 'There goes Rocinante!' Those that like it best of all are the pages; for there is no lord's antechamber where a *Don Quixote* is not to be found. If one lays it down, another will pick it up; one will pounce upon it, and another will beg for it. It affords the pleasantest and least harmful reading of any book that has been published up to now. In the whole of it there is not to be found an indecent word or a thought that is other than Catholic."

"To write in any other manner," observed Don Quixote, "would be to write lies and not the truth. Those historians who make use of falsehoods ought to be burned like the makers of counterfeit money. I do not know what could have led the author to introduce stories and episodes that are foreign to the subject matter when he had so much to write about in describing my adventures. He must, undoubtedly, have been inspired by the old saying, 'With straw or with hay[7] . . .' For, in truth, all he had to do was to record my thoughts, my sighs, my tears, my lofty purposes, and my undertakings, and he would have had a volume bigger or at least as big as that which the works of El Tostado[8] would make. To sum the matter up, Señor Bachelor, it is my opinion that, in composing histories or books of any sort, a great deal of judgment and ripe understanding is called for. To say and write witty and amusing things is the mark of great genius. The cleverest character in a comedy is the clown, since he who would make himself out to be a simpleton cannot be one. History is a near-sacred thing, for it must be true, and where the truth is, there is God. And yet there are those who compose books and toss them out into the world as if they were no more than fritters."

"There is no book so bad," opined the bachelor, "that there is not some good in it."

"Doubtless that is so," replied Don Quixote, "but it very often happens

---

4. The story, a tragic tale about a jealousy-ridden husband, occupies several chapters of Part I. Here, as elsewhere in this chapter, Cervantes echoes criticism currently aimed at his book.   **5.** Has jumbled together things of different kinds.   **6.** Unidentified.   **7.** The proverb concludes either "the mattress is filled" or "I fill my belly."   **8.** Alonso de Madrigal, bishop of Ávila, a prolific author of devotional works.

that those who have won in advance a great and well-deserved reputation for their writings, lose it in whole or in part when they give their works to the printer."

"The reason for it," said Sansón, "is that, printed works being read at leisure, their faults are the more readily apparent, and the greater the reputation of the author the more closely are they scrutinized. Men famous for their genius, great poets, illustrious historians, are almost always envied by those who take a special delight in criticizing the writings of others without having produced anything of their own."

"That is not to be wondered at," said Don Quixote, "for there are many theologians who are not good enough for the pulpit but who are very good indeed when it comes to detecting the faults or excesses of those who preach."

"All of this is very true, Señor Don Quixote," replied Carrasco, "but, all the same, I could wish that these self-appointed censors were a bit more forbearing and less hypercritical; I wish they would pay a little less attention to the spots on the bright sun of the work that occasions their fault-finding. For if *aliquando bonus dormitat Homerus,*[9] let them consider how much of his time he spent awake, shedding the light of his genius with a minimum of shade. It well may be that what to them seems a flaw is but one of those moles which sometimes add to the beauty of a face. In any event, I insist that he who has a book printed runs a very great risk, inasmuch as it is an utter impossibility to write it in such a manner that it will please all who read it."

"This book about me must have pleased very few," remarked Don Quixote.

"Quite the contrary," said Sansón, "for just as *stultorum infinitus est numerus,*[1] so the number of those who have enjoyed this history is likewise infinite. Some, to be sure, have complained of the author's forgetfulness, seeing that he neglected to make it plain who the thief was who stole Sancho's gray;[2] for it is not stated there, but merely implied, that the ass was stolen; and, a little further on, we find the knight mounted on the same beast, although it has not made its reappearance in the story. They also say that the author forgot to tell us what Sancho did with those hundred crowns that he found in the valise on the Sierra Morena, as nothing more is said of them and there are many who would like to know how he disposed of the money or how he spent it. This is one of the serious omissions to be found in the work."

To this Sancho replied, "I, Señor Sansón, do not feel like giving any account or accounting just now; for I feel a little weak in my stomach, and if I don't do something about it by taking a few swigs of the old stuff, I'll be sitting on St. Lucy's thorn.[3] I have some of it at home, and my old woman is waiting for me. After I've had my dinner, I'll come back and answer any questions your Grace or anybody else wants to ask me, whether it's about the loss of the ass or the spending of the hundred crowns."

And without waiting for a reply or saying another word, he went on home. Don Quixote urged the bachelor to stay and take potluck with him, and Sansón accepted the invitation and remained. In addition to the knight's ordinary fare, they had a couple of pigeons, and at table their talk was of chivalry and feats of arms.

---

9. Good Homer sometimes nods too (Latin); Horace, *Art of Poetry,* line 359.　　**1.** Infinite is the number of fools (Latin).　　**2.** In Part I, chap. 23.　　**3.** I shall be weak and exhausted.

[A Victorious Duel]

CHAPTER 12

Of the strange adventure that befell the valiant Don Quixote with the fearless Knight of the Mirrors.[1]

The night following the encounter with Death was spent by Don Quixote and his squire beneath some tall and shady trees,[2] the knight having been persuaded to eat a little from the stock of provisions carried by the gray.

"Sir," said Sancho, in the course of their repast, "how foolish I'd have been if I had chosen the spoils from your Grace's first adventure rather than the foals from the three mares.[3] Truly, truly, a sparrow in the hand is worth more than a vulture on the wing."[4]

"And yet, Sancho," replied Don Quixote, "if you had but let me attack them as I wished to do, you would at least have had as spoils the Empress's gold crown and Cupid's painted wings;[5] for I should have taken them whether or no and placed them in your hands."

"The crowns and scepters of stage emperors," remarked Sancho, "were never known to be of pure gold; they are always of tinsel or tinplate."

"That is the truth," said Don Quixote, "for it is only right that the accessories of a drama should be fictitious and not real, like the play itself. Speaking of that, Sancho, I would have you look kindly upon the art of the theater and, as a consequence, upon those who write the pieces and perform in them, for they all render a service of great value to the State by holding up a mirror for us at each step that we take, wherein we may observe, vividly depicted, all the varied aspects of human life; and I may add that there is nothing that shows us more clearly, by similitude, what we are and what we ought to be than do plays and players.

"Tell me, have you not seen some comedy in which kings, emperors, pontiffs, knights, ladies, and numerous other characters are introduced? One plays the ruffian, another the cheat, this one a merchant and that one a soldier, while yet another is the fool who is not so foolish as he appears, and still another the one of whom love has made a fool. Yet when the play is over and they have taken off their players' garments, all the actors are once more equal."

"Yes," replied Sancho, "I have seen all that."

"Well," continued Don Quixote, "the same thing happens in the comedy that we call life, where some play the part of emperors, others that of pontiffs—in short, all the characters that a drama may have—but when it is all over, that is to say, when life is done, death takes from each the garb that differentiates him, and all at last are equal in the grave."

"It is a fine comparison," Sancho admitted, "though not so new but that I

---

1. Until he earns this title (in chap. 15), he will be referred to as the Knight of the Wood. 2. Don Quixote and his squire are now in the woody region around El Toboso, Dulcinea's town. Sancho has been sent to look for his knight's lady and has saved the day by pretending to see the beautiful damsel in a "village wench, and not a pretty one at that, for she was round-faced and snub-nosed." But by his imaginative lie he has succeeded, as he had planned, in setting in motion Don Quixote's belief in spells and enchantments: enemy magicians, envious of him, have hidden his lady's splendor only from his sight. While the knight was still under the shock of this experience, farther along their way he and his squire have met a group of itinerant players dressed in their proper costumes for a religious play, *The Parliament of Death.* 3. Don Quixote has promised them to Sancho as a reward for bringing news of Dulcinea. 4. I.e., a bird in the hand is worth two in the bush. 5. The Empress and Cupid were characters in *The Parliament of Death.*

have heard it many times before. It reminds me of that other one, about the game of chess. So long as the game lasts, each piece has its special qualities, but when it is over they are all mixed and jumbled together and put into a bag, which is to the chess pieces what the grave is to life."

"Every day, Sancho," said Don Quixote, "you are becoming less stupid and more sensible."

"It must be that some of your Grace's good sense is sticking to me," was Sancho's answer. "I am like a piece of land that of itself is dry and barren, but if you scatter manure over it and cultivate it, it will bear good fruit. By this I mean to say that your Grace's conversation is the manure that has been cast upon the barren land of my dry wit; the time that I spend in your service, associating with you, does the cultivating; and as a result of it all, I hope to bring forth blessed fruits by not departing, slipping, or sliding, from those paths of good breeding which your Grace has marked out for me in my parched understanding."

Don Quixote had to laugh at this affected speech of Sancho's, but he could not help perceiving that what the squire had said about his improvement was true enough; for every now and then the servant would speak in a manner that astonished his master. It must be admitted, however, that most of the time when he tried to use fine language, he would tumble from the mountain of his simple-mindedness into the abyss of his ignorance. It was when he was quoting old saws and sayings, whether or not they had anything to do with the subject under discussion, that he was at his best, displaying upon such occasions a prodigious memory, as will already have been seen and noted in the course of this history.

With such talk as this they spent a good part of the night. Then Sancho felt a desire to draw down the curtains of his eyes, as he was in the habit of saying when he wished to sleep, and, unsaddling his mount, he turned him loose to graze at will on the abundant grass. If he did not remove Rocinante's saddle, this was due to his master's express command; for when they had taken the field and were not sleeping under a roof, the hack was under no circumstances to be stripped. This was in accordance with an old and established custom which knights-errant faithfully observed: the bridle and saddlebow might be removed, but beware of touching the saddle itself! Guided by this precept, Sancho now gave Rocinante the same freedom that the ass enjoyed.

The close friendship that existed between the two animals was a most unusual one, so remarkable indeed that it has become a tradition handed down from father to son, and the author of this veracious chronicle even wrote a number of special chapters on the subject, although, in order to preserve the decency and decorum that are fitting in so heroic an account, he chose to omit them in the final version. But he forgets himself once in a while and goes on to tell us how the two beasts when they were together would hasten to scratch each other, and how, when they were tired and their bellies were full, Rocinante would lay his long neck over that of the ass—it extended more than a half a yard on the other side—and the pair would then stand there gazing pensively at the ground for as much as three whole days at a time, or at least until someone came for them or hunger compelled them to seek nourishment.

I may tell you that I have heard it said that the author of this history, in one of his writings, has compared the friendship of Rocinante and the gray to that of Nisus and Euryalus and that of Pylades and Orestes;[6] and if this be true, it shows for the edification of all what great friends these two peace-loving animals were, and should be enough to make men ashamed, who are so inept at preserving friendship with one another. For this reason it has been said:

> There is no friend for friend,
> Reeds to lances turn[7] . . .

And there was the other poet who sang:

> Between friend and friend the bug[8] . . .

Let no one think that the author has gone out of his way in comparing the friendship of animals with that of men; for human beings have received valuable lessons from the beasts and have learned many important things from them. From the stork they have learned the use of clysters; the dog has taught them the salutary effects of vomiting as well as a lesson in gratitude; the cranes have taught them vigilance, the ants foresight, the elephants modesty, and the horse loyalty.[9]

Sancho had at last fallen asleep at the foot of a cork tree, while Don Quixote was slumbering beneath a sturdy oak. Very little time had passed when the knight was awakened by a noise behind him, and, starting up, he began looking about him and listening to see if he could make out where it came from. Then he caught sight of two men on horseback, one of whom, slipping down from the saddle, said to the other, "Dismount, my friend, and unbridle the horses; for there seems to be plenty of grass around here for them and sufficient silence and solitude for my amorous thoughts."

Saying this, he stretched himself out on the ground, and as he flung himself down the armor that he wore made such a noise that Don Quixote knew at once, for a certainty, that he must be a knight-errant. Going over to Sancho, who was still sleeping, he shook him by the arm and with no little effort managed to get him awake.

"Brother Sancho," he said to him in a low voice, "we have an adventure on our hands."

"God give us a good one," said Sancho. "And where, my master, may her Ladyship, Mistress Adventure, be?"

"Where, Sancho?" replied Don Quixote. "Turn your eyes and look, and you will see stretched out over there a knight-errant who, so far as I can make out, is not any too happy; for I saw him fling himself from his horse to the ground with a certain show of despondency, and as he fell his armor rattled."

"Well," said Sancho, "and how does your Grace make this out to be an adventure?"

"I would not say," the knight answered him, "that this is an adventure in itself, but rather the beginning of one, for that is the way they start. But listen; he seems to be tuning a lute or guitar, and from the way he is spitting and clearing his throat he must be getting ready to sing something."

6. Famous examples of friendship in Virgil's *Aeneid* and in Greek tradition and drama. 7. From a popular ballad. 8. The Spanish "a bug in the eye" implies keeping a watchful eye on somebody. 9. All folkloristic beliefs about the virtues of animals.

"Faith, so he is," said Sancho. "He must be some lovesick knight."

"There are no knights-errant that are not lovesick," Don Quixote informed him. "Let us listen to him, and the thread of his song will lead us to the yarn-ball of his thoughts; for out of the abundance of the heart the mouth speaketh."

Sancho would have liked to reply to his master, but the voice of the Knight of the Wood, which was neither very good nor very bad, kept him from it; and as the two of them listened attentively, they heard the following:

Sonnet

Show me, O lady, the pattern of thy will,
That mine may take that very form and shape;
For my will in thine own I fain would drape,
Each slightest wish of thine I would fulfill.
If thou wouldst have me silence this dead ill   5
Of which I'm dying now, prepare the crape!
Or if I must another manner ape,
Then let Love's self display his rhyming skill.
Of opposites I am made, that's manifest:
In part soft wax, in part hard-diamond fire;   10
Yet to Love's laws my heart I do adjust,
And, hard or soft, I offer thee this breast:
Print or engrave there what thou may'st desire,
And I'll preserve it in eternal trust.[1]

With an *Ay!* that appeared to be wrung from the very depths of his heart, the Knight of the Wood brought his song to a close, and then after a brief pause began speaking in a grief-stricken voice that was piteous to hear.

"O most beautiful and most ungrateful woman in all the world!" he cried, "how is it possible, O most serene Casildea de Vandalia,[2] for you to permit this captive knight of yours to waste away and perish in constant wanderings, amid rude toils and bitter hardships? Is it not enough that I have compelled all the knights of Navarre, all those of León, all the Tartessians and Castilians, and, finally, all those of La Mancha, to confess that there is no beauty anywhere that can rival yours?"

"That is not so!" cried Don Quixote at this point. "I am of La Mancha, and I have never confessed, I never could nor would confess a thing so prejudicial to the beauty of my lady. The knight whom you see there, Sancho, is raving; but let us listen and perhaps he will tell us more."

"That he will," replied Sancho, "for at the rate he is carrying on, he is good for a month at a stretch."

This did not prove to be the case, however; for when the Knight of the Wood heard voices near him, he cut short his lamentations and rose to his feet.

"Who goes there?" he called in a loud but courteous tone. "What kind of people are you? Are you, perchance, numbered among the happy or among the afflicted?"

---

1. The poem intentionally follows affected conventions of the time.   2. The Knight of the Wood's counterpart to Don Quixote's Dulcinea del Toboso.

"Among the afflicted," was Don Quixote's response.

"Then come to me," said the one of the Wood, "and, in doing so, know that you come to sorrow's self and the very essence of affliction."

Upon receiving so gentle and courteous an answer, Don Quixote and Sancho as well went over to him, whereupon the sorrowing one took the Manchegan's arm.

"Sit down here, Sir Knight," he continued, "for in order to know that you are one of those who follow the profession of knight-errantry, it is enough for me to have found you in this place where solitude and serenity keep you company, such a spot being the natural bed and proper dwelling of wandering men of arms."

"A knight I am," replied Don Quixote, "and of the profession that you mention; and though sorrows, troubles, and misfortunes have made my heart their abode, this does not mean that compassion for the woes of others has been banished from it. From your song a while ago I gather that your misfortunes are due to love—the love you bear that ungrateful fair one whom you named in your lamentations."

As they conversed in this manner, they sat together upon the hard earth, very peaceably and companionably, as if at daybreak they were not going to break each other's heads.

"Sir Knight," inquired the one of the Wood, "are you by any chance in love?"

"By mischance I am," said Don Quixote, "although the ills that come from well-placed affection should be looked upon as favors rather than as misfortunes."

"That is the truth," the Knight of the Wood agreed, "if it were not that the loved one's scorn disturbs our reason and understanding; for when it is excessive scorn appears as vengeance."

"I was never scorned by my lady," said Don Quixote.

"No, certainly not," said Sancho, who was standing near by, "for my lady is gentle as a ewe lamb and soft as butter."

"Is he your squire?" asked the one of the Wood.

"He is," replied Don Quixote.

"I never saw a squire," said the one of the Wood, "who dared to speak while his master was talking. At least, there is mine over there; he is as big as your father, and it cannot be proved that he has ever opened his lips while I was conversing."

"Well, upon my word," said Sancho, "I have spoken, and I will speak in front of any other as good—but never mind; it only makes it worse to stir it."

The Knight of the Wood's squire now seized Sancho's arm. "Come along," he said, "let the two of us go where we can talk all we like, squire fashion, and leave these gentlemen our masters to come to lance blows as they tell each other the story of their loves; for you may rest assured, daybreak will find them still at it."

"Let us, by all means," said Sancho, "and I will tell your Grace who I am, so that you may be able to see for yourself whether or not I am to be numbered among the dozen most talkative squires."

With this, the pair went off to one side, and there then took place between them a conversation that was as droll as the one between their masters was solemn.

CHAPTER 13

In which is continued the adventure of the Knight of the Wood, together with the shrewd, highly original, and amicable conversation that took place between the two squires.

The knights and the squires had now separated, the latter to tell their life stories, the former to talk of their loves; but the history first relates the conversation of the servants and then goes on to report that of the masters. We are told that, after they had gone some little distance from where the others were, the one who served the Knight of the Wood began speaking to Sancho as follows:

"It is a hard life that we lead and live, *Señor mio,* those of us who are squires to knights-errant. It is certainly true that we eat our bread in the sweat of our faces, which is one of the curses that God put upon our first parents."[3]

"It might also be said," added Sancho, "that we eat it in the chill of our bodies, for who endures more heat and cold than we wretched ones who wait upon these wandering men of arms? It would not be so bad if we did eat once in a while, for troubles are less where there is bread; but as it is, we sometimes go for a day or two without breaking our fast, unless we feed on the wind that blows."

"But all this," said the other, "may very well be put up with, by reason of the hope we have of being rewarded; for if a knight is not too unlucky, his squire after a little while will find himself the governor of some fine island or prosperous earldom."

"I," replied Sancho, "have told my master that I would be satisfied with the governorship of an island, and he is so noble and so generous that he has promised it to me on many different occasions."

"In return for my services," said the Squire of the Wood, "I'd be content with a canonry. My master has already appointed me to one—and what a canonry!"

"Then he must be a churchly knight," said Sancho, "and in a position to grant favors of that sort to his faithful squire; but mine is a layman, pure and simple, although, as I recall, certain shrewd and, as I see it, scheming persons did advise him to try to become an archbishop. However, he did not want to be anything but an emperor. And there I was, all the time trembling for fear he would take it into his head to enter the Church, since I was not educated enough to hold any benefices. For I may as well tell your Grace that, though I look like a man, I am no more than a beast where holy orders are concerned."

"That is where you are making a mistake," the Squire of the Wood assured him. "Not all island governments are desirable. Some of them are misshapen bits of land, some are poor, others are gloomy, and, in short, the best of them lays a heavy burden of care and trouble upon the shoulders of the unfortunate one to whose lot it falls. It would be far better if we who follow this cursed trade were to go back to our homes and there engage in pleasanter occupations, such as hunting or fishing, for example; for where is there in

---

3. Cf. Genesis 3.19. "In the sweat of thy face shalt thou eat bread, till thou return unto the ground."

this world a squire so poor that he does not have a hack, a couple of grey-hounds, and a fishing rod to provide him with sport in his own village?"

"I don't lack any of those," replied Sancho. "It is true, I have no hack, but I do have an ass that is worth twice as much as my master's horse. God send me a bad Easter, and let it be the next one that comes, if I would make a trade, even though he gave me four fanegas[4] of barley to boot. Your Grace will laugh at the price I put on my gray—for that is the color of the beast. As to greyhounds, I shan't want for them, as there are plenty and to spare in my village. And, anyway, there is more pleasure in hunting when someone else pays for it."

"Really and truly, Sir Squire," said the one of the Wood, "I have made up my mind and resolved to have no more to do with the mad whims of these knights; I intend to retire to my village and bring up my little ones—I have three of them, and they are like oriental pearls."

"I have two of them," said Sancho, "that might be presented to the Pope in person, especially one of my girls that I am bringing up to be a countess, God willing, in spite of what her mother says."

"And how old is this young lady that is destined to be a countess?"

"Fifteen," replied Sancho, "or a couple of years more or less. But she is tall as a lance, fresh as an April morning, and strong as a porter."

"Those," remarked the one of the Wood, "are qualifications that fit her to be not merely a countess but a nymph of the verdant wildwood. O whore's daughter of a whore! What strength the she-rogue must have!"

Sancho was a bit put out by this. "She is not a whore," he said, "nor was her mother before her, nor will either of them ever be, please God, so long as I live. And you might speak more courteously. For one who has been brought up among knights-errant, who are the soul of courtesy, those words are not very becoming."

"Oh, how little your Grace knows about compliments, Sir Squire!" the one of the Wood exclaimed. "Are you not aware that when some knight gives a good lance thrust to the bull in the plaza, or when a person does anything remarkably well, it is the custom for the crowd to cry out, 'Well done, whore-son rascal!' and that what appears to be vituperation in such a case is in reality high praise? Sir, I would bid you disown those sons or daughters who do nothing to cause such praise to be bestowed upon their parents."

"I would indeed disown them if they didn't," replied Sancho, "and so your Grace may go ahead and call me, my children, and my wife all the whores in the world if you like, for everything that they say and do deserves the very highest praise. And in order that I may see them all again, I pray God to deliver me from mortal sin, or, what amounts to the same thing, from this dangerous calling of squire, seeing that I have fallen into it a second time, decoyed and deceived by a purse of a hundred ducats that I found one day in the heart of the Sierra Morena.[5] The devil is always holding up a bag full of doubloons in front of my eyes, here, there—no, not here, but there—everywhere, until it seems to me at every step I take that I am touching it with my hand, hugging it, carrying it off home with me, investing it, drawing an income from it, and living on it like a prince. And while I am thinking such thoughts, all the hardships I have to put up with serving this crack-

4. About 1.6 bushels.   5. When Don Quixote retired there in Part I, chap. 23.

brained master of mine, who is more of a madman than a knight, seem to me light and easy to bear."

"That," observed the Squire of the Wood, "is why it is they say that avarice bursts the bag. But, speaking of madmen, there is no greater one in all this world than my master; for he is one of those of whom it is said, 'The cares of others kill the ass.' Because another knight has lost his senses, he has to play mad too[6] and go hunting for that which, when he finds it, may fly up in his snout."

"Is he in love, maybe?"

"Yes, with a certain Casildea de Vandalia, the rawest[7] and best-roasted lady to be found anywhere on earth; but her rawness is not the foot he limps on, for he has other and greater schemes rumbling in his bowels, as you will hear tell before many hours have gone by."

"There is no road so smooth," said Sancho, "that it does not have some hole or rut to make you stumble. In other houses they cook horse beans, in mine they boil them by the kettleful.[8] Madness has more companions and attendants than good sense does. But if it is true what they say, that company in trouble brings relief, I may take comfort from your Grace, since you serve a master as foolish as my own."

"Foolish but brave," the one of the Wood corrected him, "and more of a rogue than anything else."

"That is not true of my master," replied Sancho. "I can assure you there is nothing of the rogue about him; he is as open and aboveboard as a wine pitcher and would not harm anyone but does good to all. There is no malice in his make-up, and a child could make him believe it was night at midday. For that very reason I love him with all my heart and cannot bring myself to leave him, no matter how many foolish things he does."

"But, nevertheless, good sir and brother," said the Squire of the Wood, "with the blind leading the blind, both are in danger of falling into the pit. It would be better for us to get out of all this as quickly as we can and return to our old haunts; for those that go seeking adventures do not always find good ones."

Sancho kept clearing his throat from time to time, and his saliva seemed rather viscous and dry; seeing which, the woodland squire said to him, "It looks to me as if we have been talking so much that our tongues are cleaving to our palates, but I have a loosener over there, hanging from the bow of my saddle, and a pretty good one it is." With this, he got up and went over to his horse and came back a moment later with a big flask of wine and a meat pie half a yard in diameter. This is no exaggeration, for the pasty in question was made of a hutch-rabbit of such a size that Sancho took it to be a goat, or at the very least a kid.

"And are you in the habit of carrying this with you, Señor?" he asked.

"What do you think?" replied the other. "Am I by any chance one of your wood-and-water[9] squires? I carry better rations on the flanks of my horse than a general does when he takes the field."

Sancho ate without any urging, gulping down mouthfuls that were like the knots on a tether, as they sat there in the dark.

---

6. In the Sierra Morena, Don Quixote had decided to imitate Amadís de Gaul and Ariosto's Roland "by playing the part of a desperate and raving madman" as a consequence of love.   7. The Spanish has a pun on *crudo*, meaning both "raw" and "cruel."   8. Meaning that his misfortunes always come in large quantities.   9. Of low quality.

"You are a squire of the right sort," he said, "loyal and true, and you live in grand style as shown by this feast, which I would almost say was produced by magic. You are not like me, poor wretch, who have in my saddlebags only a morsel of cheese so hard you could crack a giant's skull with it, three or four dozen carob beans, and a few nuts. For this I have my master to thank, who believes in observing the rule that knights-errant should nourish and sustain themselves on nothing but dried fruits and the herbs of the field."

"Upon my word, brother," said the other squire, "my stomach was not made for thistles, wild pears, and woodland herbs. Let our masters observe those knightly laws and traditions and eat what their rules prescribe; I carry a hamper of food and a flask on my saddlebow, whether they like it or not. And speaking of that flask, how I love it! There is scarcely a minute in the day that I'm not hugging and kissing it, over and over again."

As he said this, he placed the wine bag in Sancho's hands, who put it to his mouth, threw his head back, and sat there gazing up at the stars for a quarter of an hour. Then, when he had finished drinking, he let his head loll on one side and heaved a deep sigh.

"The whoreson rascal!" he exclaimed, "that's a fine vintage for you!"

"There!" cried the Squire of the Wood, as he heard the epithet Sancho had used, "do you see how you have praised this wine by calling it 'whoreson'?"

"I grant you," replied Sancho, "that it is no insult to call anyone a son of a whore so long as you really do mean to praise him. But tell me, sir, in the name of what you love most, is this the wine of Ciudad Real?"[1]

"What a winetaster you are! It comes from nowhere else, and it's a few years old, at that."

"Leave it to me," said Sancho, "and never fear, I'll show you how much I know about it. Would you believe me, Sir Squire, I have such a great natural instinct in this matter of wines that I have but to smell a vintage and I will tell you the country where it was grown, from what kind of grapes, what it tastes like, and how good it is, and everything that has to do with it. There is nothing so unusual about this, however, seeing that on my father's side were two of the best winetasters La Mancha has known in many a year, in proof of which, listen to the story of what happened to them.

"The two were given a sample of wine from a certain vat and asked to state its condition and quality and determine whether it was good or bad. One of them tasted it with the tip of his tongue while the other merely brought it up to his nose. The first man said that it tasted of iron, the second that it smelled of Cordovan leather. The owner insisted that the vat was clean and that there could be nothing in the wine to give it a flavor of leather or of iron, but, nevertheless, the two famous winetasters stood their ground. Time went by, and when they came to clean out the vat they found in it a small key attached to a leather strap. And so your Grace may see for yourself whether or not one who comes of that kind of stock has a right to give his opinion in such cases."

"And for that very reason," said the Squire of the Wood, "I maintain that we ought to stop going about in search of adventures. Seeing that we have loaves, let us not go looking for cakes, but return to our cottages, for God will find us there if He so wills."

---

1. The main town in La Mancha and the center of a wine region.

"I mean to stay with my master," Sancho replied, "until he reaches Saragossa, but after that we will come to an understanding."

The short of the matter is, the two worthy squires talked so much and drank so much that sleep had to tie their tongues and moderate their thirst, since to quench the latter was impossible. Clinging to the wine flask, which was almost empty by now, and with half-chewed morsels of food in their mouths, they both slept peacefully; and we shall leave them there as we go on to relate what took place between the Knight of the Wood and the Knight of the Mournful Countenance.

CHAPTER 14

Wherein is continued the adventure of the Knight of the Wood.

In the course of the long conversation that took place between Don Quixote and the Knight of the Wood, the history informs us that the latter addressed the following remarks to the Manchegan:

"In short, Sir Knight, I would have you know that my destiny, or, more properly speaking, my own free choice, has led me to fall in love with the peerless Casildea de Vandalia. I call her peerless for the reason that she has no equal as regards either her bodily proportions or her very great beauty. This Casildea, then, of whom I am telling you, repaid my worthy affections and honorable intentions by forcing me, as Hercules[2] was forced by his stepmother, to incur many and diverse perils; and each time as I overcame one of them she would promise me that with the next one I should have that which I desired; but instead my labors have continued, forming a chain whose links I am no longer able to count, nor can I say which will be the last one, that shall mark the beginning of the realization of my hopes.

"One time she sent me forth to challenge that famous giantess of Seville, known as La Giralda,[3] who is as strong and brave as if made of brass, and who without moving from the spot where she stands is the most changeable and fickle woman in the world. I came, I saw, I conquered her, I made her stand still and point in one direction only, and for more than a week nothing but north winds blew. Then, there was that other time when Casildea sent me to lift those ancient stones, the mighty Bulls of Guisando,[4] an enterprise that had better have been entrusted to porters than to knights. On another occasion she commanded me to hurl myself down into the Cabra chasm[5]—an unheard-of and terribly dangerous undertaking—and bring her back a detailed account of what lay concealed in that deep and gloomy pit. I rendered La Giralda motionless, I lifted the Bulls of Guisando, and I threw myself into the abyss and brought to light what was hidden in its depths; yet my hopes are dead—how dead!—while her commands and her scorn are as lively as can be.

"Finally, she commanded me to ride through all the provinces of Spain and compel all the knights-errant whom I met with to confess that she is the most beautiful woman now living and that I am the most enamored man of arms that is to be found anywhere in the world. In fulfillment of this behest

2. Son of Zeus and Alcmena; he was persecuted by Zeus's wife, Hera.   3. Actually a statue on the Moorish belfry of the cathedral at Seville.   4. Statues representing animals and supposedly marking a place where Caesar defeated Pompey.   5. Possibly an ancient mine in the Sierra de Cabra near Cordova.

I have already traveled over the greater part of these realms and have vanquished many knights who have dared to contradict me. But the one whom I am proudest to have overcome in single combat is that famous gentleman, Don Quixote de la Mancha; for I made him confess that my Casildea is more beautiful than his Dulcinea, and by achieving such a conquest I reckon that I have conquered all the others on the face of the earth, seeing that this same Don Quixote had himself routed them. Accordingly, when I vanquished him, his fame, glory, and honor passed over and were transferred to my person.

> The brighter is the conquered one's lost crown,
> The greater is the conqueror's renown.[6]

Thus, the innumerable exploits of the said Don Quixote are now set down to my account and are indeed my own.'

Don Quixote was astounded as he listened to the Knight of the Wood, and was about to tell him any number of times that he lied; the words were on the tip of his tongue, but he held them back as best he could, thinking that he would bring the other to confess with his own lips that what he had said was a lie. And so it was quite calmly that he now replied to him.

"Sir Knight," he began, "as to the assertion that your Grace has conquered most of the knights-errant in Spain and even in all the world, I have nothing to say, but that you have vanquished Don Quixote de la Mancha, I am inclined to doubt. It may be that it was someone else who resembled him, although there are very few that do."

"What do you mean?" replied the one of the Wood. "I swear by the heavens above that I did fight with Don Quixote and that I overcame him and forced him to yield. He is a tall man, with a dried-up face, long, lean legs, graying hair, an eagle-like nose somewhat hooked, and a big, black, drooping mustache. He takes the field under the name of the Knight of the Mournful Countenance, he has for squire a peasant named Sancho Panza, and he rides a famous steed called Rocinante. Lastly, the lady of his heart is a certain Dulcinea del Toboso, once upon a time known as Aldonza Lorenzo, just as my own lady, whose name is Casildea and who is an Andalusian by birth, is called by me Casildea de Vandalia. If all this is not sufficient to show that I speak the truth, here is my sword which shall make incredulity itself believe."

"Calm yourself, Sir Knight," replied Don Quixote, "and listen to what I have to say to you. You must know that this Don Quixote of whom you speak is the best friend that I have in the world, so great a friend that I may say that I feel toward him as I do toward my own self; and from all that you have told me, the very definite and accurate details that you have given me, I cannot doubt that he is the one whom you have conquered. On the other hand, the sight of my eyes and the touch of my hands assure me that he could not possibly be the one, unless some enchanter who is his enemy—for he has many, and one in particular who delights in persecuting him—may have assumed the knight's form and then permitted himself to be routed, by way of defrauding Don Quixote of the fame which his high deeds of chivalry have earned for him throughout the known world. To show you how

6. From Alonso de Ercilla y Zúñiga's *Araucana,* a poem about the Spanish struggle against the Araucanian Indians of Chile.

true this may be, I will inform you that not more than a couple of days ago those same enemy magicians transformed the figure and person of the beauteous Dulcinea del Toboso into a low and mean village lass, and it is possible that they have done something of the same sort to the knight who is her lover. And if all this does not suffice to convince you of the truth of what I say, here is Don Quixote himself who will maintain it by force of arms, on foot or on horseback, or in any way you like."

Saying this, he rose and laid hold of his sword, and waited to see what the Knight of the Wood's decision would be. That worthy now replied in a voice as calm as the one Don Quixote had used.

"Pledges," he said, "do not distress one who is sure of his ability to pay. He who was able to overcome you when you were transformed, Señor Don Quixote, may hope to bring you to your knees when you are your own proper self. But inasmuch as it is not fitting that knights should perform their feats of arms in the darkness, like ruffians and highwaymen, let us wait until it is day in order that the sun may behold what we do. And the condition governing our encounter shall be that the one who is vanquished must submit to the will of his conqueror and perform all those things that are commanded of him, provided they are such as are in keeping with the state of knighthood."

"With that condition and understanding," said Don Quixote, "I shall be satisfied."

With this, they went off to where their squires were, only to find them snoring away as hard as when sleep had first overtaken them. Awakening the pair, they ordered them to look to the horses; for as soon as the sun was up the two knights meant to stage an arduous and bloody single-handed combat. At this news Sancho was astonished and terrified, since, as a result of what the other squire had told him of the Knight of the Wood's prowess, he was led to fear for his master's safety. Nevertheless, he and his friend now went to seek the mounts without saying a word, and they found the animals all together, for by this time the two horses and the ass had smelled one another out. On the way the Squire of the Wood turned to Sancho and addressed him as follows:

"I must inform you, brother, that it is the custom of the fighters of Andalusia, when they are godfathers in any combat, not to remain idly by, with folded hands, while their godsons fight it out. I tell you this by way of warning you that while our masters are settling matters, we, too, shall have to come to blows and hack each other to bits."

"The custom, Sir Squire," replied Sancho, "may be all very well among the fighters and ruffians that you mention, but with the squires of knights-errant it is not to be thought of. At least, I have never heard my master speak of any such custom, and he knows all the laws of chivalry by heart. But granting that it is true and that there is a law which states in so many words that squires must fight while their masters do, I have no intention of obeying it but rather will pay whatever penalty is laid on peaceable-minded ones like myself, for I am sure it cannot be more than a couple of pounds of wax,[7] and that would be less expensive than the lint which it would take to heal my head—I can already see it split in two. What's more, it's out of the question for me to fight since I have no sword nor did I ever in my life carry one."

7. In some confraternities, penalties were paid in wax, presumably to make church candles.

"That," said the one of the Wood, "is something that is easily remedied. I have here two linen bags of the same size. You take one and I'll take the other and we will fight that way, on equal terms."

"So be it, by all means," said Sancho, "for that will simply knock the dust out of us without wounding us."

"But that's not the way it's to be,' said the other squire. "Inside the bags, to keep the wind from blowing them away, we will put a half-dozen nice smooth pebbles of the same weight, and so we'll be able to give each other a good pounding without doing ourselves any real harm or damage."

"Body of my father!" cried Sancho, "just look, will you, at the marten and sable and wads of carded cotton that he's stuffing into those bags so that we won't get our heads cracked or our bones crushed to a pulp. But I am telling you, *Señor mio,* that even though you fill them with silken pellets, I don't mean to fight. Let our masters fight and make the best of it, but as for us, let us drink and live; for time will see to ending our lives without any help on our part by way of bringing them to a close before they have reached their proper season and fall from ripeness."

"Nevertheless," replied the Squire of the Wood, "fight we must, if only for half an hour."

"No," Sancho insisted, "that I will not do. I will not be so impolite or so ungrateful as to pick any quarrel however slight with one whose food and drink I've shared. And, moreover, who in the devil could bring himself to fight in cold blood, when he's not angry or vexed in any way?"

"I can take care of that, right enough," said the one of the Wood. "Before we begin, I will come up to your Grace as nicely as you please and give you three or four punches that will stretch you out at my feet; and that will surely be enough to awaken your anger, even though it's sleeping sounder than a dormouse."

"And I," said Sancho, "have another idea that's every bit as good as yours. I will take a big club, and before your Grace has had a chance to awaken my anger I will put yours to sleep with such mighty whacks that if it wakes at all it will be in the other world; for it is known there that I am not the man to let my face be mussed by anyone, and let each look out for the arrow.[8] But the best thing to do would be to leave one's anger to its slumbers, for no one knows the heart of any other, he who comes for wool may go back shorn, and God bless peace and curse all strife. If a hunted cat when surrounded and cornered turns into a lion, God knows what I who am a man might not become. And so from this time forth I am warning you, Sir Squire, that all the harm and damage that may result from our quarrel will be upon your head."

"Very well," the one of the Wood replied, "God will send the dawn and we shall make out somehow."

At that moment gay-colored birds of all sorts began warbling in the trees and with their merry and varied songs appeared to be greeting and welcoming the fresh-dawning day, which already at the gates and on the balconies of the east was revealing its beautiful face as it shook out from its hair an infinite number of liquid pearls. Bathed in this gentle moisture, the grass seemed to shed a pearly spray, the willows distilled a savory manna, the fountains

---

8. A proverbial expression from archery: let each one take care of his or her own arrow. Other obviously proverbial expressions follow, as is typical of Sancho's speech.

laughed, the brooks murmured, the woods were glad, and the meadows put on their finest raiment. The first thing that Sancho Panza beheld, as soon as it was light enough to tell one object from another, was the Squire of the Wood's nose, which was so big as to cast into the shade all the rest of his body. In addition to being of enormous size, it is said to have been hooked in the middle and all covered with warts of a mulberry hue, like eggplant; it hung down for a couple of inches below his mouth, and the size, color, warts, and shape of this organ gave his face so ugly an appearance that Sancho began trembling hand and foot like a child with convulsions and made up his mind then and there that he would take a couple of hundred punches before he would let his anger be awakened to a point where he would fight with this monster.

Don Quixote in the meanwhile was surveying his opponent, who had already adjusted and closed his helmet so that it was impossible to make out what he looked like. It was apparent, however, that he was not very tall and was stockily built. Over his armor he wore a coat of some kind or other made of what appeared to be the finest cloth of gold, all bespangled with glittering mirrors that resembled little moons and that gave him a most gallant and festive air, while above his helmet were a large number of waving plumes, green, white, and yellow in color. His lance, which was leaning against a tree, was very long and stout and had a steel point of more than a palm in length. Don Quixote took all this in, and from what he observed concluded that his opponent must be of tremendous strength, but he was not for this reason filled with fear as Sancho Panza was. Rather, he proceeded to address the Knight of the Mirrors, quite boldly and in a highbred manner.

"Sir Knight," he said, "if in your eagerness to fight you have not lost your courtesy, I would beg you to be so good as to raise your visor a little in order that I may see if your face is as handsome as your trappings."

"Whether you come out of this emprise the victor or the vanquished, Sir Knight," he of the Mirrors replied, "there will be ample time and opportunity for you to have a sight of me. If I do not now gratify your desire, it is because it seems to me that I should be doing a very great wrong to the beauteous Casildea de Vandalia by wasting the time it would take me to raise my visor before having forced you to confess that I am right in my contention, with which you are well acquainted."

"Well, then," said Don Quixote, "while we are mounting our steeds you might at least inform me if I am that knight of La Mancha whom you say you conquered."

"To that our[9] answer," said he of the Mirrors, "is that you are as like the knight I overcame as one egg is like another; but since you assert that you are persecuted by enchanters, I should not venture to state positively that you are the one in question."

"All of which," said Don Quixote, "is sufficient to convince me that you are laboring under a misapprehension; but in order to relieve you of it once and for all, let them bring our steeds, and in less time than you would spend in lifting your visor, if God, my lady, and my arm give me strength, I will see your face and you shall see that I am not the vanquished knight you take me to be."

---

9. Note the dignified, "majestic" plural form.

With this, they cut short their conversation and mounted, and, turning Rocinante around, Don Quixote began measuring off the proper length of field for a run against his opponent as he of the Mirrors did the same. But the Knight of La Mancha had not gone twenty paces when he heard his adversary calling to him, whereupon each of them turned halfway and he of the Mirrors spoke.

"I must remind you, Sir Knight," he said, "of the condition under which we fight, which is that the vanquished, as I have said before, shall place himself wholly at the disposition of the victor."

"I am aware of that," replied Don Quixote, "not forgetting the provision that the behest laid upon the vanquished shall not exceed the bounds of chivalry."

"Agreed," said the Knight of the Mirrors.

At that moment Don Quixote caught sight of the other squire's weird nose and was as greatly astonished by it as Sancho had been. Indeed, he took the fellow for some monster, or some new kind of human being wholly unlike those that people this world. As he saw his master riding away down the field preparatory to the tilt, Sancho was alarmed; for he did not like to be left alone with the big-nosed individual, fearing that one powerful swipe of that protuberance against his own nose would end the battle so far as he was concerned and he would be lying stretched out on the ground, from fear if not from the force of the blow.

He accordingly ran after the knight, clinging to one of Rocinante's stirrup straps, and when he thought it was time for Don Quixote to whirl about and bear down upon his opponent, he called to him and said, "Señor mio, I beg your Grace, before you turn for the charge, to help me up into that cork tree yonder where I can watch the encounter which your Grace is going to have with this knight better than I can from the ground and in a way that is much more to my liking."

"I rather think, Sancho," said Don Quixote, "that what you wish to do is to mount a platform where you can see the bulls without any danger to yourself."

"The truth of the matter is," Sancho admitted, "the monstrous nose on that squire has given me such a fright that I don't dare stay near him."

"It is indeed of such a sort," his master assured him, "that if I were not the person I am, I myself should be frightened. And so, come, I will help you up."

While Don Quixote tarried to see Sancho ensconced in the cork tree, the Knight of the Mirrors measured as much ground as seemed to him necessary and then, assuming that his adversary had done the same, without waiting for sound of trumpet or any other signal, he wheeled his horse, which was no swifter nor any more impressive-looking than Rocinante, and bore down upon his enemy at a mild trot; but when he saw that the Manchegan was busy helping his squire, he reined in his mount and came to a stop midway in his course, for which his horse was extremely grateful, being no longer able to stir a single step. To Don Quixote, on the other hand, it seemed as if his enemy was flying, and digging his spurs with all his might into Rocinante's lean flanks he caused that animal to run a bit for the first and only time, according to the history, for on all other occasions a simple trot had represented his utmost speed. And so it was that, with an unheard-of-fury, the Knight of the Mournful Countenance came down upon the Knight of the Mirrors as the latter sat there sinking his spurs all the way up to the buttons without being able to persuade his horse to budge a single inch from the spot where he had come to a sudden standstill.

It was at this fortunate moment, while his adversary was in such a predicament, that Don Quixote fell upon him, quite unmindful of the fact that the other knight was having trouble with his mount and either was unable or did not have time to put his lance at rest. The upshot of it was, he encountered him with such force that, much against his will, the Knight of the Mirrors went rolling over his horse's flanks and tumbled to the ground, where as a result of his terrific fall he lay as if dead, without moving hand or foot.

No sooner did Sancho perceive what had happened than he slipped down from the cork tree and ran up as fast as he could to where his master was. Dismounting from Rocinante, Don Quixote now stood over the Knight of the Mirrors, and undoing the helmet straps to see if the man was dead, or to give him air in case he was alive, he beheld—who can say what he beheld without creating astonishment, wonder, and amazement in those who hear the tale? The history tells us that it was the very countenance, form, aspect, physiognomy, effigy, and image of the bachelor Sansón Carrasco!

"Come, Sancho," he cried in a loud voice, "and see what is to be seen but is not to be believed. Hasten, my son, and learn what magic can do and how great is the power of wizards and enchanters."

Sancho came, and the moment his eyes fell on the bachelor Carrasco's face he began crossing and blessing himself a countless number of times. Meanwhile, the overthrown knight gave no signs of life.

"If you ask me, master," said Sancho, "I would say that the best thing for your Grace to do is to run his sword down the mouth of this one who appears to be the bachelor Carrasco; maybe by so doing you would be killing one of your enemies, the enchanters."

"That is not a bad idea," replied Don Quixote, "for the fewer enemies the better." And, drawing his sword, he was about to act upon Sancho's advice and counsel when the Knight of the Mirrors' squire came up to them, now minus the nose which had made him so ugly.

"Look well what you are doing, Don Quixote!" he cried. "The one who lies there at your feet is your Grace's friend, the bachelor Sansón Carrasco, and I am his squire."

"And where is your nose?" inquired Sancho, who was surprised to see him without that deformity.

"Here in my pocket," was the reply. And, thrusting his hand into his coat, he drew out a nose of varnished pasteboard of the make that has been described. Studying him more and more closely, Sancho finally exclaimed, in a voice that was filled with amazement, "Holy Mary preserve me! And is this not my neighbor and crony, Tomé Cecial?"

"That is who I am!" replied the de-nosed squire, "your good friend Tomé Cecial, Sancho Panza. I will tell you presently of the means and snares and falsehoods that brought me here. But, for the present, I beg and entreat your master not to lay hands on, mistreat, wound, or slay the Knight of the Mirrors whom he now has at his feet; for without any doubt it is the rash and ill-advised bachelor Sansón Carrasco, our fellow villager."

The Knight of the Mirrors now recovered consciousness, and, seeing this,

Don Quixote at once placed the naked point of his sword above the face of the vanquished one.

"Dead you are, knight," he said, "unless you confess that the peerless Dulcinea del Toboso is more beautiful than your Casildea de Vandalia. And what is more, you will have to promise that, should you survive this encounter and the fall you have had, you will go to the city of El Toboso and present yourself to her in my behalf, that she may do with you as she may see fit. And in case she leaves you free to follow your own will, you are to return to seek me out—the trail of my exploits will serve as a guide to bring you wherever I may be—and tell me all that has taken place between you and her. These conditions are in conformity with those that we arranged before our combat and they do not go beyond the bounds of knight-errantry."

"I confess," said the fallen knight, "that the tattered and filthy shoe of the lady Dulcinea del Toboso is of greater worth than the badly combed if clean beard of Casildea, and I promise to go to her presence and return to yours and to give you a complete and detailed account concerning anything you may wish to know."

"Another thing," added Don Quixote, "that you will have to confess and believe is that the knight you conquered was not and could not have been Don Quixote de la Mancha, but was some other that resembled him, just as I am convinced that you, though you appear to be the bachelor Sansón Carrasco, are another person in his form and likeness who has been put here by my enemies to induce me to restrain and moderate the impetuosity of my wrath and make a gentle use of my glorious victory."

"I confess, think, and feel as you feel, think, and believe," replied the lamed knight. "Permit me to rise, I beg of you, if the jolt I received in my fall will let me do so, for I am in very bad shape."

Don Quixote and Tomé Cecial the squire now helped him to his feet. As for Sancho, he could not take his eyes off Tomé but kept asking him one question after another, and although the answers he received afforded clear enough proof that the man was really his fellow townsman, the fear that had been aroused in him by his master's words—about the enchanters' having transformed the Knight of the Mirrors into the bachelor Sansón Carrasco—prevented him from believing the truth that was apparent to his eyes. The short of it is, both master and servant were left with this delusion as the other ill-errant knight and his squire, in no pleasant state of mind, took their departure with the object of looking for some village where they might be able to apply poultices and splints to the bachelor's battered ribs.

Don Quixote and Sancho then resumed their journey along the road to Saragossa, and here for the time being the history leaves them in order to give an account of who the Knight of the Mirrors and his long-nosed squire really were.

CHAPTER 15

Wherein is told and revealed who the Knight of the Mirrors and his squire were.

Don Quixote went off very happy, self-satisfied, and vainglorious at having achieved a victory over so valiant a knight as he imagined the one of the Mirrors to be, from whose knightly word he hoped to learn whether or not the spell which had been put upon his lady was still in effect; for, unless he chose to forfeit his honor, the vanquished contender must of necessity return and give an account of what had happened in the course of his interview with her. But Don Quixote was of one mind, the Knight of the Mirrors of another, for, as has been stated, the latter's only thought at the moment was to find some village where plasters were available.

The history goes on to state that when the bachelor Sansón Carrasco advised Don Quixote to resume his feats of chivalry, after having desisted from them for a while, this action was taken as the result of a conference which he had held with the curate and the barber as to the means to be adopted in persuading the knight to remain quietly at home and cease agitating himself over his unfortunate adventures. It had been Carrasco's suggestion, to which they had unanimously agreed, that they let Don Quixote sally forth, since it appeared to be impossible to prevent his doing so, and that Sansón should then take to the road as a knight-errant and pick a quarrel and do battle with him. There would be no difficulty about finding a pretext, and then the bachelor knight would overcome him (which was looked upon as easy of accomplishment), having first entered into a pact to the effect that the vanquished should remain at the mercy and bidding of his conqueror. The behest in this case was to be that the fallen one should return to his village and home and not leave it for the space of two years or until further orders were given him, it being a certainty that, once having been overcome, Don Quixote would fulfill the agreement, in order not to contravene or fail to obey the laws of chivalry. And it was possible that in the course of his seclusion he would forget his fancies, or they would at least have an opportunity to seek some suitable cure for his madness.

Sansón agreed to undertake this, and Tomé Cecial, Sancho's friend and neighbor, a merry but featherbrained chap, offered to go along as squire. Sansón then proceeded to arm himself in the manner that has been described, while Tomé disguised his nose with the aforementioned mask so that his crony would not recognize him when they met. Thus equipped, they followed the same route as Don Quixote and had almost caught up with him by the time he had the adventure with the Cart of Death. They finally overtook him in the wood, where those events occurred with which the attentive reader is already familiar; and if it had not been for the knight's extraordinary fancies, which led him to believe that the bachelor was not the bachelor, the said bachelor might have been prevented from ever attaining his degree of licentiate, as a result of having found no nests where he thought to find birds.

Seeing how ill they had succeeded in their undertaking and what an end they had reached, Tomé Cecial now addressed his master.

"Surely, Señor Sansón Carrasco," he said, "we have had our deserts. It is easy enough to plan and embark upon an enterprise, but most of the time it's hard to get out of it. Don Quixote is a madman and we are sane, yet he goes away sound and laughing while your Grace is left here, battered and sorrowful. I wish you would tell me now who is the crazier: the one who is so because he cannot help it, or he who turns crazy of his own free will?"

"The difference between the two," replied Sansón, "lies in this: that the one who cannot help being crazy will be so always, whereas the one who is a madman by choice can leave off being one whenever he so desires."

"Well," said Tomé Cecial, "since that is the way it is, and since I chose to be crazy when I became your Grace's squire, by the same reasoning I now choose to stop being insane and to return to my home."

"That is your affair," said Sansón, "but to imagine that I am going back before I have given Don Quixote a good thrashing is senseless; and what will urge me on now is not any desire to see him recover his wits, but rather a thirst for vengeance; for with the terrible pain that I have in my ribs, you can't expect me to feel very charitable."

Conversing in this manner they kept on until they reached a village where it was their luck to find a bonesetter to take care of poor Sansón. Tomé Cecial then left him and returned home, while the bachelor meditated plans for revenge. The history has more to say of him in due time, but for the present it goes on to make merry with Don Quixote.

CHAPTER 16

Of what happened to Don Quixote upon his meeting with a prudent gentleman of La Mancha.

With that feeling of happiness and vainglorious self-satisfaction that has been mentioned, Don Quixote continued on his way, imagining himself to be, as a result of the victory he had just achieved, the most valiant knight-errant of the age. Whatever adventures might befall him from then on he regarded as already accomplished and brought to a fortunate conclusion. He thought little now of enchanters and enchantments and was unmindful of the innumerable beatings he had received in the course of his knightly wanderings, of the volley of pebbles that had knocked out half his teeth, of the ungratefulness of the galley slaves and the audacity of the Yanguesans whose poles had fallen upon his body like rain. In short, he told himself, if he could but find the means, manner, or way of freeing his lady Dulcinea of the spell that had been put upon her, he would not envy the greatest good fortune that the most fortunate of knights-errant in ages past had ever by any possibility attained.

He was still wholly wrapped up in these thoughts when Sancho spoke to him.

"Isn't it strange, sir, that I can still see in front of my eyes the huge and monstrous nose of my old crony, Tomé Cecial?"

"And do you by any chance believe, Sancho, that the Knight of the Mirrors was the bachelor Sansón Carrasco and that his squire was your friend Tomé?"

"I don't know what to say to that," replied Sancho. "All I know is that the things he told me about my home, my wife and young ones, could not have come from anybody else; and the face, too, once you took the nose away, was the same as Tomé Cecial's, which I have seen many times in our village, right next door to my own house, and the tone of voice was the same also."

"Let us reason the matter out, Sancho," said Don Quixote. "Look at it this way: how can it be thought that the bachelor Sansón Carrasco would come as a knight-errant, equipped with offensive and defensive armor, to contend with me? Am I, perchance, his enemy? Have I given him any occasion to cherish a grudge against me? Am I a rival of his? Or can it be jealousy of the fame I have acquired that has led him to take up the profession of arms?"

"Well, then, sir," Sancho answered him, "how are we to explain the fact that the knight was so like the bachelor and his squire like my friend? And if this was a magic spell, as your Grace has said, was there no other pair in the world whose likeness they might have taken?"

"It is all a scheme and a plot," replied Don Quixote, "on the part of those wicked magicians who are persecuting me and who, foreseeing that I would be the victor in the combat, saw to it that the conquered knight should display the face of my friend the bachelor, so that the affection which I bear him would come between my fallen enemy and the edge of my sword and might of my arm, to temper the righteous indignation of my heart. In that way, he who had sought by falsehood and deceits to take my life, would be left to go on living. As proof of all this, Sancho, experience, which neither lies nor deceives, has already taught you how easy it is for enchanters to change one countenance into another, making the beautiful ugly and the ugly beautiful. It was not two days ago that you beheld the peerless Dulcinea's beauty and elegance in its entirety and natural form, while I saw only the repulsive features of a low and ignorant peasant girl with cataracts over her eyes and a foul smell in her mouth. And if the perverse enchanter was bold enough to effect so vile a transformation as this, there is certainly no cause for wonderment at what he has done in the case of Sansón Carrasco and your friend, all by way of snatching my glorious victory out of my hands. But in spite of it all, I find consolation in the fact that, whatever the shape he may have chosen to assume, I have laid my enemy low."

"God knows what the truth of it all may be," was Sancho's comment. Knowing as he did that Dulcinea's transformation had been due to his own scheming and plotting, he was not taken in by his master's delusions. He was at a loss for a reply, however, lest he say something that would reveal his own trickery.

As they were carrying on this conversation, they were overtaken by a man who, following the same road, was coming along behind them. He was mounted on a handsome flea-bitten mare and wore a hooded greatcoat of fine green cloth trimmed in tawny velvet and a cap of the same material, while the trappings of his steed, which was accoutered for the field, were green and mulberry in hue, his saddle being of the *jineta*[1] mode. From his broad green and gold shoulder strap there dangled a Moorish cutlass, and his half-boots were of the same make as the baldric. His spurs were not gilded but were covered with highly polished green lacquer, so that harmonizing as they did with the rest of his apparel, they seemed more appropriate than if they had been of purest gold. As he came up, he greeted the pair courteously and, spurring his mare, was about to ride on past when Don Quixote called to him.

"Gallant sir," he said, "If your Grace is going our way and is not in a hurry, it would be a favor to us if we might travel together."

"The truth is," replied the stranger, "I should not have ridden past you if I had not been afraid that the company of my mare would excite your horse."

"In that case, sir," Sancho spoke up, "you may as well rein in, for this horse of ours is the most virtuous and well mannered of any that there is. Never on such an occasion has he done anything that was not right—the only time

1. It has a high pommel and short stirrups.

he did misbehave, my master and I suffered for it aplenty. And so, I say again, your Grace may slow up if you like; for even if you offered him your mare on a couple of platters, he'd never try to mount her."

With this, the other traveler drew rein, being greatly astonished at Don Quixote's face and figure. For the knight was now riding along without his helmet, which was carried by Sancho like a piece of luggage on the back of his gray, in front of the packsaddle. If the green-clad gentleman stared hard at his new-found companion, the latter returned his gaze with an even greater intensity. He impressed Don Quixote as being a man of good judgment, around fifty years of age, with hair that was slightly graying and an aquiline nose, while the expression of his countenance was half humorous, half serious. In short, both his person and his accouterments indicated that he was an individual of some worth.

As for the man in green's impression of Don Quixote de la Mancha, he was thinking that he had never before seen any human being that resembled this one. He could not but marvel at the knight's long neck, his tall frame, and the leanness and the sallowness of his face, as well as his armor and his grave bearing, the whole constituting a sight such as had not been seen for many a day in those parts. Don Quixote in turn was quite conscious of the attentiveness with which the traveler was studying him and could tell from the man's astonished look how curious he was; and so, being very courteous and fond of pleasing everyone, he proceeded to anticipate any questions that might be asked him.

"I am aware," he said, "that my appearance must strike your Grace as being very strange and out of the ordinary, and for that reason I am not surprised at your wonderment. But your Grace will cease to wonder when I tell you, as I am telling you now, that I am a knight, one of those

> Of whom it is folks say,
> They to adventures go.

I have left my native health, mortgaged my estate, given up my comfortable life, and cast myself into fortune's arms for her to do with me what she will. It has been my desire to revive a knight-errantry that is now dead, and for some time past, stumbling here and falling there, now throwing myself down headlong and then rising up once more, I have been able in good part to carry out my design by succoring widows, protecting damsels, and aiding the fallen, the orphans, and the young, all of which is the proper and natural duty of knights-errant. As a result, owing to my many valiant and Christian exploits, I have been deemed worthy of visiting in printed form nearly all the nations of the world. Thirty thousand copies of my history have been published, and, unless Heaven forbid, they will print thirty million of them.

"In short, to put it all into a few words, or even one, I will tell you that I am Don Quixote de la Mancha, otherwise known as the Knight of the Mournful Countenance. Granted that self-praise is degrading, there still are times when I must praise myself, that is to say, when there is no one else present to speak in my behalf. And so, good sir, neither this steed nor this lance nor this buckler nor this squire of mine, nor all the armor that I wear and arms I carry, nor the sallowness of my complexion, nor my leanness and gauntness, should any longer astonish you, now that you know who I am and what the profession is that I follow."

Having thus spoken, Don Quixote fell silent, and the man in green was so slow in replying that it seemed as if he was at a loss for words. Finally, however, after a considerable while, he brought himself to the point of speaking.

"You were correct, Sir Knight," he said, "about my astonishment and my curiosity, but you have not succeeded in removing the wonderment that the sight of you has aroused in me. You say that, knowing who you are, I should not wonder any more, but such is not the case, for I am now more amazed than ever. How can it be that there are knights-errant in the world today and that histories of them are actually printed? I find it hard to convince myself that at the present time there is anyone on earth who goes about aiding widows, protecting damsels, defending the honor of wives, and succoring orphans, and I should never have believed it had I not beheld your Grace with my own eyes. Thank Heaven for that book that your Grace tells me has been published concerning your true and exalted deeds of chivalry, as it should cast into oblivion all the innumerable stories of fictitious knights-errant with which the world is filled, greatly to the detriment of good morals and the prejudice and discredit of legitimate histories."

"As to whether the stories of knights-errant are fictitious or not," observed Don Quixote, "there is much that remains to be said."

"Why," replied the gentleman in green, "is there anyone who can doubt that such tales are false?"

"I doubt it," was the knight's answer, "but let the matter rest there. If our journey lasts long enough, I trust with God's help to be able to show your Grace that you are wrong in going along with those who hold it to be a certainty that they are not true."

From this last remark the traveler was led to suspect that Don Quixote must be some kind of crackbrain, and he was waiting for him to confirm the impression by further observations of the same sort; but before they could get off on another subject, the knight, seeing that he had given an account of his own station in life, turned to the stranger and politely inquired who his companion might be.

"I, Sir Knight of the Mournful Countenance," replied the one in the green-colored greatcoat, "am a gentleman, and a native of the village where, please God, we are going to dine today. I am more than moderately rich, and my name is Don Diego de Miranda. I spend my life with my wife and children and with my friends. My occupations are hunting and fishing, though I keep neither falcon nor hounds but only a tame partridge[2] and a bold ferret or two. I am the owner of about six dozen books, some of them in Spanish, others in Latin, including both histories and devotional works. As for books of chivalry, they have not as yet crossed the threshold of my door. My own preference is for profane rather than devotional writings, such as afford an innocent amusement, charming us by their style and arousing and holding our interest by their inventiveness, although I must say there are very few of that sort to be found in Spain.

"Sometimes," the man in green continued, "I dine with my friends and neighbors, and I often invite them to my house. My meals are wholesome and well prepared and there is always plenty to eat. I do not care for gossip,

2. Used as a decoy.

nor will I permit it in my presence. I am not lynx-eyed and do not pry into the lives and doings of others. I hear mass every day and share my substance with the poor, but make no parade of my good works lest hypocrisy and vainglory, those enemies that so imperceptibly take possession of the most modest heart, should find their way into mine. I try to make peace between those who are at strife. I am the devoted servant of Our Lady, and my trust is in the infinite mercy of God Our Savior."

Sancho had listened most attentively to the gentleman's account of his mode of life, and inasmuch as it seemed to him that this was a good and holy way to live and that the one who followed such a pattern ought to be able to work miracles, he now jumped down from his gray's back and, running over to seize the stranger's right stirrup, began kissing the feet of the man in green with a show of devotion that bordered on tears.

"Why are you doing that, brother?" the gentleman asked him. "What is the meaning of these kisses?"

"Let me kiss your feet," Sancho insisted, "for if I am not mistaken, your Grace is the first saint riding *jineta* fashion that I have seen in all the days of my life."

"I am not a saint," the gentleman assured him, "but a great sinner. It is you, brother, who are the saint; for you must be a good man, judging by the simplicity of heart that you show."

Sancho then went back to his packsaddle, having evoked a laugh from the depths of his master's melancholy and given Don Diego fresh cause for astonishment.

Don Quixote thereupon inquired of the newcomer how many children he had, remarking as he did so that the ancient philosophers, who were without a true knowledge of God, believed that mankind's greatest good lay in the gifts of nature, in those of fortune, and in having many friends and many and worthy sons.

"I, Señor Don Quixote," replied the gentleman, "have a son without whom I should, perhaps, be happier than I am. It is not that he is bad, but rather that he is not as good as I should like him to be. He is eighteen years old, and for six of those years he has been at Salamanca studying the Greek and Latin languages. When I desired him to pass on to other branches of learning, I found him so immersed in the science of Poetry (if it can be called such) that it was not possible to interest him in the Law, which I wanted him to study, nor in Theology, the queen of them all. My wish was that he might be an honor to his family; for in this age in which we are living our monarchs are in the habit of highly rewarding those forms of learning that are good and virtuous, since learning without virtue is like pearls on a dung-hill. But he spends the whole day trying to decide whether such and such a verse of Homer's *Iliad* is well conceived or not, whether or not Martial is immodest in a certain epigram, whether certain lines of Vergil are to be understood in this way or in that. In short, he spends all of his time with the books written by those poets whom I have mentioned and with those of Horace, Persius, Juvenal, and Tibullus. As for our own moderns, he sets little store by them, and yet, for all his disdain of Spanish poetry, he is at this moment racking his brains in an effort to compose a gloss on a quatrain that was sent him from Salamanca and which, I fancy, is for some literary tournament."

To all this Don Quixote made the following answer:

"Children, sir, are out of their parents' bowels and so are to be loved whether they be good or bad, just as we love those that gave us life. It is for parents to bring up their offspring, from the time they are infants, in the paths of virtue, good breeding, proper conduct, and Christian morality, in order that, when they are grown, they may be a staff to the old age of the ones that bore them and an honor to their own posterity. As to compelling them to study a particular branch of learning, I am not so sure as to that, though there may be no harm in trying to persuade them to do so. But where there is no need to study *pane lucrando*[3]—where Heaven has provided them with parents that can supply their daily bread—I should be in favor of permitting them to follow that course to which they are most inclined; and although poetry may be more pleasurable than useful, it is not one of those pursuits that bring dishonor upon those who engage in them.

"Poetry in my opinion, my dear sir," he went on, "is a young and tender maid of surpassing beauty, who has many other damsels (that is to say, the other disciplines) whose duty it is to bedeck, embellish, and adorn her. She may call upon all of them for service, and all of them in turn depend upon her nod. She is not one to be rudely handled, nor dragged through the streets, nor exposed at street corners, in the market place, or in the private nooks of palaces. She is fashioned through an alchemy of such power that he who knows how to make use of it will be able to convert her into the purest gold of inestimable price. Possessing her, he must keep her within bounds and not permit her to run wild in bawdy satires or soulless sonnets. She is not to be put up for sale in any manner, unless it be in the form of heroic poems, pity-inspiring tragedies, or pleasing and ingenious comedies. Let mountebanks keep hands off her, and the ignorant mob as well, which is incapable of recognizing or appreciating the treasures that are locked within her. And do not think, sir, that I apply that term 'mob' solely to plebeians and those of low estate; for anyone who is ignorant, whether he be lord or prince, may, and should, be included in the vulgar herd.

"But," Don Quixote continued, "he who possesses the gift of poetry and who makes the use of it that I have indicated, shall become famous and his name shall be honored among all the civilized nations of the world. You have stated, sir, that your son does not greatly care for poetry written in our Spanish tongue, and in that I am inclined to think he is somewhat mistaken. My reason for saying so is this: the great Homer did not write in Latin, for the reason that he was a Greek, and Vergil did not write in Greek since he was a Latin. In a word, all the poets of antiquity wrote in the language which they had imbibed with their mother's milk and did not go searching after foreign ones to express their loftiest conceptions. This being so, it would be well if the same custom were to be adopted by all nations, the German poet being no longer looked down upon because he writes in German, nor the Castilian or the Basque for employing his native speech.

"As for your son, I fancy, sir, that his quarrel is not so much with Spanish poetry as with those poets who have no other tongue or discipline at their command such as would help to awaken their natural gift; and yet, here, too, he may be wrong. There is an opinion, and a true one, to the effect that 'the

3. Earning one's bread (Latin).

poet is born,' that is to say, it is as a poet that he comes forth from his mother's womb, and with the propensity that has been bestowed upon him by Heaven, without study or artifice, he produces those compositions that attest the truth of the line: 'Est deus in nobis,'[4] etc. I further maintain that the born poet who is aided by art will have a great advantage over the one who by art alone would become a poet, the reason being that art does not go beyond, but merely perfects, nature; and so it is that, by combining nature with art and art with nature, the finished poet is produced.

"In conclusion, then, my dear sir, my advice to you would be to let your son go where his star beckons him; for being a good student as he must be, and having already successfully mounted the first step on the stairway of learning, which is that of languages, he will be able to continue of his own accord to the very peak of humane letters, an accomplishment that is altogether becoming in a gentleman, one that adorns, honors, and distinguishes him as much as the miter does the bishop or his flowing robe the learned jurisconsult. Your Grace well may reprove your son, should he compose satires that reflect upon the honor of other persons; in that case, punish him and tear them up. But should he compose discourses in the manner of Horace, in which he reprehends vice in general as that poet so elegantly does, then praise him by all means; for it is permitted the poet to write verses in which he inveighs against envy and the other vices as well, and to lash out at the vicious without, however, designating any particular individual. On the other hand, there are poets who for the sake of uttering something malicious would run the risk of being banished to the shores of Pontus.[5]

"If the poet be chaste where his own manners are concerned, he would likewise be modest in his verses, for the pen is the tongue of the mind, and whatever thoughts are engendered there are bound to appear in his writings. When kings and princes behold the marvelous art of poetry as practiced by prudent, virtuous, and serious-minded subjects of their realm, they honor, esteem, and reward those persons and crown them with the leaves of the tree that is never struck by lightning[6]—as if to show that those who are crowned and adorned with such wreaths are not to be assailed by anyone."

The gentleman in the green-colored greatcoat was vastly astonished by this speech of Don Quixote's and was rapidly altering the opinion he had previously held, to the effect that his companion was but a crackbrain. In the middle of the long discourse, which was not greatly to his liking, Sancho had left the highway to go seek a little milk from some shepherds who were draining the udders of their ewes near by. Extremely well pleased with the knight's sound sense and excellent reasoning, the gentleman was about to resume the conversation when, raising his head, Don Quixote caught sight of a cart flying royal flags that was coming toward them down the road and, thinking it must be a fresh adventure, began calling to Sancho in a loud voice to bring him his helmet. Whereupon Sancho hastily left the shepherds and spurred his gray until he was once more alongside his master, who was now about to encounter a dreadful and bewildering ordeal.

---

4. There is a god in us (Latin); Ovid's *Fasti* 6.5.   5. As Ovid was by Augustus in A.D. 8.   6. The laurel.

[*"For I Well Know the Meaning of Valor"*]

CHAPTER 17

*Wherein Don Quixote's unimaginable courage reaches its highest point,
together with the adventure of the lions and its happy ending.*

The history relates that, when Don Quixote called to Sancho to bring him
his helmet, the squire was busy buying some curds from the shepherds and,
flustered by his master's great haste, did not know what to do with them or
how to carry them. Having already paid for the curds, he did not care to lose
them, and so he decided to put them into the headpiece, and, acting upon
this happy inspiration, he returned to see what was wanted of him.

"Give me that helmet," said the knight; "for either I know little about
adventures or here is one where I am going to need my armor."

Upon hearing this, the gentleman in the green-colored greatcoat looked
around in all directions but could see nothing except the cart that was
approaching them, decked out with two or three flags which indicated that
the vehicle in question must be conveying his Majesty's property. He
remarked as much to Don Quixote, but the latter paid no attention, for he
was always convinced that whatever happened to him meant adventures and
more adventures.

"Forewarned is forearmed," he said. "I lose nothing by being prepared,
knowing as I do that I have enemies both visible and invisible and cannot
tell when or where or in what form they will attack me."

Turning to Sancho, he asked for his helmet again, and as there was no
time to shake out the curds, the squire had to hand it to him as it was. Don
Quixote took it and, without noticing what was in it, hastily clapped it on his
head; and forthwith, as a result of the pressure on the curds, the whey began
running down all over his face and beard, at which he was very much startled.

"What is this, Sancho?" he cried. "I think my head must be softening or
my brains melting, or else I am sweating from head to foot. If sweat it be, I
assure you it is not from fear, though I can well believe that the adventure
which now awaits me is a terrible one indeed. Give me something with which
to wipe my face, if you have anything, for this perspiration is so abundant
that it blinds me."

Sancho said nothing but gave him a cloth and at the same time gave thanks
to God that his master had not discovered what the trouble was. Don Quixote
wiped his face and then took off his helmet to see what it was that made his
head feel so cool. Catching sight of that watery white mass, he lifted it to
his nose and smelled it.

"By the life of my lady Dulcinea del Toboso!" he exclaimed. "Those are
curds that you have put there, you treacherous, brazen, ill-mannered squire!"

To this Sancho replied, very calmly and with a straight face, "If they are
curds, give them to me, your Grace, so that I can eat them. But no, let the
devil eat them, for he must be the one who did it. Do you think I would be
so bold as to soil your Grace's helmet? Upon my word, master, by the understanding that God has given me, I, too, must have enchanters who are persecuting me as your Grace's creature and one of his members, and they are
the ones who put that filthy mess there to make you lose your patience and

your temper and cause you to whack my ribs as you are in the habit of doing. Well, this time, I must say, they have missed the mark; for I trust my master's good sense to tell him that I have neither curds nor milk nor anything of the kind, and if I did have, I'd put it in my stomach and not in that helmet."

"That may very well be," said Don Quixote.

Don Diego was observing all this and was more astonished than ever, especially when, after he had wiped his head, face, beard, and helmet, Don Quixote once more donned the piece of armor and, settling himself in the stirrups, proceeded to adjust his sword and fix his lance.

"Come what may, here I stand, ready to take on Satan himself in person!" shouted the knight.

The cart with the flags had come up to them by this time, accompanied only by a driver riding one of the mules and a man seated up in front.

"Where are you going, brothers?" Don Quixote called out as he placed himself in the path of the cart. "What conveyance is this, what do you carry in it, and what is the meaning of those flags?"

"The cart is mine," replied the driver, "and in it are two fierce lions in cages which the governor of Oran is sending to court as a present for his Majesty. The flags are those of our lord the King, as a sign that his property goes here."

"And are the lions large?" inquired Don Quixote.

It was the man sitting at the door of the cage who answered him. "The largest," he said, "that ever were sent from Africa to Spain. I am the lion-keeper and I have brought back others, but never any like these. They are male and female. The male is in this first cage, the female in the one behind. They are hungry right now, for they have had nothing to eat today; and so we'd be obliged if your Grace would get out of the way, for we must hasten on to the place where we are to feed them."

"Lion whelps against me?" said Don Quixote with a slight smile. "Lion whelps against me? And at such an hour? Then, by God, those gentlemen who sent them shall see whether I am the man to be frightened by lions. Get down, my good fellow, and since you are the lionkeeper, open the cages and turn those beasts out for me; and in the middle of this plain I will teach them who Don Quixote de la Mancha is, notwithstanding and in spite of the enchanters who are responsible for their being here."

"So," said the gentleman to himself as he heard this, "our worthy knight has revealed himself. It must indeed be true that the curds have softened his skull and mellowed his brains."

At this point Sancho approached him. "For God's sake, sir," he said, "do something to keep my master from fighting those lions. For if he does, they're going to tear us all to bits."

"Is your master, then, so insane," the gentleman asked, "that you fear and believe he means to tackle those fierce animals?"

"It is not that he is insane," replied Sancho, "but, rather, foolhardy."

"Very well," said the gentleman, "I will put a stop to it." And going up to Don Quixote, who was still urging the lionkeeper to open the cages, he said, "Sir Knight, knights-errant should undertake only those adventures that afford some hope of a successful outcome, not those that are utterly hopeless to begin with; for valor when it turns to temerity has in it more of madness than of bravery. Moreover, these lions have no thought of attacking your

Grace but are a present to his Majesty, and it would not be well to detain them or interfere with their journey."

"My dear sir," answered Don Quixote, "you had best go mind your tame partridge and that bold ferret of yours and let each one attend to his own business. This is my affair, and I know whether these gentlemen, the lions, have come to attack me or not." He then turned to the lionkeeper. "I swear, Sir Rascal, if you do not open those cages at once, I'll pin you to the cart with this lance!"

Perceiving how determined the armed phantom was, the driver now spoke up. "Good sir," he said, "will your Grace please be so kind as to let me unhitch the mules and take them to a safe place before you turn those lions loose? For if they kill them for me, I am ruined for life, since the mules and cart are all the property I own."

"O man of little faith!" said Don Quixote. "Get down and unhitch your mules if you like, but you will soon see that it was quite unnecessary and that you might have spared yourself the trouble."

The driver did so, in great haste, as the lionkeeper began shouting, "I want you all to witness that I am being compelled against my will to open the cages and turn the lions out, and I further warn this gentleman that he will be responsible for all the harm and damage the beasts may do, plus my wages and my fees. You other gentlemen take cover before I open the doors; I am sure they will not do any harm to me."

Once more Don Diego sought to persuade his companion not to commit such an act of madness, as it was tempting God to undertake anything so foolish as that; but Don Quixote's only answer was that he knew what he was doing. And when the gentleman in green insisted that he was sure the knight was laboring under a delusion and ought to consider the matter well, the latter cut him short.

"Well, then, sir," he said, "if your Grace does not care to be a spectator at what you believe is going to turn out to be a tragedy, all you have to do is to spur your flea-bitten mare and seek safety."

Hearing this, Sancho with tears in his eyes again begged him to give up the undertaking, in comparison with which the adventure of the windmills and the dreadful one at the fulling mills—indeed, all the exploits his master had ever in the course of his life undertaken—were but bread and cakes.

"Look, sir," Sancho went on, "there is no enchantment here nor anything of the sort. Through the bars and chinks of that cage I have seen a real lion's claw, and judging by the size of it, the lion that it belongs to is bigger than a mountain."

"Fear, at any rate," said Don Quixote, "will make him look bigger to you than half the world. Retire, Sancho, and leave me, and if I die here, you know our ancient pact: you are to repair to Dulcinea—I say no more."

To this he added other remarks that took away any hope they had that he might not go through with his insane plan. The gentleman in the green-colored greatcoat was of a mind to resist him but saw that he was no match for the knight in the matter of arms. Then, too, it did not seem to him the part of wisdom to fight it out with a madman; for Don Quixote now impressed him as being quite mad in every way. Accordingly, while the knight was repeating his threats to the lionkeeper, Don Diego spurred his mare, Sancho his gray, and the driver his mules, all of them seeking to put as great a distance as possible between themselves and the cart before the lions broke loose.

Sancho already was bewailing his master's death, which he was convinced was bound to come from the lions" claws, and at the same time he cursed his fate and called it an unlucky hour in which he had taken it into his head to serve such a one. But despite his tears and lamentations, he did not leave off thrashing his gray in an effort to leave the cart behind them. When the lionkeeper saw that those who had fled were a good distance away, he once more entreated and warned Don Quixote as he had warned and entreated him before, but the answer he received was that he might save his breath as it would do him no good and he had best hurry and obey. In the space of time that it took the keeper to open the first cage, Don Quixote considered the question as to whether it would be well to give battle on foot or on horseback. He finally decided that he would do better on foot, as he feared that Rocinante would become frightened at sight of the lions; and so, leaping down from his horse, he fixed his lance, braced his buckler, and drew his sword, and then advanced with marvelous daring and great resoluteness until he stood directly in front of the cart, meanwhile commending himself to God with all his heart and then to his lady Dulcinea.

Upon reaching this point, the reader should know, the author of our veracious history indulges in the following exclamatory passage:

"O great-souled Don Quixote de la Mancha, thou whose courage is beyond all praise, mirror wherein all the valiant of the world may behold themselves, a new and second Don Manuel de León,[1] once the glory and the honor of Spanish knighthood! With what words shall I relate thy terrifying exploit, how render it credible to the ages that are to come? What eulogies do not belong to thee of right, even though they consist of hyperbole piled upon hyperbole? On foot and singlehanded, intrepid and with greathearted valor, armed but with a sword, and not one of the keen-edged Little Dog[2] make, and with a shield that was not of gleaming and polished steel, thou didst stand and wait for the two fiercest lions that ever the African forests bred! Thy deeds shall be thy praise, O valorous Manchegan; I leave them to speak for thee, since words fail me with which to extol them."

Here the author leaves off his exclamations and resumes the thread of the story.

Seeing Don Quixote posed there before him and perceiving that, unless he wished to incur the bold knight's indignation there was nothing for him to do but release the male lion, the keeper now opened the first cage, and it could be seen at once how extraordinarily big and horribly ugly the beast was. The first thing the recumbent animal did was to turn round, put out a claw, and stretch himself all over. Then he opened his mouth and yawned very slowly, after which he put out a tongue that was nearly two palms in length and with it licked the dust out of his eyes and washed his face. Having done this, he stuck his head outside the cage and gazed about him in all directions. His eyes were now like live coals and his appearance and demeanor were such as to strike terror in temerity itself. But Don Quixote merely stared at him attentively, waiting for him to descend from the cart so

1. Don Manuel Ponce de León, a paragon of gallantry and courtesy, from the time of Ferdinand and Isabella. 2. The trademark of a famous armorer of Toledo and Saragossa.

that they could come to grips, for the knight was determined to hack the brute to pieces, such was the extent of his unheard-of madness.

The lion, however, proved to be courteous rather than arrogant and was in no mood for childish bravado. After having gazed first in one direction and then in another, as has been said, he turned his back and presented his hind parts to Don Quixote and then very calmly and peaceably lay down and stretched himself out once more in his cage. At this, Don Quixote ordered the keeper to stir him up with a stick in order to irritate him and drive him out.

"That I will not do," the keeper replied, "for if I stir him, I will be the first one he will tear to bits. Be satisfied with what you have already accomplished, Sir Knight, which leaves nothing more to be said on the score of valor, and do not go tempting your fortune a second time. The door was open and the lion could have gone out if he had chosen; since he has not done so up to now, that means he will stay where he is all day long. Your Grace's stout-heartedness has been well established; for no brave fighter, as I see it, is obliged to do more than challenge his enemy and wait for him in the field; his adversary, if he does not come, is the one who is disgraced and the one who awaits him gains the crown of victory."

"That is the truth," said Don Quixote. "Shut the door, my friend, and bear me witness as best you can with regard to what you have seen me do here. I would have you certify: that you opened the door for the lion, that I waited for him and he did not come out, that I continued to wait and still he stayed there, and finally went back and lay down. I am under no further obligation. Away with enchantments, and God uphold the right, the truth, and true chivalry! So close the door, as I have told you, while I signal to the fugitives in order that they who were not present may hear of this exploit from your lips."

The keeper did as he was commanded, and Don Quixote, taking the cloth with which he had dried his face after the rain of curds, fastened it to the point of his lance and began summoning the runaways, who, all in a body with the gentleman in green bringing up the rear, were still fleeing and turning around to look back at every step. Sancho was the first to see the white cloth.

"May they slay me," he said, "if my master hasn't conquered those fierce beasts, for he's calling to us."

They all stopped and made sure that the one who was doing the signaling was indeed Don Quixote, and then, losing some of their fear, they little by little made their way back to a point where they could distinctly hear what the knight was saying. At last they returned to the cart, and as they drew near Don Quixote spoke to the driver.

"You may come back, brother, hitch your mules, and continue your journey. And you, Sancho, may give each of them two gold crowns to recompense them for the delay they have suffered on my account."

"That I will, right enough," said Sancho. "But what has become of the lions? Are they dead or alive?"

The keeper thereupon, in leisurely fashion and in full detail, proceeded to tell them how the encounter had ended, taking pains to stress to the best of his ability the valor displayed by Don Quixote, at sight of whom the lion had been so cowed that he was unwilling to leave his cage, though the door had been left open quite a while. The fellow went on to state that the knight had wanted him to stir the lion up and force him out, but had finally been convinced that this would be tempting God and so, much to his displeasure and against his will, had permitted the door to be closed.

"What do you think of that, Sancho?" asked Don Quixote. "Are there any spells that can withstand true gallantry? The enchanters may take my luck away, but to deprive me of my strength and courage is an impossibility."

Sancho then bestowed the crowns, the driver hitched his mules, and the lionkeeper kissed Don Quixote's hands for the favor received, promising that, when he reached the court, he would relate this brave exploit to the king himself.

"In that case," replied Don Quixote, "if his Majesty by any chance should inquire who it was that performed it, you are to say that it was the Knight of the Lions; for that is the name by which I wish to be known from now on, thus changing, exchanging, altering, and converting the one I have previously borne, that of Knight of the Mournful Countenance; in which respect I am but following the old custom of knights-errant, who changed their names whenever they liked or found it convenient to do so."

With this, the cart continued on its way, and Don Quixote, Sancho, and the gentleman in the green-colored greatcoat likewise resumed their journey. During all this time Don Diego de Miranda had not uttered a word but was wholly taken up with observing what Don Quixote did and listening to what he had to say. The knight impressed him as being a crazy sane man and an insane one on the verge of sanity. The gentleman did not happen to be familiar with the first part of our history, but if he had read it he would have ceased to wonder at such talk and conduct, for he would then have known what kind of madness this was. Remaining as he did in ignorance of his companion's malady, he took him now for a sensible individual and now for a madman, since what Don Quixote said was coherent, elegantly phrased, and to the point, whereas his actions were nonsensical, foolhardy, and downright silly. What greater madness could there be, Don Diego asked himself, than to don a helmet filled with curds and then persuade oneself that enchanters were softening one's cranium? What could be more rashly absurd than to wish to fight lions by sheer strength alone? He was roused from these thoughts, this inward soliloquy, by the sound of Don Quixote's voice.

"Undoubtedly, Señor Don Diego de Miranda, your Grace must take me for a fool and a madman, am I not right? And it would be small wonder if such were the case, seeing that my deeds give evidence of nothing else. But, nevertheless, I would advise your Grace that I am neither so mad nor so lacking in wit as I must appear to you to be. A gaily caparisoned knight giving a fortunate lance thrust to a fierce bull in the middle of a great square makes a pleasing appearance in the eyes of his king. The same is true of a knight clad in shining armor as he paces the lists in front of the ladies in some joyous tournament. It is true of all those knights who, by means of military exercises or what appear to be such, divert and entertain and, if one may say so, honor the courts of princes. But the best showing of all is made by a knight-errant who, traversing deserts and solitudes, crossroads, forests, and mountains, goes seeking dangerous adventures with the intention of bringing them to a happy and successful conclusion, and solely for the purpose of winning a glorious and enduring renown.

"More impressive, I repeat, is the knight-errant succoring a widow in some unpopulated place than a courtly man of arms making love to a damsel in the city. All knights have their special callings: let the courtier wait upon the ladies and lend luster by his liveries to his sovereign's palace; let him nourish impoverished gentlemen with the splendid fare of his table; let him give tourneys and show himself truly great, generous, and magnificent and a good Christian above all, thus fulfilling his particular obligations. But the knight-errant's case is different.

"Let the latter seek out the nooks and corners of the world; let him enter into the most intricate of labyrinths; let him attempt the impossible at every step; let him endure on desolate highlands the burning rays of the midsummer sun and in winter the harsh inclemencies of wind and frost; let no lions inspire him with fear, no monsters frighten him, no dragons terrify him, for to seek them out, attack them, and conquer them all is his chief and legitimate occupation. Accordingly, I whose lot it is to be numbered among the knights-errant cannot fail to attempt anything that appears to me to fall within the scope of my duties, just as I attacked those lions a while ago even though I knew it to be an exceedingly rash thing to do, for that was a matter that directly concerned me.

"For I well know the meaning of valor: namely, a virtue that lies between the two extremes of cowardice on the one hand and temerity on the other. It is, nonetheless, better for the brave man to carry his bravery to the point of rashness than for him to sink into cowardice. Even as it is easier for the prodigal to become a generous man than it is for the miser, so is it easier for the foolhardy to become truly brave than it is for the coward to attain valor. And in this matter of adventures, you may believe me, Señor Don Diego, it is better to lose by a card too many than a card too few, and 'Such and such a knight is temerarious and overbold' sounds better to the ear than 'That knight is timid and a coward.'"

"I must assure you, Señor Don Quixote," replied Don Diego, "that everything your Grace has said and done will stand the test of reason; and it is my opinion that if the laws and ordinances of knight-errantry were to be lost, they would be found again in your Grace's bosom, which is their depository and storehouse. But it is growing late; let us hasten to my village and my home, where your Grace shall rest from your recent exertions; for if the body is not tired the spirit may be, and that sometimes results in bodily fatigue.'

"I accept your offer as a great favor and an honor, Señor Don Diego," was the knight's reply. And, by spurring their mounts more than they had up to then, they arrived at the village around two in the afternoon and came to the house that was occupied by Don Diego, whom Don Quixote had dubbed the Knight of the Green-colored Greatcoat.

[Last Duel]

CHAPTER 64

Which treats of the adventure that caused Don Quixote the most sorrow of all those that have thus far befallen him.

* * * One morning, as Don Quixote went for a ride along the beach,[1] clad in full armor—for, as he was fond of saying, that was his only ornament, his only rest the fight, and, accordingly, he was never without it for a moment— he saw approaching him a horseman similarly arrayed from head to foot and with a brightly shining moon blazoned upon his shield.

As soon as he had come within earshot the stranger cried out to Don Quixote in a loud voice. "O illustrious knight, the never to be sufficiently praised Don Quixote de la Mancha, I am the Knight of the White Moon whose incomparable exploits you will perhaps recall. I come to contend with you and try the might of my arm, with the purpose of having you acknowledge and confess that my lady, whoever she may be, is beyond comparison more beautiful than your own Dulcinea del Toboso. If you will admit the truth of this fully and freely, you will escape death and I shall be spared the trouble of inflicting it upon you. On the other hand, if you choose to fight and I should overcome you, I ask no other satisfaction than that, laying down your arms and seeking no further adventures, you retire to your own village for the space of a year, during which time you are not to lay hand to sword but are to dwell peacefully and tranquilly, enjoying a beneficial rest that shall redound to the betterment of your worldly fortunes and the salvation of your soul. But if you are the victor, then my head shall be at your disposal, my arms and steed shall be the spoils, and the fame of my exploits shall go to increase your own renown. Consider well which is the better course and let me have your answer at once, for today is all the time I have for the dispatching of this business."

Don Quixote was amazed at the knight's arrogance as well as at the nature of the challenge, but it was with a calm and stern demeanor that he replied to him.

"Knight of the White Moon," he said, "of whose exploits up to now I have never heard, I will venture to take an oath that you have not once laid eyes upon the illustrious Dulcinea; for I am quite certain that if you had beheld her you would not be staking your all upon such an issue, since the sight of her would have convinced you that there never has been, and never can be, any beauty to compare with hers. I do not say that you lie, I simply say that you are mistaken; and so I accept your challenge with the conditions you have laid down, and at once, before this day you have fixed upon shall have ended. The only exception I make is with regard to the fame of your deeds being added to my renown, since I do not know what the character of your exploits has been and am quite content with my own, such as they are. Take,

---

1. Don Quixote and Sancho, after numberless encounters and experiences (of which the most prominent have been Don Quixote's descent into the cave of Montesinos and their residence at the castle of the playful ducal couple who give Sancho the "governorship of an island" for ten days), are now in Barcelona. Famous as they are, they meet the viceroy and the nobles; their host is Don Antonio Moreno, "a gentleman of wealth and discernment who was fond of amusing himself in an innocent and kindly way."

then, whichever side of the field you like, and I will take up my position, and may St. Peter bless what God may give."

Now, as it happened, the Knight of the White Moon was seen by some of the townspeople, who informed the viceroy that he was there, talking to Don Quixote de la Mancha. Believing this to be a new adventure arranged by Don Antonio Moreno or some other gentleman of the place, the viceroy at once hastened down to the beach, accompanied by a large retinue, including Don Antonio, and they arrived just as Don Quixote was wheeling Rocinante to measure off the necessary stretch of field. When the viceroy perceived that they were about to engage in combat, he at once interposed and inquired of them what it was that impelled them thus to do battle all of a sudden.

The Knight of the White Moon replied that it was a matter of beauty and precedence and briefly repeated what he had said to Don Quixote, explaining the terms to which both parties had agreed. The viceroy then went up to Don Antonio and asked him if he knew any such knight as this or if it was some joke that they were playing, but the answer that he received left him more puzzled than ever; for Don Antonio did not know who the knight was, nor could he say as to whether this was a real encounter or not. The viceroy, accordingly, was doubtful about letting them proceed, but inasmuch as he could not bring himself to believe that it was anything more than a jest, he withdrew to one side, saying, "Sir Knights, if there is nothing for it but to confess or die, and if Señor Don Quixote's mind is made up and your Grace, the Knight of the White Moon, is even more firmly resolved, then fall to it in the name of God and may He bestow the victory."

The Knight of the White Moon thanked the viceroy most courteously and in well-chosen words for the permission which had been granted them, and Don Quixote did the same, whereupon the latter, commending himself with all his heart to Heaven and to his lady Dulcinea, as was his custom at the beginning of a fray, fell back a little farther down the field as he saw his adversary doing the same. And then, without blare of trumpet or other war-like instrument to give them the signal for the attack, both at the same instant wheeled their steeds about and returned for the charge. Being mounted upon the swifter horse, the Knight of the White Moon met Don Quixote two-thirds of the way and with such tremendous force that, without touching his opponent with his lance (which, it seemed, he deliberately held aloft) he brought both Rocinante and his rider to the ground in an exceedingly perilous fall. At once the victor leaped down and placed his lance at Don Quixote's visor.

"You are vanquished, O knight! Nay, more, you are dead unless you make confession in accordance with the conditions governing our encounter."

Stunned and battered, Don Quixote did not so much as raise his visor but in a faint, wan voice, as if speaking from the grave, he said, "Dulcinea del Toboso is the most beautiful woman in the world and I the most unhappy knight upon the face of this earth. It is not right that my weakness should serve to defraud the truth. Drive home your lance, O knight, and take my life since you already have deprived me of my honor."

"That I most certainly shall not do," said the one of the White Moon. "Let the fame of my lady Dulcinea del Toboso's beauty live on undiminished. As for me, I shall be content if the great Don Quixote will retire to his village for a year or until such a time as I may specify, as was agreed upon between us before joining battle."

The viceroy, Don Antonio, and all the many others who were present heard this, and they also heard Don Quixote's response, which was to the effect that, seeing nothing was asked of him that was prejudicial to Dulcinea, he would fulfill all the other conditions like a true and punctilious knight. The one of the White Moon thereupon turned and with a bow to the viceroy rode back to the city at a mild canter. The viceroy promptly dispatched Don Antonio to follow him and make every effort to find out who he was; and, in the meanwhile, they lifted Don Quixote up and uncovered his face, which held no sign of color and was bathed in perspiration. Rocinante, however, was in so sorry a state that he was unable to stir for the present.

Brokenhearted over the turn that events had taken, Sancho did not know what to say or do. It seemed to him that all this was something that was happening in a dream and that everything was the result of magic. He saw his master surrender, heard him consent not to take up arms again for a year to come as the light of his glorious exploits faded into darkness. At the same time his own hopes, based upon the fresh promises that had been made him, were whirled away like smoke before the wind. He feared that Rocinante was maimed for life, his master's bones permanently dislocated—it would have been a bit of luck if his madness also had been jolted out of him.[2]

Finally, in a hand litter which the viceroy had them bring, they bore the knight back to town. The viceroy himself then returned, for he was very anxious to ascertain who the Knight of the White Moon was who had left Don Quixote in so lamentable a condition.

CHAPTER 65

Wherein is revealed who the Knight of the White Moon was.

The Knight of the White Moon was followed not only by Don Antonio Moreno, but by a throng of small boys as well, who kept after him until the doors of one of the city's hostelries had closed behind him. A squire came out to meet him and remove his armor, for which purpose the victor proceeded to shut himself up in a lower room, in the company of Don Antonio, who had also entered the inn and whose bread would not bake until he had learned the knight's identity. Perceiving that the gentleman had no intention of leaving him, he of the White Moon then spoke.

"Sir," he said, "I am well aware that you have come to find out who I am; and, seeing that there is no denying you the information that you seek, while my servant here is removing my armor I will tell you the exact truth of the matter. I would have you know, sir, that I am the bachelor Sansón Carrasco from the same village as Don Quixote de la Mancha, whose madness and absurdities inspire pity in all of us who know him and in none more than me. And so, being convinced that his salvation lay in his returning home for a period of rest in his own house, I formed a plan for bringing him back.

"It was three months ago that I took to the road as a knight-errant, calling myself the Knight of the Mirrors, with the object of fighting and overcoming him without doing him any harm, intending first to lay down the condition that the vanquished was to yield to the victor's will. What I meant to ask of

---

2. The Spanish has an untranslatable pun on *deslocado*, which means "out of joint" ("dislocated") and also "cured of madness" (from *loco*, "mad").

him—for I looked upon him as conquered from the start—was that he should return to his village and not leave it for a whole year, in the course of which time he might be cured. Fate, however, ordained things otherwise; for he was the one who conquered me and overthrew me from my horse, and thus my plan came to naught. He continued on his wanderings, and I went home, defeated, humiliated, and bruised from my fall, which was quite a dangerous one. But I did not for this reason give up the idea of hunting him up once more and vanquishing him as you have seen me do today.

"Since he is the soul of honor when it comes to observing the ordinances of knight-errantry, there is not the slightest doubt that he will keep the promise he has given me and fulfill his obligations. And that, sir, is all that I need to tell you concerning what has happened. I beg you not to disclose my secret or reveal my identity to Don Quixote, in order that my well-intentioned scheme may be carried out and a man of excellent judgment be brought back to his senses—for a sensible man he would be, once rid of the follies of chivalry."

"My dear sir," exclaimed Don Antonio, "may God forgive you for the wrong you have done the world by seeking to deprive it of its most charming madman! Do you not see that the benefit accomplished by restoring Don Quixote to his senses can never equal the pleasure which others derive from his vagaries? But it is my opinion that all the trouble to which the Señor Bachelor has put himself will not suffice to cure a man who is so hopelessly insane; and if it were not uncharitable, I would say let Don Quixote never be cured, since with his return to health we lose not only his own drolleries but also those of his squire, Sancho Panza, for either of the two is capable of turning melancholy itself into joy and merriment. Nevertheless, I will keep silent and tell him nothing, that I may see whether or not I am right in my suspicion that Señor Carrasco's efforts will prove to have been of no avail."

The bachelor replied that, all in all, things looked very favorable and he hoped for a fortunate outcome. With this, he took his leave of Don Antonio, after offering to render him any service that he could; and, having had his armor tied up and placed upon a mule's back, he rode out of the city that same day on the same horse on which he had gone into battle, returning to his native province without anything happening to him that is worthy of being set down in this veracious chronicle.

[Homecoming and Death]

CHAPTER 73

Of the omens that Don Quixote encountered upon entering his village, with other incidents that embellish and lend credence to this great history.

As they entered the village, Cid Hamete informs us, Don Quixote caught sight of two lads on the communal threshing floor who were engaged in a dispute.

"Don't let it worry you, Periquillo," one of them was saying to the other; "you'll never lay eyes on it again as long as you live."

Hearing this, Don Quixote turned to Sancho. "Did you mark what that boy said, my friend?" he asked. " 'You'll never lay eyes on it[1] again . . .' "

"Well," replied Sancho, "what difference does it make what he said?"

"What difference?" said Don Quixote. "Don't you see that, applied to the one I love, it means I shall never again see Dulcinea."

Sancho was about to answer him when his attention was distracted by a hare that came flying across the fields pursued by a large number of hunters with their greyhounds. The frightened animal took refuge by huddling down beneath the donkey, whereupon Sancho reached out his hand and caught it and presented it to his master.

"*Malum signum, malum signum,*"[2] the knight was muttering to himself. "A hare flees, the hounds pursue it, Dulcinea appears not."

"It is very strange to hear your Grace talk like that," said Sancho. "Let us suppose that this hare *is* Dulcinea del Toboso and the hounds pursuing it are those wicked enchanters that transformed her into a peasant lass; she flees, I catch her and turn her over to your Grace, you hold her in your arms and caress her. Is that a bad sign? What ill omen can you find in it?"

The two lads who had been quarreling now came up to have a look at the hare, and Sancho asked them what their dispute was about. To this the one who had uttered the words "You'll never lay eyes on it again as long as you live," replied that he had taken a cricket cage from the other boy and had no intention of returning it ever. Sancho then brought out from his pocket four cuartos and gave them to the lad in exchange for the cage, which he placed in Don Quixote's hands.

"There, master," he said, "these omens are broken and destroyed, and to my way of thinking, even though I may be a dunce, they have no more to do with what is going to happen to us than the clouds of yesteryear. If I am not mistaken, I have heard our curate say that sensible persons of the Christian faith should pay no heed to such foolish things, and you yourself in the past have given me to understand that all those Christians who are guided by omens are fools. But there is no need to waste a lot of words on the subject; come, let us go on and enter our village."

The hunters at this point came up and asked for the hare, and Don Quixote gave it to them. Continuing on their way, the returning pair encountered the curate and the bachelor Carrrasco, who were strolling in a small meadow on the outskirts of the town as they read their breviaries. And here it should be mentioned that Sancho Panza, by way of sumpter cloth, had thrown over his gray and the bundle of armor it bore the flame-covered buckram robe in which they had dressed the squire at the duke's castle, on the night that witnessed Altisidora's[3] resurrection; and he had also fitted the miter over the donkey's head, the result being the weirdest transformation and the most bizarrely appareled ass that ever were seen in this world. The curate and the bachelor recognized the pair at once and came forward to receive them with open arms. Don Quixote dismounted and gave them both a warm embrace; meanwhile, the small boys (boys are like lynxes in that nothing escapes them), having spied the ass's miter, ran up for a closer view.

1. The same as *her* in the Spanish, because the reference is to a cricket cage, which is a feminine noun. Hence Don Quixote's inference concerning Dulcinea. 2. Meeting a hare is considered an ill omen (Latin)—that is, a bad sign. 3. A girl in the duke's castle, where Don Quixote and Sancho were guests for a time. She dramatically pretended to be in love with Don Quixote.

"Come, lads," they cried, "and see Sancho Panza's ass trigged out finer than Mingo,[4] and Don Quixote's beast is skinnier than ever!"

Finally, surrounded by the urchins and accompanied by the curate and the bachelor, they entered the village and made their way to Don Quixote's house, where they found the housekeeper and the niece standing in the doorway, for the news of their return had preceded them. Teresa Panza, Sancho's wife, had also heard of it, and, half naked and disheveled, dragging her daughter Sanchica by the hand, she hastened to greet her husband and was disappointed when she saw him, for he did not look to her as well fitted out as a governor ought to be.

"How does it come, my husband," she said, "that you return like this, tramping and footsore? You look more like a vagabond than you do like a governor."

"Be quiet, Teresa," Sancho admonished her, "for very often there are stakes where there is no bacon. Come on home with me and you will hear marvels. I am bringing money with me, which is the thing that matters, money earned by my own efforts and without harm to anyone."

"You just bring along the money, my good husband," said Teresa, "and whether you got it here or there, or by whatever means, you will not be introducing any new custom into the world."

Sanchica then embraced her father and asked him if he had brought her anything, for she had been looking forward to his coming as to the showers in May. And so, with his wife holding him by the hand while his daughter kept one arm about his waist and at the same time led the gray, Sancho went home, leaving Don Quixote under his own roof in the company of niece and housekeeper, the curate and the barber.

Without regard to time or season, the knight at once drew his guests to one side and in a few words informed them of how he had been overcome in battle and had given his promise not to leave his village for a year, a promise that he meant to observe most scrupulously, without violating it in the slightest degree, as every knight-errant was obliged to do by the laws of chivalry. He accordingly meant to spend that year as a shepherd,[5] he said, amid the solitude of the fields, where he might give free rein to his amorous fancies as he practiced the virtues of the pastoral life; and he further begged them, if they were not too greatly occupied and more urgent matters did not prevent their doing so, to consent to be his companions. He would purchase a flock sufficiently large to justify their calling themselves shepherds; and, moreover, he would have them know, the most important thing of all had been taken care of, for he had hit upon names that would suit them marvelously well. When the curate asked him what these names were, Don Quixote replied that he himself would be known as "the shepherd Quixotiz," the bachelor as "the shepherd Carrascón," the curate as "the shepherd Curiambro," and Sancho Panza as "the shepherd Pancino."

Both his listeners were dismayed at the new form which his madness had assumed. However, in order that he might not go faring forth from the village on another of his expeditions (for they hoped that in the course of the year

---

4. The allusion is to the opening lines of *Mingo Revulgo* (fifteenth century), a satire.   5. Because the knight-errant's life has been forbidden him by his defeat, Don Quixote for a time plans to live according to another and no less "literary" code, that of the pastoral. The following paragraphs, especially through the bachelor Carrasco, refer humorously to some of the conventions of pastoral literature.

he would be cured), they decided to fall in with his new plan and approve it as being a wise one, and they even agreed to be his companions in the calling he proposed to adopt.

"What's more," remarked Sansón Carrasco, "I am a very famous poet, as everyone knows, and at every turn I will be composing pastoral or courtly verses or whatever may come to mind, by way of a diversion for us as we wander in those lonely places; but what is most necessary of all, my dear sirs, is that each one of us should choose the name of the shepherd lass to whom he means to dedicate his songs, so that we may not leave a tree, however hard its bark may be, where their names are not inscribed and engraved as is the custom with lovelorn shepherds."

"That is exactly what we should do," replied Don Quixote, "although, for my part, I am relieved of the necessity of looking for an imaginary shepherdess, seeing that I have the peerless Dulcinea del Toboso, glory of these brookside regions, adornment of these meadows, beauty's mainstay, cream of the Graces—in short, one to whom all praise is well becoming however hyperbolical it may be."

"That is right," said the curate, "but we will seek out some shepherd maids that are easily handled, who if they do not square with us will fit in the corners."

"And," added Sansón Carrasco, "if we run out of names we will give them those that we find printed in books the world over: such as Fílida, Amarilis, Diana, Flérida, Galatea, and Belisarda; for since these are for sale in the market place, we can buy them and make them our own. If my lady, or, rather, my shepherdess, should be chance be called Ana, I will celebrate her charms under the name of Anarda; if she is Francisca, she will become Francenia; if Lucía, Luscinda; for it all amounts to the same thing. And Sancho Panza, if he enters this confraternity, may compose verses to his wife, Teresa Panza, under the name of Teresaina."

Don Quixote had to laugh at this, and the curate then went on to heap extravagant praise upon him for his noble resolution which did him so much credit, and once again he offered to keep the knight company whenever he could spare the time from the duties of his office. With this, they took their leave of him, advising and beseeching him to take care of his health and to eat plentifully of the proper food.

As fate would have it, the niece and the housekeeper had overheard the conversation of the three men, and as soon as the visitors had left they both descended upon Don Quixote.

"What is the meaning of this, my uncle? Here we were thinking your Grace had come home to lead a quiet and respectable life, and do you mean to tell us you are going to get yourself involved in fresh complications—

> Young shepherd, thou who comest here,
> Young shepherd, thou who goest there . . .[6]

For, to tell the truth, the barley is too hard now to make shepherds' pipes of it."[7]

"And how," said the housekeeper, "is your Grace going to stand the midday heat in summer, the winter cold, the howling of the wolves out there in the

6. From a ballad.   7. A proverb.

fields? You certainly cannot endure it. That is an occupation for robust men, cut out and bred for such a calling almost from their swaddling clothes. Setting one evil over against another, it is better to be a knight-errant than a shepherd. Look, sir, take my advice, for I am not stuffed with bread and wine when I give it to you but am fasting and am going on fifty years of age: stay at home, attend to your affairs, go often to confession, be charitable to the poor, and let it be upon my soul if any harm comes to you as a result of it."

"Be quiet, daughters," said Don Quixote. "I know very well what I must do. Take me up to bed, for I do not feel very well; and you may be sure of one thing: whether I am a knight-errant now or a shepherd to be, I never will fail to look after your needs as you will see when the time comes."

And good daughters that they unquestionably were, the housekeeper and the niece helped him up to bed, where they gave him something to eat and made him as comfortable as they could.

CHAPTER 74

Of how Don Quixote fell sick, of the will that he made, and of the manner of his death.

Inasmuch as nothing that is human is eternal but is ever declining from its beginning to its close, this being especially true of the lives of men, and since Don Quixote was not endowed by Heaven with the privilege of staying the downward course of things, his own end came when he was least expecting it. Whether it was owing to melancholy occasioned by the defeat he had suffered, or was, simply, the will of Heaven which had so ordained it, he was taken with a fever that kept him in bed for a week, during which time his friends, the curate, the bachelor, and the barber, visited him frequently, while Sancho Panza, his faithful squire, never left his bedside.

Believing that the knight's condition was due to sorrow over his downfall and disappointment at not having been able to accomplish the disenchantment and liberation of Dulcinea, Sancho and the others endeavored to cheer him up in every possible way. The bachelor urged him to take heart and get up from bed that he might begin his pastoral life, adding that he himself had already composed an eclogue that would cast in the shade all that Sannazaro[8] had ever written, and had purchased with his own money from a herdsman of Quintanar two fine dogs to guard the flock, one of them named Barcino and the other Butrón. All this, however, did not serve to relieve Don Quixote's sadness; whereupon his friends called in the doctor, who took his pulse and was not very well satisfied with it. In any case, the physician told them, they should attend to the health of his soul as that of his body was in grave danger.

Don Quixote received this news calmly enough, but not so his housekeeper, niece, and squire, who began weeping bitterly, as if he were already lying dead in front of them. It was the doctor's opinion that melancholy and depression were putting an end to his patient's life. The knight then requested them to leave him alone as he wished to sleep a little, and they

---

8. Jacopo Sannazaro (1456–1530), Italian poet, whose *Arcadia* is one of the milestones in the pastoral tradition.

complied. He slept for more than six hours at a stretch, as the saying is, and so soundly that the housekeeper and niece thought he would never wake.

At last he did, however, and at once cried out in a loud voice, "Blessed be Almighty God who has given me so many blessings! Truly His mercy is boundless and is not limited or restrained by the sins of men."

The niece listened carefully to what her uncle said, and it seemed to her that he was speaking more rationally than was his wont, at least during his illness.

"Sir," she said to him, "what does your Grace mean? Has something occurred that we know nothing about? What is this talk of mercy and sins?"

"The mercy that I speak of," replied Don Quixote, "is that which God is showing me at this moment—in spite of my sins, as I have said. My mind now is clear, unencumbered by those misty shadows of ignorance that were cast over it by my bitter and continual reading of those hateful books of chivalry. I see through all the nonsense and fraud contained in them, and my only regret is that my disillusionment has come so late, leaving me no time to make any sort of amends by reading those that are the light of the soul. I find myself, niece, at the point of death, and I would die in such a way as not to leave the impression of a life so bad that I shall be remembered as a madman; for even though I have been one, I do not wish to confirm it on my deathbed. And so, my dear, call in my good friends: the curate, the bachelor Sansón Carrasco, and Master Nicholas the barber; for I want to confess my sins and make my last will and testament."

The niece, however, was relieved of this errand, for the three of them came in just then.

"I have good news for you, kind sirs," said Don Quixote the moment he saw them. "I am no longer Don Quixote de la Mancha but Alonso Quijano, whose mode of life won for him the name of 'Good.' I am the enemy of Amadis of Gaul and all his innumerable progeny; for those profane stories dealing with knight-errantry are odious to me, and I realize how foolish I was and the danger I courted in reading them; but I am in my right senses now and I abominate them."

Hearing this, they all three were convinced that some new kind of madness must have laid hold of him.

"Why, Señor Don Quixote!" exclaimed Sansón. "What makes you talk like that, just when we have received news that my lady Dulcinea is disenchanted? And just when we are on the verge of becoming shepherds so that we may spend the rest of our lives in singing like a lot of princes, why does your Grace choose to turn hermit? Say no more, in Heaven's name, but be sensible and forget these idle tales."

"Tales of that kind," said Don Quixote, "have been the truth for me in the past, and to my detriment, but with Heaven's aid I trust to turn them to my profit now that I am dying. For I feel, gentlemen, that death is very near; so, leave all jesting aside and bring me a confessor for my sins and a notary to draw up my will. In such straits as these a man cannot trifle with his soul. Accordingly, while the Señor Curate is hearing my confession, let the notary be summoned."

Amazed at his words, they gazed at one another in some perplexity, yet they could not but believe him. One of the signs that led them to think he was dying was this quick return from madness to sanity and all the additional things he had to say, so well reasoned and well put and so becoming in a Christian that none of them could any longer doubt that he was in full possession of his faculties. Sending the others out of the room, the curate stayed behind to confess him, and before long the bachelor returned with the notary and Sancho Panza, who had been informed of his master's condition, and who, finding the housekeeper and the niece in tears, began weeping with them. When the confession was over, the curate came out.

"It is true enough," he said, "that Alonso Quijano the Good is dying, and it is also true that he is a sane man. It would be well for us to go in now while he makes his will."

At this news the housekeeper, niece, and the good squire Sancho Panza were so overcome with emotion that the tears burst forth from their eyes and their bosoms heaved with sobs; for, as has been stated more than once, whether Don Quixote was plain Alonso Quijano the Good or Don Quixote de la Mancha, he was always of a kindly and pleasant disposition and for this reason was beloved not only by the members of his household but by all who knew him.

The notary had entered along with the others, and as soon as the preamble had been attended to and the dying man had commended his soul to his Maker with all those Christian formalities that are called for in such a case, they came to the matter of bequests, with Don Quixote dictating as follows:

"ITEM. With regard to Sancho Panza, whom, in my madness, I appointed to be my squire, and who has in his possession a certain sum of money belonging to me: inasmuch as there has been a standing account between us, of debits and credits, it is my will that he shall not be asked to give any accounting whatsoever of this sum, but if any be left over after he has had payment for what I owe him, the balance, which will amount to very little, shall be his, and much good may it do him. If when I was mad I was responsible for his being given the governorship of an island, now that I am of sound mind I would present him with a kingdom if it were in my power, for his simplicity of mind and loyal conduct merit no less."

At this point he turned to Sancho. "Forgive me, my friend," he said, "for having caused you to appear as mad as I by leading you to fall into the same error, that of believing that there are still knights-errant in the world."

"Ah, master," cried Sancho through his tears, "don't die, your Grace, but take my advice and go on living for many years to come; for the greatest madness that a man can be guilty of in this life is to die without good reason, without anyone's killing him, slain only by the hands of melancholy. Look you, don't be lazy but get up from this bed and let us go out into the fields clad as shepherds as we agreed to do. Who knows but behind some bush we may come upon the lady Dulcinea, as disenchanted as you could wish. If it is because of worry over your defeat that you are dying, put the blame on me by saying that the reason for your being overthrown was that I had not properly fastened Rocinante's girth. For the matter of that, your Grace knows from reading your books of chivalry that it is a common thing for certain knights to overthrow others, and he who is vanquished today will be the victor tomorrow."

"That is right," said Sansón, "the worthy Sancho speaks the truth."

"Not so fast, gentlemen," said Don Quixote. "In last year's nests there are no birds this year. I was mad and now I am sane; I was Don Quixote de la Mancha, and now I am, as I have said, Alonso Quijano the Good. May my repentance and the truth I now speak restore to me the place I once held in your esteem. And now, let the notary proceed:

"ITEM. I bequeath my entire estate, without reservation, to my niece Antonia Quijana, here present, after the necessary deductions shall have been made from the most available portion of it to satisfy the bequests that I have stipulated. The first payment shall be to my housekeeper for the wages due her, with twenty ducats over to buy her a dress. And I hereby appoint the Señor Curate and the Señor Bachelor Sansón Carrasco to be my executors.

"ITEM. It is my will that if my niece Antonia Quijana should see fit to marry, it shall be to a man who does not know what books of chivalry are; and if it shall be established that he is acquainted with such books and my niece still insists on marrying him, then she shall lose all that I have bequeathed her and my executors shall apply her portion to works of charity as they may see fit.

"ITEM. I entreat the aforementioned gentlemen, my executors, if by good fortune they should come to know the author who is said to have composed a history now going the rounds under the title of *Second Part of the Exploits of Don Quixote de la Mancha,* to beg his forgiveness in my behalf, as earnestly as they can, since it was I who unthinkingly led him to set down so many and such great absurdities as are to be found in it; for I leave this life with a feeling of remorse at having provided him with the occasion for putting them into writing."

The will ended here, and Don Quixote, stretching himself at length in the bed, fainted away. They all were alarmed at this and hastened to aid him. The same thing happened very frequently in the course of the three days of life that remained to him after he had made his will. The household was in a state of excitement, but with it all the niece continued to eat her meals, the housekeeper had her drink, and Sancho Panza was in good spirits; for this business of inheriting property effaces or mitigates the sorrow which the heir ought to feel and causes him to forget.

Death came at last for Don Quixote, after he had received all the sacraments and once more, with many forceful arguments, had expressed his abomination of books of chivalry. The notary who was present remarked that in none of those books had he read of any knight-errant dying in his own bed so peacefully and in so Christian a manner. And thus, amid the tears and lamentations of those present, he gave up the ghost; that is to say, he died. Perceiving that their friend was no more, the curate asked the notary to be a witness to the fact that Alonso Quijano the Good, commonly known as Don Quixote, was truly dead, this being necessary in order that some author other than Cid Hamete Benengeli might not have the opportunity of falsely resurrecting him and writing endless histories of his exploits.

Such was the end of the Ingenious Gentleman of La Mancha, whose birthplace Cid Hamete was unwilling to designate exactly in order that all the towns and villages of La Mancha might contend among themselves for the right to adopt him and claim him as their own, just as the seven cities of Greece did in the case of Homer. The lamentations of Sancho and those of Don Quixote's niece and his housekeeper, as well as the original epitaphs that were composed for his tomb, will not be recorded here, but mention may be made of the verses by Sansón Carrasco:

> Here lies a gentleman bold
> Who was so very brave
> He went to lengths untold,
> And on the brink of the grave
> Death had on him no hold.
> By the world he set small store—
> He frightened it to the core—
> Yet somehow, by Fate's plan,
> Though he'd lived a crazy man,
> When he died he was sane once more.

LOPE DE VEGA
1562–1635

One of the great dramatists of the Spanish golden age, Lope Félix de Vega Carpio achieved such enormous popularity and admiration that his very name became a synonym for excellence. The impact of his art on drama was no less impressive: his method of composing three-act plays with comic or serious subplots came to dominate Spanish drama well into the eighteenth century. The importance of his dramatic legacy far exceeded his own estimation of it: Lope did not consider plays to be serious art and openly admitted that he wrote for money and for the pleasure of the people. He claimed to have composed some fifteen hundred plays (an early biographer puts the figure at eighteen hundred), and many of the thousands of characters he created were based on favorite types he frequently recycled.

Born in Madrid, Lope led a life spectacularly complicated by his three passionate loves: women, religion, and Spain, which was emerging as a nation. Married twice, Lope had at least sixteen children (six in wedlock) and affairs so numerous that some biographical sketches arrange his life by his serial (and overlapping) cohabitation with the women he celebrated in verse. Religious faith played a serious role in his private and public lives: Lope took holy orders in 1614, was elected a judge by the Spanish Inquisition, and served as an official censor. In 1622 Pope Urban VIII made him a member of the Order of St. John of Jerusalem and an honorary doctor of theology. His career in the Church and participation in the Inquisition suggest how intimately tied religious and national feeling were in Lope's mind. His devotion to Spain also led him to fight in two battles, one of them against England with the Spanish Armada. When he died in 1635, the nation mourned him with a nine-day funeral in Madrid.

Lope's dramatic art reflects his various passions. He wrote brilliant sacred plays in addition to his comedies. He created strong female characters, such as Laurencia, the heroine of the play presented in this anthology: she not only makes the most influential speech in a town council but also, when she turns from politics to romance, speaks a complete sonnet (she is the only female character in the history of Spanish drama to do so). Lope's efforts to link his plays to the idea of Spain as a nation are, perhaps, the clearest evidence of a consistent dramatic project in his many plays. He believed that plays should deal with historically important issues, such as "the events, wars, peace, counsels, fortune, change, prosperity, the decline of kingdoms and epochs of great empires and monarchies" (*The Bell of Aragon*). In his mock-epic, *The*

Cat-fight, he associates his subjects more specifically with the land and institutions of Spain: her woods, fields, trees, and flowers and "the arms and laws that maintain kingdoms and kings."

Lope's *Fuente Ovejuna* (Sheepwell) is a comedy. Charm and humor characterize its scenes, peasant characters, and dialogue, and the play ends in a jubilant affirmation of community and social order. It also has serious political dimensions and stages a daring foray into questions about law and government. Rape is the crime that finally drives the long-suffering people of Fuente Ovejuna to rise up and kill the abusive Comendador, Fernán Gómez de Guzmán, who lives in (and off) their small pastoral village. As the aristocratic Guzmán mistreats Fuente Ovejuna's councilmen, seduces and harasses its women, and imposes burdensome taxes, the villagers' thoughts turn to social contracts, law, and justice. They finally take action when the Comendador interrupts the wedding of a young couple, Frondoso and Laurencia, strips the mayor of his office, seizes Laurencia, and arrests Frondoso: they attack his household and throw the Comendador from a window to land upon the swords and spears of the women below. While the villagers celebrate by composing songs and parading raucously with Guzmán's head on a pole, word of the bloody rebellion reaches the Spanish kings, who send a judge to interrogate the villagers and administer justice. Aware of the legal consequences of their actions, the community resolves to stand by each other: even under torture, the men, women, and children of Fuente Ovejuna have one answer to the zealous judge's demand to learn the names of those responsible: "Everyone—Fuente Ovejuna did it." Left with the options of destroying the entire village or issuing a general pardon, the king chooses clemency. In the play's final scene, the villagers joyfully submit themselves to the rule of the Catholic kings—none other than the historical Ferdinand and Isabella, who completed the Reconquest of Spain, sent Christopher Columbus to America in 1492, and launched Spain's reputation as the most powerful empire of the sixteenth century.

Lope did not invent the subject of *Fuente Ovejuna:* he drew on historical events that took place in the small pastoral village in the province of Córdoba. His principal source, the chronicle history of Fray Francisco de Rades y Andrada, records that the Comendador "committed great injuries and dishonors to the people of the village, taking their daughters and wives by force, and robbing their households to maintain his soldiers." At length the villagers, calling out "long live Kings Ferdinand and Isabel, and death to traitors and bad Christians," rebelled, refused to hear the Comendador's promises of restitution, and killed him along with fourteen of his men. After his death, according to the chronicle, "they pulled his beard out by the roots with great cruelty, and broke his teeth with the pommels of their swords," mutilated the body, carried his head on a pole, refused him a Christian burial, and robbed his household. Had a single villager collapsed under torture and identified the ringleaders in order to save his or her own skin, the events at Fuente Ovejuna would be chronicled as a lurid and bloody uprising during a period of widespread cultural upheaval in Spanish history. But since each was willing to die for the others, they left a memorable and even proverbial example of resistance and solidarity. The phrase "Fuente Ovejuna lo hizo" ("Sheepwell did it") became proverbial for a dedication to community and democratic process.

Lope shows considerable sympathy for his peasants, who are goaded into their seditious frenzy. Left to their own devices, the villagers are law-abiding and peaceable: even the names of the lead characters, Frondoso ("leafy") and Laurencia ("laurel"), associate them with the most nonviolent aspects of nature. Lope's spotlight shines on the Comendador's abuses—including reports of a gang rape, brutal beatings, and the administration of an ink enema to a hapless peasant (a bizarre punishment, perhaps suggesting the censorship of writing). The attempted rape of Laurencia, the play's most dynamic and articulate character, is Lope's invention, and it plays a decisive role in defining the nature of the political violence that Guzmán perpetrates on the entire village: first, rape was an inalterable dishonor to a woman and to her father and husband, and second, it represents, in a most visceral way, Guzmán's violent disregard for consent, the key term in all social contracts. The assault shocks Laurencia into a hair-raising harangue at the town council, where she spurs the dishonored villagers to revenge. The murder scene, which follows, is fast-paced, giddy, and carnivalesque. Questions of moral interpretation are left to performance, which might emphasize either the spirit of liberation or the spirit of dangerous transgression. Lope acknowledges the more ghoulish details from the chronicle, but places them in the biased report that Flores, the Comendador's bully and pimp, makes to the Catholic kings. What compels Lope's imagination is the villagers' redemptive commitment to community. Lope uses the historical event and example to raise fundamental questions of political philosophy: does authority come from above (God) or below (the people)? is government based on a social contract? do laborers have the right to honor? are the people, if governed cruelly, entitled to revoke their consent or to resist by violence? Lope, who was no political radical, suggests that government without popular consent and mutual respect is morally bankrupt.

Through the story of Sheepwell, Lope explores political issues that gained national importance when Ferdinand of Aragon and Isabella of Castile married, paving the way to the union of Spain despite the different political traditions of Aragon and Castile. The rebellion of Fuente Ovejuna took place in 1476, seven years after Ferdinand and Isabella secretly married in hopes of uniting the Crowns of Aragon and Castile and two years after Isabella declared herself queen of Castile, following the death of her half-brother, Henry IV. At the time of the villagers' uprising, the security of the Catholic kings and the political destiny of Spain itself hung in the balance, in part because Isabella's was not the only (or even the best) claim to the Crown of Castile. In 1476 Ferdinand and Isabella were at war with Alfonso V of Portugal and his wife, Juana, alleged to be the daughter of Henry IV. Moreover, it was by no means clear how the Crowns of Castile and Aragon would reconcile the radically opposed forms of government that each province traditionally upheld. Castile espoused monarchical absolutism, a theory of power holding that the king is above the law and that "what pleases the king *is* law." The Castilian monarchy was locked in a struggle with its most powerful aristocratic families, the dynasties of Mendoza, Enríquez, and Guzmán (from which the Comendador comes). Aragon, on the other hand, rejoiced in its constitutional government, which strongly emphasized the reciprocal obligations of the monarch and his subjects. The Aragonese oath of allegiance ran "We who are as good as you swear to you, who are no better than we, to accept you as our king and sovereign lord, provided that you observe all our liberties and laws; but if not, not." To the Aragonese the liberties of subjects outstripped the prerogatives of the monarch. The events at Fuente Ovejuna coincided with the rise to power of the Catholic kings, giving Lope an opportunity to explore both the ideal form of government and Spain's future as a powerful empire. Controversy never hurt the box office, Lope knew, and so he brought to the stage political debates over dominion by consent, divine right, and force.

Lope dedicates his play's subplot to Ferdinand and Isabella. Fuente Ovejuna is under siege, and so is the Royal City (*Ciudad Real*) of Castile; Laurencia's honor is under assault, and so is Isabella's authority. Until the end of the play, when the villagers meet the Catholic kings, the sole figure to pass between the two plots is Fernán Gómez de Guzmán: when the Comendador is not brutalizing the villagers of Fuente Ovejuna, he is on the battlefield fighting against Ferdinand and Isabella. Guzmán belongs to the chivalric order of Calatrava, one of the three great military and religious orders established in the twelfth century to bring about the Reconquest of Spain, following the Arab invasion of 711. Lope's Guzmán perfectly embodies the ethos of the aristocratic *hidalgo*: "a man who lived for war, who could do the impossible through sheer physical courage and a constant effort of the will, who conducted his relations with others according to a strictly regulated code of honor, and who reserved his respect for the man who had won riches by force of arms rather than by the sweat of manual labor," as one historian puts it.

The rapacious and arrogant style of dominion exemplified by Lope's Guzmán contrasts with the military and judicial policies of the Catholic kings, whom Lope celebrates as prudent, just, and respectful of law. Guzmán abuses the idea, central to the theory of monarchical absolutism, that "what pleases the king is law." He speaks of ownership of his subjects, seduces and rapes his female subjects, and attempts to dissolve the local administration of law when he strips the mayor of office and orders the villagers to vacate the central plaza. In the play's very first scene, Guzmán greets the young Maestre of the chivalric Order of Calatrava with the blunt assertion "You owe me a lot," and proceeds to manipulate the youth into attacking the Royal City. Guzmán violates the reciprocal obligations governing the relationship of the good king and his subjects: he contemptuously rejects the suggestion that he owes anything to the villagers of Fuente Ovejuna, and it is in the role of bad counselor that he coerces the powerful but impressionable Maestre of the Order of Calatrava. The Catholic kings, on the other hand, later exemplify the magnanimous and prudential nature of good kings: they pardon the Maestre for his assault on the Royal City and direct his aggression toward wars beneficial to Spain and befitting the traditions of his Order, crusades against the Arabs. Guzmán's moral and military opposition to the idealized Catholic kings suggests that the villagers of Fuente Ovejuna are justified in their cry "Death to bad Christians and traitors."

Guzmán is not the only figure in Lope's play to wed dramatic stereotype to controversial concepts in political theory. So do the young lovers, Laurencia and Frondoso, who are both stock types from comedy and initially act like the intelligent, beautiful, unattainable young woman and the good-hearted, callow, fashion-happy young man who adores her. The characters soon reveal how they vary from their stereotypes, however. Because she has known only the Comendador's attempts to entrap her, Laurencia at first disdains love. She understandably insists that love is merely self-interest, while Frondoso, who views her coldness in purely conventional terms, seems oddly unaware that he inhabits a politically mired world and not a standard comedy. Frondoso soon learns what love requires of him: while he and Laurencia are in the woods debating about love, the Comendador, who has been out hunting deer, appears and decides to "hunt" Laurencia instead. If he is to prevent her rape, Frondoso must come out from his hiding place, pick up the Comendador's discarded crossbow, and threaten his life. Heroic and ethical but illegal, Frondoso's act wins Laurencia's love and the Comendador's murderous enmity. The Comendador's abuses habitually force peasants—and otherwise typical comic characters—to think strenuously about the nature of social contracts. The peasants conclude that those who govern owe a debt to those who serve and that communal bonds are formed by love: the willingness to enter into a social relationship and to treat the interest of others as one's own. This is the lesson that gives the villagers the courage to protect their community despite torture. In Lope's play, love is both the erotic mainstay of comedy and the harmonizing principle of government: in matters of the heart and of law, the subject must have the right to consent.

Walter Cohen, *Drama of a Nation: Public Theater and Renaissance England and Spain* (1985), Donald R. Larson, *The Honor Plays of Lope de Vega* (1977), Robert L. Fiore, *Drama and Ethos: Natural-Law Ethics in Spanish Golden Age Theater* (1975), and Edward M. Wilson and Duncan Moir, *The Golden Age: Drama 1492–1700* (1971), present useful and illuminating studies of Lope de Vega's work and its relation to Spanish theater in general. J. B. Hall, *Lope de Vega: Fuenteovejuna* (1985), presents a detailed study of the play. J. H. Elliott's *Imperial Spain 1469–1716* (1963), is an indispensable study of Spanish history and politics.

PRONOUNCING GLOSSARY

The following list uses common English syllables and stress accents to provide rough equivalents of selected words whose pronunciation may be unfamiliar to the general reader. Note that in Castilian Spanish, as opposed to the Spanish spoken in the Americas, *d* is pronounced as *th*.

Cimbranos: *seem-brah'nos*

Ciudad Real: *see-oo-dthahth' ray-ahl'*

Comendador: *koh-men-da-thor'*

Cuadrado: *kwah-drah'thoh*

Fernán Gómez de Guzman: *fer-nahn' goh'mez day gus'mahn*

Frondoso: *frohn-doh'so*

Fuente Ovejuna: *fu-en'tay o-vay-hu'nah*

Jacinta: *ha-seen'tah*

Juan Chamorro: *hwan cha-mor'roh*

Juan Rojo: *hwan ro'hoh*

Laurencia: *lau-ren'see-ah*

Leon: *lay-own'*

Lope de Vega: *loh'pay duh vay'gah*

Maestre of Calatrava: *ma-e'stray of cah-lah-trah'vah*

Manrique: *man-ree'kay*

maravedíes: *mah-rah-vay-dee'es*

Ortuño: *or-tun'yoh*

Pascuala: *pas-kwahlah*

Rodrigo Téllez Girón: *ro-dree'goh tay'-yez hi-rohn'*

Villena: *vi-yay'nah*

Fuente Ovejuna[1]

CHARACTERS

Queen ISABELLA of Castile
KING Ferdinand of Aragon
Rodrigo Téllez Girón, MAESTRE *of the religious and military Order of Calatrava*
Fernán Gómez de Guzmán, COMENDADOR *Mayor of the Order of Calatrava*
Don MANRIQUE
A JUDGE
Two COUNCILMEN *of Ciudad Real*
ORTUÑO ⎱ *servants of the Comendador*
FLORES ⎰
ESTEBAN ⎱ *Mayors of Fuente Ovejuna*
ALONSO ⎰
LAURENCIA ⎱
JACINTA ⎰ *peasant girls*
PASCUALA ⎰
JUAN ROJO, *Councilman of Fuente Ovejuna, a peasant*
Another COUNCILMAN *of Fuente Ovejuna*
FRONDOSO ⎱
MENGO ⎰ *peasants*
BARRILDO ⎰
LEONELO, *Licentiate of Law*
CIMBRANOS, *a soldier*
A BOY
PEASANTS, *men and women*
MUSICIANS
SOLDIERS

Time: 1476

1. Translated by Angel Flores and Muriel Kittel.

ACT I

Hall of the MAESTRE *of the Order of Calatrava, in Almagro.*[2]

[*Enter the* COMENDADOR[3] *and his servants,* FLORES *and* ORTUÑO.]

COMENDADOR   Does the Maestre[4] know that I am here?

FLORES   He does, my lord.

ORTUÑO   The Maestre is becoming more mature.

COMENDADOR   Does he know that I am Fernán Gómez de Guzmán?

FLORES   He's only a boy—you mustn't be surprised if he doesn't.

COMENDADOR   Nevertheless he must know that I am the Comendador.

ORTUÑO   There are those who advise him to be discourteous.

COMENDADOR   That will win him little love. Courtesy is the key to good will, while thoughtless discourtesy is the way to make enemies.

ORTUÑO   If we but realized how it makes us hated and despised by everyone we would rather die than be discourteous.

FLORES   What a nuisance discourtesy is: among equals it's foolish and toward inferiors it's tyrannical. In this case it only means that the boy has not learned what it is to be loved.

COMENDADOR   The obligation he took upon himself when he accepted his sword and the Cross of Calatrava[5] was placed on his breast should have been enough to teach him courtesy.

FLORES   If he has been prejudiced against you you'll soon find out.

ORTUÑO   Why don't you leave if you're in doubt?

COMENDADOR   I wish to see what he is like.

[*Enter the* MAESTRE *of Calatrava and retinue.*]

MAESTRE   Pardon me, Fernán Gómez de Guzmán; I only just heard that you had come. Forgive me if I have kept you waiting.

COMENDADOR   I have just cause for complaint. Both my love for you and my rank entitle me to better treatment—for you are the Maestre of Calatrava and I your Comendador and your servant.

MAESTRE   I did not know of your welcome arrival—let me embrace you again.

COMENDADOR   You owe me a great deal; I have risked my life to settle your many difficulties. I even managed to persuade the Pope to increase your age.[6]

MAESTRE   That is true, and by the holy cross which we both proudly bear on our breasts I shall repay you in love, and honor you as my own father.

COMENDADOR   I am satisfied that you will.

MAESTRE   What news of the war?

COMENDADOR   Listen carefully, and I will tell you where your duty lies.

MAESTRE   I am listening; tell me.

COMENDADOR   Maestre Don Rodrigo Téllez Girón, I need hardly remind you how your brave father resigned his high position as Maestre to you eight years ago, and appointed Don Juan Pacheco, the Grand Maestre of Santiago, to be your coadjutor, nor how kings and comendadors confirmed and swore to his act, and the Pope [Pius II][7] and his successor

---

2. Region of Spain.   3. Captain.   4. Master.   5. One of three military and religious (chivalric) orders.   6. Increased on papal authority for the purpose of holding the office of Maestre.   7. Material added for clarity has been placed in brackets throughout the play.

Paul agreed to it in their bulls; no, what I have come to tell you is this: now that Pacheco is dead and you, in spite of your youth, have sole control of the government, now is the time for you to take up arms for the honor of your family. Since the death of Henry IV your relatives have supported the cause of Don Alonso, King of Portugal, who claims the throne of Castile through his wife Juana.[8] Ferdinand, the great prince of Aragon, makes a similar claim through his wife Isabella.[9] But your relatives do not consider Ferdinand's rights to be as clear as those of Juana—who is now in your cousin's power. So I advise you to rally the knights of Calatrava in Almagro and to capture Ciudad Real,[1] which stands on the frontier between Andalusia and Castile. You will not need many men, because the enemy can count only on their neighbors and a few noblemen who support Isabella and consider Ferdinand their legitimate king. It will be wonderful if you, Rodrigo, if you, a youth, can astonish those who say that this cross is too heavy for your young shoulders. Emulate the counts of Urueña from whom you spring, and who from the height of their fame seem to be challenging you with the laurels they have won; emulate the marquises of Villena and those other captains who are so numerous that the wings of fame are not strong enough to bear them. Unsheathe your white sword, dye it red in battle till it matches the cross upon your breast. For I cannot call you the Maestre of the Red Cross as long as your sword is white: both the sword you bear and the cross you wear must be red. And you, mighty Girón, must add the crowning glory to the immortal fame of your ancestors.

MAESTRE   Fernán Gómez, you may be sure that I side with my family in this dispute, for I am convinced that they are right. And as I translate my conviction into action at Ciudad Real you will see me tearing the city walls down with the violence of a thunderbolt. I know that I am young—but do not think that my courage died with my uncle's death. I will unsheathe my white sword and its brilliance shall become the color of the cross, bathed in red blood.

But tell me, where do you live, and do you have any soldiers?

COMENDADOR   A few—but they are faithful and they will fight like lions. I live in Fuente Ovejuna, where the people are skilled in agriculture and husbandry rather than in the arts of war.

MAESTRE   And you live there, you say?

COMENDADOR   I do. I chose a house on my estate to stay in during these troubled times. Now see that all your people go into action with you— let no man stay behind!

MAESTRE   You shall see me today on horseback, bearing my lance on high.

[*Exeunt* COMENDADOR *and* MAESTRE.]

A public square in Fuente Ovejuna.

[*Enter* LAURENCIA *and* PASCUALA.]

LAURENCIA   I hoped he would never come back.

PASCUALA   I must say I thought you'd be more distressed at the news.

8. Illegitimate daughter of Henry IV, wife of Alonso of Portugal, and Isabella's rival claimant to the throne of Castile.   9. Isabella of Castile (1451–1501) and Ferdinand of Aragon (1452–1516), called the Catholic kings.   1. Royal City.

LAURENCIA   I hoped to God I'd never see him again.

PASCUALA   I have seen women just as adamant as you, Laurencia, if not more so—and yet, underneath, their hearts were as soft as butter.

LAURENCIA   Well, is there an oak tree as hard as I am?

PASCUALA   Be careful. No one should boast that he'll never thirst for water.

LAURENCIA   But I do. And I'll maintain it against the world. What good would it do me to love Fernán? Do you think I would marry him?

PASCUALA   Of course not.

LAURENCIA   Well then, I condemn infamy. Too many girls hereabouts have trusted the Comendador only to be ruined by him.

PASCUALA   All the same it will be a miracle if you escape him.

LAURENCIA   You don't understand, Pascuala. He has been after me for a month now, but he has only been wasting his time. His emissary, Flores, and that blustering fool Ortuño have come to show me a blouse, a necklace, a hat, and have told me so many wonderful stories about their lord and master that they have succeeded in frightening me but not in moving my heart.

PASCUALA   Where did they talk to you?

LAURENCIA   Down there by the brook, about six days ago.

PASCUALA   It looks as if they are trying to deceive you, Laurencia.

LAURENCIA   Deceive me?

PASCUALA   If not you, then the priest.

LAURENCIA   I may be a young chicken, but I'm too tough for His Highness. Pascuala, I would far rather put a slice of ham on the fire in the early morning and eat it with my homemade bread and a glass of wine stolen from my mother, and then at noon to smell a piece of beef boiling with cabbage and eat it ravenously, or, if I have had a trying day, marry an eggplant to some bacon; and in the evening, while cooking the supper, go and pick a handful of grapes from the vines (God save them from the hail) and afterwards dine on chopped meat with oil and pepper, and so happily to bed murmuring "Lead us not into temptation"—I would much rather this than all the wiles and tricks of scoundrels. For after all, all they want after giving us so much trouble is their pleasure at night and our sorrow in the morning.

PASCUALA   You are right, Laurencia, for as soon as they tire of love they are more ungrateful than the sparrows are to the peasants. In winter when the fields are frozen hard the sparrows fly down from the roofs, and saying "Sweet Sweet," hop right on to the dining table for crumbs, but as soon as the cold is over and the fields are again in bloom they no longer come down saying "Sweet Sweet," but stay hopping on the roof, mocking us with their calls. Men are the same; when they need us nothing can be sweeter than they—we are their life, their soul, their heart, their all—but as soon as they tire of us their sweetness disappears and their wooing phrases become a mockery.

LAURENCIA   The moral of which is: trust no man, Pascuala.

PASCUALA   That's what I say.

[*Enter* MENGO, BARRILDO, *and* FRONDOSO.]

FRONDOSO   You are wrong, Barrildo, in this argument.

BARRILDO   Well never mind, here's somebody who will settle the matter.

MENGO   Let's have an understanding before we reach them: if I'm right, then each of you gives me a present as a reward.

BARRILDO   All right. But if you lose, what will you give?

MENGO   I'll give my boxwood rebec,[2] which I value more than a barn.

BARRILDO   That's fine.

FRONDOSO   Let's approach them. God bless you, fair ladies.

LAURENCIA   You call us ladies, Frondoso?

FRONDOSO   We want to keep up with the times. In these days all bachelors are licentiates; the blind are one-eyed; the cross-eyed merely squint; and the lame have only a sprained ankle. The unscrupulous are called honest; the ignorant, clever; and the braggart, brave. A large mouth is described as luscious, a small eye as sharp. The pettifogger[3] is called diligent; the busybody, charming; the charlatan, sympathetic; the deadly bore, gallant. The cowardly become valiant; the hard-headed, vivacious; coxcombs are comrades; fools, broad-minded; malcontents, philosophers. Baldness is identified with authority, foolish chatter with wit. People with tumors have only a slight cold, and those who are arrogant are circumspect; the shifty are constant; and the humpbacked, just slightly bent. This, in short—the enumeration could go on indefinitely—was the sort of thing I did in calling you ladies. I merely followed the fashion of the day.

LAURENCIA   In the city, Frondoso, such words are used in courtesy: discourteous tongues use a severer and more acrimonious vocabulary.

FRONDOSO   I should like to hear it.

LAURENCIA   It's the very opposite of yours. The serious-minded are called bores: the unfortunate, lucky; the even-tempered, melancholy; and anyone who expresses disapproval is hateful. Those who offer good advice are importunate; the liberal-minded are dull-witted; the just, unjust; and the pious, weak-kneed. In this language the faithful become inconstant; the courteous, flatterers; the charitable, hypocrites; and the good Christians, frauds. Anyone who has won a well-deserved reward is called fortunate; truth becomes impudence; patience, cowardice; and misfortune, retribution. The modest woman is foolish; the beautiful and chaste, unnatural; and the honorable woman is called. . . . But enough! This reply should be sufficient.

MENGO   You little devil!

LAURENCIA   What an elegant expression.

MENGO   I bet the priest poured handfuls of salt on her when he christened her.

LAURENCIA   What was the argument that brought you here, if we may ask?

FRONDOSO   Listen, Laurencia.

LAURENCIA   Speak.

FRONDOSO   Lend me your ear, Laurencia.

LAURENCIA   Lend it to you? Why, I'll give it to you right now.

FRONDOSO   I trust your discretion.

LAURENCIA   Well, what was the wager about?

FRONDOSO   Barrildo and I wagered against Mengo.

LAURENCIA   And what does Mengo claim?

2. Stringed instrument.   3. Unscrupulous lawyer.

BARRILDO It is something that he insists on denying, although it is plainly a fact.

MENGO I deny it because I know better.

LAURENCIA But what is it?

BARRILDO He claims that love does not exist.

LAURENCIA Many people think that.

BARRILDO Many people do, but it's foolish. Without love not even the world could exist.

MENGO I don't know how to philosophize; as for reading, I wish I could! But I say that if the elements of Nature live in eternal conflict, then our bodies, which receive from them food, anger, melancholy, phlegm, and blood, must also be at war with each other.

BARRILDO The world here and beyond, Mengo, is perfect harmony. Harmony is pure love, for love is complete agreement.

MENGO As far as the natural world goes, I do not deny it. There is love which rules all things through an obligating interrelationship. I have never denied that each person has love proportionate to his humour— my hand will protect me from the blow aimed at my face, my foot will protect me from harm by enabling me to flee danger, my eyelids will protect my eyes from threatening specks—such is love in nature.

PASCUALA What are you trying to prove, then?

MENGO That individuals love only themselves.

PASCUALA Pardon me, Mengo, for telling you that you lie. For it is a lie. The intensity with which a man loves a woman or an animal its mate . . .

MENGO I call that self-love, not love. What is love?

LAURENCIA A desire for beauty.

MENGO And why does love seek beauty?

LAURENCIA To enjoy it.

MENGO That's just what I believe. Is not such enjoyment selfish?

LAURENCIA That's right.

MENGO Therefore a person seeks that which brings him joy.

LAURENCIA That is true.

MENGO Hence there is no love but the kind I speak of, the one I pursue for my personal pleasure, and which I enjoy.

BARRILDO One day the priest said in a sermon that there was a man named Plato who taught how to love, and that this man loved only the soul and the virtues of the beloved.

PASCUALA You have raised a question which the wise men in their schools and academies cannot solve.

LAURENCIA He speaks the truth; do not try to refute his argument. Be thankful, Mengo, that Heaven made you without love.

MENGO Are you in love?

LAURENCIA I love my honor.

FRONDOSO May God punish you with jealousy.

BARRILDO Who has won the wager then?

PASCUALA Go to the sacristan with your dispute, for either he or the priest will give you the best answer. Laurencia does not love deeply, and as for me, I have little experience. How are we to pass judgment?

FRONDOSO What can be a better judgment than her disdain?

[*Enter* FLORES.]

FLORES   God be with you!

PASCUALA   Here is the Comendador's servant.

LAURENCIA   His goshawk,[4] you mean. Where do *you* come from, my good friend?

FLORES   Don't you see my soldier's uniform?

LAURENCIA   Is Don Fernán coming back?

FLORES   Yes, the war is over, and though it has cost us some blood and some friends, we are victorious.

FRONDOSO   Tell us what happened.

FLORES   Who could do that better than I? I saw everything. For his campaign against this city, which is now called Ciudad Real [Royal City], the valiant Maestre raised an army of two thousand brave infantry from among his vassals and three hundred cavalry from laymen and friars. For even those who belong to Holy Orders are obliged to fight for their emblem of the red cross—provided, of course, that the war is against the Moors. The high-spirited youth rode out to battle wearing a green coat embroidered with golden scrolls; the sleeves were fastened with six hooks, so that only his gauntlets showed beneath them. His horse was a dappled roan, bred on the banks of the Betis, drinking its waters and grazing on its lush grass. Its tailpiece was decorated with buckskin straps, the curled panache with white knots that matched the snowflakes covering its mane. Our lord, Fernán Gómez, rode at the Maestre's side on a powerful honey-colored horse with black legs and mane and a white muzzle. Over a Turkish coat of mail he wore a magnificent breast-and-back plate with orange fringes and resplendent with gold and pearls. His white plumes seemed to shower orange blossoms on his bronze helmet. His red and white band flashed on his arm as he brandished an ash tree for a lance, making himself feared even in Granada. The city rushed to arms; the inhabitants apparently did not come out to fight but stayed within the city walls to defend their property. But in spite of the strong resistance the Maestre entered the city. He ordered the rebels and those who had flagrantly dishonored him to be beheaded, and the lower classes were gagged and whipped in public. He remained in the city and is so feared and loved that people prophesy great things for him. They say that a young man who has fought so gloriously and punished so severely all in a short time must one day fall on fertile Africa like a thunderbolt, and bring many blue moons under the red cross. He made so many gifts to the Comendador and his followers that he might have been disposing of his own estate rather than despoiling a city. But now the music sounds. The Comendador comes. Welcome him with festivity, for good will is one of the most precious of a victor's laurels.

   [*Enter the* COMENDADOR *and* ORTUÑO; MUSICIANS; JUAN ROJO, ESTEBAN, *and* ALONSO, *elders of the town.*]

MUSICIANS [*Singing*]

> Welcome, Comendador,
> Conqueror of lands and men!
> Long live the Guzmanes!
> Long live the Girones!

4. Large hawk.

> In peacetime gracious,
> Gentle his reasoning,
> When fighting the Moors
> Strong as an oak.
> From Ciudad Real
> He comes victorious,
> Bearing to Fuente Ovejuna
> Its banners in triumph.
> Long live Fernán Gómez,
> Long live the hero!

COMENDADOR   Citizens of Fuente Ovejuna, I am most grateful to you for the love you show me.

ALONSO   It is but a small part of the love we feel, and no matter how great our love it is less than you deserve.

ESTEBAN   Fuente Ovejuna and its elders, whom you have honored with your presence, beg you to accept a humble gift. In these carts, sir, we bring you an expression of gratitude rather than a display of wealth. There are two baskets filled with earthenware; a flock of geese that stretch their heads out of their nets to praise your valor in battle; ten salted hogs, prize specimens, more precious than amber; and a hundred pairs of capons and hens, which leave the cocks of the neighboring villages desolate. You will find no arms, no horses, no harnesses studded with pure gold. The only gold is the love your vassals feel towards you. And for purity you could find nothing greater than those twelve skins of wine. That wine could give warmth and courage to your soldiers even unclothed in the dead of winter; it will be as important as steel in the defense of your walls. I leave unmentioned the cheese and other victuals: they are a fitting tribute from our people to you. May you and yours enjoy our gifts.

COMENDADOR   I am very grateful to you for all of them. Go now and rest.

ESTEBAN   Feel at home in this town, my lord! I wish the reeds of mace and sedge that we placed on our doors to celebrate your triumphs were oriental pearls. You deserve such tribute and more.

COMENDADOR   Thank you, gentlemen. God be with you.

ESTEBAN   Singers, sing again.

MUSICIANS [*Singing*]

> Welcome, Comendador,
> Conqueror of lands and men!

[*Exeunt elders and* MUSICIANS.]

COMENDADOR   You two wait.

LAURENCIA   What is Your Lordship's pleasure?

COMENDADOR   You scorned me a few days ago, didn't you?

LAURENCIA   Is he speaking to you, Pascuala?

PASCUALA   I should say not—not to me!

COMENDADOR   I am talking to you, beautiful wildcat, and to the other girl too. Are you not mine, both of you?

PASCUALA   Yes, sir, to a certain extent.

COMENDADOR   Go into the house. There are men inside, so you need not fear.

LAURENCIA   If the elders accompany us—I am the daughter of one of them—it will be all right for us to go in too, but not otherwise.
COMENDADOR   Flores!
FLORES   Sir?
COMENDADOR   Why do they hesitate to do what I command?
FLORES   Come along, girls, come right in.
LAURENCIA   Let me go!
FLORES   Come in, girl, don't be silly.
PASCUALA   So that you can lock us in? No thank you!
FLORES   Come on. He wants to show you his spoils of war.
COMENDADOR [*Aside to* ORTUÑO]   Lock the door after them.
        [*Exit* COMENDADOR.]
LAURENCIA   Flores, let us pass.
ORTUÑO   Aren't you part of the gifts of the village?
PASCUALA   That's what you think! Out of my way, fool, before I . . .
FLORES   Leave them alone. They're too unreasonable.
LAURENCIA   Isn't your master satisfied with all the meat given to him today?
ORTUÑO   He seems to prefer yours.
LAURENCIA   Then he can starve!
        [*Exeunt* LAURENCIA *and* PASCUALA.]
FLORES   A fine message for us to bring! He'll swear at us when we appear before him empty-handed.
ORTUÑO   That's a risk servants always run. When he realizes the situation he'll either calm down or else leave at once.

Chamber of the Catholic Kings, in Medina del Campo

        [*Enter* KING *Ferdinand of Aragon, Queen* ISABELLA, MANRIQUE, *and attendants.*]
ISABELLA   I think it would be wise to be prepared, Your Majesty—especially since Don Alfonso of Portugal is encamped there. It is better for us to strike the first blow than to wait for the enemy to attack us.
KING   We can depend on Navarre and Aragon for assistance, and I'm trying to reorganize things in Castile so as to ensure our success there.
ISABELLA   I'm confident your plan will succeed.
MANRIQUE   Two councilmen from Ciudad Real seek audience with Your Majesty.
KING   Let it be granted them.
        [*Enter two* COUNCILMEN *of Ciudad Real.*]
1ST COUNCILMAN   Most Catholic King of Aragon, whom God has sent to Castile to protect us, we appear as humble petitioners before you to beg the assistance of your great valor for our city of Ciudad Real. We are proud to consider ourselves your vassals, a privilege granted us by a royal charter but which an unkind fate threatens to take away. Don Rodrigo Téllez Girón, famous for the valiant actions that belie his youth, and ambitious to augment his power, recently laid close siege to our city. We prepared to meet his attack with bravery, and resisted his forces so fiercely that rivers of blood streamed from our innumerable dead. He finally conquered us—but only because of the advice and assistance

given him by Fernán Gómez. Girón remains in possession of our city, and unless we can remedy our disaster soon we will have to acknowledge ourselves his vassals against our will.

KING   Where is Fernán Gómez now?

2ND COUNCILMAN   In Fuente Ovejuna, I think. That is his native town and his home is there. But the truth is, his subjects are far from contented.

KING   Do you have a leader?

2ND COUNCILMAN   No, we have none, Your Majesty. Not one nobleman escaped imprisonment, injury, or death.

ISABELLA   This matter requires swift action, for delay will only work to the advantage of the impudent Girón. Furthermore the King of Portugal will soon realize that he can use him to gain entry to Extremadura, and so cause us much damage.

KING   Don Manrique, leave at once with two companies. Be relentless in avenging the wrongs this city has suffered. Let the Count of Cabra[5] go with you. The Cordovan is recognized by everyone as a brave soldier. This is the best plan for the moment.

MANRIQUE   I think the plan is an excellent one. As long as I live, his excesses shall be curbed.

ISABELLA   With your help we are sure to succeed.

The countryside near Fuente Ovejuna.

[*Enter* LAURENCIA *and* FRONDOSO.]

LAURENCIA   You are very stubborn, Frondoso. I left the brook with my washing only half wrung out, so as to give no occasion for gossip—yet you persist in following me. It seems that everyone in town is saying that you are running after me and I after you. And because you are the sort of fellow who struts about and shows off his clothes, which are more fashionable and expensive than other people's, all the girls and boys in the countryside think there must be something between us. They are all waiting for the day when Juan Chamorro will put down his flute and lead us to the altar. I wish they would occupy their minds with things that are more their business—why don't they imagine that their granaries are bursting with red wheat, or that their wine jars are full of dregs? Their gossip annoys me, but not so much that it keeps me awake at night.

FRONDOSO   Your disdain and beauty are so great, Laurencia, that when I see you and listen to you I fear they will kill me. You know that my only wish is to become your husband: is it fair then to reward my love in this way?

LAURENCIA   I know no other way.

FRONDOSO   Can you feel no pity for my troubled mind, no sympathy for my sad condition when you know I cannot eat or drink or sleep for thinking of you? Is it possible that such a gentle face can hide so much unkindness? Heavens! you'll drive me mad.

LAURENCIA   Why don't you take medicine for your condition, Frondoso?

FRONDOSO   You are the only medicine I need, Laurencia. Come with me

5. Diego Fernández de Córdoba (1438–1487) was the first to use this title.

to the altar, and let us live like turtle doves, billing and cooing, after the church has blessed us.

LAURENCIA You had better ask my uncle, Juan Rojo. I'm not passionately in love with you . . . but there is hope that I might be in time.

FRONDOSO Oh—here comes the Comendador!

LAURENCIA He must be hunting deer. Hide behind these bushes.

FRONDOSO I will. But I'll be full of jealousy.

[*Enter the* COMENDADOR.]

COMENDADOR This is good luck. My chase of the timid fawn has led me to a lovely doe instead.

LAURENCIA I was resting a bit from my washing. By Your Lordship's leave I'll return to the brook.

COMENDADOR Such disdain, fair Laurencia, is an insult to the beauty Heaven gave you; it turns you into a monster. On other occasions you have succeeded in eluding my desires—but now we are alone in these solitary fields where no one can help you. Now, with no one to witness, you cannot be so stubborn and so proud, you cannot turn your face away without loving me. Did not Salustiana, the wife of Pedro Redondo, surrender to me—and Martín del Pozo's wife, too, only two days after her wedding?

LAURENCIA These women, sir, had had others before you, and knew the road to pleasure only too well. Many men have enjoyed *their* favors. Go, pursue your deer, and God be with you. You persecute me so that were it not for the cross you wear I should think you were the devil.

COMENDADOR You little spitfire! [*Aside*] I had better put my bow down and take her by force.

LAURENCIA What? . . . What are you doing? Are you mad?

[*Enter* FRONDOSO, *who picks up the bow.*]

COMENDADOR Don't struggle. It won't help you.

FRONDOSO [*Aside*] I'll pick up his bow, but I hope I don't have to use it.

COMENDADOR Come on, you might as well give in now.

LAURENCIA Heaven help me now!

COMENDADOR We are alone. Don't be afraid.

FRONDOSO Generous Comendador, leave the girl alone. For much as I respect the cross on your breast, it will not stop me from aiming this bow at you if you do not let her go.

COMENDADOR You dog, you peasant slave!

FRONDOSO There's no dog here. Laurencia, go quickly now.

LAURENCIA Take care of yourself, Frondoso.

FRONDOSO Run . . .

[*Exit* LAURENCIA.]

COMENDADOR What a fool I was to put down my sword so as not to frighten my quarry!

FRONDOSO Do you realize, sir, that I have only to touch this string to bring you down like a bird?

COMENDADOR She's gone. You damned, treacherous villain. Put that bow down, put it down, I say.

FRONDOSO Put it down? Why? So that you can shoot me? No, love is deaf, remember, and hears nothing when it comes into its own.

COMENDADOR Do you think a knight surrenders to a peasant?

Shoot, you villain, shoot and be damned, or I'll break the law of chivalry.
FRONDOSO   No, not that. I'm satisfied with my station in life and since I
must preserve my life, I'll take your bow with me.
   [*Exit* FRONDOSO.]
COMENDADOR   What a strange experience! But I'll avenge this insult and
remove this obstacle. . . . But to let him go! My god, how humiliating!

ACT II

The Plaza of Fuente Ovejuna.

   [*Enter* ESTEBAN *and* 1ST COUNCILMAN.]
ESTEBAN   I don't think any more grain should be taken out of our community granaries, even though they are full right now. It's getting late in
the year, and the harvest looks poor. I think it's better to have provisions
stored up in case of emergency—though I know some people have other
ideas.
1ST COUNCILMAN   I agree with you. And I've always tried to administer
the land along such peaceable ways.
ESTEBAN   Well, let's tell Fernán Gómez what we think about it. We
shouldn't let those astrologers, who are so ignorant of the future, persuade us that they know all the secrets that are only God's business. They
pretend to be as learned as the theologians the way they mix up the past
and the future—but if you ask them anything about the immediate present they are completely at a loss. Do they have the clouds and the course
of the sun, the moon, and the stars locked up at home that they can tell
us what is happening up there and what is going to bring us grief? At
seed time they levy tax on us; give us just so much wheat, oats and
vegetables, pumpkins, cucumbers, mustard. . . . Then they tell us someone has died, and later we discover it happened in Transylvania; they tell
us that wine will be scarce and beer plentiful—somewhere in Germany;
that cherries will freeze in Gascony, or hordes of tigers will prowl through
Hircania. Their final prophecy is that whether we sow or not the year
will end in December!
   [*Enter the licentiate* LEONELO *and* BARRILDO.]
LEONELO   You won't be awarded the hickory stick to beat the other stu-
dents with, for it's already been won by somebody else.
BARRILDO   How did you get on at Salamanca?
LEONELO   That's a long story.
BARRILDO   You must be a very learned man by now.
LEONELO   No, I'm not even a barber. The things I was telling you about
happen all the time in the school I was at.
BARRILDO   At least you are a scholar now.
LEONELO   Well, I've tried to learn things that are important.
BARRILDO   Anyone who has seen so many printed books is bound to think
he is wise.
LEONELO   Froth and confusion are the chief results of so much reading
matter. Even the most voracious reader gets sick of seeing so many titles.
I admit that printing has saved many talented writers from oblivion, and
enshrined their works above the ravages of time. Printing circulates their

books and makes them known. Gutenberg, a famous German from Mainz, is responsible for this invention. But many men who used to have a high reputation are no longer taken seriously now that their works have been printed. Some people put their ignorance in print, passing it off as wisdom; others inspired by envy write down their crazy ideas and send them into the world under the name of their enemies.

BARRILDO   That's a disgraceful practice.

LEONELO   Well, it's natural for ignorant people to want to discredit scholars.

BARRILDO   But in spite of all this, Leonelo, you must admit that printing is important.

LEONELO   The world got on very well without it for a good many centuries—and no Saint Jerome or Saint Augustine has appeared since we have had it.

BARRILDO   Take it easy, Leonelo. You're getting all worked up about this printing business.

[*Enter* JUAN ROJO *and another* PEASANT.]

JUAN ROJO   Four farms put together would not raise one dowry, if they're all like the one we've just seen. It's obvious that both the land and the people are in a state of chaos.

PEASANT   What's the news of the Comendador?—don't get excited now.

JUAN ROJO   How he tried to take advantage of Laurencia in this very field!

PEASANT   That lascivious brute! I'd like to see him hanging from that olive tree! . . .

[*Enter* COMENDADOR, ORTUÑO, *and* FLORES.]

COMENDADOR   Good day to you all!

COUNCILMAN   Your Lordship!

COMENDADOR   Please don't get up.

ESTEBAN   You sit down, my lord. We would rather stand.

COMENDADOR   Do sit down.

ESTEBAN   Honor can only be rendered by those who have it themselves.

COMENDADOR   Sit down, and let us talk things over calmly.

ESTEBAN   Has Your Lordship seen the hound I sent you?

COMENDADOR   Mayor, my servants are all amazed by its great speed.

ESTEBAN   It really is a wonderful animal. It can overtake any culprit or coward who is trying to escape.

COMENDADOR   I wish you would send it after a hare that keeps eluding me.

ESTEBAN   I'd be glad to. Whereabouts is this hare?

COMENDADOR   It's your daughter.

ESTEBAN   My daughter!

COMENDADOR   Yes.

ESTEBAN   But is she worth your while?

COMENDADOR   Intervene in my favor, Mayor, for God's sake.

ESTEBAN   What has she done?

COMENDADOR   She's determined to hurt me—while the wife of a nobleman here in town is dying for an opportunity to see me.

ESTEBAN   Then she would do wrong—and you do yourself no good to talk so flippantly.

COMENDADOR   My, my, what a circumspect peasant! Flores, give him a copy of the *Politics* and tell him to read Aristotle.

ESTEBAN   My lord, the town's desire is to live peaceably under you. You must remember that there are many honorable persons living in Fuente Ovejuna.

LEONELO   Did you ever hear such impudence as this Comendador's?

COMENDADOR   Have I said anything to offend you, Councilman?

COUNCILMAN   Your pronouncements are unjust, my lord, and not worth uttering. It is unfair to try to take away our honor.

COMENDADOR   Honor? Do you have honor? Listen to the saintly friars of Calatrava!

COUNCILMAN   Some people may boast of the cross you awarded them, but their blood is not as pure as you may think.

COMENDADOR   Do I sully mine by mixing it with yours?

COUNCILMAN   Evil will sully it rather than cleanse it.

COMENDADOR   However that may be, your women are honored by it.

ESTEBAN   Such words are dishonorable.

COMENDADOR   What boors these peasants are! Ah, give me the cities, where nobody hinders the pleasures of lofty men. Husbands are glad when we make love to their wives.

ESTEBAN   They certainly should not be. Do you expect us to suffer such tribulations as readily? There is a God in the cities too, and punishment falls swiftly.

COMENDADOR   Get out of here!

ESTEBAN   Are you talking to us?

COMENDADOR   Get off the Plaza immediately. I don't want to see any of you around here.

ESTEBAN   We're going.

COMENDADOR   Not in a group like that . . .

FLORES   I beg of you to control yourself.

COMENDADOR   These peasants will gossip in groups behind my back.

ORTUÑO   Have a little patience.

COMENDADOR   I marvel that I have so much. Let each man go alone to his own house.

LEONELO   Good Heavens! Will the peasants stomach that?

ESTEBAN   I'm going this way.

　　　　　[*Exeunt* PEASANTS.]

COMENDADOR   What do you think of those fellows?

ORTUÑO   You don't seem to be able to hide your emotions, yet you refuse to sense the ill feeling around you.

COMENDADOR   But are these fellows my equals?

FLORES   It's not a question of equality.

COMENDADOR   Is that peasant to keep my bow unpunished?

FLORES   Last night I thought I saw him by Laurencia's door and I gave him a slash from ear to ear—but it was someone else.

COMENDADOR   I wonder where that Frondoso is now?

FLORES   They say he's around.

COMENDADOR   So that's it. The villain who tried to murder me is allowed to go about scot-free.

FLORES   Don't worry. Sooner or later he'll fall into the snare like a stray bird, or be caught on the hook like a fish.

COMENDADOR   But imagine—a peasant, a boy, to threaten me with my own crossbow, me, a captain whose sword made Cordova and Granada tremble! Flores, the world is coming to an end!

FLORES   Blame it on love.

ORTUÑO   I suppose you spared him for friendship's sake.

COMENDADOR   I have acted out of friendship, Ortuño, else I should have ransacked the town in a couple of hours. However, I plan to withhold my vengeance until the right moment arrives. And now—what news of Pascuala?

FLORES   She says she's about to get married.

COMENDADOR   Is she going to that length?

FLORES   In other words, she's sending you to where you'll be paid in cash.

COMENDADOR   What about Olalla?

ORTUÑO   Her reply is charming.

COMENDADOR   She's a gay young thing. What does she say?

ORTUÑO   She says her husband follows her around all the time because he's jealous of my messages and your visits, but as soon as she manages to allay his fears you'll be the first to see her.

COMENDADOR   Fine! Keep an eye on the old man.

ORTUÑO   You'd better be careful.

COMENDADOR   What news from Inés?

FLORES   Which Inés?

COMENDADOR   The wife of Antón.

FLORES   She's ready when you are. I spoke to her in her back yard, through which you may go whenever you wish.

COMENDADOR   Easy girls I love dearly and repay poorly. Flores, if they only knew their worth! . . .

FLORES   To conquer without a struggle nullifies the joy of victory. A quick surrender impairs the pleasure of love making. But, as the philosophers say, there are women as hungry for men as form is for matter, so you shouldn't be surprised if things are the way they are.

COMENDADOR   A man who is maddened by love congratulates himself when girls fall easily to him, but later he regrets it. For however much we desire things we soon forget them, even the most thoughtful of us, if we have gotten them cheaply.

[*Enter* CIMBRANOS, *a soldier.*]

CIMBRANOS   Is the Comendador here?

ORTUÑO   Don't you see him before you?

CIMBRANOS   Oh, valiant Fernán Gómez! Change your green cap for your shining helmet, and your cloak for a coat of mail! For the Maestre of Santiago and the Count of Cabra are attacking Rodrigo Girón, and laying siege to Ciudad Real in the name of the Queen of Castile. All that we won at so much cost in blood and men may soon be lost again. Already the banners of Aragon with their castles, lions and bars, can be seen above the high towers of the city. Though the King of Portugal has paid homage to Girón, the Maestre of Calatrava may have to return to Almagro in defeat. Mount your horse, my lord, your presence alone will force the enemy back to Castile.

COMENDADOR   Stop. That's enough. Ortuño, order a trumpet to sound at
once in the Plaza. Tell me, how many soldiers do I have?

ORTUÑO   Fifty, I believe, sir.

COMENDADOR   Order them to horse.

CIMBRANOS   Ciudad Real will fall to the King if you do not hurry.

COMENDADOR   Never fear, that shall not happen!

    [*Exeunt all.*]

Open country near Fuente Ovejuna.

    [*Enter* MENGO, LAURENCIA, *and* PASCUALA, *running.*]

PASCUALA   Please don't leave us.

MENGO   Why? What are you afraid of?

LAURENCIA   Well, Mengo, we prefer to go to the village in groups when
we don't have a man to go with us. We're afraid of meeting the
Comendador.

MENGO   What a cruel and importunate devil that man is.

LAURENCIA   He never stops pestering us.

MENGO   I wish God would strike him with a thunderbolt and put an end
to his wickedness.

LAURENCIA   He's a bloodthirsty beast that poisons and infects the whole
countryside.

MENGO   I hear that in trying to protect you, here in the meadow, Frondoso
aimed his crossbow at the Comendador.

LAURENCIA   I used to hate men, Mengo, but since that day I've looked at
them with different eyes. Frondoso acted so gallantly! But I'm afraid it
may cost him his life.

MENGO   He'll be forced to leave the village.

LAURENCIA   I keep telling him to go away, although I love him dearly now.
But he answers all such counsel with anger and contempt—and all the
while the Comendador threatens to hang him by the feet.

PASCUALA   I'd like to see that Comendador carried off by the plague!

MENGO   I'd rather kill him with a mean stone. By God, if I threw a stone
at him that I have up at the sheepfold, it would hit him so hard it would
crush his skull in. The Comendador is more vicious than that old Roman,
Sabalus.

LAURENCIA   You mean Heliogabalus, who was more wicked than a beast.

MENGO   Well, Galván or whoever it was—I don't know too much about
history—the Comendador surpasses him in wickedness. Can anyone be
more despicable then Fernán Gómez?

PASCUALA   No one can compare with him. You'd think he'd sucked his
cruelty from a tigress.

    [*Enter* JACINTA.]

JACINTA   If friendship means anything, in God's name help me now!

LAURENCIA   What's happened, Jacinta, my friend?

PASCUALA   Both of us are your friends.

JACINTA   Some of the Comendador's attendants are trying to take me to
him. They're on their way to Ciudad Real, but they're acting more like
villains than soldiers.

LAURENCIA May God protect you, Jacinta! If the Comendador is bold with you he'll be cruel to me.
　　[*Exit* LAURENCIA.]
PASCUALA Jacinta, I'm not a man, so I can't defend you.
　　[*Exit* PASCUALA.]
MENGO But I have both strength and reputation. Stand beside me, Jacinta.
JACINTA Have you any arms?
MENGO Yes, those that Nature gave me.
JACINTA I wish you were armed.
MENGO Never mind, Jacinta. There are plenty of stones around here.
　　[*Enter* FLORES *and* ORTUÑO.]
FLORES So you thought you could get away from us, did you?
JACINTA Mengo, I'm dead with fear.
MENGO Gentlemen, this is a poor peasant girl . . .
ORTUÑO Oh, have you decided to defend young women?
MENGO I'm merely asking for mercy. I'm her relative, and I hope to be able to keep her near me.
FLORES Kill him off!
MENGO By God, if you make me mad and I take out my sling, your life will be in danger!
　　[*Enter the* COMENDADOR *and* CIMBRANOS.]
COMENDADOR What's all this? Do I have to get off my horse for some petty quarrel?
FLORES You ought to destroy this miserable village for all the joy it brings you. These wretched peasants have dared to challenge our arms.
MENGO My lord, if injustice can move you to pity, punish these soldiers who in your name are forcing this girl to leave her husband and honest parents. Grant me permission to take her home.
COMENDADOR I will grant them permission to punish you. Drop that sling!
MENGO My lord!
COMENDADOR Flores, Ortuño, Cimbranos, tie his hands with it.
MENGO Is this your justice?
COMENDADOR What do Fuente Ovejuna and its peasants think of me?
MENGO My lord, how have I or Fuente Ovejuna offended you?
FLORES Shall I kill him?
COMENDADOR Don't soil your arms with such trash. Keep them for better things.
ORTUÑO What are your orders?
COMENDADOR Flog him. Tie him to that oak tree and beat him with the reins.
MENGO Pity, my lord, have pity, for you are a nobleman!
COMENDADOR Flog him till the rivets fall from the leather.
MENGO My God. For such ugly deeds, uglier punishments.
　　[*Exeunt* MENGO, FLORES, *and* ORTUÑO.]
COMENDADOR Now my girl, why were you running away? Do you prefer a peasant to a nobleman?
JACINTA Can you restore the honor which your attendants have taken from me in bringing me to you?

COMENDADOR   Do you mean to say your honor has been lost because I wanted to take you away?

JACINTA   Yes. For I have an honest father who, if he does not equal you in birth, surpasses you in virtue.

COMENDADOR   All these troubles around this village, where peasants defy their betters, scarcely help to soothe my temper. Come along here now!

JACINTA   With whom?

COMENDADOR   With me.

JACINTA   You had better think over what you're doing.

COMENDADOR   I have thought it over, and it's so much the worse for you. Instead of keeping you for myself, I shall give you to my whole army.

JACINTA   No power on earth can inflict such an outrage on me while I live.

COMENDADOR   Get a move on now, girl.

JACINTA   Sir, have pity!

COMENDADOR   There is no pity.

JACINTA   I appeal from your cruelty to divine justice.

   [*Exit* COMENDADOR, *hauling her out.*]

Esteban's house.

   [*Enter* LAURENCIA *and* FRONDOSO.]

LAURENCIA   Are you not aware of your danger, that you dare to come here?

FRONDOSO   My daring is proof of my love for you. From that hill I saw the Comendador riding away, and since I have complete confidence in you all my fear left with him. I hope he never comes back!

LAURENCIA   Don't curse him—for the more one wishes a person to die the longer he lives.

FRONDOSO   In that case may he live a thousand years, and so by wishing him well let's hope his end will be certain. . . . Tell me, Laurencia, has my fondness for you affected you at all? Is my loyalty safely entrusted? You know that the entire village thinks we are made for each other. Won't you forget your modesty and say definitely yes or no?

LAURENCIA   My answer to you and to the village is—yes!

FRONDOSO   I could kiss your feet for such an answer! You give me new life . . . let me tell you now how much I love you.

LAURENCIA   Save your compliments and speak to my father, Frondoso, for that's the important thing now. Look, there he comes with my uncle. Be calm and confident, Frondoso, for this meeting will determine whether I'm to be your wife or no.

FRONDOSO   I put my trust in God.

   [LAURENCIA *hides herself. Enter* ESTEBAN *and the* COUNCILMAN.]

ESTEBAN   The Comendador's visit has aroused the whole town. His behavior was most regrettable, to say the least. Everybody was shocked, and poor Jacinta is bearing the brunt of his madness.

COUNCILMAN   Before long Spain will be rendering obedience to the Catholic Kings, as they are called. The Maestre of Santiago has been appointed Captain General, and is already coming on horseback to free Ciudad Real from Girón. . . . I'm very sorry about Jacinta, who is an honest girl.

ESTEBAN   The Comendador also had Mengo flogged.

COUNCILMAN   Yes. His flesh is blacker than ink or a black cloth.

ESTEBAN   Please, no more—it makes my blood boil when I think of his disgusting behavior and reputation. What good is my Mayor's staff against that?

COUNCILMAN   It was his servants who did it. Why should you be so upset?

ESTEBAN   Shall I tell you something else? I have been told that one day Pedro Redondo's wife was found down there in the depth of the valley. He had abused her and then turned her over to his soldiers.

COUNCILMAN   Listen, I hear something. . . . Who's there?

FRONDOSO   It is I, Frondoso, waiting for permission to come in.

ESTEBAN   You need no permission, Frondoso, to enter my house. You owe your life to your father, but your upbringing to me. I love you like my own son.

FRONDOSO   Sir, trusting that love, I want to ask a favor. You know whose son I am.

ESTEBAN   Did that crazy Fernán Gómez hurt you?

FRONDOSO   Not a little.

ESTEBAN   My heart told me so.

FRONDOSO   You have shown me so much affection that I feel free to make a confession to you. I love Laurencia, and wish to become her husband. Forgive me if I have been too hasty. I'm afraid I've been very bold.

ESTEBAN   You have come just at the right moment, Frondoso, and you will prolong my life, for this touches the fear nearest my heart. I thank God that you have come to save my honor, and I thank you for your love and the purity of your intentions. But I think it only right to tell your father of this first. As soon as he approves I will give my consent too. How happy I shall be if this marriage takes place.

COUNCILMAN   You should ask the girl about him before you accept him.

ESTEBAN   Don't worry about that. The matter is settled; for they discussed it beforehand, I'm sure. If you like, Frondoso, we might talk about the dowry, for I'm planning to give you some *maravedíes*.[6]

FRONDOSO   I'm not concerned about that. I don't need a dowry.

COUNCILMAN   You should be grateful that he doesn't ask you for it in wineskins.

ESTEBAN   I'll ask Laurencia what she would like to do and then let you know.

FRONDOSO   That's fair. It's a good idea to consult everybody concerned.

ESTEBAN   Daughter! . . . Laurencia!

LAURENCIA   Yes, father.

ESTEBAN   You see how quickly she replies. Laurencia, come here a minute. What would you say if your friend Gila were to marry Frondoso, who is as honest a young man as one could find in Fuente Ovejuna?

LAURENCIA   Is Gila thinking of getting married?

ESTEBAN   Why yes, if someone can be found who would be a worthy match for her.

LAURENCIA   My answer is yes.

ESTEBAN   I would say yes too—except that Gila is ugly, and it would be much better if Frondoso became your husband, Laurencia.

LAURENCIA   In spite of your years, you are still a flatterer, father.

---

6. Denomination of currency.

ESTEBAN   Do you love him?

LAURENCIA   I am fond of him, and he returns my affection, but you were saying . . .

ESTEBAN   Shall I say yes to him?

LAURENCIA   Yes, say it for me, sir.

ESTEBAN   I? Well, then I have the keys. It's settled then. Let's go to his father.

COUNCILMAN   Yes, let's go.

ESTEBAN   What shall we tell him about the dowry, son? I can afford to give you 4000 *maravedíes.*

FRONDOSO   Do you want to offend me, sir?

ESTEBAN   Come, come, my boy, you'll get over that attitude in a day or two. Even if you don't need it now, a dowry will come in handy later on.
    [*Exeunt* ESTEBAN *and* COUNCILMAN.]

LAURENCIA   Tell me, Frondoso, are you happy?

FRONDOSO   Happy? I'm afraid I'll go crazy with so much joy and happiness. My heart is so overflowing that my eyes are swimming with joy when I look at you, Laurencia, and realize that you, sweet treasure, will be mine.
    [*Exeunt* LAURENCIA *and* FRONDOSO.]

Meadow near Ciudad Real.

[*Enter the* MAESTRE, *the* COMENDADOR, FLORES, *and* ORTUÑO.]

COMENDADOR   Fly, sir! There's no hope for us.

MAESTRE   The walls were weak and the enemy strong.

COMENDADOR   They have paid dearly for it, though, in blood and lives.

MAESTRE   And they will not be able to boast that our banner of Calatrava is among their spoils. That alone would have been enough to honor their enterprise.

COMENDADOR   Your plans are ruined now, Girón.

MAESTRE   What can I do if Fate in its blindness raises a man aloft one day only to strike him down the next?

VOICES BACKSTAGE   Victory for the Kings of Castile!

MAESTRE   They're decorating the battlements with lights now, and hanging out pennants of victory from the windows in the high towers.

COMENDADOR   They do that because they have paid heavily in blood—it's really more a sign of tragedy than a celebration.

MAESTRE   Fernán Gómez, I'm going back to Calatrava.

COMENDADOR   And I to Fuente Ovejuna. Now you have to think of either defending your relatives or paying homage to the Catholic King.

MAESTRE   I'll write to you about my plans.

COMENDADOR   Time will tell you what to do.

MAESTRE   Ah, years full of the bitterness of time's betrayals!
    [*Exeunt.*]

A meadow near Fuente Ovejuna.

[*Enter the wedding train*: MUSICIANS, MENGO, FRONDOSO, LAURENCIA, PASCUALA, BARRILDO, ESTEBAN, *and* JUAN ROJO.]

MUSICIANS [*Singing*]

> Long live the bride and groom!
> Many long and happy years to them.

MENGO It has not been very difficult for you to sing.

BARRILDO You could have done better yourself, couldn't you?

FRONDOSO Mengo knows more about whippings now than songs.

MENGO Don't be surprised if I tell you that there's someone in the valley to whom the Comendador . . .

BARRILDO Don't say it. That brutal assassin has assailed everyone's honor.

MENGO It was bad enough for a hundred soldiers to whip me that day when all I had was a sling. It must have been unbearable for that man to whom they gave an enema of dye and herbs—I won't mention his name, but he was an honorable man.

BARRILDO It was done in jest, I suppose . . .

MENGO This was no joke. Enemas are desirable sometimes, but I would rather die than undergo one like that.

FRONDOSO Please sing us a song—if you have anything worth listening to.

MENGO

> God grant the bride and groom long life
> Free from envy and jealous strife,
> And when their span of years is past,
> May they be united at the last.
> God grant the bride and groom long life!

FRONDOSO Heaven curse the poet who conceived such a poem!

BARRILDO It was rather a sloppy job.

MENGO This makes me think of something about the whole crew of poets. Have you seen a baker making crullers? He throws the pieces of dough into the boiling oil until the pot is full. Some buns come out puffed up, others twisted and funnily shaped, some lean to the left, others to the right, some are well fried, others are burnt. Well, I think of a poet composing his verses in much the same way that the baker works on his dough. He hastily throws words into his pot of paper, confident that the honey will conceal what may turn out ridiculous or absurd. But when he tries to sell his poem no one wants it and the confectioner is forced to eat it himself.

BARRILDO Stop your foolishness now, and let the bride and groom speak.

LAURENCIA Give us your hands to kiss.

JUAN ROJO Do you ask to kiss my hand, Laurencia? You and Frondoso had better ask to kiss your father's first.

ESTEBAN Rojo, I ask Heaven's blessing on her and her husband for ever.

FRONDOSO Give us your blessing, both of you.

JUAN ROJO Let the bells ring, and everyone celebrate the union of Laurencia and Frondoso.

MUSICIANS [*Singing*]

> To the valley of Fuente Ovejuna
> Came the maid with the flowing hair.
> A knight of Calatrava
> Followed her to the valley here.
> Amid the shrubs she hid herself,
> Disturbed by shame and fear.

With the branches she covered herself,
Feigning she had not seen him,
But the knight of Calatrava drew near:
"Why are you hiding, fair maiden,
Know you not that my keen desire
Can pierce the thickest wall?"
She made curtains of the branches
Confused by shame and fear.
But love passes sea and mountain:
"Why are you hiding, fair maiden,
Know you not that my keen desire
Can pierce the thickest wall?"

[*Enter the* COMENDADOR, FLORES, ORTUÑO, *and* CIMBRANOS.]

COMENDADOR   Silence! You will all remain quietly where you are.

JUAN ROJO   This is not a game, my lord, and your orders will be obeyed. Won't you join us? Why do you come in such a bellicose manner? Are you our conqueror? But what am I saying . . .

FRONDOSO   I'm a dead man. Heaven help me!

LAURENCIA   Quickly, Frondoso, escape this way.

COMENDADOR   No. Arrest him, and tie him up.

JUAN ROJO   Yield to them, my boy, and go quietly to prison.

FRONDOSO   Do you want them to kill me?

JUAN ROJO   Why?

COMENDADOR   I am not a man to murder people without reason. If I were, these soldiers would have run him through by now. I'm ordering him to be taken to jail where his own father will pronounce sentence on him.

PASCUALA   Sir, a wedding is in progress here now.

COMENDADOR   What is that to me? Is he the only person in town who counts?

PASCUALA   If he offended you, pardon him, as becomes your rank.

COMENDADOR   Pascuala, it is nothing that concerns me personally. He has offended the Maestre Téllez Girón, whom God preserve. He acted counter to his orders and his honor, and must be punished as an example. Otherwise others may rebel too. Don't you know that one day this boy aimed a crossbow at the very heart of the Comendador, Mayor? Loyal vassals you are indeed!

ESTEBAN   As his father-in-law I feel I must come to his defence. I think it only natural that a man, especially a man in love, should challenge you for trying to take away his girl—what else could he do?

COMENDADOR   You are a fool, Mayor.

ESTEBAN   In your opinion, my lord!

COMENDADOR   I had no intention of taking away his girl—for she was not his.

ESTEBAN   You had the thought, and that is enough. There are kings in Castile who are drawing up new rules to prevent disorder. And they will do wrong if, after the wars, they tolerate in the towns and country districts such powerful men wearing those huge crosses on their chests. Those crosses were meant for royal breasts, and only kings should wear them.

COMENDADOR   Wrest the mayor's staff from him!

ESTEBAN Take it, sir, it is yours to keep.

COMENDADOR I'll strike him with it as if he were an unbroken horse.

ESTEBAN You are my lord, and I must bear it: strike, then.

PASCUALA Shame on you! Striking an old man!

LAURENCIA You strike him because he is my father—what injury do you avenge in this way?

COMENDADOR Arrest her, and let ten soldiers guard her.

[*Exeunt* COMENDADOR *and his men.*]

ESTEBAN May Heaven visit justice upon him!

[*Exit* ESTEBAN.]

PASCUALA The wedding has become a mourning.

[*Exit* PASCUALA.]

BARRILDO Is there not one of us who can speak?

MENGO I've already had a sound whipping and I'm covered with wales— let someone else anger him this time.

JUAN ROJO Let us all take counsel.

MENGO I advise everybody to keep quiet. He made my posterior look like a piece of salmon.

[*Exeunt all.*]

ACT III

A room in the Town Hall of Fuente Ovejuna.

[*Enter* ESTEBAN, ALONSO, *and* BARRILDO.]

ESTEBAN Has everybody come to the meeting?

BARRILDO Some people are absent.

ESTEBAN Then our danger is more serious.

BARRILDO Nearly all the town has been warned.

ESTEBAN With Frondoso imprisoned in the tower, and my daughter Laurencia in such peril, if God, in his mercy, does not come to our help . . .

[*Enter* JUAN ROJO *and the* COUNCILMAN.]

JUAN ROJO What are you shouting about, Esteban? Don't you know secrecy is all important now?

ESTEBAN I wonder I'm not shouting even louder!

[*Enter* MENGO.]

MENGO I want to join in this meeting.

ESTEBAN With tears streaming down my beard, I ask you, honest farmers, what funeral rites can we give to a country without honor—a country that is lost? And if our honor is indeed lost, which of us can perform such rites, when there is not one among us who has not been dishonored? Answer me now, is there anyone here whose life, whose deep life of honor, is still intact? Are we not all of us in mourning for each other now? If all is lost, what is there to wait for? What is this misfortune that has overtaken us?

JUAN ROJO The blackest ever known. . . . But it has just been announced that the Kings of Castile have concluded a victorious peace, and will soon arrive in Cordova. Let us send two Councilmen to that city to kneel at their feet and ask their help.

BARRILDO But King Ferdinand, who has conquered so many enemies, is

still busy making war, and will not be able to help us now while he's in
the midst of battles. We must find some other way out.

COUNCILMAN   If you want my opinion, I suggest we leave the town.

JUAN ROJO   But how can we do that on such short notice?

MENGO   If I understand the situation at all, this meeting will cost us a
good many lives.

COUNCILMAN   The mast of patience has been torn from us, and now we
are a ship driven before a storm of fear. They have brutally abducted the
daughter of the good man who rules our community, and unjustly broken
the staff of office over his head. What slave was ever treated worse?

JUAN ROJO   What do you want the people to do?

COUNCILMAN   Die, or give death to the tyrants, for we are many and they
are few.

BARRILDO   What? Raise our weapons against our lord and master!

ESTEBAN   Except for God, the King's our only lord and master, not these
inhuman, barbarous men. If God is behind our rightful anger, what have
we to lose?

MENGO   Let us be a little more cautious. I'm here to speak for the humblest peasants who always have to bear the brunt of any trouble—and I
want to represent their fears prudently.

JUAN ROJO   Our misfortunes have prepared us to sacrifice our lives, so
what are we waiting for? Our houses and vineyards have been burned
down. They are tyrants and we must have our revenge.

[*Enter* LAURENCIA, *her hair dishevelled.*]

LAURENCIA   Let me come in, for I sorely need the advice of men! Do you
know me?

ESTEBAN   God in Heaven, is that my daughter?

JUAN ROJO   Don't you recognize your Laurencia?

LAURENCIA   Yes, I am Laurencia, but so changed that looking at me you
still doubt it.

ESTEBAN   My daughter!

LAURENCIA   Don't call me your daughter!

ESTEBAN   Why not, my dear? Why not?

LAURENCIA   For many reasons—but chiefly because you let me be carried
off by tyrants, by the traitors who rule over us, without attempting to
avenge me. I was not yet Frondoso's wife, so you cannot say my husband
should have defended me; this was my father's duty as long as the wedding had not been consummated; just as a nobleman about to purchase
a jewel need not pay for it if it is lost while still in the merchant's keeping.
From under your very eyes, Fernán Gómez dragged me to his house, and
you let the wolf carry the sheep like the cowardly shepherd you are. Can
you conceive what I suffered at his hands?—the daggers pointed at my
breast, the flatteries, threats, insults, and lies used to make my chastity
yield to his fierce desires? Does not my bruised and bleeding face, my
dishevelled hair tell you anything? Are you not good men?—not fathers
and relatives? Do not your hearts sink to see me so grievously betrayed?
. . . Oh, you are sheep; how well named the village of Fuente Ovejuna
[Sheepwell]. Give me weapons and let me fight, since you are but things
of stone or metal, since you are but tigers—no, not tigers, for tigers
fiercely attack those who steal their offspring, killing the hunters before

they can escape. You were born timid rabbits; you are infidels, not Spaniards. Chicken-hearted, you permit other men to abuse your women. Put
knitting in your scabbards—what need have you of swords? By the living
God, I swear that your women will avenge those tyrants and stone you
all, you spinning girls, you sodomites, you effeminate cowards. Tomorrow
deck yourselves in our bonnets and skirts, and beautify yourselves with
our cosmetics. The Comendador will hang Frondoso from a merlon[7] of
the tower, without let or trial, and presently he will string you all up. And
I shall be glad—you race of half-men—that this honorable town will be
rid of effeminates, and the age of Amazons will return, to the eternal
amazement of the world.

ESTEBAN   Daughter, I will not stay to hear such names. I shall go now,
even if I have to fight the whole world.

JUAN ROJO   I will go with you, in spite of the enemy's power.

COUNCILMAN   We shall die together.

BARRILDO   Let us hang a cloth from a stick to fly in the wind, and death
to the traitors.

JUAN ROJO   What shall our orders be?

MENGO   To kill the Comendador without order. To rally the whole town
around us: let us all agree to kill the tyrants.

ESTEBAN   Take with you swords, lances, crossbows, pikes, and sticks.

MENGO   Long live the Kings, our only lords and masters!

ALL   Long live the Kings!

MENGO   Death to the traitor tyrants!

ALL   Death to the tyrants!

    [*Exeunt all but* LAURENCIA.]

LAURENCIA   Go—God will be with you! Come, women of the town, your
honor will be avenged—rally round me!

    [*Enter* PASCUALA, JACINTA, *and other women.*]

PASCUALA   What is happening? What are you shouting about?

LAURENCIA   Can't you see how they're on their way to kill Fernán Gómez?
Every man, boy, and child is rushing furiously to do his duty. Is it fair
that the men alone should have the glory of a day like this, when we
women have the greater grievances?

JACINTA   Tell us your plans then.

LAURENCIA   I propose that we all band together and perform a deed that
will shake the world. Jacinta, your great injury will be our guide.

JACINTA   No more than yours.

LAURENCIA   Pascuala, you be our standard bearer.

PASCUALA   I'll be a good one. I'll put a cloth on a lance and we'll have a
flag in the wind.

LAURENCIA   There's no time for that. We'll wave our caps for banners.

PASCUALA   Let's appoint a captain.

LAURENCIA   We don't need one.

PASCUALA   Why not?

LAURENCIA   Because when my courage is up, we don't need any Cids or
Rodamontes.

    [*Exeunt all.*]

---

7. One of the toothlike projections atop a castle or fortress.

Hall in the castle of the COMENDADOR.

[*Enter* FRONDOSO, *his hands tied,* FLORES, CIMBRANOS, ORTUÑO, *and the* COMENDADOR.]

COMENDADOR   I want him hung by the cord that binds his wrists, so that his punishment may be the more severe.

FRONDOSO   How this will add to your descendants' honor, my lord!

COMENDADOR   Hang him from the highest merlon.

FRONDOSO   It was never my intention to kill you.

FLORES   Do you hear that noise outside?
        [*Alarum.*]

COMENDADOR   What can it be?

FLORES   It looks as if the villagers are planning to stay your sentence, my lord.

ORTUÑO   They are breaking down the doors!
        [*Alarum.*]

COMENDADOR   The door of my house? The seat of the Commandry?

FRONDOSO   The whole town is here!

JUAN ROJO [*Within*]   Break them down, smash them in, burn, destroy!

ORTUÑO   It's hard to stop a riot once it gets started.

COMENDADOR   The town against me!

FLORES   And their fury has driven them to tear down all the doors.

COMENDADOR   Untie him. And you, Frondoso, go and calm down the peasant mayor.

FRONDOSO   I'm going, sir—love has spurred them to action.
        [*Exit* FRONDOSO.]

MENGO [*Within*]   Long live Ferdinand and Isabella, and down with the tyrants!

FLORES   In God's name, my lord, don't let them find you here.

COMENDADOR   If they persist—why, this room is strong and well protected. They will soon turn back.

FLORES   When villages with a grievance decide to rise against their rulers they never turn back until they have shed blood and taken their revenge.

COMENDADOR   We'll face this mob with our weapons, using this door as a portcullis.

FRONDOSO [*Within*]   Long live Fuente Ovejuna!

COMENDADOR   What a leader! I'll take care of his bravery!

FLORES   My lord, I marvel at yours.
        [*Enter* ESTEBAN *and the* PEASANTS.]

ESTEBAN   There's the tyrant and his accomplices! Long live Fuente Ovejuna, death to the tyrants!

COMENDADOR   Wait, my people!

ALL   Wrongs never wait.

COMENDADOR   Tell me your wrongs, and, on a knight's honor, I'll set them right.

ALL   Long live Fuente Ovejuna! Long live King Ferdinand! Death to bad Christians and traitors!

COMENDADOR   Will you not hear me? It is I who address you, I, your lord.

ALL   Our lords are the Catholic Kings.

COMENDADOR   Wait.

ALL   Long live Fuente Ovejuna, and death to Fernán Gómez!
    [*Exeunt all. Enter* LAURENCIA, PASCUALA, JACINTA, *and other women, armed.*]

LAURENCIA   You brave soldiers, no longer women, wait here in this place of vantage.

PASCUALA   Only women know how to take revenge. We shall drink the enemy's blood.

JACINTA   Let us pierce his corpse with our lances.

PASCUALA   Agreed.

ESTEBAN [*Within*]   Die, treacherous Comendador!

COMENDADOR   I die. O God, in Thy clemency, have mercy on me!

BARRILDO [*Within*]   Here's Flores.

MENGO   Get that scoundrel! He's the one who gave me a thousand whippings.

FRONDOSO [*Within*]   I shan't consider myself avenged until I've pulled out his soul.

LAURENCIA   There's no excuse for not going in.

PASCUALA   Calm yourself. We had better guard the door.

BARRILDO [*Within*]   I am not moved. Don't come to me with tears now, you fops.

LAURENCIA   Pascuala, I'm going in; I don't care to keep my sword in its scabbard.
    [*Exit* LAURENCIA.]

BARRILDO [*Within*]   Here's Ortuño.

FRONDOSO [*Within*]   Slash his face!
    [*Enter* FLORES, *fleeing, pursued by* MENGO.]

FLORES   Pity, Mengo! I'm not to blame!

MENGO   O no? Not for being a pimp, you scoundrel, not for having whipped me?

PASCUALA   Mengo, give him to us women, we'll. . . . Hurry, Mengo!

MENGO   Fine, you can have him—no punishment could be worse!

PASCUALA   We'll avenge the whippings he gave you.

MENGO   That's fine!

JACINTA   Come on, death to the traitor!

FLORES   To die at the hands of women!

JACINTA   Don't you like it?

PASCUALA   Is that why you're weeping?

JACINTA   Die, you panderer to his pleasures!

PASCUALA   Die, you traitor!

FLORES   Pity, women, *pity!*
    [*Enter* ORTUÑO, *pursued by* LAURENCIA.]

ORTUÑO   You know I have had nothing at all to do with it . . .

LAURENCIA   I know you! Come on, women, dye your conquering weapons in their vile blood.

PASCUALA   I'll die killing!

ALL   Long live Fuente Ovejuna! Long live King Ferdinand!
    [*Exeunt all.*]

Room of the Catholic Kings, at Toro.

    [*Enter* KING *Ferdinand, Queen* ISABELLA, *and the Maestre Don* MANRIQUE.]

MANRIQUE   We planned our attack so well that we carried it out without any setback. There was little resistance—even if they had tried to organize any, it would have been weak. Cabra has remained there to guard the place in case of counterattack.

KING   That was a wise decision, and I am glad that he is in charge of operations. Now we can be sure that Alfonso, who is trying to seize power in Portugal, will not be able to harm us. It is fortunate that Cabra is stationed there and that he is making a good show, for in this way he protects us from any danger and, by acting as a loyal sentinel, works for the good of the kingdom.

[*Enter* FLORES, *wounded.*]

FLORES   Catholic King Ferdinand, upon whom Heaven has bestowed the Crown of Castile, excellent gentleman that you are—listen to the worst cruelty that a man could ever behold from sunrise to sunset.

KING   Calm yourself!

FLORES   Supreme Sovereign, my wounds forbid me to delay in reporting my sad case, for my life is ebbing away. I come from Fuente Ovejuna, where, with ruthless heart, the inhabitants of that village have deprived their lord and master of his life. Fernán Gómez has been murdered by his perfidious subjects, indignant vassals who dared attack him for but a trivial cause. The mob called him tyrant and, inflamed by the power of the epithet, committed this despicable crime: they broke into his house and having no faith that he, a perfect gentleman, would right all their wrongs, would not listen to him, but with impatient fury pierced his chest which bore the cross of Calatrava with a thousand cruel wounds and threw him from the lofty windows onto the pikes and lances of the women in the street below. They carried him away, dead, and competed with one another in pulling his beard and hair, and recklessly slashing his face. In fact their constantly growing fury was so great, that some cuts went from ear to ear. They blotted out his coat-of-arms with their pikes and loudly proclaimed that they wanted to replace it with your royal coat-of-arms since those of the Comendador offended them. They sacked his house as if it were the enemy's and joyfully divided the spoils among themselves. All this I witnessed from my hiding place, for my cruel fate did not grant me death at such a time. Thus I remained all day in hiding until nightfall, when I was able to slip away furtively to come to render you this account. Sire, since you are just, see that a just punishment is administered to the brutal culprits who have perpetrated such an outrage.

KING   You may rest assured that the culprits will not go without due punishment. The unfortunate event is of such magnitude that I am astonished; I will send a judge to investigate the case and punish the culprits as an example to all. A captain will accompany him for his protection, for such great offence requires exemplary punishment. In the meantime your wounds will be cared for.

[*Exeunt all.*]

The countryside.

[*Enter* PEASANTS, *both men and women, with* FERNÁN GÓMEZ's *head on a lance.*]

MUSICIANS [*Singing*]
> Long live Isabella and Ferdinand
> And death to the tyrants!

BARRILDO   Sing us a song, Frondoso.

FRONDOSO   Here goes, and if it limps let some critic fix it.
> Long live fair Isabella
> And Ferdinand of Aragon.
> He is made for her
> And she is meant for him.
> May St. Michael guide them
> To Heaven by the hand . . .
> Long live Isabella and Ferdinand
> And death to the tyrants!

LAURENCIA   Now it's your turn, Barrildo.

BARRILDO   Listen to this, for I've been working on it.

PASCUALA   If you say it with feeling, it's going to be good.

BARRILDO
> Long live the famous kings
> For they are victorious.
> They'll be our lords
> Happy and glorious.
> May they conquer always
> All giants and dwarfs . . .
> And death to the tyrants!

MUSICIANS [*Singing*]
> Long live Isabella and Ferdinand
> And death to the tyrants!

LAURENCIA   Now it's your turn, Mengo.

FRONDOSO   Yes, Mengo.

MENGO   I'm a most gifted poet, you know.

PASCUALA   You mean a poet with a bruised backside.

MENGO
> I was whipped on a Sunday morning
> My back still feels the pain
> But the Christian Kings are coming
> There'll be no tyrants here again.

MUSICIANS   Long live the Kings!

ESTEBAN   Take away that head!

MENGO   He has the face of one who has been hanged.

[JUAN ROJO *brings in a scutcheon*[8] *with the royal arms.*]

COUNCILMAN   The scutcheon has arrived.

ESTEBAN   Let's see it.

JUAN ROJO   Where shall we place it?

COUNCILMAN   Here, in the Town Hall.

ESTEBAN   What a beautiful scutcheon!

BARRILDO   What joy!

FRONDOSO   A new day is dawning for us, and that's our sun.

---

8. Shieldlike object.

ESTEBAN

> Long live Castile and Leon
> And the bars of Aragon.
> Down with tyranny!

People of Fuente Ovejuna, listen to the words of an old man whose life has been blameless. The Kings will want to investigate what has happened, and this they will do soon. So agree now among yourselves on what to say.

FRONDOSO   What is your advice?

ESTEBAN   To die saying Fuente Ovejuna and nothing else.

FRONDOSO   That's fine! Fuente Ovejuna did it!

ESTEBAN   Do you want to answer in that way?

ALL   Yes.

ESTEBAN   Well then, I'd like to play the role of questioner—let's rehearse! Mengo, pretend that you are the one being grilled.

MENGO   Can't you pick on someone else, someone more emaciated?

ESTEBAN   But this is all make believe.

MENGO   All right, go ahead!

ESTEBAN   Who killed the Comendador?

MENGO   Fuente Ovejuna did it!

ESTEBAN   You dog, I'm going to torture you.

MENGO   I don't care—even if you kill me.

ESTEBAN   Confess, you scoundrel.

MENGO   I am ready to confess.

ESTEBAN   Well, then, who did it?

MENGO   Fuente Ovejuna.

ESTEBAN   Bind him tighter.

MENGO   That will make no difference.

ESTEBAN   To hell with the trial then!

[Enter the COUNCILMAN.]

COUNCILMAN   What are you doing here?

FRONDOSO   What has happened, Cuadrado?

COUNCILMAN   The questioner is here.

ESTEBAN   Send him in.

COUNCILMAN   A captain is with him.

ESTEBAN   Who cares? Let the devil himself come in: you know your answer.

COUNCILMAN   They are going around town arresting people.

ESTEBAN   There's nothing to fear. Who killed the Commendador, Mengo?

MENGO   Who? Fuente Ovejuna.

[Exeunt all.]

Room of the MAESTRE *of* CALATRAVA, *at Almagro.*

[Enter the MAESTRE and a SOLDIER.]

MAESTRE   What a horrible thing to have happened! Melancholy was his end. I could murder you for bringing me such news.

SOLDIER   Sir, I'm but a messenger. I did not intend to annoy you.

MAESTRE   That a town should become so fierce and wrathful, that it would dare to do such a thing! It's incredible! I'll go there with a hundred men and raze the town to the ground, blotting out even the memory of its inhabitants.

SOLDIER   Calm yourself, sir. They have given themselves up to the King and the most important thing for you is not to enrage him.

MAESTRE   How can they give themselves up to the King? Are they not the vassals of the Comendador?

SOLDIER   That, sir, you'll have to thrash out with the King.

MAESTRE   Thrash it out? No, for the King placed the land in his hands and it is the King's. He is the Sovereign Lord and as such I recognize him. The fact that they have given themselves up to the King soothes my anger. My wisest course is to see him, even if I am at fault. He will pardon me on account of my youth. I am ashamed to go—but my honor demands that I do so and I shall not forget my dignity.

[*Exeunt the* MAESTRE *and* SOLDIER.]

Public square.

[*Enter* LAURENCIA.]

LAURENCIA

>Loving, to suspect one's love will suffer pain
>Becomes an added suffering of love;
>To fear that pain great harm to him may prove
>Brings new torture to the heart again.
>
>Devotion, watching eagerly, would fain
>Give way to worry, worm of love;
>For the heart is rare that does not bend or move
>When fear his threat on the belov'd has lain.
>
>I love my husband with a love that does not tire;
>But now I live and move beneath
>The fear that fate may take away his breath.
>His good is all the end of my desire.
>
>If he is present, certain is my grief;
>If he is absent, certain is my death.

[*Enter* FRONDOSO.]

FRONDOSO   Laurencia!

LAURENCIA   My dear husband! How do you dare to come here?

FRONDOSO   Does my loving care for you give you such worries?

LAURENCIA   My love, take care of yourself. I am afraid something may happen to you.

FRONDOSO   It would displease God, Laurencia, if I made you unhappy.

LAURENCIA   You have seen what has happened to your friends and the ferocious rage of that judge. Save yourself, and fly from danger!

FRONDOSO   Would you expect cowardice from me? Do not advise me to escape. It is inconceivable that in order to avoid harm I should forgo seeing you and betray my friends and my own blood at this tragic moment.

[*Cries within.*]

I hear cries. If I am not mistaken, they are from someone put to the torture. Listen carefully!

[*The* JUDGE *speaks within, and is answered.*]

JUDGE   Tell me the truth, old man.

FRONDOSO   Laurencia, they are torturing an old man!

LAURENCIA   What cruelty!

ESTEBAN   Let me go a moment.

JUDGE   Let him go. Now, tell me, who murdered Fernán?

ESTEBAN   Fuente Ovejuna killed him.

LAURENCIA   Father, I will make your name immortal!

FRONDOSO   What courage!

JUDGE   Take that boy. Pup, speak up! I know you know. What? You refuse? Tighten the screws.[9]

BOY   Fuente Ovejuna, sir.

JUDGE   By the life of the King, I'll hang the lot of you, you peasants, with my own hands! Who killed the Comendador?

FRONDOSO   They're racking the child, and he answers that way . . .

LAURENCIA   What a brave village!

FRONDOSO   Brave and strong.

JUDGE   Put that woman, over there, in the chair. Tighten it up!

LAURENCIA   He's blind with rage.

JUDGE   You see this chair, peasants, this means death to you all! Who killed the Comendador?

PASCUALA   Fuente Ovejuna, sir.

JUDGE   Tighter!

FRONDOSO   I hadn't imagined . . .

LAURENCIA   Pascuala will not tell him, Frondoso.

FRONDOSO   Even the children deny it!

JUDGE   They seem to be delighted. Tighter!

PASCUALA   Merciful God!

JUDGE   Tighter, you bastard! Are you deaf?

PASCUALA   Fuente Ovejuna killed him.

JUDGE   Bring me someone a bit bigger—that fat one, half stripped already!

LAURENCIA   Poor Mengo! That must be Mengo!

FRONDOSO   I'm afraid he'll break down.

MENGO   Oh . . . Oh . . .

JUDGE   Give it to him!

MENGO   Oh . . .

JUDGE   Need any help?

MENGO   Oh . . . Oh . . .

JUDGE   Peasant, who killed the Comendador?

MENGO   Oh . . . I'll tell, sir . . .

JUDGE   Release him a bit.

FRONDOSO   He's confessing!

JUDGE   Now, hard, on the back!

MENGO   Wait, I'll tell all . . .

JUDGE   Who killed him?

MENGO   Sir, Fuente Ovejuna.

---

9. Instrument of torture.

JUDGE   Did you ever see such scoundrels? They make fun of pain. The ones I was surest of lie most emphatically. Dismiss them: I'm exhausted.

FRONDOSO   Oh, Mengo, God bless you! I was stiff with fear—but you have rid me of it.

[*Enter* MENGO, BARRILDO, *and the* COUNCILMAN.]

BARRILDO   Long live Mengo!

COUNCILMAN   Well he may . . .

BARRILDO   Mengo, bravo!

FRONDOSO   That's what I say.

MENGO   Oh . . . Oh . . .

BARRILDO   Drink and eat, my friend . . .

MENGO   Oh . . . Oh . . . What's that?

BARRILDO   Sweet cider.

MENGO   Oh . . . Oh . . .

FRONDOSO   Something for him to drink!

BARRILDO   Right away!

FRONDOSO   He quaffs it well! That's better, now.

LAURENCIA   Give him a little more.

MENGO   Oh . . . Oh . . .

BARRILDO   This glass, for me.

LAURENCIA   Solemnly he drinks it!

FRONDOSO   A good denial gets a good drink.

BARRILDO   Want another glass?

MENGO   Oh . . . Oh . . . Yes, yes.

FRONDOSO   Drink it down; you deserve it.

LAURENCIA   A drink for each turn of the rack.

FRONDOSO   Cover him up, he'll freeze to death.

BARRILDO   Want some more?

MENGO   Three more. Oh . . . Oh . . .

FRONDOSO   He's asking for the wine . . .

BARRILDO   Yes, there's a boy, drink deep. What's the matter now?

MENGO   It's a bit sour. Oh, I'm catching cold.

FRONDOSO   Here, drink this, it's better. Who killed the Comendador?

MENGO   Fuente Ovejuna killed him . . .

[*Exeunt* MENGO, BARRILDO, *and the* COUNCILMAN.]

FRONDOSO   He deserves more than they can give him. But tell me, my love, who killed the Comendador?

LAURENCIA   Little Fuente Ovejuna, my dear.

FRONDOSO   Who did?

LAURENCIA   You bully, you torturer! I say Fuente Ovejuna did it.

FRONDOSO   What about me? How do *I* kill *you*?

LAURENCIA   With love, sweet love, with lots of love.

Room of the Kings, at Tordesillas.

[*Enter the* KING *and queen* (ISABELLA).]

ISABELLA   I did not expect to find you here, but my luck is good.

KING   The pleasure of seeing you lends new glory to my eyes. I was on my way to Portugal and I had to stop here.

ISABELLA   Your Majesty's plans are always wise.

KING How did you leave Castile?

ISABELLA Quiet and peaceful.

KING No wonder, if you were the peacemaker.

    [*Enter Don* MANRIQUE.]

MANRIQUE The Maestre of Calatrava, who has just arrived, begs audience.

ISABELLA I wanted very much to see him.

MANRIQUE I swear, Madame, that although young in years, he is a most valiant soldier.

    [*Exit Don* MANRIQUE, *and enter the* MAESTRE.]

MAESTRE Rodrigo Téllez Girón, Maestre of Calatrava, who never tires of praising you, humbly kneels before you and asks your pardon. I admit that I have been deceived and that, ill-advised, I may have transgressed in my loyalty to you. Fernán's counsel deceived me and for that reason I humbly beg forgiveness. And if I am deserving of this royal favor, I pledge to serve you from now on; in the present campaign which you are undertaking against Granada, where you are now going, I promise to show the valor of my sword. No sooner will I unsheathe it, bringing fierce suffering to the enemy, than I will hoist my red crosses on the loftiest merlon of the battlements. In serving you I will employ five hundred soldiers, and I promise on my honor nevermore to displease you.

KING Rise, Maestre. It is enough that you have come for me to welcome you royally.

MAESTRE You are a consolation to a troubled soul.

ISABELLA You speak with the same undaunted courage with which you act.

MAESTRE You are a beautiful Esther, and you a divine Xerxes.

    [*Enter* MANRIQUE.]

MANRIQUE Sir, the judge you sent to Fuente Ovejuna has returned and he asks to see you.

KING [*To the* MAESTRE] Be the judge of these aggressors.

MAESTRE If I were not in your presence, Sire, I'd certainly teach them how to kill Comendadores.

KING That is no longer necessary.

ISABELLA God willing, I hope this power lies with you.

    [*Enter* JUDGE.]

JUDGE I went to Fuente Ovejuna, as you commanded, and carried out my assignment with special care and diligence. After due investigation, I cannot produce a single written page of evidence, for to my question: "Who killed the Comendador?" the people answered with one accord: "Fuente Ovejuna did it." Three hundred persons were put to torture, quite ruthlessly, and I assure you, Sire, that I could get no more out of them than this. Even children, only ten years old, were put to the rack, but to no avail—neither did flatteries nor deceits do the least good. And since it is so hopeless to reach any conclusion: either you must pardon them all or kill the entire village. And now the whole town has come to corroborate in person what they have told me. You will be able to find out from them.

KING Let them come in.

    [*Enter the two mayors,* ESTEBAN *and* ALONSO, FRONDOSO, *and* PEASANTS, *men and women.*]

LAURENCIA   Are those the rulers?

FRONDOSO   Yes, they are the powerful sovereigns of Castile.

LAURENCIA   Upon my faith, they are beautiful! May Saint Anthony bless them!

ISABELLA   Are these the aggressors?

ESTEBAN   Fuente Ovejuna, Your Majesty, who humbly kneel before you, ready to serve you. We have suffered from the fierce tyranny and cruelty of the dead Comendador, who showered insults upon us—and committed untold evil. He was bereft of all mercy, and did not hesitate to steal our property and rape our women.

FRONDOSO   He went so far as to take away from me this girl, whom Heaven has granted to me and who has made me so blissful that no human being can compete with me in joy. He snatched her away to his house on my wedding night, as if she were his property, and if she had not known how to protect herself, she, who is virtue personified, would have paid dearly, as you can well imagine.

MENGO   Is it not my turn to talk? If you grant me permission you will be astonished to learn how he treated me. Because I went to defend a girl whom his insolent servants were about to abuse, that perverse Nero handled me so roughly that he left my posterior like a slice of salmon. Three men beat my buttocks so relentlessly that I believe I still bear some wales. To heal my bruises I have had to use more powders and myrtleberries than my farm is worth.

ESTEBAN   Sire, we want to be your vassals. You are our King and in your defense we have borne arms. We trust in your clemency and hope that you believe in our innocence.

KING   Though the crime is grave, I am forced to pardon it since no indictment is set down. And since I am responsible for you, the village will remain under my jurisdiction until such time as a new Comendador appears to inherit it.

FRONDOSO   Your Majesty speaks with great wisdom. And at this point, worthy audience, ends the play FUENTE OVEJUNA.

WILLIAM SHAKESPEARE
1564–1616

William Shakespeare was born in the rural community of Stratford-upon-Avon in Warwickshire. His father, John Shakespeare, was a glover and, when William was born, prominent in the town's government. Little is known of Shakespeare's early life, although it is likely that he received an education at the good local grammar school and certain that he married Anne Hathaway, about seven years his senior, when he was eighteen. The couple had three children, Susanna (1583) and the twins Judith and Hamnet (1585). By 1592 Shakespeare was in London, rapidly becoming the "greatest shake-scene" around, in the irritated words of a rival who envied Shakespeare's ability to impress audiences despite his lack of a university education. Shakespeare soon became a shareholder in a prominent players' company that claimed the Lord Chamberlain as patron and the tragic actor Richard Burbage and the comedian

Will Kempe as members. Composing dramas that drew on the strengths of his repertory company, Shakespeare brought to the English stage such famous characters as Falstaff and Prince Hal, Hamlet and Ophelia, Othello and Desdemona, and King Lear.

The company originally performed at the Theatre, north of the city of London, where its actor-owner, James Burbage, faced steady opposition from the puritanical city officials who sought to close the theaters, which they considered to be hotbeds of immorality. Burbage conceived of a means to escape civic legislation against theatrical performances, and secretly moved the boards of his playhouse across the river Thames to the south bank; with these planks he constructed the Globe, the theater most often associated with Shakespeare's name. The Globe was open to all social classes: anyone who wished could enter the theater by paying a penny, and at the cost of another, get a bench, cushion, and protection (in the boxes) from inclement weather. Shakespeare, who began his career as a player, found his calling as a playwright and his fortune as a shareholder in his company. His financial successes enabled him to purchase the title of gentleman for his father, a purchase that made Shakespeare himself officially a "gentleman born."

The influence of Shakespeare's plays on the course of English literature is matched only by the King James translation of the Bible. In his time, Shakespeare garnered the interest of two British monarchs (Elizabeth I and James I), the love of popular audiences, and the respect of such tough critics as the poet and playwright Ben Jonson. After Shakespeare's death in 1616, when his friends and colleagues John Heminges and Henry Condell collected his plays into one volume (the *First Folio*), Ben Jonson wrote a magnificent verse memorial to the rival whose wit had seemed almost too fertile for the good of his art. In a poem that introduces the collected plays, Jonson praises Shakespeare as a poet who was "the Soule of the Age" and "Not of an age, but for all time!" Jonson's insistence that Shakespeare transcended the age he simultaneously embodied is paradoxical. For Jonson, however, great artists immortalize their nations and epochs. In his view, the publication of Shakespeare's plays in the form of a book meant that the entire age of "Eliza, and our James" would enter triumphantly into world history: "Triumph, my Britain, thou hast one to show, / To whom all scenes of Europe homage owe." Shakespeare himself may have suspected that his dramatic works would eventually be counted as cultural arts, but he always kept his eye on more humble and material successes. When he retired to Stratford-upon-Avon in 1612, he lived a quiet life in the house he had built (New House) from the savings he had accumulated while working in London's premiere playhouse.

The great *Tragedy of Othello, the Moor of Venice* (about 1604) was first performed at the beginning of the reign of James I, who became the patron of Shakespeare's acting company, now called the King's Men. For *Othello*, Shakespeare adapted a simple and unpleasant tale from Giraldi Cinthio's *Hecatommithi* (1565) in which a nameless Moor, duped into believing that his Venetian wife has committed adultery, murders her in a jealous rage. Shakespeare's play questions the social stereotype of the passionate Moor that Cinthio's story confirms. Shakespeare, moreover, tests and explores the very notion of identity: how do individuals' histories and imaginations affect who they are? how does Othello's eventful life—as soldier, former slave, black man, Christian convert, instrument of war, object of imaginative wonder, and perpetual outsider in his adopted home of Venice—influence who he is? and how do his stories about his exotic past transform the ways in which his audiences perceive him and conceive of their own lives?

At the outset of Shakespeare's play, Othello, a Moor and general in the Venetian Republic's army, has eloped with a beautiful noblewoman, Desdemona, whose father (Brabanzio) rushes to the Venetian Senate to challenge the marriage. The play allows the uncomfortable suspicion that Othello escapes judgment because the Senate has already commissioned him to defend the Venetian stronghold in Cyprus from the Turks. Othello's name remains uncleared until Desdemona herself testifies to her passionate consent to the marriage and gains permission to join her husband on his military expedition. If audiences hope that Othello will display his heroism in combat with the Turks, all such expectations are dashed when a violent storm disables and scatters the Turkish ships. As characters gather on the shores of Cyprus (mythical home of Venus, goddess of love) to await the safe landing of Desdemona and Othello, the idea of military combat shifts to the erotic relations between Desdemona and Othello: Desdemona is Othello's "fair warrior" and "our great captain's captain." The erotic images anticipate the couple's deferred nuptial celebrations and, ominously, the fatal transformation of Othello's love into murderous jealousy. Under Iago's malicious influence, Othello loses faith in himself and in Desdemona, and he strangles her "in her bed, even the bed she hath contaminated." When he learns the truth of Desdemona's innocence at the play's end, Othello asks to be remembered romantically as a man "who loved not wisely, but too well." Finally, he stabs himself, falls upon the bed that dominates the final act, and dies "upon a kiss."

Central to the tragedy are questions of motive. Iago's "motiveless malignancy"—a phrase coined by Samuel Taylor Coleridge—is famously mysterious, but is by no means the play's only puzzle. Othello himself struck early critics as a glorified fool: Thomas Rymer, writing in 1693, ridiculed the idea that such a trifle as a lost handkerchief—Othello's first gift to Desdemona—could turn the mind of a genuinely tragic hero against his wife. For this post-Enlightenment critic, a handkerchief held none of the mystical significance that it might for Renaissance audiences, who regarded magical talismans and religious relics as potent signs of the supernatural. During the play, however, the "mystery" that baffles Desdemona's father and finally Othello himself is how the beautiful, intelligent, and virtuous Desdemona could have felt such an ardent passion for Othello in the first place: "A maiden never bold. / Of spirit so still and quiet that her motion / Blushed at herself—and she in spite of nature, / Of years, of country, credit, everything, / To fall in love with what she feared to look on!" The differences in age, nationality, and social status, normally so disastrous, fade next to the "everything" that is Othello's race.

Shakespeare does not approach racial stereotypes strictly in terms of the race discourses of the English Renaissance. Instead, he presents all of his characters in relation to older, more limited dramatic ideas of character type. The dramatic traditions against which he defines his tragedy and characters are the medieval morality play and Roman new comedy. Roman comedy, of which *Pseudolus* is an outstanding example, draws its cast of characters from social types: in a common scenario, a clever servant circumvents the efforts of an irate father to prevent the boy from getting the girl. Although Shakespeare introduces these theatrical types in several of his early comedies, it is startling to see them frolicking about a tragedy dealing with betrayal, mad jealously, loss of identity, divorce, and murder. In *Othello*, which begins with a marriage (usually the point at which comedy ends), comic types have tragic purposes: the clever servant conspires to divorce the husband from the wife and see to it that marriage ends in a murder-suicide.

A second set of character types from new comedy is the braggart soldier and his flatterer. Iago casts himself as a cross between the clever servant and parasitic flatterer: he is, he says, one of those servants who, "trimmed in forms and visages of duty, / Keep yet their hearts attending on themselves." At the same time, he characterizes Othello as the swaggering soldier, filled with "bombast circumstance, / Horribly stuffed with epithets of war." Despite Iago's efforts to diminish Othello in the first scenes, Shakespeare's hero, when he at last appears, transcends the degrading stereotypes. When Brabanzio and his men attempt to apprehend him, one line from Othello stops his antagonists in their tracks: "Keep up your bright swords," he commands, "for the dew will rust 'em." The implicit boast is magnificent: only a warrior assured of victory has the power to refuse a challenge.

Shakespeare's use of stock types from comedy supplies a dramatic counterpart to the cultural stereotypes about race that Iago mobilizes at the outset of the play. Shakespeare's audiences must wait to learn the name of the man who is the subject of all Iago's bitter dialogues. Othello is first an anonymous "he," then a sarcastic "his Moorship." The "Moor" is the least charged of Iago's inventive and scabrous terms: he is also "the thick-lips," "an old black ram," a "Barbary horse," and "the devil." Othello goes unnamed, in fact, until the third scene, when he arrives at the Senate council chambers, where the Venetian senators await his military aid.

Against the backdrop of stock comic types, Shakespeare's tragic characters emerge as complex yet painfully vulnerable to manipulation and stereotyping. Brabanzio, for example, acts the part of the "irate father" only after Iago has stuffed his ears with racial slurs and sexually degrading images of his daughter and Othello: "Your heart is burst, you have lost half your soul. / Even now, now, very now, an old black ram / Is tupping your white ewe," Iago says, and "your daughter and the Moor are now making the beast with two backs." Unmentioned and unmentionable, Othello's blackness fuels the formerly levelheaded Brabanzio's hysteria when Iago tells him, "You'll have your daughter covered with a Barbary horse, you'll have your nephews neigh to you, you'll have coursers for cousins and gennets for germans" (Spanish horses for blood relatives). Soon Brabanzio views Othello, the man who was his beloved friend, in terms of racial prejudice, as an animal and a barbarian.

A second dramatic tradition at work in *Othello* is the medieval morality play, in which the forces of good and evil do battle for the soul of Everyman. To a certain extent, Othello acts as an Everyman, Desdemona as his good angel, and Iago as the charismatic villain known as the Vice. Shakespeare turns the morality play's allegorical battle for the soul (*psychomachia*) into a psychological struggle within Othello, who is torn between his faith in Desdemona and his radical doubts and insecurities. At the end of the play, Othello looks toward Iago's feet, half expecting to see the hooves that will furnish a supernatural explanation for his malice, and seeks to learn of "that demi-devil, / What he hath thus ensnared my soul and body?" Simultaneously, Desdemona appears to Othello as an angel: "O ill-starred wench! / Pale as thy smock! When we shall meet at count [Judgment Day] / This look of thine will hurl my soul from heaven / And friends will snatch at it." Othello sees around him the signs of a morality play gone hideously wrong. Yet an explanation of his downfall in metaphysical terms distorts the entirely human character of his tragedy. To view Iago as a demi-devil is to mystify his power and deny the human and social origins of his malevolence. To view Desdemona as an angel is to idealize her at the cost of her humanity and sexuality. For Othello, the cold, pale body of Desdemona painfully testifies to the purity of her once suspect sexuality: "Cold, cold, my girl, / Even like thy chastity." Othello's idealism is tragically at odds with his wife's passionate sexuality.

The medieval Vice was no supernatural agent: he represented an evil shared by the entire community, and he performs onstage in a way that affirms his intimate connection with the audience. While the protagonist (Everyman in the morality play and the tragic hero in Shakespeare's dramas) dominates center stage, Vice hogs the sidelines and the area downstage (close to the audience). Whereas Shakespearean tragic heroes speak soliloquies—extended monologues "overheard" by the audience—Vicefigures like Iago directly address the audience in lively, confidential, and humorous terms. The medieval Vice is expected to pun, joke, and deflate the high-flown ideals represented by other characters—the exact behavioral trademarks of Iago. Iago, however, takes none of the carnivalesque delight enjoyed by Vice: his character does not invite most actors to play him with sprightly, cackling, hand-rubbing glee. Like Vice, however, Iago represents a communal evil: cultural hatreds and bigotry, including racial prejudice, misogyny (hatred or fear of women), elitism, and smug nationalism. These are the ingredients of Iago's verbal poison, which are the jokes and corrupting "medicine" he imagines himself pouring into others' ears.

Does Iago deserve the dubious credit for engineering the alienation of Othello from Desdemona? Many readers and playgoers detect ambivalence in Othello's admiring description of Desdemona as his "fair warrior," even without Iago's suggestion that "our general's wife is now the general" and that Desdemona has become "our captain's captain." Desdemona first appears as a warrior when she listens to the epic story of Othello's life, with its

> disastrous chances,
> Of moving accidents by flood and field,
> Of hairbreadth scapes i'th'imminent deadly breach,
> Of being taken by the insolent foe
> And sold to slavery . . .

Othello recalls that Desdemona would come and "with a greedy ear, / Devour up [his] discourse" and enigmatically wish that "heaven had made her such a man." After vicariously participating in Othello's life, does Desdemona desire the man for a husband, or does she wish to be that heroic man herself? What range of feelings might Othello experience as he beholds his "fair warrior"?

In the magnificent, demanding act 3, scene 3, Iago persuades Othello to denigrate his own body as an object of sexual pleasure. Othello at first puts up a mild defense of Desdemona—"She had eyes and chose me." But he soon concedes that her eyes were led by something less than reason: he agrees when Iago insinuates that "when she seemed to shake and fear your looks, / She loved them most." Iago overtly suggests that she is adulterous but, more damningly, slyly insinuates that her passion for Othello is itself perverse. Almost effortlessly, he racializes Othello's view of himself and Desdemona, and before the scene's end, Othello is conjuring the resources of his racially marked body as if it contains the powers of hell:

> Arise, black vengeance, from the hollow hell.
> Yield up, O love, thy crown and hearted throne
> To tyrannous hate! Swell, bosom, with thy freight,
> For 'tis of aspics' tongues.

The scene ends with the symbolic divorce of Othello from Desdemona: he and Iago kneel and exchange a "sacred vow" that concludes with Iago's haunting line "I am your own forever." In this parody of the marriage ceremony, Iago exemplifies the etymological meaning of his name, "the supplanter."

Passion seems to animate and threaten the couple's marriage. Iago asserts that Desdemona's power over Othello is so absolute that he would "renounce his baptism" for her; Othello appears to confirm the extraordinary claim when he says of her, admiringly, "Excellent wretch! Perdition catch my soul / But I do love thee, And when I love thee not, / Chaos is come again." The image of chaos, the universe's natural randomness before the introduction of creative order, illuminates the psychological and linguistic incoherence into which Othello falls in the moments of the play that most try an actor's skills.

Othello exhibits an idolatrous love for Desdemona even as he prepares to murder her. In the eloquent, troublingly erotic soliloquy that begins the final scene, Othello says he will "not shed her blood, / Nor scar that whiter skin of hers than snow, / And smooth as monumental alabaster." Here, as elsewhere, Othello feels ambivalently attracted to her sexual vitality (the "rose" he will pluck) and to the artificial, statuelike qualities of her vulnerable, sleeping body. Only when she is dead can Othello safely adore Desdemona as an image of chaste purity. Unlike Pygmalion, who fell in love with his own statue and rejoiced when Venus brought the marble image to life, Othello imaginatively transforms a vibrant, sexual woman into a marble image of chastity.

Anthony Burgess, *Shakespeare* (1970), is an informed and imaginative biography. William Schoenbaum, *William Shakespeare: A Compact Documentary Life* (1977), is the standard reference. On the theatrical companies and players, Muriel Bradbrook,

The Rise of the Common Player (1964), and Andrew Gurr, *The Shakespearean Stage, 1574–1642*, 3rd ed. (1992), are recommended. Huston Diehl, *Staging Reform, Reforming the Stage* (1997), contains a strong reading of Othello's relationship to Reformation ideas about idolatry and the imagination. Janet Adelman, *Suffocating Mothers* (1992), discusses Othello's tendency to regard Desdemona as the source of his very being. Karen Newman studies the links between women and race in the chapter " 'And wash the Ethiop white': Femininity and the Monstrous in *Othello*" of *Fashioning Femininity* (1991). Carol Thomas Neely analyzes the sexual double standard of the play from the perspective of Emilia in *Broken Rituals in Shakespeare's Plays* (1985). G. K. Hunter, "Othello and Color Prejudice," in *Dramatic Identities and Cultural Tradition* (1978), remains one of the finest studies of race discourse and the play itself. Maynard Mack, "The Jacobean Shakespeare: Some Observations on the Construction of the Tragedies," in *Stratford-upon-Avon Studies: Jacobean Theatre*, vol. 1 (1960), ed. John Russell Brown and Bernard Harris, is an indispensable survey of Shakespeare's writing in his later period.

The Tragedy of Othello the Moor of Venice

CHARACTERS

OTHELLO, *the Moor of Venice*
DESDEMONA, *his wife*
Michael CASSIO, *his lieutenant*
BIANCA, *a courtesan, in love with Cassio*
IAGO, *the Moor's ensign*
EMILIA, *Iago's wife*
A CLOWN, *a servant of Othello*
The DUKE *of Venice*
BRABANZIO, *Desdemona's father, a senator of Venice*

GRAZIANO, *Brabanzio's brother*
LODOVICO, *kinsman of Brabanzio*
SENATORS *of Venice*
RODERIGO, *a Venetian gentleman, in love with Desdemona*
MONTANO, *Governor of Cyprus*
A HERALD
A MESSENGER
Attendants, officers, sailors, gentlemen of Cyprus, musicians

1.1

[*Enter* IAGO *and* RODERIGO.]

RODERIGO Tush, never tell me! I take it much unkindly
  That thou, Iago, who hast had my purse
  As if the strings were thine, shouldst know of this.[1]
IAGO 'Sblood,[2] but you'll not hear me!
  If ever I did dream of such a matter, abhor me.   5
RODERIGO Thou told'st me thou didst hold him in thy hate,
IAGO Despise me
  If I do not. Three great ones of the city,
  In personal suit to make me his lieutenant,
  Off-capped[3] to him; and by the faith of man   10
  I know my price, I am worth no worse a place.
  But he, as loving his own pride and purposes,
  Evades them with a bombast circumstance[4]
  Horribly stuffed with epithets of war,[5]

1. The marriage of Desdemona and Othello.   2. By God's blood.   3. Respectfully took their hats off.   4. Pompous speech.   5. Heroic adjectives.

Nonsuits[6] my mediators; for 'Certes,' says he,   15
'I have already chose my officer.'
And what was he?
Forsooth, a great arithmetician,[7]
One Michael Cassio, a Florentine,
A fellow almost damned in a fair wife,[8]   20
That never set a squadron in the field
Nor the division of a battle knows
More than a spinster—unless the bookish theoric,
Wherein the togaed consuls can propose
As masterly as he. Mere prattle without practice   25
Is all his soldiership; but he, sir, had th'election,
And I—of whom his eyes had seen the proof
At Rhodes, at Cyprus, and on other grounds
Christened and heathen—must be beleed[9] and calmed
By debitor and creditor. This counter-caster,[1]   30
He in good time must his lieutenant be,
And I—God bless the mark!—his Moorship's ensign.[2]
RODERIGO By heaven, I rather would have been his hangman.
IAGO Why, there's no remedy. 'Tis the curse of his hangman.
Preferment goes by letter and affection,   35
And not by old gradation,[3] where each second
Stood heir to th' first. Now, sir, be judge yourself
Whether I in any just term am affined[4]
To love the Moor.
RODERIGO I would not follow him then.   40
IAGO O sir, content you.
I follow him to serve my turn upon him.
We cannot all be masters, nor all masters
Cannot be truly followed. You shall mark
Many a duteous and knee-crooking knave   45
That, doting on his own obsequious bondage,
Wears out his time much like his master's ass
For naught but provender, and when he's old, cashiered.
Whip me such honest knaves. Others there are
Who, trimmed in forms and visages of duty,   50
Keep yet their hearts attending on themselves,
And, throwing but shows of service on their lords,
Do well thrive by 'em, and when they have lined their coats,
Do themselves homage. These fellows have some soul,
And such a one do I profess myself—for, sir,   55
It is as sure as you are Roderigo,
Were I the Moor I would not be Iago.
In following him I follow but myself.
Heaven is my judge, not I for love and duty,
But seeming so for my peculiar[5] end.   60
For when my outward action doth demonstrate.

6. Dismisses (legal metaphor).   7. Theorist.   8. He is not married in the play, although he is in
Shakespeare's source.   9. "Had the wind taken out my sails."   1. Accountant.   2. Standard-
bearer.   3. Seniority.   4. Contracted.   5. Personal.

The native act and figure of my heart
In compliment extern,[6] 'tis not long after
But I will wear my heart upon my sleeve
For daws to peck at. I am not what I am.   65
RODERIGO   What a full fortune does the thick-lips owe[7]
    If he can carry't thus!
IAGO   Call up her father,
    Rouse him, make after him, poison his delight,
    Proclaim him in the streets; incense her kinsmen,
    And, though he in a fertile climate dwell,   70
    Plague him with flies. Though that his joy be joy,
    Yet throw such chances of vexation on't
    As it may lose some colour.
RODERIGO   Here is her father's house. I'll call aloud.
IAGO   Do, with like timorous[8] accent and dire yell   75
    As when, by night and negligence, the fire
    Is spied in populous cities.
RODERIGO [calling]   What ho, Brabanzio, Signor Brabanzio, ho!
IAGO [calling]   Awake, what ho, Brabanzio, thieves, thieves, thieves!
    Look to your house, your daughter, and your bags.   80
    Thieves, thieves!
        [Enter BRABANZIO in his nightgown at a window above.]
BRABANZIO   What is the reason of this terrible summons?
    What is the matter there?
RODERIGO   Signor, is all your family within?
IAGO   Are your doors locked?
BRABANZIO   Why, wherefore ask you this?   85
IAGO   'Swounds,[9] sir, you're robbed. For shame, put on your gown.
    Your heart is burst, you have lost half your soul.
    Even now, now, very now, an old black ram
    Is tupping your white ewe. Arise, arise!
    Awake the snorting citizens with the bell,   90
    Or else the devil will make a grandsire of you.
    Arise, I say.
BRABANZIO   What, have you lost your wits?
RODERIGO   Most reverend signor, do you know my voice?
BRABANZIO   Not I. What are you?
RODERIGO   My name is Roderigo.   95
BRABANZIO   The worser welcome.
    I have charged thee not to haunt about my doors.
    In honest plainness thou hast heard me say
    My daughter is not for thee, and now in madness,
    Being full of supper and distempering[1] draughts,   100
    Upon malicious bravery dost thou come
    To start[2] my quiet.
RODERIGO   Sir, sir, sir.
BRABANZIO   But thou must needs be sure

---

6. On the outside.   7. Own.   8. Intimidating.   9. By God's wounds.   1. Intoxicating.
2. Upset.

My spirits and my place[3] have in their power   105
To make this bitter to thee.

RODERIGO   Patience, good sir.

BRABANZIO   What tell'st thou me of robbing? This is Venice.
My house is not a grange.[4]

RODERIGO   Most grave Brabanzio,
In simple and pure soul I come to you.

IAGO [to BRABANZIO]   'Swounds, sir, you are one of those that will not   110
serve God if the devil bid you. Because we come to do you service
and you think we are ruffians, you'll have your daughter covered with
a Barbary horse, you'll have your nephews neigh to you, you'll have
coursers for cousins and jennets for germans.[5]

BRABANZIO   What profane wretch art thou?   115

IAGO   I am one, sir, that comes to tell you your daughter and the
Moor are now making the beast with two backs.

BRABANZIO   Thou art a villain.

IAGO   You are a senator.

BRABANZIO   This thou shalt answer. I know thee, Roderigo.

RODERIGO   Sir, I will answer anything. But I beseech you,   120
If't be your pleasure and most wise consent—
As partly I find it is—that your fair daughter,
At this odd-even[6] and dull watch o'th' night,
Transported with no worse nor better guard
But with a knave of common hire, a gondolier,   125
To the gross clasps of a lascivious Moor—
If this be known to you, and your allowance,
We then have done you bold and saucy wrongs.
But if you know not this, my manners tell me
We have your wrong rebuke. Do not believe   130
That, from the sense of all civility,
I thus would play and trifle with your reverence.
Your daughter, if you have not given her leave,
I say again hath made a gross revolt,
Tying her duty, beauty, wit, and fortunes   135
In an extravagant[7] and wheeling stranger
Of here and everywhere. Straight satisfy yourself.
If she be in her chamber or your house,
Let loose on me the justice of the state
For thus deluding you.

BRABANZIO [calling]   Strike on the tinder, ho!   140
Give me a taper call up all my people.
This accident[8] is not unlike my dream;
Belief of it oppresses me already.
Light, I say, light!   [Exit.]

IAGO   Farewell, for I must leave you.
It seems not meet nor wholesome to my place   145
To be produced—as, if I stay, I shall—

---

3. Social position.   4. House in the wilderness.   5. Blood relations. *Barbary*: Arabian. *Coursers*: horses. *Jennets*: Spanish horses.   6. Neither morning nor night.   7. Wandering.   8. Chance circumstance.

Against the Moor, for I do know the state,
However this may gall him with some check,[9]
Cannot with safety cast[1] him, for he's embarked
With such loud reason to the Cyprus wars,   150
Which even now stands in act,[2] that, for their souls,
Another of his fathom[3] they have none
To lead their business, in which regard—
Though I do hate him as I do hell pains—
Yet for necessity of present life   155
I must show out a flag and sign of love,
Which is indeed but sign. That you shall surely find him,
Lead to the Sagittary[4] the raisèd search,
And there will I be with him. So farewell.   [Exit.]
       [Enter below BRABANZIO in his nightgown, and servants with
       torches.]
BRABANZIO   It is too true an evil. Gone she is,   160
And what's to come of my despisèd time
Is naught but bitterness. Now, Roderigo,
Where didst thou see her?—O unhappy girl!—
With the Moor, sayst thou?—Who would be a father?—
How didst thou know 'twas she?—O, she deceives me   165
Past thought!—What said she to you? [To servants] Get more tapers,
Raise all my kindred.   [Exit one or more.]
   [To RODERIGO]   Are they married, think you?
RODERIGO   Truly, I think they are.
BRABANZIO   O heaven, how got she out? O, treason of the blood!
Fathers, from hence trust not your daughters' minds   170
By what you see them act. Is there not charms
By which the property[5] of youth and maidhood
May be abused? Have you not read, Roderigo,
Of some such thing?
RODERIGO   Yes, sir, I have indeed.
BRABANZIO [to servants]   Call up my brother. [To RODERIGO] O, would you
       had had her.   175
   [To servants] Some one way, some another.   [Exit one or more.]
   [To RODERIGO   Do you know.
Where we may apprehend her and the Moor?
RODERIGO   I think I can discover him, if you please
To get good guard and go along with me.
BRABANZIO   Pray you lead on. At every house I'll call;   180
I may command at most. [Calling] Get weapons, ho,
And raise some special officers of night.
On, good Roderigo. I will deserve your pains.[6]   [Exeunt.]

1.2

       [Enter OTHELLO, IAGO, and attendants with torches.]
IAGO   Though in the trade of war I have slain men,

_____
9. Setback.   1. Dismiss.   2. Is happening.   3. Depth of skill.   4. Name of an inn.   5. Character.   6. I will make it worth your trouble.

Yet do I hold it very stuff o'th' conscience
To do no contrived murder. I lack iniquity,
Sometime, to do me service. Nine or ten times
I had thought to've yerked[7] him here, under the ribs.   5
OTHELLO   'Tis better as it is.
IAGO   Nay, but he prated,
And spoke such scurvy and provoking terms
Against your honour
That, with the little godliness I have,
I did full hard forbear him. But I pray you, sir,   10
Are you fast married? Be assured of this:
That the magnifico[8] is much beloved,
And hath in his effect a voice potential
As double as the Duke's.[9] He will divorce you,
Or put upon you what restraint or grievance   15
The law, with all his might to enforce it on,
Will give him cable.[1]
OTHELLO   Let him do his spite.
My services which I have done the signory[2]
Shall out-tongue his complaints. 'Tis yet to know—
Which, when I know that boasting is an honour,   20
I shall promulgate—I fetch my life and being
From men of royal siege,[3] and my demerits
May speak unbonneted to as proud a fortune
As this that I have reached.[4] For know, Iago,
But that I love the gentle Desdemona   25
I would not my unhousèd[5] free condition
Put into circumscription and confine
For the seas' worth.
        [*Enter* CASSIO *and officers, with torches.*]
                        But look, what lights come yond?
IAGO   Those are the raisèd father and his friends.
You were best go in.
OTHELLO   Not I. I must be found.   30
My parts, my title, and my perfect soul[6]
Shall manifest me rightly. Is it they?
IAGO   By Janus, I think no.
OTHELLO   The servants of the Duke, and my lieutenant!
The goodness of the night upon you, friends.   35
What is the news?
CASSIO   The Duke does greet you, general,
And he requires your haste-post-haste appearance
Even on the instant.
OTHELLO   What is the matter, think you?
CASSIO   Something from Cyprus, as I may divine;
It is a business of some heat. The galleys   40
Have sent a dozen sequent messengers

---

7. Stabbed.   8. Nobleman.   9. Can be twice as influential as the Duke.   1. Means.   2. Rulers
of Venice.   3. Descent.   4. My merits, which need no self-effacing, are equal to my marriage.
5. Unconfined.   6. Guiltless conscience.

This very night at one another's heels,
And many of the consuls, raised and met,
Are at the Duke's already. You have been hotly called for,
When, being not at your lodging to be found,   45
The senate sent about three several quests
To search you out.
OTHELLO   'Tis well I am found by you.
  I will but spend a word here in the house
  And go with you.   [*Exit.*]
CASSIO   Ensign, what makes he here?
IAGO   Faith, he tonight hath boarded a land-carrack.[7]   50
  If it prove lawful prize, he's made for ever.
CASSIO   I do not understand.
IAGO   He's married.
CASSIO   To who?
            [*Enter* BRABANZIO, RODERIGO, *and* OFFICERS, *with lights and
            weapons.*]
IAGO   Marry,[8] to—
            [*Enter* OTHELLO.]
  [*To* OTHELLO] Come, captain, will you go?
OTHELLO   Have with you.
CASSIO   Here comes another troop to seek for you.   55
IAGO   It is Brabanzio. General, be advised.
  He comes to bad intent.
OTHELLO   Holla, stand, there!
RODERIGO [*to* BRABANZIO]   Signor, it is the Moor.
BRABANZIO   Down with him, thief!
IAGO [*drawing his sword*]   You, Roderigo? Come, sir, I am for you.
OTHELLO   Keep up your bright swords, for the dew will rust 'em.   60
  [*To* BRABANZIO] Good signor, you shall more command with years
  Than with your weapons.
BRABANZIO   O thou foul thief, where hast thou stowed my daughter?
  Damned as thou art, thou hast enchanted her,
  For I'll refer me to all things of sense,[9]   65
  If she in chains of magic were not bound,
  Whether a maid so tender, fair, and happy,
  So opposite to marriage that she shunned
  The wealthy curlèd darlings of our nation,
  Would ever have, t'incur a general mock,   70
  Run from her guardage to the sooty bosom
  Of such a thing as thou—to fear, not to delight.
  Judge me the world if 'tis not gross in sense.[1]
  That thou hast practised on[2] her with foul charms,
  Abused her delicate youth with drugs or minerals   75
  That weakens motion.[3] I'll have't disputed on.
  'Tis probable, and palpable to thinking.
  I therefore apprehend and do attach[4] thee

7. Treasure ship.   8. By Mary.   9. Make use of natural reason.   1. Obvious.   2. Manipulated.
3. The will.   4. Arrest.

For an abuser of the world, a practiser
Of arts inhibited and out of warrant.[5]   80
[*To* OFFICERS] Lay hold upon him. If he do resist,
Subdue him at his peril.
OTHELLO   Hold your hands,
Both you of my inclining and the rest.
Were it my cue to fight, I should have known it
Without a prompter. Whither will you that I go   85
To answer this your charge?
BRABANZIO   To prison, till fit time
Of law and course of direct session
Call thee to answer.
OTHELLO   What if I do obey?
How may the Duke be therewith satisfied,
Whose messengers are here about my side   90
Upon some present business of the state
To bring me to him?
OFFICER [*to* BRABANZIO]   'Tis true, most worthy signor.
The Duke's in council, and your noble self,
I am sure, is sent for.
BRABANZIO   How, the Duke in council?
In this time of the night? Bring him away.   95
Mine's not an idle cause. The Duke himself,
Or any of my brothers of the state,
Cannot but feel this wrong as 'twere their own;
For if such actions may have passage free,
Bondslaves and pagans shall our statesmen be.   [*Exeunt.*] 100

1.3

[*Enter the* DUKE *and* SENATORS *set at a table, with lights and*
OFFICERS.]

DUKE   There is no composition in these news
That gives them credit.[6]
FIRST SENATOR   Indeed, they are disproportioned.
My letters say a hundred and seven galleys.
DUKE   And mine a hundred-forty.
SECOND SENATOR   And mine two hundred.
But though they jump not on a just account[7]—   5
As, in these cases, where the aim reports
'Tis oft with difference—yet do they all confirm
A Turkish fleet, and bearing up to Cyprus.
DUKE   Nay, it is possible enough to judgement.
I do not so secure me in the error,   10
But the main article I do approve
In fearful sense.[8]
SAILOR [*within*]   What ho, what ho, what ho!

---

5. Prohibited and illegal.   6. The consensus of the reports makes them believable.   7. Exact number.
Jump: agree.   8. The tale is believable, and the numerical errors do not make me doubt the overall report,
which I fear.

[*Enter a* SAILOR.]

OFFICER   A messenger from the galleys.

DUKE   Now, what's the business?

SAILOR   The Turkish preparation makes for Rhodes.
So was I bid report here to the state   15
By Signor Angelo.

DUKE [*to* SENATORS]   How say you by this change?

FIRST SENATOR   This cannot be,
By no assay of reason—'tis a pageant
To keep us in false gaze⁹ When we consider   20
The importancy of Cyprus to the Turk,
And let ourselves again but understand
That, as it more concerns the Turk than Rhodes,
So may he with more facile question¹ bear it,
For that it stands not in such warlike brace,²   25
But altogether lacks th'abilities
That Rhodes is dressed in—if we make thought of this,
We must not think the Turk is so unskilful
To leave that latest which concerns him first,
Neglecting an attempt of ease and gain   30
To wake and wage a danger profitless.

DUKE   Nay, in all confidence, he's not for Rhodes.

OFFICER   Here is more news.

          [*Enter a* MESSENGER.]

MESSENGER   The Ottomites, reverend and gracious,
Steering with due course toward the Isle of Rhodes,   35
Have there injointed them with an after fleet.

FIRST SENATOR   Ay, so I thought. How many, as you guess?

MESSENGER   Of thirty sail, and now they do restem
Their backward course, bearing with frank appearance
Their purposes toward Cyprus. Signor Montano,   40
Your trusty and most valiant servitor,
With his free duty recommend³ you thus,
And prays you to believe him.

DUKE   'Tis certain then for Cyprus.
Marcus Luccicos, is not he in town?

FIRST SENATOR   He's now in Florence.   45

DUKE   Write from us to him post-post-haste. Dispatch.

          [*Enter* BRABANZIO, OTHELLO, RODERIGO, IAGO, CASSIO, *and*
          officers.]

FIRST SENATOR   Here comes Brabanzio and the valiant Moor.

DUKE   Valiant Othello, we must straight employ you
Against the general enemy Ottoman.
[*To* BRABANZIO] I did not see you. Welcome, gentle signor   50
We lacked your counsel and your help tonight.

BRABANZIO   So did I yours. Good your grace, pardon me.
Neither my place, nor aught I heard of business,

---

9. Show to distract us.   1. Easy conflict.   2. Military preparation.   3. Informs. *Free duty:* unforced
respect.

Hath raised me from my bed, nor doth the general care
Take hold on me; for my particular grief   55
Is of so floodgate and o'erbearing nature
That it engluts and swallows other sorrows,
And it is still itself.
DUKE   Why, what's the matter?
BRABANZIO   My daughter, O, my daughter!
SENATORS   Dead?
BRABANZIO   Ay, to me.
She is abused, stol'n from me, and corrupted   60
By spells and medicines bought of mountebanks.[4]
For nature so preposterously to err,
Being not deficient, blind, or lame of sense,
Sans witchcraft could not.
DUKE   Whoe'er he be that in this foul proceeding   65
Hath thus beguiled your daughter of herself
And you of her, the bloody book of law
You shall yourself read in the bitter letter
After your own sense, yea, though our proper son
Stood in your action.[5]
BRABANZIO   Humbly I thank your grace.   70
Here is the man, this Moor, whom now it seems
Your special mandate for the state affairs
Hath hither brought.
SENATORS   We are very sorry for't.
DUKE [to OTHELLO]   What in your own part can you say to this?
BRABANZIO   Nothing but this is so.   75
OTHELLO   Most potent, grave, and reverend signors,
My very noble and approved[6] good masters,
That I have ta'en away this old man's daughter,
It is most true, true I have married her.
The very head and front[7] of my offending
Hath this extent, no more. Rude am I in my speech,   80
And little blessed with the soft phrase of peace,
For since these arms of mine had seven years' pith[8]
Till now some nine moons wasted,[9] they have used
Their dearest[1] action in the tented field,   85
And little of this great world can I speak
More than pertains to feats of broils and battle.
And therefore little shall I grace my cause
In speaking for myself. Yet, by your gracious patience,
I will a round unvarnished tale deliver   90
Of my whole course of love, what drugs, what charms,
What conjuration and what mighty magic—
For such proceeding I am charged withal—
I won his daughter.

---

4. Frauds.   5. Suit. *Proper:* own.   6. Tested.   7. Form and gist (i.e., it was a marriage, not a
rape).   8. Strength.   9. Past.   1. Most significant.

BRABANZIO   A maiden never bold.
Of spirit so still and quiet that her motion   95
Blushed at herself[2]—and she in spite of nature,
Of years, of country, credit, everything,
To fall in love with what she feared to look on!
It is a judgement maimed and most imperfect
That will confess perfection so could err   100
Against all rules of nature, and must be driven
To find out practices of cunning hell
Why this should be. I therefore vouch again
That with some mixtures powerful o'er the blood,
Or with some dram conjured to this effect,   105
He wrought upon her.
DUKE   To vouch this is no proof
Without more wider and more overt test
Than these thin habits and poor likelihoods
Of modern seeming[3] do prefer against him.
A SENATOR   But Othello, speak.   110
Did you by indirect and forcèd courses
Subdue and poison this young maid's affections,
Or came it by request and such fair question[4]
As soul to soul affordeth?
OTHELLO   I do beseech you,
Send for the lady to the Sagittary,   115
And let her speak of me before her father.
If you do find me foul in her report,
The trust, the office I do hold of you
Not only take away, but let your sentence
Even fall upon my life.
DUKE [to OFFICERS]   Fetch Desdemona hither.   120
OTHELLO   Ensign, conduct them. You best know the place.

                [*Exit* IAGO *with two or three officers.*]

And till she come, as truly as to heaven
I do confess the vices of my blood,
So justly to your grave ears I'll present
How I did thrive in this fair lady's love,   125
And she is mine.
DUKE   Say it, Othello.
OTHELLO   Her father loved me, oft invited me,
Still questioned me the story of my life
From year to year, the battles, sieges, fortunes
That I have passed.   130
I ran it through even from my boyish days
To th' very moment that he bade me tell it,
Wherein I spoke of most disastrous chances,
Of moving accidents by flood and field,
Of hair-breadth scapes i'th' imminent deadly breach,   135

---

2. She blushed at her own movement.   3. Common appearance. *Thin habits*: clothing.   4. Inquiry.

Of being taken by the insolent foe
And sold to slavery, of my redemption thence,
And portance[5] in my traveller's history,
Wherein of antres vast and deserts idle,[6]
Rough quarries, rocks, and hills whose heads touch heaven,   140
It was my hint to speak. Such was my process,
And of the cannibals that each other eat,
The Anthropophagi,[7] and men whose heads
Do grow beneath their shoulders. These things to hear
Would Desdemona seriously incline,   145
But still the house affairs would draw her thence,
Which ever as she could with haste dispatch
She'd come again, and with a greedy ear
Devour up my discourse; which I observing,
Took once a pliant hour, and found good means   150
To draw from her a prayer of earnest heart
That I would all my pilgrimage dilate,[8]
Whereof by parcels she had something heard,
But not intentively:[9] I did consent,
And often did beguile her of her tears   155
When I did speak of some distressful stroke
That my youth suffered. My story being done,
She gave me for my pains a world of kisses.
She swore in faith 'twas strange, 'twas passing[1] strange,
'Twas pitiful, 'twas wondrous pitiful.   160
She wished she had not heard it, yet she wished
That heaven had made her such a man. She thankèd me,
And bade me, if I had a friend that loved her,
I should but teach him how to tell my story,
And that would woo her. Upon this hint I spake.   165
She loved me for the dangers I had passed,
And I loved her that she did pity them.
This only is the witchcraft I have used.
     [Enter DESDEMONA, IAGO, and attendants.]
Here comes the lady. Let her witness it.
DUKE   I think this tale would win my daughter, too—   170
   Good Brabanzio,
Take up this mangled matter at the best.[2]
Men do their broken weapons rather use
Than their bare hands.
BRABANZIO   I pray you hear her speak.
If she confess that she was half the wooer,   175
Destruction on my head if my bad blame
Light on the man! Come hither, gentle mistress.
Do you perceive in all this noble company
Where most you owe obedience?
DESDEMONA   My noble father,

5. Conduct.   6. Empty. *Antres:* caves.   7. Man-eaters.   8. Narrate fully.   9. Intently.   1. Surpassingly.   2. I.e., make the best of it.

I do perceive here a divided duty.   180
To you I am bound for life and education.
My life and education both do learn me
How to respect you. You are the lord of duty,
I am hitherto your daughter. But here's my husband,
And so much duty as my mother showed   185
To you, preferring you before her father,
So much I challenge that I may profess
Due to the Moor my lord.
BRABANZIO   God b'wi'you, I ha' done.
  Please it your grace, on to the state affairs.
  I had rather to adopt a child than get[3] it.   190
  Come hither, Moor.
  I here do give thee that with all my heart
  Which, but thou hast already, with all my heart
  I would keep from thee. [*To* DESDEMONA] For your sake,[4] jewel,
  I am glad at soul I have no other child,   195
  For thy escape would teach me tyranny,
  To hang clogs on 'em. I have done, my lord.
DUKE   Let me speak like yourself, and lay a sentence[5]
  Which, as a grece[6] or step, may help these lovers
  Into your favour.   200
  When remedies are past, the griefs are ended
  By seeing the worst which late on hopes depended[7]
  To mourn a mischief that is past and gone
  Is the next way to draw new mischief on.
  What cannot be preserved when fortune takes,   205
  Patience her injury a mockery makes.
  The robbed that smiles steals something from the thief;
  He robs himself that spends a bootless[8] grief.
BRABANZIO   So let the Turk of Cyprus us beguile,
  We lose it not so long as we can smile   210
  He bears the sentence well that nothing bears
  But the free comfort which from thence he hears,
  But he bears both the sentence and the sorrow
  That, to pay grief, must of poor patience borrow.
  These sentences, to sugar or to gall,   215
  Being strong on both sides, are equivocal.
  But words are words. I never yet did hear
  That the bruisèd heart was piercèd through the ear.
  I humbly beseech you proceed to th'affairs of state.
DUKE   The Turk with a most mighty preparation makes for Cyprus.   220
  Othello, the fortitude of the place is best known to you, and though
  we have there a substitute of most allowed sufficiency,[9] yet opinion,
  a more sovereign mistress of effects, throws a more safer voice on
  you. You must therefore be content to slubber the gloss of your new
  fortunes with this more stubborn and boisterous[1] expedition.   225

---

3. Beget.   4. On your account.   5. Speak of maxim.   6. Stair.   7. Previously clung to hope.
8. Ineffective.   9. Ability. *Fortitude*: strength. *Substitute*: deputy.   1. Rough. *Slubber*: smear.

OTHELLO   The tyrant custom, most grave senators,
  Hath made the flinty and steel couch of war
  My thrice-driven[2] bed of down. I do agnize[3]
  A natural and prompt alacrity
  I find in hardness, and do undertake   230
  This present wars against the Ottomites.
  Most humbly therefore bending to your state,
  I crave fit disposition for my wife,
  Due reference of place and exhibition,
  With such accommodation and besort   235
  As levels with[4] her breeding.
DUKE   Why, at her father's!
BRABANZIO   I will not have it so.
OTHELLO   Nor I.
DESDEMONA   Nor would I there reside,   240
  To put my father in impatient thoughts
  By being in his eye. Most gracious Duke,
  To my unfolding lend your prosperous ear,
  And let me find a charter[5] in your voice
  T'assist my simpleness.
DUKE   What would you, Desdemona?   245
DESDEMONA   That I did love the Moor to live with him,
  My downright violence and storm of fortunes
  May trumpet to the world. My heart's subdued
  Even to the very quality of my lord.
  I saw Othello's visage in his mind,   250
  And to his honours and his valiant parts
  Did I my soul and fortunes consecrate;
  So that, dear lords, if I be left behind,
  A moth of peace, and he go to the war,
  The rites[6] for why I love him are bereft me,   255
  And I a heavy interim shall support
  By his dear absence. Let me go with him.
OTHELLO [to the DUKE]   Let her have your voice.[7]
  Vouch with me heaven, I therefor beg it not
  To please the palate of my appetite,   260
  Nor to comply with heat—the young affects
  In me defunct—and proper satisfaction,[8]
  But to be free and bounteous to her mind;
  And heaven defend your good souls that you think
  I will your serious and great business scant   265
  When she is with me. No, when light-winged toys
  Of feathered Cupid seel with wanton dullness
  My speculative and officed instruments,[9]
  That my disports corrupt and taint my business,

---

2. Winnowed three times.   3. Recognize.   4. Is appropriate to. *Exhibition*: financial support.
5. Permission. *Unfolding*: explanation. *Prosperous*: granting.   6. Marriage rites.   7. Approval.
8. I.e., consummation of marriage rites. *Heat*: lust. *Affects*: passions.   9. Clear-sightedness. *Seel*: sew
up (like a falcon's eyes). *Wanton*: lustful.

Let housewives make a skillet of my helm,   270
 And all indign and base adversities
 Make head against my estimation.[1]
DUKE   Be it as you shall privately determine,
 Either for her stay or going. Th'affair cries haste,
 And speed must answer it.
A SENATOR [to OTHELLO]   You must away tonight.   275
DESDEMONA   Tonight, my lord?
DUKE   This night.
OTHELLO   With all my heart.
DUKE   At nine i'th' morning here we'll meet again.
 Othello, leave some officer behind,
 And he shall our commission bring to you,
 And such things else of quality and respect   280
 As doth import you.
OTHELLO   So please your grace, my ensign.
 A man he is of honesty and trust.
 To his conveyance I assign my wife,
 With what else needful your good grace shall think
 To be sent after me.
DUKE   Let it be so.   285
 Good night to everyone. [To BRABANZIO] And, noble signor,
 If virtue no delighted beauty lack,
 Your son-in-law is far more fair than black.
A SENATOR   Adieu, brave Moor. Use Desdemona well.
BRABANZIO   Look to her, Moor, if thou hast eyes to see.   290
 She has deceived her father, and may thee.
        [Exeunt DUKE, BRABANZIO, CASSIO, SENATORS, and officers.]
OTHELLO   My life upon her faith. Honest Iago,
 My Desdemona must I leave to thee.
 I prithee let thy wife attend on her,
 And bring them after in the best advantage.[2]   295
 Come, Desdemona. I have but an hour
 Of love, of worldly matter and direction
 To spend with thee. We must obey the time.
          [Exeunt OTHELLO the Moor and DESDEMONA.]
RODERIGO   Iago.
IAGO   What sayst thou, noble heart?   300
RODERIGO   What will I do, think'st thou?
IAGO   Why, go to bed and sleep.
RODERIGO   I will incontinently[3] drown myself.
IAGO   If thou dost, I shall never love thee after. Why, thou silly
 gentleman!   305
RODERIGO   It is silliness to live when to live is torment; and then have
 we a prescription to die when death is our physician.
IAGO   O, villainous! I ha' looked upon the world for four times seven
 years, and since I could distinguish betwixt a benefit and an injury

---

1. Reputation. *Indign:* unworthy. *Make head:* rebel.   2. At the next opportunity.   3. Directly.

I never found man that knew how to love himself. Ere I would say I would drown myself for the love of a guinea-hen, I would change my humanity with a baboon. 310

RODERIGO What should I do? I confess it is my shame to be so fond, but it is not in my virtue to amend it.

IAGO Virtue?[4] A fig! 'Tis in ourselves that we are thus or thus. Our bodies are our gardens, to the which our wills are gardeners; so that if we will plant nettles or sow lettuce, set hyssop and weed up thyme, supply it with one gender of herbs or distract it with many, either to have it sterile with idleness or manured with industry, why, the power and corrigible[5] authority of this lies in our wills. If the beam of our lives had not one scale of reason to peise another of sensuality, the blood and baseness of our natures would conduct us to most preposterous conclusions. But we have reason to cool our raging motions, our carnal stings, our unbitted lusts; whereof I take this that you call love to be a sect or scion.[6] 315 320 325

RODERIGO It cannot be.

IAGO It is merely a lust of the blood and a permission of the will. Come, be a man. Drown thyself? Drown cats and blind puppies. I have professed me thy friend, and I confess me knit to thy deserving with cables of perdurable toughness. I could never better stead[7] thee than now. Put money in thy purse. Follow thou the wars, defeat thy favour with an usurped[8] beard. I say, put money in thy purse. It cannot be long that Desdemona should continue her love to the Moor—put money in thy purse—nor he his to her. It was a violent commencement in her, and thou shalt see an answerable sequestra- tion[9]—put but money in thy purse. These Moors are changeable in their wills—fill thy purse with money. The food that to him now is as luscious as locusts shall be to him shortly as bitter as coloquin- tida.[1] She must change for youth. When she is sated with his body, she will find the error of her choice. Therefore put money in thy purse. If thou wilt needs damn thyself, do it a more delicate way than drowning. Make all the money thou canst. If sanctimony and a frail vow betwixt an erring[2] barbarian and a super-subtle Venetian be not too hard for my wits and all the tribe of hell, thou shalt enjoy her; therefore make money. A pox o' drowning thyself—it is clean out of the way. Seek thou rather to be hanged in compassing[3] thy joy than to be drowned and go without her. 330 335 340 345

RODERIGO Wilt thou be fast to my hopes if I depend on the issue?

IAGO Thou art sure of me. Go, make money. I have told thee often, and I re-tell thee again and again, I hate the Moor. My cause is hearted, thine hath no less reason. Let us be conjunctive[4] in our revenge against him. If thou canst cuckold him, thou dost thyself a pleasure, me a sport. There are many events in the womb of time, which will be delivered. Traverse, go, provide thy money. We will have more of this tomorrow. Adieu. 350 355

---

4. Power, strength. 5. Corrective. 6. Shoot. *Unbitted:* unrestrained. 7. Serve. 8. False. *Defeat thy favor:* disguise your face. 9. Similar end. 1. Laxative made from bitter apples. *Locusts:* sweet fruit. 2. *Wandering. Sanctimony:* sacred bond (of marriage). 3. Achieving. 4. United. *Hearted:* heartfelt.

RODERIGO   Where shall we meet i'th' morning?
IAGO   At my lodging.
RODERIGO   I'll be with thee betimes.
IAGO   Go to, farewell—
  Do you hear, Roderigo?
RODERIGO   I'll sell all my land.   [*Exit.*]
IAGO   Thus do I ever make my fool my purse—
  For I mine own gained knowledge should profane   360
  If I would time expend with such a snipe.[5]
  But for my sport and profit. I hate the Moor,
  And it is thought abroad that 'twixt my sheets
  He has done my office. I know not if't be true,
  But I, for mere suspicion in that kind,   365
  Will do as if for surety.[6] He holds me well:
  The better shall my purpose work on him.
  Cassio's a proper[7] man. Let me see now,
  To get his place, and to plume up my will
  In double knavery—how, how? Let's see.   370
  After some time to abuse Othello's ears
  That he is too familiar with his wife;
  He hath a person and a smooth dispose
  To be suspected, framed[8] to make women false.
  The Moor is of a free and open nature,   375
  That thinks men honest that but seem to be so,
  And will as tenderly be led by th' nose
  As asses are.
  I ha't. It is ingendered. Hell and night
  Must bring this monstrous birth to the world's light.   [*Exit.*]   380

2.1

[*Enter below* MONTANO, *Governor of Cyprus; two other* GENTLEMEN
above.]

MONTANO   What from the cape can you discern at sea?
FIRST GENTLEMAN   Nothing at all. It is a high-wrought flood.
  I cannot 'twixt the heaven and the main
  Descry a sail.
MONTANO   Methinks the wind hath spoke aloud at land.   5
  A fuller blast ne'er shook our battlements.
  If it ha' ruffianed so upon the sea,
  What ribs of oak, when mountains melt on them,
  Can hold the mortise?[9] What shall we hear of this?
SECOND GENTLEMAN   A segregation[1] of the Turkish fleet;   10
  For do but stand upon the foaming shore,
  The chidden billow seems to pelt the clouds,
  The wind-shaked surge with high and monstrous mane[2]
  Seems to cast water on the burning Bear

---

5. Dupe. *Gained knowledge:* experience.   6. Certainty.   7. Handsome.   8. Designed. *Dispose:*
manner.   9. Joints.   1. Separation.   2. Ocean.

And quench the guards of th' ever-fixèd Pole.[3]   15
I never did like molestation view
On the enchafèd flood.
MONTANO   If that the Turkish fleet
  Be not ensheltered and embayed, they are drowned.
  It is impossible to bear it out.
          [*Enter a* THIRD GENTLEMAN.]
THIRD GENTLEMAN   News, lads! Our wars are done.   20
  The desperate tempest hath so banged the Turks
  That their designment halts. A noble ship of Venice
  Hath seen a grievous wrack and sufferance[4]
  On most part of their fleet.
MONTANO   How, is this true?   25
THIRD GENTLEMAN   The ship is here put in,
  A Veronessa. Michael Cassio,
  Lieutenant to the warlike Moor Othello,
  Is come on shore; the Moor himself at sea,
  And is in full commission here for Cyprus.   30
MONTANO   I am glad on't; 'tis a worthy governor.
THIRD GENTLEMAN   But this same Cassio, though he speak of comfort
  Touching the Turkish loss, yet he looks sadly,
  And prays the Moor be safe, for they were parted
  With foul and violent tempest.
MONTANO   Pray heavens he be,   35
  For I have served him, and the man commands
  Like a full soldier. Let's to the sea-side, ho!—
  As well to see the vessel that's come in
  As to throw out our eyes for brave Othello,
  Even till we make the main and th' aerial blue   40
  An indistinct regard.[5]
THIRD GENTLEMAN   Come, let's do so,
  For every minute is expectancy
  Of more arrivance.[6]
          [*Enter* CASSIO.]
CASSIO   Thanks, you the valiant of this warlike isle
  That so approve the Moor! O, let the heavens   45
  Give him defence against the elements,
  For I have lost him on a dangerous sea
MONTANO   Is he well shipped?
CASSIO   His barque is stoutly timbered, and his pilot
  Of very expert and approved allowance.[7]   50
  Therefore my hopes, not surfeited to death,
  Stand in bold cure.[8]
VOICES [*within*]   A sail, a sail, a sail!
CASSIO   What noise?
A GENTLEMAN   The town is empty. On the brow o'th' sea
  Stand ranks of people, and they cry 'A sail!'   55

3. North Star. *Bear:* Ursa Minor.   4. Damage.   5. The ocean and the sky become indistinguishable.   6. Arrivals.   7. Experienced reputation.   8. Not dangerously excessive, are likely to be restored.

CASSIO   My hopes do shape him for the governor.
    [*A shot.*]
A GENTLEMAN   They do discharge their shot of courtesy—
  Our friends, at least.
CASSIO   I pray you, sir, go forth,
  And give us truth who 'tis that is arrived.
A GENTLEMAN   I shall.   [*Exit.*]   60
MONTANO   But, good lieutenant, is your general wived?
CASSIO   Most fortunately. He hath achieved a maid
  That paragons description and wild fame
  On that excels the quirks of blazoning pens,
  And in th' essential vesture of creation   65
  Does tire the engineer.[9]
      [*Enter* GENTLEMAN.]
                    How now, who has put in?
A GENTLEMAN   'Tis one Iago, ensign to the general.
CASSIO   He's had most favourable and happy speed.
  Tempests themselves, high seas, and howling winds,
  The guttered rocks and congregated sands,   70
  Traitors ensteeped to enclog the guiltless keel,
  As having sense of beauty do omit
  Their mortal[1] natures, letting go safely by
  The divine Desdemona.
MONTANO   What is she?
CASSIO   She that I spake of, our great captain's captain,   75
  Left in the conduct of the bold Iago,
  Whose footing here anticipates our thoughts
  A sennight's[2] speed. Great Jove, Othello guard,
  And swell his sail with thine own powerful breath,
  That he may bless this bay with his tall ship,   80
  Make love's quick pants in Desdemona's arms,
  Give renewed fire to our extincted spirits,
  And bring all Cyprus comfort.
      [*Enter* DESDEMONA, IAGO, EMILIA, *and* RODERIGO.]
                       O, behold,
  The riches of the ship is come on shore!
  You men of Cyprus, let her have your knees.   85
      [MONTANO *and the* GENTLEMEN *make curtsy to* DESDEMONA.]
  Hail to thee, lady, and the grace of heaven
  Before, behind thee, and on every hand
  Enwheel thee round!
DESDEMONA   I thank you, valiant Cassio.
  What tidings can you tell me of my lord?
CASSIO   He is not yet arrived, nor know I aught   90
  But that he's well and will be shortly here.
DESDEMONA   O, but I fear—how lost you company?

---

9. Her nature wears out the witty poet. *Paragons:* outdoes. *Wild fame:* extravagant praise. *Blazoning pens:*
i.e., those of Petrarchan poets.   1. Deadly. *Guttered:* jagged. *Congregated:* heaped. *Ensteeped:* submerged.   2. Week's. *Footing:* arrival.

CASSIO   The great contention of the sea and skies
   Parted our fellowship.
VOICES [*within*]   A sail, a sail!   95
CASSIO   But hark, a sail.
   [*A shot.*]
A GENTLEMAN   They give their greeting to the citadel.
   This likewise is a friend.
CASSIO   See for the news.   [*Exit* GENTLEMAN.]
   Good ensign, you are welcome. [*Kissing* EMILIA.] Welcome, mistress.
   Let it not gall your patience, good Iago,   100
   That I extend my manners. 'Tis my breeding[3]
   That gives me this bold show of courtesy.
IAGO   Sir, would she give you so much of her lips
   As of her tongue she oft bestows on me,
   You would have enough.   105
DESDEMONA   Alas, she has no speech!
IAGO   In faith, too much.
   I find it still when I ha' leave to sleep.[4]
   Marry, before your ladyship, I grant,
   She puts her tongue a little in her heart,   110
   And chides with thinking.
EMILIA   You ha' little cause to say so.
IAGO   Come on, come on. You are pictures out of door,
   Bells in your parlours; wildcats in your kitchens,
   Saints in your injuries; devils being offended,
   Players in your housewifery, and hussies in your beds.[5]   115
DESDEMONA   O, fie upon thee, slanderer!
IAGO   Nay, it is true, or else I am a Turk.
   You rise to play and go to bed to work.
EMILIA   You shall not write my praise.
IAGO   No, let me not.
DESDEMONA   What wouldst write of me, if thou shouldst praise me? 120
IAGO   O, gentle lady, do not put me to't,
   For I am nothing if not critical.
DESDEMONA   Come on, essay—there's one gone to the harbour?
IAGO   Ay, madam.
DESDEMONA   I am not merry, but I do beguile   125
   The thing I am by seeming otherwise.
   Come, how wouldst thou praise me?
IAGO   I am about it, but indeed my invention
   Comes from my pate as birdlime does from frieze[6]
   It plucks out brains and all. But my muse labours,   130
   And thus she is delivered:
   If she be fair and wise, fairness and wit,
   The one's for use, the other useth it.
DESDEMONA   Well praised! How if she be black[7] and witty?
IAGO   If she be black and thereto have a wit,   135

---

3. Training.   4. She talks even when she gives me permission to sleep.   5. You pretend to do the housekeeping and work hard only in bed. *Pictures:* models. *Injuries:* when you wrong others.   6. Sticky matter from rough cloth.   7. Brunette.

She'll find a white that shall her blackness fit.

DESDEMONA Worse and worse.

EMILIA How if fair and foolish?

IAGO She never yet was foolish that was fair.
For even her folly helped her to an heir.

DESDEMONA These are old fond[8] paradoxes, to make fools laugh i'th' 140
alehouse.
What miserable praise hast thou for her
That's foul and foolish?

IAGO There's none so foul and foolish thereunto,
But does foul pranks which fair and wise ones do.   145

DESDEMONA O heavy ignorance! Thou praisest the worst best. But
what praise couldst thou bestow on a deserving woman indeed—one
that, in the authority of her merit, did justly put on the vouch of very
malice itself?[9]

IAGO She that was ever fair and never proud,   150
Had tongue at will and yet was never loud,
Never lacked gold and yet went never gay,
Fled from her wish, and yet said 'Now I may';
She that, being angered, her revenge being nigh,
Bade her wrong stay and her displeasure fly;   155
She that in wisdom never was so frail
To change the cod's head for the salmon's tail;[1]
She that could think and ne'er disclose her mind,
See suitors following, and not look behind—
She was a wight,[2] if ever such wights were—   160

DESDEMONA To do what?

IAGO To suckle fools, and chronicle small beer.[3]

DESDEMONA O most lame and impotent conclusion! Do not learn of
him, Emilia, though he be thy husband. How say you, Cassio, is he
not a most profane and liberal[4] counsellor?   165

CASSIO He speaks home,[5] madam. You may relish him more in the
soldier than in the scholar.

[CASSIO *and* DESDEMONA *talk apart.*]

IAGO [*aside*] He takes her by the palm. Ay, well said—whisper. With
as little a web as this will I ensnare as great a fly as Cassio. Ay, smile
upon her, do. I will gyve thee in thine own courtship. You say true, 170
'tis so indeed. If such tricks as these strip you out of your lieuten-
antry, it had been better you had not kissed your three fingers so oft,
which now again you are most apt to play the sir in. Very good, well
kissed, an excellent curtsy, 'tis so indeed; yet again your fingers to
your lips? Would they were clyster-pipes[6] for your sake.   175

[*Trumpets within.*]

[*Aloud*] The Moor—I know his trumpet.

CASSIO 'Tis truly so.

DESDEMONA Let's meet him and receive him.

CASSIO Lo where he comes!

8. Foolish. 9. One whose virtue elicits approval even from the malicious. 1. Exchange something valuable for something worthless. 2. Being. 3. Keep household accounts. 4. Free and easy. 5. Speaks frankly. 6. Enema tubes.

[*Enter* OTHELLO *and attendants.*]
OTHELLO [*to* DESDEMONA]   O my fair warrior!
DESDEMONA   My dear Othello.
OTHELLO   It gives me wonder great as my content
   To see you here before me. O my soul's joy,   180
   If after every tempest come such calms,
   May the winds blow till they have wakened death,
   And let the labouring barque climb hills of seas
   Olympus-high, and duck again as low
   As hell's from heaven. If it were now to die   185
   'Twere now to be most happy, for I fear
   My soul hath her content so absolute
   That not another comfort like to this
   Succeeds in unknown fate.
DESDEMONA   The heavens forbid
   But that our loves and comforts should increase   190
   Even as our days do grow.
OTHELLO   Amen to that, sweet powers!
   I cannot speak enough of this content.
   It stops me here, it is too much of joy.
   And this, [*they kiss*] and this, the greatest discords be
   That e'er our hearts shall make.
IAGO [*aside*]   O, you are well tuned now,   195
   But I'll set down the pegs[7] that make this music,
   As honest as I am.
OTHELLO   Come, let us to the castle.
   News, friends: our wars are done, the Turks are drowned.
   How does my old acquaintance of this isle?—
   Honey, you shall be well desired in Cyprus,   200
   I have found great love amongst them. O my sweet,
   I prattle out of fashion, and I dote
   In mine own comforts. I prithee, good Iago,
   Go to the bay and disembark my coffers.
   Bring thou the master to the citadel.   205
   He is a good one, and his worthiness
   Does challenge[8] much respect. Come, Desdemona.—
   Once more, well met at Cyprus!
      [*Exeunt* OTHELLO *and* DESDEMONA *with all but* IAGO *and*
      RODERIGO.]
IAGO [*to an attendant as he goes out*]   Do thou meet me presently at
   the harbour. [*To* RODERIGO] Come hither. If thou beest valiant—as   210
   they say base men being in love have then a nobility in their natures
   more than is native to them—list me. The lieutenant tonight watches
   on the court of guard.[9] First, I must tell thee this: Desdemona is
   directly in love with him.
RODERIGO   With him? Why, 'tis not possible!   215
IAGO   Lay thy finger thus, and let thy soul be instructed. Mark me
   with what violence she first loved the Moor, but for bragging and

---

7. I.e., that control the pitch on string instruments.   8. Require.   9. Guardhouse.

telling her fantastical lies. To love him still for prating?—let not thy discreet heart think it. Her eye must be fed, and what delight shall she have to look on the devil? When the blood is made dull with the 220 act of sport, there should be again to inflame it, and to give satiety a fresh appetite, loveliness in favour, sympathy in years, manners, and beauties, all which the Moor is defective in. Now, for want of these required conveniences,[1] her delicate tenderness will find itself abused, begin to heave the gorge,[2] disrelish and abhor the Moor. 225 Very nature will instruct her in it and compel her to some second choice. Now, sir, this granted—as it is a most pregnant[3] and unforced position—who stands so eminent in the degree of this fortune as Cassio does?—a knave very voluble, no further conscionable than in putting on the mere form of civil and humane seeming for the 230 better compass of his salt and most hidden loose[4] affection. Why, none; why, none—a slipper[5] and subtle knave, a finder of occasion, that has an eye can stamp and counterfeit advantages, though true advantage never present itself, a devilish knave! Besides, the knave is handsome, young, and hath all those requisites in him that folly 235 and green minds look after. A pestilent complete knave, and the woman hath found him already.

RODERIGO I cannot believe that in her. She's full of most blessed condition.

IAGO Blessed fig's end! The wine she drinks is made of grapes. If she 240 had been blessed, she would never have loved the Moor. Blessed pudding! Didst thou not see her paddle with the palm of his hand? Didst not mark that?

RODERIGO Yes, that I did, but that was but courtesy.

IAGO Lechery, by this hand; an index[6] and obscure prologue to the 245 history of lust and foul thoughts. They met so near with their lips that their breaths embraced together. Villainous thoughts, Roderigo! When these mutualities so marshal the way, hard at hand comes the master and main exercise, th'incorporate[7] conclusion. Pish! But, sir, be you ruled by me. I have brought you from Venice. Watch you 250 tonight. For the command, I'll lay't upon you. Cassio knows you not; I'll not be far from you. Do you find some occasion to anger Cassio, either by speaking too loud, or tainting[8] his discipline, or from what other course you please, which the time shall more favourably minister. 255

RODERIGO Well.

IAGO Sir, he's rash and very sudden in choler,[9] and haply may strike at you. Provoke him that he may, for even out of that will I cause these of Cyprus to mutiny, whose qualification shall come into no true taste[1] again but by the displanting of Cassio. So shall you have 260 a shorter journey to your desires by the means I shall then have to prefer them, and the impediment most profitably removed, without the which there were no expectation of our prosperity.

RODERIGO I will do this, if you can bring it to any opportunity.

1. Agreements, points in common. *Favour*: appearance.   2. Vomit.   3. Obvious.   4. Morally easy. *Conscionable*: conscience-bound. *Humane*: polite. *Salt*: lecherous.   5. Slippery.   6. Guide. 7. Sexual.   8. Disparaging.   9. Anger.   1. Pacification will not be brought about.

IAGO   I warrant thee. Meet me by and by at the citadel. I must fetch   265
   his necessaries ashore. Farewell.
RODERIGO   Adieu.   [*Exit.*]
IAGO   That Cassio loves her, I do well believe it.
   That she loves him, 'tis apt and of great credit.
   The Moor—howbe't that I endure him not—   270
   Is of a constant, loving, noble nature,
   And I dare think he'll prove to Desdemona
   A most dear[2] husband. Now I do love her too,
   Not out of absolute lust—though peradventure,[3]
   I stand accountant for as great a sin—   275
   But partly led to diet[4] my revenge
   For that I do suspect the lusty Moor
   Hath leapt into my seat, the thought whereof
   Doth, like a poisonous mineral, gnaw my inwards;
   And nothing can or shall content my soul   280
   Till I am evened with him, wife for wife—
   Or failing so, yet that I put the Moor
   At least into a jealousy so strong
   That judgement cannot cure, which thing to do,
   If this poor trash of Venice whom I trace   285
   For his quick hunting stand the putting on
   I'll have our Michael Cassio on the hip,
   Abuse him to the Moor in the rank garb[5]—
   For I fear Cassio with my nightcap, too—
   Make the Moor thank me, love me, and reward me   290
   For making him egregiously an ass,
   And practising upon[6] his peace and quiet
   Even to madness. 'Tis here, but yet confused
   Knavery's plain face is never seen till used.   [*Exit.*]

2.2

[*Enter Othello's* HERALD *reading a proclamation.*]
HERALD   It is Othello's pleasure—our noble and valiant general—
   that, upon certain tidings now arrived importing the mere perdition[7]
   of the Turkish fleet, every man put himself into triumph: some to
   dance, some to make bonfires, each man to what sport and revels
   his addiction[8] leads him; for besides these beneficial news, it is the   5
   celebration of his nuptial. So much was his pleasure should be proclaimed. All offices[9] are open, and there is full liberty of feasting
   from this present hour of five till the bell have told eleven. Heaven
   bless the isle of Cyprus and our noble general, Othello!   [*Exit.*]

2.3

[*Enter* OTHELLO, DESDEMONA, CASSIO, *and attendants.*]
OTHELLO   Good Michael, look you to the guard tonight.

---

2. Expensive.   3. By chance. *Absolute:* pure.   4. Feed.   5. Style.   6. Scheming to destroy, in
Machiavellian fashion.   7. Absolute destruction.   8. Inclination.   9. Kitchens.

Let's teach ourselves that honourable stop
Not to outsport discretion.

CASSIO   Iago hath direction what to do,
But notwithstanding, with my personal eye   5
Will I look to't.

OTHELLO   Iago is most honest.
Michael, good night. Tomorrow with your earliest
Let me have speech with you. [*To* DESDEMONA] Come, my dear love,
The purchase made, the fruits are to ensue.
That profit's yet to come 'tween me and you.   10
[*To* CASSIO] Good night.

          [*Exeunt* OTHELLO, DESDEMONA *and attendants.—Enter* IAGO.]

CASSIO   Welcome, Iago. We must to the watch.

IAGO   Not this hour, lieutenant; 'tis not yet ten o'th' clock. Our general
cast[1] us thus early for the love of his Desdemona, who let us not
therefore blame. He hath not yet made wanton the night with her,   15
and she is sport for Jove.

CASSIO   She's a most exquisite lady.

IAGO   And I'll warrant her full of game.

CASSIO   Indeed, she's a most fresh and delicate creature.

IAGO   What an eye she has! Methinks it sounds a parley to provoca-   20
tion.

CASSIO   An inviting eye, and yet, methinks, right modest.

IAGO   And when she speaks, is it not an alarum[2] to love?

CASSIO   She is indeed perfection.

IAGO   Well, happiness to their sheets. Come, lieutenant. I have a   25
stoup[3] of wine, and here without are a brace of Cyprus gallants that
would fain have a measure to the health of black Othello.

CASSIO   Not tonight, good Iago. I have very poor and unhappy brains
for drinking. I could well wish courtesy would invent some other
custom of entertainment.   30

IAGO   O, they are our friends! But one cup. I'll drink for you.

CASSIO   I ha' drunk but one cup tonight, and that was craftily qualified,[4] too, and behold what innovation it makes here! I am infortu-
nate in the infirmity, and dare not task my weakness with any more.

IAGO   What, man, 'tis a night of revels, the gallants desire it!   35

CASSIO   Where are they?

IAGO   Here at the door. I pray you call them in.

CASSIO   I'll do't, but it dislikes me.   [*Exit.*]

IAGO   If I can fasten but one cup upon him,
With that which he hath drunk tonight already   40
He'll be as full of quarrel and offence
As my young mistress' dog. Now my sick fool Roderigo,
Whom love hath turned almost the wrong side out,
To Desdemona hath tonight caroused
Potations pottle-deep,[5] and he's to watch,   45
Three else[6] of Cyprus—noble swelling spirits

---

1. Dismissed.   **2.** Military call to action.   **3.** Two-quart tankard.   **4.** Watered down.   **5.** To the
bottom.   **6.** Others.

That hold their honours in a wary distance,[7]
The very elements of this warlike isle—
Have I tonight flustered with flowing cups,
And they watch too. Now 'mongst this flock of drunkards   50
Am I to put our Cassio in some action
That may offend the isle.

    [*Enter* MONTANA, CASSIO, GENTLEMEN, *and servants with wine.*]
                            But here they come.
If consequence do but approve my dream,
My boat sails freely both with wind and stream.

CASSIO   Fore God, they have given me a rouse[8] already.   55
MONTANO   God faith, a little one; not past a pint,
  As I am a soldier.
IAGO   Some wine, ho!
    [*Sings*]
            And let me the cannikin[9] clink, clink,
            And let me the cannikin clink.
               A soldier's a man,   60
               O, man' life's but a span,
             Why then, let a soldier drink.
  Some wine, boys!
CASSIO   Fore God, an excellent song.
IAGO   I learned it in England, where indeed they are most potent in   65
  potting. Your Dane, your German, and your swag-bellied[1] Hollan-
  der—drink, ho!—are nothing to your English.
CASSIO   Is your Englishman so exquisite in his drinking?
IAGO   Why, he drinks you with facility your Dane dead drunk. He
  sweats not to overthrow your Almain. He gives your Hollander a   70
  vomit ere the next pottle can be filled.
CASSIO   To the health of our general!
MONTANO   I am for it, lieutenant, and I'll do you justice.
IAGO   O sweet England!
    [*Sings*]
            King Stephen was and a worthy peer,   75
              His breeches cost him but a crown;
            He held them sixpence all too dear,
              With that he called the tailor lown.[2]
            He was a wight of high renown,
              And thou art but of low degree   80
            'Tis pride that pulls the country down,
              Then take thy auld cloak about thee.
  Some wine, ho!
CASSIO   Fore God, this is a more exquisite song than the other.
IAGO   Will you hear't again?   85
CASSIO   No, for I hold him to be unworthy of his place that does those
  things. Well, God's above all, and there be souls must be saved, and
  there be souls must not be saved.

---

7. Are jealous of their honor.   8. Drink.   9. Drinking vessel.   1. Big-bellied.   2. Lout, oaf.

IAGO   It's true, good lieutenant.

CASSIO   For mine own part—no offence to the general, nor any man   90
of quality—I hope to be saved.

IAGO   And so do I too, lieutenant.

CASSIO   Ay, but, by your leave, not before me. The lieutenant is to be
saved before the ensign. Let's ha' no more of this. Let's to our affairs.
God forgive us our sins. Gentlemen, let's look to our business. Do   95
not think, gentlemen, I am drunk. This is my ensign, this is my right
hand, and this is my left. I am not drunk now. I can stand well
enough, and I speak well enough.

GENTLEMEN   Excellent well.

CASSIO   Why, very well then. You must not think then that I am   100
drunk.   [Exit.]

MONTANO   To th' platform, masters. Come, let's set the watch.
                                              [Exeunt GENTLEMEN.]

IAGO   You see this fellow that is gone before—
He's a soldier fit to stand by Caesar
And give direction; and do but see his vice.   105
'Tis to his virtue a just equinox,[3]
The one as long as th'other. 'Tis pity of him.
I fear the trust Othello puts him in,
On some odd time of his infirmity,
Will shake this island.

MONTANO   But is he often thus?   110

IAGO   'Tis evermore his prologue to his sleep
He'll watch the horologe[4] a double set
If drink rock not his cradle.

MONTANO   It were well
The general were put in mind of it.
Perhaps he sees it not, or his good nature   115
Prizes the virtue that appears in Cassio
And looks not on his evils. Is not this true?
            [Enter RODERIGO.]

IAGO [aside]   How now, Roderigo!
I pray you after the lieutenant, go.   [Exit RODERIGO.]

MONTANO   And 'tis great pity that the noble Moor   120
Should hazard such a place as his own second
With one of an engraffed[5] infirmity.
It were an honest action to say so
To the Moor.

IAGO   Not I, for this fair island!
I do love Cassio well, and would do much   125
To cure him of this evil.

VOICES [within]   Help, help!

IAGO   But hark, what noise?
            [Enter CASSIO, driving in RIDERIGO.]

CASSIO   'Swounds, you rogue, you rascal!

3. Precise balance.   4. Clock.   5. Rooted.

MONTANO   What's the matter, lieutenant?

CASSIO   A knave teach me my duty?—I'll beat the knave into a   130
twiggen[6] bottle.

RODERIGO   Beat me?

CASSIO   Dost thou prate, rogue?

MONTANO   Nay, good lieutenant, I pray you, sir, hold your hand.

CASSIO   Let me go, sir, or I'll knock you o'er the mazard.[7]   135

MONTANO   Come, come, you're drunk.

CASSIO   Drunk?

     [*They fight.*]

IAGO [*to* RODERIGO]   Away, I say. Go out and cry a mutiny

                                [*Exit* RODERIGO.]

Nay, good lieutenant. God's will, gentlemen!

Help, ho! Lieutenant! Sir! Montano! Sir!   140

Help, masters. Here's a goodly watch indeed.

     [*A bell rung.*]

Who's that which rings the bell? Diablo,[8] ho!

The town will rise. God's will, lieutenant, hold.

You'll be ashamed for ever.

     [*Enter* OTHELLO *and attendants, with weapons.*]

OTHELLO   What is the matter here?

MONTANO   'Swounds, I bleed still. I am hurt to th' death. [*Attacking*

     CASSIO] He dies.   145

OTHELLO   Hold, for your lives!

IAGO   Hold, ho, lieutenant, sir, Montano, gentlemen!

Have you forgot all place of sense and duty?

Hold, the general speaks to you. Hold, hold, for shame.

OTHELLO   Why, how now, ho? From whence ariseth this?   150

Are we turned Turks, and to ourselves do that

Which heaven hath forbid the Ottomites?

For Christian shame, put by this barbarous brawl.

He that stirs next to carve for his own rage

Holds his soul light. He dies upon his motion.   155

Silence that dreadful bell—it frights the isle

From her propriety.[9]

     [*Bell stops.*]

                 What is the matter, masters?

Honest Iago, that looks dead with grieving,

Speak. Who began this? On thy love I charge thee.

IAGO   I do not know. Friends all but now, even now,   160

In quarter[1] and in terms like bride and groom,

Devesting them for bed; and then but now—

As if some planet had unwitted men—

Swords out, and tilting one at others' breasts

In opposition bloody. I cannot speak   165

Any beginning to this peevish odds,[2]

And would in action glorious I had lost

---

6. Wicker-covered.   7. Head (image transferred, figuratively, from a drinking cup).   8. The Devil.
9. Order.   1. On duty.   2. Argument.

Those legs that brought me to a part of it.
OTHELLO   How comes it, Michael, you are thus forgot?
CASSIO   I pray you pardon me. I cannot speak.   170
OTHELLO   Worthy Montano, you were wont be civil.
  The gravity and stillness of your youth
  The world hath noted, and your name is great
  In mouths of wisest censure. What's the matter,
  That you unlace your reputation thus,   175
  And spend your rich opinion³ for the name
  Of a night-brawler? Give me answer to it.
MONTANO   Worthy Othello, I am hurt to danger.
  Your officer Iago can inform you,
  While I spare speech—which something now offends me—   180
  Of all that I do know; nor know I aught
  By me that's said or done amiss this night,
  Unless self-charity be sometimes a vice,
  And to defend ourselves it be a sin
  When violence assails us.
OTHELLO   Now, by heaven,   185
  My blood begins my safer guides to rule,
  And passion, having my best judgment collied,⁴
  Essays to lead the way. 'Swounds, if I stir,
  Or do but lift this arm, the best of you
  Shall sink in my rebuke. Give me to know   190
  How this foul rout began, who set it on,
  And he that is approved in this offence,
  Though he had twinned with me, both at a birth,
  Shall lose me. What, in a town of war
  Yet wild, the people's hearts brimful of fear,   195
  To manage private and domestic quarrel
  In night, and on the court and guard of safety!
  'Tis monstrous. Iago, who began't?
MONTANO [to IAGO]   If partially affined⁵ or leagued in office
  Thou dost deliver more or less than truth,   200
  Thou art no soldier.
IAGO   Touch me not so near.
  I had rather ha' this tongue cut from my mouth
  Than it should do offence to Michael Cassio.
  Yet I persuade myself to speak the truth
  Shall nothing wrong him. This it is, general.   205
  Montano and myself being in speech,
  There comes a fellow crying out for help,
  And Cassio following him with determined sword
  To execute upon him. Sir, this gentleman
  Steps in to Cassio, and entreats his pause.   210
  Myself the crying fellow did pursue,
  Lest by his clamour, as it so fell out,
  The town might fall in fright. He, swift, of foot,

---

3. Reputation. *Censure:* judgment. *Unlace:* undo.   **4.** Darkened.   **5.** Kindred.

Outran my purpose, and I returned, the rather
For that I heard the clink and fall of swords   215
And Cassio high in oath, which till tonight
I ne'er might say before. When I came back—
For this was brief—I found them close together
At blow and thrust, even as again they were
When you yourself did part them.   220
More of this matter cannot I report,
But men are men. The best sometimes forget.
Though Cassio did some little wrong to him,
As men in rage strike those that wish them best,
Yet surely Cassio, I believe, received   225
From him that fled some strange indignity
Which patience could not pass.[6]
OTHELLO   I know, Iago,
Thy honesty and love doth mince this matter,
Making it light to Cassio. Cassio, I love thee,
But never more be officer of mine.   230
    [Enter DESDEMONA, attended.]
Look if my gentle love be not raised up.
I'll make thee an example.,
DESDEMONA   What is the matter, dear?
OTHELLO   All's well now, sweeting.
Come away to bed. [To MONTANO] Sir, for your hurts   235
Myself will be your surgeon. [To attendants] Lead him off.
        [Exeunt attendants with MONTANO.]
Iago, look with care about the town,
And silence those whom this vile brawl distracted.
Come, Desdemona. 'Tis the soldier's life
To have their balmy slumbers waked with strife.   240
      [Exeunt OTHELLO the Moor, DESDEMONA, and attendants.]
IAGO   What, are you hurt, lieutenant?
CASSIO   Ay, past all surgery
IAGO   Marry, God forbid.
CASSIO   Reputation, reputation, reputation—O, I ha' lost my reputa-
tion, I ha' lost the immortal part of myself, and what remains is   245
bestial! My reputation, Iago, my reputation.
IAGO   As I am an honest man, I thought you had received some bodily
wound. There is more sense in that than in reputation. Reputation
is an idle and most false imposition, oft got without merit and lost
without deserving. You have lost no reputation at all unless you   250
repute yourself such a loser. What, man, there are more ways to
recover the general again. You are but now cast in his mood[7]—a
punishment more in policy[8] than in malice, even so as one would
beat his offenceless dog to affright an imperious lion. Sue to him
again, and he's yours.   255
CASSIO   I will rather sue to be despised than to deceive so good a

6. Endure.   7. Fired in his anger.   8. Political expedience.

commander with so slight, so drunken, and so indiscreet an officer. Drunk, and speak parrot, and squabble? Swagger, swear, and discourse fustian[9] with one's own shadow? O thou invisible spirit of wine, if thou hast no name to be known by, let us call thee devil.　260

IAGO　What was he that you followed with your sword? What had he done to you?

CASSIO　I know not.

IAGO　Is't possible?

CASSIO　I remember a mass of things, but nothing distinctly; a quarrel,　265 but nothing wherefore. O God, that men should put an enemy in their mouths to steal away their brains! That we should with joy, pleasance, revel, and applause transform ourselves into beasts!

IAGO　Why, but you are now well enough. How came you thus recovered?　270

CASSIO　It hath pleased the devil drunkenness to give place to the devil wrath. One unperfectness shows me another, to make me frankly despise myself.

IAGO　Come, you are too severe a moraller. As the time, the place, and the condition of this country stands, I could heartily wish this　275 had not befallen; but since it is as it is, mend it for your own good.

CASSIO　I will ask him for my place again. He shall tell me I am a drunkard. Had I as many mouths as Hydra,[1] such an answer would stop them all. To be now a sensible man, by and by a fool, and presently a beast! O, strange! Every inordinate cup is unblessed, and　280 the ingredient is a devil.

IAGO　Come, come. Good wine is a good familiar creature, if it be well used. Exclaim no more against it. And, good lieutenant, I think you think I love you.

CASSIO　I have well approved it, sir—I drunk?　285

IAGO　You or any man living may be drunk at a time, man. I'll tell you what you shall do. Our general's wife is now the general. I may say so in this respect, for that he hath devoted and given up himself to the contemplation, mark, and denotement[2] of her parts and graces. Confess yourself freely to her. Importune her help to put you in your　290 place again. She is of so free, so kind, so apt, so blessed a disposition, she holds it a vice in her goodness not to do more than she is requested. This broken joint between you and her husband entreat her to splinter,[3] and, my fortunes against any lay[4] worth naming, this crack of your love shall grow stronger than it was before.　295

CASSIO　You advise me well.

IAGO　I protest, in the sincerity of love and honest kindness.

CASSIO　I think it freely, and betimes in the morning I will beseech the virtuous Desdemona to undertake for me. I am desperate of my fortunes if they check me here.　300

IAGO　You are in the right. Good night, lieutenant. I must to the watch.

CASSIO　Good night, honest Iago.　　　　　　　　　　　　　　　[*Exit.*]

---

9. Coarsely. *Speak parrot*: mimic.　1. Mythical many-headed beast, capable of regenerating severed heads.　2. Observation.　3. Splint.　4. Bet.

IAGO   And what's he then that says I play the villain,
    When this advice is free I give, and honest,
    Probal[5] to thinking, and indeed the course   305
    To win the Moor again? For 'tis most easy
    Th'inclining Desdemona to subdue
    In any honest suit. She's framed as fruitful
    As the free elements,[6] and then for her
    To win the Moor, were't to renounce his baptism,   310
    All seals and symbols of redeemèd sin,
    His soul is so enfettered to her love
    That she may make, unmake, do what she list,
    Even as her appetite shall play the god
    With his weak function.[7] How am I then a villain,   315
    To counsel Cassio to this parallel course
    Directly to his good? Divinity of hell:
    When devils will the blackest sins put on,
    They do suggest at first with heavenly shows,
    As I do now; for whiles this honest fool   320
    Plies Desdemona to repair his fortune,
    And she for him pleads strongly to the Moor,
    I'll pour this pestilence into his ear:
    That she repeals him[8] for her body's lust,
    And by how much she strives to do him good   325
    She shall undo her credit with the Moor.
    So will I turn her virtue into pitch,
    And out of her own goodness make the net
    That shall enmesh them all.
          [*Enter* RODERIGO.]
                        How now, Roderigo?

RODERIGO   I do follow here in the chase, not like a hound that hunts,   330
but one that fills up the cry.[9] My money is almost spent, I ha' been
tonight exceedingly well cudgelled, and I think theissue will be I shall
have so much experience for my pains: and so, with no money at all
and a little more wit, return again to Venice.

IAGO   How poor are they that ha' not patience!   335
    What wound did ever heal but by degrees?
    Thou know'st we work by wit and not by witchcraft,
    And wit depends on dilatory time.
    Does't not go well? Cassio hath beaten thee,
    And thou by that small hurt has cashiered Cassio.   340
    Though other things grow fair against the sun,
    Yet fruits that blossom first will first be ripe.
    Content thyself a while. By the mass, 'tis morning.
    Pleasure and action make the hours seem short.
    Retire thee. Go where thou art billeted.   345
    Away, I say. Thou shalt know more hereafter.
    Nay, get thee gone.   [*Exit* RODERIGO.]

---

5. Logical, likely.   6. Unconstrained nature. *Fruitful:* generous.   7. Easily moved passion. *Appetite:* sexual desire.   8. Calls for his return.   9. One of the baying hounds.

Two things are to be done.
My wife must move for[1] Cassio to her mistress.
I'll set her on.
Myself a while to draw the Moor apart.   350
And bring him jump[2] when he may Cassio find
Soliciting his wife. Ay, that's the way.
Dull not device by coldness and delay.   [*Exit.*]

3.1

[*Enter* CASSIO *with* MUSICIANS.]

CASSIO   Masters, play here—I will content your pains[3]—
        Something that's brief, and bid 'Good morrow, general'.
        [*Music. Enter* CLOWN.]
CLOWN   Why, masters, ha' your instruments been in Naples,[4] that
        they speak i'th' nose thus?
MUSICIAN   How, sir, how?   5
CLOWN   Are these, I pray you, wind instruments?[5]
MUSICIAN   Ay, marry are they, sir.
CLOWN   O, thereby hangs a tail.
MUSICIAN   Whereby hangs a tale, sir?
CLOWN   Marry, sir, by many a wind instrument that I know. But mas-   10
        ters, here's money for you, and the general so likes your music that
        he desires you, for love's sake, to make no more noise with it.
MUSICIAN   Well, sir, we will not.
CLOWN   If you have any music that may not be heard, to't again; but,
        as they say, to hear music the general does not greatly care.   15
MUSICIAN   We ha' none such, sir.
CLOWN   Then put up your pipes in your bag, for I'll away. Go, vanish
        into air, away.   [*Exeunt* MUSICIANS.]
CASSIO   Dost thou hear, my honest friend?
CLOWN   No, I hear not your honest friend, I hear you.   20
CASSIO   Prithee, keep up thy quillets.[6] There's a poor piece of gold for
        thee. If the gentlewoman that attends the general's wife be stirring,
        tell her there's one Cassio entreats her a little favour of speech. Wilt
        thou do this?
CLOWN   She is stirring, sir. If she will stir hither, I shall seem to notify   25
        unto her.
CASSIO   Do, good my friend.   [*Exit* CLOWN.]
        [*Enter* IAGO.]
                            In happy time, Iago.
IAGO   You ha' not been abed, then.
CASSIO   Why, no. The day had broke
        Before we parted. I ha' made bold, Iago,
        To send in to your wife. My suit to her   30
        Is that she will to virtuous Desdemona
        Procure me some access.

1. Side with.   2. Exactly.   3. Reward your efforts.   4. Nasal wind instruments; bodily parts
with syphilis contracted in Naples.   5. With the reference to tail/tale below; a pun on flatulence.
6. Quibbles, puns.

IAGO I'll send her to you presently,
  And I'll devise a mean to draw the Moor
  Out of the way, that your converse and business   35
  May be more free.
CASSIO   I humbly thank you for't.   [*Exit* IAGO.]
  I never knew a Florentine[7] more kind and honest.
      [*Enter* EMILIA.]
EMILIA Good morrow, good lieutenant. I am sorry
  For your displeasure, but all will sure be well.
  The general and his wife are talking of it,   40
  And she speaks for you stoutly. The Moor replies
  That he you hurt is of great fame in Cyprus,
  And great affinity,[8] and that in wholesome wisdom
  He might not but refuse you. But he protests he loves you,
  And needs no other suitor but his likings   45
  To take the saf'st occasion by the front
  To bring you in again.
CASSIO   Yet I beseech you,
  If you think fit, or that it may be done,
  Give me advantage of some brief discourse
  With Desdemon alone.
EMILIA   Pray you come in.   50
  I will bestow you where you shall have time
  To speak your bosom[9] freely.
CASSIO   I am much bound to you.
                                    [*Exeunt.*]

                        3.2

      [*Enter* OTHELLO, IAGO, *and* GENTLEMEN.]
OTHELLO These letters give, Iago, to the pilot,
  And by him do my duties to the senate.
  That done, I will be walking on the works.
  Repair there to me.
IAGO   Well, my good lord, I'll do't.   [*Exit.*]
OTHELLO This fortification, gentlemen—shall we see't?   5
A GENTLEMAN We'll wait upon your lordship.   [*Exeunt.*]

                        3.3

      [*Enter* DESDEMONA, CASSIO *and* EMILIA.]
DESDEMONA Be thou assured, good Cassio, I will do
  All my abilities in they behalf.
EMILIA Good madam, do. I warrant it grieves my husband
  As if the cause were his.
DESDEMONA O, that's an honest fellow. Do not doubt, Cassio,   5
  But I will have my lord and you again
  As friendly as you were.
CASSIO   Bounteous madam,

---

7. One from Cassio's own city-state.   8. Kinship.   9. Mind.

Whatever shall become of Michael Cassio
He's never anything but your true servant.

DESDEMONA   I know't. I thank you. You do love my lord.   10
You have known him long, and be you well assured
He shall in strangeness stand no farther off
Than in a politic distance.[1]

CASSIO   Ay, but, lady,
That policy may either last so long,
Or feed upon such nice[2] and wat'rish diet,   15
Or breed itself so out of circumstance,
That, I being absent and my place supplied,[3]
My general will forget my love and service.

DESDEMONA   Do not doubt[4] that. Before Emilia here
I give thee warrant of thy place. Assure thee,   20
If I do vow a friendship I'll perform it
To the last article. My lord shall never rest.
I'll watch him tame,[5] and talk him out of patience.
His bed shall seem a school, his board a shrift.[6]
I'll intermingle everything he does   25
With Cassio's suit. Therefore be merry, Cassio,
For thy solicitor shall rather die
Than give they cause away.

[*Enter* OTHELLO *and* IAGO.]

EMILIA   Madam, here comes my lord.

CASSIO   Madam, I'll take my leave.

DESDEMONA   Why, stay, and hear me speak.

CASSIO   Madam, not now. I am very ill at ease,   30
Unfit for mine own purposes.

DESDEMONA   Well, do your discretion.   [*Exit* CASSIO.]

IAGO   Ha! I like not that.

OTHELLO   What dost thou say?

IAGO   Nothing, my lord. Or if, I know not what.   35

OTHELLO   Was not that Cassio parted from my wife?

IAGO   Cassio, my lord? No, sure, I cannot think it,
That he would steal away so guilty-like
Seeing your coming.

OTHELLO   I do believe 'twas he.   40

DESDEMONA   How now, my lord?
I have been talking with a suitor here,
A man that languishes in your displeasure.

OTHELLO   Who is't you mean?

DESDEMONA   Why, your lieutenant, Cassio; good my lord,   45
If I have any grace or power to move you,
His present reconciliation take;
For if he be not one that truly loves you,
That errs in ignorance and not in cunning,
I have no judgement in an honest face.   50

---

1. He shall seem only as distant as he must for political reasons.   2. Finicky.   3. Filled.   4. Have
doubts about.   5. Make him docile by keeping him awake.   6. Confessional.

I prithee call him back.

OTHELLO   Went he hence now?

DESDEMONA   Yes, faith, so humbled
That he hath left part of his grief with me
To suffer with him. Good love, call him back.   55

OTHELLO   Not now, sweet Desdemon. Some other time.

DESDEMONA   But shall't be shortly?

OTHELLO   The sooner, sweet, for you.

DESDEMONA   Shall't be tonight at supper?

OTHELLO   No, not tonight.

DESDEMONA   Tomorrow dinner, then?

OTHELLO   I shall not dine at home.
I meet the captains at the citadel.   60

DESDEMONA   Why then, tomorrow night, or Tuesday morn,
On Tuesday noon, or night, on Wednesday morn—
I prithee name the time, but let it not
Exceed three days. In faith, he's penitent,
And yet his trespass, in our common reason—   65
Save that, they say, the wars must make example
Out of her best—is not almost a fault
T'incur a private check.[7] When shall he come?
Tell me, Othello. I wonder in my soul
What you would ask me that I should deny,   70
Or stand so mamm'ring[8] on? What, Michael Cassio,
That came a-wooing with you, and so many a time
When I have spoke of you dispraisingly
Hath ta'en your part—to have so much to-do
To bring him in? By'r Lady, I could do much.   75

OTHELLO   Prithee, no more. Let him come when he will.
I will deny thee nothing.

DESDEMONA   Why, this is not a boon.
'Tis as I should entreat you wear your gloves,
Or feed on nourishing dishes, or keep you warm,
Or sue to you to do a peculiar profit   80
To your own person. Nay, when I have a suit
Wherein I mean to touch your love indeed,
It shall be full of poise[9] and difficult weight,
And fearful to be granted.

OTHELLO   I will deny thee nothing,
Whereon I do beseech thee grant me this: 85
To leave me but a little to myself.

DESDEMONA   Shall I deny you? No. Farewell, my lord.

OTHELLO   Farewell, my Desdemona. I'll come to thee straight.

DESDEMONA   Emilia, come. [To OTHELLO] Be as your fancies teach
you. Whate'er you be, I am obedient.   90

                        [Exeunt DESDEMONA and EMILIA.]

OTHELLO   Excellent wretch! Perdition catch my soul
But I do love thee, and when I love thee not,

7. Reprimand.   8. Hesitating.   9. Weight.

Chaos is come again.

IAGO   My noble lord.

OTHELLO   What dost thou say, Iago?   95

IAGO   Did Michael Cassio, when you wooed my lady,
    Know of your love?

OTHELLO   He did, from first to last. Why dost thou ask?

IAGO   But for a satisfaction of my thought.
    No further harm

OTHELLO   Why of thy thought, Iago?   100

IAGO   I did not think he had been acquainted with her.

OTHELLO   O yes, and went between us very oft.

IAGO   Indeed?

OTHELLO   Indeed? Ay, indeed. Discern'st thou aught in that?
    Is he not honest?   105

IAGO   Honest, my lord?

OTHELLO   Honest? Ay, honest.

IAGO   My lord, for aught I know.

OTHELLO   What dost thou think?

IAGO   Think, my lord?

OTHELLO   'Think, my lord?' By heaven, thou echo'st me   110
    As if there were some monster in thy thought
    Too hideous to be shown! Thou dost mean something.
    I heard thee say even now thou liked'st not that,
    When Cassio left my wife. What didst not like?
    And when I told thee he was of my counsel   115
    In my whole course of wooing, thou cried'st 'Indeed?'
    And didst contract and purse thy brow together
    As if thou then hadst shut up in thy brain
    Some horrible conceit.[1] If thou dost love me,
    Show me thy thought.   120

IAGO   My lord, you know I love you.

OTHELLO   I think thou dost,
    And for I know thou'rt full of love and honesty,
    And weigh'st thy words before thou giv'st them breath,
    Therefore these stops[2] of thine fright me the more;   125
    For such things in a false disloyal knave
    Are tricks of custom, but in a man that's just,
    They're close dilations,[3] working from the heart
    That passion cannot rule.

IAGO   For Michael Cassio.
    I dare be sworn I think that he is honest.   130

OTHELLO   I think so too.

IAGO   Men should be what they seem,
    Or those that be not, would they might seem none.

OTHELLO   Certain, men should be what they seem.

IAGO   Why then, I think Cassio's an honest man.

OTHELLO   Nay, yet there's more in this.   135
    I prithee speak to me as to thy thinkings,

1. Idea.   2. Hesitations and interruptions   3. Unfoldings. *Of custom:* habitual.

As thou dost ruminate, and give thy worst of thoughts
The worst of words.

IAGO   Good my lord, pardon me.
   Though I am bound to every act of duty,
   I am not bound to that all slaves are free to.   140
   Utter my thoughts? Why, say they are vile and false,
   As where's that palace whereinto foul things
   Sometimes intrude not? Who has that breast so pure
   But some uncleanly apprehensions
   Keep leets and law-days,[4] and in sessions sit   145
   With meditations lawful?

OTHELLO   Thou dost conspire against thy friend, Iago,
   If thou but think'st him wronged and mak'st his ear
   A stranger to thy thoughts.

IAGO   I do beseech you,
   Though I perchance am vicious in my guess—   150
   As I confess it is my nature's plague
   To spy into abuses, and oft my jealousy
   Shapes faults that are not—that your wisdom then,
   From one that so imperfectly conceits,
   Would take no notice nor build yourself a trouble   155
   Out of his scattering and unsure observance.
   It were not for your quiet nor your good,
   Nor for my manhood, honesty, and wisdom,
   To let you know my thoughts.

OTHELLO   What dost thou mean?

IAGO   Good name in man and woman, dear my lord,   160
   Is the immediate jewel of their souls.
   Who steals my purse steals trash; 'tis something, nothing;
   'Twas mine, 'tis his, and has been slave to thousands.
   But he that filches from me my good name
   Robs me of that which not enriches him   165
   And makes me poor indeed.

OTHELLO   By heaven, I'll know thy thoughts.

IAGO   You cannot, if my heart were in your hand;
   Nor shall not whilst 'tis in my custody.

OTHELLO   Ha!

IAGO   O, beware, my lord, of jealousy.
   It is the green-eyed monster which doth mock   170
   The meat it feeds on. That cuckold lives in bliss
   Who, certain of his fate, loves not his wronger.
   But O, what damnèd minutes tells he o'er
   Who dotes yet doubts, suspects yet fondly[5] loves!

OTHELLO   O misery!   175

IAGO   Poor and content is rich, and rich enough,
   But riches fineless[6] is as poor as winter
   To him that ever fears he shall be poor.

---

4. Meetings of local courts.   5. Foolishly. *Tells:* counts.   6. Endless.

Good God the souls of all my tribe defend
From jealousy!
OTHELLO   Why, why is this?   180
  Think'st thou I'd make a life of jealousy,
  To follow still the changes of the moon
  With fresh suspicions? No, to be once in doubt
  Is once to be resolved. Exchange me for a goat
  When I shall turn the business of my soul   185
  To such exsufflicate and blowed[7] surmises
  Matching thy inference. 'Tis not to make me jealous
  To say my wife is fair, feeds well, loves company,
  Is free of speech, sings, plays, and dances well.
  Where virtue is, these are more virtuous,   190
  Nor from mine own weak merits will I draw
  The smallest fear or doubt of her revolt,
  For she had eyes and chose me. No, Iago,
  I'll see before I doubt; when I doubt, prove;
  And on the proof, there is no more but this: 195
  Away at once with love or jealousy.
IAGO   I am glad of this, for now I shall have reason
  To show the love and duty that I bear you
  With franker spirit. Therefore, as I am bound,
  Receive it from me. I speak not yet of proof.   200
  Look to your wife. Observe her well with Cassio.
  Wear your eyes thus: not jealous, nor secure.
  I would not have your free and noble nature
  Out of self-bounty[8] be abused. Look to't.
  I know our country disposition well.   205
  In Venice they do let God see the pranks
  They dare not show their husbands; their best conscience
  Is not to leave't undone, but keep't unknown.
OTHELLO   Dost thou say so?
IAGO   She did deceive her father, marrying you,   210
  And when she seemed to shake and fear your looks
  She loved them most.
OTHELLO   And so she did.
IAGO   Why, go to, then.
  She that so young could give out such a seeming,
  To seel her father's eyes up close as oak,[9]
  He thought 'twas witchcraft! But I am much to blame.   215
  I humbly do beseech you of your pardon
  For too much loving you.
OTHELLO   I am bound to thee for ever.
IAGO   I see this hath a little dashed your spirits.
OTHELLO   Not a jot, not a jot.
IAGO   I'faith, I fear it has.
  I hope you will consider what is spoke   220

7. Inflated and overblown.   8. Characteristic generosity.   9. Stitch up tightly.

Comes from my love. But I do see you're moved.
I am to pray you not to strain my speech
To grosser issues, nor to larger reach[1]
Than to suspicion.

OTHELLO   I will not.   225

IAGO   Should you do so, my lord,
My speech should fall into such vile success
Which my thoughts aimed not. Cassio's my worthy friend.
My lord, I see you're moved.

OTHELLO   No, not much moved.
I do not think but Desdemona's honest.   230

IAGO   Long live she so, and long live you to think so!

OTHELLO   And yet how nature, erring from itself—

IAGO   Ay, there's the point; as, to be bold with you,
Not to affect many proposèd matches
Of her own clime, complexion, and degree,[2]   235
Whereto we see in all things nature tends.
Foh, one may smell in such a will most rank,
Foul disproportions, thoughts unnatural!
But pardon me. I do not in position
Distinctly[3] speak of her, though I may fear   240
Her will, recoiling to her better judgement,
May fall to match you with her country forms
And happily[4] repent.

OTHELLO   Farewell, farewell.
If more thou dost perceive, let me know more.
Set on thy wife to observe. Leave me, Iago.   245

IAGO [going]   My lord, I take my leave.

OTHELLO   Why did I marry? This honest creature doubtless
Sees and knows more, much more, than he unfolds.

IAGO [returning]   My lord, I would I might entreat your honour
To scan this thing no farther. Leave it to time.   250
Although 'tis fit that Cassio have his place—
For sure he fills it up with great ability—
Yet, if you please to hold him off a while,
You shall by that perceive him and his means.
Note if your lady strain his entertainment[5]   255
With any strong or vehement importunity.
Much will be seen in that. In the mean time,
Let me be thought too busy in my fears—
As worthy cause I have to fear I am—
And hold her free, I do beseech your honour.   260

OTHELLO   Fear not my government.[6]

IAGO   I once more take my leave.

                                        [Exit.]

OTHELLO   This fellow's of exceeding honesty,
And knows all qualities with a learned spirit

---

1. Extent. *Strain*: stretch.   2. Rank.   3. Directly. *Position*: argumentative posture.   4. By chance.
Fall to match: happen to coincide with. *Country forms*: the manner of her countrywomen, with a pun on
female genitals.   5. Push for his reinstatement.   6. I.e., of his own feelings.

Of human dealings. If I do prove her haggard,
Though that her jesses were my dear heart-strings   265
I'd whistle her off and let her down the wind⁷
To prey at fortune. Haply for I am black,
And have not those soft parts of conversation
That chamberers⁸ have; or for I am declined
Into the vale of years—yet that's not much—   270
She's gone. I am abused, and my relief
Must be to loathe her. O curse of marriage,
That we can call these delicate creatures ours
And not their appetites! I had rather be a toad
And live upon the vapour of a dungeon   275
Than keep a corner in the thing I love
For others' uses. Yet 'tis the plague of great ones;
Prerogatived are they less than the base.
'Tis destiny unshunnable, like death.
Even then this forkèd plague is fated to us   280
When we do quicken.⁹
　　　　[Enter DESDEMONA and EMILIA.]
　　　　　　　　Look where she comes.
If she be false, O then heaven mocks itself!
I'll not believe't.
DESDEMONA　　　How now, my dear Othello?
Your dinner, and the generous islanders
By you invited, do attend¹ your presence.   285
OTHELLO　I am to blame.
DESDEMONA　Why do you speak so faintly? Are you not well?
OTHELLO　I have a pain upon my forehead here.
DESDEMONA　Faith, that's with watching. 'Twill away again.
Let me but bind it hard, within this hour   290
It will be well.
OTHELLO　　　Your napkin is too little.
　　　　[He puts the napkin from him. It drops.]
Let it alone. Come, I'll go in with you.
DESDEMONA　I am very sorry that you are not well.
　　　　　　　　[Exeunt OTHELLO and DESDEMONA.]
EMILIA [taking up the napkin]　I am glad I have found this napkin.
This was her first remembrance from the Moor.   295
My wayward husband hath a hundred times
Wooed me to steal it, but she so loves the token—
For he conjured her she should ever keep it—
That she reserves it evermore about her
To kiss and talk to. I'll ha' the work ta'en out,²   300
And give't Iago. What he will do with it,
Heaven knows, not I.
I nothing, but to please his fantasy.³
　　　　[Enter IAGO.]

7. Set her free. Qualities: natures. Haggard: wild hawk. Jesses: hawk's leg-straps.　8. Courtiers. Haply
for: perhaps because.　9. Are born; grow sexually excited. Forkèd plague: cuckold's horns and women's
forked legs.　1. Await.　2. Pattern copied.　3. Fancy, desire. I nothing: I wish nothing.

IAGO How now, what do you here alone?

EMILIA Do not you chide. I have a thing for you.   305

IAGO You have a thing for me? It is a common thing.

EMILIA Ha?

IAGO To have a foolish wife.

EMILIA O, is that all? What will you give me now
    For that same handkerchief?   310

IAGO What handkerchief?

EMILIA What handkerchief?
    Why, that the Moor first gave to Desdemona,
    That which so often you did bid me steal.

IAGO Hast stol'n it from her?   315

EMILIA No, faith, she let it drop by negligence,
    And to th'advantage[4] I, being here, took't up.
    Look, here 'tis.

IAGO   A good wench! Give it me.

EMILIA What will you do with it, that you have been so earnest
    To have me filch it?

IAGO   Why, what is that to you?   320
    [He takes the napkin.]

EMILIA If it be not for some purpose of import,
    Give't me again. Poor lady, she'll run mad
    When she shall lack it.

IAGO Be not acknown on't.[5] I have use for it. Go, leave me.

                                        [Exit EMILIA.]
    I will in Cassio's lodging lose this napkin,   325
    And let him find it. Trifles light as air
    Are to the jealous confirmations strong
    As proofs of holy writ. This may do something.
    The Moor already changes with my poison.
    Dangerous conceits are in their natures poisons,   330
    Which at the first are scarce found to distaste,
    But, with a little[6] act upon the blood.
    Burn like the mines of sulphur.
        [Enter OTHELLO.]
                              I did say so.
    Look where he comes. Not poppy nor mandragora[7]
    Nor all the drowsy syrups of the world   335
    Shall ever medicine thee to that sweet sleep
    Which thou owedst[8] yesterday.

OTHELLO Ha, ha, false to me?

IAGO Why, how now, general? No more of that.

OTHELLO Avaunt, be gone. Thou hast set me on the rack.   340
    I swear 'tis better to be much abused
    Than but to know't a little.

IAGO   How now, my lord?

OTHELLO What sense had I of her stol'n hours of lust?

---

4. Luckily.   5. Act as if you know nothing.   6. After a short while.   7. Sleeping potions.
8. Possessed.

I saw't not, thought it not; it harmed not me.
I slept the next night well, fed well, was free and merry.   345
I found not Cassio's kisses on her lips.
He that is robbed, not wanting[9] what is stol'n,
Let him not know't and he's not robbed at all.

IAGO   I am sorry to hear this.

OTHELLO   I had been happy if the general camp,   350
Pioneers[1] and all, had tasted her sweet body,
So I had nothing known. O, now for ever
Farewell the tranquil mind, farewell content,
Farewell the plumèd troops and the big wars
That makes ambition virtue! O, farewell,   355
Farewell the neighing steed and the shrill trump,
The spirit-stirring drum, th'ear-piercing fife,
The royal banner, and all quality,
Pride, pomp, and circumstance of glorious war!
And O, you mortal engines whose rude throats   360
Th'immortal Jove's dread clamours counterfeit,[2]
Farewell! Othello's occupation's gone.

IAGO   Is't possible, my lord?

OTHELLO [taking IAGO by the throat]   Villain, be sure thou prove my
    love a whore.
Be sure of it. Give me the ocular proof,   365
Or, by the worth of mine eternal soul,
Thou hadst been better have been born a dog
Than answer my waked wrath.

IAGO   Is't come to this?

OTHELLO   Make me to see't, or at the least so prove it
That the probation[3] bear no hinge nor loop   370
To hang a doubt on, or woe upon thy life.

IAGO   My noble lord.

OTHELLO   If thou dost slander her and torture me,
Never pray more; abandon all remorse,
On horror's head horrors accumulate,   375
Do deeds to make heaven weep, all earth amazed,
For nothing canst thou to damnation add
Greater than that.

IAGO   O grace, O heaven forgive me!
Are you a man? Have you a soul or sense?
God buy you, take mine office. O wretched fool,   380
That lov'st to make thine honesty a vice!
O monstrous world, take note, take note, O world,
To be direct and honest is not safe!
I thank you for this profit, and from hence
I'll love no friend, sith[4] love breeds such offence.   385

OTHELLO   Nay, stay. Thou shouldst be honest.

IAGO   I should be wise, for honesty's a fool,

---

9. Missing.   1. Manual laborers in the army.   2. False thunder. *Circumstance:* pageantry. *Engines:*
cannons.   3. Test.   4. Since.

And loses that it works for.

OTHELLO   By the world,
I think my wife be honest, and think she is not.
I think that thou art just, and think thou art not.
I'll have some proof. My name, that was as fresh   390
As Dian's[5] visage, is now begrimed and black
As mine own face. If there be cords, or knives,
Poison, or fire, or suffocating streams,
I'll not endure it. Would I were satisfied!   395

IAGO   I see, sir, you are eaten up with passion.
I do repent me that I put it to you.
You would be satisfied?

OTHELLO   Would? Nay, and I will.

IAGO   And may. But how, how satisfied, my lord?
Would you, the supervisor,[6] grossly gape on,   400
Behold her topped?

OTHELLO   Death and damnation! O!

IAGO   It were a tedious difficulty, I think,
To bring them to that prospect.[7] Damn them then
If ever mortal eyes do see them bolster[8]
More than their own! What then, how then?   405
What shall I say? Where's satisfaction?
It is impossible you should see this,
Were they as prime as goats, as hot as monkeys,
As salt as wolves in pride,[9] and fools as gross
As ignorance made drunk. But yet I say,   410
If imputation, and strong circumstances
Which lead directly to the door of truth,
Will give you satisfaction, you might ha't.

OTHELLO   Give me a living reason she's disloyal.

IAGO   I do not like the office,[1]   415
But sith I am entered in this cause so far,
Pricked[2] to't by foolish honesty and love,
I will go on. I lay with Cassio lately,
And being troubled with a raging tooth,
I could not sleep. There are a kind of men   420
So loose of soul that in their sleeps
Will mutter their affairs. One of this kind is Cassio.
In sleep I heard him say 'Sweet Desdemona,
Let us be wary, let us hide our loves',
And then, sir, would he grip and wring my hand,   425
Cry 'O, sweet creature!', then kiss me hard,
As if he plucked up kisses by the roots,
That grew upon my lips, lay his leg o'er my thigh,
And sigh, and kiss, and then cry, 'Cursèd fate.
That gave thee to the Moor!'   430

OTHELLO   O, monstrous, monstrous!

---

5. Goddess of the moon and virginity.   6. Voyeur.   7. Spectacle. *Tedious:* demandingly.   8. Share
a pillow? support each other's bodies as pillows?   9. Heat. *Prime:* horny. *Salt:* lustful.   1. Job.
2. Driven.

IAGO   Nay, this was but his dream.
OTHELLO   But this denoted a foregone conclusion.
IAGO   'Tis a shrewd doubt,[3] though it be but a dream,
   And this may help to thicken other proofs   435
   That do demonstrate[4] thinly.
OTHELLO   I'll tear her all to pieces.
IAGO   Nay, yet be wise; yet we see nothing done.
   She may be honest yet. Tell me but this:
   Have you not sometimes seen a handkerchief
   Spotted with strawberries in your wife's hand?   440
OTHELLO   I gave her such a one. 'Twas my first gift.
IAGO   I know not that, but such a handkerchief—
   I am sure it was your wife's—did I today
   See Cassio wipe his beard with.
OTHELLO   If it be that—
IAGO   If it be that, or any that was hers,   445
   It speaks against her with the other proofs.
OTHELLO   O that the slave had forty thousand lives!
   One is too poor, too weak for my revenge.
   Now do I see 'tis true. Look here, Iago.
   All my fond love thus do I blow to heaven—'tis gone.   450
   Arise, black vengeance, from the hollow hell.
   Yield up, O love, thy crown and hearted throne
   To tyrannous hate! Swell, bosom, with thy freight,
   For 'tis of aspics' tongues.
IAGO   Yet be content.[5]
OTHELLO   O, blood, blood, blood!
IAGO   Patience, I say. Your mind may change.   455
OTHELLO   Never, Iago. Like to the Pontic Sea,[6]
   Whose icy current and compulsive course
   Ne'er knows retiring ebb, but keeps due on
   To the Propontic and the Hellespont,
   Even so my bloody thoughts with violent pace   460
   Shall ne'er look back, ne'er ebb to humble love,
   Till that a capable and wide revenge
   Swallow them up.
      [He kneels.]
                     Now, by yon marble heaven,
   In the due reverence of a sacred vow
   I here engage my words.
IAGO   Do not rise yet.   465
      [IAGO kneels.]
   Witness you ever-burning lights above,
   You elements that clip[7] us round about,
   Witness that here Iago doth give up
   The execution[8] of his wit, hands, heart
   To wronged Othello's service. Let him command,   470
   And to obey shall be in me remorse[9]

3. Guess.   4. Appear.   5. Patient.   6. Black Sea.   7. Embrace.   8. Agency.   9. Pity.

What bloody business ever.
    [*They rise.*]
OTHELLO   I greet thy love;
  Not with vain thanks, but with acceptance bounteous,
  And will upon the instant put thee to't.[1]
  Within these three days let me hear thee say   475
  That Cassio's not alive.
IAGO   My friend is dead.
  'Tis done at your request; but let her live.
OTHELLO   Damn her, lewd minx! O, damn her, damn her!
  Come, go with me apart. I will withdraw
  To furnish me with some swift means of death   480
  For the fair devil. Now art thou my lieutenant.
IAGO   I am your own for ever.   [*Exeunt.*]

3.4

    [*Enter* DESDEMONA, EMILIA, *and the* CLOWN.]
DESDEMONA   Do you know, sirrah, where Lieutenant Cassio lies?
CLOWN   I dare not say he lies[2] anywhere.
DESDEMONA   Why, man?
CLOWN   He's a soldier, and for me to say a soldier lies, 'tis stabbing.
DESDEMONA   Go to. Where lodges he?   5
CLOWN   To tell you where he lodges is to tell you where I lie.
DESDEMONA   Can anything be made of this?
CLOWN   I know not where he lodges, and for me to devise a lodging
  and say he lies here, or he lies there, were to lie in mine own throat.[3]
DESDEMONA   Can you enquire him out, and be edified[4] by report?   10
CLOWN   I will catechize the world for him; that is, make questions,
  and by them answer.
DESDEMONA   Seek him, bid him come hither, tell him I have moved[5]
  my lord on his behalf, and hope all will be well.
CLOWN   To do this is within the compass[6] of man's wit, and therefore   15
  I will attempt the doing it.   [*Exit.*]
DESDEMONA   Where should I lose the handkerchief, Emilia?
EMILIA   I know not, madam.
DESDEMONA   Believe me, I had rather have lost my purse
  Full of crusadoes,[7] and but my noble Moor   20
  Is true of mind, and made of no such baseness
  As jealous creatures are, it were enough
  To put him to ill thinking.
EMILIA   Is he not jealous?
DESDEMONA   Who, he? I think the sun where he was born
  Drew all such humours[8] from him.
    [*Enter* OTHELLO.]
EMILIA   Look where he comes.   25
DESDEMONA   I will not leave him now till Cassio
  Be called to him. How is't with you, my lord?

1. Set you about the business.   2. Dwells.   3. Lie from the heart.   4. Informed.   5. Influenced.   6. Scope.   7. Portuguese gold coins.   8. Qualities.

OTHELLO   Well, my good lady. [*Beside*] O hardness to dissemble!—
    How do you, Desdemona?
DESDEMONA   Well, my good lord.
OTHELLO   Give me your hand. This hand is moist, my lady.   30
DESDEMONA   It hath felt no age, nor known no sorrow
OTHELLO   This argues fruitfulness and liberal[9] heart.
    Hot, hot and moist—this hand of yours requires
    A sequester[1] from liberty; fasting, and prayer,
    Much castigation, exercise devout,   35
    For here's a young and sweating devil here
    That commonly rebels. 'Tis a good hand,
    A frank one.
DESDEMONA   You may indeed say so,
    For 'twas that hand that gave away my heart.   40
OTHELLO   A liberal hand. The hearts of old gave hands,
    But our new heraldry[2] is hands, not hearts.
DESDEMONA   I cannot speak of this. Come now, your promise.
OTHELLO   What promise, chuck?
DESDEMONA   I have sent to bid Cassio come speak with you.   45
OTHELLO   I have a salt and sorry rheum[3] offends me.
    Lend me thy handkerchief.
DESDEMONA [*offering a handkerchief*]   Here, my lord.
OTHELLO   That which I gave you.
DESDEMONA   I have it not about me.
OTHELLO   Not?   50
DESDEMONA   No, faith, my lord.
OTHELLO   That's a fault. That handkerchief
    Did an Egyptian to my mother give.
    She was a charmer,[4] and could almost read
    The thoughts of people. She told her, while she kept it.
    'Twould make her amiable,[5] and subdue my father   55
    Entirely to her love; but if she lost it,
    Or made a gift of it, my father's eye
    Should hold her loathèd, and his spirits should hunt
    After new fancies. She, dying, gave it me,
    And bid me, when my fate would have me wived,   60
    To give it her. I did so, and take heed on't.
    Make it a darling, like your precious eye.
    To lose't or give't away were such perdition
    As nothing else could match.
DESDEMONA   Is't possible?
OTHELLO   'Tis true. There's magic in the web[6] of it.   65
    A sibyl that had numbered in the world
    The sun to course two hundred compasses
    In her prophetic fury sewed the work.
    The worms were hallowed that did breed the silk,
    And it was dyed in mummy,[7] which the skilful   70

---

9. Generous or libidinous.   1. Removal.   2. Heraldic emblems.   3. Cold.   4. Sorceress.
5. Lovable.   6. Weaving.   7. Liquid drained from embalmed bodies. *Fury:* passion.

Conserved of maidens' hearts.
DESDEMONA   I'faith, is't true?
OTHELLO   Most veritable. Therefore look to't well.
DESDEMONA   Then would to God that I had never seen it!
OTHELLO   Ha, wherefore?
DESDEMONA   Why do you speak so startingly and rash?   75
OTHELLO   Is't lost? Is't gone? Speak, is't out o'th' way?
DESDEMONA   Heaven bless us!
OTHELLO   Say you?
DESDEMONA   It is not lost, but what an if it were?
OTHELLO   How?   80
DESDEMONA   I say it is not lost.
OTHELLO   Fetch't, let me see't.
DESDEMONA   Why, so I can, sir, but I will not now.
   This is a trick to put me from my suit.
   Pray you let Cassio be received again.
OTHELLO   Fetch me the handkerchief. My mind misgives.   85
DESDEMONA   Come, come, you'll never meet a more sufficient[8] man.
OTHELLO   The handkerchief.
DESDEMONA   I pray, talk me of Cassio.
OTHELLO   The handkerchief.
DESDEMONA   A man that all his time
   Hath founded his good fortunes on your love,
   Shared dangers with you—   90
OTHELLO   The handkerchief.
DESDEMONA   I'faith, you are to blame.
OTHELLO   'Swounds!   [Exit.]
EMILIA   Is not this man jealous?
DESDEMONA   I ne'er saw this before.
   Sure there's some wonder in this handkerchief.   95
   I am most unhappy in the loss of it.
EMILIA   'Tis not a year or two shows us a man.
   They are all but stomachs, and we all but food.
   They eat us hungrily, and when they are full,
   They belch us.
      [Enter IAGO and CASSIO.]
                        Look you, Cassio and my husband.   100
IAGO [to CASSIO]   There is no other way. 'Tis she must do't,
   And lo, the happiness! Go and importune her.
DESDEMONA   How now, good Cassio? What's the news with you?
CASSIO   Madam, my former suit. I do beseech you
   That by your virtuous means I may again   105
   Exist and be a member of his love
   Whom I, with all the office[9] of my heart,
   Entirely honour. I would not be delayed.
   If my offence be of such mortal kind
   That nor my service past, nor present sorrows,   110
   Nor purposed merit in futurity

8. Able.   9. Duty.

Can ransom me into his love again,
But to know so must be my benefit.[1]
So shall I clothe me in a forced content,
And shut myself up in some other course   115
To fortune's alms.
DESDEMONA   Alas, thrice-gentle Cassio!
My advocation[2] is not now in tune.
My lord is not my lord, nor should I know him
Were he in favour[3] as in humour altered.
So help me every spirit sanctified   120
As I have spoken for you all my best.
And stood within the blank[4] of his displeasure
For my free speech! You must a while be patient.
What I can do I will, and more I will
Than for myself I dare. Let that suffice you.   125
IAGO   Is my lord angry?
EMILIA   He went hence but now,
And certainly in strange unquietness.
IAGO   Can he be angry? I have seen the cannon
When it hath blown his ranks into the air,
And, like the devil, from his very arm   130
Puffed his own brother; and is he angry?
Something of moment then. I will go meet him.
There's matter in't indeed, if he be angry.
DESDEMONA   I prithee do so.   [*Exit* IAGO.]
                   Something sure of state
Either from Venice or some unhatched practice[5]   135
Made demonstrable here in Cyprus to him,
Hath puddled[6] his clear spirit; and in such cases
Men's natures wrangle with inferior things,
Though great ones are their object. 'Tis even so;
For let our finger ache and it indues[7]   140
Our other, healthful members even to a sense
Of pain. Nay, we must think men are not gods,
Nor of them look for such observancy
As fits the bridal. Beshrew me much, Emilia,
I was—unhandsome warrior as I am—   145
Arraiging his unkindness with my soul;
But now I find I had suborned the witness,
And he's indicted falsely.
EMILIA   Pray heaven it be
State matters, as you think, and no conception
Nor no jealous toy[8] concerning you.   150
DESDEMONA   Alas the day, I never gave him cause.
EMILIA   But jealous souls will not be answered so.
They are not ever jealous for the cause,
But jealous for they're jealous. It is a monster

---

1. Profit.   2. Advocacy.   3. Countenance.   4. Bull's-eye of a target.   5. Undisclosed stratagem.
6. Muddied.   7. Leads.   8. Trivial matter.

Begot upon itself, born on itself. 155
DESDEMONA   Heaven keep the monster from Othello's mind.
EMILIA   Lady, amen.
DESDEMONA   I will go seek him. Cassio, walk here about.
    If I do find him fit[9] I'll move your suit,
    And seek to effect it to my uttermost. 160
CASSIO   I humbly thank your ladyship.

                            [*Exeunt* DESDEMONA *and* EMILIA.]
        [*Enter* BIANCA.]
BIANCA   Save you, friend Cassio.
CASSIO   What make you from home?
    How is't with you, my most fair Bianca?
    I'faith, sweet love, I was coming to your house.
BIANCA   And I was going to your lodging, Cassio. 165
    What, keep a week away? Seven days and nights,
    Eightscore-eight hours, and lovers' absent hours
    More tedious than the dial eightscore times!
    O weary reckoning![1]
CASSIO   Pardon me, Bianca.
    I have this while with leaden thoughts been pressed, 170
    But I shall in a more continuate time
    Strike off this score[2] of absence. Sweet Bianca,
    Take me this work out.
        [*He gives her Desdemona's napkin.*]
BIANCA   O Cassio, whence came this?
    This is some token from a newer friend.
    To the felt absence now I feel a cause. 175
    Is't come to this? Well, well.
CASSIO   Go to, woman.
    Throw your vile guesses in the devil's teeth,
    From whence you have them. You are jealous now
    That this is from some mistress, some remembrance.
    No, by my faith, Bianca.
BIANCA   Why, whose is it? 180
CASSIO   I know not, neither. I found it in my chamber.
    I like the work well. Ere it be demanded[3]—
    As like enough it will—I would have it copied.
    Take it, and do't, and leave me for this time.
BIANCA   Leave you? Wherefore? 185
CASSIO   I do attend here on the general,
    And think it no addition, nor my wish,
    To have him see me womaned.
BIANCA   Why, I pray you?
CASSIO   Not that I love you not.
BIANCA   But that you do not love me.
    I pray you bring[4] me on the way a little, 190
    And say if I shall see you soon at night.
CASSIO   'Tis but a little way that I can bring you,

---

9. Suited.   1. Account.   2. Debt. *Continuate:* undisturbed.   3. Asked after.   4. Accompany.

For I attend here; but I'll see you soon.
BIANCA   'Tis very good. I must be circumstanced.[5]

[*Exeunt.*]

4.1

[*Enter* IAGO *and* OTHELLO.]

IAGO   Will you think so?
OTHELLO   Think so, Iago?
IAGO   What, to kiss in private?
OTHELLO   An unauthorized[6] kiss.
IAGO   Or to be naked with her friend in bed
  An hour or more, not meaning any harm?
OTHELLO   Naked in bed, Iago, and not mean harm?   5
  It is hypocrisy against the devil.
  They that mean virtuously and yet do so.
  The devil their virtue tempts, and they tempt heaven.
IAGO   If they do nothing, 'tis a venial slip.
  But if I give my wife a handkerchief—   10
OTHELLO   What then?
IAGO   Why then,'tis hers, my lord, and being hers,
  She may, I think, bestow't on any man.
OTHELLO   She is protectress of her honour, too.
  May she give that?   15
IAGO   Her honour is an essence that's not seen.
  They have it very oft that have it not.
  But for the handkerchief—
OTHELLO   By heaven, I would most gladly have forgot it.
  Thou said'st—O, it comes o'er my memory   20
  As doth the raven[7] o'er the infectious house,
  Boding to all!—he had my handkerchief.
IAGO   Ay, what of that?
OTHELLO   That's not so good now.
IAGO   What if I had said I had seen him do you wrong,
  Or heard him say—as knaves be such abroad,[8]   25
  Who having by their own importune suit
  Or voluntary dotage[9] of some mistress
  Convincèd or supplied[1] them, cannot choose
  But they must blab—
OTHELLO   Hath he said anything?
IAGO   He hath, my lord. But, be you well assured,   30
  No more than he'll unswear.
OTHELLO   What hath he said?
IAGO   Faith, that he did—I know not what he did.
OTHELLO   What, what?
IAGO   Lie—
OTHELLO   With her?
IAGO   With her, on her, what you will.

---

5. Given excuses, or be content with the circumstances.   6. I.e., adulterous.   7. Harbinger of death
and carrier of infection.   8. Out and about.   9. Foolishness of the will.   1. Conquered or satisfied.

OTHELLO   Lie with her? Lie on her? We say 'lie on her' when they
   belie her. Lie with her? 'Swounds, that's fulsome![2] Handkerchief—   35
   confessions—handkerchief. To confess and be hanged for his
   labour. First to be hanged and then to confess! I tremble at it. Nature
   would not invest herself in such shadowing passion without some
   instruction. It is not words that shakes me thus. Pish! Noses, ears,
   and lips! Is't possible? Confess? Handkerchief? O devil!   40
      [He falls down in a trance.]
IAGO   Work on; my medicine works. Thus credulous fools are caught,
   And many worthy and chaste dames even thus,
   All guiltless, meet reproach. What ho, my lord!
   My lord, I say. Othello!
      [Enter CASSIO.]
                              How now, Cassio?
CASSIO   What's the matter?   45
IAGO   My lord is fall'n into an epilepsy.
   This is his second fit. He had one yesterday.
CASSIO   Rub him about the temples.
IAGO
   The lethargy[3] must have his quiet course.
   If not, he foams at mouth, and by and by   50
   Breaks out to savage madness. Look, he stirs.
   Do you withdraw yourself a little while,
   He will recover straight. When he is gone
   I would on great occasion[4] speak with you.   [Exit CASSIO.]
   How is it, general? Have you not hurt your head?   55
OTHELLO   Dost thou mock me?[5]
IAGO   I mock you not, by heaven.
   Would you would bear your fortune like a man.
OTHELLO   A hornèd man's a monster and a beast.
IAGO   There's many a beast then in a populous city,
   And many a civil monster.   60
OTHELLO   Did he confess it?
IAGO   Good sir, be a man.
   Think every bearded fellow that's but yoked
   May draw[6] with you. There's millions now alive
   That nightly lie in those unproper beds   65
   Which they dare swear peculiar.[7] Your case is better.
   O, 'tis the spite of hell, the fiend's arch-mock,
   To lip a wanton in a secure couch
   And to suppose her chaste! No, let me know,
   And knowing what I am, I know what she shall be.   70
OTHELLO   O, thou art wise, 'tis certain.
IAGO   Stand you a while apart
   Confine yourself but in a patient list.[8]
   Whilst you were here, o'erwhelmèd with your grief—
   A passion most unsuiting such a man—

---

2. Nauseating.   3. Coma.   4. Serious business.   5. I.e., about the cuckold's horns.   6. Drag (a
burden). *Yoked:* i.e., in marriage.   7. Their own. *Unproper:* not exclusively their own.   8. Bounds of
patience.

Cassio came hither. I shifted him away,⁹ 75
And laid good 'scuse upon your ecstasy,⁹
Bade him anon return and here speak with me,
The which he promised. Do but encave yourself,
And mark the fleers, the gibes and notable¹ scorns
That dwell in every region of his face. 80
For I will make him tell the tale anew,
Where, how, how oft, how long ago, and when
He hath and is again to cope your wife.
I say, but mark his gesture. Marry, patience.
Or I shall say you're all-in-all in spleen,² 85
And nothing of a man.
OTHELLO   Dost thou hear, Iago?
I will be found most cunning in my patience,
But—dost thou hear?—most bloody.
IAGO   That's not amiss,
But yet keep time in all. Will you withdraw?
        [OTHELLO *stands apart*.]
Now will I question Cassio of Bianca, 90
A hussy that by selling her desires
Buys herself bread and cloth. It is a creature
That dotes on Cassio—as 'tis the strumpet's plague
To beguile many and be beguiled by one.
He, when he hears of her, cannot restrain 95
From the excess of laughter.
        [*Enter* CASSIO.]
                            Here he comes.
As he shall smile, Othello shall go mad;
And his unbookish jealousy must conster³
Poor Cassio's smiles, gestures, and light behaviours
Quite in the wrong. How do you now, lieutenant? 100
CASSIO   The worser that you give me the addition⁴
    Whose want even kills me.
IAGO   Ply Desdemona well and you are sure on't.
    Now, if this suit lay in Bianca's power,
    How quickly should you speed! 105
CASSIO [*laughing*]   Alas, poor caitiff!⁵
OTHELLO [*aside*]   Look how he laughs already.
IAGO   I never knew a woman love man so.
CASSIO   Alas, poor rogue! I think i'faith she loves me.
OTHELLO [*aside*]   Now he denies it faintly, and laughs it out. 110
IAGO   Do you hear, Cassio?
OTHELLO [*aside*]   Now he importunes him
    To tell it o'er. Go to, well said, well said.
IAGO   She gives it out that you shall marry her.
    Do you intend it?
CASSIO   Ha, ha, ha!

9. Trance. *Shifted him away*: made him go away.   1. *Obvious. Encave*: hide. *Fleers*: jeers.   2. A rage.
3. Construe. *Unbookish*: unlearned.   4. Title.   5. Wretch.

OTHELLO [*aside*]   Do ye triumph, Roman, do you triumph?   115

CASSIO   I marry! What a customer?[6] Prithee, bear some charity to my wit—do not think it so unwholesome. Ha, ha, ha!

OTHELLO [*aside*]   So, so, so, so. They laugh that wins.

IAGO   Faith, the cry goes that you marry her.

CASSIO   Prithee, say true.   120

IAGO   I am a very villain else.

OTHELLO [*aside*]   Ha' you scored[7] me? Well.

CASSIO   This is the monkey's own giving out. She is persuaded I will marry her out of her own love and flattery, not out of my promise.

OTHELLO [*aside*]   Iago beckons me. Now he begins the story.   125
   [OTHELLO *draws closer.*]

CASSIO   She was here even now. She haunts me in every place. I was the other day talking on the sea-bank with certain Venetians, and thither comes the bauble,[8] and falls me thus about my neck.

OTHELLO [*aside*]   Crying 'O dear Cassio!' as it were. His gesture imports it.   130

CASSIO   So hangs and lolls and weeps upon me, so shakes and pulls me—ha, ha, ha!

OTHELLO [*aside*]   Now he tells how she plucked him to my chamber. O I see that nose of yours, but not that dog I shall throw it to!

CASSIO   Well, I must leave her company.   135
   [*Enter* BIANCA.]

IAGO   Before me,[9] look where she comes.

CASSIO   'Tis such another fitchew![1] Marry, a perfumed one. [*To* BIANCA] What do you mean by this haunting of me?

BIANCA   Let the devil and his dam haunt you. What did you mean by that same handkerchief you gave me even now? I was a fine fool to   140 take it. I must take out the whole work—a likely piece of work, that you should find it in your chamber and know not who left it there. This is some minx's token, and I must take out the work. There, give it your hobby-horse.[2] [*Giving* CASSIO *the napkin*] Wheresoever you had it, I'll take out no work on't.   145

CASSIO   How now, my sweet Bianca, how now, how now?

OTHELLO [*aside*]   By heaven, that should be my handkerchief.

BIANCA   An you'll come to supper tonight, you may. An you will not, come when you are next prepared for.[3] [*Exit.*]

IAGO   After her, after her.   150

CASSIO   Faith, I must, she'll rail in the streets else.

IAGO   Will you sup there?

CASSIO   Faith, I intend so.

IAGO   Well, I may chance to see you, for I would very fain speak with you.   155

CASSIO   Prithee, come, will you?

IAGO   Go to, say no more.   [*Exit* CASSIO.]

OTHELLO   How shall I murder him, Iago?

IAGO   Did you perceive how he laughed at his vice?

6. Merchant; in this case, prostitute.   7. Defaced.   8. Toy.   9. I.e., "speak of the devil."   1. Polecat.   2. Easy woman.   3. Invited (i.e., never).

OTHELLO O Iago! 160

IAGO And did you see the handkerchief?

OTHELLO Was that mine?

IAGO Yours, by this hand. And to see how he prizes the foolish woman your wife. She gave it him, and he hath given it his whore.

OTHELLO I would have him nine years a-killing. A fine woman, a fair 165
woman, a sweet woman.

IAGO Nay, you must forget that.

OTHELLO Ay, let her rot and perish, and be damned tonight, for she shall not live. No, my heart is turned to stone; I strike it, and it hurts my hand. O, the world hath not a sweeter creature! She might lie by 170
an emperor's side, and command him tasks.

IAGO Nay, that's not your way.[4]

OTHELLO Hang her, I do but say what she is—so delicate with her needle, an admirable musician. O, she will sing the savageness out of a bear! Of so high and plenteous wit and invention.[5] 175

IAGO She's the worse for all this.

OTHELLO O, a thousand, a thousand times! And then of so gentle a condition.

IAGO Ay, too gentle.[6]

OTHELLO Nay, that's certain. But yet the pity of it, Iago. O, Iago, the 180
pity of it, Iago!

IAGO If you are so fond over her iniquity, give her patent to offend; for if it touch[7] not you, it comes near nobody.

OTHELLO I will chop her into messes.[8] Cuckold me!

IAGO O, 'tis foul in her. 185

OTHELLO With mine officer.

IAGO That's fouler.

OTHELLO Get me some poison, Iago, this night. I'll not expostulate with her, lest her body and beauty unprovide my mind[9] again. This night, Iago. 190

IAGO Do it not with poison. Strangle her in her bed, even the bed she hath contaminated.

OTHELLO Good, good, the justice of it pleases, very good.

IAGO And for Cassio, let me be his undertaker.[1] You shall hear more by midnight. 195

OTHELLO Excellent good.

[A trumpet.]

What trumpet is that same?

IAGO I warrant, something from Venice.

[Enter LODOVICO, DESDEMONA, and attendants.]

'Tis Lodovico. This comes from the Duke. See, your wife's with him.

LODOVICO God save the worthy general. 200

OTHELLO With all my heart,[2] sir.

LODOVICO [giving OTHELLO a letter] The Duke and the senators of Venice greet you.

OTHELLO I kiss the instrument of their pleasures.

---

4. Path 5. Creativity 6. Noble in rank, naturally kind 7. Bothers 8. Pieces. 9. Overthrow my determination. 1. Assassin. 2. I.e., welcome.

[*He reads the letter.*]

DESDEMONA   And what's the news; good cousin Lodovico?   205
IAGO [*to* LODOVICO]   I am very glad to see you, signor. Welcome to Cyprus.
LODOVICO   I thank you. How does Lieutenant Cassio?
IAGO   Lives, sir.
DESDEMONA   Cousin, there's fall'n between him and my lord
   An unkind[3] breach. But you shall make all well.   210
OTHELLO   Are you sure of that?
DESDEMONA   My lord.
OTHELLO [*reads*]   'This fail you not to do as you will'—
LODOVICO   He did not call, he's busy in the paper.
   Is there division 'twixt my lord and Cassio?   215
DESDEMONA   A most unhappy one. I would do much
   T'atone[4] them, for the love I bear to Cassio.
OTHELLO   Fire and brimstone!
DESDEMONA   My lord?
OTHELLO   Are you wise?
DESDEMONA   What, is he angry?
LODOVICO   Maybe the letter moved him,
   For, as I think, they do command him home,   220
   Deputing Cassio in his government.[5]
DESDEMONA   By my troth, I am glad on't.
OTHELLO   Indeed!
DESDEMONA   My lord?
OTHELLO [*to* DESDEMONA]   I am glad to see you mad.   225
DESDEMONA   Why, sweet Othello!
OTHELLO   Devil!
   [*He strikes her.*]
DESDEMONA   I have not deserved this.
LODOVICO   My lord, this would not be believed in Venice,
   Though I should swear I saw't. 'Tis very much.   230
   Make her amends, she weeps.
OTHELLO   O, devil, devil!
   If that the earth could teem with woman's tears.
   Each drop she falls would prove a crocodile.[6]
   Out of my sight!
DESDEMONA [*going*]   I will not stay to offend you.   235
LODOVICO   Truly, an obedient lady.
   I do beseech your lordship call her back.
OTHELLO   Mistress!
DESDEMONA [*returning*]   My lord?
OTHELLO [*to* LODOVICO]   What would you with her, sir?   240
LODOVICO   Who, I, my lord?
OTHELLO   Ay, you did wish that I would make her turn.
   Sir, she can turn and turn, and yet go on
   And turn again, and she can weep, sir, weep,
   And she's obedient, as you say, obedient,   245
   Very obedient. [*To* DESDEMONA] Proceed you in your tears.

---

3. Unnatural.   4. Bring them to accord.   5. Office.   6. I.e., false tears. *Teem:* breed. *Falls:* lets fall.

[*To* LODOVICO] Concerning this, sir—[*To* DESDEMONA] O well painted
  passion!
[*To* LODOVICO] I am commanded home. [*To* DESDEMONA] Get you
  away.
I'll send for you anon. [*To* LODOVICO] Sir, I obey the mandate,
And will return to Venice. [*To* DESDEMONA] Hence, avaunt!   250
                                        [*Exit* DESDEMONA.]
[*To* LODOVICO] Cassio shall have my place, and, sir, tonight
I do entreat that we may sup together.
You are welcome, sir, to Cyprus. Goats and monkeys![7]   [*Exit.*]
LODOVICO Is this the noble Moor whom our full senate
  Call all-in-all sufficient? Is this the nature   255
  Whom passion could not shake, whose solid virtue
  The shot of accident nor dart of chance
  Could neither graze nor pierce?
IAGO   He is much changed.
LODOVICO Are his wits safe? Is he not light of brain?
IAGO He's that he is. I may not breathe my censure   260
  What he might be. If what he might he is not,
  I would to heaven he were.
LODOVICO   What, strike his wife!
IAGO Faith, that was not so well. Yet would I knew
  That stroke would prove the worst.
LODOVICO   Is it his use,[8]
  Or did the letters work upon his blood   265
  And new-create his fault?
IAGO   Alas, alas.
  It is not honesty in me to speak
  What I have seen and known. You shall observe him,
  And his own courses[9] will denote him so
  That I may save my speech. Do but go after,   270
  And mark how he continues.
LODOVICO I am sorry that I am deceived in him.   [*Exeunt.*]

4.2

[*Enter* OTHELLO *and* EMILIA.]
OTHELLO You have seen nothing then?
EMILIA Nor ever heard, nor ever did suspect.
OTHELLO Yes, you have seen Cassio and she together.
EMILIA But then I saw no harm, and then I heard
  Each syllable that breath made up between 'em.   5
OTHELLO What, did they never whisper?
EMILIA Never, my lord.
OTHELLO Nor send you out o'th' way?
EMILIA Never.
OTHELLO To fetch her fan, her gloves, her mask, nor nothing?   10
EMILIA Never, my lord.

7. Lecherous animals.   8. Custom.   9. Actions.

OTHELLO   That's strange.

EMILIA   I durst, my lord, to wager she is honest,
Lay down my soul at stake.[1] If you think other,
Remove your thought; it doth abuse your bosom.   15
If any wretch ha' put this in your head,
Let heaven requite it with the serpent's curse,[2]
For if she be not honest, chaste, and true,
There's no man happy; the purest of their wives
Is foul as slander.

OTHELLO   Bid her come hither. Go.   [*Exit* EMILIA.]   20
She says enough, yet she's a simple bawd[3]
That cannot say as much. This is a subtle whore,
A closet lock and key of villainous secrets,
And yet she'll kneel and pray—I ha' seen her do't.

[*Enter* DESDEMONA *and* EMILIA.]

DESDEMONA   My lord, what is your will?

OTHELLO   Pray you, chuck, come hither.   25

DESDEMONA   What is your pleasure?

OTHELLO   Let me see your eyes.
Look in my face.

DESDEMONA   What horrible fancy's this?

OTHELLO [*to* EMILIA]   Some of your function,[4] mistress.
Leave procreants alone, and shut the door,   30
Cough or cry 'Hem' if anybody come.
Your mystery, your mystery[5]—nay, dispatch.   [*Exit* EMILIA.]

DESDEMONA   Upon my knees, what doth your speech import?
I understand a fury in your words,
But not the words.

OTHELLO   Why, what art thou?   35

DESDEMONA   Your wife, my lord, your true and loyal wife.

OTHELLO   Come, swear it, damn thyself,
Lest, being like one of heaven, the devils themselves
Should fear to seize thee. Therefore be double-damned:
Swear thou art honest.

DESDEMONA   Heaven doth truly know it.   40

OTHELLO   Heaven truly knows that thou art false as hell.

DESDEMONA   To whom, my lord? With whom? How am I false?

OTHELLO [*weeping*]   Ah, Desdemon, away, away, away!

DESDEMONA   Alas, the heavy day! Why do you weep?
Am I the motive of these tears, my lord?   45
If haply[6] you my father do suspect
An instrument of this your calling back,
Lay not your blame on me. If you have lost him,
I have lost him too.

OTHELLO   Had it pleased God
To try me with affliction; had He rained   50
All kind of sores and shames on my bare head,

---

1. As the bet.   2. God's curse on the serpent after the Fall.   3. Procuress, female pimp.   4. Go about your business.   5. Trade, occupation.   6. By chance. *Motive:* cause.

Steeped[7] me in poverty to the very lips,
Given to captivity me and my utmost hopes,
I should have found in some place of my soul
A drop of patience. But, alas, to make me   55
The fixèd figure for the time of scorn
To point his slow and moving finger at—
Yet could I bear that too, well, very well.
But there where I have garnered[8] up my heart,
Where either I must live or bear no life,   60
The fountain from the which my current runs
Or else dries up—to be discarded thence,
Or keep it as a cistern for foul toads
To knot and gender[9] in! Turn thy complexion there,
Patience, thou young and rose-lipped cherubin,   65
Ay, here look grim as hell.
DESDEMONA   I hope my noble lord esteems me honest.
OTHELLO   O, ay—as summer flies are in the shambles,
That quicken even with blowing.[1] O thou weed,
Who art so lovely fair, and smell'st so sweet,   70
That the sense aches at thee—would thou hadst ne'er been
    born!
DESDEMONA   Alas, what ignorant[2] sin have I committed?
OTHELLO   Was this fair paper, this most goodly book,
Made to write 'whore' upon? What committed?
Committed? O thou public commoner,[3]   75
I should make very forges of my cheeks,
That would to cinders burn up modesty,
Did I but speak thy deeds. What committed?
Heaven stops the nose at it, and the moon winks;
The bawdy wind, that kisses all it meets,   80
Is hushed within the hollow mine of earth
And will not hear't. What committed?
DESDEMONA   By heaven, you do me wrong.
OTHELLO   Are not you a strumpet?
DESDEMONA   No, as I am a Christian.   85
If to preserve this vessel for my lord
From any other foul unlawful touch
Be not to be a strumpet, I am none.
OTHELLO   What, not a whore?
DESDEMONA   No, as I shall be saved.
OTHELLO   Is't possible?   90
DESDEMONA   O heaven forgive us!
OTHELLO   I cry you mercy then.
I took you for that cunning whore of Venice
That married with Othello. [Calling] You, mistress,
That have the office opposite to Saint Peter.   95
And keeps the gate of hell,

---

7. Submerged.   8. Stored.   9. Copulate.   1. Laying their eggs. *Shambles:* meat and fish stalls.
Quicken: conceive.   2. Unwitting.   3. Prostitute.

[*Enter* EMILIA.]

you, you, ay, you.

We ha' done our course. [*Giving money*] There's money for your pains.

I pray you, turn the key and keep our counsel. [*Exit.*]

EMILIA   Alas, what does this gentleman conceive?

How do you, madam? How do you, my good lady?   100

DESDEMONA   Faith, half asleep.

EMILIA   Good madam, what's the matter with my lord?

DESDEMONA   With who?

EMILIA   Why; with my lord, madam.

DESDEMONA   Who is thy Lord?

EMILIA   He that is yours, sweet lady.

DESDEMONA   I ha' none. Do not talk to me, Emilia.   105

I cannot weep, nor answers have I none

But what should go by water.[4] Prithee tonight

Lay on my bed my wedding sheets, remember.

And call thy husband hither.

EMILIA   Here's a change indeed.   [*Exit.*]

DESDEMONA   'Tis meet I should be used so, very meet.   110

How have I been behaved, that he might stick

The small'st opinion on my least misuse[5]

        [*Enter* IAGO *and* EMILIA.]

IAGO   What is your pleasure, madam? How is't with you?

DESDEMONA   I cannot tell. Those that do teach young babes

Do it with gentle means and easy tasks.   115

He might ha' chid me so, for, in good faith,

I am a child to chiding.

IAGO   What is the matter, lady?

EMILIA   Alas, Iago, my lord hath so bewhored her,

Thrown such despite[6] and heavy terms upon her,

That true hearts cannot bear it.   120

DESDEMONA   Am I that name, Iago?

IAGO   What name, fair lady?

DESDEMONA   Such as she said my lord did say I was.

EMILIA   He called her whore. A beggar in his drink

Could not have laid such terms upon his callet.[7]   125

IAGO   Why did he so?

DESDEMONA   I do not know. I am sure I am none such.

IAGO   Do not weep, do not weep. Alas the day!

EMILIA   Hath she forsook so many noble matches,

Her father and her country and her friends,   130

To be called whore? Would it not make one weep?

DESDEMONA   It is my wretched fortune.

IAGO   Beshrew[8] him for't.

How comes this trick upon him?

DESDEMONA   Nay, heaven doth know.

EMILIA   I will be hanged if some eternal villain,

4. Tears.   5. Apply the least criticism to my smallest fault.   6. Contempt.   7. Slut.   8. Curse.

Some busy and insinuating rogue, 135
Some cogging,[9] cozening slave, to get some office,
Have not devised this slander, I will be hanged else.

IAGO Fie, there is no such man. It is impossible.

DESDEMONA If any such there be, heaven pardon him.

EMILIA A halter pardon him, and hell gnaw his bones! 140
Why should he call her whore? Who keeps her company?
What place, what time, what form, what likelihood?
The Moor's abused by some most villainous knave,
Some base, notorious knave, some scurvy fellow.
O heaven, that such companions thou'dst unfold,[1] 145
And put in every honest hand a whip
To lash the rascals naked through the world,
Even from the east to th' west!

IAGO   Speak within door.[2]

EMILIA O, fie upon them. Some such squire[3] he was
That turned your wit the seamy side without, 150
And made you to suspect me with the Moor.

IAGO You are a fool. Go to.

DESDEMONA   O God, Iago,
What shall I do to win my lord again?
Good friend, go to him; for by this light of heaven,
I know not how I lost him.
      [She kneels.]
                    Here I kneel. 155
If e'er my will did trespass 'gainst his love,
Either in discourse of thought or actual deed,
Or that mine eyes, mine ears, or any sense
Delighted them in any other form,
Or that I do not yet, and ever did, 160
And ever will—though he do shake me off
To beggarly divorcement—love him dearly,
Comfort forswear me. Unkindness may do much,
And his unkindness may defeat[4] my life,
But never taint my love.
      [She rises.]
                    I cannot say 'whore'. 165
It does abhor me now I speak the word.
To do the act that might the addition earn,
Not the world's mass of vanity could make me.

IAGO I pray you, be content. 'Tis but his humour.[5]
The business of the state does him offence, 170
And he does chide with you.

DESDEMONA If 'twere no other!

IAGO It is but so, I warrant.
      [Flourish within.]
Hark how these instruments summon you to supper.

---

9. Cheating. 1. Reveal. 2. Circumspectly. 3. Servant. 4. Ruin. 5. Mood.

The messengers of Venice stays the meat.[6]   175
Go in, and weep not. All things shall be well.
    [*Exeunt* DESDEMONA *and* EMILIA.—*Enter* RODERIGO.]
How now, Roderigo?

RODERIGO I do not find that thou deal'st justly with me.

IAGO What in the contrary?

RODERIGO Every day thou daff'st[7] me with some device, Iago, and   180
rather, as it seems to me now, keep'st from me all conveniency[8] than
suppliest me with the least advantage of hope. I will indeed no longer
endure it, nor am I yet persuaded to put up[9] in peace what already
I have foolishly suffered.

IAGO Will you hear me, Roderigo?   185

RODERIGO Faith, I have heard too much, for your words and performances are no kin together.

IAGO You charge me most unjustly.

RODERIGO With naught but truth. I have wasted myself out of my
means. The jewels you have had from me to deliver Desdemona   190
would half have corrupted a votarist.[1] You have told me she hath
received 'em and returned me expectations and comforts of sudden
respect[2] and acquaintance, but I find none.

IAGO Well, go to, very well.

RODERIGO 'Very well', 'go to'! I cannot go to, man, nor 'tis not very   195
well. Nay, I think it is scurvy, and begin to find myself fopped[3] in it.

IAGO Very well.

RODERIGO I tell you 'tis not very well. I will make myself known to
Desdemona. If she will return me my jewels, I will give over my suit
and repent my unlawful solicitation. If not, assure yourself I will seek   200
satisfaction of you.

IAGO You have said now.

RODERIGO Ay, and said nothing but what I protest[4] intendment of
doing.

IAGO Why, now I see there's mettle[5] in thee, and even from this   205
instant do build on thee a better opinion than ever before. Give me
thy hand, Roderigo. Thou hast taken against me a most just exception, but yet I protest I have dealt most directly[6] in thy affair.

RODERIGO It hath not appeared.

IAGO I grant, indeed, it hath not appeared, and your suspicion is not   210
without wit and judgement. But, Roderigo, if thou hast that in thee
indeed which I have greater reason to believe now than ever—I mean
purpose, courage, and valour—this night show it. If thou the next
night following enjoy not Desdemona, take me from this world with
treachery, and devise engines for[7] my life.   215

RODERIGO Well, what is it? Is it within reason and compass?[8]

IAGO Sir, there is especial commission come from Venice to depute
Cassio in Othello's place.

RODERIGO Is that true? Why then, Othello and Desdemona return
again to Venice.   220

---

6. Await dinner. 7. Put me off. 8. Opportunity. 9. Tolerate. 1. Vestal virgin. 2. Instant
regard. 3. Made a fool. 4. Insist. 5. Spirit. 6. Straightforwardly. *Exception:* criticism.
7. Plots against. 8. Possibility.

IAGO   O no, he goes into Mauritania, and takes away with him the fair
   Desdemona, unless his abode be lingered here by some accident,
   wherein none can be so determinate⁹ as the removing of Cassio.
RODERIGO   How do you mean 'removing' of him?
IAGO   Why, by making him uncapable of Othello's place—knocking   225
   out his brains.
RODERIGO   And that you would have me to do.
IAGO   Ay, if you dare do yourself a profit and a right. He sups tonight
   with a harlotry, and thither will I go to him. He knows not yet of his
   honourable fortune. If you will watch his going thence, which I will   230
   fashion to fall out¹ between twelve and one, you may take him at
   your pleasure. I will be near, to second² your attempt, and he shall
   fall between us. Come, stand not amazed at it, but go along with me.
   I will show you such a necessity in his death that you shall think
   yourself bound to put it on him. It is now high supper-time, and the   235
   night grows to waste. About it.
RODERIGO   I will hear further reason for this.
IAGO   And you shall be satisfied.   [*Exeunt.*]

4.3

   [*Enter* OTHELLO, DESDEMONA, LODOVICO, EMILIA, *and attendants.*]
LODOVICO   I do beseech you, sir, trouble yourself no further.
OTHELLO   O, pardon me, 'twill do me good to walk.
LODOVICO [*to* DESDEMONA]   Madam, good night. I humbly thank
   your ladyship.
DESDEMONA   Your honour is most welcome.
OTHELLO   Will you walk, sir?
   O, Desdemona!   5
DESDEMONA   My lord?
OTHELLO   Get you to bed on th'instant. I will be returned forthwith.
   Dismiss your attendant there. Look't be done.
DESDEMONA   I will, my lord.
                          [*Exeunt* OTHELLO, LODOVICO, *and attendants.*]
EMILIA   How goes it now? He looks gentler than he did.   10
DESDEMONA   He says he will return incontinent.³
   He hath commanded me to go to bed,
   And bid me to dismiss you.
EMILIA   Dismiss me?
DESDEMONA   It was his bidding. Therefore, good Emilia,
   Give me my nightly wearing, and adieu.   15
   We must not now displease him.
EMILIA   I would you had never seen him.
DESDEMONA   So would not I. My love doth so approve him
   That even his stubbornness, his checks,⁴ his frowns—
   Prithee unpin me—have grace and favour in them.   20
      [EMILIA *helps* DESDEMONA *to undress.*]
EMILIA   I have laid those sheets you bade me on the bed.

9. Decisive.   1. Take place.   2. Assist.   3. Directly.   4. Rebukes.

DESDEMONA   All's one.[5] Good faith, how foolish are our minds!
    If I do die before thee, prithee shroud me
    In one of these same sheets.
EMILIA   Come, come, you talk.
DESDEMONA   My mother had a maid called Barbary.   25
    She was in love, and he she loved proved mad
    And did forsake her. She had a song of willow.
    An old thing 'twas, but it expressed her fortune,
    And she died singing it. That song tonight
    Will not go from my mind. I have much to do   30
    But to go hang my head all at one side
    And sing it, like poor Barbary. Prithee, dispatch.
EMILIA   Shall I go fetch your nightgown?
DESDEMONA   No. Unpin me here.
    This Lodovico is a proper[6] man.
EMILIA   A very handsome man.
DESDEMONA   He speaks well.   35
EMILIA   I know a lady in Venice would have walked barefoot to Pal-
    estine for a touch of his nether lip.
DESDEMONA [sings]   'The poor soul sat sighing by a sycamore tree,
        Sing all a green willow.
    Her hand on her bosom, her head on her knee,   40
        Sing willow, willow, willow.
    The fresh streams ran by her and murmured her moans,
        Sing willow, willow, willow.
    Her salt tears fell from her and softened the stones,
        Sing willow'—   45
    Lay by these.—
                    'willow, willow.'
    Prithee, hie thee. He'll come anon.[7]
    'Sing all a green willow must be my garland.
    'Let nobody blame him, his scorn I approve'—   50
    Nay, that's not next. Hark, who is't that knocks?
EMILIA   It's the wind.
DESDEMONA [sings]   'I called my love false love, but what said he then?
        Sing willow, willow, willow.
    If I court more women, you'll couch with more men.'   55
    So, get thee gone. Good night. Mine eyes do itch.
    Doth that bode weeping?
EMILIA   'Tis neither here nor there.
DESDEMONA   I have heard it said so. O, these men, these men!
    Dost thou in conscience think—tell me, Emilia—
    That there be women do abuse their husbands   60
    In such gross kind?
EMILIA   There be some such, no question.
DESDEMONA   Wouldst thou do such a deed for all the world?
EMILIA   Why, would not you?
DESDEMONA   No, by this heavenly light.

5. No matter.   6. Handsome.   7. Soon. Hie: hurry.

EMILIA Nor I neither, by this heavenly light. I might do't as well
    i'th'dark.   65
DESDEMONA Wouldst thou do such a deed for all the world?
EMILIA The world's a huge thing. It is a great price for a small vice.
DESDEMONA In truth, I think thou wouldst not.
EMILIA In truth, I think I should, and undo't when I had done. Marry,
    I would not do such a thing for a joint ring, nor for measures of lawn, 70
    nor for gowns, petticoats, nor caps, nor any petty exhibition;[8] but for
    all the whole world? Ud's[9] pity, who would not make her husband a
    cuckold to make him a monarch? I should venture purgatory for't.
DESDEMONA Beshrew me if I would do such a wrong
    For the whole world.   75
EMILIA Why, the wrong is but a wrong i'th' world, and having the
    world for your labour, 'tis a wrong in your own world, and you might
    quickly make it right.
DESDEMONA I do not think there is any such woman.
EMILIA Yes, a dozen, and as many   80
    To th' vantage as would store[1] the world they played for.
    But I do think it is their husbands' faults
    If wives do fall. Say that they slack their duties,
    And pour our treasures into foreign laps[2]
    Or else break out in peevish jealousies,   85
    Throwing restraint upon us; or say they strike us,
    Or scant our former having in despite:[3]
    Why, we have galls; and though we have some grace,
    Yet have we some revenge. Let husbands know
    Their wives have sense like them. They see, and smell,   90
    And have their palates both for sweet and sour,
    As husbands have. What is it that they do
    When they change[4] us for others? Is it sport?
    I think it is. And doth affection[5] breed it?
    I think it doth. Is't frailty that thus errs?   95
    It is so, too. And have not we affections,
    Desires for sport, and frailty, as men have?
    Then let them use us well, else let them know
    The ills we do, their ills instruct us so.
DESDEMONA Good night, good night. God me such uses send   100
    Not to pick bad from bad, but by bad mend![6]   [*Exeunt.*]

5.1

[*Enter* IAGO *and* RODERIGO.]
IAGO Here, stand behind this bulk. Straight will he come.
    Wear thy good rapier bare, and put it home.[7]
    Quick, quick, fear nothing. I'll be at thy elbow.
    It makes us or it mars us. Think on that,

---

8. Payment. *Joint ring:* ring with two halves. *Lawn:* linen.   9. God's.   1. And as many more as it would
take to fill.   2. I.e., make love to other women. *Duties:* marital duties.   3. I.e., limit our spending out
of spite.   4. Exchange.   5. Desire.   6. Not to adopt bad practices but to learn good behavior from
them. *Uses:* habits.   7. I.e., stab him. *Bulk:* stall shop.

And fix most firm thy resolution. 5

RODERIGO Be near at hand. I may miscarry in't.

IAGO Here at thy hand. Be bold, and take thy stand.

RODERIGO [*aside*] I have no great devotion to the deed,
And yet he hath given me satisfying reasons.
'Tis but a man gone. Forth my sword—he dies! 10

IAGO [*aside*] I have rubbed this young quat almost to the sense⁸
And he grows angry. Now, whether he kill Cassio
Or Cassio him, or each do kill the other,
Every way makes my gain. Live Roderigo,
He calls me to a restitution large 15
Of gold and jewels that I bobbed⁹ from him
As gifts to Desdemona.
It must not be. If Cassio do remain,
He hath a daily beauty in his life
That makes me ugly; and besides, the Moor 20
May unfold me to him—there stand I in much peril.
No, he must die. But so, I hear him coming.
          [*Enter* CASSIO.]

RODERIGO I know his gait, 'tis he. [*Attacking* CASSIO] Villain, thou diest.

CASSIO That thrust had been mine enemy indeed,
But that my coat¹ is better than thou know'st. 25
I will make proof² of thine.
          [*He stabs* RODERIGO, *who falls*.]

RODERIGO   O, I am slain!
          [IAGO *wounds* CASSIO *in the leg from behind. Exit* IAGO.]

CASSIO [*falling*] I am maimed for ever. Help, ho, murder, murder!
          [*Enter* OTHELLO *above*.]

OTHELLO The voice of Cassio. Iago keeps his word.

RODERIGO O, villain that I am!

OTHELLO It is even so. 30

CASSIO O, help, ho! Light, a surgeon!

OTHELLO 'Tis he. O brave Iago, honest and just,
That hast such noble sense of thy friend's wrong—
Thou teachest me. Minion, your dear lies dead,
And your unblessed fate hies.³ Strumpet, I come. 35
Forth of⁴ my heart those charms, thine eyes, are blotted.
Thy bed, lust-stained, shall with lust's blood be spotted.
          [*Exit.—Enter* LODOVICO *and* GRAZIANO.]

CASSIO What ho, no watch, no passage?⁵ Murder, murder!

GRAZIANO 'Tis some mischance. The voice is very direful.

CASSIO O, help! 40

LODOVICO Hark.

RODERIGO O wretched villain!

LODOVICO Two or three groan. 'Tis heavy⁶ night.
These may be counterfeits. Let's think't unsafe
To come into⁷ the cry without more help. 45

8. To the quick. *Quat*: pimple.　9. Stole.　1. Protective armor.　2. Test.　3. Hurries on. *Min-ion*: derisive word for sweetheart, i.e., a sexual plaything.　4. Out of.　5. Passersby.　6. Dark.
7. Approach.

RODERIGO. Nobody come? Then shall I bleed to death.
    [*Enter* IAGO *with a light.*]
LODOVICO. Hark.
GRAZIANO   Here's one comes in his shirt, with light and weapons.
IAGO   Who's there? Whose noise is this that cries on murder?
LODOVICO   We do not know.
IAGO   Do not you hear a cry?   50
CASSIO   Here, here. For heaven's sake, help me.
IAGO   What's the matter?
GRAZIANO [*to* LODOVICO]   This is Othello's ensign, as I take it.
LODOVICO   The same indeed; a very valiant fellow.
IAGO [*to* CASSIO]   What are you here that cry so grievously?
CASSIO   Iago—O, I am spoiled, undone by villains.   55
   Give me some help.
IAGO   O me, lieutenant, what villains have done this?
CASSIO   I think that one of them is hereabout
   And cannot make away.
IAGO   O treacherous villains!
   [*To* LODOVICO *and* GRAZIANO] What are you there? Come in and give
     some help.   60
RODERIGO   O, help me there!
CASSIO   That's one of 'em.
IAGO [*stabbing* RODERIGO]   O murderous slave! O villain!
RODERIGO   O damned Iago! O inhuman dog!
IAGO   Kill me i'th' dark? Where be these bloody thieves?   65
   How silent is this town! Ho, murder, murder!
   [*To* LODOVICO *and* GRAZIANO] What may you be? Are you of good or
     evil?
LODOVICO   As you shall prove us, praise us.
IAGO   Signor Lodovico.
LODOVICO   He, sir.
IAGO   I cry you mercy. Here's Cassio hurt by villains.   70
GRAZIANO   Cassio?
IAGO   How is't, brother?
CASSIO   My leg is cut in two.
IAGO   Marry, heaven forbid!
   Light, gentlemen. I'll bind it with my shirt.   75
     [*Enter* BIANCA.]
BIANCA   What is the matter, ho? Who is't that cried?
IAGO   Who is't that cried?
BIANCA   O my dear Cassio,
   My sweet Cassio, O, Cassio, Cassio!
IAGO   O notable strumpet! Cassio, may you suspect
   Who they should be that have thus mangled you?   80
CASSIO   No.
GRAZIANO   I am sorry to find you thus. I have been to seek you.
IAGO   Lend me a garter. So. O for a chair,
   To bear him easily hence!
BIANCA   Alas, he faints. O, Cassio, Cassio, Cassio!   85
IAGO   Gentlemen all, I do suspect this trash

To be a party in this injury.
Patience a while, good Cassio. Come, come,
Lend me a light. [*Going to* RODERIGO] Know we this face or no?
Alas, my friend, and my dear countryman.   90
Roderigo? No—yes, sure—O heaven, Roderigo!

GRAZIANO   What, of Venice?

IAGO   Even he, sir. Did you know him?

GRAZIANO   Know him? Ay.

IAGO   Signor Graziano, I cry your gentle pardon.   95
These bloody accidents must excuse my manners
That so neglected you.

GRAZIANO   I am glad to see you.

IAGO   How do you, Cassio? O, a chair, a chair![8]

GRAZIANO   Roderigo.

IAGO   He, he, 'tis he.
[*Enter attendants with a chair.*]
O, that's well said, the chair!   100
Some good man bear him carefully from hence.
I'll fetch the general's surgeon. [*To* BIANCA] For you, mistress,
Save you your labour. He that lies slain here, Cassio,
Was my dear friend. What malice was between you?

CASSIO   None in the world, nor do I know the man.   105

IAGO [*to* BIANCA]   What, look you pale? [*To attendants*] O, bear him out
o'th' air.
[*To* LODOVICO *and* GRAZIANO] Stay you, good gentlemen.
[*Exeunt attendants with* CASSIO *in the chair and with Roderigo's
body.*]
[*To* BIANCA]   Look you pale, mistress?
[*To* LODOVICO *and* GRAZIANO] Do you perceive the ghastness[9] of her eye?
[*To* BIANCA] Nay, an[1] you stare we shall hear more anon.
[*To* LODOVICO *and* GRAZIANO] Behold her well; I pray you look upon
her.   110
Do you see, gentlemen? Nay, guiltiness
Will speak, though tongues were out of use.
[*Enter* EMILIA.]

EMILIA   Alas, what is the matter? What is the matter, husband?

IAGO   Cassio hath here been set on in the dark
By Roderigo and fellows that are scaped.   115
He's almost slain, and Roderigo dead.

EMILIA   Alas, good gentleman! Alas, good Cassio!

IAGO   This is the fruits of whoring. Prithee, Emilia,
Go know of Cassio where he supped tonight.
[*To* BIANCA] What, do you shake at that?   120

BIANCA   He supped at my house, but I therefore shake not.

IAGO   O, did he so? I charge you go with me.

EMILIA [*to* BIANCA]   O, fie upon thee, strumpet!

BIANCA   I am no strumpet, but of life as honest
As you that thus abuse me.

8. Litter.   9. Terror.   1. If.

EMILIA   As I? Fough, fie upon thee!   125
IAGO   Kind gentlemen, let's go see poor Cassio dressed.
    [*To* BIANCA] Come, mistress, you must tell's another tale.
    Emilia, run you to the citadel
    And tell my lord and lady what hath happed.
    Will you go on afore?   [*Exit* EMILIA.]
    [*Aside*]   This is the night   130
    That either makes me or fordoes² me quite.   [*Exeunt.*]

5.2

    [*Enter* OTHELLO *with a light. He draws back a curtain, revealing*
    DESDEMONA *asleep in her bed.*]
OTHELLO   It is the cause,³ it is the cause, my soul.
    Let me not name it to you, you chaste stars.
    It is the cause. Yet I'll not shed her blood,
    Nor scar that whiter skin of hers than snow,
    And smooth as monumental alabaster.⁴   5
    Yet she must die, else she'll betray more men.
    Put out the light, and then put out the light.⁵
    If I quench thee, thou flaming minister,⁶
    I can again thy former light restore
    Should I repent me; but once put out thy light.   10
    Thou cunning's⁷ pattern of excelling nature,
    I know not where is that Promethean heat
    That can thy light relume.⁸ When I have plucked thy rose
    I cannot give it vital growth again.
    It needs must wither. I'll smell thee on the tree.   15
        [*He kisses her.*]
    O balmy breath, that dost almost persuade
    Justice to break her sword! One more, one more.
    Be thus when thou art dead, and I will kill thee
    And love thee after. One more, and that's the last.
        [*He kisses her.*]
    So sweet was ne'er so fatal. I must weep,   20
    But they are cruel tears. This sorrow's heavenly,
    It strikes where it doth love. She wakes.
DESDEMONA   Who's there? Othello?
OTHELLO   Ay, Desdemona.
DESDEMONA   Will you come to bed, my lord?   25
OTHELLO   Have you prayed tonight, Desdemon?
DESDEMONA   Ay, my lord.
OTHELLO   If you bethink yourself of any crime
    Unreconciled as yet to heaven and grace,
    Solicit for it straight.   30
DESDEMONA   Alack, my lord, what may you mean by that?

2. Undoes.   3. Desdemona's infidelity.   4. Stone used in tombs and in Petrarchan descriptions of
the female body.   5. Othello compares the light of his torch to Desdemona's life.   6. Light that serves
me.   7. Most intricate, artful.   8. Relight. *Promethean heat:* divine fire (in Greek myth, Prometheus
stole fire from the heavens; one tradition holds that he gave it to humankind, another that he mingled it
with clay to create humankind).

OTHELLO   Well, do it, and be brief. I will walk by.[9]
  I would not kill thy unpreparèd spirit.
  No, heavens forfend! I would not kill thy soul.
DESDEMONA   Talk you of killing?
OTHELLO   Ay, I do.
DESDEMONA   Then heaven   35
  Have mercy on me.
OTHELLO   Amen, with all my heart.
DESDEMONA   If you say so, I hope you will not kill me.
OTHELLO   Hum!
DESDEMONA   And yet I fear you, for you're fatal then
  When your eyes roll so. Why I should fear I know not,   40
  Since guiltiness I know not, but yet I feel I fear.
OTHELLO   Think on thy sins.
DESDEMONA   They are loves I bear to you.
OTHELLO   Ay, and for that thou diest.
DESDEMONA   That death's unnatural that kills for loving.   45
  Alas, why gnaw you so your nether lip?
  Some bloody passion shakes your very frame.
  These are portents, but yet I hope, I hope
  They do not point on me.
OTHELLO   Peace, and be still.
DESDEMONA   I will so. What's the matter?
OTHELLO   That handkerchief   50
  Which I so loved and gave thee, thou gav'st to Cassio.
DESDEMONA   No, by my life and soul. Send for the man
  And ask him.
OTHELLO   Sweet soul, take heed, take heed of perjury.
  Thou art on thy deathbed.   55
DESDEMONA   Ay, but not yet to die.
OTHELLO   Presently.
  Therefore confess thee freely of thy sin,
  For to deny each article with oath
  Cannot remove nor choke the strong conception   60
  That I do groan withal.[1] Thou art to die.
DESDEMONA   Then Lord have mercy on me.
OTHELLO   I say amen.
DESDEMONA   And have you mercy, too. I never did
  Offend you in my life, never loved Cassio
  But with such general warranty of heaven   65
  As I might love. I never gave him token.
OTHELLO   By heaven, I saw my handkerchief in's hand.
  O perjured woman! Thou dost stone[2] my heart,
  And makes me call what I intend to do
  A murder, which I thought a sacrifice.   70
  I saw the handkerchief.
DESDEMONA   He found it, then.

9. Nearby.   1. Remove the suspicion growing within me (the image is from pregnancy and abortion).
Article: item (in a legalistic sense).   2. Harden.

I never gave it him. Send for him hither.
Let him confess a truth.
OTHELLO   He hath confessed.
DESDEMONA   What, my lord?
OTHELLO   That he hath usèd thee.
DESDEMONA   How, unlawfully?   75
OTHELLO   Ay.
DESDEMONA   He will not say so.
OTHELLO   No, his mouth is stopped.
Honest Iago hath ta'en order for't.[3]
DESDEMONA   O, my fear interprets! What, is he dead?   80
OTHELLO   Had all his hairs been lives, my great revenge
Had stomach[4] for 'em all.
DESDEMONA [weeping]   Alas, he is betrayed, and I undone.
OTHELLO   Out, strumpet! Weep'st thou for him to my face?
DESDEMONA   O, banish me, my lord, but kill me not.   85
OTHELLO [attacking her]   Down, strumpet.
DESDEMONA   Kill me tomorrow; let me live tonight.
OTHELLO   Nay, an you strive—
DESDEMONA   But half an hour.
OTHELLO   Being done, there is no pause.   90
DESDEMONA   But while I say one prayer.
OTHELLO   It is too late.
        [He smothers her.]
DESDEMONA   O Lord, Lord, Lord!
        [EMILIA at the door.]
EMILIA [within]   My lord, what ho, my lord, my lord!
OTHELLO   What noise is this? Not dead? Not yet quite dead?   95
I that am cruel am yet merciful.
I would not have thee linger in thy pain.
So, so.
EMILIA [within]   What ho, my lord, my lord!
OTHELLO   Who's there?
EMILIA [within]   O, good my lord, I would speak a word with you.
OTHELLO [calling]   Yes.—'Tis Emilia. [Calling] By and by!—She's
        dead.   100
'Tis like she comes to speak of Cassio's death.
The noise was high.[5] Ha! No more moving.
Still as the grave. Shall she come in? Were't good?
I think she stirs again. No. What's best to do?
If she come in, she'll sure speak to my wife.   105
My wife, my wife! What wife? I ha' no wife.
O insupportable, O heavy hour!
Methinks it should be now a huge eclipse
Of sun and moon, and that th'affrighted globe
Should yawn at alteration.[6]
EMILIA [within]   I do beseech you   110

3. Been commissioned to do it.   4. Appetite.   5. Loud.   6. Gape at the change (i.e., undergo an earthquake).

That I may speak with you. O, good my lord!
OTHELLO   I had forgot thee.—O, come in, Emilia.—
Soft,[7] by and by. Let me the curtains draw.
    [He closes the bed-curtains.]
Where art thou?
    [He opens the door. Enter EMILIA.]
        What's the matter with thee now?
EMILIA   O my good lord, yonder's foul murder's done.   115
OTHELLO   What, now?
EMILIA   But[8] now, my lord.
OTHELLO   It is the very error[9] of the moon,
  She comes more nearer earth than she was wont,
  And makes men mad.   120
EMILIA   Cassio, my lord, hath killed a young Venetian
  Called Roderigo.
OTHELLO   Roderigo killed
  And Cassio killed?
EMILIA   No, Cassio is not killed.
OTHELLO   Not Cassio killed? Then murder's out of tune,
  And sweet revenge grows harsh.   125
DESDEMONA   O, falsely, falsely murdered!
EMILIA   O Lord, what cry is that?
OTHELLO   That? What?
EMILIA   Out and alas, that was my lady's voice!
    [She opens the bed-curtains.]
Help, help, ho, help! O lady, speak again!   130
Sweet Desdemona, O sweet mistress, speak!
DESDEMONA   A guiltless death I die.
EMILIA   O, who hath done this deed?
DESDEMONA   Nobody, I myself. Farewell.
Commend me to my kind lord. O, farewell!   *[She dies.]*
OTHELLO   Why, how should she be murdered?
EMILIA   Alas, who knows?   135
OTHELLO   You heard her say herself it was not I.
EMILIA   She said so, I must needs report the truth.
OTHELLO   She's like a liar gone to burning hell.
'Twas I that killed her.
EMILIA   O, the more angel she, and you the blacker devil!   140
OTHELLO   She turned to folly, and she was a whore.
EMILIA   Thou dost belie her, and thou art a devil.
OTHELLO   She was false as water.
EMILIA   Thou art rash as fire
To say that she was false. O, she was heavenly true!
OTHELLO   Cassio did top her. Ask thy husband else.[1]   145
O, I were damned beneath all depth in hell
But that I did proceed upon just grounds
To this extremity! Thy husband knew it all.

7. Quiet.   8. Just.   9. Wandering.   1. If you don't believe it.

EMILIA My husband?
OTHELLO   Thy husband.
EMILIA   That she was false to wedlock?
OTHELLO Ay, with Cassio. Had she been true,   150
  If heaven would make me such another world
  Of one entire and perfect chrysolite[2]
  I'd not have sold her for it.
EMILIA   My husband?
OTHELLO Ay,'twas he that told me on her first.
  An honest man he is, and hates the slime   155
  That sticks on filthy deeds.
EMILIA   My husband?
OTHELLO What needs this interance?[3] Woman, I say thy husband.
EMILIA O mistress, villainy hath made mocks with love.
  My husband say she was false?
OTHELLO   He, woman.
  I say thy husband. Dost understand the word?   160
  My friend, thy husband, honest, honest Iago.
EMILIA If he say so, may his pernicious soul
  Rot half a grain a day. He lies to th' heart.
  She was too fond of her most filthy bargain.
OTHELLO Ha?   165
EMILIA Do thy worst.
  This deed of thine is no more worthy heaven
  Than thou wast worthy her.
OTHELLO   Peace, you were best.[4]
EMILIA Thou hast not half that power to do me harm
  As I have to be hurt. O gull,[5] O dolt,   170
  As ignorant as dirt! Thou hast done a deed—
  I care not for thy sword, I'll make thee known
  Though I lost twenty lives. Help, help, ho! Help!
  The Moor hath killed my mistress. Murder, murder!
      [*Enter* MONTANO, GRAZIANO, *and* IAGO.]
MONTANO What is the matter? How now, general?   175
EMILIA O, are you come, Iago? You have done well,
  That men must lay their murders on your neck.
GRAZIANO What is the matter?
EMILIA [*to* IAGO] Disprove this villain if thou beest a man.
  He says thou told'st him that his wife was false.   180
  I know thou didst not. Thou'rt not such a villain.
  Speak, for my heart is full.
IAGO I told him what I thought, and told no more
  Than what he found himself was apt and true.
EMILIA But did you ever tell him she was false?   185
IAGO I did.
EMILIA You told a lie, an odious, damnèd lie,
  Upon my soul a lie, a wicked lie.

---

2. Topaz. 3. Repetition. 4. You had better be quiet. 5. Dupe.

She false with Cassio? Did you say with Cassio?

IAGO   With Cassio, mistress. Go to, charm[6] your tongue.   190

EMILIA   I will not charm my tongue. I am bound to speak.
My mistress here lies murdered in her bed.

MONTANO AND GRAZIANO   O heavens forfend!

EMILIA [to IAGO]   And your reports have set the murder on.

OTHELLO   Nay, stare not, masters. It is true indeed.   195

GRAZIANO   'Tis a strange truth.

MONTANO   O monstrous act!

EMILIA   Villainy, villainy, villainy!
I think upon't, I think. I smell't. O villainy!
I thought so then. I'll kill myself for grief.
O villainy, villainy!   200

IAGO   What, are you mad? I charge you get you home.

EMILIA   Good gentlemen, let me have leave to speak.
'Tis proper I obey him, but not now.
Perchance, Iago, I will ne'er go home.

OTHELLO   O, O, O!
          [OTHELLO falls on the bed.]

EMILIA   Nay, lay thee down and roar,   205
For thou hast killed the sweetest innocent
That e'er did lift up eye.

OTHELLO [rising]   O, she was foul!
[To GRAZIANO] I scarce did know you, uncle. There lies your niece,
Whose breath indeed these hands have newly stopped.
I know this act shows[7] horrible and grim.   210

GRAZIANO   Poor Desdemon, I am glad thy father's dead.
Thy match was mortal to him, and pure grief
Shore his old thread in twain.[8] Did he live now
This sight would make him do a desperate turn,
Yea, curse his better angel from his side,   215
And fall to reprobance.[9]

OTHELLO   'Tis pitiful. But yet Iago knows
That she with Cassio hath the act of shame
A thousand times committed. Cassio confessed it,
And she did gratify his amorous works   220
With that recognizance[1] and pledge of love
Which I first gave her. I saw it in his hand.
It was a handkerchief, an antique token
My father gave my mother.

EMILIA   O God! O heavenly God!

IAGO   'Swounds, hold your peace!

EMILIA   'Twill out, 'twill out. I peace?   225
No, I will speak as liberal as the north.[2]
Let heaven, and men, and devils, let 'em all,
All, all cry shame against me, yet I'll speak.

IAGO   Be wise and get you home.

---

6. Silence.   7. Appears.   8. Cut the thread of his life in two.   9. Damnation (suicide was a damnable sin). *Turn:* deed.   1. Sign.   2. As freely as the north wind.

EMILIA   I will not.   230
   [IAGO *draws his sword.*]
GRAZIANO [*to* IAGO]   Fie, your sword upon a woman?
EMILIA   O thou dull Moor, that handkerchief thou speak'st of
 I found by fortune and did give my husband,
 For often, with a solemn earnestness—
 More than indeed belonged to such a trifle—   235
 He begged of me to steal't.
IAGO   Villainous whore!
EMILIA   She give it Cassio? No, alas, I found it,
 And I did give't my husband.
IAGO   Filth, thou liest.
EMILIA   By heaven I do not, I do not, gentlemen.
 O murderous coxcomb![3] What should such a fool   240
 Do with so good a wife?
OTHELLO   Are there no stones[4] in heaven
 But what serves for the thunder? Precious[5] villain!
   [*The Moor runs at* IAGO. MONTANO *disarms* OTHELLO. IAGO *wounds
   his wife.*]
GRAZIANO   The woman falls. Sure he hath killed his wife.
EMILIA   Ay, ay. O, lay me by my mistress' side!   [*Exit* IAGO.]
GRAZIANO   He's gone, but his wife's killed.   245
MONTANO   'Tis a notorious villain. Take you this weapon
 Which I have here recovered from the Moor.
 Come, guard the door without. Let him not pass,
 But kill him rather. I'll after that same villain,
 For 'tis a damnèd slave.   [*Exeunt* MONTANO *and* GRAZIANO.]
OTHELLO   I am not valiant neither,   250
 But every puny whipster[6] gets my sword.
 But why should honour outlive honesty?
 Let it go all.
EMILIA   What did thy song bode, lady?
 Hark, canst thou hear me? I will play the swan,
 And die in music. [*Sings*] 'Willow, willow, willow.'—   255
 Moor, she was chaste. She loved thee, cruel Moor.
 So come my soul to bliss as I speak true.
 So, speaking as I think, alas, I die.   [*She dies.*]
OTHELLO   I have another weapon in this chamber.
 It was a sword of Spain, the ice-brook's temper.[7]   260
 O, here it is. [*Calling*] Uncle, I must come forth.
GRAZIANO [*within*]   If thou attempt it, it will cost thee dear.
 Thou hast no weapon, and perforce must suffer.
OTHELLO   Look in upon me then, and speak with me.
 Or, naked[8] as I am, I will assault thee.   265
   [*Enter* GRAZIANO.]
GRAZIANO   What is the matter?
OTHELLO   Behold, I have a weapon;

---

3. Fool. **4.** Thunderbolts. **5.** Extreme. **6.** Trifling person. **7.** Tempered in icy water.
8. Defenseless.

A better never did itself sustain
Upon a soldier's thigh. I have seen the day
That, with this little arm and this good sword,
I have made my way through more impediments   270
Than twenty times your stop.[9] But O, vain boast!
Who can control his fate? 'Tis not so now.
Be not afraid, though you do see me weaponed.
Here is my journey's end, here is my butt.
And very sea-mark of my utmost sail.[1]   275
Do you go back dismayed? 'Tis a lost fear.
Man but a rush[2] against Othello's breast
And he retires. Where should Othello go?
[To DESDEMONA] Now, how dost thou look now? O ill-starred wench,
Pale as thy smock! When we shall meet at count[3]   280
This look of thine will hurl my soul from heaven,
And fiends will snatch at it.
      [He touches her.]
                            Cold, cold, my girl,
Even like thy chastity. O cursèd, cursèd slave!
Whip me, ye devils,
From the possession of this heavenly sight: 285
Blow me about in winds, roast me in sulphur,
Wash me in steep-down gulfs of liquid fire!
O Desdemon! Dead Desdemon! Dead! O! O!
      [Enter LODOVICO, MONTANO, IAGO guarded by officers, with CASSIO
      in a chair.]
LODOVICO   Where is this rash and most unfortunate man?
OTHELLO   That's he that was Othello. Here I am.   290
LODOVICO   Where is that viper? Bring the villain forth.
OTHELLO   I look down towards his feet,[4] but that's a fable.
      [To IAGO] If that thou beest a devil I cannot kill thee.
          [He wounds IAGO.]
LODOVICO   Wrench his sword from him.
      [Officers disarm OTHELLO.]
IAGO   I bleed, sir, but not killed.
OTHELLO   I am not sorry, neither. I'd have thee live,   295
For in my sense[5] 'tis happiness to die.
LODOVICO   O thou Othello, that was once so good,
Fall'n in the practice[6] of a cursèd slave,
What shall be said to thee?
OTHELLO   Why, anything;
An honourable murderer, if you will,   300
For naught I did in hate, but all in honour.
LODOVICO   This wretch hath part confessed his villainy.
Did you and he consent in Cassio's death?
OTHELLO   Ay.
CASSIO   Dear general, I never gave you cause.   305

---

9. What would stop you.   1. Marker of my farthest voyage. Butt: goal.   2. Aim only a reed.
3. Judgment Day.   4. I.e., to see if Iago has devil's hooves.   5. Opinion.   6. Plot.

OTHELLO I do believe it, and I ask your pardon.
  Will you, I pray, demand that demi-devil
  Why he hath thus ensnared my soul and body?
IAGO Demand me nothing. What you know, you know.
  From this time forth I never will speak word.   310
LODOVICO [to IAGO] What, not to pray?
GRAZIANO [to IAGO] Torments[7] will ope your lips.
OTHELLO Well, thou dost best.
LODOVICO Sir, you shall understand what hath befall'n,
  Which as, I think, you know not. Here is a letter,   315
  Found in the pocket of the slain Roderigo,
  And here another. The one of them imports
  The death of Cassio, to be undertook
  By Roderigo.
OTHELLO O villain!   320
CASSIO Most heathenish and most gross.
LODOVICO Now here's another discontented paper
  Found in his pocket too, and this it seems
  Roderigo meant to've sent this damnèd villain,
  But that, belike,[8] Iago in the interim   325
  Came in and satisfied him.
OTHELLO [to IAGO] O thou pernicious caitiff![9]
  How came you, Cassio, by that handkerchief
  That was my wife's?
CASSIO   I found it in my chamber,
  And he himself confessed it, but even now,   330
  That there he dropped it for a special purpose
  Which wrought to his desire.
OTHELLO   O fool, fool, fool!
CASSIO There is besides in Roderigo's letter
  How he upbraids Iago, that he made him
  Brave[1] me upon the watch, whereon it came   335
  That I was cast;[2] and even but now he spake
  After long seeming dead, Iago hurt him,
  Iago set him on.
LODOVICO [to OTHELLO] You must forsake this room and go with us.
  Your power and your command is taken off,   340
  And Cassio rules in Cyprus. For this slave,
  If there be any cunning cruelty
  That can torment him much and hold him long,
  It shall be his. You shall close[3] prisoner rest
  Till that the nature of your fault be known   345
  To the Venetian state. [To officers] Come, bring away.
OTHELLO Soft you, a word or two before you go.
  I have done the state some service, and they know't.
  No more of that. I pray you, in your letters,
  When you shall these unlucky deeds relate,   350
  Speak of me as I am. Nothing extenuate,

---

7. Tortures. 8. Perhaps. 9. Wretch. 1. Insult. 2. Dismissed. 3. Tightly constrained.

Nor set down aught in malice. Then must you speak
Of one that loved not wisely but too well,
Of one not easily jealous but, being wrought,
Perplexed in the extreme; of one whose hand,   355
Like the base Indian, threw a pearl away
Richer than all his tribe;[4] of one whose subdued[5] eyes,
Albeit unusèd to the melting mood,
Drops tears as fast as the Arabian trees
Their medicinable gum.[6] Set you down this,   360
And say besides that in Aleppo once,
Where a malignant and a turbaned Turk
Beat a Venetian and traduced the state,
I took by th' throat the circumcisèd dog
And smote him thus.   365
          [*He stabs himself.*]
LODOVICO   O bloody period![7]
GRAZIANO   All that is spoke is marred.
OTHELLO [*to* DESDEMONA]   I kissed thee ere I killed thee. No way but this:
    Killing myself, to die upon a kiss. [*He kisses* DESDEMONA *and dies.*]
CASSIO   This did I fear, but thought he had no weapon,   370
    For he was great of heart.
LODOVICO [*to* IAGO]   O Spartan dog,
    More fell[8] than anguish, hunger, or the sea,
    Look on the tragic loading of this bed.
    This is thy work. The object poisons sight.
    Let it be hid.
          [*They close the bed-curtains.*]
                Graziano, keep the house,   375
    And seize upon the fortunes of the Moor,
    For they succeed on you. [*To* CASSIO] To you, Lord Governor.
    Remains the censure[9] of this hellish villain.
    The time, the place, the torture. O, enforce it!
    Myself will straight aboard, and to the state   380
    This heavy act with heavy heart relate.   [*Exeunt with Emilia's body.*]

4. *Indian . . . tribe:* Shakespeare's plays exist in early printed editions (known as quartos) and as gathered in a large volume (known as a folio). This line is from the Quarto text of *Othello.* The Folio text reads *Judean* instead of *Indian.* While both words imply "unbeliever," Indian suggests ignorance of the pearl's value, and Judean may suggest willful refusal of it.   5. I.e., with tears.   6. Balm.   7. Sentence.
8. Cruel. *Spartan:* brutal; reference to the harsh customs of ancient Sparta.   9. Punishment.

JOHN MILTON
1608–1674

The poetic achievement of John Milton is generally regarded as the last flourishing of Christian humanism in Renaissance England; in his poetic work, the Renaissance commitment to classical revival and the Reformation emphasis on the Bible came together. Milton's late position allowed him both to "outdo" the grand epic tradition on its own terms and to criticize its pagan roots. As he well knew, Renaissance epic poets, like Christian humanists, struggled in varying degrees with their mixed allegiances to classical learning and to Christianity. To Christian scholars, the strain of serving the two masters of secular knowledge and religious faith could be distracting: even the Church father St. Jerome (ca. 347–419 or 420) had a dream in which God denounced him with the charge "You are not a Christian: you are a Ciceronian." In *Paradise Lost*, Milton attempts to resolve the conflict between the seductions of the classics and the imperatives of Christianity: he tells the biblical story of the Fall, and to this authoritative plot he subordinates the classical materials of the epic tradition. What is more, when he wishes to "body forth" the material, tactile richness of beauty—in, for example, the Garden of Eden, Eve, and the snake—he heightens the classicism of his verse. Concentrating classical allusions on the physically sensuous and psychologically disruptive elements of his poem, he allows his classical material to appear in sumptuous glory and, simultaneously, under restraint by the highest authority, the Bible. To an extent, the curbs Milton imposes on his classical sources distract attention from his equally assertive handling of the Bible; yet he does not shy away from telling a highly individual version of the story of "man's first disobedience." The story of Genesis, in which Adam and Eve broke God's prohibition and ate from the tree of knowledge, suggested to Milton an opportunity to expound his own ideas about liberty, knowledge, doubt, sexuality, and marriage.

Milton's life divides conveniently into three stages: a period of long study, which culminated in the great pastoral elegy *Lycidas* (1637) and his travels on the Continent (1638–39), where he met important literary figures in addition to the astronomer Galileo; his long involvement in doctrinal and political controversy and his service as Latin secretary to Oliver Cromwell's Council of State (1640–60); and, after the restoration of the English monarchy and his banishment from politics, the more solitary and disillusioned years in which Milton (totally blind since 1651) produced his major poetic works, *Paradise Lost* (1667), *Paradise Regained* (1671), and *Samson Agonistes* (1671).

Born in London on December 9, 1608, he received an excellent education at St. Paul's in London and Christ's College, Cambridge, where he prepared for a career in the ministry. He received his B.A. in 1629 and his M.A. in 1632, but did not take holy orders (due to his growing dissatisfaction with Church of England hierarchy). Instead, he lived reclusively at his father's estate at Horton, near Windsor, where he continued his studies and followed his dream curriculum of science and the new discoveries, mathematics, Greek and Latin authors, music, the systematic research of world history, and volumes upon volumes of poetry. In his view, his intensive studies were preparing him for the poet's role as moral leader: whoever hopes to write well, he wrote in an autobiographical sketch, "ought himself to be a true poem, that is, a composition and pattern of the best and honorablest things; not presuming to sing high praises of heroic men or famous Cities, unless he have in himself the experience and the practice of all that is praiseworthy." The complete identification of poet and poem, reading and experience, indicates how important it was to Milton to be morally "fit," not just technically skilled, to compose epic verse.

Politics and not poems were on Milton's mind, however, when he returned from his travels in Italy. Word had reached him that political trouble was brewing at home (the beginnings of the Puritan Revolt), and he returned to London, where he inserted himself into the political controversies by writing pamphlets that he hoped would inspire debate. Some of his political arguments shaped the concepts of religious, civil, and domestic liberties that he explores in *Paradise Lost* (1667). His most notable tract, *Areopagitica* (1644), opposed censorship of the press and took to task the parliamentary government (his own party) for trying to restrict the opposition: Parliament was historically bound to defend the liberties of the people, and Milton could not abide its lapse in principle. Throughout his public career he forcefully insisted on popular liberty from arbitrary rule, and he had gone so far as to defend, in print, the execution of his king (Charles I was executed in 1641). How could he justify regicide? Law, he felt, should arise from the reasoning conscience of the individual Christian; to deprive individuals of the free exercise of their reason called for violent resistance.

His most notorious prose writings, however, were directly inspired by his failed marriage and earned him the epithet "the Divorcer": at thirty-two he married the seventeen-year-old Mary Powell, who left him after six weeks. In the argumentative Milton, this event inspired considerable thought and print concerning the grounds of marriage. He complained bitterly of the English law that permitted divorce only to those who had not consummated their marriages and protested that the law left unhappy couples to "grind in the mill of an undelighted and servile copulation" (anything worth saying is worth saying grandly). Without depth of conversation, he argued, men and women were not joined in a genuine marriage. God, he claimed, meant spouses to be spiritual helpmeets and partners in "civil fellowship." In *Paradise Lost,* where Adam and Eve make love without shame and converse with delight, he illustrates his ideal of marriage. Conversation and the "sweet intercourse / Of looks and smiles" turn out to be the essential ingredients of a successful marriage. They are, Milton's Adam says, the way that human beings cope with their fundamental loneliness. When Adam asks God for a companion, he claims that man needs "conversation with his like to help / Or solace his defects" (his lonely distance from God). This loneliness is so intense that even after Eve falls, Adam affirms his need for her (although it means severing himself from God): "with thee / Certain my resolution is to die; / How can I live without thee, how forgo / Thy sweet converse and love so dearly joined?"

Milton's chief source for *Paradise Lost* is the biblical account of Creation, Eden, the Fall, and the expulsion of Adam and Eve from paradise. From the first three chapters of Genesis, he forged twelve capacious books of epic verse, which he fleshed out with his vast knowledge of the classics, history, theology, and science. He had long wanted to write something lasting and once considered composing an epic on King Arthur. Had he written a chivalric romance, he would have inserted himself directly into Virgil's imperial tradition. He began his work on *Paradise Lost,* however, after his banishment from public life: Restoration England had "fallen on evil days," and to his mind no longer had political glory to celebrate. Politically disappointed in the failure of republican government and the reinstatement of monarchy in England, he had reason to look skeptically on the imperial and romance epic tradition he once loved. In fact, he casts Satan as his empire-builder, colonizer, and merchant-adventurer, the positions that Aeneas holds in Virgil's epic. More generally, he asserts the superiority of his own subject over the epic tradition stemming from Homer and Virgil: it is, he declares, "Not less but more heroic than the wrath / Of stern Achilles" or "rage / of Turnus," the Latin warrior Aeneas must defeat in order to found Rome. He goes on to scorn the kind of medieval romance that he once planned to compose: "with long and tedious havoc" these tales have merely "*fabled* knights / In battles *feigned.*" His own tale, by implicit contrast, is genuinely historical and heroic. While epic poets assert their continuity with cultural origins, Milton characteristically insists that his own poem disrupts the heroic tradition. *Paradise Lost* alone, he implies, is genuinely concerned with historical origins and is wholly original as creative verse.

Milton's attitude toward the recovery of truth, as his confidence in his poem suggests, is paradoxically traditional and radical. The poet is at once committed to the recovery of biblical truth and determined to smash the trite conventions through which truths have passed to successive generations. When his poem first appeared, it scandalized and bewildered the reading public. Even his verse style was shocking evidence of his radicalism: the rhyming couplets and stanzas that defined English verse for many readers were nowhere to be found, and in their place were rolling periodic sentences of unrhymed verse (iambic pentameter). His rejection of rhyme so upset his contemporaries that he added a brief note explaining and defending his practice: "This neglect then of Rime so little is to be taken for a defect, though it may seem so perhaps to vulgar Readers, that it rather is to be esteem'd an example set, the first in *English*, of ancient liberty recover'd to Heroic Poem from the troublesome and modern bondage of Riming." Milton proclaimed his heroic break from literary tradition and his victorious recovery of an ancient poetic practice. More momentously, he described his poetic innovation as a politically significant act: he was liberating the intellect from bondage and restoring ancient liberties. He had destroyed the shackles of convention (rhymes)and rescued intellectual freedom, and he did it for his reader. And since liberty is meaningless unless exercised vigorously, he intended every sentence and verse line of his poem to be challenging.

Since Milton set out to innovate in verse, revolutionize interpretation, and liberate the intellect, we might suspect that he chose the wrong text: the choice of Adam and Eve to seek knowledge at the cost of their obedience to God. In fact, the status of knowledge is a central, and not fully resolved, problem in *Paradise Lost*. In *Areopagitica*, Milton argued that virtue is meaningful only when gained and tested by experience. Goodness based on mere ignorance of evil, for him, seems inferior to the reasoned choice of the good over a known and alluring evil. He speculated that the Fall caused a change in the way that human beings gained knowledge. In Eden humanity knew only good; after the Fall, humanity knew good by distinguishing it from evil. "What wisdom can there be to choose, what continence to forbear without the knowledge of evil?" he asked. "I cannot praise a fugitive and cloistered virtue, unexercised and unbreathed, that never sallies out and sees her adversary."

This is the position that the more cautious Milton of *Paradise Lost* places in the mouth of his "Adventurous" Eve just before the Fall. Eve, always more independent than Adam, wants to work alone in another part of the Garden, and when she suspects that her husband mistrusts her ability to withstand the temptations of Satan by herself, she grows adamant about facing a trial, should Satan come her way: "what is Faith, Love, Virtue unassay'd / Alone, without exterior help sustain'd?" Like the younger and rasher Milton, she considers such virtue "but a name" or an abstraction rather than an inner quality; she rejects the idea that her obedience has any significance if it is maintained only by "exterior help." If she is to enjoy a reputation for virtue, she wants it to arise from a personal history of her experiences and trials.

Adam, by contrast, seems curious and anxious about his relationship to knowledge. In his conversations with God and with the angel Raphael, he reveals how inquisitive he is about himself, Eve, the world around him, and above all, the mysterious heavens. To Raphael he expresses doubts about the excesses of God's Creation: why are there so many superior heavenly bodies revolving about the Earth? The "needless" superfluity and abundance of Creation indicate mysterious purposes that make Adam question his centrality to the cosmos. When Raphael warns him that "Heav'n is for thee too high / To know what passes there; be lowly wise; / Think only what concerns thee and thy being; / Dream not of other Worlds," Adam declares himself "cleared of doubt." He assures the angel (or himself) that it is better to be "freed from intricacies" and "perplexing" and "wand'ring" thoughts that "rove" endlessly until "warn'd, or by experience taught," the imagination learns to "not to know." Although the difference between receiving a warning and learning by experience is great, Adam falls back on the traditionalist position about knowledge, summed up in the caution to "be lowly wise": don't analyze (etymologically, to "break things apart" logically) or use empirical observation to make inquiries that can lead only to hypothesis and speculation. Expound what you know to be true; do not theorize about "high" matters from "low" or material observation (i.e., use inductive reasoning): receive, do not create your own body of wisdom.

It is a truism of the classical tradition that the beauty of temptresses (like Homer's Circe and Ariosto's Alcina) has a disruptive power over epic heroes who otherwise display Stoic constancy and integrity (literally, "wholeness"). To a limited extent, this model of heroic manhood threatened by female corruption applies to *Paradise Lost*.

The telling difference is that for Milton, the "kindly rupture" of sexual experience relates to the acquisition of knowledge and can therefore be rejected only at great personal cost to the hero. After Adam has agreed to be "lowly wise," he admits to Raphael that sexual passion, like the superabundant universe, troubles him because it is overwhelming. When he approaches his wife's "loveliness," he says,

> so absolute she seems
> And in herself complete, so well to know
> Her own, that what she wills to do or say,
> Seems wisest, virtuousest, discreetest, best . . .

Adam repeats his error of inductive reasoning: based on the empirical evidence of sight and touch, he wonders if Eve is in fact "one intended first, not after made / Occasionally." Although no less an authority than God tells him that Eve is "inferior" and "subject" to him, Adam cannot ignore his own experience. His social and spiritual interactions with Eve "subject not," he notes, but passion does, and Adam wants to know what to make of this unorthodox fact.

Through Adam's appealing inquisitiveness, Milton's readers learn an answer to a further question about sex that they might have been afraid to ask: do angels make love? Raphael, who has just reproached Adam for his own "vehement" response to sexuality, blushes and admits that they do. His blush is as revealing as his affirmation: do heavenly beings, as much as earthly ones, experience a "kindly rupture" of passion? A blush, after all, is an involuntary sign of a powerful internal fluctuation. If angels make love and blush about their rapture, then sexuality is not an evil in *Paradise Lost*—and indeed Milton has no patience for the patristic tradition that condemns sexuality as degrading. For Milton, sexuality is instead a powerful testimony to the *unfallen*, if ambiguous, quest for knowledge through experience.

And what of Milton the epic poet: does he, too, experience ruptures in his self-assertiveness? Freeing the individual believer from received wisdom is an anxious, as well as heroic, activity for Milton. In his invocations to his heavenly muse, he raises the awkward question of the source of his poetic inspiration: in book 9, for example, he mentions his "Celestial Patroness, who deigns / Her nightly visitation unimplor'd, / And dictates to me slumb'ring, or inspires / Easy my unpremeditated Verse." From her, he hopes to gain what he calls "answerable style"—poetic expression that echoes the revelation he has received. He boasts that he does not have to ask for his inspiration (as Homer and Virgil did), yet he does not assert its legitimacy. At the end of this invocation, in fact, Milton acknowledges his doubts and fears that "all be mine, / Not Hers who brings it nightly to my Ear." If he is to retell the story of the Bible in what he calls "answerable style," his imagination must be guided by heavenly authority. If his personal revelation is false, perhaps Milton will have to "answer" to his God. His style must be innovative, or it will merely recycle flawed and human-generated conventions; but it must not be "invented" by the poet himself. When Milton reflects on the ambiguous source of his inspiration, he acknowledges the anxiety of a radical Protestant who believes in the principle of personal revelation but cannot confirm it outside his own experience. He fascinatingly returns, in effect, to the basic tension that Christian humanists experienced between recovering truth (through scholarly discoveries) and revolutionizing it (by breaking with tradition).

Milton's achievements in *Paradise Lost* include his powerful rendering of human spiritual need and its relationship to domestic life. His poem might be considered "adventurous" in its explorations of the rational, sexual, and emotional psychologies that lead his Adam and Eve to fall, although it is also uncompromising about the fatal error of the Fall. Milton committed himself intellectually to disrupting the received wisdom of the classics and the Church in order to discover truths verifiable by experience. In the story of Genesis he discovers questions central to the Renaissance and Reformation: how do we know things? to what extent should "external help" such as warnings govern us? how much more rewarding—and dangerous—is the wisdom of experience? can we learn from vicarious experiences, such as sympathy and interpretation (a possibility that enlarges the moral role of art)? Milton, who wished to break the bonds constraining the intellectual and imaginative possibilities of his readers, bestowed on them what must regarded, paradoxically, as the burden of interpretive liberty: Milton works to make the reading of *Paradise Lost* a simultaneously demanding and highly personal experience.

The standard biography is William Riley Parker, *Milton: A Biography*, 2 vols. (1981). Annabel Patterson, ed., *John Milton* (1992), and David Quint, *Epic and Empire: Politics and Generic Form from Virgil to Milton* (1993), offer useful recent studies of Milton. Rewarding essays can also be found in *Re-membering Milton: Essays on the Texts and Traditions* (1987), edited by Mary Nyquist and Margaret W. Ferguson. Barbara Kiefer Lewalski, *Paradise Lost and the Rhetoric of Literary Forms* (1985), offers a lucid and comprehensive study of Milton's uses of literary genre. Patricia Parker discusses Milton's suggestive linkage of doubt, the romance form, and Eve in a chapter of *Inescapable Romance* (1975). Stanley Fish directs attention to the role of readers' responses in determining or creating meaning in *Surprised by Sin: The Reader in Paradise Lost* (1967). A Bartlett Giamatti, *The Earthly Paradise and the Renaissance Epic* (1966), analyzes the "coalescence of classical and Christian material" in the poem. Robert Crosman, *Reading Paradise Lost* (1980), is a helpful introduction for first-time readers of Milton's poem.

From Paradise Lost

FROM BOOK 1

["This Great Argument"]

Of man's first disobedience, and the fruit[1]
Of that forbidden tree whose mortal taste[2]
Brought death into the world, and all our woe,
With loss of Eden, till one greater Man[3]
Restore us, and regain the blissful seat,   5
Sing, Heavenly Muse,[4] that, on the secret top
Of Oreb, or of Sinai, didst inspire
That shepherd who first taught the chosen seed[5]
In the beginning how the Heavens and Earth
Rose out of Chaos: or, if Sion hill   10
Delight thee more, and Siloa's brook that flowed
Fast by the oracle of God,[6] I thence
Invoke thy aid to my adventurous[7] song,
That with no middle flight intends to soar

1. The apple itself, and also the consequences of Adam and Eve's disobedience.　2. The tasting of which brought mortality into the world.　3. Christ.　4. The opening invocation to the muse who will inspire (*sing* to) the poet is a regular feature of epic poems. Milton's heavenly muse elsewhere in the poem (7.1) is given the name of the mythological Urania; in another passage (9.21) she is given the adjective *celestial*. Both words—of Greek and Latin derivation, respectively—mean "heavenly." Clearly and typically, in Milton's heavenly muse pagan elements and images are adopted and given new substance within the framework of Judeo-Christian culture and beliefs.　5. The Hebrew people.　Oreb and Sinai designate the mountain where God spoke to Moses (*that shepherd*), who in Genesis taught the Hebrew people the story of the Creation.　6. The Temple. The biblical localities suggested here as haunts for Milton's muse are emblematic of his certainty about the higher nature of his theme compared with the epic subjects of pagan antiquity. The fact that *Siloa's brook* is flowing by the Temple suggests the holy nature of Milton's subject.　7. Perilous, as the poet is daring something new (see line 16).

Above th' Aonian mount,[8] while it pursues 15
Things unattempted yet in prose or rhyme.
And chiefly thou, O Spirit,[9] that dost prefer
Before all temples th' upright heart and pure,
Instruct me,[1] for thou know'st; thou from the first
Wast present, and, with mighty wings outspread, 20
Dovelike sat'st brooding[2] on the vast abyss,
And mad'st it pregnant: what in me is dark
Illumine; what is low, raise and support;
That, to the height of this great argument,[3]
I may assert[4] Eternal Providence, 25
And justify the ways of God[5] to men.

FROM BOOK 4

The Argument

Satan now in prospect of Eden, and nigh the place where he must now attempt the bold enterprise which he undertook alone against God and man, falls into many doubts with himself, and many passions, fear, envy, and despair; but at length confirms himself in evil, journeys on to Paradise, whose outward prospect and situation is described, overleaps the bounds, sits in the shape of a cormorant on the Tree of Life, as highest in the Garden to look about him. The Garden described; Satan's first sight of Adam and Eve; his wonder at their excellent form and happy state, but with resolution to work their fall; overhears their discourse, thence gathers that the Tree of Knowledge was forbidden them to eat of, under penalty of death; and thereon intends to found his temptation, by seducing them to transgress: then leaves them a while, to know further of their state by some other means. Meanwhile Uriel descending on a sunbeam warns Gabriel, who had in charge the gate of Paradise, that some evil Spirit had escaped the deep, and passed at noon by his sphere in the shape of a good angel down to Paradise, discovered after by his furious gestures in the mount. Gabriel promises to find him ere morning. Night coming on, Adam and Eve discourse of going to their rest: their bower described; their evening worship. Gabriel drawing forth his bands of nightwatch to walk the round of Paradise, appoints two strong angels to Adam's bower, lest the evil Spirit should be there doing some harm to Adam or Eve sleeping; there they find him at the ear of Eve, tempting her in a dream, and bring him, though unwilling, to Gabriel; by whom questioned, he scornfully answers, prepares resistance, but hindered by a sign from heaven, flies out of Paradise.

---

8. Helicon, the Greek mountain that was the seat of the Nine Muses. The spring Aganippe, which gives poetic power, and an altar of Zeus were part of that landscape (compare the location of Siloa's brook, lines 11–12).   9. Described in Milton's Latin treatise on Christian doctrine as "that impulse or voice of God by which the prophets were inspired," the Spirit is a further source of inspiration over and above the heavenly muse.   1. The poet asks not for song but for knowledge (*instruct me*) and identifies the Spirit with the Spirit of God that "moved upon the face of the waters" (Genesis 1.2).   2. As a bird hatching eggs. The image is pursued in line 22 with *pregnant*. *Dovelike*: the traditional figuration of the Holy Spirit (for example, Luke 3.22: "the Holy Ghost descended in a bodily shape like a dove").   3. Subject, theme.   4. Champion, vindicate.   5. Demonstrate the justice of the course of God's providence.

[Satan's Entry into Paradise; Adam and Eve in Their Bower]

O for that warning voice which he[6] who saw
Th' Apocalypse heard cry in Heaven aloud,
Then when the dragon, put to second rout,
Came furious down to be revenged on men,
Woe to the inhabitants on Earth! that now,　　　　　5
While time was, our first parents had been warned
The coming of their secret foe, and scaped,
Haply so scaped, his mortal snare! For now
Satan, now first inflamed with rage, came down,
The tempter ere th' accuser of mankind,　　　　　10
To wreak on innocent frail man his loss
Of that first battle, and his flight to Hell.
Yet not rejoicing in his speed though bold
Far off and fearless, nor with cause to boast,
Begins his dire attempt; which nigh the birth　　　　　15
Now rolling, boils in his tumultuous breast,
And like a devilish engine[7] back recoils
Upon himself. Horror and doubt distract
His troubled thoughts, and from the bottom stir
The Hell within him; for within him Hell　　　　　20
He brings, and round about him, nor from Hell
One step no more than from himself can fly
By change of place. Now conscience wakes despair
That slumbered, wakes the bitter memory
Of what he was, what is, and what must be　　　　　25
Worse; of worse deeds worse sufferings must ensue.
Sometimes towards Eden, which now in his view
Lay pleasant, his grieved look he fixes sad;
Sometimes towards heaven and the full-blazing sun,
Which now sat high in his meridian tower;　　　　　30
Then, much revolving, thus in sighs began:
　"O thou that with surpassing glory crowned
Look'st from thy sole dominion like the god
Of this new world—at whose sight all the stars
Hide their diminished heads—to thee I call,　　　　　35
But with no friendly voice, and add thy name,
O sun, to tell thee how I hate thy beams,
That bring to my remembrance from what state
I fell, how glorious once above thy sphere,
Till pride and worse ambition threw me down,　　　　　40
Warring in Heaven against Heaven's matchless King!
Ah, wherefore? He deserved no such return
From me, whom he created what I was
In that bright eminence, and with his good
Upbraided none; nor was his service hard.　　　　　45
What could be less than to afford him praise,
The easiest recompense, and pay him thanks,

6. St. John, author of Revelation.　　7. A cannon.

How due! Yet all his good proved ill in me,
And wrought but malice. Lifted up so high,
I'sdained[8] subjection, and thought one step higher   50
Would set me highest, and in a moment quit
The debt immense of endless gratitude,
So burdensome, still paying, still to owe,
Forgetful what from him I still received;
And understood not that a grateful mind   55
By owing owes not, but still pays, at once
Indebted and discharged—what burden then?
O had his powerful destiny ordained
Me some inferior angel, I had stood
Then happy; no unbounded hope had raised   60
Ambition. Yet why not? Some other power
As great might have aspired, and me, though mean,
Drawn to his part. But other powers as great
Fell not, but stand unshaken, from within
Or from without to all temptations armed!   65
Hadst thou the same free will and power to stand?
Thou hadst. Whom hast thou then, or what, to accuse,
But Heaven's free love dealt equally to all?
Be then his love accursed, since, love or hate,
To me alike it deals eternal woe.   70
Nay, cursed be thou; since against his thy will
Chose freely what it now so justly rues.
Me miserable! which way shall I fly
Infinite wrath and infinite despair?
Which way I fly is Hell; myself am Hell;   75
And in the lowest deep a lower deep
Still threatening to devour me opens wide,
To which the Hell I suffer seems a Heaven.
O then at last relent! Is there no place
Left for repentance, none for pardon left?   80
None left but by submission; and that word
Disdain forbids me, and my dread of shame
Among the spirits beneath, whom I seduced
With other promises and other vaunts
Than to submit, boasting I could subdue   85
Th' omnipotent. Ay me! they little know
How dearly I abide that boast so vain,
Under what torments inwardly I groan.
While they adore me on the throne of Hell,
With diadem and scepter high advanced,   90
The lower still I fall, only supreme
In misery: such joy ambition finds!
But say I could repent and could obtain
By act of grace my former state, how soon
Would height recall high thoughts, how soon unsay   95
What feigned submission swore! Ease would recant
Vows made in pain, as violent and void.

8. Disdained.

For never can true reconcilement grow
Where wounds of deadly hate have pierced so deep;
Which would but lead me to a worse relapse 100
And heavier fall: so should I purchase dear
Short intermission, bought with double smart.
This knows my punisher; therefore as far
From granting he, as I from begging, peace.
All hope excluded thus, behold, instead 105
Of us outcast, exiled, his new delight,
Mankind created, and for him this world!
So farewell hope, and with hope farewell fear,
Farewell remorse! All good to me is lost;
Evil, be thou my good: by thee at least 110
Divided empire with Heaven's king I hold,
By thee, and more than half perhaps will reign;
As man ere long, and this new world, shall know."
   Thus while he spake, each passion dimmed his face,
Thrice changed with pale—ire, envy, and despair; 115
Which marred his borrowed visage, and betrayed
Him counterfeit, if any eye beheld:
For heavenly minds from such distempers foul
Are ever clear. Whereof he soon aware
Each perturbation smoothed with outward calm, 120
Artificer of fraud; and was the first
That practiced falsehood under saintly show,
Deep malice to conceal, couched with revenge:
Yet not enough had practiced to deceive
Uriel,[9] once warned; whose eye pursued him down 125
The way he went, and on th' Assyrian mount[1]
Saw him disfigured, more than could befall
Spirit of happy sort: his gestures fierce
He marked and mad demeanor, then alone,
As he supposed, all unobserved, unseen. 130
   So on he fares, and to the border comes
Of Eden, where delicious Paradise,
Now nearer, crowns with her enclosure green
As with a rural mound the champaign head
Of a steep wilderness, whose hairy sides 135
With thicket overgrown, grotesque and wild,
Access denied; and overhead up grew
Insuperable height of loftiest shade,
Cedar, and pine, and fir, and branching palm,
A sylvan scene, and as the ranks ascend 140
Shade above shade, a woody theater
Of stateliest view. Yet higher than their tops
The verdurous wall of Paradise up sprung;
Which to our general sire gave prospect large
Into his nether empire neighboring round. 145
And higher than that wall a circling row

9. An angel set to guard Eden from Satan's assault.   1. Niphates, a mountain on the border of Armenia
and Assyria.

Of goodliest trees loaden with fairest fruit,
Blossoms and fruits at once of golden hue,
Appeared, with gay enameled colors mixed;
On which the sun more glad impressed his beams   150
Than in fair evening cloud, or humid bow,
When God hath showered the earth: so lovely seemed
That landscape. And of pure now purer air
Meets his approach, and to the heart inspires
Vernal delight and joy, able to drive[2]   155
All sadness but despair. Now gentle gales,
Fanning their odoriferous wings, dispense
Native perfumes, and whisper whence they stole
Those balmy spoils. As when to them who sail
Beyond the Cape of Hope, and now are past   160
Mozambic, off at sea northeast winds blow
Sabean[3] odors from the spicy shore
Of Araby the Blest, with such delay
Well pleased they slack their course, and many a league
Cheered with the grateful smell old Ocean smiles;   165
So entertained those odorous sweets the fiend
Who came their bane, though with them better pleased
Than Asmodëus[4] with the fishy fume
That drove him, though enamored, from the spouse
Of Tobit's son,[5] and with a vengeance sent   170
From Media post to Egypt, there fast bound.
    Now to th' ascent of that steep savage hill
Satan had journeyed on, pensive and slow;
But further way found none; so thick entwined,
As one continued brake, the undergrowth   175
Of shrubs and tangling bushes had perplexed
All path of man or beast that passed that way.
One gate there only was, and that looked east
On th' other side; which when th' arch-felon saw,
Due entrance he disdained, and in contempt   180
At one slight bound high overleaped all bound
Of hill or highest wall, and sheer within
Lights on his feet. As when a prowling wolf,
Whom hunger drives to seek new haunt for prey,
Watching where shepherds pen their flocks at eve   185
In hurdled cotes amid the field secure,
Leaps o'er the fence with ease into the fold;
Or as a thief, bent to unhoard the cash
Of some rich burgher, whose substantial doors,
Cross-barred and bolted fast, fear no assault,   190
In at the window climbs, or o'er the tiles;
So clomb this first grand thief into God's fold:
So since into his church lewd hirelings climb.
Thence up he flew, and on the Tree of Life,
The middle tree and highest there that grew,   195

2. Drive out.   3. Sheba of the Bible. Mozambique was an important Portuguese province in the trade
route. Milton joins biblical, classical, and modern sources to describe the exotic pleasures of Eden.
4. Demon lover of Sara in the Apocryphal Book of Tobit.   5. Tobias.

Sat like a cormorant; yet not true life
Thereby regained, but sat devising death
To them who lived; nor on the virtue thought
Of that life-giving plant, but only used
For prospect, what, well used, had been the pledge   200
Of immortality. So little knows
Any, but God alone, to value right
The good before him, but perverts best things
To worst abuse, or to their meanest use.
   Beneath him with new wonder now he views   205
To all delight of human sense exposed
In narrow room Nature's whole wealth; yea more,
A Heaven on Earth; for blissful Paradise
Of God the garden was, by him in the east
Of Eden planted. Eden stretched her line   210
From Auran eastward to the royal towers
Of great Seleucia, built by Grecian kings,
Or where the sons of Eden long before
Dwelt in Telassar.[6] In this pleasant soil
His far more pleasant garden God ordained.   215
Out of the fertile ground he caused to grow
All trees of noblest kind for sight, smell, taste;
And all amid them stood the Tree of Life,
High eminent, blooming ambrosial fruit
Of vegetable gold; and next to life,   220
Our death, the Tree of Knowledge, grew fast by—
Knowledge of good bought dear by knowing ill.
Southward through Eden went a river large,
Nor changed his course, but through the shaggy hill
Passed underneath engulfed; for God had thrown   225
That mountain, as his garden-mold, high raised
Upon the rapid current, which, through veins
Of porous earth with kindly thirst up drawn,
Rose a fresh fountain, and with many a rill
Watered the garden; thence united fell   230
Down the steep glade, and met the nether flood,
Which from his darksome passage now appears,
And now, divided into four main streams,
Runs diverse, wandering many a famous realm
And country, whereof here needs no account;   235
But rather to tell how, if art could tell,
How from that sapphire fount the crispèd brooks,
Rolling on orient pearl and sands of gold,
With mazy error under pendant shades
Ran nectar, visiting each plant, and fed   240
Flowers worthy of Paradise; which not nice art
In beds and curious knots, but Nature boon
Poured forth profuse on hill and dale and plain,
Both where the morning sun first warmly smote
The open field, and where the unpierced shade   245

6. City in Eden.

Embrowned the noontide bowers. Thus was this place,
A happy rural seat of various view:
Groves whose rich trees wept odorous gums and balm;
Others whose fruit, burnished with golden rind,
Hung amiable—Hesperian fables[7] true,   250
If true, here only—and of delicious taste.
Betwixt them lawns, or level downs, and flocks
Grazing the tender herb, were interposed,
Or palmy hillock; or the flowery lap
Of some irriguous valley spread her store,   255
Flowers of all hue, and without thorn the rose.
Another side, umbrageous grots and caves
Of cool recess, o'er which the mantling vine
Lays forth her purple grape, and gently creeps
Luxuriant; meanwhile murmuring waters fall   260
Down the slope hills dispersed, or in a lake,
That to the fringèd bank with myrtle crowned
Her crystal mirror holds, unite their streams.
The birds their choir apply; airs, vernal airs,
Breathing the smell of field and grove, attune   265
The trembling leaves, while universal Pan,[8]
Knit with the Graces and the Hours in dance,
Led on th' eternal spring. Not that fair field
Of Enna, where Proserpin gathering flowers,
Herself a fairer flower, by gloomy Dis   270
Was gathered, which cost Ceres all that pain
To seek her through the world;[9] nor that sweet grove
Of Daphne, by Orontes and th' inspired
Castalian spring,[1] might with this Paradise
Of Eden strive; nor that Nyseian isle,   275
Girt with the river Triton, where old Cham,
Whom Gentiles Ammon call and Libyan Jove,
Hid Amalthea and her florid son
Young Bacchus from his stepdame Rhea's eye;[2]
Nor where Abassin kings their issue guard,   280
Mount Amara (though this by some supposed
True Paradise), under the Ethiop line[3]
By Nilus' head, enclosed with shining rock,
A whole day's journey high, but wide remote
From this Assyrian[4] garden, where the fiend   285
Saw undelighted all delight, all kind
Of living creatures, new to sight and strange.
Two of far nobler shape, erect and tall,
Godlike erect, with native honor clad

---

7. In Ovid's *Metamorphoses* 10, a dragon guarded the golden apples on the islands known as the Hesperides.   8. A pastoral god whose name Renaissance mythographers took from the Greek *pas* or *pan*, meaning "all" (or "universal").   9. In Ovid's *Fasti* 4, Dis, the god of the underworld, abducts Proserpine, daughter of Ceres (the goddess of the Earth's natural fecundity). Because she eats seven seeds of a pomegranate in the underworld, Proserpine must remain there seven months of each year, during which time Ceres mourns and blights the Earth.   1. The groves of Daphne by the river Orontes in Syria had a temple to Apollo and a spring named after the Castalian spring of Parnassus.   2. Ammon, king of Libya, had an affair with the nymph Amalthea, who bore the god Bacchus; Ammon hid the child from his jealous wife, Rhea, on the island of Nysa. Ammon was identified with the Libyan Jove and with Ham, or Cham, son of Noah.   3. I.e., on the equator in Abyssinia.   4. The Garden was near the Euphrates in Assyria.

In naked majesty, seemed lords of all,   290
And worthy seemed; for in their looks divine
The image of their glorious Maker shone,
Truth, wisdom, sanctitude severe and pure—
Severe, but in true filial freedom placed,
Whence true authority in men; though both   295
Not equal, as their sex not equal seemed;[5]
For contemplation he and valor formed,
For softness she and sweet attractive grace;
He for God only, she for God in him.[6]
His fair large front and eye sublime declared   300
Absolute rule;[7] and hyacinthine locks
Round from his parted forelock manly hung
Clustering, but not beneath his shoulders broad:
She, as a veil down to the slender waist,
Her unadornèd golden tresses wore   305
Disheveled, but in wanton ringlets waved
As the vine curls her tendrils, which implied
Subjection,[8] but required with gentle sway,
And by her yielded, by him best received,
Yielded with coy submission, modest pride,   310
And sweet, reluctant, amorous delay.
Nor those mysterious parts were then concealed;
Then was not guilty shame. Dishonest shame
Of Nature's works, honor dishonorable,
Sin-bred, how have ye troubled all mankind   315
With shows instead, mere shows of seeming pure,
And banished from man's life his happiest life,
Simplicity and spotless innocence!
So passed they naked on, nor shunned the sight
Of God or angel, for they thought no ill;   320
So hand in hand they passed, the loveliest pair
That ever since in love's embraces met:
Adam the goodliest man of men since born
His sons; the fairest of her daughters Eve.
Under a tuft of shade that on a green   325
Stood whispering soft, by a fresh fountain-side,
They sat them down; and after no more toil
Of their sweet gardening labor than sufficed
To recommend cool Zephyr,[9] and made ease
More easy, wholesome thirst and appetite   330
More grateful, to their supper fruits they fell,
Nectarine fruits which the compliant boughs
Yielded them, sidelong as they sat recline
On the soft downy bank damasked[1] with flowers.
The savory pulp they chew, and in the rind   335

---

5. Milton includes both biblical accounts of creation, beginning with Genesis 1.27: "So God created man in his own image, in the image of God created he him; male and female created he them." He next uses the account of creating Eve from Adam's rib.   6. "The head of every man is Christ; and the head of the woman is the man" (1 Corinthians 11.3).   7. Adam's body "declares" the political theory associated with monarchical absolutism.   8. Eve's body "implies" the subjection that fulfills Adam's "Absolute rule," but negotiates the distribution of "Authority in men." In *Tetrachordon*, Milton writes of the "golden dependence of [male] headship and [female] subjection" in marriage.   9. West wind.   1. Richly patterned.

Still as they thirsted scoop the brimming stream;
Nor gentle purpose, nor endearing smiles
Wanted, nor youthful dalliance, as beseems
Fair couple linked in happy nuptial league,
Alone as they. About them frisking played   340
All beasts of th' earth, since wild, and of all chase
In wood or wilderness, forest or den.
Sporting the lion ramped, and in his paw
Dandled the kid; bears, tigers, ounces, pards,[2]
Gamboled before them; th' unwieldy elephant   345
To make them mirth used all his might, and wreathed
His lithe proboscis;[3] close the serpent sly,
Insinuating, wove with Gordian twine
His braided train, and of his fatal guile
Gave proof unheeded. Others on the grass   350
Couched, and now filled with pasture gazing sat,
Or bedward ruminating; for the sun,
Declined, was hasting now with prone career
To th' ocean isles, and in th' ascending scale
Of heaven the stars that usher evening rose: 355
When Satan, still in gaze as first he stood,
Scarce thus at length failed speech recovered sad:
   "O Hell! what do mine eyes with grief behold?
Into our room of bliss thus high advanced
Creatures of other mold, Earth-born perhaps,   360
Not spirits, yet to heavenly spirits bright
Little inferior; whom my thoughts pursue
With wonder, and could love; so lively shines
In them divine resemblance, and such grace
The hand that formed them on their shape hath poured.   365
Ah! gentle pair, ye little think how nigh
Your change approaches, when all these delights
Will vanish, and deliver ye to woe,
More woe, the more your taste is now of joy:
Happy, but for so happy ill secured   370
Long to continue, and this high seat, your Heaven,
Ill fenced for Heaven to keep out such a foe
As now is entered; yet no purposed foe
To you, whom I could pity thus forlorn,
Though I unpitied. League with you I seek,   375
And mutual amity so strait, so close,
That I with you must dwell, or you with me,
Henceforth. My dwelling, haply, may not please,
Like this fair Paradise, your sense; yet such
Accept your Maker's work; he gave it me,   380
Which I as freely give. Hell shall unfold,
To entertain you two, her widest gates,
And send forth all her kings; there will be room,
Not like these narrow limits, to receive
Your numerous offspring; if no better place,   385

2. Lynxes and leopards.   3. Trunk.

Thank him who puts me, loath, to this revenge
On you, who wrong me not, for him who wronged.
And should I at your harmless innocence
Melt, as I do, yet public reason just—
Honor and empire with revenge enlarged   390
By conquering this new world—compels me now
To do what else, though damned, I should abhor.
    So spake the fiend, and with necessity,
The tyrant's plea, excused his devilish deeds.
Then from his lofty stand on that high tree   395
Down he alights among the sportful herd
Of those four-footed kinds, himself now one,
Now other, as their shape served best his end
Nearer to view his prey, and unespied
To mark what of their state he more might learn   400
By word or action marked. About them round
A lion now he stalks with fiery glare;
Then as a tiger, who by chance hath spied
In some purlieu⁴ two gentle fawns at play,
Straight couches close; then, rising, changes oft 405
His couchant⁵ watch, as one who chose his ground,
Whence rushing he might surest seize them both
Gripped in each paw; when Adam first of men
To first of women Eve thus moving speech,
Turned him all ear to hear new utterance flow.   410
    "Sole partner and sole part of all these joys,
Dearer thyself than all; needs must the power
That made us, and for us this ample world,
Be infinitely good, and of his good
As liberal and free as infinite,   415
That raised us from the dust and placed us here
In all this happiness, who at his hand
Have nothing merited, nor can perform
Aught of which he hath need; he who requires
From us no other service than to keep   420
This one, this easy charge, of all the trees
In Paradise that bear delicious fruit
So various, not to taste that only Tree
Of Knowledge, planted by the Tree of Life,
So near grows death to life, whate'er death is,   425
Some dreadful thing, no doubt; for well thou know'st
God hath pronounced it death to taste that tree,
The only sign of our obedience left
Among so many signs of power and rule
Conferred upon us, and dominion given   430
Over all other creatures that possess
Earth, air, and sea. Then let us not think hard
One easy prohibition, who enjoy
Free leave so large to all things else, and choice
Unlimited of manifold delights;   435

4. Region on the outskirts of a given area.   5. From heraldry: lying down with the head raised.

But let us ever praise him, and extol
His bounty, following our delightful task
To prune these growing plants and tend these flowers,
Which were it toilsome, yet with thee were sweet."
   To whom thus Eve replied: "O thou for whom   440
And from whom I was formed flesh of thy flesh,
And without whom am to no end, my guide
And head, what thou hast said is just and right.
For we to him indeed all praises owe
And daily thanks, I chiefly who enjoy   445
So far the happier lot, enjoying thee
Preeminent by so much odds, while thou
Like consort to thyself canst nowhere find.
That day I oft remember, when from sleep
I first awaked, and found myself reposed   450
Under a shade on flowers, much wondering where
And what I was, whence thither brought, and how.
Not distant far from thence a murmuring sound
Of waters issued from a cave and spread
Into a liquid plain, then stood unmoved,   455
Pure as th' expanse of heaven; I thither went
With unexperienced thought, and laid me down
On the green bank, to look into the clear
Smooth lake that to me seemed another sky.
As I bent down to look, just opposite,   460
A shape within the wat'ry gleam appeared,
Bending to look on me. I started back,
It started back; but pleased I soon returned,
Pleased it returned as soon with answering looks
Of sympathy and love. There I had fixed   465
Mine eyes till now, and pined with vain desire,[6]
Had not a voice thus warned me: 'What thou seest,
What there thou seest, fair creature, is thyself;
With thee it came and goes. But follow me,
And I will bring thee where no shadow stays   470
Thy coming, and thy soft embraces, he
Whose image thou art, him thou shalt enjoy
Inseparably thine, to him shalt bear
Multitudes like thyself, and thence be called
Mother of human race.'[7] What could I do   475
But follow straight, invisibly thus led?
Till I espied thee, fair indeed and tall
Under a platan, yet methought[8] less fair,
Less winning soft, less amiably mild
Than that smooth wat'ry image. Back I turned;   480
Thou following cried'st aloud, 'Return, fair Eve,
Whom fli'st thou? whom thou fli'st, of him thou art,
His flesh, his bone; to give thee being I lent
Out of my side to thee, nearest my heart,

---

6. Like Ovid's Narcissus in *Metamorphoses* 3.339–510, Eve falls in love with her image; unlike Narcissus, she is led by God's voice to Adam, whose image she is.   7. Eve means "Mother of all things living" (11.159).   8. It seemed to me. A platan is a plane tree.

Substantial life, to have thee by my side   485
Henceforth an individual solace dear.
Part of my soul I seek thee, and thee claim
My other half.' With that, thy gentle hand
Seized mine, I yielded, and from that time see
How beauty is excelled by manly grace   490
And wisdom, which alone is truly fair."
    So spake our general mother, and with eyes
Of conjugal attraction unreproved
And meek surrender, half embracing leaned
On our first father; half her swelling breast   495
Naked met his under the flowing gold
Of her loose tresses hid. He in delight
Both of her beauty and submissive charms
Smiled with superior love, as Jupiter
On Juno smiles,[9] when he impregns the clouds   500
That shed May flowers, and pressed her matron lip
With kisses pure. Aside the Devil turned
For envy, yet with jealous leer malign
Eyed them askance, and to himself thus plained:
    "Sight hateful, sight tormenting! thus these two   505
Imparadised in one another's arms,
The happier Eden, shall enjoy their fill
Of bliss on bliss, while I to Hell am thrust,
Where neither joy nor love, but fierce desire,
Among our other torments not the least,   510
Still unfulfilled with pain of longing pines.
Yet let me not forget what I have gained
From their own mouths: all is not theirs, it seems.
One fatal tree there stands, of knowledge called,
Forbidden them to taste. Knowledge forbidden?   515
Suspicious, reasonless. Why should their lord
Envy them that? Can it be sin to know,
Can it be death? and do they only stand
By ignorance, is that their happy state,
The proof of their obedience and their faith?   520
O fair foundation laid whereon to build
Their ruin! Hence I will excite their minds
With more desire to know, and to reject
Envious commands, invented with design
To keep them low whom knowledge might exalt   525
Equal with gods. Aspiring to be such,
They taste and die; what likelier can ensue?
But first with narrow search I must walk round
This garden, and no corner leave unspied;
A chance but chance may lead where I may meet   530
Some wandering spirit of Heaven, by fountain side
Or in thick shade retired, from him to draw
What further would be learnt. Live while ye may,

---

9. In Greco-Roman mythology, Jupiter is king of the gods and Juno is his sister and wife. The marital hierarchies of the pagan gods and of the human couple differ. While Jupiter reigns (and rains) supreme, Adam and Eve enjoy "give and take." Adam smiles *with superior love*, yet Eve is physically "on top."

Yet happy pair; enjoy, till I return,
Short pleasures, for long woes are to succeed."   535

*   *   *

FROM BOOK 8

The Argument

Adam inquires concerning celestial motions, is doubtfully answered, and
exhorted to search rather things more worthy of knowledge: Adam assents,
and still desirous to detain Raphael, relates to him what he remembered
since his own creation, his placing in Paradise, his talk with God concerning
solitude and fit society, his first meeting and nuptials with Eve, his discourse
with the angel thereupon; who after admonitions repeated departs.

[Adam Describes His Own Creation and That of Eve; Having Repeated His Warning, the Angel Departs]

*   *   *

"Solicit not thy thoughts with matters hid,[1]
Leave them to God above, him serve and fear;
Of other creatures, as him pleases best,
Wherever placed, let him dispose: joy thou   170
In what he gives thee, this Paradise
And they fair Eve; heaven is for thee too high
To know what passes there; be lowly wise:
Think only what concerns thee and thy being;
Dream not of other worlds, what creatures there   175
Live, in what state, condition or degree,
Contented that thus far hath been revealed
Not of earth only but of highest heaven."
     To whom thus Adam cleared of doubt, replied.
"How fully hast thou satisfied me, pure   180
Intelligence of heaven, angel serene,
And freed from intricacies, taught to live,
The easiest way, nor with perplexing thoughts
To interrupt the sweet of life, from which
God hath bid dwell far off all anxious cares,   185
And not molest us, unless we ourselves
Seek them with wandering thoughts, and notions vain.
But apt the mind or fancy is to rove
Unchecked, and of her roving is no end;
Till warned, or by experience taught, she learn,   190
That not to know at large of things remote
From use, obscure and subtle, but to know
That which before us lies in daily life,
Is the prime wisdom, what is more is fume,
Or emptiness, or find impertinence,   195

---

1. In conversation with the angel Raphael, Adam has asked questions about astronomy and expressed
uncertainty about divine intention.

And renders us in things that most concern
Unpracticed, unprepared, and still to seek.
Therefore from this high pitch let us descend
A lower flight, and speak of things at hand
Useful, whence haply mention may arise   200
Of something not unseasonable to ask
By sufferance, and they wonted favor deigned.
Thee I have heard relating what was done
Ere my remembrance: now hear me relate
My story, which perhaps thou hast not heard;   205
And Day is yet not spent; till then thou seest
How subtly to detain thee I devise,
Inviting thee to hear while I relate,
Fond, were it not in hope of thy reply:
For while I sit with thee, I seem in heaven,   210
And sweeter thy discourse is to my ear
Then fruits of palm-tree pleasantest to thirst
And hunger both, from labor, at the hour
Of sweet repast; they satiate, and soon fill,
Though pleasant, but thy words with grace divine   215
Imbued, bring to their sweetness no satiety."
   To whom thus Raphael answered heavenly meek.
"Nor are thy lips ungraceful, sire of men,
Nor tongue ineloquent; for God on thee
Abundantly his gifts hath also poured   220
Inward and outward both, his image fair:
Speaking or mute all comeliness and grace
Attends thee, and each word, each motion forms.
Nor less think we in heaven of thee on earth
Than of our fellow servant, and inquire   225
Gladly into the ways of God with man:
For God we see hath honored thee, and set
On man his equal love: say therefore on;
For I that day was absent, as befell,
Bound on a voyage uncouth and obscure,   230
Far on excursion toward the gates of hell;[2]
Squared in full legion (such command we had)
To see that none thence issued forth a spy,
Or enemy, while God was in his work,
Lest he incensed at such eruption bold,   235
Destruction with creation might have mixed.
Nor that they durst without his leave attempt,
But us he sends upon his high behests
For state, as sovereign king, and to inure
Our prompt obedience. Fast we found, fast shut   240
The dismal gates, and barricadoed strong;
But long ere our approaching heard within
Noise, other then the sound of dance or song,
Torment, and loud lament, and furious rage.

---

2. God sent Raphael to watch the gates of hell and prevent Satan from disturbing Him during the Creation of the world.

Glad we returned up to the coasts of light   245
Ere Sabbath evening: so we had in charge.
But thy relation now; for I attend,
Pleased with thy words no less than thou with mine."
    So spake the godlike power, and thus our sire:
"For man to tell how human life began   250
Is hard; for who himself beginning knew?
Desire with thee still longer to converse
Induced me. As new waked from soundest sleep,
Soft on the flowery herb I found me laid
In balmy sweat, which with his beams the sun   255
Soon dried, and on the reeking³ moisture fed.
Straight toward heaven my wondering eyes I turned,
And gazed a while the ample sky, till raised
By quick instinctive motion up I sprung
As thitherward endeavoring, and upright   260
Stood on my feet; about me round I saw
Hill, dale, and shady woods, and sunny plains
And liquid lapse of murmuring streams; by these,
Creatures that lived and moved, and walked or flew,
Birds on the branches warbling. All things smiled;   265
With fragrance and with joy my heart o'erflowed.
Myself I then perused, and limb by limb
Surveyed, and sometimes went and sometimes ran
With supple joints as lively vigor led:
But who I was, or where, or from what cause,   270
Knew not. To speak I tried, and forthwith spake,
My tongue obeyed, and readily could name
Whate'er I saw. 'Thou sun,' said I, 'fair light,
And thou enlightened earth, so fresh and gay,
Ye hills and dales, ye rivers, woods, and plains,   275
And ye that live and move, fair creatures, tell,
Tell, if ye saw, how came I thus, how here?
Not of myself; by some great maker, then,
In goodness and in power preëminent.
Tell me how may I know him, how adore,   280
From whom I have that thus I move and live,
And feel that I am happier than I know.'
    "While thus I called, and strayed I knew not whither
From where I first drew air and first beheld
This happy light, when answer none returned,   285
On a green shady bank profuse of flowers
Pensive I sat me down; there gentle sleep
First found me and with soft oppression seized
My drowsèd sense—untroubled, though I thought
I then was passing to my former state   290
Insensible, and forthwith to dissolve;
When suddenly stood at my head a dream,
Whose inward apparition gently moved
My fancy to believe I yet had being
And lived. One came, methought, of shape divine,   295

3. Steaming.

And said, 'Thy mansion wants thee, Adam, rise,
First man, of men innumerable ordained
First father; called by thee I come thy guide
To the garden of bliss, thy seat prepared.'
So saying, by the hand he took me raised,   300
And over fields and waters, as in air
Smooth sliding without step, last led me up
A woody mountain whose high top was plain,
A circuit wide, enclosed, with goodliest trees
Planted, with walks and bowers, that what I saw   305
Of earth before scarce pleasant seemed. Each tree
Loaden with fairest fruit that hung to the eye
Tempting, stirred in me sudden appetite
To pluck and eat; whereat I waked, and found
Before mine eyes all real, as the dream   310
Had lively shadowed. Here had new begun
My wandering, had not he who was my guide
Up hither, from among the trees appeared,
Presence divine. Rejoicing, but with awe,
In adoration at his feet I fell   315
Submiss: he reared me, and, 'Whom thou soughtest I am,'
Said mildly, 'author⁴ of all this thou seest
Above or round about thee or beneath.
This Paradise I give thee, count it thine
To till and keep, and of the fruit to eat.   320
Of every tree that in the garden grows
Eat freely with glad heart; fear here no dearth.
But of the tree whose operation brings
Knowledge of good and ill, which I have set
The pledge of thy obedience and thy faith   325
Amid the garden by the Tree of Life,
Remember what I warn thee, shun to taste
And shun the bitter consequence: for know
The day thou eat'st thereof, my sole command
Transgressed, inevitably thou shalt die,   330
From that day mortal, and this happy state
Shalt lose, expelled from hence into a world
Of woe and sorrow.' Sternly he pronounced
The rigid interdiction, which resounds
Yet dreadful in mine ear, though in my choice   335
Not to incur; but soon his clear aspèct
Returned, and gracious purpose thus renewed:
'Not only these fair bounds, but all the Earth
To thee and to thy race I give; as lords
Possess it, and all things that therein live,   340
Or live in sea or air, beast, fish, and fowl.
In sign whereof each bird and beast behold
After their kinds; I bring them to receive
From thee their names, and pay thee fealty
With low subjection; understand the same   345
Of fish within their watery residence,

4. Creator, augmenter.

Not hither summoned, since they cannot change
Their element to draw the thinner air.'
As thus he spake, each bird and beast behold
Approaching two and two, these cowering low   350
With blandishment, each bird stooped on his wing.
I named them as they passed, and understood
Their nature, with such knowledge God endued
My sudden apprehension. But in these
I found not what methought I wanted[5] still,   355
And to the heavenly vision thus presumed:
    " 'O by what name, for thou above all these,
Above mankind, or aught than mankind higher,
Surpassest far my naming, how may I
Adore thee, author of this universe   360
And all this good to man, for whose well-being
So amply and with hands so liberal
Thou hast provided all things? But with me
I see not who partakes. In solitude
What happiness? Who can enjoy alone,   365
Or all enjoying, what contentment find?'
Thus I presumptuous; and the vision bright,
As with a smile more brightened, thus replied:
    " 'What callest thou solitude? Is not the earth
With various living creatures, and the air,   370
Replenished, and all these at thy command
To come and play before thee? Knowest thou not
Their language and their ways? They also know
And reason not contemptibly; with these
Find pastime and bear rule; thy realm is large.'   375
So spake the universal Lord, and seemed
So ordering. I with leave of speech implored
And humble deprecation, thus replied:
" 'Let not my words offend thee, heavenly power,
My maker; be propitious while I speak.   380
Hast thou not made me here thy substitute,
And these inferior far beneath me set?
Among unequals what society
Can sort, what harmony or true delight?
Which must be mutual, in proportion due   385
Given and received. But in disparity,
The one intense, the other still remiss,
Cannot well suit with either, but soon prove
Tedious alike. Of fellowship I speak
Such as I seek, fit to participate   390
All rational delight, wherein the brute
Cannot be human consort. They rejoice
Each with their kind, lion with lioness;
So fitly them in pairs thou hast combined:
Much less can bird with beast, or fish with fowl   395
So well converse, nor with the ox the ape;

5. Desired, lacked.

Worse then can man with beast, and least of all.'
"Whereto the Almighty answered, not displeased:
'A nice and subtle happiness I see
Thou to thyself proposest, in the choice   400
Of thy associates, Adam, and wilt taste
No pleasure, though in pleasure, solitary.
What thinkest thou then of me and this my state?
Seem I to thee sufficiently possessed
Of happiness or not? who am alone   405
From all eternity, for none I know
Second to me or like, equal much less.
How have I then with whom to hold converse
Save with the creatures which I made, and those
To me inferior, infinite descents   410
Beneath what other creatures are to thee?'
"He ceased, I lowly answered: 'To attain
The height and depth of thy eternal ways
All human thoughts come short, supreme of things.
Thou in thyself art perfect, and in thee   415
Is no deficience found; not so is man,
But in degree, the cause of his desire
By conversation with his like to help
Or solace his defects. No need that thou
Shouldst propagate, already infinite,   420
And through all number absolute, though one.
But man by number is to manifest
His single imperfection, and beget
Like of his like, his image multiplied,
In unity defective, which requires   425
Collateral[6] love and dearest amity.
Thou in thy secrecy although alone,
Best with thyself accompanied, seekest not
Social communication; yet, so pleased,
Canst raise thy creature to what height thou wilt   430
Of union or communion, deified;
I by conversing cannot these erect
From prone, nor in their ways complacence find.'
Thus I emboldened spake, and freedom used
Permissive, and acceptance found, which gained   435
This answer from the gracious voice divine:
" 'Thus far to try thee, Adam, I was pleased,
And find thee knowing, not of beasts alone
Which thou hast rightly named, but of thyself,
Expressing well the spirit within thee free,   440
My image, not imparted to the brute,
Whose fellowship, therefore unmeet for thee,
Good reason was thou freely shouldst dislike;
And be so minded still. I, ere thou spak'st,
Knew it not good for man to be alone,   445
And no such company as then thou sawest

6. Equal, with a pun on Latin *latus, lateris*, the "side" from which Eve will be formed.

Intended thee, for trial only brought,
To see how thou couldst judge of fit and meet.
What next I bring shall please thee, be assured:
Thy likeness, thy fit help, thy other self,   450
Thy wish exactly to thy heart's desire.'
    "He ended, or I heard no more, for now,
My earthly by his heavenly overpowered
Which it had long stood under, strained to the height
In that celestial colloquy sublime,   455
As with an object that excels the sense
Dazzled and spent, sunk down and sought repair
Of sleep, which instantly fell on me, called
By nature as in aid, and closed mine eyes.
Mine eyes he closed, but open left the cell   460
Of fancy,[7] my internal sight, by which
Abstract as in a trance methought I saw,
Though sleeping, where I lay, and saw the shape
Still glorious before whom awake I stood;
Who stooping opened my left side, and took   465
From thence a rib, with cordial[8] spirits warm
And life-blood streaming fresh. Wide was the wound,
But suddenly with flesh filled up and healed.
The rib he formed and fashioned with his hands;
Under his forming hands a creature grew,   470
Manlike, but different sex, so lovely fair
That what seemed fair in all the world seemed now
Mean, or in her summed up, in her contained,
And in her looks, which from that time infused
Sweetness into my heart, unfelt before,   475
And into all things from her air inspired
The spirit of love and amorous delight.
She disappeared, and left me dark; I waked
To find her or forever to deplore
Her loss, and other pleasures all abjure;   480
When out of hope, behold her, not far off,
Such as I saw her in my dream, adorned
With what all Earth or Heaven could bestow
To make her amiable. On she came,
Led by her heavenly maker, though unseen,   485
And guided by his voice, nor uninformed
Of nuptial sanctity and marriage rites.
Grace was in all her steps, heaven in her eye,
In every gesture dignity and love.
I overjoyed could not forbear aloud: 490
    " 'This turn hath made amends; thou hast fulfilled
Thy words, Creator bounteous and benign,
Giver of all things fair, but fairest this
Of all thy gifts; nor enviest. I now see
Bone of my bone, flesh of my flesh, my self   495
Before me; woman is her name, of man

---

7. Imagination.   8. From the Latin *cors, cordis*, relating to the heart.

Extracted; for this cause he shall forego
Father and mother, and to his wife adhere,
And they shall be one flesh, one heart, one soul.'
    "She heard me thus, and though divinely brought,   500
Yet innocence and virgin modesty,
Her virtue and the conscience of her worth
That would be wooed and not unsought be won,
Not obvious, not obtrusive, but retired,
The more desirable—or, to say all,   505
Nature herself, though pure of sinful thought,
Wrought in her so that, seeing me, she turned.
I followed her; she what was honor knew,
And with obsequious⁹ majesty approved
My pleaded reason. To the nuptial bower   510
I led her blushing like the morn. All heaven
And happy constellations on that hour
Shed their selectest influence; the earth
Gave sign of gratulation,¹ and each hill;
Joyous the birds; fresh gales and gentle airs   515
Whispered it to the woods, and from their wings
Flung rose, flung odors from the spicy shrub,
Disporting, till the amorous bird of night
Sung spousal, and bid haste the evening star
On his hill-top, to light the bridal lamp.   520
    "Thus have I told thee all my state, and brought
My story to the sum of earthly bliss
Which I enjoy, and must confess to find
In all things else delight indeed, but such
As, used or not, works in the mind no change,   525
Nor vehement² desire—these delicacies
I mean of taste, sight, smell, herbs, fruits, and flowers,
Walks and the melody of birds. But here,
Far otherwise, transported I behold,
Transported touch; here passion first I felt,   530
Commotion strange, in all enjoyments else
Superior and unmoved, here only weak
Against the charm of beauty's powerful glance.
Or nature failed in me and left some part
Not proof enough such object to sustain,   535
Or from my side subducting³ took perhaps
More than enough; at least on her bestowed
Too much of ornament, in outward show
Elaborate, of inward less exact.
For well I understand in the prime end   540
Of nature her th' inferior, in the mind
And inward faculties which most excel,
In outward also her resembling less
His image who made both, and less expressing
The character of that dominion given   545

9. Obedient ("following," literally), displaying the essential virtue of the wife.   1. Congratulation.
2. Overpowering, distracting.   3. Taking away.

O'er other creatures. Yet when I approach
Her loveliness, so absolute she seems
And in herself complete, so well to know
Her own, that what she wills to do or say
Seems wisest, virtuousest, discreetest, best.   550
All higher knowledge in her presence falls
Degraded; wisdom in discourse with her
Loses discountenanced, and like folly shows;
Authority and reason on her wait
As one intended first, not after made   555
Occasionally;⁴ and to consùmmate all,
Greatness of mind and nobleness their seat
Build in her loveliest, and create an awe
About her as a guard angelic placed."
   To whom the Angel with contracted brow: 560
"Accuse not nature, she hath done her part;
Do thou but thine, and be not diffident
Of wisdom; she deserts thee not if thou
Dismiss not her when most thou need'st her nigh
By àttributing overmuch to things   565
Less excellent, as thou thyself perceiv'st.
For what admir'st thou, what transports thee so?
An outside? Fair no doubt, and worthy well
Thy cherishing, thy honoring, and thy love;
Not thy subjection. Weigh her with thyself,   570
Then value. Ofttimes nothing profits more
Then self-esteem, grounded on just and right
Well managed. Of that skill the more thou know'st,
The more she will acknowledge thee her head,
And to realities yield all her shows—   575
Made so adorn for thy delight the more,
So aweful⁵ that with honor thou may'st love
Thy mate, who sees when thou art seen least wise.
But if the sense of touch whereby mankind
Is propagated seem such dear delight   580
Beyond all other, think the same vouchsafed
To cattle and each beast; which would not be
To them made common and divulged if aught
Therein enjoyed were worthy to subdue
The soul of man, or passion in him move.   585
What higher in her society thou find'st
Attractive, human, rational—love still;
In loving thou dost well, in passion not,
Wherein true love consists not. Love refines
The thoughts, and heart enlarges, hath his seat   590
In reason, and is judicious, is the scale
By which to heavenly love thou may'st ascend,
Not sunk in carnal pleasure, for which cause
Among the beasts no mate for thee was found."
   To whom thus half abashed Adam replied: 595

---

4. For a particular purpose or occasion, i.e., Adam's request for a companion.   5. Awe-inspiring.

"Neither her outside formed so fair, nor aught
In procreation common to all kinds
(Though higher of the genial[6] bed by far
And with mysterious reverence I deem)
So much delights me as those graceful acts,   600
Those thousand decencies that daily flow
From all her words and actions, mixed with love
And sweet compliance, which declare unfeigned
Union of mind, or in us both one soul,
Harmony to behold in wedded pair   605
More grateful than harmonious sound to the ear.
Yet these subject not; I to thee disclose
What inward thence I feel, not therefore foiled,
Who meet with various objects from the sense
Variously representing; yet still free   610
Approve the best, and follow what I approve.
      "To love thou balm'st me not, for love thou say'st
Leads up to Heaven, is both the way and guide;
Bear with me then, if lawful what I ask:
Love not the heavenly spirits, and how their love   615
Express they, by looks only, or do they mix
Irradiance, virtual or immediate touch?"
      To whom the Angel with a smile that glowed
Celestial rosy red, love's proper hue,
Answered: "Let it suffice thee that thou know'st   620
Us happy, and without love no happiness.
Whatever pure thou in the body enjoy'st
(And pure thou wert created), we enjoy
In eminence, and obstacle find none
Of membrane, joint, or limb, exclusive bars.   625
Easier than air with air, if spirits embrace,
Total they mix, union of pure with pure
Desiring; nor restrained conveyance need
As flesh to mix with flesh, or soul with soul.
But I can now no more; the parting sun   630
Beyond the earth's green cape and verdant isles
Hesperian sets, my signal to depart.
Be strong, live happy, and love, but first of all
His whom to love is to obey, and keep
His great command; take heed lest passion sway   635
Thy judgment to do aught which else free will
Would not admit; thine and of all thy sons
The weal or woe in thee is placed: beware.
I in thy persevering shall rejoice,
And all the blest. Stand fast; to stand or fall   640
Free in thine own arbitrement[7] it lies.
Perfect within, no outward aid require;
And all temptation to transgress repel."
      So saying, he arose; whom Adam thus
Followed with benediction: "Since to part,   645

6. Procreative.   7. Judgment.

Go, heavenly guest, ethereal messenger,
Sent from whose sovereign goodness I adore.
Gentle to me and affable[8] hath been
Thy condescension, and shall be honored ever
With grateful memory. Thou to mankind   650
Be good and friendly still, and oft return."
　So parted they, the Angel up to Heaven
From the thick shade, and Adam to his bower.

BOOK 9

The Argument

　Satan, having compassed the Earth, with meditated guile returns as a mist
by night into Paradise; enters into the serpent sleeping. Adam and Eve in
the morning go forth to their labors, which Eve proposes to divide in several
places, each laboring apart: Adam consents not, alleging the danger lest that
enemy of whom they were forewarned should attempt her found alone. Eve,
loath to be thought not circumspect or firm enough, urges her going apart,
the rather desirous to make trial of her strength; Adam at last yields. The
serpent finds her alone: his subtle approach, first gazing, then speaking, with
much flattery extolling Eve above all other creatures. Eve, wondering to hear
the serpent speak, asks how he attained to human speech and such understanding not till now; the serpent answers that by tasting of a certain tree in
the garden he attained both to speech and reason, till then void of both. Eve
requires him to bring her to that tree, and finds it to be the Tree of Knowledge
forbidden: the serpent, now grown bolder, with many wiles and arguments
induces her at length to eat. She, pleased with the taste, deliberates a while
whether to impart thereof to Adam or not; at last brings him of the fruit;
relates what persuaded her to eat thereof. Adam, at first amazed, but perceiving her lost, resolves, through vehemence of love, to perish with her,
and, extenuating the trespass, eats also of the fruit. The effects thereof in
them both; they seek to cover their nakedness; then fall to variance and
accusation of one another.

[Temptation and Fall]

No more of talk where God or angel guest[9]
With man, as with his friend, familiar used
To sit indulgent, and with him partake
Rural repast, permitting him the while
Venial[1] discourse unblamed. I now must change   5
Those notes to tragic; foul distrust, and breach
Disloyal, on the part of man, revolt
And disobedience; on the part of Heaven,
Now alienated, distance and distaste,
Anger and just rebuke, and judgment given,   10
That brought into this world a world of woe,

---

8. Easy to converse with.　9. Raphael, the "affable archangel," who in preceding books (5–8) has sat
with Adam sharing "rural repast" and discoursing on such highly relevant matters as Lucifer's fall, the
Creation, the structure of the universe. To him, Adam has told of the warning he has received from God
not to touch the Tree of Knowledge.　1. Unblemished.

Sin and her shadow Death, and Misery,
Death's harbinger. Sad task! yet argument
Not less but more heroic than the wrath
Of stern Achilles on his foe pursued   15
Thrice fugitive about Troy wall;[2] or rage
Of Turnus for Lavinia disespoused;[3]
Or Neptune's ire, or Juno's, that so long
Perplexed the Greek, and Cytherea's son:[4]
If answerable style I can obtain   20
Of my celestial Patroness,[5] who deigns
Her nightly visitation unimplored,
And dictates to me slumbering, or inspires
Easy my unpremeditated[6] verse,
Since first this subject for heroic song   25
Pleased me,[7] long choosing and beginning late,
Not sedulous by nature to indite
War, hitherto the only argument
Heroic deemed, chief mastery to dissect[8]
With long and tedious havoc fabled knights   30
In battles feigned (the better fortitude
Of patience and heroic martyrdom
Unsung), or to describe races and games,[9]
Or tilting furniture, emblazoned shields,
Impresses quaint, caparisons and steeds,   35
Bases[1] and tinsel trappings, gorgeous knights
At joust and tournament; then marshaled feast
Served up in hall with sewers and seneschals:[2]
The skill of artifice or office mean;
Not that which justly gives heroic name   40
To person or to poem. Me,[3] of these
Nor skilled nor studious, higher argument
Remains, sufficient of itself to raise
That name, unless an age too late, or cold
Climate, or years, damp my intended wing[4]   45
Depressed; and much they may if all be mine,
Not hers who brings it nightly to my ear.
    The sun was sunk, and after him the star
Of Hesperus, whose office is to bring
Twilight upon the Earth, short arbiter   50
'Twixt day and night, and now from end to end

2. At the end of the *Iliad* Achilles, whose *wrath* is the subject announced in the first line of the epic, will chase his enemy, the Trojan Hector, three times around the walls of Troy before killing him.   3. In Virgil's *Aeneid*, Lavinia, fated to be Aeneas's wife, had earlier been promised to King Turnus.   4. In the *Odyssey* Neptune (Poseidon) is the god hostile to Odysseus (*the Greek*). In the *Aeneid* the hero is persecuted by the wrath of the goddess Juno, who had quarreled with Aeneas's mother, Cytherea (Venus).   5. Urania, originally the Muse of astronomy. To Milton she is the source of *celestial* inspiration. *Answerable*: suitable.   6. In other passages of the poem, Milton refers to inspiration coming to him at night or at early dawn, with spontaneous (*unpremeditated*) ease.   7. The choice of his present heroic theme had occurred early, as had the rejection of the kind of subject matter described in the following lines.   8. To analyze but also to cut up; a possible allusion to the abundance of bloody battle wounds described in classical epics.   9. There are long descriptions of games in the *Iliad* (23) and in the *Aeneid* (10).   1. Skirtlike housings for warhorses. *Tilting furniture*: the paraphernalia of arms tournaments. *Impresses*: fancy emblems on shields.   2. Attendants at meals and stewards in noble households.   3. To me.   4. The notion that nordic climates *damp* (benumb) human wit was accepted by Milton and is as old as Aristotle. *That name*: that of epic poet. *An age too late*: a time no longer fit for epic poetry.

Night's hemisphere had veiled the horizon round,
When Satan, who late fled before the threats
Of Gabriel out of Eden,[5] now improved
In meditated fraud and malice, bent
On man's destruction, mauger[6] what might hap 55
Of heavier on himself, fearless returned.
By night he fled, and at midnight returned
From compassing the Earth—cautious of day
Since Uriel, regent of the sun, descried 60
His entrance, and forewarned the Cherubim[7]
That kept their watch. Thence, full of anguish, driven,
The space of seven continued nights he rode
With darkness; thrice the equinoctial line
He circled, four times crossed the car of Night 65
From pole to pole, traversing each colure;[8]
On the eighth returned, and on the coast averse[9]
From entrance or cherubic watch by stealth
Found unsuspected way. There was a place
(Now not, though sin, not time, first wrought the change) 70
Where Tigris, at the foot of Paradise,[1]
Into a gulf shot under ground, till part
Rose up a fountain by the Tree of Life.
In with the river sunk, and with it rose,
Satan, involved in rising mist; then sought 75
Where to lie hid. Sea he had searched and land
From Eden over Pontus, and the pool
Maeotis, up beyond the river Ob;[2]
Downward as far antarctic; and, in length,
West from Orontes to the ocean barred 80
At Darien,[3] thence to the land where flows
Ganges and Indus.[4] Thus the orb he roamed
With narrow search, and with inspection deep
Considered every creature, which of all
Most opportune might serve his wiles, and found 85
The serpent subtlest beast of all the field.[5]
Him, after long debate, irresolute
Of thoughts revolved, his final sentence chose
Fit vessel, fittest imp[6] of fraud, in whom
To enter, and his dark suggestions hide 90
From sharpest sight; for in the wily snake
Whatever sleights none would suspicious mark,
As from his wit and native subtlety
Proceeding, which, in other beasts observed,
Doubt[7] might beget of diabolic power 95

5. As described in the conclusion of book 4.   6. In spite of.   7. Gabriel's troops. Uriel (whose name means "fire of God") is, according to Milton, *regent of the sun* and heat. In book 4, he warns Gabriel and his troops against Satan entering Eden.   8. A celestial circle that crosses the poles. Satan manages always to stay on the dark side of the Earth by circling it three times along the equator (*the equinoctial line*) and twice on each of the two colures.   9. The side opposite the gate guarded by Gabriel.   1. Cf. Genesis 2.10: "And a river went out of Eden to water the garden."   2. Siberian river flowing into the Arctic Ocean. *Pontus:* the Black Sea. *Maeotis:* the Sea of Azov.   3. The Isthmus of Panama. *Orontes:* a river in Syria.   4. Rivers in India.   5. Cf. Genesis 3.1: "Now the serpent was more subtil than any beast of the field."   6. Offspring, with a devilish connotation. *Sentence:* decision.   7. Suspicion.

Active within beyond the sense of brute.
Thus he resolved, but first from inward grief
His bursting passion into plaints thus poured:
   "O Earth, how like to Heaven, if not preferred
More justly, seat worthier of Gods, as built   100
With second thought, reforming what was old!
For what God, after better, worse would build?
Terrestrial Heaven, danced round by other Heavens,
That shine, yet bear their bright officious[8] lamps,
Light above light, for thee alone, as seems,   105
In thee concent'ring all their precious beams
Of sacred influence! As God in Heaven
Is center, yet extends to all, so thou
Cent'ring receiv'st from all those orbs; in thee,
Not in themselves, all their known virtue appears,   110
Productive in herb, plant, and nobler birth
Of creatures animate with gradual life
Of growth, sense, reason, all summed up in man.[9]
With what delight could I have walked thee round,
If I could joy in aught; sweet interchange   115
Of hill and valley, rivers, woods, and plains,
Now land, now sea, and shores with forest crowned,
Rocks, dens, and caves! But I in none of these
Find place or refuge; and the more I see
Pleasures about me, so much more I feel   120
Torment within me, as from the hateful siege[1]
Of contraries; all good to me becomes
Bane,[2] and in Heaven much worse would be my state.
But neither here seek I, no, nor in Heaven,
To dwell, unless by mastering Heaven's Supreme;   125
Nor hope to be myself less miserable
By what I seek, but others to make such
As I, though thereby worse to me redound.
For only in destroying I find ease
To my relentless thoughts, and him[3] destroyed,   130
Or won to what may work his utter loss,
For whom all this was made, all this[4] will soon
Follow, as to him linked in weal or woe:
In woe then, that destruction wide may range!
To me shall be the glory sole among   135
The infernal Powers, in one day to have marred
What he, Almighty styled, six nights and days
Continued making, and who knows how long
Before had been contriving? though perhaps
Not longer than since I in one night freed   140
From servitude in glorious well-nigh half
Th' angelic name,[5] and thinner left the throng
Of his adorers. He, to be avenged,
And to repair his numbers thus impaired,

---

8. Performing their function.   9. What Adam called (5.509) "the scale of Nature" ascends from the
vegetable order (pure growth), to the animal (sensation), to the human (the two, plus reason).   1. Seat,
place.   2. Poison.   3. Man.   4. All of created nature.   5. Family, clan.

Whether such virtue,[6] spent of old, now failed 145
More angels to create (if they at least
Are his created),[7] or to spite us more,
Determined to advance into our room
A creature formed of earth, and him endow,
Exalted from so base original, 150
With heavenly spoils, our spoils. What he decreed
He effected; man he made, and for him built
Magnificent this World, and Earth his seat,
Him lord pronounced, and, O indignity!
Subjected to his service angel-wings 155
And flaming ministers, to watch and tend
Their earthy charge. Of these the vigilance
I dread, and to elude, thus wrapt in mist
Of midnight vapor, glide obscure, and pry
In every bush and brake, where hap may find 160
The serpent sleeping, in whose mazy folds
To hide me, and the dark intent I bring.
O foul descent! that I, who erst contended
With Gods to sit the highest, am now constrained
Into a beast, and, mixed with bestial slime, 165
This essence[8] to incarnate and imbrute,
That to the height of deity aspired!
But what will not ambition and revenge
Descend to? Who aspires must down as low
As high he soared, obnoxious,[9] first or last, 170
To basest things. Revenge, at first though sweet,
Bitter ere long back on itself recoils.
Let it; I reck not, so it light well aimed,
Since higher[1] I fall short, on him who next
Provokes my envy, this new favorite 175
Of Heaven, this man of clay, son of despite,
Whom, us the more to spite, his Maker raised
From dust: spite then with spite is best repaid.'
    So saying, through each thicket, dank or dry,
Like a black mist low-creeping, he held on 180
His midnight search, where soonest he might find
The serpent. Him fast sleeping soon he found,
In labyrinth of many a round self-rolled,
His head the midst, well stored with subtle wiles:
Not yet in horrid shade or dismal den, 185
Nor nocent[2] yet, but on the grassy herb,
Fearless, unfeared, he slept. In at his mouth
The devil entered, and his brutal sense,
In heart or head, possessing soon inspired
With act intelligential; but his sleep 190
Disturbed not, waiting close[3] th' approach of morn.
    Now, whenas sacred light began to dawn

6. Power, force.   7. Inciting the angels to rebellion, Satan pretended that they were not God's creation, but "self-begot" (5.860).   8. The supernatural substance of which he considers himself to be made.   9. Exposed to.   1. Against God. *I reck not:* I don't mind.   2. Harmful.   3. Hidden. *Act intelligental:* intellectual activity.

In Eden on the humid flowers, that breathed
Their morning incense, when all things that breathe
From th' Earth's great altar send up silent praise 195
To the Creator, and his nostrils fill
With grateful smell, forth came the human pair,
And joined their vocal worship to the choir
Of creatures wanting[4] voice; that done, partake
The season, prime for sweetest scents and airs; 200
Then còmmune how that day they best may ply
Their growing work; for much their work outgrew
The hands' dispatch of two gardening so wide:
And Eve first to her husband thus began:
     "Adam, well may we labor still[5] to dress 205
This garden, still to tend plant, herb, and flower,
Our pleasant task enjoined; but, till more hands
Aid us, the work under our labor grows,
Luxurious by restraint: what we by day
Lop overgrown, or prune, or prop, or bind, 210
One night or two with wanton growth derides,
Tending to wild. Thou, therefore, now advise,
Or hear what to my mind first thoughts present.
Let us divide our labors; thou where choice
Leads thee, or where most needs, whether to wind 215
The woodbine round this arbor, or direct
The clasping ivy where to climb; while I
In yonder spring[6] of roses intermixed
With myrtle find what to redress till noon.
For, while so near each other thus all day 220
Our task we choose, what wonder if so near
Looks intervene and smiles, or objects new
Casual discourse draw on, which intermits
Our day's work, brought to little, though begun
Early, and th' hour of supper comes unearned!" 225
To whom mild answer Adam thus returned:
"Sole Eve, associate sole, to me beyond
Compare above all living creatures dear!
Well hast thou motioned,[7] well thy thoughts employed
How we might best fulfil the work which here 230
God hath assigned us, nor of me shalt pass
Unpraised; for nothing lovelier can be found
In woman than to study household good,
And good works in her husband to promote.
Yet not so strictly hath our Lord imposed 235
Labor as to debar us when we need
Refreshment, whether food or talk between,
Food of the mind, or this sweet intercourse
Of looks and smiles; for smiles from reason flow,
To brute denied, and are of love the food, 240
Love, not the lowest end[8] of human life.
For not to irksome toil, but to delight,

4. Lacking. 5. Constantly. 6. Thicket, grove. 7. Suggested. 8. Object.

He made us, and delight to reason joined.
These paths and bowers doubt not but our joint hands
Will keep from wilderness⁹ with ease, as wide   245
As we need walk, till younger hands ere long
Assist us. But, if much converse perhaps
Thee satiate, to short absence I could yield;
For solitude sometimes is best society,
And short retirement urges sweet return.   250
But other doubt possesses me, lest harm
Befall thee, severed from me; for thou know'st
What hath been warned us, what malicious foe,
Envying our happiness, and of his own
Despairing, seeks to work us woe and shame   255
By sly assault, and somewhere nigh at hand
Watches, no doubt, with greedy hope to find
His wish and best adventage, us asunder,
Hopeless to circumvent us joined, where each
To other speedy aid might lend at need.   260
Whether his first design be to withdraw
Our fealty from God, or to disturb
Conjugal love, than which perhaps no bliss
Enjoyed by us excites his envy more;
Or this, or worse,¹ leave not the faithful side   265
That gave thee being, still shades thee and protects.
The wife, where danger or dishonor lurks,
Safest and seemliest by her husband stays,
Who guards her, or with her the worst endures."
    To whom the virgin² majesty of Eve,   270
As one who loves, and some unkindness meets,
With sweet austere composure thus replied:
    "Offspring of Heaven and Earth, and all Earth's lord!
That such an enemy we have, who seeks
Our ruin, both by thee informed I learn,   275
And from the parting angel³ overheard,
As in a shady nook I stood behind,
Just then returned at shut of evening flowers.
But that thou shouldst my firmness therefore doubt
To God or thee, because we have a foe   280
May tempt it, I expected not to hear.
His violence thou fear'st not, being such
As we, not capable of death or pain,
Can either not receive, or can repel.
His fraud is, then, thy fear; which plain infers   285
Thy equal fear that my firm faith and love
Can by his fraud be shaken or seduced:
Thoughts, which how found they harbor in thy breast,
Adam, misthought of her to thee so dear?"⁴
    To whom, with healing words, Adam replied: 290
"Daughter of God and man, immortal Eve,

---

9. Wildness.   1. Whether his design be this or something even worse.   2. Pure, sinless.
3. Raphael.   4. A misjudgment (*misthought*) of me.

For such thou art, from sin and blame entire;[5]
Not diffident of thee do I dissuade
Thy absence from my sight, but to avoid
Th' attempt itself, intended by our foe.   295
For he who tempts, though in vain, at least asperses[6]
The tempted with dishonor foul, supposed
Not incorruptible of faith,[7] not proof
Against temptation. Thou thyself with scorn
And anger wouldst resent the offered wrong,   300
Though ineffectual found; misdeem not, then,
If such affront I labor to avert
From thee alone, which on us both at once
The enemy, though bold, will hardly dare;
Or, daring, first on me th' assault shall light.   305
Nor thou his malice and false guile contemn—
Subtle he needs must be who could seduce
Angles—nor think superfluous others' aid.
I from the influence of thy looks receive
Access in every virtue;[8] in thy sight   310
More wise, more watchful, stronger, if need were
Of outward strength; while shame, thou looking on,
Shame to be overcome or overreached,[9]
Would utmost vigor raise, and raised unite.
Why shouldst not thou like sense[1] within thee feel   315
When I am present, and thy trial choose
With me, best witness of thy virtue tried?"
    So spake domestic Adam in his care
And matrimonial love; but Eve, who thought
Less[2] àttributed to her faith sincere,   320
Thus her reply with accent sweet renewed:
    "If this be our condition, thus to dwell
In narrow circuit straitened by a foe,
Subtle or violent, we not endued[3]
Single with like defence wherever met,   325
How are we happy, still in fear of harm?
But harm precedes not sin: only our foe
Tempting affronts us with his foul esteem
Of our integrity: his foul esteem
Sticks no dishonor on our front,[4] but turns   330
Foul on himself; then wherefore shunned or feared
By us, who rather double honor gain
From his surmise proved false, find peace within,
Favor from Heaven, our witness, from th' event?
And what is faith, love, virtue, unassayed   335
Alone, without exterior help sustained?[5]
Let us not then suspect our happy state
Left so imperfect by the Maker wise
As not secure to single or combined.
Frail is our happiness, if this be so;   340

5. Intact.   6. Literally, sprinkles.   7. Faithfulness, loyalty.   8. Increased strength.   9. Outdone.
1. Sensation.   2. Less than she deserves.   3. Endowed. *Straitened:* confined.   4. Brow.
5. Without being put to test by outside forces.

And Eden were no Eden, thus exposed."
   To whom thus Adam fervently replied:
"O woman, best are all things as the will
Of God ordained them; his creating hand
Nothing imperfect or deficient left   345
Of all that he created, much less man,
Or aught that might his happy state secure,
Secure from outward force. Within himself
The danger lies, yet lies within his power;
Against his will he can receive no harm.   350
But God left free the will; for what obeys
Reason is free; and reason he made right,
But bid her well beware, and still erect,[6]
Lest, by some fair appearing good surprised,
She dictate false, and misinform the will   355
To do what God expressly hath forbid.
Not then mistrust, but tender love, enjoins
That I should mind[7] thee oft; and mind thou me.
Firm we subsist, yet possible to swerve,
Since reason not impossibly may meet   360
Some specious object by the foe suborned,[8]
And fall into deception unaware,
Not keeping strictest watch, as she was warned.
Seek not temptation, then, which to avoid
Were better, and most likely if from me   365
Thou sever not: trial will come unsought.
Wouldst thou approve[9] thy constancy, approve
First thy obedience; th' other who can know,
Not seeing thee attempted, who attest?
But if thou think trial unsought may find   370
Us both securer[1] than thus warned thou seem'st,
Go; for thy stay, not free, absents thee more.
Go in thy native innocence; rely
On what thou hast of virtue; summon all;
For God towards thee hath done his part: do thine."   375
   So spake the patriarch of mankind; but Eve
Persisted; yet submiss,[2] though last, replied:
   "With thy permission, then, and thus forewarned,
Chiefly by what thy own last reasoning words
Touched only, that our trial, when least sought,   380
May find us both perhaps far less prepared,
The willinger I go, nor much expect
A foe so proud will first the weaker seek;
So bent, the more shall shame him his repulse.'
Thus saying, from her husband's hand her hand   385
Soft she withdrew, and like a wood nymph light,
Oread or dryad, or of Delia's train,[3]

---

6. On the alert against temptation, because God has "created Man free and able enough to have withstood his Tempter" (3.Argument).   7. Remind.   8. Procured for treacherous purposes.   9. Give proof, test.   1. Less careful, less alert to danger.   2. Submissive. Eve's submissiveness, however, is qualified by Adam's reluctant tone as he agrees to let her go and by the fact that it is she who speaks the final words of their dialogue.   3. Delia (born on the island of Delos) is the goddess Diana (Artemis), the huntress, with her train of nymphs. In Greek mythology the oreads were mountain nymphs and the dryads were wood nymphs.

Betook her to the groves, but Delia's self
In gait surpassed and goddesslike deport,
Though not as she with bow and quiver armed,   390
But with such gardening tools as art yet rude,
Guiltless of fire[4] had formed, or angels brought.
To Pales, or Pomona, thus adorned,
Likest she seemed, Pomona when she fled
Vertumnus, or to Ceres in her prime,   395
Yet virgin of Proserpina from Jove.[5]
Her long with ardent look his eye pursued
Delighted, but desiring more her stay.
Oft he to her his charge of quick return
Repeated; she to him as oft engaged   400
To be returned by noon amid the bower,
And all things in best order to invite
Noontide repast, or afternoon's repose.
O much deceived, much failing, hapless Eve,
Of[6] thy presumed return! Event perverse!   405
Thou never from that hour in Paradise
Found'st either sweet repast, or sound repose;
Such ambush hid among sweet flowers and shades
Waited with hellish rancor imminent[7]
To intercept thy way, or send thee back   410
Despoiled of innocence, of faith, of bliss.
For now, and since first break of dawn, the fiend,
Mere serpent in appearance, forth was come,
And on his quest, where likeliest he might find
The only two of mankind, but in them   415
The whole included race, his purposed prey.
In bower and field he sought, where any tuft
Of grove or garden-plot more[8] pleasant lay,
Their tendance[9] or plantation for delight;
By fountain or by shady rivulet   420
He sought them both, but wished his hap might find
Eve separate; he wished, but not with hope
Of what so seldom chanced; when to his wish,
Beyond his hope, Eve separate he spies,
Veiled in a cloud of fragrance, where she stood,   425
Half spied, so thick the roses bushing round
About her glowed, oft stooping to support
Each flower of slender stalk, whose head though gay
Carnation, purple, azure, or specked with gold,
Hung drooping unsustained, them she upstays   430
Gently with myrtle band, mindless the while
Herself, though fairest unsupported flower,
From her best prop so far, and storm so nigh.
Nearer he drew, and many a walk traversed
Of stateliest covert, cedar, pine, or palm;   435

---

4. The ability to produce fire will become necessary only after the Fall (cf. 10.1070–82).   5. In practical-minded Roman mythology, Pales and Pomona are deities who preside over flocks and fruit, respectively. Ceres is the goddess of agriculture in general. Both Pomona and Ceres are presented here in virginal youth: Pomona fleeing from her suitor Vertumnus (another agriculture deity), and Ceres before the time when Jove (Jupiter) made her the mother of Proserpina.   6. About.   7. Ominously ready.   8. Particularly.   9. A spot that they tended.

Then voluble and bold, now hid, now seen
Among thick-woven arborets and flowers
Embordered on each bank, the hand¹ of Eve:
Spot more delicious than those gardens feigned²
Or of revived Adonis, or renowned   440
Alcinous, host of old Laertes' son,³
Or that, not mystic, where the sapient king
Held dalliance with his fair Egyptian spouse.⁴
Much he the place admired, the person more.
As one who long in populous city pent,   445
Where houses thick and sewers annoy⁵ the air,
Forth issuing on a summer's morn to breathe
Among the pleasant villages and farms
Adjoined, from each thing met conceives delight,
The smell of grain, or tedded⁶ grass, or kine,   450
Or dairy, each rural sight, each rural sound:
If chance with nymphlike step fair virgin pass,
What pleasing seemed, for her⁷ now pleases more,
She most, and in her look sums⁸ all delight.
Such pleasure took the serpent to behold   455
This flowery plat,⁹the sweet recess of Eve
Thus early, thus alone; her heavenly form
Angelic, but more soft, and feminine,
Her graceful innocence, her every air
Of gesture or least action overawed   460
His malice, and with rapine¹ sweet bereaved
His fierceness of the fierce intent it brought:
That space the evil one abstracted² stood
From his own evil, and for the time remained
Stupidly good, of enmity disarmed,   465
Of guile, of hate, of envy, of revenge.
But the hot Hell that always in him burns,
Though in mid Heaven, soon ended his delight,
And tortures him now more, the more he sees
Of pleasure not for him ordained: then soon   470
Fierce hate he recollects, and all his thoughts
Of mischief, gratulating,³ thus excites:
    "Thoughts, whither have ye led me? with what sweet
Compulsion thus transported to forget
What hither brought us? hate, not love, nor hope   475
Of Paradise for Hell, hope here to taste
Of pleasure, but all pleasure to destroy,
Save what⁴ is in destroying; other joy
To me is lost. Then let me not let pass
Occasion which now smiles; behold alone   480

1. Handiwork. *Voluble:* rolling. *Arborets:* shrubs. *Embordered on each bank:* bordering a walk.
2. Imagined by the poets (cf. 9.31).   3. Odysseus. Alcinous was the king of the Phaeacians. His perpetually flowering garden is described in the *Odyssey*. (7) *Of revived Adonis:* the mythical garden where
Aphrodite (Venus) nursed her lover Adonis, wounded by a boar. The most famous description of the garden,
certainly known to Milton, is in Spenser's *Faerie Queene* 3.   4. Pharaoh's daughter (see 1 Kings 3.1).
Not mystic: not mythical like the previous "feigned" gardens of pagan antiquity. *Sapient king:* Solomon.   5. Make noisome, pollute.   6. Spread out for drying.   7. Because of her. *If chance:* if it
should happen that.   8. Rounds out and brings to perfection.   9. Plot.   1. Theft.   2. Drawn
off, separated.   3. Rejoicing.   4. Whatever pleasure.

The woman, opportune to all attempts,[5]
Her husband, for I view far round, not nigh,
Whose higher intellectual more I shun,
And strength, of courage haughty, and of limb
Heroic built, though of terrestrial mold.[6]   485
Foe not informidable, exempt from wound,
I not; so much hath Hell debased, and pain
Enfeebled me, to what I was in Heaven.
She fair, divinely fair, fit love for gods,
Not terrible, though terror be in love   490
And beauty, not approached by stronger hate,[7]
Hate stronger, under show of love well feigned,
The way which to her ruin now I tend."
    So spake the enemy of mankind, enclosed
In serpent, inmate bad, and toward Eve   495
Addressed his way, not with indented wave,[8]
Prone on the ground, as since, but on his rear,
Circular base of rising folds, that towered
Fold above fold a surging maze; his head
Crested aloft, and carbuncle[9] his eyes;   500
With burnished neck of verdant gold, erect
Amidst his circling spires, that on the grass
Floated redundant.[1] Pleasing was his shape,
And lovely; never since of serpent kind
Lovelier, not those that in Illyria changed   505
Hermione and Cadmus,[2] or the god
In Epidaurus;[3] nor to which transformed
Ammonian Jove, or Capitoline was seen,
He with Olympias, this with her who bore
Scipio, the height of Rome.[4] With tract oblique   510
At first, as one who sought access, but feared
To interrupt, sidelong he works his way.
As when a ship by skillful steersman wrought
Nigh river's mouth or foreland, where the wind
Veers oft, as oft so steers, and shifts her sail: 515
So varied he, and of his tortuous train
Curled many a wanton wreath in sight of Eve,
To lure her eye: she busied heard the sound
Of rustling leaves, but minded not, as used
To such disport before her through the field,   520
From every beast, more duteous at her call,
Than at Circean call the herd disguised.[5]

---

5. In the appropriate situation for Satan's attempts on her.   6. Formed of earth.   7. If not
approached, and counteracted, by hate.   8. Zigzagging.   9. Fiery red.   1. In great abundance.
Spires: coils, loops.   2. Those that Hermione and Cadmus were turned into. Cadmus, the founder of
Thebes, and his wife Hermione (Harmonia), according to their story as told by Ovid (*Metamorphoses* 4.562–
602), were transformed into snakes when they retired to Illyria after much family tragedy.   3. The place
in Greece where Aesculapius, the god of medicine, had his major temple and appeared to worshipers in
the form of an erect, flashy-eyed serpent (Ovid's *Metamorphoses* 15.622–744).   4. According to hero-
deifying legends, Jove, in his personification as Jupiter Ammon (a mingling of Greco-Roman and Egyptian
cults), loved Princess Olympias and became the father of Alexander the Great. As the Capitoline Jupiter
(worshiped in the major Roman temple on the Capitol), he fathered Scipio, the supreme hero (*the height*)
of Rome's African wars. In both cases, the father god appeared in the form of a snake.   5. The enchantress Circe, in the *Odyssey* (10), is surrounded by subjected beasts and transforms some of the hero's companions into swine.

He bolder now, uncalled before her stood:
But as in gaze admiring; oft he bowed
His turret[6] crest, and sleek enameled neck, 525
Fawning, and licked the ground whereon she trod.
His gentle dumb expression turned at length
The eye of Eve to mark his play: he, glad
Of her attention gained, with serpent tongue
Organic, or impulse of vocal air,[7] 530
His fraudulent temptation thus began.
  "Wonder not, sovereign mistress, if perhaps
Thou canst, who art sole wonder; much less arm
Thy looks, the heaven of mildness, with disdain,
Displeased that I approach thee thus, and gaze 535
Insatiate, I thus single, nor have feared
Thy awful brow, more awful thus retired.
Fairest resemblance of thy Maker fair,
Thee all things living gaze on, all things thine
By gift, and thy celestial beauty adore 540
With ravishment beheld, there best beheld
Where universally admired: but here
In this enclosure wild, these beasts among,
Beholders rude, and shallow[8] to discern
Half what in thee is fair, one man except, 545
Who sees thee? (and what is one?) who shouldst be seen
A goddess among gods, adored and served
By angels numberless, thy daily train."
  So glozed the tempter, and his proem[9] tuned;
Into the heart of Eve his words made way, 550
Though at the voice much marveling: at length,
Not unamazed, she thus in answer spake.
"What may this mean? Language of man pronounced
By tongue of brute, and human sense expressed?
The first at least of these I thought denied 555
To beasts, whom God on their creation-day
Created mute to all articulate sound;
The latter I demur, for in their looks
Much reason,[1] and in their actions oft appears.
Thee, serpent, subtlest beast of all the field 560
I knew, but not with human voice endued:
Redouble then this miracle, and say,
How cam'st thou speakable of mute,[2] and how
To me so friendly grown above the rest
Of brutal kind, that daily are in sight? 565
Say, for such wonder claims attention due."
  To whom the guileful tempter thus replied:
"Empress of this fair world, resplendent Eve!
Easy to me it is to tell thee all
What thou command'st and right thou shouldst be obeyed: 570

---

6. Towering. 7. Producing a voice either by using his serpent's (*organic*) tongue or by some more direct impulse on the air. 8. Mentally inadequate. 9. Preamble, introduction. *Glozed*: flattered. 1. Eve, well acquainted with animals, which are *duteous at her call* (line 521), questions the notion (*I demur*) that they are wholly deprived of *human sense and reason*. 2. How did you acquire speech after being dumb?

I was at first as other beasts that graze
The trodden herb, of abject thoughts and low,
As was my food, nor aught but food discerned
Or sex, and apprehended nothing high:
Till on a day, roving the field, I chanced   575
A goodly tree far distant to behold
Loaden with fruit of fairest colors mixed,
Ruddy and gold; I nearer drew to gaze;
When from the boughs a savory odor blown,
Grateful to appetite, more pleased my sense   580
Than smell of sweetest fennel, or the teats
Of ewe or goat dropping with milk[3] at even,
Unsucked of lamb or kid, that tend their play.
To satisfy the sharp desire I had
Of tasting those fair apples, I resolved   585
Not to defer: hunger and thirst at once,
Powerful persuaders, quickened at the scent
Of that alluring fruit, urged me so keen.
About the mossy trunk I wound me soon,
For, high from ground, the branches would require   590
Thy utmost reach, or Adam's: round the tree
All other beasts that saw, with like desire
Longing and envying stood, but could not reach.
Amid the tree now got, where plenty hung
Tempting so nigh, to pluck and eat my fill   595
I spared not; for such pleasure till that hour
At feed or fountain never had I found.
Sated at length, ere long I might perceive
Strange alteration in me, to degree
Of reason[4] in my inward powers, and speech   600
Wanted not long, though to this shape retained.[5]
Thenceforth to speculations high or deep
I turned my thoughts, and with capacious mind
Considered all things visible in Heaven,
Or Earth, or middle, all things fair and good: 605
But all that fair[6] and good in thy divine
Semblance, and in thy beauty's heavenly ray
United I beheld: no fair to thine
Equivalent or second, which compelled
Me thus, though importune perhaps, to come   610
And gaze, and worship thee of right declared
Sovereign of creatures, universal dame."[7]
   So talked the spirited[8] sly snake: and Eve
Yet more amazed, unwary thus replied:
   "Serpent, thy overpraising leaves in doubt   615
The virtue of that fruit, in thee first proved.
But say, where grows the tree, from hence how far?
For many are the trees of God that grow

---

3. According to old folklore, snakes were fond of fennel, which was supposed to sharpen their eyesight, and of goat's milk.   4. To the point of acquiring the faculty of reason.   5. Restrained, kept to his outward appearance. *Wanted not long*: the faculty of speech soon followed.   6. Fairness, beauty. *Middle*: the air.   7. Mistress of this world.   8. Possessed by an evil spirit.

In Paradise, and various, yet unknown
To us; in such abundance lies our choice,   620
As leaves a greater store of fruit untouched,
Still hanging incorruptible, till men
Grow up to their provision, and more hands
Help to disburden Nature of her bearth."[9]
    To whom the wily adder, blithe and glad: 625
"Empress, the way is ready, and not long,
Beyond a row of myrtles, on a flat,
Fast by a fountain, one small thicket past
Of blowing[1] myrrh and balm: if thou accept
My conduct, I can bring thee thither soon."   630
    "Lead then," said Eve. He leading swiftly rolled
In tangles, and made intricate seem straight,
To mischief swift. Hope elevates, and joy
Brightens his crest; as when a wandering fire
Compact of unctuous vapor,[2] which the night   635
Condenses, and the cold environs round,
Kindled through agitation to a flame
(Which oft, they say, some evil spirit attends),
Hovering and blazing with delusive light,
Misleads th' amazed night-wanderer from his way   640
To bogs and mires, and oft through pond or pool,
There swallowed up and lost, from succor far:
So glistered the dire snake, and into fraud
Led Eve our credulous mother, to the tree
Of prohibition,[3] root of all our woe: 645
Which when she saw, thus to her guide she spake:
    "Serpent, we might have spared our coming hither,
Fruitless to me, though fruit be here to excess,
The credit of whose virtue rest with thee;[4]
Wondrous indeed, if cause of such effects!   650
But of this tree we may not taste nor touch:
God so commanded, and left that command
Sole daughter of his voice; the rest,[5] we live
Law to ourselves; our reason is our law."
    To whom the tempter guilefully replied: 655
"Indeed? Hath God then said that of the fruit
Of all these garden trees ye shall not eat,
Yet lords declared of all in Earth or air?"
To whom thus Eve, yet sinless: "Of the fruit
Of each tree in the garden we may eat,   660
But of the fruit of this fair tree amidst
The garden, God hath said, 'Ye shall not eat
Thereof, nor shall yet touch it, lest ye die.' "
    She scarce had said, though brief, when now more bold,
The tempter, but with show of zeal and love   665

9. Products.   1. Blossoming.   2. Composed of greasy vapor. *Wandering fire:* will-o'-the-wisp, a light
attributed to marsh gas.   3. The forbidden Tree of Knowledge.   4. Because the forbidden tree is as
good as fruitless to Eve, the only proof of its power (*virtue*) will remain with the Serpent.   5. For the
rest. *Sole daughter of his voice:* translation from the Hebrew of God's command, described as "one easy
prohibition" (4.433).

To man, and indignation at his wrong,
New part puts on, and as to passion moved,
Fluctuates disturbed, yet comely, and in act
Raised,[6] as of some great matter to begin.
As when of old some orator renowned   670
In Athens or free Rome, where eloquence
Flourished, since mute, to some great cause addressed,
Stood in himself collected, while each part,[7]
Motion, each act, won audience ere the tongue,
Sometimes in height began, as no delay   675
Of preface brooking,[8] through his zeal of right.
So standing, moving, or to height upgrown
The tempter all impassioned thus began:
    "O sacred, wise, and wisdom-giving plant,
Mother of science![9] now I feel thy power   680
Within me clear, not only to discern
Things in their causes, but to trace the ways
Of highest agents, deemed however wise.
Queen of this universe! do not believe
Those rigid threats of death. Ye shall not die;   685
How should ye? By the fruit? it gives you life
To[1] knowledge; by the Threatener? look on me,
Me who have touched and tasted, yet both live,
And life more perfect have attained than Fate
Meant me, by venturing higher than my lot.   690
Shall that be shut to man, which to the beast
Is open? Or will God incense his ire
For such a petty trespass, and not praise
Rather your dauntless virtue, whom the pain
Of death denounced, whatever thing death be,   695
Deterred not from achieving what might lead
To happier life, knowledge of good and evil?
Of good, how just! Of evil, if what is evil
Be real, why not known, since easier shunned?
God therefore cannot hurt ye, and be just;   700
Not just, not God; not feared then, nor obeyed:
Your fear itself of death removes the fear.[2]
Why then was this forbid? Why but to awe,
Why but to keep ye low and ignorant,
His worshipers? He knows that in the day   705
Ye eat thereof, your eyes that seem so clear,
Yet are but dim, shall perfectly be then
Opened and cleared, and ye shall be as gods,
Knowing both good and evil, as they know.
That ye should be as gods, since I as man,   710
Internal man,[3] is but proportion meet,
I, of brute, human; ye, of human, gods.

6. Assuming the orator's posture. *New part:* new role, as of an actor in drama. *Fluctuates:* undulates his body.   7. Of the body.   8. Plunging into the middle of the subject (*in medias res*), without any preamble.   9. Knowledge.   1. As well as.   2. The Serpent's captious argument is that God is by definition just, but because a death-giving God would not be just, he would not be God; consequently, he would not have to be feared and obeyed.   3. The Serpent has acquired human faculties although his outer form has remained unchanged (compare *inward,* line 600).

So ye shall die perhaps, by putting off
Human, to put on gods:[4] death to be wished,
Though threatened, which no worse than this can bring. 715
And what are gods that man may not become
As they, participating godlike food?
The gods are first, and that advantage use
On our belief, that all from them proceeds.
I question it; for this fair Earth I see, 720
Warmed by the sun, producing every kind,
Them nothing: If they[5] all things, who enclosed
Knowledge of good and evil in this tree,
That whoso eats thereof forthwith attains
Wisdom without their leave? And wherein lies 725
Th' offense, that man should thus attain to know?
What can your knowledge hurt him, or this tree
Impart against his will if all be his?
Or is it envy, and can envy dwell
In heavenly breasts? These, these, and many more 730
Causes import[6] your need of this fair fruit.
Goddess humane, reach then, and freely taste!"
      He ended, and his words, replete with guile,
Into her heart too easy entrance won:
Fixed on the fruit she gazed, which to behold 735
Might tempt alone, and in her ears the sound
Yet rung of his persuasive words, impregned[7]
With reason, to her seeming, and with truth;
Meanwhile the hour of noon drew on, and waked
An eager appetite, raised by the smell 740
So savory of that fruit, which with desire,
Inclinable[8] now grown to touch or taste,
Solicited her longing eye; yet first
Pausing a while, thus to herself she mused:
      "Great are thy virtues, doubtless, best of fruits, 745
Though kept from man, and worthy to be admired,
Whose taste, too long forborne, at first assay
Gave elocution to the mute, and taught
The tongue not made for speech to speak thy praise:
Thy praise he also who forbids they use, 750
Conceals not from us, naming thee the Tree
Of Knowledge, knowledge both of good and evil;
Forbids us then to taste; but his forbidding
Commends thee more, while it infers[9] the good
By thee communicated, and our want: 755
For good unknown, sure is not had, or had
And yet unknown, is as not had at all.
In plain[1] then, what forbids he but to know?
Forbids us good, forbids us to be wise!
Such prohibitions bind not.[2] But if Death 760

4. Divinity. *Human:* humanity.   5. If they produced.   6. Imply, indicate.   7. Impregnated, filled.
8. Favorably disposed.   9. Implies.   1. In plain words.   2. Eve, who has learned from the Serpent
the art of sophistical argument, claims that God himself, by naming the tree, has indicated the *good* in it,
but a *good unknown* is as nothing. Besides, forbidding the experience of the Tree of Knowledge is forbidding
humanity *to be wise;* hence the prohibition is not binding.

Bind us with after-bands, what profits then
Our inward freedom?[3] In the day we eat
Of this fair fruit, our doom is, we shall die.
How dies the serpent? He hath eaten and lives,
And knows, and speaks, and reasons, and discerns,   765
Irrational till then. For us alone
Was death invented? Or to us denied
This intellectual food, for beasts reserved?
For beasts it seems: yet that one beast which first
Hath tasted, envies not, but brings with joy   770
The good befallen him, author unsuspect,[4]
Friendly to man, far from deceit or guile.
What fear I then, rather what know to fear
Under this ignorance of good and evil,[5]
Of God or death, of law or penalty?   775
Here grows the cure of all, this fruit divine,
Fair to the eye, inviting to the taste,
Of virtue[6] to make wise: what hinders then
To reach, and feed at once both body and mind?"
    So saying, her rash hand in evil hour,   780
Forth reaching to the fruit, she plucked, she eat.[7]
Earth felt the wound, and Nature from her seat
Sighing through all her works gave signs[8] of woe,
That all was lost. Back to the thicket slunk
The guilty serpent, and well might, for Eve   785
Intent now wholly on her taste, naught else
Regarded; such delight till then, as seemed,
In fruit she never tasted, whether true
Or fancied so, through expectation high
Of knowledge; nor was godhead from her thought.[9]   790
Greedily she engorged without restraint,
And knew not eating[1] death: satiate at length,
And heightened as with wine, jocund and boon,[2]
Thus to herself she pleasingly began:
    "O sovereign, virtuous, precious of all trees   795
In Paradise! of operation blest
To sapience, hitherto obscured, infamed,[3]
And thy fair fruit let hang, as to no end
Created; but henceforth my early care,
Not without song each morning, and due praise   800
Shall tend thee, and the fertile burden ease
Of thy full branches offered free to all;
Till dieted by thee I grow mature
In knowledge, as the gods who all things know;
Though others envy what they cannot give: 805
For had the gift been theirs, it had not here
Thus grown.[4] Experience, next to thee I owe,
Best guide; not following thee I had remained

3. Death would constitute a later bond (after-bands), after God has granted free will (inward freedom).   4. An unsuspectable authority on the subject.   5. Having no knowledge of good and evil, Eve
doesn't know what is to be feared.   6. With the power.   7. Ate.   8. Omens, metaphorically given
as—and punning with—the sighs of Nature; forebodings of disaster.   9. She thought of acquiring divinity.   1. That she was eating.   2. Cheerful.   3. Made famous. Blest to sapience: endowed with the
power to give wisdom.   4. Eve has adopted the Serpent's argument (cf. lines 720–30).

In ignorance; thou open'st Wisdom's way,
And giv'st access, though secret she retire.   810
And I perhaps am secret; Heaven is high,
High and remote to see from thence distinct
Each thing on Earth; and other care perhaps
May have diverted from continual watch
Our great Forbidder, safe⁵ with all his spies   815
About him. But to Adam in what sort⁶
Shall I appear? Shall I to him make known
As yet my change, and give him to partake
Full happiness with me, or rather not,
But keep the odds⁷ of knowledge in my power   820
Without copartner? so to add what wants
In female sex, the more to draw his love,
And render me more equal, and perhaps,
A thing not undesirable, sometime
Superior: for, inferior, who is free?   825
This may be well: but what if God have seen
And death ensue? Then I shall be no more,
And Adam, wedded to another Eve,
Shall live with her enjoying, I extinct;
A death to think. Confirmed then I resolve,   830
Adam shall share with me in bliss or woe:
So dear I love him, that with him all deaths
I could endure, without him live no life."⁸
    So saying, from the tree her step she turned,
But first low reverence done, as to the power   835
That dwelt within, whose presence had infused
Into the plant sciential⁹ sap, derived
From nectar, drink of gods. Adam the while
Waiting desirous her return, had wove
Of choicest flowers a garland to adorn   840
Her tresses, and her rural labors crown,
As reapers oft are wont their harvest queen.
Great joy he promised to his thoughts, and new
Solace in her return, so long delayed:
Yet oft his heart, divine of¹ something ill,   845
Misgave him; he the faltering measure² felt;
And forth to meet her went, the way she took
That morn when first they parted. By the Tree
Of Knowledge he must pass; there he her met,
Scarce from the tree returning; in her hand   850
A bough of fairest fruit that downy smiled,
New gathered, and ambrosial smell diffused.
To him she hastened, in her face excuse

---

5. Not dangerous.   6. Manner.   7. Advantage.   8. In these crucial lines Eve's thoughts are shown
moving through three stages: first, the idea of not sharing her knowledge with Adam, so as to enhance her
own power, with the gratuitous notion that lesser power brings no freedom at all; then jealously at the
thought of her own possible death and Adam *wedded to another Eve;* finally, with an opportune resurgence
of *love,* the resolve to be with Adam *in bliss or woe,* i.e., to make him her partner in sin. Thus the passage
is centrally representative of Milton's characterization of Eve in her relation to Adam and possibly of some
of the poet's own conceptions of women in general (cf. lines 377–84, 869–85, and 1155–61).   9. Infus-
ing knowledge.   1. *Divine of:* divining, foreseeing.   2. Irregularity of heartbeats.

Came prologue, and apology to prompt,[3]
Which with bland words at will she thus addressed: 855
    "Hast thou not wondered, Adam, at my stay?
Thee I have missed, and thought it long, deprived
Thy presence, agony of love till now
Not felt, nor shall be twice; for never more
Mean I to try, what rash untried I sought, 860
The pain of absence from thy sight. But strange
Hath been the cause, and wonderful to hear:
This tree is not as we are told, a tree
Of danger tasted,[4] nor to evil unknown
Opening the way, but of divine effect 865
To open eyes, and make them gods who taste;
And hath been tasted such.[5] The serpent wise,
Or not restrained as we, or not obeying,
Hath eaten of the fruit, and is become,
Not dead, as we are threatened, but thenceforth 870
Endued with human voice and human sense,
Reasoning to admiration,[6] and with me
Persuasively hath so prevailed, that I
Have also tasted, and have also found
Th' effects to correspond, opener mine eyes, 875
Dim erst, dilated spirits, ampler heart,
And growing up to godhead; which for thee
Chiefly I sought, without thee can despise.
For bliss, as thou hast part, to me is bliss,
Tedious, unshared with thee, and odious soon. 880
Thou therefore also taste, that equal lot
May join us, equal joy, as equal love;
Lest, thou not tasting, different degree[7]
Disjoin us, and I then too late renounce
Deity for thee, when Fate will not permit."[8] 885
    Thus Eve with countenance blithe her story told;
But in her cheek distemper[9] flushing glowed.
On th' other side, Adam, soon as he heard
The fatal trespass done by Eve, amazed,
Astonied stood and blank, while horror chill 890
Ran through his veins, and all his joints relaxed;[1]
From his slack hand the garland wreathed for Eve
Down dropped, and all the faded roses shed.
Speechless he stood and pale, till thus at length
First to himself he inward silence broke: 895
    "O fairest of creation, last and best
Of all God's works, creature in whom excelled
Whatever can to sight or thought be formed,
Holy, divine, good, amiable, or sweet!
How art thou lost, how on a sudden lost, 900

---

3. A pleading expression on her face came as an introduction (the *prologue* to a play) to prepare for (*prompt*) the formal *apology*. 4. When tasted. 5. Has been proved by tasting. 6. Admirably. 7. A difference in rank between us. 8. Cf. lines 825–33. 9. Disharmony in the body's humors, disease. 1. Slackened. *Astonied:* stunned.

Defaced, deflowered, and now to death devote?[2]
Rather how hast thou yielded to transgress
The strict forbiddance, how to violate
The sacred fruit forbidden! Some cursèd fraud
Of enemy hath beguiled thee, yet unknown,[3]   905
And me with thee hath ruined, for with thee
Certain my resolution is to die.
How can I live without thee, how forgo
Thy sweet converse and love so dearly joined,
To live again in these wild woods forlorn?   910
Should God create another Eve, and I
Another rib afford, yet loss of thee
Would never from my heart; no, no! I feel
The link of nature draw me: flesh of flesh,
Bone of my bone thou art, and from thy state   915
Mine never shall be parted, bliss or woe."
　　So having said, as one from sad dismay
Recomforted, and after thoughts disturbed
Submitting to what seemed remediless,
Thus in calm mood his words to Eve he turned: 920
　　"Bold deed thou hast presumed, adventurous Eve
And peril great provoked, who thus hath dared
Had it been only coveting to eye
That sacred fruit, sacred to abstinence,
Much more to taste it, under ban to touch.   925
But past who can recall, or done undo?
Not God omnipotent, nor Fate! Yet so
Perhaps thou shalt not die, perhaps the fact
Is not so heinous now, foretasted fruit,
Profaned first by the serpent, by him first   930
Made common and unhallowed ere our taste,
Nor yet on him found deadly; he yet lives,
Lives, as thou saidst, and gains to live as man
Higher degree of life: inducement strong
To us, as likely, tasting, to attain   935
Proportional[4] ascent, which cannot be
But to be gods, or angels, demigods.
Nor can I think that God, Creator wise,
Though threatening, will in earnest so destroy
Us his prime creatures, dignified so high,   940
Set over all his works, which in our fall,
For us created, needs with us must fail,
Dependent made; so God shall uncreate,
Be frustrate, do, undo, and labor lose;
Not well conceived of God,[5] who, though his power   945
Creation could repeat, yet would be loath
Us to abolish, lest the adversary
Triùmph and say: 'Fickle their state whom God
Most favors; who can please him long? Me first

---

2. Doomed.　　3. Unknown enemy.　　4. Proportionate to our human status (compare the Serpent's argument, lines 710–12).　　5. That would be a wrong conception of God.

He ruined, now mankind; whom will he next?'   950
Matter of scorn, not to be given the foe.
However, I with thee have fixed my lot.
Certain[6] to undergo like doom: if death
Consort with thee, death is to me as life;
So forcible within my heart I feel   955
The bond of nature draw me to my own,
My own in thee, for what thou art is mine;
Our state cannot be severed; we are one,
One flesh; to lose thee were to lose myself."
    So Adam, and thus Eve to him replied: 960
"O glorious trial of exceeding love,
Illustrious evidence, example high!
Engaging me to emulate; but short
Of thy perfection, how shall I attain,
Adam? from whose dear side I boast me sprung,   965
And gladly of our union hear thee speak,
One heart, one soul in both; whereof good proof
This day affords, declaring thee resolved,
Rather than death or aught than death more dread
Shall separate us, linked in love so dear,   970
To undergo with me one guilt, one crime,
If any be, of tasting this fair fruit;
Whose virtue (for of good still good proceeds,
Direct, or by occasion)[7] hath presented
This happy trial of thy love, which else   975
So eminently never had been known.
Were it[8] I thought death menaced would ensue
This my attempt, I would sustain alone
The worst, and not persuade thee, rather die
Deserted, than oblige[9] thee with a fact   980
Pernicious to thy peace, chiefly assured
Remarkably so late of thy so true,
So faithful love unequaled; but I feel
Far otherwise th' event;[1] not death, but life
Augmented, opened eyes, new hopes, new joys,   985
Taste so divine, that what of sweet before
Hath touched my sense, flat seems to this, and harsh.
On my experience, Adam, freely taste,
And fear of death deliver to the winds."
    So saying, she embraced him, and for joy   990
Tenderly wept, much won that he his love
Had so ennobled, as of choice to incur
Divine displeasure for her sake, or death.
In recompense (for such compliance bad
Such recompense best merits), from the bough   995
She gave him of that fair enticing fruit
With liberal hand; he scrupled not to eat,
Against his better knowledge, not deceived,[2]

6. Resolved.   7. Indirectly.   8. If.   9. Involve Adam in her guilty action.   1. The eventual consequence of her transgression.   2. Adam, unlike Eve, acts in full consciousness, not having been *deceived* by the Serpent.

But fondly overcome with female charm.
Earth trembled from her entrails, as again 1000
In pangs, and Nature gave a second groan.
Sky lowered, and muttering thunder, some sad drops
Wept at completing of the mortal sin
Original; while Adam took no thought,
Eating his fill, nor Eve to iterate 1005
Her former trespass feared, the more to soothe
Him with her loved society; that now
As with new wine intoxicated both,
They swim in mirth, and fancy that they feel
Divinity within them breeding wings 1010
Wherewith to scorn the Earth. But that false fruit
Far other operation first displayed,
Carnal desire inflaming; he on Eve
Began to cast lascivious eyes, she him
As wantonly repaid; in lust they burn, 1015
Till Adam thus 'gan Eve to dalliance move:
    "Eve, now I see thou art exact of taste,
And elegant, of sapience[3] no small part,
Since to each meaning savor we apply,
And palate call judicious. I the praise 1020
Yield thee, so well this day thou hast purveyed.
Much pleasure we have lost, while we abstained
From this delightful fruit, nor known till now
True relish, tasting; if such pleasure be
In things to us forbidden, it might be wished, 1025
For[4] this one tree had been forbidden ten.
But come; so well refreshed, now let us play,
As meet is, after such delicious fare;
For never did thy beauty, since the day
I saw thee first and wedded thee, adorned 1030
With all perfections, so enflame my sense
With ardor to enjoy thee, fairer now
Than ever, bounty of this virtuous[5] tree."
    So said he, and forbore not glance or toy
Of[6] amorous intent, well understood 1035
Of Eve, whose eye darted contagious fire.
Her hand he seized, and to a shady bank,
Thick overhead with verdant roof embowered
He led her, nothing loath; flowers were the couch,
Pansies, and violets, and asphodel, 1040
And hyacinth, Earth's freshest, softest lap.
There they their fill of love and love's disport
Took largely, of their mutual guilt the seal,
The solace of their sin, till dewy sleep
Oppressed them, wearied with their amorous play. 1045
    Soon as the force of that fallacious fruit,
That with exhilarating vapor bland

---

3. In both meanings—"wisdom" and "taste." Both *sapience* and *savor* (line 1019) are from the Latin *sapere*.
Elegant: choosy, refined. 4. Instead of. 5. Endowed with special power (compare lines 649 and
778). 6. With. *Toy*: toying, playing.

About their spirits had played, and inmost powers
Made err, was now exhaled, and grosser sleep
Bred of unkindly fumes,[7] with conscious dreams   1050
Encumbered, now had left them, up they rose
As from unrest, and each the other viewing,
Soon found their eyes how opened, and their minds
How darkened. Innocence, that as a veil
Had shadowed them from knowing ill, was gone;   1055
Just confidence, and native righteousness,
And honor from about them, naked left
To guilty Shame; he covered, but his robe
Uncovered more. So rose the Danite[8] strong,
Hercùlean Samson, from the harlot-lap   1060
Of Philìstean Dàlilàh, and waked
Shorn of his strength;[9] they destitute and bare
Of all their virtue. Silent, and in face
Confounded, long they sat, as strucken mute;
Till Adam, though not less than Eve abashed,   1065
At length gave utterance to these words constrained:
     "O Eve, in evil hour thou didst give ear
To that false worm,[1] of whomsoever taught
To counterfeit man's voice, true in our fall,
False in our promised rising; since our eyes   1070
Opened we find indeed, and find we know
Both good and evil, good lost, and evil got:
Bad fruit of knowledge, if this be to know,
Which leaves us naked thus, of honor void,
Of innocence, of faith, of purity,   1075
Our wonted ornaments now soiled and stained,
And in our faces evident the signs
Of foul concupiscence; whence evil store,
Even shame, the last[2] of evils; of the first
Be sure then. How shall I behold the face   1080
Henceforth of God or angel, erst with joy
And rapture so oft beheld? Those heavenly shapes
Will dazzle now this earthly[3] with their blaze
Insufferably bright. O might I here
In solitude live savage, in some glade   1085
Obscured, where highest woods, impenetrable
To star or sunlight, spread their umbrage broad,
And brown[4] as evening! Cover me, ye pines,
Ye cedars, with innumerable boughs
Hide me, where I may never see them[5] more!   1090
But let us now, as in[6] bad plight, devise
What best may for the present serve to hide
The parts of each from other, that seem most
To shame obnoxious,[7] and unseemliest seen;

7. Unnatural exhalations.   8. Of the tribe of Dan. Shame (personified) covered them, but his cover
(*robe*) only made them aware of their nakedness (*uncovered more*).   9. See Judges 16.4–20.   1. I.e.,
the Serpent, now disparaged.   2. Extreme, ultimate. *Evil store*: an abundance of evils.   3. Adam's
now earthly nature and sense.   4. Dark.   5. The *heavenly shapes* (line 1082).   6. As we are in.
7. Exposed to.

Some tree whose broad smooth leaves together sewed, 1095
And girded on our loins, may cover round
Those middle parts, that this newcomer, Shame,
There sit not, and reproach us as unclean."
    So counseled he, and both together went
Into the thickest wood; there soon they chose 1100
The figtree, not that kind for fruit renowned
But such as at this day, to Indians known,
In Malabar or Deccan[8] spreads her arms
Branching so broad and long, that in the ground
The bended twigs take root, and daughters grow 1105
About the mother tree, a pillared shade
High overarched, and echoing walks between;
There oft the Indian herdsman, shunning heat,
Shelters in cool, and tends his pasturing herds
At loopholes cut through thickest shade. Those leaves 1110
They gathered, broad as Amazonian targe,[9]
And with what skill they had, together sewed,
To gird their waist; vain covering, if to hide
Their guilt and dreaded shame! O how unlike
To that first naked glory! Such of late 1115
Columbus found th' American, so girt
With feathered cincture,[1] naked else and wild
Among the trees on isles and woody shores.
Thus fenced, and, as they thought, their shame in part
Covered, but not at rest or ease of mind, 1120
They sat them down to weep; nor only tears
Rained at their eyes, but high winds worse within
Began to rise, high passions, anger, hate,
Mistrust, suspicion, discord, and shook sore
Their inward state of mind, calm region once 1125
And full of peace, now tossed and turbulent:
For Understanding ruled not, and the Will
Heard not her lore, both in subjection now
To sensual Appetite, who, from beneath
Usurping over sovereign Reason, claimed 1130
Superior sway.[2] From thus distempered breast,
Adam, estranged in look and altered style,
Speech intermitted thus to Eve renewed:
    "Would thou hadst hearkened to my words, and stayed
With me, as I besought thee, when that strange 1135
Desire of wandering, this unhappy morn,
I know not whence possessed thee! we had then
Remained still happy, not as now, despoiled
Of all our good, shamed, naked, miserable.
Let none henceforth seek needless cause to approve 1140
The faith they owe;[3] when earnestly they seek

---

8. In southern India. *Figtree*: identified as the banyan or Indian fig tree, also classified in botany as *Ficus religiosa*.   9. Shield. The Amazons were women warriors in Greco-Roman myth (and in Virgil's *Aeneid*). Actually the tree's leaf is small; Milton's inaccurate notion comes from contemporary sources and goes back to antiquity.   1. Belt.   2. The victory of *Sensual Appetite* over *Reason* (cf. line 113 and n. 9, p. 2223) and over humankind's free will (compare lines 351ff.)—humanity's distinguishing traits—summarizes the history of the Fall.   3. Own. *Approve*: prove by testing.

Such proof, conclude, they then begin to fail."
   To whom, soon moved with touch of blame, thus Eve:
"What words have passed thy lips, Adam severe?
Imput'st thou that to my default, or will   1145
Of wandering, as thou call'st it, which who knows
But might as ill have happened, thou being by,
Or to thyself perhaps? Hadst thou been there,
Or here th' attempt, thou couldst not have discerned
Fraud in the serpent, speaking as he spake;   1150
No ground of enmity between us known,
Why he should mean me ill, or seek to harm?
Was I to have never parted from thy side?
As good have grown there still a lifeless rib.
Being as I am, why didst not thou, the head,   1155
Command me absolutely not to go,
Going into such danger, as thou saidst?
Too facile then, thou didst not much gainsay,
Nay, didst permit, approve, and fair dismiss.
Hadst thou been firm and fixed in thy dissent,   1160
Neither had I transgressed, nor thou with me."[4]
   To whom, then first incensed, Adam replied:
"Is this the love, is this the recompense
Of mine to thee, ingrateful Eve, expressed[5]
Immutable when thou were lost, not I,   1165
Who might have lived and joyed immortal bliss,
Yet willingly chose rather death with thee?
And am I now upbraided as the cause
Of thy transgressing? not enough severe,
It seems, in thy restraint![6] What could I more?   1170
I warned thee, I admonished thee, foretold
The danger, and the lurking enemy
That lay in wait; beyond this had been force,
And force upon free will hath here no place.
But confidence then bore thee on, secure   1175
Either to meet no danger, or to find
Matter of glorious trial and perhaps
I also erred in overmuch admiring
What seemed in thee so perfect, that I thought
No evil durst attempt thee! but I rue   1180
That error now, which is become my crime,
And thou th' accuser. Thus it shall befall
Him who, to worth in women overtrusting,
Lets her will rule; restraint she will not brook,[7]
And, left to herself, if evil thence ensue,   1185
She first his weak indulgence will accuse."
   Thus they in mutual accusation spent
The fruitless hours, but neither self-condemning;
And of their vain contést appeared no end.

---

4. The notion of man's authority over woman—recognized by Milton's Eve (e.g., in 4.442–43: "my guide / and head") and echoing St. Paul (1 Corinthians 11.3: "the head of the woman is the man") is here used by her to make Adam her equal in guilt, accusing him of indulgence in letting her go (*too facile*).
5. Demonstrated, proved.   6. In restraining Eve.   7. Put up with.

FROM BOOK 10

The Argument

Man's transgression known, the guardian Angels forsake Paradise, and return up to Heaven to approve their vigilance, and are approved; God declaring that the entrance of Satan could not be by them prevented. He sends his Son to judge the transgressors; who descends, and gives sentence accordingly; then, in pity, clothes them both, and reascends. Sin and Death, sitting till then at the gates of Hell, by wondrous sympathy feeling the success of Satan in this new World, and the sin by Man there committed, resolve to sit no longer confined in Hell, but to follow Satan, their sire, up to the place of Man: to make the way easier from Hell to this World to and fro, they pave a broad highway or bridge over Chaos, according to the track that Satan first made; then, preparing for Earth, they meet him, proud of his success, returning to Hell; their mutual gratulation. Satan arrives at Pandemonium; in full assembly relates, with boasting, his success against Man; instead of applause is entertained with a general hiss by all his audience, transformed, with himself also, suddenly into Serpents, according to his doom given in Paradise; then, deluded with a show of the Forbidden Tree springing up before them, they, greedily reaching to take of the fruit, chew dust and bitter ashes. The proceedings of Sin and Death: God foretells the final victory of his Son over them, and the renewing of all things; but, for the present, commands his Angels to make several alterations in the Heavens and Elements. Adam, more and more perceiving his fallen condition, heavily bewails,[8] rejects the condolement of Eve; she persists, and at length appeases him: then, to evade the curse likely to fall on their offspring, proposes to Adam violent ways; which he approves not, but, conceiving better hope, puts her in mind of the late promise made them, that her seed should be revenged on the Serpent, and exhorts her, with him, to seek peace of the offended Deity by repentance and supplication.

[Acceptance, Reconciliation, Hope]

                        * * * Thus began
Outrage from lifeless things; but Discord first,
Daughter of Sin, among th' irrational
Death introduced through fierce antipathy:[9]
Beast now with beast 'gan war, and fowl with fowl,   710
And fish with fish: to graze the herb all leaving,
Devoured each other; nor stood much in awe
Of man, but fled him, or with countenance grim
Glared on him passing. These were from without
The growing miseries, which Adam saw   715
Already in part, though hid in gloomiest shade,
To sorrow abandoned, but worse felt within,
And in a troubled sea of passion tossed,
Thus to disburden sought with sad complaint:

---

8. The selection printed here starts toward the end of Adam's long lamentation.   9. I.e., Discord introduced death to the irrational (beasts) through antipathy; Milton paves the way for the role of sympathy in reconciling Adam to Eve.

"O miserable of happy! Is this the end 720
Of this new glorious world, and me so late
The glory of that glory? who now, become
Accursed of blessèd, hide me from the face
Of God, whom to behold was then my height
Of happiness! Yet well, if here would end 725
The misery; I deserved it, and would bear
My own deservings; but this will not serve.
All that I eat or drink, or shall beget,
Is propagated curse.[1] O voice, once heard
Delightfully, 'Increase and multiply,' 730
Now death to hear! for what can I increase
Or multiply, but curses on my head?
Who of all ages to succeed, but, feeling
The evil on him brought by me, will curse
My head: 'Ill fare our ancestor impure! 735
For this we may thank Adam!' but his thanks
Shall be the execration;[2] so besides
Mine own that bide upon me, all from me
Shall with a fierce reflux on me redound,
On me, as on their natural center, light 740
Heavy, though in their place. O fleeting joys
Of Paradise, dear bought with lasting woes!
Did I request thee, Maker, from my clay
To mold me man? Did I solicit thee
From darkness to promote me, or here place 745
In this delicious garden? As my will
Concurred not to my being, it were but right
And equal to reduce me to my dust,
Desirous to resign and render back
All I received, unable to perform 750
Thy terms too hard, by which I was to hold
The good I sought not. To the loss of that,
Sufficient penalty, why hast thou added
The sense of endless woes? Inexplicable
Thy justice seems; yet to say truth, too late 755
I thus contèst; then should have been refused
Those terms whatever, when they were proposed.
Thou didst accept them; wilt thou enjoy the good,
Then cavil[3] the conditions? And though God
Made thee without thy leave, what if thy son 760
Prove disobedient, and reproved, retort,
'Wherefore didst thou beget me? I sought it not.'
Wouldst thou admit for his contempt of thee
That proud excuse? Yet him not thy election,
But natural necessity begot. 765
God made thee of choice his own, and of his own
To serve him; thy reward was of his grace;
Thy punishment then justly is at his will.

---

1. Eating, drinking, and procreating all increase or extend God's curse.   2. I.e., posterity's curses on Adam.   3. Raise petty objections.

Be it so, for I submit; his doom is fair,[4]
That dust I am and shall to dust return.   770
O welcome hour whenever! Why delays
His hand to execute what his decree
Fixed on this day? Why do I overlive?
Why am I mocked with death, and lengthened out
To deathless pain? How gladly would I meet   775
Mortality, my sentence, and be earth
Insensible! how glad would lay me down
As in my mother's lap![5] here I should rest
And sleep secure; his dreadful voice no more
Would thunder in my ears; no fear of worse   780
To me and to my offspring would torment me
With cruel expectation. Yet one doubt
Pursues me still, lest all I cannot die;
Lest that pure breath of life, the spirit of man
Which God inspired, cannot together perish   785
With this corporeal clod; then, in the grave,
Or in some other dismal place, who knows
But I shall die a living death? O thought
Horrid, if true![6] Yet why? It was but breath
Of life that sinned; what dies but what had life   790
And sin? the body properly hath neither.
All of me then shall die: let this appease
The doubt, since human reach no further knows.
For though the Lord of all be infinite,
Is his wrath also? Be it, man is not so,   795
But mortal doomed. How can he exercise
Wrath without end on man whom death must end?
Can he make deathless death? That were to make
Strange contradiction, which to God himself
Impossible is held, as argument   800
Of weakness, not of power.[7] Will he draw out,
For anger's sake, finite to infinite
In punished man, to satisfy his rigor
Satisfied never? That were to extend
His sentence beyond dust and Nature's law;   805
By which all causes else according still
To the reception of their matter act,
Not to th' extent of their own sphere.[8] But say
That death be not one stroke, as I supposed,
Bereaving sense, but endless misery   810

4. In his inner debate, Adam has just been arguing to himself that God created us "of choice his own, / and of his own to serve him." Hence in the same way as reward "was of his [God's] grace," so punishment "justly is at his will" and, therefore, acceptable.   5. I.e., the Earth (in 11.536, Michael, addressing Adam, calls the Earth "thy mother's lap"), probably an echo of Job 3.   6. Adam fears that the soul, breathed (*inspired*) into the *corporeal clod* at Creation, may be immortal and so suffer a *living death* in the grave.   7. Adam corrects himself, arguing (as Milton did in his theological writings) that because only the spirit (*breath of life,* line 784) sinned it shall die with the body (and, implicitly, await resurrection). Otherwise, according to the same theological line of thinking, there would be *strange contradiction,* an inadmissable sign of weakness in God.   8. Once body and spirit die, further punishment is impossible. According to *Nature's law* the power of all agents, God excepted (*all causes else*), cannot be exercised to its utmost (the *extent of their own sphere*) but is limited by the capacity for *reception* that the object of that power possesses.

From this day onward, which I feel begun
Both in me and without[9] me, and so last
To perpetuity—Ay me! that fear
Comes thundering back with dreadful revolution
On my defenseless head! Both death and I   815
Am found eternal, and incorporate both:[1]
Nor I on my part single; in me all
Posterity stands cursed. Fair patrimony
That I must leave ye, sons! O, were I able
To waste it all myself, and leave ye none!   820
So disinherited, how would ye bless
Me, now your curse! Ah, why should all mankind
For one man's fault thus guiltless be condemned,
If guiltless? But from me what can proceed,
But all corrupt, both mind and will depraved,   825
Not to do only, but to will the same
With me? How can they then acquitted stand
In sight of God?[2] Him, after all disputes,
Forced I absolve. All my evasions vain
And reasonings, though through mazes, lead me still   830
But to my own conviction: first and last
On me, me only, as the source and spring
Of all corruption, all the blame lights due;
So might the wrath! Fond[3] wish! Couldst thou support
That burden, heavier than the earth to bear;   835
Than all the world much heavier, though divided
With that bad woman? Thus, what thou desir'st,
And what thou fear'st, alike destroys all hope[4]
Of refuge, and concludes thee miserable
Beyond all past example[5] and future;   840
To Satan only like, both crime and doom.[6]
O Conscience! into what abyss of fears
And horrors hast thou driven me; out of which
I find no way, from deep to deeper plunged!"

    Thus Adam to himself lamented loud   845
Through the still night, not now, as ere man fell,
Wholesome and cool and mild, but with black air
Accompanied, with damps and dreadful gloom;
Which to his evil conscience represented
All things with double terror. On the ground   850
Outstretched he lay, on the cold ground, and oft
Cursed his creation; Death as oft accused
Of tardy execution, since denounced
The day of his offense. "Why comes not Death,"
Said he, "with one thrice-àcceptàble stroke   855

---

9. Outside. *Bereaving sense*: removing all sensory powers.   1. The use of *am*, the singular form, stresses Adam's concentration on himself and on the fact that he and death are now united in one body (*incorporate*).   2. Inheriting Adam's original sin, his descendants, like him (*with me*), are going to act sinfully by their own free will.   3. Foolish.   4. Actually, by his desperate self-accusation and by wanting to assume, alone, the burden of guilt, Adam is shown to be already on the way to full repentance and to his own regeneration.   5. That of the fallen angels. *Concludes thee*: demonstrates that you are.   6. The comparison is clearly invalid, Adam's remorse and repentant despair being opposite to Satan's choice, as seen, for example, in 4.109–10: "Farewell remorse! All good to me is lost; / Evil, be thou my good."

To end me? Shall Truth fail to keep her word,
Justice divine not hasten to be just?
But Death comes not at call; Justice divine
Mends not her slowest pace for prayers or cries.
O woods, O fountains, hillocks, dales, and bowers!   860
With other echo late I taught your shades
To answer, and resound far other song."
Whom thus afflicted when sad Eve beheld,
Desolate where she sat, approaching nigh,
Soft words to his fierce passion she essayed;   865
But her with stern regard he thus repelled:
   "Out of my sight, thou serpent! that name best
Befits thee, with him leagued, thyself as false
And hateful: nothing wants, but that thy shape,
Like his, and color serpentine, may show   870
Thy inward fraud, to warn all creatures from thee
Henceforth; lest that too heavenly form, pretended[7]
To hellish falsehood, snare them. But for thee
I had persisted happy, had not thy pride
And wandering vanity, when least was safe,   875
Rejected my forewarning, and disdained
Not to be trusted, longing to be seen
Though by the devil himself, him overweening
To overreach,[8] but, with the serpent meeting,
Fooled and beguiled; by him thou, I by thee,   880
To trust thee from my side, imagined wise,
Constant, mature, proof against all assaults;
And understood not all was but a show
Rather than solid virtue, all but a rib
Crooked by nature—bent, as now appears,   885
More to the part sinìster—from me drawn;
Well if thrown out, as supernumerary
To my just number found![9] Oh, why did God,
Creator wise, that peopled highest Heaven
With spirits masculine, create at last   890
This novelty on earth, this fair defect
Of nature, and not fill the world at once
With men, as angels, without feminine;
Or find some other way to generate
Mankind?[1] This mischief had not then befallen,   895
And more that shall befall—innumerable
Disturbances on earth through female snares,
And strait conjunction with this sex. For either
He never shall find out fit mate, but such
As some misfortune brings him, or mistake;   900
Or whom he wishes most shall seldom gain,
Through her perverseness, but shall see her gained

7. Put up as a screen.   8. Overestimating your power to outwit him.   9. Folklore has it that the rib from which Eve was created was an extra rib on Adam's left (Latin: *sinister*) side. Note double meaning of *sinister*.   1. Adam's frenzied speech belongs to a tradition of misogynistic rhetoric that goes back to antiquity. These lines, in particular, seem to echo Euripides' *Hippolytus*, lines 617–20 (Euripides was one of Milton's favorite poets).

By a far worse, or, if she love, withheld
By parents, or his happiest choice too late
Shall meet, already linked and wedlock-bound 905
To a fell[2] adversary, his hate or shame:
Which infinite calamity shall cause
To human life, and household peace confound."
    He added not, and from her turned; but Eve,
Not so repulsed, with tears that ceased not flowing, 910
And tresses all disordered, at his feet
Fell humble, and, embracing them, besought
His peace, and thus proceeded in her plaint:
    "Forsake me not thus, Adam! witness Heaven
What love sincere and reverence in my heart 915
I bear thee, and unweeting have offended,
Unhappily deceived! Thy suppliant[3]
I beg, and clasp thy knees; bereave me not,
Whereon I live, thy gentle looks, thy aid,
Thy counsel in this uttermost distress, 920
My only strength and stay: forlorn of thee,
Whither shall I betake me, where subsist?
While yet we live, scarce one short hour perhaps,
Between us two let there be peace; both joining,
As joined in injuries, one enmity 925
Against a foe by doom express assigned us,
That cruel serpent. On me exercise not
Thy hatred for this misery befallen;
On me already lost, me than thyself
More miserable. Both have sinned, but thou 930
Against God only; I against God and thee,
And to the place of judgment will return,
There with my cries importune Heaven, that all
The sentence, from thy head removed, may light
On me, sole cause to thee of all this woe, 935
Me, me only, just object of his ire."
    She ended weeping; and her lowly plight,
Immovable[4] till peace obtained from fault
Acknowledged and deplored, in Adam wrought
Commiseration. Soon his heart relented 940
Towards her, his life so late and sole delight,
Now at his feet submissive in distress,
Creature so fair his reconcilement seeking,
His counsel, whom she had displeased, his aid;
As one disarmed, his anger all he lost, 945
And thus with peaceful words upraised her soon:
    "Unwary, and too desirous, as before,
So now, of what thou know'st not,[5] who desir'st
The punishment all on thyself! Alas!
Bear thine own first, ill able to sustain 950

---

2. Fierce, bitter. *Already linked:* i.e., when he is already linked.   3. As thy suppliant. *Unweeting:* unknowingly.   4. Modifies both Eve in her lowly posture of repentance and Adam in his first reluctance to forgive.   5. Once more Eve is *too desirous* of the unknown, but her situation and her tone are now totally different—as are those of Adam, whose *counsel* and *aid* she has sought.

His full wrath, whose thou feel'st as yet least part,[6]
And my displeasure bear'st so ill. If prayers
Could alter high decrees, I to that place
Would speed before thee, and be louder heard,
That on my head all might be visited,   955
Thy frailty and infirmer sex forgiven,
To me committed, and by me exposed.[7]
But rise; let us no more contend, nor blame
Each other, blamed enough elsewhere,[8] but strive
In offices of love, how we may lighten   960
Each other's burden in our share of woe;
Since this day's death denounced, if aught I see,
Will prove no sudden, but a slow-paced evil,
A long day's dying to augment our pain,
And to our seed (O hapless seed!) derived."[9]   965
    To whom thus Eve, recovering heart, replied:—
"Adam, by sad experiment I know
How little weight my words with thee can find,
Found so erroneous, thence by just event
Found so unfortunate. Nevertheless,   970
Restored by thee, vile as I am, to place
Of new acceptance, hopeful to regain
Thy love, the sole contentment of my heart,
Living or dying from thee I will not hide
What thoughts in my unquiet breast are risen,   975
Tending to some relief of our extremes,
Or end, though sharp and sad, yet tolerable,
As in our evils,[1] and of easier choice.
If care of our descent[2] perplex us most,
Which must be born to certain woe, devoured   980
By Death at last (and miserable it is
To be to others cause of misery,
Our own begotten, and of our loins to bring
Into this cursed world a woeful race,
That, after wretched life, must be at last   985
Food for so foul a monster), in thy power
It lies, yet ere conception, to prevent
The race unblest, to being yet unbegot.[3]
Childless thou art; childless remain. So Death
Shall be deceived his glut,[4] and with us two   990
Be forced to satisfy his ravenous maw.
But, if thou judge it hard and difficult,
Conversing, looking, loving, to abstain
From love's due rites, nuptial embraces sweet,
And with desire to languish without hope   995
Before the present object[5] languishing
With like desire—which would be misery

6. Eve would not be able to bear the weight of God's full wrath, of which she has until now experienced only the smallest part.   7. In the present atmosphere of reconciliation, Adam seems to accept Eve's earlier charge (see n. 4, p. 2245); now he blames himself for having exposed her to temptation.   8. I.e., at the place of judgment (see also lines 932, 953, and 1098–99).   9. Transmitted.   1. We being in such evils.   2. Descendants, lineage.   3. To forestall, by abstinence, the birth of descendants.   4. Shall be cheated of its fill.   5. Eve herself, object of Adam's love, and now in his presence.

And torment less than none of what we dread—
Then, both our selves and seed at once to free
From what we fear for both, let us make short; 1000
Let us seek Death, or, he not found, supply
With our own hands his office on ourselves.
Why stand we longer shivering under fears
That show no end but death, and have the power,
Of many ways to die the shortest choosing 1005
Destruction with destruction to destroy?"[6]
    She ended here, or vehement despair
Broke off the rest; so much of death her thoughts
Had entertained as dyed her cheeks with pale.
But Adam, with such counsel nothing swayed, 1010
To better hopes his more attentive mind
Laboring had raised, and thus to Eve replied:—
    "Eve, thy contempt of life and pleasure seems
To argue in thee something more sublime
And excellent than what thy mind contemns: 1015
But self-destruction therefore sought refutes
That excellence thought in thee, and implies
Not thy contempt, but anguish and regret
For loss of life and pleasure overloved.[7]
Or, if thou covet death, as utmost end 1020
Of misery, so thinking to evade
The penalty pronounced, doubt not but God
Hath wiselier armed his vengeful ire than so
To be forestalled. Much more I fear lest death
So snatched will not exempt us from the pain 1025
We are by doom to pay; rather such acts
Of contumacy will provoke the Highest
To make death in us live. Then let us seek
Some safer resolution—which methinks
I have in view, calling to mind with heed 1030
Part of our sentence,[8] that thy seed shall bruise
The Serpent's head. Piteous amends! unless
Be meant whom I conjecture,[9] our grand foe,
Satan, who in the Serpent hath contrived
Against us this deceit. To crush his head 1035
Would be revenge indeed—which will be lost
By death brought on ourselves, or childless days
Resolved as thou proposest; so our foe
Shall scape his punishment ordained, and we
Instead shall double ours upon our heads. 1040
No more be mentioned, then, of violence

6. Destroy destruction (Death's power to destroy future mankind) by destroying ourselves now.   7. The suicide project excludes (*refutes*) the idea that Eve be contemptuous of life and pleasure in view of *something more sublime;* it rather implies *anguish and regret* at the thought of losing those goods.   8. Earlier in this book ("The Argument" and lines 163–208) the Lord gives sentence on the Serpent and the transgressors. The references here are to that passage, which is quite literally based on Genesis 30 (esp. lines 179–81; "Between thee and the Woman I will put / Enmity, and between thine and her seed; / Her seed shall bruise thy head, thou bruise his heel").   9. The notion that Satan spoke through the Serpent was not at first given to humanity (lines 170–71: "Concerned not Man. . . . / Nor altered his offense"). Adam is late in coming to that conclusion (*I conjecture*), and on it he bases the following eloquent argument in favor of survival, hope, procreation, and activity.

Against ourselves, and wilful barrenness
That cuts us off from hope, and savors only
Rancor and pride, impatience and despite,
Reluctance[1] against God and his just yoke   1045
Laid on our necks. Remember with what mild
And gracious temper he both heard and judged,
Without wrath or reviling. We expected
Immediate dissolution, which we thought
Was meant by death that day; when, lo! to thee   1050
Pains only in child-bearing were foretold,
And bringing forth, soon recompensed with joy,
Fruit of thy womb. On me the curse aslope
Glanced on the ground.[2] With labor I must earn
My bread; what harm: Idleness had been worse;   1055
My labor will sustain me; and, lest cold
Or heat should injure us, his timely care
Hath, unbesought, provided, and his hands
Clothed us unworthy, pitying while he judged.
How much more, if we pray him, will his ear   1060
Be open, and his heart to pity incline,
And teach us further by what means to shun
The inclement seasons, rain, ice, hail, and snow!
Which now the sky, with various face, begins
To show us in this mountain,[3] while the winds   1065
Blow moist and keen, shattering the graceful locks
Of these fair spreading trees; which bids us seek
Some better shroud, some better warmth to cherish
Our limbs benumbed—ere this diurnal star
Leave cold the night, how we his gathered beams   1070
Reflected may with matter sere foment,[4]
Or by collision of two bodies grind
The air attrite to fire;[5] as late the clouds,
Justling, or pushed with winds, rude in their shock,
Tine the slant lightning, whose thwart[6] flame, driven down, 1075
Kindles the gummy bark of fir or pine,
And sends a comfortable heat from far,
Which might supply the Sun. Such fire to use,
And what may else be remedy or cure
To evils which our own misdeeds have wrought,   1080
He will instruct us praying,[7] and of grace

---

1. Resistance, opposition.   2. The curse descending (*aslope*) on Adam took an oblique course (*glanced*)
toward the ground. Thus Adam is not only accepting the Lord's sentence (in lines 201–02 and 205; "Curs'd
is the ground for thy sake; thou in sorrow / Shalt eat thereof all the days of thy life; / . . . In the sweat of
thy face thou shalt eat bread") but turning it into a project for an active life after the Fall.   3. In his
description of *delicious Paradise* (4.132–58), Milton situates it on a high plateau at the top of a "steep
wilderness" that denies access to the "enclosure green" and its "Insuperable height of loftiest shade, / Cedar,
and pine, and fir, and branching palm, / A sylvan scene, and as the ranks ascend / Shade above shade, a
woody theater / Of stateliest view" where "gentle gales / . . . dispense / Native perfumes, and whisper whence
they stole / Those balmy spoils." That stately and blissful order is now disrupted, and after the radical
alterations in the heavens and in the elements that God has commanded, Adam is preparing to cope with
the hardships and challenges of his mortal state in a time-conditioned universe of seasonal changes, dawns
and sunset, heat and ice, and shattering winds.   4. Heat, warm. *Diurnal star*: day star, the sun. *How*:
seek how.   5. The implied belief is that rubbing two *bodies* (as two flints) against each other, the air thus
"ground down by the attrition (*attrite*) turns into fire.   6. Passing across the sky. *Tine*: kindle; that fire
was produced by lighting is one of the ancient theories about its origin on Earth.   7. If we pray to him.

Beseeching him; so as we need not fear
To pass commodiously this life, sustained
By him with many comforts, till we end
In dust, our final rest and native home.   1085
What better can we do, than to the place
Repairing where he judged us, prostrate fall
Before him reverent, and there confess
Humbly our faults, and pardon beg, with tears
Watering the ground, and with our sighs the air   1090
Frequenting,[8] sent from hearts contrite, in sign
Of sorrow unfeigned and humiliation meek?
Undoubtedly he will relent, and turn
From his displeasure, in whose look serene,
When angry most he seemed and most severe,   1095
What else but favor, grace, and mercy shone?"
    So spake our Father penitent; nor Eve
Felt less remorse. They, forthwith to the place
Repairing where he judged them, prostrate fell
Before him reverent, and both confessed   1100
Humbly their faults, and pardon begged, with tears
Watering the ground, and with their sighs the air
Frequenting, sent from hearts contrite, in sign
Of sorrow unfeigned and humiliation meek.

FROM BOOK 12

["The World Was All before Them"]

Summary   After God's acceptance of the transgressors' prayers and the decree
that "they must no longer abide in Paradise" (11, "The Argument"), Michael the
archangel, with a band of cherubim, has been sent "to dispossess them." After Eve's
lamentation and his own pleading, Adam has submitted; Michael has led him up to
a high hill where, in a mixture of prophecy and instruction, he has set "before him
in vision" the future of mankind, from Cain and Abel through Noah (11) and the
prophets, thus coming "by degrees to explain who that Seed of Woman shall be which
was promised Adam and Eve in the Fall: his incarnation, death, resurrection, and
ascension; the state of the Church till his second coming" (12, "The Argument").
Toward the close of his speech, Michael has recommended the exercise of the basic
Christian virtues, culminating in love, "By name to come called Charity, the soul /
Of all the rest: then will thou not be loath / To leave this Paradise, but shalt possess
/ A Paradise within thee, happier far" (12.584–87). Michael has just ended his long
speech.

*   *   *

    He ended, and they both descend the hill.
Descended, Adam to the bower where Eve
Lay sleeping[9] ran before, but found her waked;
And thus with words not sad she him received:
    "Whence thou return'st and whither went'st, I know;   610
For God is also in sleep, and dreams[1] advise,

8. Filling.   9. Michael has just said to Adam (lines 594–97): "Go, waken Eve; / Her also I with gentle
dreams have calmed, / Portending good, and all her spirits composed / To meek submission."   1. The
fact that Adam was granted a vision and Eve a dream may symbolize a difference in the mode of perception
between man and woman; at any rate, both are God's revelations.

Which he hath sent propitious, some great good
Presaging, since, with sorrow and heart's distress
Wearied, I fell asleep. But now lead on;
In me is no delay; with thee to go   615
Is to stay here; without thee here to stay
Is to go hence unwilling; thou to me
Art all things under Heaven, all places thou,
Who for my willful crime art banished hence.
This further consolation yet secure   620
I carry hence: though all by me is lost,
Such favor I unworthy am vouchsafed,
By me the Promised Seed shall all restore."
    So spake our mother Eve; and Adam heard
Well pleased, but answered not; for now too nigh   625
Th' archangel stood, and from the other hill[2]
To their fixed station, all in bright array,
The cherubim descended; on the ground
Gliding meteorous, as evening mist
Risen from a river o'er the marish[3] glides,   630
And gathers ground fast at the laborer's heel
Homeward returning. High in front advanced,[4]
The brandished sword of God before them blazed,
Fierce as a comet; which with torrid heat,
And vapor as the Libyan air adust,[5]   635
Began to parch that temperate clime; whereat
In either hand the hastening angel caught
Our lingering parents, and to th' eastern gate[6]
Led them direct, and down the cliff as fast
To the subjected[7] plain; then disappeared.   640
They, looking back, all th' eastern side beheld
Of Paradise, so late their happy seat,
Waved over by that flaming brand;[8] the gate
With dreadful faces thronged and fiery arms.
Some natural tears they dropped, but wiped them soon;   645
The world was all before them, where to choose
Their place of rest,[9] and Providence their guide.
They, hand in hand, with wandering steps and slow,
Through Eden took their solitary way.

---

2. The hill that Michael had pointed out to Adam in lines 590–93: "and, see! the guards, / By me encamped
on yonder hill, expect / Their motion, at whose front a flaming sword, / In signal of remove, waves fiercely
round."   **3.** Marsh.   **4.** Raised high, carried like a banner.   **5.** Burned up, as the air of the Sahara
Desert in Libya.   **6.** *The eastern gate* of Eden, guarded by Gabriel, was described earlier (4. 543–47): "It
was a rock / Of alabaster, piled up to the clouds, / Conspicuous far, winding with one ascent / Accessible
from earth, one entrance high; / The rest was craggy cliff."   **7.** Lying below.   **8.** Here meaning sword,
but also conveying the image of burning (*flaming*). *Seat:* abode.   **9.** Not, of course, a place of repose,
but their new, earthly abode.

A Note on Translation

Reading literature in translation is a pleasure on which it is fruitless to frown. The purist may insist that we ought always read in the original languages, and we know ideally that this is true. But it is a counsel of perfection, quite impractical even for the purist, since no one in a lifetime can master all the languages whose literatures it would be a joy to explore. Master languages as fast as we may, we shall always have to read to some extent in translation, and this means we must be alert to what we are about: if in reading a work of literature in translation we are not reading the "original," what precisely are we reading? This is a question of great complexity, to which justice cannot be done in a brief note, but the following sketch of some of the considerations may be helpful.

One of the memorable scenes of ancient literature is the meeting of Hector and Andromache in book 6 of Homer's *Iliad*. Hector, leader and mainstay of the armies defending Troy, is implored by his wife, Andromache, to withdraw within the city walls and carry on the defense from there, where his life will not be constantly at hazard. In Homer's text her opening words to him are these: δαιμόνιε, φθίσει σε τὸ σὸν μένος (daimonie, phthisei se to son menos). How should they be translated into English?

Here is how they have actually been translated into English by capable translators, at various periods, in verse and prose:

1. George Chapman, 1598:

> O noblest in desire,
> Thy mind, inflamed with others' good, will set thy self on fire.

2. John Dryden, 1693:

> Thy dauntless heart (which I foresee too late),
> Too daring man, will urge thee to thy fate.

3. Alexander Pope, 1715:

> Too daring Prince! . . . .
> For sure such courage length of life denies,
> And thou must fall, thy virtue's sacrifice.

4. William Cowper, 1791:

> Thy own great courage will cut short thy days,
> My noble Hector . . .

5. Lang, Leaf, and Myers, 1883 (prose):

Dear my lord, this thy hardihood will undo thee. . . .

6. A. T. Murray, 1924 (prose):

Ah, my husband, this prowess of thine will be thy doom. . . .

7. E. V. Rieu, 1950 (prose):

"Hector," she said, "you are possessed. This bravery of yours will be your end."

8. I. A. Richards, 1950 (prose):

"Strange man," she said, "your courage will be your destruction."

9. Richmond Lattimore, 1951:

Dearest,
Your own great strength will be your death. . . .

10. Robert Fitzgerald, 1979:

O my wild one, your bravery will be
Your own undoing!

11. Robert Fagles, 1990:

reckless one,
Your own fiery courage will destroy you!

From these strikingly different renderings of the same six words, certain facts about the nature of translation begin to emerge. We notice, for one thing, that Homer's word μένος (menos) is diversified by the translators into "mind," "dauntless heart," "such courage," "great courage," "hardihood," "prowess," "bravery," "courage," "great strength," "bravery," and "fiery courage." The word has in fact all these possibilities. Used of things, it normally means "force"; of animals, "fierceness" or "brute strength" or (in the case of horses) "mettle"; of men and women, "passion" or "spirit" or even "purpose." Homer's application of it in the present case points our attention equally— whatever particular sense we may imagine Andromache to have uppermost—to Hector's force, strength, fierceness in battle, spirited heart and mind. But since English has no matching term of like inclusiveness, the passage as the translators give it to us reflects this lack and we find one attribute singled out to the exclusion of the rest.

Here then is the first and most crucial fact about any work of literature read in translation. It cannot escape the linguistic characteristics of the language into which it is turned: the grammatical, syntactical, lexical, and phonetic boundaries that constitute collectively the individuality or "genius" of that language. A Greek play or a Russian novel in English will be governed first of all by the resources of the English language, resources that are certain to be in every instance very different, as the efforts with μένος show, from those of the original.

Turning from μένος to δαιμόνιε (daimonie) in Homer's clause, we encounter a second crucial fact about translations. Nobody knows exactly what shade of meaning δαιμονιε had for Homer. In later writers the word normally suggests divinity, something miraculous, wondrous; but in Homer it appears as a vocative of address for both chieftain and commoner, man and wife. The coloring one gives it must, therefore, be determined either by the way one thinks a Greek wife of Homer's era might actually address her husband (a subject on which we have no information whatever) or in the way one thinks it suitable for a hero's wife to address her husband in an epic poem, that is to say, a highly stylized and formal work. In general, the translators of our century have abandoned formality to stress the intimacy; the wifeliness; and, especially in Lattimore's case, a certain chiding tenderness, in Andromache's appeal: (6) "Ah, my husband," (7) "Hector" (with perhaps a hint, in "you are possessed," of the alarmed distaste with which wives have so often viewed their husbands' bellicose moods), (8) "Strange man," (9) "Dearest," (10) "O my wild one" (mixing an almost motherly admiration with reproach and concern), and (11) "reckless one." On the other hand, the older translators have obviously removed Andromache to an epic or heroic distance from her beloved, whence she sees and kindles to his selfless courage, acknowledging, even in the moment of pleading with him to be otherwise, his moral grandeur and the tragic destiny this too certainly implies: (1) "O noblest in desire, . . . inflamed by others' good"; (2) "Thy dauntless heart (which I foresee too late), / Too daring man"; (3) "Too daring Prince! . . . / And thou must fall, thy virtue's sacrifice"; (4) "My noble Hector." Even the less specific "Dear my lord" of Lang, Leaf, and Myers looks in the same direction because of its echo of the speech of countless Shakespearean men and women who have shared this powerful moral sense: "Dear my lord, make me acquainted with your cause of grief"; "Perseverance, dear my lord, keeps honor bright"; etc.

The fact about translation that emerges from all this is that just as the translated work reflects the individuality of the language it is turned into, so it reflects the individuality of the age in which it is made, and the age will permeate it everywhere like yeast in dough. We think of one kind of permeation when we think of the governing verse forms and attitudes toward verse at a given epoch. In Chapman's time, experiments seeking an "heroic" verse form for English were widespread, and accordingly he tries a "fourteener" couplet (two rhymed lines of seven stresses each) in his *Iliad* and a pentameter couplet in his *Odyssey*. When Dryden and Pope wrote, a closed pentameter couplet had become established as the heroic form par excellence. By Cowper's day, thanks largely to the prestige of *Paradise Lost*, the couplet had gone out of fashion for narrative poetry in favor of blank verse. Our age, inclining to prose and in verse to proselike informalities and relaxations, has, predictably, produced half a dozen excellent prose translations of the *Iliad* but only three in verse (by Fagles, Lattimore, and Fitzgerald), all relying on rhythms that are much of the time closer to the verse of William Carlos Williams and some of the prose of novelists like Faulkner than to the swift firm tread of Homer's Greek. For if it is true that what we translate from a given work is what, wearing the spectacles of our time, we see in it, it is also true that we see in it what we have the power to translate.

Of course, there are other effects of the translator's epoch on a translation besides those exercised by contemporary taste in verse and verse forms. Chapman writes in a great age of poetic metaphor and, therefore, almost instinctively translates his understanding of Homer's verb φθίσει (phthisei, "to cause to wane, consume, waste, pine") into metaphorical terms of flame, presenting his Hector to us as a man of burning generosity who will be consumed by his very ardor. This is a conception rooted in large part in the psychology of the Elizabethans, who had the habit of speaking of the soul as "fire," of one of the four temperaments as "fiery," of even the more material bodily processes, like digestion, as if they were carried on by the heat of fire ("concoction," "decoction"). It is rooted too in that characteristic Renaissance élan so unforgettably expressed in characters such as Tamburlaine and Dr. Faustus, the former of whom exclaims to the stars above:

> . . . I, the chiefest lamp of all the earth,
> First rising in the East with mild aspect,
> But fixèd now in the meridian line,
> Will send up fire to your turning spheres,
> And cause the sun to borrow light of you. . . .

Pope and Dryden, by contrast, write to audiences for whom strong metaphor has become suspect. They, therefore, reject the fire image (which we must recall is not present in the Greek) in favor of a form of speech more congenial to their age, the *sententia* or aphorism, and give it extra vitality by making it the scene of a miniature drama: in Dryden's case, the hero's dauntless heart "urges" him (in the double sense of physical as well as moral pressure) to his fate; in Pope's, the hero's courage, like a judge, "denies" continuance of life, with the consequence that he "falls"—and here Pope's second line suggests analogy to the sacrificial animal—the victim of his own essential nature, of what he is.

To pose even more graphically the pressures that a translator's period brings, consider the following lines from Hector's reply to Andromache's appeal that he withdraw, first in Chapman's Elizabethan version, then in Lattimore's twentieth-century one:

Chapman, 1598:

> The spirit I did first breathe
> Did never teach me that—much less since the contempt of death
> Was settled in me, and my mind knew what a Worthy was,
> Whose office is to lead in fight and give no danger pass
> Without improvement. In this fire must Hector's trial shine.
> Here must his country, father, friends be in him made divine.

Lattimore, 1951:

> and the spirit will not let me, since I have learned to be valiant
> and to fight always among the foremost ranks of the Trojans,
> winning for my own self great glory, and for my father.

If one may exaggerate to make a necessary point, the world of Henry V and Othello suddenly gives way here to our own, a world whose discomfort with any form of heroic self-assertion is remarkably mirrored in the burial of Homer's key terms (*spirit, valiant, fight, foremost, glory*)—five out of twenty-two words in the original, five out of thirty-six in the translation—in a cushioning huddle of harmless sounds.

Besides the two factors so far mentioned (language and period) as affecting the character of a translation, there is inevitably a third—the translator, with a particular degree of talent; a personal way of regarding the work to be translated; a special hierarchy of values, moral, aesthetic, metaphysical (which may or may not be summed up in a "worldview"); and a unique style or lack of it. But this influence all readers are likely to bear in mind, and it needs no laboring here. That, for example, two translators of Hamlet, one a Freudian, the other a Jungian, will produce impressively different translations is obvious from the fact that when Freudian and Jungian argue about the play in English they often seem to have different plays in mind.

We can now return to the question from which we started. After all allowances have been made for language, age, and individual translator, is anything of the original left? What, in short, does the reader of translations read? Let it be said at once that in utility prose—prose whose function is mainly referential—the reader who reads a translation reads everything that matters. "Nicht Rauchen," "Défense de Fumer," and "No Smoking," posted in a railway car, make their point, and the differences between them in sound and form have no significance for us in that context. Since the prose of a treatise and of most fiction is preponderantly referential, we rightly feel, when we have paid close attention to Cervantes or Montaigne or Machiavelli or Tolstoy in a good English translation, that we have had roughly the same experience as a native Spaniard, Frenchman, Italian, or Russian. But *roughly* is the correct word; for good prose points iconically *to* itself as well as referentially beyond itself, and everything that it points to in itself in the original (rhythms, sounds, idioms, wordplay, etc.) must alter radically in being translated. The best analogy is to imagine a Van Gogh painting reproduced in the medium of tempera, etching, or engraving: the "picture" remains, but the intricate interanimation of volumes with colorings with brushstrokes has disappeared.

When we move on to poetry, even in its longer narrative and dramatic forms—plays like *Oedipus,* poems like the *Iliad* or *The Divine Comedy*—our situation as English readers worsens appreciably, as the many unlike versions of Andromache's appeal to Hector make very clear. But, again, only appreciably. True, this is the point at which the fact that a translation is *always* an interpretation explodes irresistibly on our attention; but if it is the best translation of its time, like Robert Fagles's translation of the *Iliad* for our time, the result will be not only a sensitive interpretation but also a work with intrinsic interest in its own right—at very best, a true work of art, a new poem. In these longer works, moreover, even if the translation is uninspired, many distinctive structural features—plot, setting, characters, meetings, partings, confrontations, and specific episodes generally—survive virtually unchanged. It is only when the shorter, primarily lyrical forms of poetry are presented that the reader of translations faces insuperable disadvantage. In these forms, the referential aspect of language has a tendency to disappear into, or, more often, draw its real meaning and accreditation from, the iconic aspect. Let us look for just a moment at a brief poem by Federico García Lorca and its English translation (by Stephen Spender and J. L. Gili):

> ¡Alto pinar!
> Cuatro palomas por el aire van.
>
> Cuatro palomas
> vuelan y tornan.
> Llevan heridas
> sus cuatro sombras.
>
> ¡Bajo pinar!
> Cuatro palomas en la tierra están.

> the pine trees:
> Four pigeons go through the air.
>
> Four pigeons
> fly and turn round.
> They carry wounded
> their four shadows.
>
> Below the pine trees:
> Four pigeons lie on the earth.

In this translation the referential sense of the English words follows with remarkable exactness the referential sense of the Spanish words they replace. But the life of Lorca's poem does not lie in that sense. It lies in such matters as the abruptness, like an intake of breath at a sudden revelation, of the two exclamatory lines (1 and 7), which then exhale musically in images of flight and death; or as the echoings of *palomas* in *heridas* and *sombras*, bringing together (as in fact the hunter's gun has done) these unrelated nouns and the unrelated experiences they stand for in a sequence that seems, momentarily, to have all the logic of a tragic action, in which *doves* become *wounds* become *shadows*, or as the external and internal rhyming among the five verbs, as though all motion must (as in fact it must) end with *están*.

Since none of this can be brought over into another tongue (least of all Lorca's rhythms), the translator must decide between leaving a reader to wonder why Lorca is a poet to be bothered about at all and making a new but true poem, whose merit will almost certainly be in inverse ratio to its likeness to the original. Samuel Johnson made such a poem in translating Horace's famous *Diffugere nives*, and so did A. E. Housman. If we juxtapose the last two stanzas of each translation, and the corresponding Latin, we can see at a glance that each has the consistency and inner life of a genuine poem and that neither of them (even if we consider only what is obvious to the eye, the line-lengths) is very close to Horace:

> Cum semel occideris, et de te splendida Minos
>   fecerit arbitria,
> non, Torquate, genus, non te facundia, non te
>   restituet pietas.

> Infernis neque enim tenebris Diana pudicum
> liberat Hippolytum
> nec Lethaea valet Theseus abrumpere caro
> vincula Pirithoo.

Johnson:

> Not you, Torquatus, boast of Rome,
> When Minos once has fixed your doom,
> Or eloquence, or splendid birth,
> Or virtue, shall restore to earth.
> Hippolytus, unjustly slain,
> Diana calls to life in vain;
> Nor can the might of Theseus rend
> The chains of hell that hold his friend.

Housman:

> When thou descendest once the shades among,
>   The stern assize and equal judgment o'er,
> Not thy long lineage nor thy golden tongue,
>   No, nor thy righteousness, shall friend thee more.
>
> Night holds Hippolytus the pure of stain,
>   Diana steads him nothing, he must stay;
> And Theseus leaves Pirithous in the chain
>   The love of comrades cannot take away.

The truth of the matter is that when the translator of short poems chooses to be literal, most or all of the poetry is lost; and when the translator succeeds in forging a new poetry, most or all of the original author is lost.

The best practical advice for those of us who must read poems in English translations is to focus intently on the images and dramatic scenes these poems evoke and ask ourselves what there is in them or in their effect on each other that produces each poem's particular electricity. To that extent, we can compensate for a part of our losses, learn something positive about the immense explosive powers of imagery, and rest easy in the secure knowledge that translation even in the mode of the short poem brings us (despite losses) closer to the work itself than not reading it at all. "To a thousand cavils," said Samuel Johnson, "one answer is sufficient; the purpose of a writer is to be read, and the criticism which would destroy the power of pleasing must be blown aside." Johnson was defending Pope's Homer for those marks of its own time and place that make it the great interpretation it is, but Johnson's exhilarating common sense applies equally to the problem we are considering here. Literature is to be read, and the criticism that would destroy the reader's power to make some form of contact with much of the world's great writing must indeed be blown aside.

MAYNARD MACK

Judah Halevi: *Summer* ("The earth, like a girl, sipped the rains") translated by William M. Davis from *An Anthology of Medieval Lyrics*, edited by Angel Flores. Copyright © 1962 by Angel Flores.

Hildegard of Bingen: *A Hymn to St. Maximinus* ("The dove peered in") from THE MEDIEVAL LYRIC, THIRD EDITION, by Peter Dronke (Cambridge: D. S. Brewer, 1996). Reprinted by permission of the publisher.

Homer: selections from THE ILIAD by Homer, translated by Robert Fagles. Translation copyright © 1990 by Robert Fagles. Introduction and Notes copyright © 1990 by Bernard Knox. Used by permission of Viking Penguin, a division of Penguin Putnam, Inc. THE ODYSSEY, by Homer, translated by Robert Fitzgerald. Copyright © 1961, 1963 by Robert Fitzgerald and renewed 1989 by Benedict R. C. Fitzgerald. Reprinted by permission of Vintage Books, a division of Random House, Inc.

The Koran: selections from THE KORAN, translated by N. J. Dawood (Penguin Classics, 1956, Fifth revised edition, 1990). Copyright © 1956, 1959, 1966, 1968, 1974, 1990 by N. J. Dawood. Reproduced by permission of Penguin Books, Ltd.

Lucian: from SELECTED SATIRES OF LUCIAN by Lionel Casson. Copyright © 1962 by Lionel Casson. Used by permission of Doubleday, a division of Bantam Doubleday Dell Publishing Group, Inc.

Niccolò Machiavelli: from THE PRINCE AND OTHER WORKS, translated by Allan H. Gilbert, Hendricks House, Inc., Publishers, Putney, VT. Reprinted by permission of the publisher.

Marie de France: *Lanval* and *Laüstic* from THE LAIS OF MARIE DE FRANCE, translated by Glyn S. Burgess and Keith Busby (Penguin Classics, 1986). Copyright © 1986 by Glyn S. Burgess and Keith Busby. Reproduced by permission of Penguin Books, Ltd.

Michel de Montaigne: selections reprinted from THE COMPLETE ESSAYS OF MONTAIGNE, translated by Donald M. Frame, by the permission of the publishers, Stanford University Press. Copyright © 1958 by the Board of Trustees of the Leland Stanford Junior University.

Heinrich von Morungen: *The Wound of Love* ("She has wounded me") from THE MEDIEVAL LYRIC, THIRD EDITION, by Peter Dronke (Cambridge: D. S. Brewer, 1996). Reprinted by permission of the publisher.

Marguerite de Navarre: selections from THE HEPTAMERON by Marguerite de Navarre, translated by P. A. Chilton (Penguin Classics, 1984). Copyright © 1984 by P. A. Chilton. Reproduced by permission of Penguin Books, Ltd.

Ovid: excerpts from THE METAMORPHOSES OF OVID: A NEW VERSE TRANSLATION, English translation copyright © 1993 by Allen Mandelbaum. Reprinted by permission of Harcourt Brace & Company.

Francis Petrarch: Sonnets 1, 3, 34, 78, 126, 189 from PETRARCH'S LYRIC POEMS translated by Robert Durling (Cambridge, Mass: Harvard University Press). Copyright © 1976 by Robert Durling. Reprinted by permission of the publisher. Sonnet 61 from THE SONNETS OF PETRARCH by Joseph Auslander, translator. Copyright © 1931 by Longmans, Green and Co. Reprinted by permission of David McKay Co., Inc, a division of Random House, Inc. Sonnet 62 translated by Bernard Bergonzi. Reprinted by permission of the translator.

Petronius: *Dinner with Trimalchio* from THE SATYRICON, translated by J. P. Sullivan. Copyright © 1965 by J. P. Sullivan. Reprinted by permission of David Higham Associates.

Christine de Pizan: *Alone in Martyrdom* ("Alone in martyrdom I have been left") translated by Muriel Kittel, from *An Anthology of Medieval Lyrics*, edited by Angel Flores. Copyright © 1962 by Angel Flores. Reprinted by permission of the translator.

Plautus: *Pseudolus* from THREE COMEDIES: MILES GLORIOSIS, PSEUDOLUS, RUDENS. Copyright © 1991. Used by permission of Cornell University Press.

Rabbi Ephraim ben Jacob: *The Sacrifice of Issac*, excerpt from THE LAST TRIAL: ON THE LEGENDS AND LORE OF THE COMMAND TO OFFER ABRAHAM AS A SACRIFICE by Shalom Spiegel, translated with an introduction by Judah Goldin (Woodstock, VT: Jewish Lights Publishing, 1993). $17. 95 + $3.50 s/h. Order by mail or call 800–962-4544. Permission granted by Jewish Lights Publishing, P. O. Box 237, Woodstock, VT 05091.

François Rabelais: selections from GARGANTUA AND PANTAGRUEL, translated by Burton Raffel, translation copyright © 1990 by W. W. Norton & Company, Inc. Reprinted by permission of W. W. Norton & Company, Inc.

Ibn Arfaʿ Raʾsuh: *The Singing Lute* ("The lute trills the most wondrous melodies") from HISPANO-ARABIC POETRY: A STUDENT ANTHOLOGY, edited by James T. Monroe (Berkeley: University of California Press). Copyright © 1974 by The Regents of the University of California. Reprinted by permission.

Jaufré Rudel: *Love Song* ("When the nightingale in the leaves") from THE POETRY OF CERCAMON AND JAUFRÉ RUDEL, edited and translated by George Wolf and Roy Rosenstein. Reprinted by permission of Garland Press.

Sappho: selections from *Throned in Splendor* from GREEK LYRICS, translated by Richmond Lattimore. Reprinted by permission of the University of Chicago Press.

William Shakespeare: *Othello* from THE OXFORD SHAKESPEARE, edited by Stanley Wells and Gary Taylor. Copyright © 1988. Reprinted by permission of Oxford University Press.

Sir Gawain and the Green Knight: SIR GAWAIN AND THE GREEN KNIGHT, A NEW VERSE TRANSLATION by Marie Borroff, translator. Copyright © 1967 by W. W. Norton & Company, Inc. Reprinted by permission of W. W. Norton & Company, Inc.

Song of Roland: THE SONG OF ROLAND, by Frederick Goldin, translator. Copyright © 1978 by W. W. Norton & Company, Inc. Reprinted by permission of W. W. Norton & Company, Inc.

Sophocles: *Oedipus the King* from THREE THEBAN PLAYS by Sophocles, translated by Robert Fagles. Translation copyright © 1982 by Robert Fagles. Used by permission of Viking Penguin, a division of Penguin Books USA, Inc.

Walahfrid Strabo: *Elegy on Reichenau* from POETRY OF THE CAROLINIAN RENAISSANCE, edited by Peter Godman. Copyright © 1987. Reprinted by permission of Gerald Duckworth & Co., Ltd.

Thorstein the Staff-Struck: from HRAFNKEL'S SAGA AND OTHER ICELANDIC STORIES, translated by Hermann Palsson (Penguin Classics, 1971). Copyright © 1970 by Hermann Palsson. Reproduced by permission of Penguin Books, Ltd.

The Thousand and One Nights: from THE THOUSAND AND ONE NIGHTS by Husain Haddawy, translator. Copyright © 1990 by W. W. Norton & Company. Reprinted by permission of W. W. Norton & Company, Inc.

The Trial of Renard: FROM RENARD THE FOX: THE ADVENTURES OF AN EPIC HERO, translated by Patricia Terry. Copyright © 1992 by The Regents of the University of California. Reprinted by permission of the University of California Press.

Lope de Vega: *Fuente Ovejuna* from MASTERPIECES OF THE SPANISH GOLDEN AGE, translated by Angel Flores and Muriel Kittel. Reprinted by permission of Juan Flores.

François Villon: from *The Testament*. From THE POEMS OF FRANÇOIS VILLON, translated by Galway Kinnell. Copyright © 1965, 1977 by Galway Kinnell. Reprinted by permission of Houghton Mifflin Co. All rights reserved.

Virgil: selections from THE AENEID, translated by Robert Fitzgerald. Translation copyright © 1980, 1982, 1983 by Robert Fitzgerald. Reprinted by permission of Random House, Inc.

Walther von der Vogelweide: *Dancing Girl* (" 'Lady, accept this garland' ") from THE MEDIEVAL LYRIC, THIRD EDITION, by Peter Dronke (Cambridge: D. S. Brewer, 1996). Reprinted by permission of the publisher.

William IX, duke of Aquitaine: *Spring Song* ("In the sweetness of new spring") from THE MEDIEVAL LYRIC, THIRD EDITION, by Peter Dronke (Cambridge: D. S. Brewer, 1996). Reprinted by permission of the publisher.

Every effort has been made to contact the copyright holders of each of the selections. Rights holders of any selections not credited should contact W. W. Norton & Company, Inc., 500 Fifth Avenue, New York, NY 10110, in order for a correction to be made in the next reprinting of our work.

Index